D1601798

Encyclopedia of Ukraine

Encyclopedia of

UKRAINE

VOLUME II

G-K

Edited by

†VOLODYMYR KUBIJOVYČ

Published for the Canadian Institute of Ukrainian Studies,
the Shevchenko Scientific Society (Sarcelles, France), and
the Canadian Foundation for Ukrainian Studies

UNIVERSITY OF TORONTO PRESS
Toronto Buffalo London

Canadian Cataloguing in Publication Data
Main entry under title:
Encyclopedia of Ukraine

Revision of: Entsyklopediia ukraïnoznavstva.
'Published for the Canadian Institute of Ukrainian Studies, the Shevchenko Scientific Society (Sarcelles, France), and the Canadian Foundation for Ukrainian Studies'
Includes bibliographies.
Partial contents: Map & gazeteer volume – v. 1. A-F – v. 2. G-K.
ISBN 0-8020-3444-6 (v. 2).

1. Ukraine – Dictionaries and encyclopedias.
2. Ukraine – Gazeteers.
I. Kubijovyč, V. (Volodymyr), 1900–85
II. Canadian Institute of Ukrainian Studies.
III. Naukove tovarystvo imeny Shevchenka.
IV. Canadian Foundation for Ukrainian Studies.
V. Title: Entsyklopediia ukraïnoznavstva.

DK508.E52 1984 947'.71'003 C84-099336-6

Design on front cover by Jacques Hnizdovsky

The publication of this volume

has been made possible in part

through a grant from the Province of Saskatchewan

in recognition of the contributions of Ukrainian pioneers

to the development of the province.

EDITORIAL STAFF

Boris Balan	*Project Co-ordinator; Manuscript Editor*
Roman Senkus	*Chief Manuscript Editor*
Taras Zakydalsky	*Manuscript Editor*
Roma Yanchinski	*Editorial and Research Assistant*
Mary Pasieka	*Word Processor; Secretary*
Ivan Ochrymowicz	*Word Processor; Translator in Sarcelles*
Yury Boshyk	*Manuscript Editor, 1987*
George Kostiuk	*Computing Consultant*
Daria Markus	*Cataloguer in Sarcelles, 1983*
Bohdan Nebesio; Marko Stech; Olenka Syrotynska; Zenon Washchuk; Andrij Wynnyckyj	*Editorial Assistants*

CONTRIBUTORS

M. Adams; O. Andriewsky; R. Andrushkiw; B. Balan; V.N. Bandera; M. Baziuk; I. Bekerman; O. Bilaniuk; A. Bilynsky; B.R. Bociurkiw; M. Bohachevsky-Chomiak; Y. Boshyk; M. Busko; M. Chubaty; D. Chyzhevsky; B. Czajkowskyj; M. Dobriansky; V. Doroshenko; V. Fedorchuk; J. Fedynskyj; A. Feldman; C. Freeland; V. Haievsky; B. Halaichuk; J.-P. Himka; M. Hlobenko; M. Hnatiukivsky; J. Hnizdovsky; V. Holubnychy; V. Holubovych; O. Horbach; S. Hordynsky; A. Humesky; P. Isaiv; V. Ivanys; P. Kachur; I. Khoma; A. Kipa; I. Kleiner; I. Koropeckyj; I. Korovytsky; I. Koshelivets; B. Kravtsiv; B. Krawchenko; W. Krucko; V. Kubijovyč; F. Kushnirsky; I. Kuzych-Berezovsky; T. Lapychak; W. Lencyk; V. Lev; G.S.N. Luckyj; P.R. Magocsi; S. Maksudov; V. Markus; D. Marples; O. Martynovych; B. Medwidsky; V. Mezentsev; F. Miller; M. Miller; R. Miz; I. Myhul; K. Mytrovych; B. Nebesio; P. Odarchenko; O. Ohloblyn; L. Okinshevych; L. Onyshkevych; Ya. Pasternak; N. Pavliuc; V. Pavlovsky; A. Pekar; P. Petrenko; V. Petryshyn; V. Pliushch; V. Polishchuk; V. Popovych; S. Protsiuk; N. Pylypiuk; J. Reshetar; V. Revutsky; D. Saunders; R. Savytsky; H. Schultz; R. Senkus; L. Shankovsky; G.Y. Shevelov; V. Shuhaievsky; O. Shulhyn; V. Sichynsky; P. Sodol; R. Solchanyk; B. Somchynsky; C. Spolsky; M. Stakhiv; I. Stebelsky; M. Stech; D.H. Struk; B. Struminsky; O. Subtelny; L. Szuch; S. Trofimenko; K. Turkalo; A. Velyky; W. Veryha; A. Vincenz; I. Vlasovsky; I. Vytanovych; A. Woronka; W. Wowk; B. Wynar; L. Wynar; W. Wytwycky; R. Yanchinski; S. Yaniv; V. Yaniv; M. Yurkevich; T. Zakydalsky; E. Zharsky; M. Zhdan; A. Zhukovsky; O. Zinkevych; D. Zlepko

G

Gabro, Jaroslav, b 31 July 1919 in Chicago, d 28 March 1980 in Chicago. Ukrainian Catholic bishop. A graduate of the Catholic University of America and St Joseph's Seminary in Washington, DC, he was ordained in 1945. In 1961 he was consecrated bishop of the new Chicago eparchy for Ukrainians. He established a number of missions and the eparchial weekly *Nova Zoria* (The New Star). His introduction of the Gregorian calendar in 1964 aroused much controversy and led to the founding of the dissident ss Volodymyr and Olga parish.

Gabrusevych, Ivan [Gabrusevyč] (pseuds John, Irten), 1902–44. Political leader and activist of the nationalist movement in Western Ukraine. Gabrusevych belonged to the radical wing of the Ukrainian Military Organization and to the Organization of Ukrainian Nationalists. In 1930 he was a regional leader of the latter organization. As a member and leader of the Union of Ukrainian Nationalist Youth, he conducted agitational work and propaganda among Ukrainian youth. In 1929 Gabrusevych published the underground political journal *Iunak*, and in 1930 helped organize acts of sabotage against the Polish government. After a brief arrest and imprisonment, he left Western Ukraine in 1932 and stayed in Germany until the Nazi-Soviet invasion of Poland. He was arrested by the Gestapo during the Second World War and died in the Sachsenhausen concentration camp.

Gadzinsky, Volodymyr [Gadzins'kyj] (pseuds Yosyf Hrikh, Oskar Reding, Trylsky), b 21 August 1888 in Cracow, d 11 August 1932 in Odessa. Poet and critic. From 1919 he lived in Soviet Ukraine, where he worked as an editor and belonged to the writers' organizations *Hart and the All-Ukrainian Association of Proletarian Writers. His literary output consists of the poetry collections (mainly narrative poems) *Z dorohy* (From the Road, 1922), *Ainshtain, Zemlia* (Einstein, Earth, 1925), *USSR* (Ukrainian SSR, 1925), *Zaklyk chervonoho renesansu* (The Call of the Red Renaissance, 1926), and *Ne – abstrakty* (Not – Abstracts, 1927); the novelette *Kinets'* (The End, 1927); and two books of literary polemics, reviews, and criticism: *Na bezkrovnomu fronti* (On the Bloodless Front, 1926) and *Fragmenty stykhiï* (Fragments of the Elemental Force, 1927). Persecuted during the Stalinist terror, he committed suicide.

Gaganets, Yosyf [Gaganec', Josyf], b 10 April 1793 in Vyslok Velykyi near Sianik, Galicia, d 22 December 1875 in Prešov. Greek Catholic bishop. After studying theology at the Trnava academy, he was ordained in 1817 and served as a village priest. He became canon (1835), vicar capitular (1841), and bishop (1843) of Prešov eparchy. As bishop, he opposed Magyarization and promoted the Byzantine rite and the Ukrainian language. He founded many parish schools and institutions and

Ivan Gabrusevych

Bishop Yosyf Gaganets

built a new episcopal residence and cathedral. He urged his priests (he ordained 237) to pay more attention to their parishioners' secular problems. In 1846 he obtained regular state incomes for his clergy. His support of Ukrainian autonomy and his pro-Habsburg stance during the Revolution of 1848–9 resulted in attempts by Hungarian circles to have him removed from office. For his loyalty to the crown he was appointed counselor to the Austrian court in 1868.

Gagauzy. An ethnic group native to southern *Bessarabia, which now constitutes parts of the Moldavian SSR and Odessa oblast. Origins of the Gagauzy are uncertain. Their ancestors were either Turkic Oghuz or Cumans who settled in *Dobrudja in the Middle Ages, or perhaps Bulgarians who were forcibly Turkified from the 14th century onward. Although they speak Turkic, they are Orthodox, not Moslem, and are culturally close to Bulgarians, with whom they migrated to Bessarabia in the first half of the 19th century during the Turkish-Russian wars. A part of the Gagauzy resettled in the 1860s from Bessarabia to the vicinity of Berdianske on the Azov coast, and in 1908–14 to Central Asia. In 1970, 156,600 Gagauzy lived in the USSR, 26,400 of them in Ukraine and 125,000 in Moldavia. In 1979, 173,200 Gagauzy lived in the USSR. The majority are rural (82 percent in Ukraine in 1970) and have retained Gagauz as their mother tongue (89 percent in 1979).

Galagan. Surname of a Cossack *starshyna* family, which originated with Col Hnat *Galagan (d 1748) and his brother Semen, acting colonel of Myrhorod during the Crimean campaign of 1736. Other notable members of the family were Hryhorii (1716–77), colonel of Pryluka (1739–63) and a participant in Russian campaigns against the Turks and Prussians, and Hryhorii *Galagan, a civic leader.

With the death of the latter's son Pavlo (1853–69) the Galagan line came to an end.

Galagan, Hnat, b ?, d 1748 in Pryluka. In 1706 he was elected colonel at the Zaporozhian Sich and served under I. Mazepa as a colonel of a mercenary regiment. In 1708 he joined the side of Peter I against Mazepa. On 14 May 1709 he helped the Russian army to raze the Zaporozhian Sich, for which he was generously rewarded by the tsar. He served as colonel of Chyhyryn (1709–14) and Pryluka (1714–39) and was known as a careerist and oppressive exploiter of peasants.

Hryhorii Galagan

Volodymyr Galan

Galagan, Hryhorii, b 15 August 1819 in Kiev, d 25 September 1888 in Kiev. Ukrainophile civic leader, ethnographer, and patron of Ukrainian culture. A large landholder in the Poltava and Chernihiv regions, he was personally acquainted with T. Shevchenko, M. Maksymovych, P. Kulish, V. Antonovych, and many members of the *Hromada of Kiev. As a judge and a member of government agencies preparing and supervising the 1861 reforms and, from 1882, as a member of the State Council, he defended the interests of the Ukrainian peasantry. From 1865 until his death he was an active promoter of zemstvos. In Sokyryntsi, Pryluka county, he opened and subsidized the first peasant savings and loans association in Ukraine. He initiated and financially assisted the creation of elementary schools in Pryluka county and, in 1874, the Pryluka gymnasium. In memory of his son Pavlo, he founded *Galagan College in Kiev in 1871. A great benefactor and patron of the arts, he had buildings constructed in the traditional Ukrainian style, bought art works (including some by T. Shevchenko), supported the development of choral singing and *vertep* drama, and financially contributed to the journal *Kievskaia starina*. In 1873–5 he was president of the *Southwestern Branch of the Imperial Russian Geographic Society.

Galagan College (Kolegiia Pavla Galagana). Preparatory boarding school in Kiev founded on 1 October 1871 by H. *Galagan in memory of his deceased son Pavlo. The college was under the supervision of Kiev University and had four grades. In contrast to regular secondary schools it treated modern languages, drawing, and choir singing, but not Greek, as compulsory subjects. It also offered enriched courses in mathematics and Russian. Its extensive library was based on M. Markevych's collection. Fifty to sixty students per year studied at the

Galagan College

college in a family atmosphere, about half of them supported by the Galagan Foundation. Admission was restricted to boys of the Orthodox faith and preference was given to applicants from Pryluka county. Many of the school's graduates, including A. *Krymsky, went on to play important roles in Ukrainian scholarship and culture. Under the Soviet regime the college was turned into a *labor school in 1920.

Galan, Volodymyr (Gallan, Walter), b 3 April 1893 in Hlyniany, Peremyshliany county, Galicia, d 5 July 1978 in Philadelphia. Civic leader and banking executive. Galan studied law and economics in Lviv, Prague (LL D 1922), and Philadelphia. During the First World War he served in the Austrian army and then commanded a unit known as the Battery of Death in the Ukrainian Galician Army. In 1923 he immigrated to the United States. He was a founder and president (1929–40) of the United Ukrainian American Organizations of Philadelphia and helped to establish the Ukrainian Congress Committee of America. After chairing the Relief Committee for Carpatho-Ukraine (1938–9), Galan was a founder, executive director (1947–55), and president (1955–) of the *United Ukrainian American Relief Committee. He was also a founder and president of the United Ukrainian Veterans of America. He contributed many articles to the Ukrainian press and wrote a book of war memoirs, *Bateriia smerty* (The Battery of Death, 1968).

Galaţi. VIII-9. City (1980 pop 261,000) and district center in southeastern Rumania, situated at the confluence of the Danube and Seret rivers. Nearby the Prut River joins the Danube. Galaţi is an important trade and industrial center, inland port, and naval base. The largest shipyard in Rumania is found there. In the late 11th and 12th centuries it was known as Malyi Halych and played an important role in Galicia's trade with Bulgaria, the Byzantines, the Italian cities, and the Orient. From the early 16th century to 1829 it was an important Ottoman port, and from 1834 to 1883 a free port. Hetman I. Mazepa died and was buried there in St George's Cathedral.

Galay, Theodore (Ted), b 16 July 1941 in Beausejour, Manitoba. Playwright. Educated at the universities of Manitoba and British Columbia (PH D), Galay teaches mathematics at Vancouver Community College. His plays focus on ethnic identity and generational conflict. His one-act plays *After Baba's Funeral* (1979) and *Sweet and Sour Pickles* (1980) won the Best Play Award at the Theatre Ontario '80 Festival and the Drama Award of the Canadian Authors' Association in 1981. These were followed by *The Grabowski Girls* (1983), *Tsymbaly* (1985), which won the Jessie Award for Best Original Play in Vancouver in 1984–5, and *Primrose School District 109* (1985).

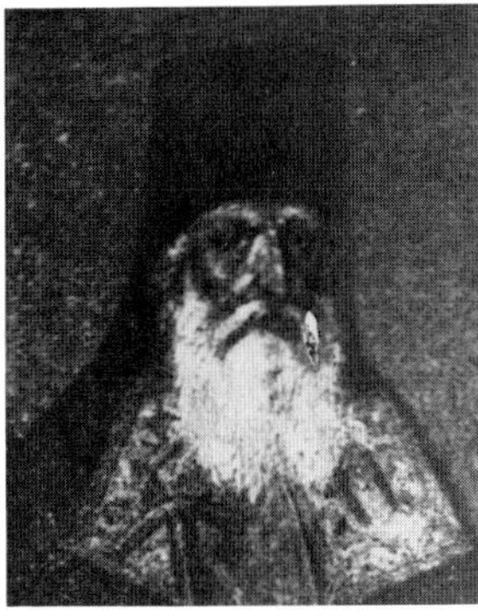

Archimandrite Ioanikii Galiatovsky

Galiatovsky, Ioanikii [Galjatovs'kyj, Ioanikij], b ?, d 12 January 1688 in Chernihiv. Writer and Orthodox church leader. Galiatovsky was educated at the Kievan College, then lectured there (1650–69) and served as its rector (from 1657) and hegumen of the Kiev Epiphany Brotherhood monastery. From 1669 he was archimandrite of the Yeletskyi Dormition Monastery in Chernihiv. He was a renowned orator and the author of a collection of sermons, *Kliuch razumieniia* (The Key of Understanding, 1659, 1663), which included 'Nauka, albo sposob zlozhenia kazania' (Teaching, or the Manner of Composing a Sermon, 1659) explaining the theory of baroque sermons. He also wrote baroque poetry, a collection of stories about the miracles wrought by the Virgin Mary, *Nebo novoie* (The New Heaven, 1665), and several polemical treatises in Polish attacking the Church Union of Berestia, Judaism, and Islam, including *Łabędź z piórami swemi* (The Swan with Its Feathers, 1679), *Alphabetum rozmaitym Heretykom ...* (A Primer for Various Heretics, 1681), and *Alkoran Machometow* (The Muslims' Koran, 1683).

BIBLIOGRAPHY
Sumtsov, N. 'Ioannikii Galiatovskii,' KS, 1884, nos 1–4
Bida, K. *Ioanikii Galiatovs'kyi i ioho 'Kliuch Razuminiia'* (Rome 1975)
Haliatovs'kyi, I. *Kliuch rozuminnia* (Kiev 1985)

Galicia (Ukrainian: Halychyna). A historical region in southwestern Ukraine. Its ethnic Ukrainian territory occupies the basins of the upper and middle Dniester, the upper Prut and Buh, and most of the Sian, and has an area of 55,700 sq km. Its population was 5,824,100 in 1939. The name is derived from that of the city *Halych.

Location and territory. Galicia lies in the middle of the European landmass between the Black and Baltic seas, to which it is linked by the rivers Dniester and Prut, and the Buh and Sian respectively. It is linked to the rest of Ukraine by land routes only. It is bounded by Poland in the west, *Transcarpathia and the *Lemko region in the southwest, *Bukovyna in the southeast, *Podilia in the east, *Volhynia in the northeast, and the *Kholm region in the northwest. Its location on the crossroads to the seas led its expansionist foreign neighbors, especially Poland and Hungary, to strive repeatedly to gain control of Galicia.

Galicia's location protected it from the incursions of Asiatic nomadic peoples and facilitated contact with the rest of Europe. After the demise of Kiev as the capital of Rus' and the decline of the Varangian trade routes, the main trade route linking the Baltic Sea with the Black Sea and Byzantium passed through Galicia. Because of its distance from the Eurasian steppe, medieval Rus'-Ukrainian statehood survived there as the Principality of *Galicia-Volhynia for another century after the sack of Kiev by the Mongols in 1240. The principality provided refuge to the people from other parts of Rus' who had fled the Mongol invasion. It thus became a reservoir of Ukrainian population, much of which later remigrated to the east. With the decline of commerce in the Black Sea Basin in the 16th century, Galicia lost its importance as the link with the Baltic. Its peripheral role vis-à-vis developments in Ukraine during the period of the *Hetman state rendered it relatively insignificant.

Only the southern, natural frontier of Galicia – shaped by the Carpathian Mountains – remained unchanged.

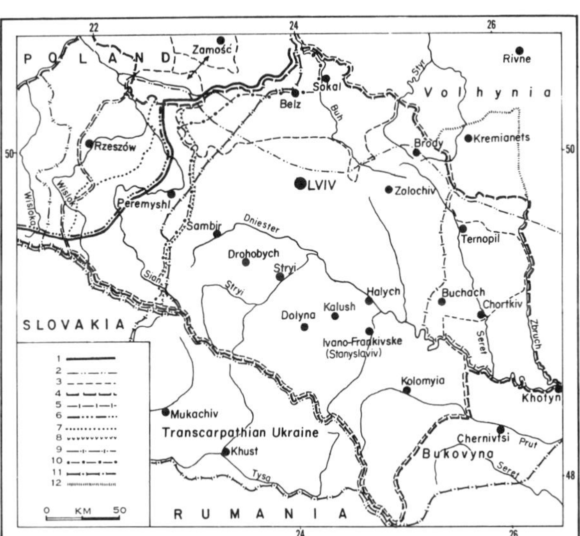

GALICIA

1. Ukrainian Galicia (and the territory of the Western Ukrainian National Republic in 1918–20)
2. Boundaries of Halych principality
3. Boundaries of Rus' and Belz voivodeships under Polish rule (to 1772)
4. Boundaries of Galicia under Austrian rule (1772–1918)
5. Western boundary of the Ternopil region under Russian rule (1809–15)
6. Ukrainian-Polish ethnic boundary
7. Jurisdictional boundary between the Lviv and Cracow appellate courts
8. Curzon Line
9. Boundary between Lviv and Cracow voivodeships
10. Western and northern boundaries of District Galicia during the German occupation (1941–4)
11. Current border of the Ukrainian SSR, Poland, Czechoslovakia, and Rumania
12. Boundary of Kremianets district within Ternopil oblast (1939–44)

The rulers of the Principality of Galicia-Volhynia had extended the eastern frontier past the Zbruch River and into the steppe; at one time (end of 12th century), they ruled lands as far south as the lower Danube. Under Polish rule (1340–1772) Galicia constituted first Rus' land (*Regnum Russiae*) and then from 1434 *Rus' voivodeship (palatinate) and the western part of *Podilia voivodeship.

Under Austrian rule (1772–1918), Galicia was bounded in the east by the Zbruch River, and in the southeast, as it had been under Poland, by the Cheremosh and Dniester rivers. After the final partition of Poland in 1795 and territorial adjustments in 1809 during the Napoleonic wars, the administrative territory of Austrian Galicia also encompassed the western, Polish ethnographic part of Galicia – the area west of the jurisdictional boundary between the Lviv and Cracow higher crownland courts, which ran along the western limits of Sianik, Brzozów, Peremyshl, and Jarosław counties. Thus, Galicia embraced almost all the territory of the former Rus' voivodeship, the southern part of Belz voivodeship, and small parts of Podilia and Volhynia voivodeships, as well as some Polish ethnic lands. From 1787 to 1849 and again in 1859–61, Bukovyna was also administratively part of Galicia. From 1809 to 1815, the Ternopil region was occupied by Russia. The *Western Ukrainian National Republic (1918–19) encompassed all of Ukrainian Galicia and, for a short time, the Ukrainian parts of Bukovyna and Transcarpathia. Under interwar Poland Ukrainian Galicia consisted of Lviv, Stanyslaviv, and Ternopil voivodeships. During the Nazi occupation (1941–4) it constituted the so-called Galicia district of the *Generalgouvernement. In 1945 the west and northwestern borderlands of Ukrainian Galicia became part of Poland. The remaining territory was divided among four Soviet oblasts: *Lviv, Drohobych (incorporated in 1959 into Lviv oblast), Stanyslaviv (renamed *Ivano-Frankivske in 1962), and *Ternopil.

Physical geography. Galicia is not a biotope, but consists of several natural regions: (1) the *Carpathian Mountains; (2) the upper *Sian region and *Subcarpathia; and (3) the upland chain of *Roztochia, *Opilia, Podilia, and *Pokutia, which are separated by the *Buh Depression from the southern fringe of the *Volhynia-Kholm Upland. No other part of Ukraine has such a large variety of landforms (mountains, foothills, plateaus, and glacial depressions) in so small an area. Galicia's *climate changes gradually from maritime in the northwest to continental in the east, mountain in the south, and Black Sea coastal in the southeast. There are corresponding vegetation zones: mountain forest and alpine meadow in the Carpathians, mixed forest in the west, and *forest-steppe in the east. The eastern perimeter of the beech and fir forests runs through Galicia.

Prehistory. The oldest inhabitants of Galicia migrated into the Dniester Basin from southern Ukraine during the Middle Paleolithic. The remains of a few settlements of the *Mousterian culture (Bilche-Zolote, Bukivna, Zalishchyky-Pecherna, Kasperivtsi) have been uncovered there. Upper Paleolithic Aurignacian peoples relatively densely populated the basin between present-day Ivano-Frankivske and Bukovyna, as well as southern Podilia. In the Mesolithic, northern Galicia between the rivers Sian and Buh was sparsely populated. In the Neolithic and Eneolithic, the northeast was inhabited by agricultural tribes of the so-called Buh culture. The Dniester Basin and part of western Podilia were inhabited by people of the *Trypilian culture. The first migrating peoples from Silesia arrived, bringing with them pottery decorated with linear bands. They were followed by seminomadic Nordic tribes of the Corded Ware culture. A Nordic tribe that buried its dead in stone slab-cists settled in the Buh Basin and spread into western Podilia.

In the Bronze Age, seminomadic peoples from the west forced a part of the autochthons in the Buh Basin to resettle in Polisia. Later, they penetrated into the region between the Dniester and the Carpathian Mountains, where they came into contact with bronze-making tribes from Transcarpathia, and a mixed variant of the *Komariv culture arose. In the middle Dniester Basin the Trypilian culture continued. In the 13th and 14th centuries BC, the first wave of the ancestors of the western proto-Slavs from Silesia penetrated into the lower Sian Basin; these tribes of the *Lusatian culture occupied the western bank of the Sian as far north as its confluence with the Tanew River.

In the Iron Age, agricultural tribes migrated back from Polisia into the upper Buh Basin and gave rise to the *Vysotske culture. In the Dniester Basin the *Thracian Hallstatt culture developed. In western Podilia, the so-called Scythian Ploughmen, who were most likely proto-Slavic tribes of the *Chornyi Lis culture, made their appearance. At the end of the La Tène period, a second wave of western proto-Slavs, the *Venedi, penetrated into the Dniester Basin and western Podilia. The *Lypytsia culture arose; it is perhaps connected with the *Getae who settled in the upper Dniester Basin, particularly after the Roman occupation of Dacia.

Galicia in the era of European tribal migration (AD 300–700) is not well known; a few proto-Slavic hamlets with gray, wheel-turned pottery and barrows with the cremated remains of the ancestors of the Tivertsians have been uncovered. Many archeological remains of the Princely era have been found, however: eg, fortified towns, settlements, burial grounds, architectural remains (the ruins of the Dormition Cathedral and other churches in Halych and *Krylos), and the *Zbruch idol. Evidence of foreign in-migration can be found in various localities: eg, ancient Magyar barrows near Krylos, Varangian barrows in the ancient town of *Plisnesk, caches of Varangian arms, medieval foreign coins, and Cuman *stone *baby*.

History

The Princely era. In the second half of the first millennium AD, the Buh, Sian, and Dniester basins were inhabited by tribes of *Buzhanians, *Dulibians, *White Croatians, and *Tivertsians. Their fortified towns – *Terebovlia, *Halych, *Zvenyhorod, *Peremyshl, and others – flourished because of their location on trade routes linking the Baltic with the Black Sea and Kiev with Cracow, Prague, and Regensburg. This region was first mentioned in the medieval chronicle *Povist' vremennykh lit* (Tale of Bygone Years), which described Grand Prince *Volodymyr the Great's war with the Poles in 981 and his annexation of the Peremyshl and *Cherven towns to Kievan Rus'. In 992, Volodymyr marched on the White Croatians and annexed Subcarpathia. Thus, by the end of the 10th century all of Galicia's territory was part of *Kievan Rus', and it shared its political, social, economic, religious, and cultural development.

After the death of Grand Prince *Yaroslav the Wise in

1054, Kievan Rus' began to fall apart into its component principalities. From 1084 Yaroslav's great-grandsons, *Riuryk, *Volodar, and *Vasylko Rostyslavych, ruled the lands of Peremyshl, Zvenyhorod, and Terebovlia. Volodar's son, *Volodymyrko, inherited the Zvenyhorod land in 1124, the Peremyshl land in 1129, and the Terebovlia and Halych lands in 1141; he made Halych his capital. Volodymyrko's son, *Yaroslav Osmomysl, the pre-eminent prince of the Rostyslavych dynasty, enlarged Halych principality during his reign (1153–87) to encompass all the lands between the Carpathian Mountains and the Dniester River as far south as the lower Danube. Trade and salt mining stimulated the rise of a powerful boyar estate in Galicia. The *boyars often opposed the policies and plans of the Galician princes and undermined their rule by provoking internal strife and supporting foreign intervention. When *Volodymyr Yaroslavych, the last prince of the Rostyslavych dynasty, died in 1199, the boyars invited Prince *Roman Mstyslavych of Volhynia to take the throne.

Roman united Galicia with Volhynia and thus created the Principality of Galicia-Volhynia. It was ruled by the Romanovych dynasty until 1340. The period from 1205 to 1238 in the Galician-Volhynian state was one of further intervention by Hungary and Poland, of internal strife among the appanage princes and the boyars, and hence of economic decline. During the reign of *Danylo Romanovych (1238–64), however, Galicia-Volhynia flourished, despite the Mongol invasion of 1240–1. Danylo promoted the development of existing towns and built new ones (Lviv, Kholm, and others), furthered the status of his allies (the burghers), and subdued the rebellious boyars. Using diplomacy and dynastic ties with Europe's rulers, he strove to stem the Mongol expansion. The Galicia-Volhynian state flourished under Danylo's successors. In 1272 Lviv became the capital, and in 1303 *Halych metropoly was founded. But resurgent boyar defiance, the Mongol presence, and the territorial ambitions of Poland and Hungary took their toll. The Romanovych dynasty came to an end in 1340 when boyars poisoned Prince *Yurii II Boleslav, and rivalry among the rulers of Poland, Hungary, Lithuania, and the Mongols for possession of Galicia and Volhynia ensued.

The Polish era. The struggle lasted until 1387. In 1340 King *Casimir III the Great of Poland attacked Lviv and departed with the Galician-Volhynian regalia. A boyar oligarchy ruled Galicia under the leadership of D. *Dedko until 1349, when Casimir again invaded and progressively occupied it. In 1370 Casimir's nephew, Louis I of Hungary, also became the king of Poland; he appointed Prince *Władysław Opolczyk in 1372 and Hungarian vicegerents from 1378 to govern Galicia. After the marriage of Grand Duke *Jagiełło of Lithuania and Louis's daughter, Queen *Jadwiga of Poland, and the resulting dynastic union in 1386, an agreement was reached whereby Galicia and the Kholm region were acquired from Hungary by Poland, and Volhynia became part of the Grand Duchy of Lithuania.

Under Polish rule, Galicia was known at first as the 'Rus' land' or 'Red Rus'' and was administered by a starosta, or vicegerent, appointed by the king. Roman Catholic dioceses were established in Peremyshl, Halych, and Kholm and were granted large estates and government subsidies. In 1365 a Catholic archdiocese was founded in Halych; it was transferred to Lviv in 1414. In the early 15th century, the region was renamed Rus' voivodeship. Its capital became Lviv, and it was divided into four lands: Lviv, Halych, Peremyshl, and Sianik; in the 16th century, the Kholm land was also incorporated. In 1434, *Rus' law was abolished in Galicia and replaced by *Polish law and the Polish administrative system. Land was distributed among the nobility, who proceeded to build up latifundia and to subject and exploit the peasants.

Major social changes occurred in Galicia. Boyars who refused to convert to Catholicism forfeited their estates. Many resettled in the Lithuanian lands; those who did not became impoverished, déclassé petty nobles and, with time, commoners. Certain boyars received royal privileges; they gradually renounced their Orthodox faith and stopped speaking Ukrainian, and became instead Polonized Catholics. The tendency to assimilate permeated all of Galicia's upper strata and was particularly prominent in the second half of the 16th century; by the end of the 17th century most of the Ukrainian nobility had become Polonized. At the same time Ukrainian merchants and artisans were deprived of their rights by the now favored Polish Catholic burghers who colonized the towns and received official positions and privileges granted solely to them by *Magdeburg law. Polish government circles encouraged the inflow of Polish and foreign nobles and Catholic peasants into Galicia. The number of Poles, Germans, Armenians, and (later) Jews increased in the towns, where they established separate communities. The government's discrimination and limitations imposed by the guilds on the Ukrainian burghers provoked them to form *brotherhoods to defend their rights towards the end of the 16th century.

In the 16th century corvée (see *Serfdom) was introduced in the Polish Commonwealth. This excessive exploitation of peasant labor, which in many cases became actual slavery, led to peasant uprisings, among them the *Mukha rebellion of 1490–2. Many peasants also escaped from the oppression to the steppe frontier of central Ukraine.

The Orthodox church, which had the support of the Ukrainian masses, had played an important role in Galicia. Yet the separate existence of Halych metropoly had been opposed from 1330 on by the metropolitans of Kiev, who resided in Moscow. Halych metropoly therefore had no hierarch in the years 1355–70 and was abolished in 1401. Halych eparchy had no bishop from 1406 to 1539. At the end of the 16th century, in response to the Roman Catholic threat as well as the Reformation, a Ukrainian Orthodox religious and cultural revival began. The defense of Ukrainian interests was assumed by the aforementioned brotherhoods. One of the first was the *Lviv Dormition Brotherhood, which existed as early as 1463, but whose earnest activity began in the 1580s, when it received Stauropegion status and founded a school, printing press, and hospital. Brotherhoods were founded in many other towns in Galicia using the one in Lviv as the model. Because of the brotherhoods, Galicia became an important center of Ukrainian cultural and religious life. The Lviv brotherhood, for example, nurtured such major Ukrainian figures as P. Sahaidachny, Y. Boretsky, Ye. Pletenetsky, Z. Kopystensky, and P. Mohyla.

After the 1596 Church Union of *Berestia established the Ruthenian Uniate church, a long period of bitter internal strife between the Ukrainian Orthodox opponents of the union and its Uniate supporters ensued. (See *Church history, *Polemical literature.) The Orthodox church lost its official status, which was not restored by the Polish king until 1632, and Galicia's role as the bastion of Ukrainian Orthodoxy was eclipsed. When the efforts of the leaders of the Hetman state to unite all the Ukrainian territories failed, the Orthodox hierarchs in Galicia and the Lviv brotherhood accepted the church union, and in 1709 Uniate Catholicism became the only faith practiced by Galicia's Ukrainians.

Under Polish rule, many Ukrainians in Galicia who opposed the Polish state's and nobles' restrictions, interdictions, and oppression fled to the east, where they participated in the organized life and events of central and eastern Ukraine and the Zaporozhian Cossacks. (Hetman P. *Sahaidachny, for example, was from Galicia.) When Hetman B. Khmelnytsky's army entered Galicia in 1648, 1649, and 1655 during the *Cossack-Polish War, Galicia's Ukrainians organized the Pokutia rebellion against the Poles in 1648, joined Khmelnytsky's forces, and many retreated with them. After the war there were other manifestations of support for pan-Ukrainian political unity by Galicia's Ukrainians, but not on a mass scale. Galicia remained primarily a theater where the Cossack and Polish armies clashed; consequently, much of its population fled and settled in the Hetman state and Slobidska Ukraine.

In the Polish era, popular reaction to Polish rule and oppression in Galicia also took the form of social banditry. The brigands, called *opryshoks, were particularly active in Subcarpathia and Pokutia from the 16th to the 19th century; their most famous leader was O. *Dovbush. From the second half of the 17th century, Poland experienced a series of wars and political, social, and economic crises leading to a general weakening of the regime that its neighbors (Austria, Prussia, and Russia) exploited. In 1772 the first partition of Poland occurred, and Galicia was annexed by the Austrian Empire.

The Austrian era. Austria laid claim to Galicia on the grounds that its empress, Maria Theresa, was also the queen of Hungary, which had occupied the Principality of Galicia-Volhynia in 1214–21 and 1370–87. The new Austrian province, called the Kingdom of Galicia and Lodomeria, had an area of some 83,000 sq km and around 2,800,000 inhabitants (in 1786). This artificial union of ethnic Ukrainian lands (with huge Polish latifundia) and Polish lands gave rise to constant disputes between the Poles and the Ukrainians under Austrian rule.

During their reigns, Austria's *Maria Theresa (1740–80) and *Joseph II (1780–90) introduced reforms to regulate landlord-peasant relations and improve the education of the clergy. In 1786 Austrian codes replaced Polish law and the *dietines were replaced by an assembly of estates composed of the magnates, nobility, and clergy, which had no real powers. All the power was placed in the hands of the Austrian bureaucracy and the imperial governor in Lemberg (Lviv). In 1782, personal subjection of the peasants was abolished and serfdom was introduced, whereby the peasantry received certain personal and property rights; this, however, was not well enforced following Joseph's death.

In general, Galicia under Austrian rule was an undeveloped and backward agricultural province that provided food products and conscripts for the empire. The new state boundaries had cut it off from the old trade routes and natural markets, resulting in the decline of its towns. But Austrian rule proved favorable to the Ukrainians' religious life and education. In 1774, the Uniate church was officially renamed the *Greek Catholic church; it and its clergy were granted the same rights and privileges as the (Polish) Roman Catholic church. Halych metropoly was reinstated in 1807 with its see in Lviv; it consisted of *Lviv and *Peremyshl eparchies. A Greek Catholic seminary, the *Barbareum (1774–84), was founded in Vienna by Maria Theresa to give the clergy a proper education. The *Greek Catholic Theological Seminary was founded in Lviv in 1783, and a special school, *Studium Ruthenum (1787–1809), was established at *Lviv University (founded in 1784) to train candidates for the priesthood who did not know Latin. These institutions prepared the future leaders of the Ukrainian cultural and national revival in Galicia, which occurred despite the fact that under the regime of State Chancellor K. von Metternich Austrian policy towards cultural and social emancipation in outlying provinces had changed for the worse. Under Leopold II, Ukrainian primary schools were abolished where Polish or German ones existed; by 1792 instruction in Ukrainian and Greek Catholic religion was very limited; and in 1812 compulsory education, introduced by Joseph II, was abolished. Lectures at Lviv University (which was closed from 1805 to 1817) were given in German and Latin, and Polish was the language of the primary schools. To counteract these developments, the church under Metropolitan M. *Levytsky began founding Ukrainian-language parochial schools, which were approved by the emperor in 1818. (See also *Education.)

Under the impact of *Romanticism and developments in Russian-ruled Ukraine and in other Slavic countries, a Ukrainian cultural and national renaissance began in Galicia in the 1820s. It was initiated by the seminary students M. *Shashkevych, Ya. *Holovatsky, and I. *Vahylevych, who were known as the *Ruthenian Triad; they published the first Galician Ukrainian miscellany, **Rusalka dnistrovaia* (The Dniester Water Nymph), in 1837. This renaissance reached it apogee in the *Revolution of 1848–9. On 22 April 1848 Governor F. *Stadion announced the abolition of serfdom in Galicia on the basis of an imperial decree. In May, elections to the first Austrian parliament were held. Thirty-nine Ukrainian deputies were elected, and they soon began demanding social reforms and the division of Galicia along national (Ukrainian and Polish) lines.

The main representative of Galician Ukrainian national aspirations became the *Supreme Ruthenian Council, which was founded in Lviv in May 1848. In its manifesto, the council proclaimed the unity of Galicia's Ukrainians with the rest of the Ukrainian people and demanded the creation of a separate crownland (province) in the Austrian Empire consisting of the Ukrainian parts of Galicia, Bukovyna, and Transcarpathia. It published the first Ukrainian newspaper, **Zoria halyts'ka.* Its representatives participated in the *Slavic Congress in Prague in June 1848, where the Ukrainians were recognized as a separate people. The council also organized a national guard, a *people's militia, and the *Ruthenian Battalion of Mountain Riflemen. The existence of the council challenged the Polish claim that Galicia was part of Poland, and Polish leaders tried to undermine the council's position by creating a pro-Polish body consisting of nobles and Polonophile intellectuals – the *Ruthenian Congress, which published the newspaper **Dnewnyk Ruskij*. During the revolution, two cultural and educational institutions, the *People's Home in Lviv and the *Halytsko-Ruska Matytsia society, were founded, and the *Congress of Ruthenian Scholars was held.

The various political and cultural activities ended with the suppression of the revolution, aided by the intervention of the Russian army in Hungary. The government of Emperor *Francis Joseph I (1848–1916) tightened its grip throughout the empire, re-established centralized rule, and introduced neoabsolutist policies. The Supreme Ruthenian Council was forced to dissolve in 1851. The Polish leaders in Galicia came to an agreement with the government whereby in exchange for their support they would have a free hand in administering the province. The devoted servant of Vienna, A. *Gołuchowski, was appointed governor (from 1865 vicegerent) of Galicia in 1849; he governed, with a few interruptions, until 1875. Gołuchowski was opposed to all Ukrainian national aspirations and Galicia's territorial division. He filled the ranks of the civil service in Galicia with Poles and Polonized Lviv University. The actions of the government disillusioned a section of the Ukrainian intelligentsia and contributed to the growth of the *Russophiles who claimed an affinity between the language of Galicia's Ukrainians and Russian. Their clerical-conservative leaders initially had a general, vague sympathy for tsarist Russia. These *Old Ruthenians, as they called themselves, cultivated a macaronic, artificial idiom called **yazychiie* by its opponents and opposed the use of the Ukrainian vernacular, which was being promoted by their opponents, the Ukrainophile *Populists. The Russophiles took control of the Halytsko-Ruska Matytsia society, the *Stauropegion Institute, and the People's Home, and created the *Kachkovsky Society in 1874. They also published the newspaper **Slovo*, the popular monthly **Nauka*, the semimonthly **Russkaia rada* and *Besieda*, and other periodicals.

The Young Ruthenians – the young, secular intellectuals of Galicia, many of whom were teachers – organized the Populist movement in reaction to the cultural and political orientation of the Russophiles. They believed in the existence of a Ukrainian nation and considered themselves to be part of it, and they championed the use of the vernacular in schools and in literature. They maintained close ties with intellectuals in Russian-ruled Ukraine, including P. Kulish, M. Kostomarov, O. Konysky, M. Drahomanov, V. Antonovych, and M. Hrushevsky. Inspired by the ideas expressed in the poetry of T. Shevchenko, the ideology of the *Cyril and Methodius Brotherhood, and the work of the *Hromada of Kiev, the Populists organized the *Ruska Besida cultural society in 1861, the *Prosvita educational society in 1868, and, with the co-operation and financial aid of Ukrainians under Russian rule, the literary Shevchenko Society in Lviv (later the *Shevchenko Scientific Society) in 1873. They began publishing various periodicals, including the widely read **Pravda*, **Dilo*, and **Zoria*. In the late 1870s a bitter struggle arose between the Russophile and Populist camps, in which the latter, supported by the students (among them I. *Franko and M. *Pavlyk) and the majority of the Ukrainian intelligentsia, emerged victorious. Thereafter the Russophiles lost most of their popular support and became peripheral to cultural developments. The support given to the Populists by leaders from Russian-ruled Ukraine, especially M. Drahomanov, helped secure their victory.

After 10 years of neoabsolutism, the constitutional period began in the Austrian state in February 1861, when the emperor issued a special patent creating a bicameral central parliament – consisting of a house of lords and a house of representatives – and provincial diets. Initially representatives to the central parliament were designated by the provincial diets, but from 1873 they were elected by four curiae: the large landowners, chambers of commerce, municipalities, and everyone else, primarily rural communities. In 1897 a fifth curia was created in which virtually every literate male could vote, and in 1907 the curiae were abolished and universal male suffrage was introduced. Greek Catholic bishops were ex-officio members of the upper house. In the lower house the number of Ukrainian members varied, the highest being 49, in 1861, and the lowest 3, in 1879. Even though the Ukrainians constituted half of the population of Austrian Galicia, their share in the diet was never more than a third, and often much less, owing to Polish control of the provincial administration and to electoral manipulation. The Ukrainian members of the central parliament and the Galician diet (in Lviv) constantly demanded the administrative and political division of Galicia along national lines, universal suffrage instead of the curial system, the expansion of the Ukrainian secondary-school network, and the creation of a Ukrainian university in Lviv.

After serfdom was abolished in 1848, the peasantry owned only tiny subsistence holdings. Until 1900, up to 40 percent of the arable land remained in the hands of the large landowners. The gentry claimed ownership of pastures and forests and the peasants no longer had the right of use, which they had previously according to the traditional 'servitudes,' but now had to pay for their use. The Polish nobility strongly opposed any improvement of the peasants' condition and the equitable distribution of land. As their population rapidly increased, the peasants were forced to subdivide their small holdings even further and to earn money by working on estates. This led to a series of agrarian strikes, the largest of which occurred in July–August 1902 with the participation of some 200,000 peasants. To alleviate the condition of the peasantry, the Populist intelligentsia strove to develop a strong *co-operative movement, *credit unions, and insurance companies. But for many impoverished peasants, even these efforts were insufficient. Beginning in the 1880s, a mass *emigration began, mainly to the United States, Canada, Brazil, and Argentina; by 1914, some 380,000 Ukrainians had left Galicia.

In the period 1867–1914, Ukrainian cultural and, to some extent, political life in Galicia underwent a remarkable growth. After the *Ems Ukase prohibited Ukrainian publications in Russian-ruled Ukraine in 1876, Galicia became the 'Piedmont' of the Ukrainian movement. Much emphasis was placed on education as the basis of national consciousness and as the means of fostering new leaders, and significant progress in this field was made, especially in the decade before the First World War. By 1914 there were 2,500 public Ukrainian-language primary schools, but only 16 gymnasiums (10 of them private) and 10 teachers' colleges. At Lviv University, 10 chairs held lectures in Ukrainian; the Chair of Ukrainian

History directed by M. *Hrushevsky was particularly important.

The Austrian government's efforts in 1890–4 to bring about a Polish-Ukrainian compromise (the so-called *New Era) because of the threat of war with Russia benefited the Poles more than the Ukrainians and did not gain popular support. It resulted, however, in a regrouping of Ukrainian political forces. The *Ukrainian Radical party (RP) was founded in 1890. The champion of agrarian socialism and anticlericalism, it opposed the policy of the New Era and the Populists who supported it. In 1895, influenced by Yu. Bachynsky's *Ukraïna Irredenta,* the RP adopted the principle of Ukrainian independence. In 1899, the majority of the Populists and certain Radicals founded the *National Democratic party (NDP). Advocating pan-Ukrainian independence as the final goal, this coalition party promoted democratic nationalism, social reform, and autonomy of the Ukrainian lands within the Austro-Hungarian Empire. Also in 1899, the socialist faction of the RP broke away and founded the *Ukrainian Social Democratic party (USDP). It pursued the goal of organizing Ukrainian workers in trade unions. In elections to the central parliament and the Galician diet, the NDP usually got about 60 percent of the Ukrainian popular vote, the RP, about 30 percent, and the USDP, about 8 percent.

In 1900, A. *Sheptytsky became the new Greek Catholic metropolitan. Under his direction the Greek Catholic church became a staunch supporter of the Ukrainian national cause, and the priests played a much more active role in civic life. At the time, Ukrainian organized life flourished because of the efforts of the Prosvita society, the sports and youth organizations *Sich and *Sokil, and the various economic and co-operative associations. Ukrainian-Polish differences were manifested by Ukrainian obstructionism in the diet, election campaign violence, Polish support of the Russophiles, Polish opposition to electoral reform, open hostility of the Poles to the creation of a separate Ukrainian university in Lviv, and student demonstrations and violence. Ethnic relations deteriorated to the extent that in 1908 the anti-Ukrainian Galician vicegerent A. Potocki was assassinated by the student M. Sichynsky. In this period international tensions came to play an important role in Galicia's domestic affairs. Worried about the impact of the Ukrainian national movement in Galicia on the population of its Ukrainian gubernias, the tsarist regime channeled much more funds to the movement's opponents in Galicia, the Russophiles, who disseminated pro-Russian propaganda in their press. The threat of a European war had existed since 1908, and on 7 December 1912, 200 leading members of the NDP, RP, and USDP met in Lviv to discuss the international crisis caused by the Balkan War. They issued a declaration reaffirming the loyalty of Galicia's Ukrainians to Austria (this loyalty was suspected by the authorities because of the Russophiles' activity) and stating that in the event of war the Ukrainians would actively support Austria against Russia, the greatest enemy of the Ukrainian people.

When the First World War broke out, the Ukrainian parties founded the Supreme Ukrainian Council in August 1914 in Lviv. Headed by K. Levytsky, the leader of the NDP, it called for struggle against Russia as a means of liberating Ukraine and sponsored the creation of a legion of volunteers, the *Ukrainian Sich Riflemen, within the Austrian army. In fall 1914, Russian forces occupied most of Galicia. Ukrainian organizations and the Ukrainian language were outlawed, and thousands of prominent Ukrainians, including Metropolitan A. Sheptytsky, were arrested and deported to the east. During the Austrian retreat tens of thousands of Ukrainians suspected, rightly or wrongly, of sympathizing with Russia or being Russian agents were summarily executed; thousands were deported to internment camps, of which *Talerhof near Graz was the largest.

The Russian occupational administration under G. Bobrinsky pursued a policy of Russification with the co-operation of local Russophiles. Ukrainian leaders who had avoided deportation fled westward, mostly to Vienna. There, in May 1915, the *General Ukrainian Council (GUC) was founded as the highest political representation of Ukrainians in the Austrian Empire. It consisted not only of 24 Galician and 7 Bukovynian representatives, but also of 3 members of the *Union for the Liberation of Ukraine, an organization of political émigrés from Russian-ruled Ukraine. In spring 1915, Austrian armies reoccupied most of Galicia, except for a strip of land between the Seret and Zbruch rivers. The GUC strove to obtain territorial autonomy for the Ukrainians of Galicia, but the Austrian regime sided with the Polish conservatives who proposed a Polish state consisting of Congress Poland and Galicia linked with the Habsburg monarchy by ties similar to those between Austria and Hungary. The Ukrainian parliamentary deputies in Vienna, headed by Ye. *Petrushevych, spoke out against the Polish proposal, demanding a separate Galician Ukrainian province and the guarantee of national autonomy well before the end of the war. The establishment of an autonomous Ukrainian government in Central Ukraine in 1917 – the *Central Rada in Kiev – encouraged the Galician Ukrainian deputies to demand autonomy and, in late 1918, independence and the union of Galicia with the *Ukrainian National Republic. Galician autonomy was demanded by the Ukrainian delegation during negotiations of the Peace Treaty of *Brest-Litovsk with the Central Powers and was the subject of a secret additional agreement between the UNR and the Austro-Hungarian government signed on 9 February 1918.

The period of Western Ukrainian statehood. Before the collapse of the Habsburg state, Galician and Bukovynian political leaders – the members of parliament and the provincial diets and party delegates – gathered in Lviv on 18 October 1918 and created a constituent assembly, the *Ukrainian National Rada. Headed by Ye. Petrushevych, it proclaimed a Ukrainian state on the territories of Galicia, northern Bukovyna, and Ukrainian Transcarpathia. On 1 November, the Rada seized the government buildings in Lviv and in the county towns of Galicia, thus bringing to an end nearly 150 years of Austrian rule. On 9 November, the Rada defined the structure of the new Western Ukrainian National Republic (ZUNR) and elected its executive body – the *State Secretariat headed by K. Levytsky. From the start, the ZUNR encountered stubborn opposition from the Poles, and heavy fighting ensued. On 21 November, the Rada was forced to quit Lviv and move to Ternopil and, in late December, to Stanyslaviv. The ZUNR began negotiating unification with the UNR, and on 3 January 1919 the Rada ratified the law on unification. The union of the two states was officially proclaimed in Kiev on 22 January 1919 and confirmed by the pan-Ukrainian *Labor Congress there.

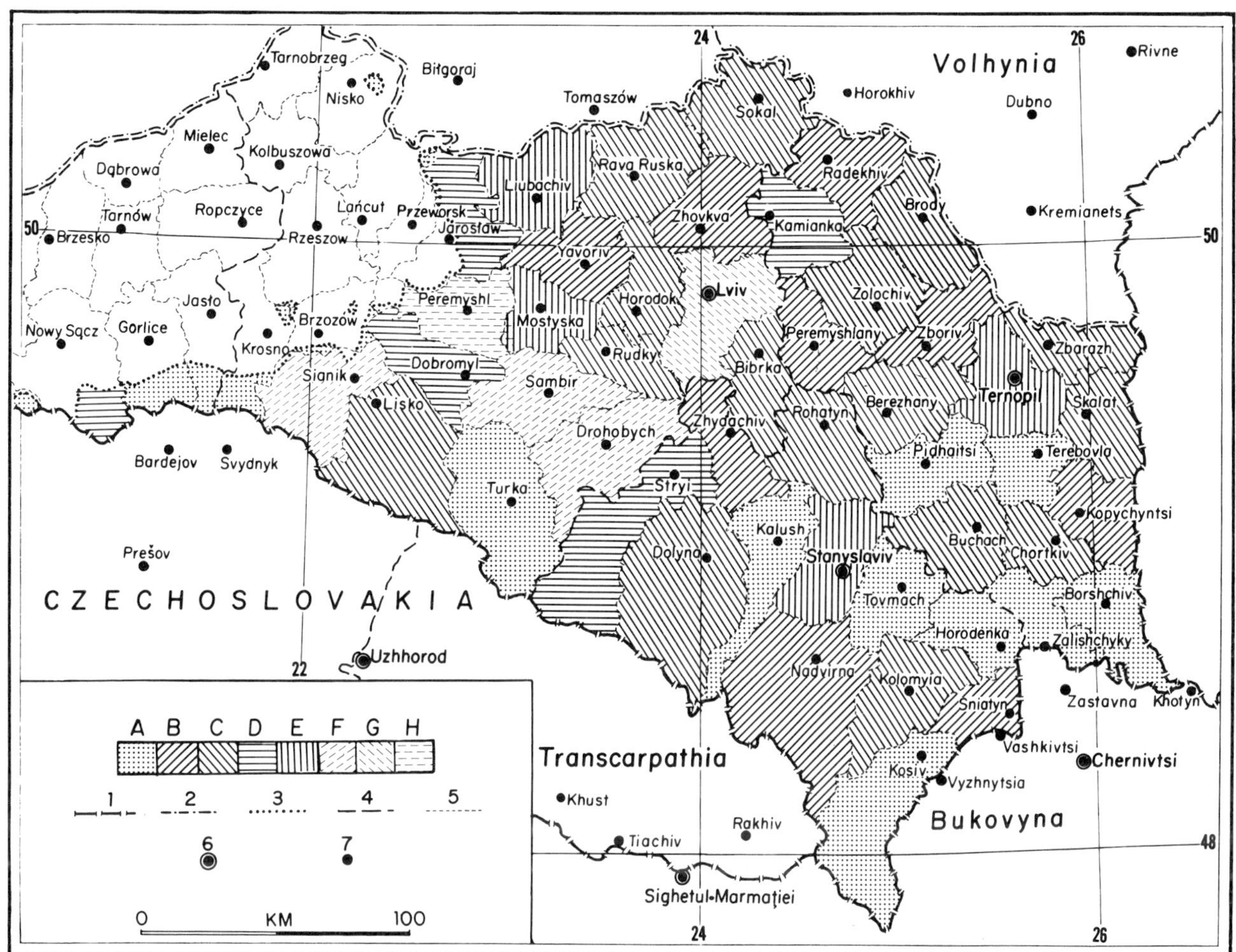

GALICIA IN THE 1920S

*Population with Ukrainian as the mother tongue**

A. 85 percent and over
B. 80–84.9 percent
C. 75–79.9 percent
D. 70–74.9 percent
E. 65–69.9 percent
F. 60–64.9 percent
G. 55–59.9 percent
H. 50–54.9 percent

*Including Roman Catholic Ukrainians and Ukrainianized Poles

1. State borders
2. Boundaries of Galicia within the Austrian Empire
3. Ukrainian-Polish ethnic boundary
4. Voivodeship boundaries
5. County boundaries
6. Voivodeship capitals
7. County towns

National unification did not change the situation in Galicia where the administration remained in local Ukrainian hands (see *Dictatorship of the Western Province of the Ukrainian National Republic), and the *Ukrainian Galician Army (UHA) continued fighting the advancing Polish army, reinforced by the divisions of Gen J. *Haller. The *Ukrainian-Polish War in Galicia lasted until July 1919, when the Ukrainian government and the UHA were forced to retreat east across the Zbruch River. The UHA fought alongside the *Army of the UNR against the Red Army (see *Ukrainian-Soviet War). The ZUNR government under Ye. Petrushevych went into exile in late 1919 and continued a diplomatic struggle from Vienna and Paris for the independence of Galicia and its recognition by the Entente Powers. During the Red Army's offensive against Poland in Galicia, the *Galician Socialist Soviet Republic existed from July to September 1920 and was headed by a Moscow-backed provisional government – the *Galician Revolutionary Committee led by V. Zatonsky. Poland emerged victorious in the Polish-Soviet War, and its occupation of Galicia and western Volhynia was recognized in the Peace Treaty of *Riga in March 1921. In March 1923 the *Conference of Ambassadors accepted that Ukrainian Galicia was part of Poland but with the proviso that Galicia would retain a certain degree of autonomy. This proviso was never honored by the interwar Polish government.

Galicia within interwar Poland, 1919–39. Well before the final international recognition of Galicia as part of Poland, Galicia was being administered as an integral part of Poland. In 1920 Galicia's diet was formally abolished. Galicia was divided among the voivodeships of Cracow, Lviv, Stanyslaviv, and Ternopil; the latter three constituted 'Eastern Little Poland,' and its Ukrainian inhabitants were officially referred to as Ruthenians (*Rusini*). The Ukrainians were subjected to a regime of terror – mass arrests, imprisonment in concentration camps, deportation, and the outlawing of Ukrainian organizations and periodicals. Ukrainians' access to government employment was denied. The region was left in a state of economic stagnation (made worse by wartime destruction), and the plight of the landless peasants was exacerbated by the officially promoted colonization of Galicia by ethnic Polish peasants.

The Ukrainians reacted by refusing to recognize the Polish regime. They boycotted the census of Galicia taken on 30 September 1921 and the 1922 elections to the Polish Sejm and Senate. The Ukrainian Labor, Radical, Social Democratic, and Christian Social parties joined forces in the *Interparty Council (1919–23), which decided what lawful tactics to use against Polish policies and protested against the Polish occupation. Because Ukrainians were effectively excluded from Lviv University in the early 1920s and the university's Ukrainian chairs and lectureships were abolished, the Ukrainians organized various clandestine courses and then the *Lviv (Underground) Ukrainian University (1921–5). Revolutionary nationalist struggle against the regime took the form of the underground *Ukrainian Military Organization (UVO), led by Ye. Konovalets, beginning in 1920.

In 1923, Ukrainian political tactics toward the regime began to change. Old parties were reconstituted, and new ones were formed. From 1925 the *Ukrainian National Democratic Alliance (UNDO) continued in the pragmatic tradition of the prewar National Democratic party and the *Ukrainian Labor party (1919–25) to obtain certain advantages for the Ukrainians. It dominated several central cultural-educational and economic institutions – Prosvita society, the Audit Union of Ukrainian Co-operatives, the Tsentrosoiuz union of farming and trade associations, and the Dnister fire-insurance association – and controlled the influential daily *Dilo*. The Ukrainian Socialist Radical party replaced the Ukrainian Radical party in 1926. The Ukrainian Social Democratic party became pro-Soviet in 1923, was suppressed in 1924, and was revived in 1928 as a member of the Second International. Various parties of the *Christian Social Movement remained active throughout the period. The Sovietophile *Sel-Rob (Ukrainian Peasants' and Workers' Socialist Alliance) was founded in 1926, split into two factions in 1927, and was suppressed in 1932. Its majority supported the illegal, underground *Communist Party of Western Ukraine, founded in 1919 as the Communist Party of Eastern Galicia, which advocated Galicia's unification with Soviet Ukraine. After the party split in 1927 into a national-Communist majority (which was expelled from the *Communist International in 1928) and a Stalinist minority, it lost much of its support. The underground *Organization of Ukrainian Nationalists replaced the UVO in 1929. Its leader remained Ye. Konovalets, and its main base of support, as well as its main area of activity, was in Galicia. The Polish government responded to the revolutionary sabotage of the UVO-OUN and Ukrainian opposition to the regime with the military and police *Pacification of Galicia in the fall of 1930 – the destruction of Ukrainian institutional property, brutalization of Ukrainian leaders and activists, and mass arrests. This did not deter the OUN, which intensified its anti-Polish activity and assassinated the Polish minister of internal affairs, B. Pieracki, in 1934, giving the regime the pretext to establish the *Bereza Kartuzka concentration camp and to arrest and convict various OUN leaders, including S. *Bandera and M. *Lebed.

The legal activity of the Ukrainian parties in Galicia in the Polish Sejm and Senate from 1928 did not produce significant results. The UNDO's efforts at reaching a Polish-Ukrainian compromise in the 1930s – the so-called *Normalization – were inconclusive, because of the chauvinistic attitude of the Polish authorities and society at large and the increasingly authoritarian and repressive policies of the military rule under J. *Piłsudski.

Ukrainian culture and education suffered under interwar Polish rule. In 1921 education in Poland was centralized, and in 1924 Ukrainian and Polish schools were unified and made bilingual. By the 1930s many of these schools were Polish. To counterbalance the Polonization of education, Ukrainians began opening private schools with the help of the *Ridna Shkola Ukrainian pedagogical society. In the latter half of the 1930s, nearly 60 percent of all Ukrainian gymnasiums, teachers' colleges, and vocational schools, with about 40 percent of all Ukrainian students, were privately run. Between the wars, the co-operative movement became better organized and helped the Ukrainian farmers and farm workers – the majority of the Ukrainian population – to withstand economic instability and the Great Depression. The leading co-operative institutions were the *Audit Union of Ukrainian Co-operatives, the *Tsentrosoiuz union, the *Maslosoiuz dairy association, the *Silskyi Hospodar farmers' association, and the *Union of Ukrainian Merchants and Entrepreneurs. They and other groups, such as the rapidly expanding women's movement and its organization, *Union of Ukrainian Women, also contributed a great deal to the cultural development of Galicia's Ukrainians.

As in the Austrian era, the Ukrainians continued to maintain their own scholarly life, literature, press, and book publishing. The leading scholarly institutions were the Shevchenko Scientific Society and the *Ukrainian Theological Scholarly Society, both of which published books and serials. Important scholarly, political, and cultural works were also published in the Basilian Fathers' **Analecta Ordinis S. Basilii Magni / Zapysky ChSVV* and in the leading Galician journal, **Literaturno-naukovyi vistnyk*, which in 1932 was replaced by **Vistnyk*, edited by the influential D. *Dontsov.

The Second World War. On the basis of the secret *Molotov-Ribbentrop Pact, which divided Eastern Europe into German and Soviet spheres of influence on 23 August 1939, Galicia east of the Sian River was occupied by the Red Army between 17 and 23 September after Germany invaded Poland on 1 September. Soviet-style elections were held on 22 October to a *People's Assembly of Western Ukraine, which in turn 'requested' the incorporation of the region into Soviet Ukraine. This request was ratified by the Supreme Soviet of the USSR on 1 November. A Soviet administration was immediately set up in Galicia. The new regime introduced fundamental changes – collectivization of agriculture, the nationalization of industry, the reorganization of the educational system on the Soviet model, albeit with Ukrainian as the language of instruction, the abolition of all existing Ukrainian institutions and periodicals, and the curtailment of the churches' activities. On 4 December Galicia was divided into four oblasts: Lviv, Drohobych, Stanyslaviv, and Ternopil. Many Ukrainian political and cultural leaders managed to flee west across the Sian and Buh rivers into the German-held *Generalgouvernement of Poland, but many others did not. Thousands were arrested and deported to the east or died in prisons.

Germany broke the non-aggression pact and invaded the USSR on 22 June 1941. The German army took Lviv on 30 June 1941 and overran all of Galicia in July. Before they retreated, the Soviets executed some 10,000 Ukrainians who had been imprisoned in Galicia.

On 30 June 1941 in Lviv, the *Bandera faction of OUN, which had organized the *Legion of Ukrainian Nationalists to fight with the Germans against the Bolsheviks, proclaimed the re-establishment of the Ukrainian state in Western Ukraine and formed the *Ukrainian State Administration under Ya. Stetsko. This government was suppressed by the Germans on 12 July, and its members and leading OUN members were arrested.

On 1 August, Galicia became the fifth district of the Generalgouvernement. The German annexation was protested by the *Ukrainian National Council (UNC), a public body representing Galicia's Ukrainians that was founded in Lviv on 30 July and headed by K. Levytsky (the honorary president was Metropolitan A. Sheptytsky). The UNC in Lviv was suppressed in March 1942 after Metropolitan Sheptytsky sent a letter to Himmler protesting against the Germans' persecution of the Jews. The *Ukrainian Regional Committee, founded in September 1941, remained the only legal civic umbrella institution; its general secretary was K. Pankivsky. In March 1942, the functions of the committee were taken over by the *Ukrainian Central Committee (UCC) based in Cracow, which had represented Ukrainians in the Generalgouvernement since 1940; V. *Kubijovyč was its president, and Pankivsky became the vice-president. Ukrainian civic, cultural, and educational institutions were allowed by the German authorities (Gov Gen H. *Frank and Gov O. *Wächter) within the framework of the UCC. Besides organizing the Ukrainians economically and culturally and overseeing relief work, the UCC was instrumental in the creation of the volunteer *Division Galizien in April 1943.

Compared to other Ukrainian territories under Nazi rule, Galicia was relatively better off. Nonetheless, the regime there was very severe: acts aimed at gaining political independence were forbidden; all opposition was brutally suppressed; and the vast majority of Galicia's Jews and Gypsies, as well as many Ukrainians, were murdered or sent to Nazi death camps. From June 1943, the *Ukrainian Insurgent Army (UPA) engaged in guerrilla warfare from its bases in the Carpathian Mountains against both the Germans and S. *Kovpak's Soviet partisans. As the Germans began retreating from Galicia, leaving Ternopil in April 1944, Lviv and Stanyslaviv in July, and Drohobych in August, the UPA and its political leadership, the *Ukrainian Supreme Liberation Council, continued their struggle against the advancing Red Army.

The Soviet period. When the USSR reoccupied all of Galicia in the fall of 1944, the prewar Soviet regime was reinstalled. The mass persecution of Ukrainians who had cooperated with the German regime or had fought for Ukrainian sovereignty (ie, members of the OUN and soldiers of the UPA and the Division Galizien) ensued. Many Ukrainians were executed, and many others were sentenced to maximum terms in labor camps or deported to Soviet Asia. The official attitude towards the Ukrainian Catholic church was one of extreme hostility. Metropolitan A. Sheptytsky died on 1 November 1944. The hierarchs of the church, including the new metropolitan, Y. Slipy, were arrested on 11 April 1945 and sentenced to long terms in prison, where most of them died. The Soviet-staged *Sobor of the Greek Catholic Church held in Lviv on 8–10 March 1946 renounced the Church Union of Berestia and decreed the abolition of the Ukrainian Catholic church and its 'reunification' with the Russian Orthodox church. Priests who refused to submit to these changes were imprisoned and/or deported. Well before the Soviet takeover, a large number of the Galician Ukrainian intelligentsia had fled westward. When the war ended, they became *displaced persons in Germany.

According to a Soviet-Polish agreement made in Moscow on 16 August 1945, the border between Polish- and Soviet-occupied Galicia ran along the *Curzon Line; thus the Sian region (including Peremyshl) and the Kholm and Lemko regions were ceded to Poland. Soon after, Poles living on Soviet territory were resettled in Poland, and most of the Ukrainians living in the above regions were forcibly resettled in the Soviet Ukraine or in the regions newly acquired by Poland from Germany. In 1951 the border between Poland and Lviv oblast was slightly modified. The forcible depopulation of Ukrainians in the border regions was calculated to destroy the social base of the UPA, which continued its activity in the Carpathian Mountains until the mid-1950s.

Because of the profound political, administrative, cultural, religious, social, economic, and demographic changes that have occurred under Soviet rule, historical Galicia has ceased to exist. The name is no longer used officially; instead, 'Western Ukraine' is now used to designate the territory of former Galicia (Lviv, Ternopil, and Ivano-Frankivske oblasts) together with western Volhynia (Volhynia and Rivne oblasts), northern Bukovyna (Chernivtsi oblast), and Transcarpathia (Transcarpathia oblast).

Population. Galicia has long been the most densely populated part of Ukraine. Although in 1939 it constituted only 6 percent of all Ukrainian ethnic territory, it had 10.5 percent of the latter's total population and almost 10 percent of all Ukrainians. Galicia was already densely populated during the Princely era. Most densely populated were the vicinities of Peremyshl, Lviv, and Halych. From the 13th to the 16th century, the population increased because of the influx of Ukrainians from the east and Polish colonists from the west. From the 15th to the 18th century Galicia also experienced population losses, caused primarily by the peasantry's flight from serfdom to the steppe frontier. After the Austrian annexation, this large-scale flight was stemmed because the Russian-Austrian border now separated Galicia from the rest of Ukraine, and the population rose steadily. It increased by 45 percent between 1869 and 1910. This growth was interrupted only by mass emigration, beginning in the 1890s. In 1939, the average population density in Galicia was 104 per sq km; in the belt between Peremyshl and Pokutia it was as high as 150 per sq km. The urban population grew slowly, from 19 percent in 1900 to 23 percent in 1931; the greatest growth occurred in Lviv and in the towns of the *Drohobych-Boryslav Industrial Region. The cities with over 20,000 inhabitants in 1931 (their 1984 pop is given in parentheses) were Lviv, 316,000 (728,000); Stanyslaviv (Ivano-Frankivske), 60,000 (200,000); Peremyshl 51,000 (61,000); Boryslav, 42,000 (34,000 in 1968); Ternopil, 36,000 (175,000); Kolomyia, 33,000 (59,000); Drohobych, 33,000 (73,000); Stryi, 31,000 (60,000); and Sambir, 22,000 (32,000 in 1975).

Until the Second World War, Galicia was one of the most overpopulated agrarian regions in Europe, with 101 agriculturalists per 100 ha of arable land (the corresponding figure for all of Ukraine was 54, for Germany, 51, and for Holland, 70). In the last 100 years, certain demographic trends can be singled out: (a) until 1890, a small annual growth (around 1.1 percent) and a high mortality rate; (b) from 1890 to 1914, an average annual natural increase of 14–15 per 1,000 inhabitants (in 1911–13, the birth rate was 40.3 and the mortality rate was 25.9 per 1,000), mass emigration overseas (a total of 380,000 persons), a high rate of seasonal migration for work (up to 100,000 annually), and an influx of Poles into the towns and the countryside; (c) from 1914 to 1921, a population decline of 12 percent; (d) from 1920 to 1939, a sharp decline in natural growth (eg, in 1938 there were 23.9 births and 15.6 deaths per 1,000 inhabitants) and a decrease in emigration (a total of 120,000) and in the influx of Poles; (e) from 1939 to 1945, continued decline in natural growth, the almost total extermination of the Jewish population, the resettlement of the Ukrainian and Polish populations on either side of the new, postwar Soviet-Polish border, the emigration of over 100,000 Ukrainians to the West, and the deportation of an unknown but large number of Ukrainians to the Soviet east; and (f) in the postwar period, a nearly normal rate of natural increase, *migration of part of the population to other Soviet regions (particularly to the Donbas and the virgin lands of Central Asia), intensive *urbanization, and a large influx of Russians.

Because of centuries-long Polish expansion there, Galicia was the first region of Ukraine to cease being purely Ukrainian; this process transpired first in the towns and later in the most fertile areas of the countryside. The percentage of Poles and/or Roman Catholics increased because their in-migration occurred at the same time as the mass emigration of Ukrainians. In the period 1880–1939 the number of Roman Catholics rose from 19.9 to 25 percent, while the number of Greek Catholics and Jews fell from 66.8 to 64.4 percent and 12.3 to 9.8 percent respectively. An intermediate ethnic category arose, the so-called **Latynnyky* (Ukrainian-speaking Roman Catholics), ie, either Ukrainians who had converted to Roman Catholicism or the descendants of Polish colonists who had to a large degree assimilated into the Ukrainian milieu. A smaller transitional category consisted of Ukrainian Catholics living in a Polish milieu who had become linguistically Polonized (mainly in the western borderlands and in Lviv).

It has been estimated by V. Kubijovyč (1983) that on 1 January 1939 Galicia had a population of 5,824,100, consisting (percentages are given in parentheses) of 3,727,600 Ukrainians (64.1); 16,400 Polish-speaking Ukrainian Greek Catholics (0.3); 947,500 Poles (16.2), of whom 72,300 (1.2) arrived in the years 1920–39; 515,100 *Latynnyky* (8.8); 569,300 Jews (9.8); and 49,000 Germans and other ethnic minorities (0.8).

Economy. In the Princely era, the economic base of Galicia changed gradually from hunting and utilization of forest resources to agriculture. At the time, grain, as well as hides and wax, was already being exported to Byzantium. Trade in salt mined in Subcarpathia was of particular economic importance. It was exported west via the Sian River and east to Kiev via land trade routes. From the 12th century, Galicia played the role of intermediary in the trade between the West and the Black Sea. In the 15th and 16th centuries, an economy based on the **filvarok* developed; the nobility exploited the peasantry in order to export as much grain, beef, wax, and timber products as possible to the rest of Europe. At the same time the salt industry grew, and other industries, such as liquor distilling, brewing, and arms manufacturing (in Lviv), arose. In the 16th century, trade with lands to the east became more difficult; the cities and towns declined because of the detrimental policies of the Polish nobility. Incessant wars and the oppression of the Ukrainian burghers and peasantry resulted in the impoverishment of the population. When Austria annexed Galicia in 1772, it was a poor, backward, and overpopulated land.

Under Austria, Galicia's depressed economy only minimally improved. Its recovery was hindered by a thoroughly unhealthy agrarian system (which did not change even after the abolition of serfdom) and by Austrian economic policies that maintained Galicia as a primarily agricultural internal colony from which the western Austrian provinces could draw cheap farm produce and timber and which they could use as a ready market for their manufactured goods (particularly textiles). Small industrial enterprises (most of them in the hands of landowners), such as textile factories, foundries, glass works, salt mines, paper mills, and sugar refineries, that had been productive in the first half of the 19th century declined thereafter because they were unable to compete with the industries of the western provinces and could not modernize because of a lack of capital, the absence of indigenous coal and iron ore, the long distance from Austria's industrial centers, and poor commercial and communication links with the rest of Ukraine. Only the food industry (distilling and milling by small enterprises) and, beginning in the 1850s, the *petroleum industry were developed in Galicia, and only the latter attracted foreign investment. Intensive agriculture could not develop because the peasants had little land, which was further parceled among the family members, and no capital, while the large landowners preferred to maintain the status quo and showed no initiative. Only emigration saved the peasants from destitution; with the exception of Transcarpathia, this process was more significant in Galicia than anywhere else in Ukraine.

Under interwar Poland, Galicia's economic state became even worse. Rural overpopulation increased because of a decline in emigration and the mass influx of Polish colonists, and industry deteriorated even further. The situation of the Ukrainian population became even more precarious with its exclusion from jobs in the civil service and in Polish-owned enterprises. Only through self-organization, especially through the co-operative movement, were the Ukrainians able to avoid economic ruin.

The postwar Soviet annexation placed Galicia's economy on a par with that of the rest of Ukraine. Agriculture was collectivized, and intensive cultivation of industrial crops, mainly sugar beets and corn, was introduced. Great changes occurred in the industrial sector by way of the large-scale exploitation of energy resources and the introduction of new industries.

In general Galicia's economy had been neglected for centuries, and its economic potential – based on its generally good farmland and propitious climate (milder and more humid than in other parts of Ukraine), sources of energy (rivers, petroleum, natural gas, timber, peat, lignite, and anthracite), and abundant labor supply – has been underdeveloped. As late as 1931, for example, 74.6 percent of the population (88 percent of the Ukrainians) were still engaged in agriculture, while only 10.9 percent (5.8 percent) were engaged in industry, 4.7 percent (1.7 percent) in trade and transport, and 9.8 percent (4.4 percent) in other professions. Arable land and farmsteads took up 52 percent of the territory; pastures, grassland, and meadows, 18 percent; forest, 25 percent; and other land, 5 percent. In the Carpathian Mountains forest took up 43 percent; pastures and meadows, 35 percent; and arable land, only 16 percent. In eastern Galician Podilia and Pokutia, arable land took up 77 percent. In Roztochia, western Galician Podilia, and Subcarpathia, arable land took up 50 percent (25 percent was forest and 20 percent was meadows and pastures).

Before the Second World War, Galicia had a sown area of 2,540,000 ha, of which 470,000 ha (18.5 percent) were devoted to wheat, 520,000 ha (20.5 percent) to rye, 220,000 ha (8.7 percent) to barley, 390,000 ha (15.4 percent) to oats, 80,000 ha (3.2 percent) to corn, 60,000 ha (2.4 percent) to buckwheat, 20,000 ha (0.8 percent) to millet, 440,000 ha (17.3 percent) to potatoes, 260,000 ha (10.2 percent) to fodder crops, and 50,000 ha (2.0 percent) to industrial crops (of which sugar beets took up 11,000 ha; flax, 13,000 ha; hemp, 15,000 ha; and rape, 5,000 ha). After the war, the area sown with industrial crops (especially with sugar beets and corn) was increased. In the Carpathian Mountains, oats and potatoes predominated; corn predominated in Pokutia and southeast Podilia; and more wheat than rye was grown in Pokutia, eastern Podilia, and Sokal county.

The poverty of the peasantry is reflected by their holdings in the 1930s. Landowning peasants together possessed only 55 percent of the land, including forests and pastures (80 percent of the arable land); 52 percent of the peasants had less than 2 ha each, 37 percent had from 2 to 5 ha, and only 11 percent had more than 5 ha. Landlessness was rampant and constantly increasing. Consequently, intensive crop growing was not possible, and harvest yields were very low, on the average 5,000 kg of grain and 5,500 kg of potatoes per ha. Even though the population had barely enough food for its own use (before the war, an annual per capita average of 90 kg of wheat and rye, 70 kg of other grain, and 395 kg of potatoes), 200,000 t of wheat and barley were annually exported from Galicia, and only a small amount of rye flour was imported. Animal husbandry was practiced more intensively and constituted the basis of the peasant budget. In 1936, for example (figures in parentheses are per 100 ha of arable land and per 100 inhabitants), 649,000 (17, 11) horses, 1,602,000 (42, 28) head of cattle, of which 1,116,000 were cows, 648,000 (17, 11) pigs, and 387,000 (10, 7) goats and sheep were raised. In general the livestock density in relation to the farmland area in Galicia was greater than elsewhere in Ukraine, and the population's livestock supply was adequate. Horticulture, orcharding (including viticulture in southeast Podilia), and beekeeping played a secondary role.

Industry in Galicia before 1945 was less developed than elsewhere in Ukraine. Manufacturing was based on the processing of indigenous raw materials, including agricultural products, timber, petroleum, and potassium salts; there was practically no textile industry or metallurgy. Therefore the prewar industrial work force was small (with a maximum of 44,000 in 1938), only 2.2 percent of Galicia's hydroelectric capacity was exploited, and electrification proceeded very slowly. Low-grade lignite was mined around Kolomyia, Rava-Ruska, Zhovkva, and Zolochiv, but not on a large scale because of competition from Silesia's coal companies (see *Subcarpathian Lignite Region). Petroleum extraction near Boryslav, Bytkiv, Nadvirna, and elsewhere in the *Subcarpathian Petroleum and Natural Gas Region was 2,100,000 t (5 percent of world production) in 1909; it fell to 717,000 t in 1938. The natural-gas industry arose in 1923 and was centered in *Dashava, which supplied gas to towns in Subcarpathia; in 1938 215 million cu m of gas were extracted. Salt mines near Drohobych, Dobromyl, Bolekhiv, and Dolyna produced in the prewar years a mere 40,000 t, or 2 percent of Ukraine's salt. Ozocerite was mined near Boryslav, Truskavets, Starunia, and Dzvyniach; its production fell from 12,300 t in 1885 to 600 t in 1938. The mining of potassium salt near Stebnyk and Kalush increased, reaching 567,000 t in 1938. The lumber industry in Subcarpathia was well developed; two-thirds of its products were exported. The food industry was underdeveloped; it produced primarily flour, beer, liquor, meat and dairy products, and beet sugar (only three sugar refineries existed before the war). The building-materials industry produced, on a limited scale, glass (in Lviv and Stryi), plaster of paris and lime (in the Dniester Basin), bricks, and tiles. Light industry was not developed enough to supply the population's needs; small companies manufactured leather, wadding, quilts, curtains, shoes, and clothing accessories. Machine building was not well developed; it was based in Lviv and Sianik.

Before the Soviet period artisans and the cottage industry played an important role in Galicia, especially in the Hutsul region. *Health resorts, *mineral waters, and spas, most of them in the Carpathian Mountains, attracted thousands of visitors. The network of railroads and highways was denser than elsewhere in Ukraine, but most roads were in a state of disrepair. Rivers were used merely to float timber to sawmills. (For the economy of postwar Galicia, see *Ivano-Frankivske oblast, *Lviv oblast, and *Ternopil oblast.)

BIBLIOGRAPHY

Zubritskii, D. *Kritiko-istoricheskaia povest' vremennykh let Chervonoi, ili Galitskoi Rusi* (Moscow 1845)

Sharanevych, Y. *Ystoriia Halytsko-Volodymyrskoy Rusy ot naidavniishykh vremen do roku 1453* (Lviv 1863)

Levytskyi, I. *Halytsko-ruskaia bybliohrafiia XIX-ho stolitiia s uvzhliadneniiem ruskykh izdanii poiavyvshykhsia v Uhorshchyni i Bukovyni (1801–1886)*, 2 vols (Lviv 1888, 1895)

Zanevych, I. [Terlets'kyi, O.]. *Znesenie panshchyny v Halychyni: Prychynok do istoriï suspil'noho zhytia i suspil'nykh pohliadiv 1830–1848 rr.* (Lviv 1895)

Die österreichisch-ungarische Monarchie in Wort und Bild, 12: *Galizien* (Vienna 1898)

Franko, I. (ed). *Materiialy do kul'turnoï istoriï Halyts'koï Rusy XVIII i XIX viku* (Lviv 1902)
Mises, L. von. *Die Entwicklung des gutsherrlich-bäuerlichen Verhältnisses in Galizien (1772–1848)* (Vienna 1902)
Bujak, F. *Galicya*, 2 vols (Lviv 1908–9)
Krevets'kyi, I. 'Halychyna v druhii polovyni XVIII v.,' *ZNTSh*, 91 (Lviv 1909)
Baran, S. *Statystyka seredn'oho shkil'nytstva u Skhidnii Halychyni v rr. 1848–1898* (Lviv 1910)
Franko, I. *Panshchyna i ïï skasuvannia v 1848 r. v Halychyni* (Lviv 1913)
Bujak, F. *Rozwój gospodarczy Galicyi (1772–1914)* (Lviv 1917)
Doroshenko, D. 'Rosiis'ka okupatsiia Halychyny 1914–1916 rr.,' *Nashe mynule*, 1 (Kiev 1918)
Doroshenko, V. 'Zakhidn'o-ukraïns'ka Narodna Respublika,' *LNV*, 1919, nos 1–3
Studyns'kyi, K. (ed). 'Materiialy dlia istoriï kul'turnoho zhyttia v Halychyni v 1795–1857 rr.,' *URA*, 13–14 (Lviv 1920)
Lozyns'kyi, M. *Halychyna v rr. 1918–1920* (Vienna 1922, New York 1970)
Vozniak, M. *Iak probudylosia ukraïns'ke narodnie zhyttia v Halychyni za Avstriï* (Lviv 1924)
Levyts'kyi, K. *Istoriia politychnoï dumky halyts'kykh ukraïntsiv 1848–1914*, 2 vols (Lviv 1926–7)
Shymonovych, I. *Halychyna: Ekonomichno-statystychna rozvidka* (Kiev 1928)
Levyts'kyi, K. *Istoriia vyzvol'nykh zmahan' halyts'kykh ukraïntsiv z chasu svitovoï viiny*, 3 vols (Lviv 1929–30)
Kuz'ma, O. *Lystopadovi dni 1918 r.* (Lviv 1931, New York 1960)
Pasternak, Ia. *Korotka arkheolohiia zakhidno-ukraïns'kykh zemel'* (Lviv 1932)
Andrusiak, M. *Geneza i kharakter halyts'koho rusofil'stva v XIX–XX st.* (Prague 1941)
Barvins'kyi, B. *Korotka istoriia Halychyny* (Lviv 1941)
Baran, S. *Zemel'ni spravy v Halychyni* (Augsburg 1948)
Matsiak, V. *Halyts'ko-Volyns'ka derzhava 1290–1340 rr. u novykh doslidakh* (Augsburg 1948)
Pashuto, V. *Ocherki po istorii Galitsko-Volynskoi Rusi* (Moscow 1950)
Kieniewicz, S. (ed). *Galicja w dobie autonomicznej (1850–1914): Wybór tekstów* (Wrocław 1952)
Babii, B. *Vozz'iednannia Zakhidnoï Ukraïny z Ukraïns'koiu RSR* (Kiev 1954)
Materialy i doslidzhennia z arkheolohiï Prykarpattia i Volyni, 1–5 (Kiev 1954–64)
Tyrowicz, M. (ed). *Galicja od pierwszego rozbioru do wiosny ludów 1772–1849: Wybór tekstów źródłowych* (Cracow 1956)
Z istoriï Zakhidnoukraïns'kykh zemel', 1–8 (Kiev 1957–63)
Najdus, W. *Szkice z historii Galicji*, 2 vols (Warsaw 1958–60)
Grzybowski, K. *Galicja 1848–1914: Historia ustroju politycznego na tle historii ustroju Austrii* (Cracow 1959)
Herbil's'kyi, H. *Peredova suspil'na dumka v Halychyni (30-i–seredyna 40-ykh rokiv XIX stolittia)* (Lviv 1959)
Kravets', M. *Narysy robitnychoho rukhu v Zakhidnii Ukraïni v 1921–1939 rr.* (Kiev 1959)
Kompaniiets', I. *Stanovyshche i borot'ba trudiashchykh mas Halychyny, Bukovyny ta Zakarpattia na pochatku XX st. (1900–1919 roky)* (Kiev 1960)
Sokhotskyi, I. (ed). *Istorychni postati Halychyny XIX–XX st.* (New York-Paris-Sidney-Toronto 1961)
Steblii, F. *Borot'ba selian skhidnoï Halychyny proty feodal'noho hnitu v pershii polovyni XIX st.* (Kiev 1961)
Rozdolski, R. *Stosunki poddańcze w dawnej Galicji*, 2 vols (Warsaw 1962)
Hornowa, E. *Stosunki ekonomiczno-społeczne w miastach ziemi Halickiej w latach 1590–1648* (Opole 1963)
Herbil's'kyi, H. *Rozvytok prohresyvnykh idei v Halychyni u pershii polovyni XIX st. (do 1848 r.)* (Lviv 1964)
Kravets', M. *Selianstvo Skhidnoï Halychyny i Pivnichnoï Bukovyny u druhii polovyni XIX st.* (Lviv 1964)
Kosachevskaia, E. *Vostochnaia Galitsiia nakanune i v period revoliutsii 1848 g.* (Lviv 1965)
Sviezhyns'kyi, P. *Ahrarni vidnosyny na Zakhidnii Ukraïni v kintsi XIX–na pochatku XX st.* (Lviv 1966)
Bohachevsky-Chomiak, M. *The Spring of a Nation: The Ukrainians in Eastern Galicia in 1848* (Philadelphia 1967)
Hornowa, E. *Ukraiński obóz postępowy i jego współpraca z polską lewicą społeczną w Galicji 1876–1895* (Wrocław 1968)
Grodziski, S. *Historia ustroju społeczno-politycznego Galicji 1772–1848* (Wrocław-Warsaw-Cracow-Gdańsk 1971)
Baran, V. *Ranni slov'iany mizh Dnistrom i Pryp'iattiu* (Kiev 1972)
Hrabovets'kyi, V. *Zakhidnoukraïns'ki zemli v period narodno-vyzvol'noï viiny 1648–1654* (Kiev 1972)
Chernysh, O. (ed). *Starodavnie naselennia Prykarpattia i Volyni (Doba pervisnoobshchynnoho ladu)* (Kiev 1974)
Serhiienko, H. (ed). *Klasova borot'ba selianstva skhidnoï Halychyny (1772–1849): Dokumenty i materialy* (Kiev 1974)
Glassl, H. *Das österreichische Einrichtungswerk in Galizien (1772–1790)* (Wiesbaden 1975)
Horn, M. *Osadnictwo miejskie na Rusi Czerwonej w latach 1501–1648* (Opole 1977)
Sirka, A. *The Nationality Question in Austrian Education: The Case of Ukrainians in Galicia, 1867–1914* (Frankfurt am Main 1979)
Chernysh, O. et al (eds). *Arkheolohichni pam'iatky Prykarpattia i Volyni kam'ianoho viku* (Kiev 1981)
Markovits, A.; Sysyn, F. (eds). *Nationbuilding and the Politics of Nationalism: Essays on Austrian Galicia* (Cambridge, Mass 1982)
Himka, J.-P. *Socialism in Galicia: The Emergence of Polish Social Democracy and Ukrainian Radicalism (1860–1890)* (Cambridge, Mass 1983)
Kubiiovych, V. *Etnichni hrupy pivdennozakhidnoï Ukraïny (Halychyny) na 1.1.1939: Natsional'na statystyka i etnohrafichna karta* (Wiesbaden 1983)
Magocsi, P. *Galicia: A Historical Survey and Bibliographic Guide* (Toronto-Buffalo-London 1983)
Kozik, J. *The Ukrainian National Movement in Galicia: 1815–1849* (Edmonton 1986)

V. Kubijovyč, Ya. Pasternak, I. Vytanovych, A. Zhukovsky

Galicia Division. See Division Galizien.

Galician Army. See Ukrainian Galician Army.

Galician Battalion of the Sich Riflemen. See Sich Riflemen.

Galician metropoly. See Halych metropoly.

Galician Revolutionary Committee (Halytskyi revoliutsiinyi komitet or Halrevkom). Provisional Soviet government that briefly governed Galicia during its occupation by the Red Army in the summer of 1920. The committee was set up on 8 July 1920 in Kharkiv on V. Lenin's orders. When the Red Army troops captured eastern Galicia, the Halrevkom established itself in Ternopil on 1 August and began to issue decrees replacing existing political, legal, social, and economic institutions with Soviet ones. It created 18 departments to administer the new state called the *Galician Socialist Soviet Republic. The chairman of the committee was V. *Zatonsky and the secretary was I. Nemolovsky – both natives of eastern Ukraine, unfamiliar with conditions in Galicia. The other key members were three Galician Ukrainians – M. Baran (vice-chairman), F. Konar (replaced soon by A. Baral), and M. Levytsky – and a Galician Pole, K. Litwinowicz. Later, new members, such as M. Havryliv, M. Kozoris, I. Siiak, and I. Kulyk, were added to the committee. When the Red Army retreated under the pressure of Ukrainian and Polish forces, the committee left Galicia and was dissolved on 23 September 1920. Most of its members stayed in Soviet Ukraine, where in the 1930s some were arrested and liquidated as 'enemies of the people.'

W. Veryha

Galician Socialist Soviet Republic (Halytska Sotsiialistychna Radianska Respublika). Short-lived state set up during the Polish-Soviet War in Soviet-occupied Galicia. The Galician SSR was proclaimed on 15 July 1920 as the Red Army approached the eastern border of Galicia. On 1 August a *Galician Revolutionary Committee was established in Ternopil as the provisional government of the new state and set about reconstructing the political, social, and economic system in the territory under its control. It declared the separation of church and state and began expropriating large landholdings, nationalizing factories and businesses, and dissolving the 'bourgeois' legal system. It imposed monetary levies on the wealthy and food requisitions on the peasants. The expropriated estates and church lands were not distributed among poor, landless peasants, but were to be turned over to state farms. The committee further prohibited private trade between town and country. Public order was maintained by the Cheka.

At its height the Galician SSR encompassed 14 complete counties and parts of several other counties in eastern Galicia. Its western boundary ran from the Dniester River northwest along the Rohatyn-Bibrka line, passing east of Lviv and west of Kamianka-Strumylova (now Kamianka-Buzka) and Sokal, and then continuing along the Buh River. Its territory covered 18,000 sq km, or about a third of Galicia's area, and its population was approximately 1,800,000. The government maintained itself in Ternopil for approximately 50 days.

Young Galicians who initially volunteered for the Red Army quickly discovered that neither it nor the new state was Ukrainian. The committee that officially formed the government, and its communist officials, received their orders from Moscow. Hence, Galician Ukrainians regarded the regime as a foreign one.

By the end of September Soviet forces were expelled from Galicia by Polish and UNR units. This marked the end of the Galician SSR, which was an artificial Bolshevik creation.

BIBLIOGRAPHY
Kul'chyts'kyi, V. *Halyts'ka Sotsialistychna Radians'ka Respublika u 1920 r.* (Lviv 1965)
Tyshchyk, B. *Halyts'ka Sotsialistychna Radians'ka Respublika (1920 r.)* (Lviv 1970)
Veryha, V. *Halyts'ka Sotsiialistychna Soviets'ka Respublika (1920 r.)* (New York-Toronto-Paris-Melbourne 1986)

W. Veryha

Galician-Bukovynian Committee (Halytsko-Bukovynskyi komitet). Organization founded in Kiev in July–August 1917 to provide relief to Ukrainian prisoners of war and refugees from Galicia and Bukovyna. Its members were mostly from Western Ukraine: D. Levytsky, V. Okhrymovych, M. Shukhevych, M. Sabat, M. Baltarovych, and I. Herasymovych. Thanks to the committee's efforts, at the end of 1917 a Ukrainian Catholic church was built on Pavlovska Street in Kiev, and on 13 November 1917 the Galician Battalion of Sich Riflemen was founded.

Galician-Ruthenian Matytsia society. See Halytsko-Ruska Matytsia society.

Galician-Volhynian Chronicle. A medieval chronicle covering the years 1201–91 in the history of the Principality of Galicia-Volhynia, written in the late 1280s and preserved in the *Hypatian Chronicle compilation. An important source to the history of southwestern Rus' (Western Ukraine), it continues the record of events begun in **Povist' vremennykh lit* (The Tale of Bygone Years) and the *Kiev Chronicle. The chronology presented in individual historical narratives was introduced in the later redactions of the original (at least five) on which the general compilation was based.

The chronicle consists of a Galician section, written in Halych, encompassing events from 1201 to 1261 and centering primarily on the reign of Prince Danylo Romanovych; and a Volhynian section, written probably in Volodymyr, encompassing events in Volhynia from 1262 to 1292 during the reigns of Prince Vasylko Romanovych and his son Volodymyr and their relations with the rulers of Lithuania and Poland. The anonymous authors evaluate events and individuals from the standpoint of the need for a unified Rus' and thus for strong princes, who counteract the centrifugal actions of rebellious boyars; the authors also defend the Galician-Volhynian princes' claims to the Kievan throne. The chronicle is a valuable literary monument, whose ornamental narrative style is reminiscent of that found in **Slovo o polku Ihorevi* (The Tale of Ihor's Campaign).

BIBLIOGRAPHY
Hrushevs'kyi, M. 'Khronol'ogiia podii Halyts'ko-volyns'koï litopysy,' *ZNTSh*, 41 (1901)
Hens'ors'kyi, A. *Halyts'ko-Volyns'kyi litopys (Protses skladannia; redaktsiï i redaktory)* (Kiev 1958)
– *Halyts'ko-Volyns'kyi litopys (Leksychni, frazeolohichni ta stylistychni osoblyvosti)* (Kiev 1961)
The Hypatian Codex, II: The Galician-Volhynian Chronicle, trans G. Perfecky (Munich 1973)

A. Zhukovsky

Galician-Volhynian state. See Galicia-Volhynia, Principality of.

Galicia-Volhynia, Principality of. A state founded in 1199 by *Roman Mstyslavych, the prince of Volhynia from 1170, who united Galicia and Volhynia under his rule. The Romanovych line ruled the state until its demise in 1340.

After the death of Grand Prince Yaroslav the Wise of Kiev in 1054, Kievan Rus' had disintegrated into 5 and then 13 separate principalities, including those of Halych (see *Galicia) and *Volodymyr-Volynskyi (Volhynia). Roman took Halych after the death of *Volodymyr Yaroslavych and in 1202 occupied Kiev with its domains as far east as the Dnieper River, thereby creating a powerful state in western Rus'. Like other princes before and after him, he had to contend with a rebellious Galician boyar oligarchy throughout his reign. He died in battle at Zawichost against Prince Leszek of Cracow. Interminable boyar rebellions arose, which Leszek and Andrew II of Hungary exploited, and in 1214 they occupied Peremyshl and Halych. In 1221 Prince *Mstyslav Mstyslavych of Novgorod drove the Hungarians from Halych, where he ruled with difficulty until 1228.

The rebellions and wars lasted until 1238, when Roman's son, *Danylo Romanovych, having consolidated his rule in Volhynia, finally seized Galicia. After subduing the boyars in 1241–2 and defeating the Chernihiv princes and their Polish and Hungarian allies at Yaroslav in 1245, Danylo consolidated his control of Galicia. He took Hrodna, Slonim, and other Chorna Rus' towns from Lithuania in the north in 1250–2 and extended his rule beyond Kiev in the east. Because of Danylo's close alliance with his brother *Vasylko Romanovych, who ruled Volodymyr from 1241 to 1269, the Galician-Volhynian state attained the apex of its power during his reign. After the enormous destruction wreaked by the Mongol invasion of Rus' in 1239–41, Danylo was forced to pledge allegiance to Khan Batu of the Golden Horde in 1246. He strove, however, to rid his realm of the Mongol yoke by attempting, unsuccessfully, to establish military alliances with other European rulers. In internal affairs, Danylo depended on the support of the burghers. During his reign the cities of Lviv and Kholm were founded. After the Mongols razed Halych in 1241, Kholm became the new capital.

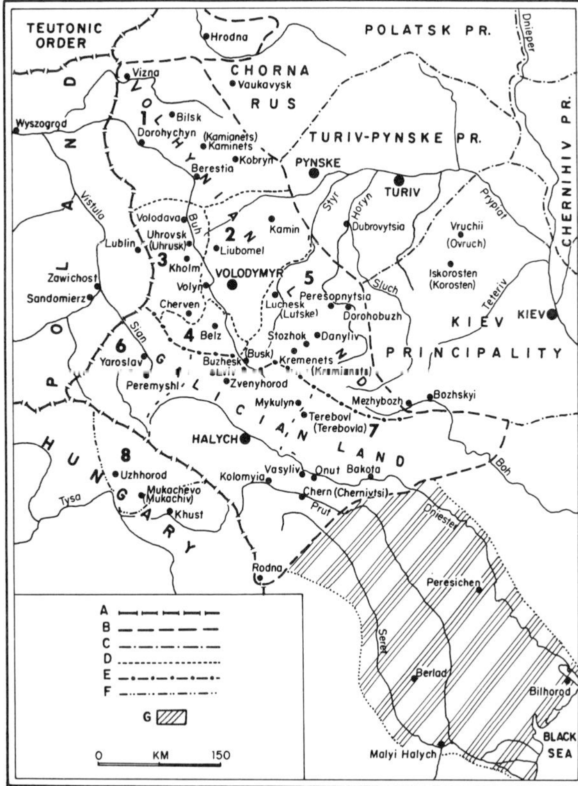

PRINCIPALITY OF GALICIA-VOLHYNIA CA 1300

A. Boundaries of Rus'
B. Boundaries of the Principality of Galicia-Volhynia
C. Principality boundaries
D. Boundaries of appanage principalities and lands
E. Northmost boundary of Mongol control
F. Boundary of Transcarpathian land (1280–1320)
G. Lands controlled by Galician princes and captured by the Mongols

1. Berestia land
2. Volodymyr-Volynskyi principality proper
3. Cherven-Kholm land
4. Belz land
5. Luchesk (Lutske) principality
6. Peremyshl principality and land
7. Terebovl (Terebovlia) principality and land
8. Transcarpathian land

Danylo died in 1264. His son and successor, *Lev I Danylovych (1264–1301), accepted Mongol suzerainty. Lev made Lviv the new capital in 1272 and took part of Transcarpathia, including Mukachiv, from the Hungarians in 1280 and the Lublin land from the Poles ca 1292. His son and successor, *Yurii Lvovych (1301–15), formally reunited Galicia and Volhynia and succeeded in getting *Halych metropoly established, but lost Transcarpathia and the Lublin land. His sons, *Lev II and Andrii Yuriiovych, ruled together from 1315 to 1323. They encouraged commerce and colonization by foreign merchants (see *Germans). The brothers joined forces with Polish princes to fight the Mongols and possibly perished in battle. The last prince, *Yurii II Boleslav (1323–40), the nephew of Yurii Lvovych, also encouraged foreign colonization, which led to conflicts with the boyars, who poisoned him and offered the throne to the Lithuanian prince *Liubartas. That same year *Casimir III the Great of Poland attacked Lviv, and the period of Lithuanian-Polish rivalry over Galicia-Volhynia began.

Because the powerful and influential *boyars constantly competed for power with the princes, certain tendencies toward *feudalism existed in the principality, unlike in other parts of Ukraine. Trade with other Rus' principalities, Hungary, Poland, Bohemia, the Holy Roman Empire, Lithuania, Bulgaria, and the Byzantine Empire was developed, and the principality prospered. It also flourished culturally, as evidenced by architectural remains and various chronicles, especially the *Galician-Volhynian Chronicle. With the death of Yurii II, it ceased existing as a separate state, and with it the Princely era in Ukraine came to an end. Over 80 towns and cities were located in the principality.

BIBLIOGRAPHY
Zubritskii, D. *Istoriia drevniago Galitsko-russkago kniazhestva*, 3 vols (Lviv 1852–5)
Sharanevych, I. *Istoriia Halytsko-Volodymyrskoi Rusy ot naidavniishykh vremen do roku 1453* (Lviv 1863)
Linnichenko, I. *Cherty iz istorii soslovii Iugo-Zapadnoi (Galitskoi) Rusi XIV–XV st.* (Moscow 1894)
Pashuto, V. *Ocherki po istorii Galitsko-Volynskoi Rusi* (Moscow 1950)
Hrytsak, P. *Halyts'ko-Volyns'ka derzhava* (New York 1958)
Kryp'iakevych, I. *Halyts'ko-Volyns'ke kniazivstvo* (Kiev 1984)
Kotliar, N. *Formirovanie territorii i vozniknovenie gorodov Galitsko-Volynskoi Rusi IX–XIII vv.* (Kiev 1985)

A. Zhukovsky

Gallicisms. Words and expressions borrowed from the French language or coined on the French pattern. In the second half of the 18th and the first third of the 19th century Gallicisms acquired currency in the language of the Russian and Polish upper classes. This stimulated their widespread adoption into Ukrainian. Many French terms entered Ukrainian via Polish; eg, *cyvil'nyj* (from the French *civil*), *cytryna* (*citron*), *kravatka* (*cravate*), *parada* (*parade*), and *teren* (*terrain*). Gallicisms adopted from Russian include *ataka* (*attaque*), *bjuro* (*bureau*), *odekol'on* (*eau de Cologne*), *pal'to* (*paletot*), and *portfel'* (*portefeuille*). Often a Gallicism would enter Ukrainian from both Polish and Russian. Typically Gallicisms refer to the theater and the fine arts: *antrakt* (*entracte*), *balet* (*ballet*), *bjust* (*buste*), *parter* (*parterre*), *pejzaž* (*paysage*); to everyday life and fashion: *vaza* (*vase*), *bljuza* (*blouse*), *kotleta* (*côtelette*), *ljampa* (*lampe*), *restoran* (*restaurant*); to military affairs: *avangard* (*avant-garde*), *artylerija* (*artillerie*), *batal'jon* (*bataillon*), *brygada* (*brigade*), *kanonada* (*canonnade*); and to social and political life and psychology: *buržuazija* (*bourgeoisie*), *parljament* (*parlement*), *entuzijazm* (*enthousiasme*), *interes* (*intérêt*). Relatively few Gallicisms are related to technology: *monter* (*monteur*), *resora* (*ressort*). Literary Ukrainian phraseology contains many French loan translations; for example, *blyskučyj uspix* (*succès brillant*), *vytončenyj smak* (*goût raffiné*), *maty misce* (*avoir lieu*). Many words restored from or based on Greek or Latin also entered Ukrainian via French in the 18th and 19th centuries.

G.Y. Shevelov

Games. Many popular games originated in the distant past and are part of the folk tradition. Not included in this category and not discussed here are games of foreign origin that were once played only by the upper strata of society (eg, sophisticated card and board games), school games learned from textbooks as part of school programs, or athletic games of recent origin (eg, soccer, hockey, and volleyball).

In Ukraine numerous folk games have been played by the people from early childhood to old age since time immemorial. However, they have not been adequately described or studied and have been regarded for the most part as part of *children's folklore, *folk customs, *folk dance, folk theater, folk teachings, and physical education.

Playing and games originated in primitive antiquity and are an expression of the play instinct. They are universal and cross-cultural. The vast majority of games pass from the adults' repertoire to that of children. The basic nature of games – as imitations of adult practices – has been preserved to the present. Preschool-age children are receptive to nursery rhymes, songs, and jingles (*zabavlianky* or *utishky*) recited by adults that accompany babies' games. Very common in Ukrainian folklore, they are acted out by the adult using specific rhythmic movements, handling of the infant's face, fingers, and toes, representative gestures, and mimicking. Their language is simple and is adapted to the child's level of understanding; alliteration, assonance, exclamation, use of diminutives, and onomatopoeia are the prevalent devices. The content is linear and happy. Repetition, particularly that of opening words, is frequently used. *Zabavlianky* reflect the feelings and expectations of adults, chiefly of mothers.

There are several distinct groups: the *hoidalky* – short refrains that are recited while rocking a child in a cradle and begin with the word *hoida* or *khyti*; *chukalky* – refrains beginning with the words *chuk, chuky, hop,* or *hutsy* that are recited while bouncing a child on the knee or foot; and *nastyrlyvi kazochky* (persistent tales) or *bezknonechni zabavlianky* (endless jingles). A number of *zabavlianky*, such as 'Ïde, ïde pan, pan, na konyku sam, sam' (A noble rides, a noble rides, on a horse alone, alone), are accompanied by imitations of riding a horse. Others have a dialogue structure consisting of numerous questions and answers. The characters in all of them are usually people and animals found in the child's immediate environment: parents and grandparents, crows, magpies, horses, cats, mice, hares, sparrows, hens, and roosters.

From the age of three children have traditionally played games that imitate domestic life. Children who tend sheep or cattle play in the pasture, where they imitate agricultural tasks such as ploughing, planting, haying, and harvesting. School-age children (6–12-year-olds) play more complex chasing, running, and catching games requiring some organization into teams and the observance of certain rudimentary, unformulated rules and prohibitions. Leaders are chosen by common agreement, by testing skill, and by counting out using incantatory verbal formulas.

Mimicry of family rituals, such as baptisms, weddings, and funerals (using dolls, rarely children), is popular among children of all ages. The imitation of betrothals and weddings by older children has erotic overtones. Sometimes the mimicking is very accurate, particularly the details of rituals. Such games are usually played by girls. Boys usually play more physical and competitive games, such as 'war,' using handmade toy weapons. They also enjoy target games, guessing games, sledding, walking on stilts, playing on homemade swings and seesaws, and mumblety-peg. All of these games, of course, are universal, and have been played not only in Ukraine. Other universal games, with widely accepted rules, have included *dovha loza* (leapfrog), *okhotnyk i zaitsi* (hide-and-seek), *kovinky* (field hockey), *panas* (blindman's bluff), *dzhut* (hot cockles), and numerous ballgames (*krynytsia, obizhka, korol*).

Today folk games in Ukraine, as in other countries, have been replaced by athletic games. The games played by children and juveniles are greatly influenced by films and television. Children play at Cowboys and Indians, Dovbush, cosmonauts, spies, sailors, and other celluloid heroes.

Traditionally children's games have required minimal equipment – sticks, stones, and potsherds. These serve as anything the children imagine them to be. Children love to make dolls, boats, wagons, watermills, sleds, necklaces, garlands, and simple wind and percussion musical instruments, thus imitating adults. Parents rarely make toys for their children, and store-bought toys have been unheard of among peasant children.

Figurative, dramatic playacting, mostly of a ritualistic nature, has constituted a distinct group of traditional folk games. It simulates particular events, acts, plants, animals, or objects using simple movements, dances (**khorovody*), songs, and elements of acting, and has been executed according to fixed notions. Most playacting has been done by young, unmarried adults and has been connected with calendric rites, most importantly those of the spring. The original, magical function of these games eventually became transformed into an erotic one, which was preserved until recent times. Gradually, the connection between figurative playacting and calendric rites disappeared.

The genetic tie of figurative games with the prehistoric period was emphasized in the early ethnographic literature, but recent researchers have shown that most of them originated in the 17th to 19th century. Many games were associated with pre-Lenten festivities (masquerading as the opposite sex or as representations of various occupations, parading with straw or wooden figures, etc), St John's feast (witch games), St Andrew's feast (love charms, flax sowing), and Christmas (the 'goat,' caroling with a star, parading with an 'aurochs,' etc). In the Christmas cycle a special group of plays dealt with the birth of Christ: 'Bethlehem' and the **vertep*, the former with actors, the latter with puppets.

Playacting had an important place in traditional wedding rituals; they include the mock kidnapping of the bride, sung dialogues between the groom's and the bride's retinues, the attempt to substitute another girl for the bride, and circling the wedding guests' houses on the second or third day of the wedding carrying a zoomorphic or anthropomorphic figure.

At evening parties (*vechernytsi*) figurative games such as 'horrors,' 'old man and woman,' 'Gypsy,' and 'confession' were played by young people. Games such as 'rooster' and 'tug-of-war' emphasized physical strength.

Funeral games, which were most widespread in the Hutsul region, were a class in themselves. They were played by young people at night during the prefuneral wake. Their original purpose was to propitiate the dead. Several dozen have been counted, including such games as 'shovels,' 'pear,' 'mill,' 'rooster,' and 'gander.' Many of them ended with a boy kissing a girl; their erotic undertone is obvious. Sometimes the deceased figured in the games. Today such games have virtually disappeared, for they clash with modern attitudes to funerals.

Because folk games have been passed on orally, they have been open to variation and improvisation. Because certain original, ancient words or properties were misunderstood, the content of dramatic games, in particular, changed considerably over time.

The oldest general descriptions of Ukrainian folk games are found in the writings of the Polish ethnographers Ł. Gołębiowski (1831), W. Zaleski (1833), and Z. Pauli (1839–40), and the Ukrainian K. Sementovsky (1843). More detailed, though limited, descriptions were written in the second half of the 19th century by Ya. Holovatsky, P. Chubynsky, M. Markevych, B. Hrinchenko, O. Kolberg, P. Ivanov, V. Yastrebov, S. Isaievych, Kh. Yashchurzhynsky, A. Wankl, Yu. Kakovsky, and M. Derlytsia. M. Kostomarov, O. Potebnia, A. Veselovsky, E. Anichkov, E. Pokrovsky, and V. Kharuzina wrote about folk games from a Romantic perspective.

In the early part of the 20th century, important contributions to the study of games were made by F. Vovk, K. Kvitka, V. Hnatiuk, Z. Kuzelia, and P. Bogatyrev. In his *Pobut selians'koï dytyny* (Folkways of the Peasant Child, 1929), N. Zahlada gave a sociological analysis of Ukrainian folk games. Since the Second World War, many new descriptions of Ukrainian folk games have appeared in the works of O. Voropai, O. Dei, and A. Kutser. Studies in the context of ritual folklore have been written by O. Zilynsky, O. Dei, and L. Hratsianska, and in the context of children's folklore by V. Boiko and H. Dovzhenok. But no definitive study of folk games, or even a comprehensive collection or rigid classification of them, has appeared in Soviet Ukraine or abroad.

BIBLIOGRAPHY

Tereshchenko, A. *Byt russkogo naroda* (St Petersburg 1847)

Ivanov, P. *Igry krest'ianskikh detei v Kupianskom uezde* (Kharkiv 1890)

Pokrovskii, E. *Detskie igry* (Moscow 1895)

Kuzelia, Z. 'Dytyna v zvychaiakh i viruvanniakh ukraïns'koho narodu: Materiialy z poludnevoï Kyïvshchyny,' *MUE*, 8–9 (1906–7)

– 'Posyzhenie i zabavy pry mertsi v ukraïns'kim pokhoronnim obriadi,' *ZNTSh*, 121–2 (1914–15)

Zahlada, N. *Pobut selians'koï dytyny: Materiialy do monohrafiï s. Starosillia* (Kiev 1929)

Vsevolodskii-Gerngross, V.; Kovaleva, V.; Stepanova, E. (eds). *Igry narodov SSSR* (Moscow-Leningrad 1933)

Dei, O. (ed). *Ihry ta pisni: Vesniano-litnia poeziia trudovoho roku* (Kiev 1963)

Zilynskij, O. 'Stare lidove hry u zapadnich a východních Slovanu.' Candidate's diss., Charles University, Prague 1965

Kutser, A. *Hei, ditochky, daite ruchky: Narodni dytiachi hry ukraïntsiv Chekhoslovachchyny* (Prešov 1972)

Dovzhenok, H. *Fol'klorna poeziia dytynstva* (Kiev 1981)

Dovzhenok, H. (ed). *Dytiachyi fol'klor: Kolyskovi pisni ta zabavlianky* (Kiev 1984)

M. Hnatiukivsky

Gamow, George, b 4 March 1904 in Odessa, d 19 August 1968 in Boulder, Colorado. American physicist. On his mother's side he was a descendant of the Ukrainian Lebedynets family. He studied in Odessa and Leningrad. As a visiting fellow (1928–31) in Göttingen, Copenhagen, and Cambridge, he contributed to the early development of quantum theory, notably by explaining the radioactive alpha decay. He left the USSR in 1933 and in 1934 accepted a professorial appointment in theoretical physics at George Washington University in Washington, DC. During this period he and E. Teller jointly made substantial contributions to the theory of beta decay. Gamow did pioneering work in cosmology and biophysics as well as nuclear physics. From 1956 till his death he was a professor of physics at the University of Colorado.

Garlic (*Allium sativum*; Ukrainian: *chasnyk*). Pungent bulbous plant used as an aliment, and as an important seasoning and preservative. Its function as medicine and charm in folk life was based on a belief in its sympathetic and contiguous powers: its pungency suggested that it could repulse pain and illness. Because of its chemical constituents, it was a successful remedy for certain diseases. Garlic has been used as a charm during pregnancy and at baptisms and weddings. Pregnant Hutsul women wore a man's shirt with a head of garlic tied to it to fend off the 'evil eye.' A head of garlic was attached to an infant's baptismal cloth for the same purpose. Boiko and Lemko brides wove garlic into their wedding garland. Garlic was worn widely during epidemics of cholera, typhus fever, and the plague. According to popular belief, human and animal ailments were caused by witchcraft; hence, the use of garlic in folk medicine was accompanied by incantations. The sign of a cross or a triangle was made three times with a knife in a bowl of water with three heads of garlic in it to the accompaniment of a suitable incantation, and the water was applied to the body as a remedy for sharp skeletal pains and muscular cramps. Cows that did not produce milk had garlic rubbed between their horns and on the udder. Because garlic was believed to be a potent substance, those who handled it had to take certain precautionary measures. Winter garlic, for example, could not be planted on a Saturday, otherwise a member of the farmer's family would die.

B. Medwidsky

Gartner, Theodor, b 4 November 1843 in Vienna, d 29 April 1925 in Innsbruck. German philologist; a professor at Chernivtsi University. Together with S. Smal-Stotsky he wrote a Ukrainian school grammar (1893, 4th edn 1928), which was widely used in Austrian-ruled Ukraine, and the scholarly *Grammatik der ruthenischen (ukrainischen) Sprache* (1913). He favored a phonetic spelling in the discussions on orthography in Western Ukraine.

Gas industry. See Natural gas industry.

Gattenberger, Konstantin, b 28 December 1843 in St Petersburg, d 30 May 1893 in Kharkiv. Russian economist and jurist of Swiss origin. A graduate of the faculty of law at Kharkiv University (1866), he taught criminal law at the university from 1868 until his death. He was a follower of J.S. Mill and, as a liberal, opposed socialism but recognized the shortcomings of capitalism and looked to trade unions, not co-operatives, for improvements in the living standard of workers. His chief works were *Vliianie russkogo zakonodatel'stva na torgovyi i bankovyi kredit* (The Influence of Russian Legislation on Commercial and Bank Credit, 1870), his doctoral thesis *Zakonodatel'stvo i birzhevaia spekuliatsiia* (Legislation and Stock-Market Speculation, 1872), and *Venskii krizis 1873 g.* (The Vienna Crisis of 1873, 1877).

Gawroński, Franciszek (pen name Rawita), b 4 November 1845 in Stepashky, Haisyn county, Podilia gubernia, d 16 April 1930 in Józefów, Poland. Polish agronomist, writer, publicist, and historian. He wrote several historical novellas with Ukrainian themes and articles on Ukrainian literature. At first he was sympathetic to the Ukrainian cause, but gradually he became hostile to it. His anti-Ukrainian attitude is expressed most vividly in *Historia ruchów hajdamackich w 18 w.* (A History of Haidamaka Movements in the 18th Century, 2 vols, 1899, 1901), *Bohdan Chmielnicki* (Bohdan Khmelnytsky, 2 vols, 1908–9), and *Kozaczyzna ukrainna w Rzeczypospolitej Polskiej* (Borderland Cossacks in the Polish Commonwealth, 1923).

Gazette de Léopol

Gazette de Léopol. A weekly French newspaper edited and published by Chevalier Ossoudi in 1776 in Lviv. It was one of the first newspapers published on Ukrainian territory; 52 issues appeared.

Gdańsk (German: Danzig). City in Poland (1980 pop 448,000). A historically important commercial-industrial center and port on the Baltic Sea. Towards the end of the 13th century, its merchants established trade relations with Rus'. From 1919 to 1939, according to the Treaty of Versailles, it was a free city in customs union with Poland, which also controlled its foreign relations. Since 1945 Gdańsk has been part of the Polish People's Republic.

From 1922 to 1945 a few hundred Ukrainians, mainly from Galicia, studied at the Danzig Polytechnic. They had their own Osnova Union of Ukrainian Students, the fraternities Halych, Zarevo, and Chornomore, the socialist Drahomanov Hromada and Franko Society, the Smoloskyp chemistry students' circle, and the Surma choir. The first ordinary congress of the Central Union of Ukrainian Students was held in Danzig in July 1923. Ukrainian student activity peaked in the mid-1920s, but the number of students subsequently dwindled because of economic difficulties.

In 1947, as part of the Polish state's policy to depopulate the Polish-Ukrainian borderland of its indigenous Ukrainians, some 10,000 Ukrainians from the *Sian region were forcibly resettled in Gdańsk voivodeship. Since 1956 the second-largest branch (400 members) of the *Ukrainian Social and Cultural Society in Poland has been located in Gdańsk; it has held youth fairs and, in 1983 and 1985 in nearby Sopot, festivals of Ukrainian song. Ukrainian was taught at Gdańsk University in 1983–5.

BIBLIOGRAPHY
Guldon, Z. *Związki handlowe dóbr magnackich na Prawobrzeżnej Ukrainie z Gdańskiem w XVIII wieku* (Toruń 1966)
Shyprykevych, V. (ed). *Propam'iatna knyha dantsigeriv: Istorychni narysy ta spomyny kolyshnikh studentiv Politekhniky Vil'noho Mista Dantsigu, 1921–1945* (Philadelphia-Toronto-New York 1979)

Nikolai Ge

Ge, Nikolai (also: Gay, Gué), b 27 February 1831 in Voronezh, Russia, d 13 April 1894 at Ivanovskyi khutir (now the village of Shevchenko), Bakhmach county, Chernihiv gubernia. Russian painter of French origin; one of the founders of the *Peredvizhniki group of Russian populist painters. Ge studied at the universities of Kiev (1847) and St Petersburg (1848–9), and at the St Petersburg Art Academy (1850–7), where he became a professor in 1863. Ge's realistic works are characterized by their psychological depth; his early works show the influence of his teacher K. Briullov and A. Ivanov. Ge executed many paintings on historical subjects, portraits (including one of M. Kostomarov, 1870), a self-portrait (1892–3), several Italian landscapes, and a famous cycle of works on New Testament themes exhibiting the influence of L. Tolstoy's ideas. From 1876 Ge lived in the Chernihiv region, where he spread Tolstoy's ideas among the peasants and took a keen interest in Ukrainian culture, particularly the works of T. Shevchenko. Many of his later paintings have Ukrainian peasants and landscapes as their subjects. Ge helped establish M. Murashko's *Kiev Drawing School. Large collections of his works are in the Kiev Museum of Russian Painting and the Tretiakov Gallery in Moscow.

Gebei, Petro [Gebej], b 20 July 1864 in Kalnyk, Bereg county, Transcarpathia, d 26 April 1931 in Uzhhorod. Greek Catholic bishop, educator, and civic figure. He completed his theological studies in the Budapest Central Seminary (1889), and began teaching canon law at the Uzhhorod Eparchial Seminary, later becoming its rector. In 1927 he was consecrated bishop of the Mukachiv Eparchy. In 1918–19 he was active in the Ruthenian People's Council, which sought Ukrainian national and religious autonomy both from the Hungarian and the Czechoslovak regimes. In 1925 he created the Central Chancellery for the Defense of the Faith, which successfully stemmed the mass conversions to Orthodoxy, defended his church's rights, and convinced the Czechoslovak state to restore confiscated properties to the church. A popular bishop, he had a populist orientation and belonged to both the Prosvita and the Dukhnovych societies.

Gebus-Baranetska, Stefaniia [Gebus-Baranec'ka, Stefanija], b 19 December 1905 in Peremyshl, Galicia. Painter and graphics artist. Gebus-Baranetska studied at the Lviv Art School (1926–9) and at the Lviv Polytechnical Institute (1928–33). She taught graphic art, weaving, and composition in various art schools in Lviv. She is best known for her woodcuts, landscapes, and bookplates. Her work is realistic in style and draws on Ukrainian folk art and themes: eg, *Shepherd* (1935), *Washerwoman* (1935), *Folk Dances* (1937), and *Kosiv Potters* (1956). Gebus-Baranetska is the subject of a monograph by A. Viunyk (1968).

Gediminas (Ukrainian: Gedymin), ca 1275–ca 1340. Grand duke of Lithuania from 1316. During his reign most of Belorussia and the Ukrainian territories of Turiv-Pynske and northern Volhynia were incorporated into the Grand Duchy of Lithuania. Gediminas called himself 'rex lithauanorum et multorum ruthenorum.' Through dynastic alliances he controlled or influenced many other realms. His brother Theodore ruled Kiev principality, his daughter Euphemia (Ofka) married Prince *Yurii II Boleslav of Volhynia in 1331, and through marriage his son *Liubartas became the prince of Galicia-Volhynia in 1340.

Gedroits, Kostiantyn [Gedrojc, Kostjantyn], b 6 April 1872 in Bendery, Moldavia, d 5 October 1932 in Moscow. Soil scientist, agrochemist; full VUAN member from 1930. A graduate of the St Petersburg Forestry Institute (1898) and St Petersburg University (1903), he became professor at the Forestry Institute in 1918. He was one of the founders and then a director (1922–30) of the agrochemical department of the Nosivka Agricultural Research Station

Kostiantyn Gedroits

Tyt Gembytsky

in the Chernihiv region. For many years he edited *Zhurnal opytnoi agronomii*. Among his scientific contributions are an explanation of the role of colloids in the formation and fertility of soils, a theory of the origin of solonetz soils and of their amelioration, and new chemical methods of soil analysis. His most important publications are *Uchenie o poglotitel'noi sposobnosti pochv* (The Theory of the Adsorptive Capacity of Soils, 4th edn 1933) and *Khimicheskii analiz pochv* (The Chemical Analysis of Soils, 4th edn 1935).

Gembytsky, Tyt [Gembyc'kyj], b 15 January 1842 in Liulyntsi, Vinnytsia county, Podilia gubernia, d 23 January 1908 in Lviv. Stage actor and director. In 1867 he founded a troupe that toured Right-Bank Ukraine. From 1869 he worked as an actor and director at the Ruska Besida theater in Lviv, where he appeared in many roles, including the mayor in N. Gogol's *Inspector General*, Martyn in I. Karpenko-Kary's *Martyn Borulia*, and Leiba in I. Tobilevych's *Zhydivka-vykhrestka* (The Baptized Jewess). He wrote a historical survey of the founding and development of Ukrainian theater in Galicia (1904) and translated Russian and West European plays into Ukrainian.

Gendarmes. See Police.

Gender (Ukrainian: *rid*). Modern Ukrainian preserves the category of grammatical gender, inherited via Common Slavic from Indo-European. Every noun in the singular (sing) is assigned to one of the three genders – masculine (m), feminine (f), or neuter (n) – but is not inflected as adjectives are.

The specific gender is determined by the ending of the noun in the nominative (nom) case sing in conjunction with the declensional type. Most m nouns have a zero ending in the nom sing, with the ending *-a* or *-u* in the genitive (gen) sing; f nouns end in *-a* or a (functionally) soft consonant in the nom sing, and in *-y* or *-i* in the gen sing; n nouns end in *-o*, *-e*, or *-a* in the nom sing, and in *-a* or *-y* in the gen sing, with minor complications. Semantic factors also influence gender: the names of males are usually m nouns regardless of the ending, and female names are f nouns.

Although gender in nouns is a classificatory category, in adjectives it is inflectional. Singular adjectives agree in gender with the nouns they modify. Gender distinctions in the nominative and accusative cases of the plural disappeared by the 15th century, and in the other cases of the plural by the 17th. Because in the singular of nouns gender is a live category, loan words in Ukrainian are either assigned a gender according to their ending (eg, m *bar* [bar], from the German f noun *die Bar*), or preserve the gender of the original language while adapting the appropriate ending for such a gender in Ukrainian (eg, f noun *akcija*, from the French f noun *action*).

G.Y. Shevelov

Genealogical vine of the Sviatopolk-Chetvertynsky princely family, from an engraving in *Teraturhima* (1638)

Genealogy. An auxiliary historical discipline that deals with family history and the lineage of individuals. It is closely related to *heraldry and diplomatics. Interest in genealogy was already evident in the Princely era (for example, in Nestor the Chronicler), but as a discipline it developed only during the Cossack period of the 17th and 18th century, when members of the Cossack *starshyna* began tracing their lineages. The most important contributions to Ukrainian genealogy have been made by O. Lazarevsky, H. Myloradovych, J. Wolff, and V. Modzalevsky. In the course of their research, other historians have also uncovered valuable genealogical information; these include O. Bodiansky, M. Kostomarov, P. Yefymenko, V. Lypynsky, M. Hrushevsky, D. Bahalii, I. Krypiakevych, B. Krupnytsky, O. Ohloblyn, and V. Seniutovych-Berezhny. There is a wealth of information on Ukrainian pedigrees at the Archives of the Department of Heraldry in Leningrad and at the Central Historical Archive in Kiev; the holdings of the latter have been partly published. Today genealogy is not a flourishing discipline in Soviet Ukraine. Since all vital records are under police control, access to them is most difficult. A genealogical section has been created (1984) as part of the Ukrainian Museum in New York to help Ukrainians in North America in tracing their family histories.

BIBLIOGRAPHY

Lazarevskii, A. 'Ocherki malorossiiskikh familii. Materialy k istorii obshchestva v XVII i XVIII vv.' *Russkii arkhiv*, 1875, nos 1–3; 1876, no. 3
– 'Liudi staroi Malorossii,' KS, 1882, nos 1, 3, 8; 1884, no. 1; 1885, no. 5; 1886, nos 1, 7; 1887, nos 6–8; 1888, no. 10; 1893, no. 11
Modzalevskii, V. *Malorossiiskii rodoslovnik*, 4 vols (Kiev 1908–14)
Ohloblyn, O. *Liudy staroï Ukraïny* (Munich 1959)
Himka, J.-P.; Swyripa, F. *Researching Ukrainian Family History* (Edmonton 1984)
Rumiantseva, V. 'Deiaki pidsumky rozvytku henealohiï,' *UIZh*, 1987, no. 3

M. Miller

General chancellor (*heneralnyi pysar*). The title of a senior member of the *General Officer Staff in the Hetman state who managed the *General Military Chancellery and supervised the hetman's domestic and foreign correspondence. The office was filled by an educated person who knew several languages and diplomatic protocol and had administrative experience, usually as a scribe or a regimental chancellor. He performed many senior diplomatic functions, guarded the state seal, supervised the state archives, and signed the hetman's decrees in his absence. He also supervised the preparation of all decrees, charters, and land grants by his many subordinates, prepared the agenda of meetings of the council of the General Officer Staff, and performed other tasks assigned to him by the hetman. The general chancellors I. Vyhovsky (1648–57), P. Teteria (1660–3), and P. Orlyk (1706–9) later became hetmans.

The title was revived in 1917 under the Central Rada to designate the state functionary who, in a ministerial capacity, guarded the state seal and documents. The post was held by P. Khrystiuk (28 June–3 September 1917), O. Lototsky (3 September–November 1917), and I. Mirny (November 1917–22 January 1918). Thereafter the post was called state secretary.

General Court (Heneralnyi sud). The highest judicial body in the UNR, enacted by the Central Rada on 17 December 1917. The General Court was empowered to rule on legal matters arising in the UNR that prior to the 1917 Revolution had been adjudicated by the Russian Senate. The court had three divisions – criminal, civil, and administrative – and a prosecutors' office. On 15 January and 2 April 1918 the Central Rada appointed the following as judges of the General Court: P. Achkasov, O. Butovsky, A. Margolin, D. Markovych, Popov, Pukhtynsky, M. Radchenko, O. Khrutsky, S. Shelukhyn, H. Shyianov, A. Viazlov, and P. Yatsenko. On 8 July 1918 the General Court was transformed by the Hetman government into the *State Senate.

General flag-bearer (*heneralnyi khorunzhyi*). Title of a low-ranking member of the *General Officer Staff in the Hetman state. His role was primarily ceremonial: to carry the great military banner (*viiskova khoruhva*) on important occasions. He also performed political, diplomatic, and military tasks assigned to him by the hetman and could serve as acting hetman.

General judge (*heneralnyi suddia*). Title of the military judge of the Cossacks and, from 1648 to 1782, of a member of the *General Officer Staff of the Hetman state. From 1654 there were usually two general judges, who collectively headed the General Court, the appellate court of the Hetman state. Most general judges had no legal experience. In addition to their judicial responsibility they also performed executive, advisory, and military functions and served as acting hetmans and diplomatic envoys. Hetman I. Samoilovych was a general judge in 1669–72.

General land survey. From 1766 to the mid-19th century, the tsarist government carried out several general land surveys throughout the Russian Empire, including Ukraine, for the purpose of establishing the boundaries of villages and towns, state lands, and various private landholdings. In the Poltava and Chernihiv regions surveys were begun in the 1760s. In Slobidska Ukraine a survey was conducted in 1769–81, in Katerynoslav and Kherson gubernias in 1798–1828, and in Tavriia gubernia in 1829–43. By means of these surveys the right of peasants to occupy land freely – a right based on customary law – was abrogated, the properties of the old owners or of new owners who had received estates from the state in the course of the surveys were consolidated, and the number of communal lands and scattered estates was sharply reduced. The surveyors produced plans of individual holdings, which were used to prepare county maps and gubernial atlases, and economic descriptions of the various land units surveyed. The documents of the general land surveys served as the legal basis of property relations until the 1917 Revolution.

General Little Russian Court (Heneralnyi malorosiiskyi sud). The highest judicial body in Left-Bank Ukraine from 1797 to 1831. It consisted of a civil and a criminal division and functioned as an appellate court in Little Russia gubernia. Its two judges and ten jurors were elected by the gentry for three-year terms. Located in Chernihiv throughout its existence, the court was subordinated to the *Russian Senate.

General Military Chancellery (Heneralna viiskova kantseliariia). The central administrative body in the Hetman state from 1648 to 1764 through which the hetmans exercised their military and civil authority. The chancellery was directed by the *general chancellor and supervised all affairs, maintained the state archives and registers, prepared the hetman's decrees, charters, and land grants, and resolved disputes regarding membership in the Cossack estate. Regimental chancellors were trained at the chancellery, and the *General Officer Staff held its meetings on its premises, which were located in the same town as the hetman's residence (Chyhyryn, Hadiache, Baturyn, Hlukhiv). In 1720 its financial and judicial powers were abrogated by Peter I, and it was reorganized according to the collegial principle.

General Military Council (Heneralna viiskova rada). A principal political body in the Hetman state from 1648 to 1750. It assumed the functions of the Cossack Council, the ruling body of the Zaporozhian Sich, and the general Cossack councils (see *Chorna rada*); elected the hetman and senior Cossack *starshyna*; and debated and resolved all (domestic and external) political, administrative, judicial, and military affairs. The council was an example of direct, popular self-rule, similar to the medieval **viche*. All members of the Cossack estate could participate in it (at times delegations representing burghers, and even peasants, took part); thus the council involved several thousand people. There was no one place of assembly; the most frequent gathering places were by the Rosava River southwest of Kiev and in Pereiaslav. During the *Cossack-Polish War, the council was the supreme legislative body. By a show of hands, it sanctioned the alliance with Muscovy in Pereiaslav (see *Pereiaslav Treaty of 1654), with Sweden in Korsun in 1657, and with Turkey in Korsun in 1669. Its powers often coincided and competed with those of the hetman and the *Council of Officers, and in the late 17th century its governing powers were lost to them. Thereafter it convened only to sanction ceremonially the election of a new hetman.

General Military Court (Heneralnyi viiskovyi sud). The highest judicial body in the Hetman state. It was formed in 1654 during B. Khmelnytsky's hetmancy and was based on the Cossack company and regimental courts. The hetman was its president, but in practice one of the two *general judges, the hetman's permanent deputy, normally presided over it. The court was a collegial institution, consisting also of other members of the *General Officer Staff and of *notable military fellows, who served on the bench in important cases. Usually, however, only one judge heard a case; he was aided by a judicial scribe. For those disagreeing with regimental or company court rulings, the General Military Court served as an appellate court; for members of the General Officer Staff and individuals under the hetman's special protection it served as a court of the first instance. Decisions of the court could be appealed only to the hetman. In the 18th century the court came under the jurisdiction of the *General Military Chancellery. In 1764 it was subordinated to the *Little Russian Collegium. The Russian government formally abolished the court in 1781, when it reorganized the Hetman state into three vicegerencies, but the court continued functioning until 1790.

General Officer Staff (Heneralna starshyna). The *hetman's senior officers in the Hetman state (1648–1782). Its members were the *general quartermaster, two *general judges, the *general chancellor, *general treasurer, two *general osauls, the *general flag-bearer, and the *general standard-bearer. They were elected by either a general Cossack council or the *Council of Officers or were appointed by the hetman or, after 1725, the Russian government. All these titles, except for the general treasurer, existed before 1648, when they designated the most senior officers in the Cossack army.

After 1648 these officers constituted a council (similar to a cabinet) that advised the hetman on the conduct of all affairs, helped formulate and execute policy, planned and directed military affairs, and ruled the state during an interregnum or in the hetman's absence; at times the council acted as the highest appellate court (eg, for charges of treason). Individual officers presided over the central administrative, judicial, and financial institutions or were personal deputies and envoys of the hetman. Their importance grew as the hetman's authority was eroded from 1709 by the Russian government, and by the mid-

18th century they were in the forefront of the movement among the Cossack *starshyna* for incorporation into the Russian imperial gentry. The members of the General Officer Staff were remunerated for their services either by large land grants, or money, or in kind.

BIBLIOGRAPHY
Gajecky, G. *The Cossack Administration of the Hetmanate*, 2 vols (Cambridge, Mass 1978)

General osaul (*heneralnyi osaul*). Title of a senior officer in the Cossack army and, after 1648, of a member of the *General Officer Staff in the Hetman state. As a rule, there were two general osauls. Their primary role was military: supervising the army's condition, commanding large detachments in wartime, managing muster rolls, directing the army engineers, commanding mercenary troops, and occasionally serving as acting hetman. They also served as the hetman's envoys, supervised matters of internal security (including reconnaissance and the suppression of mutinies), and conducted annual regimental musters and inspections. Four hetmans were former general osauls: P. Doroshenko (1663–4), D. Mnohohrishny (1668), I. Mazepa (1682–7), and I. Skoropadsky (1701–6).

General quartermaster (*heneralnyi oboznyi*). Title of the head of the *General Officer Staff in the Hetman state, who also commanded the army artillery and was responsible for army munitions, supplies, and transport. As the highest official after the hetman, he served as chief executive during an interregnum, as acting hetman, and, on occasion, as the hetman's special foreign envoy. He also managed all military affairs in the *General Military Chancellery.

General Secretariat of the Central Rada (Heneralnyi Sekretariiat Ukrainskoi Tsentralnoi Rady). Chief executive body of the UNR from 28 June 1917 to 22 January 1918. Five days after the proclamation of the First *Universal the Executive Committee (later Little Rada) of the *Central Rada accepted a proposal of the Ukrainian Party of Socialist Revolutionaries (UPSR) and formed the General Secretariat as a coalition 'cabinet' of Ukraine's autonomous government. At first the General Secretariat consisted of eight general secretaries and a general chancellor. Its chairman and general secretary (sec) for internal affairs was V. *Vynnychenko (Ukrainian Social Democratic Workers' party [USDRP]); the general chancellor was P. Khrystiuk (UPSR). The other general secretaries were: sec of finance Kh. Baranovsky (a nonpartisan co-operative leader); sec of nationalities S. Yefremov (Ukrainian Party of Socialists-Federalists [UPSF]) and (from 10 July 1917) O. Shulhyn (UPSF); sec for military affairs S. Petliura (USDRP); sec for agrarian affairs B. Martos (USDRP); sec of justice V. Sadovsky (USDRP); sec of education I. Steshenko (an independent); and sec of food supply M. Stasiuk (UPSR). The USDRP held a majority of the portfolios.

In Ukrainian circles early opinion on the role of the General Secretariat differed. Some thought it was to lay the groundwork for autonomy; others thought it was to exercise the powers of government. In non-Ukrainian circles it was regarded with great hostility. On 9 July 1917, the General Secretariat published a declaration that

General Secretariat of the Central Rada: (sitting, from left) S. Petliura, S. Yefremov, V. Vynnychenko, Kh. Baranovsky, I. Steshenko; (standing, from left) V. Sadovsky, B. Martos, M. Stasiuk, P. Khrystiuk

defined it as 'the executive body of the Central Rada.' Negotiations between the Central Rada and the Russian *Provisional Government on 11–13 July 1917 led to the latter's recognition of the General Secretariat as the highest executive power on Ukrainian territory. It was agreed that the Central Rada would be expanded to include representatives of the national minorities in Ukraine and that members of the General Secretariat, chosen from Central Rada deputies, would be confirmed by the Provisional Government. The General Secretariat was to be responsible to the Rada. By the end of July the Central Rada was enlarged by representatives of the national minorities and workers' deputies elected by the First *All-Ukrainian Workers' Congress. This change was reflected in a new General Secretariat to which five portfolios were added. V. Holubovych (UPSR) became sec of transport; A. Zarubin (Russian Socialist-Revolutionary), sec of postal and telegraph services; and M. Rafes (Jewish Bund), general controller. Two portfolios reserved for Russian Social Democrats – trade and industry, and labor – remained vacant. Three undersecretaries for nationalities were created in the General Secretariat: one for Jewish affairs, filled by M. Silberfarb (United Jewish Socialist Workers' party), one for Polish affairs, filled by M. Mickiewicz (Polish Democratic Center party), and one for Russian affairs, which remained vacant for a time.

After long hesitation the Central Rada accepted the 'Provisional Instruction to the General Secretariat' issued on 17 August 1917 by the Provisional Government. According to this decree the General Secretariat, reduced from 14 to 8 general secretaries (not counting the chancellor), was to be the highest organ of the Provisional Government in the regional administration of Ukraine and was to be appointed by the Provisional Government on the recommendation of the Central Rada. After a long, heated debate the Central Rada accepted these humiliating conditions. V. Vynnychenko resigned under severe criticism by the UPSR, and D. Doroshenko was asked to form a new General Secretariat. When he failed, V. Vynnychenko assumed the task and by September 3 completed it. On 14 September the Provisional Government confirmed the new General Secretariat. It consisted of V. Vynnychenko, chairman and sec for internal affairs; I. Steshenko, sec of education; M. Tuhan-Baranovsky (UPSF), sec of finance; O. Shulhyn, sec for nationalities;

M. Silberfarb and M. Mickiewicz, undersecretaries; M. Savchenko-Bilsky (UPSR sympathizer), sec for agrarian affairs; A. Zarubin, general controller; O. Lototsky (UPSF), general chancellor; and P. Stebnytsky (UPSF), UNR commissioner to the Provisional Government. On 10 October 1917 the program of the General Secretariat was presented to the Little Rada. Its general purpose was stated to be 'the unification of all Ukrainian territories and the entire Ukrainian people in one autonomous entity.'

After the Bolsheviks had overthrown the Provisional Government and UNR troops had taken control of Kiev, the Central Rada, with the encouragement of the Third *All-Ukrainian Military Congress, enlarged the General Secretariat by adding the following portfolios: food supply, assumed by M. Kovalevsky (UPSR); military affairs, S. Petliura; labor, M. Porsh (USDRP); trade and industry, V. Holubovych; justice, M. Tkachenko (USDRP); transport, V. Yeshchenko (Ukrainian Party of Socialists-Independentists); and postal and telegraph services, A. Zarubin. D. Odinets (Russian Popular Socialist party) was appointed undersecretary for Russian affairs. After the proclamation of the Third *Universal on 20 November 1917, the membership of the General Secretariat changed again: M. Tuhan-Baranovsky (temporarily replaced by V. Mazurenko), M. Savchenko-Bilsky, A. Zarubin, and O. Lototsky resigned. On 6 January 1918, S. Petliura left the General Secretariat. After further changes in early January 1918, the General Secretariat was left with the following members: V. Vynnychenko, chairman and sec for internal affairs; M. Tkachenko, sec of justice; M. Porsh, sec for military affairs and labor; O. Zhukovsky (UPSR), undersecretary for military affairs; O. Zarudny (UPSR), sec for agrarian affairs; M. Kovalevsky, sec for food supply; O. Shulhyn, sec of foreign affairs; V. Yeshchenko, sec of transport; M. Shapoval (UPSR), sec of postal and telegraph services; D. Antonovych (USDRP), sec for naval affairs; V. Mazurenko (USDRP), acting sec of finance; V. Holubovych, sec of trade and industry; I. Steshenko, sec of education; D. Odinets, undersecretary for Russian affairs; M. Silberfarb, undersecretary for Jewish affairs; M. Mickiewicz, undersecretary for Polish affairs; A. Zolotarev (Jewish Bund), general controller; and I. Mirny, acting general chancellor. The Fourth *Universal, proclaimed on 25 January 1918 (the document, however, was dated 22 January), transformed the General Secretariat into the *Council of National Ministers of the UNR.

BIBLIOGRAPHY

Khrystiuk, P. *Zamitky i materiialy do istoriï ukraïns'koï revoliutsiï 1917–1920 rr.*, vol 2 (Vienna 1921, New York 1969)
Zolotarev, A. *Iz istoriï Tsentral'noï Ukraïns'koï Rady – 1917* (Kharkiv 1922)
Doroshenko, D. *Istoriia Ukraïny 1917–1923 rr.*, vol 1: *Doba Tsentral'noï Rady* (Uzhhorod 1932, New York 1954)
Pidhainy, O. *The Formation of the Ukrainian Republic* (Toronto-New York 1966)
Zozulia, Ia. (ed). *Velyka Ukraïns'ka revoliutsiia: Kalendar istorychnykh podii za liutyi 1917 roku – berezen' 1918 roku* (New York 1967)
Reshetar Jr, J. *The Ukrainian Revolution, 1917–1920: A Study in Nationalism* (Princeton 1952, New York 1972)
Hunczak, T. (ed). *The Ukraine, 1917–1921: A Study in Revolution* (Cambridge, Mass 1977)

O. Shulhyn, A. Zhukovsky

General Staff of the UNR Army (Heneralnyi shtab Armii UNR). Organized in November 1917 by the General Secretariat of Military Affairs of the UNR, it was patterned on the General Staff of the Russian imperial army. While at first it had several departments, after reorganization the number was reduced to two – the organizational department and the quartermaster's department – run by assistants to the chief of staff. During its brief existence the general staff dealt mostly with organizational, not operational, matters. It drafted mobilization plans and organizational schemes, organized military schools, and prepared field manuals. Gen B. Bobrovsky was chief of general staff until March 1918, when he was succeeded by Col O. Slyvynsky. In February 1919, when the Directory of the UNR retreated from Kiev, the officers of the general staff were reassigned to the Active Army Staff. (See *Army of the Ukrainian National Republic.)

General standard-bearer (*heneralnyi bunchuzhnyi*). A senior official in the Hetman state of the 17th and 18th centuries and member of the *General Officer Staff. Formally he was responsible for safeguarding and displaying the symbol of the hetman's authority – the *bunchuk*, a standard consisting of a staff topped by an orb or spearhead and decorated with a horsetail or tassels – during ceremonies and military campaigns. He carried out various military, diplomatic, and judicial tasks assigned to him by the hetman.

General *starshyna*. See General Officer Staff.

General Survey of Landholdings (Heneralne slidstvo o maietnostiakh). A census of landowners, holdings, and peasants in Left-Bank Ukraine conducted in 1729–31 on the orders of Hetman D. Apostol with the object of establishing the rightful titles to properties and halting any further distribution of rank estates into hereditary ones. Titles were awarded for service by the Russian government, the hetmans, and, frequently, regimental colonels and were held in trust. The survey divided properties into rank estates, estates awarded on merit, town estates, free estates, disputed estates, and monastic estates. It resulted in the discovery that no more than a third of the peasants remained free commoners, the other two-thirds being subjects of the holders of rank, private, or monastic estates. After the survey the number of rank estates declined, while the number of large, permanent estates owned by the Cossack *starshyna* or monasteries increased.

General treasurer (*heneralnyi pidskarbii*). Title of a senior officer in the Hetman state, who became a member of the *General Officer Staff in 1728. His primary responsibility was to supervise government finances and to collect revenues through taxes, rents, and licenses. He also fulfilled other tasks assigned to him by the hetman.

General Ukrainian Council (Zahalna ukrainska rada). Ukrainian interparty political organization formed on 5 May 1915 in Vienna out of the Galician *Supreme Ukrainian Council by enlarging its mandate and membership. The General Ukrainian Council was to represent Ukrainians during the war, and was to be its chief spokesman within Austria-Hungary. The council consisted of 34 members. Galicia was represented by 24 delegates (most were from the National Democratic party, but a number were from the Ukrainian Radical party and 1 was from

General Ukrainian Council, 5 May 1915: (sitting, from left) T. Drachynsky, V. Bachynsky, M. Hankevych, M. Vasylko, K. Levytsky, Ye. Petrushevych, L. Bachynsky, Ye. Olesnytsky, V. Paneiko; (standing, from left) I. Bobersky, V. Doroshenko, Yu. Bachynsky, A. Skoropys, V. Temnytsky, M. Lahodynsky, O. Nazaruk, I. Makukh, L. Levytsky, K. Trylovsky, I. Semaka, S. Holubovych, V. Yasenytsk, Ya. Vesolovsky, O. Popovych, S. Baran, O. Onyshkevych

the Ukrainian Social Democratic party), Bukovyna by 7 delegates (5 from the National Democratic party, and 1 each from the Ukrainian Social Democratic party and the Ukrainian People's party), and Russian-ruled Ukraine by 3 delegates from the Union for the Liberation of Ukraine. Individual membership in the council changed frequently.

According to the council's program, Ukrainian territories under Russian rule were to form an independent Ukrainian state while the Ukrainian territories under Austria-Hungary were to become merely autonomous and unified into a single Ukrainian region. The presidium was the executive body of the council. It consisted of a president (K. Levytsky), three vice-presidents (M. Vasylko, L. Bachynsky, replaced later by Ya. Vesolovsky, and M. Hankevych, replaced later by V. Temnytsky), a deputy from the Union for the Liberation of Ukraine (O. Skoropys-Yoltukhovsky, replaced by M. Melenevsky), and a secretary (V. Temnytsky). Ye. Olesnytsky, S. Rudnytsky, S. Tomashivsky, S. Dnistriansky, and L. Tsehelsky served as special advisers to the council. The imperial manifesto of 4 November 1916, which established the Polish Kingdom and sanctioned an autonomous, Polish-dominated Galicia within Austria-Hungary, undermined the position of the council; subsequently, leadership in Ukrainian political life passed to the Ukrainian parliamentary representation.

BIBLIOGRAPHY
Pam'iatkova knyzhka Soiuzu vyzvolennia Ukraïny (Vienna 1917)
Levyts'kyi, K. *Istoriia vyzvol'nykh zmahan' halyts'kykh ukraïntsiv z chasu svitovoï viiny*, 3 vols (Lviv 1929–30)

A. Zhukovsky

General Ukrainian Non-Party Democratic Organization (Zahalna ukrainska bezpartiina demokratychna orhanizatsiia, aka the Ukrainian General Organization [Ukrainska zahalna orhanizatsiia]). A clandestine cultural organization founded in Kiev in the fall of 1897 on the initiative of O. *Konysky and V. *Antonovych. Many of its first members also belonged to a *hromada or the *Brotherhood of Taras. With about 150 members in 1901, it was enlarged and reorganized into an association of 3–10-member autonomous groups that held periodic congresses every three years to elect the executive. Most of its energy was devoted to publishing: it maintained the Vik publishing house and the Kievskaia Starina bookstore. It also encouraged the student, zemstvo, and co-operative movement, helped persecuted Ukrainian activists, and agitated for the use of the Ukrainian language in the schools. In 1903 it organized a Kotliarevsky jubilee in Poltava. In 1904 the organization adopted a full political program and changed its name to the *Ukrainian Democratic party, demanding national autonomy for Ukrainians and other nationalities within a federated Russia and radical economic and social reforms. In the following year it merged with the Ukrainian Radical party to form the *Ukrainian Democratic Radical party (UDRP), which lasted to 1907. In 1908 the groups which previously had belonged to the General Ukrainian Non-Party Democratic Organization and the UDRP established a similar secret association, the *Society of Ukrainian Progressives, which in 1917 became the Ukrainian Party of Socialist Federalists. The most important members of the organization were V. Antonovych, P. Zhytetsky, M. Lysenko, I. Shrah, Ye. Chykalenko, M. Hrushevsky, B. Hrinchenko, I. Steshenko, Ye. Tymchenko, M. Kononenko, O. Cherniakhivsky, O. Borodai, S. Yefremov, M. Mikhnovsky, O. Rusov, T. Rylsky, V. Berenshtam, and O. Lototsky.

BIBLIOGRAPHY
Iefremov, S. *Z hromads'koho zhyttia na Ukraïni* (Kiev 1909)
Doroshenko, V. *Ukraïnstvo v Rosiï* (Vienna 1916)
Chykalenko, Ie. *Spohady (1861–1907)* (Lviv 1925–6; 2nd edn, New York 1955)

Y. Boshyk, V. Doroshenko

Generalgouvernement. Political administrative entity comprising the central part of Poland occupied by Nazi Germany in 1939–45 but not incorporated directly into the Third Reich. The capital of the Generalgouvernement was Cracow. It was created by Hitler's declaration of 12 October 1939 and was essentially a German colony with a totalitarian regime and only minimal rights for the local population. The Nazis persecuted the inhabitants and deported hundreds of thousands of people to work as forced laborers in Germany. Initially composed of Kielce, Cracow, Lublin, and parts of Łódź and Warsaw voivodeships, it had an area of 95,000 sq km and a population of some 12 million. The Generalgouvernement included the borderlands of Western Ukraine – Podlachia and the Lemko, Kholm, and part of the Sian regions; covering some 16,000 sq km, these territories had 1.2 million inhabitants of whom 525,000 were Ukrainians and 170,000 were Ukrainian-speaking Roman Catholics (*latynnyky*).

After Germany invaded the USSR, Galicia (the voivodeships of Lviv, Stanyslaviv, and Ternopil) was annexed to the Generalgouvernement on 1 August 1941, increasing its territory to 145,000 sq km and its population to 18 million. Ukrainian territories in the expanded Generalgouvernement covered 63,000 sq km with a population of over 7 million, of which the total number of Ukrainians was nearly 4 million, excluding 500,000 *latynnyky*.

The organization of the Generalgouvernement resembled that of a centralized administrative unit of the Third Reich but was closer to that of a directly occupied territory (eg, *Reichskommissariat Ukraine) than to a pseudostate formation like the Protectorate of Bohemia and Moravia. All power was in the hands of the Nazi governor-general H. *Frank, who acted directly on Hitler's orders and was accountable to him alone. All responsible po-

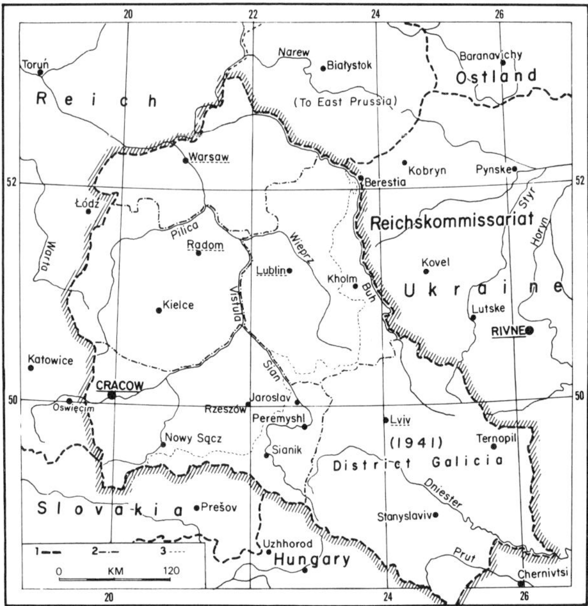

THE GENERALGOUVERNEMENT

1. Borders of the Generalgouvernement
2. District borders; district capitals underscored with dots
3. Polish-Ukrainian ethnic boundary

sitions in the administration were staffed by Germans; Polish and Ukrainian officials were used only in minor capacities. The central administration consisted of 12 (later 14) main departments and a Secretariat of State. The territory was divided into five districts, each with a corresponding administrative structure. Limited local self-rule existed, although officials and members of consultatory councils were appointed, and the Führerprinzip was adopted everywhere. Ukrainians were in a minority in the Cracow and Lublin districts but formed the majority in the 'Distrikt Galizien,' governed by O. *Wächter.

Galicia was annexed to the Generalgouvernement against the will of the Ukrainian population, dashing all hopes that the Ukrainians may have had to statehood and to political independence. The local language (Ukrainian or Polish) was used together with German in the courts, local administration, and schools. In order to promote cultural and welfare activities, and to stimulate some areas of the economy, the *Ukrainian Central Committee (1939–45) was created in Cracow and the *Ukrainian Regional Committee (1941–2) was founded in Lviv. These social institutions were controlled by the Germans.

BIBLIOGRAPHY

Kubiiovych, V. *Ukraïntsi v Heneral'nii Hubernii, 1939–1941: Istoriia Ukraïns'koho Tsentral'noho Komitetu* (Chicago 1975)

Gross, J. *Polish Society under German Occupation: The Generalgouvernement, 1939–1944* (Princeton 1979)

V. Kubijovyč, V. Markus

Genetics. Branch of biology dealing with the inheritance of characters in living organisms. It is concerned with the principles of the mutation, conservation, transfer, and expression of information contained in genes. Because both physicochemical and behavioral characteristics depend to a large extent on an organism's genetic structure, genetics underlies all other biological disciplines and has had a great influence on their development. It is central to studies of populations, evolution, speciation, and phylogeny, as well as to much of biochemistry and cytology. G. Mendel, who in 1865 first formulated the basic laws of the transmission of hereditary traits and postulated discrete units of heredity to account for these laws, is recognized as the founder of genetics, although the science began to develop only in the early 20th century when Mendel's works were rediscovered. In 1912 A. Sapiehin began to teach genetics at New Russia (Odessa) University.

In Ukraine Mendelian genetics began to develop in the early 1920s as the new ideas from Western Europe were introduced by the Ukrainian cytologist H. Levytsky. Adopting T. Morgan's chromosomal theory of heredity in 1922, H. Levytsky popularized cytogenetics and other recent discoveries in genetics. In 1923 the Commission of Experimental Biology and Genetics was set up at the VUAN to co-ordinate research in genetics and selection in Ukraine. Its chairman was I. Shmalhauzen, who worked in the Department of Experimental Zoology at the VUAN Institute of Zoology and Biology on certain phenogenetic traits and the development of vertebrates. In 1934 a genetics department, headed by I. Ahol, was established at this institute. Its most important research dealt with radiation-induced mutations in drosophila (P. Sytko and P. Khranovsky) and the effects of X-rays on chicken spermatozoa and embryos (N. Tarnavsky). In 1937 under S. Hershenzon's leadership the department turned to research on chemically induced mutations, the mutagenic effect of exogenic DNA, and the role of genetic polymorphism in speciation. Besides Hershenzon, P. Rokytsky and T. Dobzhansky did early research in population genetics in Ukraine. Among Ukrainian biologists who made contributions to applied genetics and selection before the Second World War were M. Vetukhiv, H. Karpechenko, V. Remeslo, and M. Ivanov.

From the mid-1930s Mendelian genetics in the USSR came under increasing attack by T. *Lysenko and his supporters in the scientific community and the Communist party. Defenders of the discipline were dismissed from their posts and some (I. Ahol, H. Karpechenko, and H. Levytsky) were even arrested and perished in prison. In 1948 Lysenkoism was established as the official Soviet position in biology. Hundreds of Soviet scientists were dismissed or demoted, departments and institutes of genetics were closed down, and books on genetics were destroyed. For 16 years Lysenko and his followers enjoyed virtually complete control over Soviet biology and agronomy and immunity from criticism. The downfall of their staunch supporter N. Khrushchev in 1964 exposed them to strong criticism from the scientific community and led to a rapid loss of influence.

The rebirth of genetics in Ukraine is closely associated with S. Hershenzon, who survived the repeated purges of Lysenko's opponents without abandoning genetic research. In the 1950s he pioneered the development of molecular genetics in Ukraine. Genetic research at the AN URSR was expanded significantly in 1968 when the Sector of Molecular Biology and Genetics was organized. In 1973 it was converted into the Institute of Molecular Biology and Genetics. As acting director of the new institute, Hershenzon promoted the development of genetic engineering. The mutagenic activity of viruses and exogenous DNA continues to be studied. The transfer of bacterial genes into the cells of higher organisms and the fermentative synthesis of genes outside the organism are investigated. A number of genes have been synthesized by V. Kavsan and A. Ryndich using the method of inverse transcription from RNA to DNA. The biological effects of transplanting embryos at an early stage of development have been studied by V. Evsikov, L. Morozova, and T. Titok. The institute applies genetic techniques to improve plant and animal varieties and to detect and correct genetic defects in human cells. Research in genetics is also conducted at the USSR Academy of Medical Sciences *Institute of Gerontology and at the AN URSR institutes of zoology and botany. The principal journal in the field of genetics, *Tsitologiia i genetika*, has been published in Russian since 1967. (See also *Biology and *Botany.)

C. Spolsky

Geneva. City (1985 pop 160,000) on the Rhône River in *Switzerland. Administrative and commercial center of Geneva canton, European headquarters of the UN World Health Organization and other international organizations. As the home to scores of Ukrainian émigrés from the Russian Empire and Austria-Hungary in the late 19th and early 20th century, it was a center of Ukrainian political and cultural life. M. *Drahomanov, a resident from 1876 to 1889, published the journal **Hromada* in Geneva and helped to establish the Ukrainska Drukarnia press there; directed by A. Liakhotsky, it released numerous books, journals, and pamphlets from 1876 to 1918, including many classics of Ukrainian literature and important political tracts. From 1878 to 1881 M. Pavlyk, S. Podolynsky, F. Vovk, M. Ziber, and other Ukrainian socialists collaborated with Drahomanov in Geneva. A number of Ukrainian political figures and journalists have been permanent or temporary residents of Geneva: eg, Ye. Konovalets (1930–6), L. Yurkevych, P. Chyzhevsky, M. Lozynsky, E. Batchinsky, M. Yeremiiv, M. Kushnir, M. Rudnytska, and M. Trotsky. The Ukrainian Red Cross, the Ukraina student organization, the Ukrainian Relief Committee, and the French-language bulletin *Ofinor* had offices there. Today a very small Ukrainian community (about 20 members) exists in Geneva. The city museum owns a portrait of Diderot by D. Levytsky.

BIBLIOGRAPHY
Hrushevs'kyi, M. *Z pochatkiv ukraïns'koho sotsiialistychnoho rukhu: M. Drahomaniv i zhenevs'kyi sotsiialistychnyi hurtok* (Vienna 1922)

Genghis Khan (né Temüjin), b 1155, 1162, or 1167, d 18 August 1227. One of the world's great conquerors. At the turn of the 13th century he united all the nomadic Mongol tribes in a centralized, despotic, military state and then plundered and subjugated neighboring peoples. After proclaiming himself 'universal ruler' in 1206, his armies conquered Siberia (1207), northern China (1211–15), Central Asia (1218–21), and Caucasia. By 1221 they had reached the Crimea. In 1223 the Mongols invaded Rus' after crushing at the *Kalka River the allied forces of the southern Rus' princes and the Cumans. Then they attacked the Volga Bulgars. Genghis Khan's successors continued to raid Asia and Europe. His grandson *Batu Khan laid waste to Rus' in 1237–42, and with his *Golden Horde maintained supremacy over it for many years.

BIBLIOGRAPHY
Vernadsky, G. *The Mongols and Russia* (New Haven 1953)
Grousset, R. *Conqueror of the World* (New York 1966)

Kyrylo Genik

Genik, Kyrylo (Cyril), né Genyk-Berezovsky [Genyk-Berezovs'kyj], b 1857 in Bereziv Nyzhnii, Kolomyia county, Galicia, d 12 February 1925 in Winnipeg. Pioneer community leader. Genik briefly studied law at the University of Chernivtsi. In 1880 he established a school in his native village. Acquainted with prominent radicals, including I. Franko and M. Pavlyk, he was arrested in 1880 after socialist writings were found in his home. In 1896 he led a contingent of settlers to Canada. One of the first educated Ukrainians to settle in Canada, he was employed by the Department of the Interior as an immigration officer (1897–1911) in Winnipeg. From 1897 Genik contributed articles to the Ukrainian-American newspaper *Svoboda* in which he encouraged Ukrainians to join workingmen's associations and insisted that religious life focus on moral improvement rather than ritual and tradition. In 1899 he organized the first Ukrainian urban reading association in Canada, and in 1903 helped to establish the newspaper **Kanadiis'kyi farmer*. He also participated in the founding of the *Independent Greek church. Shunned by radical circles as a suspected agent of the Liberal party and discredited among conservatives for his religious views, Genik gradually withdrew from Ukrainian life after 1905.

Genocchi, Giovanni, b 30 July 1860 in Ravenna, Italy, d 6 June 1926 in Rome. Missionary, specialist in oriental languages, and biblical scholar. After serving as a member of the apostolic legation in Syria and Istanbul and as a missionary, Genocchi was appointed in 1920 by Pope Benedict XV apostolic visitator (with diplomatic powers) to Ukraine. He was prevented from visiting Ukraine and carried out his duties mostly in Poland. In 1923 he became apostolic visitator to Galicia, assisted by Rev I. Buchko as secretary. Genocchi's diplomatic mission is described in two articles by Rev I. Khoma in *Analecta Ordinis S. Basilii Magni*, 3, nos 1–4 (1958–60).

Genocide. A crime against humanity consisting of the deliberate, systematic destruction of entire racial, national, ethnic, or religious groups. Genocide has been practiced throughout history. In the 20th century, the Turkish genocide of the Armenians in 1915–17 was the first instance. The best-known genocides were perpetrated by the Nazi regime during the Second World War, especially against the *Jews and *Gypsies, in Germany and the occupied countries. The term was in fact coined by R. Lemkin in 1944 to describe the Nazi destruction of nations during the war.

Ukrainians have been subjected to genocide under the Soviet regime, especially during the Stalinist *terror, the Second World War, and most notably in the man-made *famine of 1932–3, which afflicted Ukraine, northern Caucasia, and the Volga German ASSR. The genocidal intent of the Soviet authorities is confirmed by the geographic extent of the famine, which affected only certain national groups and especially the Ukrainians; the official Soviet policy of forced grain procurement throughout this period and the speed with which the famine abated after that policy was abandoned; the official rejection of all Western offers of assistance; and especially the continued Soviet export of grain throughout the period. Despite the existence of sufficient food reserves and satisfactory harvests, food was not released to the people and consequently 7 to 10 million people perished, either from starvation or from diseases caused by severe malnutrition. In the case of Ukraine the famine was calculated to destroy the indigenous culture by decimating the nation.

Soviet historians and leaders have denied the existence of any famine in 1932–3, although they have infrequently referred to 'difficulties in the food situation' in the early 1930s, which have been attributed to natural causes and the dislocations resulting from *collectivization and industrialization; these explanations were generally accepted by many contemporary Western observers and later historians. This is due, at least partly, to the fact that Stalin, unlike Hitler, never articulated a genocidal policy vis-à-vis the Ukrainians.

Genocide was recognized as a crime under international law in 1946 under the impact of the revelations at the Nuremberg trials. In 1948, the General Assembly of the United Nations approved the Convention on the Prevention and Punishment of the Crime of Genocide. It went into effect in 1951, but no court of international jurisdiction was created, and international sanctions against violators of the convention have been largely ineffective. The Ukrainian SSR signed and ratified the convention in 1954.

BIBLIOGRAPHY

Deker, N.; Lebed, A. (eds). *Genocide in the USSR: Studies in Group Destruction.* Institute for the Study of the USSR (Munich), series 1, no. 40 (July 1958)

Kamenetsky, I. *Secret Nazi Plans for Eastern Europe: A Study of Lebensraum Policies* (New York 1961)

Conquest, R. *The Nation Killers: The Soviet Deportation of Nationalities* (London 1970)

Horowitz, I. *Taking Lives: Genocide and State Power* (New Brunswick, NJ and London 1980)

Kuper, L. *Genocide: Its Political Use in the Twentieth Century* (Harmondsworth 1981)

Porter, J. (ed). *Genocide and Human Rights: A Global Anthology* (Washington 1982)

Charny, I. (ed). *Toward the Understanding and Prevention of Genocide: Proceedings of the International Conference on the Holocaust and Genocide* (Boulder, Colo 1984)

Kuper, L. *The Prevention of Genocide* (New Haven and London 1985)

Conquest, R. *The Harvest of Sorrow: Soviet Collectivization and the Terror-Famine* (Edmonton and New York 1986)

Serbyn, R.; Krawchenko, B. (eds). *Famine in Ukraine, 1932–1933* (Edmonton 1986)

Genre painting. A style of painting characterized by the depiction of scenes from everyday life. Ukrainian genre painting usually depicts village life. Scenes from everyday life are already found in Scythian art and in the frescoes of St Sophia Cathedral in Kiev (11th century). By definition, however, genre painting is associated with European easel painting, which dates back to the late Middle Ages in the West and the 18th century in Ukraine. Early examples of genre painting in Ukraine include works by V. Shternberg (*Easter in Ukraine*), I. Soshenko (*Boys Fishing*), and T. Shevchenko (*In the Apiary* and *Peasant Family*). With the rise of the *Peredvizhniki group of painters in the late 19th century, genre painting came to enjoy great popularity in the Russian Empire, including Ukraine. At that time K. Trutovsky (*Ukrainian Market* and *Girls at the Well*), I. Repin (*Vechernytsi* and *Village Musicians*), M. Bodarevsky (*Wedding in Ukraine*), and M. Pymonenko (*On the Stile*) were among the more prominent genre painters. Later works depicting everyday life were painted by, among others, P. Martynovych, I. Izhakevych, F. Krasytsky, A. Zhdakha, F. Krychevsky, I. Severyn, O. Murashko, and A. Petrytsky, many of whom were associated with the Peredvizhniki, and by the Western Ukrainians O. Kulchytska, I. Trush, M. Ivasiuk, Y. Bokshay, O. Kurylas, and V. Yarotsky.

In the first half of the 20th century, with the influence of Western experimentalism, genre painting declined in Western Ukraine and often appeared simply as a pretext to formal stylization, especially in graphic arts. Examples of this include the historical works of E. Kozak, M. Butovych, and H. Mazepa. In Soviet Ukraine, the first works depicting contemporary Soviet life were painted by O. Pavlenko (*Village Consultation*), K. Trokhymenko (*The Felling of Oaks*), V. Korovchynsky (*Laying Out a Newspaper*), S. Prokhorov (*Women's Section, Village Commune,* and *The Homeless*), I. Padalka (*Harvesting Eggplants*), and others. In the 1930s, in addition to village life, industrial themes also became popular subjects for genre painting (eg, K. Trokhymenko's *Kadry Dniprobudu*), while war scenes became a dominant theme during and after the Second World War (eg, A. Cherkasky's *Tragedy on the Dnieper* and Ye. Svitlychny's *Meeting in the Hospital*). More recently, prominent painters in this style have included V. Chekaniuk (*First Acquaintance* and *Siberian Morning*), V. Patyk, O. Maksymenko (*Before Sowing*), S. Hryhoriev (*Enrollment in the Komsomol*), V. Ovchynnykov (*Call to Strike*), M. Bozhiy, and T. Yablonska. In the USSR, genre painting is widely propagated as the expression of socialist realism. Among emigrants, M. Dmytrenko and D. Potoroka have specialized in genre painting.

J. Hnizdovsky

Gensorsky, Antin [Gens'ors'kyj], b 1890 in Bolestrashychi, Peremyshl county, Galicia, d 15 June 1970 in Lviv. Historian of the Ukrainian language. He graduated from St Petersburg University in 1913. After the First World War he worked as a teacher and in the library of the People's Home in Lviv. From 1939 he taught at Lviv

University, and in 1949–63 he was a senior scholarly associate at the Institute of Social Sciences of the Academy of Sciences in Lviv. He is the author of studies on Ukrainian-Polish linguistic relations in the 13th century and the linguistic influence of Ukrainian on Russian, and of a series of detailed studies on the makeup, paleography, language, and style of the *Galician-Volhynian Chronicle. He was a cocompiler and coeditor of the Polish-Ukrainian dictionary (1958–60).

Gentry. See Nobility.

Genyk-Berezovska, Zina [Genyk-Berezovs'ka], b 11 April 1928 in Solopisky near Prague. Specialist in Ukrainian literature. After graduating from Prague University in 1953, she taught Ukrainian literature there until 1960. Later she became a research associate of the Czechoslovak Academy of Sciences. She is the author of many articles in Czech and Ukrainian on H. Skovoroda, T. Shevchenko, I. Franko, and M. Pavlyk, and on modern Ukrainian writers and poets such as O. Dovzhenko, Yu. Yanovsky, P. Fylypovych, and the *Shestydesiatnyky, and has published surveys of contemporary Ukrainian drama and poetry.

Genyk-Berezovsky, Kyrylo. See Genik, Kyrylo.

Genyk-Berezovsky, Yuliian [Genyk-Berezovs'kyj, Julijan], b 20 June 1906 in Bereziv Nyzhnii, Kolomyia county, Galicia, d 16 November 1952 in Toronto. Literary recitalist; member of the Shevchenko Scientific Society. He taught Ukrainian at Cracow University and, after 1945, Ukrainian, Russian, and Polish at the universities of Graz and Toronto. He was renowned for his recitations of the works of such writers as V. Stefanyk, O. Fedkovych, M. Cheremshyna, and B. Lepky, both in Western Ukraine and in the diaspora.

Geobotany. See Phytogeography.

Geochemistry. Study of the distribution and migration of chemical elements and their isotopes in the various geospheres (solid earth, hydrosphere, and atmosphere). It covers such diverse topics as mineral exploration by geochemical prospecting, environmental pollution, hydrology, climatology, mineral phase equilibria, radiometric dating, origin of life, and paleoclimatology. Geochemical approaches supplement geological studies. They are important in discovering mineral deposits and fossil fuels for commercial exploitation. In Ukraine pioneering work in the field was done by V. *Vernadsky. Geochemical research is conducted at the Institute of Geochemistry and the Physics of Minerals and at the *Institute of Geological Sciences and the Geochemistry of Combustible Materials, both of the Academy of Sciences of the Ukrainian SSR.

Geographic Society of the Ukrainian SSR (Heohrafichne tovarystvo URSR). A scholarly and professional organization devoted to the study of theoretical and practical matters in the field of geography. Founded in 1947 as a branch of the Geographic Society of the USSR, since 1958 it has been affiliated with the AN URSR. In 1978 it had 6,850 members – including scientists, professors, environmentalists, and school teachers – in 27 branches. The central office is in Kiev. The society has 17 subject sections, among them: physical geography, economic geography, geomorphology, cartography, hydrology, meteorology and climatology, regional studies and tourism, and conservation. The most important tasks of the society include studying natural conditions and resources in Ukraine to ensure more rational development and the most convenient placement of industry, environmental protection, the popularization of geography, and the improvement of education. The society organizes conferences and congresses, and publishes scholarly collections.

Geography. The study of the spatial variation and interrelation of physical, biological, and social phenomena on the earth's surface. A broad and general field of knowledge, it is divided into various narrower branches of science: physical geography includes geomorphology and biogeography (phytogeography and zoogeography); human geography incorporates ethnogeography, population geography (*demography), *economic geography, political geography, urban geography, historical geography, and regional geography. Related disciplines include geodesy, *cartography, *geology, *soil science, ecology, *climatology and meteorology, *hydrology, and *oceanography.

The earliest geographic accounts of what is today Ukraine were written by Greek scholars. Herodotus (ca 484–ca 425 BC) described the natural environment and the population of the Black Sea region. His account was corroborated and supplemented by Hippocrates (ca 460–ca 377 BC). In their works, two eminent Greek geographers of the ancient world, Strabo (64 BC–after AD 23) and Ptolemy (2nd century AD), and the Roman naturalist Pliny the Elder (AD 23–79) devoted some attention to the Black Sea region.

In the 10th century, the Byzantine scholar Constantine VII Porphyrogenitus and Arab travelers, such as Ibn Faḍlan, described Rus' in their writings. Much geographic information can be found in the chronicle *Povist' vremennykh lit* (Tale of Bygone Years), the richest source for the history and geography of 12th-century Rus'. From the 13th century onward, descriptions of Ukraine were provided by western-European travelers: in the 13th century by the papal envoy G. da Pian del Carpini and the envoy of Louis IX of France, William of Rubrouck; in the 15th century by the French minister G. de Lannoy and the Venetian noble J. Barbaro; and in 1523–4 by A. Campense in his report on Muscovy to Pope Clement VII.

Several important geographic sources on Ukraine were written in the early-modern period. The 'Two Sarmatias' by Maciej of Miechów (1517) was translated into several languages and remained for many years a basic source of knowledge about Eastern Europe. The German S. von Herberstein's account of his 1517 and 1526 travels in Muscovy, Lithuania, and Ukraine was published in 1549. The travel accounts of Michalo Lituanus (1550, publ 1615), Blaise de Vigenère (publ 1573), and E. Lassota von Steblau (1594, publ 1854, 1866) contain much valuable information about Ukraine. Less important, but still valuable, are descriptions of Poland and Ukraine written by the Poles M. Kromer (1577) and M. Stryjkowski (1573). In the 17th century the most important works dealing with Ukraine's geography were G. Le Vasseur de *Beauplan's *Description of Ukraine* (1650, 1660, 1661) and his maps (1:1,800,000 and 1:452,000).

The Cossack Hetman state established by B. Khmelnytsky attracted many foreign visitors, some of whom included geographic descriptions in the accounts of their trips. Most were envoys: for example, the Venetian A. Vimina (1650, publ 1650, 1890); Paul of Aleppo, the secretary to Patriarch Macarius III of Antioch (1654 and 1656, publ 1896–1900); K. Hildebrandt, a Swedish legate in 1656–7 (publ 1937); the Swedish officer Weihe (ca 1709, publ 1907); and the Dane J. Just (1711).

The first census books of the towns and counties of Left-Bank Ukraine, containing a wealth of historical and geographical information, and the 'chertezh' maps of Ukraine appeared in the second half of the 17th century. The Don and Azov regions' topography was mapped at the end of the 17th century, and Left-Bank Ukraine's in the 1730s. These maps were used in preparing the atlas of Russia published by the Imperial Academy of Sciences in St Petersburg in 1745. In the 18th century the first systematic geographic descriptions of Ukraine were commissioned by the Russian government. At the same time the first systematic topographic surveys were begun. In the latter half of the 18th century Russian officers charted the coast of the Azov and Black seas and the mouths of the Dnieper, Dniester, and Danube rivers. After the Russian annexation of Southern Ukraine (New Russia), the Imperial Academy of Sciences organized expeditions to study this territory. German scholars, such as J. Güldenstädt (in 1768 and 1773–4), P. Pallas (in 1793–4 and 1796), and S. Gmelin (in 1768–9), played key roles in these expeditions. The results of the research conducted appeared in numerous records and publications. In 1781–2 V. Zuev studied the lower Dnieper, Dniester, and Boh basins. Later, in 1837, A. Demidov led a research expedition to the Crimea and the Donbas, which he described in a 4-volume account published in Paris in 1841–2.

The *Rumiantsev census of 1765–9 yielded valuable geographic information, as did several economic-statistical surveys of Left-Bank Ukraine, including O. Shafonsky's topographic and geographic surveys of Chernihiv vicegerency (1786, publ 1851) and the Kharkiv region (1788), K. German's survey of Tavriia (1807), and D. Zhuravsky's survey of the Kiev region (1852). Sections on Ukraine appeared in the geographic, statistical, and nature surveys of the Russian Empire by A. Büsching, Kh. Chebotarev (1776), I. Hackmann, S. Pleshcheev (1786), and notably J. Georgi (3 vols, 1797–1802). By the late 18th century fairly accurate topographical maps had been prepared in Russia and Austria.

The foundations of geography as an independent, modern science were laid in the early 19th century by the German scholars A. von Humboldt and C. Ritter. Modern geography in the strict sense was unknown in 19th-century Russia and Ukraine. Its main branches – geomorphology and human geography – were not developed, and what passed for geography consisted mostly of a description of the earth, ie, of the sum total of geographical data. At the same time, however, certain branches of geography, such as climatology and meteorology, hydrogeography and oceanography, and phytogeography and zoogeography, developed independently. The Imperial Russian Geographic Society, which was founded in St Petersburg in 1845, primarily explored and studied the as yet unknown territories of the empire in Asia and conducted research in geology, ethnography, and statistics. In Ukraine, the *Southwestern Branch of the society existed only in the years 1873–6, and it was not until the 1880s that geography chairs were established at the universities of Kharkiv, Lviv, and Chernivtsi.

Studies in geography were usually written by specialists in related fields working in Ukraine. The statistician P. Köppen, for example, produced an ethnographic map of European Russia (1851) and studied the physical geography of southern Ukraine and the Crimea. J. Kohl, a German geographer, wrote *Reisen in Südrussland* (1847). Research in geomorphology was conducted mostly by geologists, such as N. Borysiak, K. Feofilaktov, A. Gurov, V. Laskarev, I. Levakovsky, I. Sintsov, N. Sokolov, G. Tanfilev, and P. Tutkovsky. Research in climatology and meteorology was conducted by P. Brounov, O. Klosovsky, B. Sreznevsky, and others. M. Maksymovych studied hydrology. Important contributions were made by the soil scientists V. Dokuchaev and Yu. Vysotsky, and the phytogeographers A. Krasnov, J. Paczoski, and G. Tanfilev. Materials on the geography of Ukraine were published in regional and topographic series, such as *Materialy dlia geografii i statistiki Rossii*, **Trudy etnografichesko-statisticheskoi ekspeditsii v Zapadno-Russkii krai* (1872–8), and particularly volumes 2, 7, 9, and 14 of *Rosiia: Polnoe geograficheskoe opisanie nashego otechestva* (1899–1914) edited by V. Semenov, as well as in such reference works as *Geograficheskо-statisticheskii slovar' Rossiiskoi Imperii* (Geographical-Statistical Dictionary of the Russian Empire, 5 vols, 1863–85), and *Słownik geograficzny Królestwa Polskiego i innych krajów słowiańskich* (Geographical Dictionary of the Kingdom of Poland and Other Slavic Countries, 15 vols, 1880–1900). *Die österreichisch-ungarische Monarchie in Wort und Bild*, of which vol 12 (1898) was devoted to Galicia and vol 13 (1899) to Bukovyna, was a useful reference tool to Western Ukraine. In Galicia geographic research was conducted at first by German and (mostly) Polish specialists, such as H. Stupnicki, K. Schmedes, J. Jandaurek, A. Rehman, and E. Romer.

Most scholars before the First World War regarded Ukraine's territories as integral parts of Russia, Poland, or Austria-Hungary; they did not envision Ukraine as a unified whole. The famous French geographer E. Reclus, however, who had been influenced by M. Drahomanov, presented the Ukrainians as a distinct entity in his multivolume work. The best prewar account of Ukraine's physical geography appeared in G. Tanfilev's four-volume geography of Russia (1916–24).

The beginnings of modern Ukrainian geography date from the first decade of the 20th century and are connected with the scholarly activity of the Mathematics–Natural Science–Medicine Section of the Shevchenko Scientific Society in Lviv and that of S. *Rudnytsky, the acknowledged father of Ukrainian geography and author of the first geographic works in Ukrainian. During and immediately after the First World War Rudnytsky wrote works mostly on the geomorphology of the Carpathian Mountains and of Podilia; he produced the first study of Ukrainian geographic terminology and prepared the first geographic conspectus of Ukraine's national territories, which also examined the various branches of geography; he made a survey of the ethnogeography and political geography of Ukraine, and prepared the first and only textbook on Ukraine's geography in a foreign language – *Ukraina, Land und Volk* (1916; English transl:

Ukraine: The Land and Its People, 1918). The first maps of all of Ukraine's territories were also prepared by him.

In the 1920s the flourishing growth of research on Ukraine's natural world at the All-Ukrainian Academy of Sciences (VUAN) did not embrace geography to any great extent. As before the First World War, geographic research was conducted mostly as a sideline by specialists in related disciplines, particularly in geology. The geologist P. Tutkovsky, for example, produced the first comprehensive description of Ukraine's landforms (1924). Research in economic geography was more advanced: in the 1920s several textbooks on Ukraine's economic geography were written by such specialists as I. Feshchenko-Chopivsky, K. Vobly, O. Sukhov, and P. Fomin. Finally, in 1927 the Ukrainian Scientific Research Institute of Geography and Cartography was established in Kharkiv. Its founders hoped to make it the center of geographic studies in Soviet Ukraine. S. Rudnytsky came from Prague at the invitation of the Soviet government to direct the institute; at the beginning of the 1930s he was also appointed to the newly created chair of geography at VUAN. Associates of the institute included such scholars as M. Dmytriiev, V. Butsura, and K. Dubniak. The institute published two volumes of its journal *Zapysky* and several maps before it was abolished in 1934 and Rudnytsky was exiled for 'propagating nationalism and fascism in geography.' Thus the Stalinist terror resulted in the decline of geography as an independent science.

Except for Kiev and Kharkiv universities, no postsecondary school in Soviet Ukraine in the interwar period had a geography department. (A Geographic Institute was founded in 1917; directed by P. Tutkovsky, it became part of Kiev University in 1919.) As before the First World War, Ukrainian-language works dealing with geography continued to be written mostly by geologists. Contributions on Ukraine's geomorphology were written by R. Virzhykovsky, M. Dmytriiev, H. Zakrevska, V. Krokos, B. Lichkov, and S. Sobolev. V. Herynovych (who was persecuted in the 1930s) and H. Velychko, an urban geographer, researched the human geography of Podilia. Geographic methodology was studied by K. Dubniak. Besides the scholars who were active before the Second World War, L. Danylov, M. Danylevsky, A. Ohiievsky, Ye. Oppokiv, and others contributed to climatology and hydrology. Research in biogeography was conducted by D. Zerov, Ye. Lavrenko, Yu. Kleopov, O. Fomin, O. Yanata, M. Sharleman, and others. H. Makhiv studied soil science, and he, Tutkovsky, Fomin, and Yanata contributed works on regionalization and in regional studies. Most of these works appeared before the Stalinist suppression of Ukrainian studies and were a significant contribution to the geography of Ukraine.

In interwar Western Ukraine geographical research was conducted in Lviv by Polish scholars, such as E. Romer, A. Zierhoffer, and J. Czyżewski of the Geographic Institute at Lviv University, and by the Geographic Commission of the Shevchenko Scientific Society, which was chaired by V. Kubijovyč, a specialist in the human geography of the Carpathian region and the demography of Ukraine. Yu. Poliansky's geological research, particularly on Podilia, touched on questions of geography. Among the geographers associated with the commission were M. Dolnytsky (who lived and taught in Prague), M. Kulytsky, V. Ohonovsky, S. Pashkevych, O. Stepaniv-Dashkevych, I. Teslia, and I. Fediv.

Since the 1930s geography in the Ukrainian SSR has been subservient to Soviet economic policy, and the political aims and economic programs of the Communist party have directly influenced not only the scientific pursuits of Ukrainian geographers, but also geography as a science. During the Stalin period Soviet geography was severely circumscribed. To legitimize his grandiose economic plans, which demanded extraordinary effort, Stalin proclaimed that it was incorrect to connect the economic laws of development with nature's physical processes. Consequently Soviet geography was divided into two separate systems of science – the physical sciences and the economic sciences (ie, physical geography and economic geography). The division of theoretical work into narrow specialties and the underestimation of the practical value of geography resulted in major blunders in the utilization of natural resources.

N. Khrushchev's economic reforms, which introduced decentralization and regional administration, induced the enthusiastic study of *economic regionalization, a discussion on integrating the physical and economic aspects of the environment in research, and even the proposal that geography be treated as a unified science. Khrushchev's ambitious plans, however, were questioned by specialists, and to preserve party discipline the concept of geography as a unified science was rejected officially.

After Khrushchev's ouster L. Brezhnev's cautious policies and the party's appeals to make better use of natural resources, to protect the environment, and to plan economic complexes more efficiently obliged physical geographers to focus on the influence of human activity on the natural world, and allowed economic geographers to assess natural environment as an important factor in economic development. The study of labor resources, urban and regional planning, and the interaction between human groups and the environment pointed out the need for an understanding of sociological processes. As a result of the emphasis placed on the social aspects of development in the plans of the CPSU, economic geography was officially renamed socioeconomic geography at the 1980 congress of the Geographic Society of the USSR.

Geography in Soviet Ukraine has developed through similar stages to that in the USSR as a whole. It has not been directed, however, as in Moscow or to some extent in Leningrad, toward the development of theory or a broader range of problems, but toward the republic's internal, practical needs. With the aim of improving agriculture, work has been undertaken in the study of natural-territorial complexes, the production of large-scale soil maps, the assessment of soils and the compilation of a land cadastre, the testing of countermeasures against soil erosion, waterlogging, droughts, and hot, dry wind action, studies of the thermal and water regime of Ukraine, particularly in areas of agricultural irrigation, the introduction of agroclimatic regionalization, and the assessment of natural resources. To meet the demands of industry and economic development in general, work on economic regionalization and research on territorial production complexes, on the geography of separate branches of the economy, and on human and urban geography by research institutes, planning institutes, and university geography departments has been promoted.

The Stalinist terror decimated the number of geographers in Ukraine, and new specialists were trained only after the Second World War, when geography chairs were established at many higher educational institutions and geography faculties were created at Kiev, Kharkiv, Lviv, Odessa, Chernivtsi, and Symferopil universities. Because of the shortage of Ukrainian geographers, many graduates of Moscow University received teaching appointments in Ukraine. Later, candidates of geographic sciences from Kiev University were hired by the faculties of some universities, by pedagogical and economic institutes, and by research agencies in Ukraine.

Geographic research has been conducted not only at the universities, but also by the Ukrainian Geological Committee (est 1918), the Ukrainian Geodetic Administration (est 1919), the Ukrainian Hydrometeorological Service (est 1921), the Ukrainian Hydrometeorological Institute (est 1953), the Council (previously Commission) for the Study of the Productive Resources of the Ukrainian SSR (est 1934), the AN URSR institutes of Economics, Geological Sciences, Botany, Zoology, Hydrobiology, the Biology of Southern Seas, Marine Hydrophysics, and Geophysics, and such Ukrainian planning and research institutes as the Institute of Soil Science and Agrochemistry, the Institute of City Planning, the Institute of Water Management Construction, the Institute of Land Regulation, and the Institute of the Coal, Ore, Petroleum, and Gas Industries. The Sector of Geography was established in 1964 at the AN URSR Institute of Geological Sciences; since 1982 it has been a section of the Institute of Marine Hydrophysics. Its six departments have adopted a multifaceted research program, but an authoritative institute of geography like the one that existed in Kharkiv from 1927 to 1934 has not been re-established.

The Geographic Society of the USSR, which superseded the Imperial Russian Geographic Society, co-ordinated and popularized geographic research in the Soviet Union. In 1947 it established a branch in Kiev, with 27 city and oblast departments. In 1959 this branch was named the Ukrainian Geographic Society; in 1964 it was renamed the *Geographic Society of the Ukrainian SSR.

From 1935 to 1953 geographic works published in Soviet Ukraine had small pressruns and were written almost without exception in Russian. After Stalin's death the number of Ukrainian-language publications increased, and new periodicals, monographs, and atlases appeared. Monograph publications in the physical and biological branches of geography have been more numerous and of a better quality than those in the human and social branches. Many good monographs and textbooks in geomorphology, in particular, have been written by such scholars as V. Bondarchuk, K. Herenchuk, A. Lanko, O. Marynych, P. Tsys, and M. Veklych. Many monographs in *climatology, hydrography, soil science, and phytogeography have also appeared. The first volumes in a series of attractive, well-researched monographs on the natural environment of Ukraine's oblasts have been published under the general editorship of O. Marynych in Kiev and K. Herenchuk in Lviv. *Ukraina i Moldaviia* (Ukraine and Moldavia, 1972), edited by O. Marynych and M. Palamarchuk, is a solid contribution to the all-Union series *Prirodnye usloviia i estestvennye resursy SSSR* (The Natural Conditions and Natural Resources of the USSR).

Human geography in Soviet Ukraine has been dominated by economic geography, and most textbooks have been surveys of physical and economic geography. They include O. Dibrova's *Heohrafiia Ukraïns'koï RSR* (Geography of the Ukrainian SSR, 1954, 2nd edn 1958), and a recent text with the same title edited by M. Pistun and Ye. Shypovych (1982). M. Palamarchuk's *Ekonomichna heohrafiia Ukraïns'koï RSR* (Economic Geography of the Ukrainian SSR, 1975) is used as a handbook by teachers. The large work published by the AN URSR Institute of Economics, *Narysy ekonomichnoï heohrafiï URSR* (Studies of the Economic Geography of the Ukrainian SSR, 2 vols, 1949, 1952), has not yet been surpassed by any other publications, including the two all-Union series, each of which has two volumes devoted to Ukraine (Moscow 1957–8 and 1969). Most monographs in economic geography, by such authors as O. Davydenko, H. Hradov, I. Mukomel, M. Palamarchuk, Ye. Pitiurenko, V. Popovkin, and F. Zastavny, are devoted mostly to the development of economic regions, territorial specialization, industrial complexes, or urban systems.

Human geography, in which ethnographic, sociological, historical, and political factors play an important role, does not exist in the USSR. Research on the history of population shifts and migration, particularly in southern Ukraine, has been conducted by demographers or historians, such as E. Druzhinina, V. Kabuzan, and H. Makhnova. Similarly, ethnographers, and not geographers, study regional and ethnic traits, interethnic relations, and the interrelationship between ethnicity and the natural environment. Only a few monographs have been published on these subjects, several of them by V. Naulko.

Geographic periodicals reflect the skewed and fragmented state of geography in Soviet Ukraine. Until 1956 articles on physical geography dominated in university serial publications. Since then research in other areas has developed, particularly in economic geography. The Ukrainian Branch of the Geographic Society began publishing *Heohrafichnyi zbirnyk* in 1956, and its Lviv, Kharkiv, Crimea, Chernivtsi, Dnipropetrovske, and Melitopil departments have published their own series and bulletins in Ukrainian or Russian. Several important serial publications and interagency series have appeared: Kiev University's *Naukovi zapysky Kyïvs'koho universytetu: Trudy heohrafichnoho fakul'tetu* (1950–), *Visnyk Kyïvs'koho universytetu: Seriia heolohiï ta heohrafiï* (1958–), *Rozmishchennia produktyvnykh syl Ukraïns'koï RSR: Mizhvidomchyi naukovyi zbirnyk* (1964–), and *Ekonomichna heohrafiia: Mizhvidomchyi naukovyi zbirnyk* (1966–); Lviv University's *Visnyk L'vivs'koho universytetu: Seriia heohrafichna* (1962–); Kharkiv University's *Ekonomicheskaia geografiia: Respublikanskii mezhvedomstvennyi nauchnyi sbornik* (1964–); *Heohrafichni doslidzhennia na Ukraïni* (1969–), published jointly by the AN URSR and the Geographic Society; *Demohrafichni doslidzhennia: Respublikans'kyi mizhvidomchyi naukovyi zbirnyk* (1970–) of the AN URSR Institute of Economics; *Fizychna heohrafiia ta heomorfolohiia: Mizhvidomchyi naukovyi zbirnyk* (1970–); *Ukraïns'kyi istoryko-heohrafichnyi zbirnyk* (1971–) of the AN URSR Institute of History; and *Problemy heohrafichnoï nauky v Ukraïns'kii RSR* (1972–) of the AN URSR Sector of Geography. Geographic serials have not flourished, however. After a few years many have been discontinued, while the leading interagency collections *Ekonomichna heohrafiia* and *Fizychna heohrafiia i heomorfolohiia* have been published, like *Geodeziia, kartografiia i aerofotos"emka: Respublikanskii mezhvedomstvennyi nauchno-tekhnicheskii sbornik* (1964), in Russian since 1977.

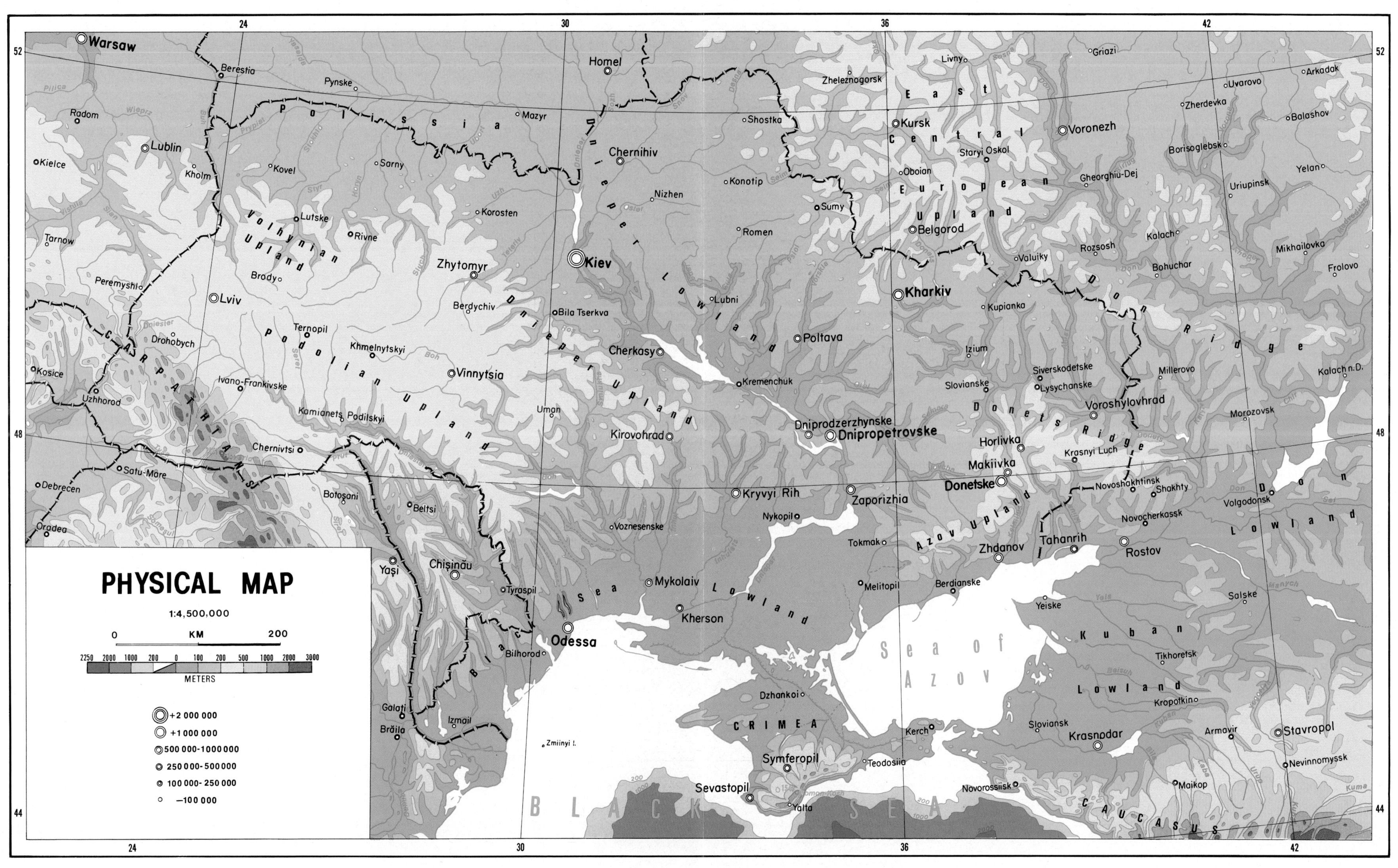

PHYSICAL MAP
1:4,500,000
0 KM 200
2250 2000 1000 200 0 100 200 500 1000 2000 3000
METERS
+2 000 000
+1 000 000
500 000-1000 000
250 000-500 000
100 000-250 000
–100 000
Warsaw
Berestia
Pynske
Homel
Radom
Lublin
Kielce
Kholm
Kovel
Sarny
Mazyr
Polissia
Chernihiv
Nizhen
Shostka
Konotip
Romen
Sumy
Kursk
Oboian
Staryi Oskol
Belgorod
Voronezh
East Central European Upland
Zheleznogorsk
Livny
Griazi
Uvarovo
Arkadak
Zherdevka
Balashov
Borisoglebsk
Gheorghiu-Dej
Uriupinsk
Yelan
Kalach
Rozsosh
Mikhailovka
Frolovo
Bohuchar
Valuiky
Tarnow
Lutske
Rivne
Korosten
Volhynian Upland
Brody
Zhytomyr
Kiev
Dnieper Lowland
Peremyshl
Lviv
Berdychiv
Bila Tserkva
Lubni
Kharkiv
Kupianka
Don Ridge
Ternopil
Drohobych
Podolian Upland
Khmelnytskyi
Vinnytsia
Cherkasy
Dnieper Upland
Poltava
Izium
Kremenchuk
Sloviansk
Siverskodonetske
Lysychanske
Millerovo
Kalach n.D.
Kosice
Uzhhorod
CARPATHIANS
Ivano-Frankivske
Kamianets Podilskyi
Uman
Voroshylovhrad
Donets Ridge
Morozovsk
Kirovohrad
Dniprodzerzhynske
Dnipropetrovske
Horlivka
Krasnyi Luch
Chernivtsi
Makiivka
Satu-Mare
Debrecen
Botoşani
Kryvyi Rih
Zaporizhia
Donetske
Novoshakhtinsk
Shakhty
Volgodonsk
Don Lowland
Beltsi
Nykopil
Oradea
Voznesenske
Novocherkassk
Azov Upland
Tokmak
Zhdanov
Tahanrih
Rostov
Yaşi
Chişinău
Mykolaiv
Melitopil
Berdianske
Tyraspil
Sea Lowland
Kherson
Yeiske
Salske
Black
Odessa
Sea of Azov
Kuban
Bilhorod
Tikhoretsk
Dzhankoi
Lowland
Galati
Kropotkino
Izmail
Brăila
CRIMEA
Kerch
Sloviansk
Krasnodar
Armavir
Stavropol
Zmiinyi I.
Symferopil
Teodosiia
Nevinnomyssk
Sevastopil
Yalta
Novorossiisk
Maikop
BLACK SEA
CAUCASUS
24
30
36
42
52
48
44

BIBLIOGRAPHY
Tanfil'ev, G. *Geografiia Rossii. Chast' 1. Vvedenie: Istoriia issledovaniia, uchrezhdeniia i izdaniia, kartografiia* (Odessa 1916)
Sichynsky, V. *Ukraine in Foreign Comments and Descriptions from the VIth to the XXth Century* (New York 1953)
Prykladni pytannia heohrafiï Ukraïns'koï SSR (Kiev 1964)
Baranskii, N., et al (eds). *Ekonomicheskaia geografiia v SSSR: Istoriia i sovremennoe razvitie* (Moscow 1965)
Suchasni problemy heohrafichnoï nauky v Ukraïns'kii RSR (Kiev 1966)
Problemy heohrafichnoï nauky v Ukraïns'kii RSR, nos 1–3 (Kiev 1972–5)
Teoretychni i prykladni pytannia heohrafiï (Kiev 1972)
Ocherki istorii geograficheskoi nauki v SSSR (Moscow 1976)
V. Kubijovyč, I. Stebelsky

Geography of Ukraine, physical. From a geographical viewpoint Ukraine consists not only of the Ukrainian SSR but also of the adjacent lands inhabited predominantly by Ukrainians (see national and ethnic *territory). It lies between 44°30′ and 52°50′ north latitude and between 20°30′ and 42°00′ east longitude, and extends from the Tysa River, the mouth of the Danube, the Black Sea, and the Caucasus Mountains in the south to Narev River, the swamps of Polisia, and the upper reaches of the Desna River in the north; and from the Poprad, Sian, and Vepr rivers and the Bilovezha Forest in the west to the semideserts between the Don River and the Caspian Sea in the east.

Ukraine is one of the natural regions of Eastern Europe. It differs from neighboring regions by a series of gradations without any sharp breaks. From the standpoint of geology (see *Geology of Ukraine), the core of the natural region consists of the Ukrainian Shield. Occupying the southwestern part of the East European Platform, Ukraine serves as a transition to the Mediterranean Geosyncline in the south. The Ukrainian part underwent greater and more recent tectonic disturbance than the rest of the East European Platform. The southern frame of Ukraine consists of the Carpathian-Crimean-Caucasian Folded Zone; its northern and northeastern frame, of the Don-Dnieper Aulacogen; its western frame, of the Lviv Trough and the Lviv-Lublin Depression; and its eastern frame, which merges with the Voronezh Crystalline Massif in the north and the Black Sea–Caspian Sea Divide in the south, of the Azov-Kuban Depression.

The relief is superimposed on this geological framework. It consists mostly of flat to gently rolling lowland, a legacy of the long period of stability of the East European Platform. Since mountains rising above 1,000 m occupy only 1.5 percent of Ukrainian territory, the mean elevation for Ukraine is 207 m.

Ukraine's relief is characterized by parallel, non-continuous belts of mountains, depressions, uplands, and lowlands that extend from west to east. Five belts may be distinguished: (1) the belt of folded mountains in the south consisting of the Carpathian, Crimean, and Caucasus mountains, which is bounded in the south by the Tysa Lowland and the Black Sea Depression, while the mountain ranges are separated from each other by the Moldavian Plain, the Black Sea, and the narrow Kerch Strait; (2) the belt of submontane and southern depressions lying north of the mountains and consisting of the Sian, Dniester (Subcarpathia), Black Sea, Azov, Lower-Don, and Kuban lowlands; (3) the compact belt of uplands north of the depressions, extending from the upper Vistula River in the west to the Donets River in the east, and consisting of the Roztochia, Opilia, Volhynia-Kholm, Podilia, Pokutia-Bessarabia, and Dnieper uplands, the Zaporozhian and Donets ridges, and the Azov Upland; (4) the belt of northern lowlands, which includes Podlachia and the Polisia, Chernihiv, Dnieper, and Donets lowlands; and (5) the separate system in the northeast consisting of the southern spurs of the Central (East European Central or Central Russian) Upland and of the Don Lowland, both of which have a meridional orientation.

The drainage system, which cuts across the relief belts, unifies Ukraine in the north-south direction. Most of the rivers flow into the Black and Azov seas. The drainage basins of the Dniester, Boh, and Kuban lie entirely within Ukrainian territory, as does most of the Dnieper and some of the Don Basin. Only the upper reaches of the Buh, Sian, and other tributaries of the Vistula, which flows into the Baltic Sea, lie within Ukraine.

Fluvial processes (erosion, transportation, and deposition of materials by water) were the chief agents that shaped Ukraine's landforms. As is evident from the substantial deposits of loess throughout Ukraine, except for Polisia and mountain slopes, Ukraine remained beyond the reach of the continental ice sheet during the Pleistocene glaciation. It was only in the Riss (or Dnieper) stage, when glaciation was at its height, that the ice cap covered Polisia and sent lobes down the Dnieper and Don lowlands. The continental ice sheet was a formidable source of meltwater that left huge ravines and valleys as it flowed south.

Glaciation left a distinct imprint on the landforms only in northwestern Ukraine. On territory that was covered by or adjacent to the ice sheet three types of landforms emerged: (1) ground moraine, which formed under the ice; (2) terminal moraine, which formed at the edge of the ice; and (3) outwash plain, formed by braided streams of meltwater extending well beyond the ice sheet. Ground moraine landforms are most common in Polisia and less so in the Desna Basin. In the Dnieper Lowland southeast of Kiev they are covered by a veneer of loess. Terminal moraine deposits are limited to northwestern Ukraine: to the region near Lake Svytiaz north of Kovel, and to a gentle arc from Verkhy through Volodymyrets and Vysotske. Outwash plains are found in the northern part of the Chernihiv Lowland, the southern part of Polisia, interspersed among the moraines of Polisia and Podlachia, and in the western part of Subcarpathia. They were formed by meltwaters from the continental ice sheet northwest of them and from mountain glaciers in the Carpathians. Drying winds caused erosion of the light-textured surface and formed sand dunes, many of which are anchored by vegetation.

Aeolian processes were particularly intensive during the glacial stages of the Pleistocene, when strong, dry winds removed fine particles from the bare periglacial surfaces and deposited them further south in sheltered valleys or in areas with more substantial vegetation. Thus loess accumulated throughout most of Ukraine. The deepest deposits (25–50 m) were left on the oldest uplands and on high river terraces that were least prone to erosion. Wind and water continued to modify the loess layer. In the Black Sea and Kuban lowlands, where the climate is drier and hot, dry winds are common, some of the shallow depressions or **pody* were formed probably by the wind.

Fluvial processes are still the dominant relief-shaping force. In the mountains swift streams cut deep valleys, undermine slopes causing slides, and in flood carry coarse sediment downstream. Traces of ice erosion such as U-shaped valleys, cirques, and horns can be found only at the higher elevations of the Carpathian and Crimean mountains, and in the Caucasus (where glaciers still exist). Little remains of the terminal moraines, many of which were removed or modified by the fluvial processes. The highest uplands are deeply incised by rivers and streams. Even lower uplands, which are covered with loess, are susceptible to erosion that forms gullies and ravines. In the lowlands, water erosion is negligible and deposition prevails. Slow-flowing rivers form braided streams with many islands.

*Climate, which includes the forces of erosion and affects the development of *soils, *flora, and *fauna, is a major landscape-forming factor. The climate of Ukraine is temperate, cool, and semicontinental. It differs considerably from that of adjacent regions (the Central European climate of Poland, the East European continental climate of the Moscow region, and the subarid climate of the Caspian Lowland), and constitutes a transitional stage to the Mediterranean climate.

Precipitation and temperature vary inversely in Ukraine. A moisture surplus (compared to the amount necessary for secure crop production) is encountered only in the Carpathians and at the higher elevations of the Caucasus and Crimean mountains. In low-lying areas moisture decreases from north to south: northwestern and northern Ukraine receive an adequate amount; central Ukraine, a varying amount; and south-central Ukraine, the Donets Upland, and the Kuban Lowland, an inadequate amount. Dry conditions prevail in the northern Crimea, the Black Sea Lowland, the Donets Lowland, and the Lower-Don Lowland.

The zonation of moisture balance is reflected in the zonation of soils, natural vegetation (before it was cleared for farming), and wildlife. In northern and northwestern Ukraine gray, acid podzol soils developed on sandy fluvio-glacial deposits under a canopy of coniferous and mixed forests that provide a habitat for a fauna common to the Central European forests. The zone of unstable moisture conditions was conducive to the development, on a loess base, of gray forest soils under broadleaf groves (usually at higher elevations), typical chernozems under meadow steppe, and degraded chernozems under forests that had replaced meadows. Forest and grassland fauna intermingled in this transitional zone of forest-steppe. In the zone of moisture deficiency to the south of the forest-steppe a complex of common chernozems developed on a loess base and under a grassy meadow steppe. The dry Black Sea Lowland was covered with a narrow-leaved grassy steppe, which is associated with southern chernozems and chestnut soils. The fauna of both steppe zones was the typical fauna of the temperate grassland biome.

While moisture balance serves as the major controlling factor in the latitudinal zonation of soils, flora, and fauna, the increasing severity of winters from west to east limits the longitudinal distribution of plants, particularly of broadleaf tree species. Thus the English yew is limited to the westernmost extreme of Ukraine, the hornbeam does not grow beyond the Poltava-Homel line in the east, and Ukraine's border region in the Lower-Don Lowland, with its severe winter and shallow snow cover, marks the eastern limit of winter wheat. The increasing continentality of the climate towards the east, including the depth of ground freezing, results in corresponding modifications of the soil.

Mountains are characterized by a vertical zonation of climate, soils, vegetation, and fauna. Most species of the fauna inhabiting the *Carpathian Mountains are common to the middle-European forests; those in the *Crimean Mountains, a mixture of Mediterranean and endemic species; and those in the Caucasus, a mixture of species from Asia and Europe.

From the standpoint of climate, flora, and fauna, Ukraine is unique. It is the only country in Europe with a predominantly meadow natural vegetation (associated with the forest-steppe and the adjacent meadow steppe) that merges gradually with the forest vegetation in the northwest, the steppe vegetation in the south and east, and the Mediterranean vegetation on the Black Sea shore. (See also *Forest belt, *Forest-steppe, *Regions of Ukraine, *Rivers, *Steppe, and *Water resources.)

BIBLIOGRAPHY

Rudnyts'kyi, S. *Osnovy zemleznannia Ukraïny*, 1 (Lviv 1924)
Kubiiovych, V. (ed). *Heohrafiia ukraïns'kykh i sumezhnykh zemel'*, 2nd edn (Cracow-Lviv 1943)
Lan'ko, A.; Marynych, O.; Shcherban', M. *Fizychna heohrafiia Ukraïns'koï RSR* (Kiev 1969)
Marynych, O.; Lan'ko, A.; Shcherban', M.; Shyshchenko, P. *Fizychna heohrafiia Ukraïns'koï RSR* (Kiev 1982)

I. Stebelsky

Geological Prospecting, Ukrainian Scientific Research Institute of. See Ukrainian Scientific Research Institute of Geological Prospecting.

Geological Sciences, Institute of the Academy of Sciences of the Ukrainian SSR. See Institute of Geological Sciences of the Academy of Sciences of the Ukrainian SSR.

Geologicheskii zhurnal (Geological Journal). Scientific bimonthly published in Kiev by the AN URSR Division of Earth Sciences and the Ministry of Geology of the Ukrainian SSR. It first appeared in 1932 under the title *Zhurnal heoloho-heohrafichnoho tsyklu*. In 1934 it continued under the title *Heolohichnyi zhurnal*, published by the AN URSR Institute of Geological Sciences. Its frequency was increased in 1958 from four to six issues per year. In 1963 the Division of Earth Sciences and the Ministry of Geology assumed responsibility for it. Since 1978 the journal has appeared only in Russian under the present title.

Geology. A science dealing with the structure, composition, and history of the earth's crust. Its major divisions are structural geology (the study of rock geometry and deformation); petrology, mineralogy, crystallography, and geochemistry (dealing with the physical and chemical properties of rock); geotectonics (the study of the structure and movement of the earth's crust); historical geology (the study of the historical origins of the earth's crust and its surface); stratigraphy (the study of rock layers and their formation); paleontology (the study of fossils); economic geology (the study of deposits of useful minerals); hydrogeology (the study of groundwater); engineering geology (the study of geological factors affecting man-made structures); and geophysics (the study of the physical parameters of earth). Because its results are of great economic importance, geological research and the preparation of geological maps often are undertaken by special state institutes. The emergence of geology as a science dates back to the second half of the 18th century.

The first geological explorations in Ukraine were conducted after the 1750s by the Russian Academy of Sciences. The researchers (P. Pallas, S. Gmelin, J. Güldenstädt, and J. Georgi), who were of German origin, studied various aspects of Southern Ukraine, the Crimea, and Caucasia. Beginning in the 1820s, the development of geology and a realization of its practical importance led to the undertaking of more precise surveys. In the 1830s the first detailed descriptions and geological maps of the Donets Basin were made by E. Kovalevsky, O. Ivanytsky, A. Oliveri, and by the expedition organized by A. Demidov. The first geological maps of Ukrainian territories included those of G. Gelmersen (1841), R. Murchison (1845), and A. Meiendorf (1849).

Until 1834 geological research in the Russian Empire was overseen by the Department of Mining and Salt Affairs, then by the General Staff of the Corps of Mining Engineers, and from 1882 by the Geological Committee in St Petersburg, which stressed particularly the development of geological cartography. Departments of geology, including mineralogy and petrology, were established at Kharkiv (under I. Levakovsky), Kiev (under K. Feofilaktov), and Odessa universities, and then at the Mining Institute in Katerynoslav. In the second half of the 19th century, also engaged in geological research were N. Borysiak, O. Hurov, I. Levakovsky, N. Krishtafovich, M. Klemm, and P. Piatnytsky in Kharkiv; M. Andrusiv, P. Armashevsky, V. Luchytsky, and N. Shmalhauzen in Kiev; I. Syntsov and V. Laskarev in Odessa; and N. Lebedev in Katerynoslav. In addition members of the St Petersburg Geological Committee, such as N. Barbot de Marni, conducted geological research in Ukraine in the 1860s, as did N. Sokolov and L. Lutugin in the 1880s. In the 1880s geological surveys and in the 1890s the preparation of the 10-verst geological map of European Russia stimulated research. Studies on Ukraine's geology were published by the universities and the Geological Committee (in its *Trudy*, *Izvestiia*, and *Materialy*). In the 1860s the serial *Sbornik materialov, otnosiashchikhsia k geologii Iuzhnoi Rossii* began to appear in Kharkiv.

Before 1917 the geology of central and eastern Ukraine was studied more than that of any other part of the Russian Empire. This was mostly a result of the need to assess the mineral resources of the Donets Basin, the Kryvyi Rih Iron-Ore Basin, and the Nykopil Manganese Basin. Some prominent geologists who worked in Ukraine, and their areas of specialization, were F. Chernyshev, N. Borysiak, N. Yakovlev, and L. Lutugin (Donets Basin), K. Feofilaktov (Poltava and Kiev regions), P. Piatnytsky (Kryvyi Rih Basin), V. Laskarev (Southern Ukraine, Ukrainian Shield, Volhynia), N. Sokolov (Lower Triassic deposits in Southern Ukraine), I. Levakovsky, O. Hurov (Left-Bank Ukraine, Donets Basin), M. Andrusiv (Neogene deposits), P. Armashevsky (Left-Bank Ukraine), A. Mikhalsky (Podilia), P. Tutkovsky (Volhynia and Polisia), and Ye. Oppokiv (Polisia). V. Dokuchaev studied the Quaternary deposits of Southern Ukraine and A. Karpinsky worked on the tectonics of Ukraine in the context of Eastern Europe.

In Western Ukraine geological research was conducted first by official institutions: the Geological Institute in Vienna, and later the Polish Academy of Sciences in Cracow (1873–). From 1887 to 1911 the academy's Physiographic Commission published a major geological atlas of Galicia (1:75,000) with an explanatory text. In Lviv the Polish Copernicus Society of Naturalists published geological research in its periodical *Kosmos*. Geology was taught at Lviv University and then at the Lviv Polytechnic. Some research was begun at the Mathematical-Scientific-Medical Section of the Shevchenko Scientific Society. Noted specialists in the geology of Western Ukraine included V. Uhlig and R. Tietze (Carpathian Mountains), J. Siemiradzki and W. Teisseyre of Lviv University, J. Niedźwiedzki of the Lviv Polytechnic, R. Zuber, A. Alth, F. Bieniasz, W. Łoziński, and M. Łomnicki.

After the First World War geological research in Ukrainian territory under Polish rule was directed by the State Geological Institute, which had a branch in Galicia – the Boryslav Station for Petroleum Prospecting. Among Polish geologists who studied Ukrainian lands were K. Tołwiński (map of the eastern Carpathian Mountains, 1:200,000), B. Świderski, H. Teisseyre, and W. Rogala (mostly the eastern Carpathians). Ukrainian geologists such as Yu. Poliansky (loess in Podilia, diluvium in Polisia), S. Pasternak (mineralogy), and I. Oleksyshyn (Miocene in Podilia) were associates of the Shevchenko Scientific Society.

In Transcarpathia geological research was overseen by the Czechoslovak Geological Institute. S. Rudnytsky, a Ukrainian geographer, made some contributions to geology.

In Soviet Ukraine geology developed rapidly in the 1920s. Most of the research was concentrated in the VUAN, whose first president was the renowned mineralogist V. Vernadsky. Within the academy's physical-mathematical division a chair of geology, a geology cabinet, a geology section, and the Commission for the Study of the Natural Resources of Ukraine were established. All of these bodies were directed by P. *Tutkovsky. The geology section published its own periodical, *Ukraïns'ki heolohichni visti*. In 1917 a group of scholars led by V. Luchytsky and B. Lichkov organized in Kiev the Ukrainian Geological Committee, on the model of the St Petersburg Geological Committee. In 1922 the committee was reconstituted as an autonomous branch of the latter committee. It published the journal *Visnyk*. The main task of the committee was to carry out geological surveys and to assess the mineral resources of Ukraine.

In 1926 the Geological Institute was established to coordinate the work of the various VUAN bodies, as well as several government-sponsored research centers. Directed by P. Tutkovsky, and then by V. Riznychenko, the institute published the journal *Trudy* (5 vols, 1928–34). Geologists who worked in the above-mentioned institutions included V. Krokos, Ye. Oppokiv, M. Bezborodko (Ukrainian Shield), V. Chyrvynsky, H. Zakrevska, R. Virzhykovsky (Podilia), O. Kaptarenko-Chernousova, and M. Melnyk. Geological work was conducted also in postsecondary schools and scientific institutes in Kharkiv, Odessa, Dnipropetrovske, Mykolaiv, and Kamianets-Podilskyi. Geologists working in Ukraine published their studies, mostly regional geologies, in Ukrainian, usually in the publications of the VUAN. P. Tutkovsky and F. Polonsky compiled the first Ukrainian geological dictionary.

During the 1930s, as the Academy of Sciences was reorganized, geology in Ukraine regressed. The geological institutions in Kiev were reorganized into the AN URSR *Institute of Geological Sciences and geological research was restricted to areas of immediate use – mineral prospecting, hydrogeology, and engineering geology. At the same time, Russian replaced Ukrainian as the primary language of the discipline in Ukraine. In 1929 the Geological Committee was transformed into a branch of the Chief Geological Surveys Administration, which was responsible to the USSR Supreme Council of the National Economy. This body assumed responsibility for most geological exploration in Ukraine. Later this role was assumed by the Committee for Geological Affairs at the USSR Council of People's Commissars, and since 1946 by the USSR Ministry of Geology, which was renamed in 1953 the Ministry of Geology and the Conservation of Mineral Resources. Some research was carried out by the Ukrainian branches of all-Union research institutions under the ministries of the petroleum industry, coal industry, and heavy industry.

Geological surveying, particularly of mining regions, developed rapidly. The entire Ukrainian SSR was mapped on the scale of 1:420,000 and then 1:200,000. Maps of the Donets, Kryvyi Rih, and Nykopil basins, and the Carpathian Mountains were prepared on the scales of 1:42,000, 1:50,000, 1:25,000, and even larger.

Geology chairs and departments were established at universities, polytechnics, and mining and agricultural institutes to train professional geologists. In the 1930s the largest geological institute was the Institute of Geological Prospecting in Kiev, which in 1935 had an enrollment of 1,159 and a faculty of 62. The universities published many geological collections, mostly in Russian.

In the interwar period chairs of geology and mineralogy were established at the Ukrainian Free University in Prague and at the Ukrainian Husbandry Academy in Poděbrady. The faculty included such émigré Ukrainian geologists as F. Shvets, O. Orlov, and A. Cherniavsky.

After the war Kiev, Lviv, and Kharkiv became the main centers for geological research. Geological exploration was placed under one state organization, which in 1965 became the Ministry of Geology of the Ukrainian SSR. Continuous prospecting by its 12 geological and geophysical trusts has led to higher estimates of coal reserves in the Donbas and iron-ore reserves in the Kryvyi Rih Basin, and to the discovery of coal, gas, petroleum, iron ore, magnesium, titanium, and other useful minerals. Seven specialized geological research institutes and the geological faculties at institutions of higher learning have also increased knowledge of the geology of Ukraine. But most research is conducted at such institutes of the AN URSR as the Institute of Geological Sciences, the *Institute of the Geochemistry and Physics of Minerals, the *Institute of Geophysics, the Institute of the *Geology and Geochemistry of Combustible Minerals, and the *Marine Hydrophysical Institute.

Except for such work as that of I. Chebanenko, who proposed a theory of the earth's geological development, most research has been oriented to the practical goals of the five-year plans. The need to expand petroleum and natural-gas reserves prompted research on new types of structures containing hydrocarbons, on methods of prognosis (V. Havrysh), on the distribution of these structures in the Dnieper-Donets Depression and the Black Sea Shelf (H. Dolenko), on seismic detection techniques, and on methods of extraction. Similarly, the need for rare ferrous and non-ferrous metals sparked considerable research on the structure of the Ukrainian Shield (V. Bondarchuk, Yu. Dovhal, G. Kaliaev, and O. Slenzak) and on ore-forming processes. Some research on earthquake prediction, explosion prevention in mines, and groundwater utilization has also been done. Complex geological studies of regions have been very common. Geologists who began making scholarly contributions to the geology of Ukraine after the war include V. Bondarchuk (Polisia, Dnieper-Donets Depression, Carpathian Mountains); M. Bezborodko, L. Lunhershauzen, K. Makov, M. Mirchynk, K. Novyk, N. Pimenova, V. Selsky, and M. Svitalsky; M. Semenenko, and D. Soboliev (Ukrainian Shield); P. Stepanov (Donets Basin); L. Tkachuk (Carpathian Mountains); O. Kaptarenko-Chernousova; and N. Shatsky. Almost all of them contributed to regional geology. More recent researchers of the geology of Ukraine are M. Balukhovsky (Dnieper-Donets Depression); A. Drannik (Ovruch Ridge); B. Hurevych (Moldavian Platform); V. Kaliuzhny (deep rock mineral-bearing fluids); V. Khomenko (Transcarpathian Depression); D. Khrushchov (salt deposits in the Carpathian Foredeep); V. Kityk (salt tectonics of the Dnieper-Donets Depression); I. Maidanovych (Donbas); B. Merlych (hydrology of Transcarpathia); M. Muratov and V. Pchelintsev (the Crimea); O. Petrichenko (salt deposits of the Carpathian Foredeep); O. Vialov (tectonics of the Carpathians and stratigraphy of the Volhynia-Podilia Platform); and A. Radzivill, P. Bukatchuk, Ye. Lazarenko, and B. Volovnyk (Volhynia-Podilia Platform).

Until the mid-1960s many geological publications appeared in Ukrainian. Two landmark reference works were published – V. Bondarchuk's *Heolohiia Ukraïny* (Geology of Ukraine, 1959) and *Atlas paleoheohrafichnykh kart Ukraïns'koï i Moldavs'koï RSR* (Atlas of Paleographic Maps of the Ukrainian SSR and Moldavian SSR, 1960). A major series, *Stratyhrafiia URSR*, was started in 1963, but the 11 planned volumes were never completed. Since 1963 no comparable major work on Ukraine has been undertaken, and technical literature has been published almost exclusively in Russian. Even *Heolohichnyi zhurnal*, the AN URSR geological periodical from 1934, changed from Ukrainian to Russian in 1978.

BIBLIOGRAPHY

Sovetskaia geologiia za 30 let (1917–1947) (Moscow 1947)

Novik, E.; Permiakov, V.; Kovalenko, E. *Istoriia geologicheskikh issledovanii Donetskogo kamennougol'nogo basseina (1700–1917)* (Kiev 1960)

Kleopov, I. *Geologicheskii Komitet 1882–1929 gg.: Istoriia geologii v Rossii* (Moscow 1964)

Popov, V. 'Uspekhi v izuchenii geologicheskogo stroeniia i mineral'nykh resursov Ukrainy,' *Sovetskaia geologiia*, 1967, no. 12

Geologi vysshikh uchebnykh zavedenii Iuzhnoi Rossii (Moscow 1972)

Batiushkova, I., et al. *Istoriia geologii* (Moscow 1973)

Paton, B., et al (eds). *Istoriia Akademii nauk Ukrainskoi SSR* (Kiev 1979)

Tikhomirov, V. *Geologiia v Akademii nauk (ot Lomonosova do Karpinskogo)* (Moscow 1979)
Storchak, P. 'Razvitie mineral'no-syr'evoi bazy geologicheskoi nauki Ukrainy,' *Sovetskaia geologiia*, 1983, no. 10
V. Kubijovyč, I. Stebelsky

Geology of Ukraine. The geological framework of Ukraine consists of two major regions: (1) the southwestern part of the Precambrian East European Platform (centered on the Ukrainian Shield) with adjoining fragments of the Hercynian Platform, and (2) the Carpathian-Crimean-Caucasian Folded Zone, which is part of the Mediterranean Geosyncline. The first represents a portion of the ancestral European landmass that has displayed no tectonism since the end of the Paleozoic Era some 570 million years ago. Previously, in the Archean and Proterozoic eras this area was so intensively folded and subjected to magmatic intrusions that it became very rigid and resistant to subsequent orogenic movement. This craton, however, experienced epeirogenic movements, consisting of broad, reversible, and slow uplift, and subsidence. The former exposed the surface to erosion; the latter, accompanied by submergence, led to the accumulation of sediments that covered the Precambrian rocks to various depths.

The Ukrainian Shield (I) forms the central core of the platform part of Ukraine. It extends in crescent form from Polisia south and southeastward to the vicinity of the coast of the Sea of Azov. Covered by a thin (5–15 m) veneer of Quaternary deposits, these intensively folded Precambrian metamorphic, intrusive, and extrusive rocks are exposed by streams and rivers in an area that, since the Proterozoic Era, has experienced differential uplift.

By contrast, the surrounding parts of the platform experienced various degrees of relative subsidence, downwarping, and accumulation of sedimentary deposits. To the west, southwest, and south the Precambrian rocks lie 1–3 km below the surface of the Volhynia-Podilia Platform (XII), the Bessarabian Platform (XIV), and the Black Sea Platform, whose basement slopes southward towards the Black Sea Depression (XV). West of the Volhynia-Podilia Platform, the Precambrian basement dips below the Lviv Trough (XI) to 6–7 km and continues northwestward under the Lviv-Lublin Depression (VIII). To the north and northeast the Precambrian basement lies 1 km below the Pynske Trough (XIII) and, except for the Chernihiv Arch (IV), again drops precipitously towards the northeast to as much as 10–12 km below the surface of the Dnieper-Donets Trough (V), and then reemerges to the northeast as the Voronezh Crystalline Massif (II). Southeast of the Dnieper-Donets Trough Hercynian tectonic activity becomes evident in the Donets Suborogen (VI) and even more so in the folded structure of the Donets Basin (VII). Because this chain of troughs, extending from the Donets Basin to the Prypiat Trough, underwent some folding like a geosyncline but then again became part of the East European Platform, it is considered transitional and was called an 'aulacogen' by N. Shatsky.

The Carpathian-Crimean-Caucasian Folded Zone belongs to the Alpine mountain-building phase of the Tertiary Period. However, it contains rocks that reveal older tectonic activity, such as the early-to-mid-Paleozoic Caledonian orogeny, and touches the remaining fragments of the Hercynian Platform, which are also part of the Mediterranean Geosyncline. The main components of this zone are the intensively folded and raised structures of the Carpathian, Crimean, and Caucasus mountains. They are bounded to the northeast and the north by their respective foredeeps, including the Carpathian Foredeep, the Moldavian Depression (XVa), the Karkinitska Trough (XVb), and the Azov-Kuban Depression (XVc). At both the northwestern and the southeastern ends the Carpathians and their foredeeps are offset by two Hercynian orogens – the Kielce-Sandomierz Ridge (X) in Poland and the Dobrudja orogen (XVI) south of the Danube. Remnants of Hercynian orogens also make up the Scythian Platform, which manifests itself as the central part of the Crimea and, east of the Sea of Azov, the Azov-Kuban Depression and the Stavropil Uplift.

Geological history. The oldest deposits that form the foundation of the East European Platform occur at shallow depths only within the Ukrainian Shield. Their intensive exploration and study has revealed a complex history that is not yet fully understood. The Ukrainian Shield rocks, dating from 750 to 3,650 million years ago, are mostly metamorphic in origin consisting of gneisses, migmatites, and metabasites. Less than 10 percent of them are magmatic rocks, among which granitoids predominate.

Archean. In the history of the formation of the Ukrainian Shield several successive geosynclinal and platform stages are distinguished. Extensive volcanic processes and the accumulation of very thick sedimentary effusive deposits characterize the earliest recorded stages of the Archean Era. Subsequent folding, intrusive magmatism, and metamorphism produced the strata of gneiss and migmatite, which are oriented mainly in the northwesterly direction. Three complexes are distinguished in this series: the Dnieper complex (gneisses, amphibolites, and migmatites separated by intrusions of granite in the central part of the shield), the Podilia-Berdychiv complex (gneiss), and the Teteriv-Boh complex (gneiss-migmatite). The Teteriv-Boh gneisses are major repositories of graphite. The ultrabasic deposits are associated with the occurrence of chrome, nickel, cobalt, and copper.

Proterozoic. After another mountain-building period the Kryvyi Rih group was deposited in a subgeosyncline that was subsequently folded with its axis in a southerly orientation. The group consists of the Inhul-Inhulets series of biotite, biotite-amphibole, and pyroxene-rich granitic gneisses, the metabasite series of metamorphosed volcanic rocks, and the Saksahan series of arkosic sandstones, phyllites, talc-chlorite schists, clays, marbles, and vast jaspilitic iron-ore deposits.

Subsequently, the Ukrainian Shield underwent erosion and peneplanation. There are no known platform sediment accumulations on it, however, except for the rare Ovruchian series. Located in the northwestern part of the shield, it contains conglomerates, quartzites, sandstones, and pyrophyllitic schists. Concurrently and subsequently, the shield experienced fracture dislocations, intrusions, and effusions. These processes gave rise to the Korosten complex (gabbro and rapakivi-like granite containing titanium-rich ilmenite) in the northwestern Korosten and central Novomyrhorod parts of the shield, and the syenite complex (parts of the Donets Ridge) near the Sea of Azov. They also caused the blocks, into which the shield was fragmented along its axis and perpendicular to it, to rise or subside relative to one another and

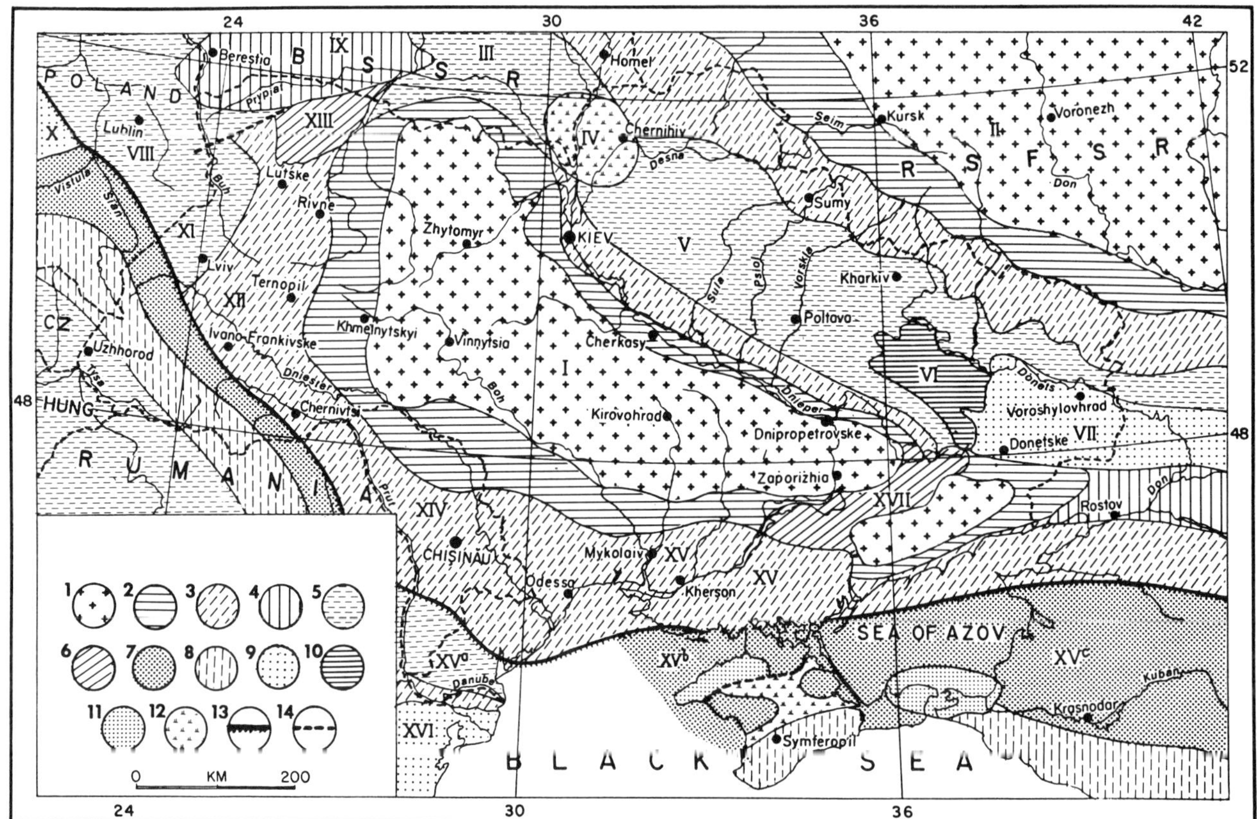

GEOLOGY: TECTONIC SCHEME OF UKRAINE AND ADJOINING TERRITORIES

1. Crystalline massifs
2. Slopes of crystalline massifs
3. Slopes, depressions, and troughs
4. Areas of rather shallow depths (to some 1,000 m) of the Precambrian foundation
5. Depressions and troughs
6. Depressions within the Ukrainian Shield
7. Foredeeps
8. Meganticlines of the Carpathians, the Crimea, and the Caucasus
9. Hercynian orogens
10. Hercynian suborogens
11. Central uplifts (Alpine)
12. Transversal arches
13. Boundary of the East European Platform
14. Volhynia and Tarkhankut faults

I. Ukrainian Shield
II. Voronezh Crystalline Massif
III. Prypiat Trough
IV. Chernihiv Arch
V. Dnieper-Donets Trough
VI. Donets Suborogen
VII. Donets Basin
VIII. Lviv-Lublin Depression
IX. Volhynia-Berestia Uplift
X. Kielce-Sandomierz Ridge
XI. Lviv Trough
XII. Volhynia-Podilia Platform
XIII. Pynske Trough
XIV. Bessarabian Platform
XV. Black Sea Depression, including
  XVa. Moldavian Depression
  XVb. Karkinitska Trough
  XVc. Azov-Kuban Depression
XVI. Dobrudja Orogen
XVII. Orikhiv-Huliai Pole Trough

to form a checkerboard pattern of exposed Archean and Proterozoic deposits as peneplanation continued. Mineralization along the fractures, particularly at their intersection, provided for the occurrence of lead. Weathering of crystalline rocks such as granite resulted in the formation of kaolin. Towards the end of the Proterozoic Era a transgression from the west left Riphean deposits of sandstone near Ostrih.

Paleozoic. This era was marked by the beginning of subsidence around the Ukrainian Shield, marine transgression, and the accumulation of sedimentary deposits. After a recession in the early Cambrian, when terrigenous clays and sands were deposited, the West European Sea encroached again, accumulating clays with phosphate rock, argillites, siltstones, and sandstones in Volhynia and Podilia. These were overlain by Ordovician limestones and, after a phase of uplift and erosion, with Silurian limestones, dolomites, shales, and marls, including pelites, arkoses, and sandstones. Deposits also occurred in the geosyncline that spread through the Carpathian and Caucasus zones, but the Caledonian folding towards the end of the Silurian Period modified the deposits into the Marmara metamorphic rocks that were preserved in the Carpathians (south of Rakhiv) and the phyllites and quartzites of the western Caucasus.

In the beginning of the Devonian Period sand was deposited in lagoons to become the Old Red Sandstone of Podilia. Continued marine transgression in the middle Devonian, however, provided for the accumulation of dolomites, limestones, and sandstones in Volhynia and Podilia. Particularly thick limestone deposits were laid down in the Carpathian Zone; limestones, clays, sandstones, and conglomerates in the Crimean and Caucasus zones; and sandstones, dolomites, limestones, gypsum, and rock salt, which formed into domes that served as traps for petroleum and natural gas, in the Dnieper-Donets Trough. Iron-bearing sandstones and shales were deposited in the Donbas. Towards the end of the Devonian Period, the Hercynian folding known as the Breton phase was associated with volcanism in the Dnieper-Donets Trough and the Donbas, and with the intrusions of granite in the Caucasus.

At the beginning of the Carboniferous Period marine transgression from the east into the Dnieper-Donets Trough and from the west into the Lviv Trough contributed to thick shale and limestone deposits. By the middle Carboniferous Period marine sedimentation changed to lagoon deposition alternating with terrestrial deposition of plant material that turned into coal. Many layers of shale, sandstones, limestones, and coal seams produced up to 12 km of Carboniferous deposits in the Donbas. A less complete record survived in the Dnieper-Donets Trough and the Lviv Trough in the west.

In the Permian Period Ukraine was mostly dry land. Submergence was confined mostly to the south. Marine transgression in the Donbas and the Dnieper-Donets Trough contributed to the deposition of what became sandstone, limestone, dolomite, gypsum, and rock salt, which later domed upward into Mesozoic strata, forming traps for petroleum and gas. The Lower Permian deposits consisted of conglomerates, sandstones, and dolomites in the Caucasus, and outliers of conglomerates, dolomites, quartzites, and sandstones in the Crimean and Carpathian zones.

Mesozoic. Beginning with the Triassic Period, continental conditions prevailed. Only in the south did marine transgression provide for the accumulation of a series of conglomerates, gray-green phyllites, and limestone-dolomites in the Carpathian Zone, dark gray mica schists and sandstones with limestone lenses in the Crimean Zone, and shales, sandstones, and limestones in the Caucasus Zone. Lacustrine colored clays, alluvial sandstones, and marls were deposited in the Dnieper-Donets Trough. The end of the Triassic Period was marked in the Donbas, Crimea, and Caucasia by a crustal disturbance known as the Old Cimmerian folding. Upwarping of the dome-like anticline in the Donbas triggered the release of mercury-bearing fluids from the magma below through fissures into the porous layers of Carboniferous sandstone and produced commercial concentrations of mercury.

In the Jurassic Period the sea in the south deepened and widened until by the Late Jurassic Period it also covered part of the Donbas and the entire Dnieper-Donets Trough. Clays, later interbedded with limestone and oolitic iron-bearing sandstone, were deposited here. In the Carpathian-Dobrudja region the continental deposits were replaced with marine shales and limestones. In the Crimean and Caucasus zones, however, volcanic activity added tuff and lava to the marine deposits of shales, limestones, and dolomites. Volcanism was associated with the New Cimmerian folding, which towards the end of the Jurassic Period affected both the Crimean and Caucasus zones and the Donbas.

Among the Mesozoic deposits the most widespread were the Cretaceous ones. They involved the deposition of conglomerates, sandstones, shales, and marls (collectively known as flysh) into the geosyncline of the Carpathian Zone. In the Crimean and Caucasus zones, however, limestone was deposited. By the Middle Cretaceous Period the sea invaded the Dnieper-Donets Trough from the north and then inundated Podilia and Volhynia, leaving as major islands the Ukrainian Shield and the Donets Ridge. Under these conditions thick strata of carbonate-rich sediments consisting of chalk, marls, limestone, and phosphate-rich sediments were deposited in deeper water, while glauconite sands were laid down along the shores of the remaining islands. The Cretaceous Period was brought to a close with folding in the Donbas, which also marked the beginning of the Alpine folding in the Carpathian-Crimea-Caucasian Zone and led to the regression of the sea.

Cenozoic. The Tertiary Period was marked by the emergence of the Carpathian and Caucasus mountains. By the end of the period the principal topographic landforms and drainage patterns of Ukraine emerged. But during the Paleogene (the earlier epoch of the Tertiary Period), flysh, including oil-bearing shale, was still being deposited in the Carpathian Zone. In the flysh were trapped many useful minerals, including oil and natural gas. Along the Black Sea Platform (the Crimean and Caucasus zones) sandstones and shales, with occasional lenses of phosphate rock, alternated with the prevailing limestone deposits. The Dnieper-Donets Trough was accumulating alternating layers of clays and sands with occasional marls. In the late Eocene (the latter half of the Paleogene Period) a shallow sea even covered much of the central part of the Ukrainian Shield, reworking in places the weathered surface to form small concentrations of bauxite, and leaving behind a veneer of sand, clay, sandstone, and marl.

By the Neogene Epoch of the Tertiary Period the Carpathians emerged as overlapping folds, leaving a narrow body of water, which gradually retreated to the southwest, in the foredeep. In the permeable strata the folds retained commercial deposits of petroleum. Clays, sands, and limestones with rock salt, potassium salts, gypsum, anhydrite, oil, ozocerite, and sulfur were deposited in the intramontane basins and the foredeep. On the south side of the Carpathians the Pannonian Massif sank below the sea, while a ring of volcanoes released great masses of effusives (andesites, dacites, and rhyolites) to form the inner side of the Carpathian Arc. Volcanic eruptions ejected tuff, which was deposited along with clays in the Pannonian Basin. The Crimean Mountains, already established during the New Cimmerian folding at the end of the Jurassic Period, were raised to higher elevations. Large quantities of iron ore were deposited near Kerch. The Caucasus, an archipelago in the Paleogene Period, emerged from the sea as a mountain range. Deposits of petroleum and gas were trapped in the folds. Sediments from the Caucasus, chiefly in the form of clays and sands, were deposited in the Azov-Kuban Depression. The shallow sea retreated from the southeastern part of the Ukrainian Shield, leaving behind bottom deposits of limestone, sand, and clay, bog deposits of lignite, and, along the shore, major concentrations of manganese and titanium.

In the Quaternary Period the Black Sea assumed its present configuration. When drainage into the Mediterranean Sea through the Dardanelles and Bosporus was established, the base level of erosion dropped and deep valleys, which are evident in Ukraine's landscape today, began to be carved by widely meandering streams. As the climate cooled, a series of glacial and interglacial stages provided the last major imprint on the surface deposits of Ukraine. Of the last four glacial ages (Günz, Mindel, Riss, and Würm), all were associated with glacial scour and deposition in the Caucasus, and the last two with minor mountain glaciation in the Carpathians. During the glacial stages deep loess deposits covered nearly three-fourths of Ukraine. During the Riss stage the continental ice sheet modified the surface with scouring and left moraine deposits in the north and down the Dnieper Lowland to Kremenchuk. Its meltwaters left outwash deposits in Polisia. Meanwhile, epeirogenic movements slowly raised the Carpathian, Crimean, and, particularly, the Caucasus Mountains, as well as the Podilian Plateau, the Bessarabian Upland, and the Right-Bank Upland, thus accelerating the erosion processes. At the same time the Black Sea and the Black Sea Lowland continued to subside. This led to the formation of limans. In Polisia peat bogs and small deposits of bog iron ore formed because of impeded drainage.

BIBLIOGRAPHY
Geologiia SSSR, 5, 8, 18 (Moscow 1958, 1974, 1986)
Bondarchuk, V. *Heolohiia Ukraïny* (Kiev 1959)
Atlas paleoheohrafichnykh kart Ukraïns'koï i Moldavs'koï RSR (Kiev 1960)
Bondarchuk, V. *Tektonika Karpat* (Kiev 1962)
Geokhronologiia dokembriia Ukrainy (Kiev 1965)
Bondarchuk, V. *Heolohiia rodovyshch korysnykh kopalyn Ukraïny* (Kiev 1966)
Nalivkin, D. *Geology of the USSR* (Edinburgh and Toronto 1973)
Geologiia Bol'shogo Kavkaza (Moscow 1976)
Osnovnye cherty tektoniki Ukrainy (Kiev 1978)

I. Stebelsky

Geophysics. Study of the earth's physical properties and of the physical processes in the different geospheres. The three major branches of geophysics are solid-earth physics, hydrospheric physics, and atmospheric physics. Some of the branches of the first are gravimetry, geodesy, seismology, geomagnetism, and geothermal studies; of the second, oceanography and land hydrology; and of the third, aeronomy, meteorology, climatology, atmospheric optics and radiotransmission, stratospheric and ionospheric physics.

In Ukraine important contributors to the development of geophysics were V. *Selsky and S. *Subbotin. The chief center of geophysical research is the AN URSR *Institute of Geophysics. The movement of the magnetic poles and motions within the earth's interior are measured at the academy's Poltava Gravimetric Observatory. Geophysical research is conducted also at several universities and specialized institutions in Ukraine.

Geophysics, Institute of the Academy of Sciences of the Ukrainian SSR. See Institute of Geophysics of the Academy of Sciences of the Ukrainian SSR.

Georgia (Georgian: Sakartvelo). A country in central Transcaucasia lying on the coast of the Black Sea. The capital city is Tbilisi (called Tiflis until 1936). In 1921 Soviet rule was established in Georgia. On 13 December 1922 it became part of the Transcaucasian Soviet Federated Socialist Republic. On 5 December 1936 Georgia became a union republic, encompassing the Abkhaz ASSR, Adzhar ASSR, and the South-Ossetian Autonomous oblast. Its area is 69,700 sq km; in 1979 its population was 4,993,200, consisting of Georgians (69 percent), Ossetians (3), Abkhazians (2), Armenians (9), Russians (7), Azerbaidzhanians (5), Greeks (2), Ukrainians (1), Jews, Kurds, and others. Of the 45,000 Ukrainians there, only 53 percent considered Ukrainian to be their mother tongue. Of the 3,570,500 Georgians in the USSR in 1979, 89,400 lived in the Russian SFSR; 16,300 lived in Ukraine; 11,400 in Azerbaijan SSR; and 3,445,000 in the Georgian SSR. Ninety-eight percent of all Georgians in the USSR consider Georgian to be their mother tongue.

Georgia has been a distinct country for two millennia. During the reign of Queen Tamara (1184–1213) it was one of the mightiest states in the Near East. Iranian and Turkish aggression compelled Erekle II to accept Russian suzerainty in 1783. In 1801–10 Russia annexed Georgia, and its royal house was replaced by military governors. Anti-Russian uprisings took place there in 1804, 1812, 1820, 1835, 1840, and 1857. After the fall of the tsarist regime, Georgia experienced a national revival. On 26 May 1918 its Menshevik-dominated national council proclaimed an independent Georgian Democratic Republic; it survived until it was invaded by Soviet troops in February 1921.

Until the 19th century contacts between Ukrainians and Georgians were sporadic and temporary. In the Princely era economic relations existed for a brief while between Georgia and Tmutorokan principality. In 1154 the grand prince of Kiev, Iziaslav Mstyslavych, married Rusudan, the daughter of Dimitri I of Georgia. Thirty years later, Queen Tamara married Yurii, the son of Prince Andrei Bogoliubskii. In the 17th and 18th centuries Cossacks and Georgians occasionally fought the Turks together, and Cossacks fled to Georgia from Turkish captivity. The works of P. Mohyla, D. Tuptalo, and T. Prokopovych were translated into Georgian and widely read. From 1743 many Georgian noble families were granted estates in the Hetman state. These nobles married members of the Ukrainian Cossack *starshyna* and the Ukrainian nobility. In 1738 the Georgian poet D. *Guramishvili settled in the Myrhorod region.

In the first half of the 19th century Ukrainians began living in Georgia, either as exiles or as part of the Russian military or civil service. In the 1860s and 1870s many Georgians began studying at higher schools in Ukraine, particularly at the Kiev Theological Academy. Among them was the writer and teacher Ya. Gogebashvili, who first raised the idea of translating Ukrainian literature into Georgian. Many Georgians remained in Ukraine as lawyers, physicians, or bureaucrats, and formed little communities in the larger towns. Several Georgian figures who graduated from higher schools in Kiev or Kharkiv – L. Ketskhoveli, Sh. Chitadze, Yasamani (M.

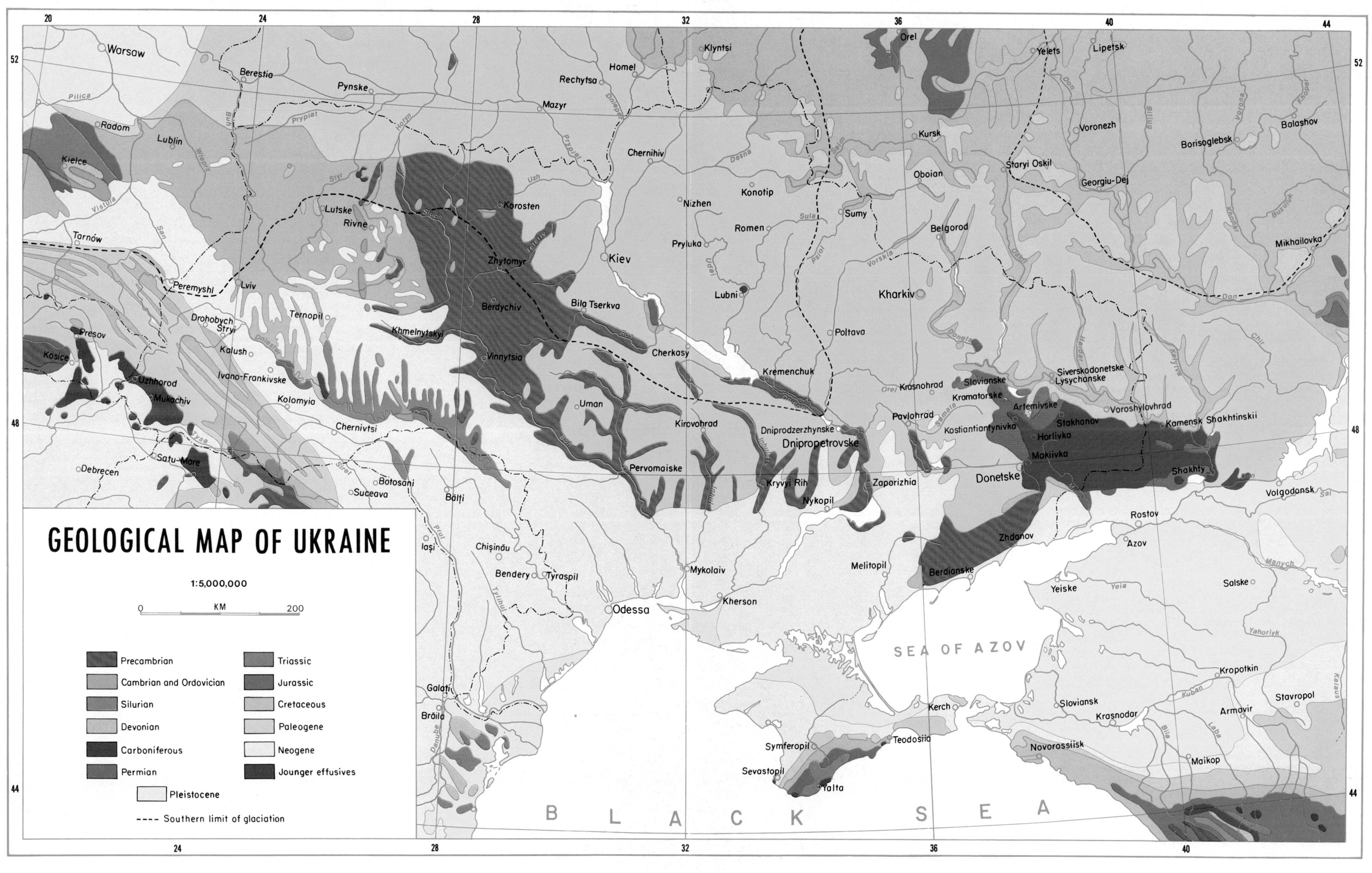
GEOLOGICAL MAP OF UKRAINE
1:5,000,000
0 KM 200
Precambrian
Cambrian and Ordovician
Silurian
Devonian
Carboniferous
Permian
Triassic
Jurassic
Cretaceous
Paleogene
Neogene
Jounger effusives
Pleistocene
Southern limit of glaciation
20
24
28
32
36
40
44
52
48
Warsaw
Berestia
Pynske
Rechytsa
Homel
Klyntsi
Orel
Yelets
Lipetsk
Mazyr
Radom
Lublin
Kielce
Tarnów
Chernihiv
Kursk
Voronezh
Balashov
Borisoglebsk
Staryi Oskil
Oboian
Georgiu-Dej
Nizhen
Konotip
Korosten
Lutske
Rivne
Romen
Sumy
Belgorod
Pryluka
Zhytomyr
Kiev
Mikhailovka
Peremyshl
Lviv
Kharkiv
Lubni
Berdychiv
Bila Tserkva
Ternopil
Drohobych
Stryi
Poltava
Presov
Khmelnytskyi
Kalush
Kosice
Vinnytsia
Cherkasy
Ivano-Frankivske
Kremenchuk
Siverskodonetske
Lysychanske
Uzhhorod
Mukachiv
Kolomyia
Uman
Krasnohrad
Slovianske
Kramatorske
Artemivske
Voroshylovhrad
Chernivtsi
Kirovohrad
Pavlohrad
Kostiantiantynivka
Stakhanov
Kamensk Shakhtinskii
Dniprodzerzhynske
Dnipropetrovske
Horlivka
Makiivka
Satu-Mare
Debrecen
Pervomaiske
Donetske
Shakhty
Botosani
Suceava
Kryvyi Rih
Zaporizhia
Nykopil
Volgodonsk
Bălti
Rostov
Zhdanov
Iași
Chișinău
Azov
Bendery
Tyraspil
Mykolaiv
Melitopil
Berdianske
Yeiske
Salske
Kherson
Odessa
SEA OF AZOV
Kropotkin
Galati
Brăila
Kerch
Sloviansk
Krasnodar
Armavir
Stavropol
Symferopil
Teodosiia
Novorossiisk
Sevastopil
Yalta
Maikop
B L A C K S E A
Vistula
Pilica
Buh
Prypiat
Horyn
Styr
Uzh
Sluch
Teteriv
Dnieper
Desna
Seim
Sula
Psiol
Vorskla
Oskil
Don
Khoper
Vorona
Bitiug
Buzuluk
Khopior
Chir
Donets
Samara
Orel
Inhulets
Inhul
Boh
Dniester
San
Tysa
Siret
Prut
Danube
Tylihul
Manych
Yeia
Yahorlyk
Kuban
Laba
Belaia
Kalaus
Sal

Kintsurashvili), N. Gambarashvili, and N. Lomouri – popularized Ukrainian literature in the Georgian press.

The noted Georgian poet A. *Tsereteli (1840–1915), who knew T. Shevchenko personally and greatly admired his work, did much to promote Ukrainian-Georgian contacts. The first Georgian translation of a poem by Shevchenko – 'Naimychka' (The Servant Girl), by N. Lomouri – was published in 1881. Translations of several other poems appeared in the following decades, as did articles about Shevchenko, and they had a significant influence on Tsereteli and other writers. The Georgians demonstrated their appreciation for Shevchenko in articles and translations on the occasion of the quinquagenary of his death in 1911 and the centenary of his birth in 1914. They protested against the government ban on commemorations of his centennial.

Other Ukrainian writers were also translated into Georgian, and Ukrainian scholars became involved in Georgian studies. Translations of I. Kotliarevsky, H. Kvitka-Osnovianenko, M. Kotsiubynsky, and I. Franko by various writers appeared in Georgian journals in the late 19th and early 20th century. During their long stay in Caucasia, M. Hulak and O. Navrotsky, both of them former members of the Cyril and Methodius Brotherhood, promoted understanding between the two peoples. Hulak worked in Kutais and Tiflis as a teacher in 1863–86 and wrote about Georgian literature. Navrotsky lived in Yerevan and worked on a Ukrainian translation of Sh. Rustaveli's *Man in the Tiger Skin*. Lesia Ukrainka lived with her husband, K. Kvitka, in Georgia for the greater part of 1903–13; during this period she wrote some of her finest plays. In the 1890s D. Mordovets wrote several historical novels set in Georgia. From the 1880s Ukrainian scholars, such as M. Sumtsov, O. Potebnia, and A. Krymsky, visited Georgia and studied its history, literature, and culture.

Ukrainian plays were staged in Georgia beginning in 1845, when the Yatsenko troupe visited Tiflis. In 1889 M. Starytsky's troupe and in 1890 M. Kropyvnytsky's troupe toured Georgia and were well received. In the early 20th century a Ukrainian troupe directed by M. Biliaieva existed in Tiflis; it staged over 45 plays between 1902 and 1919. The first Ukrainian translations of Georgian literature were of I. Chavchavadze's poems by O. Lototsky and B. Hrinchenko in 1893 in the Lviv journal *Pravda* and by P. Hrabovsky in 1897 in the Lviv paper *Zoria*.

The Georgians and the Ukrainians often collaborated in the struggle for national liberation. In 1906 their deputies to the First Russian State Duma joined the *Autonomists' Union. Its Ukrainian vice-chairman was I. Shrah, and his Georgian counterpart was Prince V. Gelovani. In the Fourth State Duma the Menshevik leader N. Chkheidze spoke out against the religious and cultural persecution of Ukrainians in Russian-occupied Galicia. After the February Revolution Georgians took part in the congress of nationalities of Russia held in Kiev on 23–28 September 1917 by the Central Rada. In 1918 diplomatic relations were established between the Ukrainian Hetman government and the Georgian republic. On 5 December 1918 the Ukrainian Hetman and Georgian governments, represented by S. Borodaievsky and V. Tevzaiia respectively, signed an agreement on consular exchange, trade, sea use, and transit rights. The Ukrainian consul general was stationed in Tiflis. Ukrainian consulates in Batumi and Gagra remained in operation until the end of 1920. Prof V. Tevzaiia headed the Georgian mission in Kiev. Abroad, Ukrainians and Georgians have worked together in such political bodies as the *Promethean movement, the *Anti-Bolshevik Bloc of Nations, and the *Paris Bloc.

Under the Soviet regime, Ukrainian-Georgian relations have been allowed to develop only in the cultural sphere. Visits to Georgia by Ukrainian writers and to Ukraine by Georgian writers have become a tradition. Since the 1920s the Dumka State Kapelle, the Berezil theater, the Franko Theater, and other troupes have staged performances in Georgia, and the Rustaveli Theater, the Mardzhanishvili Theater, and other ensembles have toured Ukraine. Articles on Ukrainian-Georgian relations appeared in the journal *Skhidnyi svit* in 1927–31. The monuments to D. Guramishvili in Myrhorod (1949) and to Lesia Ukrainka in Surami (1952) were erected as official expressions of friendship between the two peoples.

Literary translation is well developed in both literatures. The first book of Georgian literature translated into Ukrainian was a novella by M. Dgebundze-Pularia in 1929. Besides many individual poems and novellas, large editions of T. Shevchenko's poetry appeared in Georgian in 1939, 1952, and 1961. In the 1940s I. Franko's works, including 'Moisei' (Moses), were translated. In 1949 and 1952 collections of Lesia Ukrainka's works were published in translation. The contributors were such well-known Georgian writers as S. Chikovani, K. Lortkipanidze, I. Mosashvili, A. Mashashvili, I. Abashidze, R. Gvetadze, V. Gaprindashvili, S. Shanshiashvili, and A. Kurateli. The works of many Soviet Ukrainian writers – M. Bazhan, P. Tychyna, M. Rylsky, O. Dovzhenko, V. Sosiura, M. Kulish, P. Panch, I. Kocherha, O. Korniichuk, O. Honchar, and others – have been translated into Georgian. M. Bazhan has translated the Georgian classics: Sh. Rustaveli's *Man in the Tiger Skin* in 1950 and D. Guramishvili's *Davitiiani* in 1955. The works of Georgian writers N. Baratashvili, I. Chavchavadze, A. Tsereteli, A. Kazbegi, Sh. Dadiani, G. Leonidze, S. Chikovani, Yasamani, N. Lordkipanidze, I. Abashidze, D. Shengelaia, K. Kaladze, I. Mosashvili, D. Gulia, G. Tabidze, and others have been translated by M. Bazhan, M. Rylsky, L. Pervomaisky, I. Kulyk, Ye. Pluzhnyk, O. Oles, A. Malyshko, P. Voronko, M. Nahnybida, O. Novytsky, S. Kryzhanivsky, G. Namoradze, and others.

Some Ukrainians from the Kuban moved to Georgia in the 1930s, fleeing the man-made famine of 1933. The Ukrainian population of Georgia thus grew from 14,4000 in 1926 to 46,000 in 1939. The largest concentration of Ukrainians in Georgia is in Tbilisi (11,000 in 1959).

BIBLIOGRAPHY

Dymnyi, M. *Ukraïna hostem u Hruziï* (Kharkiv 1931)
Halaichuk, B. *Pro Hruziiu i hruzyniv* (Lviv 1936)
Novytsky, O. (ed). *Raiduzhnymy mostamy: Ukraïns'ko-hruzyns'ki literaturni zv'iazky* (Kiev 1968)
Skaba, A., et al (eds). *Iz istorii ukrainsko-gruzinskikh sviazei* (Kiev 1971)
Bakanidze, O. *Hruzyns'ko-ukraïns'ki literaturno-khudozhni zv'iazky* (Kiev 1985)

M. Hlobenko, A. Zhukovsky

Georgievsky, Evlogii [Georgijevskij, Evlogij] (secular name: Vasilii), b 10 April 1868 in Somovo, Odoev county, Tula gubernia, d 8 August 1946 in Paris. Russian Orthodox metropolitan. In 1902 he was appointed bishop of Lublin and in 1905 bishop of Kholm. A staunch monarchist and leader of the Union of the Russian People, he served as a deputy to the Second and Third Russian state dumas. Through his influence the Kholm region was established as a separate gubernia. In 1914 he was elevated to archbishop of Volhynia. As administrator of church affairs in Russian-occupied Galicia (1914–15), he persecuted the Ukrainian Catholic church and tried to impose Russian Orthodoxy in the region. At the beginning of 1918 he took part in the All-Ukrainian Church Sobor in Kiev. Despite his anti-Ukrainian attitude, during the Hetman government he sat on the Supreme Church Council. Under the Directory of the UNR he was arrested and exiled to the Basilian monastery in Buchach. With the defeat of the Whites he immigrated to Serbia and became administrator of Russian parishes in Western Europe and then metropolitan. His memoirs *Put' moei zhizni* (My Life's Path, 1947) contain interesting details about the Kholm region and Volhynia.

Gerbel, Nikolai [Gerbel', Nikolaj], b 8 December 1827 in Tver, Russia, d 20 March 1883 in St Petersburg. Russian poet, translator, and publisher; the first Russian translator of T. Shevchenko's poetry. Gerbel first met Shevchenko in 1846 at the Nizhen Lyceum. In 1860 he edited and published Shevchenko's *Kobzar* in Russian (rev edn 1869 and 1876). The anthology *Poeziia slavian* (Poetry of the Slavs, 1871), also published by Gerbel, contained translations of several Ukrainian poets and a survey of Ukrainian poetry by M. Kostomarov.

Gerbel, Sergei [Gerbel', Sergej], b and d ? Political leader and government official. Gerbel was a landowner from the Kherson region who was governor of Kharkiv gubernia until the Revolution of 1917. In the summer of 1918 he became minister of food provisions in the Hetman government, retaining this position in the cabinet formed by F. Lyzohub in October 1918. When the Hetman government proclaimed its federation with Russia on 14 November, Gerbel became prime minister and minister of agrarian affairs. He held these positions until 14 December 1918.

Gerken-Rusova, Natalia, b 14 June 1897 in Kiev. Scenographer, painter, and journalist. She studied art in Kiev under M. Boichuk, V. Krychevsky, and H. Narbut. She continued her studies in Florence, Nice, and Paris, where she graduated from the Ecole Nationale des Beaux Arts in 1927, and worked as a set designer in Paris, Prague, Brno, Bratislava, and Bucharest. She lived in Bucharest with her husband Yu. *Rusov from 1930 to 1941; there she also worked as an interior decorator for the king of Rumania. She is the author of *Heroïchnyi teatr* (The Heroic Theater, 1939, 1957), the plays *Shevchenko u Repninykh* (Shevchenko at the Repnins, 1947) and *Sviato dvokh epokh* (The Fete of Two Epochs, 1949), and articles in émigré periodicals. Her art works have been exhibited several times in Europe. Since the war she has lived in Montreal.

German Labor Front (Deutsche Arbeitsfront or DAF). A compulsory organization of employers and employees set up in 1934 by the Nazi regime after its abolition of trade unions (1933); it had departments for foreign workers. In 1941 a special DAF department – Betreuungstelle für ukrainische Arbeiter – for Ukrainian conscript workers from the *Generalgouvernement and from countries allied with Germany was established; its head office was in Berlin. K. Graebe, assisted by B. Bilynkevych, was in charge of the department. Through offices in Berlin, Dresden, Breslau (now Wrocław), Hamburg, Hannover, Frankfurt, Munich, Vienna, and Stuttgart, Ukrainian DAF officials provided social and, to a lesser extent, cultural services for thousands of Ukrainian laborers in 15 German provinces. These officials co-operated closely with Ukrainian civic organizations in Germany – the Ukrainian National Alliance and the Ukrainian Hromada – in serving the workers' cultural needs and defending their limited rights. Under A. Kishka's supervision the Ukrainian officials of the Reich Food Office (Reichsnährstand) looked after the needs of farm workers. From 1942 to 1945 *Visti*, a newspaper for industrial workers, was published in Berlin under H. Stetsiuk's editorship; it was followed in 1943 by *Zemlia*, a weekly for farm workers edited by S. Nykorovych.

V. Maruniak

Germanic law. A designation covering the customary and civil laws of the various Germanic peoples from the time of the ancient tribes to the modern period of nationhood. In Ukraine, Germanic law (GL) has usually been identified with *Magdeburg law (municipal autonomy), but it embraces many other legal institutions, norms, and traditions. Medieval collections of GL, such as the *Sachsenspiegel* and later codifications, were translated or revised by the Poles (eg, B. Groicki in 1558–9) and were thus known in Ukraine. They had some influence on the *Lithuanian Statute and legal practices in the Lithuanian-Ruthenian and Hetman states.

GL was brought to Ukraine under Poland and Lithuania by *Germans, who founded self-governing farming settlements and urban communities. An enterprising German would pay a lord or the state a sum of money for the right to found a colony under GL. This tenant, called the *lokator* or *osadchyi*, would normally be appointed the **soltys* – the lord's steward and village administrator. He was granted privileges for his feudal services: land, part of the money rent collected for the lord from the settlers, the right to demand certain corvée labor, freedom to build a mill or tavern, and the exclusive right to judge the settlers.

In the 14th century Polish nobles began purchasing the *soltys* titles and privileges from the original holding families. The new Polish owners abolished rural self-government under GL and introduced large-scale corvée. Only on crown and church estates did a measure of self-government remain. In the villages, GL had coexisted with traditional *Rus' law, which had given its inhabitants greater economic security and a degree of self-government. In the late 15th and the 16th century the distinction between the two laws disappeared; certain forms of GL (the *soltys*, fiefs) were combined with the practices of Rus' law. This process was accompanied by the total abrogation of village self-rule and the imposition of *serfdom.

BIBLIOGRAPHY

Halban, A. *Zur Geschichte des deutschen Rechtes in Podolien, Wolhynien und der Ukraine* (Berlin 1896)
Jakowliw, A. *Das deutsche Recht in der Ukraine und seine*

Einflüsse auf das ukrainische Recht im 16.–18. Jahrhundert (Leipzig 1942)
Kuras, S. *Przywileje prawa niemieckiego miast i wsi małopolskich XIV–XV wieku* (Warsaw 1971)

M. Chubaty, R. Senkus

Germanisms. Words and expressions borrowed from the Germanic languages. The Ukrainian language inherited some Germanisms from Common Slavic, which had adopted some loan words from the Common Germanic, Gothic, and Balkan-Germanic languages. These words are part of the vocabulary of military-political and trade relations, material culture, and partly Christian practice; for example, *meč* (sword), *polk* (regiment), *knjaz'* (prince), *korol'* (king), *lyxva* (usury), *cjata* (a coin), *xyža* (hut), *morkva* (carrot), and *pip* (priest). Very few loan words from Old Swedish entered Ukrainian; they include *ščohla* (mast), *stjah* (flag), and *kodola* (hawser). A large number of Germanisms from Low and High German were absorbed in the 14th and 15th centuries, some directly, but mostly via Polish. At that time German craftsmen emigrated in large numbers to Poland and settled in towns in western Ukraine. Some Germanisms were also introduced by Jewish settlers. The loan words of this period are mostly part of the vocabulary of the skilled trades, commerce, guilds, and municipal self-government. Some general and abstract terms were also adopted. These borrowings include *sljusar* (locksmith), *druk* (print), *xutro* (fur), *cal'* (inch), *rynok* (market), *vuxnal'* (horseshoe nail), *ratuša* (town hall), *djakuvaty* (to thank), *rjatuvaty* (to save), and *smak* (taste). From the 18th to the 20th century Germanisms became widespread in the Ukrainian spoken in Galicia and Bukovyna under Austrian rule. Some of them, for example, *strajk* (strike), *mušlja* (shell), and *tran* (whale oil), and such calques as *zlovžyvannja* (misuse, based on *Missbrauch*), *zabezpečennja* (security, based on *Versicherung*), *muzyka majbutn'oho* (a castle in the air, from *Zukunftmusik*), made their way into the standard language. But most remained merely local expressions; for example, *l'os* (lottery ticket), *fajnyj* (fine), and such syntactic constructions as *tikaty pered kym* (to run away before one), *dumaty na ščo* (to think on something). The quantity and choice of Germanisms in Ukrainian bring the language closer to the West Slavic languages.

G.Y. Shevelov

Germans. Until 1940 the fourth-largest ethnic minority in the Ukrainian lands. Very few Germans live in Ukraine today.

The Princely era. The presence of Germans in Ukraine was first recorded when Christianity was introduced in the 10th century, as merchants, members of German legations, clerics, and travelers began visiting Ukraine. At the same time that German and Ukrainian princely families established dynastic ties through marriage in the 11th and 12th centuries, Germans from Regensburg, Vienna, Mainz, and Lubeck founded small but discrete communities in Ukraine and engaged in commerce in the towns, particularly in Kiev, Volodymyr-Volynskyi, and Lutske. The presence of German merchants in Kiev during the latter half of the 12th and in the 13th century is mentioned in the Hypatian Chronicle.

A more significant influx of Germans, particularly in western Ukraine, occurred only after the Mongol invasion of Rus' in 1240–1 and the destruction of many towns. The princes of Galicia-Volhynia, imitating their Polish and Hungarian counterparts, invited Germans to rebuild the razed towns and develop trade and crafts by granting the Germans various privileges (eg, temporary tax exemptions), a large degree of autonomy, and the retention of their own legal system based on *Magdeburg law. As early as the mid-13th century, King Danylo Romanovych invited German merchants and manufacturers to newly founded Kholm, and such centers as Volodymyr-Volynskyi, Lutske, Lviv, Peremyshl, Sianik were settled thereafter. From 1270 to 1290, the mayors of Volodymyr-Volynskyi and Lutske were German. During his reign (1324–40), Prince Yurii II Boleslav, in particular, promoted the settlement of Germans in Galicia.

In Transcarpathia, German colonization had begun under Hungarian rule in the 12th century in the Ukrainian-Slovak ethnic borderland. In the 13th century, Levoča, Bardejov, Košice, and other towns there were founded by Germans, many of whom later resettled in Prešov, Uzhhorod, Mukachiv, Berehove, Khust, and, in the 14th century, Tiachiv, Vyshkove, and Dovhe Pole. The Hungarian kings accorded the Germans many privileges but obliged them to pay for land.

The Lithuanian-Polish period. German colonization intensified after the annexation of Galicia by Poland and of Volhynia and Podolia by Lithuania. It was stimulated by the granting of Magdeburg law and other privileges by the new rulers to many western Ukrainian towns. It was in these towns that Germans first settled and played an important role. From 1352 to 1550, for example, the Germans were so influential in Lviv that the mayor and most of the town councillors were elected from among them and official books and documents were written in German. New German settlers continually moved into Galicia's towns. From the late 14th century, German colonization spread into the towns of Volhynia and Podilia. The first Catholic bishops of Peremyshl, Lviv, Kholm, and Kamianets-Podilskyi were German.

German peasant colonization was markedly weaker. Until the 15th century it was limited to the Sian and Lviv regions. Peasant settlements were also granted special privileges including self-government by *Germanic law. Most of the colonists of this period came from Silesia.

German migration into Ukraine's towns declined in the mid-15th century, with only professionals and artisans arriving thereafter. Owing to the centuries-old German influence, many of Ukraine's towns resembled those of central Europe architecturally and economically and in the way they were governed. Many *Germanisms had entered the language of government, commerce, the crafts, the trade guilds, and construction. The influence of German colonization was so strong that Ukrainian burghers were occasionally forced out.

With the decline of colonization, many Germans in Ukraine became Polonized. This process, which began in the villages and smaller, isolated towns and spread to the larger towns and cities, such as Lviv, was aided by the fact that the Germans and the Poles shared a common faith – Roman Catholicism. It led ultimately to the consolidation of Polish influence in western and Right-Bank Ukraine. Only a negligible number of Germans became Ukrainianized.

In Bukovyna, German settlement was sporadic; it originated mainly in Transylvania and Galicia. After the 15th

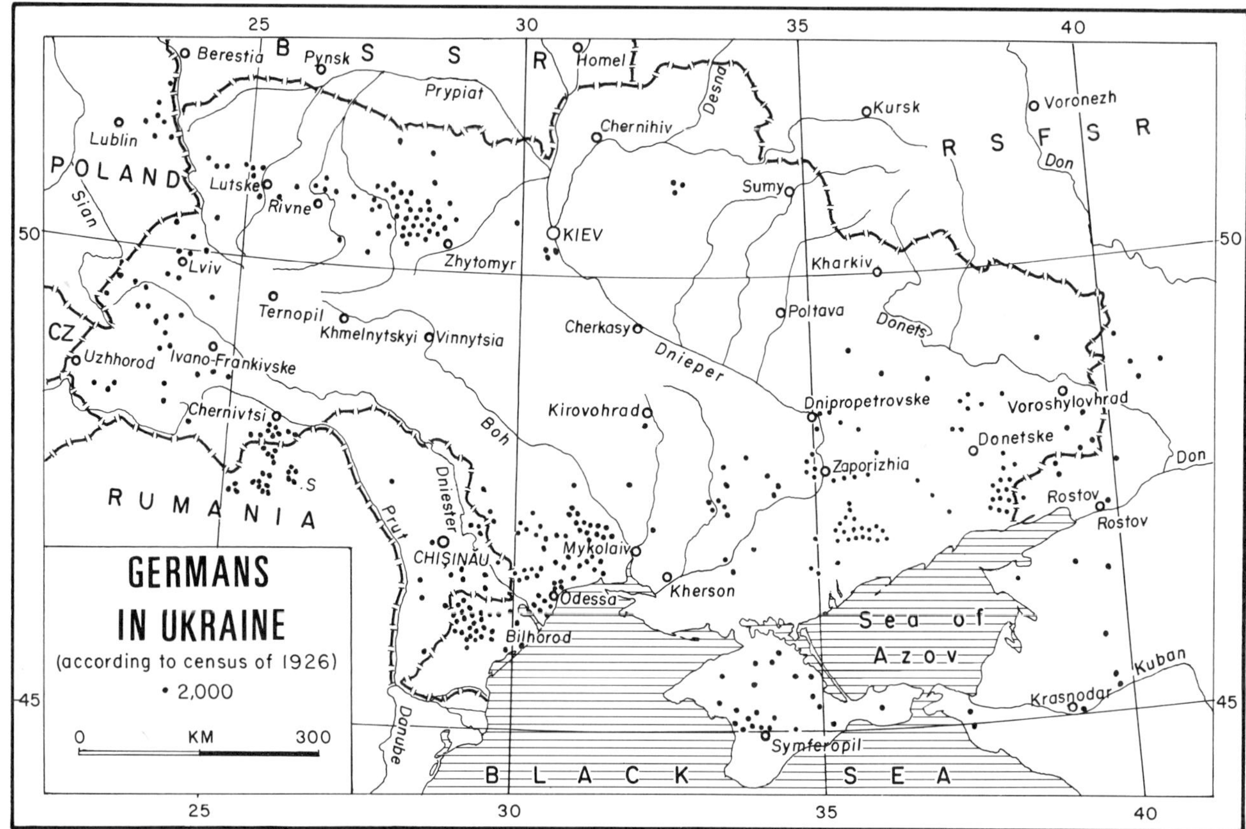

century, Germans took part in the development of the towns of Seret and Suceava and in commercial ties with Lviv.

The Hetman state. A separate German group on Ukrainian soil consisted of the soldiers and officers who served in various Polish and Lithuanian military formations. During the Cossack-Polish War in particular, the Polish army employed a considerable number of German mercenaries who played a decisive role in the Battle of Berestechko (1651).

In Left-Bank and Dnieper Ukraine, German merchants and manufacturers (mainly from the Danzig region) became more numerous in the 16th and the first half of the 17th century. They leased and exploited large estates, particularly in the Korostyshiv area, and established potash and smalt factories. In the Hetman state of the 17th and 18th centuries, considerable numbers of German artisans, who worked as managers or skilled workers in factories, agricultural specialists, architects, doctors, professional soldiers, and teachers, settled in the towns and on the Cossack *starshyna* estates. German mercenaries were employed by hetmans I. Vyhovsky and P. Doroshenko. They also served in the Russian army and in garrisons in Ukraine, particularly after the Battle of Poltava (1709). In the 18th century, German artisans, civil servants, and doctors formed permanent colonies in the cities (especially in Kiev) of the Hetman state. Some of these colonies still existed in the 20th century.

Prominent figures of German origin in Ukraine in the 17th and 18th centuries were the church leader I. *Gizel, the theologian and military engineer A. *Zörnikau, the architects J. *Baptist and J.-G. *Schädel, and the general osaul of artillery F. von *Königsek. Some Germans (mostly army officers) married into the Cossack *starshyna*, acquired estates, and settled down permanently in Ukraine, eg, the Hampfs, Lammsdorfs, Brinckens, Ritters, and Pols (O. *Pol was prominent in the Katerynoslav region).

1760–1914. In the second half of the 18th century, the Ukrainian territories under both Russian and Austrian rule were settled by a new wave of German colonists, as a few manufacturers and a large number of artisans responded to invitations by Polish magnates to settle in the towns of Right-Bank Ukraine and to work in various factories. Their number grew in the first half of the 19th century in Right-Bank and Left-Bank Ukraine, particularly in the Poltava region.

Large numbers of German farmers colonized the unpopulated expanses of *Southern Ukraine; they were attracted by the decrees of Catherine II (1763–4) and Alexander I (1804) granting them free land, freedom of religion, local autonomy, tax exemptions for 10 to 30 years, immunity from military service, interest-free loans, and the right to buy additional land. In Left-Bank Ukraine, a few small German colonies were established – in the Chernihiv region near Borzna in 1765–7 and near Krolevets in 1770. Through special agreements in 1789–90, *Mennonites settled the lands of the former Zaporozhian Host – Khortytsia Island and its vicinity near Katerynoslav.

Beginning in the early 19th century, many more Germans settled in Southern Ukraine. They came mainly from the war-torn, depressed, and overpopulated rural areas of southwest Germany (Baden, Würtemberg, Alsace, Hesse, the Palatinate), West Prussia and the Danzig area, and the Congress Kingdom of Poland. Large colonies also arose in southern Bessarabia (Akkerman county) after its annexation by Russia in 1812, and in Kherson, Katerynoslav, and Tavriia gubernias and the Tahanrih region. A few thousand Germans settled in the Kuban and the Stavropil region of Subcaucasia. According to the 1897 census, 292,500 Germans lived in Akkerman county and in Kherson, Katerynoslav, and Tavriia gubernias (4.6 percent of these regions' population). In 1911 German sources gave the number as 489,000 (42.6 percent Evangelicals, 36.7 percent Catholics, and 20.7 percent Mennonites).

A German church in the Crimea (1902)

A second large group of Germans settled in Volhynia. The first settlers were Mennonites brought in by the Polish gentry towards the end of the 18th century; most later migrated to Southern Ukraine. In 1860 about 5,000 Germans lived in 35 colonies in Volhynia, and their number grew after the serfs were emancipated and the local Polish gentry began importing labor and renting or selling their land. Smaller numbers were also invited to work the land confiscated from the Poles who had participated in the 1863 insurrection. By 1871, 28,600 Germans lived in 139 colonies in Volhynia. The greatest influx occurred after 1883. According to the 1897 census, 171,000 Germans lived in Volhynia gubernia in over 550 villages. In 1914, their number was estimated at 241,000 (66,000 in Zhytomyr county, 53,000 in Novohrad-Volynskyi county, 43,000 in Lutske county, 35,000 in Rivne county, 22,000 in Volodymyr-Volynskyi county, and 10,000 in Dubno county). Most came from Poland, and almost all were Evangelicals. Germans also settled in Podlachia and Kholm bordering on Volhynia. In 1914, Kholm county numbered 25,800 Germans (13.3 percent of the population) and Volodava county, 5,700 (4.7 percent).

In 1914, 784,100 Germans lived in the Russian-ruled Ukrainian compact ethnic territories and composed 2 percent of their population: 430,400 lived in the gubernias of Southern Ukraine, 272,100 lived in Volhynia and the Kholm region, and 81,600 lived elsewhere. They constituted either large compact islands among the indigenous population or small settlements (colonies), or lived on farmsteads. Even when the influx abated, the German population continued to increase because of a high birth rate. The number of German colonies in Southern Ukraine grew from 384 in 1890 to 966 in 1914. Buying up increasingly more land from the gentry, the Germans owned 3.8 million desiatins by 1911, including such huge estates as that of the Falz-Fein family (200,000 desiatins). Only about a tenth of the Germans lived in towns (10,000 in Odessa in 1897).

The Germans lived apart from the Ukrainians and were distinguished by their language, religion, folkways, folklore, dress, village architecture, higher economic status (especially in the south), and level of education. They had extensive rights of self-rule and settled their internal affairs democratically, choosing their own councils, teachers, and pastors. German was the official language in their colonies; these were grouped into districts, governed by central administrations in Katerynoslav (1800–22), Kishinev (1822–33), and Odessa (1833–71), which were subordinated directly to the Ministry of Internal Affairs in St Petersburg. The privileges granted after 1763 were abolished in 1871, and Russian became the official language in 1875. Thereafter many Germans, especially Mennonites, emigrated to the New World.

A German colony in the Crimea

The colonies were organized around the churches, which ran German-language religious primary schools. Secondary schools and teachers' seminaries also existed, with a *Realschule* in Odessa. After 1905 German-language private high schools were founded. The Germans also had their own philanthropic institutions, societies, hospitals, press (eg, the daily *Odessauer Zeitung* [1863–1914] and the Catholic daily *Deutsche Rundschau* [1906–14]), and publishers, particularly of almanacs and calendars.

Generally the Germans maintained their national identity and language despite the lack of links with their homeland. It was only in the towns that some Russification occurred. Relations between the Ukrainians and the German colonists were limited to neighborly contacts, the adoption of sophisticated methods of German agriculture, and the hiring of Ukrainians as seasonal workers. Many Germans took part in Ukraine's industrial development. Because of German influence, *Evangelical Christians, particularly *Stundists, grew in numbers among the Ukrainian population in the latter half of the 19th century.

Beginning in the 19th century many scholars of German descent taught at universities and colleges in Ukraine. Among the more renowned were the physicist N. *Shiller (Schiller), the mathematician H. (G.) *Pfeiffer, the astronomer R. *Fogel (Vogel), the chemist N. Bunge, the botanists W. *Besser, E.-R. *Trautfetter, and I. *Schmalhausen, the physiologist A. *Walter, the medical scientists M. Dieterichs and G. Rein, the lawyer O. *Eikhelman, the economist N. *Bunge, the philologists I. Neukirch, F. Knauer, I. Letsius, and B. Varneke, the archeologist E. Stern, and the art historians F. Schmit and F. *Ernst. The Ukrainian poet Yu. *Klen was also of German descent.

Considerably fewer Germans colonized Austrian-ruled Western Ukraine. After the annexation of Galicia (1772) and Bukovyna (1774) by Austria, the Germanization policies of the new regime brought German civil servants and farmers, the latter being encouraged to settle in the eastern borderlands by patents from Maria Theresa (1774) and Joseph II (1781) that granted privileges to the Catholics and the Evangelicals through land grants and exemption from military service and taxes. Because of indigenous rural overpopulation the influx was relatively small. Of the 249 German settlements (mostly small villages or village suburbs) in Galicia at the turn of the 20th century, 134 had been founded during the reign of Joseph II. Small-scale colonization occurred until the 1840s.

The German settlers in Galicia came from Baden, Württemberg, Hesse, the Palatinate, and, in the first half of the 19th century, northwestern Bohemia. They settled mostly in Subcarpathia or the Lviv region.

After Galicia was granted autonomy in 1861, its administration was taken over by the Poles and the official language became Polish. Many German civil servants emigrated; others became Polonized. The German farming colonies, however, did not undergo major losses. In 1914 there were 47,600 Germans in Galicia (0.9 percent of the population); 5,900 of them lived in Lviv. Half were Evangelicals and half Roman Catholics.

In Bukovyna, the German colonization was considerably greater than in Galicia as a result of the low population density and the poorly developed towns. Germans and Germanized Jews settled mostly in the towns, which soon acquired a German character. Because Germans held the highest government posts and German was the official language until 1918, their influence was greater than their numbers warranted. In 1910, 21,100 Germans (4.6 percent of the population) lived in the Ukrainian parts of Bukovyna. Its capital, *Chernivtsi, had the largest urban concentration of Germans on Ukrainian ethnic territory and was the only 'German' city in Ukraine.

In Transcarpathia, the old German colonies began to wane in the 16th century, and most Germans became Magyarized. An insignificant number of settlers arrived in 1723 and 1748, when the village of Pausching near Mukachiv was founded. It is the only locality in Ukraine where the descendants of the original German settlers live today. Other Germans arrived in 1765–77 and in the early 19th century. In 1914 about 6,000 Germans lived in Transcarpathia; they were mostly farmers (mainly in the vicinity of Mukachiv) or lumberjacks and foresters in the Carpathian Mountains.

The First World War and the Revolution. On the eve of the First World War, 859,000 Germans (1.9 percent of the population) lived on Ukrainian soil: 784,100 in the Russian Empire and 74,700 in Austria-Hungary. During the war Germans living in the Russian Empire experienced restrictions, hostility, and even persecution. In 1915, 150,000 Germans living in Volhynia and the Kholm region were deported, mostly to Siberia, and only a fraction returned to their homes after the war.

In 1917–20, the attitude of Ukraine's Germans to the UNR and Ukrainian independence was mainly one of indifference. Even so, some high-ranking officers in the UNR Army were of German descent (eg, Gen S. Delvig). Galicia's Germans, in contrast, actively collaborated with the Western Ukrainian National Republic and had representatives in the Ukrainian National Rada; many Galician-born Germans who had been Austrian army officers joined the Ukrainian Galician Army (eg, Lt Col A. Bizanz, Capt H. Koch, Gen A. Kraus). Bukovyna's Germans, however, openly supported its annexation by Rumania and the new Rumanian regime.

The First World War and the years of revolutionary turmoil led to a drastic reduction in the number of Germans in Ukraine. In Southern Ukraine many German farmers were victims of pogroms by the anarchist forces of N. *Makhno in 1919 as well as of the 1921–2 famine; a large number fled to Germany and then emigrated to North America, while others assimilated in the towns. As a result, the German population in Ukraine's compact territories fell from 872,000 in 1914 to 514,000 in 1926. The greatest losses occurred in Volhynia gubernia and Radomyshl county of Kiev gubernia, where Germans decreased from 250,000 in 1914 to 108,000 in 1926; and in the Kholm region, where they fell from 35,000 to 13,000.

The interwar years. According to the 1926 Soviet census, 514,000 Germans lived in the Ukrainian ethnic territories of the USSR: 394,000 (1.4 percent of the total population), of which 34,300 (8.7 percent) were urban, lived in Soviet Ukraine; 43,600 (6.1 percent) lived in the Crimea; and 80,000 lived in northern Caucasia. Ukrainian territories under Poland had 87,000 Germans (1931); those under Rumania had 36,000 (1930); and those under Czechoslovakia had 13,000 (1930). In 1932, the total number of Germans on all of Ukrainian compact territory was 610,000 (1.2 percent of the total population); together with the mixed ethnic territories the number rose to 720,000 (1.3 percent of the total population).

In the Ukrainian SSR in 1928–9, there were six German raions and 244 German village soviets. The Germans had their own schools (including a pedagogical institute in Odessa), publishing houses, press, and cultural institutions. During the *collectivization drive of 1929–30 and the *famine of 1932–3, the German farmers suffered enormously; many thousands were branded *kulaks and were persecuted, dispossessed, and deported to Soviet Asia. Their way of life was uprooted, their churches and other institutions were shut down, and their national raions and village soviets were abolished. Finally, in the 1936–8 Stalinist terror most of the Soviet German intelligentsia (clerics, writers, teachers, scholars, doctors) perished. To save themselves, many Germans fled their villages and disappeared into the towns.

In contrast to the prewar period, German organized life in interwar Western Ukraine, particularly in Volhynia (48,000 Germans in 1930), improved because many Germans established closer ties with their ancestral homeland. Germans under Polish rule co-operated with Ukrainians (eg, in the Bloc of National Minorities during elections to the Polish Senate and Sejm in 1922 and 1928). In Bukovyna, however, the Germans supported the ruling Rumanian parties.

The Second World War. On the basis of German Soviet treaties, many Germans living in Soviet-annexed Galicia, Volhynia, and the Kholm region were allowed to move to Germany after the 1939 partition of Poland. In 1940, when the USSR occupied Bukovyna and Bessarabia, the Germans living there were also repatriated. After the Soviet-German war broke out in 1941, the Soviet authorities, beginning on 21 August, deported about 100,000 Germans living in the Crimea and Left-Bank Ukraine to northern Caucasia, and thence to Kazakhstan; they did not have time, however, to deport those in Right-Bank Ukraine and in the Odessa region. During the Nazi occupation, the latter had *Volksdeutscher status and numerous privileges not granted to Ukrainians. Some joined military, police, and paramilitary formations and thus became collaborators in the brutal policy of the *Reichskommisariat Ukraine. This created considerable animosity between Ukrainians and Germans in Ukraine.

As the German army retreated from Ukraine in 1943 and 1944, some 350,000 Germans were evacuated to the Warthegau region of West Prussia and thence to Germany. After the Soviet army occupied part of Germany in 1945, some 250,000 Germans from Ukraine were deported and confined in labor camps in Soviet Asia. On 13 December 1955, they were amnestied and allowed to live anywhere in the USSR except their former homes. In 1964, after pressure from the West German government, the Soviet Germans were exonerated of wartime treason. Many have since assimilated, and many others have emigrated to West Germany. According to the 1970 Soviet census, only 29,900 Germans lived in Ukraine. Their number today is unknown, Soviet sources being purposely silent. (See also *Austria, *Germany, *Volga German ASSR.)

BIBLIOGRAPHY
Klaus, I. *Nashie kolonii: Opyty i materialy po istorii i statistike inostrannoi kolonizatsii v Rossii* (St Petersburg 1869, Cambridge 1972)
Kaindl, R. *Geschichte der Deutschen in der Karpathenländern*, 3 vols (Gotha 1907–11)
Pisarevskii, G. *Iz istorii inostrannoi kolonizatsii v Rossii v XVIII veke* (Moscow 1909)
Shelukhin, S. *Nemetskaia kolonizatsiia na iuge Rossii* (Odessa 1915)
Zokler, T. *Das Deutschtum in Galizien* (Dresden 1917)
Winter, E. *Das Deutschtum in der Slovakei und in Karpathorussland* (Münster 1925–6)
Stumpp, K. *Die deutschen Kolonien in Schwarzmeergebiet dem früheren Neu-(Süd)-Russland* (Stuttgart 1926)
Schirmunski, V. *Die deutschen Kolonien in der Ukraine: Geschichte, Mundarten, Volkslied, Volkskunde* (Moscow-Kharkiv 1928)
Kuhn, W. *Die jungen deutschen Sprachinseln in Galizien: Ein Beitrag zur Methode der Sprachinselforschung* (Münster 1930)
Karasek-Langer, A.; Lück, K. *Die deutschen Siedlungen in Wolhynien* (Plauen 1931)
Lang, F. *Buchenland: Hundertfünfzig Jahre Deutschtum in der Bukowina* (Munich 1961)
Müller, S. *Von der Ansiedlung bis zur Umsiedlung: Das Deutschtum Galiziens, insbesondere Lembergs, 1772–1940* (Marburg-Lahn 1961)
Keller, P. *The German Colonies in South Russia, 1804–1904*, 2 vols (Saskatoon 1968–73)
Giesinger, A. *From Catherine to Khrushchev: The Story of Russia's Germans* (Battleford, Sask 1974)
Stumpp, K. *The German Russians: Two Centuries of Pioneering* (Bonn-Brussels-New York 1978)
Kozauer, N. *Die Karpaten-Ukraine zwischen den beiden Weltkriegen, unter besonderer Berücksichtigung der deutschen Bevölkerung* (Esslingen 1979)
Stumpp, K. *The Emigration from Germany to Russia in the Years 1763 to 1862* (Lincoln, Neb 1982)
Buchsweiler, M. *Volksdeutsche in der Ukraine am Vorabend und Beginn des Zweiten Weltkriegs – ein Fall doppelter Loyalität?* (Gerlingen 1984)
Fleischhauer, I. *Die Deutschen im Zarenreich: 200 Jahre deutsch-russischer Kulturgemeinschaft* (Stuttgart 1986)

V. Kubijovyč

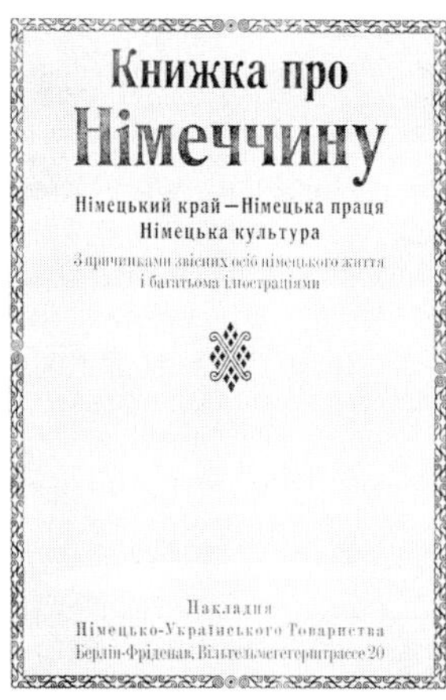

Book about Germany published by the German-Ukrainian Society

German-Ukrainian Society (Deutsch-Ukrainische Gesellschaft). A society for cultivating German-Ukrainian political, economic, and cultural relations, founded in March 1918 in Berlin by P. Rohrbach (its first president) and A. Schmidt (its first general secretary). The society's journal – *Die Ukraine* (40 issues, 1918–26) – contained valuable information about Ukraine. On H. Prokopchuk's initiative the society was revived in Munich in 1948. Since then the following have served as presidents: K. Bensch, K. Graebe, F. Roeder, O. Poebing, H. Prohaska, and E. Blauss. In 1960 it merged with the Herder German-Ukrainian Society, which had also been established in Munich in 1948 by such proponents of Ukrainian-German understanding as H. Koch, E. Mittich, and I. Mirchuk. In the years 1952–6 and 1962–8 the society published 44 issues of **Ukraine in Vergangenheit und Gegenwart* (editor: H. Prokopchuk). It also published a few dozen monographs on Ukrainian émigrés in Germany and organized lectures, art exhibits, and commemorative concerts. Since the 1970s the society has been inactive.

BIBLIOGRAPHY
Deutsch-Ukrainische Herder-Gesellschaft. *Dem Andenken Paul Rohrbachs: Ein Beitrag zur osteuropäischen Problematik* (Munich 1959)

Germany. The largest country in Central Europe, covering, until 1914, an area of 540,520 sq km. After Germany's defeat in the First World War, the Treaty of Versailles in 1919 reduced its territory to 472,030 sq km. In 1945, after its defeat in the Second World War, Germany was occupied by the Allied forces, and the Potsdam Conference left Germany with 356,270 sq km. In 1949 the United States, British, and French occupation zones became the Federal Republic of Germany (1985 pop est 60,940,000) with an area of 248,680 sq km and Bonn as the new capital; the Soviet zone became the German Democratic Republic (1985 pop est 16,703,000) with an area of 108,330 sq km and East Berlin as the capital.

Although Germany and Ukraine never shared a common border, the historical states on their territories and their peoples have had various ties since the 9th century. The closeness and distance of these ties have been affected by geopolitics, particularly by the centuries-old domination of Ukraine by Poland and Russia.

The Middle Ages. The first record of contacts dates from 18 May 838, when 'Rhos' accompanied a Byzantine legation to Ingelheim on the Rhine, the capital of Louis I the Pious. Most historians agree that the 'Rhos' were Varangians in the service of Rus'. In the 9th century, active economic relations were established between Kiev and *Regensburg via Cracow, Prague, and other towns in Poland, Moravia, and Bohemia on the main trade route between Europe and the Orient. The Franks furnished arms and other metal products, glass, ceramics, wine, cloth, and jewelry in exchange for furs, honey, wax, silver, potash, horses, and slaves from Rus'. In order to control this trade, King Louis the German (843–76) issued customs regulations in Raffelstetten, Bavaria, in which merchants from Rus' ('Rugi') are mentioned. Similar customs measures were issued by King Louis the Child in 903–7. In the 10th century, Theophilus, a monk from Helmershausen near Paderborn, Saxony, noted that 'Rus' is particularly talented in enamelling.' The records of Regensburg's merchants of 1191 refer to trade with 'Ruzarii.' Economic relations between Rus' and Regensburg were intensive until the 13th century, when the Mongol invasions and the impact of Italian merchant fleets in east-west trade led to a general decline in relations between Ukraine and Germany.

Through the activity of religious missionaries from the 10th century onward, church ties between Germany and Ukraine were established. Princess Olha dispatched emissaries in 959 to King Otto I the Great with a request to send priests and a bishop to Kiev. Around 961, the monk Adalbert from Trier arrived in Kiev as bishop, but he soon fled, having incurred the enmity of Olha's son, the pagan grand prince Sviatoslav I. Sviatoslav's son Yaropolk I (972–ca 978) tried to maintain friendly relations with Emperor Otto II; his envoys attended the great assembly in Quedlimburg in 973, where they solicited German aid against Polish expansion. His brother Volodymyr the Great (ca 980–1015) also pursued a friendly orientation toward Germany. Having married Anna, the sister of the Byzantine emperor Basil II, in 990, he became the brother-in-law of Anna's sister Theophano, the wife of Otto II. Emperor Henry II (1002–24) tried to obtain the support of Rus' in his protracted war against Bolesław I the Brave of Poland. The war forced Archbishop Bruno of Querfurt to abandon his mission among the Prussians; instead he pursued the conversion of the Pechenegs, during which he was received by Volodymyr in Kiev in 1007 and 1008. Bruno's letter to Henry is the oldest extant German written reference to Rus'.

His wife Anna having died in 1011, Volodymyr the Great married (in 1012) the daughter of Count Kuno von Enningen (and granddaughter of Otto I and Henry II). Although this marriage should have strengthened the ties of Rus' with Germany, the opposite, in fact, happened, because Bolesław I negotiated a pact with Henry II at Merseburg in 1013, and German troops helped Bolesław to invade Rus' and occupy the Cherven towns. After Volodymyr's death, the rivalry between his sons Sviatopolk and Yaroslav the Wise for the Kievan throne resulted in the interference of the rulers of Poland and Germany in the affairs of Rus'. The joint campaign of Sviatopolk and Bolesław against Yaroslav and the capture of Kiev in 1018 are described in the chronicle of Bishop *Thietmar of Merseburg. After consolidating his rule, Yaroslav entered into an alliance with Emperor Conrad II, and during the renewed Polish-German war he annexed the town of Belz (1030) and the Cherven towns (1031) with German consent. Emperor Henry III received Yaroslav's envoys in Allstedt, Thuringia, in 1040, and negotiated trade and political agreements with them. In 1043 Yaroslav offered his daughter's hand in marriage to Henry, but the offer was refused. Nonetheless, cordial relations between the Kievan state and Germany were maintained. In 1061 Henry IV gave asylum to Yaroslav's daughter Anastasiia, the wife of King Andrew I of Hungary, and sent legations to her brother Grand Prince Iziaslav Yaroslavych.

Marriages between the members of the reigning families of Germany and Rus' facilitated the political relationships between the two states. From the 11th to the 13th century, at least 12 such marriages took place. A son of Yaroslav the Wise, Sviatoslav II, the prince of Chernihiv (1054–73) and grand prince of Kiev (1073–6), married the daughter of Count Etheler of Dithmarschen. Another of Yaroslav's sons, Volodymyr, the prince of Novgorod (1034–52), was married to Oda, the daughter of Count Leopold of Stade. In 1073, another son, Grand Prince Iziaslav Yaroslavych, was forced to flee from Kiev by his brother Sviatoslav. He went to Poland and thence to Mainz to the court of Henry IV, where he appealed to Henry to help him recover the throne of Kiev from his brother. Henry sent an envoy, Bishop Burchardt of Trier, to Kiev to Sviatoslav, who in turn offered the king many precious gifts. In Germany, Iziaslav and his son Yaropolk stayed with the margrave of Thuringia, and Yaropolk married Kunigunde, the daughter of Count Otto of Orlamünde-Reichlingen. When Iziaslav failed to receive help from Henry, he sent Yaropolk with an appeal to Henry's foe, Pope Gregory VII; his plea is recorded in the Trier Psalter, which contains miniatures depicting Yaropolk's family. As the prince of Volodymyr-Volynskyi (1078–87), Yaropolk maintained personal ties with German noble houses, and his daughter married a German count. In 1089 in Cologne, Henry IV married Yevpraksiia (Praxedis Adelheid), the eldest daughter of Grand Prince Vsevolod Yaroslavych and widow of Henry, the margrave of Saxony. Through this union, Henry hoped to gain Vsevolod's political and financial support.

In the 12th century the Kievan state began to decline as a result of the internecine wars, and its constituent principalities developed on their own. From the latter half of the 12th century, the princes of Halych (Galicia) and Volodymyr (Volhynia) increased their contacts with the West. After Béla III of Hungary invaded his realm in 1189, Prince Volodymyr Yaroslavych of Halych sought refuge at the court of Emperor Frederick I Barbarossa, who received him 'with great respect' and together with Prince Casimir II the Just of Cracow helped him regain his throne. Volodymyr's successor, Roman Mstyslavych – the founder of the united Principality of Galicia-Volhynia – was involved in the wars between the German houses of Welf and Hohenstaufen and was killed in 1205 in the Battle of Zawichost against Leszek the White of

Cracow while he was an ally of King Philip of Swabia. The marriage in 1252 of Roman, the son of the Galician-Volhynian prince Danylo Romanovych, to Gertrude of Babenberg, heiress to the Austrian duchy, opened up the possibility for a Ukrainian dynasty to rule Austria. The duchy was seized by King Otakar II of Bohemia, however, and Roman was forced to flee Austria. Prince Danylo and his successors formed alliances with the *Teutonic Knights in Prussia and Livonia in order to counter the territorial ambitions of Poland and Lithuania. They also encouraged the colonization of their realm by *Germans, whose influx into the towns made it possible for the latter to receive the privileges of *Magdeburg law. Thus, from the mid-13th century on, the western Ukrainian lands of Galicia, Volhynia, and the Kholm region found themselves in the German cultural and economic sphere of influence. Entire German rural communities were established there, and for some time they were governed according to *Germanic law.

Kievan Rus' and the Principality of Galicia-Volhynia maintained ties with Germany in order to have an ally against Poland. The political balance of forces in the Rus'-Polish-German triangle was the constant aim of the Ukrainian rulers and at the same time an important factor in the political life of Europe as a whole. When medieval Ukrainian statehood came to an end in 1340, Ukraine's territories were incorporated into the Lithuanian-Ruthenian and Polish states, under which (particularly after the Union of *Krevo in 1386) the Ukrainians' autonomy was increasingly limited and they were forced to participate in the Polish-Lithuanian wars with the Teutonic Knights. Thus, at the Battle of Grunwald (1410), where the knights were decisively defeated, 9 of the 15 regiments in the Polish army were from Galicia and Podilia, and 6 of the 17 regiments in the Lithuanian army were from Volhynia and Polisia. After this victory, trading towns began developing on the Baltic littoral, and they became an outlet for Ukraine's products.

The 15th century to 1917. In this long period, when the Ukrainians were essentially stateless, Ukrainian-German relations were primarily manifested in the cultural sphere. In the 16th century, with the advent of the Reformation, Ukrainians began studying at German universities. A. Pronsky, the son of a Kiev voivode, studied at Heidelberg in the mid-16th century; in the 17th century many students from Volhynia (eg, the brothers A. and Kh. Seniuta and I. Malyshko) and Podilia (eg, P. Bokhynytsky) also studied there. The registers of the University of Leipzig from the mid-16th to the late 17th century contain a few dozen 'Ruthenian' students, including natives of Lviv (F. Bernatovych), Buchach (P. Yazlovetsky), and Volhynia (I. Herburt); in the 18th century, students from Russian-ruled Ukraine (H. Kozytsky from Kiev, M. Motonis from Nizhen), including the sons of Cossacks (the brothers Ostrohradsky, A. Bezborodko) and M. Smotrytsky, also studied there. Soon after Königsberg (Kaliningrad) University was founded in 1544, Ukrainians from Galicia and Podilia (K. Besky, the Zernytsky brothers, M. Danylovych, H. and M. Sakharovsky, I. Valovych, S. Biletsky) were among the first students. In the 18th century, I. Kant's lectures there were attended by S. Husarevsky, the brothers Tumansky, Hornovsky, and Leontovych, V. Beliavsky, O. Karasevsky, M. Shcherbak, and I. Khmelnytsky, a descendant of Hetman B. Khmelnytsky. Ukrainians also studied at the universities of Göttingen, Cologne, Kiel, Leiden, Jena, Wittenberg, Halle, and Breslau (Wrocław). Graduates of the Kievan Mohyla Academy studied medicine at Strassburg (Strasbourg) University in the 18th century (M. Terekhovsky, O. Shumliansky, M. Karpynsky, N. Ambodyk-Maksymovych).

As the power of the Zaporozhian Cossacks grew, so did their fame. In 1594, Emperor Rudolf II sent a legation under E. *Lassota von Steblau to the Zaporozhian Sich to solicit the Cossacks' aid in stemming Ottoman expansion in Europe; Lassota's diary of his trip is a valuable source about the history and geography of Ukraine. To encourage the Cossacks to join the anti-Turkish coalition, Rudolf offered them his banner as a symbol of his imperial protection over them. This displeased the Poles, who, in the Battle of Solonytsia near Lubni in 1596, defeated the Cossack rebels led by S. Nalyvaiko and captured the banner. Thus ended this short-lived attempt at German-Cossack collaboration.

During the Polish-Cossack wars of the first half of the 17th century, Brandenburg-Prussia, as Poland's fief, was obliged to aid Poland militarily. In 1635, a German garrison stationed at the Kodak fortress had the task of stopping fugitives from reaching the Sich.

The Cossack-Polish War of 1648–57 waged during the hetmancy of B. Khmelnytsky weakened Poland considerably and gave Duke Frederick William of Brandenburg-Prussia the opportunity to break away from Poland. In mid-1649 and 1651 a rumor spread throughout Poland that Frederick had come to an agreement with Khmelnytsky through the mediation of Prince György II Rákóczi of Transylvania. But it was only in 1655 that Frederick instructed his envoy U.G. von Somnitz to conclude such an agreement. In October 1656 Khmelnytsky joined the Swedish-Transylvanian-Brandenburg coalition against Poland. In June 1657 the Swedish envoy Daniel Oliveberg de Graecani Atheniensis arrived in Chyhyryn with Frederick's proposal to conclude a treaty of friendship, to which Khmelnytsky responded affirmatively. Negotiations continued in 1657–8, even after Khmelnytsky's death. Once Frederick had obtained complete independence from Poland, he assumed the role of mediator in peace negotiations between Poland and the Cossacks. But he also sent his envoy A. Achilles-Meyn to Hetman I. Vyhovsky to explore the possibility of a 'Protestant-Cossack alliance' in the event of conflict with Poland. Vyhovsky and his adviser Yu. Nemyrych reacted favorably, since the proposal, if it had been implemented, would have guaranteed independence for both sides from Poland and from Muscovy.

At the same time Austria feared the expansion of its imperial enemies Turkey and Sweden and any rapprochement between them and Khmelnytsky. In early 1657 Emperor Ferdinand III sent a legation headed by Archbishop P. Parchevich to Chyhyryn to promote a reconciliation between Poland and the Cossacks and to negotiate a coalition against Turkey. Khmelnytsky received the envoy with full honors and promised to halt the joint Cossack-Transylvanian offensive against Poland (he did not keep his promise).

Contacts between Ukrainian hetmans and Austrian and German rulers continued. For example, Hetman I. Mazepa corresponded in 1707 with Emperor Joseph I about receiving the title of imperial prince. Mazepa's émigré successor, P. Orlyk, conducted diplomatic correspondence with Augustus II of Saxony, met with Baron A. von Bernsdorf, the chief minister of George I, in Hannover, and stayed under Habsburg protection in 1721 in Breslau, where he met and gained the sympathy of Duke Charles Frederick of Holstein. His son H. Orlyk was accepted into Augustus's own regiment in Dresden. Mazepa's nephew A. Voinarovsky fled to Germany after Mazepa's defeat and lived in Hamburg, where he was abducted by Russian agents in 1716.

German-Ukrainian relations were manifested not only in the diplomatic sphere. Thousands of Cossacks served as mercenaries in the Habsburg army during the Thirty Years' War, and over 20,000 served in the Polish army that liberated Vienna from the Turks in 1683.

During the hetmancy of I. Mazepa (1687–1709), Ukraine's cultural and economic contacts with Germany were expanded. A large part of Ukraine's raw materials and agricultural products was exported to Prussia, Silesia, and other German lands, and Danzig and Breslau became important centers for Ukraine's export trade; Breslau also supplied Ukraine with many books and periodicals. From the 18th century, Kievan artisans and merchants sold German-made products and exported their own to Saxony and Prussia.

Ukrainians continued to study at German universities. Many others, including H. Skovoroda, sojourned in Germany. The German press, such as Leipzig's *Leipziger Post* and *Europäische Fama*, Berlin's *Mercurius*, *Postilion*, *Fama*, and *Relations-Courier*, and Hamburg's *Historische Remarques über die neuesten Sachen in Europa*, reported on events in Ukraine. Several 17th-century German historians wrote about Ukraine, including J. *Pastorius, author of *Bellum Scythico-Cosacicum* (1652), S. von Puffendorf, and J. *Herbinius. In the late 18th century, the explorers and naturalists J. *Güldenstädt, P. *Pallas, K. Hablitz, and S. Gmelin wrote valuable descriptions of Southern Ukraine, and the Austrian historian J.-C. *Engel wrote two of the first scholarly accounts of Ukrainian history.

After the first partition of Poland in 1772, Austria occupied *Galicia and, in 1774, *Bukovyna. Under Austrian rule the population of these lands was subjected to the evils of Germanization and foreign domination, but it also benefited from living under a relatively liberal regime (compared to Ukraine under Russian rule) and being exposed to the achievements of Germano-Austrian culture.

With the erosion of Ukrainian autonomy and finally its abolition under Russian rule in the second half of the 18th century, direct German-Ukrainian political relations declined but did not entirely disappear. In 1791, for example, V. *Kapnist was sent on a secret mission to Berlin by a group of Ukrainian noble patriots to solicit support for a Ukrainian rebellion in the event of a Prussian-Russian war.

In the 19th century, the Germans were only marginally aware of the Ukrainian national revival, despite the fact that it was initially inspired by the ideas of the German philosopher J. *Herder, and only a few Germans took an active interest in Ukrainian affairs. In 1861 the second secretary of the Prussian embassy in St Petersburg, K. von Schlötzer, sent a report to the Foreign Office in Berlin in which he described and supported 'Little Russian' separatist sentiments. In 1888 the Prussian philosopher E. von Hartmann, in his article 'Russland und Europa' (*Gegenwart*, 33, nos 1–3), called for the creation of an independent 'Kingdom of Kiev' in order to weaken Russia. Nevertheless, the official Prussian position until 1914 towards the dismemberment of the Russian Empire and Ukrainian independence was reserved and at times even hostile.

From the second half of the 19th century until the First World War, intensive maritime trade between Germany and Ukraine took place. Wheat, sugar beets, and mineral ores were exported to Germany, and agricultural machinery, chemicals, and textiles were imported into Ukraine. The investment and influence of German capital in the industries and mines of Russian-ruled Ukraine was significant.

In the cultural sphere, certain German and Austrian writers took an interest in Ukrainian literature, particularly in T. Shevchenko (H.-L. Zunk, J.-G. Obrist [*Taras Grigoriewicz Szewczenko, ein kleinrussischer Dichter*, 1870], K.-E. Franzos, W. Kawerau, W. Umlauf, G. Karpeles, J. Hart, A. Seelieb, J. Virginia, A.-M. Bosch, W. Fischer), and surveys of Ukrainian literature were published in German encyclopedias. I. Franko translated German literature into Ukrainian and informed the German-speaking world about Ukrainian affairs (some of these writings were republished in *Ivan Franko. Beiträge zur Geschichte und Kultur der Ukraine*, Berlin 1963). The works of Shevchenko, Franko, O. Kobylianska, V. Stefanyk, and other writers were also translated into German. Ukrainian political émigrés maintained contacts with German revolutionaries; eg, S. Podolynsky and M. Ziber corresponded with K. Marx, and they read each other's works.

The First World War and the Ukrainian Revolution. With the outbreak of German-Russian hostilities, German policy towards Ukraine changed completely. Although the Ukrainian problem did not figure prominently in German plans for the East until 1916, German and Austrian military and diplomatic circles secretly began aiding the *Union for the Liberation of Ukraine (SVU) – an organization founded by émigrés from Russian-ruled Ukraine that promoted the idea of an independent Ukrainian state – as a means of undermining Russia. The SVU had its headquarters in Vienna from August 1914; when the Austrians reduced their support in favor of the Poles, the SVU moved to Berlin in spring 1915. In spring 1918 the Germans permitted the creation of two Ukrainian divisions, the so-called *Bluecoats, from among the Ukrainians in the Russian army who were German prisoners of war. (In 1915 the Austrians had permitted the organization of two special camps for Ukrainian prisoners, and three similar German camps had been established later that year.)

During the war certain German historians and publicists wrote studies and articles about the threat of Russian expansion, while supporting the idea of Ukrainian independence and underlining the importance of the Ukrainian question for Germany and for world politics as a whole. The most prominent were P. *Rohrbach, one of Germany's best-informed eastern experts, K. Nötzel (*Die Unabhängigkeit der Ukraine als einzige Rettung vor der russischen Gefahr*, 1915), G. Cleinow (*Das Problem der Ukraina*, 1915), and O. Kessler (*Die Ukraine. Beiträge zur Geschichte, Kultur und Volkswirtschaft*, 1916). In December 1915, the German society Ukraine was formed in Berlin; headed by Gen K. Gebsattel, it published its own organ, *Osteuropäische Zukunft* (editor F. Schupp). The Ukrainian question was treated in the compendium *Die Ukraine* (1916) (particularly in F. Schupp's article 'Die Ukraine,

Deutschlands Brücke zum Morgenland'), in P. Ostwald's *Die Ukraine und die ukrainische Bewegung* (1916), A. Schmidt's *Das Ziel Russlands* (1916), and A. Penck's article 'Die Ukraine' in *Zeitschrift der Gesellschaft für Erdkunde zu Berlin* (1916). While most of Germany's eastern experts advocated playing the Ukrainian card, German and Austrian governing circles favored the creation of a Polish kingdom to counter Russia.

The February Revolution of 1917 in the Russian Empire and the creation of the Ukrainian Central Rada in Kiev caught the German government off guard. The German supporters of the Ukrainian movement, Rohrbach, Schmidt, Schupp, and others, continued and even stepped up their activity in the hope of influencing German public and government opinion about the importance of an independent Ukrainian state. The German and Austrian governments continued funding the SVU and subsidized Ukrainian political publications, but they failed to attract the support of the UNR leaders. Nonetheless, Germany and the other Central Powers, as a result of developments in the war and the Allied blockade, were obliged to deal with the UNR and to negotiate the Peace Treaty of *Brest-Litovsk with the UNR separately from their treaty with Soviet Russia. The treaty was signed on 9 February 1918, and the UNR and Germany exchanged ambassadors, and the German government ratified the treaty on 24 July 1918.

In order to ensure delivery of Ukrainian grain and other foodstuffs as negotiated in the treaty, the Germans offered military aid to help clear the territories of the UNR of Bolshevik forces; the UNR leaders responded favorably. Between 19 February and early April 1918, a 800,000-strong German-Austrian army under the command of Field Marshal H. von *Eichhorn occupied all of Ukraine. But the interference of the German high command in Ukrainian affairs, its seizure of the transportation network, and the arbitrary and brutal requisitioning methods of the German and Austrian forces in Ukraine led to a conflict with the UNR Central Rada. This, in turn, led to the German-backed monarchist coup d'état of Gen P. *Skoropadsky on 29 April 1918. Earlier in the month Gen W. *Groener, chief of staff of the German high command, and the German ambassador P. Mumm von Schwarzenstein had come to terms with Skoropadsky concerning future German-Ukrainian collaboration. The agreement, which gave the Germans a free hand in trade and raw-materials procurement and strengthened German control of Ukraine (by then viewed by the Germans as their satellite), considerably restricted the actions of Skoropadsky's *Hetman government. The population deeply resented the German military overlordship and responded to it with peasant risings and partisan warfare. After Skoropadsky met with Emperor William II in Berlin from 4 to 17 September 1918, and new agreements were made, German policy toward the Hetman regime became friendlier and more co-operative. But by then it was too late: two months later Germany capitulated and began withdrawing its troops from Ukraine. During the Austro-German occupation of 1918, Ukraine supplied 42,000 – 75,000 carloads (roughly 840,000 to 1.5 million tonnes) of foodstuffs to Germany and Austria.

During the period of the Central Rada, the Ukrainian ambassador to Germany was O. Sevriuk. The Hetman government's ambassador was F. Shteingel. After the *Directory of the UNR overthrew Skoropadsky, the ambassador was M. Porsh, who was succeeded in 1920 by M. Vasylko. The German plenipotentiary in Kiev from January 1919 was O. Meissner. From 1919 to 1921 the Western Ukrainian National Republic (ZUNR) was represented in Germany by R. Smal-Stotsky. V. Orenchuk was the UNR consul in Munich from 1919 to 1922. From 1921 to 1923 V. Aussem was the first representative of the Ukrainian SSR in Berlin.

The press of the day extensively covered the Brest-Litovsk treaty and the German occupation of Ukraine in 1918. Valuable memoirs of the period have been written by several key German and Austrian figures – generals M. Hoffmann, E. von Ludendorff, and W. Groener, R. von Kühlmann, O. von Czernin, and others.

In March 1918, the *German-Ukrainian Society was formed, headed by P. Rohrbach and A. Schmidt; it was critical of German policy in Ukraine, including the engineering of Skoropadsky's coup.

The interwar years. After the USSR and Germany signed the Treaty of Rapallo and the Berlin Agreement in 1922, economic relations between Soviet Ukraine and Germany were normalized. Germany and Ukraine became major trade partners, and German workers and experts helped to rebuild Ukraine's industries. A Soviet Ukrainian trade delegation was established in Berlin, and a German counterpart was located in Kharkiv. The People's Commissariat of Education of Ukraine, which created a bureau in Berlin in 1922, bought German books for Ukraine's libraries and supervised scientific and cultural co-operation, exchanges, and contacts. In the years 1925–8 over 400 Ukrainian scholars made official research trips to Germany. In 1925, scholarly and book exchanges were established between the VUAN and the Bavarian Academy of Sciences in Munich. The VUAN social-economic division had close ties with Berlin University. In the 1920s, Soviet Ukrainian writers, filmmakers, actors, opera singers, and musicians, including P. Tychyna, I. Mykytenko, M. Khvylovy, O. Dovzhenko, H. Yura, L. Kurbas, M. Boichuk, V. Sedliar, V. Meller, V. Polishchuk, and O. Dosvitny, toured Germany, and German cultural figures visited and performed in Ukraine.

The German-Ukrainian Society continued its activity, and its members' writings influenced the eastern policies of the Weimar Republic. Among the society's publications were the journal *Die Ukraine* (40 issues, 1918–26) and *Knyzhka pro Nimechchynu* (Book about Germany, 1920) edited by A. Schmidt and Z. Kuzelia. On the initiative of P. Skoropadsky and with the backing of the Ukrainian Refugee Aid Society and the Society for the Advancement of Ukrainian Culture and Knowledge (and, from 1931, the German Ministry of Education), the *Ukrainian Scientific Institute in Berlin was founded in 1926 to foster Ukrainian scholarship, provide and publish information about Ukraine, and conduct and publish research about Ukraine's relations with the West, particularly with Germany. From 1934 the institute was a state institution; it was affiliated with Berlin University until 1938.

Among the more active German Ukrainian specialists were H. *Koch, who studied Ukrainian church history; P. Rohrbach, the author of *Deutschlands Ukraine Politik* (1918); T. von Biberstein, the author of *Die ukrainische Frage: Die Ukraine vor und nach dem Weltkrieg im Lichte der neuesten wissenschaftlichen Quellen* (1934); and particularly A. Schmidt, who in his articles and the book *Ukraine, Land der Zukunft* (1939) promoted the idea of an independent Ukraine as being in the interest of Germany itself. Schmidt's orientation ran counter to A. *Hitler's expansionist and racist views, however, and his works were not allowed to circulate in 1941.

1. International borders
2. Boundaries of West German states and East German districts
3. West and East German capitals

The Second World War. The real intentions of Nazi Germany vis-à-vis Ukraine first became evident in March 1939, when it occupied Bohemia and Moravia and sanctioned the Hungarian annexation of Carpatho-Ukraine, which in 1938 had acquired national autonomy as part of the Czechoslovak Republic. In August 1939 Germany and the USSR signed the *Molotov-Ribbentrop Pact, according to which the USSR occupied most of Polish-ruled Western Ukraine after Germany invaded Poland in September. In the western Ukrainian borderlands that were incorporated into the Nazi *Generalgouvernement of Poland after the invasion, minimal cultural and social activity was allowed within the framework of the *Ukrainian Central Committee. In June 1940, the USSR took northern Bukovyna and Bessarabia from Rumania with German assent.

In June 1941, the Germans quickly overran most of Ukraine. Many Ukrainians greeted the Germans as their liberators from Soviet oppression, but this attitude soon changed as Nazi policy became evident. In July the new, Nazi, totalitarian regime suppressed the attempt to re-establish a Ukrainian state after the *Proclamation of Ukrainian Statehood in Lviv by leaders of the Bandera faction of the OUN on 30 June and placed many OUN leaders in *concentration camps. On 1 August, Galicia was incorporated as a district of the Generalgouvernement. The *Reichskommissariat Ukraine was created on 20 August on the territory of Right-Bank Ukraine and large parts of central Left-Bank Ukraine; it was governed by E. *Koch from Rivne. Northern Bukovyna, parts of Bessarabia, and so-called *Transnistria were administered by Axis Rumania.

At the start of the Second World War, Ukrainians considered the Germans as partners in their struggle to free Ukraine from Soviet Russian domination. But from the summer of 1941 Nazi Germany began treating Ukraine as its colony (*Lebensraum*). The initial somewhat positive attitude toward Ukrainians as expressed by A. *Rosenberg gave way to the extreme policies of Hitler, H. Himmler, and E. Koch. Although conditions were somewhat better for Ukrainians who found themselves under the Generalgouvernement, in general all Ukrainians were treated by the Nazi regime as a subhuman (*Untermenschen*) work pool. Most Ukrainians therefore actively or passively resisted Nazi policies in Ukraine and paid dearly for this resistance.

During the German wartime occupation, 6.8 million inhabitants of Ukraine perished as a consequence of the German-Soviet war or of German terror and the Holocaust; more than 700 cities and towns and over 28,000 villages were destroyed. Between two and three million Ukrainians were deported as *Ostarbeiter, or slave laborers, to the Third Reich. All oppositionist and independentist groups, such as the *Ukrainian national councils founded in Lviv in July and in Kiev in October 1941, the *Organization of Ukrainian Nationalists, and its expeditionary groups, were brutally persecuted, and the organized Ukrainian nationalist movement became an anti-German underground that contributed to Germany's defeat on the Eastern Front. From 1941, groups of Ukrainian partisans led by T. *Borovets in Volhynia and Polisia engaged in guerrilla warfare against both the German and the Soviet military (including the Soviet partisans). From 1943 this guerrilla warfare was spearheaded in Western Ukraine by the *Ukrainian Insurgent Army. In 1943, however, a Ukrainian volunteer formation, the *Division Galizien, was created as part of the German armed forces on the Soviet front; it was supported by the Ukrainians not as a German unit, but as the core of the armed forces in a future independent Ukraine. From August 1943 the Soviet offensive in Ukraine gained momentum, but it was only in October 1944 that the last German forces retreated from Ukrainian soil.

The postwar period. Since the Second World War, Ukraine has had official economic and cultural ties primarily with the Soviet client state of East Germany. The nature and extent of these ties are decided in Moscow. In 1958, a Ukrainian section, headed by I. Bilodid, of the Society for Soviet-German Friendship and Cultural Relations was founded in Kiev. The inhumane and destructive policies of the Nazi regime in Ukraine have tainted the perception of Germans in Soviet Ukraine. West Germany, in particular, is viewed negatively from the Soviet perspective as the successor to the Third Reich and an enemy because of its NATO affiliation; this has precluded any meaningful co-operation between Bonn and Kiev. Nonetheless, in 1986 the governments of the West German Federal Republic and the USSR agreed to open a German consulate in Kiev and a Soviet one in Munich. Other Ukrainian-German relations exist in West Germany as a result of the presence of émigrés and displaced persons who took refuge there after the war.

In 1948 the German-Ukrainian Society was revived in Munich. Between 1952 and 1958 it published 44 issues of the journal *Ukraine in Vergangenheit und Gegenwart* (editor H. Prokopchuk) and several books. In 1960 the society was merged with the *Herder German-Ukrainian Society, which was founded in Munich on the initiative of I. Mirchuk and H. Koch in 1948.

Ukrainian Studies Building in Munich, home of the Ukrainian Free University, the Shevchenko Scientific Society, and the Ukrainian Technical and Husbandry Institute

In 1946, the *Ukrainian Free University (UVU), which from 1921 to 1945 was located in Prague, was re-established in Munich. The *Shevchenko Scientific Society – the leading scholarly society in Western Ukraine from 1873 to 1939 – was revived in Munich in 1947, and the *Ukrainian Technical and Husbandry Institute – the correspondence school of the Ukrainian Husbandry Academy in Poděbrady, Bohemia, from 1932 to 1945 – was revived in Regensburg in 1945. In order to facilitate contacts with German academic circles, these three institutions formed the *Association for the Advancement of Ukrainian Studies in 1962.

Ukrainians in Germany

To 1939. Until 1914, Ukrainians came to Germany on an individual basis and only temporarily, as visitors or as students; eg, M. Lysenko studied at the Leipzig Conservatory and A. Sheptytsky, the future metropolitan, studied at Breslau University. From the late 19th century, certain Ukrainian artists have gone to Germany to study and to improve their technique (eg, M. Ivasiuk, M. Sosenko, I. Trush, Yu. Narbut, O. Murashko, M. Parashchuk, Ye. Lipetsky, D. Horniatkevych). Thousands of Ukrainians from Austrian-ruled Western Ukraine went there for seasonal work. The club Ukraina was founded in Hamburg in 1908. During the First World War, Germany was home to members of the SVU and other expatriates, who were involved in relief work on behalf of some 200,000 Ukrainian soldiers in the Russian army interned in German prisoner-of-war camps near *Wetzlar, *Rastatt, and *Salzwedel. From 1918 to 1921, the UNR and the Ukrainian State (the Hetman government) had an embassy and numerous missions in Berlin.

In 1919, relatively small numbers of political refugees who had taken part in the Ukrainian struggle for independence began settling in Germany. *Berlin became the center of Ukrainian activity. The *Ukrainska Hromada society was founded there in 1919; at first a non-partisan society, it became the center of the Hetmanite movement. In 1933 the *Ukrainian National Alliance was founded in Berlin; an OUN affiliate from 1937, it became a powerful civic organization. Two major Ukrainian publishing houses existed in Berlin: Ya. Orenstein's *Ukrainska Nakladnia (1919–33) and *Ukrainske Slovo (1921–6), directed by Z. Kuzelia. There were also several smaller publishers. Several Ukrainian newspapers and periodicals were published there, including **Ukraïns'ke slovo* (1921–4), **Ukraïns'kyi prapor* (1923–31), **Osteuropäische Korrespondenz* (1926–30), and *Ukrainischer Pressedienst / Ukraïns'ka presova sluzhba* (1931–9) (bulletins of the *Ukrainian Press Service).

A few hundred Ukrainian émigré students attended German universities. In 1921 they organized the Association of Ukrainian Students in Germany; branches, as well as independent student societies, were created in Berlin, Königsberg, Kiel, Göttingen, Breslau, Danzig (*Gdansk), and elsewhere. In 1924 an umbrella organization, called from 1925 the Union of Ukrainian Student Organizations in Germany and Danzig, was founded; in 1939 it was renamed the National Union of Ukrainian Student Organizations in Germany and in 1941 the *Nationalist Organization of Ukrainian Students.

Emigré leaders, such as Hetman P. Skoropadsky, Ye. Petrushevych, the president of the Western Ukrainian National Republic, and Ye. Konovalets, the head of the Ukrainian Military Organization, lived in Berlin with their close associates. From 1919 I. Poltavets-Ostrianytsia, the leader of the Free Cossacks, lived in Munich. In 1927 a Ukrainian Greek-Catholic parish was created in Berlin; in 1940 its pastor, P. Verhun, became the apostolic visitator for Ukrainian Catholics in Germany, and a parish was also created in Munich. In the 1930s a Ukrainian Orthodox parish also existed in Berlin.

The Second World War. On the eve of the war about 10,000 Ukrainians lived in Germany. They were joined by Ukrainians fleeing from Hungarian-occupied Transcarpathia in 1938. After Poland fell in 1939, Ukrainians – former soldiers in the Polish army, inhabitants of the Generalgouvernement, and refugees fleeing the Soviet occupation of Western Ukraine – found their way to Germany. During the German-Soviet war of 1941–5, hundreds of thousands of Ukrainians in the Soviet army who had been captured or surrendered were interned in Germany and brutally treated; many of them died in the prison camps. In pursuit of *Lebensraum*, and to ease the labor shortage caused by conscription, and to keep the German economy going, millions of foreigners were recruited or forcibly deported to work in Germany. Beginning in 1940 certain Ukrainians in the Generalgouvernement went to work in Germany voluntarily; many more were taken forcibly, as were between two and three million Ostarbeiter from Soviet Ukraine. The latter, in particular, were treated as *Untermenschen*, had no rights, and were subjected to extremely poor living and working conditions and harsh treatment, including beatings, executions, and incarceration in concentration camps for any infractions. Only in late 1944, after the Germans had retreated from Ukraine, did the Nazi regime attempt to moderate its attitude towards the Ostarbeiter as a whole. The Ukrainian Ostarbeiter were allowed to have a Ukrainian custodial agency, the Ukrainische Betreuungsstelle, headed by O. Semenenko (the former mayor of Kharkiv), which looked after their cultural needs. From 1941 Ukrainian workers in Germany from the territory of the Generalgouvernement were represented and aided by the Berlin bureau (directed by A. Figol) of the *Ukrainian Central Committee. With the wartime increase of the number of Ukrainians in Germany, the two major Ukrainian civic organizations already existing there expanded.

The nationalist Ukrainian National Alliance (headed by T. Omelchenko) by 1942 had 42,000 members in 1,268 branches; it published the newspaper *Ukraïns'kyi visnyk. The Hetmanite Ukrainska Hromada had over 6,000 members and published the newspaper *Ukraïns'ka diisnist'. An official German agency, the *Ukrainian Institution of Trust (Ukrainische Vertrauenstelle im Deutschen Reich, headed by M. Sushko), kept a register of Ukrainians in Germany and issued identity papers. As a result of its efforts, the *German Labor Front created a department to take care of the Ukrainian workers' social and cultural needs.

The postwar period. At the end of the war, some 2.5 to 3 million Ukrainians found themselves in Germany. Most were forcibly repatriated to the USSR during 1945 (see *Repatriation). Thus, at the beginning of 1946 only about 180,000 Ukrainians remained in Germany – after the Poles, the second largest national group of *displaced persons. Most of them were resettled within five years in Belgium, France, Great Britain, and later the United States, Canada, Brazil, Australia, and elsewhere overseas. Because of *emigration, the number of Ukrainians in Germany fell to 140,000 in 1947, 111,000 in 1948, 86,000 in 1949, and 55,000 in 1950.

The Ukrainian displaced persons camp near Augsburg, 1947

In 1947 most Ukrainians were housed in 134 displaced persons camps; a minority lived in private dwellings. The largest concentrations of Ukrainians were in the regions of Bavaria (66,000), Baden (9,400), and Hesse (8,200) in the American occupation zone; Lower Saxony (10,800), north Rhineland-Westphalia (6,800), Schleswig-Holstein (1,500), and Hamburg (3,200) in the British zone; and Rhineland Pfalz (3,300) and Württemberg (2,200) in the French zone. In 1946–7, the camps with large numbers of Ukrainians were: in the American zone, Regensburg (4,660), Mittenwald-Jäger-Kaserne (2,890), Augsburg-Somme-Kaserne (2,640), Munich-Freimann (2,580), Cornberg (2,340), Ellwangen (2,330), Ettlingen (2,150), Berchtesgaden-'Orlyk' (2,110), Bayreuth (2,170), Munich-Schleissheim (2,020), Aschaffenburg-Pionier-Kaserne (2,000), Neu-Ulm (1,930), Mainz-Kastel (1,800), Dillingen (1,660), Stuttgart-Zufenhausen (1,580), Aschaffenburg-Artillerie-Kaserne (1,450), Bamberg (1,380), Aschaffenburg-Lagerde (1,300), Aschaffenburg-Bois Brule (1,300), Karlsruhe (1,300), Ingolstadt (1,280), Mittenwald-Pionier-Kaserne (1,190), Stephanskirchen (1,170), Pforzheim (1,130), Neumarkt (1,070), Reiterzeich (970), Landshut (900), Erlangen (810), Ludwigsburg (800), and Munich-Laim (720); in the British zone, Hannover-'Lysenko' (3,430), Heidenau (3,030), Rheine (1,910), Münster-Lager (1,530), Mülheim-Ruhr (1,440), Hallendorf (1,420), Bathorn (1,350), Lintorf (1,320), Goslar (1,200), Hamburg-Falkenberg (1,110), Burgdorf (970), Braunschweig (900), Bielefeld (850), Delmenhorst (800), Korigen (740), Göttingen (680), and Godenau (650); and in the French zone, Gneisenau (1,370), Bad Kreuznach (670), Landstuhl (610), and Trier (530).

Since 1950. When mass resettlement came to a halt at the beginning of the 1950s, only about 20,000 Ukrainians remained in West Germany (most were elderly or disabled and not eligible for resettlement). When the camps were closed down, these persons were registered as stateless, granted rights (excluding political rights) equal to those of the German population, and integrated into German society. Most of the employable Ukrainians moved into urban-industrial areas. In 1970, 8,700 (44 percent) of the Ukrainians lived in Bavaria, 3,500 (18 percent) in Baden-Württemberg, 3,300 (16 percent) in Hesse, 1,550 (7.3 percent) in Westphalia, 1,450 (7.2 percent) in Lower Saxony, 500 (2.3 percent) in Hamburg, 400 (2 percent) in Bremen, and about 600 (3 percent) elsewhere. Eighty percent of the employable Ukrainians worked in industry and construction, 5 percent worked in agriculture, and 3 percent worked for Ukrainian civic organizations and community enterprises. After the war a small number of Ukrainians started up their own businesses and private enterprises. Some Ukrainians are professionals (doctors, dentists, engineers, lawyers, teachers, professors, etc).

Most Ukrainians in West Germany (67 percent) are Byzantine Catholics, a third (31 percent) are Orthodox, and 2 percent belong to other denominations. In 1948 the Catholics had 39 communities and 151 priests, the Orthodox had 38 communities and 99 priests, and the Evangelicals had 17 communities and 19 ministers. By 1949, the number had declined to 21 Catholic communities and 48 priests, 23 Orthodox communities and 52 priests, and 12 Evangelical communities and 12 ministers. In 1980, there were 21 Catholic communities ministered to by 26 priests and 20 Orthodox communities with 10 priests. The Ukrainian Catholic church in Germany became an exarchate in 1959. Headed by Bishop P. *Kornyliak, it consists today of four deaneries with about 13,000 faithful. The Ukrainian Autocephalous Orthodox church (UAOC) was headed by Metropolitan N. *Abramovych; he was succeeded by Archbishop O. Ivaniuk, who was succeeded in 1981 by Archbishop A. *Dubliansky. The administrator of the UAOC in Germany is Archpresbyter P. Dubytsky. A part of the Orthodox faithful belong to the Ukrainian Autocephalous Orthodox Church (Conciliar).

In the immediate postwar period, there were five institutions of higher education – the Ukrainian Free University, the Ukrainian Technical and Husbandry Institute, the *Ukrainian Higher School of Economics (1945–51), the *Theological Academy of the UAOC in Munich, and the Ukrainian Catholic Theological Seminary in Hirschberg (1946–9) – with a total of 1,270 students and 314 professors/lecturers. With the departure of most of the Ukrainians the network of Ukrainian schools fell apart, and Saturday schools were created to provide children with a Ukrainian education. The latter are supervised by the *Central Representation of the Ukrainian Emigration in Germany, an umbrella civic body created in 1945. The number of Ukrainian schools and nursery schools has decreased: in 1955 there were 41 Saturday schools and 24 nursery schools, but in 1970 there were only 20 and 3 respectively.

From 1945 to 1951, the Ukrainians' civic, cultural, professional, and political activity was very dynamic. They had 41 organizations with 638 local branches and 58,000 members; 44 publishing houses, which issued 147 periodicals and over 700 books; 31 orchestras and bands, 60 choirs, and 54 amateur theatrical groups. Among the professional groups were the theatrical troupes directed by V. Blavatsky and Y. Hirniak, the choirs conducted by N. Horodovenko and V. Bozhyk, and the Ukrainian Bandurist Chorus directed by H. Kytasty. Various professional and co-operative associations also existed. Artists, musicians, and writers had their own organizations, the most prominent being *MUR – the Artistic Ukrainian Movement. There was also an Association of Ukrainian Journalists. The 2,300 postsecondary students in 1947 were members of well-organized, active Ukrainian student communities, and from 1946 to 1952 the *Central Union of Ukrainian Students had its headquarters in Munich. The scholarly Ukrainian Free Academy of Sciences and the *Shevchenko Scientific Society were based in Germany for a few years after the war until most of their members were resettled.

Since the Second World War, *Munich has been the center not only of Ukrainian cultural, scholarly, and civic activity, but also of most of the Ukrainian émigré political organizations in West Germany, such as the *Ukrainian National Council, the *Government-in-exile of the Ukrainian National Republic, and the *Anti-Bolshevik Bloc of Nations. The OUN leaders S. *Bandera and L. *Rebet were killed by Soviet agents while living in Munich. Since the war several Ukrainian publishing houses have been located in Germany: Suchasnist, *Ukrainske Vydavnytstvo, Logos, Dniprova Khvylia, Verlag Ukraine of the German-Ukrainian Society, *Molode Zhyttia, Khrystyianskyi Holos, the M. Orest Institute of Literature, Na Hori, and Ukrainski Visti. Together, in the years 1951–80 they published some 220 titles.

Two Ukrainian weeklies – **Shliakh peremohy* and **Khrystyians'kyi holos* – the monthly journal **Suchasnist'*, and the UAOC quarterly **Ridna tserkva* still appear in Germany. The newspapers **Meta* and **Ukraïns'ki visti* were recently transferred to the United States. Such periodicals as **Ukraïns'ka trybuna, *Suchasna Ukraïna, *Ukraïns'kyi samostiinyk, *Vpered, Ukraïns'kyi zbirnyk, and Ukrainian Review* of the *Institute for the Study of the USSR, **Digest of the Soviet Ukrainian Press*, and **Ukraïna i svit* (Hannover) have ceased publication.

Various civic, cultural, religious, youth, and student organizations have existed in West Germany since the war. All of the organizations are constituent members of the Central Representation of the Ukrainian Emigration in Germany. Some scholars who remained in West Germany have taught at universities: D. Chyzhevsky at Heidelberg, O. Horbach at Frankfurt, Yu. Blokhyn, A. Bilynsky, H. Nakonechna, and M. Antokhii at Munich, D. Zlepko at Bonn, and B. Osadchuk at the Free University of Berlin. Several Ukrainians have systematically provided the German press with information about Ukraine and the Ukrainians: the Sovietologists B. Levytsky and B. Osadchuk, and the literary specialist and translator A.H. Horbach.

Many other émigrés who remained in Germany have left their mark in the life of the Ukrainian community in many spheres – in politics: A. and M. Livytsky, S. Baran, I. Mazepa, V. Vytvytsky, S. Dovhal, I. Bahriany, Ya. and S. Stetsko, L. and D. Rebet, B. Kordiuk, D. Andriievsky, O. Boidunyk, M. Kapustiansky, V. Dolenko, F. Pigido, and Ya. Makovetsky; in scholarship: I. Mirchuk, Yu. Paneiko, V. Oreletsky, Yu. Boiko-Blokhyn, V. Yaniv, B. Krupnytsky, N. Polonska-Vasylenko, P. Zaitsev, Ye. Glovinsky, Yu. Studynsky, M. Miller, P. Kurinny, O. Horbach, P. Fedenko, I. Hrynokh, M. Hotsii, H. Vaskovych, and Z. Sokoliuk at the Ukrainian Free University, and B. Ivanytsky, P. Savytsky, R. Yendyk, M. Korzhan, I. Maistrenko, and A. Figol at the Ukrainian Technical and Husbandry Institute; in literature and literary scholarship: M. Orest, E. Andiievska, I. Kachurovsky, I. Kostetsky, V. Derzhavyn, I. Koshelivets, and O. Hrytsai; in art: H. Kruk, V. Vardashko, V. Strelnikov, and V. Sazonov; in journalism: Z. Pelensky, V. Stakhiv, M. Konovalets, M. Styranka, H. Horbach, V. Maruniak, and H. Prokopchuk; in social-cultural work: Yu. Pavlykovsky, V. Pliushch, A. Melnyk, V. Didovych (now archbishop), S. Mudryk, I. Zheguts, V. Lenyk, and Yu. Kavlachuk.

The generation of Ukrainians raised in Germany after the war has by and large been assimilated by its host society. Many individuals can no longer speak Ukrainian and take no part in community life. This process has particularly affected the offspring of mixed marriages and individuals living in cities where there is no organized community.

Germans who have contributed to the field of Ukrainian studies in the postwar period include G. Stadtmüller, E. Koschmieder, A. Schmaus, H. Rheinfelder, N. Lobkowicz, J. Madey, T. Rhode, L. Müller, F. Heyer, G. Horn, E. Völkl, H. Glassel, and B. Gröschel in West Germany; and E. Winter, E. Reissner, B. Widera, L. Richter, and M. Wegner in East Germany.

BIBLIOGRAPHY

Vasil'evskii, V. 'Drevniaia torgovlia Kieva s Regensburgom,' *ZhMNP*, no. 258 (July 1888)

Halban, A. *Zur Geshchichte des deutschen Rechtes in Podolien, Wolhynien und der Ukraine* (Berlin 1896)

Goetz, L. *Das Kiever Höhlenkloster als Kulturzentrum des vormongolischen Russlands* (Passau 1904)

Ediger, T. *Russlands älteste Beziehungen zu Deutschland, Frankreich und der römischen Kurie* (Halle 1911)

Goetz, L. *Deutsch-russische Handelsverträge des Mittelalters* (Hamburg 1916)

Olianchyn, D. 'Iz materiialiv do ukraïns'ko-nimets'kykh politychnykh znosyn druh. polov. XVII. v.,' *Abhandlungen des Ukrainischen Wissenschaftlichen Institutes in Berlin*, 1 (1927)

Shaitan, M. 'Germaniia i Kiev v XI v.,' *Letopis' Arkheograficheskoi komissii za 1926 god*, 34 (Leningrad 1927)

Los'kyi, I. 'Ukraïntsi na studiiakh v Nimechchyni v XVI–XVIII st.,' *ZNTSh*, 151 (1931)

Mirtschuk, I. *Deutsche Philosophie in der Ukraine* (Munich 1939)

Doroschenko, D. *Die Ukraine und das Reich: Neun Jahrhunderte deutsch-ukrainischer Beziehungen im Spiegel der deutschen Wissenschaft und Literatur* (Leipzig 1941)

Antonowytsch, D. *Deutsche Einflüsse auf die ukrainische Kunst* (Leipzig 1942)
Kamenetsky, I. *Hitler's Occupation of Ukraine, 1941–1944: A Study of Totalitarian Imperialism* (Milwaukee 1956)
Dallin, A. *German Rule in Russia: A Study of Occupation Policies* (London 1957; rev edn Boulder, Colo 1981)
Ilnytzkyj, R. *Deutschland und die Ukraine, 1934–1945. Tatsachen europäischer Ostpolitik: Ein Vorbericht*, 2 vols (Munich 1958)
Prokoptschuk, G. *Ukrainer in München und in der Bundesrepublik*, 2 vols (Munich 1958–9)
Zastavenko, H. *Krakh nimets'koï interventsiï na Ukraïni v 1918 rotsi* (Kiev 1959)
Reitlinger, G. *The House Built on Sand: The Conflicts of German Policy in Russia, 1939–1945* (New York 1960, Westport, Conn 1975)
Kamenetsky, I. *Secret Nazi Plans for Eastern Europe: A Study of Lebensraum Policies* (New York 1961)
Rohrbach, P. *Von Brest Litowsk bis Jalta: Ein Vierteljahrhundert Osteuropa* (Munich 1961)
Kulinych, I. *Ukraïna v zaharbnyts'kykh planakh nimets'koho imperializmu* (Kiev 1963)
Nimets'ko-fashysts'kyi okupatsiinyi rezhym na Ukraïni: Zbirnyk dokumentiv i materialiv (Kiev 1963)
Pan'kivs'kyi, K. *Roky nimets'koï okupatsiï, 1941–1944* (New York 1965, 2nd edn 1983)
Deutschland-Sowjetunion: Aus fünf Jahrzehnten kultureller Zusammenarbeit (Berlin 1966)
Kulinych, I. *Ekonomichni ta kul'turni zv'iazky Ukraïns'koï RSR z Nimets'koiu Demokratychnoiu Respublikoiu (1949–1965)* (Kiev 1966)
Prokoptschuk, G. *Deutsche-Ukrainische Gesellschaft, 1918–1968* (Munich 1968)
Pashuto, V. *Vneshniaia politika Drevnei Rusi* (Moscow 1968)
Kulinych, I. *Ukraïns'ko-nimets'ki istorychni zv'iazky* (Kiev 1969)
Jacobson, H.A. (ed). *Misstrauische Nachbarn: Deutsche Ostpolitik 1919–1970* (Düsseldorf 1970)
Borowsky, P. *Deutsche Ukrainepolitik 1918 unter besonderer Berücksichtigung der Wirtschaftsfragen* (Lübeck-Hamburg 1970)
Fedyshyn, O. *Germany's Drive to the East and the Ukrainian Revolution, 1917–1918* (New Brunswick, NJ 1971)
Zelenets'kyi, O. (ed). *Na hromads'kii nyvi (do 25-littia TsPUEN)* (Munich 1971)
Torzecki, R. *Kwestia ukraińska w polityce III Rzeszy, 1933–1945* (Warsaw 1972)
Lemke, H.; Widera, B. (eds). *Russisch-deutsche Beziehungen von der Kiever Rus' bis zur Oktoberrevolution* (Berlin 1976)
Mirchuk, P. *In the German Mills of Death* (New York 1976)
Maruniak, V. *Ukraïns'ka emigratsiia v Nimechchyni i Avstriï po druhii svitovii viini, 1: Roky 1945–1951* (Munich 1985)
Boshyk, Y. (ed). *Ukraine during World War II. History and Its Aftermath: A Symposium* (Edmonton 1986)

A. Zhukovsky

Gerontology. Branch of science dealing with the phenomenon of aging in living beings, including man. Gerontology includes the study of the biology and pathology of aging, diseases and debilities of the aged and medical care for old people (geriatrics), and the social aspects of aging. Research encompasses not only medical and scientific methods of prolonging life and improving the quality of life in old age, but also addresses public policies affecting the aged. Some interest in the problem of aging can be detected among practitioners of the healing arts in Kievan Rus', who observed and noted the characteristic symptoms of aging. Concern for the aged increased after the introduction of Christianity; Grand Prince Volodymyr the Great decreed that every church establish an almshouse, and every monastery a settlement for the aged. Later, nobles, hetmans, and then the tsar's treasury were responsible for maintaining such institutions. In 1712 Peter I ordered the establishment of poorhouses for old people throughout the Russian Empire, including its Ukrainian possessions. In 1864 they were placed under the *zemstvos, and from 1870, at least partly, under municipal governments.

Beginning in the 18th and 19th centuries, individual physicians in Ukraine began studying aspects of the pathology of aging. The first scientific school of gerontology, not only in Ukraine but in the entire Russian Empire, was founded by I. *Mechnikov in 1886 in Odessa. He developed a theory on aging and claimed that the process could be controlled by means of a proper diet and surgery. In Kiev, M. *Strazhesko devoted much attention to gerontological and geriatric problems. Like his teacher V. Obraztsov (1849–1920), he distinguished physiological and pathological aging, and emphasized the dominant role of the central nervous system in all physiological and pathological processes.

After the 1917 Revolution the first important gerontological schools in the USSR arose in Ukraine. One of them was founded by the pathophysiologist O. *Bohomolets, who in 1931 established the Institute of Experimental Biology and Pathology in Kiev. In 1938 Bohomolets helped organize a large conference in Kiev on aging and longevity, the first such conference in the USSR. Its proceedings were published by the AN URSR in a collection titled *Starost'* (Old Age, 1940). A second major school of gerontology emerged at the Institute of Biology of Kharkiv University under the biochemist O. *Nahorny.

After the war gerontological research was resumed in Kiev by students of Bohomolets, and in Kharkiv by Nahorny and his school. In 1950 Nahorny's book *Starenie i prodlenie zhizni* (Aging and the Prolongation of Life) appeared. In the following year Bohomolets's students under the direction of Yu. Spasokukotsky carried out a clinical-physiological survey of about 11,000 old people throughout Ukraine (except the Crimea). This survey involved the participation of over 1,500 medical workers. In the second half of the 1950s similar surveys were begun for the entire USSR.

In fall 1958 the *Institute of Gerontology of the USSR Academy of Medical Sciences was established in Kiev. Under its directors M. *Horiev (N. Gorev) and D. *Chebotarov, it has co-ordinated all gerontological and geriatric research and practical work in the USSR. In 1959 the institute established geriatric cabinets at polyclinics in Kiev, and in 1960 at polyclinics in Kharkiv. At the same time it carried out a USSR-wide survey of people over 80 years of age. In 1961 the institute sponsored a conference with over 400 participants from all parts of the USSR; the impact of the conference was so great that the goal of extending life expectancy by means of social, economic, and medical measures was added to the CPSU program.

In 1963 a USSR conference on aging and a symposium of World Health Organization gerontologists were held in Kiev, and the USSR Association of Gerontologists and Geriatricians was founded. A 1964 symposium 'Way of Life and Human Aging' was followed by the establishment of new gerontological and geriatric institutions in various cities of the USSR and of the Chair of Gerontology at the Kiev Institute for the Upgrading of Physicians. In subsequent years international gerontological courses (1965, 1967), an international symposium on kinetic activity and aging (1968), and the Ninth International Gerontological Congress (1972), the proceedings of which were published in English, were held in Kiev. Many Ukrainian scientists have contributed to the development of gerontology; they include O. Makarchenko, M. Mankivsky, O. Mints, E. Podrushniak, I. Bazylevych, and (in Rumania) V. Jucovschi (Zhukovsky).

BIBLIOGRAPHY
Schulz, H. *Die Entwicklung der Gerontologie in der UdSSR* (Hamburg 1961)
– 'Historical Survey of Soviet Gerontology and Geriatrics,' *Review of Soviet Medical Sciences*, 1966, no. 2
– 'Die Wissenschaft vom Alter,' *Sowjet Studien*, no. 23 (1967)
Leading Problems of Soviet Gerontology, ed D. Chebotarev et al (Kiev 1972)

H. Schulz

Gerovsky, Georgii [Gerovskij, Georgij], b 6 October 1886 in Lviv, d 1959 near Prešov, Slovakia. Linguist specializing in the dialects of Transcarpathia, who graduated from the universities of Leipzig and Saratov. He was a grandson of A. *Dobriansky, whose Russophile tradition he continued. Opposed to Ukrainian being the standard language of the region, Gerovsky promoted Russian and attacked I. *Pankevych and his Ukrainian grammar (1930). He wrote articles on the history, literature, and language of Transcarpathia and a survey of Transcarpathian dialects in the Czechoslovak compendium *Československá vlastivěda* (vol 3, 1934), which is rich in factual material but marred by his Russophile views. In his last years Gerovsky taught Russian language and literature at Prešov University.

Yaroslava Gerulak: *Athena and Zeus* (terra-cotta)

Gerulak, Yaroslava [Geruljak, Jaroslava], b 5 May 1933 in Stopnica, near Kielce, Poland. Artist. Gerulak studied at Siena Heights College, Northwestern University, and the Art Institute of Chicago, and taught at Manhattanville College in Purchase, New York (1955–7). She is a member of the Association of Ukrainian Artists of America and has exhibited in Paris, New York, Toronto, and other cities. Gerulak works in a number of mediums; of special interest are her ceramic sculptures, in which she depicts mythical and folklore themes in both archaic and modern forms (eg, *Young Neptune on a Fish, Prince Ihor, Sun on a Bicycle*).

Gestapo (abbreviation of Geheime Staatspolizei). Secret police of Nazi Germany. Created in 1933, it became an adjunct to H. Himmler's SS and developed into the most dreaded Nazi security agency, using its virtually unlimited powers to uncover, imprison, and kill 'enemies of the Reich.'

After the signing of the Molotov-Ribbentrop pact the Gestapo collaborated with the NKVD in persecuting political opponents. Following the invasion of the USSR, Gestapo officials headed the SS mobile killer squads (*Einsatzgruppen*) that murdered Jews in the occupied territories; they also organized the deportation of Jews to extermination camps. The Gestapo's other principal wartime function was to suppress resistance movements throughout Europe. In 1939–40 Gestapo agents arrested members of the UNR government-in-exile in Warsaw and Paris. When the Ukrainian nationalist movement began to oppose German policy, the Gestapo imprisoned leaders of the OUN (Bandera faction) and killed leading OUN (Melnyk faction) figures in Zhytomyr and Kiev (including I. Irliavsky, I. Rohach, and O. Teliha). It conducted mass arrests and executions of rank-and-file nationalists and played a leading role in terrorizing the population during the Nazi occupation of Ukraine.

Getae. North Thracian tribes, also called Dacians, that in the 5th century BC inhabited the lower Danube region. From the 4th century BC, they occupied the area south of the Carpathian Mountains from Dobrudja to the Dniester River. About 60–50 BC, their king Burebistas united them and the neighboring Boii and Tauri into a powerful Getic-Dacian kingdom, which fell apart after his death. In AD 106, the Getae were subdued by Rome. Many of them were killed or driven northward, and their territories were incorporated into the Roman provinces of Moesia and Dacia.

Lev Gets

Gets, Lev [Gec] (Getz, Leon), b 13 April 1896 in Lviv, d 16 December 1971 in Cracow. Painter and graphic artist. Gets studied with I. Levynsky and O. Novakivsky in Lviv and at the Cracow Academy of Art (1919–23). He was a member of the Association of Independent Ukrainian Artists, and exhibited with this group in Lviv, Prague, Berlin, and Rome. After the Second World War, Gets became a professor at the Academy of Art in Cracow (1950–8). His earlier works include *[Sich] Rifleman's Anthology 1915–18* (over 500 drawings and sketches), a cycle of drawings from his stay in the Polish concentration camp at Dąbie, many drawings of Sianik, and over 100 works depicting the life of the Lemkos. His Cracow period includes almost 500 drawings of the old architecture of Cracow. Now housed in the city's historical museum,

100 of these were published as an album titled *Dawne dziedzińce i podwórza Krakowa w rysunkach Leona Getza* (Old Courts and Courtyards of Cracow in the Drawings of Leon Getz, 1958). The influence of symbolism imparts to his realistic paintings and drawings a surreal quality. Gets is the subject of a monograph by P. Kovzhun (1939).

Giannini, Amadeo, b 19 September 1886 in Naples, d 19 December 1960 in Rome. Italian jurist, specialist in international law, diplomat, senator, professor of Rome University, expert on East European affairs. He was a founder of the Institute of Eastern Europe, president of the Central State Archive in Rome, director of the Department of Commercial Affairs at the Foreign Ministry (1937–42), president of the Italian-Ukrainian Friendship Society (from 1952), and a full member of the Shevchenko Scientific Society (from 1955). He wrote numerous books on diplomatic history and international law and many publicistic works on contemporary Eastern Europe.

Giliarov, Aleksei [Giljarov], b 20 December 1855 in Moscow, d 7 December 1938 in Kiev. Philosopher; from 1922 full member of the AN URSR. Giliarov graduated from Moscow University and was a professor at Kiev University from 1891. As a Platonist he held that philosophy was not a science but a striving to reconcile the truth of reason with the truth of the heart. Besides studies of the Greek sophists and of Platonism, he wrote *Znachenie filosofii* (The Significance of Philosophy, 1888) and *Filosofiia v ee sushchestve, znachenii i istorii* (Philosophy in Its Essence, Meaning, and History, 2 vols, 1916–19). In his unfinished work *Skhema istorii filosofii v osveshchenii istoricheskogo materializma* (A Schema of the History of Philosophy in the Light of Historical Materialism, 1926–7) he attempted to revise his philosophical outlook to accommodate Marxism. He was also a student of literature, chemistry, psychology, and physiology.

Girei (Girāy). A dynasty of Crimean khans from the 15th to the 18th century, founded ca 1434 by Haji-Girei (d 1466) who, with the disintegration of the *Golden Horde, proclaimed himself the ruler of an independent Crimean Khanate. In 1475, Mengli-Girei became a vassal of the Turkish sultan. The name Girei is linked with large, continual raids on Ukraine, involving pillaging and burning of villages and the capture of slaves. *Islam-Girei III formed a pact with Hetman B. Khmelnytsky against Poland. In 1783, the last of the Gireis, Shagin-Girei, was forced to abdicate and the Crimea was annexed to the Russian Empire (see *Crimea).

Girsa, Václav, b 28 November 1875 in Shepetivka, Zaslav county, Volhynia gubernia, d 1942? Czech political figure. After completing his medical studies in 1900, he worked as a physician in Kiev. In 1917–18 he was a leading figure in the Czech movement in Ukraine and assisted in the organization of the Czechoslovak Legion. From 1921 to 1928 he directed a department of the Czechoslovak foreign ministry, and he then worked in the diplomatic service. Girsa headed relief programs for Ukrainian immigrants in Czechoslovakia. With his help a number of Ukrainian scientific and cultural institutions were established, including the Union of Ukrainian Physicians.

Inokentii Gizel

Gizel, Innokentii [Gizel', Innokentij], b ca 1600 in East Prussia, d 28 November 1683 in Kiev. Orthodox church and cultural figure of German descent. After graduating from the Kievan College (later the *Kievan Mohyla Academy) in 1642, Gizel continued his studies at the Zamostia Academy and abroad. From 1646 to 1656, he was the hegumen of a number of Kievan monasteries, as well as a professor of philosophy and rector of the Kievan College (1645–56). As archimandrite of the Kievan Cave Monastery (1656–83), he was director of its printing house. In the 1650s he participated in negotiations with Russian church leaders on the status of the Ukrainian Orthodox church. He may have been responsible for the publication of the *Kievan Cave Patericon in 1661 and 1678, and the author of the **Sinopsis* (1674), the first handbook of Ukrainian history. Gizel wrote a textbook of general philosophy, *Opus totius philosophiae* (1647), for his courses and *Myr s Bohom choloviku* (Man's Peace with God, 1669, 1671), which summarized his views of contemporary ethical and religious standards. He also wrote several polemical works against Catholicism. One of the most erudite scholars of the Kievan College, Gizel was referred to by his contemporaries as the 'Aristotle' of Kiev. He is the subject of an extensive biography by M. Sumtsov in *Kievskaia starina*, 1884, no. 10.

Gizhytska, Zoia [Gižyc'ka, Zoja], 1895–1935. Botanist, mycologist. Gizhytska was the head of the mycology laboratory at the Institute of Botany of the VUAN. A number of her articles on mycology and phytopathology were published in *Visnyk Kyïvs'koho botanichnoho sadu*. Persecuted by the Soviet authorities, she committed suicide.

Glagolitic alphabet. An old Slavic script in which the most ancient Old Church Slavonic manuscripts were written. Its origin has been disputed for a long time but it was most likely invented by *St Cyril, who also included some Hebrew letters. Under Byzantine influence it was soon replaced by the *Cyrillic alphabet, which in the shape of most letters was patterned on the Greek alphabet. There is no information on the systematic use of Glagolitic in Kievan Rus', although individual Glagolitic letters and short Glagolitic insertions occasionally occur in 15 (according to G. Ilinsky) East Slavic manuscripts of the 11th to 15th centuries, two of which are from Ukraine.

Glass, art. Branch of decorative applied art and of the *glass industry, producing glassware, sculptures, stained glass, small mosaics, architectural details, and bijouterie. In the 10th–13th centuries polychrome and gilt smalts, decorated religious objects, chimes, glass ornaments, colored windowpanes, and figural drinking vessels were produced in Ukraine at such localities as Kiev and Kolodiazhyn, Volhynia. The earliest techniques of shaping glass were drawing and casting. At the turn of the 10th century glassblowing was mastered. Later, refining by double melting was used to produce clear, transparent glass. Surviving glassware from the 10th–13th centuries shows that there were two types of products: cheap glassware made of ordinary green glass or Waldglas, and expensive glassware made of valuable white or crystal glass. The glassware was decorated with monochrome or polychrome glass thread or ribbon which was applied to form spirals, wavy lines, or geometric designs. In later centuries this remained the basic ornament of Ukrainian glass products. In the 16th–19th centuries the main glassmaking areas were the Lviv (Belz, Liubachiv) and Chernihiv regions.

The manufacture of artistic glass reached its highest state of development in the 18th and beginning of the 19th century. New, well-equipped glassworks were built. The cylindrical technique of making plate glass was mastered, and new methods of working and decorating glass, such as enameling, cutting, engraving, and gilding, were adopted. A Ukrainian style, consisting essentially of a close link between the form of the object and its decoration, evolved. Figural products were a unique feature of Ukrainian art glass: bottles and cylindrical containers were shaped as animals or birds, or as grotesque figures from folktales and proverbs. Bowl-baskets made of thin applied glass and candelabra with filigree ornamentation were a specialty of Volhynia. The Lviv region (Zhovkva) specialized in glass chandeliers. Many kinds of decoration were used in the 18th–19th centuries: molded applied ornaments (geometric designs, small figures), enamel painting on thin-walled products (mostly floral motifs and sometimes thematic representations), oil painting, which was related to folk wall painting (mostly floral motifs), incision of floral patterns (sunflowers, daisies) by means of round or oval notches, engraving (portraits, coats-of-arms), and gilding.

In the second half of the 19th century the manufacture of art glass began to decline because of competition from factory-made goods. It was only in the 1930s that glass-

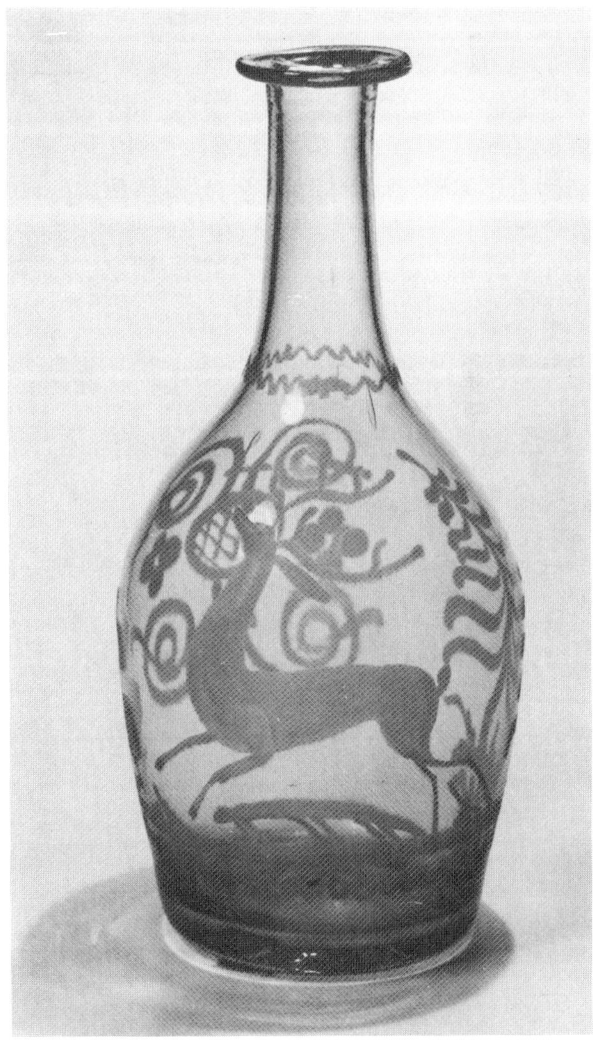

Glass art: (*above*) ram, 18th century, free-blown colorless glass (Kiev Museum of Ukrainian Decorative Folk Art); (*right*) decanter, early 19th century, engraved free-blown colorless glass (Ukrainian State Museum of Ethnography and Crafts, Lviv)

works in Soviet Ukraine began to produce art glass such as the ruby *Kremlin Stars* (1937) and the crystal fountain for the Soviet pavilion at the New York World's Fair (1939), which were made at the Kostiantynivka Avtosklo Plant. Art glass was increasingly used in architecture and in decorative applied art. The art of stained glass was revived. Most stained-glass windows were assembled at glassworks factories in Kiev and Kostiantynivka. The best-known works of the period were *The Council of Pereiaslav*, a window designed by G. Yun, V. Davidov, and S. Kyrychenko for Ukraine's pavilion at the USSR Exhibition of the Achievements of the National Economy, and *Friendship of Nations*, designed by A. Mysin and others. Since the 1950s, the manufacture of unique articles used in exhibits, prizes, and souvenirs has been emphasized. Cutting and deep-etching of layered-glass products (the so-called Gallé technique) are commonly used. Today most art glass and cut glass is manufactured at the Kiev Art Glass Plant and the Raiduha Production Association in Lviv, which since 1962 includes the Lviv No. 1 Glass Factory, the Stryi Glass Factory, and five smaller enterprises. Some specialized factories in Zhdanov, Dnipropetrovske, Dzerzhynske (Romanivka), Artemivka, and Shchyrets also produce glass products. The glass shop of the Lviv Ceramics and Sculpture Factory has been producing free-blown glass since the 1950s. Most of the glass artists at these plants are graduates of Lviv Institute of Applied and Decorative Arts. The more prominent ones are I. Apollonov, A. Balabin, A. Bokotei, O. Bohuslavsky, S. Holembovska, I. Zarytsky, O. Lasovsky, Z. Masliak, Ye. Meri, L. Mytiaieva, H. Palamar, and M. Tarnavsky. Among folk craftsmen who work in glass are B. Valko, P. Dumych, R. Zhuk, Ya. Matsiievsky, M. Pavlovsky, V. Pohrebny, and I. Chaban. Adapting traditional glassware designs, these artists create household and decorative glassware, mostly for mass production, as well as small glass sculptures.

The Kiev Museum of Ukrainian Folk Decorative Art, the Ukrainian State Museum of Ethnography and Crafts in Lviv, the Sumy Museum of Art, the historical museums of Kiev, Lviv, and Chernihiv, the regional museums of Lutske (collection of 15th–17th century art glass) and Kremianets, the Leningrad Museum of the Ethnography of the Peoples of the USSR, and the Moscow Historical Museum all maintain collections of Ukrainian artistic glass.

Glass art: figurines by Y. Matsiievsky (artist's collection)

BIBLIOGRAPHY

Rozhankivs'kyi, V. *Ukraïns'ke khudozhnie sklo* (Kiev 1959)

Suchasne ukraïns'ke khudozhnie sklo. Fotoal'bom (Kiev 1980)

Glass industry. Branch of industry that produces glass and various glass products such as construction glass (window glass, glass blocks, glass tubes), container glass (bottles, jars), laboratory glassware, light bulbs and vacuum tubes, household glassware (tableware, mirrors), electrical components (insulators, capacitors, resistors), medical glassware, optical glass, glass fibers, and art glass.

Raw materials for making glass are readily available in Ukraine. There are large deposits of quartz sand with a high silica content (at least 90 percent), which is the chief constituent of glass. The best-known deposits are located in Avdiivka (Donetske oblast), Novoselivka (Kharkiv oblast), Rokytne (Rivne oblast), Hlyboke (Chernihiv oblast), and Lviv. The annual output of quartz sand is about 2 million t, enough to meet domestic demand and to provide surplus for export. Other minerals needed for glass production such as soda, lime, gypsum, and potash are also found in Ukraine.

In ancient times glass products such as ornaments and then tableware were imported to Ukraine from Greece and the Near East, and later from the Roman Empire and Byzantium. In the 11th–13th centuries glass and glass products, mostly for decorative purposes, began to be produced domestically in Kiev (near the Church of the Tithes and the Kievan Cave Monastery), Chernihiv, Liubech, and Halych. After the Mongol invasion glassmaking declined. Its revival in the 14th–16th centuries saw a shift of its main centers from the larger cities to forest regions with readily available fuel and sand. In the mid-16th century glass was made in the districts of Belz, Liubachiv (near Potylych), and Horodok. Artisan workshops were replaced by small, factory-like glassworks. In the 17th century such enterprises appeared in the districts of Lviv and Mukachiv, the Kiev region, Volhynia, Left-Bank Ukraine, and Slobidska Ukraine. By the end of century there were 25 glassworks in Left-Bank Ukraine, established by entrepreneurs or by leaseholding craftsmen on the estates of magnates, nobles, monasteries, or (on the Left Bank) Cossack officers. Some of these enterprises were run by the same family – eg, the Los, Bilozersky, Bohynsky, Skabychevsky, and Chumak families – for many generations. With support from landowners, many of whom owned glassworks, and the Hetman administration, particularly under I. Mazepa, the industry expanded. Its output consisted mostly of window glass, glassware, particularly apothecary glassware, bottles, cut glass, and optical glass, some of which was exported to Russia, Belorussia, Poland, and the Baltic countries.

In the 18th century glass manufacturing grew quickly, particularly in the Chernihiv region. At various times a total of nearly 100 glassworks operated in Left-Bank

Ukraine. In the second half of the 18th century a number of glass factories known as *manufaktury* were set up by large landowners such as K. Rozumovsky, P. Rumiantsev, and P. Zavadovsky. Their assorted products, particularly cut glass and artistic glass, were in great demand at home and abroad. At the beginning of the 19th century there were about 40 glassworks in Ukraine, employing about 1,000 workers. Most were in Volhynia, where wood fuel was abundant. In the middle of the century glass production declined, following which began a period of concentration, when larger and more productive enterprises, organized on a capitalist basis, were established. Thus, in 1883 in Right-Bank Ukraine 30 glassworks employing 458 workers produced glass and glass products worth 180,000 rubles, while in 1900, 20 glassworks with 2,711 workers produced output worth 1,549,000 rubles. Most of the production consisted of household and apothecary glassware, tiles, and lamp components. Most enterprises, particularly the largest ones, were owned by merchants, including many Jews. On the eve of the First World War there were 17 glass factories in Right-Bank Ukraine with an annual output worth 2 million rubles. The largest of them were located in Rokytne, Ovruch county (500 workers, 700,000 rubles' worth of output), and Romanivka, Novohrad-Volynskyi county (400 workers, 200,000 rubles' worth of output), both in Volhynia gubernia, and in Myrcha, Kiev county (195 workers, 126,000 rubles' worth of output). Large glass factories using fossil fuel also appeared in the Donbas at the end of the 19th century. The largest were in Kostiantynivka and Lysychanske. By 1913 the Donbas accounted for two-thirds of Ukraine's glass output. Altogether there were about 40 glass factories in Ukraine: 10 in the Donbas and 15 in Volhynia. They produced 6,700,000 t of glass.

Glass output in Soviet Ukraine (in 1,000 sq m)

	1970	1980	1983
Window glass	51,315	39,912	49,041
Polished glass	1,685	4,578	4,914
Wired glass	2,867	3,012	2,923
Tempered, unpolished glass	1,183	1,789	1,850
Unpolished safety glass	102	63	–

During the First World War and the Revolution the glass industry declined. It began to recover during the 1920s, and by 1928–9 in Right-Bank Ukraine there were 14 glass plants with 5,398 workers producing output worth 9,100,000 rubles. The industry was reconstructed and modernized twice: during the industrialization drive in the 1930s and after the Second World War. New plants were built and new products were introduced. Production became more concentrated: the number of plants diminished from 70 in 1940 to 60 in 1971 to under 40 in 1981, while from 1940 to 1971 output increased by a factor of 4. The largest plants are in Kostiantynivka, Lysychanske, Lviv, Kherson, Kerch, Odessa, Bucha (Kiev oblast), and Kiev. Today Ukraine produces sheet glass, shaped glass, glass blocks, glazed glass, wired glass, patterned glass, heat-resistant glass, safety glass, tempered glass, mosaic tiles, marbled glass, aventurine glass, and fine glassware. Research on the scientific and technical aspects of glassmaking is done at the Kiev Branch of the Scientific Research Institute of Glass in Moscow and at the Scientific Research Institute of Glass at the Kostiantynivka Avtosklo Plant. In 1983 Ukraine accounted for 19.9 percent of the USSR glass output.

BIBLIOGRAPHY

Kuprits, A. *O stekol'noi promyshlennosti Volynskoi gubernii* (Kiev 1911)

Modzalevs'kyi, V. *Huty na Chernihivshchyni* (Kiev 1926)

Hahenmeister, V. *Hutne sklo Podillia* (Kamianets-Podilskyi 1931)

Ponomar'ov, O. *Rozvytok kapitalistychnykh vidnosyn u promyslovosti Ukraïny XVIII st.* (Lviv 1971)

Petriakova, F. *Ukraïns'ke hutne sklo* (Kiev 1975)

V. Kubijovyč, O. Ohloblyn

Glauberman, Abba, b 1917 in Warsaw, d ? Solid state physicist. A graduate of Odessa University (1939), he taught physics at Lviv University. In 1966 he was appointed director of the Scientific Research Institute of Physics at Odessa University. Among his publications is an advanced textbook, *Kvantova mekhanika* (Quantum Mechanics, 1962), one of the few Soviet textbooks of its kind published in Ukrainian.

Glavche, Egor [Glavče, Jegor], b 21 January 1871 in Kishinev, Bessarabia, d 17 August 1919 in Odessa. Dermatologist and venereologist. A graduate of Moscow University (1895), from 1900 he worked as a physician in Odessa and played a leading role in the fight against venereal disease. He did research on prophylactic measures, gave public lectures on venereal disease and prostitution, and recruited and trained physicians in dermatovenereology. In 1917 he established the first polyclinic for dermatovenereological and urogenital diseases in the Russian Empire, at which he treated patients free of charge. In 1922 the clinic was converted into the Odessa Scientific Research Institute of Dermatology and Venereology. Glavche published a number of books on syphilis and its treatment, including his doctoral thesis *Limfaticheskie zhelezy i sifilis* (The Lymph Glands and Syphilis, 1916).

Glavlit (Glavnoe upravlenie po delam literatury i izdatelstv [Chief Administration for Literary and Publishing Affairs]; Ukrainian: Holovlit). Most powerful censorship agency in the USSR. It was established under the People's Commissariat of Education in June 1922 by the RSFSR Council of People's Commissars to maintain ideological orthodoxy and to prevent breaches of state security in the media. Restricted in its powers at first, by the 1930s it attained almost total control over publishing activity: it approves new publishing houses and periodicals, appointments to all positions in publishing, and all published materials. It also controls radio and television broadcasting, film and theater productions, musical performances and recordings, public lectures, art exhibits, advertising and labeling, and the import and export of published material. Glavlit compiles lists of proscribed works, subjects, and information. Besides military and economic secrets, sensitive matters have included natural disasters and accidents in the Soviet Union, salaries of top officials, jamming of foreign radio broadcasts, and the operations of Glavlit itself. A few years after Stalin's death the agency's official name was changed to Glavnoe upravlenie po okhrane gosudarstvennykh tain v pechati (Chief Administration for the Preservation of State Secrets in the Press) and in 1966 it was brought directly under the USSR Council of Ministers. The old acronym is still used, however.

I. Koshelivets

Gleb. See Hlib.

Glière, Reinhold, b 11 January 1875 in Kiev, d 23 June 1956 in Moscow. Conductor, composer, and teacher of Belgian Jewish descent. A graduate of the Kiev School of Music and the Moscow Conservatory, he was a professor (1913–20) and director (from 1914) of the Kiev Conservatory. Among Glière's pupils were the composers L. Revutsky, B. Liatoshynsky, and P. Kozytsky. He edited and orchestrated M. Lysenko's operettas *Natalka Poltavka* (Natalka from Poltava) and *Chornomortsi* (Black Sea Cossacks), K. Stetsenko's *Haidamaky* (Haidamakas) and the cantata *Shevchenkovi* (To Shevchenko), and rewrote the orchestration for S. Hulak-Artemovsky's *Zaporozhets za Dunaiem* (Zaporozhian Cossack beyond the Danube). He composed over 500 works in a variety of genres, including the symphony *Illia Muromets* (1909–11) dedicated to the hero of the Kiev *bylyna* cycle, the symphonic tableau *Zaporozhtsi* (Zaporozhian Cossacks, 1921) inspired by I. Repin's painting, the symphonic poem *Zapovit* (Testament, 1939–41) dedicated to T. Shevchenko, and the ballet *Taras Bulba* (1951–2).

Globular Amphora culture. Archeological culture of the Eneolithic period that was widespread in territories now comprising East Germany, Czechoslovakia, Poland, Ukraine (only the Volhynia and Podilia regions), and Moldavia. Today three variants of the culture are distinguished: the Western (covering Germany, Czechoslovakia, and Western Poland), Central (Poland), and Eastern (Ukraine and Moldavia). In Ukraine the Volhynian version is distinct from the Podilian. Since the end of the 19th century about 70 burial sites, but no settlements, have been discovered in Ukraine. The dead were buried in a flexed position in rectangular sarcophaguses built of stone slabs. Group burials of what appear to be whole families were common. Cremation was rare. Various pieces of earthenware such as amphoras, tools such as stone axes and wedges, and ornaments were buried with the dead. The amphoras had a globular body, cylindrical neck, two to four handles, and a flat or concave bottom. The tribes of the Globular Amphora culture lived in large patriarchal families and practiced animal husbandry and perhaps plant cultivation.

Glovinsky, Yevhen [Glovins'kyj, Jevhen], b 1 November 1894 in Rzhyshchiv, Kiev gubernia, d 7 July 1964 in Munich. Economist and civic figure. An artillery officer in the UNR army, he emigrated in 1922 to Czechoslovakia. In 1927 he received a degree in economic engineering from the Ukrainian Husbandry Academy in Poděbrady. From 1930 to 1939 he was a secretary and research associate of the Ukrainian Scientific Institute (UNI) in Warsaw. In 1944 he fled west from the Soviet advance to Bohemia and then to Austria, where he lived in a displaced persons camp near Salzburg. In 1949 he settled in Munich, where he became a professor of the Ukrainian Technical and Husbandry Institute and the Ukrainian

Yevhen Glovinsky

Free University (1952) and a full member of the Shevchenko Scientific Society (1953) and member of the editorial board of its *Entsyklopedia ukraïnoznavstva* (Encyclopedia of Ukraine). In the interwar years he was active in émigré student and engineering organizations. After the war he was the representative of the Ukrainian National State Union party to the Ukrainian National Council, where he served as deputy chairman and member of the presidium. Glovinsky is the author of articles on Ukraine's economy in the collections of the UNI and in postwar émigré and Western Sovietological journals, and of the study *Finansy USSR* (Finances of the Ukrainian SSR, 1939).

Gmina (Polish term derived from the German *Gemeinde*). Smallest administrative territorial unit borrowed by the Poles from the Germans during the period of German colonization in the 13th and 14th centuries, and corresponding to the Ukrainian **hromada* or the Russian *volost*. Under the Polish Commonwealth a *gmina* consisted usually of a village belonging to a single landlord and run by an elected council and reeve (Polish *wójt*, Ukrainian *viit*). In Galicia under Austrian rule it was administered by an elected council and an executive selected by the council. A *viit* headed the executive and held office for three (from 1884 or six) years. The council and its executive were responsible for road maintenance, care of the poor, and issuing ordinances. They also participated in tax collecting and census taking. The *gmina* court and its elected assessors settled disputes and maintained order. In interwar Poland a *gmina* could consist of a village, small town, or several villages (called *gmina zbiorowa*).

Gmünd. Town (1985 pop 6,400) in Lower Austria on the Czechoslovak border. During the First World War a camp housing Ukrainian refugees from the Russian occupation of Galicia and Ukrainians forcibly deported by the Austrian authorities for their Russophile tendencies was located there. It had its own Ukrainian schools (including a gymnasium), and cultural and social institutions. Harsh living conditions led to a high mortality rate. From 1914 to 1917 the camp held some 14,000 Ukrainians.

Gnedich, Nikolai [Gnedič, Nikolaj] (Hnidych, Mykola), b 13 February 1784 in Poltava, d 15 February 1833 in St Petersburg. Russian writer and translator of Ukrainian descent. He was educated at the Poltava Theological Seminary, Kharkiv College, and Moscow University. He translated a collection of modern Greek folk songs (1825), J. Schiller's *Die Verschwörung des Fiesko zu Genua*, and

Voltaire's *Tancrède*, but is best known for his translation in hexameters of Homer's *Iliad* (1829). Gnedich dedicated a number of poems, such as 'Lastivka' (The Swallow), to Ukraine, and wrote some poetry in Ukrainian. His poetry, plays, and prose works contain elements of classicism and sentimentalism.

Gneiss. A metamorphic foliated rock formed from sedimentary (paragneiss) or magmatic (orthogneiss) rock at considerable depths in the earth's crust under high temperatures and pressure. Containing quartz, feldspar, and mica, along with *granite it is a basic rock of the Ukrainian Crystalline Shield. It is found also in the Maramureş-Bukovynian Upland. Gneiss is used mostly as aggregate, paving stone, and facing material.

Goat farming. Branch of animal husbandry that raises goats for their milk, meat, hide, and wool. It has been practiced in Ukraine since the Neolithic period. The distribution of goat farming is similar to that of *sheep farming, but its economic importance is much less. In 1916 there were 554,000 goats in Ukraine (as defined by present boundaries), in contrast to 6,850,000 sheep. In 1928 there were only 53,000 goats in Soviet Ukraine. The collectivization of the 1930s led to a sharp increase in the population of goats, which are easy to raise and often replaced cows. By 1935 there were 215,000 goats in Soviet Ukraine, 209,000 of them privately owned. Goat farming was concentrated in industrialized areas such as the Kharkiv region and the Donbas. In 1933 in Western Ukraine there were 37,000 goats in Galicia and Volhynia, 20,000 in Transcarpathia, and 7,000 in Bukovyna (1932). In Soviet Ukraine there were 625,000 goats in 1941, 1,209,000 in 1956, 696,000 in 1966, 252,000 in 1976, and 293,000 in 1984. Today goats are raised only on private plots, mostly in Transcarpathia, Odessa, Ivano-Frankivske, and Poltava oblasts. Dairy breeds predominate.

Goby (Gobiidae; Ukrainian: *bychok*). Common name for fish of various species in the family Gobiidae, order Perciformes. In Ukraine, Gobiidae are found in the Black and Azov seas and their estuaries, in rivers draining into the Black Sea, and in rivers of the Crimea. Some species are found only in the sea basins. As all species are edible, commercial goby fishing and canning are important, well-developed industries along the Black and Azov seacoasts. There are some 53 species in 19 genera in the family, of which 9 genera are found in Ukraine. The main commercial species in the Black and Azov seas is *Neogobius melanostomus* (round goby; Ukrainian: *bychok-kruhlok*).

GOELRO or **State Commission for the Electrification of Russia.** A Soviet Russian commission established in 1920 to plan the rapid expansion of *electric power production. The commission's plan provided for the construction, in the course of 10 to 15 years, of 20 thermal and 10 hydroelectric power stations with a total capacity of 1.75 million kW in various regions of Russia and Ukraine as the basis of the subsequent industrialization process.

The building of power stations in Ukraine according to the plan was co-ordinated in Ukraine by the Commission for the Electrification of Ukraine (est 1921), as well as by various other committees and building trusts. Nine power stations were to be built in Ukraine (thermal ones, such as the Shterivka, Lysychanske, and Izium stations, and hydroelectric ones, such as the Dnieper and Boh stations). The GOERLO plan also provided for the construction of coal-and-gas power stations. Ukrainian officials hoped that the output of Dnieper hydroelectric stations in particular would be used to deliver cheap electricity to the villages and further the industrialization of the largely agricultural Right-Bank Ukraine. However, the GOELRO plan did not address these issues, and instead focused on the reconstruction of the Donbas's metallurgical and chemical industry, the electrification of the Moscow–Kharkiv–Yuzivka (today Donetske) railway, and the creation of an unobstructed water route on the Dnieper River betweeen Kiev and Kherson. In 1932, of 40 regional electric power stations completed, five were in Ukraine, including the *Dnieper Hydroelectric Station, the largest electric power station in Europe. The aggregate capacity of the stations in Ukraine was 480,000 kW.

I. Myhul

Goetz, Leopold Karl, b 7 October 1868 in Karlsruhe, d 2 April 1931 in Bonn. German church and law historian; professor at Bonn University from 1902. Among his works are several dealing with Kievan Rus': *Das Kiever Höhlenkloster als Kulturzentrum des vormongolischen Russlands* (1904), *Kirchenrechtliche und kulturgeschichtliche Denkmäler Altrusslands nebst Geschichte des russischen Kirchenrechts* (1905), *Staat und Kirche in Altrussland: Kiever Periode, 988–1249* (1908). He also translated and edited the German version of **Ruskaia Pravda: Das russische Recht* (4 vols, 1910–13).

Nikolai Gogol; portrait by A. Ivanov (1841)

Gogol, Nikolai [Gogol', Nikolaj] (Ukrainian: Hohol, Mykola), b 1 April 1809 in Velyki Sorochyntsi, Myrhorod county, Poltava gubernia, d 4 March 1852 in Moscow. The most famous Russian writer of Ukrainian origin. Having graduated from the Nizhen gymnasium, he left for St Petersburg in 1828 armed with a manuscript and hope for a successful literary career. His aspirations were abruptly arrested by extremely negative criticism of his sentimentally Romantic narrative poem *Hans Kuechelgarten*, which he published at his own expense in 1829 and copies of which he subsequently bought out and destroyed. He tried to survive economically by working as a bureaucrat, a teacher at a boarding school for daughters of the nobility, and very briefly as a lecturer of history at St Petersburg University. In 1836 he left Russia and, except for two brief eight-month intervals (1838–9, 1841–

2), he lived abroad, mostly in Rome, until 1849, when he returned via Palestine to Russia.

While working as a minor civil servant, Gogol spent his free time composing short stories based on his observations and memories of life in Ukraine. The first two volumes of these stories, *Vechera na khutore bliz Dikan'ki* (Evenings on a Farm near Dykanka, 1831–2), brought him immediate fame. Hiding behind the authorial mask of Rudy Panko the beekeeper, Gogol managed to portray a world where fantasy and reality intermingle in the prism of the worldly-wise but unsophisticated narrator, and thus Ukraine becomes at once fanciful, humorous, nostalgic, and somewhat poignant in its quaintness.

In his second two-volume collection of Ukrainian stories, *Mirgorod* (Myrhorod, 1835), containing the first version of his famous historical novelette *Taras Bul'ba*, Gogol's nostalgic tone gives way to a more satiric view of his native land. In the same year he also published *Arabeski* (Arabesques, 1835), in which his stories dealing with the world of the St Petersburg civil servant first appeared. Simultaneously he turned to writing drama and published his great *Revizor* (The Inspector-General, 1835), which needed the approval of the emperor to be staged in 1836. This was followed by his second completed play, *Zhenit'ba* (The Marriage, 1835), and the famous satirical story *Nos* (The Nose, 1835). His other plays remained unfinished.

The staging of *The Inspector-General* did not produce the result Gogol intended. Shattered by the fact that his idea of the moral influence of true art (artistically formulated in the story 'Portret' [The Portrait] in *Arabeski*) did not have the desired effect, he left Russia. The years abroad were less productive. Gogol devoted himself to his epic work, *Mertvye dushi* (Dead Souls, 1842), but managed to finish successfully only the first of three intended parts. He also wrote his famous story *Shinel'* (The Overcoat, 1841), and revised *Taras Bul'ba* and 'Portret.' In 1845 he wrote his didactic essays, *Vybrannye mesta iz perepiski s druziami* (Selected Passages from Correspondence with Friends, 1847). Disillusioned by the attacks that followed this publication, Gogol blamed himself for being incapable of producing morally ennobling art. His attempt at preparing himself morally for his task of 'serving God and humanity' sent him first on a pilgrimage to Jerusalem; finally, under the influence of a religious fanatic, Rev M. Konstantinovsky, who demanded that he enter a monastery and destroy his 'evil' art, Gogol burned the second part of *Dead Souls*, refused all food, and stayed in bed until his death.

His works have been published by P. Kulish (6 vols, 1857), N. Tikhonravov, and V. Shenrok (7 vols, 1889–96). The fullest edition is that published by the USSR Academy of Sciences (14 vols, 1940–52). His letters were published by Kulish, Shenrok (in 4 vols, 1901), and V. Gippius. Gogol's collection of about 1,000 Ukrainian folk songs was used by M. Maksymovych and published by G. Georgievsky in 1908. His collection of materials for a Ukrainian dictionary is included in the collected works prepared by Gippius. There are numerous Ukrainian translations of Gogol's individual works and two editions of selected works, of which the most recent appeared in 1952 (3 vols).

Gogol's works display different variations of the Romantic style and a masterly use of metaphor, hyperbole, and ironic grotesque. His language is exceptionally rhythmic and euphonic. He was the first writer of the so-called Ukrainian school in Russian literature to employ a host of lexical and syntactic Ukrainianisms, primarily to play with various stylistic levels from the vulgar to the pathetic. Some of his Ukrainian stories are the earliest examples of the Russian naturalist school, which combined Romantic ideology with a negative, 'low' depiction of everyday life. Gogol's writings were frequently imitated by such Ukrainian writers as H. Kvitka-Osnovianenko, P. Kulish, and O. Storozhenko, and by such writers of the Ukrainian school in Russian literature as Ye. Hrebinka; Gogol's influence was felt in the early writings of I. Turgenev, F. Dostoevsky, V. Sollogub, and by the Russian Symbolists F. Sologub, A. Remizov, and A. Bely.

There are hundreds of translations of Gogol's works, and he is recognized as one of the greatest writers of the 19th century. His ideological writings provoked a prolonged controversy. His *Vybrannye mesta* was criticized severely by the Russian Westernizers (eg, V. Belinsky), who valued in the works of his naturalist period mainly the satire on Russian life. A popular schematic biography of Gogol spread the idea that he experienced a religious crisis abroad. It was only in the 20th century that serious studies of the formal qualities of Gogol were written (by I. Mandelshtam), and a more analytic approach to his world outlook was taken. D. Merezhkovsky studied Gogol as a religious thinker. V. Zenkovsky detected in Gogol all the basic ideas for which Dostoevsky later gained fame, as well as the same Romantic psychology. V. Gippius, following Zenkovsky to some extent, described Gogol's development as a conflict between his aesthetic and religious outlook. In the 1920s Russian Formalists (Yu. Tynianov, B. Eikhenbaum, V. Vinogradov) often used Gogol's works as the material for formulating their theories. Some recent (eg, S. Karlinsky's) studies have concentrated on the sexual conflicts inherent in Gogol's personality and reflected in his works. Other scholars have emphasized the consistency of his outlook throughout his life.

Gogol's relation to Ukraine is a controversial issue. His indifference to the Ukrainian question was sharply condemned by the critics S. Yefremov and, even more severely, Ye. Malaniuk in the 1920s. P. Fylypovych and V. Doroshenko stressed the importance of Ukrainian elements in Gogol's writings and the contribution his Rusian works made to the development of a Ukrainian national identity. The whole question of Gogol's ambivalent attitude toward Ukraine received a very thorough analysis in G. Luckyj's *Between Gogol' and Ševčenko* (1971).

BIBLIOGRAPHY

Shenrok, V. *Materialy dlia biografii Gogolia*, 4 vols (Moscow 1892–98)
Mandel'shtam, I. *O kharaktere gogolevskogo stilia* (Helsinki 1902)
Ovsianiko-Kulikovskii, D. 'N.V. Gogol',' in *Sobranie sochinenii*, 1 (St Petersburg 1910)
Slonimskii, A. *Tekhnika komicheskogo u Gogolia* (Petrograd 1923)
Gippius, V. *Gogol'* (Leningrad 1924)
– *Gogol' i natural'naia shkola* (Leningrad 1925)
Vinogradov, V. *Etiudy o stile Gogolia* (Leningrad 1926)
Belyi, A. *Masterstvo Gogolia* (Moscow-Leningrad 1934)
Literaturnoe nasledstvo, 58 (Moscow 1952)
Remizov, A. *Ogon' veshchii* (Paris 1954)
Fylypovych, P. *Hohol' ta Ukraïna* (Winnipeg 1954)

Ravliuk, M. (ed). *Hohol' i ukraïns'ka literatura* XIX *st.* (Kiev 1954)
Krutikova, N. *Hohol' ta ukraïns'ka literatura (30–80 rr.* XIX *storichchia)* (Kiev 1957)
Nabokov, V. *Nikolai Gogol* (New York 1959)
Luckyj, G. *Between Gogol' and Ševčenko: Polarity in the Literary Ukraine, 1798–1847* (Munich 1971)
Maguire, R. (ed). *Gogol in the Twentieth Century: Eleven Essays* (Princeton 1974)
Karlinsky, S. *The Sexual Labyrinth of Nikolai Gogol* (Cambridge, Mass and London 1976)
Fanger, D. *The Creation of Nikolai Gogol* (Cambridge, Mass and London 1979)
Peace, R. *The Enigma of Gogol: An Examination of the Writings of N.V. Gogol and Their Place in the Russian Literary Tradition* (Cambridge 1981)
Ukraïns'ki narodni pisni v zapysakh Mykoly Hoholia (Kiev 1985)
D. Chyzhevsky, D.H. Struk

Bishop Pavlo Goidych

Solomon Goldelman

Goidych, Pavlo Petro [Gojdyč], b 17 July 1888 in Ruski Pekliany in the Prešov region, d 17 July 1960 in Leopoldov, Slovakia. Greek Catholic bishop, church and cultural figure. He was ordained in 1911 after studying theology in Prešov and Budapest. He worked in the Prešov eparchy administration from 1914 until 1922, when he entered the Basilian Chernecha Hora Monastery near Mukachiv. In 1927 he was appointed bishop-administrator and in 1940 ordinary bishop of *Prešov eparchy. The eparchy flourished under Goidych's care: he founded monasteries, a gymnasium, a bursa, and the Blahovisnyk publishing house, promoted charities, and resisted the Slovakization of the Ukrainian minority. His arrest in June 1950 and mock trial in January 1951 for 'espionage and treason' in Bratislava marked the first step in the abolition of the Greek Catholic church in Czechoslovakia. He died in Leopoldov prison. After the restoration of the Greek Catholic church in 1968, his remains were transferred to the Prešov Cathedral.

BIBLIOGRAPHY

J.E. Pavel Gojdic, ČSSV*, jepiskop prjaševsky (1927–1947)* (Prešov 1947)
Pekar, A. *Bishop P. Gojdich,* OSBM *– Confessor of Our Times* (Pittsburgh 1980)
A. Pekar

Goldelman, Solomon, b 5 December 1885 in Soroka, Bessarabia, d 3 January 1974 in Jerusalem. Jewish and Ukrainian scholar and political figure; an economist by profession. He studied at the Kiev Commercial Institute (1907–13) and then worked there (1913–15) and for the Union of Zemstvos (1915–17). From June 1917 to April 1918 he represented the socialist Zionist party Po'alei Zion in the Central Rada and the Little Rada. Under the Hetman government he lived in Odessa, where he edited *Unser Leben*, a Po'alei Zion daily. In December 1918 he was appointed acting minister of labor and acting secretary for national minorities in the UNR Directory's government. Until February 1919 he also served as deputy to S. Ostapenko, the minister of trade and industry; from August to April 1920 he was deputy minister of labor in I. Mazepa's cabinet.

In mid-1920 Goldelman immigrated to Vienna. In 1922 he helped organize the *Ukrainian Husbandry Academy in Poděbrady; he taught there and at the Ukrainian Technical and Husbandry Institute until 1939, when he immigrated to Palestine. He maintained close ties with Ukrainian émigré institutions and promoted Ukrainian-Jewish co-operation to the end of his life. Goldelman wrote in Ukrainian an exhaustive study on the theory of stock companies (1925) and textbooks on economics and industrial policy (1923), international economic policy (1924), and the economics of industry (1934). He also wrote many articles, in Ukrainian, Yiddish, Hebrew, Russian, and German, on economics and politics, as well as the books *Lysty zhydivs'koho sotsiial-demokrata pro Ukraïnu ...* (Letters of a Jewish Social Democrat about Ukraine ..., 1921, repr 1964), *Löst der Kommunismus die Jüdenfrage? ...* (1937), *Zhydivs'ka natsional'na avtonomiia na Ukraïni, 1917–1920* (Jewish National Autonomy in Ukraine, 1917–1920, 1963, 2nd edn 1967, English trans 1968), and *Jüden-Bauern in der Ukraine ...* (1973).

BIBLIOGRAPHY

Bykovs'kyi, L. *Solomon Izrailevych Goldelman, 1885–1974: Bio-bibliohrafichni materiialy* (Denver-Jerusalem 1976)
Bykovsky, L. *Solomon I. Goldelman: A Portrait of a Politician and Educator (1885–1974)* (New York-Toronto-Munich 1980)
A. Zhukovsky

Golden Charter. A fictitious proclamation, which according to popular legend was issued by Catherine II, calling upon the Orthodox population of Right-Bank Ukraine to take up arms against the Poles and Jews and to help the Russian forces to expel the Polish authorities. It was spread orally and in handwritten copies, particularly during the *Koliivshchyna rebellion of 1768. It was propagated by M. Znachko-Yavorsky, the hegumen of the Motronynskyi Monastery near Chyhyryn, and was used by M. Zalizniak and other rebel leaders.

Golden Gate (Zoloti vorota). One of the most important architectural and historical monuments remaining from the Kievan Rus' period. Located in the southwestern part of ancient Kiev, the Golden Gate (GG) was begun in 1037 during the reign of Yaroslav the Wise. It was constructed at about the same time as St Sophia Cathedral and the upper city fortifications, and functioned as the main triumphal entrance and as a defendable portal to the fortified section of the city. The GG was built of brick and stone and consisted of a tower with a vaulted passageway (12 m high and up to 7.5 m wide), topped by a platform for guards and the small Church of the Annunciation. The passageway probably had a wooden or gilded gate, and there may have been turrets on the

Golden Gate: remnants

Golden Gate: restored

tower. The origin of the gate's name is unknown. It may have been named for the roof of the church, which was possibly covered with gold, for the copper fittings or gilt of the gate in the passageway, or for the Golden Gate of Constantinople. It served as the model for a gate built in Vladimir in the 1160s by Prince Andrei Bogoliubskii.

In 1240 the GG was partially destroyed by the Mongols; however, it remained in use as a portal until the middle of the 16th century. Such 15th- and 16th-century travelers as Paul of Aleppo and E. Lasotta von Steblau mentioned it in their writings, and a drawing (1651) by the Dutch artist A. Van Westerfeld shows the remains of the church. In 1648, after their victory over the Poles, Hetman B. *Khmelnytsky and his army made their triumphal entrance into Kiev through the GG. In 1750 the gate's remains were covered with earth. The ruins were excavated in 1832 by the archeologist K. *Lokhvytsky, and the structure was reinforced with a metal framework. Of the original GG only the brick and stone walls and portions of the arch remain. On the outside of the walls can be seen impressions left by the oak-beam framework of the walls that encircled the old city. Based on archeological excavations, scholars have created various models of the original GG, which was last restored in the early 1980s. A book about the GG, by S. Vysotsky, was published in Kiev in 1982.

Golden Horde. A Mongol-Tatar state founded about 1242 on the Volga River and lasting until the 15th century. Its first capital Sarai, founded by *Batu Khan, was near Astrakhan. The state was founded after the *Mongols had overrun much of Rus' and extended even into Poland and Hungary. Neighboring Rus' principalities became vassals of the Golden Horde. Prince *Danylo Romanovych strove in vain to form a coalition of European nations to combat the Golden Horde. After reaching its zenith in the mid-14th century, when it covered much of central Asia, the Golden Horde began to decline, losing control over its peripheries. In the 15th century it disintegrated into several independent khanates, including the *Crimean Khanate. (See also *Tatars.)

Golden-Domed St Michael's Monastery. See St Michael's Golden-Domed Monastery.

Oleksander Goldman

Goldman, Oleksander, b 3 February 1884 in Warsaw, d 30 December 1971 in Kiev. Solid-state physicist; from 1929 full member of the AN URSR. A graduate of Leipzig (1908) and Kiev (1909) universities, he worked for several years in Leningrad and then in 1918 joined the faculty of the Kiev Polytechnical Institute. In 1923 he organized and became director of the Chair of Physics in Kiev, one of the first physics research centers in Ukraine. When the chair was reorganized into the Kiev Scientific Research Institute of Physics in 1929 (now the AN URSR Institute of Physics), he was appointed director. In 1927 he founded the journal *Fizychni zapysky*, which played an important role in the advancement of physics in Ukraine and the develpment of Ukrainian terminology in the field. Goldman was one of the first researchers in Ukraine to study the properties of semiconductors, in particular rectification and metal-semiconductor contacts. He also carried out extensive research in electroluminescence.

Goldsmithery. See Jewelry.

Golitsyn, Vasilii [Golicyn, Vasilij], 1643–1714. Russian prince and diplomat, adviser and confidant of the Russian regent *Sofiia Alekseevna (1682–9) and initiator of the *Eternal Peace of 1686 with Poland. He led Russian campaigns against the Crimean Tatars in 1687 and 1689. In the unsuccessful campaign of 1687, 50,000 Cossacks took part, many of whom lost their lives after the Tatars set fire to the steppe. The blame was placed on Hetman I. *Samoilovych, and Golitsyn with the support of a part of the Cossack *starshyna* had him deposed and exiled. Golitsyn supported the candidacy of I. *Mazepa as the new hetman. The campaign of 1689, led jointly by Golitsyn and Mazepa, was also not successful, and Golitsyn was removed from office when Peter I became tsar.

Gololobov, Yurii, b 2 September 1930 in Moscow. Organic chemist; since 1976 corresponding member of the AN URSR. A graduate of the Moscow Chemical-Technical Institute (1953), he worked in different chemical institutes of the USSR Academy of Sciences in Moscow. In 1970 he was appointed chairman of a department of the AN URSR Institute of Organic Chemistry. His research deals with the synthesis of organophosphorus compounds and their chemical and biological properties, with the practical goal of finding ways to produce new pesticides, complexing agents, and medicines.

Golovin, Pavel, b 3 July 1885 in Izhevskoe, Riazan gubernia, d 22 January 1964 in Kiev. Chemist; from 1939 corresponding member of the AN URSR. A graduate of the Moscow Higher Technical School, he worked as an engineer and lecturer in Moscow. In 1932 he moved to Kiev, where he worked for six years at the Central Sugar Institute and then directed the Laboratory of Carbohydrate Chemistry and Technology at the AN URSR Institute of Organic Chemistry. At the same time he lectured at the Kiev Technological Institute of the Food Industry. He published over 90 papers, mostly on the chemistry of sugars and on food-processing technology.

Golubev, Stepan, b 1849, d 8 November 1920 in Kiev. Church historian. He taught at Kiev University and the Kiev Theological Academy. Among his many works are *Kievskii mitropolit Petr Mogila i ego spodvizhniki* (The Kiev Metropolitan Petro Mohyla and His Champions, 2 vols, 1883, 1898), *Istoriia Kievskoi Dukhovnoi Akademii: Period do-Mogilianskii* (The History of the Kiev Theological Academy: The Pre-Mohyla Period, 1886), and *Kievskaia Akademiia v kontse XVII i nachale XVIII st.* (The Kiev Academy at the End of the 17th and the Beginning of the 18th Century, 1901). Many of his articles on Ukrainian cultural and church history of the 16th to 18th centuries appeared in *Kievskaia starina, Arkhiv Iugo-Zapadnoi Rossii, Trudy Kievskoi Dukhovnoi Akademii,* and *Chteniia Istoricheskogo obshchestva Nestora Letopistsa.* He compiled and edited *Materialy dlia istorii zapadno-russkoi pravoslavnoi Tserkvi (XVI i XVII st.)* (Materials on the History of the West Russian Orthodox Church [The 16th and 17th Centuries], 1879, 1891), a volume with the same title for the 18th century (1895), and *Pamiatniki literaturnoi polemiki pravoslavnykh iuzhnorusstsev s latino-uniatami* (Monuments of the Literary Polemics of the Orthodox South Russians with the Latin-Rite Uniates, 3 vols, 1887, 1893, 1914).

A. Zhukovsky

Golubinsky, Evgenii [Golubinskii, Evgenij], b 12 March 1834, d 20 January 1912. Russian church historian. From 1861 he taught at the Moscow Theological Academy, becoming a professor in 1881, and was a member of the Historical Society of Nestor the Chronicler. In 1903 he was elected to the Russian Academy of Sciences. His major works are *Istoriia russkoi tserkvi* (The History of the Russian Church, 2 vols, 4 parts, 1880–1911, repr 1969), which contains valuable information about the Ukrainian church to the middle of the 15th century, and *Istoriia kanonizatsii sviatykh v Russkoi Tserkvi* (A History of Canonization in the Russian Church, 1902, repr 1969). He is also the author of many articles in Moscow theological journals. His harsh criticism of generally accepted views and the originality of his works influenced the historiography of the Russian church.

Golubovsky, Petr [Golubovskii, Pjotr], b 28 June 1857 in Minusinsk, Enisei gubernia, d 31 March 1907 in Kiev. Russian historian; student of V. Antonovych. He chaired the Department of Russian History at Kiev University. He wrote a number of monographs on medieval Ukraine and Belorussia; eg, *Istoriia Severskoi zemli do poloviny XIV stoletiia* (History of the Novhorod-Siverskyi Land to the Mid-14th Century, 1882), *Pechenegi, torki, i polovtsy do nashestviia tatar: Istoriia iuzhno-russkikh stepei IX–XIII vv* (The Pechenegs, Torks, and Cumans before the Tatar Invasion: A History of the Southern Rus' Steppes in the 9th–13th Centuries, 1884), and *Istoriia Smolenskoi zemli do nachala XV v.* (History of the Smolensk Land to the Beginning of the 15th Century, 1895). He also published many articles in *Kievskaia starina.*

Gołuchowski, Agenor, b 8 February 1812 in Skala, Borshchiv circle, Galicia, d 3 August 1875 in Skala. Polish count and Austrian statesman. He was the vicegerent of Galicia in 1849–59, 1866–7, and 1871–5, the Austrian minister of internal affairs in 1859, and minister of state in 1860. He resisted the efforts of Galicia's Ukrainians to gain equal national and social rights with the Poles. He pressed for the abolition of the Chair of Ukrainian Language at Lviv University, the introduction of a Latin script for the Ukrainians, and the adoption of the Gregorian calendar by the Ukrainian church. During his term in office he promoted home rule for Galicia's Poles, and the Galician civil service and Lviv University were Polonized, ending the era of Germanization.

Roman Gonsett

Gonsett, Roman [Gons'kyj], b 1891 in Zelena, Brody county, Galicia, d 25 June 1951 in North Hollywood, California. Inventor. After immigrating to Canada in 1907, Gonsett began experimenting with electricity in Edmonton. He moved to Chicago in 1916 and settled in Los Angeles during the 1920s. With his son, Faust, he worked on the development of the 'walkie-talkie' and patented almost 100 inventions, many in the field of two-way and mobile radio equipment. Contracts received from the US Department of National Defense and Security during the Second World War led to the establishment of the Gonsett Company. Gonsett bequeathed his library to the University of Alberta, Edmonton, as well as funds for the purchase of Ukrainian books. An artifact collection of his inventions is housed in the Provincial Museum of Alberta.

Gonta, Ivan, b ? in Rozsishky near Uman, Bratslav voivodeship, d 1768 in Serby (now Gontivka) near Mohyliv, Kamianets-Podilskyi voivodeship. One of the leaders of the *Koliivshchyna rebellion. A captain in the Cossack household militia of F. Potocki, the voivode of Kiev, in Uman from 1757, he was ordered to attack the approaching Haidamaka forces led by M. *Zalizniak. Instead, he and his militia joined the rebels, and the joint forces captured and ravaged Uman on 21 June 1768, massacring Polish nobles, Jews, and Uniates. Gonta was proclaimed colonel of Uman. Fearing that the rebellion would spread into their domain, the Russian government sent a regiment of Don Cossacks to Uman to suppress it. Its colonel, Gurev, tricked the rebels into believing he sided with them. He invited them to a banquet, at which about 900 of them were seized and handed over to the Polish crown hetman, K. Branicki. Before being executed, Gonta and others were tortured cruelly for several days. Parts of his body were nailed to gallows in 14 towns. Many folk songs and legends were composed about him, and he is one of the heroes in T. Shevchenko's long poem *Haidamaky* (The Haidamakas).

Ivan Gonta

Good Friday, Church of (Piatnytska Tserkva; also Tserkva sv. Paraskevy). An important architectural monument of the Kievan Rus' period in Chernihiv, built near the site of a former market in the late 12th or early 13th century. The church differs from others in Chernihiv by its finish, ornamentation, and the structure of its vault. Its general shape is square. The church has three naves (8.2 m by 12.5 m) and three apses, with four supporting pillars, which carry the weight of the vault and one cupola. The interior is distinctive for its sense of great spaciousness. Restorations in the Ukrainian Baroque style were made to the church in 1670 and in the 1690s (probably by the architect I. Zarudny), and paid for by the colonel of Chernihiv regiment, V. Dunin-Borkovsky. In the 17th century a convent was attached to the church, but it burned down in 1750. In the 1820s a bell tower, designed by the architect A. Kartashevsky, was built for the church; the tower was torn down during restorations. The church, damaged in 1941, was restored after the Second World War under the direction of P. Baranovsky.

Church of Good Friday in Chernihiv (12th–13th century)

Church of Good Friday in Lviv

Good Friday, Church of (Piatnytska Tserkva; also Tserkva sv. Paraskevy). An important architectural and historical monument in Lviv, located at the foot of Zamkova Hora mountain in the center of the old city. The church's construction was paid for by the Moldavian hospodar V. *Lupu, and several Moldavian rulers are buried in the church. Built in the early 1640s on the site of previous churches, the present structure is made of unfinished stone blocks. Such features as small, highly placed windows, thick walls, and embrasures emphasize the fortress-like aspects of its architecture. The church combines elements of many styles, in particular Gothic and the late Renaissance: its interior lines are severe and laconic, but enlivened by a highly ornamented iconostasis.

The great value of the church lies in the masterpieces of Lviv painters and woodcarvers of the early 17th century adorning it. Of particular note is the five-tiered Renaissance iconostasis (a sixth row was added in 1870, to give a total of 70 icons), with Baroque gates topped by a crucifix. The richest and most elaborate part of the iconostasis is the portal with an icon of Christ the Archpriest over the arch. The icons added in 1870 (ss Cyril and Methodius, ss Olha and Volodymyr, St Nicholas, and St John Chrysostom) were painted by A. Kachmarsky. The vault and walls of the presbytery are decorated with late 18th-century frescoes by L. *Dolynsky. The church has been damaged several times; it was last restored in 1908.

Goose (genus *Anser*; Ukrainian: *huska*). Order Anseriformes, family Anatidae. Although all four species in the genus *Anser* ('true' geese) are found in Ukraine, only *A. anser* (synonym: *A. cinereus*; common: grey or greylag goose; Ukrainian: *sira huska*) and *A. fabalis* (bean goose; Ukrainian: *humennyk*) breed there. *A. albifrons* (syn: *A. casarca*; white-fronted goose; Ukrainian: *biloloba huska* or *kozarka*) and *A. erythropus* (lesser white-fronted goose, squeaking goose; Ukrainian: *piskulka, mala kozarka*) migrate through Ukraine; in warm years small numbers of both species winter on the Black Sea coast and in Crimea. Domesticated goose, *A. anser domesticus*, was derived from the native gray goose, and is an important commercial food source because of its efficient and fast growth rate. The best-known breeds of domesticated goose in Ukraine include the Toulouse, Emden, Great Gray, Camomile, Kholmohory, Pereiaslav, and West Ukrainian breeds.

Gorbunov, Borys, b 4 February 1901 in Kiev, d 28 July 1944 in Kiev. Specialist in structural mechanics and welding; corresponding member of the AN URSR from 1939. He worked at various institutes of the Academy of Sciences contributing to the analysis of the stability of bridge structures, the strength of welding joints, and the strength of materials. Together with Ye. Paton he contributed to the theory of welded bridge structures.

Gorgany Mountains. The central part of the Carpathian *Beskyds, situated between the Mizunka River in the west and the Prut River in the east, and between the limits of the Carpathian Mountains in the north and the Middle-Carpathian Depression in the south. Covering an area of approximately 2,500 sq km, the Gorgany are the least accessible and least populated part of the Ukrainian Carpathians. They are formed mostly of hard and resistant sandstones. The transverse valleys of the Mizunka, Svicha, Chechva, Limnytsia, Bystrytsia Nadvirnianska, Bystrytsia Solotvynska, and Prut rivers dissecting the longitudinal ridges have transformed the latticed structure of the mountains into a feathered, and sometimes insular, form.

The elevation of the mountains increases from 1,400 m in the west (Mt Gorgan Vyshkivskyi at 1,448 m) to 1,800 m in the Limnytsia Basin (the peaks: Grofa at 1,748 m, Popadia at 1,742 m, Syvulia at 1,836 m, Ihrovyshche at 1,807 m, and Vysoka at 1,805 m) and then decreases towards the east (the peaks: Doboshanka at 1,760 m, Syniak at 1,664 m, and Khomiak at 1,544 m). The peaks, which are often separated from one another by deep ravines, are more differentiated than the peaks in other parts of the Beskyds. Extensive fields (up to 5 sq km) of sandstone boulders (the result of wind erosion) cover the higher peaks, particularly their southern slopes, and weak traces of past glaciation are found on the highest slopes. River valleys in the Gorgany are deeply incised (up to 1,000 m) and narrow and their slopes are steep. The rivers have an irregular flow, which is often interrupted by rapids and falls (eg, the Bukhtovets and Prut rivers). The Gorgany remain largely forested. Eighty percent of their total area is covered by forests consisting mostly of spruce; mixed forests are found only on the periphery and in Transcarpathia. Above the upper forest line (at 1,450–1,550 m) Swiss mountain pine is more widespread than in other parts of the Ukrainian Carpathians. Because of this and the sandstone fields, mountain meadows seldom occur in the Gorgany. The Beskyds lying between the two arms of the Middle-Carpathian Depression represent a transitional form between the landscape of the Gorgany and that of the Polonynian Beskyd. This is particularly evident in the basin of the upper Tereblia River in Transcarpathia (the peaks: Kanch, 1,583 m; Strimba, 1,723 m; Streminis, 1,599 m).

Because of their inhospitable environment, the Gorgany are very sparsely populated. In the western and central Gorgany, inhabited by the *Boikos, villages are situated mostly on the mountain periphery; the interior is penetrated only by settlements of the *Hutsuls in the Bystrytsia Nadvirnianska and Prut river valleys. The towns of *Nadvirna and *Diliatyn are located on the periphery. Non-Ukrainians – Jews, Poles, and Germans – appeared in this region in the 19th century when the forests began to be commercially exploited; in 1939 they composed close to 10 percent of the total population. These minorities are no longer found there.

The forests are the principal natural resource of the Gorgany. Their exploitation was facilitated in the late 19th century by the construction of a dense network of narrow-gauge track on which timber was transported to large lumber mills in Vyhoda, Broshniv-Osada, Nadvirna, and other towns. A small petroleum industry was located in Bytkiv, Pasichna, and Ripne. The health resorts of the Prut River valley – Vorokhta, Yaremcha, Yamne, Mykulychyn, and others – acquired a nationwide reputation; their development was facilitated by the only railroad in the Gorgany, which links the Prut River valley with Transcarpathia through the Tatarskyi Pass.

V. Kubijovyč

Gorlice (Ukrainian: Horlytsi [Horlyci]). IV-2. County town (1983 pop 26,300) in Poland, situated on the Ropa River in the Low Beskyd foothills. Until 1946 the southern part of Gorlice county was within Ukrainian ethnic territory (the western part of the *Lemko region). In 1939, 27,000 of the county's 29,000 inhabitants were Ukrainian. In 1945–6 most of them were forcibly resettled in the western oblasts of Soviet Ukraine or in the western regions of Poland newly acquired from Germany.

Gorodtsov, Vasilii [Gorodcov, Vasilij] , b 11 March 1860 in Dubrovichi, Riazan gubernia, Russia, d 3 February 1945 in Moscow. Russian archeologist. A professor at Moscow University from 1918, he studied the monuments of various epochs from the Paleolithic period to medieval times, developed a periodization scheme for the Bronze Age in eastern Europe, and was the first to note the distinct features of the *Middle-Dnieper culture. He conducted archeological excavations in the Crimea and in the Poltava, Kharkiv, and Donets regions. His numerous works (over 200) on archeology, ethnography, and historical geography laid the foundation for much of Soviet archeological writing, field research, and methodology; they include widely used textbooks on the archeology of primitive society (1908) and on ancient folkways (1910), and a book on the Stone Age (1923).

Semen Goruk

Goruk, Semen, b 13 September 1873 in Sniatyn, Galicia, d 1920 ? Senior officer of the Ukrainian Galician Army. Active in prewar paramilitary organizations in Galicia, Goruk became commander of a company (August 1914) and then of a battalion (March 1915) of the Ukrainian Sich Riflemen. On 30 September 1916, he was captured by the Russian army and spent the remainder of the war as a prisoner. On 5 November 1918 he became the chief of staff of the Ukrainian Galician Army, and on 10 December 1918 he was transferred to the Secretariat of Military Affairs, serving as its personnel officer until he returned to work in the General Staff. On 1 January 1919, Goruk was promoted to the rank of major. In April 1920, while commanding a unit of the Ukrainian Galician army, he was captured by the Bolsheviks in Kiev and incarcerated on the Solovets Islands.

Gospel. See Bible.

Gosplan. See State Planning Committee.

Goszczyński, Seweryn, b 4 November 1801 in Illintsi, Lypovets county, Kiev gubernia, d 25 February 1876 in Lviv. Polish Romantic poet, publicist, and political activist; a leading member of the *Ukrainian school in Polish literature. His narrative poem *Zamek Kaniowski* (Kaniv Castle, 1828) depicts the Haidamaka rebellion of 1768. The influence of Ukrainian folklore and history is evident in the versified novella *Król zamczyska* (King of the Castle, 1842) and other poems. His collected works (4 vols) appeared in Lviv in 1911; his biography, by B. Suchodolski, was published in 1927.

Gothic style. Dominant artistic style of Western and Central Europe in the Middle Ages. In architecture it is characterized by pointed arches and ribbed vaults supported by vertical shafts and buttresses. The pointed arch was known along the Black Sea coast in the early Christian period and was reintroduced to Ukraine in the 14th–15th centuries from Western and Southern Europe. Gothic architecture was relatively rare in the 14th–16th centuries, and was restricted mainly to Western Ukraine, where it served as a transitory style. It was used mainly in castles and fortifications such as those in Khotyn, Lutske, Kamianets, Mezhybizh, and Nevytske, and in Makovytsia in Transcarpathia. Elements of the Gothic style are also found in churches in Rohatyn, Sutkivtsi, Ostrih, and Derman, and more frequently in Roman Catholic churches such as the Lviv Cathedral and the church in Vyzhniany near Zolochiv. The Gothic style can be discerned in the domes of wooden churches in the Khust region of Transcarpathia – eg, St Parasceve's Church (17th century) in Oleksandrivka and St Nicholas's Church (1779) in Danylove. The naturalistic trend in Gothic art had an influence on Ukrainian monumental and iconographic painting, on engraving and handicrafts, and especially on metalworking and jewelry making in the 15th–17th centuries.

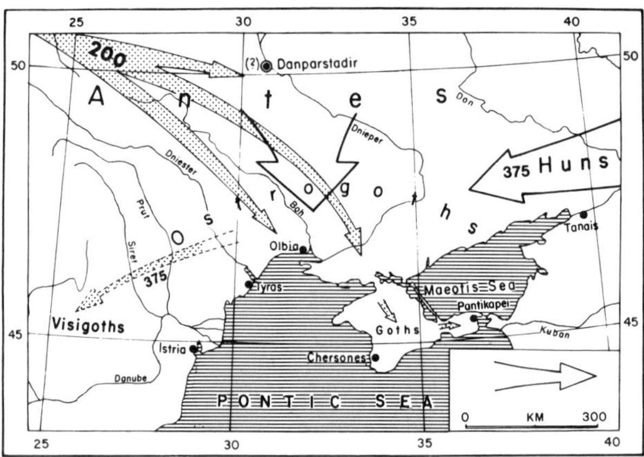

GOTHS IN UKRAINE

Goths. The name of ancient Germanic tribes that migrated from southern Scandinavia and in the 1st century AD inhabited the southeast coast of the Baltic Sea and the Vistula River basin. In the second half of the 2nd century they began migrating south and reached the Black Sea, where they intermixed with local Scythians and Sarmatians and established a tribal state. From the middle of the 3rd century they raided the Roman provinces, forcing the Romans to abandon Dacia in 271. Internal divisions resulted in the creation of two realms: that of the Ostrogoths, from the Donets River and the

Kuban to the Dniester River, and that of the Visigoths, between the Dniester and the Danube rivers. The Ostrogoths captured the Black Sea states of Olbia, Tyras, and the Bosporan Kingdom and established a large empire, which reached its zenith during the reign of King Ermanaric (350–75). In the 4th century the Goths adopted Arian Christianity, and their bishop, Ulfilas, translated the Bible into Gothic (extant portions are known as the *Codex Argenteus*). In 375 the Huns conquered the Ostrogothic state. Some Ostrogoths remained behind in the Crimea, where they managed to survive until the 17th century, but most moved into Thrace, and later into Pannonia and, in 455, into Italy. They ruled Italy from 493 to 526; in 554 they were dispersed by Emperor Justinian and disappeared. Gothic metal products and goldware were distributed widely throughout Eastern Europe, and with their great migration the Goths brought their metalworking skills to Western Europe. The artistic style they introduced is known as the Merovingian or Gothic style.

BIBLIOGRAPHY

Braun, F. *Razyskaniia v oblasti Goto-slavianskikh otnoshenii* (St Petersburg 1899)

Vasiliev, A. *The Goths in Crimea* (Cambridge, Mass 1936)

Iordan [Jordanes]. *O proiskhozhdenii i deianiiakh gotov,* trans E. Skrzhinskaia (Moscow 1960)

Burns, T. *A History of the Ostrogoths* (Bloomington 1984)

A. Zhukovsky

Gouzenko, Igor [Guzenko, Ihor], b 13 January 1919 in Rohachiv, Volhynia gubernia, d late June 1982 near Toronto. Soviet defector. Educated at the Moscow Military Intelligence Academy, Gouzenko was assigned in 1943 to the Soviet embassy in Ottawa as a cipher clerk. In September 1945 he defected with documents on Soviet espionage activities aimed particularly at Western atomic bomb secrets. His information led to the arrest and conviction of atomic physicists A.N. May and K. Fuchs. In Canada 10 of 18 persons charged with espionage, including Communist-Progressive MP F. Rose, were convicted. Gouzenko wrote two books: his memoirs *This Was My Choice* (1948) and the novel *The Fall of a Titan* (1954).

Governing Council of the Hetman Office (Pravlenie getmanskogo uriada). A provisional government in the Hetman state of Left-Bank Ukraine from 1734 to 1750. After the death of Hetman D. *Apostol, the tsarist government forbade the election of a new hetman. In order to further limit Ukrainian *autonomy, Empress Anna Ivanovna assigned the Hetman's functions to an appointed council of three Russian officials and three members of the Cossack *starshyna,* who were to rule according to Ukrainian customary law, the empress's decrees, and the *Reshitel'nye punkty,* the constitution imposed in the Hetman state by Russia in 1728. Although all members were to have equal authority, the council was actually ruled by Prince A. Shakhovskoi until 1737, briefly by Prince I. Bariatinsky, and then by Gen I. Bibikov until 1745 with secret instructions from the empress to further subjugate Ukraine. The senior Ukrainian member of the council was General Quartermaster Ya. Lyzohub. Other Ukrainian members included General Judge M. Zabila, General Osaul F. Lysenko, and General Treasurer A. Markovych. The council's decisions could be overruled by the Chancellery of Little Russian Affairs of the Russian Senate, to which the council was subordinated. During the council's rule, Ukraine bore the brunt of the economic destruction and population losses wreaked by the Russo-Turkish War of 1735–9. The council existed until Empress Elizabeth I restored the *General Military Chancellery and K. *Rozumovsky was appointed hetman in 1750.

Government, municipal. See Municipal government.

Government borrowing. See State loans.

Government-in-exile of the Ukrainian National Republic (Uriad Ukrainskoi Narodnoi Respubliky v ekzyli). The government institutions of the UNR were evacuated first partly (end of 1919) and then totally (1920) from Ukraine as Bolshevik troops occupied the country. Most of the institutions were relocated in Tarnów, Poland, and a few in Częstochowa. Later they were moved to Warsaw, Paris, and Prague.

The UNR government-in-exile was based on the Law on the Temporary Supreme Authority and the Legislative System of the UNR and the Law on the State People's Council, which were adopted by the *Directory of the UNR in Ukraine on 12 November 1920. These acts, which were based on the resolutions of the *Labor Congress, transferred legislative powers and ultimate authority over the government to the State People's Council. But until this council would be convened, its functions were assigned to the UNR Council of National Ministers, while the Directory, or more precisely its head, was empowered to act as the supreme state authority: to approve laws, treaties, appointments, foreign representation, etc. If the Directory head became unable to carry out these responsibilities, they would be transferred to a special college, and if this college could not be convened, they would be assumed by the head of the Council of National Ministers.

Apart from the shortlived *Council of the Republic in Tarnów, which consisted of representatives of political parties, professional associations, and cultural organizations, there was no legislative body among the state institutions in exile. It was only in 1947 that the *Ukrainian National Council was formed to act as a parliament in exile, with authority to elect succeeding governments.

Until 25 May 1926 the head of the Directory, and hence of the state, was S. *Petliura. After Petliura's death this office was assumed by A. *Livytsky, and in 1939–40 by V. *Prokopovych. The Council of National Ministers was headed in exile by A. Livytsky (1920–1 and 1922–6), P. *Pylypchuk (1921–2), V. Prokopovych (1926–39), O. *Shulhyn (1939–40), and K. *Pankivsky (1945–8). The government-in-exile suspended activities during the Second World War, but A. Livytsky, as head of the Directory, signed various petitions to the German government. After the war the composition of the government changed as activists of several Western Ukrainian political parties and of civic organizations from Soviet Ukraine joined the government.

The government-in-exile never established itself as the sole political center for Ukrainians in the diaspora: it was opposed both by parties active in the UNR during the struggle for Ukrainian independence and in interwar Western Ukraine. Often, the government was treated as just another party, whose members were labeled '*uenerivtsi*.' The government's strongest support came from the Ukrainian Radical Democratic party (see *Ukrainian Party of Socialists-Federalists), which provided most of the government officials. The Ukrainian Social Democratic Workers' party did not join the government, but recognized its legitimacy. In contrast, the Ukrainian Party of Socialist Revolutionaries, led by M. Shapoval, strongly opposed the government, as did the Hetmanite *Ukrainian Union of Agrarians-Statists and the *Organization of Ukrainian Nationalists. The attitude of political circles from Galicia, particularly of the *Ukrainian National Democratic Alliance, changed from rejection (because of the Treaty of *Warsaw), to indifference, and finally to co-operation on specific political and civic issues.

The government acted through a number of ministries and institutions. External affairs – the sphere of most intensive activity – were overseen by A. *Nikovsky, and then by O. Shulhyn (until 1946). At first the government maintained UNR diplomatic representatives in a number of countries, among them K. Matsiievych in Rumania, A. Livytsky in Poland, M. Slavinsky in Czechoslovakia, R. Smal-Stotsky in Germany, M. Vasylko in Switzerland, V. Mursky in Turkey, and O. Shulhyn in France. Except for France, all the missions in those countries were abolished at the beginning of the 1920s. As head of the mission in Paris and later as minister for foreign affairs, O. Shulhyn maintained contact with the *League of Nations, where he protested against the Bolshevik occupation of Ukraine, Soviet diplomatic initiatives, and the Stalinist terror and man-made famine in Ukraine. The government-in-exile conducted some of its activities in foreign affairs through the Ukrainian Association for the League of Nations and, from 1933 to 1939, through a permanent secretariat in Geneva, run by M. *Livytsky. It was also active in organizing the *Promethean movement among émigrés from countries occupied by Soviet Russia.

The government-in-exile devoted special attention to military organs, which were responsible for training military personnel, organizing former soldiers, and maintaining clandestine contacts with supporters in Soviet Ukraine. These were overseen by V. *Salsky, the minister of military affairs (to 1940), and by Generals O. *Udovychenko, M. *Bezruchko, V. *Petriv, and M. *Omelianovych-Pavlenko. Some UNR officers worked under special contract for the Polish army and received Polish military training. To promote the military profession the government organized the Ukrainian Military History Society and published journals such as *Tabor* and *Za derzhavnist'* as well as other literature.

In civic and cultural spheres the UNR government-in-exile acted through various associations that supported it: the *Union of Ukrainian Emigré Organizations in France, the *Ukrainian Central Committee in Warsaw, the *Public Relief Committee of Ukrainian Emigrants in Rumania, the *Ukrainian Alliance in Czechoslovakia, and others. Their work was co-ordinated by the *Supreme Emigration Council headed by O. Shulhyn. The *Petliura Ukrainian Library (est 1926) in Paris preserved UNR archives. In 1938 the government founded the *Ukrainian Mohylo-Mazepian Academy of Arts and Sciences. Thanks to the efforts of the government-in-exile, the Polish government set up the *Ukrainian Scientific Institute in Warsaw. The weekly **Tryzub*, published in Paris from 1925 to 1940, was an unofficial publication of the government-in-exile. An important source of support for the government was the Brotherhood of Ukrainian Statism, founded in Ukraine during the struggle for independence. Composed of civic leaders and intellectuals organized in a number of clandestine branches, members of the brotherhood met regularly to review the work of the government and to discuss changes in its composition and other matters.

After the Second World War the head of the Directory, A. Livytsky, reorganized the UNR government-in-exile. Thus, in 1947 the *Ukrainian National Council was set up as a pre-parliament of the UNR state center in exile to continue the ideological and legal tradition of the UNR government.

BIBLIOGRAPHY
Iakovliv, A. 'Osnovy konstytutsiï UNR,' *Tryzub*, nos 114–15 (1928)
Shul'hyn, O. *Derzhavnist' chy haidamachchyna?* (Paris 1931)
Shapoval, M. 'Liakhomaniia,' *Nasha doba* (1931)
Shul'hyn, O. *Bez terytoriï: Ideolohiia ta chyn uriadu UNR na chuzhyni* (Paris 1934)
Sal's'kyi, V. 'Shliakhy borot'by,' *Tryzub*, nos 174–7 (1940)
Livyts'kyi, M. *DTs UNR v ekzyli mizh 1920 i 1940 rokamy* (Munich-Philadelphia 1984)

A. Zhukovsky

Governor (*hubernator*). The ruler of a *gubernia in Russia appointed by the tsar, usually from amongst the nobility. At the beginning of the 19th century, some gubernias (eg, Kiev, Podilia, and Little Russia) had military governors; this position also existed in certain ports (eg, Mykolaiv) and in the Kuban and other Cossack territories. The governor was responsible for the judicial system, police, finances, and general administration of the gubernia, and supervised the autonomous *zemstvos. He was accountable to the minister of internal affairs, although some governors were supervised by a *governor-general. The nature of the position changed constantly, depending on the needs of the state and the personalities of the individuals involved. After the 1917 Revolution, the gubernias were ruled by *gubernial commissioners during the period of the Central Rada and by gubernial elders (*starosty*) during the Hetman government. Several governors were appointed when the Russian army occupied Galicia and Bukovyna during the First World War.

The head of autonomous Subcarpathian Ruthenia (1920–38) was also called a governor and was appointed by the president of Czechoslovakia. This was mostly a figurehead position, as his authority was limited by the central government and real power was in the hands of a Czech vice-governor.

Governor-general (*heneral-hubernator*). A high-ranking official in the civil or military administration in Russia who supervised several *gubernias or *vicegerencies, or had other special duties. Since he was accountable only to the tsar and the Senate, a governor-general had large discretionary powers. From the beginning of the 18th century, the title of governor-general was given to the commanders of the Russian armies in Ukraine; they also had considerable influence in civil matters, especially in Kiev. After the abolition of the Hetman state in 1764, P. *Rumiantsev-Zadunaisky was appointed president of the Little Russian Collegium and governor-general of Little Russia. After a series of administrative territorial changes resulting from the abolition of the Cossack regiments and the introduction of the provincial reforms, Little Russia general-gubernia was re-established in 1802. It lasted until 1835, and for much of this period the post was occupied by N. *Repnin. Kharkiv general-gubernia, comprising Kharkiv and Voronezh gubernias, existed from 1775 until 1796. In 1832 Kiev general-gubernia was established, comprising the Right-Bank gubernias of Kiev, Podilia, and Volhynia. D. *Bibikov used this post (1837–52) to further the Russification of the area. It survived the longest of all the general-gubernias in Ukraine, lasting until 1914. The New Russia general-gubernia (1797–1874) consisted of the steppe gubernias of Kherson, Katerynoslav, and Tavriia, and, for shorter periods, Bessarabia and the Kuban. Others were of a temporary nature, eg, Odessa general-gubernia (1905–8), formed because of a state of war or political upheavals in a given region.

The title of governor-general was given to the chief civilian administrator of Galicia and Bukovyna when they were occupied by Russian armies in 1914–17. The administrative center was in Chernivtsi. The first person to serve in this post was Count G. Bobrynsky, followed in 1916 by Gen V. Trepov. In April 1917 this post was taken over by D. Doroshenko.

V. Markus

Gowda, Michael [Govda, Myxajlo], b 8 November 1874 in Vetlyn, Jarosław county, Galicia, d 8 July 1953 in Edmonton. To avoid military service Gowda immigrated to Canada and settled in Alberta in 1898. Employed as an interpreter by an Edmonton retailer, he published articles and poems in the Ukrainian-American newspaper *Svoboda*, urging the public to support education. He was one of the founders of the first Ukrainian reading club in Edmonton and one of the leaders of the Federation of Ukrainian Socialist Democrats of Canada. In 1913 he and seven other Ukrainians ran as independents for the Alberta legislature.

Goy, Luba [Goj, Ljuba], b 8 November 1945 in Haltern, Germany. Actress and comedienne. Goy came to Canada with her parents in 1951 and settled in Ottawa. She studied at the National Theatre School in Montreal (1967–70). She has performed at Stratford's Third Stage, with the Stratford Festival's National Arts Centre Company and The Jest Society. Since the mid-1970s Goy has been a regular on CBC radio and TV's satirical review 'The Royal Canadian Air Farce,' for which she has been a cowinner of three ACTRA awards. She has performed across Canada in *Just a Kommedia* (written by N. Rylsky), a play on growing up Ukrainian in Canada.

GPU (Gosudarstvennoe politicheskoe upravlenie; in Ukrainian: DPU or Derzhavne politychne upravlinnia [State Political Administration]). Organ of Soviet security police created on 6 February 1922 in place of the *Cheka. Unlike its predecessor, the GPU was a regular agency operating within a legal framework under the control of the People's Commissariat of Internal Affairs. Its functions were espionage, suppression of counter-revolutionary activity, and protection of the borders and railways. In Ukraine a republican GPU directed by V. Balytsky was set up by the 22 March 1922 resolution of the All-Ukrainian Central Executive Committee. With the founding of the USSR, all the republican GPUs were brought under a new central agency, the OGPU (Obedinennoe gosudarstvennoe politicheskoe upravlenie [Unified State Political Administration]), in November 1923. The status of the agency was raised to that of a separate commissariat directly under the USSR Council of People's Commissars. For the first time the secret police was recognized as a permanent and legitimate feature of the Soviet system and was fixed in the constitution. In spite of its legal position the OGPU continued to be used as an instrument of Party policy. F. *Dzerzhinsky stayed on as its director and in 1926 was succeeded by his deputy, V. Menzhinsky (1926–34). In the republics the OGPU had its subsidiary organs and a representative on the republican councils of people's commissars. In 1924 the GPU in Ukraine became a people's commissariat of the Ukrainian SSR. It was headed by V. Balytsky, who sat on the republic's Council of People's Commissars. Branches were organized at the gubernia, okruha, and oblast levels. At first the GPU and OGPU were denied the punitive powers of the Cheka, and retained only investigative and examining powers. By the end of the 1920s, however, the OGPU reclaimed all the extraordinary powers of its predecessor. Sentences were passed without trial and in camera, as in the Cheka period, by the so-called Separate Council of the GPU in Ukraine, or by the Judicial Collegium of the OGPU in Moscow. Like the Cheka the OGPU used ruthless terror against members or suspected sympathizers of any opposition within or outside the Party. It fabricated conspiracies, staged show trials, carried out mass arrests, ran the system of corrective labor camps, and provided forced labor for large-scale projects. In Ukraine the GPU mopped up what remained of the insurgent movement (1922–3), organized the trial of the Union for the Liberation of Ukraine (1929–30), directed mass repressions during collectivization (1929–33), exterminated activists of the Ukrainian Autocephalous Orthodox church and Ukrainian cultural leaders, and suppressed various Party deviations (see *Terror). In 1934, after G. Yagoda became head of the agency, the OGPU was reorganized into the *NKVD.

Grabar, Igor. See Hrabar, Ihor.

Grabar (Hrabar), Vladimir, b 22 January 1865 in Vienna, d 26 November 1956 in Moscow. Specialist in the history and theory of international law; brother of I. Hrabar (Grabar). As a child Grabar lived near Prešov in the home of his grandfather A. *Dobriansky. In 1871 he emigrated to Russia to join his father E. Grabar, a lawyer and member of the Hungarian parliament who had been forced to become a political émigré. After studies at Galagan College and graduation from Moscow University (1888), he taught at the universities of Tartu (1893–1918), Voronezh (1919–22), and Moscow (1922–4). An associate of the Institute of Law of the USSR Academy of Sciences and a full member of the AN URSR from 1926, he was a legal adviser to the Soviet Commissariat of Foreign Trade (1922–9) and the Soviet delegation at the Conference of Lausanne (1922–3). His many works in Russian, Ukrainian, French, and German include *Rimskoe pravo v istorii mezhdunarodno-pravovykh uchenii: Elementy mezhdunarodnogo prava v trudakh legistov XII–XIV vv.* (Roman Law in the History of International-Law Doctrines: Elements of International Law in the Works of 12th- to 14th-Century Legists, 1901) and *Materialy k istorii literatury mezhdunarodnogo prava v Rossii (1647–1917)* (Materials on the History of the Literature of International Law in Russia [1647–1917], 1958).

Grabowicz, George [Hrabovyč, Hryhorij], b 12 October 1943 in Cracow, Poland. Literary scholar. Grabowicz received his PH D from Harvard University in 1975, and since then has been a professor at that university, where he holds the Dmytro Čyževs'kyj Chair of Ukrainian Literature. He is the author of articles on literary history and theory, as well as the books *Toward a History of Ukrainian Literature* (1981) and *The Poet as Mythmaker: A Study of Symbolic Meaning in Taras Ševčenko* (1982).

Grabowski, Michał, b 25 September 1804 in Zolotiiv (now part of Rivne), Volhynia, d 19 November 1863 in Warsaw. Polish Romantic writer and literary critic. A friend of P. Kulish, he contributed to his ethnographic collection **Zapiski o Iuzhnoi Rusi* (Notes on Southern Rus') and influenced Kulish's views on the Cossacks. A notable member of the *Ukrainian school in Polish literature, he wrote historical novelettes with Ukrainian subject matter, such as *Koliszczyzna i stepy* (The Koliivshchyna Rebellion and the Steppes, 1838) and *Stanica Hulajpolska* (The Huliai-Pole Station, 1840–1), and contributed to *Obozrenie mogil, valov i gorodishch Kievskoi gubernii* (Survey of Kurhans, Battlements, and Fortified Cities of Kiev Gubernia, 1848) as well as to several other compendiums of historical, ethnographic, and archeological studies, including *Ukraina dawna i teraźniejsza* (Ukraine Ancient and Contemporary, 1850).

Grabski, Stanisław, b 5 April 1871 in Borowa, Łowicz county, Warsaw gubernia, d 6 May 1949 in Sulejówek near Warsaw. Polish economist and political figure, a leader of the National Democracy party. He was professor at Lviv (1910–39) and Warsaw (1946–9) universities. From 1919 to 1927 he served as deputy to the Sejm, and in 1923 and 1925–6 as minister of religious faiths and education. He favored a pro-Russian policy. Grabski was the author of the so-called *Lex Grabski*, passed on 31 July 1924, concerning the unification of Polish and Ukrainian schools into bilingual schools with Polish as the language of instruction unless the census figures (25 percent Ukrainian population) warranted a referendum on the language of instruction. This resulted in a virtual disappearance of Ukrainian schooling, the number of schools teaching in Ukrainian falling from 2,426 in 1921–2 to 745 in 1927–8.

Grądzki, Samuel (Grondski), b ?, d ca 1672 in Galicia. Polish diplomat and historian. In 1655 he participated in negotiations between King Jan II Casimir Vasa and Hetman B. Khmelnytsky. A year later he served as envoy of Charles X Gustavus of Sweden to Khmelnytsky, and then as representative of Prince György II Rákóczy of Transylvania in negotiations with Col A. Zhdanovych of the Kiev Cossack regiment. His *Historia belli Cosacco-Polonici authore Samuele Grondski de Grondi conscripta anno 1675* (published in Hungary in 1789) is a valuable source of information on the Khmelnytsky period.

Graebe, Kurt, b 9 February 1874 in Karniszewo, Gniezno county, Poland, d 8 August 1952 in Munich. German political figure in interwar Poland; from 1922 to 1930 a member of the Polish Sejm. Graebe co-operated with Ukrainian deputies in organizing a Bloc of National Minorities in the Sejm and at the *Congress of National Minorities in Geneva. During the Second World War, as head of a department of the *German Labor Front, he was responsible for the welfare of Western Ukrainian workers in Germany. In 1951–2 he was president of the *German-Ukrainian Society.

Graffiti. Inscriptions or drawings usually scratched on pillars and walls. The oldest known graffiti in Ukraine were found during the excavations of the sites of the *ancient states on the Northern Black Sea coast. The best described are those in the St Sophia Cathedral in Kiev (dating from ca 1042 onwards). Other important graffiti (12th century) were discovered in a cave of the Kievan Cave Monastery. Graffiti are important for linguists and historians because they often reveal the spoken language, everyday life, and important events of a period. Although useful also for the study of archeology, paleography, art history, and onomastics, they should be approached with caution, as occasionally people from outside regions and countries, often pilgrims, drew them. Ukrainians may have left graffiti outside of Ukraine; for example, at the Hagia Sophia in Constantinople. Ukrainian graffiti have been discovered, studied, and published by I. Sreznevsky (1881), I. Tolstoi (1953), S. Vysotsky (*Drevnerusskie nadpisi Sofii Kievskoi* [Old Rus' Inscriptions in the St Sophia Cathedral of Kiev, 1966]; *Srednevekovye nadpisi Sofii Kievskoi* [Medieval Inscriptions in the St Sofia Cathedral of Kiev, 1976]), and others.

Grain procurement. The means by which the state obtains large grain reserves to feed the armed forces, the civil service, and the industrial work force, to use as export, and to be fully able to satisfy the consumption needs of the population. In contrast to purchase on the open market, procurement is compulsory in nature and involves a fixed, stable, and, as a rule, low price.

Grain procurement was introduced by the tsarist regime during the First World War. The Ministry of Agriculture and a special board of food supply procured grain at fixed prices that were, at first, higher than the market prices. Rampant inflation and speculation caused an increase in the market prices, however, and farmers

Cyrillic graffiti on a wall of the St Sophia Cathedral in Kiev

became reluctant to sell grain to the state. The authorities then resorted to requisitioning, which aroused deep discontent among the peasantry. In 1914–15, the state procured 41.7 percent of the grain available on the open market; in 1915–16, 51.3 percent; and in 1916–17, 67.9 percent. Even though it possessed two-thirds of all marketable grain on the eve of the revolution, the state was unable to supply the population adequately.

During the period of *War Communism the Bolshevik state applied the policy of forced grain expropriation on a massive scale. A *surplus appropriation system (*prodrazverstka*) was introduced, whereby each peasant household was ordered to turn over its food surplus to the state at a fixed price. As a result of rampant inflation and the lack of manufactured market goods, however, money lost its value, and state payments for grain deliveries became worthless; when they were finally abolished the farmers did not even notice it. In March 1919 the *prodrazverstka* (Ukrainian: *prodrozkladka*) was extended to Ukraine. It was implemented with the help of *committees of poor peasants, armed workers' detachments, and the Cheka, which seized grain and punished the 'hoarders.' The peasants, left with almost no food, naturally resisted, and armed struggle ensued between the Soviet regime and the peasants and among the peasants themselves. Peasant partisans resisted and attacked the Reds and the Whites throughout Ukraine, and until the Red Army emerged victorious, the Ukrainian peasantry combated the *prodrazverstka* via armed struggle, the black market, reduced sowings, and concealment.

In 1920–1, when the main anti-Bolshevik forces had been defeated, Ukrainian grain deliveries to the Soviet state amounted to 2.6 million t out of a gross harvest of about 8.6 million t. This expropriation, combined with drought and reduced sowings, led to the *famine of 1921–2 and millions of deaths in the five southern gubernias of Ukraine. Faced with declining productivity and mass unrest, the authorities decided to replace the *prodrazverstka* with a less stringent *tax in kind. This shift marked the beginning of the *New Economic Policy and the restoration of the private sector in small-scale trade and industry. In 1921–2 grain deliveries to the state amounted to 1.9 million t, parts of which were used to create local reserves. In 1924 compulsory deliveries of food supplies were abandoned and were replaced by a monetary tax.

The period of freedom from compulsory deliveries of grain and other farm products did not last long. In January 1928 they were reinstituted. Peasants were forced to sell grain at a fixed low price; in Ukraine in 1927–8 they were paid 7 rubles per 100 kg of wheat, and in 1928–9, 8.30 rubles (the free market price was 11 and 26 rubles respectively). Peasants who refused to surrender their grain to the state were charged under article 127 of the Criminal Code of the Ukrainian SSR with speculation and concealment of goods, which were punishable by one year of imprisonment and the confiscation of property. A quarter of the grain obtained in this way was distributed free to the rural poor to gain their support for *collectivization and for punitive measures against the peasants (*kulaks), who were held responsible for the shortages.

The peasants responded to the reintroduction of compulsory deliveries by decreasing productivity. This, in turn, provoked the state to implement new, drastic measures, such as grain seizures, arrests, and confiscation. At the 11th Congress of the CP(B)U in 1930, it was stated that in only 22 of Ukraine's 41 okruhas, 33,000 peasant households were prosecuted and their property confiscated. In order to give the compulsory deliveries a legalistic semblance, seeded land was declared to be under contract.

In contrast to common practice, however, the contracts were not entered into voluntarily by the peasantry and the state did not assume any obligations, such as supplying seed, equipment, or goods. Directives for the procurement plan came from the center, were confirmed at a general meeting of the poor peasants or of all the inhabitants of a village, and then were vigorously implemented by local officials, who were given the authority to impose fines up to five times the imposed quota for late or incomplete grain delivery and even to confiscate the property of uncooperative peasants. Deliveries were officially viewed as the 'natural' fulfillment of the agricultural tax and of other obligations, which were numerous by the late 1920s – self-assessment, compulsory insurance, obligatory loans for the consolidation of peasant holdings, and obligatory industrialization loans – and often exceeded a peasant family's total income.

After collectivization began, extremely high delivery quotas were levied to compensate for earlier shortfalls. When the kulaks and other peasants refused or were unable to meet them, practically all their grain stocks were confiscated. After the 'liquidation of the kulaks as a class,' the *collective and state farms assumed the burden of grain deliveries. Peasant opposition to collectivization caused agricultural production to decline dramatically, yet the state continued to demand delivery of the same and even greater grain quotas (see table).

Before collectivization the peasants had surrendered less than a fifth of their harvest to the state. In 1929–30 the state increased the share to 30 percent for the USSR as a whole and 40 percent for Ukraine. In fact, the state received an even higher percentage because harvest yields were distorted. In January 1933, CP(B)U General Secretary S. Kosior referred to the previously standard methods of estimating harvests as 'kulak arithmetic' and urged party workers to ignore them. The Central Statistical Administration had been abolished, many noted statisticians and other critics had been arrested, and officials were thus able to demand excessive procurements using an artificial device called 'biological yield.' For example, the real USSR harvest in 1933 was 68.4 million t, whereas the biological harvest was estimated at 89.8 million t. Consequently delivery plans were increased to impossible levels.

This state of affairs led to the terrible, man-made famine of 1932–3 (see *Genocide). Special detachments of urban activists searched the homes of collective and independent farmers and seized all the grain they could find to fulfill the delivery quota. Peasants were forbidden to save grain for seed, feed, or even human comsumption; all of it was removed. Even so, the excessive delivery plans imposed in Ukraine could not be fulfilled. As punishment, individual villages, rural soviets, and even raions were blacklisted and deprived of commodities, all institutions in them were closed down, trade was prohibited, and the population's livestock was confiscated for next year's meat delivery. All these measures resulted in several million deaths from starvation and related diseases in Ukraine. At the time, the absolute priority of

Gross harvests and state procurements of grain

	Gross harvest (in million t)	Procurements and purchases (in million t)	Procurements as a percentage of harvests	Contribution to total USSR procurements (%)
RUSSIAN EMPIRE AND USSR				
1913	86.5	18.9	21.9	
1921	42.3	3.8	8.9	
1922	50.3	6.9	13.8	
1925–28	73.7	13.3	18.0	
1929–33	69.9	21.0	30.0	
1934–39	72.3	30.1	41.6	
1946–50	64.8	27.9	43.1	
1951–55	88.5	34.2	38.6	
1956–60	121.5	47.9	39.4	
1961–65	130.3	51.6	39.6	
1966–70	167.6	66.0	39.4	
1971–75	181.6	67.6	37.2	
1976–80	189.1	77.7	41.1	
UKRAINE				
1913	18.0*	5.0*	27.8	26.5
1921	8.6	2.6	30.2	68.4
1922	10.2	1.7	16.7	24.6
1925–28	16.8	3.1	18.5	23.3
1929–33	17.1	6.9	40.4	32.9
1934–39	18.1	8.2	45.3	27.2
1946–50	16.9	7.7	45.6	27.6
1951–55	23.3	9.1	39.1	26.6
1956–60	23.9	7.0	29.3	14.6
1961–65	29.3	11.0	37.5	21.3
1966–70	33.4	11.1	33.2	16.8
1971–75	40.0	14.0	35.0	20.7
1976–80	43.2	14.0	32.4	18.0

*Average for 1911–15

state procurements was enacted. In mid-1933 the state issued a compulsory procurement decree. According to it, collective farms in Ukraine had to deliver 3,100 kg of grain from every ha of seeded land that was not worked by a *machine-tractor station (MTS), and 2,500 kg from every ha that was worked by an MTS. The state received even more grain – approx 20 percent of the harvest (150–200 kg/ha) paid by each collective farm to the MTS for its services. The delivery quotas of independent and collective farmers with *private plots were even higher. In general, quotas were not based on the harvest, and nonfulfillment resulted in fines, expropriation, imprisonment, and deportation.

The 1933 decree guaranteed that collective farmers had the right to freely dispose of all grain left over after the collective farms had fulfilled their obligations to the state and had made full provision for seed, reserve, and feed funds. The quantity of grain taken by the state was so great, however, that in most cases, after fulfilling their deliveries and stocking their funds, the collective farms had no surplus. The payments in kind to the MTS changed several times in subsequent years. In 1937–9 the rate was 45–50 percent of all grain collected and depended on the harvest and the type of work done; in 1954–7 the rate was fixed at 220 kg per ha of arable (instead of sowed) land. Besides procuring most of its grain by compulsory means, the state also purchased a smaller amount (10–15 percent) from the collective farmers at above-quota prices. In 1939, for example, the procurement price paid for wheat was 9.42 rubles per 100 kg, while the above-quota price was 23.97 rubles per 100 kg. Procurement prices barely changed for over 20 years and became divorced completely from real costs and values. Thus, in 1953 the state paid 10 kopecks for 1 kg of wheat, whereas it sold 1 kg of flour for 5 rubles. This disparity discouraged incentive and productivity. From time to time enormous procurements would leave the rural population without grain and famine would again flare up, as it did in 1946 in most of the oblasts of Ukraine and Moldavia.

When the Germans occupied Ukraine during the Second World War they left largely intact the entire Soviet collective- and state-farm system. In some regions of Ukraine, grain quotas imposed by the Nazis on collective farms were double the 1941 Soviet norm. Between 1941 and 1944 over 80 percent of the six million tons of grain requisitioned by the Reich from the occupied territories of the USSR came from Ukraine. After J. Stalin's death the Soviet procurement system began to change. The September 1953 CC CPSU plenum raised the purchase prices of grain significantly and reduced the quotas of compulsory deliveries. Even more important changes took place in 1958 and 1965: the purchase prices were raised by a large factor, a bonus of 50 percent for deliveries above the quota was established, payment in kind for MTS services was abolished, and the MTS were finally disbanded. Purchase prices began varying regionally across the USSR. In 1968, for example, the average price of wheat was 68 rubles per t; in southern Ukraine it was 65 rubles on collective farms and 28.5 rubles on state farms; in the Soviet Far East it was 121 rubles. These changes resulted in increased productivity, larger harvests, and larger purchases in the 1960s. At the same time Ukraine's contribution to the general procurement plan was lowered, and the percentage of the grain taken from Ukrainian peasants fell (see table).

In the last 15 years, however, the situation has again become more complex. At first gross harvests ceased to increase; then they began to decline. As a result, official data about harvests have not been published. In order to remedy this state of affairs, the authorities have conducted various experiments in the countryside. But compulsory deliveries of grain and other farm products to the state have not been abolished. (See also *Agricultural procurement.)

BIBLIOGRAPHY
Materialy po istorii sel'skogo khoziaistva i krest'ianstva SSSR, 3 (Moscow 1959)
Kononenko, K. *Ukraïna i Rossiia: Sotsiial'no-ekonomichni pidstavy ukraïns'koï natsional'noï ideï, 1917–1969* (Munich 1965)
Moshkov, Iu. *Zernovaia problema v gody sploshnoi kollektivizatsii* (Moscow 1966)
Tseny i tarify (Moscow 1969)

V. Kubijovyč, S. Maksudov

Grain production. Major branch of agriculture producing grain cultures. In 1984, 15,695,000 ha in Ukraine were devoted to grain crops; this accounted for 47.6 percent of Ukraine's arable land and for 13 percent of the land under grain in the USSR. Similar percentages held in the 1960s and 1970s, but earlier the picture was different. In 1913 (within present-day boundaries) the area devoted to grain in Ukraine equaled 24,700,000 ha, or 88 percent of the total cultivated land area in Ukraine and 23.6 percent of the land under grain in the USSR.

The structure of grain production in Ukraine has changed significantly in the course of history, as a result not only of climatic and economic conditions but also of government policy. Grain growing has been practiced in Ukraine since the Neolithic period: in the Trypilian culture, grains, chiefly *millet, spring *wheat, and *barley, were a staple of the diet. In the Hallstatt period (1000–500 BC) *rye appeared; then in the 1st century AD *buckwheat and finally *oats. From the mid-7th century BC to the 4th century AD, the Black Sea region of Ukraine was an important source of grain for Greece and Asia Minor. During the Slavic period the most important grain was millet. In the second half of the 1st millennium AD rye became a staple, along with wheat and barley. The introduction of winter varieties made possible a partial transition to a two-year, and even a three-year, rotation system. In the Princely era grain production met the demands of the local population and provided a surplus for export to the Crimea and Byzantium in the south and to Novgorod in the north. After the Mongol invasion grain production temporarily declined. In the 14th and 15th centuries the cultivation of oats continued to expand. The state collected oats as tribute to meet the need of its army for horse fodder. By the end of the 15th century Ukraine regained its status of bread basket as the Polish-Lithuanian Commonwealth began to export grain to the rest of Europe, particularly to Holland. Nobles set up **filvarky* to bring more land under cultivation and to increase corvée. The grain was transported by river to the Baltic Sea. First Western Ukraine, drained by the Buh and Sian basins, and then in the 16th and 17th centuries the Boh and Dnieper regions, served as the source of export grain. As Left-Bank and Slobidska Ukraine were colonized in the 17th century, the area under grain cultivation expanded. In these regions, however, grain production was not commercial.

A new period in the history of grain production began at the end of the 18th century when the Russian Empire reached the coast of the Black Sea and rapid settlement proceeded on the steppes. In southern Ukraine, land under cultivation increased quickly from 880,000 ha at the beginning of the 18th century to 6,000,000 in 1860, ie, from 4.5 percent to 34 percent of the total land area. The importance of Ukraine's grain production grew particularly after the 1860s, when the demand for grain in Turkey, Greece, and the industrial countries of Europe (Britain, Germany, and Holland) rose and the construction of railroads in the 1870s facilitated export through Black Sea ports. The land area devoted to grain in Russian-ruled Ukraine expanded from 18,150,000 ha in 1881 to 22,770,000 in 1913. In Subcaucasia it expanded from 3,740,000 ha in 1898 to 7,370,000 in 1913. The proportion of commercial grain varieties increased: from 1881 to 1913, the percentage of all land under wheat and barley increased from 35 and 16 to 38 and 25 percent respectively, while the percentage of land under rye decreased from 26 to 18. These changes occurred mostly in southern Ukraine. There the main trends in farming were the opening of the entire steppe to cultivation; the abandonment of the fallow-land system; the concentration on grain production, with grain crops taking up 96 percent of the total sown area; the specialization in spring wheat and barley, which accounted for 75 percent of the land under grain; the mechanization of agriculture; relatively low yields; and finally, a rise in commercial agriculture, with 50 percent of the harvest being exported. In Right-Bank Ukraine grain farming was more intensive. The three-field system was being replaced by the four-field system; all grains were grown, although winter wheat and rye received preference; and yields were higher because of the introduction of sugar beets, which permitted some crop rotation and thus led to a stabilization and then decrease in the amount of land under grain between 1881 and 1913 by 5 percent. Grain exports barely reached 20 percent of the harvest because of higher population density. In Western Ukraine crop rotation was more widespread, and only 70–80 percent of all arable land was under grain. While yields at the end of the 19th century (especially in Galicia) were fairly high, the greater population density and relatively small area sown with grain kept exports insignificant; there was also little specialization in grains. Grain farming conditions in Subcaucasia were similar to those in southern Ukraine, while conditions in Left-Bank Ukraine were transitional between those of Right-Bank Ukraine and the steppe. In northern Ukraine rye and oats were the chief grains. The three-field system there was being replaced by the many-field rotation system. The region was not self-sufficient in grain.

In Ukraine as a whole, the expansion in the land area devoted to grain and increasing yields resulted in rising gross harvests, which increased more rapidly than the population, and hence ever-larger grain surpluses. During the First World War grain production underwent fundamental changes as exports stopped entirely and the military's demand for feed grain rose sharply. Thus, the area seeded with barley in Ukraine and northern Caucasia increased from 3,235,500 ha in 1913 to 3,633,300 ha in 1916, or to 36.5 percent of all the land devoted to barley in the empire. The area devoted to oats and groat cultures also increased, while the area devoted to wheat decreased slightly. Despite shortages of farm labor and machinery, the proportion of winter wheat to spring wheat grown in Ukraine continued to rise. This indicated that in general Ukrainian farmers were well off and could afford substantial labor and capital investments. The rising price of grain, which more than doubled, improved the living standard of the middle and prosperous peasant. During 1917–21 the entire farming system was transformed radically: the large estates were divided among the peasants; landholdings were generally equalized; the use of forests became free; seed supply to farmers was diminished sharply; and Bolshevik food appropriation detachments were sent into the villages. While the average peasant family saw an improvement in its farm buildings and the size of its landholdings and livestock herd, it was threatened by the forcible grain requisitions and the peasants reduced the area seeded with grain. In 1921 increasing grain confiscation by the state (see *War Communism) and crop failure in the south led to *famine. With the introduction of the *New Economic Policy agricultural production began to rise rapidly.

The *collectivization drive led to a sharp decline in grain production. The total sown area in Ukraine was reduced; yields and gross harvests fell. The imposition of drastic grain delivery quotas by the state resulted in the man-made famine of 1932–3, during which millions died, and in serious undernourishment of the peasantry in subsequent years. By establishing collective and state farms, the state gained control over all grain production. Henceforth, only state functionaries could decide what would be sown and when, and when it would be harvested. All of this restructuring undermined production. At the same time the structure of grain production continued to change as winter wheat and corn became the predominant grains; by 1957 they accounted for 62 percent of the land devoted to grains, whereas in 1913 they had accounted for only 38 percent.

The production of wheat, the principal staple of the diet in Ukraine, is concentrated on large farms in Odessa, Mykolaiv, Kherson, Kirovohrad, and Crimea oblasts. To increase yields wheat is preceded by perennial grasses and legume crops. Sowing wheat on bare fallow, a widespread practice in the 1940s and 1950s, is rare today. Barley is the second most-important grain in Ukraine today and the chief spring crop. Like wheat, barley is mostly grown in the southern oblasts and on relatively large farms. It is used primarily in industry and as animal feed. Corn not only is grown for its grain but is also important as green fodder, which is used as silage. In the 1960s, under N. Khrushchev's influence, corn was introduced by compulsion throughout the USSR and in Ukraine came to take up almost one-third of the total sown area. Recently, the importance of corn grain has fallen dramatically and its cultivation is limited to the traditional southern and western regions. Rye, which at one time was Ukraine's principal grain, accounted for some 2 percent of the total sown area in 1983. It continues to be an important crop only in the northern and western oblasts – Chernihiv, Zhytomyr, Vinnytsia, and Volhynia – and is grown on relatively small tracts. This reduction in rye production is attributable to the higher yields, resistance, and adaptability of the new wheat varieties, as well as to government policies.

*Legume cultures have steadily gained importance as an integral part of the crop-rotation system and as fodder crop. The amount of land area devoted to grain is increasing very slowly because of the expansion of potato, vegetable, beet, and industrial crops, and also because the four-field rotation system is being replaced by the five-field system. (See table 1.)

In the mid-19th century backward farming methods kept grain yields very low. Thus, in the 1860s–1880s the yield in the southern (steppe) regions was 3.0–3.1 centners per ha, on the Left Bank 3.8–4.1, and on the Right Bank 4.7–5.4. Subsequently, yields rose significantly, so

TABLE 1
Area sown with grains and legumes (in thousand ha)

	1913	1940	1950	1960	1970	1980	1983
Total sown area	27,952	31,336	30,656	33,547	32,782	33,578	33,157
ALL GRAINS	24,696	21,385	20,047	13,729	15,518	16,473	15,783
Winter grains	7,626	10,116	9,300	5,160	6,904	8,992	6,952
wheat	3,088	6,317	5,383	3,691	5,960	8,000	5,862
rye	4,517	3,685	3,905	1,347	832	799	745
barley	21	114	12	122	112	193	345
Spring grains	17,070	11,269	10,747	8,569	8,614	7,481	8,831
wheat	5,770	901	1,168	261	70	31	18
barley	5,824	3,987	2,744	2,421	3,258	3,281	3,608
oats	2,923	2,282	1,797	872	811	707	691
corn	853	1,560	2,757	3,037	2,262	1,498	2,021
millet	525	955	556	772	521	341	389
buckwheat	698	723	634	393	364	345	348
rice	–	2	2	0	32	37	35
LEGUMES	438	836	766	787	1,280	1,194	1,649
peas	–	358	224	419	975	1,033	1,453
vetch and vetch mixtures for seed	–	252	316	142	131	65	91

TABLE 2
Grain yields in centners per ha

	1913	1940	1950	1960	1970	1975	1976–80
All grains	9.4	12.4	10.2	15.8	23.4	20.4	26.1
Winter wheat	11.8	12.1	11.1	17.5	26.0	22.9	30.1
Winter rye	10.1	11.1	11.1	10.6	14.1	14.2	17.8
Winter barley	10.1	11.1	11.1	10.6	14.1	14.2	26.7
Spring wheat	7.5	8.4	6.1	12.6	19.1	15.3	23.5
Spring barley	9.3	14.2	7.8	17.9	24.5	18.3	24.1
Oats	10.4	12.1	8.9	13.3	20.8	13.2	15.4
Corn	10.2	16.3	15.2	18.1	27.9	24.5	29.0
Millet	9.6	14.7	6.5	13.9	13.3	12.9	14.6
Buckwheat	5.7	8.0	4.8	6.2	7.8	5.4	10.5
Rice	–	28.8	10.9	22.5	51.2	56.1	37.1
Legumes	8.6	10.3	7.6	12.7	16.5	16.5	19.7

that in 1900–10 the steppe produced 5.9 centners per ha, the Left Bank 6.9, and the Right Bank 9.6. In Galicia at the time grain yields were somewhat higher, while in Bukovyna and Transcarpathia they were only slightly higher or about the same as in Russian-ruled Ukraine. In 1913 the average yield in Ukraine as a whole was 9.4 centners per ha (see table 2). The yield of the principal grains was similar to yields in the United States in this period, and greater than those in Canada.

After the revolution the average yield fell somewhat to 8.5–8.9 centners per ha in good harvest years (1923, 1926, 1927) and to 6–7 centners per ha in bad harvest years (1924, 1928). During the collectivization period yields declined, but because of the disruption of the statistics-gathering system, it is difficult to establish exactly by how much. In 1931 the yield was about 8.7 centners per ha; in 1932, 6.6 centners per ha; and in 1933, 7.5 centners per ha. In 1934–5 it did not exceed 6–7 centners per ha, and in 1936 it began to rise. In Galicia, the average yield of the principal grains in 1934–8 was 10.1 centners per ha, while in Volhynia it reached 11.4 centners per ha. From the mid-1950s to the end of the 1960s wheat and barley yields improved considerably, approaching those of the United States and Canada, although the corn yield was only half of North America's. In recent years, although the yield of grain crops in Ukraine is significantly higher than in other grain-producing regions of the USSR, Ukraine's yields have not been rising. In 1975, for example, the grain yield in Ukraine was 20 centners per ha, while the average yield for the USSR was 10.9 centners per ha. At the same time Ukraine's yield of the more important grain crops is below that of other grain-growing countries. In 1975 Hungary produced 38.2 centners per ha, Poland and Romania 24.5, and Czechoslovakia 33.3. The lack of any progress in grain yields during the last decade is a cause of great concern.

In 1913 the gross grain harvest in Russian-ruled Ukraine was 23 million t or 28 percent of the entire harvest in the empire. Of this, the wheat harvest of 8 million accounted for 15 percent of world production. From 1909 to 1913, after meeting domestic demands for food (230 kg of wheat and rye, and 290 kg of all grains per person per year), feed, and seed, Russian-ruled Ukrainian territories exported annually 8 million t of grain, or one-third of their total harvest. This amounted to 80 percent of the grain exports of the empire and 21 percent of world exports. The nine Ukrainian gubernias supplied 6.7 million t (including 3.9 million t by steppe Ukraine), and Kuban supplied 1.4 million t. Ukraine exported more wheat than any other country in the world: 4.3 million t (20 percent of world exports) compared to the United States' 2.7 million t or Argentina's 2.6 million t. Ukraine's barley exports of 2.7 million t accounted for 43 percent of world exports. Ukraine's export of other grains (600,000 t) was not very important. Twenty percent of Ukraine's grain products was sold within the Russian Empire, mostly as flour, while 80 percent was sold abroad, mostly to Germany (barley, wheat), Italy (wheat), Britain, France, and Greece. From 1909 to 1911 the average annual export of grain and flour from the nine Ukrainian gubernias alone was valued at 368 million rubles, or 46.5 percent of the value of all their exports.

After the outbreak of the First World War gross harvests declined, and during 1917–21 they fell catastrophically. In 1921 the gross harvest came to 8.5, and in 1922, 10.5 million t. In 1925–7, 17–18 million t of grain were harvested annually, while in 1932 and 1934 the harvest probably did not exceed 12 million t, and taking into account losses during harvesting, must have been even lower. In 1933 and 1935 harvests were close to 17, and after 1936 remained at about 20 million t. Ukraine's share of the total grain production of the USSR increased in the prewar period to about one-third. However, Ukraine's share of world production fell significantly: in 1938 the republic's wheat harvest amounted to only 5 percent of the world harvest.

From 1946 to 1950 Ukraine produced annually about 17 million t of grain. N. Khrushchev's reforms in the mid-1950s resulted in considerably larger harvests. From 1951 to 1960 they were generally 23–24 million t; from 1961 to 1970, 31 million t; and from 1971 to 1980, 42 million t. The average annual harvest from 1976 to 1980 was 43 million t, or almost double the 1913 harvest. At the same time *grain procurements were reduced because of the vigorous development of animal husbandry. Ukraine's share in world grain production continues to decline (see table 3). At the end of the 1970s the republic produced only 3–3.5 percent of the world's wheat, less than one-fourth of that produced by the United States.

Since 1980, Ukraine and other regions of the USSR have experienced a crisis in grain farming. Gross harvests are no longer increasing, in spite of the intensive use of machinery, fertilizers, chemicals, and plant breeding. Obviously, this is due to the structural defects of the

TABLE 3
Gross grain harvests in thousands of t

	1913	1940	1950	1960	1970	1971	1976–80
All grains	23,157	26,420	20,448	21,790	36,392	33,803	43,151
Wheat	7,970	8,407	6,701	6,788	15,606	18,247	21,968
Rye	4,540	4,097	4,334	1,425	1,176	1,107	1,278
Barley	5,444	5,789	2,159	4,528	8,288	7,576	10,642
Oats	3,026	2,765	1,604	1,160	1,682	1,054	1,492
Corn	870	2,550	4,177	5,531	6,337	3,080	4,353
Millet	502	1,400	1,059	688	694	435	517
Buckwheat	400	581	303	250	285	133	330
Rice	–	5	2	0.4	165	217	142

Soviet agricultural system – lack of incentive for the farming population to improve production – and to soil exhaustion. To achieve the growth rates similar to those of the so-called green revolution, major reforms in farm production and management are necessary. (See also *Agriculture.)

BIBLIOGRAPHY
Narodne hospodarstvo USRR: *Statystychnyi dovidnyk* (Kiev 1935)
Sotsialisticheskoe sel'skoe khoziaistvo Sovetskoi Ukrainy (Kiev 1939)
Karnaukhova, E. *Razmeshchenie sel'skogo khoziaistva Rossii v period kapitalizma, 1860–1914 gg.* (Moscow 1951)
Ocherki razvitiia narodnogo khoziaistva Ukrainskoi SSR (Moscow 1954)
Hurzhii, I. *Rozklad feodal'no-kriposnyts'koï systemy v sil's'komu hospodarstvi Ukraïny pershoï polovyny* XIX *st.* (Kiev 1954)
Arkhimovych, O. 'Zernovi kul'tury v Ukraïni,' *Ukraïns'kyi zbirnyk,* no. 4 (1955)
Posevnye ploshchadi SSSR. *Statisticheskii sbornik,* vol 1 (Moscow 1957)
Bondarenko, V. *Razvitie obshchestvennogo khoziaistva kolkhozov Ukrainy v gody dovoennykh piatiletok* (Kiev 1957)
Materialy po istorii sel'skogo khoziaistva i krest'ianstva SSSR (Moscow 1959)
Narodnoe khoziaistvo SSSR *v 1983 g.* (Moscow 1984)

V. Kubijovyč, S. Maksudov

Grains. The most important group of cultivated plants whose seeds are used as a staple of the human diet, animal feed, and raw material in many industries. The grains are divided into cereals and legumes. Most cereals, including wheat, rye, barley, rice, oats, and corn, belong to the botanical family Gramineae; buckwheat is a member of the family Polygonaceae.

Grain crops have a long history in Ukraine. Evidence suggests that as early as the Neolithic period, in the 5th to 4th centuries BC, wheat, barley, and millet were grown along the Buh and Dniester rivers. In 1913 (within the present boundaries of Ukraine) 24,696,000 ha were devoted to growing grain, or 88 percent of the total cultivated land area in Ukraine. In 1983 the figure was 15,783,000 ha or 48 percent of the area under cultivation in Ukraine. In 1913 the gross grain harvest in Ukraine was 23,157,000 t; in 1980, 38,100,000 t. In 1980 Ukraine accounted for 20 percent of the USSR's gross grain harvest. The average yield of grain crops in Ukraine was 9.4 centners per ha in 1913 and 23.1 centners per ha in 1980. The most important grain crop in Ukraine is winter wheat, followed by spring barley, corn, and peas (see *Grain production).

B. Krawchenko

Grammar. The study of the formation of words, their inflections (morphology), and their functions and relations in the sentence (syntax). The first grammar known in Ukraine was an anonymous translation and adaptation of an unfinished Greek grammatical treatise – 'O osmikh" chastikh" slova, elika pishem" i gl[ago]lem"' (On the Eight Parts of Speech as Written and Spoken), the authorship of which was attributed without foundation in the Middle Ages to St John of Damascus and then to Ioann, the exarch of Bulgaria. The oldest extant manuscript copies of this grammar date from the 16th century and deal only with four parts of speech: the noun, verb, participle, and article. A 15th-century treatise on letters by the Bulgarian Serbian scholar Constantine the Grammarian from Kostenec was also used, though less widely, at the time. 'On the Eight Parts of Speech' became the model for the first Ukrainian printed grammars – I. Fedorovych's primer (1574) and **Khramatyka sloven'ska iazyka* (Grammar of the Slavic Language, 1586). It also had some impact on the more original, larger grammars of the late 16th and early 17th century, whose authors were part of the movement to restore and purify Church Slavonic. The most important were the Greek grammar **Adelphotes* (1591) and the grammars of L. Zyzanii (1596) and M. Smotrytsky (1619); the latter definitely influenced the form of Church Slavonic language in Ukraine, Russia, Serbia, and Croatia. None of these grammars dealt with the vernacular, but only with the language of church ritual and theological writings.

The philosophical-rationalist grammar that became influential in Western Europe at that time had a very limited impact in Ukraine because of the cultural dominance of the church in the 17th century and the general decline of cultural life in the 18th century. Even in the first half of the 19th century ecclesiastical, bookish traditions prevailed in Galicia and Transcarpathia. The grammars of M. Luchkai (1830), Y. Levytsky (1834), and I. Vahylevych (1845) still retained much of the Church Slavonic tradition. The influence of the Romantic approach spread slowly; it was applied hesitantly at first in the grammars of O. Pavlovsky (written before 1805 and published in 1818), I. Mohylnytsky (written before 1824), and Y. Lozynsky (written before 1833 and published in 1846). Thereafter the Romantic approach, which focused on the distinctive features of the folk vernacular as the immutable expressions of the 'spirit of a people,' became a long-standing tradition in Ukrainian grammar and led to an insistence on the preservation and development in the language of all that was 'native' and 'natural' at the expense of that which was 'bookish,' 'false.'

ГРАММАТІКА
СЛОВЕНСКА.
Съставленна, Лаврентіемъ
Зизаніемъ.

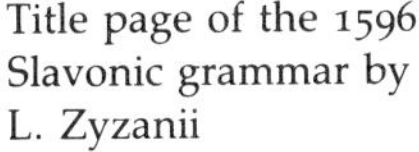
Title page of the 1596 Slavonic grammar by L. Zyzanii

Title page of the 1918 Ukrainian grammar by V. Simovych

The positivist-comparative approach to the study of the Slavic languages, including Ukrainian, began spreading after the publication of *Vergleichende Grammatik der slavischen Sprachen* (vol 1, 1852) by the Serbian scholar F. Miklosich. This new approach was combined with the Romantic one in O. Ohonovsky's *Studien auf dem Gebiete der ruthenischen Sprache* (1880); in P. Zhytetsky's *Ocherk zvukovoi istorii malorusskogo narechiia* (Outline of the Historical Phonology of the Little Russian Dialect, 1876); in the first Galician Ukrainian school grammars, by M. Osadtsa (1862, 1864, 1876), H. Shashkevych (1865), P. Diachan (1865), and O. Partytsky (1873); and even in the first school grammars in Russian-ruled Ukraine, which were permitted to appear after 1905, by P. Zalozny (pt 1, 1906, 1912, 1917; pt 2, 1913), H. Sherstiuk (pt 1, 1907, 1912, 1917; pt 2, 1909, 1917), Ye. Tymchenko (1907, 1917), A. Krymsky (1907), I. Nechui-Levytsky (1914), and O. Kurylo (1917). While O. Potebnia transcended the eclectic, Romantic, and positivist (neogrammarian) combination of approaches found in the books of his predecessors in his synthesizing works on historical syntax, S. Smal-Stotsky and T. Gartner attempted, in their *Grammatik der ruthenischen (ukrainischen) Sprache* (1913), to defend the essentially Romantic approach by means of the neogrammarian method, in a rather mechanical way.

During the period from 1917 to 1933 in Soviet Ukraine, when the Ukrainian literary language underwent substantial standardization, the Romantic approach became more and more obviously puristic. This is evident in such works as O. Kurylo's *Uvahy do suchasnoï ukraïns'koï literaturnoï movy* (Commentaries on the Contemporary Ukrainian Literary Language, 1920, 1923, 1925), V. Simovych's Ukrainian grammars (1919, 1921), I. Ohiienko's *Chystota i pravyl'nist' ukraïns'koï movy* (The Purity and Correctness of the Ukrainian Language, 1925), and especially in S. Smerechynsky's *Narysy z ukraïns'koï syntaksy* (Essays on Ukrainian Syntax, 1932) and Ye. Tymchenko's monographs on functions of grammatical cases (1913–28). In this period most grammar textbooks were also written from the purist perspective (eg, by H. Ivanytsia, M. Hladky, O. Kurylo, P. Horetsky, I. Shalia). A less radically romantic and puristic approach is represented in O. Syniavsky's works, such as *Normy ukraïns'koï literaturnoï movy* (The Norms of the Ukrainian Literary Language, 1931), in *Pidvyshchenyi kurs ukraïns'koï movy* (An Advanced Course in the Ukrainian Language, 1930, prepared by L. Bulakhovsky's followers and edited by him), and in textbooks by O. Syniavsky, M. Sulyma, M. Yohansen, M. Nakonechny, and others.

In the early 1930s such scholars as O. Kurylo and O. Syniavsky became interested in structural linguistics, but this development was cut short by the Stalinist suppression of Ukrainian culture. It has been manifested outside Ukraine, however, in V. Simovych's articles and in Yu. Sherekh's (Shevelov's) *Narys suchasnoï ukraïns'koï literaturnoï movy* (An Outline of the Contemporary Ukrainian Standard Language, 1951). In Ukraine the compulsory method in grammar since the 1930s has been based on a combination of revived logicist-rationalist theory and political propaganda; most books of that time have served to Russify the Ukrainian literary language. The best works published there in the past 50 years are *Kurs suchasnoï ukraïns'koï literaturnoï movy* (A Course in the Contemporary Ukrainian Literary Language, 1951), edited by L. Bulakhovsky, and three volumes of *Suchasna ukraïns'ka literaturna mova* (The Contemporary Ukrainian Literary Language, 1969–72), edited by I. Bilodid. (See also *Lexicology, *Linguistics, and *Syntax.)

G.Y. Shevelov

Grand hetman (*hetman velykyi* or *hetman zemskyi*). Chief military commander in the Grand Duchy of Lithuania. Usually the palatine of Vilnius, originally he was appointed to command only during military campaigns. The formation of armies, their armament, and the state's defense were the responsibility of the *Council of Lords; his duties began after the armies had assembled and concerned such matters as discipline, strategy, and organization; he led the soldiers into battle. The Ukrainian prince K. *Ostrozky (1463–1533) is the first man documented with the title of grand hetman (1497). In the early 16th century the position became a permanent one. In 1568 the grand hetman was given the right to raise money for the maintenance of the army and became the minister of defense, assisted by a field hetman. Until the Union of *Lublin in 1569 he was also a member of the Council of Lords. Poland had an equivalent office, called royal grand hetman.

Grand prince (*velykyi kniaz*). Title of the prince who headed the Riurykid senior princes of Kievan Rus'. From the 10th to the 13th century the title was assumed, as a rule, by the rulers of Kiev. The powers of the grand prince over other princes were limited. In practical terms they consisted of the ability to convene princely congresses, hold supreme command during military campaigns, and exert influence in the appointment of bishops. These powers were gradually constricted, mirroring the collapse of the political order in Kievan Rus' and its fragmentation into appanage principalities. By the end of the 12th century the title itself was used by many other princes and by the second half of the 13th century the Kievan princes had completely lost the right to the name. The title passed to the princes of Galicia-Volhynia and Suzdal-Vladimir.

The title was also frequently claimed by senior princes of other eastern Slavic lands. From the 12th to the 16th century it was adopted by the supreme rulers of Lithuania. After the Union of *Lublin in 1569, the Polish king was also the grand prince of Lithuania. In Russia, after the liquidation of the other principalities, the title was used by the Muscovite princes to signify the supreme ruler of all the Russian lands. The title was used there until 1547, when Grand Prince Ivan IV the Terrible assumed the appellation of tsar. From 1797 until 1886 'grand prince' was used by the tsar's sons, brothers, grandsons, great-grandsons, and great-great-grandsons through the male line. From 1886 to 1917 the use of the title was limited to the tsar's sons, brothers, and nephews.

Granite. A medium- or coarse-grained igneous rock that is rich in quartz, feldspar, and mica. The most common plutonic rock of the earth's crust, granite is valued as a building stone; its better varieties are used for ornamentation. In Ukraine granite and *gneiss are the basic rocks of the *Ukrainian Crystalline Shield; there, in the river valleys, outcrops of granite form a unique landscape. Many varieties of granite, differing in composition, origin, physical properties, color, and economic value, are found in Ukraine. Before the Second World War Ukraine accounted for 25 percent of the granite produced in the USSR. Granite is quarried near Klesiv in Rivne oblast (gray and pink granites); at Novohrad-Volynskyi, Korostyshiv, and Korosten in Zhytomyr oblast and Sudylkiv in Khmelnytskyi oblast (red granite); in the Vinnytsia-Hnivan region (dark-gray granite); along the Ros River (Pohrebyshche, Horodyshche, Bila Tserkva, and Bohuslav); in the Uman-Talne region of Cherkasy oblast; and near Kremenchuk and in the Yanchivske-Natalivka deposit in Zaporizhia oblast. Deposits in the southern Boh River region and the Azov Upland are little exploited because of their distance from transportation facilities.

Alexander Granovsky

Granovsky, Alexander [Hranovs'kyj, Oleksander] (full name: Neprytsky-Hranovsky), b 4 November 1887 in Berezhtsi, Kremianets county, Volhynia gubernia, d 4 November 1976 in St Paul, Minnesota. Zoologist, publicist, community leader, and poet. Granovsky studied at the Kiev Commercial Institute (1909–10) before immigrating to the United States in 1913. He continued his studies at the Sorbonne and University of Wisconsin (PH D, 1926) and taught entomology and economic zoology at the universities of Wisconsin (1922–30) and Minnesota (1930–56). He wrote numerous scientific articles and was a worldwide authority on the biology and taxonomy of the Aphididae, two species of which were named after him: *Calaphis granovskyi* and *Drephanaphis granovskyi*. He also pioneered in studies of insect transmission of plant diseases and was the first entomologist in the United States to carry out large-scale field testing of the insecticide DDT for control of potato insects.

Granovsky was a full member of the Shevchenko Scientific Society and the Ukrainian Academy of Arts and Sciences in the US, president (1935–63) of the Organization for the Rebirth of Ukraine, and member of the senate of the OUN. He was a founding member of and held various positions (from 1944) in the Ukrainian Congress Committee of America. He is the author of many political essays and books, including *Ukraine's Case for Independence* (1940), *Vil'na Ukraïna neobkhidna dlia postiinoho myru* (A Free Ukraine Is Necessary for a Lasting Peace, 1945), and *Na shliakhu do derzhavnosty* (On the Road to Statehood, 1965). His modernist poetry first appeared in the Kiev journals *Ukraïns'ka khata* and *Ridnyi krai*. He wrote seven collections of poetry (1910–14, 1953–64).

C. Spolsky

Grape growing. See Viticulture.

Grapes (*Vitis*; Ukrainian: *vynohrad*). A group of shrubs and vines in the genus *Vitis*. Five species occur in Ukraine; these include the sole native European species, *V. vinifera* L. 1753; an Asian species, *V. amurensis* Rupr. 1859; and three New World species, *V. berlandieri* Planchon 1880, *V. rupestris* Scheele 1848, and *V. vulpina* L. 1753. *V. vinifera* consists of two subspecies, *V. v. sylvestris* (= *V. sylvestris* Gmelin) and *V. v. vinifera* (= *V. v. sativa* Hegi). All cultivated European varieties belong to the subspecies *V. v. vinifera* and were derived, at least in part, by selection from the subspecies *V. v. sylvestris*, although recent hybridization between the two subspecies, as well as with the New World species, makes the taxonomy somewhat confusing. New World species are used as phylloxera-resistant root stocks for cultivars of *V. v. vinifera* or of hybrids between the latter and New World species. Of the 100 or so varieties of *V. v. vinifera* in Ukraine, the most common ones are white and pink shasla, Hamburg muscat, Rhine riesling, pearl of Saba, Matiash yanosh, and Alexandrian muscat.

Grapes are used in making wine, brandy, vodka, alcohol, vinegar, aldehyde, grape juice, syrup, raisins, and jams and are eaten fresh. In the USSR some varieties are considered to have medicinal value in the treatment of anemia, metabolic disorders, and stomach and kidney ailments. Roasted seeds are used as a coffee substitute. Seed oil is used as food, in soap manufacture, and as a fuel. Because of the economic importance of grapes in both agriculture and industry, much effort since 1936 has been put into improving *viticulture. The Ukrainian Scientific Research Institute of Viticulture and Wine Making in Odessa is the main research institution in this field; some research is also carried out in the departments of viticulture of the Odessa and the Crimea agricultural institutes.

C. Spolsky

Graphic art. A form of pictorial art that is predominantly linear in effect and includes original drawings and *illuminations as well as reproductions, such as book *illustrations, *bookplates, *posters, and prints, that are made by various printing techniques (woodcut, engraving, etching, aquatint, *lithography, and the like).

In Ukraine, from the 11th to the 16th century manu-

1

2

3

4

5

6

7

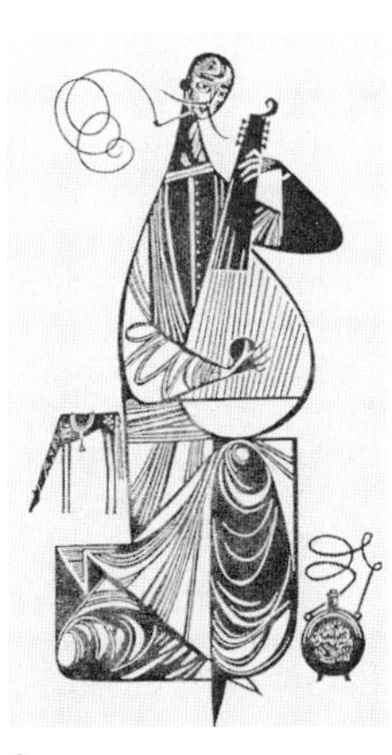

8

9

GRAPHIC ART 1) P. Kovzhun, cover for I. Franko's *Iz dniv zhurby*, 1922. 2) P. Kovzhun, sample initials. 3) I. Ostafiichuk, illustration for *Vona-zemlia* by V. Stefanyk, 1968. 4) J. Hnizdovsky, illustration for *Slovo o polku Ihorevim*, 1950. 5) H. Yakutovych, illustration (woodcut) for *Tini zabutykh predkiv* by M. Kotsiubynsky. 6) O. Hubariev, illustration (linocut) to a Transcarpathian ballad, 1966. 7) R. Lisovsky, cover for *Svitlist'* by Yu. Lypa. 8) M. Levytsky, *Kozak Mamai* (linocut). 9) A. Bazylevych, illustration for *Eneïda* by I. Kotliarevsky.

script books were ornamented with headpieces, initials, tailpieces, and illuminations. Many of these features appeared as well in the first printed books. Lviv became the first center of printing and graphic art after I. *Fedorovych established his printing house there in 1573. One of the first influential engravers was L. Fylypovych-Pukhalsky. Graphic-art centers also arose at presses established in Ostrih, Volhynia (where the Ostrih Bible was published in 1581), in Striatyn and Krylos in Galicia, and finally in Kiev at the highly advanced engraving shop of the Kievan Cave Monastery Press. In the first half of the 17th century T. Petrovych of Kiev, who illustrated the Discourses of St John the Evangelist (1623), and A. Klyryk of Lviv were renowned engravers; other craftsmen are only known by their first name – eg, Luka or Illia – or by the initials they left on their engravings.

Beginning in the second half of the 17th century, in addition to religious themes, secular and everyday subjects, portraits, town plans, etc were depicted in graphic form. Realism, which came to Ukraine with the Renaissance and baroque art, fundamentally changed graphic art. During the Ukrainian baroque period, which coincided with the Hetman state, engraving became highly developed, utilizing not only new forms, but also allegory, symbolism, heraldry, and very ornate decoration. These characteristics suited the belligerency and dynamism of the Cossack era, whose apogee during the hetmancy of I. Mazepa defined the artistic fashion for the late 17th and early 18th centuries. At this time, graphic art began to be used for purposes other than book publishing. An interesting new form, the so-called *tezy* – large graphics on paper or silk, dedicated to famous political or church figures with their portraits and elaborate poetical dedications – became popular.

The turn of the 18th century saw the emergence of the first engraved landscapes – eg, D. Sinkevych's view of the Krekhiv Monastery (1699) – as well as the first engravings with historical themes – eg, N. Zubrytsky's depiction of the siege of Pochaiv (1704). Zubrytsky produced 67 engravings for **Ifika iieropolitika* (1712). He, Sinkevych, and other baroque engravers (eg, Ye. Zavadovsky) came from Western Ukraine. But the main center remained Kiev: engraving was taught at the Kievan Mohyla Academy and the Kievan Cave Monastery Press, whose students were often sent to study abroad, especially in Germany. The most famous Kievan craftsman of the time was the portraitist and illustrator O. Tarasevych (active from 1667 to 1720). His pupil D. Haliakhovsky produced the great *teza* with the portrait of I. Mazepa. Other notable craftsmen were Z. Samoilovych, I. Shchyrsky, L. Tarasevych, I. Strelbytsky, and I. Myhura, who was known for his very personal style incorporating folk art motifs. All these craftsmen were in great demand in Poland, Lithuania, Belorussia, Moldavia, and Muscovy.

After the defeat of Mazepa in 1709, cultural life in Ukraine declined because of Russian political restrictions and the migration of Ukrainian intellectuals and artists to St Petersburg. Nevertheless, Kiev still had such craftsmen as A. Kozachkivsky and especially H. Levytsky, the most prominent Ukrainian engraver of the 18th century who created the large *teza* of Archbishop R. Zaborovsky (1739). In Western Ukraine, particularly in Pochaiv, Volhynia, renowned engravers included Y. and A. Gochemsky and F. Strelbytsky.

Lithography, which was developed in Europe in the 1790s, was taken up by Ukrainian artists in Lviv in 1822, in Kiev from 1828, and later in Odessa and other centers. Etching as a technique was made popular by T. Shevchenko, who in 1844 published an album of six etchings, *Zhivopisnaia Ukraina* (Picturesque Ukraine), and later executed numerous portraits, landscapes, and illustrations. Shevchenko was also a pioneer in modern aquatint.

The 1863 and 1876 Russian prohibitions against Ukrainian-language publications delayed the further development of graphic arts in Ukraine. Conditions improved somewhat at the beginning of the 20th century, and new graphic artists and illustrators appeared, such as I. Izhakevych, S. Vasylkivsky, M. Samokysh, O. Slastion, A. Zhdakha, and in Lviv, O. Kulchytska. All of them were largely influenced by realism. V. Krychevsky first explored the possibilities of a new style, combining elements of traditional Ukrainian printing with popular folk motives and using the latest graphic technology, particularly in book publishing.

The major craftsman of modern Ukrainian graphic art was Yu. *Narbut, who became renowned in St Petersburg in the Russian circle Mir Iskusstva and its journal *Apollon*. After the 1917 Revolution, he returned to Kiev, where he made his most significant contributions to the development of Ukrainian graphic art. His designs of official UNR bank notes, postage stamps, seals, and book decorations are among the finest achievements of Ukrainian graphic art (see *Currency). In these and other works, Narbut aimed at a synthesis of Ukrainian baroque graphic traditions with a modern approach and flowing, rhythmic linearity. At the newly established Ukrainian State Academy of Arts in Kiev, he taught his craft to such artists as L. Lozovsky, M. Kyrnarsky, and R. Lisovsky.

Graphic art was also nurtured by M. Boichuk, who advocated the continuation of Ukrainian artistic traditions, particularly Byzantine ones, through modern art forms; his followers include his wife S. Nalepinska, I. Padalka, O. Sakhnovska, M. Kotliarevska, V. Sedliar, and O. Dovhal. The realist style was espoused by the talented and prolific V. *Kasiian, who produced many engravings and illustrations on political and labor themes; as a professor at the Kharkiv and Kiev art institutes, he had a major influence on the development of socialist realism in graphic art. Other artists such as A. Sereda, A. Strakhov, L. Khyzhynsky, H. Pustoviit, and B. Kriukov also contributed to the development of Soviet Ukrainian graphic art in the 1920s and 1930s.

In interwar Polish-ruled Galicia, there arose in Lviv an important group of graphic artists who were closely connected with artists in other European cities. The more prominent of these were P. Kovzhun, who was well known for his cubist and constructivist book designs, M. Butovych, R. Lisovsky, P. Kholodny Jr, N. Khasevych, V. Tsymbal, V. Masiutyn, H. Mazepa, and E. Kozak. The Lviv exhibit of Ukrainian graphic art in 1932 was one of the biggest events of its kind, with 1,392 works from all branches of the graphic arts, including works by artists from Soviet Ukraine. Ukrainian graphic artists also exhibited in various Western European cities; eg, in Berlin at the State Art Library in 1933 and in Rome in 1938.

Since the Second World War all graphic art in Ukraine has had to conform to the official style of socialist realism and has been used as an instrument in political and economic propaganda. It was only during the brief thaw after Stalin's death that Western influences were allowed. In the last decade a number of new talented artists have attempted to expand the boundaries of socialist realism while remaining faithful to the tradition of the Kasiian school. The more prominent postwar artists of the prerevolutionary generation are M. Derehus, O. Pashchenko, and V. Lytvynenko. Artists born after the revolution include S. Adamovych, A. Bazylevych, O. Danchenko, H. Havrylenko, O. Hubariev, S. Karaffa-Korbut, V. Kutkin, I. Ostafiichuk, V. Panfilov, V. Perevalsky, I. Pryntsevsky, and H. Yakutovych.

After the Second World War many Ukrainian artists emigrated to the West, especially to North and South America, where they continued to make important contributions: eg, J. Hnizdovsky, who settled in the United States and achieved international prominence with his woodcuts, P. Andrusiv, V. Balias, M. Butovych, M. Dmytrenko, I. Keivan, E. Kozak, P. Kholodny Jr, M. Levytsky, H. Mazepa, and V. Tsymbal. A postwar generation of Western graphic artists of Ukrainian origin, including B. Bozhemsky, L. Hutsaliuk, A. Lysak, R. Logush, A. Maday, A. Olenska-Petryshyn, Z. Onyshkevych, and B. Pachovsky, has also arisen; it has been joined by recent Soviet émigrés such as R. Bahautdyn, Yu. Lytvyn, V. Makarenko, and V. Strelnikov. (See also *Art, *Illumination, *Illustration, and *Printing.)

BIBLIOGRAPHY
Makarenko, M. *Ornamentatsiia ukraïns'koï knyzhky XVI–XVII vv.* (Kiev 1926)
Popov, P. *Materiialy do slovnyka ukraïns'kykh graveriv* (Kiev 1926; addendum 1927)
Ksylohrafichni doshky Lavrs'koho muzeiu (Kiev 1927)
Kataloh hrafichnoï vystavky ANUM (Lviv 1932)
Antonowytsch, D. *Katalog der Ausstellung ukrainischer Graphik* (Berlin 1933)
Sichyns'kyi, V. *Istoriia ukraïns'koho graverstva XVI–XVII st.* (Lviv 1937)
Hrafika v bunkrakh UPA (Philadelphia 1952)
Kataloh vystavky mysttsiv suchasnoï ukraïns'koï knyzhnoï hrafiky (Toronto 1956)
Vrona, I. *Ukraïns'ka radians'ka hrafika* (Kiev 1958)
Zapasko, Ia. *Ornamental'ne oformlennia ukraïns'koï rukopysnoï knyhy* (Kiev 1960)
Kasiian, V.; Turchenko, Iu. *Ukraïns'ka dozhovtneva realistychna hrafika* (Kiev 1961)
Turchenko, Iu. *Ukraïns'kyi estamp* (Kiev 1964)
Stepovyk, D. *Vydatni pam'iatky ukraïns'koho hraverstva XVII stolittia* (Kiev 1970)
Ketsalo, Z. (comp). *Hrafika L'vova* (Kiev 1971)
Ovdiienko, O. *Knyzhkove mystetstvo na Ukraïni, 1917–1974* (Kiev 1974)
Lohvyn, H. *Z hlybyn: Davnia knyzhkova miniatiura XI–XVIII stolit'* (Kiev 1974)
Stepovyk, D. *Oleksandr Tarasevych: Stanovlennia ukraïns'koï shkoly hraviury na metali* (Kiev 1975)
Fomenko, V. *Hryhorii Levyts'kyi i ukraïns'ka hraviura* (Kiev 1976)
Stepovyk, D. *Ukraïns'ka hrafika XVI–XVIII stolit': Evoliutsiia obraznoï systemy* (Kiev 1982)

S. Hordynsky

Graphite (Ukrainian: *hrafit*). A naturally occurring form of carbon having high electrical conductivity, chemical inertness, and lubricity. It is widely used in metallurgical, chemical, nuclear, electrotechnical, and other industries. Ukraine is the major producer of graphite for the USSR. It is found in crystalline veins in Precambrian gneisses, primarily in three regions: western Kirovohrad oblast (the Zavallia deposit, with current reserves of 25 million t), the Kryvyi Rih region around Petrivske (with reserves of 7.5 million t), and near Staryi Krym in southern Donets oblast (with reserves of 3.4 million t). Ukrainian graphite is very flaky, the ores containing concentrations of 17–70 percent. In Ukraine there are two enrichment plants, which process the ore from neighboring mines, in Zavallia and Staryi Krym.

Gratovich, Eugene [Gratovyč, Jevhen], b 26 September 1941 in Alchevske, Luhanske oblast. Violinist, educator. He studied violin with J. Heifetz, and completed his music studies at the Boston Conservatory and Boston University (DMA 1968). At age 16 he was appointed soloist with the Philadelphia Orchestra. For his debut at Carnegie Hall, New York, in 1976 he performed works by J. Carpenter, C. Ives, A. von Webern, and S. Prokofiev. He has taught music at De Paul University and at the universities of Missouri and California–San Diego. In 1979 he recorded an album with V. Baley and B. Turetzky, *20th Century Ukrainian Violin Music*. He is a leading authority on, and performer of, C. Ives.

Grave, Dmytro, b 6 September 1863 in Kirillov, Novgorod gubernia, d 19 December 1939 in Kiev. Mathematician; from 1919 full member of the AN URSR, from 1923 full member of the Shevchenko Scientific Society, and from 1929 honorary member of the Academy of Sciences of the USSR. After obtaining a doctorate from St Petersburg University in 1897, he was first a professor at Kharkiv University (till 1899) and then at Kiev University (till 1939). From 1934 to 1939 he was also director of the AN URSR Institute of Mathematics in Kiev, where he made important contributions to Galois theory, the theory of ideals, number theory, the three-body problem, and equations of the 5th degree. Later, he contributed to the advancement of applied mathematics, mathematical physics, and mechanics. Grave is regarded as the founder of the Kiev school of algebra, which became the center of algebraic studies for the entire USSR. Besides numerous research articles, Grave wrote several books, including *Teoriia konechnykh grupp* (The Theory of Finite Groups, 1908), *Kurs algebraicheskogo analiza* (A Course of Algebraic Analysis, 1910), and *Teoreticheskaia mekhanika na osnove tekhniki* (Theoretical Mechanics Based on Technology, 1932).

Gray Ukrainian cattle. See Great horned cattle.

Graycoats (Sirozhupannyky). The popular name of an infantry division formed by the Austrian army in Volodymyr-Volynskyi during March–August 1918. Recruited from among Ukrainian prisoners of war in Austria, it was officially designated the First Rifle-Cossack Division, under the command of Col I. Perlyk. It was composed of four infantry regiments and various other combat and support units, with a total strength of 6,140. On 28 August 1918, the Graycoats were transferred to the Ukrainian Hetman government army and stationed in the vicinity of Konotip. In October 1918, the division was reduced in strength, but during the November insurrection it declared its allegiance to the UNR Directory and was reinforced with insurgents. Reorganized in December 1918 as the Gray Division of the *Army of the

The Graycoat Division on parade, Kiev, 15 August 1918

UNR and placed under the command of Gen A. Puzytsky, it fought against Bolshevik forces on the Ovruch–Korosten–Berdychiv line. In April 1919 it was expanded into a corps unit of two infantry divisions and transferred to the Polish front, where in May it was decimated in combat against the Polish army. Subsequently, the unit was reformed as the 4th Gray Division with a strength of 700, then reduced to a brigade of the 2nd Volhynian Division; it participated in combat until November 1920. Other commanders of the Graycoats included Otaman Palii, Lt Col Abaza, Gen Martyniuk, and Col Handzha.

Graywolves Company of the Ukrainian Insurgent Army (Sotnia Siromantsi). A combat unit of the UPA in Galicia, organized in October 1943 near Dolyna in the Carpathian Mountains, in the 4th UPA Military District (MD – Stanyslaviv region) of UPA-West. It was initially commanded by Lt D. *Karpenko. In November 1943, the Graywolves was assigned to the 3rd MD (Ternopil region) and sent northwest to the 2nd MD (Lviv region) to fight against the Polish Home Army in the Rava-Ruska area. The Graywolves operated in that area from April through August 1944, and then returned to the 3rd MD. On 30 September 1944, the Graywolves played a key role in a battle with a motorized NKVD battalion near Univ (now Mizhhiria), Peremyshliany county. For the remainder of 1944, the company participated in almost continuous armed combat, culminating on 17 December 1944 in a successful attack on Novi Strilyshcha. Lt Kosach committed suicide in March 1946 when his bunker was discovered by Soviet security forces, and the last skirmish attributed to the Graywolves occurred on 15 July 1946. During the summer of 1947, the company was officially demobilized. It was one of the few UPA units that integrated soldiers from various parts of Ukraine.

P.R. Sodol

Graz. City in Austria (1984 pop 246,000), capital of Styria province. A Ukrainian community, mostly of students from Galicia and Bukovyna, was established there in the late 19th century. The Rus' mutual aid association was organized there in 1895 and renamed the Ukrainian students' society *Sich in 1910. The 50 Ukrainian students in Graz after the First World War grew to about 200 after the Second World War, when many displaced persons enrolled at the university; they published the journal *Students'kyi klych* in 1947. Ukrainian language and literature were taught at Graz University. From 1945 to 1949 a Ukrainian refugee representation in Styria, directed by V. Tymtsiurak, was based there. Today the Ukrainian community in Graz is very small. The history of Ukrainian student life has been documented in the collection *Ukraïn'skyi Grats-Leoben* (Ukrainian Graz-Leoben, 1985), edited by M. Chyrovsky.

Grazhda

Grazhda. Archaic form of an enclosed, rectangular farmstead constructed of logs. It consisted of a house with a steep two- or four-sided roof and a veranda and windows facing the yard, and such farm buildings as a storehouse, stable, sheepfold, sty, separate root cellar, shelter annex, and woodshed. The buildings were arranged in such a way as to protect the yard from snow and predators. *Grazhdy* were common in the Carpathian Mountains, particularly in the Hutsul region. Examples of them have been preserved at the Ukrainian SSR (Kiev), Lviv, and Transcarpathian (Uzhhorod) museums of folk architecture and folkways. The *zymivka*, *zymarka*, and *salash* are simplified winter variants of the *grazhda*. The *grazhda* is related to the so-called Etruscan house, which is known to have been used as early as the 8th century BC. F. Vovk believed that the *grazhda* is the oldest form of Ukrainian residential building, and traced back to it the whole evolution of farmsteads in Ukraine.

BIBLIOGRAPHY
Sičinskyj, V. *Dřevěné stavby v Karpatské oblasti* (Prague 1940)

Grazhdanka alphabet. See Hrazhdanka alphabet.

Great Britain (official name: United Kingdom of Great Britain and Northern Ireland). A constitutional monarchy, its territory covers 244,100 sq km, and its population in 1985 was 56,520,000, including about 30,000 Ukrainians. The capital is London.

Ukrainian-British contacts. At first, relations between Ukraine and Great Britain were sporadic. According to the sagas, after Canute's conquest of England in 1016 the sons of the English king Edmund II found refuge in Kiev. *Gytha, the daughter of King Harold II, was married to Prince Volodymyr Monomakh and brought an English retinue with her to Kiev. Besides dynastic ties, there was some trade between the two countries. In the 12th century a Scottish monastery and church were built in Kiev. For the next few centuries, however, British-Ukrainian relations were interrupted. In the 15th century grain and lumber began to be exported via the Baltic Sea from Ukraine to Britain. At the beginning of the 17th century the noble Yu. *Nemyrych studied at Oxford and Cambridge.

In the 17th century English readers began to take an interest in the Cossacks, receiving much of their information through the English legation in Turkey. R. Knolles, in his *The Generall Historie of the Turks* (1603), described Cossack naval expeditions on the Black Sea. English official circles were especially interested in the Cossacks as potential allies in their conflict with the European Catholic states, including Poland-Lithuania, in the early 17th century. Newspapers such as *Mercurius Politicus, London Gazette, The Moderate Intelligencer,* and *Several Proceedings* informed the English public about developments in Ukraine under B. Khmelnytsky and subsequent hetmans. The diary of P. Gordon, a Scottish general of the Russian army, contained much interesting information about Ukraine. Other early sources of information about Ukraine included E. Browne's translation of P. Chevalier's *Histoire de la guerre des Cosaques contre la Pologne* titled *A Discourse of the Origin, Countrey, Manners, Governement and Religion of the Cossacks ...* (1672), P. Heylyn's world geography (1666), A. Tyler's *Memoires of John the Great ... Present King of Poland ...* (1685), Fr P. D'Alerac's *Les Anecdotes de Pologne* (English edn 1700), and F. Tellow's *The Ancient and Present State of Moskovy ...* (1698). A collection of letters by the personal physician to the Polish king John III, B. Connor, to various English dignitaries was published in 1690 as *The History of Poland ...* One of these letters, to William, Duke of Devonshire and Lord Steward, contained an especially detailed description of Ukraine and the Cossacks.

In the 18th century Peter I's victory over Charles XII of Sweden and Hetman I. Mazepa at the Battle of Poltava (1709) again aroused the British public's interest in Ukraine. British diplomats and envoys, who were alarmed by the growth of Russian power, followed closely developments in Ukraine, and especially Ukrainian independence sentiments. P. Orlyk, the émigré hetman of Ukraine, maintained contacts with British government circles. A translation of G. de Beauplan's *Description d'Ukranie,* published in J. Churchill's collection of travel accounts (1704), was widely read. J. James, J. Marshall, E. Clarke, and others wrote descriptions of Ukraine in the 18th and early 19th century. Lord Byron's romantic tale *Mazeppa: A Poem* (1819) did much to popularize the famous hetman in the 19th century. At the end of the 18th century the British government defended non-Catholics who were being persecuted in the Polish Commonwealth.

In the 1860s British economic ties with Ukraine expanded. The New Russia Ironworks Company (est 1870), founded by J. Hughes and funded mostly by British capital, provided strong competition for Belgian, French, and Russian companies. In the 1870s it established a metallurgical plant in Bakhmut county, which used Donbas coal to process iron ore brought in from Kryvyi Rih. By the turn of the century it was one of the largest providers of iron and metal products for both the imperial Russian economy and for export. Meanwhile, in Galicia several petroleum consortiums were organized to exploit the resources in the Drohobych region: the Anglo-Austrian Society in Tustanovychi (est 1906), the Anglo-Polish Trade Society (est 1908), and the English Stock Company in Lviv (est 1912). From 1904 R. Zalozetsky-Sas acted as honorary British consul in Lviv. Around the turn of the century Britain was a major consumer of Ukrainian grain and sugar (as much as one-third of all Ukrainian exports of the latter), as well as of substantial quantities of livestock and iron ore.

In the second half of the 19th century English works on Ukrainian folklore and literature began to appear in print; eg, W. Morfill's articles on T. Shevchenko, E. Voynich's collection of Shevchenko translations (1911), and later works by R. Seton-Watson, A. Toynbee, W. Napier, and C. Macartney. The journal *Athenaeum* published some articles and reviews of Ukrainian subjects, including a description of the Kiev branch of the Russian Geographical Society by M. Drahomanov. Between 1912 and 1915 G. *Raffalovich (pseud: Bedwin Sands), a Jew from Ukraine, advocated Ukrainian independence in his numerous journalistic writings until he was forced to leave Britain, having been accused of pro-German sympathies. Raffalovich also translated M. Hrushevsky's *The Historical Evolution of the Ukrainian Problem* (London 1915). After the Second World War W. Matthews, a Slavist, and the historian H. Seton-Watson published studies on Ukraine.

The attitude of the British government to Ukrainian independence was reserved, but not hostile. In December 1917 J.P. Bagge was sent to Kiev to represent Great Britain in the UNR. The UNR Directory sent a diplomatic mission to Great Britain – headed by M. Stakhovsky and then by A. Margolin and Ya. Olesnytsky – but it did not receive official recognition from Britain. The mission of the Western Ukrainian National Republic also was not formally recognized. The work of these missions was limited to informing the British public about Ukrainian affairs and to preparing several memorandums. The British government actively supported the White armies of generals A. Denikin and P. Wrangel.

During the Paris Peace Conference various solutions to the problem of eastern (Ukrainian) Galicia were considered by the British government, including its incorporation into Czechoslovakia or a non-Bolshevik Russia and its inclusion as an autonomous territory in the Polish Republic. The *Curzon Line, which was proposed by the British foreign secretary, Lord G. Curzon, was adopted by the Allied Supreme Council as Poland's eastern border, and after the Yalta Conference (1945) it became the basis of the Polish-Ukrainian border.

During the interwar period protests against anti-Ukrainian policies of the Polish authorities were often voiced in Britain. The British press, and particularly the *Manchester Guardian,* criticized the so-called *Pacification. An objective report on the campaign by M. Sheepshanks, the general secretary of the International Women's Union who visited eastern Galicia immediately after the Pacification, appeared in the *Manchester Guardian Weekly*. The British consul in Warsaw spent much of the autumn of 1930 in Lviv, keeping his government informed of events in Galicia. On 5 October 1932 a group of 32 MP's and five members of the House of Lords submitted the 'Petition to the League of Nations concerning the Ukrainian Minority in Poland and the Question of the Establishment of an Autonomous Regime in the Territory Known as Eastern Galicia ...'

In 1933 the British government became even more interested in Ukraine. Its missions in Warsaw and Moscow were instructed to follow closely Ukrainian affairs. M. Muggeridge, an English correspondent in Moscow, sent in accurate reports on the man-made *famine in Ukraine. Questions about the famine were raised in the House of Commons. For much of this period T. Philipps, the British relief commissioner in 'South Russia' in 1921, was one of the more influential British officials who was knowledgeable about Ukrainian affairs.

From 1932 to 1939 V. *Kaye-Kysilevsky directed the Ukrainian Press Bureau in London, which was financed by Ya. Makohin. In 1933–5 Ye. Liakhovych acted as the representative of the OUN in London and in the late 1930s the Ukrainian Canadian S. Davidovich ran the Ukrainian Information Bureau there. A group of Hetmanite supporters published *The Investigator*, an English-language information bulletin edited by V. Korostovets.

In 1935 the Anglo-Ukrainian Committee was formed in London to promote the cause of Ukrainian independence. Its members included Lord Dickinson, Mrs Dugdale, G. Gooch, L. Lawton, F. Lincoln, C. Macartney, Col C. L'Estrange Malone, G. le M. Mander, Sir W. Napier, and M. Sheepshanks.

After the Second World War the British government supported the Soviet annexation of Galicia. In a House of Commons debate on 21 February 1945, A. Eden argued that the annexation would strengthen Ukraine's political and ethnic unity. In 1947 and 1950 the British government tried to establish diplomatic relations with the Ukrainian SSR, but it could not gain the approval of the Soviet authorities in Moscow.

In the 1950s the Scottish League for European Freedom in Edinburgh, headed by D. Stewart, maintained close ties with the *Anti-Bolshevik Bloc of Nations and the OUN (Bandera faction), and in its publications supported the idea of Ukrainian independence. A number of English politicians were members of the Anglo-Ukrainian Society, which was organized by A. *Herbert. In 1951 some House of Commons members proposed that a Ukrainian radio program on the BBC be established, but failed to win majority support. In the 1960s the Anglo-Ukrainian Mazeppa Society was founded.

Ukrainians in Great Britain. There were a few Ukrainians in Great Britain before 1939: members of diplomatic missions from the period of Ukrainian independence, a group of political émigrés, and a small number of students. There was also a community of Ukrainian workers in Manchester, who in 1893 on their way to North America had decided to stay in England. By 1912 the community numbered 500. Most of them immigrated to the United States before the outbreak of war in 1914. Those who remained worked mostly as tailors and had their own Ukrainian Club (est 1929). After the fall of France in 1940 some Ukrainian soldiers in the Polish army went to England. During the Second World War a representative of the Government-in-exile of the UNR, V. Solovii, was active in London. D. Skoropadsky, a leader of the Hetmanite movement, lived in London during the war.

Ukrainians appeared in Britian in larger numbers during and immediately after the war. Among them were soldiers of the Canadian armed forces and of the Polish army, some of them evacuated from France but most (about 6,000 members of Gen W. Anders's corps) brought in from Italy. The first Ukrainians in the *Division Galizien (eventually totaling 8,361 men) arrived as contract laborers in Britain from the British POW camp in Rimini, Italy in April 1947. In June the so-called European Voluntary Workers who were recruited by special commissions in the British zones in Germany and Austria began to arrive; within two years 21,000–24,000 Ukrainians, including about 5,000 women, came in under this classification. People with higher education were not admitted, and elderly people were accepted very reluctantly. About 2,000 Ukrainian women from Yugoslavia and Poland were admitted in subsequent years on invitation from prospective husbands. Ukrainian men married Italian, German, and Irish women, but rarely English women. At the beginning of the 1950s Ukrainians began to emigrate from Britain to North America. Eventually, 8,000–10,000 individuals left.

Ukrainian veterans of the Polish army were treated on a par with Poles and Englishmen; they had a free choice of occupation and residence. Members of the Division

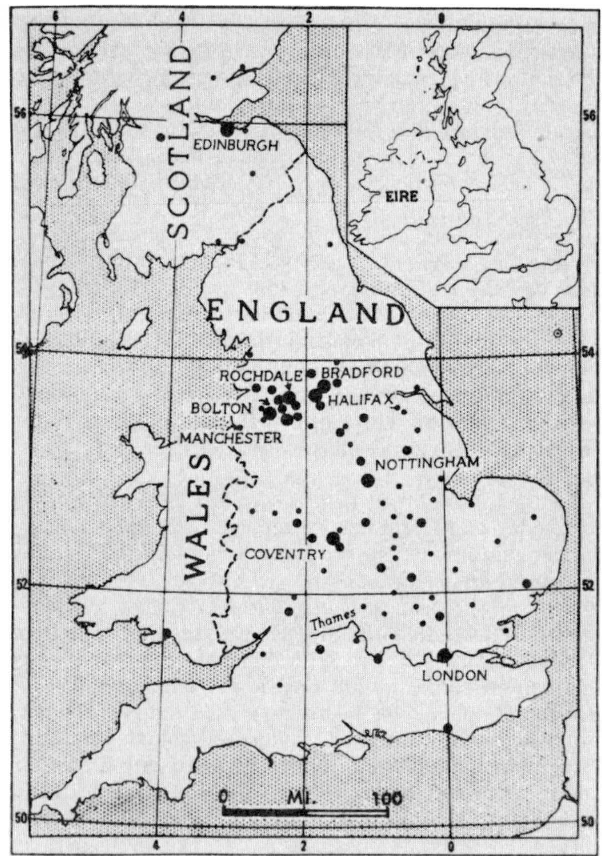

Major concentrations of Ukrainians in Great Britain

Galizien, however, continued to be treated as prisoners, living in hostels and working as farm laborers; only at the end of 1948 and the beginning of 1949 were they freed from their obligations and restrictions and allowed to work and live where they desired. The European Voluntary Workers were contracted for three years of regimented labor on farms, in textile factories or coal mines, as hospital orderlies, or as domestic help, after which they too became free workers. All foreign workers received the same wages as British workers. Ukrainians tended to move from the farms into the cities, taking jobs as unskilled labor in transport (railways and buses) and the textile, coal, and construction industries. Many with some secondary education tried to upgrade their education to qualify for a white-collar job. Women tended to work as nurses. Ukrainians of the younger generation (born in Britain) usually do not attend university and are satisfied with a secondary education and vocational training. A large proportion of them, particularly women, work as teachers or as office clerks. Only a few (600–800) have completed university studies and become professionals. In 1983 S. Terlecky, a Ukrainian, was elected as a Conservative to the House of Commons.

The overwhelming majority of Ukrainians in Britain (75–80 percent) own their own homes, and 5–7 percent own more than one house. Relatively few postwar immigrants – usually only those with some education – have applied for British citizenship; Ukrainians born in Britain have become citizens automatically. In general, Ukrainians have a good reputation among the British: they are believed to be thrifty, enterprising, hard working, and conscientious. They are also quick to attain a decent standard of living. Two-thirds of Ukrainian immigrants in Britain are Galicians; the rest come from other parts of Ukraine.

The territorial distribution of Ukrainians in Britain has changed dramatically. Immediately after the war, about 10,000 Ukrainians lived in Scotland, but by 1980 at most 1,000 remained there. There are almost no Ukrainians in northern Wales or in Northern Ireland, and only 250–300 in southern Wales. Ukrainians are concentrated mostly in London and in central England – in Manchester and vicinity (Rochdale, Bolton, Bury); in the textile region of Leeds, Bradford, Halifax, and Huddersfield; in the heavy-industry region of Birmingham, Coventry, and Wolverhampton; and in Nottingham and Leicester. In 1985 there were about 1,500 Ukrainians in London, 2,000 in Nottingham, 2,000 in Bradford, and 4,000 in metropolitan Manchester.

Religion. Of the 30,000 Ukrainians in Great Britain in 1985, 3,500–4,000 were Orthodox, 21,000–22,000 were Ukrainian Catholic, and the rest belonged to other denominations or to none at all.

The first Ukrainian priests were chaplains of the Canadian armed forces – Rev S. Savchuk (Orthodox) and Rev M. Horoshko (Catholic) – who arrived in the summer of 1944. In 1946 Rev J. Jean, a Basilian monk, was sent from Canada. Ukrainian Catholics in Britain came under the jurisdiction of the apostolic visitator of Ukrainians in Western Europe. From the end of 1946 this office was held by Bishop I. Buchko, who visited England in early 1947 and, with the co-operation of the British hierarchy, established the organizational structure for Ukrainian Catholics. Rev J. Jean, who later became general vicar, was appointed to the London parish and assigned eight

Ukrainian Catholic Cathedral in London

priests (four former chaplains of the Division Galizien, two former chaplains of Anders's corps, and two priests sent from Rome) to serve all of Britain. The first church was established in London in Saffron Hill, and congregational centers were set up in Manchester, Nottingham, Rochdale, Bradford, Cambridge, and Edinburgh. The arrival of more priests from Germany increased the total number to 17. In 1949 Rev V. Malanchuk became vicar-general; he was succeeded in 1950 by Rev O. Malynovsky and in 1957 by Rev P. Maliuga. An exarchate (from 1967 an apostolic exarchate), initially headed by the archbishop of Westminster, W. Godfrey, was set up for Ukrainians in 1957. In 1961 he was replaced by Bishop A. Horniak. A large Ukrainian Catholic cathedral was opened in the following year in the Mayfair district of London. In 1985 the exarchate encompassed 16 churches and 13 priests in England and Scotland.

Two priests and their congregations remain outside the jurisdiction of the exarch because of a major controversy that developed in the 1970s between Bishop Horniak and Archbishop Major Y. Slipy over the problem of a Ukrainian Catholic patriarchate. They formed first the Central Committee for a Ukrainian Catholic Patriarchate and then the Ukrainian Catholic Patriarchate Lay Association, which in 1985 represented 75 branches and 16 member organizations with about 5,000 members.

Most Orthodox Ukrainians in Britain belong to the Western European Metropolitanate of the *Ukrainian Autocephalous Orthodox church. The first Orthodox congregations arose in the 1940s when about 5,000 Orthodox laymen and a number of priests arrived from Germany as European voluntary workers. An administrative board for England headed by Rev I. Hubarzhevsky and then by Rev S. Molchanivsky was elected. A Ukrainian Orthodox bishop for Great Britain – V. Didovych – was not appointed until 1983. Since 1948 over 30 priests have ministered to the Ukrainian Orthodox in England. Today there are eight priests and two deacons. There are five Orthodox churches but 18 parish centers. Parishes that do not have their own churches conduct services in Anglican churches. In 1977 a Ukrainian Orthodox cathedral, religious center, and episcopal residence were established in London.

In the 1960s and 1970s a small number of Orthodox Ukrainians belonged to the Ukrainian Autocephalous Orthodox Church (Conciliar), which was led by Rev I. Hubarzhevsky. A number of congregations of the All-Ukrainian Evangelical Baptist Fellowship are still active in Britain.

Civic and political organizations. During the Second World War the *Ukrainian Canadian Servicemen's Association was established in London. It, in turn, organized the *Central Ukrainian Relief Bureau to assist the *displaced persons in Europe. In January 1946 the *Association of Ukrainians in Great Britain (SUB) was organized, mostly by Ukrainian soldiers of the Polish army. By the beginning of 1947 its membership numbered 1,430. As the influx of refugees from Europe increased, SUB membership grew rapidly and by 1949 reached 22,000. A power struggle within the association culminated in the victory of the OUN (Bandera faction) at the convention of March 1949, and the secession of the defeated minorities, who formed the *Federation of Ukrainians in Great Britain. This schism in the Ukrainian community of Great Britain has had a decisive influence in almost all facets of community life.

SUB remains the largest Ukrainian organization in Britain: almost 27,000 people have passed through its ranks. At the end of 1984 it had 58 branches, 12 local chapters, and a membership of 16,700. Other important organizations include the *Ukrainian Former Combatants in Great Britain, which in the 1950s had a membership of 4,000 and in 1986 still had 1,740 members and 50 branches; the Bandera faction's *Ukrainian Youth Association (est 1948), which once claimed a membership of close to 5,000 and in 1986 still had about 3,000 members; and the *Association of Ukrainian Women in Great Britain, with 2,500–2,800 members. The *Plast Ukrainian scouting organization was established in Great Britain in 1950; in 1985 it had 215 members.

Every Ukrainian émigré political party has some sympathizers in Great Britain, but the most numerous and active force consists of supporters of the Bandera faction. Adherents of this group have gained control of most Ukrainian organizations, the press, and economic institutions (several co-operative unions) in Great Britain. Supporters of the Hetmanite movement, which had some influence while D. Skoropadsky was alive, have collaborated with the Bandera faction. The Federation of Ukrainians in Great Britain is controlled by the OUN (Melnyk faction). In the past the Ukrainian Revolutionary Democratic party, which controlled the Petliura Legion, and the supporters of the *Ukrainian National Council, who formed the Ukrainian Association of Great Britain, had some influence in the Ukrainian community. The Ukrainian-Polish Society, of which K. Zelenko is copresident, has a membership of 190 and is still politically active.

Education. In the immediate postwar years there were few Ukrainian children of school age in Great Britain. Their numbers began to increase from the end of the 1950s as children born in Britain reached school age. Ukrainian schools were organized by SUB, the Union of Ukrainian Teachers and Instructors (est 1955), and a few other associations. By the mid-1960s there were 45 Ukrainian Saturday schools, with a total enrollment of about 3,000. At the same time there were 15 Ukrainian nurseries with about 200 children. Up to 230 individuals taught in these institutions. Eventually, the number of students and schools declined: by 1984 there were 14 schools with an enrollment of 350. Most teachers now are graduates of Ukrainian Saturday schools. Since 1980 the teachers' union has been headed by B. Marchenko.

The number of Ukrainian students attending British post-secondary schools peaked in the 1970s: in 1973 it was over 700. The Ukrainian Student Club at the time had over 100 members. The Ukrainian Graduate Society, whose membership consists of recent graduates of higher schools, conducts cultural and social activities at an academic level. In 1979 a branch of the Ukrainian Catholic University was set up in London.

Literature, art, music, and science. There are not many Ukrainian intellectuals or writers in England. Some of the writers who lived there are V. Shaian, S. Fostun (president of the Society of Ukrainian Litterateurs since 1976), and the poets B. Bora (Shkandrii), H. Mazurenko, and A. Lehit. The English poet V. Rich has translated Ukrainian literature. Several Ukrainian émigré scholars have worked in England: the archeologist V. Shcherbakivsky, the historian P. Fedenko, the forester O. Paramoniv, the biochemist M. Zakomorny, and the Slavist V. Swoboda. Well-known artists have included the painters V. Perebyinis, H. Mazurenko, and R. Hluvko; the graphic artists R. Lisovsky and I. Voloshchak; and the enamelist M. Ladyk.

The best Ukrainian choir in Great Britain is Homin (formerly Burlaka) in Manchester, which won first prize at an international competition in Llangollen, Wales; its conductors have been Ye. Pasika (until 1965) and Ya. Babuniak. The Orlyk dance ensemble, directed by P. Dnistrovyk and M. Babych, has received international recognition. A number of dance and instrumental ensembles are supported by local branches of the Ukrainian Youth Association. V. Lutsiv, a bandura player and impresario, is also active in Ukrainian musical life.

Publishing. The Ukrainian Publishers, Ltd has been an important publisher for the Bandera faction not only in Britain, but in the West as a whole. The firm has published SUB weekly **Ukraïns'ka dumka*, the journals **Vyzvol'nyi shliakh*, **Ukrainian Review*, and *Holos molodi*, and belletristic and publicistic works. The veterans' quarterly **Surmach* still appears, but the socialist journal *Nashe slovo* and the monarchist newspaper *Ranok* were short-lived. A number of religious periodicals have been published in England: the Catholic journal *Nasha tserkva* (1953–75), the Orthodox *Vidomosti Heneral'noho tserkovnoho upravlinnia UAPTs* (since 1950), and the Baptist quarterly *Visnyk spasinnia* (since 1949). A group of Ukrainian students and graduates known as the Vitrage Society published the journal *Vitrazh* (1977–83).

General features and prospects. From its beginning the Ukrainian community in Great Britain had some distinctive features: it consisted mostly of young men who had served the cause of Ukrainian independence during the Second World War. Because of their age and political experience, the first generation of emigrants was extremely active, in comparison with other emigrant groups, in community affairs: almost 80 percent of all Ukrainians belonged to Ukrainian organizations and churches. The high degree of political commitment facilitated the dominance of the community by radicals. Furthermore, the religious conflict within the Catholic church had a detrimental effect on the community. As a result of a shortage of Ukrainian women, quite a few postwar imigrant men remained single and the number of mixed marriages was high, making it difficult to maintain the Ukrainian language and culture among the second generation. Consequently a relatively small proportion of young people of Ukrainian origin attend Ukrainian schools and belong to Ukrainian youth organizations today, and the process of linguistic assimilation has advanced quite far.

With the passing of the older generation, the dynamism of the Ukrainian community has declined in the 1980s. This is evident from the falling membership of Ukrainian organizations and the declining circulation of the Ukrainian press. And the occupational profile of the Ukrainian community is changing: the younger generation is entering the professions and is advancing beyond its elders in economic status. Those who remain conscious of their ethnic identity continue to participate in community life, which is changing in form and content.

BIBLIOGRAPHY

Borshak, E. 'Early Relations between England and Ukraine,' *Slavonic Review*, no. 28 (1931–2)

Wynar, L. 'The Question of Anglo-Ukrainian Relations in the Middle of the Seventeenth Century,' AUA, 7, nos 21–2 (1958)

Nerhood, H. (comp). *To Russia and Return: An Annotated Bibliography of Travelers' English-Language Accounts of Russia from the Ninth Century to the Present* (Columbus, Ohio 1968)

Danyliv, T. *Kudy ide nasha hromada u Velykobritanii* (Munich 1970)

Zelenko, K. 'Velykobritaniia i Ukraïna,' in *Ievhen Konovalets' ta ioho doba* (Munich 1974)

Petryshyn, R. 'Ukraïntsi v Velykobritanii,' in *Ukraïns'ki poselennia: Dovidnyk*, ed A. Milianych et al (New York 1980)

– 'Britain's Ukrainian Community: A Study of the Political Dimension in Ethnic Development.' PH D diss, University of Bristol 1980

Luciuk, L.Y. *Heroes of Their Day: The Reminiscences of Bohdan Panchuk* (Toronto 1983)

Saunders, D. 'Aliens in Britain and the Empire during the First World War,' in *Loyalties in Conflict: Ukrainians in Canada during the Great War*, eds F. Swyripa and J. Thompson (Edmonton 1983)

M.D. Dobriansky

Great Horde. See Tatars.

Great horned cattle (*Bos taurus;* Ukrainian: *velyka rohata khudoba*). Species of domestic cow, *Bos taurus*, which originated most probably from the extinct wild *aurochs and was domesticated a few thousand years ago. Great horned cattle are an important source of milk, meat, and leather and, previously, of fertilizer and draft power as well. They are particularly valued for high milk productivity (up to 8.2 kg of good-quality milk per day).

The main breeds of great horned cattle in Ukraine are the Simmental, Red Steppe, Lebedyn, Spotted Black, Gray Ukrainian, White-headed Ukrainian, Red Polish,

Great horned cow

and Carpathian Brown. Of these, the Simmental and Red Steppe breeds constitute 80 percent of the cattle on collective and state farms. The Simmental, a meat and dairy breed developed in Switzerland, was introduced in Ukraine in the second half of the 19th century. The crossing of Simmental bulls with Gray Ukrainian cows produced a Ukrainian subbreed of Simmentals. The Red Steppe, one of the better dairy breeds, was developed in Ukraine in the first half of the 19th century by crossing various dairy breeds from Germany with local breeds, mainly the Gray Ukrainian, followed by inbreeding and selection for milk yield and red coat. The Lebedyn, recognized as a specific breed in 1950, was developed in Sumy oblast by crossing local cows, mainly the Gray Ukrainian, with bulls of the Suisse (Swiss Brown) breed. It is bred in Sumy, Kharkiv, and Chernihiv oblasts. The Spotted Black, recognized as a separate dairy breed in 1959, was developed by crossing local cattle with Ostfriesian and some other derived Dutch breeds. The breed is raised mostly in Khmelnytskyi, Zhytomyr, Kiev, Poltava, Volhynia, Rivne, and Lviv oblasts. The Gray Ukrainian, a meat and dairy breed distinguished by good health and endurance, is reared mainly in Poltava and Dnipropetrovske oblasts. It is highly valued for developing and improving new breeds. The White-headed Ukrainian, a dairy breed, was developed in the 19th century in Ukraine by crossing the Polisia breed with the Spotted Black Dutch breed. It is bred in Zhytomyr, Khmelnytskyi, and Kiev oblasts. The Red Polish, a dairy breed developed at the end of the 19th century in Poland from central European red cattle, is raised mostly in Volhynia, Ternopil, Rivne, and Lviv oblasts. It is very similar to, but smaller than, the Red Steppe breed. The Carpathian Brown, a meat and dairy breed, was developed in the Carpathian region in the first half of the 20th century. A mountain breed raised chiefly in the Carpathian oblasts, it is also used for improving local breeds of cattle in Armenia and the Asian republics of the USSR. (See also *Cattle raising.)

C. Spolsky

Great Russian Office (Velikorossiiskii prikaz). An institution of the Muscovite central government in the 17th and 18th centuries. Its function from 1688 was to control and supervise the Cossack regiments in Left-Bank Ukraine that were not part of the Hetman state, ie, Okhtyrka, Sumy, Izium, and Kharkiv regiments. It also administered the Cossack population in Slobidska Ukraine. The office was located in Moscow and was responsible to the Posolskii prikaz, the central office for foreign affairs.

Grecisms. See Hellenisms.

Greece. Republic situated in the southern Balkan Peninsula and on neighboring islands of the Ionian and Aegean seas. Its land area is 132,000 sq km, and its population in 1985 was 9,967,000. The capital is Athens (1981 pop 886,000). Greece became an independent state in 1829. From 1832 to 1974 it was a constitutional monarchy; since then it has been a republic.

Because of Ukraine's dependent status, political, economic, and even cultural contacts between Ukraine and Greece have been sporadic and short-lived. From the mid-19th century the Greek merchant navy played an active role in servicing Ukrainian ports. But there has never been significant trade between the two countries. From January to April 1919, over 23,000 Greek troops were part of the Allied interventionist forces and occupied areas around Odessa, elsewhere in southern Ukraine, and in the Crimea. From March 1919 to July 1920 a diplomatic mission represented the UNR in Athens; it was headed by F. Matushevsky and, after his death in October 1919, by M. Levytsky. A Greek consul was based in Kiev until August 1918. During the Soviet period minor cultural contacts have existed between Greece and Ukraine.

Greek themes are found in the works of such Ukrainian writers as M. Kostomarov and Ya. Shchoholiv in the 19th century and M. Rylsky, M. Zerov, B. Ten, and L. Pervomaisky in the 20th century. Translations of works by M. Ludemis, N. Kazantzakis, K. Kodzas, Y. Ritsos, E. Alexiou, and other writers have been published in Ukraine. The works of T. Shevchenko (ed E. Alexiou, 1964), Lesia Ukrainka, and I. Franko (trans S. Mavroidi-Papadaki) have been translated into Greek. Today the leading Hellenists in Ukraine are A. Biletsky (classical philology) and T. Chernyshova (modern Greek at Kiev University). (See also *Ancient states on the northern Black Sea coast, *Byzantine Empire, and *Greeks.)

A. Zhukovsky

Greek art. In Ukraine Greek art objects are found mostly along the Black Sea coast and in the Crimea. Examples of ancient Greek art from the 7th–6th century BC to the 2nd–3rd century AD have been found at the sites of former Greek colonies such as Tyras, Olbia, Chersonese Taurica, Theodosia, Panticapaeum, Phanagoria, Taman, and Gorgippia. The most prominent influence is that of the Ionian colonists from Asia Minor, particularly from Miletos, Priene, and Herakleia. But samples of Athenian art dating back to the 5th century BC are also present.

Greek art attained its widest influence in the 4th–3rd century BC, although it reached some regions only in the Hellenistic period. Its influence spread as far as the Kiev, Kharkiv, Poltava, and Zaporizhia regions, Podilia, and Galicia, and left its mark on the art and crafts of the local populations such as the Scythians, Sarmatians, Alans, Roxolani, and Antes. At the same time these autochthons influenced Greek art in the Black Sea colonies, especially the clothing, women's ornaments, and jewelry of the colonists. The fusion of Greek and indigenous elements resulted in an art particular to the Greek colonies in Ukraine.

Greek art in Ukraine: vase, 5th–4th century BC, from Phanagoria in the Crimea

Greek cities on the Black Sea coast were surrounded by walls with gates and towers; those of Olbia, Ilurat, and Chersonese Taurica are well preserved. Within the walls there were fine civic buildings, temples, and private homes with pools and fountains. The foundations of some of these have been preserved. Excavations of various types of graves, including vaulted graves built of wedge-shaped stone that were unknown in Greece, have yielded much information about Greek construction methods. The burial chambers of the kurhans Zolota Mohyla (near Symferopil) and Tsarskyi Kurhan (near Kerch), dating back to the 4th century BC, are masterpieces of construction.

A few sculptural remnants, which are not older than the 4th century BC, have been found. A number of better-preserved fragments from the Hellenistic period, carved in the style of Praxiteles, Polyclitus, or Scopas, were found in Olbia (a marble statue of Artemis) and Chersonese Taurica. A larger number of grave stelai with carved or painted representations of the deceased and the tools of their trade have been preserved. A Chersonese stele with a portrait of a youth is a unique relic of 5th-century carving. Marble reliefs depicting the exploits of Hercules, Dionysius, Silenus, Satyrs, and Maenades date back to the 2nd century AD. Many terra-cotta statuettes associated with the cults of Demeter, Astarte, and Aphrodite or depicting everyday activities and scenes have been found. Ceramic products with figures painted in the so-called black and red style have been discovered in Olbia, Kerch, and Smila. Ceramic griffons, eagles, sphinxes, etc, display eastern and local artistic features. From the scenes that are engraved on the famous gold vase from the *Kul Oba kurhan and the silver amphora from the *Chortomlyk kurhan, it is evident that the artists were familiar with everyday life of the Scythians or Roxolani. The artistic etchings on bronze articles, mostly from Olbia, are in the Ionic style and probably were made locally. Objects made later are decorated in the style of the Hellenistic and Roman period.

There is a large variety of fine jewelry such as gold earrings with pendants, masks, bracelets, and rings with precious stones. Pontic coins of the 4th century BC from Panticapaeum are considered to be the highest achievements of ancient engraving. Many Greek art objects were lost at the end of the 18th and during the 19th century because of the negligence of Russian authorities. Only a small part of the art treasures have been preserved in the Hermitage museum in Leningrad and in Kiev and Odessa museums.

BIBLIOGRAPHY
Rostovtsev, M. *Antichnaia dekorativnaia zhivopis' na iuge Rossii* (St Petersburg 1913)
Farmakovskii, B. *Ol'viia* (Moscow 1915)
Blavatskii, V. *Iskusstvo Severnogo Prichernomor'ia antichnoi epokhi* (Moscow 1947)
Gaidukevich, V. *Bosporskoe tsarstvo* (Moscow-Leningrad 1949)
Mongait, A. *Classical Cities of the North Coast of the Black Sea. Archeology in the USSR* (London 1961)

V. Sichynsky

Greek Catholic church. The historical name given to churches in the eastern half of the Roman Empire or in lands culturally dependent on the Byzantine Empire that gave allegiance to Rome but at the same time maintained many of their traditional Eastern religious customs. Some of these emerged in the early centuries of the Christian era, although most arose after the split between Eastern Orthodoxy and Western Catholicism in 1054.

Ideally, the Roman church was a universal cultural and religious entity without any national connotations whereas the Slavic and other churches in the East (Russian, Ukrainian-Belorussian, Bulgarian, Rumanian, etc) were culturally (and usually administratively) dependent on Byzantium and were thus viewed as 'Greek' churches practicing the Greek rite. Ukrainian Christians in the 16th and 17th centuries called themselves 'people of the Greek-Eastern rite.' The Church Union of *Berestia (1596), with its pragmatic though only partial solutions to the problems of church unity, attempted to overcome the divisions between East and West by creating a number of 'Greek' eparchies united administratively and by creed to the Roman Catholic world. The term *Graeci catholici* was coined by the Vatican to distinguish this new entity from the rest of the Eastern world – the *Graeci schismatici* or simply *Graeci.* However, as early as the 1620s, the term *Rutheni catholici* began to be used to characterize Ukrainian (and Belorussian) Catholicism, thus recognizing at least a nascent national character in these churches (Ukrainians and Belorussians not united with Rome were called *Rutheni schismatici*). These same terms were used to describe the rite of the Ukrainian churches. Similarly, the names *Rutheni uniti* and *Rutheni non uniti* or just simply *uniti* and *non uniti* were used especially by Polish religious as well as lay circles in order to underline the singularity of Ukrainian Catholicism and to imply its inferiority vis-á-vis their own Roman Catholicism. The Orthodox in Eastern Europe also used the name 'Uniate' pejoratively.

As an official appelation 'Greek Catholic' (*Griechisch-katolisch*) was introduced by the Austrian administration during the reign of Empress Maria Theresa in order to group under one name all the Eastern rite Catholics in the Austro-Hungarian Empire (ie, Ukrainians, Rumanians, Serbs, Croats, Hungarians, etc). This designation outlived the empire and was retained as the official name by its successor states. The name was also adopted in countries to which adherents of these churches emigrated. In fact, however, the appelation 'Greek' was irrational for it incorrectly implied that the liturgical language was Greek. For this reason, the Vatican now officially calls the earlier 'Greek' rite 'Byzantine,' a designation that encompasses the Albanians, Belorussians, Bulgarians, Greeks, Italians, Syrian Melchites, Hungarians, Russians, Rumanians, Slovaks, Croats, and Ukrainians regardless of their place of residence. Furthermore, the national character of these churches is also now generally recognized by Rome; thus Ukrainian Catholics are more specifically Catholics of the Ukrainian-Byzantine rite, Rumanian Catholics are Catholics of the Rumanian-Byzantine rite, and so on.

Among the various branches of the Byzantine rite, the Ukrainians are the most numerous (about 5.5 million in 1939), followed by the Rumanians (1.7 million), Hungarians (250,000), and others. The Hungarian and Slovak Byzantine-rite Catholics are mostly assimilated Ukrainians from Transcarpathia (see *Mukachiv and *Prešov eparchies). Today, although it is anachronistic to ignore the national dimension of these churches by simply referring to them as Greek Catholic, this name is still given to Ukrainian Catholics living in Poland, Czechoslovakia, and Yugoslavia where, for political reasons, the appelation 'Ukrainian' is avoided. Similarly, the term 'Greek Catholic church' is employed for Eastern-rite Catholics in Hungary. In the 1960s, the name *Ukrainian Catholic church was adopted to designate Ukrainian Catholics in the diaspora as well as the underground Ukrainian Catholic communities in the USSR.

A. Velyky

Greek Catholic Theological Academy in Lviv

Greek Catholic Theological Academy (Hreko-katolytska bohoslovska akademiia; aka Ukrainian Theological Academy). The academy was founded in Lviv in 1928 by Metropolitan A. *Sheptytsky to foster theological studies with particular emphasis on the liturgical and other particularities of the Eastern rite, the history of the union of the Ukrainian church with Rome, and Eastern dogma. It was also a school of higher education for candidates to the priesthood. The academy was to serve as the embryo of a future Ukrainian university. Organized on the same principles as Catholic universities in the West, it offered a five-year program. It had faculties of philosophy and theology, and a law faculty was to have been established in fall 1939. There were 350–400 students between 1932 and 1939, with 50–70 graduating each year, and a teaching staff of about 30 professors and lecturers. Ukrainian and Latin were the languages of instruction. The academy was directed by a rector appointed by the metropolitan from among the full professors. For the entire period of its existence the rector was Rev (later metropolitan and cardinal) Y. *Slipy.

Altogether the academy published 21 volumes of works. The history seminar published (irregularly) its *Arkhiv Seminara istorii*; the Slavic philology seminar, the semi-annual *Slovo*; and the history seminar of art, the quarterly *Mystetsvo i kul'tura*. The academy maintained a library and a museum (est 1932) with icons from the 14th to the 16th centuries. Scholars such as Metropolitan A. Sheptytsky, Bishop M. Charnetsky, reverends Y. Slipy, T. Myshkovsky, V. Laba, D. Dorozhinsky, Ya. Levytsky, M. Konrad, A. Ishchak, and Yu. Dzerovych, and laymen M. Chubaty, I. Krypiakevych, Ya. Pasternak, Yu. Poliansky, K. Chekhovych, V. Zalozetsky, and B. Kudryk served on its faculty. The academy was closed by the Soviet authorities in 1939 and again in 1944. From 1941 to 1944 it had an enrollment of 97 students. When Metropolitan Y. Slipy came to the West in 1963 he founded the *Ukrainian Catholic University in Rome and re-established the academy as its faculty of theology.

BIBLIOGRAPHY
Slipyi, I. *Hreko-Katolyts'ka Bohoslovs'ka Akademiia v pershim tr'okhlittiu isnuvannia (1928–1931)* (Lviv 1932)
Kuchabs'kyi, V. *Hreko-Katolyts'ka Bohoslovs'ka Akademiia v druhomu tr'okhlittiu svoho isnuvannia (1931–1934)* (Lviv 1935)
Hreko-Katolyts'ka Bohoslovs'ka Akademiia v tret'omu tr'okhlittiu svoho isnuvannia (1934–1937) (Lviv 1941)
Senytsia, P. *Svityl'nyk istyny: Dzherela do istoriï Ukraïns'koï Katolyts'koï Bohoslovs'koï Akademiï u L'vovi 1928/29–1944*, 3 vols (Toronto-Chicago 1973–83)

W. Lencyk

Greek Catholic Theological Seminary in Lviv (Hreko-katolytska dukhovna seminariia u Lvovi). Seminary established under Bishop P. Biliansky in 1783 by Joseph II as a general seminary to educate and train Greek Catholic clergy for the Ukrainian population of the Austrian Empire. It replaced the seminary known as the *Barbareum in Vienna. Spiritual training and education in the Eastern rite were conducted at the seminary under the supervision of the rector, while theological subjects were studied at the theological faculty of Lviv University. The program took four years to complete. In the 1880s the average annual enrollment was 200. The seminarians came from Lviv and Peremyshl eparchies. In 1845 Bishop I. Snihursky of Peremyshl established a theological seminary in Peremyshl, at which seminarians from his eparchy who had completed the first three years at the Lviv seminary could register for the final year.

After the First World War the seminary in Lviv became an archeparchial seminary. When the Polish authorities refused to respect the rights of the Ukrainian Catholic professors of the theological faculty at Lviv University, a theological faculty was established at the seminary. In 1928 this faculty was reorganized into the *Greek Catholic Theological Academy. In 1907 a seminary was opened in Stanyslaviv, and in 1921 the Peremyshl seminary began to offer a complete four-year program. The Lviv seminary, however, remained the largest seminary for Catholics of the Eastern rite, with approximately 400 students in 1935. Some of its seminarians came from other eparchies and from outside Galicia – from Bukovyna, Transcarpathia, Yugoslavia, and Bulgaria. A student association known as the Shashkevych Reading Society was active at the seminary; it published lectures, music notes, almanacs, and the journal *Katolyts'kyi vskhid* (1904–7). The seminary itself published the monograph series Asketychna biblioteka under the editorship of Rev Y. Slipy, and from 1783 maintained a valuable library and archive. Some prominent church leaders, such as A. Anhelovych, M. Skorodynsky, O. Bachynsky, H. Yakhymovych, H. Khomyshyn, Y. Botsian, T. Halushchynsky, and Y. Slipy, served as rectors of the seminary. Rev I. Chorniak was the last rector.

The seminary was housed in a building erected in 1888. It contained a chapel painted by P. Kholodny Sr (1929). The seminary also owned two old buildings, formerly owned by the Dominican Sisters, and the Church of the Holy Spirit, which was destroyed by a German bomb in 1939. The seminary was closed down by Soviet authorities in 1939, but reopened in 1941. In 1944 it was abolished permanently by the Soviet government along with the entire Ukrainian Catholic church. Its property was nationalized, and its library was transferred to the Lviv branch of the AN URSR.

BIBLIOGRAPHY
Studyns'kyi, K. *L'vivs'ka dukhovna seminariia v chasakh Markiiana Shashkevycha (1829–1843)* (Lviv 1916)
Hreko-katolyts'ka dukhovna seminariia u L'vovi, 2 vols (1935–9)

W. Lencyk

Greek Catholic Union of the USA (Soedinenie greko-kaftolicheskikh russkikh bratstv). Largest fraternal society of Transcarpathian immigrants and their descendants in the United States. It was founded in 1892 in Wilkes-Barre, Pennsylvania, to unite Carpatho-Ruthenians of the Greek Catholic faith, promote education, build churches, and support widows, orphans, and the indigent. Galician Ukrainians also belonged to the union until they set up the populist Ruthenian National Association (later the *Ukrainian National Association) in 1894. For a long time the union played a leading role in the Carpatho-Ruthenian community. In 1918–19 its support proved important for the incorporation of Transcarpathia into Czechoslovakia. The national orientation of the union was usually Russophile – although sometimes it espoused a distinct Ruthenian identity – and consistently anti-Ukrainian. At its height in 1928 the union consisted of 1,328 lodges with 120,000 members. In the 1960s it was weakened by assimilation. The term 'russkii' was dropped from its official name, and its biweekly *Messenger* (formerly *Amerikanskii russkii viestnik*) began to appear only in English. As its cultural and educational functions diminished, the union was reduced to a mere mutual benefit and insurance association. In 1985 it claimed 52,000 members in 400 lodges.

Greek loan words. See Hellenisms.

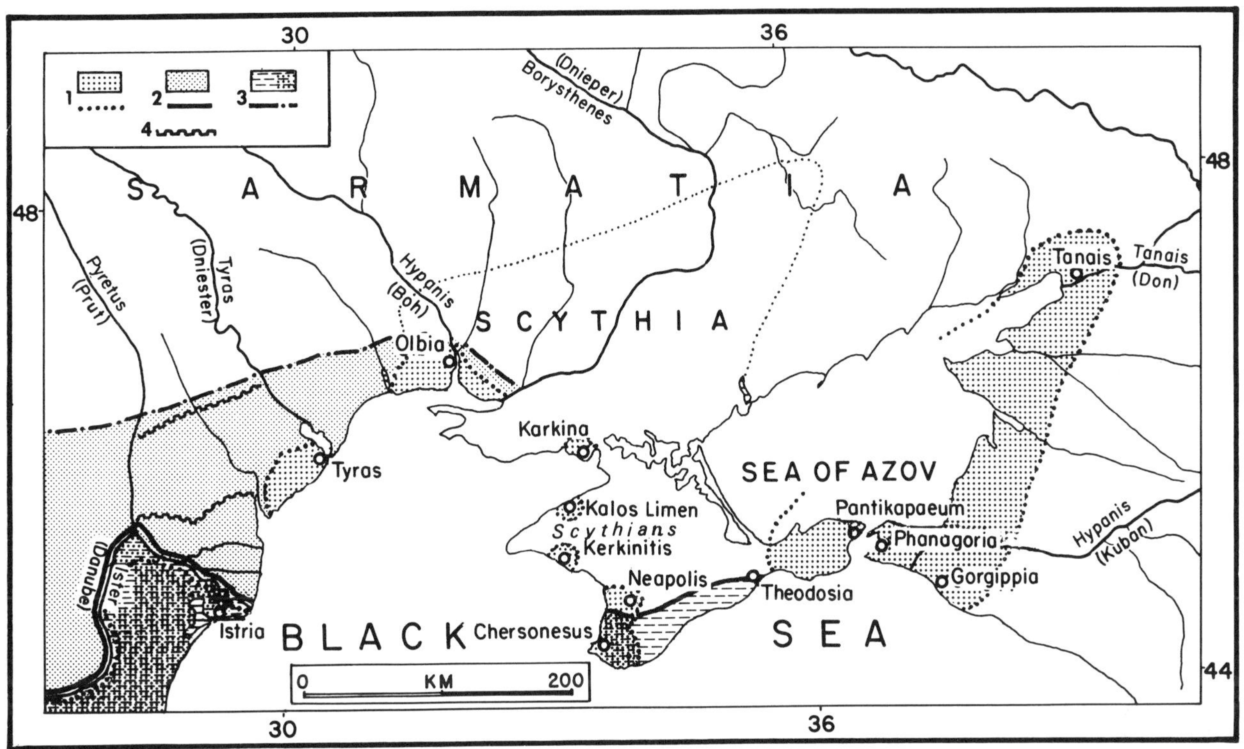

HELLENIC STATES AND COLONIES ON THE NORTHERN BLACK SEA COAST

1. Bosporan Kingdom and other Greek, Byzantine, and Roman colonies (5th century BC–4th century AD)
2. Roman expansion (1st–2nd centuries AD)
3. Territory under Byzantine control (4th–6th and 9th–11th centuries AD)
4. Trajan's Walls (98–117 AD)

Greeks (Ukrainian: *hreky*). Greeks first appeared in Ukraine about 1000 BC to trade with the peoples living on the Black Sea littoral. The first Greek (Ionian) colony was established at the end of the 7th century BC on *Berezan Island. Most others arose in the 6th century BC: *Olbia on the Boh Estuary and *Tyras on the Dniester Estuary; Theodosia (now *Teodosiia), *Panticapaeum, Myrmecium, and *Nyphaeum in the Crimea; and *Phanagoria, Cepi, and Hermonassa in the Taman Peninsula. *Chersonese Taurica, a Doric colony, arose in the Crimea in the 5th century BC. The easternmost colony, *Tanais, was founded in the 3rd century BC at the mouth of the Don River. Ceramic ware, weapons, jewelry, ornaments, oil, and wine were traded for local grain, slaves, fish, hides, and pelts, which were exported to the Greek city-states on the Aegean coast. With time the larger colonies themselves became Greco-barbarian city-states. In the 5th century BC several Greek poleis united with the indigenous peoples to create the *Bosporan Kingdom. From the 1st century BC to the 3rd century AD the Greek city-states in southern Ukraine were part of the Roman Empire. Apart from Chersonese Taurica and Panticapaeum, they were destroyed by the Huns in the 4th century.

From the 9th century on, the principalities of Rus' had close ties with the *Byzantine Empire, particularly after the adoption of Christianity from Byzantium in 988 by Grand Prince *Volodymyr the Great of Kiev. With a few exceptions the hierarchy of the Orthodox church in medieval Ukraine consisted of Greeks. Even after the fall of the empire in 1453, Ukrainian-Greek church and economic relations were maintained. But they were not of any great consequence until the end of the 16th and most of the 17th century, when Greek merchants settled in Lviv, Kamianets-Podilskyi, and other cities and participated in the activities of the Orthodox brotherhoods. As the Polish Catholic-Ukrainian Orthodox struggle intensified, Orthodox Ukrainians strengthened their ties with the patriarchs of Constantinople, who had jurisdiction over *Kiev Metropoly until 1686. In the cultural sphere, the *brotherhood schools originally had Greek-Church Slavonic curriculums. Greek scholars in Ukraine, such as *Arsenii (Arsenius) of Elasson and C. *Lucaris, and Ukrainian scholars who had direct contact with Greece, such as Kypriian of Ostrih, Friar Joseph from Mt Athos, and Hegumen I. *Boryskovych, or who were versed in the Greek language and literature, such as L. and S. Zyzanii, K. Stavrovetsky, M. Smotrytsky, and Z. Kopystensky, all played key roles in the Ukrainian cultural and religious revival, particularly in Ostrih and Lviv. The earliest textbooks were modeled on Greek examples. Each year dozens of monks came from Mt *Athos to collect alms in Ukraine.

Greek clerics often acted as advisers in Ukrainian church matters; Prince K. Ostrozky, for example, was advised by Dionysius Paleologos and Moskhopulos, who lived in Ostrih. Some Greek clergymen – for example, Patriarch Jeremias II of Constantinople, the protosyncellus Nicephorus, C. Lucaris, and M. Syrigos – came to Ukraine on special missions and took part in church events. Some of them were involved in political affairs; for example, as patriarch, C. Lucaris conducted negotiations with the Cossacks in the 1620s. There were Greeks in the upper echelons of the Hetman state: *Daniel Oliveberg de Graecani Atheniensis served as Hetman B. Khmelnytsky's envoy; and Astamatos (Ostamatenko) served as the envoy of hetmans Yu. Khmelnytsky and P. Doroshenko to Constantinople. A number of Ukrainian families of the Cossack *starshyna* or noble estate were of Greek descent: Tomara, Kapnist, Ternaviot, Levytsky, Yanzhul, Konstantynovych, Khrystoforovych, Manuilovych, Ursal, Motonis, Komburlei, Mazapet, and Mazaraka.

Greek merchants and entepreneurs prospered in Ukraine. In 1657 Hetman B. Khmelnytsky granted trading privileges to a group of Greek merchants who settled in Nizhen. The annual fairs organized by it turned *Nizhen into an emporium that retained its importance until the founding of Odessa (1794) and other Black Sea ports in the late 18th century. A sizable community of Greek traders and artisans remained in Nizhen county until the early 19th century. Greeks also lived in Pereiaslav and Kiev. In 1748 the Greek colony in Kiev established St Catherine's Monastery in the Podil district.

In the 18th century political conditions in the Russian Empire did not serve to promote Ukrainian-Greek economic relations. Religious and cultural ties continued to be maintained, however, particularly through the Kievan Mohyla Academy and other colleges (later seminaries), which attracted Greek students well into the 19th century. N. *Theotokis, who hailed from Corfu, founded the Poltava Seminary and was the archbishop of Kherson in 1779–86.

Ruins of a Greek house in Ukraine (late 18th century)

Towards the end of the 18th century the number of Greeks in Ukraine rose sharply. After protracted wars with Turkey, Russia finally gained control of the steppes in southern Ukraine and began colonizing them. Foreign settlers were offered various concessions and assistance, including exemptions from taxation and military service, unrestricted fishing rights, and material support. After the 1768–74 war ended, the Russian authorities helped several thousand Greeks who had sympathized with or fought on the Russian side during the war to emigrate from Asia Minor to the Crimea, Tahanrih, and Kherson. In 1774–83, 18,400 Greeks were forcibly resettled from the Crimea to Azov gubernia on the coast of the Sea of Azov and along the Solona and Kalmiius rivers. During the first two winters there, 4,655 died from the cold, lack of food and shelter, and disease. Those who survived built the city of Mariiupil (now *Zhdanov) and populated 22 other settlements. In 1897, 69,400 Greeks lived in Katerynoslav gubernia, most of them in the Mariiupil region. Many of them retained their distinctive Greek-Tatar dialects and folkways well into the 20th century, even though in the 1870s they lost the right to have their own schools and self-government that they had been granted in 1779. Twelve villages were settled by the so-called Greek Hellenes, who spoke a modern Greek dialect; 10 were settled by the so-called Greek Tatars, who spoke a language resembling Tatar.

A Greek woman wearing a traditional headdress (late 19th century)

Other Greeks settled in the steppe interior, particularly near the Dnieper rapids, and were among the original inhabitants of Katerynoslav (now Dnipropetrovske), Novomoskovske, and other towns. In the 1790s many emigrants from the Aegean islands settled in towns along the Black Sea littoral – Odessa, Kherson, Mykolaiv, and others. After 1812 the number of emigrants declined.

Some Greeks were organized at first into military settlements and battalions (near Odessa and Balaklava in the Crimea), but the majority turned to farming, artisanry, or trade. After the Russian-Turkish wars ended, many Phanariote boyars and officials from Moldavia and Walachia were endowed with pensions and lands by the Russian government. The Cantacuzino family, for example, received 19,000 desiatins of land near Zolotonosha, over 13,000 near Voznesenske, and up to 400 in the Romen region; Prince C. Ypsilantis received 14,000 desiatins in the Chernihiv region; and the engineer Karadzhi was granted an estate near Bohodukhiv.

Greeks played a significant role in Ukraine's commerce. At the beginning of the 19th century trade in Mariiupil, Mykolaiv, Yelysavet (now Kirovohrad), and Tahanrih was controlled by Greeks, who also played a particularly important role in the development of *Odessa as an international trade center. In 1814 the revolutionary secret society Philikí Etaireía, which in the 1820s was headed by A. and D. Ypsilantis, was established by Greek merchants in Odessa, and the city became an important center of the Greek national independence movement. Odessa's relatively small Greek community (5,070 in 1897) maintained its importance in the city's commerce, and that of Southern Ukraine as a whole, until the 1917 Revolution.

With the consolidation of Soviet power in 1920, many Greek merchants lost their properties to the state. Thousands of Greek professionals lost their jobs and many fled to Greece and other countries.

According to the 1926 Soviet census, there were 105,000 Greeks in the Ukrainian SSR, of which 64,200 lived in the Mariiupil region and 3,500 in the Odessa region. An additional 22,000 Greeks lived in the Kuban, 24,000 in the Crimea, and 10,000 in eastern Subcaucasia. In 1933, 156,000 Greeks lived on Ukraine's compact ethnographic territory, and 167,000 in all the territories inhabited wholly or in part by Ukrainians. In the USSR as a whole there were 214,000 Greeks according to the 1926 census, and 286,000 according to the 1939 census.

In 1926, 4,000 (11,500 in 1816) of the Greek inhabitants in the region between Mariiupil and Staline (now Donetske) lived in Mariiupil and constituted 10 percent of the city's population (in 1897 they constituted 30 percent); 93,000 lived in about 29 large villages, 15 of them purely Greek. Among the largest were Yalta, Manhush (now Pershotravneve), Urzuf, and Staryi Krym near the Azov coast; Sartana, Hnativka (now Starohnativka), Karan (now Hranitne), Chermalyk (now Zamozhne), Styla, and Starobesheve along the Kalmiius River; and Velykyi Yanysol (now Velyka Novosilka), Komar, Bohatyr, Staryi Kermenchyk (now Staromlynivka), and Nova Karakuba (now Krasna Poliana) in the northwest along the Mokri Yaly River. Together the Greeks accounted for 10 percent of the population in the region.

In the Crimea, about 60 percent of the Greeks lived in the cities and suburbs of Yalta, Sevastopil, Symferopil, Kerch, and Teodosiia. In the Odessa region, besides the old Greek colony (1,400) in Odessa, there was a colony (1,400) in the village of Sverdlove. There were also small Greek communities in Staline (700), Kharkiv (500), and Kiev (300). In other cities, such as Nizhen, Mykolaiv, and Dnipropetrovske, which at one time had Greek inhabitants, the Greeks had merged with the local population.

In the Kuban and eastern littoral of the Black Sea, Greeks lived in and around the coastal cities of Novorosiiske, Anapa, Helendzhyk, Tuapse, and Sochi, as well as in the interior Abynske and Krymske raions and the city of Krasnodar. Thirty-one percent of them were urban dwellers (10.3 percent in Soviet Ukraine).

A contemporary Greek house in Donetske oblast

In the 1920s and early 1930s, the Greeks had three national raions and 30 national rural soviets in Soviet Ukraine. But they were not adequately provided with education in their mother tongue, and 76 percent of all Greek children attended Russian schools (only 2 percent attended Ukrainian schools). Hence, in spite of the high literacy rate among the Greeks (64 percent in 1926), only 1 percent of them could write in Greek. During the period of Ukrainization in the 1920s, a Greek-language pedagogical tekhnikum and agricultural school existed in Mariiupil and Greek newspapers were published. During the Stalin terror the schools were closed and all nationally conscious Greek activists were repressed. The Greek poet H. *Kostoprav died in a labor camp. In the late 1920s the All-Ukrainian Scientific Association of Oriental Studies (A. Kovalivsky and others) conducted research on the Greek colonies in the Mariiupil region.

According to the 1959 census there were 104,400 Greeks in the Ukrainian SSR, 93,000 of them in Donetske oblast. Only 8 percent (81 percent in 1926) gave Greek as their mother tongue, while 89 percent (17 percent in 1926) gave Russian, and 3 percent gave Ukrainian. These language-use data were basically repeated in the 1979 census: of the 104,100 Greeks in Ukraine, only 9 percent gave Greek as their mother tongue. The cataclysmic events in Soviet history (famine, terror, war), assimilation, and Russification have contributed to the population decline and changing culture of Greeks in Ukraine.

In 1969 a small selection of H. Kostoprav's poetry was published in Kiev in Ukrainian translation. A few years later a parallel Greek-Ukrainian edition of poetry by Greeks from Donetske oblast was published.

BIBLIOGRAPHY

Kharlampovych, K. 'Narysy z istoriï hrets'koï koloniï v Nizheni (XVII–XVIII st.),' *ZIFV*, 24 (1929)

Teokharidi, T. 'Hrets'ka viis'kova kolonizatsiia na pivdni Ukraïny na prykintsi XVIII ta pochatku XIX stolittia,' *Visnyk Odes'koï komisiï kraieznavstva pry VUAN*, 4–5 (1930)

Naulko, V. *Razvitie mezhetnicheskikh sviazei na Ukraine (istoriko-etnograficheskii ocherk)* (Kiev 1975)

Herlihy, P. 'Greek Merchants in Odessa in the Nineteenth Century,' *HUS*, 3/4 (1979–80)

Zapantis, A. *Greek-Soviet Relations, 1917–1941* (Boulder 1982)

V. Kubijovyč, R. Senkus, A. Zhukovsky

Greens. See Partisan movement in Ukraine, 1918–22.

Alexander Gregorovich

Gregorovich, Alexander [Hryhorovyč, Oleksander], b 11 March 1893 in Orelets, Sniatyn county, Galicia, d 24 June 1970 in Hamilton, Ontario. Community leader. Gregorovich emigrated from Galicia in 1911 and settled in Alberta; he became one of the first Ukrainian teachers in rural Ukrainian school districts. A founding member of the *Ukrainian National Federation, he was president of its first national executive (1932–6) and its first branch in Edmonton. He served as administrator and coeditor (1934–40) of *Novyi shliakh*, and was a founder (1939) of

Nova Hromada, the first Ukrainian credit union in Canada. He cotranslated two works under the pseudonym Oreletsky: *The Black Deeds of the Kremlin* (1953) and Ivan Bahriany's novel *The Hunters and the Hunted* (1954). In 1957 he compiled and published on microfilm a scarce collection of Ukrainian scientific dictionaries that had been published in Ukraine in the 1920s.

Gregory of Nazianzus, Sermons of Saint. Gregory's 13 orations had been translated from Greek into Church Slavonic, possibly in the *Glagolitic alphabet, their East Slavic copies being perhaps the earliest extant text written in Ukraine, probably in Galicia, in the mid-11th century (376 folios). The Ukrainian copyist added to the often mistranslated Church Slavonic original many new mistakes; as a result, the text occasionally is unintelligible. The manuscript is preserved in the Leningrad Public Library. The language of the text was studied by A. Budilovich (1871), who also published the text (1875).

Gregory the Bulgarian. See Bolharyn, Hryhorii II.

Grekov, Boris, b 21 April 1882 in Myrhorod, Poltava gubernia, d 9 September 1953 in Moscow. Russian medieval historian. A professor at the universities of Leningrad and Moscow, he became a full member of the Academy of Sciences of the USSR in 1935 and the director of its institutes of History (1937–53), the History of Material Culture (1944–6), and Slavic Studies (1946–53). His major works are *Rabstvo i feodalizm v drevnei Rusi* (Slavery and Feudalism in Ancient Rus', 1934), *Kievskaia Rus'* (Kievan Rus', 1939, 1944, 1953; Ukrainian transl 1951; English transl 1959), *Kul'tura Kievskoi Rusi* (The Culture of Kievan Rus', 1944; English transl 1947), and *Krest'iane na Rusi s drevneishikh vremen do XVII veka* (Peasants in Rus' from Oldest Times to the 17th Century, 2nd edn, 2 vols, 1952–4). Writing in conformity with official Soviet views on historiography, he attempted to refute M. *Hrushevsky's and M. Pokrovsky's theories and to prove that Kievan Rus' was the common patrimony of the Russians, the Ukrainians, and the Belorussians. His collected works were published in Moscow (4 vols, 1959–60).

Vasyl Grendzha-Donsky

Petro Grigorenko

Grendzha-Donsky, Vasyl [Grendža-Dons'kyj, Vasyl'] b 23 April 1897 in Volove (now Mizhhiria), Transcarpathia, d 25 November 1974 in Bratislava, Slovakia. Writer and journalist. Grendzha-Donsky was befriended by the poet V. *Pachovsky, under whose influence he actively participated in the cultural revival of Ukrainians in Transcarpathia and was the first Transcarpathian author to write in literary Ukrainian. The editor of *Nasha zemlia* (1927–8) and *Nova svoboda* (1938–9) in Uzhhorod, he was a prolific writer in the 1920s and 1930s. His works, which are imbued with patriotic romanticism, include collections of poetry: *Kvity z terniamy* (Flowers with Thorns, 1923), *Zoloti kliuchi* (Golden Springs, 1923), *Shliakhom ternovym* (On the Thorny Path, 1924), *Tobi ridnyi kraiu* (To You, Native Land, 1936), and others; collections of short stories: *Opovidannia z karpats'kykh polonyn* (Stories from the Carpathian Meadows, 1926), *Nazustrich voli* (A Rendezvous with Freedom, 1929); the drama in verse *Ostannii bii* (The Last Battle, 1930); the historical drama *Sotnia Mocharenka* (Mocharenko's Company, 1932); and the novelettes *Il'ko Lypei, rozbiinyk* (Ilko Lypei, the Brigand, 1936) and *Petro Petrovych* (1937). In 1964 a selection of his works was published in Prešov; its title *Shliakhom ternovym* suitably summarizes the life of Grendzha-Donsky, whose national orientation often made his existence difficult under the various regimes he lived through. By 1986 the Carpathian Alliance in Washington had published seven volumes of his complete works.

D.H. Struk

Greschuk, Demetrius [Greščuk, Dmytro], b 7 November 1923 in Innisfree, Alberta. Bishop of the Ukrainian Catholic church. Educated at St Augustine's Seminary in Toronto, Greschuk was ordained in 1950 and served in the Eparchy of Edmonton (Edmonton and Calgary). In 1974 he was appointed bishop of Nazianzus and consecrated auxiliary bishop of the Ukrainian Catholic Eparchy of Edmonton. In 1984 he was appointed apostolic administrator of Edmonton and the Northwest Territories, and in 1986, bishop of Edmonton.

Gridnev, Vitalii. See Hridniev, Vitalii.

Grigorenko (Hryhorenko), Petro, b 16 October 1907 in Borysivka, Nohaiske county, Tavriia gubernia, d 21 February 1987 in New York City. Former major general in the Soviet army, military engineer, and dissident. Grigorenko attended the Kharkiv Polytechnical Institute (1929–31), the Moscow Military Engineering Academy (1931–4), and the General Staff Academy in Moscow (1937–9). Serving in the Far East after 1939, he was reprimanded in 1941 for criticizing Stalin's purge of the Red Army. A division commander on the German front (1943–5), he taught at the Frunze Military Academy in Moscow (1945–61), became head of the Faculty of Military Cybernetics, and was promoted to the rank of general in 1956.

On 7 September 1961, at a local Moscow CP conference, Grigorenko advocated democratization of the CPSU and criticized corrupt officials, the privileges of leading Communists, and the repression directed against Communist reformers. He was subsequently fired from his post, transferred to the Far East, and removed from active service. He founded (1963) the League of Struggle for the Revival of Leninism and publicly championed the right of the Crimean Tatars, deported under Stalin, to return to their homeland. Arrested in February 1964, he was committed to psychiatric prisons in 1964–5 and 1969–74. He was one of the founders of the *Ukrainian Helsinki Group (1976) and its representative to the Moscow Helsinki Group. In 1977 he left for medical treatment in the United States and was stripped of his Soviet citizenship in absentia, thus preventing his return. He is the author of over 80 works in military science, as well as dissident writings; his memoirs have appeared in Russian (1973, 1976), Ukrainian (1984), and other languages.

Grinberg, Lev, b 1790 in Volhynia, d 1850 in Warsaw. Physician. A graduate of Berlin University (1824), he practiced medicine in Kiev and Zaslav. In 1829 he was sent to do research on the plague in Bessarabia. His publications include a number of important monographs such as *Theorie der orientalischen Cholera* (1836) and *Vseobshchii terminologicheskii meditsinskii leksikon na latinskom, nemetskom i russkom iazykakh* (Universal Terminological Medical Lexicon in the Latin, German, and Russian Languages, 1839–42).

Gritchenko, Alexis. See Hryshchenko, Oleksa.

Groener, Wilhelm, b 22 November 1867 in Ludwigsburg, Württemberg, d 3 May 1939 in Bornstedt, Germany. German general; later a statesman in the Weimar Republic. The chief of staff of the German Supreme Army Command in Ukraine from March to December 1918, he was highly critical of the Central Rada and engineered Hetman P. *Skoropadsky's coup d'état of 29 April 1918. He pursued the policy of exploiting Ukraine as an occupied country, extracting from it grain, other foodstuffs, and raw materials. At his insistence the Bluecoat and Graycoat divisions, the Galician Sich Riflemen regiment, and other Ukrainian units were disarmed, and he further hindered the formation of Ukrainian military units. Later he was one of the founders of the Ukrainian Scientific Institute in Berlin and the first chairman of its board of trustees (1926–34). His memoirs were published in 1957.

Gross national income. See National income.

Gross national product. See National income.

Grossman, Vasilii, b 12 December 1905 in Berdychiv, Kiev gubernia, d 14 September 1964 in Moscow. Russian writer of Jewish origin. His writing career began in the 1930s and his literary output includes a play and several novels. Grossman was attacked during the anti-Jewish campaign in 1953; although he was later rehabilitated (a monograph on him by A. Bocharov appeared in 1970), some of his most important work has been published only in the West. His fictionalized memoirs, *Vse techet*, published abroad in 1970 (in English as *Forever Flowing* in 1972), are remarkable for their moving accounts of collectivization and the man-made *famine in Ukraine, and for the argument that Lenin, not just Stalin, was to blame for the evils of Soviet society.

Grottaferrata Monastery (also called Crypta ferrata). Founded in 1004 by Nilus of Rossano as an abbey of the Byzantine rite; its residents are Basilian monks mostly of Albanian, Greek, and Italian origin. Only a few have been Ukrainian. Located 20 km southeast of Rome, the monastery contains valuable Medieval and Renaissance masterpieces, a large library of old books, and a book-restoration laboratory. Its printing shop, established in 1909, produces Greek and Slavic liturgical books that are used by the Ukrainian Catholic church.

Group of Ukrainian National Youth (Hrupa ukrainskoi natsionalnoi molodi or HUNM). A nationalist organization founded in 1922 by soldiers of the Ukrainian Galician Army at the internment camp in Josefov, Bohemia as a result of increasing political divisions in the Ukrainian student movement. In the mid-1920s, it developed close ties to the *Ukrainian Military Organization and attempted to unite all Ukrainian émigré organizations on a nationalist platform. Its central office in Prague co-ordinated the work of many branches: in Brno, Příbram, Liberec, Bratislava, and Josefov in Czechoslovakia; in Vienna, Graz, and Leoben in Austria; and in Lviv and other towns in Galicia. The branches in Galicia reorganized themselves in 1926 into the *Union of Ukrainian Nationalist Youth. In 1929 both organizations merged with the newly founded *Organization of Ukrainian Nationalists. The monthly **Natsional'na dumka* was the official journal of HUNM. Its presidents, in chronological order, were Z. Petriv, L. Makarushka, M. Konovalets, I. Gyzha, S. Nyzhankivsky, and O. Boidunyk.

Grudziński, Stanisław, b 27 April 1852 in Vodianyky, Zvenyhorodka county, Kiev gubernia, d 3 June 1884 in Warsaw. Polish poet and writer. He studied in Kiev and translated three of T. Shevchenko's poems into Polish. His poem 'Dwie mogiły' (Two Kurhans, 1879) and collection *Powieści ukraińskie* (Ukrainian Novellas, 2 vols, 1879–80) contain depictions of the life of Ukrainian peasants.

Gubernia (*huberniia*). An administrative territorial unit in the Russian Empire. The division into gubernias was introduced by Peter I. In Ukraine, Azov and Kiev gubernias were formed in 1708; the latter existed alongside the Ukrainian regimental administrative system, which was abolished in 1764–81. The extent and status of gubernias in Ukraine changed often (see *Administrative territorial division). Most administrative, fiscal, judicial, and military institutions were headed by the *governor, although they were staffed by officials of the respective ministry. Reforms enacted in 1775–85 were intended to create an elaborate system of administration involving the representative institutions of the nobility, urban strata, and peasants. These were only partly successful, although the gubernia Gentry Assemblies (founded in 1785) had a noticeable influence on local government. Self-administrating institutions in the gubernias, the *zemstvos, began to appear in the 1860s. Towards the end of the 18th century, alongside the gubernias, the government created *vicegerencies; these later became gubernias or were included in pre-existing gubernias. In 1914, there were 10 gubernias (Chernihiv, Katerynoslav, Kharkiv, Kherson, Kholm, Kiev, Podilia, Poltava, Tavriia, and Volhynia) on Ukrainian ethnic territory, and eight (Bessarabia, Hrodna, Kursk, Lublin, Mahiliou, Minsk, Orel, and Voronezh) in ethnically mixed territories. Most gubernia administrations published an official newspaper called *Gubernskie vedomosti*. At certain times some individual gubernias were united to create general-gubernias, headed by a *governor-general. This occurred in Ukraine in the first half of the 19th century. Gubernias were in turn subdivided into counties (*povity*; Russian: *uezdy*). Gubernias were abolished in the USSR in 1925.

Gubernial commissioners (*huberniialni komisary*). Gubernial administrators who under the Russian Provisional Government replaced the *governors of the tsarist regime. In March 1917, the Provisional Government appointed the heads of the gubernia zemstvo administrations as the first commissioners. In Ukraine these officials were recognized by the Central Rada in the summer of 1917. In gubernias where the Provisional Government recognized the authority of the Central Rada, the commissioners were M. Sukovkin and then O. Salikovsky in Kiev; A. Livytsky in Poltava; M. Iskrytsky and then D. Doroshenko in Chernihiv; A. Viazlov in Volhynia; and M. Stakhovsky in Podilia. After the proclamation of the UNR in November 1917, the Ukrainian government also accepted the gubernial commissioners previously confirmed by the Provisional Government in other gubernias of the UNR. As the influence of Bolshevik soviets increased, the power of the commissioners, especially in large industrial centers such as Kharkiv, Katerynoslav, and Odessa, diminished. Counties were administered by county commissioners. When in the spring of 1918 the Central Rada returned to Kiev, it appointed its own gubernial commissioners as well as gubernial military commanders. On 14 May 1918 the commissioners were replaced by the Hetman government with 11 gubernial starostas; most of them were indifferent or even hostile to Ukrainian interests.

Mykola Gudzii

Gudzii, Mykola [Gudzij], b 3 May 1887 in Mohyliv, Podilia gubernia, d 29 October 1965 in Moscow. Literary scholar. He graduated in 1911 from Kiev University, where he studied under V. Peretts. In 1922 he was appointed professor at Moscow University; in 1945 he became a full member of the AN URSR and worked at its Institute of Literature. From 1951 to 1963 he headed the Commission on the History of Philological Sciences of the AN URSR. Gudzii wrote many studies of old and modern Ukrainian literature, including *Literatura Kievskoi Rusi i drevneishie inoslavianskie literatury* (The Literature of Kievan Rus' and the Oldest Other Slavic Literatures, 1958) and *Istoriia drevnei russkoi literatury* (A History of Old Russian Literature, 1st edn 1938, 7th edn 1966; English trans 1949, 1970), and articles on *Slovo o polku Ihorevi* (The Tale of Ihor's Campaign). He compiled the important *Khrestomatiia po drevnei russkoi literatury* (Anthology of Old Russian Literature, 1st edn 1935, 6th edn 1955), and was editor in chief of the complete edition of T. Shevchenko's works (6 vols, 1963–4) and a coeditor of the works of V. Stefanyk (3 vols, 1949–54).

Guerrilla warfare. See Partisan movement in Ukraine, 1918–22, Soviet partisans in Ukraine, 1941–5, and Ukrainian Insurgent Army.

Guild (Ukrainian: *tsekh*: German: *Zunft* or *Zech*). Closed corporate association of craftsmen working either in a single trade or in several closely related *crafts. Guilds arose and began to spread in the towns of Western Europe during the 11th and 12th centuries. The typical form of a guild as a corporation uniting the craftsmen of a trade emerged in the Middle Ages. These corporations were particularly well organized in German territories; from there, by way of Poland, they spread to Ukraine, especially in towns governed by *Magdeburg law. At first, these corporations were only professional and social organizations of craftsmen. They were especially important as charitable and mutual-benefit associations. At the same time, they defended the craftsmen's economic interests by obtaining and guarding certain exclusive rights, eliminating competition from other social groups, controlling working conditions and wages, and regulating prices and supplies. Certain trades were monopolized by the guilds, which became closed circles of members (known as brothers) maintaining strict internal discipline. Membership was made difficult to gain and was strictly controlled by the apprenticeship system. Over time, the guilds took on a political character, acting as the representative body for the craftsmen. Through the guilds, together with the patricians, merchants, and other urban strata, the craftsmen participated in the administration and governing of *cities and towns. Similar associations arose among doctors, teachers, lawyers, pharmacists, notaries, and members of other professions. In the Russian Empire these professional organizations came to be called *gildy*, while trade corporations kept the name *tsekh*.

The precursors of the guilds in Ukraine are mentioned in the Rus' chronicles and were known as trade companies (*druzhyny*), ruled by elders (*starshyny*). Little is known about their organization or function. In Ukraine, the first Western-style guilds appeared in the 14th century (eg, the cobblers' guild in Peremyshl in the 1380s). Later, well-known guilds arose in Lviv (there were 10 in 1425, 20 in 1579, and 30 in the mid-17th century). Guilds also appeared in Lutske (five in the mid-16th century), Kovel, Volodymyr, Kholm, Krasnystaw, Ternopil, and other towns. The most renowned guilds in Ukraine at the time were those of the carpenters and the goldsmiths.

In time, the guilds emerged as the basic form of association for craftsmen in towns and cities throughout Ukraine. Guilds became particularly significant in the 16th–18th centuries, when they spread from Galicia to Right-Bank Ukraine and the Hetman state. By 1552 there were 17 guilds in Kiev. The largest were the cobblers' (in 1762 it had 643 master craftsmen), the tailors' (327), the weavers' (109), the fishermen's (266), the musicians' (243), the coopers' (243), the bakers' (130), the butchers' (124), and the painters' (177).

Guild membership was limited to a trade's master craftsmen who owned necessary tools and a workshop. New members were elected to the guild subject to certain other conditions, such as the completion of an apprenticeship, the employment of a journeyman (*pidmaister* or *cheliadnyk*) and apprentice (*uchen*), the production of a masterpiece, and the payment of guild dues. These conditions were eased for the sons and sons-in-law of a master with a hereditary workshop. In addition to taking the oath of the guild, a member had to swear to respect the town's laws before the magistrates. Only master craftsmen enjoyed full rights; journeymen and apprentices were in a subordinate position and the latter were particularly exploited. Therefore, in some towns, separate organizations of journeymen were formed for self-defense and to provide mutual aid. In some cases they had their own homes (*hospody*) where they lodged under the supervision of an elderly master.

As in Western Europe, the guilds defended the economic interests of the master craftsmen, controlled prices by excluding craftsmen who were not guild members from the market, and supervised the professional ethics and standards of their members (their expertise, the quality of their products, prices, etc). The guilds were headed by an elected guild master and executive. They had their own charter, which was approved by the magistrates or in some cases by the king. Some major guilds ratified the charters of other, less-important guilds. Guilds had their representatives on the town council and other institutions of local administration, and these bodies, as well as the central government, upheld the guild's laws and decisions. In many towns the guilds helped to finance and staff the town watch, police, and fire department. The support of town councils was particularly important in the struggle between the guilds and craftsmen outside the guilds; councils fined the non-affiliated craftsmen, the so-called *partachi*, for violating guild privileges and often even confiscated their wares and arrested them. Therefore, the latter could only work in the suburbs, in small towns and villages, or on gentry estates, where the guilds did not have the right to a monopoly. In comparison with guild members, these craftsmen had very limited rights, were poorly organized, and generally were discouraged from practicing their trade.

The craftsmen within the guilds followed their own code of behavior and discipline, enforced by guild courts. They had their own elaborate rituals, treasury (the guild 'trunk'), flag, seal and emblem (the *tsekha*), and even ceremonial dress for special occasions (church feasts, funerals, banquets, official meetings, etc). Each guild also had its own coat of arms (*herb*), which depicted the respective trade. The members (*bratchyky*) of the guild celebrated religious feasts together and often undertook the upkeep of a church or a chapel, financing renovations and providing it with wax used in the services. Some guilds had private quarters; eg, in Kiev, the cobblers' guild had a building and an eatery in the Podil district. Certain guilds had their own stores for retailing their members' products. The musicians' guild in Kiev was the founder of the city's orchestra and a school of music in the 18th century. The guilds also played an important social role by providing charity and benevolent services for impoverished members and their widows and orphans.

In economic matters, conflicts arose between the guilds and the merchants or their corporations because the latter favored free enterprise and competition among craftsmen and the unrestricted access of non-guild craftsmen to the market. The gentry and nobility were also opposed to the autonomy of the guild corporations and to the 'guild coercion' that obliged craftsmen outside the guilds to renounce certain rights.

Because of their Western European origin, guilds in Ukraine were closely associated with the Roman Catholic faith, drawing members at first only from the Catholic population (Germans and Poles). Orthodox Ukrainians and Armenians were ineligible for membership unless they became Catholics or, later, Uniates, and even then they were denied full rights. It was exceptional for an Orthodox to be tolerated even as a journeyman or apprentice. In the Hetman state, however, guilds founded by Orthodox craftsmen existed. Jews were generally prohibited from joining guilds, although in time they monopolized certain trades, even as *partachi*.

In towns where Roman Catholic guilds existed, the Orthodox Ukrainians formed separate organizations, the so-called Brotherhoods. These associations were not based on trades and instead united all Orthodox burghers. Since their concerns were cultural and religious, and above all related to the defence of their nationality, they did not fulfill the same economic functions as guilds. While guilds in Western Europe were also often connected with religious life, these ties were much stronger in Ukraine. The Jews sometimes founded their own guilds with the permission of either the town council or the central government. The increase in the number of *partachi*, the beginning of industrial manufacturing, the rise in imports of manufactured goods, the internal decline of the guilds through indiscipline and the relaxation of professional standards, and the opposition of merchants and nobles all weakened the power of the guilds and finally led to the dissolution of the system in Poland.

Although guilds existed throughout the 18th century, they no longer enjoyed an economic monopoly or their previous autonomy, especially as craftsmen outside the guilds became progressively more emancipated. In 1785 in Left-Bank Ukraine, and in 1840 on the Right-Bank, the Russian government formally curtailed the autonomy of the guilds and subordinated them to local authorities. The craftsmen's activity became regulated by the guild statutes of Peter I (1722) and Catherine II (1785). Under the terms of the latter, the guild craftsmen became one of six categories of town dwellers, although at the time they did not form a separate craftsmen's class. The 1799 'Guild Charter' of Paul I and the 1802 guild reforms led to the creation of a separate craftsmen's estate. The craftsmen who gained life membership in the guilds (*vichnozapysani*) had all the rights and privileges of town dwellers and paid taxes according to services rendered and the number of workmen employed.

In general, the frequent reforms and changes in official policy reflected ambivalence on the part of the government; at the same time, the state endeavored to retain control over all social strata and to encourage the individual initiative which, it was believed, would further the development of crafts and manufacturing. These contradictions ensured that the nature and functions of the guilds changed slowly under Russian rule. At the end of the 19th century, Russian legislation began to abolish the guilds, turning them into trade associations with charitable goals (eg, in 1886, the Kiev cobblers' guild became a mutual-aid society). The guilds were finally abolished in Western Ukraine by the Austrian government in 1860 and in Russia in 1900.

BIBLIOGRAPHY

Setsinskii, E. *Materialy dlia istorii tsekhov v Podolii* (Kamianets-Podilskyi 1904)

Hrushevs'kyi, M. *Istoriia Ukraïny-Rusy*, 6 (Kiev-Lviv 1907, New York 1955)

Slabchenko, M. *Khoziaistvo Getmanshchiny v XVII–XVIII stoletiiakh*, 2: *Sud'by fabriki i promyshlennosti* (Odessa 1922)
Iershov, A. 'Do istorii tsekhiv na Livoberezhzhi XVII–XVIII vv.,' *Zapysky Nizhens'koho instytutu narodnoï osvity*, 7 (Nizhen 1926)
'Nizhyns'ki tsekhy v pershii polovyni XVII v.,' *Chernihiv i pivnichne Livoberezhzhia*, ed M. Hrushevs'kyi (Kiev 1928)
Charewiczowa, Ł. *Lwowskie organizacje zawodowe za czasów Polski przedrozbiorowej* (Lviv 1929)
Klymenko, P. *Tsekhy na Ukraïni* (Kiev 1929)
Pazhitnov, K. *Problema remeslennykh tsekhov v zakonodatel'stve russkogo absoliutizma* (Moscow 1952)
Kryp'iakevych, I. 'Borot'ba netsekhovykh remisnykiv proty tsekhiv u L'vovi (1590–1630 rr.),' *Z istorii zakhidnoukraïns'kykh zemel'*, 1 (Kiev 1957)
Kis', Ia. *Promyslovist' L'vova u period feodalizmu (XVIII–XIX st.)* (Lviv 1968)

V. Markus

Gulag. See Concentration camps.

Güldenstädt, Johann Anton, b 10 May 1745 in Riga, d 3 April 1781 in St Petersburg. German naturalist and physician. At the request of the St Petersburg Academy of Sciences Güldenstädt visited Ukraine in 1773–4 and was the first to describe carefully the flora, fauna, and soils of the Ukrainian steppe, and to explain the origin of chernozem. He also discovered a number of previously unknown small animals (molerats, a new species of suslik) and collected materials on the history of the Crimea. His writings contain detailed descriptions of the natural features, daily life, and economy of Ukraine. His most important scientific work is *Reisen durch Russland und im Caucasischen Gebirge* (2 vols, 1787, 1791).

Gumilevsky, Filaret (secular name: Konobeevsky, Dmitrii), b 23 October 1805 in Konobeev, Shatsk county, Tambov gubernia, d 9 August 1866 in Chernihiv. Russian theologian and church historian; a graduate and later rector (1835–41) of the Moscow Theological Academy. In 1848 he was appointed bishop of Kharkiv and in 1859 archbishop of Chernihiv. He founded the newspaper *Chernigovskie eparkhial'nye izvestiia*. Among his numerous publications the most significant historical works are *Istoriia russkoi tserkvi* (A History of the Russian Church, 1847–8), *Istoriko-statisticheskoe opisanie khar'kovskoi eparkhii* (A Historical-Statistical Description of Kharkiv Eparchy, 1852–9), and *Istoriko-statisticheskoe opisanie chernigovskoi eparkhii* (A Historical-Statistical Description of Chernihiv Eparchy, 1873). His most important theological works are *Pravoslavnoe dogmaticheskoe bogoslovie* (Orthodox Dogmatic Theology, 1864) and *Obzor russkoi dukhovnoi literatury* (A Review of Russian Theological Literature, 1859–63). He also wrote about the history of Slobidska Ukraine.

Gummerus, Herman, b 24 December 1877, d 18 July 1948. Finnish politician and historian. A professor at Helsinki University, he was an active supporter of Ukraine's right to independence. He maintained contact with Ukrainian revolutionary circles, particularly during the First World War, when he was the Stockholm representative of the Union of Nations Enslaved by Russia. In 1918–19 he was head of Finland's diplomatic mission in Ukraine. He is the author of many speeches and articles on Ukraine and the Swedish book *Orostider i Ukraina* (Turbulent Times in Ukraine, 1931; published in Finnish as *Ukrainan murrosajoilta*).

Herman Gummerus

Guramishvili, David [Guramišvili], b 1705 in Saguramo, Georgia, d 1 August 1792 in Myrhorod, Poltava gubernia. Georgian poet. From 1738 he served in the Russian army, retiring in 1760 to an estate granted to him near Myrhorod. His famous collection of autobiographical poetry *Davitiani* (1787), particularly the poem 'The Shepherd Katsviia,' contains descriptions of Ukrainian landscapes and elements of Ukrainian folk songs and poetry. The collection was translated into Ukrainian by M. Bazhan and published in 1955.

Gutkovsky, Klym [Gutkovs'kyj], b 18 August 1881 in Ternopil, Galicia, d 29 May 1915 in Budapest. Sports organizer, who was active in the Sich and Sokil sports organizations in Galicia and was a well-known cyclist and hiker. He discovered the stalactite caves at Kryvche village in Podilia. In 1914 he joined the Legion of the Ukrainian Sich Riflemen and organized a Hutsul company in Strabychove, Transcarpathia. After a brief training period in Khust, the company distinguished itself under his command defending Vyshkiv Pass against Russian troops in early 1915. Gutkovsky died of battle wounds in a hospital.

Gvardiiske [Gvardiis'ke]. VIII-14–15. Town smt (1977 pop 12,300) in Symferopil raion, Crimea oblast, situated on the Salhyr River. Until 1944 it was called Sarabuz. The Crimean Orcharding Research Station, a branch of the Nikita Botanical Garden, and a republican orchard-planning institute are located here. The food industry is the mainstay of the local economy.

Gymnasium. A general-education secondary school preparing students for university. Gymnasiums originated in Germany in the 16th century.

Galicia. Under the Polish Commonwealth, *education in Ukraine was parochial; the *brotherhood schools and later the *Basilian monastic order administered elementary and secondary education for Ukrainians, while the Jesuit order was primarily responsible for educating Roman Catholics. Austria's recognition of the equality of the Greek Catholic and Roman Catholic churches in the territories acquired by it from Poland in 1772 led to important educational reforms. With the dissolution of the Jesuit order in 1773, its schools in Galicia were replaced by state schools, including four gymnasiums. Most of the students were children of Polish nobles or of German or Czech officials. In 1784, however, Joseph II decreed that only gymnasium graduates would be admitted to seminaries and established Lviv University and the *Academic Gymnasium of Lviv for training Greek Catholic priests with a command of Ukrainian (Ruthenian). The medium of instruction was Latin, with German as an auxiliary language. Ukrainian was taught as a subject. In 1818 the curriculum was expanded from five to six grades; two more grades were added in 1849.

In 1849 the Supreme Ruthenian Council demanded that Ukrainian be introduced as the language of instruction in state schools located in predominantly Ukrainian areas of Galicia. While accepting the demand in principle, the central authorities postponed its implementation out of practical considerations and made Ukrainian a compulsory subject. It retained this status until 1856.

Under the constitution of 1867, the Poles gained control of Galicia's provincial government and educational system. State-funded schools, which had been overseen from 1848 by the imperial Ministry of Education and from 1855 by the consistories, were placed under the Provincial School Board. In the gymnasiums Polish replaced German as the language of instruction. Ukrainian was admitted only as a 'conditionally compulsory' subject (one's choice could not be changed later). Ukrainian was allowed as the medium of instruction only at the Academic Gymnasium of Lviv, at first only in the four lower grades; in the upper grades Polish was used until 1874. State funding for new classes or schools was granted by the Polish-dominated Galician Diet; hence Ukrainian gymnasiums and even parallel Ukrainian classes at Polish gymnasiums could not be established without a determined political struggle. By 1910 there were 35 state gymnasiums in eastern Galicia: 28 Polish, 5 (and a branch) Ukrainian, and 1 German. Thus, there was one Polish gymnasium per 60,400 Poles and one Ukrainian gymnasium per 666,000 Ukrainians. Ukrainian was the language of instruction at the following state gymnasiums: the Academic Gymnasium and its branch (est 1906) in Lviv, and the Peremyshl (parallel Ukrainian courses from 1888, an independent school from 1895), Kolomyia (parallel courses from 1893, independent from 1900), Ternopil (parallel courses from 1898, independent from 1906), and Stanyslaviv (1905) gymnasiums. Parallel Ukrainian classes were also established in the Polish gymnasiums in Berezhany (1906) and Stryi (1907).

Their access to public funding blocked by Polish authorities, Ukrainians turned to organizing privately funded schools. Most of the private Ukrainian gymnasiums were sponsored by the Ruthenian (from 1912 Ukrainian) Pedagogical Society (see *Ridna Shkola) and the *Provincial School Union. By 1914 the following towns had private gymnasiums: Kopychyntsi (1908), Yavoriv (1908), Buchach (1908), Horodenka (1909), Rohatyn (1909), Brody (1909), Peremyshliany (1909), Zbarazh (1910), Buzke (1910), Dolyna (1911), and Chortkiv (1911). For girls there were two secondary schools: a lyceum of the Ukrainian Girls' Institute in Peremyshl (1903) and the first Ukrainian gymnasium for girls run by the Basilian nuns in Lviv (1906). It was difficult to obtain accreditation for these schools from the Provincial School Board, which was controlled by the Poles. Unaccredited gymnasiums could not issue diplomas and could not apply for state support. While many private Polish gymnasiums were accepted after one or two years into the state school system, private Ukrainian schools were not and remained a heavy drain on the financial resources of the Ukrainian community. From 1908 to 1911, Ukrainian boys in Galician gymnasiums numbered 5,670–7,230, or approximately 21–23 percent of the total enrollment in all boys' gymnasiums. Meanwhile, the greater importance of private education is evidenced by the fact that in 1911–12 Ukrainian boys accounted for 33 percent of the enrollment in private gymnasiums; the respective figure for girls was approximately 8 percent. At the time Ukrainians accounted for 42 percent of the province's population.

All Ukrainian gymnasiums were of the classical type, emphasizing Latin and Greek. Their curriculum consisted of the following compulsory subjects: religion, Latin, the language of instruction (Ukrainian or Polish), world geography and history, mathematics (all taught from grades one to eight), Greek (from grade three to eight), biology (grades one, two, five, and six), and physics (grades three, four, seven, and eight). German, French, music, art, physical education, history of Austria-Hungary, stenography, and the other provincial language (Polish or Ukrainian) were electives. Few Ukrainians attended so-called realgymnasiums, which emphasized modern languages and science, or technical schools, partly because these were Polish and partly because technical education was not held in high esteem.

Ukrainian gymnasiums were closed down during the Russian occupation of Galicia (1914–17). In February 1919 the government of the Western Ukrainian National Republic nationalized some private Ukrainian gymnasiums and Ukrainianized some Polish state gymnasiums in Galicia. Thus, the number of Ukrainian state gymnasiums rose to 20. Upon conquering Galicia the Polish authorities recognized only the seven Ukrainian state gymnasiums that had existed before 1 November 1918. In 1920 the gymnasium system was reformed and the humanistic gymnasium (without the Greek language) was introduced. The Ukrainian state gymnasiums were all classical ones, but some new private gymnasiums were humanistic. By 1923 there were 14 Ukrainian gymnasiums financed by the Ukrainian Pedagogical Society (renamed Ridna Shkola in 1926) and parallel Ukrainian classes at the Polish gymnasium in Stryi. In Volhynia, annexed by Poland in 1919, there were only three coeducational private Ukrainian gymnasiums: in Lutske (1918), Kremianets (1923), and Rivne (1923). From 1924 instruction in history, geography, and Polish civics at Ukrainian gymnasiums had to be given by Polish teachers. Later some military training became compulsory as well. Ukrainian was taught to all boys at some Polish gymnasiums because of its possible usefulness in war against the USSR. In 1932 extensive gymnasium reforms were introduced: grades three to six of the old gymnasium were turned into a new four-year gymnasium, while grades seven and eight became a two-grade *lyceum. By curriculum the gymnasiums were classified into mathematico-physical, naturalistic, humanistic, classical, and other categories. By 1939 the number of Ukrainian state gymnasiums declined to 5, while the number of private gymnasiums increased to 22. Of the 27 gymnasiums, 13 were coeducational, 7 were for boys, and 7 for girls. There were also 5 state-funded and 16 private Ukrainian lyceums. At the same time there were 114 Polish gymnasiums and 106 lyceums in Galicia. The total enrollment in Ukrainian gymnasiums and lyceums was 6,000.

During the Second World War the *Generalgouvernement Ukrainian gymnasiums were established in Jarosław and Kholm. With the incorporation of Galicia into the Generalgouvernement in 1941, ten more Ukrainian gymnasiums were established. By 1942 enrollment at the 12 gymnasiums reached 7,017 students, including 2,137 girls; enrollments fell to 5,700 in the following years because of restrictions imposed by German authorities. After the second Soviet occupation of Galicia in 1944, gymnasiums were replaced with *ten-year schools. The gymnasiums in Jarosław and Kholm, which became part of Poland, were closed down by the authorities.

Transcarpathia. The first gymnasium in Transcarpathia was established at Uzhhorod as the Royal Archgymnasium (later *Uzhhorod Gymnasium) in 1778. In 1790 Latin replaced German as the language of instruction, and in 1796 Hungarian replaced Latin. The limited use of Ukrainian was permitted from 1849 to 1851 as a reward to the Ukrainians for their loyalty during the Hungarian revolution. Ukrainian was an optional subject at the Hungarian gymnasiums in Mukachiv (est 1872) and Berehove. With the incorporation of Transcarpathia into Czechoslovakia in 1919, the gymnasiums were transformed into realgymnasiums and Ukrainian was introduced as a language of instruction. By 1921–2 a fourth Ukrainian gymnasium had opened in Khust, and in 1922–3 Ukrainian students numbered 1,660. In 1936 a Ukrainian classical gymnasium was founded by the Basilians in Uzhhorod. By 1938 Subcarpathian Ruthenia had five Ukrainian (three of which offered parallel courses in Czech or Magyar), one Czech, and two Hebrew gymnasiums. In the autonomous state of Carpatho-Ukraine (October 1938–March 1939) there was one private and seven state-funded Ukrainian gymnasiums with an enrollment of 1,941 boys and 1,193 girls. Under the Hungarian occupation (1939–44) all but three Ukrainian gymnasiums were Magyarized; only the local dialect was permitted in the schools, and the term 'Ukrainian' was banned. In 1945 the Soviet school system was introduced and ten-year schools replaced gymnasiums. In the Prešov region there were three Ruthenian-Russian gymnasiums in 1945–6. Later they were transformed into Ukrainian secondary schools.

Bukovyna. The first gymnasium in Bukovyna was a German one opened in Chernivtsi in 1808. Ukrainian was offered as a subject at this school only from 1851. A second German gymnasium with parallel classes taught in Ukrainian was opened in Chernivtsi in 1896, and a similar school was established in Kitsman in 1904. There were two Ukrainian schools: a classical state gymnasium in Vyzhnytsia (1908–21) and a private realgymnasium in Vashkivtsi (from 1912). The German gymnasium in Seret introduced parallel Ukrainian courses in 1914. On the eve of the Rumanian invasion at the end of 1918 there were five Ukrainian gymnasiums (in Chernivtsi, Vyzhnytsia, Vashkivtsi, and two girls' gymnasiums in Chernivtsi and Kitsman) and three bilingual gymnasiums (in Chernivtsi, Kitsman, and Seret); their Ukrainian enrollment was 2,820. Under Rumanian rule all gymnasiums in Bukovyna were Rumanianized by 1924. When the region was incorporated into Soviet Ukraine, the gymnasiums were replaced by Soviet ten-year schools.

Russian-ruled Ukraine. The first gymnasiums appeared at the beginning of the 19th century in the larger cities: Poltava (1804), Kharkiv (1805), Chernihiv (1808), Novhorod-Siverskyi (1808), Kremianets (1812), Katerynoslav (1812), Kiev (1812), Kherson (1814), and Vinnytsia (1814). Prior to that, higher education was provided mostly by the *colleges. In time many county towns had gymnasiums. These schools were an important means of Russifying the offspring of the Cossack officer elite and assimilating them to the Russian nobility. Besides the four-year classical gymnasiums, there were two commercial gymnasiums – in Odessa (1804–17) and Tahanrih (1806–37). After the Polish insurrection of 1830–1, the Polish school system in Right-Bank Ukraine was dismantled and Russian gymnasiums were introduced. Responsibility for administering gymnasiums in Ukrainian territories was transferred from Kharkiv and Vilnius universities to school district curators. In 1864 the gymnasiums were reorganized into classical (offering both Latin and Greek), semiclassical (offering Latin only), and realgymnasiums (offering no ancient languages). Furthermore, the progymnasium, corresponding to the first four years (and later six years) of a regular gymnasium, was introduced. The gymnasium curriculum consisted of religion, Russian language, French or German, mathematics (compulsory in all seven grades), Greek and history (grades three to seven), geography (grades one to four), natural history (grades one to three), and penmanship (grades one to four). Military gymnasiums established in 1862 were converted to cadet schools in 1882. Under the school statute of 1871, ancient languages were emphasized and science was removed from the curriculum. Grade seven was extended to two years, and admission of non-nobles was severely restricted. The realgymnasium was demoted to a realschule, which prepared students for higher technical schools. Towards the end of the century the gymnasium curriculum diverged from the 1871 standard and admission requirements were eased considerably. The growth in the number of gymnasiums and progymnasiums and in their total enrollment is presented in table 1.

At the beginning of the 20th century the number of gymnasiums, especially private ones, rose sharply. Most students were local Ukrainians with a strong admixture of Poles in Right-Bank Ukraine and, in the latter half of the 19th century, Jews in the south. This is illustrated in table 3 by data on the religious composition of the student body in 1887.

Data on the social composition of the student body in 1887 show that gymnasiums basically educated young nobles and townsmen. Sons of clergy were encouraged to enter seminaries, not gymnasiums. (See table 2.)

In 1862 private seven-year girls' gymnasiums began to be organized. The Ministry of Public Education began to set up similar gymnasiums in 1870. These schools did not offer ancient languages, but had seven regular grades and an eighth grade for training elementary-school teachers and governesses. Four- and five-grade state progymnasiums were also founded. There were many more private gymnasiums than state ones. By 1887 in the Kharkiv school district there were 18 girls' gymnasiums and 40 progymnasiums with a total enrollment of 10,337, while in the Odessa school district the respective figures were 17, 18, and 6,451. Before 1917 the gymnasiums in Ukraine were entirely Russian institutions. Only two private boys' gymnasiums – V. Naumenko's in Kiev and

TABLE 1
Number of gymnasiums (G), progymnasiums (P), and students (S) in Russian-ruled Ukraine

School district	1824		1836		1847		1854		1863		1876			1887			1891		
	G	S	G	S	G	S	G	S	G	S	G	P	S	G	P	S	G	P	S
Kharkiv	12	1,153	6	1,336	7	1,808	7	1,357	7	2,702	11	10	5,136	17	12	5,641	17	10	5,177
Odessa	–	–	5	659	6	1,842	7	1,692	8	2,332	13	10	4,956	16	10	5,387	16	10	5,148
Kiev	–	–	9	3,165	11	4,151	11	3,539	11	4,841	11	6	5,882	17	7	7,514	18	6	7,174

TABLE 2
Social composition of students, 1887

School district	Nobility	Clergy	Townsmen	Peasants	Foreigners	Others
Kharkiv	2,757	340	1,925	515	104	–
Odessa	2,096	160	2,729	182	200	20
Kiev	4,183	543	2,149	395	162	82

TABLE 3
Religious background of gymnasium students, 1887

School district	Orthodox	Roman Catholic	Protestant	Jewish	Other
Kharkiv	4,907	169	123	337	42
Odessa	3,137	272	116	1,622	240
Kiev	4,910	1,567	138	885	14

Kovalchuk's in Odessa – encouraged an interest in Ukrainian culture. At the turn of the century secret Ukrainian student circles existed at gymnasiums in Kiev, Poltava, Pryluky, and Lubni.

After the February Revolution of 1917 the Russian Provisional Government permitted the opening of only two Ukrainian gymnasiums. The efforts of the UNR Secretariat of Education to Ukrainianize gymnasiums were hampered by Russified school administrators and teachers. The Ukrainian community, however, began to establish its own gymnasiums: the Shevchenko Gymnasium, the Cyril and Methodius Gymnasium, and three others in Kiev; the Kotliarevsky Gymnasium in Poltava; the Hrinchenko Gymnasium in Kharkiv; the Drahomanov Gymnasium in Odessa; and others in Katerynoslav, Kamianets, Kherson, and even in some county centers and larger villages. By the end of 1918 there were about 150 Ukrainian gymnasiums. The Ukrainian language and Ukrainian studies were taught at the established Russian gymnasiums in Ukraine. At the beginning of 1919 there were a total of 836 gymnasiums in the UNR, of which 161 were state-funded, 409 community-funded, and 266 privately funded; 474 were for boys, 362 for girls. Two Ukrainian gymnasiums were established in the Kuban. In 1920, after the Bolsheviks occupied Ukraine, the gymnasiums were converted into *labor schools.

Abroad. A number of Ukrainian gymnasiums were organized by Ukrainian émigrés; eg, in Harbin, Manchuria, in 1917 (closed down by Chinese authorities in the 1920s). After the war refugees and prisoners of war from the UNR set up a gymnasium in Kalisz, Poland (1924–34) and a realgymnasium in Prague (1925, transferred to Řevnice in 1927 and to Modřany in 1937). After the Second World War 27 DP camps in Germany and two in Austria had Ukrainian gymnasiums in 1947–8. As Ukrainians emigrated to countries with a different educational system, the Ukrainian gymnasium became all but extinct. One Ruthenian gymnasium, using the *Bačka dialect as the medium of instruction, was established in 1945 in Ruski Krstur, Serbia.

(See also *Education.)

BIBLIOGRAPHY
Buzek, J. *Rozwój stanu szkół średnich w Galicyi w ciągu ostatnich lat 50 (1859–1909)* (Lviv 1909)
Alston, P. *Education and the State in Tsarist Russia* (Stanford 1969)
Sirka, A. *The Nationality Question in Austrian Education: The Case of Ukrainians in Galicia, 1867–1914* (Frankfurt am Main 1980)

P. Polishchuk, B. Struminsky

Gymnastics. A sport involving systematic and usually rhythmic physical exercises for men and women as well as performances on special gymnastic apparatus. In Ukraine, gymnastics was first practiced in the first half of the 19th century by the youth of the nobility. The sport came from Western Europe and was widely publicized in the press as a form of physical therapy. In 1838 commanders in the Russian army were ordered to institute the use of gymnastics among the troops, but the practice did not spread. In the early 20th century Swedish-style gymnastics spread in Western Ukraine, promoted by such youth organizations as *Sokil, *Sich, and *Plast, which were modeled on the Czech Sokol movement. Towns in Russian-ruled Ukraine had Russian Sokol organizations, in which some Ukrainian youths participated. In 1913 the first All-Russian Olympiad was held in Kiev; gymnastics was included in the program.

The first years of Soviet rule in Ukraine saw the emergence of the so-called proletarian-culture movement, whose founders labeled competitive gymnastics a 'bourgeois' sport and promoted instead 'labor' gymnastics (*trudova himnastyka*). In the 1930s, sports, including gymnastics, became widespread in Ukraine since they were included in the party's program of the education of workers. Efforts were made at a number of conferences to standardize the sport by establishing set rules and criteria for competition. In 1937 all-Union regulations were adopted and Soviet athletes began to compete in international meets, although it was only in 1938–40 that gymnastics began to enjoy great success in Ukraine. In 1938, the Kiev gymnast A. Ibadulaiev became the all-round champion of the USSR.

After the Second World War, O. Myshakov was placed in charge of Ukrainian gymnastics. As a result of his training methods, the Ukrainian gymnasts M. Horokhovska, L. Latynina, N. Bocharova, V. Chukarin, B. Shakhlin, D. Leonkin, M. Nikolaeva, Yu. Titov, and P. Astakhova became world and Olympic champions in gymnastics. In four consecutive Olympic games (1952–64), Ukrainian gymnasts won a total of 27 individual or team gold medals, 17 silver, and 13 bronze, and were repeatedly world and European champions. After Myshakov was dismissed from his post gymnastics in Ukraine declined, and in the next four Olympic games (1968–80) Ukrainian gymnasts did not win a single individual gold medal. At the start of the 1980s, a revival of gymnastics began in Ukraine, with such international-class gymnasts as S. Zakharova (Kiev) and B. Makuts (Lviv). The 1985 world championships in Montreal saw O. Omelianchyk from Kiev share the title of all-round women's champion. In 1976, Ukrainian gymnast Yu. Titov was elected president of the International Gymnastics Federation.

BIBLIOGRAPHY
Himnastyka (Kiev 1956)
Latynina, L. *Soniachna molodist'* (Kiev 1958)
Shakhlin, B. *Narodzhennia peremoh* (Kiev 1962)

O. Zinkevych

György I Rákóczi. See Rákóczi I, György.

György II Rákóczi. See Rákóczi II, György.

Gypsies (Ukrainian: *tsyhany*). Gypsies (from 'Egyptians,' as they were known in the English statutes) are the descendants of wandering tribes that left northern India toward the end of the 1st millennium AD. They call themselves Rom, meaning 'Men,' and their language is known as Romani; its structure is derived from Sanskrit, and it contains Greek, Rumanian, and Slavic features. At first the Gypsies settled in Persia and Armenia. Brought to Anatolia by the Byzantines, in the 13th and 14th centuries they spread into the Balkans and Eastern Europe, and thence into Central and Western Europe. They were eventually dispersed, often by expulsion, throughout the world, in which there is today an estimated 8 to 10 million. All Gypsies who speak Romani are bilingual: besides their mother tongue they speak the language of the country in which they live.

The presence of Gypsies in Ukraine was first documented in the early 15th century (Sianik, 1428). In general, they led a closed, aloof, nomadic or semisettled way of life. In winter they usually lived in huts, wagons, and tents on the outskirts of villages. Traditionally they worked as artisans (blacksmiths, carpenters, coppersmiths), horse traders, animal trainers, and peddlers. Streetcorner entertaining, music-making, singing, dancing, conjuring, fortune-telling, begging, and petty crime were sources of supplementary income. In Left-Bank Ukraine, where they were more sedentary and wealthier than in Right-Bank Ukraine, some intermarried with Ukrainians. The nomadic Gypsies maintained their social organization and folkways, shunning non-Gypsy contacts, education, and values, often as a reaction to prevailing anti-Gypsy attitudes and persecution. Each clan (an alliance of families) elected its own chieftain. Repeated attempts by the Polish, Austrian, and Russian authorities to force the Gypsies to integrate and adopt a settled way of life proved unsuccessful. To some extent, however, the Gypsies did accept the language and faith of the dominant society, being Orthodox in most of Ukraine, Catholics in Galicia and Transcarpathia, and Moslems in the Crimea.

During the Second World War Nazi policies to exterminate the Gypsies were implemented in occupied Ukraine, as in other countries. In July 1943 the Rumanian authorities transported some 25,000 Gypsies to Transnistria, along the Boh River; about half of them perished because of brutal treatment. Estimates of the total number murdered in Europe range from 220,000 to 400,000; in Ukraine thousands were killed at Babyn Yar in Kiev, and in the Crimea, Podilia, Galicia, and Volhynia.

According to the 1926 Soviet census, there were 13,600 Gypsies in the Ukrainian SSR, 2,500 of whom lived in cities. In the Crimea there were 1,300, and in northern Caucasia, 6,800. On all of the Ukrainian ethnic territories there were close to 20,000. According to the 1970 census there were 30,100 Gypsies in the Ukrainian SSR (up from 28,000 in 1959), and 175,300 in the USSR as a whole. In 1979 there were 209,200 Gypsies in the USSR according to the census; of these, 34,500 were in Ukraine. Western experts estimate there were 480,000 in the USSR in 1980, although the estimate of the World Romani Union is considerably higher.

Gypsies are scattered throughout Ukraine, but their largest concentrations are in Transcarpathia, Crimea, and Odessa oblasts. Almost half of them live in cities. Forty percent of urban Gypsies and 35 percent of rural Gypsies consider Romani their mother tongue. With the Soviet authorities forcing the Gypsies to adopt a settled way of life (resolution in 1926 and a government decree in 1956), more are increasingly being employed in agriculture and industry.

The material culture of the Gypsies has never differed appreciably from that of the dominant society except in dress. They have, however, a rich folk tradition, with its own mythology and magic, oral literature, songs, music, and dance. Gypsy themes can be found in Ukrainian literature (particularly in the writings of S. Rudansky, M. Starytsky, I. Franko, and O. Kobylianska) and in music.

BIBLIOGRAPHY
Barannikov, A. 'Ob izuchenii tsygan SSSR,' *Izvestiia AN SSSR,* 1929, series VII, nos 5–6
German, A. *Bibliografiia o tsyganakh: Ukazatel' knig i statei s 1780 g. po 1930 g.* (Moscow 1930; Leipzig 1977)
Barannikov, O. *Ukraïns'ki tsyhany* (Kiev 1931)
– *The Ukrainian and South Russian Gypsy Dialects* (Leningrad 1933)
Ficowski, J. *Cyganie Polscy: Szkice historyczno-obyczajowe* (Warsaw 1953)
Kenrick, D.; Puxon, G. *The Destiny of Europe's Gypsies* (Sussex-London 1972)
Hancock, I. *Gypsy Slavery and Persecution* (Lewiston, NY 1986)

V. Kubijovyč, R. Senkus

Gypsum. Mineral, hydrous calcium sulfate. In nature it is usually found in a granular (alabaster), fibrous (selenite), or crystalline form. Pure gypsum is colorless and transparent; different impurities give it different colors. Gypsum is used widely in manufacturing cementing materials, paints, enamels, and glazes; in improving the soil (gypsuming); in medicine and optics. Before 1917 gypsum was produced mostly on a seasonal basis using artisan techniques. In 1913 Ukraine produced only 62,000 t, which accounted for 31 percent of the total gypsum production of the Russian Empire. By 1940 Ukraine's gypsum production reached 892,000 t, and by 1983, 956,000 t or approximately 29 percent of the USSR production. The largest deposits of gypsum lie in the Donets Basin, and were formed in the Permian period. Second in importance are the deposits along the Dniester River in Western Ukraine. Smaller deposits are located in Sumy, Poltava, and Crimea oblasts.

Gytha, dates unknown. Daughter of the last Anglo-Saxon king in England, Harold II. After Harold's death in the Battle of Hastings in 1066, she took refuge at the court of the Danish king Sweyn II. In 1074 or 1075 she became the first wife of Prince *Volodymyr Monomakh.

Gzhytsky, Volodymyr [Gzhyts'kyj], b 15 October 1895 in Ostrivets, Terebovlia county, Galicia, d 19 December 1973 in Lviv. Writer. After serving in the Ukrainian Galician Army in 1918–19, he moved to Kharkiv. He was a member of the writers' groups *Pluh and *Zakhidnia Ukraina. The history of Western Ukraine is the subject of many of his works. His novel *Chorne ozero* (The Black Lake, 1929) provoked severe official criticism because it exposed Russian colonial policies towards other nations of the USSR. In 1934 he was sent to a Soviet concentration camp. He was released and rehabilitated in 1956 and returned to Lviv. There he published, among other works, the prose collection *Povernennia* (The Return, 1958), the autobiographical novel *U shyrokyi svit* (Into the Wide World, 1960), and the novels *Opryshky* (Opryshoks, 1962), parts of which first appeared in the 1930s, *Slovo chesty* (Word of Honor, 1968), and *Karmeliuk* (1971).

Volodymyr Gzhytsky

H

Haas, Maara (née Lazechko, Myroslava), b 12 February 1920 in Winnipeg. Canadian poet and writer of Ukrainian origin. She has translated in her own poetic idiom much of T. Shevchenko's poetry and has written a television script about his life. Her best-known work is the humorous autobiographical novel *The Street Where I Live* (1976), which depicts Winnipeg's north end in the 1930s.

Habsburg dynasty. Family that ruled the Duchy (later Archduchy) of Austria from 1278. In 1526 they gained possession of the Bohemian and Hungarian kingdoms (including Transcarpathia), and from 1452 to 1806 members of the family were the emperors of the Holy Roman Empire; in the 19th century they took the title of Emperor of Austria (from 1867 the Dual Monarchy of Austria-Hungary). The Habsburgs also acquired the titles of King of Galicia and Lodomeria (Volodymeria) after the annexation of Galicia in 1772, and Prince of Bukovyna in 1849. *Maria Theresa (1740–80), *Joseph II (1780–90), Leopold II (1790–2), Francis I (1792–1835), Ferdinand I (1835–48), *Francis Joseph I (1848–1916), and Charles I (1916–18) were all Habsburgs who ruled over Galicia and Bukovyna. In general, the policy of the Habsburgs was oriented towards maintaining a centralized empire, to which end they followed the maxim of *divide et impera*. They tolerated national differences in cultural matters, but repressed any separatist movements. In socioeconomic affairs, Austria under the Habsburgs maintained the non-German provinces as internal colonies. The reign of the Habsburgs in Galicia and Bukovyna ended when the *Western Ukrainian National Republic was created on 1 November 1918 in Galicia and on 6 November 1918 in Bukovyna.

Archduke Wilhelm Habsburg-Lothringen (Vasyl Vyshyvany)

Habsburg-Lothringen, Wilhelm, b 10 February 1895 in Pula, Dalmatia (now Yugoslavia), d 1949. Austrian prince and army officer. A supporter of the Ukrainian cultural and national movement who adopted the name Vasyl Vyshyvany, Habsburg won wide popularity among Galician Ukrainians. In 1918 he commanded Austrian army units in southern Ukraine, including units of the *Ukrainian Sich Riflemen. In the autumn of 1918 his command was transferred from Oleksandrivske (now Zaporizhia) to Bukovyna. During 1919 Habsburg served as a colonel in the UNR war ministry. In August 1947 he was arrested by the MVD in Vienna and imprisoned in the USSR, where he later died. He is the subject of a biography by N. Hirniak (1956).

Hacquet, Baltazar, b 1739 or 1740 in Leconquet, Brittany, France, d 10 January 1815 in Vienna. Austrian physician and naturalist of French origin. Hacquet was a professor of natural history and medicine at Lviv University from 1787 to 1805, concentrating on the fields of geology and biology. He carried out a number of scientific expeditions to various regions of the Austrian empire, leaving descriptions of the environment, natural resources, and the customs of the inhabitants in numerous works, such as his four-volume *Neueste physikalisch-politische Reisen in den Jahren 1788 und 1789 durch die Dacischen und Sarmathischen oder Nördlichen Karpathen* (1790–6).

Hadiache or **Hadiach** [Hadjače or Hadjač]. III-14. Town (1969 pop 13,200) and raion center in Poltava oblast. Established in 1634, under the Hetman state it was a fortified regimental center (1648–9, 1672–1783). There Hetman I. Vyhovsky concluded the Treaty of *Hadiache with Poland in 1658. Under Russian rule it was a county town in Poltava gubernia (1803–1917). The scholar and civic leader M. Drahomanov was born there in 1841. The P. Prokopovych Research Station of Apiculture, an agricultural school, and a regional history museum are located there.

Hadiache, Treaty of. An agreement with Poland signed on 16 September 1658 by Hetman I. *Vyhovsky after he suppressed a revolt led by the colonel of Poltava, M. *Pushkar, and severed relations with Muscovy for its violations of the 1654 Treaty of *Pereiaslav. The Polish commission at the negotiations was led by S. Bieniewski and K. Jewłaszewski; the Ukrainian, by Yu. *Nemyrych, the architect of the treaty, and P. *Teteria.

According to the treaty, Kiev, Chernihiv, and Bratslav palatinates were to constitute the independent Grand Duchy of Rus', whose nobles and Cossack *starshyna* would be equal partners with their Polish and Lithuanian counterparts in a gentry-ruled federation under a commonly elected king. The duchy was to be governed by a hetman elected for life from among four candidates presented by the Ukrainian estates and confirmed by the king. There were to be an autonomous duchy administration, duchy senators and deputies to the common Sejm, and a separate court system, treasury, currency, and army of 30,000 registered Cossacks and 10,000 regular mercenaries, paid from public taxes. The hetman and his army were to remain faithful to the Crown and the duchy could not have diplomatic relations or enter into alliances with foreign states. The Polish and Lithuanian armies were denied the right to enter the duchy, except in the event of war, and then they would come under the hetman's command. Up to 100 worthy Cossacks in each regiment could be granted noble status. Poles who had lost their properties during the *Cossack-Polish War would have them restored, subject to the hetman's approval. A general anmesty was to be effected. The Orthodox were to enjoy the same unrestricted rights as the Catholics throughout the Commonwealth, and the Orthodox metropolitan of Kiev and the bishops of Lutske, Lviv, Peremyshl, Kholm, and Mstsislau were to sit in the common Senate. No Uniate monasteries or churches were to be built in the duchy. Two Orthodox academies (universities) – in Kiev and elsewhere – were to be opened. An unlimited number of Orthodox schools, colleges, gymnasiums, and printing presses could be established, and the freedom to publish was guaranteed.

In protracted negotiations the Ukrainian envoys strove unsuccessfully to have Volhynia, Belz, Galicia, Podilia, Pynske, Starodub, and Ovruch palatinates included in the Grand Duchy of Rus'. The treaty was finally ratified by the Sejm on 22 May 1659, but, in spite of support from the Cossack *starshyna*, Ukrainian nobles, and higher clergy, it did not find favor among the Cossack and peasant masses, which remained hostile to the restoration of de facto Polish rule and the prewar status quo, and to greater stratification among the Cossacks. Because of Vyhovsky's failures in the war with Muscovy that followed his initial victory at *Konotip in June 1659, uprisings against him, and his withdrawal from political affairs and demise, the terms of the treaty were never implemented.

BIBLIOGRAPHY
Budzynovs'kyi, V. *Hadiats'ki postuliaty i Het'man Vyhovs'kyi* (Lviv 1907)
Herasymchuk, V. 'Vyhovshchyna i Hadiats'kyi traktat,' *ZNTSh*, 89 (1909)
Hadiats'kyi dohovir mizh Ukraïnoiu i Pol'shcheiu 1658 r. (Lviv 1934)
Mishko, S. 'Hadiats'kyi dohovir,' *Vil'na Ukraïna* (Detroit), 23–4 (1959)
Kot, S. *Jerzy Niemirycz w 300-lecie Ugody Hadziackiej* (Paris 1960)
O'Brien, C. *Muscovy and the Ukraine from the Pereiaslav Agreement to the Truce of Andrusovo, 1654–1667* (Berkeley 1963)
Kamiński, A. 'The Cossack Experiment in *Szlachta* Democracy in the Polish-Lithuanian Commonwealth: The Hadiach (Hadziacz) Union,' HUS, 1, no. 2 (1977)

B. Krupnytsky

Hadzhega, Vasyl [Hadžega, Vasyl'], b 28 July 1864 in Poliana, Máramaros county, d 15 March 1938 in Uzhhorod. Greek Catholic priest (canon and archpriest) in Transcarpathia; historian, pedagogue, and civic leader; full and honorary member of the Shevchenko Scientific Society. After graduating from a seminary in Budapest and obtaining a doctorate in theology in Vienna, he became archivist of the Mukachiv Eparchy and professor at the Uzhhorod Theological Seminary. He was active in pro-Ukrainian institutions, a leading member of the Christian Popular party, and supporter of Rev A. *Voloshyn's views. As archivist, he did extensive research in the socio-economic history of Transcarpathia, and particularly in the history of the church. Many of his articles were published in the periodicals *Naukovyi zbirnyk tovarystva Prosvita v Uzhhorodi*, which he edited, and *Podkarpatskaia Rus'*, which he coedited. He also wrote a novelette, *Vyshchehrad* (1926). A complete bibliography of his works appeared in *Naukovyi zbirnyk tovarystva Prosvita v Uzhhorodi*, vols 13–14 (1938).

Vasyl Hadzhega

Hadziewicz, Rafał, b 13 October 1803 in Zamch near Biłgoraj (now Poland), d 17 September 1886 in Kielce, Poland. Classical painter and graphic artist. Having studied art in Warsaw (1822–9), Dresden and Paris (1829–31), and Italy (1831–3), he taught painting and drawing at the Art School in Cracow (1834–9), Moscow University (1839–44), and the School of Fine Arts (1844–64) and the Drawing Class (1864–71) in Warsaw. In 1871 he retired to Kielce. Hadziewicz was an eclectic painter who dealt with mythological, religious, and historical themes. He is noted for his self-portraits and portraits. His genre paintings on Ukrainian themes include *The Blind Man Playing the Guitar* and *A Ukrainian Peasant Family in the Evening around a Lamp*. Among his religious works is the well-known iconostasis (1844–6) of the Stariava village church in Mostyska county, Galicia.

Hadzinsky, Mykola [Hadzins'kyj], b 1901 in Kamianets, Brest county, Hrodna gubernia, d 4 August 1984 in Rochester, New York. Experimental physicist. A graduate of Kharkiv University, from 1932 to 1941 he chaired the Department of Physics at the Kharkiv Zootechnical Institute and did research at the Kharkiv Roentgen-Radium Institute. He contributed to the early development of nuclear physics in Kharkiv. Immigrating to Germany and in 1951 to the United States, he served as professor and chairman of the Physics Department at Wilberforce University, and then from 1955 to 1969 as professor of physics at the Rochester Institute of Technology. He was one of the leaders of the *United Hetman Organization and served as the chairman of its presidium.

Hagiography. Biographies, tales, and legends about saints, including accounts of miracles performed by them, particular episodes from their lives, and their martyrdom. These writings are among the most important monuments of old Ukrainian literature. By the 11th century there were already many translations of Greek and Latin hagiographic writings, individual lives of saints such as the Pannonian Lives of ss Cyril and Methodius, the Czech lives of St Václav and St Ludmila, and the Moravian Life of St Vitus; patericons (collections of episodes from lives of monks) such as the Patericon of Sinai, of Jerusalem, and of Rome (a redaction of Pope Gregory the Great's *Dialogues*); reading menologies (collections of lives and sermons arranged according to the church calendar, not for liturgical use but for daily reading); and prologues or synaxaries (collections similar to menologies but with abridged lives). Original works written in Ukraine include the Lives of ss Borys and Hlib (*Chtenie*) and the Life of St Theodosius of the Kievan Cave Monastery, both by Nestor the Chronicler (end of the 11th century), the beautifully composed *Skazanie* (Tale) of the murder of Borys and Hlib, and the Life of Prince Mstyslav. The lives of St Volodymyr the Great, St Olha, Mykhailo of Chernihiv, and Boyar Fedir have come down to us only in later redactions. Fragments of the Life of the Varangians Slaughtered by Pagans in Kiev, the Life of St Anthony of the Kievan Cave Monastery, and the Life of Prince Ihor of Chernihiv have been preserved in the chronicles. The *Kievan Cave Patericon, consisting of the correspondence between Bishop Simon and Brother Polycarp (1215–25) and several tales by Polycarp (1223–33), is an important monument of hagiographic literature.

Because of Western European and Polish influence, there was a revival of hagiographic literature in the 17th century. A new redaction of a two-volume prologue with versed epigrams, a Polish and a Ukrainian Church Slavonic edition of the Kievan Cave Patericon, A. Kalnofoisky's *Teraturgema*, and lives of Uniate saints, mostly in Latin, were published. P. Mohyla collected tales of a hagiographic nature that remained unpublished. Some of his material was used by I. Gizel and V. Yasynsky. D. Tuptalo's reading menology based on Slavonic and Latin literature as well as some new manuscript sources is a masterpiece of Ukrainian hagiographic literature. This work influenced the literatures of all Orthodox Slavs. In the 18th–20th centuries lives of saints assumed an official character. This is true of the lives of St Dmytro (Tuptalo), St Tikhon Zadonsky, St Innocent of Irkutsk, and Y. *Horlenko. Lives of saints are an important auxiliary source for the history of Ukraine.

BIBLIOGRAPHY

Kliuchevskii, V. *Drevnerusskie zhitiia sviatykh kak istoricheskii istochnik* (Moscow 1871)
Barsukov, N.P. *Istochniki russkoi agiografii* (St Petersburg 1882)
Hrushevs'kyi, M. *Istoriia ukraïns'koï literatury*, vols 2–3 (Kiev-Lviv 1923; 2nd edn, New York 1959)
Dublians'kyi, A. *Ukraïns'ki sviati* (Munich 1962)

D. Chyzhevsky, A. Zhukovsky

Hahilky. See *Vesnianky-hahilky*.

Hai, Oleksander [Haj], b 8 August 1914 in Katerynoslav (now Dnipropetrovske). Stage and screen actor. He began his career at the Dnipropetrovske Ukrainian Music and Drama Theater in 1929. A graduate of the Moscow Artistic Academic Theater (1936), in 1947 he joined the Lviv Ukrainian Drama Theater, where he has appeared in various plays. His film credits include the lead role in *Hryhorii Skovoroda* (1958), M. Kotsiubynsky in *Rodyna Kotsiubyns'kykh* (The Kotsiubynsky Family, 1970), and Terracini in the screen version of O. Korniichuk's play *Pam'iat' sertsia* (Memory of the Heart, 1971).

Hai-Holovko, Oleksa [Haj-Holovko] (Hay-Holowko), b 12 August 1910 in Pysarivka, Balta county, Podilia gubernia. Writer. He worked as an editor for the journal *Chervonyi shliakh* in Kharkiv and the Kiev film studio in the 1930s and was a member of the Ukrainian Writers' Union from 1933. In 1940 he moved to Lviv and during the war he worked as a forced laborer in Germany. He immigrated to England in 1948 and settled in Canada in 1949. Among his works are the collections of poetry *Shturmovi baliady* (Storming Ballads, 1934) and *Surmach* (The Bugler, 1942); the short stories *Svitannia* (Dawn, 1936) and *Odchaidushni* (The Audacious, 1959); the satirical long poem *Kokhaniiada* (The Love-in, 1947); and the autobiographical accounts *Poiedynok z dyiavolom* (Duel with the Devil, 2 vols, 1950) and *Smertel'noiu dorohoiu* (Along the Road of Death, 2 vols, 1979, 1983). His collected poetical works appeared in Toronto in 1970 and 1978.

Haida [Hajda]. Discovered in 1978 in the Carpathian foothills by an expedition of the Museum of Folk Architecture and Folkways of the Ukrainian SSR, a folk musical instrument in the form of a straight whistle flute with two movable wooden rings. It was carved from wood and decorated with elaborate and original designs. Some scholars, such as I. Shramko, believe that this instrument was directly connected with an ancient cult of a fertility god.

Haidai, Mykhailo [Hajdaj, Myxajlo], b 9 December 1878 in Dankivka khutir, Pryluky county, Chernihiv gubernia, d 9 September 1965 in Kiev. Composer, choir director, ethnographer. A conductor of various Ukrainian choirs in Vinnytsia, Moscow, and Kiev, where he conducted DUMKA (1924–7), Haidai wrote choral works and arrangements of Ukrainian folk songs. As an ethnographer, he was associated with the VUAN Ethnographic Commission (1920–33), the AN URSR Institute of Folklore (1936–41), and the Institute of Fine Arts, Folklore, and Ethnography. He transcribed over 2,000 folk songs, many of which were published in his *Zrazky narodnoï polifoniï* (Examples of Folk Polyphony, 2 vols, 1928–9).

Haidai, Zoia [Hajdaj, Zoja], b 2 June 1902 in Tambov, Russia, d 21 April 1965 in Kiev. Operatic soprano. A

Zoia Haidai

graduate of the Lysenko Music and Drama Institute in Kiev (1927), she was a soloist of the Kiev (1928–30, 1935–55) and Kharkiv (1930–4) opera and ballet theaters, and a teacher at the Kiev Conservatory (1947–65). She appeared in over 50 Ukrainian, Russian, and Western European operas, including S. Hulak-Artemovsky's *Zaporozhian Cossack beyond the Danube* (as Oksana) and M. Verykivsky's *Servant Girl* (as Hanna). She also appeared on the stage outside the USSR in such countries as China, Canada, and the United States. In 1960 L. Doroshenko wrote a biography of Haidai.

Haidamaka, Dmytro [Hajdamaka] (real name: Vertepov), b 7 February 1864 in Lukovskaia near Piatigorsk in Caucasia, d 9 May 1936 in Dnipropetrovske. Stage impresario, actor, and director. He began his acting and directing career in M. *Kropyvnytsky's troupe in 1891. From 1897 to 1917 he managed his own troupe, consisting of 40–60 actors and a choir of 30–40 people, and staged classical and contemporary plays, operas, and operettas. Thereafter he worked with various troupes, including those of the Donetske (1927–34), Leningrad, and Dnipropetrovske (1934–6) Ukrainian drama theaters.

Haidamaka. A participant in spontaneous, popular uprisings against the Polish regime in Right-Bank Ukraine in the 18th century. The term's origin is Turkish (*hajdemak*, 'to pursue'); it signifies a restless, rebellious individual. The Balkan Slavs have a corresponding term – *hajduk*. The Galician Ukrainian equivalent is *opryshok. Haidamakas were recruited from among dissatisfied peasants, fugitive serfs, hired laborers, and even artisans and burghers. They formed detachments or bands under the leadership of chieftains who collaborated to organize large-scale rebellions known as the *haidamaka uprisings. The earliest information about haidamakas comes from 1708, when rebels led by H. Pashchenko were active in Volhynia; by 1712 they had extended their operations to Podilia and the Bratslav and Kiev regions. The term was first used in a document dated 22 February 1717.

Haidamaka Battalion of Slobidska Ukraine (Haidamatskyi Kish Slobidskoi Ukrainy). Military unit formed in Kiev during December 1917 by S. *Petliura, who became its first commander. Initially composed of one infantry battalion and one artillery battery with a total strength of 300, it played a prominent role in the battle for Kiev during January and February 1918. Many of its first members were students from local military schools. In March 1918 the unit was incorporated into the Zaporozhian Corps as the 3rd Haidamaka Infantry Regiment under Col V. Sikevych. In June 1919 it was transformed into a brigade consisting of four infantry battalions and other units under Otaman O. Volokh. Later that year the unit, under Volokh's influence, mutinied against the UNR and acted independently until its destruction in 1920.

Haidamaka Cavalry Regiment (Haidamatskyi kinnyi polk im. K. Hordiienka). The first regular cavalry unit of the Army of the UNR. It originated within the Turkestan Division of the Russian army in southwestern Volhynia in late 1917 under Col V. Petriv. During January 1918 it fought its way to Kiev and participated in combat defending the Central Rada. In March 1918 the regiment was incorporated into the *Zaporozhian Corps and remained part of it until the war for Ukrainian independence ended.

Haidamaka Units of the Army of the UNR. Military formations that arose in 1917 either as a result of the officially sanctioned Ukrainianization of certain units of the Russian army, or in a spontaneous, revolutionary manner, against the will of the Russian commanders. Most of the haidamaka units disintegrated with the collapse of the Russian army. Others – such as the haidamaka battalions in Katerynoslav and Odessa, the haidamaka companies in Uman and Oleksandrivske, and the haidamaka company formed in the Finland Division of the Russian army – took part in battles with Bolshevik forces in December 1917. They were routed with heavy losses and ceased to exist. Only two haidamaka formations were incorporated within the regular Ukrainian army in February 1918: the *Haidamaka Battalion of Slobidska Ukraine and the K. Hordiienko *Haidamaka Cavalry Regiment.

Haidamaka uprisings (Haidamachchyna). Eighteenth-century popular rebellions against the social, national, and religious oppression of the Polish regime in Right-Bank Ukraine.

As corvée obligations and the abuse of power by Polish magnates and nobles and their Jewish stewards in Ukraine increased, disaffection among the common people grew; serfs, other peasants, impoverished Cossacks, artisans, petty burghers, and agricultural colonists fled from their oppressors into the steppes or forests. There they formed bands of *haidamakas, which moved swiftly from one area to another to attack their unwary enemy and disappeared again into the wilds. Zaporozhian Cossacks played leading roles as organizers of the rebel bands, which plundered and burned towns and nobles' estates, killing Roman Catholic and Uniate clerics, nobles and their agents, Jewish stewards, innkeepers, and money lenders, thereby inflicting heavy economic losses on the latifundia system. The Poles reacted by further repressing the peasantry. Haidamakas who were captured were tortured and cruelly executed. Yet the haidamakas' call for a land free from Poles, Jews, and landlords, for the abolition of serfdom, and for the free exercise of the Orthodox faith found sympathy among the peasantry and many Orthodox monks, who often provided them with shelter, supplies, and hiding places. The small Polish army in Ukraine and the magnates' household militias (consisting of Cossacks who often switched sides) found it hard to counteract them, and haidamaka raids became more and more common, thus turning into mass uprisings that covered the entire breadth of Right-Bank Ukraine.

The first general insurrection broke out in 1734 during the war for the Polish throne after the death of Augustus II. Russian troops, which had been sent to depose King *Stanisłaus I Leszczyński, were viewed as the harbingers of liberation from Polish oppression, and the masses of the Kiev region rebelled. The uprising quickly spread to Podilia and part of Volhynia, where it became particularly violent. *Verlan, the former captain of the Lubomirski family's Cossack militia in Sharhorod, became the supreme commander of the rebel army. Other leaders included S. *Chaly, who eventually betrayed the haidamakas, M. *Hryva, I. Medvid, M. Motorny, and Pysarenko. In summer 1734 the haidamakas captured several towns, including Vinnytsia, Zhvanets, Kremianets, Brody, and Zbarazh, and penetrated as far as Kamianets-Podilskyi and Lviv. The uprising was crushed by the intervention of Russian troops, after Augustus III ascended the Polish throne. Thereafter smaller haidamak rebellions continued for some time (see H. *Holy).

The second major uprising broke out in 1750 without an external stimulus, but simply as a result of the movement's increased popular support. Having organized themselves on the territory of the Zaporozhian Cossacks, the haidamakas crossed into the southern part of the Kiev palatinate. Led by M. Sukhy, P. Taran, O. Pysmenny, I. Pokoliaka, M. Teslia, Mochula, and others, they roused almost the entire populace of Right-Bank Ukraine to revolt. They captured Uman, Vinnytsia, Chyhyryn, Khvastiv, Liatychiv, Korsun, Trakhtemyriv, and other towns before the uprising was suppressed by the combined Polish noble forces of Kiev, Podilia, and Volhynia palatinates. Failure of the revolt can be attributed to the lack of co-ordination among the various haidamaka detachments, of a general plan of action, and of a common leader.

The largest and bloodiest haidamaka uprising, known as the *Koliivshchyna, broke out in 1768 in the Kiev and Bratslav regions and spread to Podilia, Volhynia, and even Subcarpathia. It was sparked by the appearance in Right-Bank Ukraine of Russian troops, sent to suppress the anti-Russian Polish noble Confederation of *Bar. The main leaders of the uprising were the Zaporozhian Cossack M. *Zalizniak and the captain of the Uman Cossack militia, I. *Gonta. Many towns were captured by the rebels, and their Polish and Jewish inhabitants were slaughtered. Again, the Poles managed to crush the uprising only with the help of Russian troops.

After 1768 haidamaka uprisings in Right-Bank Ukraine declined. Such later revolts as that led by U. *Karmaliuk, however, were not unlike the earlier ones. The haidamakas and their uprisings have been preserved in the collective memory in the form of legends and folksongs. The haidamakas, and particularly the Koliivshchyna, have been presented in a heroic light in the works of T. Shevchenko, members of the Ukrainian School in Polish literature, and such Soviet writers as I. Kocherha, M. Mushketyk, and M. Syrotiuk. They were also idealized to some extent by Ukrainian populist historians of the 19th century.

BIBLIOGRAPHY
Akty o gaidamakakh (1700–1768). Arkhiv Iugo-Zapadnoi Rossii, pt 3, vol 3 (Kiev 1876)
Antonovich, V. *Issledovanie o gaidamachestve po aktam 1700–1768 gg.* (Kiev 1876)
Rawita-Gawroński, F. *Historya ruchów hajdamackich w XVIII w.*, 2 vols (Lviv 1899, 1901)
Horban', M. *Haidamachchyna* (Kharkiv 1923)
Lola, O. *Haidamats'kyi rukh na Ukraïni 20–60 rr. XVIII st.* (Kiev 1965)
Butych, I.; Shevchenko, F. (eds). *Haidamats'kyi rukh na Ukraïni v XVIII st.: Zbirnyk dokumentiv* (Kiev 1970)
Serczyk, W. *Hajdamacy* (Cracow 1972)
Kohut, Z. 'Myths Old and New: The Haidamak Movement and the Koliivshchyna (1768) in Recent Historiography,' *HUS*, 1, no. 3 (1977)
Pelenski, J. 'The *Haidamak* Insurrections and the Old Regimes in Eastern Europe,' in *The American and European Revolutions, 1776–1848: Sociopolitical and Ideological Aspects*, ed J. Pelenski (Iowa City 1980)

B. Krupnytsky, A. Zhukovsky

Haidamaky. Radical left-wing political organization in the United States founded in 1907 with headquarters in New York and chapters in a number of cities. It published its own periodical, *Haidamaky* (1909–16), which gradually changed from a monthly to a weekly, under the editorship of M. Zhandoga, A. Petriv, and Ya. Kornat. In 1910 the organization began to provide relief and insurance services for its members. By 1914 its membership was close to 1,000. The president was I. Borodaikevych. As a national organization it was dissolved in 1918, although its Trenton chapter continued to operate until 1925. Most of its chapters joined the Ukrainian Workingmen's Association, while some joined pro-communist organizations.

Haidamaky. A popular weekly newspaper of a nationalist and democratic character that appeared in Lviv from October 1902 to 1907. The publisher was the teacher M. Petrytsky, and the editors were M. Petrytsky and A. Sembratovych (1904).

Haidarivsky, Vasyl [Hajdarivs'kyj, Vasyl'] (pen name of V. Haivoronsky), b 1 December 1908 in Kostiantynivka, in the Donbas, d 13 November 1972 in Philadelphia. Writer. A member of the literary group Zaboi and the All-Ukrainian Association of Proletarian Writers, in 1933 he was exiled but escaped and lived in hiding in Caucasia. In 1944 he moved to Lviv, and after the war he immigrated to the United States. Many of his stories appeared in Soviet, West Ukrainian, and émigré periodicals. He is the author of the story collection *A svit takyi harnyi* (And the World Is So Beautiful, 1962) and the novellas *Puhachivs'ka rudnia* (The Puhachiv Mine, 1933), *Shche odno kokhannia* (One More Love, 1946), and *Zaiachyi pastukh* (The Hare Herder, 1962).

Stepan Haiduchok

Hryhorii Haievsky

Haiduchok, Stepan [Hajdučok], b 13 March 1890 in Pidtemne, Lviv county, d 16 March 1976 in Lviv. Physical education instructor and leading figure in the sports movement in Western Ukraine. A follower of I. *Bobersky, he organized fitness programs and hiking clubs;

he was one of the first promoters of skiing and skating in Western Ukraine and wrote textbooks and numerous articles on physical education.

Haienko, Fedir [Hajenko], b 6 June 1906 in Myshuryn Rih, Verkhnodniprovske county, Katerynoslav gubernia, d 13 December 1983 in Neu-Ulm, Germany. Political leader, journalist, economist. He graduated from the Kharkiv Institute of the National Economy in 1936. After the Second World War he lived in Austria and from 1952 in Germany. A leading member of the Ukrainian Revolutionary Democratic party, he served as its general secretary (1963–7) and editor in chief of its weekly *Ukraïns'ki visti* (1973–8). For many years (1953–69) he sat on the Presidium of the Ukrainian National Council. He was a founding member of the Congress of Free Political Thought (1972–6) and a research associate of the Institute for the Study of the USSR (1954–71). His analytical articles on developments in the USSR, and particularly in Ukraine, appeared in various journals and newspapers, including *Vestnik po izucheniiu SSSR*.

Haievsky, Hryhorii [Hajevs'kyj, Hryhorij], b 26 January 1872 in Tulchyn, Bratslav county, Podilia gubernia, d 1933 in Kiev. Stage director and educator. From 1904 he taught at the Lysenko Music and Drama School in Kiev and later at the Kiev State Art Institute and other higher schools. He directed plays at the Ukrainian National Theater in Kiev (1917–18) and at the Mykhailychenko Theater in Kiev in the 1920s. Among his published works are a study *Zavdannia rezhysera* (The Task of a Stage Director, 1920) and Ukrainian translations and adaptations of works by S. Maugham and U. Sinclair.

Haievsky, Sylvestr [Hajevs'kyj, Syl'vestr] (secular name: Stepan), b 9 January 1876 in Mykhyryntsi, Starokostiantyniv county, Volhynia gubernia, d 9 September 1975 in Melbourne. Specialist in Ukrainian studies, pedagogue, and archbishop of the Ukrainian Autocephalous Orthodox church (UAOC); full member of the Shevchenko Scientific Society and the Ukrainian Academy of Arts and Sciences. He completed philological studies at Kiev University in 1912. From 1918 to 1919 he served as vice-chancellor and then as director of the general department of the State Chancellery of the UNR. In 1921 he was appointed professor of Kamianets-Podilskyi Ukrainian State University. He was arrested in 1922 and again in 1932. After his second release he spent two years in Kazakhstan and Uzbekistan and then taught at pedagogical institutes in Ukraine. On 16 May 1942 he was consecrated bishop of Lubni Eparchy. In 1949 he immigrated to Australia, where he served as acting bishop and archbishop of the UAOC for Australia and New Zealand until 1963. His chief works are *'Aleksandriia' v davnii ukraïns'kii literaturi* ('Alexandria' in Old Ukrainian Literature, 1929), *Tserkovnyi ustrii v Ukraïni* (The Structure of the Church in Ukraine, 1946), *Zapovit Mytropolyta P. Mohyly* (The Testament of Metropolitan P. Mohyla, 1947), *Frankiv 'Moisei'* (Franko's 'Moisei,' 1948), and *Beresteis'ka Uniia 1596 roku* (The Union of Berestia in 1596, 1963).

Haievsky, Valentyn [Hajevs'kyj] (pseuds: Vasyl Halaida, V. Hlushko, V. Horenko, Tahorenko), b 29 July 1902 in Kiev. Specialist in the history of Ukrainian theater, drama critic, pedagogue; son of Hryhorii *Haievsky. A graduate of Kiev University (1935) and the Kiev Theater Institute (1940), he lectured at the latter (1938–43). During the war he emigrated to Germany and in 1950 settled in the USA. His publications include studies of T. Shevchenko's association with M. Shchepkin (1939), P. Saksahansky as stage director (1939), the actor H. Yura (1940), and sketches on modern Ukrainian theater (1940), as well as over 80 articles and reviews.

Haimanova mohyla: silver embossed, engraved, and gilded cup with a frieze depicting Scythian warriors, 4th century BC

Haimanova mohyla. A large Scythian royal kurhan of the 4th century BC situated near Balky, Vasylivka raion, Zaporizhia oblast. It was excavated in 1969–70 by V. Bidzilia. Remnants of carts and a burial feast, four burials with seven human skeletons, over 250 gold ornaments, and numerous iron, bronze, wood, bone, and clay artifacts and weapons were unearthed. The most noteworthy find was a gilded silver cup with a frieze depicting Scythian warriors.

Haimanova mohyla: stamped gold plaques depicting maenads, 4th century BC

Haisyn [Hajsyn]. V-10. City (1971 pop 23,725) on the Sob River in eastern Podilia and a raion center in Vinnytsia oblast. First mentioned in 1545, from 1797 to 1917 it was a county town in Podilia gubernia. In spring 1919

Otaman A. *Volynets's partisans fought the Bolshevik Tarashcha Division in the Haisyn region. In fall 1919 the Ukrainian Sich Riflemen Brigade and units of the UNR Army fought the Fourth Corps of A. Denikin's Volunteer Army on the Huncha-Hraniv-Marianivka-Tymar-Ziatkivtsi front. The Haisyn-Bratslav partisan brigade was organized there by Otaman Volynets in the spring of 1920. Foodstuffs, kitchenware, alcohol, furniture, bricks, and clothing are produced in the city.

Haivas, Yaroslav [Hajvas, Jaroslav], b 8 January 1912 in Sosnivka, Zolochiv county, Galicia. Civic leader and political activist. Haivas was a member of the national executive of the OUN in Western Ukraine (1937–9). After the split in the OUN he joined the Melnyk faction, with which he remained until 1972. During the German occupation of Ukraine, he was a leading member of the national executive of the OUN in Reichskommissariat Ukraine (1941–4). He immigrated to Germany in 1945 and to the United States in 1950. He is the author of two memoirs, *Koly kinchaiet'sia epokha* (On the Threshold of a New Era, 1964) and *Volia tsiny ne maie* (Freedom Has No Price, 1972).

Haivazovsky, Ivan. See Aivazovsky, Ivan.

Haivoron [Hajvoron]. V-10. Town (1970 pop 14,400) and raion centre in Kirovohrad oblast, situated on the Boh River. A railway junction, it has a granite quarry and machine-building tekhnikum. The 6th-century *Haivoron settlement was excavated nearby in 1960.

Haivoron settlement. An ancient Slavic iron-working center discovered on an island in the Boh River near the town of Haivoron in Kirovohrad oblast. Excavation done in 1960–1 by V. Bidzilia revealed that the settlement was active in the 6th and 7th centuries AD. The dig uncovered 25 iron-smelting furnaces, a semi-pit dwelling, storage pits, tools, pottery, various objects of daily use, and ornaments.

Mykhailo Haivoronsky Anatol Hak

Haivoronsky, Mykhailo [Hajvorons'kyj, Myxajlo], b 15 September 1892 in Zalishchyky, Galicia, d 11 September 1949 in New York. Conductor and composer. A graduate of the Lysenko Higher Institute of Music in Lviv, he organized and conducted the Ukrainian Sich Riflemen Band (1914–19) and then served as chief bandmaster of the UNR Army. From 1920 he taught music and conducted various choirs in Lviv. In 1923 he immigrated to the United States, where he founded (1930) and conducted the United Ukrainian Chorus. He composed many Sich Riflemen songs, choral works, church music, and instrumental music for violin, string orchestra, band, and symphony orchestra. He also arranged many folk songs and compiled a number of songbooks. A monograph on him by W. Wytwycky appeared in New York in 1954.

Hajdúdorog eparchy. Greek Catholic eparchy set up in 1912 by Francis Joseph I under pressure from the Hungarian government and confirmed by Pius X. Its first seat was the town of Hajdúdorog in northeastern Hungary. Its faithful are Hungarian Catholics of the Eastern rite, primarily descendants of Magyarized Transcarpathian Ukrainians who lived in formerly Ukrainian ethnic territories or in pockets scattered among the Hungarian majority. (See *Hungary and *Transcarpathia.)

At first the Hajdúdorog eparchy encompassed 162 parishes, eight of which were transferred from the Prešov eparchy, 70 from the Mukachiv eparchy, and 83 from Rumanian eparchies in Transylvania. After 1919 most of the Rumanian eparchies became part of Rumania; hence, the eparchy consisted mostly of former Ukrainian parishes. At present the eparchy has 126 parishes, 170 priests, and about 300,000 faithful. The first bishop of Hajdúdorog eparchy was I. Miklossi and his successor was M. Dudás. Since 1975 the bishop has been I. Timkó. The present seat of the eparchy is Nyiregyhára.

Hak, Anatol (pen name of Ivan Antypenko; other pen names: Osa, Antosha Ko, Martyn Zadeka), b 20 June 1893 on a khutir near Huliai Pole, Katerynoslav gubernia, d 4 December 1980 in Philadelphia. Writer and feuilletonist. Hak was first published in a tsarist army newspaper in 1917 while serving on the Rumanian front. In the 1920s he belonged to the writers' association *Pluh and was published in various periodicals, including *Selians'ka pravda* in Kharkiv. Emigrating at the end of the Second World War, he contributed to the émigré press in Germany and, from 1949, in the United States. Hak's numerous feuilletons and satirical sketches were aimed both at the Soviet regime and at the émigrés. He is the author of nine collections of humorous stories, including *Lopans'ki raky* (The Crabs of Lopan, 1926), *Radio-invalidy* (Radio-Invalids, 1927), and *Parazyty pid mikroskopom* (Parasites under a Microscope, 1930); the novel *Moloda napruha* (The Young Force, 1933); several plays, including *Studenty* (Students, 1924), *Rodyna patsiukiv* (A Family of Rats, 1927), and *Spadkoiemtsi misis Pylypson* (The Inheritors of Mrs Pilipson, 1977); the feuilleton collections *Mizhplanetni liudy* (The Interplanetary People, 1947) and *Na dvokh trybunakh* (On Two Tribunes, 1966); and the book of memoirs *Vid Huliai-Polia do N'iu-Iorku* (From Huliai-Pole to New York, 1973), which contains a wealth of information about the literary world of the 1920s in Soviet Ukraine.

D.H. Struk

Hakkebush, Liubov [Hakkebuš, Ljubov], b 26 September 1888 in Nemyriv, Bratslav county, Podilia gubernia, d 28 May 1947 in Kiev. Prominent stage actress and teacher. She studied at the Moscow Kamernyi Thea-

Liubov Hakkebush

Bishop Yevhen Hakman

ter and appeared in amateur productions staged by the Kobzar Ukrainian club in Moscow. She first appeared on the Ukrainian stage in 1918 at the State National Theater in Kiev. From 1918 to 1926 she worked in Kiev at the State Drama Theater, the First Theater of the Ukrainian Soviet Republic, and under the direction of L. Kurbas in the Kiev Drama Theater (*Kyidramte) and the *Berezil theater. She then worked at the Ukrainian drama theaters of Odessa (1926–8, 1939–41), Kharkiv (1928–33), and Staline (Donetske, 1933–9). She also taught acting at the theaters, the music and drama institutes of Kiev (1922–6), Odessa (1926–8), and Kharkiv (1929–33), and the Kiev Institute of Theater Arts (1944–7). She appeared in over 80 leading and supporting roles in such plays as H. Ibsen's *Vikings at Helgeland*, M. Kulish's *Komuna v stepakh* (Commune in the Steppes), C. Goldoni's *La locandiera*, and Molière's *Le Bourgeois gentilhomme*. Most memorable were her renditions of Lady Macbeth in *Macbeth* and Fru Alving in Ibsen's *Ghosts*. Hakkebush's life and career are described in N. Yermakova's *Aktors'ka maisternist' Liubovy Hakkebush* (The Thespian Mastery of Liubov Hakkebush, 1979).

V. Revutsky

Hakman, Yevhen, b 1793 in Vaslovivtsi, Zastavna county, Bukovyna, d 31 March 1873 in Chernivtsi. Orthodox bishop of Bukovyna from 1834 to 1873. Hakman introduced improvements in the life of the Ukrainian Orthodox in Bukovyna. During his administration Ukrainian became the second language of the Bukovynian diocese in 1838; the educational level of the clergy was raised through the appointment of qualified theology professors; the diocese was reorganized into 12 protopresbyteries; and clergymen were granted regular salaries. In 1848 and 1849 he supported Rumanian and German petitions to the Austrian government to grant political autonomy to Bukovyna by separating it from Galicia, but opposed Rumanian efforts to create a Rumanian metropolitanate of Bukovyna, Transylvania, and the Banat. When Bukovyna was made into an autonomous crownland in 1861, he became the first marshal of the Bukovynian Diet. At the Orthodox synod in Karlovci, Slavonia, in 1864 and through his pastoral letter of 1865, he successfully opposed efforts to have his diocese subordinated to the newly created Rumanian metropolitanate of Transylvania. It was on Hakman's initiative that *Ruska Besida, the first Ukrainian civic organization in Bukovyna, was founded in 1869. In January 1873, because of his efforts the diocese became a metropolitanate, and Hakman became the first metropolitan of Bukovyna and Dalmatia. The Orthodox cathedral and the metropolitan's residence built by his orders in Chernivtsi now house Chernivtsi University. He is the author of *Nationale und Kirchliche Bestrebungen der Rumänen in der Bukowina 1848–1865* (1889). His pastoral letters were published in 1899 by S. Smal-Stotsky.

R. Yanchinski

Mykola Halahan

Halahan, Mykola, b 1882 in Trebukhiv, Oster county, Chernihiv gubernia, d ? Political and community leader, publicist. A physicist by profession, Halahan was a member (1903–5) of the Revolutionary Ukrainian party and then of Spilka. In 1917 he joined the Ukrainian Social Democratic Workers' party and became a representative of the Central Rada in the Kuban and then in Rumania (1918). During the Directory he led the Ukrainian diplomatic mission in Hungary. He immigrated to Vienna, where he headed the Ukrainian Relief Committee, and then to Prague. There he directed the Ukrainian Community Publishing Fund, organized and headed the Ukrainian Civic Committee in Czechoslovakia (1927–39), and taught at the Ukrainian gymnasium. He is the author of memoirs in four volumes (1930), books on social and political themes, and works on physics. After 1945 his fate is unknown.

Halaichuk, Bohdan [Halajčuk] (Halajczuk), b 21 July 1911 in Uhersko, Stryi county, Galicia, d 31 July 1974 in Buenos Aires. Specialist in international law, publicist, Catholic activist; full member of the Shevchenko Scientific Society and of the Ukrainian Academy of Arts and Sciences. He studied at the Catholic University of Louvain and Innsbruck University (PH D 1946). In 1949 he immigrated to Argentina. Appointed professor of international law at the Catholic Pontifical University of Argentina in 1959, he directed the Institute of Soviet Studies, which he helped to organize. In the 1970s he served as president of the Ukrainian Catholic Alliance and director of a branch of the Ukrainian Catholic University in Buenos Aires. Besides numerous journal and newspaper articles, he wrote books in international law and political science: *Los estados conquistados ante el derecho internacional* (1950), *El estado ucranio del siglo 20* (1953), *Natsiia ponevolena, ale derzhavna* (A Subjugated, but State-Possessing

Nation, 1953), and *Historia de la organización politica de Europa Oriental* (1972). In his legal works he defended the view that Soviet Ukraine is a subject of international law.

Halan, Anatol (pen name of A. Kalynovsky; other pen names: I. Eventualny, A. Chechko), b 22 August 1901 in Zemlianka, Hlukhiv county, Chernihiv gubernia. Writer and journalist. From 1924 his stories were published in Soviet Ukrainian journals. He ceased writing in 1933 and resumed only in 1946 in Austria, from where he emigrated to Argentina and then to the United States. His first poetry collection (1930) and first play (1932) were followed by eight collections of stories, three novellas, a novella in verse, a poetry collection, three collections of satires, two volumes of memoirs, and a play. Halan's prolific output is often satirical or humorous and marked by a journalistic facility and emphasis on plot at the expense of psychological depth.

Halan, Yaroslav, b 27 July 1902 in Dynów, Brzozów county, Galicia, d 25 October 1949 in Lviv. Communist journalist and writer. Before Galicia's incorporation into the Soviet Ukraine Halan was a member of the literary group *Horno and a contributor to the Lviv Sovietophile journal **Vikna*. First published in 1927, he is the author of propaganda plays – *Vantazh* (Cargo, 1928), *Veronika* (1930), *Pid zolotym orlom* (Under the Golden Eagle, 1948), and *Liubov na svitanni* (Love at Dawn, 1949) – and socialist-realist stories and pamphlets, many of them aimed against the Ukrainian nationalist and independence movement and the Ukrainian Catholic church. His pro-Soviet activities before and after the Second World War led to his assassination by Ukrainian nationalists. His life and death have been effectively exploited by the Soviet regime in its attacks on 'Ukrainian bourgeois nationalism.' Since 1964 the Halan prize has been awarded by the Writers' Union of Ukraine for the best propagandistic journalism. Halan's works in three volumes were published in Kiev in 1977–8.

Halecki, Oskar, b 26 May 1891 in Vienna, d 17 September 1973 in White Plains, New York. Polish historian and political figure. While a professor at Warsaw University (1918–39), he served as a historical expert in the Polish delegation at the Paris Peace Conference (1919). His report *Les Relations entre la Pologne et les terres lithuaniennes et ruthènes avant les partages* (1919) to the peace conference supported Polish territorial claims. In 1940 he moved to the United States, where he taught East European history at Fordham University (1944–61). He is the author of many works on medieval and early modern Polish history, including *From Florence to Brest, 1439–1596* (1958), which stresses the 'civilizing mission' of Polish Catholicism in Eastern Europe and Ukraine. His main contribution to Ukrainian historiography is *Przyłączenie Podlasia, Wołynia i Kijowszczyzny do Korony w roku 1569* (The Annexation of Podlachia, Volhynia, and the Kiev Region to the [Polish] Crown in 1569, 1915).

Haliakhovsky, Danylo [Haljaxovs'kyj], b and d ? Noted engraver. A graduate of the Kievan Mohyla Academy, he worked in Kiev from 1674 to 1709. His best-known works are two panegyric prints dedicated to metropolitans V. Yasynsky and Y. Krokovsky, a large announcement of a debate at the Kievan Mohyla Academy dedicated to I. Mazepa (1708; the unique *teza* displays the hetman's portrait and is preserved at the Krasiński Library in Warsaw), and an engraving of John the Evangelist in the Bible of the Kievan Cave Monastery (1707).

Mykhailo Halibei

Teodot Halip

Halibei, Mykhailo [Halibej, Myxajlo], b 22 August 1885 in Yezupil, Stanyslaviv county, Galicia, d 27 June 1964 in Oakland, California. Artisan, entrepreneur, and civic leader. He was a Ukrainian National Democratic party delegate at the Labor Congress in Kiev in 1919 and a member of the Ukrainian National Council of the Western Ukrainian National Republic and of the central committee of the Ukrainian National Democratic Alliance (1928–39). In the interwar years he owned a ceramic-tile works in Lviv and was active in many civic organizations including the Zoria association, the Burgher Brotherhood (cofounder and secretary, 1920–30), and the Ridna Shkola and Prosvita societies. He was a member of the board of directors of the Sokil-Batko athletic association (1920–8), the Dilo publishing association (1928–39), and various banks, co-operative associations, schools, and hospitals. He wrote several articles on the history of Lviv's Ukrainian burghers in the newspaper *Dilo*. From 1948 he lived in the United States, where he was active in community organizations.

Halich, Wasyl [Halyč, Vasyl'], b 6 April 1896 in Stribychi, Sambir county, Galicia. Historian and community leader in the United States. He received his PH D from the University of Iowa in 1934 and was a professor of history at the University of Wisconsin in Superior from 1946 to 1966. He is a full member of the Shevchenko Scientific Society. He is a pioneer of studies on Ukrainians in the United States and author of *Ukrainians in the United States* (1937, 1974).

Halip, Teodot, b 19 June 1873 in Voloka, Vashkivtsi county, Bukovyna, d 6 April 1943 in Brno, Czechoslovakia. Lawyer, civic and political leader in Bukovyna, writer and publicist. Halip was the president of the Sich Union (1904–14) and the leader of the Ukrainian Radical party in Bukovyna (1906–18). In 1911 he was elected to the Bukovynian Diet. When Rumania occupied Bukovyna in November 1918, he left for Galicia. He sat on the Ukrainian National Rada of the Western Ukrainian National Republic in Stanyslaviv, and later served as a member of the UNR diplomatic mission in Rome. From

1920 he worked as an attorney in Khust and in 1939 moved to Brno. He also lectured on criminal law at the Ukrainian Free University in Prague. Halip is an author of a collection of short stories, *Pershi zori* (First Stars, 1895); two collections of poetry, *Dumy ta pisni* (Thoughts and Songs, 1901) and *Dyka rozha* (Wild Rose, 1919); memoirs (in the newspaper *Krakivs'ki visti*, 1943); and studies of Transcarpathian customary law.

Halkin, Oleksander, b 21 July 1914 in Berdianske, Tavriia gubernia, d 22 October 1982. Physicist; full member of the AN URSR from 1965. He began his experimental research at the Ukrainian Physico-Technical Institute in 1937, two years before graduating from Kharkiv University. After the Second World War he resumed work at the same institute. In 1965 he became the director of the AN URSR Physico-Technical Institute at Donetske and a professor of Donetske University. His chief publications deal with superconductivity, acoustical properties of solids at low temperatures, dispersion of sound velocity in metals in a magnetic field, and nuclear magnetic resonance. He oversaw the construction of special radiospectrometers for probing nuclear resonance.

Halkyn, Oleksa, b 21 September 1866 in Kiev gubernia, d 1940 in Lviv. General staff officer in the Russian army and in 1918 chief of the general staff of the Ukrainian army of the Hetman government. In 1919 Halkyn was a member of the UNR high military council and during 1920–1 he headed the UNR war ministry. He was promoted to lieutenant general. He was arrested by the NKVD in Lviv in 1940 and executed.

Haller, Józef, b 13 August 1873 in Jurczyce, near Cracow, Poland, d 4 June 1960 in London. General of the Polish army which was organized in France during 1918. In April 1919 Haller and his army of six infantry divisions arrived in Warsaw with Allied directives to operate against the Red Army. However, his divisions engaged the Ukrainian Galician Army in intensive combat during May–July and succeeded in pushing it out of Galicia into central Ukraine. On 1 June 1919 Haller was promoted to full general, and he continued to hold key positions in the Polish army until 1926.

Hallstatt culture. An archeologically defined culture of the Late Bronze Age and the Early Iron Age (ca 10th–5th centuries BC). The name is derived from a burial ground discovered in 1846 near the town of Hallstatt in southwestern Austria, where objects characteristic of the period were first identified. The culture was spread throughout south-central Europe and has been identified with the Celts and Illyrians. These groups were engaged in agriculture, animal husbandry, ceramic production, and the mining of salt, copper, and iron. Their semi-fortified settlements consisted of surface and semi-pit dwellings.

Halpern, Yakiv [Hal'pern, Jakiv], b 1 January 1876 in Vilnius, d 22 December 1941 in Dnipropetrovske. Surgeon. A graduate of Kiev University (1899), he taught at the Dnipropetrovske Medical Institute from 1922 and edited (1921–41) the medical journal *Novyi khirurgicheskii arkhiv*. He wrote a number of works on stomach and digestive-tract surgery, and on blood transfusion.

Mykhailo Halushchynsky

Tyt Teodosii Halushchynsky

Halushchynsky, Mykhailo [Haluščyns'kyj, Myxajlo], b 26 September 1878 in Zvyniach, Chortkiv county, Galicia, d 25 September 1931 in Lviv. Political and cultural leader, pedagogue. After completing his studies in Lviv and Vienna he taught secondary school in Zolochiv until he became director of the Ridna Shkola gymnasium in Rohatyn in 1910. During the First World War, he was an officer of the Ukrainian Sich Riflemen (USS) and then a USS liaison officer at the Austrian High Command. After the war he taught at the Lviv (Underground) Ukrainian University. From 1923 to 1931 he was president of the Prosvita society in Lviv and editor of its educational magazine *Zhyttia i znannia*. A candidate of the Ukrainian National Democratic Alliance, in 1928 he was elected to the Polish Senate and served as its vice-president. He wrote a book of memoirs – *Z Ukraïns'kymy Sichovymy Stril'tsiamy* (Among the Ukrainian Sich Riflemen, 1934) – and a number of pedagogical works.

Halushchynsky, Tyt Teodosii [Haluščyns'kyj], b 13 April 1880 in Buchach, Galicia, d 31 August 1952 in Mundare, Alberta. Priest, biblical scholar, and church historian; brother of M. *Halushchynsky. After studying philosophy and theology at the universities of Lviv, Fribourg, Vienna (D TH, 1906), and Innsbruck, he taught at the Stanyslaviv Theological Seminary. He took monastic vows in 1908 and was appointed lecturer at Lviv University (1915) and at the Greek Catholic Theological Seminary (1920), where he also served as rector (1920–5). He was a founding member and president (1923–6) of the Ukrainian Theological Scholarly Society. In 1931 he became the spiritual adviser at St Josaphat's College in Rome. In 1949 he was elected archimandrite of the Basilian order of monks and appointed consultator to the Sacred Congregation for the Oriental Churches. Besides numerous articles on public affairs, philosophy, and theology, Halushchynsky wrote *Istoriia bibliina Staroho Zavita* (Biblical History of the Old Testament, 3 vols, 1914–34) and *De urbis Babel exordiis ac de primo in terra Sinear regno* (1917), and edited *Acta Innocentii PP. III (1198–1216) A Registris Vaticanis* (1944).

Halych [Halyč]. IV-3. City (1971 pop 4,800) at the confluence of the Lukva and Dniester rivers, raion center of Ivano-Frankivske oblast. It arose in the 14th century, some time after the Mongols destroyed princely Halych, on the site of the city's river port 5 km north of the city. By the middle of the century the town and the surrounding territory were annexed by Poland. In 1367 Halych was granted the rights of Magdeburg law and soon a castle was built to protect it against the Tatars. From the 14th century it was the see of the *Halych metropoly and from 1375 the see of a Latin-rite Catholic diocese. By the 16th century the town was one of the larger trade centers in eastern Galicia. Many of its inhabitants joined B. Khmelnytsky's rebellion. In the second half of the 17th century the castle and part of the town were destroyed by the Tatars. Henceforth Halych remained an insignificant small town. In 1772 it was acquired by Austria in the first partition of Poland. It revived somewhat toward the end of the 19th century with the construction of a railway line linking it with Lviv, Stanyslaviv, and Chernivtsi. In June 1915 the Ukrainian Sich Riflemen pushed the Russian army out of Halych. In the summer of 1919 the city witnessed several battles between the Third Corps of the Ukrainian Galician Army and the Poles. Halych's most valuable architectural monuments are the Nativity Church (built at the turn of the 14th century and restored in 1825) and the remnants of the castle.

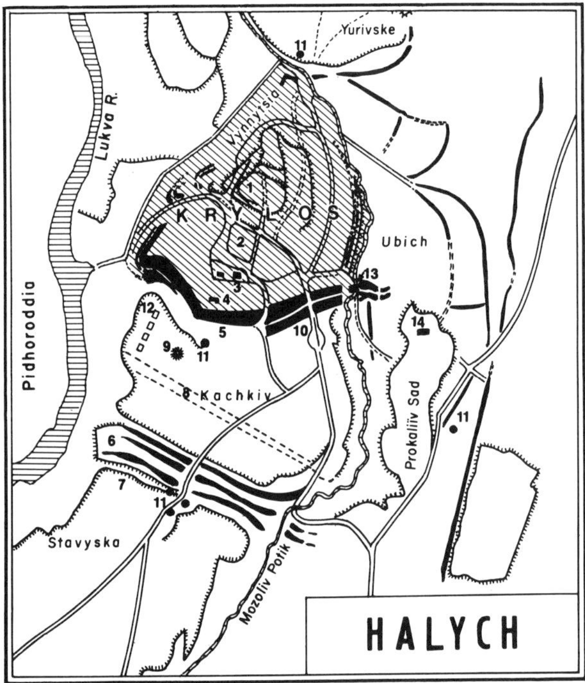

MEDIEVAL HALYCH

1. Zolotyi Tik (castle)
2. Bazaar
3. Dormition Cathedral
4. Metropolitan's palace
5. Inner walls
6. Outer walls
7. Other walls
8. Excavated walls
9. Tumulus
10. Main Gate
11. Defense towers
12. Artisans' and merchants' quarter
13. Dam on the Mozoliv Potik (stream)
14. Church of the Resurrection

Halych, princely. City located at the site of present-day *Krylos, dating back to the turn of the 9th century. An important trade and cultural center of medieval Rus', it reached the height of its power in the second half of the 12th century. The suburbs or lower town, the location of the city's river port, is now the site of modern *Halych; monasteries, churches, and small fortified settlements were also located on the city's outskirts. From 1144 it was the capital of Yaroslav Osmomysl's Principality of Galicia, and from 1199 the capital of Roman Mstyslavych's Principality of *Galicia-Volhynia. In 1238 Danylo Romanovych established his residence at Halych. Three years later the city was razed by the Mongols.

Archeological excavations of the city began in the early 20th century and continued into the 1950s. The remains of the Dormition Cathedral (built in 1157), the city walls, castle moats, and many stone buildings of the lower town have been uncovered, as have Yaroslav Osmomysl's sacrophagus and skeleton and an abundance of metal, ceramic, and glass products. At Shevchenkove village nearby the remains of St Panteleimon's Church (built in 1200) have been excavated.

Halych Gospel (1144)

Halych Gospel (1144). The oldest extant dated text written in Western Ukraine and the oldest extant tetraevangelium written in Ukraine. The text comprises 260 folios, of which folios 229–260 were added later, in the 12th or 13th century. The text was copied from a south Slavic source; the scribe introduced some features of the local dialect. The manuscript is preserved at the Moscow History Museum. It has been published in two not-quite-reliable volumes by Archimandrite Amfilokhii (Moscow, 1882–3). Its language has been studied by V. Jagić (1884), V. Le-Juge (1897), and E. Blokhina (1976).

Halych Gospel. A gospel written in Old Ukrainian between 1266 and 1301, most likely in 1288. An aprakos-evangelium of 175 folios, it was copied by the Presbyter Georgii in or near Halych from a Bulgarian original. The manuscript is preserved at the Leningrad Public Library. Fragments of it were published by A. Sobolevsky (1884), who also studied the language of the text.

Halych metropoly. A metropoly of the Ukrainian church established in 1303 in the city of Halych. From around 1156 Halych had been the see of Halych eparchy, for which a cathedral was built in 1157. When in 1299 the Kievan metropolitan Maximos transferred his see to Vladimir on the Kliazma, Prince Lev Danylovych of Galicia-Volhynia demanded the creation of a metropoly in his principality. Lev was concerned that the Kievan metropolitan would be under the influence of the Suzdal princes, and that he would be unable to devote attention to his distant eparchies. But it was only during the reign of Lev's son, Prince Yurii Lvovych, that the Byzantine emperor, Andronicus II Palaeologus, issued a bull and Patriarch Athanasios of Constantinople a charter granting the establishment of the Halych metropoly. At first it consisted of five eparchies: Volodymyr, Peremyshl, Lutske, Turiv, and Kholm. Little is known about the first metropolitan, Niphont. He was succeeded by Petro, who was consecrated metropolitan of Kiev, Halych, and all Rus' (1308–26), with residence in Moscow (see *Church, history of the Ukrainian). The third metropolitan, Gabriel, died shortly after his consecration. This initiated a period of crisis as the new metropolitan of Kiev, Theognostos, attempted to suppress the rival metropoly and consecrated Gabriel's successor Theodore as only the bishop of Halych. Theodore appealed to Patriarch John Calecas, and for a brief period succeeded in acquiring the Halych see. Finally in 1347 the Kievan metropolitan, supported by Prince Simeon of Moscow, prevailed upon the new emperor John Cantacazenus to formally abolish the Halych metropoly; in 1355 its eparchies were transferred to the newly created metropoly of Lithuania and Volhynia.

In 1370 the Polish king, Casimir II, fearing the growing Lithuanian influence in Galicia-Volhynia, dispatched a candidate named Antonii to Patriarch Philotheos for consecration as metropolitan of a renewed and autonomous Halych metropoly. The patriarch agreed, and Antonii served as metropolitan from 1371 to 1391, but with responsibility for only three eparchies. Upon Antonii's death, the Polish king Jagiełło tried to have Ivan, bishop of Lutske, named as his successor, but this time the nomination was not confirmed by the patriarch. Instead, in 1401 the Lithuanian metropolitan, *Cyprian, was confirmed as metropolitan of Kiev, Halych, and All-Rus'. At that time the Halych metropoly ceased to exist (in 1406 the eparchy too was disbanded), and responsibility for local administration was given to vicars, appointed first by the Kiev metropolitan and from 1509 by the Roman Catholic archbishop of Lviv, with the approval of the Polish king.

In 1539 the eparchy was re-established when Makarii Tuchapsky became bishop of Halych, Lviv, and Kamenets, with his see in Lviv. In 1700, under Bishop Y. Shumliansky, the eparchy accepted the Church Union of *Berestia. After the partitions of Poland, Russian repression of the Uniate church in its newly acquired territories, which included the de facto abolishment of the Uniate metropoly of Kiev, led the Uniate hierarchy to increase its efforts in securing the re-establishment of the Halych metropoly in Austria-Hungary. This was facilitated by the more tolerant religious policies of the Habsburgs. In 1806 Emperor Francis I officially supported these efforts, and on 17 April 1807 Pope Pius VII issued the bull *In Universalis Ecclesiae Regimine* restoring the Halych metropoly with two eparchies (Lviv and Peremyshl). In 1885 a new eparchy of Stanyslaviv (now part of Lviv archeparchy) was created, and in 1934 the *Lemko Apostolic Administration was separated from Peremyshl eparchy. The bishop of Peremyshl, A. Anhelovych, was consecrated as the first metropolitan. The Halych metropolitan was accorded the same rights as the metropolitan of Kiev as outlined in the 1596 bull of Pope Clement VIII, *Decet Romanum Pontificem*. A. Anhelovych was metropolitan from 1807 to 1814. He was succeeded by M. Levytsky (1816–58), H. Yakhymovych (1860–3), S. Lytvynovych (1863–9), Y. Sembratovych (1870–82), S. Sembratovych (1885–98), Yu. Sas-Kuilovsky (1899–1900), A. Sheptytsky (1900–44), and Y. Slipy (1944–84), who was arrested by the Soviet authorities in Lviv in 1945 and imprisoned until 1963 when he was permitted to immigrate to Rome. The successor of Y. Slipy, M. Liubachivsky, now resides in Rome. In the 19th and 20th centuries, the Halych metropoly was a major center of the cultural and civic life of Ukrainians in Galicia.

BIBLIOGRAPHY
Harasiewicz, M. *Annales Ecclesiae Ruthenae* (Lviv 1862)
Pelesz, J. *Geschichte der Union der Ruthenischen Kirche mit Rom*, 2 vols (Vienna 1878, 1880)
Rudovych, I. *Istoriia halytsko-l'vovskoi ieparkhiï* (Zhovkva 1902)
Amman, A. *Abriss der ostslawischen Kirchengeschichte* (Vienna 1950)
Stasiw, M. *Metropolia Haliciensis*, 2nd edn (Rome 1960)
Nazarko, I. *Kyïvs'ki i halyts'ki mytropolyty: Biohrafichni narysy (1590–1960)* (Toronto 1962)

W. Lencyk

Halych principality. See Galicia.

Halychanyn (The Galician). A semimonthly sociopolitical and literary supplement to the Russophile newspaper *Slovo*. A total of 90 issues were published in Lviv from January 1867 to 1870. The editor and publisher was B. Didytsky. *Halychanyn* appeared in *yazychie*, an artificial mixture of Ukrainian and Russian. Its contents included articles dealing with the history of Ukraine, poetry by such writers as M. Maksymovych, S. Vorobkevych, and K. Ustyianovych, as well as works by the Russian writers I. Turgenev, F. Tiutchev, and others.

Halychanyn (The Galician). Daily newspaper published in Lviv from 1893 to 1913 by Russophile Galicians subsidized by the Russian government and supported by the Polish authorities. It replaced **Halytskaia Rus'*. Its editors (V. Lutsyk, I. Pelekh, O. *Markov, and others) opposed the Ukrainian national orientation. Semimonthly supplements included *Vienochek* (1904–8), an illustrated children's magazine, and *Lemko* (1911–13), edited by H. Hanuliak and others.

Halycho-ruskii vistnyk (Galician-Ruthenian Herald). The official government newspaper for Ukrainians in the Austrian Empire. It appeared three times a week in Lviv from 2 July 1849 until February 1850. In total, 94 issues were published. It was edited by M. Ustyianovych with the assistance of I. Holovatsky, M. Kossak, and B. Didytsky. In addition to official decrees and edicts, the newspaper published articles on national and international politics, and on Ukrainian affairs, such as problems of the Ukrainian language and orthography (I.

Lozynsky and I. Levytsky) and education. Some literary works, particularly by M. Ustyianovych, were also published, as were biographies, obituaries, and reports from the homeland. In February 1850 its head office was moved to Vienna, and the name of the newpaper was changed to *Vistnyk.

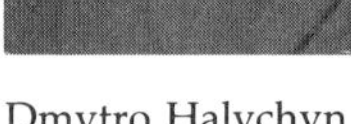

Dmytro Halychyn

Alimpii Halyk: *Portrait of a Youth* (1750s)

Halychyn, Dmytro [Halyčyn], b 30 October 1895 in Dychky, Rohatyn county, Galicia, d 26 March 1961 in New York. Prominent Ukrainian-American community leader. Having served as an officer in the Ukrainian army, he studied foreign trade at the University of Vienna before immigrating in 1923 to the United States. He served as the first president of the United Ukrainian War Veterans of America, sat on the executive of the United Ukrainian Organizations in America, and was active in the Pan-American Ukrainian Conference. He was a founder, vice-chairman (1952–6), and chairman (1956–61) of the Ukrainian Congress Committee of America. For many years he represented the Ukrainian community in the ethnic department of the national committee of the Republican party. His most important contribution was his work as supreme secretary (1933–50) and supreme president (1950–61) of the *Ukrainian National Association. During his term of office the membership of the association grew from 20,000 in 1933 to 79,000 in 1961. The Ukrainian Free University conferred an honorary doctorate in law on Halychyn.

Halychyna. See Galicia.

Halyk, Alimpii, b ca 1685 in Bohuslav, Kiev voivodeship, d May 1768 in Kiev. Icon painter and engraver. As a member (1724–44) and head (1744–55) of the Kievan Cave Monastery Icon Painting Studio, he took part in painting the interior of the monastery's Dormition Cathedral (1724–31) and the exterior of the Trinity Gate Church (1742–4). He also painted the icons of St Elizabeth's Church and Fortress (1754), of St Cyril's Monastery in Kiev (1759), and of many other churches in the Kiev region. Icon sketches, prints, and portraits bearing his signature have been preserved in the albums of the Icon Painting Studio.

Halyn, Martyrii, 1856–1943? Physician; civic leader. Halyn was a medical officer in the Russian army before joining the Army of the UNR during the struggle for Ukrainian independence. A member of the Ukrainian Scientific Society in Kiev, he supervised its work in the area of medical terminology. During the Hetman government of 1918, he was the director of the Terminology Commission of the Ministry of Public Health. In 1920 he immigrated to Rumania. He is the author of *Rosiis'ko-ukraïns'kyi medychnyi slovnyk* (Russian-Ukrainian Medical Dictionary, 1920) and *Medychnyi latyns'ko-ukraïns'kyi slovnyk* (Medical Latin-Ukrainian Dictionary, 1926). He also wrote memoirs (published in the journal *Za derzhavnist'* and separately) and a number of works on surgery.

Halytskaia Rus' (Galician Rus'). A Russophile daily newspaper, subsidized by the Russian government, that was published in Lviv from April 1891 to December 1892. It replaced *Chervonaia Rus'* (1888–91), which had been banned. It was edited by O. Avdykovsky and I. Pelekh. A total of 215 issues appeared. In a pastoral letter of 22 December 1892, the Ukrainian Galician episcopate forbade the clergy and the faithful to read and propagate the newspaper. Soon afterwards *Halytskaia Rus'* ceased publication and in its place **Halychanyn* began to appear.

Halytskii Sion. See *Ruskii Sion.*

Halytsko-Ruska Matytsia (HRM). A literary and educational society established in June 1848 in Lviv by the *Supreme Ruthenian Council. Modeled on Serbian (1826), Czech (1831), and other similar predecessors, the HRM fostered schooling and general cultural enlightenment by publishing popular-science literature, grammars, and textbooks. Rev M. Kuzemsky was its first head. In 1850 it had 193 dues-paying members, 69 of whom were priests. In 1861 its statute was ratified. In the 1860s it was taken over by the *Russophiles (Ya. Holovatsky, A. Petrushevych, B. Didytsky, and others), who promoted the use of the artificial, bookish **yazychie* language and later even Russian. Consequently, the Galician populists founded the *Prosvita society in 1868. The activity and influence of the HRM declined in the 1880s, but it continued to exist (with periods of inactivity, 1895–1900, 1909–22) until 1939. The HRM published about 60 books (15 in 1848–50, 15 in 1850–61, 26 in 1862–99, 4 in 1900–39). It also published scholarly serials: *Galitskii istoricheskii sbornik* (3 vols, 1853–60), *Naukovyi sbornik* (4 vols, 1865–8), **Literaturnyi sbornik* (15 vols, 1869–73, 1885–90, 1896–7), and *Nauchno-literaturnyi sbornik* (8 vols, 1901–2, 1904–6, 1908, 1930, 1934).

BIBLIOGRAPHY
Bendasiuk, S. 'Ucheno-literaturnoe obshchestvo Galitsko-russkaia Matitsa vo L'vove (proshloe i nastoiashchee),' *Nauchno-literaturnyi sbornik Galitsko-russkoi Matitsy*, 7 (1930)
Pashaeva, N.; Klimkova, L. 'Galitsko-russkaia Matitsa vo L'vove i ee izdatel'skaia deiatel'nost',' *Kniga*, 34 (Moscow 1977)

I. Myhul

Hamaliia. Name of several family lines, probably of different origin, extending back to Cossack times. Mykhailo was the founder of one such line. In 1649 he was registered as a Cossack of Cherkasy company and in 1662 was appointed colonel of Cherkasy regiment by Hetman

Ya. Somko. His sons, Hryhorii and Andrii, were prominent Cossack officers. The latter served, at first, as captain of Lokhvytsia company and then, under I. *Mazepa, as general osaul (1689–94). Andrii's son Mykhailo (d ca 1724) served as captain of Lokhvytsia company (1690–3), general standard-bearer (1701–4), acting colonel of Poltava (1705), and general osaul (1707–9). Because of his close ties with Mazepa, after the hetman's defeat he was forced to reside in Moscow until 1715. His brother, Antin (d 1728), was Mazepa's general osaul. In 1712 Antin was exiled to Siberia and then forced to live in Moscow until his death. Ivan (b 17 December 1699, d 21 March 1766), nephew of Mykhailo and Antin, served in various capacities under D. Apostol, and took part in campaigns against Poland and Turkey. In 1750 he became acting colonel of Myrhorod, and in 1762 general judge. Platon Hamaliia (b 28 November 1766, d 21 July 1817), the son of Yakiv, was a seaman and a scholar. A graduate of the Kievan Mohyla Academy and the Naval Academy, he served in the imperial navy and saw action against the Swedes. He began to lecture on naval theory and practice in 1793 and wrote several books on the subject. In 1808 he was elected full member of the Imperial Academy of Sciences.

O. Ohloblyn

Mykola Hamaliia

Serhii Hamchenko

Hamaliia, Mykola [Hamalija], b 17 February 1859 in Odessa, d 29 March 1949 in Moscow. Microbiologist and epidemiologist; from 1940 honorary member of the USSR Academy of Sciences, and from 1945 full member of the USSR Academy of Medical Sciences. A graduate of Odessa (New Russia) University (1880) and the Military Medical Academy in St Petersburg (1883), he worked briefly in 1886 under L. Pasteur in Paris. Later that year in Odessa Hamaliia founded, with I. Mechnikov, the first bacteriological station in the Russian Empire and performed the first rabies vaccinations. The succeeding years were devoted to research on rabies, tuberculosis, cholera, and cattle plague. He was a founder of the Bacteriological Institute in Odessa and served as its director (1899–1908). In 1901–2 he combated the plague in Odessa, and then cholera in Transcaucasia, the Volga region, and the Donbas. Hamaliia founded and edited (1910–13) *Gigiena i sanitariia*, the first journal of its kind in the Russian Empire. Then he served as director of the Vaccination Institute in Leningrad (1912–28) and of the Central Institute of Epidemiology and Bacteriology (1930–8), as chairman of the microbiology department of the Second Moscow Medical Institute (1938–49), and as honorary president of the All-Union Society of Microbiologists, Epidemiologists, and Infectionists (1939–49), which he founded. In his final years he headed a laboratory at the Institute of Epidemiology and Microbiology of the USSR Academy of Medical Sciences. Hamaliia wrote over 300 scientific works on rabies, the plague, cholera, smallpox, and other infectious diseases, and made a number of important discoveries. His collected works were published posthumously.

M. Adams

Hamaliia, Semen [Hamalija], b 12 August 1743 in Kytaihorod, Poltava regiment, d 22 May 1822 in Avdotin, Moscow gubernia. Philosopher, mystic. A graduate of the Kievan Mohyla Academy (1763) and of the Academic University in St Petersburg (1769), he taught Latin briefly at a cadet school, served as a functionary of the Imperial Senate (1770–4), and ran Count Z. Chernyshev's chancellery. He was also a member of the Society for Promoting the Translation of Foreign Books (est 1768) and the Typographic Company of Moscow (est 1784). Retiring in 1784, he devoted the rest of his years to translating the works of mystics such as J. Böhme, J. Vives, and L. Saint-Martin, and to organizing Masonic lodges. His correspondence was published in 1832 and again in 1836–9, but most of his translations remain unpublished.

Hamarnik, Yan, b 2 June 1894 in Zhytomyr, d 31 May 1937. Communist party and Red Army activist of Polish origin. In 1917 he was a member of the Kiev Communist party committee and from October 1917, a member of its revolutionary committee. In 1918–20 he was a leading member of the Odessa, Kharkiv, and Crimea party organizations, and a political commissar in the Red Army. From 1920 to 1923 he was chairman of the Odessa and then Kiev gubernia party organizations. During 1923–9 he was a CP and Red Army activist in Siberia and Belorussia, and in 1928 secretary of the CC of the Belorussian CP. Hamarnik became chief of the Red Army political department in 1929 and deputy defense minister of the USSR (1930–7). He committed suicide during the Red Army purges, but was posthumously rehabilitated.

Hamchenko, Serhii [Hamčenko, Serhij], b 7 October 1859 in Ratne, Kovel county, Volhynia, d 1934 in Zhytomyr. Archeologist. He studied at Kiev University (1876–80); in 1878 he helped V. Antonovych excavate a Rus' burial ground near Zhytomyr. His independent archeological work began in 1886. In 1900 he initiated the establishment of the Volhynia Research Society. A member of the Russian Archeological Society from 1908, in 1909–13 he conducted digs in Podilia. From 1919 he lived in Zhytomyr and worked for the Volhynian Museum. In 1926 he began working with the All-Ukrainian Archeological Committee (VUAK), of which he became vice-president in 1928. In his numerous articles and research reports in Ukrainian and Russian archeological publications Hamchenko made major contributions to research on the Trypilian, Timber-Grave, Cherniakhiv, and Zarubyntsi cultures. He conducted many digs of burial grounds and settlements in Volhynia and Podilia, as well as in Kiev and the vicinities of Cherkasy, Kremenchuk, Izium, Luhanske, Kupianske, Artemivske, Kharkiv, and the Dnieper Hydroelectric Station. He gathered around him a school of younger archeologists (I. Levytsky, F. Kozubovsky, O. Lahodovska, M. Makarevych, and others).

Hamilton. City (1981 pop 537,600) and leading industrial center in Ontario, Canada. In 1981, 11,600 of its residents were of Ukrainian origin. The first Ukrainian organizations in Hamilton were socialist – the Shevchenko Prosvita Association (1910), a branch of the Ukrainian Social Democratic Party of Canada (1915), and the Women's Educational Organization (1920). A congregation of Ukrainian Baptists had formed by 1914. The Church of the Holy Ghost, a Ukrainian Catholic church, was built in 1918. During the interwar years branches of the Ukrainian Labour-Farmer Temple Association, the Canadian Sitch Organization, the Ukrainian National Federation, the United Hetman Organization, and the Ukrainian Catholic Brotherhood of Canada were established. By 1941 there were 2,265 Ukrainians in Hamilton.

Today the Ukrainian community in Hamilton is served by three Catholic and one Orthodox parish, a Presbyterian congregation, three Ukrainian schools (one of them a Catholic day school), several youth associations, and the Ukrainian Canadian Social Services Inc.

The largest organizations are the local branches of the Ukrainian National Federation, the Canadian League for Ukraine's Liberation, and the Ukrainian Self-Reliance League of Canada. There are four Ukrainian credit unions and a branch of the Ukrainian Canadian Professional and Business Federation. The community as a whole is represented by the local office of the Ukrainian Canadian Committee.

Hamkalo, Ivan, b 1 May 1939 in Horodyshche Korolivske, Bibrka county, Galicia. Conductor and educator. Hamkalo graduated from the Lviv Conservatory in 1963. He has conducted the Lviv Oblast Ukrainian Music and Drama Theater in Drohobych (1963–5), the Donetske Symphony Orchestra (1968–70), and the orchestra of the Kiev Theater of Opera and Ballet (since 1970). He has taught at the Kiev Conservatory (1977–81) and the Kiev Institute of Culture (since 1981).

Hamorak, Yurii. See Stefanyk, Yurii.

Handziuk, Yakiv [Handzjuk, Jakiv], b 1863, d February 1918 in Kiev. Senior officer in the Ukrainian army, 1917–18. In the fall of 1917 he organized and commanded the 1st Division of the 1st Ukrainian Corps. In January 1918 he took over command of the entire corps. He was captured by Bolshevik forces in Kiev and executed.

Hankenstein Codex. An 11th–12th century Church Slavonic manuscript written in Western Ukraine and preserved at the Austrian National Library in Vienna. Also called the Ochtoechus of Vienna, it is a 289-folio liturgical anthologium. Its language, which has many local features, has been studied by S. Smal-Stotsky (1886), K. Kysilevsky (1953), and G. Shevelov (1979).

Hankevych, Klymentii [Hankevyč, Klymentij] (Hankiewicz, Clemens), b 1842 in Nastasiv, Ternopil circle, d 1924. Galician pedagogue and linguist. He wrote comparative studies on accent in Sanskrit, Greek, and Ukrainian; of greater importance because of their factual material are his descriptive works on accent in Ukrainian dialects and on folk etymology. He also wrote on the history of Slavic philosophy and psychology.

Lev Hankevych

Mykola Hankevych

Hankevych, Lev [Hankevyč], b 1 June 1881 in Staromishchyna, Skalat county, Galicia, d 14 December 1962 in New York. Political figure, publicist, and attorney. In the early 20th century he was active in socialist circles in Galicia, heading *Moloda Ukraina (1901–3) and working with the committee in exile of the Revolutionary Ukrainian Party in Lviv. He also co-operated with the Ukrainian Social Democratic Workers' party, making illegal trips to Russian-ruled Ukraine. During the First World War he collaborated with the *Union for the Liberation of Ukraine and was its emissary in Bulgaria. In 1918 he was a member of the Ukrainian National Council of the Western Ukrainian National Republic. Hankevych was an especially prominent activist in the *Ukrainian Social Democratic party (USDP) and head of its executive in 1921–3 and 1930–4. In the 1930s he gained renown as the defense counsel in political trials of OUN and Ukrainian Military Organization members in Polish courts. He was also a president of the Union of Ukrainian Lawyers in Lviv and vice-president of the Lviv Bar Association. In 1944 he immigrated to Munich and later to New York. He contributed to *Pravnychyi Vistnyk* (1910–13), coedited *Vpered* (1918–22), the journal of the USDP, and wrote publicistic essays on the history of Ukrainian socialism.

A. Zhukovsky

Hankevych, Mykola [Hankevyč], b 16 May 1867 in Sniatyn, Galicia, d 31 July 1931 in Shklo, Yavoriv county, Galicia. Political and trade-union leader. A graduate of Lviv university and a lawyer by profession, Hankeych was active in socialist circles in Galicia and played an important role in organizing Ukrainian workers. In the 1890s he published briefly the newspaper *Robitnyk*, then became a founding member of the Ukrainian Social Democratic party. During the First World War he was vice-president of the Supreme Ukrainian Council in Lviv and a founder of the General Ukrainian Council in Vienna. Hankevych edited *Volia* (1900–7), the newspaper of the Ukrainian Social Democratic party, and wrote prolifically for Polish and Ukrainian journals and newspapers. He was an active proponent of co-operation between Ukrainian and Polish socialists.

Hannover. City (1983 pop 527,500) and capital of the state of Lower Saxony, West Germany. During the Second World War many Ukrainians were conscripted to work in factories located in Hannover and its suburbs. In one such suburb, Saltzgitter, there is a monument to the memory of the many Ukrainians who died while working in the large metallurgical plant located there. In 1945–9 Hannover and its vicinity had the largest concentration of Ukrainians in northern Germany. Ukrainian displaced persons (about 5,000 in 1945 and 2,840 in 1948) were housed in the M. Lysenko camp, which served as the center of Ukrainian organizations in the British occupation zone. The camp had a nursery, a primary school, a gymnasium, and a technical school, as well as various cultural groups and civic organizations. A camp near the neighboring town of Burgdorf housed 800 Ukrainians in 1948. Today Ukrainians in Hannover number about 300. A single Ukrainian church, St Volodymyr's, serves both Ukrainian Catholic and Orthodox communities in that city.

Vsevolod Hantsov

Hantsov, Vsevolod [Hancov], b 25 November 1892 in Chernihiv, d autumn 1979 in Chernihiv. Noted linguist. After graduating from Galagan College, he studied under L. Shcherba, A. Shakhmatov, and J. Baudouin de Courtenay at St Petersburg University and taught there in 1916–17. In 1918 he was the education commissioner in Kozelets county. In October 1918 he became a professor at Kiev University. In 1920 he became the director of the VUAN Commission for Compiling a Dictionary of Spoken Ukrainian in Kiev, and from 1924 he was a coeditor of the VUAN Russian-Ukrainian dictionary. He played an active role in the Kharkiv Orthographic Commission. At the Stalinist show trial of the *Union for the Liberation of Ukraine in 1930, he was sentenced to eight years' imprisonment, which were later extended, apart from a short break in 1947, until 1956. He then returned to Chernihiv and tried to resume scholarly activity, but was prevented from doing so by I. *Bilodid. (A short article by him did appear, however, in *Radianske literaturoznavstvo*, 1966, no. 3.)

Before his arrest Hantsov worked on problems of the normalization of literary Ukrainian and on the history of Belorussian (a study of the Radziwill Chronicle, 1927), but his most important contributions were in the field of Ukrainian historical dialectology. On the basis of his analysis of Ukrainian dialects in the Chernihiv region he proposed the theory that the Ukrainian language was formed by the fusion of originally distinct dialectal groups – the southern and northern groups, of which the present-day southwestern and northern Ukrainian dialects are a continuation. This led him to reclassify Ukrainian dialects (1924) and to develop a scheme of the early history of Ukrainian. His division of Ukrainian dialects into three groups – northern, northwestern, and relatively recent southeastern (formed by the synthesis of two former groups) – provided the foundation for subsequent studies of Ukrainian dialectology. An analysis of Hantsov's works can be found in Yu. Sherekh's *Vsevolod Hantsov, Olena Kurylo* (1954).

G.Y. Shevelov

Hanulia, Yosyf [Hanulja], b 10 August 1873 in Nyzhnyi Ripashi, in the Prešov region, Transcarpathia, d 8 October 1962 in Cleveland. Transcarpathian cultural leader, writer, and Greek Catholic priest. A graduate of the Prešov Greek Catholic Seminary, Hanulia served in several parishes in Prešov eparchy, before being sent in 1904 to the United States to minister to the needs of Carpatho-Ruthenian immigrants. From 1914 until his death he served in a parish in Cleveland, Ohio. There in 1927 he helped establish the Rusin Elite Society, which published the bilingual English-Ruthenian illustrated monthly magazine *Vozhd–The Leader* (1929–30). He also served as president of the Rusin Cultural Garden Association. He founded and edited the newspaper *Rusin–The Ruthenian* (1910–16) and wrote a series of pioneering textbooks for the network of Ruthenian schools in the United States. A staunch defender of the traditions of the Greek Catholic church, he elaborated his views in his study *The Eastern Ritual* (2 vols, 1954).

Hanuliak, Hryhorii [Hanuljak, Hryhorij] (pen names: H. Marusyn, Hryts Zazulia, Hrytsko Mamalyga), b 1 March 1883 in Syniava, Sianok county, Galicia, d 29 August 1945 in Sianok. Publisher, journalist, and writer. In 1908 he began to write in the Lemko vernacular for the Russophile press (*Nauka, Halychanyn, Prikarpatskaia Rus', Volia narodu*). In the 1920s he adopted a Ukrainophile orientation. He published a collection of poems, *Vesniani sny* (Spring Dreams, 1909), and several short stories and humorous monologues. In the 1930s he wrote 10 plays for folk theaters. In 1921 he founded the publishing house Rusalka and published the popular series *Knyhozbirnia shkoliaryka* (children's stories, many of which were authored by Hanuliak), *Literarturna biblioteka, Narodna biblioteka* (both edited by S. Kalynets), and *Teatralna biblioteka* (about 150 plays for amateur theatrical groups). He also published the journals *Teatral'ne mystetstvo* (1922–5) and *Veselyi kalendar* (to 1939). Hanuliak headed the Union of Ukrainian Merchants and Entrepreneurs in Lviv (1928–34).

Hanuschak, Ben [Hanuščak], b 29 April 1930 in Earl Grey, Saskatchewan. Teacher, lawyer, and politician. A graduate of the University of Manitoba, he taught in Winnipeg and served as president of the Winnipeg Teachers' Association before entering politics. From 1966 to 1981 he was the New Democratic party (NDP) member of the Manitoba legislature for Burrows. He served as secretary of the Manitoba NDP (1966–8), speaker of the Manitoba assembly (1969–70), minister of consumer and corporate affairs (1970–3), minister of education (1971–3), minister of colleges and university affairs (1973–6), minister of continuing education and manpower (1976–7), and minister of tourism, recreation, and cultural affairs (1976–7). In February 1981 Hanuschak left the NDP, citing differences with party policy on the Canadian constitution, and became one of the founders of the Progressive party. In November 1981 he failed to win re-election to the legislature.

Hanushevsky, Mykhailo [Hanuševs'kyj, Myxajlo], b 5 December 1880 in Sukhovolia, Lviv county, Galicia, d 9 February 1962 in Uhornyky, Lviv oblast. Ukrainian Catholic priest, civic and political leader. He studied at the Greek Catholic Theological Seminary in Lviv, and philosophy and law at Lviv and Vienna universities. He was a chaplain to Metropolitan A. Sheptytsky (1905–6), but was transferred on his own request to work in small parishes throughout Galicia. One of the pioneers of the dairy and credit-union co-operative movement, Hanushevsky also organized many branches of the Prosvita Society and various health and temperance groups. In 1928 he was elected to the Polish Sejm as a representative of the Ukrainian National Democratic Alliance. In 1939 he was arrested by the Gestapo and held in prison for several months. In 1946 Hanushevsky was arrested by the Soviet authorities and sent to Siberia where he was incarcerated for 11 years.

Hanusz, Jan, b 13 July 1858 in Kolodiivka, Stanyslaviv circle, Galicia, d 26 July 1887 in Paris. Polish linguist of Ukrainian origin. His PH D dissertation (1883) at Cracow University, 'Über die Betonung der Substantiva im Kleinrussischen,' was published in 1884. From 1884 until his death he was a docent at the University of Vienna, where he taught Sanskrit, Lithuanian, and comparative and Celtic linguistics. He is the author of around 150 works, including articles on stress in Ukrainian dialects, the general character of the Ukrainian language, and the language of Armenians in Western Ukraine.

Hanzha, Ivan [Hanža], b ?, d September 1648 near Pyliavtsi, Podilia. Military leader during the time of Hetman B. Khmelnytsky. An officer in the army of the Polish magnate A. Koniecpolski, he joined the Cossack side with the outbreak of the *Cossack-Polish War in 1648. During the Battle of *Zhovti Vody, on orders from Khmelnytsky, he persuaded an army of four to five thousand registered Cossacks to abandon the Polish forces. After the Battle of Korsun he successfully led a peasant uprising against the Polish nobility in the Uman region. In the summer of 1648 he organized the Uman Regiment and became its first colonel, but died soon after in the Battle of Pyliavtsi.

Haraksim, L'udovít, b 1 August 1928 in Uzhhorod. Slovak historian, specialist in Ukrainian history. From 1956 to 1973 he worked first at the Slovak Academy of Sciences and then at the Slovak National Museum in Bratislava. His publications focus on the cultural and political life of Ukrainians in Eastern Slovakia in the 19th century. Among them is the monograph *K sociálnym a kultúrnym dejinám Ukrajincov na Slovensku do roku 1867* (On the Social and Cultural History of Ukrainians in Slovakia to 1867, 1961). Since 1972 he has not been permitted to publish.

Harald III (Hardraade or Hardruler), b 1015, d 25 September 1066 in Stamfordbridge, England. King of Norway from 1045 to 1066. After the Danish victory in the Battle of Stiklestad (1030), Harald fled to Rus'. There he headed the Varangian guard of Prince Yaroslav the Wise, whose daughter *Yelysaveta Yaroslavna he later married. Some of his poetry is extant, including a song he composed in Yelysaveta's honor, which was translated into Ukrainian by I. Franko. From Rus' he went to Constantinople, where for some 10 years he headed the Varangian guard of the Byzantine emperor Michael IV, becoming the most famous Varangian in the Byzantine service. In 1045 Harald returned through Rus' and Sweden to Norway and shared the kingdom with his nephew Magnus I; upon Magnus's death in 1047, he became sole ruler of Norway. He invaded England in 1066 and died in battle at Stamfordbridge, where the Norwegians were routed.

Harambašić, August, b 14 July 1861 in Donja-Miholjac, Slovenia, d 16 July 1911 in Stenjevac. Croatian Romantic poet. His translations of T. Shevchenko's poetry appeared in various Yugoslav journals; eight narrative poems were published as a book, together with Shevchenko's autobiography and a scholarly introduction, in 1887. He also translated Marko Vovchok's short stories, which were published with an extensive introduction in 1899.

Harapiak, Harry [Harapjak], b 17 September 1938 in Cowan, Manitoba. Politician. A railway engineman, Harapiak was elected to the Manitoba legislature in 1981 as the New Democratic party member for The Pas. In January 1985 he was appointed minister of northern affairs.

Harapnyk (The Whip). Illustrated magazine of humor and satire published irregularly from 1921 to 1935 in Edmonton and Andrew, Alberta, by T. Tomashevsky. It featured illustrations by O. Hryhorovych, Ya. Maidanyk, and L. Snaichuk. It made biting comments on labor and farm issues and on the Great Depression.

Haras, Mykola, b 1870 in Vashkivtsi, Bukovyna, d ? Civic and religious leader. Haras cofounded and headed the teacher's organization Ukrainska Shkola in Chernivtsi. He was also the leader of the Ukrainian faction at the eparchial assemblies of the Bukovynian Orthodox church (1931–8). He authored *Istorychnyi ohliad i suchasnyi stan ukraïnskoï osvity i kul'tury na Bukovyni* (Historical Survey and the Current Situation of Ukrainian Education and Culture in Bukovyna, 1934) and *Iliustrovana istoriia tovarystva Ukraïns'ka Shkola v Chernivtsiakh, 1887–1937* (An Illustrated History of the Society 'Ukrainska Shkola' in Chernivtsi, 1887–1937, 1937).

Harasevych, Andrii [Harasevyč, Andrij] (pseud: Surmach, Vasyl), b 13 August 1917 in Lviv, d 24 July 1947 while climbing Mt Wazmann near Berchtesgaden, West Germany. Poet. He began writing when still a student in Khust and Uzhhorod and his poems were published in various newspapers and periodicals there and in Lviv. While a student in Prague, he fell under the influence of the nationalist school, especially the poet O. *Olzhych; his first collection of poems, *Sonety* (Sonnets, 1941), is imbued with the then-current nationalist sentiments. Most of his poems appeared posthumously in the collection *Do vershyn* (To the Heights, 1959). Several short stories appeared in various periodicals.

Mykhailo Harasevych

Harasevych, Mykhailo [Harasevyč, Myxajlo], b 1763 in Zolochiv county, Galicia, d 1836. Baron of Neustern, church historian, and prominent Galician religious figure. He studied theology at the Barbareum in Vienna. In 1787 he was given the Chair of Pastoral Theology in Lviv, and later also taught in a Ukrainian theological institute; he was twice vicar-general of the Lviv eparchy. Through his efforts in Vienna and Rome the Galician metropoly of the Ukrainian Catholic church was restored in 1806, the Lviv *kapitula* was recognized, and the church became equal to and completely independent of the Polish Roman Catholic church. After the death of Metropolitan A. Anhelovych in August 1814, Harasevych administered the metropoly until the appointment of Metropolitan M. Levytsky in March 1816. Harasevych is the author of *Annales Ecclesiae Ruthenae* (1862), a documented history of the Ukrainian Catholic church, in which he defended the church's status from a historico-legal position.

Harasevych, Oleksander [Harasevyč], 1876–1934. Galician agronomist and pedagogue. Before the First World War Harasevych worked as an organizer of dairy co-operatives, an agriculture instructor for the Prosvita society (1904–9), and a lecturer at the Lviv teachers' seminary. He was one of the founders and a long-term president of the *Vidrodzhennia temperance society. In the 1920s he lived in Soviet Ukraine; he died in Kharkiv during the 1933–4 purge.

Harashchenko, Ivan [Haraščenko], b 5 May 1881 in Krasnyi Kut, Slovianoserbske county, Katerynoslav gubernia, d 20 March 1952 in New York. Businessman, church and civic leader. Active in the Orthodox church in Kharkiv and Slobidska Ukraine, in 1921 he was elected vice-chairman of the All-Ukrainian Orthodox Church Council in Kiev. To finance the publication of religious books, he sold all his property. For his religious activism he spent 10 years in Soviet concentration camps. He left Ukraine during the Second World War. In 1943 he became a member of the Great and Little Councils of the Ukrainian Autocephalous Orthodox Church (Conciliar). In 1950 he was ordained in West Germany and in 1951 immigrated to the United States.

Harbin. City (1982 pop 2,550,000) in northeast China, capital of Heilungkiang province. Harbin was founded in 1898 as a railway center of the Chinese Eastern Railway, which was built by Russia on Chinese territory to link the Trans-Siberian Railroad with Vladivostok. Most of the inhabitants were employees of the railway company, including mostly Russians but also Ukrainians and other nationalities. Ukrainians formed their own artistic groups and maintained close ties with Ukraine and their countrymen in the *Far East. In 1907 the Ukrainian Club was founded. After the February Revolution of 1917 the Ukrainian community in Harbin became much more active. Several new institutions such as the Ukrainian Council and the Manchurian Regional Council were created to provide political leadership in the Far East and to maintain close ties with Ukraine. In 1917 a company of Ukrainian troops was sent from Harbin to Ukraine. It was commanded by P. Tverdovsky, who returned to Harbin a year later as a consul of the UNR. A Ukrainian school and gymnasium were established on the premises of the Ukrainian Club. In 1918 the Ukrainian Orthodox parish of the Holy Protectress was organized by Rev M. Trufaniv. By 1929 it had built its own church.

From 1922 to 1931 the Ukrainian community in Harbin was isolated from other Ukrainian centers and treated unfairly by Chinese authorities, who were influenced by local Russians. The Ukrainian People's Home was confiscated and the Ukrainian schools and other institutions

Ukrainian Orthodox Chapel in the Ukrainian Club in Harbin, ca 1930

were abolished. Only the Prosvita society continued to operate under the auspices of the YMCA. It maintained a drama group and published a weekly – *Ukraïnske zhyttia*.

The fortunes of the Ukrainian community improved in 1931 when the Japanese buffer state of Manchukuo was set up. The Ukrainian People's Home was restored to the Ukrainian community. The Ukrainian Political Center assumed the leading role in Ukrainian life in Manchuria. It founded the Ukrainian Publishing Union, which published *Man'dzhurs'kyi vistnyk* (ed I. Svit, 1932–7) as well as books and brochures. From 1934 Ukrainians had their own radio programs. The Zelenyi Klyn association and the Ukrainian Youth Association merged to form the Association of Ukrainian Youth. In 1935 the Ukrainian National Colony was founded as an umbrella organization for all Ukrainian communities in *Manchuria. When Manchuria was occupied by the Soviet armies in 1945, most Ukrainians were arrested and deported and their institutions were abolished. Until then the number of Ukrainians in Harbin was close to 15,000. (See also *China.)

V. Kubijovyč

Oleksa Harbuziuk

Harbuziuk, Oleksa [Harbuzjuk], b 29 March 1920 in Berehy, Dubno county, Volhynia. Baptist pastor, church leader, and journalist. He studied theology and journalism in Germany and has lived in Chicago since 1949. From 1968 to 1972 he was president of the Ukrainian Evangelical Baptist Convention of the USA, and in 1972 he became president of the All-Ukrainian Evangelical Baptist Fellowship. He is a member of the presidium of the secretariat of the World Congress of Free Ukrainians and an executive committee member of the American Council of Christian Churches. In 1966 he began broadcasting religious programs to Ukraine and editing **Pislanets' pravdy*.

Hare (*Lepus*; Ukrainian: *zaiats*). Mammal of the family Leporidae of the order Lagomorpha. Distinguished from rabbits by physical and developmental characteristics, the hare is about 47 cm long and 1.5–4 kg in weight, depending on the species. Two species are found in Ukraine: the brown, or common hare (*L. europaeus*), most numerous in the steppe, forest-steppe, and Kuban regions, and the white, or blue hare (*L. timidus*), infrequently found in the northwestern parts of Ukraine. Hares are herbivorous and occasionally damage pastures, crops, and forest vegetation. Hare are hunted in Ukraine for their meat and fur.

Harkusha, Semen [Harkuša], b ca 1739 in Berezan, in the Homel region of Belorussia, d ? Zaporozhian Cossack, merchant, and rebel leader. Born Mykolaienko and nicknamed Harkusha at the Zaporozhian Sich, he fought in the Russian-Turkish War of 1768–74 with the Zaporozhian army, and took part in the Ochakiv and Khadzhybei campaigns. From the early 1770s on he led a group of rebels who raided gentry estates in Slobidska, Left-Bank and Right-Bank Ukraine, and Belorussia. Captured in 1773, 1778, and 1783, he escaped from prison all three times. In 1784 he was again apprehended, tortured, and sentenced to a life term of forced labor in Kherson.

Harmashiv, Vsevolod [Harmašiv], b 1868 in Mykolaiv, Kherson gubernia, d 1953 in Munich. Surgeon. From 1897 to 1914 he served as senior physician on the staff of the Kiev Military Hospital. During the war he served in the active Russian army, and then returned to the Kiev hospital with the rank of general of medical services. In 1922 Harmashiv immigrated to Czechoslovakia, where he was appointed professor of biology and hygiene at the Ukrainian Higher Pedagogical Institute in Prague. From 1930 to 1933 he was rector of the institute. He founded a number of clinical sanatoriums for emigrants in Czechoslovakia. In 1945 he moved to Germany.

Harmatii, Vasyl [Harmatij, Vasyl'], 1810–1900. Peasant leader in Galicia. Harmatii was a representative to the Austrian parliament in 1848, and later was a founder of the radical movement and a leader of the Ukrainian Radical party. His sons Luka (1866–1925) and Mykhailo (killed by the Soviets in 1939) were also members of the Ukrainian Radical party.

Harness making. See Saddle making.

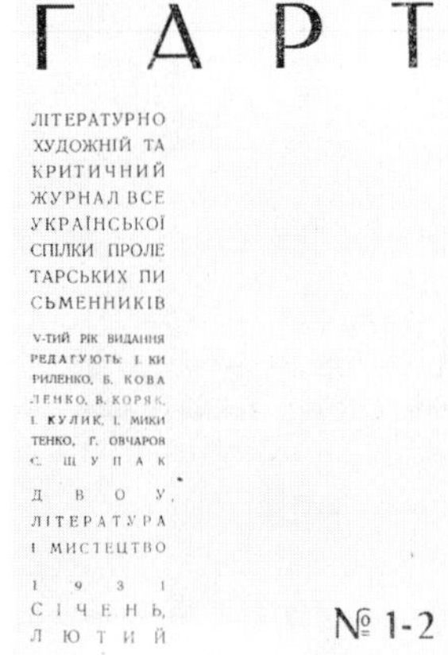

ГАРТ

ЛІТЕРАТУРНО ХУДОЖНІЙ ТА КРИТИЧНИЙ ЖУРНАЛ ВСЕ УКРАЇНСЬКОЇ СПІЛКИ ПРОЛЕ ТАРСЬКИХ ПИ СЬМЕННИКІВ

V-ТИЙ РІК ВИДАННЯ РЕДАГУЮТЬ: І. КИ РИЛЕНКО, Б. КОВА ЛЕНКО, В. КОРЯК, І. КУЛИК, І. МИКИ ТЕНКО, Г. ОВЧАРОВ С. ЩУПАК

ДВОУ, ЛІТЕРАТУРА І МИСТЕЦТВО

1931 СІЧЕНЬ, ЛЮТИЙ

№ 1-2

Hart, title page

Hart (Tempering). A literary and political monthly published in Kharkiv in the years 1927–32 by the *All-Ukrainian Association of Proletarian Writers (VUSPP), which claimed to be the direct offspring of the 'proletarian' writers' group *Hart (1923–5) and was an archenemy of the literary group *Vaplite and its successors. Among its contributors were Yu. Smolych, K. Hordiienko, I. Le, N. Zabila, I. Kyrylenko, O. Kundzich, L. Pervomaisky, O. Vlyzko, V. Sosiura, M. Dolengo, B. Kovalenko, L. Skrypnyk, I. Mykytenko, I. Kulyk, V. Koriak, Ya. Savchenko, S. Shchupak. The journal ceased publication when VUSPP was dissolved in 1932.

Hart (Tempering). An association of proletarian writers founded in Kharkiv in January 1923 by V. *Blakytny. According to its program, its purpose was 'to struggle against bourgeois art' and 'to attract the proletarian masses to literary creativity.' Branches of the association were set up in Kiev, Katerynoslav, Odessa, Kamianets-Podilskyi, and other cities. It published two almanacs: *Hart* (Kharkiv, 1924) and *Kyïv-Hart* (Kiev, 1925). Among its members were V. Ellan-Blakytny, K. Hordiienko, I. Dniprovsky, D. Falkivsky M. Yohansen, H. Koliada, O. Kopylenko, V. Koriak, H. Kotsiuba, I. Kulyk, V. Polishchuk, Ya. Savchenko, I. Senchenko, M. Kulish, V. Sosiura, P. Tychyna, M. Khvylovy. A disagreement between the adherents of its official mass orientation and the supporters of M. *Khvylovy, who advocated artistry as the goal of literary activity (the Urbino group), led to Hart's dissolution in December 1925. Khvylovy and his supporters founded the writers' group *Vaplite, while most of the other members joined the *All-Ukrainian Association of Proletarian Writers.

Harvard Ukrainian Research Institute

Harvard Ukrainian Research Institute (HURI). A research institute of Ukrainian studies at Harvard University in Cambridge, Massachusetts. It was established in June 1973 on the recommendation of the university's ad hoc Committee on Ukrainian Studies. This committee, which included professors O. Pritsak, I. Ševčenko, R. Pipes, H. Lunt, W. Weintraub, and E. Keenan, had been appointed in 1968 by the dean of the Faculty of Arts and Sciences to formulate and supervise a program for Ukrainian studies at Harvard. The founding of HURI followed the endowment of chairs in Ukrainian history (1968), literature (1973), and linguistics (1973) and the introduction of courses in Ukrainian studies in several Harvard departments. In 1974 the ad hoc committee became the Standing Committee on Ukrainian Studies, an event that marked the completion of the formal structure of Ukrainian studies at Harvard.

The goals of the institute are to support research, publications, and teaching in Ukrainian studies. HURI conducts a weekly seminar in Ukrainian studies, holds conferences, and sponsors approximately 30 research associates yearly. Publications of the Harvard Series in Ukrainian Studies include monographs, conference proceedings, documents, and offprints. HURI also publishes the scholarly journal **Harvard Ukrainian Studies* and *Minutes of the Seminar in Ukrainian Studies*. Special projects undertaken by HURI include research on the famine of 1932–3 and the publication of texts and documents relating to the millennium of Christianity in Ukraine. The institute, in conjunction with the Harvard Summer School, has offered courses in Ukrainian disciplines since 1971. HURI has on staff a Ukrainian specialist who oversees the collection of Ucrainica in the Harvard University library system, including the reference library located at the institute. From its beginnings, the director of the institute has been O. Pritsak and the associate director I. Ševčenko, except in 1977 and 1985–6, when Ševčenko served as director. F. Sysyn was appointed associate director in 1985. Financial support for HURI is provided by the *Ukrainian Studies Fund.

M. Baziuk

Harvard Ukrainian Studies. The scholarly journal of the *Harvard Ukrainian Research Institute, published quarterly in Cambridge, Massachusetts, since March 1977 under the editorship of O. Pritsak and I. Ševčenko. The journal deals primarily with history, linguistics, and literature, although related disciplines are sometimes represented. It also publishes historical documents.

Harvest rituals. Folk ceremonies dating back to ancient times and marking the opening and closing of the harvest period. These ceremonies were characterized by a sequence of magical rituals that interacted with natural processes and phenomena. The spiritualization of nature was at the essence of these rites, which could influence critically the fate of the harvest.

Zazhynky marked the commencement of harvesting and took place at the end of June or the beginning of July. In the morning, all the reapers went into the fields together. The master or village elder took off his hat, turned to the sun, and uttered a special incantation requesting the fields to surrender their harvest and to give the reapers sufficient strength with which to gather it in. In more recent times, the incantation was replaced with a prayer. Then, the mistress or a woman reputed to be lucky (called *postadnytsia* in some regions) cut the first sheaf of grain, which was called *voievoda*. Women reapers rolled around on a cleared patch of the field with the purpose of absorbing strength from the soil. The *postadnytsia* presented the master with the first sheaf after which he offered everyone liquor and food. In the evening, the *voievoda* sheaf was brought to the master's house and was placed in the icon corner where it was to stand until the end of the harvesting.

Obzhynky marked the end of the harvesting, usually at the end of July or the beginning of August. After the last clutch of grain had been cut, a solemn procession around the field took place. A clump of unreaped wheat or rye left at the edge of the field was tied into a sheaf known alternatively as 'Volos's beard,' 'Elijah's beard,' 'the Savior's beard,' 'Grandfather's beard,' 'goat,' or simply 'beard' and was left as an offering to the gods of the fields. In some regions the 'beard' was thought to contain the benevolent spirits of ancestors who would protect the fields. Thereafter the reapers walked in a procession from the fields to the master's house, carrying the last sheaf (*ostalets*). The sheaf was then presented to the master and mistress accompanied with wishes of happiness and abundance. The master carried the ceremonial gift into the house and placed it in the icon corner. A harvest feast ensued, whereupon everyone was treated to drinks and food in the house or yard. These rituals, which are very similar to wedding rituals, were accompanied with special songs (see *Harvest songs). Some elements of the *obzhynky* rituals have been revived in 'harvest feasts' that are held today in Soviet Ukraine; eg, grain garlands are carried in procession and presented to chairmen of artels or collective farms. This ceremony is followed by dancing, singing, games, or sports competitions.

BIBLIOGRAPHY
Koperzhyns'kyi, K. *Obzhynky: Obriady zboru vrozhaiu u slov'ians'kykh narodiv novoï doby rozvytku* (Odessa 1926)
Krut', Iu. *Khliborobs'ka obriadova poeziia slov'ian* (Kiev 1973)
B. Kravtsiv, M. Hnatiukivsky

Harvest songs. Class of ritual and lyric folk songs associated with the harvest period and divisible into three groups that coincided with the preparations for harvesting, the harvest itself, and the aftermath of the harvest.

Zazhynky songs accompanied the rituals at the beginning of the harvest (see *Harvest rituals) such as the tying of the first sheaf. They bestow honor upon the master and mistress and ask nature to yield its fruits and grant the reapers strength to ensure an easy and successful harvesting period.

Harvesting (*zhnyvarski*) songs were not associated with any form of ritual. They were sung while working in the fields or walking to and from the fields. Most of them spoke of the reaper's hard work from sunrise to sunset. Besides field labor, they depict relations between the farmhands and the master. Harvesting songs often address the forces of nature: they rebuke the sun for rising too early and setting too late, or ask the moon to light the way home.

Obzhynky songs are related to the rituals that close the harvest. By theme they can be divided into several subgroups: (1) finishing songs, which are connected with the reaping of the last field ('Oi, ty, nyvo, nyvon'ko' and 'Do kintsia, zhenchyky, do kintsia'); (2) songs for the tying of the 'beard' at the border of the mown field ('Borodu pololy, ruchky pokololy' and 'Oi, chyia to boroda'); (3) songs for the tying of the last sheaf and *obzhynky* garland ('Ziidy khmaron'ko z neba' and 'Kotyvsia vinochok po poliu'); (4) songs accompanying the procession to the master's cottage ('Buvai, nyvo, zdorova' and 'Shchos' u seli dym kuryt''); (5) songs for the arrival at the master's cottage ('Vyidy, panochku, vyidy' and 'Kazala nam nyvka'); and (6) songs sung in the master's house ('A v nashoho hospodaria toloka' and 'Sydyt' pan na pokuti').

The composition of harvest songs is distinct. They are remarkable for their emotive language, colorful epithets, and hyperbolic comparisons. Psychological parallelism and the personification of natural entities are typical of these songs. Their melodies are archaic and closely related to *wedding songs. Today in Ukraine the traditional harvest songs are being revived to some extent. They appear with increasing frequency in the repertoire of amateur artistic groups. However, attempts to compose new 'Soviet harvest songs' have not been very successful. Contemporary harvest songs account for only 12.5 percent of the total collection, and even these are essentially modifications of traditional songs incorporating the use of current terminology.

BIBLIOGRAPHY
Krut', Iu. (comp). *Zhnyvars'ki pisni* (Kiev 1971)
M. Hnatiukivsky

Hashynsky, Arkadii [Hašyns'kyj, Arkadij], b 29 July 1920 in Melitopil, Katerynoslav gubernia. Stage actor and teacher. A graduate of the Moscow State Institute of Theater Arts (1945), since 1948 he has worked at the Kiev Ukrainian Drama Theater and has appeared in numerous roles. He also teaches at the Kiev Institute of Theater Arts.

Hasidism (from the Hebrew *hasidim*, meaning pious, righteous). Jewish religious movement which arose in Ukraine in the 18th century in opposition to the dogmatic and ritualistic formalism of the established orthodox Judaism. It originated as a loose network of small local groups devoted to an ascetic or ecstatic way of life, practicing their own rites, and embracing a mystical world view, which was influenced to some extent by the medieval Jewish Kaballah. These groups were led by charismatic, righteous individuals, the *zaddikim*. Hasidism was a popular movement that actively preached social reform and appealed particularly to the lower classes of Jewish society.

The first Hasidic leader was Israel Ba'al Shem Tov (1700–60), who was active in Podilia and traveled to other parts of the Polish Commonwealth to propagate his ideas. He was widely reputed as a holy man with supernatural powers of healing and mystical visions. His doctrines and counsels were formulated in pithy sayings. Important early centers of Hasidism included Mezhyrich, Chornobyl, and Medzhybizh. The movement soon spread to Austria-Hungary, and Hasidic communities sprang up in Galicia, Bukovyna, and Transcarpathia. Hasidic schools and printing presses were set up in Korets, Zhytomyr, Berdychiv, Zhovkva, and other towns. Russia's code for Jews, issued in 1804, legalized Hasidism by allowing Hasidic communities to build their own synagogues and choose their own rabbis. By the mid-19th century the majority of Jews in Ukraine were Hasidic and the movement was accepted by orthodox Jewry. Hasidic folklore (songs, dances, and sayings) is rich in Ukrainian themes. From Ukraine Hasidic Jews immigrated to Palestine and to the United States. In the 20th century, as Jewish life became increasingly secularized, Hasidism declined. Its opposition to the Zionist movement diminished its political influence. During the Holocaust Hasidism was completely eradicated in Eastern Europe; only a small number of its remaining adherents managed to emigrate. M. Buber's and A. Heschel's philosophical systems are known as neo-Hasidism.

BIBLIOGRAPHY
Rabinowicz, H. *World of Hasidism* (New York 1970)
Mahler, R. *Hasidism and the Jewish Enlightenment: Their Confrontation in Galicia and Poland in the First Half of the Nineteenth Century* (Philadelphia-New York-Jerusalem 1985)
V. Markus

Hasko, Mechyslav, b 27 January 1907 in Lutske, Volhynia gubernia. A poet, prose writer, and translator. In 1925 he immigrated to the Ukrainian SSR. He graduated from the Kharkiv Institute of National Economy in 1929. He belonged to the *Zakhidnia Ukraina writers' association. His early works included the poetry collections *Obabich kordonu* (On Both Sides of the Border, 1930) and *Shliu vam svii pryvit* (I Send You My Greetings, 1931) and the long poem 'Nad aerodromom' (Over the Airfield, 1931). Repressed during the Stalin terror, he was rehabilitated in 1956. A new collection of his poems appeared in 1958, followed by *Lanky zhyttia* (The Links of Life, 1967). He has also published studies on Shevchenko – *Pro shcho rozpovidaiut' maliunky Tarasa Shevchenka* (What the Paintings of Taras Shevchenko Tell, 1970) and *U koli Shevchenkovykh ta Hoholevykh druziv* (In Shevchenko's and Gogol's Circle of Friends, 1980) – and translations from Polish and English.

Haslo (The Slogan). The monthly organ of the *Revolutionary Ukrainian party, published in Chernivtsi from March 1902 to May 1903. A total of 17 issues appeared. It was edited in Kiev and then Lviv by D. Antonovych and M. Rusov, then taken to Chernivtsi, where L. Kohut and V. Simovych supervised its publication. Most of the copies were then smuggled back into Russian-ruled Ukraine for distribution. The journal advocated social democracy and Ukrainian autonomy. It published articles on international politics and reported extensively on current affairs throughout Ukraine.

Hasyn, Oleksa (*nom de guerre*: Lytsar), b 8 July 1907 in Koniukhiv, Stryi county, Galicia, d 31 January 1949 in Lviv. Senior officer of the UPA. In 1935 he was appointed chief of the military and organizational department of the national executive of the OUN in Galicia. Hasyn was arrested several times by Polish authorities and spent a year in the Bereza Kartuzka concentration camp. In 1937 he left Poland illegally to work abroad in the military department of the OUN leadership. He completed an officer course and wrote a military textbook. A founding member of the OUN (Bandera faction), in the summer of 1941 he organized and commanded a clandestine officer school in the Lviv region. After escaping from a Gestapo prison in 1942, Hasyn served as military instructor of OUN. In 1943 he was appointed UPA deputy chief of staff, and in 1946, chief of staff. A year later he became a member of the supreme command and in 1948 was promoted to colonel. He was killed in action in Lviv.

Hattsuk, Oleksa [Hatcuk], b 14 October 1832 in Odessa, d 5 December 1891 in Moscow. Archeologist, journalist, and publisher. Hattsuk graduated from Moscow University in 1857. He was involved in the publication of the literary-scholarly monthly *Osnova in St Petersburg. Until 1875 he also contributed to the newspaper *Odesskii vestnik*. From 1875 to 1890 in Moscow he published the annual *Krestnyi kalendar'* and a political-literary-artistic weekly, popularly called *Gazeta A. Gattsuka*. He is the author of popular and scholarly articles, a version of the Ukrainian alphabet (*Ukraïns'ka abetka* 1861), and the first popular book on the prehistoric archeology of Russia and Ukraine: *Starina Russkoi zemli ...* (Antiquity of the Rus' Land ..., 1866).

Havlíček-Borovský, Karel, b 21 October 1821 in Borová (now Zbraslavice), Kutná Hora county, Bohemia, d 29 July 1856 in Prague. Czech poet and publicist. From 1842 to 1844 he taught in Lviv and Moscow and visited Kiev. He was a close acquaintance of Ya. *Holovatsky and O. *Bodiansky. He became a Slavophile and was a strong proponent of national rights for the peoples of the Austro-Hungarian Empire, including the Ukrainians. He is the author of a number of political tracts and satirical poems. His poetry was translated into Ukrainian by I. Franko.

Havrylenko, Alla, b 6 December 1934 in Kremenchuk. Ballerina. A graduate of the Kiev School of Choreography (1954), she joined the Kiev Theater of Opera and Ballet in 1955 as a soloist. She has danced the lead roles in K. Dankevych's *Lileia* (The Lily) and A. Adam's *Giselle*, Mavka in M. Skorulsky's *Lisova pisnia* (The Forest Song), Juliet in S. Prokofiev's *Romeo and Juliet*, and the White Lady in A. Glazunov's *Raymonda*.

Havryliuk, Oleksander [Havryljuk], b 23 April 1911 in Zabolottia, Biała county, Podlachia, d 22 June 1941 in Lviv. A communist writer in interwar Western Ukraine. A member of the *Horno writers' group in Lviv, he published in the journal *Vikna* and other Galician communist periodicals of the 1930s and was imprisoned by the Poles for his political activity. He became the director of the literary fund in Lviv after the Soviet occupation in 1939 and was killed during the city's bombardment by the Germans. His poetry, stories, essays, and novella *Bereza* have been published in several Soviet editions of his works.

Mykhailo Havrylko

Havrylko, Mykhailo, b 5 October 1882 in Runivshchyna, Poltava county, Poltava gubernia, d 1920? Sculptor. He studied art under F. Balavensky in Myrhorod (1899–1904), at Baron A. Shtiglits's Art School in St Petersburg (1904–5), the Cracow Academy of Arts (1907–

10), and A. Bourdelle's studio in Paris. His works include portraits such as *Hannusia* (1909); busts of the writers M. Shashkevych (1910), T. Shevchenko (1911, 1919), and Yu. Fedkovych (1913); thematic compositions such as *Banduryst*, *The Parting*, and *Cossack on a Horse*; and a well-known bas-relief medallion of T. Shevchenko (1911). He took part in four competitions for a T. Shevchenko memorial in Kiev (1910–13), but without success. His first proposal (1910) was the most interesting one: it presented the poet in Cossack dress on a high pedestal surrounded by the heroes of his poems. Later the Soviet sculptor M. Manizer augmented this composition with workers and Red Army soldiers and used it for his Shevchenko memorial in Kharkiv (1935). In 1915 Havrylko joined the Sich Riflemen, was wounded in battle, and then transferred to the *Graycoats. His last work was a bust of T. Shevchenko for the foyer of the Gogol Theater in Poltava (1919).

Havryshchuk, Mykola [Havryščuk], 1878–1942. Bukovynian primary school teacher, pedagogue, political activist. He was one of the leaders of the Social Democratic party in Bukovyna and a deputy to the Bukovynian Diet (1911–18). From 1920 he worked in Transcarpathia. He wrote textbooks on methodology such as *Metodyka pochatkovoï nauky v narodnii shkoli* (Methods of Elementary Teaching in Public School, 1913) and translated a number of German pedagogical books.

Hawrelak, William [Havreljak, Vasyl'], b 4 October 1914 in Wasel, Alberta, d 7 November 1975 in Edmonton. Entrepreneur and politician. Owner of a soft-drink company and a real-estate developer, in 1949 Hawrelak was the first Ukrainian elected to the city council of Edmonton. In 1951 he was elected mayor of Edmonton, the first Ukrainian mayor of a major Canadian city. He served three terms – 1952–9, 1963–5, and 1974–5 – and in 1956 was elected president of the Canadian Federation of Mayors. Forced to resign from office in 1959 and 1965 because of real-estate scandals, he was exonerated in the later case by the Supreme Court of Canada. Hawrelak was a member of the Ukrainian Canadian Professional and Business Federation and active in the Ukrainian Greek Orthodox church.

Bohdan Hawrylyshyn

Hawrylyshyn, Bohdan [Havrylyšyn], b 19 October 1926 in Koropets, Buchach county, Galicia. Business educator. A graduate of the University of Toronto, the Centre d'Etudes Industrielles (now the International Management Institute) in Geneva, and the University of Geneva (PH D 1975), since 1960 he has been a faculty member, and since 1968 director, of the institute. A lecturer and consultant to international organizations and corporations, he is a Fellow of the World Academy of Arts and Sciences, the International Academy of Management, and the Club of Rome. Hawrylyshyn sits on the editorial board of several professional journals and is the author of *Road Maps to the Future: Towards More Effective Societies* (1980).

Haydak, Mykola [Hajdak], b 12 May 1898 in Malyi Yanysol, Mariiupil county, Katerynoslav gubernia, d 12 August 1971 in Minnesota. Apiculturist and specialist in beekeeping; full member of the Ukrainian Academy of Arts and Sciences. He studied at Kiev University and in Prague at the Ukrainian Free University and the Czech Polytechnical Institute, graduating from the latter in 1927. In 1930 Haydak immigrated to the United States, and in 1933 he obtained his PH D in apiculture at the University of Wisconsin. He worked as a professor at the University of Minnesota until 1966. Haydak wrote a textbook on beekeeping for the Ukrainian Husbandry Academy in Poděbrady and some 220 papers dealing with apiculture.

Hayfields. Land covered by cereal (eg, timothy, ryegrass) and pulse (eg, red and pink clover) grasses that are used for various types of feed: hay, haylage, hay meal, and roughage. In 1984 the total hayland in Ukraine comprised 2,100,000 ha (4.3 percent of the republic's arable land and 6.1 percent of the USSR hayland).

About 25 percent of the hayland in Ukraine is sown; the rest is natural. Almost a half of the latter is dry land (yielding 12–15 centners per ha), and the rest is flooded (20–25 centners per ha) or low-lying (12–15 centners of acidic hay per ha). Tilled fields have a much higher yield – 80–100 centners per ha.

Hayfields are unevenly distributed throughout Ukraine. They comprise 10 percent of all farmland in Polisia and the Carpathian region, 5 percent in the forest-steppe, and 0.7 percent in the steppe. Regions with less hayland generally devote more land to other *fodder forage crops such as tubers and corn. The area of hayland in Ukraine is steadily decreasing, while the fodder crop area is increasing. In 1913, 10,000,000 ha in Ukraine were devoted to fodder crops, of which 91 percent were hayland or pastureland. In 1959 fodder crops took up 17,700,000 ha, yet hayfields and pastures accounted for only 45 percent of the area (in the USSR as a whole, hayland accounted for as much as 83 percent of all fodder cropland). This trend in Ukraine can be explained by the move to intensive livestock farming, which increases the demand for feed. Since hay is one of the least productive fodder crops, it is increasingly being replaced by other types of fodder.

C. Freeland

Hazelnut (*Corylus*; Ukrainian: *lishchyna zvychaina*; American: filbert). An important nut-bearing plant; a genus of the birch (Betulaceae) family which grows most frequently as a tall bush (2–4 m) and less frequently as a tree (7–8 m). Two species grow in Ukraine: the common or European hazel (*C. avellana*), found as brush in mixed forests in Polisia and in the forest-steppe region, and the giant hazel (*C. maxima*), cultivated in the Crimea and in eastern and southeastern Ukraine. Hazelnuts are grown commercially for food and processed for oil; the wood is used in carpentry. Hazelnut trees are planted for anti-erosion and decorative purposes throughout Ukraine.

Hazeta dlia narodnykh uchytelei (Newspaper for Elementary School Teachers). An official weekly publication of the Hungarian Ministry of National Education, which appeared in Budapest from 1868 to 1873. It was published in the languages of the nations living in Hungary – Hungarian, German, Rumanian, Slovak, Ukrainian (Ruthenian), Serbian, and Croatian – and distributed free of charge to schools in Hungary. Beginning in 1872 (issue 42), it was printed using phonetic spelling.

Hazeta shkol'na (School Newspaper). Periodical devoted to education, published semimonthly in Lviv from 27 May 1875 to the end of 1879 (from 1877 it was also a literary journal). A total of 110 issues appeared. It was published and edited by O. *Partytsky, who also was author of many articles on pedagogical, historical, and literary subjects. Contributors included O. Barvinsky, O. Ohonovsky, H. Vretsona, S. Kurylovych, O. Oryshkevych, Z. Savchynsky, and P. Zaklynsky. Literary works by such writers as T. Shevchenko, M. Shashkevych, Yu. Fedkovych, M. Vovchok, M. Ustyianovych, O. Konysky, F. Zarevych, and S. Vorobkevych were also published. The journal published articles on the methodology of teaching various subjects and on cultural and economic issues, as well as reviews, biographies, and reports from the homeland. *Hazeta shkol'na* was populist in character and advocated the use of Ukrainian in schools.

Health care. See Public health.

Health education. The system of dissemination of health, sanitation, and medical knowledge with the aim of improving conditions in the workplace and of life in general, maintaining health and longevity.

In Ukraine, early texts such as the *Izbornik* of Sviatoslav, *Fizioloh*, and *Pchola* contained advice on medicine and hygiene. In the 16th and 17th centuries such advice was dispensed in various herbals and self-healing manuals (*lechebnyky, zelnyky, vertohrady*), most of which were translations of Byzantine or Western European texts. In the 18th and 19th centuries medical knowledge was disseminated by Ukrainian medical scientists, including D. Samoilovych, K. Yahelsky, O. Shafonsky, M. Hamaliia, F. Barsuk-Moisieiev, N. Ambodyk-Maksymovych, and Ye. Mukhin. Popular medical texts were written by S. Venechansky (about the treatment of venereal diseases), Ya. Sapolovych and I. Kamenetsky (for priests and seminarians), I. Kashynsky, F. Loievsky, and O. Maslovsky.

In the Russian Empire in the 19th and early 20th centuries, Ukrainians published articles in such popular medical publications as *Drug zdraviia, Populiarnaia meditsina, Zdorov'e, Vegeterianskii vestnik, Vegeterianskoe obozrenie*, and *Zdorovaia zhizn'*. Important work in health education was done by the zemstvos (see *Zemstvo medicine) and the Pirogov Society of Russian Physicians, under whose auspices the Commission for Popular Hygiene Education was formed in 1894. Both the zemstvos and the Pirogov society published popular pamphlets on health care, including some by Ukrainian authors such as O. Yakovenko and O. Tarasenko. They were published in Ukrainian by the *Philanthropic Society for Publishing Generally Useful and Inexpensive Books in St Petersburg. Health care was taught in army units from 1861. In Kiev, public lectures in medicine were given from 1886. Other popular medical works written in the latter half of the 19th century include *Pro khvoroby i iak ïm zapobihaty* (On Diseases and Their Prevention, 1874) by S. Nis and S. Podolynsky's *Zhyttia i zdorov'ia liudei na Ukraïni* (The Life and Health of the People in Ukraine, 1879). *Zhyttia i Znannia*, the first Ukrainian-language medical journal in Russian-ruled Ukraine, was published in Poltava in 1913–14.

During the period of the struggle for Ukrainian independence health education was conducted by the Ministry of Public Health and the Ukrainian Red Cross under both the government of the UNR and the Hetman government. In the Western Ukrainian National Republic it was the responsibility of the Commissariat and Council for the Protection of Peoples' Health.

In Western Ukraine, in addition to the work done by official agencies in Galicia and Bukovyna, considerable health education was conducted by the *Prosvita society. Later, various other Ukrainian health organizations included the temperance and anti-nicotine Vidrodzhennia society (founded 1909), the Ukrainian Physicians' Society (founded 1910), the Ukrainian National Society for Child and Adolescent Care (founded 1917), and the Ukrainian Hygienic Society (founded 1929). These organizations, with their local branches, published pamphlets on health protection and hygiene, and organized lectures, displays, and other activities. In addition, magazines such as *Zdorovlie, Vidrodzhennia*, and *Narodne zdorovlia* educated the masses about health care.

In the USSR, health education is conducted by the Ministry of Health, the Ukrainian Red Cross, the Znannia Society, various cultural-enlightenment organizations, trade unions, sport associations, and universities. Health education is taught in schools. Workers in the agricultural and food industry and food services are required to conform to minimal sanitary and hygienic standards. Lectures on industrial health and hygiene are given to industrial workers. In villages there are community health schools. Systematic health education is also conducted by various institutions of preventative medicine (eg, *sanitary-epidemiological stations, hospitals) and by the military. Each oblast and raion center has a health-education council under the Ministry of Health of the Ukrainian SSR as well as buildings of sanitary education that co-ordinate health education in the various centers. In 1977 there were 86 such buildings in Ukraine. At the Ukrainian Scientific Reasearch Institute of General and Communal Hygiene there is a methodological center for health education. Medical knowledge is also spread through the press, cinema, and television. Before the Second World War, many popular health journals were published, including *Shliakh do zdorov'ia* (1925–41), *Chervonyi Khrest* (1929–41), *Iunatskyi Chervonyi Khrest*, and *Psykhohihiienu v masy* (1933–4). Recently, however, the publication of materials on health and hygiene in Ukrainian has decreased greatly. Much health education in the USSR is intended to serve the political and economic interests of the state. Besides simple health care, its goals include the propagation of a socialist lifestyle, the 'rational use of work and leisure time,' and the struggle against alcoholism, illegal drug use, and other harmful practices. Continuing problems in public health – eg, periodic outbreaks of epidemics almost unknown in developed countries, high absentee rates due to illness, and a recent and unprecedented decline in life expectancy rates – suggest that health education in Ukraine may not be particularly effective, despite the considerable resources devoted to it.

From 1945 onwards, health education among Ukrainian émigrés was conducted by the Ukrainian Red Cross in West Germany and Austria and by the Ukrainian Medical-Charitable Service, based in Munich. Some work is also done by the Ukrainian Medical Association of North America.

BIBLIOGRAPHY

Sokolov, I.; Trakhman, Ia. *Orhanizatsiia i metodyka sanitarno-osvitn'oï roboty* (Kiev 1958)

Ocherki po istorii sovetskogo sanitarnogo prosveshchenia (Moscow 1960)

Pliushch, V. *Narysy z istoriï ukraïns'koï medychnoï nauky ta osvity*, 2 vols (Munich 1970, 1983)

V. Pliushch

Health resorts and sanatoriums. Facilities for treating or preventing diseases and improving health. Health resorts are located in areas with natural curative resources such as a favorable climate, mineral springs, muds, limans, beaches, and special local foods. Although their medicinal value is sometimes questioned, health resorts are extremely popular in Ukraine and are an important component of the entire system of public-health care. Some sanatoriums and rest homes are located at health resorts. Others serve as vacation spots, although they may also offer a varied program of physiotherapy and general or specialized medical treatment.

The earliest records about curative localities in Ukraine refer to mineral springs in Transcarpathia, then under Hungarian rule. Ivan IV's envoys, returning in 1558 from Constantinople to Moscow through the Carpathian Mountains, observed that mineral baths in this region provided an effective cure for various illnesses. For many centuries local inhabitants took advantage of the curative powers of mineral springs and muds in Ukraine. Some areas in Galicia such as Shklo, Liuben Velykyi, and Nemyriv attracted visitors from abroad as early as the 17th century. In Russian-ruled Ukraine health resorts began to develop at the beginning of the 19th century on the limans near Odessa, at Slovianske and Berdianske, and particularly on the Crimean coast. Private hospitals and boarding homes with a total of up to 1,000 beds were established there. Patients bathed directly on the beach or at the spring. The first baths were built in Kuialnyk only in 1834. In the second half of the 19th century the expansion of the railway network led to the rapid development of health resorts. With the opening of the Odessa–Kuialnyk railroad in 1873 Kuialnyk was developed rapidly as a resort area. By the turn of the 20th century the resort areas in southern Ukraine provided such facilities as sanatoriums, hotels, boarding homes, and balneological hospitals, all of them private, profit-making facilities. At the same time so-called cottage districts were established in the vicinity of the larger cities. By 1917 the boarding homes (excluding those in cottage districts and hotels) in Russian-ruled Ukraine had a capacity of 2,000 boarders.

Balneological reseach was begun in Ukraine at the end of the 19th century by Y. Mochutkovsky, who founded the Odessa Balneological Society. Other contributors to the field included Ya. Bardakh and O. Veryho. In 1914 O. Shcherbak founded the Sechenov Clinical Institute of Physical Therapy in Sevastopil, which he directed for 20 years. New methods of balneotherapy (mud therapy), which won recognition abroad, were developed there.

After the Revolution of 1917 all health resorts came under the authority of the mining department of the RSFSR Supreme Council of the National Economy, and in 1918 under the People's Commissariat of Health of the RSFSR. In March 1919 all health resorts and health resort areas were nationalized, and in 1920–1 the Crimean palaces, private buildings, and cottages located in resort areas were confiscated for the purpose of converting them into sanatoriums and rest homes. The Sanatorium–Health Resort Administration of the People's Commissariat of Health of the Ukrainian SSR was set up in 1919, but it did not gain control over all-Union resort areas of Odessa, Berdianske, and Slovianske until 1925. In 1920 Ukraine's Commissariat of Health established a health resort commission, which included such members as Ye. Brukser, T. Brusylovsky, and S. Nalbandov, to oversee the development of health resorts. This commission laid the foundations of health-resort studies in Ukraine. In 1920 there were 46 general sanatoriums with 4,050 beds and a number of mud sanatoriums in Ukraine (excluding the Crimea and Western Ukraine).

In 1922 a state tuberculosis institute was founded in Yalta, at which, from 1925, research on the microclimate of the resorts on the southern coast of the Crimea was done. In 1931 this institute was reorganized into the Institute for the Climatotherapy of Tuberculosis, which in 1955 was merged with the Institute of Physiotherapy in Sevastopil to form the Scientific Research Institute of Physiotherapy and Climatotherapy in Yalta. The Scientific Research Institute of Health Resort Studies, which is the chief research institute in the field, was established in Odessa in 1928 on the basis of the All-Ukrainian Balneological Institute (Lermontov Resort), founded in 1923. The institute has four departments, four clinics, a number of research laboratories, a branch in Uzhhorod, clinical resorts in Berdianske and Truskavets, and 30 control and biochemical stations in various localities of Ukraine. It publishes the annual collection *Kurortologiia i fizioterapiia*.

By 1936 there were 359 sanatoriums and 173 rest homes with 58,923 beds in Soviet Ukraine. Twenty-five health-resort areas in Vinnytsia, Dnipropetrovske, Donetske, Kiev, Odessa, Kharkiv, and Chernihiv oblasts had been developed. Besides health facilities run by the Commissariat of Health, there were health resorts and rest homes managed by various government departments and trade unions. In this period there were three curative mud areas in Ukraine (Kuialnyk, Khadzhybei Liman, and Hola Prystan), three balneological areas (Myrhorod, Berezivski Mineralni Vody, and Shepetivka), three mixed resort areas (Slovianske, Kyrylivka, and Berdianske), and numerous climatic resort areas, such as Sosnivka, the suburbs of Kiev, Hadiache, Sharivka, and Krominne. The annexation of Western Ukraine during the Second World War greatly increased the number of resorts in Ukraine, although many were closed or damaged during the war. In 1954 the Crimea with its numerous resorts was also incorporated into Ukraine; hence, the number of sanatoriums increased to 506 (69,500 beds) and the number of rest homes to 148 (25,130 beds). In 1956 all health resorts were placed under Ukraine's Ministry of Health, and in 1960, except for tuberculosis facilities, they were transferred to the All-Union Central Council of Trade Unions. Today all health resorts and sanatoriums in Ukraine, except tuberculosis and childrens' sanatoriums, as well as a few maintained for Party and government leaders and the KGB, are overseen by the Ukrainian Health Resort Administration of the Trade Unions in Kiev. In 1970 a system classifying health resorts by union, republican, and local status was introduced. Resorts on the Crimean coast, in Truskavets, Odessa, and Berdianske, were given union status. The increase in the number of health facilities in Ukraine is depicted in table 1.

TABLE 1
Number of sanatoriums, rest homes, and resorts (number of beds, in thousands, in parentheses)

Type of facility	1970	1975	1980	1984
Sanatoriums and rest homes	1,847 (301)	2,737 (462)	2,991 (561)	3,243 (614)
Sanatoriums and boarding homes with medical care	483 (113)	486 (122)	507 (143)	508 (150)
Children's sanatoriums	202 (34)	206 (35)	210 (37)	213 (39)
Preventive sanatoriums	266 (19)	320 (26)	393 (36)	437 (41)
Rest homes and boarding homes	186 (51)	242 (77)	270 (93)	292 (98)
Rest resorts	804 (94)	1,499 (175)	1,643 (219)	1,816 (256)
Tourist resorts	108 (24)	190 (62)	178 (70)	190 (69)

Except for Lviv oblast, health resorts in western Ukraine are as yet underdeveloped. The largest number of health-care facilities is found in the Crimea and Odessa oblast. In number of health resorts, Ukraine is second only to the RSFSR in the Soviet Union. Ukraine has resorts of every type. In quantity and variety, Ukraine has some of the richest reserves of *mineral waters in the USSR. Over 500 mineral springs have been registered by the AN URSR. The largest number of springs is located in western Ukraine. The most famous resort is Truskavets in Lviv oblast. Mineral waters from its 14 springs are used in treating stomach, intestine, and liver disorders. Its unique spring called Naftusia yields water that is reputed to be effective against kidney stones. Stomach, intestine, and liver ailments as well as metabolism disorders are treated also at Poliana, Soimy, Shaian (Transcarpathia), and Morshyn (Lviv oblast). The hydrogen sulfide springs in Nemyriv, Liuben Velykyi, Shklo (Lviv oblast), and Syniak (Transcarpathia) are thought to be helpful in treating cardiovascular, gynecological, dermatological, and neurological diseases. Peat muds and ozocerite, which are found in these areas, are also used in the treatment. Transcarpathia, with over 300 springs producing carbonic, hydrogen sulfide, sodium chloride, hydrocarbonate-sodium chloride, sodium hydrocarbonate, and other waters, is well known throughout the USSR. Mineral waters with different chemical contents are found also in the Lemko region, in Ivano-Frankivske, Poltava, Kharkiv, and Crimea oblasts, and elsewhere. Radioactive mineral waters in large quantitites are available in Khmilnyk in Vinnytsia oblast, Kyrylivka and Berdianske in Zaporizhia oblast, Teterivske in Zhytomyr oblast, Bila Tserkva and Myronivka in Kiev oblast, and other places in south-central Ukraine. Resorts on the limans (Kuialnyk, Khadzhybei, and Sukhyi) and lakes of the Odessa region, on the Azov coast (Yeiske and Utliuk limans and lakes near Zhdanov and Berdianske), and in the Crimea (Saky, Chokratske, Adzhi-Hal, Syvash lakes) are famous for their mud baths. Besides muds of marine origin there are muds of continental origin on Hola Prystan Lake and Hopra Liman in Kherson oblast, Solenyi Liman in Dnipropetrovske oblast, and at Slovianske, Donetske oblast. In northwestern Ukraine there are also rich deposits of peat muds suited for medicinal use.

Climatic resorts are scattered throughout Ukraine. In the west they are located near balneological resorts. Tuberculosis is treated at mountain resorts of Ivano-Frankivske oblast such as Yaremcha, Vorokhta, and Kosiv. Staryi Krym in the Crimea is also a mountain resort. The most popular climatic resorts are the sea-bathing resorts on the southern coast of the Crimea (Alupka, Alushta, Haspra, Hurzuf, Yevpatoriia, Koreiz, Livadiia, Planetarske, Simeiz, Sudak, Teodosiia, Foros, and Yalta), and in the vicinity of Odessa (Velykyi Fontan and Zatoka). There are many climatic resorts in the coniferous and mixed forests of Kiev oblast (in Boiarka, Bucha, Verzel, Irpin, and Koncha-Zaspa), Kharkiv oblast (in Volodymyrivka, Zanky, and Komarivka), Cherkasy oblast (in Prokhorivka), Vinnytsia oblast (in Pechera and Khmilnyk), and Lviv oblast (in Briukhovychi).

The importance of rest resorts and tourist resorts is increasing steadily. Adults usually take advantage of sanatoriums and boarding homes on designated tourist routes. Young people stay in facilities maintained by the Pioneer organization and schools, and in children's recuperative facilities under the control of the Ministry of Health. The number of people using health resorts is given in table 2. In 1985, 11.4 million people made use of the various resorts, sanatoriums, and rest facilities in Ukraine. Of these 9.7 million received lengthy treatment or rest, 0.8 million received one- or two-days' rest, and 0.9 million used the sanatoriums on tourist routes during holidays. Over 5 million children and teenagers used the facilities. The normal stay at sanatoriums was 24 days to two months, and at rest homes from 12 to 24 days. Individuals usually use sanatoriums and health-resort facilities free of charge (the costs are covered by the trade unions), or else, on a physician's recommendation and with the approval of trade-union authorities, pay 30 percent of the cost. Over a million people from other republics of the USSR and from abroad make use of Ukraine's health resorts. Some 40,000 people work in these facilities, including 3,500 physicians and over 8,000 middle-level medical staff.

There are plans to distribute sanatoriums and health resorts more evenly throughout Ukraine and to increase the output of bottled mineral water. At present, about 0.5 million bottles are produced at 30 springs, and most

TABLE 2
Number of people using sanatoriums and rest homes on an annual basis, by type of facility (in thousands)

Type of facility	1970	1975	1980	1983
Sanatoriums and rest facilities	3,255	6,375	7,809	9,650
Sanatoriums and boarding homes with medical care	882	1,118	1,377	1,477
Preventive sanatoriums	203	293	453	534
Resort polyclinics on tourist routes	244	260	337	313
Rest homes and boarding homes	759	1,064	1,148	1,200
Rest resorts	424	949	1,112	1,441
Tourist resorts	743	2,691	3,382	4,685

of them are consumed outside Ukraine. Plans call for the training of more health resort physicians.

BIBLIOGRAPHY
Kurorty Ukrainskoi SSR. Eds A. Struev and R. Koraev (Kiev 1955)
Babynets', A. *Dzherela mineral'nykh vod Radians'koï Ukraïny* (Kiev 1958)
Vykorystannia pryrodnykh likuval'nykh resursiv Ukraïny (Kiev 1959)
Poltoranov, V. *Sanatorno-kurortnoe lechenie i otdykh v SSSR* (Moscow 1971)

H. Schultz

Heather (*Calluna*; Ukrainian: *veres*). Plant genus of the Ericaceae family containing one species – the Scotch heather (*C. vulgaris*). This evergreen bush reaches a height of 30–60 cm. It is closely leaved and has purplish pink, bell-shaped, honey-yielding flowers. It grows in forests (mostly pine forests), forest clearings, and peat bogs. In Ukraine heather is found in Polisia, the forest belt of the Carpathian Mountains, and Roztochia-Opilia, but rarely in the forest-steppe belt.

Heavy industry. Group of industries that turn out producer goods in contrast to light industry, which manufactures consumer goods. According to Soviet classification heavy industry includes such branches as the *electric power, *fuel, *metallurgical, *chemical, *petrochemical, *machine-building, *metalworking, *lumber, *paper, and *building-materials industries. In 1984 heavy industry accounted for 66 percent of both Ukraine's and the USSR's total industrial output. Since Stalin's industrialization drive heavy industry has been stressed more than any other branch of the Soviet economy. Soviet authorities view heavy industry as the source of raw materials, capital stock, and technology for other branches, and as the moving force in the growth of the economy as a whole.

Ukraine's share of heavy industry under the Russian Empire was very high. By the end of the 19th century a number of heavy-industry centers had sprung up in Ukraine: the *Donets Basin (coal, iron, chemicals, and machines), the *Dnieper Industrial Region (iron and nonferrous ores and metallurgy), the *Kryvyi Rih Iron-Ore Basin, and the Kharkiv region (machines and metalworking). In 1913 Ukraine produced over 90 percent of the empire's output of coke, 78 percent of its coal, 75 percent of its iron ores, 69 percent of its pig iron, and 58 percent of its steel. Yet the Ukrainian economy was still not biased towards heavy industry; its gross national product was divided almost equally between industry and agriculture. Except for the petroleum industry, which developed rapidly towards the end of the 19th century in Galicia, Western Ukraine under Austrian rule remained an industrially undeveloped region.

In the Soviet period Ukraine's heavy industry served as the basis of the accelerated industrialization of the USSR. The construction in the 1930s of the *Dnieper Hydroelectric Station, the largest station in Europe at the time, was a major achievement. Coal mining and the iron and steel industry in Ukraine, which were important for strategic as well as economic reasons, were strongly supported. The growth in producer goods was much faster than in consumer goods. With the rise of new industrial centers in the Urals and western Siberia, Ukraine's share in the total USSR output of most producer goods fell. Ukraine's heavy industry recovered slowly from the destruction it sustained during the Second World War. For most of its products, 1940 output levels were reached only in the early 1950s, when Ukraine's industry grew at a faster rate than the USSR's or the RSFSR's industry. Again producer goods were favored over consumer goods. New industries producing automobiles, electrotechnical equipment, precast reinforced-concrete structures, and other products were established. The pace of industrial growth slowed in the 1960s and 1970s.

In the early 1980s more than 85 percent of Ukraine's electric power was produced by thermal power stations, most of which burned coal. The fuel is supplied mostly by the Donets Basin and is becoming more and more difficult to extract. To reduce dependence on fossil fuels and to increase the power supply of the European part of the USSR and Eastern Europe, nuclear power stations are being rapidly constructed. In the 1981–5 period construction work on seven stations, three of which were already in operation, was under way: Chornobyl, Zaporizhia, Khmelnytskyi, Odessa, Crimean, Rivne, and southern Ukraine.

In 1983 Ukraine's output of iron ore exceeded the combined output of the United States and Canada. The metal content of Ukraine's ore is higher than that of ores from other parts of the USSR, but because of lack of proper equipment the ore is not always enriched. Obsolescent equipment is a problem that plagues the Ukrainian iron and steel industry. In recent years serious attempts have been made to modernize technology and to improve the quality of metals. To increase the output of coke, lack of which restricts the growth of the iron and steel industry, much attention is given to the substitution of low-grade for high-grade coal in its production.

Ukraine is rich in minerals: more than 7,000 deposits have been discovered and 4,000 of these have been explored. Mining is a mixed blessing, however. Of the 1.5 billion cu m of rock extracted annually, 70 percent is dumped. This is extremely harmful to the environment. Strip mining and building-materials quarrying are also contributing to environmental problems.

Ukraine's chemical industry expanded in the 1950s, and its share in the country's total industrial output has grown steadily. It is more successful in meeting agriculture's demand for fertilizers than industry's demand for synthetic materials. The petrochemical industry is relatively new to Ukraine. Automobile tires and various consumer goods began to be manufactured only 30 years ago.

TABLE 1
Ukraine's output of important heavy-industry products (percent of USSR output in parentheses)

Product group	1940	1960	1970	1980	1983
Electric power (billions of kWh)	12.4 (25.3)	53.9 (18.5)	137.6 (18.6)	236.0 (18.2)	242.9 (17.2)
Coal (millions of tonnes)	83.8 (49.6)	172.1 (42.7)	207.1 (41.2)	197.1 (34.0)	–
Rolled steel (millions of tonnes)	6.5 (49.6)	18.0 (35.3)	32.7 (35.4)	36.0 (30.4)	37.6 (30.8)
Iron ore (million of tonnes)	20.2 (67.6)	59.1 (55.8)	111.2 (56.4)	125.5 (51.3)	124.0 (50.6)
Mineral fertilizers (at 100% nutrients, millions of tonnes)	0.2 (30.0)	0.8 (25.4)	2.5 (19.1)	4.1 (16.5)	5.0 (16.8)
Chemical fibers (thousands of tonnes)	1.6 (14.5)	14.2 (6.7)	65.3 (14.7)	161.2 (15.2)	181.7 (15.9)
Metal-cutting machine tools (thousands of units)	11.7 (20.0)	20.5 (13.1)	29.6 (14.7)	32.9 (15.2)	30.2 (15.9)
Tractors (thousands of units)	10.4 (32.9)	88.0 (36.8)	147.5 (32.1)	135.6 (24.4)	134.7 (23.9)
Excavators (units)	17 (0)	3,053 (24.6)	7,741 (25.0)	9,874 (23.6)	9,435 (22.5)
Diesel locomotives (units)	1 (20.0)	1,142 (87.6)	1,390 (93.6)	1,311 (95.1)	1,306 (95.0)
Freight cars (thousands of units)	10.3 (33.3)	17.6 (48.4)	29.6 (50.8)	31.6 (50.2)	30.6 (52.4)
Paper (thousands of tonnes)	27.9 (3.3)	134.3 (5.8)	187.4 (4.5)	209.0 (4.0)	274.2 (4.8)
Cement (millions of tonnes)	1.2 (20.7)	8.1 (17.8)	17.3 (18.1)	–	–

Ukraine's machine-building and metalworking industries are among the most advanced industries in the USSR. There is virtually no branch of these industries in Ukraine that is not well developed. Their share in Ukraine's industrial output doubled between 1965 and 1985. By 1990 they will account for almost one-third of the total output. These industries are modernizing their technology.

TABLE 2
Share (in percent) of branches of heavy industry in Ukraine's industrial output (at 1982 prices)

Branch	1965	1975	1983
Electric power	3.3	3.4	3.2
Fuel	11.4	7.7	6.1
Chemical and petrochemical	3.6	5.4	6.2
Machine building and metalworking	14.5	21.2	27.4
Lumber and paper	3.1	2.7	2.7
Building materials	4.5	4.4	3.7
Total heavy industry	40.4	44.8	49.3

The growth of the lumber and paper industries in Ukraine is limited by the forest resources, which are located primarily in the Carpathian region. While lumber output declined during 1965–85, the paper industry, which imported raw materials from other Union republics, almost doubled its output.

The importance of the building-materials industry is evident from the fact that its low output has become a serious constraint on the rate of investment in Ukraine. Among its most important products are cement, precast reinforced-concrete structures, and wall materials.

According to the Twelfth Five-Year Plan (1986–90), Ukraine's total industrial output as well as its heavy-industry output is to increase by 18–21 percent. This increase entails an average annual growth rate of 3.6 percent, which is below the projected rate (4.1 percent) for the USSR as a whole. The emphasis is on electric power, iron and manganese ores, chemicals, and machines. In the machine-building and metalworking sector, higher-than-average growth rates are projected for the instruments, machine-tool, and chemical-machinery industries. Among specific products, programmed machine tools, robots, automatic machines, and computers are given the highest priority. The technological modernization of the iron and steel industry and coal mining is viewed as the key to the smooth development of Ukraine's entire heavy industry. (See also *International economic relations.)

BIBLIOGRAPHY

Koropeckyj, I. (ed). *The Ukraine within the USSR: An Economic Balance Sheet* (New York 1977)
Emel'ianov, A. (ed). *Promyshlennost' v usloviiakh razvitogo sotsializma (na primere Ukrainskoi SSR)* (Kiev 1981)

F. Kushnirsky

Heavy-machine-building industry. See Machine building.

Hebrew sources for the history of the Ukrainian language. From the time of Kievan Rus', such sources are scarce. A letter of recommendation from the Jewish community of Kiev in the first half of the 10th century contains the first-ever record of the name of the city of Kiev; the so-called Schechter text (10th century) contains references to several ethnic names in Ukraine. There are a few records from the time of the mass settlement of Jews in Ukraine, beginning in the 14th century. The number of records increased substantially in the 16th and 17th centuries. They consist mostly of rabbinical responsa (by J. Hoeschel ben Joseph, A. Rapoport, J. Sirkes, and others), but also of several Hebrew chronicles, including N. Hanover's chronicle (1653; English trans 1950) of the Cossack-Polish War. These texts contain mentions of some Ukrainian place-names. Their linguistic value is diminished by the failure of the Hebrew alphabet to render vowels.

Hegelianism. The philosophy of G. Hegel (1770–1831) was the culmination of German idealism, which at the beginning of the 19th century had a dominant influence on philosophical thought in the Russian Empire, including Ukraine. This influence can be attributed partly to the government's effort to insulate Russia from French revolutionary ideas and to encourage intellectual contacts with Germany, and partly to the strength of Eastern Christian mysticism in Russia, which in the 17th and 18th centuries readily absorbed elements of German mysticism. The mystical interpretation of reality as a dynamic, spiritual whole determined by an internal dialectic prepared the ground for German idealism. The popularity of Romanticist literature in the second quarter of the 19th century made the reading public receptive to certain ideas espoused by German idealists.

In Ukraine, as in other parts of the Russian Empire, Hegel attracted attention first among university students, then among the reading public, and finally among university faculty. In 1833 a student circle devoted to the study of German idealism, particularly Hegel, arose at Kharkiv University. Among its members were I. Sreznevsky and A. Metlynsky. In the 1840s, when a brother of N. *Stankevich (one of the first Hegel enthusiasts in Russia) studied in Kharkiv, a student circle devoted to German idealism was active there. In Kiev a student circle devoted to Hegel formed around Professor M. Kostyr, but no information about it is available. A Hegelian circle, to which I. Lashniukov belonged, arose in the 1840s at Nizhen Lyceum. From student circles Hegelian ideas spread to literary magazines and salons.

I. Borisov, rector of the Kiev Theological Academy (1830–6), encouraged the study of German idealism at the school and was a specialist on the subject. S. *Hohotsky and O. *Novytsky, two graduates of the academy who later taught philosophy at Kiev University, were strongly influenced by Hegel's historical approach and dialectical method. In his *Obozrenie sistemy filosofii Gegelia* (A Survey of Hegel's System of Philosophy, 1860) and his monumental *Filosofskii leksikon* (Philosophical Lexicon, 4 vols, 1857–73), Hohotsky recognized Hegel's system as the culmination of philosophy, but rejected his concept of the absolute and his deduction of finite subjects. By removing God and finite spirits from the scope of the dialectic, Hohotsky attempted to reconcile Hegel with theism. Novytsky's major work, *Postepennoe razvitie drevnikh filosofskikh uchenii v sviazi s razvitiem iazycheskikh verovanii* (The Gradual Development of Ancient Philosophical Doctrines in Relation to the Development of Pagan Beliefs, 4 vols, 1860–2), was greatly influenced by Hegel. K. Nevolin, who in 1829 attended Hegel's lectures in Berlin, taught law at Kiev University (1834–43) and was one of the most successful propagators of Hegelian ideas in Ukraine. A number of other professors of Kiev University were influenced by Hegel to one degree or another: M. *Ivanyshev, a specialist in state law who had studied in Berlin and had known N. Stankevich; M. Piliankevych, assistant professor of law; V. Krasov, professor of literary theory (1837–9) and a friend of N. Stankevich; M. Kostyr, professor of literary history (1839–50, then at Kharkiv University 1850–3); O. *Fedotov-Chekhovsky, a historian of law; and P. Pavlov, professor of Russian history and the history of art (1847–59). Traces of Hegelianism can be detected in the outlook of the university's first rector, M. *Maksymovych, who was influenced mostly by Schelling, and in the writings of the historian M. Kostomarov.

At Kharkiv University the most influential teacher of Hegel's philosophy of history was M. Lunin, professor of universal history (1835–44). His student, A. Roslavsky-Petrovsky, a historian and statistician, dealt with philosophical problems of history in a Hegelian spirit (1837–72). A. Metlynsky, professor of Russian literature, was influenced deeply by Hegel, particularly on the question of national culture. Two other members of the Kharkiv faculty were influenced by Hegel: A. Walicki, professor of classical philology (1835–58), and A. Paliumbetsky, professor of law (1838–76).

In Odessa A. Bakunin, a Hegelian and the brother of M. Bakunin, taught jurisprudence at the Richelieu Lyceum (1844–6). O. *Mykhnevych, professor of philosophy at the lyceum, attempted to reconcile German idealism with theism and was influenced by Hegel's historicism. Hegel's ideas were mentioned often in the lectures of K. Zelenetsky, professor of literary history (1812–58) and a follower of Schelling. At Nizhen Lyceum I. Lashniukov, professor of Russian history (1853–68), was familiar with Hegel's ideas and referred to them in his lectures, and M. *Tulov, professor of literature who had studied with O. Novytsky, was interested in Hegel.

In Austrian-ruled Galicia some acquaintance with Hegel was evident in Y. Chachkovsky's work *Versuch der Vereinigung der Wissenschaften* (pt 1, 1863), in which he proposed an original system of categories. K. Hankevych, a philologist, referred to Hegel in his attempt to define the character of Slavic philosophy.

In the 20th century the Ukrainian émigré scholar D. *Chyzhevsky explored Hegel's influence in such works as *Hegel bei den Slaven* (1934) and *Gegel' v Rossii* (Hegel in Russia, 1939). In the Ukrainian SSR P. Demchuk and V. Yurynets have studied Hegel from a Marxist viewpoint. V. Shynkaruk has made an important contribution to Hegelian studies: *Logika, dialektika i teoriia poznaniia Gegelia* (Hegel's Logic, Dialectics, and Theory of Knowledge, 1964).

Although it was quite extensive, Hegel's influence in Ukraine was not very deep. While many specific ideas were borrowed from him, no original contributions to his system were made and no new system was inspired by him.

BIBLIOGRAPHY

Chyzhevs'kyi, D. *Narysy z istoriï filosofiï na Ukraïni* (Prague 1931)

Jakowenko, B. *Hegelianismus in Russland* (Prague 1934)

D. Chyzhevsky

Hegumen (*ihumen*). Title of the superior of a small monastery in the Eastern church (the superior of a large monastery is called an *archimandrite). In the Russian Empire after the secularization of monastic properties in 1764, a hegumen was the superior of a monastery relegated to the so-called third class; first- and second-class monasteries were headed by archimandrites. The superior of a convent is called an *ihumenia*. In the Greek Catholic church the superior of all the monasteries in a given province is called a *protoihumen*. In Ukraine hegumens were influential during the Princely and Cossack eras, especially in the fields of literature and education. They participated in sobors, in the election of bishops, and occasionally in Cossack councils.

Heimanovych, Oleksander [Hejmanovyč], b 4 August 1882 in Kharkiv, d 18 April 1958 in Kharkiv. Neurologist. A graduate of Moscow University (1909), he organized a neurological center in Kharkiv during the First World War and in 1920–1 reorganized it into the Ukrainian Neurological Institute. He served as the first director of the institute and then as director of its neurological clinic and neurological laboratory (1937–53). In 1932 Heimanovych was elected vice-president of the

Ukrainian Psychoneurological Academy. Heimanovych wrote over 300 works on neuropathology, neurosurgery, infectious diseases and traumatic injuries of the central nervous system, and swelling of the brain.

Maksym Hekhter

Ivan Hel

Hekhter, Maksym [Hexter], b 1885 in the Kiev region, d 25 December 1947 in Prague. Publicist and political activist of Jewish descent. Hekhter was a member of the Revolutionary Ukrainian party and the Bund. In 1905 he was arrested for propagating Ukrainian autonomy among workers and briefly imprisoned. He worked for the journals *Rada, Literaturno-naukovyi vistnyk, Ekonomist* (1904–14), *Dilo,* and others, contributing mostly articles on socioeconomic subjects. The UNR Directory appointed him a member of its diplomatic mission to the United States in 1919, but he was unable to take up his position. In the interwar period he settled in Prague. He wrote prolifically on cultural and political life in Ukraine for the Western press, particularly for such journals as *Prager Presse* (1921–38) and *Slavische Rundschau* (1929–39).

Hel, Ivan [Hel'], b 18 July 1937 in Klitsko, Horodok county, Galicia. Political dissident. Hel was expelled from secondary school in 1952 for refusing to join the Komsomol. In 1954 he graduated from a trade school in Sambir and went to work in Lviv. In 1965 he was arrested for distributing Ukrainian samvydav. He received a sentence of three years in a labor camp, which he served in Mordovia. During this time he wrote a number of protests to Soviet officials. Released in 1968, Hel worked as a metalworker and teacher until his dismissal because of political activism. He was rearrested in 1972 and sentenced to 10 years in labor camps and 5 years in exile. He was released in 1987 and returned to Lviv.

Helias, Yaroslav [Heljas, Jaroslav], b 21 November 1916 in Terpylivka, Zbarazh county, Galicia. Stage actor and director. He made his stage debut in 1935 in the touring Tobilevych Ukrainian People's Theater in Galicia. He has worked at the Ukrainian drama theaters of Lviv (1939–49, 1958–61), Kharkiv (1949–57), Odessa (1961–3), and Ternopil (1963–74). In 1974 he was appointed chief stage director at the Transcarpathian Ukrainian Music and Drama Theater in Uzhhorod. He has directed plays by I. Franko, O. Dovzhenko, J. Słowacki, S. Petöfi, L. Zabashta, K. Čapek, and others. Some of his best roles have been Zadorozhny in I. Franko's *Ukradene shchastia* (Stolen Happiness) in 1940, Don Juan in Lesia Ukrainka's *Kaminnyi hospodar* (The Stone Host) in 1942, Hamlet in W. Shakespeare's play (1943 and 1957), Vorkaliuk in Ya. Halan's *Liubov na svitanku* (Love at Dawn) in 1952, Chatsky in A. Griboedov's *Woe from Wit* in 1948, and Vadym in O. Levada's *Faust i smert'* (Faust and Death) in 1961.

Yaroslav Helias

Hellenisms. Words and expressions borrowed from the Greek (Gk). Their number in proto-Slavic was very limited: *komora* (Gk *kamára,* 'vault'), *korabel'* (Gk *karábion,* 'ship'), and possibly *banja* (Gk *bálaneion,* 'bathhouse') and *terem* (Gk *téremnon,* 'house,' 'dwelling'). With the Christianization of Rus' many Hellenisms entered into the Old Ukrainian language, primarily via Bulgarian. Certain ones were used only in the bookish language; others, however, also became part of the vernacular. Most Hellenisms of this period were religious and ecclesiastical terms: eg, *apostol* (Gk *apóstolos,* 'apostle'), *jevanhelije* (Gk *euaggélion,* 'Gospel'), *ieretyk* (Gk *airetikós,* 'heretic'), *idol* (Gk *eídōlon,* 'idol'), *panaxyda* (Gk *pannukhída,* 'requiem'), and *janhol* (Gk *ággelos,* 'angel'); first names: eg, Vasyl' (Gk Basileios) and Sofija (Gk Sophia); and scientific terms: eg, *apostrof* (Gk *apostrophē,* 'apostrophe'), *aromat* (Gk *árōma,* 'aroma'), *astronomija* (Gk *astronomía,* 'astronomy'), *dijalekt* (Gk *diálektos,* 'dialect'), *hramatyka* (Gk *grammatikē,* 'grammar'), *dijafrahma* (Gk *diáphragma,* 'diaphragm'), *piramida* (Gk *pūramíd,* 'pyramid'), and *planeta* (Gk *plánētes,* 'planet'). Such Hellenisms as *kyparys* (Gk *kupárissos,* 'cypress'), *kyt* (Gk *kētos,* 'sea monster,' 'whale'), *okean* (Gk *Ōkeanós,* 'ocean'), *kutja* (Gk *koukkía,* 'beans,' 'seed,' a festive dish made of wheat kernels, poppy seed, and honey), *voxra* (Gk *ōkhra,* 'ochre'), possibly *ohirok* (Gk *ágouros,* 'cucumber') and *subota* (Gk *Sámbaton,* 'Saturday') were widespread. Gk calques were also widely used, eg, *vselennaia* (Gk *oikouménē,* 'universe'), *Bohorodycja* (Gk *Theotókos,* 'Mother of God'), and *blahoslovennja* (Gk *eulogía,* 'benediction'). A number of Ukrainian phrases and proverbs are of Gk origin; eg, *klyn klynom vybyvajut* ('a wedge is knocked out with a wedge') and *vyjty sukhym z vody* ('to emerge dry from the water').

A second, smaller influx of Hellenisms occurred in the 15th and 16th centuries. They were introduced through literature by Balkan refugees fleeing Turkish rule and partly by Rumanian and Bulgarian settlers and herders moving in the Carpathian region. The latter brought such words as *kolyba* (Gk *kalúbē,* 'cottage,' 'hut') and *trojanda* (Gk *triantáphullon,* 'rose'). Later (18th and 19th century) Hellenisms were part of the argot into which they penetrated from Greek merchants and settlers on the Black Sea littoral – eg, *joryj* (Gk *geraiós*, 'old') and *kimaty* (Gk *koimōmai*, 'to sleep') – and did not enter standard Ukrainian. However, many words formed from Gk elements in Western Europe have been widely used as scientific terms in Ukrainian; eg, *daktyloskopiia* (dactyloscopy) and *telefon* (telephone).

G.Y. Shevelov

Helman, Maks [Hel'man], b 10 December 1892 in Odessa. Sculptor and pedagogue. He studied in art schools in Petrograd (1916–17), Moscow (1921–2), and Leningrad, where he was a student of A. Matveev. From 1926 he was a lecturer and then a professor (1939–69) at the Kiev State Art Institute. His works on revolutionary themes include the bas-reliefs *The Barricades* and *Zymovy's Assault* (1927), the sculptures *Our Change* and *The Guardian in the Air* (1929), and the frieze on the building of the Council of People's Commissars in Kiev (1933). He is also known for his sculpted portraits of writers such as G. Shkurupii and V. Pidmohylny, and the artists V. Kasiian and M. Zankovetska.

Helsinki Accords. See Ukrainian Helsinki Group.

Hemp (*Cannabis sativa*; Ukrainian: *konoplia* or the plural *konopli*). A plant of the Cannabaceae family, or its fiber; one of the group of plants from which bast fibers are obtained. The best soils for hemp are chernozems and drained peat bogs. In Ukraine the most common sorts of hemp are Dnipropetrovske hybrids 1 and 4; the Southern maturing monoecious 1, 4, and 9; the Poltava monoecious 3; and the Southern Cherkasy. Hemp is grown primarily in Chernihiv, Cherkasy, Poltava, Sumy, Mykolaiv, Dnipropetrovske, and Odessa oblasts.

Hemp has been used in Ukraine for a very long time. Archeological evidence confirms Heredotus's observation that the Scythians used hemp as a narcotic, and it is possible that they introduced the plant into Europe. Under the Russian Empire, hemp became a very important export crop. Local processing, however, was not encouraged (see *Jute-hemp industry). The amount of land in Ukraine seeded with hemp has decreased greatly over the years, from 161,300 ha in 1901–5 to 183,000 ha in 1950, 80,000 ha in 1965, and 30,000 ha in 1982. The total yield of hemp fiber in 1982 was 43,000 t.

Hemp fiber was used by Ukrainian peasants for many purposes, but mainly for clothing. Hemp has also been used in folk medicine. The juice, flowers, and seeds were taken internally for their diuretic, pain-relieving, and sleep-inducing effects. Other uses of the plant included poultices and sutures in operations. Today hemp is used by the textile industry, for cordage (rope, twine, etc), fishnets, canvas, and upholstery and drapery materials. Its seeds contain 30–35 percent fatty oil, which is used in foods, paints, varnishes, soaps, and animal fodder. The garden variety of hemp is grown as an ornamental.

V. Kubijovyč, R. Yanchinski

Heneralna starshyna. See General Officer Staff.

Henicheske [Heničes'ke]. VII-15. City (1966 pop 18,600) and raion center in Kherson oblast, situated on the northwest coast of the Sea of Azov at the entrance to Syvash Lake. It was founded as a fort in 1784 and from 1812 was also known as Ust-Ozivske. It was a port and a trade center on the salt route that went from the Crimea north to Ukraine and Russia; at the turn of the 20th century it had one of the largest flour mills in southern Ukraine. The administration of the *Azov-Syvash Game Preserve is located there.

Henicheske salt lakes. A group of over 40 shallow saltwater lakes on Arabat Spit in the Crimea. The largest of these, Henicheske Lake (4.9 km long, up to 2.9 km wide, and up to 0.6 m deep), is exploited as a salt pan.

Henicheske Strait. A narrow, shallow strait joining Syvash Lake with the Sea of Azov off the northern tip of Arabat Spit. It is up to 150 m wide, 4 km long, and 4.6 m deep.

Henry I, b ca 1008, d 4 August 1060 at Vitry-aux-Loges, near Orléans. The king of France from 1031. In 1051 he married *Anna Yaroslavna of Kiev, the daughter of Grand Prince Yaroslav the Wise. Henry's and Anna's older son, Philip I, was the successor to Henry; their younger son, Hugh, became the count of Vermandois.

Heolohichnyi zhurnal. See *Geologicheskii zhurnal.*

Heorhii [Heorhij], ?–1079. Kievan metropolitan. Of Greek origin, Heorhii arrived in Ukraine around 1062 and became, subsequently, the seventh metropolitan of Kiev. He was the author of a polemical work, *Stiazanie s latinoiu* (Struggle against the Roman Church).

Heorhii of Zarub [Heorhij Zarubs'kyj]. A monk at the Zarub monastery, which was located near present-day Zarubyntsi, Kaniv raion, Cherkasy oblast. He is the author of an 'Instruction for Spiritual Offspring,' written probably in the late 12th or early 13th century, in which he rejects worldly pleasures, particularly entertainment by **skomorokhy* and musicians.

Heorhiivka [Heorhijivka]. V-20. Town smt (1977 pop 8,100) in Lutuhyne raion, Voroshylovhrad oblast. From the mid-18th century until 1917 it was called Konoplianivka. It has a building-materials plant and a fish-packing plant.

Heraldry. The science and art dealing with hereditary insignia distinguishing individuals, institutions, and corporations, specifically with their origin and evolution and the rules governing their forms and use. As an ancillary historical discipline, heraldry is closely related to archeology, *genealogy, paleography, numismatics, and sphragistics. (See also *Coat of arms.)

Symbolic emblems were commonly used in patriarchal societies to designate the possessions of the clan. With the rise of feudalism and the emergence of private property, emblems were used to represent individual families or houses. The oldest signs were elementary symbols such as the cross (more than 200 forms are known in heraldry), the swastika, the square, the lozenge, the circle, and other simple signs mostly symbolizing the sun. In Ukraine, letter-like signs are also known. They were probably of Gothic origin, although some may possibly be relics of ancient Slavic writing. The oldest Ukrainian emblems have been found on pottery from the 8th century, while crests and emblems of some princely and boyar families date back to the 10th century. Family emblems are mentioned frequently in *Ruskaia Pravda* (11th century), where they are called *rizy*, *mity*, and *p'iatna*. Many of these were based on a monogram of the family name. Crests of noble families were already widespread in the Galician-Volhynian Principality.

In the 15th and 16th centuries Western European heraldry – particularly in the form that it developed in Poland – began to strongly influence Ukrainian heraldry. Typical symbols such as the star, crescent, flowers, and weapons, as well as heraldic beasts and birds (eg, the lion, unicorn, horse, deer, griffin, eagle, stork, and raven), appeared in Ukrainian crests, often alongside older symbols. Most Ukrainian nobles in the Polish-Lithuanian Commonwealth (the Ostrozkys, Zaslavskys, Zbarazhskys, etc) had family crests, many of which can be found in the earliest published collections (eg, B. Paprocki's *Panosza* [1575] and *Herby rycerstwa polskiego* [1584] and J. Sibmacher's *Allgemeines grosses und vollständiges Wappenbuch* ... [1637]). In the 17th and 18th centuries many Cossack *starshyna* also adopted crests. These often stressed military motifs, and under the influence of the baroque became very elaborate. As some of these families and individuals rose to prominence in the Russian Empire, popular symbols from Russian heraldry were incorporated (eg, the crest of the Rozumovsky family includes two humble Cossacks as well as the two-headed eagle symbolizing the Russian throne). In the late 18th century many of the *starshyna* and older noble families sought to have their crests recognized by the imperial authorities.

The study of heraldry contributes to the understanding of family and national traditions and relations. Yu. Narbut illustrated several collections of Ukrainian and Russian crests, as well as the journal *Gerboved*, published in St Petersburg (1913–14). V. Lukomsky, V. Modzalevsky, and H. Mylorodovych made many contributions to heraldry in Ukraine in the early 20th century, as have the émigrés M. Bytynsky, V. Seniutovych-Berezhny, V. Shcherbakivsky, V. Sichynsky, and M. Miller. In the Ukrainian SSR in recent years heraldry has gained considerable popularity as an ancillary historical discipline.

BIBLIOGRAPHY

[Darowski-Weryha, A.] *Znaki pieczętne Rusi* (Paris 1862)
Myloradovich, G. *Gerby malorossiiskikh dvorianskikh familii* (Chernihiv 1892)
Lukomskii, V.; Modzalevskii, V. *Malorossiiskii gerbovnik* (St Petersburg 1914)
Narbut, G. *Gerby getmanov Malorossii* (Petrograd 1915)
Vvedens'kyi, A.; Diadychenko, V.; Strel's'kyi, V. *Dopomizhni istorychni dystsypliny* (Kiev 1963)
Drachuk, V. *Rasskazyvaet geral'dika* (Moscow 1977)
Rumiantseva, V. *Emblemy zemel' i gerby gorodov Levoberezhnoi Ukrainy perioda feodalizma* (Kiev 1986)

M. Miller

Herashchenko, Oleh [Heraščenko], b 12 August 1925 in Chuvalachi, Uzbek SSR. Specialist in thermodynamics; since 1976 a corresponding member of the AN URSR. A graduate of the Kiev Polytechnical Institute, in 1951 he became a research associate of the AN URSR Institute of Technical Thermophysics, and in 1974 he was appointed its director.

Herasiuta, Mykola [Herasjuta], b 18 December 1919 in Oleksandriia, Kherson gubernia. Specialist in mechanics and machine building; corresponding member of the AN URSR since 1967. Since 1952 he has taught at Dnipropetrovske University. His work is devoted to the dynamics of complex mechanical systems.

Lidiia Herasymchuk

Herasymchuk, Lidiia [Herasymčuk, Lidija], b 5 April 1922 in Kiev, d 5 December 1958 in Kiev. Ballerina. A graduate of the Kiev School of Choreography (1937), she worked as a soloist with the Kiev Opera and Ballet Theater (1935–41, 1944–58) and the Kirov Opera and Ballet Theater in Leningrad (1941–4). She appeared in numerous roles, including Marusia in A. Svechnikov's *Marusia Bohuslavka*, Venus and Mariula in K. Dankevych's *Lileia* (The Lily), and the Water Nymph in M. Skorulsky's *Lisova pisnia* (The Forest Song).

Herasymchuk, Vasyl [Herasymčuk, Vasyl'], 1880–1944. Galician historian and student of M. Hrushevsky; full member of the Shevchenko Scientific Society. He wrote primarily about Cossack history of the latter half of the 17th century. He compiled materials on the history of the Khmelnytsky period from Polish sources for the Archeographic Commission of the VUAN, but they were never published. He is the author of *Chudnivs'ka kampaniia 1660 r.* (Chudniv Campaign of 1660, 1913) and many articles in *Zapysky Naukovoho tovarystva im Shevchenka*.

Herasymenko, Kost, b 11 May 1907 in Prykhidky, Pyriatyn county, Poltava gubernia, d 27 September 1942. Poet and playwright. His first poems were published in 1925. He is the author of the poetry collections *Zrist* (Growth, 1933), *Veresen'* (September, 1935), *Pam'iat'* (Memory, 1938), *Doroha* (The Road, 1939), and *Portret* (Portrait, 1941); of the plays *Pry bytii dorozi* (By the Well-Travelled Road, 1939) and *Lehenda* (The Legend, 1941); and of the libretto to M. Verykivsky's opera *Naimychka* (The Servant Girl). A war correspondent, he was killed on the Caucasian front.

Herasymovych, Ivan [Herasymovyč], b 27 November 1876 in Halych, Galicia, d 11 May 1942 in Berlin. Educator and community leader. From 1898 Herasymovych taught in various schools in Halych county. Fired from his position by the Polish authorities for nationalist activities, he resumed teaching in Bukovyna. In Chernivtsi he founded and published the semimonthly *Promin'* (1904–7), the first Ukrainian-language teachers' journal in the Austrian Empire. In 1918–19 he was the head of the press bureau of the Supreme Command of the Ukrainian Galician Army. With the Bolshevik takeover of Ukraine he fled to Berlin, where he edited the weekly *Ukraïns'ke slovo* and wrote *Holod na Ukraïni* (Famine in Ukraine, 1922). From 1922 he lived in Lviv, where he worked in the central administration of the Ridna Shkola educational society and edited (1932–9) its journal by the same name. During the German occupation of Western Ukraine he worked in the schools department of the Ukrainian Central Committee in Cracow. He wrote textbooks and articles on educational matters.

Herasymovych, Sylvestr [Herasymovyč, Syl'vestr], b 1881, d June 1943. Co-operative organizer, Galician political leader. At the beginning of the 1920s he served as director of the Provincial Union of Farming and Trading Associations and as the Union's representative on the executive of the Provincial Audit Union. He was a founding member of the Provincial Committee for Organizing Co-operatives (est in Lviv in 1921). When the Provincial Union of Farming and Trading Associations was reorganized into *Tsentrosoiuz in 1924, Herasymovych continued as director until 1929. At the same time he sat on the executive board of *Silskyi Hospodar. In the 1930s he helped found the *Front of National Unity and headed its political collegium. He also served as an editor in the Front's publishing house *Batkivshchyna. In 1940 he was arrested by Soviet authorities and exiled to Kazakhstan.

Herbert, Auberon, b 1922, d 21 July 1974 in Dulverton, England. English journalist, defender of Soviet-occupied East-European nations. He graduated from Balliol College in Oxford. During the Second World War Herbert served as a volunteer in the Polish Corps. He was a founder (1953) and vice-president of the Anglo-Ukrainian Society. Later he was active in the Mazeppa Society. He published articles about the captive nations under Russia, particularly in the weekly *The Tablet* and in *The Daily Telegraph.*

Herbest, Benedykt, b ca 1531 in Nove Misto near Dobromyl, Galicia, d 4 March 1598 in Jarosław, Galicia. Polish Jesuit theologian and scholar. A graduate of the Cracow Academy, he was the rector of schools in Lviv (1555–8), Cracow, and Poznań, and the Jesuit college in Jarosław. An advocate of the Counter-Reformation in Western Ukraine, he actively promoted the conversion of the Ukrainian Orthodox elite to Catholicism and initiated a written polemic with H. *Smotrytsky on this topic with his brochure *Wiary kościoła rzymskiego wywody y greckiego niewolstwa historya ... dla Rusi nawrócenia pisaney* (Elucidations of the Faith of the Roman Church and the History of Greek Enslavement ... Written for the Conversion of Rus', 1586).

Herbilsky, Hryhorii [Herbil's'kyj, Hryhorij], b 14 December 1904 in Katerynoslav (now Dnipropetrovske). Historian. From 1931 to 1946 he lectured in several institutions, including Saratov and Kiev universities. He worked at Lviv University from 1946 and specialized in Galician history. He has written over 50 works, including *Ukrainskie kozatskie polki i ukrainskoe opolchenie v Otechestvennoi voine 1812 g.* (Ukrainian Cossack Regiments and the Ukrainian Levy en Masse in the Patriotic War of 1812, 1943), *Peredova suspil'na dumka v Halychyni (30-i–seredyna 40-kh rokiv XIX stolittia)* (Leading Social Thought in Galicia [1830s–mid-1840s], 1959), and *Rozvytok prohresyvnykh idei v Halychyni v pershii polovyni XIX st. (do 1848 r.)* (The Development of Progressive Ideas in Galicia in the First Half of the 19th Century [to 1848], 1964).

Herbinius, Johannes (Kapusta, Jan), b ca 1627–33 in Byczyna (Pietschen), Silesia, d March 1679 in Grudziądz, Poland. Polish-German scholar. A Lutheran minister, theologian, and pedagogue, he lived in Sweden, Denmark, Poland, and Lithuania. In 1674 he obtained materials on the Kievan Cave Monastery from its archimandrite, I. *Gizel, and used them to write *Religiosae Kijovienses Cryptae, s. Kijovia subterranea* (1675).

Jan Herburt (portrait, 1570)

Herburt, Jan Szczęsny, b 1567 probably in Bonevychi, Dobromyl county, Galicia, d 31 December 1616 in Dobromyl, Galicia. Polish community leader, publisher, and writer of Ukrainian origin. In 1611 he established his own printing press in Dobromyl. In his *Zdanie o narodzie ruskim* (A Note about the Ruthenian People, 1611) he defended the right of Ukrainians to remain Orthodox and spoke out against the imposed Church Union of Berestia of 1596. He is the author of *Victoriae Kozakorum de tartaris Tauricianis in anno 1608 narratio*; he also wrote some poetry in Ukrainian, the most famous being *Hadka Hrytsia z Fortunoiu* (Hryts's Dialogue with Fortune).

Herder, Johann Gottfried von, b 25 August 1744 in Mohrungen, East Prussia, d 18 December 1803 in Weimar. German philosopher, theologian, and writer; a theorist of the *Sturm und Drang* literary movement and an important thinker in the philosophy of history and culture. He emphasized the role of folklore in the development of literature and compiled the first anthology of folk poetry from various nations – *Volkslieder* (1778–9). His work influenced M. Maksymovych and I. Metlynsky in Ukraine.

Herder German-Ukrainian Society (Deutsch-Ukrainische Herder-Gesellschaft). Society created in Munich in 1948 to promote contacts between Ukrainian and German scholars. Its presidents were K. Graebe, H. Koch,

E. Mittich, and I. Mirchuk. In 1960 the society merged with the *German-Ukrainian Society.

Hereta, Ihor, b 25 September 1938 in Skomorokhy, Ternopil county, Galicia. Archeologist and art scholar. A graduate of Chernivtsi University, in 1962 he became a research associate of the Ternopil Regional Museum. He helped found the Ternopil Art Gallery, of which he became director in 1978, the Krushelnytska Memorial Museum in Bila, and the Kurbas Memorial Museum in Staryi Skalat. In the course of his archeological digs in Western Ukraine, Hereta discovered over 50 monuments of various epochs and cultures, but mostly of the *Cherniakhiv culture. He has compiled guides to several memorial museums and published numerous scholarly articles.

Heritage Savings and Trust. A financial institution incorporated on 1 May 1967 in Edmonton, Alberta. It was formed with support from the local Ukrainian community and its directors included W. Sereda, P. Shewchuk, P. Savaryn, and Z. Matishak. Initial shareholder capital amounted to $1,233,236 with investments primarily in mortgage, bond, and stock portfolios. It grew rapidly during the 1970s; in 1981 its total assets amounted to $142,515,111.

Yosyf Hermaize

Metropolitan Maksym Hermaniuk

Hermaize, Yosyf [Hermajze, Josyf], b 1892 in Kiev, d? Historian and political figure of Karaite origin. He was a member of the Ukrainian Social Democratic Workers' party and sat on the All-Ukrainian Council of Military Deputies and the Little Rada of the Central Rada. A graduate of, and later professor at, Kiev University, he specialized in the sociopolitical history of Ukraine. A close associate of M. Hrushevsky, he was secretary of the Historical Section of the VUAN and director of its Archeographic Commission. Arrested in 1929 and accused of belonging to the *Union for the Liberation of Ukraine, he was sentenced to six years in labor camps, which he served in Yaroslavl and on the Solovets Islands. He then settled in Saratov, but was soon rearrested and sentenced to an additional 10 years. His subsequent fate is unknown. Hermaize wrote many works, a number of them pioneering studies. His *Narysy z istorii revoliutsiinoho rukhu na Ukraïni* (Essays on the History of the Revolutionary Movement in Ukraine, vol 1, 1926) has thus far been the only monograph on the *Revolutionary Ukrainian party. He is the author of articles and collections of documents on such topics as the Koliivshchyna rebellion, the Decembrist movement in Ukraine, M. Drahomanov and V. Antonovych and Ukrainian historiography, and Ukrainian relations with the Don region in the 17th century, which appeared in the serials of the VUAN and Kiev University. He also edited the published records of the Polish investigation and trial of Koliivshchyna rebels in Kodnia (*Ukraïns'kyi arkhiv*, vol 2, 1931) and wrote introductions to P. Kulish's *Chorna rada* (Black Council, 1925), V. Vynnychenko's selected works (1927), and M. Kostomarov's *Chernihivka* (Girl from Chernihiv, 1928).

Hermaniuk, Maksym [Hermanjuk], b 30 October 1911 in Nove Selo, Zhovkva county, Galicia. Archbishop and metropolitan of the Ukrainian Catholic church in Canada; full member of the Shevchenko Scientific Society. He joined the Redemptorist order in 1933 and was ordained in 1938. He studied at Louvain University (TH D 1943). In 1948 he came to Canada as supervisor of the Ukrainian Redemptorist Vice-Province of Canada and the United States and taught at the Ukrainian Redemptorist Seminary in Waterford, Ontario, where he founded and edited the theological journal *Lohos*. In 1951 he was appointed auxiliary bishop of Winnipeg and in 1956 archbishop and metropolitan of the Ukrainian Catholic church in Canada. He took part in the Second Vatican Council (1962–5) and is a member of the Presidium of the World Congress of Free Ukrainians, of the Secretariat for Promoting Christian Unity, and of the Joint Working Group of the World Council of Churches. His publications include *La Parabole évangélique* (Louvain, 1947), *Bibliini opysy svitu v svitli suchasnoï nauky* (The Biblical Descriptions of Our World in the Light of Contemporary Science, 1950), and *Nashi zavdannia* (Our Tasks, 1960).

Hermitage (Ukrainian: *skyt*). A number of cells inhabited by monks who lived in seclusion and practiced a more exacting regime than ordinary monks. Such habitations were located at some distance from the monasteries to which they were subordinate. Eventually the distinction in regime became blurred and hermitages became merely small monasteries attached to a larger one. In Ukraine a number of monasteries had hermitages, some of them more than one hermitage. The Pochaiv Monastery, for example, had the Kozachi Mohyly and Rudnia-Pochaivska *skyty*, and the St Michael's Golden-Domed Monastery had the Teofaniia *skyt*. A few hermitages, such as the *Maniava Hermitage, were entirely independent.

Hermonassa. An ancient Greek city located on the Taman Peninsula near the present-day site of Taman, a village in Krasnodar krai, founded in the 6th century BC by Ionians and probably by Aeolitians as well. After Phanagoria, it was the second most important economic center of the Asiatic side of the *Bosporan Kingdom. Hermonassa's economy was based on agriculture, fishing, and trade. The Huns destroyed the city in the 4th century AD and in the 10th century AD the ancient Rus' city of *Tmutorokan arose on the site. In the 12th century it was an Italian trading port, known as Tamatarxa, Matarxa, or Matriga. Significant archeological excavations conducted since the 1950s have uncovered a frieze from the temple of Aphrodite and, from the 4th century BC, a buried treasure of gold Bosporan coins and a necropolis containing a marble sarcophagus shaped in the form of a Greek temple.

Herodotus, b ca 485 BC in Halicarnassus, Asia Minor, d ca 425 BC in Athens or Thurii, southern Italy. Greek historian of the Greco-Persian wars, known as the father of history. He traveled widely throughout the Middle East, North Africa, and southern and eastern Europe, including the territories of present-day Ukraine. In the fourth volume of his *History* he describes the Dnieper River, judging it to be the most useful river in the world after the Nile, and the territory, customs, and life of the Cimmerians, Taurians, Scythians, and other peoples of the region. Archeological excavations have confirmed many of his observations.

Herring (*Clupea*; Ukrainian: *oseledets'*). Small (10–50 cm) silvery fish of the family Clupeidae, widely distributed in northern waters, including the Black Sea and the Sea of Azov. There are five species of herring in Ukraine: Kerch herring, Black Sea herring, Caspian shad, Black Sea sprat, and common sprat. Herring have a great economic importance. They are eaten fresh, salted, smoked, or tinned. In the USSR they are an important part of the diet, particularly for prisoners in transport.

Hershenzon, Serhii [Heršenzon, Serhij], b 11 February 1906 in Moscow. Geneticist, one of the founders of population genetics; since 1976 full member of the AN URSR. After graduating from Moscow University in 1927, he worked consecutively at the Institute of Experimental Biology, the Timiriazev Biological Institute, and the Institute of Genetics of the USSR Academy of Sciences. In 1937 he moved to Kiev to chair the department of genetics and Darwinism at Kiev University (1937–41, 1944–8) and a department of the Institute of Zoology of the AN URSR (1937–63). After serving as assistant director of the Institute of Microbiology and Virology, in 1968 he was appointed department chairman, and in 1973 acting director of the Institute of Molecular Biology and Genetics in Kiev. In 1924–6 Hershenzon participated in the first genetic studies of natural *Drosophila* populations. In the 1930s he studied the causes of mutation and the mutagenic effect of exogenic DNA. After 1953 he did pioneering work in molecular genetics: he demonstrated that information is transcribed inversely from RNA to DNA and studied the mutagenic role of viruses in the host cell. He is the author of *Osnovy sovremennoi genetiki* (The Foundations of Contemporary Genetics, 1979) and the editor of *Tsitologiia i genetika*.

M. Adams

Hershtansky, Demian [Herštans'kyj, Dem'jan], b 1 November 1865 in Tarazh, Kremianets county, Volhynia gubernia, d 1936 in Volodymyr-Volynskyi. Volhynian civic and church leader. He was an Orthodox priest with the rank of protopresbyter and a deputy to the Polish Senate (1922–8).

Hertsa [Herca]. V-7. Town (1966 pop 1,500) in Hlyboka raion, Chernivtsi oblast. First mentioned in 1408; before being annexed by Austria in 1774 it belonged to the Principality of Moldavia. In 1918 it was annexed by Rumania, and in 1940 by the Ukrainian SSR. Most of its inhabitants are Rumanian.

Demian Hershtansky

Hertsyk, Hryhorii [Hercyk, Hryhorij], b and d ? Acting colonel of Poltava regiment in 1705 and a supporter of Hetman I. *Mazepa. After the defeat at the Battle of Poltava in 1709, he accompanied Mazepa into exile in Bendery. Under Hetman P. Orlyk, he served as general osaul. In 1715 he went with Orlyk to Stockholm. He lived there until 1719, when he was sent by the hetman to Poland to enter into relations with the Zaporozhian Cossacks and the Crimean khan. In Warsaw he was seized by Russian agents and taken to St Petersburg where he was held in the SS Peter and Paul Fortress. In 1728 he was released and permitted to live in Moscow. Records of his interrogation in St Petersburg in 1721 were printed in *Kievskaia starina*, 1883, no. 3.

Herzen, Aleksandr, b 6 April 1812 in Moscow, d 21 January 1870 in Paris. Most prominent Russian publicist and political thinker of his generation. Having left Russia in 1847, he published *Poliarnaia zvezda* and *Kolokol* in London. As a proponent of a socialistically inclined populism, he supported Ukraine's right to independence, but his personal hope was for a pan-Slavic federation. He considered Ukrainian to be a separate Slavic language, then an unusual view among Russians, and admired the poetry of T. Shevchenko. Herzen, whose journal was widely disseminated in Ukraine, was respected by the leading Ukrainian activists of the time, including T. Shevchenko, M. Kostomarov (who in 1860 contributed an article to *Kolokol* on the Ukrainian question), M. Levchenko, and V. Antonovych.

Hetman, Mykhailo [Het'man, Myxajlo] (Hethman, Michael), b 14 September 1893 in Zalistsi Novi, Zboriv county, Galicia, d 2 February 1981 in Toronto. Community leader and journalist. In the First World War he served with the Ukrainian Sich Riflemen, and in the 1920s immigrated to Canada. Active in the Ukrainian monarchist movement, from 1927 he was on the supreme council of the *Canadian Sitch Organization and on the editorial board of *Kanadiis'ka Sich* (1928–30). During the 1930s he was head (*oboznyi*) of the *United Hetman Organization. From 1937 to 1949 he edited its weekly *Ukraïns'kyi robitnyk* in Toronto. Subsequently he edited *Nasha derzhava* (1952–5) and its successor *Bat'kivshchyna*, which he cofounded.

Hetman (from the German *Hauptmann* and the Polish *hetman*: 'leader'). In the Polish Kingdom in the 16th century, local military commanders and administrators were known as hetmans. The title was also used for the supreme military commander both in Poland and in the Grand Duchy of Lithuania (see *Grand hetman). At the end of the 16th century the commander of the *Cossacks, originally known as the elder (*starshyi*), also became known as the hetman. The first Cossack hetmans included K. Kosynky, S. Nalyvaiko, P. Sahaidachny, and T. Fedorovych.

From 1648 the hetman was the head of the Cossack state (see *Hetman state). In this capacity he had broad powers as the supreme commander of the Cossack army; the chief administrator and financial officer, presiding over the state's highest administrative body, the *General Officer Staff; the top legislator; and from the end of the 17th century, the supreme judge as well. The first hetman who was also head of the state was B. *Khmelnytsky. The hetman issued administrative decrees, called *Hetman manifestos, which were binding on the whole population. His powers extended to some degree even to church affairs: he confirmed the appointment of church hierarchs and endowed bishoprics, monasteries, and sometimes churches with lands. He also appointed many officials of the state and granted land for service. The hetman represented the state in its external relations, receiving and sending out envoys and concluding treaties. With the partition of Ukrainian territories between Poland and Muscovy in the 1660s there arose competing hetmans in Right- and Left-Bank Ukraine and a prolonged period of civil war began. Right-Bank hetmans soon lost their political power, becoming simply commanders of Cossack military formations under Polish or Ottoman control.

Hetmans were elected by the *General Military Council for an unspecified term: in principle for life, but in practice for 'as long as it pleases the host.' Since their authority was not constitutionally defined, it varied greatly and depended on the personalities of the individuals involved. In general, their authority overlapped or was limited by the powers of other state institutions, such as the General Military Council and the *Council of Officers, which included senior officers and colonels of the Cossack *regiments. From the end of the 17th century the tsar of Muscovy, through his representatives at the military councils, greatly influenced the election of hetmans. In the 18th century the hetman's powers were reduced and he became more dependent on the tsar. In particular, the tsarist government deprived hetmans of the right to conduct their own foreign relations and steadily increased its control over Ukraine's internal administration. In Left-Bank Ukraine each new hetman swore an oath of allegiance to the tsar and concluded a new agreement with the tsarist government outlining his rights and responsibilities (see *Hetman articles).

The more important hetmans of all Ukraine were B. Khmelnytsky (1648–57), I. Vyhovsky (1657–9), and Yu. Khmelnytsky (1659–63). Renowned Right-Bank hetmans included P. Teteria (1663–5), P. Doroshenko (1665–76), and Yu. Khmelnytsky (1667–81 and 1685), while Left-Bank hetmans included I. Briukhovetsky (1663–8), D. Mnohohrishny (1669–72), I. Samoilovych (1672–87), I. Mazepa (1687–1709), I. Skoropadsky (1709–22), P. Polubotok (acting hetman 1722–4), D. Apostol (1727–34), and K. Rozumovsky (1750–64). After several earlier attempts, the office of hetman was finally abolished by Catherine II in 1764, and its responsibilities were assumed by the *Little Russian Collegium. Hetman rule displayed both monarchic and republican tendencies, but the former were dominant, particularly under B. Kmelnytsky, who hoped to establish a hereditary hetmancy, I. Samoilovych, and I. Mazepa. The hetman's insignia included the **bulava*, standard, flag, and seal. An officer who carried out temporarily the duties of a hetman was known as the *acting hetman. Many hetmans gained renown as patrons of Ukrainian culture by establishing monasteries and schools.

P. *Skoropadsky, the head of the Ukrainian state from April to December 1918, revived the title of hetman. (See *Hetman government.)

BIBLIOGRAPHY

Diadychenko, V. *Narysy suspil'no-politychnoho ustroiu Livoberezhnoï Ukraïny kintsia XVII–pochatku XVIII st.* (Kiev 1959)
Okinshevych, L. *Ukrainian Society and Government, 1648–1781* (Munich 1978)

L. Okinshevych

Hetman articles (*Hetmanski statti*). Legal documents that defined the prerogatives of the Cossack Hetman state in the 17th and 18th centuries and its relations with Muscovy. The first such articles were compiled as a result of negotiations between Hetman B. Khmelnytsky's emissaries and representatives of the tsar in March 1654 in Moscow (see *Pereiaslav Treaty of 1654). New articles were drawn up with the election of each new hetman. Although they were based in principle on those agreed to by Khmelnytsky, there tended to be a further erosion of the rights of the Hetman state with each new agreement. In addition to the agreement of 1654, there were the *Pereiaslav Articles of 1659 and 1674, the *Hlukhiv Articles of D. Mnohohrishny in 1669, the *Konotip Articles of I. Samoilovych in 1672, and the *Kolomak Articles of I. Mazepa in 1687. The last articles were those of D. Apostol in 1728. Thereafter Ukraine's status was determined by unilateral acts on the part of the Russian government, which increasingly diminished Ukrainian autonomy.

Hetman government. The antisocialist Ukrainian government formed after the coup d'état of Gen P. *Skoropadsky in Kiev on 29 April 1918, during which the congress of the conservative *All-Ukrainian Union of Landowners proclaimed Skoropadsky hetman of Ukraine. This coup was backed by the generals of the German and Austrian armies that occupied Ukraine after the Peace Treaty of *Brest-Litovsk and by former tsarist officers.

On the day of the coup Skoropadsky issued two edicts – Manifesto to the Entire Ukrainian Nation and Laws Concerning the Provisional State System of Ukraine – that together constituted a provisional constitution for the new regime. The *Council of National Ministers and *Central Rada of the UNR and their laws and land reforms were abolished, and the right of private land ownership was reinstated. All legislative and executive powers were transferred to the hetman, who at the same time was proclaimed commander in chief of the military. The edicts created a Council of Ministers with executive and legislative functions, to be appointed by the hetman and to be responsible solely to him. Although decrees and orders of the hetman were to be countersigned by the prime minister or another appropriate minister, the hetman was to ratify all decisions of the council, thus reinforcing his dictatorial power. Civil rights were to be guaranteed 'within the limits of the law' (ie, newspapers were strictly censored or shut down, and most public gatherings and strikes were banned), and a supreme court was to be created, with the hetman retaining the

The Great Seal of the Hetman government

authority to commute sentences. The name of the Ukrainian National Republic was changed to the Ukrainian State.

Skoropadsky appointed M. Ustymovych and, after he failed, M. *Vasylenko to form a government from representatives of moderate Ukrainian parties, particularly the *Ukrainian Party of Socialists-Federalists (UPSF). Neither succeeded because of a boycott of the undemocratic regime by the major Ukrainian political parties, including the UPSF. Nonetheless, a Council of Ministers was formed on 10 May with the following ministers (many of them Russophile): premier and minister of internal affairs, F. *Lyzohub; external affairs, D. *Doroshenko; army, A. Rogoza; finance, A. Rzhepetsky; trade, S. Gutnik; land affairs, V. Kolokoltsov; food provisions, Yu. Sokolovsky; cults, V. Zenkovsky; national health, V. Liubynsky; education, M. Vasylenko; communication, B. Butenko; justice, M. Chubynsky; labor, Yu. Vagner; state controller, Yu. Afanasev; and state secretary, I. Kistiakovsky. During the summer some changes were made in the Council of Ministers. S. Gerbel became minister of food provisions; A. Romanov, minister of justice; I. Kistiakovsky, minister of internal affairs; and S. Zavadsky, state secretary. The ministries that existed during the UNR were reorganized; most deputy ministers were replaced, although the majority of officials from the previous government remained. Local administration was entrusted to gubernial and county starostas (see *Gubernial commissioners) appointed by the hetman.

Although its social and economic policies were a failure, the Hetman government did achieve certain successes in *diplomacy in establishing a *consular service and, particularly, in education and culture. It normalized diplomatic relations with the Central Powers and several neutral countries, strengthened relations with the *Kuban, the *Don region, and *Crimea, and was even formally recognized by Soviet Russia, with which it signed a preliminary peace treaty on 12 June 1918. The government established the Ukrainian state universities of *Kiev and *Kamianets-Podilskyi; chairs of Ukrainian philology and history at the other Ukrainian universities; the Ukrainian *Academy of Sciences, a national library (today the Central Scientific Library of the AN URSR), a state archive, the *State Drama Theater, a state museum, and a state music and drama institute in Kiev; it also opened or Ukrainianized over 150 gymnasiums and made the teaching of Ukrainian language, history, and geography compulsory in Russian schools. Despite German hindrances, it made strides in the organization of an effective military force (see *Army of the UNR); many of its senior officers were, however, pro-White Russians and hostile to the Ukrainian cause.

From the very beginning, the Hetman regime was opposed by most Ukrainian organizations (see, eg, the *All-Ukrainian Union of Zemstvos). Ukrainian nationalists criticized it for the following reasons: its pro-Russian orientation; its reliance on Russians, including individuals closely identified with the tsarist regime and members of the Constitutional Democratic and Octobrist parties, to staff important positions in the government and military; its indifference to Ukrainianization of the government and to Ukrainian autonomy; and its reliance on the German army (see *Germany), which oppressed the population and exploited Ukraine economically. Socialists, meanwhile, criticized its reactionary policies, particularly its repressiveness, condoning of the landlords' terrorization of the peasantry, and unwillingness to effect comprehensive land reforms, as well as its support by the Russian capitalist *Union of Industry, Trade, Finances, and Agriculture. The peasants reacted to the regime's excesses with numerous rebellions and guerrilla warfare (eg, that directed by N. *Makhno and H. *Tiutiunnyk), arson, and assassinations (eg, of H. *Eichhorn). Soon after the coup, representatives of various Ukrainian parties, unions, and civic-cultural associations formed the Ukrainian National-State Union, later renamed the *Ukrainian National Union (UNU), to co-ordinate opposition to the Hetman government and revive Ukrainian democracy and independence.

The imminent defeat of the Central Powers, the deteriorating domestic situation, and the Bolshevik consolidation of power in Russia led to a series of political crises in the fall of 1918. Six members of the cabinet, led by D. Doroshenko, increased their efforts to Ukrainianize the regime, which included terminating German overlordship and seeking international recognition of an independent Ukrainian state. This effort was opposed by the other 10 ministers, who published a memorandum advocating the federation of Ukraine with a non-Bolshevik Russia, and stating that Ukraine's most important role was as a base of operations against the Bolsheviks. The ministers also hoped that this policy would find favor among the *Entente Powers, which supported the re-establishment of a united Russia.

At this time Skoropadsky began serious negotiations with the expanded UNU to broaden his base of support. The UNU demanded eight ministerial portfolios, the convocation of a diet, political amnesty, and the end of censorship and restrictions on freedom of speech. Although a consensus was not reached, five UPSF members of the UNU agreed to participate in the Council of Ministers. In the manifesto of 22 October, the hetman proclaimed his support of the principle of an independent Ukrainian

Kaiser Wilhelm II and Hetman Pavlo Skoropadsky

state and promised to accelerate agrarian reforms and the convocation of a diet. On 24 October a new cabinet, representing a compromise between Ukrainian nationalist and pro-Russian forces, was formed: F. Lyzohub, premier; D. Doroshenko, external affairs; A. Rogoza, military affairs; V. Reinbot, internal affairs (acting); A. Rzhepetsky, finance; O. Lototsky (UNU), religious affairs; P. Stebnytsky (UNU), education; V. Leontovych (UNU), agriculture; S. Gerbel, food provisions; A. Viazlov (UNU), justice; M. Slavinsky (UNU), labor; S. Mering, trade and industry; B. Butenko, communications; V. Liubynsky, health; S. Petrov, state controller; and S. Zavadsky, state secretary.

The final capitulation of the Central Powers (11 November 1918) and the withdrawal of their armies, the mainstay of the hetman's authority, led to a dramatic change of policy. Hoping to please the victorious Entente nations, Skoropadsky proclaimed, in his manifesto of 14 November, his intention to federate with a non-Bolshevik Russian state. At the same time he formed a new cabinet, composed mostly of Russian monarchists: premier and minister of agriculture, S. Gerbel; external affairs, Yu. Afanasev; army, D. Shchutsky; navy, A. Pokrovsky; internal affairs, I. Kistiakovsky; education, V. Naumenko; religious affairs, M. Voronovich; finance, A. Rzhepetsky; communication, V. Liandeberg; trade, S. Mering; justice, V. Reinbot; health, V. Liubynsky; labor, V. Kosynsky; food provisions, G. Glinka; and state controller, S. Petrov.

These developments triggered the popular uprising co-ordinated by the UNU. It had been prepared long in advance with the support of the *Sich Riflemen, who had defeated the hetman's forces at *Motovylivka on 18 October and had begun advancing on Kiev. On 14 December 1918, after German troops abandoned Kiev, Skoropadsky abdicated and fled to Germany, and the Council of Ministers surrendered power to the *Directory of the UNR. Some of Skoropadsky's ministers were later arrested by the new republican government.

BIBLIOGRAPHY

Khrystiuk, P. *Zamitky i materiialy do istorii ukraïns'koï revoliutsiï 1917–1920 rr.*, 3 (Vienna 1921; New York 1969)

Doroshenko, D. *Istoriia Ukraïny 1917–1923 rr.*, 2: *Ukraïns'ka Het'mans'ka Derzhava 1918 roku* (Uzhhorod 1930; New York 1954)

Dolenga, S. *Skoropadshchyna* (Warsaw 1934)

Reshetar, J. *The Ukrainian Revolution, 1917–1920: A Study in Revolution* (Princeton 1952; New York 1972)

Shapoval, M. *Het'manshchyna i Dyrektoriia: Spohady* (New York 1958)

Skliarenko, Ye. *Borot'ba trudiashchykh Ukraïny proty nimets'ko-avstriis'kykh okupantiv i Het'manshchyna v 1918 rotsi* (Kiev 1960)

Fedyshyn, O. *Germany's Drive to the East and the Ukrainian Revolution, 1917–1918* (New Brunswick, NJ 1971)

Hunczak, T. (ed). *The Ukraine, 1917–1921: A Study in Revolution* (Cambridge, Mass 1977)

B. Balan, O. Shulhyn, A. Zhukovsky

Hetman manifestos (*universaly*). Official decrees issued by the government of the Hetman state in the 17th and 18th centuries. The practice was adopted from the Polish kings, who declared their will in circular letters addressed to their subjects (*universales letterae*). Manifestos were addressed in the hetman's name to the entire population and often contained important directives or ordinances. Special manifestos were directed at specific institutions, estates, military units, settlements, or groups. Some were called instructions, particularly those that dealt with the court system: for example, the manifestos of P. Polubotok (1722), D. Apostol (1730), and K. Rozumovsky (1761–3). At times hetmans issued manifestos granting lands and peasants to Cossack officers and church institutions or confirming land ownership, as well as manifestos granting special protection or exempting certain individuals from the authority of administrative and judicial bodies. Manifestos were always confirmed by the seal of the Zaporozhian Host.

Hetman state or **Hetmanate** (Hetmanshchyna). The name of the Ukrainian Cossack state, which existed from 1648 to 1782. It came into existence as a result of the *Cossack-Polish War and the alliance of the *registered Cossacks with the Cossacks of the *Zaporozhian Sich and other segments of the Ukrainian populace. The territory of the state at the time of its first *hetman, B. *Khmelnytsky (1648–57), consisted of most of central Ukraine, ie, the territory of the former voivodeships of Kiev, Bratslav, Chernihiv, and part of Volhynia voivodeship, as well as part of Belorussia (see *Belorussian

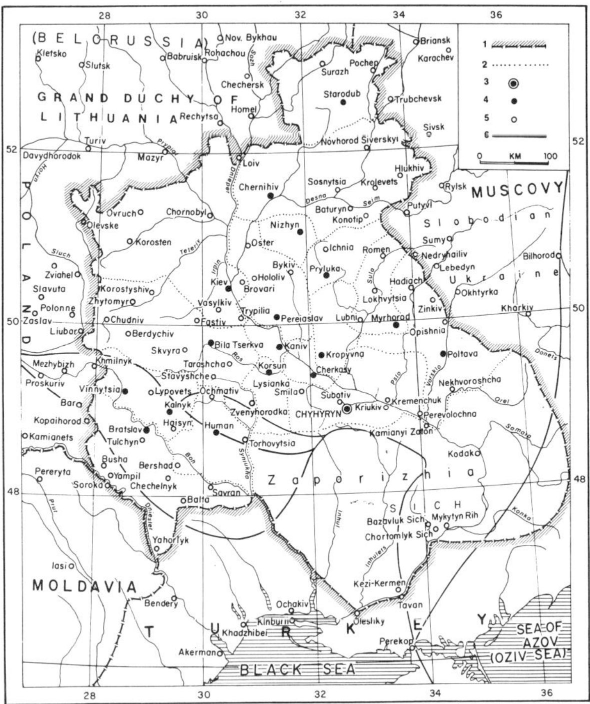

THE HETMAN STATE UNDER BOHDAN KHMELNYTSKY, CA 1650

1. State border
2. Regimental boundaries
3. Hetman's capital
4. Regimental centers
5. Other towns
6. Tatar routes

Regiment). In 1663 the Hetman state in Right-Bank Ukraine came under Polish domination, while the Left Bank came under Muscovite control. A period of civil war ensued as various Left- and Right-Bank hetmans (particularly P. *Doroshenko, Yu. *Khmelnytsky, and I. *Samoilovych), backed by their respective supporters, attempted to reestablish a unitary state. Despite these efforts, the partition of the hetmanate was confirmed by the Muscovite-Polish Treaty of *Andrusovo (1667) and the *Eternal Peace of 1686. When the Cossacks were abolished by Poland in 1700 on the Right Bank, the Hetmanate was left with only the lands of the Left Bank – Chernihiv voivodeship (together with the Starodub region) and the part of Kiev voivodship to the east of the Dnieper. The capitals of the Hetman state were Chyhyryn (1648–63), Hadiache (1663–8), Baturyn (1669–1708 and 1750–64), and Hlukhiv (1708–34). From 1654 the Hetman state was nominally a vassal of Muscovy (see Treaty of *Pereiaslav). The political relationship between the two countries was renegotiated with the election of each new hetman (see *Hetman articles), which led to the steady erosion of the Hetmanate's sovereignty.

The Hetman state exhibited elements of both republican and monarchic types of government. Because it did not have a constitution that defined the powers and prerogatives of its various institutions, these changed over time as a result of internal conflicts and the encroachments of the Russian government. The highest ruling organs were three bodies with somewhat overlapping functions: the *General Military Council, the hetman, and the *Council of Officers. The General Military Council was the institution of direct government in the 17th century and represented in theory the supreme will of the dominant group in society, the Cossacks. The hetman, meanwhile, was the head of state, commander in chief of the Cossack army, and head of the entire administrative, judicial, and military apparatus. Some hetmans recognized the ultimate authority of the military councils, while others, such as B. Khmelnytsky and particularly I. Samoilovych and I. *Mazepa, opposed it. During the reign of these hetmans, the state most resembled a monarchy with the election for life of the monarch-hetman. The Council of Officers was a semiformal advisory body that met twice a year; with time it acquired the characteristics of an estate parliament for the *Cossack *starshyna*. Other central institutions included the *General Military Chancellery, which executed the hetman's orders, and the *General Officer Staff, which functioned as the hetman's cabinet. At first this body was elected by the Council of Officers, but later it was appointed by the hetman himself, or, as the state lost its autonomy, by the Russian government. The *General Military Court, presided over by the hetman, was the supreme court of appeal.

At the local level the state was organized, on the basis of the Cossack military organization, into regiments (see *Regimental system) and companies (see *Company system). In B. Khmelnytsky's time, there were 10 Right-Bank and 7 Left-Bank regiments; later there were 10 regiments in total. The regimental and company administrations mirrored that of the central government: each regiment had a military council, colonel, and regimental council of officers, and each company a captain and council of officers. At first most officers at the local as well as central levels of administration and the judiciary were elected. Later, however, this practice declined and individuals were appointed by higher authorities or the Russian government.

The Hetmanate, particularly in the 18th century, had a social hierarchy, where an individual's political power, legal rights, and social status were determined by his membership in a particular social group or *estate. At the top of the pyramid were the senior Cossack officers (the Cossack *starshyna* and the *notable military fellows), followed by the *Cossacks, the *burghers and other town dwellers, and the *peasants. At first, after the Khmelnytsky uprising, the state was in principle composed of free citizens, although some of the peasantry (particularly the *church peasants) remained in a state of servitude. With time, however, as their obligations grew heavier, the rest of the peasantry and the rank-and-file Cossacks became impoverished, and the Hetman state became an increasingly regimented class society in which only the officer class had special privileges. Town dwellers also began to lose their political autonomy, although large cities and towns continued to be ruled under *Magdeburg law. At the same time class barriers were created: eg, it was forbidden for a peasant to become a Cossack. The legal system of the state was derived from a variety of sources, particularly the 1648 Polish edition of the Lithuanian Statute (see *Code of Laws of 1743).

In the 18th century, the increasing political control of the Hetman state by Russia precluded the independent evolution of its administrative, financial, and judicial institutions. During the reign of *Catherine II (1762–96)

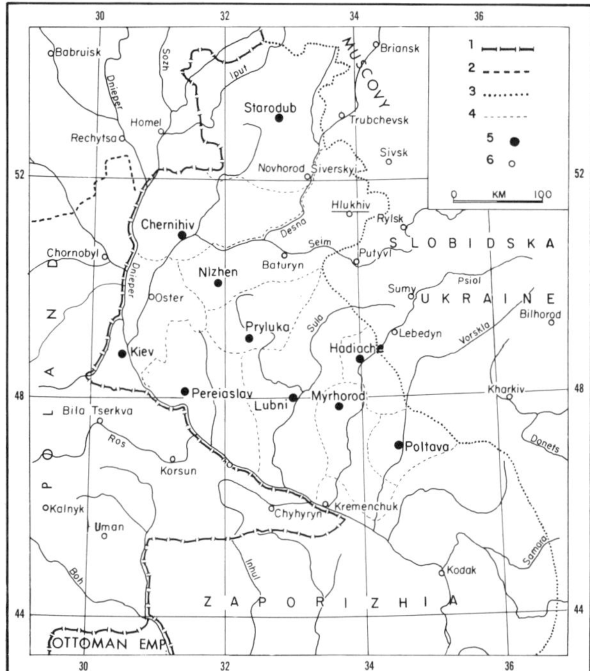

THE HETMAN STATE CA 1750

1. State boundaries (Polish, Russian, Ottoman)
2. Southern boundary of Lithuania within the Polish Commonwealth
3. Eastern limits of the Hetman state and of the lands of the Zaporozhian Cossacks
4. Territorial-administrative boundaries of the Hetman state's regiments
5. Regimental capitals
6. Other towns

Last capital of the Hetman state is underscored.

Ukrainian autonomy was progressively destroyed. After several earlier attempts, the office of hetman was finally abolished by the Russian government in 1764, and his functions were assumed by the *Little Russian Collegium. In 1782 the regiments were replaced by *vicegerencies, and Russian political and administrative institutions and practices replaced the unique institutions of the Hetmanate. At the same time the social structure of the state was recast: *serfdom was introduced, the Cossacks lost what remained of their special status, and the *starshyna* was at least partially integrated into the Russian nobility.

BIBLIOGRAPHY
Vasylenko, M. 'Z istoriï ustroiu Het'manshchyny,' *ZNTSh*, 108 (1912)
Slabchenko, M. *Opyty po istorii prava Malorossii XVII–XVIII st.* (Odessa 1911)
– *Hospodarstvo Het'manshchyny XVII–XVIII st.*, 4 vols (Odessa 1923–5)
Miakotin, V. *Ocherki sotsial'noi istorii Ukrainy v XVII–XVIII v.*, 3 vols (Prague 1924–6)
Okinshevych, L. *Tsentral'ni ustanovy Ukraïny-Het'manshchyny XVII–XVIII st.*, pt 2: *Rada starshyny* (Kiev 1930)
Diadychenko, V. *Narysy suspil'no-politychnoho ustroiu Livoberezhnoï Ukraïny kintsia XVII–pochatku XVIII st.* (Kiev 1959)
Kohut, Z. 'The Abolition of Ukrainian Autonomy (1763–1786): A Case Study in the Integration of a Non-Russian Area into the Russian Empire,' PH D diss, University of Pennsylvania, 1975
Gajecky, G. *The Cossack Administration of the Hetmanate*, 2 vols (Cambridge, Mass 1978)

L. Okinshevych, A. Zhukovsky

Hetmanite movement. See Conservatism, V. Lypynsky, Ukrainian Hetman Organization of America, Ukrainian Union of Agrarians-Statists, and United Hetman Organization.

Hets, Mykola [Hec] (Hec, Nikolas), b 20 October 1910 in Liatsko, Dobromyl county, Galicia. Journalist and civic leader. Hets studied at Lviv University. He was a coeditor of the daily *Ukraïns'ki visti* (1938–9). He immigrated to Brazil in 1947, where he edited the weekly *Khliborob* (1948–50) and the monthly *Boletim Informativo* (1950–4) in Curitiba, Paraná. He became in 1950 the secretary and in 1965 the head of the Society of Friends of Ukrainian Culture. He has done research on the history of Ukrainians in Brazil, and is the author of a monograph (1937) about the town of Dobromyl.

Hewak, Benjamin, b 12 November 1935 in Winnipeg. Jurist and community leader of Ukrainian descent. A graduate of the University of Manitoba Law School (LLB 1960), he served as crown attorney and defense counsel before being appointed in 1970 judge of the County Court, and in 1985 chief justice of the Queen's Bench in Manitoba. He has been active in the Ukrainian community as president of the Ukrainian National Youth Federation, director of the Rusalka Ukrainian Dance Ensemble, and honorary board member of the Ukrainian Cultural and Educational Centre.

Hierarchy, church. The higher orders of the *clergy (bishop, archbishop, metropolitan, patriarch) and the highest level of church authority. In Ukraine the hierarchy has played a distinct and often crucial role in civic and national life.

The Ukrainian church since its establishment has been headed by a hierarch with the title of *metropolitan, initially confirmed by and under the jurisdiction of the Patriarch of Constantinople. The metropolitan's see was Kiev, although it was at times located in other cities of Rus' (see *Kiev metropoly). The early metropolitans were Greeks; in the 250 years before the Mongol invasion, only 2 of the 20 metropolitans were of local origin. The first *bishops were also mostly Greeks, but they were gradually replaced by local people.

In Kievan Rus' hierarchs were generally recruited from among the monks of the Kievan Cave Monastery. In the 15th and 16th centuries the practice developed of appointing hierarchs from among the elite of Ukrainian society – the nobility. The method of appointment differed at various times. At first new bishops were elected by a council of bishops and then confirmed by the prince; later they were often nominated by the prince or other lay authorities – in the Polish Commonwealth the king and in the Hetmanate the hetman – or by church synods involving the participation of laymen. The Ukrainian hierarchy enjoyed great autonomy and its dependence on the ecumenical Patriarch of Constantinople was limited. In recent times, most Ukrainian Orthodox churches have become autocephalous or completely independent.

With the Mongol invasion in the mid-13th century, Kiev lost its importance as a religious center when the hierarchy fled to the west and north of Kiev metropoly. The Rus' church disintegrated into three separate provinces – the Galician, Lithuanian, and Muscovite – each headed by a metropolitan. When the Moscovite church broke away from Kiev in the 15th century, the Ukrainian hierarchy became most closely identified with the western provinces. In these territories, however, a division occurred in the hierarchy when in 1595–6 part of the Orthodox hierarchy, with the Kievan metropolitan, M. Rahoza, entered into the Church Union of *Berestia with Rome. Since that time, the two Ukrainian churches, the Orthodox and the Uniate Catholic, have each had their own hierarchies, with their own distinct histories.

With the defection of most bishops to the newly created Uniate church, the Orthodox hierarchy found itself in a minority. In 1620, however, the patriarch of Jerusalem, Theophanes, consecrated a new metropolitan and several new bishops for Ukraine. This event occurred against the wishes of the Polish authorities but was supported by the Cossack host. The succeeding several decades were marked by a remarkable revival of Orthodox Ukrainian religious and cultural life, led by the dynamic new hierarchy, particularly Metropolitan P. Mohyla. Toward the end of the 17th century, however, after the subjugation of the Kiev metropoly to the Moscow patriarch (1686), the Ukrainian Orthodox hierarchy lost its independence, and in the 19th century it essentially merged with the Russian hierarchy. From 1721 Orthodox bishops in Ukraine were nominated exclusively by the Russian *Holy Synod.

With the renaissance of the Ukrainian state (1917–20), the need arose for a separate Ukrainian hierarchy. When the Russian hierarchs refused to consecrate Ukrainian candidates as bishops, the Ukrainian hierarchy was renewed in 1921 by a non-traditional rite of consecration that was not recognized by all the faithful or other churches. This hierarchy of the newly established Ukrainian Autocephalous Orthodox church fell prey to the national-religious policy of the USSR and was physically liquidated beginning in 1929. On the eve of the Second World War there was not a single Ukrainian bishop left in the Ukrainian SSR. It was only in 1942 that a new hierarchy was consecrated for central Ukraine by bishops from Western Ukraine (Volhynia, Polisia, and the Kholm region), which had not been under Soviet rule. This hierarchy continues to exist only outside the USSR, since the church in Ukraine is again under the jurisdiction of the Russian church. In the West the Ukrainian Orthodox church is not united under a single hierarchy, but, in addition to some smaller jurisdictions, consists of three metropolies, two of which are headed (in 1986) by M. *Skrypnyk (in the United States, Europe, South America, Australia, and New Zealand) and one by V. Fedak (in Canada and Australia). Each metropoly has its own hierarchy.

The hierarchy of the Ukrainian Catholic church was created in 1595–6. After a period of rapid growth in the 17th and 18th centuries a decline began after the Russian acquisition of Right-Bank Ukraine, the major center of Ukrainian Catholicism, in the Partitions of Poland. With the intention of destroying the Uniate church, the Russian army and bureaucracy persecuted the Catholic hierarchy, especially in the period 1773–96. Nevertheless, in 1825 the Ukrainian Catholic hierarchy still consisted of a metropolitan and five bishops. It was only after Metropolitan Y. *Bulhak died that the abolition of the Union was proclaimed (1839) and the Uniate hierarchy was dissolved. Attempts to maintain the hierarchy in the western reaches of Russian-ruled Ukraine, in the Kholm region and Podlachia, were also unsuccessful, and in 1875 the Uniate church and its hierarchy were abolished there as well. The hierarchy continued to exist only beyond the borders of the Russian Empire, in Transcarpathia and Galicia, where, in 1806, the *Halych metropoly was re-established under A. Anhelovych. After the Second World War the hierarchy of the Ukrainian Catholic church was arrested and almost completely destroyed. Today in the Ukrainian SSR, only secretly consecrated Uniate hierarchs (in 1986 they numbered five to seven) can continue some activity, mostly underground. Thus, the Ukrainian Catholic hierarchy exists openly only outside the borders of the USSR. Until 1984 it was headed by the Halych metropolitan Y. *Slipy, who was succeeded by M. Liubachivsky; it consists of bishops and exarchs in the various countries in which Ukrainian emigrants have settled, as well as metropolitans who head the church provinces in Canada and the United States. (See also *Church, history of the Ukrainian; *Churches of Ukraine, structures of the; *Ukrainian Orthodox church; *Ukrainian Orthodox Church in the USA; *Ukrainian Orthodox Church of America; *Ukrainian Greek Orthodox Church in Canada; and *Ukrainian Autocephalous Orthodox church.)

BIBLIOGRAPHY
Levitskii, O. 'Iuzhnorusskie arkhierei v XV–XVII v.', *KS*, 1882, no. 2
Luzhnyts'kyi, H. *Ukraïns'ka Tserkva mizh Skhodom i Zakhodom* (Philadelphia 1954)
Vlasovs'kyi, I. *Narys istoriï Ukraïns'koï Pravoslavnoï Tserkvy*, 4 vols (South Bound Brook, NJ 1955–66)
Nazarko, I. *Kyïvs'ki i halyts'ki mytropolyty: Biohrafichni narysy (1590–1960)* (Toronto 1962)
Blažejowskyj, D. *Byzantine Kyivan Rite Metropolitanates, Eparchies and Exarchates: Nomenclature and Statistics* (Rome 1980)
I. Korovytsky

High Beskyd. Name of that part of the *Beskyds – the outer flysch belt of the Ukrainian Carpathian Mountains – lying between the imaginary line joining Turka and Boryslav in the west and the Mizunka River valley in the east, and between the limits of the Carpathians in the north and the Middle-Carpathian Depression in the south.

The High Beskyd has an area of about 2,000 sq km and begins rising from an elevation of 300–400 m. It is lowest in its northern part – the highest peak there is Mt Tsukhovyi Dil (942 m) – where a banded structure has been created by longitudinal sandstone ridges and parallel valleys, wide depressions, and small hollows (Verkhnie Synovydne and Mizunka) carved out of soft schists and clays. The rounded and uniform mountains there are quite densely populated (60 inhabitants per sq km) and deforested (24 percent of the land area is cultivated, 38 percent is pasture and hayfields, and only 35 percent is forest).

South of the longitudinal Stryi River valley the High Beskyd attains elevations of 1,100 m and up. There the highest peaks are Mt Parashka (1,271 m), Mt Zelemianka (1,267 m), and Mt Magura (1,368 m). Narrow and deep transverse valleys (such as the Opir, Sukil, and Mizunka river valleys), which intersect the longitudinal valleys, predominate. The mountain tops have a sharper definition and are often denuded. Forests consisting mostly of spruce still cover 70 percent of the area, and the population density is lower (30 inhabitants per sq km).

The High Beskyd has long been inhabited by the ethnographic group of the *Boikos. (Until 1941 Poles and Jews each constituted 10 percent of the population.) The main occupations are crop cultivation (rye, potatoes, and oats) and animal husbandry, logging and woodworking, and, in the Boryslav region, petroleum extraction. Cities (Boryslav, Bolekhiv) lie on the mountains' periphery. In the interior the main centers are Skole (woodworking), Skhidnytsia (petroleum), Verkhnie Synevidske (woodworking), and the resorts of the Opir Valley – Hrebeniv, Tukhlia, Slavske, and Zelemianka.

V. Kubijovyč

Higher Courses for Women. See Education of women and Higher educational institution.

Higher education. The highest level of formal schooling in academic, professional, or technical fields, which is accessible only to students who have completed a secondary education. The origin of higher education in Ukraine can be traced back to the confessional colleges that arose in the period of religious strife (16th–17th century). The colleges organized by the Jesuits served as a model for similar Orthodox and later Uniate schools. According to their standard curriculum, which consisted of three lower grades (infima, grammar, and syntax) and two intermediate grades (poetics and rhetoric) and required six years to complete, these schools were institutions of secondary education. Yet some of them offered courses belonging to the higher grades (philosophy, requiring three years, and theology, requiring four years) that were typical of academies. The Jesuits established a number of such higher colleges in Ukrainian and Belorussian territories: in Vilnius (est 1570, academy from 1578), Lviv (1608), Orsha (beginning of 17th century), Berestia (first quarter of the 17th century), Pynske (1633), Ostrih (1624, added philosophy in 1636), Vitsebsk (ca 1640), Dorohychyn (1661), Minsk (ca 1650, added philosophy and theology at the end of the 17th century), and Kamianets-Podilskyi (1611, added philosophy at the end of the 17th century). A full higher education could be obtained by Ukrainians only at the Jesuit-run academy in Lviv (1661–1763), Vilnius, Zamostia, or Cracow. Despite its name, the Ostrih Academy (est ca 1580 by the Orthodox Prince K. Ostrozky) did not offer a higher education. The only Orthodox college that provided a partial higher education was the Kievan Mohyla College (est 1632). In spite of a royal prohibition (1635), philosophy and theology courses were offered at the school on an irregular basis until philosophy and theology grades were permanently established as part of the curriculum in the 1680s. It was only in 1701 that the school was recognized officially as an academy (see *Kievan Mohyla Academy). Among the numerous Uniate colleges run by the Basilian order only a few – in Zhyrovichy, Buchach, and Volodymyr-Volynskyi – introduced some courses of the higher grades in the 18th century.

The first university in Ukraine – *Lviv University – was founded in 1784 by Emperor Joseph II. The language of instruction was Latin, but literary Ukrainian (Ruthenian) of the period was used in the *Studium Ruthenum, a special institute of the university for educating candidates for the Uniate priesthood. The German character of the university was underlined when German was adopted as the language of instruction in 1817. During the Revolutions of 1848–9 the Ukrainians won some concessions in university education: a Ukrainian chair in the Department of Theology was established in 1848 and the first Chair of Ukrainian (Ruthenian) Language and Literature was set up in the following year. In 1849 and 1860 the central authorities declared their intention to convert Lviv University gradually into a Ukrainian institution. Two Ukrainian chairs were set up in the law department in 1862. Under strong political pressure from the Poles, however, the central government eventually abandoned this policy: in 1871 it recognized the university as a bilingual institution by replacing German with Ukrainian and Polish as the languages of instruction, and in 1879 it approved the Polonization of the university, by accepting Polish as the language of the institution's internal administration. Although a few other Ukrainian chairs were established, the population's educational needs were not met and by the turn of the century the Ukrainians in Galicia demanded their own university. The broad campaign for a separate Ukrainian university persisted for many years and erupted occasionally into violence. Finally, in 1912 the Austrian authorities promised to establish a Ukrainian university, but were prevented from doing so by the First World War.

In Russian-ruled Ukraine a number of university projects were drawn up in the 18th century. Hetman K. Rozumovsky in 1760 proposed to establish a university in Baturyn. Under Catherine II Ukrainian deputies to the Legislative Commission of 1767–9 demanded that a university be founded in Kiev or Pereiaslav. The nobility of the Sumy and the Chernihiv regions collected funds to build universities in their respective capitals. Prince G. Potemkin fostered a plan to open a university in Katerynoslav. The first university in Russian-ruled Ukraine was finally estabished in Kharkiv in 1805 (see *Kharkiv University). The project proposed by V. *Karazyn became a reality as a result of his persistent efforts and the generosity of the local nobility. Although the language of instruction was Russian, as in all higher schools in Russian-ruled Ukraine, the university became the home of the *Kharkiv Romantic School and played an important role in the Ukrainian cultural renaissance and national awakening in the 19th century.

In 1820 the Bezborodko Gymnasium of Higher Learning, later known as the *Nizhen Lyceum, was opened in Nizhen. Its nine-year program was more demanding than that of a secondary level and compared favorably with that offered by Russian universities.

*Kiev University was founded in 1834 in place of the abolished *Kremianets Lyceum whose Polish student body had taken part in the Polish uprising of 1830. M. Maksymovych, a pioneer of Ukrainian ethnography, literary studies, and history, served as the university's first rector. The first generation of students was predominantly Polish. Eventually, Ukrainians and Russians formed a majority.

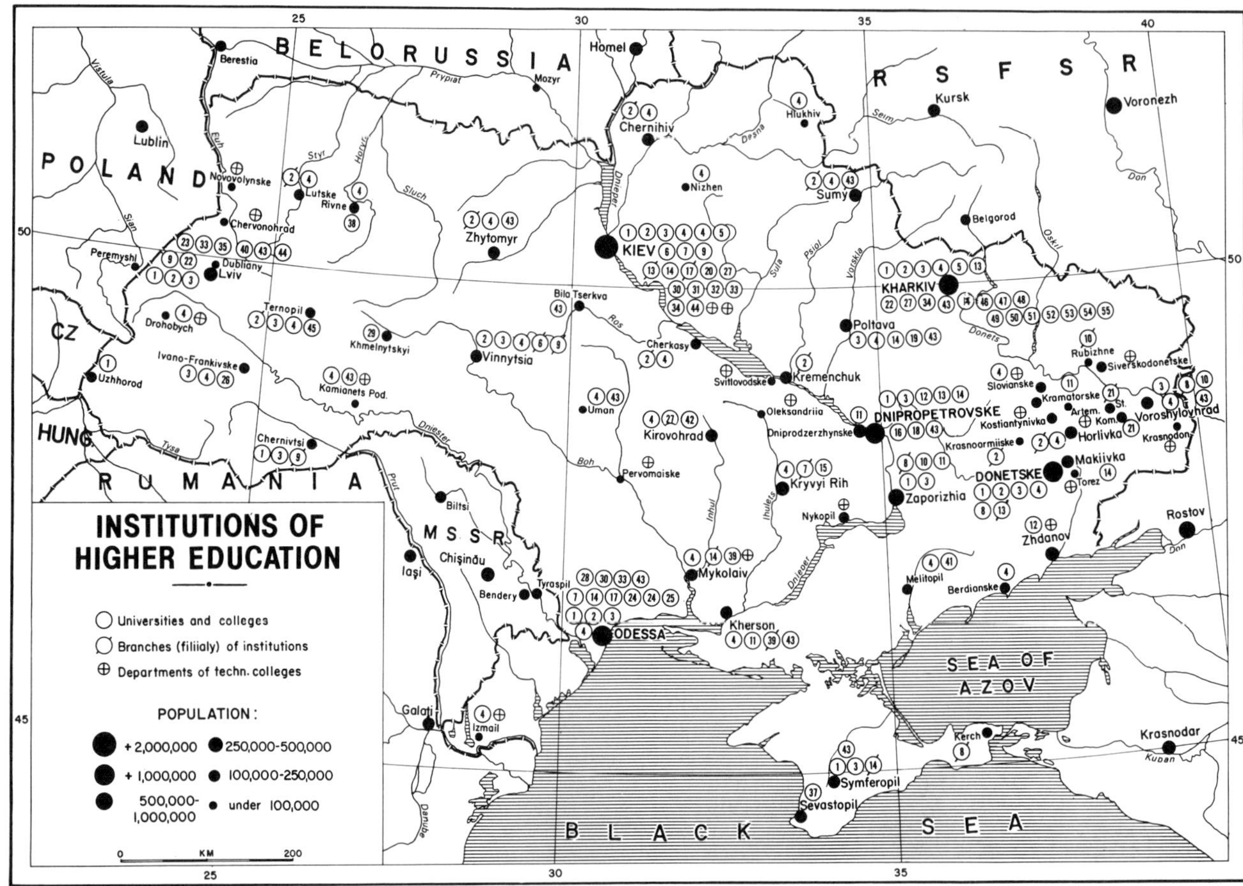

1. Universities
2. Polytechnical institutes
3. Medical institutes
4. Pedagogical institutes
5. Institutes of culture (Kiev, Kharkiv)
6. Ukrainian Agricultural Academy (Kiev)
7. Institutes of the national economy (Kiev, Odessa)
8. Donetske Institute of Soviet Trade
9. Trade and economics institutes (Kiev, Lviv)
10. Machine-building institutes (Voroshylovhrad, Zaporizhia)
11. Industrial institutes
12. Metallurgical institutes (Dnipropetrovske, Zhdanov)
13. Institutes of railway-transport engineers
14. Civil-engineering institutes
15. Kryvyi Rih Ore-Mining Institute
16. Dnipropetrovske Mining Institute
17. Odessa Electrotechnical Institute of Communication
18. Dnipropetrovske Chemical Technology Institute
19. Poltava Co-operative Institute
20. Institute of Theater Arts of the Ukrainian SSR (Kiev)
21. Komunarske Mining and Metallurgical Institute
22. Zootechnical-veterinary institutes (Lviv, Kharkiv)
23. Lviv Forestry Technological Institute
24. Odessa Institute of Naval Engineers and Odessa Higher Nautical Engineering School
25. Odessa Hydrometeorological Institute
26. Ivano-Frankivske Institute of Petroleum and Gas
27. Kharkiv Aviation Institute and Kiev Institute of Civil Aviation Engineers
28. Odessa Technological Institute of the Refrigeration Industry
29. Khmelnytskyi Technological Institute of Consumer Services
30. Technological institutes of the food industry (Kiev, Odessa)
31. Kiev Technological Institute of Light Industry
32. Kiev Art Institute
33. Conservatories (Kiev, Lviv, Odessa)
34. Automobile and road institutes (Kiev, Kharkiv)
35. Ukrainian Printing Institute (Lviv)
37. Sevastopil Instrument-Making Institute
38. Ukrainian Institute of Water Management Engineers (Rivne)
39. Mykolaiv Shipbuilding Institute
40. Lviv Institute of Applied and Decorative Arts
41. Melitopil Institute of Agricultural Mechanization
42. Kirovohrad Institute of Agricultural-Machine Building
43. Agricultural institutes
44. Institutes of physical culture (Lviv, Kiev)
45. Ternopil Finance and Economics Institute
46. Kharkiv Radioelectronics Institute
47. Kharkiv Institute of Communal Construction Engineers
48. Kharkiv Institute of Agricultural Mechanization and Electrification
49. Kharkiv Juridical Institute
50. Kharkiv Institute of Public Consumption
51. Kharkiv Industrial Engineering Institute
52. Kharkiv Industrial Design Institute
53. Kharkiv Institute of Arts
54. Kharkiv Pharmaceutical Institute
55. Ukrainian Correspondence Polytechnical Institute (Kharkiv)

Artem. = Artemivske; Kom. = Komunarske; St. = Stakhanov

The origins of higher technical education in Ukraine date back to 1844 when the Technical Academy (now the *Lviv Polytechnical Institute) was opened. The Farming Academy in Dubliany (est 1855) was the only higher agricultural school in Western Ukraine before the First World War. In Russian-ruled Ukraine the veterinary school of Kharkiv University (est 1839) was reorganized in 1851 into an independent, higher veterinary school, and then in 1873 into the Kharkiv Veterinary Institute. A number of higher technical schools were founded in the late 19th century: the Kharkiv Technological Institute (1885; see *Kharkiv Polytechnical Institute), a commercial institute in Kiev (1896), the *Kiev Polytechnical Institute (1898), and the Katerynoslav Higher Mining School (1899). In 1915 the agricultural institute in Novo-Aleksandriia (now Puławy, Poland) was evacuated to Kharkiv and reorganized into the Institute of Agriculture and Forestry.

In 1863, during the period of liberalization under Alexander II, the universities were granted limited autonomy (election of rectors and professors, reduction in administrative surveillance), concessions that were revoked in 1884. During this period another university was established in Ukraine: the New Russia University (later *Odessa University), formed in 1865 out of the Richelieu Lyceum, which until 1837 was a secondary, rather than a higher, institution of learning. In Austrian-ruled Ukraine a German university with a Chair of Ukrainian Language and Literature was established in Chernivtsi in 1875 (see *Chernivtsi University).

Higher education became accessible to women only in the second half of the 19th century (see *Education of women). In 1870 the Russian Ministry of Public Education permitted women to attend public lectures, and special courses began to be organized for them. The Higher Courses for Women were set up at Kiev University in 1878, but were closed down by the authorities in 1885. The situation improved only after the Revolution of 1905: private higher schools for women were opened in Kiev; the Higher Courses for Women at the university were revived in 1906 and were renamed the St Olha's Women's Institute in 1914; and similar private schools appeared in Odessa in 1906 and in Kharkiv in 1907. Professional education for women was available at women's medical institutes in Kiev (1910), Kharkiv (1910), Odessa (1910), and Katerynoslav (1916), and at the Froebelian pedagogical courses in Kiev and Kharkiv. From 1906 to 1909 women were permitted to attend universities.

After 1905 the question of university courses in Ukrainian studies was raised, but the authorities, supported by Russian faculty, prohibited any instruction in this field. The Russian system of higher education in Ukraine was elitist. In 1914 there were only 27,000 students attending 19 institutions of higher learning, and most of them were from the nobility.

In 1917, after the February Revolution, new higher schools appeared in Ukraine: the Ukrainian People's University in Kiev, a commercial institute and a conservatory in Kharkiv, an agricultural institute in Odessa, the *Ukrainian State Academy of Arts, and the Ukrainian Pedagogical Academy in Kiev. At the same time existing higher schools began to be Ukrainianized and chairs of Ukrainian language, literature, history, and legal history were set up at existing universities. In 1918 the Ukrainian People's University was transformed by the hetman's decree into the Ukrainian State University of Kiev (while St Vladimir University remained Russian), and new universities were set up in Katerynoslav (see *Dnipropetrovske University), Symferopil, and Kamianets-Podilskyi (see *Kamianets-Podilskyi Ukrainian State University). At the same time the Ukrainian Historical-Philological Faculty in Poltava and the Ukrainian Teachers' Institute in Zhytomyr were opened.

When the Bolsheviks came to power Ukraine's commissar of education, H. *Hrynko (1920–3), abolished the universities, transforming them into *institutes of people's education (INO), to which a number of newly created teachers' institutes were added. Among the administrative changes were the reorganization of the medical faculties of universities into separate institutes and the absorption of the faculties of law by the new institutes of the national economy. *Tekhnikums, which in Ukraine, unlike in Russia, were higher technical schools, trained narrow specialists in various technical fields. *Institutes were devoted exclusively to teaching, while research and the preparation of scholars and scientists were the responsibility of autonomous research chairs. Many subjects were taught by the laboratory-brigade method, which precluded individual testing. This system of higher education, known as the Hrynko System, was unique to Ukraine.

In Soviet Ukraine, institutions of higher education lacked any autonomy. Rectors were appointed by the people's commissar of education, and often their political credentials, rather than academic qualifications, were decisive. Access to higher education was made difficult for people of 'non-labor origin'; nonetheless, 43 percent of the students attending institutes were offspring of white-collar workers. Candidates seeking admission to higher educational establishments had to produce references from Party, trade union, or Communist Youth League organizations. Workers' faculties (*robitfaky*) were established to prepare students of worker or poor peasant origin for admission to higher education.

During the 1920s an effort was made to Ukrainianize higher education. The first step was to introduce courses with Ukrainian content: Ukrainian history, language, literature, and economic geography became compulsory for all students. The second step was to introduce Ukrainian as a language of instruction. By 1928, out of 38 institutes, 11 offered instruction only in Ukrainian and 24 in both Ukrainian and Russian, and out of 126 tekhnikums, 46 offered instruction only in Ukrainian and 34 in both Ukrainian and Russian. Beginning in 1925, a knowlege of Ukrainian became, in many regions, a condition for admission to higher education or for graduation. By 1927 these requirements applied to all higher educational establishments in Ukraine.

Ukrainians were underrepresented among students of higher education. In 1928 they accounted for 54 percent of the 33,400 students at institutes (Russians represented 16 percent, Jews 25 percent), 63 percent of the 26,900 students at tekhnikums, and 53 percent of the 9,800 students at workers' faculties. Women accounted for approximately a quarter of the enrollment at institutes. In 1925 only a third of the teaching staff in institutes and 43 percent at tekhnikums gave Ukrainian as their nationality. The lack of Ukrainian-speaking faculty and hostility to Ukrainian among Russian teachers stymied the *Ukrainization process. In addition to these difficulties, the Ukrainian system of higher education did not receive the financial support that the Russian system did from the all-Union budget. In spite of this, by 1929 Ukraine had a higher per capita enrollment in higher education than Russia did, and its rate of growth was faster than in Russia.

Between 1929 and 1934 the system of higher education in Ukraine was reorganized to conform with that in the rest of the USSR. Most institutes (technical, economic, agricultural, medical) were transferred from the jurisdiction of the People's Commissariat of Education (NKO) to that of appropriate commissariats, leaving only pedagogical and artistic institutes under the NKO. Tekhnikums in 1928 were transformed into either institutes or specialized secondary schools. In 1934 the universities in Kiev, Kharkiv, Odessa, and Dnipropetrovske were restored. The institutes of social education, of vocational education, and of political education, into which INO's were divided in 1930, were transformed into pedagogical institutes. The laboratory-brigade method was abolished and traditional requirements and teaching methods were restored. Programs, textbooks, and examinations were standardized. University and institute chairs resumed research activities that had been confined to special research chairs.

With rapid industrialization in the 1930s, higher educational facilities were expanded greatly to meet the needs of industry. The number of institutions of higher learning increased sharply from 42 in 1929 to 173 in 1940 (including correspondence schools), and the student population expanded from 40,890 to 196,800. The preferential admission of working-class and poor peasant students to higher education was gradually abandoned as the quality of graduates was stressed. Even tuition fees, a prerevolutionary practice favoring the children of the elite, were instituted from 1940 to 1956. In 1936, 44 percent of university students were offspring of white-collar workers; 40 percent, of workers; and a mere 13 percent, of peasants. In 1933 Ukrainization was halted and the Ukrainian faculty and student body of higher educational institutions were purged. As a result the proportion of Ukrainian students dropped from 55 percent in 1933 to 53 percent in 1935. The proportion of Ukrainian research staff declined from 49 percent in 1929 to 31 percent in 1934, while the proportion of Russians increased from 30 to 50 percent. Many leading Ukrainian scholars perished during the 1930s. A concerted effort was made to promote Russian language and subjects in higher education.

After the First World War the Polish authorities in Galicia abolished the Ukrainian chairs at Lviv University (even Ukrainian philology had to be taught in Polish), and restricted the admission of Ukrainian students. As a result the *Lviv (Underground) Ukrainian University was established in 1921. In 1922–3 the *Lviv (Underground) Higher Polytechnical School with a one-year curriculum was opened at the underground university. Harassed by Polish authorities and refused recognition by the Polish government, the university dissolved in 1925. Talks on the establishment of a Ukrainian state university collapsed when the Polish authorities rejected Lviv as a possible location and the Ukrainians rejected Stanyslaviv or Cracow. The *Greek Catholic Theological Academy in Lviv (est 1928) was the only officially recognized Ukrainian institution of higher learning in interwar Poland. Chairs of Ukrainian studies existed at Polish universities in Cracow and Warsaw, in addition to one at Lviv University.

After the First World War a number of Ukrainian organizations abroad founded the *Ukrainian Free University in Vienna in 1921. Having received recognition and financial support from the Czechoslovak government, it was transferred to Prague. Another higher school, the *Ukrainian Husbandry Academy (est 1922), operated in Poděbrady until 1935, when it was transformed into a correspondence school – the *Ukrainian Technical and Husbandry Institute. Both schools were evacuated to Munich just before the arrival of the Soviet Army in 1945. The *Ukrainian Higher Pedagogical Institute in Prague was supported by the Czechoslovak government from 1923 to 1933.

After the Second World War Ukraine's system of higher education expanded, but its accessibility to Ukrainians has remained a problem. New universities were established in the Ukrainian SSR: *Uzhhorod University (1945), *Donetske University (1965), *Symferopil University (1972, having been abolished in 1925), and *Zaporizhia University (1985). The universities of Lviv and Chernivtsi, and the Lviv Polytechnic (see *Lviv Polytechnical Institute), were incorporated into the Soviet system. Except for pedagogical, medical, and art schools, the institutions of higher education in Ukraine were under the direct control of the union Ministry of Higher and Specialized Secondary Education. A republican Ministry of Higher and Specialized Secondary Education, established in 1955 (only in the case of Ukraine), gave the republic a voice in the running of its higher educational system, but only until 1959, when the Union-Republic Ministry of Higher and Specialized Secondary Education was set up in Moscow. In 1965 only 50 of the 132 higher educational institutions in Ukraine were under the republic's jurisdiction. Postgraduate programs in Ukraine could only be established with Moscow's permission. It was not possible, for example, to obtain in Ukraine a doctorate in pedagogy.

At the same time pressures for the Russification of higher education in Ukraine have increased. In 1954 the compulsory entrance examination in Ukrainian, but not in Russian language and literature, was dropped. Proposals to Ukrainianize higher education put forward by Ukraine's Party leadership in 1965 were blocked by Moscow. Of the 75,027 students attending the republic's eight universities (1965), 61 percent were Ukrainian; 56 percent of the faculty were Ukrainian, but only 34 percent lectured in Ukrainian. Almost 70 percent of the subjects taught at the universities were not supplied with Ukrainian-language textbooks. The granting of degrees is under the supervision of the Supreme Attestation Commission in Moscow, which encourages postgraduate students to write their dissertations in Russian (from 1944 to 1960, 86 percent of the dissertations accepted at Lviv University were written in Russian). The preference for Russian in higher education means that Ukrainian-speaking students are disadvantaged in the competition with Russian-speaking students for admission to establishments of higher education. Furthermore, higher education in Ukraine, as throughout the Soviet Union, is biased in favor of the upper strata of society. In 1965, for example, 70 percent of first-year students at Kharkiv University were the offspring of white-collar workers; 23 percent, of workers; and only 7 percent, of collective farmers. Since Ukrainians are underrepresented in the upper stratum, this bias further restricts access to higher education for Ukrainians. As a result, although in 1956 Ukrainians accounted for 64 percent of the enrollment in higher educational institutions in Ukraine, in 1971 they accounted for only 60 percent. There is evidence of outright discrimination against Ukrainians: a secret instruction issued in 1974 restricted the admission of local students to institutions of higher learning in Western Ukraine to 25 percent of the freshman class. The percentage of women among students increased from 47 percent in 1970–1 to 54 percent in 1983–4. Under N. Khrushchev's regime (1955–64) institutions of higher education were consolidated and their number decreased. Higher education 'that did not lose contact with production,' ie, evening and extramural education, was promoted. This policy led to a decline in the quality of graduates and was reversed in 1964, after Krushchev's fall.

The territorial distribution of institutions of higher learning in Ukraine is very uneven. The major centers in 1983–4 were Kharkiv oblast (21 of 146 such institutions for all Ukraine and 15 percent of the enrollment), the city of Kiev (18 institutions and 17 percent of enrollment), Odessa oblast (15 and 10 percent), Dnipropetrovske oblast (12 and 9 percent), and Lviv oblast (12 and 8 percent). The specializations that attract the largest number of students are (in 1983–4): education and cultural studies, 15 percent; economics, 13 percent; and machine and tool building, 12 percent.

In 1984–5 Ukraine had 16 percent of all higher educational establishments and 16.6 percent of the total number of students in the USSR. At the same time Ukraine represented 18.5 percent of the USSR population.

There are two Ukrainian universities outside of Ukraine: the *Ukrainian Catholic University in Rome (est 1963) and the Ukrainian Free University in Munich. The former, however, does not have the right to confer doctoral degrees. In Canada, the United States, Australia, and Europe courses in Ukrainian studies are offered by many universities. A number of Ukrainian research institutes exist as integral parts of national university systems.

BIBLIOGRAPHY

Titov, Kh. *Stara vyshcha osvita v Kyïvs'kii Ukraïni kintsia XVI–pochatku XIX st.* (Kiev 1924)
Savych, A. *Narysy z istoriï kul'turnykh rukhiv na Ukraïni ta Bilorusi v XVI–XVIII v.* (Kiev 1929)
Krylov, I. *Systema osvity v Ukraïni (1917–1930)* (Munich 1956)
Vyshcha shkola Ukraïns'koï RSR za 50 rr., 2 vols (Kiev 1967–8)
Krawchenko, B. *Social Change and National Consciousness in Twentieth-Century Ukraine* (London 1985)

M. Hlobenko, B. Krawchenko, B. Struminsky

Higher educational institution (*vyshchyi uchbovyi zaklad* or VUZ). A calque of the Russian *vysshee uchebnoe zavedenie*; in Soviet usage the term applies to post-secondary schools of various kinds – universities, polytechnics, institutes, academies, conservatories, and higher schools. In the 1920s such institutions were called *vysh* (from *vyshchi shkoly*, 'higher schools'). Generally, they offer a four- to six-year program leading to a diploma and combine teaching with research. Some of them are devoted to upgrading the qualifications of specialists. (See also *Higher education.)

Hiliarov, Merkurii [Hiljarov, Merkurij], b 6 March 1912 in Kiev, d 2 March 1985 in Moscow. Entomologist, scientific administrator; from 1974 full member of the USSR Academy of Sciences. A graduate of Kiev University (1933), he headed a department of the All-Union Rubber Institute, and in 1944 joined his mentor I. Shmalhauzen at the Institute of Evolutionary Morphology of the USSR Academy of Sciences. From 1955 he directed the institute's laboratory of soil zoology. At the same time he taught at the Moscow Pedagogical Institute (1949–77) and then at Moscow University (1972–85). From 1959 he was president of the National Committee of Soviet Biologists, and from 1978 academic secretary of the academy's Division of General Biology. His major work in soil zoology includes the book *Zakonomernosti prisposoblenii chlenistonogikh k zhizni na sushe* (Trends in the Adaptations of Arthropods to Life on Dry Land, 1970).

Hiliarovsky, Mykhailo [Hiljarovs'kyj, Myxajlo], b 14 August 1934 in Teliatyn, Lublin voivodeship, Poland. Stage director. After graduating from the Kiev Institute of Theater Arts in 1960, he worked as a stage director in various theaters in Chernihiv, Nizhen, Drohobych (1964), Lviv, and Kiev (1961–75). In 1976 he was appointed chief stage director at the Kirovohrad Ukrainian Music and Drama Theater.

Himka, John-Paul [Xymka], b 18 May 1949 in Detroit. Historian. Educated at the University of Michigan (PH D 1977), from 1977 to 1980 he was a research associate at the Canadian Institute of Ukrainian Studies. A specialist in the social and political history of 19th-century Galicia, he was appointed (1985) assistant professor at the University of Alberta. He wrote *Socialism in Galicia: The Emergence of Polish Social Democracy and Ukrainian Radicalism (1860–1890)* (1983).

Himmler, Heinrich, b 7 October 1900 in Munich, d 23 May 1945 in Lüneburg, Germany. Nazi politician, chief of the Gestapo and later of the entire German police, and from 1943 minister of the interior. More than any other Nazi leader, he was responsible for the atrocities perpetrated by the Nazi regime. A fanatic enemy of the Slavs, in 1939 he was appointed Reichskommissar to consolidate and extend German territory in the east. Denying the Ukrainian people any rights, he conceived the plan to resettle them in Asia near and beyond the Caspian Sea and to settle Germans in Ukraine after the war. When, towards the end of the war, the Ukrainian National Committee was being formed, he advocated that non-Russian anti-Soviet forces be placed under the command of A. Vlasov. In the final hour Himmler betrayed Hitler and, avoiding arrest, was captured by the Western allies. He committed suicide by taking poison.

Hintsi settlement. An Upper Paleolithic site on the right bank of the Udai River near Hintsi, Lubni raion, Poltava oblast. It was discovered in 1871 by F. Kaminsky and was excavated in 1873, 1914–15, and 1935. Remains of mammoth-bone dwellings, storage pits, fire pits, and flint and bone tools were uncovered, some with geometric ornamentation.

Hirchak, Yevhen [Hirčak, Jevhen], b and d ? Bolshevik publicist and literary critic. He was a member of the department for the nationalities problem at the Ukrainian Institute of Marxism-Leninism and of the All-Ukrainian Association of Proletarian Writers. Two of his brochures – *Shums'kizm i rozlam v KPZU* (Shumskyism and the Split in the Communist Party of Western Ukraine, 1928) and *Khvyl'ovizm* (Khvylovyism, 1929) – attacked M. *Khvylovy. As editor of the newspaper *Bil'shovyk Ukraïny*, he wrote several articles criticizing M. Volobuiev. In *Na dva fronta v bor'be s natsionalizmom* (On Two Fronts in the Struggle with Nationalism, 1930), he exposed various ideological 'deviations.' In 1933 he was criticized for 'errors on the theoretical front' and in 1934 disappeared without trace.

Hirmologion (Ukrainian: *irmoloi, irmolohii, irmolohion*). One of the liturgical books used in the Eastern churches. It contains all the hirmoi and prayers that are to be sung during religious services and musical notations to them. The oldest extant hirmologion was preserved at the Basilian monastery in Supraśl, Poland. The first Ukrainian notated hirmologion was printed in Lviv in 1700 by the hieromonach at St George's Cathedral, Y. Horodetsky, and embellished by N. Zubrytsky and D. Sinkevych; the prolegomenon was written by Hegumen Y. Skolsky. Others were printed by the Lviv Dormition Brotherhood (1709, 1757), the Kievan Cave Monastery (1753, 1769, 1778, 1791), and in Chernihiv (1761) and Pochaiv (1766, 1775, 1792, 1794).

Hirniak, Nykyfor [Hirnjak], b 23 July 1885 in Strusiv, Terebovlia county, Galicia, d 4 March 1962 in Clifton, New Jersey. Ukrainian Galician Army officer. He commanded the replacement unit of the Legion of Ukrainian Sich Riflemen (1915–18). In 1919 he served as mobilization officer in the war ministry of the Western Ukrainian National Republic and then in the general staff of the Army of the UNR. On 1 March 1919 he was promoted to major. In 1920 he became chairman of the Revolutionary Committee of the Ukrainian Galician Army in Vinnytsia and was instrumental in concluding the temporary alliance between the remnants of the Ukrainian Galician Army and the Red Army. After 1921 he taught at the Ternopil gymnasium. He immigrated to the United States in 1949. There he wrote a number of works on the Ukrainian independence struggle, including the memoirs *Ostanii akt trahediï Ukraïns'koï Halytskoï Armiï* (The Last Act of the Tragedy of the Ukrainian Galician Army, 1959).

Hirniak, Olimpiia. See Dobrovolska, Olimpiia.

Hirniak, Yosyp [Hirnjak, Josyp], b 14 April 1895 in Strusiv, Terebovlia county, Galicia. A leading Ukrainian stage actor and director. He began his career in 1914 in an amateur troupe of the Ukrainian Sich Riflemen and then worked in the professional companies of the Ukrainska Besida Theater in Lviv (1916–18), the New Lviv Theater (1919–20), the Franko Ukrainian Drama Theater and its studio (1920–2), and the *Berezil theater in Kiev and Kharkiv (1922–33). A close associate of the influential director L. *Kurbas, Hirniak was arrested during the Stalin terror in 1933 and exiled to Chibiu in the Soviet Arctic, where he performed in the Kosolapkin Theater (1934–40). In 1942–4 he acted in and directed plays, including the first Ukrainian production of Shakespeare's *Hamlet*, at the Lviv Opera Theater. As displaced persons after the Second World War, Hirniak and his wife O. *Dobrovolska founded a Ukrainian theater studio

Yosyp Hirniak; portrait by S. Hruzbenko (1943)

in Landeck, Austria, in 1946, toured Austria and Bavaria, and continued to produce, direct, and act in many Ukrainian and West European plays after immigrating to the United States in 1949. From 1954 to 1964 he was the artistic director of the *Ukrainian Theater in America, which he helped found. As an actor, Hirniak became famous for his roles in Berezil's productions of M. Kulish's *Myna Mazailo, Narodnii Malakhii* (The People's Malakhii), *Komuna v stepakh* (Commune in the Steppes), *Maklena Grasa*, and *97*. As an actor and director he developed Kurbas's system of 'transformation' and attempted to combine the traditions of the Ukrainian *intermede with the art of the modern theater. He is the author of articles on the history of Ukrainian theater, including 'Birth and Death of the Modern Ukrainian Theater' in *Soviet Theaters 1917–1941: A Collection of Articles* (ed M. Bradshaw, 1954), and memoirs (1982).

BIBLIOGRAPHY

Khmuryi, V.; Dyvnych, Iu.; Blakytnyi, Ie. *V maskakh epokhy* (np 1948)
Boichuk, B. (ed). *Teatr-studiia Iosypa Hirniaka Olimpiï Dobrovol's'koï* (New York 1975)
Hirniak, Y. *Spomyny* (New York 1982)
Revuts'kyi, V. *Neskoreni berezil'tsi* (New York 1985)

V. Revutsky

Hirniak, Yuliian [Hirnjak, Julijan], b 8 September 1881 in Strusiv, Terebovlia county, Galicia, d 5 June 1970 in Passaic, New Jersey. Chemist, physicist, and educator; brother of Nykyfor and Yosyp *Hirniak. Yuliian taught at the branch of the *Academic Gymnasium of Lviv before and after the First World War, and in 1921–3 was a professor at the Lviv (Underground) Ukrainian University. He immigrated to the United States after the Second World War. He was a member (from 1907) of the Shevchenko Scientific Society, which published his works on theoretical chemistry and physics, and is the author of several school textbooks.

Hirny, Vasyl [Hirnyj, Vasyl'], b 14 March 1902 in Zaliska Volia, Jarosław county, Galicia, d 5 July 1981 in Lębork, Poland. Writer, journalist, and community activist. Hirny lived and worked in France in 1926–7, studied at Lviv University in 1927–32, and worked as an editor for the Lviv newspaper *Novyi chas* (1932–9). His publicistic feuilletons and literary parodies (under the pseudonym Fed Tryndyk) were published in that paper and in other Lviv periodicals; his *Literaturni parodiï* (Literary Parodies) appeared in 1936. Hirny also wrote an educational booklet for the peasantry, *Shcho diialosia v seli Molodivtsi* (What Happened in the Village of Molodivka, 1933), and a novel about Ukrainian migrant workers in France, *Rozhubleni syly* (Squandered Strengths, 1943). In 1948 he settled in Lębork near Gdańsk. From 1956 he wrote feuilletons for the Warsaw paper *Nashe slovo* and was active in the Ukrainian Social and Cultural Society in Poland.

Hirnyk, Mykola, b 7 June 1923 in Verbovets, Katerynopil raion, Cherkasy oblast. A poet and translator. He has worked as an editor for various periodicals and is the author of 15 poetry collections, including *Moia Zvenyhorodshchyna* (My Zvenyhorod Region, 1950), *Virnist'* (Fidelity, 1952), *Poezii* (Poems, 1968), *Kriz' vidstani* (Across Distances, 1969), *Odvichne, s'ohodenne* (Eternal, Today, 1973), and *Nevtoma* (Indefatigability, 1975).

Leonard Hirshman

Hirshman, Leonard [Hiršman], b 25 March 1839 in Tukums, Latvia, d 3 January 1921 in Kharkiv. Ophthalmologist. After graduating from Kharkiv University in 1860, he studied in France and Germany. In 1868 he began teaching at Kharkiv University. In 1885 he was promoted to full professor of the first ophthalmological department established at the university. Hirshman founded the first eye clinic at the university in 1870 and established and personally financed two eye hospitals, a clinic, and a school for the blind. From 1886 he served as president of the Kharkiv Medical Society. He resigned from the university in 1905 to protest repression of students by the authorities. From 1908 he directed the municipal eye hospital, which he had founded. His published works deal with the physiology of color perception, the embolism of retinal vessels, and the treatment of trachoma. The Ukrainian Scientific Research Institute for Eye Diseases in Kharkiv and an eye hospital in Leningrad have been named in his honor.

Hirske [Hirs'ke]. V-19, DB II-5. City (1970 pop 15,805) in Voroshylovhrad oblast, founded as a mining town in 1898. It is administered by the Pervomaiske city soviet. Its main industry is anthracite mining; it also has a mineral-enrichment plant and a shoe factory.

Hist. Name originating in Kievan Rus' for a certain category of merchant. In Ukraine the term was used as early as 945 and as late as the 15th century and referred to foreign merchants trading in Ukraine, to Ukrainian merchants who went abroad to trade, and, by extension, to local merchants engaging in inter-town trade. A *hist* was a merchant of considerable means and influence, distinguished from ordinary traders by the greater extent of his business, the distances over which it was conducted, and his high social status. Such merchants were accorded a number of privileges: coastal (littoral) trade rights (*Strandrecht*); precedence in competition; and the right to to be judged by their own peers and their own law. A foreign *hist* could not acquire immovables, although this right belonged to the self-administered companies of foreign merchants, which ran hospices for their members.

Historical Museum of the Ukrainian SSR

Historical Museum of the Ukrainian SSR (Derzhavnyi istorychnyi muzei Ukrainskoi RSR). One of the richest museums in Ukraine, which originated with the City Museum of Antiquities and Art, founded in 1899 by M. Biliashivsky, M. Khvoika, and D. Shcherbakivsky. In 1924 it was renamed the T.H. Shevchenko All-Ukrainian Historical Museum and in 1965 it assumed its present name. The original holdings were divided in 1936, and most of the art collection was removed to form the Kiev Museum of Ukrainian Art. The museum is located in the old city of Kiev near the ruins of the Church of the Tithes, in an area that has been declared a state reserve. It has over 600,000 exponents, including archeological, ethnographic, numismatic items, paintings, sculptures, and old manuscripts, many of which are unique. The museum is divided into the following departments: primitive society, Scythian period, Kievan Rus' era, 14th–18th century Ukraine, 19th–early 20th-century Ukraine, and three departments covering the Soviet period. It has two branches, the *Museum of Historical Treasures of the Ukrainian SSR and the Kosyi Kaponir Museum, located on the site of the Kievan Cave Fortress and devoted to the revolutionary movement in the 19th and 20th centuries. The museum has published the journal *Pratsi* since 1958.

BIBLIOGRAPHY

Kyïvs'kyi derzhavnyi istorychnyi muzei: Korotkyi dovidnyk (Kiev 1958)

Derzhavnyi istorychnyi muzei Ukraïns'koï RSR: Putivnyk (Dozhovtnevyi period) (Kiev 1966)

Historical Society of Nestor the Chronicler (Istoricheskoe obshchestvo Nestora-letopistsa). Scholarly society founded in 1873 in Kiev. Named in honor of *Nestor, the first Ukrainian chronicler (11th–12th century), it was affiliated from 1876 with Kiev University and from 1921 with the All-Ukrainian Academy of Sciences. The society's members researched the archeology and history of Ukraine, particularly the history of law, religion, and literature in Ukraine and Russia, and promoted the development of historical studies, including the auxiliary disciplines. The society organized scholarly colloquiums, and published its members' research in *Trudy* and in **Chteniia v Istoricheskom obshchestve Nestora-letopistsa*. The society also maintained a library (1,500 vols in 1892).

Among those who headed the society were such eminent scholars as V. Ikonnikov, V. Antonovych, M. Vladimirsky-Budanov, M. Dashkevych, O. Lazarevsky, and M. Vasylenko. In the decade after the 1917 Revolution the society (by then bearing the Ukrainian name Istorychne tovarystvo Nestora-litopystsia) had 212 active members, and from 1920 to 1928 approximately 300 scholarly papers were presented at its meetings. In the early 1930s the society was abolished by the Soviet government.

BIBLIOGRAPHY

Narizhnyi, S. 'Istorychne Tovarystvo Nestora Litopystsia,' UI, 1975, nos 1–4

Historical songs. A genre of folk songs that presents historical events and individuals in a generalized, artistic manner with details, names, and facts that may be inaccurate. Ukrainian historical songs appeared at the same time as the *dumas, and perhaps even preceded them. They differ from the dumas in that they describe concrete historical events and figures; their story line is less developed, their emotive range is greater, and in them the lyrical element prevails over the epic element. Their strophe is rhythmically structured and consists usually of two or four lines. The melody is encompassed in one couplet and is repeated without modification in subsequent couplets.

The oldest cycle of historical songs dates back to the 16th century and depicts the Cossacks' struggle against the Tatars and Turks; the best known are the songs about Baida (D. Vyshnevetsky) of 1564, the capture of Varna of 1605, and the siege of the Pochaiv Monastery of 1675. A second cycle consists of songs about the Cossacks' struggle against Poland; the best known are the songs about B. *Khmelnytsky, the Battle of Zhovti Vody, the Battle of Berestechko, the curse on Khmelnytsky for the Tatar captivity of 1653, and about D. *Nechai, M. *Kryvonis, and S. *Morozenko. A third cycle deals with Russian oppression and includes songs about construction work on the St Petersburg canals, the destruction of the Zaporozhian Sich, and the death of a Cossack in Russian captivity ('Stoït' iavir nad vodoiu'). A fourth cycle consists of songs about the *Haidamaka uprising and includes songs such as the ballad about the cooper's daughter (Bondarivna) and the songs about S. Chaly, M. *Zalizniak, and M. Shvachka. There is also a large corpus of songs describing Cossack daily life: the relations between a Cossack and the community, with his family, and particularly with his beloved ('Oi, pushchu ia konychen'ka'). Songs on social questions constitute a special group: they deal with the struggle among different Cossack strata ('Oi, nastupaie ta chorna khmara'), with corvée and the oppression and resistance of the common people, and include songs about U. *Karmaliuk, L. *Kobylytsia, and O. *Dovbush.

The oral tradition of Western Ukraine has preserved the memory of L. Kossuth and the Hungarian revolution of 1848, and Austria's occupation of Bosnia. There are Hutsul and Boiko songs about the First World War, sung in a **kolomyika* meter of 4 + 4 + 6 syllables, songs about emigrating to America, and songs about seasonal migrant work.

The Revolution of 1917–20 was widely reflected in new dumas and songs such as the duma about the destruction of Liutenka by the Bolsheviks ('U vivtorok vrantsirano ...'). The Second World War, in particular the UPA struggle, is also reflected in the oral tradition. Songs about recent events, however, are not circulated widely and are quickly forgotten.

The best-known annotated study of Ukrainian historical songs is the two-volume collection compiled by M. *Drahomanov and V. Antonovych, *Istoricheskie pesni malorusskogo naroda* (Historical Songs of the Little-Russian People, 1874–5). Drahomanov's later compilations of and valuable commentaries to *Novi ukraïns'ki pisni pro hromads'ki spravy* (New Ukrainian Songs on Social Topics, 1881) and *Politychni pisni ukraïns'koho narodu 18–19 st.* (Political Songs of the Ukrainian People in the 18th and 19th Centuries, 2 vols, 1883, 1885) are other valuable contributions to the study of historical songs.

BIBLIOGRAPHY

Maksimovich, M. *Ukrainskie narodnye pesni* (Moscow 1834)
Plisets'kyi, M. *Ukraïns'ki dumy ta istorychni pisni* (Moscow 1944)
Ukraïns'ki narodni dumy ta istorychni pisni (Kiev 1955)
Rodina, M. 'Istorychni pisni,' in *Ukraïns'ka narodna poetychna tvorchist'*, vol 1 (Kiev 1958)
Istorychni pisni (Kiev 1961)
Stel'makh, M. (ed). *Narodni perlyny* (Kiev 1971)
Spivanky-khroniky novyny (Kiev 1972)

P. Odarchenko, D.H. Struk

Historiography. The study of the principles, theory, and history of historical writing. Historical writing in Ukraine dates back to the earliest *chronicles of the first half of the 11th century. In time the compiling of chronicles gave way to new forms of historical writing. Since the 19th century the history of Ukraine has been studied not only by Ukrainian but also by foreign – mostly Polish and Russian – scholars, research institutions, and learned societies. At the turn of the 20th century, M. *Hrushevsky proposed the first modern scheme of Ukrainian history that traced the national historical continuity of the Ukrainian people throughout their ethnic territories and a new period in Ukrainian historiography arose, defined by the predominance of the study of Ukraine as a nation-state. Contemporary Ukrainian historical scholarship outside Soviet Ukraine consists of various currents of this approach.

The Princely era (11th–13th centuries). Chronicles were compiled in Ukraine beginning in the first half of the 11th century, mostly in Kiev – first at the Saint Sophia Cathedral and then at the Kievan Cave Monastery and the Vydubychi Monastery – but also in Chernihiv, Pereiaslav, Volhynia, and Galicia. The earliest chronicles were chronological records of current events. Soon, however, compilations of chronicles appeared. Their authors' aims were closely connected with contemporary religious and political developments. The oldest chronicle collections are the Primary Chronicle or *Povist' vremennykh lit* (up to 1111), the *Kiev Chronicle (up to 1200), and the *Galician-Volhynian Chronicle (1201–92).

The Primary Chronicle is the outstanding work of Ukrainian medieval historiography. According to traditional belief and scholarly research, particularly that of A. Shakhmatov, its author was *Nestor, a monk of the Kievan Cave Monastery. It has been preserved in numerous codices and redactions. The most important are the *Laurentian (1377) and the *Hypatian (1425) chronicles. In the latter the Kiev and the Galician-Volhynian chronicles appear as continuations of the Primary Chronicle. The first attempt at a Ukrainian translation of the Primary Chronicle with annotations for the general reader was made by V. Blyznets and published in 1982.

The Lithuanian-Polish and early Cossack periods (14th–17th centuries). Chronicle writing continued in the 14th and 15th centuries, but very few examples have survived. In the 15th century the so-called Lithuanian or western Ruthenian chronicles appeared. The oldest of these, such as the *Suprasl Chronicle, are direct continuations of the compilations of the Kievan Rus' period and reflect the old Ukrainian historical tradition. The later ones, such as the *Bykhovets Chronicle of the late 16th century, reveal the influence of new sociopolitical conditions in the Grand Duchy of Lithuania. The Ukrainian historical tradition is represented by new Ukrainian chronicles of the 16th–17th centuries, particularly by the *Hustynia and the *Lviv Chronicle.

Cultural and national developments in the 16th and 17th centuries produced a large number of polemical religious and political treatises whose authors frequently referred to historical sources to support their claims and to defend the national and religious rights of the Ukrainian people. A national-historical orientation is evident in the works of I. Vyshensky, Yu. Rohatynets, S. Zyzanii, Kh. Filalet, I. Potii, Z. Kopystensky, M. Smotrytsky, Y. Boretsky, K. Sakovych, and scholars at the *Kievan Mohyla Academy, who tried to demonstrate a direct line of continuity in the historical process of the Ukrainian people.

In the 16th and 17th centuries foreign annalists and diplomats wrote memoirs and historico-geographic descriptions of Ukraine. Among them are G. Le Vasseur de *Beauplan's *Description d'Ukranie* (1650), E. *Lassota von Steblau's diary of 1573–94, and P. *Chevalier's *Histoire de la guerre des Cosaques contre la Pologne* (1663).

The Cossack-Hetman state (17th–18th centuries). The Khmelnytsky rebellion and the formation of the Ukrainian Cossack state had a great influence on the development of Ukrainian historiography. Historical writing transcended earlier parameters of the chronicle and acquired the traits of pragmatic, synthetic history. In the second half of the 17th century such works as T. *Safonovych's *Kroinika* (Chronicle, 1672), **Sinopsis* (1674), whose author is thought to be I. *Gizel, and L. *Bobolynsky's *Litopisets sii iest' kronika …* (This Chronicle Is a Chronology …, 1699) appeared. A new category of chronicle – the so-called Cossack chronicles – was compiled in the late 17th and early 18th centuries. These surveyed the events from 1648 to ca 1700 and include the *Samovydets (Eyewitness) Chronicle, written probably by R. Rakushka, and the chronicles of H. *Hrabianka and S. *Velychko.

Historical works viewing the Princely era as the ancestor of the Hetman state were written in the 18th century: the anonymous *Kratkoe opisanie Malorossii* (A Brief Description of Little Russia) in the 1730s; P. *Symonovsky's *Kratkoe opisanie o kozatskom malorossiiskom narode i o voennykh ego delakh* (Brief Description of the Cossack Little Russian People and Their Military Exploits, 1765); S. *Lukomsky's *Sobranie istoricheskoe* (Historical Compilation, 1770); A. *Rigelman's *Letopisnoe povestvovanie o Maloi Rossii i ee narode i kazakakh voobshche* (Chronicle Narrative about Little Russia and Its People and the Cossacks in General, 1785–6); O. *Shafonsky's *Chernigovskogo namestnichestva topograficheskoe opisanie* (Topographical Description of Chernihiv Vicegerency, 1788); M. *Antonovsky's *Istoriia o Maloi Rossii* (History of Little Russia, 1799); and Ya. *Markovych's survey of Rus' up to the 11th century, *Zapiski o Malorossii, ee zhiteliakh i proizvedeniiakh* (Notes on Little Russia, Its Inhabitants, and Events, vol 1, 1798).

In the second half of the 18th century and the early 19th century Archbishop H. Konysky, H. Poletyka, F. Tumansky, A. Chepa, V. Lomykovsky, M. Bantysh-Kamensky, V. Poletyka, M. Markiv, M. Berlynsky, I. Kvitka, Metropolitan E. Bolkhovitinov, and others worked on the history of Ukraine as a whole or on specific aspects of it. In the late 18th century foreign historical works on Ukraine appeared: J.-B. *Scherer's *Annales de la Petite Russie ou histoire des cosaques-zaporogues et des cosaques de l'Ukraine ou de la Petite Russie, depuis leur origine jusqu'à nos jours* (2 vols, 1788), K. Hammerdorfer's *Geschichte der ukrainischen und saporogischen Kosaken nebst einigen Nachrichten von der Verfassung und Sitten derselben* (1789), and J.-C. *Engel's *Geschichte der Ukraine und der ukrainischen Kosaken* (1796). Towards the end of the 18th century **Istoriia Rusov* (History of the Rus'es) was written by an anonymous author. This work exerted a considerable influence on the subsequent development of Ukrainian historiography.

The 19th century. Upholding the autonomist traditions of the Hetman period, Ukrainian historians in the first half of the 19th century continued producing synthetic, general works. D. *Bantysh-Kamensky's *Istoriia Maloi Rossii …* (History of Little Russia …, 4 vols, 1822) and M. *Markevych's *Istoriia Malorossii* (History of Little Russia, 5 vols, 1842–3) were systematic surveys of the history of Ukraine from ancient times to the end of the 18th century that concentrated on the Cossack-Hetman period. Under the influence of *Romanticism, Ukrainian historians focused their attention on the history and life of the common people. This infatuation with the folk (*narodnist*) eventually developed into an identification with the socially and economically downtrodden masses. Studied at first as an object of history, the 'people' was eventually viewed as the principal agent of historical development. With some exceptions, Ukrainian historiography of the middle and second half of the 19th century is dominated by the populist school, whose influence extended into the early decades of the 20th century. It found its most vivid expression in the works of M. Maksymovych, M. Kostomarov, P. Kulish, O. Lazarevsky, and V. Antonovych.

M. *Maksymovych, who wrote numerous studies in the history of Kievan Rus', the Cossack-Hetman period, and Cossack historiography, represented Romantic populism in Ukrainian historiography. M. *Kostomarov devoted himself mostly to research on the political history of Hetman Ukraine. His monographs on the Khmelnytsky period, the period of Ruin (1657–87), and the Mazepa period, as well as his studies of hetmans I. Vyhovsky, Yu. Khmelnytsky, and P. Polubotok, and of P. Mohyla, were based on a wealth of source materials. In his distinctive, masterly style, he presented a colorful but one-sided picture of Ukraine's history in the second half of the 17th and the first quarter of the 18th century. While he vividly described various spontaneous popular movements, Kostomarov underestimated the role of the hetmans, including B. Khmelnytsky, as state-builders. His historicophilosophical studies, particularly 'Mysli o federativnom nachale v drevnei Rusi' (Thoughts on the Federative Principle in Ancient Rus') and 'Dve russkie narodnosti' (Two Rus' Peoples), had an enormous impact on the subsequent development of Ukrainian historical thought.

P. *Kulish wrote mostly on the Cossack period; his distinctive works are *Istoriia vossoedineniia Rusi* (The History of the Reunification of Rus', 3 vols, 1873–7) and *Otpadenie Malorossii ot Pol'shi, 1340–1654* (The Secession of Little Russia from Poland, 3 vols, 1888–9). O. *Lazarevsky studied the socioeconomic history of Left-Bank Ukraine in the 17th and 18th centuries. He focused on the peasantry, the Cossack *starshyna*, the nobility, land tenure and colonization, and the administrative and judicial system of the Hetman state in numerous articles and in *Opisanie Staroi Malorossii* (A Description of Old Little Russia, 3 vols, 1888, 1893, 1902).

V. *Antonovych devoted most of his research to the socioeconomic history of Right-Bank Ukraine in the 16th–18th centuries and to the political history of the Lithuanian-Ruthenian state. He wrote a number of monographs on the history of the Cossacks and the Haidamakas, the peasantry, the nobility, cities and burghers, and the church. In his *Besidy pro chasy kozats'ki na Ukraïni* (Discourses about Cossack Times in Ukraine, 1897), which was republished as *Korotka istoriia Kozachchyny* (A Short History of the Cossack Period, 1912), he presented a general survey of Cossack history. His outstanding achievement was to found the Kiev school of history, which consisted of his former students at Kiev University: D. Bahalii, I. Lynnychenko, M. Dovnar-Zapolsky, M. Dashkevych, P. Holubovsky, V. Liaskoronsky, M. and O. Hrushevsky, V. Danylevych, O. Andriiashev, P. Ivanov, N. Molchanovsky, and others.

The Kiev school laid the foundations of modern Ukrainian historiography. Antonovych was closely linked with three centers of Ukrainian historical research: the *Kiev Archeographic Commission, the *Historical Society of Nestor the Chronicler, and the learned circle that published the journal **Kievskaia starina*. Historical research was also conducted at Kiev University and at the Kiev Theological Academy, where M. Petrov, S. Golubev, F. Titov, and other professors specialized in the history of the Ukrainian church, education, and culture and published their studies in **Trudy Kievskoi dukhovnoi akademii* (1860–1917).

In the second half of the 19th century historical research on Ukraine was conducted not only in Kiev, but also at Kharkiv University and by the Kharkiv Historical-Philological Society, at Odessa University and by the Odessa Society of History and Antiquities, and in Galicia at the Stauropegion Institute in Lviv. In Odessa A. Skalkovsky studied the history of the Zaporozhian Sich and southern Ukraine. In Galicia the prominent historians were D. Zubrytsky, Rev A. Petrushevych, I. Sharanevych, Yu. Tselevych, K. Zaklynsky, A. Dobriansky, Bishop Yu. Pelesh, and Rev S. Kachala. The Halytsko-Ruska Matytsia society published several volumes of historical studies. From 1886 O. Barvinsky published a series, entitled Rus'ka istorychna biblioteka, of historical studies by various authors. Outside Ukraine M. *Drahomanov did some historical research. His historicophilosophical works such as *'Propashchyi chas – Ukraïntsi pid Moskovs'kym tsarstvom, 1654–1876* (The Lost Epoch: Ukrainians under the Muscovite Tsardom, 1654–1876, 1909) had a great influence on the development of Ukrainian historical thought.

M. Hrushevsky and the early 20th century. By the end of the 19th century Ukrainian historians could boast of having produced a substantial number of monographs. The general growth of Ukrainian culture and the rise in national consciousness created a demand for a scholarly synthesis of Ukrainian history and for popular historical works. M. Hrushevsky introduced the first scholarly scheme of the history of the Ukrainian people on all its territories. The theoretical arguments for it were formulated in his article 'Zvychaina skhema "rus'koï" istoriï i sprava ratsional'noho ukladu istoriï skhidn'oho slov'ianstva' (The Traditional Scheme of 'Russian' History and the Problem of a Rational Ordering of the History of the Eastern Slavs) in *Sbornik stattei po slavianovedeniu*, vol 1 (1904). He applied it in his monumental work *Istoriia Ukraïny-Rusy* (The History of Ukraine-Rus', 10 vols, 1898–1937). His approach won acceptance not only among Ukrainian, but also among some foreign (particularly Russian and Polish), historians. Hrushevsky presented general surveys of Ukraine's history in his popular works, which were published in various editions and languages, beginning with *Ocherk istorii ukrainskogo naroda* (An Outline of the History of the Ukrainian People) in 1904. He wrote several hundred scholarly works on Ukrainian history, historiography, and the study of sources.

Hrushevsky's conception of history, which was based on the premise that social interests override state or political interests, was closely related to that of the populist school. However, the more he delved into history, and particularly into the Cossack and Khmelnytsky period, and the more he became involved in Ukrainian political life, the more weight he attributed to state and political factors.

One of Hrushevsky's important achievements was to found a school of history in Lviv consisting of such former students of his as S. Tomashivsky, M. Korduba, I. Krypiakevych, I. Dzhydzhora, I. Krevetsky, V. Herasymchuk, B. Barvinsky, and O. Terletsky. Most of their studies, which were primarily of the Lithuanian-Polish and Cossack-Hetman periods, were published by the *Shevchenko Scientific Society (NTSh). The research promoted in Lviv was all-Ukrainian in scope and dealt with all regions of Ukraine. Consequently historians not only of Western Ukraine, but also from Russian-dominated Ukraine – O. Hrushevsky, V. Lypynsky, V. Domanytsky, M. Vasylenko, V. Modzalevsky, O. Lototsky, M. Slabchenko, V. Barvinsky, and others – contributed to the publications of the society. After the 1905 Revolution, Hrushevsky established in Kiev a new important center of historical research – the *Ukrainian Scientific Society (UNT), which published the periodicals *Zapysky UNT*, *Ukraïna*, and *Naukovyi zbirnyk*. Other scholars associated with this center were O. Levytsky, I. Kamanin, V. Shcherbyna, L. Dobrovolsky, V. Danylevych, A. Yakovliv, D. Doroshenko, M. Stadnyk, A. Berlo, Ye. Kivlitsky, and O. Shramchenko.

Historical research, mostly on Left-Bank and Slobidska Ukraine, was continued at Kharkiv University and by the Kharkiv Historical-Philological Society by D. Bahalii, D. Miller, M. Plokhynsky, V. Barvinsky, M. Maksymeiko, and others. In Odessa the university and the Odessa Society of History and Antiquities remained the main research centers. Their best-known scholars were I. Lynnychenko, M. Slabchenko, and P. Klepatsky. In Katerynoslav the Archival Commission focused on the history of the Zaporozhian Sich and southern Ukraine and published the works of such researchers as D. Yavornytsky, D. Doroshenko, and V. Bidnov. In Chernihiv the Archival Commission had such associates as V. Modzalevsky, P. Doroshenko, and A. Verzylov. I. Pavlovsky, L. Padalka, V. Parkhomenko, and others were associated with the Poltava Archival Commission. O. Fotynsky was active in Zhytomyr, and Rev Yu. Sitsynsky and P. Klymenko in Kamianets-Podilskyi. In Nizhen the local Historical Philological Society published studies by such scholars as M. Berezhkov and Yu. Maksymovych. P. Korolenko and F. Shcherbyna worked in the Kuban. The Tavriian Scholarly Archival Commission in the Crimea published studies by O. Markevych and others.

The history of Ukraine in Russian and Polish historiography. In the 19th and 20th centuries a number of foreign scholars contributed significantly to Ukrainian historiography. Most Russian and Polish historians, however, subsumed and fragmented the history of Ukraine within a scheme of history based on various concepts of the Russian or Polish states. In spite of their tendentiousness, however, Russian and Polish researchers brought forth a great deal of new documentary material, and some of them made a substantial contribution to Ukrainian historiography. Among Russian historians the most prominent investigators of Ukraine's past were S. Solovev, G. Karpov, A. Lappo-Danilevsky, A. Shakhmatov, E. Golubinsky, M. Liubavsky, A. Presniakov, M. Priselkov, V. Eingorn, P. Zhukovich, E. Shmurlo, B. Grekov, V. Picheta, and G. Vernadsky. The best Polish specialists were M. Grabowski, E. Rulikowski, J. Bartoszewicz, T. Stecki, K. Szajnocha, A. Jabłonowski, J. Rolle (Dr Antoni J.), M. Dubiecki, T. Korzon, K. Pułaski, J. Tretiak, L. Kubala, M. Handelsman, K. Chodynicki, W. Tomkiewicz, S. Kuczyński, O. Halecki, and H. Paszkiewicz.

Modern Ukrainian historiography. Building on the research of earlier periods, modern Ukrainian historians have demonstrated that there has been a historical continuity from the Princely Rus' state of the 10th–14th centuries through the Hetman state of the 17th–18th centuries to the national Ukrainian state revived in 1917–20. This tradition of national statehood has become the determining idea in modern Ukrainian historiography. Its founders were V. Lypynsky, S. Tomashivsky, and D. Doroshenko.

V. *Lypynsky studied the history of the Ukrainian nobility and devoted much attention to Hetman B. Khmelnytsky's rule. His most important works are *Szlachta ukraińska i jej udział w życiu narodu ukraińskiego* (The Ukrainian Nobility and Its Participation in the Life of the Ukrainian People, 1909), *Z dziejów Ukrainy* (On the History of Ukraine, 1912), and *Ukraïna na perelomi, 1657–9* (Ukraine at the Turning Point, 1657–9, 1920). Lypynsky believed that the task of modern Ukrainian historiography was to revive the historical tradition of the Hetman state.

S. *Tomashivsky wrote a number of important source studies of the Hetman period before turning his attention to medieval Ukraine. His *Ukraïns'ka istoriia, 1: Starynni i seredni viky* (Ukrainian History, 1: The Ancient and Medieval Periods, 1919) is a synthetic interpretation of the period.

The interwar years

Soviet Ukraine. After the brief spell of Ukrainian independence from 1917 to 1920, Ukrainain historians in Galicia, Soviet Ukraine, and abroad continued their research in spite of various unfavorable circumstances. They refined and elaborated Hrushevsky's scheme of Ukrainian history by supplementing it with the modern principle of statehood. In the 1920s historical research flourished in the Ukrainian SSR owing mostly to the efforts of M. Hrushevsky, who in 1924 became a central figure at the All-Ukrainian Academy of Sciences (VUAN) in Kiev. He edited a number of periodicals that played a key role in Ukrainian historiography – **Ukraïna* (1924–30), **Za sto lit* (1927–30), **Zapysky Istorychno-filolohichnoho viddilu VUAN* (1925–30), and *Naukovyi zbirnyk Istorychnoï sektsiï VUAN* (1924–9) – as well as the publications of the *Archeographic Commission. Besides his own works the academy published the works of his associates, such as O. Hrushevsky, Y. Hermaize, P. Klymenko, V. Danylevych, V. Shcherbyna, L. Dobrovolsky, and K. Lazarevska, and the works of his students S. Shamrai, O. Baranovych, M. Tkachenko, V. Yurkevych.

The second major centers of historical research in the 1920s were the institutions in Kiev and Kharkiv directed by D. *Bahalii. Associates and fellows of these centers contributed important studies on 17th- and 18th-century Ukraine: the works of Bahalii himself and of O. Ohloblyn (economic and political history), N. Polonska-Vasylenko (the Zaporozhian Cossacks and southern Ukraine), V. Romanovsky, V. Barvinsky, N. Mirza-Avakiants, V. Dubrovsky, O. Bahalii-Tatarynova, V. Bazylevych, M. Horban, D. Solovii, A. Kozachenko, and others. M. *Vasylenko and his associates – L. Okinshevych, I. Cherkasky, V. Novytsky, M. Tyshchenko, V. Hryshko – made significant contributions to the history of Ukrainian law and the state system, while such scholars as K. Vobly, A. Yaroshevych, and Ye. Stashevsky developed the field of economic history.

The Odessa historical center under the direction of M. *Slabchenko also accomplished important work. Besides Slabchenko himself, a specialist in socioeconomic and legal history, scholars such as Ye. Zahorovsky and O. Riabinin-Skliarevsky were active there. Other, less important, centers of Ukrainian historiography were Dnipropetrovske, with such scholars as D. *Yavornytsky and V. Parkhomenko; Poltava, with P. Klepatsky and others; Nizhen, with M. Petrovsky and A. Yershov; and Chernihiv, with P. Fedorenko and others. The Marxist historical school was centered mainly in Kharkiv and was led by M. *Yavorsky and his associates and students M. Rubach, Z. Hurevych, and M. Svidzinsky. It was rather isolated from the mainstream of Ukrainian historiography in the 1920s and 1930s.

In the 1930s the Soviet authorities dissolved almost all the historical research centers. Many historians were arrested or dismissed from work and the normal development of historical studies in Soviet Ukraine was disrupted.

Galicia and the emigration. In the interwar years many historians worked in Galicia in spite of difficult material circumstances and political restrictions. Most of them, including S. Tomashivsky, I. *Krypiakevych, M. *Korduba, O. Terletsky, V. Herasymchuk, I. Krevetsky, B. Barvinsky, M. Chubaty, M. Andrusiak, Rev Y. Skruten, and Rev T. Kostruba, were associated with the NTSh. Their works were published in *ZNTSh, Stara Ukraïna, Analecta Ordinis S. Basilii Magni*, and *Bohosloviia*. In Transcarpathia Rev V. Hadzhega and A. Hodinka conducted research, and in Bukovyna, Ye. Kozak and M. Haras.

Outside Ukraine the main émigré institutions were the Ukrainian Free University, the Ukrainian Historical-Philological Society, and the Museum of Ukraine's Struggle for Independence in Prague; the Ukrainian Scientific Institute in Berlin; and the Ukrainian Scientific Institute and the Ukrainian Military History Society in Warsaw. Many prominent Ukrainian historians became émigrés: M. Hrushevsky (until 1924), V. Lypynsky, S. Tomashivsky (for a time), D. Doroshenko, A. Yakovliv, R. Lashchenko, V. Bidnov, V. Prokopovych, E. Borschak, O. Shulhyn, B. Krupnytsky, S. Narizhny, D. Olianchyn, Mykhailo Antonovych, and I. Losky. Some of them studied archival materials in Western Europe, which hitherto had been scarcely known in Ukrainian historiography. This research resulted in the publication of valuable studies including D. *Doroshenko's synthetic works in Ukrainian history and historiography, A. *Yakovliv's historiographic studies, B. *Krupnytsky's works on I. Mazepa and P. Orlyk, E. *Borschak's studies of H. and P. Orlyk and Franco-Ukrainian relations, and D. *Olianchyn's investigations of Ukrainian-German relations in the 17th and 18th centuries.

The postwar period

Soviet Ukraine. After the war independent historical research in Ukraine was again restricted. Institutions such as the *Institute of History of the Academy of Sciences of the Ukrainian SSR were staffed by such historians of the older and Soviet generations as I. Krypiakevych, M. Petrovsky, M. Rubach, O. Baranovych, K. Huslysty, F. Yastrebov, M. Suprunenko, P. Lavrov, V. Diadychenko, F. Los, K. Stetsiuk, V. Holobutsky, I. Hurzhii, and I. Boiko. Quite a number of works on Ukrainian history were published each year, and **Ukraïns'kyi istorychnyi zhurnal* began appearing in 1957. Yet, Soviet Ukrainian historiography has been mostly subservient to the political goals and policies of the Soviet government. The interests of the Communist Russian state determine the ideology, methodology, subject-matter, and even the phraseology of the historians. The state dictates what the results of research should be and what conclusions should be drawn. Consequently the scholarly value of general historical surveys, such as *Istoriia Ukraïns'koï RSR* (History of the Ukrainian SSR, 2 vols, 1953, 1958, and in 8 vols [1977–9]), of monographs, such as I. Krypiakevych's *Bohdan Kmel'nyts'kyi* (1954), and even of collections of documents, such as *Vossoedinenie Ukrainy s Rossiei* (The Reunification of Ukraine with Russia, 3 vols, 1954), is diminished considerably.

In 1954 Hrushevsky's castigated scheme was formally replaced by the CC CPSU-approved 'Theses on the 300th Anniversary of Ukraine's Reunification with Russia' as the normative framework of historical interpretation. This new scheme is based on the officially recognized concept of one Rus' people, out of which the Russian, Ukrainian, and Belorussian nations developed. The theses on reunification thus posit a unitary Russian state and thereby rule out the existence of the Hetman state and impute a common path of national development for Russians, Belorussians, and Ukrainians culminating in tsarist Russia and now in the USSR. The few Soviet historians – M. *Braichevsky, for example – who have openly rejected this theory have been severely criticized and even repressed.

Since 1954 the only Soviet surveys of Ukrainian historiography that have appeared are M. Marchenko's *Ukraïns'ka istoriohrafiia (z davnikh chasiv do seredyny XIX st.)* (Ukrainian Historiography [from Ancient Times to the Mid-19th Century], 1959) and, a quarter of a century later, L. Kovalenko's *Istoriohrafiia istoriï URSR* (Historiography of the History of the Ukrainian SSR, 1983) and A. Santsevych's *Ukraïns'ka radians'ka istoriohrafiia (1945–1982)* (Soviet Ukrainian Historiography [1945–82], 1984). The major source of general historical information that has appeared is *Radians'ka entsyklopediia istoriï Ukraïny* (The Soviet Encyclopedia of the History of Ukraine, 4 vols, 1969–72). Several valuable annuals have been published: *Istorychni dzherela ta ïkh vykorystannia* (1966–72), *Kyïvs'ka starovyna* (1973), *Istoriohrafichni doslidzhennia v Ukraïns'kii RSR* (1968–72), and *Istorychni doslidzhennia: Vitchyzniana istoriia* (1975–).

Some of the contemporary historians in Soviet Ukraine are O. Apanovych, Ya. Dashkevych, Yu. Hamretsky, H. Herbilsky, V. Hrabovetsky, Ya. Isaievych, P. Kalenychenko, O. Karpenko, L. Kovalenko, O. Kompan, S. Korolivsky, M. Kotliar, M. Kravets, M. Leshchenko, A. Lykholat, P. Mykhailyna, I. Rybalka, A. Santsevych, P. Tolochko, V. Sarbei, A. Shlepakov, H. Serhiienko, S. Tymoshchuk, S. Vysotsky, and Ya. Zapasko.

Scholarship in the West. Among the older Ukrainian historians who found themselves in Western Europe or North America after the war were M. Andrusiak, E. Borschak, Rev A. Velyky, I. Vytanovych, M. Zhdan, P. Hrytsak, V. Hryshko, D. Doroshenko, V. Dubrovsky, B. Krupnytsky, Rev I. Nazarko, O. Ohloblyn, L. Okinshevych, D. Olianchyn, N. Polonska-Vasylenko, Rev Y. Skruten, M. Chubaty, O. Shulhyn, A. Yakovliv, K. Pankivsky, and M. Stakhiv. The chief publishers of works in history have been the Shevchenko Scientific Society, the Ukrainian Academy of Arts and Sciences, the Ukrainian Free University, and the Basilian scholarly center in Rome. Some of the outstanding publications of the immediate postwar period were E. Borschak's *La Légende historique de l'Ukraine. Istorija Rusov* (1949), B. Krupnytsky's *Het'man Danylo Apostol i ioho doba* (Hetman Danylo Apostol and His Period, 1948), L. Okinshevych's 'Znachne viis'kove tovarystvo v Ukraïni-Het'manshchyni XVII–XVIII st.' (Notable Military Fellows in Hetman Ukraine of the 17th–18th Century, *ZNTSh*, vol 157 [1948]), A. Yakovliv's 'Ukraïns'kyi kodeks 1743 roku' (The Ukrainian Code of 1743, *ZNTSh*, vol 159 [1949]), and N. Polonska-Vasylenko's *Settlement of the Southern Ukraine, 1750–1775* (AUA, vols 4–5 [1955]). Ukrainian historians have collaborated on various compendiums and journals, as well as the encyclopedias published in the West.

Many postwar Ukrainian historians outside Ukraine have worked at various universities and other institutions, where they have specialized in different areas of Ukrainian and East-European history. Historians in the United States include J. Basarab, M. Bohachevsky-Chomiak, Y. Bilinsky, N. Chirovsky, B. Dmytryshyn, O. Dombrovsky, O. Fedyshyn, G. Gajecky, S. Horak, T. Hunczak, I. Kamenetsky, R. Klymkevych, Z. Kohut, T. Mackiw, M. Palij, Ya. Pelensky, J. Reshetar, R. Solchanyk, O. Sonevytsky, P. Stercho, F. Sysyn, R. Szporluk, and L. Wynar. O. Pritsak holds the Hrushevsky Chair of Ukrainian History at Harvard University, where the Harvard Ukrainian Research Institute publishes *Harvard Ukrainian Studies*. In 1965 the Ukrainian Historical Society was founded in the United States; it publishes the journal *Ukraïns'kyi istoryk*. In Canada specialists in Ukrainian history include M. Antonovych, A. Baran, O. Gerus, J.-P. Himka, O. Pidhainy, T. Prymak, I.L. Rudnytsky, R. Serbyn, O. Subtelny, and S. Velychenko. P. Magocsi holds the Chair of Ukrainian Studies at the University of Toronto, which specializes in history. The Canadian Institute of Ukrainian Studies has published historical monographs and conference proceedings, as well as articles in its *Journal of Ukrainian Studies*. In Europe the best-known Ukrainian historians include B. Kentrzhynsky, V. Kosyk, A. Zhukovsky, D. Zlepko, and O. Vintoniak. Non-Ukrainian historians who have published significant works on Ukrainian history include A. Adams, J. Armstrong, R. Conquest, L. Gordon, J. Mace, C. Manning, and R. Sullivant in the United States; W. Allen in England; and R. Portal and G. Luciani in France. Among Polish historians who have devoted their attention to Ukrainian history are W. Serczyk, L. Podhorodecki, A. Podraza, J. Radziejowski, J. Kozik, A. Poppe, R. Torzecki, and Z. Wójcik. Russian historians have also written on Ukrainian history; among them are E. Druzhinina, G. Marakhov, V. Mavrodin, V. Pashuto, B. Rybakov, and M. Tikhomirov. (See also *Archeography and *Church, historiography of the Ukrainian.)

BIBLIOGRAPHY

Antonovich, V. *Istochniki dlia istorii Iuzhnoi i Zapadnoi Rossii* (Kiev 1881)

Klepats'kyi, P. *Ohliad dzherel do istoriï Ukraïny*, vol 1 (Kamianets-Podilskyi 1920)

Bahalii, D. *Narys ukraïns'koï istoriohrafiï*, 2 vols (Kiev 1923, 1925)

Doroshenko, D. *Ohliad ukraïns'koï istoriohrafiï* (Prague 1923)

Kryp'iakevych, I. *Ukraïns'ka istoriohrafiia* (Lviv 1923)

Kalynovych, I. 'Ukraïns'ka istorychna bibliohrafiia za 1914–1923 rr.,' *ZNTSh*, 134–5 (1924)

Krevets'kyi, I. 'Ukraïns'ka istoriohrafiia na perelomi,' *ZNTSh*, 134–5 (1924)

Andrusiak, M. 'Ukraïns'ka istoriohrafiia 1921–1930 rr.,' *Litopys Chervonoï kalyny*, 9–10 (1932)

Narizhnyi, S. 'Ukraïns'ka istoriohrafiia,' in *Ukraïns'ka zahal'na entsyklopediia*, vol 3 (Lviv-Stanyslaviv-Kolomyia 1935)

Korduba, M. *La Littérature historique soviétique ukrainienne. Compte-rendu 1917–1931* (Warsaw 1938; 2nd edn, Munich 1972)

Doroshenko, D. 'A Survey of Ukrainian Historiography' and Ohloblyn, O. 'Ukrainian Historiography 1917–1956,' AUA, 5–6 (1957)

Krupnyts'kyi, B. *Ukraïns'ka istorychna nauka pid Sovietamy (1920–1950)* (Munich 1957)

Marchenko, M. *Ukraïns'ka istoriohrafiia (z davnikh chasiv do seredyny XIX st.)* (Kiev 1959)

Kryp'iakevych, I. *Dzherala z istoriï Halychyny periodu feodalizmu (do 1772 r.)* (Kiev 1962)

Ohloblyn, O. *Dumky pro suchasnu ukraïns'ku soviets'ku istoriohrafiiu* (New York 1963)

Vynar, L. 'Ohliad istorychnoï literatury pro pochatky ukraïns'koï kozachchyny,' UI, 1965, nos 1–4

Santsevych, A. *Problemy istoriï Ukraïny pisliavoiennoho periodu v radians'kii istoriohrafiï* (Kiev 1967)

Kryp'iakevych, I. 'Narys metodyky istorychnykh doslidzhen',' *UIZh*, 1967, nos 2–4, 7–10

Pidhainy, O. *Ukrainian Historiography and the Great East-European Revolution* (Toronto and New York 1968)

Lytvynenko, M. *Dzherela istoriï Ukraïny XVIII st.* (Kharkiv 1970)

Chubatyi, M. *Ukraïns'ka istorychna nauka: Ïï rozvytok ta dosiahnennia* (Philadelphia 1971)

Diadychenko, V.; Los', F.; Sarbei, V. *Rozvytok istorychnoï nauky v Ukraïns'kii RSR (1945–1970)* (Kiev 1972)

Hurzhii, I.; Kalenychenko, P. (eds). *Rozvytok istorychnoï nauky na Ukraïni za roky radians'koï vlady* (Kiev 1973)

Mel'nyk, L. *Rozvytok naukovoho piznannia istoriï* (Kiev 1983)

Kovalenko, L. *Istoriohrafiia istoriï Ukraïns'koï RSR vid naidavnishykh chasiv do Velykoï Zhovtnevoï Sotsialistychnoï Revoliutsiï* (Kiev 1983)

Santsevych, A. *Ukraïns'ka radians'ka istoriohrafiia (1945–1982)* (Kiev 1984)

O. Ohloblyn, A. Zhukovsky

History, Institute of the Academy of Sciences of the Ukrainian SSR. See Institute of History of the Academy of Sciences of the Ukrainian SSR.

History Library of the Ukrainian SSR (Istorychna biblioteka URSR). A library in Kiev specializing in historical literature. Founded in 1939 on the basis of several religious libraries in Kiev, the building was destroyed during the Second World War and most of its books (approx 500,000 volumes) were stolen or perished. The library reopened in 1952. In 1979 its collection consisted of approximately 639,400 volumes relating to the history of the Ukrainian SSR, Marxist-Leninist theory, the history of the CPSU and the USSR, archeology, numismatics, ethnography, philosophy, the history of art and literature, and the history of religion. The department of rare books contains some 67,000 books and manuscripts of Ukrainian and foreign origin.

History of Ukraine. Information on the earliest history of Ukraine is derived from archeological records and from general descriptions of the early Slavs by Greek, Roman, and Arabic historians. Beginning with the Middle Ages, the history of the Ukrainians can be divided into discernible periods: (1) the so-called Princely era of *Kievan Rus' and the Principality of *Galicia-Volhynia; (2) the period of the *Lithuanian-Ruthenian state; (3) the period of the *Cossacks and the *Hetman state; (4) the national and cultural renaissance of the 19th century; (5) the Ukrainian nation-state of 1917–21; (6) the interwar occupation of Ukrainian territories by four foreign powers; and finally (7) the consolidation of most Ukrainian ethnic territory into a Soviet Ukrianian state. Because more than one political state often ruled Ukraine's territories simultaneously and, at times, several Ukrainian governments coexisted (eg, those of the Hetman state and of Right-Bank Ukraine), dealing with Ukraine's history presents many difficulties. Furthermore Western Ukraine experienced a historical development separate from that of central and eastern Ukraine, resulting in the evolution of the historical-political entities of *Galicia, *Volhynia, *Bukovyna, and *Transcarpathia. The only denominator unifying all of Ukraine's lands and state formations has been the Ukrainian people and its linguistic, social, cultural, and religious specificities.

The Stone Age. The oldest traces of human existence in Ukraine, dating from the early *Paleolithic Period (ca 300,000 BC) of the Stone Age, were discovered near the village of Luka-Vrublivetska on the Dniester River in 1946. Archeological evidence indicates that by the Upper Paleolithic Period (40,000–15,000 BC) almost all of Ukraine was inhabited by clans of hunters and gatherers. During the *Mesolithic Period (10,000–7,000 BC) Ukraine's inhabitants engaged in fishing, had domesticated dogs, and used the bow and arrow; the first tribal units then appeared. During the *Neolithic period (7,000–3,000 BC) primitive *agriculture and *animal husbandry arose, as did pottery and weaving. These activities developed further during the Copper and *Bronze ages.

The Copper and Bronze ages. The *Trypilian culture (first discovered in 1896), which existed from 4,000 to 2,000 BC in the Dnieper and Dniester basins of Right-Bank Ukraine, was the most advanced culture during this period on the territory of Ukraine. Many other synchronous cultures evolved from the late 4th to the early 1st millennium BC. The Left-Bank steppe and forest-steppe were inhabited by the agricultural-pastoral tribes of the *Pit-Grave, *Catacomb, *Serednyi Stih, *Marianivka, *Timber-Grave, and *Bondarykha cultures. Right-Bank Polissia and parts of the forest-steppe were the home of the *Middle-Dnieper and *Bilohrudivka cultures. The tribes of the Corded-Pottery, Funnel-Ware, *Globular-Amphora, *Trzciniec, and *Lusatian cultures inhabited Volhynia and parts of Podilia. The *Komariv, *Vysotske, and *Noua cultures evolved in the Dniester Basin, and the *Stanove culture, in Transcarpathia.

The Iron Age. During the *Iron Age, significant changes occurred in the material culture of Ukraine's inhabitants, particularly in agriculture, metallurgy, and commerce. In the early 1st millennium BC Iranian tribes – *Cimmerians – appeared on the territory of the Dnieper and Boh basins in southern Ukraine. Archeological evidence shows that they, like the tribes of the indigenous Timber-Grave, Bilohrudivka, Bondarykha, and *Chornyi Lis cultures, had iron implements. In the 8th century BC, the Cimmerians were displaced by the *Scythians, tribes of nomadic horsemen from Central Asia that intermingled with and assimilated the indigenous peoples and founded an empire that lasted until the 2nd century AD. The Scythians' political and economic hegemony in the region was established after they repulsed the invasion of King Darius of Persia in 513 BC.

From the 7th century BC, Greek city-states founded trading colonies on the northern Pontic littoral. With time these towns became independent poleis (see *Ancient states on the northern Black sea coast), which interacted and traded with the other peoples of the region, particularly the Scythians, *Taurians, *Maeotians, *Sindians, and *Getae. In the late 5th century BC, the Hellenic towns on the Kerch and Taman peninsulas of the Crimea united to form the *Bosporan Kingdom. In the 1st century BC the Hellenic states were annexed by the Romans and remained under Roman rule until the invasions of new nomadic peoples: the *Sarmatians, *Alans, and *Roxolani, Iranian-speaking tribes from Central Asia that

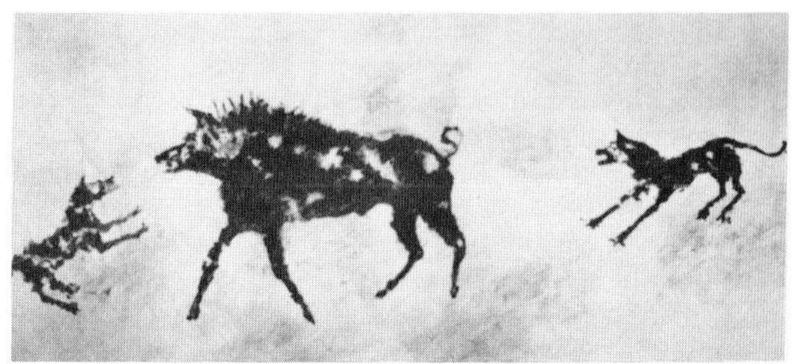

Wild Boar Hunt; detail from a wall painting in the Scythian tomb near Neapolis

had appeared in the Pontic steppes in the 4th century BC and had conquered most of the Scythians' territories by the 2nd century BC; and the *Goths, Germanic tribes that arrived in the late 2nd century AD from the Baltic region and conquered the Sarmatians and other indigenous peoples. In the 3rd century the Goths waged war against the Romans and took most of their colonies on the Pontic littoral. Gothic rule collapsed in 375 under the onslaught of the *Huns; most of the Goths fled west beyond the Danube, and only a small number remained in the Crimea.

The Hunnic invasion of Europe initiated what is known as the great migration of peoples from the East. After the Huns, the Ukrainian steppes were invaded by the Bulgars in the 5th century, the *Avars in the 6th, the *Khazars in the 7th, the Magyars in the 9th, the *Pechenegs and *Torks in the 10th and 11th, the *Cumans in the 11th and 12th, and the *Mongols in the 13th.

By the 2nd century BC, Ukraine's forest-steppe regions, Polisia, and part of the steppe were inhabited by the agricultural proto-Slavic tribes of the *Zarubyntsi culture; Western Ukraine was populated by the tribes of the *Przeworsk culture. By the 2nd century AD, the tribes of the *Cherniakhiv culture populated large parts of the Ukrainian forest-steppe. Most scholars consider the territory bounded by the middle Dnieper River, the Prypiat River, the Carpathian Mountains, and the Vistula River to be the cradle of the ancient *Slavs. By the 4th century AD, the Eastern Slavs of Ukraine had organized themselves into a tribal alliance called the *Antes, whose domain stretched from the Dniester to the Don River. In the early 6th century the Antes established relations with the *Byzantine Empire, against which they also waged war in the Balkans. Their state lasted until the 7th century, when it was destroyed by the Avars and most of the Antes fled north to resettle in the upper Dnieper Basin.

By the 6th century AD, the ancestors of the Ukrainians were divided into several tribal groups: the *Polianians on the banks of the Dnieper River around Kiev; the *Siverianians in the Desna, Seim, and Sula basins; the *Derevlianians in Polisia between the Teterev and Prypiat basins; the *Dulibians, later called *Buzhanians and *Volhynians, in the Buh Basin; the *White Croatians in Subcarpathia; the *Ulychians in the Boh Basin; and the *Tivertsians in the Dniester Basin. These tribes had ties with the proto-Belorussian *Drehovichians, the proto-Russian *Radimichians, *Viatichians, and *Krivichians, and the Baltic tribes to the north; the Bulgarian Kingdom and the Byzantine Empire to the south; the Khazar Khaganate and the Volga Bulgars to the east; and the proto-

Polish Vistulans and Mazovians, Great Moravia, and the Magyars to the west. They also traded with more distant lands via international trade routes: the route 'from the Varangians to the Greeks' linking the Baltic and Black seas mostly via the Dnieper River and thus joining Scandinavia with Byzantium; the east-west route from the Caspian Sea to Kiev and then to Cracow, Prague, and Regensburg, thus joining the Arab world with central and western Europe; and the route linking the Caspian and Baltic seas and thus the Arab world with Scandinavia. Because they lived along or at the crossroads of these important trade routes, the proto-Ukrainian tribes played an important economic and political role in eastern Europe.

The tribes shared a common proto-Slavic language and pagan beliefs. They built their agricultural settlements around wooden fortified towns. *Kiev was the capital of the Polianians; *Chernihiv, of the Siverianians; Iskorosten (*Korosten), of the Derevlianians; Volyn (Horodok on the Buh), of the Dulibians; and *Peresichen, of the Ulychians. The Polianians were the most developed of the tribes; according to the Rus' Primary Chronicle, their prince, *Kyi, founded Kiev in the late 6th century. Kiev's strategic position at the crossroads of the trade routes contributed to its rapid development into a powerful economic, cultural, and political center. The tribal princes, however, were not able to transform their tribal alliances into viable states and thus protect their independence. In the early 8th century, the Polianians and Siverians were forced to recognize the supremacy of the Khazar Khaganate and to pay tribute. In the mid-9th century, the warlike *Varangians from Scandinavia invaded and conquered the tribal territories, and established the foundations for *Kievan Rus' state with its capital in Kiev.

The Princely era. The leading role in this state until its demise some five centuries later was played by the princes (whence the name of this period). The Primary Chronicle states that the Eastern Slavs had invited the Varangians to rule over them. This source was later used to substantiate the so-called *Norman theory of the origins of Kievan Rus'. The *Riurykids, the dynasty that ruled Rus' and other East European territories until 1596, originated with the Varangian prince *Riuryk. The most outstanding Varangian ruler of Rus' was Prince *Oleh (Oleg), who succeeded Riuryk in Novgorod ca 879. In 882 he killed *Askold and Dyr and took power in Kiev, which became the capital of his realm. He then conquered most of the East Slavic tribes, thus becoming the undisputed ruler of a vast and mighty state. After consolidating his power and eliminating the influence of the Khazars on his territory, Oleh undertook an expedition against Constantinople, forcing it to sue for peace and to pay a large indemnity in 907. In 911 he concluded an advantageous trade agreement and laid the basis for permanent trade links between Rus' and the Byzantine Empire.

The efforts of Oleh's successor *Ihor (Igor, 912–45) to gain control of the northern Pontic littoral led to war with Byzantium and to a new treaty with Constantinople: the trade privileges obtained by Oleh were significantly curtailed. Throughout his reign, Ihor tried to consolidate the central power of Kiev by pacifying the rebellious neighboring tribes. The Derevlianians, who fiercely defended their autonomy, captured and killed Ihor during one of his attempts to extort tribute from them.

Ihor's widow *Olha (Olga, 945–62), who was possibly a Slav, ruled Rus' until her son Sviatoslav I Ihorevych came of age. During her reign the Slavic members of her court gained ascendancy. Olha converted to Christianity by 957. She established direct contacts with Constantinople and links with West European rulers.

*Sviatoslav (962–72), known as 'the Conqueror,' expanded the borders and might of Rus'. He waged a successful war against the Volga Bulgars and destroyed the Khazar Kaganate. The elimination of the Khazars had negative consequences, however: it opened the way for the invasion of Rus' by new Asiatic tribes. Sviatoslav expanded the frontiers of his realm to the Caucasus and then conquered the Bulgarians (967–8), establishing Pereiaslavets on the Danube. Threatened by his encroachments, Constantinople declared war on Sviatoslav. After initial victories in Macedonia, Sviatoslav was defeated and forced out of Bulgaria in 971. On his way back to Kiev with a small retinue, he was ambushed by Pecheneg mercenaries of the Byzantines near the Dnieper Rapids and died in battle.

*Yaropolk I Sviatoslavych (972–80) ruled over Kiev after his father's death. He wanted to unite the entire kingdom under his rule and succeeded in killing Oleh, but his brother Volodymyr escaped and hired Varangian mercenaries, with whose help he killed Yaropolk.

Encolpion with St Borys, from the Church of the Tithes in Kiev

*Volodymyr I the Great (980–1015) thus united under his rule the lands acquired by his predecessors and proceeded to extend his territory. He waged an ongoing struggle from 988 to 997 with the Pechenegs, who were constantly attacking Rus' towns and villages, and built a network of fortresses to protect Kiev.

After his conquests, Volodymyr ruled the largest kingdom in Europe, stretching from the Baltic Sea in the north to the Azov and Black seas in the south and the Volga River in the east to the Carpathian Mountains in the west. To administer his scattered lands, he created a dynastic seniority system of his clan and members of his retinue (*druzhyna*), in which the role of the Varangians was diminished. To give his vast domain a unifying element Volodymyr adopted Byzantine Christianity as the state religion, was baptized, and married Anna, the sister of the Byzantine emperor Basil II.

The official *Christianization of Ukraine in 988 had important consequences for the life of Kievan Rus' (see also *Church, history of the Ukrainian). The unity of the state and the authority of the grand prince were strengthened. *Byzantine art, architecture, literature, and teaching were introduced and adopted by the princes, boyars, and upper classes. Many churches and monasteries were built, and the *clergy became a powerful cultural and political force.

Line of Bishops; mosaic in the lower apse of the St Sophia Cathedral in Kiev

During his reign, Volodymyr began minting coins stamped with the symbol of a trident. In 1918 the *trident was chosen as Ukraine's national emblem.

Towards the end of his life, Volodymyr's sons Sviatopolk and Yaroslav (by then prince of Novgorod) rebelled against his authority. When Volodymyr died in 1015, a bitter struggle for hegemony ensued among his sons, which lasted till 1036 when Yaroslav established control over most of the Kievan state.

During the reign of *Yaroslav the Wise (1019–54) the Kievan state attained the height of its cultural development.

Yaroslav paid much attention to the internal organization of his state. He built fortifications to defend his steppe frontier. He promoted Christianity, established schools, and founded a library at the St Sophia Cathedral (in 1036 to commemorate his victory over the Pechenegs). During Yaroslav's reign the *Kievan Cave Monastery was founded in 1051; it became the pre-eminent center of monastic, literary, and cultural life in Rus'. Yaroslav had the customary law of Rus' codified in the **Ruskaia Pravda* in order to regulate economic and social relations, which were becoming more complex. An important development that occurred during his rule was the rise of an indigenous, Slavic political elite in the Kievan state that included such figures as Yaroslav's adviser *Dobrynia, Dobrynia's son Konstantyn (Yaroslav's lieutenant in Novgorod), and Vyshata Ostromyrych (the governor of Kiev). Thenceforth the role of the Varangians was limited, even as mercenaries. Yaroslav's influence spread far and wide because he arranged dynastic alliances with nearly all the reigning families of Europe.

Before his death in 1054, Yaroslav divided his realm among his five remaining sons. Yaroslav maintained the principle of seniority introduced by his father, according to which the eldest son inherited Kiev and the title of grand prince, while the other sons were to respect the eldest and help him administer Rus'. In the event of the death of the eldest son, his place was to be taken by the next eldest, and so forth. The seniority principle did not survive the test of time, however. As the sons and their offspring prospered in the lands they inherited, their interests conflicted with one another and with the interests of state unity. Internecine strife developed, provoking the eventual collapse of the Kievan state.

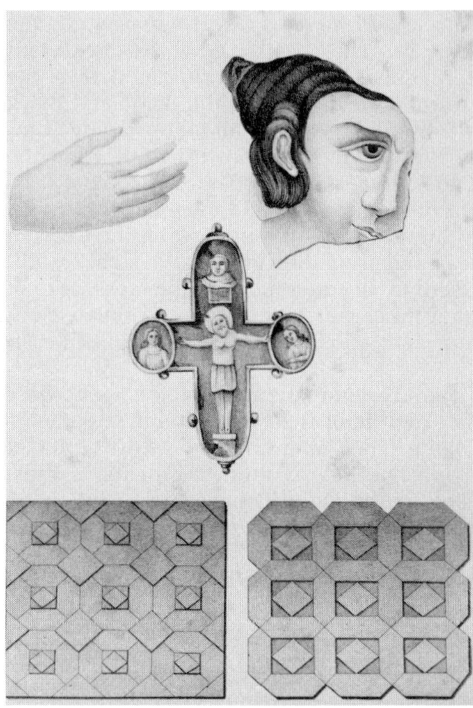

Fragments of frescoes and floors and a cross found in the ruins of the Church of the Tithes in Kiev

The last of Yaroslav's sons on the Kievan throne, *Vsevolod Yaroslavych (1078–93), directly ruled the principal lands of Rus': Kiev, Chernihiv, Pereiaslav, Smolensk, Rostov, and Suzdal. In the last years of his reign, Vsevolod's realm was administered by his son *Volodymyr Monomakh of Pereiaslav.

Vsevolod was succeeded in Kiev by his nephew *Sviatopolk II Iziaslavych (1093–1113), whose reign was distinguished by his continuous wars with the Cumans. With his cousin, Volodymyr Monomakh, Sviatopolk undertook successful expeditions against the invaders in 1103, 1109, and 1111.

The Cuman menace and ongoing wars among the princes were the subject of the 1097 *Liubech congress of princes near Kiev. Called at the initiative of Monomakh, the princes altered the principle of patrimony. It was decided that sons had the right to inherit and rule the lands of their fathers, thus annulling the seniority system created by Yaroslav the Wise, and that Rus' would be subdivided into autonomous principalities, whose rulers would, nonetheless, obey the grand prince in Kiev.

The consensus reached at Liubech was short-lived. Conflicts among the princes once again began pitting the Rostyslavych, Monomakh, and Sviatoslavych branches of the dynasty against Davyd Ihorevych and Sviatopolk. To settle the conflicts and organize campaigns against the Cumans, congresses were held at *Vytychiv (1100) and *Dolobske (1103).

The Kiev Uprising of 1068–9; miniature from the Radziwiłł Chronicle

When Sviatopolk died, the common people responded to the social and economic oppression of his regime with the *Kiev Uprising of 1113. The alarmed boyars turned to Volodymyr Monomakh to restore order and to ascend the Kievan throne. The popular Monomakh (1113–25) began his reign by amending the *Ruskaia Pravda* (see the *Statute of Volodymyr Monomakh). He was the last of the grand princes who strove to curtail the internecine wars among the princes in order to maintain the unity and might of Rus'. As before, Monomakh concentrated on combating the Cumans, whom he drove back to Caucasia and the Volga early in his reign, making the steppes safe again for Slavic colonization.

During Monomakh's reign, Rus' flourished culturally. Many churches were built, the *Kievan Cave Patericon was begun, and the writing of chronicles, hagiography, and other literature thrived. Before his death Monomakh wrote his famous testament, **Pouchennia ditiam*, a work of literary value in which he instructed his sons how to be strong and just rulers.

Skomorokhy; fresco in the south tower of the St Sophia Cathedral in Kiev

Monomakh was succeeded by his eldest son *Mstyslav I Volodymyrovych (1125–32), who inherited the lands of Kiev, Smolensk, and Novgorod; the remaining lands of Rus' were distributed among his brothers. Mystyslav's authority stemmed from his ability to organize the princes in combating the Cumans' renewed invasions. Like his father, he maintained ties with the rulers of Europe.

The political and social institutions of Kievan Rus'. From the 10th to the 12th century the Kievan state underwent significant sociopolitical changes. Volodymyr the Great was the first ruler to give Rus' political unity, by way of organized religion. The church provided him with the concepts of territorial and hierarchical organization; Byzantine notions of autocracy were adopted by him and his successors. The grand prince maintained power by his military strength, particularly through his **druzhyna* or retinue. He ruled and dispensed justice with the help of his appointed viceroys and local administrators – the **tysiatskyi*, **sotskyi* and **desiatskyi*.

Members of the *druzhyna* had a dual role: they were the prince's closest counselors in addition to constituting the elite nucleus of his army. Its senior members, recruited from among the 'better people' or those who had distinguished themselves in combat, soon acquired the status of barons called *boyars. The prince consulted on important state matters with the *Boyar Council. The **viche* (assembly) resolved all matters on behalf of the population and it became particularly important during the internecine wars of the princes for the throne of Kiev.

The privileged elite in Rus' was not a closed estate; based as it was on merit, its membership was dependent on the will of the prince. The townsfolk consisted of *burghers – mostly *merchants and craftsmen – and paupers. Most freemen were yeomen, called *smerds. A smaller category of half-free peasants were called zakups. The lowest social strata in Rus' consisted of slaves (see *slavery).

The disintegration of the Kievan state. During the reign of Mstyslav's successor and brother, Yaropolk Volodymyrovych (1132–9), widespread dynastic rivalry for the crown of the 'grand prince of Kiev and all of Rus'' arose between the *Olhovych branch of Chernihiv and the Monomakhovych clans. These internecine wars continued for a century, during which time the throne of *Kiev principality changed hands almost 50 times.

As a result of the wars, Kiev's primacy rapidly declined. In 1169 Prince Andrei Bogoliubskii of Vladimir, Rostov, and Suzdal sacked Kiev and left it in ruins. Thereafter the title of grand prince of Kiev became an empty one, and the autocratic rulers of Vladimir were a constant threat to the Ukrainian principalities of southern Rus', as were the Cumans. From the mid-12th century, *Kiev, *Polatsk, *Turiv-Pynske, Volodymyr-Volynskyi (see *Volhynia), Halych (see *Galicia), *Chernihiv, and *Pereiaslav developed as politically and economically separate units. In 1136 *Novgorod became a sovereign mercantile city-republic tied to the Baltic cities of the Hanseatic League and the Slavic hinterland and controlled by a boyar oligarchy.

Galicia assumed the leading role among the Ukrainian principalities during the reign of its prince *Volodymyrko (1124–53). The reigns of his son *Yaroslav Osmomysl (1153–87), who extended the territory of Halych principality to the Danube Delta, and grandson *Volodymyr Yaroslavych (1187–99) were marked by frequent struggles with the powerful Galician boyar oligarchy.

Volhynia gained prominence under the reign of the Monomakhovychi beginning in the 1120s. After a half-century of individual, fragmented autonomy, the appanage Volodymyr and Lutske (Lucheske) principalities and the *Berestia land were reunited under the rule of Prince *Roman Mstyslavych (1173–1205). In 1199 Roman was invited by the Galician boyars to become the ruler of Halych principality.

The historical fate of *Transcarpathia, which until the late 10th century was ruled by the Kievan state, was different. After the death of Volodymyr the Great, the Hungarian king, Stephen I, took advantage of the internecine struggles that arose in Rus' to annex Transcarpathia; except for a few short periods, it remained part of Hungary until 1918. The other western borderlands, *Bukovyna and *Bessarabia, were part of Rus' from the 10th century, and it was only after the demise of the Galician-Volhynian state that they became part of *Moldavia.

St Mark the Evangelist; miniature from the Ostromir Gospel (1056)

The Galician-Volhynian state (1199–1340). As the ruler of the newly created Principality of *Galicia-Volhynia, and particularly after he conquered the lands of Kiev principality in 1202, Roman reigned over a large and powerful state, which he defended from the Yatvingians and Cumans. When he died the boyar oligarchy took control in Galicia.

Prince Leszek of Cracow and King Andrew II of Hungary exploited the succession crisis and civil strife: Leszek occupied most of Volhynia, and Andrew placed his son Koloman on the Halych throne in 1214 as 'King of Galicia and Lodomeria.' In 1221 *Mstyslav of Novgorod, to whom the boyars had appealed for help, defeated the Hungarians, occupying the Galician throne until 1228. By 1230 *Danylo Romanovych and *Vasylko Romanovych were able to consolidate their rule in Volhynia, and in 1238 they drove the Hungarians, to whom Mstyslav had restored Galicia in 1228, from Galicia.

Yet the threat from the east continued. The Mongols entered Rus' and routed the united armies of the Rus' princes under the command of Mstyslav Mstyslavych and Danylo at the Kalka River in 1223. A large army of Mongols led by *Batu Khan invaded Rus' again in 1237, devastated the Pereiaslav and Chernihiv regions in 1239, sacked Kiev in 1240, and penetrated into Volhynia and Galicia, where it razed most of the towns, including Volodymyr and Halych in 1241.

Danylo, the outstanding ruler (1238–64) of Galicia-Volhynia, after defeating the Teutonic Knights at Dorohychyn in 1238, subduing the rebellious boyars in 1241–2, and defeating Rostyslav Mykhailovych of Chernihiv and his Polish-Hungarian allies at Yaroslav in 1245, prepared to overthrow the Mongol yoke. His attemps at forming a military coalition with the Papacy, Hungary, Poland, and Lithuania against the Mongols did not succeed, however, and in 1255 Danylo relied on his own forces to defeat the Mongols and their vassals between the Dniester and Boh rivers and in Volhynia. But the massive Mongol offensive of 1259, led by *Burundai, forced him to submit to the authority of the *Golden Horde.

The Galician-Volhynian state declined steadily under Danylo's successors *Lev I Danylovych (1264–1301), *Yurii Lvovych (1301–15), *Lev II and Andrii Yuriiovych (corulers 1315–23), and *Yurii II Boleslav (1323–40). After the death of Yurii II, rivalry among the rulers of *Poland, *Hungary, *Lithuania, and the Mongols for possession of Volhynia and Galicia ensued. The Lithuanian duke *Liubartas became the ruler of Volhynia and the Kholm region. The Polish king *Casimir III attacked Lviv in 1340, but it was not until 1349 that he was able to defeat the Galician boyars led by D. *Dedko and to occupy Galicia. Casimir's successor, Louis I of both Hungary (1342–82) and Poland (1370–82), ruled Galicia through his vicegerents, among them *Władysław Opolczyk. In 1387, Louis's daughter Queen *Jadwiga annexed Galicia and the Kholm region to Poland.

The Kievan state and the Galician-Volhynian states, referred to in Ukrainian historiography as the Princely era, lasted in Ukraine for nearly five centuries, from 860 to 1340. The Galician-Volhynian state, relatively unscathed by the Mongol onslaught, became the main repository of the traditions of the Kievan state, and the historical evolution of the Ukrainian lands remained incontrovertibly tied to that of Western civilization.

Ukraine under Lithuanian and Polish rule. While the Ukrainian principalities declined under onslaughts of the Asiatic nomads, the Grand Duchy of *Lithuania rose to prominence in the Baltic region. *Gediminas (1316–41) annexed the Belorussian and Ukrainian lands of *Chorna Rus', Vitsebsk, Minsk, Berestia, Turiv-Pynske, Volhynia, and the northern Kiev region. In 1323 Gediminas assumed the title of 'Lithuanian, Samogitian, and Ruthenian (Rus') grand duke.' To consolidate his realm, he fostered dynastic ties by marrying his daughters to Ruthenian (Belorussian and Ukrainian) princes and promoting Ruthenian culture. *Algirdas (1345–77) enlarged the grand duchy by conquering the Ukrainian lands of Chernihiv, Novhorod-Siverskyi, and, after defeating the Tatars at Syni Vody in 1363, Kiev, Pereiaslav, and Podilia.

Thus, nine-tenths of the grand duchy became composed of autonomous Ukrainian and Belorussian territories. Until 1385 the intermarriage of Ruthenian and Lithuanian princely families strengthened the Ruthenian influence in the *Lithuanian-Ruthenian state. As members of the grand duke's privy council, high-ranking military commanders, and administrators (vicegerents),

Ruthenian nobles became part of the ruling elite. Ruthenian became the official state language and Orthodoxy the prevailing religion (10 of Algirdas's 12 sons were Orthodox). Under Algirdas's son and successor Jogaila, the Lithuanian-Ruthenian state was threatened by the Teutonic Knights, Tatars, and Muscovy. To gain support Jogaila agreed to marry the Polish queen *Jadwiga, share her throne, and unite Lithuania with Poland. After the Union of *Krevo of 1385, Jogaila became King Władysław II *Jagiełło of Poland as well as remaining the grand duke of Lithuania. Although the grand duchy retained its independence, the Polish nobility made inroads there, resulting in a strong Lithuanian-Ruthenian backlash against Polonization and Catholicism.

Artifacts from the Princely era: 1) sword handle; 2) soldier's helmet; 3) prince's helmet; 4–5) silver coins of Volodymyr the Great, 10th–11th centuries; 6) coin of Prince Sviatopolk II, 11th century; 7) coin of Yaroslav the Wise, early 11th century; 8) detail from a prince's helmet; 9–11) gold and silver armbands; 12) chain from Chernihiv [from V. Sichynsky]

Opposition to this union was led by *Vytautas, whose popularity and alliance with the Teutonic Knights forced Jagiełło to recognize him in 1392 as grand duke of all Lithuanian-Ruthenian lands. Under his rule (1392–1430) the grand duchy incorporated all the lands between the Dniester and Dnieper rivers as far south as the Black Sea and reached the summit of its greatness. After his defeat by the Tatars in battle at the Vorskla River in 1399, however, Vytautas was forced to abandon his expansionist plans in the east and seek an accord with Jagiełło. The Lithuanian-Polish Union of *Horodlo of 1413 curtailed the participation of the Orthodox (and thus the Ruthenians) in governing the state and allowed only Catholics to remain in the Lithuanian state council.

Towards the end of the 15th century a new external menace arose – the Crimean Tatar Khanate, which seceded from the Golden Horde and in 1478 became a vassal of Ottoman Turkey. As the ally of Grand Prince Ivan III of Muscovy, Lithuania's enemy, Khan Mengli Girei sacked Kiev in 1482. From then on the *Tatars regularly raided and ravaged the Ukrainian lands. Lithuania was unable to prevent these raids, nor could it stop Muscovy from annexing a large part of its Ruthenian lands, including northern Chernihiv and Novhorod-Siverskyi principalities. With the support of Muscovy, certain Ruthenian princes, led by M. *Hlynsky, who proclaimed himself grand duke, rebelled against Lithuanian Catholic rule in 1508. The rebellion was quelled, however, and the *Hlynsky and other noble families fled to Muscovy. Thus ended the last attempt by the Ruthenian princes to secede from Lithuania.

Court Musicians; a miniature from the Kiev Psalter (1397)

Lithuania and Poland's ongoing wars with Muscovy and the Tatar threat during the reigns of *Alexander Jagiellończyk (1492–1506), *Sigismund I (1506–48), and *Sigismund II Augustus (1548–72) created the need for close collaboration, mutual defense, and a movement for a real, and not just dynastic, union of the two states. The Lithuanian-Ruthenian lower nobility supported unification, for it would give them the privileges and freedoms enjoyed by the *szlachta* in the Polish parliamentary monarchy. The princes and magnates opposed it, however, for it would mean the loss of their authority (see *Council of Lords). In January 1569 the Sejm in Lublin failed to reach an accord on the union, and Sigismund II annexed Podlachia, Volhynia, and the Kiev and Bratslav regions – over one-third of the grand duchy – to Poland. After further negotiations and conflicts the Union of *Lublin was signed on 1 July 1569. Thereafter Poland and Lithuania constituted a single, federated state – the Commonwealth – ruled by a jointly elected monarch; the state was to have a common Diet, foreign policy, currency, and property law. Both partners were to retain separate administrations, law courts, treasuries, armies, and laws, however. Because Poland now possessed the larger territory, it had greater representation in the Diet and thus became the dominant partner. The only Ukrainian lands left in the grand duchy were parts of the Berestia and Pynske regions.

With the Union of Lublin, the Lithuanian-Ruthenian period – the only period of full-fledged *feudalism in Ukrainian history – came to an end. Thereafter the Ukrainian lands, for the most part, constituted the Rus', Belz, Podilia, Podlachia, Volhynia, Bratslav, Kiev, and, from 1635, Chernihiv *voivodeships (palatinates) within the Polish crown. There the *Lithuanian Statute – the legal code of the Lithuanian-Ruthenian state – remained in effect, but Ukrainian as the official language was supplanted by Polish and Latin. Nevertheless Ukrainian princes continued to own large estates and thus maintained their former privileged positions. On the territory of Volhynia, in particular, there remained a large number of influential Ukrainian nobles – eg, the *Ostrozky, Vyshnevetsky, Koretsky, Kysil, Chartorysky, Chetvertynsky, Zbarazky, and Zaslavsky families. The Polish king, however, began distributing ownership charters to the 'empty' lands in Right-Bank Ukraine to a small number of Polish and Polonized Ukrainian magnates; thus arose the huge latifundia – virtually autonomous domains – of the *Potocki, *Zamoyski, *Sieniawski, Kalinowski, Tyszkiewicz, *Zbarazki (Zbarazky), Koniecpolski, and *Wiśniowiecki (Vyshnevetsky) families in Ukraine.

Kievan Cave Patericon, frontispiece (1406 redaction)

The integration of the Ukrainian lands into Poland resulted in significant national and religious transformations. Part of the relatively small Ukrainian elite, particularly the magnates, became Polonized as a result of the influence of Polish *education and of the large number of in-migrating Polish nobles and Catholic clergy (especially the *Jesuits). Even many prominent Ukrainian families, including that of Prince K. Ostrozky, a leading defender of Orthodoxy, converted to Roman Catholicism and readily adopted Polish language and culture.

Under the new regime, the noble-dominated *cities and towns grew in size and number and experienced an economic boom. It was, however, almost exclusively the Catholic German and Polish burghers who benefited from self-government by *Magdeburg law. The Orthodox Ukrainian burghers were the victims of persecution and segregation; this incited them to organize *brotherhoods in order to defend and promote their national, cultural, and corporate interests.

The *peasants gained nothing from the union. Fully subjected to the nobles and their agents, they were forced to perform increasingly more corvée labor (see *Serfdom) and were restricted in their right to move from one landlord to another. Conditions in the newly colonized lands of the Dnieper Basin were somewhat better, owing to their relative underpopulation. There, in order to attract peasant settlement, the nobles introduced the **sloboda* – an agricultural settlement whose inhabitants were exempted temporarily from feudal obligations.

The rule of the Polish 'nobles,' the Polonization, economic exploitation, and religious and national-social oppression provoked organized forms of protest: the growth of *Protestantism, particularly of the *Socinians, among the Ukrainian nobility; the above-mentioned Orthodox burgher brotherhoods and *brotherhood schools; and attempts by the déclassé Orthodox hierarchy and clergy to gain parity with their Roman Catholic counterparts, culminating in the 1596 Church Union of *Berestia and the creation of the Uniate or *Greek Catholic chuch. The church union was not accepted by the majority of the Ukrainian population, however, and many Ukrainian nobles, led by K. Ostrozky, as well as the brotherhoods actively opposed it. The religious struggles that ensued found their written expression in *polemical literature. (See also *Church, history of the Ukrainian.)

The religious struggle was only one aspect of the Ukrainian-Polish conflict. The political opposition of the Ukrainian people was also manifested by the *Cossacks – members of the various social groups (peasants, burghers, and nobles) – who escaped from their oppressors into the Commonwealth-Tatar steppe frontier.

The Cossacks. From the 15th century onward, thousands of fugitives from Polish rule and serfdom settled in this no-man's-land. To defend themselves from Tatar attacks, they organized armed groups and fortified settlements. With time they also began attacking the Tatar and Turkish settlements on the Black Sea. In 1552–4, Prince D. *Vyshnevetsky united various Cossack groups and founded a Cossack fortress on Mala Khortytsia Island south of the Dnieper Rapids. This became the first of several Cossack centers called the *Zaporozhian Sich, the nucleus of the quasi-democratic Cossack domain that became known as *Zaporizhia ('land beyond the rapids').

Seal of the Zaporozhian Cossack Host, 1622

The Cossacks' expeditions against the Tatars and Turks made them famous throughout Europe. In 1577 they marched on Moldavia to help one of their own, I. *Pidkova, become the hospodar there. In 1594, A. Komulovich and E. *Lassota von Steblau, the envoys of Pope Clement VIII and Emperor Rudolph II, enlisted Cossack mercenaries under H. *Loboda and S. *Nalyvaiko in the war against the Turks. These and other manifestations of Cossack military and political autonomy were a threat to the Polish regime, for they provoked Tatar and Turkish retaliation in Ukraine. As early as 1572, Sigismund II tried to circumscribe the Cossacks' growth and freebootery by creating a register of 300 royal Cossacks, who were granted privileges, liberties, land, and money in return for military service to the crown. The institution of these so-called *registered Cossacks, whose number increased (at times to 6,000) during Poland's wars, provoked discontent among the magnates, who opposed any ennoblement of the Cossacks, as well as social divisions and discord among the Cossacks as a whole. Those not 'registered' were officially considered peasants and subject to feudal obligations. These and other measures precipitated rebellions led by K. *Kosynsky (1591–3) and S. Nalyvaiko and H. Loboda (1594–6) (in which registered Cossacks participated) against the magnates in Ukraine. The latter rebellion in particular involved many burghers and peasants, and engulfed large parts of Right-Bank Ukraine and Belorussia; it was brutally suppressed by the crown army led by S. *Żółkiewski, and Polish oppression in Ukraine intensified.

In the first quarter of the 17th century, Poland needed the Cossacks in its wars with Turkey (in Moldavia), Sweden (in Livonia), and Muscovy. The crown therefore restored the civil rights it had abolished after the Kosynsky rebellion and reinstated the register of Cossacks. At that time the Cossacks assumed a more political role as the defenders of outlawed Orthodoxy, which cemented their ties with the burghers and peasants; the unceasing defense of their corporate rights prepared them for their future role as the vanguard of a national revolution. Hetman P. *Sahaidachny (1614–22), the renowned leader of Cossack sea expeditions against the Tatar towns in the Crimea (1606–17), succeeded in creating a disciplined, regular Cossack army. In 1618 his army took part in the campaign of Prince Władysław against Moscow, and in 1621 the united Polish-Cossack army halted the Turkish advance on central Europe at the Battle of *Khotyn. A protector of Orthodoxy, in 1621 Sahaidachny played a key role in persuading the Patriarch of Jerusalem to renew the Ukrainian Orthodox hierarchy and consecrate Y. *Boretsky as metropolitan of Kiev. Sahaidachny pursued a conciliatory policy vis-à-vis the Polish Crown. The king, however, would not recognize the new Orthodox hierarchs, and soon after Khotyn any privileges the Cossacks had been granted for their wartime role were abrogated.

Although in this period the Cossacks were cognizant of their strength, they were not united in their attitude to the Polish regime. One group, consisting of the registered Cossacks, sought a compromise with the Poles. The other, the unprivileged majority, led by O. Holub, ignored the Polish injunctions. They remained recalcitrant, and in 1624–5 even fought on land and sea against Turkey as the allies of the Crimean khan Mohamet-Girei III. The Polish king, seeing his relations with Turkey endangered, sent the crown army under S. *Koniecpolski to subdue the Zaporozhians. Hetman M. *Zhmailo and his successor M. *Doroshenko were forced to sign the *Kurukove Treaty, which limited the number of registered Cossacks to 6,000 and the Cossacks' freedom in general. But peace did not last long. The 1630 Zaporozhian rebellion, led by T. Fedorovych (Triasylo), forced the Poles to negotiate the *Pereiaslav Treaty of 1630, which increased the register to 8,000 but failed, as before, to appease the Zaporozhians, who continued their raids against the Turks.

Crest of Metropolitan Petro Mohyla, 1646

In 1632 the registered Cossacks, led by I. *Petrazhytsky-Kulaha, demanded that they, as a loyal, obedient, knightly estate, be allowed to take part in the election of the new king after the death of *Sigismund III Vasa. The Diet in Warsaw that elected *Władysław IV Vasa legalized the Orthodox church and recognized its hierarchy to mollify the Ukrainians and counter pro-Muscovite attitudes. Under P. *Mohyla, the new metropolitan of Kiev (1633–47), the Orthodox church experienced a renaissance, as did Ukrainian education, scholarship, and culture in general (see *Kievan Mohyla Academy).

King Władysław IV was much more liberal toward his Ukrainian subjects than Sigismund had been. But although the Cossacks helped him in his wars with Sweden, Muscovy (during which the Chernihiv region was annexed), and Turkey, he did not recognize their demands for increased privileges. Consequently, many Cossacks continued to flee to Zaporizhia. To stop this exodus the Polish government built a fort in *Kodak in 1635, but the Cossacks, led by Hetman I. *Sulyma, razed it. The general dissatisfaction with Polish rule resulted in a new popular uprising in 1637, led by P. *Pavliuk. The rebels were defeated in the Battle of *Kumeiky and forced to accept even greater restrictions. In the spring of 1638, a rebellion again erupted, this time on the Left Bank, under the leadership of D. *Hunia, Y. *Ostrianyn, and K. *Skydan. Having fought several battles, the rebels finally surrendered at the Starets River. After this event the number of registered Cossacks was limited to 6,000, their senior officers were appointed by the Polish nobles, the hetman was replaced by a Polish commissioner, burghers and peasants were forbidden to marry Cossacks or join their ranks, Cossacks could reside only in Chyhyryn, Korsun, or Cherkasy districts, unregistered Cossacks were outlawed, the Kodak fortress was rebuilt, and Polish garrisons were stationed throughout Ukraine.

For a decade thereafter the Polish magnate kinglets kept the Cossacks in check and intensified their exploitation and oppression of Ukrainian Orthodox peasants and burghers. This 'golden tranquility' was broken by yet another uprising, this time on a much greater scale.

The Khmelnytsky era. The great uprising of 1648 was one of the most cataclysmic events in Ukrainian history. It is difficult to find an uprising of comparable magnitude, intensity, and impact in the history of early modern Europe.

A crucial element in the revolt was the leadership of Hetman B. *Khmelnytsky (1648–57), whose exceptional organizational, military, and political talents to a large

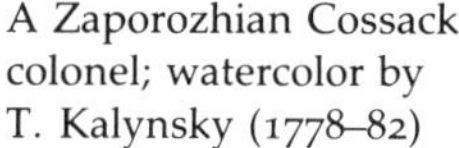

A Zaporozhian Cossack colonel; watercolor by T. Kalynsky (1778–82)

A 17th-century Ukrainian magnate; watercolor by T. Kalynsky (1778–82)

extent accounted for its success. The uprising engulfed all of Dnieper Ukraine. Polish nobles, officials, Uniates, and Jesuits were massacred or forced to flee. Jewish losses, estimated at over 50,000 during what became a decade-long *Cossack-Polish War, were especially heavy, because the *Jews, who were concentrated in Ukraine in large numbers, were seen as agents of the Polish *szlachta*. Great massacres were also perpetrated against the Ukrainian populace by the retreating Poles, led by the magnate J. *Wiśniowiecki. The Poles were crushed at the Battle of *Zhovti Vody on 16 May 1648 and again in September, at the Battle of *Pyliavtsi in Volhynia where the Cossacks were joined by the peasants en masse. Poland proper was now defenseless, but Khmelnytsky, after briefly occupying western Ukraine and besieging Lviv and Zamostia, decided, because of oncoming winter and doubts about the chances of success of a full-scale invasion of Poland, to return to Dnieper Ukraine. Upon his triumphant entry into Kiev, he declared that although he had begun the uprising for personal reasons he was now fighting for the sake of all Ukraine.

By April 1649, it was clear that Khmelnytsky was contemplating a separation of Ukraine from the Commonwealth, and the Commonwealth armies, led by the new king, *Jan II Casimir Vasa, and Prince J. Radziwiłł, launched a counteroffensive. Defeated once again at the battle of *Zboriv on 15 August, the Poles sued for peace and a treaty was signed on 18 September 1649. The Poles, however, broke the treaty in 1651 and with the help of the Tatars defeated the Cossacks at the battle of *Berestechko; and Khmelnytsky was forced to conclude the Treaty of *Bila Tserkva in September 1651. The treaty allowed the Poles to return to much of Ukraine.

Realizing that he could not defeat the Poles by military means alone and hoping to expand his political base, Khmelnytsky turned to diplomacy. In September 1650 he dispatched a large Cossack force to Moldavia in the hope of installing his son, T. *Khmelnytsky, there. The hetman envisaged the creation of a great coalition backed by the Ottomans, Tatars, and Danubian principalities and consisting of Ukraine, Transylvania, Brandenburg, Lithuania, and even Cromwell's England. His aim was to restructure the Commonwealth into an equal union of Poland, Lithuania, and Ukraine with Prince György *Rákóczi II of Transylvania as its new king. Khmelnytsky's plans suffered a great setback when the Moldavian boyars revolted and his son died in 1653. Another major setback occurred during the seige of *Zhvanets in Podilia in December 1653: Khmelnytsky was about to annihilate the army of Jan Casimir when his Tatar allies signed a separate peace with the Poles. Khmelnytsky then abandoned his orientation on the Ottomans and Tatars and drew closer to Muscovy.

Tsar Aleksei Mikhailovich agreed to help Khmelnytsky 'for the sake of the Orthodox faith,' expecting also to regain some of the lands Muscovy had previously lost to Poland, to utilize Ukraine as a buffer zone against the Ottomans, and, in general, to expand his influence. The 1654 *Pereiaslav Treaty established an alliance of Ukraine and Muscovy. The Poles responded to the new alliance by combining forces with the Tatars. A new expanded phase of conflict began. In 1654, while a combined Muscovite-Ukrainian army (see I. *Zolotarenko) scored major successes in Belorussia, the Poles and, especially, the Tatars devastated Ukraine. A year later it was Poland that experienced devastation, when the Swedes, taking advantage of the war, invaded the country. Sensing the imminent demise of the Commonwealth, György Rákóczi of Transylvania concluded an alliance with Khmelnytsky, and in January 1657 a large Ukrainian-Transylvanian force was sent into Poland to expedite its partition.

Wife of a 17th-century Ukrainian magnate; watercolor by T. Kalynsky (1778–82)

A 17th-century city woman; watercolor by T. Kalynsky (1778–82)

Khmelnytsky's foreign policy, especially his co-operation with the Swedes, who were also at war with Muscovy, raised the tsar's ire. But Khmelnytsky also had his grievances: he was bitter over the imposition of Muscovite rule in Belorussia, where the populace had expressed preference for a Cossack government; even more infuriating was the Vilnius Peace Treaty with the Poles in October 1656, which Moscow had concluded without consulting the hetman. Mutual recriminations followed, and there were signs that the hetman was reconsidering the link with Moscow. Then the Ukrainian-Transylvanian offensive in Poland collapsed. Crushed by these setbacks and already ill, Khmelnytsky died on 6 August 1657.

The Hetman state. At the time of Khmelnytsky's death, the Cossacks controlled the former palatinates of Kiev, Bratslav, and Chernihiv, an area inhabited by about 1.5 million people. About 50 percent of the land, formerly owned by the Polish crown, became the property of the Zaporozhian Host, which, in return for taxes, allocated it to self-governing peasant villages. Cossacks and Ukrainian nobles retained approximately 33 percent of the land, and the church, 17 percent. The entire area was divided into 16 military and administrative regions corresponding to the territorially based *regiments of the Cossack army (see *Regimental system). Initially, the *Cossack *starshyna* (senior officers) were elected by their units, but in time these posts often became hereditary.

At the pinnacle of the Cossack military-administrative system stood the *hetman. Assisting the hetman was the *General Officer Staff, which functioned as a general staff and a council of ministers. The formal name of the new political entity was the Zaporozhian Host; the Muscovites, however, referred to it as *Little Russia, while the Poles continued calling it Ukraine.

Hoping to establish a dynasty, Khmelnytsky had arranged for his 16-year-old son Yurii to succeed him. It soon became apparent, however, that the young boy was incapable of ruling, and I. *Vyhovsky was chosen hetman (1657–9). Vyhovsky hoped to establish an independent Ukrainian principality. His elitist and pro-Polish tendencies engendered a rebellion by the rank-and-file Cossacks and Zaporozhians, led by M. *Pushkar and Ya. *Barabash and covertly backed by Moscow. Vyhovsky emerged victorious but militarily and politically weakened. Realizing that a confrontation with Moscow was inevitable, Vyhovsky entered into negotiations with the Poles regarding the return of Ukraine to the Commonwealth. In September 1658 they concluded the Treaty of *Hadiache. Viewing the treaty as an act of war, Moscow dispatched a large army into Ukraine. In July 1658, it was crushed near Konotip by a combined force of Poles, Ukrainians, and Tatars. But Vyhovsky's politics continued to elicit opposition, and several Cossack leaders (I. *Bohun, I. *Sirko, I. *Bezpaly) rose in revolt. Realizing that his base of support was crumbling, in September 1659 the hetman fled to Poland.

The *starshyna*, hoping that the appeal of his name would help to heal internal conflicts, elected Yu. *Khmelnytsky hetman (1659–62). The Muscovites, who returned to Ukraine with another large army, forced the young hetman to renegotiate the Pereiaslav Treaty. The new pact was a major step forward in Moscow's attempts to tighten its hold on Ukraine: it increased the number of Muscovite governors and garrisons in Ukraine, forbade the hetman to maintain foreign contacts without the tsar's permission, and stipulated that election of Cossack leaders should be confirmed by Moscow. Disillusioned, Khmelnytsky went over to the Poles in 1660, helped them defeat the tsar's army at Chudniv, and signed the Treaty of *Slobodyshche. The Left-Bank regiments, led by Ya. *Somko, refused to follow Khmelnytsky, however, and remained loyal to the tsar. Unable to cope with the strife and chaos, Khmelnytsky resigned in 1663. A period of constant war and devastation began.

The Ruin. During this period, called the Ruin by contemporaries, Ukraine was divided along the Dnieper River into two spheres of influence, the Polish in *Right-Bank Ukraine and the Muscovite in *Left-Bank Ukraine and Kiev. At times, the Ottoman presence was felt in the south. All Cossack hetmans during this period were dependent on these powers for support. The hetmans' weakness stemmed largely from internal conflicts, especially the ongoing social tensions between the Cossack *starshyna* and the rank and file and the peasants, who resented the attempts of the *starshyna* to monopolize political power and impose labor obligations upon them. Consequently, political factionalism, opportunism, and adventurism became prevalent among the Cossack leaders, who were easily manipulated by Ukraine's powerful neighbors.

A 17th-century peasant girl; watercolor by T. Kalynsky (1778–82)

Two typical hetmans of the period were P. *Teteria (1663–5) on the Right Bank and I. *Briukhovetsky (1663–8) on the Left Bank. Teteria, who adhered strictly to a pro-Polish line, invaded the Left Bank together with the Poles in 1664 and urged its Cossacks to march on Moscow. When the offensive failed, Teteria and the Poles (see S. *Czarniecki) returned to the Right Bank (see I. *Popovych, *Varenytsia uprising); their brutality in quelling numerous anti-Polish uprisings aroused such animosity that Teteria was forced to abdicate and flee to Poland.

On the Left Bank, Briukhovetsky's policy toward Moscow was exceedingly conciliatory (see *Baturyn Articles). The first Ukrainian hetman to pay homage to the tsar (for which he received the title of boyar, estates, and the daughter of Prince Dolgoruky in marriage), in 1665 he signed the *Moscow Articles, which significantly increased Moscow's political, military, fiscal, and religious control. These concessions, the hetman's high-handedness, the behavior of the Muscovite governors and tax collectors, and the Treaty of *Andrusovo (1667) – an armistice that ratified the partition of Ukraine between Poland and Muscovy – infuriated the populace and led to widespread revolts against Briukhovetsky and the Muscovite garrisons. Briukhovetsky's attempts at backing away from Moscow and heading the revolt against it failed to appease the rebels, and in 1668 he was killed by an angry mob.

Kozak-Mamai; 19th-century folk painting

Election of an otaman at the Zaporozhian Sich; watercolor by T. Kalynsky (1778–82)

An attempt to preserve Cossack Ukraine from chaos and to reassert Ukrainian self-government was made by the popular colonel of Cherkasy and hetman of the Right Bank, P. *Doroshenko (1666–76). After the Poles signed the Treaty of Andrusovo, Doroshenko turned against them and resolved to unite all of Ukraine under his rule. To gain the support of the rank-and-file Cossacks, he agreed to hold frequent meetings of the General Military Council, and to free himself from overdependence on the powerful colonels, he established mercenary *Serdiuk regiments under his direct command. In fall 1667, a combined Cossack-Ottoman force compelled King Jan Casimir to grant the hetman wide-ranging authority over the Right Bank. Doroshenko then invaded the Left Bank and, after Briukhovetsky's demise in 1668, was proclaimed hetman of all Ukraine. During his absence from the Right Bank, however, the Zaporozhians proclaimed P. *Sukhovii hetman; soon after, the Poles returned and established Mykhailo *Khanenko as yet another rival hetman. Returning to confront his adversaries, Doroshenko appointed D. *Mnohohrishny acting hetman (1668–72) on the Left Bank. A Muscovite army invaded the Left Bank, however, and Mnohohrishny was forced to swear allegiance to the tsar (see *Hlukhiv Articles) in 1669.

Ukraine was divided again. Weakened, Doroshenko was forced to rely increasingly on the Ottomans. In 1672 his forces joined the huge Turkish-Tatar army that wrested Podilia away from the Poles (see *Buchach Peace Treaty of 1672), and in 1674–7 he found himself fighting on the side of the Turks against the Orthodox forces of the tsar and of the new Left Bank hetman I. Samoilovych. Compromised by his association with the Muslim occupation and the ravages of the civil war, the now unpopular Doroshenko surrendered to Samoilovych in 1676.

To replace Doroshenko in the ongoing struggle between the Porte and Moscow for the Right Bank during the *Chyhyryn campaigns of 1677–8, the Ottomans resurrected Yu. Khmelnytsky as the 'Prince of Ukraine' (1677–8, 1685). The 1681 Peace Treaty of *Bakhchesarai left much of southern Right-Bank Ukraine a deserted neutral zone between the two empires. No longer in need of Yu. Khmelnytsky, the Ottomans had him executed, and pashas governed the Right Bank from Kamianets-Podilskyi.

From 1669 the Left Bank remained under Muscovite control (see *Little Russian Office) and was spared the recurrent Ottoman, Tatar, Polish, and Muscovite invasions that devastated the once flourishing Right Bank. Although Mnohohrishny, like Briukhovetsky, was elected hetman there with Muscovite acquiesence, he did not intend to be a puppet of the tsar. This was evident from his demands that Moscow limit its military presence in the cities to Kiev, Nizhen, Pereiaslav, and Chernihiv. With the help of mercenary regiments, he managed to establish order on the Left Bank, but his constant conflicts with the increasingly entrenched *starshyna* brought about his downfall.

Mnohohrishny's successor I. *Samoilovych (1672–87) made loyalty to Moscow and cordial relations with the *starshyna* the cornerstones of his policy. He thus managed to remain hetman for an unprecedented 15 years. To win over the *starshyna,* he awarded the members generous land grants and created the so-called *fellows of the standard (a corps of junior officers), thereby encouraging the development of a hereditary elite on the Left Bank. Like all hetmans, Samoilovych attempted to extend his authority over all of Ukraine. He tightened his control over the unruly Zaporozhians, and from 1674 he fought alongside the Muscovites against Doroshenko and the Turks. Greatly disappointed by his and Muscovy's failure to conquer the devastated Right Bank, he organized the mass evacuation of its inhabitants to the Left Bank and *Slobidska Ukraine. The 1686 Polish-Muscovite *Eternal Peace and anti-Muslim coalition validated Poland's claims to the Right Bank and placed the Zaporozhian lands under the direct authority of the tsar instead of the hetman. Consequently, Samoilovych was not overly co-operative when Muscovy launched a huge invasion of the Crimea in 1687. Blamed by the Muscovite commander V. *Golitsyn and the Cossack *starshyna* for its failure, Samoilovych was deposed and exiled to Siberia.

After Poland recovered the Right Bank from Turkey in 1699 and the Zaporozhians asserted their autonomy, only about a third of the territory of the *Hetman state, or Hetmanate, that B. Khmelnytsky established remained under the authority of the hetmans. Situated now mostly on the Left Bank, the Hetmanate consisted of only 10 regiments. While the structure of Cossack self-government underwent only minor changes, major shifts occurred in the socioeconomic structure of the Left Bank. By the late 17th century, the *starshyna* had virtually excluded rank-and-file Cossacks from decision-making and higher offices, and the latter's political decline was closely

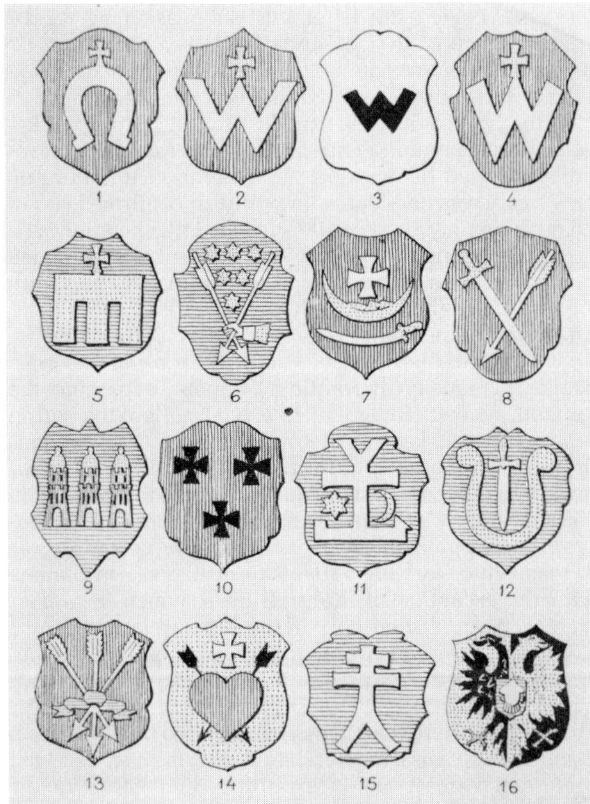

Coats of arms of Ukrainian hetmans: 1) P. Sahaidachny (1616–22); 2) B. Khmelnytsky (1648–57); 3) I. Vyhovsky (1657–9); 4) Yu. Khmelnytsky (1659–63); 5) P. Teteria (1663–5); 6) I. Briukhovetsky (1663–8); 7) P. Doroshenko (1665–76); 8) D. Mnohohrishny (1668–72); 9) M. Khanenko (1670–4); 10) I. Samoilovych (1672–87); 11) I. Mazepa (1687–1709); 12) P. Orlyk (1710–42); 13) I. Skoropadsky (1708–22); 14) P. Polubotok (1722–4); 15) D. Apostol (1727–34); 16) K. Rozumovsky (1750–64) [from V. Sichynsky]

related to their mounting economic problems. Individual Cossacks took part in the almost endless wars of the 17th and early 18th centuries at their own expense. Consequently many of them were financially ruined, and this caused a decline in the number of battle-ready Cossacks and in the size of the Cossack army. In 1700 the Hetmanate's army numbered only about 20,000 men. Moreover, the equipment, military principles, and tactics on which the Cossacks relied had become increasingly outdated. Confronted by internal weaknesses, leading a depleted military force, and disillusioned by the behavior of the Poles and Ottomans during the Ruin, most Cossack leaders no longer questioned the need to maintain links with Moscow. But they were still committed to preserving what was left of the rights guaranteed to them by the Pereiaslav Treaty of 1654.

The Mazepa era. A decisive phase in the relationship of the Hetmanate to Moscow occurred during the hetmancy of Samoilovych's successor I. *Mazepa (1687–1708/9), one of the most outstanding and controversial of all Ukrainian political leaders. For most of his years in office Mazepa pursued the traditional, pro-Muscovite policies of the Left-Bank hetmans. He continued to strengthen the *starshyna*, issuing them over 1,000 land grants (see *Kolomak Articles), but he also placed certain limits on their exploitation of the lower classes. The largess of the tsars made him one of the wealthiest landowners in Europe. Mazepa used much of his wealth to build, expand, and support many churches and religious, educational, and cultural institutions. His pro-*starshyna* policies, however, engendered discontent among the masses and the anti-elitist Zaporozhians and resulted in a dangerous but unsuccessful Tatar-supported Zaporozhian uprising led by P. Ivanenko (*Petryk) in 1692–6.

Zaporozhian icon of the Holy Protectress depicting churches funded by Hetman I. Mazepa

A cardinal principle of Mazepa's policy was the maintenance of good relations with Moscow. He developed close relations with Tsar *Peter I, energetically helping him in his 1695–6 Azov campaigns against the Tatars and Turks. He was also his adviser in Polish affairs. These close contacts helped him gain Muscovite backing for the occupation of the Right Bank in 1704 during the great anti-Polish Cossack revolt led by S. *Palii. Once again Ukraine was united under the rule of one hetman. But as the Great Northern War (1700–21), in which *Charles XII of Sweden and Peter were the main opponents, progressed, dissatisfaction with Muscovite rule spread in the Hetmanate. The Cossack regiments suffered huge losses during difficult campaigns in the Baltic region, Poland, and Saxony; the civilian populace had to support Muscovite troops and work on fortifications; and Peter's reforms threatened to eliminate Ukrainian autonomy and integrate the Cossacks into the Muscovite army. Pressured by the disgruntled *starshyna*, Mazepa began having doubts about Moscow's overlordship. In 1705 *Stanislaus I Leszczyński, Charles's Polish ally, secretly proposed to him to bring Ukraine into the Polish-Lithuanian federation. In October 1708, after the tsar informed Mazepa that he could not count on Moscow's aid should the Swedes and Poles invade Ukraine, Mazepa decided to

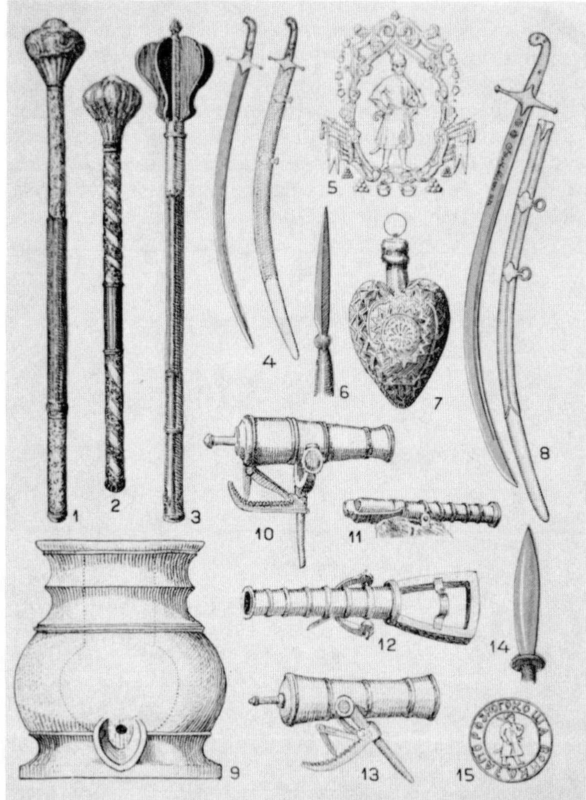

Cossack weaponry and regalia: 1–3) maces of hetmans and colonels; 4) saber; 5) insignia on the banner of the Domontovsky Regiment, 1762; 6, 14) spears; 7) gunpowder flask; 8) the saber of Hetman I. Mazepa, 1662; 9) 40-mm mortar; 10–13) cannons; 15) Cossack seal from the early 17th century [from V. Sichynsky]

join the advancing Swedes. In July 1709, Charles and Mazepa were defeated in the decisive Battle of *Poltava and fled to Ottoman Moldavia, where the aged and dejected hetman died.

About 50 leading members of the *starshyna*, almost 500 Cossacks from the Hetmanate, and over 4,000 Zaporozhians followed Mazepa to Bendery. These 'Mazepists' were the first Ukrainian émigrés. In the spring of 1710 they elected P. *Orlyk, Mazepa's general chancellor, as their hetman-in-exile. Anxious to attract potential support, Orlyk drafted the Constitution of *Bendery. With Charles's backing, he concluded anti-Muscovite alliances with the Tatars and the Porte and in January 1711 launched a combined Zaporozhian-Tatar offensive in Ukraine. After initial successes, the campaign failed.

The decline of Ukrainian autonomy

Left-Bank Ukraine. After the failure of Mazepa's plans, the absorption of the Hetmanate into the Russian Empire began in earnest. It was, however, a long, drawn-out process, which varied in tempo, because some Russian rulers were more dedicated centralizers than others and during certain times, especially in the course of war with the Ottomans, it was dangerous to antagonize the Ukrainians. To weaken Ukrainian resistance, the imperial government used a variety of divide-and-conquer techniques: it encouraged conflicts between the hetmans and the *starshyna*, cowed the latter into submission by threatening to support the peasantry, and used complaints by commoners against the Ukrainian government as an excuse to introduce Russian administrative measures.

With the acquiescence of the tsar, I. *Skoropadsky, was chosen hetman (1708–22). Several Russian innovations followed his election. In violation of tradition, no new treaty was negotiated, and the tsar confirmed Ukrainian rights only in general terms (see *Reshetylivka Articles). Peter appointed a Russian resident, accompanied by two Russian regiments, to the hetman's court with supervisory rights over the hetman and his government. The hetman's residence was moved from Baturyn to Hlukhiv, closer to the Russian border. Peter began the practice of personally appointing colonels, bypassing the hetman, while the resident received the right to confirm other officers. Many of the new colonels were Russians or other foreigners, and for the first time Russians, particularly A. Menshikov, acquired large landholdings in Ukraine (many of them expropriated from the Mazepists). Even publishing was controlled by Peter's decree of 1720, which forbade publication of all books in Ukraine with the exception of liturgical texts, which, however, were to be published only in the Russian language.

In 1719 Ukrainians were forbidden to export their grain and other products directly to the West; instead, they had to ship through Russian-controlled Riga and Arkhangelsk, where the prices were dictated by the Russian government. Russian merchants, meanwhile, received preferential treatment in exporting their goods to the Hetmanate. Tens of thousands of Cossacks were sent north to build the Ladoga canal and the new capital of St Petersburg, where many of them died. As a final blow to the autonomy of the hetman, Peter instituted the *Little Russian Collegium on 29 April 1722. Established supposedly to look after the tsar's interest by controlling finances and to hear appeals against any wrongdoings of the *starshyna*, it seriously undermined the position of the hetman. Skoropadsky protested vehemently but to no avail. Soon after its establishment he died.

While P. *Polubotok was acting hetman (1722–4), a struggle for power developed between him and Gen S. Veliaminov, the head of the Collegium. Refusing to give ground to the Collegium, Polubotok improved several aspects of the hetman government, especially the judiciary, so as to deprive Russians of an excuse for interference. To reduce peasant grievances, he pressured the *starshyna* to be less blatant in exploiting the peasantry. Polubotok's and the *starshyna*'s repeated entreaties to restore their privileges, abolish the Collegium, and appoint a hetman (see *Kolomak Petitions) angered Peter and he responded by increasing the authority of the Collegium. Soon afterward, Polubotok and his colleagues were ordered to St Petersburg and imprisoned there. Polubotok died in prison. His colleagues were pardoned after Peter's death in 1725.

With Polubotok incarcerated, the Collegium had free rein in the Hetmanate. In 1722 it introduced direct taxation of the Ukrainians. But, when Veliaminov demanded that Russians in Ukraine, and especially the influential Menshikov, also pay taxes, he lost support in St Petersburg. Moreover, the possibility of a new war with the Ottoman Empire raised the need to appease the Ukrainians. Therefore, in 1727, Emperor *Peter II, influenced by Menshikov, abolished the Collegium and sanc-

Folk dress from various regions of Ukraine: 1) typical traditional; 2) Kiev region; 3) Poltava region; 4) Kharkiv region; 5) Southern Ukraine; 6) Galicia; 7) Bukovyna; 8) Hutsul region; 9) Transcarpathia

tioned the election of a new hetman, D. *Apostol (1727–34).

The new hetman's diplomatic, military, and political prerogatives were limited. Aware that any attempt to restore the hetman's political rights was doomed, Apostol concentrated on improving the social and economic conditions. He regained, however, the right to appoint the General Officer Staff and colonels, greatly reduced the number of Russians and other foreigners in his administration, brought Kiev, long under the authority of Russian governors, under his sway, and had the number of Russian regiments in Ukraine limited to six. Thus, he slowed the process of the Hetmanate's absorption into the Russian Empire.

After Apostol's death, the new empress, *Anna Ivanovna (1730–40), forbade the election of a new hetman and established a new board, the *Governing Council of the Hetman's Office (1734–50), to rule the Ukrainians. Its first president, Prince A. Shakhovskoi, received secret instructions to spread rumors blaming the hetmans for taxes and mismanagement and to persuade Ukrainians that the abolition of the Hetmanate would be in their interest. Russian political practices, such as that of obligatory denunciation (*slovo i delo*), were introduced in Ukraine in this period. Because of the Russo-Turkish War of 1735–9, during which Ukraine served as a base, the Cossacks and peasants suffered tremendous physical and economic losses. During the council's existence the *Code of Laws of 1743, which had been begun under Apostol, was completed but never implemented.

During the reign of Empress *Elizabeth I (1741–62), her consort and (from 1742) husband O. Rozumovsky, by birth a simple Cossack who rose to the title of count, influenced her to abolish the council and restore the hetmancy with his younger brother Count K. *Rozumovsky as hetman (1750–64). The new hetman spent most of his time in St Petersburg, where he was president of the Imperial Academy of Sciences and deeply involved in court politics and governmental affairs. During his absences from Ukraine, the land was governed by the *starshyna*, thus hastening their transformation, begun in the late 17th century, into a typical hereditary, landowning, nobility. The *starshyna* persuaded Rozumovsky to issue an edict in 1760 limiting the free movement of the peasantry. A major setback, however, was the Russian abolition in 1754 of Ukrainian import and export duties, a major source of income in the Hetmanate's budget. After helping *Catherine II (1762–96) come to power, Rozumovsky returned to the Hetmanate. In October 1763 he and the *starshyna* met in council at Hlukhiv and petitioned the empress to renew the Hetmanate's lost prerogatives and to approve the creation of a noble diet modeled on the Polish Sejm. Rozumovsky also requested hereditary rights to the hetmancy for his family. Catherine, however, in line with her general policy of uniformity and centralization, and following G. *Teplov's advice, decided to abolish the legal separation of Ukraine and Russia altogether, and in 1764 she compelled Rozumovsky to resign as hetman.

The liquidation of the Hetmanate. Catherine completed the policy of centralization and institutional Russification that Peter I began in Ukraine and in other autonomous lands of the empire. In 1763 she approved the creation of *New Russia gubernia out of the lands of *New Serbia and *Slobidska Ukraine, and in 1764 she restored the Little Russian College (this time with four Russians and four Ukrainians). The task of its president, Count P. *Rumiantsev, was to eliminate Ukrainian autonomy gradually and cautiously. He neutralized the Ukrainian elite by recruiting their members into Russian service and giving them rank and promotions. In order to introduce taxation and control peasant labor in Ukraine, Catherine ordered a thorough survey of the population and resources of the Hetmanate – the *Rumiantsev census – to be carried out. An unexpected complication arose with the strong stand in defense of Ukrainian autonomy taken by the Ukrainian deputies, particularly H. *Poletyka, at the Legislative Commission Assembly of 1767.

After the Russo-Turkish War of 1768–74 and the Treaty of *Küçük Kaynarca, the liquidation of Ukrainian autonomy gained new impetus. The Zaporozhian *New Sich was destroyed by Russian troops in 1775; many of the dispersed Zaporozhians fled and established the *Danubian Sich, and the vast lands of *Southern Ukraine were incorporated into the empire as part of New Russia and Azov gubernias and developed by their governor G. *Potemkin. Catherine promoted the settlement of these largely unpopulated areas by *Germans, *Serbs, *Mennonites, *Bulgarians, and others, and the establishment of several new cities on the Black and Azov seas to attract foreign trade. By 1782 all the traditional 10 Left-Bank regiments of the Hetmanate were abolished and reconstituted as the new Kiev, Chernihiv, and Novhorod-Siverskyi vicegerencies and part of New Russia gubernia. In 1780 most of Slobidska Ukraine became part of the new Kharkiv vicegerency. The imperial bureaucracy replaced Ukrainian administrative, judicial, and fiscal institutions and social and legal norms with Russian ones. In 1783 the Cossack regiments were transformed into 10 regular cavalry regiments and the Russian system of conscription and *serfdom was extended into Ukraine. The Ukrainian elite acquiesced becaused they benefited from the changes: the 1785 charter gave them the privileges of Russian nobility (though less than half of those who registered as nobles were recognized as such). The Ukrainian church suffered a major setback under the new order: its lands and peasants were secularized, and many monasteries were closed down in 1786. The Hetmanate and the Cossack social order ceased to exist.

Right-Bank Ukraine. In 1714 Poland again regained control of the devastated and depopulated Right Bank, and a colonizing movement was organized by the Polish magnates who owned much of the land. Peasants from northwestern Ukraine, especially Volhynia, were attracted there by 15-to-20-year exemptions from corvée and other obligations. With them came Orthodox and Uniate clergy. Cossackdom, however, was not allowed to develop. The towns that were re-established were largely inhabited by Jews, who earned their living as innkeepers, artisans, and merchants. Polish gentry were largely attendants at the magnates' courts, and leaseholders or stewards managed their estates. At the peak of the social order were the few wealthy magnate families that owned huge latifundia. For much of the 18th century the Right Bank was a typical noble-dominated society, marked by lack of central authority, oligarchic politics, and extreme exploitation of the peasantry.

Without Cossacks, the peasantry was ineffective in resisting the nobility. Occasionally minor disturbances broke out, led by runaway peasants who congregated in forests and emerged to attack isolated noble estates. These so-called *Haidamakas usually enjoyed the support of the peasants; gradually, they became a serious problem for the Polish nobles, especially after the corvée exemption expired, serfdom was imposed, and religious oppression was intensified. In 1734, when Poland was involved in a conflict with Russia, the first serious *Haidamaka uprising broke out. Another major one occurred in 1750. The most widespread and bloodiest was the so-called *Koliivshchyna Rebellion of 1768, when the Poles were engaged in another war with Russia (see Confederation of *Bar). Thousands of Polish nobles, Jews, and Catholic clergy were massacred. Fearing that rebellion would spread into its possessions, the Russian government sent forces to quell it. Thus ended the last great uprising of the Ukrainian peasantry against the Polish nobles.

Russia's expansion was a dominant factor in the history of Ukraine. In the late 18th century its ruler, Catherine II, concentrated on a great drive southward to the Black Sea in order to gain access to the Mediterranean and world trade. Southern Ukraine was thus colonized and urban centers began to develop. While it was liquidating the autonomy of the Hetmanate and absorbing the lands of the Zaporozhian Sich, Russia also conquered the Crimean Khanate in 1774 and, after annexing it in 1783, gained control of the entire northern Black Sea coast. Russia interfered in Poland and influenced political developments there throughout the 18th century, ostensibly to protect its Orthodox population. In 1772, 1793, and 1795 the Commonwealth was partitioned among Russia, Austria, and Prussia. Thus, by 1795 all of Right-Bank Ukraine had been incorporated into the Russian Empire, which now controlled about 80 percent of the Ukrainian lands. The remainder were part of the Habsburg monarchy. Transcarpathia became part of the Habsburg Empire along with Hungary in 1526; Galicia was taken in in the first partition of Poland in 1772; and Bukovyna was taken from the Turks in 1774 and formally incorporated into Austria in 1787.

Social transformations. In the 17th and 18th centuries there were extensive social changes in Ukraine. On the Left Bank, the Cossack *starshyna* evolved from elective officers into a hereditary nobility. By the end of the 18th century they numbered about 2,000 adult males. Constituting less than 1 percent of the population, they controlled about 50 percent of the land (see *Rank estates). Meanwhile, the status of rank-and-file Cossacks declined drastically. Deprived of political prerogatives by the *starshyna*, they also encountered debilitating economic difficulties. Obliged to render extremely protracted, and therefore costly, military service throughout the 18th century, many of them fell into debt and lost or gave up their Cossack status and became state peasants. This downward mobility was reflected in the decline of their numbers in active military service: from 50,000 in 1650 to 30,000 in 1669 and 20,000 in 1730. Because the *starshyna* and Cossacks were not taxed, they often competed successfully with the burghers in local commerce and primitive, small-scale manufacturing and thereby undermined the prosperity of the relatively small urban stratum (about 4 percent of the population).

Even more drastic was the decline in the fortunes of the peasantry. After 1648 they became free peasants who lived in self-governing communities and owed relatively minor obligations for use of the land to the Zaporozhian Host. But as the *starshyna* accumulated more land, it constantly raised the labor obligations of the peasantry. In Mazepa's time peasants were forced to work, on the average, two days a week for local *starshyna* landowners. Within a generation the obligations rose to three days and more. The final step in the enserfment of the Left-Bank peasantry occurred in 1783, when Catherine II deprived them of the right to leave their landlords under any circumstances. With the introduction of serfdom most traces of the social upheaval and experimentation that began with the Khmelnytsky uprising disappeared, and Ukrainian society became much like the noble-dominated societies of its neighbors.

Ukraine under imperial rule. From the late 18th century to 1917–18, Ukrainians were subjected to imperial rule.

Throughout this period, the tsarist government consistently and systematically attempted to obliterate most traces of Ukrainian distinctiveness. During the reign of *Alexander I (1801–25), the Russian presence in Ukraine consisted primarily of the imperial army and bureaucracy. By the 1830s, during the reign of *Nicholas I (1825–55), the process of establishing a centralized administration throughout Ukraine was completed. The abolition of Magdeburg law in 1831 and the Lithuanian Statute in 1840 put an end to non-Russian legal influences, elected officials, and municipal self-government in Ukraine. Even the name 'Ukraine' almost disappeared from usage: the Left Bank was generally referred to as Little Russia, while the Right Bank was officially called the Southwest Territory. Among the Ukrainian elite, especially the descendants of the old Cossack *starshyna*, a 'Little Russian mentality' – a tendency to view Ukraine as a distinct but organic part of the Russian Empire – became widespread.

Although the impact of the French Revolution and the Napoleonic invasion of 1812 was minimal in Ukraine secret societies nonetheless arose there as part of the *Decembrist movement. Its members attempted unsuccessfully to stage the first revolution (1825) in the Russian Empire. In 1830 the Polish nobles on the Right Bank joined the anti-Russian rebellion that began in the Congress Kingdom of Poland. After suppressing it in 1831, the tsarist government instituted Russification policies on the Right Bank. Harshly implemented by Governor-General D. *Bibikov, they had a major impact on both the Ukrainians and Poles. To curtail the influence of the Polish nobles in society and local government, the estates of about 3,000 nobles were confiscated, and some 340,000 were deprived of their status and deported to the east. To counter Polish influence in culture and *education on the Right Bank, the Kremianets Lyceum was closed down, and a Russian University was opened in Kiev in 1834. In 1839 the numerous Uniates in the region were forced to adopt Orthodoxy (see *Church, history of the Ukrainian). To win over the Ukrainian peasantry and further alienate them from the Polish nobles, in 1847 Bibikov introduced Inventory Regulations limiting the obligations a peasant owed his landlord.

The vast majority of the approximately 2.4 million Western Ukrainians in the Habsburg Empire in the early 19th century lived in eastern *Galicia; the remainder lived in Bukovyna and Transcarpathia. Their social structure was relatively simple, for the population in eastern Galicia consisted mostly of impoverished peasantry (95 percent) and about 2,000 priestly families. The nobles in Galicia were almost all Poles or Polonized Ukrainians, and Jews made up the overwhelming majority of the small urban population. The socioeconomic development of Western Ukraine lagged behind that of Russian-ruled Ukraine. It was one of the poorest regions in all Europe. Galicia was incorporated into the Habsburg Empire during a time of major changes, and Emperor *Joseph II developed a special interest in Galicia, viewing it as a kind of laboratory for his educational, social, and economic reforms. Most notable in this respect was the transformation of the clergy into a civil service, the limitation of corvée labor, the regulation of feudal units, and the abolition of the personal dependence of peasants on the seigneur. After Joseph's death (1790), many of his reforms, especially those pertaining to the peasants, were either subverted by the nobles or rescinded by his conservative successors.

The rise of national consciousness. In Ukraine, as elsewhere in Eastern Europe, the rise of national consciousness was primarily associated with the impact of Western ideas (especially those of J. *Herder, the French Revolution, and *Romanticism) and with the birth of an *intelligentsia. The institutions of higher learning established to provide the imperial governments with well-trained bureaucrats facilitated the development of the intelligentsia. *Kharkiv University served as the intellectual center of Russian-ruled Ukraine until *Kiev University assumed this role in the 1830s. Initially, the Ukrainian intelligentsia under Russia consisted primarily of nobles by background. A small minority were priests' sons, burghers, or Cossacks. The intelligentsia's numbers were small; eg, prior to 1861 Kharkiv and Kiev universities produced a total of only about 4,300 graduates. Later, noble representation in the intelligentsia declined and that of commoners, including peasants, rose.

Indicative of the first phase of nation-building was the interest shown by the intelligentsia in the late 18th and early 19th century in Ukrainian history, *historiography, *ethnography, and *folklore. Given the central importance of the native language in the maintenance of national consciousness, the Ukrainian intelligentsia was anxious to raise its status. A significant event in this regard was the publication in 1798 of I. *Kotliarevsky's *Eneïda* (Aeneid). Despite their achievements in *literature and *scholarship, the Ukrainian intelligentsia of the early 19th century continued to view Ukraine and the Ukrainians in regionalist terms, convinced that in cultivating things Ukrainian it was also enriching the cultural heritage of Russia as a whole.

In the 1840s a new generation of Ukrainian intellectuals, now based in Kiev, emerged. Among its leaders were the historian M. *Kostomarov, the author P. *Kulish, and, most important, the poet T. *Shevchenko, whose works have exerted an unparalleled influence on Ukrainians. In 1847 the above mentioned, together with a small group of other Ukrainian intellectuals, began the political phase of nation-building by founding in Kiev the secret *Cyril and Methodius Brotherhood, which was quickly uncovered by the tsarist police. The trials and exile of its leaders marked the beginning of the long confrontation between the Ukrainian intelligentsia, which stood for national rights and social justice, and the Russian imperial authorities.

In Austrian-ruled Western Ukraine, in the early 19th century the intelligentsia was practically synonymous with the Greek Catholic *clergy – the only social group that could avail itself of higher learning. Thus, of the 43 Ukrainian-language books that appeared there between 1837 and 1850, 40 were written by priests. The first signs of interest in the native language appeared in *Peremyshl, where, in 1816, Rev I. *Mohylnytsky organized a clerical society for the purpose of disseminating culture and enlightenment and preparing simple religious texts. In the 1830s the center of nation-building activity shifted to *Lviv, where young, idealistic seminarians captivated by romantic national ideas came to the fore (see *Ruthenian Triad).

Imperial change and reforms. Nationhood became a major political issue in Western Ukraine during the *Revolution of 1848–9, which shook the Habsburg Empire and much of Europe. Confronted by uprisings in Hungary, Italy, and Vienna itself, and threatened by a Polish revolt in Galicia, the Habsburgs sought to gain popular support by abolishing serfdom and establishing parliamentary representation. These developments provided the impetus for political self-organization of Ukrainians. Rejecting the claims of the Poles to represent the entire population of Galicia, the Ukrainians established the *Supreme Ruthenian Council as their representative body and clashed with the Poles at the *Slavic Congress in Prague. Thus began a long period of Polish-Ukrainian political conflicts in Galicia. Demanding autonomy, the Ukrainians established the first Ukrainian-language newspaper (*Zoria halyts'ka*) and the popular enlightenment and publishing society *Halytsko-Ruska Matytsia, pressured the Habsburgs to establish a chair of Ukrainian philology at *Lviv University, began the construction of the *People's Home in Lviv, formed pro-Habsburg militias, and established contacts with compatriots in Bukovyna and Transcarpathia (see, eg, A. *Dobriansky). Thus, the revolutionary climate of 1848 allowed the Western Ukrainians to express and organize themselves as a distinct nation for the first time in modern history.

Russia's defeat in the *Crimean War of 1853–6 brought to the fore the empire's socioeconomic backwardness and impelled *Alexander II to introduce major reforms. The most important of these was the abolition of *serfdom in 1861. The impact of this emancipation on the Ukrainians was especially great because 42 percent of them (compared to an average of 35 percent in the Russian Empire) had been private serfs. Other reforms introduced by Alexander in the 1860s included the sale of land to state peasants; the introduction of local organs of self-government (*zemstvos) to look after education, public health, the mail, and roads; expanded accessibility to higher education; and the modernization of the *court system.

Socioeconomic changes. In the latter part of the 19th century, the economic situation in the Ukrainian countryside steadily worsened as heavy redemption payments, taxes, and lack of land impoverished the peasantry. Rapid population growth increased land hunger, and great numbers of peasants were forced to emigrate to the Asian regions of the Russian Empire (see *Emigration, *Far East, *Siberia, *Turkestan); by 1914 almost 2 million Ukrainians had settled permanently in these regions. Paradoxically, this stagnation did not prevent Ukraine from enlarging its role as the 'granary of Europe.' A small segment of the nobles, along with entrepreneurs from other classes, succeeded in transforming their estates into large, modern agribusinesses that supplied the imperial and foreign markets. In the steppe regions wheat was the main cash crop, and 90 percent of the empire's wheat exports – and 20 percent of world production – came from Ukraine. The Right Bank, where sugar beets were the chief cash crop, produced over 80 percent of the empire's sugar.

With the abolition of serfdom the way was finally cleared for industrialization and economic modernization. The first railway track was laid in 1866–71 between Odessa and Balta to facilitate the movement of grain. As the railway network grew, even more Ukrainian food and raw materials were sent northward to Russia in exchange for an unprecedented quantity of finished products. As a result, Ukraine's economy, which theretofore had been relatively distinct and self-sustaining, began to be integrated into the imperial economic system. The rapid growth of *railway transportation stimulated the demands for coal and iron. Consequently, between 1870 and 1900, and especially during the 1890s, the southeastern Ukrainian *Donets Basin, with its rich coal reserves, and *Kryvyi Rih Iron-Ore Basin became the fastest-growing industrial regions in the empire. Developed by foreign capital, with the aid of state subsidies, by 1900 these regions produced almost 70 percent of the empire's coal and most of its iron ore. In 1914 over 320,000 workers were employed here. During the 19th century Ukraine experienced much urban development. Between 1860 and 1897, the population of Odessa, the largest city, grew from 113,000 to 404,000; Kiev grew from 55,000 to 248,000 and Kharkiv from 50,000 to 174,000. In 1897, however, still only 13 percent of Ukraine's population lived in the 113 population centers officially designated as towns and cities. A crucial aspect of the industrial and urban change was that Ukrainians, who constituted 73 percent of the population in 1897, were little affected by them. They constituted 30 percent of the urban population, while Russians formed 34, Jews 27, and other national groups 9 percent of the urban total. Ukrainians were also a minority within the working class – 39 percent of the total. They were also very weakly represented in the intelligentsia: 16 percent of lawyers, 25 percent of teachers, and less than 10 percent of the writers and artists in Ukraine. Whereas at the turn of the 19th century there had been relatively few *Russians in Ukraine, by 1897 they constituted 12 percent of its inhabitants and formed the vast majority of the workers in the coal and metallurgical industries, as well as of employees in state administration. Because of especially rapid population growth among the *Jews, by the late 19th century they accounted for 8 percent of the population (compared to 4 percent for the empire as a whole) and they played a dominant role in trade and commerce in Ukraine. The Poles, who like the Jews were concentrated on the Right Bank, constituted about 6.5 percent of the population.

The emergence of nationalism and socialism. After the death of the archconservative *Nicholas I in 1855, the nascent Ukrainian movement showed new signs of life. In St Petersburg and Kiev, a new generation of Ukrainian activists, composed mostly of students, formed civic and cultural groupings called *hromadas. The St Petersburg hromada published an important journal, *Osnova*. A significant feature of the Kiev hromada was that it attracted a small group of Polish and Polonized nobles from the Right Bank who, guilt-stricken by the age-old exploitation of the Ukrainian peasantry by their class, resolved to draw closer to the masses among whom they lived. Led by V. *Antonovych and others, they called themselves *Khlopomany (peasant lovers). In the early 1860s, hromadas also appeared in Poltava, Chernihiv, Kharkiv, and Odessa, as well as St Petersburg and Moscow. Because of their advocacy of *populism and national traditions their members came to be called *Ukrainophiles.

The cultural and scholarly activities of the Ukrainophiles aroused the ire of Russian conservatives and government officials, and they were accused of fostering Ukrainian separatism. Consequently, in July 1863 P. *Valuev, the minister of the interior, banned the publication in Ukrainian of all scholarly, religious, and educational books. Soon after, the hromadas were dissolved and some Ukrainophiles were sent into internal exile. About a decade later, the Ukrainophiles, still led by V. Antonovych, surreptitiously renewed their activities. They formed the Old *Hromada of Kiev, so named to differentiate it from the new hromadas formed by students, and in 1873 they expanded their cultural activities by gaining control of the semiofficial *Southwestern Branch of the Imperial Russian Geographic Society. That same year they also convinced Countess Ye. Myloradovych and other wealthy philanthropists to fund the newly formed Shevchenko Society in Lviv.

As ties between the Ukrainian intelligentsia in the Rus-

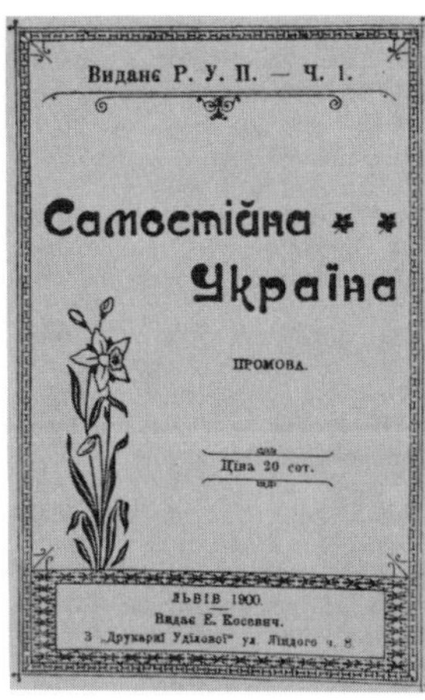
Видане Р. У. П. — Ч. 1.

Самостійна Україна

Промова.

Ціна 20 сот.

Львів 1900.
Видає Е. Косевич.
З „Друкарні Уділової" ул. Ліндого ч. 8

Title page of M. Mikhnovsky's *Samostiina Ukraïna*, 1900

sian and Austrian empires became stronger, *Galicia increasingly served as the main center of Ukrainophile activities because it was beyond the reach of tsarist restrictions. In 1876, alarmed by the growth of the Ukrainophile movement, Alexander II banned the printing and importation of Ukrainian-language publications (see *Ems Ukase). Several activists, most notably M. *Drahomanov, were forced into exile abroad. From Geneva, Drahomanov and other émigrés addressed the socioeconomic plight of the peasantry and advocated socialist ideas in the journal **Hromada*, which was smuggled into Ukraine. With the rise of radicalism among the intelligentsia in the Russian Empire in the 1870s, the question of the relationship between revolutionaries and Ukrainophiles and the 'Ukrainian question' came to the fore. Many revolutionaries in Ukraine, such as A. *Zheliabov, D. *Lyzohub, V. *Osinsky, and M. *Kybalchych, believed that it would be better for national distinctions to disappear so that a global socialist society might emerge. Consequently, a split between the socialist and more traditional Ukrainophiles occurred.

Early exponents of *Marxism in Ukraine were the economist M. *Ziber and S. *Podolynsky, a close associate of Drahomanov. But it was only in 1891–2 that the first stable Marxist group – the Russian Social Democratic Group – appeared in Kiev. A reflection of the political activism that swept through the empire beginning in the 1890s was the appearance of illegal Ukrainian political organizations and parties: the *Brotherhood of Taras (1891–8), the *General Ukrainian Non-Party Democratic Organization (1897–1904), the *Revolutionary Ukrainian party (1900–5), the *Ukrainian Socialist party (1900–3), the *Ukrainian People's party (1902–7), the *Ukrainian Democratic party (1904–5), the Ukrainian Radical party (1904–5), the Ukrainian Democratic Radical party (1905–8), the Ukrainian Social Democratic *Spilka (1904–13), the *Ukrainian Social Democratic Workers' party (1905–20), and the *Society of Ukrainian Progressives (1908–17).

The *Revolution of 1905 had an important impact on the development of the Ukrainian movement because Ukrainian-language publishing was permitted, as was freedom of association. Consequently by 1906 the number of Ukrainian-language periodicals had increased from 2 to 18, and Ukrainian publishing houses, *Prosvita cultural societies, co-operatives, and music and drama groups proliferated. These new initiatives were desperately needed to improve the cultural and educational levels of development of the Ukrainian population. In 1897 only 13 percent of Ukrainians were literate. In the wake of the revolution an imperial parliament – the State *Duma – was established, and its Ukrainian members formed a caucus within it. By 1908, however, government restrictions against the rapidly spreading Ukrainian movement had mounted again.

Despite the repression that marked the 1876–1905 period, Ukrainian scholarship made great progress (see *Historiography, *Legal scholarship, *Economic studies, *Linguistics, *Ethnography, *Folklore, *Literature studies, *Archeology, *Archeography, *Church historiography, *Geography). Ukrainian *literature flourished, many *scholarly societies were established, and by 1890 Ukrainian *theater boasted five professional troupes, each with repertoires of 20 to 30 plays that were performed with great success throughout the empire.

Developments in Western Ukraine. In 1851 the population of Galicia was 4.6 million, of which Ukrainians constituted about 50 percent, Poles 41 percent, and Jews 7 percent. By 1910 the population had almost doubled, to 8 million (Ukrainians 42 percent; Poles [and other Roman Catholics], 47 percent; Jews, 11 percent). Over 90 percent of Ukrainians were peasants. Inhabiting the poorest regions in the Habsburg Empire and vulnerable to exploitation by Polish landlords, they were extremely impoverished. Most had landholdings of less than 5 ha. Many of them were heavily in debt, usually to Jewish usurers whose interest rates (generally 52–104 percent annually, and occasionally as high as 500 percent) forced thousands of peasants to auction their land. Because industry was practically non-existent (except in the *Drohobych-Boryslav Industrial Region), there were few alternatives to rural poverty. Consequently, pressure to emigrate was great, and between 1890 and 1914 the *emigration of over 500,000 Ukrainians from Western Ukraine to the New World took place.

After 1849, when Count A. *Gołuchowski was appointed governor of the province, the political situation of the Ukrainians in Galicia deteriorated markedly. After the Austro-Hungarian compromise of 1867, the Polish nobility won total control over the recently formed (1861) Galician *Diet, and Vienna promised not to interfere in the Polish conduct of Galician affairs. Discouraged by the Polish predominance, disenchanted with the Habsburgs, and lacking confidence in the Ukrainians' ability to stand on their own, in the 1860s a large part of the West Ukrainian clerical and conservative elite, which controlled most Ukrainian institutions, looked to Russia for support. The *Russophiles' tendency to identify with the tsar and the Russian people and culture was opposed by most students, younger clergy, and members of the rising secular intelligentsia. Using Shevchenko and the Ukrainophiles in Russian-ruled Ukraine as well as the Ruthenian Triad as their models, the Galician *Populists championed the use of the vernacular, sought closer ties with the Ukrainian peasantry and its culture, and stressed the national distinctiveness of the Ukrainians. By the 1880s, however, a small group of young intelligentsia, led by I. *Franko and M. *Pavlyk, concluded that neither the Populists nor the Russophiles addressed adequately the pressing socioeconomic needs of the West Ukrainian peasantry. Greatly influenced by M. *Drahomanov, they adopted a program that combined socialism with Ukrainian national demands, and in 1890 they formed the *Ukrainian Radical party.

Despite their political disadvantages vis-à-vis the Poles,

Galicia's Ukrainians lived in a constitutional monarchy that allowed much greater freedom of association and expression than was possible in the Russian Empire. This freedom, as well as examples set by the Czechs, Germans, and Poles, led to an upsurge of organizational activity in Western Ukraine in the late 19th and early 20th centuries. A harbinger of this tendency was the *Prosvita society founded by the Populists in 1868 to spread literacy among the peasants. By 1914 it operated nearly 3,000 reading rooms and had close to 37,000 members. Later the gymnastic societies *Sokil (1894) and *Sich (1900) were founded; by 1914 they had well over 50,000 members. From the 1880s a Ukrainian *co-operative movement flourished in Western Ukraine, as did the Ukrainian *press, and by 1913 West Ukrainians could boast of having 80 periodicals, 66 of them in Galicia, 8 in Bukovyna, 4 in Transcarpathia, and 4 in Vienna and Budapest. All this activity not only addressed the cultural and socioeconomic needs of the Ukrainian masses, it also spread national consciousness and encouraged close ties between the intelligentsia (consisting usually of leaders of organizations) and the peasantry.

With the arrival in 1894 of M. *Hrushevsky from Kiev to occupy the Chair of History at Lviv University a new era in Ukrainian scholarship began, and under his direction in 1893 the Shevchenko Society was transformed into the *Shevchenko Scientific Society, a de facto academy of sciences. As various ideologies crystallized, the organizational infrastructure grew, and the need to function effectively in a parliamentary system became more pressing, the West Ukrainians formed political parties, notably the above-mentioned Ukrainian Radical party (1890–1939), the populist-independentist *National Democratic party (1899–1919), the Marxist *Ukrainian Social Democratic party (1899–1924), and the Catholic Ruthenian People's Union (1896).

As a result of the widespread educational, religious, civic, cultural, literary, and economic activity, Galicia became the bastion of the Ukrainian national movement. The Poles' increased efforts to limit it led to a rapid escalation of hostilities between the two communities, reflected in the fierce clashes between Ukrainian and Polish students at Lviv University and the assassination, in 1908, of Vicegerent A. *Potocki by the Ukrainian student M. *Sichynsky. *Bukovyna's 300,000 Ukrainians experienced an upsurge in activity similar to that of their Galician counterparts. They succeeded in establishing an effective educational system and gaining significant representation in the Viennese parliament. By contrast, the 500,000 Ukrainians in Hungarian-dominated *Transcarpathia had great difficulty in establishing their national identity because of the intense Magyarization policies of the government and strong Russophile tendencies among the tiny intelligentsia.

Ukraine in the First World War. The impact of the *World War on the Ukrainians, who were caught between major adversaries in the conflict, was immediate and devastating. About 3 million of them fought in Russia's armies, and over 250,000 served in Austria's forces. Some of the biggest battles on the eastern front occurred in Galicia, and much of Western Ukraine suffered terribly from repeated offensives and occupations. On the eve of the war, the West Ukrainians declared their loyalty to the Habsburgs. When war broke out, they formed an umbrella organization – the *Supreme Ukrainian Council in Lviv – and organized a 2,500-man volunteer legion, the *Ukrainian Sich Riflemen – the first Ukrainian military unit in modern times. In 1915 they created a co-ordinating body in Vienna – the *General Ukrainian Council – consisting of 21 Galician and 7 Bukovynian representatives and 3 members of the *Union for the Liberation of Ukraine (an organization of émigrés from Russian-ruled Ukraine who sought German and Austrian aid for the creation of an independent Ukrainian state).

A platoon of Ukrainian Sich Riflemen

As Russian armies occupied much of Galicia and Bukovyna in September 1914, the retreating Habsburg authorities, suspecting the Ukrainians of pro-Russian sympathies, arrested and executed hundreds without trial and deported over 30,000, including many Russophiles, to internment camps, such as the one near *Talerhof in Austria. Under Russian occupation, the West Ukrainians were also subjected to exceedingly harsh treatment. Intent on Russifying the population, the tsarist authorities arrested and deported thousands of Ukrainian activists, shut down Ukrainian institutions, and banned the use of Ukrainian. They also launched a campaign to liquidate the Greek Catholic church, exiling Metropolitan A. *Sheptytsky to Russia in the process. In 1915 Western Ukraine was reoccupied by Austria. In the rest of Ukraine, Ukrainian activities were almost totally suppressed until the outbreak of the Revolution of 1917.

The rebirth of Ukrainian statehood (1917–20). By the third year of the Great War, the multinational Russian, Austro-Hungarian, and Ottoman empires all showed signs of internal weakness and disintegration. In the Russian Empire, military defeats, disorganization, inflation, and serious food shortages provoked mass social discontent and unrest, which culminated in the *February Revolution of 1917 and the collapse of the monarchy. Following the abdication of Nicholas II on 15 March 1917, most of the opposition parties in the Duma banded together to form the Russian *Provisional Government. The Bolsheviks, however, who came to dominate the soviets of workers' and soldiers' deputies in Petrograd and elsewhere, refused to participate in the government. In this situation of social and economic chaos and dual political authority, the Provisional Government found it impossible to maintain control.

Taking advantage of the revolutionary situation, Ukraine's national leaders put forth not only social but also national and political demands. On 17 March 1917, the representatives of various Ukrainian political, com-

The Pedagogical Museum in Kiev, seat of the Central Rada in 1917–18

munity, cultural, and professional organizations gathered in Kiev and formed the Ukrainian *Central Rada as an all-Ukrainian representative body. On 22 March, the Rada issued an appeal to the Ukrainian people to maintain peace, establish order, and form political, cultural, and economic associations. Almost immediately a Constituent Military Council and Central Ukrainian Co-operative Committee were established, and the Prosvita society (banned in 1910) and the newspaper *Rada* (banned in 1914), now renamed **Nova rada*, were revived. The congress of co-operatives held in Kiev on 27–28 March came out in support of Ukrainian autonomy, as did a mass rally of over 100,000 people in Kiev on 1 April.

Beginning in March, various political parties were reorganized or created. The liberal *Society of Ukrainian Progressives was renamed the Union of Ukrainian Federalists-Autonomists and, in June 1917, the *Ukrainian Party of Socialists-Federalists (UPSF); led from June by S. *Yefremov, it favored autonomy within a federal Russian republic. The *Ukrainian Social Democratic Workers' party (USDWP) was revived; led by V. *Vynnychenko and S. *Petliura, it propagated the idea of Ukrainian independence. The *Ukrainian Party of Socialist Revolutionaries (UPSR) headed by M. *Kovalevsky enjoyed mass peasant support; it pushed for territorial autonomy and the nationalization of land and dominated the *Peasant Association, a mass organization that pursued the socialization of land. At the end of December 1917, the *Ukrainian Party of Socialists-Independentists (UPSI) was founded by Ukrainian patriots who were military personnel or had army backgrounds; its members (who in March 1917 had formed the *Ukrainian Military Club headed by M. *Mikhnovsky) organized Ukrainian military formations (see *Army of the UNR) and were the first to propagate the idea of an independent Ukrainian state. The small, conservative but separatist *Ukrainian Democratic Agrarian party (UDAP) was founded in May 1917 by Ukrainian landowners; its ideologist V. *Lypynsky promoted the idea of an independent monarchy ruled by a hetman and a Cossack elite. The USDRP and UPSR came to play leading roles in the Rada; the UPSF provided many of its functionaries; but the UPSI and UDAP played minor roles. Other minor parties – the *Ukrainian Labor party (ULP) and *Ukrainian Federative Democratic party – also appeared.

In Petrograd itself, a rally of over 20,000 Ukrainians, mostly soldiers, came out in support of Ukraine's autonomy. A week later the *Ukrainian National Council was established there with close links to the Rada. A similar Ukrainian Council was created in Moscow in late May.

An important event in the first phase of the Ukrainian revolution was the *All-Ukrainian National Congress convoked by the Rada (Kiev, 19–21 April 1917) whose 900 delegates recognized the Rada as the 'supreme national authority' and demanded Ukraine's autonomy, minority rights, and the participation of Ukrainian representatives in a future peace conference. The congress reorganized the Rada and elected its president (M. Hrushevsky) and vice-presidents (V. Vynnychenko and S. Yefremov). After the congress, the Rada elected from among its members an executive committee, later called the Little Rada.

Soldier, peasant, and worker organizations were also born in this period. These groups convened to proclaim their support for the Rada and elect delegates to it. The first *All-Ukrainian Military Congress (18–21 May 1917) created the Ukrainian General Military Committee headed by S. Petliura; the second congress (18–23 June 1917) organized the *Free Cossacks (volunteer units) and elected the *All-Ukrainian Council of Military Deputies to the Rada. The first *All-Ukrainian Peasant Congress (10–16 June 1917) elected the Central Committee of the Peasant Association and the *All-Ukrainian Council of Peasants' Deputies to the Rada, and the first *All-Ukrainian Workers' Congress (24–26 July 1917) elected the *All-Ukrainian Council of Workers' Deputies to the Rada.

With the revolution, all tsarist interdictions concerning the Ukrainian language were abolished and Ukrainian culture, education, and publishing flourished.

Ukraine's national minorities – the Russians, Jews, and Poles – also organized themselves. Russians continued to dominate in city elections. The Provisional Government appointed (mostly Russian) *gubernial commissioners (usually the heads of gubernial zemstvo executives) in Ukraine. Thus, in the first months of the revolution in Ukraine, dual authority – that of the Rada and the Provisional Government – existed. The Rada was also confronted in the Russified cities by the soviets of workers' and soldiers' deputies, but these had little Ukrainian support. Most non-Ukrainian political and civic organizations were hostile to the idea of Ukrainian autonomy, let alone independence.

When the Rada's autonomist demands were presented by a delegation to the Provisional Government and the Petrograd Soviet in May 1917 and rejected, the Rada issued the first of its four *universals on 23 June 1917 during the second All-Ukrainian Military Congress. It called for the creation of an elected people's assembly (diet) to ratify the laws determining the political and social order of an autonomous Ukraine. On 28 June the *General Secretariat of the Rada was established as its executive body under V. Vynnychenko.

These important steps were accepted by the majority of Ukrainians. Consequently the Russian government had to come to terms with the Rada and its demands. In its Second Universal (16 July 1917) the Rada informed the people that the final decision on Ukraine's autonomy would be made by the *All-Russian Constituent Assembly. The legal basis for Ukraine's autonomy was elaborated in the Statute of the Higher Administration of Ukraine and approved by the Little Rada on 29 July 1917. The Provisional Government, now headed by A. *Kerensky, refused to ratify the statute, however, and on 17 August it issued a 'Temporary Instruction to the General Secretariat' subordinating the General Secretariat to the Provisional Government instead of the Rada. The Rada reluctantly accepted the instruction as a temporary truce and the basis for obtaining further rights.

Ukrainian-Russian relations continued to deteriorate, as did economic conditions, military discipline, law and order, and the situation at the front. Interparty relations within the Rada and its control outside Kiev became even more unstable. Although the Rada did succeed in organizing the *Congress of the Peoples of Russia (21–28 September) and a congress of 80 gubernial and county commissioners (16–17 October), the Provisional Government continued to oppose the General Secretariat's attempts at functioning as an autonomous government.

On 7 November 1917 (25 October OS) the Bolsheviks in Petrograd overthrew the Provisional Government (see *October Revolution). Under the leadership of V. *Lenin and L. *Trotsky, they soon took power throughout most of ethnic Russia. But they were unsuccessful in Ukraine, the *Kuban, and the *Don region. The Rada condemned the coup on 8 November, but tried to remain neutral. On 10–13 November, however, battles took place in Kiev between the units of Kiev Military District, still loyal to the Provisional Government, and local Bolshevik forces. The pro-Rada First Ukrainian Regiment for the Defense of the Revolution, formed out of the delegates at the third All-Ukrainian Military Congress, intervened on the side of the Bolsheviks, and the Provisional Government's troops retreated to the Don.

The Third All-Ukrainian Military Congress in Kiev, November 1917

On 12 November the Rada created a larger, more left-leaning General Secretariat. In its Third Universal (20 November 1917), it proclaimed the creation of the *Ukrainian National Republic in federation with Russia (see *Universals of the Central Rada). The new General Secretariat also guaranteed freedom of speech, press, religion, and assembly, announced a political amnesty, and decreed that land was to be socialized without compensation. Workers were to be given control over their workplaces and production was to be state controlled. National minorities were granted *national-personal autonomy.

The elections in Ukraine to the *All-Russian Constituent Assembly (10–12 December 1917) gave majority support to the Ukrainian parties, particularly the UPSR (45.3 percent). The relations between the Rada and Bolshevik Russia deteriorated further. On 12 December, an attempted Bolshevik armed takeover in Kiev was suppressed, and Bolshevik attempts to turn the *All-Ukrainian Congress of Workers', Soldiers', and Peasants' Deputies' (17–19 December) against the Rada failed after the Council of People's Commissars in Petrograd sent an ultimatum on 17 December, demanding that the Rada allow Bolshevik forces to fight counterrevolutionaries on Ukrainian territory and that it prevent the passage of Don Cossacks leaving the southwestern front to join A. Kaledin's anti-Bolshevik army in the Don region.

The Rada rejected the Soviet Russian ultimatum and, soon after, the *Ukrainian-Soviet War broke out. The Bolsheviks proclaimed a Ukrainian soviet republic at the first All-Ukrainian Congress of Soviets in Kharkiv (11–12 December) and appointed a workers' and peasants' government (the *Peoples' Secretariat) on 30 December. A Russian Bolshevik army, aided by local rebellions, invaded Left-Bank Ukraine in January 1918 and, after the Battle of *Kruty (29 January), began advancing on Kiev. Though the Army of the UNR suppressed the Bolshevik uprising at the *Arsenal plant in Kiev (4 February), the Rada was forced to abandon Kiev and flee to Zhytomyr on 7 February.

St Sophia Square in Kiev during the proclamation of Independence, 25 January 1918

By December 1917 the Rada's leaders concluded that a separate peace treaty with the Central Powers and German military aid were the only way of saving the UNR. Since only a full-fledged independent state could conclude an international agreement, on 25 January 1918 the Rada issued its Fourth Universal (back-dated to 22 January) proclaiming Ukraine's independence. The General Secretariat was renamed the *Council of National Ministers, and 2 February was announced as the date for the convention of the *Constituent Assembly of Ukraine, elections to which had taken place on 9 January

The signing of the Peace Treaty of Brest-Litovsk, 9 February 1918

in regions not occupied by the Bolsheviks. A week later V. Vynnychenko resigned as prime minister, and on 30 January V. *Holubovych formed a new, UPSR-dominated government.

On 9 February 1918 the Peace Treaty of *Brest-Litovsk between the UNR and the Central Powers was signed, and on 19 February German-Austrian armies began their offensive against the Bolshevik-occupied lands. In early March Holubovych's government returned to Kiev, and by early April the last of the Red Army retreated from Ukraine. The German high command interfered in Ukrainian internal affairs as soon as its offensive began. Germany was interested mainly in exploiting Ukraine economically as part of its war effort, and the disorder, anti-German guerrillas, and policies of an uncooperative Ukrainian socialist government made the attainment of this goal difficult. To ensure the delivery of foodstuffs, the Germans took control of the railways. To force the recalcitrant peasants to sow their fields, Field Marshal H. von *Eichhorn issued an order on 6 April reversing the Rada's land nationalization policies, and on 25 April he formally introduced martial law. Gen W. *Groener began secret negotiations with Gen P. *Skoropadsky, a representative of conservative and landowning circles in Ukraine, about forming a new government that would be favorably disposed to the Germans' aims and policies. On 26–27 April the Ukrainian *Bluecoats divisions were disarmed and on 29 April, the day that the *Constitution of the UNR was adopted and M. Hrushevsky was elected president of the republic, a German-supported coup d'état was staged, and the congress of the *Union of Landowners proclaimed Skoropadsky 'Hetman of Ukraine.'

The Hetman government. Skoropadsky assumed all executive and legislative power and supreme command of the army and navy; only judiciary functions were left to a General Court. All laws promulgated by the Rada were abolished, and the UNR was renamed the Ukrainian State. The new regime, its legislation, and administration resembled those of tsarist times.

The first *Hetman government under Premier F. *Lyzohub included such well-known Ukrainian figures as D. *Doroshenko and M. *Vasylenko. Many of the other members belonged to Russian parties, mainly to the Russian Constitutional Democratic party; some were even Russian monarchists. The repressive, pro-German, and reactionary social and economic policies of the new regime and its (mostly Russian) collaborators engendered opposition from most of the Ukrainian political parties and the zemstvos, and led to strikes, widespread peasant rebellions and peasant guerrillas (eg, N. *Makhno and Yu. *Tiutiunnyk), arson and bombings, assassinations (eg, that of Eichhorn), and even increased support for the Bolsheviks.

Organized Ukrainian political opposition to the Hetman regime originated in May 1918, when members of the UPSI, UDAP, UPSF, ULP, and the railwaymen's and postal-telegraph unions formed the *Ukrainian National-State Union. In July this coalition was joined by the USDWP, UPSR, and various cultural, civic, labor, and professional organizations, and renamed the *Ukrainian National Union (UNU). After Germany's surrender in November 1918 and the withdrawal of its troops, the danger of a renewed Bolshevik occupation led Skoropadsky to turn to the anti-Bolshevik, but also anti-Ukrainian and pro-White, Entente Powers. To appease them he proclaimed his intention to federate with a future non-Bolshevik Russia and appointed a new cabinet made up mostly of Russian monarchists. These developments triggered the popular uprising that the UNR had been planning. Commanded by the *Directory of the UNR, the uprising was supported militarily by the *Sich Riflemen, various guerrilla detachments, thousands of peasants, and, towards the end, Ukrainian soldiers in the hetman's army. In December 1918, his military and German support gone, Skoropadsky abdicated, and the UNR was re-established in Kiev.

The period of the Directory of the UNR. On 26 December 1918 the Directory restored the legislation of the UNR (landowners' and church estates were again socialized without compensation), and in January 1919 a new Council of National Ministers of the UNR was constituted. To counter widespread pro-Bolshevik propaganda, the socialist Directory built its authority on the basis of gubernia and county labor councils of workers, peasants, and toiling intelligentsia. The Labor Congress that took place on 23–28 January 1919 in Kiev ratified the unification of the UNR and the newly created *Western Ukrainian National Republic (ZUNR) and recognized the supreme power of the Directory until the next session of the congress.

The proclamation of unification, Kiev, 22 January 1919

Upon assuming power, the Directory was faced with an extremely difficult internal and international situation. It was forced to deal with a renewed Bolshevik offensive and to continue fighting the *Ukrainian-Soviet War; to aid the ZUNR in the ongoing *Ukrainian-Polish War in Galicia; to circumvent Gen. A. *Denikin's anti-Ukrainian as well as anti-Bolshevik Volunteer Army in the Don region and hostile Rumanian forces in *Bessarabia and *Bukovyna; to contain the Franco-Greek Entente expeditionary forces that had occupied the Crimea and Odessa and were helping Denikin; and to cope with an unruly *partisan movement (eg, N. Makhno and N. *Hryhoriiv), whose activities and excesses compromised and even endangered the new government.

The only solution was to come to an agreement with either Moscow or the Allies. The failure of Premier V. Chekhivsky and Directory chairman V. Vynnychenko to arrange peace with the Bolsheviks prompted the government to accept the pro-Entente orientation proposed by S. *Petliura, the supreme military commander. On 10 February 1919, Vynnychenko and Chekhivsky resigned and Petliura became the new chairman. To facilitate negotiations with the Entente, the USDWP and UPSR withdrew from the government, and on 13 February a new cabinet, headed by S. *Ostapenko and composed mainly of ministers belonging to the UPSF, was formed. The new government tried to negotiate a common strategy against the Bolsheviks with the French commander in Odessa, Col H. Freydenberg. The plan failed because of Denikin's opposition, the population's hostility to the policies of the 'bourgeois' cabinet and its accommodation with the French, and the Entente's insistence on Petliura's resignation and French control of the army, railroads, and finances.

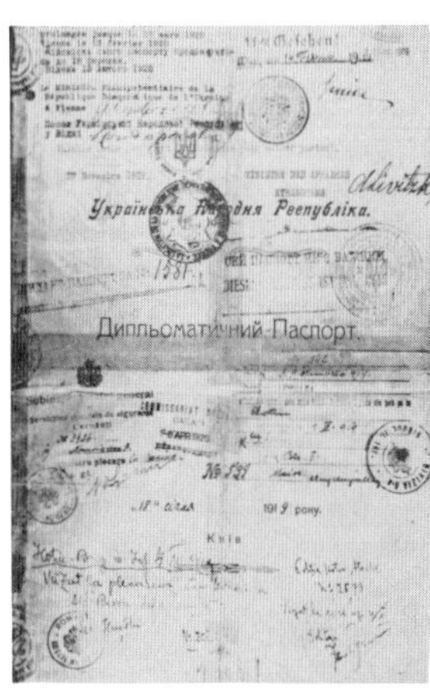
Українська Народня Республіка.
Дипльоматичний Паспорт.
1919 року.
Київ

Page from a UNR diplomatic passport

Beaten on several fronts, the government was no longer in control. Ukrainian army units became demoralized, increasingly more and more partisan otamans appeared, and the Bolshevik offensive forced the Directory to evacuate Vinnytsia. Meanwhile Otaman N. Hryhoriiv drove the Entente forces out of Kherson (10 March), Mykolaiv (15 March), and Odessa (6 April). With the Entente forces' retreat from Ukraine, Ostapenko's cabinet lost its raison d'être, and on 9 April a new cabinet, headed by B. *Martos and made up of USDWP and UPSR members, was formed in Rivne, Volhynia. The new government appealed to the populace to continue resisting the Bolshevik aggressors, reassured it that it would not turn for aid to foreign powers, and reiterated its adherence to democracy.

Between April and July, 328 anti-Bolshevik revolts took place in Ukraine. They were led by the left faction that had split from the USDWP in January and founded the *Ukrainian Social Democratic Workers' party (Independent) and by part of the UPSR; together they formed the *All-Ukrainian Revolutionary Committee, with a program of creating an independent socialist (non-Bolshevik) Ukrainian republic. The insurgent forces of otamans N. Hryhoriiv and D. *Zeleny also fought the Bolsheviks. The initial successes of the Directory in the Ukrainian-Soviet War were undermined by opposition from the UPSI and the right-wing *Ukrainian People's Republican party, which backed Otaman V. *Oskilko's abortive coup in Rivne on 29 April.

In June the government moved to Kamianets-Podilskyi, and on 27 August a new USDWP/UPSR-dominated cabinet, headed by I. *Mazepa, was constituted there. In July a joint offensive of the Army of the UNR and the *Ukrainian Galician Army (UHA) began against the Bolsheviks in Right-Bank Ukraine. Simultaneously but independently, Denikin's Volunteer Army began its offensive against the Bolsheviks in Left-Bank Ukraine. On 31 August both forces entered Kiev; to avoid armed conflict, the Ukrainian command withdrew from the city.

At this point, views among the Ukrainian leaders diverged. The Directory and the cabinet considered both the Whites and the Reds to be Ukraine's main foes; to get aid from the Entente they were prepared to form an alliance with Poland. The Ukrainians from Galicia, headed by Ye. *Petrushevych, however, considered Poland the greater enemy; they were prepared to come to terms with Denikin and thus get the support of the Entente. Meanwhile, the Entente Powers, being hostile to Ukrainian independence, began an economic blockade of Ukraine, and the Volunteer Army pursued a reactionary policy of destroying everything Ukrainian, terrorizing the populace, and restoring land to the gentry in the occupied territories.

Massive jacqueries against the Whites, led by Makhno, Zeleny, and other partisan leaders, erupted, and Petliura, to whom the Directory yielded all power on 15 September, declared war on Denikin on 24 September. A typhus epidemic, exacerbated by the lack of medical supplies owing to the Entente's blockade, annihilated up to 70 percent of the Ukrainian army (90 percent of the UHA) and decimated the populace. Consequently the UHA commander, Gen M. *Tarnavsky, signed an alliance with Denikin on 6 November, on the eve of the start of the third Soviet offensive in Ukraine. Petrushevych opposed this alliance, and on 16 November he and others in the government of the *Dictatorship of the Western Province of the UNR left Kamianets for Vienna. A day earlier, F. Shvets and A. Makarenko, two of the three remaining members of the Directory, went abroad on state business and gave Petliura authority to act in the name of the Directory. Petliura and the government and army of the UNR left Kamianets for Volhynia, and on 17 November the Poles occupied Kamianets.

In late November the Army of the UNR found itself surrounded by the Bolshevik, Polish, and White forces in Volhynia. In December the UNR government and army commanders abandoned regular warfare for partisan tactics against the Bolshevik and Denikin forces and the first *Winter Campaign began. Petliura went to Warsaw to join the vice-premier, A. *Livytsky, in trying to influence the attitude of the Entente Powers.

On 16 December the Bolsheviks occupied Kiev for the third time. By the middle of February 1920, they had forced Denikin's army out of Ukraine with the aid of UHA formations (the Red Ukrainian Galician Army), which had joined them in January. Thus, by early 1920 Volhynia and western Podilia were occupied by the Polish army, and the rest of Ukraine was under Bolshevik control.

Meanwhile, the Ukrainian emissaries in Warsaw had begun negotiations favorable to the Poles resulting in the Treaty of *Warsaw of 22 April 1920 signed by Petliura and J. *Piłsudski. The terms of the treaty, especially the surrender of the western Ukrainian territories to Poland, caused painful and profound discord among Ukrainians. As a result, Mazepa's government resigned, and a new UNR government – the last one on Ukrainian soil – was formed in May 1920 by V. *Prokopovych.

A joint offensive of the Polish-Ukrainian armies against Soviet-occupied Ukraine and Belorussia began on 24 April. On 6 May they took Kiev, but in June they were forced to retreat to Galicia and Poland proper. On 15 August the Bolsheviks were routed near Warsaw, and the joint armies of a new Polish-Ukrainian counteroffensive occupied part of Podilia by mid-October.

On 12 October the Polish government signed an armistice with the Soviets, and the 30,000-man Army of the UNR was forced to retreat on 21 November into Poland, where its soldiers were placed in *internment camps. Armed struggle against the Bolsheviks was continued by dozens of partisan groups in Podilia, Kiev, Katerynoslav, and Poltava gubernias. The insurgents, who numbered some 40,000 in late 1920, resisted Soviet rule until 1924. They were joined by UNR Army veterans from Poland under the command of Yu. *Tiutiunnyk, who operated in Volhynia and Podilia in November 1921 (the second *Winter Campaign).

The 18 March 1921 Peace Treaty of *Riga reaffirmed the Polish-Soviet armistice, established diplomatic relations between Poland and Soviet Ukraine, and legitimized Poland's annexation of Western Ukraine. The UNR parliament in exile – the *Council of the Republic – functioned in Tarnów, Poland, from February to August 1921.

The Western Ukrainian National Republic, 1918–23. The rebirth of the Western Ukrainian state was influenced strongly by the Revolution of 1917 and its aftermath in the rest of Ukraine. On 18–19 October 1918, the Ukrainian members of the Austrian parliament and the Galician and Bukovynian diets and three delegates from each Ukrainian political party in Galicia and Bukovyna constituted the *Ukrainian National Rada (UNRada) in Lviv as the representative council of the Ukrainians in Austria-Hungary and proclaimed the creation of a Ukrainian state on the territory of Galicia, northern Bukovyna, and Transcarpathia. A democratic constitution, granting proportional representation to all national minorities in the state organs, was adopted. Ye. Petrushevych was elected chairman of the UNRada, and a delegation for Galician affairs in Vienna under the direction of K. *Levytsky was formed.

On 9 November the UNRada named the new state the *Western Ukrainian National Republic (ZUNR) and the members of the Galician delegation became its first government – the *State Secretariat.

The UNRada proclaimed personal autonomy for the national minorities. Nonetheless, the Poles in Galicia were hostile to the ZUNR from the outset and mounted armed opposition to it. The *Ukrainian-Polish War began 1 November 1918. Polish forces occupied Lviv on 21 November, forcing the new government to move to Ternopil. While the Poles were backed by the might of the new Polish state, the ZUNR could only count on the military potential of Galicia's Ukrainians. Nonetheless, with the exception of Lviv, the corridor linking it with Peremyshl, and a few western counties, most of Galicia remained in Ukrainian hands. In late December, the UNRada and the government moved to Stanyslaviv. On 4 January 1919 a 10-member government executive, headed by S. *Holubovych, was appointed.

From its inception the State Secretariat was charged with the task of unifying all the Ukrainian territories into one state. On 1 December 1918 an agreement to federate had been signed by representatives of the ZUNR and UNR governments in Khvastiv; on 4 January 1919, the UNRada ratified the law of union, and on 22 January the union was proclaimed and celebrated in Kiev. Thereafter, the ZUNR was officially called the *Western Province of the UNR. Its political structure and ruling bodies were not changed, however, owing to the exigencies of the wars with Ukraine's enemies.

The UNRada promulgated various laws for the new state and sought international recognition of the ZUNR (see *Diplomacy) and an end to the war with Poland. The government devoted much of its attention to the *Paris Peace Conference and to lobbying the *Entente Powers.

By June 1919, the tide in the Ukrainian-Polish War had turned against the ZUNR and the UHA. Holubovych's government resigned, and the UNRada empowered Ye. Petrushevych to head a *Dictatorship of the Western Province of the UNR. The war continued to go badly despite the successes of the *Chortkiv offensive, and on 16–18 July UHA and the government retreated into UNR territory, leaving Galicia under Polish occupation.

While in Kamianets-Podilskyi, Ye. Petrushevych and Petliura failed to come to terms, and after the UHA was decimated by typhus and the third Soviet invasion of Ukraine began, Petrushevych left in November for Vienna, from where he and his government launched a diplomatic campaign against Poland until the *Conference of Ambassadors sanctioned the Treaty of Riga (1921) and the annexation of Galicia and western Volhynia by Poland in March 1923.

(See *Bukovyna and *Transcarpathia for the history of these regions during the years 1918–20.)

Ukraine in the interwar years

Soviet Ukraine. During the Ukrainian-Soviet War the Bolsheviks formed several short-lived governments in Ukraine (see *Communist Party of Ukraine, *Council of People's Commissars, *Donets–Kryvyi Rih Soviet Republic, *People's Secretariat, and *Provisional Workers' and Peasants' Government of Ukraine). Although, for tactical reasons, they recognized the independence of Ukraine, and the Third All-Ukrainian Congress of Soviets (Kiev, – March) adopted the first *Constitution of the Ukrainian SSR as 'an independent and sovereign state,' in reality the military, state, and Party apparatuses were directed from Moscow and dominated by foreign and anti-Ukrainian elements, who terrorized the population while imposing their rule (see *Cheka), nationalizing all industry and commerce, and enforcing a ruthless requisitioning of farm produce. The excesses of *War Communism led to the ruin of the agricultural economy and culminated in the 1921–3 *famine in Ukraine.

As a result of widespread opposition, the Bolsheviks were forced to build an indigenous power base by seeking accommodation with and incorporating the 'national communists' – the influential *Borotbists and *Ukrainian Communist party (UCP). By 1921, the forces of the UNR and Gen P. *Wrangel's White army had been defeated and the peace treaty with Poland had been signed. Soviet power was by and large secure, and Lenin introduced the *New Economic Policy (NEP). On 30 December 1922 the USSR – a multinational federation of Soviet republics – was formally constituted (see *Federalism). According to the Constitution of the USSR that was ratified by the Second Congress of Soviets on 31 January 1924, foreign relations, commerce, the military, transportation, and communications became prerogatives of the all-Union government, while the republican governments were given authority over internal and agrarian affairs, education, the judiciary, public health, and social security within their own borders. Nevertheless, the USSR remained in practice a centralized state, and directives continued to come from Moscow.

To appease the various nationalities and gain their support for Soviet rule, the Bolsheviks approved the principle of *korenizatsiia* (*indigenization) and condemned Russian chauvinism at their 12th Congress in 1923. The new *nationality policy emphasized the need for the economic development of various republics, the creation of indigenous national cadres, education in the mother tongue, de-Russification of the Party and state apparats, and even the creation of territorial military units in the individual republics. As a result, *Ukrainization was introduced in 1923 and its development had a profound impact on culture, education, and politics.

The positive changes that the NEP and Ukrainization brought about convinced certain Galician Ukrainian and émigré political figures and scholars (eg, M. Hrushevsky, A. Nikovsky, P. Khrystiuk, M. Chechel, M. Shrah, S. Rudnytsky) to return to Ukraine. These policies also generated a national *literary discussion about the direction that Ukrainian literature should take; during it the influential and popular writer M. *Khvylovy even advocated cultural (and ultimately political) independence from Moscow and an orientation toward Western civilization. Ukrainization also buttressed the position of the *Ukrainian Autocephalous Orthodox church (UAOC), which was founded in Kiev in 1921 (see *Church, history ...).

The success of Ukrainization and the national legitimacy it gave Ukraine soon threatened Moscow's hegemony and spawned a fierce struggle between its supporters and opponents in the CP(B)U. In May 1926 the People's Commissar of Education, O. *Shumsky, protested against delays in Ukrainizing the proletariat, as well as Stalin's appointment of a non-Ukrainian, L. *Kaganovich, as first secretary of the CP(B)U (1925–8). He also defended the views of Khvylovy and the *Neoclassicists, and was condemned as a 'nationalist deviationist.' His removal provoked a schism in the *Communist Party of Western Ukraine, resulting in the expulsion of its 'Shumskyist' majority from the Comintern in 1928. M. *Volobuiev's analysis of Moscow's continuing colonialist exploitation of Ukraine was also condemned as the 'economic foundation of Khvylovyism and Shumskyism.'

To undermine Ukrainization, between 1926 and 1928 over 36,000 'Shumskyists,' 'Khvylovyists,' and 'Trotskyists' were expelled from the CP(B)U. Khvylovy was forced to renounce his views, and *Vaplite – the group of writers he led and influenced – was forced to dissolve in 1928. In 1928 a campaign against the 'nationalist deviations' of the Ukrainian Marxist school of history also began, led by M. *Yavorsky. In 1930, 45 leading figures in Ukrainian scholarship, culture, and the UAOC were sentenced at the show trial of the *Union for the Liberation of Ukraine and the Association of Ukrainian Youth, which were allegedly led by S. Yefremov, V. Durdukivsky, and V. Chekhivsky. Fifteen other alleged counterrevolutionary organizations were 'uncovered' during the Stalinist *terror of the 1930s.

Towards the end of the 1920s, having defeated the various internal Party oppositions, J. *Stalin consolidated his personal power. Under his rule the USSR became an increasingly Russocentric totalitarian state administered by an all-powerful, loyal, and ruthless bureaucracy and secret police – the *GPU and *NKVD. In December 1927, the 15th Party Congress approved the introduction of *collectivization and the acceleration of industrialization and ushered in the First *Five-Year Plan (1928–33). Private industry was abolished, all commerce was nationalized, the peasants were herded into *collective farms, and impossible quotas for the delivery of grain and other foodstuffs to the state were imposed. Those who opposed these Draconian measures were deported to *concentration camps if not killed outright, and hundreds of thousands of peasants were labeled *kulaks and deported to Siberia or the Arctic.

During this undeclared but nonetheless real war against the Ukrainian nation, Moscow's henchmen V. Molotov and L. Kaganovich blamed the leaders of the CP(B)U for the collapse of agriculture and the failure of collectivization. After the harvest of 1932 was already in, armed Party brigades confiscated all peasant stock of food and grain. The resulting man-made *famine and terror in the countryside caused the deaths of over 6 million people. The demographic and cultural consequences were colossal: the Ukrainian village, with its customs and traditions, ceased to exist.

This *genocide succeeded in breaking the peasantry and thus the backbone of the Ukrainian nation and began an offensive to transform Ukrainian culture into a tool of the Russian-Soviet regime. To achieve this task, P. *Postyshev was sent into Ukraine in January 1933 as the second CP(B)U secretary and de facto dictator of Ukraine. His arrival marked the beginning of the Great Terror in Ukraine, during which all Ukrainian cultural achievements were systematically destroyed. Ukrainization was officially abolished on 22 November 1933, and *Russification in all sectors of Ukrainian life was pursued. In this war against the Ukrainian nation four-fifths of the Ukrainian cultural and intellectual elite perished. Seeing their nation ravaged by famine and terror, both Khvylovy and Mykola *Skrypnyk, themselves persecuted, committed suicide in 1933.

Throughout the 1930s the CP(B)U was extensively purged of 'Ukrainizers' and hundreds of thousands of its members disappeared. Postyshev himself was removed in 1937 during the *Yezhov terror, and in 1938 S. *Kosior, the CP(B)U first secretary (1928–38), was replaced: both were subsequently shot. In 1937, almost all the members of the CP(B)U Central Committee and Ukrainian government were liquidated, and the head of the government from 1934, P. *Liubchenko, committed suicide. By the end of the 1930s the Ukrainian population was decimated and leaderless, its culture destroyed. In 1938, Stalin appointed two loyal servitors, N. *Khrushchev and D. *Korotchenko, to head the CP(B)U and the Ukrainian government.

Western Ukraine under Poland. In the years 1919–23 in *Galicia, *Podlachia, western *Volhynia, western *Polisia, and the *Kholm, *Lemko, and *Sian regions, the Poles pursued a policy of denationalization, persecution, and repression. In 1919–20, 70,000 Ukrainians were imprisoned in concentration camps. The Galician Diet was abolished in 1920, as was Galician autonomy that had existed under Austrian rule since the late 1860s. The Ukrainian press was censored, and the Ukrainian chairs at Lviv University were closed down. The so-called *Sokal border was created to prevent contact between the Galician organizations and institutions and their counterparts in the northwest regions (Volhynia, Polisia, Podlachia, and the Kholm region).

The founding meeting of the Ukrainian Military Organization in Prague, July 1920; sitting, from left: I. Andrukh, Ye. Konovalets, V. Kuchabsky; standing, from left: ?, M. Matchak, Ya. Chyzh

The Ukrainians in Galicia responded by creating the *Lviv (Underground) Ukrainian University and a nationalist underground – the *Ukrainian Military Organization (UVO) – and by boycotting the census of 1920 and the elections of 1922. The Ukrainians in the northwest regions did not boycott the elections, however, and sent 20 representatives to the Sejm and 5 to the Senate. In March 1923 the Conference of Ambassadors sanctioned Poland's annexation of Galicia and the ZUNR government in exile was dissolved. Consequently the Galician political parties changed their strategy and began seeking accommodation with and participation in the new regime.

In 1925 the centrist *Ukrainian National Democratic Alliance (UNDO) was formed under D. Levytsky; until the Second World War it was the most popular and influential legal political party. After the Radical party was joined by Socialist Revolutionaries from Volhynia in 1926, it was renamed the Ukrainian Socialist Radical party (USRP). The *Ukrainian Social Democratic party (USDP), which was banned as communist in 1924, was revived in December 1929; neither it nor the *Ukrainian Catholic People's party, formed in 1930, had much influence or support. Sovietophile tendencies were represented by the *Ukrainian Party of Labor (1927–30) and the Ukrainian Peasants' and Workers' Socialist Alliance or *Sel-Rob (1926–32), the front organization of the clandestine *Communist Party of Western Ukraine (1923–38).

The UVO, led by Ye. *Konovalets, engaged in acts of sabotage throughout the 1920s against the Polish government and landowners, as well as against Ukrainian 'collaborators' with the regime and Sovietophiles. From the mid-1920s, new, younger members, who were not veterans of the UHA or Ukrainian Sich Riflemen, were recruited into the thinning ranks, and in 1929 the conspiratorial *Organization of Ukrainian Nationalists (OUN) was founded to take over its functions and to propagate a well-defined program and ideology of *nationalism, much of it inspired by the writings of D. *Dontsov. Konovalets became the leader of the OUN.

The Polish government maintained its anti-Ukrainian policies throughout the 1920s. In 1924 it banned the use of Ukrainian in state and self-government institutions and abolished unilingual Ukrainian schools (see *Education). Throughout the 1920s it promoted the colonization of Western Ukraine by Poles. The influx of some 200,000 Poles into the villages and some 100,000 into the towns and cities heightened Ukrainian-Polish tensions.

During the 1928 Polish elections, 46 Ukrainians were elected to the Sejm and 13 to the Senate. The deputies and senators from the UNDO and USRP, in particular, defended Ukrainian interests, declaring that they stood for a pan-Ukrainian sovereign state. Despite the government's oppressive measures, Ukrainian cultural, scholarly, civic, and co-operative life continued to develop. In fall 1930 the Piłsudski government reacted to ongoing OUN activity with military and police *pacification of Galicia. Ukrainian political, civic, and cultural figures were brutally beaten and tortured, Ukrainian institutional and private property was destroyed, and mass arrests occurred. This terror and intimidation affected the outcome of the 1930 elections: only 27 Ukrainians were elected to the Sejm and 5 to the Senate.

Polish oppression intensified in the 1930s. Municipal self-government was abolished in Galicia in 1933. Polisia and the Lemko and Kholm regions, in particular, were subjected to wholesale Polonization and forced conversion to Roman Catholicism. Hundreds of Ukrainian political prisoners were confined in the *Bereza Kartuzka concentration camp established in 1934. In 1935 a new Polish constitution reduced the powers and composition of the Sejm and the Senate, and Poland became a virtual dictatorship. Attempts by the UNDO (led by V. Mudry) at seeking the *normalization of Ukrainian-Polish relations proved unsuccessful because of Polish chauvinistic attitudes and discrimination, the regime's repressiveness, the revolutionary militancy of the OUN, and the uncompromising attitude of the *Front of National Unity, the *Union of Ukrainian Women, and other Ukrainian organizations and political parties.

Ukrainian territories under Rumanian rule. From November 1918, Ukrainians of Bukovyna, Bessarabia, and part of the Muramureş region came under Rumanian rule. Opposition to the regime was manifested by the *Khotyn uprising of 1919 and the Tatarbunary uprising of 1924. The greatest national persecution occurred in *Bukovyna, where repressive military rule lasted until 1928. The Ukrainian chairs at Chernivtsi University and most Ukrainian organizations were abolished, the Ukrainian press was forbidden, and Rumanianization of the Ukrainian Orthodox church was systematically pursued. In 1922 instruction in Ukrainian was abolished in almost all schools. To facilitate the Rumanianization of education, a 1924 law proclaimed Ukrainians to be Rumanians who had forgotten their mother tongue.

Conditions improved somewhat in 1927, and the populist *Ukrainian National party (UNP), headed by V. Zalozetsky-Sas, was founded to defend Ukrainian interests in parliament as best it could. Despite the regime's oppression, Ukrainian cultural, community, and student organizations in Bukovyna remained active and several periodicals were published, including the daily *Chas* (1928–40). Teaching in Ukrainian was allowed from 1931 to 1933.

In the 1930s, the underground OUN gained a large following among Bukovyna's students and peasants. The Nationalists published the monthly **Samostiina dumka* (1931–7) and the weekly **Samostiinist'* (1934–7). In 1938 all Ukrainian political parties were outlawed, and thereafter all manifestations of Ukrainian organized life were persecuted by the royal dictatorship.

The League of Ukrainian Nationalists in Prague; sitting, from left: M. Stsiborsky, M. Tobilevych, T. Pasichnyk-Tarnavsky, L. Kostariv, M. Zahryvny; standing, from left: Yu. Rudenko, Yu. Artiushenko, D. Pasichnyk, R. Myniv, D. Demchuk, O. Chekhivsky, K. Dudariv

Ukrainian territories under Czechoslovak rule. In 1919 the Ukrainians of Transcarpathia elected to be part of the new Czechoslovak Republic (see *Central Ruthenian People's Council and *American National Council of Uhro-Rusins), and the official region of *Subcarpathian Ruthenia was created, leaving the Prešov region as part of Slovakia. It was governed by J. Brejcha and a five-man *Directory of Subcarpathian Ruthenia (1919–20). The central government approved the use of the local language in education and other official activities. Consequently the struggle between the Ukrainophile-Populist and Russophile camps over the unresolved language question and national identity intensified. The Populists, led by Rev A. *Voloshyn and M. and Yu. *Brashchaiko, founded the *Ruthenian Agrarian party and the *Prosvita society, co-operatives, publishing houses, periodicals, and the *Plast scouting organization. The Russophiles set up their own parties, the *Dukhnovych Society, and other rival counterparts.

Seeing that the 'Ruthenians' were divided and mistrusting the Russophiles and Magyarophiles in particular, the central government did not move on the demands to create a local diet or institute autonomy in the region. Governor A. Beskyd, a Russophile, purged the administration of Ukrainians, and he and Vice-governor A. Rozsypal did much to discredit Ukrainians in the eyes of the central government.

In 1928 Subcarpathian Ruthenia became the fourth province of the Czechoslovak republic with its capital in Uzhhorod. In the 1930s many Ukrainians became Sovietophile Communists or radical nationalists in reaction to Prague's refusal to grant autonomy to the region and its support of the Russophiles, the policies of the chauvinistic Czech bureaucracy, and the effects of the depression (chronic unemployment, rural poverty, hunger).

Under the influence of the Ukrainian movement, demands for autonomy grew, but the Czech government, preoccupied with the Sudeten German crisis, deferred its implementation. After the Munich Agreement on 11 October 1938 Prague was forced to allow the creation of an autonomous Subcarpathian Ruthenian government headed by A. *Brodii and, from 26 October, A. Voloshyn. The Ukrainian movement strove to form a Carpatho-Ukrainian state incorporating the Prešov region and federated with the Czechs and the Slovaks, while most of the Russophiles supported union with Hungary. On 2 November southern Transcarpathia (including Uzhhorod, Mukachiv, and Berehove) was ceded to Hungary. Despite this loss, the Ukrainians took to building an autonomous *Carpatho-Ukraine with the aid of Galician and Bukovynian émigrés and material support from the overseas emigration. The school system was Ukrainianized, and a paramilitary force – the *Carpathian Sich – was created with OUN assistance. Elections to the *Diet of Carpatho-Ukraine were held on 12 February 1939 in which the *Ukrainian National Alliance of political parties received 86.1 percent of the vote.

The new government had to contend with Polish and Hungarian border incursions and friction with Prague, culminating in a battle between the Carpathian Sich and Czech troops under Gen L. Prchala on 14 March. In Khust on 15 March the diet proclaimed Carpatho-Ukrainian independence, ratified a constitution, elected A. Voloshyn president of the state, and confirmed a new government under Premier Yu. Revai. At that very moment Hungarian forces invaded Carpatho-Ukraine and the president and part of the government fled to Rumania.

The Ukrainian political émigrés in Europe. After the demise of the UNR, most of its government and army and many political and cultural figures sought refuge in Central and Western Europe. *Prague, *Warsaw, *Vienna, *Berlin, and *Paris became the major émigré centers, and small communities were established in *Geneva, *London, Louvain, *Rome, *Zagreb, *Bucharest, *Sofia, and Helsinki. Several political parties remained active in the emigration: the USDWP, the UPSR, the UPSF (renamed the Ukrainian Radical Democratic party), and the *Ukrainian

Commander D. Klympush with soldiers of the Carpathian Sich

Union of Agrarians-Statists. By the late 1920s the socialists, liberals, and conservatives had been largely eclipsed in the emigration, as in Galicia, by the radical nationalists of the UVO and OUN.

The *Government-in-exile of the UNR was active throughout the interwar years. The heads of its Directory were S. Petliura (1920–6), A. Livytsky (1926–39), and V. Prokopovych (1939–40). Until the early 1920s the Government-in-exile relied on the UNR diplomatic missions created in 1918–19 to lobby the Western governments.

Ukraine during the Second World War. The secret *Molotov-Ribbentrop Pact of 23 August 1939 divided Eastern Europe between Nazi *Germany and the USSR. On 1 September Germany invaded Poland, thereby beginning the Second World War, and soon it occupied Podlachia, the Kholm and Lemko regions, and Galicia west of the Sokal–Lviv–Stryi line. The Western Ukrainians offered a measured welcome to the Germans believing they would prove to be their liberators from Polish oppression. A 600-man unit consisting of OUN and Carpathian Sich members served as the intermediary between the population and the advancing German army until the end of September 1939.

In its occupied territories the Germans created the so-called *Generalgouvernement (GG) of Poland. When the Soviet armies began occupying Western Ukraine east of the Sian and Buh rivers, some 20,000 refugees fled to the GG; in 1940 they were joined by refugees from Bukovyna. There, between November 1939 and April 1940, OUN leaders organized a civic umbrella organization, and in June 1940 this *Ukrainian Central Committee (UCC), headed by V. *Kubijovyč, was sanctioned by the German authorities.

Although most of the leaders of the Western Ukrainian parties had fled to the GG, conditions there prevented them from engaging openly in political activity. Only the OUN, headed by R. Sushko, was tolerated initially by the Germans because of its prewar anti-Polish activity. In February 1940 the OUN split into two factions – one supporting the strategy and tactics of the émigré leadership, headed since August 1939 by A. *Melnyk, and the other supporting the positions of those who had directed the revolutionary struggle against the Poles in Western Ukraine, headed by S. *Bandera. In June 1941, on the eve of the German-Soviet War, both factions tried to consolidate the existing Ukrainian political forces in order to lead them in a war against the USSR and thereby establish an independent Ukraine.

Between 17 and 23 September 1939 the Soviets occupied Western Volhynia and Galicia. Soviet-style elections to a *People's Assembly of Western Ukraine were held on 22 October. After the assembly 'requested the reunification of Western Ukraine with the Ukrainian SSR,' a policy of wholesale Sovietization was introduced, accompanied by the mass arrests of Ukrainian leaders who had not managed to flee and the suppression of all Ukrainian national institutions and organizations. With the Soviet occupation, Polish domination of state and administrative institutions ceased, and Ukrainians flooded into the towns and began Ukrainianizing them. These changes, however, did not compensate for the general anti-Ukrainian Soviet oppression and terror that ensued. The Soviet authorities also deported many Polish colonists and Jews to the east.

The USSR occupied Rumanian-held northern Bukovyna and Bessarabia on 28 June 1940, and on 2 August they were officially incorporated into the USSR. The changes that ensued there were analogous to those in Western Ukraine, and Ukrainian replaced Rumanian as the official language.

The German invasion of the USSR on 22 June 1941 revealed Soviet weaknesses and the lack of popular support for the Soviet regime, especially in Ukraine. Many Soviet soldiers deserted, many more surrendered en masse, and the Germans rapidly advanced eastwards, occupying practically all of Ukraine by the end of 1941. Caught unprepared, the Soviets retreated in a disorganized fashion beyond the Urals. The NKVD executed about 15,000 Ukrainian political prisoners in Lviv, Zolochiv, Rivne, Lutske, Kiev, Kharkiv, and elsewhere. Taking advantage of the German halt on the Dnieper, Soviet authorities destroyed industrial and government buildings, food reserves, and railroads. Berdychiv, central Kiev (including Khreshchatyk), most of Kharkiv, and the Dnieper Hydroelectric Station were blown up, mines in the Donbas were flooded, and Ukraine generally suffered considerably as a result of this evacuation.

At the outset of the war, the government of the Ukrainian SSR and many institutes of the Academy of Sciences were evacuated to Ufa. For the next few years, in an attempt to gain popular support, some concessions were made to Ukrainian patriotism, including the publication of more objective accounts of Ukrainian history and more Ukrainian-language works in general.

Galicia became a GG district on 1 August 1941; most of Ukraine became part of the *Reichskommissariat Ukraine on 20 August. Rumania reoccupied northern Bukovyna, part of Bessarabia, and *Transnistria on 19 August; and Transcarpathia remained under Hungarian rule. Throughout Ukraine anti-German resistance grew when the Nazis began implementing their racial and economic policies. Before the invasion, the OUN Bandera faction had organized *Legions of Ukrainian Nationalists (Nachtigal and Rolland) to fight against the Bolsheviks, and during the invasion both OUN factions sent expeditionary groups composed of Western Ukrainians and émigrés into central and eastern Ukraine to rebuild Ukrainian political and cultural life there.

On 30 June 1941, the Bandera faction issued the *Proclamation of Ukrainian statehood in Lviv and formed the *Ukrainian State Administration headed by Ya. *Stetsko. In early July, however, the Germans arrested the administration's members and proceeded to suppress the Bandera faction and to send its members to concentration camps.

Another *Ukrainian National Council had been created in Lviv in July 1941 under the aegis of Metropolitan A. *Sheptytsky and headed by K. Levytsky; it represented the Ukrainians before the German authorities and strongly protested the incorporation of Galicia into the GG until it was banned in March 1942. In September 1941 the Germans allowed the *Ukrainian Regional Committee, headed by K. Pankivsky, to function as an umbrella body; in March 1942 its functions were taken over by the UCC in Cracow and Pankivsky became V. Kubijovyč's right hand.

On 19 September the Germans occupied Kiev. In October O. Olzhych and other Melnyk faction members formed a *Ukrainian National Council under M. Velychkivsky there as the Ukrainian political-civic center. In December the Germans suppressed the council, arrested the leading nationalists (including O. and M. Teliha, I. Rohach, I. Irliavsky, and O. Chemyrynsky), whom they executed in February 1942, and forced the Melnyk faction to go underground.

The larger part of Ukraine – the Reichskommissariat Ukraine – was under the tyrannous rule of E. *Koch. Based in Rivne, he pursued a policy of terror and extreme exploitation of the population, which was deemed subhuman. The Germans retained the Soviet collective farm system there until 1943, forbade private trade (except for local markets and co-operatives), and generally took as much food and raw materials from Ukraine as they could. Most cultural institutions and organizations were soon suppressed, and only four-year primary schools were allowed to function. The press (about 115 periodicals) was German-run or strictly controlled. Although the UAOC was tolerated, the Germans favored the Autonomous Orthodox church subordinated to the Moscow patriarch.

During the German occupation, 6.8 million people were killed in Ukraine, of whom 600,000 were Jews and 1.4 million were Soviet military personnel killed at the front or starved to death in prisoner-of-war camps. From February 1942, more than 2 million Ukrainians were deported as slave laborers to Germany (see **Ostarbeiter*). Nazi destruction and terror in Ukraine provoked general hostility and gave rise to political and military resistance. National partisans in Volhynia had organized the so-called *Polisian Sich, renamed the *Ukrainian Insurgent Army (UPA), under the command of T. *Borovets (Bulba) to fight the retreating Soviet army after the invasion. From the spring of 1942 they were fighting both the Germans and *Soviet partisans in Ukraine. From the middle of 1942 both OUN factions also had functioning guerrilla units throughout Ukraine.

After the Germans' defeat at Stalingrad in January 1943, armed resistance in Ukraine increased significantly. The Bandera-faction partisans built up their forces, disarmed the partisans supporting Borovets and the Melnyk faction, and took the name of the UPA for their own partisan units, which were under the command of R. *Shukhevych. Having forced the Germans to abandon the Volhynian countryside, in May 1943 the UPA expanded into Galicia to defeat the Soviet-partisan offensive under S. *Kovpak and to continue fighting the Germans as well as the guerrillas of the *Polish Home Army. In July 1944 the UPA commanders initiated the creation of the *Ukrainian Supreme Liberation Council as the political leadership of the pan-Ukrainian national underground, which continued its struggle against Communist rule and

Volunteers for the Division Galizien leaving for training camps, Lviv 1943

oppression until the 1950s and propagated a democratic program adopted by the Bandera faction in 1943.

By mid-1943, the Soviet offensive forced the Germans to begin their retreat from Ukraine. In Left-Bank Ukraine the Germans engaged in wholesale destruction, ruining Dnipropetrovske, Poltava, Kremenchuk, Kiev, and other cities. By spring 1944 the front was in Western Ukraine, and in July the *Division Galizien, a Ukrainian formation in the German armed forces created in 1943 and conceived by the Ukrainian organizers as the nucleus of the future army in an independent Ukraine, was largely destroyed at the Battle of *Brody. By the end of October 1944, all Ukrainian territory was again in Soviet hands.

In autumn 1944, when almost all of Ukraine had been reoccupied by the USSR, the Germans began changing their attitude to the Ukrainian question and released political leaders, including Bandera, Melnyk, Stetsko, and Borovets, from concentration camps. In March 1945 they recognized the *Ukrainian National Committee (UNC) under the leadership of Gen P. Shandruk, V. Kubijovyč, and O. Semenko as the representative body of the Ukrainians in the Third Reich. The UNC, however, was unable to do much apart from saving the remnants of the Division Galizien and uniting them with other Ukrainian formations in the German military (eg, the *Ukrainian Liberation Army) to create a *Ukrainian National Army, which surrendered to the British after Germany capitulated.

(See *Bessarabia, *Bukovyna, *Transcarpathia, and *Transnistria for an account of wartime Hungarian and Rumanian occupations.)

Postwar Ukraine

The Stalin period. Throughout the war, the Soviet propaganda machine used German excesses and atrocities to its advantage while propagating the idea of the 'Great Patriotic War against fascist aggression.' It also attracted sympathy for the Soviet cause among the Ukrainians by focusing on developments on the 'Ukrainian fronts' and fostered antipathy for the UPA and OUN by portraying them as Nazi collaborators. Pro-Soviet sympathy increased after the Soviet constitution was modified in February 1944, granting Ukraine the right to have direct relations with other countries and its own republican military formations; and again in April 1945 after the Western powers acceded to Moscow's demand that Soviet Ukraine be recognized as an independent state and a founding member of the United Nations at the San Francisco Conference. (See also *International legal status of Ukraine and *International organizations.) Meanwhile Soviet terror mounted against the nationalist enemies of the USSR in Ukraine and in Soviet-occupied Europe, as well as against other 'traitors' – Soviet soldiers who had surrendered to the Germans and Soviet citizens who were *Ostarbeiter*.

After the war, major territorial and population changes occurred in Ukraine. On 29 June 1945, Czechoslovakia ceded Carpatho-Ukraine to the USSR. On 16 August the Polish-Soviet border was established, leaving some Ukrainian ethnic territories in Poland. The Rumanian-Soviet border was confirmed in the *Paris peace treaties of 1947 as the one created in June 1940. As a result of the war, the population of Ukraine had declined by some 10.5 million (25 percent): 6.8 million had been killed or died of hunger or disease, and the remainder consisted of those who had been evacuated or deported as political prisoners to Soviet Asia and remained there and those who had been slave laborers and émigrés in the Third Reich and chose to remain in the West as *displaced persons. The *national composition of Ukraine's population changed radically during the war. Most Jews had been annihilated during the Nazi Holocaust, and most Germans who had lived in Ukraine retreated with the German army. After the war, in 1945–7 over 800,000 Poles living in Western Ukraine were resettled in Poland, and over 500,000 Ukrainians living in Poland's eastern borderlands were resettled in Ukraine (see *Resettlement). There also occurred a large in-migration of Russians into Ukrainian towns and cities, including those of Western Ukraine, and a new period of *Russification began. In the immediate postwar years thousands of Ukrainians, mainly in Western Ukraine, were tried for their political or religious activity and sent to *concentration camps. About 1.3 million slave laborers in Germany were subjected to forcible *repatriation to Ukraine; because they had had contact with the non-Soviet world, 300,000 of them were deported to Siberia, while the rest underwent political re-education.

The most pressing task faced by the Soviet regime was the reconstruction of the economy, which had been devastated during the war: 16,000 industrial enterprises, 2,000 railway stations, 28,000 collective farms, 872 state farms, 714 towns and cities, 28,000 villages, and 2 million buildings had been destroyed; 10 million people had been left homeless. More than 12 million t of agricultural products, over 14 million head of cattle and sheep, and a large amount of agricultural machinery had been taken to Germany. The Fourth Five-Year Plan (1946–50) allotted 20 percent of Soviet capital investment for the reconstruction of Ukraine; over 2,000 plants and the electric power system were rebuilt and expanded, and the natural gas industry was developed in Western Ukraine. Agriculture was revived more slowly, because of the opposition to *collectivization in Western Ukraine, the lack of farm machinery, population dislocation, a drought in 1946, and a famine in 1946–7.

The *Council of Ministers (CM) of the Ukrainian SSR replaced the Council of People's Commissars as the government in March 1946, and the CP(B)U first secretary from 1938, N. Khrushchev, also became its first chairman. Moscow replaced him as first secretary in March 1947 with L. Kaganovich, who proceeded to purge 'nationalists' from the ranks of the Ukrainian cultural intelligentsia. In December 1947, however, Khrushchev was again appointed first secretary only to be replaced in December 1949 by L. *Melnikov, who in 1949–52 had 22,175 members (3 percent) of the CP(B)U expelled for 'nationalism.' From 1947 to 1954 the CM chairman was D. *Korotchenko.

During the years that A. *Zhdanov and his ideas dominated Soviet cultural policy (1946–53), the few Ukrainian cultural and scholarly achievements of the Second World War were condemned as 'bourgeois nationalist' and suppressed. Members of various scholarly institutes and journal editorial boards were removed; works by prominent writers (eg, Yu. Yanovsky, V. Sosiura, A. Malyshko, O. Dovzhenko) who were praised for their national patriotism during the war were criticized; and books on Ukrainian history and literature published during the war were condemned and removed from circulation. Cultural and linguistic Russification was stepped up, particularly in newly annexed Western Ukraine.

An UPA detachment celebrating Easter in the forest, 1946

The greatest repression during the last years of the Stalin period took place in Western Ukraine and was directed against OUN, UPA, and Division Galizien members and the Ukrainian Catholic church (see *Church, history ...). In 1946, at the *Synod of Lviv, the Church Union of Berestia of 1596 was formally abolished against a background of terror directed at the Ukrainian Catholic hierarchy and clergy.

The postwar émigrés. After the war over 200,000 Ukrainian *displaced persons in the Allied zones of Germany and Austria chose not to return to the USSR for political reasons. From 1947 to 1952 the vast majority immigrated to the *United States, *Canada, *Australia, *Great Britain, *France, *Belgium, *Brazil, and *Argentina (see also *Emigration). Most prewar émigré and Western Ukrainian organizations, institutions, and parties were reactivated, and new parties were formed. Except for the Hetmanites, the parties co-operated from June 1948 in the new *Ukrainian National Council of the Government-in-exile of the UNR. The Foreign Representation of the *Ukrainian Supreme Liberation Council, founded in 1944, also promoted the Ukrainian national cause in the West. In 1967 a new body, the *World Congress of Free Ukrainians, was established to co-ordinate the civic and cultural activities of the Ukrainian emigration.

De-Stalinization in Ukraine, 1953–9. After Stalin died on 5 March 1953, a slow liberalization and decentralization process began in the USSR. The campaign against Ukrainian nationalism and Zionism subsided and in June 1953 Melnikov was accused of excessive Russification and replaced as CPU first secretary by O. *Kyrychenko, the first Ukrainian to occupy the post since 1922.

To gain the Ukrainians' support, the new Soviet leadership under Khrushchev honored the tricentenary of the Pereiaslav Treaty and the 'reunification' of the Ukrainian and Russian peoples in 1954 by transferring the *Crimea from the RSFSR to Ukraine.

Ukrainian representation in leading Party and government positions was increased; thus by 1 June 1954, 72 percent of the CPU Central Committee, 75 percent of the Supreme Council of the Ukrainian SSR, and 51 percent of the directors of large industrial enterprises were Ukrainian.

After the war, thousands of Western Ukrainian community leaders, OUN and UPA members, and Ukrainian Catholic clergy and faithful were sent to Soviet *concentration camps, where they were subjected to arbitrarily harsh and inhumane treatment. They responded by organizing labor *strikes, which were brutally and ruthlessly suppressed. Hundreds of Ukrainians were thus killed in the camps of Vorkuta and Norilsk in the Soviet Arctic in 1953 and Kingir, Kazakhstan, in 1954. The mass unrest, coupled with widespread expectations of change after Stalin's death, prompted the Soviet government to declare a political amnesty on 18 September 1955, and in 1956 many Ukrainians were released.

From 1955, descriptions of and protests against the excesses of the Soviet regime, concerning especially the oppression of the Ukrainian nation, were circulated by way of unofficial, uncensored documents and writings (*samvydav). The first such document was the 'Open Letter to the UNR' from Ukrainian political prisoners in the Mordovian camps. The Ukrainian intelligentsia and students began demanding cultural and intellectual freedom and social change. At the same time the crimes of the Stalin 'personality cult' were officially condemned by Khrushchev at the 20th CPSU Congress in 1956, and the Party officially adopted a policy of de-Stalinization. During the cultural 'thaw' that followed and until 1959, the Ukrainian intelligentsia fought for and achieved a relaxation of censorship and educational, cultural, and *language policy, and the *'rehabilitation' of many Ukrainian cultural figures and intellectuals banned or destroyed during the Terror.

The regime made other concessions to the Ukrainians. It lowered taxes, allowed peasants more freedom in using their private plots of land, and improved food supplies in the cities. A republican Ministry of Higher Education, *Academy of Construction and Architecture of the Ukrainian SSR, *Ukrainian Academy of Agricultural Sciences, and Union of Journalists of Ukraine were established. Economic decentralization was carried out, and the Ukrainian government assumed control of 10,000 industrial enterprises. Official attitudes towards religion hardened, however, and by 1961 a renewed *antireligious propaganda campaign had resulted in the liquidation of about half of all existing religious institutions: parishes, monasteries, seminaries.

Hopes that the liberalization would continue were dashed in 1958, when Khrushchev made the teaching of non-Russian languages optional in Russian schools in Ukraine and propaganda in favor of the Russian language was stepped up. In 1957 M. *Pidhorny had replaced Kyrychenko as first secretary. In 1959 A. *Skaba was given the task of tightening Party control over ideological work in Ukraine, and a new campaign against 'bourgeois nationalism' and 'Zionism' began.

Ukraine in the 1960s. Despite the regime's efforts to the contrary, the 'thaw' radicalized an entire postwar generation and inspired it to continue demanding changes in cultural and nationality policy and criticizing Russification and the 'fusion of nations' concept in the 1961 CPSU program. The foremost representatives of this new generation of the 1960s – the *Shestydesiatnyky writers, publicists, and artists – called for a return to truth, which brought them into conflict with the older generation of writers and officials who had risen under Stalin. In 1962 the Party decided that dissent had to be stopped, and in 1963 the Shestydesiatnyky and their ideas were publicly denounced. The intimidation and persecution silenced some of them, but others became more politicized and actively participated in the *dissident movement that erupted and continued throughout the 1960s. It was expressed in the form of petitions, protests, demonstrations, samvydav literature, workers' strikes, and even illegal political groups with secessionist programs.

In 1965 the first wave of arrests of Ukrainian dissidents (B. and M. Horyn, I. Hel, P. Zalyvakha, S. Karavansky, V. Moroz, M. Osadchy, A. Shevchuk, and others) took place, and the first major analytical dissident document – I. Dziuba's *Internationalism or Russification?* – was written. V. Chornovil distributed a commentary on the political trials of 20 dissidents, for which he himself was imprisoned in 1967–9.

From 1963 to 1972 P. *Shelest was the CPU first secretary. He defended the economic interests of Ukraine, and sided with the critics of Russification and the defenders of Ukrainian culture and language who spoke out at the Fifth Congress of the Writers' Union of Ukraine in 1966. Under Shelest a new variant of 'Ukrainization' was promoted: teaching in Ukrainian in institutions of higher education was expanded; more books in Ukrainian (including *encyclopedias) were published; the study of Ukrainian history was encouraged and new historical journals appeared; and the press published many articles of a patriotic nature.

Ukraine in the 1970s and 1980s. In 1964 L. *Brezhnev replaced Khrushchev and reasserted Moscow's centralist and Russification policies. Under him the *KGB resolutely persecuted the dissident movement throughout the USSR. In Ukraine this persecution culminated in a second wave of arrests in 1972. That same year Shelest was replaced by the more subservient V. *Shcherbytsky. Since that time Shcherbytsky has remained firmly in control in Ukraine and has followed Moscow's directives, purging the AN URSR institutes of archeology, history, literature, and philosophy in 1973, suppressing the *Ukrainian Helsinki Group and any other manifestations of political or religious dissent, and implementing Russification policies in education and scholarship. Leadership changes in Moscow since Brezhnev's death in 1982 have not fundamentally altered this course. (See *Ukrainian SSR.)

BIBLIOGRAPHY

Hrushevs'kyi, M. *Istoriia Ukraïny-Rusy*, 10 vols (Lviv-Vienna-Kiev 1898–1937; New York 1954–8)

Efimenko, A. *Istoriia ukrainskago naroda*, 2 vols (St Petersburg 1906)

Hrushevs'kyi, M. *Iliustrovana istoriia Ukraïny* (Kiev 1911, 1913, 1917; Vienna 1921)
Grushevskii, M. 'Istoriia ukrainskago naroda,' in *Ukrainskii narod v ego proshlom i nastoiashchem* (St Petersburg 1914)
Iefymenko, O. *Istoriia ukraïns'koho narodu* (Kharkiv 1922)
Iavors'kyi, M. *Narys istoriï Ukraïny*, 2 vols (Kharkiv 1925; vol 1 repr, Adelaide 1986)
Bahalii, D. *Narys istoriï Ukraïny na sotsiial'no-ekonomichnomu grunti* (Kharkiv 1928)
Iavors'kyi M. *Istoriia Ukraïny v styslomy narysi*, 3rd edn (Kharkiv 1928)
Krupnitzky, B. *Geschichte der Ukraine* (Leipzig 1939; 2nd edn, 1943)
Allen, W. *The Ukraine: A History* (Cambridge 1940; New York 1963)
Hrushevsky, M. *A History of the Ukraine* (New Haven 1940; Hamden, Conn 1970)
Huslystyi, K. et al (eds). *Narys istoriï Ukraïny* (Ufa 1942)
Petrovs'kyi, M. (ed). *Istoriia Ukraïny*, 1 (Ufa 1943)
Manning, C. *The Story of the Ukraine* (New York 1947)
Kholms'kyi, I. [Kryp'iakevych, I.]. *Istoriia Ukraïny* (Munich 1949; New York 1971)
Kasymenko, O. et al (eds). *Istoriia Ukraïns'koï RSR*, 1 (Kiev 1953, 1955)
Suprunenko, M. et al (eds). *Istoriia Ukraïns'koï RSR*, 2 (Kiev 1959)
Kostruba, T. *Narys istoriï Ukraïny* (Toronto 1961)
Kubijovyč, V. et al (eds). *Ukraine: A Concise Encyclopaedia*, 1 (Toronto 1963)
Rudnytsky, I.L. 'The Role of the Ukraine in Modern History,' in *The Development of the USSR*, ed D.W. Treadgold (Seattle–London 1964)
Diadychenko, V.; Los', F.; Spyts'kyi, V. *Istoriia Ukraïns'koï RSR* (Kiev 1965)
Istoriia robitnychoho klasu Ukraïns'koï RSR, 2 vols, ed F. Los' (vol 1), I. Hurzhii et al (vol 2) (Kiev 1967)
Istoriia selianstva Ukraïns'koï RSR, 2 vols, ed V. Diadychenko (vol 1), I. Kompaniiets' et al (vol 2) (Kiev 1967)
Istoriia Ukraïns'koï RSR, ed K. Dubyna et al, 2 vols (Kiev 1967; Russian edn 1969)
Radians'ka entsyklopediia istoriï Ukraïny, ed A. Skaba et al, 4 vols (Kiev 1969–72)
Holobuts'kyi, V. *Ekonomichna istoriia Ukraïns'koï RSR: Dozhovtnevyi period* (Kiev 1970)
Portal, R. *Russes et Ukrainiens* (Paris 1970)
Polons'ka-Vasylenko, N. *Istoriia Ukraïny*, 2 vols (Munich 1972, 1976)
Doroshenko, D. *A Survey of Ukrainian History*, ed, updated (1914–75), and intro by O. Gerus (Winnipeg 1975)
Nahayewsky, I. *History of Ukraine*, 2nd edn (Philadelphia 1975)
Istoriia Ukraïns'koï RSR, ed A. Sheveliev et al, 8 vols in 10 bks (Kiev 1977–9; Russian edn, 1981–5)
Rybalka, I. *Istoriia Ukraïns'koï RSR: Doradians'kyi period* (Kiev 1978)
Serczyk, W. *Historia Ukrainy* (Wrocław–Warsaw–Cracow–Gdańsk 1979)
Kondufor, Iu. et al (eds). *Istoriia Ukraïns'koï RSR: Korotkyi narys* (Kiev 1981)
Rudnytsky, I.L. (ed). *Rethinking Ukrainian History* (Edmonton 1981)
Rybalka, I.; Dovhopol, V. *Istoriia Ukraïns'koï RSR: Epokha sotsializmu* (Kiev 1982)
Szporluk, R. *Ukraine: A Brief History*, 2nd edn (Detroit 1982)
Istoriia narodnoho hospodarstva Ukraïns'koï RSR, ed I. Lukinov et al, 3 vols in 4 bks (Kiev 1983–)
From Kievan Rus' to Modern Ukraine: Formation of the Ukrainian Nation [M. Hrushevsky's 'The Traditional Scheme of "Russian" History and the Problem of a Rational Organization of the History of the Eastern Slavs' and O. Pritsak and J. Reshetar Jr's 'Ukraine and the Dialectics of Nation-Building'] (Cambridge, Mass 1984)

O. Subtelny, A. Zhukovsky

Hitler, Adolf, b 20 April 1889 in Braunau am Inn, Austria, d 30 April 1945 in Berlin. German dictator, founder and leader of National Socialism. In his youth Hitler absorbed the anti-Semitic and anti-Slavic prejudices of such Viennese political extremists as G. von Schönerer, leader of the Pan-German Nationalist party, and K. Lüger, leader of the Christian Socialist party. These views hardened into fanatical nationalism after Germany's defeat in the First World War. In 1921 Hitler became leader of the Nazi party. Imprisoned after an abortive putsch in 1923, he wrote the programmatic *Mein Kampf* (1925–6), in which he proclaimed his fundamental goals: to establish the dominance of the Aryan race by destroying the 'Jewish enslavers' and building a powerful German state, and to transform Russia and its dependencies into *Lebensraum* for German colonists. The Slavs, whom Hitler considered subhuman, would be enserfed or exterminated. The political crisis resulting from the depression brought Hitler to power as chancellor in 1933. He soon consolidated his dictatorship and began planning for war. In 1939 he secured Hungary's support by allowing it to overrun Carpatho-Ukraine. After the German invasion of the USSR Hitler incorporated Galicia into the *Generalgouvernement, allowed Romania to take over a large part of southwestern Ukraine (Transnistria), and called for the complete German colonization of Ukraine over a 20-year period. Rejecting A. Rosenberg's concept of a Ukrainian puppet regime, Hitler appointed E. *Koch *Reichskommissar* of Ukraine and, at conferences held at Koch's field headquarters near Vinnytsia on 22 July 1942 and 19 May 1943, gave his full support to Koch's ruthless policies. Hitler insisted that the Ukrainian population be reduced by official encouragement of abortion and contraception, as well as by the denial of health care. Ukrainians were to be given only rudimentary education in order to make them obedient slaves. The prospect of defeat did not change Hitler's views: convinced that Ukrainians were unreliable, in late March 1945 he ordered the *Division Galizien to be disarmed. As Soviet troops entered Berlin, he committed suicide.

BIBLIOGRAPHY

Hitler's Table Talk (London 1953)
Kamenetsky, I. *Hitler's Occupation of Ukraine (1941–1944): A Study of Totalitarian Imperialism* (Milwaukee 1956)
– *Secret Nazi Plans for Eastern Europe: A Study of Lebensraum Policies* (New York 1961)
Rich, N. *Hitler's War Aims*, 2 vols (New York 1973–4)

M. Yurkevich

Hiunivka kurhans. A burial site of the Bronze and early Iron ages near Hiunivka, Kamianka-Dniprovske raion, Zaporizhia oblast. Excavations carried out in 1976–7 uncovered 21 kurhans, 18 of which were built by the Scythians in the 4th–3rd century BC. The largest kurhan, known as Vyshneva Mohyla, contained many artifacts, including over 400 golden ornaments.

Hladenko, Ivan, b 3 October 1915 in Annivka, Lebedyn county, Kharkiv gubernia. Veterinarian; since 1975 member of the All-Union Academy of Agricultural Sciences. A graduate of the Kharkiv Veterinary Institute (1938), he worked as a research associate at the Ukrainian Scientific Research Institute of Experimental Veterinary Medicine and in 1957 was appointed director of the institute. His publications deal with veterinary pharmacology and toxicology.

Hladky, Hryts [Hladkyj, Hryc'], b 19 January 1893 in Chernykhivtsi, Zbarazh county, Galicia, d 14 September 1936 in Lviv. Political leader and journalist. He participated in the wars for Ukraine's independence as a captain of the UNR Army and chief of the chancellery of the Sich Riflemen Corps. After the war he was active in politics as organizer for the Ukrainian Radical party in the Lviv region. In 1922 he moved to Lutske where he helped found the Ukrainian Bank, edited a local paper, *Ukraïns'ke zhyttia*, and assisted M. Cherkavsky in publishing *Ukraïns'ka hromada*. Rejecting his party's election strategy, he joined the Ukrainian National Democratic Alliance (UNDO) in 1928 and returned to Lviv where he became editor of UNDO's newspaper *Svoboda*, chief of its national office, and chairman of the party's Lviv regional organization. Hladky committed suicide.

Hladky, Matvii [Hladkyj, Matvij], b ?, d May 1652. Colonel of Myrhorod Regiment (1648 or 1649–April 1652) and military leader in Hetman B. Khmelnytsky's army during the Cossack-Polish War 1648–54. Hladky took part in the battles of Korsun and Pyliavtsi in 1648 and in the siege of Zbarazh in 1649. In autumn 1648 he assumed command of Cossack forces fighting the army of the Lithuanian nobility in Belorussia. When the Tatars temporarily captured Khmelnytsky during the Battle of Berestechko (1651), he fulfilled the duties of hetman and acquired the reputation of being an excellent commander. After the Treaty of Bila Tserkva (1651) restored the privileges of the Polish nobles, he opposed the advance of the Polish army into Left-Bank Ukraine. According to the Samovydets Chronicle, Hladky aspired to become hetman and was executed on the orders of Khmelnytsky.

Hladky, Yaroslav [Hladkyj, Jaroslav], b 16 May 1908 in Rohatyn, Galicia. Community and scout leader. Hladky was an executive member of Plast, the Ukrainian Scouting organization, from 1928. From 1930 to 1939 he headed Plast during its illegal existence in interwar Galicia under Poland and edited its ideological journal *Vohni*. In Western Europe and then the United States after the Second World War, he was the supreme commander (1945–54) of the boy scouts in Plast, head of the Plast world executive (1954–8, 1962–6), and head of the organization's world council (1973–82).

Hladky, Yosyp [Hladkyj, Josyp], b 1789 in Melnyky, Zhytomyr voivodeship, d 17 July 1866 in Oleksandrivske (now Zaporizhia). The last otaman of the *Danubian Sich, elected in 1827. During the Russo-Turkish War, he and a group of 1,500 Danube Cossacks joined the Russian side in May 1828 at Izmail. In revenge the Turks destroyed the Sich and scattered the remaining inhabitants. Hladky and his followers were settled between Berdianske and Mariiupil, where they founded the *Azov Cossack Host; Hladky was made acting otaman of the host in 1832. In 1853 he retired with the rank of major general.

Hladylovych, Demian [Hladylovyč, Dem'jan], b 1846, d 28 January 1892. Galician civic leader. He was head of the Shevchenko Society in Lviv and one of the founders of the *Dnister society and the newspaper **Dilo*. He administered *Dilo* for many years and was instrumental in turning it into the foremost Ukrainian daily in Galicia.

Hladylovych, Ivan [Hladylovyč], 1901–1945. Political leader and journalist in Galicia. In the 1920s Hladylovych was active in the Ukrainian Catholic student movement and one of the leaders of the Union of Hetmanists-Statists, serving as editor of their organ *Khliborobs'kyi shliakh* (1932–). From the mid-1930s he was a leader of the *Front of National Unity, coediting its newspaper *Ukraïns'ki visti* in Lviv.

Hlaváček, František, b 26 November 1876 in Slavkov, Moravia, d 1974. Czech journalist, political and civic leader. He was the first translator into Czech of such Ukrainian writers as I. Franko, B. Hrinchenko, D. Mordovets, M. Vovchok, Lesia Ukrainka, and V. Hnatiuk, and the author of the first Czech study of I. Franko. At the end of the 19th century he published in the Czech press dozens of articles on Ukrainian affairs. His large study of T. Shevchenko appeared in *Národní Listy* in 1939. After the war his articles in the field of Ukrainian studies and his memoirs and correspondence with Ukrainian cultural figures were printed in Ukrainian journals and scholarly collections published in Kiev, Lviv, Prešov, Novi Sad, and Toronto.

Hlevakha [Hlevaxa]. III-11. Town smt (1977 pop 9,400) southwest of Kiev in Vasylkiv raion, Kiev oblast. Hlevakha was founded as a village in the second half of the 16th century. Battles for the control of Kiev took place there between units of the UNR Army, the Ukrainian Galician Army (UHA), and Otaman D. Zeleny and those of the Bolshevik and White Russian forces. On 29 August 1919, after a three-day battle, the First and Third Corps of the UHA and the Zaporozhian Corps of the UNR Army broke through the Bolshevik front during their advance on Kiev. Today it contains an experimental biology station of the AN URSR, and several scientific-research institutes.

Hlevakha kurhan. A large burial mound of the 6th century BC near Hlevakha, Kiev oblast. Excavations of the 12-m-high kurhan in 1950 uncovered a large, wood-paneled burial chamber containing the remains of a Scythian warrior (possibly a tribal chieftain) and of a ritually executed woman. The most notable find was a large black-glazed vessel with gold appliqué.

Hlianko, Fedir [Hljan'ko], b 15 September 1879 in Slavhorodske, Vovchanske county, Kharkiv gubernia, d 21 April 1955 in Fort Wayne, Indiana. One of the pioneers of the Ukrainian movement among the workers of Kharkiv. Before the revolution he worked with H. *Khotkevych in Kharkiv organizing Ukrainian workers and cofounding the Ukrainian workers' theater. He was elected to the Central Rada in 1917 and was a delegate to the Labor Congress in 1919. He was an active member of the Ukrainian Autocephalous Orthodox church and was imprisoned by Soviet authorities. He left the USSR during the Second World War, and in 1950 immigrated to the United States.

Hlib Volodymyrovych [Hlib Volodymyrovyč], ca 984–1015. Saint and prince. One of 12 sons of *Volodymyr the Great, in 987–9 he received from his father the city of Murom. During the internecine struggle for the throne of the Kievan grand prince after Volodymyr's death (1015) Hlib and his brother Borys were killed in 1015 on the orders of their older brother Sviatopolk – Hlib near Smolensk and Borys near Pereiaslav. In 1019, the bodies were ordered exhumed by their brother *Yaroslav the Wise, brought to Vyshhorod, and buried there in St Basil's Church. Soon afterwards, both brothers were canonized by the Orthodox church. According to O. Pritsak (*The Origin of Rus'*, vol 1, 1981) the canonization was probably promoted by the new grand prince, Yaroslav, for the purpose of legitimizing his rule and investing his dynasty with prestige and honor. For centuries, ss Borys and Hlib were greatly revered by the common people.

Hlib Yuriievych [Hlib Jurijevyč], ?–1171. Prince of Pereiaslav (1155–69) and Kiev (1169–71); son of *Yurii Dolgorukii of Suzdal and grandson of Volodymyr Monomakh. He took part in the campaigns of his father against Grand Prince *Iziaslav Mstyslavych in 1147–8. After Yurii's defeat in 1151, Hlib was allowed to keep Pereiaslav, but soon after was given Horodets (now Oster) instead. He was returned Pereiaslav after Prince Iziaslav Davydovych of Chernihiv occupied the Kievan throne in 1155. After his brother Andrei Bogoliubskii of Suzdal took Kiev in 1169, Hlib was granted Kiev and gave Pereiaslav to his son Volodymyr. Mstyslav Iziaslavych of Volhynia and Yaroslav Osmomysl of Halych attacked Hlib in 1170 and he fled to Pereiaslav, but soon after he reoccupied Kiev and held it till his death. It was during Hlib's reign that Pereiaslav principality ceased being under the control of Kiev.

Leonyd Hlibov

Mykola Hlobenko

Hlibov, Leonyd, b 5 March 1827 in Veselyi Podil, Khorol county, Poltava gubernia, d 10 November 1893 in Chernihiv. Writer, teacher, and civic figure. After graduating from the Nizhen Lyceum in 1855, he taught at the Chornyi Ostriv gymnasium and Chernihiv gymnasium from 1858. He was active in the Chernihiv Hromada and the Sunday-school movement, published popular educational books, and contributed to the St Petersburg Ukrainian journal *Osnova*. In 1861 he founded and edited the weekly **Chernigovskii listok*, in which he published articles, poetry, and stories in Ukrainian. In 1863 the tsarist authorities closed down the paper and banned his works, and Hlibov lost his teaching job and was forced to live in Nizhen under police surveillance. From 1867 to his death he was the director of the Chernihiv Zemstvo printing house.

Hlibov wrote over 40 Romantic lyrical poems in Ukrainian (mostly elegies); one, 'Zhurba' (Sorrow), was put to music by M. Lysenko and became a popular folk song. His most important works are his 107 fables, which appeared from 1853 in the press and have been published since 1863 in many editions. They are written in the vernacular and satirize contemporary life and conditions from a liberal perspective using Ukrainian motifs and folklore. Hlibov also wrote several dozen rhymed riddles for children and the farce *Do myrovoho* (To the Justice of the Peace, 1862). Studies of his life and works have been written by M. Zahirnia and B. Hrinchenko (1900) and B. Huriev (1965), among others.

I. Koshelivets

Hlibovytsky, Ivan [Hlibovyc'kyj], ?–1890. Pedagogue and Russophile civic leader in Bukovyna. As a teacher at the Chernivtsi gymnasium (1864–71) and Teachers' seminary (1872–90) he promoted **yazychie* and opposed the use of the vernacular in literature and learning. He edited *Bukovinskaia zoria* (1870–1), a liberal arts journal. Because of its artificial language and bookish style, it won little support and after the 16th issue ceased publication.

Hlibovytsky, Vasyl [Hlibovyc'kyj, Vasyl'], 1904–? Journalist, community leader in Galicia. Hlibovytsky was active in Ukrainian Catholic organizations. He was an editor of the journals *Ukraïns'ke iunatstvo* and *Lytsarstvo Presviatoï Bohorodytsi*. An organizer of the religious event Ukrainian Youth for Christ, held in 1933, he was a founder and later head of *Orly Catholic Association of Ukrainian Youth. During the Second World War he was the general secretary of the *Ukrainian Central Committee in Cracow. In 1948 he disappeared without a trace in Germany.

Hloba, Ivan, b ?, d 1791. Last chancellor (1762–75) of the Zaporozhian Sich before its destruction by Catherine II in 1775. The following year Hloba was exiled by the Russian government to a monastery near Turukhansk in Tobolsk gubernia, where he died.

Hlobenko, Mykola (pen name of M. Ohloblyn), b 19 December 1902 in Novo-Heorhiivske, Kupianka county, Kharkiv gubernia, d 29 May 1957 in Mougins, France. A literary historian and pedagogue; full member of the Shevchenko Scientific Society and the Ukrainian Academy of Arts and Sciences. After graduating from the Kharkiv Institute of People's Education in 1928, he worked as a language editor for newpapers, journals, and publishing houses and taught Ukrainian at various schools. A displaced person in Germany after the Second World War, he became (in 1947) an editor of the Munich newspaper *Ukraïns'ka trybuna* and (in 1948) a professor at the Ukrainian Free University. From 1951 he lived and worked in Sarcelles near Paris as the associate editor of the *Entsyklopediia ukraïnoznavstva* (1949–52; published in English in 1963 as vol 1 of *Ukraine: A Concise Encyclopaedia*). He is the author of large parts of the section on literature in that encyclopedia. He also wrote articles on old Ukrainian literature, most notably a study of A. Kalnofoisky's *Teraturhima* (1956). His selected essays and a bibliography of his works were reprinted in two posthumous collections: *Istoryko-literaturni statti* (Articles on Literary History, 1958) and *Z literaturnoï spadshchyny* (From the Literary Legacy, 1961).

I. Koshelivets

Hlobus. A popular, illustrated semimonthly periodical published in Kiev from November 1923 to December 1935, as a supplement first to the newspaper *Bil'shovyk,* then (from 1925) to *Proletars'ka Pravda.* It was edited by S. Shchupak with the assistance of B. Antonenko-Davydovych. The journal published stories, novellas, poems, travel reports, translations of foreign literature, and art and theater reviews. It reported on international and national events, on cultural affairs, and on developments in science and technology. *Hlobus* published the works of such writers as M. Bazhan, O. Vlyzko, M. Ivchenko, Ya. Kachura, T. Osmachka, Ye. Pluzhnyk, I. Le, H. Kosynka, Ya. Savchenko, S. Skliarenko, M. Tereshchenko, M. Rylsky, and Yu. Yanovsky, most of whom were members of the writers' group *MARS.

Hlobyne. IV-14. Town (1965 pop 14,000) and raion center in Poltava oblast, founded in the early 18th century. It is an important food-industry center.

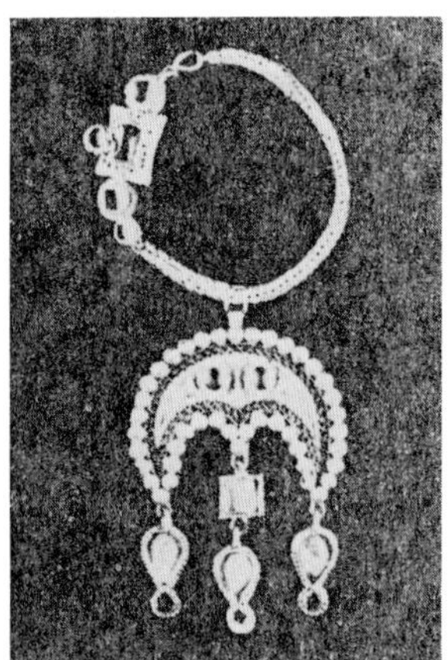

Hlodosiv hoard: woman's necklace

Hlodosiv hoard. A collection of gold and silver artifacts from the 7th century AD discovered in 1961 in an ancient chieftain's grave near Hlodosy, Novoukraina raion, Kirovohrad oblast. The hoard contained necklaces, bracelets, rings, belt buckles, earrings, medallions, weapon handles, and fragments of silver plates and other ware. The gold and silver articles together weighed over 3,600 kg. The remains of a cremated military leader, arrows, parts of a horse harness, and fragments of linen and silk were also found. A study about the hoard by A. Smilenko, *Hlodos'ki skarby,* was published in 1965.

Hlovatsky, Yakiv [Hlovac'kyj, Jakiv], b 1735 in Vinkivtsi, Podilia, d ? Icon painter; monk of the Basilian order. He painted the monastery churches in Pochaiv (1762), Buchach (1770, destroyed by fire in 1865), Zahora, and Pidhirtsi. He also did portraits of churchmen and benefactors of the Basilian order, including M. Potocki (1771).

Hlukh, Yosyp [Hlux, Josyp], b and d ? Colonel of Uman Regiment during the *Cossack-Polish War of 1648–54. In March 1651 the Cossack army under the command of Hlukh (Hlukhy) and the colonel of Poltava Regiment, M. *Pushkar, completely destroyed the advance forces of the Poles near Lypovets, forcing the Polish hetman M. *Kalinowski to lift the siege of Vinnytsia. In summer 1651 the Uman Regiment under Hlukh struck a decisive blow against the Crimean Tatars, who had betrayed their Cossack allies at the Battle of *Berestechko and who were pillaging Left-Bank Ukraine. However, at the beginning of 1654 both Hlukh and the colonel of Bila Tserkva, S. Polovets, were removed by Hetman B. Khmelnytsky on charges of incompetence, stemming from an inadequate defense of Right-Bank Ukraine against the Poles. Hlukh was temporarily restored to his position and probably remained as colonel of Uman throughout 1655. His further fate is unknown.

Hlukhiv

Hlukhiv [Hluxiv]. II-14. City (1970 pop 27,100) on the Yesman River and a raion center in Sumy oblast. Mentioned in the Hypatian Chronicle under the year 1152 as a city in Chernihiv principality, in the 13th and 14th centuries it was the capital of an appanage principality. In the 1350s the region came under Lithuanian rule; it was annexed by Muscovy in 1503 and by Poland in 1618. Part of the Hetman state from 1648 on, it was an important trade center and a company town in the Nizhen regiment. The *Hlukhiv Articles were signed here in 1669. After the destruction of *Baturyn, Hlukhiv was (during the years 1708–22 and 1727–34) the capital of the Left-Bank hetmans. During the years 1722–7 and 1764–86 it was the seat of the *Little Russian Collegium. The *Hlukhiv Singing School was established there in 1738. From 1782 it was a county town in Novhorod-Siverskyi vicegerency, and from 1802, in Chernihiv gubernia. After the 1917 Revolution Hlukhiv became part of the UNR, and in January 1919 it was occupied by Soviet forces. Today the city has the 'Elektropanel' plant and produces food, flax fiber, machinery, building materials, and woolens. Its most important institutions are the All-Union Scientific Research Institute of Fiber Plants (est 1931), a pedagogical institute (est 1874), and an agricultural tekhnikum. Among its architectural monuments are the Triumphal Arch (or Kiev Gate, built in 1744), St Nicholas's Church (1696), the Transfiguration Church (1765), and St Anastasia's Church (1884–93).

Hlukhiv Articles. An agreement in 27 points signed on 16 March 1669 in Hlukhiv by the newly elected hetman of Left-Bank Ukraine, D. *Mnohohrishny, and representatives of Muscovy, defining the political and legal relations between Left-Bank Ukraine and Muscovy. The accord, which replaced the *Moscow Articles signed by

Hetman I. Briukhovetsky, was influenced by the serious unrest in Ukraine. The agreement began by guaranteeing the Ukrainian 'rights and liberties' spelled out in the *Pereiaslav Treaty of 1654. It further specified that Muscovite voivodes were to be maintained in Kiev, Chernihiv, Nizhen, Pereiaslav, and Oster, although they could no longer interfere in local government, and it set the number of registered Cossacks at 30,000. The hetman was not given the right to maintain foreign relations, but was given some responsibility over financial affairs. The Hlukhiv Articles were published in 'Istochniki malorossiiskoi istorii,' no. 1, *Chteniia v Imperatorskom obshchestve istorii i drevnostei rossiiskikh* (1858), edited by D. Bantysh-Kamensky.

Hlukhiv Council of 1750. A council of Cossack officers that took place at Hlukhiv in February 1750 and at which, on the recommendations of Empress Elizabeth I and the Russian government, K. *Rozumovsky was elected hetman of Left-Bank Ukraine. The revival of the Hetmanate in Left-Bank Ukraine was welcomed by the Cossack *starshyna* and the population, which had suffered under the Russian officials during the rule of the *Governing Council of the Hetman Office. With the election of a hetman by the Hlukhiv Council, the autonomy of the Hetman state was partially restored.

Hlukhiv Singing School. The first school of singing in the Russian Empire, established to train singers for the royal court. It was founded in 1738 in Hlukhiv, the capital of Hetman Ukraine, and operated almost 40 years. Its usual enrollment was 20. Students were trained for two years: reading musical scores, singing, and playing the violin, *husli,* and bandura. Each year the top 10 students were sent to the court chorus in St Petersburg. The school's first conductor was F. Yavorsky. Graduates of the school included many famous Ukrainian singers, instrumentalists, and composers of the 18th century; for example, M. Berezovsky, D. Bortniansky, and A. Losenko.

Hlushchenko, Ivan [Hluščenko], b 28 July 1907 in Lysianka, Zvenyhorodka county, Kiev gubernia. Biologist; from 1956 full member of the All-Union Academy of Agricultural Sciences (VASKhNIL). A graduate of the Kharkiv Agroeconomic Institute (1930), he became one of the most ideologically strident supporters of T. *Lysenko. He joined the staff of the Institute of Genetics of the USSR Academy of Sciences in 1939 and replaced G. Karpechenko as head of its laboratory of plant genetics (1941–65). He was put in charge of a laboratory at VASKhNIL's Institute of Soil Science when Lysenko was removed from the directorship of the Institute of Genetics in 1965. Since 1976 Hlushchenko has headed the laboratory of plant development at VASKhNIL's Institute of Applied Molecular Biology and Genetics. His publications deal with vernalization, hybridization, and plant selection.

Hlushchenko, Mykola [Hluščenko] (Gloutchenko, Nicolas), b 17 September 1901 in Novomoskovske, Katerynoslav gubernia, d 31 October 1977 in Kiev. Artist. A graduate of the Academy of Art in Berlin (1924), from 1925 he worked in Paris where he immediately attracted the attention of French critics. From the Neue Sachlichkeit style of his Berlin period he changed to post-

Mykola Hlushchenko

impressionism. Besides numerous French, Italian, Dutch, and (later) Ukrainian landscapes, he also painted flowers, still life, nudes, and portraits (of O. Dovzhenko and V. Vynnychenko, as well as portraits commissioned by the Soviet government of the French writers H. Barbusse, R. Rolland, and V. Margueritte and the painter P. Signac). At the beginning of the 1930s, Hlushchenko belonged to the Association of Independent Ukrainian Artists and helped organize its large exhibition of Ukrainian, French, and Italian paintings at the Ukrainian National Museum in Lviv. In 1936 he moved to the USSR, but was allowed to live in Ukraine only after the war when his works began to reflect official approved socialist realism. In the 1960s, having come into close contact with new artistic trends on his trips abroad, he revitalized his paintings with expressive colors, and assumed a leading position among Ukrainian colorists. Hlushchenko's work was exhibited in Berlin (1924), Paris (five exhibits 1925–34), Milan (1927), Budapest (1930, 1932), Stockholm (1931), Rome (1933), Lviv (1934, 1935), Moscow (1943, 1959), Belgrade (1966, 1968), London (1966), Toronto (1967–9), and Kiev (over 10 exhibits).

BIBLIOGRAPHY
Kovzhun, P.; Hordyns'kyi, S. *Mykola Hlushchenko* (Lviv 1934)
Shpakov, A. *Mykola Petrovych Hlushchenko* (Kiev 1962)
Buhaienko, I. *Mykola Hlushchenko* (Kiev 1973)

S. Hordynsky

Hlushkevych, Mariian [Hluškevyč, Marijan], b 31 March 1877 in Dydova, Turka county, Galicia, d 17 July 1935 in Lviv. Galician community leader and lawyer. Before the First World War Hlushkevych studied in Russia, where he became an active member of the Russophile movement among Galician Ukrainians. During the war he returned to Galicia with the Russian army, and was appointed mayor of Peremyshl. After the Revolution of 1917, while living in eastern Ukraine, he gradually left the Russophiles. He returned to Galicia in 1921 and became a professor of law at the Lviv (Underground) Ukrainian University. Later, he defended Ukrainians in political trials. He was a vice-president of the Union of Ukrainian Lawyers in Lviv and an active member of the Polish Bar Association.

Hlushko, Sylvester [Hluško, Syl'vester], ca 1896–1938. Member of M. *Hrushevsky's school of Ukrainian history. He was affiliated with the Scientific Research Chair of Ukrainian History at the All-Ukrainian Academy of Sciences. Hlushko specialized in 19th- and 20th-century

Ukrainian history. He is the author of several articles and reviews on such topics as P. Kulish, M. Drahomanov, and the peasant movement in Ukraine (mostly published in *Ukraïna*, 1924–9). In 1934 he was arrested and exiled to Siberia; he perished there during the Yezhov terror of 1936–8.

Hlushko, Vasyl [Hluško, Vasyl'], b 28 August 1920 in Bohuchar, Voronezh gubernia, Russia. Geologist; corresponding member of the AN URSR since 1967. A graduate of Voronezh University (1942), from 1946 to 1953 he prospected for gas and petroleum in western Ukraine. From 1953 he served as research associate of the Ukrainian Branch of the All-Union Scientific Research Institute of the Geological Prospecting of Petroleum. In 1965 he became director of the Ukrainian Scientific Research Institute of Geological Prospecting of the Ministry of Geology of the Ukrainian SSR. His works deal with tectonics, and petroleum and gas reserves, particularly in the Carpathians.

Hlushko, Yurii [Hluško, Jurij] (pseud: Mova), b 1882? d spring 1942 in Kiev. Journalist; organizer of Ukrainian community and cultural life in the Far East. From 1918 to 1920 he was president of the Secretariat of the Far Eastern Ukrainian Territorial Council. He was arrested by the Bolsheviks in November 1922, and two years later was sentenced to three years' imprisonment. Eventually, he returned to Ukraine and lived in Kiev.

Viktor Hlushkov

Isydore Hlynka

Hlushkov, Viktor [Hluškov], b 24 August 1923 in Rostov-na-Donu, Russia, d 30 January 1982. Specialist in cybernetics, computer science, and control theory; full member of the AN URSR from 1961 and of the Academy of Sciences of the USSR from 1964. In 1957 he was appointed director of the Computing Center of the AN URSR, which in 1962 was reorganized into the Institute of Cybernetics. In 1962 he became vice-president of the AN URSR. He did seminal work in the fields of modern algebra, automata theory, digital computers, the application of cybernetics to economics, automatic control systems, and artificial intelligence. He solved the generalized 5th Gilbert Theorem. His influence on the development of computer sciences, computer manufacturing, and the automatization of production in the USSR was very important. Computer systems such as Dnepr and Mir were designed and constructed under his supervision. He is the author of a general theory of automata that has been utilized widely in computer and automatic-machine construction. Hlushkov was first to propose a radically new system of computer-assisted economic planning; many of his methods are used in the Soviet bloc today. He served as editor in chief of *Entsyklopediia kibernetyky* (Encyclopedia of Cybernetics, 2 vols, 1973), which was published in Ukrainian and Russian.

L.S. Onyshkevych

Hlyboka. v-6. Town smt (1977 pop 7,600) and raion center in Chernivtsi oblast. It was first mentioned in historical sources in 1438. From 1918 to 1940, under Rumanian rule, it was called Adîncata. Today it is a railway junction and has a food and glass industry.

Hlyniany [Hlynjany]. IV-5. Town smt (1970 pop 4,000) in Zolochiv raion, Lviv oblast, situated in the Buh Depression. First mentioned in 1379, in 1397 it was granted the right of *Magdeburg law. It has been known for its textiles and kilims since the mid-18th century. In 1919 the Ukrainian Galician Army fought several battles with the Polish army in its vicinity. Today the town has a kilim-weaving mill, a dairy, and a brick factory.

Hlynka, Anthony, b 28 May 1907 in Denysiv, Ternopil county, Galicia, d 25 April 1957 in Edmonton. Politician and community leader. In 1910 his family immigrated to Delph, Alberta. A founding member of the *Ukrainian National Federation, in the 1930s he frequently contributed to its weekly, *Novyi shliakh*. From 1935 to 1937 he edited and published an irregular anti-communist tabloid, *Klych*. As a Social Credit candidate, in 1940 and 1945 he was elected to represent Vegreville in the House of Commons. In Ottawa he criticized discrimination against Canadians of foreign extraction, spoke about an independent Ukrainian state in postwar Europe, and championed the right of Ukrainian displaced persons to settle in Canada. In the federal elections of 1949 and 1953, he lost by narrow margins to J. Decore. A collection of his articles and parliamentary speeches was published in 1982.

Hlynka, Isydore, b 17 February 1909 in Ternopil, Galicia, d 18 May 1983 in Winnipeg. Biochemist and community leader. In 1910 his family immigrated to Delph, Alberta. After graduating from the University of Alberta and the California Institute of Technology (PH D 1940), he worked for the Canadian Department of Agriculture. An authority on cereal chemistry, Hlynka developed various laboratory instruments and edited *Wheat Chemistry and Technology* (1964). For many years he sat on the presidium of the Ukrainian Canadian Committee and served as president of the Taras Shevchenko Foundation. Hlynka is the author of *The Other Canadians* (1981), a collection of articles on Canadian multiculturalism originally published during the 1970s in *Ukraïns'kyi holos* under the pseudonym of Ivan Harmata.

Hlynsky [Hlyns'kyj]. Name of a Ukrainian noble family, descended from the Tatar noble Leksad (Oleksander), who was granted Poltava in 1430 by Grand Duke Vytautas. He was also granted Hlynske near Romen (whence the family name). Prince Lev Hlynsky had four sons: Mykhailo *Hlynsky; Bohdan, the vicegerent of Cherkasy and Putyvl who in 1493 destroyed the Turkish fortress of Ochakiv; Ivan (Mamai, d 1522), the palatine of Kiev (1505–8); and Vasyl (d before 1522), the governor of Slonim and Berestia. They attained prominence at the turn of the 16th century through the influence of Mykhailo, who was close to *Alexander Jagiellończyk. The brothers led an unsuccessful rebellion (1507–8) of dissatisfied landowners against Alexander's successor, King Sigismund I, and fled to Moscow, where they received the title of boyar and large landholdings. There Vasyl's daughter Elena (Olena) married Grand Prince Vasilii III Ivanovich in 1526 and was a regent (1533–8). Vasyl's sons Yurii and Mikhail played an important role at the court of Tsar Ivan IV the Terrible, Elena's son.

Hlynsky, Mykhailo [Hlyns'kyj, Myxajlo], b ca 1460, d 15 September 1534. A member of the Ukrainian nobility. He studied in Western Europe, where he served at the court of Emperor Maximilian I and entered the military service of Prince Albert of Saxony and converted to Catholicism. Upon his return to the Commonwealth in 1497, he rose rapidly in the service of *Alexander Jagiellończyk. He was endowed with large estates in Ukraine and Belorussia and was appointed a marshal of the court (1499) and a member of the *Council of Lords of the Grand Duchy of Lithuania. The closest adviser to the grand duke, he used his influence to obtain high offices for other Ukrainian nobles. After Alexander was elected king of Poland in 1501, Hlynsky ran the affairs of Lithuania in his absence. His Ukrainian orientation incurred the hostility of the Lithuanian nobles. With the death of Alexander, his influence waned. Although he supported the election of the new king, Sigismund I, he fell from favor and was even accused of poisoning Alexander. Together with his brothers Vasyl and Ivan he led an unsuccessful uprising (1507–8) of Ukrainian and Belorussian landowners against Sigismund and the Lithuanian nobles. Subsequently the brothers fled to Muscovy, where they became boyars. During the Lithuanian-Muscovite War of 1514, Hlynsky led a large Muscovite force against Smolensk. But feeling mistreated, he began secret negotiations to switch allegiances. He was found out, accused of treason, and imprisoned in Moscow. He was released only after his niece, Elena, married Grand Prince Vasilii III Ivanovich in 1526. After Vasilii's death in 1533, Elena became regent and Hlynsky became her principal counselor but was soon accused of trying to sieze power; he was again imprisoned in 1534 and starved to death in that year.

Hlynsky, Yakym [Hlyns'kyj, Jakym], ?–1732. Eighteenth-century icon painter and gilder, representative of the Ukrainian baroque. His early works were done in Chernihiv (icon of the Holy Virgin [1716]). He is probably the painter of *Young Wife in a White Kerchief* (beginning of the 18th century). In 1723 he did the icons and gilded the iconostasis of the Dormition Cathedral of the Kievan Cave Monastery.

Hmyria, Borys [Hmyrja], b 5 August 1903 in Lebedyn, Kharkiv gubernia, d 1 August 1969 in Kiev. Opera singer (high bass). In 1939 he graduated from the Kharkiv Conservatory and became a soloist at the Kiev Theater of Opera and Ballet. His more important roles were Miroshnik in A. Dragomyzhsky's *Rusalka* (The Nymph), Mephistopheles in Gounod's *Faust*, the title role in Mussorgsky's *Boris Godunov*, and Kryvonis in K. Dankevych's *Bohdan Khmelnytsky*. He also performed chamber works. He toured Czechoslovakia, Bulgaria, Poland, China, and other countries. He is the subject of biographies by I. Stebun (1960), P. Golubev (1959), and B. Buriak (1975).

Borys Hmyria

Dmytro Hnatiuk

Hnatiuk, Dmytro [Hnatjuk], b 28 March 1925 in Mamaivtsi Stari (now Novosilka), Kitsman county, Bukovyna. Concert and opera singer (baritone). In 1951 he graduated from the Kiev Conservatory and became a soloist of the Kiev Theater of Opera and Ballet. His repertoire includes about 30 operatic roles, ranging from Ostap in *Taras Bulba* and Mykola in *Natalka Poltavka*, both by M. Lysenko, and Martyn in H. Maiboroda's *Mylana*, to the title roles in P. Tchaikovsky's *Mazepa* and *Eugen Onegin*, A. Borodin's *Prince Igor*, Verdi's *Rigoletto*, as well as Valentin in Gounod's *Faust*, Figaro in Rossini's *Barber of Seville*, and Papageno in Mozart's *The Magic Flute*. Hnatiuk has toured Australia, Africa, the United States, Canada, Japan, and other countries.

Volodymyr Hnatiuk

Hnatiuk, Volodymyr [Hnatjuk], b 9 May 1871 in Velesniv, Buchach county, Galicia, d 6 October 1926 in Lviv. Noted Slavic ethnographer, literary scholar, translator, journalist, and community figure in Western Ukraine; member of the Shevchenko Scientific Society (NTSh) in Lviv from 1899, the Imperial Academy of Sciences in St Petersburg from 1902, the Czechoslovak Folklore Society in Prague from 1905, the Society for Austrian Folk Art in Vienna, the Folklore Fellows in Helsinki, and the VUAN and the Ethnographic Society in Kiev from 1924. Hnatiuk began collecting folklore during his adolescence. He studied at Lviv University (1894–8), where he headed the Academic Hromada; his mentors there – M. *Hrushevsky and I. *Franko – became his close lifelong collaborators. From 1898 to his death he was the general secretary of NTSh. In 1898 he was elected secretary, and in 1913 chairman, of the *Ethnographic Commission of the NTSh. From 1899 he was also the secretary of the NTSh Philological Section. Hnatiuk was also an editor of and contributor to several NTSh serials: *Khronika NTSh* (66 issues in Ukrainian, 59 in German), **Etnohrafichnyi zbirnyk* (EZ, 22 vols), and **Materiialy do ukraïns'koï etnolohiï* (20 vols). While he was its general secretary, the NTSh reached the peak of its development, becoming the equivalent of an academy of sciences.

Hnatiuk also served two terms (1899–1906, 1922–6) on the editorial board of the journal *Literaturno-naukovyi vistnyk*, for which he solicited many contributions and wrote many articles and reviews on literary, political, and linguistic topics. He also contributed to *Zapysky NTSh*, *Kievskaia starina*, *Zhytie i slovo*, *Dilo*, and other Ukrainian, as well as German, Polish, and Czech, periodicals. One of the founders (in 1899), the secretary (1899–1912), and a director of the Ukrainian-Ruthenian Publishing Association, he edited over 150 of its volumes of Ukrainian and European literature, translating many of the foreign works himself. He was also an active member of the Lviv Prosvita society.

Hnatiuk maintained extensive contacts with almost all important Ukrainian and many non-Ukrainian scholars and cultural figures. Together with I. Franko and F. Vovk, he was instrumental in turning folklore collecting in Western Ukraine into a scholarly discipline; he wrote many programs and methodological guidelines for collectors, and in his *Ukraïns'ka narodna slovesnist'* (Ukrainian Folk Literature, 1916) he presented a system for recording, classifying, and publishing Ukrainian folklore.

Hnatiuk's research was focused initially on the Hungarian-ruled Ukrainians. He made five research trips (during 1895–6, 1899, 1903) to Transcarpathia and one each to Bačka (1897) and the Banat (1903), and wrote over 100 studies of their folklore, material culture, and dialects; the most important study is *Etnohrafichni materiialy z Uhors'koï Rusy* (Ethnographic Materials from Hungarian Ruthenia, vols 3, 4, 9, 25, 29, and 30 [1897–1911] of EZ). Between 1899 and 1914 he spent many summers in the Hutsul region, where he conducted ethnographic research among its inhabitants and collected many artifacts for the NTSh museum. After falling ill with tuberculosis in 1903, Hnatiuk could not engage in much fieldwork; instead he organized a correspondence network of about 800 folklorists, with whose help he compiled over two dozen unsurpassed volumes of materials that were published in the NTSh serials edited by him and in the collection *Das Geschlechtsleben des Ukrainischen Bauernvolkes* (2 vols, 1909, 1912).

Hnatiuk was an advocate of the comparative-historical approach, which he applied in his studies of folktales, fables, songs, legends, beliefs, and rituals. He also wrote valuable works about folk cookery, handicrafts, folk literature, folk architecture, demonology, and folkways. His writings on various Ukrainian dialects and argots and on normative grammar and orthography were important contributions in the field of Ukrainian linguistics. In the political sphere, Hnatiuk supported the Ukrainian Radical party and was an opponent of the Galician Russophiles and Populists.

In 1969 an ethnographic-memorial museum dedicated to Hnatiuk was opened in Velesniv; in 1971 a memorial sculpted by L. Bihanych was erected there. A monument to him was also raised at his grave at the Lychakiv Cemetery in Lviv.

BIBLIOGRAPHY
Iatsenko, M. *Volodymyr Hnatiuk (zhyttia i fol'klorystychna diial'nist')* (Kiev 1964)
Mushynka, M. *Volodymyr Hnatiuk – doslidnyk folkl'oru Zakarpattia.* Vol 190 of *ZNTSh* (Paris-Munich 1975)
Romanenchuk, B. (ed). *Volodymyr Hnatiuk: Vybrani statti pro narodnu tvorchist'. Na 110-richchia narodzhennia, 1871–1981.* Vol 201 of *ZNTSh* (New York 1981)
Mushynka, M. *Bibliohrafiia drukovanykh prats' Volodymyra Hnatiuka* (Edmonton, forthcoming)

M. Hnatiukivsky

Hnatyshak, Mykola [Hnatyšak], b 5 December 1902 in Peremyshl, d 8 November 1940 in Liebstadt, Germany. Literary scholar. He received his PH D in Slavic philology from the University of Prague in 1927 and then worked as an assistant in the Ukrainian Scientific Institute in Berlin (1927–30). In 1931 he moved to Lviv, where he became an editor of the Ukrainian Catholic weekly *Meta* and the journal *Khrystos – nasha syla*. He also contributed to the journal *Dzvony*. He emigrated to Czechoslovakia in 1939. In 1940, shortly before he died, he became a lecturer at the University of Vienna. Hnatyshak is the author of numerous articles on literary topics in periodicals and of a history of Ukrainian literature, vol 1 of which was published in 1941. In his history he formulated a new periodization of Ukrainian literature: he divided it into five old and five new periods according to predominantly formal and aesthetic styles – the Old Ukrainian, Byzantine, Late Byzantine, Renaissance, and Cossack-Baroque periods in the old, and the Pseudo-Classical, Biedermaier, Romantic, Realistic, and Modern periods in the new. His literary theory is based on roughly three principles: O. Potebnia's notion of a structural relation between the text and the word, emphasis on literary form, and an ideological aestheticism derived from national, Christian ethics. Although he was somewhat influenced by the structuralist school in Prague, he departed from its tenets in stressing the importance of the influence of the environment on the author and hence on the literary work. He judged literature by applying not only formalistic principles but also socially acceptable aesthetic norms. Because for him these norms were colored by national and Christian ethics his approach can be referred to as 'national realism.'

D.H. Struk

Hnatyshyn, Andrii [Hnatyšyn, Andrij], b 26 December 1906 in Chyzhykiv, Lviv county, Galicia. Composer and conductor. A graduate of the Lysenko Higher Institute of Music in Lviv and the Vienna Conservatory, in the 1930s he became the conductor of the choir at St Barbara's Church in Vienna. He has worked as a conductor in various theaters in Vienna and in motion pictures, and has often performed Ukrainian music on the Vienna Radio. His original compositions include over 100

Andrii Hnatyshyn

John Hnatyshyn

songs for chorus and solo written to poems by T. Shevchenko, I. Franko, and L. Ukrainka and to German poems, arrangements of folk songs for chorus, several divine liturgies and church services, an oratorio, several cantatas, an opera (*Olena*, 1980), and a number of instrumental pieces (quartet, trio, and *The Ukrainian Suite*). In recognition of his compositions the Austrian government awarded Hnatyshyn the title of professor and Pope John XXIII awarded him the Silver Cross.

Hnatyshyn, John [Hnatyšyn, Ivan], b 20 January 1907 in Vashkivtsi, Bukovyna, d 2 May 1967 in Saskatoon. Lawyer and senator. His family came to Canada in 1907 and settled near Canora, Saskatchewan. A graduate of the University of Saskatchewan, he was admitted to the bar in 1933 and was appointed Queen's Counsel in 1957. He served as president of the Saskatoon Conservative Association, provincial vice-president of the Saskatchewan Conservative party, president of the Saskatoon Bar Association, and chairman of the board of directors of the Mohyla Ukrainian Institute. In 1959 he was appointed senator.

Ray Hnatyshyn

Borys Hniedenko

Hnatyshyn, Ramon (Ray) [Hnatyšyn], b 16 March 1934 in Saskatoon. Lawyer and politician. Son of J. *Hnatyshyn. A graduate of the University of Saskatchewan, he practiced law in Saskatoon and then lectured on law at the University of Saskatchewan (1966–74). In 1973 he was appointed Queen's Counsel. As a Progressive Conservative (PC), he was elected to the House of Commons for Saskatoon West in 1974, 1979, 1980, and 1984. In the PC government of 1979–80 he served as minister of energy, mines, and resources, and as minister of state for science and technology. An opponent of capital punishment, Hnatyshyn monitored the solicitor general's department while in the PC shadow cabinet in 1983. He has served as PC government House leader (1984–5), president of the Queen's Privy Council (1985–6), and minister of justice and attorney general (1986–).

Hnidych, Mykola. See Gnedich, Nikolai.

Hnidyntsi Petroleum and Gas Field. Located near Hnidyntsi, Varva raion, Chernihiv oblast, this oil and gas field began to be worked in the 1960s. Exploratory oil drilling was completed in 1959 and extraction began in 1965. The oil lies at a depth of 1,700–1,900 m in a stratum of Lower Permian and Upper-Carboniferous sandstone. It is low in sulfur (less than 0.5 percent) and paraffin (2 percent), but high in resin (up to 28 percent). Most of the oil is pumped to the Kremenchuk Petroleum Refinery, but some of it is refined at Nadvirna, Odessa, and Polatsk, Belorussia. Gas exploration was completed in 1967 and extraction began in the following year. The gas is found at a depth of 3,200–3,270 m in a stratum of Lower-Carboniferous sandstone. It consists predominantly of methane (80 percent), ethane (9 percent), propane (4.6 percent), butane (1.3 percent), and pentane (0.25 percent). The natural gas is pumped into the Shebelynka-Kiev gas system.

Hniedenko, Borys [Hnjedenko], b 1 January 1912 in Simbirsk (now Ulianovsk), Russia. Mathematician; full member of the AN URSR from 1948. A graduate of Saratov University (1930), he served as director of the AN URSR Institute of Mathematics (1955–8) and, from 1965, as head of the University of Moscow Department of Mathematics. He has written works on the theory of probability, mathematical analysis and statistics, and the history and methodology of mathematics. He has also worked in the fields of cybernetics and computer science.

Hnivan [Hnivan']. IV-9. Town smt (1977 pop 8,000) in Tyvriv raion, Vinnytsia oblast, situated on the Boh River. It was first mentioned in 1629. It has large granite quarries, a sugar refinery (est 1877), and concrete plants.

Hnizdovsky, Jacques [Hnizdovs'kyj, Jakiv], b 27 January 1915 in Pylypche, Borshchiv county, Galicia, d 8 November 1985 in New York. Painter, engraver, and book designer. Having studied at the academies of art in Warsaw and Zagreb, he settled in the United States in 1949. In his paintings and prints he reduced objects to their primeval structure of lines and forms, and called this style 'simplified realism.' Among his oils are multifigural compositions such as *The Homeless* (1947), also known as *Displaced Persons*, portraits, landscapes, numerous still lifes, and entire series on the Paris metro, New York skyscrapers, and the Bronx brownstones. The same precision and devotion to detail is displayed in his woodcuts, which number close to 250. They include some extremely intricate works, eg, *Field* (1962), *Sunflower* (1965), and *Two Rams* (1969). Starting with a style close to Dürer's, he absorbed elements of old Ukrainian engravings,

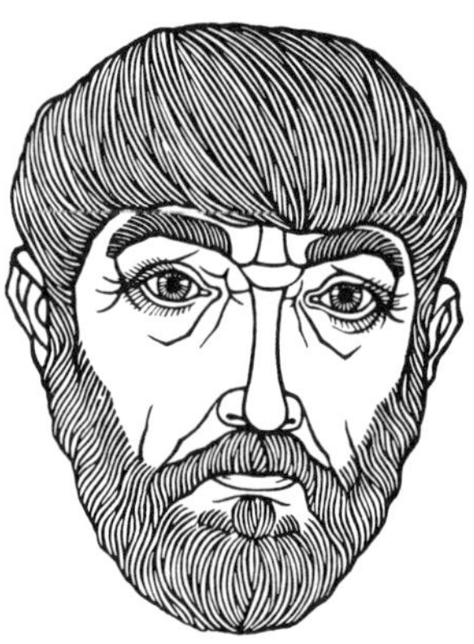

Jacques Hnizdovsky: *Self-Portrait* (woodcut, 1971)

Chinese and Japanese woodcuts, and various modern tendencies, and molded them into a personal style that brought him international recognition. Hnizdovsky illustrated many books, including *Slovo o polku Ihorevi* (The Tale of Ihor's Campaign, 1950), M. Halun Bloch's *Ukrainian Folk Tales* (1964), *Poems of Samuel Taylor Coleridge* (1967), and the album *Flora Exotica* (1972). He also designed several hundred book covers (among them the *Encyclopedia of Ukraine*) and a large number of bookplates.

Hnizdovsky began to display his work at Ukrainian exhibitions in Germany immediately after the war. One-man exhibitions of his work have been held at leading galleries in New York, New Orleans, Paris, and London. Traveling exhibits of his works were organized in the United States in 1967 and in Canada in 1973. His woodcuts have been included in group exhibits of the Society of American Graphic Artists and a number of exhibits in Europe, Asia, South America, and Africa sponsored by the US Information Agency. His works are included in the permanent collections of art museums (Boston, Cleveland, Philadelphia), museums, galleries (Winnipeg, Addison), universities (Duke, Delaware), and libraries (New York Public Library, Library of Congress), and in numerous private collections.

BIBLIOGRAPHY
Iakiv Hnizdovs'kyi (New York 1967)
Terem, no. 5 (1975)
Hnizdovsky: Woodcuts, 1944–1975, ed A.M. Tahir (Gretna, LA 1976)
Hnizdovsky: Years of Search 1950–1960 (Chicago 1978)

S. Hordynsky

Hnizna River. A left-bank tributary of the Seret River in the Podilian Upland. It is 81 km long and has a basin area of 1,110 sq km. The town of Terebovlia is located on the Hnizna.

Hnyla Lypa River. A left-bank tributary of the Dniester River in Podilia. The Hnyla Lypa is 87 km long and has a basin area of 1,320 sq km. During the First World War pitched battles between the armies of the Central Powers and Russia, and between the Ukrainian Sich Riflemen and Russian forces, were fought along its banks. On 24–28 June 1919 the Second Corps of the Ukrainian Galician Army fought Polish forces along the river, which marked the Dusaniv-Vovkiv front.

Hnyle more. See Syvash Lake.

Hnylopiat River [Hnylop'jat']. A right-bank tributary of the Teteriv River in the Dnieper River basin. It is 99 km in length and has a basin area of 1,312 sq km.

Hnylorybov, Tymofii, b 1 May 1901 in Gusevo, Donets okrug, Don Cossack province. Surgeon. A graduate

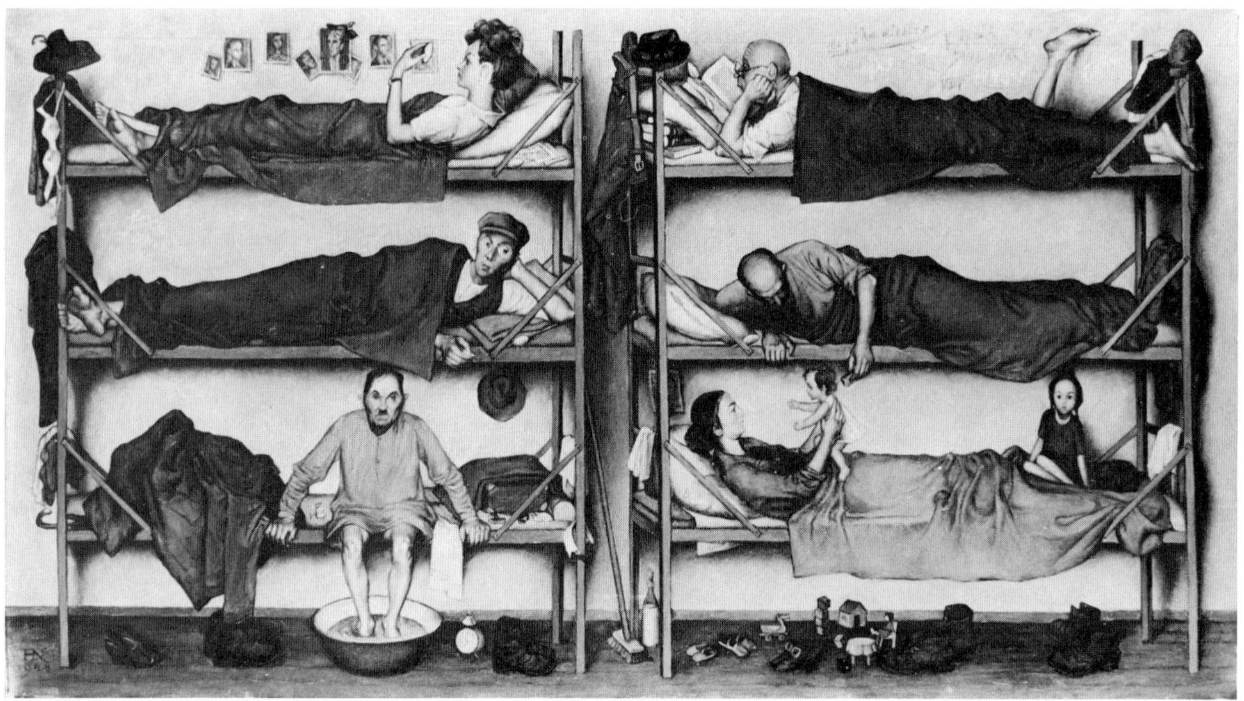

Jacques Hnizdovsky: *Displaced Persons* (oil, 1948)

of Rostov University (1925), he was appointed professor at the Dnipropetrovske Medical Institute in 1945. Most of his published works deal with restorative and cardiovascular surgery and the surgical treatment of diseases of the peripheral nervous system and endocrinal glands.

Hnylosyrov, Vasyl (also Hnylosyr), b 21 March 1836 in Poltava, d 3 November 1901 in Kaniv. Ukrainian pedagogue, journalist, and writer. While studying at Kharkiv University in the 1860s, he organized *Sunday schools and was in contact with other Ukrainian hromadas. From 1873 to 1893 he was the director of the county school in Kaniv and also looked after the grave of T. Shevchenko. He published his work under the pseudonym A. Havrysh in the journals *Osnova* and *Kievskaia starina.*

Hnylyi Tikych River [Hnylyj Tikyč]. A left-bank tributary of the Syniukha River. It flows for 157 km through the Dnieper Upland and the Boh River basin. Its own basin covers an area of 3,150 sq km. Its waters are used for domestic and industrial consumption, irrigation, and fish breeding. Three small hydroelectric stations are located on the river.

Hnylyi Yelanets River [Hnylyj Jelanec']. A left-bank tributary of the Boh River. It flows for 103 km through the Dnieper Upland and the Black Sea Lowland and has a basin area of 1,235 sq km. Its waters are used mostly for irrigation.

Hochemsky, Adam and Yosyf [Hočems'kyj]. The two brothers, whose birth and death dates are unknown, were copper and wood engravers in Pochaiv in the 18th century. Adam, who was active in the 1770s and 1780s, produced over 60 engravings, including *The Reshnivka Mother of God* (1770, 1774), *The Pochaiv Mother of God* (1773), *St Basil the Great* (1775), and *The Crucifixion* (1784) in Lahodyntsi, whose frame is decorated with interesting scenes of everyday life. He illustrated *Trefolohion* (1777) and a missal (1778). A view of Jerusalem and one of Constantinople (1778) were done by him. Yosyf was active from 1740 to the 1780s, producing nearly 130 copper etchings and woodcuts. They include illustrations to a pentecostarion (1747), a breviary (1741), a triodion (1767), and an *Apostol* (1768), scenes of the Lord's Passion, *The Sobor of the Kievan Cave Saints, The Siege of Pochaiv* (1675), and *Antimension* (1763). His personal style is particularly marked in the series of the Lord's Passion. Many of his engravings were copied and produced as popular prints.

Yosyf Hochemsky: *Joseph and His Brothers* (copper engraving, 1745)

Hockey, ice. Game played on ice by two teams, each trying to drive a rubber puck into the opponent's net. In Ukraine a form of hockey known as *bendi* (bandy), played with a ball, was played in Kharkiv as early as 1911–12. By 1922–3 the game had spread throughout the Donbas. In 1937 the first Ukrainian team (Kharkiv Silmash) took part in the competitions for the USSR cup.

The modern form of ice hockey developed first in Western Ukraine. The rules of the game were drawn up by I. Bobersky in 1906. In the early 1920s hockey teams were organized by sports associations such as Ukraina in Lviv and Dovbush in Chernivtsi. In central and eastern Ukraine modern ice hockey became popular only after the Second World War. In 1946 a republican hockey federation was established; it is a member of the all-Union Hockey Federation. Teams, which are located in most large Ukrainian cities, compete for the Soviet championship. Since 1954 Soviet teams have participated in the Olympic games, the world championships, and other international tournaments. The best Ukrainian players are attracted to Moscow to play on teams representing the USSR. Among them, E. Babych and V. Tretiak (goaltender on the Soviet Olympic team) are well known.

In the early 1980s the Kiev Sokil team gained wide popularity in Ukraine and the Soviet Union. It scored many victories in international competitions and toured Canada and the United States.

After the Second World War the team Lev in Mittenwald, Bavaria, won wide support from Ukrainian refugees in Germany. It played against German, American, Austrian, and Italian teams.

The game is popular with youngsters of Ukrainian origin in Canada and the United States. They join amateur and professional teams and many have become well known: T. Sawchuk, D. Lewicki, W. Broda, E. Nesterenko, B. Barilko, B. Mosienko, and W. Tkaczuk. J. Bucyk, V. Stasiuk, and B. Horvath of the National Hockey League's Boston Bruins became known as the 'Uke line' in the late 1950s. In the 1985–6 season there were 41 players of Ukrainian descent in the National Hockey League, the most famous being M. Bossy, D. Hawerchuk, and M. Krushelnyski.

E. Zharsky

Hodiak, John (Hodiak, Ivan), b 16 April 1914 in Pittsburgh, d 19 October 1955 in Tarzana, California. American actor of Ukrainian descent. After working as a radio announcer and actor for several years, in 1943 he made his film debut in *A Stranger in Town.* He appeared in 34 Hollywood films, of which the most important were the A. Hitchcock thriller *Lifeboat* (1944), *Sunday Dinner for a*

Soldier (1944), *A Bell for Adano* (1945), and *The Harvey Girls* (1946). Turning to the stage, he won critical acclaim for his performance as Lt Maryk in *The Caine Mutiny Court Martial* (1953). His last film role was Lt Col Thomas in *On the Threshold of Space* (1956).

Hodinka, Antonii (Antal), b 13 January 1864 in Ladomirov, Transcarpathia, d 15 July 1946 in Budapest. Historian. He was a professor of the Law Academy in Bratislava (1906–18); professor (1918–35), dean, and president at the University of Pécs; a member of the Hungarian Academy of Sciences (from 1933); and head of the Subcarpathian Learned Society in Uzhhorod (1940–4). He wrote several works, including *A Munkácsi Görög-Katholikus Püspökség Története* (History of the Mukachiv Greek-Catholic Eparchy, 1909), *A Munkácsi Görög-Szertartású Püspökség Okmánytára* (The Archives of the Mukachiv Greek-Rite Eparchy, vol 1, 1911), and *Az orosz évkönyvek magyar vonatkozásai* (The Hungarian-Related Sections of the Russian Annals, 1916). His compilation of documents pertaining to Prince F. *Koriatovych and the founding of the Mukachiv Monastery was published posthumously in *AOBM*, vols 1–2 (1950–4). He also wrote in the east Transcarpathian dialect, under the pseudonym Sokyrnytsky Syrokhman, such works as *Uttsiuznyna, gazduvstvo y proshlost' iuzhno-karpats'kykh rusynov* (The Heritage, Economy, and Past of the South-Carpathian Ruthenians, 1922).

Hodlin, Mykhailo, b 26 November 1886 in Novozybkov, Chernihiv gubernia, d 5 September 1973 in Kiev. Soil scientist. A graduate of the Kiev Polytechnical Institute (1914), he was a professor at the Kiev Agricultural Institute from 1930 and the Ukrainian Agricultural Academy from 1954. Hodlin created new methods of determining the composition of soil and its general acidity and salinity. He elaborated a soil classification system and developed a system of indicators characterizing various soil structures. He was a coauthor of *Pochvy USSR* (Soils of the Ukrainian SSR, 1951).

Hoffmann, Max, b 25 January 1869 in Homberg, d 8 July 1927 in Bad Reichenhall, Germany. German general. The chief of staff of the German eastern front from August 1916, he headed, with R. von Kühlmann, the German delegation that signed a separate treaty with the UNR at *Brest-Litovsk in February 1918.

Hog raising. Branch of animal husbandry that raises hogs for meat, lard, leather, and other products. Until 1975 it was the most important source of meat in Ukraine. Now it is second only to cattle raising.

Historically, the number of hogs in Ukraine has been subject to great fluctuations; it has fallen drastically in times of economic difficulty or during war and at other times has risen more rapidly than the population of any other livestock. In eastern and central Ukraine before 1917 hog raising was widely practiced by small and land-hungry peasant households, particularly in the central regions such as Poltava and Chernihiv. Hogs were easy to rear – they could be fed on potatoes and corn. Some were exported to Germany. During the latter part of the First World War, the total hog population in central and eastern Ukraine fell from 4.6 million to less than half this figure. With the introduction of the New Economic Policy (1923–8) and more advantageous conditions for private farming, the number of hogs tripled to approximately 7 million. From the outset of the collectivization drive communal hog farms were organized in collective and, to a lesser extent, state farms. During this period, many peasants slaughtered their livestock, including hogs, rather than give them up to the collective farms. During the man-made *famine of 1932–3, hogs were slaughtered for food or died from starvation. By 1933 there were only about 2 million hogs (28 percent of the pre-collectivization population) in Soviet Ukraine. The Model Collective-Farm Statute introduced in 1935 permitted collective-farm households to rear hogs. Hog raising on private plots soon became the leading branch of animal husbandry in Ukraine. By 1941 almost 60 percent of all hogs in the republic were raised on private plots, 31 percent on collective farms, 6 percent on state farms, and the remainder on auxiliary farms. In 1941 over 33 percent of all hogs in the USSR were bred in Ukraine. In 1940 pork accounted for over 50 percent of Ukraine's meat production. On state farms the percentage was much higher, because after 1930 pork production became their speciality. Outside Soviet Ukraine in Polish-ruled Galicia and Volhynia, there were about 1.6 million hogs in 1932. By 1936 the figure rose to 1.87 million. In northern Bukovyna and the Ukrainian parts of Bessarabia, which were under Rumanian rule, the total in 1932 stood at 204,700 hogs and in Transcarpathia it was 138,200. The most important hog-raising region before the Second World War was Polisia, with over 30 hogs per 100 ha of arable land. By 1941 the number of hogs in Soviet Ukraine had recovered from the collectivization drive and the famine; it was expanded by about 26 percent by the annexation of Western Ukraine in 1939–40. Thus at the outbreak of the German-Soviet War the total number of hogs in Ukraine exceeded 9 million. The destruction of farms and food requisitions during the war reduced the total to less than 3 million. In some oblasts – eg, Ternopil – the hog population fell by almost 90 percent. The drought and famine of 1946, which affected eastern Ukraine, reduced hog numbers even further. The prewar total was not equaled until the mid-1950s.

In the 1950s and 1960s hog raising became the most important branch of animal husbandry in Ukraine. It benefited from the enlargment of collective farms undertaken in 1950–1, and from the expansion of the sugar-refining industry, whose by-products were used as feed. Since the 1960s hog production has stagnated somewhat because of a number of factors, including adverse weather conditions in the late 1970s and early 1980s that reduced feed output. The importance of pork in Ukraine's meat production declined from 50.4 percent in 1940 to 47 percent in 1970 and to 35.4 percent in 1982. This decline mirrors closely the general situation in the USSR. In the same period the output of poultry meat and beef has increased significantly. Between 1971 and 1983 the total number of hogs on both collective farms and private plots fell, but on state farms it rose by about 4.4 percent. Even on state farms the specific weight of hog raising declined. Today pork production has retained its priority only on the private plots of collective farmers. Since 1971 the population in Ukraine has been quite stable. In 1983 it came to 21.2 million or 27 percent of the USSR total. The highest number of hogs per ha is to be found in the western and northwestern oblasts: Transcarpathia,

Chernivtsi, and Rivne; the lowest number in the steppe regions. Almost all hogs today are purebred. The main breeds are the Large White (over 80 percent), the Steppe White (over 10 percent), and the Myrhorod (over 5 percent).

Important scientific research on hog raising is conducted at the Poltava Scientific Research Institute of Hog Raising, the Scientific Research Institute of Animal Husbandry of the Forest-Steppe and Polisia of the Ukrainian SSR, the Scientific Research Institute of Land Cultivation and Animal Husbandry in the Western Regions of the Ukrainian SSR, and the Ukrainian Scientific Research Institute of Animal Husbandry of the Steppe Regions in Askaniia-Nova.

D. Marples

Hohol, Albert [Hohol'], b 27 December 1922 in Two Hills, Alberta. Educator and politician. Educated at the universities of Alberta and Oregon (PH D 1967), between 1947 and 1971 he was a teacher and superintendent of schools in Alberta. As the Progressive Conservative member of the Alberta legislature for Edmonton-Belmont (1971–9), he served as minister of manpower and labor (1971–5) and minister of advanced education and manpower (1975–9). Since 1979 he has been commissioner of the Alberta Workers' Compensation Board. He played a key role in establishing the Canadian Institute of Ukrainian Studies.

Hohol, Mykola. See Gogol, Nikolai.

Hohol, Ostap [Hohol'], ?–1679. Cossack military leader during the *Cossack-Polish War of 1648–54. A member of the Volhynian nobility, he was intermittently the colonel of Podilia (Mohyliv) regiment from 1658 until 1676 (when the regiment was dissolved). He was briefly, in 1649 and 1674, colonel of the Kalnyk (Vinnytsia) regiment. From 1676 until his death he was acting hetman of Right-Bank Ukraine.

Hohol-Yanovsky, Vasyl [Hohol'-Janovs'kyj, Vasyl'] (Gogol, Vasilii), b 1777 on the farmstead Kupchynskyi (today Hoholeve) near Myrhorod in the Poltava region, d March 1825 in nearby Kybyntsi. A landowner of Cossack *starshyna* descent and Ukrainian playwright; the father of N. *Gogol. In the 1820s he directed the theater of the noble D. *Troshchynsky on the latter's estate in the village of Kybyntsi and wrote and staged plays for it in Ukrainian. They include the *intermediia*-like comedy 'Sobaka-vivtsia' (The Dog-Sheep) and the farce 'Prostak, ili khitrost' zhenshchiny, perekhitrennaia soldatom' (The Simpleton, or the Cunning of a Woman Outwitted by a Soldier), which is similar to I. Kotliarevsky's *Moskal'-charivnyk* (The Muscovite-Sorcerer).

Hohotsky, Sylvestr [Hohots'kyj, Syl'vestr], b 17 January 1813 in Kamianets-Podilskyi, Podilia gubernia, d 11 July 1889 in Kiev. Philosopher and pedagogue. He graduated from the Kiev Theological Academy in 1837 and remained there to teach Polish and German languages and philosophy. In 1848 he was appointed professor of philosophy and in 1851 professor of pedagogy at Kiev University. Hohotsky was influenced mostly by Hegel and developed a vague theistic philosophy. His most important contribution to philosophy was *Filosofskii leksikon* (Philosophical Lexicon, 4 vols, 1857–73). At first a Ukrainophile and a contributor to **Osnova*, he later opposed the Ukrainian movement.

Hoida, Yurii [Hojda, Jurij], b 15 March 1919 in Zniatseve, Mukachiv county, Transcarpathia, d 2 June 1955 in Uzhhorod. Poet. In his many collections of poetry – *Liudy moieï zemli* (People of My Land, 1948), *Verkhovyns'ka poema* (Highland Poem, 1949), *Sontse nad Tysoiu* (Sun above the Tysa, 1950), *Vysoki dorohy* (High Roads, 1952), *Liryka* (Lyrical Poetry, 1954) – Hoida glorified the Soviet annexation of Transcarpathia.

Hola Prystan [Hola Prystan']. VII-13. Town (1983 pop 14,700) and raion center in Kherson oblast. A commercial port (since 1868) on the Konka River 20 km from the Dnieper Estuary, it was first mentioned in 1786, and fortified during the Crimean War. The site of the first state radio station in Ukraine, created in 1902 by A. Popov. The Komunar plant (boats, furniture), the Hopry mud-bath sanatorium and spa, and the museum, laboratories, and offices of the *Black Sea Nature Reserve are located there.

Holeho, Mykola, b 15 June 1914 in Khrystynivka, Kiev gubernia. Specialist in mechanics and machine building; corresponding member of the AN URSR since 1967. Having graduated from the Kiev Institute of Civil Aviation Engineers in 1938, he worked as an engineer and manager at various aviation plants. From 1954 to 1975 he was rector of the institute. In 1976 he was appointed department chairman at the AN URSR Institute for Problems of the Strength of Materials. His main publications deal with methods of increasing machine reliability and durability.

Holendry. IV-9. Village in Kalynivka raion, Vinnytsia oblast in northeastern Podilia. In 1919 the Kolomyia Brigade of the Ukrainian Galician Army defeated units of the Red Army there.

Holidays. Today in the USSR there are six statutory holidays: 1 January (New Year's Day), 8 March (International Women's Day), 1 and 2 May (International Toilers' Solidarity Days), 9 May (Victory Day), 7 and 8 November (Anniversary of the October Revolution), and 5 December (Soviet Constitution Day). In addition most employees have 15 days of paid holidays per year (1978).

The concept of a statutory (paid) holiday is a recent one and coincides with the large-scale development of wage labor. Before 1917 in Russian-ruled Ukraine, besides religious and folk holidays (see *Church holidays; *Folk calendar), certain anniversaries in the royal family were celebrated as national holidays. Under Nicholas II these holidays were the empress's saint's day (23 April), the emperor's birthday (6 May), the anniversary of the emperor's coronation (14 May), the empress's birthday (25 May), the dowager empress's birthday (14 November), the crown prince's birthday (22 November), the emperor's saint's day (6 December). The total number of religious and national holidays amounted to over 50 days a year (excluding Sundays). Not all of them were paid, however, and the number of non-working days varied from industry to industry. Most peasants and other independent producers observed religious and folk holidays at their own expense.

In the Habsburg Empire, of which Western Ukraine was a part, there were no national holidays connected with anniversaries in the royal family, although the decennial jubilees of Francis Joseph's birth and accession to the throne were marked with great fanfare. The only holidays on which labor in industry was regulated (particularly by the laws of 1885, 1895, and 1905) were religious holidays. After 1848 Ukrainians in Galicia observed the anniversary of the abolition of serfdom (3 May, OS) and, beginning in 1862, the anniversary of T. Shevchenko's death (26 February, OS). Observance of these anniversaries was voluntary.

Ukrainians outside Ukraine commemorate annually two historical events: on 22 January the Independence of Ukraine, and on 1 November the 1918 November uprising in Lviv (*Lystopadovyi zryv*). In 1981 a citizen group in Kiev declared 12 January Ukrainian Political Prisoner's Day to commemorate the mass arrests of Ukrainian dissidents that took place on 12 January 1972. This anniversary is observed by some Ukrainian communities outside the USSR and Eastern Europe, and by some individuals within the Soviet Union and its satellites.

J.-P. Himka, B. Krawchenko

Olena Holitsynska

Yevhen Holitsynsky

Holitsynska, Olena [Holicyns'ka], b 29 December 1899 in Izium, Kharkiv gubernia, d 25 March 1978 in Irvington, New Jersey. Stage actress; daughter of H. Borysohlibska. After graduating from the Lysenko Music and Drama School in Kiev, she worked at the Molodyi Teatr theater in Kiev (1918), the Ukrainska Besida Theater in Lviv (1920–41), and the Lviv Theater of Opera and Ballet (1941–4). She made guest appearances with the Berezil theater (1927), the Tobilevych Ukrainian People's Theater, and the Kotliarevsky Theater in Lviv (1938). Her repertoire consisted of heroic roles, particularly in plays by V. Vynnychenko, H. Ibsen, and Molière. She also appeared in classical operettas by J. Strauss and F. Lehár.

Holitsynsky, Yevhen [Holicyns'kyj, Jevhen], b 20 October 1878 in Kishinev, d 17 March 1932 in Prague. Chemist and political leader. He studied chemistry in Kiev and Prague. A prominent member of the *Revolutionary Ukrainian party, from 1902 he was a member of its central committee and from 1903 to 1904 he was the party's representative abroad. In 1905 he returned to Ukraine and joined the Ukrainian Social Democratic Labor party, and from 1915 to 1917 he served as liaison officer between Ukrainian activists in Kiev and the *Union for the Liberation of Ukraine. In 1917–18 Holitsynsky was a member of the Central Rada and director of the general department of the ministry of trade and industry. In 1919 he headed a special UNR mission to the United States, and later served as diplomatic envoy to Estonia. From 1923 he was docent of chemical technology at the Ukrainian Husbandry Academy in Poděbrady.

Holland. See Netherlands.

Holoborodko, Vasyl [Holoborod'ko, Vasyl'], b 1946 in Voroshylovhrad oblast. Poet. Details of his biography are skimpy. He was a miner in 1964, a student at Kiev University in 1966, and stationed as a soldier in the Far East in 1969. In 1964 several of his poems appeared in the literary periodicals *Literaturna Ukraïna* and *Dnipro*, after which he fell into official disfavor and was no longer published in Ukraine despite accolades by I. Dziuba and other critics on the uniqueness and freshness of his imagery and poetic vision. Holoborodko's vision of the world is through the prism of innocence. His poetry draws its power from a metaphorical rendering of reality in images striking by their quality of child-like magic, wonder, and naïvete. Four manuscript collections of his poems were smuggled to the West and published together in Paris in 1970 under the title *Letiuche vikontse* (The Flying Window).

Holobutsky, Volodymyr [Holobuc'kyj], b 28 July 1903 in Velykyi Bir, Surazh county, Chernihiv gubernia. Historian. Since the mid-1930s he has worked at various Soviet higher educational institutions, including Chernivtsi University (1951–4), the AN URSR Institute of History (1947–61, 1974–), and the Kiev Institute of the National Economy (1955–). His major works devoted to Ukrainian history of the 16th–19th centuries, particularly of the Cossacks, include *Chernomorskoe kazachestvo* (The Black Sea Cossacks, 1956), *Zaporozhskoe kazachestvo* (The Zaporozhian Cossacks, 1957), *Zaporiz'ka Sich v ostanni chasy svoho isnuvannia, 1734–1775* (The Zaporozhian Sich in the Last Period of Its Existence, 1734–75, 1961), and *Diplomaticheskaia istoriia osvoboditel'noi voiny ukrainskogo naroda, 1648–1654 gg.* (The Diplomatic History of the Liberation War of the Ukrainian People, 1648–54, 1962).

Holod, Roman, b 17 August 1905 in Dmytrovychi, Lviv county, Galicia, d 26 December 1966 in Toronto. Community and co-operative leader; agricultural engineer. He organized and lectured in the agricultural training program *Khliborobskyi Vyshkil Molodi and was the founder and director of the Rip, Vovna, and Shovk agricultural co-operatives in the 1930s in Lviv. During the Second World War he worked with the Ukrainian Central Committee in Cracow. After the war, first in Germany then after 1948 in Canada, he was a leader of Plast and a fund raiser for the Shevchenko Scientific Society in France.

Holohory. The western part of the northern edge of the Podolian Upland, which is known as the *Holohory-Kremianets Ridge, extending 60 km from Lviv to Zolochiv. It is dissected by tributaries of the Buh River. The highest peaks are Chortivska Cliff near Lviv (414 m) and Kamula (471 m).

Holohory-Kremianets Ridge. The northwestern part of the *Podolian Upland. The ridge falls steeply in ledges to the Buh Depression and Little Polisia. As a result of intensive erosion, it now consists of mesas dissected by river valleys, gullies, and ravines. The ridge is divided into the uplands of Holohory and Voroniaky and the Kremianets Hills.

Holos (Voice). A weekly newspaper that came out in Berlin from January 1940 to June 1945. It was edited by B. *Kravtsiv and served as the principal organ for **Ostarbeiter* and for other Ukrainians working in Germany under the Third Reich.

Holos Khrysta Cholovikoliubtsia (La Voix du Christ Ami des Hommes). A popular Catholic journal published in Louvain, Belgium, since June 1946. At first a monthly, then a bimonthly (1955–80), after a break it reappeared as a quarterly in 1984. The chief editors have been M. Hermaniuk (1946–8), S. Bozhyk (1948–69), and D. Dzvonyk (1969–80). In 1984 it became the official organ of the Ukrainian Catholic Exarchate for France and the Benelux countries.

Holos molodi (Youth Speaks). Illustrated bilingual (Ukrainian-English) monthly (later quarterly) organ of the Ukrainian National Youth Federation published in Winnipeg from 1947 to 1954. The journal, which originated in 1943 as a separate page of the newspaper **Novyi shliakh*, was intended to reach a generation that no longer spoke Ukrainian. Among its editors were B. Bociurkiw, L. Kossar, T. Tsirka, and P. Yuzyk.

Holos narodnyi (The Voice of the People). A literary-political semimonthly periodical published and edited by I. Bilous in Kolomyia from 26 October 1865 to 1868. It was the first Ukrainian newspaper in Galicia published outside Lviv. It contained historical and church calendars as well as political and historical articles by such contributors as A. Shankovsky and M. Hnatevych. It also included articles on agriculture. Folklore, reviews, obituaries, and local news were also published. *Holos narodnyi* was published in both the *hrazhdanka and Cyrillic alphabets.

Holos natsiï (The Voice of the Nation). A weekly political periodical of a nationalistic character, edited by O. Boidunyk. It appeared in Lviv in 1936–7 in place of the suppressed journal *Visti* (News), edited by B. Kravtsiv. When *Holos natsiï* was also banned, it was replaced by *Holos* (Voice, 1938–9), with B. Kravtsiv again as editor.

Holos pratsi (Voice of Labour). See *Robitnytsia*.

Holos robitnytsi (Working Woman's Voice). See *Robitnytsia*.

Holos Spasytelia (Redeemer's Voice). Religious monthly published in Ukrainian and English by the Redemptorist Fathers in Yorkton, Saskatchewan. From April 1923 to February 1928 it was called *Holos Izbavytelia*. In November 1933 it reappeared under its present name. It generally avoids controversial Ukrainian political and social issues. Among its editors have been Revs Y. Bala, I. Bala, K. Lototsky, Y. Korba, M. Shchudlo, and R. Khomiak.

Holos zhyttia (The Voice of Life). A left-wing political and literary semimonthly periodical published from 1929 to 1938 in Uzhhorod. The organ of the Union of Toiling Peasants from 1931, its editors included A. Mondok and I. Beleha.

Holoskevych, Hryhorii [Holoskevyč, Hryhorij], b 4 November 1884 in Soprunkivtsi, Nova Ushytsia county, Podilia gubernia, d autumn 1934 in Tobolsk, Siberia. Linguist. He graduated from the Kamianets-Podilskyi Theological Seminary in 1905 and studied linguistics under A. *Shakhmatov at St Petersburg University (1906–11); he was active in the Ukrainian hromada there. In 1917 he moved to Kiev and organized, with P. Zaitsev and P. Stebnytsky, the Drukar publishing house (1917–20). He was a central figure in the *Slovo publishing co-operative (1922–6). He became an associate of the VUAN in 1918 and was a coeditor of its Russian-Ukrainian dictionary (1924–8). He wrote studies on a Podilian dialect (1910) and the language of the *Eusebius Gospel (1914), and compiled the first Ukrainian orthographic dictionary (1st edn 1914; 7th edn 1931, incorporating changes codified in the 1928 orthography, repr New York 1952). He was arrested in August 1929 and at the Stalinist show trial of the *Union for the Liberation of Ukraine in 1930 he was sentenced to five years' imprisonment. After serving three years in the Yaroslavl prison he was exiled to Tobolsk, where he committed suicide.

Holota, Illia, b ?, d 27 July 1649 near Zahalle, Belorussia. Cossack leader. A colonel of the Registered Cossacks, he joined B. Khmelnytsky's rebellion in 1648. In spring 1649 he led a large Cossack detachment north of the Prypiat River, where they defeated a Lithuanian army commanded by J. Radziwiłł that had been sent to reinforce the Polish forces. For the next three months his forces participated in a series of battles with Lithuanian and Polish units. Surrounded and outnumbered by the enemy, he died in battle.

Holota, Petro (pen name of P. Melnyk), b 1902 in Balashivka (now part of Kirovohrad), d 8 November 1949 in Sniatyn, Stanyslaviv oblast. Writer. He belonged to the writers' groups *Molodniak (1926–7) and *Avanhard (1928–9). His first collections of poetry – *Ternystyi shliakh do voli i osvity* (The Thorny Path to Freedom and Education, 1921) – and of prose – *V dorozi zmahan'* (On the Road of Struggles, 1925) – were followed by a few more collections of proletarian poetry, the prose collection *Brud* (Dirt, 1929), and two novellas: *Dni iunosty* (Days of Youth, 1930) and *Skhodylo sontse* (The Sun Was Rising, 1930). Holota was repressed in the 1930s. Subsequently rehabilitated, he settled down in Sniatyn in 1945 and worked there as an editor of the raion newspaper.

Holota. Stratum of landless peasants that appeared in Ukraine at the end of the 15th century as serfdom was introduced under Polish and Lithuanian rule. The term *holota* appears in documents dating back to the 16th century. Some of these impoverished peasants resettled in the free territories of the Bratslav, Kaniv, and Cherkasy regions, where they formed a significant part of the Cossack stratum. Later, in the 16th–18th centuries, many fled to the territories of the Zaporozhian Sich, where they constituted the majority of the population. Most became poor Cossacks who worked as hired hands on the estates of wealthy Cossacks or in fishing, salt-making, or chumak enterprises. Some traveled to the Crimea, Moldavia, or Wallachia in search of work. The *holota* took part in the Cossack uprisings against the Poles and constituted a large part of B. Khmelnytsky's army in the war of 1648–57. In the 18th century it played an important role in the *Haidamaka uprisings. It ceased to exist as a separate social stratum with the introduction of serfdom under Russian rule after the destruction of the Zaporozhian Sich. The *holota* is remembered in folk songs ('Oi nastupyla ta chorna khmara') and dumas; eg, 'Duma about Cossack Holota's Duel with a Tatar' and 'Duma about Handzha Andyber.'

Holovanivske [Holovanivs'ke]. v-11. Town smt (1978 pop 6,700) and raion center in Kirovohrad oblast. It was first mentioned in 1764. It has a food, lumber, consumer, and brick industry.

Holovanivsky, Sava [Holovanivs'kyj], b 29 May 1910 in Yelysavetahradka, Oleksandriia county, Kherson gubernia. A socialist realist poet, prosaist, and playwright. He is the author of over 30 poetry collections, beginning with *Kin'my zaliznymy* (With Iron Horses, 1927); the collections *Dramy* (Dramas, 1956) and *P'iesy* (Plays, 1973); the collections of publicistic and artistic prose *Skatertiu dorizhka* (Good Riddance, 1930), *Chobit Evropy* (The Boot of Europe, 1932), *Poiedynok* (The Duel, 1941), and *Kraplia krovi* (A Drop of Blood, 1945); the novels *Vasyl' Naida* (1930), *Topolia na tomu berezi* (The Poplar on the Other Bank, 1965), and *Korsun'* (1972); and two books of articles on current affairs.

Holovashchuk, Serhii [Holovaščuk, Serhij], 30 September 1922 in Sobolivka, Radomyshl county, Kiev gubernia. Lexicographer. An associate of the AN URSR Institute of Linguistics, he has coedited its Ukrainian-Russian dictionary (vol 6, 1963), Russian-Ukrainian dictionary (3 vols, 1968, 2nd edn 1980–1), dictionary of the Ukrainian language (vols 8–11, 1977–80), and Ukrainian orthographic dictionary (1975). A proponent of bringing Ukrainian closer to Russian, he presented his theoretical views in *Perekladni slovnyky i pryntsypy ïkh ukladannia* (Bilingual Dictionaries and the Principles of Their Compilation, 1976).

Holovatiuk, Yevhen [Holovatjuk, Jevhen], b 28 September 1938 in Lozovata, Lypovets raion, Vinnytsia oblast. Stage director. A graduate of the Kiev Institute of Theater Arts (1961), he has worked at theaters in Mykolaiv, Alma-Ata, Dnipropetrovske, and Donetske. In 1976 he became chief stage director of the Donetske Ukrainian Music and Drama Theater.

Holovatsky, Ivan [Holovac'kyj], 1814–99. Civic leader and journalist; brother of Ya. *Holovatsky. Holovatsky contributed to the government newspaper *Halycho-Ruskii vistnyk* in 1849–50 and then edited its successor *Vistnyk*, published in Vienna, in 1850–1. For many years he translated Austrian law into Ukrainian and taught Russian at the University of Vienna. He published the almanac *Vinok rusynam na obzhynky* (A Garland for Ruthenians after the Harvest, 1846–7).

Holovatsky, Rodion [Holovac'kyj], b 18 October 1917 in Lviv, d 22 July 1985 in Rome. Ukrainian Catholic priest. He studied at the Lviv Theological Academy and at the Urbaniana University in Rome. From 1951 he was a parish priest in the province of Misiones in Argentina. In 1959 he was appointed chaplain of Saint Josaphat's Ukrainian Pontifical College in Rome and director of the Ukrainian department of the Vatican radio.

Yakiv Holovatsky

Holovatsky, Yakiv [Holovac'kyj, Jakiv], b 17 October 1814 in Chepeli, Zolochiv circle, Galicia, d 13 May 1888 in Vilnius. Noted historian, literary scholar, ethnographer, linguist, bibliographer, lexicographer, and poet. As a student he traversed Galicia, Bukovyna, and Transcarpathia collecting folk songs. In 1832, at Lviv University he, M. Shashkevych, and I. Vahylevych formed the *Ruthenian Triad, which published the first Galician almanac in the vernacular, **Rusalka dnistrovaia* (The Dniester Nymph, 1837), and played an important role in the Galician cultural revival. He graduated from Lviv University in 1841, and in 1843 he became a Greek-Catholic village priest. In 1848 he participated in the Congress of Ruthenian Scholars in Lviv, and from 1848 to 1867 he was the first professor of Ruthenian (Ukrainian) philology at Lviv University. Influenced by M. Pogodin's Pan-Slavist ideas, he became a *Russophile in the 1850s. Dismissed from the university for his views, in 1867 he moved to Russian-ruled Vilnius to head the archeographic commission there.

Holovatsky wrote many ethnographic and literary works; the most important are *Try vstupytel'nyie prepodavanyia o ruskoi slovesnosty* (Three Introductory Lectures on Ruthenian Literature, 1849), *Ocherk staroslavianskogo basnosloviia, ili mifologiia* (A Study of Old Slavic Fables, or Mythology, 1860), *O pervom literaturno-umstvennom dvizhenii rusinov v Galitsii ...* (On the Ruthenian's First Literary-Intellectual Movement in Galicia ..., 1865), and the particularly valuable *Narodnye pesni Galitskoi i Ugorskoi Rusi* (Folk Songs of Galician and Hungarian Ruthenia, 4 vols, 1878). His first poems, articles, and translations of Serbo-Croatian folk songs appeared in *Rusalka dnistrovaia* and in the almanac **Vinok rusynam na obzhynky* (A Garland for Ruthenians after the Harvest, 1846–7). Most of his theological, literary, and historical studies, as well as his memoirs, were published in *Naukovyi sbornik* of the Halytsko-Ruska Matytsia society, *Halychanyn*, *Slovo*, and *Vremennyk Ynstytuta Stavropyhiiskoho*.

Believing that folk vernacular is the truest expression

of a people's spirit, Holovatsky devoted much effort during his Romantic period (to 1848) to collecting and researching native linguistic data. His *Hramatyka ruskoho iazyka* (Grammar of the Ruthenian Language, 1849) was compiled from his university lectures and was modeled on A. *Vostokov's Russian grammar. His *Rozprava o iazytsi iuzhnoruskim i ieho narichiiakh* (Treatise on the South Russian Language and Its Dialects, 1849) was the first attempt at a scientific classification of Ukrainian dialects. By the time he wrote his unpublished grammar of 1851, however, Holovatsky had rejected the Romantic-national perspective; the work is written from a Russophile orientation. Thereafter his writings, including *Geograficheskii slovar' zapadnoslavianskikh i iugoslavianskikh zemel' i prilezhashchikh stran* (Geographical Dictionary of West Slavic and South Slavic Lands and Adjacent Countries, 1884), reflected the influence of Russian Pan-Slavism.

BIBLIOGRAPHY
Vavrik, V. *Iakov Fedorovich Golovatskii. Ego deiatel'nost' i znachenie v galitsko-russkoi slovesnosti* (Lviv 1925)
Humeniuk, M.; Kravchenko, I. (eds). *Shashkevych, I. Vahylevych, Ia. Holovatsky: Bibliohrafichnyi pokazhchyk* (Lviv 1962)
Pil'huk, I.; Chornopys'kyi, M. (eds). *Pys'mennyky Zakhidnoï Ukraïny 30–50-kh rokiv XIX st.* (Kiev 1965)
V. Lev, G.Y. Shevelov

Holovaty, Antin [Holovatyj], b 1744, d 19 February 1797. Military leader. Educated at the Kievan Mohyla Academy, he served as chancellor of the Zaporozhian Host and as a colonel of the *Boh Cossack Army. In 1787 he helped organize the Army of Loyal Cossacks, which was renamed *Black Sea Cossacks. His assistance to the Russian army in the Russian-Turkish War of 1787–91, particularly in the capture of Berezan fortress, gained him the tsar's favor. After the war Holovaty conducted the resettlement of the Cossacks to the Kuban region. In 1796 he was elected otaman of the Black Sea Cossacks and participated with two regiments in the Russian campaign against Persia. According to tradition, Holovaty was the author of a number of popular songs.

Holovaty, Pavlo [Holovatyj], b ca 1715, d ca 1795. Last military judge of the Zaporozhian Sich. When the Sich was razed in 1775, he was arrested, tried in St Petersburg, and exiled for life to Znamenie Monastery in Tobolsk, Siberia.

Holovchenko, Heorhii [Holovčenko, Heorhij], b 5 July 1931 in Luhanske (now Voroshylovhrad). Architect. A graduate of the Kharkiv Civil Engineering Institute (1957), he has built the Philharmonia (1962), the monument to the heroes of the Soviet Union (1965), the Drama Theater (1970), and the Oblast Trade Union Soviet, all in Voroshylovhrad. He collaborated with several sculptors in building the memorial complex to the Young Guards (1965) in Krasnodar and other monuments in the Voroshylohrad region.

Holovchenko, Ivan [Holovčenko], b 14 October 1918 in Lyman Druhyi, Kupianka county, Kharkiv gubernia. Soviet army general, political figure, and writer. After graduating from the CC CPSU Higher Party School in 1948, he held various Party posts before joining the KGB (1955–62). In 1962 he became a colonel-general and minister of internal affairs of the Ukrainian SSR. As a prosaist he debuted in 1957 with a selection of short stories, *Zapysky chekista* (A Chekist's Notes). His other works include the novels *Tretia zustrich* (The Third Meeting, 1960), *Chorna stezhka* (Black Pathway, 1961), and *Militseis'ki buval'shchyny* (Experiences in the Militia, 1974), and several novels coauthored with O. Musiienko. Holovchenko's works conform to the official style of socialist realism and deal mainly with the events of the Second World War.

Holovetsky, Dionisii [Holovec'kyi, Dionisij], b 3 November 1885 in Staryi Sambir, Sambir county, Galicia, d 4 February 1961 in Glen Cove, New York. Priest of the Basilian monastic order, specialist in canon law. He served as rector of Saint Josaphat's Ukrainian Pontifical College in Rome (1926–32). He was a member of the Codification Commission for Eastern Canon Law and a consultator of the Sacred Congregation for the Oriental Churches. A collection of Ukrainian sources of eastern law, 'Jus Particulare Ruthenorum,' published in *Codificazione Canonica Orientale. Fonti XI* (1933), was compiled by Holovetsky. In 1946–53 he taught canon law at the Catholic University of America in Washington, DC.

Holovianko, Zynovii [Holov'janko, Zynovij], b 24 November 1876 in Talova Balka, Oleksandriia county, Kherson gubernia, d 23 September 1953 in Kiev. Silviculturist and entomologist. Holovianko graduated in 1901 from the St Petersburg Forestry Institute and worked in various forestry stations in Ukraine. From 1937 to 1953 he was a professor at the Kiev Forestry Institute and was associated with the AN URSR. He founded the Darnytsia Forestry Research Station near Kiev in 1924 and headed it until 1934. He is the author of works on ecology, the morphology of insect pests and methods of combating them, and the regeneration of tree crops.

Yuliian Holovinsky

Holovinsky, Yuliian [Holovins'kyj, Julijan], b 1 December 1894 in Radymno, Peremyshl county, Galicia, d 30 September 1930 in Bibrka, Lviv county. Political and military activist. A captain in the Ukrainian Galician Army, after the struggle for Ukrainian independence he was interned in the camps at Josefov and Brno in Czechoslovakia. In the 1920s he was a cofounder and leading member of the *Ukrainian Military Organization. He organized the assassination attempt on Polish President S. Wojciechowski in 1924 and the assassination of S. Sobinski in 1926, the attack on the main Post Office in Lviv, and various other acts of sabotage. Imprisoned many times, he was finally captured and executed by the Polish police without a trial.

Andrii Holovko

Holovko, Andrii, b 3 December 1897 in Yurky, Kobeliaky county, Poltava gubernia, d 5 December 1972 in Kiev. A prominent first-generation Soviet-Ukrainian writer. Although he initially fought for Ukraine's independence as a soldier in the UNR Army, in 1920 he went over to the Red Army. Holovko began his literary career with the poetry collection *Samotsvity* (Gems, 1919), and joined the peasant writers' group *Pluh. His early prose collections – *Divchynka z shliakhu* (The Little Girl from the Road, 1923), *Chervona khustyna* (The Red Kerchief, 1924), *Mozhu* (I Can, 1926), *Pylypko* (1928), and others – were imbued with revolutionary romanticism. His novel *Bur'ian* (Weeds, 1927) depicts the arbitrariness of rural Bolshevik leaders in the first years after the 1917 Revolution. Holovko's most important work is his novel *Maty* (Mother, 1932); dealing with events in the Ukrainian countryside during the 1905–7 revolution, it was censured by Party critics as nationalist, and its second edition (1934) was revised to conform to the dictates of socialist realism. His trilogy *Artem Harmash* (1951, 1960, and 1970), which depicts events in the countryside during the October Revolution in Ukraine, is a typical Soviet literary work. Holovko's other works include the plays *V chervonykh shumakh* (In the Red Din, 1924) and *Rais'ke iabluko* (The Crabapple, 1926), the film script *Lita molodii* (Youthful Years, 1956), and the cinenovella *Skyba Ivan* (1934). His works have been republished many times; a five-volume collection appeared in 1976–7 and a bibliography of his works was prepared by T. Maievska in 1964.

I. Koshelivets

Holovko, Dmytro, b 6 November 1905 in Uman, Kiev gubernia. Master craftsman in ceramics. He studied at the Shevchenko School of Folk Art in Uman (1920–2) and the Art-Ceramics Tekhnikum in Mezhyhiria (1924–8). His works include vases and figurines using traditional Ukrainian folk pottery motifs (rams, deers, lions, etc).

Holovko, Hryhorii, b 13 October 1900 in Dibrivka, Myrhorod county, Poltava gubernia. Architect; full member of the Academy of Construction and Architecture of the Ukrainian SSR (1958–63). He graduated from the Kiev Institute of Civil Engineering in 1935. His projects include the planning of the towns of Bila Tserkva and Novohrad-Volynskyi, the design of three stations of the Kiev subway, and the building of the Institute of Hydrology and Hydrotechnology of the AN URSR in Kiev, all of which were realized in collaboration with other architects. He was a member of the editorial board of *Istoriia ukraïns'koho mystetstva* (A History of Ukrainian Art, 6 vols, 1966–70). From 1937 to 1974, he was the head of the Union of Architects of Ukraine.

Holovshchyna [holovščyna] (*poholovshchyna, holovnytstvo*). A fine imposed on a murderer and paid to the victim's relatives. In the Princely era it supplemented the **vyra*, which was paid to the prince and amounted to half a *vyra* (20 *hryvni*). According to the laws of the Lithuanian-Ruthenian and Hetman states, the payment varied with the victim's status; the penalty for killing a noble was four or five times as high as that for killing a peasant. If the murderer was punished by death, the *holovshchyna* was paid by his guarantors or accomplices.

Holovyne labradorite deposits. Principal source of labradorite in the USSR, located in Cherniakhiv raion, Zhytomyr oblast. The deposits are worked by the Zhytomyrnerudprom, an enterprise under the ministry of the building-materials industry of the Ukrainian SSR. Labradorite is used for facing buildings and constructing monuments. These deposits were known in antiquity; published information about them dates back to 1835. Holovyne labradorite was used for the Lenin Mausoleum in Moscow and the Shevchenko monument in Kharkiv.

Ambrose Holowach

Holowach, Ambrose [Holovač, Amvrozij], b 22 July 1914 in Edmonton. Politician and businessman. He won a seat in the House of Commons in 1953 and again in 1957 as the Social Credit member for Edmonton East. Defeated in the federal election of 1958, from 1959 to 1971 he represented Edmonton Centre in the Alberta legislature. In 1962 he was appointed provincial secretary, becoming the first cabinet minister of Ukrainian origin in Alberta.

Holowaty, Michael [Holovatyj, Myxajlo], b 21 November 1922 in Stanyslaviv (now Ivano-Frankivske), Galicia. Research engineer in the fields of metallurgy and mining technology. After studying at Breslau University, in 1945 he was appointed research associate at Heidelberg University. Since 1951 he has worked for the Inland Steel Co in the United States; since 1972 he has directed its research department. He is the author of numerous papers in the field of ferrous metallurgy and holds 21 US patents. He has received a number of awards for the development of tellurium steels.

Holowinsky, Ivan [Holovins'kyj], b 25 April 1927 in Zarvanytsia, Zolochiv county, Galicia. Psychologist and educator. A graduate of Salzburg University (1948), Holowinsky completed his ED D at Temple University in 1961. A professor at Rutgers University since 1966 and consultant at the Princeton Child Development Institute (1972–), Holowinsky has conducted research on comparative learning disabilities in Eastern Europe and the Soviet Union. He has written a number of articles on special education for the mentally retarded.

Hołówko, Tadeusz, b 15 September 1889 in Semipalatinsk, Turkestan, d 29 August 1931 in Truskavets, Drohobych county, Galicia. Polish socialist politician and publicist. He was a close collaborator of J. *Piłsudski and a leading proponent of Ukrainian-Polish reconciliation. He actively supported the Institute for Nationalities Research and efforts to establish a Ukrainian university in Lviv. As a member of the Sejm and director of the Eastern Department at the Polish Ministry of Foreign Affairs (1927–30), he advocated co-operation with the government-in-exile of the UNR and the *Promethean movement. He was killed by members of the OUN, which accused Hołówko of the 'spiritual disarmament' of Ukrainian society. He wrote many pamphlets and articles for the Polish press on the Ukrainian question and minorities in Poland. He is the subject of a biography by I. Werschler, *Z dziejów obozu belwederskiego: Tadeusz Hołówko, życie i działalność* (From the History of the Belvedere Camp: Tadeusz Hołówko, His Life and Work, 1984).

Holub. Cossack family line founded by Hryhorii at the beginning of the 17th century in the Chernihiv region. Its most important members were Zakhar, a military fellow (1667–90); Kost, a general standard-bearer (1678–87); and Hryhorii, a graduate of the Kievan Mohyla Academy (1699) and fellow of the standard (from 1727) who later entered a monastery on Mt Athos and assumed the name of Hurii.

Holub, Olyfer, ?–1628. Cossack hetman (1622–3). Elected after Sahaidachny's death, he failed to win the approval of the Polish king, although as a spokesman of the wealthier Cossacks he favored a moderate policy towards Poland. During his rule the Cossacks disregarded Polish policy and waged sea campaigns against Turkey. Failing to obtain guarantees of Cossack privileges from the Polish Sejm, he resigned from office. As a colonel he fought the Poles in 1625. He died in battle during a Cossack campaign against the Crimea.

Holubenko, Petro (pen name of P. Shatun), b 12 January 1907 in Derkachi, Kharkiv gubernia. Scholar, journalist, and writer. He completed his studies in the history of literature at Kharkiv University in 1941. As a displaced person after the Second World War in Germany and as a resident in the United States, he has produced studies of the Ukrainian revival of the 1920s; his book *Vaplite* (1948) and numerous articles on the writer M. *Khvylovy in the émigré press are important contributions to literary scholarship.

Holubets, Mykhailo [Holubec', Myxajlo], b 30 October 1930 in Velykyi Liubin, Horodok county, Galicia. Botanist; corresponding member of the AN URSR since 1978. Holubets graduated from the Lviv Agricultural Institute in 1953. He has worked at the Scientific Research Institute of Land Cultivation and Animal Husbandry of the Western Regions of the Ukrainian SSR (1957–62) and the AN URSR Institute of Botany (1963–70), and from 1970 to 1974 he was the director of the AN URSR Natural Science Museum in Lviv. Since 1974 he has directed the Lviv branch of the Institute of Botany. Holubets has done research in geobotany, ecology, and nature conservation.

Mykola Holubets

Holubets, Mykola [Holubec'], b 15 December 1891 in Lviv, d 22 May 1942 in Lviv. Art scholar, writer, and journalist. After studying at the Cracow Academy of Art and the universities of Vienna and Lviv, he joined the Ukrainian Sich Riflemen in 1914 and worked in its press bureau in Vienna. With V. Sichynsky, Holubets was one of the leading historians of Ukrainian art and commentators on artistic life in Galicia. In this field his main works are: *Ukraïns'ke maliarstvo XVI–XVII v. pid pokrovom Stavropihiï* (Ukrainian Painting in the 16th–17th Centuries under the Patronage of the Stauropegion Brotherhood, 1920), *Nacherk istoriï ukraïns'koho mystetstva* (An Outline of the History of Ukrainian Art, 1922), *Halyts'ke mystetstvo* (Galician Art, 1926), and the chapter on art in *Istoriia ukraïns'koï kul'tury* (History of Ukrainian Culture, 1937). He wrote analytical and perceptive booklets and articles on Ukrainian artists such as A. Archipenko (1922), T. Shevchenko (1924), L. Dolynsky (1924), P. Kholodny Senior (1926), M. Havrylko, L. Gets (1934), T. Kopystiansky, O. Kulchytska, Yu. Narbut, O. Novakivsky, I. Trush, and P. Kovzhun (1939). He was also interested in regional studies and wrote articles and booklets on the history of towns such as Lviv (guide book, 1925), Lavriv (1926–7), Belz, Buzke, Zvenyhorod (1927), Peremyshl (1928), Sokal (1929), Terebovlia (1928), Zhovkva, and medieval Halych (1937). His works appeared in various scholarly and literary-artistic journals. Holubets edited several journals: *Svit* (1917–18), *Zhyttia i mystetstvo* (1920), *Masky* (1923), *Ukraïns'ke mystetstvo* (1926), *Nedilia* (1928–31), and the daily *Chas* (1931).

In literature he appeared first as a poet. His verses were published in various journals, and several short collections of his poems such as *Fragmenty* (Fragments, 1909), *Buvaiut' khvyli* (There Are Moments, 1910), and *Moisei bezumnyi* (Mad Moses, 1914) were published in Lviv or Vienna. Later he turned to prose, composing novelettes such as *Liudy i blazni* (People and Clowns, 1927), sketches such as *Hei, vydno selo* (Hey, a Village Is in Sight, 1934), and historical novels such as *Zhovti Vody* (1937) and *Plem'ia Dzhingiskhana* (Genghis Khan's Tribe, 1938). He also translated G. Hauptmann's *Die versunkene Glocke*, H. Ibsen's *Peer Gynt*, and H. Heine's poetry.

S. Hordynsky

Holubiev, Pavlo [Holubjev], b 28 June 1883 in Bakhmut, Katerynoslav gubernia, d 3 March 1966 in Kharkiv. Teacher of vocal music. A graduate of the Kharkiv Music School (1906), from 1939 he served as professor at the Kharkiv Conservatory. Among his students was B. *Hmyria, about whom he wrote a book.

Volodymyr Holubnychy

Holubnychy, Volodymyr [Holubnyčyj], b 2 June 1936 in Sumy. Olympic and world track and field champion. A graduate of the Kiev Institute of Physical Culture (1969), he took the gold medal in the 20-km walk at the Olympics in Rome (1960) and in Mexico City (1968), the silver medal at the Olympics in Munich (1972), and the bronze medal at the Olympics in Tokyo (1964). He established two world records (1955, 1958), three USSR records, and six Ukrainian records in the 20-km walk. In 1974 he was the European champion in this event. He now coaches and teaches.

Holubnychy, Vsevolod [Holubnyčyj], b 5 June 1928 in Bohodukhiv, Kharkiv okruha, d 10 April 1977 in New York City. Economist and political figure; member of the Ukrainian Academy of Arts and Sciences in the United States. He left Ukraine with his family in 1943 and immigrated to the United States in 1951. He studied economics at Columbia University (PH D 1971) and from 1962 taught at Hunter College, City University of New York. Holubnychy was a leading member of the Ukrainian Revolutionary Democratic party, particularly of its left-wing faction, and editor of its periodicals *Iunats'ka borot'ba* and *Vpered*. He published many works on Soviet regional economics, Ukrainian-Russian economic relations, Ukrainian economic and political history, and Marxist

Vsevolod Holubnychy

Vsevolod Holubovych

economic theory and philosophy. He contributed entries to *Entsyklopediia ukraïnoznavstva* and served as its economics editor. Some of his works have been published posthumously in *Soviet Regional Economics: Selected Works of Vsevolod Holubnychy*, ed I.S. Koropeckyj (1982).

Holubovsky, Zakharii [Holubovs'kyj, Zaxarij], b 1736 in Poltava, d 1810 in Kiev. Painter, graduate of the Kiev Theological Academy and the Kievan Cave Monastery Icon Painting Studio. As head of the studio (1772–6), he took part in painting and restoring the monastery's Dormition Cathedral and directed the painting of the underground churches of the Near Caves. Of his paintings only the *Holy Martyr with a Flower in Her Hand* (end of the 18th century), a fine example of the Ukrainian baroque style, has been preserved.

Holubovych, Mykhailo [Holubovyč, Myxajlo], b 21 November 1943 in Zolotonosha, Cherkasy oblast. Stage and screen actor. A graduate of the Kiev Institute of Theater Arts (1967), he has worked since then at the Voroshylovhrad Ukrainian Music and Drama Theater and has appeared in roles such as Kolesnyk in *Poviia* (The Whore), based on P. Myrny's novel, Vasyl in M. Strarytsky's *Tsyhanka Aza* (Aza, the Gypsy Girl), Ferdinand in F. Schiller's *Kabale und Liebe*, and Terracini in O. Korniichuk's *Pam'iat' sertsia* (Memory of the Heart). He has also appeared in several Soviet films.

Holubovych, Sydir [Holubovyč], b 1875 in Tovstenke, Kopychyntsi county, Galicia, d 12 January 1938 in Lviv. Civic and political leader; lawyer. He was head of the student Academic Hromada in Lviv and later a civic activist in the Ternopil region. In 1911 he was elected to the Austrian parliament and in 1913 to the Galician Sejm, representing the National Democratic party. In 1915 he was a member of the *General Ukrainian Council. He was secretary of justice in the first government of the Western Ukrainian National Republic (1918); later he became head of the secretariat and secretary of finance, trade, and industry. After 1919 he was a leading member of the *Ukrainian Labor party, and in 1925 he participated in the founding of the Ukrainian National Democratic Alliance.

Holubovych, Vsevolod [Holubovyč], b 1885 in Poltavka, Balta county, Podilia gubernia, d ? Political figure, journalist, and engineer. A graduate of the Kiev Polytechnical Institute, he represented the *Ukrainian Party of Socialist Revolutionaries (UPSR) in the Little Rada and *General Secretariat of the UNR. In January 1918 he led the first UNR delegation, which negotiated the Peace Treaty of *Brest-Litovsk. From 30 January 1918 to Hetman P. Skoropadsky's coup of 29 April, he was the prime minister and minister of foreign affairs in the *Council of National Ministers of the UNR. He was imprisoned by the Hetman government until its overthrow in December 1918. After the UPSR split in May 1918, Holubovych remained in its centrist current. In 1919–20, he published its daily *Trudova hromada* in Kamianets-Podilskyi and Vinnytsia. In 1921 a Bolshevik tribunal sentenced him in a show trial to five years in a concentration camp together with other members of the UPSR Central Committee, but he was soon amnestied and served as the chairman of the Supreme Economic Council of the Ukrainian SSR until 1931, when he was again arrested and sentenced in the show trial of the 'Ukrainian National Center' (M. *Hrushevsky's followers) and never heard from again.

Holy, Hnat [Holyj], b and d ? Zaporozhian Cossack, haidamaka chieftain. In the 1730s and 1740s he led a detachment of haidamakas that raided the estates of Polish nobles, lessors, and merchants in the Vinnytsia and Cherkasy regions. In 1741 he executed the Polish ally S. *Chaly and in 1743 captured Zvenyhorodka. His detachment was active until 1748. Holy became a popular hero and was remembered in folk songs.

Holy Scriptures. See Bible.

Holy Synod (Sviateishii Vserossiiskii Pravitelstvuiushchii Sinod). The highest ruling body of the Orthodox church in the Russian Empire, established by Peter I in 1721 to replace the Moscow patriarchate. It was created in order to subordinate the church to secular authority. The first statutes were laid down in the Spiritual Regulation written by T. *Prokopovych in 1722. Under the Holy Synod the clergy became civil servants and the church was turned into a bureaucratic institution. While the Holy Synod was given responsibility for educational and benevolent work and certain ecclesiastical matters, its power was clearly limited; eg, it could only nominate candidates for bishop, whom the tsar then appointed. It was composed of representatives of the church hierarchy and the clergy appointed by the tsar, and was presided over by the tsar's representative, the *ober-prokuror*, whose rank from 1824 was equivalent to that of a minister. In 1764 the Holy Synod's large estates were confiscated, further undermining its independence. It continually limited any remnants of autonomy of the Kiev metropoly and opposed the use of the Ukrianian language in church schools in 1860 and 1912. When the Moscow patriarchate was re-established in 1917, the Holy Synod was abolished.

Holynsky, Mykhailo [Holyns'kyj, Myxajlo], b 2 January 1895 in Verbivtsi, Horodenka county, Galicia, d 1 December 1973 in Edmonton. Operatic tenor. In 1920 he began to study voice in Lviv and continued in Milan. After his successful debut at the Lviv opera in 1925, he appeared in Poznań, Toruń, and Warsaw. Apart from a brief trip to Berlin in 1927, Holynsky spent 1926–30 as a tenor soloist in the USSR – in Kiev, Kharkiv, Odessa, Moscow, Leningrad, and Tiflis. In the 1930s he sang in Lviv, Warsaw, and the larger cities of Galicia. During a tour of the United States and Canada, the Second World War broke out and he decided to settle in Canada. In subsequent years he gave numerous recitals and made several recordings.

Mykhailo Holynsky

Home industry. See Cottage industry.

Home rule. See Local government.

Homel oblast. Oblast (1982 pop 1,636,000) in the southeastern Belorussian SSR with an area of 40,400 sq km. Its southwestern part lies south of the Prypiat River in Polisia and within Ukrainian ethnic territory. According to the 1979 census, 0.03 percent of the oblast's population was Ukrainian. Only 48.7 percent of the Ukrainians gave Ukrainian as their mother tongue; 46 percent gave Russian and 5 percent gave Belorussian.

Homestead. See *Khutir* and Private plot.

Homiletics. The art of religious discourse and preaching of sermons, homilies, and catechetical instruction. It has been practiced in Ukraine since its *Christianization in the late 10th century, when it was employed to propagate the new religion. Slavic homilies were initially introduced from Bulgaria; new ones were then locally created or translated from the Greek. The oldest extant Rus' sermon is the panegyrical *'Slovo o zakoni i blahodati' (Sermon on Law and Grace, 1051) by the eloquent Metropolitan Ilarion. Other famous Rus' preachers were Hegumen Moisei of the Vydubychi Monastery, the author of 'Pokhvalne slovo' (Sermon of Praise, 1198), and Bishop *Cyril of Turiv (d 1182), who freely dramatized events from the Gospel and was called the 'new Chrysostom.' Alongside didactic sermons (eg, by *St Theodosius of the Caves, d 1074), describing the duties of monks, condemning paganism and social inequality, and exhorting the faithful to observe the church's teachings, a genre of Byzantine rhetoric dealing with the fine points of theology was fostered.

Homiletics in Kievan Rus' evolved until the Mongol invasion and the sacking of Kiev in the mid-13th century, after which it was continued on a lesser scale in Galicia-Volhynia, which was less affected by the invasions from the east. Translations and newly composed collections of sermons such as the **Izmarahd* (Emerald) and **Zlataia tsep*" (Golden Chain) were used. The sermons of Bishop

*Serapion of Vladimir (d 1275) dealt with the Mongol invasion and the fate of the church, and those of Metropolitan G. Tsamblak of Kiev (1415–19) elucidated the feast days. Metropolitan *Cyprian of Kiev (1376–89) translated many well-known sermons by St John Chrysostom.

The decline of homiletics between the 13th and 15th centuries in the Ukrainian church was commented on by both Catholic (P. Skarga in 1577) and Orthodox (Prince K. Ostrozky in 1593) figures.

Homiletics revived in Ukraine in the 16th century because of the influence of the Reformation and the schism in the Ukrainian church (culminating in the Church Union of *Berestia in 1596). In the religious polemics that arose between the Orthodox and the new Uniate Catholic churches, the sermons of the Orthodox hierarchs Z. *Kopystensky and M. *Smotrytsky and the Uniates I. *Potii and Y. *Kuntsevych played a central role in the development of this art.

Vade mecums in homiletics were the numerous *didactic gospels of the 16th and 17th centuries that were used not only by clerics but also by precentors and by lecturers and students at Orthodox brotherhood schools. Sermons were recited by heart by professional preachers called *kaznodii*; and among the most talented of these was the monk and teacher S. *Zyzanii. Homiletics was taught in the rhetoric classes of brotherhood schools and at Catholic colleges, and bishops put much effort into acquiring the best preachers for their cathedrals. Hegumens, who were obliged to preach sermons to their monks, were known for being proficient preachers; Y. *Zalizo was particularly famous for his homilies.

In the 17th century, sermons were delivered in bookish Belorussian-Ukrainian combined with vernacular elements, in Church Slavonic, or in Polish. Both the Orthodox and Uniate churches placed much emphasis on the clarity of sermons. Comprehensibility was recommended by the Vilnius congregation in 1636 and by I. *Vyshensky in his teachings, and it was popularized in the *trebnyky* (books of rituals) of Metropolitan P. Mohyla and Bishop H. Balaban. Sermons were usually preached after the reading of the Gospel in Uniate churches, while Orthodox priests as a rule delivered their sermons at the end of the liturgy. By the turn of the 17th century, two tendencies in homiletics were discernible: (1) the Old Ruthenian or Conservative, which adhered to traditional Greek teachings; and (2) the new or Western, which touched on contemporary questions that were relevant to the audience. A combination of the two was recommended in the Didactic Gospel of 1616, which advised not to discuss the unfathomable mysteries of the faith but 'to teach the common and uneducated people God's will and commandments.' Both tendencies were apparent in collections of sermons such as L. Baranovych's *Truby sloves propovidnykh* ... (The Trumpets of Preaching Words, 1674) and A. Radyvylovsky's *Vinets Khrystov* (Christ's Wreath, 1688). With the development of literary baroque, homiletics revived. The best example of this trend is probably I. *Galiatovsky's work on homiletics, published as part of his *Kliuch razuminiia* (Key to Understanding, 1659, 1663, 1665).

When in the late 17th century the Ukrainian Orthodox church came under the control of Moscow, the hitherto common homiletical practices of the Orthodox and Uniate churches began to diverge. Kiev's best Orthodox preachers (including Metropolitan S. *Yavorsky and Archbishop T. *Prokopovych) were brought to Moscow and St Petersburg to modernize homiletics in Russia.

As a result of systematic Russification, homiletics in the Ukrainian language progressively declined in the 19th century. Nationally conscious preachers strove occasionally to save Ukrainian homiletics, but their efforts (eg, the publications of sermons in Ukrainian by Rev V. *Hrechulevych and Rev I. Babchenko) were largely unsuccessful. In the 20th century, Archbishop P. Levytsky was punished for similar efforts, as was Bishop A. Hudko for preaching in Ukrainian in Volhynia in 1904–9.

In the Ukrainian Catholic church, the 18th century saw the continuation of developments of the previous century, and the Ukrainian bookish, and later the vernacular, language replaced Church Slavonic and Polish in homiletics. The first collections of sermons were published by the *Basilian monastic order and used to teach oratory in their schools: *Narodovishchaniie* ... (Popular Preaching, 1756) and *Simia slova Bozhiia prostym iazykom* (The Seed of God's Word in Simple Language, 1772). Of the enlightened Basilian preachers, I. Kostetsky, Hegumen K. *Srochynsky, and Yu. Dobrylovsky were well known. After the partition of the Ukrainian lands in the Polish-Lithuanian Commonwealth between Russia and Austria (1772), the Russian authorities persecuted, and by 1830 abolished, the Ukrainian Catholic church in the territory under their control. That church continued its legal existence only in Austrian-ruled Western Ukraine. There, the clergy was educated in German and Polish schools and at first preached only in Polish, especially in the larger towns.

At the turn of the 19th century, under the influence of the nascent Ukrainian national movement, the clergy in Western Ukraine began using the vernacular in their sermons and publications – eg, *Nauky parokhyial'nyia z slavenoruskoho iazyka na prostyi iazyk ruskyi perelozhennyia* (Teachings for Parishes Translated from the Slavonic-Ruthenian into the Common Ruthenian Tongue, 1794). Sermons were published in the vernacular by M. Luchkai (2 vols, 1831), T. Vytvytsky (2 vols, 1847), and A. Dobriansky (1850) and in supplements to such newspapers as *Zoria halytska* (1853–4). The theology department at Lviv University introduced Ukrainian lectures on homiletics in 1850. The level of preaching improved significantly when Yu. Pelesh's *Pastyrs'ke bohoslovia* (Pastoral Theology, 2 vols, 1876–7) was introduced as the study text. A popular lecturer on homiletics at the university and author of several collections of sermons was I. *Bartoshevsky. In the 1930s, lectures on homiletics were given at the Greek Catholic Theological Academy in Lviv and other theological seminaries. Sermons were published in the religious journals *Nyva*, *Bozhe slovo*, *Dobryi pastyr*, *Sivach*, and *Dushpastyr*. Among the more eminent preachers were Metropolitan A. Sheptytsky and bishops H. Khomyshyn and S. Ortynsky.

The Ukrainian Orthodox church was restored under the Ukrainian National Republic in 1917 and survived in Soviet Ukraine until the early 1930s. During this time homiletics was fostered by the Ukrainian Autocephalous Orthodox church (UAOC); because of the lack of printing presses, sermons were produced in typescript or in hand-copied form using duplicating machines. The UAOC created groups of 'good messengers' (*blahovisnyky*) among the clergy and laity and introduced special homiletical services. Metropolitans V. Lypkivsky and M. Boretsky were eminent UAOC preachers. Since the 1930s sermons in Soviet Ukraine have been delivered mostly in Russian (except in the Western Ukrainian regions annexed in 1944). Until 1944 the Orthodox theological seminaries in Western Ukraine taught homiletics; sermons were published in periodicals and separately in books such as Archbishop O. Hromadsky's *Slova* (Words).

Homiletics has always played a very important role in the Evangelical churches. The preachers among the *Baptists in Russian-ruled Ukraine have only used Russian, however, and Ukrainian came to dominate in sermons in Western Ukraine only in the 20th century. Despite severe restrictions by the Soviet state, Baptist homiletics has survived in Ukraine. In the United States and Canada, the Ukrainian Evangelical Christians and Baptists have published sermons and have had experienced preachers, such as pastors V. Borovsky and O. Harbuziuk.

Homiletics has developed normally outside the Soviet bloc within all the Ukrainian churches, and they have published or republished a considerable number of collections of sermons – eg, Rev K. Lototsky's (1954), Archbishop V. Malets's (1963), Metropolitan V. Lypkivsky's (1969), Rev T. Minenko's (1980), Cardinal Y. Slipy's (1981), Rev I. Figol's (1981), and Cardinal M. Liubachivsky's (1984) – and radio sermons – eg, Rev S. Mudry's (1970), I. Barchuk's (1971), and Rev M. Dyrda's (1974) – and studies and textbooks on homelitics – eg, Rev F. Kulchynsky's (1971).

BIBLIOGRAPHY
Vozniak, M. *Istoriia ukraïns'koï literatury*, 3 vols (Lviv 1920–4)
Peretts, V. 'K voprosu ob uchitel'nykh evangeliiakh XVI–XVII v.,' *Sbornik Otdeleniia russkogo iazyka i slovesnosti AN SSSR* (Leningrad 1926)
Korowicki, I. 'Stan kaznodziejstwa prawosławnego na przełomie ww. XVI–XVII w państwie Litewsko-Polskiem,' *Elpis*, 1–2 (Warsaw 1935)
Bida, K. *Ioanikii Galiatovs'kyi i ioho 'Kliuch" razuminiia'* (Rome 1975)
Ilarion [Ohiienko, I.]. *Ukraïns'ka Tserkva: Narysy z istoriï Ukraïns'koï Pravoslavnoï Tserkvy*, 2nd rev edn (Winnipeg 1982)
Podskalsky, G. *Christentum und theologische Literatur in der Kiever Rus' (988–1237)* (Munich 1982)

I. Korovytsky

Homin Ukraïny

Homin Ukraïny (Echo of Ukraine). Political weekly published in Toronto since 15 December 1948; unofficial organ of the *Canadian League for Ukraine's Liberation since August 1949. Established to publicize the resistance of the Ukrainian Insurgent Army to Soviet rule, in its political orientation it is militantly anti-communist and pro-OUN (Bandera faction). Its editors have been M. Sosnovsky (1948–9, 1951–4), R. Rakhmanny (1949–51), V. Solonynka (1954–79), A. Bedrii (1979–80), O. Matla (1980–1), and O. Romanyshyn (1981–). A monthly supplement on literature and art, edited by B. Stebelsky, has appeared since September 1955. An eight-page English-language monthly supplement, *Ukrainian Echo*, began in May 1977, edited by A. Bandera (1977–84) and I. Mytsak (1984–). In 1985 the paper's weekly circulation was 11,500.

Vadym Homoliaka

Homoliaka, Vadym [Homoljaka], b 30 October 1914 in Kiev. Composer. A student of L. Revutsky, he graduated from the Kiev Conservatory (1946) and then lectured there for two years. He has written many ballets including *The Zaporozhian Cossacks* (1954), *The Sorochyntsi Fair* (1954), *Black Gold* (1957, 2nd version 1960), *Puss in Boots* (1959), and *Oksana* (1964). He has also composed a number of symphonic poems, overtures, concertos, symphonies, and film scores.

Homosexuality. See Sexual life.

Homzyn, Borys (pseud: Newfryingpan), b 20 June 1887 on the family estate near Savran, Balta county, Podilia gubernia, d 15 November 1965 in Berlin. Writer, editor, and civic figure. After serving as an officer in the UNR Army in 1917–21, he emigrated to Prague in 1922, where he edited the student journal *Spudei* and the newspaper *Ukraïna*. In 1938 he moved to Berlin, where he was active in the Hetmanite movement and edited the journal *Natsiia v pokhodi*. Homzyn contributed articles, stories, and poems to the underground publications of OUN and later to many émigré periodicals. Only some of them have been published in separate collections, such as the collection of modernist poetry *Troizillia* (Clover, 1928) and, under his pseudonym, the book *Bol'shevyzm – orhanichne moskovs'ke iavyshche* (Bolshevism – an Inherent Muscovite Phenomenon, 1957).

Honchar, Ivan [Hončar], b 27 January 1911 in Lypianka, Chyhyryn county, Kiev gubernia. Sculptor and ethnographer. He studied at the Kiev Industrial Arts School (1927–30) and the Kiev Institute of Agrochemistry and Soil Sciences (1931–6). In the 1930s he began sculpting; he has produced such works as the statues *Shevchenko at the Precentor's* (1939), *Young Taras Shevchenko* (1950), *Lesia Ukrainka*, and *Ustym Karmeliuk* (1965), and busts of the writers A. Malyshko and O. Honchar (1949).

Having collected historical and ethnographic materials throughout Ukraine, in 1960 he set up in his apartment a private museum of over 3,000 items (tools, clothing, ceramics, icons, embroideries, Easter eggs, and old books). His 16 volumes of ethnographic materials remain unpublished.

Oles Honchar

Honchar, Oles [Hončar, Oles'], b 3 April 1918 in Sukha, Kobeliaky county, Poltava gubernia. One of the most prominent Soviet Ukrainian writers of the postwar period; a full member of the AN URSR since 1978. A Second World War veteran and graduate of Dnipropetrovske University, he has been publishing since 1938. From 1959 to 1971 he headed the Writers' Union of Ukraine. Honchar gained prominence with the novel-trilogy *Praporonostsi* (The Standard Bearers, 1947–8, English trans 1948) about the Red Army in the Second World War. His other works include the novellas *Zemlia hude* (The Earth Drones, 1947), *Mykyta Bratus'* (1951), *Shchob svityvsia vohnyk* (Let the Fire Burn, 1955), and *Bryhantyna* (The Brigantine, 1973); the novels *Tavriia* (1952), *Perekop* (1957), *Liudyna i zbroia* (Man and Arms, 1960), *Tronka* (The Sheep's Bell, 1963), *Tsyklon* (The Cyclone, 1970), *Bereh liubovi* (The Shore of Love, 1976), *Tvoia zoria* (Your Dawn, 1980), and *Sobor* (The Cathedral, 1968), which was officially censured and subsequently removed from circulation; the short-story collections *Modry kamen'* (The Modra's Rock, 1948), *Pivden'* (The South, 1951), *Chary-komyshi* (Enchantments-Rushes, 1958), and *Masha z Verkhovyny* (Masha from the Highlands, 1959); and three collections of literary articles (1972, 1978, 1980). His works have been republished many times (eg, in 6 vols in 1978–9) and translated into over 40 languages, and have been the subject of a large body of Soviet literary criticism.

I. Koshelivets

Honcharenko, Ahapii [Hončarenko, Ahapij] (real name: Humnytsky, Andrii), b 31 August 1832 in Kryvyn, Skvyra county, Kiev gubernia, d 5 May 1916 in Hayward, Alameda county, California. Orthodox priest, publicist, and first Ukrainian political émigré to the United States. A descendant of a Cossack family, he graduated from the Kiev Theological Seminary and entered the Kievan Cave Monastery. Sent to Athens in 1857 to serve as deacon at the embassy's church, he began to contribute articles to A. Herzen's *Kolokol*. He was discovered and arrested in 1860, but escaped and traveled extensively before immigrating to the United States in 1865. A subsidy from

Ahapii Honcharenko

the federal government enabled Honcharenko to establish in San Francisco a semimonthly (eventually a semiweekly) newspaper – the *Alaska Herald*, with a Russian- and Ukrainian-language supplement *Svoboda* – aimed at the inhabitants of recently purchased Alaska. He published the paper single-handedly from 1868 to 1872, glorifying the Ukrainian Cossacks, popularizing T. Shevchenko's poems, defending democracy, individual freedom, and private initiative, and attacking Russian autocracy and imperialism, the conservatism and corruption of the Russian church, and capitalist monopolies. He also prepared the *Russo-English Phrase Book* (1868) for American soldiers serving in Alaska. He retired to a farm in Hayward that he named 'Ukraina ranch.' There in the early 1900s a group of Ukrainian immigrants from Canada and Galicia organized a short-lived commune called the Ukrainian Brotherhood. M. *Pavlyk corresponded with Honcharenko and published his *Spomynky* (Recollections, 1894) in Kolomyia.

BIBLIOGRAPHY

Luciw, W.; Luciw, T. *Ahapius Honcharenko and the Alaska Herald* (Toronto 1963)

Luciw, T. *Father Agapius Honcharenko: First Ukrainian Priest in America* (New York 1970)

V. Markus

Honcharenko, Hnat [Hončarenko], b ca 1837 in Ripky, Kharkiv county, d ca 1917. One of the most famous *kobzars. Blind from childhood, he learned to play the kobza at 20–22 and wandered throughout the Kharkiv region, singing and playing *dumas, psalms, and humorous songs in the traditional manner and teaching other kobzars. He spent the last part of his life mostly in Sevastopil. In 1908 Lesia Ukrainka took Honcharenko to Yalta and, with the help of her husband K. Kvitka and O. Slastion, recorded his dumas on phonograph cylinders. F. Kolessa transcribed and published them in the collection *Melodiï ukraïns'kykh narodnykh dum* (The Melodies of Ukrainian Folk Dumas, 2 vols, 1910, 1913; repr 1969).

Honcharenko, Nina [Hončarenko], b 20 August 1919 in Pokrovtsi, Melitopil county, Tavriia gubernia. Opera singer (mezzo-soprano). A graduate of the Kiev Conservatory (1944), she was a soloist of the Kiev Theater of Opera and Ballet from 1944 to 1969. Her main roles included Amneris in Verdi's *Aïda*, Carmen in Bizet's *Car-*

(from left) Hnat Honcharenko and Ostap Borodai

men, Nastia in M. Lysenko's *Taras Bulba,* Varvara and Solomiia in K. Dankevych's *Bohdan Khmelnytsky,* and the mother in H. Maiboroda's *Arsenal.*

Honcharenko, Oleh [Hončarenko], b 18 August 1931 in Kharkiv. World-class speedskater. He won the world skating championship three times (1953, 1956, 1958), the European championship (1957), and two bronze medals at the Winter Olympics in Cortina d'Ampezzo (1956).

Hondius (de Hondt), Willem, b ca 1597 at The Hague, d ca 1658 in Danzig (now Gdańsk). Renowned Dutch copper engraver, son and pupil of H. Hondius I. Working in Danzig (1634–53), he engraved – from G.-L. Beauplan's sketches – maps of Ukraine (1640, 1648, 1650), which appeared in the latter's *Description of Ukraine.* Among his other works related to Ukraine are three portraits of Hetman B. Khmelnytsky (1651), a map of the marshes near Pynske with a dedication to Yu., V., and S. Nemyrych (1650), and the frontispiece to J. Pastorius's *Bellum Scythico-Cosacium ...* (1652).

Honennia slidom ('pursuing the trail'). One of the investigative methods practiced under Princely and Lithuanian-Ruthenian criminal law. It was applied in cases of murder or theft and was conducted by the victim or his relatives with the aid of the community. The person to whom the trail led was considered guilty unless he managed to 'divert the trail.' In the Hetman period *honennia slidom* was known as *shliakuvannia.*

Honey plants. The common name for a large group of wild and cultivated plants from whose flowers honeybees gather nectar and pollen.

Up to 1,000 different species of honey plants are known in the USSR, but only some 200 of these produce sufficient quantities of nectar and pollen to be useful in apiculture (see *Beekeeping). Honey plants commonly cultivated in Ukraine include sunflower, buckwheat, clover, mustard plant, beans, vetch, sweet clover, rape, medic, radish, many garden crops such as cucumbers, melons, grapes, and citrus plants, and almost all fruit and berry plants. Cotton, kenaf, salvia, dandelion, anise, sage, valerian, coriander, mint, wild thyme, and cornflower also serve as good sources of nectar and pollen. Trees and shrubs form another important group of honey plants, the most common being linden, maple, acacia, caragana, willow, cranberry, apricot, pear, cherry, apple, and plum trees and raspberry, gooseberry, and black-currant bushes. While most honey plants have other uses, some are cultivated specifically for their nectar and pollen (eg, phacelia, viper's bugloss, ground ivy, white dead nettle, burnet, woundwort). Some plants are only a source of pollen: hazel, alder, birch, poppy, corn, sorrel, ripple grass, and others. The cultivation of honey plants in Ukraine was first researched and promoted by P. *Prokopovych.

BIBLIOGRAPHY

Berehovyi, P. *Naiholovnishi medonosni roslyny Ukraïny* (Kiev 1959)

Polishchuk, V.; Bilous, V. *Medonosni dereva i kushchi* (Kiev 1972)

Honorsky, Rozumnyk [Honors'kyj], b 1790 in Tula, Russia, d 27 August 1819 in Kharkiv. Writer and publicist. Having studied at St Petersburg Pedagogical Institute, Honorsky became a lecturer of literature, statistics, and geography at Kharkiv University (1816). Along with E. Filomafitsky and H. Kvitka-Osnovianenko, he edited and published one of the first journals in Ukraine, **Ukrainskii vestnik* (1816–18). He also wrote poetry and a number of works on literary theory.

Hooliganism. The Soviet term for acts of disorderly conduct or disrespect for social standards. At times various 'non-conformist' deeds are also referred to as hooliganism. The crime is defined in article 206 of the Criminal Code of the Ukrainian SSR; punishment for it is dispensed by the courts or administrative procedure; eg, by the head of the local militia. Acts of petty hooliganism by minors 16 years of age or younger are punishable by fines aimed at restitution and payable by the parents. Acts of petty hooliganism by adults are punishable by detention for 10 to 15 days, corrective labor for one to two months at a fifth of one's salary, or a fine of 10 to 30 rubles. Punishment for major acts varies from a fine of 30 to 50 rubles to imprisonment or corrective labor for six months to one year. Malicious hooliganism involving resisting the militia is punishable by imprisonment for one to five years. Malicious hooliganism involving dangerous weapons is punishable by imprisonment for three to seven years.

Manifestations of political or religious opposition, such as participating in an officially unsanctioned demonstration or gathering or publicly resisting the authorities, are often branded as hooliganism. Such was the case on 21

May 1972 in Kiev, when around 50 people who gathered at T. Shevchenko's monument to sing Ukrainian songs were accused of petty hooliganism and held for 15 days. Often the authorities set up their opponents by staging street fights and acts of assault and using false witnesses who are often police agents. Thus, in recent years many dissidents and human-rights activists have been tried for hooliganism and imprisoned.

Although Soviet propaganda insists that hooliganism is typical only of Western societies, this phenomenon is quite widespread in the USSR, particularly among young people, because of a low standard of social mores and the inadequacies of the social system. Thus in 1976 hooliganism accounted for 24 percent of the total number of criminal convictions (976,000) in the USSR.

V. Markus, S. Maksudov

Hop growing. The hop (*Humulus*) is a perennial climbing herb whose dried cones are used as medicine and as beer flavoring. In Ukraine hops began to be cultivated in the 1870s under the influence of Czech colonists in the climatically suited regions of Volhynia and Kiev gubernias. By 1913, 5,000 ha were devoted to hops and the harvest reached 6,000 t. During the First World War and the Revolution production fell: in 1922 only 280 ha were seeded with hops. By 1940, however, production approached the prewar level: 5,750 ha were seeded and the yield was 0.75 t per ha. Although the area devoted to hops has increased continuously to 6,100 ha in 1964 and 6,800 ha in 1970, yields have remained low – between 0.8 and 1 t per ha. Ukraine produces up to 70 percent of the hops grown in the USSR, and most of its production is exported to breweries in other Soviet republics. Zhytomyr oblast, which accounts for 60 percent of the area devoted to hops and 70 percent of the gross harvest, is the leading hop-growing region in Ukraine.

Hopak

Hopak. An original Ukrainian folk dance of an improvised nature. Its name is derived from *hopaty*: 'to leap and stamp one's feet.' The *hopak* arose as a male dance at the Zaporozhian Sich in the 16th century and gradually spread throughout Ukraine, particularly through the Kiev region. As it spread it became transformed into a group dance performed by couples with males retaining the lead role. It has several variants: a solo dance, a group and couple dance, and in Western Ukraine a circular dance (*hopak-kolo*). Its charm and attractiveness lie in the *hopak*'s freedom of improvisation, which allows individual dancers to display their talents within a larger dance group. The basic male movements are leaps, squats, stretches on the ground and in the air, and various turns; the female movements are quick steps, bends, and turns. Solo performances in the *hopak* often involve a competition in virtuosity. Complex acrobatic movements are common in stage arrangements of the dance. The tunes to which the dance is performed vary greatly. Some of them are songs, such as 'Od Kyieva do Luben' and 'Hop, moï hrechanyky.' Others are original compositions. The tempo is fast; the beat is 2/4. The *hopak* is the culminating dance in the repertoire of almost all Ukrainian dance ensembles. It is very popular among Ukrainians outside Ukraine. *Hopak* melodies often appear in classical music: in such operas as S. Hulak-Artemovsky's *Zaporozhian Cossack beyond the Danube*, M. Lysenko's *Taras Bulba*, P. Sokalsky's *The Defense of Dubno*, and B. Yanovsky's *Black Sea Duma*; in such ballets as A. Svechnikov's *Marusia Bohuslavka* and B. Libovytsky's *Marusia*; and in A. Shtoharenko's symphonic suite *In Memory of Lesia Ukrainka*.

M. Hnatiukivsky

Hopko, Vasyl, b 21 April 1904 in Hrabské, Prešov region, Czechoslovakia, d 23 July 1976 in Prešov. Ukrainian Catholic bishop of the Prešov eparchy. Hopko studied at the Theological Seminary in Prešov and at Charles University in Prague, where he obtained a D TH. In 1934 he organized a Ukrainian Catholic parish in Prague. From 1945 he edited the journal *Blahovisnyk*. In 1947, he was consecrated as auxiliary bishop of Prešov eparchy. Upon its liquidation in 1950, Hopko was arrested and sentenced to 15 years' imprisonment. He was released in 1964 and actively participated in the attempts to restore the Prešov eparchy in 1968–9, but was not permitted to serve as its bishop.

Horák, Jiří, b 4 December 1884 in Benešov, Bohemia, d 14 August 1975 in Martin, Slovakia. Prominent Czech Slavist; full member of the Czechoslovak Academy of Sciences from 1956. A professor at Prague (1919–22, 1927–44, 1949–51) and Brno (1922–6) universities, he specialized in Ukrainian literature and folklore, most of his studies appearing in Czech ethnographic and philological journals. As the general secretary of the First Congress of Slavic Philologists (Prague 1929), Horák was instrumental in representing Ukrainian studies as an independent discipline for the first time at an international forum.

Horak, Stephan, b 23 October 1920 in Horodok, Galicia, d 20 December 1986 in Charlston, Illinois. Historian and bibliographer. A graduate of the universities of Erlangen (PH D 1949), Bonn, and Michigan, and full member of the Shevchenko Scientific Society; from 1965 he was professor of Russian and modern European history at Eastern Illinois University. Among his monographs are *Ukraine in der internationalen Politik, 1917–1953* (1957), *Poland and Her National Minorities, 1919–1939: A Case Study* (1961), and *Poland's International Affairs, 1919–1960* (1964). Bibliographic guides that he has edited or compiled include *Russia, the USSR and Eastern Europe: A Bibliographic Guide to English-Language Publications* (2 vols, 1978, 1982), *Guide to the Study of the Soviet Nationalities: Non-Russian Peoples of the USSR* (1982), and *The Soviet Union and Eastern Europe: A Bibliographic Guide ...* (1985). He was editor of the journal *Nationalities Papers* (1972–85) and the president of the Association for the Study of the Nationalities of the USSR and Eastern Europe (1973–).

Horbach, Anna Halyna [Horbač] (Horbatsch) (née Lutsiak), b 2 March 1924 in Brodina, Bukovyna. Publicist and translator. Horbach works primarily as a translator and popularizer of Ukrainian literature and as an analyst of contemporary literary developments in Ukraine, especially the literature of dissent. Her translations into German include several prose works; two anthologies of modern Ukrainian prose, *Blauer November* (1959) and *Ein Brunnen für Durstige* (1970); and Ukrainian stories for children.

Oleksa Horbach

Ivan Horbachevsky

Horbach, Oleksa [Horbač, Olexa] (Horbatsch), b 5 February 1918 in Romaniv, Bibrka county, Galicia. Linguist and philologist. A graduate of the University of Lviv, where he studied with V. Simovych, J. Janów, and Z. Stieber, he lectured at West German universities (1952–65) and became professor of Slavic Studies at the University of Frankfurt (1966–79). He wrote a dissertation and articles on social dialects in Ukrainian, as well as studies on Ukrainian, Church Slavonic, and Polish texts of the 16th–19th centuries, the most important of these being his study of the grammar by M. Smotrytsky and the lexicon by P. Berynda. He has also published descriptions of Ukrainian dialects, especially in Rumania, Slovakia, and Yugoslavia. Likewise, he has published numerous previously unpublished or inaccessible middle-Ukrainian texts as well as studies in historical lexicology, focusing on problems of etymology.

Horbachevsky, Antin [Horbačevs'kyj], b 27 January 1856 in Zarubyntsi, Zbarazh county, d 26 April 1944 in Sianik, Galicia. Lawyer and civic and political figure in Galicia. He was an active member of the populist movement and later cofounder of the Ukrainian National Democratic Alliance, as well as editor of the newspaper *Dilo* (1883–4). From 1912 to 1918 he was a member of the Austrian State Tribunal in Vienna; in 1913 he was elected to the Galician Diet. During the Western Ukrainian National Republic he was a member of the Ukrainian National Council and, in 1919, of the Ukrainian diplomatic mission in Warsaw. From 1927 to 1939 he was a senator in the Polish Senate and chairman of the Ukrainian Parliamentary Club.

Horbachevsky, Ivan [Horbačevs'kyj], b 4 October 1800 in Nizhen, Chernihiv gubernia, d 21 January 1869 in Petrovskii Zavod, Trans-Baikal province. Civic and political figure and a *Decembrist. The descendant of an impoverished Ukrainian noble family, he was an officer in the 8th Artillery Brigade in Novohrad-Volynskyi. In 1823 he became a member of the *Society of United Slavs and a representative to the Vasylkiv council of the *Southern Society. For participating in the revolt of the Chernihiv regiment, he was arrested in February 1826 and sentenced to hard labor for life; the term was later reduced to 20 years. He served the sentence in the Trans-Baikal province, where he remained until his death. He is the author of *Zapiski, Pis'ma* (Notes, Letters, 1925, 1963).

Horbachevsky, Ivan [Horbačevs'kyj], b 15 May 1854 in Zarubyntsi, Zbarazh county, Galicia, d 24 May 1942 in Prague. Biochemist, epidemiologist, political figure; full member of the Czech Academy of Sciences and from 1925 of the All-Ukrainian Academy of Sciences; honorary member of the Shevchenko Scientific Society. A graduate of Vienna University (1875), from 1883 to 1917 he was a professor at Prague University, dean of its medical faculty for four years, and university rector (1902–3). He founded the Institute of Physiology in Prague. Horbachevsky served on the Supreme Health Council in Vienna and in 1908 was appointed to the Austrian upper chamber. In 1917–18 he was the first minister of health for Austria. In 1919 he helped found the *Ukrainian Free University in Vienna. When it moved to Prague in 1922, he served as professor and rector (1923–4, 1931–5).

Horbachevsky's principal scientific contributions are in organic and physiological chemistry. He was one of the first chemists to isolate amino acids and to establish that they are protein components. His synthesis of uric acid from carbamide and glycine in 1882 marked an important breakthrough. He established how uric acid is formed in the body and studied uremia. In 1889–91 he discovered xanthineoxidase. Besides numerous scientific papers, Horbachevsky wrote a Czech textbook – *Lékařská chemie ve čtyřech dilech* (Medical Chemistry in Four Volumes, 1904–8) – and a Ukrainian textbook for advanced students – *Orhanichna khimiia* (Organic Chemistry, 1925). He devoted much thought to the development of Ukrainian chemical terminology, and also published in the areas of epidemiology, popular hygiene, and forensic medicine.

S. Trofimenko

Horbal, Mykola [Horbal'], b 6 May 1941 in Volovets, Gorlice county, Galicia. Musician, poet, and dissident.

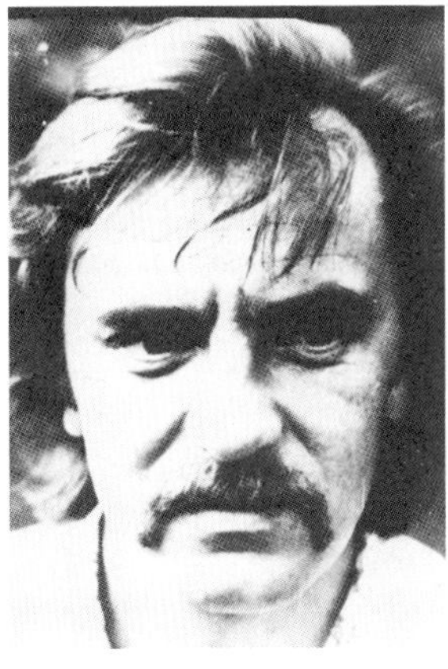

Mykola Horbal

In 1970 he was arrested and sentenced to five years in a Soviet labor camp and two years of exile for writing the long poem 'Duma.' After his release he worked as a lift operator in Kiev. For joining the *Ukrainian Helsinki Group, he was rearrested on 23 October 1979 and sentenced to another five years of hard labor. Rearrested while serving this sentence, he was condemned on 10 April 1985 to another eight years of imprisonment and three years of exile. Horbal's poetry, including *Detali pishchanoho hodynnyka* (Parts of an Hourglass, 1983), a collection of poetry and songs that are reflections upon prison life, has been published in the West.

Horban, Mykola [Horban'], b 1899 in the Poltava region, d ? Historian and writer. Among his scholarly works are *Narysy z istorii ukraïns'koï istoriohrafiï*, part 1: *Novyi spysok litopysu 'Kratkoe opisanie Malorossii'* (Essays on the History of Ukrainian Historiography, part 1: A New Redaction of the 'Short Description of Little Russia,' 1923) and articles in the periodicals and collections of the VUAN and in the journal *Chervonyi Shliakh*. His literary output consisted of the historical novelettes *Kozak i voievoda* (The Cossack and the Voivode, 1926) and *Slovo i dilo hosudareve* (The Word and Deed of the Ruler, 1930). Horban was arrested during the Stalinist terror in the early 1930s; deported to Kazakhstan, he worked there as an archivist and published several works on the history of that country and western Siberia.

Horbatsch, Anna-Halja. See Horbach, Anna Halyna.

Horbatsch, Olexa. See Horbach, Oleksa.

Volodymyr Horbovy

Horbovy, Volodymyr [Horbovyj], b 1898 in Dolyna, Galicia, d 21 May 1984 in Dolyna. Lawyer; political prisoner. Horbovy was an active member of the Ukrainian Military Organization and the OUN in the interwar period, for which he was imprisoned by the Poles in Brigidka prison in Lviv (1922) and in the Bereza Kartuzka concentration camp (1934). As a defense lawyer for Ukrainian political prisoners in Polish courts, he was best known for his defense of OUN members during the famous Warsaw trial in which 12 leading Ukrainian nationalists (including S. *Bandera) were charged with the assassination of B. Pieracki, the Polish minister of internal affairs. In June 1941 Horbovy was elected head of the Ukrainian National Committee in Cracow, and issued a manifesto calling for an independent Ukraine. He was arrested by the Germans but a year later was released on medical grounds. After the war he served as a legal adviser to the Czechoslovak Ministry of Agriculture. Horbovy was arrested by Czechoslovak authorities (1947) and in 1948 handed over to the Soviets, thereafter serving a sentence of 25 years in Soviet labor camps.

Hordiichuk, Mykola [Hordijčuk], b 9 May 1919 in Chornorudka, Skvyra county, Kiev gubernia. Ethnomusicologist. Hordiichuk is the chairman of the Department of Musicology at the AN URSR Institute of Fine Arts, Folklore, and Ethnography. He has written several monographs on prominent figures in Ukrainian music: M. Kolachevsky (1954), M. Leontovych (1956, 1974), H. Maiboroda (1963), P. Maiboroda (1964), and M. Leontovych (in Russian, 1977); as well as several surveys: *Derzhavnyi ukraïns'kyi narodnyi khor* (The Ukrainian State Folk Choir, 1951), *Sovremennaia ukrainskaia narodnaia pesnia* (The Contemporary Ukrainian Folk Song, 1964), *Symfonichna muzyka* (Symphonic Music, 1960, 1962), and *Ukraïns'ka radians'ka symfonichna muzyka* (Soviet Ukrainian Symphonic Music, 1969). Besides collecting and deciphering notations for many folk songs, he prepared a practical handbook, *Iak zapysuvaty narodnu muzyku?* (How to Record Folk Music? 1960).

Hordiienko, Dmytro [Hordijenko], b 8 December 1901 in Pluzhnyky, Pyriatyn county, Poltava gubernia, d 1 January 1974 in Pluzhnyky. A writer and journalist. Hordiienko belonged to the literary organizations Molodniak (1926–30) and Prolitfront (1930). He is the author of the poetry collections *U put'* (On the Road, 1927) and *Arky* (The Arks, 1929); eight story collections, including *Zelenyi fligel'* (The Green Wing, 1928) and *Polamani liudy* (Broken People, 1929); the novels *Tynda* (1930), *Sribnyi krai* (The Silver Land, 1931), and *Zavoiovnyky nadr* (Conquerors of the Earth's Depths, 1932); and several collections of essays. During the Stalin terror, in the mid-1930s, he was arrested and imprisoned in Siberia. He was rehabilitated after Stalin's death in 1956, and two volumes of his works were republished in 1965–6.

Hordiienko, Kost [Hordijenko, Kost'], b ? in the Poltava region, d 1733. Otaman of the Zaporozhian Sich from 1702. An enemy of Muscovy, he opposed Hetman I. Mazepa's acceptance of Russian domination. In March 1709 he arrived with 8,000 Zaporozhian Cossacks at the headquarters of the Swedish army and, with I. Mazepa's mediation, signed a treaty with Charles XII on 8 April at Velyki Budyshcha. After the Battle of Poltava he enabled Charles's and Mazepa's forces to cross the Dnieper near Perevolochna and to escape to Bendery. After Mazepa's death, Hordiienko supported P. Orlyk and in 1711 took part in Orlyk's unsuccessful campaign against Right-Bank Ukraine. After reaching an agreement with Turkey in 1712, he left Orlyk and until 1728 commanded the Oleshky Sich under the protectorate of the Crimean khan.

Hordiienko, Kost [Hordijenko, Kost'], b 3 October 1899 in Mykytyntsi, Proskuriv county, Podilia gubernia. Socialist realist writer and journalist. A member of the All-Ukrainian Association of Proletarian Writers, he wrote 21 story collections and 10 novellas, including *Avtomat* (The Automaton, 1928), *Povist' pro komunu* (Tale about a Commune, 1930), *Ataka* (The Attack, 1931), and *Skvar i*

Kost Hordiienko

Mykhailo Hordiievsky

syn (Skvar and His Son, 1935; rewritten as *Sim'ia Ostapa Tura* [Ostap Tur's Family, 1958]). His novels include *Dity zemli* (Children of the Earth, 1937; rewritten as *Zarobitchany* [Migrant Workers, 1949]) and the trilogy *Buimyr* (1939–68). Many of his works are set in the countryside of the Lebedyn region (now in Sumy oblast). Hordiienko has also written a collection of articles about literary Ukrainian, *Slovo pro slovo* (A Word about the Word, 1964), and a collection of musings and reminiscences, *Riasne slovo* (The Abundant Word, 1978).

Hordiienko, Yehor [Hordijenko, Jehor], b 1812 in Okhtyrka, Kharkiv gubernia, d 1897 in Kharkiv. Physician and civic leader. After graduating from Kharkiv University, he studied in Berlin and Paris and then taught chemistry at Kharkiv University. In the 1840s he made the first chemical analysis of the mineral waters in Slovianske. As a member of many organizations in Kharkiv and head of the city duma (1870–) and Kharkiv county zemstvo, he contributed to the development of education and the city's economy. He established the first plant for artificial mineral water in Kharkiv (1843) and wrote many articles about education, zemstvos, railroads, and peasants in the region. In his will he donated all his property to public education.

Hordiienko Haidamaka Cavalry Regiment. See Haidamaka Cavalry Regiment.

Hordiievsky, Mykhailo [Hordijevs'kyj, Myxajlo], b 5 June 1885 in the Kiev region, d ? Philosopher, Classical historian, and educator. Hordiievsky graduated from Odessa University in 1910 and became a professor there, teaching also at various schools in Odessa. He was a member of the Society of Ukrainian Progressives. During the Ukrainian Revolution of 1917–21 he was an active member of the Ukrainian Party of Socialist Revolutionaries. In the 1920s, as the head (1926–30) of the Odessa Scientific Society of the Ukrainian Academy of Sciences and of its pedagogical section, he was a leader in the implementation of the Ukrainization policy in the Odessa region. His main works include *Lesevych iako filosof* (Lesevych as a Philosopher, 1915), *Pedahohika prahmatyzmu* (The Pedagogy of Pragmatism, 1924), as well as numerous works on Pestalozzi and translations. His manuscript 'Rabstvo v starodavn'omu Rymi' (Slavery in Ancient Rome) was confiscated by the Soviet secret police before it was published. He was arrested 27 March 1938 and was probably shot.

Hordon, Volodymyr, b 25 October 1871 in Lokhvytsia, Poltava gubernia, d 3 January 1926 in Kharkiv. Specialist in civil law and procedure. In 1906 he was appointed professor of Kharkiv University, and in 1920 of the Kharkiv Institute of the National Economy. In 1925 he was elected full member of the Ukrainian Academy of Sciences. He directed the legal department of the People's Commissariat of Internal Trade of the Ukrainian SSR and took part in the preparation of the Ukrainian civil and civil-procedure codes. His chief works are *Status grazhdanskogo sudoproizvodstva* (The Status of Civil Court Procedure, 1914) and *Sistema sovetskogo torgovogo prava* (The System of Soviet Trade Law, 1924).

Sviatoslav Hordynsky: *Self-Portrait* (oil, 1960)

Hordynsky, Sviatoslav [Hordyns'kyj, Svjatoslav], b 30 December 1906 in Kolomyia, Galicia. Painter, graphic artist, poet, translator, art and literary scholar, son of Ya. *Hordynsky; member of the Ukrainian Academy of Arts and Sciences and the Shevchenko Scientific Society. He studied art at O. Novakivsky's school in Lviv, then in Berlin (1928) and in Paris at the Académie Julien and the Académie de l'Art Moderne (with F. Léger, 1929–31). Returning to Lviv, he worked as a painter and book designer. He cofounded the Association of Independent Ukrainian Artists, edited its journal *Mystetstvo*, and organized its art exhibitions (1931, 1933). Immigrating to the United States in 1947, he helped found the Ukrainian Artists' Association there, serving as its president (1956–63) and participating in its exhibitions. Since 1950 he has painted about 50 churches in North America and Europe. His wall paintings and iconostases are a synthesis of the neo-Byzantine and modernist styles.

Several of Hordynsky's poetry collections have been published: eg, *Barvy i linii* (Colors and Lines, 1933), *Viter nad poliamy* (The Wind above the Fields, 1938), *Vybrani poezii, 1933–1943* (Selected Poems, 1933–1943, 1944), and *Vohnem i smerchem* (By Fire and Whirlwind, Munich 1947). In its restraint and polish his poetry is close to that of the *Neoclassicists. He is a versatile translator: his *Poety Zakhodu* (Poets of the Western World, 1961) contains 60 verses by Roman, Italian, French, English, German, and Polish poets. He has also translated the complete works of F. Villon (1973) and K. Ryleev's *Voinarovskii*. A jubilee edition of *Slovo o polku Ihorevi* (The Tale of Ihor's Campaign, 1950), edited by Hordynsky, contains his rendering of the poem in contemporary Ukrainian. He has also done a study of the poem's relation to Ukrainian folk poetry (1963).

Hordynsky has compiled and edited albums of such artists as T. Shevchenko (1942), P. Kovzhun (1944), H. Kruk, A. Pavlos, and M. Mukhyn (1947), V. Tsymbal (1972), P. Andrusiv (1980), and H. Mazepa (1983). His most important contributions to the history of Ukrainian art are *Ukraïns'ki tserkvy v Pol'shchi* (Ukrainian Churches in Poland, 1969) and *Ukraïns'ka ikona dvanadtsiatoho–visimnadsiatoho storichchia* (The Ukrainian Icon of the 12th–18th Centuries, in English and Ukrainian 1973, in German 1981). He is also the author of numerous articles on art in various journals and newspapers. An active member of the Ukrainian community, he is the vice-president of the Slovo Association of Ukrainian Writers in Exile.

V. Popovych

Yaroslav Hordynsky

Hordynsky, Yaroslav [Hordyns'kyj, Jaroslav], b 22 August 1882 in Shklo, Yavoriv county, Galicia, d 29 October 1939 in Lviv. Pedagogue and literary scholar. Hordynsky received his PH D from Lviv University and worked as a teacher of Ukrainian language and literature in Kolomyia, and then at the Academic Gymnasium of Lviv and in the Lviv (Underground) Ukrainian University. In 1914 he became a full member of the Shevchenko Scientific Society; in 1918 he was elected deputy to the Ukrainian National Council of ZUNR. His numerous studies of such writers as V. Prokopovych, T. Shevchenko, I. Franko, and M. Khvylovy appeared in the journals *Literaturno-naukovyi vistnyk, Dzvony, My, Nasha kul'tura,* and *Ukraïna* (1924–30). His most important work was the monograph *Literaturna krytyka pidsoviets'koï Ukraïny* (Literary Criticism in Soviet Ukraine, 1939), which remains the basic published work on the literary organizations and the *Literary Discussion in Ukraine of the 1920s.

Horetsky, Petro [Horec'kyj], b 6 December 1888 in Mutyn, Krolevets county, Chernihiv gubernia, d 16 August 1972 in Kiev. Linguist. Horetsky was an associate of the Institute of the Ukrainian Scientific Language and later of the AN URSR Institute of Linguistics. He was active in Ukrainian lexicography in the 1920s (preparing a dictionary of pedagogic and psychological terms, 1928) and served as a compiler of volume four of the academy's Russian-Ukrainian dictionary (seized at the printer's before final publication). He coauthored (with I. Shalia) a grammar of the Ukrainian language (eight printings, 1926–9). Following his arrest (ca 1932) for alleged bourgeois nationalism, he was demoted to the status of a proofreader. Reinstated in the Institute of Linguistics, he took part in the preparation of the 6-volume Ukrainian-Russian dictionary (1953–63) and of the 11-volume Ukrainian dictionary (1970–80). He also wrote a survey of the history of Ukrainian lexicography (*Istoriia ukraïns'koï leksykohrafiï*, 1963).

Horiany [Horjany]. V-3. Village (1969 pop 1,300) in Uzhhorod raion, Transcarpathia oblast. First mentioned in written sources in 1250, it has extensive orchards and vineyards. Its rotunda chapel, built at the turn of the 12th century, is a valuable historical monument. The chapel's annex is decorated with frescoes painted in the 15th century.

Horiev, Mykola [Horjev], b 21 June 1900 in Kazan, Russia. Pathophysiologist; full member of the USSR Academy of Medical Sciences from 1953. A graduate of Irkutsk University (1926), for many years he headed a department of the AN URSR Institute of Physiology. He was a founder, the first director (1958–62), and then a department head at the Institute of Gerontology of the USSR Academy of Medical Sciences in Kiev. Horiev wrote close to 100 works on the physiology and pathology of blood circulation, shock, hypertrophy, myocardial infarction, arteriosclerosis, tuberculosis, kidney diseases, and gerontology.

Horka, Lavrentii, b 1671 in Lviv, d 10 April 1737 in Viatka, Russia. Writer and churchman. A graduate and then instructor at the Kiev Academy, in 1713 he was appointed hegumen of Vydubychi Monastery in Kiev and in 1722 of the Resurrection Monastery in Moscow. After consecration, he served as bishop of Astrakhan (1723–7), Ustiug (1727–31), Riazan (1731–3), and Viatka (1733–7). He wrote a treatise on poetics, *Idea artis poëseos* (1707–8), and a tragicomedy, *Iosif patriarkha* (Joseph, the Patriarch), which was staged at the Kiev Academy in 1708.

Horkusha, Fylon [Horkuša], b and d ? Cossack colonel. In the summer of 1648 he led the Cossack forces supporting the rebels in Belorussia against the Lithuanian nobility during the *Cossack-Polish War. In the spring of 1651, as the colonel of Chornobyl regiment and together with the armies of M. Nebaba and A. Zhdanovych, he defended Ukraine's borders against the offensive of the Lithuanian army led by J. Radziwiłł. In March–April 1654 he was Hetman B. Khmelnytsky's envoy to the Muscovite government. He led a Cossack army in southern Volhynia in 1657. In June–November 1658 and in 1669–70 he was colonel of Poltava regiment. His subsequent fate is not known.

Horlenko. Line of Cossack officers descended from Lazar, colonel of the Pryluky regiment intermittently from 1658 to his death in 1687. The more distinguished members of the family were D. *Horlenko, Lazar's son; Yakym (d before 1758), fellow of the standard from 1725, general flag-bearer from 1729, acting hetman in the Crimean campaign of 1737, and general judge from 1741; Y. *Horlenko; and V. *Horlenko.

Horlenko, Dmytro, b and d ? Colonel of Pryluky regiment (1692–1708) and a close associate of Hetman I. Mazepa. In 1708, with Mazepa, he switched allegiance from Tsar Peter I to King Charles XII of Sweden. After the Battle of Poltava in 1709, Horlenko fled with Mazepa to Bendery. He took part in the campaigns of Hetman P. Orlyk in Right-Bank Ukraine in 1711 and 1713. In 1715 he came into conflict with Orlyk and went to Russia, where he settled in Moscow. In 1731 he was allowed to return to Ukraine.

Nina Horlenko

Horlenko, Nina, b 1 March 1895 in Bilopillia, Kholm region, d 4 May 1964 in Philadelphia. Dramatic actress. She completed her studies at the Lysenko Music and Drama School in Kiev and began her career in M. Sadovsky's theater. In the 1920s she worked at the Kharkiv Chervonozavodskyi Ukrainian Drama Theater, and in the 1930s at the Shevchenko Theater (formerly Berezil). After the Second World War, she performed in Germany with the Ensemble of Ukrainian Actors (1946–8) and then moved to the United States. She appeared in plays by H. Sudermann, G. Hauptmann, V. Vynnychenko, and Lesia Ukrainka (*Boiarynia, Dol'ores*), and distinguished herself in the role of Ahapiia in M. Kulish's *Narodnyi Malakhii* (The People's Malakhii).

Horlenko, Vasyl, b 1 March 1853 in Yaroshivka, Romen county, Poltava gubernia, d 13 April 1907 in St Petersburg. Literary critic and art scholar. After graduating from the Sorbonne he returned to Ukraine in 1882 and maintained close ties with such Ukrainian cultural figures as M. Kostomarov, P. Myrny, P. Martynovych, M. Storozhenko, and M. Zankovetska. A frequent contributor to *Kievskaia starina*, he wrote numerous surveys of Ukrainian literature, articles about dumas, book reviews, and literary portraits of such writers as T. Shevchenko, I. Kotliarevsky, H. Kvitka-Osnovianenko, I. Nechui-Levytsky, P. Myrny, I. Franko, and Ya. Shchoholev. In these portraits he combined, under the influence of C. Sainte-Beuve and H. Taine, esthetic judgment with historical description. He also wrote studies of such Classicist artists as D. Levytsky and V. Borovykovsky. Part of Horlenko's works were collected and published in *Iuzhnorusskie ocherki i portrety* (South-Russian Sketches and Portraits, 1898), *Ukrainskie byli* (The Ukrainian Past, 1899), and *Otbleski: Zametki po slovesnosti i iskusstvu* (Reflections: Comments about Literature and Art, 1905). His letters to P. Myrny were published in 1928. A monograph about him by D. Doroshenko was published in Paris in 1934.

Bishop Yoasaf Horlenko

Horlenko, Yoasaf (secular name: Yakym), b 19 September 1705 in Pryluka, Poltava region, d 21 December 1754 in Hraivoron, Slobidska Ukraine. Church leader and writer. He was a grandson of a Pryluka colonel and on his mother's side a grandson of Hetman D. Apostol. During his studies at the Kievan Mohyla Academy he took his monastic vows, and after graduating lectured at the academy (1729–31). In 1737 he became hegumen of the *Mhar Transfiguration Monastery, and in 1748 bishop of Belgorod and Oboian (which included the later eparchies of Kharkiv, Kursk, and a part of Chernihiv). Horlenko rebuilt churches, raised the moral and educational level of the clergy, and supported Kharkiv College. He wrote a brief autobiography and a play, *Bran' chesnykh sedmi dobrodetelei z sedmi grekhami smertnimi* (The Struggle of the Seven Cardinal Virtues with the Seven Deadly Sins, 1737). He was venerated by the common people and in 1911 was canonized by the Orthodox church.

Horlivka. V-19, DB III-4. City (1984 pop 341,000) under oblast jurisdiction in Donetske oblast 40 km from Donetske, one of the most important anthracite-mining and industrial centers in the Donbas, and a railway and highway junction. Founded beginning in the mid-18th century as the villages of Hosudariv Bairak, Mykytivka, Zaitseve, and Zalizna, it is named after a Russian mining engineer who built the first coal mine there in 1867. By the early 20th century the mining settlement had developed into an important industrial center. From 10,000 inhabitants in 1898, its population grew to 30,000 in 1916, 23,100 in 1926, and 181,500 in 1939. Horlivka was devastated during the Second World War, but by 1959 its population had grown to 308,000 (46 percent of which was Ukrainian and 48 percent Russian). Since 1970 its coal industry has not expanded (until then over 10 million t of coal was produced annually); consequently its population has grown by only 6,000 since 1970. Of Horlivka's nine anthracite mines, several are among the largest in the Donbas: the Lenin, Kindrativka-Nova, Kocheharka, Komsomolets, and Gagarin mines. Also located there are five mineral-enrichment factories, the Styrol chemicals trust, a coke-chemicals plant, the Kirov machine-building plant (one of the largest coal-mining-machine manufacturers in the USSR), four mechanical repair plants, the Mykytivka mercury and dolomite plants, and the Panteleimonivka refractory-materials plant. Its food (meat, milk, wine), clothing, cloth furnishings, woodworking, and building-materials industries are all well developed. Among its educational institutions are a pedagogical institute of foreign languages (English and French), a branch of the Donetske Polytechnical Institute, six special secondary schools, 12 vocational-technical schools, a city historical museum, a mining museum, and an art museum. The city is divided into three city raions.

V. Kubijovyč

Horlivka Machine-Building Plant (Horlivskyi mashynobudivelnyi zavod im. S.M. Kirova). One of the largest plants specializing in machine building for the coal industry in the USSR. It was established by a Belgian company in 1895 in Horlivka, now in Donetske oblast. In 1928 the plant produced the first coal face-cutting machine in the USSR and in 1936, the smallest and shortest coal-cutting machine in the world, the HTK-3. By the end of the 1930s it was one of the principal producers of mining machinery for Ukraine and the USSR. Completely destroyed during the Second World War, it was reconstructed and now specializes in a wide range of shaft-mining machines. Coal combines produced there have been awarded gold medals at various international fairs. In the late 1960s the plant employed almost 2,500 workers.

Horlytsi. See Gorlice.

Horlytsia [Horlycja]. An old Ukrainian thematic dance performed by many couples, sometimes with a female (called the *horlytsia*) solo. It expresses liveliness, energy, and humor. The tempo is moderately quick; the beat is 2/4. The name of the dance is derived from the turtle-dove, which in Ukrainian folklore symbolizes faithful love.

Hornbeam (*Carpinus;* Ukrainian: *hrab*). Popular name for species of deciduous trees, less commonly bushes, belonging to the genus *Carpinus*, of the birch (Betulaceae) family. Hornbeams have smooth, gray bark, short trunks, and horizontally growing branches with ovate and double-toothed leaves. They are hardy, slow-growing trees that are used for loom shuttles, parquet floors, musical instruments, tools, fuel, and as an ornamental in parks and gardens. Two species of hornbeam occur in Ukraine: the European hornbeam (*C. betulus*), which is found predominantly in Right-Bank Ukraine, the Carpathians, and Crimea; and the eastern or little hornbeam (*C. orientalis*), also found in Crimea.

Horniatkevych, Damian [Hornjatkevyč, Dam'jan], b 13 November 1892 in Lisko, Galicia, d 3 March 1980 in Kerhonkson, New York. Painter and art scholar. As a student at the Cracow Academy of Art, he researched works by medieval Ukrainian painters in Poland (among them frescoes from 1470 in the Wawel Cathedral in Cracow) and then published his results in *Postup* (1922–4) and *Notatky z mystetstva* (1965). After graduating in 1923, he studied portrait painting in Dresden and landscape painting in Munich (1925). Returning to Galicia, he painted mostly portraits and studied folk art. In the 1930s he painted four churches – in Nastasiv, Uhniv, Nemyriv, and Vorobliachyn. A displaced person after the war, he immigrated to the United States in 1949. He was vice-president of the Ukrainian Academy of Arts and Sciences in the US and head of its fine arts section (1951–70). He

Damian Horniatkevych

continued to paint in a realist style, concentrating on landscapes. Exhibitions of his work were held in New York in 1964, 1966, and posthumously in 1981. His publications include *Taras Schewtschenko als Maler* (1964) and numerous articles on Ukrainian artists, folk art, and the history of art.

Horno (The Forge). A communist literary group in Polish-occupied Western Ukraine that was founded in Lviv in May 1929 and took over publication of the journal **Vikna* (1927–32). Headed by V. Bobynsky, P. Kozlaniuk, and S. Tudor, it had 28 founding members, including O. Havryliuk, Ya. Halan, Ya. Kondra, and S. Masliak. From 1930 Horno belonged to the Moscow-sponsored International Bureau of Revolutionary Literature. In 1933 the group was officially dissolved under pressure from the Polish authorities. It continued functioning unofficially until 1939.

Hornostaivka [Hornostajivka]. VI-14. Town smt (1983 pop 5,830) on the Dnieper River and a raion center in Kherson oblast. Founded in the 18th century, the town serves as a port on the left bank of the Kakhivka Reservoir. Food production and local services are the mainstay of its economy.

Hornovy, Osyp [Hornovyj] (pseud of O. Diakiv), b 21 June 1921 in Olesyn, Berezhany county, Galicia, d 28 November 1950 in Velykopole, Yavoriv raion, Lviv oblast. Political activist and publicist. A member of the youth movement of the OUN from the late 1930s, in 1943–4 he served on the national executive of the youth wing of the OUN (Bandera faction) and was a member of the editorial board of *Iunak* and editor of the journal *Visti* (under the pseud Yuriiv). In 1945–8 he worked in the OUN leadership's central propaganda office. From 1948 he headed the OUN national executive in Lviv region. He became a member of the OUN leadership in 1949, and a member of the Ukrainian Supreme Liberation Council and vice-chairman of its General Secretariat in 1950. Hornovy died in a battle with MVD forces. His collected works, *Ideia i chyn* (Idea and Action), were published in London in 1968; an English-language edition of his writings appeared in New York as *The USSR Unmasked* (1976).

Hornykiewicz, Oleh [Hornykevyč], b 17 November 1926 in Sychiv, Lviv county, Galicia. Biochemist and pharmacologist. A specialist in diseases of the central and peripheral nervous systems, Hornykiewicz received his MD from the University of Vienna (1951) where he was a professor from 1953 to 1967. In 1956–8 he was a British Council Scholar at Oxford University. From 1967 to 1976 he was a professor at the University of Toronto, where he concurrently headed the Department of Psychopharmacology at the Clarke Institute of Psychiatry. Since 1977 he has been professor and chairman of the Department of Biochemical Pharmacology at the University of Vienna. Hornykiewicz has received international recognition for his research on Parkinson's disease and the palliative effects of the drug L-dopa, for which he and his colleagues received the prestigious Wolf Foundation Award in Medicine (1979). Hornykiewicz is coauthor of *The Pharmacology of Psychotherapeutic Drugs* (1969).

Horod or ***Hrad.*** A fortified settlement in Kievan Rus'; in later times the word described an administrative center for a larger region. The oldest Slavic fortified settlements in Ukraine were built by the Antes in the 6th century AD. A *horod* was usually located on an easily defensible site, in a forest, by adjoining lakes or marshes, or on a high riverbank. A moat and/or an earthen wall and wooden palisade surrounded the *horod* and provided further protection. A *horod* usually consisted of two parts: the inner or upper town (**dytynets*), located within the fortifications, and the outer or lower town (*okolnyi hrad, posad, pidhoroddia,* or *pryhoroddia*), outside the walls. The latter was inhabited mostly by merchants and artisans. *Horods* varied greatly in area and population, but in the early period of Kievan Rus' they were essentially rural settlements, or citadels, serving as places of refuge for the surrounding population in times of war. Those that were well situated (eg, near rivers or in mountain passes) became trade and manufacturing centers and acquired larger populations. Many old towns in Ukraine derive their names from a fortified settlement, such as Vyshhorod, Raihorod, Uzhhorod, and Bilhorod. In Kievan Rus' these settlements were so numerous that the Varangians called it the 'land of cities' (*Gardariki*). Volodymyr the Great, Yaroslav the Wise, and Danylo Romanovych built a great number of fortified settlements. (See also *Cities and towns.)

Horodenka. v-6. City (1968 pop 9,400) and raion center in Ivano-Frankivske oblast. This Pokutia town was first mentioned in late 12th-century chronicles. By the 15th century, under Polish rule, it was a trade center. In 1668 it was granted the rights of Magdeburg law. Under Austrian (1772–1918) and Polish (1919–39) rule it was a county town. Today its largest plants are a sugar refinery and a liquor distillery.

Horodetsky, Oleksii [Horodec'kyj, Oleksij], b 30 March 1897 in Novokostychi, Samara gubernia, d 9 January 1967 in Kiev. Biophysicist, roentgenologist, and radiologist; corresponding member of the AN URSR from 1957. A graduate of Saratov University, he began his research in roentgenology in 1926, and from 1935 to 1941 taught at the Bashkir Medical Institute in Ufa. He served as head of the Department of Roentgenology and Radiology at the Kiev Institute of Postgraduate Medical Training (1944–67), and as chief roentgenologist of the Ministry of Health of the Ukrainian SSR (1945–50). In 1953–67 he headed the Biophysics Laboratory and the Roentgenological and Radiological Department of the Kiev Institute of Experimental Biology and Pathology. In the course of his research into blood disorders, cancer, cardiac function, and irradiation of living tissue, he devised several new therapeutic irradiation techniques, as well as a complex treatment for the effects of radiation exposure.

Horodetsky, Serhii-Volodymyr [Horodec'kyj, Serhij-Volodymyr], b 1885 in Podilia, d 9 April 1956 in New York. Agronomist. From 1921 to 1941 he taught agronomy at agricultural institutes in Kamianets-Podilskyi, Kiev, and Zhytomyr and worked at the Agronomic Institute of the Belorussian Academy of Sciences, from which he received a doctorate. He was also an associate of the VUAN Scientific Research Chair of Botany. After the Second World War he lived in Germany and then in the United States. In 1946 he was appointed professor of the Ukrainian Technical and Husbandry Institute and a full member of the Shevchenko Scientific Society. He published numerous scientific and popular works, including *Sil's'ke hospodarstvo Podillia pered svitovoiu viinoiu* (Agriculture in Podilia before the World War, 1929).

Horodetsky, Stepan [Horodec'kyj], b 1853 in Mezhyhirtsi, Stanyslaviv county, Galicia, d 26 November 1928 in Verbylivtsi, Rohatyn county, Galicia. Church and community leader; Greek Catholic priest. Having completed his studies in Lviv and Rome, he served as rector of the Lviv Theological Seminary, chaplain to Metropolitan S. Sembratovych, curate of Verbylivtsi, and dean of the Rohatyn chapter. In 1912 he was appointed papal chamberlain, and then vicar general and archpriest. A dedicated populist, he was an organizer of the National Democratic party, and later of the Ukrainian Labor party and of the Ukrainian National Democratic Alliance. He supported the local *Prosvita society and the Ukrainian school movement in the county, and founded the first credit union in Rohatyn. In 1925 he was elected honorary member of Prosvita.

Horodetsky, Vladyslav [Horodec'kyj], b 4 June 1863 in Sholudky, Bratslav county, Podilia gubernia, d 3 January 1930 in Teheran. Architect. A graduate of the Academy of Arts in St Petersburg (1890), he worked for many years in Kiev, where he designed such buildings as the Art and History Museum (now the Kiev Museum of Ukrainian Art) in the classical style (1897–1900), a Karaite synagogue in a Moorish style (1899–1900), a Roman Catholic church in stylized Gothic (1899–1909), and a residential building on Bankova Street (now Ordzhonikidze no. 10) (1902–3). He designed numerous schools, churches, and industrial buildings in the Kiev region, Uman, Cherkasy, and Symferopil. In 1920 he moved to Warsaw and in 1928 to Iran, where he built the royal palace and other buildings.

Horodlo, Union of. An agreement concluded on 2 October 1413 between Duke Vytautas and the nobles of Lithuania and King Jagiełło and the nobles of Poland in Horodlo, a town on the Buh River in the southern Kholm region. The agreement was intended to facilitate the complete union of Poland and Lithuania – a process begun by the Union of *Krevo – by merging the administrations of the two states and by recognizing the noble claims of the Lithuanian boyars and magnates. The preservation of the distinct offices of Polish king and Lithuanian grand duke, however (although the latter was clearly subordinate), left the issue of the complete union unresolved. Under the terms of the agreement the Catholic nobles of Lithuania were granted equality with their Polish counterparts; Orthodox (mostly Ruthenian) nobles, however, were consigned to second-class status and prohibited from full participation in state affairs.

Horodnia [Horodnja]. II-12. City (1983 pop 12,400) and, since 1923, a raion center in northern Chernihiv oblast. First mentioned in 1552, from 1635 to 1654 it was a Polish county center, from 1705 to 1782 a Cossack company town, and from 1782 to 1917 a county town. In 1848, one of the first sugar refineries in Ukraine was built there. It received city status in 1957. The city produces flax fiber, bricks, and food, dairy, and wood products, and processes labradorite.

Horodnychyi. In princely times an official who supervised the building and maintenance of towns, particularly their fortifications. During the Lithuanian-Ruthenian period the *horodnychyi* commanded the city and fortress and collected taxes from the **volost*; there were 15 such commanders in the Grand Duchy of Lithuania. From 1635 some *horodnychi* were immediately subordinate to the grand princes and the Council of Lords. In Russia and Ukraine from 1775 to 1862 the term designated a county-seat administrator, who was also head of the local police.

Horodnyk. A category of indentured peasants in Ukraine in the 14th–19th centuries. *Horodnyky* were first mentioned in documents at the end of the 14th century, although their number grew most quickly beginning in the 16th century. They owned plots that were too small to support subsistence agriculture – usually up to 2 ha in area – and little livestock. They performed corvée without draft animals. *Horodnyky* also hired themselves out temporarily to wealthy peasants, merchants, chumaks, artisans, and others. They were especially numerous in more densely settled regions, constituting approximately 25–35 percent of the peasant population of Right-Bank Ukraine in the 16th and 17th centuries. *Horodnyky* took part in numerous peasant uprisings. After the peasant reforms of 1861, most received free land allotments.

Horodok. IV-4. Town (1970 pop 12,000) and raion center in Lviv oblast, situated 30 km from Lviv on the Vereshchytsia River. First mentioned in the Hypatian Chronicle as Solianyi Horodok under the year 1213, in the 13th and 14th centuries it was an important fortified town in Galicia-Volhynia. In the early 15th century it received the rights of Magdeburg law. Destroyed by the Tatars in the 1530s, in the late 16th and early 17th centuries it flourished again as a center of trade (salt, cattle, and fish) and culture with a church brotherhood from 1591 and a school. During the Cossack-Polish War, Cossack and Muscovite troops routed S. Potocki's Polish army there in September 1655. The town was again destroyed by the Tatars in 1672. The Russian army defeated the Austrian army there in August 1914 after a six-day battle, and in February 1919 Western Ukrainian and Polish forces fought each other there for control of the Lviv-Peremyshl railway line. Today the town has clothing, food, and construction industries. Among its architectural monuments are St Nicholas's Church (1510), the wooden Church of St John the Baptist (1670), and a Roman Catholic church (15th–18th century).

Horodok. V-7. Town (1970 pop 15,000) and raion center in Khmelnytskyi oblast, situated on the Smotrych River in eastern Podilia. It was first mentioned in historical documents under the year 1392. In 1793, after the second partition of Poland, the town came under Russian rule. In April 1919 the Volhynian Group of UNR Army units fought several battles there against Bolshevik forces. It was a raion center in Proskuriv okruha (1923–30), Vinnytsia oblast (1932–7), and Kamianets-Podilskyi oblast (1937–54). Machine tools and foodstuffs are produced there.

Horodok. III-7. Village 8 km from Rivne in Volhynia. Seven Paleolithic camp sites of the early Aurignacian culture, a large workshop of Neolithic flint implements, two Eneolithic cist graves, a settlement and burial ground with Silesian-type corded ware, a 7th–8th-century fortified settlement, and four settlements and two burial grounds of the Princely era were excavated there by L. Chykalenko in 1912–16, L. Sawicki in 1923–9, M. Drewko in 1927–8, and I. Sveshnikov in 1960–1. Altogether 25 archeological monuments have been discovered. First mentioned in 1463, from the early 16th century to 1794 Horodok was the site of a monastery and an episcopal seat. An 18th-century church and bell-tower gate have also been preserved.

Horodok. V-6. A village in Zalishchyky raion, Ternopil oblast, at the junction of the Seret and Dniester rivers. Settlements of the Upper Paleolithic period, the Trypilian culture, and the 9th–7th centuries BC, as well as Scythian kurhans and a crypt of the Princely era under stone slabs, were excavated there by A. Kirkor in 1878, G. Ossowski in 1890, and T. Sulimirski in 1934.

Horodok, Battle of. A battle between the combined Cossack and Muscovite armies and the Polish army, which took place near Horodok west of Lviv on 29 September 1655. It was one of the major encounters of the *Cossack-Polish War, when Cossack and Muscovite forces began to advance on Western Ukraine and to liberate Galicia from Polish rule in the spring of 1655. In September 1655, while the armies of Hetman B. Khmelnytsky and V. Buturlin besieged Lviv, Cossack and Muscovite detachments pursued the main body of the 40,000-strong Polish army commanded by S. Potocki. In the Battle of Horodok, the Cossacks under H. Lesnytsky and the Muscovite regiments under G. Romodanovsky routed the Poles.

Horodovenko, Nestor, b 27 October 1885 in Venslav, Lokhvytsia county, Poltava gubernia, d 21 August 1964 in Montreal. Choir conductor and pedagogue. In 1917 he taught at the Second Ukrainian Gymnasium in Kiev and conducted the Kiev University choir. Later he directed the Dniprosoiuz Chorus, which subsequently became the chorus of the Kiev Department of People's Education and in 1919 *DUMKA, and served as its principal conductor from 1919 to 1938. Under his direction the chorus completed several critically acclaimed tours of Ukraine, other Soviet republics, and Western Europe. From 1930 he was also a professor and director of the

Nestor Horodovenko

conducting department at the Kiev Music Institute (later Conservatory). In 1938 he was temporarily banned from conducting for political reasons and DUMKA was reorganized. During the Second World War he directed choirs in Kiev and Lviv. After the war he conducted in Germany, and from 1949 in Montreal, where he directed the choir Ukraina. In addition to numerous Ukrainian works, Horodovenko's repertoire included Beethoven, Mozart, Verdi, Haydn, Ravel, Grieg, and Debussy.

Horodovi Cossacks. See Town Cossacks.

Horodsk or **Horodesk** [Horods'k or Horodes'k]. An ancient Rus' town situated on the Teteriv River; today the village of Horodske in Korostyshiv raion, Zhytomyr oblast. Archeological surveys and excavations conducted in 1936–7, 1939–40, 1946–7, and 1955–8 revealed that from the 9th to the 13th century Horodsk was an iron-working center whose inhabitants were engaged in farming and in making iron implements and weapons, pottery, and jewelry. The town was destroyed by the Mongols in the mid-13th century. A late Trypilian settlement (early 2nd millennium BC) also existed there.

Horodyshche [Horodyšče]. IV-12. Town (1971 pop 16,300) and raion center in Cherkasy oblast, situated on the Vilshanka River. First mentioned in the 16th century, it has a memorial museum and monument dedicated to the singer and composer S. *Hulak-Artemovsky (who was born there), a large sugar refinery (since 1848), a brewery, and a labradorite quarry. The 1771 Church of St Mary the Protectress is preserved there.

Horodyshche [Horodyšče]. III-8. Village in Shepetivka raion, Khmelnytskyi oblast. In 1957–63 the remains of an old fortified city, which some scholars believe to have been the Rus' city of Iziaslavl, were excavated there. Uncovered were burned ruins of dwellings, numerous agricultural and artisans' implements and weapons, pottery, hundreds of human skeletons, and several hoards of silver ornaments and jewelry. The city was probably founded in the late 12th century and was destroyed by the Mongols in 1241.

Horodyshche *Apostol* [Horodyšče] (aka Khrystynopil *Apostol*). A 12th-century manuscript (299 folios), copied from the original Church Slavonic in Galicia or in southern Volhynia. It represents a significant source for the study of the development of the Ukrainian language. The bulk of the manuscript is kept in the Lviv Historical Museum, but the initial eight folios are in the Central Scientific Library of the AN URSR in Kiev. The above sections have been published respectively by O. Kaluzhniatsky (1896) and S. Maslov (1910). The language has been studied by O. Kolessa (1923).

Horodyshche Gospel [Horodyšče] (aka Buchach Gospel). A Church Slavonic text copied in Ukraine, probably in southern Volhynia, in the 12th or first half of the 13th century (160 folios), now kept in the Lviv Museum of Ukrainian Art. It was utilized by I. Svientsitsky (1911) and O. Kolessa (1925) as a source in the study of the historical development of the Ukrainian language. Fragments of it were subsequently published by the latter.

Horodysky, Oleksander [Horodys'kyj], b 1 May 1930 in Kiev. Electrochemist; since 1978 full member of the AN URSR. Upon graduating from the Kiev Polytechnical Institute in 1951 he joined the Institute of General and Inorganic Chemistry of the AN URSR, and in 1973 was appointed director of the institute. He discovered a number of laws of electrochemical kinetics, developed a theory of the non-stationary state of electrochemical systems and bifunctional electrochemical systems permitting electrolysis above the solvent potential, used quantum-mechanical methods to calculate electron transfer in condensed phases, devised methods and equipment for electrochemical research, and found electrochemical ways to synthesize many inorganic materials.

Horokhiv [Horoxiv]. III-5. Town (1970 pop 5,500) and raion center in Volhynia oblast, situated on the Buh-Styr watershed in the Volhynian Upland. It was first mentioned in the Hypatian Chronicle under the year 1240. The city's food and wine industry is based on the fertile lands of the vicinity; it has two brickyards and a tool-and-die-making plant.

Horokhovatsky, Yaroslav [Horoxovac'kyj, Jaroslav], b 17 September 1925 in Oleksandriia, Kremenchuk okruha, d 28 May 1976 in Kiev. Physical chemist; from 1972 corresponding member of the AN URSR. Upon graduating from Kiev University in 1951 he joined the AN URSR Institute of Physical Chemistry. His chief publications deal with heterogeneous catalysis.

Mariia Horokhovska

Horokhovska, Mariia [Horoxovs'ka, Marija], b 17 October 1921 in Yevpatoriia, Crimean ASSR. World-class gymnast. A graduate of the Kiev Institute of Physical Culture (1956), she won two gold and five silver medals in various gymnastic individual and team events at the Olympic Games in Helsinki (1952). She won the gymnastics championship of Ukraine and the USSR several times before attaining the world championship in team events (1954). She competed as a member of the Budivelnyk team from Kharkiv and now works as a coach and teacher.

Horse breeding. Horse breeding is an important branch of *animal husbandry. Before agriculture was mechanized, the horse was the principal work animal. It also played an important role in transport and warfare, and was a significant source of meat and hide. Today horses on collective state farms are used for local transport, vegetable gardening, and livestock herding.

Horse breeding appeared in territories of the Trypilian culture as early as the Bronze Age. The horse served alongside the ox as a draft animal. For steppe nomads, particularly the Scythians, the horse was indispensable as a means of transportation and as a source of meat, milk, and hide. In the Princely era horses continued to be important in farming, and even more important in warfare (see *Cavalry). Horses then were of local stock, but some were obtained by trade or capture from steppe tribes. The princes owned large horse herds. Several horse breeds were known and some selective breeding was practiced.

During the Cossack period horse breeding developed particularly in response to military needs. In the 17th–18th centuries the hetmans took an interest in horse breeding. During I. Samoilovych's and I. Mazepa's rule large stud farms in the steppe of Nizhen regiment and in Pryluka regiment supplied the hetman's army with horses. Later, the Russian government took over some of these farms. In the Hetman state, Slobidska Ukraine, and Zaporizhia, horses were also bred by Cossack officers on large estates. By the end of the 18th century, stud farms appeared in Right-Bank Ukraine on the estates of magnates such as Branicki, Potocki, and Rzewuski.

With Russia's conquest of the southern Ukrainian steppes in the second half of the 18th century, the new settlers began to raise large horse herds on these lands and horse breeding began to assume a commercial character. As more and more of the steppe came under cultivation and grazing land decreased, and as the army's demand for horses at the same time fell, horse raising in the steppes declined. At the time, the ox was the principal draft animal for plowing the virgin steppes. In Kherson gubernia, for example, the number of horses declined from 400,000 in 1808 to 120,000 in 1861. In the second half of the 19th century, when the steppes had been brought under the plow, the ox was replaced by the swifter-moving horse and horse breeding experienced a revival. Thus, in Kherson gubernia the horse population increased to 329,000 (1.4 horses to each ox) by 1881, and to 814,000 (8.17 horses to each ox) by 1913. In all the steppe gubernias the horse population increased from 360,000 in 1861 to 1,100,000 in 1882, and to 2,100,000 in 1912. In the forest-steppe belt this process took place sooner and the growth was less dramatic – from 2,300,000 in 1883 to 3,500,000 in 1912. Altogether in 1912 there were 6,600,000 horses in territories that are now part of the Ukrainian SSR.

Although every peasant farmer wanted to own a horse, most peasant farms were too small to support one. In 1891 in the nine Russian-ruled gubernias of Ukraine 42.4 percent of peasants farms had no horse, 13.4 percent had only one horse, 23.4 percent had two horses, and 20.8 percent had three or more horses. In 1916, 89.4 percent of all horses were owned by peasants but the average number of horses per household was only 1.1. Moreover, these horses were often underfed and overworked. In Western Ukraine a similar situation prevailed even after the First World War: in Galicia (1927) 70 percent of peasant farms had one or no horse, in Transcarpathia (1925) 87.7 percent, and in Bukovyna (1925) 19.8 percent. The most important local breeds were: in Southern Ukraine, the Black Sea and Ukrainian horse developed by the Zaporozhian and Kuban Cossacks; in the southeast, the Don horse; in the north, the Polisian horse; and in the Carpathian Mountains, the Hutsul pony. Relatively few horses were purebred. The chief stud farms in Ukraine were the Derkulske (1751), Striletske (1803), Novooleksandrivka (1810), and Lymarivka (1819) farms in Starobilske county, Kharkiv gubernia, the Yanov farm in Podlachia, and the Radivtsi (Rădăuţi) farm in Bukovyna.

During the First World War and the Revolution the horse population of Ukraine (as defined by today's boundaries) declined to 4,700,000 or 71 percent of the prewar figure. A strong demand for horses led to a rapid recovery in their numbers: by 1929 there were 6,800,000 horses on Ukrainian ethnic territory, and 5,600,000 horses in the Ukrainian SSR of the time. Forced collectivization and the man-made famine of 1932–3 had a devastating impact on the horse population of Soviet Ukraine: by 1934 it dropped to 2,500,000. Since the tractor industry was in its infancy and could not replace animal power with machines, the horse shortage contributed to the agricultural crisis. Further decline in the horse population was brought about by the Second World War, the collectivization of Western Ukraine, and finally continued progress in farm mechanization. By 1951 it fell to 2,245,000, by 1970 to 1,322,000, and by 1983 to 807,000. State and collective farms owned 96 percent of the horses (1955). The highest concentration of horses was in Khmelnytskyi, Vinnytsia, Chernihiv, and Odessa oblasts.

Today, while the horse population continues to decline, horses are bred within a uniform system of state-controlled stud farms, breeding stables, stations, and hippodromes. New breeds have been developed and old ones have been improved. The main breeds in Ukraine are the Orlov and Russian trotters, the Soviet, Russian, and Percheron draft horses, and the Thoroughbred, Budenny, and Don horses. Of the various Ukrainian breeds only the Hutsul pony and the Polisia horse continue to be raised.

BIBLIOGRAPHY

Tvarynnytstvo Ukraïns'koï RSR: Statystychnyi zbirnyk (Kiev 1960)
Sil's'ke hospodarstvo URSR: Statystychnyi zbirnyk (Kiev 1970)

C. Freeland

Horseradish (*Armoracia rusticana*; Ukrainian: *khrin*). A perennial herbacious plant belonging to the mustard family (Brassicaceae or Cruciferae). Horseradish is grown throughout Ukraine. The plant has elongate or linear leaves, a long, straight, branched stem (maximum 1 m in height), and a large white root. The root and leaves are bactericidal and contain various constituents, most notably vitamin C. The root is eaten raw or cooked, and may be dried, marinated, pickled, or salted. Horseradish is a traditional Ukrainian Easter condiment. In addition to its food value, the plant has historically had a wide variety of medicinal uses in the treatment of various nutritional and pathological disorders. Ukrainian folk literature contains many references to horseradish, often as a synonym for the devil.

Alla Horska

Mykhailo Horyn

Horska, Alla [Hors'ka], b 18 September 1929 in the Crimea, d 28 November 1970 in Vasylkiv, Vasylkiv raion, Kiev oblast. Monumentalist painter, graduate of the Kiev State Art Institute, and wife of V. *Zaretsky. She was a founder and active member of the Club of Creative Youth (est 1962) in Kiev, which played an important role in the cultural movement of the 1960s. She designed the stage sets for M. Kulish's *Otak zahynuv Huska* (Thus Huska Died), whose premiere at the Lviv Ukrainian Drama Theater was banned. In 1964 she collaborated with H. Sevruk and L. Semykina on a stained-glass panel designed by P. Zalyvakha for Kiev University. Because of its unconventional style and patriotic message, the panel, which depicted an angry T. Shevchenko, was destroyed by the authorities, and Horska was expelled from the Union of Artists of the Ukrainian SSR. To find work she had to leave Kiev, but she continued to defy the authorities by protesting against their repressive measures. She was murdered in 1970. Although the crime remains officially unsolved, circumstantial evidence points to the KGB's involvement. Horska's main works are monumental internal and external paintings and mosaics decorating schools, museums, and restaurants, done in collaboration with other artists.

Horticulture. See Orcharding and fruit farming.

Horyn, Bohdan [Horyn'], b 10 February 1936 in Kniselo, Bibrka county, Galicia. Art and literary scholar, political dissident. A graduate of Lviv University (1959), he specialized in the psychology of artistic creativity and over a few years published more than 30 articles. In 1966 he was convicted of anti-Soviet agitation and propaganda and sentenced to four years in a strict-regime labor camp.

Horyn, Mykhailo [Horyn', Myxajlo], b 20 June 1930 in Kniselo, Bibrka county, Galicia. Educator, literary scholar, psychologist, and dissident. A graduate of Lviv University (1953), he taught Ukrainian language and literature, logic, and psychology in secondary schools, and then did research in the psychology and work physiology of labor. In 1966 he was accused of anti-Soviet agitation and propaganda and sentenced to six years in a strict-regime labor camp. In 1981 he was sentenced to ten years in a strict-regime camp and five years of internal exile.

Horyn River

Horyn River [Horyn']. A right-bank tributary of the Prypiat River. It has a length of 659 km, a width of 20–80 m, and a depth of up to 16 m; its basin covers an area of 27,700 sq km. The Horyn's lower stretch is navigable. The upper Horyn dissects the Volhynian Upland and the Polisia Lowland. The *Sluch River is the Horyn's largest tributary.

Hoshcha [Hošča]. III-7. Town smt (1978 pop 4,300) and raion center in Rivne oblast, situated on the Horyn River. First mentioned in the 14th century, in the late 16th century it became a center of the *Socinians in Volhynia, who established a school there in the early 17th century. To combat their influence, an Orthodox monastery with a secondary school was founded there in 1638. In the 18th century the monastery and school were taken over by the Basilians, who maintained them until 1833. The miraculous icon of the Mother of God in the Pochaiv Monastery originated in Hoshcha. Today the town produces butter, cheese, and animal feed.

Hoshiv: Basilian church on Yasna Hora mountain

Hoshiv [Hošiv]. IV-4. Village (1971 pop 1,900) in Bolekhiv raion, Ivano-Frankivske oblast. It is known for its Basilian monastery, which was built in the 1570s. The latest monastery building was constructed on Yasna Hora in 1836–7 and the latest church in 1834–42. With its miracle-working icon of the Weeping Mother of God, which since the 18th century has been popularly known as the Queen of the Carpathians, the monastery used to attract thousands of pilgrims from Galicia and Bukovyna. In 1951 the Soviet authorities abolished the monastery and converted its buildings into a hostel for indigent children. A history of the monastery, *Iasna Hora v Hoshevi* (The Luminous Mount of Hoshiv) by Rev M. Dydra, was published in New York in 1972.

Hoshkevych, Viktor [Hoškevyč], b 21 March 1860 in Kiev, d 2 March 1928 in Kherson. Archeologist and museologist. While working for the Kherson gubernia statistical committee, he did archeological research in the Kherson region. In 1890 he established a museum in Kherson with a rich archeological collection consisting mostly of Greek, Scythian, and Sarmatian materials. He published a museum newsletter and the daily Kherson newspaper *Iug* (1898–1907). He is the author of *Klady i drevnosti Khersonskoi gubernii* (Hoards and Antiquities of Kherson Gubernia, 1903) and *Drevnie gorodishcha po beregam nizovogo Dnepra* (Ancient Fortified Settlements on the Banks of the Lower Dnieper, 1913).

Hoshko, Yurii [Hoško, Jurij], b 28 April 1917 in Starychi, Peremyshl county, Galicia. Ethnographer. From 1951 to 1958 he served as director of the Lviv Historical Museum, and thereafter as director of the Ukrainian State Museum of Ethnography and Crafts (now a branch of the Institute of Fine Arts, Folklore, and Ethnography in Kiev). His chief works are *Hromads'kyi pobut robitnykiv Zakhidnoï Ukraïny, 1920–1939* (The Community Life of the Workers in Western Ukraine, 1920–1939, 1967) and *Naselennia ukraïns'kykh Karpat XV–XVII st.: Zaselennia, mihratsiï, pobut* (The Population of the Ukrainian Carpathians in the 15th–18th Century: Settlement, Migrations, Customs, 1976).

Bohdan Hoshovsky

Hoshovsky, Bohdan [Hošovs'kyj] (pseuds: Didus, B. Danylovych), b 21 August 1907 in Zolochiv, Galicia, d 21 July 1986 in Toronto. Civic figure, journalist, and writer, editor, and publisher of *children's literature. He edited the journals *Mali druzi* (1937–8, 1940–4, 1948) and *Doroha* (1937–8, 1940, 1942–4) and such book series as *Moia knyzhechka* (My Book, 1940–4) and *Doroha* (The Road, 1940–2). During the Second World War he worked for the publisher Ukrainske Vydavnytstvo. After the war he immigrated to Toronto, where he founded two publishing houses for children's literature: Nashym Ditiam and Yevshan Zillia. He cofounded and headed the Association of Ukrainian Writers for Young People, and has coedited the journal *Veselka*. Hoshovsky is the author of children's stories and articles on various topics in the Ukrainian press.

Hoshovsky, Volodymyr [Hošovs'kyj], b 25 September 1922 in Uzhhorod. Folklorist, founder of cybernetic ethnomusicology. A graduate of the Lviv Conservatory (1953), where he lectured (1961–9). He founded and directed the folk-music cabinet at the conservatory. In 1975 he became a research associate of the Arts Institute of the Academy of Sciences of the Armenian SSR in Yerevan, and compiled a cybernetic universal structural-analytical catalogue of folk songs (UNSAKAT). His chief publications are *Ukrainskie pesni Zakarpat'ia* (Ukrainian Songs of Transcarpathia, 1968) and *U istokov narodnoi muzyki slavian* (At the Sources of the Slavs' Folk Music, 1971). He has edited a Russian collection of K. Kvitka's works and a collection of papers on the algorithmic analysis of musical texts.

Hospital. Institution at which sick people are given medical and surgical treatment. The earliest hospitals developed out of hostels for pilgrims and travelers to Jerusalem that provided care for their sick guests during frequent epidemics. There were hospitals in Ukraine by the end of the 10th century. Under Prince Volodymyr the Great, free shelters, attached to monasteries and churches, for orphans, the homeless, the aged, and the sick were built. These were supported by a tithe. Metropolitan Yefrem founded several hospitals in Pereiaslav and other towns at the end of the 11th century. In the 15th–17th centuries some hospitals were maintained by the brotherhoods.

From 1775 hospitals in Russian-ruled Ukraine came under the control of social-welfare boards, managed by local administrators elected by the gentry. Small hospitals for serfs were sometimes maintained on the estates of large landowners. In this period hospitals were charitable shelters rather than treatment facilities and they were few in number. The first hospital in the modern sense of the term was a 50-bed hospital for infectious diseases established in Kiev in 1787, and the first hospital for somatic illnesses was established in 1803. During the Russian-Turkish War, a teaching hospital for training physicians operated in Yelysavethrad (now Kirovohrad) from 1788 to 1793. In this period hospitals appeared in Kremenchuk (1800), Poltava (1804), Cherkasy (1822), and a number of other towns. Gradually the local shelters were also converted into true hospitals.

With the introduction of *zemstvo medicine the number of hospitals and hospital beds throughout the Russian Empire increased rapidly after 1864. Legislation introduced in 1866 required factory owners to provide hospital facilities for employees. In 1915 in Russian-ruled Ukraine, there were 617 gubernia and county hospitals, 21 municipal hospitals, 202 factory hospitals, 47 Jewish hospitals, 4 church-run hospitals, 26 hospitals run by

Number of hospitals and beds in Ukraine, 1913–85

	1913	1932	1940	1950	1960	1970	1980	1983	1985
No. of hospitals	1,438	1,333	2,498	3,533	5,046	4,700	3,843	3,808	–
No. of beds (in thousands)	47.7	73.8	157.6	194.2	334.2	511.0	627.1	652.5	661.0
Beds per 10,000 inhabitants	13.6	17.5	37.7	52.2	80.4	107.6	125.4	129.1	130.0

volunteers, 4 run by the Red Cross, 66 private hospitals, 17 university hospitals, 16 hospitals run by the railroads, 68 prison hospitals, and 58 run by various other institutions and organizations. There were also 22 institutions for the mentally ill.

In Galicia and Bukovyna, which were under Austrian rule, hospitals were overseen until 1918 by the provincial authorities. In the 1920s and 1930s hospitals (including state, self-governing, community, and private hospitals) in Polish-ruled territories of Ukraine came under the jurisdiction of the voivodeship government.

In the Ukrainian SSR the typical hospital since 1947 consists of an inpatient and an outpatient department. Hospitals are classified as general or specialized (infectious diseases, tubercular, psychiatric, gynecological, oncological, etc), some of which are attached to institutions of higher education or scientific research institutes. General hospitals in Ukraine are officially classified in categories based on the range of services they offer and their administrative subordination. These categories include republic and oblast hospitals (offering the most comprehensive range of medical services), town and urban district hospitals, raion center hospitals, and rural district hospitals. In 1971, for the entire USSR, the average number of beds per hospital for each category was 613, 166, 156, and 31 respectively. Most hospitals in Ukraine are controlled by the republic's Ministry of Health, but some are under the jurisdiction of the USSR Ministry of Defense and such ministries as the Ministry of Transport, which retains considerable autonomy in providing health care to its employees.

The development of the hospital network in Ukraine is summarized in the accompanying table. In general, the eastern oblasts of Ukraine are best supplied with hospital beds. According to 1985 figures, Kirovohrad oblast had 143 beds per 10,000 inhabitants, the city of Kiev 138.9, Voroshylovhrad oblast 138.9, Donetske oblast 135.9, and Dnipropetrovske oblast 133.7. The worst-supplied oblasts were in the south and west: Transcarpathia (114.9), Rivne (119.4), Lviv (120.4), Odessa (123.2), Ivano-Frankivske (120.3), Zhytomyr (123.6), Kherson (124.8), Chernivtsi (124.4), and Ternopil (125.0). The low figure of 115.0 beds per 10,000 inhabitants for Kiev oblast (excluding the city of Kiev) is explained by the practice of transporting patients from various parts of the oblast to Kiev for treatment. In 1985, Ukraine, on the average, had 130 beds per 10,000 inhabitants, the RSFSR 126, and the USSR 120.8.

In 1960 over 20 percent of hospital beds were occupied by medical patients, 13 percent by surgical patients, and 10 percent by mental patients. Less than 10 percent of the beds were used by the following groups of patients: pregnant women and women in childbirth, women with gynecological disorders, children, and people with infectious diseases.

Despite the recent increases in the number of hospitals in Ukraine, especially in rural areas (by the mid-1970s almost every raion in the county had a hospital with some 250–300 beds), there are shortcomings in the system. Many hospitals are severely overcrowded – in fact, increases in the number of beds are often a result of simply placing more beds in existing facilities – and overall sanitary conditions are often primitive, with clean bedding and sterilized or disposable equipment being in short supply. In addition, claims that health care is equally accessible to everyone in society are somewhat unfounded. The best hospitals in the USSR are in Moscow, and high Party officials and employees of certain agencies (eg, the KGB and the Academy of Sciences) have access to special, and undoubtedly superior, hospital services.

BIBLIOGRAPHY

Materialy do istorii rozvytku okhorony zdorov'ia na Ukraïni (Kiev 1957)

Organizatsiia zdravokhraneniia v SSSR, 2 vols (Moscow 1958)

Ryan, M. *The Organization of Soviet Medical Care* (Oxford-London 1978)

Verkhrats'kyi, S. *Istoriia medytsyny*, 3rd edn (Kiev 1983)

T. Lapychak

Hospodar (The Farmer). The first Ukrainian educational periodical devoted to agriculture and industry. It was published semimonthly in Lviv from 10 July 1869 to 1872. The editor was S. Shekhovych, and contributors included Ye. Hlynsky and V. Ruzhytsky. It was first printed in the hrazhdanka, then in the Cyrillic, and from 1871 in the Latin alphabet.

Hospodar (The Farmer). A monthly magazine for farmers, published in Peremyshl from July 1898 to 1913. From 1902 it included the supplement *Ekonomist*. The publisher was I. Nehrebetsky and the editors I. Nehrebetsky (1898–1905) and T. Kormosh (1906–13).

Hospodar i promyshlennyk (The Farmer and Manufacturer). An illustrated semimonthly periodical devoted to agriculture, industry, and commerce, published in Stanyslaviv (now Ivano-Frankivske) from November 1879 to 1882 and then in Lviv (1883–7). A total of 163 issues appeared. Beginning with the 23rd issue in 1883 it included the supplement *Lystok hospodars'kyi*. The editor until 1885 was A. Nychai; he was succeeded by A. Hlodzynsky (1886) and V. Nahirny (1886–7). P. Bazhansky, L. Vitoshynsky, I. Horodysky, K. Kuzyk, I. Naumovych, and V. Ruzhytsky were among the main contributors.

Hospodars'ka chasopys' (The Farming Periodical). The semimonthly organ of the Silskyi Hospodar association. It appeared in Lviv from 25 January 1910 until 1918 and again in 1920. The managing editor was H. Velychko; other editors included K. Kakhnykevych (1910–18) and Yu. Pavlykovsky.

Hospodars'ko-kooperatyvnyi chasopys (The Farming-Co-operative Periodical). An official organ of the Provincial Audit Union (later the *Audit Union of Ukrainian Co-operatives), which appeared in Lviv from 1921 to 1944, with a break in 1940–1. At first it was a monthly, published for the Committee for Organizing Co-operatives by the Silskyi Hospodar association. On 10 August 1922 it became a semimonthly, and in 1925, a weekly. Its chief editors were Yu. Pavlykovsky (1921), M. Korchynsky and A. Havrylko (1922–7), Z. Pelensky (1927–30), Ye. Khraplyvy (1930–3), and V. Sofroniv-Levytsky (1933–44). It printed articles of a theoretical nature as well as educational and instructional articles on agriculture and economics, especially concerning the co-operative movement. The journal was illustrated by E. Kozak from 1927.

Hospodarstvo Ukraïny (Economy of Ukraine). Monthly economic journal published in Kharkhiv from 1924 to 1934 by the State Planning Committee of the Ukrainian SSR. The first three issues (1924–5) were published in Russian under the title *Khoziaistvo Ukrainy* but all subsequent issues appeared in Ukrainian. In 1926 the journal absorbed the Russian-language *Finansovyi biulleten'*. With the March issue of 1934 it was renamed *Sotsialistychna Ukraïna* and after the July–August issue it was discontinued. As a government publication, the journal reflected the Ukrainization policies of the 1920s. In its articles the Ukrainian economy was treated as a distinct unit whose interests did not always coincide with those of the USSR economy. With the introduction of the First Five-Year Plan in 1929 and the increased centralization of economic decision-making in Moscow, the nature of the journal changed and its quality deteriorated. In 1932 its editorial board was reprimanded for publishing articles that deviated from the Party line and several board members were persecuted. The editors were H. Hrynko, A. Dudnyk, M. Popov, and Ya. Tun. Among its contributors were well-known economists from Ukraine (such as P. Fomin, L. Yasnopolsky, and K. Vobly) and from Moscow (such as T. Khachaturov, A. Probst, and M. Volf).

Stepan Hostyniak

Hostyniak, Stepan [Hostynjak], b 20 September 1941 in the village of Zbudský Rokytov in eastern Slovakia. A leading Ukrainian poet in the Prešov region of Slovakia, he is the author of six poetry collections: *Proponuiu vam svoiu dorohu* (I Propose My Way to You, 1965), *Lyshe dvoma ochyma* (With Only Two Eyes, 1967), *Virshi* (Poems, 1972), *Buket* (Bouquet, 1979), *Seismohraf* (Seismograph, 1982), and *Anatomiia druhoho oblychchia* (The Anatomy of a Second Face, 1986). He has also published several short stories in the journal *Duklia* and elsewhere. His poetry is characterized by an almost prosaic directness. Everyday situations, objects of daily use, and simple 'feelings' provide the subject of his poems, which are most often renderings in free verse.

Hotuis' (Be Prepared). Illustrated monthly magazine for the members of the youngest age group (6–12 years) of the *Plast Ukrainian Youth Association. From January 1953 to December 1970 it was published in New York and since then in Toronto. *Hotuis'* succeeded *Novak*, which appeared after 1945 irregularly in Germany. Its editors have been L. Khraplyva (1953–70) and A. Horokhovych (1970–). Since the 1970s its circulation has declined from 1,500 to 900.

Hotvald [Hotval'd]. IV-17. Town (1976 pop 20,300), a raion center in Kharkiv oblast. Called Zmiiv until 1976, it was renamed in honor of the Czech Communist leader K. Gottwald. Zmiiv was first mentioned in the 12th century as the Zmiiske fortified settlement. Used by Prince Ihor Sviatoslavych of Novhorod-Siverskyi in his struggle with the Cumans, it was later destroyed by the Mongols. In the mid-1500s an outpost was built there, and in the 1650s the Cossacks built a fort there to defend the vicinity against the Tatars. Zmiiv was a company town of the Kharkiv regiment from 1669 to 1765. It was ravaged by the Tatars in 1688, 1689, and 1692. Its Cossacks took part in the uprisings led by I. Dzykovksy (1670) and K. Bulavin (1707–9). The St Nicholas monastery was located nearby from 1688 to 1788. Later Zmiiv was a county town in Slobidska Ukraine (1797–1835) and Kharkiv (1836–1920) gubernias. It became a raion center in 1923. It has a food industry, and machines, containers, paper products, and building materials are manufactured there.

Household tax (*podvornoe oblozhenie*). A system of direct taxation introduced in Russia in 1679, in which the basic unit taxed was the household. It replaced the tax based on the **sokha* (plough), and enlarged the tax base by including previously exempt categories of the population. The central government set the total tax to be collected from a community and the village or town administration apportioned the tax among the households according to their ability to pay. The household tax was introduced in Left-Bank Ukraine at the end of the 17th century and continued to be collected until the second half of the 18th century.

Housing. Shelter or dwellings provided for the population. In Soviet Ukraine, housing is either socialized property – ie, state (mostly urban) and collective-farm and co-operative (mostly rural) housing – or privately owned. Its ownership, use, size, and costs are governed by *housing legislation, which recognizes four categories of housing: (1) communal buildings owned and rented out by local soviets; (2) buildings leased to state agencies and civic organizations; (3) buildings built by housing-construction co-operatives; and (4) privately owned buildings.

In Ukraine the shortage of housing has been a persistent problem. Destruction during the two world wars, the expropriation of private property by the Soviet state,

Soviet housing policies and inadequacies thereof, and rapid industrialization and urbanization since the 1920s have made this problem acute.

In 1917 there was only 46.1 million sq m of housing space in Ukraine. In the first few years of the Soviet period, seven-eights of new housing was built using private capital, but this activity came to an end with the phasing-out of the New Economic Policy. During the First and Second Five-Year plans (1928–37) the construction of new housing fell by more than half (table 1). Although a 1928 law prescribed a minimum living space of 8.6 sq m per person, this minimum was not attained throughout the 1930s, when it was common for four individuals, and often two families, to share one room. The authorities were forced to rely on the private sector again, and during the Third Five-Year Plan the area of new housing tripled; 59.1 percent of it was built privately. In 1940 there was 97 million sq m of urban housing space, 48.1 million sq m of which was privately built and owned.

TABLE 1
Housing construction in the socialized and private sectors in Soviet Ukraine, 1920–85 (in millions of sq m of general housing space)

		Private		
	Socialized	Urban	Rural	Total
1920–28	5.3 (12.6%)	5.0	31.7	42.0
1929–32 (1st)*	6.6 (57.9%)	1.2	3.6	11.4
1933–37 (2nd)	6.1 (50.0%)	1.2	4.9	12.2
1938–45 (3rd)	14.4 (40.9%)	4.3	16.5	35.2
1946–50 (4th)	14.8 (32.2%)	8.2	23.0	46.0
1951–55 (5th)	15.6 (37.1%)	11.8	14.7	42.1
1956–60 (6th)	32.7 (37.4%)	23.3	31.4	87.4
1961–65 (7th)	42.6 (44.8%)	24.9	27.5	95.0
1966–70 (8th)	50.3 (52.3%)	19.6	26.2	96.1
1971–75 (9th)	58.4 (59.8%)	19.3	20.0	97.7
1976–80 (10th)	60.4 (66.5%)	18.6	11.8	90.8
1981–85 (11th)	62.8 (68.1%)	18.2	11.2	92.2

*Ordinals refer to the corresponding five-year plan.

During the Second World War almost 40 percent of Ukraine's housing was destroyed, leaving 10 million people homeless. In 1946–50 the private sector again built two-thirds of all new housing, while the state concentrated on industrial reconstruction and expansion. The continuing acute housing shortage, however, forced the state to adopt a resolution in 1957 on the development of housing construction and to implement a strategy for accelerating new housing construction. Consequently by the end of 1960 Ukraine's urban housing space increased to 203.7 million sq m, more than double the 1940 figure. In the 1960s the participation of both the socialized and private sectors in housing construction grew, and during each of the Seventh, Eighth, and Ninth Five-Year plans (1959–75) over 95 million sq m of new housing was built. In 1966–70, for the first time since the Second World War, the socialized sector produced more than half (52.3 percent) of new housing space.

During the Tenth and Eleventh Five-Year plans (1976–85) new housing construction fell to slightly over 90 million sq m per plan, of which only a third was privately built.

Capital investment in all housing has grown from 1,702 million rubles in 1960 to 2,746 million rubles in 1975 and 3,883 million rubles in 1985. Between 1961 and 1985, Ukraine's share of the total USSR *capital investment in housing from all sources was 14.0 percent, but of the state's investment in housing, only 11.8 percent. Both figures are significantly lower than the percentage of Ukraine's population in the USSR as a whole (18.6–20 percent during this period). Yet, between 1961 and 1985, 17.9 percent of all new housing and 15.8 percent of new state-financed housing in the USSR was built in Ukraine, indicating that in Ukraine housing construction costs less than in other parts of the USSR because climatic conditions are better, or the construction is of poorer quality, or both.

In 1985 the per capita amount of living space available in Ukraine was above the USSR average by 7.5 percent in urban areas and 19.6 percent in rural areas. (In the RSFSR the corresponding figures were 1.2 and 5.7 percent above the average.) Ukraine ranks fifth among the Soviet republics in living space available per urban inhabitant and seventh in living space available per rural inhabitant. Table 2 indicates that in the early 1980s two-thirds of urban housing was built by the socialized sector, nine-tenths of rural housing was built privately, and over half of all housing was privately owned. In 1985 the average amount of living space per capita in Ukraine was 15.9 sq m (17 sq m in rural areas). The amount of living space in urban centers has grown progressively, from 97.0 million sq m (6.7 sq m per capita) in 1940 to 313.1 million sq m (12.1 sq m per capita) in 1970 and 505.1 million sq m (14.9 sq m per capita) in 1985. The average size of an apartment in Ukraine increased with each five-year plan: during the Fifth (1951–5) it was 42.9 sq m, during the Ninth (1971–5) it surpassed 51 sq m, and by 1983 it reached 54.2 sq m. In official Soviet usage, 'general housing space' includes kitchens, vestibules, utility rooms, bathrooms, closets, pantries, storage rooms, and interior corridors. Hence, effective living space amounts to only 53 percent of the general housing space in Ukraine.

TABLE 2
Housing in Soviet Ukraine (in millions of sq m of general living space)

		Socialized	Private
1980 total	756.3 (100.0%)	308.6 (40.8%)	447.7 (59.2%)
Urban	440.7 (58.3%)	283.4 (64.3%)	157.3 (35.7%)
Rural	315.6 (41.7%)	25.2 (8.0%)	290.4 (92.0%)
1985 total	828.0 (100.0%)	374.5 (45.2%)	453.5 (54.8%)
Urban	505.1 (61.0%)	342.5 (67.8%)	162.6 (32.2%)
Rural	322.9 (39.0%)	32.0 (9.9%)	290.9 (90.1%)

About 80 percent of urban housing in Ukraine consists of buildings with 5 to 12 stories. In the 1960s and 1970s attempts were made, particularly in southern Ukraine, to promote the construction of less massive, Mediterranean-style complexes based on Italian models, but the Party came out in favor of monolithic high-rise complexes constructed using reinforced-concrete building systems. To accelerate this type of construction, a number of industrial complexes were set up in Kiev, Donetske, Kharkiv, Zaporizhia, Kryvyi Rih, and Voroshylovhrad. Today the basic types of housing in Ukraine are apartment buildings (about 90 percent of the stock) in which families reside permanently; hotels in which small families and individuals reside both permanently and temporarily; dormitories for students and transient singles; and special buildings for the handicapped and seniors. In large cities most new buildings have 16 or more stories, and new apartments are better equipped and larger than before.

In rural areas, the most prevalent form of housing today is single-family cottages with three to five rooms and adjacent private plots. Built by private tradesmen from local materials, in appearance and architecture they vary regionally. In the last few years the rate of rural housing construction has slowed down because of the migration of young people to urban centers.

Today the major responsibility for new housing construction is borne by the socialized sector – the state, housing-construction co-operatives, and civic organizations. In 1958 the USSR Council of Ministers decreed that co-operative housing built by local soviets, enterprises, institutions, state farms, and organizations for the use of their members should be stepped up. Buildings put up by co-operatives that date from 1924 belong to their members and cannot be sold or transferred. When a co-operative raises funds among its members to cover at least 40 percent of a project's costs, it receives state credit to cover the rest and the project is included in the state's construction plan. Materials and fixtures are then allocated to the project at the same price as those sold to state building enterprises. The operations of housing–co-operative organizations in Ukraine are regulated by a statute based on the 1958 decree of the Ukrainian Council of Ministers.

Any citizen who can cover 30 percent of an apartment's construction costs can join a co-operative. It is unlikely, however, that co-operatives will prove successful in the future. When professional building organizations put up socialized housing, their workers receive 10 percent of the constructed living space for their own use. Co-operatives cannot offer this incentive. Furthermore, their members are usually more demanding than state inspectors when it comes to quality control and incomplete work. Hence both building organizations and raion executive committees have tended to regard co-operatives as an unnecessary burden, and today co-operatives build only about 6 percent of all housing in Ukraine.

In 1958 the Ukrainian Council of Ministers passed a regulation requiring individual builders in urban centers and construction collectives formed by groups of them to put up apartment buildings or groups of single-unit dwellings, financed with the aid of state credit. Raion soviet executive committees draft and approve the charters of these collectives and usually oversee their operations, using the 1972 Council of Ministers statute regulating housing-construction co-operatives as a model. The statute grants co-operative–housing members apartments calculated at 13.65 sq m of living space per person; if this figure is exceeded, an apartment cannot contain more than one room per family member. Housing construction co-operatives have the same status as legal persons, and the housing built by them is incorporated into the individual-private sector of the housing fund of the Ukrainian SSR.

Official Soviet sources state that today about 80 percent of the population have their own apartments. Much of Ukraine's housing area, however, would be classified in the West as slums, and condemned. Several types of dwellings that are calculated into Ukraine's total housing stock can at best be described as temporary. They include (1) communal apartment buildings, in which several nuclear families that may not even be related and may be of different generations each occupy one room in an apartment and share a kitchen and bathroom; (2) dormitories and youth hostels with communal kitchens and other facilities, which are built and occupied mostly by workers and other young people who have yet to receive permanent housing, and where each resident is allotted not more (and often less) than 6 sq m of space by local authorities; and (3) makeshift barracks and shacks that are thrown up usually by shock workers at their building sites, are left standing after completion of their work, and often end up in the hands of private individuals who rebuild and sell them at inflated prices to young couples who want a modicum of privacy.

Housing construction in Ukraine is plagued with all the problems affecting Soviet industry: poor-quality and ill-fitting materials, shoddy workmanship, limited assortment, and excessive delays in completing construction. Long waiting periods as well as various forms of influence peddling add further aggravations. Even co-operatively built apartments are overpriced (costing the buyer about 15,000 rubles) and require extensive repairs before they can be occupied.

Despite the growth in housing construction in Ukraine, it has failed to keep up with the need for more housing caused by high marriage and divorce rates. That the housing problem remains acute is reflected in a recent CPU CC resolution that in the next 15 years housing construction should be increased so that each person would have approximately 18 sq m of living space, and every family of three to four members an apartment of 50–70 sq m. (See also *Construction industry.)

B. Czajkowskyj

Housing legislation. A branch of civil and administrative law regulating the ownership, rental, and exchange of dwellings (including their sale and inheritance) and the conditions and rights of their use. Article 42 of the 1978 Constitution of the Ukrainian SSR guarantees every person the right to permanent housing, be it in a private or communal dwelling. The main sources of housing law were previously the Civil Code of the Ukrainian SSR (particularly chapter 26), various government resolutions, statutes, and directives, and the regulatory acts of local agencies. Today housing law is regulated by the 'Statute on the Procedure of Assigning Living Space in the Ukrainian SSR' adopted by the Council of Ministers of the Ukrainian SSR and the Ukrainian Republican Council of Trade Unions on 20 December 1974. Instructions and rules for the use of residential buildings are issued by the Ministry of Communal Housing. In January 1983 the Housing Code of the Ukrainian SSR came into effect and it was adopted by the Supreme Soviet of the Ukrainian SSR on 30 June 1983 on the basis of the 1981 'Principles of Housing Legislation' of the USSR and its constituent republics. The code (193 articles in 7 chapters) contains all the norms of housing legislation (state, administrative, and civil law and judicial procedure) that were already operative and scattered throughout various sources, as well as several new norms that supersede

Mt Hoverlia in the Chornohora mountain group

outdated ones or fill in gaps in legislation; the latter regulate the use of privately owned housing in greater detail, as well as the exchange of living quarters, and give building owners relatively more leeway in leases (which are now not renewed automatically but must be consented to by both parties).

Privately owned buildings are limited in size to 60 sq m per family (except for very large families). Private owners have the right to private use of land that is part of the lot on which their building stands. Offices and apartments are rented out on the basis of five-year leases modeled on a lease approved by the Ministry of Communal Housing on 29 December 1962. The ministry supervises the entire housing fund (see *Housing) and partly regulates its use within the framework of USSR and republican laws. Oblast, city, and raion housing administrations are subordinated to the ministry.

Municipal soviets' housing commissions keep track of citizens' housing needs, make appropriate recommendations to their executive bodies, and generally oversee local housing conditions. The lowest rung in the local administration of large communal, official, and co-operative housing is the so-called Housing Exploitation Office found in every building since 1968, when earlier building-maintenance administrations were organized. These offices act in accordance with the 'Standard Statute on the Administration of Buildings' set down by the Ministry of Communal Housing on 2 July 1966. Housing construction co-operatives are regulated as legal entities by the Council of Ministers' statute adopted on 30 June 1985, according to which each occupant is allotted not more than 13.65 m of living space.

BIBLIOGRAPHY
Landkof, S. *Zhytlove pravo* (Kiev 1950)
Landkof, S.; Burshtein, I.; Fel'dman, A. *Zhilishchnoe zakonodatel'stvo SSSR i USSR* (Kiev 1957)
Lisnychenko, T. *Aktual'ni pytannia radians'koho zhytlovoho zakonodavstva* (Kiev 1972)
Holodnyi, M. *Poriadok kvartyrnoho obliku i nadannia zhytla* (Kiev 1977)
'Zhytlovyi kodeks Ukraïns'koï RSR,' *Radians'ke pravo*, 1983, no. 9
'Prymirnyi statut zhytlovo-budivel'noho kooperatyvu,' *Radians'ke pravo*, 1985, no. 10

V. Markus

Hoverlia [Hoverlja]. V-5. The highest mountain in Ukraine (2,061 m); part of the *Chornohora mountain group in the Ukrainian Carpathians. The springs from which the Prut River originates are found here. Hoverlia is marked by postglacial depressions and a rocky peak that gives way to jagged slopes covered with brush and then beech and coniferous forests. Its southern slopes form part of the *Carpathian Nature Reserve.

Hoverlia (4th) Group of the Ukrainian Insurgent Army (Karpatska Hrupa 4 – Hoverlia). Code name of UPA units located on the territory of the (4th) Military District of the UPA-West in Galicia. Until early 1945, this territory consisted only of the Stanyslaviv oblast and Bukovyna; later it included almost all Soviet territory south of the Dniester River – the Drohobych, Stanyslaviv, and Chernivtsi oblasts. It also conducted some operations in Transcarpathia.

From the beginning Hoverlia was the largest and most

active group in Galicia. Most of the UPA training camps in Galicia, including the 'Oleni' officer school, were situated in its mountainous territory. In 1945 Hoverlia was divided into so-called tactical sectors (*taktychni vidtynky*). The Kolomyia tactical sector (known as Hutsulshchyna), the mountainous territory of Kosiv, Kolomyia, Sniatyn, and Horodenka counties, formed a virtual UPA republic in early 1945. It reportedly contained 4 combat battalions and 12 training companies. Another 5 combat battalions were located in the Stanyslaviv tactical sector (also known as Chornyi Lis), the most famous base of UPA operations. Altogether, in early 1945 the Hoverlia Group consisted of 14 combat battalions and an assortment of companies. By the fall of 1945 their estimated total strength was 4,200 men, 80 percent of whom were assigned to the Stanyslaviv oblast. Hoverlia units constituted the bulk of the troops involved in the First (September 1945) and the Second UPA Raid (April 1946) into Czechoslovakia. During 1947–9 UPA combat units continued to operate only on Hoverlia territory. The last two actions by Hoverlia units were a raid into Rumania in June–July 1949 and the ambushing of Soviet troops in Sambir county in July–August 1949. The Hoverlia Group was commanded by Lt I. Beleilovych (*nom de guerre*: Dzvinchuk; 1943), Lt I. Butkovsky (*nom de guerre*: Hutsul; to summer 1944), Kolchak (to summer 1945), and Maj M. Tverdokhlib (*nom de guerre*: Hrim; to 1949).

BIBLIOGRAPHY

Litopys Ukraïns'koï Povstans'koï Armiï, vols 3–4: *Chornyi lis*, ed Ie. Shtendera et al (Toronto 1978–9)

P. Sodol

Hoydysh, Walter [Hojdyš, Volodymyr], b 28 May 1940 in Lublin, Poland. Aerodynamicist and research engineer who taught at New York University (1967–70) and then served as the director of Environmental Engineering Research Laboratories there. He has written numerous papers in the fields of environmental sciences and aerodynamics.

Ihor Hrabar

Hrabar, Ihor (Grabar, Igor), b 25 March 1871 in Budapest, d 16 May 1960 in Moscow. Painter and historian of art; from 1943 full member of the USSR Academy of Sciences and from 1947 of the USSR Academy of Arts. He came from a Russophile Transcarpathian family. His mother was O. *Hrabar, and he was brought up by his grandfather, A. *Dobriansky, in the village of Chertizhne, Prešov region. After graduating from the Academy of Arts in St Petersburg (1898), where he studied under I. Repin, he studied painting with A. Ažbé in Munich (1903–8). From 1910 he lived in Russia, first in St Petersburg and then in Moscow. From landscape painting in the impressionist style he turned in the 1920s to portrait painting in the official socialist-realist style. He edited and wrote some chapters of the six-volume *Istoriia russkogo iskusstva* (The History of Russian Art, 1909–16), which also contains information about Ukrainian art. In 1955 Hrabar visited Transcarpathia and donated 36 paintings to the Transcarpathian Painting Gallery in Uzhhorod. A detailed account of his work can be found in his autobiography *Moia zhizn'* (My Life, 1937).

Hrabar, Konstantyn, b 15 August 1877 and d 1938 in Uzhhorod. Transcarpathian civic and political leader; priest. From 1901 to 1921, Hrabar served in parishes in Transcarpathia. His political career began in 1919 with his election to the Diet of the Hungarian-organized autonomous province of Ruska Kraina. Disillusioned with Hungarian policies toward Transcarpathia, in May 1919 he became a member of the pro-Czech Uzhhorod Ruthenian National Council and of the delegation sent to Prague to pledge allegiance to the Czech Republic. Hrabar served as director of the Subcarpathian Bank (1921–8), and as mayor of Uzhhorod from 1928 to 1935. In 1935 he was appointed governor of Subcarpathian Ruthenia, a position he held until the establishment of autonomy in October 1938.

Hrabar, Olha, b 1846 in Transcarpathia, d ? The wife of Emanuil Hrabar, a lawyer and member of the Hungarian parliament. She was the chief defendant in the trial of Russophiles held in Lviv in 1881. Among the other defendants were her father A. *Dobriansky, I. Naumovych, and V. Ploshchansky. They were indicted for treason, for maintaining contacts between the Russophiles in Austro-Hungary and St Petersburg circles. Hrabar was acquitted of the charges against her and emigrated to Russia.

Hrabec, Stefan, b 14 January 1912 in Stanyslaviv, Galicia, d 25 December 1972 in Łódź, Poland. Polish linguist, professor at Toruń and, from 1954, Łódź universities. His contributions included studies of Ukrainian influences on the Polish language and of the toponomy of the Hutsul region. He was coauthor of *Dzieje języka ukraińskiego w zarysie* (A Historical Survey of the Ukrainian Language, 1956) and, together with P. Zwoliński, compiled a Ukrainian-Polish dictionary (1957).

Hrabets, Omelian [Hrabec', Omeljan] (*nom de guerre*: Batko), b 1 August 1911 in Nove Selo near Liubachiv, Galicia, d 10 June 1944 in Vinnytsia oblast. Prominent OUN leader and UPA commander. He organized anti-Polish demonstrations in Lviv and was incarcerated in 1938–9. In 1941 Hrabets emerged as a top leader of the OUN (Bandera faction) for mid-central Ukraine and in 1943 became commander of the UPA-South. He was killed in action against NKVD troops.

Hrabianka [Hrabjanka] (aka Hrebinka). Noble family founded by Ivan Hrabianka in the second half of the 17th century. Its more prominent representatives were Ivan's son, Hryhorii *Hrabianka, the writer Yevhen *Hrebinka, and his brother Mykola (1819–80), an architect and academician.

Hrabianka, Hryhorii [Hrabjanka, Hryhorij], 1686–1737/1738. A Cossack officer and historian. He held various offices in Hadiache regiment: judge (1717–23), quartermaster (1726–30), and colonel (1730–8). For signing and delivering the *Kolomak Petitions he was imprisoned from 1723 to 1725 in St Petersburg. He died in a campaign against the Crimean Tatars during the Russo-Turkish War. Hrabianka is the author of *Diistviia prezil'noi i ot nachala poliakov krvavshoi nebyvaloi brani Bohdana Khmelnytskoho, hetmana Zaporozhskoho s poliaky ...* (The Events of the Most Bitter and the Most Bloody War since the Origin of the Poles between Bohdan Khmelnytsky, the Zaporozhian Hetman, and the Poles ..., 1710). This work presents the history of Ukraine from ancient times to 1709; almost half of it deals with the *Cossack-Polish War of 1648–57. Hrabianka used various official documents, eyewitness accounts, chronicles, the **Sinopsis* of 1674, the writings of M. Kromer, M. Bielski, M. Stryjkowski, A. Guanini, W. Kochowski, S. Puffendorf, and other works. His chronicle is inspired by the idea of Ukrainian Cossack autonomism. He condemns those Russian voivodes who restricted Ukraine's political rights. The work is known from numerous 18th-century transcriptions. It was published in 1793 in an abridged version by F. Tumansky in *Rossiiskii magazin* and in 1854, using six different copies, by the Kiev Archeographic Commission. The censored parts of the latter version were later published in *Kievskaia starina*, vol 47 (1894). Some scholars – S. Narizhny, for example – expressed doubts about Hrabianka's authorship of the chronicle.

BIBLIOGRAPHY

Hrushevs'kyi, M. 'Ob ukrainskoi istoriografii XVIII v. Neskol'ko soobrazhenii,' in *Izvestiia AN SSSR*, 1934, no. 3

Narizhnyi, S. 'Deistviia prezelnoi brani,' in *Pratsi Ukrains'koho istorychno-filolohichnoho tovarystva v Prazi*, vol 2 (1939)

O. Ohloblyn

Hrabianka Chronicle. See Hrabianka, Hryhorii.

Hrabovetsky, Volodymyr [Hrabovec'kyj], b 24 July 1928 in Pechenizhyn, Kolomyia county, Galicia. Historian. In 1960 he was appointed senior research associate at the Department of Ukrainian History of the AN URSR Institute of Social Sciences in Lviv. His works deal mainly with Ukrainian history of the 16th–18th centuries, particularly the Carpathian *opryshoks. The more important are *Selians'kyi rukh na Prykarpatti u druhii polovyni XVII–pershii polovyni XVIII st.* (The Peasant Movement in Subcarpathia in the Second Half of the 17th and the First Half of the 18th Century, 1962) and *Antyfeodal'na borot'ba karpats'koho opryshkivstva XVI–XIX st.* (The Antifeudal Struggle of Carpathian Opryshoks in the 16th–19th Centuries, 1966).

Hrabovsky, Emilian [Hrabovs'kyj], b 20 November 1892 in Uzhhorod, d 20 October 1955 in Uzhhorod. Landscape painter and graphic artist. A graduate of the Budapest Painting Academy (1918), he produced such works as *A Mountain Landscape* (1914), *A Haystack* (1922), and *Drachyny Landscape* (1922), which depict Transcarpathian landscapes in a lyrical style. In the 1930s, when he lived in Budapest, he stopped painting. Returning to Uzhhorod, he resumed painting in the 1940s and produced such works as *A Mountain Vale* (1942), *Hoverlia* (1946), and *Mountain Meadows* (1951–3). A monograph on Hrabovsky was written by L. Shandor in 1962.

Hrabovsky, Ihor [Hrabovs'kyj], b 1 July 1934 in Mohyliv-Podilskyi, Vinnytsia oblast. Film director and screenwriter. After graduating from the Kiev Institute of Theater Arts in 1958, he worked as a film director at the Odessa Artistic Film Studio and, from 1962, at the Ukrainian Studio of Documentary Films. He became well known when his film *Kermanychi* (Helmsmen, 1965) was acclaimed by critics in London and New York. He also directed such films as *Bukovyna. 28-e lito* (Bukovyna. The 28th Summer, 1968), *Lesia Ukraïnka* (1971), *Vohnennyi shliakh* (The Fiery Road, 1974), and the trilogy *Radians'ka Ukraïna* (Soviet Ukraine, 1978).

Hrabovsky, Leonid [Hrabovs'kyj], b 28 January 1935 in Kiev. Composer. A graduate (1959) of and teacher (1961–3, 1966–8) at the Kiev Conservatory. During the 1960s he became associated with the Kiev avant-garde, a group of young Ukrainian composers, most of whom had studied with B. *Liatoshynsky. He combines elements of the folk tradition with new compositional techniques to produce original musical structures. Much of his work is inspired by Ukrainian, French, German, and Japanese poetry. It includes *Four Ukrainian Songs* (1959) for mixed chorus and orchestra; *Symphonic Frescoes* (1961) for orchestra; *The Sea* for commentator, chorus, organ, and orchestra (1970); a trio for piano, violin, and bass (1964); *Ornaments* (1969) for oboe, harp, and viola; as well as numerous pieces for voice with chamber ensembles, for piano, for violin, and for oboe.

Pavlo Hrabovsky

Hrabovsky, Pavlo [Hrabovs'kyj], b 11 September 1864 in Pushkarne, Okhtyrka county, Kharkiv gubernia, d 12 December 1902 in Tobolsk, Siberia. Poet, translator, journalist, and revolutionary. For his radical populist involvement, he was expelled from the Kharkiv Theological Seminary in 1882 and forced to live in Pushkarne under police surveillance. He was imprisoned and then exiled to Irkutsk gubernia in Siberia in 1886. In 1889, in Irkutsk, he was again imprisoned; released in 1893, he was forced to live in Viliusk, Yakutsk (from 1897), and Tobolsk (from 1899), where he died of a pulmonary illness. Hrabovsky corresponded from prison with Galicia's Ukrainians, who published his poetry and literary criticism in the journals *Zoria, Dzvinok, Pravda, Narod, Zhytie i slovo,* and *Literaturno-naukovyi vistnyk.* As a poet, he rejected 'art for art's sake' and wrote mainly social, political, and patriotic verse; he sought out consonant motifs in the works of many Russian, European, and American poets he translated. His collections of original verse – *Prolisok* (The Glade, 1894) and *Z pivnochi* (From the North, 1896) – and of translations – *Tvory Ivana Suryka* (The Works of Ivan Suryk, 1894), *Z chuzhoho polia* (From a Foreign Field, 1895), and *Dolia* (Fate, 1897) – were all published in Lviv. The collection *Kobza* and the long poem *Khoma Bahlai,* a paraphrase of R. Burns, were published in Chernihiv in 1898. Hrabovsky's works have been republished numerous times in Soviet Ukraine; three volumes of his collected works appeared in Kiev in 1959–60. Studies of his life and work have been written by O. Kyselov (1951, 1959, 1972) and Yu. Bukhalov (1957), as have many articles; a bibliography by M. Moroz appeared in 1964.

I. Koshelivets

Hradyzke [Hradyz'ke]. IV-14. Town smt (1978 pop 9,500) in Hlobyne raion, Poltava oblast. Traces of a settlement of the *Cherniakhiv culture (2nd–5th centuries AD) were found near the town. In medieval times the site was occupied by a fortified settlement (*horodyshche*), which was razed by the Tatars, and from which a later settlement derived its name – Horodyshche (changed to Hradyzke in 1789). At the turn of the 16th century the Pyvohorskyi Monastery was built nearby. In the 17th century the town's inhabitants supported Cossack uprisings against the Poles and the wars conducted by B. Khmelnytsky. A century later many of its inhabitants joined the *haidamaka uprisings. At the end of the 18th century it was a county center of Katerynoslav vicegerency and in the 19th century it declined to a small, provincial town.

Hramota. A charter or a type of legal document or writ particularly common in the Princely era and in the Lithuanian-Ruthenian period. *Hramoty* can generally be divided into three categories: those issued by a ruler or government office, conferring privileges or guaranteeing historic rights; those issued by private parties (wills, testaments, contracts); and those issued by the church. Princes used *hramoty,* for example, to confer privileges on foreign traders (Prince Andrii Yuriiovych's *hramota* of 1320) or Magdeburg rights on cities (Sianik 1339). The oldest *hramoty* found in Ukraine date back to the 12th century (Prince Mstyslav Volodymyrovych's charter of 1130).

In the Grand Duchy of Lithuania *hramoty* granted certain rights to whole segments of the population (eg, nobles or Jews) or guaranteed existing customary-law rights of individuals or groups. In the so-called *land charters grand dukes confirmed the historic rights of whole provinces, particularly Ukrainian and Belorussian, guaranteeing the traditional systems of law. Over 10 such charters from the 15th and 16th centuries, some containing references to even older writs pertaining to Volhynia, the Kiev region, Galicia, and Podlachia, have been preserved. Although these writs lost their legal force when state-wide codes such as the *Lithuanian Statute were introduced, they are nevertheless important as sources for the history of Ukrainian law.

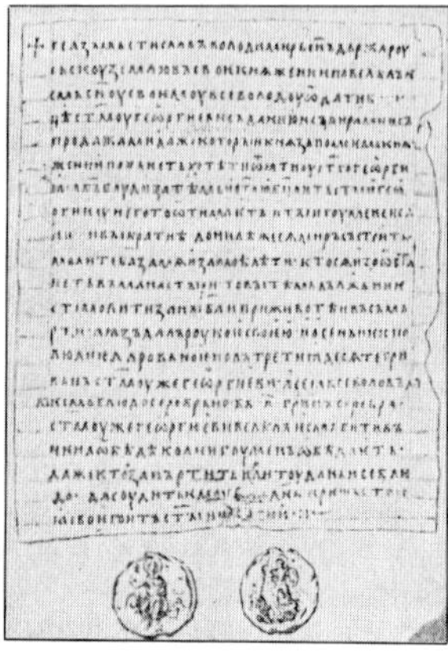

Hramota of Prince Mstyslav Volodymyrovych (ca 1130)

In the Cossack period the Russian tsars and their government offices (*prikazy*) issued various *hramoty,* particularly land deeds to Ukrainian officers loyal to the tsar and to Slobidska Ukraine regiments, often in competition with universals issued by hetmans and colonels. In 1785 Catherine II extended the Charter of the Nobility to Ukraine, thus endowing the Ukrainian upper class with the rights of the Russian gentry.

Individual documents used in church administration, particularly charters of privilege such as stauropegion granted to brotherhoods, also took the form of a *hramota.*

During the period of the Hetman government in 1918, important legal state documents such as the proclamation of a new government and a new provisional constitution, the agrarian reform act, the act of federation with Russia, and the hetman's renunciation of power were called *hramoty.*

Hramoty are important sources for the history of the Ukrainian language because of the greater similarity to the vernacular than is, for example, present in church texts. Their language has its own localized traditions characterized by variations in phraseology and orthography. No private legal *hramoty* from the period of Kievan Rus' have been preserved, except for Mstyslav's charter of 1130, which contains no striking Ukrainian linguistic features. Three charters from 1288–9 are included in the text of the Galician-Volhynian Chronicle. A more systematic collection of *hramoty* from Volhynia dating back to 1350, from Galicia dating back to 1359, and from the Kiev region dating back to 1427 has been preserved. About 100 of the earliest writs from the mid-14th to the mid-15th century were published in V. Rozov's *Ukrains'ki hramoty* (Ukrainian Charters, 1928). Their language was studied by V. Demianchuk in his *Morfolohiia ukraïns'kykh hramot XIV i pershoï polovyny XV v.* (The Morphology of Ukrainian Charters of the 14th and the First Half of the 15th Century, 1928) and by W. Kuraszkiewicz in his *Gramoty halicko-wołyńskie XIV–XV w.* (Galician-Volhynian Charters of the 14th–15th Centuries, 1934). Newer editions – M. Peshchak's *Hramoty XIV st.* (Charters of the 14th Century, 1974) and V. Rusanivsky's *Ukraïns'ki hramoty XV st.* (Ukrainian Charters of the 15th Century, 1965) – uncritically reproduce many texts from later copies or from unreliable publications. Later charters from these territories have been partially published with questionable accuracy in the series *Akty, otnosiashchiesia k istorii Iuzhnoi i Zapadnoi Rossii* (1863–92), *Akty, otnosiashchiesia k istorii Zapadnoi Rossii* (1846–53), *Akty izdavaiemye Vilen-*

skoiu arkheograficheskoiu komissieiu (1868–88), and *Zherela do istorii Ukraïny-Rusy* (1895–1900), and in the publications of gubernial archival commissions, especially in Chernihiv and Poltava.

Of some historical significance are the so-called Moldavian *hramoty* dating back to 1388 and covering the entire 15th century. They were written by Ukrainian and Rumanian scribes in the Ukrainian tradition of chancellary language in Bessarabia and Moldavia. Besides being published in earlier, unreliable editions by V. Ulianitsky and O. Kaluzhniatsky, they appeared in scholarly editions by E. Hurmuzaki (1890–1), A. Yatsimirsky (1907), M. Costąchescu (1931–3), I. Bogdan (1913, 1938), Gh. Ghibănescu (1906–26), and others. They were studied from the linguistic standpoint by I. Bogdan (1908), A. Yatsimirsky (1910), V. Yaroshenko (1931), and I. Ohiienko (1935). Extant charters from Transcarpathia date back to 1404 and have been published and studied by A. Petrov and G. Gerovsky.

G.Y. Shevelov

Hranovsky, Oleksander. See Granovsky, Alexander.

Hrazhdanka [Hraždanka]. Originally a script used for books of a non-religious nature. It consisted of Cyrillic characters somewhat modified to resemble Latin letters and reflecting a general tendency toward simplification. Although it was introduced for Russian in 1708 by order of Peter I, the hrazhdanka to some extent was influenced by the development of the Cyrillic script in Ukraine.

Hrdyna, Yaroslav, b 2 February 1871 in Plzeň, Bohemia, d 2 June 1931 in Dnipropetrovske. Specialist in applied mechanics. From 1902 to 1931 he was a professor at the Dnipropetrovske Mining Institute. He created a new branch of theoretical mechanics, the mechanics of living organisms, which later became the foundation of the mechanics of control mechanisms.

Hreben, Leonid [Hreben'], b 17 August 1888 in Krynky, Belorussia, d 10 July 1980. Veterinarian, geneticist; full member of the AN URSR from 1948. A graduate of the Moscow Agricultural Academy (1924), he was a professor at the Omsk Veterinary Institute (1930–4), and from 1934 he worked at the All-Union Institute of Animal Hybridization and Acclimatization in Askaniia Nova (now the Ukrainian Scientific Research Institute of Animal Husbandry of the Steppe Regions). A specialist in animal husbandry, Hreben (along with M. Ivanov) succeeded in developing improved breeds of the Askaniia Nova fine-wooled sheep and the Ukrainian steppe white swine, as well as introducing a new breed – the Ukrainian steppe spotted swine. Hreben wrote a number of works on selective breeding and zootechnics.

Hrebenetsky, Oleksander [Hrebenec'kyj], b 1875, d ? Teacher, political activist. A member of the Ukrainian Party of Socialists-Federalists, he took part in the Ukrainian revolution and war of independence. After the war he taught geography at the First (Shevchenko) Labor School in Kiev and worked as research associate at the Institute of the Ukrainian Scientific Language of the All-Ukrainian Academy of Sciences. In 1929 he was arrested for having been a member until 1924 of the Brotherhood of Ukrainian Statehood and a cofounder of the *Union for the Liberation of Ukraine (SVU). On 17–19 April 1930, at the show trial of SVU members, he was sentenced to death, but the sentence was commuted to six years' imprisonment. He was rearrested in the mid-1930s and his further fate is unknown.

Hrebin, Avram [Hrebin'] (also known as Hreben), b 8 September 1878 in Berezna, Chernihiv county, Chernihiv gubernia, d 21 December 1961 in Dmytrivka, Chernihiv oblast. Lira player. Having lost his sight at the age of 19, he learned the art of lira playing from the lirnyk, T. Parkhomenko. For the rest of his life he wandered throughout the Chernihiv region. He composed his own songs and set other poets' works to music. Some of his repertoire – 6 dumas, 40 songs, and a few dozen dances – has been preserved on tape at the AN URSR Institute of Fine Arts, Folklore, and Ethnography in Kiev.

Hrebinka (family). See Hrabianka.

Yevhen Hrebinka

Hrebinka, Yevhen, b 2 February 1812 at Ubizhyshche khutir near Pyriatyn in Poltava gubernia, d 15 December 1848 in St Petersburg. Romantic writer. From 1834 he lived in St Petersburg, where he taught literature in military schools and in the Institute of Mining Engineers and maintained close ties with several literary circles. He took an active part in purchasing T. Shevchenko's freedom and helped publish Shevchenko's *Kobzar* in 1840. His works in Ukrainian and Russian first appeared in journals and almanacs in 1831. In 1834 he published *Malorossiiskie prikazki* (Little Russian Proverbs) in Moscow; because of its vivid and pure language, wit, laconic style, and attention to ethnographic detail, it ranks among the best collections of fables in Ukrainian literature. He composed a number of lyrical poems, including 'Ukrainskaia melodiia' (A Ukrainian Melody, 1839) and others that became folk songs. His 1836 translation of A. Pushkin's *Poltava* is a burlesque rendition. Hrebinka also wrote prose and poems in Russian. Among them are some works with Ukrainian themes such as the Gogolesque *Rasskazy piriatintsa* (Stories of a Pyriatynian, 1837), the historical poems 'Getman Svirgovskii' (1839) and 'Bogdan' (1843), the novelette *Nezhinskii polkovnik Zolotarenko* (The Nizhen Colonel Zolotarenko, 1842), and the novel *Chaikovskii* (1843). Hrebinka is thus recognized as a leading representative of the so-called Ukrainian school in Russian literature. In 1841 he published one of the first Ukrainian almanacs, *Lastivka*. His collected works were first published in 1862. His Ukrainian works appeared in 1906 with an introduction by S. Yefremov.

BIBLIOGRAPHY
Kovalenko, G. *Evgenii Grebinka* (Chernihiv 1899)
Zubkov, S. *Ievhen Pavlovych Hrebinka: Zhyttia i tvorchist'* (Kiev 1962)
Tsyban'ova, O. *Ievhen Hrebinka* (Kiev 1972)

I. Koshelivets

Hrebinka. III-13. Town (1970 pop 12,000) and raion center in Poltava oblast, situated on the Orzhytsia River. It was founded in 1895 as a junction of the Kiev-Kharkiv railway and is named after Ye. *Hrebinka. UNR and Bolshevik troops fought each other there several times, particularly in January 1919.

Hrebinky. IV-11. Town smt (1978 pop 8,100) in Vasylkiv raion, Kiev oblast. It has a sugar refinery, a dairy, a mixed-feed plant, and an agricultural-machinery plant. An experimental farm of the All-Union Sugar Beet Institute is located there. The town was founded in the early 17th century.

Metropolitan Floriian Hrebnytsky

Hrebnytsky, Floriian [Hrebnyc'kyj, Florijan], b 1683 in the vicinity of Polatsk, Belorussia, d 1762 in Strun, near Polatsk. Leader of the Ukrainian-Belorussian Uniate church. Entering the Basilian monastic order in 1699, he completed his theological studies in Vilnius Collegium (TH D, 1710) and was appointed archbishop of Polatsk in 1717. He participated in the Synod of *Zamostia in 1720 and vigorously implemented its reforms. Between 1746 and 1748 he administered the Kievan metropolitanate and in 1748 he became metropolitan. He protested Russian discrimination against Uniates and Polish attempts to subsume the Uniates under the Roman Catholic church. On his request Pope Benedict XIV issued *Allatae sunt* (1755), reaffirming papal opposition to the conversion of eastern-rite Catholics to the Latin rite. Hrebnytsky did much to improve the education of the Uniate clergy. Thanks to his efforts, the Pope gave the Uniate church control of the Vilnius Pontifical Seminary. Hrebnytsky summoned frequent episcopal councils to strengthen unity and discipline within the church.

Hrechenko, Vasyl [Hrečenko, Vasyl'], b 30 January 1906 in Kobeliaky, Poltava gubernia, d 14 September 1967 in Kharkiv. Stage designer. A graduate of the Kharkiv Art Institute, from 1933 he worked at the Kharkiv Ukrainian Drama Theater (before 1934 the Berezil theater), where in 1944 he was appointed chief set designer. He designed sets for over 60 plays, including T. Shevchenko's *Nazar Stodolia* (1939), A. Dumas the Younger's *La Femme de Claude* (1938), *Eugénie Grandet*, based on H. de Balzac's novel (1940), Shakespeare's *Othello* (1952) and *Hamlet* (1956), I. Tobilevych's *Sava Chalyi* (1958), and L. Ukrainka's *Kaminnyi hospodar* (The Stone Master, 1966).

Hrechukha, Mykhailo [Hrečuxa, Myxajlo], b 19 September 1902 in Moshny, Cherkasy county, Kiev gubernia, d 15 May 1976 in Kiev. State and party official. He served in the party as first secretary of the Zhytomyr city and oblast committees (1938–9), as member of the republican Politburo (1938–61), and as candidate member of the CC CPSU (1956–61). In the government of the Ukrainian SSR he was president of the Supreme Soviet (1939–54) and deputy-chairman (1954–61) of the Council of Ministers.

Hrechulevych, Vasyl [Hrečulevyč, Vasyl'], b 1791 in Podilia, d 1875. Archpriest of the Kamianets-Podilskyi eparchy. He wrote a popular collection of sermons, *Propovedi na malorossiiskom iazyke* (Sermons in the Little Russian Language, 1849; 2nd edn, 1857), *Katekhizicheskiia besedy na simvol very i molitvu Gospodniu* (Catechismal Conversations on the Confession of Faith and the Lord's Prayer, 1858), *Besedy o semi tainstvakh* (Conversations on the Seven Sacraments, 1859), and two conversations *O dolzhnostiakh roditelei i detei* (On the Duties of Parents and Children, 1859). All these books, despite their titles, were written in Ukrainian and are among the few Ukrainian religious works that were approved by Russian censors.

Hrechyna, Mykhailo [Hrečyna, Myxajlo], b 11 April 1902 in Budyshche, Cherkasy county, Kiev gubernia, d 21 June 1979 in Kiev. Architect. A graduate of the Kiev State Art Institute (1930), he helped design a number of large buildings in Kiev: eg, the Dynamo Stadium (1937, reconstructed in 1956–8 and 1978–9), the Central Stadium (1937–41, reconstructed in 1967 and 1978), the Sports Palace (1960), the Chamber of Trade and Industry building (1964), and the Rus' hotel (1965–79). He also built the Tarasova Hora hotel (1961) in Kaniv. His publications include *Stadiony* (Stadiums, 1957) and articles on architecture and construction.

Oleksander Hrekov

Borys Hrinchenko

Hrekov, Oleksander, b 4 December 1875 in Sopych, Hlukhiv county, Chernihiv gubernia, d 2 December 1958 in Vienna. Ukrainian army general. In the Russian army from 1899, Hrekov graduated from the General Staff Academy in St Petersburg in 1905. During the First World War he commanded various units of the Russian army, and in 1915 was promoted to general. In the Ukrainian army from 1917 to 1919, he held a number of important posts, including division commander, deputy then minister of military affairs of the UNR, and commander of the southern front. From 9 June to 5 July 1919 he was commander in chief of the Ukrainian Galician Army and conducted the successful Chortkiv offensive for which he was promoted to major general. From 1920 he lived in Vienna, where on 30 August 1948 he was arrested by the MVD and incarcerated in Siberia. He was released and returned to Vienna on 23 December 1956.

Hrenivka settlement. A settlement of the early *Trypilian culture excavated in Hrenivka (now Lupolove), Ulianivka raion, Kirovohrad oblast in 1947–8. Uncovered were the remains of surface mud dwellings with stone doorsteps, pottery fragments, and various stone implements and weapons.

Hreze, Volodymyr, b 9 December 1915 in Moscow. Hydrobiologist; corresponding member of the AN URSR since 1967. A graduate of Kharkiv University (1939), since 1959 he has worked as director and branch head at the AN URSR Institute of the Biology of Southern Seas. Hreze specializes in saltwater and freshwater hydrobiology, including the biological activity of reservoirs, the pelagic biological structure of the Black, Mediterranean, and Caribbean seas and Atlantic Ocean, and the trophic structure of plankton in the Ionic Sea. His quantitative studies of plankton production have been used to calculate the renewal of the nutritional base of fish.

Hridniev, Vitalii [Hridnjev, Vitalij], b 7 August 1908 in Uvarovo, Tambov gubernia, Russia. Metallurgist; full member of the AN URSR since 1967. From 1930 to 1941 he worked at the Dnipropetrovske Metallurgical Institute and from 1945 to 1955 at the Kiev Polytechnical Institute. In 1955 he was appointed director of the AN URSR Institute of the Physics of Metals. He has contributed to various areas of the physics of metals: the theory of phase conversions in iron-, titanium-, and copper-based alloys; the low-temperature behavior of metals; and the theory of electro-tempering of steel.

Hrinchenko, Borys [Hrinčenko], b 9 December 1863 at Vilkhovyi Yar khutir in Kharkiv county, d 6 May 1910 in Ospedaletti, Italy. Prominent public figure, educator, writer, folklorist, and linguist. The best known of his numerous pseudonyms are P. Vartovy, V. Chaichenko, B. Vilkhivsky, and L. Yavorenko. For 10 years he taught in elementary schools in Kharkiv and Katerynoslav gubernias. He made an effort to teach children their native language and also wrote some of the first Ukrainian-language school textbooks. He was one of the founders of the *Brotherhood of Taras in 1891. In 1894 he settled in Chernihiv, where he worked at the gubernia zemstvo office and was active in the local hromada. With I. Cherevatenko's financial support, he organized there the largest publishing house in Russian-ruled Ukraine, which published 50 popular-educational books despite severe censorship. In 1902 he moved to Kiev, where the Kiev Hromada entrusted him with the task of compiling a dictionary of the Ukrainian language. In 1906 he became a coeditor of the newspaper *Hromads'ka dumka* and the journal *Nova hromada*. He founded and was first president (1906–9) of the Kiev Prosvita society. In 1904 he was a cofounder of both the *Ukrainian Radical party and the *Ukrainian Democratic party, which merged in 1905 to form the *Ukrainian Democratic Radical party (UDRP).

Hrinchenko's dedicated service to the populist cause began in the 1880s when the prospects of success appeared dimmest. It consisted mostly of journalistic and community work aimed at shaping, in Hrinchenko's words, 'out of the Ukrainian nation one nationally conscious, enlightened community' that would have access to all the achievements of culture and would overcome the gap between the common people and the intelligentsia. His later convictions were formulated in the program of the UDRP, of which he was the author. Among his publicistic works, 'Lysty z Ukraïny Naddniprians'koï' (Letters from Dnieper Ukraine, published in the Chernivtsi weekly *Bukovyna* in 1892–3 and separately in Kiev 1917 under the pseudonym P. Vartovy) is particularly important. Hrinchenko expounded his ideas, based on years of pedagogical and community work, in the books *Na besprosvetnom puti (Ob ukrainskoi shkole)* (On the Darkling Path [On Ukrainian Schools], 1906) and *Pered shyrokym svitom* (Before the Wide World, 1907), as well as in numerous articles in the popular press. He died of tuberculosis and was buried in Kiev. His funeral was a day of national mourning.

Hrinchenko's literary work was directly linked with his journalistic work and was to a large extent subservient to it. In his 50 realistic short stories and tales and particularly in his four novelettes – *Soniashnyi promin'* (The Sun Ray, 1891), *Na rozputti* (At the Crossroads, 1892), *Sered temnoï nochi* (In the Dark Night, 1901), and *Pid tykhymy verbamy* (Under the Quiet Willows, 1902) – he depicted Ukrainian peasant life while raising urgent social questions, the attitude of the intelligentsia to the peasantry, the education and denationalization of the rural population, and the relation between nationalism and radicalism or socialism. 'Sad scenes' of peasant life, dedication to the cause of the people, and the pathos of public duty are the dominant themes of his poetry, which first appeared in 1891. Some of Hrinchenko's plays are historical – *Stepovyi hist'* (The Steppe Guest, 1898) and *Sered buri* (In the Midst of a Storm, 1899). Others deal with everyday, practical issues – for example, *Nakhmarylo* (It Has Become Cloudy, 1897), *Arsen Iavorenko* (1901), and *Na novyi shliakh* (Onto a New Road, 1906). Because of their relevant social content, Hrinchenko's works were very popular in their time, but have become dated. The author's practical motivation accounts for the schematic style of his works. Hrinchenko also translated a number of works by Western European writers including J. von Goethe, F. von Schiller, G. Hauptmann, H. Ibsen, A. Schnitzler, O. Mirbeau, and D. Defoe.

Hrinchenko was a noted Ukrainian ethnographer. His major contributions in this field are the large, well-annotated collection *Etnograficheskie materialy, sobrannye v Chernigovskoi i sosednikh s nei guberniiakh* (Ethnographic Materials Collected in the Chernihiv and Neighboring Gubernias, 3 vols, 1895–9); a collection of Ukrainian folk tales and stories, *Iz ust naroda: Malorusskie rasskazy, skazki i prochee* (From the Mouths of the People: Little Russian Stories, Tales, Etc, 1900); and the first bibliographic guide, *Literatura ukrainskogo fol'klora (1777–1900)* (The Literature of Ukrainian Folklore [1777–1900], 1901).

His interest in ethnography led Hrinchenko to collect material for a dictionary. He incorporated much of this material into the 68,000-word, four-volume *Slovar ukraïns'koï movy* (Dictionary of the Ukrainian Language, 1907–9) that he edited, which contained also materials collected by P. Kulish from 1861 on, the Kiev Hromada, and the editorial board of *Kievskaia starina*. The dictionary is based on ethnographic records and excerpts from literary works published mostly between 1798 and 1870; almost all of it is documented. Until recently it was the fullest Ukrainian dictionary of its kind and one of the outstanding dictionaries in Slavic lexicology. It is prefaced by Hrinchenko's valuable survey of Ukrainian lexicography.

Hrinchenko was involved also in the development of the literary Ukrainian language. In such articles as 'Halyts'ki virshi' (Galician Poems, 1891) and 'Kil'ka sliv pro nashu literaturnu movu' (A Few Words about Our Literary Language, 1892) in *Zoria*, he objected to an excessive infiltration of Western Ukrainian elements into the standard language based on the dialects of Dnieper Ukraine. In accordance with his populist orientation, Hrinchenko took the comprehensibility of an expression to the common people as the main criterion for its acceptability. His observations on the attitude of the peasants to literary Ukrainian as well as his arguments for the free development of the Ukrainian language were presented in the book *Tiazhkym shliakhom* (Along a Difficult Road, 1906; 2nd edn, 1912). In the 1900s Hrinchenko took a more moderate position on Western Ukrainian elements in literary Ukrainian.

The fullest collection of Hrinchenko's literary works is the 10-volume set published by Knyhospilka and Rukh publishers (1926–30).

BIBLIOGRAPHY
Plevako, M. *Zhyttia ta pratsia Borysa Hrinchenka* (Kharkiv 1911)
Smilians'kyi, L. *Borys Hrinchenko. Krytychno-biohrafichnyi narys* (Kharkiv 1930)

M. Hlobenko

Mariia Hrinchenko

Mykola Hrinchenko

Hrinchenko, Mariia [Hrinčenko, Marija] (pseud: M. Zahirnia; née Gladilina), b 1863 in Bohodukhiv, Kharkiv gubernia, d 15 July 1928 in Kiev. Wife and active assistant of B. *Hrinchenko in his civic, ethnographic, and lexicographic work; author of popular brochures and books; translator into Ukrainian of works by such writers as H. Ibsen, M. Maeterlinck, H. Sudermann, M. Twain, H.C. Anderson, E. De Amicis, H. Beecher Stowe, and C. Goldoni. From 1919 she worked as a member of the VUAN Commission of the Dictionary of Contemporary Ukrainian. The second volume of the dictionary was subsequently dedicated to her memory.

Hrinchenko, Mykola [Hrinčenko], b 4 May 1888 in Kiev, d 27 November 1942 in Ufa, Bashkir ASSR. Musicologist, historian of Ukrainian music, and folklorist. A graduate of the Kiev Music School (1912) and the Kamianets-Podilskyi Ukrainian State University (1920), he taught at the Lysenko Music and Drama Institute (1925–33) and the Kiev Conservatory (1934–7). At the same time he was a research assistant of the Chair of Art Studies at the All-Ukrainian Academy of Sciences, and in the 1930s of the Institute of Ukrainian Folklore. In 1933 he was arrested and forced to renounce his 'nationalist deviations.' His publications include several monographs and about 60 articles on musicology and folklore, some of which were republished in a collection of selected works in 1959. His most important work is *Istoriia ukraïns'koï muzyky* (History of Ukrainian Music, 1922), which was republished in 1961 by the Ukrainian Music Institute in New York.

Hrinchenko, Oleksander [Hrinčenko], b 23 June 1904 in Dovhenke, Uman county, Kiev gubernia. Soil scientist. A graduate of Uman Agricultural Institute (1926), from 1929 he worked at the Kharkiv Agricultural Institute, serving as rector (1959–69) and then head of its Department of Soil Science (from 1969). Hrinchenko developed theories and practical methods of increasing the productivity of solonetz and podzol soils of the forest-steppe and the Polisia region of Ukraine.

Hrodzinsky, Andrii [Hrodzins'kyj, Andrij], b 3 December 1926 in Bila Tserkva. Botanist and plant physiologist; since 1979 full member of the AN URSR; brother of D. *Hrodzinsky. A graduate of the Bila Tserkva Agricultural Institute (1954), he joined the staff of the Institute of Botany of the AN URSR in 1957. Since 1965 he has been director of the academy's Central Republican Botanical Garden, and since 1974 academic secretary of the Division of General Biology. His research has centered on the biochemical and physiological interaction of plants in cultivated and natural ecosystems.

Hrodzinsky, Dmytro [Hrodzins'kyj], b 5 August 1929 in Bila Tserkva. Plant physiologist and biophysicist; since 1976 corresponding member of the AN URSR; brother of A. *Hrodzinsky. A graduate of the Bila Tserkva Agricultural Institute (1952) and Moscow University (1954), in 1955 he joined the staff of the Institute of Plant Physiology of the AN URSR. In 1963 he became head of its biophysics and radiobiology department and in 1974 director of the institute. His research deals with the effects of radiation on plant cells and tissues, and their mechanisms for repairing radiation damage.

Hrodzynsky, Morits [Hrodzyns'kyj, Moric], b 26 January 1887 near Berdianske, Tavriia gubernia, d 22 November 1962 in Kharkiv. Jurist, specialist in criminal law and procedure. In 1920 he began to lecture at the Kharkiv Juridical Institute. His chief works are *Obviniaemyi, ego obiazannosti i prava v protsesse* (The Accused, His Obligations and Rights in the Legal Process, 1926), *Dokazy v* *radians'komu kryminal'nomu protsesi* (Evidence in Soviet Criminal Trials, 1933), and *Kassatsionnoe i nadzornoe proizvodstvo v sovetskom ugolovnom protsesse* (Appeal and Review Procedure in Soviet Criminal Trials, 1949).

Hromada. The Ukrainian term for a commune or community – the most basic administrative-territorial unit in any one (rural) settlement. Historically the social and legal significance of the term has varied. It has also been used to refer to church-parish communities and to groups sharing property (to the exclusion of non-members). During the medieval Princely era a community was called a *verv*. Several *vervy* made up a *volost*. Other terms for communities at the time were the *desiatok* (clan), *sotnia* (larger clan), and *tysiacha* (tribe); with time these took on the same meaning as the *hromada*, *verv*, and *zemlia* ('land,' ie, 'domain') respectively, and in the end acquired additional military meanings (see *Desiatskyi and *Tysiatskyi*).

In the 14th and 15th centuries, when *Rus' law was still in effect in Galicia and the Lithuanian-Ruthenian state, many *volost hromady* existed and enjoyed wide-ranging self-rule. The head of each **dvoryshche* (an extended-family group) met with his peers (*muzhiie, liudy*) to elect the leader (*starets* or **starosta*) of a *volost*. The general assembly of a *volost* – the **kopa* – had judicial and enforcement functions (see *Community court), and members of the *volost* were collectively responsible for tax collection and apprehending and handing over wrongdoers. In introducing serfdom (see *Voloka land reform), the nobility of the 16th century broke up the *volost hromady* into individual village *hromady*. The latter retained vestiges of self-rule and fought to maintain their ancient rights, but they lost their autonomy with the advent of Polish-Lithuanian rule and the substitution of Rus' law with *Germanic law. Thereafter the *hromada* was subject to the authority of a **viit* (reeve) designated by the local demesnal owner (a noble, the church, or the king).

In the Carpathian Mountains of Galicia the pastoral *hromady* were governed by *Wallachian law; they elected their leader (*kniez*) and enjoyed self-rule for a much longer time because of their isolation and non-agricultural economy.

In Left-Bank Ukraine, *hromady* existed well into the 19th century. They were either purely Cossack, mixed (ie, consisting of Cossacks and commoners sharing the same rights but headed by a Cossack otaman), or purely peasant-village *hromady* (headed by a *viit* or *starosta*). The otaman and *viit/starosta* were elected and were responsible for convening assemblies to resolve communal matters of administration, justice, and land use.

Because the *hromady* each owned some land, they came to be known as land communities. Allotments of arable land and their subdivision were designated by the *hromada* assembly. In Ukraine, land ownership by the *hromady* diminished during the 18th century; in Russia proper, land ownership by the peasant commune (**obshchina*) had deeper roots and continued up to the 1917 Revolution. The 1861 *land reform and abolition of serfdom in the Russian Empire gave the land *hromady* new relevance: land ownership was granted not to individual peasants, but to the *hromada*, which then distributed the land and had collective responsibility for ensuring that its members paid their taxes and redemption payments. This kind of *hromada* was prevalent in Left-Bank and Southern Ukraine. Not until the *Stolypin agrarian reforms after the 1905 Revolution did private land ownership and use supersede that of the commune. This transformation occurred far more extensively in Ukraine than in Russia proper (see *Land tenure system).

Under Russian rule, the *hromada* as an administrative unit existed in the form of a 'rural society,' and throughout the 19th century it was allowed a minimum of social organization and autonomy. Until 1861, only state peasants could belong to village *hromady*; afterwards, all emancipated serfs were included. The governing bodies of the village *hromada* were the *skhod* (assembly, consisting of the village elders and 2 adult male family heads for every 10 households) and the *starosta*. The *skhod* elected the *starosta* and other officials, set taxes, and resolved various husbandry problems. Nonetheless, the village *hromada* had extremely limited self-rule and was directly supervised by various *volost* authorities. On an informal and extra-legal level the hromada also acted to preserve community solidarity and interests through social control of behavior. Community action (*samosud*) was taken against fellow villagers or outsiders who broke the law or infringed upon local customs.

Under Austrian rule, the West Ukrainian village *hromada* had much more extensive autonomy. In addition to specific functions delineated by various laws, it performed others handed down by the civil administration. The governing organs of the *hromada* were the council and the *viit*. Only adult males who paid taxes or were enumerated in the census as part of a particular professional category could take part in its elections.

During the period of Ukrainian statehood in 1917–20, self-government of the *hromady* was restored and democratized but had little opportunity to develop. Under Soviet rule, the village and municipal *hromady* were replaced in the 1920s by *rural soviets and *municipal governments.

In Western Ukraine under interwar Polish rule the village *hromada* did not, in fact, have its own government but was, in most cases, administered by an appointed government commissioner. The traditional system, however, was not officially abolished until 1933, when a new law concerning territorial self-rule was introduced and several *hromady* came to constitute a **gmina*. The *hromada* was responsible for taking care of its village's communal property and roads, and co-operating with the *gmina* authorities in cultural, agricultural, and health matters affecting the village. The head of the *hromada* – the **soltys* – and its council were elected by all inhabitants of the *hromada* who were 24 years of age or older. The election of the *soltys* was confirmed by the county head (*starosta*), and the entire *hromada* was supervised by the county office and the *gmina* head (*viit*, Polish: *wójt*), who, despite the existence of this legal framework, was frequently appointed in many Ukrainian regions by the commissioner.

In Transcarpathia, each village had a self-governing *hromada*, which elected its *starosta*. Only in matters concerning the administration of the state as a whole (under Hungary and Czechoslovakia) were several *hromady* subordinated to a district notary office.

V. Markus

Hromada (Community). A weekly newspaper published in Lutske, Volhynia, from 1922 to 1926. At first, under the editorship of A. Novynsky (1922–4), it had a general democratic character. From 22 November 1925 it was the official organ of the Ukrainian National Democratic Alliance, edited by M. Cherkavsky. Following the 43rd issue, it was suppressed by the Polish regime. It reappeared as *Ukraïns'ka hromada* and continued to be published until 1929.

Année V. HROMADA № 1.
M. Dragumanov, M. Pavlik & S. Podolinskiy
ГРОМАДА
УКРАЇНСЬКА ЧАСОПИСЬ
Рік V. Число I.
GENÈVE
1881

Hromada

Hromada. Sociopolitical and literary collection published in Geneva from 1878 to 1882 by M. *Drahomanov with the assistance of A. Liakhotsky, S. Podolynsky, F. Vovk, L. Drahomanov, and later M. Pavlyk. Altogether five volumes of the collection appeared: two in 1878 and one each in 1879, 1880, and 1882. They contained theoretical articles advocating a democratic, socialist program, surveys of socioeconomic conditions in Ukraine, literary works, and critical essays such M. Drahomanov's important essay on T. Shevchenko.

In 1881 two issues of a political journal also entitled *Hromada* appeared in Geneva. Its editors were M. Drahomanov, S. Podolynsky, and M. Pavlyk. Its platform, which accepted the necessity of a revolution, was defined more clearly than that of the collection. Besides surveys of political developments in Europe and analyses of socioeconomic conditions in Ukraine, the journal published belles lettres. In 1886 the *Hromada of Kiev, which considered Drahomanov's political commitment untimely and harmful to the Ukrainian national revival in Ukraine, broke off relations with him. Without the hromada's financial support he could no longer publish his collection or journal.

Hromada of Kiev. The most active and enduring hromada in Russian-ruled Ukraine (see *Hromadas). It was not only the chief cultural, and to some extent political, society of Ukrainian intelligentsia in Kiev but also, through its contacts with similar societies in other cities, the most important catalyst of the Ukrainian national revival of the second half of the 19th century. Although accounts vary, it was founded probably in 1859 mostly by students who felt morally obligated to improve the condition of the people through education. The first period of the hromada's history (1859–63) was devoted primarily to *Sunday-school teaching. The students who taught at the Novoe Stroenie School – O. Stoianov, P. Chubynsky, V. Torsky, and the Syniehub brothers – were among the hromada's founders. At the end of 1860 or the beginning of 1861 a **khlopoman* group consisting of V. Antonovych, T. Rylsky, K. Mykhalchuk, B. Poznansky, F. Panchenko, and others joined the hromada. The society did not have a clearly defined program or structure. As stated in its public declaration, 'Otzyv iz Kieva' (A Reply from Kiev, published in *Russkii vestnik* [1862]) signed by 21 members, the hromada rejected revolutionary activity and supported education of the peasants, the development of the Ukrainian language and literature, and separatism. In 1862, at the height of its activity, the hromada's membership reached 200, and included representatives from various social strata – the peasantry, Cossack, clergy, civil servants, burghers, and landowners – and from different nationalities – Jews and Poles as well as Ukrainians. After closing down the Sunday schools in August 1862, the authorities officially banned the hromada at the beginning of 1863. Nevertheless for a whole year it continued some of its activities, such as studying ethnography, customary law, and geography and preparing books for the masses. At the end of 1863 and the beginning of 1864 its members published a handwritten satirical magazine *Pomyinytsia* that contained information about the hromada's membership and activities. When the use of Ukrainian in print became severely restricted by P. *Valuev's circular, the hromada's level of activity declined.

Hromada of Kiev, August 1874; sitting on the floor, from left: fourth O. Rusov, fifth I. Zhytetsky; sitting on chairs, from left: M. Lysenko, M. Chubynsky, I. Nechui-Levytsky, M. Starytsky, O. Levytsky; standing, from left: second M. Drahomanov, fifth M. Kovalevsky, second from right P. Zhytetsky

The hromada renewed its activity in 1869. Its ranks were strengthened by the influx of new members, and included such cultural activists as V. Antonovych, P. Zhytetsky, M. Drahomanov, M. Lysenko, V. Berenshtam, M. Starytsky, F. Vovk, M. Ziber, P. Chubynsky, P. Kosach, V. Rubinstein, I. Rudchenko, Yu. Tsvitkovsky, and O. Rusov. The hromada met on Saturdays at the apartments of its members. It helped young peasants to get a secondary education, and then encouraged them to work as educators in the villages. Its greatest achievement was to establish the *Southwestern Branch of the Imperial Russian Geographic Society, which between 1873 and 1876 completed an astonishing amount of research in the geography, ethnography, economy, and statistics of Ukraine. Most of the hromada's members worked in the branch, among whose nearly 200 associates the most active were V. Antonovych, P. Chubynsky, and M. Drahomanov. Besides scholarly work, the hromada turned its attention to public affairs. It took over the newspaper *Kievskii telegraf, which under the editorship of its members Yu. Tsvitkovsky and M. Drahomanov (1875–6) became the hromada's unofficial organ. In 1876 the secret *Ems Ukase led to new repressions against the Kiev hromada: the Southwestern Branch and the *Kievskii telegraf* were closed down, some hromada members (M. Drahomanov and M. Ziber) were dismissed from their leading posts at Kiev University, and others (F. Vovk and S. Podolynsky) were forced to emigrate. Under the close surveillance of the authorities, the hromada reduced its activities and limited itself to strictly cultural, apolitical goals. As a result it failed to attract members from the younger generation, which began to form its own hromadas in the second half of the 1870s. To distinguish it from the new societies, the Hromada of Kiev began to be called the Old Hromada.

In the 1880s the hromada, led by V. Antonovych, again became more active in the cultural sphere. Its energies were focused on publishing a journal, **Kievskaia starina* (1882–1906), devoted to Ukrainian studies. This unofficial organ of the Old Hromada was financed by V. Symyrenko, V. Tarnovsky, and Ye. Chykalenko. At the same time the Old Hromada built a new monument on T. Shevchenko's grave in Kaniv and republished his *Kobzar* (The Minstrel, 1884). To dissociate itself from M. Drahomanov's political ideas and activities in Geneva, the hromada, which 10 years before had entrusted him with the task of informing Western Europe about Ukraine and had provided the financial support for his publications, broke off relations with him in 1886.

At the end of the 19th and the beginning of the 20th centuries the Old Hromada admitted some younger members, such as Ye. Chykalenko, O. Cherniakhivsky, I. Steshenko, S. Yefremov, L. Zhebunov, Ye. Tymchenko, and M. Levytsky, and intensified its activities. It completed the compilation of a Ukrainian dictionary that had been carried on for many years under V. Naumenko's direction, and published it under the editorship of B. Hrinchenko in 1907–9. Thanks to the hromada's initiative the *General Ukrainian Non-Party Democratic Organization was founded in 1897. Until 1917 it played an active role in organizing *Prosvita societies and some Ukrainian organizations of a national scope such as the *Society of Ukrainian Progressives.

BIBLIOGRAPHY
Miiakovskii, V. 'Kievskaia Gromada,' *Letopis' revoliutsii*, 1924, no. 4
Chykalenko, Ye. *Spohady (1861–1907)* (Lviv 1925–6; 2nd edn, New York 1955)
Riabinin-Skliarevs'kyi, O. 'Kyïvs'ka Hromada 1870-kh rr.,' *Ukraïna*, 1927, nos 1–2
Zhytets'kyi, I. 'Kyïvs'ka Hromada za 60-tykh rokiv,' *Ukraïna*, 1928, no. 1
Nazarevs'kyi, O. 'Do istoriï Kyïvs'koï Hromady 1870-kh rokiv,' *Za sto lit*, 5 (1930)
Savchenko, F. *Zaborona ukraïnstva 1876 r.* (Kharkiv-Kiev 1930; repr, Munich 1970)
Lotots'kyi, O. *Storinky mynuloho*, 3 vols (Warsaw 1932–4)
Doroshenko, D. *V. Antonovych* (Prague 1942)

A. Zhukovsky

Hromadas. Clandestine societies of Ukrainian intelligentsia that in the second half of the 19th century were the principal agents for the growth of Ukrainian national consciousness within the Russian Empire. They began to appear after the Crimean War, in the late 1850s, as part of the broad reform movement. Being illegal associations they lacked a definite organizational form, a well-defined structure and program, and a clearly delimited membership. Because of police persecution and the mobility of their members, most hromadas existed for only a few years. Even in the longer-lived ones the level of activity fluctuated considerably. Members differed in political conviction; what united them was a love for the Ukrainian language and traditions and the desire to serve the people. The general aims of the hromadas were to instill through self-education a sense of national identity in their members and to improve through popular education the living standard of the peasant masses. Members were encouraged to use Ukrainian and to study Ukrainian history, folklore, and language. They read T. Shevchenko's works and observed the anniversary of his death. Each hromada maintained a small library of illegal books and journals from abroad for the use of its members. The larger hromadas organized drama groups and choirs, and staged Ukrainian plays and concerts for the public. The hromadas were active in the *Sunday-school movement: they financed and staffed schools and prepared textbooks. They also printed educational booklets for the peasants and distributed them in the villages. Avoiding contacts with revolutionary circles, the hromadas regarded their own activities as strictly cultural and educational. It was only at the turn of the century that they began to raise political issues and to become involved in political action. With time a generational difference emerged among the hromadas: societies consisting of young people (secondary-school and university students) became known as young (*molodi*) hromadas, and those with older members became known as old (*stari*) hromadas.

Since most of the information about the hromadas is derived from personal recollections and police records, it is spotty and often contradictory. Some hromadas have left no trace behind. The first hromada, established in St Petersburg, was already active by the fall of 1858. It consisted of some former members of the *Cyril and Methodius Brotherhood, M. Kostomarov, P. Kulish, T. Shevchenko, and V. Bilozersky, V. Kokhovsky, O. Kistiakovsky, D. Kamenetsky, M. Storozhenko, M., F. and O. Lazarevsky, H. Chestakhivsky, V. Menchyts, and Ya. Kukharenko. With financial support from the landowners V. Tarnovsky and H. Galagan, works of Ukrainian writers began to be published and the journal **Osnova* appeared. St Petersburg became the center of the Ukrainian national movement at the time. Another hromada outside Ukraine sprang up at the University of Moscow in 1858–9. It maintained close ties with former members of the Cyril and Methodius Brotherhood. By the mid-1860s its membership, which included P. Kapnist and M. Rohovych, reached 60. It was uncovered by the police in 1866.

In Ukraine the most important hromada, the *Hromada of Kiev, was organized in 1859 by students who were active in the Sunday-school movement. It maintained close contact with the St Petersburg hromada. In Kharkiv a student circle that collected ethnographic material formed around O. Potebnia at the end of the 1850s, but the first hromada arose probably in 1861–2. In Poltava a hromada arose in 1858. Among its members were D. Pylchykiv, O. Konysky, M. Zhuchenko, Ye. Myloradovych, and V. Kulyk. Another hromada sprang up in Chernihiv probably at the end of 1858. Its most active members were O. Tyshchynsky, O. Markovych, L. Hlibov, and S. Nis, and its most important contribution to the development of national consciousness was the publication of **Chernigovskii listok*. The Polish Insurrection of 1863–4 led to a strong anti-Ukrainian campaign in the Russian press and to repressive measures by the government. P. *Valuev's secret circular prohibited the publication of Ukrainian books for the peasants. Ukrainian Sunday schools were closed down, and leading hromada activists such as P. Chubynsky, O. Konysky, and S. Nis were subjected to administrative banishment. These measures disrupted the activities of the hromadas for a number of years.

At the beginning of the 1870s the Hromada of Kiev with about 70 members resumed its leading role in the Ukrainian cultural revival. Its activities were disrupted again by the authorities in 1875–6. By this time a strong hromada had emerged in Odessa. Among its founding members were L. Smolensky, M. Klymovych, M. Kovalevsky, V. Malovany, and O. Andriievsky. Most of its members shared M. *Drahomanov's ideas, and some of them (Ye. Borysov, Ya. Shulhyn, D. Ovsianyko-Kulykovsky) even contributed articles to his journal **Hromada*. The society aided Drahomanov and other Ukrainian activists financially, supported Ukrainian publications in Galicia, financially helped talented individuals to gain an education, and distributed illegal literature. By the time it was crippled with a wave of arrests in 1879, the hromada in Odessa had over 100 members. Besides the Hromada of Kiev this was the only hromada that lasted for several generations.

In the 1880s those members of the Odessa hromada who had avoided exile turned to purely cultural activities. They supported the development of Ukrainian theater in southern Ukraine, published collections of the best current works by Ukrainian writers, helped M. Komarov compile *Slovar' rosiis'ko-ukraïns'kyi* (The Russian-Ukrainian Dictionary, 4 vols, 1893–8), and made an unsuccessful attempt to publish a journal. Thanks to a more tolerant governor in the Kherson gubernia, the Odessa hromada was more active at the time than the Hromada of Kiev. In the 1890s a student hromada emerged in Odessa but it did not survive long. The old hromada, under pressure from younger members, gradually became involved in some political activity. In Kiev several student hromadas sprang up in the 1880s: a study circle inspired by Drahomanov's ideas was organized by O. Dobrohraieva at the Higher Courses for Women; a political group guided by M. Kovalevsky advocated a constitutional federation and spread propaganda among students; and several smaller circles were formed at particular schools. In the 1890s L. Skachkovsky organized a hromada of theology students, which consisted of about 30 members including O. Lototsky and P. Sikorsky. In 1895 a student hromada, which included H. Lazarevsky, D. Antonovych, V. Domanytsky, and P. Kholodny, arose at Kiev University. A number of other higher schools in Kiev had their own secret hromadas. There was little contact between the old hromada, which shied away from political involvement, and the young hromadas.

In Kharkiv there was a loosely organized, informal old hromada consisting of such scholars and writers as O. Potebnia, D. Pylchykov, V. Aleksandrov, P. Yefymenko, and his wife O. Yefymenko. A student hromada headed by O. Korchak-Chepurkivsky and including members such as M. Levytsky and Ye. Chykalenko took shape in 1882. Two years later a political hromada that embraced the principles of the Cyril and Methodius Brotherhood and of M. Drahomanov was organized by V. Malovany, M. Levytsky, I. Telychenko, and N. Sokolov. Another politically oriented student hromada was founded in 1897 by D. Antonovych, Yu. Kollard, M. Rusov, B. Martos, O. Kovalenko, B. Kaminsky, L. Matsiievych, and others. By 1899 it had over 100 members, and in 1904 it merged with the illegal *Revolutionary Ukrainian party (RUP), which previously had been founded by the hromada. In Chernihiv a hromada with members such as I. Shrah, M. Kotsiubynsky, I. Konoval, and B. Hrinchenko was active at the end of the 1890s, and in Poltava a hromada was headed by M. Dmytriiev.

Outside of Ukraine a large and active student hromada existed in the 1880s in St Petersburg, whose higher schools attracted many students from Ukraine. Hromada members smuggled illegal literature into Russia, studied Drahomanov's works, organized a choir, and celebrated Shevchenko's anniversary each year. In 1886 some of its members composed a political program and formed the Ukrainian Social Revolutionaries. Towards the end of the 1890s an old hromada was formed in St Petersburg by Ye. Chykalenko, V. Leontovych, O. Borodai, P. Stebnytsky, and others.

At the beginning of the 20th century as students became more nationally conscious and politically engaged, hromadas proliferated in gymnasiums, higher schools, and universities. The Revolution of 1905 drew attention to political issues and loosened restrictions on political activity. The student hromada in Kiev had evolved into a branch of the RUP by 1904 and in 1905 was decimated by arrests. It reorganized itself in the following year and fell under the influence of the Ukrainian Social Democratic party. In 1906 new hromadas arose at Kiev University, the Higher Courses for Women, and the Kiev Polytechnic. In order to gain official recognition these societies avoided political action. The student hromada of Kharkiv (est 1907), with a membership of about 150, was a legal, chartered society. In Odessa there was a short-lived (1903–6), illegal student hromada. Outside of Ukraine the St Petersburg student hromada in 1903 united over 300 Ukrainian students belonging to various school hromadas into one organization. Almost all members (about 60) of this hromada, which was headed by V. Pavlenko, H. Bokii, and then D. Doroshenko, were members of RUP. A small student hromada in Dorpat (Tartu) (est 1898) was headed by F. Matushevsky. In Moscow the Ukrainian student hromada (est 1898) staged concerts and plays and avoided political activities. A small student hromada was organized in Warsaw by V. Lashchenko in 1901.

At the end of the 19th century efforts were made to co-ordinate the activities of the widely dispersed old and young hromadas. At the initiative of V. Antonovych and O. Konysky, a conference of members of various hromadas was held in Kiev in 1897, and the *General Ukrainian Non-Party Democratic Organization was established. In August 1898 the first Ukrainian student conference was held in Kiev and was attended by representatives of young hromadas. A year later the second conference was held. The purpose of the third conference, held in Poltava in June 1901, was to draw the student hromadas into revolutionary activity under the leadership of RUP. A fourth student conference was called in St Petersburg in 1904.

As reaction set in and restrictions on political activity were tightened, hromada members continued to be active in various cultural societies, Prosvitas, and other organizations until the Revolution of 1917. The traditional name hromada was later used by Ukrainian émigrés, particularly students, for their organizations.

BIBLIOGRAPHY
Chykalenko, Ie. *Spohady (1861–1907)* (Lviv 1925–6; 2nd edn, New York 1955)
Vozniak, M. 'Z zhyttia chernihivs'koï hromady v 1861–63 rr.,' *Ukraïna*, 1927, no. 6
Iehunova-Shcherbyna, S. 'Odes'ka hromada kintsia 1870-kh rokiv,' *Za sto lit*, 2 (1928)
Riabinin-Skliarevs'kyi, O. 'Z zhyttia odes'koï hromady 1880-kh rokiv,' *Za sto lit*, 4 (1929)
Hnip, M. *Hromads'kyi rukh 1860 rr. na Ukraïni* (Kharkiv 1930)
Lotots'kyi, O. *Storinky mynuloho*, 3 vols (Warsaw 1932–4)
Z mynuloho. Zbirnyk 2 (Warsaw 1939)
Antonovych, M. 'Koly postaly hromady?' *Naukovyi zbirnyk UVAN*, 3 (1977)
Stovba, O. 'Ukraïns'ka students'ka hromada v Moskvi 1860-kh rokiv,' *Naukovyi zbirnyk UVAN*, 3 (1977)

M. Hlobenko, T. Zakydalsky, A. Zhukovsky

Hromadianka (The Citizeness). The semimonthly sociopolitical organ of the women's organization Druzhyna Kniahyni Olhy. It was published in Lviv from October 1938 to 1939 in place of *Zhinka* (Woman) and *Ukraïnka* (Ukrainian Woman), which had been closed down by the Polish government. The editor was M. *Rudnytska.

Hromadianyn (The Citizen). The organ of the Ukrainian Radical party in Bukovyna, published in Chernivtsi from 10 January 1909 to 1911. It appeared three times a month. In total, 39 issues appeared. The publisher and chief editor was V. Budzinsky, and the editorial board included Yu. Serbyniuk, D. Makohon, I. Popovych, and I. Herasymovych.

Hromads'ka dumka (Community Thought). The first Ukrainian-language daily newspaper published in the Russian Empire. It was published in Kiev by Ye. Chykalenko, V. Symyrenko, and V. Leontovych and first appeared on 31 December 1905. The first day's run of 5,000 copies was confiscated by the authorities, but the newspaper was again allowed to continue. It was closed temporarily by the government in late January 1906 and repressed throughout its existence. The last issued appeared on 18 August 1906, following which it was finally banned by the tsarist government. It published articles on politics, economics, culture, and developments in science, as well as literary works. The chief editor was F. *Matushevsky and the editorial secretary was V. Kozlovsky. Contributors included S. Yefremov, V. Durdukivsky, B. and M. Hrinchenko, and M. Levytsky. Articles by M. Hrushevsky (on Ukrainian political thought in the 19th century), B. Hrinchenko (on education), and V. Domanytsky (review of Ukrainian press in Russia) were published, as well as publicistic articles by O. Makovei and M. Lozynsky, poems and satire by V. Samiilenko, Kh. Alchevska, M. Cherniavsky, and P. Kapelhorodsky, and belles-lettres by A. Teslenko, V. Vynnychenko, and M. Levytsky. In September 1906 the daily *Rada* succeeded *Hromads'ka dumka*.

S. Yaniv

***Hromads'ka dumka* (Lviv).** See *Dilo*.

Metropolitan Oleksii Hromadsky

Hromadsky, Oleksii [Hromads'kyj, Oleksij], b 1882 in Dokudova, northern Kholm region, d 7 May 1943 near Smyha, Volhynia. Orthodox church leader and metropolitan. A graduate of the Kiev Theological Academy (1908), he served as lecturer and rector of the Kremianets Theological Seminary (1918–22). In 1922 he became bishop of Lutske, Hrodna, and Novahrudak and in 1928 archbishop. Appointed archbishop of Kremianets and Volhynia in 1934, he supported the de-Russification of the local church and its independence from the Moscow patriarchate. Under German rule, on 18 August 1941 a sobor of bishops at Pochaiv proclaimed him metropolitan of the new *Ukrainian Autonomous Orthodox church. He then reversed his previous policy and recognized the canonical jurisdiction of the Moscow patriarchy. On 8 October 1942 he met in Pochaiv with representatives of the Ukrainian Autocephalous Orthodox church and worked out the conditions for the union of the two churches. A few months later, he was killed unintentionally in an UPA ambush. His publications include theological studies, two volumes of sermons in Ukrainian, and a historical monograph *K istorii Pravoslavnoi Tserkvi v Pol'she ... (1922–1933)* (Toward the History of the Orthodox Church in Poland ... [1922–1933], 1937).

Hromads'kyi druh (Community Friend). A radical political and literary journal edited by M. *Pavlyk with I. *Franko and the assistance of M. Drahomanov. It was published in Lviv using the *Drahomanivka alphabet. Only two issues of the journal were published (in 1878), and both were confiscated by the Austrian authorities. After its suppression, Franko and Pavlyk published the collections *Dzvin* and *Molot*.

Hromads'kyi holos (Community Voice). A popular monthly, then semimonthly (1906–9), and finally weekly (from 1910) magazine published in Lviv from 1892 to 1939, with breaks in 1914–16 and 1918–21. It was the organ of the *Ukrainian Radical party in Galicia, and then (from 1926) of the Ukrainian Socialist Radical party. Its editors included V. Budzynovsky (1892–6), I. Franko (1896–7), M. Pavlyk (1898–1903), L. Martovych (1904), and I.

Makukh (1905). Under the title *Novyi hromads'kyi holos*, its editors were I. Yaremko, P. Dumka, M. Viniarsky, P. Volosenko (1906–8), D. Katamai (1911–14), O. Nazaruk (1916–18), O. Pavliv (1922–8), and M. Stakhiv (1929–39). The more eminent contributors were I. Franko, V. Stefanyk, M. Cheremshyna, M. Shapoval, and P. Fedenko. Monthly supplements included *Sichovi visti* (1912–14, 1922–4, ed D. Katamai), *Molodi kameniari* (1928–32), and *Snip* (1936–7, ed O. Pavliv).

Hromads'kyi visnyk. See *Dilo.*

Hromashevsky, Lev [Hromaševs'kyj], b 13 October 1887 in Mykolaiv, d 1 May 1980 in Kiev. Epidemiologist; full member of the USSR Academy of Medical Sciences from 1944. Hromashevsky graduated from New Russia (Odessa) University in 1912. He worked in the department of epidemiology of the Odessa Medical Institute from 1918 to 1928, gaining recognition for his work on typhus and cholera. He then directed the Dnipropetrovske Institute of Sanitation and Bacteriology (1928–31) and the Department of Epidemiology of the Central Institute for the Training of Physicians (1931–48). From 1951 to 1963 he headed the Department of Epidemiology at the Kiev Medical Institute; he served also as the institute's assistant director from 1960 to 1970. Most of his publications deal with public health policy and with insect transmission of infectious enteric diseases and seasonal variations in the occurrence of these diseases.

Hromenko (*nom de guerre* of Duda, Mykhailo), b 1921 in Galicia, d ? Prominent UPA officer. After serving in the Nachtigall and 201 Shutzmannschaft battalions, from March 1943 he was a military instructor in various schools and units of UPA-North. For three years he commanded the 95th Company of the Peremyshl Battalion. On 11 September 1947 his company completed a long march across Czechoslovakia and arrived in West Germany, the first UPA unit to accomplish this feat. His personal account of the march was published as *U velykomu reidi* (In the Great Raid, 1956). In 1949 he was promoted to captain. In May 1950 he was sent to Ukraine with dispatches for the Ukrainian Supreme Liberation Council. Three months later he was captured by MVD agents and sentenced to 25 years in a concentration camp. Hromenko was twice awarded the Gold Cross of Combat Merit for heroism and exemplary leadership (1946 and 1950).

Hromnytsky, Pavlo [Hromnyc'kyj], b 15 December 1889 in Hromnytsia, Katerynoslav gubernia, d 23 August 1977 in Prague. Postimpressionist painter. He was a student of I. Repin and N. Dubovskoi and lived in Paris in 1922–5, where he studied with H. Matisse. From 1928 he lived in Prague except for a brief period of imprisonment in the USSR (1945–7). His works include *Poisonous Flowers* (1925), a portrait of I. Horbachevsky (1935), two portraits of O. Oles (1941, 1944) that in 1967 were presented by the painter as a gift to the Writers' Union of Ukraine, *The Builders* (1948), and *Autumn Mood* (1958). Some of Hromnytsky's paintings are found in the collections of the Tretyakov Gallery in Moscow, the Luxembourg Museum in Paris, the Kiev Museum of Ukrainian Art, the National Gallery in Prague, and the Svydnyk Museum of Ukrainian Culture in Czechoslovakia.

Hromnytsky, Sydir (Isydor) [Hromnyc'kyj], b 7 January 1850 in Zahirochko, Bibrka county, Galicia, d 17 December 1937 in Lviv. Classical philologist and civic leader in Galicia. Hromnytsky studied theology and philosophy at the University of Vienna. He taught Greek and Latin at the Ukrainian Academic Gymnasium of Lviv in 1873 and from 1878 to 1906, and in 1906–16, was the first principal of its branch in Lviv. He was a leading member of many Galician organizations, most notably *Ridna Shkola, the *Teachers' Hromada, *Ukrainska Besida, *Prosvita, the *Stauropegion Institute in Lviv, and the Provincial School Council (1914–20). He was also a member of the Lviv city council (1916–27). He was a vice-president and long-time administrator of the *Shevchenko Scientific Society (1884–1903), and an honorary member from 1886.

Hromokliia River [Hromoklija]. A right-bank tributary of the Inhul River, flowing for 102 km through the western part of the Black Sea Lowland and draining a basin of 1,545 sq km. Its waters are used for irrigation.

Hromyka or **Hromeka, Mykhailo,** b ?, d December 1651 in Korsun (now Korsun-Shevchenkivskyi, Cherkasy oblast). Colonel of Bila Tserkva regiment (1649–51). A member of the Ukrainian petty nobility, Hromyka served in the ranks of the *registered Cossacks. During the *Cossack-Polish War of 1648–51, he took part in the battles of Korsun, Zboriv, and Berestechko. He supervised the compilation of new lists of registered Cossacks, resulting from a clause in the Cossack-Polish Treaty of *Bila Tserkva signed in 1651, after the Cossacks' defeat by the Poles. The number of registered Cossacks was to be lowered to 20,000, and those excluded were to be reduced to the status of serfs. As a result the Cossacks in Korsun revolted and killed Hromyka.

Hrono (Cluster). A literary and artistic group, created in Kiev in October 1920, under the leadership of V. Polishchuk. It opposed the 'proletarian' ideology of other groups and called for a 'synthesis of existing trends' and the 'harmonious coexistence of the collective and the individual' ('Credo' in the collection *Hrono*, 1920). Other members of the group were P. Fylypovych, H. Kosynka, G. Shkurupii, V. Cherniakhivska, M. Tereshchenko, D. Zahul, K. Kotko, M. Stasenko, and the artists M. Burachek, M. Kyrnarsky, V. Levandovsky, S. Pozharsky, and H. Narbut. The group's activity was short-lived, lasting only until 1921.

Hrozin, Borys, b 16 October 1898 in Kiev, d 22 October 1962 in Kiev. Metallurgist; corresponding member of the AN URSR from 1939. He worked in various metallurgical institutes in Ukraine developing methods of studying the mechanical properties of tempered steel and of prolonging the life of machine parts, and studying the surface properties of metals. He pioneered the use of radioactive isotopes in the study of wear of machine components.

Hrubeshiv [Hrubešiv] (Polish: Hrubieszów). III-4. Town (1974 pop 16,300) and county town in Lublin voivodeship, Poland, situated on the Huchva River in the Kholm region. First mentioned in the 14th century as a royal village, in 1400 it was granted the rights of Magdeburg law. It was destroyed by the Tatars in 1498. For centuries it had been a center of Ukrainian life in the southeastern Kholm region. In 1893 it had a population of 9,600, of which 5,260 were Jews, 3,260 were Orthodox, and 1,070 were Catholic. In the interwar period Ukrainians constituted 38 percent, Ukrainian-speaking Roman Catholics 20 percent, and Poles 32 percent of the population. In May 1946 Hrubeshiv was the site of an encounter between UPA and Polish underground units and Soviet and Polish government forces. That same year most of the county's Ukrainians were forcibly resettled in the Ukrainian SSR.

Volodymyr Hrudyn

Hrudyn, Volodymyr (Groudine, Vladimir), b 1893 in Kiev, d 14 November 1980 in Philadelphia. Pianist, composer, and pedagogue. A graduate of the Kiev (R. Glière's class) and Odessa conservatories, he taught music at the Kiev Conservatory and the Lysenko Music and Drama Institute, then at the Lysenko Higher Institute of Music in Lviv, and after the Second World War in Prague, Paris, and New York. His compositions include a symphony, two orchestral and four piano suites, two concertos for piano and orchestra, two violin sonatas and one for piano, two trios, a string quartet, and some songs. Some of his piano works were published in 1962 by Paragon.

Hrudyna, Dmytro, 1898–1937. Soviet drama critic of the 1920s and 1930s. He worked briefly as an actor and later headed the theater department of the Committee for the Arts at the Council of People's Commissars of the Ukrainian SSR. In his articles, which appeared in *Krytyka, Nove mystetstvo,* and *Radians'kyi teatr,* he attacked any strivings for new artistic forms, and particularly the *Berezil theater directed by L. Kurbas. With the introduction of the Russification policy, he was arrested. He died in exile.

Hrun-Tashan River [Hrun'-Tašan']. A left-bank tributary of the Psol River in Poltava oblast, created by the confluence of the Hrun and Tashan rivers. It is 91 km long, and its basin area is 1,870 sq km.

Hrunsky, Mykola [Hruns'skyj], b 10 October 1872 in Sumy, Kharkiv gubernia, d 13 August 1951 in Kiev. Linguist, Slavist. A graduate of Kharkiv University (1896), he was appointed professor at Kiev University (1915). He published *Ocherki po istorii razrabotki sintaksisa slavianskikh iazykov* (Outlines of the History of Development of the Syntax of Slavic Languages, 2 vols, 1910–11); a number of studies of the Freising Fragments, the Kiev Glagolitic Folios, and the Glagolitic alphabet; a prose translation with commentary on *Slovo o polku Ihorevi* (1952); and a number of textbooks in Church Slavonic, the history of the Ukrainian language, and contemporary Ukrainian orthography.

Hrushetsky, Antin [Hrušec'kyj], b 1734 in Volhynia, d 1798 in Suprasl (now Poland). Painter. Trained in Kamianets-Podilskyi and Lviv, he entered the Basilian monastery in Pochaiv in 1751 as an experienced painter and devoted himself to icon painting. In 1760 he moved to Cracow, and then to Warsaw, where he did some paintings for King Stanislaus II Augustus Poniatowski, and to Suprasl, where the iconostasis that he painted has become famous. Some of his works were well known in their time: eg, *The Penitent Mary Magdalene* (1754), *The Three Kings* (1783), and *The Golden Calf* (undated). His paintings *Madonna* and *The Dance of the Nymphs* were displayed in 1894 at an exhibition in Lviv. His painting technique shows that he was familiar with post-renaissance Italian painting.

Hrushetsky, Ivan [Hrušec'kyj], b 22 August 1904 in Komyshuvakha, Verkhodniprovske county, Katerynoslav gubernia. Communist party official. After beginning his political career in the 1920s in Zaporizhia oblast, he became a deputy to the USSR Supreme Soviet in 1937 and to the Ukrainian SSR Supreme Soviet in 1938. From 1938 to 1961 he served as secretary of oblast CP(B)U executive committees in Dnipropetrovske, Stanyslaviv, Chernivtsi, Lviv, and Volhynia. He was made a member of the CC CPU in 1952 and again in 1960, and of the CC CPSU in 1961. In 1972 he became a member of the Politburo of the CPU, chairman of the Presidium of the Supreme Soviet of the Ukrainian SSR, and deputy chairman of the Presidium of the USSR Supreme Soviet. He retired from these positions in 1976.

Hrusheve Monastery. Orthodox monastery dedicated to St Michael in Hrusheve village in eastern Transcarpathia. Established in the 12th century, it obtained the right of stauropegion in 1391 and became an important religious and cultural center with a library, school, and printing press. In 1404 it was endowed with three villages: Hrusheve, Teresva, and Kryve. With the advancement of Catholicism in Transcarpathia the monastery lost its estates in 1660 and was razed during I. Thököly's uprising against the Habsburgs (ca 1680).

Hrushevska, Kateryna [Hruševs'ka], b 1900 in Lviv, d 1953 in exile, probably in Siberia. Ethnographer and

Kateryna Hrushevska

sociologist; daughter of M. Hrushevsky. In the 1920s she worked at the VUAN as head of the Commission of Historical Songs and of the Cabinet of Primitive Culture, and as secretary of the Cultural-Historical Commission. In the early 1930s she shared her father's exile in Moscow. After his death in 1934, she resumed her scholarly work as a research associate of the AN URSR Institute of Literature. Her best work was published in *Pervisne hromadianstvo ta ioho perezhytky na Ukraïni* (1926–30), a journal that she edited. She was the editor of two important collections: *Z prymityvnoï kul'tury: Rozvidky i dopovidi* (From Primitive Culture: Studies and Lectures, 1924), with a foreword by M. Hrushevsky, and *Z prymityvnoho hospodarstva* (From Primitive Economy, 1927). Her chief accomplishment was the collection *Ukraïns'ki narodni dumy: Korpus* (Ukrainian Folk Dumas: The Corpus, 2 vols, 1927, 1931); volume three of the planned six-volume set was ready for publication but was confiscated by the Soviet authorities. She also took an interest in non-Ukrainian folklore and wrote *Prymityvni opovidannia: Kazky i baiky Afryky ta Ameryky* (Primitive Stories: The Tales and Fables of Africa and America, 1923). After her father's death she prepared for publication his manuscripts, particularly the subsequent volumes of *Istoriia Ukraïny-Rusy* (The History of Ukraine-Rus') and *Istoriia ukraïns'koï literatury* (The History of Ukrainian Literature). In August 1937 Hrushevska was arrested and sent to a concentration camp in Nogaisk. Her manuscripts were destroyed. Although some of her works are approved in the Soviet Union, she has not been rehabilitated.

M. Hnatiukivsky

Hrushevska, Mariia [Hrushevs'ka, Marija] (neé Voiakovska), b ca 1870, Bohdanivka, Skalat county, Galicia, d 1953. Civic leader and pedagogue in Lviv and Kiev; the wife of M. *Hrushevsky. Hrushevska was an associate of the journal *Literaturno-naukovyi vistnyk*, in which she also published her translations of French works. In 1917 she was a member of the Central Rada and of the Ukrainian National Theater Committee.

Hrushevska-Shamrai, Hanna. See Shamrai, Hanna.

Hrushevsky, Mykhailo [Hruševʼkyj, Myxajlo], b 29 September 1866 in Kholm, d 25 November 1934 in Kislovodsk, North Caucasus krai, RSFSR. The most distinguished Ukrainian historian; principal organizer of Ukrainian scholarship, prominent civic and political leader, publicist, and writer; member of the *Shevchenko Scientific Society (NTSh) from 1894, the VUAN from 1923, and the USSR Academy of Sciences from 1929. Hrushevsky's father, Serhii, was a Slavist and pedagogue. In 1869 the family moved to the Caucasus where Hrushevsky graduated from the classical gymnasium in Tiflis (1886). While still a gymnasium student he began to write belle lettres in Ukrainian; his first publication was a story that appeared in the newspaper *Dilo* in 1885. Hrushevsky graduated in 1890 from the Historical-Philological Faculty at Kiev University where he was a student of V. *Antonovych. His first scholarly publications were 'Iuzhnorusskie gospodarskie zamki v polovine XVI v.' (South Ruthenian Feudal Castles in the Mid-16th Century), *Kievskie universitetskie izvestiia*, 1890; 'Volynskii vopros 1077–1102' (The Volhynian Question, 1077–1102), *Kievskaia starina*, no. 33 (1891); and 'Hromads'kyi rukh na Ukraïni-

Mykhailo Hrushevsky

Rusi v XIII vitsi' (The Social Movement in Ukraine-Rus' in the 13th Century), *Zapysky NTSh*, 1 (1892). He remained at Kiev University to prepare his candidate's thesis, published as *Ocherk istorii kievskoi zemli ot smerti Iaroslava do kontsa XIV veka* (A Survey of the History of the Kiev Land from the Death of Yaroslav to the End of the 14th Century, 1891), and then received a master's degree for the dissertation 'Barskoe starostvo: Istoricheskie ocherki' (The Bar County: Historical Survey), published in 1894. In 1894, on the recommendation of V. Antonovych, Hrushevsky was appointed professor of the newly created chair of Ukrainian history (officially it was called The Second Chair of Universal History, with special reference to the History of Eastern Europe) at Lviv University.

Upon arriving in Lviv Hrushevsky became active in the NTSh. He became the director of the Historical-Philosophical Section in 1894, and in 1897 he was elected president. With extraordinary energy he reorganized the NTSh, which under his leadership became akin to an academy of sciences. He collected funds, founded a library and museum, initiated scholarly contacts with a host of academic bodies, and gathered around him many scholars, including his close collaborator for many years, I. *Franko. Under Hrushevsky's editorship (1895–1913) the major journal of the NTSh, *Zapysky NTSh*, was transformed from an annual to a quarterly and then a bimonthly publication. In 1895 he established the Archeographic Commission of NTSh, which published documents and sources for Ukrainian history in its serials *Zherela do istoriï Ukraïny-Rusy* and *Pam'iatky ukraïns'ko-rus'koï movy i literatury*. Much of Hrushevsky's own work was published in these journals and later republished in *Rozvidky i materiialy do istoriï Ukraïny-Rusy* (Research and

Materials toward a History of Ukraine-Rus', 5 vols, 1896–1905). In Lviv Hrushevsky developed a school of Ukrainian history with historians such as S. Tomashivsky, O. Terletsky, M. Korduba, I. Krypiakevych, V. Herasymchuk, I. Dzhydzhora, I. Krevetsky, D. Korenets, and O. Tselevych.

In 1898, together with I. Franko and V. *Hnatiuk, he founded *Literaturno-naukovyi visnyk*, the most important forum for Ukrainian literature and political discussion of its time. Hrushevsky was also one of the organizers of the Ukrainian Publishing Association (1899) and the *Society of Friends of Ukrainian Scholarship, Literature, and Art (1904). Hrushevsky's contribution to the development of Ukrainian education in Galicia deserves particular attention. From 1908 he headed the *Teachers' Hromada and from 1910 the *Provincial School Union. Soon after arriving in Lviv he began to work towards the creation of a Ukrainian university there, beginning with the organization of popular lecture series and a summer school.

In 1898 the first volume of his monumental *Istoriia Ukraïny-Rusy* (History of Ukraine-Rus') was published in Lviv; by 1937 another nine volumes, covering Ukrainian history to 1658, had appeared in Lviv and Kiev. This work was the first major synthesis of Ukrainian history ever written. In 1904 his *Ocherk istorii ukrainskogo naroda* (Survey of the History of the Ukrainian People) was published in St Petersburg (2nd edn, 1906; 3rd edn, 1911). A general overview of Ukrainian history, this work was based on the course he had taught at the Russian Higher School of Social Studies in Paris in the spring of 1903. It was republished with some changes in a more popular form as *Iliustrovana istoriia Ukraïny* (Illustrated History of Ukraine; the first of several Ukrainian editions appeared in 1911, and a Russian version was published in 1912). Subsequently, versions of these popular histories appeared in German, French, English, Bulgarian, and Czech.

In 1904, in a collection of the Russian Imperial Academy of Sciences, *Sbornik statei po slavianovedeniiu*, vol 1, Hrushevsky published perhaps his most important essay, titled 'Zvychaina skhema "ruskoï" istoriï i sprava ratsional'noho ukladu istoriï skhidn'oho slov'ianstva' (The Traditional Scheme of 'Russian' History and the Problem of a Rational Ordering of the History of the Eastern Slavs). In this article Hrushevsky traced the history of Ukraine and of the Ukrainian people to the period of Kievan Rus' and argued that the history of the Ukrainian nation is distinct from that of the Russian both in its origin and in its political, economic, and cultural development (the German translation of the article appeared in 1935, and the English in 1952). Although the argument was rejected by most Russian historians, who believed that the modern Russian state was the only direct descendant of Kievan Rus' and did not accept that the Ukrainian nation had developed as a result of a separate and unique history, Hrushevsky's scheme and periodization of Ukrainian history was accepted, with some changes, by most Ukrainian historians, including those in Soviet Ukraine (until 1929), and in the emigration as the basic scheme of Ukrainian national historiography.

As a student and during his first years in Lviv, Hrushevsky devoted most of his energy to organizing Ukrainian scholarly and cultural life. In Kiev he worked closely with V. Antonovych, O. *Konysky, and other activists of the older generation associated with the Hromada of Kiev. In Galicia he began to play a more active role in Ukrainian political life. In 1899 he was one of the founders of the *National Democratic party, although he quit the party soon afterwards. Hrushevsky's real political activity, however, began only after the 1905 Revolution in Russia, which resulted in the easing of restrictions on Ukrainian life and the emergence of mass Ukrainian organizations and political parties. From then on Hrushevsky spent most of his time in Russian-ruled Ukraine, although he remained a professor of Lviv University until 1913.

Hrushevsky was a prolific publicist. In 1906 in St Petersburg he helped found and was a regular contributor to *Ukrainskii vestnik*, the official organ of the Ukrainian club of the State Duma. His articles on Ukrainian and international political affairs appeared in various other Ukrainian and Russian publications (especially *Literaturno-naukovyi visnyk* and *Ukrainskaia zhizn'*) and in several separate collections, including *Z bizhuchoï khvyli* (From the Current Wave, 1906), *Osvobozhdenie Rossii i ukrainskii vopros* (The Liberation of Russia and the Ukrainian Question, 1907), *Nasha polityka* (Our Politics, 1911), in which he sharply criticized the leaders of the National Democratic party in Galicia, and *Vil'na Ukraïna* (Free Ukraine, 1917).

After a brief stay in St Petersburg, Hrushevsky transferred his activities to Kiev, where in 1907 he began to publish *Literaturno-naukovyi visnyk*. In 1907 he also cofounded the *Ukrainian Scientific Society, modeled on the NTSh, serving as its first head and coeditor of its journals *Zapysky ukraïns'koho naukovoho tovarystva v Kyievi* and *Ukraïna* (from 1914). In order to foster Ukrainian national consciousness among the peasantry, Hrushevsky founded and published the popular newspaper *Selo* (1909–11); when this was closed down by the Russian government, he established *Zasiv* (1911–12). In 1908 Hrushevsky was one of the founding members of the *Society of Ukrainian Progressives, emerging as the universally acknowledged leader of the Ukrainian movement.

During the First World War, when the Russian government again clamped down on Ukrainian activities, Hrushevsky was arrested in the fall of 1914. After a two-month imprisonment in Kiev, he was exiled to Simbirsk, then to Kazan, and finally to Moscow, where he remained under police surveillance. Despite this repression he continued his scholarly work and even helped edit *Ukrainskaia zhizn'* and the Ukrainian-language weekly *Promin'*.

Hrushevsky was released from exile after the February Revolution of 1917 and he quickly emerged as the leader of the Ukrainian national revolution. On 17 March, while still in Moscow, he was elected chairman of the *Central Rada. Under his direction, this body soon became the revolutionary parliament of Ukraine. In 1917 Hrushevsky became a supporter of the newly formed *Ukrainian Party of Socialist Revolutionaries (UPSR), the majority party in the Central Rada. On 29 April 1918, he was elected president of the UNR.

A coup d'état led by P. *Skoropadsky overthrew the government of the UNR. This ended Hrushevsky's involvement in government, although he continued his political activities, especially in the UPSR, and his publicistic work (in 1918 he published the collection *Na porozi novoï Ukraïny: Hadky i mriï* [On the Threshold of a New Ukraine: Thoughts and Dreams]). In 1919 he emigrated and increased his political-publicistic activities as a member of the Foreign Delegation of the UPSR. For the next few years he traveled widely in Western Europe trying to rally support for the Ukrainian independence movement and re-establishing scholarly contacts. In 1919 he founded the *Ukrainian Sociological Institute in Vienna (later moved to Prague), which published, among others, his works *Pochatky hromadianstva (henetychna sotsiolohiia)* (The Beginnings of Society [Genetic Sociology], 1921), *Z pochatkiv ukraïns'koho sotsiialistychnoho rukhu: Mykhailo Drahomanov i zhenevs'kyi sotsiialistychnyi hurtok* (On the Beginnings of the Ukrainian Socialist Movement: Mykhailo Drahomanov and the Geneva Socialist Group, 1922), and *Z istoriï relihiinoï dumky na Ukraïni* (On the History of Religious Thought in Ukraine, 1925). He also began his monumental *Istoriia ukraïns'koï literatury* (The History of Ukrainian Literature) and edited the organ of the UPSR **Boritesia–Poborete* (1920–2). His political writings of this period show his increasing reconciliation with Communist rule in Ukraine and his desire to return to Ukraine to continue his scholarly and civic work; he was especially encouraged by the announcement of *Ukrainization and the *New Economic Policy.

In 1923 Hrushevsky was elected a full member of the VUAN and he left for Kiev in early 1924. This action was severely criticized by most of the Ukrainian political émigrés. At the VUAN, Hrushevsky soon resumed his role as the central figure in Ukrainian scholarship. He assumed leadership of the VUAN archeographic commission, organized a series of academic commissions to research Ukrainian history and folklore, and directed the training of new historians as the holder of the Chair of Modern Ukrainian History. He revived and edited **Ukraïna* (1924–30), which became the main organ of Ukrainian studies. He was also the editor of *Naukovyi zbirnyk Istorychnoï sektsiï VUAN* (1924–9) and the collections **Za sto lit* (6 vols, 1927–30), *Studiï z istoriï Ukraïny* (3 vols, 1926–30), and *Ukraïnskyi arkhiv* (3 vols, 1929–31). In Kiev, Hrushevsky continued work on his major syntheses of Ukrainian history and literature. In 1926 Ukraine solemnly celebrated Hrushevsky's 60th birthday and the 40th anniversary of his scholarly work. That same year, collaboration was renewed between the NTSh and VUAN.

Despite Hrushevsky's great achievements in this period, opposition to him grew steadily in official circles and among Marxist scholars. Increasingly, his historical scheme was rejected as 'nationalistic,' and he was criticized for not adopting the official Soviet Marxist interpretation of Ukrainian history. In 1929 these attacks increased, and Hrushevsky was progressively forced to withdraw from his work in the VUAN. In March 1931 he was exiled to Moscow. Subsequently, the institutions that he had founded at the VUAN were closed, the serials that he edited ceased publication, and most of his students and co-workers were arrested and deported. By 1934, the school of history he had founded in Soviet Ukraine was destroyed. Still, Hrushevsky remained a productive scholar in his last years, working mostly on Ukrainian historiography of the 17th and 18th centuries; his last two articles were published in periodicals of the USSR Academy of Sciences in 1932 and 1934. Eventually, the difficult conditions of life in semi-freedom abroad and the further persecutions by the Soviet regime led to a deterioration of Hrushevsky's health. He died in Kislovodsk, where he had gone for medical treatment, and was buried in Kiev in the Baikove cemetery.

Hrushevsky's historical approach was formed under the influence of his professor, V. Antonovych, as well as M. *Kostomarov, M. *Drahomanov, and later E. Durkheim. He belonged to the populist school of Ukrainian historiography and stressed the primacy of social or popular interests over the interests of the state and the nation. Later in his career, perhaps as a result of his own political activities, Hrushevsky began to attach more importance to the state and the political development of the Ukrainian nation. He rejected the *Normanist theory of early Ukrainian history, and considered the Antes the predecessors of the Ukrainian nation. Using a wide variety of sources, Hrushevsky outlined the ethnogenesis of the Ukrainian nation and established the continuity of Ukrainian historical processes, even throughout the periods of Ukrainian statelessness. His historical scheme was adopted by some non-Ukrainian historians (eg, O. Presniakov, M. Liubavsky, O. Halecki).

Hrushevsky also did considerable work in the history of literature. At first this entailed short digressions in *Istoriia Ukraïny-Rusy*; later he turned his full attention to this topic in the important *Istoriia ukraïns'koï literatury* (History of Ukrainian Literature, 5 vols, 1922–7; vols 6 and 7 remained unpublished), which examined Ukrainian literature up to the beginning of the 17th century in relation to the development of culture. He also wrote numerous articles of literary criticism and reviews. In his *Istoriia Ukraïny-Rusy*, as well as in *Kul'turno-natsional'nyi rukh na Ukraïni v XVI–XVII vitsi* (The Cultural-National Movement in Ukraine in the 16th–17th Centuries, 1912; 2nd edn, 1920) and a series of his lesser works, Hrushevsky examined the development of education, religious life, art, printing, and other facets of Ukrainian culture. A number of his works were devoted to ethnography, folklore, and sociology. Hrushevsky also worked in archeology, publishing a series of articles and attempting the first synthesis of the archeology of Ukraine in vols 1–3 of *Istoriia Ukraïny-Rusy*.

As a belletrist, Hrushevsky wrote tales, dramas, and short stories (many appeared in the collection *Pid zoriamy: Opovidannia, nacherky, zamitky, istorychni obrazy* [Under the Stars: Stories, Sketches, Notes, Historical Portraits, 1928]). In total, Hrushevsky wrote over 1,800 works. His bibliography to 1904, compiled by I. Levytsky, is given in *Naukovyi Zbirnyk prysviachenyi profesorovy Mykhailovy Hrushevs'komu uchenykamy i prykhyl'nykamy* (A Scholarly Collection Dedicated to Professor Mykhailo Hrushevsky by his Students and Friends, Lviv 1906), and a bibliography of his works from 1905 to 1928 is given in *Iuvileinyi zbirnyk na poshanu akademika Mykhaila Serhiievycha Hrushevs'koho* (A Jubilee Collection in Honor of the Academician Mykhailo Serhiievych Hrushevsky, Kiev 1929).

Hrushevsky's accomplishments, as the scholar who realized the principal task of Ukrainian historiography (ie, the synthesis of the entire Ukrainian historical process), as the organizer of Ukrainian national scholarship, and as a civic and political activist and one of the most prominent figures of the period of the liberation struggle, provoked the Bolsheviks to take a sharply negative attitude towards him, despite his return to Soviet Ukraine. The 1946 resolution of the CC of the CP(B)U, in particular, and later Soviet publications characterize him as a 'nationalist historian,' 'the ideologist of the Ukrainian counterrevolutionary bourgeoisie,' and 'the untamed enemy of Soviet rule.' The Soviet regime continues to combat

Hrushevsky's scheme and its followers in history, literature, linguistics, and other disciplines.

In 1966 Ukrainian scholarly institutions in the diaspora celebrated the centenary of Hrushevsky's birth and in 1984, the 50th anniversary of his death. On these occasions, special issues of *Ukraïns'kyi istoryk* devoted to Hrushevsky were published. In 1974 the Ukrainian Historical Society began a separate serial publication, *Hrushevskiana*, devoted to the study of the life and work of Hrushevsky. Hrushevsky wrote two short autobiographies: the first was published in Lviv in 1906 (repr, Toronto 1965) and the second in Kiev in 1926 (2nd edn with notes and intro by L. Wynar, New York 1981).

BIBLIOGRAPHY

Herasymchuk, V. 'Mykhailo Hrushevs'kyi iak istoriohraf Ukraïny,' *ZNTSh*, 133 (1922)
Bahalii, D. 'Akad. M.S. Hrushevs'kyi i ioho mistse v ukraïns'kii istoriohrafiï,' *ChSh*, 1927, no. 1
Iuvilei akademika M.S. Hrushevs'koho, 1866–1926 (Kiev 1927)
Bidlo, I. *Michal Hruševskyj* (Prague 1935)
Borschak, E. 'Mykhailo Hrushevskyj,' *Le Monde Slave*, 1935, no. 1
Krupnytsky, B. Introduction to the repr edn of *Istoriia Ukraïny-Rusy*, 1 (New York 1954)
Doroshenko, O. 'A Survey of Ukrainian Historiography' and Ohloblyn, O. 'Ukrainian Historiography 1917–1956,' AUA, 5–6 (1957)
Vynar, L. *Mykhailo Hrushevs'kyi i Naukove Tovarystvo im. Tarasa Shevchenka, 1892–1930* (Munich 1970)
Vynar, L. 'Naivydatnishyi istoryk Ukraïny Mykhailo Hrushevs'kyi,' *Suchasnist'*, 1984, no. 11; 1985, nos 1–4
Wynar, L. (ed). *Mykhailo Hrushevs'kyi, 1866–1934: Bibliographic Sources* (New York-Munich-Toronto 1985)
Prymak, T. *Mykhailo Hrushevsky and the Politics of National Culture* (Toronto 1987)

O. Ohloblyn, L. Wynar

Oleksander Hrushevsky

Hryhorii Hrushka

Hrushevsky, Oleksander [Hruševs'kyj], b 1877, d ?. Historian; brother of M. *Hrushevsky. He studied at Kiev University with V. Antonovych and was a privatdocent at the universities of Odessa, St Petersburg, and Kiev; he was one of the first to lecture in Ukrainian at Odessa University (1906). In 1918 he was appointed professor at Kiev University. He was a full member of the Ukrainian Scientific Society in Kiev and the Shevchenko Scientific Society. In the 1920s he served as director of the Historical-Geographical Commission of the VUAN and a member of the VUAN Archeographic Commission. He was exiled in 1937 during the Stalin terror and his subsequent fate is unknown. He wrote a number of historical studies, including *Pinskoe Poles'e* (Pynske Polisia, 1901), *Ocherki istorii Turovskogo kniazhestva* (Essays on the History of Turiv Principality, 1902), and *Goroda Velikogo Kniazhestva Litovskogo v XIV–XVI vv.* (Cities of the Grand Duchy of Lithuania in the 14th–16th Centuries, 1918). His numerous articles on the political, socioeconomic, and regional history of 16th–19th-century Ukraine and on Ukrainian historiography appeared in various VUAN journals, especially in *Ukraïna*. He was also the author of studies of Ukrainian writers, which were published together in *Z suchasnoï ukraïns'koï literatury* (On Contemporary Ukrainian Literature, 1909, 1918).

Hrushevsky Institute. See St John's Institute.

Hrushka, Hryhorii [Hruška, Hryhorij], b 10 September 1859 in Zarubyntsi, Ternopil circle, Galicia, d 16 April 1913 in Peniaky, Lviv county, Galicia. Greek Catholic priest and community leader. Hrushka studied theology in Rome and Lviv and immigrated to the United States in 1889, where he became a parish priest in Shenandoah, Pennsylvania, and Jersey City, New Jersey. With the intention of instilling a national consciousness among Ukrainian immigrants, he cofounded and edited (1893–5) **Svoboda*. He was also one of the organizers of the *Ukrainian National Association. In 1896 Hrushka temporarily converted to Russian Orthodoxy following a series of misunderstandings with the Latin-rite hierarchy, whose policies, in his opinion, threatened Ukrainian traditions. After leaving the United States (1900) and settling briefly in Eastern Ukraine, he returned to Galicia, disillusioned with the politics of the Russian Orthodox church. He entered a Uniate Basilian monastery, and then served as a priest in several parishes. Hrushka was the author of short stories and polemical poetry. His papers from the years 1883 to 1901, which represent a significant source on Ukrainian-American history, are held in the Manuscript Division of the Library of Congress in Washington, DC.

Hrushkevych, Teofil [Hruškevyč], b 4 August 1846 in Horozhanna Mala, Rudky county, Galicia, d 2 May 1915 at Schmidsdorf near Payerbach in Lower Austria. Galician civic leader. A gymnasium teacher, Hrushkevych organized education in the Kolomyia region (1879–89), and was director (1909–12) of the Ukrainian gymnasium in Yavoriv. He edited the journal *Uchytel'* (1890–2) and wrote several textbooks and popular brochures.

Hruzkyi Yelanchyk River [Hruz'kyj Jelančyk]. A river in Donets oblast that empties into Tahanrih Bay in the Sea of Azov. It is 91 km long, and its basin area is 1,250 sq km. The town of Novoazovske is located at its mouth.

Hruzynsky, Oleksander [Hruzyns'ky], b 22 December 1881 in Nizhen, Chernihiv gubernia, d 11 January 1951. Philologist; member of the Ukrainian Scientific Society in Kiev. In the 1920s he was a professor at the Nizhen and the Kharkiv Institute of People's Education. Persecuted in the 1930s, he left Ukraine and taught in Leningrad and Mahiliou. Eventually he returned and lived in Kiev. He is the author of articles on the 16th-century Peresopnytsia and Litky Gospels and on the works of T. Prokopovych and H. Skovoroda.

Hryd (collective noun, also *hrydba*; singular – *hryden*). The junior retainers of a prince in the Kievan Rus' period. The *hryd* performed military service and participated in the administration of princely property. They lived in separate quarters at court. The word is used in the earliest chronicles and **bylyny* and is probably of Scandinavian origin.

Michael Hryhorczuk

Hrytsko Hryhorenko

Hryhorczuk, Michael [Hryhorčuk, Myxajlo], b 28 November 1905 in Gilbert Plains, Manitoba, d 11 July 1978 in Ethelbert, Manitoba. Lawyer and politician. Son of N. Hryhorczuk. After studying at the universities of Saskatchewan and Manitoba, he practiced law and served as reeve of Ethelbert and chairman of the Ethelbert School Board. A Liberal-Progressive member for Ethelbert in the Manitoba Legislature (1949–66), he was appointed attorney general (1955–8), becoming the second cabinet minister of Ukrainian origin in Manitoba. Hryhorczuk was an active member of the Ukrainian Greek Orthodox church.

Hryhorczuk, Nicholas [Hryhorčuk, Mykola], b 17 December 1888 in Buchachky, Kolomyia county, Galicia, d 23 November 1979 in Ethelbert, Manitoba. Merchant and politician. His family came to Canada in 1897 and settled north of Dauphin, Manitoba. A prosperous lumber and implement dealer, he served as reeve of Ethelbert and in 1920 was elected to the Manitoba Legislature as the Liberal-Progressive member for Ethelbert. He was reelected in 1922, 1927, 1932, and 1941 and defeated in 1936 and 1945. For a brief period in 1936 he served as deputy speaker. He was an active member of the Ukrainian Greek Orthodox church in Canada from its inception in 1918.

Hryhorenko, Hrytsko (pen name of Oleksandra Sudovshchykova-Kosach), b March 1867 in Makarev, Kostroma gubernia, northern Russia, d 27 April 1924 in Kiev. Writer and social activist; the wife of M. *Kosach and sister-in-law of Lesia *Ukrainka. Together with Kosach and Ukrainka she was active in radical Ukrainophile student circles and the writers' circle Pleiada (1888–93). Her first collection of prose, *Nashi liudy na seli* (Our Rural People), was published in 1898. Hryhorenko's naturalistic stories depict the hardship, destitution, and moral decay of life in the Ukrainian village and in exile, and have been likened to V. Stefanyk's. She also wrote eight plays (five for children) and a collection of children's stories and plays *Ditky* (Little Children, 1918), and translated French (J. Verne), English, and Swedish literature into Ukrainian. Her complete works (in two volumes) were published in Kharkiv in 1930, and selections appeared in Kiev in 1918, 1929, and 1959.

Hryhorenko, Petro. See Grigorenko, Petro.

Hryhorenko, Yaroslav, b 12 October 1927 in Kiev. Mechanical engineer and specialist in applied mathematics; corresponding member of the AN URSR since 1978. After graduating from Kiev University (1955), Hryhorenko began working at the AN URSR Institute of Mechanics, where he has been assistant director since 1977. Since 1971 he has also been a professor at Kiev University. Hryhorenko specializes in the mechanics of casings construction and the problem of their high-tension deformation.

Hryhoriev, Serhii [Hryhorjev, Serhij], b 5 July 1910 in Luhanske, Bakhmut county, Katerynoslav gubernia. Painter and graphic artist. A graduate of the Kiev State Art Institute (1932), where he studied under F. Krychevsky and F. Krasytsky, his early works depicted children and young people: eg, *Children at the Beach* (1937), *Youth Festival* (1938), and *Portrait of a Girl* (1939). After the war he concentrated on family and school scenes such as *Young Naturalists* (1948), *Admission to the Komsomol* (1949), *Children Pouring over Books* (1969), and *Mother* (1970). He also did portraits of writers – A. Holovko (1966), A. Malyshko (1967), P. Panch (1967), and M. Bazhan (1976) – and of other cultural figures. He taught art at the Kharkiv Art Institute (1933–4) and, intermittently, at the Kiev State Art Institute (1934–60). T. Gureva (1957) and V. Afanasev (1967) have written monographs about Hryhoriev.

Hryhorii [Hryhorij], b and d ? Deacon, scribe, and illuminator of the 11th century. He copied and probably illuminated the *Ostromir Gospel (1056–7), the oldest known manuscript produced in Kievan Rus'. The prevalent view is that he lived and worked in Kiev, not Novgorod.

Hryhoriiv, Nykyfor [Hryhorijiv], b 25 February 1883 in Burty, Kaniv county, Kiev gubernia, d 5 August 1953 in New York. Civic and political figure, publicist, and pedagogue. He was a member of the Society of Ukrainian Progressives and a contributor to the journals *Rada*, *Maiak*, and *Ridnyi krai* (under the pseud H. Nash). In 1917 he became an activist of the Ukrainian Party of Socialist Revolutionaries (UPSR) and a member of the Central Rada. As president of the Council of Military Deputies for the Kiev Military Okruha, he headed the drive to Ukrainianize the army. In 1918 he served as minister of education in V. Holubovych's government and then joined the Ukrainian National Union to overthrow the Hetman government. In 1919 he was a deputy of the Labor Congress and the director of the UNR Army press service. As a member of the Central Committee of the UPSR, he headed the party's center faction and opposed the Borotbists. In 1921 Hryhoriiv immigrated to Prague, where he served as vice-president of the Ukrainian Civic Committee in Czechoslovakia and as director of the Ukrainian

Nykyfor Hryhoriiv

Sociological Institute, which he helped found. After he immigrated to the United States in 1938, he worked on *Narodna volia* and in 1949 became director of the Ukrainian service of the Voice of America. He wrote a number of journalistic works, including *Osnovy natsioznannia* (The Foundations of Nation Studies, 1940), *Ukraïns'ka natsional'na vdacha* (The Ukrainian National Character, 1941), *Derzhavoznavstvo* (State Studies, 1936), *Spohady ruïnnyka* (A Destroyer's Memoirs, 1937), and *The War and Ukrainian Democracy* (1945).

V. Markus

Hryhoriiv or **Hryhoriv, Nykyfor (Matvii)** [Hryhorijiv or Hryhor'jiv, Matvij], b ca 1885 in Zastavia, Ushytsia county, Podilia gubernia, d 27 July 1919. A Ukrainian revolutionary leader in southern Right-Bank Ukraine. A former tsarist army captain, during the UNR Directory's rebellion against the German army and the Hetman government in 1918 he led an autonomous force of 6,000–8,000 Borotbist and anarchist partisans in the Oleksandriia and Mykolaiv regions. In January 1919 Hryhoriiv rebelled against the Directory after it forbade him to move against the Allied forces. He aligned himself with the Soviet government in Kharkiv, and from February to April his army of 15,000 played a central role in the successful Bolshevik offensive against the White and Allied forces in Mykolaiv, Kherson, and Odessa. In early May 1919, however, Hryhoriiv rejected the Bolshevik order to send his forces against the Rumanians to support B. Kun's revolution in Hungary. Instead, he proclaimed himself the otaman of Ukraine and organized an anti-Bolshevik jacquerie that spread throughout Kherson and Katerynoslav gubernias before being suppressed in late May by the Red Army. Hryhoriiv and the remnants of his army then allied themselves with the anarchist army of N. Makhno, who had Hryhoriiv shot when the latter proposed that their forces take part in A. Denikin's White offensive against the Bolsheviks.

BIBLIOGRAPHY
Adams, E. *Bolsheviks in the Ukraine: The Second Campaign, 1918–1919* (New Haven and London 1963)
Palij, M. *The Anarchism of Nestor Makhno, 1918–1921: An Aspect of the Ukrainian Revolution* (Seattle and London 1976)

R. Senkus

Hryhorivka fortified settlement. An archeological site near Hryhorivka, Mohyliv-Podilskyi raion, Vinnytsia oblast, excavated in 1947–8 and 1952–3. A multi-period settlement was excavated there: from Scythian times (7th–6th centuries BC), pit and surface dwellings, pottery, and storage pits; from the period of the *Lypytsia culture (1st–3rd centuries AD), the remains of dwellings; and from the 9th–10th centuries AD, pit dwellings with stone ovens and 25 iron-smelting furnaces.

Hryhorovych, Dmytro [Hryhorovyč], b 6 February 1883 in Kiev, d 26 July 1938 in Moscow. Airplane designer, aeronautical engineer. A graduate of the Kiev Polytechnical Institute (1909), he designed some of the earliest hydroplanes, such as the flying boats M-1 (1913), M-5 (1914), and M-9 (1915), and the first fighter seaplane in the world – the M-P. He was also the designer of the I-2 fighter, the M-24 flying boat, and the ROM-2 reconnaissance seaplane. Together with N. Polikarpov, he designed the advanced fighter planes I-5 (1930) and PI-1 (1930–3).

Hryhorovych, Ivan [Hryhorovyč], b 1876 in Hnylche, Ternopil county, Galicia, d 3 April 1937 in Lviv. Actor and singer (tenor). He was a member of the Ukrainian Ruska Besida theater and appeared in its productions between 1895 and 1900. He then joined the Polish theater of T. Pawlikowski (1900–5), while occasionally accepting roles in productions in Belgrade and Zagreb. In 1907 he returned to the Ruska Besida Theater, with which he remained until 1912. His major roles included Petro in M. Lysenko's *Natalka Poltavka* and Ivan in the same composer's *Chornomortsi* (Black Sea Cossacks), Andrii in S. Hulak-Artemovsky's *Zaporozhets' za Dunaiem* (Zaporozhian Cossack beyond the Danube), Jontek in S. Moniuszko's *Halka*, and Mazaniello in D. Auber's *Muette de Portici*. He appeared in concert recitals of Ukrainian folk songs and of works by M. Lysenko, V. Matiuk, and O. Nyzhankivsky.

Hryhorovych, Ivan [Hryhorovyč], b 19 January 1911 in Chernivtsi, Bukovyna, d ? Civic and political leader in Bukovyna. As a founder of the Legion of Ukrainian Revolutionaries (1930) and of Mesnyk Ukrainy (1932), which joined the OUN, he was one of the first organizers of the nationalist movement in the region. He coedited the OUN weekly *Samostiinist'* (1934–7), and was active in the nationalist student association Zalizniak (1934–7). In 1937 he was sentenced for his political activity to three years' imprisonment by a Rumanian military tribunal. In 1941 he marched east with the *OUN Expeditionary Groups. He disappeared after being arrested in 1944 in Bucharest by the Soviets.

Hryhorovych, Vasyl [Hryhorovyč, Vasyl'], b 1786 in Pyriatyn, Kiev vicegerency, d 15 March 1865 in St Petersburg. Art scholar. A graduate of the Kiev Academy (1803), he taught esthetics and served as conference secretary at the Academy of Arts in St Petersburg (1829–59). He befriended and supported Ukrainian art students in St Petersburg. It was with his permission that T. Shevchenko attended drawing classes of the Society for the Promotion of the Arts, and he took part in purchasing Shevchenko's freedom. To commemorate the day of his liberation, Shevchenko dedicated the poem 'Haidamaky' to Hryhorovych.

Hryhorovych, Viktor [Hryhorovyč], b 12 May 1815 in Balta, Podilia gubernia, d 31 December 1876 in Yelysavethrad, Kherson gubernia. Russian Slavist of Ukrainian descent. He taught Slavic languages at the universities in Kazan (1839–49, 1854–65), Moscow (1849–54), and Odessa (1865–76). In his works he defended the theory of the Pannonian origin of Old Church Slavonic. During his expedition through Slavic countries in 1844–6 he amassed an important collection of Old Slavic manuscripts, which he donated to the university in Odessa. After his death Hryhorovych's manuscripts, notebooks, and old books were deposited at the Rumiantsev Museum in Moscow.

Hryhorovych, Yevheniia [Hryhorovyč, Jevhenija], b 17 April 1905 in Dubno, Volhynia gubernia, d 15 July 1978 in Kiev. Film director. A graduate of the Odessa Film Tekhnikum, she began to work as a film director in 1930 at the Odessa Artistic Film Studio. From 1943 she worked at the Kiev Popular Science Film Studio. Her popular documentary films include *Berezhit' khlib* (Save the Bread, 1945), *Po pivnichnii Bukovyni* (Through Northern Bukovyna, 1950), *Pam'iatnyky drevn'oï Rusy* (Monuments of Ancient Rus', 1969), and *Berezhit' ridnu pryrodu* (Preserve Our Natural Environment, 1974). She also directed the full-length movie *Oleksander Dovzhenko* (1964).

Hryhorovych-Barsky, Ivan [Hryhorovyč-Bars'kyj], b 1713 in Kiev, d 1785 in Kiev. Architect of the Ukrainian or Cossack baroque style; brother of V. *Hryhorovych-Barsky. A graduate of the Kievan Mohyla Academy, he designed many buildings in Kiev: the church and belfry of St Cyril's Monastery Church (1750–60, destroyed by the Soviet regime), the Church of the Holy Protectress (1766), the Church of St Nicholas on the Bank (1772–5), the belfry of ss Peter and Paul Monastery (1761–3), the Old Bursa of the Kievan Mohyla Academy (1778), the Hostynyi Dvir warehouse (1760s), and the Magistrat grain warehouse (1760). His work was not confined to Kiev: in Lemeshi near Chernihiv he built the Church of the Three Saints (1761), and in Kozelets, the regimental chancellery (1757) and the Church of the Nativity of the Mother of God (1752–64, in collaboration with A. Kvasov). He adapted the architectural tradition of the Eastern church to the demands of his period and created new and original buildings.

Hryhorovych-Barsky, Vasyl [Hryhorovyč-Bars'kyj, Vasyl'] (pseuds Plaka, Albov), b 1701 in Kiev, d 7 October 1747 in Kiev. Traveler and writer. He studied at the Kievan Mohyla Academy in 1715–23, and from 1723 to 1747 traveled in countries of central, eastern, and southern Europe and the Near East. He compiled a Latin grammar for Greeks and left a detailed account of the economic condition, education, customs, history, and research on artistic monuments of the countries and places he visited; the work was accompanied by 150 drawings. At first his description was circulated widely in copied manuscript form in Ukraine and Russia. The first edition was published posthumously by V. Ruban in 1778. The eighth, most complete, edition, with letters to his brother I. Hryhorovych-Barsky, appeared in four parts in 1885–7 under the editorship of N. Barsukov as *Stranstvovaniia Vasil'ia Grigorovicha-Barskogo po sviatym mestam Vostoka s 1723 po 1747 g.* (The Travels of Vasyl Hryhorovych-Barsky to the Holy Places of the East from 1723 to 1747). Hryhorovych-Barsky was buried at the Kievan Epiphany Brotherhood Monastery. Books about him have been published by V. Askochensky (1854) and I. Rodachenko (1967).

Belfry of St Cyril's Monastery in Kiev, designed by Ivan Hryhorovych-Barsky (1760) and demolished by the Soviet government in 1937

Hryhoruk, Yevhen, b 6 January 1899 in Troianka, Balta county, Kherson gubernia, d 24 October 1922 in Yalta. A revolutionary, journalist, and poet. In 1921 he became the director of the Kiev branch of the All-Ukrainian Publishing House and then the director of a department of the State Publishing House in Moscow. His propagandistic and symbolist poetry appeared in various periodicals. A volume of his collected works was published in Kharkiv in 1928. He was a persona non grata because of his *Borotbist past during the Stalin period, but his works were posthumously rehabilitated after Stalin's death and a volume of his poems was published in Kiev in 1962.

Hrymailo, Yaroslav [Hrymajlo, Jaroslav], b 2 December 1906 in Rohyntsi, Khmilnyk county, Podilia gubernia, d 1984 in Kiev. Socialist realist writer and journalist. From 1926 to 1932 he was a member of the *Molodniak writer's group and the All-Ukrainian Association of Proletarian Writers. His works, many of them for children, include 16 poetry collections, the first of which was *Vitryla pidniato* (The Sails Are Hoisted, 1930); 14 prose collections, starting with *Iuni mandrivnyky, abo Podorozh na Dniprelstan* (Young Travelers, or a Trip to the Dnieper Dam, 1930); and the novels *Syn leitenenta* (The Lieutenant's Son, 1950), *Kavaler ordena Slavy* (The Knight of the Order of Glory, 1955), *Nezakinchenyi roman* (An Unfinished Romance, 1962), and *Zacharovanyi na Skhid* (Enchanted to the East, 1971).

Hryn Ivanovych [Hryn' Ivanovyč], b ? in Zabludau, Belorussia, d ? Engraver of the 16th century. As I. *Fedorovych's helper, he was sent to learn engraving with L. *Fylypovych-Pukhalsky (1577–8). Then he worked as an engraver and type founder in Ostrih (1579–81), Vilnius (1582), and Lviv (1583).

Hrynchyshyn, Michael [Hrynčyšyn, Myxajlo], b 18 February 1929 in Buchanan, Saskatchewan. Since 1983 bishop of the Ukrainian Catholic church and apostolic exarch for Ukrainian Catholics in France. Entering the Redemptorist novitiate in 1945, he was ordained in 1952. In 1955 he earned a doctorate at the Pontifical Institute for Oriental Studies in Rome. He served as rector, professor of theology, and prefect at Redemptorist seminaries in Meadowvale, Ontario, and Yorkton, Saskatchewan, and as priest in Saskatoon, Winnipeg, and Newark, New Jersey. He was president of the Canadian section of the Ukrainian Theological Scholarly Society, editor of *Lohos* (1960–5), and superior of the Yorkton Province of the Ukrainian Redemptorist Fathers (1972–81). As postulator of Metropolitan Sheptytsky's beatification and canonization, he collected 21 volumes of the metropolitan's writings. Since 1978 he has been secretary general of the Central Millennium Jubilee Committee of the Ukrainian Catholic church.

Hrynchyshyn, Mykola [Hrynčyšyn], b 1 December 1914 in Moose Jaw, Saskatchewan. Journalist, communist activist; since 1964 member of the Central Committee of the Communist Party of Canada. Since 1936 he has worked on the staff of Ukrainian communist newspapers such as *Ukraïns'ki robitnychi visti* and *Narodna hazeta* (1937–41), and has edited *Ukraïns'ke slovo* (1952–65) and then *Zhyttia i slovo*.

Hrynevetsky, Ivan [Hrynevec'kyj], b 24 June 1850 in Sianichok, Sianik county, Galicia, d 25 January 1889 in Peremyshl. Actor, stage director. From 1869 to 1881 he appeared on the Polish stage, but at the same time worked for the Ruska Besida theater in Lviv as an actor (1874–80), stage director (from 1876), and theater director with I. Biberovych (1882–9). He improved the artistic quality of the Galician theater by combining the technical advancements of the West European theater with the principles of the ethnographic theater developed by M. Kropyvnytsky. He revitalized the repertoire of the Ruska Besida theater with current Ukrainian plays by H. Tsehlynsky, K. Ustyianovych, O. Ohonovsky, S. Vorobkevych, and Yu. Fedkovych, and with translations of such dramatists as C. Goldoni, Molière, H. Kleist, J. Schiller, and H. Sudermann. He also staged operettas by J.-R. Planquette, J. Strauss, J. Offenbach, and others. As an actor he appeared in such roles as the mayor in N. Gogol's *The Inspector General*, Tikhon in A. Ostrovsky's *Groza* (Thunderstorm), Karl Moor in J. Schiller's *Die Räuber*, and Bychok in M. Kropyvnytsky's *Hlytai, abozh pavuk* (The Profiteer, or the Spider).

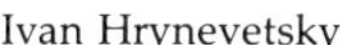

Ivan Hrynevetsky

Katria Hrynevycheva

Hrynevetsky, Stepan [Hrynevec'kyj], b 6 October 1877 in Buzke, Kamianka Strumylova county, Galicia, d 6 November 1942 in Chicago. Physician and civic leader. After completing his medical degree at the University of Vienna, and working for over eight years as an assistant and lecturer at Vienna General Hospital, he immigrated to the United States (ca 1907). Settling in Chicago, he opened a private practice and joined the staffs of St Mary of Nazareth and Billings hospitals. He also lectured at the Rush Medical College in Chicago. He was an editor of the weekly *Ukraïna* (1918–20), organizer and head of the monarchist Sich society, and editor of its journal, *Sich* (1920). He served as the Chief Otaman of the Sich movement in the United States (1920–5), but resigned after a conflict with the hetman, P. Skoropadsky. In the late 1930s Hrynevetsky organized a Ukrainian detachment in the Illinois National Guard.

Hrynevych, Feodosii [Hrynevyč, Feodosij], b 1 November 1922 in Ripna, Podilia region. Specialist in electrometry; since 1973 corresponding member of the AN URSR. After graduating from the Lviv Polytechnical Institute in 1953, he worked in various electrotechnical institutes in Ukraine and Siberia. He developed the theory and construction methods of several digital and analog measuring instruments.

Hrynevycheva, Katria [Hrynevyčeva, Katrja] (née Banakh), b 19 November 1875 in Vynnyky, Lviv county, d 27 December 1947 in Berchtesgaden, Germany. Modernist, writer, and community leader. With encouragement from V. Stefanyk and I. Franko, she began writing poetry and prose in Ukrainian, which appeared in such journals as *Literaturno-naukovyi vistnyk* and *Bukovyna* from 1893 on. From 1909 to 1911 she edited the children's magazine *Dzvinok*. From 1915 to 1917 she taught at Ukrainian internment camps in Austria and contributed to *Vistnyk Soiuzu vyzvolennia Ukraïny*. Starting in 1918 she worked for the newspaper *Ukraïns'ke slovo*. In 1922 she was elected president of the *Union of Ukrainian Women in Galicia. She is the author of short-story collections – *Legendy i opovidannia* (Legends and Short Stories, 1902), *Po dorozi v Sykhem* (On the Way to Sychem, 1923), *Nepoborni* (The Invincible, 1926, about Galician internees)

– and a few years later she wrote several historical novelettes set in the Princely era – *Sholomy v sontsi* (Helmets in the Sun, 1924, 1929), and *Shestykrylets'* (The Six-Winged One, 1935, 1936). Her works, most of which appeared first in periodicals, have not been collected. Her masterly handling of the Ukrainian language, particularly her stylizing of the folk vernacular and her sophisticated use of Ukrainian archaisms in her historical novelettes, places her among the best Ukrainian modernist prose writers. Her biography, by her son Ya. Hrynevych, was published in Toronto in 1968.

M. Hlobenko

Hrynkiv, Thomas [Hryn'kiv, Toma], b 4 August 1941 in Wilkes-Barre, Pennsylvania. Pianist and teacher. A graduate of Wilkes College and the Manhattan School of Music (MA 1967), he won a competition to play P. Tchaikovsky's First Piano Concerto with L. Stokowski, and was awarded a gold medal at the Geneva Competition (1967). He has toured the major cities of Europe and North and South America, and has made several recordings. He taught music at the Fieldstorn School and is a member of the New American Trio, the Kalyna Piano Trio, and the Audubon Quartet. His Ukrainian repertoire includes works by L. Revutsky, V. Kosenko, S. Liudkevych, and N. Nyzhankivsky.

Hryhorii Hrynko

Hrynko, Hryhorii [Hryn'ko, Hryhorii], b 30 November 1890 in Shtepivka, Lebedyn county, Kharkiv gubernia, d 15 March 1938 in Moscow. Soviet Ukrainian political figure. A member of the *Borotbists, Hrynko joined the CP(B)U in 1919 and soon became a member of the All-Ukrainian Central Executive Committee (CEC), the Council of People's Commissars, the CEC of the RSFSR, and the All-Ukrainian Military-Revolutionary Committee (1919–26). He took part in the 1919–20 Comintern-sponsored negotiations between the Borotbists and the CP(B)U concerning the merger of the two parties. During these talks, Hrynko insisted that the Ukrainian SSR should retain economic autonomy, an idea later reiterated by M. *Volobuiev. After the merger, he became the Ukrainian people's commissar of education (1920–2), in which capacity he insisted on Ukrainian cultural distinctness and made his commissariat a central political institution during the *Ukrainization period. The so-called Hrynko educational reform, which existed with some changes from 1920 to 1932, created a system of education that was radically different from that instituted in Russia by A. Lunacharsky. The Hrynko system focused on vocational-technical instruction in public education. Higher education was reorganized and geared to meet Ukraine's dire need for specialists.

Hrynko was also a member of the CP(B)U CEC (1924–7), the head of the Ukrainian State Planning Commission (1922–6), and deputy chairman of the Ukrainian Council of People's Commissars. As deputy chairman of the USSR State Planning Commission (1926–9), he insisted that Ukraine be treated as a national economic entity. In 1929 Hrynko served as USSR deputy people's commissar of agriculture, from 1930 to 1937 as USSR people's commissar of finances, and from 1934 to 1937 as a candidate member of the All-Soviet CP(B) CC and member of the Presidium of the CEC of the USSR. Arrested during the Yezhov terror in 1937, he was executed in 1938 as a 'fascist spy' after a show trial.

I. Myhul

Hrynko, Mykola [Hryn'ko], b 30 April 1920 in Kherson. Stage and film actor. From 1946 to 1955 he worked in the Zaporizhia Ukrainian Music and Drama Theater. He made his film debut in 1951. In 1963 he began working at the Kiev Artistic Film Studio. His best-known roles were Commissar Artem in *Zahybel' eskadry* (Destruction of a Squadron, 1966), Danilo Cherny in *Andrei Rublev* (1968), Anton Chekhov in *Siuzhet dlia nevelychkoho opovidannia* (A Plot for a Short Story, 1969), and Nikon in *Iaroslav Mudryi* (Yaroslav the Wise, 1982).

Hrynky [Hryn'ky]. Village formerly in Kremianets county, Volhynia, and now in Lanivtsi raion, Ternopil oblast. It became notorious in the winter of 1937–8, when the Polish Border Guard Corps and the Polish administration used force to convert its Orthodox inhabitants to the Roman Catholic faith. They succeeded in converting 116 Ukrainians. Similar incidents occurred in the neighboring villages of Lanivtsi, Bilozirka, and Yuskivtsi. This campaign had the unintended effect of strengthening national consciousness among Volhynia's Ukrainians. Polish Sejm members S. Baran and S. Tymoshenko intervened in the diet on behalf of the Orthodox population.

Hrynokh, Ivan [Hryn'ox], b 28 December 1907 in Pavliv, Radekhiv county, Galicia. Ukrainian Catholic priest, theologian, church and political leader; full member of

Rev Ivan Hrynokh

Oleksa Hryshchenko

the Shevchenko Scientific Society. A graduate of the Greek Catholic Theological Academy in Lviv (1930), he studied at Innsbruck University (D TH 1933), then at Munich University, and finally at l'Institut Catholique in Paris. Returning to Lviv in 1934, he lectured at the Theological Academy and served as spiritual adviser to Ukrainian students in Polish-ruled territories. Since 1941 Hrynokh has been active in the nationalist movement. He was a founding member and second vice-president of the Ukrainian Supreme Liberation Council in 1944, and then head of its External Representation (1946–80). In 1944–5, on behalf of the council and the UPA, he negotiated with Hungarian, Rumanian, and Polish military officials. After emigrating he served as professor at the Ukrainian Catholic Theological Seminary in Hirschberg and Culemborg, the Ukrainian Free University in Munich, and the Ukrainian Catholic University in Rome. Since 1963 he has sat on the Liturgical Commission of the Ukrainian Catholic church, and since 1969 has headed the Ukrainian Theological Scholarly Society. His publications include *Sluha Bozhyi Andrei – Blahovistnyk iednosty* (God's Servant Andrei – The Evangelist of Unity, 1961) and articles in theology and church history. A close collaborator of Cardinal Y. *Slipy, Hrynokh was appointed to the Consistory of the Lviv Archeparchy in 1978 and elevated to patriarchal archimandrite in 1982. He is an advocate of the eastern orientation assumed by the Ukrainian Catholic church and particularly the concept of a Kiev-Halych patriarchate.

V. Markus

Hryshchenko, Mykyta [Hryščenko], b 27 September 1900 in Trushky, Vasylkiv county, Kiev gubernia. Scholar and pedagogue. A graduate of the Kiev Institute of the National Economy (1926), he held the Chair of Pedagogy at Kiev University from 1958 to 1975. His chief publications are *Rozvytok narodnoï osvity na Ukraïni za roky Radians'koï vlady* (The Development of Public Education in Ukraine under the Soviet Regime, 1957) and *Spadshchyna K.D. Ushyns'koho i pytannia pedahohiky vyshchoï shkoly* (K.D. Ushynsky's Heritage and the Question of Pedagogy in Higher Schools, 1975).

Hryshchenko, Oleksa [Hryščenko] (Gritchenko, Alexis), b 2 April 1883 in Krolevets, Chernihiv gubernia, d 28 January 1977 in Vence, France. Painter and author. While specializing in biology at Kiev and Moscow universities, he studied painting with S. Sviatoslavsky in Kiev and K. Yuon in Moscow. He became involved in the modern art movement in Russia and developed close ties with two important art collectors – S. Shchukin and O. Morozov. During a brief stay in Paris in 1911 he met A. Lhote, A. Archipenko, and Le Fauconnier and became interested in cubism. From 1919 to 1921 he lived in Istanbul, where he painted hundreds of watercolors. In 1921 he moved to France. By this time he had changed his cubist style to a more dynamic expressionism, distinguished by cascades of exotic oriental colors. Hryshchenko exhibited his works in the leading art galleries of Paris (eg, Paul Guillaume, Bing, Granoff, Druet, de l'Elysée, Weil, and Bernheim-Jeune), and participated in exhibitions such as Salon des Tuileries and Salon d'Automne (member from 1930). In the 1930s his works were displayed in Lviv at exhibitions of the Association of Independent Ukrainian Artists and in a one-man show.

Oleksa Hryshchenko: *Puerto Audierne*

He became known in the United States in 1923, when the Barnes Foundation in Philadelphia acquired several of his works. After the war he had several one-man shows in New York and Philadelphia. In 1963 he established the Alexis Gritchenko Foundation, to which he donated over 70 works (now housed at the Ukrainian Institute of America in New York). His paintings are found in many museums, including the Musée National d'Art Moderne in Paris, the Royal Museum in Copenhagen, the Musée Royal in Brussels, the Museum of Modern Art in Madrid, the Museum of Montreal, and the Lviv Museum of Ukrainian Art. Many of his works are in private collections. Besides articles Hryshchenko wrote monographs on art: *O sviaziakh russkoi zhivopisi s Vizantiei i Zapadom* (The Ties of Russian Painting with Byzantium and the West, 1913) and *Russkaia ikona kak iskusstvo zhivopisi* (The Russian Icon as Painting, 1917). Hryshchenko also wrote several volumes of memoirs: *Deux ans à Constantinople* (1930, with 40 reproductions of his watercolors; Ukrainian version 1961, without reproductions); *L'Ukraine de mes jours bleus* (1957, Ukrainian version 1958); *Moï zustrichi i rozmovy z frantsuz'kymy mysttsiamy* (My Encounters and Discussions with French Artists, 1962; English translation 1968); and *Roky buri i natysku* (The Years of Storm and Stress, 1967).

BIBLIOGRAPHY
Kovzhun, P. *Hryshchenko-Gritchenko* (Lviv 1934)
Jean, R. *Alexis Gritchenko, sa vie, son oeuvre* (Paris 1948)
Charmet, R. et al. *Alexis Gritchenko* (Paris 1964)
Gritchenko – O. Hryshchenko, 1883–1977 (New York 1983)

S. Hordynsky

Hryshko, Hryhorii [Hryško, Hryhorij], b 25 January 1906 in Velykofedorivka, Oleksandriia county, Kherson gubernia, d 9 February 1959 in Kiev. Communist party official. From 1937 to 1951 he occupied several posts in the CP(B)U in Mykolaiv, Volhynia, Ternopil, and Kherson oblasts. He became a member of the CC CP(B)U in 1949, serving as secretary in 1951–2. In 1952–7 he was first secretary of the CP(B)U Kiev oblast executive committee and a candidate member of the Presidium of the CPU.

Mykhailo Hryshko

Hryshko, Mykhailo [Hryško, Myxajlo], b 27 February 1901 in Mariiupil (now Zhdanov), Katerynoslav gubernia, d 3 June 1973 in Kiev. Opera singer (baritone). A graduate of the Odessa School of Music (1926), he was soloist at the opera and ballet theaters in Odessa (1924–7), Kharkiv (1927–36), and Kiev (1936–64). In 1934–5 and 1941–4 he sang at the opera in Tbilisi. His repertoire included the roles of Mykola in M. Lysenko's *Natalka Poltavka*, Ostap in the same composer's *Taras Bulba*, Figaro in Mozart's *The Marriage of Figaro*, and the title roles in K. Dankevych's *Bohdan Khmelnytsky*, A. Borodin's *Prince Igor*, and Verdi's *Rigoletto*. A biography of Hryshko, written by I. Stebun, was published in 1958.

Hryshko, Mykola [Hryško], b 6 January 1901 in Poltava, d 3 January 1964 in Kiev. Botanist, geneticist; from 1939 full member of the AN URSR. A graduate of the Poltava (1925) and Kiev (1926) agricultural institutes, he chaired the plant genetics and selection department of the All-Union Hemp Institute of the All-Union Academy of Agricultural Sciences (1932–9) and of the Hlukhiv (then Kiev) Agricultural Institute (1932–41). He wrote one of the first Ukrainian textbooks on general genetics, *Kurs zahal'noï henetyky* (A Course in General Genetics, 1933). During the war he headed the academy's Division of Biological Sciences (1940–3) and its Botanical Institute (1939–44), and then founded and directed the Central Republican Botanical Garden (1944–58). After T. Lysenko's triumph at the All-Union Academy of Agricultural Sciences in 1948, Hryshko lost his presidency of the Division of Agricultural Sciences at the AN URSR and his professorship at Kiev University. With the resurgence of Lysenkoism in 1958, he was demoted at the Botanical Garden to senior scientific worker. He died on the eve of Lysenko's fall from power.

Hryshko, Vasyl [Hryško, Vasyl'], b 1897, d ? in Montreal. Specialist in the history of law in the Hetman state. From 1930 to 1933 Hryshko was an associate of the VUAN *Commission for the Study of the History of Western-Ruthenian and Ukrainian Law in Kiev. He taught at the Ukrainian Free University in Munich from 1946 to 1949 and was a member of the Shevchenko Scientific Society from 1947. He is the author of articles on monastic properties in the Hetman state, the institution of elect Cossacks and Cossack helpers, and the second Lithuanian Statute. He was active in the Hetmanite movement in Canada and wrote for and edited several of its publications.

Hryshko, Vasyl (Wasyl) [Hryško, Vasyl'], b 15 January 1914 in Dubno, Volhynia. Emigré political figure, publicist, and literary scholar; member of the Slovo Ukrainian Writers' Association in Exile and a corresponding member of the Ukrainian Academy of Arts and Sciences in the United States. Imprisoned by the GPU in the 1930s, he immigrated to Germany after the war and to the United States in 1949.

Hryshko has been the ideologue of the *Ukrainian Revolutionary Democratic party since 1948, its leader (1967–75), and honorary head. He is the author of memoirs, many political and literary articles in émigré periodicals, and over a dozen books, including the novella collection *Styk* (The Junction, 1933), *Anty-SSSR* (Anti-USSR, 1952), *Experience with Russia* (1956), *Moloda Ukraïna porevoliutsiinoho sorokalittia pid Sovietamy (1918–1958)* (Young Ukraine of the Postrevolutionary Forty Years under the Soviets [1918–1958], 1958), *Tretia syla, tretii shliakh, tretia revoliutsiia* (The Third Power, Third Path, Third Revolution, 1970), and *The Ukrainian Holocaust of 1933* (1983).

Hryts-Duda, Ivan [Hryc'-Duda], b 5 June 1911 in Rudlova, Prešov region, Czechoslovakia. Actor, writer, collector of folklore, pedagogue. A graduate of the teachers' seminary in Uzhhorod (1935), he taught in rural schools in Transcarpathia. He was an actor with the Nova Stsena theater in Khust (1936–9) and then helped to organize the Ukrainian National Theater in Prešov (1946–61), where he also acted and served as director. His plays, poetry, and prose were published in the periodicals *Duklia, Nove zhyttia,* and *Druzhn'o vpered,* which he also edited. He has written a collection of short stories, *Nezhody* (Discords, 1967), an epic poem in two parts, and several dramas.

Hrytsa, Sofiia [Hryca], b 5 December 1932 in Lviv. Ethnomusicologist. A graduate of the Lviv conservatory, since 1957 she has worked at the AN URSR Institute of Fine Arts, Folklore, and Ethnography. Her areas of interest are the history of Ukrainian ethnomusicology, songs of the Carpathian region, and the melodies of Ukrainian epic songs. Among her chief publications are *Filaret Mykhailovych Kolessa* (1962) and *Melos ukraïns'koï narodnoï epiky* (Melos of the Ukrainian Folk Epic, 1979). She has also compiled numerous collections, including *Naimyts'ki ta zarobitchans'ki pisni* (Servants' and Laborers' Songs, 1975).

Hrytsai, Dmytro [Hrycaj] (*nom de guerre*: Perebyinis), b 1 April 1907 in Dorozhiv, Sambir county, Galicia, d 19 December 1945 in Prague. Prominent OUN leader and UPA officer, in 1933–4 he served as chief of the military and organizational department of the national executive of the OUN in Galicia. In 1934 Hrytsai was imprisoned for two years in the Bereza Kartuzka Polish concentration camp. In 1940–2 he was chief of the military department of the OUN (Bandera faction). Arrested by the Germans in 1942, in May 1943 he was rescued from a Gestapo prison. Promoted from major to general in November 1945, he was appointed UPA chief of staff. At the end of 1945 he was entrusted with an important mission to the OUN Leadership abroad, and was captured by Czechoslovak guards while attempting to cross the border to West Germany. Hrytsai committed suicide in prison.

Dmytro Hrytsai

Hrytsai, Mykhailo [Hrycaj, Myxajlo], b 16 September 1925. Folklorist and literary scholar. For many years he held the Chair of Ukrainian Literature and was dean of the philological faculty of Kiev University. His main works are *Ukraïns'ka literatura XVI–XVIII st. i fol'klor* (Ukrainian Literature in the 16th–18th Centuries and Folklore, 1968), *Davnia ukraïns'ka poeziia ...* (Old Ukrainian Poetry ..., 1972), and *Davnia ukraïns'ka proza ...* (Old Ukrainian Prose ..., 1975).

Hrytsai, Ostap [Hrycaj], b 2 November 1881 in Kniazhpil, Dobromyl county, Galicia, d 7 May 1954 in Munich. Journalist, critic, writer, and translator. After receiving a PH D in German language and literature from the University of Vienna in 1910, he taught at the Academic Gymnasium in Lviv. He lived in Vienna from 1914 to 1945 and then in Bavaria. During the First World War he belonged to the *Union for the Liberation of Ukraine. He was a full member of the Free Ukrainian Academy of Arts and Sciences and of the Shevchenko Scientific Society. His first literary works began to appear in *Sich* in 1908. His stories and articles appeared in such publications as *Dilo, Literaturno-naukovyi vistnyk, Svoboda, Volia,* and *Ukraïns'ke slovo.* A series of his articles on Ukrainian literature and his German translations of *Slovo o polku Ihorevi* (The Tale of Ihor's Campiagn), many of T. Shevchenko's poems, and poems by other Ukrainian poets were published in the Vienna newspaper *Ukrainische Nachrichten.*

Hrytsai, Vasyl [Hrycaj, Vasyl'] (stage name of Vasyl Koltanovsky), b 1856 in Kukovychi, Chernihiv county, Chernihiv gubernia, d 2 March 1910 in Kukovychi. Actor, singer, stage director. From 1883 to 1899 he acted in the troupes of M. Kropyvnytsky, M. Starytsky, P. Saksahansky, and D. Haidamaka. Then for the next seven years he managed his own troupe. He sang tenor and later baritone parts in S. Hulak-Artemovsky's *Zaporozhets' za Dunaiem* (Zaporozhian Cossack beyond the Danube), I. Kotliarevsky's *Natalka Poltavka* (Natalka from Poltava), and M. Starytsky and M. Lysenko's *Nich pered Rizdvom* (Christmas Eve). His most successful roles were as Yurko Dovbush and Khoma in M. Starytsky's *Iurko Dovbush* and *Oi, ne khody, Hrytsiu* (Don't Go to the Party, Hryts), and Mykyta in M. Kropyvnytsky's *Dai sertsiu voliu – zavede v nevoliu* (Give the Heart Free Reign and It Will Lead You into Slavery).

Hrytsak, Yevhen [Hrycak, Jevhen], b 5 January 1890 in Peratyn, Radekhiv county, Galicia, d 23 October 1944 in Czechoslovakia. Pedagogue and linguist. A graduate of Cracow University (PH D 1913), he taught at a gymnasium in Kiev from 1917 and worked as an associate of the VUAN Terminological Commission. He returned to Galicia in 1923 and taught in Peremyshl and (from 1940) Jarosław. While fleeing to the West in 1944 he was killed at the Orem-Laz refugee camp in Slovakia by Soviet partisans. Hrytsak's publications include studies of Ukrainian word formation, onomastics, and literature, dictionaries, and grammar textbooks. His chief works are: *Z istoriï ukraïns'koho knyzhkovoho rukhu na Velykii Ukraïni, 1917–1922* (On the History of the Ukrainian Book Movement in Great Ukraine, 1917–22, 1923), *Pid chervonoiu vladoiu: Shkil'na sprava na radians'kii Ukraïni* (Under the Red Regime: Schooling in Soviet Ukraine, 1923), and a Ukrainian-Polish and Polish-Ukrainian dictionary compiled with K. Kysilevsky (1931).

Hrytsiak, Yevhen [Hrycjak, Jevhen], b 1926 in Stetseva, Sniatyn county, Galicia. Soviet political prisoner. A Red Army veteran, he was arrested in 1949 and sentenced for his wartime, nationalist student activities to 25 years in Soviet labor camps in Soviet Central Asia and Siberia. He was one of the organizers of the 1953 prisoners' revolt in the Norilsk Camp. His memoirs of the revolt were published in the West in Ukrainian in 1980 and in English in 1984 (*The Norilsk Uprising*). Hrytsiak was amnestied in 1956, rearrested in 1959, and released again in 1964. In 1977 he lost his job at a Stetseva collective farm for applying to emigrate to Israel.

Hrytsiuk, Oleksander [Hrycjuk], b 10 October 1923 in Kiev. Internist; from 1978 corresponding member of the Academy of Medical Sciences of the USSR. A graduate (1951) of, and then lecturer at the Kiev Medical Institute, he became director of the Kiev Scientific Research Institute of Clinical Medicine (1970–4), and in 1973 head of the department of hospital therapy at the Kiev Medical Institute. His publications deal with cardiology, rheumatology, and the organization of therapeutic services.

Hryva, Matvii, b and d? A Zaporozhian Cossack and one of the leaders of the *Haidamaka uprisings in Right-Bank Ukraine in the 1730s. Hryva took part in the uprising led by *Verlan. In 1734 he led a force of peasants and Zaporozhian Cossacks on Vinnytsia and laid waste to landlords' estates in the region. After the uprising was suppressed, he retreated with his men to the Zaporozhian Sich. In the fall of 1736 Hryva and his haidamakas captured Pavoloch (now in Popilnia raion, Zhytomyr oblast) and Pohrebyshche (now in Vinnytsia oblast). His subsequent fate is unknown.

Hryvnak, Andrii, b 1898, d 13 February 1969 in Szczecin, Poland. Community and political leader. Hryvnak was a member of the chief executive of the Ukrainian Socialist Radical party in Galicia and a representative to the Polish Sejm from 1933. He was also a Supreme Council member of the Union of Ukrainian Progressive Youth in Lviv and a Rohatyn county union organizer. With the Soviet invasion of Western Ukraine in 1939, Hryvnak was elected head of a village soviet. Arrested by the

Soviets (1939) and sentenced to five years' hard labor, he was released into the Soviet army in 1944. In 1945 he was demobilized and settled in Szczecin.

Hryvnia [Hryvnja]. (1) An old monetary unit, originally silver in composition, which subsequently was defined as a unit of weight and a monetary unit, either real or for counting purposes. Frequently mentioned in *Ruskaia Pravda*, the *hryvnia* was divisible into smaller denominations (see *Currency).

(2) A silver coinage meant for use as an exchange medium. In Kievan Rus' the following types of *hryvni* were known: (a) hexagonal 'Kievan' *hryvni* weighing about 160 g (11th to the mid-13th centuries); (b) hexagonal coins of a slightly different form weighing 196 g (mid-13th century); (c) rhombic coins with variations and elongated coins with flattened tongue-like ends known as 'Chernihiv' *hryvni*, weighing about 196 g (12th century); (d) stick-like coins similar to 'Novgorod' *hryvni* but weighing 155 g (mid-13th century); and (e) short, boat-like *hryvni* weighing about 196 g found in southern Ukraine, probably of Tatar origin (approx 14th century).

(3) A unit of weight (a *hryvnia* of gold or of silver approx equivalent to 409.5 g) used in the 9th and subsequent centuries, probably borrowed from the Arabic east by inhabitants of the Dnieper region.

(4) A unit of currency issued by the independent Ukrainian state (1917–20), which in 1918 legally became the primary monetary unit.

V. Shuhaievsky

Hryvniak, Yurii [Hryvnjak, Jurij], b 30 May 1912 in Velykyi Bereznyi, Transcarpathia. Ukrainian scholar, publicist, and civic leader in Czechoslovakia. His research deals mainly with prominent Ukrainians in Czechoslovakia and Ukrainian-Czech relations. He wrote a monograph on I. Puliui (1971) and articles for the Ukrainian and Czech press. He also translated some works of M. Lysenko and S. Hulak-Artemovsky into Czech.

Huba, Ihor (secular name: Ivan), b 21 June 1885 in Bandurivka, Oleksandriia county, Kherson gubernia, d 24 November 1966 in New York. Archbishop of the Ukrainian Autocephalous Orthodox church. Ordained in 1921, he served as a priest in Poland and then in Kovel, Volhynia. From 1932 he served on the Commission for Translating the Holy Scripture and Liturgical Books at the Ukrainian Scientific Institute in Warsaw. On 10 February 1942 he was consecrated bishop of Uman and then promoted to archbishop of Poltava and Kremenchuk. Emigrating in 1944, he lived in Augsburg, Germany, until 1949 when he moved to the United States, where he founded the Cathedral of the Holy Trinity in New York. In 1954, with Archbishop P. Vydybida-Rudenko he formed the Ukrainian Autocephalous Orthodox Church in Exile.

Hubarenko, Vitalii, b 13 June 1934 in Kharkiv. Composer. A graduate of the Kharkiv Conservatory (1960, D. Klebanov's class), he has taught theory and composition at the conservatory since 1961. He has composed several operas, including *The Destruction of a Squadron* (based on O. Korniichuk's play) and *Mamai*, two symphonies (1961, 1965), a symphonic poem *In Memory of Taras Shevchenko* (1962), a symphonic picture *Kupalo* (1971), some concertos for cello and flute, chamber music, vocal cycles, and songs.

Hubariev, Oleksander [Hubarjev], b 1 September 1926 in Dnipropetrovske. Graphic artist. A graduate of the Kiev State Art Institute (1955), he produced a number of linocut series such as *Folk Ballads of Transcarpathia* (1966) and *Ukrainian Songs about Love* (1967); several watercolor series such as *Through Svanetiia* (1965), *Along the Yenisei* (1966), and *Through Tuva* (1970); book illustrations; and numerous bookplates. An album of his works was published by V. Shevchuk in 1967.

Hubenko, Pavlo. See Vyshnia, Ostap.

Huberhrits, Maks [Huberhric], b 19 January 1886 in Romen, Poltava gubernia, d 6 May 1951 in Kiev. Physician; from 1948 full member of the AN URSR. A graduate of Kiev University (1911), he worked in its clinic (1911–14) and in I. Pavlov's physiological laboratory (1915–17). He headed the department of diagnosis and special pathology (1920–8) and the department of internal medicine (1928–51) of the Kiev Medical Institute. From 1945 he was also scientific director of the Institute of Nutrition of the Ministry of Public Health of the Ukrainian SSR. His publications deal with the physiology and pathology of blood circulation and metabolism.

Hubitsky, Taras [Hubic'kyj], b 1908 in Drohobych, Galicia, d 1974 in Detroit. Musician and musical director. In 1910 his parents immigrated to Canada. He received his musical education in Winnipeg and at the Royal Academy of Music in London, England, and became a leader in Ukrainian musical circles in Canada. He was a contributor to and patron of the journal *Ukraïns'ka muzyka* (1937–9), published by the Union of Ukrainian Professional Musicians in Lviv. He lived in Detroit from 1937, where he played with the symphony orchestra and founded the Detroit String Orchestra.

Hubkiv. Village in Berezne raion, Rivne oblast, situated on the Sluch River. The ruins of a 15th-century castle are found here. On 2 July 1943 German troops herded the villagers into the village church and set it on fire, killing several hundred adults and children, including the Rev Venedykt Kornytsky and the psalmist Borys Petriv.

Huchva River [Hučva] (Polish: Huczwa). A left-bank tributary of the Buh River, located in Lublin voivodeship, Poland, on Ukrainian ethnographic territory in the southern Kholm region. The Huchva is 80 km long, and its basin area is 1,431 sq km. The town of Hrubeshiv is located on the Huchva.

Huculak, Michael [Huculjak, Myxajlo], b 15 July 1894 in Novoselytsia, Dolyna county, Galicia, d 28 August 1976 in Vancouver. Educator. After the war he attended the University of Vienna (PH D 1926) and then taught secondary school in Rivne, Kalush, Vienna, Karlsfeld, and Berchtesgaden. After the Second World War he immigrated to Canada and settled in Vancouver, where he founded the Ukrainian Teachers' Association of Canada.

He is the author of *When Russia Was in America: The Alaska Boundary Treaty Negotiations, 1824–5, and the Role of Pierre de Poletica* (1971).

Hudovych [Hudovyč]. Name of a Cossack *starshyna* family. Among its members was Vasyl Hudovych (d 1764), a fellow of the standard and a general treasurer (1764) in the Hetman state. He was a member of the delegation that went to the Russian government in 1745–9 with the request to restore the Hetmanate.

Vasyl's son Ivan (1741–1820) had an illustrious career in the Russian service. He was named a count in 1797 for his exploits during the Russo-Turkish wars and as governor-general of Caucasia was appointed the military governor of Kiev and, later, Kamianets-Podilsky, with jurisdiction in Volhynia and Minsk gubernias (1798–1800). In 1807 he became a field marshal for his role in annexing and subduing Caucasia in 1806–7. In 1804 he became commander of the Russian army in Moscow and a member of the State Council. He retired in 1812. He was married to the daughter of Hetman K. Rozumovsky, Praskoviia.

Another son, Andrii (b 1731, d 24 June 1808), studied, like his brother Ivan, at the universities of Königsberg, Halle, and Leipzig. He had close ties with Prussian governing circles. He was an adjutant general and adviser to Tsar Peter III (1761–2) and took part in the diplomatic negotiations ending the Seven Years' War. After Catherine II came to power, he went into retirement, traveled abroad, and lived on his large estates in Starodub and Chernihiv regiments. He maintained close ties with members of the *Novhorod-Siverskyi patriotic circle and with V. Kapnist. For his loyalty to Peter III, his son, Tsar Paul I, made Hudovych a general and a knight in 1796. The Hudovych family had familial and social ties with most of the Ukrainian elite of the period.

O. Ohloblyn

Huietsky, Semen [Hujec'kyj], b 15 May 1902 in Zhytomyr, Volhynia gubernia, d 20 August 1974 in Kiev. Painter. A graduate of the Kiev State Art Institute (1929) and a student of F. Krychevsky and L. Kramarenko, he specialized in historic and revolutionary themes. His best-known works include *In the Last Underground* (1958–9), *On the Threshhold of Life* (1962–3), and *The Return* (1970–1). He also did still lifes, landscapes, and portraits.

Huiva River. [Hujva]. A right-bank tributary of the upper Teteriv River. The Huiva flows for 97 km through the Dnieper River basin. Its own basin has an area of 1,505 sq km.

Huklyvyi Chronicle. A chronicle, begun in 1660 and continued until 1830, that was an addition to the register of the village of Huklyvyi, now in Transcarpathia oblast. It was written in the vernacular and described political and religious events and everyday life in Transcarpathia. Its main author was the village priest, M. Hryhashii.

Hulak, Mykola, b 1822 in a village of Zolotonosha county, Poltava gubernia, d 7 June 1899 in Yelizavetpol, Azerbaijan. Educator and scholar. A graduate of Dorpat (Tartu) University (1843), he was a founder and one of the radical members of the *Cyril and Methodius Brotherhood. He was severely punished for this association by imprisonment in Schlüsselburg Fortress (1847–50) and exile in Perm (1850–5). Then he taught secondary school in southern Ukraine and Caucasia. Known for his encyclopedic knowledge, he wrote studies in history, philology, literature, and mathematics, and translated some Georgian and Azerbaijan literary works.

Mykola Hulak

Petro Hulak-Artemovsky

Hulak-Artemovsky, Petro [Hulak-Artemovs'kyj], b 27 January 1790 in Horodyshche, Kiev gubernia, d 13 October 1865 in Kharkiv. Poet, fabulist, scholar and translator of classical literature. After studying at the Kiev Theological Academy and Kharkiv University, in 1818 he was appointed lecturer of Polish at Kharkiv University, and in 1825, professor of Russian history and geography. From 1841 to 1849 he served as the university's rector. He began to publish in 1817. Familiar with the peasants' language and way of life, he wrote in the tradition of I. *Kotliarevsky, using burlesque in his fables, supplications, poems, and travesties of Horace's odes. His best-known fable, 'Pan i sobaka' (The Master and His Dog, 1818), satirizes the arbitrary brutality of the serf-owning gentry. Some of his works, such as 'Do liubky' (To My Beloved), exhibit elements of sentimentalism. His Romantic ballads, 'Rybalka' (The Fisherman) and 'Tvardovs'kyi,' are thematic borrowings from J. von Goethe and A. Mickiewicz supplemented with Ukrainian elements. His works are collected in *Tvory* (Works, 1927, with an introduction by I. Aizenshtok) and *Baiky, balady, liryka* (Fables, Ballads, Lyric Poetry, 1958, with an introduction by I. Pilhuk).

Hulak-Artemovsky, Semen [Hulak-Artemovs'kyj], b 16 February 1813 in Horodyshche, Cherkasy county, Kiev gubernia, d 17 April 1873 in Moscow. Composer, opera singer, actor, and dramatist. He was the nephew of P. Hulak-Artemovsky and a close friend of T. Shevchenko. A graduate of the Kiev Theological Seminary, he studied voice in St Petersburg and Florence (1839–42). He was noted for his dramatic talent and his powerful, rich baritone voice. From 1842 Hulak-Artemovsky was the leading soloist at the Mariinskii Theater and the Italian Opera in St Petersburg. His repertoire included over 50 operatic roles, including Ruslan in M. Glinka's *Ruslan and Liudmila*, Masetto in Mozart's *Don Giovanni*, Antonio and Lord Ashton in G. Donizetti's *Linda di Chamounix* and

Semen Hulak-Artemovsky

Oleksa Huliaiev

Lucia di Lammermoor. He wrote the comic opera *Zaporozhets' za Dunaiem* (Zaporozhian Cossack beyond the Danube, 1863), in which he sang the part of Karas; the divertissement *Ukraïns'ke vesillia* (The Ukrainian Wedding, 1851), in which he sang the father-in-law; the vaudeville *Nich na Ivan Kupala* (St John's Eve, 1852); and several songs. As an actor he appeared in roles such as Vybornyi and Chupryna in I. Kotliarevsky's *Natalka Poltavka* (Natalka from Poltava) and *Moskal'-charivnyk* (The Muscovite-Sorcerer).

BIBLIOGRAPHY
Kaufman, L. *S.S. Hulak-Artemovs'kyi* (Kiev 1962)

W. Wytwycky

Hulbyshche [Hul'byšče]. A kurhan in Chernihiv from the 10th century AD. Excavations carried out in 1872 by D. Samokvasov uncovered a large burial containing the cremated remains of a warrior and a woman; animal bones; gold, silver, and bronze buttons and buckles; bronze tableware fragments; helmets; chain-link armor; weapons, some with silver ornamentation; and other artifacts.

Hulevychivna, Yelyzaveta [Hulevyčivna, Jelyzaveta], 1575–1642. Kievan noblewoman and benefactress; wife of the marshal of Mozyr, S. Lozka. In 1615 she donated to the *Kiev Epiphany Brotherhood a building and land in the Podil district of Kiev for the establishment of an Orthodox monastery, school, hostel, and hospital. The latter part of her life was spent in Lutske, where she involved herself in the work of the Lutske Brotherhood.

Huliai-Pole [Huljaj-Pole]. VI-17. Town (1970 pop 16,200) on the Haichur River and a raion center in Zaporizhia oblast. It was founded in 1785 as a military settlement. From 1917 to 1921 it was the center of N. *Makhno's anarchist activity. The city has agricultural-machinery, automobile-repair, paint, consumer-products, food-processing, mixed-feed, and shoe plants and a historical museum.

Huliaiev, Oleksa [Huljajev], b 1 March 1863 in Kiev, d 27 November 1923 in Kiev. Jurist of civil law and specialist in Roman law; member of the All-Ukrainian Academy of Sciences. After graduating from Kiev University, he continued his studies in Berlin. He lectured at Dorpat (Tartu), Kiev (1894–1908), St Petersburg, and Moscow universities. In 1920 he was appointed professor at the Kiev Institute of the National Economy. His chief works are *Naem uslug* (Hiring of Labor, 1893) and *Russkoe grazhdanskoe pravo* (Russian Civil Law, 1913).

Hulianytsky, Hryhorii [Huljanyc'kyj, Hryhorij], b and d ? Cossack military figure and diplomat; Ukrainian nobleman from the Volhynia region. Hulianytsky was colonel of the Nizhen (1656–9) and Korsun regiments (1662). He accomplished several diplomatic missions to Russia for Hetman B. Khmelnytsky. Later he criticized Khmelnytsky's decision to seek alliances with the Ottoman Porte and Russia, becoming a leading proponent of a pro-Polish orientation by the Cossacks. He was a supporter of Hetman I. Vyhovsky, helped suppress the rebellion led by Ya. Barabash and M. Pushkar against the hetman in 1657–8, and participated in Vyhovsky's campaign to end Ukraine's alliance with Russia. Hulianytsky particularly distinguished himself in the Ukrainian victory over the Russian army at Konotip in 1659. After Vyhovsky's defeat and removal from office in 1659, Hulianytsky supported Hetman Yu. Khmelnytsky. In 1660 he helped conclude the Treaty of *Slobodyshche. In 1663–4 he took part in P. Teteria's campaign against the Russians in Left-Bank Ukraine, but was defeated in battle. Accused of treason by S. Czarniecki, he was imprisoned by the Poles in 1664. Released in 1667, he became a colonel of the Polish army in 1675.

Hůlka, Rudolf, b 15 November 1887 in Lasenice, Jindřichův Hradec county, Czechoslovakia, d 18 September 1961 in Prague. Czech economist, painter, translator, and popularizer of Ukrainian literature. In 1922 he published a postcard series of 16 sketches of wooden churches and belfries in Transcarpathia. Encouraged by V. *Hnatiuk, in the early 1920s he began to translate Ukrainian works into Czech. Of his translations, 37 books have been published and about 20 remain in manuscript form. He translated almost the complete works of V. Stefanyk, L. Martovych, M. Kotsiubynsky, and M. Cheremshyna.

Hultai, Vasyl [Hul'taj, Vasyl'] (Hultay, William), b 10 August 1900 in Hlushkiv, Horodenka county, Galicia, d 18 June 1974 in Toronto. Community leader. After serving in the UHA Army, Hultai studied at Cracow University. A member of the Ukrainian Military Organization, in 1927 he immigrated to Canada to avoid harassment by Polish police. He was a founder and head of the Ukrainian War Veterans' Association of Canada, and a founding member of the *Ukrainian National Federation, serving as chief organizer, deputy head (1938–46), head (1954–6), and first president (1956–7). He also founded the New Pathway Publishers and the Ukrainian Cultural and Educational Centre in Winnipeg.

Huly, Maksym [Hulyj], b 3 March 1905 in Nova Basan, Kozelets county, Chernihiv gubernia. Biochemist; since 1957 full member of the AN URSR. A graduate of the Kiev Veterinary-Zootechnical Institute (1929), in 1932 he became a research associate, in 1950 a department head, and in 1971 director of the Institute of Biochemistry of the AN URSR. At the same time (1944–76) he chaired the Department of Biochemistry of the Ukrainian Agricultural Academy. A member of the Presidium of the Academy of Sciences since 1957, he was its vice-president from 1958 to 1962. His publications consist of over 170 papers on metabolism, physicochemical properties of proteins, and the biosynthesis of proteins. He developed methods of isolating, purifying, and crystallizing tissue proteins that proved useful in the production of fermentation preparations for industry and medicine, methods of combating diabetes and ketosis in human beings and animals, and methods of stimulating biosynthetic processes that help to increase productivity in animal husbandry.

Huly-Hulenko, Andrii [Huluj-Hulenko, Andrij], b 1886, d 1921? Senior officer of the UNR Army. He came to prominence as an insurgent commander supporting the *Directory in southern Ukraine during 1918–19. In 1920 he commanded the 1st (Zaporozhian) Division of the UNR Army. In November 1921 he commanded the Bessarabian Group in the Second Winter Campaign, entering Ukraine from Rumania. He was captured by Bolshevik forces and probably executed.

Human. See Uman.

Human geography. The study of the spatial distribution of various human phenomena (social, cultural, economic, political, or historical), of their interrelationship, and of their relation to the physical environment. The main branches of human geography are social, cultural, political, economic, urban, population, transportation, and historical geography.

The human geography of Ukraine was founded as a scientific discipline by S. *Rudnytsky. Calling his major study *Osnovy zemleznannia Ukraïny*, Knyha 2: *Antropoheohrafiia Ukraïny* (Foundations of the Earth Science of Ukraine, vol 2: Anthropogeography of Ukraine, 1926), he borrowed the title and organizing concepts from two outstanding German geographers, C. Ritter and F. Ratzel, and the French geographer E. Reclus, who in his *Nouvelle géographie universelle* (1876–94) singled out Ukraine as a major region. He also adopted some aspects of Ratzel's environmental determinism. Rudnytsky defined Ukraine as an anthropogeograhic unit – a continuous territory inhabited by the Ukrainian nation – and justified his approach by observing that a nation's territory was more stable than the political borders. He defined a nation as a large group of people who identify themselves as members of a group, occupy a given territory for a long time, and share a common language, culture, tradition, and political aspirations.

Further contributions to the human geography of Ukraine were made by V. *Kubijovyč and his associates, who accepted Rudnytsky's definition of Ukraine, updated the data, and published the first atlas of Ukraine (1937), covering 66 topics and containing over 200 maps and diagrams. This effort was followed by *Heohrafiia ukraïns'kykh i sumezhnykh zemel'* (Geography of Ukrainian and Bordering Lands, 1943). The work not only updated Rudnytsky's data but provided more detailed discussion by specialists of the history of Ukrainian colonization of the land (I. Krypiakevych), contemporary distribution of population, population dynamics, nationalities in Ukraine and inter-ethnic relations (V. Kubijovyč), physical anthropology of Ukrainians (R. Yendyk), geography of Ukrainian language and dialects (I. Zilynsky), and a study of settlements (Kuvijovyč, M. Kulytsky).

Soviet geographers, however, rejected not only environmental determinism but also anthropogeography. They divided geography into physical geography (where interrelations among phenomena are determined by laws of physical sciences) and economic geography (where interrelations are determined by laws of economics). Specialized fields such as population geography and urban geography were developed within *economic geography. By 1982 the discipline was broadened to economic and social geography, which would incorporate all aspects of human activity in its spatial manifestations, including problems of social anthropology and human ecology.

BIBLIOGRAPHY

Rudnyts'kyi, S. *Osnovy zemleznannia Ukraïny*, 2: *Antropoheohrafiia Ukraïny* (Uzhhorod 1926)
Kubiiovych, V. (ed). *Atlas of Ukraine and Adjoining Countries* (Lviv 1937)
– *Heohrafiia ukraïnskykh i sumezhnykh zemel'* (Cracow-Lviv 1943)
Tverdokhlebov, I.; Shvets', A. 'Territorial'no-khoziaistvennaia sistema kak ob"ekt izucheniia ekonomicheskoi i sotsial'noi geografii,' *Ekonomicheskaia geografiia*, no. 32 (1982)
Vashchenko, A.; Kuz'minskaia, E. 'Nekotorye aspekty ekonomiko-geograficheskikh issledovanii v svete sovremennykh sotsial'nykh problem,' *Ekonomicheskaia geografiia*, no. 37 (1985)

I. Stebelsky

Human rights. Fundamental claims which are, or should be, legally recognized and protected to secure the fullest development of each and every individual's personality. Usually such rights are regarded as inherent in humans, ie, not conferred by positive law, and hence inalienable. The theory of human rights, first conceived of as natural rights, originated with the Greek and Roman Stoics and was developed by the Fathers of the Church, the medieval theologians, and Protestant thinkers. They were asserted in the Petition of Right (1628), the Bill of Rights (1689), the American Declaration of Independence (1776), and the French Declaration of the Rights of Man and of the Citizen (1789), and played a decisive role in the English Civil War and the American and French revolutions. In the 19th and 20th centuries some basic rights have been enshrined in the constitutions of many states and have been translated to varying degrees into legal rights. Classical rights (to life, liberty, security of person, equality before the law, private property, freedom of thought, speech, and assembly, right to representation) tended to be negative – they placed restraints on the state for the sake of individual liberty and political equality. The new rights demanded in the 20th century (to work, rest and leisure, adequate standard of living, education, social security, and participation in culture) are positive – they require the state to provide certain goods and services to ensure social equality and economic security. Since individual rights can be realized only within a given people's culture and tradition, the concept of human rights must include the rights of peoples. The right of all peoples to equality and self-determination has been widely recognized in the 20th century. The mass terror inflicted by states on their own citizens and the two world wars in this century have made human rights a leading concern of individuals, governments, and international organizations.

The League of Nations did not come forth with a comprehensive statement on human rights, but it did attempt to protect certain human rights through its Covenant and the mandate system. Some peace treaties after the First World War contained special provisions for the rights of racial, linguistic, and religious minorities (see *national minorities). A more concerted approach to human rights was made by the United Nations (UN). Its charter demands respect for human rights and fundamental freedoms as a guarantee of international co-operation and peace. In 1946 the UN Commission on Human Rights was set up under the Economic and Social Council to prepare an international bill of rights. The first part of the bill – the Universal Declaration of Human Rights – was ratified by the General Assembly on 10 December 1948. This was, in a sense, a revolutionary document: although it lacked any legal force, it set a standard by which governments could be judged by the world public. Its moral and political significance is immense. The second part of the commission's work was to prepare the International Covenant on Civil and Political Rights (1966) and the International Covenant on Economic, Social, and Cultural Rights (1966). Signatories of these treaties, including the USSR, the Belorussian SSR, and the Ukrainian SSR (19 October 1973), undertake to respect the rights specified in the first document and make progress towards realizing the rights specified in the second. Besides these general treaties the UN has adopted a number of special conventions that deal with the rights of specific categories of people such as refugees, stateless persons, women, and children. Only some of these agreements have been signed by the Ukrainian SSR: the International Convention on Elimination of All Forms of Racial Discrimination (1980), the International Convention on the Suppression and Punishment of the Crime of Apartheid (1975), and the Convention on the Non-Applicability of Statutory Limitations to War Crimes and Crimes against Humanity (1969).

The Ukrainian SSR was a member of several UN agencies in the field of human rights: the Commission on Human Rights (1946–7, 1983–5), the Special Committee on the Policies of Apartheid (from 1970), the Committee on the Elimination of Racial Discrimination (1970–1), the Commission on the Status of Women (1981–4), and the Human Rights Committee. The last was formed in 1976 to examine the reports of signatories to the Covenant on Civil and Political Rights and to deal with petitions from signatories concerning the violations of human rights in other countries. Its recommendations have a certain moral and political influence, but no legal power. In 1968 Ukraine's representative on the committee, Prof P. *Nedbailo, was the first laureate of its annual prize for work on behalf of human rights. Soviet representatives at the UN often criticize human rights violations in other countries such as South Africa, Chile, and Israel.

Human rights provisions were part of the Final Act of the Conference on Security and Co-operation in Europe, which was signed on 1 August 1975 in Helsinki by 35 countries, including the USSR but not the Ukrainian SSR. The so-called Third Basket of the agreement guarantees the fundamental freedoms and such rights as freedom of movement across borders, free exchange of ideas, emigration, and family reunification. The Soviet Union has failed to live up to its undertakings on human rights, and this has been pointed out to its representatives at the periodic review conferences on the Helsinki Accords. Besides official delegations, spokesmen of non-governmental organizations have attended these conferences in Belgrade, Madrid, and Vienna and have staged their own parallel forums. The most active Ukrainian human rights groups in the West are the Human Rights Commission of the World Congress of Free Ukrainians, the External Representation of the Ukrainian Helsinki Group, Americans for Human Rights in Ukraine, Prolog, and Smoloskyp associations. Independent organizations such as *Amnesty International and Freedom House play an important role in the worldwide struggle for human rights, including the struggle in Ukraine.

The worldwide human rights movement spread to the USSR and Eastern Europe after J. Stalin's death (see *dissident movement). Calling themselves *pravozakhystnyky* (rights defenders), Soviet dissidents exposed their government's violation of Soviet law, the Soviet constitution, and international commitments on human rights. The struggle for human rights in Ukraine entered a new phase after the mass arrests of dissidents in 1972–3 and the signing of the Helsinki Accords. In fall 1976 the *Ukrainian Helsinki Group, consisting of 10 members, arose in Kiev. During its brief existence it prepared and disseminated about 20 documents concerning human rights violations in Ukraine, including several memoranda to the signatories of the Helsinki Accords who had gathered for a review conference in Belgrade. The group was repressed and its members were severely punished. In spite of heavy sacrifices the human rights movement in Ukraine has not been crushed. Although it is now largely invisible, it occasionally displays signs of vitality. At the beginning of the 1980s, for example, the Ukrainian Committee for the Defense of the Rights of the Ukrainian Catholic Church and the Rights of the Faithful was formed under the leadership of Y. Terelia.

BIBLIOGRAPHY

Kolsyk, W. *Violation des droits de l'homme en Ukraine et en URSS* (Paris 1969)

Chalidze, V. *To Defend These Rights: Human Rights and the Soviet Union* (New York 1974)

Verba, L.; Yasen, B. (eds). *The Human Rights Movement in Ukraine: Documents of the Ukrainian Helsinki Group, 1976–80* (Baltimore-Washington-Toronto 1980)

Ovsiuk, O. *Ideolohichna borot'ba i prava liudyny* (Kiev 1982)

Zinkevych, O. (ed). *Ukraïns'ka Hel'sins'ka Hrupa, 1978–82. Dokumenty i materiialy* (Toronto-Baltimore 1983)

V. Markus

Humanism. The broad program of cultural reform inspired by the ideal of *humanitas* – the harmonious synthesis of intellectual, moral, and political virtues in a fully active life – and implemented by redirecting inquiry and education to classical studies. In reacting against the scholasticism of the medieval period, the humanists went far beyond simply reviving classical Greek and Latin and emulating the ancient writers. They reoriented man's interest from God and the afterlife to the individual and the fullest realization of his potentialities in this life. They freed men's minds from dogmatism and servility, and encouraged criticism and creativity. They offered hope of a new golden age rivaling that of Pericles and Augustus. Thus, humanism was nothing less than a total world view that constituted the intellectual underpinning of the Renaissance. Originating in the 14th century in the Italian city-states, in the 15th century it received a strong impetus from the influx of scholars and classical texts from Byzantium; towards the end of the 15th and the beginning of the 16th century it spread from Italy to the rest of Europe. Its chief patrons and supporters were the secular rulers of Europe – patricians, princes, and kings who often employed humanists as ministers and diplomats. Humanism also received some support from the Catholic church, which assimilated some of its ideas and used them in the service of faith. As a complete secular alternative to the religious culture of the medieval period, humanism has had a decisive influence on the development of Western culture.

Humanistic ideas began to enter Ukraine towards the end of the 15th century. Their main carriers were foreign visitors and Ukrainian graduates of foreign universities. Because of an active trade between Galicia and the Italian states of Genoa, Venice, and Florence, a sizable Italian colony consisting of merchants, manufacturers, bankers, technical experts, and legal advisers flourished in Lviv in the 15th and 16th centuries. One of its most influential families, the Tebaldis, had close ties with Florentine humanists. It was probably A. Tebaldi who invited the humanist F. Buonaccorsi (Callimachus Experience) to Lviv in 1470. After medieval Lviv was destroyed by fire in 1527, a new city was built largely by Italian architects in the Renaissance style.

It is evident from student registers that sons of Ukrainian (Ruthenian) nobles and burghers studied at such universities as the Sorbonne, Bologna, Padua, Prague, and Heidelberg from as early as the 14th century. In the 15th and 16th centuries Cracow University admitted about 800 Ukrainians. A number of Ukrainians educated abroad became humanist scholars and educators: Yu. *Drohobych, professor of Bologna and Cracow universities in the 1480s; Prince A. Svirsky, lecturer on Aristotle at Cracow University; Pavlo Rusyn (Paulus Ruthenus) from Krosno, teacher of Latin literature at Cracow University (1506–8) and then active among Hungarian humanists; and Lukash from Nove Misto, lecturer at Cracow University and author of a textbook in epistolography (1522).

The curriculum and methodology of the *brotherhood schools, colleges, and academies (see *Higher education) founded in Ukrainian and Belorussian territories in the 16th–18th centuries were strongly influenced by humanistic pedagogical theory and pratice. The trivium and quadrivium inherited from the medieval schools constituted merely a framework that became filled with a new content – the classical languages and literatures. Jesuit and, later, Piarist schools emphasized Latin. Orthodox schools, in contrast, at first gave primacy to Greek, without neglecting Church Slavonic and Latin, but eventually turned to Latin in order to compete more effectively in the religious arena. The program of Uniate schools, which were established in the 17th and 18th centuries, was similar to that of the Orthodox schools. Greek churchmen and scholars who had studied in Italy and were steeped in humanistic studies played an important role in the development of Orthodox schools in Ukraine; for example, *Arsenii of Elasson served as rector of the Lviv Dormition Brotherhood School, and C. *Lucaris served as lecturer at the *Ostrih Academy (M. Smotrytsky referred to him as his teacher) and as rector of the brotherhood school in Vilnius.

The clearest evidence of humanistic influences in Ukrainian literature of the late 16th and 17th centuries is found in the *polemical literature. Although the polemical tracts of such writers as Z. Kopystensky, Kh. Filatet, L. Zyzanii, H. and M. Smotrytsky, and I. Potii are devoid of the tolerant spirit that was typical of humanists, they display an intimate knowledge of classical literature, an acquaintance with recent humanistic writing, and a mastery of the rhetorical devices and dialectical techniques practiced by the humanists. I. Vyshensky, the most gifted and powerful writer among the Orthodox polemicists, employed a style closely resembling that of the humanists, while rejecting their learning and educational program. A few Western literary works of the Renaissance period were translated into Ukrainian. While literary production in the Ukrainian (Ruthenian) language was very limited at the time, some Ukrainian writers, who came to be classified as Polish humanists, wrote in Latin. Pavlo Rusyn from Krosno produced a collection of Latin poetry entitled *Carmina* (1509). S. Orikhovsky (Orichovius Ruthenus) wrote a number of political treatises, including *Fidelis Subditus* (1543) and *Quincunxie* (1564), collections of historical studies such as *Origo Polonorum* (publ posthumously 1611), and pamphlets warning against the Turkish threat. A professor of Cracow University, Tychynsky, signed his panegyrics Ticiensis Roxolanus, and Ch. Samborchyk used the pen name Vigilantius Gregorius Samboritanus Ruthenus. J. Herburt, the author of *Tabulae*, was known as Ioannis Ruthenus, and it is possible that J. Szczesny Herburt, a Polish writer who defended the Orthodox church and the Ukrainian people from the Polish Catholic offensive, was of Ukrainian origin.

The humanistic school in Polish literature, which was founded by J. Kochanowski, included some writers of Ukrainian origin and often dealt with Ukrainian themes. M. Sęp Szarzyński (1550–81), who was born in Galicia, quoted Ukrainian songs in his poetry. In his Latin poem *Roxolania* (1584), S. Klonowicz (1545–1602) depicted contemporary life in Ukraine, and Sz. Szymonowicz (1558–1629), who was born in Lviv, produced a collection of verses about peasant life in Ukraine – *Sielanki* (Peasant Idylls, 1614, 1628). The latter was imitated by Sz. (1608–29) and J. (1597–1677) Zimorowicz in their collections *Roksolanki – to jest ruskie panny* (Roxolanas – That Is, Ruthenian Girls, 1654) and *Nowe sielanki ruskie* (New Ruthenian Peasant Idylls, 1663). B. Głowacki (1543–1614), in his poem on Ivan Pidkova, praised the military prowess of the Cossacks.

Polish historical writing at the time had a humanistic inspiration. The works of Maciej z Miechowa (1457–1523), M. (1455–1575) and J. (1540–99) Bielski, M. Stryjkowski (1547–82), and S. Sarnicki (1532–97) contained much information about Ukraine (derived from extant Ukrainian chronicles) and influenced the development of Ukrainian historical writing in the 17th century.

The humanistic tradition remained a vital force in 17th- and 18th-century Ukrainian literature, which is commonly known as the Ukrainian *baroque. Poetics and rhetoric textbooks (most of which were in Latin) written by Ukrainians were based on Italian or German models. Original Ukrainian poetry and drama were heavily influenced by classical and humanist authors. Much of this literature was written in Latin by such scholars as S. Yavorsky, T. Lopatynsky, T. Prokopovych, and S. Polotsky. The centrality of the humanistic curriculum in higher education accounts for the enormous influence of humanistic studies and ideals in Ukrainian culture to the end of the 18th century.

BIBLIOGRAPHY
Hlobenko, M. 'Do pytan' vyvchennia barokkovoï doby na Ukraïni,' *Ukraïna*, 1952, no. 8
Lempicki, S. *Renesans i humanizm w Polsce* (Warsaw 1952)
Marchenko, M. *Istoriia ukraïns'koï kul'tury z naidavnishykh chasiv do seredyny* XVII *st.* (Kiev 1961)
Golenishchev-Kutuzov, I. *Gumanizm u vostochnykh slavian (Ukraina i Belorussiia)* (Moscow 1963)
Kravtsiv, B. 'Renesans i humanizm na Ukraïni,' *Suchasnist'*, 1974, no. 9
Čyževs'kyi, D. *A History of Ukrainian Literature*, trans D. Ferguson et al (Littleton, Colo 1975)
Ovsiichuk, V. *Ukraïns'ke mystetstvo druhoï polovyny* XVI–*pershoï polovyny* XVII *st.: Humanistychni ta vyzvol'ni ideï* (Kiev 1985)
K. Mytrovych, T. Zakydalsky

Humeniuk, Andrii [Humenjuk, Andrij], b 1916. Folklorist; professor at the Kiev Institute of Culture, specializing in folk songs, dance, and instrumental music. Among his chief works are *Ukraïns'ki narodni muzychni instrumenty* (Ukrainian Folk Musical Instruments, 1967), *Ukraïns'kyi narodnyi khor* (The Ukrainian Folk Choir, 1969), *Narodne khoreohrafichne mystetstvo Ukraïny* (The Folk Choreographic Art of Ukraine, 1969), and *Instrumental'na muzyka* (Instrumental Music, 1972). He also compiled a number of collections, including *Ukraïns'ki narodni tantsi* (Ukrainian Folk Dances, 1972).

Feodosii Humeniuk

Humeniuk, Feodosii [Humenjuk, Feodosij], b 1941 in Rybchyntsi, Khmilnyk raion, Vinnytsia oblast. Non-conformist painter. A graduate of the Dnipropetrovske Art School and the Leningrad Institute of Sculpture, Architecture, and Painting (1965), in 1974 he took part in the first unofficial art exhibition in Leningrad and in 1975 he and V. Makarenko organized the first avant-garde art exhibition in a private apartment in Moscow. This led to Humeniuk's expulsion from the Union of Artists of the USSR and banishment to Dnipropetrovske. His works, which tourists had managed to bring out of the USSR, were exhibited without his permission in Toronto in 1978, 1980, and 1984. Humeniuk deals with historical and religious themes through a rich system of symbols. Such canvases as *Banduryst, The Hetmans, Kozak Mamai, Christmas Eve Supper* (1977), *Shevchenko*, and *The Holy Family* (1976) express his deep love for Ukraine and her past. From a formal aspect, Humeniuk's work is closely related to M. Boichuk's monumentalist style, which combines old Byzantine traditions with folk art and modern Western styles, and remains a dominant influence in Ukraine's artistic processes.

Theodore Humeniuk

Humeniuk, Theodore [Humenjuk, Teodor], b 21 November 1891 in Potochyska, Horodenka county, Galicia, d 4 March 1978 in Toronto. Lawyer and community leader. Humeniuk went to Canada in 1908. Graduating from the Osgoode Hall Law School in 1923, he became the first Ukrainian to practice law in eastern Canada. He was one of the first Ukrainians to be appointed King's Counsel. Active in the Ukrainian Greek Orthodox church, Humeniuk was a founder and president of the Ukrainian Self-Reliance League and of its foundation. For many years he contributed articles and satirical poems to the newspaper *Ukraïns'kyi holos*. From 1941 to 1950 he served as president of the Toronto branch of the Ukrainian Canadian Committee.

Dokiia Humenna

Humenna, Dokiia, b 10 March 1904 in a suburb of Zhashkiv, Kiev gubernia. Writer. She studied literature at the Institute of People's Education in Kiev. Her first literary sketch, 'U stepu' (In the Steppe), was published in 1924, and thereafter her prose appeared in the major

Soviet Ukrainian literary journals. She belonged to the peasant writers' association *Pluh. Her travel reports, 'Lysty z stepovoï Ukraïny' (Letters from Steppe Ukraine, *Pluh*, 1928) and *Ekh, Kuban', ty Kuban' khliborodnaia* (Eh, Kuban, Kuban, You Bountiful Land, (published in *Chervonyi shliakh*, 1930, and separately, in 1931), incurred party censure. Stalinist terror forced her to remain silent until 1939. Then several stories and the novelette *Virus* (Virus, 1940) appeared, which once again brought on official censure. Escaping to Lviv during the German occupation of the USSR, she contributed her prose to the periodic press there. Emigrating after the war, she lived in DP camps in Austria and Germany where she wrote a collection of stories *Kurkul's'ka viliia* (The Kulaks' Christmas Eve, 1946) and began her famous tetralogy *Dity chumats'koho shliakhu* (Children of the Milky Way, 1948–51), which she finished after moving to New York City. Since settling in the United States, Humenna has maintained a very active literary career, publishing more that 15 books and contributing to journals and collections. Her abiding interest in feminism, prehistoric life, mythology, and archeology is evident in most of her postwar works, such as *Mana* (Delusion, 1952), *Velyke Tsabe* (The Great Tsabe, 1952), *Zolotyi pluh* (The Golden Plough, 1968). Notable also are her essays about travels in the New World, such as *Bahato neba* (A Lot of Sky, 1954), about the United States, and *Vichni vohni Alberty* (The Eternal Fires of Alberta, 1959), as well as her collection of stories *Sered khmarosiahiv* (Among the Skyscrapers, 1962).

D.H. Struk

Humenne. V-2. County center (1975 pop 23,400) of Východoslovenský kraj in eastern Slovakia. First mentioned in documents from the 14th century, today it is an administrative and cultural center. Twenty-one percent of the county's population is Ukrainian, although some Ukrainians speak only Slovak. In Humenne itself 10 percent of the inhabitants are Ukrainians. The city's gymnasium has a Ukrainian department.

Humetska, Lukiia [Humec'ka, Lukija], b 18 January 1901 in Livcha, Liubachiv county, Galicia. Philologist. A graduate of Lviv University (1929), she received her doctorate in 1956 and was the director of the linguistics section of the AN URSR Institute of Social Sciences in Lviv. A well-trained philologist, Humetska has studied primarily the Ukrainian language of the 14th and 15th centuries, writing many articles about it and a book on word formation in the official documents of that time (1958). She was the chief editor of a Polish-Ukrainian dictionary (2 vols, 1958, 1960) and a dictionary of Old Ukrainian of the 14th and 15th centuries (2 vols, 1977, 1978), and a member of the editorial boards of the 11-volume dictionary of the Ukrainian language (1970–80) and the linguistic journal *Movoznavstvo* (1967–82).

Humor. Humor plays a prominent role in all genres of Ukrainian folklore, literature, music, and art.

Many genres of folk prose are based on humor, particularly anecdotes, fables, fairy tales, stories, legends, and narratives (see *Folk oral literature). Humor is connected with ritual holidays and family customs, particularly various Easter, Kupalo, christening, and wedding rituals. *Carols and prayers often become infused with elements of parody. Humor is also manifested in proverbs, homilies, similes, and riddles.

A large component of Ukrainian *folk songs consists of so-called joking songs (*zhartivlyvi pisni*). These are songs on varying themes and subjects (especially family ties and customary relations), at the base of which lie an amusing thought, occurrence, or accident. They are always tailored to the audience. Joking songs are often intended to deride the character faults of individual family members or the community. Songs about youth are particularly common. These are often used in courtship or in acquaintance between the sexes. Songs depicting harmonious family life are very rare; rather, humorous songs focus on the 'typical' vices of men and women – tantrums, laziness, ineptitude, miserliness, inhospitability, inclination to drink, women's whims, and so on. Joking songs neither condemn nor condone unfaithfulness in marriage; particularly in songs about marriages between old men and young women and relationships between godparents, they adopt a fairly tolerant attitude. One of the largest subgroups of joking songs is the **kolomyiky*. This is almost the only genre of Ukrainian folk song that is still being created, and thus is a clear reflection of contemporary life. Both *kolomyiky* and anecdotes are frequently colored with political satire. Closely related to *kolomyiky* are so-called *blatni* songs, which deal with antisocial elements such as prostitutes, thieves, and other types of criminals. Joking songs have a specific compositional form and melody. Many take the form of a dialogue. The comic effect is achieved through such devices as contrast, hyperbole, strings of humorous details or epithets, intonation, gestures, and improvisation.

Humor also occupies an important place in folk drama, particularly in the **vertep* (puppet theater). Other mixed folklore-literary genres of the baroque period – eg, *intermedes (interludes), burlesque schoolboy's rhymes, and Cossack folk poetry – are based entirely on humor. The Cossack environment produced parodic *dumas such as 'Duma about Cossack Holota,' rhyming narratives (eg, 'Pekelnyi Marko' [Hellish Marko] and 'Vakula Chmyr'), and numerous songs that humorously portray the free Cossack lifestyle. Another subgroup of Ukrainian folklore consists of *soromitski* songs, anecdotes, and folk tales. These are of a frivolous, indecent or vulgar, and erotic nature and serve to entertain in fairly narrow circles.

The creators and disseminators of humorous works in Kievan Rus' were wandering artists: psaltimer players, jesters, and gamesters. From the 16th to the 19th centuries the primary carriers of humorous works were the *kobzars, lira players, and wandering students. Examples of Ukrainian intermedes (to the plays of Ya. Havatovych) have come down to us from the 1720s. The oldest recorded Ukrainian joking song is 'Chom, chom, chomu bosa khodysh' (Why, Why, Why Do You Go Barefoot), transcribed in 1620. Humorous stories, anecdotes, and joking songs can be found in virtually all folk anthologies from the 17th to the 20th centuries, which testifies to their great popularity. Elements of Ukrainian joking songs can be found in the works of Polish writers of the 16th and 17th centuries. Later this humor exerted a profound influence on the 'Ukrainian school' in Polish literature. Humorous works entered Ukrainian literature on a large scale through the *vertep*. Ukrainian theater of the 19th century was influenced by this genre. Humorous scenes of folk customs and rites, such as engagements, weddings, and parties, were important components of most Ukrainian comedies of the first half of the 19th century. A more sophisticated conceptualization of folk humour was provided in the works of realist dramatists such as M. Kropyvnytsky, M. Starytsky, I. Tobilevych, and I. Franko. I. Kotliarevsky's travesty of the Aeneid (*Eneïda*, 1798) and some works of N. Gogol are based entirely on Ukrainian folk humor. The *smikhomovky* (amusing sayings) of S. Rudansky and the *pobrekhenky* (little lies) of P. Hulak-Artemovsky occupy important places in the literature of Ukrainian humor. The classic exponent of humor in modern Ukrainian literature is O. Vyshnia. Humor as a device was often used by such composers as S. Hulak-Artemovsky, in *Zaporozhets za Dunaiem* (Zaporozhian Cossack beyond the Danube); M. Lysenko, in *Rizdviana nich* (Christmas Night), *Taras Bulba*, *Koza dereza* (Billy Goat's Bluff), *Eneïda*; and S. Liudkevych, in *Dovbush*. Among contemporary composers who frequently use humor are O. Bilash, I. Vymer, K. Dankevych, and H. Maiboroda. In pictorial art, comic scenes can be found in paintings of as early as the 16th–18th centuries, while in the 19th and 20th centuries humor was one of the central themes of Ukrainian painting, particularly in the works of K. Trutovsky, K. Tymonenko, E. Bukovetsky, and A. Zhdakha. Among contemporary artists who use comic elements and themes are A. Bazylevych, M. Butovych, M. Samokysh, V. Chernukha, E. Kozak, T. Yablonska, F. Krychevsky, D. Farkavec, Y. Bokshai, W. Kurelek, and N. Husar. (See also *Humoristic and satiric press.)

BIBLIOGRAPHY

Makhnovets', L. *Davnii ukraïns'kyi humor i satyra* (Kiev 1959)

Nud'ha, H. *Smiitesia na zdorovia* (Kiev 1960)

Dei, O. 'Pisennyi humor ukraïns'koho narodu,' in *Narodnopisenni zhanry* (Kiev 1977)

Myshanych, O. *Ukraïns'ka literatura druhoï polovyny XIX st. i usna narodna tvorchist'* (Kiev 1980)

M. Hnatiukivsky

Humoristic and satiric press. The humoristic press in Ukraine emerged almost at the same time as the general press. The first Ukrainian newspapers contained – in addition to chronicles of events – scholarly, literary, and satirical material. *Kharkovskii demokrit* (1816) had a humor section, while **Dnewnyk Ruskij* (1848) and the women's journal *Lada* (1853) of Lviv published humorous short stories. However, political censorship by the Russian and Austrian regimes and restrictions placed on the use of the Ukrainian language in the Russian Empire severely limited the early development of the humoristic press.

The first expressly humorous and satirical magazines appeared during the 1860s; these circulated only in manuscript form in very limited circles. *Pomyinytsia* (1863–4) was compiled by members of the Hromada of Kiev to poke fun at the opponents of the Hromada. At the Lviv Theological Seminary, A. Vakhnianyn's *Klepalo* circulated from 1860 to 1863; it was populist in orientation. More biting, and well illustrated by Yu. Dutkevych, was O. Partytsky's *Homin*. Issues of these magazines were frequently confiscated by the seminary's administration. Besides satirizing life in the seminary, they commented on community affairs and political events in contemporary Galicia. The first printed humor magazine was *Dulia*, one issue of which appeared in 1864, probably under the editorship of A. Kobyliansky. It was followed by Yu. Moroz's *Kropylo* in Kolomyia (1869) and the Russophile *Strakhopud*, first published in Vienna (1863–8) under the editorship of Y. Lyvchak, but subsequently revived in Lviv by I. Arsenych and V. Stebelsky (1872–3), S. Labash (1880–2), and O. Monchalovsky (1886–93). A. Ripai, V. Kimak, and K. Sabov's *Sova* was published in Uzhhorod and Budapest (1871), and I. Semaka's semimonthly *Lopata*, in Chernivtsi (1876).

The political differentiation of 1880–1905 and the debates between Ukrainophiles and Russophiles in Galicia provided great impetus to the development of the humoristic press. In Lviv *Zerkalo* (1882–3) and *Nove Zerkalo* (1883–5) were edited by K. Ustyianovych. Journals called *Zerkalo* appeared again in Lviv in 1889–93 (published by V. Levytsky, K. Pankivsky, and I. Krylovsky) and in 1898–1909 (published by O. Dembytsky). The weekly *Antsykhryst* (1902) was published by S. Terletsky and O. Shpytko in Chernivtsi, and I. Kuntsevych's *Komar* appeared in Lviv (1900–5).

Osa (The Wasp)

The Revolution of 1905 brought some relaxation of controls in Russian-ruled Ukraine and, along with a revival in political and cultural life, a strong interest in humor magazines. Humorous feuilletons began to appear in general newspapers. In Kiev, V. Lozynsky published *Shershen'* (1906) and P. Bohatsky published *Khrin* (1908), but these were suppressed by new restrictions and censorship. The comparatively more liberal political climate in this period in Galicia gave rise to *Osa* (1912), published by P. Odynak and with caricatures by Ya. Pstrak, and S. Terletsky's *Zhalo* (1913–14).

Koliuchky (Thorns)

The First World War brought new proscriptions on publishing in Ukrainian. At the same time, a new kind of press emerged under the auspices of the Ukrainian Sich Riflemen on the fronts, in camps for Ukrainian prisoners of war, and later in internment camps in Poland and Czechoslovakia. These journals came out irregularly and were printed on very primitive hectographs or circulated in manuscript form. The Sich Riflemen's humor magazines included *Samokhotnyk* (1915–19), published by its press bureau and edited by A. Babiuk, K. Kuzmovych, A. Lototsky, and others, and well illustrated by O. Kurylas and L. Gets; *Samopal* (1916); *USUSU* (1916–17), edited by Yu. Kalamar; *Smittia*; and *Tyfusna odnodnivka*. Magazines published in POW and internment camps included *Kharakternyk* (1920–1), edited by H. Hladky; *Promin'* (1921); *Okrip* (1921); *Polyn; Grymasa* (1921); *Komar* (1920); *Zhalo* and *Avans* published in Wadowice; *Oko* and *Sych* in Kalisz; *Lystok Ob'iav* in Pykulychi; *Blokha* and *Budiak* in Strilkiv; and *Vzad* (1919–21), illustrated by E. Kozak. Other magazines included *Lezhukh*, published in Tukholia (1921); *Koliuchky* in Częstochowa and Warsaw (1926–9); and *Kamedula*, which appeared in Liberec, Czechoslovakia (1919–20).

Under the UNR and Hetman government independent humor magazines enjoyed a brief renaissance. *Gedz* (1917–18), the weekly *Budiak*, well edited by S. Panochini (1917), and *Rep'iakhy* (1918) all appeared in Kiev. Numerous provincial newspapers also contained much humorous content. After 1920 these journals inspired similar magazines in cities with large communities of Ukrainian émigrés: in Vienna, *Ieretyk* and *Smikh*, edited by O. Oles; in Prague, *Vikhot'*, *Gedz*, *Liushnia*, *Oko*, *Rep'iakh*, *Satyrykon*, and *Ukraïns'kyi kapitalist'*; and in Poděbrady, *Absurd*, *Enei*, *Kropyva*, *Metelyk*, *Podiebradka*, *Podiebrads'ka hlidka*, and others.

The partition of Ukraine among four states dictated the character of the humoristic press in the interwar period. In Soviet Ukraine during the early 1920s, humor was placed at the service of propaganda. During NEP, when censorship was eased somewhat, some satirization of everyday and literary-artistic themes was permitted, including even sharp criticism of opposition to Ukrainization by Russified city dwellers and the Soviet bureaucracy. In the 1920s and early 1930s, popular humor magazines included *Chervonyi perets'* (1922), *Zhuk* (1923–4), *Havrylo* (1925–6), the Russian-language *V chasy dosuga*, *Novyi bich*, *Struzhki* (1922), *Krasnaia osa*, *Krasnoe zhalo* (1924), and *Uzh* (1928–9) in Kharkiv; *Bumerang* (1927) and the Russian *Tiski* (1923) in Kiev; the Russian *Bomba*, *Burzhui*, *Shpil'ka* (1918), *Krasnyi smekh* (1919), *Oblava* (1920), and *Komsomol'skii Krokodilenok* (1923) in Odessa; *Ternytsia* in Bila Tserkva; and *Zhyttia i humor* (1928) in Zhytomyr.

Perets' (Pepper)

In addition, most general literary magazines and newspapers contained satire of political and everyday life – *Znannia* (1923–35), *Sil's'kohospodars'kyi proletar* (1921–7), *Selianka Ukraïny* (1924–31), *Vsesvit* (1925–34), *Uzh* (1928–9), and especially *Bezvirnyk* (1925–35), in which satirists turned their attention to the war on religion. The satirical semimonthly **Chervonyi perets'* resumed publication in Kiev in 1927. In 1933, however, many of its collaborators were persecuted, and humor magazines in general fell victim to Stalinist repression. **Perets'*, which succeeded *Chervonyi perets'*, benefited from a temporary relaxation of censorship in 1944–5 (in the 1940s a special edition of the magazine was published for Western Ukraine), only to be severely criticized in the following year. It was even the subject of special criticism by the CC CP(B)U. Since 1953, official directives have decreed that a 'critical' course be strengthened in the entire USSR. As a result the humorous sections of newspapers and some journals (eg, the illustrated *Ukraïna*) have been expanded. Most of this humor is intended to encourage labor discipline and to combat the adoption of Western styles and habits. Many caricatures and satirical feuilletons are published in factory newspapers, and placards and posters are displayed in special cases in city streets. The most noteworthy contemporary caricaturists include V. Lytvynenko, O. Koziurenko, V. Hlyvenko, O. Dovhal, O. Dovzhenko, L. Kaplan, and A. Vasylenko. The style of their caricatures is so similar that it is often difficult to distinguish between these artists. By official decree, satire is now directed against the forces of reaction, manifestations of bourgeois and nationalist ideology, and all things that hinder the construction of communism.

In interwar Galicia, humor magazines contended with prohibitions, confiscations, and financial difficulties; only

Zyz (Cross-eyed)

by frequently changing publishers and names of publications were they able to maintain a continuity in publication before 1924. Early humor magazines of this period were *Budiak*, edited by S. Charnetsky (1921–2); *Gudz*, edited by D. Krenzhalovsky (1922); *Zhalo*, edited by P. Buniak; and *Masky* (1923), edited by M. Holubets. These were succeeded by *Zyz* (1924–33), edited by L. Lepky. The co-operation of E. Kozak ensured the high level of quality of this publication. R. Pashkivsky's *Zhorna* (1933–4) was displaced by E. Kozak's *Komar* (1933–9), which became the training ground for the humorists and caricaturists who worked with him in the emigration. Notable illustrators in the humoristic press of the period were P. Kovzhun (Ïzhak), O. Sorokhtei, P. Kholodny Jr, R. Lisovsky, and R. Chornii. Since the Second World War caricaturists such as L. Semchyshyn, V. Tsymbal, M. Levytsky, B. Kriukov, A. Klymko, M. Butovych, M. Dmytrenko, and L. Hutsaliuk also deserve mention. The satire in Galician humor magazines was directed mostly at Bolshevik policies in Soviet Ukraine, although they also satirized Ukrainian cultural and political life under Poland. Humorous material naturally was also published in the general press. The contributors included Tyberii Horobets (S. Charnetsky), Halaktion Chipka (R. Kupchynsky), Lele (L. Lepky), Fed Tryndyk (V. Hirny), Iker (I. Kernytsky), Babai (B. Nyzhankivsky), Teok (T. Kurpita), Andronik (L. Senyshyn), I. Chornobryvy, V. Sofroniv-Levytsky, and Ivan Sorokaty (Yu. Shkrumeliak).

In Transcarpathia and Bukovyna, the following humor magazines were published: *Sova* (1922–3), edited by L. Shutka, in Uzhhorod; *Ku-Ku* (1931–3) in Mukachiv; and *Shchypavka, Zhalo* (1926), *Budiak* (1930–1), and *Chortopolokh* (1936–7) in Chernivtsi.

Ïzhak (The Hedgehog)

The displaced persons camps of the post–Second World War period were fertile grounds for the development of the humoristic press. Dozens of journals and magazines appeared, although most were short-lived, irregular, and printed on primitive presses. The more important of these émigré publications were T. Kurpita's *Ïzhak*, which changed to *Ïzhak-Komar* and then *Komar* (Munich, 1946–8), and E. Kozak's **Lys Mykyta*, which is still published in the United States.

Lys Mykyta (Fox Mykyta)

In North America, the humoristic press consisted mostly of short-lived and irregular magazines that were often more popular than the daily political press. In the United States, these included *Osa* (1902–3) in Oliphant, Pennsylvania; *Molot* (1908–12, 1919–23), *Shershen'* (1908–11),

Tochylo (The Grindstone)

Osa (1912–13), *Iskra* (1917–20), *Lys Mykyta* (1920–3), *Perets'* (1923–5), *Puhach* (1925), *Smikh i pravda* (1926–8), *Boievi zharty* (1936), *Kol'ka* (1936–8), *Oko* (1939), *Mykyta* (1948–56), and E. Berezynsky's *Nove Tochylo*, all in New York; *Osa* (1918–29, 1931), *Batih* (1921), *Lys* (1950), all in Chicago; and E. Kozak's *Lys Mykyta*, published in Detroit since 1951. In Canada, P. Krat published the anti-clerical *Kadylo* (1913) and *Kropylo* (1913–18), and in Winnipeg Ya. Maidanyk published *Vuiko* (1918–27) and S. Doroshchuk published *Tochylo* (1930–47). T. Tomashivsky's *Harapnyk* (1930–5) appeared in Edmonton. Humorous almanacs such as *Humorystychnyi Kaliendar Veselyi druh* (1918–27) and *Humorystychnyi Kaliendar Vuika*(1925–32) also appeared.

In the 1930s in Buenos Aires *Shershen'* and *Batizhok* were published, and Yu. Serediak's *Mitla* appeared from

Mitla (The Broom)

1949 to 1976. In Curitiba, Brazil, *Batizhok* was published as a supplement to the newspaper *Khliborob* (1938–40). In Australia *Perets'* (1950), *Shmata* (1970–1), and *Osa* (1972) were all published, and in London, England, *Osa* appeared from 1961 to 1974.

BIBLIOGRAPHY
Babiuk, A. 'Strilets'ka presa,' *Visnyk SVU* (1917)
Hnatiuk, V. 'Rukopysni humorystychni chasopysy,' in *ZNTSh*, 130 (1920)
Chyzh, Ia. 'Pivstolittia ukraïns'koï presy v Amerytsi,' in *Kalendar Ukraïns'koho Robitnychoho Soiuzu* (Scranton 1939)
Zhyvotko, A. *Istoriia ukraïns'koï presy* (Regensburg 1946)
Butnyk-Sivers'kyi, B. 'Hazetna karykatura na Ukraïni v roky inozemnoï voiennoï interventsiï ta hromads'koï viiny,' *Ukraïns'ke mystetstvoznavstvo*, 1967, no. 1
Demchenko, E. *Satiricheskaia pressa Ukrainy, 1905–1907 gg.* (Kiev 1980)

S. Yaniv

Hunczak, Taras [Hunčak], b 13 March 1932 in Stare Misto, Pidhaitsi county, Galicia. Historian. A graduate of Fordham University and the University of Vienna (PH D 1960), since 1960 he has taught history at Rutgers University. He has edited and contributed to *Russian Imperialism from Ivan the Great to the Revolution* (1974) and *The Ukraine, 1917–1922: A Study in Revolution* (1977), and edited or coedited several collections of documents on Ukrainian history and the struggle for Ukrainian independence, including *Symon Petliura: statti, lysty, dokumenty* (Symon Petliura: Articles, Letters, Documents, vol 2, 1979), *Ukraïns'ka suspil'no-politychna dumka v 20 stolitti: Dokumenty i materiialy* (Ukrainian Social-Political Thought in the 20th Century: Documents and Materials, 3 vols, 1983), *Ukraïna i Pol'shcha v dokumentakh, 1918–1922* (Ukraine and Poland in Documents: 1918–1922, 2 vols, 1984), *The Ukrainian Revolution: Documents, 1919–1921* (1984), and 'UPA v svitli nimetskykh dokumentiv' (The UPA in Light of German Documents, in *Litopys Ukraïns'koï Povstans'koï Armiï*, vols 6–7, 1983). Since 1984 he has been the editor of the monthly *Suchasnist'*.

Hundiak, Marko [Hundjak] (secular name: Ivan), b 7 July 1895 in Pluhiv, Zolochiv county, Galicia, d 5 August 1984 in Carteret, New Jersey. Archbishop of the Ukrainian Orthodox Church in the United States. In 1913 he emigrated to the United States and studied theology at the Catholic College in Chicago. Having been ordained by Bishop N. Budka in 1919 he served in several parishes. In 1930 he went over to the Orthodox church and two years later became pastor in Carteret. In 1970 he was consecrated bishop, and in 1973 promoted to archbishop and vicar to Metropolitan Mstyslav. Besides doing pastoral and missionary work in the church, he was active in local civic affairs and coedited *Narodna volia* (1947–8).

Hunenko, Alexander, b 5 March 1937 in Romanivka, Poltava raion. Sculptor and educator. Immigrating to the United States in 1950 from Germany, he graduated from the Minneapolis College of Art and Design (BFA 1961) and the Yale University School of Art and Architecture (MFA 1963). In 1966–8 he attended the American Academy in Rome and taught at several universities, including Yale. Hunenko's early sculptures were massive and often shapeless abstract forms. Eventually, his art evolved

Alexander Hunenko: *Hadunca* (University of Colorado, Main Campus)

toward dynamic geometrized forms. The names of his works – *Hadunca, Bohunha, Taspor Alema, Poliksana,* etc – are his own fanciful inventions. He regards his art as 'public' and useful. His purpose is to humanize the barren cityscapes. His sculptures have been exhibited at numerous group and one-man shows, and have been acquired by the Walker Art Center in Minneapolis, the Minneapolis Institute of Arts, the Ukrainian Institute of Modern Art in Chicago, and numerous college and private collections.

Hungarian loan words. Terms borrowed by Ukrainian from the Hungarian language – a member of the Finno-Ugric linguistic group of the Uralic language family. The Hungarians appeared in east Slavic territories between 884 and 898, but no Hungarian loan words from this period have been preserved in Ukrainian. In the centuries succeeding the Hungarian settlement in the Carpathian Basin and its further expansion into Ukrainian lands south of the Carpathians, many Hungarian terms were absorbed into the language of Transcarpathian Ukrainians, particularly in the 16th century. Some of these loan words entered other, mostly western, dialects of the Ukrainian language, and a few made their way into standard Ukrainian, for example, *gazda* (master, Transcarpathian Ukrainian from the 13th century), *barda,* or *bartka,* or *balta* (axe, from the 13th–14th century), *legin'* (young man), *ganč* or *gandža* (flaw), *čyžmy* (boots), *puhar* (large cup, from the 16th century), and the Lviv term *batjar* (hooligan, from the 18th century) from the Hungarian *betyár*. Some Hungarian loan words may have come into literary Ukrainian recently and independently of Transcarpathian dialects; for example, *husar* (huszár, in Transcarpathian Ukrainian from the 15th century), *čardaš* (czardas), *papryka* (red pepper), *hajduk* (rebel, 19th century), and *guljaš* (goulash). However, most Hungarian loan words never spread beyond the Transcarpathian, mainly southwestern, dialects; for example, *marha* (property, livestock), *arsag* (state, state road), *varoš* (city), *katuna* (warrior), *bytjukh* (illness), *šuha* (never, adopted not later than the 13th century), *baršun* (velvet, 14th century), *kelčyx* (food, expenses, 15th century), *papuči* (slippers), *garadyči* (steps, 16th century), *pryjš* (winepress, 17th century), *galyba* (disorder, scandal, 18th century), and *krumpli* (potatoes, 19th century). These terms are now gradually disappearing from the dialects.

BIBLIOGRAPHY

Lizanec, P. *Magyar-ukrán nyelvi kapcsolatok* (Budapest 1970)

Lyzanets', P. *Uhorsko-ukraïns'ki mizhmovni kontakty (Na materiali ukraïns'kykh hovoriv Zakarpattia)* (Uzhhorod 1970)

Rot, A. *Vengersko-vostochnoslavianskie iazykovye kontakty* (Budapest 1973)

Lyzanets', P. *Atlas leksychnykh madiaryzmiv ta ïkh vidpovidnykiv v ukraïns'kykh hovorakh Zakarpats'koï oblasti* URSR (Budapest 1976)

Lizanets, P. *Vengerskie zaimstvovaniia v ukrainskikh govorakh Zakarpatia* (Budapest 1976)

Mokan', A. 'Leksicheskie ungarizmy v maramoroshskikh ukrainskikh govorakh Zakarpatskoi oblasti,' *Voprosy finno-ugorskoi filologii,* 1977, no. 3

Hungarians (Ukrainian: *madiary, uhortsi*). A Finno-Ugric people known ethnically as Magyars. They constitute the basic population of *Hungary (96 percent of 10.7 million in 1985) and minority populations in Rumania (8 percent in 1983), Yugoslavia (2 percent in 1981), Czechoslovakia (4 percent in 1980), Ukraine, Austria, and other Western countries, for a total of 14.4 million worldwide. Most Hungarians are Catholic (68 percent, of which 3 percent are Byzantine Catholic) or Protestant (25 percent, mostly Calvinist).

The Magyars migrated to the steppe regions of contemporary Ukraine as vassals of the Khazars from their ancestral homeland between the Volga River and the Ural Mountains. In the late 9th century they briefly formed a federation of seven tribes (Etelköz) in the interstice of the Boh, Dniester, Prut, and Seret rivers before being driven westward by the Pechenegs and Volga Bulgars across the Carpathian Mountains. Led by Árpád, they destroyed the Moravian Empire in 906 and occupied Pannonia, where they subdued and assimilated the local Slavic population. Their first king, Stephen (997–1038), converted them to Christianity and laid the foundations for the strong, centralized state of Hungary, to which the Ukrainian lands of *Transcarpathia belonged until the 20th century.

Of the Hungarians in Soviet Ukraine today (164,400 in 1979), most (158,400) live in *Transcarpathia oblast, where they constitute a substantial minority (13.7 percent, down from 15.6 percent in 1970). They comprise most of the inhabitants of Berehove raion, half of the population of Vynohradiv raion, sizable groups in Uzhhorod and Mukachiv raions, and smaller groups in Tiachiv, Khust, and Rakhiv raions. Most Hungarians in Ukraine (96.7 percent in 1979) have retained their mother tongue as their first language. In 1970 only 34 percent of Hungarians in Ukraine were urban dwellers.

Hungarian linguistic, social, and cultural influence in Transcarpathia spanned several centuries. Consequently many Ukrainians there, mainly urban dwellers and the intelligentsia, became Magyarized. The reverse process occurred only very rarely. Surprisingly, however, despite the forced Magyarization of names in the 19th and 20th centuries, many Hungarians have Ukrainian surnames, and Slavic loan words, including Ukrainian ones, exist in the Hungarian language. The oldest borrowings are terms of social organization – eg, *király* (Ukrainian: *korol'*, 'king'), *ispán* (*pan*, 'lord, leader'), *szabad* (*svobidnyi*, 'free'), *csald* (*cheliad'*, 'family'), *szolga* (*sluha*, 'servant'); and church words – eg, *barát* (*brat*, 'brother, friar'), *kereszt* (*khrest*, 'cross'), *szombat* (*subota*, 'Saturday'). *Hungarian loan words have also entered the Ukrainian language. Both the Hungarians and Ukrainians in their common borderlands have influenced each other's folkways, folklore, and folk culture.

The Hungarians of Transcarpathia oblast benefit from fairly broad minority rights in education, the mass media, and publishing. Two Hungarian-language oblast newspapers – *Kárpáti igaz szó* and *Kárpátontuli Ifjúság* – and a raion newspaper in Berehove – *Vörös Zászló* – are published there. In the 1970s, there were 15 secondary and 125 elementary schools in the oblast with Hungarian as the language of instruction. Plays are performed in Hungarian in Berehove, and there is a Hungarian language section in the philological faculty of Uzhhorod University. The Karpaty publishing house issues books in Hungarian for local schools and exports calendars and translations of Ukrainian literature to Hungary.

V. Markus

Hungary (Magyarország). A landlocked country in the Danube Basin of Eastern Europe sharing a common border with Soviet Ukraine of 105 km. Its capital is Budapest. Until its partition in 1920 so-called greater Hungary had an area of 325,400 square km and a population of over 21 million consisting of *Hungarians and several other nationalities, including the Ukrainians of *Transcarpathia. The Hungarian People's Republic (est 1946) is a Soviet-bloc country with an area of 93,000 sq km. Its population in 1985 was over 10.6 million.

Relations with Ukraine. During their migration westward to the lands they now inhabit, the ancient Hungarians (Magyars) came into contact with the Ukrainian tribes of Kievan Rus' and even passed through Kiev in the late 9th century. Hungarian warriors are known to have served in the retinues of various Rus' princes. After Grand Prince Volodymyr the Great of Kiev died in 1015, King Stephen I of Hungary extended his realm to Transcarpathia. The generally amicable political and economic relations between medieval Hungary and the Kievan state were strengthened by dynastic ties. Volodymyr the Great's daughter Premyslava married Stephen's cousin and rival, Duke Vászoly. From 1034 to 1046 two of Vászoly's sons lived in exile in Kiev; one of them, later King Andrew I, married Anastasiia-Agmunda, the daughter of Grand Prince Yaroslav the Wise. During the reigns of Andrew (1046–60) and his son Salomon (1063–74), Rus' influence at the Hungarian royal court and in Hungarian cultural and religious life (particularly in spreading Byzantine Christianity) grew. Grand Prince Sviatopolk Iziaslavych's daughter Predslava married Duke Álmos in 1104. Yevfimiia, the daughter of Grand Prince Volodymyr Monomakh, married King *Kálmán I (1095–1116) in 1112. Suspecting her of adultery, Kálmán banished Yevfimiia to Kiev, where in 1113 she gave birth to a son, Borys, whom Kálmán refused to recognize as his. From 1131 until his death in battle in 1155, Borys was a pretender to the Hungarian throne. His last opponent, King Géza II, married Yevfrosyniia, the daughter of Grand Prince Mstyslav I Volodymyrovych, in 1145.

The Galician princes of Rus' initially had good relations with Hungary, but they were eventually forced to confront Hungary's intrusion into the internecine wars of Rus' and its encroachment into their lands. In 1099 the Rostyslavych princes defeated Kálmán's army at the Vihor River near Peremyshl, and in 1151 Prince Volodymyrko Volodarevych routed the Hungarian troops supporting his enemy, Grand Prince Iziaslav Mstyslavych, at Dorohobuzh. In 1188 King Béla III (1172–96) seized Halych and declared himself king of Galicia, but in the ensuing conflict he was forced to withdraw in 1190. Prince Roman Mstyslavych was supported by the future King Andrew II (1205–35) in his efforts to consolidate his rule in Halych and Volodymyr-Volynskyi principalties. In 1205 Roman's widow Anna turned to Andrew for help in securing the united principality for her young sons Danylo and Vasylko from the intervening Novhorod-Siverskyi princes. Andrew, however, proclaimed himself 'king of Galicia and Lodomeriia,' although he did give Anna and Danylo refuge at his court. In 1211 Andrew's forces helped the Galician boyars defeat the Novhorod-Siverskyi princes Roman, Sviatoslav, and Volodymyr Ihorevych. In 1215 Andrew's son Kálmán II was crowned king of Galicia on the basis of an agreement to partition Galicia between Andrew and Prince Leszko of Cracow in Spiš in 1214; he ruled there with great opposition and difficulty until being driven out by Prince Mstyslav Mstyslavych in 1219 and again in 1221.

In 1225 Andrew's son Andrew married Mstyslav's daughter Maria and was given Peremyshl. From 1226 the Hungarians again tried to conquer Galicia with the help of pro-Hungarian Galician boyars. Danylo defeated them at Halych in 1230 and 1233, but even after his decisive victory in the Battle of Yaroslav in 1245, the Hungarian kings continued using the title of 'king of Galicia and Lodomeriia.' In 1247 King Béla IV made peace with Danylo; his daughter Constance married Danylo's son Lev I, and Danylo helped Béla in his war with Austria. Lev extended his domain into Transcarpathia, and Ukrainian rule in the Mukachiv region lasted for 50 years. Lev's grandchildren Lev II and Andrii Yuriiovych were unsuccessful candidates for the Hungarian throne that Charles Robert ascended in 1308. King Louis the Great (1342–82) helped Poland contend with Lithuania over Galicia; after he became the Polish king in 1370, Galicia was governed by Władysław Opolczyk and Hungarian viceroys until 1387, when it was finally taken over by the Poles.

After the Galician-Volhynian state collapsed in the late 14th century, and particularly after most of Hungary came under Ottoman rule in the 16th century, Hungarian-Ukrainian relations were negligible. It was not until the 17th century that relations were revived between the Cossack Hetman state and the autonomous principality of *Transylvania; in the latter the Ukrainians of Transcarpathia took part in a number of Hungarian uprisings and wars with Austria.

Hungary's earlier contention for Galicia, its occasional rule there, and its dynastic links with its Ukrainian rulers gave the Habsburgs of Austria, who ruled most of Hungary from 1699, the legal argument for claiming Galicia during the partition of Poland in 1772, and they assumed the title 'Rex Galiciae et Lodomeriae.' Under the Austrian Empire, Ukrainian-Hungarian relations were determined by the dominant and repressive role the Hungarians played in governing Transcarpathia. The anti-Habsburg Hungarian national movement was also hostile to most other national minorities in the empire and to their aspirations (except those of the Poles), and thus did not arouse much sympathy among the Ukrainian masses. Consequently, during the *Revolution of 1848–9, Ukrainians (whether as conscripts in the Russian army that intervened in Hungary or as members of the *National Guard) found themselves in the antirevolutionary, pro-Habsburg camp. The empire's Ukrainians did not benefit from the 1867 Austro-Hungarian Compromise and the creation of the dual monarchy. As Hungarian chauvinistic policies in Transcarpathia and Hungarian-Polish amity grew, even more Ukrainians were drawn into the pro-Habsburg or pro-Russian (see *Russophiles) camps.

In the 20th century, the presence of Hungarian military forces on Ukrainian soil during the two world wars left memories of severe repression amidst the populace. During the First World War, the anti-Russian, émigré Union for the Liberation of Ukraine propagated the idea of Ukrainian independence in Hungary and won the support of a small number of prominent Hungarians (who did not view Transcarpathia as part of Ukraine). A popular journal, *Ukránia*, was edited and published in Budapest in 1916–17 by H. Strypsky. After the war, in 1919 and 1920, the UNR and Western Ukrainian National Republic (ZUNR) had diplomatic missions in Budapest, headed by M. Halahan and Ya. Biberovych respectively. The ZUNR government had trade relations with Hungary, to which it mainly exported oil, and formally appeared neutral on the question of Transcarpathia while supporting the movement for its inclusion in the Ukrainian state.

During the Communist regime of B. Kun in Hungary (March–August 1919), a newspaper, *Chervona Ukraïna*, was published for Ukrainian soldiers in prisoner-of-war and internment camps. The Soviet Russian government attempted to come to the aid of the Hungarian Communists, but its efforts were blocked by the Ukrainian Galician Army, UNR forces, and the anti-Bolshevik uprising led by N. Hryhoriiv. With the demise of the 'Soviet Republic' in Hungary, some of its supporters immigrated to the Soviet Ukraine.

Perhaps because of historical antipathy, very few Ukrainian political émigrés lived in interwar Hungary, despite the anti-Bolshevik sentiments prevailing there. Most Magyarized or pro-Hungarian Transcarpathian intellectuals did, however, and formed their own political organization opposed to Czechoslovak irredentism. Among the Trancarpathian intellectuals active in Hungary in the interwar period were the historian A. *Hodinka and the Slavists S. *Bonkáló and H. *Strypsky.

Since the Second World War there has been a measure of co-operation between Hungarian and Ukrainian émigrés in the West. Gen F. Farkas headed the Council of the Anti-Bolshevik Bloc of Nations, and Hungarian publicists have had their articles published in the Ukrainian émigré press.

Relations with Soviet Ukraine. As Nazi Germany's ally, Hungary declared war on the USSR on 23 June 1941 and dispatched an expeditionary force to the Eastern front. A Hungarian occupational authority functioned briefly in southeast Galicia. The main Hungarian forces (two divisions) were annihilated during the Soviet Voronezh offensive in 1943. While retreating through territory controlled by the Ukrainian Insurgent Army in April 1944, the Hungarian command entered into a neutrality and aid agreement with the latter.

Between September 1944 and April 1945 Hungary was completely occupied by Soviet armies and forced to surrender. Transcarpathia, which Hungary had taken from Czechoslovakia in 1938–9, was ceded to Soviet Ukraine. Hungary's defeat was sealed in the Paris peace treaties of 10 February 1947, which imposed on it 200 million dollars in reparations payable to the USSR.

Soviet-Hungarian agreements in 1945 and 1948 integrated Hungary's economy with the Soviet Union's, and in 1949 it became a member state of the *Council for Mutual Economic Assistance. About 30 percent of Hungary's exports go to the USSR. Ukraine imports steam locomotives, communications and medical equipment, textiles, footwear, breeding livestock, and food products from Hungary. Of Soviet exports to Hungary, Ukraine provides almost 100 percent of the iron ore, coke, and coal, 81 percent of the hydroelectric power, 80 percent of the manganese, and 58 percent of the ferrous metals. Ukraine also exports lumber, heavy machinery, and industrial equipment to Hungary. Hydroelectric power is transmitted to Hungary by the Mir system through Mukachiv, and oil and natural gas are transferred via the Druzhba and Bratstvo pipelines. The main railway transit center for Hungarian-Soviet import/export trade is Chop on the Hungarian-Ukrainian-Czechoslovak border. The Danube also serves as a trade conduit.

Official ties of friendship and co-operation have been established between the Hungarian counties and Ukrainian oblasts of Csongrád-Odessa, Zala-Kherson, Baranya-Lviv, Szabolc-Szatmár-Transcarpathia, Bács-Kiskun-Crimea, and Fejer-Voroshylovhrad, and between the cities Szeged-Odessa and Pécs-Lviv.

Ukrainian-Hungarian cultural relations. The highlights of these relations outside Transcarpathia include H. Skovoroda's stay in Hungary in 1745–50 and the publication of the first Galician-Ukrainian almanac, **Rusalka Dnistrovaia*, in Buda in 1837. Otherwise, cultural contacts were minimal. The Transcarpathian figures Yu. *Zhatkovych and H. Strypsky began translating Ukrainian literature into Hungarian in the early 20th century, and already before the First World War, works of Hungarian literature (by S. Petőfi, J. Arany, M. Jókai, K. Mikszáth) had been translated into Ukrainian by P. Hrabovsky, M. Cheremshyna, and I. Franko. Works by Hungarian Communist writers about life in Transcarpathia appeared in Soviet Ukraine in the 1920s, including those of M. Zalka, E. Madarász, and B. Illés. In the 1920s and 1930s V. Sosiura and L. Pervomaisky translated Hungarian literary works into Ukrainian; the latter also wrote a cycle of poetry entitled 'Uhors'ka rapsodiia' (Hungarian Rhapsody, 1936).

The creation of a chair of Ukrainian language at Budapest University in 1945 marked the beginning of systematic scholarly and scientific co-operation. Kiev University has established official relations with Debrecen University, and Uzhhorod University with Szeged University and the Nyíregyháza Pedagogical Institute. Academic exchanges and co-operation exist between the AN URSR and the Hungarian Academy of Sciences. G. Rado is a prominent Hungarian specialist in Ukrainian studies and translator of Ukrainian literature. V. Scher has written on Ukrainian literature, and J. Perényi has written several studies on Transcarpathia's history. The writer S. Weöres has translated many of T. Shevchenko's poems for the 1953 Hungarian edition of the *Kobzar*; and A. Hidas has published several translations of Shevchenko's poems and a selection of M. Kotsiubynsky's stories. Other notable Hungarian translators of Ukrainian literature include E. Grigašsy, Zs. Ráb, and S. Karig. M. Bazhan, D. Pavlychko, I. Drach, V. Korotych, Yu. Shkrobynets, I. Chendei, M. Tomchanii, S. Panko, M. Lukash, and others have translated Hungarian literature into Ukrainian. In 1972 the Debrecen journal *Alföld* devoted two of its issues to modern Ukrainian literature.

Since the 1950s Ukrainian and Hungarian singers, choirs, orchestras, bands, and dance, theater, and opera companies have toured each other's country. In 1960 the first Ukrainian Culture Week was celebrated in Budapest, and in 1965 the first Ukrainian culture days were celebrated throughout Hungary. The first Hungarian culture days were celebrated in Ukraine in 1959. A few hundred Hungarian students study each year at Ukrainian postsecondary schools (240 in 1968), but few Ukrainians study in Hungary. Exhibits of Hungarian art are mounted in Ukraine and vice versa, and the Transcarpathian Art Museum in Uzhhorod has a large collection of works by Hungarian painters, particularly M. Munkácsy and S. Hollosi (under whom Yu. Narbut studied).

The Hungarian composer F. Liszt used Ukrainian folk motifs in some of his works, particularly in the symphonic poem *Mazepa*. B. Bartok performed in Odessa and Kharkiv in 1929, collected and arranged Ukrainian folk melodies, and corresponded with F. Kolessa and K. Kvitka.

Ukrainians in Hungary. Only a few thousand Ukrainians live in Hungary today (about 3,000 in 1960). They are mainly Ukrainians from Transcarpathia who remained after 1945 and their offspring; they have no organized community life. Ethnographic islands with certain Ukrainian linguistic and cultural traits exist in certain regions of Hungary; they are remnants of now completely assimilated settlements that were still identifiable as ethnically Ukrainian in the 18th and 19th centuries. These settlements were populated by Ukrainians and Slovaks who had fled during the Turkish invasions into the Hungarian lowlands, and by a small number of Transcarpathian participants in the 1848 Revolution. Although they constituted majorities in certain villages, they never constituted more than 4 or 5 percent of the population of any particular county. In 1836–40 there were approx 35,000–40,000 Ukrainians living in Borsod, Abaúj, Zemplén, Szatmár, Bereg, and Makó counties in 21 wholly Ukrainian, 28 Ukrainian-Hungarian, 1 Ukrainian-Hungarian-German, 2 Ukrainian-Slovak, and 2 Ukrainian-Slovak-Hungarian villages. The number of Byzantine-Catholics in these counties was markedly greater than the number of Ukrainians; most likely many of them were assimilated Ukrainians in addition to Byzantine Catholic Hungarians, Serbs, Greeks, and Rumanians. The southernmost settlement of Ukrainians was the city of Makó close to the Rumanian border, which served as a transfer point for Transcarpathians migrating to the *Bačka region in present-day Yugoslavia.

Hungarian assimilation pressures were intensified from the mid-19th century with the Magyarization of the Byzantine Catholic church after the founding of *Hajdúdorog eparchy and after the Hungarian Republic was created in 1918, when the population of the Ukrainian ethnographic islands was completely isolated from their compatriots in Czechoslovak-ruled Transcarpathia and an administration for the Byzantine Catholics of Borsod county was established in Miskolc. The introduction of the use of Hungarian in the liturgy resulted in the almost total assimilation of the remaining Ukrainians in Hungary. Today only the elderly in certain villages still understand Ukrainian. Extant traces of Ukrainian folkways and folklore and the existence of Ukrainian surnames and even certain religious traditions hint at the origin of these people. In the 1960s, E. Bálecki of Budapest University investigated the dialect of the village of Komloska in Abaúj county. In the mid-1970s, Bishop Y. Segedii of Zagreb visited various Ukrainian settlements in Hungary and documented a number of indicators of Ukrainian identity he found there.

BIBLIOGRAPHY

Marchenko, H.; Hranchak, I. *Uhors'ka Radians'ka Respublika 1919 roku ta ïi mizhnarodne znachennia* (Uzhhorod 1959)

Shevchenko, F. (ed). *Ukraïns'ko-uhors'ki istorychni zv'iazky* (Kiev 1964)

Pashuto, V. *Vneshniaia politika Drevnei Rusi* (Moscow 1968)

Lavrinenko, Iu. *Ukrainskaia SSR v sovetsko-vengerskikh ekonomicheskikh otnosheniiakh* (Kiev 1969)

Rado, G. *Szomszédunk-Ukrájna* (Budapest 1969)

Rusyn, O. *Rozvytok i zmitsnennia radians'ko-uhors'koho ekonomichnoho spivrobitnytstva 1945–1969 rr.* (Lviv 1970)

Slov'ians'ko-uhors'ki mizhmovni ta literaturni zv'iazky (Uzhhorod 1970)

Ukraïns'ka RSR u radians'ko-uhors'komu spivrobitnytstvi (1945–70) (Kiev 1972)

Kovach, A. 'Ukrainski (ruski) ostrova u siverno–vostochnoi chasti neshei Madiarskei u XVIII–XIX veku,' *Nova dumka*, nos 7–8 (Vukovar 1974)

Segedii, I. 'Z kraïny moïkh predkiv,' *Khrystiians'kyi kalendar na 1978* (Ruski Krstur 1977)

Varadi-Shternberh, Ia. *Spadshchyna stolit': Doslidzhennia v haluzi rosiis'ko-uhors'kykh i ukraïns'ko-uhors'kykh zv'iazkiv* (Uzhhorod 1979)

V. Markus

Hunia, Dmytro [Hunja], b and d ? A leader of the Cossack peasant uprisings against the Polish nobility. In 1637 he took part in P. Pavliuk's rebellion. After its defeat at *Kumeiky and Borovytsia near Chyhyryn, he and other rebels retreated to the Zaporozhian Sich, where the Cossacks elected Hunia hetman. At the beginning of 1638 his forces routed the Polish expedition of registered Cossacks sent to subdue the Sich. In the spring of 1638 Hunia joined the uprising led by K. Skydan and Ya. *Ostrianyn. After its defeat at Zhovnyn, Ostrianyn's forces retreated to Slobidska Ukraine. The remaining Cossacks continued the fight under Hunia. In the spring of 1640 Hunia led a campaign of Zaporozhian and Don Cossacks against Turkey. His subsequent fate is unknown.

Hunkevych, Dmytro [Hun'kevyč], b 30 September 1893 in Lysovychi, Dolyna county, Galicia, d 4 February 1953 in Toronto. Playwright. Hunkevych immigrated to North America in 1909 and eventually settled in Winnipeg, where in his spare time he wrote children's stories and over 20 plays. Most of his plays, especially *Zhertvy temnoty* (Victims of Darkness, 1924) and *Krovavi perly* (Bloodstained Pearls, 1926), deal with social disintegration and the exploitation of immigrants in North America.

Huns (also known as Hunni). A nomadic pastoral people renowned for their military prowess who originated in northern China and then migrated to Central Asia. In the 2nd century AD they appeared in the steppes on the northern coast of the Black Sea. In the second half of the 4th century they began a massive migration into Central Europe, initiating the period of the great migrations of peoples into Europe from Asia. In 375 they defeated the *Goths and the *Alans and sacked most of the Greek colonies on the Black Sea coast. In the 5th century they moved to Pannonia (an area west of the Danube, now Hungary and northern Yugoslavia), followed by some Goths, Alans, and *Antes. There, under the leadership of Attila, the Huns reached the height of their power. Attila's domain stretched from the Volga to the Rhine and the northern shores of the Black Sea, known as Pontic Scythia. After Attila's death in 453, the Hun kingdom quickly disintegrated. Some of the tribes returned to the northern shores of the Azov Sea, where they were known by various names until the 6th century.

Hunter, Alexander Jardine, b 1868 in Leith, Ontario, d 25 August 1940 in Teulon, Manitoba. Medical doctor and missionary. Educated at the University of Toronto, in 1902 Hunter was sent as a medical missionary to Teulon, Manitoba, by the Presbyterian Board of Home Missions. Until his retirement in 1927, he served among Ukrainian immigrants in the Interlake district. Concerned with converting Ukrainians to Protestantism, Hunter grew to respect Ukrainian culture, acquired fluency in Ukrainian, and published a free translation of 23 poems by T. Shevchenko, *The Kobzar of the Ukraine* (1922). Coeditor of **Kanadiis'kyi ranok* from its inception in 1920 until his death, Hunter also wrote *A Friendly Adventure* (1929), a memoir of his missionary work.

Hunting. The taking of wild animals and birds for meat, skins, or fur. Hunting was prevalent in Ukraine from the Paleolithic era, and in prehistoric times constituted one of the chief sources, along with fishing, of livelihood for the population. With the development of agriculture, hunting lost much of its economic importance and gradually came to be considered a form of entertainment, acquiring the characteristics of a sport.

During the Princely era, the prince and his retinue hunted big game such as bison, auroch, moose, deer, bear, lynx, wild boar, and tarpan. Hunting was considered entertainment and a kind of military training, but it also had the function of gathering meat and skins. Scenes from the princes' hunts are depicted on the walls of St Sophia Cathedral in Kiev. Small-game hunting had great economic importance, particularly the hunting of martin, ermine, otter, sable, beaver, and other animals that yield expensive fur. Furs were a major export of Kievan Rus'. Hunting was practiced by large segments of the population, including monks. Except for the prince and his retinue, all hunters paid a special hunting tax or *lovche*. Princes and nobles usually hunted on horseback, killing a cornered animal with a bow, spear, sling, ax, or knife. Large animals were also caught in pits and traps (*doly* or *samolovky*), while small fur-bearing animals and birds were caught in snares and nets (*teneta* or *perevisy*), or with trained falcons and hawks. Sometimes dogs were used to corner the animals or chase them into the traps.

Hunting played a particularly important role in the

Bear Hunt; fresco in the north tower of the St Sophia Cathedral in Kiev

economic life of the Zaporozhian Cossacks. However, colonization, deforestation, the increased cultivation of land in central and eastern Ukraine, and the introduction of firearms in the 15th and 16th centuries contributed to a rapid depletion of game fauna. With the drastic reduction of large hoofed animals by the 16th century, hunting for the fur industry, particularly of beaver and otter, remained the only commercially significant form of hunting. The fauna of southern Ukraine, which had been marked by a rich diversity of species, was quickly depleted by the settlement of the steppes in the mid-18th century.

Hunting has been officially regulated from historical times, but early legislation (eg, in *Ruskaia Pravda* of the 11th century, the Lithuanian Statute of the 16th century, and the Code of Laws of 1743) was concerned only with trespassing on hunting property. Laws regulating the methods of hunting and the protection of certain species by the designation of specific hunting season were not enacted until the second half of the 19th century (1892 in Russian-ruled Ukraine and 1875, 1896, and 1909 in Galicia).

In the Ukrainian SSR hunting is under the jurisdiction of the Chief Administration of Game Management, the Ministry of Forest Management of the Ukrainian SSR, and several civic organizations (eg, the Ukrainian Association of Hunters and Fishermen). Before the Second World War, official policy encouraged commercial hunting. Since then, most emphasis has been placed on ensuring an adequate wildlife base for sport hunting. This has included the establishment of *nature reserves and wildlife refuges, the setting of quotas, the designation of limited hunting seasons, and the destruction of harmful predators. Today, only the hunting of fur-bearing animals is commercially significant (see *Fur industry). In 1969 the Council of Ministers of the Ukrainian SSR adopted the all-Union 'Decree on Hunting and the Hunting Industry in the Ukrainian SSR' as the basic legislation concerning hunting.

For the most part, hunting has remained the preserve of the privileged circles of Ukrainian society: the gentry and the bourgeoisie before the Revolution, government officials, military officers, and Party members under Soviet rule. However, illegal hunting or poaching is widespread, perhaps even accounting for the deaths of more animals than legalized hunting. During the Revolution and both world wars, huntable fauna decreased dramatically in population. In Western Ukraine, despite harsh laws restricting hunting, the wildlife population has declined, mostly because of the destruction of forests. In the Carpathian Mountains in particular, the number of deer and wild boar has decreased catastrophically, while the number of predatory animals, such as wolves, has increased.

As a result of human activities, some species have become extinct or have emigrated from Ukraine, while others have become rare and their habitat severely restricted (see *Fauna). Most of these species are protected by law, and an absolute ban has been imposed on the hunting of bears, beavers, and desmans. In total, 31 mammals are classified as huntable in the Ukrainian SSR, of which 13 have commercial significance. Close to 90 species of birds are also hunted.

The following mammals are hunted on a large scale (figures refer to the approximate annual kill): gray hare (in the 1960s 1 million, and in the 1970s 0.5 million), fox (in the 1960s 100,000, and in the 1970s 20,000–30,000), red deer (250–350), chamois (2,000), and wild boar (2,000). Fur-bearing animals hunted include the muskrat (in the 1960s 85,000, and in the 1970s 20,000–30,000), martin (4,000), and raccoon (until the 1970s 100,000, since then only a few thousand per year). Mink and otter are taken in small numbers. So-called second-class furs, obtained from the destruction of gophers, moles, wolves, and other pests and harmful animals, are also used commercially. Hunted fowl in Ukraine include ducks, snipes, coots, and corncrakes.

In order to increase the game population in Ukraine, several species have been acclimatized or reacclimatized (the muskrat, raccoon, spotted deer, mountain sheep, beaver, white hare, sable, pheasant, rock partridge). However, the breeding of exotic animals in the wild disrupts the biocenotic balance of endemic fauna, and in some instances raises the possibility of bastardization. In some cases, acclimatized species (eg, the racoon and the muskrat) are pests.

The scientific aspects of hunting are studied at the AN URSR Institute of Zoology, the Ukrainian Scientific Research Institute of Forest Management and Agroforest Amelioration and its Carpathian branch, and at chairs of zoology at various institutes of higher education.

Until 1939 there existed a number of hunting associations in Galicia, including Vatra in Stanyslaviv and Tur in Lviv. In Soviet Ukraine, the All-Ukrainian Association of Hunters and Fishermen was established in 1923. It existed until the mid-1930s and published the journals *Ukraïns'kyi myslyvets' i rybalka* (1925–32) and *Radians'kyi myslyvets' ta rybalka* (1927–30). In 1947 the Ukrainian Association of Hunters and Fishermen was formed. It has branches at the oblast and raion levels and a membership of over 300,000. Currently, there are no Ukrainian-language hunting magazines. Large collections of hunting trophies, originally collected mainly by nobles, are today found in several museums (particularly the Natural Science Museum of the AN URSR in Lviv).

BIBLIOGRAPHY
Averin, V. *Myslyvstvo* (Kharkiv 1927)
Myhulin, O. *Zviri URSR* (Kiev 1938)
Sokur, I. *Ssavtsi fauny Ukraïny i ïkh hospodars'ke znachennia* (Kiev 1960)
Kornieiev, O. *Myslyvstvo – haluz' narodnoho hospodarstva* (Kiev 1964)
Dovidnyk myslyvtsia ta rybalky (Kiev 1972)
Okhota (Kiev 1976)
Pryroda Ukraïny ta ïi okhorona (Kiev 1976)

B. Luchakovsky, E. Zharsky

Hurby, Battle of. Engagement fought by the Ukrainian Insurgent Army (UPA) and special NKVD troops on 24 April 1944 near Hurby village, southeast of Dubno in Volhynia. This was the largest battle between the UPA and Soviet forces. In early 1944 the forested region between Dubno and Kremianets became the principal base of the UPA-South, which operated just behind the Soviet 1st Ukrainian Front commanded by Marshal G. Zhukov. On 21 April about 30,000 NKVD Internal Troops under the general command of Maj Gen S. Marchenkov encircled about 5,000 UPA fighters. As the circle tightened, UPA units attempted to break out. By 23 April, after several major skirmishes, the main body of insurgents was surrounded near Hurby. Led by Brig Comm Yasen, the UPA troops had well-prepared defensive positions and were armed with light infantry weapons, heavy machine guns, 120-mm mortars, and light artillery.

The Soviet attack began early on 24 April and continued until late at night. The NKVD rifle brigades were supported by artillery, tanks, and airplanes. During the night UPA units broke through the primary encirclement in several directions and during the next two days came into contact with NKVD blocking units. Wounded insurgents and civilians hiding in the forests were summarily executed by their Soviet captors.

According to NKVD reports the operation involved 26 battles or major skirmishes and captured arms included 1 airplane, 7 artillery pieces, 15 mortars, 47 machine guns, a printing press, 120 wagons with horses, ammunition, and food supplies. According to UPA estimates Soviet losses were over 800.

P. Sodol

Hurevych, Borys [Hurevyč], b 23 February 1937 in Kiev. Middleweight wrestler and Olympic champion. A graduate of the Kiev Institute of Physical Culture (1969), he won the gold medal at the Olympic Games in Mexico City (1968), the world championship (1967, 1969), and the European championship (1967, 1970) in freestyle wrestling. He was champion of Ukraine and the USSR a number of times. Now he trains other wrestlers. Known for his sportsmanship, he was chosen by Ye. Vuchetych as the model for the sculpture *We Shall Beat Our Swords into Ploughshares,* which stands beside the United Nations Building in New York.

Hurevych, Hryhorii [Hurevyč, Hryhorij], b 20 September 1898 in Homel, Belorussia, d 6 July 1969 in Kharkiv. Surgeon. A graduate of the Kiev Medical Academy (1920), he headed the surgery department of the Vinnytsia Medical Institute (1934–9) and then worked at the Kharkiv Medical and Stomatological Institute (1950–69). His published works deal with problems of surgical endocrinology, blood transfusion, and general and military field surgery.

Hurevych, Zinovii [Hurevyč, Zinovij], b 1898 in Hlukhiv, Sumy oblast. Specialist in social hygiene. A graduate of the Kharkiv Medical Institute (1924), he also taught there. He wrote over 100 works, among them *Koronarna khvoroba* (Coronary Disease, 1963), and coauthored several pioneering studies of sexual behavior, the most significant being *Stateve zhyttia selianky* (The Sexual Life of the Peasant Woman, 1931, with A. Vorozhbyt), *Problemy statevoho zhyttia* (Problems of Sexual Life, 1930, with F. Grosser), and *Suchasne stateve zhyttia* (Contemporary Sexual Life, 1928, with F. Grosser), the German translation of which was reprinted in *Zeitschrift für Sexualwissenschaft*, vol 15, no. 8, 1929.

Hurhula, Iryna, b 3 May 1904 in Bolekhiv, Dolyna county, Galicia, d 20 May 1967 in Lviv. Art scholar. A graduate of Lviv University, she joined the staff of the National Museum in Lviv in 1923 and of the Ukrainian State Museum of Crafts (now the Ukrainian State Museum of Ethnography and Crafts) in 1944. For a time she served as director of the latter museum. She is the author of *Narodne mystetstvo zakhidnykh oblastei Ukraïny* (Folk Art of the Western Oblasts of Ukraine, 1966) and the coauthor of *Narodni maistry* (Folk Craftsmen, 1959) and *Vbrannia* (Dress, 1961). She did the annotations in O. Kulchytska's *Narodnyi odiah zakhidnykh oblastei URSR* (Folk Costumes of the Western Oblasts of the Ukrainian SSR, 1959) and wrote scholarly and popular articles on Ukrainian folk art, guide books, catalogues, and booklets.

Hurkevych, Volodymyr [Hurkevyč], 1871–1937. Lawyer and political and cultural leader in the Sambir region. Hurkevych was a member of the chief executive of the Ukrainian Radical party. He was a founder and the first president of the *Boikivshchyna ethnographic museum in Sambir and the author of articles on the history of the Boiko region.

Hurko, Bohdan, b 21 March 1916 in Krakovets, Yavoriv county, Galicia. Mechanical engineer and inventor. He studied engineering in Lviv, in Graz, Austria, and in Louisville, Kentucky. After immigrating to the United States he worked for several appliance companies and from 1957 to 1972 taught at the University of Louisville. He holds 33 US and foreign patents. His patent for a self-cleaning oven is licensed by most appliance manufacturers around the world.

Hurmuzaki, Eudoxiu, 1812–74. Rumanian baron, historian, and politician. A Ukrainophobic Rumanian chauvinist, he founded the anti-Ukrainian Party of Patriots in Bukovyna and developed a theory of 'Ukrainianized Rumanians.' He petitioned the Austrian government in 1848–9 to separate Bukovyna from Galicia and unite it with Transylvania. He published and edited the German- and Rumanian-language newspaper *Bucovina* (1848–52) and wrote historical works on Rumania and Bukovyna, including *Fragmente zur Geschichte der Rumänen* (5 vols, 1878–86) and *Slavisierung der Bukowina* (1900). He started the collection of historical documents on the Rumanians known as *Colecţia Hurmuzaki* (44 vols, 1874–99), of which he collected 11 volumes. This collection contains some materials on the history of Ukraine.

Hursky, Jacob [Hurs'kyj, Jakiv], b 4 November 1923 in Zholdaky, Chernihiv gubernia. Linguist. After the Second World War he immigrated to the United States and received his PH D from the University of Pennsylvania (1957). He is currently a professor at the University of Syracuse. He is noted for his studies in Ukrainian anthroponymics, specifically on peculiarities of Cossack family names in the 17th century and on the language of 16th-century texts.

Hursky, Valerian [Hurs'kyj], b 29 September 1874 in Kharkiv, d 24 November 1934 in Kharkiv. Silviculturist. A graduate of St Petersburg Forestry Institute (1898), he supervised amelioration work in forests in the Kharkiv and Poltava regions (1903–19) where, under his direction, pine stands of about 20,000 ha were planted. From 1921 he headed the Department of Amelioration of the Kharkiv Agricultural and Forestry Institute (now the Kharkiv Agricultural Institute). From 1931 he was an associate of the Ukrainian Scientific Research Institute of Forest Management and Agroforest Amelioration. He has written works on the reforestation of sandy regions and the creation of anti-erosion forestry belts.

Hurtuimosia (Let Us Gather). An irregular journal of military and civic affairs, published in Prague from 1929 to 1938. Twenty-four issues appeared, including a special issue dedicated to S. *Petliura. The journal supported the *Government-in-exile of the UNR. The editors were V. Fylonovych and M. Bytynsky. Articles and memoirs were contributed by D. Herodot, O. Dotsenko, P. Zlenko, V. Kushch, V. Petriv, V. Salsky, S. Siropolko, P. Shandruk, A. Yakovliv, and others.

Hurvych, Iryna [Hurvyč, Iryna], b 17 June 1911 in Letychiv, Podilia gubernia. Film director. After graduating from the Kiev Art Institute in 1934 she worked at the Kiev Artistic Film Studio. From 1940 she worked at the Kiev Popular Science Film Studio, where she began to direct films in 1959. Her films include *Iak zhinky cholovikiv prodavaly* (How Wives Sold Their Husbands, 1972) and *Teplyi khlib* (Warm Bread, 1973).

Huryn, Ivan, b 7 May 1905 in Bziv, Pereiaslav county, Poltava gubernia. Folklore collector. A secondary school teacher, he wrote down over 5,000 songs and riddles. He also collected materials on folk customs, handicrafts, dialects, and Czech folklore in the Rivne region. He is the author or compiler of numerous books and articles, including *Slovnyk ukraïns'kykh rym* (Dictionary of Ukrainian Rhymes, 1979), which he coauthored with A. Buriachok. Many of Huryn's collected materials are deposited at the AN URSR Institute of Fine Arts, Folklore, and Ethnography.

Hurzhii, Ivan [Huržij], b 28 September 1915 in Khudiaky, Cherkasy county, Kiev gubernia, d 31 October 1971 in Kiev. Historian; corresponding member of the AN URSR from 1958. From 1948 he worked at the Institute of History of the AN URSR, as a senior research associate, professor and holder of the chairs of Feudal History (1955–8), and of Historiography and Source Studies (1969–71), and assistant director (1958–71). His works deal with the socioeconomic history of Ukraine in the 18th and 19th centuries. They include *Zarodzhennia robitnychoho klasu Ukraïny (Kinets XVIII–persha polovyna XIX st.)* (The Birth of Ukraine's Working Class [Late 18th–First Half of the 19th Century], 1958), *Rozvytok tovarnoho vyrobnytstva i torhivli* *na Ukraïni (z kintsia XVIII st. do 1861 r.)* (The Development of Manufacturing and Trade in Ukraine [from the End of the 18th Century to 1861], 1962), and *Ukraïna v systemi vserosiis'koho rynku 60–90-kh rokiv XIX st.* (Ukraine in the All-Russian Market System in the 1860s–1890s, 1968). A bibliography of his works was published in 1965.

Hurzuf

Hurzuf. IX-15. Town smt (1978 pop 10,600) located 16 km from Yalta on the southeast coast of the Crimea and administered by the Yalta city soviet. Protected from the north and northeast by the Hurzuf Yaila Plateau, the town is a popular health and tourist resort and a grape-growing center. It was originally a Tatar village. A Byzantine fortress was built there in the 6th century; it was rebuilt in the 14th century by the Genoese (they called their colony Grasui and Gorzanium). The ruins of the fortress, a palace, and park have been preserved.

Husar, Natalka, b 22 July 1951 in Newark, New Jersey. Artist. Educated at Rutgers University, Husar has lived in Toronto since 1973. She has completed a number of corporate commissions and participated in several group and individual exhibits in Toronto and Edmonton, including 'The Golden Form' (1977), 'Faces-Facades' (1980), and 'Beyond the Irony Curtain' (1986). Husar works in a variety of mediums – porcelain and plexiglass, acrylics, and clay – and is noted for her satirical portrayals of Ukrainian Canadian life.

Husaruk, Eugène, b 2 March 1932 in Warsaw. Violinist, conductor. Coming to Canada in 1949, he studied music at the McGill Conservatory of Music in Montreal, the Vienna Academy, and the Accademia Chigiana of Siena. In 1957 he joined the Montreal Symphony Orchestra (MSO) and in 1968, as MSO soloist, he premiered G. Fiala's *Divertimento Concertanie*. During the 1977–8 and 1979–80 seasons he served as the MSO concertmaster. He played principal violin in the recording of S. Gellman's *Mythos II*, and has appeared as concertmaster with several radio and television orchestras and as a member of a number of prominent Canadian ensembles and chamber orchestras.

Natalka Husar: *Mama's Boy* (acrylic on canvas, 1985)

Húsek, Jan, b 17 October 1884 in Ostrožská Nová Ves, Uherske Hradiste county, Bohemia, d 6 December 1973 in Brno. Czech historian, linguist, and ethnographer; specialist on the nationality question in Transcarpathian Ukraine and the Prešov region. In his most important work, *Národopisná hranice mezi Slováky a Karpatorusy* (The Ethnic Boundary between the Slovaks and the Carpatho-Rusyns, 1925), Húsek proved that there were 278 Ukrainian villages and 94,000 Ukrainian inhabitants in the region. His ethnographic chart is still relevant.

Hushalevych, Ivan [Hušalevyč], b 4 December 1823, Paushivka, Chortkiv county, Galicia, d 2 June 1903 in Lviv. Priest, publicist, and writer. As a student at the

Ivan Hushalevych

Lviv Greek Catholic seminary, Hushalevych wrote the song 'Myr vam, brattia, vsim prynosym,' which was recognized in 1848 by the Supreme Ruthenian Council in Lviv as the anthem of Galician Ukrainians. After graduating (1849), Hushalevych taught Ukrainian and catechism at the Academic Gymnasium of Lviv, with the exception of a few brief intervals, until his retirement (1889). In 1849 he began publishing *Pchola*, the first Ukrainian literary-scholarly journal in Galicia. From 1850 to 1853 he edited the newspaper *Zoria Halytska*, and in 1863–4 he worked on the educational periodical *Dom i shkola*. By the 1850s he had begun to adopt a Russophile political orientation, which included a rejection of the written Ukrainian language in favor of **yazychie*. Hushalevych was a deputy to the Galician Diet (1861–70), serving as a delegate to the State Council in Vienna (1867–70). In addition to writing poetry, he also wrote dramas for the Ukrainian theater in Galicia, and his operetta *Pidhiriany* (1879), set to music by M. Verbytsky, was popular in Western Ukraine.

Hushalevych, Yevhen [Hušalevyč, Jevhen], b 28 November 1864 in Lviv, d 29 May 1907 in Cologne. Opera singer (tenor); the son of I. *Hushalevych. He studied music at the Vienna Conservatory (1888–91) and performed in the opera theaters of Bratislava, Berlin, Brno, Prague, Budapest, Warsaw, Lviv, and other cities. He played the leading roles in Wagner's *Tannhäuser*, *Lohengrin*, and *The Flying Dutchman*; in G. Meyerbeer's *The Huguenots* and *The Prophet*; in Rossini's *Barber of Seville*; and in Verdi's *Troubadour*. He also gave recitals of works by M. Lysenko and arrangements of Ukrainian folk songs.

Hushlak, Gerald [Hušlak], b 15 February 1945 in Edmonton. Artist and educator. A graduate of the Royal College of Art in London, England (MFA), Hushlak has taught painting at the University of Calgary since 1975. His work is found in numerous galleries, including the San Francisco Museum of Modern Art and the Smithsonian Institute in Washington, DC. Winner of the Purchase Award at the 1977 World Print Competition, Hushlak has made major innovations in drawing and printmaking by using computer-controlled drafting machines that permit an exact determination of visual effects to construct drawings.

Husiak, Dariia [Husjak, Darija], b 1924. Political prisoner. Husiak was a liaison officer for the central executive of the Organization of Ukrainian Nationalists in the 1940s. Arrested by the KGB in 1950, she received a 25-year sentence, serving 19 years of her sentence in prison and the remainder in a concentration camp. She was released in 1975.

Husiatyn [Husjatyn]. IV-7. Town smt (1978 pop 2,800) and raion center in Ternopil oblast, situated on the west bank of the Zbruch River. It was first mentioned in 1559, the year it was granted the rights of Magdeburg law. Under Austrian rule (1772–1918) a Galician county town, it grew because it was located on the Austrian-Russian border. Eventually it declined, and its population fell from 6,000 in 1910 to 3,000 by 1931. From April to June 1919 the Ukrainian Galician Army (UHA) fought several battles against Bolshevik forces there, and in July the UHA battled the Poles there before it retreated beyond the Zbruch. The architectural monuments include the ruins of a 17th-century castle, St Onuphrius's Church (16th century), a town hall and a synagogue built in the Renaissance style (17th century), and a Bernardine monastery and church (16th century).

Husli (aka *husli-psaltyr*). A stringed instrument very similar to a psaltery, widely known among the Slavic nations since ancient times. In Ukraine during the medieval period it consisted of a shallow, harp-shaped box strung with a variable number of strings. It was held horizontally on the lap and played by plucking the strings with bare fingers. Later, it assumed a trapezial form, and in the 18th century it was enlarged into an instrument resembling a clavichord. It is still used as a folk instrument.

Huslysty, Kost [Huslystyj, Kost'], b 18 September 1902 in Zaporizhia, d 21 February 1973 in Kiev. Historian and ethnographer; from 1969 a corresponding member of the AN URSR. He worked in research institutions in Kharkiv and Kiev (1928–36), at the AN URSR Institute of History, and from 1954 at the Institute of Fine Arts, Folklore, and Ethnography. In the 1960s he played an important role in the revival of Ukrainian ethnography and history. The more important of his works are *Koliivshchyna* (1947), *Voprosy istorii Ukrainy i etnicheskogo razvitiia ukrainskogo naroda* (Problems in the History of Ukraine and the Ethnic Development of the Ukrainian People, 1963), and *Do pytannia utvorennia ukraïns'koï natsiï* (On the Question of the Formation of the Ukrainian Nation, 1967).

Hustynia Chronicle. A 17th-century chronicle compiled at the *Hustynia Trinity Monastery. The original is no longer extant, but a copy has been preserved, transcribed in the vernacular by the monk-priest M. Losytsky, at the monastery. Its author and date of compilation have not been established. The historian A. Yershov thought that the work was written between 1623 and 1627 by Z. *Kopystensky.

The main text of the chronicle is an account of Ukrainian history from the times of Kievan Rus' to 1597. Although much of the information given is based on Polish, Lithuanian, Byzantine, old Rus', and other chronicles, it is also an original history of contemporary conditions in Ukraine, its ties with Russia, the politics of the Lithuanian grand princes, the nobility of Poland and Turkey, and the depredations of the Turks and Tatars. The chronicle ends with chapters on the origin of the Cossacks, the introduction of the Gregorian Calendar, and the

Church Union of *Berestia. An outstanding monument of 17th-century Ukrainian historiography, its text was published in *Polnoe sobranie russkikh letopisei* (The Complete Collection of Rus' Chronicles, vol 2, 1845). A modern Ukrainian version was published in Kiev in 1985.

Hustynia Trinity Monastery

Hustynia Trinity Monastery. A men's monastery founded by the monk Ioasaf before 1612 on the domains of Prince M. Korybut-Vyshnevetsky in Hustynia village in the Poltava region. Its construction was completed by Metropolitan I. Kopynsky and financed by Princess R. Vyshnevetska. In 1636 the monastery burned down and was abandoned. It was rebuilt in 1639 by Hegumen I. Torsky on Metropolitan P. Mohyla's orders. During the rebellion in 1648 it was abandoned by the monks. Hetman B. Khmelnytsky took it under his protection and patronage. Its land endowment was confirmed by his wife's decree of 1655. After another fire in 1671, Hetman I. Samoilovych built a new Trinity Church. Another stone church – the Dormition Church – was added later by Hetman I. Mazepa. In the 17th century the *Hustynia Chronicle was written at the monastery. Towards the end of the 18th century Hustynia Monastery was one of the richest monasteries in Ukraine. In 1786, however, the Russian government secularized its land, and in 1793 closed it down. It was reopened in 1844. Princess V. Repnina renovated the Dormition Church and buried her father in it. In 1845 T. Shevchenko visited the monastery and painted three watercolors of it. The monastery was closed by Soviet authorities.

Hutsa, Yurii. See Venelin, Yurii.

Hutsailo, Yevhen [Hucajlo, Jevhen], 1880–1928. Pedagogue, political activist in Bukovyna, a founder of the regional branch of the Ukrainian Social Democratic party. During the First World War he was an active member of the Union for the Liberation of Ukraine and helped organize educational and cultural programs for Ukrainian prisoners of war in Germany. In 1918 he was a coeditor of the Social Democratic paper *Vpered* in Lviv. After the war he immigrated to the Ukrainian SSR and worked in the field of education in Kharkiv.

Liuboslav Hutsaliuk: *City in the Sun* (oil, 1957)

Hutsaliuk, Liuboslav [Hucaljuk, Ljuboslav], b 2 April 1923 in Lviv. Painter and graphic artist. He studied art at E. Kozak's studio in Berchtesgaden (1946–9), at the Cooper Union Art School in New York (1949–54), and at the Campanella Academy in Rome. His first important exhibition took place in 1959 in Paris, and was followed by exhibitions in Milan (1959), New York (1962, 1966, 1968), Paris (1963, 1976), and Boston (1973). He is a member of the Audubon Artists, La Société des Artistes Indépendants de Paris, and the Ukrainian Artists' Association in the United States. Hutsaliuk enjoys experimenting with colors. He uses a spatula as well as a brush, and his paintings often look like multicolored mosaics. His style is expressionist, but often contains elements of other styles. Its power is derived chiefly from a rich and well-disciplined palette that combines Ukrainian Eastern dynamism with the mannerism of French painting. Hutsaliuk also does graphic art, mainly book illustrations. His satirical cartoons and caricatures have appeared in the journal *Lys Mykyta* since 1954.

Hutsalo, Yevhen [Hucalo, Jevhen], b 14 January 1937 in Staryi Zhyvotiv (today Novozhyvotiv), Illintsi raion, Vinnytsia oblast. A prominent Soviet Ukrainian writer since the 1960s. A graduate of the Nizhen Pedagogical

Yevhen Hutsalo

Institute (1959), he was first published in 1960 and is the author of over 25 novella and short-story collections, several of them for children. They include *Liudy sered liudei* (People among People, 1962), *Iabluka z osinnoho sadu* (Apples from an Autumn Orchard, 1964), *Olen' Avhust* (The Stag Avhust, 1965), *Proletily koni* (The Horses Flew By, 1966), *Rodynne vohnyshche* (The Family Hearth, 1968), *Poliuvannia z honchym psom* (Hunting with a Hound, 1980), and *Opovidannia z Ternivky* (Stories from Ternivka, 1982). Considered in the 1960s one of the Shestydesiatnyky – the postwar generation of writers and cultural activists who rejected Stalinist methods and ideology and pushed for cultural and political liberalization – he subsequently chose the safe life of an official writer over one of opposition to the regime. Hutsalo's works are noted for their detail, lyrical descriptions of nature, psychological portraits, and abundant use of the rural vernacular. He is also the author of a trilogy of novels – *Pozychenyi cholovik* (The Borrowed Man, 1982), *Pryvatne zhyttia fenomena* (The Private Life of a Phenomenon, 1982), and *Parad planet* (Parade of Planets, 1984) – and, since 1981, three poetry collections.

I. Koshelivets

Hutsul Alps (Ukrainian: Hutsulski Alpy). A mountain group, also called the Rakhiv Mountains, composing the westernmost part of the *Maramureş-Bukovynian Upland; it is situated between the Bila Tysa River valley in the north and the Ruskova River valley in the south. Because of their considerable height (over 1,900 m), geological structure (gneiss, crystalline schists, limestones, and pyroclastic deposits), deep valleys, and distinct glacial forms, the Hutsul Alps are the most variegated and picturesque of the Ukrainian Carpathians. Their peaks are pointed and their slopes are steep and rocky. The ridge consists of two mountain groups: (1) Mt Pip Ivan (1,946 m), a massive gneiss pyramid, and (2) Mt Farcau (1,961 m), a conical basalt mountain, and the limestone Mt Mykhailyk (1,920 m). Above the spruce forests covering the mountain slopes lie extensive meadows, scrubs of pine, and rock fields. The population is concentrated in the valleys of the Bila Tysa (Bohdan), Tysa (Rakhiv), and Ruskova (Ruska Poliana and Ruske Kryve) rivers.

Hutsul Beskyd (Ukrainian: Hutsulskyi Beskyd). A part of the mountain system of the *Beskyds situated between the Prut River valley in the west, the Suceava River valley in the southeast, the outer limits of the Carpathians in the northeast, and the Zhabie-Selietyn Depression in the southwest. It rises steeply from its base (300–400 m) above Subcarpathia, and its peaks attain heights of 800 m at its periphery to 1,500 m in its interior. The Hutsul Beskyd is highest in the southwest, where such peaks as Mt Luchyna (1,464 m), Mt Hordii (1,478 m), Mt Kamenystyi (1,369 m), and Mt Ihrets (1,313 m) are located. Its topography, with its well-defined crests, is similar to that of the neighboring *Gorgany. As in the other Beskyds, a latticed structure is formed there by longitudinal ridges, which alternate with parallel valleys, and the transverse valleys of the Prut, Cheremosh, Suceava, Pistynka, and Seret rivers. As in other parts of the Carpathians inhabited by the *Hutsuls, settlements there are scattered and can be found at the highest altitudes. Towns, such as Diliatyn, Pechenizhyn, Pystyn, Kosiv, Kuty, and Vyzhnytsia, are situated in the foothills. Many of the forests have been cleared and replaced by extensive pastures and hayfields, and animal husbandry is the main form of agriculture. Historically the western, Galician, part of the Hutsul Beskyd has been more densely settled and more deforested; in the eastern, Bukovynian, part the erstwhile prevalence of large estates obstructed free colonization. In the Galician part cultivated land constitutes 9 percent, hayfields and pastures 54 percent, and forest 34 percent of the total land area; the population density is 72 per sq km. In the Bukovynian part the respective figures are 8 percent, 26 percent, and 64 percent, and the density is 47 per sq km.

V. Kubijovyč

Hutsul dialect. One of the southwestern dialects of the Ukrainian language, related to the *Boiko dialect, the Middle-Transcarpathian dialects, and particularly the *Bukovyna-Pokutia dialects. From the 17th century the most archaic dialects found along the Cheremosh River have spread to the upper Tysa River and to Bukovyna, resulting in a narrow belt of Hutsul to Middle-Transcarpathian transitional dialects found along the Ruskova River. The interaction of Hutsul and Dniester dialects in Pokutia gave rise to the Pokutian dialect. According to the chronicles, the Tivertsians (and Ulychians) left their Black Sea settlements in search of lands that were free of nomad raids. They migrated westward into Transylvania and northwestward into Pokutia. On the basis of this statement historians and linguists such as A. Shakhmatov, T. Lehr-Spławiński, and J. Janów claimed that the Hutsuls were the descendants of the above-mentioned Tivertsians who had absorbed a large influx of Rumanians in the 13th–14th centuries. The strong linguistic, particularly lexical, influence of Rumanian on the Hutsul dialect is attributable to the fact that the Ukrainian Slavs inhabited the valleys while the Wallachian herdsmen held the mountain meadows of the same region. No scientific evidence exists to support N. Iorga's hypothesis that the Hutsuls are Ukrainianized Rumanians.

The characteristic features of the Hutsul dialect are: (1) *i* from *ē*, *ō* (*n'is: nesty, nosa* [to carry, nose]); but, along the Cheremosh River also *u*, *ü* from *ō* (*vyn, vÿn* for *vin* [he]), particularly after labials; (2) the palatalized hushing sibilants (*č'ort* [devil], *š'um* [noise]) and the transformation of the groups *šč*, *ždž* into *š'š'*, *ž'ž'* (*š'š'o* for *ščo* [what], *dož'ž'ú* for *došču* [rain, gen sing]); (3) the retention of the 'Central European' or semi-soft *l* (*molbokó* [milk]) and of the soft syllable-final *r'* (*pýsar'* [scribe]) or in place of the proto-Slavic *ŕ̥* (*ver'x* [top]); (4) the soft articulation of the groups: *k'y, g'y, x'y, k'e, g'e, x'e (rúk'y* [hands], *sux'é* [dry]); (5) the transformation of *'a* (and less frequently the old *ja*) into *'ê (jê) (ž'êl'* for *žal'* [pity], *pjêk'* for *p'iat'* [five], *jêvir* for *javir* [maple], *bojêty sy, bojáty sy* for *bojatysja* [to fear]); (6) the absence of the epenthetic *l'* after labials (*róbju*, but: *robl^{b}ényj* [made]); (7) dorsal articulation of palatized *t', d'* as *k', g' (k'ílo* for *tilo* [body], *g'id* for *did* [grandfather]); (8) the coronal (Poltavian) articulation of palatalized dentals *s^b, z^b, c^b, dz^b*; (9) the dispalatalization of the word-final *s', z' (ces* for *cej* [this], *kriz* for *kriz'* [throughout]) and *c', s'* in suffixes: *-ec, -yca, -ck'yj, -sk'yj (xl^{b}ópec* [boy]; *mol^{b}odýca* [young wife]; *pánck'yj* [master's]; *xl^{b}ópsk'yj* [peasant's]) but in the southwest *-c^{b}k'yj, -s^{b}k'yj*; (10) the lowered articulation of the stressed *y* close to *e* (*syen* [son]); the articulation of *e* next to *r* approaches *a* (*tré^{a}ba* for *treba* [need]); (11) the absence of lengthened consonants in combinations of the type: *z^{b}íl'e* for *zillja* [herbs]), (12) the articulation of the prefix *vy-* as *vi-* (*vibrau* for *vybraŭ* [chose]); (13) the clear distinction between the case endings of hard and soft nouns *(zeml^{b}éu* [earth, inst sing] – *rukóŭ* [hand, inst sing]; *na koný* [horse, loc sing – *na stol'í* [table, loc sing; *ého* [this, gen sing] – *tóho* [that, gen sing]; *sýneho* [blue, gen sing] – *dóbroho* [good, gen sing]); (14) the extensive use of *-iŭ (-yŭ)* in the genitive plural of feminine nouns (*bdž'ól'iŭ* [of bees], *cér'kviŭ* [of churches]); (15) the enclitic forms of pronouns: *my, ty, sy* for *meni* [I, dat sing], *tobi* [you, dat sing], *sobi* [reflexive, dat sing]; *mn'y, n'y, mjy, mi* for *mene* [I, gen sing]; *k'y* for *tebe* [you, gen sing; *sy* for *sebe* [reflexive, dat sing]; (16) verb forms of the type: *berét* [takes] – *berút* [they take]; *pytájet, pytat* [asks] (along the Cheremosh River), *pytájut* [they ask]; *xódyt* [walks] – *xóg'e* for *xodjat'* [they walk]; *berémo, berém* (in the east), *beréme* [we take] (in the northwest); the past tense: *xodýŭ sme, -jes; xodýl^{b}y smo* (in the east: *xodýl^{b}ym*), *-ste* [I, you walked]; conditional: *xodýŭ byx* [I would walk]; future tense: *mu xodýty* [I will walk] (less frequently: *búdu xodyty*); *xóg'u* [I walk], *nós'u* [I carry], *výž'u* [I see], *xóž'u* [I walk]; (17) omission of syllables after the stress in the vocative of proper names: *Ju*! for *Jurku, Pará*! for *Parasko*. Rumanian loan words are common in the southeast and Hungarian loan words in the west.

O. Horbach

Hutsul region (Hutsulshchyna). A region in the southeasternmost part of the Carpathian Mountains of Galicia, Bukovyna, and Transcarpathia (the basins of the upper Prut, upper Suceava, upper Bystrytsia Nadvirnianska, and upper Tysa valleys), inhabited by Ukrainian highlanders called *Hutsuls. Except for eight settlements in Rumania, the Hutsul region lies within the present-day borders of the Ukrainian SSR.

The earliest studies of the region and its inhabitants were written in the 1790s by B. Hacquet, professor of Lviv University, and in the first half of the 19th century by I. Vahylevych, Ya. Holovatsky, and such Polish scholars as K. Milewski, K. Wójcicki, A. Bielowski, I. Czerwiński, S. Staszic, and W. Pol. Since the second half of the 19th century much research on the history, dialect, folklore, and ethnography of the region has been produced by Ukrainian (Ya. Holovatsky, I. Franko, V. Hnatiuk, S. Vytvytsky, O. Ohonovsky, F. Vovk, A. Onyshchuk, F. Kolessa, I. Verkhratsky, V. Kobrynsky, I. Krypiakevych, R. Harasymchuk, V. Shukhevych, V. Kubijovyč, O. and A.-H. Horbach, and others), Polish (J. Turczyński, O. Kolberg, A. Kirkor, I. Kopernicki, K. Kosiński, and others), Czech (J. Král, D. Krandžalov, J. Podolák), Russian (P. Bogatyrev), German (R. Kaindl), Rumanian (I. Pătruț), and Hungarian (B. Gunda) scholars. The region has also served as the subject or setting of many literary works, notably those by Yu. Fedkovych, H. Khotkevych, Lesia Ukrainka, V. Stefanyk, M. Cheremshyna, M. Kotsiubynsky, O. Kobylianska, P. Shekeryk-Donykiv, M. Lomatsky, U. Samchuk, V. Grendzha-Donsky, J. Korzeniowski, S. Vincenz, and Z. Kudejar.

In the southeast the Hutsul region borders on ethnic Rumanian lands; in the west, on the region of the *Boikos; in the north, on the region of the Subcarpathian *Pidhiriany; and in the southwest, on long-cultivated Transcarpathian Ukrainian lands. The inhabitants of the villages of Ruska Poliana, Kryve, and Ruskova in the Ruskova Valley of the Maramureş region in Rumania and Kobyletska Poliana, Velykyi Bychkiv, Rosishka, Luh, and Verkhnie Vodiane (formerly Vyshnia Apsha) in Transcarpathia oblast display some Hutsul linguistic and ethnographic features. The accompanying table shows the area and population of the region in 1939 excluding these villages.

The region is located in the most elevated and picturesque part of the Ukrainian Carpathians: (from the northeast to the southwest) (1) the *Hutsul Beskyd and part of the adjacent *Gorgany; (2) the *Zhabie-Selietyn Depression; (3) the high *Svydivets and *Chornohora and lower Kukul, Krynta, and Liudova Baba mountain groups of the *Polonynian Beskyd; and (4) the *Maramureş-Bukovynian Upland, which includes the *Hutsul Alps and the *Chyvchyn Mountains. The gently sloping mountains are densely populated, and the land there is cultivated to a considerable height owing to the moderating climatic influence of the Black Sea and the massiveness of the ranges, which make summers in the region warmer than in other parts of the Carpathians. Highland pastures (*polonyny*) are widespread, and herding, particularly of sheep, has traditionally been widely practiced.

In 1939 the population of the Hutsul region consisted of Ukrainians (89 percent), Jews (7.5 percent), Poles (in Galicia, 2 percent), Rumanians (in Bukovyna, 0.5 percent), and Czechs (in Transcarpathia, 1 percent). Ar-

The Hutsul region in 1939

	No. of communities	Area (sq km)	Population	No. of Ukrainians
In Galicia	44	2,900	94,000	87,000
In Bukovyna	28	2,200	45,000	37,000
In Transcarpathia	8	1,400	36,000	32,000
Total	80	6,500	175,000	156,000

Hutsul church in Yasinia

Hutsul ceramic oven

menians, who at one time played an important economic role in the region, Germans, Hungarians, and Gypsies accounted for a tiny fraction of the population; the latter concentrated in the small towns and the resort centers of the Prut Valley and disappeared almost completely by the end of the Second World War. Ninety-five percent of the population is rural, and only the small towns of Verkhovyna (formerly Zhabie), Rakhiv, Yasinia, Putyliv, Vorokhta, and Yaremche lie within the region proper; the last two are important resort centers in the Prut Valley. The average population density is 27 per sq km. The most densely populated (70 per sq km) are the Zhabie-Selietyn Depression and most of the Hutsul Beskyd, where lumbering has left only a third of the area forested. The Galician part of the region is more densely populated than the Bukovynian or Transcarpathian parts, where the earlier existence of large latifundia impeded free settlement.

Herding and animal husbandry, traditionally the chief occupations in the Hutsul region, have determined the forms and uniqueness of the settlements that have existed there. These have been characterized by their dispersal, high altitude (1,100–1,600 m and, in the case of Hostovets, 1,700 m), transhumant (groups of remote herdsmen's huts [*stai*] and corrals in the *polonyny*) and seasonal (*zymivky*, *litovyshcha*) nature, and ongoing transformation from temporary pastoral colonies into permanent settlements (particularly in the Galician part).

Crop cultivation has been practically non-existent in the region: farmland accounts for barely 4 percent of the total area (it constitutes 25 percent in the Boiko region and 35 percent in the Lemko region), while mountain meadows and hayfields account for 33 percent and forest for 59 percent. For centuries the inhabitants exchanged meat, dairy products, and wool for grain from Pokutia and the Maramureş region. Beekeeping, hunting, trap-

Vorynnia, a Hutsul rail-fence

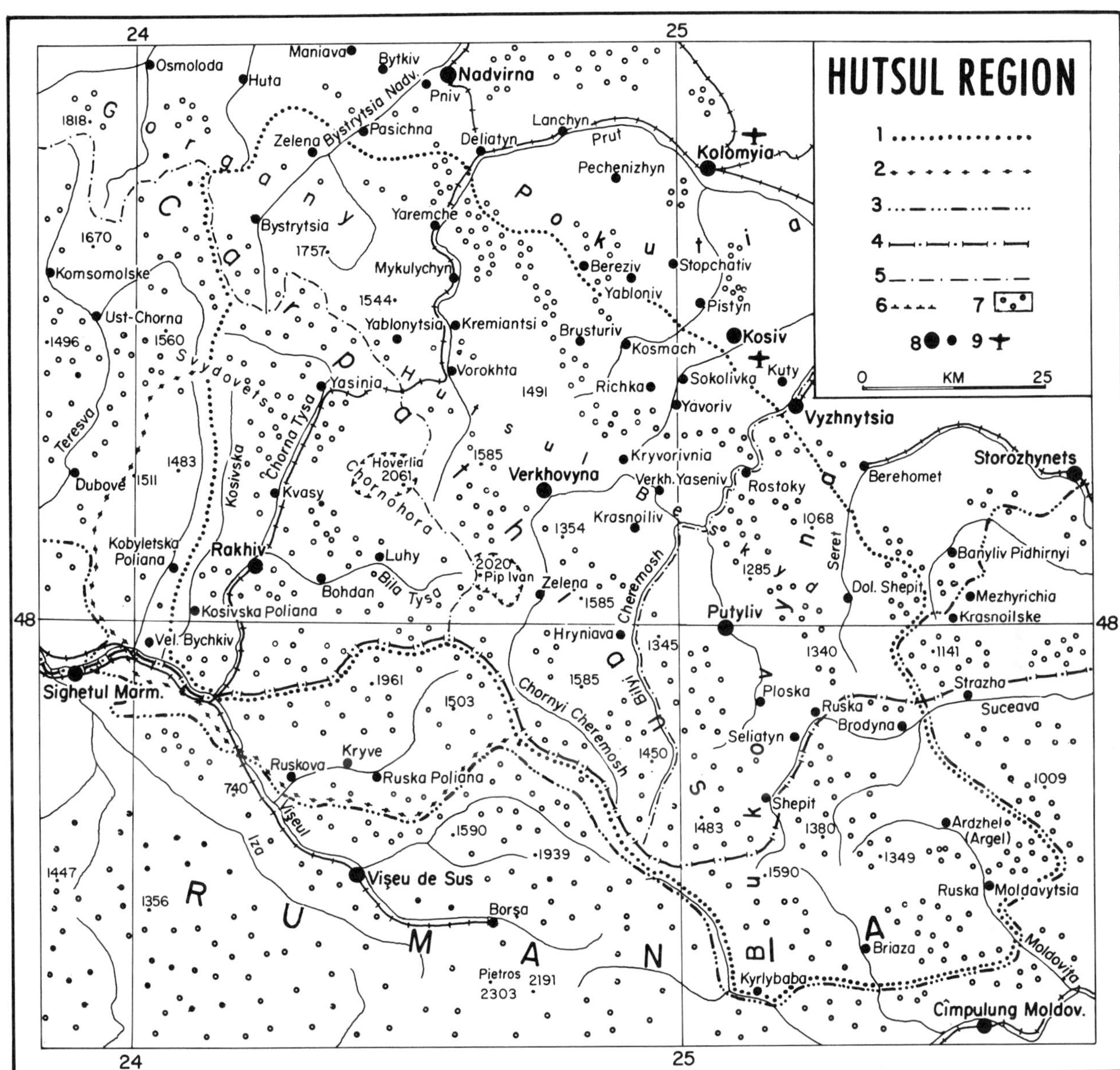

1. Boundary of the Hutsul region
2. Boundary of transitional ethnographic territory
3. Ukrainian-Rumanian ethnic border
4. Border of the Ukrainian SSR
5. Oblast borders
6. Boundaries of the Carpathian Nature Reserve
7. Forested areas
8. Raion centers and other settlements
9. Airports

ping, fishing, salt mining, and domestic crafts – woodworking, weaving, furriery, tanning, and handicrafts – were auxiliary occupations. Commerce was conducted primarily by Armenians and Jews in the piedmont towns. In the second half of the 19th century the region's economy declined because of its remoteness from railway lines, the redistribution of land and impoverishment of the peasantry, and the latter's inability to compete with factories in producing and selling goods. Eventually, seasonal logging work, often outside the region, became the chief occupation of most Hutsuls. Crop cultivation, primarily of potatoes, corn, barley, and flax but also of oats and rye, remained primitive. The development of resorts, mostly in the Prut Valley but also in the Tysa Valley, was of little benefit to the indigenous population. Large-scale handicraft enterprises, such as the Hutsulske Mystetstvo co-operative in Kosiv, only began developing in the interwar period. The Transcarpathian part of the region enjoyed the quickest rate of economic development under the Czechoslovak Republic, while the Bukovynian part completely stagnated under interwar Rumania. Since the Second World War the primary industries of the Hutsul region have continued to be animal husbandry, lumbering, and wood processing, and health-resort services and artistic-handicrafts manufacturing have remained the main secondary industries.

V. Kubijovyč, N. Pavliuc

Hutsul Song and Dance Ensemble (Hutsulskyi ansambl pisni i tantsiv). An ensemble founded in 1940 in Stanyslaviv (now Ivano-Frankivske) consisting of a choir, dance troupe, and an orchestra of folk instruments. The ensemble performs and promotes the study of folk songs and dances of the Hutsul region. It also performs works by various Ukrainian and foreign composers. The ensemble's directors have included M. Hrynyshyn and V. Derevianko (1970–).

Hutsul Theater; H. Khotkevych is in the center.

Hutsul Theater (Hutsulskyi teatr). Amateur drama group of Hutsul peasants, organized in 1910 by H. *Khotkevych at the Sich Home in Krasnoilia, Kosiv county. In 1911–12 the group, which had 40 members (including L. *Kurbas) and an orchestra of Hutsul folk musicians, toured the villages and towns of Galicia and Bukovyna. It also performed in Lviv, Cracow, and Chernivtsi. Its repertoire included ethnographic plays written by Khotkevych: *Hutsul's'kyi rik* (The Hutsul Year) and *Neproste* (Non-Simple); *Dovbush*, a dramatization of the legend about the folk hero; *Praktykovanyi zhovnir* (The Experienced Soldier); and *Antin Revizorchuk*, a reworking of J. Korzeniowski's *Karpaccy górale* (Carpathian Highlanders). In 1913–14 Khotkevych tried to organize a tour of Russian-ruled Ukraine for the group but military events stopped it and the ensemble dissolved. For most of its existence the Hutsul Theater was directed by O. Remez.

BIBLIOGRAPHY

Charnetskyj, S. *Narys istoriï ukraïns'koho teatru v Halychyni* (Lviv 1934)

Shekeryk, P. 'Pershyi hutsul's'kyi teatr opered' svitovoi voinov,' in *Kalendar hutsul's'kyi na rik 1937* (Warsaw 1936)

V. Revutsky

Hutsuls (Ukrainian: *hutsuly*). An ethnographic group of Ukrainian pastoral highlanders inhabiting the *Hutsul region in the Carpathian Mountains. According to K. Milewski and J. Korzeniowski, the name *hutsul* was originally *kochul* ('nomad,' cf literary Ukrainian *kochovyk*), which became *kotsul* and then *hotsul*, and referred to inhabitants of Rus' who fled from the Mongol invasion into the Carpathians. Other scholars (eg, I. Vahylevych) believed that the name derives from a subtribe of the Cumans or Pechenegs – the ancient Turkic Utsians or Uzians – who fled from the Mongols into the mountains. S. Vytvytsky proposed that the name derives from Hetsylo, the brother of Prince Rostislav of Moravia, or from the name of a tribe allied with the Ostrogoths – the Horulians-Hutsians. Since the 19th century the most widely accepted view (held by Ya. Holovatsky, O. Kaluzhniatsky, I. Ohonovsky, I. Krypiakevych, V. Hnatiuk, I. Pătruţ, and others) has been that the name comes from the Rumanian word for brigand, *hoţul/hoţ*. The Soviet scholar B. Kobyliansky claimed that the Hutsuls are descended from the Slavic tribe of the Ulychians who resettled in the Carpathians. Based on the first written mention of the name (1816), S. Hrabec and V. Hrabovetsky believe the name is of recent origin and that it was originally a nickname given to the region's inhabitants by the neighboring Boikos.

Hutsuls on the way to a market in town

Archeological evidence of human existence in the region dates back 100,000 years. Certain localities (eg, Kosiv) were settled as early as the Neolithic Period (6,000–4,000 BC), and the so-called Carpathian kurhans excavated in the late 19th and early 20th centuries in river valleys around Kolomyia and Kosiv revealed distinct evidence of the Dacian and Cherniakhiv cultures. The Slavic *White Croatians inhabited the region in the first millennium AD; with the rise of Kievan Rus', they became vassals of the new state. Place-names in the region's valleys – eg, Kniazhdvir on the Prut River, Kniazhe on the Cheremosh River, Kniazhyi Forest near Bereziv Vyzhnii, and Boiarske Pasture in Zelena – indicate that the region was settled during the period of Kievan Rus' and the Principality of Galicia-Volhynia (9th–13th centuries). References to salt mines in the region ('Kolomyia salt') are found in the Galician-Volhynian Chronicle, and the earliest recorded mention of a settlement there (1367) is that of the salt-mining center of Utoropy. Many other Hutsul settlements and monasteries are mentioned in charters and municipal and land documents beginning in the 15th century: eg, Bereziv (1412), Pystyn (1416), Kosiv (1424), Luh (1439), Pechenizhyn (1443), Kuty (1449),

Hutsul wedding party

Vyzhnytsia (1450), and Pniv (1454). The population grew as increasingly more peasants fled into the mountains to escape serfdom, and by the mid-19th century there were over 100 Hutsul villages and 10 noble-owned towns in the region.

Although the overwhelmingly peasant Hutsuls came to be dominated and oppressed by Polish magnates and Hungarian nobles, a Ukrainian petty nobility arose in Bereziv. They and their peasant brethren took part in the *Mukha rebellion against Poland (1490–2), and in 1509 and the 1530s they aided the Moldavians in their wars with the Poles. Local, spontaneous Hutsul peasant rebellions against noble oppression became recurring phenomena. Hutsuls are known to have participated in the Cossack-peasant rebellion led by S. Nalyvaiko, and Hutsul names have been found on the lists of registered Cossacks. Hutsuls also took part in the Cossack-Polish War of 1648–54, most notably in the uprising against the Poles in Pokutia led by S. *Vysochan in 1654 and the siege of the Polish castle in Pniv. From the mid-16th century to the 1870s bands of brigands called *opryshoks, which came to play the role of avengers of the wrongs inflicted on the common people by the magnates and their agents, operated freely throughout the Hutsul region.

Under Austrian rule, numerous local Hutsul uprisings against the oppressive landowners continued; the most significant were those led or inspired by L. *Kobylytsia throughout the 1840s. Since the 19th century, the national awakening of the Hutsuls, like their history in general, has been conditioned by developments in *Galicia, *Bukovyna, and *Transcarpathia, of which the Hutsul region is a part.

Literacy among the Hutsuls remained low until the 20th century; the first elementary school in the region was established only in 1816, in Pechenizhyn. The most significant growth of national consciousness among the Hutsuls occurred after the rise of the popular Ukrainian Radical party in Galicia and Bukovyna in the 1890s and the establishment of branches of the Sich physical-culture society in the Hutsul centers by Yu. Solomiichuk-Yuzenchuk in the 1900s. Many Hutsuls filled the ranks of the Ukrainian Sich Riflemen in 1914–15 and took part in the wars for Ukrainian independence of 1918–20. On 7 January 1919 a Hutsul force drove the Hungarian garrison from Yasinia. With the aid of a company of Sich Riflemen, it occupied Sighet on 14–16 January, and on 5 February a Hutsul Republic was proclaimed in Transcarpathia. Its 4-man Ukrainian government and 42-member Hutsul Council were headed by S. *Klochurak. The republic lasted until 11 June, when Rumanian troops occupied the area.

Hutsul pottery

The Hutsuls are distinguished from other ethnographic groups in the Carpathians by their colorful, richly ornamented folk dress, which today is worn only on festive occasions. Outer garments of both sexes consist of a black or dark red coat (*serdak*), a linen blouse or shirt with multicolored embroidery or glass beads, and a short, sleeveless white sheepskin jacket (*kozhushyna* or *kyptar*) often ornamented with appliqués of leather, embroidery, and string, and mirror inlays. Men wear a broad-rimmed hat (*krysania*) decorated with colored string and plumes, a sheepskin hat in winter, a long shirt over narrow linen trousers, and a wide (*remin*) or narrow (*cheres*) belt with purses and brass ornamentation over the shirt. Women wear a wraparound skirt (*zapaska* or *horbotka*) and a headband (*namitka*) or colorful kerchief (*khustka*). Footwear consists of leather moccasins laced above the ankle.

The Hutsuls are renowned for their artistic *wood carving and inlaying of wooden objects with contrasting wood, brass, silver, bone, mother-of-pearl, and glass beads; their ceramics; their handmade jewelry, ornaments, and implements of brass, leather, and bone; their vibrant handwoven textiles and *kilim weaving; and particularly their embroidery, *Easter eggs, and distinctive wooden *folk architecture. The churches in Vorokhta, Kniazhdvir, Kryvorivnia, Yasinia, Zelena, and Verbovets are fine examples of the Hutsul style. The Hutsul farmstead (*grazhda) is also notable for its features.

There are rich collections of Hutsul handicrafts and folk art in the Ukrainian State Museum of Ethnography and Crafts in Lviv, the Chernivtsi Regional Museum, ethnographic museums in Uzhhorod, Vienna, and Budapest, and particularly the *Kolomyia Museum of Hutsul Folk Art.

The Hutsuls' rich folklore and folkways and the *Hutsul dialect have been preserved to this century. They are not only recorded and described in scholarly studies,

Hutsul musicians

but are also depicted in the literary works of Yu. Fedkovych, I. Franko, M. Kotsiubynsky, M. Cheremshyna, H. Khotkevych, O. Kobylianska, and many other writers. The Hutsul folk tradition is rich in songs, many of which valorize the deeds of the opryshoks, particularly O. *Dovbush, and the Rumanian popular rebel, G. Pintea. The Hutsuls also have distinctive folk music and dances. Their **kolomyiky* and **troisti muzyky* have gained popularity far beyond the Hutsul region. Since parts of the Hutsul region have a mixed Ukrainian-Rumanian population, certain cultural features of the Rumanian and other Balkan peoples are discernible among the Hutsuls. Their instrumental music, for example, is very rhythmic, like that of the Balkan region. The most popular Hutsul folk dances are the fast-paced *hutsulka* and, around Rakhiv, the *trybushanka*.

Hutsul immigrants in the West have established societies in Great Britain, Chicago, Philadelphia, Buffalo, Cleveland, Toronto, Oshawa, and Hamilton, which have occasionally held joint conferences and congresses and in 1985 federated in the Ukrainian World Alliance of Hutsuls. The Chicago Chornohora society has published the journal *Hutsuliia*, edited by M. Domashevsky, who also directs the Hutsul Research Institute and has published two volumes of a history of the Hutsul region.

BIBLIOGRAPHY
Hacquet, B. *Neueste physikalisch-politische Reisen ... durch die ... Nördlichen Karpathen*, 4 vols (Nuremberg 1790–6)
Witwicki, S. *O Hucułach: Rys historyczny* (Lviv 1873)
Kaindl, R. *Die Huzulen: Ihr Leben, ihre Sitten und ihre Volksüberlieferung* (Vienna 1894)
Shukhevych, V. *Hutsul'shchyna*, 5 vols (Lviv 1899–1908); Polish edn: W. Szuchiewicz, *Huculszczyzna*, 4 vols (Cracow 1902–8)
Kryp'iakevych, I. 'Z istoriï Hutsul'shchyny,' LNV, 80–2 (1923)
Kubijowicz, W. *Życie pasterskie w Beskidach wschodnich* (Cracow 1926)
Kondracki, M. *Muzyka Huculszczyzny* (Warsaw 1935)
Ossendowski, F. *Huculszczyzna. Gorgany i Czarnohora* (Poznan 1936)
Hrabec, S. *Nazwy geograficzne Huculszczyzny* (Cracow 1950)
Kolberg, O. *Ruś Karpacka*, 2 vols (Wrocław-Poznan 1970–1)
Vincenz, A. de. *Traité d'anthroponymie houtzoule* (Munich 1970)
Domashevs'kyi, M. (ed). *Istoriia Hutsul'shchyny*, vols 1–2 (Chicago 1975, 1986)
Mandybura, M. *Polonyns'ke hospodarstvo Hutsul'shchyny druhoï polovyny XIX–30-kh rokiv XX st.* (Kiev 1978)
Senkiv, I. *Die Hirtenkultur der Huzulen: Eine volkskundliche Studie* (Marburg/Lahn 1981)
Hrabovets'kyi, V. *Hutsul'shchyna XIII–XIX stolit': Istorychnyi narys* (Kiev 1982)
Vincenz, S. *On the High Uplands: Sagas, Songs, Tales and Legends of the Carpathians*, trans H. Stevens (New York nd)

N. Pavliuc, V. Sichynsky, S. Vincenz

Hutyn Mountains (Hutynski hory). The southern part of the *Volcanic Ukrainian Carpathians. Lying south of the Tysa River on the Ukrainian-Rumanian border in Transcarpathia, they close off the Maramureş Basin in the southwest. The mountains constitute a gently sloping, densely forested ridge about 50 km long. Their peaks range from 900 to 1,100 m in altitude.

Hutyria, Viktor [Hutyrja], b 11 September 1910 in Syniavske, Don Cossack Province, d 21 October 1983. Petrochemist; full member of the AN URSR from 1961, member of its presidium (1961–3, 1974–), and vice-president (1963–74). After graduating from the Azerbaijan Petroleum Institute in 1932, he worked for 25 years in various capacities at the Azerbaijan Petroleum Research Institute. From 1959 to 1963 he chaired the department of petrochemistry at the academy's Institute of Macromolecular Chemistry, and from 1974 he was in charge of the department of petrochemistry at the academy's Institute of Physical-Organic and Carbon Chemistry. He published much on the petroleum deposits in Azerbaijan and Ukraine, and on the catalytic processes of hydrocarbon transformation. He did research on catalytic petroleum cracking, the synthesis of aluminosilicate catalysts, the synthesis of ethanol from ethylene on an industrial scale, and the composition of the oil from the Baku fields.

Huz, Oleksander [Huz'], b 29 January 1939 in Ichnia, Chernihiv oblast. Materials scientist; since 1978 full member of the AN URSR. A graduate of Kiev University (1961), in 1976 he was appointed director of the AN URSR Institute of Mechanics. As a specialist in the mechanics of hard deformative bodies, he has contributed to the theory of stability of composite materials and structural elements and developed new methods of non-destructive testing of composite materials.

Huz, Petro [Huz'], b 7 October 1898 in Liutenka, Hadiache county, Poltava gubernia, d 2 May 1959 in Liutenka. Kobzar. Having lost his sight in early childhood, he learned to play the bandura from M. *Kravchenko and became an active kobzar after the Revolution, giving concerts in villages and cities throughout Ukraine. In 1940 he joined the State Ethnographic Ensemble of Bandurysts. Besides the traditional kobzar songs, his repertoire included Soviet 'folk' songs, some of which were of his own composition.

Huzar, Liubomyr, b 26 February 1933 in Lviv. Hieromonach of the Studite order. Emigrating in 1944, he eventually settled in the United States. After completing his studies at the Catholic University of America in Washington and at the Pontifical Urban University in Rome (1972), he lectured on eastern theology at the latter. A close collaborator of Cardinal Y. Slipy, in 1978 he was appointed archimandrite of St Theodore Monastery in Castelgandolfo, and in 1985 protosyncellus of the Lviv archeparchy.

Huzar, Olha (née Pavliukh), b 1885 in Vienna, d ? Feminist leader and journalist in Bukovyna. She was vice-president (1921–3) and president (1930–2) of the Womens' Hromada society and president of the Myronosytsi social-aid society. In the 1930s she contributed to journals such as *Ridnyi krai* and *Literaturno-naukovyi vistnyk,* and edited a women's page in *Chas* (1934–6). She also translated German and French literature. In 1942 she was sentenced by a Rumanian court to five years' imprisonment for her community activities. In 1945 she was imprisoned in Chernivtsi by the Soviets and disappeared without trace.

Huzar, Yevhen, 1854–1918. Galician church and community leader, writer. Huzar was a catechist and educator who organized Ukrainian domestic workers in Lviv. He wrote textbooks on such topics as hagiography and church history.

Huzhova, Vira [Hužova], b 18 January 1898 in Kiev, d 6 December 1974 in Kiev. Opera and concert singer (soprano). A graduate of the Kiev Conservatory (1919), from 1924 to 1950 she was a soloist with Kiev, Kharkiv, Baku, Tbilisi, and Odessa operas. Her repertoire of nearly 40 roles included Odarka in S. Hulak-Artemovsky's *Zaporozhets za Dunaiem* (Zaporozhian Cossack beyond the Danube), Yaroslavna in A. Borodin's *Prince Igor,* Tatiana in P. Tchaikovsky's *Eugene Onegin,* Hanna in H. Zhukovsky's *Mest,* and the title roles in Verdi's *Aïda* and Puccini's *Tosca.* From 1950 to 1961 she also taught at the Kiev Conservatory. Her memoirs were published in 1971.

Hvozdyk, Kyrylo, b 22 June 1895 in Rebedailivka, Chyhyryn county, Kiev gubernia. Easel painter and monumentalist. In the 1920s he studied under M. *Boichuk at the Kiev State Art Institute and belonged to the Association of Revolutionary Art of Ukraine. He took part in painting the murals of the Peasant Sanatorium in Odessa (1928). He also depicted some scenes of peasant life such as *The Shepherd* (1928), *Radio in the Village* (1929), *Harvest Festival,* and *The Police Search.* In the 1930s he was arrested and exiled.

Hydrobiology, Institute of the Academy of Sciences of the Ukrainian SSR. See Institute of Hydrobiology of the Academy of Sciences of the Ukrainian SSR.

Hydrology. Study of the distribution, properties, and circulation of the earth's waters. In practice it is limited to inland waters – rivers and streams, lakes, marshes, groundwater, and snow. The discovery, use, management, and conservation of water resources are all in the province of hydrology. Because of their economic importance, a substantial amount of government-sponsored research on Ukraine's inland waters was done in the 19th century. This work resulted in a number of significant publications such as *Gidrografiia Rossii* (Hydrography of Russia, 6 vols, 1844–9), which contains much material on Ukraine, and M. Maksymovych's *Dnepr i ego bassein* (The Dnieper and Its Basin, 1901).

In the 1920s, as the hydroelectric potential and the economic importance of water resources increased sharply, hydrologic research in Ukraine expanded. In 1922 a chair of hydrology was established at the Kiev Polytechnical Institute, which in 1926 was reorganized into the Scientific Research Institute of Water Resources of Ukraine. The institute was directed by Ye. Oppokiv and published its *Visti* in Ukrainian. In 1934 it was incorporated into the All-Ukrainian Academy of Sciences and subjected to several reorganizations: in 1938 it became the Institute of Hydrology, in 1944 the Institute of Hydrology and Hydrotechnology (with a Russian-language *Izvestiia*), and in 1963 the Institute of Hydromechanics. The institute's journal, *Hidromekhanika,* appeared in Ukrainian in the 1960s, and now appears in Russian as *Gidromekhanika.* The institute has made significant contributions to the theory and application of hydrology in developing, controlling, and preserving the water resources of Ukraine. Other institutions where significant hydrologic research is carried out are the Marine Hydrophysical Institute of the AN URSR, the Institute of Hydrobiology of the AN URSR, the Ukrainian Hydrometeorological Scientific Research Institute (established in 1953 on the basis of the Kiev Hydrological Observatory and the Kiev Hydrophysical Observatory) and its field stations, the Ukrainian Scientific Research Institute of Hydrotechnology and Soil Melioration (established in 1929 in Kiev by the People's Commissariat of Agriculture) with its several field stations, and a number of research groups at higher educational institutions.

O. Bilaniuk

Hydromechanics, Institute of the Academy of Sciences of the Ukrainian SSR. See Institute of Hydromechanics of the Academy of Sciences of the Ukrainian SSR.

Hydrometeorology. See Hydrology.

Hygiene. A branch of medicine that deals with the diverse influences of the environment on the health of humans, their life span, and capabilities for work. Hygiene aims to develop methods for preventing and combatting disease. It is especially concerned with the prevention of epidemics and communicable diseases and, more recently, with health conditions in the workplace and home. It is closely related to other scientific disciplines, particularly physiology, pathology, bacteriology, *epidemiology, clinical medicine, toxicology, ecology, and demography. The practical application of knowledge gained by the study of hygiene is called *sanitation. Hygienic research constitutes an important basis for preventive medicine and has important implications for public policy. It can be divided into several categories: communal (dealing with housing conditions), alimentary, personal, social, pediatric, labor, military, and others.

Hygiene is one of the most ancient sciences. During the period of Kievan Rus', the chronicles and other early texts, such as the *Izbornik* of Sviatoslav (11th century), contained many tips for hygiene based on folk knowledge. The level of sanitary culture was quite advanced for those times. Various herbals and self-healing manuals (*lichebnyky, zilnyky, travnyky*), which were common in the Middle Ages, contained advice with regard to drinking water, personal cleanliness, preparation of meals, cleanliness of cooking and eating utensils, care of clothing and bedding, etc. The writings of Princess Yevpraksiia-Zoia (12th century) contain advice on the treatment of various diseases, the airing of rooms, bathing, nutrition, hygienic measures for children, and sexual hygiene. By the 16th and 17th centuries, a number of medical guides with instructions on hygiene were popular. From the 16th century, isolation of the infectiously ill was practiced. The first quarantine was established in 1740 near Kiev.

In the 18th century, Ukrainian physicians such as D. Samoilovych, N. Ambodyk-Maksymovych, Ye. Mukhin, and Kh. Barsuk-Moisieiev, as well as Russian physicians such as S. Zybelin and M. Mudrov, made important contributions to hygiene and to the containment of epidemics in Ukraine. They also popularized the practice of disinfection and vaccination.

The development of the science of hygiene was accompanied by the introduction of legislation concerning sanitary practices. In Russian-ruled Ukraine these included decrees concerning the paving of city streets, the appointment of city controllers of sanitation, and the regulation of sanitary practices in the sale of food. In the 19th century, the frequent cholera outbreaks and other epidemics had a major influence on the development of hygiene. They prompted the reorganization of large cities and considerable advancement in the scientific study of hygiene. By the late 19th century, questions of personal hygiene and preventive medicine became secondary to general societal protection of health. Aspects of hygiene were researched and taught in the medical faculties of Kharkiv and Kiev universities from their establishment in 1805 and 1834 respectively, while separate chairs of hygiene, among the first in all of Europe, were founded at Kiev in 1871 and at Kharkiv in 1873. A major contribution to experimental hygiene was made by V. *Subbotin, the first professor of hygiene at Kiev University. He also authored a popular textbook on hygiene for students and medical doctors, and established a hygienic laboratory (1875). The first professor of hygiene at Kharkiv was A. Yakoby; he was succeeded by I. Skvortsov.

Beginning in the 1860s many zemstvo physicians did important work in the fields of sanitation and preventive medicine (see *zemstvo medicine). In the 19th and early 20th centuries hygiene and sanitation were not yet clearly differentiated. Individual physicians and associations often combined scientific study of hygiene with the development and enforcement of sanitary norms and considerable community involvement in the popularization of health care. In fact, most of the early chairs of hygiene at the universities were officially called chairs of hygiene and medical police or chairs of public health. This facilitated the definition of practical indicators and regulations for public health in the areas of communal health, labor, nutrition, and the like. Hygienists worked in close contact with epidemiologists, bacteriologists, and pathologists such as I. Mechnikov, O. Bezredka, M. Hamaliia, D. Zabolotny, T. Minkh, V. Vysokovych, and V. Podvysotsky. Several important contributions to hygiene in this period were made by O. Korchak-Chepurkivsky, a former zemstvo physician who taught hygiene in the medical faculty of Kiev University (after 1921 the Kiev Medical Institute) from 1903 to 1934, and who held leading positions in hygiene at the VUAN from 1921.

The Revolution of 1917 and the succeeding struggle for Ukrainian independence caused a drastic decline in sanitary and hygienic conditions. After the consolidation of Soviet rule in Ukraine, hygiene, along with all other branches of medicine, came under the jurisdiction of the state. The reorganization of existing medical schools in the 1920s, and the establishment of new ones in several cities in the 1930s, greatly furthered the development of hygiene. In 1934–6 entire faculties of sanitation and hygiene were established in a number of medical institutes, with several chairs where various aspects of hygiene were studied and taught. Special attention was given to problems of labor and alimentary hygiene. In this period, important contributions to hygiene were made by O. *Marzieiev, head of the sanitary-epidemiological administration of the Ukrainian SSR Commissariat of Public Health (1922–35) and professor of hygiene at Kharkiv and Kiev universities. He founded and headed (1931–56) the Ukrainian Institute of Communal Hygiene, which was primarily concerned with problems of housing and living conditions. This institute is now located in Kiev and is called the Scientific Research Institute of General and Communal Hygiene. Research in hygiene is also conducted at a scientific research institute of alimentary hygiene in Kiev and at four scientific research institutes of the hygiene of labor and prophylactic medicine (in Kiev, Kharkiv, Donetske, and Kryvyi Rih). In the 1920s and 1930s several institutions of the AN URSR conducted research in hygiene, including the chair of hygiene and sanitation held by O. Korchak-Chepurkivsky. Much attention was given to medical statistics, prophylactic medicine, and epidemiology.

In Western Ukraine, the research and teaching of hygiene was limited before 1939. Organizations such as the Prosvita and Vidrodzhennia societies did much to encourage hygienic measures, as did numerous physicians. In interwar Galicia, a branch of the Polish State Institute of Hygiene was established in Lviv. Research at this institute focused primarily on problems of bacteriology and epidemiology, as well as issues in communal hygiene.

BIBLIOGRAPHY

Ocherk istorii meditsinskoi nauki i zdravookhraneniia na Ukraine (Kiev 1954)
Sorok let sovetskogo zdravookhraneniia (Moscow 1957)
Pliushch, V. *Narysy z istoriï ukraïns'koï medychnoï nauky ta osvity*, 2 vols (Munich 1970, 1983)

Grando, A. *Razvitie gigieny v Ukrainskoi SSR* (Kiev 1975)
Gabovich, R. *Gigiena* (Moscow 1977)
60 let sovetskogo zdravookhraneniia (Moscow 1977)

H. Schultz

Hykavy, Onufrii [Hykavyj], b 1885 in Peremyliv, Husiatyn county, Galicia, d 4 May 1945 in Winnipeg. Teacher, journalist, and community leader. Hykavy immigrated to Canada in 1902 and became a Ukrainian bilingual teacher in rural Manitoba (1907–13). In 1910 he published *Zbirnyk baiok* (Collection of Tales), one of the first collections of Ukrainian children's literature in Canada. An editor of the newspaper **Kanadiis'kyi farmer* (1913–32, 1944–5), his editorials in 1917 were instrumental in the formation of the *Ukrainian Greek Orthodox Church in Canada.

Hynylevych, Hryhorii [Hynylevyč, Hryhorij], b 5 February 1809 in Yavoriv, Galicia, d 30 November 1871 in Peremyshl. Clergyman, writer, and leader of the Greek Catholic church. A member of the church consistory, he was in charge of schools in the Peremyshl eparchy and rector of the Peremyshl Greek Catholic Theological Seminary. In 1848 he headed the Ukrainian delegation to the Slavic Congress in Prague, at which he defended the distinctiveness of the Ukrainian people from the Poles and the Russians. As a deputy to the Galician Diet, he demanded the division of Galicia into Ukrainian and Polish parts and obtained the first government subsidy for a Ukrainian cultural institution – the Ruska Besida theater. The graduates of the Peremyshl seminary dedicated their first almanac, titled *Lirvak z nad Siana* (The Lira Player from the Sian, 1852), to Hynylevych.

Hynylevych, Yaroslav [Hynylevyč, Jaroslav], b 9 April 1891 in Shumiach, Turka county, Galicia, d 14 October 1980 in Munich. Physician and civic leader. A graduate of Lviv University (1916), he served as a physician in the Austrian and then in the Ukrainian Galician Army (1918–20). He was Metropolitan A. Sheptytsky's private physician. In 1939 he became professor of medicine at Lviv University and two years later at the Lviv Medical Institute. Emigrating in 1944, he settled in Munich. From 1951 he was president of the Ukrainian Medical-Charitable Service. In 1964 Hynylevych received the title of Knight-Commander of the Order of St Sylvester from Pope Paul VI.

Hypanis. The name of both the Boh and the Kuban rivers in the works of such classical authors as Herodotus, Strabo, Dionysius, Ptolemy, Stephanus Byzantinus, and Ovid.

Hypatian Chronicle. Compendium of three *chronicles: Nestor's **Povist' vremmenykh lit* (Tale of Bygone Years, ca 1110) with some alterations, particularly at the end of the text, the *Kiev Chronicle of the 12th century, and the *Galician-Volhynian Chronicle. The oldest redaction of the compendium, dating back to the early 15th century, was discovered by N. Karamzin at the Hypatian Monastery in Kostroma, Russia. There are two more redactions from the 16th century, the first of which was probably written in Belorussia. The best sources of information about the Hypatian Chronicle are M. *Hrushevsky's works *Istoriia Ukraïny-Rusy* (The History of Ukraine-Rus', vol 3) and *Istoriia ukraïns'koï literatury* (History of Ukrainian Literature), and works by A. Shakhmatov, V. Pashuto, D. Chyzhevsky, M. Priselkov, I. Eremin, and N. Berezhkov. It was published by the Imperial Archeographic Commission as *Ipat'evskaia letopis'* (The Hypatian Chronicle) in *Polnoe sobranie russkikh letopisei* (The Full Collection of Rus' Chronicles, vol 2, 1843), republished in a second edition as *Letopis' po Ipatskomu spisku* (The Chronicle According to the Hypatian Redaction, 1871), and again republished as part of the second edition of the complete collection under the title *Ipat'evskaia letopis'* (The Hypatian Chronicle, 1908). It was republished incomplete again by A. Shakhmatov in his third edition of the *Polnoe sobranie russkikh letopisei* (vol 2, 1923). After the removal of several north Russian features such as the spelling of *ě* in place of the strong ь, the Hypatian Chronicle displays, though unsystematically, several features of Old Ukrainian. Consequently, of all chronicles it is the most important source for studies of Old Ukrainian. Variations between Church Slavonic and Old Ukrainian components in the text were generally motivated by stylistic considerations.

Hzhytsky, Stepan [Hžyc'kyj], b 14 January 1900 in Ostrivets, Ternopil county, Galicia, d 19 August 1976 in Lviv. Biochemist; from 1951 corresponding member of the AN URSR. A graduate of the Lviv Academy of Veterinary Medicine (1929), he became lecturer in biochemistry at the academy, and in 1951 chairman of the biochemistry department at the Scientific Research Institute of Land Cultivation and Animal Husbandry of the Western Regions of the Ukrainian SSR. In 1960 he was the supervisor of the metabolism laboratory of the Ukrainian Scientific Research Institute of the Physiology and Biochemistry of Farm Animals. He specialized in the treatment of metabolic disorders in farm animals, and proposed a hypothesis on the etiology and pathogenesis of chronic hematuria in cattle.

I

Iaşi (Jassy). VI-8. The principal city (1977 pop 269,500) in northeastern Rumania and a county center. It was first mentioned in the 11th century as Yaskyi Torh on the Rus' trade route between Kamianets-Podilskyi and Bilhorod-Dnistrovskyi. From 1434 Iaşi was the residence of the Moldavian prince-regent. From 1565 to 1862 it was the capital of Moldavia.

In November 1577, the Cossack otaman I. Pidkova occupied Iaşi and proclaimed himself hospodar of Moldavia. In 1594, Iaşi was captured by the Cossack forces of S. Nalyvaiko and H. Loboda. The Battle of *Cecora in 1620 took place near Iaşi. Under Moldavia's ruler V. Lupu (1634–53), Iaşi had close ties with Ukraine. In 1640 professors S. Pochatsky and I. Yevlevych of Kiev College founded an orthodox college there, at which Metropolitan P. Mohyla of Kiev had a complete printing press installed in 1641. In September 1642 a council of Ukrainian, Greek, and Moldavian Orthodox theologians was held in Iaşi; it ratified Metropolitan Mohyla's confession of the faith. During the Cossack-Polish War, in 1650 the Cossack forces under T. Khmelnytsky and Col D. Nechai occupied Iaşi. In 1652 Khmelnytsky married Lupu's daughter there and in May 1653, he defeated a Polish-Wallachian-Transylvanian army there. Hetman P. Orlyk lived in Iaşi towards the end of his life and died there in 1742. A Russian-Turkish peace, confirming Russia's annexation of the lands between the Boh and Dniester rivers and of the Crimea, was signed in Iaşi in 1791. In November 1918 representatives of the Entente Powers met in Iaşi to plan a military intervention with the Volunteer Army in Ukraine. The Hetman government sent a delegation headed by I. Korostovets to the talks. From 1928 to 1936 Ukrainian students from Bukovyna and Bessarabia at Iaşi University had their own club, Hromada. In January 1942, a Rumanian court martial in Iaşi tried 12 Bukovynians (among them O. Huzar, M. Zybachynsky, and Yu. Furman) for Ukrainian irredentism and sentenced them to terms of hard labor.

A. Zhukovsky

Ibn-Baṭṭūtah (Batutah), b 24 February 1304 in Tangier, d 1368 in Fès. Arab traveler and merchant. From 1325 to 1353 he visited many countries of Europe, Asia, and Africa, including the southern regions of present-day Ukraine. He left a valuable account of his travels, an English translation of which was published in 1958.

Ibn-Faḍlān, Ahmad, b and d ? Arab writer and traveler of the first half of the 10th century. In 921–2, as secretary of the Bagdad caliph's legation, he completed a trip from Baghdad through Bukhara and Khorezm to the Volga Bulgars. Portions of his report on the trip are extant; in them he gives valuable information about the life and beliefs of various tribes then living on the territory of Ukraine and in the Black Sea and Caucasus regions. A. Kovalivsky's study of Ibn-Faḍlān's account was published in 1956.

Ibn-Hawqal, b and d ? Arab geographer, merchant, and traveler of the 10th century. He is the author of a narrative (977), in which he retells the story of the three kinds of Rus' people and gives a description of Kiev. He mentions the rout of the Volga Bulgars and the Khazars by the people of Rus' ca 969, possibly by the Kievan prince, Sviatoslav I Ihorevych.

Ibn-Khordādhbih, b ca 820, d ca 912. Geographer and writer of Persian origin. He was the first Arab writer known to have written about the eastern Slavs. He is the author of a narrative (847) in which he mentions the trade routes and the visits of Rus' merchants to Baghdad.

Ichnia [Ičnja]. III-13. City (1983 pop 18,000) in the Dnieper Lowland and a raion center in Chernihiv oblast. First mentioned in the early 13th century, in 1648–9 it was a regiment center, and from 1649 to 1781 a company town of Pryluka regiment. Under tsarist rule it played no administrative role. Since the 18th century it has been known for its artistic ceramics. From the 1830s on, a textile industry developed there, and after 1861 it became an important grain-trading center. Today its main industry is food production. A branch of the Pryluka Artistic Wares Factory and a historical museum are located there.

Ichniansky, Myroslav [Ičnjans'kyj] (pen name of Ivan Kmeta), b 23 August 1901 in Ichnia, Chernihiv gubernia. Poet, writer, and pastor. His first two collections of poetry, *Arfa* (The Harp, 1925) and *Narodni melodii* (Folk Melodies, 1927), were published in Ukraine. Since emigrating to Canada in 1929 (he moved to the United States in 1940), he has produced several more collections: *Fragmenty* (Fragments, 1929), *Lira emigranta* (An Emigrant's Lyre, 1936), *Chasha zolota* (The Golden Chalice, 1964), *Kryla nad morem* (Wings over the Sea, 1970), *Zahravy vechirni* (Evening Sunsets, 1976), and the long poem *Rik dvotysiachnyi* (The Year 2000, 1979). He has also translated British poetry into Ukrainian. One of his prose works, *Huragan* (1936), has been translated into English as *The Hurricane: A Tale of Evangelism in the USSR*, 1939).

Icon. An image depicting a holy personage or scene in the stylized Byzantine manner, and venerated in the Eastern Christian churches. The image can be executed in different media; hence, the term 'icon' can be applied to mural paintings, frescoes, or mosaics, tapestries or embroideries, enamels, and low reliefs carved in marble, ivory, or stone or cast in metal. The typical icon, however, is a portable painting on a wooden panel, and it is this form of icon that is discussed here (for other forms see *Fresco painting, *Mosaic, and *Enamel).

Technique. The earliest technique of icon painting was encaustic, but the traditional and most common technique is tempera. The paint – an emulsion of mineral pigments (ochers, siennas, umbers, or green earth), egg yolk, and water – is applied with a brush to a panel prepared in a special way. The panel of well-dried linden, birch, poplar, alder, pine, or cypress is 3–4 cm thick. To prevent warping it is reinforced with two hardwood slats inserted in grooves on the reverse side. The face side is slightly hollowed to obtain a concave surface surrounded by a protective border, usually 3 cm wide and scored to provide a better gluing base. It is then covered with canvas, to which several layers of gesso (plaster or powdered alabaster mixed with fish glue) are applied. When an even, smooth surface has been produced, an outline of the painting is traced on it with charcoal or scratched into it with a needle. Gold leaf is fixed to designated areas before painting begins. The paint is applied in successive layers from dark to light tones; then the figures are outlined and, finally, certain areas are highlighted with whitener. After drying, the painting is covered with a special varnish consisting of linseed oil and crystalline resins to protect it from dust and humidity. The varnish imparts depth and richness to the pale tones of tempera but, eventually, becomes dark with dirt. Traditionally cleaned with a vinegar and ammonia solution, the varnish is now treated with chemical solutions that are capable of restoring the original brilliance and depth to the colors.

History. With the introduction of Christianity in the 10th century, Byzantine icons and icon painters began to be imported into Ukraine. According to the Primary Chronicle, Volodymyr the Great ordered icons for the Church of the Tithes from Chersonesus. In the following century an indigenous school of icon painting developed in Kiev. By the turn of the century the *Kievan Cave Monastery Icon Painting Studio could boast of such renowned painters as *Hryhorii and *Olimpii, who are mentioned in the monastery's Patericon. In the 12th century the studio's influence was felt throughout Rus' – in Galicia, Volhynia, Novgorod, Suzdal, and Yaroslavl. Its distinctive style of painting resembled closely the style of contemporary mosaics in Kiev. Because of their destructibility by fire and desirability as war booty, many icons perished. No Kievan icons from the 11th century, and only a few from the 12th, have survived to our day. The oldest surviving masterpieces of the Kiev school include *The Mother of God Great Panagia*, a large icon done probably by Olimpii and donated by Volodymyr Monomakh to a church in Rostov; *St Demetrius of Thessalonica*, a 12th-century icon that belonged to the Dormition Church in Dmitrov; *St Nicholas with Saints on the Borders* (turn of the 12th century); *The Mother of God of the Caves* or *The Svensk Mother of God*, a late 13th-century copy of an earlier Kievan icon done for Prince Roman; and *Ihor's Mother of God*, a 13th-century work that disappeared from the Kievan Cave Monastery during the Second World War. There are also a number of icons that belong to the Kiev tradition of icon painting, but may have been produced in centers other than Kiev. The most important of these are works that were probably produced by the Novgorod school according to Kievan models: *The Ustiug Annunciation* (12th century), *The Archangel Gabriel* or *The Angel with Golden Hair* (12th), and *ss Borys and Hlib* (12th–13th). The famous *Vyshhorod Mother of God*, later known as *The Vladimir Mother of God*, is not a Kievan but a Greek icon that was brought in 1134 from Constantinople to Vyshhorod, and taken to Vladimir by Andrei Bogoliubskii in 1155.

With the rise of the Galician-Volhynian state in the 13th century, a Galician tradition of icon painting arose. The earliest Galician icons that have survived are from the 14th century. We can assume that earlier icons were painted in a style similar to that of Kievan icons. The chief icon painting schools in Galicia were those of Peremyshl and Lviv. Each of them had many branches scattered throughout the Carpathian region as far east as Transcarpathia. Numerous samples of their work dating back to the early 15th century have been preserved. Although works of this period are unsigned and undated, some of them are distinctive enough to be attributed to particular studios and masters. Some icons were painted by monks, but most were done by highly trained secular craftsmen or self-taught folk artists. Municipal archives in Peremyshl contain references to icon painters such as Vladyka (1393–4), Matvii (1431–51), T. Drobysh (1443–50), and Yakiv (1443–51), and those in Lviv refer to Stanyslav (1404–12), Ivan and Luka (1406–25), and Andrii (1443–8). Galician icons of the 15th century are characterized by their pure, almost classical, style. The figures are balanced perfectly with the background. The drawing is delicate and refined, and its lines are rhythmic. The forms tend to be rounded. Full-bodied reds, greens, and blues contrast strongly with the prevalent muted colors. The background is monotonic and peaceful, usually light ocher or bluish gray. Gold is used only for the halo. Designs are carved on the halo and, towards the end of the century, in the background. The finest surviving examples of this style are *The Nativity of the Mother of God* from Vanivka, *The Passion of Christ* from Zdvyzhennia, *The Archangel Michael* and *The Archangel Gabriel* from Dalova, *ss Cosmas and Damian* from Tylych, *Christ the Teacher* from Mylyk, *The Mother of God with the Prophets* from Pidhorodtsi, *The Last Judgment* from Mshanets, *St Nicholas with Scenes from His Life* from Radruzh, and *The Mother of God Hodegetria* from Krasiv. Fourteenth-century icons such as *St George the Dragon-Slayer* from Stanylia and *The Dormition of the Mother of God* from Zhukotyn are quite distinct in style. Their simplified figures are flat and have a clear outline. Little is known about icon painting in Volhynia, but the early 14th-century *Mother of God from Lutsk* shows that Volhynian icons were similar to contemporary Galician ones.

In the 16th century Lviv became the main center of icon painting. The names of many masters whose works have not been identified have come down to us in the municipal archives: M. Vorobii (1524–75), Khoma (1536–49), Fedir (1539–64), V. Vorobii (1575), and L. Pukhala (1575–1611) and his sons Ivanko and Oleksander. A number of towns near Lviv (Staryi Sambir, Stryi, Yavoriv, and Rohatyn) developed their own schools. The style evolved towards a greater emphasis of the graphic element, which became typical of Ukrainian icons: figures began to be circumscribed with a distinct line. With a heavier application of whitener, forms became more plastic and rounded. The colors became livelier. The background was colored solid gold or silver and was ornamented with engraved or impressed geometric designs. Among the numerous icons that survive from this period, the finest samples of the Peremyshl school are

ICONS 1) Prince Ihor's icon of the Theotokos (13th century; formerly at the Kievan Cave Monastery Museum). 2) St Nicholas (16th century, from Transcarpathia; Bardejov Museum, Slovakia). 3) The Last Judgment (16th century, Peremyshl school; Lviv Museum of Ukrainian Art). 4) ss Luke and Simon (16th century, from Rohatyn; Lviv Museum of Ukrainian Art). 5) The Dormition of the Virgin Mary (1705, by Y. Kondzelevych; Lviv Museum of Ukrainian Art). 6) The Holy Protectress with portraits of Metropolitan D. Balaban and Hetman B. Khmelnytsky (17th century; Kiev Museum of Ukrainian Art). 7) Detail from the Pidhorodtsi Theotokos (15th century; Lviv Museum of Ukrainian Art). 8) The Vyshhorod (Vladimir) Theotokos (12th century; Tretiakov Gallery, Moscow). 9) The Máriapócs Theotokos (ascribed to Pylypenko, 1731; Kiev Museum of Ukrainian Art). 10) Belzebub: detail from the Last Judgment (17th century; Museum of Ukrainian Culture, Svidník, Slovakia).

ICONS 1) The Vyshhorod (Vladimir) Theotokos (early 12th century; Tretiakov Gallery, Moscow). 2) Orant (Kiev school, early 12th century; Tretiakov Gallery, Moscow). 3) The Last Judgment (16th century, from Rivne [Sernie], Transcarpathia; Museum of Ukrainian Culture, Svidník, Slovakia). 4) Christ in Glory (early 16th century, from Dolyna, Galicia; Lviv Museum of Ukrainian Art). 5) The Virgin Odigitria with the Apostles (15th century, from Novosiltsi, Galicia; Sanok Museum, Poland). 6) The Mandylion (14th–15th century, from Krempna, Lemko region; Sanok Museum, Poland). 7) Destruction of Sodom: detail from an icon of St Michael Archangel (16th century; Bardejov Museum, Slovakia). 8) ss Juliana and Anastasia (18th-century baroque icon from Konotip). 9) The Theotokos with Christ (18th century; Kiev Museum of Ukrainian Art). 10) The Holy Protectress (19th-century folk painting on glass; Ukrainian Museum, Stamford, Conn).

The Nativity of Christ and *The Passion of Christ* from Trushevychi, *The Annunciation* from Dalova, *The Adoration of the Magi* from Busovysko, *The Archangel Michael* from Ilnyk, *The Dormition of the Mother of God* (signed by Oleksii) from Smilnyk, *Christ with the Twelve Apostles* and *The Nativity of the Mother of God* (both by Dmytrii) from Dolyna, and *The Mother of God* from Florynka. The Lviv school produced such masterpieces as *The Crucifixion with Attending Women* from Borshchovychi, *The Transfiguration* and *The Archangel Michael* from Yabloniv, *St Parasceve* from Krushelnytsia, *The Nativity of the Mother of God* and *The Descent into Hell* from Vyshenka, *The Last Judgment* and *St Mark* from Kamianka-Buzka, and *ss Borys and Hlib* and *The Crucifixion* from Potelych. Galician artists kept abreast of developments in the Balkans, Novgorod and Moscow in the north, and Western Europe, but it is difficult to pinpoint any concrete borrowings.

The first painters' guild in Lviv was organized in 1596 and its membership was restricted at first to Catholics. By the mid-17th century, however, Ukrainian (Orthodox) artists made their way to the top offices in the guild. Specializing in portrait and icon painting, masters were highly skilled artists who had spent several years abroad. The leading Ukrainian painters in Lviv were F. Senkovych, M. Petrakhnovych, and S. Korunka. A number of provincial schools of icon painting achieved a wide reputation. There were several studios in Rybotychi that combined elements of the traditional icon with elements of Western engraving and left such works as *The Last Judgment* and *The Nativity of Christ*. The town of Sudova Vyshnia produced several outstanding painters: I. Brodlakovych, Yatsko Vyshensky, and Ivan the Painter. I. Rutkovych worked in Zhovkva, and Y. Kondzelevych (b in Zhovkva) worked at the Maniava Hermitage. A strong tendency towards realism in Galician icon painting can be attributed to the influence of Western Europe. The personages in the icons became individualized and the background became filled with natural landscapes. Color contrasts were toned down to obtain gentle transitions. Oil paints were introduced in the second half of the century, usually in combination with tempera. Elements of realism are clearly marked in such icons as *The Last Supper* (1638) from the Dormition Cathedral in Lviv and *The Nativity of the Mother of God* (mid-17th century) from the Church of Good Friday in Lviv, and the icons of the Church of the Holy Spirit in Rohatyn.

At the beginning of the 17th century icon painting began to revive in eastern Ukraine. Its patrons were not only the church but also the rising Cossack elite. The new baroque churches in Kiev, Chernihiv, and other centers of the Cossack state were decorated with elaborate iconostases. The Kievan Cave Monastery became the leading center of icon painting. In the new icons the severe Byzantine style gave way to the dynamic, luxurious, and expressive style of the baroque. The icon of the Mother of God as the Protectress is typical of this period. It depicts the Mother of God covering with her mantle the patrons of the church and other dignitaries of the time. Some examples of this icon portray such hetmans as B. Khmelnytsky, D. Apostol, and P. Polubotok with their wives and families. *The Zaporozhian Protectress*, which was executed in a simple, primitive style, presents the Mother of God with the leaders of the Zaporozhian Host.

By the second half of the 18th century the icon evolved into an ordinary painting on a biblical theme and disappeared as a distinctive art form. This evolution is apparent in the work of V. *Borovykovsky and L. *Dolynsky. At the beginning of the 20th century, Ukrainian icon painting was revived in a neo-Byzantine form, represented by M. *Boichuk and his 'monumentalist' school, as well as by M. Sosenko, P. Kholodny Sr, M. Osinchuk, V. Diadyniuk, and others. Since 1948, in the United States, Canada, Europe, and Australia, many churches and iconostases have been decorated in this style by painters such as M. Osinchuk, P. Andrusiv, P. Kholodny Jr, S. Hordynsky, M. Dmytrenko, I. Denysenko, M. Bilynsky, M. Levytsky, Ya. Hnizdovsky, and M. Bidniak. Among the contemporary painters of icons are A. Solohub, M. Mor, the Studite monk Yu. Mokrytsky, and O. Mazuryk.

Research. The systematic study of icons began only in the mid-19th century. At first icons were viewed simply as archeological objects or a form of handicraft. It was only in the 20th century that they have been approached as artistic objects. This is largely attributable to new restoration techniques, which for the first time uncovered the rich colors and complex composition of old icons, and to improvements in reproduction technology, which made comparative studies possible. The first centers of icon research were Kiev, with its small but valuable icon collections at the City Museum and the Museum of the Theological Academy, and Lviv, with its rich collections at the National Museum and the Stauropegion Museum. Comparative analysis has shown that old Ukrainian icons, while based on Byzantine models in theme and style, possessed distinctive national traits and were organically rooted in Ukrainian spirituality.

BIBLIOGRAPHY

Holubets', M. *Ukraïns'ke maliarstvo XVI–XVII st. pid pokrovom Stavropigiï* (Lviv 1920)

Svientsits'kyi, I. *Ikony Halyts'koï Ukraïny XV–XVI vikiv* (Lviv 1929)

Bazhan, M. (ed). *Istoriia ukraïns'koho mystetstva v shesty tomakh*, vols 1–3 (Kiev 1966–8)

Hordyns'kyi, S. *Ukraïns'ka ikona, 12–18 storichchia* (Philadelphia 1973)

Lohvyn, H.; Miliaieva, L.; Svientsits'ka, V. *Ukraïns'kyi seredn'ovichnyi zhyvopys* (Kiev 1976)

S. Hordynsky

Iconography. A study that identifies, describes, classifies, and interprets symbols, themes, and subject matter in the visual arts. It originated in Europe in the 16th century, when it concentrated on collecting emblems and symbols from classical literature. Viewed as a handmaid of archeology, in the 18th century it consisted of the classification of subjects in ancient monuments. In the next century it became independent of archeology and concentrated mostly on the use and meaning of symbols in Christian art. In Ukraine, iconographical studies of saints venerated by Ukrainians were published by M. Batih, F. Bilous, M. Dragan, M. Holubets, S. Hordynsky, D. Horniatkevych, P. Kholodny, N. Kondakov, Ya. Konstantynovych, L. Miliaieva, Rev Yu. Mokrytsky, M. Osinchuk, H. Pavlutsky, V. Peshchansky, Rev I. Pavlyk, K. Shyrotsky, M. Sokolowski, M. Sumtsov, I. Svientsitsky, V. Svientsitska, and P. Zholtovsky.

Iconostasis. A solid wooden, stone, or metal screen separating the sanctuary from the nave in Eastern Chris-

ICONOSTASES 1) The Good Friday Church in Lviv (1644). 2) St Nicholas's Military Cathedral in Kiev (1696). 3) St George's Cathedral at the Vydubychi Monastery in Kiev (late 17th century). 4) The Dormition Cathedral at the Yeletskyi Monastery in Chernihiv (1670). 5) St Barbara's Ukrainian Catholic Church in Vienna (late 18th century). 6) St Nicholas's Cathedral in Nizhen (1730s). 7) The Holy Protectress Church in Novhorod-Siverskyi (1766). 8) St John the Baptist Ukrainian Catholic Church in Newark, New Jersey (modern transparent iconostasis by S. Hordynsky). [Note: numbers 2, 3, 4, 6, and 7 have all been destroyed.]

tian churches. Of varying height, it consists of rows of columns and icons. It extends the width of the sanctuary and has three entrances: the large Royal Gates at the center and the smaller Deacon Doors on each side. The Royal Gates are hung with a curtain. Western churches, whether Catholic or Protestant, have a low barrier instead of an iconostasis. The iconostasis evolved in Byzantium in the 9th–11th centuries.

The icons of the iconostasis are separated by columns and are arranged in several rows. The number of icons and ranges can vary. Usually, a full iconostasis contains over 50 icons set in four to six rows, but simpler (one- or two-story) and more elaborate (seven-story) iconostases are known. The lowest range consists of the icons on the Royal Gates depicting the Annunciation and the four evangelists, and of the full-length icons of the Savior (right of the gates) and the Mother of God (left of the gates), of the church's patron saint, and of the more venerated saints. In the second row immediately above the Royal Gates, the Last Supper is depicted, flanked by icons of the 12 main holy days of the church year. The third row consists of the Supplication or Deesis at the center and icons of the apostles. In the fourth tier the prophets are displayed, with the patriarchs or Christ's Passion above. The iconstasis is topped by a cross with an image of Christ on it. The icons are set in a structure of finely carved and gilded columns and beams. The ornamental motif consists usually of interwoven grapevines.

In Ukraine the earliest iconostases were low, consisting of only two tiers. Their further development was conditioned by the development of wooden architecture and the decline of the art of mosaics. By the 14th–15th centuries the typical structure of the two- and three-tiered iconostasis was established. From a simple support for icons the iconostasis evolved by the 17th–18th centuries into an elaborate product of several arts: architecture, sculpture, and painting. It grew in both size and complexity as a fifth and even sixth tier was added. The earliest surviving iconostases date back to the beginning of the 17th century. They include M. Petrakhnovych's iconostasis (1637) of the Dormition Church in Lviv, the iconostases of the Church of Good Friday (1644) in Lviv and the Church of the Holy Spirit (1650) in Rohatyn, the Bohorodchany iconostasis, which was painted by Y. Kondzelevych for the Maniava Hermitage in 1705 and was later transferred to a church in Bohorodchany, and I. Rutkovych's iconostases in Volytsia-Derevlianska (1680–2), Volia-Vysotska, and the Church of Christ's Nativity in Zhovkva (1697–9). Very little remains of the rich iconostases in central Ukraine. Many of the older iconostases, including those admired in 1665 by Paul of Aleppo (in the Dormition Church of the Kievan Cave Monastery and in the churches in Vasylkiv, Trypilia, and Pryluka), were replaced by more modern baroque structures, which were eventually destroyed by the Soviets. The only surviving example of the grand baroque iconostases financed by the hetmans and Cossack officers is the iconostasis of the Transfiguration Church in Sorochyntsi (1732), which measures 17 m in height and 20 m in width. The most important monuments of Ukrainian art destroyed in the 1930s by the Soviet regime are the iconostases of the following churches: the Dormition Cathedral of the Yeletskyi Monastery (1670) in Chernihiv, one of the largest iconostases in Ukraine; the Church of the Nativity of the Mother of God (1684) of the Molchany Monastery near Putyvl; the Transfiguration Cathedral (1684) in Izium; *St Nicholas's Military Cathedral (1696) in Kiev (seven tiers, 15.5 m high and 22 m wide); St George's Cathedral of the Vydubychi Monastery (1700s) in Kiev; the Cathedral of the Elevation of the Cross (1709) in Poltava; St Michael's Golden-Domed Cathedral (1719) in Kiev; St Nicholas's Cathedral (1734) in Nizhen; St Nicholas's Church (1730s), the Church of the Holy Spirit (1746), and the Church of the Holy Protectress (1760s), all in Romen; the Trinity Cathedral (1740) of the *Trinity–St Elijah Monastery in Chernihiv; the Trinity Cathedral (18th century) of the *Hustynia Trinity Monastery; the Church of Christ's Ascension (1761) in Berezna; St Nicholas's Cathedral (1765) in Mhar Monastery; the Church of the Holy Protectress (1766) in Novhorod-Siverskyi; and the Dormition Cathedral (1775) in Mezhyrich. Other than a few icons from the Novhorod-Siverskyi, Berezna, and Mezhyrich churches, all that remains of the destroyed iconostases are old, prerevolutionary sketches or photographs, often of poor quality. Any reference to the destruction of these masterpieces in Soviet publications is prohibited. Today the art of the iconostasis is cultivated only outside Ukraine. Such artists as S. Hordynsky, P. Kholodny Jr, M. Osinchuk, and M. Levytsky have adorned many Ukrainian churches in the United States, Canada, South America, Western Europe, and Australia with iconostases of various styles from the strictly traditional to the modern.

BIBLIOGRAPHY
Dzieduszyński, W. *Ikonostas Bohordczański* (Lviv 1886)
Konstantynowycz, J. *Ikonostasis. Studien und Forschungen* (Lviv 1939)
Drahan, M. *Ukraïns'ka dekoratyvna riz'ba XVI–XVIII st.* (Kiev 1970)

S. Hordynsky, I. Korovytsky

Ideia i chyn (Idea and Deed). Underground organ of the Leadership of the Organization of Ukrainian Nationalists (Bandera faction) in Western Ukraine. It was published from 1942 to 1946 and edited by D. Maivsky.

Idyll. A poetic work depicting the tranquil, happy life of simple folk – usually peasants or shepherds – in an idealized natural setting. Often this kind of poetry is called pastoral or bucolic. As a definite literary form, the idyll survived until the classicist period, but idyllic motifs were frequently used in later periods. In Ukrainian literature the idyll as a definite literary form has few examples. O. Lobysevych's 18th-century burlesque imitations of Virgil's *Eclogues* have not survived. Given the predominance of national and social themes, instances of idyllic motifs in modern Ukrainian literature are infrequent. They appear in L. Borovykovsky's 'Podrazhaniie Horatsiiu' (Imitation of Horace); in T. Shevchenko's 'Sadok vyshnevyi kolo khaty' ('The Cherry Orchard by the House') and in certain depictions in some of his other poems; in P. Kulish's 'Orysia'; from time to time in Ukrainian prose and drama beginning with the works of H. Kvitka-Osnovianenko; and in certain works of the *Neoclassicists, particularly the early poetry of M. Rylsky. They are also found in the works of poets and writers of the 'Ukrainian schools' in Polish and Russian literature and in particular foreign works with Ukrainian themes:

Polish idylls (especially those by S. Szymonowicz), N. Gogol's short stories, Russian literary depictions of travels through Ukraine, and B. Zaleski's and A. Tolstoi's poetry.

D. Chyzhevsky, D.H. Struk

Iednist' (Unity). A weekly newspaper published in Adelaide (Australia) from 1949 to 1956. It supported the politics of the UNR Government-in-exile. Its founder and chief editor was Ya. Lohyn.

Ievanhel's'ka pravda (Evangelical Truth). Religious monthly published from 1940 to 1979 in Toronto by the Ukrainian Evangelical Alliance of North America. Its editor was M. Fesenko. Besides religious articles it published articles on social and political issues and works by Ukrainian poets and writers. Some articles appeared in English.

Ievanhel's'kyi ranok (Evangelical Morning). An evangelical Christian monthly journal published since 1961 by the Ukrainian Evangelical Alliance of North America in Toronto and Detroit. It also has an English-language supplement, *The Ukrainian Christian Herald.* Its predecessors were the weekly **Ranok* (from 1905) and the monthly **Kanadiiskyi ranok* in Edmonton (1920–61). The editor in chief from 1961 to 1987 was V. Borovsky.

Ifika ieropolitika: copper etching by I. Fylypovych (1760)

Ifika ieropolitika. An illustrated philosophical-moralistic work on 67 subjects pertaining to ethics, morality, philosophy, and educational foundations, published by the Kievan Cave Monastery Press in 1712 and the Lviv Dormition Brotherhood Press in 1760. Illustrations were executed by N. Zubrytsky in the Kiev edition and by I. Fylypovych in the Lviv edition. Under each allegorical illustration (Truth, Shame, Humility, Gentleness, etc) there was a verse of four or (less often) six lines. The book's author is unknown; he was probably a monk at the Kievan Cave Monastery.

Ihnatiienko, Varfolomii [Ihnatijenko, Varfolomij], b 25 August 1892 in Ozeriany, Lokhvytsia county, Poltava gubernia, d 7 December 1943. Bibliographer. He worked at the Ukrainian Scientific Research Institute of Bibliology and directed the bibliographic department in 1923–31. He wrote *Ukraïns'ka presa 1916–23* (The Ukrainian Press 1916–23, 1926) and *Bibliohrafiia ukraïns'koï presy za sto lit, 1816–1916* (Bibliography of the Ukrainian Press, 1816–1916, 1930). He also contributed many articles to the journals *Bibliohrafichni visti, Knyha,* and *Zhyttia i revoliutsiia.*

Ihnatovych, Hnat [Ihnatovyč] (stage name of H. Balinsky), b 17 November 1898 in Nemyriv, Bratslav county, Podilia gubernia, d 16 January 1978 in Uzhhorod. Stage director, actor, and teacher. He studied with L. *Kurbas at the Molodyi Teatr theater (1918–19) and appeared in the productions of the Kiev Drama (1920–2) and Berezil (1922–5) theaters. He also directed the 1924 Berezil production of E. Toller's *Masse-Mensch.* Thereafter he taught at the Kiev (1924–8) and Kharkiv (1928–34) music and drama institutes and at the acting school of the Kiev Artistic Film Studio (1934–46). From 1946 to 1963 he served, with breaks, as the artistic director of the Transcarpathian Ukrainian Music and Drama Theater in Uzhhorod. There he directed many plays by Ukrainian, Russian, and European playwrights. Ihnatovych appeared in such roles as Yarema in *Haidamaky* (based on T. Shevchenko's poem), the millionaire's son in G. Kaiser's *Gas 1,* and Macduff in Shakespeare's *Macbeth.*

Ihnatovych, Volodymyr [Ihnatovyč], 1883–1928. Cultural and political figure of the early 20th century. A member of the *Hromada of Kiev, in December 1917 he helped found the *Ukrainian Federative Democratic party, which advocated an autonomous Ukraine within a federated state. Under the Hetman government he was director of the Ukrainian State Bank, and sat on the financial commission of the Ukrainian delegation that negotiated peace with Soviet Russia. In November 1918 he concluded an agreement with the Kuban government on financial transactions.

Ihor, b ca 877, d 945. Grand prince of Kievan Rus' from 912. According to the Rus' Primary Chronicle, Ihor was the son of *Riuryk, but he could have been his grandson. During his rule the Turkic Pechenegs attacked Rus' in 915 and 920, Slavic tribes still separate from the Kievan state were subjugated, and Byzantine influence in Rus' increased. In 913–14 he led an expedition to the Caspian Sea, which ended in a rout by the Khazars. He attacked Byzantium in 941 but his fleet was repulsed by 'Greek fire'; his forces then ravaged the coast of Asia Minor during their retreat. In 943–5 Ihor waged a successful campaign in Caucasian Albania against the Caliphate and occupied the capital of Berdaa before his army was forced to retreat because of an epidemic of dysentery. In 945 he concluded a trade agreement with Byzantium, promising not to attack Byzantine towns in the Crimea and to help them to repel Black Bulgars. During his reign he waged war on the 'rebellious' Slavic tribes of the Derevlianians and Ulychians and took the city of Peresichen. He was killed by the Derevlianians of Korosten while attempting to extort excessive tribute. His death was avenged by his wife *Olha, whom he had married in 904. At Ihor's death, 20 Rus' princes recognized the supremacy of Kiev.

Ihor Olhovych [Ihor Ol'hovyč], b ?, d 1147. Prince of Novhorod-Siverskyi and, after the death of his brother *Vsevolod Olhovych, grand prince of Kiev from 1146.

The son of Oleh Sviatoslavych, founder of the Olhovych dynasty, he took part in the internecine princely struggles on the side of the rulers of Chernihiv. Only days after he inherited Kiev the commoners, unhappy with the oppressive reign of the Olhovyches begun under Vsevolod, rebelled. The Kievan boyars offered Kiev to *Iziaslav Mstyslavych of Pereiaslav, who came and defeated Ihor's army in battle. Ihor was imprisoned in St John's Monastery in Pereiaslav. Falling ill, he took monastic vows and was allowed to live in St Theodore's Monastery in Kiev. He was beaten to death by a mob incited by news of Iziaslav's intentions to declare war on the Chernihiv princes. He was buried in Chernihiv and later canonized as a martyr.

Ihor Sviatoslavych [Ihor Svjatoslavyč], 1151–1202. Prince of Novhorod-Siverskyi (1178–98) and Chernihiv (1198–1202). The son of Sviatoslav Olhovych of Chernihiv, he took part in the war of Andrei Bogoliubskii against Grand Prince Mstyslav Iziaslavych of Kiev in 1169. The *Cumans' marauding attacks in southern Rus' forced him to join other princes in fighting the nomads. In 1185 he organized a campaign without the knowledge of the grand prince of Kiev; his army, after an initial victory, was surrounded on the Kaiala River and routed. Ihor was captured but managed to escape. This event is the subject of the epic tale **Slovo o polku Ihorevi* (The Lay of Ihor's Campaign). After Ihor's defeat the Cumans ravaged the Pereiaslav region.

Ihren camp sites. Several Neolithic camp sites dating from the late 5th to the early 4th century BC discovered in the southern part of Dnipropetrovske on a peninsula at the mouth of the Samara River. Excavations carried out in the 1930s revealed flint and bone tools, fragments of clay and stone pottery, remnants of dwellings, burials, and other artifacts attributed to the Dnieper-Donets, *Surskyi-Dnieper, and *Serednii Stih cultures.

Ikonnikov, Vladimir, b 21 December 1841 in Kiev, d 26 November 1923 in Kiev. Historian and academician of the Russian Academy of Sciences from 1914 and VUAN from 1920. Ikonnikov finished his studies at Kiev University in 1865. From 1866 to 1871 he taught at Kharkiv University, various gymnasiums in Odessa, and Odessa University, and from 1871 at Kiev University. He received his doctorate in 1869 for his dissertation on the cultural influence of Byzantium in Rus'. Ikonnikov was one of the founders and the president (1874–7 and 1893–5) of the *Historical Society of Nestor the Chronicler. From 1873 to 1913 he was the chief editor of *Universitetskie izvestiia* at Kiev University; in 1904 he was made head of the *Kiev Archeographic Commission. He is the author of a number of scholarly works, many of which appeared in *Kievskaia starina*. His most important work is the encyclopedic two-volume *Opyt russkoi istoriografii i ee protivniki* (Study of Russian Historiography and Its Opponents, 1891, 1908; the manuscript of the third volume is in the Central Library of the Academy of Sciences of the Ukrainian SSR). His major work on Ukrainian history is *Kiev v 1654–1855 gg: Istoricheskii ocherk* (Kiev in 1654–1855: A Historical Survey, 1904).

Ikva River. A right-bank tributary of the Styr River. The Ikva flows for 155 km through Podilia and the Volhynian Upland and has a basin area of 2,250 sq km. Its upper stretch near Kremianets and Dubno lies in a picturesque valley.

Ilarion, b ?, d before 1054 in Kiev. Eminent church and literary figure of the 11th century; the first non-Greek metropolitan of Kiev. Ilarion was a priest in Berestove near Kiev when in 1051, according to the wish of Yaroslav the Wise, an episcopal sobor elected him metropolitan. He codified the laws governing church life and defended the independence of the Rus' church from the Byzantine hierarchy. A brilliant preacher and talented writer, Ilarion is credited with four works: *Slovo o zakoni i blahodati* (Sermon on Law and Grace, before 1052), a prayer, a confession of faith, and a short collection of instructions for priests. The first work has been preserved in more than 50 redactions of the 15th and 16th centuries, and had an important influence on Ukrainian and other Slavic literatures.

BIBLIOGRAPHY
Müller, L. *Des Metropoliten Ilarion Lobrede auf Vladimir den Heiligen und Glaubensbekenntnis* (Wiesbaden 1962)
Moldovan, A. *'Slovo o zakone i blagodati' Ilariona* (Kiev 1984)

Ilarion. See Ohiienko, Ivan.

Ilchenko, Oleksander [Il'čenko], b 4 June 1909 in Kharkiv. Writer and wartime journalist. Beginning with *Dniprel'stan* (The Dnieper Dam, 1932), he has written 10 prose collections, 3 plays, and the novels *Peterburz'ka osin'* (Autumn in St Petersburg, 1941), about T. Shevchenko, *Zvychainyi khlopets'* (An Ordinary Boy, 1947), *Neapolitanka* (The Girl from Naples, 1963), and the folkloric *Kozatskomu rodu nema perevodu, abo zh Mamai i chuzha molodytsia* (Cossack Kind Will Never Die, or Mamai and Another's Young Wife, 1958). His works in two volumes were published in 1979.

Ilin, Vasyl [Il'jin, Vasyl'], b 14 January 1901 in Kiev, d 13 July 1963 in Kiev. Ukrainian linguist and lexicographer. He served as senior research associate and scientific secretary of the Institute of Linguistics of the AN URSR, and as editor of vols 3 and 4 of the Ukrainian-Russian dictionary (in 6 vols; 1961) and of *Leksykohrafichnyi biuleten* (1958–63). He is the author of studies in the morphology of modern standard Ukrainian and in the history of standard Ukrainian, as well as of numerous articles on the language of T. Shevchenko, all in the spirit of bringing Ukrainian closer to Russian. In editing the language in the six-volume edition of T. Shevchenko's works Ilin falsified the original by introducing the Russian pronounciation of Church Slavonicisms.

Ilinsky, Grigorii [Il'inskij, Grigorij], b 23 March 1876 in St Petersburg, d 1937? Russian linguist of Ukrainian descent. A graduate of St Petersburg and Kiev universities (1911), he served as docent of Kharkiv University (1907–9) and then as professor at the Nizhen Historical-Philological Institute (1909–18), Saratov University (1920–7), and Moscow University (from 1927). He wrote works on comparative Slavic phonology and morphology, summarized in his *Praslavianskaia grammatica* (Grammar of Common Slavic, 1916), on Slavic etymology, and on problems in the historical development of individual Slavic languages, including Ukrainian (the assimilation of vowels in Ukrainian, lengthening of consonants in words such as *zillia* [herbs], the imperative, and Ukrainian etymologies). Many of his studies of Ukrainian were published in periodicals of the Ukrainian Academy of Sciences and in *Ridna mova* (Warsaw). His work is characterized by an excessive emphasis on sound alternation with little attention to the historical background of linguistic developments or linguistic geography; it also tends to underrate foreign influences. A victim of Stalinist repression in the 1930s, Ilinsky died in prison.

Iliustrovana Ukraïna (Illustrated Ukraine). A literary, art, and popular scientific journal published semimonthly in Lviv in 1913–14. Its chief editor was I. Krypiakevych; he was assisted by D. Katamai. The journal embraced authors and readers from all parts of Ukraine. Poetry and prose contributors included Kh. Alchevska, M. Vorony, O. Zhurlyva, B. Lepky, Ya. Mamontov, V. Masliak, V. Pachovsky, Ya. Savchenko, and H. Chuprynka. Historical and scholarly works and literary and art reviews were published by M. Vozniak, O. Hrytsai, M. Yevshan, R. Zaklynsky, O. Nazariiv, F. Riznychenko, M. Shumytsky, Ya. Strukhmanchuk, and others. Community and political events were reported, and the journal contained theater and music reviews as well as translations of world literature; supplements serialized V. Hugo's *Quatre-vingt treize* and H.G. Wells's *The Time Machine*. Thirty-four issues appeared before publication ceased because of the war.

Ilkevych, Hryhorii [Il'kevyč, Hryhorij], b 13 October 1803 in Nove Selo, Zhovkva circle, Galicia, d 1841 in Horodenka, Kolomyia circle, Galicia. Folklorist and ethnographer. A gymnasium teacher in Kolomyia (1824–35) and Horodenka (1835–41), he published a collection of 2,715 Western Ukrainian folk sayings and riddles, *Halytskii prypovidky i zahadky zibrani Hryhorym Il'kevychom* (Galician Proverbs and Riddles Collected by Hryhorii Ilkevych, 1841). From 1836 to 1840 he also wrote a number of articles on ethnography. Parts of his major work, *Zbirnyk ukraïns'kykh istorychnykh pisen'* (Collection of Ukrainian Historical Songs), were published in **Rusalka dnistrovaia* (1837) and in anthologies edited by Ya. Holovatsky and W. Zalieski, but most of it remains unpublished.

Illia [Illja] (aka Iliia), b and d ? A 17th-century wood engraver. A monk at St Onuphrius Monastery, in the 1630s he worked as an engraver in Lviv. From 1640 to about 1680 he worked at the Kievan Cave Monastery Press. During his career he produced about 600 woodcuts for illustrations, title pages, headpieces, and prints. His work decorated such books as the Anthologion (Lviv 1638, 1643); the *Apostol* (Lviv 1639, 1654); the Octoechos (Lviv 1640); the Triodion (Kiev 1640, 1648); the Pentecostarion (Lviv 1642); the Psalter (Kiev 1644); the Octoechos (Lviv 1644); the Euchologion of P. Mohyla (Kiev 1646), one of the finest examples of Ukrainian book design of the time; the Nomocanon (Lviv 1646); the Kievan Cave Patericon (Kiev 1661, 1678); and L. Baranovych's *Mech dukhovnyi* (The Spiritual Sword, 1666) and A. Radyvylovsky's *Ohorodok Marii Bohorodytsi* (The Garden of Mary, the Mother of God, 1676). Two albums of his woodcuts were published in Kiev in the 1640s, and a collection of 132 of his biblical illustrations appeared at the end of the 17th century. Illia was a master of the thematic woodcut. His illustrations depict daily life, landscapes, buildings, and famous monks of the Kievan Cave Monastery.

Woodcut from the Kievan Cave Patericon by Illia

Illiashevych [Illjaševyč] (Eliiashevych). Name of a family of Lviv burghers that in the 18th and 19th centuries played an important role in the *Stauropegion Brotherhood. The more prominent members of the family were Yurii (d 1735), elder of the brotherhood in 1722–35; Vasyl, elder and in 1756 mayor of Lviv; and Oleksander (d 1825), vice-elder and author of one of the first histories of the brotherhood (1825).

Illichivske [Illičivs'ke]. VII-11. City in Odessa oblast, situated on the right shore of Sukhyi Liman about 30 km south of Odessa. Having one of the largest ports on the Black Sea, it has been under direct oblast jurisdiction since 1973, when it became a city. Established as a settlement called Buhovi Khutory in the late 18th century, it was renamed Illichivka in 1929 and acquired its present name in 1952, when it became a town (smt). It is a rapidly growing city with a young population (average age in the late 1970s was 24) consisting of longshoremen, shipbuilders, and merchant marines. The city has container ports, shipyards, and a reinforced-concrete plant. Its docks became a port separate from Odessa's in 1961.

Illienko, Vadym [Illjenko], b 3 July 1932 in Novomoskovske, Dnipropetrovske oblast. Cinematographer; the brother of Yu. *Illienko. After graduating from the All-Union Institute of Cinematography in 1955, he shot his first films at the Kiev Artistic Film Studio: *Hory klychut'* (The Mountains Are Calling, 1956) and *Zvychaina rich* (An Ordinary Thing, 1958). From 1958 to 1961 he worked at the Yalta Artistic Film Studio. After returning to the Kiev studio he has filmed, among other movies, *Oleksa Dovbush* (1961), *Za dvoma zaitsiamy* (After Two Hares, 1962), *Vechir na Ivana Kupala* (The Eve of Ivan Kupalo, 1967), *Sviato pechenoï kartopli* (Feast of Baked Potatoes, 1977), and *Try hil'zy anhliis'koho karabinu* (Three Cartridges for an English Carbine, 1983).

Illienko, Yurii [Illjenko, Jurij], b 18 July 1936 in Cherkasy. Cinematographer and screen director; the brother of V. *Illienko. A graduate of the All-Union Institute of Cinematography (1960), he has worked at the Yalta Artistic Film Studio and, since 1965, at the Kiev Artistic Film Studio. He also teaches at the Kiev Institute of Theater Arts. His camera work in S. Paradzhanov's *Tini zabutykh predkiv* (Shadows of Forgotten Ancestors, 1964) earned him an award at the 1965 international film festival in Mar del Plata, Argentina. His *Proshchaite holuby* (Goodbye, Pigeons, 1960), made in fulfillment of degree requirements, was approved for general distribution in the USSR. He made his debut as a director with his adaptation of N. Gogol's stories *Vechir na Ivana Kupala* (The Eve of Ivan Kupalo, 1967). Then he scripted and directed such films as *Bilyi ptakh z chornoiu oznakoiu* (White Bird with a Black Mark, 1972), which won a gold medal at the Moscow International Film Festival; *Vsuperech vs'omu* (Contrary to Everything, 1973); *Lisova pisnia – Mavka* (The Forest Song – Mavka, 1981), an adaptation of Lesia Ukrainka's play; and *Lehenda pro kniahyniu Ol'hu* (The Legend of Princess Olha, 1983), the first part of a planned trilogy on Kievan Rus'. Illienko's highly personal cinema is deeply rooted in Ukrainian history and folklore. His original cinematographic style uses subjective camera and explores the potentialities of color.

Illinska, Varvara [Illins'ka], b 19 November 1920 in Izhevsk, Udmurt ASSR. Archeologist. A specialist on the Scythian period, since 1945 she has worked at the Institute of Archeology of the AN URSR. She is the author of numerous articles and several books, including *Skify dneprovskogo lesostepnogo Levoberezh'ia* (The Scythians in the Forest-Steppe on the Dnieper's Left Bank, 1968) and *Ranneskifskie kurgany basseina r. Tiasmin (VII–VI vv do n.e.)* (Early Scythian Kurhans of the Tiasmyn River Basin [7th–6th Century BC], 1975), and a coauthor of the chapter on the Scythian period in vol 2 of *Arkheolohiia Ukraïns'koï RSR* (The Archeology of the Ukrainian SSR, 1971).

Illintsi [Illinci]. IV-10. Town smt (1978 pop 4,100) on the Sob River and a raion center in Vinnytsia oblast. Until the late 19th century it was called Lintsi. A castle was located there from the 14th to 17th centuries. The town has a sugar refinery and a local museum.

Illiteracy. See Literacy.

Illumination. Colored illustration and decoration of early manuscripts. The illuminations contained in imported Greek and Bulgarian manuscripts served as models for the illuminators of the first books written in Ukraine.

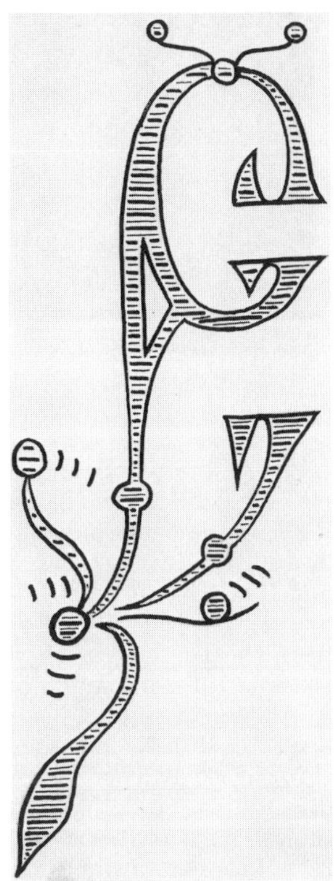

Sample initial

The three illuminations (of the Evangelists John, Luke, and Mark) in the Ostromir Gospel (1056–7) and the eight (including an image of Christ and a portrait of Prince Sviatoslav and his family) in the *Izbornik* of Sviatoslav (1073) are painted in vivid colors and gold in the Byzantine style and are embellished with a geometric and plant ornament that shows traces of local influence. The five illuminations in Princess Gertrude's Psalter (1078–87), including a portrait of her son Yaropolk with his wife Irena and depictions of the Mother of God enthroned, of Christ's Nativity, and of the Crucifixion with the Evangelists, are done in a Byzantine-Romanesque style that suggests they originated in Western Ukraine. Besides illustrations these manuscripts contained purely decorative artwork: the headpieces, tailpieces, and initials consisted of interlacing flowers, leaves, and geometric figures.

The illuminations produced in the 12th and 13th centuries, mostly in the western regions of Ukraine, are more modest in form. They are found in such manu-

Headpiece from the *Apostol* printed by I. Fedorovych (Lviv, 1574)

Initials from a Pochaiv missal (1775)

scripts as the Dobryla Gospel (1164), the Khrystynopil *Apostol* (12th–13th centuries), the Halych Gospel (1266), the Peremyshl Gospel (beginning of the 13th century), the Buchach Gospel (13th century), the Instructions of St Ephraem of Syria (1492), and the Kiev (or Spiridon) Psalter (1397). Their themes vary: they depict saints, battles, landscapes, and allegories. The Discourses of St Gregory the Theologian have a remarkable miniature of Christ.

The crowning work of the 14th century is the Kiev Psalter of 1397 with 226 sheets adorned with 293 masterful miniatures. The decorative interlace is influenced by neo-Byzantine and Balkan styles and incorporates teratological motifs. To the 15th century belong the Radziwiłł Chronicles, with 618 miniatures that are copies of a massive Kievan historical work from the 12th–13th centuries. Also remaining from the 15th century are fine Gospels from Halych, Serniv, and Mukachiv.

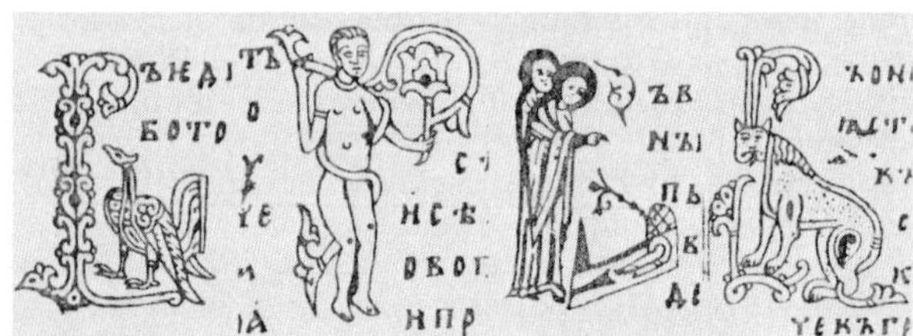

Initials from the St George Monastery Gospel (12th century)

Renaissance influences are detectable in the illuminations of later manuscripts such as the Gospel of the Kievan Cave Monastery (1538), the Khyshevych Gospel (1546), the Kholm Gospel (mid-16th century), the Zahoriv *Apostol* (1554), a mid-16th-century missal illuminated by Master Andrii, the Peresopnytsia Gospel (1556–61) illuminated by Mykhailo Vasylovych from Sianik, the Stryi Gospel (1594), and the Kermanych Gospel (1596). Besides Renaissance elements, folk designs appear in the headpieces and tailpieces of 16th- and 17th-century manuscripts.

Baroque motifs appeared in the illuminations done in the second half of the 17th and the beginning of the 18th century. Fine examples of this type are found in the Kievan Cave Patericon (copied in Hadiache in 1658), L. Baranovych's Missal (1665), A. Radyvylovsky's *Ohorodok Marii Bohoroditsy* (The Garden of Mary, the Mother of God, 1676), Y. Shumliansky's *Zertsalo* (Mirror, 1686), several hirmologions (1679, 1721, 1747, 1777), a missal (1718), and an *Apostol* (1727). Headpieces, initials, and tailpieces

Miniature from the Peresopnytsia Gospel (1556–61)

became more elaborate, and were dominated by fantastic plant motifs.

BIBLIOGRAPHY
Svientsits'kyi, I. *Prykrasy rukopysiv Halyts'koï Ukraïny XVI v.*, 3 issues (Zhovkva 1922–3)
Zholtovs'kyi, P. *Ukraïns'ka rukopysna knyha ta ïï ozdoblennia* (Kharkiv 1926)
Zapasko, Ia. *Ornamental'ne oformlennia ukraïns'koï rukopysnoï knyhy* (Kiev 1960)
Svirin, A.N. *Iskusstvo knigi drevnei Rusi* (Moscow 1964)
Lohvin, H. *Into the Deep Past: Miniatures and Ornaments in Old Manuscripts of the 11th–18th Centuries* (Kiev 1977)

S. Hordynsky

Illustration. Pictorial representation that elucidates or adorns the text of a book or magazine. Besides illustrations in the strict sense, also included are purely ornamental devices such as the headpiece, initial, and tailpiece.

In the 11th–16th centuries, before the introduction of printing, manuscripts produced in Ukraine were adorned with *illuminations. With the invention of printing, the various forms of printmaking were used first for the reproduction of illustrations in books. The earliest books printed in Ukraine were illustrated with *woodcuts, a technique that continued to be employed by printers into the 18th century. I. Fedorovych's *Apostol* (Lviv 1574), the first book to be printed in Ukraine, contains a fine frontispiece of St Luke the Evangelist. The ornamental headpieces, initials, and tailpieces that appear in his books were influenced by the illuminations in Ukrainian manuscripts and the designs in Cyrillic books printed earlier in Prague and Venice, and in turn had an influence on the ornamentation of Ukrainian books. Some of the artists employed by I. Fedorovych were I. Fylypovych-Pukhalsky, Hryn Ivanovych, and an unidentified 'W.S.' (the signature on the frontispiece in the *Apostol*). In the 17th century many printing presses were established in Ukraine and the demand for illustrators increased. Among the best-known woodcut illustrators of the time were P. Berynda, Illia, A. Klyryk, T. Petrovych, Prokopii, I. Reklinsky, M. Semeniv, D. Sinkevych, T. Zemka, Ye. Zavadovsky, and N. Zubrytsky. The thematic range of illustrations expanded from religious to historical, genre, and portrait. Their style was influenced by the Renaissance and then the baroque.

Copper engraving began to be used in book printing at the end of the 17th century and, thanks to its flexibility and precision, became the dominant illustration medium in the 18th century. Among the first engravers in Ukraine were L. Tarasevych and O. Tarasevych (who also introduced etching into Ukraine), Z. Samoilovych, I. Strelbytsky, I. Shchyrsky, and N. Zubrytsky, the illustrator of **Ifika iieropolitika*. In the 18th century the foremost Ukrainian engravers were A. and Y. Hochemsky, M. Karnovsky, A. Kozachkovsky, H. Levytsky (the greatest master of the century), Makarii, I. Myhura, T. Rakovetsky, F. Strelbytsky, and H. Tepchehorsky. Some of them excelled not only in engraving, but also in etching and mezzotint. The baroque introduced new allegorical and symbolic themes into illustrations. At the turn of the 17th century landscape illustrations (by D. Sinkevych) and battle scenes (by N. Zubrytsky) began to appear. Spiraling branches and acanthus leaves as well as elements of folk art were employed in the elaborate ornamentation that embellished the printed page. The engraving shop at the Kievan Cave Monastery Printing House was the leading center for book illustration in Ukraine. Ukrainian illustrators were in great demand in Poland, Lithuania, Belorussia, Moldavia, and Muscovy in this period.

Towards the end of the 18th century the art of illustration was influenced by *classicism. Although engraving and etching continued to be widely used (eg, by F. Strelbytsky), a new technique of illustration – *lithography – was introduced in the early 19th century. Because it was less expensive, easier to use, and more flexible than other techniques, it quickly became the favorite medium among illustrators. Masters of the technique included K. Trutovsky, M. Mikeshin, Y. Svoboda, O. Slastion, and V. Timm.

At the end of the 19th and the beginning of the 20th century photomechanical methods of reproduction were perfected, making it possible to base illustrations not only on prints but also on pen drawings and watercolors. Some of the leading Ukrainian illustrators of the 20th century are I. Izhakevych, M. Samokysh, O. Kulchytska, Yu. Narbut, V. Krychevsky Sr, E. Kozak, V. Kasiian, O. Sudomora, B. Kriukov, M. Derehus, M. Dmytrenko, and P. Andrusiv. Many of them have illustrated classics of Ukrainian literature. Some others who have contributed to this field are O. Dovhal, I. Ostafiichuk, H. Pustoviit, V. Sedliar, and O. Sakhnovska. B. Kriukov, S. Levytska, and V. Masiutyn have illustrated some classics of world literature. Among the most recognized modern designers of headpieces and tailpieces are Yu. Narbut, A. Sereda, P. Kovzhun, M. Butovych, V. Kasiian, V. Krychevsky Sr, J. Hnizdovsky, P. Andrusiv, M. Aleksiiv, and H. Yakutovych.

The most extensively illustrated literature is children's books and magazines. Some of the best-known artists in this area are E. Kozak, O. Kulchytska, O. Kurylas, O. Sudomora, P. Andrusiv, M. Levytsky, H. Mazepa, P. Kholodny, V. Lytvynenko, L. Dzholos, Ye. Soloviov, A. Rieznychenko, and T. Yablonska.

BIBLIOGRAPHY

Makarenko, M. *Ornamentatsiia ukraïns'koï knyzhky XVI–XVII st.* (Kiev 1926)

Shpakov, A. *Khudozhnyk i knyha* (Kiev 1973)

Ovdiienko, O. *Knyzhkove mystetstvo na Ukraïni 1917–1974* (Lviv 1974)

S. Hordynsky

Ilnytsia [Il'nycja]. V-4. Town smt (1978 pop 7,900) in Irshava raion, Transcarpathia oblast. It was first mentioned in 1450. Its lignite deposits have been mined since 1865. Existing mines were built mostly after 1945. Machine parts are also produced there.

Ilnytsky, Luka [Il'nyc'kyj], b and d ? Community leader. In the 1870s he was a member of the Kiev Hromada and of the Southwestern Branch of the Imperial Russian Geographic Society, for which he collected ethnographic data. Ilnytsky had a bookstore and publishing house in Kiev. He published a number of Ukrainian works for the Hromada during a brief period of liberalization in the 1880s.

Ilnytsky, Oleksander [Il'nyc'kyj], b 1889 in Chornyi Ardiv, Ugocsa county, Transcarpathia, d 1947. Canon of the Greek Catholic church and political leader in Transcarpathia. Ordained in 1914, he served in the administration of the Mukachiv eparchy and by 1930 rose to the rank of canon. He edited several church journals: *Dushpastyr* (1924–33), *Myssiinyi vistnyk* (1931–8), and *Dobryi pastyr* (1932–42). Ilnytsky defended a separate Rusyn nationality, distinct from Ukrainian and Russian. Welcoming the Hungarian regime in 1939, he was appointed chief adviser to the commissioner for Subcarpathia (1939–44), chairman of the Subcarpathian Academy of Sciences (1942–4), and member of the upper house of the Hungarian parliament (1939–44). After Bishop O. Stoika's death in 1943, Ilnytsky became capitular vicar of the Mukachiv eparchy. In 1946 he was tried by the Soviets for collaborating with the Hungarians and found guilty of treason. He died in prison.

Ilnytsky, Roman [Il'nyc'kyj], b 18 June 1915 in Kryvche, Borshchiv county, Galicia. A journalist and political activist. He studied at Lviv and Columbia universities. In July 1941 he was a member of the Provisional Ukrainian Government in Lviv; he was then arrested by the Gestapo and deported to Sachsenhausen concentration camp, where he was interned from 1942 to 1944. In 1945–7 he was the general secretary of the Central Representation of the Ukrainian Emigration in Germany and published the weekly *Chas* (1945–9) in Fürth. He was also the head of the Association of the Free Press of Central and Eastern Europe and the general secretary of the International Committee of Displaced Persons and Political Refugees. He contributed to the paper *Ukraïns'kyi samostiinyk* and was its chief editor in 1955–6. From 1954 he was active in the OUN (Abroad) (OUN[Z]) and in 1957–8 the head of its political council. In 1957 Ilnytsky immigrated to the United States. He was the cofounder of the Ukrainian Democratic Movement and its president in 1976–82. Since 1982 he has been vice-chairman of the Ukrainian Supreme Liberation Council. His major works are *The Free Press of the Suppressed Nations* (1950), *Deutschland und die Ukraine, 1934–1945* (2 vols, 1955–6), *Orhanizatsiia Ukraïns'kykh Natsionalistiv v Ukraïni, OUN(Z) i ZCh OUN* (The Organization of Ukrainian Nationalists in Ukraine, OUN[Z] and ZCh OUN, 1962), and *Pryznachennia ukraïntsiv v Amerytsi* (The Destiny of Ukrainians in America, 1965).

S. Yaniv

Rev Vasyl Ilnytsky

Ilnytsky, Vasyl [Il'nyc'kyj, Vasyl'], b 22 April 1823 in Pidpechary, Stanyslaviv county, Galicia, d 15 April 1895 in Pidpechary. Ukrainian Catholic priest, pedagogue, historian, and writer. A graduate of Lviv and Vienna universities, he was consecrated in 1848. That same year he became a member of the Supreme Ruthenian Council. From 1868 to 1892 he was principal of the Academic Gymnasium of Lviv. Using pseudonyms, such as Denys, Denys iz-nad Sereta, and Podolianyn, Ilnytsky published many popular articles on the history of Rus' and Cossack Ukraine, and several monographs such as *Starodavnyi Zvenihorod* (Ancient Zvenyhorod, 1861), *Starodavna Trebovlia* (Ancient Terebovlia, 1862), and *Perehliad iuzhnoruskoi istorii od r. 1337–1450* (A Survey of South-Ruthenian History from 1337 to 1450, 1875). He also wrote popular accounts of his travels and novelettes such as *Rohnida-Horislava: Povist' istoricheska s x stolitiia (979–986)* (Rohnida-Horyslava: A Historical Novelette from the 10th Century [979–986], 1860), *Horbatyi: Povist' nachertana na pidstavi znaidenoho pamiatnyka* (The Hunchback: A Novelette Based on a Discovered Monument, 1877), and *Svaty* (The In-Laws).

Ilnytsky, Volodymyr [Il'nyc'kyj], b 1887 in Pidhaitsi, Galicia, d 12 May 1942. Lawyer and community leader in the Drohobych region. He was the founder and head of *Pidoima (1923–39), an association that represented Ukrainians on whose land petroleum had been discovered. He organized private education and was an activist in the *Front of National Unity from 1933. In 1939 he was arrested by the Bolsheviks. Sentenced to 10 years' imprisonment, he died en route to a labor camp in Central Asia.

Ilovaiske [Ilovajs'ke]. VI-19, DB IV-4. City (1970 pop 19,700) in Donetske oblast administered by the Khartsyzke city soviet. It was founded as a railway station in 1869 and is an important railway junction in the southern Donbas.

Ilurat. A city of the *Bosporan Kingdom founded in the 1st century AD. Its ruins still stand near Ivanivka in Lenine raion, Crimea oblast, 17 km southwest of Kerch. Excavations conducted since 1948 have revealed that the city was fortified with strong triple walls and towers. The remains of stone buildings and straight, paved streets have been uncovered. The city's inhabitants were mostly Hellenized Scythian and Sarmatian military settlers. Its ruins provide a vivid picture of the Greco-Scythian culture of the Bosporan Kingdom. The city was destroyed by the Goths in the 260s.

Iman (since 1973, called Dalnerechensk). A city in Primore krai in the Soviet Far East. Iman and its vicinity were settled by Ukrainians (42 percent of the population in 1926). In 1917–22 it was one of the centers of the Ukrainian movement in the Far East, with a local Ukrainian council (1918) and a Ukrainian National Committee (1920–2).

Immigration. During the Princely era, immigrants in Rus'-Ukraine were few; they were mostly Armenian, Greek, Polish, and Jewish merchants who settled in the larger towns. In the Principality of Galicia-Volhynia, the immigrants were mostly Poles and German artisans. Other immigrants included prisoners of war who were occasionally freed and allowed to settle in Ukraine (ie, Pechenegs, Torks, Cumans, and Yotvingians). During the periods of Lithuanian and Polish rule in the 14th and 15th centuries, in Western Ukraine immigration of Armenians and Germans increased, and Italian and Greek merchants began settling in the larger towns. In the 15th and 16th centuries a large immigration of Jews occurred. It was not as massive or as significant as that of the Poles, however, who colonized Galicia and, after the Union of Lublin in 1569, the fertile lands of Podilia, Right-Bank Ukraine, and, in the first half of the 17th century, Left-Bank Ukraine. Thereafter the Jews and the Poles were the principal national minorities in Ukraine until the early 19th century.

During the period of the *Cossack-Polish War and the Hetman state of the mid-17th to the mid-18th century, immigration in Ukraine was minimal because of political turmoil. As the domination of Ukraine by Muscovy and its successor the Russian Empire grew from the late 17th century, so did the immigration of Russians. From the mid-18th century the tsarist government promoted the colonization of *Southern Ukraine by Serbs (in so-called *New Serbia and *Sloviano-Serbia), Germans, Greeks, Bulgarians, and Moldavians. After Ukraine was partitioned between the Russian and Austrian empires in the late 18th century, the immigration of Poles and Jews into its central and eastern lands ceased. The influx of Russians increased constantly throughout the 19th century, particularly in the cities and in the industrial centers of the Donets Basin. In the latter half of the 19th century, some 200,000 German, Czech, and Polish farmers settled on the parceled lands of the former Polish latifundia in Volhynia. In central and eastern Ukraine during the period 1890–1930, some two million immigrants, mostly Russians, arrived. According to the 1926 census, 23 percent of Soviet Ukraine's population consisted of immigrants, most of them Russians; 941,000 other foreigners were in Ukraine at the time of the census (70 percent of them were residing in urban centers).

In Western Ukraine under Austrian-Hungarian rule, small numbers of Germans arrived in the late 18th and early 19th centuries. Throughout the 19th century large numbers of Poles settled in Galicia and Bukovyna, mainly in the cities, in the Drohobych-Boryslav Industrial Region, and on the lands of the former Polish latifundia. This influx coincided with the mass *emigration of Western Ukrainians, who were forced to leave because of rural overpopulation. More Poles (some 300,000) immigrated to Western Ukraine under interwar Polish rule. In the interwar period, some 30,000 Czechs settled in Transcarpathia, and a sizable number of Rumanians moved to northern Bukovyna and northern Bessarabia.

Since the 1930s, the mass immigration of Russians to the urban centers and industrial regions of Soviet Ukraine has intensified. It has been encouraged by the Soviet authorities, who have pursued a policy of *Russification while destroying millions of Ukrainians during the *famine, political repression, and deportations of the Stalinist terror. Since the Second World War the number of immigrants other than Russians in Ukraine has declined considerably. The number of Russians who have immigrated to Ukraine in the past half-century has been estimated at eight million.

(For details about Ukraine's national minorities, see *Armenians, *Belorussians, *Bulgarians, *Czechs, *Germans, *Greeks, *Gypsies, *Hungarians, *Jews, *Moldavians, *Poles, *Rumanians, *Russians, *Serbia, *Slovaks, and *Tatars.)

BIBLIOGRAPHY
Bagalei, D. 'Kolonizatsiia Novorossiiskogo kraia i pervye shagi ego po puti kul'tury,' KS nos 4–7 (1889)
Shelukhin, S. *Nemetskaia kolonizatsiia na Iuge Rossii* (Odessa 1915)
Khomenko, A. *Naselennia Ukraïny 1897–1927* (Kharkiv 1929)
Hirshfeld, A. *Mihratsiini protsesy na Ukraïni* (Kharkiv 1930)
Dimitrov, D. *Bolgarskoe pereselenie v Ukrainu i Krym: Sbornik rabot studentov-vydvizhentsev i nauchnykh rabotnikov* (Leningrad 1931)
Kubiiovych, V. *Terytoriia i liudnist' ukraïns'kykh zemel'* (Lviv 1935)
Dashkevich, Ia. *Armianskie kolonii na Ukraine v istochnikakh i literature XV–XIX vekov* (Erevan 1962)
Naulko, V. *Etnichnyi sklad naselennia Ukraïns'koï RSR* (Kiev 1965)
– *Heohrafichne rozmishchennia narodiv v URSR* (Kiev 1966)

V. Kubijovyč

Imperialism. The process of territorial expansion by a state and its establishment of formal sovereignty or domination over subordinate political entities and societies that differ culturally and ethnically from it. The term frequently connotes oppression and exploitation and the fusion of militarism and colonialism.

Ukraine has been the victim of imperialism on the part of its neighbors. Poland, for example, took the western and central Ukrainian lands and all of Belorussia as a result of the union of Poland and Lithuania (1385) when the Lithuanian ruler Jagiełło married the Polish queen Jadwiga. The most persistent form of imperialism from which Ukraine has suffered has been practiced by the Russian Empire and the Soviet Union, beginning with the policy of expansion and aggrandizement adopted by the Muscovite State in annexing neighboring principalities, especially Novgorod in 1478, and continuing with the subjugation of the Kazan Tatar Khanate in 1552 and the penetration and annexation of Siberia in 1649. Muscovy obtained the opportunity to penetrate eastern and central Ukraine with the Treaty of *Pereiaslav (1654), under the guise of aiding the Ukrainian Hetman state that proclaimed its independence from Polish rule in 1648. The renaming of the Muscovite State as the Russian Empire (1721) reflected growing imperial ambitions that included the Russian annexation of Belorussia and the Right-Bank Ukrainian territories and Volhynia in the last quarter of the 18th century, with the partitioning of the Commonwealth of Poland. The Crimea was annexed in 1783 and Bessarabia in 1812.

Other forms of imperialism undertaken at the expense of Ukraine included that of the Habsburg dynasty's acquisition of Galicia in 1772 and Bukovyna in 1774. Hungarian claims to non-Magyar 'lands of the crown of St Steven' included Carpatho-Ukraine and Slovakia. In the Second World War Ukraine was an object of Nazi Germany's eastward drive for empire and suffered for three years as a battleground for the competing Nazi and Soviet imperialisms.

Imperialism is the outgrowth of various domestic and external circumstances. Muscovite and Russian imperialism was facilitated by the development of autocratic rule and an absolutist political order in the Muscovite State that its rulers acquired while collecting tribute from other principalities on behalf of the Mongol-Tatar authorities. Marx and Engels developed the concept of 'Oriental despotism' and used it to characterize the Muscovite State and Russia. The subjugation of alien peoples meant that the Muscovite State acquired a diverse population that prevented its future development into a conventional nation-state and impelled it on the course of an empire. Empire-building was also facilitated by taking advantage of opportunities, filling power vacuums, and selecting weakened victims whose subjugation involved little risk. Thus, in the 19th and 20th centuries the Russian Empire expanded in East Asia at the expense of a weakened China that could not defend itself, but this expansion also provoked the ire of Japan and led to Russia's military defeat in 1905. Russian imperialism also sought to take advantage of the balance of power when it participated in the partition of Poland, when it proposed to Great Britain the partition of the Ottoman Empire, and when it annexed Western Ukraine and Belorussia under the 1939 Nazi-Soviet Pact. The Russian quest for empire was sustained by a seemingly unending and obsessive search for 'security' by means of annexing contiguous territories and then penetrating into adjacent territories in order to ensure the security of the most recent acquisition.

Russian imperialism has relied heavily on Russian nationalist historiography that had its origins in the imperial designs of Peter I. The official political doctrine of *autocracy promoted Russian imperialism. Russian historians have sought to justify expansionism, wars, and colonization as a natural and 'legitimate' process of development. The Russian claim to the history of Kievan Rus' was designed to broaden the historical and geographical claim of Muscovy and St Petersburg, which would have been reduced if Novgorod rather than Kiev were deemed the precursor of 'Russia.' The principal exception in Russian historiography was M. Pokrovsky, a Russian Marxist historian who criticized Russia's depredations against subject peoples and regarded Russian expansionism as a consequence of the state's failure to deal with domestic problems. Pokrovsky's writings were banned as part of Stalin's revival of Russian nationalism and subsequently remained in official disfavor.

Rationalization of empire has been provided by the adoption of a messianic role and civilizing mission as evidenced by the idea of Moscow being the *Third Rome, and in the views of such Russian *Slavophiles as F. Dostoevsky, N. Danilevsky, A. Khomiakov, and F. Tiutchev. Slavophilism depicted Russia as 'truth-possessing' and morally superior, as historically destined to redeem humankind. It claimed universality and easily developed into Pan-Slavism, which advocated Russian subjugation of other Slavic (and non-Slavic) peoples, even when they possessed older cultures that were more highly developed than that of the Russians. Justification was also sought in the obsession with obtaining Constantinople and in reviving a reduced Byzantine Empire as part of the Russian imperial plan by delivering the Balkan Christian peoples from Ottoman rule.

Russian expansionism also sought justification in the view that its purpose was the acquisition of 'warmwater ports.' This rationale does not explain Muscovy's acquisition of Siberia, and it ignores the fact that Russia had acquired an ice-free port at Murmansk as early as the 13th century but did not develop it until 1915. The theory was used to rationalize the Soviet claim to Dairen and Port Arthur in Manchuria at the 1945 Yalta Conference.

Ukraine has played a vital role in Russian imperialism. It has served as a *place d'armes* for the acquisition of Russian naval power in the Black Sea, and it has enabled the Soviet Union to exert political and military pressure against Poland, Czechoslovakia, Hungary, the Balkans, and Turkey. Ukraine's strategic position and its economic and human resources have been used to enhance Soviet Russian military capabilities.

BIBLIOGRAPHY

Thornton, A. *Doctrines of Imperialism* (New York 1965)
Seton-Watson, H. *The New Imperialism* (New York 1971)
Cohen, B. *The Question of Imperialism* (New York 1973)
Hunczak, T. (ed). *Russian Imperialism from Ivan the Great to the Revolution* (New Brunswick, NJ 1974)
Pap, M. (ed). *Russian Empire: Some Aspects of Tsarist and Soviet Colonial Practice* (Cleveland 1985)

J. Reshetar

Impressionism. An important movement in painting that arose in France in the late 1860s and is linked with artists such as C. Monet, C. Pissarro, A. Renoir, and A. Sisley, who sought to capture with short strokes of unmixed pigment the play of sunlight on objects. The name of the movement was derived from C. Monet's *Impressions: Sunrise* (1872). Impressionism had a strong influence on Ukrainian painting. The first Ukrainian impressionists appeared at the end of the 19th century and were graduates of the Cracow Academy of Fine Arts, where they had studied under J. Stanisławski, L. Wyczólkowski, and J. Fałat. O. Novakivsky, who later embraced a symbolic expressionism reminiscent of V. van Gogh and F. Hodler, was one of the first Ukrainian impressionists. I. Trush, who preferred to work with grayed colors, adopted impressionism only partly. M. Burachek captured the sunbathed colors of the Ukrainian steppe. M. Zhuk and I. Severyn introduced decorative elements into their impressionist works. Impressionism was a major trend in Ukrainian painting until the early 1930s. Its leading exponents were O. Murashko, V. and F. Krychevsky, P. Kholodny Sr (landscapes and portraits), M. Hlushchenko, and O. Shovkunenko. Then M. Dmytrenko, M. Nedilko, M. Krychevsky, and M. Moroz continued the tradition of Ukrainian impressionism.

Impressionism gave rise to Neo-impressionism, which attempted to base painting on scientific theory; Post-impressionism, which cultivated the esthetics of color; and Pointillism, which broke down colors into their elementary hues and distributed them in mosaic-like patterns. S. Borachok, M. Radysh, and V. Khmeliuk may be included among the Neo-impressionists and Post-impressionists. With the imposition of socialist realism in the 1930s, impressionism in Soviet Ukraine was condemned as decadent and proscribed, although its influence in the better Ukrainian painters is evident.

Impressionist sculptors such as A. Rodin avoided sharp outlines and excessive detail in order to convey a general impression of the object. The leading Ukrainian exponents of this trend were M. Parashchuk, M. Havrylko, B. Kratko, S. Lytvynenko, and A. Pavlos.

Impressionism left its imprint also on music and literature. In music it strove to convey intimate and subtle moods. V. Barvinsky was a typical representative of this trend in music. Impressionism in literature is a manner of writing whereby the author does not try to represent reality objectively but to capture the impressions derived from it. The writer frequently centers his attention on the mental life of a character by simply registering his impressions or sensations instead of interpreting experience. The representive impressionist writers in Ukrainian prose are M. Kotsiubynsky, V. Stefanyk, H. Kosynka, and M. Khvylovy (although he shows traces of expressionism), and in poetry O. Oles. Impressionism often was linked with other literary trends such as Symbolism (D. Zahul) and Neoromanticism (V. Sosiura).

S. Hordynsky

Imstycheve [Imstyčeve]. Village (1980 pop 2,800) in Irshava raion, Transcarpathia oblast. It was first mentioned in the 15th century. The village was famous for its monastery, founded in 1661 by Bishop I. Zeikan of Mukachiv and visited by many pilgrims. In the 18th century it became a Basilian monastery. It was closed by the Soviets in 1946.

Incantation (Ukrainian: *zaklynannia*). The use of chanted, spoken, or written formulas to bind spiritual powers to certain actions that will accomplish a desired goal. Incantations in Ukrainian folklore can be classified into several groups according to their purpose. (1) Productive incantations to bring success in mushroom picking, hunting, fishing, beekeeping, and crop harvesting, ensure rainfall, clear away clouds, and destroy pests. (2) Defensive incantations to ward off or combat evil spirits that cause illnesses. (3) Family incantations to ensure personal and family happiness and prosperity, and success in love, marriage, and in giving birth. (4) Social or communal incantations to secure a superior's favor or success in litigation, and ward off fines, wounds or death in war, and epidemics in the community. (5) Malevolent incantations to inflict psychological suffering, illness, or death on an enemy in revenge for such wrongdoings as jilting, libel, robbery, and slaughter of livestock.

Incantations are one of the oldest genres of folklore. They originated in pre-Christian societies and reflect an anthropomorphic and magical world view. Later, they absorbed elements of the Christian religion such as petitions to Jesus Christ, the Virgin Mary, and various saints. Although folklorists deny this, incantations are still used in Ukraine today. It is interesting to note that there is no mention of incantations in the latest (1983) Soviet textbook on Ukrainian folklore for post-secondary schools, although a separate chapter was devoted to this topic in all previous editions.

BIBLIOGRAPHY

Efimenko, P. *Sbornik malorossiiskikh zaklinanii* (Moscow 1874)
Antonovych, V. *Chary na Ukraïni* (Lviv 1905)
Novitskii, Ia. *Malorusskie narodnye zagovory, zaklinaniia, molitvy i retsepty* (Katerynoslav 1913)

M. Hnatiukivsky

Incomplete secondary school (*nepovna serednia shkola*). In Soviet Ukraine an incomplete general secondary education was provided by *seven-year schools until 1959, and then by *eight-year schools.

Incunabula (from the Latin: 'cradles'). The first books produced after the invention of typography in 1440 to 1500. Most incunabulas dealt with religious subjects and were printed in Latin. The text did not have spacing between paragraphs or between words. Initials and decorative frames were hand painted and there were no title pages or page numbers. Information about the book was given in the epilogue.

The first publications of a secular nature appeared in 1470. The first book in Old Slavonic was *Mysal*, printed in 1483 in *Glagolitic and *Cyrillic by the printers S. Fiol (1491) and Makarii (1494–5). During the 15th century about 35,000–40,000 editions (excluding broadsides) were printed. It is estimated that some 500,000 copies have been preserved. The largest collections can be found in the British Library in London, the National Library in Paris, the Bavarian State Library in Munich, and the Vatican Library in Rome. In the USSR there are approximately 10,000. Of this number about 750 editions are to be found in the Ukrainian SSR: 516 are in the Central Scientific Library of the AN URSR, 46 in the Library of Lviv University, 42 in the Lviv Scientific Library of the AN URSR, 24 in the libraries of Uzhhorod University, 18 in Kharkiv University, and 15 in the Lviv Museum of Ukrainian Art.

Since 1904 an international commission in Berlin has been keeping a register of incunabulas and, since 1924, it has published *A Catalogue of Incunabulas*, of which eight volumes have appeared. As of 1985, the following catalogs of incunabulas have been published in Ukraine: F. Maksymenko's *Pershodruky (inkunabuly) Naukovoï Biblioteky L'vivs'koho Universytetu* (First Prints [Incunabulas] of the Scientific Library of Lviv University, 1958), E. Aleksandrovich's *Inkunabuli Tsentralnoi biblioteki Khar'kovskogo universiteta: Katalog* (Incunabulas at the Central Library of Kharkiv University: A Catalogue, 1962), B. Zdanevych's *Kataloh inkunabul* (A Catalogue of Incunabulas, Kiev, 1974), P. Lutsyk's *Inkunabuly L'vivs'koï Naukovoï biblioteky im. V. Stefanyka AN URSR* (The Incunabulas at the V. Stefanyk Lviv Scientific Library of the AN URSR, 1974), and Yu. Sak's *Inkunabuly biblioteky Uzhhorods'koho derzhavnoho universytetu* (The Incunabulas of the Library of the Uzhhorod State University, 1974).

Y. Boshyk, S. Yaniv

Independence, Struggle for (1917–20). The term used to describe the political, military, and diplomatic activities to achieve Ukrainian statehood in all Ukrainian territories. At first this struggle concerned the central Ukrainian territories, which, until 1917, were part of the Russian Empire. Following the *February Revolution of 1917, three Ukrainian state formations were established in central Ukraine. On 17 March the *Central Rada, headed by M. *Hrushevsky, was created in Kiev. The state-founding proclamations of the Central Rada were the four *universals: the First (23 June 1917) proclaimed Ukrainian autonomy; the Second (16 July) stated the agreement and the reciprocal recognition between the Central Rada and the *Provisional Government; the Third (20 November) created the *Ukrainian National Republic (UNR); and the Fourth, dated 22 January 1918, declared the independence and sovereignty of the UNR on 25 January 1918. The session of the Central Rada on 29 April 1918 ratified the constitution of the UNR and elected M. Hrushevsky president. That same day, however, a coup d'état was staged with the support of the Germans by conservative circles at the congress of the *All-Ukrainian Union of Landowners of Ukraine. Gen P. *Skoropadsky was proclaimed hetman of the *Ukrainian State, which replaced the UNR. The hetman decreed the 'Laws for the Provisional Regime in Ukraine,' which annulled the previous legal status and all laws of the UNR, and formed the *Hetman government.

The Ukrainian political formations that opposed the hetman formed the *Ukrainian National Union at the beginning of August 1918 and on 13 November they appointed the *Directory of the UNR, headed by V. Vynnychenko. Following P. Skoropadsky's 14 November 1918 proclamation of the federation of Ukraine with Russia, the Directory began an anti-hetman uprising that culminated on 14 December in the restoration of the republican rule of the UNR.

The Directory introduced the labor principle of rule with the *Labor Congress as the highest legislative body and with the *Council of National Ministers of the UNR as the executive organ. On 11 February 1919 V. Vynnychenko stepped down as head of the Directory and his post was taken over by S. *Petliura, who also became *supreme otaman of the *Army of the UNR. He occupied these positions until his death on 25 May 1926.

In the western Ukrainian lands that formed part of the Austro-Hungarian Empire, the *Ukrainian National Rada (UNRada) was formed in Lviv on 18–19 October 1918 and proclaimed a Ukrainian state on the territory of Galicia, northern Bukovyna, and Transcarpathia. It assumed power in Galicia on 1 November 1918 and in the Ukrainian part of Bukovyna on 6 November. On 9 November the UNRada announced the establishment of the *Western Ukrainian National Republic (ZUNR) and formed a government, the *State Secretariat of the ZUNR, headed by K. *Levytsky. On 22 January 1919 the union of the ZUNR with the UNR was solemnly proclaimed in Kiev; following this event, the ZUNR officially became the *Western Province of the UNR. On 9 June 1919 the UNRada appointed Ye. *Petrushevych plenipotentiary dictator of the ZUNR.

The essential military forces in Central Ukraine were volunteer army formations, among which the best were the regular units of the *Sich Riflemen. These units formed the Army of the Ukrainian National Republic, which defended the Ukrainian state against the Bolshevik Red Guards units, which came from Russia or were formed in Ukraine, as well as against the White armies of A. *Denikin and P. *Wrangel. Alongside the regular Ukrainian army formations, the *Partisan movement in Ukraine (1918–22), consisting of spontaneously formed, uncoordinated, often anarchic (see N. *Makhno) units led by local otamans, fought for the national and social goals of the revolution, although they did not share the ambitions of Ukrainian statehood.

In Western Ukraine the struggle for Ukraine's liberation was led by the *Ukrainian Sich Riflemen, who were first part of the Austro-Hungarian army and later incorporated into the *Ukrainian Galician Army (UHA), which was the regular army of the ZUNR. It defended the Western Ukrainian state from invasion by Poland (see *Ukrainian-Polish War). Later, together with the Army of the UNR, UHA fought against the Bolsheviks and the Whites.

The UNR and the Ukrainian state were intensely active in *diplomacy and were recognized by several states. A delegation from the UNR signed the Peace Treaty of *Brest-Litovsk with the Central Powers.

Under the pressure of unfavorable conditions at the front, the Directory signed the Treaty of *Warsaw with Poland in April 1920, and the two began a joint advance against the Soviet army in Ukraine (see *Ukrainian-Soviet War). Under Bolshevik pressure the Army of the UNR retreated from Ukraine on 21 November to Poland. The last organized military encounter of the struggle for Ukrainian independence was the second *Winter Campaign led by Yu. *Tiutiunnyk, although the partisan struggle continued for some time. The *Government-in-exile of the UNR continued the political battle for independence throughout the interwar period.

BIBLIOGRAPHY
Vynnychenko, V. *Vidrodzhennia natsiï*, 3 vols (Kiev-Vienna 1920)
Khrystiuk, P. *Zamitky i materially do istoriï ukraïns'koï revoliutsiï 1917–1920 rr.*, 4 vols (Vienna 1921–2)
Levyts'kyi, K. *Istoriia vyzvol'nykh zmahan' halyts'kykh ukraïntsiv v chasi svitovoï viiny 1914–1918 rr.* (Lviv 1928)
Mazepa, I. *Ukraïna v ohni i buri revoliutsiï 1917–1921*, 3 vols (Prague 1942, Munich 1950)
Reshetar, J. *The Ukrainian Revolution, 1917–1920: A Study in Nationalism* (Princeton 1952; New York 1972)
Udovychenko, O. *Ukraïna u viini za derzhavnist': Istoriia orhanizatziï i boiovykh dii ukraïns'kykh zbroinykh syl 1917–1921* (Winnipeg 1954)
Hunczak, T. (ed). *The Ukraine, 1917–1921: A Study in Revolution* (Cambridge, Mass 1977)

A. Zhukovsky

The first consistory of the Independent Greek church; Bishop Seraphim is in the center.

Independent Greek church. A church established in Winnipeg in 1903–4 through the efforts of K. *Genik, I. *Bodrug, and I. Negrich. Adherents of the anticlerical tradition of the Ukrainian Radical party, Genik and Bodrug opposed Russian Orthodox and Roman Catholic missionaries, whom they accused of favoring ritual and tradition over moral and ethical principles in religious life. Influenced by Presbyterian theologians at Manitoba College, they established the new church to act as a bridge to Protestantism. The Byzantine rite was retained, but the administration of the church was to be democratic with its ministry espousing evangelical principles. In 1905 a weekly, **Ranok*, was established, and classes for ministers were organized at Manitoba College. By 1907 the church had 24 Ukrainian ministers and missionaries, some gymnasium or university graduates from Galicia, but mostly poorly educated men, formerly associated with the eccentric Bishop *Seraphim (Ustvolsky). Subsidized by the Presbyterians, the new clergy served some 3,500 families, mainly in rural Manitoba and Saskatchewan. In Alberta the Edmonton congregation was the most reformed. After 1910 popular support waned as Protestant reforms were introduced into the liturgy. Growth was also checked by the traditionalism of most Ukrainian peasant immigrants, divisions within the ranks of the clergy, the revitalization of Ukrainian Catholic forces after Metropolitan A. *Sheptytsky's 1910 visit to Canada, and deteriorating relations with the Presbyterian sponsors.

To the Presbyterians, the conversion to Protestantism was the first step toward absorption into a culturally homogeneous English-speaking Canadian nation. When the mass of Ukrainian converts failed to appear, the Presbyterians abandoned the project in 1912. Nineteen ministers and missionaries, but not Bodrug, converted to Presbyterianism, although only a few remained within the Presbyterian (and later the United Church) fold permanently.

O. Martynovych

Independent Social Democratic Youth Association (Nezalezhna sotsiial-demokratychna spilka molodi). Youth organization of the Independent Social Democratic Party of Ukraine. It was active in Soviet Ukraine in 1919–20 and opposed the *Communist Youth League of Ukraine. In 1920 it merged with the *Communist Youth Association. Its members later joined the *Ukrainian Communist party.

Independentists. See Ukrainian Social Democratic Workers' Party (Independentists).

Indigenization (*korenizatsiia*). A policy adopted by the Twelfth Congress of the Russian Communist party (17–25 April 1923) but only partially and briefly implemented. Acknowledging that the tsarist Russian government had oppressed and exploited its non-Russian subjects and caused their inequality, and that vestiges of these practices remained in the USSR, the congress resolved to rectify this condition by encouraging the economic and cultural development of the non-Russian Soviet republics with the aim of making them equals of the Russian RSFSR. Accordingly, leading political, economic, and cultural cadres in each republic were to be recruited from among the local, indigenous population. The policy involved wide-ranging reforms: the strengthening of local cadres, the use of national languages in education and government, the de-Russification of the state apparat, the fostering of national cultures, and even the creation of national-republican armies. The congress condemned not only local nationalism but also Russian chauvinism, which was deemed to be more pernicious.

Indigenization was bitterly opposed by the 'imperialist' elements in the party and Soviet government. Consequently, it did not persist and public mention of it has been avoided.

The implementation of indigenization was different in each republic. In Ukraine it was called *Ukrainization, which was quite successful, despite the opposition of Russian chauvinist functionaries, until its abolition in 1933.

BIBLIOGRAPHY
Skrypnyk, M. *Statti i promovy, 2: Natsional'ne pytannia* (Kharkiv 1929)
Kommunisticheskaia Partiia Sovetskogo Soiuza v rezoliutsiiakh i resheniiakh s"ezdov, konferentsii i plenumov TsK, 1: 1898–1925 (Moscow 1953)
Dvenadtsatyi s"ezd RKP(b), 17–25 aprelia 1923 goda: Stenograficheskii otchet (Moscow 1968)
Dzyuba, I. *Internationalism or Russification?* (London 1968)

A. Zhukovsky

Industrial crops. A term applied to agricultural crops that serve as basic raw materials for various industries. Sometimes also called technical crops, they require extensive off-farm processing in order to be efficiently utilized. Industrial crops grown in Ukraine include oil-bearing crops (sunflower, castor bean, seed flax [for linseed oil], soybean), sugar crops (beet), volatile-oil-bearing crops (coriander, mint, rose, salvia), fiber crops (flax [for linen], hemp), and others (hops, tobacco). Some of these have been cultivated in Ukraine for many centuries (flax, hemp), others since the 19th century (sunflower, sugar beet, hops), and some only in more recent years.

Under Soviet rule, cotton, caoutchouc, and kenaf were introduced, but natural conditions in Ukraine proved unfavorable and these crops are no longer raised. In 1940, for example, cotton was grown on 238,000 ha (8.5 percent of the industrial crop area), but within a decade it had been phased out.

A rapid expansion of areas allocated to industrial-crop production, particularly sugar beets and sunflowers, occurred in the 1950s and 1960s (see table 2). The areas were stabilized during the 1970s, but since 1980 they have declined slightly because of unfavorable economic conditions and shortfalls in agrotechnology and labor.

Industrial-crop production has generally mirrored hectarage expansion and, to a lesser extent, higher yields. During the 1970s and 1980s, however, the output of industrial crops fluctuated widely (see table 1). This was particularly true of sugar beets. In 1976, for example, the sugar-beet harvest set a new record of 61.8 million t, 23.5 million t (62 percent) more than in 1975. Relative to leading producer countries, Ukraine's rank in sugar-beet production in 1981–4 was as follows: Ukraine (at annual average of 43.9 million t) = 100.0, the USSR = 170.3, France = 62.1, the United States = 47.0, and West Germany = 44.1. In sunflower-seed production: Ukraine (at 2.3 million t) = 100.0, the USSR = 214.2, Argentina =

TABLE 1
Soviet Ukraine's industrial-crop production, in million t

	1913	1940	1950	1960	1970	1980	1985
Sugar beets	9.337	13.052	14.624	31.761	46.309	48.841	43.569
Sunflowers	0.071	0.946	0.727	1.664	2.654	2.257	2.287
Fiber flax	0.004	0.019	0.012	0.074	0.089	0.092	0.118
Hemp	–	0.047	0.027	0.019	0.023	0.008	0.009

TABLE 2
Soviet Ukraine's industrial crops (in million ha with % of all crops in parentheses)

	1913	1940	1950	1960	1970	1980	1985
Total area	0.904 (3.2)	2.699 (8.6)	2.890 (9.4)	3.574 (10.7)	3.939 (12.0)	4.071 (12.1)	3.669 (11.2)
Sugar beets	0.558 (2.0)	0.820 (2.6)	0.828 (2.7)	1.457 (4.3)	1.659 (5.1)	1.775 (5.3)	1.641 (5.0)
Sunflowers	0.076 (0.3)	0.720 (2.3)	0.894 (2.9)	1.505 (4.5)	1.710 (5.2)	1.683 (5.0)	1.480 (4.5)
Fiber flax	0.016 (0.1)	0.118 (0.4)	0.126 (0.4)	0.223 (0.7)	0.230 (0.7)	0.226 (0.7)	0.211 (0.6)
Hemp	0.127 (0.5)	0.200 (0.6)	0.183 (0.6)	0.098 (0.3)	0.063 (0.2)	0.031 (0.1)	0.022 (0.1)

82.1, the United States = 65.6, and China = 44.7. In fiber-flax production: Ukraine (at 103,000 t) = 100.0, the USSR = 376.7, China = 86.4, France = 60.2, and Poland = 32.0.

Industrial crops are grown in all of Ukraine's geoclimatic zones. The forest-steppe zone, with favorable soils and moisture, produces the greatest quantity, particularly of sugar beets, but also of sunflowers, tobacco, and hemp. Oil crops, especially sunflowers, are raised primarily in the relatively dry steppe zone. Fiber flax, hops, and hemp are produced in the more humid Polisia region, while roses and some tobacco are grown in the sunny Crimea.

I. Kuzych-Berezovsky

Industry. An important economic sector, subdivided into branches including *electric power; *fuel; ferrous *metallurgical; non-ferrous metallurgical; chemical and *petrochemical; *machine building and metalworking; *lumber, *woodworking, and *paper; *building-materials; *construction; *glass and china; *light; *food; microbiological; medical; *flour milling and *mixed-feed; and *printing industries.

History to the mid-19th century. As human civilization developed on the territory of Ukraine, so did various non-agricultural economic activities (see *Crafts). Small-scale manufacture in Ukraine began developing in the 17th century. The Polish-ruled regions of Western and Right-Bank Ukraine remained economically backward agricultural lands, where the population (four-fifths serfs) eked out a subsistence form of living; their meager demand for non-agricultural goods was satisfied by a widespread *cottage industry. The needs of the nobility, their retainers, and the burghers were met primarily by goods imported from abroad and by products crafted by domestic artisans, many of them *Germans, *Jews, and *Armenians.

In Left-Bank and *Slobidska Ukraine, however, conditions for industrial development were relatively favorable. Low population density, greater personal freedoms, and fertile land there fostered a higher standard of living and a concomitant increase in the demand for manufactured products, particularly in the growing towns and cities. This demand was met less by imports and increasingly by local production stimulated by the mercantilist policies of the hetmans. Such policies, especially by I. Mazepa and, after the demise of the Hetman state, by certain Russian tsars, led to a growth in the manufacture of saltpeter, salt, window glass, crude iron, distilled liquor, and woolen textiles. These products not only were sold on the domestic market, but were also exported to Russia and other countries. Several large enterprises were founded in the early 18th century: a textile factory in Putyvl, a tobacco plant in Okhtyrka, sail-and-linen plants in Pochep and Sheptaky, a gunpowder plant in Shostka, and silk plants in Kiev and Nizhen.

After southern Ukraine was incorporated into the Russian Empire in the second half of the 18th century, the tsarist government promoted its settlement by granting land to both nobles and peasants. The rapid agricultural development was not accompanied by any immediate industrial growth, although some industry was developed in a few of the new port cities, such as Odessa, Kherson, and Azov.

INDUSTRY

Mining and extraction

A. Anthracite
B. Lignite
C. Peat
D. Petroleum
E. Natural gas
F. Iron ores
G. Manganese ores
H. Mercury ores
I. Graphite
J. Nickel and chromite ores
K. Ozokerite
L. Salt
M. Potassium salt
N. Flux limestones
O. Kaolinites
P. Refractories
Q. Sulfur

Manufacturing and processing

1. Ferrous metals
2. Non-ferrous metals
3. Machine building and metalworking
4. Energy-generating machinery
5. Electrical machinery
6. Machine tools and instruments
7. Railroad machinery
8. Ships (including repairs)
9. Automobiles
10. Tractors and agricultural machinery
11. Chemicals
12. Mineral fertilizers
13. Artificial and synthetic fibers
14. Petroleum
15. Wood products and paper
16. Building materials
17. Cement
18. Glass, porcelain, and china
19. Textiles
20. Clothing
21. Leather, furs, and footwear
22. Food
23. Fishing and canned fish
24. Canned fruit and vegetables
25. Wines

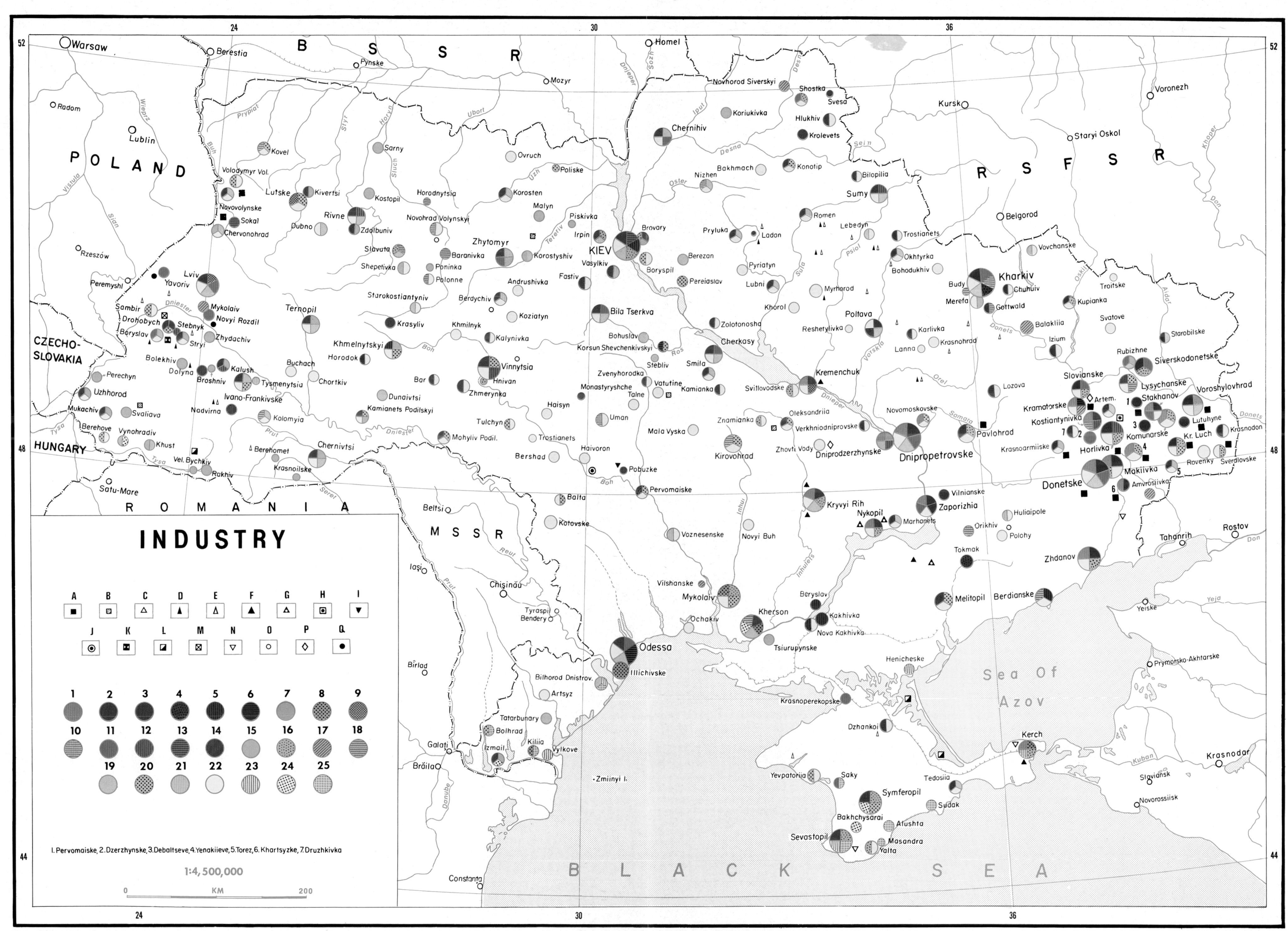
INDUSTRY
A B C D E F G H I
J K L M N O P Q
1 2 3 4 5 6 7 8 9
10 11 12 13 14 15 16 17 18
19 20 21 22 23 24 25
1. Pervomaiske, 2. Dzerzhynske, 3. Debaltseve, 4. Yenakiieve, 5. Torez, 6. Khartsyzke, 7. Druzhkivka
1:4,500,000
0 KM 200
B S S R
POLAND
R S F S R
CZECHO-SLOVAKIA
HUNGARY
ROMANIA
M S S R
Sea of Azov
B L A C K S E A
Warsaw
Berestia
Pynske
Homel
Mozyr
Radom
Lublin
Rzeszów
Peremyshl
Kursk
Voronezh
Staryi Oskol
Belgorod
Rostov
Krasnodar
Novorossiisk
Yeiske
Chișinău
Iași
Bîrlad
Galați
Brăila
Constanța
Satu-Mare
KIEV
Lviv
Kharkiv
Odessa
Dnipropetrovske
Donetske
Zaporizhia
Kryvyi Rih
Mykolaiv
Kherson
Poltava
Sumy
Chernihiv
Zhytomyr
Vinnytsia
Khmelnytskyi
Ternopil
Rivne
Lutske
Chernivtsi
Uzhhorod
Ivano-Frankivske
Kirovohrad
Cherkasy
Kremenchuk
Voroshylovhrad
Zhdanov
Melitopil
Berdianske
Symferopil
Sevastopil
Kerch
Yalta
Horlivka
Makiivka
Kramatorske
Slovianske
Lysychanske
Sieverskodonetske
Kostiantynivka
Stakhanov
Komunarske
Kr. Luch
Pavlohrad
Nykopil
Marhanets
Nova Kakhivka
Kakhivka
Izmail
Bilhorod Dnistrov.
Illichivske
Bila Tserkva
Uman
Shostka
Konotip
Kovel
Korosten
Berdychiv
Mukachiv
Drohobych
Stryi
Kalush
Kolomyia
Kamianets Podilskyi
Zmiinyi I.
Dnieper
Dniester
Danube
Desna
Prut
Boh
Don
Donets

Modern industrial development in Ukraine began at the end of the 18th century. The tsarist government in St Petersburg established new factories and managed them or leased them to private entrepreneurs. Industrial enterprises were also founded by the landowning nobles, especially on the Right Bank, to process agricultural raw material – sugar refineries, distilleries, and flour mills. Between 1825 and 1860, the number of mechanized plants in the nine Ukrainian gubernias of the Russian Empire increased from 674 to 2,709, the number of industrial workers grew from 15,200 to 85,800, and the value of output rose from 15.7 to 34.4 million rubles. In 1860, Ukraine accounted for 17.6 percent of the empire's plants, 15.1 percent of its workers, and 11.8 percent of the value of its output. Kiev gubernia, with its various consumer-goods industries in Kiev and sugar refineries in the countryside, was the most developed and accounted for 38 percent of Ukraine's workers and 42 percent of its output. Kharkiv and Chernihiv gubernias were second and third in terms of industrial development.

The mid-19th century to 1914. The turning point in the economic modernization of Ukraine and of the Russian Empire as a whole was the abolition of *serfdom in 1861. This measure was motivated by the need for a solid economic foundation for the empire's political aspirations, ie, a modernized agricultural system, greater labor mobility and industrial growth, and increased financial liquidity. Of particular importance for Ukraine's economy was the construction of railroads during the 1870s and 1880s. The railroads brought many benefits through low-cost transportation. Cheaper coal from the Donbas and iron ore from the Kryvyi Rih Basin led to phenomenal growth in ferrous metallurgy and related industries. Cheaper transport stimulated exports of grain, other agricultural products, and various industrial products (sugar, spirits, coal, rails). Railroad expansion gave impetus to industries ancillary to railroad construction. Finally the linking of Right- and Left-Bank Ukraine with southern Ukraine integrated the various Ukrainian regions into an economic entity, a national economy, and gave rise to common economic interests that were occasionally different from those of other parts of the Russian Empire.

To ensure the attainment of the emancipation reform's objectives, the central government intensified its intervention in economic life by introducing tariffs on certain products and thus facilitating their production at home, subsidizing certain enterprises, reducing taxes on others, and introducing the gold standard. The last measure in part increased foreign investment in the empire, while the convenient location of rich mineral resources attracted it into Ukraine. Thus, by 1913, Ukraine – which accounted for less than one-fifth of the empire's industrial output – was the recipient of about one-third of all foreign *investment in the empire. Prior to the First World War, foreign-owned (mainly French, British, and Belgian) companies produced 70 percent of Ukraine's coal, 67 percent of its pig iron, 58 percent of its steel, and 100 percent of its machinery (see *Capitalism). The sugar industry was a notable exception: it was overwhelmingly owned by local producers, many of them Ukrainian (such as the Yakhnenko, Symyrenko, Kharytonenko, Tereshchenko, Kandyba, and Arandarenko families).

Ukraine's industry expanded particularly rapidly during the last third of the 19th century. Between 1860 and 1895, the number of enterprises increased from 2,147 to 30,310, the number of workers from 85,800 to 205,300, and output from 47.2 to 260.9 million rubles. Table 1 shows the growth in output of some important products during this period. This remarkable growth was interrupted by the European economic crisis of 1900–3. Growth resumed soon after, however, with a noticeable shift in emphasis from the production of producer goods to that of consumer goods. The recovery is reflected in the increase in the number of industrial workers, from 354,700 in 1902 to 631,400 in 1914.

TABLE 1
Growth of some important products in the nine Ukrainian gubernias of the Russian Empire

Coal	1860–90	12.36 %	
Iron ore	1870–90	18.4 %	
Pig iron	1880–90	23.7 %	
Rolled steel	1880–90	19.8 %	
Metalworking and machine building	1865–90	11.1 %	
Granulated sugar	1881/2–89/90	6.1 %	
Bricks	1865–95	6.0 %	
Woolen textiles	1865–95	9.0 %	decrease

One of the characteristics of Ukraine's industrial development was its skewed structure. The extractive, industrial-materials, and food-products branches were generally better developed than the branches producing finished goods (see table 2). The tsarist government's policies and Ukraine's resource endowment explain the unbalanced structure of Ukraine's industry. The railroad network and transportation tariffs facilitated the export of Ukraine's rich mineral, industrial, and agricultural raw materials resources to manufacturing centers in central Russia, mainly those of Moscow and St Petersburg, and customs duties favored the export of similar products abroad. This retarded the production of capital equipment and consumer goods in Ukraine.

The weight of the extractive and industrial-materials branches determined the regional distribution of Ukraine's industry; the regions that experienced growth were those with the necessary resources for the development of these branches. Table 2 illustrates the distribution of industrial output in 1910 within the present borders of Soviet Ukraine. The most developed was Katerynoslav gubernia in the southeast, mainly as a result of the rich mineral resources and ferrous metallurgy of the Donbas and the Katerynoslav and Kryvyi Rih regions. Mining, metallurgy, and some machine building in the southeast were supplemented by flour milling and some machine building on the Black Sea littoral. In the southwest (the Right Bank) and the northeast (the northern Left Bank), food processing (predominantly of beet sugar, but also of flour and liquor) was the leading industry.

Austrian-ruled Galicia, Transcarpathia, and Bukovyna were industrially less advanced than Russian-ruled Ukraine. Petroleum extraction was of great importance in Galicia at the turn of the century, while woodworking predominated in Transcarpathia and Bukovyna.

The interwar period. Ukraine's industry was severely damaged during the First World War and the 1917–20 struggle for Ukrainian independence. After the consolidation of Soviet rule, reconstruction during the period of the *New Economic Policy proceeded swiftly, and Ukraine's industry regained its prewar output level by

TABLE 2
Structure of industrial output in Ukraine in 1910 (within the present boundaries of the Ukrainian SSR)

Industrial region*	Branch distribution (% of region)									
	% of Ukraine as a whole	Mining and metallurgy	Metalworking and machine building	Woodworking	Food: Total	Food: Sugar	Chemicals	Textiles	Other
Southeast	33.0	38.6	39.3	0.4	18.3	0.4	2.9	0.1	0.4
Southwest	23.6	1.3	5.0	3.3	85.3	56.3	0.7	0.4	4.0
Northeast	17.1	2.0	6.3	3.4	82.0	36.3	1.0	3.1	2.2
Black Sea	12.8	0.6	12.4	2.5	53.7	10.5	3.0	1.3	26.5
Western Ukraine	13.5	28.4	13.3	22.7	20.0	–	5.3	3.2	7.1
Ukraine as a whole	100.0	22.3	13.6	4.8	49.5	19.5	2.3	1.3	6.2

*Including the smaller territorial subdivisions of Yuzivka, Luhanske, Mariiupil, and Katerynoslav in the southeast; Kiev, Zhytomyr, Rivne, Berdychiv, Kamianets-Podilskyi, Vinnytsia in the southwest; Kharkiv, Chernihiv, Sumy, and Poltava in the northeast; Odessa, Kherson, Mykolaiv, Sevastopil, Teodosiia, Symferopil on the Black Sea; and Lviv, Boryslav, Drohobych, Chernivtsi, and Mukachiv in Western Ukraine.

1928. The first two *five-year plans (1928–32 and 1933–7) were crucial for Ukraine's future industrial development: the planning and management system and industrialization objectives introduced at that time have largely remained in force to this day. According to official Soviet statistics, which tend to bias indexes upwards, the output of Ukraine's large-scale industry (the bulk of all industry) increased 5.5 times between 1928 and 1937. According to revised Western estimates, Ukraine's total industrial output between the two benchmark years increased 3.4 times; the output of machine building and metalworking increased 6.1 times; of other producer-goods branches, 3.1 times; of the food industry, 1.4 times; and of light industry, 3.0 times.

Table 3 reflects the remarkable growth of Soviet Ukrainian industry during the years 1928–40. It also illustrates the general Soviet approach toward industrialization: the emphasis on the production of producer goods over consumer goods and the shift in importance of producer-goods production from Ukraine to some Russian regions, mainly in the Urals and western Siberia, during this period. Ukraine's share of the USSR total declined chiefly in producer-goods production between the two benchmark years, while its shares in production of certain comsumer goods increased.

The rapid increases in industrial output took place mainly because of increases in inputs. The growth of resource productivity was negligible. The number of workers increased between 1929 and 1940 from 855,000 to 2,213,000, or 2.6 times. The increase in fixed assets was also considerable, because 47.9 percent of Ukraine's total investment was allocated to industry during the First Five-Year Plan, 46.7 percent during the Second Five-Year Plan, and 42.6 percent during the first three and one-half years of the Third Five-Year Plan. As a result, several important heavy-industry enterprises were constructed during this period, including the Kharkiv Tractor Plant, the Dnieper Hydroelectric Station, the Zuivka, Siverskodonetske, and Kryvyi Rih state regional power stations, the metallurgical plants Azovstal in Mariiupil (now Zhdanov) and Zaporizhstal in Zaporizhia, and machine-building plants in Kiev and Kramatorske. As their locations indicate, industrialization efforts were concentrated in the regions with abundant raw materials – the Donbas and Dnipropetrovske oblast – and the demographically and politically important metropolitan centers of Kharkiv and Kiev.

TABLE 3
Growth of Ukraine's industry 1928–40

	Index 1940 (1928 = 100)	Ukr SSR as % of total production in the USSR: 1928	1940
PRODUCER GOODS			
Pig iron	408.4	71.9	64.7
Steel ingots	371.0	56.7	48.8
Rolled steel	326.8	58.1	49.7
Coke	393.1	95.7	74.5
Iron ore	427.5	77.0	67.6
Coal	337.4	69.9	50.5
Electric power	983.3	25.2	25.7
Mineral fertilizers	1,775.4	41.9	31.3
Soda ash	246.6	81.6	81.0
Industrial lumber	520.0	2.4	4.4
Plywood	125.8	14.3	4.3
Paper	135.4	7.2	3.4
Cement	410.1	16.1	21.5
Building bricks	243.2	25.6	21.5
Window glass	164.5	31.5	34.2
Machine building and metalworking (revised data)	564.7	17.5	19.6
CONSUMER GOODS			
Granulated sugar	151.8	78.1	73.0
Fish, marine animals, whales	311.2	5.3	9.9
Butter	378.4	10.7	14.8
Vegetable oil	339.1	10.4	19.9
Confectioneries	883.9	21.9	24.3
Salt	170.7	50.6	22.1
Cotton fabrics	690.0	0.1	0.3
Woolen fabrics	611.0	2.3	10.0
Hosiery	827.1 (1927–8 = 100)	14.2	16.4
Knit underwear	376.0 (1928–9 = 100)	11.7	24.4
Leather footwear	329.0 (1929 = 100)	16.1	19.3

Ukraine's share in the output and employment in the

TABLE 4
Ukrainian SSR's industry as a percentage of the industry of the USSR

FIXED CAPITAL	
10 October 1928	21.1
1 January 1938	20.7
EMPLOYMENT	
1928	20.4
1937	18.0
1940 (incl Western Ukraine)	20.2
INVESTMENT	
First Five-Year Plan, 1928–32	20.5
Second Five-Year Plan, 1933–7	18.4
Third Five-Year Plan, 1938–mid-1941	14.9

TABLE 5
Indexes of industrial growth in Ukrainian SSR and the USSR

	1940	1945	1950	1965	1985
Ukraine	100	26	115	555	1,692
USSR	100	92	173	791	2,547

TABLE 6
The growth rates of Soviet Ukraine's industry

1950–55	13.9
1955–60	10.7
1960–65	8.8
1965–70	8.4
1970–75	7.1
1975–80	3.9
1980–85	3.5

TABLE 7
Postwar growth rates of individual branches of industry

	1950–65 (%)	1965–85 (%)
Total industry	11.1	5.7
Electric power	14.0	5.9
Fuels	7.0	2.2
Machine building and metalworking	15.5	9.5
Ferrous metallurgy	9.6	2.9
Lumber, woodworking, cellulose, paper	6.8	5.1
Chemicals	17.7	8.6
Building materials	14.5	4.5
Glass, china, earthenware	11.0	8.0 (1965–84)
Light industry	9.3	6.0
Food industry	9.5	3.5
Flour, grist, mixed feed	5.8	5.8 (1965–84)

industry of the USSR did not change noticeably between the benchmark years (see table 4). But its share of investment declined steadily, reflecting the determination of the Soviet leadership to develop the Asian parts of the RSFSR, primarily because of the availability of the rich resources there and defense considerations. While this policy – which is still in force – may be justified in terms of long-term development and for reasons of defense, it was economically inefficient during the interwar period. Capital productivity was higher in practically all of the industrial branches in Ukraine than in the favored Asian regions. The industrial development of Galicia under Poland, Transcarpathia under Czechoslovakia, and Bukovyna under Rumania stagnated during this period.

The postwar period. Because of Ukraine's geographical location, its industry was severely damaged during the Second World War. At the beginning of the hostilities, the Soviet authorities dismantled and evacuated 544 complete plants eastward, primarily to western Siberia, with the intention of reassembling them for use in the war effort against the Germans. Because of poor organization and the lack of supplementary inputs, only a small portion of these enterprises were actually put into operation. The remaining equipment and machinery were either included in the existing enterprises or remained unutilized, while unevacuated enterprises were systematically destroyed by the retreating Soviet authorities. The Germans were both unable and unwilling to revive industrial activity during their occupation of Ukraine, and whatever was still usable they destroyed prior to the return of the Red Army. According to Soviet statistics, the damage incurred by Ukraine's industry during the war amounted to 44 billion rubles (in 1941 prices); 16,150 industrial enterprises were completely destroyed or extensively damaged. It is difficult to apportion exactly the responsibility for this destruction, but it is safe to assume that the Soviet authorities were no less culpable than the Germans.

The main Soviet objective during the early postwar years was the speedy reconstruction of industry, even at the expense of other economic sectors. Because of great sacrifices by the population, the prewar level of output was already exceeded by 1950 (see table 5). Reconstruction was facilitated by installing machinery and equipment taken by the USSR as reparations from its former enemies. There is no indication that any of the assets of Ukraine's industry that were evacuated at the beginning of the war were ever returned.

A trend of constantly declining growth rates can be observed in Ukraine during the postwar period, as in all of industry in the USSR. The decline has been particularly sharp since the mid-1970s (see table 6). The growth rates of individual industrial branches during the years 1950–65 and 1965–85 are presented in table 7. The growth of the traditional branches of Ukraine's industry – fuels (especially coal mining), ferrous metallurgy, and food processing – slowed down relatively more than that of other branches. Soviet statistics have tended to bias growth rates upwards, especially during the early postwar years, and give a growth rate for Ukraine's industry of almost 13 percent between 1950 and 1958. Although revised Western estimates show it was closer to 9 percent, even this lesser figure can be considered robust by world standards. Industry's share in Ukraine's net material product varied between 48.1 percent in 1960 and 50.5 percent in 1975. According to a Western estimate, its share in the gross national product was 39.3 percent in 1970. Ukraine has not regained its prewar position within the entire industry of the USSR, however, even though the growth rates of its industry and that of the USSR as a whole have been almost identical during the 1950–85 period (8.0 percent), because Ukraine suffered much more from the war than the rest of the USSR.

The development of Ukraine's industry during the postwar period can be summarized by using the indicators in table 8. The growth of output in the years 1965–

TABLE 8
Growth of output and input and Ukraine's shares in USSR industry during the postwar period

	Growth rates (%)			Ukraine as % of Soviet economy		
	1950	1950–65	1965–85	1950	1965	1985
Output (in billion rubles)	135.9	11.1	5.7	17.8	18.7	18.6
Employment (in thousands)	2,509.0	4.8	1.9	16.4	18.4	19.4
Fixed capital (in billion rubles)	32.0 (1965)	NA	7.2	NA	18.4	16.7

NOTE: The total Soviet investment in Ukraine was 16.1% in 1951–60, 15.5% in 1961–70, 14.5% in 1971–80, and 15.1% in 1981–5.

85 was almost half that of the years 1950–65, although Ukraine's shares in the USSR for the three benchmark years did not change appreciably. The slowdown in output growth in Ukraine could be attributed largely to a slowdown in the expansion of inputs (labor and capital) rather than to the productivity. Employment growth fell sharply from 4.8 percent per annum over 1950–85 to only 1.9 percent over 1965–85. Also, the share of Soviet investment in Ukraine diminished steadily after 1960 (table 8). Since Soviet fixed-capital growth declined after 1960, the declining Ukrainian share of investment means Ukrainian fixed-capital growth fell even more than the Soviet total.

Some reasons for the slowdown of industry during the last two decades are applicable to the entire USSR, including Ukraine. First, in view of the declining rate of entrants into the labor force and the continued high rate of capital formation, diminishing returns to capital are being experienced. Second, a decline in resource productivity – the result of inefficient and centralized planning and management, including a defective incentive structure – is often suggested as a cause of slowdown. There are also factors that are specific to Ukraine: depleted fuel (coal, oil, gas) reserves and the rising cost of their extraction, exhausted hydro energy sources, a water shortage, and an imbalance between the supply of agricultural raw materials and the necessary processing facilities. Perhaps of greatest importance is the relatively declining allocation by the central planners of investment in the economy of Ukraine, including its industry (table 8). As a result, new technological processes and the modernization of the industrial structure cannot be fully introduced in Ukraine. Instead, the allocation of investment to develop the Asian parts of the RSFSR, which began in the early 1930s, has been intensified since the mid-1960s (eg, the construction of several territorial production complexes in Siberia and the Baikal-Amur Railway Trunk Line). From the standpoint of the entire Soviet economy, such investment distribution may be inefficient. According to various Western studies, the productivity of capital and of total resources has been higher for most of the postwar period in Ukraine than in the RSFSR, although a reversal in this trend seems to have been taking place since the mid-1960s.

Several changes in the planning, management, and incentive structure of industry were introduced in the USSR during the postwar period. The system established under Stalin in the late 1920s and early 1930s was characterized by a strict centralization of decision-making powers in the hands of planners and union ministries in Moscow. The resulting stifling of local initiative proved to be detrimental to economic growth during the 1950s. The economic reforms of 1957 shifted the locus of decision-making from Moscow to regional authorities (see *Regional economic councils) and, in some measure, the republics. But this relatively decentralized system was replaced in 1965 by one that revived the ministerial structure and, at the same time, allocated greater powers to individual enterprises. Because the subsequent performance of industry was unsatisfactory, the prerogatives of enterprises were gradually abrogated. A so-called economic experiment was introduced in 1983, according to which some planning and managerial powers, primarily with respect to the wage bill and incentive funds, were allocated to five ministries in Moscow and some republics (the Ministry of the Food Industry in Ukraine). What the outcome of this experiment will be is as yet unclear. It is safe to say that all these reforms have not exerted a differential effect on Ukraine's industrial performance. The 1957–65 period of regional economic councils was, however, somewhat conducive to a limited widening of the Soviet Ukrainian government's autonomy.

In view of present-day conditions in Ukraine, Soviet leaders have formulated a specific approach toward Ukraine's industrial development in recent official documents, which state that Ukraine should specialize in energy-, investment-, and water-saving branches and processes. The decline in coal production should be arrested, nuclear-energy generation should be expanded, and various energy-saving measures should be undertaken; new investment should be allocated to prominent branches such as coal and ferrous metallurgy only for reconstruction and not for the construction of new facilities; Ukraine's industry should become specialized in (1) machine building (electricity-generating equipment, metal lathes, and livestock- and animal-feeds machinery), (2) certain skilled, labor-intensive industries (automobiles, computers, electrical and radio technology, and ball bearings), and (3) the output of certain raw and industrial materials (iron and manganese ores, electric

TABLE 9
Investment in Ukraine's industrial branches for selected years (1958–83)

	1958	1970	1983
Total industry	100.0	100.0	100.0
Energy and fuels	10.0	12.8	9.3
Machine building and metalworking	19.7	17.1	27.4
Industrial materials	28.8	29.6	28.9
Consumer goods	41.5	40.5	34.4

power, gas, superphosphate) for export, primarily to the European Comecon countries; and new facilities for processing export products and imports should be constructed near the Black Sea ports. It appears that such an investment policy has been followed in the past, especially since 1970 (see table 9). Of all branches, only machine building has received more investment, while the decline of investment in fuels and food processing has been quite pronounced.

Table 10 presents the growth in output of individual products between 1940 and 1985 and their shares in the USSR for the benchmark years. The data by and large

TABLE 10
Ukraine's output of selected products

	1940		1965		1985	
	Ukr. SSR as % of USSR	Index (1940 = 100)	Ukr. SSR as % of USSR	Index (1940 = 100)	Ukr. SSR as % of USSR	Units
FUEL AND ENERGY						
Electric energy	25.5	762.9	18.7	2,191.6	17.6	272.0 kWh
Coal	59.6	231.9	47.1	235.2	41.3	197.1 mil t (1980)
INDUSTRIAL MATERIALS						
Steel	48.6	415.7	40.6	603.4	36.3	53.7 mil t (1980)
Rolled steel	49.0	464.3	42.2	668.2	34.9	37.7 mil t
Iron ore	67.6	415.3	54.7	594.7	48.4	120.0 mil t
Mineral fertilizers	28.1	746.2	21.4	2,393.4	15.1	5.1 mil t
Sulfuric acid	25.6	463.6	22.2	1,013.5	15.7	4.1 mil t
Caustic soda	81.1	195.9	29.7	281.1	23.9	1.2 mil t
Soda ash	44.3	183.1	11.9	644.1	16.4	499.8 th t
Chemical fibers	SA*	100.0	10.8	374.5	11.8	164.8 th t
Lumber	3.2	160.3	3.3	135.9	2.9	10.6 mil cu m
Plywood	4.0	500.3	8.9	609.0	9.4	190.0 th t cu m
Paper	3.3	594.6	5.1	932.5	5.0	299.2 th t
Cellulose	4.7	2,725.0	2.4	3,760.7	1.3	105.3 th t
Cement	21.5	1,013.2	17.0	1,844.2	18.4	22.5 mil t (1975)
Bricks	21.5	504.5	22.1	560.1	21.8	9.0 mil
Reinforced concrete	NA	100.0	16.5	232.3	15.7	21.5 mil cu m
Window glass	33.5	301.3	24.3	330.1	20.8	50.5 mil sq m
MACHINE BUILDING						
Large electric machines	SA	100.0	37.9	163.8	23.8	9,500
Metal lathes	20.0	212.8	13.4	265.8	17.1	31,100
Automation equipment	NA	100.0 (1970)	25.4	419.3	24.9	1,190.8 mil rubles
Computation equipment	NA	100.0 (1970)	17.4	2,358.1	24.6	1,033.9 mil rubles
Agricultural machinery	NA	100.0	12.1	298.7 (1970 = 100)	12.2	800.6 mil rubles
Tractors	32.9	1,137.5	33.3	1,306.7	23.2	135,900
Excavators	SA	100.0	28.7	161.3	23.5	10,000
Bulldozers	SA	100.0	42.0	153.9	31.8	13,000
Railway freight cars	33.3	176.7	46.0	173.6	50.2	31,600 (1980)
Automobiles	2.8 (1950)	320.8	9.5	1,128.4	9.4	206,200 (1980)
CONSUMER PRODUCTS						
Hose	16.2	340.7	20.0	488.4	20.3	387.8 mil pairs
Underwear	23.9	485.8	20.6	785.8	19.5	238.1 mil pairs
Knitwear	20.4	271.7	17.3	677.5	16.0	81.5 mil items
Apparel	NA	100.0	19.0	171.9 (1970 = 100)	19.7	5,124.5 mil rubles
Leather shoes	19.2	233.6	19.6	455.1	23.6	185.7 mil pairs
Sugar	73.0	423.2	60.6	395.4	52.9	6,247 th t
Meat	19.4	370.2	21.3	787.6	21.8	2,355 th t
Butter	13.2	843.8	26.2	1,171.8	25.7	3,902 th t
Canned food	30.3	490.6	23.4	1,173.4	22.1	3,978 mil cans
Bicycles	SA	100.0	20.4	104.9	16.4	743,000
Refrigerators	SA	100.0	16.8	263.5	12.7	743,000
Radios	SA	100.0	10.7	52.5	3.3	291,000
Televisions	NA	100.0	14.2	590.8	32.7	3,067
Cameras	9.1	421.1	12.9	814.2	12.6	263,000
Furniture	NA	100.0	21.2	353.0	18.7	1,403.6 mil rubles

*SA = small amounts; NA = not available

confirm previous findings in value and aggregate terms: the recent slowdown in the growth rate of all industry, a change in the structure of Ukraine's industry with an emphasis on machine building, and the decreasing share of Ukraine's output in the overwhelming majority of products in the USSR. Ukraine is an important world producer of various industrial products. For example, in 1983 Ukraine ranked 1st in the world in the output of manganese ore, 2nd in iron ore, 3rd in tractors, 4th in sugar and crude steel, 5th in TV sets, 6th in butter, and (in 1975) 8th in cement. It lagged behind, however, in the output of other commodities, particularly of consumer goods; eg, it ranked 17th in automobile production, and its output of chemical fibers and paper was surpassed by virtually all the industrialized countries.

Ukraine's industrial growth during the postwar period has been low in comparison with that of other Soviet republics: it was 11.1 percent per year between 1950 and 1965 and 5.7 percent between 1965 and 1985 (9.8 and 5.8 percent respectively in the case of the RSFSR), thereby ranking Ukraine 9th and 11th among the 15 republics during the respective periods. At the same time, Ukraine's population increase – of 21.4 percent – was the lowest among the republics between 1959 and 1985. As a result, Ukraine's industrial output per capita has slipped from 4th place in 1960 to 6th place in 1985 among the 15 republics.

Ukraine's oblasts differ substantially in terms of the index of industrial output per capita (see table 11). They can be classified into four groups: (1) five highly industrialized oblasts (an index above 115) located in the Donets-Dnieper Region (see also *Donets Basin and *Dnieper Industrial Region); (2) eight oblasts with an average level of industrialization (an index between 80 and 115); (3) six oblasts with a below-average level of industrialization (an index between 65 and 79); and (4) six poorly industrialized oblasts (an index below 65). The least industrially developed region in Ukraine is the southwest. The data in table 11 reflect a tendency toward a decrease in interoblast inequality. For example, the ratio between the indexes of the most and least developed oblasts decreased from 5.1 to 3.4 between 1965 and 1978, primarily as a result of the relatively greater allocation of industrial investment to the western oblasts. Investment in Chernivtsi, Rivne, Ternopil, and Khmelnytskyi oblasts was 2.2 times, and in Volhynia oblast 7.5 times, larger in 1978 than in 1965, while investment in the Donets-Dnieper region's oblasts increased by only 68 percent during the same period. In spite of this progress, 63 percent of Ukraine's industrial assets and 54 percent of its workers were still located in the Donets-Dnieper region in 1979, while the corresponding percentages were 27 and 35 for the southwestern region and 10 and 11 for the southern region. The respective population shares were 42, 44, and 14 percent.

The uneven distribution of Ukraine's industry continues to result from its unbalanced structure, ie, the favoring of heavy industry before and even more after the 1917 Revolution. Since the necessary raw materials and subsequently industrial materials were readily available in the Donets-Dnieper region, heavy industry grew there. The necessary raw materials for the development of other industrial branches were distributed less unevenly throughout Ukraine; as a result, the distribution of these branches is also less uneven than that of heavy industry.

TABLE 11
Levels of development of Ukrainian SSR economic regions

	1965	1978
UKRAINIAN SSR	100.0	100.0
DONETS-DNIEPER REGION	141.5	128.8
Dnipropetrovske oblast	184.3	157.6
Donetske oblast	169.2	129.2
Kharkiv oblast	137.9	132.2
Kirovohrad oblast	65.7	76.2
Poltava oblast	77.7	96.3
Sumy oblast	74.8	83.6
Voroshylovhrad oblast	141.1	126.2
Zaporizhia oblast	167.9	169.5
SOUTHWESTERN REGION	62.2	77.9
Cherkasy oblast	65.0	75.6
Chernihiv oblast	65.7	80.7
Chernivtsi oblast	64.1	65.9
Ivano-Frankivske oblast	44.3	69.8
Khmelnytskyi oblast	46.1	62.5
Kiev oblast	95.9	110.1
Lviv oblast	83.4	100.5
Rivne oblast	46.2	61.2
Ternopil oblast	33.2	50.6
Vinnytsia oblast	54.0	63.9
Volhynia oblast	39.7	49.6
Transcarpathia oblast	44.3	62.3
Zhytomyr oblast	57.0	66.3
SOUTHERN REGION	92.1	81.7
Crimea oblast	91.5	78.5
Kherson oblast	90.0	89.0
Mykolaiv oblast	77.7	84.0
Odessa oblast	100.2	80.1

BIBLIOGRAPHY

Ivanys, V. *Promyslovist' Ukraïny i Pivnichnoho Kavkazu* (Warsaw 1937)

Holubnychy, V. *The Industrial Output of the Ukraine, 1913–1956: A Statistical Analysis* (Munich 1957)

Seredenko, M. (ed). *Promyslovist' Radians'koï Ukraïny za 40 rokiv (1917–1957)* (Kiev 1957)

Kononenko, K. *Ukraine and Russia: A History of the Economic Relations between Ukraine and Russia (1654–1917)* (Milwaukee 1958)

Nesterenko, O. *Rozvytok promyslovosti na Ukraïni*, 3 vols (Kiev 1959–66)

Korets'kyi, L.; Palamarchuk, M. *Heohrafiia promyslovosti Ukraïns'koï RSR* (Kiev 1967)

Koropeckyj, I.S. *Location Problems in Soviet Industry before World War II: The Case of the Ukraine* (Chapel Hill 1971)

Ohloblyn, O. *A History of Ukrainian Industry* (Munich 1971)

Voloboi, P.; Popovkin, V. *Problemy terytorial'noï spetsializatsiï i kompleksnoho rozvytku narodnoho hospodarstva Ukraïns'koï RSR* (Kiev 1972)

Senkiw, R. 'The Growth of Industrial Production in Ukraine, 1945–71,' PH D diss (University of Virginia 1974)

Crisp, O. *Studies in the Russian Economy before 1914* (New York 1976)

Koropeckyj, I.S. (ed). *The Ukraine within the USSR: An Economic Balance Sheet* (New York 1977)

Koropeckyj, I.S.; Schroeder, G. (eds). *Economics of Soviet Regions* (New York 1981)

Kravets', O. *Knyha z istoriï fabryk ta zavodiv Radians'koï Ukraïny (1921–1980)* (Kiev 1982)

I.S. Koropeckyj

Indyshevsky, Stepan [Indyševs'kyj], b 1892 in Stanyslaviv, Galicia, d 1938. Engineer and military leader. Until 1914 he was an organizer of the Sich movement. During the war for Ukraine's independence he served on the General Staff of the Sich Riflemen Corps and organized the army's technical units. After the war he spent two years in Transcarpathia and in 1925 moved to Kharkiv. He was killed during the Yezhov purges.

Indyshevsky, Yaroslav [Indyševs'kyj, Jaroslav], b 1895, d 31 May 1937 in Prague. Captain in the Legion of Ukrainian Sich Riflemen. In 1919 he served in Vienna as military attaché of the legation of the Western Ukrainian National Republic. After the war he joined the Ukrainian Military Organization and served as its regional commander for Western Ukraine (1924–6).

Infantry (*pikhota*). The oldest and proportionally the largest branch of the army; it conducts combat operations on its own or with the support of other branches. During the Middle Ages in Ukraine the small princely retinue was usually mounted, but in wartime the bulk of the troops consisted of footmen armed with bows and pikes. In the 17th century the Cossacks were known as the best infantry in Europe. In the 20th century, the Ukrainian armies consisted mostly of infantry, and the UPA (1943–9) was basically a light infantry.

Inheritance law. A division of civil law dealing with the transfer of possessions of deceased individuals to their heirs. During the Kievan Rus' period, inheritance was strictly determined by family ties, and only family members could be heirs. The person leaving an inheritance could have some influence over how it was to be divided, but could not assign it to non-family members. If an individual left no offspring, the inheritance went to the principality, by default. The form of a will (see *Dukhivnytsia*) was usually oral, delivered in the presence of family members. The detailed laws of inheritance encoded in the *Ruskaia Pravda* distinguished between the rights of inheritance of *smerdy* (slaves or commoners) and boyars (nobles or barons), and outlined the rights of the widow.

Under the Lithuanian Statute, inheritance continued to be determined by family ties. However, both fluid and static assets acquired during a lifetime could be assigned to non-family members. Some classes of individuals were forbidden to compose wills, and only legally empowered individuals could receive inherited goods or assets. There were also restrictions imposed on inheritances by women, servants, and some classes of peasantry.

The reforms brought about during the Cossack era were later modified by the Code of 1743, which allowed for inheritance by illegitimate offspring of assets acquired during the bequeathers' lifetime.

After the abolition of the Hetmanate, Russian authorities in 1835 established the primacy of the *Svod zakonov Rossiiskoi Imperii*, with some adjustments in the Poltava and Chernihiv gubernias to ensure congruence with earlier civil law. This system of laws was based on sequential order of inheritance of offspring, widow, parents, followed by brothers and sisters. In Galicia under Austria and then Poland the Austrian civil code of 1811 was enforced. Under this code, the bequeather was empowered to distribute assets to mainly one individual or to many, as long as the bequeather respected the rights of all legally entitled members of the family. This law ensured universality of distribution by automatically legally entitling certain members of the family to certain portions of the estate, irrespective of the will of the bequeather or primary heir.

During the years of Ukrainian statehood, previous laws (Russian and Austrian) concerning inheritance remained in force. After the Bolshevik Revolution all such laws were annulled by decree of the Council of Peoples' Commissars of the Ukrainian SSR on 3 November 1919. However, agriculturally based assets not exceeding 10,000 rubles could remain as family possessions and were not confiscated by the state. This system continued through the NEP period in various modified forms.

Under the Civil Code of the Ukrainian SSR of 16 December 1922, rights of inheritance were limited to direct descendants (children, grandchildren, and great-grandchildren), the widow, relatives who were unable to work, and the impoverished who were dependants of the deceased one year prior to his death. The inheritance was to be divided equally among all beneficiaries named above. The testator had the right to rearrange the distribution of assets in a will, or to specifically exclude a particular individual, but not to assign them to legally unentitled persons.

In 1928 all offspring 18 years of age or under were entitled to three-fourths of the assets of the deceased. An individual had the right to leave his possessions to the state, to the Party, and to community (but not religious) organizations. In 1945 the circle of inheritors was expanded to include siblings.

The legislation currently operative in matters of inheritance consists of the general foundations for civil law of the USSR and the Civil Code of the Ukrainian SSR, enacted on 18 July 1963 (chapter VII, articles 524–564). The first rank of inheritors legally entitled to equal parts of the inheritance are children, spouses, and parents of the deceased. Grandchildren can be inheritors if the parents of the deceased are not alive. In the event of the absence of inheritors of the first rank, siblings are entitled to equal portions, as are the grandparents. Every citizen is entitled to leave his assets divided among any number of individuals. The compulsory portion of assets to be given to children who have not reached the age of majority or are not able to work (this includes adopted children), spouse, parents, and dependants is two-thirds. In the event of the lack of these primary inheritors, all assets become the property of the state. Inheritors also become responsible for debts incurred by the testator. In the event of the death of a member of a collective farm, the assets pass to the legally defined inheritors. Specific regulations apply to division of assets deposited in various state savings treasuries and funds. Inheritance fees in the Ukrainian SSR are now fixed at 10 percent of the value of the inherited assets.

If the testator and the inheritors live in different countries, then inheritance is divided according to the laws of the country of residence of the deceased. Purportedly, the inherited assets pass untouched to the inheritors in the USSR or vice versa. According to this principle of international private law, the Soviet legal organs assiduously search for possible inheritances coming to their citizens and, to this end, have established broad legal contacts with the countries of destination of emigrants from the Soviet Union.

BIBLIOGRAPHY
Antymonov, B.; Grave, K. *Sovetskoe nasledstvennoe pravo* (Moscow 1955)
Hordon, M. *Radians'ke tsyvil'ne pravo* (Kharkiv 1966)
– *Nasledovanie po zakonu i po zaveschchaniiu* (Moscow 1967)
Iakymenko, O.; Baru; M., Hordon, M. (eds). *Tsyvil'nyi kodeks Ukraïns'koï RSR, Naukovo-praktychnyi komentarii* (Kiev 1971)
Nikitiuk, P. *Nasledstvennoe pravo i nasledstvennyi protsess* (Kishinev 1973)

J. Fedynskyj

Inhul River. A left-bank tributary of the Boh River, which it joins at Mykolaiv. The Inhul is 354 km long (30 km of which are floodplains) and has a basin area of 9,890 sq km. The upper Inhul flows through the Dnieper Upland and forms a narrow river bed in the granite base. In its middle stretch the river enters the Black Sea Lowland. The Inhul freezes in December and thaws in March. Its waters are used for domestic consumption and irrigation.

Inhulets [Inhulec']. VI-14. City (1970 pop 32,000) in Dnipropetrovske oblast, situated on the Inhulets River in the *Kryvyi Rih Iron-ore Basin and administered by a raion soviet of the city of *Kryvyi Rih. Inhulets was founded in the early 20th century as a mining town. In 1956 it received city status. The largest plant in the city is the Inhulets Mining and Enrichment Complex. The city also produces food and road-construction materials.

Inhulets Irrigation System. Built in 1951–63, this is one of the first irrigation systems in Ukraine. It is located on the right bank of the Dnieper River and in the basin of the Inhulets River, a tributary of the Dnieper. The system covers an area of 175,000 ha and supplies 62,700 ha of agricultural land in Mykolaiv and Kherson oblasts. The water from the Dnieper is diverted for 83 km upstream along the Inhulets by means of a pumping station that raises the water 60 m through two pipelines to a reservoir. From there it flows into the main canal, which conducts it 53 km along the northern limits of the irrigation system. Then it is fed into distribution canals (465 km total length), which transfer it to irrigation ditches (1,263 km total length). The drainage and waste-water disposal network consists of 600 km of conduits. About 4,000 hydrotechnical installations are used to distribute the water to the fields. Of the supply and irrigation canals, 1,100 km are concrete-lined. The October Reservoir (capacity 31.5 million cu m), which supplies Mykolaiv with drinking water, is an integral part of the Inhulets Irrigation System.

Inhulets River [Inhulec']. A right-bank tributary of the lower Dnieper River, with a length of 550 km and a basin area of 14,460 sq km. Its upper stretch lies in the Dnieper Upland, its lower stretch in the Black Sea Lowland. The river freezes in December and thaws in March. Its water volume varies. The Inhulets is accessible to small craft for 110 km upstream. The river supplies the *Inhulets Irrigation System. Its flow is regulated by nine reservoirs.

Initsiatyvnyky (Initiators). An action group of Baptists in the USSR that organized the dissident Council of Churches of Evangelical Christians-Baptists (CCECB). The Initsiatyvnyky date from 1960 when, in the course of N. Krushchev's antireligious campaign, the officially recognized and controlled All-Union Council of Evangelical Christians-Baptists (AUCECB) acceded to illegal Soviet demands for further restrictions on its proselytizing and baptism, including the exclusion of children from religious services. Led at the time by A. Prokofev (hence one of the early Soviet designations for the group was the Prokofevtsy) and G. Kriuchkov (the present head of the CCECB, in hiding), the Initsiatyvnyky unsuccessfully demanded the convocation of an extraordinary congress of the AUCECB. Known in 1962 as the 'Organizing Committee,' the group's members were subjected to public slander, police harassment, and numerous arrests and trials on trumped-up charges; nevertheless, in 1963 their protests compelled the AUCECB to withdraw some of the most objectionable 'self-restrictions' on Evangelical Christian-Baptist activities. By 1965, however, the unregistered Initsiatyvnyky congregations broke completely from the AUCECB and formed the CCECB, a decentralized and very successful underground religious organization with its own clandestine facilities for mass publication (it runs the Christian Press) and for the distribution of periodicals such as *Bratskii listok* and *Vestnik istiny*, Bibles, hymnbooks, and other religious literature. Although Soviet authorities prohibited the AUCECB from publishing in Ukrainian, since 1975 the CCECB has published the New Testament and two hymnbooks in Ukrainian.

In 1964 the mounting Soviet arrests of Initsiatyvnyky led to the formation of the Council of Relatives of Imprisoned Evangelical Christians-Baptists. This group publishes the *Biuleten Soveta rodstvennikov uznikov EkhB* (130 issues by 1985), which regularly reports on the persecution of Evangelical Christians-Baptists. According to its report for 1985, 143 dissident Baptists were held in prison, labor camps, psychiatric prisons, or internal exile; during the year, 52 followers of the CCECB were sentenced by Soviet courts. In 1985, the CCECB following was estimated at 2,000 congregations with some 100,000 baptized members. Among the members and the persecuted of the CCECB, Ukrainians constitute the largest national group.

In 1979, the imprisoned general secretary of the CCECB, Pastor G. Vins of Kiev, was expelled to the United States in an exchange for Soviet spies. Since 1980, he has headed the International Representation of the CCECB, headquartered in the United States.

BIBLIOGRAPHY
Bourdeaux, M. *Religious Ferment in Russia: Protestant Opposition to Soviet Religious Policy* (London 1968)
Sawatsky, W. *Soviet Evangelicals since World War II* (Scottdale, PA and Kitchener, Ont 1981)

B.R. Bociurkiw

Inkerman. A cliff in the Crimea near Sevastopil on the Chorna River. A Taurian settlement of the 9th century BC and a late Scythian burial ground of the 4th century AD were excavated there in the late 1940s. From the 6th to the 15th centuries the stronghold of Kalamita existed there; many of its dwellings and churches were built inside caves. In 1427 it became a port of the southwest-Crimean principality of Theodoro (Mangup). In 1475, Kalamita was captured by the Turks and renamed Inkerman. On 5 November 1854, a Russian army was routed there by the British-French forces besieging Sevastopil during the Crimean War.

Inkerman

Inkizhinov, Valerii [Inkižinov, Valerij], b 25 March 1895 in Irkutsk, Russia, d 27 September 1973 in Brunoy (Essonne), France. Actor and director. A Kirghiz by birth, he studied acting at the V. Meyerhold theater school. In 1919 he began to direct plays and to appear in films. During the 1926–7 season in Kharkiv he directed two productions of the *Berezil theater: *Sadie*, a dramatization of S. Maugham's 'Rain' by J. Colton and C. Randolph, and W. Gilbert and A. Sullivan's *The Mikado*, which included a number of skits on Kharkiv life by M. Khvylovy, M. Yohansen, and O. Vyshnia. As a film actor he is best known for his lead roles in *Potomok Chingis-Khana* (known in English as *Storm over Asia*, 1928) and *Kometa* (The Comet, 1930). Immigrating in 1930 to Germany and then to France, he continued to act in films, but played secondary roles.

Inlay: round wooden box by I. Semeniuk

Inlay. Ornamentation produced by embedding pieces of material such as bone, wood, straw, mother-of-pearl, glass, or metal in a surface of a different color or type. In Ukraine, inlay techniques have been used for many centuries. In 17th-century Hutsul wood carvings, crushed coal was rubbed into the incisions to enhance the contrast between the design and the background. In the 19th century, other types of inlay were developed in the Hutsul region; eg, M. *Mehedyniuk introduced colored-bead inlay, and V. *Devdiuk introduced intarsia, and metal and mother-of-pearl inlays. These techniques were used also by such master craftsmen as M. and V. Shkribliak and Yu., S., and P. *Korpaniuk. In the 1920s O. *Saienko introduced pure and dyed straw inlay.

Inlay: wooden plate by Yu. Korpaniuk

Inner Carpathian Valley. A wide, longitudinal valley in the eastern Carpathian Mountains stretching for 150 km between the *Polonynian Beskyd and the *Volcanic Ukrainian Carpathians. For the most part the valley follows the course of the small tributaries of the main transverse rivers of Transcarpathia, starting in the northwest in Slovakia at the Chirocha River, a tributary of the Laborets, and ending in the southeast at the Rika River. From there it broadens out into the wide *Maramureş Basin. Most of the valley lies at an altitude of 150–300 m. It rises to 450 m only at the valley passes. Because of suitable natural conditions, much of the valley is farmland and densely settled. Towns and raion centers – Snyna, Velykyi Bereznyi, Perechyn, and Svaliava – are located where the valley meets the main transverse river valleys.

Innitzer, Theodor, b 25 December 1875 in Vejprty, Bohemia, d 9 October 1955 in Vienna. Archbishop of Vienna (from 1932) and cardinal (from 1933). Ordained in 1902, he taught the New Testament at Vienna University (1913–32) and served as Austrian minister of social welfare (1929–30). A sympathetic supporter of Ukrainians, in the 1920s he helped Ukrainian émigrés in Austria through the Ukrainian Religious Committee in Vienna, and in 1933 he organized international relief for the starving population of Soviet Ukraine. As ordinary for the Greek Catholic congregations in Austria, in 1945 he appointed M. Hornykevych as their vicar-general.

Innocent IV, Pope (secular name: Sinibaldo Fieschi), b ca 1200 in Genoa, d 7 December 1254 in Naples. He was elected pope in 1243, and in 1245 at the General Council of Lyons called for a crusade to defend eastern Europe against the Tatar invasion, and for negotiations with the Eastern church to end the schism. Archbishop P. *Akerovych from Rus' took part in the council. To establish his influence in eastern Europe the pope made contacts with princes Danylo and Vasylko, the rulers of Galicia-Volhynia, through G. da Pian del Carpini, his emissary to the Mongols. In 1246–7 he corresponded with Danylo about an anti-Tatar coalition and church union. In 1253 Archimandrite Opizo brought Danylo a royal crown from the pope. Although Innocent IV issued a bull calling for a crusade against the Tatars, the campaign did not take place. The pope's letters to the Galician-Volhynian princes have been published in *Documenta Pontificum Romanorum Historiam Ucrainae Illustrantia (1075–1700)*, vol 1 (1953).

Innsbruck. City (1984 pop 117,000) on the Inn River in western Austria and capital of the Tirol federal state. In the summer of 1945, 4,000 Ukrainian displaced persons lived there, but most of them fled to Bavaria, whence they immigrated to North America. Innsbruck was the first center of the *Ukrainian Central Relief Alliance in Austria. Until 1951 Innsbruck had a Ukrainian Catholic and a Ukrainian Orthodox parish, a Ukrainian gymnasium, an Association of Ukrainians in the Tirol and Vorarlberg, and the Brotherhood of St Andrew. Some 450 Ukrainians studied at its university; they formed a Ukrainian student club (headed by M. Denysiuk) and published the irregular journals *Students'kyi shliakh, Zveno, Stezhi,* and *Na varti.* Before the Second World War the future Cardinal Y. Slipy and Archbishop I. Buchko were among the Ukrainians who studied at the Jesuit Theological Academy in Innsbruck. Today some 100 Ukrainians live in Innsbruck and its vicinity.

INO. See Institutes of people's education.

Inozemtsev, Aleksandr, b 1889 in Siberia, d 1948 in Munich. Russian Orthodox churchman. As bishop (from 1922) and later archbishop of Pynske and Podilia, he worked for more than 25 years with Ukrainians. In 1941, together with Bishop P. Sikorsky, he asked Metropolitan D. Valedinsky to assume spiritual responsibility over the Orthodox church in Ukraine. He participated in the consecration of bishops for the Ukrainian Autocephalous Orthodox church in February 1942 and served as the first chairman of the church's Synod of Bishops. In 1944 he immigrated to Germany.

Insabato, Enrico, b 21 September 1878 in Bologna, d 6 March 1963. Italian political activist and publicist, expert on Arabian and Ukrainian affairs, and supporter of Ukrainian independence. As a result of Insabato's efforts, the Italian premier, V. Orlando, agreed to send 80,000 Ukrainian prisoners of war to combat the Bolshevik invasion of 1917–18, but this was blocked by the French premier, G. Clemenceau, who feared the Ukrainians would be used against the Poles. Elected by the Italian Peasant's party to Parliament, Insabato vigorously opposed Mussolini's recognition of the Bolshevik regime. He was an executive member of the Ukrainian-Italian Friendship Association and an active member of the Shevchenko Scientific Society (from 1955). He was the author of many publicistic essays, including *Ucraina e la Chiesa Cattolica* (1933) and *Ucraina: Populazione e economia* (1938).

Inscriptions. Written matter carved, scratched, or painted on hard or durable materials. The study of inscriptions (*epigraphy) provides linguists with data on linguistic phenomena of a given period. Inscriptions appear in great numbers in Ukraine. The earliest date back to the 7th century BC when Greek colonies sprang up on the Black Sea coast, but these are irrelevant to the history of the Ukrainian language. The oldest inscriptions pertaining to the history of Ukraine appeared with the introduction of Christianity and of the Cyrillic alphabet in Ukraine. They include the name and the title of Queen Anna Yaroslavna of France written on a charter (1063), an invocatory text on a Chernihiv *hryvnia* of the 11th century, an inscription on the goblet of Prince Volodymyr of Chernihiv (before 1151), and an inscription on the cross of Princess Yevfrosyniia of Polatsk made by a Kievan artisan in 1161. Inscriptions on coins are known from the time of Volodymyr the Great (ca 980–1015) and Prince Sviatopolk (1015–19). Inscriptions on seals are known from the late 10th century on (see *Sphragistics). In later periods the number of inscriptions on various objects increased substantially. (See also *Graffiti.)

Insignia. See Regalia.

Institut zur Erforschung der UdSSR. See Institute for the Study of the USSR.

Institute, Physical-Technical, of the Academy of Sciences of the Ukrainian SSR. See Physical-Technical Institute of the Academy of Sciences of the Ukrainian SSR.

Institute for Demography and Sanitation Statistics of the Academy of Sciences of the Ukrainian SSR. See Demography.

Institute for Nationalities Research (Polish: Instytut Badań Spraw Narodowościowych; Ukrainian: Instytut doslidiv natsional'nykh sprav). A research institute in Warsaw that existed from 1921 to 1939. It sponsored research, organized public lectures and seminars, and published numerous research reports, primarily on the national minorities in interwar Poland (Ukrainians, Belorussians, etc), but also on the general problem of minorities in Europe and on Polish communities outside Poland. The institute was headed by several associates of J. Piłsudski: L. Wasilewski, T. Hołówko, S. Thugutt, and S. Paprocki. Its organ from 1927 was **Sprawy narodowościowe*. Major contributions to the study of Ukrainians in Galicia were made by prominent Ukrainian coworkers of the institute such as M. Kovalevsky and B. Rzhepetsky.

Institute for Nuclear Research of the Academy of Sciences of the Ukrainian SSR (Instytut yadernykh doslidzhen AN URSR). An institute established in 1970 as an outgrowth of six nuclear-research departments at the AN URSR *Institute of Physics. Its scientists (217 in 1980) are involved in research and development in theoretical and experimental low- and medium-energy nuclear physics, nuclear spectroscopy, nuclear-power technology, radiation physics, materials science, and plasma physics. The institute has a staff of close to 700 in 21 departments (1 in Uzhhorod); it operates two cyclotrons, an experimental nuclear reactor, several advanced computers, a design section, and a graduate program. Its directors have been M. Pasichnyk (1970–3) and O. Niemets (1974–).

Institute for Problems of Machine Building of the Academy of Sciences of the Ukrainian SSR (Instytut problem mashynobuduvannia AN URSR). A technological institute established in Kharkiv in 1972 to replace a branch of the AN URSR *Institute of Technical Thermophysics. It has 16 departments, 4 laboratories, a computer center, a technological-design bureau, and a developmental production center. Its scientists (167 in 1980) conduct research in the fields of mechanical engineering, solid-state and fluid mechanics, applied and theoretical mathematics and computer science, hydroelectric and nuclear energy, machine reliability, internal-combustion machines, and various aspects of machine building. The institute publishes the periodical *Problemy mashinostroeniia*. Its director is A. Pidhorny.

Institute for Problems of Materials Science of the Academy of Sciences of the Ukrainian SSR (Instytut problem materialoznavstva AN URSR). A technological institute in Kiev, formed in 1955 from the AN URSR special alloys laboratory under I. Frantsevych. Until 1964 it was called the Institute of Metal Ceramics and Special Alloys. The institute has 28 departments, 5 laboratories, a design office, a pilot plant, and a graduate program. Its scientists (668 in 1980) are engaged in x-ray and electromagnetic analysis, solid-state physics and chemistry, structural studies and materials design, and technology. The institute is the world's leading research center of powder metallurgy; it co-ordinates the work of 432 concerns and 39 government agencies in this field throughout the USSR, and publishes the journal *Poroshkovaia metallurgiia / Powder Metallurgy* (1961–). It has designed and supervised the construction of over 100 metallurgical concerns, including the largest powder-metallurgy factory in the world in Brovary, and plants in Zaporizhia, Donetske, Poltava, and Yerevan. It is also the leading Soviet research center for electric heating appliances, and the center of Ukraine's solar-energy research. The institute's directors have been I. *Frantsevych (1955–73) and V. Trefilov (1973–).

Institute for Problems of Modeling in Energetics. See Institute of Electrodynamics.

Institute for Problems of the Strength of Materials of the Academy of Sciences of the Ukrainian SSR (Instytut problem mitsnosti materialiv AN URSR). A unique Soviet technological institute, directed by H. Pysarenko. It was established in Kiev in 1966 out of the Strength of Materials Section (formed in 1951) of the AN URSR Institute for Problems of Materials Sciences. It has 13 departments, a laboratory, a design office, a pilot plant, and a graduate program. Its scientists (164 in 1980) focus on investigating failure of mechanisms, experimental and theoretical reliability prediction, and calculation and evaluation of the strength of various structural materials under extreme conditions. The results of this research are applied in the nuclear industry, cryogenics, gas pipelines, and machine building. Research results are published in the institute's journal *Problems of Strength / Problemy prochnosti* (1969–).

Institute for the Study of the USSR (Instytut dlia vyvchennia SSSR; German: Institute zur Erforschung der UDSSR). An American-sponsored research institute founded in Munich in July 1950 by a group of émigré scholars from the Soviet Union. Originally called the Institute for the Study of the Culture and History of the USSR, the institute's aim was to conduct research on various aspects of the state and society of the USSR, especially the nationalities question. The first president of its Learned Council was B. Martos. Other prominent members were A. Yakovliv, I. Bakalo, M. Miller, P. Kurinny, and B. Krupnytsky. The institute had a varied publication program of periodicals, monographs, and conference proceedings in several languages, including the journals *Ukraïns'kyi zbirnyk* (17 issues, 1954–60) and *Ukrainian Review* (9 issues, 1955–60). Among its publications were works by P. Fedenko, V. Holubnychy, H. Kostiuk, N. Polonska-Vasylenko, D. Solovei, and other Ukrainian scholars. By 1960 it had 45 full and 29 corresponding members. The institute was dissolved in June 1972.

Institute of Applied Mathematics and Mechanics of the Academy of Sciences of the Ukrainian SSR (Instytut prykladnoi matematyky i mekhaniky AN URSR). A scientific research institute established in 1970 in Donetske, succeeding the academy's Donetske Computing Center (est 1965). It has a staff of over 120 in nine departments, where mathematical physics, solid-state dynamics, multivariable differential equations, function theory, probability theory, mathematical statistics, applied mechanics, elasticity theory, and other technical subjects are studied. Much of the research is focused on computer applications in industrial programs and automation systems. The directors of the institute have been I. Danyliuk (1965–74), A. Bogomolov (1974–7), and I. Skrypnyk. The institute publishes the periodic compendiums *Mekhanika tverdogo tela* and *Teoriia sluchainykh protsessov* and has a graduate program and a control-system design center.

Institute of Archeology of the Academy of Sciences of the Ukrainian SSR (Instytut arkheolohii AN URSR). A research institute established in 1938 in Kiev. Its forerunners include the Kiev Archeological Institute (1917–24), the *All-Ukrainian Archeological Committee (1923–34), and the Institute of the History of Material Culture of the Academy of Sciences of the Ukrainian SSR (1934–8). The institute co-ordinates all written and field research in archeology and ancient history in Ukraine. In 1970 a separate branch for the study of Kiev's archeology was created. At the present time the institute has 12 departments and 4 sectors. Two preserve areas – Olviia (est 1952) near Parutyne, Ochakiv raion, Mykolaiv oblast, and Kamiana Mohyla (est 1954) near Terpinnia, Melitopil raion, Zaporizhia oblast – are maintained by the institute. The institute has published specialized monographs and collections and several serials: *Arkheolohiia* (1st series, 24 vols, 1947–70; 2nd series, 48 vols, 1971–84), *Arkheolohichni pam'iatky URSR* (13 vols, 1949–63), *Kratkie soobshcheniia Instituta arkheologii AN URSR* (12 issues, 1952–62), and *Arkheologicheskie issledovaniia na Ukraine* (4 issues, 1967–72). In 1985 it had a staff of 130 scholars. In 1984 a history of the institute was published in Kiev. (See also *Archeology.)

Institute of Biochemistry of the Academy of Sciences of the Ukrainian SSR (Instytut biokhimii im. O.V. Palladina AN URSR). Research institute founded in Kharkiv in 1925 on the basis of the Chair of Physiology at the Kharkiv Agricultural Institute. Originally it was called the Ukrainian Biochemical Institute. Since 1931 it has been part of the AN URSR in Kiev. The institute primarily conducts and publishes research in molecular biology and animal and human biochemistry. In 1969 a branch was established in Lviv. In 1980 it had 10 departments, 8 laboratories, and a staff of 502 (125 scholars). A number of prominent biochemists have worked or are working at the institute: O. Palladin, who founded one of the largest Soviet schools of biochemistry and whose name the institute now carries, D. Ferdman, M. Huly, V. Belitser, and R. Chahovets. Its current director is V. Lishko. The institute published the journal *Naukovi zapysky Ukraïns'koho biokhimichnoho instytutu* beginning in 1926. In 1934 it was replaced by *Ukraïns'kyi biokhimichnyi zhurnal*, which was published until 1978. A bimonthly journal – *Ukrainskii biokhimicheskii zhurnal* – and a periodical collection – *Biokhimiia zhivotnykh i cheloveka* – are now published in Russian by the institute.

Institute of Botany of the Academy of Sciences of the Ukrainian SSR (Instytut botaniky im. M.H. Kholodnoho AN URSR). Research institute founded in 1921 as the Botanical Cabinet and Herbarium of the Ukrainian Academy of Sciences in Kiev. In 1931 it was merged with the Scientific Research Institute of Botany of the People's Commissariat of Education of the Ukrainian SSR, and in 1971 it was given its present name, to honor the prominent botanist M. Kholodny. The institute conducts and publishes research on the vegetation of Ukraine and its protection and use in agriculture and medicine, and on plant physiology and biochemistry, geobotany, systematics, and ecology. Directed by K. Sytnyk, in 1980 it had a staff of over 400 (172 scholars) in 14 departments, 4 of which are part of a branch of the institute in Lviv (founded in 1973), 2 laboratories, and an experimental field laboratory. It manages the *Ukrainian Steppe Nature Reserve and since 1921 has published a bimonthly journal – **Ukraïns'kyi botanichnyi zhurnal* – and monographs, of which the most valuable have been *Vyznachnyk roslyn URSR* (Field Guide to the Plants of the Ukrainian SSR, 1950), **Flora URSR* (The Flora of the Ukrainian SSR, 12 vols, 1936–65), *Roslynnist' URSR* (The Vegetation of the Ukrainian SSR, 4 vols, 1968–73), and *Vyznachnyk hrybiv Ukraïny* (Field Guide to the Fungi of Ukraine, 5 vols, 1967–79). (See also *Botany.)

Institute of Colloidal Chemistry and Hydrochemistry of the Academy of Sciences of the Ukrainian SSR. See Chemistry.

Institute of Cybernetics of the Academy of Sciences of the Ukrainian SSR (Instytut kibernetyky AN URSR im. V.M. Hlushkova). A major scientific research institute established in Kiev in 1962, succeeding the AN URSR Computing Center (est 1957). It has a staff of over 2,000 in 52 departments, 27 laboratories, and its own powerful computing center. It also has a design center with a staff of 2,000 and its own pilot plant. Research is focused on computer programming and design, automation and systems theory and design, economic, technical, biological, and medical cybernetics, control systems, robotics, and mathematical economics. The institute's associates have designed and constructed the MIR, Promin, Dnepr, Kiev, Iskra, Ros, and other computers, including the first Soviet microcomputers. The institute publishes the semimonthly journals **Kibernetika* (1965–), *Avtomatika* (1963–), and *Upravliaiushchie sistemy i mashiny* (1972–), and the periodic compendiums *Kibernetika i vychislitel'naia tekhnika* and *Naukovedenie i informatika*. It also prepared and published the first Soviet encyclopedia of cybernetics (2 vols, 1973–4), in Ukrainian. Its directors have been V. *Hlushkov (1962–82) and V. Mykhalevych.

Institute of Economics of the Academy of Sciences of the Ukrainian SSR (Instytut ekonomiky AN URSR). Research institute founded in Kiev in 1936 on the basis of the Agroeconomics Institute of the All-Ukrainian Association of Marxist-Leninist Scientific Research Institutes (VUAMLIN). In 1938 the Institute of Demography and Health Statistics of the academy was incorporated into it. The institute conducts and publishes research in political economy, planning and economic management, Ukraine's economic growth and development, industrial economics, statistics and demography, Ukraine's economic history, and economic thought in Ukraine. With its branches in Lviv, Kharkiv, and Odessa (established in 1964, 1965, and 1970 respectively), in 1980 it consisted of 30 departments with a staff of 1,080 (287 scholars). The institute operates three computer centers and trains graduate economists. Its current director is (since 1976) I. Lukinov. It publishes monographs and collections, two interagency serials – *Istoriia narodnoho hospodarstva ta ekonomichnoï dumky Ukraïns'koi RSR* (1965–) and *Demohrafichni doslidzhennia* (1969–) – and, since 1958, the journal **Ekonomika Radians'koï Ukraïny*. (See also *Demography, *Economic geography, *Economic press, and *Economic studies.)

Institute of Electric Welding of the Academy of Sciences of the Ukrainian SSR (Instytut electrozvariuvannia AN URSR im. Ye.O. Patona). A major Soviet scientific research institute established in Kiev in 1934. Probably the world's most important center of research in electric-arc welding and special electrometallurgy, it has attracted some of the foremost scientists in these fields, including I. Pokhodnia and V. Lebedev. The institute has pioneered many applications in welding technology, many of which are used worldwide; it has granted over 30 major foreign licenses; and it participated in the world's first experiments in cutting and welding metal in outer space, on the Soiuz 6 space station (1969). The institute publishes the monthly journal *Avtomaticheskaia svarka* and the compendium *Problemy spetsiial'noi elektrometallurgii*, and has a graduate program and a permanent

UN seminar for engineers from the developing countries. Its directors have been Ye. *Paton (1934–53) and his son B. *Paton. It has a staff of over 2,000 in 43 departments and laboratories, and over 4,700 employees in its experimental technological design center and two experimental plants (electromachine building and welded materials).

Institute of Electrodynamics of the Academy of Sciences of the Ukrainian SSR (Instytut electrodynamiky AN URSR). A research institute founded in Kiev in 1947, succeeding the electrotechnical branch of the Institute of Energetics. Until 1963 it was called the Institute of Electrotechnology. Research at the institute is focused on electromagnetic energy generation, conversion, and transmission, energy systems, energy measuring devices and generators, electronics, and computing systems. The institute has a staff of over 750 in 15 departments and an experimental production center with over 200 employees. During the years 1949–51 its staff constructed the MEOM, the first digital computer outside the United States. In 1957 the computer-design section became the AN URSR Computing Center, and in 1962 the *Institute of Cybernetics. The institute has been directed by S. Lebedev (1947–52), A. Nesterenko (1952–9), O. Miliakh (1959–73), and A. Shydlovsky. It has a graduate program and publishes the periodic compendium *Problemy tekhnicheskoi elektrodinamiki*.

The Sector of Electronics and Modeling was created within the institute in 1971. In 1981 it became the new Institute for Problems of Modeling in Energetics. Its staff, in 14 departments directed by G. Pukhov, studies mainly analog and digital control systems and automatization and their application in energetics, electronics, and the aviation industry. The new institute publishes the periodic compendium *Gibridnye vychislitel'nye mashiny i kompleksy*. It has a branch devoted to electric-energy magnetohydrodynamic generators.

L. Onyshkevych

Institute of Fine Arts, Folklore, and Ethnography of the Academy of Sciences of the Ukrainian SSR (Instytut mystetstvoznavstva, folkloru ta etnohrafii im. M.T. Rylskoho AN URSR). A leading research institute. Founded in 1936 as the Institute of Ukrainian Folklore, it replaced the abolished VUAN *Ethnographic Commission, *Cabinet of Anthropology and Ethnology, Cabinet of Musical Ethnography, Cabinet of Primitive Culture, Chair of Ukraine's History, and Commission for Historical Songs. Some of these had been incorporated into the new Institute of the History of Material Culture (1934–8), which had its own folkloristic-ethnographic section with a museum and cabinet of musical ethnography (headed by V. Kharkiv).

The Institute of Ukrainian Folklore had three sectors: oral folklore, headed by M. Nahorny (1937–9) and M. Pavlii (1939–41); musical folklore, headed by M. Haidai (1936–7), P. Kozytsky (1937–8), and M. Hrinchenko (1938–41); and financial resources. Its first director was the former deputy commissar of education, A. Khvylia. He was replaced in 1939 by Yu. Sokolov, who was brought in from Moscow University and elected a full member of the AN URSR. In the prewar Stalinist period its main focus was the collection and study of new 'Soviet' folklore and providing assistance to those who created it. Folk tales, legends, myths, and other traditional folk genres were deemed 'vestiges of capitalism.'

After the Soviet occupation of Galicia, in November 1939 a branch of the institute was created out of the abolished ethnographic section of the Shevchenko Scientific Society and headed by F. *Kolessa. After the outbreak of the German-Soviet War, in July 1941 the institute was evacuated to Ufa, Bashkiria, where it was reduced to a department of the AN URSR Institute of Social Sciences with a staff of two. In June 1942 the Institute of Folk Creativity and Art was formed there under the directorship of M. Hrinchenko and, after his death in November, M. *Rylsky.

From August 1943 to March 1944 the institute operated from Moscow, and in March 1944 it was substantially reorganized and re-established in Kiev under its current name. M. Rylsky remained its director until his death in 1964, when the institute was named in his honor. His successors have been M. Syvachenko (1964–73) and S. Zubkov (1974–). In 1982 a branch of the institute was created in Lviv out of the Ukrainian State Museum of Ethnography and Crafts; it is directed by Yu. Hoshko.

The institute's policies and research have largely been subject to non-scholarly, Soviet political considerations; this bias has been reflected in many of its publications.

Today the institute has 10 research departments: musicology, theater studies, cinema studies, visual art, art theory, the theoretical problems of the artistic development of the masses, folkloristics, Slavic folkloristics, ethnography, and Soviet holidays and rituals. In accordance with Soviet nationality policy, it promotes and publishes research on the Ukrainian arts and ethnography in the context of contemporary interethnic relations in the USSR and the Soviet bloc and their mutual 'enrichment' and 'internationalization.' Emphasis has been placed on the study of working-class culture, historical ethnography, the culture and folkways of the inhabitants of the Carpathian Mountains, and museology. The institute has published the periodicals **Ukraïns'kyi fol'klor* (1937–9), *Narodna tvorchist'* (1939–41), and **Narodna tvorchist' ta etnohrafiia* (1957–). Its most important project, however, has been a 35-volume series Ukraïns'ka narodna tvorchist' (Ukrainian Folk Creativity), of which 23 volumes have been published. Multiple-author, three-volume histories of Ukrainian decorative and applied folk art, Ukrainian classical music, and Ukrainian cinema will be published in the near future. In 1986 the institute had a staff of 151 of which 97 were scholarly associates.

(See also *Art studies and research, *Ethnography, *Musicology, and *Theater studies.)

M. Hnatiukivsky

Institute of Gas of the Academy of Sciences of the Ukrainian SSR. See Chemistry.

Institute of General and Inorganic Chemistry of the Academy of Sciences of the Ukrainian SSR. See Chemistry.

Institute of Geological Sciences of the Academy of Sciences of the Ukrainian SSR (Instytut heolohichnykh nauk AN URSR). An institute formed in Kiev in 1926 from the merger of several geological sections of the VUAN and of the People's Commissariat of Education.

Until 1934 it was called the Geological Institute, and then, until 1939, the Institute of Geology. The institute has 16 departments, 3 laboratories, a geological museum (est 1927), a library, a branch in Kryvyi Rih (est 1972), a research drilling ship, and an experimental pilot plant (est 1980). Its Lviv branch (1939–41, 1944–50) became the *Institute of the Geology and Geochemistry of Fossil Fuels. The Ukrainian Paleontological Society, the Ukrainian Stratigraphic Committee, and the republican scientific councils on hydrology and engineering geology and on the geology of seas and oceans are affiliated with the institute.

The institute's scientists (144 in 1980) conduct research in general, Precambrian, marine, and petroleum geology, geotectonics, lithology, stratigraphy, hydrogeology, and paleontology. They systematically study Ukraine's territory and seas with the aim of locating new mineral deposits and have written theoretical studies on the volcanic formation of islands, comparative planetology, and the mathematical modeling of shock-wave effect on mineral transformations. Much theoretical and applied work has been done in hydrogeology (the location and tapping of underground water resources near major Ukrainian urban centers, the rational use of water, and soil amelioration). The institute's members also participate in international studies of oceans. Research areas that have recently been developed include coal and marine geology, the modeling of geological heat- and mass-transfer processes, and the application of aerogeology and cosmic geology as a prospecting tool.

Research results have been published as monographs and in the journal *Geologicheskii zhurnal* (1934–). The institute's directors have all been prominent geologists: P. Tutkovsky (1926–30), V. Riznychenko (1930–2), M. Svitalsky (1934–7), Ye. Burkser (1938–9), B. Chernyshov (1939–46), V. Luchytsky (1947–9), A. Babynets (1949–53), V. Bondarchuk (1953–63), V. Porfirev (1963–8), Ye. Lazarenko (1969–71), V. Didkovsky (1971–7), and E. Shniukov (1977–).

S. Trofimenko

Institute of Geophysics of the Academy of Sciences of the Ukrainian SSR (Instytut heofizyky im. S.I. Subbotina AN URSR). A scientific institute established in Kiev in 1960 as an outgrowth of the work of the AN URSR Institute of Geological Sciences. The institute has 9 departments, a technological design office, 8 laboratories, 10 seismic stations, 2 magnetometric stations, 2 magnetic observatories, and an astrophysical observatory. Since 1964 the *Poltava Gravimetric Observatory has been subordinate to it. In the USSR it leads the way in the interpretation of geological-geophysical data and in the development of a gravitational model of the earth's crust. Its scientists (129 in 1980) study the structure, composition, formation, tectonic movements, and changes in the earth's crust and mantle, using seismic, gravimetric, magnetometric, radiation, and satellite survey methods; detailed mapping of the earth's gravitational, thermal, electric, and magnetic fields; radioactive dating and paleomagnetism; and theoretical geophysics (including mathematical modeling). The development and improvement of research methodology, technology, and instrumentation and the computerization of data collection and processing are important components of the institute's work. The institute publishes the bimonthly journal *Geofizicheskii sbornik*. Its directors have been S. Subbotin (1960–76) and A. Chekunov (1976–).

Institute of Geotechnical Mechanics of the Academy of Sciences of the Ukrainian SSR (Instytut heotekhnichnoi mekhaniky AN URSR). An institute in Dnipropetrovske formed in 1967 out of a branch (est 1962) of the AN URSR *Institute of Mechanics. It has 13 departments, a laboratory, a special construction-technology bureau, and a pilot plant. Its scientists (136 in 1982) study geological processes related to mining and develop the technological basis for the mining industry in Ukraine. The institute's directors have been M. Poliakov (1967–75) and V. Poturaev (1975–).

Institute of Gerontology of the Academy of Medical Sciences of the USSR (Instytut herontolohii AMN SRSR). A scientific research institute established in Kiev in the fall of 1958 for the purpose of studying medical, pathological, and social aspects of aging. Its chief founder and first director was M. *Horiev, who in 1962 was succeeded by D. *Chebotarov. As the only such institution in the USSR, it is responsible for co-ordinating and overseeing all gerontological and geriatric research and clinical work in the Soviet Union and the socialist countries. It is the largest center for gerontological research in Europe and a member of the World Health Organization network. The institute administers major studies and surveys of aging in the USSR, and regularly sponsors all-Union and international conferences, symposia, and courses. The institute has 5 departments, 12 laboratories, 4 clinical divisions, and a polyclinic. Its staff numbers 600. The monthly journal *Gerontologiia i geriatriia* is published by the institute.

Institute of History of the Academy of Sciences of the Ukrainian SSR (Instytut istorii AN URSR). Research institute established in 1936 out of various liquidated institutions of the VUAN and the Ukrainian Institute of Marxism-Leninism (UIML). Both the institute and its predecessors have played a seminal role in historical scholarship in Ukraine.

The antecedents of the institute were the Historical Section and its chairs and commissions, and the *Historical Society of Nestor the Chronicler in the VUAN historical-philological division. By 1924 the section had a Chair of Ukrainian History (directed by M. *Hrushevsky) in Kiev and another (directed by D. *Bahalii) in Kharkiv, and several other chairs. The activity of the first was most diverse, and it became the central institution of historical research, co-ordinating the work of almost all the other historical institutions and historians affiliated with the VUAN; it also published *Studiï z istoriï Ukraïny* (3 vols, 1926–30). The Historical Section published the journal **Ukraïna* (1924–32) and six issues of *Kul'turno-istorychnyi zbirnyk* (1924–9). Its Cultural History Commission published *Pervisne hromadianstvo ta ioho perezhytky na Ukraïni* (6 vols, 1926–9) under the editorship of K. *Hrushevska. The Commission for Compiling a Historical-Geographical Dictionary of Ukraine published *Istorychno-heohrafichnyi zbirnyk* (4 vols, 1927–31) under the editorship of O. Hrushevsky. Four commissions were engaged in regional history. The first (headed by V. *Shcherbyna) conducted research on Kiev and Right-Bank Ukraine; the second (headed by O. *Hermaize), on Left-

Bank Ukraine; the third (headed by M. *Tkachenko), on Southern Ukraine; and the fourth (headed by F. *Savchenko), on Western Ukraine. Each of them published or had prepared collections of research. The Archeographic Commission (directed by O. Hermaize) published *Ukraïns'kyi arkheohrafichnyi zbirnyk* (3 vols, 1926–30) and a volume of *Ukraïns'kyi arkhiv* (1929).

Volumes 6, 11, 17, 20, and 24 of the **Zapysky Istorychno-filolohichnoho viddilu* VUAN were solely devoted to history and were subtitled *Pratsi* of the Historical Section. Besides serials, most of them edited by M. Hrushevsky, the section published collections of articles on the Decembrist movement in Ukraine (2 vols, 1926, 1930) and Ukraine's socioeconomic history (1932), festschrifts for D. Bahalii (1927) and M. Hrushevsky (1928–9), and books by Bahalii, Hrushevsky, P. Klymenko, O. Baranovych, I. Dzhydzhora, V. Levynsky, F. Savchenko, and O. Hermaize.

From 1922 the institute's antecedents at the UIML in Kharkiv were the department, chair, and cabinet of Ukrainian history headed by M. *Skrypnyk and M. *Yavorsky. In 1931 the UIML became part of the new *All-Ukrainian Association of Marxist-Leninist Institutes (VUAMLIN), and an Institute of History was established there; the latter published a one-volume history of Ukraine in 1932.

The invaluable work of all these institutions was cut short during the Stalinist terror of the early 1930s. Many historians were killed or sent to the GULAG; the historical-philological division was closed down; and virtually all research and publishing were halted. A Historical-Archeological Institute, headed by F. Kozubovsky and then I. *Kravchenko, was established in 1934 to fight 'Ukrainian bourgeois historiography.' In 1936 it was merged with the VUAMLIN Institute of History to form the Institute of History of Ukraine in the Division of Social Sciences of the newly created AN URSR. Thenceforth the institute propagated a Stalinist, Russian chauvinist historiography. It was headed briefly by A. Saradzhev and then S. Belousov (1936–41). In 1940, a branch of the institute was opened in Lviv in newly annexed Galicia on the foundation of the liquidated historicophilosophical section of the Shevchenko Scientific Society; the branch was headed by I. Krypiakevych until 1941. Between 1936 and 1941 the institute had only 16 scholarly associates.

After Germany invaded Soviet Ukraine in 1941, the institute was evacuated to Ufa, Bashkiria, and merged with the Institute of Archeology to form the Institute of History and Archeology under M. Petrovsky (1942–7). From 1943 to 1944 the institute was based in Moscow. Upon its return to Kiev it was reorganized in 1944 and again in 1952. The activities of the Lviv branch were revived as part of the AN URSR *Institute of Social Sciences there. In 1947 the institute was condemned for fostering Ukrainian nationalism, and the little work that was done diminished even further under the new director, O. *Kasymenko (1947–64). Little of lasting value was published in the years 1934–54.

During the post-Stalin thaw, however, the institute became one of the focal points of the Soviet Ukrainian cultural revival; a great deal of new research on Ukrainian history was conducted, and many fundamental Stalinist historiographic concepts were criticized and modified. In the 1960s a non-official historiography evolved (see, eg, M. *Braichevsky), which even rejected these concepts. At the time K. Dubyna was the institute's director (1964–7). The institute was again condemned for fostering nationalism in the early 1970s. During the KGB clampdown against the Ukrainian *dissident movement in 1972, some historians at the institute were fired (eg, Ya. Dzyra); others were blacklisted and even arrested; and even the CPU watchdog at the institute, A. Skaba (1968–73), was replaced by A. Shevelev (1973–8), under whom the topics that could be researched were severely limited. Since 1979, however, under the current director, Yu. Kondufor, some relaxation has been discernible.

In 1978 a section of the institute and subdivisions of the AN URSR Institute of Economics formed the new *Institute of Social and Economic Problems of Foreign Countries. Today the Institute of History consists of 17 departments, whose approx 100 scholars study the history of Ukraine, historiography, sources, ancillary historical disciplines, Ukraine's relations with foreign countries, regional history, the history of the socialist countries, the history of science, the history of technology, the Ukrainian diaspora, and the international-workers and national-liberation movements. Between 1936 and 1986 it published nearly 8,500 monographs, collections of articles and documents, textbooks, and brochures; many of them, however, are devoid of real scholarly value. The institute's major periodicals have been *Naukovi zapysky Instytutu istorii* (13 vols, 1943–60) and **Ukraïns'kyi istorychnyi zhurnal* (bimonthly from 1956, monthly since 1965). A history of the institute (1936–86) by A. Santsevych and N. Komarenko was published in Russian in Kiev in 1986. (See also *Archeography and *Historiography.)

I. Myhul, R. Senkus

Institute of Hydrobiology of the Academy Sciences of the Ukrainian SSR (Instytut hidrobiolohii AN URSR). A research institute in Kiev established in 1939 on the basis of the AN URSR Dnieper Biological Station (est 1909). It has 13 departments, 3 laboratories, 4 experimental bases and stations, 2 large research ships, and a small fleet of vessels. Its scientists (over 100 in 1985) conduct research in hydrobiology, limnology, ichthyology, hydrochemistry, water management and ecology, algology, toxicology, and parasitology; they study the biological resources and industrial pollution of Ukraine's water bodies and canals and develop methods for improving or correcting them. The institute publishes the bimonthly journal *Gidrobiologicheskii zhurnal* (1965–). Its directors have been Ya. Roll (1939–59), O. Topachevsky (1959–73), L. Sirenko (1974–5), V. Maliuk (1975–9), and V. Romanenko (1979–).

Institute of Hydromechanics of the Academy of Sciences of the Ukrainian SSR (Instytut hidromekhaniky AN URSR). A research institute founded in Kiev in 1926 on the basis of the Chair of Hydrology of the Kiev Polytechnical Institute as the Institute of Water Management of the Council of People's Commissars of the Ukrainian SSR. It became part of the AN URSR in 1934 and was restructured and renamed the Institute of Hydrology in 1938 and the Institute of Hydrology and Hydrotechnology in 1944. It received its present name in 1963. The institute has a staff of around 400 in 10 departments, devoted to various aspects of hydraulics, hydromechanics, water filtration, water conservation, hydraulic structures, and hydrodynamics. It also has an experimental production center with 100 employees, and a computer center. Research performed at the institute has been widely used throughout the USSR (eg, in the construction of hydroelectric stations and irrigation and drainage systems, in long-distance water transport in the polar regions, and in fighting erosion). The institute has been directed by Ye. Opokov (1926–37), A. Ohiievsky (1937–9), H. Sukhomel (1940–58), M. Didkovsky (1958–65), G. Logvinovich (1966–71), O. Oliinyk (1972–81), and A. Fedorovsky. It publishes the republican interagency compendiums *Gidromekhanika* and *Bionika*.

Institute of Jewish Culture of the All-Ukrainian Academy of Sciences (Instytut ievreiskoi kultury pry VUAN). An institution founded in Kiev in November 1926 to co-ordinate and promote Yiddish pedagogy and scholarship and Jewish studies in Soviet Ukraine. It was originally a Chair of Jewish Culture. Its first director was the philologist and Jewish civic figure N. Shtif. In 1919 a Hebraist Historical-Archeographic Commission had been established at the VUAN under A. Krymsky; its real leader, however, was I. Galant. The commission published articles in Ukrainian learned journals and collections and its own *Zbirnyk prats'* (2 vols, 1928–9) before being abolished in 1929. It was then that the Chair of Jewish Culture, under the direction of Y. Liberberg, was upgraded into an institute.

The institute had a sizable staff (30 in 1929, over 100 in 1934) and consisted of eight sections: philology (headed by N. Shtif and then E. Spivak), history (Y. Liberberg and then A. Margolis), literature (N. Oyslender and then M. Wiener), pedagogy-pedology (Y. Yakhinson), socio-economic (I. Weizblit, from 1930), bibliology (A. Kvitny); ethnography (M. Wiener), and Birobidzhan studies (from 1934). It had a large library (based on that of the former Jewish Historical-Ethnographic Society, est 1908), an archive (including that of the Society for the Spread of Enlightenment among the Jews of Russia, est 1863), a bibliographic center, a press archive, and a graduate program. A branch in Odessa, with the historian S. Borovoi as head, was short-lived (1928–9). The institute worked closely with official Jewish scholarly institutions in Moscow and Minsk.

With the demise of the policy of *Ukrainization and the onslaught of Stalinism, the institute suffered persecution (eg, the harassment of Shtif [d 1933] and the removal of Weizblit in 1931 and Oystender in 1932). Nonetheless, from 1931 to 1936 it was the leading Jewish scholarly institution in the USSR. In 1934 Liberberg and many other members of the institute immigrated to the new Jewish Autonomous oblast in Birobidzhan, and G. Gorokhov became the new director. In 1936 the institute was suddenly closed down, and Gorokhov and most of its other staff were arrested as 'Trotskyists' and 'Zionists.' In late 1936 the institute was replaced by a downgraded Cabinet for the Study of Soviet Jewish Literature, Language, and Folklore under E. Spivak. In 1949, during the Zhdanov purge of Jewish culture, the cabinet was liquidated and its members were arrested.

Important publications of the institute and the cabinet are the journals *Di Yidishe Shprach* (24 issues, 1927–30), *Shriftn* (1 vol, 1928), and the quarterly *Visnshaft un revoliutsye* (1934–6); a bibliological collection (1930); I. Weizblit's study of Jewish population dynamics in Ukraine in 1897–1926 (1930); A. Yuditsky's history of the Jewish bourgeoisie in Russia in the first half of the 19th century (1931); M. Berehovsky's book on Yiddish musical folklore (1934); and M. Wiener's history of 19th-century Yiddish literature (1940). The institute also published several Yiddish dictionaries and sponsored all-Union conferences on Jewish socioeconomic research (1931) and the Hebrew language (1934).

R. Senkus

Institute of Linguistics of the Academy of Sciences of the Ukrainian SSR (Instytut movoznavstva AN URSR im. O.O. Potebni). An institute established in Kiev in 1930 to co-ordinate all linguistic research in Soviet Ukraine after the liquidation of the various linguistic departments of the VUAN. It was created to give scholarly legitimacy to the Stalinist policy of linguistic *Russification at a time when Ukrainian studies and the social sciences and humanities in general were being muzzled, nationally conscious Ukrainian academics were being persecuted, and strict controls were being imposed on all research and publications. Under the directorship of N. *Kahanovych (1933–7), the institute issued unmitigated attacks on the previous directors and authors of linguistic research, many of whom were repressed, and began publishing terminological bulletins and dictionaries adapted to Russian terminology to supplant those prepared by the abolished *Institute of the Ukrainian Scientific Language of the VUAN (see *Terminology). From 1934 to 1939 it published 16 issues of the serial *Movoznavstvo*, made up chiefly of unscholarly, defamatory articles. Upon Kahanovych's arrest, the new director became M. *Kalynovych (1937–41), who initiated the publication of the irregular *Naukovi zapysky: Movoznavstvo* (18 vols, 1941, 1946–63), in which some articles were published in Russian. After the Soviet occupation of Galicia, a branch of the institute was created in Lviv in 1940.

During the Soviet-German War, the institute's staff was evacuated to Ufa (1941–4), where it constituted the language section of a unified Institute of Language and Literature that published two volumes of its own *Naukovi zapysky* up to 1946. After the war the institute's Lviv branch became a department of the (Lviv) *Institute of Social Sciences of the AN URSR under the supervision of I. *Svientsitsky (1945–56). The institute itself was reinstated and acquired a new director – L. *Bulakhovsky (1944–61) – under whom its publishing program expanded in the 1950s. Since that time the institute has published the serials *Dialektolohichnyi biuleten'* (9 issues, 1949–62) and *Leksykohrafichnyi biuleten'* (9 issues, 1951–63); an official bimonthly journal, **Movoznavstvo* (since 1967); and numerous monographs, textbooks, and collections of articles in the various branches of *linguistics, including *dialectology, *etymology, *grammar, *lexicology, *lexicography, *linguistic geography, *onomastics, *stylistics, and *syntax. Recently two very important multivolume publications were undertaken by the institute: the three-volume *Atlas ukraïns'koï movy* (Atlas of the Ukrainian Language, vol 1, 1984) and the seven-volume *Etymolohichnyi slovnyk ukraïns'koï movy* (Etymological Dictionary of the Ukrainian Language, vol 1, 1982; vol 2, 1985). It has also continued to publish the requisite amount of propaganda about the linguistic affinity and interaction of the Ukrainian and Russian languages, mirroring Soviet *nationality policy.

From 1962 to 1981 the institute's director was I. *Bilodid, under whom a Russian department was created in 1971 to propagate linguistic Russification. Since 1981 the director has been V. *Rusanivsky.

Currently the institute consists of 110 scholars in 7 departments: theory and history of Ukrainian, general and Slavic linguistics, comparative and Romance and Germanic linguistics, Russian, lexicology and lexicography, culture of speech, and structural-mathematical linguistics. It also has a dialectology and onomastics group and a working group of the Committee on Scientific Terminology. An Onomastic Commission studies the origin and function of proper names and works on transcription, the orthography of proper names, and renaming. Other Soviet commissions of the International Committee of Slavists (eg, the commissions on Lexicography and Lexicology and on Linguistic Terminology) use it as a base. A book about the institute appeared in Kiev in 1975.

O. Horbach

Institute of Literature of the Academy of Sciences of the Ukrainian SSR (Instytut literatury im. T.H. Shevchenka AN URSR). A research institute where research on the history of Ukrainian literature, particularly on the works of T. *Shevchenko, is conducted and published. It was founded in Kharkiv in 1926 as the Taras Shevchenko Scientific Research Institute. A proposal to create this type of an institute at the Academy of Sciences in Kiev was made originally by S. Yefremov, but the institute was initially attached to the People's Commissariat of Education and placed under the direction of party writers – S. Pylypenko, V. Koriak, and A. Richytsky. Prominent literary specialists such as S. Yefremov, O. Doroshkevych, B. Yakubsky, P. Fylypovych, V. Miiakovsky, V. Derzhavyn, V. Petrov, and M. Plevako took part in the institute's projects and publications until the late 1920s. The first director was D. *Bahalii (1926–32). During the first few years of the institute's existence, significant research on Shevchenko was carried out, but in the early 1930s his works began to be falsified to fit preconceived interpretations, as exemplified by the writings of Ye. *Shabliovsky, who was appointed director of the institute in 1934. This practice culminated in the tendentious doctrine that T. Shevchenko was a 'revolutionary democrat' and a disciple of V. Belinsky, N. Chernyshevsky, and other Russian thinkers. In 1936 the institute was transferred from the Commissariat of Education to the Academy of Sciences in Kiev and called the Shevchenko Institute of Ukrainian Literature. The poet P. Tychyna was appointed director. In 1944 he was replaced by the scholar O. Biletsky. In 1941, after the German invasion, the institute was evacuated to Ufa, where it was part of the Institute of Language and Literature of the Academy of Sciences until it was moved back to Kiev in 1944. In 1952 it received its present name.

Since 1944 the institute has been the co-ordinating center for all literary studies in Soviet Ukraine. Besides the 1939 five-volume and the 1949 ten-volume collection of Shevchenko's works, the institute has published numerous monographs and collections on Shevchenko by D. Kosaryk, I. Pilhuk, Ye. Nenadkevych, Ye. Kyryliuk, Ye. Shabliovsky, O. Biletsky, O. Deich, and others. The political bias of many of these studies diminishes considerably their scholarly value. The same is true of the studies that were published on the centenary of I. Franko's birth in 1955 by M. Vozniak and in 1956 by O. Biletsky, I. Bass, O. Kyselov, and others.

Possessing a huge collection of manuscripts (over 100,000), after the war the institute published a series of 'collected' works by Ukraine's classical writers: V. Stefanyk (3 vols, 1949–54), Lesia Ukrainka (5 vols, 1951–6 and 12 vols, 1975–9), I. Kotliarevsky (2 vols, 1952–3), P. Myrny (5 vols, 1954–6), Marko Vovchok (6 vols, 1955–6), and I. Franko (20 vols, 1950–6). Unfortunately, the selection of materials is at times falsified or bowdlerized and the introductions and commentaries in these collections are often incomplete and tendentious in their approach.

While O. *Biletsky was the director (1944–61), one could perceive in the institute's publications an obvious attempt to view the history of Ukrainian literature in relation to the development of world literature. Under the directors M. *Shamota (1961–78) and I. *Dzeverin (1978–), however, the party line has been reaffirmed and, in general, research of a propagandistic, rather than scholarly, nature has been published, focusing on the theory of socialist realism, the guiding influence of Russian literature on Ukrainian literature, and the like.

The preparation of surveys and textbooks of Ukrainian literature has been a central function of the institute. A Chrestomathy of Old Ukrainian Literature (pub in 1949, 1952, and 1967) and a two-volume history of Ukrainian literature (ed O. Biletsky and others, pub in 1950) were ready for publication in 1941, but did not appear because of the war. S. Maslov and Ye. Kyryliuk's *Narys istoriï ukraïns'koï literatury* (Outline History of Ukrainian Literature, 1945) was criticized harshly in 1946 for being 'nationalistic' and was withdrawn from circulation. In 1954 a new outline history in Ukrainian and Russian appeared. Adhering to the Stalinist conception of Ukrainian culture, it gave a completely distorted account of the development of Ukrainian literature. The first volume of *Istoriia ukraïns'koï literatury* (A History of Ukrainian Literature, eds O. Biletsky, M. Bernshtein, and M. Gudzii, 1954) was written in the same spirit. The second volume, dealing with the Soviet period, avoided mentioning many banned and repressed writers; its account of the early Soviet period was so poor and incomplete that the volume was withdrawn from circulation and extensively revised before being republished in 1957. An eight-volume (nine-book) history of Ukrainian literature was published between 1967 and 1971, and a two-volume history is to appear in the 1980s. One of the largest projects planned by the institute, in collaboration with the publishers of the Ukrainian Soviet Encyclopedia, is the publication of a five-volume Ukrainian literature encyclopedia. The publication of 50 vols of I. Franko's works (vol 1, 1976) is to be completed in this decade.

Since becoming the co-ordinating center for literary research in Soviet Ukraine, the institute has expanded significantly. Today it consists of eight sections: old Ukrainian literature, prerevolutionary Ukrainian literature, Soviet Ukrainian literature, Russian literature, literature of the Slavic peoples in the people's democracies and other foreign literatures, Shevchenko studies, literary theory (primarily socialist realism), and manuscripts and textual criticisms. The institute has a staff of 133, 90 of them scholars. Twenty have doctoral degrees (7 are corresponding members of the Academy of Sciences) and 63 are candidates of sciences. Since 1938 the institute has published **Radians'ke literaturoznavstvo* as its official periodical (since 1957 as a monthly journal). Since the war a branch of the institute has been located in Lviv, where such scholars as M. Vozniak, F. Kolessa, K. Studynsky, and V. Shchurat were affiliated during its early years. From 1948 to 1965 it published twelve collections of articles and materials on I. Franko. (See also *Literature studies.)

I. Koshelivets

Institute of Macromolecular Chemistry of the Academy of Sciences of the Ukrainian SSR. See Chemistry.

Institute of Marx-Engels-Lenin. See Institute of Party History.

Institute of Mathematics of the Academy of Sciences of the Ukrainian SSR (Instytut matematyky AN URSR). An institute established in 1934 out of three VUAN mathematical commissions chaired by D. Grave, Yu. Pfeiffer, and M. Kravchuk. Since that time it has been the main center of mathematical research in Ukraine.

Under its first director, D. *Grave (1934–9), the institute was the center of Soviet algebraic studies. Under its second director, M. *Lavrentev (1939–41), several distinguished Polish mathematicians of the well-known Lviv school (eg, S. Banach and his students, S. Mazur, V. Orlicz, and J. Schauder) became affiliated with the institute after the Soviet occupation of Western Ukraine. During the Second World War the institute was directed by Yu. Pfeiffer (1941–4) and was evacuated to Ufa and then Moscow. It was re-established in Kiev under its former director M. Lavrentev (1944–9). M. *Krylov's and N. *Bogoliubov's earlier joint work in non-linear mechanics was further developed after the war by Bogoliubov, his students O. Parasiuk and D. Shirkov, and Yu. Mytropolsky and Y. Shtokalo. Under the directors A. Ishlinsky (1949–55), B. Hniedenko (1955–8), and Yu. Mytropolsky (1958–), research has concentrated on the theory of asymptotic methods in non-linear mechanics, asymptotic and operational methods for special classes of linear and non-linear equations, mathematical methods in quantum field theory, functional analysis, differential equations, complex variables, the theory of conformal maps, the application of analysis methods, approximation methods, mechanics theory, and elasticity theory. Some work has been done in such areas of pure mathematics as algebraic and differential topology, differential geometry, and contemporary abstract algebra.

The institute has 13 departments and over 200 mathematicians. It has published the journals *Zhurnal Instytutu matematyky AN URSR* (1934–8), *Zbirnyk prats' Instytutu matematyky AN URSR* (1938–48), and *Ukrainskii matematicheskii zhurnal* (1949–). (See also *Mathematics.)

W.V. Petryshyn

Institute of Mechanics of the Academy of Sciences of the Ukrainian SSR (Instytut mekhaniky AN URSR). A research institute founded in Kiev in 1919. It was called the Institute of Technical Mechanics until 1929 and the Institute of Construction Mechanics until 1959. Research by its staff of 600 in 16 departments is focused on statics and dynamics, the theory of elasticity, physics of membranes, construction and thermal mechanics, fatigue of materials, theory of machines, composite materials, theory of non-linear vibrations, and related areas. The results of the institute's research have been widely utilized in the USSR. The institute publishes the monthly journal of applied mechanics *Prikladnaia mekhanika* and the periodic compendium *Teplovye napriazheniia v elementakh konstruktsii* and has a graduate program. It has been directed by S. Tymoshenko (1919–20), D. Grave (1921), K. Siminsky (1921–32), S. Serensen (1932–40), M. Kornoukhov (1940–4), F. Bieliankin (1944–58), G. Savin (1958–9), A. Kovalenko (1959–65), V. Kononenko (1965–75), and O. Huz.

In 1968 a section of the institute was established in Dnipropetrovske. In 1979 it became the new Institute of Technical Mechanics, directed by V. Pylypenko. Research by its staff of over 450 in 11 departments and a special technological design office is focused on the dynamics of complex mechanical systems, particularly in rail and air transport. The new institute also has an experimental manufacturing enterprise and a computer center.

L. Onyshkevych

Institute of Metal Physics of the Academy of Sciences of the Ukrainian SSR (Instytut metalofizyky AN URSR). A scientific-technological institute founded in Kiev in 1955 from the AN URSR Laboratory of Metal Physics (est 1945). It has 15 departments, 8 laboratories, a computer center, a technological-design office, and a pilot plant. Its scientists (217 in 1980) carry out studies in theoretical and experimental solid-state physics, particularly the physics of metals and alloys. It has been headed by G. Kurdiumov (1945–51), V. Danylov (1951–4), A. Smirnov (1955), V. Hridniev (1955–85), and V. Bariakhtar (1985–).

Institute of Organic Chemistry of the Academy of Sciences of the Ukrainian SSR. See Chemistry.

Institute of Party History of the Central Committee of the Communist Party of Ukraine (Instytut istorii partii TsK KPU). A branch of the Institute of Marxism-Leninism of the CC CPSU located in Kiev. It conducts and publishes research on the history of the CPU; prepares and publishes translations of the classics of Marxism-Leninism; maintains the Party archives and a specialized library in Party history; and oversees oblast Party committee archives and the Kiev and Lviv branches of the Central Lenin Museum.

The institute is the offspring mainly of the All-Ukrainian Commission for [the Study of] the History of the October Revolution and the Communist Party (Bolshevik) of Ukraine and, to some extent, the Ukrainian Institute of Marxism-Leninism (UIML), which were established originally to provide Marxist counterparts to the traditional historical scholarship of the All-Ukrainian Academy of Sciences.

The commission was founded in Kharkiv in 1921 and subordinated to the Central Executive Committee of the CP(B)U in 1922. Its organ, **Litopys revoliutsii* (1922–33), was published in Russian until 1927. In 1929 the commission was restructured and renamed the Institute of Party History and the October Revolution in Ukraine. In 1934 this institute was moved to Kiev.

The UIML was established in Kharkiv in 1922–3; until

1924 it was known as the Ukrainian Institute of Marxism and Marxist Studies. Proclaimed officially in 1925 to be the center of Marxist thought and scholarship in Ukraine, it aspired to become the republican counterpart of the Communist Academy in Moscow. M. *Skrypnyk was its main Party patron and director of its chair on the nationality question. M. Yavorsky was the head of its historical section. The institute published the journal **Prapor Marksyzmu* (1927–31). In 1931 the CP(B)U accused the UIML of nationalist deviationism. It was broken up into autonomous units that together formed the *All-Ukrainian Association of Marxist-Leninist Scientific Research Institutes (VUAMLIN). In 1936 some sections of VUAMLIN were incorporated into what is now known as the *Institute of History of the AN URSR, and in 1939 the remaining departments were merged with the Institute of Party History and the October Revolution in Ukraine to form the Ukrainian Branch of the Institute of Marx-Engels-Lenin of the CC of the All-Russian Communist Party (Bolshevik). This body assumed the new name, Institute of Party History of the CC CPU, in 1956.

Among the institute's numerous recent publications are *Komunistychna partiia Ukraïny v rezoliutsiiakh z'ïzdiv, konferentsiï i plenumiv TsK* (The Communist Party of Ukraine in the Resolutions of Congresses, Conferences, and Plenums of the CC, 1976–7) and *Narysy istoriï komunistychnoï partiï Ukraïny* (Outlines of the History of the Communist Party of Ukraine, 4 edns). It also publishes the journal **Ukraïns'kyi istorychnyi zhurnal* in collaboration with the Institute of History. Since 1956 its directors have been P. Pavliuk and V. Yurchuk (1974–).

I. Myhul

Institute of Philosophy of the Academy of Sciences of the Ukrainian SSR (Instytut filosofii AN URSR). Principal center for philosophical studies in Ukraine, founded in November 1946 to conduct and co-ordinate research in philosophy and to prepare specialists in the field. In the 1920s and 1930s some work in philosophy was done at the AN URSR by the Historical-Literary Society of the historical-philological division, the Chair of the History of Philosophy and Law in the social-economic division, the Chair of Marxism-Leninism, and the Commission of Philosophy. Staffed by over 120 researchers, the institute has 15 departments, some of which have little to do with philosophy: dialectical materialism, historical materialism, philosophical questions of scientific communism, history of philosophical and social thought in Ukraine, logic of scientific knowledge, philosophical questions of the natural sciences, esthetics, scientific atheism, contemporary philosophy abroad, theoretical problems of ethnic relations and proletarian internationalism, philosophical problems of social psychology, sociological research on labor and on social and professional guidance, and sociopsychological problems of management. Since the 1960s there has been a strong emphasis on research with an immediate practical application in education, the economy, or the building of a communist society. Its most important and interesting philosophical contributions have been in the fields of philosophy of science and the history of philosophy in Ukraine. Among the leading specialists in the first area are M. Omelianovsky, P. Kopnin, P. Dyshlevy, and M. Popovych, and in the second area, D. Ostrianyn, V. Nichyk, and I. Tabachnikov. The institute's publication of scholarly editions of the collected works of H. Skovoroda (1961, 2nd edn 1973) and the translated works of T. Prokopovych (1979–81), and some textbooks from philosophy courses given at the Kievan Mohyla Academy in the 17th and 18th centuries, have a lasting significance for the history of philosophy. In 1973 it published the first Ukrainian *Filosofs'kyi slovnyk* (Philosophical Dictionary). Besides monographs, collections of essays, and pamphlets, the institute published annually *Naukovi zapysky Instytutu filosofiï* (7 vols, 1951–61) and continues to publish the Ukrainian-language bimonthly *Filosofs'ka dumka* (since 1969). The institute's directors have been M. Omelianovsky (1946–52), D. Ostrianyn (1952–62), P. Kopnin (1962–8), and V. Shynkaruk (since 1968).

T. Zakydalsky

Institute of Physical Chemistry of the Academy of Sciences of the Ukrainian SSR. See Chemistry.

Institute of Physical-Organic Chemistry and Coal Chemistry of the Academy of Sciences of the Ukrainian SSR (Instytut fizyko-orhanichnoi khimii ta vuhlekhimii AN URSR). A scientific institute established in Donetske in 1975 out of the Donetske branch of physical-organic chemistry of the AN URSR Institute of Physical Chemistry. It has 13 departments, a petrochemical branch in Kiev, and a pilot plant. Its scientists (110 in 1980) study kinetics and the mechanism of organic reactions, coal-based and organic synthesis, and catalysis by organometallic and organic compounds; they develop new physicochemical methods for the study of coal and oil and their components, and for converting them into chemical intermediates and fuels. The institute has been directed by L. Lytvynenko (1975–83) and A. Popov (1983–).

Institute of Physics of the Academy of Sciences of the Ukrainian SSR (Instytut fizyky AN URSR). A scientific institute established in Kiev in 1929 as the Kiev Research Institute of Physics out of the physics chair of the Kiev Polytechnical Institute. Incorporated into the VUAN in 1932, it was renamed in 1936. It has 12 departments, 2 laboratories, a graduate program, a technological-design office, and a production enterprise. Its scientists (216 in 1980) conduct research in solid-state physics, surface physics, plasma physics, quantum electronics, quantum optics, new types of tunable lasers and lasers of extreme-narrow spectral lines, and the development of new research instrumentation. Some of the research previously conducted at the institute is now done at the AN URSR institutes for Nuclear Research, of Semiconductors, of Metal Physics, and of Theoretical Physics. The institute has been directed by O. Goldman (1929–38), Ye. Myseliuk (1938–41), G. Pfeiffer (1941–4), O. Leipunsky (1944–9), M. Pasichnyk (1949–65), A. Prykhotko (1965–70), and M. Shpak (1970–). (See also *Physics.)

Institute of Physiology of the Academy of Sciences of the Ukrainian SSR (Instytut fiziolohii im. O.O. Bohomoltsia AN URSR). A research institute established in Kiev in 1953 out of the Institute of Experimental Biology and Physiology of the Ministry of Health Protection (est 1930) and the AN URSR Institute of Clinical Physiology (est 1934). It has 14 departments, 9 laboratories, and a research-production enterprise. Its scientists (159 in 1980) do research on the *physiology and pathophysiology of higher nervous activity, cellular processes, and the blood-vascular system, and develop drugs and methods for curing nervous, mental, heart, and digestive disorders and diseases. The institute publishes the journals *Fiziologicheskii zhurnal* (1955–) and *Neirofiziologiia* (1969–). Its directors have been A. Vorobiov (1953–5), O. Makarchenko (1955–66), and P. Kostiuk (1966–).

Institute of Radio Physics and Electronics of the Academy of Sciences of the Ukrainian SSR (Instytut radiofizyky i elektroniky AN URSR). A scientific institute founded in Kharkiv in 1955 out of a division of the AN URSR *Physical-Technical Institute. It has 16 departments, 2 laboratories, an experimental-production enterprise, and a research-design office. Its scientists (209 in 1980) study millimeter and submillimeter radio waves, electromagnetic transmission, wave refraction, diffraction, and absorption, radio astronomy, high-frequency properties of solid materials, biophysics, and semiconductor physics; they have made significant contributions in the fields of radiometry, quantum electronics, acoustic lasers, plasma physics, and radio propagation. The institute's radio astronomy division built the electronically controlled UTR-2 radio telescope; at the time of its construction (1970), it was the most powerful instrument of its type in the northern hemisphere. With the aid of this and other radio telescopes, fundamental research has been performed on pulsars and the sun's corona. The institute has designed and manufactured various radio and electric apparatuses and measuring instruments that are used throughout the USSR. It has been directed by O. Usykov (1955–73) and V. Shestopalov (1973–).

L. Onyshkevych

Institute of Semiconductors of the Academy of Sciences of the Ukrainian SSR (Instytut napivprovidnykiv AN URSR). A scientific institute established in Kiev in 1960 out of two departments and a laboratory of the AN URSR Institute of Physics. It has 17 departments, several laboratories, a technological-design office, a graduate program, and a pilot plant. Its scientists (380 in 1980) study interaction of electromagnetic radiation with semiconductors (eg, photoelectric and optical instruments and solid-state lasers), radiospectroscopy, surface phenomena, and crystal structure and defects, and design semiconductor devices. Their contributions have been applied to electron microscopy, transducers for petrochemical studies, cryogenics, and optoelectronics. The institute publishes the serial collections *Kvantovaia elektronika* and *Poluprovodnikovaia tekhnika i mikroelektronika*. It has been directed by V. Lashkarov (1960–70) and O. Snitko (1970–).

Institute of Social and Economic Problems of Foreign Countries of the Academy of Sciences of the Ukrainian SSR (Instytut sotsialnykh i ekonomichnykh problem zarubizhnykh krain AN URSR). An institute established in 1978 within the AN URSR Social Sciences Section as the principal republican policy-oriented research center in the field of international affairs. It forms a part of the academy's Department of Economics and is divided into three sections with 11 departments (one in Uzhhorod and one in Chernivtsi). The institute's main areas of research include national problems in foreign countries and questions of ideology; migration processes abroad and the situation of the Ukrainian emigration; and the struggle against 'foreign organizations of Ukrainian bourgeois nationalists and Zionist centers.' It is responsible for co-ordinating the work of Ukrainian social scientists in the area of counterpropaganda. In recent years, its efforts in this regard have been subjected to serious criticism. The institute has published over 40 monographs and collections of articles and publishes (since 1981) a quarterly, *Zarubezhnyi mir: sotsial'no-politicheskie i ekonomicheskie problemy*. It has a research staff of approximately 50 individuals and since 1978 its director has been A. Shlepakov.

Institute of Social Sciences of the Academy of Sciences of the Ukrainian SSR (Instytut suspilnykh nauk AN URSR). The institute was organized in 1951 out of the Lviv branches of the academy's institutes of economics, history, archeology, literature, and linguistics. These branches had been established in 1940–1 in place of the dissolved Shevchenko Scientific Society and were restored in 1945. From 1963 to 1969 the institute came under the jurisdiction of the Ukrainian SSR Ministry of Higher and Secondary Special Education. Then it became part of the Social Sciences Section of the Academy of Sciences. Its directors have been O. Nesterenko, I. Krypiakevych, M. Oleksiuk, V. Chuhaiev, and M. Bryk. During the cultural revival of the 1960s the institute became one of the main centers of interdisciplinary studies in Western Ukraine, particularly in history, archeology, folklore, ethnography, and economics. It published a number of collections, including *Materialy i doslidzhennia z arkheolohiï Prykarpattia i Volyni* (Materials and Research in the Archeology of Subcarpathia and Volhynia, 5 vols, 1954–64) and *Z istoriï zakhidnoukraïns'kykh zemel'* (From the History of Western Ukrainian Lands, 5 vols, 1957–60), which was continued as *Z istoriï Ukraïns'koï RSR* (From the History of the Ukrainian SSR, 3 vols, 1962–3). The institute also publishes monographs and collective works on the history of material culture, on ancient populations of Subcarpathia and Volhynia, on Ukrainian historical lexicology and lexicography (including an important two-volume dictionary of Old Ukrainian, 1977–8), on paleolithic monuments of the Dniester region, and on the archeology of Galicia. After suffering a decline during the repressions of the 1970s, the institute recently has experienced a revival. It is organized in seven departments and has an academic staff of over 70 individuals.

I. Myhul

Institute of State and Law of the Academy of Sciences of the Ukrainian SSR (Instytut derzhavy i prava AN URSR). Research institution of the Academy of Sciences formed in 1969 out of the Sector of State and Law (est 1949). It comes under the Division of History, Philosophy, and Law. The institute is organized into six departments: theory and history of the state and law, Soviet construction, the management of the state and economy, socialist legality and criminology, problems of Ukraine's involvement in international law, and comparative state studies. There are also several councils devoted to specific problems. The institute has the task of co-ordinating research in the field of juridical sciences in Ukraine. It also provides graduate studies in its various departments. During the cultural revival of the 1960s an attempt was made to develop the history of the Soviet

Ukrainian state and law. Since the early 1970s the institute has concentrated on problems of economic management, socialist construction, and Soviet procuratorial and investigative practice. Its most important publications include *Narysy z istorii derzhavy i prava Ukraïns'koï RSR* (A Survey of the History of State and Law of the Ukrainian SSR, 1957), *Istoriia derzhavy i prava Ukraïns'koï RSR (1917–1967)* (The History of the State and Law of the Ukrainian SSR [1917–1967], 2 vols, 1967), and several collections of documents on the history of the international relations of the Ukrainian SSR. Since 1958 the institute has published the journal *Radians'ke pravo* in collaboration with the Ministry of Justice of the Ukrainian SSR, the Supreme Court, and the republican procurator's office. The institute's directors have been V. Koretsky and B. Babii, and currently it has an academic staff of over 60 individuals.

I. Myhul

Institute of Superhard Materials of the Academy of Sciences of the Ukrainian SSR (Instytut nadtverdykh materialiv AN URSR). A scientific institute established in Kiev in 1961; in 1972 it became part of the academy. It has 20 departments and laboratories, a technological-design office, a pilot plant, and a graduate program. Its scientists (270 in 1980) study the formation of diamonds and other superhard crystals, their properties and synthesis, and their various industrial and scientific applications. They have developed a technology for synthesizing artificial industrial diamonds; supervised the construction of production facilities for superhard materials, machines, and instruments in Poltava, Yerevan, Lviv, and elsewhere; invented new superhard materials (eg, Slavutych); pioneered the CVD method of growing thin films of diamond; and synthesized a new industrial diamond (AV) using explosive methods. Use of the institute's inventions has been licensed to various foreign countries. The institute publishes the journal *Sverkhtverdye materialy* (1979–) and the periodical collection *Sinteticheskie almazy*. It has been directed by V. Bakul (1961–77) and M. Novykov (1977–).

L. Onyshkevych

Institute of Technical Thermophysics of the Academy of Sciences of the Ukrainian SSR (Instytut tekhnichnoi teplofizyky AN URSR). A technological institute established in Kiev in 1947 out of several departments of the AN URSR Institute of Energetics (est 1939); until 1963 it was called the Institute of Thermoenergetics. It has 5 sections, 18 departments, 2 research-and-design technological offices, 2 research-production enterprises, and a pilot plant. Its scientists (268 in 1980) study the practical problems of thermodynamics, the development of new energy sources, air pollution, thermal problems in nuclear-power and mining technology, and thermal exchange. The research results are used at over 500 Soviet concerns. The institute publishes the bimonthly journal *Promyshlennaia teplotekhnika* (1979–) and the periodical collections *Teplofizika i teplotekhnika* and *Problemy kontrolia i zashchita atmosfery ot zagriazneniia*. It has been directed by I. Shvets (1947–52, 1954–5), V. Tolubynsky (1953–4, 1963–72), G. Shchegolev (1955–63), H. Babukha (1972–3), O. Herashchenko (1974–83), and A. Dolinsky (1983–).

Institute of the Biology of Southern Seas of the Academy of Sciences of the Ukrainian SSR (Instytut biolohii pivdennykh moriv im. O.O. Kovalevskoho AN URSR). Research institute founded in 1963 in Sevastopil on the basis of the Sevastopil, Karadag (Teodosiia), and (in 1964) Odessa biological stations. With its branches in Odessa and Teodosiia (the Karadag branch), it consisted in 1980 of 586 employees (159 scholars) in 11 departments, 21 laboratories, and it operated 3 exploration ships (in 1976). It conducts and publishes research in marine biology and ecology, the development and protection of marine resources, marine pollution, and the economic exploitation of the marine environment. Since 1977 the director of the institute has been V. Zaika.

Institute of the Economics of Industry of the Academy of Sciences of the Ukrainian SSR (Instytut ekonomiky promyslovosti AN URSR). Research institute in Donetske founded in 1969 on the basis of the Donetske industrial-economics branch of the Institute of Economics. Research in the institute's 11 departments (1 is located in Zaporizhia) focuses on computer technology and econometrics and their application in industry, and on problems in production management and planning. The institute has branches in Dnipropetrovske, where research concentrates on the metallurgical industry, and Voroshylovhrad, and operates a computer center in Donetske. In 1985 the staff numbered approximately 350. The institute has been headed by O. Alymov (1969–73) and M. Chumachenko (1973–).

Institute of the Geochemistry and Physics of Minerals of the Academy of Sciences of the Ukrainian SSR (Instytut heokhimii i fizyky mineraliv AN URSR). A scientific institute founded in Kiev in 1969 from the Geochemistry, Mineralogy, Petrography, and Ore Deposits Sector and the Metallogenesis Sector of the AN URSR Institute of Geological Sciences. It has 16 departments, a metallogenesis sector, several laboratories, and a research pilot plant. Its scientists (200 in 1980) conduct fundamental research in geochemistry, mineralogy, petrology, and metallogenesis. They study the nature and properties of minerals (using crystallochemistry and mineral physics) and the geology and geochemistry of Ukraine's ore and mineral deposits; establish criteria for prospecting; and scientifically predict deposit locations. The institute is a leading Soviet institution in geochronology; it has produced a catalogue and map of the isotopic dates and strata in the Ukrainian Shield. Its scientists' research in metallogenesis and ore formation has resulted in discoveries of significant titanium deposits. The institute publishes four research annuals. Its directors have been M. Semenko (1969–77) and M. Shcherbak (1977–).

S. Trofimenko

Institute of the Geology and Geochemistry of Fossil Fuels of the Academy of Sciences of the Ukrainian SSR (Instytut heolohii i heokhimii horiuchykh kopalyn AN URSR). A scientific institute established in 1951 in Lviv, replacing a branch of the AN URSR Institute of Geological Sciences. Until 1962 it was called the Institute of the Geology of Useful Minerals. The institute has 10 departments and 7 laboratories. Its scientists (123 in 1980) study the theoretical and practical problems of geology, geochemistry, and geophysics relating to the genesis and structure of fossil fuels and their migration and accumulation in deep and shallow strata; and assess the potential of Ukraine's coal, gas, and oil, and sulfur deposits, develop new technology in relation to these, and make recommendations for their rational industrial exploitation. The institute leads the way in Soviet studies of endogenous mineral formation, based on inclusions; its scientists have created an evolutionary model of physicochemical conditions of mineralogenesis in pegmatite and metasomatite granite inclusions, which forms the basis for locating valuable minerals. Since 1965 the institute has published the serial *Geologiia i geokhimiia goriuchikh iskopaemykh*. Its directors have been V. Porfirev (1951–63), H. Dolenko (1963–82), and R. Kucher (1982–).

S. Trofimenko

Institute of the History of Material Culture. See Institute of Archeology of the Academy of Sciences of the Ukrainian SSR.

Institute of the History of Ukrainian Culture. See Scientific Research Institute of the History of Ukrainian Culture.

Institute of the Ukrainian Scientific Language (Instytut ukrainskoi naukovoi movy or IUNM). An institute of the VUAN formed in 1921 after the consolidation of the Terminological Commission of the Ukrainian Scientific Society in Kiev and the Orthographic-Terminological Commission of the Historical-Philological Division of the VUAN. It consisted of departments of law (chaired by I. Cherkasky), natural science (P. Tutkovsky, Kh. Polonsky), technology (K. Turkalo), agriculture (K. Osmak), and economics (H. Kryvchenko). Its first director was A. Krymsky; its secretaries were M. Liubynsky (until 1925) and H. Kholodny, who later became its second director. The IUNM flourished from 1925 to 1928, when it employed up to 25 scholars. From 1923 to 1930 it published over 20 terminological dictionaries in the fields of chemistry, geology, mathematics, administrative language, anatomy, zoology, botany, pedagogy, natural science, communal economy, construction, technology, and military affairs (see *Terminology). It also published two issues of *Visnyk IUNM* (1928–30) and a manual (1928) for collecting natural-science terminological materials. In 1930 Kholodny and seven IUNM associates were defendants in the show trial of the *Union for the Liberation of Ukraine and imprisoned; the work of IUNM was condemned as nationalistic wrecking and the IUNM was abolished and replaced by the *Institute of Linguistics of the AN URSR.

K. Turkalo

Institute of Theoretical Physics of the Academy of Sciences of the Ukrainian SSR (Instytut teoretychnoi fizyky AN URSR). A research institute established in Kiev in 1966 out of the theoretical division of the AN URSR Institute of Physics. It has 14 departments, a graduate program, and a branch in Lviv. Its scientists (120 in 1980) conduct fundamental research in the fields of solid-state physics, nuclear and particle theory, statistical physics, chaos dynamics, plasma physics, and quantum biophysics. The institute publishes in Russian the periodical collection *Fizika molekul*. It has been directed by N. Bogoliubov (1966–72) and O. Davydov (1973–). The institute's halls are decorated with I. Marchuk's ceramic bas-reliefs and mosaics depicting motifs from Ukrainian cultural history.

Institute of Zoology of the Academy of Sciences of the Ukrainian SSR (Instytut zoolohii AN URSR). The co-ordinating center of zoological research in Ukraine, established in Kiev in 1930 out of the VUAN zoology museum (est 1919) and the F.Z. Omelchenko Biology Institute (est 1919 as a laboratory); until 1938 it was called the Institute of Zoology and Biology. The institute has 12 departments and 3 laboratories and experimental bases; it runs the *Black Sea Nature Reserve. Its scientists (144 in 1980) do research on the systematics and evolution of animal and plant organisms, parasitology, ecology, and the problems of utilization and conservation of the animal world. The institute publishes the serial *Zbirnyk prats' zoolohichnoho muzeiu* (1926–), the multivolume reference work **Fauna Ukraïny* (The Fauna of Ukraine, 1956–), and the bimonthly journal *Vestnik zoologii* (1967–). Its directors have been I. Shmalhauzen (1930–41), D. Tretiakov (1944–8), O. Markevych (1948–50), V. Kasianenko (1950–63), P. Mazhuha (1963–5), I. Pidoplichko (1965–73), and V. Topachevsky (1973–). (See also *Zoology.)

Institutes. In Imperial Russia the term was applied to certain research institutions and to boarding schools for children of the nobility. Before 1918 there were 12 institutes in Ukraine. From 1920, when universities were abolished, to 1933, when they were restored, institutes were the principal type of higher educational institution in Soviet Ukraine. Since then most *higher educational institutions other than universities have been called institutes. In 1982 there were 45 technological, 15 medical, 13 agricultural, 8 pedagogical, 7 economic and law, 3 art, and 1 physical education institutes in Ukraine. Similar educational institutions are known also as academies and higher schools. Scientific research institutes not only conduct basic research in the natural and social sciences but also prepare specialists in the different fields. Some of them (58 in 1977) belong to the system of the *Academy of Sciences of the Ukrainian SSR, while others come under various ministries. Details about the latter are kept secret. Regional scientific centers of the Academy of Sciences (Dnipropetrovske, Donetske, Western, Northwestern, Northeastern, and Southern) co-ordinate the work of the various research institutes and bring it into closer relation with industry.

Institutes for daughters of the nobility *(instytuty blahorodnykh divyts)*. Boarding schools for noble girls between the ages of 12 and 17 in prerevolutionary Russia. They were loosely patterned on the Smolnyi Institute in St Petersburg (est 1764), the first school of this type in Russia. Such schools were introduced in Russian-ruled Ukraine, partly as an alternative to Roman Catholic convent schools, which were Polish in spirit. The first institute for noble girls in Ukraine was established in Kharkiv in 1812. It was followed by similar ones in Poltava (1817), Odessa (1828), Kerch (1835), and Kiev (1838). Their purpose was moral, rather than academic, education: to prepare young women for their role as wives and mothers. Emphasis was placed on the social graces, French language, music, drawing, dancing, and handicrafts. Some instruction in literature, history, and religion was also included. An optional one-year course in pedagogy was sometimes offered. The girls were supervised and watched closely under an oppressive regime. Ukrainian teachers, who were usually men, sometimes managed to introduce local Ukrainian flavor into the curriculum. By the end of the 19th century the program of the institutes was updated to reflect the standards of secondary education.

M. Bohachevska-Chomiak

Institutes of culture (*instytuty kultury*). Higher educational institutions in the USSR that train librarians, bibliographers, and cultural-educational workers such as club managers and amateur choir, orchestra, and drama-group directors. They were organized out of former library science institutes. Their program for full-time students requires four years, and for part-time students five years of study. In 1979 there were 17 institutes of culture in the USSR, three of which were in Ukraine: in Kiev (with a branch in Mykolaiv), Kharkiv, and Rivne.

Institutes of foreign languages (*instytuty inozemnykh mov*). Pedagogical institutes that train teachers of foreign languages for higher educational institutions and upgrade the qualifications of language teachers. Today there are two such institutes in Ukraine: the Kiev Pedagogical Institute of Foreign Languages (est 1948) and the Horlivka Pedagogical Institute of Foreign Languages (est 1949 in Bila Tserkva and moved to Horlivka in 1954). The former has six departments: English, French, German, Spanish, Russian (for foreign students), and professional development. The latter has two: English and French.

Institutes of people's education (*instytuty narodnoi osvity*, INO). Higher pedagogical schools introduced in 1920 by H. *Hrynko in place of universities as part of his general reform of the educational system of the Ukrainian SSR. They were formed out of the physical-mathematical-scientific and the historical-philological faculties of abolished universities and from teachers' institutes. INOs were divided into two faculties: the faculty of social education with a three-year program to prepare teachers for the upper grades of seven-year schools, and the faculty of professional education with a four-year program to prepare teachers for vocational schools. The faculties were subdivided into various departments. In 1929 there were 12 INOs: in Kiev, Kharkiv, Odessa, Dnipropetrovske, Nizhen, Poltava, Kamianets-Podilskyi, Zhytomyr, Mykolaiv, Kherson, Chernihiv, and Luhanske. Their total enrollment was 6,200, Ukrainians accounting for 65 percent. Most of the institutes published their own journals. In 1930 they were split up into more specialized institutions – *institutes of social education, *institutes of professional education, and institutes of political education.

Institutes of professional education (*instytuty profesiinoi osvity*). Higher educational establishments with three faculties (social sciences, physics-mathematics, agriculture-biology) that existed in the Ukrainian SSR from 1930 to 1933. Based on the faculties of professional education of the former *institutes of people's education, their four-year program trained lecturers for *tekhnikums, *workers' faculties, and other technical schools. In 1933 they were incorporated into the reorganized university system.

Institutes of social education (*instytuty sotsialnoho vykhovannia*). Post-secondary pedagogical institutions organized in 1930 in the Ukrainian SSR out of the faculties of social education of the *institutes of people's education. They offered three-year programs that qualified graduates to teach in seven-year schools or pedagogical tekhnikums, or to supervise children's clubs. The Kharkiv Institute of Social Education was the first institute to obtain a department for the protection of minors and a department for instructors of people's education. In 1933 the institutes of social education were reorganized into *pedagogical institutes.

Instructional literature. A genre of oratorical, didactic prose that was popular in ancient and medieval times in Europe. There are many translated and original works of this genre in Old Ukrainian literature – speeches, discourses, and homilies. Among translated works the oldest are the instructions of Xenophon and Theodora in the *Izbornik* of Sviatoslav (1076). Of the original works the most important are Prince Volodymyr Monomakh's *Pouchennia ditiam* (Instructions to My Children), Ilarion's *'Slovo o zakoni i blahodati' (Sermon on Law and Grace), the sermons and instructions of Cyril of Turiv, the 'Poucheniie o liubvi' (Instructions on Love) attributed to Klym Smoliatych, and the instructions of Luka Zhydiata and of Serapion of Vladimir. Some anonymous works were also widely known: 'Slovo o pravdi i nepravdi' (A Sermon on Truth and Falsehood), 'Slovo o linyvim i sonlyvim' (A Sermon on a Lazy and Sleepy Man), a sermon on parental respect, and others. The nature of poetry in *Ifika ieropolitika* (1712) was also instructional. Works of instructional literature typically consist of an appeal to children or the faithful to live righteously, learn, work hard, be merciful toward others, and live humbly and simply.

Instrumental music. In Ukraine, as in Western Europe, instrumental music developed considerably later than vocal music. The earliest works of instrumental music date back to the second half of the 18th century with the sonata for violin and harpsichord by M. Berezovsky and numerous compositions by D. Bortniansky: several piano sonatas, three violin sonatas, a quartet, a quintet, and the *Symphony in B-flat major*. A major contribution to Ukrainian instrumental music was made by M. *Lysenko, who wrote a number of piano compositions (*Ukrainian Suite* [1869]), two rhapsodies based on themes from Ukrainian folk songs, a sonata, and the *Heroic Scherzo*, works for piano and violin, a trio, and a quartet. A contemporary of Lysenko, M. Kolachevsky, composed works for the piano and a symphony in four movements. At the beginning of the 20th century many instrumental works, especially for piano, were composed by Ya. Stepovy, S. Liudkevych, V. Barvinsky, L. Revutsky, and V. Kosenko. Since then, instrumental music in all its forms (solo, *chamber, and orchestra music) has been the most popular style of music among Ukrainian composers.

BIBLIOGRAPHY

Dremliuha, M. *Ukraïns'ka fortepiianna muzyka* (Kiev 1958)
Borovyk, M. *Ukraïns'kyi radians'kyi kamerno-instrumental'nyi ansambl'* (Kiev 1968)
Hordiichuk, M. *Ukraïns'ka radians'ka symfonichna muzyka* (Kiev 1969)

W. Wytwycky

Instytut Badań Spraw Narodowościowych. See Institute for Nationalities Research.

Instytut doslidiv Volyni. See Research Institute of Volyn.

Insurance. A form of risk sharing. In return for paying premiums to an insurance fund, insured individuals or legal persons are guaranteed compensation for specific types of damage to their material or personal interests. Obligatory social-insurance coverage is administered in much the same manner in both Soviet-type and capitalist economies. The organization of optional forms of insurance differs in two principal ways. First, the financial power of Western insurance firms is incompatible with the Soviet bloc's economic structure. Hence, all forms of insurance in Ukraine are administered by the state, which is not obliged to keep a minimum percentage of insurance funds on hand and uses premiums to finance a variety of social and economic programs. The second difference is the absence of Western civil-damage laws and the attendant need for liability insurance. Consequently a greater burden is placed on compensatory forms of insurance. Some groups, however, are shortchanged in the interplay between the state as the employer, the state as the producer, and the welfare state. Collective farmers, for example, can neither receive benefits for which disabled state employees qualify nor sue for damages if, for instance, a state-manufactured auger malfunctions.

The earliest form of indemnity in Ukraine, as set down in the *Ruskaia Pravda*, was the payment of damages or **vyra* in cases of manslaughter of a member of a community or of his or her murder by an unknown assailant. Three characteristics of the *vyra* evoke modern forms of insurance: it was linked to a citizen's death; liability was shared by all of the community's members; and it was paid out in installments over a number of years.

Modern forms of insurance did not develop in Ukraine until the late 18th century, when Russian- and foreign-owned joint-stock associations and mutual-insurance companies arose in the Russian Empire. The tsarist government tried to oust the foreign companies and to control the insurance (especially property insurance) business. In 1827 it gave the newly formed private First Russian Insurance Company a monopoly on fire insurance in some of the empire's cities, including Odessa. The Second Russian Fire Insurance Company (est 1835) was given an insurance monopoly in the 9 Ukrainian gubernias and 31 others, excluding the cities there.

In cities such as Poltava, Kharkiv, Kherson, Kiev, and Odessa, mutual fire-insurance companies became very successful. The Kiev Mutual Fire Insurance Company for Beet-Sugar Factories and Refineries was established in 1872. In 1864 legislation gave the newly formed zemstvos responsibility for farm insurance in the Left-Bank and steppe gubernias. Where there were no zemstvos (eg, in Kiev, Volhynia, and Podilia gubernias), state-run insurance institutions operated. A minimum level of insurance coverage was compulsory for everyone. Life insurance was organized by railway workers' pension funds and state-run savings banks.

Similar types of insurance companies developed in Western Ukraine on the basis of the Austrian imperial patent of 1852. Initially all insurance companies there were foreign owned. In 1892 the first Ukrainian fire-and-theft insurance company, *Dnister, was founded in Lviv. From 1911, with the establishment of the *Karpatiia mutual-insurance company, Ukrainians could buy life insurance from a Ukrainian company as well. From 1935 to 1939 the business of these two companies was hindered by the granting of a monopoly on fire insurance to a Polish company.

After the Revolution of 1917, co-operative insurance companies – which had been almost non-existent under tsarism – flourished in Ukraine. In 1918 the *Strakhsoiuz All-Ukrainian Insurance Union was formed; one of the chief functions it performed was conducting a vote at its general meetings on how many insurance payments each member co-operative should be obliged to make. During the period of War Communism (1919–21) the state took control of insurance. In 1921 it provided coverage for workers and employees (and extended it to all citizens in 1922), liquidated the Strakhsoiuz and all other insurance companies, and nationalized their assets. This extreme measure was softened in 1922, when co-operatives were allowed to provide mutual insurance of movable property and goods under the auspices of the All-Ukrainian Co-operative Insurance Union (Koopstrakh). The Koopstrakh prospered (from 1926–7 its guarantees totaled 672.2 million rubles) until it, too, was liquidated in 1930. From 1925 a central agency in Moscow – the Chief Administration of State Insurance (Gosstrakh) of the Ministry of Finance of the USSR – administered all insurance matters. All farmers were obliged to purchase fire, livestock, disease, hail damage, and transportation-accident insurance from the state. During collectivization, however, the Gosstrakh refused to indemnify peasant households on the grounds that livestock, buildings, and machines were being intentionally destroyed to keep them from falling into the hands of the collective farms.

In 1956 the Soviet insurance system was reformed. On the premise that insurance was basically a way for small bodies to share risks that they could not afford to take alone, the state opted out of all insurance schemes. In 1958 the insurance system was decentralized, and the Gosstrakh became a separate department whose functions were restricted to co-ordinating its branches in each of the republics. The Gosstrakh of the Ukrainian SSR, or Derzhstrakh, which is responsible to the republican Ministry of Finance, became the body that oversees insurance in Ukraine. In 1958 it spent 401.1 million rubles on insurance (41.2 percent on temporary disability, 15.3 percent on maternity and childcare, 9.2 percent on sanatoriums and other medical expenses, 2.6 percent on children's services, and 1.0 percent on other expenses).

In Soviet Ukraine today two types of insurance exist: property and personal. The property of collective and state farms and other agricultural enterprises and privately owned buildings and cattle must be insured. *Social insurance and travel insurance (except when using municipal transit and intraoblast buses) are also obligatory. Collective farms can purchase optional insurance on their livestock, crops, and equipment. The main forms of optional insurance for individuals are household, property, livestock, life, disability, accident, and child insurance. Soviet citizens and foreign-trade bodies functioning abroad are insured by the Administration of Foreign Insurance (Inderzhstrakh) of the Ministry of Finance of the USSR.

BIBLIOGRAPHY
Mukhin, I. *Derzhavne strakhuvannia v SRSR* (Kiev 1961)
Schütte, E. *Das Versicherungswesen der Sowjet-Union ohne Berücksichtigung der Sozialversicherung. Mit einem Rückblick auf das vorrevolutionäre Erbe* (Berlin 1966)
Reitman, L. *Lichnoe strakhovanie v SSSR* (Moscow 1969)
Motylev, L. *Gosudarstvennoe strakhovanie v SSSR i problemy ego razvitiia* (Moscow 1972)
Tagiev, G. *Razvitie gosudarstvennogo strakhovaniia v SSSR (1917–1977 gg.)* (Moscow 1978)
Pleshkova, A. (ed). *Fond gosudarstvennogo strakhovaniia v SSSR* (Moscow 1984)

A. Bilynsky, C. Freeland

Intarsia: wooden plate depicting Hetman B. Khmelnytsky

Intarsia. A pictorial or ornamental mosaic consisting of wood pieces of various colors and textures inlaid in a wood surface. Developed in Italy in the 15th century, in the latter half of the 18th century intarsia became a popular method for decorating furniture, tableware, musical instruments, and religious objects in the western parts of Ukraine. Since the 19th century it has been used mostly in Hutsul handicrafts. Intarsia was used first in Hutsul wood carving by V. *Devdiuk. Besides traditional geometric ornamentation, since 1945 various propagandistic Soviet themes and portraits of a few Ukrainian historical figures have been done with intarsia.

Intelligentsia. A collective name for those who play a leading role in the cultural, social, and intellectual life in a society, from the Latin word *intelligentia* ('intelligence') from *intellegere* ('to perceive, understand, comprehend'). In Ukrainian and Russian the term (*inteligentsiia, intelligentsiia*) is a general abstract noun based on the noun *inteligent, intelligent* ('intellectual'). Contemporary sociological usage, however, often distinguishes between the intelligentsia – a broad social group consisting of professionally trained specialists – and intellectuals – a subcategory of the former that includes only those who serve as culture-bearers and the custodians of the tradition of creative and critical thinking about society's problems.

The word 'intelligentsia' is widely thought to be of mid-19th-century Russian origin, when it referred to a small educated minority whose members came from all sections of society, but mainly from the *nobility and urban bourgeoisie (*burghers). During the 19th century the term was also often used to describe only those educated individuals who aspired to independent thinking, questioned traditional values and the status quo, and sought radical social and political changes (eg, the Slavophiles and Westernizers, and later the Populists, socialists, and Marxists).

In Soviet Ukraine the intelligentsia is defined as 'a social group comprising individuals professionally involved in creative mental work, in the development and dissemination of culture, or in fulfilling specific administrative functions in production or other spheres of social life.' This broad definition includes almost all individuals employed in occupations requiring some post-secondary education, ie, professional scientists, engineers, teachers, physicians, librarians, academics, writers, artists, and supervisory personnel in industry and the state administration. Unlike the workers and collective farmers, who are said to constitute a class, the intelligentsia is considered to be a social group. However, some Western analysts and unofficial Soviet theorists have argued that part of the intelligentsia – ie, those in the political, military, and police hierarchy – do, in fact, constitute a new ruling class.

In modern times the intelligentsia has played a prominent role in anticolonial and national movements, particularly of nations that have lost their traditional ruling class (eg, the nobility) and whose economic development has been so weak that it has failed to produce significant indigenous bourgeois, petit-bourgeois, merchant, or artisan groups. In other national movements the petite bourgeoisie (eg, the Czech) or the gentry (eg, the Polish or Hungarian) played a leadership role, but in Ukraine leadership of the national movement went by default to the intelligentsia, because the other groups were missing in the social structure of the Ukrainian nation. The fact that until recently the Ukrainian intelligentsia was a small group hindered the development of national consciousness and the national movement.

The intelligentsia emerged as a separate social stratum in Russian-ruled Ukraine in the first half of the 19th century. Its ranks were initially filled by the sons of the minor gentry, who, finding no outlet in agriculture and commerce, sought positions in the service of the empire as petty officials and clerks, junior military and naval officers, or educators. Every modest modernizing step, eg, the growth of industry or the educational system, increased the size of the indigenous intelligentsia. The emancipation of the peasantry in 1861, which hastened its differentiation, provided an additional stimulus for the growth of its cadres. In the 1870s, the richer peasants, like their gentry predecessors, began pushing their sons to acquire some education.

Because of the preponderance of impoverished peasants in Ukraine's social structure and an educational system that was elitist and linguistically Russian, the nationally conscious Ukrainian intelligentsia represented but a tiny layer of the population. According to the 1897 census, out of a total population of 23.4 million in the nine Ukrainian gubernias, only 24,000 individuals had some form of tertiary education, and only 17,000 had specialized secondary training. The vast majority of this intelligentsia was not Ukrainian, but Russian, Jewish, or Polish. Moreover, because of socioeconomic and political pressures, many members of the intelligentsia with Ukrainian backgrounds had become Russified. For example, only 16 percent of the lawyers, less than a quarter of the teachers, and only 10 percent of the writers and artists in Ukraine claimed Ukrainian nationality in 1897. Of the 127,000 people enumerated in the census as having occupations involving intellectual labor, less than a third were Ukrainian.

The first formal sociopolitical organization of the nationally conscious Ukrainian intelligentsia – the secret *Cyril and Methodius Brotherhood – existed briefly (1846–7) before being suppressed. From the late 1850s to the 1890s, the clandestine *hromadas were its main organizations. In the late 19th century, the Ukrainian intelligentsia turned to organizing *Prosvita societies, a *co-operative movement, and revolutionary political *parties. From the 1917 Revolution to 1921 the national movement and the struggle for Ukrainian *autonomy and independence were headed largely by the intelligentsia.

In Western Ukraine the emergence of an intelligentsia was the result of the educational reforms of the Habsburg enlightened absolutists *Maria Theresa (1740–80) and her coruler and successor *Joseph II (1765–90). They established theological seminaries in Vienna, Lviv, Uzhhorod, and Chernivtsi to provide the Ukrainian clergy with a higher education; they also founded Lviv University and gymnasia in Lviv and Uzhhorod (a gymnasium was founded in Chernivtsi in 1808). In both Galicia and Transcarpathia these institutions very rapidly produced a Ukrainian intelligentsia. In the case of Transcarpathia there was even an overproduction of intelligentsia relative to the needs of the region, and a number of Ukrainian intellectuals immigrated to the Russian Empire, where they enjoyed considerable success (eg, P. Lodii, I. Orlai, and Yu. Venelyn). Although this new intelligentsia was primarily clerical, it included a secular component from the start, especially in Transcarpathia; a Ukrainian secular intelligentsia was unambiguously in evidence in Galicia by the 1840s. The development of a Ukrainian intelligentsia proceeded much more slowly in Bukovyna, since the Habsburgs did not take as much care to educate the Orthodox clergy there as they did to educate the Greek Catholic clergy in the rest of Western Ukraine.

During the Revolution of 1848 it was primarily the Galician clergy that assumed leadership of the *Supreme Ruthenian Council, the representative political body of Western Ukraine. Nonetheless, the secular intelligentsia (often of clerical social backgrounds) played a considerable role: Ukrainians employed in the civil service made up 32 percent of the council's membership; university and gymnasium students, 10 percent; and educators and writers, each 5 percent.

The constitutional restructuring of the Habsburg Empire in the late 1860s had a major impact on the west-Ukrainian intelligentsia. The Compromise of 1867 between Austria and Hungary led to the forcible Magyarization of the church, bureaucracy, and educational institutions in Transcarpathia, decimating and weakening the local Ukrainian intelligentsia. In 1910 only 0.8 percent of Transcarpathia's Ukrainians were employed as teachers, notaries, lawyers, priests, journalists, or in the military.

Although the Ukrainian intelligentsia in Galicia was subject to pressures of Polonization after the Austro-Hungarian Compromise, these pressures were more than counterbalanced by the civil rights guaranteed under the Austrian constitution of 1867. As in Transcarpathia, only 0.7 to 0.8 percent of the Ukrainian population was employed in the bureaucracy and liberal professions in 1900, yet there were several crucial differences. First, the Galician Ukrainian intelligentsia achieved a relatively high aggregate number (over 6,000 by the early 1870s, and over 20,000 by the turn of the century), which enabled it to undertake ambitious projects (such as the establishment of an academy – the *Shevchenko Scientific Society – in 1893 and the publication of 43 periodicals, including several daily newspapers, by 1910). Second, as a result of the liberties constitutionally guaranteed in Austria but absent in the Russian Empire and Hungary, members of the intelligentsia were able to work almost exclusively in the Ukrainian language, whether as clergymen, journalists, lawyers, or professors. Thus, although the Galician intelligentsia was smaller in absolute numbers than the Ukrainian intelligentsia in the Russian Empire and roughly equal in proportionate size to the Transcarpathian, it had a freedom of national intellectual action that made a significant qualitative difference. Finally, unlike its counterpart in Russian-ruled Ukraine and Transcarpathia, it had the opportunity to link up with the masses of the Ukrainian population, the peasantry, in a well-organized national movement. The intelligentsia discovered very early on that the leadership of a mass national movement produced tangible benefits for itself, such as the expansion of the Ukrainian-language educational system at all levels and entrance into government and parliamentary careers for its members. It established manifold institutions to link up with the masses, the first and most important of which was the popular educational *Prosvita society (during the first seven years of its existence, 1868–74, Prosvita had a membership consisting primarily of clergy [33 percent], lawyers and civil servants [25 percent], educators [20 percent], and students [10 percent]). The connections forged between the intelligentsia and the peasantry during the half-century preceding the 1917 Revolution made the revolutionary movement in Galicia more disciplined and unified than that in Russian-ruled Ukraine.

The growth of a Ukrainian intelligentsia in Bukovyna was a phenomenon of the late 19th and early 20th centuries. Key moments in its development were the establishment of Chernivtsi University in 1875 (a quarter of its students were Ukrainian in 1914) and the rapid expansion of the elementary educational system in the early 20th century. The emerging Bukovynian intelligentsia worked very closely with its Galician counterpart, many of whose methods and institutions it copied.

In the wake of the defeat of the Ukrainian national forces in the Ukrainian-Soviet War of 1917–21, many members of the Ukrainian intelligentsia immigrated to *Poland, *Czechoslovakia, *Germany, and *France. Those who remained in Soviet Ukraine had their activity and employment opportunities circumscribed by the Bolshevik authorities. After the *New Economic Policy and the introduction of *Ukrainization in the 1920s, the Bolsheviks were forced to pursue a policy of detente with the Ukrainian intelligentsia. Remaining suspicious of it, the Bolsheviks were nonetheless forced to enlist its support to hasten the economic, social, and educational development of the republic. During the relatively liberal period of 1923–9 the Ukrainian intelligentsia seized whatever opportunities were available and spearheaded the cultural and national renaissance of that period.

The growth of the state apparat, the Ukrainization of public institutions, and the expansion of the educational system greatly contributed towards expanding the size of the indigenous intelligentsia. Thus the number of employees in the educational system grew from 70,131 in 1926 to 111,135 in 1929, and the percentage of Ukrainians in it increased from 65 to 72. Between 1926 and 1929 the number of individuals engaged in other forms of intellectual work expanded from 255,223 in 1926 to 397,701 in 1929, and the representation of Ukrainians from 52 to 58 percent. In 1923 only 23 percent of civil servants in the republic were Ukrainian, but by 1926 the figure had risen to 54 percent.

In 1928, as Ukrainization was drawing to a close with the rise of Stalinist totalitarianism, the intelligentsia received its first major blow with the show trial of 'bourgeois specialists' in the Shakhty region. This was followed by arrests and the show trial of members of the intelligentsia accused of belonging to a so-called *Union for the Liberation of Ukraine. The purpose of these campaigns was to intimidate and silence the members of the intelligentsia who had led the intellectual, cultural, and national revival of the 1920s.

During the Soviet industrialization drive of the 1930s the intelligentsia of Ukraine, especially technical personnel, experienced rapid growth. Thus, the number of engineers and technical staff increased from 25,000 in 1926 to 123,000 in 1936. The majority of the members of this new scientific and technical intelligentsia were former workers and peasants who had been given an education and promoted to positions of responsibility. Very little information on changes in the national composition of the intelligentsia during the 1930s has come to light. Data that are available suggest that although in absolute numbers Ukrainians registered an increase, their percentage in the intelligentsia remained static or declined. A comparison of 1929 and 1939 data shows that the Ukrainians' share of intellectual occupations declined from 58 percent to 56 percent.

The Stalinist terror of the 1930s took a heavy toll of the Ukrainian intelligentsia. It is estimated that 80 percent of Ukraine's writers and creative intelligentsia were eliminated. As a result of the 1933–4 purge, for instance, the proportion of Ukrainians among the staff of research institutes in Soviet Ukraine dropped from 50 percent of the total in 1929 to 31 per cent in 1934, whereas the share of Russians increased from 30 to 50 percent in the same period.

In the interwar period the situations of the Ukrainian intelligentsia in the three regions of Western Ukraine were almost the reverse of what they had been in the late 19th and early 20th centuries. Now the development of the intelligentsia was retarded in both Galicia and Bukovyna, while in Transcarpathia a Ukrainian intelligentsia flourished. In both Poland and Rumania, to which Galicia and Bukovyna were annexed after the defeat of the Ukrainian national revolution, chauvinistic government policies excluded Ukrainians from employment in the civil service, discriminated against them at all educational levels (but particularly at the university level), drastically reduced or abolished state subsidies for Ukrainian intellectual and cultural institutions, and reduced the status of the Ukrainian language. As a result of these policies, exacerbated later by the effects of the Depression, most of the Ukrainian intelligentsia found its talents underutilized. Outstanding scholars ended up teaching in secondary schools or made ends meet by writing for the popular press. Many ambitious young intellectuals were fortunate to find employment as bookkeepers with the co-operative movement. This frustration of the Ukrainian intelligentsia in interwar Galicia and Bukovyna was a prime factor inclining it to political extremism in the 1930s.

By contrast, the situation in Transcarpathia was quite favorable. The new Czechoslovak regime expanded the educational system dramatically, deliberately recruited Ukrainians to the lower levels of the civil service, and did not discriminate against the Ukrainian language. Thus, by 1930 in Transcarpathia 13,670 Ukrainians (2.5 percent of the total Ukrainian population) were employed in the bureaucracy and liberal professions.

During the Second World War, many members of the Soviet Ukrainian intelligentsia were evacuated to Central Asia in the face of the advancing German army. The Nazis unleashed a wave of terror against the remaining intelligentsia, in keeping with H. Himmler's orders that 'the entire Ukrainian intelligentsia must be decimated ... Do away with it and the leaderless mass would become obedient.'

In the postwar period, the demands of scientific and technological development have necessitated the rapid numerical growth of the intelligentsia. Thus, the gainfully employed intelligentsia in Soviet Ukraine has grown from 513,000 in 1941 to 3,269,000 in 1970 and 5,958,000 in 1983. (The totals for the USSR are 2,401,000, 16,841,000, and 31,628,000 in the respective years.) Included in these figures are individuals who have only completed specialized secondary educations (3,430,000 in Ukraine and 18,141,000 in the USSR in 1983). Some sociologists argue that, properly speaking, the intelligentsia consists only of persons with a tertiary education. Using this criterion, the gainfully employed intelligentsia in 1983 numbered 13,487,000 in the USSR and 2,528,000 in Ukraine (53 percent of it women). In Ukraine engineers are the single largest group within the intelligentsia with tertiary educations – 1,085,000 in 1983.

It is possible to ascertain the Ukrainians' share of the intelligentsia as a whole (those gainfully employed, students, and pensioners) for 1970: the 1.1 million Ukrainians who belonged to the intelligentsia (with tertiary educations) represented 54.7 percent of the total group in the republic. In the case of the intelligentsia as a whole (including those with specialized secondary educations), 63.1 percent, or 2.6 million, were Ukrainian. Data on the national composition of specialists – defined as all those with higher or specialized secondary educations gainfully employed in the national economy – show that the Ukrainians' share in this occupational group dropped slightly, from 63.5 percent in 1960 to 63.2 percent in 1970. Since in 1970 Ukrainians represented 75 percent of the republic's total population, these figures indicate a serious underrepresentation of Ukrainians in the intelligentsia of Soviet Ukraine. This problem is itself tied to difficulties in the *social mobility of Ukrainians.

In the contemporary period the intelligentsia has remained the most active element in society promoting Ukrainian national demands. Indicative of this is the fact that the large majority of dissidents in Soviet Ukraine are members of the intelligentsia.

BIBLIOGRAPHY
Leikina-Svirskaia, V. *Intelligentsiia v Rossii vo vtoroi polovine XIX veka* (Moscow 1971)
Churchward, L.G. *The Soviet Intelligentsia: An Essay on the Social Structure and Roles of Soviet Intellectuals during the 1960s* (London and Boston 1973)
Bailes, K.E. *Technology and Society under Lenin and Stalin: Origins of the Soviet Technical Intelligentsia, 1917–1941* (Princeton 1978)
Magocsi, P.R. *The Shaping of a National Identity: Subcarpathian Rus', 1848–1948* (Cambridge, Mass and London 1978)
Krawchenko, B. *Social Change and National Consciousness in Twentieth-Century Ukraine* (London 1985)
Tkachova, L. *Intelihentsiia Radians'koï Ukraïny v period pobudovy osnov sotsializmu* (Kiev 1985)
Kozik, J. *The Ukrainian National Movement in Galicia: 1815–1849*, ed L.D. Orton (Edmonton 1986)

J.-P. Himka, B. Krawchenko

Inter-Allied Commission. See Ukrainian-Polish War in Galicia, 1918–19.

Intermarriage. See Marriage.

Intermede (Ukrainian: *intermediia*). A short comic or satiric sketch that was performed between acts of serious plays. The first known intermede was performed in 15th-century England during a play by H. Medwall.

The first two intermedes in Ukraine are found in the publication of J. *Gawatowicz's Polish tragedy about the death of John the Baptist (1619). The plots of intermedes were not related to the subject of the plays in which they occurred and were often written by different authors. Reflecting the social, political, and religious relations of their time, they were mostly anecdotes with one-dimensional, stereotyped characters: Cossacks, peasants, Gypsies, Poles, Jews, Russian soldiers, and Belorussians. The characters often spoke a mixture of various languages, although the Ukrainian ones spoke in the pure vernacular. M. Dovhalevsky was a master of Ukrainian intermedes; he wrote up to five versified intermedes for each of his Christmas and Easter dramas (1736–7). Five intermedes were performed during H. Konysky's tragic comedy *Voskresenie mertvykh* (Resurrection of the Dead, 1747), and seven or eight during the anonymous Ukrainian play *Stefanotokos* staged in Novgorod in 1742. References to other non-extant intermedes exist. The influence of intermedes is seen in the works of I. Nekrashchevych, in Christmas puppet plays (the **vertep*), in humorous verses of the 18th century, and in 19th-century Ukrainian comedies. An analysis and a selection of texts is found in M. Vozniak's *Pochatky ukraïns'koï komediï* (Beginnings of Ukrainian Comedy, 1919, repr 1955).

D. Chyzhevsky

Internal passport. See Passport system.

International Commission for the Study of the Folk Culture of the Carpathians and Balkans (Mizhnarodna komisiia po vyvchenniu narodnoi kultury Karpat i Balkanu). An international organization founded in 1959 and called until 1976 the International Commission for the Study of the Folk Culture of the Carpathians. Initiated by Czech and Polish ethnographers, it has co-ordinated ethnographic and other research on the Carpathian and (later) northern Balkan regions by Bulgarian, Czechoslovak, Polish, Rumanian, Soviet, and Yugoslavian scholars. The nucleus of the commission's Soviet section (headed by Yu. Bromlei from Moscow) is made up of Ukrainian scholars from Kiev, Lviv, Uzhhorod, and Chernivtsi. The commission's administrative center (until 1990) is located in Bratislava; its general secretary is V. Frolec from Brno. The commission publishes the periodical *Carpatobalcanica* (*Carpatica* until 1977); 15 issues, with articles in Russian, German, English, and French, appeared by 1985. Every national section has its own serial; the Soviet one is *Karpatskii sbornik*, published by the USSR Institute of Ethnography, of which 3 issues have appeared since 1972.

In the 1960s the commission's main focus was the preparation of comprehensive bibliographic tools. This work culminated in the three-volume *Bibliographia etnographica carpatobalcanica* (Brno 1981–5). A Ukrainian bibliography, Ya. Prylypko's *Ukraïns'ke radians'ke karpatoznavstvo* (Soviet Ukrainian Carpathology), was published in Kiev in 1972.

Every national section publishes monographs. Soviet Ukrainian works include those by Yu. *Hoshko (1976), R. *Kyrchiv (1978), M. Mandybura (1978; see bibliography in *Hutsuls), T. Hontar (*Narodne kharchuvannia ukraïntsiv Karpat* [The Folk Diet of the Carpathians' Ukrainians, 1979]), Z. Boltarovych (*Narodne likuvannia ukraïntsiv Karpat kintsia XIX–pochatku XX st.* [Folk Medicine of the Carpathians' Ukrainians at the End of the 19th–Beginning of the 20th Century, 1980]), V. *Hrabovetsky (1982), and M. Sopolyha (*Narodne zhytlo ukraïntsiv Skhidnoï Slovachchyny* [The Folk Dwelling of the Ukrainians of Eastern Slovakia, 1983]); and many historical-ethnographic collections, such as the 23-author *Boikivshchyna* (The Boiko Region, 1983) edited by Yu. Hoshko et al.

The commission regularly holds conferences, seminars, and deliberations. Some have taken place in Ukraine; the most noteworthy are the conference on the Culture and Folkways of the Population of the Ukrainian Carpathians (Uzhhorod 1972) and on the 25th anniversary of the commission (Lviv 1984).

BIBLIOGRAPHY
Porits'kyi, A. 'Mizhnarodna komisiia po vyvchenniu kul'tury narodiv Karpat,' *NTE*, 1961, no. 3
Kutel'makh, K.; Pavliuk, S. 'Karpato-balkanika: Problemy i perspektyvy,' *NTE*, 1985, no. 3
Slovenský národopis, 1985, no. 4

M. Hnatiukivsky

International economic relations. Ukraine has been involved extensively in *foreign trade in addition to internal trade with other Soviet republics. Moreover, except for the brief reconstruction period after the Second World War, it has been a net supplier of capital and human resources for the development of the vast Asian regions of the USSR. The outflow of capital funds is reflected in Ukraine's annual *budgets and corresponds to the net export surpluses in its *balance of payments.

Ukraine's interaction with the rest of the world has also included the exchange of technological knowledge and the transfer of voluntary and, at times, forced skilled and unskilled labor. During the 1950s, it contributed capital equipment, technical know-how, and human resources for the construction of Nowa Huta and other industrial projects in Poland. It has played a similar role in Soviet aid to India, Cuba, and countries in Africa and Asia. Some 10,000 foreign students and trainees are educated in Ukraine annually.

During the early years of collectivization and during the 1940s in Western Ukraine, the Soviet authorities deported hundreds of thousands of Ukrainians in order both to destroy opposition to the Soviet regime and to provide a source of forced labor for the planned development of Kazakhstan's 'virgin lands,' Siberia's gold mines, and other natural resources in Soviet Asia. Subsequently, the Soviet system of education and job placement has encouraged the out-migration of Ukrainians to other parts of the USSR and the influx of non-native personnel into Ukraine. Consequently there has been a steady rise in the number of non-Ukrainians in Ukraine's urban and industrial centers.

As a founding member of the United Nations, Ukraine has participated in such UN bodies as the International Labour Organisation, the UN Conference on Trade and Development, the UN Industrial Development Organization, the Economic Commission for Europe, the Statistical Commission, and the Natural Resources Committee. It has been a signatory of over 120 international agreements and conventions; those dealing with economic matters include the Convention Concerning the Protection of Wages, the International Constitution of the Universal Postal Union, the Statute of the International Atomic Energy Commission, and the Agreement on the Danube Commission. But while Soviet Ukraine partakes formally in the above international institutions and contributes technical personnel and funds for their operation, it does not have the autonomy to represent its own socioeconomic interests. Ukraine lacks a voice even in the Soviet-bloc *Council for Mutual Economic Assistance (Comecon), although its production plans, transportation network, natural-gas pipelines, and electricity grids are more integrated with the neighboring socialist countries than are those of the rest of the USSR.

Most East European countries have consulates in Kiev, and several countries have them in Odessa. The United States is in the process of establishing a consulate in Kiev for the protection of American tourists and commercial interests.

During the *New Economic Policy system of the 1920s, Ukraine was allowed some autonomy in external trade. But the subsequent Soviet centralized system of planning, Moscow's monopoly in foreign trade and banking, and a lack of its own diplomatic network have obscured Ukraine's international identity in spite of its continued substantial interaction with the world economy.

Economic historians have documented the involvement of Ukraine – with its rich human and natural resources and important geopolitical location – in international commerce. Hoards of ancient Greek, Roman, Arab, and Persian coins unearthed in Ukraine confirm that international transit and direct trade existed there already in pre-Christian times. The Rus' chronicles provide extensive evidence about Ukraine's foreign trade and describe the laws, treaties, and political conditions of commerce under the rulers of Kievan Rus' and the Principality of Galicia-Volhynia. Domestic and international trade declined during the Mongol invasions from the mid-13th through the 14th centuries, but revived under Lithuanian and Polish rule. Ukraine was drawn into the international grain trade through the Baltic port of *Gdańsk and continued to supply the growing European markets with agricultural staples also under the Hetman state of the mid-17th to mid-18th century. When Ukraine progressively lost its autonomy under Russian domination, its foreign trade became increasingly constrained by tsarist mercantilist policies.

During the millennium prior to Soviet rule, a special role in Ukraine's international commerce and finance was played by its *cities. They were often self-governed, and they usually welcomed and protected the *Armenians, *Germans, *Jews, *Greeks, and other foreign merchants and their permanent settlements. Foreign artisans (see *Crafts) and artists also provided vital links with the countries to the west. Thus Greek architects introduced stone construction in Ukraine (eg, the St Sophia Cathedral in Kiev, 1037–54), Italian masters enhanced the Renaissance architecture of Lviv during the 16th and 17th centuries, and foreign engineers (eg, the Frenchman G. Le Vasseur de *Beauplan) supervised the construction of many castles and fortifications during the 17th century. During the 19th century, Belgian, French, and other foreign capital (see *Capitalism and *Industry) contributed greatly to the industrialization of Ukraine, while Ukraine's balance of trade generated substantial surpluses that were used to service the external debts of the Russian Empire. Meanwhile, Western Ukraine under Austro-Hungarian (1772–1918) and Polish (1921–39) rule was a peripheral region in relation to the pertinent ruling metropolis and hence at a disadvantage in international trade and finance.

Several political-economic theories can be applied in interpreting the subordinate status of Ukraine and the other subjugated nations in the Russian Empire and in its successor the Soviet Union. Lenin argued that Russian *imperialism before the October Revolution was a manifestation of monopoly capitalism, and he condemned the persistence of 'Great Russian chauvinism' even after the Bolsheviks gained power. H. Seton-Watson and V. Holubnychy regarded Ukraine as the victim of an imperialism driven by Russia's sociopolitical and economic objectives. W. Kolarz, D. Solovei, and B. Wynar interpreted Ukraine's status as that of a colony. The economists M. Volobuiev and Z. Melnyk have analyzed Ukraine's financial exploitation through Moscow's control of taxation and expenditures that involve unrequited requisitions of huge budgetary surpluses by the central government. Finally, V.N. Bandera has adapted and elaborated J. Galtung's structuralist theory of imperialism to explain the institutionalized mechanisms of control and exploitation of Ukraine as a weak periphery by Russia as a dominant metropolis. By not allowing Ukraine to engage directly in trade and other international transactions, the central authorities have deprived it of the profits and other benefits it could derive from international specialization and related activities.

BIBLIOGRAPHY

Volobuiev, M. 'Do problemy ukraïns'koï ekonomiky,' *Bil'shovyk Ukraïny*, 1929, nos 2–3

Kobers'kyi, K. *Ukraïna v svitovomu hospodarstvi* (Prague 1933)

Kolarz, W. *Russia and Her Colonies* (New York 1952)

Osechyns'kyi, V. *Halychyna pid hnitom Avstro-Uhorshchyny v epokhu imperializmu* (Lviv 1954)
Wynar, B. 'The Establishment of Soviet Colonialism in Ukraine,' *UQ*, Spring 1957
Solovei, D. *Ukraïna v systemi soviets'koho koloniializmu* (Munich 1959)
Kulinych, I.; Peters, I. *Ekonomichne spivrobitnytstvo Ukraïns'koï RSR z kraïnamy sotsializmu* (Kiev 1962)
Seton-Watson, H. 'Moscow's Imperialism,' *Problems of Communism*, January–February 1964
Committee on the Judiciary, United States Senate. *The Soviet Empire: A Study in Discrimination and Abuse of Power* (Washington 1965)
Holubnychy, V. 'Some Economic Aspects of Relations among the Soviet Republics,' in *Ethnic Minorities in the Soviet Union*, ed E. Goldhagen (New York 1968)
– 'Ukraïna v systemi vserosiis'koho, evropeis'koho i svitovoho hospodarstva,' *Ukraïns'kyi samostiinyk*, nos 145, 146 (1969)
Polons'ka-Vasylenko, N. *Istoriia Ukraïny*, 2 vols (Munich 1972)
Vasilenko, V.; Lukashuk, I. *The Ukrainian SSR in Contemporary International Relations* (Kiev 1975)
Chirovsky, N.Fr. *An Introduction to Ukrainian History*, 3 vols (New York 1981–6)
Dereviankin, T. et al (eds). *Istoriia narodnoho hospodarstva Ukraïns'koï RSR*, 3 vols (Kiev 1983–6)
Bandera, W. 'Międzynarodowe stosunki gospodarcze w cieniu dominacji rosyjskiej,' *Sucasnist: Zeszyt w języku polskim*, no. 1–2 (Munich 1985)

V.N. Bandera

International Free Academy of Arts and Sciences (Académie internationale libre des sciences et des lettres). An academy of émigré scholars from central and eastern European countries (excluding Russia) under Communist control. Established in Paris in 1951 at O. *Shulhyn's initiative, in 1970 the academy had 330 members. Fifty-two of the members were Ukrainian. Its presidents have been C. Antoniade and C. Marinescu, and its vice-presidents, O. Shulhyn and O. Kulchytsky. Accounts of the academy's scholarly conferences and assemblies have been published in its French-language *Bulletin* (5 issues have appeared). Since 1970 the academy has not been very active.

International legal status of Ukraine. International law is the body of laws and principles that governs relations between states and other entities that carry an international personality. It arose toward the end of the Middle Ages with the emergence of modern nation-states. Since the 17th century it has developed as a separate branch of law and an important discipline in the study of international relations.

The question of a state's international status may be examined within the framework of current theories of international law, or in the light of whatever fragmentary norms of international law existed at a given time. The central issues that need to be addressed are the extent to which a state is sovereign (see *Sovereignty) and whether that state or entity is recognized by the world community as a subject of international law (ie, does it have an international personality?). A state's international personality is measured by its recognized international legal liability and by its legal capacity to engage in international relations – including the negotiation of treaties, legation (the sending and receiving of diplomatic missions), membership in international organizations, and legitimate waging of war and concluding of peace.

The international status of Ukraine in the modern period is the subject of considerable controversy from the viewpoint of international law. This controversy has arisen because of Ukraine's dependence on other states, and because of the long intervals of Ukrainian statelessness in this period. At first, the *Hetman state, and to a certain degree before that the Zaporozhian Sich (see *Zaporizhia), had a distinct international personality – they engaged in diplomatic relations and entered into mutually binding treaties with foreign powers. The nature of Ukraine's later dependence on Muscovy, or the dependence of separate regions of Ukraine on the Polish Commonwealth or the Ottoman Empire, is difficult to describe using classical definitions of international law. Historical and legal interpretations of the Muscovite-Ukrainian Treaty of *Pereiaslav (1654) and the subsequent agreements between the hetman and the tsar (see *Hetman articles), and the nature of the resulting relationship between the two countries, have varied. Some scholars see in them the complete incorporation of the Hetman state into Muscovy, although the former may have retained some internal autonomy. Others have variously described the relationship as a 'personal union' or a 'real union' between the two states, or simply a military alliance, while still others have characterized the Hetmanate from the second half of the 17th century as a vassal or protectorate of Muscovy. In any case, whatever independence the Hetman state enjoyed at first was gradually lost, and with that its international personality declined until it disappeared completely after I. Mazepa's defeat by Peter I at the Battle of *Poltava.

The question of Ukraine's international status became an issue again only in the 20th century with the reestablishment of a Ukrainian state in the form of the *Ukrainian National Republic. The subsequent de jure or de facto recognition of the various governments of the UNR and the *Hetman government by a total of 23 states and the establishment of diplomatic relations with a number of these governments (see *Diplomacy and *Consular service), their status as signatories to international *treaties (esp the Treaty of *Brest-Litovsk and the Treaty of *Warsaw), and their acknowledged right as a sovereign state to wage war against foreign aggressors, all confirm these governments' international personality.

The early international status of the Ukrainian SSR is more problematic. Its independent international status was affirmed by the fact that it was recognized by countries such as Poland, Czechoslovakia, Turkey, Austria, and Germany; that it maintained a foreign affairs commissariat and diplomatic service; and that it negotiated treaties, including the Peace Treaty of *Riga. Attempts were also made in a series of diplomatic notes to make the Ukrainian SSR appear as a separate belligerent in the Soviet-Polish War of 1920–1 and in the conflict with the Western Allies and Rumania during their intervention in the Russian Civil War. A major obstacle to its full recognition by the international community, however, was the issue of its sovereignty. The legal relationship between Russia and Ukraine before 1923 is difficult to characterize. Although formally the Ukrainian SSR was an independent Soviet republic, in reality its relationship to the RSFSR was based on a unique sort of federal system (see *Federalism), predicated mostly on the resolution of the All-Ukrainian Central Executive Committee of 1 June 1919 establishing a military and economic alliance between the two Soviet republics, and the so-called workers'-peasants' treaty between the Ukrainian SSR and the RSFSR of 28 December 1920. Unlike the governments of the UNR and the *Hetman government, which asserted their sovereignty in their official proclamations (see *Universals of the Central Rada) and were clearly accorded international legitimacy, the government of the Ukrainian SSR did little to reinforce its image as an autonomous state and hence its international personality. Moreover, the existence of the *Government-in-exile of the UNR served to undermine the international legitimacy of the Ukrainian SSR.

The incorporation of Ukraine into the USSR in 1922 ended its competency in defense and foreign affairs and formally united all the Soviet republics into a single 'federal state.' The subsequent Soviet constitutions of 1924 and 1936 (see *Constitution of the Ukrainian SSR) introduced a centralized political system and made foreign affairs the exclusive prerogative of the Union government, although in the 1936 and 1977 constitutions the Ukrainian SSR was simultaneously guaranteed the legal right to *secession.

Constitutional reforms introduced in February 1944 had a fundamental impact on the international status of the Ukrainian SSR. It formally reacquired the right to legation, although it has not as yet established diplomatic relations with any country. A foreign affairs commissariat was re-established (since 1946 the Ministry of Foreign Affairs), and Ukraine began to participate in the negotiation of foreign treaties, specifically the peace talks that ended the Second World War (see *Paris Peace Treaty of 1947), where the Ukrainian SSR was granted the status of an Allied state and even claimed war damages. In theory Ukraine was also guaranteed the right to its own military formations, but none were ever organized and this prerogative was eventually abrogated by the 1977 constitution. At the same time, however, the constitutional amendments specified that the Union government reserved for itself the right to 'regulate the general order of the relations of union republics with foreign states.' This condition has made it difficult to characterize the status of the republics even within the context of Soviet law.

Two major unresolved questions in international legal theory are: can the constituent parts of a federal state possess an international personality, and can they be considered the subjects of international law? The implications of the debate over these issues for the international status of the Ukrainian SSR are obvious. While most Soviet (eg, S. Krylov and V. Koretsky) and even some Western scholars believe that the Ukrainian SSR enjoys sovereignty, even within the federal Soviet state, and therefore can be considered the subject of international law, their arguments are rejected by other jurists and scholars.

Another measure of a country's international personality is its membership in *international organizations. The government of the UNR did not belong to any official international organizations, with the brief exception of a commission that regulated shipping on the Black Sea in 1918; its application in 1920 to join the League of Nations could not be considered before Ukraine was overrun by the Bolsheviks. The Ukrainian SSR did not begin to participate formally in international organizations until 1945, when it joined the United Nations (UN) as one of its founding members. According to the theory of 'collective recognition' advanced by some scholars, Soviet Ukraine's membership in the UN implies its recognition by all of the organization's founding members and, therefore, its general recognition by the world community. Most countries, however, including the United States, reject this interpretation and argue that their acceptance of the Ukrainian and Belorussian SSR as members of the UN does not imply a general and full recognition, but only a limited 'functional recognition' extended specifically to their role in the organization. With the exception of the UN and its various agencies, the Ukrainian SSR does not belong to any major international organizations. It does not even belong as a separate state to the various associations of socialist states, such as the *Council for Mutual Economic Assistance or the Warsaw Pact. (See also *International economic relations and *Ukrainian Soviet Socialist Republic.)

BIBLIOGRAPHY

Halajczuk, B. *El estado ucranio del siglo 20* (Buenos Aires 1953)

Korets'kyi, V. 'Rozkvit suverenitetu ukraïns'koï radians'koï derzhavy v skladi SRSR,' *Vistnyk AN URSR*, no. 8 (Kiev 1954)

Yakemchuk, R. *L'Ukraine en droit international* (Louvain 1954)

Markus, V. *L' Ukraine soviétique dans les relations internationales et son statut en droit international, 1918–23* (Paris 1959)

Bilinsky, Y. 'The Ukrainian SSR in International Affairs after World War II,' *AUA*, 9, no. 1–2 (New York 1961)

Halajczuk, B. 'The Soviet Ukraine as a Subject of International Law,' *UAU*, 9, no. 1–2 (New York 1961)

Halaichuk, B. 'Pravo legatsiï URSR,' *Suchasnist'*, no. 12 (1964)

Ukrainskaia SSR i zarubezhnye sotsialisticheskie strany (Kiev 1965)

Sosnovs'kyi, M. *Ukraïna na mizhnarodnii areni, 1945–65* (Toronto 1966)

Mizhnarodne pravo (Kiev 1971)

Vasylenko, V. *Pravovi aspekty uchasti Ukraïns'koï RSR u mizhnarodnykh vidnosynakh* (Kiev 1984)

International organizations. Non-profit organizations that draw their membership from at least three countries and conduct operations in at least three countries. The main types of international organizations are intergovernmental organizations (IGO) established by governments through multilateral treaties, and non-governmental organizations (NGO) composed of either national associations in various fields (political, professional, trade, religious, cultural, or sport) or individuals from different countries who seek to improve co-operation and understanding among peoples. Ukrainian world organizations, which represent only Ukrainian associations or individuals from different countries, are not discussed here. There has been a proliferation of international organizations in the 20th century, which, for this reason, has been called the century of international association. Ukrainians as a stateless people took part and continue to take part in some NGO. The Ukrainian SSR is a member of several IGO.

In 1905 the leaders of non-Russian nationalities within the Russian Empire founded the *Autonomists' Union in St Petersburg, the first international organization of its kind in Russia. The *Congress of the Peoples of Russia, which on M. *Hrushevsky's initiative was convened in Kiev in September 1917, elected a committee to co-ordinate the struggle of non-Russian nations for a federation, but did not give rise to a permanent organization. Ukrainian organizations abroad sought contacts with other national groups to promote the cause of Ukrainian independence. As early as 1918 Ukrainians in North America helped found the Central European Democratic Union, headed by T. Masaryk. The Federation of Ukrainians in the United States, as well as a separate representation of Carpatho-Ukrainian immigrants, joined the union. In 1919 the Ukrainian National Committee together with Lithuanian, Latvian, and Estonian organizations formed the League of Four Nations in the United States.

In 1920, under very difficult conditions, the UNR government applied for membership in the *League of Nations, but before the application could be approved the government was forced into exile. However, two émigré organizations – the Ukrainian Association for the League of Nations and the Western Ukrainian Association of the League of Nations – worked closely with the International Federation of League of Nations Societies. In 1934 the USSR joined the League of Nations and was seated on some of its subordinate agencies. The Ukrainian SSR, however, because of its complete subservience to Moscow, did not belong to any IGO during the interwar period.

The situation changed in 1945 when the Ukrainian SSR was permitted to play a limited role in the field of foreign relations. To strengthen the position of the Soviet bloc in the new intergovernmental organizations that arose after the war and, partly, to satisfy the national aspirations of Ukrainians, the USSR demanded that Ukraine and Belorussia be reorganized as founding members of the United Nations (UN).

As a UN member, Ukraine has the right to nominate and elect judges of the International Court of Justice in The Hague. The Ukrainian jurist V. Koretsky served on the court as a judge (1961–70) and vice-chairman (1967–70). In 1962 Soviet Ukraine joined the Permanent Court of Arbitration, founded in 1899 in The Hague, and gained the right to nominate four members to a permanent panel of arbitrators from which parties to a dispute select a tribunal to settle their dispute. Among the UN agencies (see accompanying table) to which it belongs, Ukraine has been most active in the United Nations Educational, Scientific, and Cultural Organization (UNESCO) and in the International Labour Organisation (ILO). Although the Ukrainian SSR is not a member of some specialized agencies of the UN such as the International Civil Aviation Organization and the International Maritime Organization, Ukraine has taken part in some of their conferences and has signed the conventions prepared by the conferences. The Ministry of Foreign Affairs in Kiev, which has a separate department for international organizations, keeps in touch with the international organizations to which Ukraine belongs or with which it co-operates. Ukraine maintains permanent missions at the UN in New York, at the UN European headquarters in Geneva, at UNESCO in Paris, and at the UN agencies in Vienna (See also *International economic relations). Ukraine's position on various issues taken up by these agencies is determined entirely by the USSR government. Ukraine is a signatory of a number of conventions prepared by these organizations, particularly by the International Labour Organisation (see *Treaties).

The Ukrainian SSR does not belong as a separate entity to the Soviet-bloc intergovernmental organizations of which the USSR is a member, although these organizations are sponsored by the USSR; eg, the Warsaw Treaty Organization, the Comecon, the International Investment Bank, and the International Centre for Scientific and Technical Information. Ukraine is not a separate member of the Danube Commission set up in 1948 by the Belgrade Convention, although Ukraine signed the original convention. The Ukrainian SSR is not even represented in pro-Soviet political NGO such as the World Peace Council, on whose presidium O. Korniichuk served as representative of the USSR, not of Ukraine. Ukraine's application to the Inter-Parliamentary Union (est in 1888) was rejected, although a Soviet parliamentary group was admitted in 1955.

After the First World War, in spite of their nongovernmental status, Ukrainian émigré organizations, particularly political ones, were very active on the international stage. UNR circles in Warsaw, for example,

Ukraine in UN agencies

Organization	Founding date	Admission date	Headquarters
COUNCILS			
UN Economic and Social Council	1946	1946, 1977	Geneva, New York
SPECIAL BODIES OF THE GENERAL ASSEMBLY			
UN Children's Fund	1946	1958	New York
UN Conference on Trade and Development	1964	1972	Geneva
UN Development Program	1965	1965	New York
UN Environment Program	1972	1981	Nairobi
SPECIALIZED AGENCIES			
International Telecommunication Union	1865	1947	Geneva
World Meteorological Organization	1873	1948	Geneva
Universal Postal Union	1874	1947	Berne
International Labour Organisation	1919	1954	Geneva
World Health Organization	1946	1946	Geneva
UN Educational, Scientific, and Cultural Organization	1946	1954	Paris
International Atomic Energy Agency	1956	1957	Vienna
UN Industrial Development Organization	1966	1966	Vienna
World Intellectual Property Organization	1967	1970	Geneva

organized the *Promethean movement, which embraced the nations subjugated by the Soviet Union. Besides a Promethean club, the Friendship Committee of the Peoples of Caucasia, Turkestan, and Ukraine was active in Paris and published *La Revue de Prométhée* (1938–9). As members of Polish, Rumanian, or Czechoslovak delegations, Ukrainian parliamentarians took part in the work and the congresses of the Inter-Parliamentary Union. Ukrainian political leaders in Poland and Rumania attended the *Congress of National Minorities.

After the Second World War, Ukrainian political organizations were active members, and often cofounders, of several organizations representing Central and East European and Asian nations in a common struggle against Soviet domination; eg, the *Anti-Bolshevik Bloc of Nations, the *Freedom International, and the League for the Liberation of Nations of the USSR (the so-called *Paris Bloc). The Ukrainian Movement for a Federated Europe (est 1961 in Paris) was a member of the European Center for Federalist Action.

Ukrainian socialist parties were the first party organizations to establish extensive contacts with similar parties or movements in other countries. Thus in 1919–20 the Ukrainian Party of Socialist Revolutionaries and the Ukrainian Social Democratic Workers' party (USDRP), and in the interwar years the USDRP alone, belonged to the *Socialist International. Since 1950 the unified Ukrainian Socialist party has been a member of the Socialist Union of Central-Eastern Europe. Ukrainian Communist parties – the CP(B)U and the Communist Party of Western Ukraine – joined the *Communist International in 1919 but remained members only during the 1920s. The *Ukrainian Communist party and the Borotbists were not admitted to the International. The CPU was not a member of the Information Bureau of Communist and Workers' Parties (1947–56), nor did it take part in a series of consultative conferences of communist and workers' parties convened by Moscow in the 1960s–1970s. In relations with communist parties outside the USSR the CPSU represents all the Soviet republican party organizations.

Ukrainian non-political organizations also established ties with non-governmental organizations in their fields. As early as 1920 the *National Council of Ukrainian Women joined the International Council of Women (a federation of national women's organizations founded in 1888), and in 1925 took part in its Washington congress. As a representative of a stateless nation, it was expelled from the federation in 1928. The *Union of Ukrainian Women in Lviv was admitted in 1923 to the International Alliance of Women (a federation of women's organizations founded in 1904 to fight for women's suffrage) and participated in its congresses. In the interwar years Ukrainian women formed a section of the Women's International League for Peace and Freedom. After the Second World War the International Alliance of Women did not renew the membership of associations whose national constituency lay within the Soviet bloc, but it gave associate status to the *World Federation of Ukrainian Women's Organizations. In 1950 the federation became a member of the World Movement of Mothers. (See also *Women's movement.)

Ukrainian students took an active part in international life through the *Central Union of Ukrainian Students (TseSUS), which in 1922 became a special member of the International Confederation of Students and was also a member of the International Students' League and the International Students' Aid. Before and after the Second World War, TseSUS participated in a series of international students' congresses and exhibitions. The students of Soviet Ukraine have no national organization other than the Communist Youth League of Ukraine, which does not participate in any NGO. Only the Student Council of the USSR belongs to the pro-Communist International Union of Students.

Before the Revolution and during Ukraine's independence Ukrainian trade union organizations did not belong to any international unions. At first the trade unions of the Ukrainian SSR were members of the Red International of Trade Unions (Profintern). After 1945 only the All-Union Central Trade Union, not the republican unions of Ukraine, has been a member of the pro-Communist World Federation of Trade Unions. In 1949 the Confederation of Free Ukrainian Trade Organizations was founded in Paris. Its membership included the *Union of Ukrainian Workers of France and the Union of Ukrainian Workers of Belgium, and the confederation itself was a member of the International Federation of Christian Trade Unions (est 1920). On the confederation's initiative in 1951, the International Federation of Christian Workers in Exile was founded in Paris. In the 1950s it represented the emigrant trade unions of 12 national groups from Central and Eastern Europe.

Ukrainian co-operative organizations became active in international organizations rather early. The Kharkiv co-operative leader, M. Ballin, was one of the founders of the International Co-operative Alliance (est 1895 in London). A number of Ukrainian co-operative activists took part in its congresses, and some (S. Borodaievsky and B. Martos) were members of the International Institute for Co-operative Studies. The Narodna Torhovlia co-operative union, the Provincial Audit Union (later the Audit Union of Ukrainian Co-operatives), and in 1917–20 the Dniprosoiuz co-operative association were full members of the alliance. Since 1921 the national co-operative associations of the Ukrainian SSR have been represented by the all-Union Tsentrosoiuz in Moscow.

Ukrainian Catholic associations belonged to a number of international organizations, usually as full members. Soon after its creation the Obnova Society of Ukrainian Catholic Students joined the Pax Romana International Movement of Catholic Students and the association of Slavic Catholic organizations Slavia Catholica. After the war Obnova was the chief founder of the Alliance of Exiled Catholic Student Organizations of Central and Eastern Europe, while the Ukrainian Catholic Academic Alliance Obnova was a founding member of the Pax Romana International Catholic Movement for Intellectual and Cultural Affairs. The *Ukrainian Christian Movement participates in international congresses and is a member of the International Council of Catholic Men (Unum Omnes). No Ukrainian religious organization or church, whether Catholic, Orthodox, or Protestant, is a member of the World Council of Churches. Only the Russian Orthodox church and the All-Union Soviet of Christians and Baptists, which claim to represent the faithful in Ukraine, are members of the union. The metropolitan of Kiev, Filaret Denysenko, is an active representative of the Russian Orthodox church on the international scene. The Ukrainian Exarchate of the Russian Orthodox church in Kiev has a department of external relations.

In the cultural field the *Ukrainian Academic Committee (est 1924 in Prague) co-operated with international learned societies such as the International Committee on Intellectual Co-operation of the League of Nations in Geneva and the Institute of Intellectual Co-operation in Paris. After the Second World War, Ukrainian and other émigré scholars founded the *International Free Academy of Arts and Sciences in Paris. Ukrainian Soviet scholars are represented in international associations devoted to particular disciplines not by their own republican committees but by all-Union committees. The only exception to this rule is the International Association for the Study and Dissemination of Slav Cultures, founded by UNESCO in 1976, where Ukrainian Slavists are represented by a committee of the AN URSR. In 1968 efforts were made in Prešov, Czechoslovakia, to form an association of teachers of Ukrainian similar to the International Association of Teachers of Russian Language and Literature, but the project was opposed by Soviet officials.

In the late 1920s and at the beginning of the 1930s, Ukrainian Soviet writers belonged to international proletarian literary unions, and in 1930 the Second Congress of Proletarian Writers was held in Kharkiv. Apart from this, Ukrainian cultural life in the USSR has been completely isolated, especially since 1945, from international organizations. In 1954 the Soviet government introduced a policy of so-called cultural exchange. Many USSR organizations are members of international bodies, but Ukrainian republican organizations and institutions are not permitted to hold separate memberships or to participate directly in the work of such bodies. Furthermore, Ukrainian scholars or cultural workers are rarely appointed to the Soviet delegations. Ukraine does not have a separate membership even in pro-Communist international organizations such as the International Association of Democratic Lawyers, the Women's International Democratic Federation, or the International Organization of Journalists. Since the late 1950s some Ukrainian émigré writers have been active in the international PEN club.

In the interwar period Ukrainian journalists belonged to foreign press associations in west-European capitals – eg, the Union of Foreign Journalists in Berlin, which was headed by Z. Kuzelia. In 1945 Ukrainian journalists in West Germany played an instrumental role in setting up the Union of the Free Press, which published the monthly *Freie Pressekorrespondenz*. Members of the Association of Ukrainian Journalists in Germany and of the Society of Ukrainian Journalists and Writers in Great Britain helped found the International Federation of Free Journalists in 1948. Since 1957 the Association of the Ukrainian Catholic Press has been a full member of the International Catholic Union of the Press, whose board of directors included V. Yaniv.

Soviet Ukrainian youth and sport organizations are not members of international organizations. Although in 1945 a separate delegation represented the Ukrainian SSR at the First Congress of the World Federation of Democratic Youth in London, later only the Committee of Youth Organizations of the USSR became a member of the federation. A similar republican committee for Ukraine, founded in 1956, does not engage in any international activity and does not belong to any international organization. The Ukrainian SSR is not a member of the Olympic Committee, although Ukrainian sportsmen participate in the *Olympic Games. Before the Second World War the *Plast Ukrainian Youth Association was the only Western Ukrainian or émigré youth organization to take part in international activity. Because the Boy Scouts International Bureau did not recognize scouting organizations of stateless nations, Plast could participate in jamborees and international conferences only as part of some other national scouting association. In the 1950s Ukrainians participated, either individually or as members of the national organizations of their adopted countries, in some conferences of the World Assembly of Youth. As for charitable associations, the *Ukrainian Red Cross (est 1918) worked through its liaison officer in Geneva with the International Red Cross, but after 1920 failed to win full membership because it represented a stateless nation. The *United Ukrainian American Relief Committee (est 1944), with headquarters in Philadelphia and a European office in Munich, and the *Central Ukrainian Relief Bureau in England worked closely with international organizations such as the *United Nations Relief and Rehabilitation Administration (1946), the *International Refugee Organization (1947–52), the Provisional Intergovernmental Committee for the Movement of Migrants from Europe (est 1951), and the UN High Commissioner for Refugees (from 1952). After the Second World War Ukrainian emigration agencies belonged to various international refugee organizations such as the Zentralverband der ausländischen Flüchtlinge in der Bundesrepublik Deutschland, which had about 20 member-associations representing various national groups, including the *Central Representation of the Ukrainian Emigration in Germany.

Ukrainian émigrés take part in the work of non-governmental organizations to inform the non-Ukrainian public about the Ukrainian cause (see *Press and information bureaus abroad) and to win recognition for Ukraine as an important factor in world politics.

BIBLIOGRAPHY

Ukraïns'ka RSR na mizhnarodnii areni (Kiev 1963, 1966, 1977, 1981, 1984)

Batiuk, V. *Ukraïna v Mizhnarodnii Orhanizatsiï Pratsi* (Kiev 1968)

Sawczuk, K. *The Ukraine in the United Nations Organization: A Study in Soviet Foreign Policy, 1944–1950* (New York-London 1975)

Ukraïns'ka RSR u mizhnarodnykh orhanizatsiiakh. Dovidnyk (Kiev 1984)

V. Markus

International Refugee Organization (IRO). A temporary agency of the United Nations (UN) that assisted refugees and *displaced persons in Europe and Asia after the Second World War. The organization, which was headquartered in Geneva, was formally established in December 1946 by a resolution of the UN General Assembly. Eventually, 18 countries ratified the IRO's constitution and joined the organization; these countries also provided its operating funds. The USSR and its satellites refused to join, however, because the organization mostly cared for refugees from Eastern Europe who found themselves in the British, American, and French zones of occupation and who, for political reasons, refused to return to their country of origin (see *Repatriation). The total number of people under the protection of the IRO was around 1,600,000, including some 200,000 Ukrainians. The IRO began operation in July 1947 when it took over administration of the *displaced persons camps, where most refugees lived, from the *United Nations Relief and Rehabilitation Administration. In addition to administering camps, the IRO aided in the voluntary repatriation of refugees (although very few people were repatriated after 1946) and helped the remainder to settle permanently in European or other countries; it also succeeded the Intergovernmental Committee on Refugees as the international body with legal responsibility for refugees. Many countries (Australia, Canada, the United States, and South American countries) accepted IRO-sponsored immigrants under special legislation. In total, some 1,000,000 people were resettled overseas, among them about 114,000 Ukrainians. When the IRO ended its activity in Europe in 1952, about 100,000 refugees remained in camps in West Germany and Austria. These countries, with the help of international organizations, assumed responsibility for the material well-being of the displaced persons and gave them the status of refugees. International legal responsibility for the refugees fell to the UN High Commission for Refugees in Geneva, the successor of the IRO. During its existence a small number of Ukrainians were employed at the middle and lower levels of the IRO administration in Germany and Austria.

V. Markus

Internationalism. An ideological and sociopolitical movement predicated on the ideal of co-operation between free and equal societies. According to this ideal, international co-operation and solidarity is more important than national interest. The modern form of internationalism arose from the liberal and democratic ideals of the French Revolution. With the birth of socialism, internationalism was given a theoretical basis by such thinkers as K. Marx, F. Engels, P. Proudhon, K. Kautsky, and R. Luxembourg, and an organizational form by various international socialist groups (see *Socialist International) towards the end of the 19th century.

In Ukraine, internationalism first developed after the French Revolution in Ukrainian masonic circles (see *Freemasonry) and in the thinking of the *Decembrists. Ukrainian Slavophilism, particularly that of the *Cyril and Methodius Brotherhood, emphasized the co-operation, equality, and brotherhood of nations, primarily among the Slavs. The first theoretical expression of internationalism in Ukrainian appeared in the works of M. *Drahomanov: *Vol'nyi soiuz / Vil'na spilka* (A Voluntary Union, 1884), 'Shevchenko, ukraïnofily i sotsializm' (Shevchenko, the Ukrainophiles, and Socialism, 1879), and *Istoricheskaia Pol'sha i velikorusskaia demokratiia* (Historical Poland and Great Russian Democracy, 1881–2). He tied his conception of internationalism to 'Europeanism' and federalism. The precondition for international co-operation was, for Drahomanov, recognition of the principle that 'every nation is to be its own master.'

Internationalism was prominent in the political thinking and literature of the Ukrainian left towards the end of the 19th century and beginning of the 20th, and included I. Franko, M. Pavlyk, and S. Podolynsky among its advocates. The Ukrainian socialist parties (the Ukrainian Social Democratic Workers' party, Ukrainian Party of Socialist Revolutionaries, and Ukrainian Radical party) saw it as one of the main components of Ukrainian politics. A wing of the Ukrainian Party of Socialist Revolutionaries adopted the name Internationalists in 1918–19. Ukrainian liberal parties such as the Ukrainian National Democratic Party, the Ukrainian Party of Socialists-Federalists, and the Ukrainian National Democratic Alliance also developed conceptions of liberal internationalism.

Internationalism also played an important part in the development of the communist movement and, in particular, came to be the focus of debate between Russian and Ukrainian communists. The *Borotbists and the Ukrainian Communist party adopted the principles of internationalism in their struggles against Russian centralism, Russian domination of the USSR, and state chauvinism. Russian Bolsheviks, in contrast, considered Ukrainian national communism an obstruction to internationalism. This same problem arose in the crisis of the Western Ukrainian Communist party in 1926–30 and prompted the intervention of the Communist International. Ukrainian communists of the above-mentioned movements adhered to the classic Marxist interpretation of internationalism, ie, the equality and solidarity of proletarian movements. It was enshrined in the first constitution of the Ukrainian SSR as a clause concerning the world federation of Soviet republics, of which the Ukrainian SSR was to be a member.

The concept of internationalism changed under Stalin. Its traditional meaning was replaced by Russian national egoism and chauvinism, a trend that persists to the present day. Domestically, internationalism in the USSR is identified with the promotion of positive attitudes towards Russian language, culture, and political centralization. Externally, it signified uncritical support for Soviet foreign policy. Ukrainian writers such as Ivan Dziuba (in his work *Internationalism or Russification?* [1965]) have criticized this distortion. (See also *Marxism.)

B. Krawchenko

Internationalists. The name of a leftist group formed in early 1918 within the Ukrainian Party of Socialist Revolutionaries. During the Fourth Party Congress in May 1918, the Internationalists constituted a majority in the Central Committee. They conducted propaganda through their underground organ *Borot'ba* (hence the subsequent name of the party, *Borotbists) and worked towards the revolutionary overthrow of the *Hetman government.

Internationals. See Communist International and Socialist International.

Internment camps. Civilian internment camps were established in Canada during the First World War. Ukrainians formed the largest contingent of the nearly 6,000 interned as Austro-Hungarian nationals because they were considered to be potentially disloyal. Camps were established in Spirit Lake (Quebec), Petawawa and Kapuskasing (Ontario), Brandon (Manitoba), Banff and Jasper (Alberta), and Vernon (British Columbia). The Ukrainian internees were employed in building roads, erecting and repairing buildings, and cleaning and draining land.

In Poland, soldiers of the Army of the UNR were first interned in Łańcut, in late 1919 following the collapse of the Ukrainian front, although some military units were organized from the internees and returned to central Ukraine to continue fighting the Red Army. After the final defeat of the UNR armies in November 1920, approx 20,000 men crossed into Polish territory, where they were interned in several camps. The larger camps included those in Łańcut, Aleksandrów Kujawski, and *Kalisz. Smaller camps were located at *Tuchola, Wadowice, and Piotrków. In mid-1921, those interned at Łańcut were transferred to Strzałkowo, and in late 1921, those at Aleksandrów were transferred to Szczepiórno. The latter camp, as well as the neighboring one in Kalisz, remained open until August 1924.

Conditions in the internment camps in Poland were hard, but cultural and educational life in the camps was quite developed. Technical courses were provided for the illiterate; various schools were formed and a people's university was established at Łańcut; choirs, theater groups, and other art and performance groups were active, as were religious organizations; and various publications were issued.

The administration of the camps was in Ukrainian hands. Officials of the Government-in-exile of the UNR conducted officer training and instruction in military theory, and several veterans' organizations were founded.

The internment camps in Kalisz and Szczepiórno were second to *Warsaw as the largest centers of Ukrainian cultural life in Poland. The number of soldiers in these internment camps declined progressively. Many left for Czechoslovakia to study, and others went to France to work. After the closure of the camps, the veterans were given the status of political émigrés in Poland.

Following the end of hostilities, most remaining units of the *Ukrainian Galician Army (UHA) made their way to Czechoslovakia, where they were interned. Sections of the *Mountain and *Sambir brigades and the Krukenychi Group were separated from the main forces of the UHA in May 1919 and forced to retreat into Transcarpathia, where they were disarmed and transferred to the camp at Deutsch-Gabel. The Czechoslovak authorities were sympathetic to the UHA soldiers and officers as long as the border disputes with Poland remained unresolved and they believed that the UHA could be used against the Poles. They issued full army rations and pay comparable to that of the Czechoslovak army, and granted all internees freedom of movement. Passes to Prague could be obtained on producing Ukrainian Army identification. Gen A. *Kravs's group was interned at *Liberec on 10 September 1920, after it had left the Dniester front and crossed Transcarpathia with 300 officers and 500 men. They were joined by another 130 officers and men who arrived from the Italian POW camp at Monte Cassino. In April 1921 the 4,000 internees from Liberec and Deutsch-Gabel were transferred to *Josefov. The camp there remained operative until 1926.

The number of soldiers in internment camps began to decrease in 1921, when the government formed workers' brigades (70 such brigades were formed in various towns throughout Czechoslovakia in 1921). Some returned to Galicia after 1923 when it was ceded to Poland by international agreement. Most officers traveled to study in *Prague, *Poděbrady (at the Ukrainian Husbandry Academy), Brno, and Příbram. After the closure of the Josefov camp, veterans were granted political immigrant status and some took Czechoslovak citizenship. Various military training programs, technical courses, literacy programs, general higher education courses, as well as general social and cultural activity such as choirs, libraries, publishing concerns, and theater groups, all formed part of the life in the internment camps.

BIBLIOGRAPHY
Narizhnyi, S. *Ukraïns'ka emigratsiia* (Prague 1942)
Motyl, A.J. *The Turn to the Right: The Ideological Origins and Development of Ukrainian Nationalism 1919–1929* (Boulder, Colo 1980)
Melnycky, P. 'The Internment of Ukrainians in Canada,' in *Loyalties in Conflict: Ukrainians in Canada during the Great War*, eds F. Swyripa and J.H. Thompson (Edmonton 1983)

Y. Boshyk, L. Shankovsky

Interparty Council (Mizhpartiina rada). A political body founded in 1919 in Lviv after the *Ukrainian-Polish War. It co-ordinated the legal struggle of the Ukrainian Labor (formerly National Democratic), Ukrainian Radical, Ukrainian Social Democratic, and Christian Social parties against the Polish occupation of Galicia. The council's chairmen were V. Bachynsky and, later, A. Kurovets. It had close ties with Ye. Petrushevych's Government-in-exile of the Western Ukrainian National Republic and funded the clandestine Ukrainian Military Organization. In January 1922 the Social Democratic party adopted a pro-Soviet platform. In March 1923 the Allied Conference of Ambassadors recognized Poland's annexation of Galicia and the Government-in-exile was dissolved. Consequently, in May 1923 the Radical party left the council, a schism developed in the Labor party, and the council fell apart.

Intourist. All-Union company established in 1929 to handle foreign tourism in the USSR. It arranges tours for foreign visitors to the USSR and for Soviet citizens traveling abroad. It operates hotels, motels, camping grounds, and tours in the USSR. Its headquarters are in Moscow, and it has branches in 28 countries, including Ukraine. According to Western intelligence sources, Intourist is under the control of the Second Chief Directorate of the *KGB.

Investment. Narrowly defined as the addition to an economy's stock of physical capital – factories, equipment, transport, housing, and so on – necessary for an economy to produce more goods and services for a growing population. Economic analysts also use a broader definition that includes accumulation of inventories. The level of investment in an economy is generally determined by the level of its savings. With respect to a region within a national economy, the levels of investment and savings may differ, since savings generated in one region may be invested in another region.

Investment, particularly in *industry, was intensified greatly in Russian-ruled Ukraine during the second half of the 19th century, primarily as a result of (1) the construction of railroads linking Ukraine's regions with each other and its entire economy with the rest of the Russian Empire and, through the ports on the Black and Azov seas, with other countries; (2) the expansion of heavy industry, primarily in the Donbas and the Kryvyi Rih Iron-ore Basin; and (3) the spread of food-processing industries throughout Ukraine. The investment that took place there was typical of a developing economy – elements of a free market and significant government involvement in economic activity. The bulk of private investment in industry was made by Belgian, French, and British capitalists (see *Capitalism). Besides investing in enterprises owned by the royal family, the tsarist government invested in such large-scale projects as the construction of a railway network and the development of a military-industrial complex, using excessive taxation and loans from the public, including foreigners, as its source of funds.

Under Soviet rule the nature of investment changed. In Ukraine, as in the rest of the USSR, private investment in most production activities was outlawed. Thus, in the early 1980s private investment represented less than 3 percent of total investment in the Ukrainian economy, and it was limited to co-operative apartments in the cities and small houses in the countryside. In contrast to market economies, Soviet planned investment determines centrally the level of savings, often by restricting personal consumption.

Government investment in all sectors of Soviet Ukraine's economy, such as collective agriculture, is regulated by ministries and state planning committees in Kiev and Moscow. Investment appropriations are included in annual and five-year economic plans on the basis of submitted proposals. A proposal for an investment project may be initiated by an enterprise, an intermediate administrative organ, or a ministry. In all cases, a thorough justification is required, and the necessary condition is the existence of an excessive demand for a specific good or service. The decision-making process in investment is a complex one. All proposals, along with technological and economic documentation, are examined at several administrative levels – supposedly to filter out the most valuable proposals and to reduce the number of those for further consideration. Final decisions are made by the party authorities in Moscow. Upon final approval, funds are appropriated to the project and a contractor is assigned. Budget constraints do not play an important role in determining the annual ceiling on total investment in the USSR, but rather the capacity of the construction industry and the availability of new machines and equipment.

Using the state budget and decentralized sources, investment is distributed among the sectors of the Soviet economy and individual regions, including the union republics. As a result, regional investment may be greater or less than its savings. Examples of the former include Soviet Asiatic regions, which have enjoyed an excess of investment over savings during the postwar period. Ukraine, in contrast, has experienced a loss of a part of its savings to other parts of the USSR. Table 2 shows investment in Ukraine in the Soviet period, including its percentage of total Soviet investment. Tables 1 and 3 give the breakdown of total investment by sector of the economy and of industrial investment by product group. In the 1920–85 period, Ukraine received 15.4 percent of all Soviet investment, while accounting for slightly less than one-fifth of the USSR population. Although these are average estimates, there is a distinct tendency for the investment percentages to decline over time, except for the reconstruction periods between 1918 and 1928 and between 1946 and 1950, when Ukraine's share in total Soviet investment approached its population share. Because of declining birth rates in Ukraine, the proportion of its population in the USSR has also declined, although at a slower pace than investment. Thus, in 1959 per capita investment in Ukraine amounted to 84 percent of per capita investment in the USSR, and by 1985 it dropped to only 77 percent.

The slowdown of per capita investment in Ukraine especially affects the consumer. Because such industries in Ukraine as machine building, mining, and ferrous metallurgy are of prime importance to the Soviet interests, they are more protected against lowering investment than the consumer-goods sector, which must absorb the burden. Municipal services, water supply, sewage,

TABLE 2
Investment in Ukraine's economy, 1918–85

Period	Billion rubles	% of USSR investment
1918–40	10.0	16.2
1951–55	17.1	16.5
1956–60	32.6	16.9
1961–65	47.3	16.9
1966–70	66.5	16.7
1971–75	89.5	15.9
1976–80	105.7	14.7
1981–85	117.0	13.9
Total	498.1	15.4

TABLE 3
Industrial investment by product group in Ukraine's economy (%)

Product group	1966–70	1971–5	1979
Electric power	9.3	9.0	7.7
Coal	16.2	14.0	14.4
Crude oil and gas	7.4	7.0	8.7
Ferrous metals	18.1	15.0	16.6
Chemicals and petrochemicals	9.4	10.0	9.2
Machines and metalworking	16.7	22.0	14.7
Wood and paper	1.3	2.0	1.2
Building materials	4.7	4.0	1.9
Textiles and apparel	3.5	4.0	1.9
Food	9.3	8.0	7.1

TABLE 1
Investment by sector in Ukraine's economy (%)

Sector	1918–40	1956–60	1961–5	1966–70	1971–5	1976–80	1981–5
Industry	38.1	38.7	38.8	37.7	37.1	38.1	38.8
Agriculture	9.3	15.6	16.6	17.8	20.9	21.2	19.7
Construction	0.9	2.5	2.2	2.6	2.8	2.8	2.5
Transportation and communications	16.2	8.3	11.5	10.6	11.0	11.0	10.8
Residential construction	19.0	22.2	16.9	15.3	14.0	13.4	14.5
Trade services	16.5	12.7	14.0	16.0	14.2	13.5	13.7

and road infrastructure have the lowest investment priority. Local party and administrative authorities are even required to assist in these areas with their own investment sources, such as the profits from lotteries, free services of military personnel, and free weekend labor by citizens. Medical facilities and public-transportation and communications systems also do not receive enough investment. Although housing and day-care facilities seem to be accorded higher priorities because they are considered important for keeping workers on the job, they are also subject to shortages, which cannot be eased without accelerated investment.

Two examples illustrate the relative situation in Ukraine and the RSFSR. In the years 1981–4 annual per capita investment in residential construction in Ukraine was 65 rubles. In the RSFSR it was 96 rubles, ie, almost one and one half times greater. In the same period annual per capita investment in the trade and service sectors was 62 and 106 rubles, respectively, or 70 percent larger. Moreover, the official Soviet information used in these examples does not take into account investment in housing and in services by collective farms in the RSFSR, thus underestimating the latter's total investment for those purposes.

Although investment in heavy industry has been given a high priority in Ukraine, its efficiency has not satisfied the authorities for many reasons, one being that there has existed a discrepancy between annual investment and the amount of new capital stock put into operation. Since investment is free of charge, there exists pressure on the part of plant managers to initiate new investment projects. But because of the limited capacity of the Soviet construction industry, at a large number of construction sites the average duration of individual projects has been 10–12 years – double the normative term approved by the authorities. To accelerate the completion of investment projects, the decision was made to reduce their number drastically in the 1986–90 Five-Year Plan and even to abandon certain construction projects started previously.

Two other developments aimed at increasing the efficiency of investment are related to the composition of new capital stock and the distribution of investment funds among different types of projects. Production capital stock consists of structures and machines. To increase the working capacity of new plants, attempts were made in the last two decades to make the capital less structure-intensive and more machine-intensive. Thus, in the years 1970–85 the proportion of investment allotted to equipment in Ukraine was raised from 29 to 39 percent, and it has been decided to continue this policy in the 1986–90 plan. Another development involves the shift in investment priorities from new construction to the renovation and modernization of existing plants. In the years 1979–84 the proportion of investment in renovating and modernizing Ukrainian industry rose from 35 to 41 percent, but it is still viewed as insufficient. According to the planning authorities, relative to investment in new construction, investment in renovation pays off three times faster, requires a 27 percent shorter project duration, and has an output-to-capital ratio 1.5 times higher. The 1986–90 Five-Year Plan has called for directing half of industrial investment into renovation. Rapid innovation and the introduction of advanced machines are considered the key to raising the efficiency of industrial investment.

BIBLIOGRAPHY
Emel'ianov, A., et al. *Promyshlennost' v usloviiakh razvitogo sotsializma (na primere Ukrainskoi SSR)* (Kiev 1981)
Gillula, J. 'The Growth and Structure of Fixed Capital,' in I.S. Koropeckyj and G. Schroeder (eds), *Economics of Soviet Regions* (New York 1981)
Kushnirsky, F. *Soviet Economic Planning, 1965–1980* (Boulder, Colo 1982)

F. Kushnirsky

Ioan II, ?–1089. Metropolitan of Kiev from 1077 to 1089. A Greek by birth, he was famous for his erudition and administrative ability. He wrote a letter to Pope Clement III (first published in 1854), responding to the pope's attempt to establish contact with the Eastern hierarchs, and a collection of canonical instructions (first published in 1815).

Ioan IV, ?–1166. Metropolitan of Kiev from 1164 to 1166. A Greek by birth, he was sent to Kiev by the Patriarch of Constantinople against the wishes of Prince Rostyslav Mstyslavych, who wanted a metropolitan of Ukrainian origin.

Iorga, Nicolai, b 17 June 1871 in Botoşani, Moldavia, d 28 November 1940, near Sinaia, Rumania. Historian and premier of Rumania in 1931–2. Iorga was a member of the Rumanian parliament for many years. In his historical works he denied that Ukrainians were indigenous to Bukovyna and Bessarabia, considering them Ukrainianized Rumanians or migrants from Galicia. He tendentiously examined Rumanian-Ukrainian relations, promoted assimilation, and advanced the claims of Rumania to Transnistria.

Iracema (also Iraputan). A town in the municipality of Itaiópolis, Santa Catarina state, in southern Brazil. The location of one of the oldest Ukrainian settlements in Brazil, it was settled ca 1895–6 by approx 200 Ukrainian families. A Basilian monastery was established there, as well as an active parish embracing 12 other church communities. Altogether, there are about 6,000 Ukrainians in the area, most of them farmers.

Iranian peoples. The east Aryan group of peoples of the Indo-European family that today inhabit Iran, Soviet Central Asia and Transcaucasia, Afghanistan, and parts of Pakistan, Turkey, and Iraq. In ancient times they also inhabited southeastern Europe. During the 1st millennia BC and AD Ukraine was inhabited consecutively by the Iranian-speaking *Cimmerians, *Scythians, *Sarmatians, *Alans, and Irano-Turkic *Khazars. These peoples interacted with the indigenous proto-Slavs and influenced their cultural development.

Iranianisms. The earliest Iranianisms are words borrowed from the languages of such northern Iranian nomadic tribes as the Scythians, Sarmatians, and Alans, which from the 6th century BC came into contact with Slavs in southern Ukraine and later with early Ukrainian tribes. Iranianisms are common in east-Slavic languages. Ukrainian examples include *topir* (axe), *sobaka* (dog), *xom'jak* (hamster), *morda* (snout), *raj* (paradise), *vyrij* (warm region), *Xors;* names of rivers, eg, *Don, Dnipro, Dnister, Kuban';* and names of tribes, eg, *xorvaty* (Croatians), *jasy* (Ossetes), and *kasohy* (Circassians). After the 12th century many middle and modern Persian Iranianisms entered Ukrainian as Turkisms – primarily terms for apparel, orcharding, and commerce, such as *bazar* (bazaar) and *majdan* (square) – and into Transcarpathian dialects as *Hungarian loan words – *vašar* (market), *orsak* (state). Many etymologists recognize Iranian influences in several religious or mythological expressions in Ukrainian, such as *Boh* (God), *dyv* (wonder), and *svjatyj* (holy); however, these are not to be considered direct borrowings from Iranian languages.

Irchan, Myroslav [Irčan] (pen name of Andrii Babiuk), b 14 July 1897 in Piadyky, Kolomyia county, Galicia, d 1937? Writer. From 1923 to 1929 he lived in Winnipeg, where he edited pro-Communist periodicals of the Ukrainian Labour-Farmer Temple Association – *Robitnytsia* and *Svit molodi* – and founded the writers' group Zaokeanskyi Hart, which was affiliated with the Kharkiv-based proletarian writers' organization *Hart. From 1929 he lived in Kharkiv, where he headed the organization of Western Ukrainian Communist émigré writers *Zakhidnia Ukraina and edited its monthly journal until its demise in 1933. Irchan was arrested during the Yezhov terror and disappeared. He was posthumously rehabilitated. He is the author of about two dozen collections of prose, dealing mainly with the Ukrainian-Polish War and the tribulations of Ukrainian peasant life in Galicia and the New World. Irchan also wrote 11 plays (7 of them in Winnipeg) on similar themes, which were quite popular in their day among Ukrainian Canadians. They include *Buntar* (The Rebel, 1922), *Rodyna shchitkariv* (The Family of Brush Makers, 1923), *Dvanadsiat'* (The Twelve, 1923), *Pidzemna Halychyna* (Underground Galicia, 1926), *Radii* (Radium, 1928), and *Pliatsdarm* (The Battle Zone, 1933). He is also the author of two volumes of memoirs about the Ukrainian-Polish War, *Trahediia Pershoho Travnia* (The Tragedy of the First of May, 1923) and *V bur'ianakh* (In the Weeds, 1925).

Irchan has been the subject of a substantial body of Soviet Ukrainian literary scholarship, including monographs by L. Novychenko (1958), V. Vlasenko and P. Kravchuk (1960), and L. Melnychuk-Luchko (1963), and a bibliography by V. Mashotas (1961). A two-volume selection of his works was published in Kiev in 1958.

I. Koshelivets, R. Senkus

Irkutsk. City (1982 pop 575,000) and oblast capital in Siberia, situated at the confluence of the Irkut and Angara rivers. A Russian fort was built there in 1661. A town was founded in 1686; it became an eparchial see in 1727, a gubernia capital in 1764, and the residence of the governor-general of Siberia in 1803 and of eastern Siberia in 1822. Under the tsars it was a place of political exile. The Ukrainians I. *Kulchytsky (1727–31) and I. *Nerunovych (1732–47) were bishops there; they were renowned for their missionary and educational activity among the Buriats and other Siberian peoples. In 1728 Kulchytsky reorganized the local school. Among its teachers were the exiled professors of the Kievan Mohyla Academy, Archimandrite P. Malynovsky and I. Maksymovych. Many Ukrainian settlers in *Siberia and the *Far East passed through Irkutsk, and a Ukrainian *vertep* has been preserved there. Today Irkutsk is an important industrial, scientific, and cultural center, port, and railway junction. According to the 1979 census, 90,800 Ukrainians lived in Irkutsk oblast; 42,600 stated Ukrainian was their mother tongue.

Irliavsky, Ivan [Irljavs'kyj] (pen name of I. Roshko), b 1919 in Irliava, Ung county, Transcarpathia, d 21 February 1942 in Kiev. Poet of the nationalist school. While living in Prague, he contributed to nationalist periodicals. His poetry collections are *Holos Sribnoï Zemli* (The Voice of the Silver Land, 1939), *Moia vesna* (My Spring, 1940), *Veresen'* (September, 1941), and *Brosti* (Buds, 1942). In 1941 he joined the *OUN expeditionary groups and went to Kiev, where he became the secretary of a writers' union headed by O. Teliha. He was executed by the Gestapo together with Teliha and other writers who refused to collaborate with the German occupational regime.

IRO. See International Refugee Organization.

Iron Age. A cultural-technological era in the development of humankind following the *Bronze Age in the 1st millennium BC that was characterized by the diffusion of iron and steel implements and weapons. In western and central Europe it consisted of the *Hallstatt (800–500 BC) and La Tène (500–1 BC) phases. This periodization is applicable only in Western Ukraine, which was penetrated by the *Thracian Hallstatt and Celtic La Tène cultures. The Iron Age in the rest of Ukraine is divided into three periods: the *Cimmerian or Pre-Scythian (8th and 7th centuries BC), the *Scythian (7th to 3rd centuries BC), and the Sarmatian (3rd century BC to 4th century AD).

The oldest extant evidence of iron use in Ukraine dates from the late 2nd millennium BC. It was, however, only in the 8th and 7th centuries BC that iron metallurgy was developed and basic tools and weapons began to be made of iron and steel in Ukraine. Stone implements were displaced; bronze implements, however, continued to be widely used well into the Cimmerian and Scythian periods. The unrivaled predominance of iron implements and weapons and the flourishing of iron metallurgy in Ukraine began only toward the end of the Iron Age.

The use of iron tools stimulated the development of agriculture, crafts, trade, and human progress as a whole. In the early Iron Age the population of the Eurasian steppe turned to what was, for that time, a more productive form of animal husbandry: nomadism. It was then that the migration of peoples, and hence frequent armed conflicts, occurred. On Ukraine's territory great tribal alliances coalesced, the earliest state formations emerged, and proto-urban fortified settlements and true ancient cities appeared. In the 7th century BC the Greeks began the colonization of the northern Black Sea littoral and the establishment of city-states there (see *Ancient states on the northern Black Sea coast). At the beginning of the Iron Age the territory and population of Ukraine entered the historical arena. In this epoch the population of Ukraine established economic and cultural contacts with the civilizations of the ancient world and was described by Assyrian, Greek, and Roman writers.

In the 8th and 7th centuries BC Ukraine's steppe was inhabited by seminomadic Cimmerian tribes, which archeologists identify with the *Timber-Grave culture. In the Cimmerian phase the forest-steppe between the Dnieper and Dniester rivers was occupied by the seden-

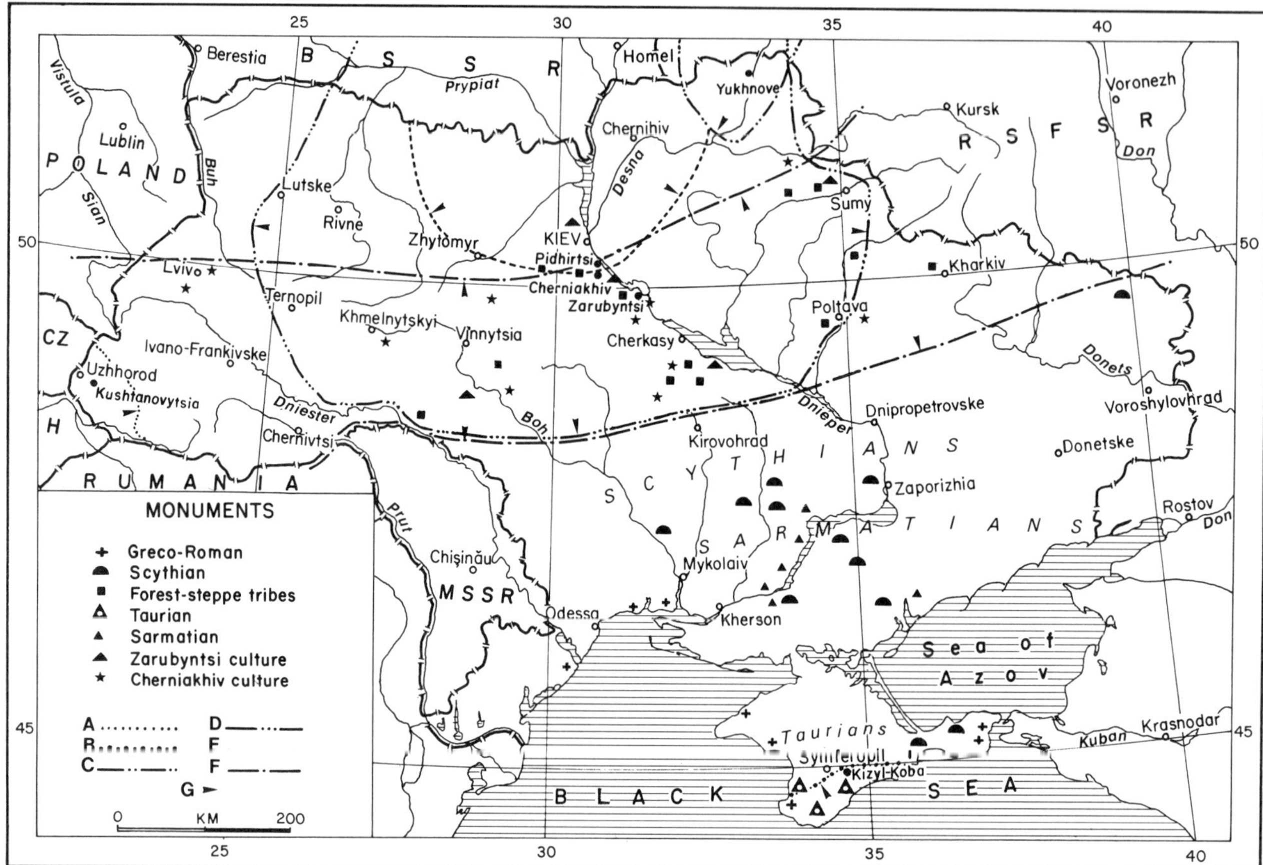

IRON AGE

A. Kushtanovytsia culture
B. Kizyl-Koba culture
C. Yukhnove culture
D. Zarubyntsi culture
E. Mylohrad-Pidhirtsi culture
F. Cherniakhiv culture
G. Direction of a culture's expansion

tary agricultural tribes of the *Chornyi Lis culture, descendants of the Bronze Age *Bilohrudivka culture. Many scholars consider the Chornyi Lis and Bilohrudivka tribes to be the indigenous proto-East Slavic population of Ukraine. Contemporaries of the Cimmerians in Galicia and Volhynia were the tribes of the *Lusatian culture; believed to have been the ancestors of the Western Slavs, they came from the territory of Poland during the late Bronze Age. From the 11th to the 6th centuries BC the upper Buh Basin was populated by the tribes of the *Vysotske culture – descendants of both the Lusatian and Chornyi Lis tribes – while western Podilia, Bukovyna, and Transcarpathia were influenced by tribes of the Thracian Hallstatt culture created by the *Getae and Dacians.

In the 7th century BC the Scythians penetrated into Ukraine's territory, drove out the Cimmerians, and established a large empire. It has been posited that the agricultural tribes of the Right-Bank forest-steppe called 'Scythian plowmen' by Herodotus were in fact descendants of the proto-Slavic Chornyi Lis culture that adopted the culture of the dominant 'Royal Scythians.' The forest zone bordering on Scythia was inhabited by ancient Baltic tribes of the *Mylohrad-Pidhirtsi culture in the upper Dnieper Basin and the *Yukhnove culture in the middle Desna Basin. The Crimean mountains were the home of the Kizyl-Koba culture of the *Taurians. In Transcarpathia, descendants of the Thracian Hallstatt culture constituted the *Kushtanovytsia culture in the 6th to 3rd centuries BC. In the course of the 2nd and 1st centuries BC the indigenous Thracian and proto-Slavic population of Transcarpathia, western Podilia, Bukovyna, Galicia, and Volhynia intermingled with the Celtic tribes of the La Tène culture that spread there from central Europe.

In the 3rd and 2nd centuries BC the Sarmatians displaced the Scythians from most of the Ukrainian steppe, and the Scythians remaining in the lower Dnieper Basin and the Crimean steppe founded so-called Little Scythia with its capital at *Neapolis near present-day Symferopil. In the 1st century BC the Getae expanded into the lower Dnieper and the Dniester basins. During the next three centuries they and the Dacians created the *Lypytsia culture in the upper Dniester Basin. In the forest-steppe between the Dniester and Dnieper rivers the *Zarubyntsi culture, considered by most scholars to have been proto-Slavic, flourished from the 3rd century BC through the 1st century AD until it was destroyed by the Sarmatians' expansion into the middle Dnieper Basin. Its remnants, pushed into the upper Dnieper Basin, together with Bal-

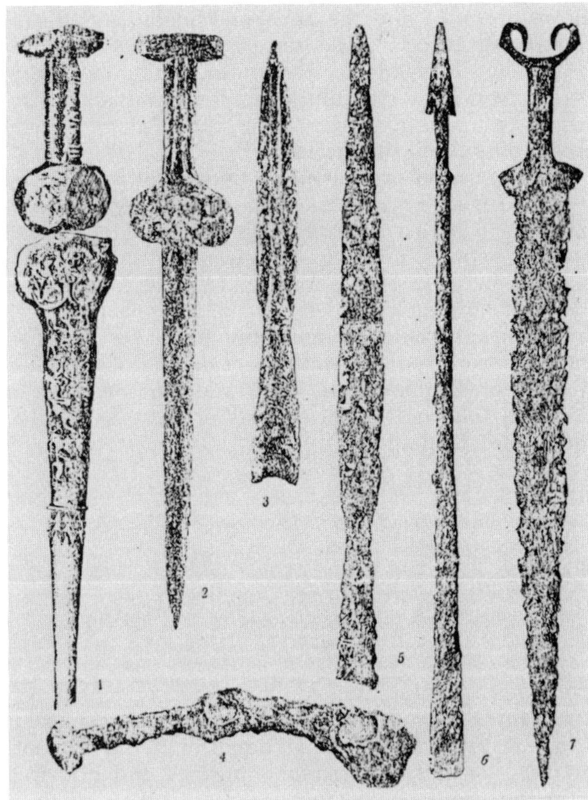
Scythian iron weapons found in 6th-to-4th-century BC burial sites in the middle Dnieper region; drawing according to Ya. Pasternak, 1961

tic tribes created the Kievan culture of the 2nd to 4th centuries AD. In the forest-steppe and steppe zones between the Dniester and Donets rivers in the 2nd to 5th centuries AD, the multiethnic (Sarmatian, Scythian, Thracian, and proto-Slavic) *Cherniakhiv culture emerged under the strong influence of the neighboring Roman provinces of the Danube Basin. At that time Subcarpathia was dominated by the Carpathian Burial-Mound culture of the Thracian Carpi. In the 3rd and 4th centuries AD the ancestors of the Western Slavs and Germanic Vandals – the tribes of the *Przeworsk culture – and Germanic *Goths and Gepidae penetrated from the Baltic region and the Vistula Basin into the Cherniakhiv and Carpathian Burial-Mound cultural zones. The Goths moved on into the northern Black Sea littoral, where in the late 4th century AD they, the Sarmatians, the tribes of the Cherniakhiv culture, and the remaining Hellenic city-states were conquered by the invading Turkic *Huns. The ensuing decline and desertion of the core territory of Ukraine in the late 4th and 5th centuries AD ended the Iron Age there.

BIBLIOGRAPHY
Liapushkin, I. *Dneprovskoe lesostepnoe levoberezh'e v epohu zheleza*, vol 104 of *Materialy i issledovaniia po arkheologii SSSR* (Moscow-Leningrad 1961)
Pasternak, Ia. *Arkheolohiia Ukraïny* (Toronto 1961)
Terenozhkin, A. *Predskifskii period na dneprovskom Pravoberezh'e* (Kiev 1961)
Sulimirski, T. *Prehistoric Russia* (London 1970)
Arkheolohiia Ukraïns'koï RSR, vols 2–3 (Kiev 1971, 1975)
V. Mezentsev

Iron Division. See Third Iron Rifle Division of the Army of the UNR.

Iron industry. A branch of mining involving the extraction of *iron ore and its processing for use in the steel and other branches of the *metallurgical industry. Iron smelting existed in Ukraine as far back as the 5th century BC. Although quite widespread in Kievan Rus', its output was not sufficient to satisfy domestic demand. During the 15th century, iron production was revived. Iron ore found in shallow mines or at the bottom of bogs and lakes was brought to the surface using crude water-pumping systems and windlasses, and was smelted in primitive furnaces fanned by bellows. Production was concentrated in the well-forested (and therefore fuel-rich) Polisia, Volhynia, and, to a lesser extent, Galicia, Bukovyna, and Transcarpathia. The ores were generally low grade; therefore higher-grade ores and ready-made iron products were imported, primarily from the alpine regions of Europe, Hungary, and (later) Muscovy.

A short-lived growth in Ukraine's iron industry occurred after the introduction of the blast furnace in the Kiev region, Volhynia, and Polisia in the 18th century. Its subsequent decline in these regions was caused by the depletion of accessible mines, the destruction of the forests, the shortage of cheap labor after the emancipation of the peasant, and competition from the iron industry of the Urals. The number of productive iron mines fell from 500 in the late 18th century to 61 in 1853.

Small, medium-grade iron-ore deposits in the Donbas were first mined in the late 18th century. Abundant local coal resources facilitated the growth of the Donbas metallurgical industry. Output remained relatively small,

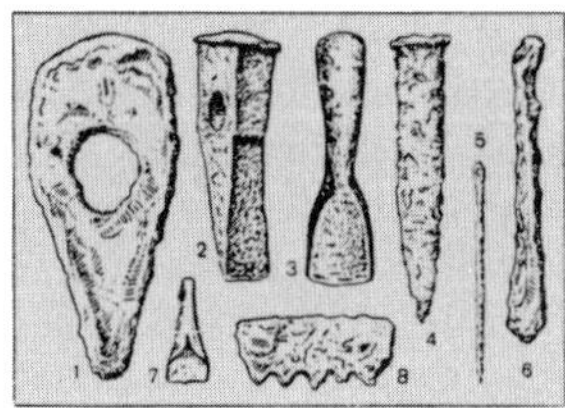
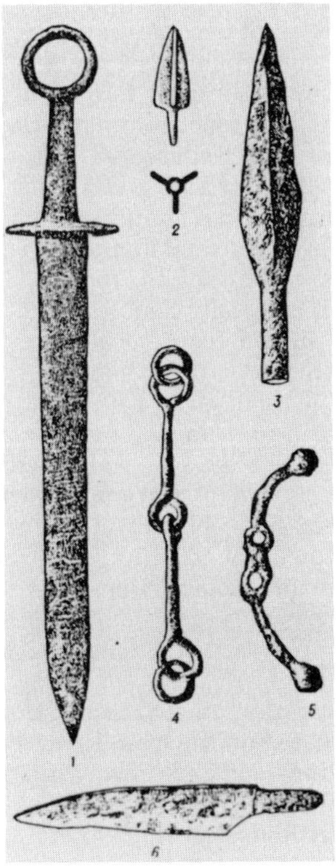
(*above*) Scythian iron tools; drawing according to B. Shramko, 1970
(*left*) Sarmatian iron weapons and bridle piece; drawing according to M. Viazmitina, 1971

Ukraine's iron industry, 1880–1984

Year	Output of iron ore (in million t)	% of Ukraine's output in total: the Russian Empire* to 1913, USSR after
1880	0.07	7.1
1890	0.38	19.8
1900	3.44	56.5
1910	4.26	73.5
1913	6.87	74.7
1920	4.7	77.0
1932	8.4	69.8
1940	20.2	67.6
1950	21.0	53.0
1960	59.1	55.8
1970	111.2	56.9
1984	122.8	49.7

*Russian Empire using present boundaries of USSR.

however, accounting in 1880 for 7 percent of the Russian Empire's total. A radical change in Ukraine's iron industry occurred with the development of the *Kryvyi Rih Iron-ore Basin (Kryvbas) in the early 1880s and the construction of the First Catherinian Railroad linking it and the *Dnieper Industrial Region with the Donbas and its high-grade coal in the 1880s. The proximity of the Dnieper's water route and the Black Sea ports was conducive to the export of ores, and foreign (mostly French) investment brought about the introduction of modern technology in iron mining. As a result, Ukraine became the leading producer of iron ore in the empire (see the accompanying table), outstripping the Urals by 1897. The Kryvbas accounted for about 95 percent of Ukraine's output. In 1913 Ukraine produced 6 percent of Europe's and 3.5 percent of the world's iron ore and was the world's fourth-largest producer, preceded only by the United States, France, and Germany. The iron industry employed about 25,000 workers and exported about one-fifth of its output, mostly to Germany and Poland.

Ukraine's iron industry declined drastically during the First World War and collapsed completely during the years 1919–21. By the late 1920s, however, it had regained its prewar level (see the table), and it grew rapidly during the interwar years. By 1940, output was almost triple that of 1913, although its share of the USSR total had declined slightly because of the construction of the Ural-Kuznetsk Basin Industrial Complex. The Kryvyi Rih Basin remained Ukraine's most important producer of iron ore; production there was concentrated in eight large mines.

Devastated during the Second World War, Ukraine's iron industry was rebuilt and regained its prewar level of production by 1950. The Kryvbas continues to account for about 90 percent of Ukraine's iron-ore production. The second most important (but much smaller) producer is the *Kerch Iron-ore Basin. To prepare low-grade ores for industrial use, enriching plants have been constructed. The first was that of the *Komysh-Buruny Iron-ore Complex near Kerch, which began production in 1936. After the war the *Southern (1955), *New Kryvyi Rih (1959), Central (1961), *Northern (1963), and Inhulets (1965) mineral-enrichment complexes began operating in or near Kryvyi Rih. Iron ore has also been extracted since the war from the *Kremenchuk and Bilozerka iron-ore regions and processed by the *Zaporizhia Iron-ore Complex since 1969 and the Dnieper Mineral Enrichment Complex in Komsomolske since 1970.

Ukraine's iron industry has continued to grow during the postwar period. Output increased almost sixfold between 1950 and 1984 (see table), but its share of total Soviet output fell significantly.

Ukraine's iron ore (about 30 percent of total Soviet reserves) is an important commodity in Soviet foreign trade. In 1970 it accounted for 98.1 percent of total Soviet iron-ore exports, most of which were sent to the European Comecon countries for use in the development of their metallurgical industries. Ukraine's iron-ore thus plays an important role in the integration of the economies of the Comecon countries with the economy of the USSR. At present, Ukraine is the world's leading producer of iron ore, followed by other parts of the USSR, China, Brazil, and Australia.

BIBLIOGRAPHY

Zheleznorudnaia promyshlennost' Ukrainskoi SSR: Tekhniko-ekonomicheskii obzor (Kiev 1964)

Orlovs'kyi, B. *Zalizorudna promyslovist' Ukraïny v dorevoliutsiinyi period: Istoryko-ekonomichnyi narys* (Kiev 1974)

Syrevaia baza chernoi metallurgii Ukrainskoi SSR (Kiev 1974)

I.S. Koropeckyj, V. Kubijovyč, S. Protsiuk

Iron ores. A natural mineral formation containing iron compounds from which iron is industrially extracted. Iron ores vary in their mineral composition, iron content, amount of useful and harmful impurities, and industrial properties. Their main types are classified according to their dominant mineral compound and geological formation. The ores found in Ukraine are hematite (Fe_2O_3), magnetite (Fe_3O_4), siderite ($FeCO_3$), brown and bog iron ores containing hydrous ferric oxides ($Fe_2O_3{\cdot}nH_2O$), and ferruginous quartzites. For industrial purposes a distinction is made between poor and rich ores, the latter containing more than 46 percent iron. When high-grade ores are inaccessible or exhausted, it becomes necessary to separate and discard unusable materials from low-grade ores. The processes of upgrading are termed beneficiation and are accomplished by leaching and drying, flotation, agglomeration, or magnetic separation. Harmful impurities, such as sulfur, phosphorus, and arsenic, may degrade the quality of an ore, necessitating the addition of different ores in order to prepare it for industrial use. The mixture of manganese, chromium, nickel, titanium, vanadium, and cobalt is usually beneficial.

Ukraine's total reserves of proved economically minable iron ore were officially estimated at 18.8 billion t (in 1968), constituting 32 percent of total Soviet reserves (21 percent of high-grade reserves), and an additional 7.2 billion t whose exploitation has yet to be assessed. There are 79 iron-ore deposits in Ukraine. The four main ones are the *Kryvyi Rih (Dnipropetrovske oblast) and *Kerch (Crimea) iron-ore basins and the *Kremenchuk (Poltava oblast) and Bilozerka (Zaporizhia oblast) iron-ore regions. (See also *Iron industry.)

B. Somchynsky

Irpin [Irpin']. III-11. City (1970 pop 25,300) under the jurisdiction of Kiev oblast, situated on the Irpin River 27 km from Kiev. It was founded in 1902 as a railway junction. Today it is a popular health-resort town. In February 1918, when the Central Rada returned to Kiev, Irpin was the site of several battles between the Sich

Riflemen and Bolshevik forces, and in late 1918, of clashes between the UNR Black Sea Battalion and Hetman government units. Today its main industries are building-materials manufacturing and machine building: it has one of the largest brick-and-tile plants in Ukraine, a wall-materials and industrial-plastics complex, and a plant that produces machines for the local peat industry. Furniture and leather goods are also manufactured there.

Irpin Drainage and Irrigation System. A drainage and irrigation system constructed in 1947–53 (and improved in 1974) on the floodlands of the Irpin River and its tributaries. The system consists of two reservoirs (with a total capacity of 17,500,000 cu m), a 128-km canal with 9 locks regulating one of the branches of the Irpin, a 612-km drainage network with 810 regulatory locks, and 16 pumping stations. The whole system encompasses about 8,000 ha, of which 7,400 ha are under cultivation.

Irpin River [Irpin']. A right-bank tributary of the Dnieper River, 162 km in length and draining a basin of 3,340 sq km. The Irpin's marshes protected Kiev from the west, and hence had a strategic importance. The Treaty of Andrusovo (1667) and the Eternal Peace of 1686 designated the Irpin as the border between the Russian and Polish states. Retreating from Kiev in early February 1919, the UNR Army came to a halt at the Irpin. There in the summer of 1919 the Rava-Ruske (6th) Brigade of the Ukrainian Galician Army crushed the last Bolshevik resistance outside Kiev and captured 2,000 prisoners as well as rich spoils. In 1947–53 the *Irpin Drainage and Irrigation System was built in the river's floodplains.

Irrigation. The artificial application of water to land, primarily for agricultural purposes, using surface water from streams, rivers, and storage lakes, or subsurface water from aquifers. Water is transported by canals and pipelines using gravity flow supplemented by pumping and then distributed through smaller ditches or pipelines to farms, where it is applied by means of flood or furrow systems. Sprinklers have been increasingly used, because they decrease the loss of water through evaporation.

Before 1917 only 17,400 ha of land were irrigated in Ukraine, mostly in southern Ukraine. By 1940, 89,700 ha were irrigated, primarily by small local streams, rivers, ponds, lakes, and artesian wells. In the 1950s the construction of large irrigation systems using the waters of reservoirs created by the *Dnieper Cascade of Hydroelectric Stations was begun. The most important were the *Inhulets, *Krasnoznamianka, and Kamianyi Pod irrigations systems. Smaller ones were created in the Crimea (the *Salhyr Irrigation System) and near the Dniester Estuary. By 1968, 53 systems irrigated 747,900 ha of Ukraine's arable land in Crimea, Kherson, Dnipropetrovske, Donetske, Mykolaiv, Odessa, Zaporizhia, Voroshylovhrad, Kiev, Kharkiv, and Kirovohrad oblasts.

In 1966 a large-scale program of irrigating Ukraine's southern oblasts, where the land was most fertile but

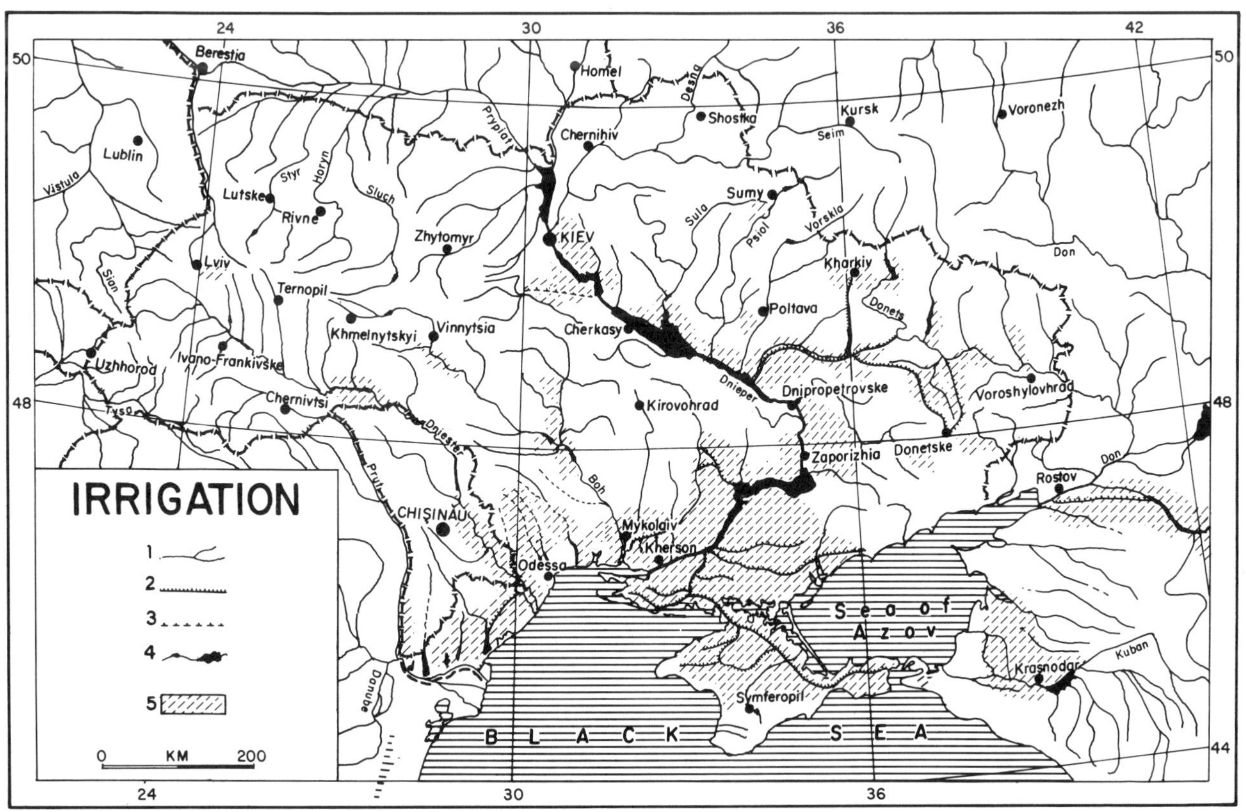

1. Rivers
2. Irrigation canals
3. Underground irrigation canal
4. Reservoirs
5. Irrigated lands

precipitation scarce, was begun. Since that time the amount of land irrigated has grown by approximately 120,000 ha per year. It totaled 2,384,000 ha in 1984. Since irrigation has become a major factor in increasing grain yield, the irrigation of 8–9 million ha in Ukraine has been projected. In the late 1960s, 41 percent of Ukraine's irrigated land was devoted to fodder crops and only 22.5 percent to grain crops. Since then most of newly irrigated land has been used for grain cultivation. Between 6 and 7 percent of Ukraine's arable land is now under irrigation.

A whole series of new systems has contributed to the increase in irrigated land. The most important is in the *North Crimean Canal, which extends 400 km from the *Kakhivka Reservoir to Kerch and irrigated 228,000 ha (in 1980) of steppe land in Kherson and northern Crimea oblasts. Others include the *Kakhivka, *Dnieper-Donbas Canal, *Chaplynka, Northern Rohachyk, Lower Dnieser, Bortnyky, and Frunze irrigation systems.

Since 1965 irrigation has been the most important water consumer in Ukraine. It was estimated to consume 10.4 cu km per yr (42.8 percent) of the water from the Dnieper River in 1980. Since Ukraine has the greatest per capita water deficit in the USSR, the conflicting demands of municipal, industrial, and agricultural users have become an acute problem. Irrigation is both affected by and results in water *pollution. Crops may be damaged by salt concentrations from industrial pollution or continual irrigation, which raises the groundwater level and results in soil salinization. The Zaporizhia Iron-ore Complex has poisoned the irrigation systems of the Rohachyk and Vasylivska rivers. In other cases, irrigation systems have been polluted by fertilizers, fine soil particles, and decaying organic matter.

Water shortage has also increased as a result of the use of poor technical equipment in irrigation. The use of ditches instead of sprinklers results in evaporation losses, while use of unlined beds leads to excessive drainage losses. The increasing use of cement beds, closed pipelines, and sprinklers should promote water conservation in the future.

Ukraine has become the object of a major water-diversion scheme that would involve the transfer of 16–23 cu km per yr of water northward from the Danube to irrigate 2.6–4.6 million ha in the Dnieper Basin. The first step through Sasyk Lake was completed in 1983, but because of uncoordinated planning and insufficient research the irrigation of the Budzhak steppe resulted in soil salinization, making the area infertile. The continuing controversy over large-scale diversion schemes has put the completion of this project in doubt.

B. Somchynsky

Irshava [Iršava]. v-4. Town smt (1978 pop 6,300) on the Irshava River at the foot of the Volcanic Ukrainian Carpathians and a raion center in Transcarpathia oblast. It was first mentioned in 1341. It has an abrasives plant, an industrial-machine-repair plant, several food-processing plants, a cotton-textiles mills, and a furniture factory. Lignite coal, limestone, and marble are mined in its vicinity.

Isaievych, Yaroslav [Isajevyč, Jaroslav], b 7 March 1936 in Verba, Dubno county, Volhynia. Historian. In 1959 he was appointed research associate of the Institute of Social Sciences of the Academy of Sciences in Lviv. He is the author of numerous works on the cultural and economic history of Galicia up to the 18th century (particularly the history of towns and of printing). His major works are *Bratstva ta ïkh rol' v rozvytku ukraïns'koï kul'tury XVI–XVIII st.* (Brotherhoods and Their Role in the Development of Ukrainian Culture in the 16th–18th Century, 1966), *Dzherela z istoriï ukraïns'koï kul'tury doby feodalizmu XVI–XVIII st.* (Sources on the History of Ukrainian Culture in the Feudal Period of the 16th–18th Century, 1972), *Istoriia knigopechataniia na Ukraine i ego rol' v mezhslavianskikh kul'turnykh sviaziakh (XVI–pervaia polovina XVII st.)* (The History of Book Printing in Ukraine and Its Role in Inter-Slavic Cultural Relations [16th–First Half of the 17th Century], 1977), *Prichinki pervopechatnika* (Contributions of the First Printer, 1981), and biographies of Yu. *Drohobych (1972) and I. *Fedorovych (1975).

Petro Isaiv

Isaiv, Petro [Isajiv], b 26 June 1905 in Lisky, Kolomyia county, Galicia, d 23 February 1973 in Philadelphia. Historian, pedagogue, and journalist. A graduate of Lviv University (MA 1931) and the Ukrainian Free University (PH D 1947), he taught secondary school in Lviv and edited the journals *Molode zhyttia* (1927–9) and *Dzvony* (1931–9). During the war he headed the educational department of the Ukrainian Central Committee and edited *Ukraïns'ka shkola* (1942–3). In 1944 he immigrated to Germany and in 1949 to the United States. Isaiv served as head of the executive of the *Obnova academic society, edited the weekly *Shliakh* (1949–63), and was active in Ukrainian education. On the strength of his scholarly contributions he was elected full member of the Schevchenko Scientific Society (1952) and professor of the Ukrainian Catholic University (1965). His publications include numerous articles, particularly on Ukrainian church history, entries in *Entsyklopediia ukraïnoznavstva,* and the monograph *Prychyny upadku ukraïns'koï derzhavy v kniazhi i kozats'ki chasy* (The Causes of the Fall of the Ukrainian State in Princely and Cossack Times, 1975).

Isajiw, Wsevolod [Isajiv, Vsevolod], b 6 November 1933 in Lviv, Galicia. Sociologist. Educated at La Salle College and the Catholic University of America (PH D 1967), he has taught at St John's University, the University of Windsor, and, since 1970, the University of Toronto. He has written *Causation and Functionalism in Sociology* (1968) and various articles, and has edited a number of books, including *Ukrainians in American and Canadian Society* (1976) and *Identities: The Impact of Eth-*

nicity on Canadian Society (1977). He was president of the Canadian Ethnic Studies Association (1973–7).

Ishchak, Andrii [Iščak, Andrij], b 23 September 1887 in Mykolaiv, Zhydachiv county, Galicia, d 26 June 1941 in Lviv. Ukrainian Catholic priest, educator, and theologian; full member of the Shevchenko Scientific Society (1935). During the First World War he served as an army chaplain. In 1918 he became prefect of the Greek Catholic Seminary, and then taught canon law and Eastern dogmatics at the Greek Catholic Theological Academy (1928–39). He published a number of historical and theological studies such as 'Uniini i avtokefal'ni zmahannia na ukraïns'kykh zemliakh vid Danyla do Izydora' (Uniate and Autocephalous Strife in Ukrainian Lands from Danylo to Isidore, *Bohosloviia* [1923, 1924, 1927]), 'De Zacharia Kopystenskyj eiusque Palinodia' (*Bohosloviia* [1930–1]), and 'Dohmatyka nez'iedynenoho Skhodu' (Dogmatics of the Non-united East, *Pratsi Hreko-Katolyts'koï bohoslovs'koï akademiï* [1936]). He was shot by Soviet airmen at the outbreak of the German-Soviet War.

Ishchenko, Ivan [Iščenko], b 17 July 1891 in Pustovarivka, Skvyra county, Kiev gubernia, d 21 November 1975 in Kiev. Surgeon; from 1945 corresponding member of the AN URSR. A graduate of Kiev University (1917), he was the chief surgeon of the Kiev Military Hospital (1944–54) and a department head at the Kiev Medical Institute. His publications deal with problems of clinical and experimental surgery, particularly with abdominal surgery, shock, and organ transplantation.

Ishchenko, Oleksii [Iščenko, Oleksij], ?–1811. Kiev silversmith of the late 18th and early 19th centuries. A master craftsman with his own shop, he did his most important work for the Kievan Cave and St Michael's Golden-Domed monasteries. His works, signed with the initials 'AI,' include the silver Royal Gates of the Church of the Elevation of the Cross (1784), two icon vestments (1784), a copper book for a gospel with 11 enamel medallions (1785), a copper altarpiece for St Michael's Golden-Domed Monastery, a silver vestment for an icon of St Barbara (1790), and a silver plate (1791). He also gilded a dome of the Dormition Cathedral of the Kievan Cave Monastery (1780). Many other works by Ishchenko have not been preserved.

Ishchuk, Arsen [Iščuk], b 22 June 1908 in Horodok, Berdychiv county, Kiev gubernia, d 21 December 1982 in Kiev. Literature scholar and prosaist. From 1937 he taught at Kiev University and served there as a dean and prorector. He wrote monographs on Lesia Ukrainka (1950), P. Tychyna (1954), and V. Mynko (1957), the collections *Statti pro radians'ku literaturu* (Articles about Soviet Literature, 1958) and *Na shliakhu postupu* (On the Road of Progress, 1968), and the novel-chronicle *Verbivchany* (The Villagers of Verbivka, 3 vols, 1961–75).

Ishlinsky, Aleksandr [Išlinskij], b 6 August 1913 in Moscow. Specialist in mechanics; full member of the AN URSR since 1948 and of the Academy of Sciences of USSR since 1960. From 1948 to 1955 he served as director of the Institute of Mathematics of AN URSR and professor at Kiev University. He has also taught at Moscow University and served as director of its Institute of Mechanics. In 1964 he became director of the Institute for Problems of Mechanics of the AN URSR. His contributions to mechanics include a theoretical basis for a space gyroscope.

Metropolitan Isidore

Isidore, b ca 1380–90, d 27 April 1463 in Rome. Metropolitan of Kiev. A Greek by birth, in 1436 he was consecrated metropolitan of Rus' by the Patriarch of Constantinople, Joseph II. He favored a church union with Rome and in 1439, at the Council of Ferrara-Florence, he signed the union of the Greek and Latin rite churches (see *Florence, Church Union of). In 1440, as legate of Pope Eugenius IV, he traveled throughout Ukraine proclaiming the union. In 1441 he went to Moscow, the seat of the Kievan metropolitanate. There, however, his proclamation of the union was opposed by the prince and the hierarchy. He was briefly imprisoned but escaped and fled to Ukraine, where, having lost most of his support, he remained for only a short time before returning to Rome. In Rome he was appointed a cardinal and became known as *Cardinalis Rutheni*. He abandoned the title of metropolitan of Rus' in ca 1445–8, but he continued his efforts on behalf of the Ukrainian church, making several trips to Constantinople and even to Rus'. He died in Rome and was buried in the Vatican Basilica. His sermons were published by the Pontifical Institute of Oriental Studies in Rome in 1971.

Iskra, Ivan, b ? d 26 July 1708 in Borshchahivka (now in Vinnytsia oblast). Colonel of Poltava regiment from 1696 to 1703; the grandson of Ya. Ostrianyn. Iskra took part in the Russian campaign of 1696 against the Turkish fortresses on the lower Dnieper River, as acting hetman of the Cossack regiments. In 1700 he led a large Cossack force against the Swedes in Livonia during the Northern War. He opposed Hetman I. *Mazepa's separatist plans, and in 1703 Mazepa deposed him. In August 1707 Iskra and the general judge V. *Kochubei denounced Mazepa to Tsar Peter I. Trusting Mazepa and finding no evidence to prove their accusations, Peter had Iskra and Kochubei arrested, returned to Ukraine, and beheaded. They are buried at the Kievan Cave Monastery.

Iskrytsky [Iskryc'kyj]. Name of a noble family in the Chernihiv region. Mykhailo, a Kievan noble of the mid-17th century, married Eva Morzhkovska, the sister of Hetman P. Teteria. His son, Vasyl (d 1696, buried in Lviv), was a Notable Companion of the Zaporizhian Host (1659). Vasyl's daughter, Uliana (Olena, d 29 October

1742), married Hetman D. Apostol. Several other Iskrytskys were famous civic leaders in the Chernihiv region in the 18th to 20th centuries, including Hryhorii, who was marshal of the nobility in Novhorod-Siverskyi vicegerency (1788–93), and Petro, who served as general flagbearer under Hetman K. Rozumovsky (1760–2).

Iskusstvo v Iuzhnoi Rossii (Art in Southern Russia). Monthly devoted to pictorial art and architecture that was published in Kiev in 1913–14 as the continuation of *Iskusstvo i pechatnoe delo* (1909–10) and *Iskusstvo; Zhivopis'; Grafika; Khudozhestvennaia pechat'* (1911–12). It published articles on the history of world art and particularly on the history of Ukrainian art, the traditions of Ukrainian folk art, and the contemporary artistic schools in Ukraine. Among its contributors were N. Ge, F. Ernst, P. Martynovych, O. Novytsky, M. Petrov, K. Shyrotsky, and M. Vrubel.

Islam-Girei III (Islām Girāy), 1604–June 1654. Khan of the Crimean Tatars in 1644–54 and an untrustworthy ally of Hetman B. *Khmelnytsky in the *Cossack-Polish War of 1648–57. While in Ukraine, his forces pillaged towns and villages, and carried off the inhabitants as slaves. Islam-Girei III deserted Khmelnytsky thrice – at the battles of *Zboriv (1649) and *Berestechko (1651) and the siege of *Zhvanets (1653) – each time entering into a separate peace agreement with the Polish king Jan II Casimir Vasa. He played both sides in the conflict to his own advantage. Consequently, Khmelnytsky turned to Muscovy for aid and signed the Treaty of *Pereiaslav with the tsar in 1654. According to a Ukrainian legend, a Ukrainian woman slave avenged the destruction wrought in her country by the Tatars by poisoning Islam-Girei.

Ispravnik. Name of an official on the county level in the Russian Empire. *Ispravniki* were introduced by Catherine II in 1775. At first they were county heads elected from among the local nobility. From 1862 they were appointed by the gubernia governor and their functions were expanded to include supervision of the county police and prisons and membership in various county committees and commissions. In 1874 they became members of the county bureaus for peasant affairs. They were responsible directly to the governor, and their police authority in the county, except in those towns that had their own police force, was practically unrestricted. (See also *Police.)

Israel. Jewish state established on the territories of British-controlled Palestine on 14 May 1948. In 1986, the population of Israel (not including territories occupied in 1967) was 4,381,000, of which 83 percent were Jews and 17 percent non-Jews. Of the latter, 77 percent were Moslems, 13.5 percent Christians, and approx 9 percent Druze. Approximately 1.2 million Arabs live in territories occupied by Israel since 1967. The official capital of Israel is Jerusalem.

Historical ties between Palestine and Ukraine were based on religious motives. The Holy Land drew pilgrims from Ukraine as far back as the 11th century (see also *Jerusalem). Hetman I. Mazepa contributed generously to monasteries and churches in the Holy Land. During the Second World War, some Ukrainians who were in the Polish army stayed on what is now Israeli territory. Today, in the city of Nazareth there is an outpost (*stanytsia*) of the Ukrainian Catholic church.

Jews from Ukraine played an important part in both the world Zionist movement and in the creation of the Israeli state. The leader of the Hibbat Zion, L. Pinsker, who called for the creation of a Jewish state, was born in Tomashiv, in the Kholm region, and was educated in Odessa. Also of Ukrainian origin are the greatest theoretician of Socialist Zionism, B. Borochov; the founder and theoretician of anti-Socialist Zionism, V. *Zhabotinsky; the founder of modern Hebraic literature and the greatest Jewish poet, Hayyim Nahman Bialik; the second president of Israel, I. Ben-Zvi; former prime minister G. Meir; former acting prime minister and minister of foreign affairs M. Sharett; the founder of Israeli industry A. Shenkar; and others in all branches of political, social, economic, and cultural life.

Jews emigrated from Ukraine to Palestine in larger numbers at the beginning of the Zionist movement, in the late 19th century. In 1971 a relatively large exodus of Jews from Ukraine (as well as from other parts of the USSR) to Israel began. Close to 100,000 Jews emigrated from Ukraine but less than half of these settled in Israel, most making their way to the United States and Canada. The accompanying table gives figures for the number of Jews who emigrated from Ukraine by city (from which over 1000 emigrated).

City of origin of Jewish emigrants from Ukraine

City	Number of Jewish emigrants (1968–81)	Number immigrating to Israel	% of total emigrants
Kiev	23,666	4,734	20
Kharkiv	3,969	577	14.5
Odessa	24,794	4,249	17.1
Lviv	8,237	3,480	42.3
Chernivtsi	17,868	16,361	91.6
Mukachiv	1,085	1,024	94.4

The percentage of Jews who, having emigrated from Ukraine, went to Israel is larger for those cities in which the Jews were not so Russified and denationalized. Many Ukrainians of mixed marriages and parentage also emigrated.

Today in Israel, the newly arrived emigrants from Ukraine constitute a significant percentage of engineers, doctors, and industrial workers. There are a few kibbutzim with a majority of Jews from Ukraine. Some immigrants are members of the Association for Jewish-Ukrainian Contacts, which publishes the journal *Diialohy*. The greatest concentrations of Jews from Ukraine are in the Tel Aviv area, Beer-Sheva, Jerusalem, and Haifa.

BIBLIOGRAPHY

Gitelman, Z. *Becoming Israelis: Political Resocialization of Soviet and American Immigrants* (New York 1982)

Šnaton Statisti Leisrael (Jerusalem 1984)

Facts about Israel (Jerusalem 1985)

I. Kleiner, V. Markus

Istanbul. The largest city (1984 pop 2,854,000) in Turkey. Its old city (Stamboul) stands on a triangular peninsula between Europe and Asia washed by 'the three seas': the Bosporus, the Golden Horn, and the Sea of Marmara. The Golden Horn inlet separates the original old city from the 'newer' (10th century on) city of Beyoglu (formerly Galatia-Pera) to the north. The Bosporus separates European Istanbul from its Asian districts of Üsküdar (formerly Scutari and Chrysopolis) and Kadiköy (Chalcedon). Istanbul is a renowned port and political and cultural center. It was the capital of the Byzantine and Ottoman empires and, until 1923, of the Turkish Republic. It has many Byzantine and Turkish architectural monuments (churches, mosques, and palaces), learned societies, research institutes, museums, libraries, and newspapers; a university (est 1453), technical university, and academy of fine arts; other post-secondary schools; and a palace of culture.

The site of the ancient Greek colony of *Byzantium was founded on the Bosporus ca 660 BC and came under Persian, Athenian, Spartan, Macedonian, and Roman rule. In 324 AD, after defeating his rival Licinius, Emperor Constantine the Great made Byzantium his capital. Renamed Constantinople, it became one of the world's most powerful, beautiful, and wealthy cities. In 381, the city became the seat of a patriarch who was second only to the bishop of Rome. Because of its central role in the *Byzantine Empire, its geopolitical location, and its wealth, Constantinople became an object of conquest by the Persians and Avars (626), the Arabs (674–8, 717–18), the Bulgars (813, 913), the Pechenegs (1090–1), and Kievan Rus'.

Varangian-Rus' forces first besieged Constantinople in 860; the sieges of the Kievan princes Oleh I (907), Ihor Olhovych (944), and Volodymyr Yaroslavych (1043) followed. But there were also amicable relations between Constantinople and Kiev. In 957, for example, Emperor Constantine Porphyrogenitus welcomed the visit of Princess Olha with much pomp and circumstance. In the 11th and 12th centuries, banished Rus' princes sought refuge there; in 1129 five Polatsk princes banished by Grand Prince Mstyslav I Volodymyrovych settled there with their families. Rus' warriors served in Constantinople; in the 11th century, there was a retinue of them at the emperor's court. Rus' merchants received special privileges in Constantinople, as laid down in the treaties of 911, 944, and 971; they were allowed to live in a separate quarter near St Mamant's Monastery. From that time on merchants from Constantinople also traded in Ukraine.

Constantinople – called Tsargrad or Tsarhorod ('The Emperor's City') by the Slavs – played an important role in the Christianization of Ukraine in 988 and the subsequent history of the Ukrainian *church. From 1037 to 1686, Kiev metropoly was under the canonical jurisdiction of the Patriarch of Constantinople, who appointed its metropolitans. Patriarchs who had a particularly important influence on church affairs in Ukraine were Jeremiah II (1589–95), who granted the right of stauropegion to the Lviv, Kiev, and Lutske brotherhoods; Parthenius, who ratified Metropolitan P. Mohyla's Orthodox Confession of the Faith (1643); Dionysius IV, who placed Kiev metropoly under the jurisdiction of the Patriarch of Moscow (1686); and Gregory VII, who confirmed the autocephaly of the Orthodox church in Poland (1924). Many Ukrainian pilgrims on their way to the Holy Land passed through Constantinople, which was considered a holy city; some of them, such as Hegumen Danylo of Chernihiv (ca 1113), the Nizhen monk I. Vyshensky (1708), the Chyhyryn monk Serapion (1749), and V. Hryhorovych-Barsky (1723), left accounts of their stay there.

Together with Christianity, *Byzantine art and law were brought to Ukraine from Constantinople. The *architecture of Kiev under Volodymyr the Great and Yaroslav the Wise used Constantinople as the model. Churches (especially the *St Sophia Cathedral), palaces, and the *Golden Gate were built and embellished by Byzantine craftsmen and painters. The most famous Rus' icon, the Vyshhorod *Theotokos*, was painted by artists from Constantinople.

Constantinople was sacked by the Crusaders in 1204, and the ensuing dismemberment of the Byzantine Empire, Latin rule (1204–61), Turkish expansion, and foreign occupations and sieges led to the city's political and economic decline. Finally, in 1453 the Ottoman sultan Mehmed II seized Constantinople and massacred its population. The city was then repeopled and rebuilt. From 1457, as Istanbul, it was the capital of the Ottoman Empire and enjoyed centuries of peace and prosperity.

Under the Ottomans, decisions made in Istanbul influenced the fate of much of southeastern Europe, including most of Ukraine (see *Turkey). During the numerous raids of Turkey's vassals, the Crimean Tatars, into Ukraine, thousands of Ukrainians were captured and shipped to the slave market in Istanbul; among them was Roksoliana, who ca 1520 became the wife of Sultan Süleyman I. The Cossacks combated the Turks and Tatars; their leader Prince D. Vyshnevetsky was captured and executed in Istanbul in 1563. Under and after Hetman P. Sahaidachny the Cossacks were strong and daring enough to sail across the Black Sea and pillage the environs of Istanbul in 1615, 1620, and thrice in 1624, releasing Cossacks and other Christians from Turkish captivity. During the Polish-Ottoman Battle of Cecora, the future hetman B. Khmelnytsky was captured and held prisoner in Istanbul (1620–2). At the start of the Cossack-Polish War (1648), Khmelnytsky's emissary, Col P. Dzhalalii, concluded an alliance at the Porte. Hetman P. Doroshenko had residents at the Porte from 1666. In 1672, Yu. Khmelnytsky was captured by the Tatars and taken to Istanbul; he lived there as the archimandrite of a Greek monastery for six years before becoming the hetman of Right-Bank Ukraine.

During the First World War, the *Union for the Liberation of Ukraine had its representatives, headed by M. Melenevsky, in Istanbul. After the 1918 Peace Treaty of Brest Litovsk, envoys of the Ukrainian Hetman government (M. Sukovkin in 1918) and the UNR Directory (O. Lototsky in 1919–20 and J. Tokarzewski-Karaszewicz in 1920–1) resided in Istanbul. In 1919–21 the Ukrainian artist O. Hryshchenko also lived there. After the Armistice of 11 November 1918, 300 Ukrainians in the Austrian army who had surrendered on the Western front were brought to Istanbul and allowed to return home through the intervention of the Ukrainian envoy. In 1921–35, a representative of the UNR Government-in-exile, V. Mursky, resided in Istanbul. After the Second World War, until the late 1940s, there was a small but active Ukrainian community in Istanbul, headed by M. Zabila.

BIBLIOGRAPHY
Barsov, T. *Konstantinopol'skii patriarkh i ego vlast' nad russkoiu tserkoviiu* (St Petersburg 1878; repr, The Hague 1968)
Kondakov, N. *Vizantiiskie tserkvi i pamiatniki Konstantinopolia* (Odessa 1887)
Lotots'kyi, O. *Storinky mynuloho,* 4: *V Tsarhorodi* (Warsaw 1939)
Levchenko, M. *Ocherki po istorii russko-vizantiiskikh otnoshenii* (Moscow 1956)
Hornykevych, T. *Viden', Tsarhorod, Ateny: Podorozhni zapysky* (Munich 1964)

A. Zhukovsky

Istoriia narodnoho hospodarstva ta ekonomichnoï dumky Ukraïns'koï RSR (History of the National Economy and Economic Thought in the Ukrainian SSR). A scholarly series published since 1965 by the AN URSR Institute of Economics in Kiev. Since its establishment the editor has been T. Derev'iankin. It contains articles on the latest research in Ukrainian economic history and history of economic thought. Twenty issues have been published (to 1986), but the number of copies printed is gradually decreasing: from 1,000 in 1974 to 890 in 1984.

Istoriia Rusov (History of the Rus' People). An important document of Ukrainian political thought from the end of the 18th or beginning of the 19th century, of unknown authorship. It vividly depicts the development of Ukraine, its people, and statehood from the remote past to 1769, focusing mostly on the periods of the *Cossacks, B. *Khmelnytsky, and the *Hetman state. The historical outlook embodied in the work is that of traditional Cossack historiography. The underlying principle of *Istoriia Rusov* is that each nation has a natural, moral, and historical right to an independent political development; its main theme is the struggle of the Ukrainian nation against foreign (Russian or Polish) domination. The author made ample use of contemporary historical sources and supplemented them with various legends, personal recollections, and 18th-century archival materials. It was not the writer's intention, however, to present an objective history of Ukraine; rather, he presented history as he believed it should have been. According to E. *Borschak, *Istoriia Rusov* is a historical legend, a political exposition in a historical form. It is written in the Russian literary language of the time with a large admixture of Ukrainian words. Because of censorship, the author often concealed his true thoughts or attributed them to historical personalities by quoting fictitious speeches or correspondence.

The authorship of the book has not been determined. Archbishop H. Konysky was first thought to be the author, but this hypothesis was later rejected. Many historians, including V. Ikonnikov, O. Lazarevsky, M. Vasylenko, and D. Doroshenko, claimed that the author was Hryhorii *Poletyka. Others, among them V. Horlenko, A. Yershov, and E. Borschak, held that it was Poletyka's son, Vasyl. M. Hrushevsky suggested that the work was coauthored by father and son. Several specialists – M. Slabchenko, P. Klepatsky, A. Yakovliv, and M. Vozniak – proposed that the author was O. *Bezborodko. Other names have been suggested, including N. *Repnin (by M. Drahomanov), V. *Lukashevych (by M. Petrovsky), and O. *Lobysevych. Some scholars claim the work was written in the 1760s–1770s (Lazarevsky, Doroshenko, Slabchenko, Vozniak); others give the 1790s as the date (Yakovliv, B. Krupnytsky); still others suggest it was written as late as 1815–25 (Horlenko, Yershov, Borschak). The book probably originated in the Novhorod-Siverskyi region, was copied several times, and edited again sometime between 1815 and 1822. The author, or authors, of *Istoriia Rusov* belonged to the *Novhorod-Siverskyi patriotic circle and were connected with Prince O. Bezborodko by official, personal, and ideological-political interests.

Istoriia Rusov was first mentioned in 1825. For a long time the work circulated in manuscript. It was extremely popular and had a strong influence on the development of Ukrainian historiography in the 19th century. The historical-literary works of M. Markevych, Ye. Hrebinka, I. Sreznevsky, N. Gogol, A. Metlynsky, M. Kostomarov, P. Kulish, and, above all, T. Shevchenko were based on *Istoriia Rusov*.

The work was published first by O. *Bodiansky in *Chteniia v Imperatorskom obshchestve istorii i drevnostei rossiiskikh* (1846) and in a separate edition. A Ukrainian translation by V. Davydenko, edited and introduced by O. *Ohloblyn, was published in 1956 in New York.

BIBLIOGRAPHY
Doroshenko, D. '*Istoriia Rusov* iak pam'iatka ukraïns'koï politychnoï dumky druhoï polovyny 18 v.,' *Khliborobs'ka Ukraïna*, vol 3 (1921)
Iakovliv, A. 'Do pytannia pro avtora *Istoriï Rusiv*,' *ZNTSh* 154 (1937)
Vozniak, M. *Psevdo-Konys'kyi i Psevdo-Poletyka ('Istoriia Rusov' u literaturi i nautsi)* (Lviv-Kiev 1939)
Borschak, E. *La légende historique de l'Ukraine. Istoriia Rusov* (Paris 1949)
Ohloblyn, O. 'Where Was *Istoriya Rusov* Written?' *AUA* 3 (1953)
Yakovliv, A. '*Istoriya Rusov* and Its Author,' *AUA* 3 (1953)
Shevel'ov, Iu. '*Istoriia Rusov* ochyma movoznavtsia,' in *Zbirnyk na poshanu prof. d-ra O. Ohloblyna* (New York 1977)

O. Ohloblyn

Italy. A country (1985 pop 52,079,000) in southern Europe occupying the Apennine Peninsula and the islands of Sicily and Sardinia. It has an area of 301,277 sq km. Individual Italian states freed themselves from foreign rule beginning in the early Middle Ages, but Italy did not become a united kingdom until the mid-19th century. Since 1871 Rome has been its capital. A Fascist dictatorship between 1922 and 1945, Italy became a republic in 1946.

In the 12th and 13th centuries AD, Italian merchants appeared in Kiev, and from the 12th to the 15th century, Venice, Genoa, and Pisa had commercial relations with the lands of the Crimea and southern Ukraine. Genoa and Venice established trading colonies on the northern Pontic and Azov coasts and in the Crimea – Kaffa (Teodosiia), which even had its own bishopric, Soldaia (*Sudak), Cembalo (Balaklava), Tana (Oziv), Bosporo (Kerch), Moncastro (Bilhorod-Dnistrovskyi), Matrega (Tmutorokan), Copa, Mapa, and Bata. From there, Italian corporations and individual merchants engaged in transit trade with the lands of Ukraine, Muscovy, Poland, Caucasia, Persia, India, and China. To obtain and maintain these colonies on the Black and Azov seas, Genoa and Venice waged war with each other and with the Crimean Tatars. The strongest center was Genoese-controlled Kaffa; before it was razed by the Turks in 1475, a thriving international market in slaves taken during Tatar raids into Ukraine and Caucasia operated there.

Relations between Italy and Rus' date from the 10th century onward, when various popes sent legations to the princes of Kiev and Galicia-Volhynia to negotiate a religious union or (later) an anti-Mongol coalition or both (see, eg, *Danylo Romanovych and Church Union of *Florence and Rome).

International trade routes between Europe and the Orient passed through Ukraine. In the 15th century, Italian merchants and artisans began settling in Lviv and other Western Ukrainian towns under Polish rule. There they specialized in trade and banking, opened schools of commerce, and introduced the ideas of *humanism and the *Renaissance. Italian craftsmen, architects, and painters built and embellished churches and palaces; eg, the Dormition Church (by Pietro Italus from Lugano and Paolo Romanus), the Korniakt Building (by P. di Barbone and P. Dominici), the Golden Rose Synagogue (by the Italian known as P. Shchaslyvy), and the *Black Building (by the Italian known as P. Krasovsky) in Lviv. In Transcarpathia, as well, Italian influence is apparent in the architecture and frescoes of the rotunda in the village of Horiany, one of the many villages owned, together with Uzhhorod, between 1322 and 1691 by the Italian Drughet family, which founded Uzhhorod College. During the Renaissance individual Ukrainians studied in Italy and brought Italian ideas, literature, and culture back with them to Ukraine. One of them, Yu. *Drohobych, became a professor and rector at Bologna University.

Italian-Ukrainian political relations did not exist in Ukraine under Polish rule until the Cossack period. In 1646 the Venetian emissary G.A. Vimina Bellanese visited Hetman B. Khmelnytsky in Chyhyryn to try to persuade him to join a military coalition against Turkey. Vimina published an account of the Cossack-Polish War in Venice in 1671.

There was significant Italian influence on Ukrainian literature, painting, architecture, and music in the baroque, rococo, and classicist periods. Such architects as S. Bracci, B. *Rastrelli, A. Rinaldi, and G. *Quarenghi built palaces and churches in Kiev, Baturyn, Kozelets, and elsewhere in central Ukraine. At the same time Ukrainian artists and composers studied in Italy; eg, A. Losenko, I. Martos, O. Biliavsky, V. Bereza, D. Bortniansky, and M. Berezovsky. Many other Ukrainians visited Italy in the 17th and 18th centuries; some left accounts of their travels; eg, H. Skybynsky, Hieromonach T. Kaplonsky, V. Hryhorovych-Barsky, and T. Prokopovych, who studied in Rome (1699–1701). Apparently, H. Skovoroda also visited Italy.

Around the time of the Church Union of *Berestia (1596), close ties existed between the Ukrainian church and the Vatican, and religious representatives were exchanged. Soon after, a permanent presence of Ukrainian and Belorussian Uniate clergy was established at the Vatican in Rome, and it has lasted to this day.

In the 1820s and 1830s the Italian duke Charles of Bourbon-Parma resided in Vienna; there he became acquainted with the Ukrainian Greek Catholic priests at St Barbara's Church and became such an enthusiast of the Eastern rite that he built a Greek Catholic church at his home in Lucca. Three Transcarpathian priests – the writers M. Luchkai and later the brothers A. and O. Labants – stayed as guests there several years. In the 1840s and 1850s Rev V. *Terletsky tried to influence the Vatican's policies concerning Poland and Ukraine. Throughout the 19th century, Ukrainians from Galicia and Bukovyna in the Austrian imperial army were posted on the territory of northern Italy and took part in battles against the Italians. Their experiences are portrayed in the Romantic works of A. Mohylnytsky, M. Ustyianovych, and particularly Yu. Fedkovych. In the second half of the 19th century, such Ukrainian writers and poets as P. Kulish, Marko Vovchok, Lesia Ukrainka, B. Hrinchenko, and M. Kotsiubynsky visited Italy; their sojourns there are reflected in their works. Ukrainian painters of the 19th century also studied in or visited Italy; eg, N. Ge, I. Repin, P. Boryspolets (d 1880 in Rome), R. Hadziewicz, K. Ustyianovych, A. Mokrytsky, V. Orlovsky, I. Shapovalenko, S. Vasylkivsky, and O. Murashko.

In 1873, the Florentine journal *Rivista Europea* printed M. Drahomanov's article on Ukrainian literature and the cultural movement under Russia and Austria; this was the first detailed information in Italian about the Ukrainian national movement. In 1908–9, M. Hrushevsky published a series of interesting accounts of his trip to Italy in *Literaturno-naukovyi vistnyk*. Around the turn of the century the poet P. Karmansky studied in Rome; there are many Italian themes in his works, and he translated contemporary Italian poets. Other Ukrainian writers – I. Franko, V. Shchurat, M. Vorony, V. Samiilenko, P. Hrabovsky – also translated Italian literature. Franko wrote a study of Dante (republished in Kiev in 1965).

The influence of Italian theater and opera in Ukraine has been discernible since the late 18th century. In the early 19th century, the magnate Y. Illinsky produced an Italian opera at his estate in Romaniv, Volhynia, using singers brought from St Petersburg. In 1811, an Italian comic opera was produced in Odessa. Italian opera troupes performed in Kiev in 1847 and 1863–5 and in Poltava and Odessa in the 1850s. Several Ukrainians studied singing in Italy. The tenor M. *Ivanov sang in the world premiere of G. Rossini's *Stabat Mater* (1842).

During the First World War, Ukrainians in the Austro-Hungarian army fought on the Italian front. Many of them died at the Battle of the Piave. Thousands (60,000 according to some estimates) were held in prisoner-of-war camps on the island of Asinara and near Cassino and Arquata. The Italian member of parliament E. Insabato tried to have them sent to Ukraine to fight the Bolsheviks. His efforts failed because of French opposition, and they were freed only in 1921 and returned to Poland. In 1919–20, diplomatic missions of the UNR (headed by D. Antonovych and V. Mazurenko) and the Western Ukrainian National Republic (headed by O. Kolessa and V. Bandrivsky) were sent to Italy; Italy did not recognize the Ukrainian state, however, and they acted only in an unofficial capacity. A military delegation headed by O. Sevriuk and his deputy I. Kossak intervened in Italy on behalf of the prisoners of war. The UNR mission published the weekly *La Voce dell'Ucraina* (edited by M. Yeremiiv).

In the interwar years, several Ukrainian political and cultural figures lived in Rome: Ye. Onatsky, M. Yeremiiv, J. Tokarzewski-Karaszewicz, Ye. Konovalets, M. Lypovetska, and the painters I. Kurakh, S. Mako, R. Lisovsky, and H. Mazepa. In 1938 an exhibit of 374 works by 41 artists took place there. Several dozen gymnasium and theology students studied at the Salesian center in

Turin, and Basilian monks from Galicia began living at the *Grottaferrata Monastery near Rome. Contacts with the Fascist authorities were maintained mainly by the OUN, which held its second great congress in Italy in 1939. This did not deter the Mussolini government, however, from supporting Hungary's claim to Carpatho-Ukraine in 1938–9.

During the Second World War, an Italian expeditionary corps commanded by Gen G. Messe fought on the Eastern front in Ukraine. In May and June 1944, the Polish Expeditionary Corps under Gen W. Anders fought in the Allied campaign against the Germans between Naples and Rome. It became famous for its capture of the stronghold on Monte Cassino. Several dozen of the 2,000 Ukrainians in the corps are buried in the military cemetery at the foot of the mountain.

At the war's end in 1945, some 15,000 Ukrainians found themselves in Italy. Most were soldiers in the *Division Galizien who had surrendered to the British and were interned in prisoner-of-war camps near Bellaria and then near Rimini. A small number consisted of refugees in displaced persons camps near Naples (Caserta, Capua, and elsewhere); later, Ukrainian refugees from Yugoslavia stayed for a short time in a camp near Trieste. The prisoners and refugees were helped partially by the Ukrainian Relief Committee in Rome, founded on the initiative of Bishop I. *Buchko. In 1947, the prisoners of war were transported as contract laborers to Great Britain, whence many of them, like most refugees, emigrated to the New World.

Since the late 1940s only a small community of Ukrainian Catholic clergy, students, and a few individuals has existed in and near Rome, where *St Josaphat's Ukrainian Pontifical College (est 1897), the Ukrainian Minor Pontifical Seminary (est 1954), and the *Ukrainian Catholic University (est 1963) are located. Since the war Rome has been the main center of the *Basilian monastic order and the Ukrainian Catholic church in general. In Castel Gandolfo, outside Rome, a Studite monastery was founded in 1965 by Cardinal Y. Slipy. The villa of St Andrew, bought in 1929 by Metropolitan A. Sheptytsky, has been a rest home for seminarians. Elsewhere in Italy, Rev I. Khomenko lived and worked on the translation of the Bible on the Isle of Capri.

To familiarize Italians with Ukraine, an Italian-Ukrainian Friendship Society was founded in 1952 by V. Fedoronchuk; its chairman was Ambassador A. Giannini. Other notable Italian friends of the Ukrainians were Senator R. Ciasca, E. Insabato, Prince G. Alliata, and G. Bernabei. In 1954–6, the journal *Ucraina* was published in Italian. In 1951 the Italian state radio began broadcasting daily in Ukrainian; the broadcasts have been directed by V. Fedoronchuk (until 1975), Rev V. Sapeliak, and Rev R. Saba. The Vatican radio also broadcasts daily programs in Ukrainian. Ukrainian has been taught at the universities of Naples and Rome. The Milanese journal *L'Altra Europa* (formerly *Russia Christiana*) has often published articles on Ukrainian subjects, especially about religious dissent in Ukraine.

Italian-Ukrainian cultural and literary relations have continued in the 20th century. The Ukrainian Futurists followed closely the activities and writings of their Italian counterparts. Since the 1920s, a substantial body of Italian literature has been translated into Ukrainian. Dante's *Divine Comedy* has been translated by I. Franko, M. Rylsky and P. Karmansky, Ye. Drobiazko (1968, 1976), and more recently by the émigrés I. Kachurovsky and (in a prose version) B. Lonchyna; a translation of Dante's *Vita nuova* appeared in 1965. Petrarch's works have been translated by M. Zerov, I. Steshenko, I. Kachurovsky, and D. Palamarchuk. Translations of Boccaccio's *Decameron* were published in 1928 and 1969. Michelangelo's sonatas have been translated by M. Bazhan, I. Drach, and D. Pavlychko. In 1958 an anthology of Italian contemporary poetry was published in Kiev. Translations have been published separately or in the journal *Vsesvit*; they include works by A. Negri, G. Leoparde, G. Verga, C. Goldoni, E. De Amicis, G. di Lampedusa, G. Piovone, A. Moravia, E. Vittorini, I. Calvino, C. Pavese, C. Malaparte, D. Rodari, E. Montale, P.P. Pasolini, and others. Some Ukrainian literature, particularly T. Shevchenko's, has been translated and studied in Italy.

At the turn of the 20th century, the Ukrainian opera singers O. Myshuha and S. Krushelnytska trained in Italy and were acclaimed for their performances at the Rome Opera and La Scala in Milan. The singer I. Steshenko also trained in Italy. Since the 1960s, Soviet Ukrainian opera singers, including R. Babak, Ye. Miroshnychenko, A. Solovianenko, M. Ohrenych, and M. Kondratiuk, have trained at La Scala.

Over the centuries the Ukrainian language has acquired many Italian words and expressions. Many are *Latinisms, but others have been borrowed from modern Italian. The first loan words were ecclesiastical and religious terms; later ones were terms of finance, trade, warfare, sailing, art, music, theater, architecture, and daily life.

BIBLIOGRAPHY

Hordyns'kyi, Ia. 'Ukraïna i Italiia: Ohliad vzaiemyn do 1914 r.,' *Zbirnyk zakhodoznavstva*, 2, ed F. Savchenko (Kharkiv-Kiev 1930)

Lonchyna, T. 'Ukraïntsi v Italiï ta Vatykani,' in *Ukraïns'ki poselennia: Dovidnyk*, ed A. Milianych et al (New York 1980)

Varvartsev, N. *Ukraina v rossiisko-ital'ianskikh obshchestvennykh i kul'turnykh sviaziakh* (Kiev 1986)

V. Fedoronchuk, V. Markus

Itil. Capital of the Khazar kaganate (see *Khazars) in the 8th to 10th centuries, situated at the mouth of the Volga River, not far from present-day Astrakhan. Itil was an important commercial center because of its favorable location at the crossroads of the Volga River trade route and the overland trade route between Europe and Central Asia. The diverse population of Itil included many Slavic merchants. It was razed by Sviatoslav I Ihorevych in 965.

Itinerant tutors (*mandrivni diaky*). In 17th- and 18th-century Ukraine wandering graduates or older students of theological seminaries or brotherhood schools and, occasionally, clergymen without positions who supported themselves by private tutoring or short-term school teaching, and by entertaining the common people with humorous verses, comic skits, or *vertep* plays. The common people also called them *pyvorizy* (beer guzzlers). The works written by itinerant tutors include mostly burlesque poems, versified travesties, parodies, satires, humorous dialogues, *vertep* dramas, and lyric poetry. As a transitional stage from religious to secular literature, they occupy an important place in the development of Ukrainian literature. Relatively few works of this type – eg, the autobiography of I. Turchynovsky, the poem about Rev Nehrebetsky, and the poem about Kyryk – and authors' names – I. Turchynovsky, M. Mazalevsky, K. Zynoviiv, and V. Barsky – have come down to us.

The itinerant tutor appears as a literary persona in the intermedes of M. Dovhalevsky, and later in the works of N. Gogol, V. Narizhny, H. Kvitka-Osnovianenko, and I. Tobilevych. The language and style used by itinerant tutors influenced such writers as I. Nekrashevych and I. Kotliarevsky, as well as Kotliarevsky's imitators in the early 19th century. The works of itinerant tutors have been studied by I. Franko, M. Petrov, P. Zhytetsky, P. Yefymenko, O. Biletsky, and P. Popov.

BIBLIOGRAPHY
Zhytets'kyi, P. *'Eneïda' Kotliarevs'koho v zv'iazku z ohliadom ukraïns'koï literatury XVIII stolittia* (Kiev 1919)
Bilets'kyi, O. (ed). *Khrestomatiia davn'oï ukraïns'koï literatury* (Kiev 1949)

D. Chyzhevsky

Iunak (Youth). Illustrated monthly magazine for members of the *Plast Ukrainian Youth Association between the ages of 12 and 18. The successor to *Molode zhyttia*, *Doroha*, and *Na slidi*, which served the same age group in interwar Western Ukraine and postwar Germany, *Iunak* began to appear in Toronto in January 1963. It contains articles on a broad range of topics written in a concise, clear style and richly illustrated with sketches and photographs. Its editors have been L. Onyshkevych (1963–7) and O. Kuzmovych (1968–).

Ivakh, Onufrii. See Ewach, Honore.

Ivakhiv, Vasyl [Ivaxiv, Vasyl'] (pseuds: Som, Sonar), b 1912 in Podusiv, Peremyshliany county, Galicia, d 13 May 1943 near Kolky, Volhynia. Senior *UPA officer. A longtime OUN member, he was active in 1940–1 in the Bandera faction of the Galician underground. In the subsequent year he organized and conducted various military courses for the OUN. In March 1943, Ivakhiv was sent to Volhynia by M. Lebed to bring the rapidly growing insurgency movement under unified command. He became the first chief of staff of the insurgent forces organized by the Bandera faction, and conducted negotiations with T. Borovets to unify peacefully all insurgent units under one UPA command. Before he could accomplish this act, he was killed in combat with German units. He was awarded posthumously the rank of lieutenant colonel.

Ivakhnenko, Oleksii [Ivaxnenko, Oleksij], b 30 March 1913 in Kobeliaky, Poltava gubernia. Cyberneticist; since 1961 corresponding member of the AN URSR. He worked at several of the academy's institutes before being appointed in 1962 chairman of a department in the Institute of Cybernetics. His Ukrainian language book *Kibernetychni systemy z kombinovanym keruvanniam* (Cybernetic Systems in Automated Management, 1963) was the first significant work on cybernetics published in the Ukrainian SSR. His other works deal with several areas of technical cybernetics such as self-organizing systems theory, automatic-control theory, and mathematical modeling for forecasting and control.

Ivakin, Yurii, b 6 January 1917 in Katerynoslav (now Dnipropetrovske), d 1983. Literary scholar, feuilletonist, and satirist. He received a doctorate in philology from Kiev University in 1940. In 1946 he became a candidate and later an associate of the AN URSR Institute of Literature. His writing career began in 1947 with the satirical collection *Perets'* (Pepper). Several other collections have appeared, including *Parnas'kyi tsyrul'nyk* (The Barber of Parnassus, 1970), *Parodiï* (Parodies, 1971), and *Vid velykoho do smishnoho* (From the Sublime to the Ridiculous, 1979). His main contribution, however, lies in his studies of T. Shevchenko: *Satyra Shevchenka* (Shevchenko's Satire, 1959), *Styl' politychnoï poeziï Shevchenka* (The Style of Shevchenko's Political Poetry, 1961), as well as two volumes of commentaries to Shevchenko's **Kobzar* (1964 – poetry written before 1847; and 1968 – poetry from 1847 to 1861).

Ivan Rostyslavych. See Berladnyk, Ivan Rostyslavych.

Ivanchenko, Fedir [Ivančenko], b 12 October 1918 in Velykyi Vystrop, Lebedyn county, Kharkiv gubernia. Metallurgist; corresponding member of the AN URSR since 1982. A graduate of the Dnipropetrovske Metallurgical Institute (1945), he has been a professor of mechanics at Kiev Polytechnical Institute since 1969. Ivanchenko is one of the founders of a branch of mechanics known as heavy machinery mechanics and has developed new theories and methods of energy-exchange calculations in the design of metallurgical machines.

Ivanchenko (Ivanova) Raisa [Ivančenko, Rajisa], b 30 November 1934 in Huliai-Pole, Zaporizhia oblast. Writer and historian at Kiev University. She is the author of the prose collections *Liubyty ne prosto* (To Love Is Not Simple, 1976) and *Ne rozmynys' iz soboiu* (Do Not Part Ways with Yourself, 1980); the novel *Peredchuttia vesny* (Premonition of Spring, 1970); the historical novels *Kliatva* (The Curse, 1971, 1985, about M. Drahomanov), *Hniv Peruna* (The Wrath of Perun, 1982), and *Zoloti stremena* (Golden Stirrups, 1984, about King Danylo); and scholary works, including *Mykhailo Drahomanov u suspil'no-politychnomu rusi Rosiï ta Ukraïny (II polovyna XIX st.)* (M. Drahomanov in the Sociopolitical Movement in Russia and Ukraine in the Second Half of the 19th Century, 1971), which was severely criticized by the Party.

Ivanchov, Fedir [Ivančov], b 17 October 1916 in Fogarash (now Zubivka), Mukachiv county, Transcarpathia. Ukrainian writer and satirist in Slovakia. A member of the Communist Party of Czechoslovakia since 1948, he has been a teacher and an editor. Before the war he wrote two plays and a collection of short stories in Russian. He is the author of several Ukrainian collections of socialist-realist stories about life in Transcarpathia: *Pidiimaiet'sia khliborob* (The Farmer Is Rising, 1954), *Otaki dila* (Such Matters, 1957), *Hrishni dushi* (Sinful Souls, 1961), *Dorohamy zhyttia* (Along the Roads of Life, 1976), and *Liudy v stroiu* (People in the Ranks, 1977). From 1960 to 1971 he was the editor-in-chief of the magazine *Duklia*. A study of his life and work by M. Roman was published in Prešov in 1976.

Ivaneiko, M. See Shlemkevych, Mykola.

Ivanenko, Dmytro, b 29 July 1904 in Poltava, Poltava gubernia. Theoretical physicist; brother of O. *Ivanenko. After graduating from Leningrad University (1927), he worked at a number of scientific institutes in Leningrad, Kharkiv, Tomsk, Sverdlovsk, and Kiev. In 1942 he was appointed professor at Moscow University, and in 1949 he became an associate of the USSR Institute of the History of Science and Technology. He has made important contributions to the field of nuclear physics, cosmic radiation, gravitation, quantum mechanics, and mathematics. In 1929 he developed, with V. Fok, the theory of the parallel transfer of electron spinor wave functions. In 1932 he advanced the hypothesis that the atomic nucleus is composed of protons and neutrons. Simultaneously with I. Tamm (1934–6), he laid the foundations of the theory of specific nuclear forces, and then in parallel with I. Pomeranchuk and A. Sokolov (1944–8) he worked out the theory of electromagnetic radiation emitted by accelerated electrons. He proposed a new linear matrix geometry and non-linear spinor equations.

Ivanenko, Oksana, b 13 April 1906 in Poltava. Writer. After graduating from the Kharkiv Institute of People's Education (1926), she taught homeless juvenile delinquents at the Gorky Colony near Kharkiv and edited the children's monthly *Barvinok*. Since 1930 she has published over 40 collections of children's prose, most of which were republished in *Tvory* (Works, 5 vols, 1966–8); three novellas; and the biographical novels *Tarasovi shliakhy* (The Paths of Taras, 1961, about T. Shevchenko) and *Mariia* (1973, about Marko Vovchok). She also translated the tales of H.C. Andersen and the Grimm brothers into Ukrainian. A study of her life and works, by I. Shkarovska, appeared in 1969.

Ivanenko, Petro. See Petryk, Petro.

Ivane-Puste settlement. A Scythian settlement of the 6th–5th century BC. It was discovered in Ivane-Puste, Borshchiv county, Galicia, in 1935 and excavated in 1958–62. The remains of surface dwellings with ovens and open fireplaces, various farm implements, and fragments of pottery were found at the site. The inhabitants of the settlement were herdsmen and ploughmen.

Ivanets, Ivan [Ivanec'], b 1893 in Novosilky Hostynni, Rudky county, Galicia, d 10 March 1946 in Solikamsk, Perm oblast, RSFSR. Painter and graphic artist. During the war for Ukraine's independence Ivanets headed the Press Office of the Legion of Ukrainian Sich Riflemen, and then served on the legion's staff as attaché on gas warfare. A graduate of the Ukrainian Studio of Plastic Arts in Prague (1927), he worked as an illustrator, mostly for the Chervona Kalyna publishing house in Lviv. In 1942–4 he was president of the Association of Plastic Artists in Lviv. Arrested by the Soviets in Cracow in 1945, he was deported to Solikamsk. Ivanets painted battle scenes and landscapes, and wrote many articles on art.

Ivan-Horod. A fortified settlement of the 12th and early 13th century in Kiev principality near the present town of Rzhyshchiv in Kiev oblast. First mentioned in the chronicles in 1151. Standing south of Kiev, it protected the capital from the steppe nomads. In 1223 it was destroyed by the Tatars. Excavations in 1960–6 uncovered the ruins of log fortifications and dwellings, pottery kilns, smithy implements, weapons, tools, various ornamental objects, and animal bones and bread grains.

Ivanivka. V-19, DB III-5. Town smt (1978 pop 10,400) in Antratsyt raion, Voroshylovhrad oblast. Founded in 1771, it has an industrial-machinery plant, a brewery, and a local food industry.

Ivanivka. VI-11. Agricultural town smt (1978 pop 2,900) and raion center in Odessa oblast on the Velykyi Kuialnyk River. It was founded as Malobaranivka in 1793; from 1858 to 1946 it was called Yanivka.

Ivanivka. VII-15. Town smt (1983 pop 5,100) on the Velyka Kalha River in the Black Sea Lowland and a raion center in Kherson oblast. It was founded in 1820. Its inhabitants are employed in agriculture and food processing.

Ivankivtsi settlement. An early Slavic settlement of the *Cherniakhiv culture (4th–6th century AD) discovered outside Ivankivtsi, Nova Ushytsia raion, Khmelnytskyi oblast. Investigations in 1951–2 and 1959–61 uncovered the remains of surface dwellings and storage pits, fragments of pottery, traces of iron working, iron knives, bronze fibulae, and silver Roman coins. Three granite idols that were discovered there are preserved at the Kamianets-Podilskyi and Chernivtsi regional museums.

Ivano-Frankivske [Ivano-Frankivs'ke]. V-5. City (1985 pop 210,000), raion center and capital of *Ivano-Frankivske oblast, an important railway and highway junction, and now the second-largest city in Galicia. Called Stanyslaviv until 1939 and Stanislav until 1962, it is situated in Subcarpathia near the confluence of the Bystrytsia Nadvirnianska and Bystrytsia Solotvynska rivers.

Stanyslaviv was founded in 1662 on the site of the former village of Zabolotiv by the Polish magnate A. Potocki, who named it after his son, Stanisław. In 1663 it was granted the rights of Magdeburg law. The town was well protected by walls and a citadel (restored in the mid-18th century) and was densely built up. Potocki's palace was completed there in 1672 and the town hall in 1695. After the Turks captured Kamianets-Podilskyi in 1672, Stanyslaviv protected the southeastern borders of the Polish Commonwealth from the Turks and Tatars. In 1677 the Armenian community there received special privileges; thenceforth the town had two municipal councils – one for the Ukrainians and Poles and one for the Armenians. Shortly after its founding, Jews began settling there.

As a result of Armenian commerce, the town was an important trade and manufacturing center from the late 17th to the mid-18th century. Fairs were held regularly where Moldavian, Hungarian, Silesian, and Austrian goods were traded for locally produced leather and fur products. Stanyslaviv was also a flourishing cultural center. A branch of the Cracow Academy was established there in 1669; in 1722 it was converted into a Jesuit college. In 1732 the town's population was 3,321 (45 percent Ukrainian and Polish, 44 percent Jewish, and 10 percent Armenian). Later many Armenians out-migrated, and their self-government came to an end in 1769. In the 18th century, the town's development was hindered by frequent wars. During the Great Northern War Hetman I. Mazepa's forces occupied it in 1706–7, and during the Confederation of *Bar it was thrice taken by Russian troops. Plagues decimated the populace in 1705, 1730, and 1770.

In 1772 Stanyslaviv came under Austrian rule and became a circle and (from 1867) county center. In 1801 the state assumed ownership of the town from the Potockis, and its fortifications were torn down in 1809–12. During the *Spring of Nations in 1848, the Ukrainians there organized a circle council as a branch of the *Supreme Ruthenian Council in Lviv and, in the circle itself, peasant militia units and a company of 'Ruthenian Riflemen' to fight the Hungarian and Polish insurgents.

The construction of a railway junction in 1866 stimulated the city's growth. Its population increased from 11,000 in 1849 to 18,600 by 1880 despite a major fire in 1868. By 1886 it had about 30 small industrial enterprises.

The appointment of a Greek Catholic bishop to *Stanyslaviv eparchy (1885) and the establishment of a Ukrainian-language state gymnasium (1905, under the direction of M. Sabat) were milestones for the town's Ukrainians. Stanyslaviv's population continued to grow rapidly, reaching 33,400 by 1910. In 1925, after Knihynyn-Koloniia, which was originally a German settlement, and the

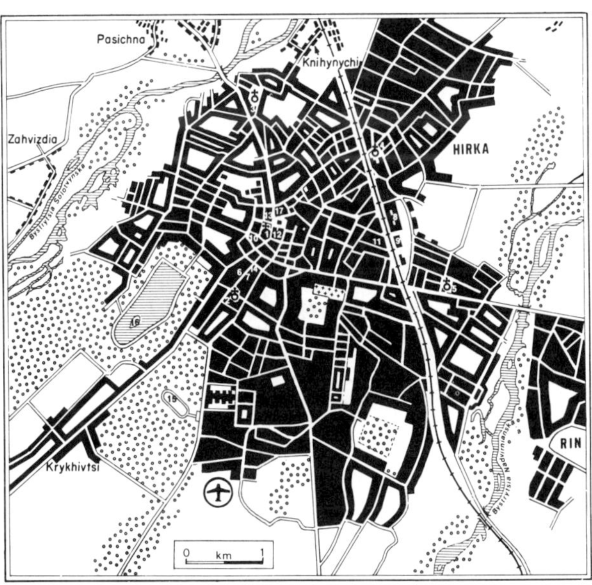

IVANO-FRANKIVSKE

1–5. Ukrainian Catholic churches
6. Episcopal residence until 1945
7. Pedagogical Institute (former theological seminary)
8. Railway station
9. Bus terminal
10. Medical Institute
11. Institute of Petroleum and Gas
12. Ukrainian Music and Drama Theater
13. Regional Museum
14. Philharmonic
15. Stadium
16. Lake
17. Collective-farm market

Knihynyn-Selo had been incorporated, its population reached 54,000 (this included a 3,500-man garrison).

During the First World War Stanyslaviv was close to the front and in 1916–17 suffered much damage. From December 1918 to May 1919 it served as the capital of the *Western Ukrainian National Republic (ZUNR). On 3 January 1919 the Ukrainian National Rada began holding its sessions there; on that day it passed the law on the unification of the ZUNR and the Ukrainian National Republic.

From May 1919 to September 1939 the city was under Polish rule and was one of the larger industrial centers in Galicia. Its main industries were locomotive and railway-car maintenance, petroleum refining, tanning, machine building, food processing, and woodworking. The city was a voivodeship capital (1921–39) and an important cultural center for its three principal nationalities. In 1939 its population of 64,000 included 12,000 Ukrainians (19 percent), 23,500 Poles (37 percent), 26,500 Jews (41 percent), and 2,000 Germans (3 percent).

Stanyslaviv was an important Ukrainian religious, cultural, and educational center with a Ukrainian Greek Catholic seminary, a theological lyceum, three parishes, and three monasteries. Secondary education was provided by four Ukrainian (two state and two private) and seven Polish gymnasiums. A music school, established in 1902 by D. Sichynsky and Ye. Yakubovych, became in 1921 a branch of the Lysenko Higher Institute of Music in Lviv. The city played an important role in Ukrainian musical life. A Boian choir society was organized there in 1894. The noted musicians D. Sichynsky, O. Zalesky, and Ya. Barnych worked there. Several dozen Ukrainian social and cultural organizations – such as the main office of the *Skala Catholic reading halls, a branch of the *Prosvita society (est 1877), artistic, religious, economic, professional, sports, and charitable associations – were active in Stanyslaviv. On the initiative of N. *Kobrynska the first Ukrainian women's society – the Society of Ruthenian Women – was founded there in 1884, and the first women's almanac – **Pershyi vinok* – was published there in 1887. A congress of *Sich societies took place there in 1910, and a Ukrainian Women's Congress was held there in 1934. The amateur *Tobilevych Ukrainian People's Theater was established in 1911; in 1927 it became a permanent theater under the direction of M. Bentsal and the sponsorship of K. Vyshnevsky. Stanyslaviv was also an important publishing center: between 1879 and 1944, 43 periodicals were published there; most of them were short-lived. The most important were the economic biweekly *Hospodar i promyshlennyk* (1879–82), the monthly for precentors *Diakovskii hlas"* (1895–1914, called from 1910 *Holos diakiv*), and *Visnyk Stanyslavivs'koï ieparkhiï* (1886–1939). No Ukrainian general or political newspaper, including *Stanyslavivs'ki visty* (1912–13), was published for more than two years, but a Polish weekly, *Kurjer Stanisławowski*, came out, with a few short interruptions, from 1886 to 1939. The Ukrainian press developed rapidly while Stanyslaviv was the capital of the ZUNR: 12 newspapers and magazines, including the government daily *Republyka* (1919), appeared there. During the 1920s Bystrytsia was a major publishing house and in book production the city stood fifth in Galicia; by 1939 about 150 books had been published there.

During the Second World War Stanyslaviv was under Soviet (1939–41) and German (1941–4) occupation. Soviet

Ivano-Frankivske

rule after July 1944 led to mass repression, particularly in 1945–6. Because of the liquidation of Jews under the Nazi regime, the postwar resettlement of the Poles, and the influx of Russians, the national composition of the city's population changed; in the 1959 census Ukrainians accounted for 67 percent of the total population of 66,000, Russians for 25 percent, and others (mostly Jews and Poles) for 8 percent.

After the war the city's industries were rebuilt and expanded. Today there are 45 enterprises, producing consumer items, instruments, tools and equipment (particularly for petroleum and gas extraction and refining), reinforced concrete, and glass products.

The main educational institutions in Ivano-Frankivske are institutes of pedagogy, medicine, and petroleum and gas; nine specialized secondary schools; and six vocational-technical schools. Among its scientific institutions are the Carpathian Branch of the Ukrainian Scientific Research Institute of Forest Management and Agroforest Amelioration and the Planning and Design Technological Institute of the Ministry of the Forest Industry of the Ukrainian SSR. Located in the city are the *Ivano-Frankivske Ukrainian Music and Drama Theater and a puppet theater; an oblast philharmonic; the *Hutsul Song and Dance Ensemble; oblast archives with documents dating back to the 18th century; the *Ivano-Frankivske Regional Museum; two oblast newspapers, *Prykarpats'ka pravda* and *Komsomol's'kyi prapor*; and an oblast radio and TV station. Among the city's architectural monuments are the city hall (now the regional museum, rebuilt in 1870), the former Jesuit college and church (1729), a former Armenian baroque church with two steeples (1763), and remnants of the city walls. In the late 19th century the city center shifted southeast from the 'old town.' The eastern and northern districts of the city were densely built up. According to the general city plan of 1955, which was later modified, the old districts were to be reconstructed and new ones created. The city has many parks and a 38-ha artificial lake in the southwest. Ivano-Frankivske is 'closed' to foreigners.

BIBLIOGRAPHY

Barącz, S. *Pamiątki miasta Stanisławowa* (Lviv 1858)
Ploshchanskii, V. 'Halytsko-russkii horod Stanyslavov po dostovirnym ystochnykam,' *Naukovyi sbornyk Halytsko-russkoi Matytsy*, 4 (Lviv 1868)
Szarłowski, A. *Stanisławów i powiat Stanisławowski pod względem historycznym i geograficzno-statystycznym* (Stanyslaviv 1887)
Holubkov, M.; Sichkar, H. *Ivano-Frankivs'k* (Lviv 1963)
Davydova, Iu. *Ivano-Frankivshchyna v mynulomu i teper* (Uzhhorod 1968)
Istoriia mist i sil: Ivano-Frankivs'ka oblast' (Kiev 1971)
Kravtsiv, B. (ed). *Al'manakh stanyslavivs'koï zemli* (New York, Toronto, and Munich 1975)

P. Isaiv, V. Kubijovyč

Ivano-Frankivske Institute of Petroleum and Gas (Ivano-frankivskyi instytut nafty i hazu). Technical school of higher education under the Ministry of Higher and Specialized Secondary Education of the Ukrainian SSR. Formed in 1967 out of a branch of the Lviv Polytechnical Institute, it consists of nine departments such as geology, mechanical engineering, and automatization. It has a graduate program, an evening school, and a correspondence school. In 1979 its enrollment was 7,500.

Ivano-Frankivske Medical Institute (Ivano-Frankivskyi medychnyi instytut). A teaching institute under the jurisdiction of the Ministry of Health of the Ukrainian SSR. Established in 1945, it includes a therapy and a stomatology department, a graduate school, and a preparatory program. In 1979 its enrollment was 2,500. The institute publishes a collection titled *Mikroelementy v medytsyni*.

Ivano-Frankivske oblast. An administrative region in Western Ukraine, established on 4 December 1939. Until

1962 it was called Stanyslaviv oblast. Its area is 13,900 sq km, and its population 1,374,600 (1986). The oblast has 14 raions, 352 rural soviets, 13 cities, and 26 towns (smt). The capital is Ivano-Frankivske (formerly Stanyslaviv).

Physical geography. The *Carpathian Mountains in the west and southeast cover nearly one-half of the oblast's territory. The highest ranges are the *Gorgany (with a maximum elevation of over 1,800 m) and *Chornohora (reaching 2,000 m). The middle part of the oblast, stretching from the Carpathian Mountains to the Dniester River valley, lies in the Dniester Lowland. The land rises again to the northeast as part of the Opilia Upland and to the southeast as the Pokutia-Bessarabia Upland. In the north the soil is mostly eroded chernozem, gray forest podzol, and deep chernozem; in Subcarpathia it is primarily clay or peat podzolic; in the Carpathians, brown soils and mountain meadow soils predominate; and in the river valleys, meadow and bog soils are common. Forests (mainly beech, fir, and pine in the mountains and oak, sycamore, and ash in the lowlands) cover 35 percent of the oblast's territory. The rich mineral resources of the oblast include oil, natural gas, potassium salts, common salts, ozokerite, brown coal, bituminous shales, phosphorite, marl, limestone, graphite, and mineral water springs. The principal rivers are the Dniester – with its tributaries the Bystrytsia, Limnytsia, and Svirzh (on the right bank) and the Hnyla Lypa and Svicha (on the left bank) – and the Prut with its tributaries the Licha, Rybnytsia, and Cheremosh. The climate of the oblast is temperate-continental: temperatures average −5.1°C in January and 18.8°C in July. Temperatures are considerably lower in the mountains. The annual precipitation is 500–800 mm (800–1,100 mm in the mountains), and the growing season lasts 150–165 days a year.

History. Until the 12th century, the territories of the present oblast formed part of the Principality of Kiev. From the middle of the 12th century, these territories were successively part of the Galician, Volodymyr-Volynskyi, and Galician-Volhynian principalities. In the 14th century they came under Lithuanian and then Polish rule as part of the Polish-Lithuanian Commonwealth. The area was acquired by Austria in the 18th-century Polish partitions. A part of the Western Ukrainian National Republic following the First World War, the territories then came under Polish rule after the defeat of the former, as part of Stanyslaviv county. They were annexed by the USSR in 1939 as Stanyslaviv oblast, and Soviet rule was re-established in 1944.

Population. The average population density in 1986 was 98.9 people per sq km. The proportion of the urban population is rising steadily: it was 27.6 percent of the total population in 1965 and 42 percent in 1986. The total population of the oblast increased 14.5 percent in that same period. The ethnic composition of the population in 1979 (1959 figures in parentheses) was Ukrainians 95.2 (94.8) percent, Russians 3.7 (3.4) percent, and Poles 1 (0.9) percent. In 1984, three cities had a population of over 50,000: Ivano-Frankivske (200,000), Kalush (64,000), and Kolomyia (59,000).

Economy. Ivano-Frankivske oblast is an agrarian-industrial region. The major industries involve the processing of local petroleum, mineral, forest, and agricultural resources. Most industrial development has occurred since the Second World War.

Industry. Industry in Ivano-Frankivske utilizes the energy resources in the oblast: natural and coal gas, peat, and electricity generated at the regional power plant in Burshtyna. In 1983 light industry accounted for 22 percent of the gross value of production in the oblast. This was followed by machine building and metalworking (14.3 percent), the chemical industry (approx 13.7 percent), the food industry (13.1 percent), and the forestry (including woodworking and furniture making) industry (12.9 percent). Petroleum and natural-gas production, important industries in the interwar period, have steadily declined in importance as resources have been depleted. Light industry in the oblast includes leather tanning and processing (in Ivano-Frankivske and Bolekhiv), fur processing (Tysmennytsia), knitting (Ivano-Frankivske), weaving and brush production (Kolomyia), and artisanal industries such as woodcarving, incrustation, carpet weaving, and embroidery (Ivano-Frankivske, Kosiv, Kolomyia, Verkhovyna, Kuty). The machine-building and metalworking industry, centered mainly in the city of Ivano-Frankivske, specializes in the manufacture of control and regulatory apparatuses, agricultural machinery, mechanical presses, and electrotechnical and oil-industry machinery, and in the fitting and maintenance of locomotives. The chemical and petrochemical industries (in Ivano-Frankivske, Nadvirna, Kalush, and Vyhoda) produce potassium derivatives, vinyl chlorides, aerosols, butane, propane, edible paraffin, carbamic and polychlorovinyl tars, and synthetic oils. Sugar refining is the most important branch of the food industry (in Horodenka and Bovshiv). It is followed by the dairy, meat, baking and distilling, brewing, tobacco-curing, canning, and confectionary industries (in Ivano-Frankivske, Kolomyia, Kalush, and Sniatyn). The forestry industry is centered in Nadvirna, Bolekhiv, Verkhovyna, Broshniv-Osada, and Vyhoda; furniture manufacturing is based in Ivano-Frankivske, Sniatyn, and Bolekhiv; and the paper industry is concentrated mainly in Kolomyia. Oil and gas are extracted in Dolyna, Nadvirna, Bytkiv, and Bohorodchany. In 1968 the oblast accounted for 19 percent of all the gas extracted in the Ukrainian SSR.

Agriculture. Both crop cultivation and animal husbandry are practiced in Ivanko-Frankivske. In 1983 there were 168 collective farms (252 in 1971) and 30 state farms (20 in 1971). The total arable land in the oblast is 609,000 ha (1983); of this 68.9 percent is cultivated, 16.4 percent is pastureland, 12.3 percent is hayfields, and 2.4 percent is used for other purposes. The total seeded area is 428,000 ha; in 1978, of the total seeded area of 430,000 ha, 176,300 ha (41 percent) was devoted to grain crops, 149,600 ha (34.8 percent) to fodder, 57,200 ha (13.3 percent) to fruits and vegetables, and 46,900 ha (10.9 percent) to industrial crops. The principal grains are winter wheat (79,900 ha) and barley (50,000 ha). Sugar beets account for about one-half of the total area devoted to industrial crops; other industrial crops grown in the oblast include flax and tobacco. Orchards and berry patches covered 24,100 ha in 1978; the principal fruits harvested are apples, pears, plums, and cherries. Walnuts are also grown.

Animal husbandry is well developed in the oblast, particularly in the hilly and mountainous regions. It consists mainly of dairy- and beef-cattle farming. In 1972 there were some 533,400 head of cattle, including 229,200 milk cows. The main breeds of cattle are the Simmenthal, Spotted Black, and Carpathian Brown. There were also some 267,700 hogs in 1972 (the Large White, the Long-eared White, and the Myrhorod) and 116,300 sheep and goats. Fishing is also practiced.

Transport. The oblast has 479 km of railways. The main railway junctions are Ivano-Frankivske, Kolomyia, and Diliatyn. The main lines are those from Lviv to Ivano-Frankivske and from Ivano-Frankivske to Kolomyia, Kalush, and Diliatyn. There are some 5,800 km of motor roads, 4,400 km of which are hard surfaced. The more important trunk roads link Ivano-Frankivske with Lviv, Kolomyia–Chernivtsi, Diliatyn–Rakhiv, Stryi–Mukachiv–Uzhhorod, and Kolomyia–Kosiv–Verkhovyna. There is also an airport in Ivano-Frankivske. The Soiuz gas pipeline passes through the oblast and the Braterstvo pipeline originates there.

BIBLIOGRAPHY
Pro sotsialistychni peretvorennia na Stanislavshchyni (Stanyslaviv 1957)
Rozkvit ekonomiky zakhidnykh oblastei URSR (1939–1964 rr.) (Lviv 1964)
Istoriia mist i sil Ukraïns'koï RSR: Ivano-Frankivs'ka oblast' (Kiev 1971)
Koval'chak, H. (ed). *Industrial'nyi rozvytok zakhidnykh oblastei Ukraïny v period komunistychnoho budivnytstva* (Kiev 1973)
Pryroda Ivano-Frankivs'koï oblasti (Lviv 1973)
Sotsial'ni peretvorennia u radians'komu seli: Na prykladi sil zakhidnykh oblastei Ukraïns'koï RSR (Kiev 1976)

B. Balan, I. Myhul

Ivano-Frankivske Pedagogical Institute (Ivano-Frankivskyi derzhavnyi pedahohichnyi instytut im. V.S. Stefanyka). A higher teaching institute under the jurisdiction of the Ministry of Education of the Ukrainian SSR. Founded in 1940 as a teachers' college, it was transformed in 1950 into a pedagogical institute. In 1982 it had seven departments: philology (Ukrainian and Russian languages and literatures), foreign languages, physics and mathematics, elementary education, music education, history, and principals' upgrading. In 1979 its enrollment was 4,539. The regular program requires five years of study; only the music education program requires four.

Ivano-Frankivske Regional Museum (Ivano-Frankivskyi kraieznavchyi muzei). Museum founded in 1940 on the basis of several existing collections in Stanyslaviv (now Ivano-Frankivske), including the Zhabivsky 'Hutsulshchyna' Museum. Many of the museum's over 84,000 exponents (as of 1979) relate to the uprising led by Hetman B. Khmelnytsky, the popular rebellion led by O. Dovbush, the activities of the Communist Party of Western Ukraine, and the Second World War. The museum has several branches: the Krylos Regional Museum, the I. Franko Literary-Memorial Museum in Kryvorivnia, the Museum of Partisan Glory in Yaremcha, the L. Martovych Literary-Memorial Museum in Torhovytsia, and the Ivano-Frankivske Museum of the History of Religion and Atheism.

Ivano-Frankivske Ukrainian Music and Drama Theater (Ivano-Frankivskyi ukrainskyi muzychno-dramatychnyi teatr im I. Franka). The theater was organized in Stanyslaviv (now Ivano-Frankivske) in 1939 out of several Galician troupes (I. Kohutiak's, Y. Stadnyk's) employing actors from central and eastern Ukraine. During the German occupation (1941–4) it functioned under the

Ivano-Frankivske Ukrainian Music and Drama Theater

Ukrainian Central Committee. It resumed activities in 1945 after the Second World War. In the first period its repertoire included Soviet plays such as O. Korniichuk's *Platon Krechet* and K. Trenev's *Liubov Iarova*. During the German occupation Yu. Kosach's *Obloha* (The Siege) and *Marsh chernihivs'koho polku* (March of the Chernihiv Regiment), as well as the operatic version of I. Kotliarevsky's *Natalka Poltavka* (Natalka from Poltava), were staged. Since 1945 its better productions have included adaptations of I. Franko's *Dlia domashn'oho vohnyshcha* (For the Home Hearth) and N. Gogol's *Strashnaia mest'* (The Terrible Revenge), as well as A. Khyzhniak's *Danylo Halyts'kyi* (Danylo of Halych) and D. Pavlychko's *Zolotorohyi olen'* (The Deer with Golden Horns). O. Yakovliv, M. Ravytsky, and V. Smoliak have served as directors of the theater, and D. Narbut as set designer.

Ivanopil [Ivanopil']. IV-9. Town smt (1978 pop 5,800) in Chudniv raion, Zhytomyr oblast. Founded in the 17th century, until 1946 it was called Yanushpil (Januszpol). It has a sugar refinery.

Ivanov, Andrei, b 28 October 1888 in Kukshevo, Kostroma gubernia, Russia, d 10 June 1927 in Moscow. Rus-

Ivano-Frankivske Regional Museum

sian communist activist in Ukraine. In 1916 he headed the Bolshevik group in the arsenal factory in Kiev. He was head of the revolutionary council and one of the leaders of the January 1918 revolt against the Ukrainian Central Rada in Kiev. In 1918 he was a member of the Presidium of the Central Executive Committee of Soviets in Ukraine and People's Commissar of Internal Affairs in the Ukrainian Soviet government. From 1919 to 1925 he headed the Kiev, Kharkiv, and Odessa provincial executive committees and from 1923 was a member of the Politburo of the CP(B)U.

Ivanov, Andrii, b 30 December 1900 in Zamość, Poland, d 1 October 1970 in Moscow. Baritone singer. A graduate of N. Lund's Singing Studio in Kiev (1924), he sang in the Azerbaijan (1926–8), Odessa (1928–31), and Sverdlovsk (1931–4) opera and ballet theaters. In 1934 he became a soloist at the Kiev Theater of Opera and Ballet, and in 1950 he moved to Moscow to sing at the Bolshoi Theater. His main roles were Igor in A. Borodin's *Prince Igor*, Rigoletto in G. Verdi's *Rigoletto*, the Sultan in S. Hulak-Artemovsky's *Zaporozhian Cossack beyond the Danube*, Onegin in P. Tchaikovsky's *Eugene Onegin*, and Shchors in B. Liatoshynsky's *Shchors*. He also gave concerts in Hungary, Austria, England, Germany, and Czechoslovakia.

Ivanov, Ihor, b 26 July 1928 in Kiev, d 8 August 1980 in Kiev. Architect. A graduate of the Kiev Civil-Engineering Institute (1955), he designed such major buildings as the Kiev Hotel (1973) in Kiev, the Black Sea Hotel (1973) in Odessa, the Medical Institute (1976) in Kishinev, and the Intourist Hotel (1978) in Kharkiv. He also oversaw the reconstruction of the October Revolution Square (1977) and Obolon residential development (1977) in Kiev.

Ivanov, Ivan, b 21 November 1918 in Ramene, East Prussia. Specialist in mechanics; since 1978 corresponding member of the AN URSR. Since 1966 he has worked at the Dnipropetrovske Branch of the academy's Institute of Mechanics. He has done important research in gas dynamics, heat exchange, strength of materials, and reliability of mechanical structures.

Ivanov, Leonid, b 16 April 1913 in Katerynoslav, d 29 November 1972 in Kharkiv. Literary scholar. He taught at the universities of Dnipropetrovske (from 1940) and Kharkiv (from 1968). His publications dealing with the relations between Ukrainian and foreign literatures include *Mikhail Kotsiubinskii* (1956), *Zarubizhna literatura 1871–1917 rr.* (Foreign Literature, 1871–1917, 1959), a book on R. Rolland (1960), and numerous articles about M. Kotsiubynsky.

Ivanov, Mikhail, b 2 October 1871 in Yalta, Tavriia gubernia, d 29 October 1935 in Moscow. Animal breeder; in 1935 elected full member of the All-Union Academy of Agricultural Sciences. After graduating from the Kharkiv Veterinary Institute (1897) and studying breeding techniques abroad, he joined the institute's faculty in 1900. In 1914 he was appointed professor at the Moscow Agricultural Institute, where he taught to the end of his life. He organized and directed (1925–35) the zootechnical experimental breeding station at the Askaniia-Nova

Mikhail Ivanov

Nature Reserve. There he conducted experiments in animal acclimatization and hybridization, introducing his own methods of producing new breeds and improving existing breeds. The Askaniia sheep and the Ukrainian Steppe White hog were bred by Ivanov. In 1956 the breeding station was named in his honor.

Ivanov, Mykola (Ivanoff, Nicolai), b 22 October 1810 in Voronizh, Sumy county, Kharkiv gubernia, d 19 July 1880 in Bologna, Italy. Operatic tenor, one of the best representatives of the Halican School of bel canto. From 1820 he sang in the Imperial Court Kapelle under the tutelage of M. Glinka, who in 1830 took him to Italy to study singing. In 1832 Ivanov made his debut in Naples as Percy in G. Donizetti's *Anna Bolena*, and then sang in Paris, London, and Milan. In 1842 he appeared in the world premiere of G. Rossini's arrangement of the poem *Stabat Mater Dolorosa*, conducted by G. Donizetti. His better-known operatic roles included Edgardo in G. Donizetti's *Lucia di Lammermoor* and Rodrigo in G. Rossini's *Othello*. His performance of Ukrainian folk songs, which he enjoyed singing, made a great impression on H. Berlioz. He retired in 1852 and lived in Bologna.

Ivanov, Oleksander, b 1836 in Tavriia gubernia, d 26 September 1880 in Kiev. Ophthalmologist. A graduate of the medical faculty of Moscow University (1859), from 1867 he worked at the Kiev Military Hospital. In 1869 he was appointed professor of the new department of eye diseases at Kiev University. His publications deal with eye anatomy, the dislocation of the lens, and inflammation and swelling of the retina and optic nerve.

Ivanov, Petro, b 1837 in Chuhuiv, Zmiiv county, Kharkiv gubernia, d 1926. Ethnographer. Ivanov was a teacher and principal of the county school in Kupianka, and then an inspector of public schools (1877–84). He collected ethnographic materials and some biological data on the Kupianka and Starobilske regions. His articles on the fauna of the Kupianka region appeared in *Trudy* of the Kharkiv Society of Naturalists. Several of his longer articles were published also as separate works; for instance, *Zhizn' i pover'ia krest'ian Kupianskogo uezda, Khar'kovskoi gubernii* (The Life and Beliefs of the Peasants of Kupianka County, Kharkiv Gubernia, 1907), *Igry krest'ianskikh detei v Kupianskom uezde* (The Games of Peasant Children in Kupianka County, 1889), and *Iz oblasti malorusskikh narodnykh legend* (From the Realm of Little Russian Folk Legends, 1894).

Ivanov, Vadym, b 30 April 1892 in Mariiupil, Katerynoslav gubernia, d 15 January 1962 in Kiev. Physician; from 1957 full member of AN URSR and from 1953 full member of the USSR Academy of Medical Sciences. After graduating from Kiev University (1916), he worked in its clinics under F. Yanovsky. He was appointed professor and department chairman at the Second Kiev Medical Institute in 1933 and at the Kiev Medical Institute in 1944. From 1953 he chaired the Department of Clinical Physiology at the AN URSR Institute of Physiology. Ivanov was a leading gastrointestinal and pulmonary specialist, and author of over 80 publications.

Ivanov, Viktor, b 31 January 1909 in Koziatyn, Berdychiv county, Kiev gubernia, d 18 June 1981 in Kiev. Screen director, actor, and writer. After graduating from the All-Union Institute of Cinematography in 1936, he worked at the Kiev Artistic Film Studio. In the 1950s he also worked at film studios in Sverdlovsk, Vilnius, and Kaunas. His directing credits, combined in many cases with acting credits, include *Pryhoda z pidzhakom Tarapun'ky* (The Adventure with Tarapunka's Jacket, 1955), *Shel'menko-denshchyk* (Shelmenko the Orderly, 1957), *Oleksa Dovbush* (1961), *Za dvoma zaitsiamy* (After Two Hares, 1962), *Kliuchi vid neba* (Keys to Heaven, 1965), and *Snihove vesillia* (Snow Wedding, 1980).

Ivanov, Yevhen, b 24 February 1873 in Monashka, eastern Siberia, d 27 October 1929. Archivist. A student of D. Bahalii at Kharkiv University, in 1897 he was appointed archivist of the Kharkiv Historical Archive. From 1909 to 1918 he was the secretary of the Kharkiv Historical Philological Society. From 1920 he worked at the Central Historical Archive in Kharkiv. An expert on 17th- and 18th-century manuscripts, he is the author of articles on archival science and the history of Left-Bank Ukraine. He coedited the journal *Arkhivna sprava*.

Ivanychi [Ivanyči]. III-5. Town smt (1978 pop 6,400) and raion center in Volhynia oblast, situated where Volhynia, Galicia, and the Kholm region meet. First mentioned in 1545, it was under Polish (1569–1795, 1920–39) and Russian (1795–1917) rule. Its main industry is food processing.

Ivanychuk, Roman [Ivanyčuk], b 27 May 1929 in Trach, Kolomyia county, Galicia. Popular Soviet Ukrainian writer. His works include the prose collections *Prut nese kryhu* (The Prut Carries Blocks of Ice, 1958), *Ne rubaite iaseniv!* (Don't Fell Ash Trees! 1961), *Pid sklepinniam khramu* (Beneath the Vault of the Temple, 1961), *Topolyna zametil'* (The Poplar Blizzard, 1965), *Dim na hori* (The House on the Hill, 1969), and *Na perevali* (At the Mountain Pass, 1981); the novels *Zharin'* (The Heat Wave, 1964), *Spraha* (Thirst, 1967), *Misto* (The City, 1977), and *S'ome nebo* (Seventh Heaven, 1985); and the historical novels *Mal'vy* (Hollyhocks, 1969), *Cherlene vyno* (Burgundy Wine, 1977), *Manuskrypt z vulytsi Rus'koï* (Manuscript from Ruska Street, 1979), *Voda z kameniu* (Water from Stone, 1981), and *Chetvertyi vymir* (The Fourth Dimension, 1984). Ivanychuk has been criticized for idealizing Ukraine's historical past in his works, and his *Mal'vy* was later banned.

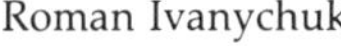
Roman Ivanychuk

Vasyl Ivanys

Ivanys, Vasyl, b 3 April 1888 in Stanytsia Nastasivka, Temriutsk district, in the Kuban, d 28 November 1974 in Toronto. Economist and civic leader. He studied economics at the Moscow Commercial Institute and engineering at the Novocherkassk Polytechnical Institute (1911–15). After the February Revolution Ivanys supported the *Kuban faction that demanded independence for the region and had close ties with the Central Rada in Kiev. He was a member of the Kuban Rada from 1918, minister of trade and industry in 1919, and prime minister of the Kuban government and acting otaman of the Kuban army in 1920. As an émigré in Czechoslovakia Ivanys was one of the founders and later a professor (1927–) of the Ukrainian Husbandry Academy in Poděbrady, then at the Ukrainian Technical and Husbandry Institute (UTHI) (1932–). He published extensively on the natural and industrial resources of Ukraine and North Caucasia, including the monographs *Promyslovist' Ukraïny i Pivnichnoho Kavkazu* (The Industry of Ukraine and North Caucasia, 1937) and *Energetychne hospodarstvo Ukraïny ta Pivnichnoho Kavkazu* (The Energy Industry of Ukraine and North Caucasia, 1934), and several works on the Kuban, including *Borot'ba Kubani za nezalezhnist'* (Kuban's Struggle for Independence, 1968). In 1945–8 Ivanys headed the UTHI in Regensburg. In Canada from 1948, he played an active role in the Shevchenko Scientific Society and in the Brotherhood of St Volodymyr in Toronto. His memoirs, in five volumes, were published as *Stezhkamy zhyttia* (The Paths of Life, 1958–62).

Y. Boshyk

Ivanyshev, Mykola [Ivanyšev], b 17 November 1811 in Kiev, d 26 October 1874 in Kiev. Historian and jurist. After completing his theological studies in Kiev and law studies in Berlin, Prague, and Kiev, in 1840 he was appointed professor of Kiev University. He served as dean of its law faculty (1848–62) and from 1862 to 1865 as rector of the university. He was one of the founders and chairmen of the Kiev Archeographic Commission and of the Kiev Central Archive of Old Documents, and the editor of many of their publications. In 1845 Ivanyshev excavated Perepiatykha kurhan in the Kiev region (with T. Shevchenko as draftsman on the project). He wrote a number of works in the history of Ukrainian law, including *Soderzhanie postanovlenii dvorianskikh provintsial'nykh seimov v Iugo-Zapadnoi Rossii* (Contents of Resolutions of Provincial Gentry Assemblies in Southwestern Russia, 1861) and *O drevnikh sel'skikh obshchinakh v Iugo-Zapadnoi Rossii* (On Old Peasant Communes in Southwestern Russia, 1863). He also wrote studies of the church union based on documents in the Kiev archive and studies of Bohemian state law. In his law studies he was an adherent of the historical school. Ivanyshev is the subject of a biography by A. Romanovich-Slavatinsky (1876), and a collection of his works, edited by Romanovich-Slavantinsky and K. Tsarevsky, was published in 1876.

Ivanytsia, Hryhorii [Ivanycja, Hryhorij], 1892–193? Pedagogue. In the 1920s Ivanytsia was a professor at the Kiev Institute of People's Education, the secretary of the VUAN Pedagogical Commission, and coeditor of the journal *Radians'ka osvita*. He is the author of articles on the methodology of teaching Ukrainian language and literature, readers, and textbooks, including one on Ukrainian for Russian speakers (1925, 2nd edn 1927). A defendant in the Stalinist show trial of 'members' of the *Union for the Liberation of Ukraine in 1930, he died in a Soviet labor camp.

Borys Ivanytsky

Ivan Ivasiuk

Ivanytsky, Borys [Ivanyc'kyj], b 21 March 1878 in Sumy, Kharkiv gubernia, d 4 April 1953 in Detroit. Civic leader and prominent dendrologist; the founder of Ukrainian forestry science and a full member of the Shevchenko Scientific Society and the Ukrainian Academy of Arts and Sciences. He graduated from the Imperial Forestry Institute in St Petersburg (1902) and then worked in state forests throughout Ukraine. In 1917 he was one of the organizers of the Forestry Department of the UNR Ministry of Agriculture and from the end of 1918 director of the department. In 1919–20, he was lecturer at the Kamianets-Podilskyi Ukrainian State University. In 1921 he immigrated to Czechoslovakia. There he was one of the organizers, a professor, and rector (1928–32) of the Ukrainian Husbandry Academy in Poděbrady and the first president of the Ukrainian Technical and Husbandry Institute (1932–6). In 1944 he moved to Regensburg, where he helped re-establish the Ukrainian Technical and Husbandry Institute in 1945, serving again as president (1947–52). In Germany he was also involved in Ukrainian civic life and was elected chairman of the presidium of the Ukrainian National Council. Most of Ivanytsky's publications are devoted to the environment, history, and economy of Ukrainian forests. They include *Lisy i lisove hospodarstvo na Ukraïni* (Forests and Forest Exploitation in Ukraine, 2 vols, 1936, 1939) and the textbooks *Kurs lisivnytstva* (A Course in Forestry, 1922), *Dendrolohiia* (Dendrology, 1924), and *Die Entwaldung der Ukraine* (1928).

A. Zhukovsky

Ivanytsky, Hryhorii [Ivanyc'kyj, Hryhorij], 1881–1918. A political and civic leader. He studied at the Poltava Theological Seminary, where he was a member of the student hromada. Later he joined the Revolutionary Ukrainian party and then the Ukrainian Social Democratic Workers' party in the Poltava region. In April 1917, during the Russian occupation of Western Ukraine, Ivanytsky was appointed commissar of Vyzhnytsia county in Bukovyna. He was assassinated by pro-Bolshevik sailors in Odessa in April 1918 while negotiating with non-Ukrainian democratic circles for the government of the UNR.

Ivanytsky, Teodor [Ivanyc'kyj], b 1860, d 7 July 1935 in Chernivtsi. Bukovynian teacher and civic figure. From 1911 to 1918 he was a representative from the National Democratic party to the Bukovynian provincial diet. From 1912 to 1920 he headed the Selianska Kasa savings association in Chernivtsi, and from 1927 he was a member of the executive of the *Ukrainian National party, the sole legal Ukrainian party in Bukovyna under Rumanian rule. In 1929 he founded and then directed the Chas publishing house, which issued the Chernivtsi daily **Chas*.

Ivanytsky-Vasylenko, Serhii [Ivanyc'kyj-Vasylenko, Serhij], b 15 February 1883 in Zolotonosha, Poltava gubernia, d 1938? Historian of Ukrainian law, cofounder and secretary of the VUAN Commission for the Study of the History of Western Ruthenian and Ukrainian Law in Kiev during the 1920s. Areas of his research and study included the history of *Magdeburg law in Ukraine and the use of land by the aristocracy in the Hetman state. Together with L. *Okinshevych, he compiled a bibliography of Lithuanian-Ruthenian law and a guide to materials on the history of Ukraine in *Polnoe sobranie zakonov Rosiiskoi Imperii*. He translated many works on Polish legal history.

Ivashutych, Oleksander [Ivašutyč], b 15 October 1900 in Kiev, d 18 January 1970 in Kharkiv. Stage actor and director. In 1919 he debuted at the Kiev Second Raion Ukrainian Drama Theater. He appeared in the productions of the Berezil theater (1922–6) in Kiev, the Odessa State Drama Theater (1927–9), and the Kharkiv Musical Comedy Theater (1929–41). From 1945 he worked in the Kharkiv Musical Comedy Theater as a director, and appeared in many operettas, including O. Riabov's *Night in May*, *Wedding in Malynivka*, and J. Strauss the Younger's *Gypsy Baron*, and staged O. Riabov's *Sorochyntsi Fair*, C. Lecocq's *Giroflé-Girofla*, and U. Gadzhibekov's *Vendor of Hand-made Goods*.

Ivasiuk, Ivan [Ivasjuk], b 1879 in Khotyn county, Bessarabia, d 31 October 1933 in Prague. Teacher, co-operative organizer, and civic and political figure in the Kuban. He was a teacher in the Katerynoslav region and the Kuban. For eight years before the 1917 Revolution he was the director of the Tsentrosoiuz co-operative bank in Katerynodar. In 1920 he became finance minister in V. Ivanys's Kuban regional government. He emigrated that year to Czechoslovakia, and from 1923 he lectured at the Ukrainian Husbandry Academy in Poděbrady. His published works include studies on banking and co-operatives, a textbook on co-operative accounting, the book *Kredytova kooperatsiia na Ukraïni* (Credit Co-operatives in Ukraine, 1933), and the economic survey *Kuban'* (1925).

Mykola Ivasiuk

Ivasiuk, Mykola [Ivasjuk], b 28 April 1865 in Zastavna, Bukovyna, d 1930? Realist painter. A student of the Vienna (1884–9) and Munich (1890–6) art academies, he organized the first Ukrainian art school in Chernivtsi (1899–1908), then worked in Lviv, Vienna, and Prague. In 1925 he accepted an invitation to teach at the Kiev State Art Institute. His most important works deal with historical themes: *Khmelnytsky at Zboriv* (1893), *The Battle of Khotyn* (1903), *Khmelnytsky's Entry into Kiev* (1912), and *Bohun at Berestechko* (1919). He also painted a large number of genre scenes and portraits (of O. Kobylianska, Yu. Fedkovych, I. Franko, T. Shevchenko, O. Myshuha, and self-portraits). Ivasiuk is a representative of the academic style of the Vienna-Munich school at the end of the 19th century. The Ukrainian Cossack theme, which is prominent in Ivasiuk's work, was popular at the time in Polish and Russian painting. After working for a few years in Kiev, he was arrested by the secret police and disappeared.

Volodymyr Ivasiuk

Mykhailo Ivchenko

Ivasiuk, Volodymyr [Ivasjuk], b 4 April 1949 in Kitsman, Chernivtsi oblast, d ca 1 May 1979 near Lviv. Composer. From 1972 he studied music under A. Kos-Anatolsky at the Lviv Conservatory. Although he composed piano and cello pieces, Ivasiuk is best known for his songs, which number about 50. His first song, 'Vidlitaly zhuravli' (The Cranes Were Leaving), was released in 1965. In some cases – eg, in 'Lysh raz tsvite liubov' (Love Blooms but Once), 'Balada pro mal'vy' (Ballad about Hollyhocks), and 'Ia – tvoie krylo' (I am Your Wing) – he composed the melody only; in others – eg, in 'Dva persteni' (Two Rings), 'Vodohrai' (Water Fountain), 'Pisnia bude pomizh nas' (A Song Will Be among Us), and 'Chervona ruta' (Red Rue) – both the melody and lyrics. Ivasiuk's tunes are a blend of Ukrainian folk and contemporary popular music. He was one of the most popular songwriters in Ukraine. His mutilated body was discovered in a woods outside Lviv about three weeks after he had been murdered. The circumstantial evidence points to the KGB as the perpetrator of the slaying. Ivasiuk's funeral was attended by over 10,000 people.

Ivchenko, Liudmyla. See Kovalenko, Liudmyla.

Ivchenko, Mykhailo [Ivčenko, Myxajlo], b 1890 in Pryluka county, Poltava gubernia, d 1939 in Ordzhonikidze, RSFSR. Writer. Before the 1917 Revolution he worked as a statistician in the Poltava region and wrote articles on economics, natural science, and the national question for periodicals such as *Rada* and *Khutorianyn*. A Soviet 'fellow traveler' in the 1920s he was the author of the impressionistic prose collections *Shumy vesniani* (The Murmurs of Spring, 1919), *Imlystoiu rikoiu* (Along the Misty River, 1926), *Porvanoiu dorohoiu* (Along the Broken Road, 1927), and *Zemli dzvoniat'* (The Lands Peal, 1928). His most significant work, the novel *Robitni syly* (The Work Forces, 1929), portrays allegorically the fostering of national consciousness. A defendant at the show trial of the *Union for the Liberation of Ukraine in 1930, he received a conditional sentence and was exiled to Ossetia; the circumstances of his death are unknown.

Ivchenko, Oleksander [Ivčenko], b 23 November 1903 in Velykyi Tokmak, Tavriia gubernia, d 30 June 1968 in Zaporizhia. Aeronautical engineer specializing in engine design; full member of the AN URSR from 1964. After working in industry, he joined the staff of the Research and Design Bureau of the Kharkiv Aviation Institute in 1945. He designed a number of piston engines for agricultural and passenger planes, the first Soviet piston and gas turbine engines for helicopters, and some highly reliable turboprop engines for passenger and transport planes.

Ivchenko, Viktor [Ivčenko], b 2 November 1912 in Bohodukhiv, Kharkiv gubernia, d 6 September 1972 in Kiev. Film director. A graduate of the Kiev Institute of Theater Arts (1937), Ivchenko first worked as an actor and director in the Lviv Ukrainian Drama Theater. In 1953 he began to work as a film director at the Kiev Artistic Film Studio. There he produced such films as *Dolia Maryny* (Maryna's Fate, 1953, with I. Shmaruk), *Shliakh do sertsia* (The Way to the Heart, 1970), and *Sofiia Hrushko* (1971). Ivchenko's works are characterized by a theatrical style of filmmaking. He has also adapted such classics of Ukrainian literature as T. Shevchenko's *Nazar Stodola* (with H. Chukhrai, 1955) and Lesia Ukrainka's *Lisova pisnia* (The Forest Song, 1961).

Ivliv, Trokhym, 1880–1938 ? Opera singer (bass) and stage actor. A member of D. Haidamaka's and M. Yaroshenko's troupes, the Ukrainska Besida theater (1909–10), the Sadovsky Theater in Kiev (from 1910), the Vinnytsia Drama Theater (1920–3), and the Kharkiv Touring Opera Company (from 1928), he appeared in such operas as S. Moniuszko's *Halka*, M. Arkas's *Kateryna*, D. Sichynsky's *Roksoliana*, and M. Lysenko's *Eneïda* (Aeneid), and in such plays as M. Kropyvnytsky's *Vii* and J. Słowacki's *Mazepa*.

Izarsky, Oleksa [Izars'kyj], b 30 August 1919 in Poltava. Writer. A graduate of Kiev University, he emigrated to the United States after the Second World War. He has contributed prose to various émigré journals and is the author of several novels – *Ranok* (Morning, 1963), *Viktor i Lialia* (Victor and Lialia, 1965), *Chudo v Myslovytsiakh* (Miracle in Myslovytsi, 1967), *Kyïv* (Kiev, 1971), *Saksons'ka zyma* (A Saxon Winter, 1972), *Poltava* (1977), *Lito nad ozerom* (Summer on the Lake, 1981) – and the study *Ril'ke na Ukraïni* (Rilke in Ukraine, 1952).

Izbekov, Volodymyr, b 20 July 1881 in Pogromnoe, Saratov gubernia, d 20 March 1963. Inorganic chemist; from 1939 corresponding member of the AN URSR. Upon graduating from Yurev University, he joined the faculty of the Kiev Polytechnical Institute (1909–62). He chaired the departments of inorganic chemistry of the Institute of Chemistry of the Academy of Sciences of the Ukrainian SSR (1933–41) and of Kiev University (1933–41, 1944–50). His publications deal with the electrochemistry of molten salts, the industrial conversion of raw minerals, and the recovery of rare metals from industrial wastes.

Izbornik (*s"bornik, sbornik", sobornik"*). A Church Slavonic liturgical book with dates of the various religious services throughout the year, sometimes with the liturgical texts included; or a collection of texts from various sources. Many of the collections were translated from Byzantine variants. The **Izbornik* of Sviatoslav (1073) and the collection of homilies **Zlatostrui*, for example, were translations. Other collections, such as the **Izbornik* of Sviatoslav (1076) and the book of homilies **Izmarahd*, probably originated in Ukraine. Some collections were only supplemented with materials of Ukrainian origin: for example, *Torzhestvennik*, a book of homilies for feast days, was supplemented by the sermons of *Cyril of Turiv. From the 16th to 18th centuries numerous private compilations of various texts appeared, particularly collections of verses and stories. In modern times the term *izbornik* is no longer used.

***Izbornik* of Sviatoslav (1073).** Manuscript written in the **ustav* script consisting of 266 two-column, illustrated parchment folios. It was discovered in 1887 by K. Kalaidovich in the Resurrection Monastery of the New Jerusalem near Moscow and is preserved at the Moscow Historical Museum. A unique theological compendium, it contains excerpts from the works of the Fathers of the Church, a chronology, a survey of poetic figures and tropes, articles on grammar, logic, and philosophy, parables, riddles, and the first list of books forbidden in Ukraine. An interesting illumination of the family of Prince Sviatoslav Yaroslavych, for whom the work was prepared, was inserted. A translation of the original Greek collection was done in Church Slavonic in eastern Bulgaria for King Simeon (893–927), to whom there is a dedication in the preface. This text was merely copied in Kiev, and Sviatoslav's name was substituted for Simeon's. The copyists – two monks, one of whom was called 'Ioan the Precentor' – introduced certain phonetic Ukrainianisms. A facsimile edition of the manuscript was published using phototype in 1880 with an introduction by G. Karpov. One-third of the manuscript was prepared for printing with Greek and Latin texts by O. Bodiansky and published in 1856–66 and republished in *Chteniia v Imperatorskom obshchestve istorii i drevnostei rossiiskikh* in 1882. A new edition of the collection was published in Moscow in 1977. A. Rozenfeld's study of its language appeared in *Russkii filologicheskii vestnik*, vol 41 (1899).

O. Horbach

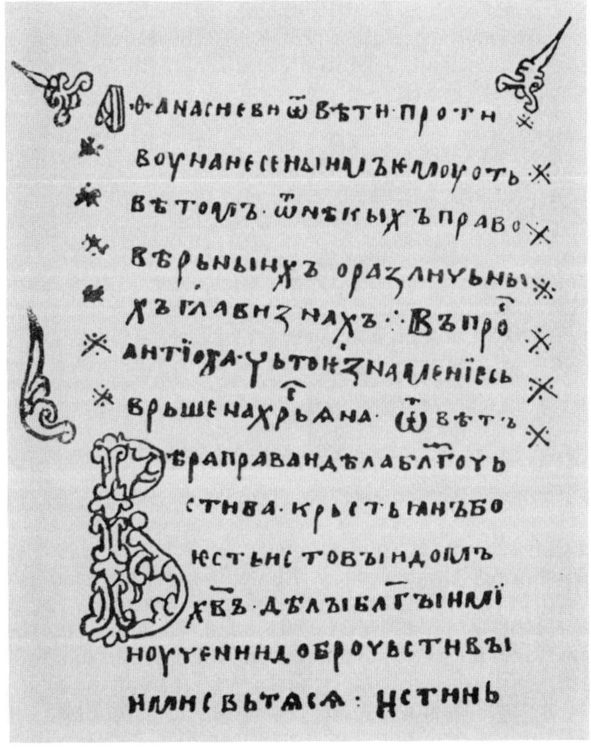

Izbornik of Sviatoslav (1076)

***Izbornik* of Sviatoslav (1076).** A manuscript of 176 two-column quarto sheets compiled by an unknown monk named Ioan of Kiev from 'many princely books' during the reign of Prince Sviatoslav Yaroslavych. It contains general moral instructions, aphorisms, and interpretations of the Holy Scripture. Some scholars (A. Popov, I. Budovnits) assert that some of the material was compiled in Kiev. The language of the collection contains phonetic, morphological, and lexical Ukrainianisms. V. Shimanovsky published the manuscript in *K istorii drevnerusskikh govorov* (On the History of Ancient Rus' Dialects, 1887) and separately in 1894. Corrections to the text were pointed out by S. Kulbakin in *Zhurnal Ministerstva narodnogo prosveshcheniia*, 1898, no. 2, and by V. Bobrov in *Russkii filologicheskii vestnik*, vols 47–8 (1902). A new edition of the collection came out in 1965. The work is also called the Shcherbatov *Izbornik* after the Russian historian A. Shcherbatov, who in the 18th century owned the manuscript, and the Hermitage *Izbornik* after the imperial public library (now the Leningrad Public Library) where it was deposited after Shcherbatov's death.

Izhakevych, Halyna [Jižakevyč], b 23 April 1919 in Kiev. Linguist. A graduate of Kiev University (1944), she has worked as a research associate of the AN URSR Institute of Linguistics, becoming the first head of the institute's Russian department in 1971. She specializes in Ukrainian-Russian linguistic relations, particularly in the comparison of the structure of the two languages, constantly emphasizing the allegedly beneficial influence of Russian on Ukrainian. She has published numerous articles and books, including *Ukraïns'ko-rosiis'ki movni zv'iazky radians'koho chasu* (Ukrainian-Russian Linguistic Contacts of the Soviet Period, 1969), and has edited collective symposia such as *Funktsionirovanie russkogo iazyka v blizkorodstvennom iazykovom okruzhenii* (The Functioning of the Russian Language in a Close Linguistic Family Environment, 1981).

Ivan Izhakevych

Izhakevych, Ivan [Jižakevyč], b 18 January 1864 in Vyshnopil, Uman county, Kiev gubernia, d 19 January 1962 in Kiev. Realist painter and graphic artist, one of the most popular artists in Ukraine. He studied art at the Kievan Cave Monastery Icon Painting Studio (1876–82), the Kiev Drawing School (1882–4), and the St Petersburg Academy of Arts (1884–8). In 1883–4 he took part in the restoration of the 12th-century frescoes in St Cyril's Church in Kiev, and later (1904–8) painted the refectory and the All-Saints Church of the Kievan Cave Monastery. A prolific illustrator, he worked for Russian journals at the time when Ukrainian ones were forbidden, and often referred to Ukrainian themes. In the 1890s he illustrated some of T. Shevchenko's poetry, such as 'Prychynna' (The Blighted Girl), 'Haidamaky' (The Haidamakas), and 'Kateryna.' In the 1920s he did easel paintings on themes from T. Shevchenko's poetry, and at the end of the 1930s a series of illustrations and the cover for the jubilee edition of *Kobzar* (The Minstrel, 1940). Many of his illustrations of Shevchenko's works were printed separately as postcards. Izhakevych also illustrated the works of Lesia Ukrainka, N. Gogol, M. Kotsiubynsky, H. Kvitka-Osnovianenko, I. Franko, V. Stefanyk, and I. Kotliarevsky. By style he belongs to the Populist School of the second half of the 19th century.

BIBLIOGRAPHY
Kovalevs'ka, M. *I.S. Ïzhakevych* (Kiev 1949)
Ivan Sydorovych Ïzhakevych. Al'bom (Kiev 1964)

S. Hordynsky

Izhevsky, Vasilii [Iževskii, Vasilij], b 16 June 1863 in Riazan, d 23 October 1926 in Kiev. Metallurgist. From 1889 to 1926 he taught at the Kiev Polytechnical Institute. He worked on problems of smelting, metallography, electrometallurgy, and thermal processing, and developed several electric furnaces, a gas generator, and a number of metallurgical processes.

Izhoi (from the Old Ukrainian *hoity*, 'to comfort' or 'to live'). Category of déclaseé people in Kievan Rus' who retained their free status. According to the church laws laid down by Prince Vsevolod Mstyslavych in the 12th century, the *izhoi* consisted of illiterate sons of priests, **kholopy* who had bought their freedom but had no means of subsistence, bankrupt merchants, and even princes who had lost their properties and inheritances. Many *izhoi* lived under the protection of the church, but most, especially the more numerous *kholopy*, settled on land that they did not own and became dependent on the landowner. *Izhoi* are mentioned in *Ruskaia Pravda*. By the 14th century *izhoi* had ceased to exist as a separate estate but the term was still used into the 15th century for the payment that *kholopy* made to purchase their release. In the Lithuanian-Ruthenian state the *lezni liudy* corresponded to the *izhoi*.

Iziaslav or **Zaslav** [Iz'jaslav]. III-7. Town (1981 pop 14,300) and raion center in Khmelnytskyi oblast, situated in southeastern Volhynia. Founded in 987, from the 14th century it belonged to the Ostrozky princes, from the 16th century to the Zaslavsky princes, and from 1673 to the Sangushko princes. In 1754 it was granted the rights of Magdeburg law. Under Russian rule it was a vicegerency capital (1793–5) and a county town in Volhynia gubernia (1796–1917). Among its architectural monuments are a castle and a Roman Catholic cathedral from the 16th century; the city walls, with a gate and towers; and a palace from the 17th century.

Iziaslav Mstyslavych [Iz'jaslav Mstyslavyč], b ca 1097, d 13 November 1154. Grand prince of Kiev; the son of Mstyslav Volodymyrovych of Novgorod and grandson of Volodymyr Monomakh. Having ruled for a time in Kursk, Polatsk, Pereiaslav, Turiv and Pynske, and Volodymyr-Volynskyi, he seized the throne of Kiev in 1146 from *Ihor Olhovych after the death of *Vsevolod Olhovych. His main opponent was his uncle, Prince *Yurii Dolgorukii of Suzdal, who defeated him in battle at Pereiaslav and forced him out of Kiev in 1149. Iziaslav fled to Volhynia, but managed to recapture Kiev after defeating Yurii in battle in 1150 and 1151; he ruled it thereafter with his uncle *Viacheslav Volodymyrovych. Iziaslav was an energetic and popular ruler who wanted to put an end to the subordination of the Rus' church to the patriarch in Constantinople. Under his protection and without the patriarch's approval, the bishops of Rus'-Ukraine elected a Ukrainian, Klym *Smoliatych, as Kiev metropolitan in 1147. After his death the dynastic struggle for the Kievan throne continued.

Iziaslav Volodymyrovych [Iz'jaslav Volodymyrovyč], b and d ? A prince of the Olhovych dynasty of Chernihiv, son of Volodymyr Ihorevych of Putyvl and grandson of Ihor Sviatoslavych of Chernihiv. In 1211 he was prince of Terebovlia. During the struggle among the princes of southern Rus' for the thrones of Kiev and Halych, Iziaslav was a close ally of *Mykhailo Vsevolodovych of Chernihiv. He pillaged Halych principality in 1233, and in 1235 he helped Mykhailo to defeat *Volodymyr Riurykovych of Kiev and *Danylo Romanovych of Halych near Torcheske, to take Kiev, and to drive Danylo from Halych. Iziaslav became the prince of Kamianets in Volhynia. A Mongol vassal from 1240, his fate after he was captured by Danylo in 1255 is unknown.

Iziaslav Yaroslavych [Iz'jaslav Jaroslavyč], b 1024, d 3 October 1078. Grand prince of Kiev intermittently from 1054 to 1078; the eldest son of *Yaroslav the Wise. Before inheriting the throne of Kiev from his father, Iziaslav ruled Turiv. In the 1060s he brought most of the Rus' territories west of the Dnieper River under his control. For refusing them arms to fight invading Cumans, the inhabitants of Kiev revolted in 1068. He fled to Poland and with the aid of his brother-in-law and cousin, *Bolesław II, took Kiev a year later from Vseslav Briachyslavych of Polatsk. When his brothers *Sviatoslav II and *Vsevolod Yaroslavych of Chernihiv marched on Kiev in 1073, its inhabitants refused to support Iziaslav and he was forced to flee abroad. He sought help in 1075 from Emperor Henry IV of Germany and Pope Gregory VII, but his efforts were in vain. In 1077, after Sviatoslav, who ruled Kiev, died and was succeeded by Vsevolod, Iziaslav marched on Kiev with Polish troops. Vsevolod renounced his throne and retired to Chernihiv. Iziaslav died in battle helping Vsevolod recapture Chernihiv from Sviatoslav's son Oleh and his Cuman allies.

Izium [Izjum]. IV-18, DB I-2. City (1982 pop 61,000) under oblast jurisdiction and raion center in Kharkiv oblast, situated in a picturesque setting at the foot of Kremianets Mountain on the right bank of the Donets River. A settlement was established there in the second quarter of the 17th century; in 1681 it was fortified by Kharkiv regiment's Col H. Donets, and the fortress served as an important defense outpost against Tatar incursions. From 1685 to 1765 Izium was a regimental capital in Slobidska Ukraine. It was a county town in Kharkiv vicegerency (1780–6) and in Slobidska Ukraine (1796–1835) and Kharkiv (1835–1917) gubernias. Because of its importance as an industrial and commercial center between Kharkiv and the Donets Basin, it has expanded rapidly (1926 pop 12,000; 1959 pop 38,000; 1970 pop 52,000). Its plants produce optical equipment, machine parts, reinforced-concrete structures, construction materials, and foodstuffs. Among its architectural monuments are the Transfiguration Cathedral (1684) and St Nicholas's Church (1809–23).

Izium Road (Iziumskyi shliakh). One of the branches of the *Murava Road, which in the 16th to 18th centuries linked Left-Bank Ukraine with Slobidska Ukraine and Muscovy. It was a major trade artery and one of the routes used by the Crimean and Nogay Tatars for their raids on central Ukraine. The Izium Road branched off from the Murava Road near the headwaters of the Orel River, crossed the Donets River near the town of Izium, and followed the right bank of the Oskil River north. It rejoined the Murava Road in the area between the Oskil, Psiol, Vorsklo, and Dinets rivers. The building of the Bilhorod Line of fortresses in the 1630s and the settlement of Slobidska Ukraine by the Cossaks ended the Tatar raids along the road.

Iziumov, Ovsii [Izjumov, Ovsij], b 1898, d ? in Kazakhstan. Linguist, lexicographer. He compiled three popular dictionaries: *Slovnyk rosiis'ko-ukraïns'kyi* (A Russian-Ukrainian Dictionary, 3 edns, 1926, 1927), *Ukraïns'ko-rosiis'kyi slovnyk* (A Ukrainian-Russian Dictionary, 1930), and *Pravopysnyi slovnyk* (An Orthographic Dictionary, 1931), which diverged in some respects from the standard established by the State Orthographic Commission of Kharkiv in 1929. He wrote works on Ukrainian word formation and courses in Ukrainian grammar. He was a coauthor of *Slovnyk chuzhomovnykh sliv* (A Dictionary of Foreign Words, 1932). He was arrested during the Yezhov terror in 1937 and reportedly died in exile.

Izmail [Izmajil]. VIII-9. City (1984 pop 87,000) under oblast jurisdiction and raion center in Odessa oblast; an important commercial port on the left bank of the Kiliia Channel of the Danube Delta, situated about 80 km from the Black Sea. Originally called Smil, from 1484 to 1812 and from 1856 to 1877 it belonged to the Turks, who fortified the town and built a large citadel there. The Cossacks attacked it in 1603, 1609, 1610, and 1630, and pillaged it in 1632. In 1770, 1790, and 1809 it was captured by Russian armies. From 1812 to 1856 and from 1877 to 1917 Izmail belonged to Russia and was a country town in Bessarabia. From 1918 to 1940 and from 1941 to 1944 it belonged to Rumania. In 1940–1 and from 1944 to 1954 it was an oblast capital. Today the city's industries repair ships, process fish, and produce canned food and industrial equipment. Among its architectural monuments are a 16th-century mosque and three early 19th-century churches.

Izmailov, Mykola [Izmajlov], b 22 June 1907 in Sukhumi, Georgia, d 2 October 1961 in Kharkiv. Electrochemist, from 1957 corresponding member of the AN URSR. A graduate of the Kharkiv Tekhnikum of Economics and Finance (1926), he did most of his scientific work at Kharkiv University. At the same time (1929–61) he did research at the Kharkiv Chemical and Pharmaceutical Institute. His many publications deal mainly with the electrochemistry of solutions. He developed a quantitative theory of electrolyte dissociation in solution and of their adsorption from solution. He was the first to develop two-dimensional chromatography, and he demonstrated the effect of solvent on the relative strength of acids and bases.

Izmailovych, Dmytro [Izmajlovyč], b 1890 in Yuryntsi, Proskuriv county, Podilia gubernia, d October 1976 in Rio de Janeiro. Painter. In 1919 he immigrated to Turkey and in 1927 to Rio de Janeiro, where he devoted himself to painting. His works include madonnas in the Byzantine icon style, paintings of natives in northern Brazil, and portraits of famous Brazilian writers. He also painted churches. His style changed gradually from a realistic to an abstract one. Izmailovych exhibited his works in Athens, Paris, New York, Rio de Janeiro, São Paolo, and Curitiba.

Izmarahd (Emerald). An anthology of about 150 homilies compiled in the 14th century by authors such as SS

John Chrysostom, Basil the Great, Gregory I, Theodosius of the Caves, and Cyril of Turiv. Fragments of this anthology were published by V. Peretts (1929); the language was studied by Peretts and O. Trebin (1910).

Izmarahd. Publishing house and lending library in Lviv, owned by M. Matchak (1923–39). It published the complete collection of M. Cheremshyna's and V. Stefanyk's works, an artistic collection of bookplates, an anthology of contemporary Ukrainian poetry edited and prefaced by Ye. Pelensky, and the works of young writers as well as classics for schoolchildren.

J

Jabłonowski, Aleksander, b 19 April 1829 in Goźlin, near Warsaw, d 22 August 1913 in Odessa. Polish historian and ethnographer. He studied at the universities of Kiev (1847–9) and Dorpat (Tartu, 1849–52). Together with A. Pawiński, he published *Źródła Dziejowe* (Historical Sources), an important series of documents relating to the history of the Polish Commonwealth. Several volumes were devoted to Right-Bank Ukraine and included his introductory articles. He also wrote a number of articles on Ukrainian history for such Polish scholarly journals as *Ateneum* and *Kwartalnik Historyczny*, and two monographs: *Akademia Kijowsko-mohilańska: Zarys historyczny na tle rozwoju ogólnego cywilizacyi zachodniej na Rusi* (The Kievan Mohyla Academy: A Historical Essay on the Development of Western Civilization in Ruthenia, 1900) and *Historya Rusi południowej do upadku Rzeczypospolitej polskiej* (The History of Southern Ruthenia to the Fall of the Polish Commonwealth, 1912). In these works he exaggerated the influence of Polish culture on Ukrainian. He also argued that a Ukrainian state never existed and strongly criticized the role of the Cossacks. His collected works, *Pisma Aleksandra Jabłonowskiego* (The Writings of Aleksander Jabłonowski), were published in Warsaw in seven volumes (1910–13); the first four volumes are devoted to Ukrainian history.

Jackiw, Roman [Jac'kiv], b 8 November 1939 in Lubliniec, Katowice voivodeship, Poland. American physicist of Ukrainian descent. After teaching for three years at Harvard University, in 1969 he joined the faculty of the Massachusetts Institute of Technology. He has made substantial contributions to field theory and has coauthored several advanced textbooks in physics: *Intermediate Quantum Mechanics* (1968), *Lectures on Current Algebra and Its Applications* (1972), and *Dynamical Gauge Symmetry Breaking* (1982).

Jacyk, Peter. See Yatsyk, Petro.

Jadwiga (Hedwig), b ca 1374, d 17 July 1399 in Cracow. The queen of Poland from 1384. With the support of the anti-Hungarian Polish nobility, she succeeded her father, King Louis I, in Poland, while her sister Maria became the queen of Hungary. The Polish nobles rejected the personal union of Poland and Hungary and brought about the annulment of Jadwiga's betrothal to Duke William of Habsburg in 1385, and in 1386 she married Grand Duke Jogaila (*Jagiełło) of Lithuania, with whom the nobles had negotiated the politically advantageous Union of *Krevo in 1385. In 1387, Jadwiga and the Poles embarked on a campaign to regain Galicia, which Hungary had ruled since 1378. By promising privileges to the nobility, burghers, and clergy, they took Peremyshl and Lviv without a conflict, and met with only sporadic opposition from the Hungarian palatine Benedict elsewhere. Thenceforth, until the partition of Poland in 1772, Galicia remained under Polish rule.

Jagić, Vatroslav, b 6 July 1838 in Varaždin, Croatia, d 5 August 1923 in Vienna. Noted philologist; founder of modern Slavistics. Croatian by descent, Jagić graduated from the University of Vienna in 1860, and after a stay in Zagreb became professor at the universities of Odessa (1871–4), Berlin (1874–80), St Petersburg (1880–6), and Vienna (1886–1908). He was a member of several academies – such as those of Zagreb (from 1866), St Petersburg (from 1880), and Vienna (from 1886) – and of the Shevchenko Scientific Society (from 1903). Jagić had a command of all the Slavic languages. The journal that he founded and edited, *Archiv für slavische Philologie* (1876–1920) – often referred to as Jagić's *Archiv* – became the most authoritative forum for Slavic studies in the world. His contributions to research on Old Church Slavonic (summarized in his *Entstehungsgeschichte der kirchenslavischen Sprache*, 1913), including his demonstration that Macedonian was the basis of this language and that its first alphabet was Glagolitic, are relevant also for the history of the eastern Slavic languages and literatures. In his *Razsuzhdeniia iuzhnoslavianskoi i russkoi stariny o tserkovno-slavianskom iazyke* (Deliberations of the South-Slavic and Russian Antiquity on the Church Slavonic Language, 1896) he published and commented on texts that determined early grammatical approaches to Slavic, while in *Istoriia slavianskoi filologii* (History of Slavic Philology, 1910) he presented a detailed synthetic survey of Slavic philology, including Ukrainian, through the 19th century. In his works on 'Old Russian' – 'Chetyre kritiko-paleograficheskiia stati' (Four Critico-Paleographic Articles, 1884), and particularly *Kriticheskie zametki po istorii russkogo iazyka* (Critical Comments on the History of the Russian Language, 1889), which resulted from his disagreement with O. Sobolevsky's views – he gave a broad and objective picture of Old Ukrainian phonology and morphology, even though he believed in the existence of a common Old Russian language. His extended reviews of P. Zhytetsky's *Ocherk zvukovoi istorii malorusskogo narechiia* (Outline of the Phonological History of the Little Russian Dialect, 1876) made a further contribution to the history of Ukrainian. His characterization of the Bačka and Banat dialects enriched Ukrainian dialectology.

BIBLIOGRAPHY

Materialy dlia biograficheskogo slovaria deistivel'nykh chlenov Imperatorskoi akademii nauk, vol 2 (Petrograd 1917)

Demianchuk, V. *Hnat (Vatroslav) Jagić, 1838–1923* (Kiev 1924)

Kombol, M. *Vatroslav Jagić: Izbrani kraći spisi* (Zagreb 1948)

G.Y. Shevelov

Jagiełło (Lithuanian: Jogaila; Ukrainian: Yahailo), b ca 1351 in Vilnius, d 1 June 1434 in Horodok near Lviv. Grand duke of Lithuania (1377–81, 1382–92) and king of Poland (1386–1434), known as Władysław II. The son of *Algirdas, he was the founder of a dynasty that ruled Poland until 1572. He concluded the Union of *Krevo between the ruling houses of Poland and Lithuania in 1385 and, after marrying Queen *Jadwiga in 1386, he was crowned king. In 1387 he officially made Lithuania a Catholic country. In 1392 he relinquished Lithuania to his cousin *Vytautas, although he formally remained grand duke. At the Battle of Grunwald (Tannenberg) in 1410, Jagiełło and Vytautas's Polish-Lithuanian-Ruthenian and other forces won a decisive victory over the Teutonic Knights. After Vytautas's death he fought his brother *Švitrigaila over Podilia (1430–2). Under Jagiełło the annexation of Galicia by Poland was completed, the Polish gentry was granted greater property rights, and Lithuania and Ukraine were drawn into the Polish sphere of political and cultural influence. Viceroys replaced many hereditary princes as local rulers, and Catholic nobles had a privileged status.

Jagiellon dynasty. Dynasty of Polish and Lithuanian monarchs, who ruled much of east-central Europe in the 15th and 16th centuries. The dynasty originated with Grand Duke Jogaila (*Jagiełło) of Lithuania, who became King Władysław II of Poland (1386–1434) by marrying Queen *Jadwiga. His successors were his sons *Władysław III Warneńczyk of Poland (1434–44) and Hungary (1440–4) and *Casimir IV Jagiellończyk of Lithuania (1440–92) and Poland (1447–92); Casimir's sons John Albert of Poland (1492–1501), Alexander I of Lithuania (1492–1506) and Poland (1501–6), and *Sigismund I of Poland and Lithuania (1506–48); and Sigismund's son *Sigismund II Augustus of Poland and Lithuania (1548–72), with whom the Polish-Lithuanian dynasty came to an end. Casimir's fourth son, Władysław, was the king of Bohemia (1471–1516) and Hungary (1516–26); he was succeeded by his son Louis II (1516–26).

In Ukraine, Jagiellon rule was marked by the liquidation of the last independent (appanage) Lithuanian-Ruthenian principalities, the consolidation of Polish rule in the western Ukrainian lands, intensive Polonization, the imposition of Roman Catholicism and *Germanic and *Magdeburg law, urban growth, significant economic development, and the enserfment of the peasantry.

Jakóbiec, Marian, b 8 September 1910 in Hynovychi, Berezhany county, Galicia. Polish Slavist and literary critic. Educated at Lviv, Prague, and Belgrade universities, in 1947 he was appointed professor at Wrocław University. He was the vice-president of the Polish-Soviet Institute, editor of the journal *Slavia orientalis*, and the vice-president of the Institute of Slavic Studies of the Polish Academy of Sciences. Jakóbiec wrote many studies on Slavic literatures and, particularly, on the relations between Ukrainian and Polish literature. His major works on Ukrainian literature are *Iwan Franko* (1958) and *Literatura ukraińska: Wypisy* (Ukrainian Literature: An Anthology, 1963; coauthored with T. Holyńska-Baranowa), and lengthy introductions to Polish translations of *The Tale of Ihor's Campaign* (1950) and the selected works of M. Kotsiubynsky (1954), I. Franko (1955), and T. Shevchenko (1955). He also wrote many articles on Ukrainian poets such as Shevchenko, Franko, M. Rylsky, and Lesia Ukrainka.

Jakobson, Roman, b 11 October 1896 in Moscow, d 18 July 1982 in Cambridge, Massachusetts. American linguist and philologist of Jewish-Russian descent. He studied at Moscow University, and received his doctorate from Prague University. He was a professor at several universities: Brno (1933–9), Columbia (1943–9), Harvard (from 1949), and the Massachusetts Institute of Technology (from 1957). Along with V. Mathesius and N. Trubetzkoy he founded the so-called Prague school of linguistics, which developed the phonemic principle in both synchronic and historical linguistics, and the concept of linguistic leagues, ie, similarities in the development of adjacent languages independently of their genetic interrelations. During his stay in the United States Jakobson revised the notion of phoneme, defining it as a bundle of distinctive features, 12 in number, that are common to all languages of the world. The search for universals, often at the cost of ignoring the peculiarities of individual languages, is typical of his conceptual approach. In this spirit he also attempted to build a theory of a Slavic conjugation based on a single stem, to develop a general case theory, and to derive Slavic versification systems from a common source. In this approach factual evidence was often sacrificed to theoretic consistency. Accordingly, in his *Remarques sur l'évolution phonologique du russe comparée à celle des autres langues slaves* (1929) only the phonological development of Russian and Serbo-Croatian is held to be motivated, while the rest of the Slavic languages, including Ukrainian, appear to be devoid of independent development, but determined by either Russian or Serbo-Croatian tendencies. Transferred to the political sphere, this attitude resulted in an attack on the policy of *Ukrainization and on its promoters (1934). Similarly, Jakobson's article on the imperative in Ukrainian (1965) is an attempt to play down the peculiarities of this form. In 1952–4 Jakobson argued against A. Mazon for the authenticity of **Slovo o polku Ihorevi*.

BIBLIOGRAPHY

Roman Jakobson: A Bibliography (The Hague 1971)
Holenstein, E. *Roman Jakobson's Approach to Language: Phenomenological Structuralism* (Bloomington, Ind 1976)

G.Y. Shevelov

Jan II Casimir Vasa, b 22 March 1609 in Cracow, d 16 December 1672 in Nevers, France. King of Poland and grand duke of Lithuania in 1648–68; the son of Sigismund III Vasa. The last ruler of the Vasa dynasty to occupy the Polish and Lithuanian thrones, Jan was elected king after the death of his brother Władysław IV. During his reign the Polish magnates pressed him to expend Poland's resources on winning the *Cossack-Polish War of 1648–57. In 1649 and 1651, he personally directed military campaigns against Hetman B. Khmelnytsky and the Cossacks in Ukraine. After the Treaty of *Pereiaslav of 1654 placed Ukraine under Muscovite protection, he was forced into a long war with Muscovy (1654–67). This further exhausted Poland, as did internal discord and the war with Sweden and its allies (1655–60). Jan concluded the Treaty of *Hadiache with Hetman I. Vyhovsky in 1658 and the Treaty of *Andrusovo with Muscovy in 1667. His attempts at strengthening royal absolutism caused a mutiny among the gentry, who forced him to abdicate in 1668 and to go to France.

Jan III Sobieski, b 17 August 1629 in Olesko, Galicia, d 17 June 1696 in Wilanów, Poland. King of Poland and grand duke of Lithuania in 1674–96. The son of Jakub, the castellan of Cracow, he fought in the Cossack-Polish War, at the battles of Zboriv (1649) and Berestechko (1651), and was severely wounded. He participated in Poland's wars with the Cossacks, Tatars, Muscovy, Sweden, and Turkey, becoming the field hetman in 1666 and grand hetman in 1668. Opposed to the reign of Michael Wiśniowiecki, he was elected king upon the latter's death. During his reign he concentrated on waging war against Turkey, becoming famous for his defense of Lviv in 1675. By the Treaty of *Zhuravno (1676) he recovered large parts of Ukraine from Turkey, but without Podilia. He led the army of Poland, in which there were many Ukrainian Cossacks, that forced the Turks to lift the siege of Vienna in 1683. In 1684 he allowed the Cossacks to resettle the devasted lands in Right-Bank Ukraine. He continued his war with Turkey until 1691, attempting unsuccessfully to occupy Moldavia and Wallachia and thus to secure Poland's access to the Black Sea. In 1686 he concluded the *Eternal Peace with Muscovy. Jan tried to introduce a hereditary, absolute monarchy and other reforms but failed because of opposition from the senate, diet, and allies.

Janissaries (Turkish: *yeniçeri;* Ukrainian: *yanychary*). Members of an elite infantry corps in the Ottoman Empire, established by Sultan Murad I (1360–89). They were recruited from prisoners of war and later, using the *devşirme* system, from Christian youths (Serbs, Bulgarians, and others) in the empire who were converted to Islam. Raised in the spirit of religious fanaticism, celibacy, and blind obedience to the sultan, they constituted three highly disciplined divisions numbering up to 40,000 men under the command of an *aga*. The janissaries became a powerful military and political force and one of the pillars of the Turkish sultans' personal rule. In the late 17th century, the celibacy rule and other restrictions on them were relaxed. From the 16th century, they frequently interfered in state affairs and staged palace coups. The corps was abolished in 1826 after it mutinied, and was massacred by order of Sultan Mahmud II. In the Ukrainian vernacular, the term *yanychar* connotes a renegade who faithfully and ardently serves a foreign power.

Janiw, Wolodymyr. See Yaniv, Volodymyr.

Janów, Jan, b 22 November 1888 in Moshkivtsi, Kalush county, Galicia, d 17 December 1952 in Cracow. Polish philologist, dialectologist, educator; from 1946 full member of the Polish Academy of Sciences. A graduate of Lviv University (1913), he served as professor of Lviv (1927–45) and then of Cracow University (1945–52). Janów wrote a number of works on Polish and Ukrainian philology and dialectology including *Gwara małoruska Moszkowiec i Siwki Naddniestrzańskiej* ... (The Little-Ruthenian Dialect of Moshkivtsi and Sivka-on-Dniester ..., 1926), *Z fonetyki gwar rusińskich* (From the Phonetics of Ruthenian Dialects, 1928), and *Legendarno-apokryficzne opowieści ruskie o męce Chrystusa z uwzględnieniem zabytków staropolskich* (Ruthenian Legendary and Apocryphal Tales on Christ's Passion Taking into Account Old Polish Sources, 1931). He also wrote extensive introductions to S. Piskorski's *Żywot Barlaama i Jozafata* (The Life of Barlaam and Josaphat, 1935) and J. Malecki-Sandecki's *Ewangeliarz z początku XVI w* ... (The Gospel from the Beginning of the 16th Century ..., 1947).

Japan (Nippon, Nihon). An Asian country (1985 pop 121,000,000) occupying an archipelago consisting of four main islands (Hokkaido, Honshu, Kyushu, and Shikoku), the Ryukus, and thousands of minor islands in the northwestern Pacific Ocean; it has an area of 377,801 sq km.

The Karmeliuk-Kamensky troupe in Japan, 1915

Ukrainian-Japanese relations are a 20th-century phenomenon. The first contacts occurred during the Russo-Japanese War of 1904–5, during which Sen J. Russell of Hawaii (M. Sudzylovsky), a former medical student at Kiev University, went to Japan and organized relief for captured tsarist troops (many of them Ukrainians) and published a periodical for them. The theatrical troupe of K. Karmeliuk-Kamensky, which often toured Ukrainian settlements in the Russian Far East and China, also performed in Tokyo, Kobe, Yokohama, and Kamakura in 1916. As a result of the efforts of the Russian consul in Japan, the Ukrainian Y. Hashkevych, an Oriental Institute was established in Vladivostok; Japanese was taught there. Ukrainian students at the institute later lived in Japan: B. Vobly was the UNR government's representative there. Neznaiko, a Ukrainian from the Far East, studied at the Orthodox seminary in Tokyo. An Orthodox mission existed at the Russian consulate in Hakodate and, from 1872, in Tokyo; one of its priests in Tokyo was the Ukrainian S. Hlibov. The kobzar and Esperantist V. Yeroshenko taught in Tokyo (1914–21) and wrote poetry, stories, fairy tales, and plays in Japanese.

In early July 1917 an attaché from the Japanese embassy in Petrograd visited the Ukrainian Central Rada in Kiev, and in November 1917 Japan opened a military mission there, headed by Gen Takayanachi. A Japanese consulate in Odessa oversaw shipping between Odessa and the Far East. Japan had a representative in the *Conference of Ambassadors that recognized Poland's rule of Galicia in 1923.

The Allied military intervention in the Russian *Far

East in 1918 involved over 120,000 Japanese troops, who occupied territories with large Ukrainian populations, including the cities of Vladivostok, Nikolsk (Ussuriisk), Khabarovsk, Blagoveshchensk, and Chita. From 1920 to November 1922 these territories constituted the *Far Eastern Republic, which was a Japanese protectorate. When the republic was occupied by Soviet forces, some 200 Ukrainian activists were arrested; 24, including P. Horovy, Yu. Hlushko-Mova, V. Kyiovych, M. Pyrohiv, and V. Kozak, were tried in Chita in 1923–4 as separatists and Japanese collaborators.

Many Ukrainians in the Far East fled from Soviet rule to *Harbin, Manchuria, which was occupied by Japan in 1931 (see *China). The Ukrainians in Harbin had frequent contacts with the Japanese military authorities, who restored to them the building of the Ukrainian Club that had been confiscated by the Chinese and allowed the newspaper *Man'dzhurs'kyi vistnyk* (1932–7, ed I. Svit) to be published and several Ukrainian community organizations to function. The Japanese liaison officer K. Horie frequently interceded on behalf of the Ukrainians there. In the late 1920s and 1930s, UNR émigrés had contacts with Japanese officials in Europe. In Warsaw, Gen V. Salsky influenced the views of the Japanese military attaché, Col Yanagita; the latter was later transferred to Hsinking, where he helped the Ukrainians in Manchukuo in their dealings with the authorities.

In the 1930s, the OUN had political and military contacts with the Japanese, who were interested in furthering anti-Soviet activity in the Far East. In 1934 a few OUN operatives went from Europe via Tokyo to Harbin. There they became active in the Ukrainian community and conducted secret political work in the Soviet Far East. The OUN members B. Markiv, R. Korda-Fedoriv, and M. Mytliuk created the Ukrainian Far Eastern Sich youth organization in Harbin. In 1937 the Japanese authorities sided openly with émigré Russian fascist organizations and circumscribed the activity of most of the Ukrainian organizations, except for the Ukrainian National Colony in Manchukuo. However, they allowed the Ukrainians in Shanghai to publish the newspaper *Ukraïns'kyi holos na Dalekomu skhodi* (1941–4, ed M. Milko) and to organize a Ukrainian National Committee.

Japanese-Ukrainian cultural contacts have been mainly literary. In Japan the best-known Ukrainian writer has been T. Shevchenko. The fullest Japanese collection of his poetry (26 poems), translated by T. Shibuya, S. Komatsu, T. Murai, H. Tadzawa, and T. Kinoshita, appeared in Tokyo in 1964. Several articles about him have also appeared. In 1961, an Association for Shevchenko Studies was established, and meetings of Soviet Ukrainian and Japanese writers took place on the 100th anniversary of Shevchenko's death and the 150th anniversary of his birth. A few works by I. Franko, Lesia Ukrainka, P. Tychyna, and M. Stelmakh have also been translated into Japanese.

Some Japanese literature has been translated into Ukrainian; eg, A. Lototsky's *Iapons'ki kazky* (Japanese Fairy Tales, 1926), S. Tokunaga's *Street without Sunshine* (1932) and *Silent Mountains* (1954), W. Hosoi's *Kodji the Textile Worker*, and T. Kobayashi's *The Crabmeat Factory Ship* (1934). Translations of Japanese literature were published in 1961 in an anthology of Oriental literature edited by A. Kovalivsky. The émigré I. Shankovsky published a collection of 100 13th-century Japanese court poems in Ukrainian translation.

In the 1920s, Japanese language and literature were taught at Kharkiv University, which published F. Pushchenko's Japanese grammar in 1926. Also in 1926, the All-Ukrainian Scientific Association for Oriental Studies (VUNAS) was established in Kharkiv, with branches in Kiev and Odessa; F. Pushchenko was the director of the Japanese section. Articles in Japanese studies and translations appeared in *Biuleten' VUNAS* (1926–8) and in the journal *Skhidnyi svit* (1927–31). In 1931, translations of 26 classical Japanese poems were published in a collection with an introductory essay by O. Kremena.

Outside Ukraine, S. Levynsky, who worked at the Polish consulate in Harbin, Peking, and Saigon from 1935 to 1946, published an account of his travels, *Z iapons'koho domu* (From a Japanese Home, 1932). V. Odynets studied at the Oriental Institute in Harbin and later taught East European history at Hsinking University. He and A. Dibrova, with the help of S. Levynsky, I. Svit, and several Japanese linguists, compiled a Ukrainian-Japanese dictionary (ed Y. Saburo, Harbin 1944). The Council of the Ukrainian National Colony in Harbin published the anthology *Dalekyi skhid* (The Far East), which included translations of Japanese poetry and articles on Japanese folkways and education.

Since the Second World War, notable Soviet Ukrainian Japanese specialists have included Ya. Pobilenky and I. Chyrko. In Japan, specialists in Ukrainian literature have been S. Fukuoka at Hokkaido University, K. Komatsu at the Institute of Foreign Languages in Kobe, and S. Kimura at Tokyo University. K. Nakai has written on Ukrainian history. Ukraine has been studied within the framework of Soviet and East European studies.

BIBLIOGRAPHY
Svit, I. *Ukraïns'ko-iapons'ki vzaiemyny 1903–1945* (New York 1972)

A. Zhukovsky

Jargon. A vocabulary or idiom understood only by members of a specific occupational or social group (eg, tramps, kobzars, hawkers, sailors, prostitutes, beggars, thieves) which is used by them as a means of mutual identification and differentiation from the rest of society. Because of their emotivity, many words and expressions of various jargons have become part of urban *slang.

The devices of word formation in Ukrainian jargons consist of (1) the interpolation of a syllable, such as *kry-* or *šu-*, between syllables of a standard word, eg, *'kry-pi-kry-du'* from *pidu* ('I will go'); (2) the deformation of a standard word by (a) aphaeresis, eg, *'ašoxa'* from *kaša* ('kasha'), (b) metathesis, eg *'Lykačiv'* from *'Lyčakiv'*, or (c) prothesis, eg, *'šmurnyj'* from *durnyj* ('stupid'); (3) metaphoric and metonymic substitutions, eg, *cybulja* ('onion') for *hodynnyk* ('watch'); and (4) the adoption of loan words (mainly from Yiddish, Romany, and modern Greek) that are often used figuratively, eg, *oxvés* ('icon,' 'picture,' or 'God') and *oxcijos* (a hundred-unit banknote) from the Greek *o theos* ('God'). Devices 1 and 2 were used mostly in occupational jargons of the 19th and early 20th century.

The phonetics and grammar of a jargon are not independent; they are taken from the local general speech.

For example, the jargon of Buchach's *lirnyks was based on the Dniester dialect, while that of Ternopil's and Vinnytsia's was based on the Podilia dialect; Lviv's slang was based on the Polonized dialect as used there, while jargons of Odessa, Kiev, and Kharkiv were based on Russified parlance used in those cities. The jargons spoken in parts of Ukraine bordering on Poland, eastern Belorussia, and Russia's Voronezh region can be traced back to the 17th century. In Ukraine various jargons were first recorded in the second half of the 19th century. These records include those of Kharkiv's beggars by V. Ivanov; of eastern Podilia's lirnyks by V. Borzhkovsky; of Ternopil's lirnyks by K. Studynsky; of Buchach's lirnyks by V. Hnatiuk; of Novyi Ropsk's (in Chernihiv gubernia) fullers by F. Nykolaichyk; of Chernihiv's blind beggars by P. Tikhanov; of thieves and hooligans by V. Trakhtenberg and V. Bets; of the homeless and school children by V. Petrov, V. Shchepotev, and V. Straten; of criminals by V. Popov (in Kiev, 1912) and A. Kurka (in Lviv, 1896).

BIBLIOGRAPHY
Borzhkovskii, V. 'Lirniki,' KS, 1889, no. 9
Hnatiuk, V. 'Lirnyky. Lirnyts'ki pisni, molytvy, slova, zvistky i t.p. pro lirnykiv povitu Buchats'koho,' EZ (1896)
Jagić, V. 'Die Geheimsprachen bei den Slaven,' *Sitzungsberichte der Wiener Akademie der Wissenschaften, Phil.-Hist. Kl.*, 1 (1896)
Iazyk i literatura, 7 (1931) (articles by B. Larin, M. Fridman, A. Barannikov, and N. Dmitriev)
Straten, V. 'Argo i argotizmy,' *Trudy komissii po russkomu iazyku*, 1 (1931)
Horbach, O. 'Argot in Ukraine,' *Proceedings of the Shevchenko Scientific Society, Philological Section*, 1 (1952)

O. Horbach

Jarosław (Ukrainian: Yaroslav). III-3. City (1982 pop 36,100) and county center in Przemyśl voivodeship, Poland, on the Sian River. Named after Grand Prince Yaroslav the Wise of Kiev, it was first mentioned in 1152 during the reign of Prince Volodymyrko of Halych. In 1245 the Battle of *Yaroslav took place there, during which the army of Prince Danylo Romanovych of Volhynia defeated that of Rostyslav Mykhailovych of Chernihiv and his Hungarian and Galician boyar allies. In the mid-14th century the city came under Polish rule. Granted the right of Magdeburg Law in 1375, it was an important trade center in the 15th–17th centuries. A Jesuit college was founded there in 1575. In 1722 it came under Austrian rule; from 1856 it was a county center. Destroyed during the First World War, from 1919 to 1939 it belonged to Poland. In 1939 Ukrainians composed 16 percent of the city's and 75 percent of the county's population. Under the German occupation (1939–44), a branch of the *Ukrainian Central Committee was active there; it established Ukrainian shops, a co-operative union, a gymnasium, a trade school, a People's Home, and a Farmer's Bank. The Greek-Catholic auxiliary bishop H. Lakota was based there, and the city was the center of the Ukrainian Relief Committee in the Sian region. In 1946 the UPA fought Polish partisans and government troops in the Jarosław region, but it was unable to prevent the wholesale deportation of the county's Ukrainian population to northwest Poland. Since that time the population of Jarosław and its county has been almost entirely Polish.

BIBLIOGRAPHY
Wagner, W. *Handel dawnego Jarosława do połowy XVII w.* (Lviv 1929)
Wondaś, A. *Szkice do dziejów Jarosławia*, 3 vols (Jarosław 1934–6)
Gottfried, K. *Ilustrowany przewodnik po Jarosławiu* (Jarosław 1937)
Semchyshyn, M.; Borodach, V. (eds). *Iaroslavshchyna i Zasiannia 1031–1947: Istorychno-memuarnyi zbirnyk* (New York-Paris-Sydney-Toronto 1986)

M. Stech

Jary, Riko, b 14 April 1898 in Rjysion, Austria, d 20 May 1969 in Austria. Journalist; military and political leader of mixed Ukrainian-Austrian background. In 1929 he became a founding member of the OUN and treasurer of the Leadership of Ukrainian Nationalists. He served as the main contact between the Ukrainian Military Organization and OUN and the Abwehr (German military intelligence) and organized military and security training for Ukrainian nationalists. In March 1939, he arranged the delivery of arms by Germany to Ukrainian insurgents in Transcarpathia, and in 1939–40 he co-ordinated the assistance provided by the Abwehr to Ukrainian military formations. Jary initiated contacts between S. *Bandera and the Abwehr in November 1940 and became a member of the OUN (Bandera faction). Saved once from arrest by the Gestapo by the intervention of the chief of German intelligence, Admiral W. Canaris, he was finally arrested in 1942 and held under house arrest from February 1943 in Semering near Vienna. After the war, he lived in Austria. Jary's role in the nationalist movement is the subject of some controversy; however, allegations that he and his wife Olly (née Spiegelvogel) co-operated with the Third Communist International and speculation that they were Bolshevik agents remain unsubstantiated.

D. Zlepko

Jassy. See Iaşi.

Jean, Josaphat Joseph, b 19 March 1885 in Saint-Fabien near Rimouski, Quebec, d 8 June 1972 in Grimsby, Ontario. Missionary priest. Upon graduating from the Grand Séminaire of Montreal, Jean was ordained in 1910 and departed for Galicia to study Ukrainian and the Eastern rite in preparation for his work among Ukrainian settlers in western Canada. In 1912 he organized a school in Sifton, Manitoba, and served at a number of Ukrainian missions in St Boniface diocese. In the following year he returned to Galicia and entered the Basilian monastic order. During the war he served as a priest and chaplain of the Ukrainian Galician Army. In June 1919 he was appointed special secretary to the president of the Western Ukrainian National Republic (ZUNR). Then he served as a member of the ZUNR diplomatic corps in Warsaw, the Ukrainian delegation to the Riga Peace Conference, and the Ukrainian mission in Geneva. In 1923 Jean was sent to Bosnia by Metropolitan A. Sheptytsky to establish a Studite monastery for the Ukrainians in the region, but encountered strong government opposition to the plan. Returning to Canada in 1925, he established Shepticky village (today Lac Castagnier) near Abitibi, Quebec, for emigrants from Galicia and Ukrainian refugees from Bosnia. The colony of some 50 families failed, however, and Jean served as priest in Ukrainian parishes of Montreal

(1931–45). Immediately after the war he worked in London and Paris aiding Ukrainian refugees and promoting immigration to Canada. He returned to Mundare in 1949 to teach at the Basilian novitiate. His valuable collection of rare books and historical documents is preserved in Mundare.

Jedlička, Aloiz, b 14 December 1821 in Kukleny, Bohemia, d 15 September 1894 in Poltava. Ukrainian composer, folklorist, and pedagogue of Czech origin. After studying at the Prague Conservatory (1837–42), he moved to Ukraine. In 1845 he became acquainted with T. Shevchenko. From 1848 to 1892 he taught piano at the Poltava Institute for Daughters of the Nobility, where he also organized a choir. His piano pieces such as 'Leaf from an Album,' 'Kerchief,' 'Recollections of Poltava,' and 'Flowers of Ukraine' are based on Ukrainian folk music. He collected Ukrainian folk songs and published them in two collections: *Sobranie malorossiiskikh narodnykh pesen* (A Collection of Little Russian Folk Songs, 1861) and *Sto malorossiisskikh narodnykh pesen* (A Hundred Little Russian Folk Songs, 1869). He also did arrangements of folk songs and edited the musical score of I. Kotliarevsky's *Natalka Poltavka* (Natalka from Poltava). Several works of Ukrainian poets were set to music by Jedlička.

Jedlnia privileges. Decree issued in 1430 by the Polish king Władysław II Jagiełło in the village of Jedlnia in Kielce voivodeship. It granted the nobility important rights such as the inviolability of the individual and his property without a court decision. These rights were to apply in Ruthenian lands as well. The decree provided for the incorporation of the Grand Duchy of Lithuania in the Kingdom of Poland. The implementation of the decree finally replaced the old Ukrainian law in Galicia with Polish law.

Jędrzejewicz, Jerzy, b 2 March 1902 in Bawaria, Końskie county, Poland, d 19 November 1975 in Warsaw. Polish writer, translator, and literary critic. A professor of literature at Warsaw University, his finest contribution to Ukrainian studies was a biographical novel about T. Shevchenko titled *Noce ukraińskie albo rodowód geniusza* (Ukrainian Nights or the Biography of a Genius, 1966), which was a best seller in Poland and was republished twice (1970, 1972). A Ukrainian translation by Ye. Roslytsky appeared in Toronto in 1980. Jędrzejewicz translated over 30 novels, over 20 dramas, and many poems from Ukrainian, Russian, Italian, and German to Polish. His translations of Ukrainian literature include a two-volume collection of M. Kotsiubynsky's works (1954), M. Rylsky's *Shopen* (Chopin, 1947), T. Shevchenko's *Progulka s udovol'stviem i ne bez morali* (A Trip with Pleasure and Not without a Moral, 1960), a book of selected poetry by T. Shevchenko (1972), and a book of short stories by Ye. Hutsalo. He also wrote articles on Shevchenko, Kotsiubynsky, Hutsalo, and others.

Jehovah's Witnesses. A theocratic millennarian religious sect that began in the United States in the 19th century and has since spread to much of the world, including Ukraine. It is most widely represented there in Donetske, Mykolaiv, Trancarpathia, and Chernivtsi oblasts. It also has a strong following in the Kuban.

Since the Witnesses are illegal in the USSR, they operate secretly at the local, district, and regional levels. The local level cells are made up of 5–15 people. During their meetings they study literature published by the sect's headquarters in New York. They themselves publish the underground Ukrainian-language journal *Vartova bashnia*. They recruit from among ordinary Soviet people and are especially successful with the desperate and disillusioned.

Throughout their history in the USSR, the Witnesses have been severely persecuted because their doctrine is perceived to be anti-Soviet. Because their leadership is based in the United States, they have also been accused of being a front for espionage. Both J. Stalin and N. Khrushchev conducted major Soviet-wide campaigns against the sect (in 1951, 7,000 Witnesses were reportedly in prison or exile) and there continue to be frequent reports of the trial and imprisonment of Witnesses. However, the movement appears to be remarkably resilient; some well-informed observers believe that the Soviet branch of the Jehovah's Witnesses is one of the strongest in the world.

O. Zinkevych

Jensen, Alfred, b 30 September 1859 in Fors, near Gävle, Sweden, d 15 September 1921 in Vienna. Prominent Swedish Slavist. He wrote articles on T. Shevchenko in Swedish and a book in German, *Taras Schewtschenko: Ein ukrainisches Dichterleben* (1916), and translated some of his poems into Swedish. In 1909 he visited Ukraine and became personally acquainted with I. Franko and M. Kotsiubynsky; his translation of two of the latter's stories appeared in 1909 (*I vilt äktenskap*). Jensen produced a monograph on Hetman I. Mazepa in 1909 and studies of Hetman P. Orlyk and the Voinarovsky family. In 1921 he edited a Swedish collection on Ukrainians, which was published in the Nationernas Bibliotek series as *Ukrainarna*. A member of the Shevchenko Scientific Society from 1911, he contributed many articles to its periodicals and followed closely Ukrainian academic activities, about which he informed the Swedish public.

Jer (pronounced *yer*). Originally, the name for two letters of the Glagolitic and Cyrillic alphabets: ъ and ь in Cyrillic. The origin of the name is unknown; possibly, it was derived from the jargon name of a bird (a type of swallow) whose shape in flight resembles the shape of the Glagolitic letters. The jers as sounds arose ca 800 AD in Common Slavic from the short *u* and *i* respectively. In their subsequent development in Proto-Ukrainian the jers split into weak and strong depending on their position in the word; namely, they became strong if followed in the next syllable by a weak jer. The strong jers developed into *o* and *e* respectively, while the weak jers underwent reduction and were lost ca 1150. Thus, the disyllabic words *sъnъ* ('sleep') and *dьnь* ('day') of late Common Slavic became *son* and *den'* in modern Ukrainian. The letter ь is still used in the Ukrainian alphabet; not as a vowel, however, but as a 'soft sign' to indicate palatalization of the preceding consonant.

Jerlicz, Joachim, b 19 May 1598 in Kolentsi, eastern Volhynia, d after 1673. Polish chronicler of Ukrainian noble descent. A monk at the Kievan Cave Monastery, he joined the Polish army and fought in the *Cossack-Polish War. In 1648, while hiding in the Kievan Cave

Monastery, he began a chronicle covering the years 1620 to April 1673. While it is virulently anti-Cossack in tone and considerably distorts events of the period, the chronicle nonetheless provides useful information about the war. It was first published in Warsaw as *Latopisiec albo kroniczka różnych spraw i dziejów* (Chronicle of Various Matters and Events, 2 vols, 1853).

Jerusalem. Ancient city (1986 pop 420,000) claimed as the capital by Israel, and regarded as a holy city by Jews, Christians, and Moslems. The earliest historical references to Jerusalem date back to the middle of the 2nd millennium BC and describe it as the capital of Jewish kings. The city has been destroyed twice – by the Babylonians in 587 BC and by the Romans in 70 AD.

As the site of Christ's life, death, and resurrection, Jerusalem and Palestine have attracted for many centuries pilgrims from Ukraine. Many of them left memoirs and accounts of their travels, which have been studied extensively. One of the first pilgrims from Ukraine to visit Jerusalem was *Danylo, the hegumen of a Chernihiv monastery, who wrote a widely known account of his pilgrimage in 1106–8. In the 15th century Arsenii of Thessalonica wrote an account of his pilgrimage to the Holy Land. In 1590–3 Danylo of Korsun, the archimandrite of a monastery in the Hrodna region, lived in Jerusalem and left an account entitled *Peregrinatsiia ili put do Ierusalimu ...* (The Pilgrimage or Voyage to Jerusalem ..., publ 1906), which imitated closely Hegumen Danylo's earlier work. More Ukrainian pilgrims visited the Holy Land at the beginning of the 18th century. Two monks of the Novhorod-Siverskyi Monastery of the Transfiguration, Makarii and Sylvestr, left some notes on their journey in 1704. A hieromonach of the Borys and Hlib Monastery in Chernihiv eparchy described his pilgrimage of 1707–9 in *Puteshestvie ieromonakha Ippolita Vishenskogo v Ierusalim, na Sinai i Afon* (The Travels of the Hieromonach Ipolit Vyshensky to Jerusalem, Sinai, and Mt Athos, publ 1914). At about the same time (1712–14) Varlaam Linytsky, a hieromonach of the Kievan Cave Monastery, visited Jerusalem and left some notes on his stay.

The noted 18th-century traveler V. Hryhorovych-Barsky visited many countries in Europe and the Near East, and left four illustrated volumes of recollections entitled *Stranstvovan'iia Vasil'ia Grigorovicha-Barskogo po sviatym mestam Vostoka s 1723 po 1747 g.* (The Travels of Vasyl Hryhorovych-Barsky to the Holy Places of the East from 1723 to 1747, 1885–7). He spent about five months in Jerusalem itself studying and sketching various sites associated with Christ's life, which he describes in detail. Separion, a monk of the Motronynskyi Holy Trinity Monastery near Chyhyryn, described his 1749 trip to Jerusalem in his *Putnik ili puteshestvie vo sviatuiu zemliu ...* (The Trip or Travels to the Holy Land ..., publ 1873).

Pilgrimages to Jerusalem and the Holy Land continued in the 19th century, and a number of accounts were written by pilgrims from Western Ukraine. V. *Terletsky described his two-year travels in the Near East in his two-volume *Zapiski vtorogo poklonicheskogo puteshestviia z Rima v Ierusalim ...* (Notes on the Second Pilgrim Voyage from Rome to Jerusalem ..., 1861). L. Turiansky, a Galician, wrote a sketch of his visit to the Holy Land titled *Opys z ust palomnyka* (A Description from a Pilgrim's Mouth, 1886). Rev A. Poliansky's recollections of his pilgrimage were published also in 1886. A little later Rev T. Dutkevych's *Podorozh do Ierusalymu* (Journey to Jerusalem, 1899) was published in Kolomyia. In 1900 the Rev B. Kyrchiv organized pilgrimages to the Holy Land.

Metropolitan A. Sheptytsky visited Jerusalem and the Holy Land in 1904 and in 1906, when he was accompanied by 505 pilgrims. This group of pilgrims established a chapel at the Austrian hospital and donated liturgical books, rare vestments, and a golden chalice to it. The metropolitan and his group were received by the Patriarch of Jerusalem. Rev Yu. Dzerovych wrote an account of this pilgrimage titled *Propamiatna knyha Pershoho Rus'ko-narodnoho palomnytstva v Sviatu Zemliu vid 5 do 28 veresnia 1906* (A Commemorative Book of the First Ruthenian Popular Pilgrimage to the Holy Land from 5 to 28 of September 1906, 1907). In the interwar period various political and bureaucratic complications discouraged organized pilgrimages and no Ukrainian group visited the Holy Land. In 1933 Y. Slipy, who was rector of the Greek Catholic Theological Seminary at the time, traveled to the Holy Land and later wrote *Palomnytstvo do Sviatoï Zemli* (A Pilgrimage to the Holy Land, 1935). Since the Second World War Ukrainians in the West have made a number of pilgrimages to Jerusalem. Yu. Fedoriv and M. Zhyzhka have both published accounts of their trips.

A silver plate (106 by 83 cm) with an engraving of Christ's entombment was donated by Hetman I. Mazepa ca 1707 to the Church of the Lord's Resurrection, which is part of the building complex known as the Church of the Holy Sepulchre. This gift has been preserved there and is still used as an altar covering. Otaman P. Kalnyshevsky is also known to have sent precious gifts to the Church of the Holy Sepulchre.

A. Olesnytsky, a professor of the Kiev Theological Academy and specialist in biblical archeology, published many studies in his field including *Sviataia Zemlia* (The Holy Land, 2 vols, 1875–6). During the Second World War Ukrainian pilgrims donated a tablet with an inscription of the Lord's Prayer in Ukrainian and Church Slavonic to the Pater Noster Church on the Mount of Olives.

In 1979 the public Committee for Jewish-Ukrainian Cooperation, which published the journal *Contact*, was set up in Jerusalem. In 1981 a splinter group of the committee founded the Society of Ukrainian-Jewish Contacts. It publishes a quarterly bulletin *Diialohy*, edited by Ya. Suslensky. Yad Vashem's list of righteous gentiles who risked their lives to save Jews in the Holocaust includes 60 Ukrainians. On 13 May 1985 a monument to the Jewish-Ukrainian and Ukrainian victims of Nazism and Russian Bolshevism, donated by Yu. Dyba, was unveiled near the Tomb of King David on Mount Zion. A few months later it was destroyed by anti-Ukrainian extremists.

A. Zhukovsky

Jesenská, Růžena, b 17 June 1863, d 14 July 1940. Czech writer and translator. Her translations of 28 poems by T. Shevchenko, together with her long introduction, were published in 1900. She also translated several poems by I. Franko, Lesia Ukrainka, and B. Lepky.

Jesuits (Societas Jesu). Roman Catholic monastic order founded in 1534 by I. Loyola and approved in 1540 by Pope Paul III. Organized originally to convert Moslems, it became the chief instrument of the Counter-Reformation. It defended and spread the Catholic faith through missions, research, publication, and education. The Jesuits often played an important political role. In 1773 Pope Clement XIV disbanded the order, but it continued its activities in the Russian Empire under the protection of Catherine II. Restored in 1814 by Pope Pius VII, it was expelled from Russia in 1820. The only Ukrainian territory in which the Jesuits continued to operate was Galicia.

Introduced to Poland by Cardinal S. Hosius in the mid-16th century, the Jesuits extended their influence throughout Ukrainian and Belorussian territories. They founded *colleges and academies that were emulated by the Orthodox and Uniates. The schools consisted of two levels: the lower with five grades, and the higher with two grades (see *Higher education). There were 23 Jesuit colleges in Ukrainian territory. The most important ones were the college in Yaroslav (est 1574, enrollment in 1600 approx 60), Lviv (est 1608), Lutske (1614 enrollment approx 400), Kamianets-Podilskyi (est 1611), Vinnytsia, Bar, Berestia, Peremyshl (est 1570), Pynske (est 1633), and Kiev (est 1647). Some of them also taught Ruthenian. The sons of many Ukrainian noble families attended these colleges and the Jesuit Academy in Vilnius (est 1570). Ukrainian clergy were often graduates of Jesuit seminaries. Through their schools the Jesuits succeeded in converting large numbers of Ukrainians and Belorussians to Roman Catholicism and in Polonizing them. Prince K. Ostrozky's sons and J. Wiśniowiecki (Vyshnevetsky), for example, became Roman Catholics.

The Jesuits, particularly P. Skarga, B. Herbest, and the papal legate A. Possevino, actively promoted the Church Union of *Berestia. Because of their enormous political influence at court and among the Polish nobility and their accumulation of landholdings (including the estates of the Ostrozky family left to them by Princess A. Ostrozka), the Jesuits drew the enmity of the Ukrainian people, and particularly of the Cossacks. During the *Cossack-Polish War they were persecuted and driven from Ukraine. In various treaties with the Poles the Cossacks demanded that the Jesuits be expelled from Ukrainian territory. Uniate metropolitans frequently petitioned the Pope to stop the Jesuit practice of converting Uniates to Roman Catholicism.

In 1781, after the abolition of the Jesuit order, the Polish Commission of National Education transferred the Jesuit college in Bar, and various Jesuit buildings in Ovruch, Ostrih, and Volodymyr-Volynskyi, to the Basilian monastic order. In the 19th century the restored Jesuits established monasteries in the larger cities of Galicia such as Lviv, Ternopil, and Stanyslaviv, a boarding school and gymnasium in Khyriv, and a pilgrimage site called Kokhavyna.

In 1882 Pope Leo XIII assigned to the Jesuits the task of reforming the Basilian order. Here the most important work was done by H. Jackowski, K. Szczepkowski, and K. Baudiss. After 1920 an eastern branch of the order was organized in Poland. Its centers were Albertin in Belorussia and Dubno in Volhynia, where the Jesuits ran a pontifical seminary. The most prominent figures of this branch were J. Urban, the editor of the bimonthly *Oriens*, W. Dąbrowski, and the Spaniard J. Morillo, the publisher of the journal *Oriente Europeo*.

The Jesuits took part in the attempts to bring about a union between the Orthodox of Transcarpathia and Rome; however, because of their policy of conversion to Roman Catholicism and Magyarization, the Jesuits failed in their efforts.

The Jesuit order produced some outstanding historians of the Eastern church such as A. Ammann. Ukrainian members of the order include Rev S. Tyshkevych, the son of M. Tyshkevych. Some prominent leaders of the Ukrainian Catholic church, including Y. Slipy, K. Bohachevsky, V. Laba, I. Stakh, and A. Ishchak, were graduates of Jesuit universities in Europe. A number of American universities and colleges at which Ukrainians teach or study are run by the Jesuits.

BIBLIOGRAPHY

Pelesz, J. *Geschichte der Union der ruthenischen Kirche mit Rom* (Würzburg-Vienna 1878–80)

Załęski, S. *Jezuici w Polsce*, 5 vols (Lviv-Cracow 1900–6)

W. Lencyk

Jeunes Amis de l'Ukraine. See Organization of Ukrainian Youth in France.

Jewelry and ornamentation. Jewelry consists of objects of adornment valued for their craftsmanship and the rarity of their components. One of the oldest art forms, jewelry making in Ukraine dates to the Paleolithic period, when bones and wood were used to fashion decorative items. Ornamentation refers to the crafting of various objects (eg, chalices, book bindings, weapons) and their embellishment with gems and precious metals, particularly gold and silver.

Jewelry making and fine metalworking were well developed in the *ancient states on the northern Black Sea coast. For the inhabitants of the Greek colonies, jewelry, made mostly of bronze, played an important economic role and was widely traded. Many *Scythian artifacts, dating back to the 7th–2nd centuries BC, have been found in grave sites in southern Ukraine. The Scythians created fine jewelry and developed their own 'animalistic style,' depicting running or fighting animals on plaques of gold or silver. Outstanding examples of Scythian handiwork include a silver amphora found in the *Chortomlyk kurhan, a gold pectoral from the *Krasnokutskyi kurhan, and a gold quiver and bow cover found near Melitopol.

In Kievan Rus', the craft of enameling enjoyed great popularity and reached a high level of development (see *Enamel). The artisans of Kiev, Kaniv, Chernihiv, and elsewhere made elaborate diadems, earrings, necklaces, rings, and pendants. They also used their skills in fashioning religious artifacts: chalices, censers, crosses, and ornamental bindings on Gospels and other church books. A unique silver-covered bull's horn was uncovered in the 10th century *Chorna Mohyla. Many precious metals and stones were imported to Rus' from Central Asia and the Caucasus. The Mongol invasion in the 13th century led to a temporary decline in crafts throughout much of Ukraine.

In the 14th–16th centuries, the main centers of goldsmithing, silversmithing, and jewelry making in Ukraine were Kiev, Lviv, Kamianets-Podilskyi, and Chernihiv. A Kievan guild of goldsmiths existed from at least 1518, and the names of 28 Lviv goldsmiths from the 15th century are known today. In this period Western Europe replaced Byzantium as the main source of influence on Ukrainian ornamentation; many artisans were of foreign (particularly German and Armenian) origin, especially

Jewelry and ornaments: 1–13) rings and earrings; 14) mirror; 15) part of a necklace; 16–17) enamel earrings (Kievan Rus'); 18) bells; 19–20) water spouts; 21) golden candelabra (Kievan Rus') [from V. Sichynsky]

in the cities of Western Ukraine. The most important artifacts of the 16th century were religious ones. Designs became extremely elaborate, marked by the generous use of precious ornaments. At the same time, precious metals and gems began to be used in making household articles such as plates and flatware, and in embellishing weapons. The wealthy Right-Bank nobility provided a large market for luxury items. In the late 17th century, with the emergence of a Cossack elite, new centers of jewelry making and ornamentation developed in the Left Bank. Separate guilds of goldsmiths were established in Pryluka (1749), Chernihiv (1786), and Nizhen (1786). In this period Ukrainian artisans mastered almost all the major techniques in working with precious metals, including pouring, engraving, embossing, and inlaying. Outstanding examples of jewelry and ornamentation include the encolpion by the Kievan artisan Fedir (1655), the silver-bound Gospel by the Romny craftsmen A. Ivanovych and A. Peliakovsky (1688), and work by I. Ravych, I. Biletsky, and M. Yurevych. Gold and silver were often used to emboss iconostases and individual icons, and Cossack officers generously endowed many churches and monasteries with expensive ornaments.

From the end of the 18th century, jewelry making and ornamentation declined steadily in Ukraine. It was only in 1878 that the first modern jeweler began manufacturing jewelry in Kiev. Now in Ukraine there are five jewelry factories, which generally produce poor-quality items for mass markets. The richest collections of old Ukrainian jewelry and ornaments are found in the Museum of Historical Treasures of the Ukrainian SSR, the Historical Museum of the Ukrainian SSR, the Kiev Museum of Ukrainian Art, and the Hermitage in Leningrad.

BIBLIOGRAPHY

Shcherbakivs'kyi, D. *Ukraïns'ke mystetstvo* (Lviv-Kiev 1913)
Pavluts'kyi, H. *Istoriia ukraïns'koho ornamentu* (Kiev 1927)
Petrenko, M. *Ukraïns'ke zolotarstvo XVI–XVIII st.* (Kiev 1970)

B. Balan

Jewish Battalion of the Ukrainian Galician Army (Zhydivskyi kurin UHA). The battalion was formed from Jewish militia units in the city of Ternopil during June 1919 as part of the *Ukrainian Galician Army (UHA). It was commanded by Lieutenant S. Leimberg and initially was under direct operational control of I Corps Headquarters. The battalion reached a total strength of 1,200 soldiers, who were organized into four infantry companies, one machine-gun company, one engineer company, and other units. After basic training in Ostapie, Skalat county, the battalion was sent to the Polish front and was in combat from 14 July 1919. During the withdrawal of the UHA to the east, the battalion initially had responsibility for rearguard security and later participated in combat against Bolshevik forces in Proskuriv (Khmelnytskyi) and captured the town of Mykhalpil (Mykhailivka). In Vinnytsia the battalion's mission was to secure the city and the headquarters of I Corps. In the march on Kiev in late August 1919 the battalion was attached to the 6th Brigade with the mission of gaining and securing the rail station at Sviatoshyne. In September 1919 the battalion was temporarily stationed in Berdychiv, where its actions in securing the town gained wide support among the local people. After transfer to Vinnytsia in late autumn 1919, the battalion was so decimated by the typhus epidemic that it was disbanded and its surviving soldiers were reassigned to other UHA units.

P.R. Sodol

Jews (Ukrainian: *zhydy, ievreï*). Jews first settled on Ukrainian territories in the 4th century BC in the Crimea and among the Greek colonies on the northeast coast of the Black Sea. From there they migrated to the valleys of the three major rivers – the Volga, Don, and Dnieper – where they maintained active economic and diplomatic relations with Byzantium, Persia, and the Khazar kaganate (see *Khazars). The latter empire consisted of Turkic tribes that converted to Judaism in about 740 AD. In the aftermath of Khazaria's conquest in 964 by the Kievan prince *Sviatoslav I, Khazarian Jews settled in Kiev, the Crimea (see *Karaites), and the Caucasus.

Throughout the 11th and 12th centuries Khazarian Jews steadily migrated northwards. In Ukraine the Jewish population developed a distinct presence. In Kiev they settled in their own district called *Zhydove, the entrance to which was called the *Zhydivski vorota* (Jewish gate). Jews fleeing the Crusaders came to Ukraine as well, and the first western-European Jews began to arrive from Germany, probably in the 11th century.

The Kievan princes Iziaslav and Sviatopolk II, Prince

Danylo Romanovych of Galicia, and the Volhynian prince Volodymyr Vasylkovych were well disposed to their Jewish subjects and assisted their activities in trade and finance. Jews were also appointed to administrative and financial posts. However, as in other parts of Europe, this benevolent treatment was not consistent. During an uprising in 1113 the Zhydove district was ransacked, and during the rule of *Volodymyr Monomakh Jews were expelled from Kiev. The Mongol conquest of the Crimea and of Kievan Rus' strengthened commercial relations, and brought peace and prosperity to the Jewish community up to the time of the Tatar-Lithuanian War (1396–99).

The expulsion of the Jews from the states and cities of Western and Central Europe in the 13th–15th centuries led Jews to flee eastward, to Austria, Hungary, Bohemia, Moravia, Poland, and the Ottoman Empire. By 1500, Jews living in Ukrainian lands under Polish rule could be found in 23 towns and constituted one-third of all Jews in the Polish kingdom. The central European Jews (*ashkenazim*) spoke Yiddish (a German dialect), wore distinctive dress, and lived apart from the local population, either in separate districts or ghettos of cities, or in small, predominantly Jewish, settlements (*shtetl*). They were usually poorer than the earliest Jewish immigrants to Ukraine. Barred from owning land and from the professions, the majority of Jews were engaged in modest occupations, as artisans and in petty trade. Protected by the Polish monarchs against hostile nobles and urban dwellers, Jews were directly subordinate to the king, paying a separate tax for which they were collectively responsible. In return, royal decrees (dating back as early as 1264) allowed the Jews to govern themselves. In 1495 King Alexander Jagiellończyk established autonomous local governments (see *Kahal), with jurisdiction over schools, welfare, the lower judiciary, and religious affairs. From the mid-16th century to 1763 the central institution of Jewish life in the Polish kingdom was the Council of the Four Lands (Great Poland, 'Little Poland,' Chervona Rus' [Galicia], and Volhynia). The council met semiannually (later irregularly), with the site alternating between Jarosław and Lublin, to apportion the responsibility for taxes and decide on matters of concern to the Jewish community.

In the late 15th century Jews from Poland and Germany began arriving in Ukrainian territories under Lithuanian rule (especially the Kievan region and Podilia). Kiev became a famous center of Jewish religious education. This period was also one of suffering for both the indigenous and the Jewish populations because of the Tatar raids. In 1482 many Jews were seized by the Tatars and sold into slavery in the Crimea.

The largest migration of Jews to Ukrainian territories took place in the last quarter of the 16th century. Some came from other parts of Poland and Lithuania to settle the newly opened areas; others from as far as Italy and Germany. In 1569, with the creation of the Polish-Lithuanian Commonwealth (see Union of *Lublin) and the transfer of Ukraine from Lithuanian to Polish administration, vast areas of Ukraine were opened to colonization and to commercial agricultural development for trade with Western Europe. Between 1569 and 1648 the number of Jews in Ukraine increased from about 4,000 to nearly 51,325, dispersed among 115 towns and settlements in the voivodeships of Kiev, Podilia, Volhynia, and Bratslav. If the older Jewish community in the Ruthenian and Belz voivodeships is included, at the turn of the century there were 120,000 Jews in Ukrainian territories, out of an estimated total population of 2 to 5 million. This rapid increase was a result not only of migration but also of natural population growth.

Jews began taking advantage of the new professional and economic opportunities in the frontier territories of Ukraine. As Polish and Lithuanian nobles accumulated more land, Jews came to act as their middlemen, providing indispensible services to the absentee and local lords as leaseholders of large estates, tax collectors (see *Tax farming), estate stewards (with the right to administer justice, including the death penalty), business agents, and operators and managers of inns, dairies, mills, lumber yards, and distilleries. In trade, they supplanted Armenians and competed with urban Ukrainians. Jews came to be perceived as the immediate overlords of the peasantry and the most important competitors to the urban Christian Orthodox population.

The situation of the Jewish population became increasingly vulnerable in the early 17th century. Dissatisfaction with the difficult conditions on the part of the enserfed peasantry, the *Cossacks, and urban Orthodox Ukrainians led to the 1648 uprising under B. *Khmelnytsky. Polish landowners, Catholics, and Jews were the main victims of the uprising. In many cities, particularly in the Podilia and Volhynia regions and Left-Bank Ukraine, the Jewish population was decimated. Jewish eyewitness chroniclers (eg, Nathan Hanover) estimate the figure of casualties between 100,000 and 120,000. In light of the estimated size of the Jewish population in Ukraine in 1648 (ca 51,000), this figure reflects rather the trauma of the experience and not the actual numbers. Nonetheless Jews, perceived as representatives of the Polish landlords, suffered greatly during the uprising. To escape persecution, some Jews converted to Christianity.

The status of Jews was very different in the Russian-dominated *Hetman state. The Russian government was opposed to Jewish immigration and, beginning with Peter I, forbade Jews from settling in Left-Bank Ukraine. Nevertheless, because the economic value of Jewish settlers was recognized by officials of the Hetmanate, the decrees issued by St Petersburg for the expulsion of Jews from Left-Bank Ukraine were not always enforced, and several petitions were addressed to St Petersburg requesting permission to allow Jews in. Most Jews, however, lived in Right-Bank Ukraine, which remained under Polish control until 1772.

The economic hardship of the peasantry and the intensified national and religious oppression by Poland in these areas caused popular unrest that came to be directed also against Jews. This unrest was manifested in the *Haidamaka uprisings, and especially the *Koliivshchyna rebellion of 1768, when 50,000–60,000 Jews perished out of a total Jewish population of about 300,000 in Right-Bank Ukraine. Nevertheless, Jewish immigration to Ukraine continued throughout the 18th century, and while most Jews lived in poverty, some began to acquire great wealth.

After the partition of Poland in the late 18th century, the presence of 900,000 Jews on what was now Russian imperial territory forced the Russian government to abandon its previous policy of exclusion of Jews from Russia proper. In 1772 (and 1791, 1804, 1835) the government established a territorial region called the *Pale of Settlement beyond which Jewish settlement was prohibited. In Ukraine this area included almost all the former Polish-controlled territories; the Left-Bank gubernias of Chernihiv and Poltava, except for the crown hamlets; New Russia gubernia; Kiev gubernia, but not the city; and Bessarabia (1812). The Pale existed, with some special criteria permitting individual Jews to live outside it, until 1915.

During the reign of Alexander I (1801–25) the position of Jews initially improved as restrictions on their movement and enrollment in schools were eased and official anti-Semitic propaganda abated. Economically, Jews prospered in Southern Ukraine, where they played a major role in the grain trade; they acquired an especially strong presence in such commercial centers as *Odessa, *Kremenchuk, and *Berdychiv. In 1817 Jews owned 30 percent of the factories in Russian-ruled Ukraine. Towards the end of Alexander's rule, however, state-sponsored conversion attempts and expulsions from certain areas were encouraged.

Under Nicholas I (1825–55) official persecution of the Jews increased dramatically. Of the 1,200 laws affecting Jews between 1649 and 1881, more than half were instituted during his reign. Among these provisions were compulsory military service for Jews (1827), including the conscription of children; expulsions from cities (Kiev, Kherson, and Sevastopil); abolition of the kahal (1844); banning of the public use of Hebrew and Yiddish; aggressive conversion measures; and further travel and settlement restrictions (1835). In 1844 a decree was issued that created new Jewish schools similar to the parish and district schools and that aimed to assimilate the Jews.

Jews benefited from the brief period of liberalism that initially characterized the reign of Alexander II (1855–81). With the rise of the Jewish emancipation movement a few restrictions were loosened: some Jews – among them merchants of the first guild (1859), university graduates (1861), and various categories of artisans and tradesmen (1865) – were granted freedom of movement; and conscription of Jews into the army was placed on the same basis as for other subjects of the empire (1856), which included the abolition of the conscription of children. By 1872 Jews were actively engaged in the major industries in Ukraine: they comprised 90 percent of all those occupied in distilling and 32 percent in the sugar industry. But with the Odessa pogrom in 1871, the momentum for reform was quickly reversed, especially after the assassination of the tsar, and new laws restricting Jewish economic activity were introduced. In 1873, the rabbinical college in Zhytomyr was transformed by the authorities into a secular school.

The reign of the tsar's successors, Alexander III (1881–96) and Nicholas II (1896–1917), ushered in an era of state-supported *pogroms (1881–2, 1903, 1905), charges of ritual murder in the *Beilis affair (1913), expulsions from Kiev (1886) and Moscow (1891), and stricter segregation of the Jewish population within the Pale (1882). Wide-scale pogroms took place in October 1905, when in one month 690 pogroms were carried out in 28 gubernias (of which 329 pogroms were in Chernihiv gubernia alone). Many of these outbursts were encouraged by the anti-Semitic *Black Hundreds movement.

The government limited educational opportunities in 1887 and again in 1907 by placing a quota on Jews to be admitted to secondary schools and universities: 10 percent within the Pale, 3 percent in Moscow and St Petersburg, and 5 percent in the rest of the empire. Jews could be admitted to the bar only with permission of the minister of justice (1887), and they could not vote in district *zemstvo assembly elections (1890), even though they were obliged to pay zemstvo taxes. Economically, Jews were deprived of an important source of livelihood when the government forbade them to acquire property outside towns or large villages (1882), forcing them into the cities, and again (1894) when the state declared a monopoly on the sale of spirits, refusing Jews licences to sell spirits (see *Propination). The desperate economic position of Jews in the Pale was reflected in the fact that 30 percent had to be supported by philanthropic relief. In essence, the Jews never achieved or were never granted emancipation under tsarist Russian rule.

The reaction to these repressive measures and activities was a dramatic increase in Jewish emigration to North America, increased support for the *Zionist movement (the largest Jewish political movement by 1917), and active participation in all-Russian revolutionary or Jewish socialist political parties. Among the latter were the *Bund and the smaller Jewish Socialist Labor Party, Zionist Socialist Labor Party, and Poale Zion.

During the First World War more than 500,000 Jews were deported from the military zones, and as the Russian army defeats increased, so the position of the Jews deteriorated. They were accused of being spies and traitors and of undermining the regime.

In Austria-Hungary, Jews did not receive rights equal to those of the general population until 1868. Until then, their rights were limited by the Josephine patents, which sought to assimilate Jews and to involve them in agriculture. When Galicia (1772) and Bukovyna (1774) were incorporated into the Austro-Hungarian Empire, most Jews in Galicia were concentrated in the eastern part of this crown land. They made up about 11 percent of the population of Galicia both in 1869 (575,433) and in 1900 (811,183). Sixty percent of Jews were engaged in trade and commerce in an area where 75 percent of the population (and 94 percent of Ukrainians) earned its livelihood from agriculture and forestry. Jews formed an absolute majority in many important trading centers, such as *Brody on the Russian border. Jews figured prominently as officials attached to the estates (stewards, overseers, labor recruiters); as storekeepers, leaseholders of Polish estates, and tavernkeepers; as officials in local government; and in the working class (as workers in the oil industry centered in the *Drohobych-Boryslav Industrial Region).

Only about 60 percent of eastern Galicia's Jews lived in cities and towns. Jews in rural areas represented a sizable portion of Galicia's Jewish population, and they were an anomaly in comparison to Jewish demographic patterns elsewhere. Both in terms of their numbers and because of their precarious position as middlemen between lord and peasant, rural Jews were often the scapegoats for dissatisfaction and resentment. Many among the non-Jewish population shared a hostile view of Jews as exploiters and servants of the Polish nobility and landowners, even though the vast majority of Jews lived in poverty, like their Ukrainian neighbors. In contrast to conditions in the Russian Empire, however, there were no pogroms; rather, the social and economic character of this antagonism was expressed in political and economic competition. As a vulnerable minority, Jews in Galicia usually voted with the ruling Polish nation, and throughout the second half of the 19th century Poles and Jews worked closely during the elections to parliament. After universal male suffrage was proclaimed in 1907, some Jews (especially supporters of the Zionist movement) allied themselves with Ukrainian political parties.

The collapse of tsarism in March 1917 soon brought emancipation for the Jews in the Russian Empire. On 20 March the Provisional Government declared that Jews were now equal citizens; they were not, however, granted national minority status or autonomy.

In Ukraine, the *Central Rada established in March 1917 decided in late July to invite the minority nationalities (Russians, Poles, and Jews) to join its ranks. As a result, 50 Jews, from all the major parties, joined the Central Rada and 5 joined the Little Rada. The Jewish parties were also represented in the *General Secretariat (later the *Council of National Ministers of the UNR). M. Rafes, a Bundist, took on the post of general controller. Within the secretariat of nationalities, departments were set up for each minority and M. Silberfarb, of the United Jewish Socialist Workers' party, was appointed undersecretary for Jewish affairs. He became general secretary for Jewish affairs, with ministerial ranking, on the formation of the UNR (20 November 1917), and then minister for Jewish affairs when the proclamation of Ukrainian independence was issued (25 January 1918). Responsibility for Jewish affairs under the Central Rada thus passed from a department (undersecretariat) to a secretariat and then to a ministry. An advisory council representing the main Jewish parties was formed on 10 October 1917 and the Provisional National Council of the Jews of Ukraine convened in November 1918. Yiddish was one of the languages used by the Central Rada on its official currency and in proclamations, and the law on *national-personal autonomy gave non-Ukrainian nationalities the right to manage their national life independently. However, during the regime of Hetman P. Skoropadsky (see *Hetman government), this law was rescinded (9 July 1918) and the Ministry of Jewish Affairs abolished.

Under the *Directory, the Ministry of Jewish Affairs (headed at first by A. Revutsky) was re-established, and the law on national-personal autonomy was re-enacted. From April 1919, as the Directory was forced to move constantly westwards, the minister of Jewish affairs was P. Krasny. Other Jews who occupied prominent positions in the Central Rada or Directory governments were S. *Goldelman, a deputy minister of trade and industry and of labor, and A. *Margolin, a member of the Ukrainian Party of Socialists-Federalists who was deputy minister of foreign affairs and a diplomatic representative in London and at the Paris Peace talks. Several prominent Zionists also supported Ukrainian autonomy, including V. *Zhabotinsky, D. Pasmanik, and J. Schechtman.

The Central Rada government was the first in history to grant Jews autonomy (see *National minorities), and its relationship with Jewish political parties was generally amicable. All Jewish parties in the Central Rada voted for the creation of the UNR and, because they were categorically opposed to the Bolsheviks, saw the Republic as the only remaining parliamentary democracy. The subsequent declaration of independence, however, was opposed by the Bund, and the other Jewish parties, including the Zionists, abstained from voting. In general, the mainstream Jewish public did not respond positively to the Central Rada and Jews preferred a united all-Russian government to better represent the interests of the Jewish minority. Neither was there full confidence in the Ukrainian government's ability or willingness to halt the spread of pogroms in Ukraine and to organize a strong military presence.

The scale of the pogroms during the revolution in Ukraine was devastating for the Jewish population. The Whites (see A. *Denikin), peasant bands, otamans, and some units of the UNR Army, having regarded Jews as pro-Bolshevik, all took part in these atrocities, as did the anarchists (see N. *Makhno) and the Red Army. However, just before the formation of the Directory, elections to the Jewish communal councils indicated that of the 270,497 votes cast, 66 percent were for non-socialist parties (Orthodox and Zionist), while 34 percent voted for socialist party representatives.

The government and high command of the UNR Army tried to combat the instigators of the pogroms. Orders were issued imposing courts-martial for pogromists and some executions were carried out. The government assisted pogrom survivors and co-operated with both the Jewish community and foreign representatives in investigations of the pogroms.

In Galicia, Jews were neutral in the Polish-Ukrainian conflict but later supported the *Western Ukrainian National Republic government. They were granted equality and national rights, including permission to create their own police units. Some Jews served in the ranks of the Ukrainian Galician Army (see *Jewish Battalion).

The consolidation of Bolshevik rule brought the Jewish community both hardships and opportunities. Under *War Communism (1918–21), when free commerce was banned and private businesses nationalized, Jews suffered great economic setbacks. Moreover, the Bolsheviks seemed determined to destroy the last vestiges of organized Jewish life. In April 1919 they abolished most community organizations. As part of their general antireligious campaign they also closed down many synagogues and outlawed religious and Hebrew education. In Ukraine the Bolsheviks pursued a vigorous anti-Yiddish policy aimed at assimilating Jews; eg, the number of Yiddish books published declined from 274 in 1919 to 40 in 1923.

At the same time, formal and informal restrictions against Jewish participation in government and administration were abolished, especially for those who chose the path of assimilation. Special Jewish sections (the so-called *yevsektsii*) were formed within the Party to facilitate Jewish participation, and it was often these groups that most strongly attacked the Zionist and traditional Jewish parties. Individual Jews benefited from the pro-Russian and pro-urban orientation of the Party, and many became part of the system, especially in education, the economy, and the middle echelons of the Party administration and government. Although only one-half of 1 percent of the total Jewish population joined the Bolshevik party, they constituted a large percentage of all Bolsheviks in Ukraine, in 1922 approx 13.6 percent of the CP(B)U. Fully 15.5 percent of the delegates to the 5th and 7th all-Ukrainian Congress of Soviets in 1921 and 1922 were of Jewish origin.

In an effort to consolidate the regime and broaden its support among the non-Russian nations, the Bolsheviks instituted a number of important changes in 1923. As a solution to the 'nationalities problem' the policy of *indigenization was adopted. This policy encouraged the use of national languages and the recruitment of non-Russians into the Party, education, and the government. It is difficult to judge what effect the Ukrainian version of indigenization, *Ukrainization, had on Ukraine's Jewish population. Since only 0.9 percent of all Ukrainian Jews (in 1926) declared their mother tongue to be Ukrainian, the introduction of Ukrainian as the official language certainly limited their opportunities in the Party, government, and scholarship. Moreover, the active recruitment of Ukrainians meant that the Jewish proportion would decline in these sectors. In 1923 Jews constituted 47.4 percent of students at higher educational institutions, but in 1929, only 23.3 percent, and their percentage in the CP(B)U fell from 13.6 in 1923 to 11.2 in 1926. Yet, in a speech to the 15th Congress of the Russian CP(B) in December 1927, S. Ordzhonikidze, the head of the Central Control Commission of the Party, reported that Jews still constituted 22.6 percent of the governmental machinery in Ukraine and 30.3 percent in the city of Kiev. The first secretary of the CC CP(B)U from 1925 to 1926, L. *Kaganovich, was of Jewish descent. In the end, Ukrainization was only a partial success, and it was finally abandoned in 1933 in favor of strict *Russification.

Indigenization brought obvious benefits to the Jews as well. Jewish culture flourished in Ukraine, and several Yiddish theaters, institutes, periodical publications, and schools were established. Soviets in which the official language was Yiddish were established to administer the Jewish population: there were 117 such Soviets in 1926 and 156 by 1931. Moreover, Yiddish-language courts were set up, and the government offered a variety of services in Yiddish.

The *New Economic Policy (NEP), which was introduced in 1921 to allow for some measure of private capitalist activity, was another significant development for the Jewish community. Many Jewish artisans re-established their private shops and at least 13 percent of all Ukrainian Jews became involved in commerce (1926). According to the census of 1926, fully 78.5 percent of all private factories in Ukraine under NEP were Jewish owned. This situation was short-lived. In the second half of the 1920s the Soviet authorities increasingly cut back on private capitalism, and NEP was for all practical purposes stopped by 1930.

In the 1920s the Soviet regime placed a major emphasis on changing the traditional social and economic structure of Jewish life, primarily by encouraging Jews to become engaged in agriculture. Jewish agricultural colonies had existed in Ukraine, especially Southern Ukraine, from the late 18th century. In 1924 the Soviet government set up two official bodies to promote Jewish rural settlement; they were assisted by the American Jewish Joint Distribution Committee, which provided funds and machinery. From 69,000 in 1926, the number of Jewish farmers in the Ukrainian SSR increased to 172,000 in 1931; of these, 37,000 lived on colonies established under Soviet rule. One of the goals of some Jewish community leaders was the establishment of a Jewish territorial unit – an *autonomous oblast or even *autonomous soviet socialist republic – on Ukrainian territory. As a first step, three Jewish raions were established: Kalinindorf (in Kherson okruha), founded in 1927; Novozlatopil (Zaporizhia okruha), in 1929; and Stalindorf (Kryvyi Rih okruha), in 1930. Eventually this plan was abandoned, at least partly because of the opposition of Ukrainian government leaders who feared the truncation of their republic; instead, in 1934 the Birobidzhan Jewish Autonomous oblast was established in the Far East. In the second half of the 1930s, most Jews left these agricultural colonies, either for Birobidzhan or for the cities.

The end of indigenization brought an end to the renaissance of organized Jewish life in the USSR. The Yiddish-language governmental institutions, the *yevsektsii*, the Yiddish writers' organizations, and many major cultural and scholarly institutions (eg, the *Institute of Jewish Culture in Kiev) were closed down, and the formal support given by the regime to Jewish developments was replaced by a growing official anti-Semitism. Many Jewish activists fell victims to the Stalinist terror of the 1930s.

In Western Ukraine during the interwar period strong economic competition from Ukrainian co-operatives and from private commercial and industrial firms eroded the economic base of Jewish life in Poland, Czechoslovakia, and Rumania. The Polish government, and such Polish anti-Semitic groups as Rozwój, initiated anti-Jewish measures and activities. Despite the perception of economic antagonism between Jews and Ukrainians, there was some political co-operation: eg, in the 1922 and 1928 elections to the Polish Parliament, when Ukrainian and Jewish parties joined the coalition Bloc of National Minorities, and in the elections to the Czechoslovak and Rumanian parliaments. Repressive Polish measures against Ukrainians and the co-operation of some Jewish leaders with the Polish government led to resentment of the Jews.

The first Soviet occupation of Western Ukraine (1939–41) followed the pattern already established in the USSR. On the one hand, Jewish national and cultural rights were limited, traditional institutions were abolished, and the economy was restructured and nationalized, bringing great hardships to artisans and merchants. On the other, individual Jews were given better opportunities as the official quotas, limiting their access to education and the professions, were abolished. Overall, many Jews welcomed the Soviet occupation, as it brought an end to the official anti-Semitism of the Polish regime and staved off the threat of Nazi occupation.

The German occupation of Ukraine during the Second World War – and, indeed, the entire war period – was a tragedy for Ukrainian Jews. Within the enlarged 1941 boundaries of the Soviet Union, 2.5 of the 4.8 million Jews were killed. In Western Ukraine only 2 percent (17,000) of the entire Jewish population survived. The destruction of Jews began in fall 1941, initially in central Ukraine and then in Western Ukraine. In Kiev alone, 35,000–70,000 Jews were murdered at *Babyn Yar. Mass murder of Jews was carried out throughout Ukraine in 1942–4. Apart from the involvement of individuals and some organized auxiliary units, the Ukrainian population did not take part in these genocidal actions. Despite the penalty of death for aiding Jews, a number of Ukrainians, among them Metropolitan A. *Sheptytsky, tried to save Jews.

The Jewish population suffered severe discrimination in the postwar years. The crackdown on Jewish community life intensified as the teaching of Hebrew was

prohibited, the Yiddish theater was abolished, Yiddish publications were suspended, hundreds of Jewish leaders were arrested (1948), and Yiddish writers were imprisoned. Twenty-four of the more prominent leaders and writers in the USSR were executed after a secret trial in August 1952. In 1953 Stalin's persecutions came to a head with the so-called doctors' plot, in which nine doctors, six of them Jewish, were accused of conspiring with Western powers to poison Soviet leaders. Thousands of Jews were removed from official posts, particularly from the armed forces and security services, and their role in the Party was reduced. In higher educational institutions quotas were imposed on the numbers of Jewish students admitted.

After Stalin's death the situation for individual Jews improved somewhat, but the assimilatory campaign and repression of Jewish culture and religion continued. Anti-Semitism in the guise of 'anti-Zionism' became, and continues to be, part of Soviet internal and foreign policy. Soviet Ukrainian educational institutions are also used in this campaign; for example, the AN URSR in 1963 published T. Kichko's anti-Semitic pamphlet, *Judaism without Embellishment*. Only about 60 synagogues have survived into the 1980s in the USSR, and, of these, more than half are in the Georgian Republic.

After the 1967 Six-Day War in the Middle East and the emergence of the *dissident movement in the Soviet Union, a strong Jewish emigration movement arose. In the 1970s there was a massive emigration of Jews from Ukraine to the West, including *Israel and North America. Between 1970 and 1980, 250,000 Soviet citizens emigrated on Israeli visas. By 1980 severe restrictions were placed on Jewish emigration; it is estimated that in 1981 alone, approx 40,000 were refused permission to emigrate.

Ukrainian dissidents, including I. Dziuba, S. Karavansky, Ye. Sverstiuk, V. Chornovil, L. Pliushch, and P. Grigorenko, have worked with Jewish activists (eg. E. Kuznetsov, A. Shifrin, A. Radygin, and Y. Zigels) in advocating Jewish-Ukrainian co-operation. *Ukraïns'kyi visnyk*, the Ukrainian **samvydav* journal, continuously reported on the persecution of Jewish activists.

In 1979 Ukrainian Jewish émigrés in Israel formed the Public Committee for Jewish-Ukrainian Cooperation, which in 1981 became the Society of Jewish-Ukrainian Relations, headed by Ya. Suslensky. Even earlier, in the 1950s, a commission of Jewish-Ukrainian affairs was established at the Ukrainian Academy of Arts and Sciences in New York, and in 1953 the Association to Perpetuate the Memory of Ukrainian Jews was formed in New York, headed by M. Osherovych.

Demography. At the end of the 19th century there were approx 3 million Jews living in ethnographic Ukrainian territories (see table 1). Ukraine at that time had the highest concentration of Jews in the world, with some 30 percent of the total world population of Jewry (1.3 million Jews lived in Poland and 1.2 million in Lithuania and Belorussia). In the eight Ukrainian gubernias of Russian-ruled Ukraine in 1897, 43.3 percent of all Jews worked in commerce, 32.2 in crafts and industry, 7.3 in private services, 5.8 in public services (including the liberal professions), 3.7 in communication, 2.9 in agriculture, and 4.8 in no permanent occupation.

TABLE 1
Jews in Ukraine, 1897 and 1900

Region	No. in 1,000s	% of total population
Russian Empire (1897)	2,245	7.4
Austria–Hungary (1900)	730	13.0
Galicia	610	12.8
Transcarpathia	55	11.2
Bukovyna	65	15.6
Total (1897)	2,950	8.3
Within the current boundaries of the Ukrainian SSR	2,680	9.3

Almost 60 percent of Ukrainian Jews lived in cities and constituted one-third of the urban population of the country (see *Cities and towns). Because of their confinement to the Pale, the Dnieper River served as a major demographic demarcation line. In Western and Right-Bank Ukraine, Jews made up 10–15 percent of the population, but in Left-Bank Ukraine, only 4–6 percent. In most cities of Western and Right-Bank Ukraine they constituted a relative majority (40 percent on average), while they formed an absolute majority in such cities as Berdychiv (78 percent), Uman (58 percent), and Bila Tserkva (53 percent).

The First World War and the subsequent upheavals of 1917–21 in the central and western lands led to a significant decrease in the Jewish population as a result of casualties and a sizable emigration. The abolition of the Pale of Settlement enabled Jews to move to other parts of the old Russian Empire as well as to eastern Ukraine and the Kuban region. As a result, the Jewish population in Ukrainian territories decreased from 8.3 percent of the total population in 1897 to 5.5 percent in 1926. (Jewish population distribution is given in table 2.)

Overall, the greatest percentage decreases occurred in Right-Bank Ukraine, while the greatest increases occurred in Slobidska Ukraine (particularly in Kharkiv). The distribution of Jewish population by geographic region for 1897 and 1926 is given in table 3.

Demographic data for the Ukrainian SSR in 1926 illustrate the high rates of Jewish urbanization: 26 percent of the total Jewish population lived in villages, 51.6 percent lived in cities of 100,000 or less, and 22.2 percent lived in cities with a population of more than 100,000. Moreover, the concentration of Jews in medium- and large-sized cities, a process that began in the 19th century, continued. Between 1897 and 1926, the number of Jews decreased by 33 percent in villages and by 22 percent in towns of less than 20,000; meanwhile, their number increased by 7 percent in cities of 20,000 to 100,000 and by 106 percent in cities of over 100,000. In 1897, 27.4 percent of Ukraine's urban population was Jewish; in 1926, 22.8 percent.

The cities with the largest populations of Jews in 1926 (1897 figures in parentheses) were Odessa, 154,000 or 36.5 percent of the total population (140,000, 34.8 percent); Kiev, 140,500 or 27.3 percent (31,800, 12.8); Kharkiv, 81,500 or 19.5 percent (11,000, 6.3); and Dnipropetrovske, 62,000 or 26.7 percent (40,000, 35.5). In 1931 Lviv's Jewish population numbered 98,000 or 31.9 percent (in 1900 the respective figures were 44,300 and 26.5), and in Chernivtsi, 42,600 or 37.9 percent (21,600 or 32.8 percent). Before the First World War, Odessa had the third-largest Jewish population in the world after New York and Warsaw. According to the 1926 Soviet Ukrainian census, the distribution of the Jews by occupation was as follows: 20.6 percent in arts and crafts, 20.6 in public services (administrative work), 15.3 workers, 13.3 in commerce, 9.2 in agriculture, 1.6 in liberal professions, 8.9 unemployed, 7.3 of no profession; the rest were classified in a miscellaneous category. The proportion of Jews in economic administration was 40.6 percent, and in medical-sanitary administration, 31.9 percent.

The use, and even the knowledge, of Yiddish began

TABLE 2
Jews in Ukraine, 1926–33

Region	No. in 1,000s	% of total population
Ukrainian SSR (1926)	1,580	5.4
Poland (1931)	932[1]	10.1
Rumania (1930)	129[2]	10.4
Czechoslovakia (1930)	89	12.1
All Ukrainian ethnographic territories (1933)	2,980	5.5
Ukrainian SSR within current borders	2,720	6.5

1 In Galicia 556,000 (10.3 percent), in Volhynia and Polisia 307,000 (10.3), and in the Kholm and Podlachia regions 69,000 (9.2)
2 In Bukovyna 55,000 (11.9) and in Bessarabia 68,000 (9.1)

TABLE 3
Distribution of Jews by geographic region

Region	1897 in 1000s	1897 %	1926 in 1000s	1926 %	% in cities/villages
Western Ukraine	1,120	13.1	1,020	10.3	38.0/4.6
Central Ukraine	1,475	13.5	1,210	8.4	31.6/3.2
Left-Bank Ukraine	330	4.6	360	3.2	18.8/0.5
Slobidska region and Donbas	25	0.5	140	1.6	7.4/0.1
The Caucasus	–	–	10	0.2	0.9/ –
All ethnographic Ukrainian territories	2,950	8.3	2,740	5.5	21.5/1.8

to decline sharply in the 20th century, particularly in larger cities: in 1926 only 76 percent of Jews in the Ukrainian SSR claimed Yiddish as their mother tongue (70 percent of the urban and 95 percent of the rural population), while 23 percent listed Russian and barely 1 percent listed Ukrainian. The extent of Russification is evidenced by the fact that only 16 percent had no written knowledge of Russian and as many as 31 percent had no written knowledge of Yiddish (78 percent could not write in Ukrainian).

On the eve of the Second World War there were about 3 million Jews in Ukrainian lands; they constituted 20 percent of the total world Jewish population and 60 percent of the Jewish population of the USSR. During the war the Germans murdered most of the Jews in the territories they occupied. The only ones who survived were those who had been saved by Ukrainians at the risk of their own lives or were evacuated to the eastern reaches of the USSR before the German advance, and some in Transcarpathia, Bessarabia, and Bukovyna, where there was no direct German occupation, and where the deportation and extermination of the Jewish population was not as complete.

TABLE 4
Jews in Ukraine, 1959 and 1970, in 1,000s

	1959	1970
City of Kiev	154	152
Odessa oblast	121	117
Kharkiv oblast	84	76
Dnipropetrovske oblast	73	69
Vinnytsia oblast	50	42
Donetske oblast	43	40
Chernivtsi oblast	42	37
Zhytomyr oblast	42	36
Lviv oblast	30	28
Crimean oblast	26	26

Since the Second World War the Jewish population in the Ukrainian SSR has declined steadily. In the 20 years from 1959 to 1979 it decreased by 24.5 percent, from 840,000 in 1959 to 777,000 in 1970 (which constituted 1.65 percent of the population of Ukraine, and 36.1 percent of the total Soviet Jewish population) and 634,000 in 1979. This decline has been caused by low birth rates, the rise in intermarriages, and, since 1971, mass emigration. Table 4 shows the present distribution of Jews in Kiev and in oblasts in which they number more than 20,000. Jews now live almost exclusively in provincial centers and in larger cities. They are virtually absent in towns and villages.

Cultural life. From the very beginning of mass Jewish settlement in Ukraine, Jewish cultural and religious life was highly developed. The impressive stone synagogues throughout Ukraine serve as interesting historical monuments to Jewish material culture. The more notable ones, such as those in Volhynia (in Dubno, Lutske, and Liubomyl), date back to the 16th–18th centuries. The Cossack uprisings of the 17th century, the destruction wrought by the *Cossack-Polish War of 1648–57, and the general social and economic dislocations of the era initiated a period of great change for the Jewish population of Ukraine. Many Jewish scholars fled to the West, where they founded Talmudic centers in Holland, Germany, and Bohemia. Religious disillusionment spread and many Jews sought solace in a variety of ascetic or mystical movements. *Hasidism, which was founded in Ukraine by Israel Ba'al Shem Tov, became the dominant religious trend in Western Ukraine. In the late 18th century the *Haskalah* or Enlightenment movement, inspired by Moses Mendelssohn, emerged. Adherents of this movement sought a synthesis of Jewish religious tradition with the demands of modern life. The Enlightenment movement later fostered the spread of Zionism, which had many adherents in Ukraine.

The rebirth of Hebrew and its application to modern life also originated with Jews from Ukraine. Ahad Ha-Am (1856–1927), who was born in the Kiev region, is considered the founder of 'cultural' or 'Spiritual' Zionism. Also of Ukrainian origin are the famous Hebrew lyric poet Hayyim Nahman Bialik (1873–1934) and the poet Saul Tchernichowsky (1875–1943). The brilliant tradition of Yiddish culture in the 16th–18th centuries was continued in Ukraine by Shalom Aleichem (Rabinovitz, 1859–1916), who profoundly influenced an entire generation of Jewish writers. After 1920 Chernivtsi became an important center of Jewish culture.

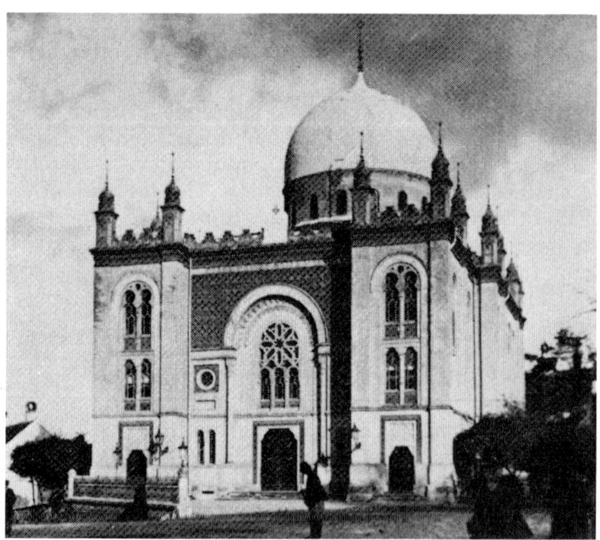

Synagogue in Chernivtsi

The Jewish press developed rapidly from the mid-19th century. The first serials, published in Russian and Yiddish, appeared in Odessa; they included *Rassvet* (1860) and *Zion* (1861). In the early 20th century in Galicia, the Jewish daily *Chwila* and a number of other periodicals were established in Lviv.

In the Ukrainian SSR during the period 1923–34, Jews benefited from the granting of national rights and freedom for cultural development. Yiddish was recognized as an official language and used in administrative matters in Jewish soviets. Many Jewish periodicals were established; eg, *Stern*, the official organ of the CC CPU and the All-Ukrainian Council of Trade Unions. All laws and government directives were also published in Yiddish. In the Ukrainian SSR in 1925 there were 393 trade and technical schools in which the language of instruction was Yiddish, attended by 61,400 students or one-third of the total Jewish student population. There were four

Jewish pedagogical institutes and separate departments in the Institute of People's Education in Odessa. In 1928, 69,000 students attended 475 Jewish schools, and by 1931 there were 831 schools and 94,000 students. The closing of Jewish schools began in 1933–4, at the same time as the abolition of Ukrainization. By the start of the Second World War, the Jewish educational system had, for all practical purposes, been abolished.

The higher academic institutions devoted to the study of Jewish culture included the VUAN Hebraic Historical-Archeographic Commission and Chair of Jewish Culture, which became the Institute of Jewish Culture in 1929. The All-Ukrainian Mendele Mokher Seforim Museum of Jewish culture was established in Odessa, while the Central Jewish Library was located in Kiev.

Jewish theaters, which had been prominent in the theatrical and artistic life of prerevolutionary Ukraine, continued to exist under Soviet rule. In 1922 permanent Jewish theaters were organized in Kiev and Odessa, and a Jewish department of the Kiev Institute of Theater Arts was established in 1934. Many Jewish poets and writers became active in the 1920s, publishing in Yiddish, including L. Kvitko, I. Fefer, D. Feldman, D. Nister, Kh. Hildin, and A. Reizin. Their works were translated into Ukrainian by P. Tychyna, M. Rylsky, and others. Jewish cultural activists were subjected to the same wave of repressions in the 1930s as were directed at Ukrainians and many Jewish institutions were closed by the authorities. After the Second World War all expressions of Jewish culture were stifled in Ukraine. From 1950 to 1952 a number of Jewish writers and cultural activists were murdered by the NKVD, among them D. Bergelson, D. Hofstein, P. Markish, I. Fefer, L. Kvitko, P. Kaganovich-Nistor, and A. Kushnirov.

Ukrainian themes are found in the works of Jewish writers active in Ukraine, such as M. Mokher Seforim (1836–1917), Shalom Aleichem, Sh. Frug, Sh. Asch, and B. Horowitz, and among those active in the diaspora, such as H.N. Bialik, Sh. Bikel, and R. Korn.

A number of Jewish writers became part of the general Ukrainian literary process: the poets L. Pervomaisky, S. Holovanivsky, I. Kulyk, A. Katsnelson; the prose writers N. Rybak, L. Smiliansky; the dramatist L. Yukhvid; the literary historians and critics Ye. Aizenshtok, A. Leites, S. Shchupak, I. Stebun (Katsnelson), O. Borshchahivsky, Ye. Adelheim, and A. Hozenpud. Also active in Ukrainian circles were the historians Y. Hermaize and S. Borovoi and the linguist O. Kurylo. Many of the above were repressed during the purges in the 1930s. In the 1970s and 1980s, the poets L. Kyselov and M. Fishbein (the latter emigrated to the West in 1979) also wrote in Ukrainian.

Two of the more prominent translators of Ukrainian poetry were D. Hofstein, who published translations of Shevchenko's poetry in 1937, and A. Klein, who published a collection of translations of Ukrainian folk works in Kolomyia, in 1936. An important role in the popularization of Ukrainian literature was played by Ya. Orenstein, the founder and owner of Ukrainska Nakladnia, a publishing house based in Kolomyia and Berlin. It was established in 1903 and in the next 30 years published hundreds of Ukrainian titles.

An interesting development was the attempt made by Jewish émigrés to establish a Ukrainian theater in the United States. In Philadelphia, I. Ginzberg led a Jewish-Ukrainian acting company in 1910–12, I. Elgard (Izydor Elgardiv) led a touring theater group in 1916–17, and D. Medovy led his own Jewish-Ukrainian theatrical company in 1917–28. All of them staged Ukrainian plays and helped popularize them.

The unique nature of Jewish-Ukrainian relations is reflected in the Ukrainian oral tradition. The popular song of the traditional spring cycle *Ïde ïde Zel'man* hearkens back to the days when Jews held leases on Ukrainian churches. Motifs on Jewish privileges appeared frequently in the *dumas. One of the so-called younger dumas is called *Zhydivski utysky* (Jewish Oppressions). In various **vertep* dramas and *intermedes the sympathetic and comic figure of the Jew appears with the Zaporozhian cossack, the noble, and the Gypsy. Among the many Ukrainian authors who have portrayed Jews have been T. Shevchenko, I. Franko, S. Rudansky, Ya. Shchoholiv, T. Borduliak, M. Levytsky, M. Kotsiubynsky, V. Vynnychenko, O. Oles, A. Liubchenko, L. Pervomaisky, M. Khvylovy, B. Antonenko-Davydovych, Ya. Hrymailo, and Yu. Smolych.

Today the role of Jews in Ukraine has significantly decreased, although they remain the second largest minority after the Russians. (See also *Anti-Semitism.)

BIBLIOGRAPHY

Dubnow, S. *History of the Jews in Russia and Poland from the Earliest Times until the Present Day*, 3 vols (Philadelphia 1916–20)

Mytsiuk, O. *Agraryzatsiia zhydivstva Ukraïny na tli zahal'noï ekonomiky* (Prague 1933)

Levitas, I. *The Jewish Community in Russia, 1772–1844* (New York 1943)

Greenberg, L. *The Jews in Russia: The Struggle for Emancipation*, 2 vols (New Haven 1944, 1951)

Baron, S. *A Social and Religious History of the Jews*, 2nd rev edn, 17 vols (New York 1952–78)

– *The Russian Jew under Tsars and Soviets* (New York 1964)

Ukrainians and Jews: A Symposium (New York 1966)

Goldelman, S. *Jewish National Autonomy in Ukraine 1917–1920* (Chicago 1968)

Kochan, L. (ed). *The Jews in Soviet Russia since 1917* (New York 1970)

Gitelman, Z. *Jewish Nationality and Soviet Politics: The Jewish Section of the CPSU* (Princeton 1972)

Weinryb, B.D. 'The Hebrew Chronicles on Bohdan Khmel'-nyts'kyi and the Cossack-Polish War,' *HUS*, vol 1, no. 2 (June 1977)

Frankel, J. *Prophecy and Politics: Socialism, Nationalism, and the Russian Jews, 1862–1917* (New York 1981)

Levitats, I. *The Jewish Community in Russia, 1844–1917* (Jerusalem 1981)

Redlich, S. 'Jews,' in *Guide to the Study of the Soviet Nationalities: Non-Russian Peoples of the USSR*, ed by S. Horak (Littleton, Colo 1982)

Mendelsohn, E. *The Jews of East Central Europe between the World Wars* (Bloomington, Ind 1983)

Pinkus. B. *The Soviet Government and the Jews, 1918–1967: A Documented Study* (Cambridge 1984)

Goldberg, J. *Jewish Privileges in the Polish Commonwealth* (London 1985)

Aster, H.; Potichnyj, P. (eds). *Jewish-Ukrainian Relations in Historical Perspective* (Edmonton 1987)

V. Kubijovyč, V. Markus

Jimson weed (*Datura stramonium*; Ukrainian: *durman*). A poisonous annual weed of the potato family (Solanaceae), 1–2 m in height, with white or pale violet trumpet-shaped flowers and a round, spiny fruit. It grows throughout Ukraine. Its toxicity is due to atropine and other alkaloids. Jimson weed leaves are used medicinally as a sedative. Some varieties of the plant are used decoratively.

Jireček, Josef, b 9 October 1825 in Vysoké Mýto, Bohemia, d 25 November 1888 in Prague. Czech historian, philologist, and political figure. Jireček coedited or wrote several school textbooks for the various nationalities of the Austrian Empire. In 1859 he was appointed by the Austrian Ministry of Education to design a system for the Latin transcription of Ukrainian (see *Alphabet war). His proposal was published as *Über den Vorschlag das Ruthenische mit lateinischen Schriftzeichen zu schreiben* (1859). Although it was approved by the government and A. Gołuchowski, the governor general of Galicia, it was resisted by Galician Ukrainians as a form of Polonization and was never generally adopted. The materials on the Alphabet war were published in *Die ruthenische Sprach- und Schriftfrage in Galizien* (1861).

Joachim V. Patriarch of Antioch ca 1581–92. He was commissioned by the Constantinople Patriarch, Jeremiah II, to report on the status of the Kievan metropoly. In 1586 he visited Lviv and confirmed the new statute of the Lviv Dormition Brotherhood on behalf of Jeremiah granting the right of *stauropegion (direct subordination to a patriarch instead of a local bishop). This statute became the model for other Ukrainian brotherhoods.

John XXIII, Pope (secular name: Angello Roncalli), b 25 November 1881 in Sotto il Monte, Italy, d 3 June 1963 in Rome. As pope his greatest achievement was the calling of the Second Vatican Council, which opened in 1962 and closed after his death. The most important of his seven encyclicals were *Mater et Magistra* (1961) and *Pacem in terris* (1963). Through secret diplomacy John secured in 1963 the release from Siberia of Metropolitan Y. *Slipy, whom in 1960 he had designated cardinal *in pectore*. Furthermore he appointed Rev A. Velyky secretary of the Preparatory Commission for the Oriental Churches, and then of the Vatican Council Commission for the Oriental Churches. In April 1963 John raised the Ukrainian Lesser Seminary in Rome to the status of a pontifical college.

John-Paul II (secular name: Karol Wojtyła), b 18 May 1920 in Wadowice, Poland. The first Slavic pope, elected in October 1978. He is one of the first popes to speak openly about human rights violations in Communist countries and to defend the existence of the Catholic church, including the Ukrainian, in the USSR. Fluent in Ukrainian, during his frequent trips he has met many Ukrainian faithful, to whom he has issued addresses emphasizing the importance of maintaining rites, traditions, and national culture. In March 1979 he addressed an important letter to Cardinal Y. Slipy inaugurating the jubilee of the Millennium of the Baptism of Rus'-Ukraine. This letter drew a formal protest from the Moscow Patriarchate. In December 1979, along with Y. Slipy, he consecrated Rev M. Liubachivsky as archbishop. John-Paul II has recognized the legitimacy of regular and electoral synods of Ukrainian Catholic bishops. In 1980 he appointed M. Liubachivsky archbishop and co-adjutor of Lviv eparchy with the right of succession to Y. Slipy; Liubachivsky had been nominated by an extraordinary synod of Ukrainian bishops. In 1980 John-Paul II named a Ukrainian, Archbishop M. Marusyn, as secretary of the *Congregation of Eastern Churches, and in 1985 he elevated Liubachivsky to cardinal.

I. Khoma

Joint-stock company. A manufacturing or trading association in which the stock is divided into shares and the share owners bear a limited liability to the amount of their investment. Profits are distributed in the form of dividends proportionally to the shareholder's investment and irrespective of his function in the process of production.

In Ukraine the first joint-stock companies appeared at the end of the 18th century. By the 1860s they were quite common in the metallurgical and coal industries of the Donbas, and were financed mostly by foreign capital. Some of the more important joint-stock companies were the Cockerill-Dnieper Metallurgical Association, the Donets Company in Druzhkivka, the Central Donets Company in Almazna, and the *Prodamet and *Produgol syndicates. In 1911 joint-stock companies owned 5.3 percent of all manufacturing concerns and produced 60 percent of Ukraine's industrial output. By 1913 the shares in rail and urban transportation and other industries were worth 97 million rubles. One of the first Ukrainian joint-stock companies to appear in Western Ukraine was the *Narodna Torhovlia consumer co-operative (est 1883) in Lviv. During the NEP period the central government in Moscow used joint-stock companies as one of the means to control industry and trade in Soviet Ukraine. Thus the Radio Company created in Moscow in 1924 expanded its operations in 1925 to Kharkiv and Kiev, and then in 1927 to Dnipropetrovske, Artemivske, Staline, and Odessa. Beginning in 1928 joint-stock companies were replaced with state associations controlled by the appropriate Soviet commissariats. After the Second World War joint-stock companies, in which the Soviet Union had a controlling interest, were established in several East European countries. In the 1960s joint-stock companies with a limited participation of large Western firms began to reappear in the USSR.

L. Szuch

Jordanes or **Jordanis.** A 6th-century Goth historian. He was the secretary of the military leader of the Alans, Gunthigis (Baza). He is the author of the chronicle *De origine actibusque Getarum* (551), a basic source on the history of the *Goths, the Huns, and the tribes north of the Black Sea that contains valuable information about the ancient Slavs. The definitive edition of the work was published in *Monumentae Germaniae Historica*, vol 5 (1882).

Josefov. A town in Bohemia, Czechoslovakia. Between April 1921 and 1923 an internment camp for soldiers of the *Ukrainian Galician Army was located there. It was established following the liquidation of two previous internment camps in *Deutsch-Gabel and *Liberec. The internees formed a separate Ukrainian Brigade of approximately 4,000 men. They supported the Western Ukrainian National Republic (ZUNR) and filled the role of its exile army. The officers organized the Fighting Organization of Galicia, which was later transformed into the Ukrainian Military Organization Representation in Czechoslovakia, based in Prague and headed by Lt I.

*Rudnytsky. A demanding cultural-educational program was provided by members of the Cultural-Educational Committee. In 1922 the committee had 1,176 members in and outside the camp. The committee was seen as the center of all cultural and educational work for the ZUNR soldiers in Czechoslovakia.

In 1923, after Polish-Czechoslovak relations improved and the Galician question was settled internationally, the camp was gradually liquidated. Some of the internees returned to Galicia, but the majority obtained political immigrant status and remained in Czechoslovakia.

BIBLIOGRAPHY
Narizhnyi, S. *Ukraïns'ka emigratsiia* (Prague 1942)
Motyl, A.J. *The Turn to the Right: The Ideological Origins and Development of Ukrainian Nationalism 1919–1929* (Boulder, Colo 1980)

Y. Boshyk

Joseph II, b 13 March 1741 in Vienna, d 20 February 1790 in Vienna. Emperor of the Holy Roman Empire (1765–90), which he ruled together with his mother *Maria Theresa until 1780. During his rule, Austria annexed *Galicia (1772) during the first partition of Poland and acquired *Bukovyna (1774) from Turkey. Joseph concluded a formal alliance with Catherine II of Russia, forcing Austria to enter the Russo-Turkish War in 1788. An enlightened absolutist, he accelerated the reforms begun by Maria Theresa, which were aimed at strengthening the Habsburg Empire politically, economically, and militarily. Many of them benefited his Ukrainian subjects. To integrate Austria's multinational lands into a unitary state, a carefully controlled and centrally co-ordinated bureaucracy was put in charge of all branches of the administration and a police force with extensive powers was introduced. German became the official language in 1784 to facilitate the work of the central authority and to bind the empire. The Toleration Patent, which established religious equality before the law, was issued in 1781 in the belief that the loyalty of non-Catholics would thus be secured. To diminish the power of the Catholic church and raise revenue for the state, nearly 900 monasteries (including many Basilian ones) were dissolved in 1782; their properties were transformed into schools, philanthropic institutions, government buildings, army barracks, and even prisons. The priesthood was transformed into a civil service paid by the state (which dramatically improved the economic situation of the Greek Catholic clergy), bishops were deprived of much of their authority, and Greek Catholic priests received rights equal to those of the Roman clergy. *Lviv University and the *Greek Catholic Theological Seminary were opened in 1784, and the affiliated *Studium Ruthenum for Ukrainian priests was founded in 1787. Joseph's agrarian legislation of the 1780s did much to improve conditions for the Ukrainian peasantry. Among his major reforms were the limitation of corvée labor on the seigneurial estates to three days a week, the regulation of other feudal rents, and the abolition of the status of personal dependence on the seigneur (*Leibeigenschaft*). Joseph encouraged new agricultural methods and the colonization of Galicia by Germans. Equality before the law was promoted by the regulation of criminal procedures, the introduction of new law courts and new codes of civil law (1786), and criminal law (1787); the latter abolished torture, the death penalty, and brutal punishments. Joseph's reforms caused widespread unrest and even revolt (in the Netherlands and Hungary), and many of them were repealed even before his death. However, they did break the all-powerful position of the Polish nobility in Galicia and stimulated the rise of a Ukrainian intelligentsia.

BIBLIOGRAPHY
Rosdolsky, R. *Die grosse Steuer- und Agrarreform Josefs II: Ein Kapitel zur österreichischen Wirtschaftsgeschichte* (Warsaw 1961)

R. Senkus

Joukovsky, Arkadii. See Zhukovsky, Arkadii.

Journal of Ukrainian Studies. A semiannual interdisciplinary journal of Ukrainian studies, published since autumn 1976 by the *Canadian Institute of Ukrainian Studies. The managing editor was R. Senkus from 1976 to 1986; M. Yurkevich succeeded him in 1986.

Journalism. See Press.

Journals. See Periodicals.

Józewski, Henryk, b 1892 in Kiev, d 23 April 1981 in Warsaw. Polish political leader. From 1914 to 1920 he was a member of the Supreme Command of the 3rd (Ukrainian) Section of the underground Polish Military Organization. During the joint Ukrainian-Polish Kiev Campaign in 1920 he served as deputy minister of the interior in S. Petliura's government. With J. Piłsudski's rise to power he returned to politics and in 1928 became voivode of Volhynia. As minister of the interior from December 1929 to June 1930, he introduced a differentiated nationalities policy that was tailored to the specific conditions in different regions. Resuming his previous post in Volhynia, Józewski tried to overcome the animosity between Poles and Ukrainians and to gain the political support of the Ukrainian community. His educational and administrative reforms favored Ukrainian participation in the cultural and political life of Volhynia. While closing down some organizations such as Plast, he permitted others to be founded. In 1930 he formed a special committee to promote understanding between the Ukrainian Orthodox and the Polish Roman Catholic churches. With the support of UNR activists, he established the *Volhynian Ukrainian Alliance. Some of its members, including P. Pevny, S. Tymoshenko, and S. Skrypnyk, won seats in the Polish Sejm and Senate and formed a separate Ukrainian parliamentary representation. Józewski failed to win the confidence of the Ukrainian population and came under attack from the local Poles and the army. In 1938 he was transferred from Volhynia to Łódź.

BIBLIOGRAPHY
Chojnowski, A. *Koncepcje polityki narodowościowej rządów polskich w latach 1921–1939* (Wrocław 1979)

M. Stech

Juba, Stephen [Dzjuba, Stepan], b 1 July 1914 in Winnipeg. Politician and businessman. During the 1930s he established a successful distributing firm in Winnipeg. Between 1953 and 1959 he sat in the Manitoba legislature as an independent member for Logan. From 1956 until his retirement in 1977 he was mayor of Winnipeg, the first non-Anglo and non-Celt to hold this office. Juba cultivated a populist image by living modestly and breaking with the rigid formalities of his office. He introduced Sunday sports and more liberal liquor laws, and brought the 1967 Pan-American Games to Winnipeg. In 1973 he twinned Winnipeg with Lviv. Juba was appointed to the Order of Canada in 1970.

Judaizers. A religious sect of an obscure origin and nature that arose in the late 15th century in Novgorod and Moscow principalities. According to a chronicle, the sect was founded in Novgorod by Skhariia, a Jewish merchant who arrived from Kiev with Prince Mykhailo Olelkovych in 1471 and converted two Orthodox priests to his faith. According to some scholars the sect first arose in Ukraine. Its beliefs were more closely related to Western rationalist heresies, which were known in Novgorod, than to Judaism. The Judaizers emphasized the Old Testament, celebrated Easter on the Passover, and kept the Sabbath. They rejected the church hierarchy, monasticism, icon worship, and the sacraments of Christ, and denied his divinity, the trinitarian nature of God, and the immortality of the soul. The earliest Slavonic translations of philosophical works such as the *Lectures of Moses the Egyptian (Maimonidean Logic)*, A. Ghazali's *Introduction to Philosophy*, and *Secreta Secretorum* are attributed to adherents of the sect. The Judaizers spread to Moscow, where the sect gained adherents among the church hierarchy and protectors around the tsar's family. Having been condemned by the church, the sect was severely persecuted. Remnants of it fled to Lithuania and Poland, and their descendants were resettled by Tsar Nicholas I on Ukrainian territories along the Black Sea and in Transcaucasia. In the 18th century, Judaizing tendencies appeared among several Russian sects which were unrelated to the 15th-century Judaizers. At the beginning of the 19th century a sect of sabbath observers was discovered in Voronezh gubernia on Ukraine's northern border. In 1825 various restrictions and burdens were placed on the sect; these were not lifted until 1884.

BIBLIOGRAPHY
Chyzhevsky, D. *Narysy z istoriï filosofiï na Ukraïni* (Prague 1931)
Kazakova, N.; Lur'e, Ia. *Antifeodal'nye ereticheskie dvizheniia na Rusi XIV– nachala XVI veka* (Moscow 1955)

I. Korovytsky

Judge. See Court system.

Judicial procedure. See Civil procedure and Criminal procedure.

Judicial system. See Court system.

Juliette (stage name of Julia Sysak-Cavazzi), b 26 August 1927 in St Vital, Manitoba. Singer and entertainer of Ukrainian origin. She began to sing professionally at 13 and made her debut on CBC radio at 15. In 1954 she began to appear regularly on CBC-TV as 'Our Pet, Juliette.' Her program 'Juliette' (1956–66) was one of Canada's most popular TV shows. Later she did TV specials and hosted two CBC-TV talk shows, 'After Noon' (1969–71) and 'Juliette and Friends' (1973–5). She has recorded for RCA Camden. In 1975 she was appointed to the Order of Canada.

Juniper (*Juniperus*; Ukrainian: *yalivets*). Genus of evergreen trees and shrubs belonging to the cypress family. Nine out of about 70 species of juniper grow in Ukraine. The common juniper (*J. communis*) is widespread in the Carpathians, Polissia, and the northern forest-steppe belt. Its bluish cones are used to flavour foods and alcoholic beverages. Oil of juniper, which is obtained from the wood and leaves of several species, is used in cosmetics and medicines such as diuretics. The eastern red cedar (*J. virginiana*), savin (*J. sabina*), and Chinese juniper (*J. chinensis*) are cultivated as ornamental trees and their rot-resistant wood is used in furniture making.

Jurassic Period. See Geology of Ukraine.

Jury. See Trial by jury.

Justice of the peace. A non-professional judge who serves as an independent judicial agent in the settling of minor civil and criminal matters. This office has existed as an institution in Western Europe and England since the 14th century. In the Russian Empire, justices of the peace were introduced after the judicial reforms of 1864. Local county or city assemblies, consisting of citizens who owned property or were educated, elected the justices to three-year terms, subject to Senate ratification. In Right-Bank Ukrainian gubernias (Kiev, Volhynia, and Podilia), justices of the peace were appointed by the minister of justice. An act of 1899 abolished the office, except in large cities (Kharkiv and Odessa). In 1912 the office was re-established, and justices remained active until the 1917 Revolution.

Jute-hemp industry. A branch of the textile industry that processes hemp and jute fibers to make sacks, rope, twine, cordage, and other goods. Until the 20th century hemp processing was mostly a cottage industry and was confined to the hemp-growing regions, particularly the Chernihiv region. Yet in the late 17th and early 18th centuries hemp was the second-greatest export of Left-Bank Ukraine. Despite the crippling effect of Petrine mercantilist policies on the hemp trade, hemp processing remained one of the most important sectors in an industrially underdeveloped Ukraine. In the 19th century the industry expanded rapidly in southern Ukraine. It was close to sources of raw materials (the hemp-growing steppes and jute-exporting India), and to markets such as the Black Sea ports. In 1828 there were three privately owned rope factories in Odessa. At the end of the century the two largest jute-hemp enterprises in Ukraine were the *Odessa Jute Factory, which manufactured jute products and paper and employed 1,100 workers, and the Kharkiv Plant of Sack and Cord Products, which processed only jute and employed 300 workers. The former accounted for 70 percent, and the latter for 20 percent, of the jute production in Russian-ruled Ukraine. In 1913, 105,000 ha of land were devoted to hemp. Ukraine's output of jute and hemp products was worth 14.3 million rubles (in 1925–7 prices) and constituted 20 percent of the empire's output. In Austrian-ruled Ukraine 22,000 ha of land was devoted to hemp in 1913; however, there was almost no jute-hemp industry in Western Ukraine because of competition from Polish industry.

Under Soviet rule the jute-hemp industry underwent some important changes: cottage enterprises were replaced by large factories, and by the 1930s jute ceased to be imported and the industry became limited to domestically grown hemp and to kenaf, which was grown in the Asian republics. The First World War and the Revolution also had a devastating effect on the jute-hemp industry: in 1920 production was only 28.9 percent of the 1913 level. After recovering somewhat in the 1920s the industry was set back by the collectivization drive. Between 1927 and 1934 the land area devoted to hemp decreased from 174,000 ha to 25,000 ha (in Western Ukraine it increased from 26,000 ha [1929] to 30,000 ha [1933]). By 1940 the area devoted to hemp reached 200,000 ha and the value of the output of Ukraine's 27 jute-hemp factories increased from 25.4 million rubles (1927–8) to 88 million rubles. The jute-hemp industry accounted for 4.1 percent of Ukraine's light-industry output and for 28.6 percent of the USSR jute-hemp production.

Although interwar production levels were reached by 1955 (23,000 t), the jute-hemp industry has declined since then. The area sown to hemp dropped steadily after the Second World War and amounted to only 29,000 ha in 1984. The gross output of raw hemp has not declined as sharply as the sown area, because the traditional central-Russian varieties of hemp have been replaced with higher-yielding southern varieties. In 1984 the area sown to southern hemp, which yields 24.0 centners per ha, was twice the area sown to central-Russian hemp, which yields 6.3 centners per ha. In 1940 the areas were approximately equal. The main shortcoming of southern hemp is its low yield of oilseed. However, because seed harvesting requires manual picking, the cultivation of hemp for seed is diminishing. The gross harvests of hemp have decreased from a peak of 222,000 t in 1955 to 37,000 t in 1984. As the decreasing output of hemp yarn (from 34,600 t in 1970 to 15,400 t in 1984) shows, the jute-hemp industry is diminishing in importance. Kharkiv, Odessa, and Kirovohrad are the main centers for jute-hemp processing. As in earlier times, Western Ukraine has no jute-hemp industry.

C. Freeland, B. Wynar

Juvenile delinquency. Antisocial or criminal acts such as violence and vandalism committed by minors. In Ukraine, as in the whole Soviet Union, this is a serious social problem.

Individuals over 16 years of age, and juveniles over 14 who have committed particularly dangerous acts such as murder, robbery, and malicious hooliganism, are subject to criminal prosecution. The criminal code of the Ukrainian SSR and of the other Soviet republics treats youth as a mitigating circumstance. Criminals under 18 years of age cannot be executed or sentenced to more then 10 years' imprisonment. They are confined in special correctional labor colonies for juveniles.

Such lenient treatment was not always extended to juvenile delinquents. The Criminal Code of 1926 permitted children 12 years of age to be tried. The 7 April 1935 decree of the USSR Central Executive Committee and the Soviet of People's Commissars required that all punitive measures, including execution, be applied to 12-year-olds. The law of 31 May 1941 emphasized that children over 12 years should be prosecuted not only for premeditated crimes but also for unintentional harm due to carelessness. According to the law on misappropriating socialist property, children could be imprisoned for picking an apple in a collective-farm orchard or digging up a potato in the field, and particularly large numbers of children ended up in prison. The introduction of legal penalties for lateness for work led to the harsh treatment of many children. Even absenteeism from factory-plant schools was punished with six months' imprisonment. Child criminals, as A. Solzhenitsyn points out, adjusted quickly to camp life and became part of the criminal underworld. It was only after Stalin's death that the laws against juvenile delinquency were humanized somewhat. By the decree of 24 April 1954 the majority of juveniles who were serving their first sentence and had completed a third of it were released.

Crimes by children up to 14 years of age, minor crimes by juveniles 14–16 years of age, and various misdemeanors by 16- to 18-year-olds such as petty speculation, truancy, and refusal to work are examined by municipal and raion commissions for juvenile affairs. These commissions can either censure a young wrongdoer or his parents, impose a fine on them, or send the offender to a special psychiatric or educational institution (special school or special vocational-technical school).

Although crime statistics are not published in the Soviet Union, one can assert that juvenile delinquency is widespread. A handbook on legal statistics says that juveniles up to 18 years of age account for 7 percent of all sentences. This is equivalent to the proportion of 14- to 18-year-olds in the population. But since the juvenile sentences in question pertain only to serious crimes, which usually account for 10–15 percent of all crimes, the true number of offences by juveniles is probably 7–10 times as high and close to the total number of crimes by adults. There is also evidence to suggest that recidivism is high among juvenile offenders.

Most juvenile delinquents in the USSR are boys (93 percent); many are either out of school or enrolled in technical schools. In the prewar and the immediate postwar periods the main cause of child crime was undoubtedly homelessness, which resulted from the dislocations and high loss of life in the Revolution and the First World War, the *famine of 1931–3 in Ukraine, and the mass terror (see *Children, homeless). Today, one of the main causes of delinquency is a lack of parental supervision. In almost all families both parents work, and there are many single-parent families because of a high rate of divorce and the birth of many children to single mothers. Other important factors in juvenile delinquency are the harmful influence of idle youngsters and the lack of gainful employment and other prospects. The most prevalent juvenile offenses are hooliganism, robbery, theft, and fighting. Crimes of unmotivated brutality are not infrequent. (See *Hooliganism.)

BIBLIOGRAPHY

Connor, W. *Deviance in Soviet Society: Crime, Delinquency, and Alcoholism* (New York and London 1972)

S. Maksudov

K

Kabachkiv, Ivan [Kabačkiv], b 6 October 1874 in Veremiivka, Zolotonosha county, Poltava gubernia, d 2 December 1962 in New York. Economist and lawyer; full member of the Ukrainian Academy of Arts and Sciences in the United States. A graduate of St Petersburg University's Faculty of Law, before 1917 he held several positions in the Imperial Ministry of Finance. From 1919 to 1920 he served as a state auditor of the UNR, and after that in the UNR Government-in-exile. From 1925 to 1934 he lectured at the Higher Pedagogical Institute in Prague and in 1944 he was appointed lecturer and eventually professor of the Ukrainian Free University in Munich. He emigrated to the United States in 1949. His published works deal with the structure of the government budget in Czechoslovakia and in Ukraine, and with the USSR tax system.

Kabachok, Volodymyr [Kabačok], 1885–1937? Kobza player and artistic director of the Poltava Banduryst Kapelle (1923–33). In 1934 he was arrested and exiled to Kolyma, where he died.

Stepan Kachala

Kachala, Stepan [Kačala], b 1815 in Firmiiv, Berezhany county, Galicia, d 1888 in Shelpaky, Zbarazh county, Galicia. Ukrainian Catholic priest and political leader. A populist, he was a founding member of the *Halytsko-Ruska Matytsia (1848) and the Narodnyi Dim in Lviv (1849). He was one of the Ukrainian representatives at the Slavic Congress in Prague in 1848. Kachala was elected to the Galician Sejm in 1861 and to the Imperial Parliament in Vienna in 1873. He was a founding member and president of the Shevchenko Literary Society (later the Shevchenko Scientific Society) and the *Prosvita society. He wrote popular brochures on political and social subjects and the book *Polityka Polaków względem Rusi* (The Politics of the Poles with Regard to Ruthenia, 1879), which appeared in Ukrainian as *Korotka istoriia Rusy* (A Short History of Ruthenia, 1886).

Kachanivka [Kačanivka]. III-13. Health resort in Ichnia raion, Chernihiv oblast. Because of its mild climate, Kachanivka has a tuberculosis sanatorium. A palace was built there by P. Rumiantsev-Zadunaisky, which in the 1770s became the estate of the Tarnovsky family. In the 19th century many noted writers, such as N. Gogol, T. Shevchenko, and Marko Vovchok, visited Kachanivka. A rich collection of Ukrainian antiquities and documents connected with T. Shevchenko was transferred eventually from Kachanivka to the Chernihiv State Historical Museum.

Kachenovsky, Dmitrii [Kačenovskij, Dmitrij], b 30 December 1827 in Karachev, Orel gubernia, d 2 January 1873 in Kharkiv. Specialist in international law and the history of political institutions. A graduate of Kharkiv University, where he was appointed to the Chair of International Law (1849) and subsequently promoted to professor (1859). His *O kaperakh i prizovom sudoproizvodstve* (1855), which was published in London in English translation as *Prize-Law, Particularly with Reference to the Duties and Obligations of Belligerents and Neutrals* (1867), was instrumental in the inclusion of several articles on humanizing naval warfare and banning privateering in the Declaration of Paris (1856). In his *Kurs mezhdunarodnogo prava* (A Course in International Law, 1863–6) he severely criticized positivist theories of international law. He raised the issue of codifying international law and contributed to the founding in 1873 of the Institute of International Law in Ghent, Belgium.

Kachenovsky, Mikhail [Kačenovskij, Mixail], b 12 November 1775 in Kharkiv, d 3 March 1842. Russian historian and literary critic of Ukrainian and Greek origin. He finished his studies at Kharkiv College in 1789. From 1805 to 1830 (with minor intervals) he edited and published the journal *Vestnik Evropy*. From 1810 he was a professor at Moscow University and in 1837 he became its rector. Kachenovsky opposed the nationalist views of N. *Karamzin and was a founder of the skeptical school in Russian historiography. He questioned the authenticity of many works of the Kievan period – including *Povist' vremennykh lit* (Tale of Bygone Years), *Slovo o polku Ihorevi* (The Tale of Ihor's Campaign), and *Ruskaia Pravda* (Rus' Law) – believing them to be written at a later date. This provoked others to analyze these monuments in detail. He was convinced that Kievan Rus' did not have its own literature, commerce, laws, or currency and that these were imported from Germany in the 14th century.

Kachkovsky, Mykhailo [Kačkovs'kyj, Myxajlo], b 1802 in Dubno, Łańcut county, Galicia, d 20 August 1872 in Kronstadt, Russia. Galician cultural figure of a populist outlook. A judge by profession, he endorsed the Austrian regime and worked within its confines to promote the cultural and educational advancement of the Ukrainian people. He provided financial support to writers and publications of both cultural camps in Galicia – the Old Ruthenians (Russophiles) and the Populists. The Russophile newspaper *Slovo* (1861–87) in Lviv received large subsidies from him. He encouraged the development of literature in the local Ukrainian vernacular by rewarding writers, particularly students, with monetary prizes. In his will he left about 80,000 guilders to set up a foundation at the *People's Home in Lviv for awarding prizes for literary works written in the local Ukrainian language and for supporting periodical publications. Upon retiring Kachkovsky set out on an extended tour of Russia, in the course of which he succumbed to cholera. Although he had never been a Russophile, a society created by Russophiles in 1874 as a counterweight to the Prosvita society was named after Kachkovsky because he had supported some Old-Ruthenian causes (see *Kachkovsky Society).

Kachkovsky Society (Obshchestvo im. M. Kachkovskogo). A cultural and educational society named in honor of M. *Kachkovsky that was founded in 1874 in Kolomyia by Galician Russophiles led by Rev I. *Naumovych. It was modeled on the populist *Prosvita society (est 1868), and its purpose was to enlighten the common people. In 1876 its head office was moved to Lviv. The society had branch offices in county towns and libraries in villages. Its main activity was publishing inexpensive religious books, calendars, farming manuals, and popular entertaining novels. From 1930 its monthly booklets were known as Narodnaia Biblioteka. I. Naumovych's works came out separately in seven editions. Some of these publications were written in the local Ukrainian vernacular, and others in the artificial *yazychie. The society also reprinted the works of Russian writers. Besides publishing, it organized practical courses on farming and co-operation. In 1924 *Nauka*, which was founded by I. Naumovych in 1871, became the official journal of the society. Despite its large financial reserves, the society's importance diminished with the decline of the Russophile movement. In 1914 it had only about 300 reading rooms, compared to 2,944 of the Prosvita society, and in 1936 its membership was 5,975, compared to Prosvita's 306,000 (1935). The society's presidents were Rev I. Naumovych, Rev T. Pavlykiv, B. Didytsky, and P. Svystun before the First World War, and A. Aleksevych, M. Hlushkevych, Ya. Verbytsky, and A. Kopystiansky after the war.

BIBLIOGRAPHY

Andrusiak, M. *Geneza i kharakter halyts'koho rusofil'stva v XIX–XX st.* (Prague 1941)

A. Zhukovsky

Kachmar, Vasyl [Kačmar, Vasyl'], b 20 August 1904 in Viisko, Dobromyl county, Galicia. Journalist, OUN leader, and Catholic activist. He was imprisoned in the Polish penal camp Bereza Kartuzka for his political activities. He served as an editor on *Ukraïns'kyi holos* in Peremyshl (1930–2), *Nash prapor* in Lviv (1936–9), and *Krakivs'ki visti* (1939–40). After the Second World War he immigrated to Germany and in 1949 to the United States. In the mid-1960s he was a founder and the first chairman of the Ukrainian Patriarchal Society in the United States. Kachmar wrote many articles and brochures on religious subjects.

Kachmar, Volodymyr [Kačmar], b 18 March 1893 in Lviv, d December 1964 in Cracow. Bass opera singer; educator. He made his debut at the Lviv Opera in 1919. In 1924–5 he sang at La Scala in Milan. Kachmar taught singing at the Lviv Conservatory (1938–41, 1944–6) and then at the State Higher School of Music in Cracow (1946–64). His repertoire included Godunov in M. Mussorgsky's *Boris Godunov*, Ramfis in G. Verdi's *Aida*, and Zbigniew in S. Moniuszko's *The Haunted Castle*. His concert repertoire often included Ukrainian vocal works.

Kachor, Andrii [Kačor, Andrij], b 13 December 1908 in Borshchovychi, Lviv county, Galicia. Economist and co-operative organizer. Active in the co-operative movement since 1928, until 1944 he worked as an organizer of the co-operative Maslosoiuz and auditor of the Audit Union of Ukrainian Co-operatives in Lviv. He edited *Hospodars'ko-kooperatyvne zhyttia*, the organ of the Alliance of Ukrainian Co-operators in Germany (1947–8). After emigrating to Canada in 1950, he published studies on the Ukrainian co-operative movement including *Ukraïns'ka molochars'ka Kooperatsiia v Zakhidnii Ukraïni* (Ukrainian Dairy Co-operatives in Western Ukraine, 1949).

Kachura, Borys [Kačura], b 1 September 1930 in Tulchyn, Vinnytsia oblast. Soviet political figure. Since 1963 he has worked in the Party administration. He was second secretary (1974–6) then first secretary (1976–82) of the Donetske Oblast Party Committee. In 1971 he was elected a candidate member of the CC CPU and in 1976 he became a full member of the CC CPU and of the CC CPSU. Also in 1976 he became a candidate member, and in 1981 a full member, of the CPU Politburo. In 1982 he was appointed a secretary of the CC CPU with special responsibility for energy. Since 1975 he has also been a member of the presidium of the Supreme Soviet of the Ukrainian SSR.

Kachura, Yakiv [Kačura, Jakiv], b 21 October 1897 in Yurkivka, Bratslav county, Podilia gubernia, d October 1943. Writer. His works were first published in 1923 and he became a member of the writers' group *Pluh and the All-Ukrainian Association of Proletarian Writers. He is the author of several collections of stories dealing with the war, the Revolution, and contemporary life, as well as the novels *Chad* (Fumes, 1929) and *Ol'ha* (1931) and the Stalinist historical novella *Ivan Bohun* (1940). A Soviet war correspondent from 1941, Kachura was captured by the Germans in May 1942 and died in a concentration camp in the Donbas. His selected works (2 vols) were published in 1958; a critical biography by B. Buriak appeared in 1962.

Kachurovsky, Ihor [Kačurovs'kyj], b 1 September 1918 in Nizhen, Chernihiv gubernia. Writer and literary scholar. A graduate of the Kursk Pedagogical Institute (1941), he fled to Austria in 1944. In 1948 he immigrated to Argentina, where he edited the monthly *Porohy* in Buenos Aires. In 1969 he moved to Munich; since 1979 he has taught at the Ukrainian Free University there, from 1982 as a professor. As a poet, Kachurovsky is considered a suc-

Ihor Kachurovsky

cessor to the *Neoclassicists of the 1920s; he is the author of the collections *Nad svitlym dzherelom* (At the Lustrous Source, 1948), *V dalekii havani* (In the Faraway Haven, 1956), and *Pisnia pro bilyi parus* (Song about the White Sail, 1971) and the long poem *Selo* (The Village, 1960). His well-received novels include *Shliakh nevidomoho* (The Path of the Stranger, 1956; English: *Because Deserters Are Immortal*, 1979), *Zaliznyi kurkul'* (The Iron Kulak, 1959), and *Dim nad krucheiu* (The House on the Cliff, 1966). As a literary scholar, Kachurovsky has written articles about Ukrainian writers and literature, and the books *Strofika* (Versification, 1967), *Fonika* (Phonics, 1984), and *Narys komparatyvnoi metryky* (Outline of Comparative Metrics, 1985). He has also edited collections of Ukrainian poetry and translated Italian, Spanish, French, Russian, Polish, Belorussian, and Dutch poetry into Ukrainian, including a selection from Petrarch (1982).

I. Koshelivets

Kadets. See Constitutional Democratic party.

Kadiivka. See Stakhanov.

Kadylo (The Censer). Satirical tabloid, edited and published irregularly from 1913 to 1918 by P. *Krat in Winnipeg, Vancouver, and finally, Toronto. From a socialist viewpoint the illustrated periodical lampooned the Catholic and Orthodox clergy, satirized the Ukrainian Canadian intelligentsia, and condemned the tsarist autocracy in the Russian Empire. It serialized several of Krat's satirical works and featured political cartoons, including caricatures of prominent Ukrainian-Canadian figures. At least 25 issues appeared. *Kropylo*, published by Krat in Winnipeg shortly before *Kadylo* appeared, was very similar to its successor.

Kaffa. See Teodosiia.

Kaganovich, Lazar [Kaganovič], b 22 November 1893 in Kabany, Kiev county, Kiev gubernia. Bolshevik and Soviet political leader of Jewish descent. Joining the Bolshevik party in 1911, he organized trade unions in various towns of Ukraine. During the revolutionary period he held important Party posts in Belorussia (1917), Russia (1918–20), and Turkestan (1920–1). Transferred to Moscow, he worked in the central agencies of the Russian Communist Party (Bolshevik) (CP[B]). By 1925 he became a member of the CC CP(B), and by 1930 a member of the Politburo. Because of his unconditional loyalty, Kaganovich was used by Stalin for the most repugnant and ruthless tasks. As first secretary of the CC CP(B)U (1925–8), he was responsible for crushing O. *Shumsky's opposition while maintaining the appearance of *Ukrainization. Upon his return to Moscow he was appointed to the Party Secretariat, where he had a decisive influence on Ukrainian affairs. In 1933, as director of the agricultural department of the CC of the All-Union CP(B), he set up the political departments of the machine-tractor stations and helped V. Molotov organize the forced collectivization of Ukraine by terror and famine. From 1935 to 1944 Kaganovich held various government posts in Moscow. In 1947, he was again appointed first secretary of the CC CP(B)U and was assigned the task of pacifying Ukraine. After J. Stalin's death in 1953, he rose to first deputy premier of the USSR and member of the Presidium, but four years later lost all his government and Party posts, and even his Party membership, for participating in an abortive attempt to oust N. Khrushchev from power. He was later rehabilitated.

V. Holubovych, V. Markus

Kahal or **Qahal.** A Hebrew term meaning 'assembly' or 'community' referring to the autonomous governments of Jewish communities in the Polish-Lithuanian Commonwealth and the Russian Empire. Kahals emerged on Ukrainian territories under Polish rule in the early 16th century, when they were formed to administer the collective taxation of the Jews in the Commonwealth. Each community had a single kahal, although some smaller communities were placed under the jurisdiction of larger ones. In internal affairs they enjoyed virtual political autonomy: they regulated local commerce, education, the treatment of transients, hygiene and sanitation, and relations between landlords and tenants, and administered charity. Local rabbis were under their authority, and kahal courts ruled on almost all religious and secular disputes according to Jewish law. They also had the power to expel members from the synagogue, placing them outside the law. Representatives from the kahals participated in the annual meetings of the central Jewish organ in the Polish Kingdom, the Council of the Four Lands.

Kahals had at least 8 members in the smallest and 22–35 members in medium-sized communities. The executive consisted usually of 4 elders (*rashim*) and 3–5 'honorary' members (*tuvim*); they, the rabbi, and some other officials with specific responsibilities (eg, judges) were paid by the kahal. The executive was elected by the community. Initially, everyone was enfranchised, and the kahals defended the interests of all Jews, but over time the wealthy and privileged came to dominate these groups and used their powers to ensure their positions. In the 18th century many Jews began calling for abolition of kahals, especially as they were increasingly drawn into the struggles between the various religious movements and political groupings. Many kahals became indebted.

After the Polish partitions the influence of kahals within the Russian Empire progressively declined as the state assumed more direct power over Jews. In 1827, however, they were given the added responsibility of providing conscripts for the army. In 1844 they were officially abolished by the tsarist regime in Ukraine and most of the rest of the empire; they continued to exist only in the

Baltic region. Afterwards, Jewish communities were given jurisdiction only over religious and charitable affairs, and occasionally over education.

P. Kachur

Kahalnyk River [Kahal'nyk]. A river flowing for 134 km through the Kuban Lowland and draining a basin of 5,080 sq km. The Kahalnyk empties into Tahanrih Bay of the Sea of Azov.

Kahanovych, Naum [Kahanovyč], b and d ? Linguist. His articles and reviews in *Prapor marksyzmu* and *Krytyka* at the beginning of the 1930s initiated a broad campaign against Ukrainian linguistics of the 1920s, characterizing it first as an expression of populism and then as an expression of 'Ukrainian bourgeois nationalism.' From 1933 to 1937 he was a corresponding member of the AN URSR, the director of the AN URSR *Institute of Linguistics, the editor of the journal *Movoznavstvo*, the compiler of a school textbook of Ukrainian, and the de facto dictator in the field of Ukrainian linguistics. He used his position to Russify ruthlessly literary Ukrainian and to discredit Ukrainian linguists. In 1937 he was arrested and reportedly executed.

Kaharlyk. IV-11. Town (1970 pop 10,900) and raion center in Kiev oblast, situated on the Rosava River in the Dnieper Upland. The ruins of 11th–13th-century fortifications and a park with 19th-century gardens are found there. Its industries produce foodstuffs, mixed feed, asphalt, and artistic wares.

Kaiala River [Kajala]. River mentioned in the Rus' epic **Slovo o polku Ihorevi* (Tale of Ihor's Campaign) as the place where the Cumans routed the army of Prince *Ihor Sviatoslavych in 1075. Possibly it is the present-day Kalmiius River.

Kaindl, Raimund Friedrich, b 31 August 1866 in Chernivtsi, d 15 March 1930 in Graz, Austria. German historian, ethnographer, and archeologist; full member of the Shevchenko Scientific Society from 1914. A graduate of Chernivtsi University and a professor there (1901–14) and at Graz University (from 1915), he was an important scholar of the history of Bukovyna and the ethnography of the Hutsuls, as well as the history and ethnography of the Germans in Eastern Europe. Kaindl refuted the views of Rumanian historians who questioned the autochthonous origins of Ukrainians in Bukovyna. Of his numerous works relating to Ukrainian studies the most important are *Die Ruthenen in der Bukowina* (1889–90, coauthor A. Manastyrsky), *Die Huzulen* (1893), *Geschichte der Bukowina* (3 vols, 1896–1903), *Die Ethnographie der Huzulen* (1897), *Das Ansiedlungswesen in der Bukowina seit der Besitzergreifung durch Österreich* (1902), *Geschichte der Deutschen in der Karpathenländern* (3 vols, 1906–11), and *Geschichte der Stadt Czernowitz* (1908).

Kakhivka [Kaxivka]. VII-14. City (1979 pop 39,000), raion center, and river port in Kherson oblast, situated on the left bank of the Dnieper River. Established in 1791 as a village, it grew into an important grain and wool trading town; the largest employment exchange for agricultural laborers in southern Ukraine was located there in the late 19th century. Electric-welding and irrigation equipment, reinforced-concrete materials, furniture, and food products are manufactured there. Since 1957 a museum, and since 1964 a branch of the AN URSR Institute of Electric Welding, have been located there.

Kakhivka Hydroelectric Station. The second-largest and southernmost of the *Dnieper Cascade of Hydroelectric Stations. It was built in the years 1950–6, 12 km southwest of the city of Kakhivka, in Kherson oblast. Each of its six generators provides 58,500 kW; together they produce an annual average of 1.4 billion kWh of energy. A highway and railway traverse the station's 3.84-km dam complex, which holds back the waters of the *Kakhivka Reservoir. The city of *Nova Kakhivka has arisen next to the station.

Kakhivka Irrigation System. One of the largest irrigation systems in the USSR. It provides water to the dry steppe farmland of Kherson and Zaporizhia oblast. Construction of the system began in 1967. The planned irrigation area of 260,000 ha was increased in 1979 to 784,000 ha. The system's source of water is the *Kakhivka Reservoir, from which water is channeled via the Kakhivka Canal (130 km), the Sirohozhy Canal (114 km), the Chaplynka Canal (42 km), a network of interfarm supply and field canals (total 192 km), and 65 waterworks. In 1979, 110,000 ha of the irrigated land was cultivated.

Kakhivka Reservoir. A huge reservoir created in 1956 after the dam of the *Kakhivka Hydroelectric Station was built on the lower Dnieper River. It is 240 km long and up to 23 km wide and has a surface area of 2,155 sq km, a volume of 18.2 cu km, and an average depth of 8.4 m. Its level varies from 3 to 26 m. Its waters supply hydroelectric stations, the *Krasnoznamianka and *Kakhivka irrigation systems, industrial plants, freshwater-fish farms, and the *North Crimean and *Dnieper–Kryvyi Rih canals. The reservoir has created a deep-water route, allowing sea ships to sail up the Dnieper. (See map on page 402.)

Kakhnykevych, Kyrylo [Kaxnykevyč], b 1850 in Kolomyia, Galicia, d 27 May 1926 in Lviv. Journalist and civic figure. A graduate of the University of Vienna (1876) and the Vienna Higher School of Agriculture, he taught school and then worked on the editorial staff of *Dilo* (1884–90). For many years he was the editor of *Narodna Chasopys'* (1891–1914, 1918), the Ukrainian supplement to the government daily *Gazeta Lwowska*. A member of the board of directors of *Silskyi Hospodar, he edited its semimonthly *Hospodars'ka chasopys'* (1910–18) and its book series Hospodarska Biblioteka (Farming Library). At the same time he translated literary pieces from various European languages for *Hospodars'ka chasopys'* and wrote popular booklets on farming, which were published by the Prosvita society and Silskyi Hospodar.

Kalach [Kalač]. III-21. Town (1971 pop 19,000) on the Podgornaia River in Voronezh oblast, RSFSR. Founded in the early 18th century, it has a machinery plant and a food industry. According to the 1926 census Ukrainians constituted 84 percent of its population.

Kalachevsky, Mykhailo [Kalačevs'kyj, Myxajlo], b 26 September 1851 in Popivka, Kremenchuk county, Kher-

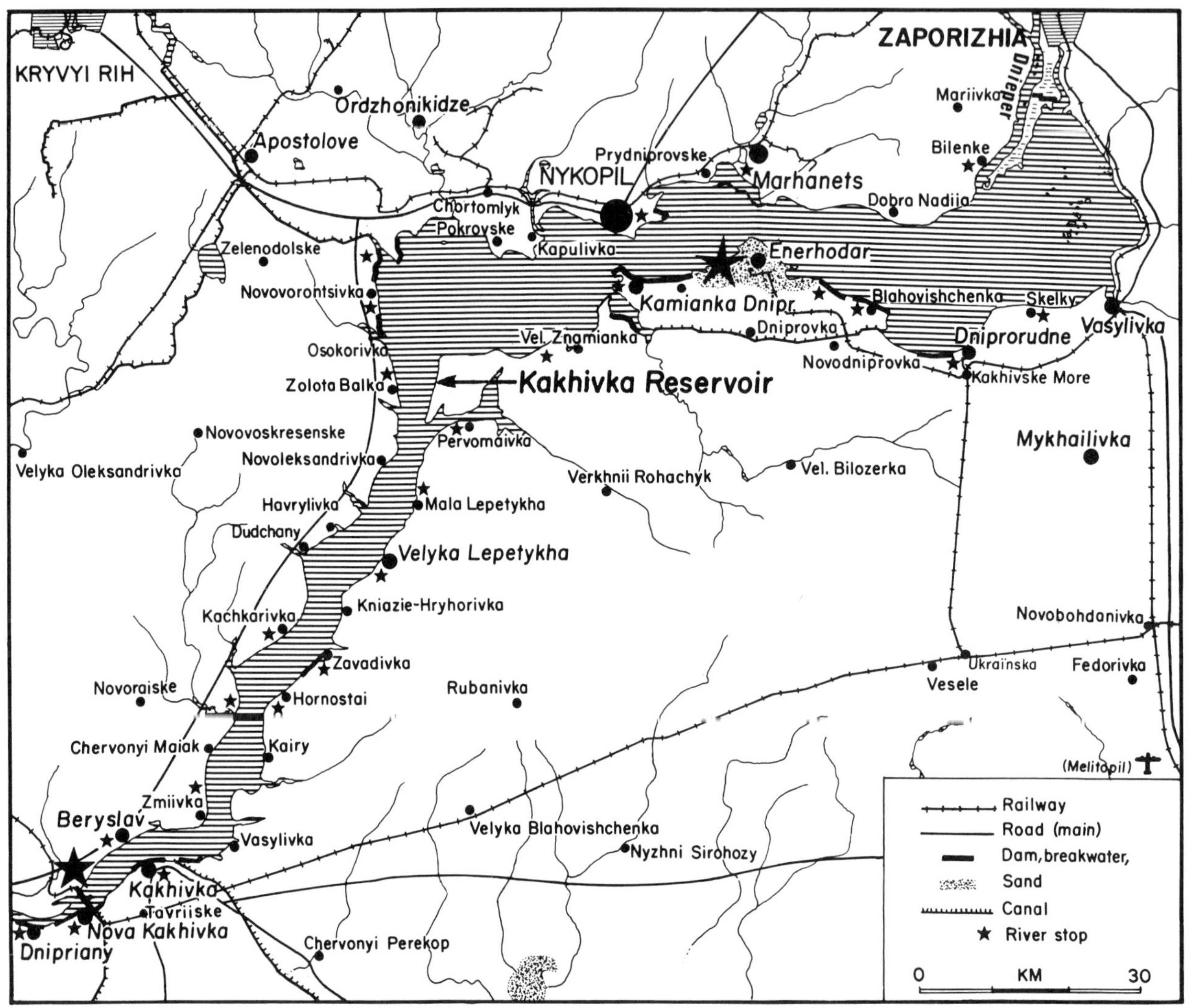

KAKHIVKA RESERVOIR

Large star indicates Enerhodar Atomic Energy Station.

son gubernia, d 1910–12 in Kremenchuk. Composer; by profession a lawyer. A graduate of the Leipzig Conservatory (1876), he settled in Kremenchuk and was active in its musical life, organizing concerts and music groups. His compositions include *The Ukrainian Symphony* (1876), based on Ukrainian folk melodies; a string quartet; piano pieces; a requiem; and 19 songs. M. Hordiichuk has published two monographs on him (Kiev, 1954 and 1963).

Kalakut. A pejorative term used in *Podlachia and sometimes in the Kholm region to denote Ukrainians who had become assimilated as Poles. *Kalakuty* spoke Ukrainian but were Roman Catholics.

Kalamitska Bay (Kalamitska zatoka). A bay of the Black Sea on the western coast of the Crimea, between the capes of Tarkhankut and Khersones. The city of *Yevpatoriia is situated on the bay.

Kalanchak [Kalančak]. VII-14. Town smt (1983 pop 9,900) and raion center in Kherson oblast, situated on the Kalanchak River. It was founded in 1794 as a settlement of exiled participants in the *Turbai uprising. Its inhabitants are employed mainly in agriculture.

Kalannyky or ***Kalanni liudy.*** A category of unfree people in Galicia in the period of the so-called *Lithuanian-Ruthenian law (15th and 16th centuries). They were attached to the land, most frequently on state or church properties. They paid a quitrent but could dispose of their own possessions and appear in court as witnesses. In some places they lived in entire settlements. Their status was similar to that of the **zakupy* in Kievan Rus' and the peasant **otchychi* under Lithuanian rule.

Kalba, Semen [Kal'ba], b 22 October 1911 in Mozolivka, Nadvirna county, Galicia. Lawyer and community leader. Educated at Lviv University, the Institut des Recherches Economiques in Louvain, and the Ukrainian Free University in Prague (LLD 1943), after the war Kalba practiced law in the French occupation zone of Germany and represented the United Ukrainian Relief Committee (ZUADK) and the Ukrainian Canadian Relief Fund before French and German authorities. He emigrated to the United States in 1950 but returned to Europe two years later as the European director of ZUADK. Later he served as executive director of the Ukrainian Canadian Committee (1966–81).

Halyna Kalchenko

Kalchenko, Halyna [Kal'čenko], b 4 February 1926 in Borzna, Chernihiv region, d 11 March 1975 in Kiev. Sculptor. A graduate of the Kiev State Art Institute (1953) and a student of Mykhailo *Lysenko, she worked mostly in bronze and marble. Her works consist chiefly of statues such as those of M. Leontovych in Tulchyn (1970), S. Hulak-Artemovsky in Horodyshche (1971), Lesia Ukrainka (1973) in Kiev, and I. Kotliarevsky (1974) in Kiev, and portraits such as those of K. Dankevych, O. Kobylianska, L. Revutsky, Ya. Stepovy, and B. Rudenko.

Kalchenko, Nykyfor [Kal'čenko], b 27 January 1906 in Koshmanivka, Poltava gubernia. Soviet state and party official. In the 1930s Kalchenko participated in the collectivization drive in Kharkiv oblast. He was a candidate (1938–40) and a full (1940–76) member of the CC CP(B)U, and a candidate (1952–6, 1966–76) and a full (1956–66) member of the CC CPSU. From 1952 to 1976 he was a member of the Politburo of the CPU. He was in charge of various Ukrainian government ministries: economic crops (1946–7), state farms (1947–50), agriculture (1950–2), and procurements (1961–5). He also served as deputy chairman (1952–4, 1961–76) and chairman (1954–61) of the Council of Ministers of the Ukrainian SSR.

Kalenychenko, Ivan [Kalenyčenko], b 1805 in Sumy, Kharkiv gubernia, d 1876. Physician, botanist, and zoologist. Kalenychenko graduated from Kharkiv University in 1829 and worked as a physician. From 1838 to 1864 he taught biology and held the Chair of Physiology and Pathology at Kharkiv University. Kalenychenko's wide interests included plant taxonomy (*Daphne, Crataegus*), entomology, and medicine. During his expeditions to the Caucasus and France he collected a large herbarium, which he donated to Kharkiv University. Kalenychenko published over 40 scientific works in Latin and French. Some plants were named after him (eg, *Euphorbia kaliniczenkoï*).

Kalenychenko, Luka [Kalenyčenko], b 20 February 1898 in Karlivka, Kostiantynohrad county, Poltava gubernia, d 5 August 1968 in Kiev. Restoration specialist and art scholar. A graduate of the Myrhorod Art School (1918) and the Kiev Art Institute (1931), in 1938 he organized the first central research and restoration studio in Ukraine. In Kiev he oversaw the restoration of the paintings of St Volodymyr's Cathedral (1946–52), the Church of St Cyril's Monastery (1950), St Andrew's Cathedral (1951–2), and St Sophia Cathedral (1952–68). He described his work on the frescoes and mosaics of the latter in an article published in *Iskusstvo* in 1958. His publications include articles on art history and a monograph on O. Shovkunenko published in 1947.

Kalenychenko, Nina [Kalenyčenko], b 9 March 1922 in Myrhorod, Poltava oblast. Literary scholar. She has written several studies on Ukrainian literature, most notably *Ukraïns'ka proza pochatku XX st.* (Ukrainian Prose at the Turn of the 20th Century, 1964). The life and work of M. Kotsiubynsky has been the subject of articles and monographs by her, including *Mykhailo Kotsiubyns'kyi* (1956) and *Velykyi sontsepoklonnyk* (The Great Sun Worshipper, 1967).

Kaliannyk, Ivan [Kaljannyk] (pen name of I. Kaliannikov), b 20 March 1911 in Diatkovo, Orel gubernia, Russia, d 10 April 1939. Poet of Russian origin. He belonged to the *Prolitfront writers' association. Although his poetry glorified Ukraine's industrialization, it was attacked for being 'nationalist.' He wrote several collections of poetry among which *Strum* (The Current, 1931), *Vysoka put'* (The Lofty Path, 1932), and *Hordist'* (Pride, 1936) are most notable. Collections of his poems appeared posthumously in 1959, 1962, and 1967.

Kalinin, Kostiantyn, b 29 December 1889 in Valuiky, Voronezh gubernia, d 21 April 1940 in Voronezh. Aeronautical engineer and airplane designer. A graduate of the Kiev Polytechnical Institute, he headed the Design Bureau of the Kiev Aviation Plant and in 1926 was put in charge of the Design Bureau of the new Kharkiv Plant of Research Aircraft Building. He designed the first five models of the K series of passenger planes (1925–9), the 120-seat K-7 airliner (1930–3), the K-12 tailless bomber (1937), and the K-13 special-purpose bomber (1938). Reportedly, he was purged during the 1930s for Ukrainian bourgeois nationalism and died in prison.

Kalinowski, Marcin, b ? d 2 June 1652 near Batih, now Chetvertynivka, in Trostianets raion, Vinnytsia oblast. Polish magnate with considerable landholdings in Ukraine. From 1635 he was the voivode of Chernihiv, from 1646 the Polish field hetman, and from 1651 the royal grand hetman. During the *Cossack-Polish War, in the Battle of *Korsun in 1648, he was captured by the Cossacks, who handed him over to the Crimean Tatars.

Having paid a large ransom, he returned to Poland from the Crimea in 1650. In February 1651 he attacked towns in Podilia and laid siege to Vinnytsia. After the Cossacks' defeat at the Battle of *Berestechko and the subsequent Treaty of *Bila Tserkva in 1651, he took revenge on the Ukrainian populace in the Bratslav and Chernihiv regions. At the Battle of *Batih in 1652 the Polish forces led by him were completely routed, and he himself perished.

Kalishevsky, Yevfimii [Kališevs'kyj, Jevfimij] (secular name: Yukhym), 1892–? Bishop of the Ukrainian Autocephalous Orthodox church. He was consecrated in 1922 and served in Cherkasy (1922–9) and Odessa (1929–30) eparchies. Arrested in 1936 (1930 according to some sources) and deported, his subsequent fate is unknown.

Kalisz. A city (1977 pop 95,100) and county center in Poznań voivodeship, Poland. In the 1920s and 1930s it was an important Ukrainian émigré center. An internment camp for UNR soldiers who had crossed into Poland existed there from 1920 to 1924. Cultural and educational activity – schools, courses, publishing houses, theater, V. Avramenko's folk-dance school, irregular periodicals of short duration, and the literary monthly *Veselka* (1922–3) – flourished in the camp. After 1924 the community's life was centered in an area of camp 10 called Ukrainska Stanytsia, where such institutions as the Society of UNR Army Soldiers, the Ukrainian Association of Disabled Veterans, and the Shevchenko Gymnasium (1921–37) were located. The latter had a total enrollment of 1,000 and graduated 130 students during its existence. The monthly *Ukraïns'kyi invalid* was published there from 1925 to 1931. The Ukrainian Military History Society, with its annual *Za derzhavnist'* (1929–35), and the military journal *Tabor* (1923–6) were located in Kalisz before being transferred to Warsaw. About 1,500 Ukrainians remained in Kalisz and its vicinity in the 1930s.

Kaliuzhny, Denys [Kaljužnyj], b 16 October 1900 on the khutir Kaliuzhnyi in Lebedyn county, Kharkiv gubernia, d 24 June 1976 in Kiev. Hygienist and educator; corresponding member of the USSR Academy of Medical Sciences from 1961. A graduate of the Kharkiv Medical Institute (1926), from 1932 to 1973 he worked at the Kiev Research Institute of General and Communal Hygiene, directing it from 1956 to 1971. From 1933 to 1970 he also taught at post-secondary schools in Kharkiv and Kiev. He was one of the first to research industrial pollution in Ukraine.

Kaliuzhny, Naum [Kaljužnyj] (real name: Sheitelmann), b 1885 in Myrhorod county, Poltava gubernia, d ? Journalist; communist leader of Jewish descent. An active Borotbist, he participated in the process of forming the Ukrainian SSR. He edited the Borotbist newspaper *Proletars'kaia pravda* and later the official newspaper of the CP(B)U *Selians'ka bidnota* and the journal *Chervonyi shliakh*. From 1921 to 1926 Kaliuzhny worked at the consulate of the Ukrainian SSR in Prague, and then at the Soviet embassy in Prague, where he was active in the Soviet propaganda campaign aimed at Ukrainian students in Czechoslovakia. Most of the students who were induced to return to Ukraine were later arrested and executed. Kaliuzhny himself was arrested in 1933 and disappeared without trace.

Kaliuzhny, Oleksander [Kaljužnyj], b 1896, d ? Cameraman. From 1926 he worked at the Odessa Film Factory of the All-Ukrainian Photo-Cinema Administration shooting films such as *Pidozrilyi bahazh* (Suspicious Baggage, 1926), *Synii paket* (The Blue Package, 1926), *Benia Kryk* (1927), *Naperedodni* (On the Eve, 1928), *Mertva petlia* (The Dead Noose, 1929), *Pravo na zhinku* (The Right to a Wife, 1930), and *Karmeliuk* (1931). Attacked for formalism, he was arrested in the 1930s and disappeared without trace.

Kalka River. A small river, 88 km long and draining a basin of 1,260 sq km, that flows into the Kalmiius River in the Azov steppe. Today it is called the Kalchyk or Kalets River. It was the site of the first battle between the armies of the princes of southern Rus' and the invading Mongol-Tatar hordes of Genghis Khan. Because of lack of leadership and the plight of their Cuman allies, the Rus' forces were routed on the banks of the river in 1223 after a three-day battle. After the battle the Mongols ravaged the southern frontier of Rus' before returning to the Volga region.

Kálmán, b ca 1070, d 3 February 1116. King of Hungary from 1095. He married Yefimiia, the daughter of Prince Volodymyr Monomakh. During his rule, he seized Dalmatia, Croatia, and part of Transcarpathia. In 1099, as the ally of Sviatopolk II Iziaslavych of Kiev, he was defeated in battle near Peremyshl by the united armies of the princes Volodar and Vasylko Rostyslavych of Galicia and Khan Boniak and the Cumans.

Kalmiius or **Kalmius River** [Kal'mijus]. A river dissecting the Donets Ridge and emptying into the Sea of Azov. It is 210 km long and has a basin area of 5,070 sq km. This unnavigable river supplies the northwestern Donbas with water for domestic and industrial use. The upper Kalmiius is connected to the Donets River by the Donets-Donbas Canal. Four reservoirs have been built on the river.

Kalmyk ASSR. An autonomous republic (1982 pop 304,000) in the Russian RSFSR, lying in the west Caspian Depression. Its territory, most of which is semidesert, covers 75,900 sq km. The capital is Elista. A Kalmyk autonomous oblast was established in 1920; it became an autonomous republic in 1935. The republic was abolished in 1943 for alleged wartime collaboration with the Germans by the Kalmyks, who were deported en masse to eastern Siberia. They were allowed to return beginning in 1956, and the autonomous oblast and republic were reconstituted in 1957 and 1958 respectively. In 1926 its national composition was 75.6 percent Kalmyk, 10.1 percent Russian, and 10.3 percent Ukrainian. Ukrainian peasants began settling in Kalmykia's arable western part in the late 19th century; there they constituted 21 percent of the population in 1926. In 1979 Kalmyks constituted 41.5 percent, Russians 42.6 percent, and Ukrainians 1.3 percent of the population; only 40.5 percent of the population was urban.

Kalnofoisky, Atanasii [Kal'nofojs'kyj, Atanasij], b and d ? A 17th-century monk who was ordered by Metropolitan P. *Mohyla to record the wondrous events that occurred at the Kievan Cave Monastery in the immediate past. The result was the Polish work *Teratourgema lubo* *cuda, ktore były tak w samym święto cudotwornym Monastyru Pieczarskim, Kiiowskim* ... (Teraturgima, or the Miracles That Did Occur So in the Very Miraculous Kievan Cave Monastery ..., 1638). This work was analyzed in detail by M. *Hlobenko in an article in *Zbirnyk 'Ukraïns'koï literaturnoï hazety'* (1956).

Kalnyn, Liudmila [Kalnyn', Ljudmila], b ? Russian linguist. Kalnyn is an associate of the Institute of Slavic and Balkan Studies at the Academy of Sciences of the USSR. After studying Slavic historical phonology, Kalnyn turned to the investigation of Slavic dialects, especially Ukrainian ones. In this field she has published many articles and the monograph *Opyt modelirovaniia sistemy ukrainskogo dialektnogo iazyka* (An Attempt at Modeling the System of Ukrainian Dialectal Language, 1973). On the basis of her fieldwork in several villages where the Boiko, Hutsul, and Sian dialects are spoken, as well as in some Polisian villages with a transitional Ukrainian-Belorussian dialect, she constructs generalized models of the dialects and compares them with each other and with some Slavic languages to arrive at a typology of dialectal speech. She has also studied such dialectal phenomena as sandhi, voicing and devoicing of consonants, and syllable boundaries.

Petro Kalnyshevsky; medal by V. Masiutyn

Kalnyshevsky, Petro [Kalnyševs'kyj], b 1690, d 31 October 1803 in Solovki, Arkhangelsk. The last kish otaman of the New Sich (1762, 1765–75). An able administrator and diplomat, he did much for the economic and cultural development of Zaporizhia and the defense of its independence. He encouraged the colonization of Zaporizhian territory and the expansion of grain production and trade. Several times he was sent as an envoy to St Petersburg to defend the territorial rights of Zaporizhia from encroachment by the Russian government and the foreign army colonies that were established in southern Ukraine (New Serbia and Slovian-Serbia). He did not succeed, however, in preventing the ultimate destruction of the Sich in 1775. In 1776 he was exiled to a monastery on the *Solovets Islands, where he was kept a prisoner in extremely difficult conditions until his release in 1801. After his release, he became a monk there at the age of 110.

Kalos Limen. An ancient Greek city founded in the 4th century BC on the west littoral of the Crimea. Its ruins are located 1.5 km northwest of the present-day village of Chornomorske (formerly Ak-Mechet) in Crimea oblast. The site was excavated six times between 1837 and 1959. Uncovered were the remains of defensive walls, towers, and buildings; amphorae, and pottery; grain mortars; millstones; and terra-cotta figurines. In the 4th–3rd century BC the town was ruled by the city state *Chersonese Taurica. It was subsequently controlled by the Scythians and later destroyed at the end of the second century BC. The upper layers of the site contained remains of other cultures, dating from the 1st through the 3rd centuries AD and from medieval times. A necropolis with kurhans is located near the ruins. (See also *Ak-Mechet burial site.)

Kalush [Kaluš]. IV-5. City (1984 pop 64,000) and raion center, in and under the jurisdiction of Ivano-Frankivske oblast, situated in the Kalush Depression on the Syvka River. First mentioned in the Galician-Volhynian Chronicle under the year 1241, in 1549 it received the rights of Magdeburg law. Under Austrian and Polish rule Kalush was a county town. Its rapid growth in the early 19th century was conditioned by rock-salt mining in its vicinity. As salt production fell the town declined, and in the latter half of the 19th century the population grew very little (1857 pop 8,000; 1914 pop 9,000). Its fortunes improved with the development of potassium-salt extraction and processing, and its population grew to 40,700 by 1970. Today the city's major industries are the Khlorvinil chemical-metallurgical conglomerate, a reinforced-concrete complex, and a metalworking complex. A branch of the All-Union Scientific Research Institute of Halurgy and a chemical-technology tekhnikum are located there.

Kalush-Holyn potassium deposits. One of the largest deposits of potassium salts in Ukraine, covering an area of 80 sq km. The deposits, which are Miocene sediments of the Subcarpathian Foredeep, are located in Kalush raion, Ivano-Frankivske oblast, at a depth of 15–1,000 m. The seams range from a few centimeters to 40 m in thickness and consist of such minerals as rock salt (halite), kainite, sylvite, carnallite, anhydrite, and polyhalite. Most of the mining is underground, but some surface mining has been introduced recently. Rock salt has been mined in this area since the 15th century.

Kaluzhniatsky, Omelian [Kalužnjac'kyj, Omeljan] (Kałużniacki), b 23 January 1845 in Turie, Sambir circle, Galicia, d 3 July 1914 in Chernivtsi. Slavist and Slavic paleographer; corresponding member of the Russian Imperial Academy of Sciences from 1891. After studying at Lviv and Vienna universities, he was professor at Chernivtsi University (1875–1914). He published several Old Ukrainian and Old Bulgarian monuments such as the Putna Gospel and the Horodyshche *Apostol*, and did much research on the influence of Church Slavonic on Rumanian. He also wrote the monograph *Obzor slaviano-russkikh pamiatnikov iazyka i pis'ma nakhodiashchikhsia v bibliotekakh i arkhivakh l'vovskikh* (A Survey of Slavonic-

Russian Monuments of Language and Literature Found in Lviv Libraries and Archives, 1878).

Kalyn, Andrii, b 3 May 1908 in Horinchove, near Khust, Transcarpathia, d 11 December 1979. Foremost folk storyteller in Transcarpathia. In 1946 his narration of 120 tales and many other oral prose works were transcribed. Most of them appeared in the book *Zakarpats'ki kazky Andriia Kalyna* (The Transcarpathian Tales of Andrii Kalyn, 1955) and in a number of collections and anthologies. Collections of his tales were also published in Russian (1957, 1960) and Czech (1958).

Kalyn, Volodymyr, b 19 September 1896 in Lviv, d 14 January 1923 in Ternopil. Stage actor with a varied repertoire. He worked with L. *Kurbas in the Ternopilski Teatralni Vechory theater (1915–17), Molodyi Teatr (1917–19), the First Theater of the Ukrainian Soviet Republic (1919), the New Lviv Theater (1920), and the Kyidramte (1920–2). His repertoire included such roles as Stepan and Koval in M. Kropyvnytsky's *Nevil'nyk* (The Prisoner), Leiba and Gonta in Kurbas's adaptation of T. Shevchenko's *Haidamaky* (The Haidamakas), Macduff in W. Shakespeare's *Macbeth,* Schigorski in M. Halbe's *Jugend,* Cavaliere di Ripafratta in C. Goldoni's *La Locandiera,* and Podkolosin in N. Gogol's *Zhenit'ba* (The Wedding).

Kalyna, Volodymyr, b 18 August 1896 in Kolokolyn, Rohatyn county, Galicia, d 5 November 1965 in New York. Physicist, mathematician, educator; full member of the Shevchenko Scientific Society. In 1914 he joined the Ukrainian Sich Riflemen (USS), and by 1918 rose to company commander, then adjutant of the First Kurin. After the war he completed his studies at Graz University (PH D 1929) and returned to Lviv, where he taught mathematics and physics. Settling in the United States after the Second World War, he chaired the School Council of the Ukrainian Congress Committee of America and was active in other Ukrainian organizations. His publications include a study of the suspension of paint particles in emulsions, articles on the USS, and war memoirs titled *Kurin' Smerty USS* (The Death Kurin of the Ukrainian Sich Riflemen).

Kalyna. See Viburnum.

Kalyna Co-operative. The oldest Ukrainian consumer co-operative in Canada, incorporated in 1940 in Winnipeg. It was originally founded by the Ukrainian Riflemen's Hromada on the model of the Chervona Kalyna Publishing Co-operative in Lviv. At first it served as the exclusive Canadian agent for several Ukrainian publishers in Europe and sold embroidered clothing and handicrafts. Among its early organizers were V. Topolnytsky, S. Tsybulsky, P. Shulha, D. Gerych, P. Ustash, O. Tarnovetsky, and I. Bobersky. After the Second World War the co-operative began to sell various home furnishings, appliances, musical instruments, and other items, and in 1949 it established an automobile and home insurance agency.

Kalynets, Ihor [Kalynec'], b 9 July 1939 in Khodoriv, Lviv oblast. Poet. A graduate of Lviv University (1961), Kalynets was employed at the Lviv Oblast State Archive. In 1972 he and his wife were victims of a wave of political

Ihor Kalynets

arrests. Both were imprisoned, he for 'anti-Soviet activity' (ie, because his poetry had been published in the West) to six years in labor camp and three years of exile. In May–June 1974 Kalynets took part in a hunger strike of political prisoners in a Perm region labor camp; later he signed several appeals from political prisoners to the authorities. Since his release from exile in Chita oblast in 1981, Kalynets has lived in Lviv, his poetic muse silenced.

Inspired by the imagistic verse of B.I. *Antonych, Kalynets developed his poetry into the finest exponent of modern Ukrainian 'engagé' lyricism. He employs images that are often primeval and a vocabulary that is rich in cultural allusions while using a prosodic cadence that is contemporary. Only a few of his poems have been officially published in Ukraine, in journals in the early 1960s. His collection *Vohon' Kupala* (The Fire of Kupalo) was published in Kiev in 1966 but was immediately suppressed and all copies were confiscated. Since that time his poetry has been blacklisted in the USSR and he has been published only in the West: the collections *Poezii z Ukraïny* (Poems from Ukraine, 1970), *Pidsumovuiuchy movchannia* (Summing up Silence, 1971), *Koronuvannia opudala* (The Crowning of a Scarecrow, 1972), and *Vohon' Kupala* (1975; reprint of the confiscated 1966 edition). Some poems have been translated into German and French as the collections *Bilanz des Schweigens* (1975) and *Les balladins du sel* (1980).

D.H. Struk

Kalynets, Iryna [Kalynec'] (née Stasiv), b 6 December 1940 in Western Ukraine. Dissident; wife of I. *Kalynets. A graduate of Lviv University, she taught Ukrainian literature and language at the Lviv Polytechnical Institute and published children's stories and verses. An active defender of V. *Moroz in 1970 and a founding member of the Committee in Defense of N. *Strokata in 1971, she was arrested in Lviv in January 1972 and sentenced in August for anti-Soviet agitation and propaganda to six years in prison and three years of exile. In the Mordovian labor camps, where she served her sentence, she joined protests against camp conditions and made demands for the recognition of political prisoners. After serving her term of exile in Chita oblast, she was released in 1981 and returned to Lviv.

Kalynivka. IV-9. Town smt (1978 pop 16,100) and raion center in Vinnytsia oblast, situated on the Zherd River in eastern Podilia. It was founded in the early 18th century.

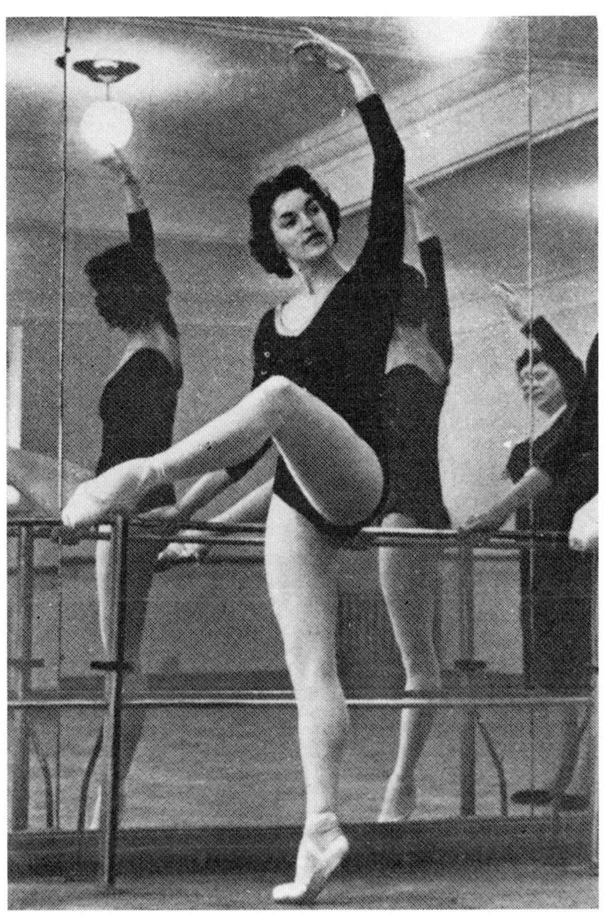

Valentyna Kalynovska

Kalynovska, Valentyna [Kalynovs'ka], b 28 July 1938 in Kiev. Ballerina. After graduating from the Kiev Choreography School in 1957, she joined the Kiev Theater of Opera and Ballet. She appeared in such roles as Varia in V. Homoliaka's *Black Gold*, Palahna in V. Kyreiko's *Shadows of Forgotten Ancestors*, Donna Anna in V. Hubarenko's *The Stone Master*, the title roles in G. Bizet's *Carmen*, R. Shchedrin's *Carmen Suite*, and A. Glazunov's *Raymonda*, the Mistress of the Copper Mountain in S. Prokofiev's *The Stone Flower*, and Odette-Odile in P. Tchaikovsky's *Swan Lake*.

Kalynovsky, Hryhorii [Kalynovs'kyj, Hryhorij], b ? in Krolevets, Chernihiv region, d ? A tsarist army officer, he published the first separate Ukrainian ethnographic study: a description of Ukrainian wedding rituals (St Petersburg 1777). A modern Ukrainian translation was published in the collection *Vesillia* (Wedding), vol 1 (Kiev 1970).

Kalynovych, Fedir [Kalynovyč], b 1 March 1891 in Hanivtsi, Rohatyn county, d ? A mathematician in Kiev. An associate of the VUAN Institute of the Ukrainian Scientific Language, he compiled a Ukrainian dictionary of mathematical terminology (3 parts, 1925–6, 1931; the last part with H. Kholodny).

Kalynovych, Ivan [Kalynovyč], b 28 November 1885 in Lviv, d 12 November 1927 in Lviv. Bibliographer, publisher, and political figure. He was a founder of the Vsesvitna Biblioteka publishing house in Zolochiv and editor of the newspapers *Drohobyts'kyi Lystok* (1919) and the Lviv *Nashe Slovo* (1927). He wrote numerous bibliographies that appeared in journals such as *Knyzhka* (1921–3) and *Nova Ukraïna* (1923) and in the calendars of the Prosvita society (1924–6). His bibliography of works on Ukraine in foreign languages and publications appeared in *Kul'tura* in Lviv and *Ukraïna* in Kiev (1925, 1927). He published an index to the publications of the Prosvita society (1924) and separate bibliographies of Ukrainian studies (1924) and sources on the history of the Ukrainian Sich Riflemen (1924). Kalynovych also prepared a catalogue of over 300,000 index cards on Ukrainian bibliography; it is now located in the Lviv Scientific Library of the AN URSR. In 1918–19, Kalynovych was a deputy to the Ukrainian National Council of the Western Ukrainian National Republic and a representative to the Labor Congress in Kiev.

Kalynovych, Mykhailo [Kalynovyč, Myxajlo], b 13 October 1888 in Zhakhnivka, Bratslav county, Podilia gubernia, d 16 January 1949 in Kiev. Linguist; full member of the AN URSR from 1939. A graduate of Kiev University (1912) and professor there from 1916, he also worked at the AN URSR Institute of Linguistics from 1924, serving as director from 1939 to 1941. He published works in general linguistics, including *Vstup do movoznavstva* (Introduction to Linguistics, 1939; 2nd edn, 1947), studies of modern French literature, and translations from Sanskrit. He also served as the editor in chief of a Russian-Ukrainian dictionary (80,000 words, 1948) compiled in the official spirit of Russification.

Kalynovych, Volodymyr [Kalynovyč], b 1884, d 1945 in Dresden, Germany. Educator and publicist. He was the author of German grammars and articles on educational themes and the publisher of the newspaper *Ukrainische Blätter* (Vienna 1918) and the journals *Ukraïna* (Kiev 1919) and *Ukraïns'ka shkola* (Lviv 1925). Kalynovych and his wife and daughter were killed during the Allied bombing of Dresden.

Kalynsky, Tymofii [Kalyns'kyj, Tymofij], b early 1740s, d after 1809. Civic leader; artist. Descended from old

Tymofii Kalynsky: *Zaporozhian Cossacks Dancing* (watercolor, 1778–82)

Ukrainian gentry in Right-Bank Ukraine and educated at the Kievan Mohyla Academy, he served in various provincial chancelleries. He wrote several legal and historical memoranda, only some of which have been published, defending the noble status not only of the Ukrainian gentry but also of the Cossacks. In 1778–82 he painted some 30 large watercolors depicting members of the various estates in their characteristic dress. These works were preserved at the Imperial Society of History and Russian Antiquities in Moscow and were reproduced in A. *Rigelman's *Letopisnoe povestvovanie o Maloi Rossii i ee narode i kazakakh voobshche* (A Chronicle Account of Little Russia, Its People, and the Cossacks in General, 1847).

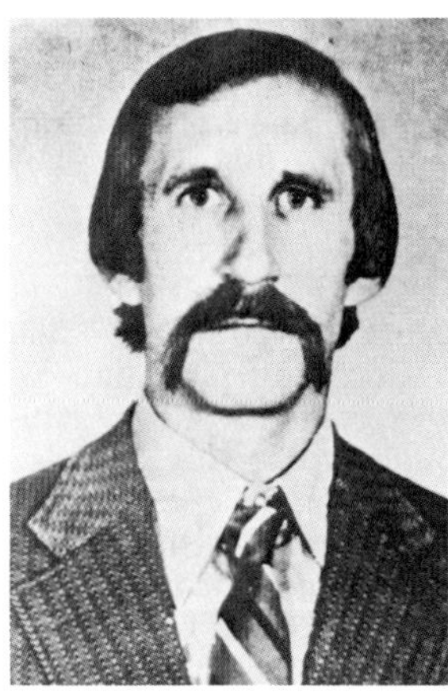

Vitalii Kalynychenko

Kalynychenko, Vitalii [Kalynyčenko, Vitalij], b 1935. Dissident. Employed as an engineer in Leningrad, in 1966 he attempted to cross the Finnish border and was punished for this act of 'treason' with 10 years in prison. Having served his sentence, he lived in Dnipropetrovske, where he joined the *Ukrainian Helsinki Group. He was arrested in November 1979 and sentenced for anti-Soviet agitation and propaganda to 10 years in prison and 5 years of exile.

Kalytovska, Marta [Kalytovs'ka], b 22 October 1916 in Stryi, Galicia. Poet, journalist, and translator. She studied at Louvain University in Belgium. Now residing in France, she contributes to émigré periodicals and has written two collections of gentle, personal lyrics: *Liryka* (Lyrics, 1955) and *Rymy i ne-rymy* (Rhymes and Nonrhymes, 1959). She also writes poetry in French and in 1974 published *Dix lettres à Sophie*, a slim collection of poems dedicated to the writer S. Yablonska, whose memoirs she has collected and edited in a Ukrainian and a French edition. She has also translated German, French, and Spanish literature into Ukrainian.

Kalytovsky, Omelian [Kalytovs'kyj, Omeljan], b 1855 in Butyny, Zhovkva circle, Galicia, d 18 March 1924 in Lviv. Pedagogue. A graduate of Lviv University, he taught at the Ukrainian Academic Gymnasium in Lviv, (1878–1900) and was the principal of the new Ukrainian gymnasium in Ternopil (1900–7). He was the author of schoolbooks and articles on historical and educational topics in the newspapers *Dilo* and *Zoria* (he edited the latter in 1886).

Kalytva Ridge. A landmark on the right bank of the Orel River in Tsarychanka raion, Dnipropetrovske oblast; it is 82 m high, 5 km long, and 3 km wide.

Kamanin, Ivan, b 1850 in Dymer, Kiev county, Kiev gubernia, d 1921. Historian, archivist, and paleographer. A graduate of Kiev University (1872), where he studied under V. Antonovych and M. Drahomanov, Kamanin was a specialist in 16th- and 17th-century Ukrainian history. From 1883 he worked at and then directed the Kiev Central Archive of Old Acts. He helped compile and edit the series **Arkhiv Iugo-Zapadnoi Rossii*, and was a member of the VUAN Commission for the Study of the History of Western Ruthenian and Ukrainian Law. His monographs, some of which also appeared in *Kievskaia starina* and *Chteniia v Istoricheskom obshchestve Nestora-letopistsa*, include *Ocherk getmanstva P. Sagaidachnogo* (An Essay on the Hetmanate of P. Sahaidachny, 1901), *K voprosu o kozachestve do Bogdana Khmel'nitskogo* (On the Problem of the Cossacks up to the Time of Bohdan Khmelnytsky, 1894), and *Poslednie gody samoupravleniia Kieva po Magdeburskomu pravu* (The Last Years of Kiev's Self-Government under Magdeburg Law, 1888). He also published many important collections of documents, especially on the history of the Khmelnytsky uprising, and such valuable studies of Ukrainian paleography as *Paleograficheskii Izbornik* (Paleographic Collection, 1909) and *Vodiani znaky na paperi ukraïns'kykh dokumentiv XVI i XVII vv. (1566–1651)* (Watermarks on the Paper of Ukrainian Documents of the 16th and 17th Centuries [1566–1651], with O. Vitvytska, 1923).

A. Zhukovsky

Kamchatka oblast. An administrative region of the RSFSR consisting of Kamchatka Peninsula and part of the mainland along the Pacific coast. The mountainous, volcanic country has a cold humid climate. Its area is 472,300 sq km and its 1986 population was 435,000, 358,000 of which was urban. The oblast capital is Petropavlovsk-Kamchatskii (1986 pop 248,000). According to the 1979 census, Ukrainians account for 7 percent of the population. The main industries are fishing, lumbering, canning, woodworking, and boat building. Little is known about the labor camps, in which Ukrainians constitute a high proportion of the inmates. The camps, at least six in number, belong to the Dalstroi system. Their inmates are employed in logging, mining, construction of military facilities, and submarine repairs.

Kamenetsky, Danylo [Kamenec'kyj], 1830–81. Publisher, folklorist, and civic figure. An active member of the St Petersburg Hromada, he managed P. Kulish's printing press and the journal **Osnova*. Thanks to his capable assistance, T. Shevchenko's *Kobzar* (1860), Marko Vovchok's *Narodni opovidannia* (Folk Stories, 1857), and other Ukrainian literary works appeared in print. Kamenetsky introduced popular booklets for the common people that were known as *metelyky*. He collected Ukrainian folk songs and published a collection of them entitled *Ukraïns'ki pisni z holosamy* (Ukrainian Songs with Music, 1861).

Kamenetsky, Ihor [Kamenec'kyj], b 2 January 1927 in Rohatyn, Galicia. Political scientist. He immigrated to the United States in 1949 and received a PH D in political science from the University of Illinois, Urbana, in 1957. He has been a professor at Central Michigan University since 1957, specializing in comparative government and international relations. His major works are *Hitler's Occupation of Ukraine 1941–1944: A Study of Totalitarian Imperialism* (1956) and *Secret Nazi Plans for Eastern Europe: A Study of Lebensraum Policy* (1961).

Kameniar (Stonecutter). A republican publishing house of the State Committee of the Ukrainian SSR for Publishing, Printing, and the Book Trade. It was established in Lviv in 1939 as a book-editing firm and in 1940 became part of the Vilna Ukraina newspaper and magazine publishing house. In 1950 this firm was reorganized into the Lviv Oblast Book and Journal Publishing House, which in 1964 was turned into a republican publishing house and was named Kameniar. It published the journals *Literatura i mystetstvo* (1940–1), *Radians'kyi L'viv* (1945–51), and *Zhovten'* (1951–present). Its book publications include literary works of writers from Western Ukraine (mainly Lviv), children's literature and translations, regional studies, art books, and guidebooks for historical sites and museums. Many of its publications are political propaganda brochures for mass distribution.

Kameniari (Stonecutters). A semimonthly newspaper published by the Free Organization of Ukrainian Teachers in Bukovyna from 1908 to 1914 in Chernivtsi. It was edited first by O. Ivanytsky and then by I. Karbulytsky and L. Yasinchuk. It was revived after the war and began to appear from 15 February 1921 under the editorship of I. Danylevych. Besides professional and educational questions, the paper discussed broader social and political issues; it reached a wide public. Its contributors included Z. Kuzelia, O. Remez, K. Danyliuk, M. Milkovych, V. Kmitsykevych, and M. Korduba. In early November 1922 the paper was banned by the Rumanian authorities.

Kameniari (Stonecutters). A monthly magazine published by the Union of Ukrainian Progressive Youth from 1932 to 1939 in Lviv. Its editors were I. Luchyshyn and P. Kostiuk.

Kameniari. See Union of Ukrainian Progressive Youth.

Kamiana baba. See Stone *baba*.

Kamiana Mohyla. A knoll of sandstone deposits from the Miocene epoch resembling a large kurhan, situated near Terpinia, Melitopil raion, Zaporizhia oblast. Beneath it several caves have been discovered containing petroglyphs of wild bulls, wolves, horses, and other animals, human beings, and geometric patterns dating back to the Upper Paleolithic and Mesolithic periods and the Bronze Age, when this was a site of religious worship. The caves were discovered by M. Veselovsky in 1890 and were investigated in 1936–8, the 1950s, and the 1970s. Neolithic campsites were also excavated nearby.

Kamianets [Kam'janec']. I-4. Town smt (1972 pop 5,100) and raion center in Brest oblast, Belorussian SSR. Its previous name was Kamianets Lytovskyi. The town was founded in 1276 by Prince Volodymyr Vasylkovych of Volhynia. In the early 14th century it became part of the Grand Duchy of Lithuania. By the mid-17th century it had declined to an insignificant village. Of its former fortifications, only the medieval White Tower has been preserved. Kamianets and its environs are on Ukrainian ethnic territory, and in the Peace Treaty of Brest-Litovsk (1918) they were recognized as a part of Ukraine.

Kamianets-Podilskyi [Kam'ianec'-Podil's'kyj]. V-7. City (1985 pop 97,000) under oblast jurisdiction and raion center of Khmelnytskyi oblast, situated picturesquely on the Smotrych River in eastern Podilia.

First mentioned in an Armenian chronicle of the 11th century, when it belonged to Halych principality, the town was destroyed by the Mongols in 1240. In the 1360s it fell under the rule of the Lithuanian Koriiatovych princes. In 1430 Poland gained control of the town; in 1432 it was granted the rights of Magdeburg law; and in 1463 it became the capital of Podilia voivodeship. Under the Poles it grew into a center of international trade and artisanry, second only to Lviv. Its wooden Rus' fortress was replaced in the 15th and 16th centuries by a large stone citadel, and the city was well fortified with walls and towers. It protected the southeastern frontier of the Polish Commonwealth from the Tatars and Turks. In 1463 Kamianets was proclaimed a royal city and was granted duty-free status.

Citadel in Kamianets-Podilskyi (14th–17th century)

The city's first inhabitants were Ukrainians and Armenians; eventually many Poles and Jews settled there. The Ukrainian, Armenian, and Lithuanian-Polish burghers each had municipal self-government, beginning in the Lithuanian period. Under the Poles, however, the Ukrainian citizens saw their rights diminished: in 1534 they were forced to live outside the city walls, and in 1670 the Ukrainian municipal council (*magistrat*) was united with the Polish council, in effect annulling Ukrainian self-government. During the *Cossack-Polish War the city was besieged by Cossack forces in 1648, 1651, and 1655. In 1672 the city was captured by Hetman P. Doroshenko and his Turkish allies; it remained in Turkish hands until 1699, when it was restored, with the rest of Podilia, to Poland by the Treaty of Karlowitz.

Under the Turks the city declined economically and demographically. Slow growth resumed under Russian rule in 1793. The city was a Russian vicegerency (1795–7) and gubernia (1797–1917) capital. In 1812 its citadel, which had been strengthened by the Turks, was dismantled. Because of the absence of a railway link (established only in 1914) the city remained primarily a center of trade and artisanship, with very little industry. Its population grew from 3,450 in 1793 (a third of what it had been in the mid-16th century) to 16,000 in 1820,

22,800 in 1860, 37,000 in 1893, and 50,000 on the eve of the First World War. It played a far greater role as the cultural capital of Podilia: an Orthodox brotherhood school had been established there in 1589; many prominent figures – eg, M. Leontovych, A. Svydnytsky, M. Kotsiubynsky, and S. Rudansky – studied at its theological seminary (est 1805); it had one of the first *Prosvita societies in Russian-ruled Ukraine; it was the home of a historical-archeological society and a historical-archeological museum, founded in 1890 by Ye. Sitsinsky; and it had 10 secondary schools and a theater.

Town hall in Kamianets-Podilskyi (16th–18th century)

Under Ukrainian rule (1917–20) the *Kamianets-Podilskyi Ukrainian State University was established there in the summer of 1918 by the Hetman government. In 1919 and 1920 the city served on several occasions as the seat of the Directory of the UNR and the government of the Western Ukrainian National Republic.

In November 1920 the city fell under Soviet rule and functioned as an okruha (1923–30) and oblast (1937–41) capital. After the destruction it had suffered during the First World War and Revolution, which was repeated during the Second World War, the city grew very slowly until the 1960s. In 1926 it had a population of 32,100, consisting of Ukrainians (45 percent), Jews (40 percent), Russians (7 percent), and Poles (6 percent). By 1959 its population had grown to 40,000, by 1970 to 57,000, and by 1979 to 84,000. In 1959 Ukrainians made up 71 percent of its population, Russians 21 percent, Poles 5 percent, and Jews 3 percent.

Today the city's industries produce auto parts, farm machinery, electrical machines and equipment, cables, tools, woodworking instruments, reinforced-concrete structures, asphalt, concrete, wall materials, cement, food products, furniture, textiles, and clothing. The city has a pedagogical institute (est 1921), an agricultural institute (est 1921), seven specialized secondary schools, three technical schools, a historical museum (since 1919), a botanical garden (est 1930), and a dendrological park.

The city's old town lies on a high plateau within a loop formed by the Smotrych River. Since 1948 it has been an all-Union state historical preserve. Located there are centuries-old narrow, winding streets and buildings, the citadel, which was separated from the rest of the town by a deep ravine and controlled access to it, remnants of the city walls, several towers, and the fortified Ruska and Polska gates.

Other architectural monuments have also been preserved in the city: the town hall (16th–18th century), St Nicholas's Church (1280, the oldest Armenian church in Ukraine), the Church of St John the Baptist (16th century), the Church of SS Peter and Paul (15th–16th century), a late Renaissance Dominican church, the Catholic Gothic cathedral (late 15th century) with a minaret added in the Turkish period, and a number of Renaissance and baroque buildings.

BIBLIOGRAPHY
Setsinskii, E. *Gorod Kamenets-Podol'skii* (Kiev 1895)
Plamenyts'ka, Ie.; Vynokur, I.; Khotiun, H.; Medvedovs'kyi, I. *Kam'ianets' Podil's'kyi* (Kiev 1968)
Kam'ianets' Podil's'kyi: Putivnyk (Lviv 1970)

V. Kubijovyč

Kamianets-Podilskyi Agricultural Institute (Kamianets-Podilskyi silskohospodarskyi instytut). An institution of higher learning under the Ministry of Agriculture of the USSR. It was separated from the Kamianets-Podilskyi Ukrainian State University and turned into an independent institution in 1921. In the 1920s all lectures were given in Ukrainian. In 1924–8 the institute published five volumes of *Zapysky*. At the end of the 1920s and during the 1930s many of its faculty, including M. Velychkivsky, I. Oliinyk, V. Khranevych, O. Melnyk, S. Pliuiko, N. Homorak, M. Herashchenko, P. Nalyvaiko, and V. Zhyvan, were arrested and imprisoned. Today the institute has six faculties: agronomy, zoological engineering, veterinary science, economics, agricultural mechanization, and upgrading for farm managers and specialists. The institute has a graduate program. The enrollment in 1979 was 5,300, of which 2,360 were correspondence students.

Kamianets-Podilskyi Historical Museum and Preserve (Kamianets-Podilskyi istorychnyi muzei-zapovidnyk). A museum and preserve that dates back to the Depository of Antiquities established in 1890 by the Podilia Church Historical Archeological Society. Many of the old manuscripts and exponents from the original museum were transferred to Kiev in the 1930s or destroyed during the Second World War. After the war the museum was reopened and reorganized. Today its collection (some 89,000 items in 1979) is housed in three historic buildings: articles relating to the history of the city and Podilia are located in the remains of the 14th-century castle; the division of the history of religion and atheism is housed in the 15th-century Roman Catholic cathedral; and the fine-art collections are housed in the 16th-century town hall. In recent years the museum and preserve has been developed as a major tourist center.

Kamianets-Podilskyi oblast. See Khmelnytskyi oblast.

Kamianets-Podilskyi Pedagogical Institute (Kamianets-Podilskyi derzhavnyi pedahohichnyi instytut im. V. Zatonskoho). An institution of higher education under the Education Ministry of the Ukrainian SSR. It was formed in 1948 out of the Kamianets-Podilskyi Teachers' Institute (1935–48), whose origin can be traced back to the Kamianets-Podilskyi Ukrainian State University (1918–21), the Kamianets-Podilskyi Institute of People's Education (1921–30), and the Kamianets-Podilskyi Institute of Social Education (1930–4). The institute has (1982) six faculties: philology, history, physical education, physics and mathematics, elementary education, and part-time studies. The regular program is four years, but in the faculties of history, physics and mathematics, and part-time studies it is five. In 1979 the enrollment was 3,700.

Kamianets-Podilskyi Ukrainian State University (Kamianets-Podilskyi derzhavnyi ukrainskyi universytet). An institution of higher education founded in the period of Ukraine's independence. It was organized thanks to the initiative of gubernial zemstvo and municipal council leaders such as O. Pashchenko, V. Prykhodko, K. Solukha, and O. Shulminsky, and was chartered by Hetman P. Skoropadsky on 22 October 1918. I. *Ohiienko, one of the university's organizers, became rector. It was divided into five faculties: history and philology (headed by L. Biletsky), natural sciences and mathematics (headed by P. Buczyński), theology (headed by V. Bidnov), law (opened in fall 1919 and headed by Kh. Lebid-Yurchyk), and agriculture (opened in fall 1919 and headed by S. Bachynsky). By summer 1920 there were 65 scholars – including 11 professors and 25 docents – on the faculty, and the enrollment, 80 percent of which was Ukrainian, reached 1,400. Besides the names mentioned above, the more prominent faculty members included D. Doroshenko, M. Drai-Khmara, M. Fedorov, P. Klymenko, O. Mytsiuk, M. Plevako, S. Ostapenko, M. Vikul, and the chaplain, Archpriest Yu. Sitsinsky. When the Bolsheviks gained control of the city at the end of 1920, the theology and law faculties were abolished. In the following year the other faculties were separated and reorganized into the Kamianets-Podilskyi Institute of People's Education and the Kamianets-Podilskyi Agricultural Institute. Some of the professors emigrated and joined the faculties of Ukrainian higher schools in Prague or the staff of Ukrainian research institutes in Warsaw and Berlin. Others stayed behind and continued to teach at the new institutes. Many of them were purged in the 1930s and disappeared in prison or exile.

Kamiani Mohyly Nature Reserve (Zapovidnyk Kamiani Mohyly). A branch of the *Ukrainian Steppe Nature Reserve. Covering an area of 356 ha, the reserve lies in the Azov Upland near Rozivka, Volodarske raion, Donetske oblast. Rising up to 150 m above the surrounding steppe, it constitutes a miniature highland region built of gray granite, gneiss, and syenite and overlaid by a rocky steppe with many endemic plant species. The reserve was founded in 1927 and became a state reserve under the jurisdiction of the Academy of Sciences in 1951.

Kamianka [Kam'janka]. IV-13. Town (1972 pop 14,600) and raion center in Cherkasy oblast, situated on the Tiasmyn River. It was founded in the early 17th century. Its industries produce machinery, building materials, foodstuffs, and alcohol.

Kamianka [Kam'janka]. V-9. Town smt (1972 pop 12,500) and raion center in the Moldavian SSR, situated on the left bank of the Dniester River. Viticulture and fruit growing are the main occupations in the region. According to the 1926 census, Ukrainians constituted 46.6 percent and Rumanians 38.4 percent of the population in Kamianka raion.

Kamianka Dormition Monastery. A monastery located on the Snov River, near Kamianka khutir, Novozybkov county, in northern Chernihiv gubernia. It was founded in 1681 by the local starosta I. Bolkhovsky with funds provided by Hetman I. Mazepa. Originally a men's monastery, it was closed in 1764 and reopened in 1786 as a convent. The convent was closed permanently after the Revolution of 1917. Its cathedral housed a famous icon of the Mother of God.

Kamianka fortified settlement (Kamianske horodyshche). The ruins of a large (almost 12 km long) fortified settlement located on the left (east) bank of the Dnieper River opposite the present-day city of Nykopil in Zaporizhia oblast. The site was excavated by D. Serdiukov in 1899–1900 and by B. Grakov in 1938–41 and 1944–50. Large, wooden ground dwellings and pit dwellings and an acropolis were excavated. This trading and metalworking center was probably Ateas's capital. It is the largest Scythian settlement discovered in Ukraine after *Bilske. Beyond its walls other settlements of that and later periods and a burial ground of the *Cherniakhiv culture were found. The inhabitants of the settlement engaged in farming, animal herding, and trade, particularly with the Hellenic colonies on the Black Sea coast. The settlement was abandoned, except for the acropolis, in the 3rd century BC. At the beginning of the 18th century the fortress Kamianyi Zaton was built on the site by Peter I to defend against Tatar incursions. Most of the ruins are now submerged by the Kakhivka Reservoir. The settlement has been described in books by B. Grakov (1954) and I. Griaznov (1978).

Kamianka-Buzka [Kam'janka-Buz'ka]. III-5. City (1968 pop 9,200) and raion center on the Buh River in Lviv oblast. It was first mentioned as the village of Dymoshyn in 1406. In the 1440s it was renamed Kaminka, and in 1485 Kaminka Strumylova, after Yu. Strumylo, Lviv's palatine and the town's former starosta, who had a castle built and obtained the right of Magdeburg law for the town in 1471. The town became an important crafts and trading center situated on the routes from Kiev and Volhynia to Lviv and Poland. It was destroyed during the Cossack-Polish War of 1648–57. Under Austrian rule it lost the right of Magdeburg law in 1786 and declined. From 1867 to 1939 it was a county center. It had a Prosvita society from 1892 and a People's Home from 1911. In 1939 its population was 9,600 (3,100 Ukrainian, 3,850 Jews, and 2,550 Poles); 5,830 (including virtually all of the Jews) were killed during the war, and 3,200 were forcibly taken to work in Germany. Under Soviet rule it received its present name in 1944. Parquetry (famous throughout the USSR), lumber, clothing, linen, bricks, and food products are made there. The city's Church of the Nativity of the Virgin Mary (1882) and wooden St Nicholas's Church (1667) have been preserved. The Basilian Sisters' Annunciation Monastery existed there until 1782.

Kamianka-Dniprovska [Kam'janka-Dniprovs'ka]. VI-15. Town (1972 pop 16,900) on the left bank of the Kakhivka Reservoir and a raion center in Zaporizhia oblast. Founded in 1793, until 1920 it was called Mala Znamianka. Near the city the large Scythian *Kamianka fortified settlement of the late 5th to the late 3rd centuries BC was discovered.

Kamianske. See Dniprodzerzhynske.

Kamieński, Franciszek, b 9 October 1851 in Lublin, d 16 September 1912 in Warsaw. Polish botanist. Kamieński studied at Warsaw (1870–1) and Strasbourg (PH D 1875) universities, then taught botany at Lviv University, the Lviv Polytechnical Institute, and the Lviv Higher Veterinary School (1877–83). In 1888 he became a professor at Odessa University and from 1895 he also directed the Odessa Botanical Garden. Kamieński published over 40 scientific works in plant anatomy and morphology and floristics. He also researched the flora of Crimea, grape diseases, and the adaptability of osiers in southern Ukraine. He became famous for his description of the phenomenon of mycorrhiza (1880) and his studies on Indian pipe (*Monotropa uniflora*).

Kamin-Koshyrskyi [Kamin'-Košyrs'kyj]. II-5. Town (1970 pop 6,300) and raion center in Volhynia oblast, situated on the Tsyr River in western Polisia. First mentioned as Kosher in historical sources under the year 1196, it received the rights of Magdeburg law in 1430. Logging and woodworking are its main industries. The wooden Church of the Nativity, built in 1723, is preserved there.

Kaminka-Strumylova. See Kamianka-Buzka.

Kaminka-Strumylova Gospel. A manuscript gospel transcribed from a south-Slavic source in 1411 in Kaminka-Strumylova (now Kamianka-Buzka), a town on the Buh river in the Galician-Volhynian Principality. It is preserved in the Central Scientific Library in Kiev. Its language contains some traces of Volhynian dialects. The work was described by G. Kryzhanovsky in *Rukopisnye evangeliia v kievskikh knigokhranilishchakh* (Manuscript Gospels in Kievan Libraries, 1889), and its language was analyzed by him in an article published in *Volynskie eparkhial'nye vedomosti*, 1886, nos 17–18.

Kaminsky, Anatol [Kamins'kyj, Anatol'], b 17 May 1925 in Koshliaky, Zbarazh county, Galicia. Publicist and political figure. A graduate of the Ukrainian Free University in Munich and the London School of Economics and Political Science, he is a contributor to *Ukraïns'kyi samostiinyk* and *Suchasnist'*. He is a member of the Political Council of the OUN, and since 1982 of the Presidium of the External Representation of the *Ukrainian Supreme Liberation Council. Having worked many years for the *Prolog Research Corporation in New York, in 1984 he became editor in chief of the Ukrainian desk at Radio Liberty in Munich. As a publicist he has written several books on the political struggle for Ukrainian independence: *Na novomu etapi* (On a New Standpoint, 1965), *Za suchasnu kontseptsiiu ukraïns'koï revoliutsiï* (For a Contemporary Concept of the Ukrainian Revolution, 1970), *Dynamika vyzvol'noï borot'by* (Dynamics of Liberation Struggle, 1973), and *Do perspektyv nashoï polityky* (Toward a Perspective on Our Politics, 1977).

Kaminsky, Andrii [Kamins'kyj, Andrij] (pseud: Pidesha), b 1873 in Galicia, d 1957 in Yugoslavia and buried in Maribor. Priest, pedagogue, and publicist. From 1906 to 1918 he was a coeditor of the newspaper *Svoboda* in the United States. After the First World War he settled in Yugoslavia and in his writings propagated Slavophile ideas, particularly the idea of Ukrainian and Russian cooperation against Polish and German expansionism in Eastern Europe. He wrote a novel about student life, *Vostok i Zapad* (The East and the West, 1903), and numerous popular political booklets such as *Halychchyna piiemontom* (Galicia as the Piedmont, 1924), *Zahadka Ukraïny i Halychchyny* (The Riddle of Ukraine and Galicia, 1927), *Narodnyky i obshcherosy* (Populists and All-Russians, 1930), and *Synteza ukraïnstva i rusofil'stva* (The Synthesis of Ukrainianism and Russophilism, 1937).

Kaminsky, Bonifatii [Kamins'kyj, Bonifatij], b 1873? in Pryluka, Poltava gubernia, d 1919 in Kiev. Community and political leader. He was one of the founders of the Revolutionary Ukrainian party and later a member of the Ukrainian Social Democratic Workers' party. He worked for the Kherson zemstvo (1914–17) and then for the All-Ukrainian Zemstvo Union.

Kaminsky, Fedir [Kamins'kyj], b 1845 in Minsk gubernia, d 1 April 1891 in Kruhlyk, Lubni county, Poltava gubernia. Archeologist. Kaminsky studied at Kiev University and then worked as a teacher in Pereiaslav, Khorol, Lubni, and Pryluky. In 1873 he was the first to excavate a Paleolithic site in Ukraine, at *Hintsi in the Poltava region. His discoveries were published in the proceedings (*Trudy*) of the Third Archeological Congress in Kiev, and sparked interest in the study of Paleolithic monuments in Eastern Europe. He also excavated monuments in the region of Lubni, particularly Scythian kurhans. He contributed articles to the journal *Kievskaia starina*.

Kaminsky, Viacheslav [Kamins'kyj, Vjačeslav], 1869–1938? Ethnographer; a specialist in Ukrainian customary law. For over 10 years he was the secretary of the VUAN Commission for the Study of Ukraine's Customary Law. Kaminsky contributed articles to the commission's series *Pratsi Komisiï* ... and to the journals *Etnohrafichnyi visnyk* and *Zapysky Istorychno-filolohichnoho viddilu VUAN*; a separate collection of his essays appeared as *Narysy zvychaievoho prava Ukraïny* (Sketches of the Customary Law of Ukraine, 1928). Kaminsky was arrested by the Soviet authorities in 1934 and died in prison.

Kaminsky, Yosyf [Kamins'kyj, Josyf], b 17 November 1878 in Rakovec nad Odnavou, Zemplén county, Hungary, d 1944 in Uzhhorod, Transcarpathia. Priest, editor, lawyer; pro-Hungarian political leader. In 1920 he helped found the opposition Autonomous Agricultural Union, but in 1923 went over to the pro-government Agrarian party and won a seat in parliament (1924–5). Turning against the regime, he returned to the Autonomous Agricultural Union and published his own paper, *Karpatorusskii golos* (1932–4), and edited calendars for the Dukhnovych Society. In 1939, upon Hungary's occupation of Transcarpathia, he was appointed to the Upper House of the Hungarian Parliament. He disappeared when the Red Army entered Hungary in 1944. Besides some brief studies on local history, his publications include *Natsional'noe samosoznanie nashego naroda* (The National Self-consciousness of Our People, 1925) and *Istoriia Tsentral'noi russkoi narodnoi rady* (A History of the Central Russian People's Council, 1927).

Kampov, Pavlo, b 21 September 1929 in Dilok, Transcarpathia. Dissident. A graduate of Uzhhorod University

(1952), he taught mathematics at the university. In 1970 he stood as an unofficial candidate in the elections to the Supreme Soviet of the Ukrainian SSR. He was arrested and sentenced to six years in prison and three years of exile for his booklet *Dvadtsiat' piat' rokiv nadii i rozcharuvan'* (Twenty-five Years of Hopes and Disappointments). Because of severe illness, he was released in 1977, two years before completing his term. In 1981 he was arrested again and sentenced to 10 years in prison and 3 years of exile. He became almost totally blind at the Lviv labor camp. His *samvydav* book *Vykhovuvaty liudei dobrymy* (To Educate People to Be Good) and his letters, protests, and appeals to the authorities are widely circulated in Ukraine.

Kamula. IV-5. A hill situated southeast of Lviv in the western part of the *Holohory and marking the highest point (471 m) of the Podolian Upland.

Kanada (Canada). Weekly newspaper published from 2 September 1913 to 4 January 1915 in Winnipeg by the Ruthenian Publishing Company, which was organized by such prominent Ukrainian members of the Conservative party as T. Stefanyk, P. Gigeichuk, and H. Bodnar. Its editors were I. Sluzar and N. Bachynsky. The paper was subsidized by the Conservative party in Manitoba, and it portrayed the party as a friend of the Ukrainian farmer. *Kanada* attacked vehemently all Ukrainian leaders and organizations except for Bishop N. Budka and the Ukrainian Catholic church. Its most known contributor was P. *Karmansky.

Kanadiis'ka Sich (The Canadian Sitch). Ukrainian monthly published from 15 April 1928 to 15 August 1930 in Winnipeg by the *Canadian Sitch Organization and edited by V. Bosy. The paper propagated a monarchist ideology based on the writings of V. *Lypynsky, and featured an English-language section under the motto 'Work and Order.' Altogether 19 issues were published.

Kanadiiskaia nyva (The Canadian Field). A Russophile religious and political fortnightly published from September 1908 to 1910 in Winnipeg and from 1909 also in Edmonton. The publisher and editor was Hegumen A. Chekhovtsev, who was assisted by M. Gowda. An organ of the Russian Orthodox Mission in Canada, the purpose of the newspaper was to attract Orthodox, and even Catholic, Ukrainians to the Russian church and to gain their support for the tsarist regime. It was printed in Ukrainian with Russian transliteration.

Kanadiiskaia pravoslavnaia Rus' (Canadian Orthodox Rus'). An anti-Ukrainian religious and political fortnightly published from 28 September 1916 to 1917 in Winnipeg by the Russian Orthodox Mission in Canada. The tabloid was printed mainly in Russian with a few articles in Ukrainian. It contained mostly political articles by Archimandrite A. Fylypovsky and V. Hladyk, which denied the distinctiveness of the Ukrainian people and propagated Russian patriotism. The paper's appearance marked the beginning of independence for the Russian Orthodox Church in Canada.

Kanadiis'kyi farmer (Canadian Farmer). First Ukrainian-language newspaper in Canada, published weekly

15193
КАНАДИЙСКІЙ ФАРМЕР
CANADIAN FARMER

Kanadiis'kyi farmer

in Winnipeg from 12 November 1903 to 9 November 1981. Its first owner was the North West Publishing Company formed by K. Genik, I. Bodrug, and I. Negrich. During its first decade it was subsidized by the Liberal party, and it maintained essentially a pro-Liberal policy until 1963. An advocate of Ukraine's independence, the paper was a staunch opponent of Communism and a strong supporter of the Ukrainian Canadian Committee. Except for a brief period (1928–32) when it belonged to the National Press, a pro-Conservative group led by H. Kurdydyk and L. Biberovych, it was owned from 1913 to 1973 by F. Dojaček and his sons. In 1966 an American edition of the paper, *Vil'nyi svit*, appeared. In the fall of 1973 it was purchased by Trident Press, the publisher of *Ukraïns'kyi holos*, with which it was amalgamated in 1981. Its editors included I. Negrich, O. Megas, A. Novak, O. Hykavy (1913–32, 1944–5), M. Hykavy (1945–61), M. Shkavrytko (1963–73), B. Martynovych (1974–8), and Yu. Mulyk-Lutsyk (1978–81). Between 1929 and 1969 the circulation was approximately 15,000.

Kanadiis'kyi ranok (Canadian Morning). Ukrainian religious newspaper published from 19 October 1920 to 31 August 1961. It was set up through the merger of the Methodist *Kanadyiets'* and the Presbyterian **Ranok*. Subsidized by the United Church of Canada, until 1932 the paper appeared monthly and thereafter semimonthly. It followed a moderate editorial policy and covered not only religious issues but also cultural and social developments in Canada and Ukraine. Among its editors were D. Pyrch, Z. Bychynsky, M. Karabut, M. Berezynsky, I. Kovalevych, and L. Standret. When the United Church withdrew its support, the Ukrainian Evangelical Alliance of North America assumed responsibility for it and changed its name to **Ievanhel's'kyi ranok*.

Kanadiis'kyi rusyn. See *Kanadiis'kyi ukraïnets'*.

Kanadiis'kyi ukraïnets' (Canadian Ukrainian). Ukrainian Catholic weekly inspired by Metropolitan A. Sheptytsky. It began publication on 27 May 1911 in Winnipeg under the name *Kanadiis'kyi rusyn* (Canadian Ruthenian). Financed until 1916 by St Boniface diocese under Archbishop A. Langevin, it sought to neutralize the influence of Protestant, Russian Orthodox, and secular ideas within the Ukrainian Canadian community. Supported by Bishop N. Budka, it was an important organ of the Ukrainian Catholic church. In April 1919 it was renamed *Kanadiis'kyi ukraïnets'*. Burdened with debts resulting from costly libel suits by the Ukrainian Greek Orthodox church during the 1920s, it was sold to a private company in 1927. The last issue appeared on 11 March 1931. Among its editors were M. Syroidiv, O. Sushko, I. Petrushevych, Rev M. Zalitach, Rev P. Oleksiv, R. Kremar, I. Rudachek, T. Martsiniv, A. Zahariichuk, V. Bosy, and V. Biberovych.

Kanadyiets' (The Canadian). Religious newspaper published semimonthly from January 1912 to June 1920 in Edmonton. It was edited by M. Belegai and subsidized by the Methodist church. The paper contained expositions of the Bible, articles on the history of Protestantism, attacks on the Catholic church, and practical information for farmers. It paid little attention to developments in Ukraine or in Ukrainian-Canadian communities and, therefore, found few readers. In 1920 it was merged with the Presbyterian paper **Ranok* to form **Kanadiis'kyi ranok*.

Kandyba. Name of a Cossack *starshyna* family originally from Right-Bank Ukraine that later settled in the Konotip region. Andronyk's descendants Semen, Mykhailo, and Petro all served as captains of Pishchane company in Cherkasy regiment in the mid-18th century. Fedir was colonel of Korsun regiment (1669–72), captain of Konotip regiment (from 1681), and then Nizhen regimental quartermaster (1698–1700). He participated in the Chyhyryn (1677–8) and Crimean (1687, 1689) campaigns against the Turks. His son Andronyk (Andrii, d 1730) was captain of Konotip regiment (1698–1707), colonel of the Korsun regiment (1708–9), and later general judge (1729). He was interned in Moscow from 1710 to 1715 for supporting I. Mazepa's alliance with Sweden against Russia.

Ivan Kandyba

Kandyba, Ivan, b 7 July 1930 in Stoino, Podlachia (now in Poland). Dissident, active in the national and human rights movements in Ukraine. A graduate of Lviv University, he practiced law until his arrest in 1961. He was accused of treason and anti-Soviet agitation and propaganda for having organized with L. *Lukianenko the Ukrainian Workers' and Peasants' Union and having raised the issue of Ukraine's right to secede from the USSR. Kandyba served 15 years in strict-regime labor camps in Mordovia. His account of his trial and similar political trials in the 1950s, titled *Za pravdu i spravedlyvist'* (For Truth and Justice), was smuggled out of prison and published in the West. After being released in 1976, Kandyba made every effort to emigrate. In 1976 he became a founding member of the *Ukrainian Helsinki Group. This led to his arrest in 1977 and to the maximum sentence of 10 years in prison and 5 years of exile for anti-Soviet agitation and propaganda.

Kandyba, Oleh. See Olzhych, Oleh.

Kandyba, Oleksander. See Oles, Oleksander.

Kaniuk, Serhii [Kanjuk, Serhij], b 15 July 1880 in Khlivyshche, Kitsman county, Bukovyna, d 15 March 1945 in Karaganda, Kazakhstan. Bukovynian political leader and publicist. By profession a teacher and an inspector of primary schools, he led the left wing of the Social Democratic party of Bukovyna. In 1918 he helped organize the Communist Party of Bukovyna. He was the publisher and editor of the pro-Soviet weeklies *Volia narodu* (1919–20) and *Hromada* (1921), which appeared in Chernivtsi. In 1922 he immigrated to the Ukrainian SSR, where he served in the People's Commissariat of Education. Kaniuk's publications include brochures in defense of Bukovynian Ukrainians such as *Pid chobotom rumuns'kykh boiar* (Under the Heel of Rumanian Boyars, 1930) and *Bukovyna v rumuns'kii nevoli* (Bukovyna in Rumanian Captivity, 1930), short stories, and pedagogical articles. In the 1930s he was imprisoned and died in a labor camp.

Kaniv: Shevchenko Museum (designed by V. Krychevsky and P. Kostyrko, 1934–7)

Kaniv. IV-12. City (1971 pop 18,800) under oblast jurisdiction, raion center in Cherkasy oblast, situated on the right bank of the Dnieper River (now the Kaniv Reservoir). One of the most important cities in Kievan Rus', it was mentioned in the Kievan Cave Patericon as existing in the last half of the 11th century. Kaniv arose on the site of, or near, the fortified city of *Roden. From the middle of the 12th century it was an important trade center on the Dnieper route to Constantinople (until the latter's capture by the Turks in 1453), the residence of various appanage princes and of Mstyslav Mstyslavych and Roman Mstyslavych, and a fortress defending the frontier of Rus' and traders from Cuman invaders. Under Lithuanian rule (1362–1596) it was governed by *starostas. In 1556 it was granted the rights of Magdeburg law. In the Cossack period it was a regimental center (1637–78). Under Russian rule (from 1793) it was a county town in Kiev gubernia (1838–1917). In the summer of 1920 UNR and Bolshevik forces fought each other there. Kaniv was also a raion center in Kiev gubernia (1923–5), Cherkasy okruha (1925–30), and Kiev oblast (1932–54). Today food production, an electromechanical plant, and the *Kaniv Hydroelectric Station are the mainstays of the city's economy. Located there are a cultural-educational school, a vocational-technical school, and a museum of decorative folk art. St George's (or Dormition) Cathedral, built in

1144 by Vsevolod Olhovych, has been preserved there to this day. The *Kaniv Museum-Preserve, where T. Shevchenko is buried, the *Kaniv Nature and Historical Reserve, and the archeological sites of *Kniazha Hora and the *Kaniv settlement are located nearby.

V. Kubijovyč

Kaniv Hills. A range of hills, 3–9 km wide, forming the eastern edge of the Dnieper Upland. They extend a distance of 70 km, from Trakhtemyriv to the mouth of the Ros River, and are clearly demarcated from the rest of the Dnieper Upland. The hills are 80–255 m high and descend steeply (down to 160 m) to the Dnieper River. They consist of Triassic, chalk, and Tertiary strata that were dislocated by the Dnieper glacier and are dissected by numerous ravines. Their slopes are covered with forest. The *Kaniv Nature and Historical Reserve and the *Kaniv Museum-Preserve, where T. Shevchenko is buried, are located there.

Kaniv Hydroelectric Station. One of stations of the Dnieper Cascade of Hydroelectric Stations, built near Kaniv between 1963 and 1975. Its 24 turbine generators (total capacity: 444,000 kW) produce an annual average output of 323 million kWh.

Kaniv Museum-Preserve (Kanivskyi muzei-zapovidnyk 'Mohyla T.H. Shevchenka'). A park containing the grave of Ukraine's greatest poet and national figure, T. *Shevchenko, and a museum dedicated to his memory, located near the city of Kaniv on Tarasova (formerly Chernecha) Hill. A monument by K. Tereshchenko was first erected on Shevchenko's grave in 1923. The park was created in 1925 by government decree. In 1939 a new, bronze monument to the poet by the sculptor M. Manizer was erected, and the museum, designed by the architects V. Krychevsky and P. Kostyrko, was opened. Destroyed during the Second World War by the German army, the museum and the monument were rebuilt. Both are major tourist attractions.

Kaniv Museum-Preserve: Monument to Taras Shevchenko

Kaniv Nature and Historical Reserve (Kanivskyi pryrodnycho-istorychnyi zapovidnyk). A reserve located on the right bank of the Dnieper River near Kaniv in Cherkasy oblast. Established in 1931 as the National Forest Steppe Reserve, it was renamed the Middle Dnieper National Reserve in 1934 and the Kaniv Biogeographical Reserve in 1939 before assuming its present name in 1948. It has an area of 1,035 ha. The reserve is located in the northern part of the Ukrainian *forest-steppe region in the *Kaniv Hills. Forests, mainly elm and oak, predominate. The hills are broken by deep ravines, where several geological strata, containing fossils of some extinct plants and animals, are visible. The fauna of the reserve is typical of the forest-steppe; the most common animals are roe deer, badger, and marten. Approximately 275 species of birds are also found there. The Kaniv reserve is rich in historical artifacts. Archeological research has uncovered artifacts from the late Paleolithic and Neolithic eras, the Trypilian culture, and Scythian settlements, and some traces of Antes and Polianian tombs.

Kaniv Reservoir. A reservoir created in 1972 by the dams of the Kaniv Hydroelectric Station on the Dnieper River. It is 162 km long and up to 5 km wide and has a

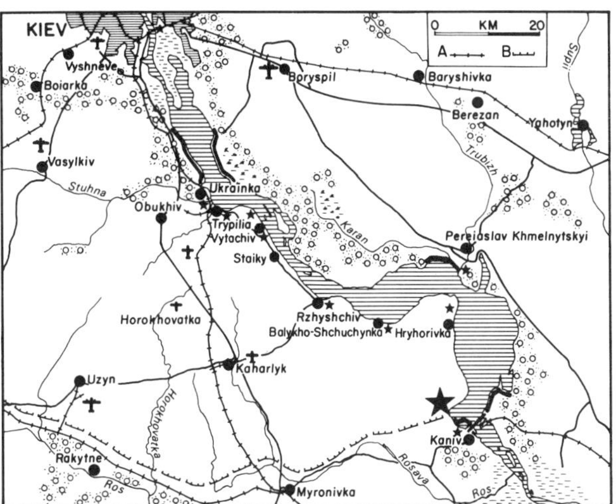

KANIV RESERVOIR

A. Railway line
B. Kaniv–Bila Tserkva underground canal

Large star indicates hydroelectric station; small stars are river ports.

surface area of 675 sq km, a volume of 2.6 cu km, and an average depth of 5.5 m. Together with the *Kakhivka and *Kiev reservoirs it has created a deep-water route on the Dnieper, allowing sea ships to sail upstream as far as the Prypiat River.

Kaniv settlement. An ancient Slavic settlement dating back to the 7th–9th centuries AD, situated along the right bank of the Dnieper River near the city of Kaniv. Excavations carried out in 1957–62 uncovered the remains of pit dwellings and semi-pit dwellings containing ovens and sleeping platforms, fragments of pottery ware and farm implements, iron knives, fishing hooks, arrowheads, and bronze and glass ornaments. The inhabitants of the settlement lived by farming and herding, supplemented by hunting and fishing, and practiced pottery and metalworking.

Kantemyrivka settlements and burial site. Early Slavic settlements and burial ground of the *Cherniakhiv culture (2nd–6th centuries AD), situated near Kantemyrivka, Chutove raion, Poltava oblast. Excavations of the site in 1924 and 1948 uncovered the remains of a storage shed, three kurhans with a catacomb, a niche, and a pit burial, and 10 other graves. Remnants of earthen and glass ware, bone combs, bronze fibulas and buckles, glass counters, gold ornaments, and iron fishing rods were found in the graves.

Kantianism. The distinctive system of philosophy developed by I. Kant (1724–1804). In Ukraine it received some attention, but never gained much of a following among thinkers. Information on Kant's philosophy was disseminated mostly by followers of F. Schelling and G. Hegel (see *Hegelianism) such as J. Schad in Kharkiv. Some of Kant's doctrines were expounded by P. Lodii in his *Logicheskie nastavleniia rukovodstvuiushchiia k poznaniiu i razlichiiu istinnogo ot lozhnogo* (Logical Rules Leading to the Understanding of and Distinction between Truth and Falsehood, 1915) and by V. Dovhovych in his *Extractus systematis Kantiani* (manuscript). In the 1830s and 1840s Kant's philosophy was studied at the Kiev Theological Academy from a historical point of view. Graduates of the academy such as S. Hohotsky and P. Yurkevych devoted some attention to Kant: the first wrote *Kriticheskii vzgliad na filosofiiu Kanta* (A Critical View of Kant's Philosophy, 1847) and the second 'Razum po ucheniiu Platona i opyt po ucheniiu Kanta' (Reason According to Plato's Teaching and Experience According to Kant's Teaching, 1865). Towards the end of the century two professors of Kiev University analyzed certain Kantian doctrines: A. Kozlov published *Genesis teorii prostranstva i vremeni Kanta* (The Genesis of Kant's Theory of Space and Time, 1884) and G. Chelpanov published *Istoriia osnovnykh voprosov etiki* (History of the Fundamental Problems of Ethics, 1897). Kant had a certain positivist influence on the later works of V. Lesevych. Some work on Kant was done at Odessa University: professor M. Lange discussed Kant in his *Istoriia nravstvennykh idei XIX v.* (History of Moral Ideas of the 19th Century, 1888), and M. Hordiievsky published 'Kriticheskii razbor dvukh pervykh antinomii Kanta' (A Critical Analysis of Kant's First Two Antinomies, 1910) in the university's *Zapiski*. B. Kistiakovsky's theory of method in the social sciences owes much to modern German Kantianism. A Ukrainian translation of Kant's *Prolegomena to Any Future Metaphysics*, edited and introduced by I. Mirchuk, was published in 1930.

D. Chyzhevsky, T. Zakydalsky

Kaolin. A soft white clay consisting of the mineral kaolinite and varying amounts of other minerals. It is used in the making of porcelain, china, refractories, paper, rubber, paint, cosmetics, and many other products. Kaolin is widespread in the Ukrainian Crystalline Shield, and small deposits are found in Transcarpathia and Subcarpathia. Of about 1,000 deposits in Ukraine, only 12 are mined. The largest ones are near Hlukhivtsi in Vinnytsia oblast, Prosiana in Dnipropetrovske oblast, and Polohy in Zaporizhia oblast. Kaolins mined in Ukraine account for 85 percent of all Soviet production.

Pylyp Kapelhorodsky

Kapelhorodsky, Pylyp [Kapel'horods'kyj], b 26 November 1882 in Horodyshche, Lebedyn county, Kharkiv gubernia, d 21 November 1942. Writer and journalist. A student at the Poltava Theological Seminary (1897–1902), he was persecuted for his revolutionary activity by the tsarist authorities. From 1904 he lived in the Kuban and worked as a teacher and journalist. After the 1917 Revolution he returned to Ukraine. In the 1920s he worked for newspapers in Lubni and Poltava and belonged to the peasant writers' organization Pluh. His first poems were published in the 1905 almanac *Persha lastivka*. In 1907 his book *Ukraïntsi na Kubani* (Ukrainians in the Kuban) and the poetry collection *Vidhuky zhyttia* (Echoes of Life) appeared. In the late 1920s he published three short collections of satirical and humorous prose and the novella *Neporozuminnia* (Misunderstanding, 1928). His novel-chronicle about the revolution in the Kuban, *Shurhan*, appeared in 1932. Kapelhorodsky was repressed during the *Yezhov terror and rehabilitated after J. Stalin's death. A collection of his works was published in Kiev in 1961.

Kapelle (Ukrainian: *kapelia*). An ensemble of singers or instrumentalists or both. Kapellen originated in Ukraine in the 15th century as church-choir ensembles. In the 16th and 17th centuries, choral-instrumental or purely instrumental kapellen, performing both sacred and secular music, appeared. From the 16th century on, choral kapellen were organized at the bursas (residences) of brotherhood schools and at metropolitans' cathedrals. Manor kapellen, primarily at the palaces of hetmans, arose in the 17th century. During the 19th and early 20th centuries, itinerant choral ensembles were organized by such composers and conductors as M. Lysenko, Ya. Kalishevsky, H. Davydovsky, and K. Stetsenko. Professional ensembles, which emerged later, included the *Ukrainian Republican Kapelle (1919–21, conductor O. Koshyts), the DUMKA choral kapelle (1919–), the Poltava Banduryst Kapelle (1925–35), the State Ukrainian Choir in Kharkiv (DUKh, 1920s), the Kiev Banduryst Kapelle (1918–35), the State Banduryst Kapelle of the Ukrainian SSR (1935–) in Kiev, and the Ukrainian Bandurist Chorus in Detroit. Among the best-known amateur ensembles are those of the Kiev Polytechnical Institute and the Donets Railroad.

Kapishovsky, Vasyl [Kapišovs'kyj, Vasyl'], b 7 July 1914 in Komloš (now Chmelova) in the Bardejov district in Eastern Slovakia. Pedagogue and Communist Party activist. He has been a Party functionary since 1945. From 1946 to 1948 he directed Ukrainian schools in Slovakia. He has also been a delegate to the Slovak national council and, since 1969, a delegate to the federal national congress. From 1963 to 1968 he headed the Central Committee of the *Cultural Association of Ukrainian Workers in Czechoslovakia. After the Soviet invasion in 1968 he was accused of 'bourgeois nationalism.' He has written several socioeconomic studies and cultural histories of the Ukrainian minority in the Prešov region, including *Skhidnia Slovachchyna vchora i s'ohodni* (Eastern Slovakia, Past and Present, 1983).

Kapitula, Dmytro, b 14 October 1873 in Sviatkova Velyka, Jasło county, Galicia, d 25 December 1953 in McAdoo, Pennysylvania. One of the first Ukrainian community leaders in the United States. Settling in the United States in 1888, he served as president of the *Ukrainian National Association (1908–17) and then as chairman of its auditing committee (1933–53). He was one of the founding members of the Ukrainian Congress Committee of America.

Kapka, Dmytro (real name: Kapkunov), b 7 November 1898 in Kiev, d 23 October 1977 in Kiev. Comic actor. He began to perform on the stage of the State People's Theater in 1918 and then sang in the choir DUMKA. He studied film acting in Warsaw. From 1923 to 1964, except for the 1930s, he worked in the cinema, appearing in such roles as Smith in *Pidozrilyi bahazh* (Suspicious Baggage, 1926), the doll merchant in *Iahidky kokhannia* (The Berries of Love, 1926), Matnia in *Mykola Dzheria* (1927), Kozhukh in *Bohdan Khmel'nyts'kyi* (1941), and Tkach in *Vechori na khutori bilia Dykan'ky* (Evenings at the Khutir near Dykanka, 1961).

Kapkan, Yurii, 1875–? Senior officer of the UNR Army. A lieutenant colonel in the Russian army and author of a field manual on machine guns, he joined the Ukrainian army in the spring of 1917. Promoted to colonel, he commanded the *Khmelnytsky Regiment and the First Serdiuk Division. At the end of 1917 he was in charge of the Ukrainian forces at the Bolshevik front. In 1919 he served as an infantry inspector of the UNR Army.

Kapnist. Name of a noble family that owned estates in Left-Bank Ukraine. Its members used the title of count, which was granted to their Greek ancestor Stomatello Kapnissis in Venice in 1702; it was not recognized in Russia until the 1870s. Stomatello's brother (?) Basilio (?–1757) enrolled as Vasyl Kapnist in the Russian army during the 1711 Prut campaign of Tsar Peter I. He became a captain in Izium regiment in 1726, the colonel of Myrhorod regiment in 1737, and brigadier of the Slobidska Ukraine regiments in 1751. He was killed during the Seven Years' War near Gross Jägersdorf in East Prussia. Three of his sons – Mykola, Petro, and Vasyl – were Ukrainian patriots. Mykola became the marshal of the Katerynoslav gubernia nobility in 1795. Petro (ca 1750–1826) was a guard officer who lived abroad for 20 years; he returned to Ukraine a convinced republican and established a 'republic' on his estate in the village of Turbaitsi, Khorol county. Vasyl *Kapnist was a famous poet and civic leader. One of Vasyl's sons, Ivan (ca 1794–1860), was the marshal of the Poltava gubernia nobility and a friend of Prince M. Repnin. He took part in designing a project for the renewal of Ukrainian Cossack regiments in 1831. Later he became the governor of Smolensk and of Moscow. Oleksa (ca 1796–1869), marshal of the nobility of Myrhorod county and a friend of T. Shevchenko, and Semen (ca 1791–1843), the marshal of Kremenchuk county, were involved in the Decembrist movement.

O. Ohloblyn

Vasyl Kapnist

Kapnist, Vasyl, b 23 February 1758 in Obukhivka, Myrhorod regiment, d 9 November 1823 in Kybyntsi, Poltava gubernia. Noted poet; civic and political figure. He served as marshal of the nobility for Myrhorod county in 1782 and for Kiev gubernia in 1785–7. In 1782 he composed 'Oda na rabstvo' (Ode on Slavery) protesting the Russian government's abolition of Ukraine's autonomy. During the Russian empire's two-front war with Turkey and Sweden his plan for reviving volunteer Cossack regiments in Ukraine, drafted in 1788, was not implemented by the tsarist government. In 1791 Ukrainian patriotic circles, probably from Novhorod-Siverskyi, entrusted him with secret negotiations in Berlin for Prussian aid in the event of a Russian-Prussian war and a possible Cossack rebellion against Russia, but he did not obtain a definite commitment. His comedy *Iabeda* (Calumny, 1798) condemned Russia's centralist policy in Ukraine. As general judge (1802) and marshal for Poltava gubernia (from 1820), he defended Ukrainian interests, especially during the Napoleonic invasion of 1812–13 when 15 Cossack regiments were re-established and when Cossacks were exempted from the draft and various taxes. In this period he wrote lyrical poetry, modeling himself on classical poets such as Horace. He also translated *Slovo o polku Ihorevi* (The Tale of Ihor's Campaign) into Russian, adding an interesting commentary emphasizing the poem's Ukrainian origin and distinctive Ukrainian qualities. His collected works were published in 1796, 1806, 1849, and 1960.

BIBLIOGRAPHY
Berkov, P. *V.V. Kapnist* (Moscow-Leningrad 1950)
Ohloblyn, O. 'Vasyl' Kapnist,' *Literaturno-naukovyi zbirnyk* UVAN, vol 1 (New York 1952)
Matsai, A. *'Iabeda' V.V. Kapnista* (Kiev 1958)

O. Ohloblyn

Petro Kapshuchenko: *Spanish Dance*

Kapshuchenko, Petro [Kapšučenko] (Kapschutenko, Pedro or Peter), b 27 September 1915 in Ukraine. Sculptor specializing in miniatures. He studied art in Ukraine and Germany. Immigrating in 1949 to Argentina, he won recognition for his work and was elected honorary member of the Universidad Libre de Humanidades in Buenos Aires. In 1963 he settled in Philadelphia, USA, where he took part in many Ukrainian exhibits. His one-man shows in 1973 at the Museum of Fine Arts in Springfield, Massachusetts, and at the Washington County Museum, Hagerstown, Maryland, introduced him to the wider American public. Most of his works deal with contemporary everyday life (eg, *Mexican Roundup, Spanish Dance, Old Woman Sewing*, and *Street Musician*), but some have a religious (eg, *Blessing of St John*) or historical (eg, *Kozak with Bandura* and *Hopak*) theme. His monumental works include the statue of Metropolitan V. Lypkivsky at the Ukrainian Orthodox Center in South Bound Brook, New Jersey. Kapshuchenko's style is very expressive and often humorous.

Kaptarenko-Chornousova, Olha [Kaptarenko-Čornousova, Ol'ha], b 21 May 1899 in Nova Ivanivka, Bessarabia. Geologist and paleontologist. She graduated from the Kamianets-Podilskyi Institute of People's Education in 1923 and received her doctorate from the Institute of Geological Sciences of the AN URSR in 1947. From 1928 Kaptarenko-Chornousova was an associate and from 1947 a department head of the Institute of Geological Sciences of the AN URSR. Her scientific works deal with the study of rhizopods, stratigraphy, and paleontology of the Jurassic, cretaceous, and paleogene seams of Ukraine.

Kapto, Oleksander, b 14 April 1933 in Vyshchetarasivka, Tomakivka county, Dnipropetrovske oblast. Communist Party activist. From 1957 he worked in the Communist Youth League of Ukraine, editing its newspaper *Komsomol'skoe znamia* (1963–6) and serving as second and then first secretary of the Central Committee (1966–72). After a brief term as secretary of the Kiev city committee of the CPU, he was appointed secretary of the Kiev oblast committee (1972–9). Since 1979 he has been a secretary of the CC CPU and a candidate member of the Politburo.

Kapusta, Lavrin, b and d ? Otaman of Chyhyryn, and one of the men in charge of intelligence for Hetman B. Khmelnytsky. He investigated a circle of spies working for the Poles, which included a number of people close to the hetman; among them was Khmelnytsky's second wife, M. Czaplińska. He uncovered Col M. Fedorovych's plot to overthrow the hetman and the assassination plans of the Polish spy J. Smiarowski. Kapusta also carried out important diplomatic assignments. In September–October 1653 he was sent by Khmelnytsky to Moscow to urge the tsar to begin his campaign against Poland. In 1657 he was sent on a mission to Constantinople.

Kapustiansky, Ivan [Kapustjans'kyj], b 1894 in Zhovtneve in the Poltava region, d 1939? Literary scholar and journalist. A graduate of the Nizhen Historical-Philological Institute, he taught at the Poltava Institute of People's Education (1921–5) and then was a graduate student at the Kharkiv Institute of People's Education and a scholarly associate of the Shevchenko Institute of Literature in Kharkiv. In 1923 he joined the peasant writers' organization Pluh. His literary, pedagogical, and publicistic articles appeared in Soviet Ukrainian periodicals; reprinted separately were *Sotsiial'na pisnia na ukraïns'komu grunti* (The Social Song on Ukrainian Soil, 1924) and *Uchytel'stvo v ukraïns'kii literaturi* (Teachers in Ukrainian Literature, 1925). He also wrote the monograph *Valeriian Polishchuk* (1925). In 1934 he disappeared in the GULAG.

Kapustiansky, Mykola [Kapustjans'kyj], b 1 February 1879 in Chumaky, Katerynoslav gubernia, d 19 February 1969 in Munich. Senior officer of the Ukrainian army in 1917–20 and member of the OUN Leadership. A graduate of the General Staff Academy in St Petersburg (1912), he fought in the Russian-Japanese War and the First World

Mykola Kapustiansky

War, and by 1917 reached the rank of colonel. After the Revolution he joined the Ukrainian units of the Russian army and served as their delegate to the Second All-Ukrainian Military Congress. In August 1917 he was appointed chief of staff of the First Division of the First Ukrainian Corps, and in early 1918 chief of staff of the southwestern front. Under the Directory, he served as operations chief and then as general quartermaster of the UNR Army. In 1920 he was promoted to brigadier general. After the war he emigrated to Poland and then France, where he organized and headed the *Ukrainian National Union. Kapustiansky was a founder of the OUN and a member of its Leadership (1929–69). In 1935–6 he visited Ukrainian communities in the United States and Canada to gain support for the OUN. During the Second World War he served as vice-president of the Ukrainian National Council in Kiev, and was imprisoned by the Germans. After the war he was the first chief of the military section of the Government-in-exile of the UNR. He wrote *Pokhid ukraïns'kykh armii na Kyïv-Odesu v 1919 rotsi* (The March of Ukrainian Armies on Kiev-Odessa in 1919; 1922, 2nd edn 1946) and numerous articles on military affairs.

P. Sodol

Kapynos (Kupynos), Voitykh, ?–ca 1610. Architect. From 1582 he was listed as a master in the Lviv builders' guild register. In 1597 he joined his father-in-law, P. Romanus, in building the famous Dormition Church in Lviv.

Karabelesh, Andrii [Karabeleš, Andrij], b 24 September 1906 in Tybava (now in Svaliava raion), Transcarpathia, d there 4 September 1964. Russophile poet and writer. In the 1930s he worked as a teacher in Transcarpathia. From 1941 to 1945 he was imprisoned in German concentration camps. After the war he became a professor at Prešov University. Writing only in Russian, he remained outside the mainstream Ukrainian revival in eastern Slovakia. He authored the collections *Izbranye proizvedeniia* (Collected Works, 1928), *V luchakh rassveta* (In Dawn's Rays, 1929), *Na smertel'nom rubezhe (Zapiski iz fashists'kikh kontslagerei)* (On the Verge of Death [Notes from Fascist Concentration Camps], 1953), and *V Karpatakh* (In the Carpathians, 1955).

Karabinevych, Apolinariia [Karabinevyč, Apolinarija] (née Lopukhovych; stage name: Liucia Barvinok), b 8 October 1896 in Chernihiv, d 22 August 1971 in Rochester, New York. Character actress and stage director. She began her acting career in the O. Sukhodolsky and O. Mitkevych troupes. From 1920 to 1939 she worked as an actress and stage director in the Galician touring company known as the Sadovsky Ukrainian Drama Theater, and then became artistic director of the Ternopil Oblast State Ukrainian Drama Theater (1939–41). Her repertoire included Kylyna in O. Sukhodolsky's *Khmara* (The Cloud), Hanna in O. Barvinsky's *Het'man Polubotok*, and Khyvria in M. Starytsky's *Sorochyns'kyi iarmarok* (The Sorochyntsi Fair). Having left Ukraine before the war's end, she immigrated to the United States in 1949.

Karabinevych, Opanas [Karabinevyč], b 1892?, d 1970? in Lviv. Stage actor and director. From 1924 to 1939 he was the director of the Galician touring company known as the Sadovsky Ukrainian Drama Theater, which specialized in ethnographic and historical plays. During the Soviet occupation of Galicia in 1939–41, he reorganized this company into the Ternopil Oblast State Ukrainian Drama Theater. Later, he was assigned to a collective-farm theater in Berezhany. After serving a long term as a prisoner of conscience, he was released in the 1960s and returned to Lviv.

Karabi-Yaila [Karabi-Jajla]. The largest tablelike massif in the main range of the *Crimean Mountains.

Karabynevych, Mykolai [Karabynevyč, Mykolaj], b 1888 in the Podilia region, d 1932? Bishop of the Ukrainian Autocephalous Orthodox church. He graduated from the Podilia Theological Seminary and was ordained in 1911. In 1923 he was consecrated bishop of Mohyliv-Podilia and in 1931 he became bishop of Uman. He contributed to the journal *Tserkva i Zhyttia* (1927). In 1932 he was arrested and shot in Moscow (according to some sources he was executed in 1935).

Karabyts, Ivan [Karabyc'], b 17 January 1945 in Yalta, Pershotravneve raion, Donetske oblast. Composer and conductor. A graduate of the Kiev Conservatory (1971) and a student of B. *Liatoshynsky and M. Skoryk, he conducted the Song and Dance Ensemble of the Kiev Military Okruha (1968–74). His compositions include a cycle of 24 preludes for piano, a piano trio, 3 symphonies, 3 song cycles for voice and piano (including *Pastels* to the words of P. Tychyna), the oratorio *Charming the Fire*, a cantata based on H. Skovoroda's poem collection *Sad bozhestvennykh pisen'* (The Garden of Divine Songs), and film scores.

Karachai-Cherkess Autonomous oblast. An autonomous region in *Stavropol krai, situated on the northern slopes of the Caucasus. Established in 1922, it has an area of 14,100 sq km and population of 369,000 (1979), consisting of Karachais (30 percent), Cherkessians (9 percent), Russians (45 percent), Abazinians (7 percent), Nogais (3 percent), Ukrainians, Greeks, and Ossetians. In 1926 there were 2,800 Ukrainians (0.4 percent of the population); in 1970 there were 4,800 (0.1 percent), of whom 68 percent were urban dwellers. The Cherkessians had their own national district in 1926–8 and autonomous oblast in 1928–57. In 1944 the entire Karachai population was deported to Soviet Central Asia for alleged collaboration with the Germans in August 1942–January 1943. Many died in transit. In 1957 the Karachais were allowed to return to their homeland, and the Karachai-Cherkess Autonomous oblast was reinstated.

Kara-Dag. IX-16. A volcanic ridge, up to 577 m in elevation, lying in the eastern part of the *Crimean Mountains on the coast of the Black Sea, into which it drops abruptly in ledges. The lower slopes of the Kara-Dag are forested with oak, hornbeam, and ash, and the upper slopes are covered with steppe vegetation. In 1907–14 the Kara-Dag Biological Station, which later became the Kara-Dag branch of the Institute of the Biology of Southern Seas of the Academy of Sciences of the Ukrainian SSR, was set up to study the biology of the Kara-Dag.

Kara-Dag Nature Reserve (Karadagskyi zapovidnyk AN URSR). A reserve in the Crimea established in 1979 to study the physical geography of the *Kara-Dag Mountains and to conserve their natural resources (soils, flora, and fauna). From 1907 to 1979 the Kara-Dag Biological Station fulfilled this role.

Karadžić, Vuk, b 6 November 1787 in Tršić, Serbia, d 6 February 1864 in Vienna. Eminent Serbian philologist, folklorist, and historian; the founder of modern literary Serbian. He published the first grammar, alphabet, and phonetic orthography of vernacular Serbian; the influence of M. *Smotrytsky's grammar on this work is considerable. In 1814 he also published the first collection of Serbian folk songs. Thereafter he devoted himself to promoting the adoption of vernacular Serbian as the literary language and collecting Serbian folklore. His orthography was officially adopted in Serbia in 1868. Karadžić's pioneering contributions – opposed by both Serbian conservatives and Austrian censors – had a profound impact on 19th-century Ukrainian intellectuals, particularly M. Shashkevych, Ya. Holovatsky, I. Vahylevych, O. Barvinsky, and Ye. Zhelekhivsky in Galicia and M. Maksymovych, A. Metlynsky, and T. Shevchenko in Russian-ruled Ukraine, who used them as a model and inspiration for their own work; they translated some of his writings into Ukrainian. While living in Vienna, Karadžić became a close friend of the Galician journalist I. Holovatsky. In 1819 he visited Kiev, Chernivtsi, and Lviv and became acquainted with several Ukrainian cultural figures. Later he corresponded with and influenced O. Bodiansky and I. Sreznevsky, who wrote his biography (1846). He was elected a full member of the Odessa Society of History and Antiquities (1842) and the Austrian (1848), Prussian (1850), and Russian (1851) academies of sciences, and an honorary member of the Kharkiv University Council (1846).

BIBLIOGRAPHY
Kyryliuk, Ie. *Vuk Karadzhych i ukraïns'ka kul'tura* (Kiev 1978)

M. Hnatiukivsky

Karaffa-Korbut, Sofiia, b 23 August 1924 in Lviv. Graphic artist. A graduate of the Lviv Institute of Applied and Decorative Arts (1953) and a student of R. Selsky and V. Manastyrsky, she specializes in printmaking and book illustrations. Her favorite technique is the linocut. Her works include colored linocuts such as *Verkhovyna Spring* (1962) and *Fairy Tale* (1963), based on Lesia Ukrainka's *Lisova pisnia* (The Forest Song); a series of prints based on T. Shevchenko's historical poems (1963–6); linocut illustrations to I. Franko's poem 'Ivan Vyshensky'

Sofiia Karaffa-Korbut: woodcut (1969)

and novelette *Boryslav smiiet'sia* (Boryslav Is Laughing, 1964–5); and illustrations for many children's books. Combining elements of modern art and folk art, she is one of the most talented and original graphic artists in Ukraine, and a worthy continuator of the Lviv graphic arts school founded by P. *Kovzhun and M. *Butovych.

Karaganda oblast. An administrative region in the central part of Kazakhstan. Its climate is dry and continental, and its chief natural resource is coal. The oblast has an area of 85,400 sq km and a population (1986) of 1,354,000. Ukrainians account for about 8.3 percent of the population (112,400). The proportion of Ukrainians is much higher in the Karlag, a large system of labor camps established before the Second World War. The system consists of 27 departments, and each department has several camps. The inmates work in coal mining, construction, and farming.

Karagodeuashkh kurhan. A large Scythian kurhan near Krymska stanytsia, Krasnodar krai, containing the richest treasures of all known kurhans from the 4th–3rd century BC in the Kuban. Excavations in 1888 revealed two stone burial chambers with corridors. The main chamber, which was adorned with frescoes, contained the remains of a warrior, arms, gold ornaments, a gold coin, and earthen, bronze, and silver ware. In the corridor of the second chamber the remains of a young woman in luxurious ritual dress and of a funeral feast, a carriage, and two horse skeletons were found. This kurhan resembles the Scythian royal kurhans of the lower Dnieper region.

Karaimovych, Illiash [Karajimovyč, Illjaš], b? d 4 May 1648 in Kamianyi Zaton (near present-day Dniprovokamianka, Verkhnodniprovske raion, Dnipropetrovske oblast). Leader of the *registered Cossacks. He was their acting hetman in the Novhorod-Siverskyi region during the Polish-Muscovite War in 1634. In 1637 he was made colonel of Pereiaslav. In April 1648 Karaimovych and I. Barabash led the 4,000–5,000 registered Cossacks accompanying the Polish forces sent to crush the Cossack rebellion begun by Hetman B. *Khmelnytsky at the Zaporozhian Sich. On the way, the registered Cossacks held a general council at which Karaimovych, Barabash, and their pro-Polish supporters were killed. Under F. Dzhalalii and B. Topyha, Cossacks joined the rebels on 12 May 1648 near *Zhovti Vody and took part in the battle there a few days later.

Karaites (Ukrainian: *Karaimy*). A non-Talmudic Jewish sect acknowledging no authority except the Holy Scriptures. It arose in the 8th century. Karaites in Ukraine are ethnically Turkish, probably descendants of Khazarian Jews (see *Khazars). They began settling in the Crimea (especially in *Chufut-Kaleh) sometime after the 9th century, and in Lithuania, near Trakai and Vilnius, in the 17th century; from there some moved to Western Ukraine, settling near Lutske and Halych. Until the 20th century they lived in small, tight-knit communities, where they maintained their Turkic language and customs. In 1863 they were officially recognized in the Russian Empire as a distinct ethnic group and exempted from the laws that applied to Jews. From 1837 the Karaim Religious Board in Yevpatoriia administered the Karaite community. Yet, their numbers continued to decline through assimilation. In the USSR they are considered to be a separate nationality. Their number there has fallen steadily, from 8,324 in 1926 to just 3,341 in 1979. In 1970 there were 2,596 in the Crimea. They are also found in Volhynia and Odessa oblasts. Their language belongs to the Kipchak group of Turkish, although the Karaites in Western Ukraine and elsewhere have their own dialects. Now, most use Russian.

Karamzin, Nikolai, b 12 December 1766 in Mikhailovka, Simbirsk gubernia, Russia, d 3 June 1826 in St Petersburg. Russian historian, publicist, and writer; the founder of the sentimental school in Russian literature. At the request of Tsar Alexander I, he wrote *Istoriia gosudarstva rossiiskogo* (The History of the Russian State, 12 vols, 1816–29), up to the year 1611, which, although it contains a wealth of documentary material, identifies the history of Russia with the history of the Russian state and autocracy. He was a proponent of the *Normanist theory of the origin of Kievan Rus' and wrote about Rus' as the historical heritage of Russia. Among those who aided Karamzin's research was the Ukrainian historian M. *Bantysh-Kamensky. Karamazin's views formed the basis of much of official 19th-century Russian historiography.

Karanovych, Dariia [Karanovyč, Darija], b 18 October 1908 in Kolomyia, Galicia. Pianist and pedagogue; daughter of Ya. *Hordynsky. She studied with V. Barvinsky at the Lysenko Higher Institute of Music in Lviv, with P. Weingarten and E. von Sauer in Vienna, and with E. Steuermann at the Vienna Academy of Music. She gave concerts in Vienna, Lviv, Warsaw, Salzburg, Berlin, and Prague and played for Vienna and Salzburg radio. Since 1953 she has been teaching in New York at the Ukrainian Music Institute of America, of which she has served as president (1967–70, 1986–). Her extensive piano repertoire is rich in Ukrainian works. In 1985 she released a record of piano music by Ukrainian composers such as M. Lysenko, V. Barvinsky, N. Nyzhankivsky, and L. Revutsky.

Karas, Yosyp [Karas', Josyp], b 5 October 1918 in Khorol, Poltava region. Landscape painter. A graduate of the Kharkiv Art Institute (1948), he lectured at the institute until 1957. In 1969 he began to teach at the Kharkiv Industrial Design Institute. His works include *Hay Making* (1950), *Close to Autumn* (1954), *Native Fields* (1960–1), *Endless Fields* (1964), *The Last Hectares* (1972), and *Ukrainian Wheat* (1977).

Joan Karasevich

Karasevich, Joan [Karasevyč, Ivanna], b 12 November 1937 in Winnipeg. Singer and actress. A graduate of the National Theatre School of Canada, at the 1965 Stratford Festival Karasevich became the first actress to receive the Tyrone Guthrie Award. Besides appearing frequently at Ukrainian concerts, she has written and staged two productions dealing with the Ukrainian experience in Canada, and created the role of Anna in the production 'Just a Kommedia' (1984). Karasevich has also performed in films and on radio and television, including the role of Anna in *The Newcomers*, about Ukrainian immigrants in the 1920s.

Karatnytsky, Modest [Karatnyc'kyj], b 1858 in Galicia, d 30 November 1940 in Lviv. Jurist, civic leader. He was president of the Society of Ukrainian Lawyers and of the Land Mortgage Bank in Lviv. After the First World War he presided over the circuit court in Berezhany. A firm believer in the advancement of the Ukrainian cause, he headed the Ukrainian National Society for Child and Adolescent Care and supported the Plast Ukrainian Youth Association.

Karavaiv, Volodymyr, b 9 March 1864 and d 7 January 1939 in Kiev. Ukrainian zoologist and traveler. After graduating from Kiev University, Karavaiv was a scientist there from 1890 to 1919. He was one of the founders of the Zoological Museum of the AN URSR (1919) and its director (1926–34). He participated in numerous scientific expeditions throughout Ukraine, to the Caucasus, Africa, and Asia. He donated detailed descriptions of the expeditions as well as collections of animals and insects, especially ants, to the Zoological Museum of the AN URSR. Karavaiv is best known for his works on myrmecophilism. His other scientific works deal with ants, crayfish, and radiolaria.

Karavan. A Scythian fortified settlement of the late 5th to early 2nd centuries BC discovered near Karavan, Derhachi raion, Kharkiv oblast. Excavations carried out in 1954–5 uncovered the remains of fortifications, clay and wood surface dwellings, ceramics, and the bones of domestic and wild animals. Miniature clay vessels, a fragment of an anthropomorphic statuette, clay 'breads,' and 170 clay models of grains found by a sacrificial altar and in an ash mound were probably associated with a Scythian agricultural cult.

Sviatoslav Karavansky

Vasyl Karazyn

Karavansky, Sviatoslav [Karavans'kyj, Svjatoslav], b 24 December 1920 in Odessa. Poet, translator, dissident. Because he had fought for Ukraine's independence during the Second World War, he was sentenced in 1945 to 25 years in prison. After serving 17 years in the labor camps of Kolyma, Magadan, and Mordovia, he was released and returned to Odessa. His poems, translations, and articles appeared in the Soviet press. His protests against Russification and official abuses led to his arrest in 1965, and the revocation of his amnesty. Before he had served his term, he was sentenced to another five years. Although he had joined the *Ukrainian Helsinki Group at the beginning of 1979 he was released in the fall and forced to emigrate with his wife, N. *Strokata. Since his arrival in the United States, he has published several collections of original and translated poems: *Sutychka z taifunom* (Encounter with a Typhoon, 1980), *Moie remeslo* (My Trade, 1981), *Iaryna z horodu Khomy Chereshni* (Vegetables from the Garden of Khoma Chereshnia, 1981), and *Humorystychnyi samvydav* (A Humorous Self-Publishing, 1982).

Karazyn, Vasyl, b 10 February 1773 in Kruchyk, near Bohodukhiv, Slobidska Ukraine, d 16 November 1842 in Mykolaiv. Civic leader, economist, and inventor, of Greek noble descent. Karazyn studied mining and metallurgy in St Petersburg and then secretly traveled to Western Europe to continue his studies. A committed liberal, he tirelessly worked to reform the Russian Empire. In a series of letters and memoranda to influential officials and the tsar, he urged the establishment of a constitutional monarchy in the empire and the abolition of serfdom. His most important achievements were in the field of education. As the director of schools in the Ministry of Education (1801–4) he began reforming the educational system along Western lines. He also convinced the nobility and merchants of Slobidska Ukraine to establish and fund *Kharkiv University. His progressive ideas, however, eventually led him to fall into disfavor in official circles, and he was imprisoned in Shlisselburg Fortress (1820–1) and confined to his estate for many years.

Karazyn's political and economic theories helped to lay the basis for Ukrainian territorial autonomy. He strongly criticized policies that encouraged the concentration of industry and manufacturing in central Russia, policies which reduced Ukraine to a simple supplier of raw materials for the imperial economy. He also stressed the need to expand foreign trade and to improve agricultural practices by introducing new grain varieties, potatoes, and other crops, and abandoning the three-field rotation system. He devoted considerable energy to developing agricultural and metallurgical machinery. His inventions include steam heating and drying machines and machines used in saltpeter extraction. He founded and headed (1811–18) the Philotechnical Society, which popularized his scientific ideas and promoted the modernization of agriculture. Karazyn also made several important contributions to *climatology and meteorology and established one of the first meteorological stations in the empire. In total, he wrote over 60 articles and studies; his collected works *Sochineniia, pis'ma i bumagi V.N. Karazina* were published in 1910 (ed D. Bahalii).

BIBLIOGRAPHY
Danilevskii, G.P. 'Vasilii Nazar'evich Kazarin,' *Sochineniia G.P. Danilevskogo*, vol 21 (St Petersburg 1901)
Flynn, J. 'V.N. Karazin, the Gentry, and Kharkov University,' *SR*, 28 (1969), no. 2
Lavrinenko, Iu. *Vasyl' Karazyn – arkhitekt vidrodzhennia. Materialy i dumky do 200-littia z dnia narodzhennia 1773–1973* (Munich 1975)

B. Balan, A. Zhukovsky

Karbovanets [Karbovanec']. The Ukrainian equivalent of the Russian *ruble. The term was first used for the main unit of paper *currency in the independent Ukrainian state of 1917–20.

Karbulytsky, Iliarii [Karbulyc'kyj, Iljarij], b 5 September 1880 in Voloka, Vyzhnytsia county, Bukovyna, d 31 January 1961 in Chernivtsi. Teacher, political leader, and publicist. An elementary school teacher by training, he was editor of the teachers' journal *Promin'* (1904–7) and newspaper *Kameniari* (1908–14). For a time he edited the Kreitsarova Biblioteka (Kreutzer Library, 1902–8) book series for children. Besides many articles, he wrote a historical study, *Rozvii narodn'oho shkil'nytstva na Bukovyni* (The Development of Public Schools in Bukovyna, 1907), and a play about the Hutsuls, *Zradnyk* (The Traitor, 1936). An active member of the Ukrainian National party, in 1937 he was elected to its executive board. After the war he was imprisoned by the Soviets for 12 years in labor camps in the RSFSR.

Karger, Mikhail, b 30 May 1903 in Kazan, Russia, d 26 August 1976 in Leningrad. Archeologist and art scholar. Specializing in the archeology of Kievan Rus', he excavated architectural monuments in such cities and towns as Kiev, Novgorod, Pereiaslav-Khmelnytskyi, Halych, and Volodymyr-Volynskyi. He wrote dozens of archeological articles and the books *Arkheologicheskie issledovaniia drevnego Kieva: Otchety i materialy (1938–1947 gg.)* (Archeological Investigations of Ancient Kiev: Reports and Materials [1938–1947], 1950) and *Drevnii Kiev* ... (Ancient Kiev ..., 2 vols, 1958, 1961), and coauthored *Istoriia kul'tury drevnei Rusi* (A History of the Culture of Ancient Rus', 2 vols, 1948, 1951).

Karhalsky, Serhii [Karhal's'kyj, Serhij] (real surname: Slynko), b July 1889 in Odessa, d 1938 in a Soviet labor camp. Stage actor and director. A graduate of Mochalova's Odessa Drama School, from 1912 he worked in Russian provincial troupes in Ukraine. In 1919 he joined the First Theater of the Ukrainian Soviet Republic in Kiev, and in 1922 the Berezil theater. He was an organizer and the director (1925–8) of the First Ukrainian State Opera in Kharkiv. Then he worked as a stage director at the Ukrainian opera in Kharkiv and Kiev and at the Second Ukrainian Touring Opera in Vinnytsia. From 1935 to 1937 he was chief stage director at the Kiev Theater of Musical Comedy. His actor's repertoire included the Dam Wrecker in Lesia Ukrainka's *Lisova pisnia* (The Forest Song), Banquo in W. Shakespeare's *Macbeth*, Lacey Granitch in L. Kurbas's adaptation of U. Sinclair's *Jimmie Higgins*, and Figaro in P. Beaumarchais's *Le Mariage de Figaro*. He directed operas such as M. Lysenko's *Taras Bulba* (1928), A. Vakhnianyn's *Kupalo* (1929), V. Kostenko's *Karmeliuk* (1931), and the Ukrainian versions of A. Dargomyzhsky's *Rusalka* (1931), A. Borodin's *Prince Igor*, and C. Zeller's *The Bird Dealer* (1936).

Karkhut, Spyridon [Karxut], b 30 September 1869 in Novosilka Kostinkova, Borshchiv county, Galicia, d 14 March 1931 in Lviv. Ukrainian Catholic priest, educator, civic leader. He was ordained in 1892 and graduated from Lviv University (PH D 1914). He was a teacher of classical philology at the Ukrainian Academic Gymnasium in Lviv (1906–28) and then professor of Old Church Slavonic at the Theological Academy in Lviv (1928–31). In 1929–30 he was also the dean of the Faculty of Theology at the academy. Karkhut was the author of *Hramatyka ukraïns'koï tserkovno-slovians'koï movy* (The Grammar of the Ukrainian Church Slavonic Language, 1927).

Karkhut, Vasyl [Karxut, Vasyl'], b July 1905 in Markivtsi, Tovmach county, Galicia, d 9 October 1980 in Lviv. Physician, writer, and civic leader. Upon graduating from Lviv University (1932), he practiced medicine in Volhynia. When *Plast was banned in 1930, he organized clandestine units for young tradesmen and edited the Plast magazine *Vohni*. He wrote short stories for young people and a novel, *Vistria v temriavi* (A Blade in the Darkness, 1934; repr 1941 under the title *Polumianyi vykhor* [The Flaming Whirlwind]). In the mid-1930s he served two years in the Polish concentration camp of Bereza Kartuzka. After the war he spent 18 years in Soviet labor camps. Released in 1963, he practiced medicine in a village near Sniatyn and compiled a handbook on medicinal plants, *Liky navkolo nas* (Remedies around Us, 1975).

Karlivka. IV-16. Town (1980 pop 17,000) and raion center in Poltava oblast, situated on the Orchyk River in the Dnieper Lowland. It was founded in the 1740s. Its machine-building plants supply food-processing and distilling industries.

Karlo-Marksove. V-19, DB III-4. An smt (1979 pop 15,000) in the Donets Basin in Donetske oblast, under the jurisdiction of the Yenakiieve city soviet. Established in 1783, until 1924 it was called Sofiivka. Located there is a coal mine opened in 1858.

Karmaliuk, Pavlo [Karmaljuk], b 6 January 1908 in Osivtsi, Radomyshl county, Kiev gubernia, d 1986 in Lviv. Operatic baritone. A graduate of the Kiev Conservatory (1941) and a student of D. Yevtushenko, in 1944 he joined the Lviv Theater of Opera and Ballet. From 1950 he taught singing at the Lviv Conservatory. His repertoire included Rigoletto in G. Verdi's *Rigoletto*, Figaro in G. Rossini's *Barber of Seville*, Onegin in P. Tchaikovsky's *Eugene Onegin*, Igor in A. Borodin's *Prince Igor*, Ostap in M. Lysenko's *Taras Bulba*, Bohdan in K. Dankevych's *Bohdan Khmelnytsky*, and Maksym in A. Kos-Anatolsky's *The Sky's Glow*. He also performed as a chamber singer.

Ustym Karmaliuk

Karmaliuk, Ustym [Karmaljuk], b 10 March 1787 in Holovchyntsi (now Karmaliukove), Lityn county, d 22 October 1835 in Shliakhovi Korychyntsi (now Korychyntsi), Liatychiv county, Podilia gubernia. Ukrainian folk hero, the 'last haidamaka.' Karmaliuk (Karmeliuk) was born a serf. Sent into the army in 1812 by his landowner, Karmaliuk fled the army and, together with other deserters, organized rebel bands, which he led in attacks on landowners and merchants. He was captured in 1814, sentenced in Kamianets-Podilskyi to 500 blows while running a gauntlet, and sent to a military unit in the Crimea. On his way he escaped and again organized a peasant rebellion, which from 1814 to 1828 encompassed a significant portion of Lityn, Liatychiv, and Proskuriv counties in Podilia gubernia, attracting not only peasants, but also army deserters and the urban poor. The rebellion occurred at a time when serfdom in the Russian Empire had become commercially profitable and was at its most repressive and exploitative stage of development; landowners had increased the amount of compulsory peasant labor to as much as six days a week. This social oppression also had a national dimension in Podilia, where most of the magnates were Polish.

Karmaliuk's struggle was at its height in 1830–5, when

it spread from Podilia into the neighboring regions of Kiev, Volhynia, and Bessarabia and involved up to 20,000 peasants. Approximately 1,000 raids were made by the rebels on landowners' estates. Whatever was captured in the attacks was distributed among the village poor, who always gave Karmaliuk refuge and help. To quell the uprising, the tsarist government quartered units of soldiers in the regions where peasant unrest was strongest. Karmaliuk was apprehended and sentenced four times to hard labor in Siberia, but each time he managed to escape and return to lead a rebellion. He was killed in an ambush by the nobleman Rutkowski. Karmaliuk's struggle against oppression has been immortalized in many Ukrainian sayings and folk songs ('Za Sybirom sontse skhodyt'' [The Sun Rises beyond Siberia]), in literature (Marko Vovchok, M. Starytsky, S. Vasylchenko, V. Kucher), and in music (V. Kostenko).

BIBLIOGRAPHY
Ustym Karmaliuk. Zbirnyk dokumentiv (Kiev 1948)
Hurzhii, I. *Ustym Karmaliuk* (Kiev 1955)

Petro Karmansky

Karmansky, Petro [Karmans'kyj] (pseuds: Petro Hirky, Les Mohylnytsky), b 29 May 1878 in Chesaniv, Galicia, d 16 April 1956 in Lviv. Poet, civic leader, and journalist. Karmansky was a prominent member of the modernist group *Moloda Muza, and his early collections of poetry – *Z teky samovbyvtsia* (From the Briefcase of a Suicide, 1899), *Oi liuli smutku* (Sleep Sadness, Sleep, 1906), *Bludni vohni* (Will-o-the-Wisp, 1907), *Plyvem po moriu t'my* (We Sail on the Sea of Darkness, 1909), and *Al fresco* (1917) – reflect the typical *fin-de-siècle* ennui and pessimism of the modernist poets throughout Europe. His particular idiom is characterized by the frequent use of religious imagery – an influence of his studies at the Collegium Ruthenum in Rome – and the often satiric tone provoked by the estrangement between the brooding modernist poet and 'callous' society. Discontent did not leave him even when he tried to work within the needs of the society by being a high-school teacher, then a representative in the diplomatic missions of the Western Ukrainian National Republic to Rome, the United States, Canada, and Brazil, and finally an editor (1922–5). After the Soviet occupation of Western Ukraine, Karmansky lectured at Lviv University and wrote two collections distinguished by their official optimism: *Do sontsia* (Toward the Sun, 1941) and *Po iasnii dorozi* (On the Bright Road, 1952). Karmansky was also a proficient translator. Of his numerous translations (primarily from Italian) *The Divine Comedy* (translated together with M. *Rylsky) is the most ambitious. Toward the end of his life he wrote memoirs of his experiences abroad as well as virulent attacks against Ukrainian 'bourgeois nationalists' and the Vatican.

D.H. Struk

Karmazyn-Kakovsky, Vsevolod [Karmazyn-Kakovs'kyj], b 16 September 1898 in Creteşti, Iaşi county, Rumania. Art scholar and landscape architect. He taught at several universities – in Kharkiv (1931–41), Odessa (1942–4), and Iaşi (1945–65) – and worked as a research associate at the Institute of History and Archeology of the Rumanian Academy of Social and Political Sciences. He designed sanatorium gardens and was responsible for landscaping of some resorts on the Black Sea and the botanical garden of Iaşi University. Since 1972 he has been living in Munich. His publications include over 300 works, most of them in Rumanian dealing with the curative effects of landscapes. He has written some articles and monographs in Ukrainian on the history of Ukrainian art; eg, *Ukraïns'ka narodna arkhitektura* (Ukrainian Folk Architecture, 1972) and *Mystetstvo lemkivs'koï tserkvy* (The Art of the Lemko Church, 1975).

Karmeliuk-Kamensky, Kostiantyn [Karmeljuk-Kamens'kyj, Kostjantyn], b 1858 in Koziatyn, Berdychiv county, Kiev gubernia, d 1932 in Harbin, Manchuria. Stage actor and director. He organized a Ukrainian theatrical troupe that, starting in 1904, toured Caucasia, Turkestan, Siberia, and the Far East (1912). In 1916 it toured Japan (Kobe, Tokyo, Yokohama, and Kamakura) and China (Shanghai), and in the following year it visited Ussuriisk and Vladivostok. Its repertoire included I. Kotliarevsky's *Natalka Poltavka* (Natalka from Poltava), M. Kropyvnytsky's *Vii*, M. Starytsky's *Tsyhanka Aza* (Aza, the Gypsy Girl), and O. Sukhodolsky's *Khmara* (The Cloud). In 1918 the troupe broke up, but many of its members remained in the Far East and joined other drama groups.

Karnaukhivka [Kanauxivka]. V-15. Town smt (1979 pop 8,200) located on the right bank of the Dnieper River in Dnipropetrovske oblast. The settlement was established in 1737 and is now under the jurisdiction of the Bahlii raion soviet in Dniprodzerzhynske. Most of its inhabitants work in Dniprodzerzhynske or Dnipropetrovske.

Karnovsky, Mykhailo [Karnovs'kyj, Myxajlo], b and d ? Printmaker and book illustrator of the early 18th century. A representative of O. Tarasevych's school of copper engraving, he was educated probably at the Chernihiv College and the Kievan Mohyla College. From 1701 to 1710 he worked as an engraver at the Printing House in Moscow. Karnovsky is known for his illustrations of L. Magnitsky's first arithmetic textbook (1703), including a fine frontispiece depicting Pythagoras and Archimedes, the *teza* posters in honor of Metropolitan Y. Krokovsky (1706) and the patriarchal *locum tenens* S. Yavorsky (1708), and a print of the Kievan Cave Mother of God among the Stars. Karnovsky and other Ukrainian engravers introduced the traditions of Ukrainian graphic art to Russia and influenced the development of Russian engraving.

Karovets, Makarii [Karovec', Makarij], b 1873 in Galicia, d 1944 in Bratislava. Ukrainian Catholic priest of the Basilian order, writer, and journalist. Karovets was a chaplain of the Ukrainian Sich Riflemen and lived in Soviet-ruled Ukraine until the late 1920s. After he returned to Galicia he wrote *Velyka reforma Chyna sv. Vasyliia Velykoho* (The Great Reform of the Order of St Basil the Great, 4 vols, 1932–8) and articles on historical, social, and religious issues.

Karpat' (The Carpathian). A religious educational weekly, published in Uzhhorod from 20 June 1873 to 13 April 1886 by the eparchial administration and the Society of St Basil the Great. It was edited by M. Homychkov with the assistance of O. Homychkov. The paper had a pro-Hungarian profile. It came out in Russian-Ukrainian *yazychie. A Hungarian supplement was added in 1875–7. From 1882 most of the articles were published in Hungarian. Its main contributors were O. Popovych, A. Kralytsky, I. Sylvai, Ye. Fentsyk, I. Rakovsky, Yu. Stavrovsky-Popradov, M. Beskyd, and T. Zlotsky. Besides religious articles, the paper published official announcements, news from correspondents, feuilletons, and belles-lettres. Later, it reprinted articles from the Budapest, Moscow, St Petersburg, and Odessa press. It contained much information about Transcarpathian Ukrainians.

Karpatiia. A mutual life-insurance company that operated in Lviv from 1911 to 1939. In 1939 its capital reserve was 220,000 zlotys ($41,800), and its insurance fund amounted to one million zlotys ($190,000). B. Yaniv, the first director, was succeeded by I. Gyzha in 1930. L. Makarushka served as assistant director.

Karpatorusskii golos (Carpathoruthenian Voice). A Russophile daily, then weekly, newspaper published in Uzhhorod from 1932 to 1934 and from 1938 to 1944. Because of its opposition to the Czechoslovak government, it was banned, and was replaced by *Nash karpatorusskii golos* (1934–5). It resumed publication under Hungarian rule. Its publishers were Y. Kaminsky and S. Fentsyk, and its editor was V. Labanich.

Karpats'ka pravda (Carpathian Truth). A weekly newspaper of the Transcarpathian Regional Committee of the Czechoslovak Communist party published in Mukachiv in 1920–38. From 1920 to 1921 it was titled *Pravda* and was published in *yazychie. From 1925 it appeared in literary Ukrainian. Its editors were I. Mondok, P. Boichuk, and O. Borkaniuk. In October 1938 the paper was banned by the Czechoslovak government. It resumed publication in November 1944 as the daily *Zakarpats'ka pravda*.

Karpatskyi soiuz. See Carpathian Alliance.

Karpaty (Carpathians). A publishing house in Uzhhorod under the jurisdiction of the State Committee of the Ukrainian SSR for Publishing, Printing, and the Book Trade. Founded in 1945 as the Transcarpathian Book-Newspaper Publishers, it changed names several times before assuming its present name in 1964; it became an oblast-level publisher in 1951 and a republic-level publisher in 1964 serving Transcarpathia, Ivano-Frankivske, and Chernivtsi oblasts. At first, Karpaty published Ukrainian literary works and regional guides; now its production includes political, art, technical, agricultural, and folklore books. It has collaborated with Hungarian firms in publishing Hungarian translations of Ukrainian and Russian classics and other books since 1958, and has copublished books with Slovak publishers since 1975. Karpaty also publishes in Moldavian, and produces tourist guides in various languages. In 1979, it's total pressrun was more than 2 million.

Karpeka, Volodymyr, b 31 May 1877 in Kiev, d ? Jurist; educator. In 1917 he served on the faculty of Kiev University. In 1930 he taught history of law at the Kiev Agricultural Institute. His publications in economics and law include 'Perevaha vydatkiv iak pryntsyp derzhavnoho hospodarstva' (Deficit Spending as a Principle of State Economics, 1929). He was arrested in 1937 and disappeared without trace.

Karpeko, Oleksander, 1891–? Educator. In the 1920s he taught at the Nizhen Institute of People's Education and was, for a while, its rector. He was the deputy director of the Department of Agitation and Propaganda of the CC CP(B)U in 1930, the deputy people's commissar of education of the Ukrainian SSR in 1932–3, and the head of the All-Ukrainian Radio Committee. He was arrested during the Stalinist terror in 1934, and his further fate is unknown.

Karpenko, Dmytro (nom de guerre: Yastrub), b 1920 in Poltava gubernia, d 17 December 1944 in Strilyska Novi, Drohobych oblast. Prominent UPA field commander. A lieutenant of a Red Army tank unit, in 1943 he joined the OUN in the Odessa region. Advancing quickly in rank, he became commander of the Siromantsi Company, which in November 1943 was assigned to the Ternopil Military District. In the spring and summer of 1944 Karpenko fought the Polish Home Army and Soviet partisans in the Rava-Ruska area. Returning to his base in September, he rose to battalion commander and fought several large battles with the NKVD Internal Troops, including the Battle of Univ on 30 September. Killed in action, he was awarded posthumously the rank of captain and the Gold Cross of Combat Merit First Class. Karpenko was the first officer to receive this medal.

Karpenko, Heorhii, b 6 June 1910 in Tomsk, Russia, d 15 November 1977 in Lviv. Specialist in materials mechanics; full member of the AN URSR from 1967. From 1946 to 1950 he was scientific secretary of the Presidium of AN URSR, and then director of the academy's Institute of Mechanical Engineering and Automation (1952–71), which in 1964 was renamed the Physical Mechanics Institute. He did pioneering work on the physicochemical mechanics of materials, contributing new theories of corrosion fatigue and hydrogen brittleness in steel.

Karpenko, Oleksander, b 1896 in Lypova Dolyna, Hadiache county, Poltava gubernia. Agronomist. A graduate of the Kiev Polytechnical Institute (1928), he taught at the Kiev Institute for the Mechanization and Electrification of Agriculture and worked at the Ukrainian Research Institute of Agricultural Machine Building

(1930–6). From 1936 to 1950 he headed the Sowing Machinery Laboratory of the All-Union Institute for the Mechanization and Electrification of Agriculture in Moscow. He wrote over 120 articles on such topics as agricultural machines and equipment, the mechanization of fieldwork, and the technology of farming in dry regions.

Karpenko, Oleksander, b 15 June 1921 in Sloboda village in the Chernihiv region. Historian. He taught in higher educational institutions from 1944 to 1949, and worked in Lviv from 1949 to 1960 as an associate of the Institute of Social Sciences of the AN URSR. He was criticized for his attempts to restore the ZUNR as a legitimate subject of research. In 1960 he received a position at Lviv University. His works deal with the history of Poland and Western Ukraine, and the 1920s in Soviet Ukraine. One of his chief works is *Imperialistychna interventsiia na Ukraïni 1918–20* (The Imperialist Intervention in Ukraine in 1918–20, 1964).

Karpenko, Yurii, b ? Linguist. In 1956 he became affiliated with Chernivtsi University and later with Odessa University. After a series of articles on the history of Ukrainian numerals, he published studies of toponyms, especially the hydronyms of Bukovyna, the Lower Dniester Basin, and the Odessa region. His research was summarized in the monograph *Toponimiia Bukovyny* (Toponymy of Bukovyna, 1973) and the collective work that he edited, *Hidronimy Nyzhn'oho Podnistrovia* (Hydronyms of the Lower Dniester Region, 1981). In *Vstup do movoznavstva* (Introduction to Linguistics, 1983) he describes the various trends in modern linguistics.

Ivan Karpenko-Kary

Karpenko-Kary, Ivan [Karpenko-Karyj] (pen name of Ivan Tobilevych), b 29 September 1845 in Arsenivka, Bobrynets county, Kherson gubernia, d 15 September 1907 in Berlin. Famous Ukrainian actor and playwright; the brother of the theater figures P. *Saksahansky, M. *Sadovsky, and M. *Sadovska-Barilotti. From the age of 14 he worked as a clerk (from 1869 as a police secretary in Yelysavethrad). In 1863 he met M. *Kropyvnytsky and with him became involved in producing amateur theater in Yelysavethrad. In 1883 he lost his job for his involvement with Ukrainian revolutionaries and for procuring passports for them and joined M. *Starytsky's troupe. In 1884 he was exiled to Novocherkassk; returning to Ukraine in 1886, he lived under police surveillance until 1889. From 1887 until his illness in 1904 he lived on his farmstead, wrote, and worked as a stage actor and director, mostly in the traveling troupe of his brother P. Saksahansky. He was acclaimed for his principal dramatic and comic roles in many Ukrainian plays, some of them his own. He was buried on his farmstead near Yelysavethrad (now Kirovohrad); the memorial museum-preserve Khutir Nadiia was opened there in 1956.

Karpenko-Kary was renowned as a playwright. He began writing quite late in life: his first story, *Novobranets* (The New Conscript), and first play appeared in 1883. Altogether he wrote 18 frequently produced plays: the satiric comedies *Rozumnyi i duren'* (The Wise Man and the Fool, 1885), *Martyn Borulia* (1886), *Chumaky* (Chumaks, 1897), *Sto tysiach* (One Hundred Thousand, 1889), *Khaziaïn* (The Master, 1900), *Suieta* (Vanity, 1902), and *Zhyteiske more* (The Sea of Life, 1904); the dramas *Burlaka* (The Vagabond, 1883), *Pidpanky* (The Status Seekers, 1883), *Naimychka* (The Servant Girl, 1885), *Beztalanna* (The Fortuneless Maiden, 1886), *Bat'kova kazka* (The Father's Tale, 1892), and *Ponad Dniprom* (Along the Dnieper, 1897); and the historical ethnographic plays *Bondarivna* (The Cooper's Daughter, 1884), *Palyvoda XVIII st.* (A Madcap of the 18th Century, 1893), *Lykha iskra pole spalyt' i sama shchezne* (The Evil Spark Will Burn the Field and Itself Disappear, 1896), *Sava Chalyi* (1899), and *Handzia* (1902).

While realistically and perceptively portraying life and social relations in the village, Karpenko-Kary also reflected in his plays the impact of colonialism in Russian-ruled Ukraine: land poverty and rural overpopulation, and the ignorance and evil deeds of the peasant in a position of authority (in *Burlaka*), the rich peasant (Kalytka in *Sto tysiach*), and the large landowner (Terentii Puzyr in *Khaziaïn*).

Some of Karpenko-Kary's plays were an important step forward in Ukrainian theater. In them he abandoned the sentimental populist-ethnographic approach and melodramatic, operatic forms; instead he highlighted social relations and conflicts and concentrated on psychological portrayal and character development, thereby creating the finest examples of turn-of-the-century Ukrainian didactic plays about peasant life and laying the foundations of modern Ukrainian theater. His plays are still often produced in Ukraine. His works have been republished many times; the most complete editions are *Tvory* (Works, 6 vols, 1929–31), *P'iesy* (Plays, 1949), and *Tvory* (Works, 3 vols, 1960–1).

BIBLIOGRAPHY

Iefremov, S. *Karpenko-Karyi* (Kiev 1924)
Tobilevych, S. *Zhyttia I. Tobilevycha* (Kiev 1948)
Stetsenko, L. *I. Karpenko-Karyi (I.K. Tobilevych): Zhyttia i tvorcha diial'nist'* (Kiev 1957)
Kravchenko, Zh. *Karpenko-Karyi: Anotovanyi bibliohrafichnyi pokazhchyk* (Odessa 1958)
Skrypnyk I. *Ivan Karpenko-Karyi: Literaturnyi portret* (Kiev 1960)
Tsyban'ova, O. *Litopys zhyttia i tvorchosti I. Karpenka-Karoho (I.K. Tobilevycha)* (Kiev 1967)

I. Koshelivets

Karpenko-Krynytsia, Petro [Karpenko-Krynycja] (pseud of Petro Horban), b 22 December 1917 in Baklanova Muraviika near Chernihiv. Poet and journalist. He began writing in 1938. In 1950 he immigrated to the United States. Karpenko-Krynytsia's first collections of poetry reflect the romantic heroism of the Ukrainian national struggle during the Second World War; they include *Hrymliat' dorohy* (The Roads Are Thundering, 1942), *Polum'iana zemlia* (The Flaming Earth, 1947), *Pidniati vitryla* (Raised Sails, 1950), and *Soldaty moho legionu* (The Soldiers of My Legion, 1951). A notable stylistic change occurred in his last three poetry collections (especially in the genre of the lyrical longer poem) *Poemy* (Poems, 1954), *Povernennia druha* (The Return of a Friend, 1958), and *Indiians'ki baliady* (Indian Ballads, 1968).

Karpiak, Volodymyr [Karp'jak], b 28 July 1909 in Peremyshl, Galicia, d 19 January 1972 in Philadelphia. Stage actor and operetta tenor. From 1934 to 1939 he acted in various theaters in Galicia such as the Tobilevych Ukrainian People's Theater, the Kotliarevsky Theater, and the Lesia Ukrainka Ukrainian Drama Theater and, during the war, at the Lviv Opera Theater. Having immigrated to West Germany, he belonged to the Ensemble of Ukrainian Actors. In 1950 he settled in Philadelphia, where in 1963 he joined the Teatr u Piatnytsiu company. His repertoire included Sándor, Paganini, and Józsi in F. Lehár's *Where the Lark Sings, Paganini,* and *Gypsy Love.*

Karpov, Gennadii, b 14 February 1839, d 6 May 1890. Russian historian. He studied with S. *Solovev at Moscow University. In 1870–1 he was a professor at Kharkiv University and then lived in Moscow. He is the author of works on 17th-century Ukraine, among them *Kriticheskii obzor razrabotki glavnykh russkikh istochnikov do istorii Malorossii otnosiashchikhsia za vremia 1654–1672 gg.* (A Critical Survey of the Treatment of Major Russian Sources on the History of Little Russia in the Years 1651–1672, 1870), *Kostomarov kak istorik Malorossii* (Kostomarov as a Historian of Little Russia, 1871), and *Nachalo istoricheskoi deiatel'nosti Bogdana Khmel'nitskogo* (The Beginning of the Historical Activity of B. Khmelnytsky, 1873). He also edited **Akty, otnosiashchiesia k istorii Iuzhnoi i Zapadnoi Rossii* (vols 10, 14, 15) and the *Izbornyk* of Sviatoslav of 1073, published in 1880. Although written from a biased Russian imperialist perspective, his works contain a wealth of documentary material on the history of Ukraine. A bibliography of his works is found in *AUA*, 5–6 (1957).

Karpovych, Leontii [Karpovyč, Leontij] (secular name: Lonhyn), b 1580? in the Pynske region, d October 1620. Orthodox church leader, pedagogue, and polemist. He studied at the Ostrih Academy, then became rector of the brotherhood school in Vilnius. A defender of the Orthodox church, he condemned the Church Union of *Berestia. While working at the Vilnius monastery press (1610), he was involved in the publication of M. Smotrytsky's antiunion work, *Trenos;* for this he was imprisoned for two years. After his release he was the founder and archimandrite of the Holy Spirit Monastery in Vilnius (1613–20) and then was elected bishop of Volodymyr and Berestia but died before being consecrated. A renowned preacher and polemist, he authored *Kazan'e dvoe* (Two Sermons, 1615) and *Kazanie na pogrzebie kniazia Wasila Wasilewicza Galiczyna* (Sermon at the Grave of Prince Vasyl Vasylovych of Galicia, 1619), and wrote prefaces to the collections *Vertohrad dushevnyi* (A Spiritual Garden, 1620) and *Sviatoho Ioanna Zlatoustaho ...* (St John Chrysostom ..., 1620).

Karpukhin, Petro [Karpuxin], b 26 September 1902 in Makiivka, Bakhmut county, Katerynoslav gubernia, d 31 May 1974 in Kharkiv. Organic chemist; from 1939 corresponding member of the AN URSR. After graduating from the Kharkiv Chemical-Technological Institute (1926), he taught there for many years. He specialized in the synthesis of organic dyes out of coal tar and published over 80 papers on the subject.

Karpynsky, Oleksander [Karpyns'kyj], b 1869 in Biała Podlaska in Podlachia, d 1929 in Rivne. Civic and political leader. Under the tsarist regime he served as a judge in Chernihiv. In the revolutionary period he was deputy minister of internal affairs in V. Vynnychenko's cabinet (1918), a member of the Council of the Ministry of Foreign Affairs of the Hetman government, and then adviser to the UNR diplomatic mission in Warsaw (1919–20). After the war he practiced law in Rivne and headed the local Prosvita society. From 1922 to 1928 he served as deputy to the Polish Senate and as president of the Ukrainian Senate Club in Warsaw.

Karsky, Evfimii [Karskij, Evfimij], b 1 January 1861 in Lasha, Belorussia, d 29 April 1931 in Leningrad. Linguist. Karsky was a professor at Warsaw (1894–1916) and then Petrograd (later Leningrad) universities (1916–28), and editor of *Russkii filologicheskii vestnik.* In addition to fundamental works in the history and dialectology of Belorussian and the history of Belorussian literature, he wrote studies of Old Church Slavonic texts and the syntax of the Laurentian Chronicle and published critical editions of the Laurentian Chronicle, *Ruskaia Pravda,* and a Ukrainian Lucidarius of the 17th century. His important textbook *Slavianskaia kirillovskaia paleografiia* (Slavic Cyrillic Paleography) was published in 1928. Karsky also published materials on southern Ukrainian dialects, and gave a general survey of Ukrainian dialects in *Russkaia dialektologiia* (Russian Dialectology, 1924). A bibliography of his publications appeared in *Izvestiia Akademii nauk SSSR, Otdel obshchestvennykh nauk* (1932).

Karst. Terrain consisting of soluble rock such as limestone or gypsum and characterized by barren, rocky ground, sinkholes, precipices, caves, and underground streams and lakes. The term is derived from the Karst, a limestone plateau in the Dinaric Alps of Yugoslavia. In Ukraine karst features are most prominent in regions built of Upper Jurassic limestones, such as the Crimean Mountains (particularly the *Yaila plateaus) and the Podilian *Tovtry; of gypsum, such as southwestern Podilia and Pokutia; or of marls, such as southwestern Podilia and Volhynia. They are much less prominent in the southern Donbas and the Central Upland. In Caucasia karst features are widespread in the Black Sea littoral and Rocky Caucasus ranges.

Kartvelishvili, Lavrentii [Kartvelišvili, Lavrentij], b 28 April 1890 in Samtredia, Georgia, d 22 August 1938. Bolshevik leader. In 1918 he became a member of the All-Ukrainian Party Provisional Committee and served in the Red Army in the Odessa region. In the 1920s and 1930s he served in various party positions in Ukraine, Russia, and Georgia. In 1929–30 he was second secretary of the CC CP(B)U and a member of its Politburo and Organizational Bureau. He perished in the political purges of the 1930s and was rehabilitated in the 1950s.

Kasha, Michael [Kaša, Myxajlo], b 6 December 1920 in Elizabeth, New Jersey. Physical chemist of Ukrainian descent; member of the US National Academy of Sciences. A graduate of the universities of Michigan and California (PH D 1945), since 1951 he has been a professor at Florida State University and director of the Institute of Molecular Biophysics (1960–). Kasha has published extensively in the areas of molecular biophysics, emission spectroscopy of molecules, classification of electronic transitions, radiationless transitions, theoretical photochemistry, and molecular excitons and energy transfer.

Andrii Kashchenko

Mykola Kashchenko

Kashchenko, Andrii [Kaščenko, Andrij], b 1858 on the Veselyi khutir, Oleksandrivske county, Katerynoslav gubernia, d 29 March 1921. Writer. He began writing in 1883, but became known only after the Revolution of 1905, when the ban on Ukrainian publishing in Russian-ruled Ukraine was lifted. He is the author of many stories and novellas, most set in the Cossack period. Although they have little literary value and are historically inaccurate, because of their easy and romantic representation of Ukraine's past they became extremely popular and played an important didactic role, instilling a fundamental sense of Ukrainian patriotism in their peasant and young readers. Consequently they have been banned in Soviet Ukraine; numerous editions, however, appeared in interwar Galicia.

Kashchenko, Mykola [Kaščenko], b 7 May 1855 at Veselyi khutir, Oleksandrivske county, Katerynoslav gubernia, d 29 March 1935 in Kiev. Biologist, embryologist, and plant breeder; from 1919 full member of the Ukrainian Academy of Sciences. A graduate (1880) of Kharkiv University, he taught at Tomsk University (1895–1912) and then at the Kiev Polytechnical Institute. He directed the Acclimatization Garden in Kiev (1914–35) and the Zoological Museum of the Ukrainian Academy of Sciences (1919–26), both of which he had organized. Kashchenko contributed to many areas of biology. His pioneering studies in pathological embryology included microscopic analysis of human embryonic terata. He wrote many taxonomic works on Siberian fauna and acclimatized many medicinal, industrial, decorative, and edible plants (pears, apricots, grapes) to Ukraine and Siberia. A biography of him by N. Konotopets was published in Kiev in 1980.

Kashchenko, Vasyl [Kaščenko, Vasyl'], b 1812, d 15 December 1894. Horticulturalist and forester. For over 50 years he developed new fruit trees at his estate Pryiut in Katerynoslav gubernia. He was one of the first agronomists in the Russian Empire to introduce shelterbelts and urged their application in steppe farming.

Kashshai, Antin [Kaššaj], b 24 February 1921 in Dubrynych near Perechyn, Transcarpathia. Landscape painter. A student of Y. *Bokshai, Kashshai is known for such works as *Winter in the Carpathian Mountains* (1952), *First Snowfall* (1952), *The Mountain Pass* (1954), *Under the Mountain Meadows* (1963), *October* (1970), and *A Misty Morning* (1979). A book about him was written by G. Ostrovsky in 1962.

Kashynsky, Pavlo [Kašyns'kyj], b 25 September 1890 in Kiev, d 3 January 1980 in Munich. Publisher, publicist, and educator. He was head of the Brotherhood of Independentists in Kiev. He served as principal of Ukrainian secondary schools in Kiev and Dashiv (1917), Kiev (1918), Vienna (1942–5), and Munich (1946–53). For many years Kashynsky was director of the Vernyhora publishing society in Kiev (1916–21), Vienna (1918–23, 1939–), and Munich (1946–8). From 1925 to 1935 he published and edited *Österuropäischer Pressedienst* in Vienna.

Kasianenko, Hryhorii [Kasjanenko, Hryhorij], 1891–? Aeronautical engineer and political leader. During the period of Ukrainian independence he was a member of the Central Rada and the Committee for the Defense of the Revolution. Under the Soviet regime he worked as an engineer in the aircraft industry. He perished during the Stalinist terror of the 1930s.

Volodymyr Kasianenko

Kasianenko, Volodymyr [Kas'janenko], b 16 November 1901 in Velykyi Yanysol, Mariiupil county, Katerynoslav gubernia, d 18 January 1981 in Kiev. Anatomist; from 1951 a full member of the AN URSR. He graduated from the Kiev Veterinary Institute in 1926 and worked there until 1950 as professor (from 1938) and head of the division of evolutionary morphology. Then he worked at the Institute of Zoology of the AN URSR as institute director (1950–63) and consultant (1964–81). Most of Kasianenko's research dealt with the evolution and anatomy of muscle and bone structures in mammalian limbs.

Kasianenko, Yevhen [Kasjanenko, Jevhen], 1889–? Political leader and journalist. During the revolutionary period he sat on the Central Rada (1917–18) as a representative of the Ukrainian Social Democratic Workers' party. As a member of the party's left wing led by Ye. Neronovych, he went over to the Bolsheviks and joined the CP(B)U. He edited various publications, including the semiofficial organ of the government *Visti Vseukraïns'koho tsentral'noho vykonavchoho komitetu*. He disappeared in the late 1930s during the Party purges in Ukraine.

Kasianov, Oleksander [Kas'janov], b 23 February 1906 in Kharkiv, d 23 September 1961 in Kharkiv. Architect; corresponding member of the Academy of Construction and Architecture of the Ukrainian SSR. A graduate of the Kharkiv Art Institute (1930), he was Kharkiv's chief architect (1943–50) and director of the Institute of Urban Planning of the Academy of Construction and Architecture. He helped draft the general plans for Kharkiv, Chernihiv, Kamianets-Podilskyi, Lviv, and Voroshylovhrad. Kasianov edited the journal *Budivnytstvo i arkhitektura* and wrote books on city planning: *Misto maibutn'oho* (The City of the Future, 1957) and *Radian'ke mistobudivnytstvo na Ukraïni* (Soviet Urban Planning in Ukraine, 1955).

Vasyl Kasiian: *Self-Portrait* (1931)

Kasiian, Vasyl [Kasijan, Vasyl'], b 1 January 1896 in Mykulyntsi, Stanyslaviv county, Galicia, d 26 June 1976 in Kiev. Graphic artist of the realist school; from 1947 full member of the USSR Academy of Arts and the Academy of Architecture of the Ukrainian SSR. A graduate of the Prague Academy of Arts (1926) and a student of M. Švabinský, he assumed Soviet citizenship and in 1927 immigrated to the Ukrainian SSR, where he taught at the Kiev State Art Institute (1927–30 and 1944–76), the Ukrainian Printing Institute in Kharkiv (1930–7), and the Kharkiv Institute of Arts (1938–41). A prolific and versatile artist, he excelled in all the graphic techniques – wood engraving, copper engraving, linocut, and lithography – as well as pen drawing and watercolors. During his Prague period Kasiian dealt with social themes, depicting the poverty and hard life of the lower classes in Europe. Coming to Ukraine, he created several series of propaganda wood and copper engravings about collective-farm life, the building of the Dnieper Hydroelectric Station, mining in the Donbas, and the building of the Kiev Metro. He also devoted a series of engravings to V. Lenin and to J. Stalin (almost 50 works). Following N. Khrushchev's condemnation of the personality cult, Kasiian destroyed whole portfolios of his engravings of Stalin. The most valuable part of his rich, technically flawless legacy consists of the works on industrial themes, which document the economic transformation of Ukraine, and the illustrations to works by T. Shevchenko, Lesia Ukrainka, I. Franko, M. Kotsiubynsky, V. Stefanyk, and O. Kobylianska. Socialist realism, which Kasiian defended in his articles, led him to adopt elements of naturalism and had a detrimental effect on his later work. He wrote many works on graphic techniques, and collaborated with Yu. Turchenko on a study of T. Shevchenko's graphic works. He was the editor of *Taras Shevchenko: Mystets'ka spadshchyna* (Taras Shevchenko: The Artistic Legacy, 4 vols, 1961–4), which contains all of Shevchenko's known works, and a coeditor of the six-volume *Istoriia ukraïns'koho mystetstva* (History of Ukrainian Art, 1966–8). From 1927 Kasiian's numerous artistic works were displayed at one-man exhibitions, including six in Kiev, three in Kharkiv, two in Odessa, and one each in Lviv, Moscow, Prague, and Bucharest. His works were included in most official Soviet exhibitions abroad, including the Venice Biennale.

BIBLIOGRAPHY
Portnov, H. *Vasyl' Illich Kasiian* (Kiev 1962)
Kostiuk, S. *Vasyl' Kasiian. Bibliohrafichnyi pokazhchyk* (Lviv 1976)
Vladych, L. *Vasyl' Kasiian* (Kiev 1978)

S. Hordynsky

Kasperovych, Mykola [Kasperovyč], b 1885 in Kozelets, Chernihiv gubernia, d 1934? Painter and art restorer. A friend and student of M. *Boichuk, he studied art in Paris and in 1910 took part in a group exhibit of Boichuk's students at the Salon des Indépendents. From 1914 he oversaw the restoration work at museums in Chernihiv and in 1924 became director of the Restoration Studio of the Kievan Cave Monastery Museum of Cults and Customs. When the monastery was closed in 1926, he was appointed director of the Restoration Studio of the All-Ukrainian Museum Village, located on the grounds of the monastery and encompassing the collections of several important museums. Besides conserving art objects, the studio conducted systematic research in the history of Ukrainian painting. When the museum village was abolished in 1934, Kasperovych was arrested and disappeared without a trace.

Kasymenko, Oleksander, b 23 June 1905 in Velyka Burimka, Zolotonosha county, Poltava guberniia, d 13 January 1971 in Kiev. Soviet historian and Party functionary. From 1931 he taught at Kiev University. From 1933 to 1947 he held various Party posts. In 1946 he was a member of the Soviet Ukrainian delegation at the Paris Peace Conference. From 1947 to 1964 he served as director of the Institute of History at the Academy of Sciences of the Ukrainian SSR and editor of many of its publications. His works are written in a propagandistic manner and deal mostly with Ukrainian-Russian relations.

Katamai, Bohdan [Katamaj], b 10 August 1911 in Yamnytsia, Stanyslaviv county, Galicia. Journalist, editor, and civic leader. Arriving in the United States in 1930, he became a founder and the first president of the Ukrainian Catholic Youth League in America. In 1934 he was elected president of the Society of Mazepists and editor of its monthly journal *Holos Mazepyntsiv*. Returning to Galicia in 1936, he worked as an editor on the newspaper *Ukraïns'ki visti*. With the outbreak of war he returned to the United States, and became editor (1943–50) of the newspaper *Ameryka*, which he transformed into a daily. At the same time, Katamai served on the executive of the Ukrainian Congress Committee of America (1941–50) and on the board of directors of the United Ukrainian American Relief Committee (1947–9).

Katamai, Dmytro [Katamaj], b 1886 in Yamnytsia, Stanyslaviv county, Galicia, d 3 April 1935 in Vienna. Political and civic figure. He sat on the executive committee of the Ukrainian Radical party and edited its weekly *Hromads'kyi holos* (1911–14). In 1913 he founded the literary and scientific monthly *Iliustrovana Ukraïna*. Before the First World War, Katamai was an organizer of the Sich movement. During the war he served as secretary (1914–17) on the Combat Executive of the Ukrainian Sich Riflemen (USS) and as a lieutenant colonel in the Army of the UNR. He designed the *mazepynka* cap, known originally as the *katamaivka*, which was part of the USS uniform.

Katerynodar. See Krasnodar.

Katerynopil [Katerynopil']. V-11. Town smt (1979 pop 6,800) and raion center in Cherkasy oblast. First mentioned in the mid-16th century as the town of Kalnyboloto. From 1648 to 1712 it was a company town in Korsun regiment. In 1793 it came under Russian rule; it was renamed in 1795. From 1795 it was a county town (from 1797 in Kiev gubernia). Bricks and animal feed are produced there.

Katerynoslav. See Dnipropetrovske.

Katerynoslav Cossack Army. A military formation centered between the Boh and Inhul rivers in southern Ukraine. It was formed in 1787 by Russian Gen G. *Potemkin from two former units of the *Boh Cossack Army and local peasants and military colonists to defend southern Ukraine against the Turks and to fight in the Russian-Turkish War (1787–91). The subsequent conscription of merchants, artisans, and Old Believers from the region increased the size of the army to some 50,000, including 10,000 active soldiers organized in 10 regiments. The army gained renown in battles against the Turks at Akerman (Bilhorod-Dnistrovskyi). The Katerynoslav Cossack Army was disbanded in 1796. In 1802 some 3,000 of the former Cossacks were resettled in the Kuban, where they joined the *Kuban Cossack Host.

Katerynoslav group (Ukrainian: Katerynoslavtsi). The popular name for the Donets–Kryvyi Rih Basin regional organization of the Russian Social Democratic Workers' Party (Bolshevik) (RSDRP[B]), created in the summer of 1917 with centers in Kharkiv and Katerynoslav. The largest Bolshevik organization in Ukraine, its leaders included E. Kviring, Ya. Yakovlev, and Artem (F. Sergeev). Located in the industrial center of Ukraine, with its concentration of Russian or Russified workers, the group consistently and adamantly defended a centralist position on the question of Party and state organization. It considered Ukraine to be an integral part of Russia and opposed the idea of a separate Soviet Ukrainian republic and the establishment of an autonomous Ukrainian Communist party with a single party center. In 1918 it was behind the formation of the *Donets–Kryvyi Rih Soviet Republic. Throughout the Revolution the members had serious disagreements with the Kiev-based wing of the Bolshevik party, which was generally more conscious of the strength of Ukrainian national sentiment and therefore recognized the need to compromise with pro-Ukrainian forces and establish a distinct all-Ukrainian party. When the Moscow Bolshevik leadership eventually sided with the Kievan wing, the Katerynoslav group was forced to dissolve and was incorporated into the *Communist Party of Ukraine (Bolshevik).

Katerynoslav gubernia. An administrative-territorial unit in Russian-ruled Ukraine. Katerynoslav (Russian: Ekaterinoslav) – today *Dnipropetrovske – was the capital. In 1764 *New Russia gubernia had been created to administer much of Southern Ukraine, including the lands of the Zaporozhian Host after the destruction of the New Sich in 1775. It was replaced by Katerynoslav vicegerency in 1783 but was reinstated in 1796. In 1802 its territory was divided among the newly created Mykolaiv (from 1803 *Kherson), *Tavriia, and Katerynoslav gubernias. Katerynoslav gubernia consisted of Katerynoslav and Verkhnodniprovske counties west of the Dnieper, and Bakhmut, Novomoskovske, Oleksandrivske, Pavlohrad, Slovianoserbske, and Rostov counties east of the river; in 1874 Oleksandrivske county was divided to create Mariiupil county, and in 1887 Rostov county was transferred to the Don Cossack province. The gubernia's population was 662,000 in 1811, 902,400 in 1851, 1,204,800 in 1863, and 1,792,800 in 1885; the vast majority were peasants. From the second half of the 19th century the gubernia was the coal-mining and metallurgical center of Ukraine, incorporating the *Dnieper Industrial Region and the *Donets Basin. Consequently its population multiplied, increasing by 1897 to 2,113,700 (69.5 percent Ukrainian, 18.2 percent Russian, 4.2 percent Jewish, 4 percent German, 2.3 percent Greek, 1.1 percent Tatar). In 1924 it had 3,424,100 (13.6 percent urban) inhabitants, living in 5,165 settlements, 36 of them cities and towns; close to half were non-Ukrainian, and the largest social category was that of workers (25 percent). Under Soviet rule the gubernia was abolished in 1925, and its territory (76,912 sq km) was divided among seven okruhas: Katerynoslav, Oleksandrivske, Berdianske, Zaporizhia, Kryvyi Rih, Melitopil, and Pavlohrad.

I. Myhul, R. Senkus

Katolyts'kyi Vskhid (Catholic Dawn). A quarterly published from 1904 to 1907 in Lviv by the Vlasna Pomich Bohosloviv society. It consisted of theological studies, news about theologians, and the first literary efforts of young writers. The editor was Rev H. Plakyda.

Katonin, Yevhen, b 5 April 1889 in Odessa, d 27 February 1984 in Kiev. Architect; from 1948 full member of the Academy of Architecture of the Ukrainian SSR and then of the Academy of Construction and Architecture of the Ukrainian SSR (1956–64). A graduate of the All-Russian Academy of Arts in Petrograd (1918), he was appointed lecturer (1922) and then professor (1937) at the academy. In 1948 he joined the faculty of the Kiev State Art Institute. As an architect he helped design the Victory Park in Leningrad, the Kiev Station of the Moscow Metro, and the Vokzalna Station of the Kiev Metro. He also worked as a graphic artist.

Katsap [kacap]. Derogatory name applied to Russians by Ukrainians. It is used often in the folk tradition and literature. P. Kulish wrote about T. Shevchenko: 'He made us despise the Muscovites ... We called them *katsapy*.' Marko Vovchok wrote: 'The market was seething with bustle ..., the hucksters were jabbering, the gypsies swearing, the *katsapy* railing.' The word can also be found in the works of T. Shevchenko, P. Myrny, A. Svydnytsky, S. Rudnytsky, and D. Bedzyk. According to some scholars (A. Brückner, M. Vasmer) *katsap* is derived from the Ukrainian *tsap* (goat); according to others (A. Krymsky, D. Yavornytsky) it comes from the Tatar *kassap* (butcher).

Katsnelson, Abram [Kacnel'son], b 14 January 1914 in Horodnia, Chernihiv gubernia. Poet and literary critic. He graduated from Kiev University in 1941 with a degree in the theory of literature. His first collection of poems, *Krapli sontsia* (Droplets of the Sun, 1935), was followed by many other collections of rather average Soviet lyrical poetry – *Dostyhaiut' plody* (The Fruits Are Ripening, 1938), *Riast* (Corydalis, 1940), *Perednii krai* (The First Land, 1947), *V im'ja zhyttia* (In the Name of Life, 1953) – as well as the novelette in verse *Posered buri* (Amidst a Storm, 1963). His contribution as a literary scholar to poetics is notable, and his numerous articles have been published as separate collections of essays: *Krasa i syla virshovanoho slova* (The Beauty and Strength of the Poetic Word, 1963), *Pravdyva iskra Prometeia* (The True Spark of Prometheus, 1968), *Pro poeziiu i poetiv* (About Poetry and Poets, 1972), and *Pro poeziiu* (About Poetry, 1977). The essays range from studies of individual poets or poems to general analyses of poetic language and tropes.

Kavaleridze, Ivan, b 26 April 1887 at Ladanskyi khutir in Kharkiv gubernia, d 3 December 1978 in Kiev. Sculptor, film director, dramatist, and screenwriter. He studied art at the Kiev Art School (1907–9), the St Petersburg Academy of Arts (1909–10), and with N. Aronson in Paris (1910–11). His sculptures include busts of famous people such as F. Chaliapin (1909), and over 100 monuments in various cities of Ukraine: eg, the monument to Princess Olha in Kiev (1911), which was destroyed in 1934; the Shevchenko monuments in Kiev (1918), Romen (1918), Poltava (1925), and Sumy (1926); and the Skovoroda monuments in Lokhvytsia (1922) and Kiev (1977). In the 1920s his work was influenced by Cubism. His group

Ivan Kavaleridze: *Don Quixote*

compositions – *Bohdan Khmelnytsky Sends the Kobza Players into the Villages* (1954), *A. Buchma in the Role of M. Zadorozhny* (1954), and *Prometheus* (1962) – are somewhat stylized.

In 1928 he became interested in filmmaking. He scripted and directed a number of innovative historical films marked by stylization and monumentalism: *Zlyva* (The Downpour, 1929), *Perekop* (1930), *Koliïvshchyna* (1933), and *Prometei* (Prometheus, 1936). Accused of 'nationalist deviation' and formalism, he was forced to turn to popular themes and a simplified style. He adapted the operas *Natalka Poltavka* (Natalka from Poltava, 1936) and *Zaporozhets' za Dunaiem* (Zaporozhian Cossack beyond the Danube, 1938) for film. After the Second World War he directed the films *Hryhorii Skovoroda* (1960) and *Poviia* (The Strumpet, 1961) based on P. Myrny's novel.

A retrospective exhibit of his sculptures was held in 1962. He wrote several heroic dramas: *Votaniv mech* (Wotan's Sword, 1966), *Perekop* (1967), and *Persha borozna* (The First Furrow, 1969).

BIBLIOGRAPHY
Nimenko, A. *Kavaleridze – skul'ptor* (Kiev 1967)
Zinych, S.; Kapel'horods'ka, N. *Ivan Kavaleridze* (Kiev 1971)
V. Revutsky

Kavetsky, Rostyslav [Kavec'kyj], b 1 December 1899 in Samara, Russia, d 12 October 1978 in Kiev. Oncologist. A graduate of Samara University (1925); from 1951 full member of the AN URSR. At the Academy of Sciences of the Ukrainian SSR he directed its Institute of Clinical

Rostyslav Kavetsky

Vladimir Kaye-Kysilewsky

Physiology (1946–51) and served as head of its biological sciences division (1952–61, 1963–6). He was a founder and the first director of the Kiev Institute of Experimental and Clinical Oncology of the republic's Ministry of Public Health (from 1970, the AN URSR Institute for Problems of Oncology). Kavetsky was a leading cancer specialist. His research dealt with the role of the nervous and endocrine systems in tumor growth.

Kavunnyk, Danylo. See Vellansky, Danylo.

Kaye-Kysilewsky, Vladimir [Kysilevs'kyj, Volodymyr], b 4 August 1896 in Kolomyia, Galicia, d 30 July 1976 in Ottawa. Historian and civil servant; son of O. *Kysilevska. During the First World War he served with the Ukrainian Sich Riflemen and the Ukrainian Galician Army. After the war he studied history at Vienna University (PH D 1924). Having emigrated to Canada in 1925, he became editor of the newspapers *Zakhidni visti* in Edmonton (1928–30) and *Ukraïna* in Chicago (1931). While working as director of the Ukrainian Press Bureau in London, England (1931–40), he completed his doctoral studies at the School of Slavonic and East European Studies (1933–6). He returned to Canada in 1940 and, eventually, worked for the Department of National War Services as a liaison officer with ethnic groups. He played an advisory role in the formation of the Ukrainian Canadian Committee. After the war he continued his career in the civil service and taught history and Slavic studies at the University of Ottawa (1948–60). In 1954 he was elected first president of the Canadian Association of Slavists. Kaye-Kysilewsky wrote *Early Ukrainian Settlements in Canada, 1895–1900* (1964) and compiled the *Dictionary of Ukrainian Canadian Biography: Pioneer Settlers of Manitoba 1891–1900* (1975). In 1974 he was appointed to the Order of Canada.

Kazakhstan or **Kazakh Soviet Socialist Republic.** The second-largest republic (1986 pop 16,028,000) in the USSR, with an area of 2,717,300 sq km. It is bounded by the Volga region and the Caspian Sea on the west, the Sinkiang Uighur Autonomous region of the People's Republic of China on the east, the Ural Mountains and western Siberia on the north, and the Central Asian Soviet republics of Turkmenistan, Uzbekistan, and Kirgizia on the south. The capital is Alma-Ata (1986 pop 1,088,000). The republic has 19 oblasts, 222 raions, 83 cities, and 204 towns (smt). In 1986, 57.5 percent of the population was urban. The northern and northeastern parts of Kazakhstan have been settled by Ukrainians, and today, based on estimates of cumulative immigration, almost 26 percent of the republic's population is of Ukrainian origin.

Kazakhstan is essentially a tableland, much of which is covered by deserts or semideserts. Its western and southwestern parts consist of the Caspian Depression and the Ustiurt Plateau. Farther east, the Ural Plateau separates the Caspian Depression from the vast Turan Plain, in the south of which lies the Aral Sea. The north is part of the West Siberian Plain. Central Kazakhstan is an undulating upland. In the east and southeast, the desert expanses are bounded by the Altai, Tarbagatai, and Dzhungarian Alatau mountains and the northern and western ranges of the Tian Shan.

A narrow belt of forest-steppe with chernozem soils – a continuation of the Siberian forest-steppe – stretches across northern Kazakhstan. Farther south lies a wide steppe belt with chernozem and chestnut-brown soils and a belt of infertile deserts and semideserts. In the southern and eastern piedmont lies another belt of fertile steppes with loess soils. Only the forest-steppe and steppe belts and the larger river valleys (where irrigation and reclamation are feasible) are arable.

Kazakhstan was originally populated by nomadic Turkic tribes, out of which the Kazakh hordes and khanate evolved in the 15th century. Russian penetration began in the 1730s, and by the 1860s all of Kazakhstan had been annexed. The first Slavic settlers were Cossacks.

Beginning in the last two decades of the 19th century, northern Kazakhstan, along with the adjacent parts of Siberia and the Urals, attracted the largest number of Russian and Ukrainian agricultural settlers (see *Emigration). In 1897 there were 37,700 Ukrainians there. More than a million settlers had arrived by 1916. Before the 1917 Revolution the eastern parts of Kazakhstan were within the Steppe and *Turkestan general-gubernias. After occupying Central Asia, the Bolshevik authorities set up various autonomous oblasts and republics in the region. In 1920 the territory settled by the Kazakhs became the Kirgiz Autonomous SSR; in 1925 it was renamed the Kazakh Autonomous SSR. In 1936 the Kazakh SSR – an artificial entity that does not correspond to either historical or (in the north) ethnographic developments – was constituted.

Beginning in the 1880s the nature of Kazakhstan's economy changed from one of nomadic herding to a settled herding and farming type. In the late 1920s a mixed economy based on the mining of more than 90 ferrous and non-ferrous metals and coal began to develop. Since 1954 cultivation of the 'virgin lands' (which saw the influx of over half a million Ukrainians) has made agriculture an important branch of the economy. Today Kazakhstan is one of the main regions of grain growing (wheat, millet, rice) and sheep and cattle farming in the USSR. It is the principal Soviet supplier of chromite and non-ferrous metals (silver, gold, copper, lead, zinc, titanium, magnesium, rare and precious metals) and the third most important supplier of coking coal (the Karaganda and other basins). Its electric-power, chemical, petroleum and natural-gas extraction and refining, machine-building, clothing, and food industries are not insignificant.

As the country's economic structure has changed, so has its population. In the 1926 census the population of Kazakhstan was 6,503,000, with Kazakhs constituting 57.1 percent, Ukrainians 13.2 percent, and Russians 19.7 percent. Collectivization, famine, and Stalinist repressions caused a decline in the population in general and of Kazakhs in particular. According to the unreliable 1939 census, Kazakhstan's population was 6,094,000, a decline of some 7 percent from the 1926 figure. The total number of Kazakhs in the republic between 1926 and 1939 dropped by 35 percent. In 1939 Kazakhs constituted 38.2 percent of the population and Ukrainians, 10.8 percent. In 1959 the population of Kazakhstan was 9,310,000; Kazakhs accounted for 30 percent and Ukrainians, 8.2 percent. In 1979 Kazakhs constituted 36 percent, Russians 40.8 percent, Ukrainians 6.1 percent, and Germans 6 percent of the population.

The Kazakhs have remained primarily a rural people. In 1970 only 26 percent of them lived in urban centers, and the Kazakhs constituted only 17 percent of the republic's urban population (Russians constituted 58 percent) and 23 percent of its specialists. In 1959 only 19 percent of the republic's working class was Kazakh. Despite being a minority in their own republic, the Kazakhs have maintained their national identity. In 1979, 99 percent of them considered Kazakh their mother tongue.

In 1979 there were 898,000 Ukrainians in Kazakhstan; in 1970, 933,000. The actual number of Ukrainians or inhabitants of Ukrainian origin – if one extrapolates from pre-Soviet emigration data and the 1926 census – should be much higher, from 3 to 4 million. In 1979, only 41.3 percent of those who identified themselves as Ukrainians considered Ukrainian to be their mother tongue; 58.6 percent considered it to be Russian. Ukrainians have lived mostly in the agricultural regions of the north and the southeast piedmont. The territories they have inhabited form, along with the adjacent areas of western *Siberia, the *Urals, and the northern *Kirgiz SSR, a compact region of Ukrainian settlement – like the *Far East – in Asia. Ukrainians settlers have called this region Siryi Klyn (the Gray Wedge) or Sira Ukraina (Gray Ukraine).

Ukrainian-Kazakh relations have been mainly cultural and have been associated primarily with the figure of T. Shevchenko, who was exiled to Kazakhstan (1848–57). Kazakh themes and subjects occur in several poems and stories he wrote there and in the 200 paintings and drawings he executed as a member of an expedition to the Aral Sea in 1848–9. In 1939 the port on the Caspian Sea in Mangyshlak oblast in whose fortress Shevchenko was forced to live in 1850–7 was renamed Fort Shevchenko in his honor; a Shevchenko Memorial Museum was founded there. The Kazakh State Art Gallery in Alma-Ata was also named in Shevchenko's honor in 1939; paintings by Shevchenko and exhibits dealing with Ukrainian-Kazakh cultural ties are housed there. A Kazakh edition of Shevchenko's *Kobzar* was published in 1935, and several editions of his works have been published in Kazakh since then; 17 Kazakh poets prepared the 1964 edition. The Kazakh scholar T. Beisov published a monograph on Shevchenko in Kazakhstan in 1952, and the Academy of Sciences of the Kazakh SSR published a collection of essays about Shevchenko in 1964. Many articles about him have also been written; he has appeared in Kazakh artworks and literature; and the Kazakh film studio released a film about him.

Works by other Ukrainian writers (I. Franko, Lesia Ukrainka, P. Tychyna, M. Bazhan, O. Honchar, M. Stelmakh, and others) have been translated into Kazakh and published in separate editions, anthologies, and journals. Works by Kazakh writers (Abai Kunanbaiev, Dzhambul Dzhabaiev, M. Auezov, G. Mustafin, G. Musrepov, S. Mukanov, and others) have been translated into Ukrainian. Kazakhstan has been the setting of works by O. Desniak, O. Donchenko, T. Masenko, Yu. Smolych, I. Senchenko, N. Zabila, and other Ukrainian writers.

During the Second World War many Ukrainians lived as evacuees in Kazakhstan; among them were the artist A. Petrytsky, the sculptor M. Lysenko, the composer M. Skorulsky (who composed a quintet based on the works of Abai Kunanbaiev), and the companies of the Kiev Ukrainian Drama Theater (in Semipalatinsk), the Kiev Russian Drama Theater (in Karaganda), and the theaters of Poltava, Dnipropetrovske, Luhanske, and other cities. The faculty members of the Kiev Agricultural Institute worked at the Kazakh Agricultural Institute in Alma-Alta, while those of Kiev and Kharkiv universities were consolidated into one Ukrainian State University, which took over the buildings of the Kzyl-Orda Pedagogical Institute.

From the early 19th century the tsarist authorities exiled their political opponents to Kazakhstan. This practice has been continued in the Soviet period. In the 1930s and 1940s, in particular, thousands of Ukrainians were sent to *concentration camps around Karaganda (the Karlag system), where many of them died. Those who survived were not allowed to return to Ukraine, and many remained in Kazakhstan.

BIBLIOGRAPHY

Korbut, S. *Siryi Klyn i ukraïns'ka kolonizatsiina sprava* (Lviv 1937)
Demko, G. *The Russian Colonization of Kazakhstan, 1896–1916* (Bloomington and The Hague 1969)
Marunchak, M. *Ukraïntsi v SSSR poza kordonamy URSR* (Winnipeg 1974)
Koishibaeva, R. *Kazakhsko-ukrainskie literaturnye sviazi* (Alma-Ata 1977)
Alekseenko, N. *Naselenie dorevoliutsionnogo Kazakhstana (chislennost', razmeshchenie, sostav, 1870–1914 gg.)* (Alma-Ata 1981)
Bekmakhanova, N. *Mnogonatsional'noe naselenie Kazakhstana v epokhu kapitalizma: 60-e gody XIX veka–1917 g.* (Moscow 1986)

B. Krawchenko, V. Kubijovyč, A. Zhukovsky

Kazanets, Ivan [Kazanec'], b 12 October 1918 in Lotsmanska Kamianka (now a part of Dnipropetrovske), Katerynoslav gubernia. Government and Communist Party leader. He was first secretary of the Stalin oblast Communist Party of Ukraine committee (1953–60) and second secretary (1960–3) and a member of the Presidium of the CC CPU (1960–5). From 1963 to 1965 he served as head of the Council of Ministers of the Ukrainian SSR and then as minister of metallurgy of the USSR.

Kazanka. VI-13. Town smt (1978 pop 8,500) and raion center in Mykolaiv oblast, situated on the Vysun River in the Black Sea Lowland. Founded in the early 19th century, it has a food industry and a regional museum.

Kazennyi Torets River [Kazennyj Torec']. A right-tributary of the Donets River, the Kazennyi Torets flows for 134 km through the northwestern Donets Basin and drains a basin of 5,410 sq km. Its waters supply industry and are used for irrigation.

Kazka, Arkadii, b 24 September 1890 in Sedniv, Chernihiv gubernia, d 1933. Poet. Supporting himself by teaching, he was published, beginning in 1919, in such journals as *Literaturno-naukovyi visnyk, Nova hromada,* and *Chervonyi shliakh.* In 1928 he joined the writers' group *Pluh. A collection of his poetry, 'Lamentabile,' remains unpublished. Kazka cultivated the classical forms of the sonnet, triolet, and rondeau. He committed suicide in an NKVD prison in Odessa.

Bohdan Kazymyra

Volodymyr Kedrovsky

Kazymyra, Bohdan, b 19 October 1913 in Cherniiv, Stanyslaviv county, Galicia. Historian, educator, journalist. A graduate of Louvain University (1935), the Greek Catholic Theological Academy in Lviv (1941), and Vienna University (PH D 1955), he taught sociology at the Theological Academy in Lviv (1935–9, 1942–4). In 1948 he established and directed the Ukrainian Press Bureau in Brussels and lectured at the Ukrainian theological seminary in Culemborg, Holland. Settling in Canada in 1950, he organized the Ukrainian Press Bureau in Edmonton and edited the monthly *Katolyts'ka aktsiia* (1950–5). Since then he has worked as a librarian and archivist. In 1963 he was appointed professor of sociology at the Ukrainian Catholic University in Rome. Kazymyra's publications include numerous articles in history and sociology and pamphlets on the history of the Ukrainian Catholic church in Canada.

Kedrovsky, Volodymyr [Kedrovs'kyj], b 13 August 1890 in the Kherson region, d 13 March 1970 in New York. Journalist; military and political activist. He was a member of the Central Committee of the Ukrainian Party of Socialist Revolutionaries and an organizer of the Ukrainian armed forces during the Ukrainian struggle for independence of 1917–20. Elected vice-president of the *Ukrainian Military Committee, Kedrovsky was a member of the Central Rada, serving as the UNR undersecretary of war in 1917 and as chief inspector of the UNR armed forces in 1919. In 1920 he was appointed ambassador to the Baltic republics. He immigrated to Vienna in 1921, where he was the head of the Ukrainian League of Nations Association until 1924 and active in the Association of Ukrainian Journalists in Europe. In 1926 he immigrated to the United States. He was coeditor of the daily newspaper *Svoboda* (1926–33) and chief of the Ukrainian section of Voice of America (1955–63). His memoirs, *Obrysy mynuloho* (Sketches of the Past) and *1917-yi rik* (The Year 1917, vol 1), were published in 1966.

Ivan Kedryn

Ivan Keivan: *Self-portrait*

Kedryn, Ivan (pen name of Ivan Rudnytsky), b 22 April 1896 in Khodoriv, Bibrka county, Galicia. A prominent journalist and political leader; full member of the Shevchenko Scientific Society. He is the brother of Milena, Mykhailo, and Anton Rudnytsky. A graduate of Vienna University (1923), he worked on the staff of the journal *Volia* in Vienna (1920–2) and the newspaper *Dilo* in Lviv (1922–39). For a time he served as *Dilo*'s Warsaw correspondent (1926–36) and as the first press attaché of the Ukrainian Parliamentary Representation in Warsaw (1925–31). In 1937–9 he was *Dilo*'s editor for political affairs. As a veteran of the UNR Army and a leading member of the Ukrainian National Democratic Alliance (UNDO), he was responsible for liaison between the UNDO and Col Ye. Konovalets of the OUN, and between the UNDO and the UNR Government-in-exile. In 1944 he immigrated to Austria, where he headed the Ukrainian Central Relief Alliance in Austria (1946–9). Having settled in the United States in 1949, he served for many years on the editorial board of *Svoboda*. He was president of United Ukrainian War Veterans in America and coeditor of its *Visti kombatanta*. Kedryn has edited various collections and almanacs, including the history of the Sich Riflemen *Zoloti Vorota* (The Golden Gates, 1937). His more important works are *Beresteis'kyi myr: Spomyny i materiialy* (The Peace Treaty of Brest-Litovsk: Recollections and Materials, 1928), *Prychyny upadku Pol'shchi* (The Causes of Poland's Fall, 1940), *Paraleli z istorii Ukraïny* (Parallels in the History of Ukraine, 1971), a book of memoirs, *Zhyttia – podiï – liudy* (Life – Events – People, 1976), and a collection of selected articles, *U mezhakh zatsikavlennia* (Within the Range of [My] Interests, 1986). As a journalist he wrote numerous articles for the Ukrainian, Polish, German, and English press on a wide range of topics, including Ukrainian political and community life, world politics, and cultural developments.

S. Yaniv

Kehychivka [Kehyčivka]. IV-16. Town smt (1979 pop 7,500) and raion center in Kharkiv oblast. Founded in the late 19th century, it has a food industry. Natural gas is extracted in the raion.

Keivan, Ivan [Kejvan] (Keywan), b 16 September 1907 in Karliv, Sniatyn county, Galicia. Painter, graphic artist, and art scholar. Completing his art studies at the Cracow (1928–9) and Warsaw (1932–7) academies of fine art and the Ukrainian Art School in Lviv (1937), he taught art at the Ukrainian gymnasium in Kolomyia and after the war at Ukrainian schools in Germany. Since 1949 he has been living in Edmonton, Canada, where he helped found the Ukrainian Association of Artists. He has done a series of large portraits – which includes portraits of I. Franko, T. Osmachka, V. Lesych, and the artist's wife – and a self-portrait. His publications include many articles and a number of monographs: *Taras Shevchenko – obrazotvorchyi mystets'* (T. Shevchenko as a Plastic Artist, 1964), *Volodymyr Sichyns'kyi* (1957), *Dmytro Antonovych* (1966), and *Ukraïns'ke obrazotvorche mystetstvo* (Ukrainian Fine Arts, 1984). His oil paintings and graphic works have been exhibited in Lviv, Warsaw, Paris, Munich, Amsterdam, and various cities in Canada and the United States.

Keller, Fedor, b 1857, d 20 December 1918 in Kiev. Russian count and army general. In 1914 as commander of the Tenth Cavalry Division of the Russian army, he ordered pogroms of the Ukrainian population in Galicia. In 1918 Hetman P. Skoropadsky appointed him supreme commander of the Ukrainian armed forces. During the uprising against the hetman regime, Keller was captured by troops loyal to the Directory and killed in an escape attempt.

Kelmentsi [Kel'menci]. V-7. Town smt (1979 pop 6,900) and raion center in Chernivtsi oblast, situated in the Khotyn region of northern Bessarabia. First mentioned in 1559.

Kempe, Lavrentii, b 22 August 1901 in Volodarka, Skvyra county, Kiev gubernia, d 27 January 1981 in Toronto. Character actor. From 1921 he worked with various Galician touring companies, the Tobilevych Ukrainian People's Theater in Stanyslaviv (1928), Y. Stadnyk's company, O. Karabinevych's company in Volhynia, and the Franko Ukrainian Theater in Stanyslaviv (1940–4). Emigrating from Ukraine during the war, he was active in the Ukrainian theater in Austria and from 1949 in Canada. Kempe's repertoire included Shostenko and Nevidomy in Yu. Kosach's *Obloha* (The Siege) and *Marsh chernihivs'koho polku* (The March of the Chernihiv Regiment), respectively. In Toronto he directed and appeared in operettas such as Ya. Barnych's *Hutsulka Ksenia* (Ksenia, the Hutsul Girl) and *Sharika*.

Kentrzhynsky, Bohdan [Kentržyns'kyj] (Kentrschynskyj), b 22 February 1919 in Rivne, Volhynia gubernia, d 23 May 1969 in Stockholm. Political figure, publicist, and historian. During the Second World War he was the official representative of the OUN (Melnyk faction) in Finland. From 1945 he headed the Ukrainian Information Bureau (UIB) in Stockholm and acted as the Scandinavian representative of the Executive of the Ukrainian National Council. For many years he was a member of the Leadership of Ukrainian Nationalists (PUN). From 1957 he lectured on history at Stockholm University and served as research associate of the Swedish Royal Academy. Based on his research in Scandinavian archives, he wrote a number of important articles on the Khmelnytsky and Mazepa periods, which were published in *Karolinska Förbundets Arsbok*, and a monograph *Mazepa* (1962). He also wrote several popular histories of Ukraine: *Kampen om Ukrainas självständighet* (1942), *Sanningen om Ukraina* (1943), and *Katajaisena kasvaa vapautemme* (1944).

Kerch, Oksana [Kerč] (pen name of Yaroslava Kulish), b 24 October 1911 in Przeworsk, Galicia. Writer. After the Second World War she emigrated to Argentina, where she wrote the novel *Al'batrosy* (Albatrosses, 1957). After moving to the United States she wrote the novels *Narechenyi* (The Fiancé, 1965) and *Takyi dovhyi rik* (Such a Long Year, 1971). She has also contributed many reviews and articles to Ukrainian periodicals.

Kerch: the dromos of the Royal kurhan (4th century BC)

Kerch [Kerč]. VIII-17. City (1985 pop 168,000) under oblast jurisdiction and port in the eastern Crimea. It is divided into three city raions and is an important transportation center.

Kerch originated in the 6th century BC as the Greek colony of *Panticapaeum, which in the succeeding century became the capital of the *Bosporan Kingdom. From the middle of the 1st century BC it was under Roman

Kerch: wall painting in the vault of the Royal kurhan (4th century BC)

and then Byzantine control. It suffered severely from barbarian invasions and was devastated by the Huns in AD 375. From the 10th to the 12th century the Slavic settlement of Korchev, which belonged to *Tmutorokan principality, was a center of trade between Rus' and the Crimea, Caucasia, and the Orient. In the 14th and 15th centuries the Genoese colony of Cerco (Cerchio) was established there, which in the late 15th century passed to the Turks, who built a citadel there. By the Peace Treaty of *Küçük Kaynarca in 1774, Kerch and the neighboring fortress of Yenikale (built in 1706) were ceded to Russia.

Because of its location, from 1821 Kerch developed into an important trade and fishing port. Its population grew from 8,230 in 1840 to 34,780 in 1897. It was looted by the British during the Crimean War in 1855. After suffering a decline during the First World War and the civil war (1926 pop 34,600), the city resumed its growth in the late 1920s with the expansion of various industries, iron ore and metallurgy in particular, and by 1939 its population had reached 104,500. Severely damaged during the Second World War it has been completely rebuilt.

Kerch is the center of the *Kerch Iron-ore Basin, the base of a fishing fleet, and an important fish-processing center for numerous varieties of fish products. Shipbuilding, building-materials manufacturing, food processing, and light industry also play a significant role in the city's economy. Its port handles agglomerate produced by the Komysh-Burunskyi Iron-ore Complex, iron pipes, coal, building materials, grain, and fish. Its railway ferry links the Crimea with Caucasia. The city has research institutes of fish farming and oceanography, a metallurgical and shipbuilding tekhnikum, a medical school, and six vocational-technical schools. Its large history and archeology museum (est 1826) has a valuable collection reflecting the region's past. Its most impressive architectural monuments are Demeter's Vault with Greek mythological frescoes (1st century AD), the Church of St John the Baptist (10th century, with murals from the 13th–14th century), and the Yenikale fortress. Located nearby are several ancient kurhans and excavated cities.

V. Kubijovyč

Kerch Iron-ore Basin. A group of iron-ore deposits in the northern and eastern parts of the Kerch Peninsula with an area over 250 sq km and estimated reserves of 8 billion t (0.3 percent of Ukraine's total reserves). Two-thirds of the reserves consists of tobacco ores, and one-third of the more valuable brown ores. The latter have an iron content of approximately 37 percent and some harmful impurities; hence, these ores must be subjected to concentration and chemical treatment. Iron-ore seams extend no deeper than 100–160 m and can be easily strip-mined.

The Kerch deposits began to be mined at the end of the 19th century. In 1913, 370,000 t or 5 percent of Ukraine's iron ore was mined in Kerch. The industry employed 3,000 workers. During the 1920s production was low: in 1928 only 51,000 t were mined. When the *Komysh-Buruny Iron-ore Complex was built in the 1930s, the industry expanded rapidly and by 1940 reached an output of 1.3 million t. After the Second World War the mines were reopened only in 1951. In 1955 their output was 2.6 million t and in 1975 it peaked at 4.8 million t (3.9 percent of Ukraine's output). As the brown ores became depleted and grave problems were encountered in upgrading the tobacco ores, production declined to 3.5 million t (2.9 percent of Ukraine's output) by 1984.

An integrated iron and steel mill in Kerch was uneconomical and was not rebuilt after the Second World War. The ore mined in the Kerch Peninsula is shipped across the Sea of Azov to the *Zhdanov Azovstal Metallurgical Plant.

B. Somchynsky

Kerch Peninsula. A 3,000-sq-km, riverless peninsula in the eastern Crimea, connected to it by the 17-km Parapach Isthmus. It is washed by the Sea of Azov to the north, the Black Sea to the south, and the Kerch Strait to the east. The rich *Kerch Iron-ore Basin is found there. The soils are mainly chestnut alkaline; chernozems are found in pockets in the north and southeast. The vegetation is mostly of the treeless steppe variety. Ruins of the ancient *Bosporan Kingdom are located on the coast. The main city in the peninsula is Kerch. The peninsula's hilly northern parts consist of calcites, marls, and sandstone; saline lakes (from which salt is extracted) and many mud volcanoes are found there. Its southern part is steppe land.

Kerch Strait. Known in ancient times as the Cimmerian Bosporus, the strait is situated between the Kerch Peninsula of the Crimea and the Taman Peninsula of the Kuban and joins the Black and Azov seas. Its length is 41 km; its width, 4–15 km; and its depth, 5–13 m. The strait is an important navigation route. For two months of the year it is covered by ice floes. A railway ferry and other boat services maintain communications between its two shores.

Kerensky, Aleksandr [Kerenskij], b 4 May 1881 in Simbirsk (now Ulianovsk), Russia, d 11 June 1970 in New York. Russian statesman during the 1917 Revolution. He became the minister of justice in the Russian *Provisional Government in March 1917 and the minister of war in May 1917. On 12 July he became prime minister. He fled from Russia during the Bolshevik takeover in November and lived in London and Paris. In 1940 he moved to the United States.

Kerensky had criticized the tsarist regime's nationalities policy and its persecution of the Ukrainian language. However, as prime minister his primary concern was to keep the Russian Empire intact. As the Ukrainian government, the *Central Rada, grew stronger and more inclined toward independence for Ukraine, Kerensky became more opposed to it. As war minister he had banned the Second *All-Ukrainian Military Congress that met in June 1917; as prime minister he was forced to recognize the legitimacy of its decisions and to withdraw his ban. After the declaration of the First *Universal, he had no choice but to negotiate with the Rada's *General Secretariat in July 1917 and to recognize the Rada and the autonomy of Ukraine. The last months of his government were marked by a steady deterioration in Ukrainian-Russian relations and the political situation in Russia in general.

Kerkinitidis. An Ionic polis founded at the turn of the 5th century BC on the western coast of the Crimea on the site of present-day Yevpatoriia. It flourished in the

4th and 3rd centuries BC, when it came under the control of *Chersonese Taurica. It was destroyed by the Huns in the 4th century AD. Excavations carried out in 1917–18, 1929, and 1950 uncovered a part of the city wall, streets, and the remains of buildings.

Ivan Kernytsky

Kernytsky, Ivan [Kernyc'kyj], b 30 September 1909 in Hai, Lviv county, Galicia, d 9 April 1979 in Lviv. Ukrainian linguist. A research associate of the AN URSR Institute of Social Sciences specializing in Middle Ukrainian, he devoted his attention particularly to the morphology of 16th-century Ukrainian. He is the author of numerous articles in this field and a monograph, *Systema slovozminy v ukraïns'kii movi na materialakh pamiatok XVI v.* (The Inflectional System of Ukrainian Based on the Materials of 16th-Century Monuments, 1967). He also studied the Lemko dialect and published Lemko texts from the 16th and 17th centuries in *Akty sela Odrekhova* (Documents of the Village of Odrekhiv, 1970). He was coeditor of *Slovnyk staroukraïns'koï movy XIV–XV st.* (Dictionary of Old Ukrainian of the 14th–15th Centuries, 1977–8).

Kernytsky, Ivan [Kernyc'kyj] (pseuds: Iker, Gzyms, Papai), b 12 September 1913 in Sukhodil, Bibrka county, Galicia, d 15 February 1984 in New York. Writer and feuilletonist. He began as a staff writer for *Nash prapor* in Lviv (1933–9) and worked also as a correspondent and feuilletonist for other periodicals in Ukraine, in displaced persons camps, and, after 1949, in the United States, mainly for the daily *Svoboda*. He was also the coeditor of the humor magazine *Lys Mykyta*. Although he wrote several comedies, his main work consisted of humorous short stories and novelettes, including *Sviatoivans'ki vohni* (The Fires of St John's Eve, 1934), *Tsyhans'kymy dorohamy* (Along Gypsy Roads, 1947), *Heroi peredmistia* (The Suburban Hero, 1958), and *Budni i nedilia* (Weekdays and Sunday, 1973).

KGB (Komitet gosudarstvennoi bezopasnosti; in Ukrainian: KDB or Komitet derzhavnoi bezpeky [Committee for State Security]). Soviet political police in charge of intelligence at home and abroad as well as the security of the borders, atomic installations, and weapons programs. Legally, a government agency responsible to the USSR Council of Ministers, it is in reality the Party's instrument of control over political life in the Soviet Union. It was established as a separate agency on 13 March 1954 to break up the power of the Ministry of Internal Affairs (MVD), and its authority was restricted to matters of state security. Coming directly after L. Beria's thwarted attempt to use the security system under his control to establish himself as J. Stalin's successor, the reorganization of the security machine had the purpose of ensuring the Party's control over it and preventing it from ever again threatening the principle of collective leadership. KGB heads are *ex officio* members of the Council of Ministers. The KGB remains the Soviet security organization to the present time; thus, it has lasted longer than any previous political police force (*Cheka, *GPU, OGPU, *NKVD, *MGB).

The agency consists of three levels: the central organs under the USSR Council of Ministers, the republican organs under the republican council of ministers, and the local organs in oblasts, krais, cities, and raions. It is a complex organization, divided into four main directorates: the First has charge of all intelligence operations abroad, the Second controls the activities of the Soviet people and foreigners in the USSR, the next, numbered as the Fifth (est 1969), deals with ideological opponents and dissidents, and the unnumbered Border Guards Directorate watches over the borders. The main directorates are supported by seven independent directorates (sections) and six independent departments, which are subdivided into a host of smaller units. The number of people employed by the agency is estimated at over 100,000.

The first chairman of the KGB was I. Serov, who played an important role in N. Khrushchev's rise to power. In Ukraine the agency was headed by V. Nikitchenko. A new emphasis on legality reduced the power of the secret police to organize mass terror without depriving the police of arbitrary power over individuals. Many inmates, mostly non-political prisoners of corrective labor camps, were released, and conditions in the camps were improved. Strikes and revolts in the camps from 1953 to 1956 were ruthlessly crushed, but were followed also by some reforms. The KGB made a concerted effort to deny nationalist émigré groups any influence within the USSR and to paralyze them by destroying their leadership and demoralizing their members. The execution in May 1954 of V. *Okhrymovych, an underground organizer sent into Ukraine by the OUN, set the stage for a wave of trials of former OUN members and a broad propaganda campaign against the OUN and the Ukrainian Catholic church in Western Ukraine. In Munich the two leaders of the OUN L. *Rebet (1957) and S. *Bandera (1959) were assassinated by the KGB agent B. Stashynsky. In 1960 V. Kuk, R. *Shukhevych's successor in command of the UPA, appealed to Ukrainians abroad to give up their struggle against the Soviet regime and to return to Ukraine, and M. Matviieiko, the former head of the security section of the OUN (Bandera faction), turned out to be an *agent provocateur*. In spite of some liberalization, Soviet citizens could not discuss important political issues outside official forums. Any attempts to organize political groups without state approval were suppressed and the organizers were punished severely. In Ukraine the KGB uncovered several such groups: the 'United Party for the Liberation of Ukraine' in 1957, the 'Ukrainian National Committee,' and the 'Ukrainian Workers' and Peasants' League,' both in 1961.

Under the chairmanship of A. Shelepin (1958–61) and V. Semichastny (1961–7), the KGB became more sophisticated in its methods of repression. The new criminal code of 1958 introduced a new, vaguely defined crime against the state – 'anti-Soviet agitation and propaganda' – which became widely used by the KGB to give an appearance of legality to political oppressions. Although victims no longer disappeared without warning or trace, the trials were contrived and closely controlled by the police. Physical torture was much reduced, but various psychological pressures were exploited to the full. The detention of political opponents in mental hospitals to obviate the inconveniences of public trial became an increasingly favored method of repression. A gamut of less severe measures from police harassment and searches to loss of residency or job was instituted as means of greater intimidation. Furthermore, the 'heroic tradition' of the secret police and its current exploits were glorified in the mass media. The agency was given an air of omniscience and invincibility.

The Twenty-Second CPSU Congress (1961) led to bold demands for further de-Stalinization. In Ukraine the intelligentsia called for a complete exposure of past crimes and a reversal of the Russification policy. In the mid-1960s the KGB struck at the Ukrainian cultural movement, arresting over 20 young intellectuals in Ukraine. A year later, more than 70 Ukrainians were arrested and harshly punished for circulating *samvydav* literature. Far from intimidating the young intelligentsia, the trials produced the opposite effect.

The new chairman of the KGB, Yu. *Andropov (1967–82), responded to the rising tide of protest in the wake of the invasion of Czechoslovakia in 1968 with arrests, trials, and forcible psychiatric treatment. In July 1970 V. Nikitchenko was replaced by V. *Fedorchuk as chairman of the Ukrainian KGB and the agency intensified its activity in Ukraine. Its ranks increased greatly. To discredit the *dissident movement, a strong propaganda campaign was launched linking the dissidents with nationalist circles abroad. The trial of Ya. Dobosh, a Belgian citizen of Ukrainian origin, on a charge of anti-Soviet activities served as the pretext for another wave of arrests in Ukraine in early 1972. The most common charge was 'anti-Soviet agitation and propaganda.' The next major operation of the KGB was directed against the *Ukrainian Helsinki Group, established on 9 November 1976 in Kiev. Its members were harassed and then arrested, many of them on false criminal charges such as rape, theft, and drug trafficking. In spite of loud protests from abroad, they were given maximal sentences. With the arrest of dissidents and the virtually automatic resentencing of those who had completed their terms, the dissident movement in Ukraine was severely crippled. In the 1970s and 1980s the KGB also devoted some attention to religious groups. The KGB largely controlled the activities of the official Russian Orthodox church and persecuted the Evangelical Christian Baptists and Roman Catholics as well as the banned Greek Catholic church. In the 1960s the KGB launched a propaganda campaign against the Jewish faith.

Changes in the KGB leadership in the 1980s had little effect on the organization's established policies and practices. In May 1982 V. Fedorchuk was promoted to the top post in the union agency and his republican post was assumed by S. Mukha. In December 1982 V. Chebrikov replaced Fedorchuk. Alongside the Party and the armed forces, the KGB remains one of the principal power bases in Soviet society. In spite of M. Gorbachev's emphasis on legality and openness, the KGB has retained its arbitrary powers and continues to operate outside the law and beyond public scrutiny.

BIBLIOGRAPHY
Levytsky, B. *The Uses of Terror: The Soviet Secret Police 1917–1970* (New York 1972)
Corson, W.R.; Crowley, R.T. *The New KGB: Engine of Soviet Power* (New York 1985)

M. Stech

Khabarovsk: Third Ukrainian Far Eastern Congress, 7–12 April 1918; the head of the congress, Yu. Mova, is in the center wearing a hat.

Khabarovsk [Xabarovsk]. Capital (1982 pop 553,000) of Khabarovsk krai and principal city of the Soviet *Far East. It was founded in 1858 as a military outpost called Khabarovka. The present name was adopted in 1893. At the beginning of the 1880s it had more than 4,000 inhabitants. Since then its population has grown rapidly, reaching 15,000 in 1897, 49,700 in 1926, 207,300 in 1939, 322,700 in 1959, and 436,000 in 1970. Situated on the Amur River near its confluence with the Ussuri River, the city is an important transport junction and industrial center (machine building, metalworking, petroleum refining, woodworking, food processing, and light industries). It is located in an ethnically mixed region, called Zelenyi Klyn by its Ukrainian inhabitants. According to the 1926 census, 3,800 or 7.3 percent of the city's inhabitants were Ukrainian; in 1970 about 30,000 or 6.8 percent were Ukrainian. Together with Vladivostok, Khabarovsk was the most important center of Ukrainian settlement in Zelenyi Klyn. Ukrainian organizations flourished there during the Revolution of 1917–22. The second and third *Far Eastern Ukrainian congresses were held in Khabarovsk, and a number of Ukrainian newspapers – *Khvyli Ukraïny*, *Ranok*, and *Nova Ukraïna* – were published there. After Soviet occupation in 1922, Ukrainian political activities ceased, but cultural activities, under Soviet control of course, continued. Since the mid-1930s intensive, officially promoted Russification has taken its toll among the large and growing Ukrainian population.

V. Kubijovyč

Khabarovsk krai. An administrative region of the RSFSR on the Pacific coast. Covering 824,600 sq km, it has (1986) a population of 1,760,000, 79.5 percent of which is urban. According to the 1979 census, 86.6 percent of the population is Russian and 5.8 percent is Ukrainian. Judging by the 1926 census, according to which Ukrainians accounted for 23 percent of the population, the number of people of Ukrainian descent is much higher. The number of political prisoners, many of them Ukrainians, who are held in the labor camps scattered throughout the region is unknown. They are forced to work in logging.

Khadzhybei Estuary (Khadzhybeisky lyman). VIII-11. An estuary on the northwest coast of the Black Sea near Odessa. Separated from the sea by a 4.5-km-wide sandbank, the estuary is 31 km long, 0.5–2.5 km wide, and up to 2.5 m deep. It covers an area of 70 sq km. The purported curative properties of its black silt led to the establishment of the Khadzhybei health resort on its shore. The Malyi Kuialnyk River empties into the estuary.

Khalansky, Ivan [Xalans'kyj], b 1749 in Khalan, Slobidska Ukraine, d ca 1825 in Novhorod-Siverskyi, Chernihiv gubernia. Cultural figure and organizer of education, a member of the *Novhorod-Siverskyi patriotic circle. After serving in the imperial bureaucracy in St Petersburg (from 1774), in 1778 he entered military service, becoming quartermaster (1780) and then captain (1782) of a Ukrainian Hussar regiment. He became the procurator first of the Novhorod-Siverskyi Upper Court in 1784 and then of the Upper Lord Court (1790–5). From 1789 Khalansky devoted himself to the cause of public education in Novhorod-Siverskyi, Starodub, Hlukhiv, and Chernihiv, introducing many reforms in educational practices. In 1805 he founded and became the first director of *Novhorod-Siverskyi Gymnasium.

Khalansky, Mykhailo [Xalans'kyj, Myxajlo], b 13 November 1857 in Raskhovets, Shchigry county, Kursk gubernia, Russia, d 12 April 1910 in Kharkiv. Literary historian and ethnographer; corresponding member of the Russian Academy of Sciences. He studied at the universities of Kharkiv and St Petersburg. In 1891 he was appointed professor of the Chair of Russian Language and Literature at Kharkiv University. His research was greatly influenced by O. *Potebnia and dealt with the *bylyny*, South and East Slavic epic poetry and legends, dumas, and literary monuments of the Rus' period. His many publications include *Velikorusskie byliny Kievskogo tsikla* (Russian *Bylyny* of the Kievan Cycle, 1885), 'Iuzhno-slavianskie skazaniia o Kraleviche Marke v sviazi s proizvedeniiami russkogo bylevogo eposa' (South Slavic Legends about Prince Mark in Relation to the Works of the Russian *Bylyna* Epic, *Russkii filologicheskii vestnik*, 1892–6), and *Ekskursiia v oblast' drevnikh rukopisei i staropechatnykh izdanii* (An Excursion into the Realm of Early Manuscripts and Old Printed Works, 1900–2).

Khalupnyk. Category of peasant in territories ruled by Poland and the Grand Duchy of Lithuania and later by the Austrian and Russian empires. Peasants lost their land as a result of the **Voloka* land reform of 1557 to the Polish nobility and magnates and were left only with their own houses (*khalupy*, hence the name) and small land allotments. Deprived of their livelihood, *khalupnyky* were forced to become hired laborers on the **filvarok*, or artisans, or to seek work in the cities. In addition, they performed compulsory labor for the lord (25 days a year of 'pedestrian corvée,' ie, without the use of draft animals) and other services. In the Russian Empire of the late 18th and early 19th centuries, the growth of serfdom increased the number of *khalupnyky*. They numbered 7.5 percent of peasant households in Right-Bank Ukraine in 1848 and 24 per cent in Left-Bank Ukraine in 1859. After the abolition of serfdom in 1861 they did not receive land but remained farm laborers or were forced to migrate to the city in search of work.

Khamula, Mykhailo [Xamula, Myxajlo], b 28 September 1885 in Bortkiv, Zolochiv county, Galicia, d 25 November 1969 in New York. Businessman. He was the owner of a large-scale kilim and woven-products factory in Hlyniany. His products were designed by Ukrainian artists such as S. Borachok, M. Butovych, V. Diadyniuk, and P. Kholodny and won many awards at exhibitions. He was commercially represented in many cities of Western Europe and the United States. In 1939 Khamula's factory was nationalized by the Soviet authorities. He emigrated during the Second World War and in 1950 settled in the United States. His memoirs, *Hlyniany, misto moïkh kylymiv* (Hlyniany, Town of My Kilims), were published in 1969.

Khandrykov, Mytrofan [Xandrykov], b 1 January 1837 in Moscow, d 7 August 1915. Astronomer and geodesist; corresponding member of the Russian Imperial Academy of Sciences from 1896. A graduate of Moscow University (1858), from 1870 he was a professor at Kiev University and the director of the Kiev Astronomical Observatory (to 1901). His main contributions were in theoretical and descriptive astronomy, particularly the computation of the orbits of planets and comets and prediction of eclipses. He is the author of numerous works, including the three-volume *Sistema astronomii* (The System of Astronomy, 1875–7).

Khanenko [Xanenko]. Cossack officer family established by Stepan Khanenko, who at the beginning of the 17th century joined the Zaporozhian Sich. Prominent political leaders of the Hetman state and important cultural figures of the 19th–20th centuries came from this family. In the late 1650s Mykhailo *Khanenko, Stepan's son, attained the office of colonel of Uman regiment, and later became hetman of Right-Bank Ukraine (1669–74) and P. *Doroshenko's opponent. One of Stepan's grandsons, Fedir (d 1744), became quartermaster of Kiev regiment, while another, Danylo, became acting colonel of Lubni regiment and took part in a joint Russian campaign against the Tatars; he perished at the siege of Kizi-Kermen in 1697. Danylo married the daughter of General Quartermaster I. *Lomykovsky. Mykola *Khanenko (1693–1760), Danylo's son, was a prominent political and diplomatic figure of the *Hetman state. Among his sons the most successful was Vasyl (ca 1730–?), who studied in Hlukhiv, St Petersburg, and Kiel, and served from 1752 to 1762 as cavalry captain of the Holstein Corps in St Petersburg and abroad, and as personal adjutant of Peter III. In 1762 he resigned his military commission and settled in Lotaky village in Starodub regiment on an estate granted to him by Hetman K. Rozumovsky. He was one of the largest landowners of the Hetman state. Vasyl's younger brother, Ivan (1743–ca 1797), after studying in St Petersburg, was appointed *fellow of the standard in 1767 and fought in the Russo-Turkish War of 1768–74. Later he served as Count P. Rumiantsev's personal adjutant. In 1783, having retired from military service, he was marshal of the nobility for Pohar county. His extensive landholdings consisted of villages in Pohar and Starodub counties. Towards the end of his life he resumed military office as lieutenant-colonel of the Hlukhiv Rifle Regiment. His wife, Sofiia Horlenko, was the great-granddaughter of Hetman D. Apostol. Ivan's older son, Oleksander (ca 1776–1830), served under the patronage of the chancellor, Prince O. *Bezborodko, as a court councilor at the Collegium of Foreign Affairs from 1799. In 1800 he was appointed secretary to the Russian legation in London. Eventually, he retired to his estate in Surazh county and was elected marshal of the county nobility. He also belonged to a Ukrainian autonomist circle (see *Autonomy). Ivan's grandson, Mykhailo (1818–52), served in the 1840s as marshal of the nobility of Novhorod-Siverskyi county, and was interested in Ukrainian history. He wrote articles on the economy of the northern Chernihiv region. Mykhailo's brother Oleksander *Khanenko (ca 1816–95) wrote a number of historical studies. A third brother, Ivan (1817–91), published materials on Surazh county. The son of Ivan Ivanovych, Bohdan (1848–1917), was a noted art collector, archeologist, and art patron.

BIBLIOGRAPHY
Bodianskii, O. 'Istoricheskoe svedenie o general'nom khorunzhem Nikolae Daniloviche Khanenke,' *Chteniia v Imperatorskom obshchestve istorii i drevnostei rossiiskikh*, 1 (1858)
Lazarevskii, O. 'Predislovie k Dnevniku Nikolaia Khanenko,' *KS*, no. 3 (1884)
Titov, A. 'Dnevnik Nikolaia Khanenko,' *KS*, nos 7–8 (1896)
Modzalevskii, V. *Malorossiiskii rodoslovnik*, vols 1–4 (1908–14)
Ohloblyn, O. *Khanenky. Storinka z istorii ukraïns'koho avtonomizmu 18 st.* (Kiel 1949)
– *'Khanenky,' Liudy staroï Ukraïny* (Munich 1959)

A. Zhukovsky

Khanenko, Bohdan [Xanenko], b 23 January 1848 on the Khanenko family estate in Chernihiv region, d 8 June 1917 in Kiev. Collector of Ukrainian antiques and art, archeologist, and arts patron, honorary member of the St Petersburg Academy of Arts. A great-grandson of Mykola Khanenko and son of I. Khanenko, he was president of the All-Russian Union of Industrialists and a permanent member of the State Council. Most of his archeological and art collection was donated to the Museum of Arts in Kiev, which later formed the foundation of the VUAN Museum of Art (now the Kiev Museum of Western and Eastern Art). Khanenko financed his own archeological digs, mostly in the Kiev region, and with the assistance of his wife, Varvara, published a six-volume catalogue of the discovered treasures titled *Drevnosti Pridneprov'ia Chernogo moria i poberezhiia* (Antiquities of the Dnieper Region and the Coast of the Black Sea, 1899–1907). He was a member of the Archeological Commission, the Historical Society of Nestor the Chronicler, and other scientific societies.

Khanenko, Mykhailo [Xanenko, Myxajlo], ca 1620–80. Hetman of Right-Bank Ukraine from 1669/70 to 1674. As colonel of the Uman regiment in 1656–60 and 1664–9, he supported the pro-Polish orientation of hetmans Yu. Khmelnytsky and P. Teteria. In 1668 he sided with the Zaporozhian Cossack faction that, with Crimean Tatar support, opposed the authority of Hetman P. *Doroshenko in Right-Bank Ukraine and tried to replace him with P. *Sukhovii. In July 1669, after Sukhovii was decisively defeated by Doroshenko, Khanenko was proclaimed hetman at a council of three Right-Bank regiments in Uman. Continuing the struggle against Doroshenko, he was defeated in battle at Stebliv on 29 October 1669. On 2 September 1670 Khanenko's envoys concluded a treaty with the Poles at Ostrih in which Khanenko received Polish recognition and military aid, after agreeing to swear fealty to the Polish king, to limit his rule only to a small part of the Right Bank, and to extend autonomy only to the Cossack stratum. Khanenko lost several more battles in his war with Doroshenko. In 1674, after the forces of the Moscow-supported hetman of Left-Bank Ukraine, I. *Samoilovych, crossed the Dnieper River to fight Doroshenko and were joined by most of the Right-Bank regiments, Khanenko relinquished his power to Samoilovych in exchange for estates in Left-Bank Ukraine. Later he was accused of conducting secret talks with the Poles in 1677–8, and the tsar ordered Samoilovych to imprison Khanenko in Baturyn. Khanenko succeeded in establishing his innocence, but he died shortly after.

Mykhailo Khanenko

A. Zhukovsky

Khanenko, Mykola [Xanenko], b 6 December 1693, d 27 January 1760 in Hlukhiv. Noted political figure and statesman of the *Hetman state; general flag-bearer, diplomat, memoirist. The son of Col D. Khanenko, he was educated at the Kievan Mohyla Academy and then at the Lviv Dormition Brotherhood School. In 1710 he entered military service. In 1717 he was appointed military secretary, and in 1721 assistant *general chancellor.

He enjoyed the confidence of hetmans I. Skoropadsky and P. *Polubotok. In May 1723 Polubotok sent him to St Petersburg as a member of a delegation requesting permission to elect a new hetman. In response, both Khanenko and Polubotok were imprisoned in the Peter and Paul Fortress.

On Khanenko's return to Ukraine in 1726, he was appointed judge (1727–38) and then quartermaster of the Starodub regiment. During the Russo-Turkish War (1735–9), he saw action in the Crimea and was rewarded for his service with the office of *general standard-bearer in 1738. Two years later he became a member of the *General Court, and then in 1741 he received the office of *general flag-bearer, which he held until shortly before his death.

Khanenko was a member of the Commission for Translating and Codifying Little-Russian Law Books, which produced the *Code of Laws of 1743. Under Hetman K.

*Rozumovsky, Khanenko was one of the leading officials of the *General Military Chancellery. His correspondence with his son, Vasyl, which was published in part in *Chernigovskie gubernskie vedomosti* (1852) and in his *Dnevniki* (Diaries; from 1719 to 1754), is a valuable source for Ukraine's history. *Dnevnik* for 1727–52 was published in *Kievskaia starina*, vols 8–16 (1884–6); *Dnevnik* for 1719–21 and *Partikuliarnii zhurnal* (Journal of Particulars) for 1754 were also published in *Kievskaia starina* (1896); *Dnevnik* for 1732–3 appeared in *Chernigovskie eparkhial'nye izvestie* (1865); and *Diariush, ili zhurnal* (Diary or Journal) for 1722 was published by O. Bodiansky in *Chteniia v Imperatorskom obshchestve istorii i drevnostei rossiiskikh*, bk 1 (1858). Khanenko left a rich archive of valuable historical materials: Ukrainian–Russian treaties (known as *Hetman Articles), constitutions of Polish Sejms, 17th–18th-century tsarist ukases, official and family records, the Constitution of *Bendery, and a manuscript, 'Kratkoe opisanie Malorossiiskogo kraia' (A Brief Description of the Little-Russian Land).

A. Zhukovsky

Khanenko, Oleksander [Xanenko], 1805/16–1895. Civic figure, historian, and collector of Ukrainian antiquities. In the 1840s he served as marshal of the nobility of Surazh county in Chernihiv gubernia. In 1858 he was appointed to the Chernihiv Gubernia Committee for the Improvement of the Peasants' Condition, and later he was active in implementing the reforms of 1861. In 1860 he became a member of the Land Survey Chamber in Chernihiv. He is the author of the valuable *Istoricheskii ocherk mezhevykh uchrezhdenii v Malorossii* (A Historical Outline of Land-Surveying Institutions in Little Russia, 1870) and of historical articles in *Chernigovskie gubernskie vedomosti* and elsewhere. His articles on the town of Pohar (1871), St T. Uhlytsky, the history of several localities in Chernihiv Gubernia (1887), and the documents of the Khanenko family (1887) also appeared as separate brochures. Khanenko amassed a large collection of 17th- and 18th-century books printed in Kiev and Chernihiv.

Kharchenko, Vasyl [Xarčenko, Vasyl'], b 14 January 1910 in Kamianka, Chyhyryn county, Kiev gubernia, d 26 October 1971 in Kiev. Stage director and pedagogue. Graduating from the Lysenko Music and Drama Institute in Kiev (1933), he worked as an actor and stage director at the Zankovetska Ukrainian Drama Theater in Zaporizhia, which in 1944 became the Lviv Ukrainian Drama Theater. After the war he was artistic director of the Lviv Young Spectator's Theater (1947–52), and chief stage director of the Lviv Theater of Opera and Ballet (1952–6), the Kiev Ukrainian Drama Theater, and the Kiev Operetta Theater (1957–60). From 1956 Kharchenko taught at the Kiev Institute of Theater Arts. He directed plays such as W. Shakespeare's *Othello*, I. Kocherha's *Svichchyne vesillia* (Svichka's Wedding), and L. Smiliansky's *Muzhyts'kyi posol* (The Peasant Deputy); and such operas as K. Dankevych's *Bohdan Khmelnytsky*, G. Verdi's *Othello*, and M. Arkas's *Kateryna*.

Kharchuk, Borys [Xarčuk], b 13 September 1931 in Lozy, Kremianets county, Volhynia. Writer. Since 1957 he has published 13 collections of stories and novelle and the novels *Volyn'* (Volhynia, 4 vols, 1959–65), *Maidan* (The Square, 1970), *Khlib nasushchnyi* (Daily Bread, 1976), *Dovha hora* (The Long Hill, 1979), and *Krevniaky* (Relatives, 1985). Many of his works are set in rural Volhynia before, during, and after the Second World War.

Kharkevych, Edvard [Xarkevyč], b 23 February 1855 in Stanyslaviv, Galicia, d 24 September 1913 in Lviv. Educator, Germanist, and classical philologist. Kharkevych was a director (1895–1909) of the *Academic Gymnasium of Lviv and established a second branch of that institution. He headed (1896–1902) the Ukrainian Pedagogical Society, the forerunner of the *Ridna Shkola society, and in 1898 founded the first private Ukrainian secondary school for girls in Lviv. He also created and headed a financial aid society, Ruslan, to help needy students further their education.

Kharkiv, Oleksander [Xarkiv], b 1 March 1897 in Kremenchuk, Poltava gubernia, d 14 September 1939 in Stryi, Galicia. Monumentalist painter and graphic artist. After serving in the UNR Army in 1918–20, he settled in Western Ukraine. Upon graduating from the Cracow Academy of Arts in 1925, Kharkiv did restoration work on the polychrome murals of Wawel Castle and the frescoes of the Jagiełło Library in Cracow. He taught art at secondary schools in Yavoriv, where he helped found the Yavorivshchyna Museum. From 1934 he taught art in Stryi and collaborated with the Verkhovyna Museum. As an artist he painted churches and iconstases in the Byzantine style, landscapes, and portraits (Countess Dębicka, Ukrainian hetmans), and designed bookplates. Some of his work was exhibited at the World's Fair in Chicago in 1933. Kharkiv was shot by the Polish underground.

Kharkiv. A literary almanac of the Kharkiv oblast branch of the Writers' Union of Ukraine. Eight issues were published between 1952 and 1955 in Kharkiv. Besides literary works, it contained literary criticism, publicistic articles, a chronicle of literary and artistic events, and a section for young writers. Its contributors included such writers as P. Panch, I. Muratov, I. Vyrhan, Yu. Shovkoplias, and V. Kochevsky. In January 1956 the almanac was replaced by the journal **Prapor*.

Kharkiv [Xarkiv]. III-17. Ukraine's second-largest city (1985 pop 1,554,000) and the capital of Kharkiv oblast, situated at the confluence of the Lopan, Udy, and Kharkiv rivers; the historic capital of *Slobidska Ukraine, it is an important industrial, communications, scientific, and cultural center. From 1920 to 1934 it was the capital of Soviet Ukraine. Kharkiv's proximity to the Donets Basin and its location at the intersection of the trade routes between Russia and the Black Sea and central Ukraine and Caucasia have facilitated its economic growth. The city is over 300 sq km in area and is divided into nine raions: Chervonozavodskyi, Dzerzhynskyi, Frunzenskyi, Kominternivskyi, Kyivskyi, Leninskyi, Moskovskyi, Ordzhonikidzevskyi, and Zhovtnevyi.

Origins. Kharkiv's name is most likely derived from the Kharkiv River. The Russian historian N. Aristov believed it was derived from the Cuman settlement of Sharukan, which existed on the territory of the present-day city. According to popular legend, the city is named after a Cossack, Kharko.

History. Kharkiv's vicinity has been settled since the 2nd millennium BC. Bronze Age settlements, Scythian kurhans (6th–3rd centuries BC), and Sarmatian relics (2nd–1st centuries BC) have been excavated there. Relics of the *Cherniakhiv culture (2nd–5th centuries AD) have been unearthed in the city, and the Donets fortified Slavic settlement of the early Middle Ages has been excavated nearby.

From the 12th to the 17th century the large territory around present-day Kharkiv was wild steppe dominated by the Cumans and then by the Tatars. From the early 17th century the territory belonged formally to Muscovy, which stationed frontier garrisons there and sent out scouts and explorers to reconnoiter and map the region. Later, networks of fortifications against the Crimean and Nogay Tatars – the Bilhorod, Izium, and *Ukrainian lines – were built, and non-serf villages (*slobody*, hence the name 'Slobidska Ukraine') and more numerous settlements of refugees from the war-torn Hetman state and Right-Bank and Western Ukraine sprang up. By the mid-17th century several such settlements existed in Kharkiv's vicinity.

The generally accepted date of Kharkiv's founding is 1654/5, when Ukrainian Cossacks led by I. Karkach built a fortified settlement on the plateau surrounded by the Kharkiv and Lopan rivers. A fortress was completed in 1659. Although they were formally under the jurisdiction of a Muscovite military governor, as military frontiersmen the Cossacks were allowed to be self-governing, according to 'Cherkessian custom,' with the right of free settlement, enterprise, and trade, until the reign of Peter I. In 1655 the population of Kharkiv was about 2,000, including about 600 Cossacks.

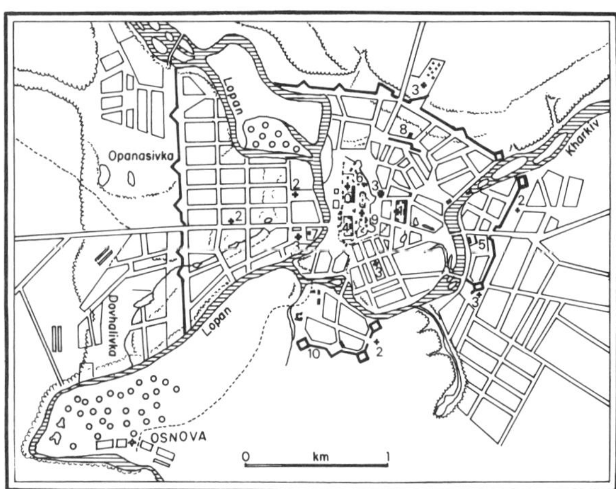

KHARKIV IN 1787

0. College and monastery
1. School
2. Wooden churches
3. Parish churches (stone)
4. Residence of governor-general
5. Post office
6. Bank
7. State pharmacy
8. Food warehouse
9. Gubernia administration building
10. Walls of fortress

For the remainder of the 17th and most of the 18th century Kharkiv remained a defensive outpost; the Russian garrison and artisans and merchants lived within the fortress, but most of the Cossack population lived outside in nearby expanding *slobody* and engaged in farming, fishing, beekeeping, and barter trade. From 1659 to 1765 Kharkiv was the capital of *Kharkiv regiment, one of the largest Cossack administrative and military units in Slobidska Ukraine. In 1660–2 a new citadel, with administrative buildings (a governor's house) and churches, was built.

18th century to 1917. By the 18th century, the outside fortress had expanded beyond the Lopan and Kharkiv rivers. Alarmed by Hetman I. Mazepa's uprising and the rebellious Don Cossacks during the Russian-Swedish War, Peter I had Kharkiv's fortifications enlarged in 1708 and imposed restrictions and taxes on the Cossack population.

In 1724 the town had 61 streets and 1,300 courtyards. In 1732 its male population was 3,700, 2,500 of whom were Cossacks. The town changed gradually from a military outpost into a trading center as the borders of the Russian state shifted southward. Tatars still attacked the fortress (12 times between 1672 and 1738), however, and devastated the *slobody*. Russia's wars with Turkey, Sweden, and Poland drained the town of its Cossack population and burdened it economically. Much of the town was destroyed by a fire in 1733, and its population was decimated by plague in 1738 and 1741. Kharkiv nonetheless revived and grew because of its economically advantageous location, which facilitated its advancement as a cultural center. During the 18th century Kharkiv's annual fairs (four in the 18th and five in the 19th century) attracted increasingly more merchants not only from Kiev but also from the Baltic, central Russia, the Crimea, Poland, Silesia, Moldavia, and Germany. *Kharkiv College was founded in 1734; until the founding of Kharkiv University in 1805, it was the best educational institution in Slobidska Ukraine. In 1789 two public schools were opened. In 1765 the Russian government abolished the Cossack regimental system in Slobidska Ukraine.

As the capital of the new Slobidska Ukraine gubernia (1765–80) and then Kharkiv vicegerency (1780–96), again of Slobidska Ukraine gubernia (1796–1835), and *Kharkiv gubernia (1835–1925), Kharkiv prospered. From 1835 to 1882 it was also the seat of the governor-general of three gubernias: Kharkiv, Poltava, and Chernihiv. The social differentiation that had begun in Kharkiv and the frontier society of Slobidska Ukraine in the 17th century accelerated greatly in the late 18th: the Cossack *starshyna* was incorporated into the Russian nobility, the rank-and-file Cossacks were reduced in status to military settlers equal to state peasants, and hitherto free peasants became serfs. The merchants and petty artisans organized themselves into Russian-type guilds and emerged as distinct classes.

Under the governors and vicegerents (to whom the city administration was subject from 1787) Kharkiv was developed according to imperial standards of urban architecture, which were set in St Petersburg. New government, commercial, and private stone buildings were erected, some of them – the cathedral of the Holy Protectress Monastery (1689), the governor's house (1766–77), the stone office building (begun in 1785), and the Dormition Cathedral (1783) – within the fortified town. From 1776 to 1810 P. Yaroslavsky designed many of the city's buildings.

Kharkiv: Tevelev Square

In 1799 *Kharkiv eparchy was constituted. From the reign of Paul I (1796–1801) to the 1890s, Kharkiv was also the center of a military district, with a high concentration of military personnel and their families. After the legal reforms of 1867, Kharkiv became the seat of a high court whose jurisdiction exceeded the gubernia's boundaries.

With the founding of *Kharkiv University and the university press in 1805 (through the efforts of V. *Karazyn and Kharkiv's Ukrainian nobility), the city also became an important educational and publishing center in Ukraine and the Russian Empire as a whole. In the 19th century four boys' gymnasiums, six secondary schools, a Realschule, a post-secondary veterinary institute (1873, replacing a veterinary school founded in 1839), a post-secondary technological institute (1885), and secondary commercial, technical, skilled-trade, agricultural, railway, music, art, and zemstvo midwifery schools were opened in the city. By the turn of the 20th century there were 60 societies there, including a philotechnical (1811), scientific (1813), Bible (1816), folklore (1817), philanthropic (1843), medical (1861), Red Cross (1876), Orthodox missionary (1876), and orphanage society (1874). The *Kharkiv Literacy Society (1869) was one of the most successful of its kind in Ukraine. The city also had an art school (1861), stock exchange (1867), opera house (1874), music school (1883), museum (1886), and public library (1886). A nobles' assembly (1815–20), military academy (1825–8), theater (1840–3), technological institute (1879–85), duma building (1885), and many new commercial and private buildings were constructed. From the 1890s O. Beketov designed numerous buildings in the modern style. In 1913 the art school building was built in the Ukrainian style by K. Zhukov.

Municipal services, however, were inadequate, and Kharkiv was known as a 'dirty city.' Until the 1830s its streets were unpaved and impassable in wet weather. The water from the rivers running through the city was undrinkable; an aqueduct was built only in 1881 and enlarged in 1912–13, when a water tower supplying the main streets was erected. Residents of side streets and suburbs had to rely on wells. Construction of a sewage system was begun only in 1912. Gas lighting was introduced in the 1880s, and electric lighting in 1898 (on the city's outskirts). From 1882 a horse-drawn trolley line, which from 1886 was owned by a Belgian stock company, operated on the central streets. The first tramway was laid in 1906. Medical care was also inadequate. In 1878 there were only four hospitals in the city; in 1901 there were only eight hospitals and 390 doctors.

The city's population grew almost twentyfold in the 19th century: from 11,000 in 1787 to 23,000 in 1837, 35,600 in 1856, 50,300 in 1861, 128,500 in 1881, 174,000 in 1897, 198,300 in 1901, and 244,700 in 1914. Most of the increase after 1861 was due not to natural growth but to municipal annexation and particularly the influx of Russian workers, merchants, tradesmen, and civil servants. According to the 1897 census, over two-thirds of Kharkiv's residents were born in Ukraine. Because of the impact of Russification, however, only 25 percent of the residents stated that Ukrainian was their native language.

In 1855 Kharkiv had 212 small primitive manufacturing enterprises with a total of 4,256 workers (2,460 of them serfs) producing carriages, bricks, beer, tanned leather, wool, tobacco, soap, wax, rendered fat, wadding, copper and iron goods, lead shot, consumer items, and vegetable oil. Kharkiv's industries and commerce expanded rapidly after the emancipation of the peasants and particularly after the railway reached the city in 1868. Between 1871 and 1900 the number of factories and plants increased from 79 to 259 (the number of machine-building and metalworking plants from 12 to 59). In 1900 there were over 12,000 workers and 22,700 artisans in the city. By 1904 there were 106 officially registered factories and 1,112 lesser enterprises employing a total of 17,000 workers in the city. In 1917 there were over 150 factories and over 35,000 workers. Because of primitive working and living conditions, economic exploitation, and political oppression, workers' unrest was a common occurrence in Kharkiv from the 1870s.

From the 1810s Kharkiv was an important center of the Ukrainian cultural renaissance. Many of the first Ukrainian linguistic, ethnographic, historical, and modern literary works were published there. Published also were the first periodicals in Russian-ruled Ukraine: the weekly newspaper *Khar'kovskii ezhenedel'nik* (1812), the satirical journal *Khar'kovskii demokrit* (1816), the cultural-political monthly *Ukrainskii vestnik* (1816–19), the weekly *Khar'kovskie izvestiia* (1817–23), the agricultural journal *Ukrainskii domovod* (1817), and the scholarly-literary journal *Ukrainskii zhurnal* (1824–5 at Kharkiv University). Key Ukrainian cultural figures lived and worked in Kharkiv: H. Kvitka-Osnovianenko, P. Hulak-Artemovsky, L. Borovykovsky, I. Sreznevsky, M. Petrenko, O. Korsun, A. Metlynsky, Ya. Shchoholiv, and M. Kostomarov; many of them belonged to the *Kharkiv Romantic School. Several of the earliest Ukrainian miscellanies were also published in Kharkiv: *Ukrainskii al'manakh* (1831), *Utrenniaia* zvezda (1833), *Ukrainskii sbornik* (1838, 1841), *Snip* (1841), and *Molodyk* (1843–4). Russian newspapers in Kharkiv – *Khar'kovskie gubernskie vedomosti* (1838–1915), *Khar'kovskie eparkhial'nye vedomosti* (1867–83), *Khar'kov* (1877–80), *Iuzhnyi krai* (1880–1917), and *Khar'kovskii listok* (1898–?) – also covered developments in Ukrainian cultural life. (By the turn of the 20th century, 3 dailies and 16 other periodicals were being published in Kharkiv.)

The first professional theater troupe in Ukraine was established in Kharkiv in 1789, but it was not until 1842 that L. Mlotkovsky opened a theater building there. H. Kvitka-Osnovianenko directed the Kharkiv theater in 1812–18 and staged his plays there. M. Shchepkin, I. Dreisig, and K. Solenyk and the Stein troupe (1823–36) appeared on the Kharkiv stage. The earliest Ukrainian plays were

Kharkiv: Gagarin Avenue

performed there, including the original production of I. Kotliarevsky's *Natalka Poltavka* (Natalka from Poltava) in 1821. In the 1880s and 1890s the Ukrainian troupes of M. Kropyvnytsky, M. Sadovsky, P. Saksahansky, and M. Zankovetska performed in Kharkiv, and in 1901 H. Khotkevych organized the first Ukrainian workers' theater there. Ukrainian cinema originated in Kharkiv in the late 1890s, with the short documentaries of A. *Fedetsky. Many artists lived in Kharkiv, including D. Bezperchy, S. Vasylkivsky, M. Tkachenko, M. Raievska-Ivanova, P. Levchenko, M. Berkos, I. Skolov, and M. Samokysha. In 1906 an art society was founded there.

Various revolutionary groups had adherents in Kharkiv. In 1856–8 the *Kharkiv-Kiev Secret Society was active there, as were anarchist-populist cells of Zemlia i Volia and Narodnaia Volia beginning in the 1860s. K. Alchevska, the wife of the Kharkiv industrialist O. Alchevsky, funded and ran the famous *Kharkiv Women's Sunday School from 1862 to 1919, until 1870 secretly. The liberal members of the region's *zemstvos conducted legal, educational, medical, agronomical, co-operative, and social work among the masses from 1864; in 1878 a secret zemstvo conference took place in Kharkiv. From the 1890s various Marxist socialist groups and cells of the Russian Social Democratic Workers' party were active in the city. At the turn of the 20th century and during the Revolution of 1905 the Mensheviks organized and led workers' strikes and demonstrations; they were the most popular of the revolutionary groups.

Kharkiv's Ukrainian intelligentsia (eg, P. Lobko, O. Potebnia, V. Mova, and F. Pavlovsky) was involved in the secret Kharkiv Hromada from the early 1860s. From 1906 to 1916 the Kvitka-Osnovianenko Ukrainian Club (later the Prosvita society) was active in the city, and a co-operative publishing house published books in Ukrainian. Members of gentry families of Cossack *starshyna* descent – the Donets-Zakharzhevskys, Shydlovskys, and Alchevskys, to name a few – contributed much to the economic and architectural development of the city. M. Mikhnovsky, a lawyer in Kharkiv, was one of the founders of the *Brotherhood of Taras; his advocacy of a program for an independent Ukraine resulted in the founding of the *Revolutionary Ukrainian party at a Kharkiv student meeting in 1900. In 1906 the Ukrainian-language newspaper for peasants, *Porada* (ed M. Lobodovsky), came out in Kharkiv. Other prominent Ukrainian scholars and civic and literary figures lived in Kharkiv in the late 19th and early 20th century: D. Bahalii (later the university rector and head of the city council), M. Sumtsov, D. Yavornytsky, I. Bilokonsky, I. Manzhura, P. Hrabovsky, and B. Hrinchenko.

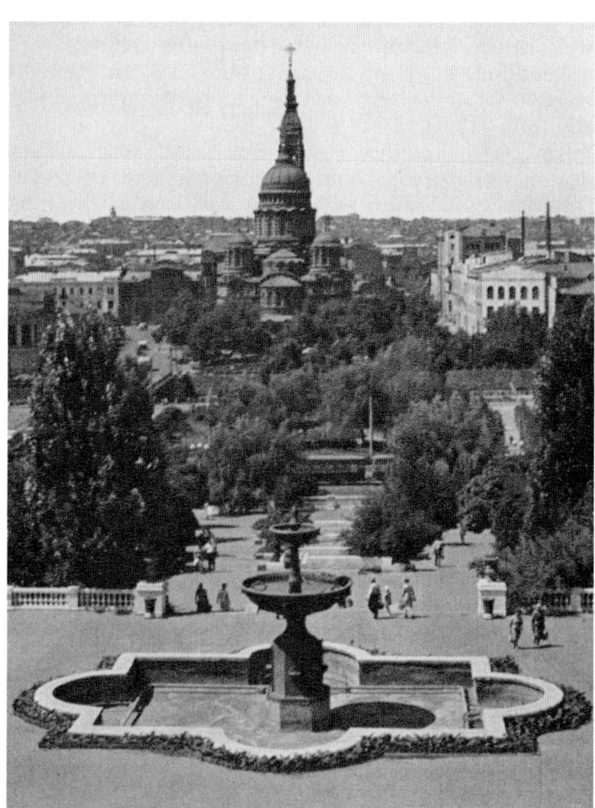

Kharkiv: Khalturin Descent, Cascade Square

1917–20. After the 1917 February Revolution Kharkiv was governed by the gubernial commissioner of the Russian Provisional Government, the city duma, and the zemstvos. Workers' soviets dominated by Russian Mensheviks and Socialist Revolutionaries attempted to seize power, particularly after the October Revolution. Many of the Ukrainian residents supported the *Central Rada in Kiev; to influence developments in the Russified city and to provide leadership for the Ukrainian population of the region, they held a congress and formed a Ukrainian Gubernial Council, headed by a man called Rubas, in late April 1917. A gubernial peasant congress was held in June, and a congress of Slobidska Ukraine's Prosvita societies was held in Kharkiv in August. A Ridna Shkola society was created to promote the Ukrainization of elementary schools. New Ukrainian newspapers – the weekly *Ridne slovo*, the Social Democratic triweekly *Robitnyk*, and the socialist daily *Nova hromada* – appeared in 1917–18.

The Central Rada's first two universals (decrees) did not explicitly extend its authority to the Kharkiv region, but the Third Universal (7 November 1917) – which proclaimed the existence of the UNR – did so without defining the republic's borders, and Ukrainized regiments were stationed in the city. But Kharkiv's proximity to Russia proper and to the Donbas, which were both under Bolshevik control, sealed the city's fate. In late November 1917 units of Russian Red Guards and Bolshevized sailors from the Baltic region reached the city. On 10 December, with the help of local Bolsheviks, they disarmed the UNR and the Russian anti-Bolshevik troops there. On 24–25 December an 'All-Ukrainian Congress of Soviets' convened in Kharkiv. It elected a Soviet government of Ukraine – the *People's Secretariat – which remained there until February 1918, when the city became the capital of the *Donets–Kryvyi Rih Soviet Republic. German units and the UNR Zaporozhian Division under P. Bolbochan's command took Kharkiv from the Bolsheviks on 19 April 1918. Col O. Shapoval was appointed the gubernial commander there. Many local Ukrainians joined the Zaporozhian Division, which was enlarged into a corps.

Under the *Hetman government a gubernial starosta, P. Zalesky, resided in Kharkiv until 2 July, when he was removed for his anti-Ukrainian actions. The Hrinchenko Gymnasium (directed by M. Plevako) was set up, and other schools were Ukrainized. The government shut down the opposition newspaper *Narodne dilo*. In November 1918 the city was taken by troops of the UNR *Directory. On 3 January 1919 it was recaptured by the Bolsheviks. A. Denikin's Volunteer Army occupied the city on 25 June and held it until 11 December.

1920–41. After Denikin's defeat by the Red Army, Kharkiv became the capital of Soviet Ukraine. The All-Ukrainian Central Executive Committee, the Council of People's Commissars, and the central offices of the CP(B)U, commissariats, trade unions, and republican organizations and periodicals were located in Kharkiv from 1920 to 1934. Central co-operative institutions were also based there until they were shut down in the early 1930s. In the early 1920s some diplomatic missions and consulates were also opened there. The Ukrainian Autocephalous Orthodox church flourished in Kharkiv from 1923 to 1926, when Archbishop O. Yareshchenko was arrested by the GPU. As part of the policy of *Ukrainization, post-secondary Soviet schools, including the *Kharkiv Institute of People's Education (1921–30), the Institute of the National Economy, and the Artem Communist University, were Ukrainized in the 1920s. Because of frequent reorganization, the number of post-secondary schools in Kharkiv grew: there were 10 in the early 1920s, 23 in 1931, and 36 in 1940 (with an enrollment of 31,000). In 1926 some faculties of the old Technological Institute were reorganized into separate machine-building, chemical-technology, and electrotechnical institutes; after the Second World War these were amalgamated again in the *Kharkiv Polytechnical Institute. The university, which was abolished in 1920, was reopened in 1932. The Ukrainian School of Red Officers was opened in Kharkiv in 1920; it was closed down in the early 1930s with the abandonment of Ukrainization.

From 1920 to 1934 many important scientific institutions were located in Kharkiv: the Scientific Committee of Ukraine, the Agricultural Scientific Committee of Ukraine, the Central Historical Archive, the Central Statistical Administration of Ukraine, the Central Archival Administration of the Ukrainian SSR, the All-Ukrainian Agronomic Society, the All-Ukrainian Association of Oriental Studies, and the All-Ukrainian Association of Marxist-Leninist Scientific Research Institutes. Important contributions to Ukrainian studies were made by the scholars of the Ukrainian Scientific Research Institute of Geography and Cartography, the Scientific Research Institute of the History of Ukrainian Culture, the Chair of the History of Ukraine, and the Shevchenko Institute of Literature; most of these scholars became victims of the Stalinist terror.

A number of museums were opened, including the All-Ukrainian Historical Museum, the Museum of Slobidska Ukraine, the Museum of Social Culture, and the Museum of Ukrainian Art. Large publishing houses such as the State Publishing House of Ukraine, Proletarii, and Radianskyi Selianyn, and the co-operative publishers Knyhospilka and Rukh (which were closed down eventually), were located there. The Ukrainian Book Chamber ran a wide range of operations. Important artists' and writers' associations such as Pluh, Hart, Vaplite, Nova Generatsiia, the All-Ukrainian Association of Proletarian Writers, and Prolitfront were active until 1932, when all associations were dissolved. A single Writers' Union of Ukraine was established in Kharkiv in 1934 at the First Ukrainian Writers' Congress. In 1930 the Second International Conference of Revolutionary Writers was held there. Several important cultural periodicals were published in Kharkiv: *Chervonyi shliakh, Hart, Pluh, Vaplite, Literaturnyi iarmarok, Vsesvit, Foto-kino*, and *Nove mystetstvo*. Important Ukrainian theaters existed there: the Kharkiv Children's Theater (1922–41), the Franko Theater (1923–6, transferred to Kiev), the Ukrainian People's Theater (1924–8), the Kharkiv Theater of Opera and Ballet (1925–), the Berezil Theater (1926–33, transferred from Kiev), the Veselyi Proletar Theater (1926–ca 1933), the Kharkiv Chervonozavodskyi Ukrainian Drama Theater (1927–33), the Kharkiv Theater of Musical Comedy (1929–), and the Kharkiv Theater of the Revolution (1931–7). Actors were trained at a music and drama institute (1923–34). In 1940 there were 14 theaters in Kharkiv, including several amateur ones.

As the capital of Soviet Ukraine, Kharkiv was developed more intensively than other cities. Its area grew substantially, from 141 sq km in 1924 to 272 sq km in

1939. The Derzhprom complex of high-rise office buildings (1925–9, designed by S. Serafimov, S. Kravets, and M. Felger) – the new administrative center – was built near Dzerzhinsky Square. The Electromechanical Plant's Palace of Culture (now the building of the Kharkiv Chervonozavodskyi Ukrainian Drama Theater), decorated with frescoes by M. *Boichuk, V. Sedliar, and I. Padalka that were later destroyed, was erected on Povstannia Square (1933–8). In 1930–4 the Design Building (now a university building) and Co-operative Building were built. New industrial plants were constructed and prerevolutionary ones were reconstructed and modernized. To house the rapidly growing population, apartment subdivisions (Novyi Pobut, Chervonyi Promin, Studentske Mistechko) were constructed. The tramway network was extended and bus and trolleybus lines were introduced. The reconstruction of industries destroyed during the 1917 Revolution and subsequent Ukrainian-Russian wars was followed by accelerated industrialization. In 1931 the huge *Kharkiv Tractor Plant went into production; in 1933, the Kharkiv Machine-Tool Plant; and in 1934, the Kharkiv Turbine Plant. Prerevolutionary plants such as the electromechanical (est 1887), cable (1890), motor (1882), and transport-machine-building (1885) increased their output. In 1930 the Kharkiv Regional Electric Station began supplying the city with electricity. By 1937 the output of Kharkiv's industries was 35 times greater than in 1913.

As new buildings went up, many structures of historical or cultural value were senselessly destroyed in the 1930s, including most of the baroque churches: St Nicholas's Cathedral of the Ukrainian Autocephalous Orthodox church, the Church of the Myrrhophores, St Demetrius's Church, and the Church of the Nativity (a fortified Cossack church).

Kharkiv: Cathedral of the Holy Protectress (1689)

During the 1920s the impact of Ukrainization on Kharkiv had been great. In the early 1930s this policy was abandoned, and after the Stalinist suppression of Ukrainian institutions and cultural figures, the man-made *famine of 1932–3, intensified Russification, and the transfer of the capital to Kiev in 1934, Kharkiv lost much of its Ukrainian character.

1941–3. During the Second World War Kharkiv suffered extensive damage. As the German armies advanced toward the city, the Soviet authorities dismantled and evacuated many of the factories and institutions and over 400,000 of the inhabitants to Soviet Asia. Thousands of prisoners in Kharkiv's NKVD prisons were executed during the retreat, and all of the city's railway tracks and yards, power stations, water-supply systems, and other utilities were dynamited. The Germans took Kharkiv on 25 October 1941. Since the city was within the front zone, it remained under direct German military control. The Ukrainians who remained in Kharkiv were allowed to establish a city council; it was chaired by O. Kramarenko (rector of the Kharkiv Polytechnical Institute) until he was executed by the Germans in 1942 and then by O. Semenenko until 1943. Other institutions, such as a city bank, an oblast administration (headed by M. Vetukhiv), consumer association (A. Yaremenko), Prosvita society (V. Dubrovsky), Ukrainian Civic Committee (V. Dolenko), newspaper (*Nova Ukraïna*, ed V. Tsarynnyk) and journal (*Literaturnyi zasiv*), and a revived Ukrainian Autocephalous Orthodox church (Metropolitan T. Buldovsky), were allowed to function. A Ukrainian nationalist underground (led by M. Kononenko) was active in the city until its key figures were suppressed.

During the 22-month German occupation, thousands of Kharkiv's inhabitants died of hunger, disease, and cold (14,000 in the first three months of 1942 alone). Thousands of nationalist activists and real and suspected Soviet partisans and their supporters were shot or hanged by the Gestapo. Many Jews were murdered. By the time the Germans abandoned Kharkiv they had killed 100,000 people and forcibly transported 60,000 to Germany as *ostarbeiter*. Soviet forces recaptured Kharkiv on 16 February 1943, held it until 15 March, and finally established permanent control there on 23 August. At that time the population of the city was between 160,000 and 192,000. The Soviet special police squads (SMERSH) proceeded to shoot or imprison real and suspected German collaborators and Ukrainian nationalist supporters.

Postwar Kharkiv. Reconstruction of the city began almost immediately and continued for some years after the war. Since the war, apartment subdivisions (eg, Saltivka, Pavlove Pole, Oleksiivka, Danylivka, Kholodna Hora, Selektsiina Stantsiia, and Chervona Bavariia) have been built up to house the burgeoning population. Municipal utilities have been improved: buildings were supplied with natural gas from the Shebelynka deposit in 1956, a new aqueduct from the Krasnopavlivka Reservoir was built, tramway routes have been increased to 33, bus routes to over 50, and trolleybus routes to 36. The local rivers have been cleaned up. In 1968–75 the first line of the Kharkiv Metro (17.3 km long, with 13 stations) was built; in 1978 a second line was begun, and a third line is being planned. The commercial network, educational facilities, and health-care system have all been expanded. In Kharkiv's vicinity several sanatoriums, rest homes, and resorts have been opened. In 1976 there were

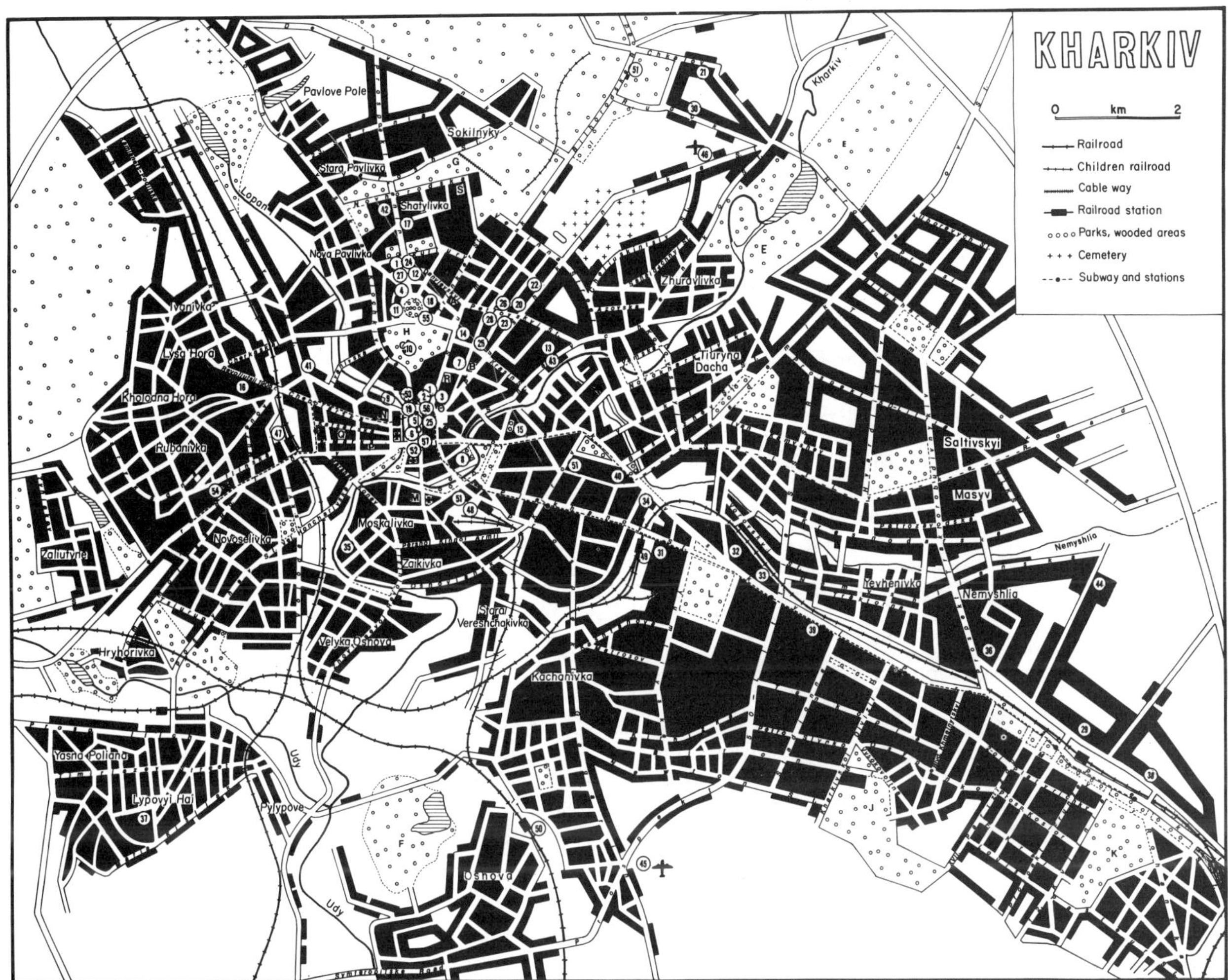

1. Ukrainian Drama Theater
2. Theater of Opera and Ballet
3. Philharmonic
4. Television studio
5. Conservatory
6. Historical-Regional Museum
7. Art Gallery
8. Korolenko Library
9. Institute of Culture
10. Astronomical Observatory
11. University
12. Medical Institute
13. Polytechnical Institute
14. Civil-Engineering Institute
15. Institute of Railway-Transport Engineers
16. Institute of Communal-Construction Engineers
17. Institute of Automatics and Cybernetics
18. Military Academy
19. Institute of Arts
20. Juridical Institute
21. Aviation Institute
22. Pharmaceutical Institute
23. Automobile and Road Institute
24. Radioelectronics Institute
25. Pedagogical Institute
26. Institute of Agricultural Mechanization and Electrification
27. Industrial Engineering Institute
28. Book Palace of the Ukrainian SSR
29. Tractor Plant
30. Aircraft Plant
31. Transport-Machinery Plant
32. Electrotechnical Plant
33. Turbine Plant
34. Serp i Molot Plant (agricultural machinery)
35. Svitlo Shakhtaria Plant (mineshaft lighting equipment)
36. Pivdennkabel Plant (cables)
37. Rope Plant
38. Tile Plant
39. Air-Conditioner Plant
40. Bicycle Plant
41. Machine-Tool Plant
42. Chemical-Reagents Plant
43. Pharmaceuticals Plant
44. Elektrovazhmash Plant (heavy electrical machinery)
45. Civil airport
46. Military airport
47. Pivdenna railway station
48. Levada railway station
49. Balashhivska railway station
50. Osnova railway station
51. Bus stations
52. Annunciation Cathedral
53. Dormition Cathedral
54. Kholmohory Church
55. Dzerzhinsky Square
56. Soviet Ukraine Square
57. Rosa Luxemburg Square

A. Natural Science Museum
B. Art Museum
C. Planetarium
D. Historical Museum
E. Zhuravlivka Hydropark
F. Osnova Meadow Park
G. University Botanical Garden
H. Shevchenko Park
I. Hryhorivka Woods
J. Park of the 50th Anniversary of the USSR
K. Park of the 40th Anniversary of the Komsomol
L. Artem Park
M. Circus
N. Central Department Store
O. Puppet Theater
P. Young Spectator's Theater
Q. Theater of Musical Comedy
R. Russian Drama Theater
S. Dynamo Sport Complex

about 7,000 physicians and 70 hospitals (with about 60,000 beds) in Kharkiv.

Today there are over 2,500 streets and 26 squares in the city. There are 110 parks, the largest being Gorky Park, Shevchenko Garden (with a zoo), Artem Park, the Forest Park, the University Botanical Garden, and Maiakovsky Park.

Kharkiv's role as a transportation hub has grown. Railway lines radiate from it in eight directions. The largest station is Pivdenna. The city is connected by air with the major cities of Ukraine and the Soviet Union; the present airport was built in 1954. The suburban and intercity bus network has 290 routes.

Population. In the Soviet period, as earlier, Kharkiv's population has grown steadily, from 285,000 in 1919 to 417,000 in 1926 (the third-largest city, after Kiev and Odessa, in Ukraine). By 1926 Ukrainians formed a relative majority at 38 percent, compared to Russians (37 percent) and Jews (19.5 percent); in 1897 the corresponding figures were 29, 60, and 6 percent. The population continued growing in the 1920s and 1930s, mostly because of the influx of peasants; in 1939 it was 833,000. As a result the city's area more than doubled between 1910 (67 sq km) and 1924 (141 sq km), and doubled again by 1939 (272 sq km). Since the drastic decline during the Second World War, the population has increased significantly: from 192,000 in 1943 to 672,000 in 1946, 856,000 in 1953, 953,000 in 1959, 1,223,000 in 1970, and 1,554,000 in 1985. In 1939 and 1959 the ethnic composition figures for the city were: Ukrainians, 49 and 48 percent; Russian, 33 and 40 percent; and Jews, 16 and 9 percent. Russification has been quite detrimental: in the 1959 census, only 64.1 percent of Kharkiv's Ukrainians stated that Ukrainian was their native language; today there would probably be even fewer.

Economy. Kharkiv is one of the largest industrial centers in both Ukraine and the USSR, with over 250 enterprises. It is third in machine building and metalworking after Moscow and Leningrad, with such large plants as the Kharkiv Tractor Plant, Transport Machine-Building Plant, Electromechanical Plant, Machine-Building Plant (mining machines), Motor Plant, Electrotechnical Plant (electric motors), Machine-Tool Plant, Turbine Plant, Aircraft Plant, Bicycle Plant, Elektrovazhmash Plant (turbogenerators), Cable Plant, and Bearing Plant. Also manufactured there are hydraulic lifts, refrigerators, construction equipment, automobiles, electronic, mining, and medical equipment, television sets, cameras, plastics, chemicals, paints, cosmetics, and pharmaceuticals. The woodworking, furniture, building-materials, construction, and printing industries are well developed. The food industry includes a confectionery association, breweries, a vegetable-oil and animal-fat processing complex, and a meat-packing complex. Clothing, textiles, leather, footwear (the largest factory in Ukraine), and rope are the main products of light industry. The number of industrial workers in the city was over 350,000 in 1961 and 500,000 in 1980.

Education, science, and culture. Kharkiv has been a major cultural and scientific center in Soviet Ukraine, second only to Kiev. In 1982 there were 20 post-secondary schools in Kharkiv: Kharkiv University, the Kharkiv Polytechnical, Agricultural, Medical, Juridical, Industrial Design, Pedagogical, Industrial Engineering, Civil Engineering, Automobile and Roads, Radioelectronics, Aviation, Pharmaceutical, and Zootechnical-Veterinary institutes; and the Kharkiv institutes of Agricultural Mechanization and Electrification, Communal-Construction Engineers, Railway-Transport Engineers, Public Consumption, Culture, and Arts. The former Kharkiv Conservatory (1923–63) and Theater Institute (1939–63) now constitute the Institute of Arts. In 1982 the city had 188 elementary, 38 specialized secondary, and 46 secondary vocational-technical schools; about 150 research and planning and design institutes affiliated with post-secondary schools, the CPU, or ministries; and 6 research institutes constituting the Northeastern Scientific Center of the AN URSR. Since the early 1930s and particularly after the Second World War, Russification in Kharkiv's schools and research institutions has been intense. A good half of its Writers' Union members write only in Russian.

The city's other prominent scholarly institutions are the Kharkiv Astronomical Observatory, Mathematical Society, Scientific Library (nearly six million volumes), University Library (over three million volumes), Scientific Medical Library, Oblast Archive, Historical Museum, Art Museum, and the Natural Science Museum. The city supports an oblast philharmonic, circus, and 6 professional theaters: the Kharkiv Theater of Opera and Ballet, Ukrainian Drama Theater, Russian Drama Theater, Young Spectator's Theater, Theater of Musical Comedy, and puppet theater; only the first two stage productions in Ukrainian. The public enjoys the use of the large Ukraina cinema and concert hall, 22 other cinemas, 249 libraries, 38 community-run museums, a sports palace, water sports palace, 5 parks of culture and recreation, 2 stadiums, and the Mala Pivdenna children's railroad. There are 65 hospitals in the city.

The following newspapers and journals are published in Kharkiv: the oblast newspapers *Sotsialistychna Kharkivshchyna* (from 1934), *Lenins'ka zmina* (1938), and *Krasnoe znamia* (1958); the city newspaper *Vechirnii Kharkiv / Vechernii Khar'kov* (from 1963 in Ukrainian, from 1983 in both Ukrainian and Russian); and the monthly journal *Prapor* (1956). The Prapor and Vyshcha Shkola publishing houses, Book Chamber of the Ukrainian SSR, Sotsialistychna Kharkivshchyna Publishing House and Printing Complex, and Frunze Book Factory are involved in publishing and printing. Two television channels are available: a Russian all-Union one and a republican-oblast one in both Ukrainian and Russian. In 1979 a new telecenter was established.

The city is ornamented with a large number of monuments, many of them dedicated to Soviet leaders and heroes and victims of the Second World War. Monuments to Ukrainian cultural figures include those of T. Shevchenko (1935), M. Kotsiubynsky (1957), V. Karazyn (1905), and N. Gogol (1909). Prerevolutionary architectural monuments include the cathedrals of the Holy Protectress (1689) and Dormition (1771, damaged in the mid-1930s), an 18th-century palace, and the former bishop's residence (now the Historical Museum).

BIBLIOGRAPHY

Karpov, V. *Khar'kovskaia starina* (Kharkiv 1900)

Gusev, A. *Khar'kov, ego proshloe i nastoiashchee* (Kharkiv 1902)

Bagalei, D.; Miller, D. *Istoriia goroda Khar'kova za 250 let ego sushchestvovaniia (s 1655-go po 1905-yi god)*, 2 vols (Kharkiv 1905, 1912)

Al'bovskii, E. *Khar'kovskie kazaki* (St Petersburg 1914)
Ivolhin, I. *Staryi Kharkiv* (Kharkiv 1920)
Taranushenko, S. *Stari khaty Kharkova* (Kharkiv 1922)
Kas'ianov, O. *Kharkiv: Istorychno-arkhitekturnyi narys* (Kiev 1956)
Diachenko, M.; Rozin, S.; Riabko, V. *Kharkiv: Mistsia istorychnykh podii, pam'iatnyky i zaklady kul'tury, vydatni diiachi* (Kharkiv 1957)
Istoriia mist i sil URSR: *Kharkivs'ka oblast'* (Kiev 1967; Russian edn 1976)
Myklashevs'kyi, I. *Muzychna i teatral'na kul'tura Kharkova kintsia* XVIII*–pershoï polovyny* XIX *st.* (Kiev 1967)
Danylov, V. *Kharkiv* (Kiev 1968)
Kurman, M.; Lebedinskii, I. *Naseleniie bol'shogo sotsialisticheskogo goroda* (Moscow 1968)
D'iachenko, N. *Ulitsy i ploshchadi Khar'kova* (Kharkiv 1974, 1977)
Semenko, O. *Kharkiv, Kharkiv ...* (New York 1976)
Alferov, I.; Antonov, V.; Liubarskii, R. *Formirovanie gorodskoi sredy (Na primere Khar'kova)* (Moscow 1977)
Sokil, V. 'Zdaleka do blyz'koho,' *Suchasnist'*, 1981, no. 2
Andreeva, G.; Oleinik, V. *Znakom'tes' – Khar'kov: Putevoditel'* (Kharkiv 1982)

V. Markus, R. Senkus

Kharkiv Agricultural Institute (Kharkivskyi silskohospodarskyi instytut im. V.V. Dokuchaieva). A higher educational institution supervised by the Ministry of Agriculture of the USSR. Its origins stem from the Agronomy Institute founded in Marymont near Warsaw in 1816, which was renamed the Institute of Agriculture and Forestry in 1840, moved to Puławy, Poland, in 1869, and evacuated to Kharkiv in 1914. It has been known by its present name since 1921. The institute has faculties of agronomy, plant protection, soil science and agrochemistry, economics, land-management engineering, architecture and farm construction, and one for the upgrading of agricultural specialists, a correspondence school, a graduate school, and two teaching and research farms. In 1976–7 it had over 5,500 students, 32 chairs, 310 teachers, a library with over 450,000 volumes, and about 100 cabinets and laboratories.

Kharkiv Art Institute. See Kharkiv Industrial Design Institute.

Kharkiv Art Museum (Kharkivskyi khudozhnii muzei). One of the most important museums in Ukraine. Founded in 1920, it has been reorganized and renamed several times since then. At first known as the Kharkiv Museum of Church History, it consisted basically of the antiquarian collections of Kharkiv and Volhynia eparchies and the art collection of Kharkiv University. Its holdings were enriched with precious religious articles that were acquired in the course of registering historical objects belonging to the churches and monasteries of the Kharkiv region. In 1922 the museum was renamed the Kharkiv Museum of Ukrainian Art. It consisted of three departments: architecture, sculpture, and painting. The last encompassed medieval mural paintings, 16th–19th-century icons, portraits, folk paintings, and 19th–20th-century paintings. In 1931 the plastic arts collection was separated from the museum to form the National Ukrainian Painting Gallery. During the 1930s the museum was closed to the public. After the war it resumed operations in 1944. From 1949 to 1965 it was known as the Kharkiv State Museum of Fine Art, and since 1965 by its present name. The exhibits, which occupy 25 halls, are divided into five sections: prerevolutionary Ukrainian and Russian art, Soviet art, foreign art (very meager), and decorative and applied art. The works of noted Ukrainian masters such as V. Borovykovsky, D. Levytsky, A. Losenko, and I. Aivazovsky are displayed in the Russian art section. A collection of S. Vasylkivsky's works, as well as paintings by P. Martynovych, P. Levchenko, M. Berkos, D. Bezperchy, M. Tkachenko, and T. Shevchenko (a self-portrait), forms an important part of the Ukrainian section. A separate hall is devoted to I. Repin's works, including one version of his famous painting *The Zaporozhian Cossacks Writing a Letter to the Sultan*. In the Soviet art section, Ukrainian and Russian artists are exhibited side by side, including such noted Ukrainian artists as M. Samokysha, M. Burachek, O. Slastion, F. Krychevsky, O. Murashko, M. Derehus, I. Izhakevych, Yu. Narbut, M. Pymonenko, and T. Yablonska. In the 1980s, the museum possessed nearly 20,000 art works. The Kharkiv Art Museum organizes one-man, thematic, and touring exhibitions. The museum building was designed by O. Beketov. An album of the museum with a Ukrainian, Russian, and English text was published in 1983.

S. Hordynsky

Kharkiv Astronomical Observatory (Kharkivska astronomichna observatoriia). A research facility of Kharkiv University. Largely because of the efforts of H. Levytsky, the astronomical cabinet (est 1808) was reorganized in 1888 into an observatory with its own building and proper equipment. The observatory is equipped with a meridian circle, a spectrohelioscope, a 700-mm optical telescope, and other instruments. The chief areas of research are astronometry, the physics of the moon, planets, and solar activity, and optical methods of processing astronomical data. The first photographs of the other side of the moon were processed, and a map and catalogue were prepared, at the observatory. Noted astronomers such as L. Struve, M. Yevdokymov, B. Ostashchenko-Kudriavtsev, and M. Barabashov have worked there.

Kharkiv Automobile and Roads Institute (Kharkivskyi avtomobilno-dorozhnyi instytut im. Komsomolu Ukrainy). A technical institution of higher education under the jurisdiction of the Ministry of Higher and Specialized Secondary Education of the Ukrainian SSR. Formed in 1930 out of the road-building departments of several technical institutes, it has departments of automobile engineering, mechanical engineering, road construction, and industrial engineering, as well as an evening and correspondence school. It offers a graduate program and a qualifications upgrading program. Its enrollment in 1984 was over 6,800.

Kharkiv Aviation Institute (Kharkivskyi aviiatsiinyi instytut im. M. Zhukovskoho). A technical institution of higher education under the jurisdiction of the USSR Ministry of Higher and Specialized Secondary Education. Formed in 1930 out of the aviation department of the Kharkiv Polytechnical Institute, it has departments of airplane construction, aviation instruments, motors, control systems, and radiotechnology as well as an evening and a graduate school and an airplane-design office.

Noted engineers such as O. Antonov, A. Liulka, and Yu. Proskura have worked at the institute. In 1983 its enrollment was over 8,000.

Kharkiv Chervonozavodskyi Ukrainian Drama Theater (Kharkivskyi chervonozavodskyi derzhavnyi ukrainskyi dramatychnyi teatr). A theater established in 1927 in the Chervonozavodskyi district in Kharkiv. Its first artistic director was O. Zaharov, who was succeeded in 1928 by V. Vasylko. L. Klishcheiev was the stage director, and B. Kosariev and Yu. Magner were the set designers. Many of its original actors came from the Shevchenko Ukrainian Drama Theater. The company included such names as Ye. Zarnytska, M. Petlishenko, L. Hakkebush, V. Masliuchenko, Y. Maiak, M. Tahaiv, I. Tverdokhlib, and A. Kramarenko. Its repertoire consisted mostly of Soviet plays by I. Mykytenko, Ya. Mamontov, M. Irchan, L. Pervomaisky, and I. Kocherha, but included also L. Starytska-Cherniakhivska's *Rozbiinyk Karmeliuk* (The Highwayman Karmeliuk), V. Vynnychenko's *Hrikh* (Sin), E. O'Neill's *Desire under the Elms*, and *Vovcha Zhraia* (Wolf Pack), based on J. London's novel. Following L. Kurbas's example, in 1928 V. Vasylko formed an acting and directing laboratory. After being attacked for constructivism, the theater was disbanded in 1933. Some of its staff were transferred to Staline (now Donetske), where they formed the core of the new Staline Ukrainian Drama Theater.

V. Revutsky

Kharkiv Civil-Engineering Institute (Kharkivskyi inzhenerno-budivelnyi instytut). A technical institution of higher education under the jurisdiction of the Ministry of Higher and Specialized Secondary Education of the Ukrainian USSR. Formed in 1930 out of the construction department of the Kharkiv Technological Institute and the architecture department of the Kharkiv Art Institute, it has departments of architecture, construction, mechanics-technology, and sanitary engineering as well as an evening, correspondence, and graduate school. Its enrollment in 1984 was about 4,000.

Kharkiv College (Kharkivskyi kolehium). One of the most important religious secondary schools in the Russian Empire in the 18th century. It was founded originally (1722) as an eparchial seminary in Belgorod by Bishop Ye. Tykhorsky, and was transferred to Kharkiv in 1726 by Prince M. Golitsyn. Modeled on the Kievan Mohyla Academy, the seminary provided at first the kind of general education that was demanded of candidates for priesthood. Its six-grade curriculum stressed the Slavonic, Greek, and Latin languages; hence the seminary became known as the Slavonic-Greek-Latin School. In 1734 it assumed the title of college, and quickly attained a reputation for learning, second only to the Kievan Mohyla Academy. To attract students interested in a civil career, Bishop P. Smelech introduced in 1737 mathematics, French, and German, and invited foreign instructors to teach these subjects. It was transformed into the Kharkiv Theological Seminary in 1817 and thereafter provided only ecclesiastical education. In 1765 supplementary classes in French, German, mathematics, drafting, engineering, artillery, and geodesy were introduced for secular students. Physics and natural history were added in 1795, and agriculture and medicine at the beginning of the 19th century. Instruction took place mainly in Latin. The enrollment in 1727 was close to 400 and later rose as high as 800. The faculty included some famous artists and thinkers: I. Sabluchok, A. Vedel, and H. Skovoroda (1759–66). Many of the college's graduates gained distinction as church leaders, scholars, or cultural figures: N. Gnedich, M. Kachenovsky, Y. Mukhin, T. Smilivsky, and P. Yaroslavsky, among others. With the opening of Kharkiv University in 1805, the college's role in secular education declined. In 1817 the college was again converted into a theological seminary.

D. Saunders

Kharkiv Conservatory (Kharkivska konservatoriia). A higher school of music under the Ministry of Culture of the Ukrainian SSR. It was formed in 1917 out of the Kharkiv Music School (est 1883). In 1924 the conservatory was reorganized into the Kharkiv Music and Drama Institute and was reconstituted 10 years later out of the institute's music faculty. The conservatory consisted of eight faculties: piano, orchestra, folk instruments, singing, chorus conducting, musicology, composition, and music research. Evening and correspondence courses were offered. Its faculty included S. Bohatyrov, who raised a whole generation of composers such as D. Klebanov, M. Koliada, Yu. Meitus, V. Nakhabin, M. Tits, M. Fomenko, and A. Shtoharenko. In 1963 the conservatory was turned into the music faculty of the new Kharkiv Institute of Arts.

Kharkiv Electromechanical Plant (Kharkivskyi elektromekhanichnyi zavod or KhEMZ). A large industrial complex established in Kharkiv in 1915. During the Second World War it was evacuated east and its production machinery was used to equip five new factories in various parts of the USSR. Its buildings in Kharkiv were demolished. By 1950 the plant had been rebuilt, and in 1976 it was reorganized into an industrial complex. Its production consists mostly of large electric machines (200–25,000 kW), electric motors, transformers, automatic switches, and consumer products.

Kharkiv eparchy. An Orthodox eparchy founded in 1799 and comprising the territory of Slobidska Ukraine (later Kharkiv) gubernia. Until 1836 the bishops were officially titled Bishop of Slobidska Ukraine and Kharkiv, later Bishop of Kharkiv and Okhtyrka. Now the eparchy comprises only Kharkiv oblast, and the bishop is titled Bishop of Kharkiv and Bohodukhiv. The eparchy published a semimonthly newsletter, *Khar'kovskie Eparkhial'nye Vedomosti* (1867–83), succeeded by *Listok Khar'kovskoi Eparkhii* (1884–1917), and the religious journal *Vera i Razum*, which all contained important material on the history of the Ukrainian church. Before the 1917 Revolution there were six men's and six women's monasteries in the eparchy and 1009 priests (1913). In the 1920s a 'regional church' or eparchy of the *Ukrainian Autocephalous Orthodox church was established in Kharkiv, and the church's monthly journal, *Tserkva i Zhyttia*, was published there. A representation of the *All-Ukrainian Orthodox Church Council was also established. The more renowned hierarchs of the eparchy were Archbishops I. *Borisov, F. *Humilevsky, and M. *Bulgakov.

Kharkiv gubernia. An administrative-territorial unit in Russian-ruled *Slobidska Ukraine. *Kharkiv was the capital. In 1765 Slobidska Ukraine gubernia superseded the abolished Cossack regiments of Izium, Okhtyrka, Ostrohozke, Sumy, and Kharkiv. It was replaced by Kharkiv vicegerency in 1780 but restored in 1796 and renamed Kharkiv gubernia in 1835. From 1835 the gubernia consisted of 11 counties: Bohodukhiv, Izium, Kharkiv, Kupianka, Lebedyn, Okhtyrka, Starobilske, Sumy, Valky, Vovchanske, Zmiiv. In 1773 the gubernia had a male population of 666,000 living in 670 settlements; 58.6 percent consisted of Cossacks and military settlers, and 34 percent of peasants. The total population was 1,030,000 (90 percent peasant) in 1811, 1,590,900 in 1863, and 2,492,300 (18 percent urban) in 1897 (Ukrainians represented 82.7 percent; Russians, 16.3 percent). In 1924 the population was 2,728,400 (20 percent urban, of which only 55 percent was Ukrainian). The gubernia was primarily an agricultural region. Industry was underdeveloped and consisted mainly of beet-sugar processing, distilling, brewing, and metalworking. The gubernia was abolished in 1925, and its territory (36,727 sq km) was divided among Izium, Kupianka, Starobilske, Sumy, and Kharkiv okruhas; most of it made up *Kharkiv oblast in 1932.

R. Senkus

Kharkiv Historical Museum

Kharkiv Historical Museum (Kharkivskyi istorychnyi muzei). One of the richest museums in Ukraine. Its origin goes back to the City Museum of Industry and Art founded in 1886 on the initiative of H. *Danylevsky. In 1920 the Skovoroda Museum of Slobidska Ukraine was formed out of this museum, the contents of the exhibition of Far Eastern Art and Ethnography of the Seventh Archeological Congress (1902), which had been kept by Kharkiv University, and the museum collection of the Kharkiv Historical-Philological Society. M. Sumtsov, one of its founders, became the museum's director. In the 1930s, during the suppression of Ukrainian learning, the museum was closed. It was reopened only after the Second World War and was renamed. Today the museum consists of four departments: archeology, pre-Soviet history, Soviet history, and Soviet-Czechoslovak friendship (located in Sokolove village near Kharkiv). Its holdings amount to about 200,000 articles. Besides archeological treasures such as V. *Gorodtsev's finds in the Izium region, the relics of a Saltiv burial site (8th–10th centuries), and the memorials from a fortified settlement in the Donets region (9th–12th centuries), it has a collection of articles from the early history of Kharkiv and numismatic, ethnographic, arms, flag, and art collections. From the Soviet period it has collections of propaganda materials, weapons, and memorabilia of Bolshevik leaders.

Kharkiv Historical-Philological Society (Kharkovskoe istoriko-filologicheskoe obshchestvo). Scholarly society founded at Kharkiv University in 1876, whose objective was to study Left-Bank and Slobidska Ukraine and subsequently carry on educational and cultural work. The Kharkiv society, along with a number of other official Ukrainian scientific societies, focused exclusively upon scholarly subjects following a period of increased intolerance that culminated in the *Ems ukase in 1876. The society's members consisted of lecturers from the university and other educational institutions and the local intelligentsia, among them such prominent figures as D. Bahalii, V. Buzeskul, O. and P. Yefymenko, O. Rusov, D. Yavornytsky, B. Liapunov, D. Ovsianyko-Kulykovsky, M. Khalansky, M. Hrunsky, V. Rezanov, Ya. Novytsky, V. Barvinsky, O. Vetukhiv, Ye. Ivanov, I. Manzhura, and O. Biletsky. The presidents of the society were V. Nadler (1877–8), O. Potebnia (1878–90), M. Drinov (1890–7), and M. Sumtsov (1897–1918). The society founded an archive (1880), containing significant documentation from the period of the hetmanate before 1782 and the *Little Russian Collegium, an ethnographic museum, and two libraries. It organized archeological and ethnographic expeditions, describing them in its various serial publications: *Sbornik Khar'kovskogo Istoriko-filologicheskogo obshchestva* (21 vols, 1886–1914), *Trudy* (7 vols, 1893–1902), and *Vestnik* (5 issues, 1911–14). The society ceased to function under Soviet rule in 1919. Its archive is now located at the Central State Historical Archive of the Ukrainian SSR.

Kharkiv Industrial Design Institute

Kharkiv Industrial Design Institute (Kharkivskyi khudozhno-promyslovyi instytut). A five-year art school under the Ministry of Higher and Specialized Secondary Education of the Ukrainian SSR. It was formed in 1963 out of the Kharkiv Art Institute (1927–63). The institute has two faculties: industrial design and interior design. The former is subdivided into such departments as the design of industrial furnishings, of transportation means, and of consumer goods, industrial graphics, and packaging. The second consists of such departments as the design of interiors, exhibits, advertisements, and small architectural forms, and monumental-decorative art. The enrollment is close to 650 per year.

Kharkiv Industrial-Engineering Institute (Kharkivskyi inzhenerno-ekonomichnyi instytut). A technical institution of higher education under the jurisdiction of the Ministry of Higher and Specialized Secondary Education of the Ukrainian SSR. Formed in 1930 out of the industry department of the Kharkiv Institute of the National Economy, it has a number of departments: machine-building, economics, chemistry, information processing, and labor management. It offers a graduate program and has an evening and a correspondence school. In 1984 its enrollment was about 5,000.

Kharkiv Institute of Arts (Kharkivskyi instytut mystetstv im. I. Kotliarevskoho). An institution of higher learning under the jurisdiction of the Ministry of Culture of the Ukrainian SSR. It was formed in 1963 out of the Kharkiv Conservatory and the Kharkiv Theater Institute. The institute has 10 faculties: stage acting, puppetry acting, stage directing, theater studies, piano, vocal music, folk instruments, orchestra, choir conducting, and theory and history. Its regular program for performing artists and drama or music teachers requires four years to complete; its correspondence and evening programs require one or two years more. Well-known actors such as O. Serdiuk and L. Tarabarynov have served on its faculty. The enrollment is over 800.

Kharkiv Institute of Culture (Kharkivskyi instytut kultury). An institution of higher learning under the Ministry of Culture of the Ukrainian SSR. Organized in 1929 out of the faculty of political education of the Kharkiv Institute of People's Education, it was reorganized and renamed several times before assuming its present form and name in 1966. Its task is to train librarians, bibliographers, and cultural-educational workers (organizers of clubs and directors of amateur ensembles). It has two departments – library science, and culture and education, both with a four-year program – and a correspondence school. The institute publishes collections of papers: *Bibliotekarstvo i bibliohrafiia* and *Kulturno-osvitnia robota*. In 1984 its enrollment was about 4,000.

Kharkiv Institute of People's Education (Kharkivskyi instytut narodnoi osvity im. O. Potebni or KhINO). A post-secondary educational institution organized in 1921 out of *Kharkiv University. It had three faculties: professional education, social education, and political education, each with a four-year program. For many years its principal was M. Havryliv. In 1925 its enrollment was almost 2,000 and in 1930 over 3,000. The faculty in 1925 had 205 members. In the 1920s KhINO underwent *Ukrainization. In 1932–3 Kharkiv University was restored by merging the KhINO, the Institute of the National Economy, and faculties of several other institutes.

Kharkiv Institute of Railway-Transport Engineers (Kharkivskyi instytut inzheneriv zaliznychnoho transportu im. S. Kirova). A post-secondary technical school under the jurisdiction of the Ministry of Roads of the USSR. In 1930 it succeeded the Kharkiv Railroad School established in the 1880s. The institute has five daytime faculties (mechanics; construction; automation, telemechanics, and communications; transportation management; and economics), an evening faculty, a correspondence faculty, an upgrading faculty, a graduate program, and a library with over 500,000 volumes. Branches of the institute are located in Donetske and Kiev. In 1983/4 it had 8,500 students. Between 1930 and 1983 over 36,000 engineers completed its 5–6-year program.

Kharkiv Juridical Institute (Kharkivskyi yurydychnyi instytut). An institution of higher education for the training of lawyers and legal staff. Its origins stem from the Faculty of Law of Kharkiv University, which in 1920 became a faculty of the Kharkiv Institute of the National Economy and in 1930 was reorganized into the separate Institute of Soviet Construction and Law. In 1935 it received its present name. The only juridical institute in Ukraine, in the 1970s its annual enrollment was over 4,000, most in correspondence and evening programs. The institute has 17 chairs, a graduate school, and a library with over 300,000 volumes. Well-known jurists – eg, M. Paliienko, V. and M. Hordon, V. Koretsky, M. Maksymeiko, P. Nedbailo, and S. Vilniansky – have been part of its faculty.

Kharkiv Literacy Society (Kharkivske tovarystvo dlia poshyrennia v narodi hramotnosti or Kharkivske tovarystvo hramotnosti). Society established in 1869 on the initiative of several Kharkiv university faculty members, especially N. Beketov, M. Sumtsov, V. Danylevsky, and D. Bahalii. The society drew on broad public support to develop programs and schools to promote literacy and education in the whole gubernia. Loosely connected to similar societies in other regions, it supported the founding of four separate Sunday literacy schools for men and women, trade schools, programs on personal hygiene, handicrafts courses, and five small circulating libraries. In 1903 it acquired a building to house its headquarters, a museum of visual teaching aids, and a library. In 1912 it sponsored the publication of the multivolume *Narodnaia entsiklopediia nauchnykh i prikladnykh znanii* (People's Encyclopedia of Scientific and Practical Knowledge). After the 1905 Revolution it began sponsoring public discussions on current political affairs. Its activities were severely curtailed during the First World War, and after the 1917 Revolution its work was taken over by the Ukrainian Scientific and Technical Society and the Ukrainian Commissariat of Education.

M. Bohachevsky-Chomiak

Kharkiv Machine-Tool Plant (Kharkivskyi verstatobudivnyi zavod im. S.V. Kosiora). One of the largest plants of the machine-tool industry in Ukraine, built in 1933. It was destroyed during the Second World War and rebuilt by the early 1950s. The plant has 14 primary and auxiliary shops such as the foundry, modeling, smithy, and assembly shops. Its basic production consists of automatic and semiautomatic machine tools, automatic conveyer belts, and large, medium, and special cylinder-and-cone grinding machines. Machine tools produced there are exported throughout the USSR and Eastern Europe.

Kharkiv Mathematics Society (Kharkivske matematychne tovarystvo). Society founded in 1879 at Kharkiv

University to promote the study of mathematics. The organizer and first president was V. Imshenetsky. Since 1947 it has had two sections: scientific research and pedagogy. The society published protocols of its meetings from 1879 to 1888 and the journal *Soobshcheniia Khar'kovskogo matematicheskogo obshchestva* from 1888 to 1956. Since then, it has published a journal together with the mathematics department of Kharkiv University in the series *Uchenye zapiski Khar'kovskogo universiteta*. Its members have included O. Grave, A. Liapunov, and V. Steklov.

Kharkiv Medical Institute

Kharkiv Medical Institute (Kharkivskyi medychnyi instytut). A post-secondary institution in Kharkiv under the jurisdiction of the Ministry of Health Protection of the Ukrainian SSR. It originated as the Faculty of Medicine (est 1805) at Kharkiv University, which was merged with the Kharkiv Women's Medical Institute (est 1910) to form a medical academy in 1920 and the institute in 1921. A second institute was created in 1935; it was merged with the first in 1943. The institute has four faculties (therapeutics, pediatrics, hygiene, stomatology), a preparatory department, and a graduate program. In 1984 it had over 5,000 students in a six-year program; 60 chairs; a central research laboratory; laboratories devoted to cardiology, virology, ophthalmic microsurgery, and the female reproductive system; four research museums; and a research library with over 620,000 volumes. Since 1935 the institute has published collections of scientific papers. It has graduated about 40,000 physicians and medical scientists. Some of the prominent medical scientists who have taught there are V. Danylevsky, V. Vorobiov, V. Protopopov, G. Folbort, O. Cherkes, V. Belousov, M. Bokarius, I. Hryshchenko, V. Derkach, B. Zadorozhny, H. Karavanov, Ye. Popov, M. Sytenko, N. Trinkler, V. Prykhodko, Yu. Orlenko, N. Tytarenko, V. Matvieieva, O. Nalbat, R. Synelnykov, M. Solovev, and A. Utevsky.

Kharkiv Motor Plant (Kharkivskyi motorbudivnyi zavod 'Serp i molot'). A large agricultural-machinery manufacturing plant based on a factory founded in 1875 by M. Helferich and a Belgian industrial trust. In the interwar period the plant produced tractor parts, threshing machines, and other agricultural machines. Largely destroyed during the Second World War, it was rebuilt beginning in 1943. Since the 1960s the factory has specialized in producing motors for tractors and combines.

Kharkiv oblast. An administrative region in northeastern Ukraine, formed on 27 February 1932. Its area is 31,400 sq km; in 1986 its population was 3,146,900. The oblast has 25 raions, 328 rural soviets, 16 cities, and 62 towns (smt). The capital is Kharkiv.

Physical geography. The oblast is essentially located in the Dnieper Lowland; only its northern part is in the Central Russian Upland. The vegetation is of the steppe and forest-steppe variety. The oblast's northwestern forest-steppe has medium-humus chernozem, dark-gray podzolized, and podzolized chernozem soils. Its eastern and southern steppe has ordinary medium-humus chernozems and, in the river valleys, soddy, weakly podzolized meadow-chernozem and also marshy soils. Forests cover 11 percent of the oblast. Large deposits of petroleum, natural gas, peat, anthracite, lignite, rock salt, iron ores, phosphates, limestone, marls, ordinary and quartzose sands, chalk, refractory clays, zinc, and ocher are located there.

The largest rivers are the Donets; its right-bank tributaries the Udy, Kharkiv, Lopan, Mozh, Chepil, and Bereka; its left-bank tributaries the Vovcha, Velykyi Burluk, Voloska Balakliika, and Oskil; and the Merlia, Orel, Orelka, Berestova, Brytai, and Bahata rivers of the Dnieper Basin. Mineral springs and several small lakes are found in the oblast; most of the lakes are in the Donets marshlands (Lyman, Borove, Bile, Lebiazhe, Chaika). The climate is temperate-continental, with an average temperature in January of −7 to −8°C and in July of 20–21.5°C. The annual precipitation ranges from 457 mm in the east to 568 mm in the west. Dry spells occur in the summer, and dry winds and dust storms in the spring.

History. The oblast's territories once belonged to the Kievan and Chernihiv lands of Kievan Rus'. With the Mongol invasions of the 13th century they were largely unsettled and constituted part of the so-called Dyke Pole (Loca Deserta). In the 16th century they became nominally part of Muscovy. Ukrainian Cossacks and Russian peasants began settling there, and they became part of *Slobidska Ukraine. In the 17th and 18th centuries they constituted parts of the Kharkiv and Izium regiments. From 1765 they were under direct Russian rule, as part of Slobidska Ukraine gubernia (1765–80, 1796–1835), Kharkiv vicegerency (1780–96), and Kharkiv gubernia (1835–1917). After the February Revolution of 1917, they changed hands several times among the UNR, the Hetman government, the Directory of the UNR, the Bolsheviks, and the Whites. Under Soviet rule from 1920, the gubernia was abolished in 1925 and replaced by Kharkiv, Izium, Kupianka, and Sumy okruhas. In 1932 these okruhas were replaced by Kharkiv oblast. Its borders were modified several times; in 1937 parts of it were incorporated into the newly created Poltava oblast, and in 1939, Sumy oblast.

Population. The oblast's population did not grow because of the many deaths and deportations that occurred during the Stalinist terror, the man-made *famine of 1932–3, and the Second World War. In 1965 it was 2,650,000. Between 1965 and 1984, however, it increased by 18 percent. In 1965, the average density was 75 inhabitants per sq km; in 1984 it was 99.5. The proportion of urban dwellers grew from about 25 percent in the mid-1920s to 53 percent in 1939, 69 percent in 1970, and 78 percent in 1986. Ukrainians made up only 68.8 percent of the population in 1959 and 64.2 percent in 1979; Russians,

26 percent and 31.8 percent; and Jews, 3.3 percent and 2.1 percent. Linguistic Russification is well advanced: in 1979 only 80.5 percent of the oblast's Ukrainians claimed Ukrainian as their first language, and only 52.2 percent of the population as a whole did. The most populous cities are Kharkiv, Izium, Lozova, Chuhuiv, Kupianka, Balakliia, and Liubotyn.

Industry. The oblast is one of the most industrialized in the USSR. In 1983, the main industries were machine building and metalworking (51 percent of gross output), food (15.3 percent), light industry (14.3 percent), and building materials (3.5 percent). Machine building, metallurgy, and metalworking are concentrated in *Kharkiv; secondary plants are found in Kupianka, Chuhuiv, Lozova, Derhachi, Paniutyne, and Izium. The oblast is the primary producer in Ukraine of confectioneries. Other branches of the food industry manufacture sugar products (in Kharkiv, Kupianka, Savyntsi), meat products (Kharkiv, Vovchanske, Kupianka, Krasnohrad, Izium, Chuhuiv, Bohodukhiv), flour and groats (Kharkiv, Krasnohrad, Lozova, Barvinkove), dairy products, vegetable oil, tobacco, beer, and spirits.

Light industry is also concentrated in Kharkiv, where plants produce clothing, textiles, footwear, and leather goods; other plants are found in Valky, Vilshany, Kupianka, Krasnohrad, Bohodukhiv, Komarivka, Liubotyn, and Lozova. Porcelain and ceramic tiles are made in Budy and Balakliia; wood products, furniture, and cellulose, in Kharkiv, Merefa, Izium, Chuhuiv, Hotvald, Derhachi, Vilshany, Zmiiv, and Rohan. The printing industry is concentrated in Kharkiv. Chemicals, pharmaceuticals, and cosmetics are made in Kharkiv and Pervomaiske; medical equipment, in Kharkiv and Izium. Building materials (cement, asbestos, bricks, slates, lime, reinforced-concrete materials, and glass) are made in Kharkiv, Balakliia, and Merefa. Natural gas extracted from the deposits at *Shebelynka, Kehychivka, Yefremivka, Melykhivka, Khrestyshche, Sosnivka, and elsewhere is the oblast's main source of fuel. Power is produced by large hydroelectric stations in Zmiiv and Eskhar and several thermal stations.

Agriculture. Grains, vegetables, fruits, and fodder and industrial crops are grown, and farm animals are raised at 274 collective and 158 state farms (in 1983). In 1983 there was 2,673,000 ha of farmland in the oblast; 90.5 percent (2,418,000 ha) was being used: of the latter 82.5 percent (1,994,000 ha) for crops, 11.9 percent (287,000 ha) as pasture, and 4.0 percent (95,000 ha) as hayfields. Of the total cropland, 1,853,000 ha (93 percent) were sown; 97,300 ha were irrigated, and 8,700 ha were drained. The main grain crops are winter wheat (40 percent), summer barley, corn, millet, and buckwheat. The main industrial crops are sunflowers and sugar beets (46 percent). Fodder crops consist of beets, roots, and grasses. Animal husbandry accounts for 55.6 percent of the agricultural output; cattle farming prevails, but hogs, poultry, rabbits, honey bees, and fish are also raised.

Transportation. In 1976 the oblast had 1,520 km of railway, of which 907 km was electric. Trunk lines crossing the oblast include the Moscow–Kharkiv–Sevastopil, Briansk–Kharkiv–Zhdanov, Moscow–Kharkiv–Donetske, and Lviv–Kiev–Poltava–Kharkiv–Kupianka–Valuiky lines. The major junctions are Kharkiv, Lozova, Kupianka, Krasnohrad, Merefa, and Liubotyn. In 1983 there were 8,300 km of roads, of which 6,600 were paved. The major highways include Moscow–Kharkiv–Symferopil and Kiev–Kharkiv–Rostov-na-Donu. An airport is located near Kharkiv.

BIBLIOGRAPHY

Istoriia mist i sil Ukraïns'koï RSR: *Kharkivs'ka oblast'* (Kiev 1967; Russian edn 1976)

I. Myhul, R. Senkus

Kharkiv Painting School (Kharkivska maliuvalna shkola). Founded in 1869 as a private art school by M. *Raievska-Ivanova, it was reorganized in 1896 into the City Painting School. In 1912 it was turned into a secondary art school whose graduates were admitted to the art academies. Its teachers and patrons included P. Levchenko, S. Vasylkivsky, I. Repin, and M. Fedorov. In 1921 the Kharkiv Art School was transformed into a higher art institution, the Kharkiv Art Tekhnikum, which in 1927–8 was renamed the Kharkiv Art Institute and included a vocational art school.

Kharkiv Pedagogical Institute

Kharkiv Polytechnical Institute

Kharkiv Pedagogical Institute (Kharkivskyi derzhavnyi pedahohichnyi instytut im. H. Skovorody). An institution of higher learning for preparing secondary-school teachers, under the Ministry of Education of the Ukrainian SSR. It was formed in 1933 out of the Kharkiv Institute of Social Education, which had been organized in 1931 out of the faculty of social education of the Kharkiv Institute of People's Education. It consists of five faculties: philology, physics and mathematics, natural science, preparation of elementary-school teachers, and physical education. The institute has a correspondence school and a graduate program. Its undergraduate program requires four or five years to complete. The total enrollment in 1983–4 was 4,700.

Kharkiv Polytechnical Institute (Kharkivskyi politekhnichnyi instytut im. V. Lenina). An institution of higher education under the Ministry of Higher and Specialized Secondary Education of the Ukrainian SSR, and one of the leading technical schools of the USSR. It was formed in 1929 out of the Kharkiv Technological Institute, which was founded in 1885. In 1930 it was replaced by a number of specialized institutes – mechanical, electrical, chemical, civil engineering, and aviation – but it was restored in 1949. It has 13 faculties – including the faculties of machine building, electric power, metallurgy, farm machinery, engineering and physics, and automatization – and over 100 laboratories. A graduate program and several upgrading programs are offered to postgraduates. The regular undergraduate program requires five years to complete. Branches of the institute exist in Sumy and Kremenchuk. In 1984 the enrollment was about 24,000. In 1952 its journal *Ucheni zapysky / Uchenye zapiski* was renamed *Visnyk*, and in 1976 it began to be published in Russian as *Vestnik*.

Kharkiv regiment. An administrative and military unit in *Slobidska Ukraine centered in Kharkiv. It was formed in 1659–60 by Cossacks and peasants from Right- and Left-Bank Ukraine and occupied the sparsely populated territory between the Bakhmutka, Merla, Uda, and Orel rivers. In 1685, a separate Izium regiment was detached. The regiment's territory was crossed by the *Murava Road and was often raided by Crimean and Nogay Tatars. Kharkiv regiment comprised 18 companies (in 1680 – 1715). In 1732 it had a population of 75,000 in 135 settlements. Its most prominent colonel was I. *Sirko (1664–5 and 1667). The regiment fought in the Russian-Turkish and Russian-Swedish wars of the late 17th and 18th centuries. It was abolished in 1765 and its territory became part of Slobidska Ukraine gubernia. Some of the Cossacks were organized into a regular lancer unit while the rest lost their remaining Cossack privileges.

Kharkiv Romantic School. A group of young poets who were professors or students at Kharkiv University in the 1830s–1840s. The term 'school' was proposed by A. *Shamrai, who researched and published their poetry. The school's main representatives were I. Sreznevsky, A. Metlynsky, M. Kostomarov, L. Borovykovsky, M. Petrenko, and O. Shpyhotsky. Like young poets of other nations in the Romantic period, they were imbued with an incipient national consciousness, which prompted them to study the ethnography of their people. While collecting, publishing, and imitating folk songs, legends, and stories, the Kharkiv romantics developed their own, predominantly historical, themes. As a result of their ethnographic interest, their view of the common people differed from the patronizing attitude of their predecessors I. Kotliarevsky and H. Kvitka-Osnovianenko. Instead of treating the people as naive children of nature, they saw in them a source of spiritual renewal and strength and poetic inspiration. This new view was shared even by those who, like A. Metlynsky, were cowed by the suppression of the *Cyril and Methodius Brotherhood and did not believe in the feasibility of a national renaissance of the Ukrainian people. Without entirely overcoming the traditional inclination toward verbosity, the Kharkiv romantics nonetheless rejected the literary burlesque cultivated by the previous generation and reminded educated Ukrainians that, as P. Kulish wrote, their 'native language exists not only for the purpose of berating the shiftless peasant.' This new attitude towards the people later gave rise to a Ukrainian messianism, which was articulated in M. Kostomarov's **Knyhy bytiia ukraïns'koho narodu* (Books of the Genesis of the Ukrainian People).

BIBLIOGRAPHY

Shamrai, A. (ed). *Kharkivs'ka shkola romantykiv*, 3 vols (Kharkiv 1930)

Luckyj, G. *Between Gogol' and Ševčenko: Polarity in the Literary Ukraine, 1797–1847* (Munich 1971)

P. Petrenko

Kharkiv Scientific Society (Kharkivske naukove tovarystvo). A society uniting researchers and lecturers from various institutions of higher learning in Kharkiv founded in 1924. Its six sections (technology, natural science, medicine, agriculture, education, and linguistics-literature) published their own annual reports and journals: eg, *Visnyk pryrodoznavstva* (1927–31), *Biuleten' Postiinoï komisiï vyvchannia krovianykh uhrupovan'* (4 issues, 1927–30), and *Naukovo-tekhnichnyi visnyk* (over 90 issues from 1926 to 1936). The society also published its own periodical and annual report – *Biuleten'* (9 issues, 1927–8) and *Zvit pro diialnist'* (1924–6). Among its more prominent collaborators were S. Rudnytsky, V. Rubashkin, M. Bilousiv, M. Barabashov, and O. Yanata. In the mid-1930s the society was dissolved and its sections were merged with other institutes.

Kharkiv Society of Naturalists (Kharkivske tovarystvo doslidnykiv pryrody). Society established in 1869 at Kharkiv University to promote the study of the natural sciences and research on the natural resources and geology of the Kharkiv region and southern Ukraine. Its membership increased from 40 in 1869 to 108 in 1897 and 212 in 1927. In 1914 the society established the Donetske Hydrobiological Station. It published the journal *Trudy obshchestva ispytatelei prirody pri Khar'kovskom universitete* (Works of the Society of Naturalists at Kharkiv University, 1869–1925 in Russian and 1927–30 in Ukrainian). The society ceased to exist in 1930.

Kharkiv Theater Institute (Kharkivskyi derzhavnyi teatralnyi instytut). A higher school set up in 1939 for training stage actors and directors. It was formed out of the Kharkiv Theater School, which had arisen in 1934 out of the Kharkiv Music and Drama Institute (est 1923 as a result of the reorganization of the Kharkiv Conservatory). Until 1934 L. *Kurbas's system of training was used, while Kurbas himself and some of his students (V. Vasylko, H. Ihnatovych, B. Tiahno, M. Verkhatsky, and L. Hakkebush) served on the faculty. The longest-serving members on the institute's faculty were I. Marianenko (1925–34, 1934–41, and 1944–61) and M. Krushelnytsky (1946–52). During the Second World War the Kharkiv Theater Institute operated in Saratov as the Ukrainian department of the Moscow Institute of Theater Arts. Returning to Kharkiv in 1943, it resumed work as a branch of the Kiev Institute of Theater Arts, and in 1945 became an independent institute. In 1963 the Kharkiv Theater Institute was abolished and was replaced by two faculties – acting and directing – in the new Kharkiv Institute of Arts.

Kharkiv Theater of Musical Comedy (Kharkivskyi teatr muzychnoi komedii). Founded in 1929, it is the oldest Ukrainian operetta theater. Its inauguration, which coincided with the Ukrainization of the Odessa Opera, was celebrated as a victory for the state's *Ukrainization policy. At first the company concentrated on classical operettas, rendering them, thanks to the influence of L. *Kurbas's school, in an experimental style. It staged such musicals as J. Offenbach's *Orpheus in the Underworld*, S.

Hulak-Artemovsky's *Zaporozhian Cossack beyond the Danube,* and J. Strauss's *Gypsy Baron.* Since 1936 the theater has served as a laboratory of the new Ukrainian operetta. Its more successful productions include O. Riabov's *Wedding at Malynivka,* D. Klebanov's and V. Nakhabin's *The Amorous Guest,* S. Zhdanov's *Palyvoda* (The Madcap), K. Bents's *Starry Nights,* H. Finarovsky's *Palm Island,* and O. Sandler's *At Dawn.* Its stage directors were M. Avakh, Ya. Bortnyk, and B. Balaban; its conductors, B. Kryzhanivsky and B. Cheboksarov; its choreographer, V. Verkhovynets; and its soloists, V. Novynska, D. Ponomarenko, and O. Ivashutych. During the Second World War the theater was evacuated to Uzbekistan; it returned to Kharkiv in 1945. Since then its most successful productions have been those of classical Viennese operettas.

V. Revutsky

Kharkiv Theater of Opera and Ballet

Kharkiv Theater of Opera and Ballet (Kharkivskyi derzhavnyi akademichnyi teatr opery ta baletu im. M. Lysenka). The first Ukrainian opera theater with a resident company. It was founded in 1925 as the Ukrainian Capital Opera, and received its current name in 1944. The first permanent opera company in Kharkiv arose in 1880, and it became the first company to stage M. Lysenko's Ukrainian operas *Christmas Night* (1883) and *The Drowned Maiden* (1885). In 1918 the company became known as the People's Opera, and in 1920 as the Russian State Opera. By 1934 the theater had produced 32 operas and 11 ballets, including B. Liatoshynsky's *The Golden Ring,* V. Kostenko's *Karmeliuk,* A. Vakhnianyn's *Kupalo,* M. Lysenko's *Taras Bulba,* O. Chyshko's *Apple Blossom Captivity,* and the Ukrainized versions of A. Dargomyzhsky's *The Water Nymph* and A. Borodin's *Prince Igor.* The ballets produced there included B. Yanovsky's *Ferenji* and M. Verykivsky's *The Nobleman Kanovsky,* in which the choreographer V. Lytvynenko combined for the first time elements of classical ballet and Ukrainian folk dances. Many masterpieces of Russian and world opera were produced; eg, E. Wolf-Ferrari's *The Jewels of the Madonna* and G. Puccini's *Turandot.* In 1934–41 new productions of S. Hulak-Artemovsky's *Zaporozhian Cossack beyond the Danube* and M. Lysenko's *Natalka from Poltava* were staged. During this period G. Meyerbeer's *The Huguenots* was one of the more successful productions of a classical opera. In 1941–5, the company worked in Chita and, later, collaborated with the Kiev Opera in Irkutsk. After 1945 the company's opera repertoire included M. Verykivsky's *The Servant Girl* and K. Dankevych's *Bohdan Khmelnytsky* and *Nazar Stodolia;* its ballet repertoire consisted of such productions as V. Nakhabin's *Danko, Tavriia, The Burgher from Tuscany,* and *Spring Tale,* and K. Dankevych's *The Lily.* In the 1970s the number of Ukrainian operas and ballets in the theater's repertoire was minimal: a new production of *Taras Bulba* (sets by A. Petrytsky) was directed by V. Skliarenko, and M. Skorulsky's ballet *The Forest Song* (1970, 1980) and V. Hubarenko's *The Stone Master* (1972, 1974) were performed. The opera's stage directors have included S. Karhalsky, D. Smolych, M. Foregger, M. Stefanovych, and V. Skliarenko. Among its stage designers have been A. Petrytsky, O. Khvostenko-Khvostov, D. Ovcharenko, and L. Bratchenko. A. Pazovsky, V. Tolba, Ye. Dyshchenko, I. Zak, and Ya. Skybynsky worked at the opera as conductors, and K. Holeizovsky, P. Virsky, M. Moiseiev, P. Yorkyn, V. Lytvynenko, and V. Shkilko as choreographers. Among its better-known opera soloists have been V. Budnevych, M. Hryshko, B. Hmyria, I. Patorzhynsky, Yu. Kyporenko-Domansky, M. Donets, I. Kuchenko, M. Mykysha, V. Huzhova, Y. Chervoniuk, and M. Lytvynenko-Volhemut. Its ballet soloists have included V. Dulenko, A. Yarygina, S. Kolyvanova, O. Sobol, and T. Popesku.

V. Revutsky

Kharkiv Theater of the Revolution (Kharkivskyi derzhavnyi teatr revoliutsii). An affiliate of the All-Ukrainian Association of Proletarian Writers, it was founded in 1931 to counteract the influence of *Berezil theater. The company consisted of actors from the Odessa Ukrainian Drama Theater of the Revolution, from other Kharkiv theaters, and from the Kiev Ukrainian Drama Theater. Its artistic director was M. Tereshchenko; its literary director, I. Mykytenko; its composers, M. Verykivsky and B. Yanovsky; its choreographer, P. Virsky; and its stage designers, A. Petrytsky and B. Kosariev. Its actors included Yu. Shumsky, V. Varetska, M. Dykova, P. Stoliarenko-Muratev, V. Sokyrko, V. Masliuchenko, and P. Mikhnevych. The repertoire consisted of such plays as I. Mykytenko's *Marusia Shurai, Solo na fleiti* (A Flute Solo), and *Divchata nashoï kraïny* (The Girls of Our Country), I. Kocherha's *Maistry chasu* (Masters of Time), and A. Afinogenov's *Strakh* (Fear). After the closing of *Berezil, the Kharkiv Theater of the Revolution was merged in 1937 with the Kharkiv Theater of Working Youth to form the Kharkiv Lenin Komsomol Theater. In 1940 the latter was transferred to Bukovyna and was renamed the Chernivtsi Oblast Ukrainian Music and Drama Theater.

V. Revutsky

Kharkiv Tractor Plant (Kharkivskyi traktornyi zavod im. S. Ordzhonikidze). The largest plant of its kind in Soviet Ukraine. Constructed in 1930–1, it produced wheel-drive (from 1931) and caterpillar (from 1937) tractors. During the Second World War the plant was dismantled and evacuated to Rubtsovsk in Siberia. It was rebuilt in Kharkiv from 1944 to 1949. Beginning in 1949 diesel caterpillar tractors, such as the DT-54, and small wheel-drive tractors (the KhTZ-7, DT-14, and DT-20) were built there. Today the plant's 50 departments produce mainly the fast-moving caterpillar tractors T-74 and T-150, the 3-ton wheel-drive T-150K, the small garden tractor T-25, en-

Kharkiv Tractor Plant

gines, and parts, which are used throughout the USSR and the Comecon countries.

Kharkiv Transport Machine-Building Plant (Kharkivskyi zavod transportnoho mashynobuduvannia im. V.O. Malysheva). One of the oldest and largest heavy-machine-building plants in Ukraine. It was founded in 1895 by the Russian Steam Locomotive and Machine Company. During the Second World War the plant was dismantled and evacuated to the Urals. It was rebuilt beginning in 1943. The plant produced steam locomotives, boilers, and agricultural machines from 1897, internal-combustion engines from 1913, and diesel engines from the 1920s. Since 1947 powerful locomotives – most recently the 2TE-40 Ukraina – have been built there. The plant also specializes in building diesel generators.

Kharkiv Turbine Plant (Kharkivskyi turbinnyi zavod im. S.M. Kirova). One of the largest power-generating-machinery plants in Ukraine. Completed in 1934, in 1941 it was dismantled and evacuated to the Urals. The plant was rebuilt in Kharkiv in 1944 and modernized several times. It produces steam, hydraulic, and gas turbines, mainly 100,000 to 1,000,000 kW steam turbines for thermal, hydro (since 1954), and nuclear (since 1975) power stations, which are used throughout the USSR and abroad.

Kharkiv Ukrainian Drama Theater (Kharkivskyi ukrainskyi dramatychnyi teatr im. T. Shevchenka). A national theater founded in 1935 out of remnants of the suppressed *Berezil theater as an explicit negation of the latter. The chief features of the new theater's policy were the adoption of socialist realism, a preference for Russian Soviet plays in its repertoire, an imitation of the Kiev Ukrainian Drama Theater, a predilection for O. *Korniichuk among Ukrainian playwrights, and the restriction of its Western European repertoire to 19th-century classics. By decree of the People's Commissariat of Education, M. Krushelnytsky was appointed director of the Berezil theater in October 1933 and retained this position in the new theater until 1952. He was succeeded by B. Nord (1952–7), a product of the Moscow Artistic Academic Theater, O. *Serdiuk (1957–62), and V. Krainychenko (1962–4). Thereafter, the theater gradually regressed to a repertoire of contemporary socialist-realist plays, populist-realist classics, and increasingly frequent guest performances staged by Russian directors of K. Stanislavsky's school. The theater's stage directors included H. Kononenko (1965–9), a postwar graduate of

Kharkiv Ukrainian Drama Theater

the Kharkiv Institute of Arts, V. Ohloblyn (1967–71), of the Moscow school, and later B. Meshkis (1971–4), A. Litko (1974–9), and O. Bieliatsky. Among the more memorable plays produced by the company after the war were V. Mynko's *Ne nazyvaiuchy prizvyshch* (Without Naming Names), H. Ibsen's *Ghosts*, W, Shakespeare's *Hamlet* (1956), O. Kolomiiet's *Planeta Speranta* (Planet Speranta, 1966), I. Kavaleridze's *Perekop*, M. Kulish's *Patetychna sonata* (The Sonata Pathétique, 1972), and W. Shakespeare's *Richard III* (1976). The theater's stage designers included V. Meller, V. Hrechenko, D. Vlasiuk, H. Batii, O. Kostiuchenko, V. Kravets, and T. Medvid. Besides the former Berezil actors (A. Buchma, D. Antonovych, I. Marianenko, L. Dubovyk, Ye. Bondarenko, N. Uzhvii, S. Fedortseva, and V. Chystiakova), the company included such actors as L. Krynytska, N. Herasymova, N. Lykho, R. Kolosova, S. Chybisova, L. Popova, O. Svystunova, L. Bykov, A. Litko, V. Shestopalov, V. Maliar, A. Dzvonarchuk, V. Ivchenko, and L. Tarabarynov.

V. Revutsky

Kharkiv University (Kharkivskyi derzhavnyi universytet im. A.M. Gorkoho). The first university in Russian-ruled Ukrainian territory. It was founded in 1805 on the initiative of V. *Karazyn, and with the financial support of the local nobility, burghers, and the municipal council. The university enjoyed a broad autonomy: its highest governing body was the Professorial Council, which elected the rector and all the professors. Count S. Potocki was appointed curator of the university, and the first rector was the philologist I. Rizhsky. During the first decade the faculty consisted mostly of foreign scholars, the majority of whom were German. The more noted ones were the philosopher J. Schad and the historian D. Rommel.

During the 19th century the university consisted of four faculties: physics-mathematics, history-philology, law, and medicine. A veterinary school, which was added to the medical faculty in 1839, became an independent institute in 1850. The university was provided with a surgical laboratory and clinic; art, astronomy, physics, technology, zoology, and mineralogy cabinets; a botanical garden; a library; and a printing press. The Philotechnical Society (est 1811) and the Kharkiv Learned

Society (est 1812) admitted not only university professors but also interested members of the public. The first periodicals in eastern Ukraine, including *Khar'kovskii ezhenedel'nik* (1812), *Ukrainskii vestnik* (1816–19), and *Ukrainskii zhurnal* (1824–5), were published by cultural circles closely connected with the university. In the 1830s a number of professors and students of Kharkiv University formed a literary group known as the *Kharkiv Romantic School. Until 1832 the university oversaw the whole educational system in Slobidska Ukraine. In the first 30 years of its existence Kharkiv University was an important cultural force in Ukraine. It introduced Western ideas and trends and recognized the cultural significance of Ukrainian folklore. Its cultural role declined as the university's autonomy was abolished.

In 1835 a new charter strengthened the power of the centralized bureaucracy. A government-approved curator and rector were put in charge of the university. By 1848 all publications and even lectures were subjected to censorship. Scholars were prohibited from traveling abroad. After the death of Nicholas I the restrictions were lifted gradually. The new charter of 1863 enlarged the powers of the Professorial Council and the rector. Funds for museums and libraries, and particularly for scientific research, were increased greatly. These changes inaugurated the university's golden age of scholarship. Its professors made some important contributions to various sciences. In the early 1860s the faculty numbered about 50 and the enrollment was 425. Several learned societies with a broad membership promoted research: the *Kharkiv Society of Naturalists (est 1869), the *Kharkiv Historical-Philological Society (est 1876), and the *Kharkiv Mathematics Society (est 1879). The university began to publish its *Zapiski* in 1874. During the period of reaction after the assassination of Alexander II, the university's autonomy was again severely restricted. In 1884 the Ministry of Education acquired control over appointments and even the curriculum. In spite of political interference, studies in Ukrainian history, literature, and language continued to expand. The Kharkiv Historical-Philological Society published a wealth of materials in these fields. Many professors of the university became active in the city's cultural institutions, such as the public library and the Literacy Society. Enrollment rose, reaching some 1,500 in 1887. Student *hromadas sprang up and became involved in political activities. The Revolution of 1905 led to an easing of government controls and a quickening of the development of national consciousness. On the initiative of M. Sumtsov, D. Bahalii, and A. Zaikevych, the Professorial Council issued a memorandum in 1905 recommending an end to the censorship of Ukrainian publications. Although the Ministry of Education rejected in 1906 the rector's proposal to set up a chair of Ukrainian history and a chair of Ukrainian literature and language, it permitted a course in the history of 'Little Russian' literature. The course was conducted in the following year by M. Sumtsov in Ukrainian, as were D. Bahalii's and M. Khalansky's courses in Ukrainian history and the history of the Ukrainian language. In 1905 the university conferred honorary doc-

Kharkiv University

torates on M. Hrushevsky and I. Franko, and in 1910 on O. Yefymenko. Enrollment grew rapidly from 1,486 in 1904 to 3,450 in 1907.

The building complex housing the university changed little during the 19th century. In the second half of the century, I. Kharytonenko financed the construction of a medical building and a student residence. During D. Bahalii's rectorship at the beginning of the 20th century, additional facilities were built.

Before 1917 the more notable professors of Kharkiv University were the philologists I. Sreznevsky, N. and P. Lavrovsky, O. Potebnia, and S. Kulbakin; the ethnographers A. Metlynsky and M. Sumtsov; the historians D. Bahalii and V. Buzeskul; the jurists and sociologists I. Tymkovsky, D. Kachenovsky, and M. Kovalevsky; the economist V. Levytsky; the statisticians A. Roslavsky-Petrovsky and P. Köppen; the mathematicians A. Liapunov and T. Osypovsky; the physicists M. Pylchykov and D. Rozhansky; the chemists N. Beketov, V. Tymofieiev, and O. Danylevsky; the botanists V. Palladin and A. Krasnov; and the geologists N. Borysiak and I. Levakovsky. Among the professors of medicine were M. Trinkler, V. Vorobiov, V. Krylov, and N. Melnikov-Razvedenkov.

During the revolutionary period of 1917–20 the predominantly Russian faculty recognized the linguistic and cultural rights of the Ukrainian people but resisted the idea of political independence. Control of the university changed several times before the Bolsheviks finally established their power in Kharkiv. In 1920 the university was reorganized into various institutes such as the Academy of Theoretical Sciences (in 1921 turned into the Kharkiv Institute of People's Education), the Kharkiv Medical Institute, and the Kharkiv Institute of the National Economy. In the early 1920s research in Ukrainian history, literature, and language developed vigorously, but in the late 1920s and early 1930s almost all the scholars in Ukrainian studies were arrested. P. Ritter perished in prison. Others were exiled, many of them never to return: S. Taranushenko, A. Kovalevsky, A. Shamrai, Yu. Savchenko, P. Petrenko, I. Kapustiansky, K. Nimchynov, B. Tkachenko, N. Mirza-Avakiants, M. Yohansen, I. Troian, O. Matviienko, M. Plevako, and O. Syniavsky. In 1933 the institutes were consolidated into one university with seven faculties: physics-mathematics, chemistry, biology, geology-geography, literature-linguistics, history (including the philosophy department), and economics (including the economic geography department). Eight research institutes were brought under the university and large funds were provided to stimulate research. In 1936 the university was named after the Russian writer M. Gorky although he had never been connected with it in any way. Its enrollment rose from 1,900 in 1933–4 to 2,900 in 1938–9, but few students specialized in Ukrainian studies. During the Second World War the university was evacuated to Kzyl-Orda in Kazakhstan.

A number of noted professors who worked at Kharkiv University before the Revolution stayed on its faculty under the Soviet regime. They were joined by some other prominent faculty members: the mathematicians S. Bernshtein, N. Akhiiezer, V. Marchenko, D. Syntsov, A. Sushkevych, and O. Pohorielov; the physicists O. Akhiiezer, A. Walter, Ye. Lifshyts, and A. Zhelykhivsky; the astronomer M. Barabashov; the physiologists O. Nahorny and V. Nikitin; the biochemist V. Zalesky; the geologist D. Soboliev; the economist O. Liberman; the classicist A. Kotsevalov; the literary scholar O. Biletsky; and the linguist L. Bulakhovsky. Some faculty members of Kharkiv University, such as A. Kotsevalov, O. Paradynsky, V. Derzhavyn, M. Hlobenko, and Yu. Shevelov, emigrated after 1943. After the war the biologist I. Bulankin was for a long term the non-elected rector.

Today Kharkiv University has 11 faculties: mechanics-mathematics, physics, physics-technology, radio-physics, chemistry, biology, geology-geography, economics, history, philology, and foreign languages. It also has a graduate school, evening school, and correspondence courses. There are 4 research institutes, dozens of laboratories, an astronomical observatory, a botanical garden, 4 museums, a central library, and 50 departmental libraries. The enrollment (1983–4) is 11,000 and the faculty numbers about 700. According to social origin (1968), 55 percent of the students came from white-collar, 30 percent from worker, and 15 percent from peasant families. Out of the 777 lecturers (1965), only 104 or 13 percent lectured in Ukrainian.

BIBLIOGRAPHY

Bagalei, D. *Opyt istorii Khar'kovskogo universiteta*, 2 vols (Kharkiv 1893, 1904)

Bagalei, D.; Sumtsov, N.; Buzeskul, V. *Kratkii ocherk istorii Khar'kovskogo universiteta za pervye sto let ego sushchestvovaniia* (Kharkiv 1905)

Khar'kovskii Gosudarstvennyi Universitet im. A. Gor'kogo za 150 let (Kharkiv 1955)

V. Markus

Kharkiv Women's Sunday School (Kharkivska zhinocha nedilna shkola). One of the first and most important institutions of adult education not only in Ukraine but in the Russian Empire. It was founded by Khrystyna *Alchevska in 1862 as a literacy school for women, mostly working-class women, and for many years it was the only school of its kind in the entire Russian Empire. Before its official opening in 1870, it operated illegally at the home of its founder. Instruction was free and the minimum age of admission was 10. By the 1890s the enrollment reached over 450. For four hours on Sundays the students were taught elementary-school subjects and read the works of Ukrainian writers, particularly of T. Shevchenko. With her teaching staff Alchevska worked out a methodology for adult education that stressed the use of literary works instead of primers, close student-teacher contact, discussion instead of rote learning, and student involvement in curriculum planning. Convinced that students should be taught in the language that they know best, Alchevska taught in Ukrainian until it was banned. The school's teachers compiled a bibliographic guide for adult students, *Chto chitat' narodu* (What the People Should Read, 3 vols, 1884–1906), and a teaching manual for instructors, *Kniga vzroslykh* (Book for Adults, 3 vols, 1899–1900). Funded by private donations, the school existed for over 50 years and served as a model for literacy schools throughout Ukraine and Russia.

M. Bohachevsky-Chomiak

Kharkiv Young Spectator's Theater (Kharkivskyi teatr yunoho hliadacha im. Leninskoho komsomolu). One of the first theaters for young spectators in Ukraine. It was founded in 1920 on the initiative of the Kharkiv Higher Theater School, and was reorganized several times – into the Fairy-Tale Theater, the First State Theater for Children, and the Gorky Young Spectator's Theater (1933–44) – before it was transferred to Lviv. It was only in 1960 that a new theater for young spectators was formed in Kharkiv out of the oblast music and drama theater. At first its plays were produced only in Russian, but since 1925 they have been produced in both Ukrainian and Russian. From a teaching and demonstrating theater it evolved, eventually, into a professional theater. Besides Ukrainian, Russian, and world classics, its repertoire includes contemporary Soviet plays, often on political themes. Among its directors have been V. Skliarenko, M. Verkhatsky, V. Vilner, and L. Klishcheiev, and its stage sets have been designed by B. Kosariev. Its repertoire consists of such plays as M. Kropyvnytsky's *Doky sontse ziide, rosa ochi vyist'* (By the Time the Sun Rises, the Dew Will Burn out the Eyes), V. Sukhodolsky's *Iunist' Tarasa* (Taras's Youth), N. Gogol's *Zhenit'ba* (The Marriage), J. Molière's *Les Fourberies de Scapin*, and F. Schiller's *Kabale und Liebe*.

V. Revutsky

Kharkiv Zootechnical-Veterinary Institute (Kharkivskyi zooveterynarnyi instytut im. M. Borysenka). A post-secondary institution under the jurisdiction of the Ministry of Agriculture of the USSR, located in the town of Mala Danylivka north of Kharkiv. It was established in 1960 by merging the Kharkiv Veterinary (est 1851) and Zootechnical (est 1922) institutes. The institute has faculties of zootechnics; veterinary medicine; preparation by correspondence; foreign students; and the upgrading of veterinarians, collective and state farm directors, and agricultural lecturers. It has 23 chairs, a graduate program, 2 research farms, and a library with over 385,000 volumes. In 1983 the institute had over 2,000 full-time and 1,700 correspondence students. It publishes collections of scientific articles.

Kharkiv-Kiev Secret Society (Kharkivsko-kyivske taiemne tovarystvo). Secret conspiratorial political organization founded by students at Kharkiv University in 1856. It represented a fusion of two Kharkiv groups that had formed independently; the originators of the first group were Ya. Bekman, M. Muravsky, P. Yefymenko, and P. Zavadsky, and the second group was composed of wealthy noble students as represented by N. Raevsky. The society's objectives were the overthrow of tsarist autocracy, emancipation of the peasants, and the establishment of a republican government in the Russian Empire. The society distributed banned works, anti-tsarist leaflets, and manuscript journals, among them *Svobodnoe slovo* (The Free Word, Kharkiv) and *Glasnost'* (Suffrage, Kiev). Its members established *Sunday schools among the workers and artisans and maintained contacts with other underground circles. In April 1858 the society instigated student protests in Kharkiv, resulting in the expulsion of the majority of its members. They subsequently moved to Kiev, where they founded a similar group and continued their activities. In late 1859 the society had more than 100 members. In January–February 1860, 22 of its members were arrested and exiled. Later that year the society ceased to exist. Several of the society's members joined the revolutionary organization *Zemlia i Volia.

Khar'kov (Kharkiv). A daily newspaper devoted to literature and politics that was published in Kharkiv from 1877 to 1880. It followed closely the activities of the local zemstvo. Its contributors included O. Bodiansky, D. Kachenovsky, and M. Sumtsov.

Khar'kovskie izvestiia (Kharkiv News). A weekly newspaper published in Kharkiv from 1817 to 1823. Published and edited at first by A. Verbytsky, in 1819 it was placed under the jurisdiction of the Council of Kharkiv University. P. Hulak-Artemovsky, E. Filomafitsky, A. Sklabovsky, and O. Kunytsky served as editors appointed by the council. The newspaper printed news about the theater, reviews of new publications, statistical reports, and sketches of everyday life in Kharkiv. It published the poems of H. Kvitka-Osnovianenko in Ukrainian.

Khar'kovskii demokrit (Kharkiv Democrat). The first satirical magazine in Ukraine. It was published monthly in Kharkiv in 1816 by V. Maslovych, who was also its editor. Its contributors included I. Sreznevsky, O. Somov, A. Sklabovsky, R. Honorsky, F. Zelensky, and D. Yaroslavsky. H. *Kvitka-Osnovianenko made his debut as a poet and satirical feuilletonist in the magazine. It published some of the first Ukrainian-language works to appear in the periodical press. The butt of its criticism was the social conditions in the Russian Empire. Altogether, six issues appeared.

Kostiantyn Kharlampovych

Kharlampovych, Kostiantyn [Xarlampovyč], b 30 July 1870 in Rohachi, Berestia county, Hrodna gubernia, d 23 March 1932. Historian; corresponding member of the Imperial Academy of Sciences from 1916 and full member of the VUAN from 1920. A graduate of the St Petersburg Theological Academy (1894), he was a privatdocent (from 1899) and then professor (1909–21) at Kazan University. Kharlampovych was a specialist in church history and culture and education in the 16th to 18th centuries. Although he was forced to live in Moscow in the 1920s, he actively participated in the work of the VUAN, contributing numerous articles to the journal *Ukraïna*, and was a member of the VUAN Archeographic Commission. His monographs and major studies include *Zapadnorusskie pravoslavnye shkoly XVI i nachala XVII veka* (Western Ruthenian Orthodox Schools in the 16th and Early 17th Centuries, 1898), 'Zapadnorusskie tserkovnye bratstva i ikh prosvetitel'naia deiatel'nost' v kontse XVI i nachale XVII v' (Western Ruthenian Church Brotherhoods and Their Educational Activities in the Late 16th and 17th Centuries, *Khristiianskoe chtenie*, 1899), *Malorossiiskoe vliianie na velikorusskuiu tserkovnuiu zhizn'* (Little Russian Influence on Great Russian Church Life, 1914), 'Narysy z istoriï hrets'koï koloniï XVII–XVIII st. v Nizhyni' (Sketches from the History of the Greek Colony of the 17th–18th Centuries in Nizhen, *Zapysky Istorychno-filolohichnoho viddilu VUAN*, 24 [1929]). Kharlampovych also contributed articles to such journals as *Kievskaia Starina* and *Volynskie Eparkhial'nye vedomosti*. In 1929 he was expelled from the VUAN for political reasons, and to this day he is rarely mentioned in official Soviet histories of the academy. He is the subject of a biography by K. Bidnov (Warsaw 1933).

A. Zhukovsky

Khartsiiev, Vasyl [Xarcijev, Vasyl'], b 12 January 1866 in Katerynoslav (now Dnipropetrovske), d 29 November 1937 in Kharkiv. Linguist and literary theorist. A graduate of Kharkiv University (1890), he taught at gymnasiums in Kharkiv, Katerynoslav, and Yelysavethrad (later Kirovohrad), and from 1929 at the Yelysavethrad Pedagogical Institute. He wrote articles in linguistics, literary theory, and language teaching methods. A student of O. *Potebnia, his main achievement was to publish Potebnia's uncompleted, unpublished manuscripts, particularly the third volume of *Iz zapisok po russkoi grammatike* (From Notes on Russian Grammar, 1899), and to popularize his ideas.

Khartsyzke [Xartyz'ke]. V-19, DB III-4. City (1986 pop 68,000) under oblast jurisdiction in Donetske oblast. Established as a railroad station and coal-mining settlement in 1869, it has grown substantially since the Second World War. In 1897 its population was 674; in 1912, 1,500; in 1923, 3,000; in 1931, 8,300; in 1963, 38,000. From 1923 to 1962 it was a raion center. Its several plants produce large-diameter steel pipes, steel wire and cables, machinery, armatures, metal products, and food concentrates.

Kharytonenko, Ivan [Xarytonenko], b 1820 in Nyzhnia Syrovatka, Sumy county, Kharkiv gubernia, d 12 December 1891. Landowner, industrialist, philanthropist. He owned five sugar-beet refineries in Kharkiv gubernia and was one of the wealthiest sugar factory owners in Ukraine. From 1890 he was a leading member of the Kiev Refined-Sugar Syndicate. Kharytonenko funded a childrens' home, a student residence at Kharkiv University, and a church in Nyzhnia Syrovatka.

Khasevych, Nil [Xasevyč] (noms de guerre: D. Bei, Bei-Zot), b 1905 in Diuksyn, Rivne country, Volhynia gubernia, d 1952. Graphic artist. As a student of the Warsaw Academy of Arts (1925–37), he belonged to the Ukrainian art circle Spokii. Specializing in bookplates produced by the woodcut technique, he participated in many exhibitions, particularly in the Berlin and Prague exhibitions of Ukrainian graphic art and in the International Exhibition of Woodcuts in Warsaw (1936–7). Joining the UPA in 1943, he worked as an underground artist designing and illustrating its publications. Two albums of his work have been published: *Ekslibrys Nila Khasevycha* (Bookplates by Nil Khasevych, 1939) and *Hrafika v bunkrakh UPA* (Graphic Art in the Bunkers of the UPA, 1952). He was killed by Soviet counterinsurgency forces.

Nil Khasevych: *Sleeping Boy* (woodcut)

Khata (Home). A literary almanac edited and published by P. *Kulish in St Petersburg in 1860 in two printings. The almanac contained a selection of T. Shevchenko's poetry, published under the heading 'Kobzars'kyi hostynets'' (The Kobzar's Gift), fables by Ye. Hrebinka, and poems by Ya. Shchoholev and P. Kuzmenko. Furthermore, it published O. Psol's poems (unsigned) dedicated to the persecuted members of the *Cyril and Methodius Brotherhood, and particularly to T. Shevchenko. A play by P. Kulish, *Kolii* (Kolii Rebels), and a number of short stories were included: M. Vovchok's 'Chary' (Charms), P. Kulish's 'Sira kobyla' (The Gray Mare), H. Barvinok's 'Lykho ne bez dobra' (Evil Is Not without Good), 'Voseny lito' (Summer in Autumn), and 'Try sl'ozy divochi' (A Girls' Three Tears), and M. Nomys's 'Did Myna i baba Mynykha' (Grandpa Myna and Grandma Mynykha).

Khata (Home). The first Ukrainian magazine in Canada. It was an illustrated monthly devoted to literature, politics, and current issues. Published in Winnipeg in 1911–12, it folded after the sixth issue. Its editor was J. *Krett, and contributors included the best Ukrainian writers in Canada at the time: P. Krat-Ternenko, O. Zherebko, O. Boian, P. Kazan, and V. Kudryk. The magazine also published established writers in Ukraine such as H. Khotkevych, B. Hrinchenko, and O. Kovalenko. Translations of J. London were very popular. Articles on education, co-operatives, and political questions, as well as materials on the history of Ukrainians in Canada, were an important part of its contents.

Khataevich, Mendel [Xatajevič, Mendel'], b 22 March 1893 in Homel, Belorussia, d 1 February 1939. Bolshevik leader and Soviet official. Joining the Russian Social Democratic Workers' party (Bolshevik) in 1913, he worked on provincial Party committees in Belorussia and Samara gubernia during the 1917 Revolution. In 1923–4 he was secretary of the Odessa Gubernia Committee of the CP(B)U and then held Party posts outside Ukraine. In October 1932 he became secretary of the CC CP(B)U, and in January

1933 secretary of the Dnipropetrovske Oblast Party Committee as well. In 1937 he was second secretary of the CP(B)U. An influential Party official, he carried out J. Stalin's orders in collectivizing Ukrainian farming and organizing the man-made *famine of 1932–3. Arrested in 1937, he died in prison; he was later rehabilitated by N. Khrushchev.

Khaustov, Pavlo [Xaustov], b 14 November 1882 in Sharinovske, Tomsk gubernia, d 26 September 1949 in Kiev. Architect. A graduate of the Moscow (1915) and Kiev (1933) civil-engineering institutes, he oversaw the drafting of the development plans for the Zaporizhia metropolitan area, Kiev, Yasynuvata, Voroshylovhrad, and Bila Tserkva. His publications deal with urban planning and include articles on the planning of Zaporizhia and Kiev.

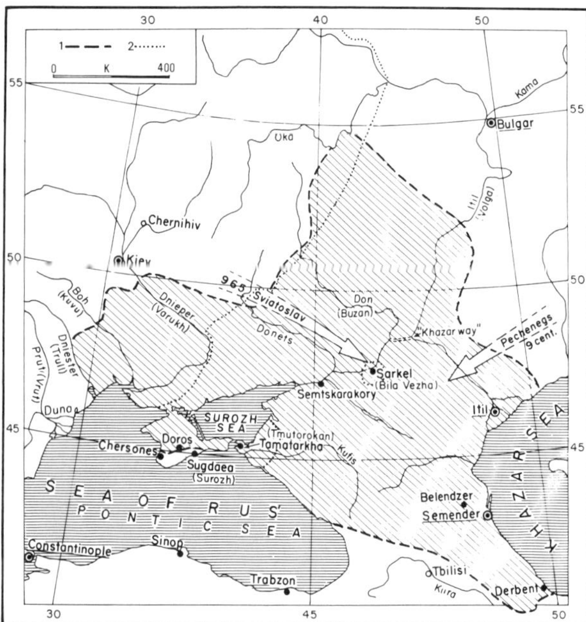

KHAZAR KAGANATE

1. Borders in the 8th century
2. The eastern limits of Kievan Rus' and its colonies in the 10th century

Khazars (Ukrainian: *khozary*). Seminomadic, Turkic-speaking people that appeared in southeastern Europe after the expulsion of the *Huns in the 4th century and lived in the area until the 11th century. They were the eastern neighbors of the eastern Slavic tribes and then of Kievan Rus'. There are various hypotheses on the origin of the Khazars; they considered themselves close to the Bulgars, Oghuz, and Avars. The territory first settled by them encompassed the Caspian steppes between the Sulak River and the lower Don River. At first the Khazars were nomads and herders, but eventually some of them turned to farming and especially trade.

From the second half of the 6th century the Khazars were ruled by the western Turkic kaganate. After the dissolution of the kaganate in the middle of the 7th century, the Khazars conquered some of the Bulgar and other Caucasian (eg, *Alans) and Slavic tribes, and established the Khazar kaganate, the first state in eastern Europe. The supreme sovereign was the kagan, the high priest, but the actual ruler was the vicegerent or assistant kagan. The kaganate's first capital was Semender (Samandar) in northern Daghestan. In the mid-8th century, under pressure from the Arabs to the south, the capital was transferred to *Itil on the Volga River, near present-day Astrakhan. Itil became an important trade center between East and West. In 835 the fortified city of Sarkil was built on the Don River with the help of Byzantine craftsmen. Among its inhabitants were many Rus', Greek, Iranian, and central-Asian merchants.

The Khazar kaganate reached its zenith in the late 8th century when it gained control over northern Caucasia, the Azov steppe, and most of eastern Europe up to the Dnieper River. The proto-Ukrainian Siverianians and Polianians paid tribute to the Khazars. The kaganate dominated the trade routes between the Far East and Byzantium and between the Arabic Empire and the Slavic territories and Scandinavia to the north. Until the mid-10th century, Khazar trade with these centers was interrupted only by intermittent wars between these same powers.

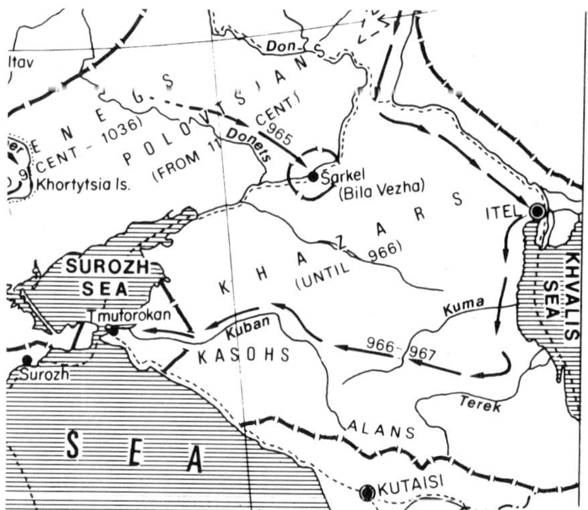

Khazars; arrow shows campaign of Prince Sviatoslav I.

At the beginning of the 8th century, Jews from Iran and Byzantium settled among the Khazars in northern Daghestan. Although some Khazars soon converted to Judaism, it was only at the beginning of the 9th century that Kagan Obadiah proclaimed non-Talmudic Judaism the state religion. Prior to that (ca 735), Arabs had invaded the kaganate and forced some members of the ruling class to adopt Islam. Meanwhile, Byzantium tried to convert the Khazars to Christianity: in 860–1 St Cyril conducted a mission among them and a metropoly with seven eparchies was organized. The Khazars even played a role in spreading Christianity in Rus' before its official conversion under Volodymyr the Great. All of these faiths coexisted peacefully on Khazar territory.

In the late 9th century the Black Sea steppes (southern Ukraine) that were under Khazar control were invaded by the *Pechenegs, whose incessant raids on the kaganate considerably weakened the Khazar state. From the late 9th century Kievan Rus' also emerged as a major opponent. According to the chronicles, Askold and Dyr's Varangian troops liberated Kiev from the Khazars in 862, and in 883–5 Prince Oleh freed the Polianians and Siverianians from Khazar rule. Prince Ihor's army twice (913–14 and 943–4) marched through Khazarian territory to the Caspian Sea and brought back rich booty. In his 941 campaign against Byzantium, however, Ihor received support from the kaganate and there were Christian Khazars among his warriors.

In 964–5 Prince Sviatoslav I Ihorevych inflicted the final blow to the Khazar state: he destroyed Itil and Semender, and annexed Sarkil and the northwestern part of Khazar territory to Rus' (see *Tmutorokan principality). This action proved to be detrimental to Rus', which became vulnerable to constant nomadic invasions from the east. In 985 Volodymyr the Great defeated the Bulgars and Khazars and forced them to pay tribute. The Khazars are last mentioned in the chronicles under the year 1079 when they conspired to seize Prince Oleh Sviatoslavych in Tmutorokan and hand him over to the Byzantine emperor. After the fall of the kaganate, the Khazars gradually intermixed with the Turkic and *Cuman populations and eventually disappeared as a distinct people.

BIBLIOGRAPHY
Rybakov, B. 'K voprosu o roli Khazarskogo kaganatu v istorii Rusi,' *Sovetskaia arkheologiia*, 18 (1953)
Dunlop, D. *The History of the Jewish Khazars* (New York 1954)
Artamonov, M. *Istoriia khazar* (Leningrad 1962)
Pletneva, S. *Khazary* (Moscow 1976)
Pritsak, O. 'The Khazar Kingdom's Conversion to Judaism,' HUS, 2 (1978), no. 3

A. Zhukovsky

Kherson [Xerson]. VII-13. Oblast capital (1985 pop 346,000), a large sea and river port and railway terminus.

Kherson in the late 18th century; painting by F. Alekseev

Kherson: shipyard

The town, with a fortress, admiralty, and shipyard, was founded in 1778 on the site of the Russian fortress Aleksandr-shants (1737–9) and was named after the ancient city of *Chersonese Taurica. Its construction was completed rapidly using thousands of conscripted sailors, laborers, soldiers, prisoners, and serfs. In 1783 the first warship of the Russian Black Sea fleet was launched there. In 1784 Kherson became a county town and in 1803 a gubernia capital. Shipbuilding, commerce, and shipping (particularly the export of grain and lumber to western Europe) were the cornerstones of its economy. With the deepening of the Dnieper Estuary waterway at the turn of the 20th century, Kherson's role as an export port increased. A railway link was established in 1907. The city's manufacturing sector (food and wool processing, machine building, and pig-iron founding) remained secondary. Its population grew from 2,000 in 1799 to 23,650 in 1846, 43,900 in 1859, 59,100 in 1897, and 81,000 in 1913.

In the second half of the 19th century, Kherson became a cultural center with a teacher's seminary and public library (1872), an archeological museum (est 1890 by V. Hoshkevych), a gubernia scholarly archival commission

Kherson: grain elevators

(1898), a people's home and a branch of the imperial music society (1905), and the daily *Iug* (est 1897, ed V. Hoshkevych). The writers Dniprova Chaika, M. Cherniavsky, and I. Karpenko-Kary lived and worked in the city.

During 1917–20, Kherson was occupied by various forces: Ukrainian, Bolshevik, French, White, and Polish. As a consequence of several years of war and destruction, its population fell (74,500 in 1920). It decreased radically to 41,300 in 1923, probably as a result of the 1921 *famine, but then rose steadily, reaching 58,800 in 1926 and 97,200 in 1939. The city was an okruha capital from 1923 to 1932. It suffered devastation and great population loss during the Second World War. In 1944 it became an oblast capital. After the war the city and its economy were rebuilt and expanded. Its population grew to 158,000 in 1959 and 261,000 in 1970. Its ethnic composition has changed, particularly since the war. In 1897, 1926, and 1959, the percentage of Ukrainians was, respectively, 19.6, 36, and 63; of Russians, 47.2, 36, and 29; of Jews, 29.1, 26, and 6.

Kherson is an important industrial center. Of its 56 large enterprises, the most important are the Petrovsky Combine Plant, the Comintern Shipbuilding and Repairs Complex, the Kuibyshev Ship Repair Complex, and the Kherson Cotton Manufacturing Complex (one of the largest textile plants in the USSR). Kherson's port facilities handle a large volume of exports and imports from many countries around the world.

Kherson is also a scientific and cultural center. Located there are 4 institutes; 15 post-secondary vocational and technical schools; an oblast library, philharmonic, and theater; a regional-history and an art museum; the oblast newspaper *Naddniprians'ka pravda*; and the Ukrainian Scientific Research Institute of Irrigation Farming. Among its 316 cultural and historical monuments are the remnants of the fortress walls and gates (dismantled in 1835), the Black Sea Hospital (designed by A. Zakharov and built in 1803–10), the naval arsenal (18th century), and the Cathedral of the Transfiguration (1781).

BIBLIOGRAPHY
Babashov, Iu. *Kherson* (Kiev 1964)
Kherson za 50 rokiv radians'koï vlady, 1917–1967 (Odessa 1966)
Sergeeva, G.; Arkhipov, E. *Kherson* (Kiev 1968)
Kherson. Putevoditel' (Symferopil 1977)
Khersonu 200 let. 1778–1978: Sbornik dokumentov i materialov (Kiev 1978)
Mel'nikov, A.; et al (eds). *Istoriia gorodov i sel Ukrainskoi SSR: Khersonskaia oblast'* (Kiev 1983)

V. Kubijovyč

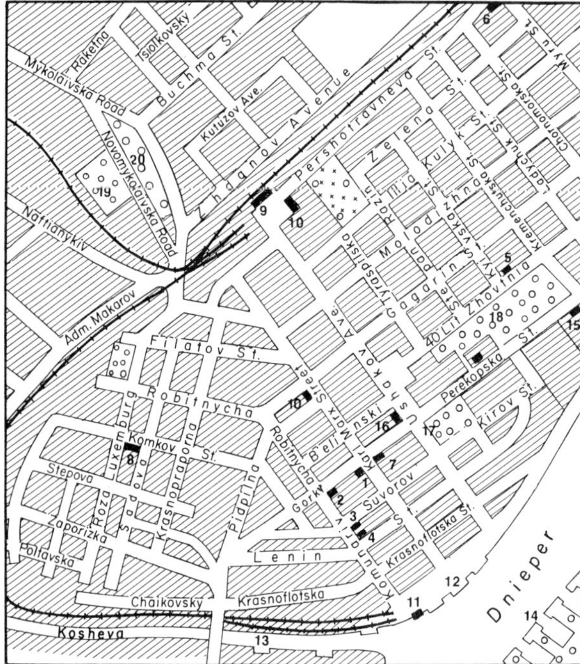

KHERSON

1. Oblast Ukrainian Music and Drama Theater
2. Oblast Philharmonic
3. Planetarium
4. Art Museum
5. Pedagogical Institute
6. Industrial Institute
7. Branch of the Mykolaiv Shipbuilding Institute
8. Agricultural Institute
9. Railway station
10. Bus stations
11. Dnieper Sea and River station
12. Commercial port
13. Naval port and shipyards
14. Wharfs
15. Former residence of the poet M. Cherniavsky
16. Building in which the first state telegraph station in Ukraine was installed in 1902
17. Site of the former fortress
18. Komsomol Park
19. Botanical garden
20. Park of the 50th Anniversary of the October Revolution

Kherson Cotton Textile Manufacturing Complex

Kherson Cotton Textile Manufacturing Complex (Khersonskyi bavovnianyi kombinat). One of the largest textile plants of the USSR. Construction of the complex began in 1952. The first section went into operation in 1961; the second in 1964. The complex consists of three spinning and weaving factories and a finishing mill. Utilizing cotton and synthetic rayon staple fiber as raw materials, it produces various types of fabrics for upholstery and articles of clothing, pile fabrics, and terry-cloth goods. The complex produces 388,000 t of yarn and 194,300,000 running m of fabric per year (1976). The value of its total annual production is 387,000,000 rubles. Many countries import its fabrics.

Kherson eparchy. An Orthodox eparchy, founded in 1837, with its see in Odessa (hence it is officially called Kherson and Odessa eparchy). Before the Revolution of 1917, the territory of Kherson eparchy corresponded to Kherson gubernia; until 1859 it also included Tavriia gubernia and was known as Kherson and Tavriia eparchy. Now it comprises the Odessa, Mykolaiv, and Kherson oblasts (Voroshylovhrad eparchy, which includes Voroshylovhrad and Donetske oblasts, is temporarily under its jurisdiction). Before the Revolution there were two mens' and three womens' monasteries and 815 priests (1913). An eparchial newsletter, *Khersonkie Eparkhial'nye Vedomosti*, was published semimonthly from 1860. Now, there is only one monastery for men and one for women. Since 1945, the only theological seminary in the Ukrainian SSR has been located in Odessa.

Kherson gubernia. An administrative-territorial unit in Russian-ruled Southern Ukraine between the Dnieper and Dniester rivers. One of the three new gubernias created after *New Russia gubernia was abolished in 1802, it was called Mykolaiv gubernia until 1803, when Kherson became the new capital. From 1809 the gubernia had five counties: Kherson, Oleksandriia, Olviopil, Tyraspil, and Yelysavethrad. Odessa county was added in 1825. A seventh county – Bobrynets – existed from 1828 to 1865. Ananiv replaced Olviopil as a county center in 1834. The cities of Odessa and Mykolaiv (in 1803–61) and their vicinity were governed separately: Odessa by a *gradonachalnik* answerable directly to the tsar and (from 1822) the governor-general of New Russia and Bessarabia, and Mykolaiv by a military governor. A third of the population (military settlers, admiralty settlements, foreign colonists) was subject to martial law until 1858.

The gubernia had a population of about 245,000 in 1812, 893,000 in 1851, 1,330,000 in 1863, 2,027,000 in 1885, 2,733,600 in 1897, and 3,744,600 in 1914. In the 1850s it consisted of Ukrainians (68–75 percent), Rumanians (8–11 percent), Russians (3–7 percent), Jews (6 percent), Germans (4 percent), Bulgarians (2 percent), Serbs, Greeks, and Gypsies. In 1914 Ukrainians composed only 53 percent of the population, while Russians made up 22 percent and Jews 12 percent. Urban dwellers made up 10–20 percent of the population until the 1850s; in 1897 they composed almost 30 percent. In-migration accounted for much of the population growth; eg, in 1897, 46 percent of the population was born outside of the gubernia. The gubernia's, economy was predominantly agricultural. Thousands of agricultural laborers from the other Ukrainian gubernias found work there during the grain harvest. Industry, consisting primarily of flour milling, distilling, metalworking, iron mining, beet-sugar processing, and brick making, was underdeveloped.

Under Soviet rule, in 1920 the gubernia's territory (70,600 sq km) was divided to form the new Odessa gubernia. Kherson gubernia was renamed Mykolaiv gubernia in 1921 and amalgamated with Odessa gubernia in 1922. In 1925 Odessa gubernia was abolished, and its territory was divided into six okruhas: Kherson, Kryvyi Rih, Mykolaiv, Odessa, Pershomaiske, and Zinoviivske. In 1932 much of this territory was incorporated into the new Odessa oblast, which was divided to form Mykolaiv oblast in 1937. The latter was divided in 1944 to form the new Kherson oblast.

I. Myhul, R. Senkus

Kherson oblast. An administrative region (1986 pop 1,220,000) in southern Ukraine, formed on 30 March 1944. It covers an area of 28,500 sq km, divided among 18 raions, 237 rural soviets, 9 cities, and 30 towns (smt). The capital is *Kherson.

Physical geography. The oblast is located in the steppe of the Black Sea Lowland on both banks of the Dnieper River directly north of the Black Sea and the Sea of Azov. The land is flat and dissected by ravines and small depressions. Its jagged coastline is dotted with shallow saltwater lakes, limans, bays, spits, and sandy islands. In its northern part the soils are mostly low-humus chernozems; in the south they are mostly of the dark-chestnut alkaline variety. Virgin steppe flora and fauna are preserved at the *Askaniia-Nova and *Black Sea nature reserves and five other conservation sites. Limestone, marl, kaolin, and sand deposits abound. Salt and curative muds are extracted from Lake Syvash and the coastal lakes. The principal rivers in the oblast are the Dnieper and its tributary the Inhulets; they supply the Kakhivka, Krasnoznamianka, and Inhulets irrigation systems . The Kakhivka Reservoir and Hydroelectric Station are located on the Dnieper. The climate is temperate-continental, with an average temperature of −4°C in January and 22.5°C in July. The average annual precipitation is 300 mm in the south and 420 mm in the north. Winters are mild, with little snowfall; summers are hot and dry, with dust storms and droughts.

History. In ancient times the oblast's territory was populated by Scythians and Sarmatians. Later it was nominally ruled by Kievan Rus' and Lithuania. In the 15th century it came under Crimean Tatar rule. After the Russo-Turkish War of 1768–74, it was annexed by Russia and colonized (see *Southern Ukraine) as part of New Russia gubernia (1774–83, 1797–1803) and Katerynoslav vicegerency (1783–96). In 1803 it was divided between *Kherson gubernia (1803–1921) on the Dnieper's right bank and *Tavriia gubernia (1802–1918) on the left bank. Under Soviet rule it became part of Mykolaiv gubernia in 1921, Odessa gubernia in 1922, Kherson and Melitopil okruhas in 1925, Odessa oblast in 1932, and Mykolaiv oblast in 1937.

Population. The population of the oblast increased by 46 percent between 1959 and 1984. Urbanization has been primarily a postwar phenomenon, rising from about 15 percent of the population in the early 1930s to 51 percent in 1965 and 61 percent in 1986. The average population density in 1986 was, at 42.8 inhabitants per sq km, still the lowest in Ukraine. The percentage of Ukrainians has dropped from 81.1 in 1965 to 76.7 in 1979, while that of Russians has risen from 15.6 to 19.5. The oblast's largest cities are Kherson and Nova Kakhivka.

Industry. The oblast's main industries are machine building and metalworking (30.6 percent of all output), light industry (23.1 percent), food production (20.7 percent), and fuel production (10.5 percent). In Kherson, large cargo ships, tankers, and other seacraft are built and repaired, and agricultural machines (combines, tractors), irrigation equipment, electric measuring devices, and electric equipment are made. Industrial engines and generators are made in Nova Kakhivka; electric-welding equipment, in Kakhivka. The food industry consists of canning (Kherson, Skadovske), flour milling (Kherson, Kakhivka, Henicheske, Tsiurupynske, Skadovske, Beryslav), meat packing (Kherson, Novotroitske, Nova

Kakhivka), wine making (Kherson, Nova Kakhivka, Beryslav, Henicheske, Tsiurupynske), sea fishing, and the making of dairy products, vegetable oil, and feed. Petroleum is refined in Kherson. Cellulose for paper is processed in Tsiurupynske. The Kherson Fiberglass-Container Plant is the largest of its kind in the USSR. In light industry, textile production predominates (see *Kherson Cotton Textile Manufacturing Complex); shoes and clothing are made in Kherson, Henicheske, and Tsiurupynske. Reinforced concrete, asphalt, bricks, and other building materials are made in Kherson, Nova Kakhivka, and Kakhivka; lime, in Bila Krynytsia and Arkhanhelske. Energy is provided by the Kakhivka Hydroelectric Station, the Kherson Thermoelectric Central Station, and several regional thermal stations using imported coal, oil, and gas.

Kherson oblast: land irrigation

Agriculture. In 1983 there were 147 collective farms and 145 state farms. They had at their disposal 2,190,000 ha of land; 1,964,000 ha were used directly for agriculture: of this 88.8 percent was cultivated, 7.9 percent was pasture, and 0.7 percent was hayfield. Irrigated land constituted 397,100 ha (70,000 ha in 1963). The main crops were winter wheat (53 percent of the land sown with grains), sunflowers (62.5 percent of the land sown with industrial crops), corn, barley, legumes, rice, millet, castor beans, alfalfa, tomatoes, peppers, eggplants, squash, and melons. (Of the total cultivated area in 1976, grain crops took up 48 percent; fodder crops, 39.2 percent; industrial crops, 8.1 percent; and garden vegetables, melons, and potatoes, 4.4 percent.) Vineyards took up 26,700 ha, and fruit orchards (apricots, peaches, cherries, quinces, plums, apples, pears), 15,600 ha. Animal husbandry (56.4 percent of the total value of agricultural output) consists primarily of dairy and beef cattle farming, but also of pig, sheep, poultry, fish, and silkworm farming.

Transportation. In 1983 there were 456 km of railroads. Trunk lines crossing the oblast include the Kherson–Dnipropetrovske, Kherson–Symferopil, and Kherson–Mykolaiv lines. Kherson and Kakhivka are the main junctions. There are 5,300 km of roads, of which 4,500 are paved. The main highways crossing the oblast are Moscow–Symferopil and Rostov–Odessa-Reni. Kherson has an airport. Kherson, Skadovske, and Henicheske are important seaports; ships sailing up the Dnieper stop at the river ports of Kherson, Nova Kakhivka, Beryslav, and Velyka Lepetykha.

BIBLIOGRAPHY

Istoriia mist i sil Ukraïns'koï RSR: Khersons'ka oblast' (Kiev 1973; Russian edn 1983)

I. Myhul, R. Senkus

Kherson Regional Museum (Khersonskyi kraieznavchyi muzei). A museum organized in 1963 after the merger of the Kherson Historico-Archeological Museum with the Kherson Natural Historical Museum. The first museum had contained the collections of two earlier museums, a local archeological museum founded by V. Hoshkevych in 1890 and a historical museum organized by J. Paczoski in 1899. Now the museum has three sections, with over 100,000 exponents (1984), covering the region's natural history, prerevolutionary history, and history under Soviet rule. It is especially rich in archeological artifacts uncovered near the village of Berezna and in the excavations of the ancient Greek colony of Olbia. The Kherson Regional Museum has branches in Kakhivka, Henicheske, Beryslav, and Tsiurupynske.

Khersones Historical-Archeological Museum (Khersoneskyi istoryko-arkheolohichnyi muzei-zapovidnyk u Sevastopoli). Called originally a 'depository of local antiquities,' the museum was established in 1892 at a former monastery to house the archeological artifacts discovered during the excavation of the old Greek city of *Chersonese Taurica. The museum contains about 200,000 items from the 5th century BC to the 15th century AD and displays about 5,000 of these as well as an epigraphic and numismatic collection, multicolored ceiling paintings (4th–3rd century BC), mosaics, ceramics, and remnants of the city's architectural features. The museum publishes research news in *Khersonesskii sbornik* (1926–59) and *Soobshcheniia Khersonesskogo muzeia*.

Khinkulov, Leonid [Xinkulov], b 1 January 1912 in Kiev. Literary scholar and critic of the Stalinist generation specializing in Ukrainian-Russian literary relations. He is the author of more than a dozen books in Russian and Ukrainian, including two on M. Gorky and Ukraine (1961, 1963), four on T. Shevchenko (1957, 1960, 1962, 1963), and one on famous writers who visited Kiev (1982).

Khira, Oleksander [Xira], b 17 January 1897 in Vilkhivtsi, Transcarpathia, d 26 May 1983 in Karaganda, Kazakhstan. Ukrainian Catholic bishop. A graduate of the Central Seminary in Budapest (1920), from 1924 to 1947 he taught canon law, church history, and moral and pastoral theology at the Mukachiv Theological Seminary. In 1934 he was appointed rector of the seminary, but he was dismissed in 1939 by the Hungarian authorities for his pro-Ukrainian activities. He was secretly consecrated bishop in 1945 by T. Romzha, whom he succeeded as bishop of Mukachiv eparchy in 1947. In 1949 he was arrested by the Soviet authorities and imprisoned in labor camps in Central Asia. He was released in 1956 and returned to Vilkhivtsi, but in 1957 he was forbidden to live in Ukraine and exiled to Kazakhstan. There he ministered to Germans, Lithuanians, Poles, and, unofficially, Ukrainians. In 1978 the local Soviet authorities

Oleksander Khira

registered his parish and gave him permission to build a church in Karaganda.

Khliborob (Farmer). A popular semimonthly (later monthly) published in Lviv and Kolomyia from April 1891 to September 1895 by the *Ukrainian Radical party. Its editors were I. Franko, M. Pavlyk, and S. Danylovych. The paper discussed sociopolitical and economic issues affecting the rural population. It published articles by M. Drahomanov, I. Herasymovych, V. Stefanyk, and L. Martovych, as well as literary works by I. Franko, L. Martovych, and V. Korolenko.

Khliborob (Farmer). A popular semimonthly newspaper for farmers published in Chernivtsi from 1904 to 1913 by the Council of Regional Culture for the Crownland of Bukovyna. Its editor was S. *Smal-Stotsky.

Khliborob (Farmer). The first newspaper in Russian-ruled Ukraine to appear in Ukrainian. A weekly aimed at farmers and peasants, it was published without official permission in Lubni, Poltava gubernia, in November and December 1905 by the local Ukrainian hromada. Its editor was M. Shemet. The fourth issue was confiscated, and with the appearance of the fifth issue the paper was banned by the authorities. Its maximum circulation was estimated to be 5,000.

Khliborob (Farmer). An illustrated semimonthly devoted to co-operative affairs and farming, which was published in Kharkiv from 1907 to 1918 by the Kharkiv Society of Agriculture. It came out in both Ukrainian and Russian and its editor was S. Kuznetsov.

Khliborob (Farmer). A weekly newpaper of a nationalist orientation published in Curitiba, Brazil, from 1938 to 1941 and from 1948 to 1974, when it was replaced by a monthly bulletin. It was a continuation of the weekly *Ukraïns'kyi khliborob*, which had been founded in Porto Uniao in 1924 by P. *Karmansky and transferred to Curitiba in 1935. Both papers were published by the Ukrainian Union, which in 1938 was reorganized into the Union for Agricultural Education. In 1931 *Ukraïns'kyi khliborob* published a Portuguese supplement *Vida Ukraina*, and in 1938–40 *Khliborob* had a humor supplement *Batizhok*. Before 1941 the more noted editors of the two papers were P. Karmansky, V. Kuts, I. Paliatynsky, and I. Horachuk. From 1948 the editors were M. Hets, S. Plakhtyn, and O. Vashchenko.

Khliborob Ukraïny (Farmer of Ukraine). A popular monthly journal published since 1963 in Kiev by the Ministry for the Production and Delivery of Agricultural Products of the Ukrainian SSR. It is the successor to *Kolhospne selo*, which in 1949 replaced *Kolhospnyk Ukraïny* (est 1939). It publishes articles dealing with soil cultivation, economics, farm mechanization, and labor management. It also publishes advice on specific problems of production.

Khliborobs'ka molod' (Farm Youth). An educational monthly published from 1934 to 1939 in Lviv by the *Khliborobskyi Vyshkil Molodi organization, which was affiliated with the Silskyi Hospodar society. Its editor was Ye. Khraplyvy.

Khliborobs'ka pravda (Farmer's Truth). A political weekly newspaper published irregularly in Chernivtsi from 1924 to 1938. In 1923 it came out under the title *Khliborob* (Farmer). Until 1930 it described itself as the official paper of the Rumanian National Farmer's party, and then of the Ukrainian Farmer's party (although no such party existed). It supported official Rumanian policy and attacked the Ukrainian National party. The publisher and editor was K. Krakaliia. Among its contributors were H. Andriiashchuk, S. Nykorovych-Hnidy (who also edited its literary and scholarly supplement and the women's page in 1935), O. Kovalsky, and I. Bordeiny.

Khliborobs'ka Ukraïna (Agrarian Ukraine). An ideological, irregular collection published from 1920 to 1925 in Vienna by the Ukrainian Union of Agrarians-Statists (USKhD). Five volumes appeared, edited by V. *Lypynsky. They contained his fundamental political treatise 'Lysty do brativ khliborobiv' (Letters to Brother Agrarians) and his polemical articles such as 'Poklykannia variahiv' (The Calling of the Varangians) and 'Orhanizatsiia Khliborobiv' (The Organization of Agrarians); D. Doroshenko's analyses of the events of 1918 in Ukraine, and particularly of Ukraine's foreign policy; S. Tomashivsky's theoretical articles 'Istoriia i polityka' (History and Politics) and 'Vlada i kul'tura' (Power and Culture); and M. Tymofiiv's studies of Ukraine's economic potential and of the role played by Jews in its economy. E. Borshchak, D. Olianchyn, and O. Skoropys-Yoltukhovsky contributed articles on history, while S. Shemet wrote on the development of the Ukrainian Democratic Agrarian party and on current activities of the USKhD abroad. Extracts from the memoirs of P. *Skoropadsky were published in one of the volumes. When the USKhD dissolved, the collection ceased to appear. Later it reappeared as a publication of the Brotherhood of Ukrainian Classocrats-Monarchists Hetmanites in Prague (2 vols, 1931 and 1933).

Khliborobsko-osvitnii soiuz. See Union for Agricultural Education.

Khliborobskyi Vyshkil Molodi (Agricultural Training for Youth or KhVM). An organization for young farmers set up in 1932 by the *Silskyi Hospodar society in Lviv. It consisted of young (age 12–18) male, female, or mixed groups affiliated with local Silskyi Hospodar circles, to replace the rural farming schools in Galicia. Its founder was Ye. *Khraplyvy. Assisted by agronomists and community activists, he developed a program for the KhVM and published it in the form of a handbook, *Iak pratsiuvaty v Khliborobs'komu vyshkoli molodi* (How to Work in the Khliborobskyi Vyshkil Molodi, 3 edns). The training lasted four years: theoretical courses were taught in the fall and winter, practical instruction (competitions) was given in spring and summer. The main purpose of this training was to upgrade the skills of young farmers and to inculcate a sense of social responsibility and national pride in them. Besides Ye. Khraplyvy, the leading organizers were V. Tomashivsky, H. Eliiashevsky, V. Dmytrenko, R. Holod, and P. Zeleny. The organization published the monthly *Khliborobs'ka molod'*. By 1938 it encompassed 1,180 groups in 550 villages with a total membership of 13,080 men and 840 women. Instructors supervised the work in the villages, while county agronomists oversaw the work in the counties. During the first Soviet occupation the KhVM was closed down, but in 1941 the German authorities permitted it to resume its activities. When Soviet forces recaptured Galicia in 1944, it was dissolved.

V. Kubijovyč

Khlopomany; standing, from left: O. Khoinovsky, V. Vasylevsky, V. Vynarsky; sitting, from left: T. Rylsky, V. Antonovych

Khlopoman. Adherent of a populist movement of Ukrainian students and intelligentsia in Right-Bank Ukraine in the 1850s–1860s. The derogatory Polish term *'chłopoman,'* meaning lover of the peasantry, was adopted eventually by those who propagated the notion of 'love for the simple Ukrainian people.' The movement, which was greatly influenced by French socialists (P-J. Proudhon, L-A. Blanqui) and democratic populism, originated among students of Kiev University who belonged to the Polonized nobility. Recognizing the duty to serve 'the people among whom one lives,' they turned away from Polish student organizations and established a Ukrainian society. The *khlopoman* movement also had an impact on young people in Left-Bank Ukraine, particularly in Kharkiv, Poltava, Chernihiv, and Odessa. The movement's founders included V. Antonovych, T. Rylsky, B. Poznansky, K. Mykhalchuk, P. Zhytetsky, and P. Chubynsky. V. *Antonovych articulated its ideological principles and basic program. In replying to Polish accusations of treason and defection, he rejected the Polish nobility's social order and Jesuitism as alien to the 'spirit of our people and harmful to its life,' and encouraged his contemporaries to love the people, to expiate the sins of their fathers towards the people by actively serving them. Charged with collaborating with Russian revolutionaries, the *khlopomany* published a denial, 'Otzyv iz Kieva' (A Reply from Kiev), in *Sovremennaia letopis'*, vol 11 (Moscow 1862). The 21 signatories of this statement rejected revolutionary methods and declared that their sole concern was to educate the recently emancipated peasantry. They also refuted the charge of separatism, arguing that separatism could have no practical significance for a mostly illiterate people. A cautious attitude towards the authorities and the conviction that educational and cultural progress must precede political action prompted them to emphasize the apolitical nature of the movement.

The *khlopomany* operated strictly within the law to avoid any suspicion of revolutionary activity. From 1859 they were active in the *Hromada of Kiev. They helped found *Sunday schools and contributed to the journal **Osnova*. During summer vacations they organized tours of Ukraine, known as 'going to the people,' to acquire knowledge of the land and its people. Because of their cultural and educational work, the *khlopomany* were falsely accused by Russian reactionary circles of being politically implicated in the Polish rebellion of 1863. Despite the repressive conditions that followed, including the implementation of the Valuev ukase (see P. *Valuev), they continued to participate in the work of the Hromada of Kiev and in other community efforts.

BIBLIOGRAPHY
Antonovich, V. 'Moia ispoved',' *Osnova*, 1 (1862)
Drahomanov, M. 'Do istoriï ukraïns'kykh khlopomaniv u 1860 rr.,' *Zhytie i slovo*, 1895, no. 3
Antonovych, V. 'Avtobiohrafichni zapysky,' LNV, 1908, nos 7–9
Lipiński, W. *Szlachta na Ukrainie* (Cracow 1909)
Poznanskii, B. 'Vospominaniia,' *Ukrainskaia zhizn'*, 1914, nos 8–10
Mytsiuk, O. *Ukraïns'ki khlopomany* (Chernivtsi 1933)
Doroshenko, D. *Volodymyr Antonovych, ioho zhyttia i naukova ta hromads'ka diial'nist'* (Prague 1942)
Suspil'no-politychnyi rukh na Ukraïni v 1863–1864 rr.: Materialy i dokumenty (Kiev 1964)
Tabiś, J. *Polacy na uniwersytecie Kijowskim 1834–63* (Cracow 1974)

A. Zhukovsky

Khlysts. Members of a mystical Orthodox sect that arose in the mid-17th century at the same time as the *Old Believer movement. The sect was characterized by an extremely conservative devotion to ritual and the liturgy. Suffering severe persecution in Russia, many Khlysts fled to Ukraine in the 1860s. Their communities (called *korabli*, 'ships') survived in the Kiev, Podilia, Poltava, Kharkiv, and Kuban regions, and elsewhere until the 1930s. In Ukraine the Khlysts were called *shalaputy*, although they called themselves *Bozhi liudy* (God's people). The main tenets of their religion were contained in 12 commandments; in particular, they believed that divinity could enter a human being for leading a saintly life. The Khlyst creed never became popular among Ukrainians. D. Tuptalo was the first Ukrainian author to mention them in his works.

Vasyl Khmeliuk: *Rue de Poteau* (oil)

Khmeliuk, Vasyl [Xmeljuk, Vasyl'], b 31 July 1903 in Cherniatyn, Volhynia gubernia, d 2 November 1986 in Paris. Postimpressionist painter and poet. He studied art at the Cracow Academy of Arts and at the Ukrainian Studio of Plastic Arts in Prague. In 1928 he settled in Paris, where his work attracted the attention of prominent collectors, such as A. Vollard and S. Shchukin, and appeared at well-known galleries. In the 1930s his paintings were exhibited also in England, Italy, and Switzerland. From 1943 he was associated with the Durand-Ruel Gallery, which organized exhibitions for him in Paris, New York, and other cities. His works, done in strong contrasting colors, include paintings of flowers, still lifes, landscapes, and portraits. They can be found in museums in Paris, London, Stockholm, Lviv, and Lucerne, in the collection of Oxford University, and in private collections. Three collections of Khmeliuk's experimental poetry have been published in Prague: *Hin* (Instinct, 1926), *Osinnie sontse* (The Autumn Sun, 1928), and *1926, 1928, 1923* (1928).

Khmelnytsky, Bohdan (Fedir) Zinovii [Xmel'nyc'kyj], b ca 1595–6, d 6 August 1657 in Chyhyryn. Hetman of the Zaporozhian Host from 1648 to 1657, founder of the *Hetman state (1648–1782). By birth he belonged to the Ukrainian lesser nobility and bore the Massalski, and later the Abdank, coat of arms. His father, M. *Khmelnytsky, served as an officer under the Polish crown hetman S. Żółkiewski and his mother, according to some sources, was of Cossack descent. Kmelnytsky's place of birth has not been determined for certain. Little more is known about Khmelnytsky's education. Apparently, he received his elementary schooling in Ukrainian and his secondary and higher education in Polish at a Jesuit college, possibly in Jarosław, but more probably in Lviv. He completed his schooling before 1620 and acquired a broad knowledge of world history and fluency in Polish and Latin. Later he acquired a knowledge of Turkish,

Hetman Bohdan Khmelnytsky, portrait in the Kievan Cave Monastery (destroyed)

Tatar, and French. The Battle of *Cecora (1620), in which he lost his father and was captured by the Turks, was his first military action. After spending two years in Istanbul, he was ransomed by his mother and returned to Ukraine.

There is no reliable information about Khmelnytsky's activities from 1622 to 1637. All later accounts of his exploits in wars against the Tatars, Turks, and Russians (1632–4) have no documentary foundation. Only one fact is certain – that in the 1620s he joined the *registered Cossacks. Sometime between 1625 and 1627 he married Hanna Somko, a Cossack's daughter from Pereiaslav, and settled on his patrimonial estate in Subotiv near Chyhyryn. By 1637 he attained the high office of military chancellor. His signature appeared on the capitulation agreement signed at Borovytsia on 24 December 1637 that marked the end of a Cossack rebellion.

There are grounds to believe that Khmelnytsky belonged to the faction of officers that favored an understanding between the *Zaporozhian Host and Poland. Subsequent events, however, dashed any hopes of reconciliation. By the Ordinance of 1638 the Polish king revoked the autonomy of the Zaporozhian Host and placed the registered Cossacks under the direct authority of the Polish military command in Ukraine. The office of military chancellor, which Khmelnytsky had held, was abolished and Khmelnytsky was demoted to a captain of Chyhyryn regiment. In the fall of 1638 he visited Warsaw with a Cossack delegation to petition King Władysław IV Vasa to restore the former Cossack privileges.

In the next few years Khmelnytsky devoted his attention mostly to his estates in the Chyhyryn region, but in 1645 he served with a detachment of 2,000–2,500 Cossacks in France, and probably took part in the siege of Dunkirk. By this time his reputation for leadership was such that King Władysław, in putting together a coalition of Poland, Venice, and other states against Turkey, turned to him to obtain the support of the Zaporozhian Cossacks. In April 1646 he was one of the Cossack envoys in Warsaw with whom the king discussed plans for the impending war. These events contributed to his reputation in Ukraine, Poland, and abroad, and provided him with wide military and political contacts.

Khmelnytsky, however, had been regarded with suspicion for many years by the Polish magnates in Ukraine who were politically opposed to King Władysław. The new landowners of the Chyhyryn region, A. Koniecpolski, Crown Hetman S. Żółkiewski, and his son, Crown Flag-bearer Aleksander, treated Khmelnytsky with particular hostility. With the collusion of the Chyhyryn assistant vicegerent D. Czapliński, who bore some personal grudge against Khmelnytsky, they conspired to deprive Khmelnytsky of his Subotiv estate. In spite of the fact that Khmelnytsky received a royal title to Subotiv in 1646, Czapliński raided the estate, seized movable property, and disrupted the manor's economy. At the same time Czapliński's servants severely beat Khmelnytsky's small son at the marketplace in Chyhyryn. Under these conditions of violence and terror Khmelnytsky's wife died in 1647, and towards the end of the year A. Koniecpolski ordered Khmelnytsky's arrest and execution. It was only the help and the surety put up by his friends among the Chyhyryn officers, and particularly by Col S. Krychevsky, that saved Khmelnytsky from death. At the end of December 1647 he departed for Zaporizhia with a small (300–500-man) detachment. There he was elected *hetman. This event marked the beginning of a new Cossack uprising, which quickly turned into a national revolution (see *Cossack-Polish War).

Khmelnytsky was married three times. His first wife, who was the mother of all his children, died prematurely. His second wife, Matrona, whom he married in early 1649, was the former wife of his enemy D. Czapliński. In 1651 while Khmelnytsky was away on a military campaign, she was executed for conspiracy and adultery by his son Tymish. In the summer of 1651 Khmelnytsky married Hanna Zolotarenko, a Cossack woman from Korsun and the widow of Col Pylyp (Pylypets). Surviving him by many years, she entered a monastery in 1671 and adopted the religious name of Anastasiia. Khmelnytsky had two sons and four daughters. His older son, Tymish *Khmelnytsky, died on 15 September 1653 in the siege of the Moldavian fortress of Suceava. The younger son, Yurii (Yuras) *Khmelnytsky, was elected during his father's lifetime heir apparent under I. Vyhovsky's regency. Eventually, Yurii twice held the office of hetman. Khmelnytsky's daughter Kateryna (Olena) was married to D. Vyhovsky, and after his death in Muscovite captivity she married Hetman P. Teteria. The second daughter, Stepaniia, was the wife of I. Nechai, who died in Muscovite exile. She later became a nun in Kiev. The names of the other two daughters are unknown. One of them was married to Capt Hlyzko of Korsun regiment, who died in 1655 fighting against Poland. The other was married in 1654 to L. Movchan, a Cossack from Novhorod-Siverskyi. Khmelnytsky's line died out at the end of the 17th century. The Khmelnytskys were numerous in Left-Bank Ukraine and Russia but were of a different lineage. Khmelnytsky was buried on 25 August 1657 in St Elijah's Church in Subotiv, which he himself had built.

Khmelnytsky's greatest achievement in the process of national revolution was the Cossack Hetman state of the Zaporozhian Host (1648–1782). His statesmanship was demonstrated in all areas of state-building – in the military, administration, finance, economics, and culture. With political acumen he invested the Zaporozhian Host under the leadership of its hetman with supreme power in the new Ukrainian state, and unified all the estates of Ukrainian society under his authority. Khmelnytsky not only built a government system and developed military and civilian administrators, including I. Vyhovsky, P. Teteria, D. and I. Nechai, I. Bohun, H. Hulianytsky, and S. Mrozovytsky-Morozenko, out of Cossack officers and Ukrainian nobles, but also established an elite within the Cossack-Hetman state. In spite of setbacks and difficulties, this elite preserved and maintained its gains in the face of Muscovy's invasion and against Polish and Turkish claims almost to the end of the 18th century.

Khmelnytsky's Realm (Khmelnychchyna). The national uprising of 1648–57 headed by B. Khmelnytsky liberated a large part of Ukrainian territory from Poland and established a Cossack-Hetman state that was abolished only in the 1780s (see *Hetman state). Khmelnytsky's uprising induced some changes in the political system of eastern Europe, and brought about certain changes in the socioeconomic structure of Cossack Ukraine. It gave rise to a new elite of Cossack officers

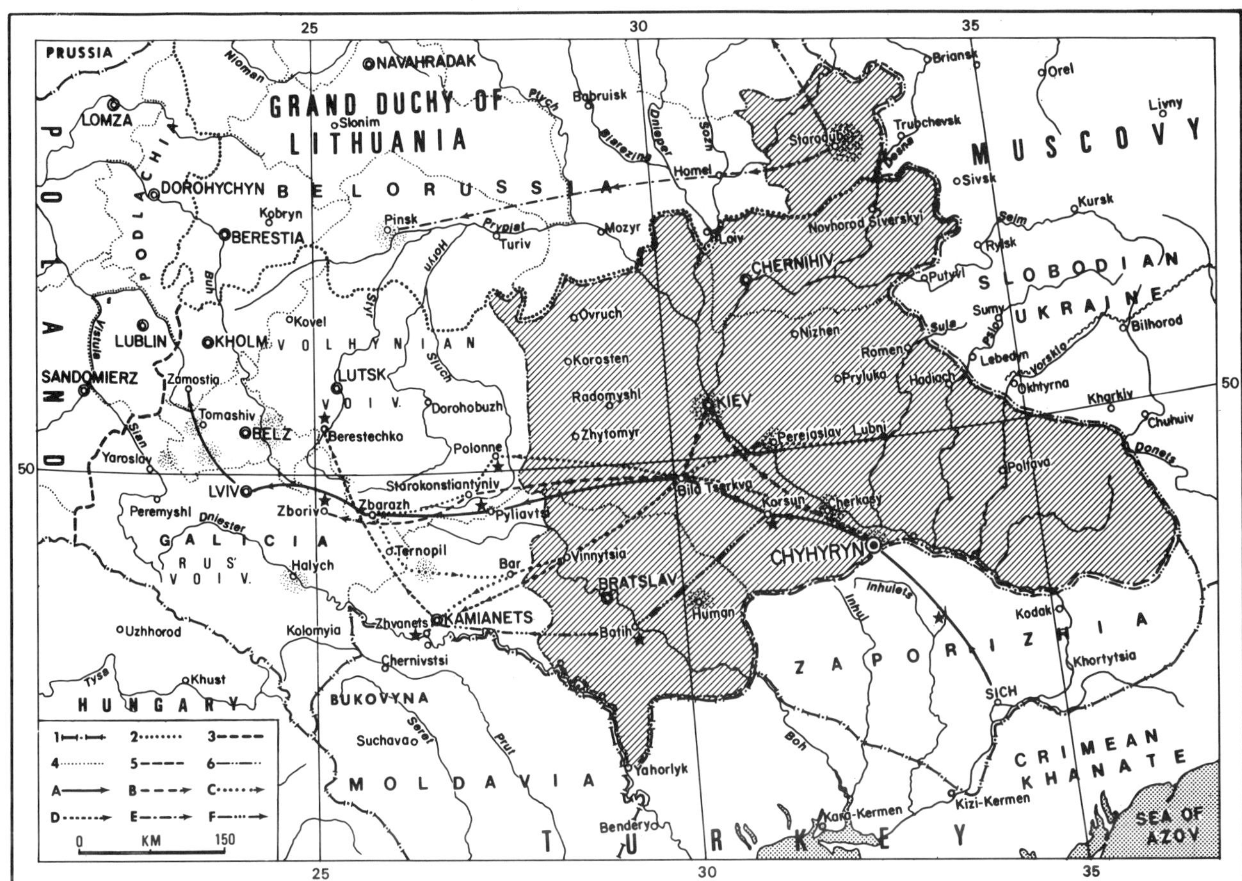

UKRAINE UNDER BOHDAN KHMELNYTSKY

1. Border of the Kingdom of Poland in 1648
2. Boundary between the Polish Commonwealth and the Grand Duchy of Lithuania
3. Westernmost limit of Ukrainian ethnic territory
4. Voivodeship (palatinate) boundaries
5. Northernmost limit of the lands of the Zaporozhian Cossacks
6. Border of the Hetman state according to the 1649 Treaty of Zboriv

A. Khmelnytsky's first campaign (1648)
B. Second campaign (1649)
C. M. Kryvonis's campaign (1648)
D. Khmelnytsky's third campaign (1650)
E. I. Zolotarenko's campaign (1654)
F. Cossack campaign of 1652

The stars mark main battles of the Cossack-Polish War, and the speckled areas mark local rebellions.

that eventually, in the 18th century, evolved into a Ukrainian variant of the Polish nobility and, in the 19th century, into a Ukrainian variant of the Russian nobility.

The Cossack state, or '*kozatske panstvo*,' emerged long before the Khmelnytsky period. According to historians such as I. Krypiakevych, N. Polonska-Vasylenko, and L. Okinshevych, a Ukrainian Cossack state – the Zaporozhian Sich – was established as early as the 16th century. V. Lypynsky believed that the Cossacks 'in a nationally alien Poland slowly became a state within a state.' But the Sich and the Cossack estate were only embryonic forms of the Cossack state that was established in the 17th century on old Cossack territories – the Dnieper region, including Kiev – and on the recently colonized southern Left-Bank Ukraine. The Cossacks claimed these lands as their own by right of conquest and use. From the time of Hetman P. Konashevych-*Sahaidachny, Cossackdom as a 'state within a state' became absorbed into the Cossack world view. This view was accepted in Poland and in Western Europe, particularly in Sweden and Transylvania; eg, in 1628 Prince Bethlen-Gábor of Transylavania said: 'The Cossack people can secede from Poland and build its separate Commonwealth ... if only it finds for its struggle a wise and noble leader and organizer.' Khmelnytsky turned out to be that leader.

The first reports about Khmelnytsky's uprising and his alliance with the Turks and Crimean Tatars informed the Polish government that this was more than just a rebellion. Both Crown Hetman M. Potocki and A. Kysil, the voivode of Bratslav who was knowledgeable in Ukrainian affairs, wrote in March and May 1648 respectively that the Cossacks 'absolutely want to rule in Ukraine' and that Khmelnytsky 'will form a new duchy.'

In Ukrainian political circles there were different ideas on the structure of the new state. Among the Orthodox nobility and higher clergy the conception that two sov-

Entrance of Hetman Khmelnytsky into Kiev, 1649 by M. Ivasiuk (oil, 1949)

ereigns – the Kiev metropolitan and the hetman of the Zaporozhian Host – would enter into relations with Poland was quite popular. But Khmelnytsky's military victories in 1648–9 and his triumphal entry into Kiev in 1648, at which he was hailed as 'the Moses, savior, redeemer, and liberator of the Rus' people from Polish captivity ... the illustrious ruler of Rus',' weighed on the side of a Cossack state. In February 1649 during negotiations with a Polish delegation headed by A. Kysil in Pereiaslav, Khmelnytsky declared that he was 'the sole Rus' autocrat' and that he had 'enough power in Ukraine, Podilia, and Volhynia ... in my land and principality stretching as far as Lviv, Kholm, and Halych.' It became clear to the Polish envoys that Khmelnytsky had 'denied Ukraine and all Rus' to the Poles.' A Vilnius panegyric in Khmelnytsky's honor (1650–1) asserted: 'While in Poland it is King John Casimir, in Rus' it is Hetman Bohdan Khmelnytsky.'

Khmelnytsky claimed the divine right to rule over Cossacks as early as 29 July 1648, when in a letter to a Muscovite voivode he titled himself 'Bohdan Khmelnytsky, by Divine grace hetman with the Zaporozhian Host.' This formula was repeated in all official Cossack documents. In a letter from the Hlukhiv captain, S. Veichyk, to the Sevsk voivode, Prince T. Shcherbatov, written on 22 April 1651, the following title is used: 'By God's grace our Great Ruler, Sir Bohdan Khmelnytsky, the Hetman of the entire Zaporozhian Host.' Foreigners addressing Khmelnytsky titled him 'Illustrissimus Princeps' or 'Dux.' Greek metropolitans who visited Ukraine in 1650 prayed for him during the liturgy as 'the Ruler and Hetman of the Great Rus'.' The Turkish sultan called him a prince and monarch, and other foreign rulers called him 'illustrissimus dux.'

The *Pereiaslav Treaty of 1654 did not change the political status of Ukraine, or the title or authority of its hetman. Although the presence of a Russian garrison in Kiev and the tsar's new title 'Tsar of Little Russia, Grand Prince of Kiev and Chernihiv' laid symbolic claim of Muscovite supremacy in Ukraine, the 'Zaporozhian Host' remained a separate, independent state known as the Rus' state, or *Hosudarstvo rosiiske*, as it was called by B. Khmelnytsky in his letter of 17 February 1654 to the tsar. In Muscovite sources it was called the Little-Russian state (*Malorossiiskoe gosudarstvo*). It had its own head of state – the hetman of the Zaporozhian Host, elected for life – its own government and army, foreign policy, legislature and judiciary, finances, and independent religious and cultural life.

Khmelnytsky retained full state powers in both internal and external affairs. The hetman continued to be 'the master and hetman' of the Ukrainian state, 'the supreme ruler and master of our fatherland,' as he was called in official Ukrainian documents. Metropolitan S. Kosiv referred to him in 1654 as 'the leader and commander of our land.' Khmelnytsky referred to himself as 'the master of the entire Rus' land' (1655) and as 'Clementia divina Generalis Dux Exercituum Zaporoviensium' (letter to C. Şerban, the ruler of Wallachia, 1657). General Chancellor I. Vyhovsky described Khmelnytsky to a Transylvanian envoy in 1657 thus: 'As the tsar is a tsar in his realm, so the hetman is a prince or king in his domain.' Ukraine's status as a sovereign state received international recognition. The Korsun Treaty of Alliance with Sweden of 6 October 1657 recognized Ukraine as 'a free people, subject to no one' (*pro libera gente et nulli subjecta*).

Khmelnytsky's Cossack state can be regarded as a new political entity – 'Ukraine of the Zaporozhian Host,' as it was known in Moscow – or as a restoration of the old Rus' state (*Hosudarstvo rosiiskoie*, as Khmelnytsky called it in his letter to the tsar of 17 February 1654). In all his negotiations with Sweden and Transylvania, Khmelnytsky demanded that his claims 'to all old Ukraine, or Rus' (Roxolania), wherever the Greek faith and their language still exist, as far as the Vistula River,' be recognized.

The issue of the legitimate historical boundaries of the Cossack state brought the Belorussian question to the forefront of Ukrainian politics. The Zaporozhian Cossacks were interested in Belorussia as early as the 16th century, as is evident from H. Loboda's and S. Nalyvaiko's campaigns. Khmelnytsky paid close attention to Belorussia from the very beginning of his uprising. He supported the Cossack movement led by K. Poklonsky in eastern Belorussia. A Belorussian regiment under the control of the Zaporozhian Host existed in 1655–7. In 1656 Khmelnytsky took under his protection Slutsk principality, which belonged to Prince B. Radziwiłł, then in 1657 Staryi Bykhau, granting it the right to free trade with Ukraine, and finally, on 8 July 1657, at the request of the Pynske nobility, Pynske, Mazyr, and Turau counties. These actions greatly disturbed Muscovy, which began, in V. Lypynsky's words, 'the struggle of two Rus'es over the third Rus'.' Although B. Khmelnytsky's death put an end to Ukraine's expansion into Belorussian territory, the tradition of a 'Rus' state' was preserved in the policies of I. Vyhovsky, and traces of it can be found even later.

BIBLIOGRAPHY

Hrushevs'kyi, M. *Istoriia Ukraïny-Rusy*, vols 8, 9 (Kiev 1907, 1931; repr, New York 1954, 1957)
Kubala, L. *Szkice historyczne: Wojna moskiewska* (Warsaw 1910)
Lipiński, W. *Z dziejów Ukrainy* (Cracow 1912; 2nd edn in his *Tvory*, vol 2, Philadelphia 1980)
Kubala, L. *Wojna szwedska* (Lviv 1913)
– *Wojna brandenburska i najazd Rakoczego* (Lviv 1917)
Lypyns'kyi, V. *Ukraïna na perelomi* (Vienna 1920; 2nd edn, New York 1954)
Kryp'iakevych, I. 'Studiï nad derzhavoiu Bohdana Khmel'nyts'koho,' *ZNTSH*, vols 139–40, 144–5, 147, 151 (1926–7, 1931)

Petrovs'kyi, M. *Vyzvol'na viina ukraïns'koho narodu proty hnitu shliakhets'koï Pol'shchi i pryiednannia Ukraïny do Rosiï 1648–54 rr.* (Kiev 1940)
Vernadsky, G. *Bohdan, Hetman of Ukraine* (New Haven 1941)
Iakovliv, A. *Dohovir Het'mana Bohdana Khmel'nyts'koho z moskovs'kym tsarem Oleksiiem Mykhailovychem 1654 r.* (New York 1954)
Kryp'iakevych, I. *Bohdan Khmel'nyts'kyi* (Kiev 1954)
Ohloblyn, O. *Dumky pro Khmel'nychchynu* (New York 1957)
Shevchenko, F. *Politychni ta ekonomichni zv'iazky Ukraïny z Rosiieiu v seredyni XVII st.* (Kiev 1959)
Ohloblyn, O. *Problema derzhavnoï vlady na Ukraïni za Khmel'nychchyny i Pereiaslavs'ka uhoda 1654 r.* (Munich-New York 1960)
Golobutskii, V. *Diplomaticheskaia istoriia osvoboditel'noi voiny ukrainskogo naroda 1648–54 gg.* (Kiev 1962)
Kryp'iakevych, I. 'Administratyvnyi podil Ukraïny 1648–54 rr.' *Istorychni dzherela ta ïkh vykorystannia*, vol 2 (Kiev 1966)
Wójcik, Z. *Dzikie pola w ogniu*, 3rd edn (Warsaw 1968)
Shevchenko, F. 'Istorychne mynule v otsintsi B. Khmel'nyts'koho,' *Ukraïns'kyi istorychnyi zhurnal*, 12 (1970)
Zlepko, D. *Der grosse Kosakenaufstand 1648 gegen die polnische Herrschaft* (Wiesbaden 1980)
Zagorovskii, L. *Rossiia, Rech' Pospolitaia i Shvetsiia v seredine XVII veka* (Moscow 1981)

O. Ohloblyn

Khmelnytsky, Ivan [Xmel'nyc'kyj], b January 1742, d 13 January 1794. Philosopher. After graduating from the Kievan Mohyla Academy, he attended Königsberg University where he received a doctorate for his *Razsudzhenie ob osnovaniiakh filosofskikh* (Discourse on Philosophical Foundations, 1762). Settling in St Petersburg, Khmelnytsky wrote several original works including *Razsuzhdenie o rabstve po zakonam estestvennym i pravu vsenarodnomu* (Discourse on Slavery according to Natural Law and Universal Customary Law) and translated a number of scholarly books including one by J. Comenius. His chief works, which were written in Latin, survive only in Russian translation. Khmelnytsky's philosophical views were strongly influenced by C. Wolff and G. Leibniz.

Khmelnytsky, Mykhailo [Xmel'nyc'kyj, Myxajlo], b ?, d October 1620. The father of B. *Khmelnytsky, he was a petty Orthodox nobleman probably from the village of Khmelnyk in the Peremyshl region. As a young man he worked at the court of Crown Hetman S. Żółkiewski in Zhovkva and then at the court of Ya. Danylovych, the starosta of Chyhyryn and Korsun. In the Chyhyryn region, he established a number of new settlements, acquired his own estate in Subotiv, and eventually became vice-starosta. He maintained close links with the Zaporozhian Cossacks. During the Polish-Turkish War of 1620–1, Khmelnytsky commanded a detachment of volunteers from Chyhyryn in S. Żółkiewski's army in the Moldavian campaign. He died while fighting the Tatars at the Battle of *Cecora.

Khmelnytsky, Tymish [Xmel'nyc'kyj, Tymiš], b 1632, d 15 September 1653. The eldest son of B. *Khmelnytsky. In February-March 1648, his father left him as a hostage with the Crimean khan, Islam-Girei, to guarantee their alliance. Later, as captain of Chyhyryn company, he distinguished himself as a capable commander in the Cossack-Polish War. In 1650 he led a large Cossack-Tatar army against Moldavia, forcing the hospodar of Moldavia, V. *Lupu, to abandon his co-operation with the Poles and form an alliance with the Cossacks instead. To strengthen this alliance, Lupu promised his daughter, Roksana *Lupu, in marriage to Khmelnytsky, who led (in 1652) another army into Moldavia and married Roksana. During this campaign his army participated in the Battle of *Batih, where the Cossacks scored a decisive victory over the Poles. These developments made Moldavia's neighbors uneasy; Prince György Rákóczi II of Transylvania and hospodar Matei Basarab of Wallachia, fearing the growth of Cossack influence in the region, supported a revolt by Moldavian boyars against Lupu. Khmelnytsky led another Cossack army to Lupu's defense. In May 1653, after early victories at Iasy and Focšani, his army was defeated at Finta (17 May). That autumn Khmelnytsky came a second time to help his father-in-law; however, this time he was killed in battle in Suceava. His death ended his father's attempts to develop a Cossack-Moldavian alliance as the cornerstone of his foreign policy.

Tymish Khmelnytsky

Hetman Yurii Khmelnytsky

BIBLIOGRAPHY
Vengrzhenovskii, S. 'Svad'ba Timosha Khmel'nitskago (epizod iz istorii malorussko-moldavskikh otnoshenii),' *KS*, 1897, nos 3 and 5

A. Zhukovsky

Khmelnytsky, Yurii [Xmel'nyc'kyj, Jurij] (aka Khmelnychenko, Yuras), 1641–85. Hetman of Ukraine (1657, 1659–63) and hetman of the Right Bank (1677–81, 1685); the younger son of B. *Khmelnytsky. His father, who hoped to establish a hereditary hetmancy, designated him as his successor after the death of his older son, Tymish. Although this was opposed by many Cossacks, who favored an elected hetmancy or had their own ambitions to become hetman, Yurii was initially chosen hetman while his father was still alive. At the Cossack Council in Chyhyryn in August 1657, however, after his father's death, when it became clear that the 16-year-old was incapable of governing on his own, the Cossacks elected I. *Vyhovsky as hetman. Subsequently, however, Vyhovsky lost the support of the Cossacks and abdicated in September 1659. Khmelnytsky was again elected hetman of Ukraine, supported primarily by the pro-Muscovite Cossack families who opposed Vyhovsky's pro-Polish policies (see the Treaty of *Hadiache).

Capitalizing on the anarchy that was developing in Ukraine and Khmelnytsky's inexperience and weakness, the Muscovite government and its plenipotentiary Prince A. Trubetskoi forced Khmelnytsky to ratify the *Pereiaslav Articles of 1659, which limited the sovereign rights of Ukraine, giving Moscow the power to appoint its own voivodes and to keep garrisons in six Ukrainian towns. This treaty greatly angered most Cossacks. In 1660, when the Muscovite army on whose side the Cossacks were obliged to fight in the war against Poland was defeated, the Cossacks went over to the Poles and the Muscovites were forced to surrender at Chudniv. In October 1660, Khmelnytsky concluded the Treaty of *Slobodyshche with the Poles, dissolving the alliance with Moscow and restoring the union with Poland, and annulling the Pereiaslav articles. This treaty, approved by the Cossack Council in Korsun, was opposed by some Left-Bank regiments led by Ya. Somko and by the Cossacks of the Zaporozhian Sich led by I. Briukhovetsky, who favored a pro-Moscow orientation. Khmelnytsky, unable to control the situation, abdicated at the beginning of 1663 and became a monk, taking the name Gedeon. The emergence of both pro-Polish and pro-Muscovite forces in Ukraine, led by competing hetmans, led to the partition of the Cossack state into Left- and Right-Bank Ukraine and initiated the period of Ukrainian history known as the Ruin.

In 1664, the Polish government accused Khmelnytsky of treason and arrested him. When he was released in 1667, he entered an Uman monastery where in 1670 (1673 according to some sources) he was captured by Crimean Tatars and taken to Istanbul. After a period of imprisonment, Khmelnytsky became the archimandrite of a Greek monastery. Eventually, the Turks attempted to use him to consolidate their rule over Right-Bank Ukraine. In 1677, Khmelnytsky was allowed to return to Ukraine, where he proclaimed himself Prince of Little Russia-Ukraine and Commander-in-Chief of the Zaporozhian Host, and established his capital in Nemyriv. In 1678–9, with the help of Tatar and Turkish troops, he attempted to annex the Left Bank. Once again, however, he proved to be incompetent and alienated even some of his closest collaborators. The southern Right Bank became depopulated as the population fled east beyond the Dnieper to escape his oppressive rule and the constant fighting between the Turks, Cossacks, Muscovites, and Poles. Following these failures, and the reconcilement between Moscow, Turkey, and the Crimean Khanate, Khmelnytsky was again deposed as hetman. In 1685, he proclaimed himself hetman once more, but after half a year he was executed at Kamianets-Podilskyi for disobeying Turkish orders. Yu. Khmelnytsky was a weak, unbalanced individual whose activities proved detrimental to the course of Ukrainian history and attempts at establishing a Ukrainian state.

BIBLIOGRAPHY

Antonovych, V.; Bets, V. *Istoricheskie deiateli Iugo-zapadnoi Rosii* (Kiev 1883)

Kostomarov, M. *Het'manuvannia Vyhovs'koho i Iuriia Khmel'nyts'koho* (Ternopil 1892)

Herasymchuk, V. 'Vyhovs'kyi i Iurii Khmel'nyts'kyi,' *ZNTSh*, 59–60 (1904)

Rawita-Gawroński, F. *Ostatni Chmielniczenko (Zarys monograficzny) 1640–1679* (Poznan 1919)

A. Zhukovsky

Khmelnytsky Regiment (Pershyi ukrainskyi kozachyi im. hetmana B. Khmelnytskoho polk, aka Bohdanivtsi). Organized with the help of Gen M. Khodorovych and proclaimed on 1 May 1917 by Ukrainian soldiers of the Kiev étape station, it became the first regular unit of the Ukrainian army. The regiment consisted of 16 companies with 3,600 men. From August to November it served at the front as part of the Tenth Infantry Division. In April 1918 the regiment was renamed the Third Khmelnytsky Zaporozhian Infantry Regiment and assigned to the Zaporozhian Corps. Its commanders were Capt D. Putnyk-Hrebeniuk, Lt Col Yu. Kapkan, Lt Col Yu. Lastovchenko, Col O. Shapoval, Lt Col M. Lubianytsky, Col S. Lazurenko, and Col I. Kyrychenko. The regiment fought for Ukraine's independence until the end of 1920.

Khmelnytskyi

Khmelnytskyi [Xmel'nyc'kyj]. IV-7. City (1985 pop 217,000), the capital of Khmelnytskyi oblast. Until 1954 it was called Proskuriv, when it was renamed to honor hetman B. Khmelnytsky. First mentioned as the Polish royal outpost of Ploskyriv (Polish: Płoskirów) in 1493, it was fortified in the 16th century. Its inhabitants took part in the Cossack-Polish wars and in the Haidamaka rebellions. In 1780 the town was renamed Proskuriv. In 1793 it came under Russian rule and became a county center (from 1797 in Podilia gubernia).

From 1917 to November 1920 Proskuriv was controlled much of the time by the UNR. Under Soviet rule from 1920, it became an okruha center (1923–30, 1935–7) and then an oblast capital (in 1941 and 1944–54 of Kamianets-Podilskyi oblast). The Second World War brought about radical changes in the national composition of its population: the Ukrainians rose from 39 percent in 1926 to 53 in 1959, and Russians from 7 to 21 percent, while Jews fell from 42 to 10 percent, and Poles from 10 to 7 percent.

Until the Soviet period the city's economy was based on sugar refining, grain markets, and cottage industries. Today Khmelnytskyi is a rail junction and an important industrial center. Over 50 enterprises produce various machines, transformers and substations, thermoplastics machinery, auto and tractor parts, metal-stamping and pressing equipment, dairy, sugar, and meat products, furniture, footwear, clothing, leather goods, chemical products, reinforced-concrete products, and bricks.

Located in the city are a technological institute of consumer services; three tekhnikums (autoelectromechanical, Soviet trade, and co-operative); three specialized secondary schools (music, pedagogy, and medicine); a regional museum (est 1925); an oblast Ukrainian music and drama theater, a puppet theater, and a philharmonic orchestra; and the oblast newpaper *Radianske Podillia*.

BIBLIOGRAPHY
Humeniuk, S. *Svidky istorychnykh podii: Rozpovid' pro pam'iatni mistsia m. Khmel'nyts'koho* (Lviv 1970)
Istoriia mist i sil Ukraïns'koï RSR. Khmel'nyts'ka oblast' (Kiev 1971)

V. Kubijovyč

Khmelnytskyi oblast. An administrative region (1986 pop 1,527,700) in Podilia in Right-Bank Ukraine, formed on 22 September 1937. The oblast covers an area of 20,600 sq km; it has 20 raions, 465 rural soviets, 12 cities, and 25 towns (smt). Since 1941 the capital has been *Khmelnytskyi; until 1954 it was called Proskuriv.

Physical geography. The oblast is located in the forest-steppe of the central part of the Volhynia-Podilia Upland. Its undulating plain is dissected by many river valleys and is terraced in the northeast; in the south belts of canyons, limestone hills, cliffs, and ridges (the *Tovtry) occur. The topsoil consists of loess and loess-like loamy deposits. The central part of the oblast has mainly low-humus chernozems; the south, podzolized chernozems and gray and light-gray podzolized soils; and the north, a mixture of soddy podzolized, carbonate, and chernozem soils. Forests cover 13 percent of the oblast's area; in the north they are mostly pine, with some birch and aspen, while in the south they consist of oak, hornbeam, linden, ash, hazel, and other deciduous trees. Reforestation is occurring in the south (20,300 ha in 1973–84). Deposits of limestone, gypsum, chalk, kaolin, bentonite, dolomite, and granite are widespread, and there are small phosphorite and peat deposits and several mineral springs. There are 165 rivers longer than 10 km. They are part of the Dnieper Basin in the north (the tributaries Khomora, Horyn, and Sluch), the Boh Basin in the east (the Buzhok, Vovk, and Ikva), and the Dniester Basin in the south (the Dniester, Zbruch, Zhvanchyk, Smotrych, Ushytsia, Ternava, Muksha, Kalius, and Studenytsia). There are many ponds and 44 small reservoirs. The climate is temperate-continental, with an average temperature of −5.5°C in January and 18.5°C in July. The annual precipitation is 576–628 mm. Native flora and fauna are protected in 13 estate conservation areas and numerous other areas.

History. Already settled in the early Stone Age, from the 9th century the oblast's territory belonged to Kievan Rus'; from the mid-12th century it was part of the principality of Galicia and then Galicia-Volhynia. In the 13th century parts of it came under Mongol rule. In the 14th century it belonged to Lithuania, and from the 1430s, to Poland (from the 1460s as part of *Podilia voivodeship). In the 17th century, most of it was taken by the Turks but returned to Poland at the end of the century. It was annexed by the Russian Empire in 1793 and divided between *Volhynia and *Podilia gubernias in 1797. Under Soviet rule, it was partitioned among Kamianets-Podilskyi, Proskuriv, and Shepetivka okruhas in 1925 and became part of Vinnytsia oblast in 1932. In 1937 it constituted the new Kamianets-Podilskyi oblast, which was renamed Khmelnytskyi oblast in 1954.

Population. The population of the oblast has not grown. In 1926 the three okruhas now composing the oblast had a population of 1,774,000. During the man-made *famine of 1932–3, 15–20 percent of the population died. Much of the sizable Jewish population (eg, 8 percent of Proskuriv okruha in 1926) was annihilated by the Germans during the Second World War, and many Poles (10.2 percent of Proskuriv okruha in 1926) were resettled in Poland after the war. The oblast's population decreased by 6 percent between 1963 (its high point, at 1,627,000) and 1984. The increase in the urban population has been primarily a phenomenon of the 1970s. In 1959, only 24 percent of the population was urban; in 1971, 28 percent; and by 1986, 44 percent. The average population density has decreased: from 88 inhabitants per sq km (in the three okruhas) in 1926 to 79 in 1959 and 74.5 in 1984. Ukrainians composed 90.1 percent of the population in 1959 and 90.8 percent in 1979; Russians, 3.8 and 4.9 percent; Poles, 4.3 and 2.8 percent; and Jews, 1.2 percent (in 1959) and 1.0 percent (in 1970). In 1979, 98.7 percent of the oblast's Ukrainians and 80 percent of the Poles claimed Ukrainian as their first language; only 6 percent of the entire population claimed Russian. The largest cities are Khmelnytskyi and Kamianets-Podilskyi.

Industry. The oblast specializes in food processing (34.6 percent of gross industrial output in 1983); machine building and metalworking (31.9 percent); light industry (13.9 percent); building-materials manufacturing (7.7 percent); and lumbering, cellulose and paper making, woodworking, and furniture making (4.6 percent). In 1983 the oblast's 16 sugar refineries (in Teofipol, Volochyske, Horodok, Yasne, and Starokostiantyniv) produced 8.4 percent of Ukraine's beet sugar. Vegetable and fruit canneries are found in Kamianets-Podilskyi, Medzhybizh, Nova Ushytsia, Vinkivtsi, and Sataniv; confectionery plants, in Khmelnytskyi, Zinkiv, and Slavuta; large dairies, in Khmelnytskyi, Kamianets-Podilskyi, Shepetivka, Starokostiantyniv, and Dunaivtsi; meat-packing plants, in Khmelnytskyi, Kamianets-Podilskyi, and Shepetivka; breweries, in Khmelnytskyi, Slavuta, and Zinkiv; and flour mills, in Bohdanivtsi, Volochyske, Kamianets-Podilskyi, Slavuta, and Polonne. There are 27 feed plants.

Machine tools are made in Kamianets-Podilskyi, Khmelnytskyi, and Horodok; electronic equipment and electric machinery, in Kamianets-Podilskyi and Khmelnytskyi; agricultural machines, in Khmelnytskyi, Kamianets-Podilskyi, and Shepetivka; and equipment for the food industry, in Krasyliv. Textiles are made in Kamianets-Podilskyi, Dunaivtsi, and Slavuta; clothing, in Kamianets-Podilskyi, Khmelnytskyi, and Chornyi Ostriv; leather goods, in Khmelnytskyi and Kamianets-Podilskyi; and wood products, in Shepetivka, Slavuta, Iziaslav, Dunaivtsi, Vovkovyntsi, and Liatychiv. Reinforced-concrete materials are made in Khmelnytskyi, Kamianets-Podilskyi, and Slavuta; exterior tiles and drywall, in Kamianets-Podilskyi; drainpipes, in Romanyny; asphalt and concrete, in Khmelnytskyi; cement, in Kamianets-Podilskyi; ceramic tiles and glass products, in Slavuta; china, in Polonne; gravel and tar paper, in Slavuta; lime, in Zakupane and Humentsi; and refractories, in Burtyn. There are 13 brick plants in the oblast.

Agriculture. In 1983 there were 437 collective and 34 state farms in the oblast. They had at their disposal 1,790,000 ha of land, of which 1,568,000 ha was farmland; of the latter, 88.5 percent was cultivated, 5.3 percent was hayfield, and 3.1 percent was pasture. Of the seeded land (1,397,000 ha), 5.1 percent consisted of grain crops; 28.1 percent, of fodder crops; 12.8 percent, of industrial crops; and 8 percent, of garden vegetables, melons, and potatoes. Orchards and berry fields occupied 64,600 ha. The principal grain crops are winter wheat (45.7 percent), spring barley (19.7 percent), corn (7 percent), and buckwheat (3 percent). The principal fodder crops are corn, grasses, clover, and alfalfa. The principal industrial crop is sugar beets (81.9 percent in 1970). Sunflowers, medicinal plants, and tobacco are also grown. Animal husbandry consists primarily of dairy and beef cattle and pig farming. Poultry farming, beekeeping, and pond fishing are secondary.

Transportation. In 1983 there were 732 km of railroad in the oblast. The main trunk lines crossing it are the Kiev–Lviv and Kiev–Kamianets-Podilskyi. There are 7,000 km of roads, of which 6,000 are paved. The main highways are Kiev–Lviv, Khmelnytskyi–Chernivtsi, and Vinnytsia–Rivne. There is a domestic airport near Khmelnytskyi.

BIBLIOGRAPHY
Verkhovnyi, O. *Khmel'nyts'ka oblast' (Heohrafichnyi narys)* (Kiev 1960)
Istoriia mist i sil Ukraïns'koï RSR: Khmel'nyts'ka oblast' (Kiev 1971)

I. Myhul, R. Senkus

Khmelnytskyi Ukrainian Music and Drama Theater (Khmelnytskyi ukrainskyi muzychno-dramatychnyi teatr im. H.I. Petrovskoho). Founded in 1931 in Novocherkassk as the North Caucasia Regional Ukrainian Drama Theater, it was transferred to Ukraine and in 1934 became the Vinnytsia Touring Workers' and Collective Farmers' Theater. In 1938 it was renamed the Kamianets-Podilskyi Oblast Theater, and in 1954 it was transferred to Khmelnytskyi and assigned its current name. During the Second World War, the company toured the Far East and the northern fronts. For many years it operated under the tutelage of the Kiev Ukrainian Drama Theater, which lent it stage directors and actors such as H. Yura, K. Koshevsky, A. Buchma, and Yu. Shumsky. At first its repertoire consisted of Ukrainian classics, which in the 1940s were supplemented with Russian and Soviet plays and in the 1950s with the works of European dramatists including C. Goldoni, B. Brecht, F. García Lorca, and W. Shakespeare.

Khmil, Ivan [Xmil'], b 16 October 1923 in Stari Shepelychi, Kiev oblast. Historian. A graduate of Kiev University (1951), he was the chief editor of the AN URSR publishing house (1960–3) and a functionary at the UN Secretariat in New York (1965–71). Since 1971 he has worked at the AN URSR Institute of History. He is the author of monographs on the diplomatic activity of the Ukrainian SSR from 1917 to 1920 (1962) and anticommunism in the United States (1975).

Khmilevsky, Prokop [Xmilevs'kyj], b ca 1600 in the Mazowsze region, Poland, d 1664 in the Derman Monastery, Volhynia. Basilian monk and bishop of Peremyshl. He studied in Braunsberg, Prussia. In 1639 he was rector of the ecclesiastic school in Volodymyr-Volynskyi and archimandrite of the Dubno Monastery. In 1651 he was appointed coadjutor of Peremyshl eparchy, and in the next year he succeeded A. *Krupetsky as bishop of Peremyshl, Sambir, and Sianik. At about the same time he became archimandrite of Derman Monastery and was given responsibility for administering Lutske eparchy. Khmilevsky was bitterly opposed by the Orthodox bishop of Peremyshl, A. *Vynnytsky, who refused to permit the spread of the Church Union into the eparchy. He was never allowed to occupy his see and remained in Volhynia until his death.

Khmilnyk

Khmilnyk [Xmil'nyk]. IV-8. City (1974 pop 20,000) and raion center in Vinnytsia oblast. First mentioned in 1362, when it came under Lithuanian rule; from 1434 to 1793, with interruptions, Khmilnyk belonged to the Polish Commonwealth. In 1448 it was granted the rights of Magdeburg law. Growing slowly because of repeated Tatar attacks, in 1534 it was fortified. Its inhabitants participated in the 1594–6 and 1637 Cossack rebellions against Poland, and from 1648 to 1667 it was part of the Hetman state. Under Turkish rule (1672–9) the town declined. Annexed by Russia in 1793, from 1797 to 1804 it was a county center in Podilia gubernia. In 1923 it became a raion center. Earlier the city's population consisted mostly of Jews (56 percent in 1926) and Ukrainians (41 percent). In 1959 only 2 percent of the population was Jewish; Ukrainians constituted 92 percent. Over 50,000 people annually visit the city's sanatoriums and health resorts, where radioactive mineral waters (discovered in 1934) and peat baths are used to treat various physical disorders.

Khmilnyk Chronicle (Khmilnytskyi litopys). A monument of Ukrainian historiography and literature dating from the middle of the 17th century. It is one of the so-called Cossack chronicles and was probably written in the town of Khmilnyk in Podilia. The anonymous author described events in Khmilnyk and Right-Bank Ukraine in the period 1636–50, including the Cossack uprisings of 1636–8 led by P. *Pavliuk and K. Skydan, the devastation of Podilia by Tatar and Turkish raids, and the first years of B. *Khmelnytsky's rebellion: the battles at *Zhovti Vody, *Korsun, and *Pyliavtsy, the defeats of the Polish armies in Podilia, and the victories of M. Kryvonis at Nemyriv, Makhnivka, Zhyvotiv, Berdychiv, and Tulchyn. The chronicle also contains valuable information on everyday life in the 17th century, such as descriptions of agricultural practices and the availability and prices of various commodities in Khmilnyk. The Khmilnyk Chronicle was published with an introduction by O. Levytsky in *Letopis' Samovidtsa po novootkrytym spiskam …* (The Samovydets Chronicle According to Recently Discovered Manuscripts …, Kiev, 1878). It has also been researched by V. Ikonnikov.

Khmury, Vasyl [Xmuryj, Vasyl'] (real name: Butenko), b 1896 in Rashivka, Hadiache county, Poltava gubernia, d ? Journalist; art and theater critic. A graduate of the Sorochyntsi Teachers' Seminary, in the 1920s and 1930s he edited the journal *Nove mystetstvo*, worked in the Rukh co-operative publishing house in Kharkiv, and contributed articles on the theater, cinema, and art to the newspaper *Visti VUTsKV* and its weekly supplement *Kul'tura i pobut*, and to the journals *Chervonyi shliakh* and *Sil's'kyi teatr*. He wrote the text to A. Petrytsky's *Teatral'ni stroï* (Theater Costumes, 1929) and a number of books: *Notatky pro teatr, kino i prostorove mystetstvo* (Notes on the Theater, Cinema, and Spatial Art, 1930), *Iosyp Hirniak* (1931), and *Mar'ian Krushel'nyts'kyi* (1931). Khmury was arrested in 1937 and disappeared without trace.

Khodchenko, Pavlo [Xodčenko], b 15 January 1880 in Lukianivka, near Mykolaiv, d 11 January 1967 in Kiev. Writer. He is the author of the novels *Na khutori* (On the Khutir, 1929), *Sorochyns'ka trahediia* (The Sorochyntsi Tragedy, 1940–57), *Stepova khvylia* (The Steppe Wave, 1945), and *Zrostannia* (Growing up, 1956); several plays; and the memoirs *Vyprobovuvannia zrilosti* (Testing Maturity, 1958) and *Dosvitni zahravy* (The Twilight Glow, 1967).

Khodetsky, Starion [Xodec'kyj], b 21 February 1821 in Symferopil, Tavriia gubernia, d 10 February 1887 in Kiev. Biologist, forester, educator. A graduate of St Petersburg University (1842), he studied abroad and then gave public lectures on agriculture. From 1854 to 1878 he held the Chair of Agriculture and Forestry at Kiev University and edited (1863–73) *Universitetskie izvestiia*. He wrote a number of studies on farming in Russia and animal husbandry, and several farming manuals. He developed the first Russian nomenclature for wool (1847), and proposed a number of methods for steppe afforestation.

Khodoriv [Xodoriv]. IV-5. Town (1971 pop 10,200) in Zhydachiv raion, Lviv oblast, situated on the Luh River on the western fringes of Podilia. First mentioned in 1394 as the village of Khodoriv-stav or Khodorostav, in 1772 it came under Austrian rule. A railway link was established in 1866, and in the 1890s the town became an important railway junction. During the Ukrainian-Polish War of 1918–19 the supreme headquarters of the Ukrainian Galician Army was located there. Under Soviet rule it has been a raion center in now-defunct Drohobych oblast (1940–1, 1944–59) and in Lviv oblast (1959–63). The town's sugar refinery (est 1913) was one of the largest in interwar Poland.

Khodorovsky, Hryhorii [Xodorovs'kyj, Hryhorij] (real name: Moroz-Khodorovsky), b 2 December 1853 in Kokhnivka, Zolotonosha county, Poltava gubernia, d 1 July 1927 in Sevastopil. Pianist, composer, and pedagogue. Having studied at the Leipzig (1865–9) and St Petersburg (1870–2) conservatories, he served under F. Liszt for one year as choirmaster in Weimar. Then he taught piano at the music school of the Russian Music Society in Kiev (1875–94), and in 1913 was appointed professor at the Kiev conservatory. After the 1917 Revolution he moved to Sevastopil, where he organized a people's conservatory. Khodorovsky composed piano music, including the *Ukrainian Rhapsody*, and under the pseudonym Konstantinov, arranged Ukrainian folk songs for piano. K. Kvitka and L. Revutsky were his students.

Khodorovych, Mykola [Xodorovyč], b 18 December 1857 in Kiev, d 1936 in Prague. General. After graduating from the Imperial General Staff Academy in St Petersburg, he served in various regions of the Russian Empire. During the Russo-Japanese War he was promoted to major general. He was chief of staff (July 1914–1915) and then commander-in-chief (1915–17) of the Kiev Military District. In this capacity he organized the Jan Hus legion out of Czech and Slovak prisoners of war. In late 1917 he was instrumental in the formation of the *Khmelnytsky Regiment (Bohdanivtsi) of the UNR Army out of Ukrainians serving in the Russian army. After the First World War he was granted asylum by the Czechoslovak government and moved to Prague.

Khodyka, Fedir [Xodyka] (aka Kobyzevych), b ca 1550, d January 1625 in Kiev. Member of the city council of Kiev in 1592–1613, and Kiev magistrate in 1613–18 and 1621–5. Khodyka was a wealthy textile merchant and Polish sympathizer whose policies were highly repressive toward the Ukrainian Orthodox population. He supported the increase of Polish power in Ukraine by such measures as the building up of a Polish garrison in Kiev at the expense of the Ukrainian inhabitants. At the end of 1624, with the aid of the Uniate priest I. Yuzefovych and Catholicized administrators, he began to close down Kievan Orthodox churches and hand them over to the Uniates, although he did prevent the seizure of St Sophia Cathedral and the Vydubychi Monastery. In a significant show of solidarity the townspeople and a large contingent of Zaporozhian Cossacks under the leadership of A. Lazorenko and Ya. Chyhrynets reopened the churches and drowned Khodyka and Yuzefovych in the Dnieper River.

Khoinatsky, Andrii [Xojnac'kyj, Andrij], 1836–88. Orthodox church leader, pedagogue, and church historian. A graduate of the Kiev Theological Academy, he taught at the Kremianets Theological Seminary and then became a lecturer in theology at the Nizhen Historical-Philological Institute. Khoinatsky specialized in the history of the church in Volhynia, especially the Pochaiv Monastery and the Church Union, and folk rites and beliefs. In addition to numerous journal articles, he wrote *Zapadnorusskaia Tserkovnaia Uniia v eia Bogosluzhenii i obriadakh* (The Western Ruthenian Church Union in Its Liturgies and Rites, 1871) and *Ocherki iz istorii Pravoslavnoi Tserkvy i drevnego blagochestiia na Volyni* (Outlines on the History of the Orthodox Church and Early Religiosity in Volhynia, 1878); a revised version of his *Pochaevskaia Uspenskaia Lavra* (The Pochaiv Dormition Monastery) appeared posthumously in 1897.

Khokhol [xoxol]. A derogatory Russian term for Ukrainians. *Khokhol* literally means a sheaf or tuft of cereal stalks and is derived from an old Slavic word. As a term used to describe Ukrainians, it may have originally referred to the customary tufts of hair worn by the Cossacks, called *oseledtsi*. Although it was primarily used by Russians to denigrate Ukrainians, at times, especially in the 19th century, it was used by Ukrainians as a term of self-identification. In these contexts, the term *khokhol* has appeared in Ukrainian literature, mainly in historical literary works by such writers as O. Dovzhenko ('Eh, you, *khokhol*. You would only joke') and Z. Tulub ('Our *khokhly* always wear moustaches'). In the 20th century the term began to be used by Ukrainians as a scornful epithet for Russified Ukrainians.

Kholm [Xolm] (Polish: Chełm). II-4. The principal city (1977 pop 49,000) of the *Kholm region, situated on the steep bank of the Uherka River, a tributary of the Buh River; since 1975 the capital of Chełm voivodeship in Poland. The date of its origin is unknown. In 1237 Prince Danylo Romanovych of Volhynia built a castle there and reinforced the town with stone walls and with defensive towers in the neighboring villages of Bilavyne and Stovp. As a result Kholm withstood the Mongol invasion of 1240. At that time the trade route linking Rus' via Galicia with the Mediterranean lost its importance because of Constantinople's decline and the Mongols' control of the steppes and was supplanted by the route linking western Rus' via the Buh and Vistula with the Baltic ports and the realm of the Teutonic Knights. Because Kholm was located on the latter route, after also becoming the ruler of Galicia, Danylo made it his capital and the see of *Kholm eparchy.

As the capital of Galicia-Volhynia (until 1272) and then of an appanage principality, the town withstood another Mongol siege (1261) but suffered greatly during the Lithuanian-Polish-Hungarian wars for control of Galicia-Volhynia in the 14th century before being annexed by Poland in 1387. In 1392 the city obtained the rights of Magdeburg law, which were later supplemented with royal privileges. From 1484 it and the Kholm land were part of Rus' voivodeship. From the mid-15th century Kholm was an important trade center. Yet in 1612 it had only 2,200 inhabitants, 800 of whom were Jews. As an eparchial see and religious-educational center, it had some cultural influence. From the mid-17th century Kholm declined because of Poland's continual wars. In 1648 it was captured and briefly held by the Cossack army of Hetman B. Khmelnytsky. Later it was ravaged by Swedish and Muscovite troops, particularly during the Great Northern War (1700–21). In the late 18th century its population was only 2,500 (over 1,000 Jews, 1,000 Poles, and only 200 Uniate Ukrainians).

After the Third Partition of Poland the town belonged to Austria (1795–1807), the Grand Duchy of Warsaw (1807–12), the Congress Kingdom of Poland (1812–32), and Russia (1832–1917). It remained a small Polonized county capital and trade center with a predominantly Jewish population (in 1860, 2,480 of its 3,600 inhabitants were Jews). Its importance was as the see of a Uniate eparchy. In the second half of the 19th century, Russians, mostly civil servants, began settling in Kholm. In 1873 it had a population of 5,595, consisting of 263 Orthodox (Russians), 530 Uniates (Ukrainians), 1,294 Roman Catholics (Poles), and 1,503 Jews. By 1911 its population had grown to 21,425, consisting of 5,181 Orthodox (Ukrainians and Russians), 3,820 Roman Catholics (Poles), 12,100 Jews, and 315 Lutherans (Germans). With the abolition of the Uniate church and the influx of Russian Orthodox clergy, Russian influence grew, and Kholm became the center of Russification in the Kholm region, with several Russian secondary schools and a theological seminary. During the brief liberal period after the Revolution of 1905 the city's Ukrainian inhabitants were able to establish the Enlightenment Society of Kholm Rus' (which published the bilingual Ukrainian-Russian journal *Brats'ka besida*) and a *Prosvita society, but after *Kholm gubernia was formed in 1912, Russification pressures increased with the rise in the number of Russian functionaries in the city.

Kholm: Cathedral of the Nativity of the Virgin Mary

During the First World War almost all of Kholm's Ukrainians and Russians were evacuated east in 1915, before its capture by the Austrian army. Many Ukrainians returned in 1920–2, those who had been in the UNR with a developed national identity. Under interwar Polish rule (1921–39) the city was a minor center of Ukrainian life. The region's cultural-educational *Ridna Khata society was centered there. Published there were the pro-Soviet and Socialist weeklies *Nashe zhyttia* (1921–8), *Selians'kyi shliakh* (1937–8), and *Nove zhyttia* (1927–8), calendars, and other materials. In the late 1920s, however, these activities and publications were suppressed by the Polish authorities, as was Ukrainian church life (the city's Orthodox cathedral and cemetery were desecrated by the Poles and closed down as early as 1919).

After Germany invaded Poland in 1939, Kholm was part of the *Generalgouvernement and experienced a resurgence of Ukrainian activity to which refugees from Soviet-occupied Galicia made an important contribution. A Ukrainian Committee and Provisional Church Council were formed. Thanks to the efforts of the *Ukrainian Central Committee in Cracow the Orthodox cathedral was restored to the Ukrainians, and Kholm became the see of the new Kholm-Podlachia eparchy; its archbishop, I. *Ohiienko, established a small seminary there. A Ukrainian Relief Committee was also active there. Ukrainian schools (including a gymnasium, a technical school, and two trade schools), educational and artistic groups, a drama troupe, co-operatives, and various private businesses were allowed to function. This revival was cut short by the Soviet and Polish Communist occupation in July 1944. Many of Kholm's active Ukrainians fled west to Germany and emigrated after the war to the New World. The majority of those who stayed behind were forcibly resettled in 1946 by the Polish authorities in the former German territories of western Poland. Today only a small number of Ukrainians live in Kholm, where they have an Orthodox parish.

The city's most important architectural monument is the Cathedral of the Mother of God built by Prince Danylo in the mid-13th century on Castle Hill. Rebuilt after being destroyed by fire in 1256, at the end of the 16th century it became the residence of the Uniate bishop. It underwent major alterations in 1638–40 under Bishop M. Terletsky and was renovated in 1735–56 in the style of the late baroque. Minor alterations were made in 1874–8 after it became an Orthodox church. Its iconostasis, many icons, and several murals were destroyed by the Poles in 1919, after which it belonged to the Roman Catholic church. Further changes were made after the building was restored to the Orthodox church in 1940, and again after it was taken over once more by the Roman Catholic church in 1946. The miraculous medieval icon of the Theotokos has been preserved in the cathedral. Other architectural monuments in the city include the Orthodox Church of the Holy Spirit (1849), a Roman Catholic church in the late rococo style (1753–63) designed by P. Fontana, and the monastery of the Franciscan Reformaci (1736–40, rebuilt in the 19th century). The city's museum contains many masterpieces of church art.

BIBLIOGRAPHY
Batiushkov, M. *Kholmskaia Rus'* (St Petersburg 1887)
Czernicki, K. *Chełm, przeszłość i pamiątki* (Kholm 1936)
Sichyns'kyi, V. *Misto Kholm* (Cracow 1941); repr in *Nadbuzhanshchyna: Istorychno-memuarnyi zbirnyk*, 1, ed M. Martyniuk et al (New York-Paris-Sydney-Toronto 1986)
Pasternak, Ie. *Narys istoriï Kholmshchyny i Pidliashshia (Novishi chasy)* (Winnipeg-Toronto 1968)
Zimmer, B. *Miasto Chełm: Zarys historyczny* (Warsaw-Cracow 1974)

V. Kubijovyč

Kholm eparchy. An eparchy founded in the first half of the 13th century by prince Danylo Romanovych of Galicia-Volhynia in the *Kholm region and Podlachia. The see was in Uhrusk until ca 1240, when it was transferred to Kholm. Kholm eparchy was under the Kievan metropolitan except for a short period in the 14th century, when it was part of Halych metropoly. From the mid-14th century it was known as Kholm and Belz eparchy. The eparchy's hierarchy joined the Church Union of *Berestia in 1596, although Orthodox forces continued to fight for control of the eparchy for several decades. The more renowned Uniate bishops were D. *Zbiruisky (1585–1603), who accepted the Church Union, M. *Terletsky (1630–49), who defended the Uniate church against Latinizing clergy, Ya. *Susha (1652–87), F. Volodkovych (1731–56), and M. Rylko (1759–84). During their tenures, Kholm eparchy had a theological seminary, a school for training deacons, and three monasteries (in Kholm, Yablochyn, and Turkovychi).

Kholm eparchy was divided in the First Polish Partition of Poland in 1772: the north, including Kholm, remained under Poland while the south was annexed by Austria. The entire eparchy became part of the Grand Duchy of Warsaw in 1809, and part of the Russian-ruled Polish Kingdom in 1815. Its location within the semiautonomous kingdom allowed it to remain a Uniate eparchy throughout the first half of the 19th century when Tsar Nicholas I was destroying the Uniate Church in Russia and forcing its followers to convert to Orthodoxy. In 1807 it was again placed under the jurisdiction of Halych metropoly, and in 1830 it was directly subordinated to the Vatican.

From its inception, Khlolm eparchy was faced with strong Latinizing and Polonizing pressures, because of its proximity to Poland. A Roman Catholic diocese of Kholm existed from the 19th century and it attracted many followers from among Polonized Ukrainians. Under Bishop F. Tsikhanovsky (1810–28), the number of Uniate parishes fell from 317 to 278. In the mid-19th century, the Russian authorities again began pressuring the bishops to return to Orthodoxy. When Bishop I. Kaminsky resisted, he was dismissed and the Russophile Y. Voitsitsky (1866–8) was appointed administrator of the eparchy. He maintained a pro-Russian policy and recruited Russophile priests from Galicia for the eparchy. When the Vatican refused to recognize Voitsitsky as bishop, the tsarist authorities agreed to the appointment of a new bishop, M. Kuzemsky (1868–71), a canon from Lviv. He attempted to stop the Latinization but at the same time remained loyal to Rome. In 1875 the authorities appointed M. Popel, a supporter of Orthodoxy from Galicia, administrator of the eparchy. On 18 February 1875, on behalf of the Kholm clergy and consistory, Popel formally requested the admission of 120 parishes into the Orthodox church. As a result of widespread opposition to this move in the eparchy, 74 priests were deported to Siberia, 60 priests were expelled to Galicia, scores of faithful were killed, and some 600 were also deported to Siberia.

After the abolition of the Church Union, Kholm eparchy was incorporated within the Warsaw Orthodox eparchy, which was renamed Kholm and Warsaw eparchy, and Popel became the vicar-general of Kholm. In 1902 E. *Georgievsky became bishop of Kholm, and in 1905 Kholm eparchy again became a separate entity, headed by Georgievsky. The great resentment on the part of the clergy and faithful to the forced conversion to Orthodoxy is evidenced by the mass conversions to Roman Catholicism in the eparchy after the granting of some religious freedom by the authorities in 1905.

After the First World War, Kholm eparchy was incorporated into Warsaw eparchy, headed by D. *Valedynsky. Although the cathedral in Kholm was given to the Roman Catholic church by the Polish authorities in 1919 and Russians controlled the Orthodox church in Poland, the Kholm region became a major center of Ukrainian Orthodoxy, and many religious publications were issued in Ukrainian there. Under the German occupation during the Second World War, Kholm cathedral was returned to Orthodox Ukrainians and Kholm eparchy, officially called Kholm and Podlachia eparchy, was reestablished (with I. Ohiienko as bishop) and Ukrainianized. In 1943 it was raised to the status of a metropoly; at that time it had 91 parishes. Kholm eparchy was finally abolished when it became part of Poland after the Second World War.

BIBLIOGRAPHY

Pelesz, J. *Geschichte der Union der Ruthenischen Kirche mit Rom*, 1 (Vienna 1878)

Likowski, E. *Dzieje Kościoła Unickiego na Litwie i Rusi w XVIII–XIX wieku*, 2nd edn (Warsaw 1906)

Sonevyts'kyi, L. 'Ukraïns'kyi iepyskopat Peremys'koï i Kholms'koï eparkhiï v XV–XVI st.,' *ZChVV*, 1 (1955), no. 6; repr in L. Sonevyts'kyi, *Studiï z istoriï Ukraïny* (Paris-New York-Sydney-Toronto 1982)

Vlasovs'kyi, I. *Narys istoriï Ukraïns'koï Pravoslavnoï Tserkvy*, 3 (Bound Brook, NJ 1957)

Glinka, L. 'Diocesia Ucraino-Cattolica di Cholm,' *AOBM* 1 (1975), no. 34

W. Lencyk

Kholm Gospel. A 167-sheet gospel written in the late 13th century, probably in Kholm. Its Church Slavonic language is distinguished by Ukrainian phonetic features. An excerpt from the work appeared in A. Sobolevsky's *Ocherki iz istorii russkogo iazyka* (Outlines on the History of the Russian Language, 1884). The gospel is preserved in the Lenin Library in Moscow.

Kholm gubernia. An administrative-territorial unit in the Russian Empire, created in 1912 out of the eastern borderlands of Lublin and Siedlce gubernias of the Congress Kingdom of Poland. The capital was Kholm. The gubernia's territory (10,456 sq km) was divided among six counties: Kholm, Biała Podlaska, Volodava, Hrubeshiv, Tomaszów, and Konstantyniv. Its population (841,800 in 1914) consisted of Ukrainians (53.2 percent), Poles (23.9 percent), Jews (15.4 percent), Russians (3.7 percent), and Germans (3.7 percent). During the First World War it was under martial law. From 1918 to 1920 its territory was part of the UNR. In 1921 it was ceded by Soviet Russia to Poland. (See *Kholm region.)

Kholm region (Kholmshchyna). A historical-geographical land west of the Buh River, bordering on the Polish Lublin region in the west, Volhynia in the east, Podlachia in the north, and Galicia in the south. The boundary between Siedlce and Lublin gubernias of the Russian Empire can be taken as the boundary between the Kholm region (Kholm, Hrubeshiv, Krasnystaw, Tomaszów, Zamość, and Biłgoraj counties) and Podlachia (Biała Podlaska, Volodava, Konstantyniv, and Radzyń Podlaski counties). In the interwar period the Kholm region within Lublin voivodeship had an area of 7,270 sq km. The name of the region, which has also been called Kholm Rus', the Transbuh region (Zabuzhia), and Transbuh Rus', has often been extended to include *Podlachia, because the latter was part of *Kholm eparchy and (from 1912 to 1917) *Kholm gubernia; except for northern Podlachia, which was part of Bielsk Podlaski county in Hrodna gubernia, the two regions have shared a common history since 1795.

Because it was a borderland, the Kholm region did not develop strong ties with the rest of Ukraine's territories, and until the 20th century its Ukrainian population had a relatively weak sense of national identity. The reign of Prince *Danylo Romanovych of Galicia-Volhynia was the exception: being on the periphery of the Mongol invasion, the region enjoyed relative peace and prosperity, and Danylo made *Kholm, its major city, his capital. Its proximity to Poland, however, made the region susceptible to Polish influences and facilitated its Polonization, beginning in the 14th century. Thereafter the history of both the Kholm region and Podlachia unfolded in a manner that was unique for Ukraine's lands, particularly in

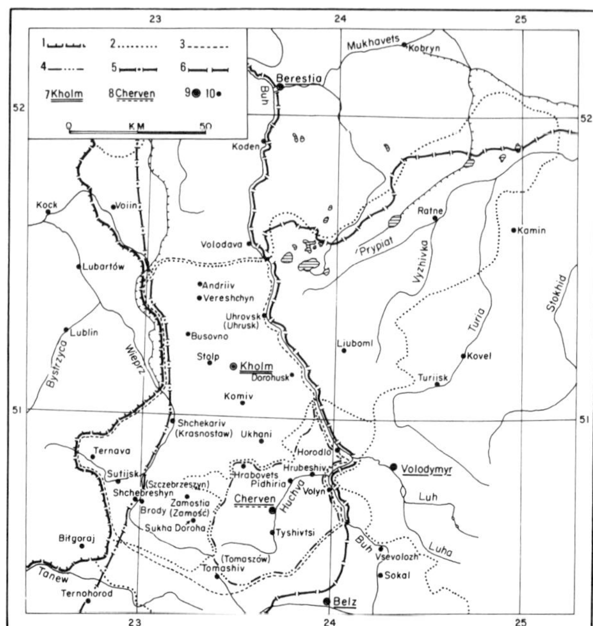

KHOLM REGION

1. Western boundary of Rus' (10th–14th centuries)
2. Kholm land in the late 14th–15th centuries
3. Borders of the territory of the Cherven towns in the 10th–12th centuries
4. Cherven principality in 1210
5. Border of the UNR according to the 1918 Peace Treaty of Brest-Litovsk
6. Present Polish-Ukrainian border
7. Capital of the Kholm land
8. Capital of Cherven principality
9. Capitals of principalities and lands
10. Other settlements

the religious sphere. Since 1921 they have belonged to Poland; since 1975 they have constituted most of Chełm, Zamość, and Biała Podlaska voivodeships and the southern part of Białystok voivodeship. After the Second World War most of the Ukrainian population was forcibly resettled by the Polish authorities, and few Ukrainians live there today.

Physical geography. Most of the Kholm region lies in the western part of the *Volhynia-Kholm Upland. Its gently undulating plain has an average altitude of 200–250 m and is built on a chalk foundation overlain with Tertiary strata, loess, and fertile soils (chernozems around Hrubeshiv). The region's small northern and northeastern parts lie in the medium-fertile Podlachia Lowland into which the descent (20–40 m) from the upland forms a distinct step. The southwest lies in the less fertile *Sian Lowland. The rivers are part of the large Vistula Basin; they include the Buh with its tributaries the Uherka and Huchva, the Wieprz with the Bystrzyca, and the Sian's tributary, the Tanew.

The region's climate is transitional between continental and oceanic. Winters are mild: in Kholm the median January temperature is −4.4°C. Summers are temperate: in Kholm the median July temperature is 18.5°C. The average annual temperature is 7.4°C. In neighboring Lublin there are 137 clear days per year and the annual precipitation is 546 mm, mainly in summer (250 mm). Almost all of the region belongs to the central-European mixed-forest zone. The eastern limit of the beech, fir, larch, and hornbeam and northwestern limit of the spruce run through it and Podlachia. At one time large forests covered the southwest. The region's soils are of the sandy (20 percent), loess (20 percent), chernozem (10 percent), loam (12 percent), peat-and-bog (16 percent), and pine-forest (15 percent) variety.

History

To 1815. The Kholm region has been inhabited since the Upper Paleolithic period. In the early medieval period it was settled by the East Slavic *Dulibians. From the second half of the 10th century it was ruled by the Volhynian princes of Kievan Rus' (see *Cherven towns), and from the 13th century to 1340, by the Principality of Galicia-Volhynia. Its southern part constituted the historical *Belz land. In the 14th century territorial wars for control of the region raged. It was held by Lithuania (1340–77) and Hungary (1377–87) before Poland consolidated its four-century rule there. In the 15th century almost all of the region was part of the Kholm land, which was divided into Kholm and Krasnystaw counties; it was governed from Kholm by a castellan appointed by the palatine of Rus' voivodeship in Lviv. In 1648, during the Cossack-Polish War, the army of Hetman B. Khmelnytsky captured Kholm and Zamostia (Zamość) and briefly held the Kholm region and Podlachia. In the 1650s and in 1704–10 Polish-Swedish battles took place there.

Under Polish rule the region's upper social strata succumbed to Polonization, which was bolstered by the influx of Polish colonists there and, in even greater numbers, in Podlachia. The Uniate church played a leading role in the region's cultural and educational life, beginning in the 17th century. The Kholm Uniate brotherhood and Basilian monks ran church schools; Bishop M. Terletsky founded a Uniate gymnasium in Kholm in 1639; and Bishop M. Ryllo founded a Uniate seminary there in 1760. After the Third Partition of Poland in 1795, the region and Podlachia were annexed by Austria. From 1809 to 1814 they were part of the Grand Napoleonic Duchy of Warsaw; from 1815 to 1832, the Congress Kingdom of Poland; and from 1832 to 1917, the Russian Empire.

1815–1914. As part of the Congress Kingdom, the Kholm region and Podlachia were governed by Poles, and linguistic and religious Polonization increased. The Greek Catholic (Uniate) church was the only bulwark against complete assimilation. The region's nobles and magnates of Ukrainian descent had long been Polonized, however, and only the Ukrainian peasants remained loyal to the Uniate church and its clergy. Consequently even the Uniate church was unable to withstand the pressures of Romanization, and its clergy modified its structure by introducing chapters (see *Canon), corrupted its ritual with such Roman trappings as organ music and monstrances, had iconostases removed, and delivered sermons in Polish. Thus the Uniate church in the Kholm region came to resemble the Roman Catholic church more than it did its counterpart in Galicia. Unlike the Galician clergy, few priests in the Kholm region and Podlachia had a higher education. Some spoke only Polish and did not know Church Slavonic, and they and their families regarded themselves as Poles. The failure of the Polish Insurrection of 1830 did not diminish Polish influence in the Kholm region and Podlachia, for the laws, official language, and administration in Russian-ruled Poland remained Polish. In 1839 the Uniate church was outlawed in the Russian Empire except in the Kholm region and Podlachia; there it continued to be tolerated but was closely supervised by the Russian viceroy in Warsaw, who influenced the nomination of bishops. At the same time, the church was able to retain some measure of Ukrainianness because of the presence of Galician-born priests there and because the metropolitan of Halych still had some say in the election of its bishops, even after Kholm eparchy was subordinated directly to the Vatican in 1830. The position of the church deteriorated after the defeat of the Polish Insurrection of 1863–4, which some local Uniate clergy supported and many priests' sons joined. The tsarist regime in Poland became more repressive, replaced Polish with Russian as the language of government and education, and brought many Russian bureaucrats and colonists into the region. To counteract Polish influence, in 1875 it abolished the Uniate church there, incorporating its 120 parishes into the new Kholm-Warsaw Orthodox eparchy. Around 100,000 of the Uniate faithful, particularly in Podlachia, refused to become Orthodox, and the tsarist authorities resorted to police and military violence, mass arrests, exile to Siberia, and even killing to suppress religious opposition. Only 59 of 214 Uniate clergy embraced the Orthodox faith; 74 others were exiled, and 66 were expelled to Galicia. At the same time, some Greek Catholic clergy from Galicia voluntarily converted and became Orthodox parish priests in the region, and many teachers from central Ukraine moved there and disseminated Ukrainian populist ideas among the peasantry.

Religious and ethnic relations in the region changed during the Russian Revolution of 1905, when Tsar Nicholas II issued an ukase on religious tolerance. Because the Uniate church was still outlawed, 170,000 of 450,000 'Orthodox' converted to Roman Catholicism by 1908; many peasants were blackmailed and coerced by Polish landowners to do so. This conversion resulted in another upsurge of Polonization, particularly among the younger people. As a result the region's population was split into three groups: the nationally conscious Ukrainian-speaking Orthodox, the ethnic Polish Roman Catholics, and the Ukrainian-speaking converts, who by and large lacked a clear sense of national identity and were contemptuously called *'Kalakuty' or 'Pereketsi' (turncoats) by the first group.

Alarmed by the conversions, the Russian Holy Synod created a separate Orthodox eparchy under Bishop E. Georgievsky. To counteract Catholicism and Polonization, Georgievsky allowed the use of certain local liturgical customs and sermons in Ukrainian. At the turn of the 20th century the state of education in the Kholm region was better than in the central and eastern regions of Ukraine. A relatively dense network of elementary schools was in place and teachers were trained at pedagogical seminaries in Kholm and Biała Podlaska and the Kholm Theological Seminary. After the Revolution of 1905 the Ukrainian national movement found adherents among many of these teachers. From 1905 O. Spolitak and O. Losky published several popular booklets and one issue of the confiscated newspaper *Buh* in Hrubeshiv. The Popular Enlightenment Society of Kholm Rus' published books, the Russian and Ukrainian weekly *Bratska besida* (ed M. Kobryn), and the popular *Kholmskii narodnyi kalendar*. The Kholm Orthodox Brotherhood (est 1885) published the daily *Kholmskaia Rus'* (1912–17).

To undermine Polish influence, local Orthodox circles (particularly the Kholm Brotherhood) proposed that the Kholm region become a separate gubernia. After many public hearings, written submissions, and debates in the Russian State Duma, where the gubernial project was opposed not only by the Polish caucus but also by the deputies of other national minorities (except the Ukrainians), the Kadets, and the socialists, the bill creating Kholm gubernia was passed and enacted by the tsar on 23 June 1912. The gubernia was formed out of the Ukrainian-populated parts of Lublin and Siedlce gubernias; its borders were delineated on the basis of V. Frantsev's ethnographic maps. It was placed under the direct jurisdiction of the Ministry of Internal Affairs in St Petersburg, but its school system came under the supervision of the Kiev school superintendent. The outbreak of the First World War prevented the law from being fully implemented.

1915–19. In August 1915 the Kholm region and Podlachia became a theater of war. Having already deported all German colonists into the Russian hinterland, before its retreat the Russian army conducted a mass evacuation of the region's population. Fearful of Polish persecution if they remained, almost all Russians and Ukrainians left voluntarily. Only the Poles and practically all the Kalakuty stayed behind. During its retreat the Russian army burned down almost all the Ukrainian villages. After the retreat only 25,000 Ukrainians remained – 15,000 in the Kholm region and 10,000 in Podlachia.

Under the Austrian occupation, Ukrainian cultural and educational activity in the Kholm region was ruled out because of the small Ukrainian population and because the Austrian authorities, who were influenced by the Poles, forbade it. In Podlachia, however, which was occupied by the Germans, the *Union for the Liberation of Ukraine was allowed to open Ukrainian schools in early 1917, and the Ukrainian Hromada in Biała Podlaska was allowed to publish the newspaper *Ridne slovo* (1917–19).

The 300,000 evacuees from the Kholm region and Podlachia suffered severe hardships during their chaotic evacuation to the east. Most of them lost their belongings on the way, and many succumbed to disease. Eventually the tsarist authorities set up relief committees to help them resettle in the Volga region or in Central Asia. Most worked as farm laborers; because of their agrarian skills, they managed to live reasonably well. Being displaced among Russians made the refugees aware that they were not Russian. The Revolution of 1917 and the creation of the *Central Rada in Kiev had an even greater impact on their national consciousness. In spring 1917 they held a number of local congresses in various places of the empire and chose 276 delegates to the All-People's Congress of the Kholm Region. Held in Kiev on 7–12 September 1917, the congress resolved that the people of the Kholm region were Ukrainian and should be part of Ukraine and elected a Kholm Gubernia Executive Committee whose members – O. Vasylenko, Rev A. Mateiuk, T. Olesiiuk, A. Duda, S. Liubarsky, K. Dmytriiuk, and M. Shketyn – automatically became delegates to the Central Rada.

On 27 November 1917 the Central Rada adopted the resolution proposed by the Kholm delegates that the Kholm region and Podlachia were an integral part of the UNR and placed all the evacuees and their institutions under the protection of the *General Secretariat, which was to establish political and administrative order in these regions. The Peace Treaty of *Brest-Litovsk, signed by the UNR and the Central Powers on 9 February 1918, recognized the Kholm region and Podlachia region, defined roughly by the borders of Kholm gubernia, as part of the UNR. This recognition provoked widespread Polish protest even in the Austrian Parliament. Ukrainian commissioners (O. Skoropys-Yoltykhovsky, K. Dmytriiuk) were sent to establish order in the regions, and the evacuees slowly began returning home. There they met with concerted Polish opposition, tacitly supported by the Austrian authorities.

After the Central Powers capitulated, German troops were evacuated in December 1918, and in February 1919 Polish units occupied the Kholm region and Podlachia. Skoropys-Yoltukhovsky and many Ukrainian teachers and leaders were imprisoned. Of the 389 Orthodox churches there in 1914, 149 were transferred to the Polish Catholic church; 111 were desecrated, looted, and closed down; and 79 were destroyed during the war or after by the Polish authorities.

1920–39. During the Polish-Soviet War of 1920 the Kholm region and Podlachia were briefly occupied by Soviet troops in August. Polish rule of these regions was affirmed by the Polish-Soviet Peace Treaty of *Riga. By 1922 many Ukrainian evacuees had returned to their devastated villages, even though the Polish authorities had made it difficult for them, particularly the Ukrainian intelligentsia, to do so. Because of Polish enmity, many remained in the USSR. Altogether, the number of Ukrainians in the region was about 120,000, or a third less than it had been in 1914.

In the interwar period no other Ukrainian territory under Polish rule was subjected to as much official Polonizing pressure as were the Kholm region and Podlachia within Lublin voivodeship. The schools were exclusively Polish, many of the prewar Ukrainian Orthodox churches were given to the Polish Catholic church, the land was distributed to the many Polish colonists who were brought in, and concerted efforts were made to convert the Orthodox to the newly fabricated 'Roman Catholic church of the Eastern Rite.' Yet the Ukrainians managed to set up their own community institutions, including the cultural-educational *Ridna Khata society with 125 branches, co-operatives (which came under the Audit Union of Ukrainian Co-operatives in Lviv), the newspaper *Nashe zhyttia*, and prayer houses to replace the churches that were not allowed to reopen by the authorities. They demonstrated their political unity in the 1922 Polish elections and, despite gerrymandering, managed to elect P. Vasynchuk, Y. Skrypa, S. Liubarsky, S. Makivka, A. Vasynchuk, and Ya. Voitiuk to the Sejm and I. Pasternak to the Senate. From 1926 the Polish regime became more authoritarian and repressive. It closed down the Ridna Khata society in 1930, prohibited Ukrainian theater and press, cut off the co-operative movement's links with Lviv, and instituted police surveillance and persecution of activists, many of them members of the Communist Party of Western Ukraine or the Ukrainian National Democratic Alliance. Democratic Sejm elections were rendered impossible, and in 1928 only one Ukrainian was elected. Hundreds of citizens were imprisoned, many of them on trumped-up charges of being subversive communists. The only Ukrainian institution that was not outlawed was the Orthodox church, but even it was forced to use Polish as the official language of publication, religious instruction, and sermons. Its clergy was closely watched by the police, and many nationally conscious priests were relieved of their duties and not allowed to minister to their flocks. In late 1937 the Polish authorities began a mass demolition of Orthodox churches as 'superflous entities'; by 1938, of 389 Orthodox churches in the Kholm region and Podlachia in 1914, 149 had become Roman Catholic churches and 189 had been wantonly destroyed by the Polish authorities (112 in 1938 alone). In the late 1930s the authorities tacitly condoned another means of repression against the Ukrainians: armed Polish gangs ('krakusy') that attacked Ukrainian homes and destroyed property.

1939–44. Two weeks after Germany invaded Poland in September 1939, German troops had occupied all of the Kholm region and Podlachia, which became part of the Lublin district of the occupied *Generalgouvernement of Poland. The Germans tolerated Ukrainian cultural activity, and in the larger Ukrainian communities various civic organizations sprang up within the first few weeks of the occupation. They organized refugee relief, defended the interests of the Ukrainian population before the authorities, established a network of Ukrainian schools, revived the branches of the Ridna Khata society and Ukrainian co-operatives, and took back many Orthodox churches that had been Romanized by the Poles. Local Ukrainians were assisted in this work by about 1,500 to 2,000 refugees from the Soviet-occupied Western Ukrainian territories and liberated political prisoners from Polish prisons and concentration camps, living in Lublin and other cities, where they worked as clerks in the German administration, agents of co-operatives, teachers, and community leaders. From 1940 a sizable number of refugee clergymen from Bukovyna performed pastoral functions in the region's Orthodox church. At the same time the German authorities resettled all indigenous Germans in western Poland and replaced them with Poles deported from there, thus increasing the local Polish population. In addition according to a German-Soviet repatriation agreement, about 5,000 indigenous Ukrainians were allowed to emigrate to Soviet Ukraine in 1940.

Soon after the occupation began, Ukrainian committees were created in Biłgoraj, Ternohorod, Tomaszów, Zamość, Hrubeshiv, Kholm, Lublin, Volodava, Krasnystaw, and Biała Podlaska. A Central Kholm Committee was established in Kholm to oversee all Ukrainian activity, but in practice it limited itself to that of Kholm and Volodava counties. The most influential local leaders were A. Pavliuk (chairman of the Central Kholm Committee), S. Liubarsky, V. Kosonotsky, V. Ostrovsky, O. Rochniak in Zamość, I. Pasternak in Biała Podlaska, and T. Olesiiuk in Volodava. By November 1940 all the Ukrainian committees recognized the authority of an umbrella committee in Cracow headed by V. Kubijovyč which from June was called the *Ukrainian Central Committee (UCC), and the local committees became known as Ukrainian relief committees.

During the German occupation, the Ukrainian church underwent a revival. On 5 November 1939 a Provisional Orthodox Church Council already existed in Kholm, and soon a separate administration of the Orthodox church, led by Rev I. Levchuk and with Rev M. Maliuzhynsky as vicar general, was functioning. By the beginning of 1940 the number of Orthodox parishes had increased from 51 to 91. The restoration of the Kholm Cathedral to the Orthodox church on 19 May 1940 symbolized an end to Polish religious domination in the region. Representations by the UCC on behalf of the church before the German authorities led to the official sanctioning of the restored Ukrainian Autocephalous Orthodox church and the restoration of Kholm eparchy (as the Kholm-Podlachia eparchy) and the consecration of Prof I. Ohiienko as archbishop of Kholm.

For the first time in the Kholm region and Podlachia, Ukrainian became the language of instruction in a network of elementary schools, the secondary technical and trade schools in Kholm, and the commercial schools in Volodava, Biała Podlaska, and Hrubeshiv. A Ukrainian gymnasium (with as many as 625 students) in Kholm and student residences in Kholm, Biała Podlaska, and Volodava were opened. Correspondence courses were organized by *Ukrainian educational societies allowed by Germans. Local co-operatives were subordinated to county unions and an audit union in Lublin. Public Ukrainian activity was co-ordinated locally by the Ukrainian relief committees. A significant number of Ukrainians lived and worked in Lublin; there V. Tymtsiurak and, from 1941, L. Holeiko represented the UCC before the district governor. B. Hlibovytsky and Ye. Pasternak in Biała Podlaska, M. Strutynsky in Hrubeshiv, and R. Perfetsky in Zamość were noted local Ukrainian relief committee leaders. Thus Ukrainian national life flourished in the region as it never had before. Problems arose, however, with the Kalakuty, most of whom were indifferent to the Ukrainian organizational efforts.

After most of the Galician refugees returned to Galicia when it was occupied by the Germans in the summer of 1941, Ukrainian activity in the Kholm region and Podlachia began declining. In 1942 the anti-German Polish nationalist underground, later known as the *Polish Home

Army, also began a campaign of terror against the Ukrainians, burning down their villages and murdering the inhabitants. In Hrubeshiv county, the Ukrainians responded by organizing Samooborona (self-defense) units that had links with the UPA. In 1943 the chairman of the Hrubeshiv relief committee, M. Strutynsky, the former senator I. *Pasternak, the Samooborona commanders Ya. Halchevsky-Voinarovsky and Yu. Lukashchuk, and other Ukrainian leaders were assassinated by the Polish underground. In 1943 the Germans began forcibly deporting the inhabitants of many Polish and Ukrainian villages in Zamość and Tomaszów counties with the aim of resettling Germans there and undermining the popular base of the undergrounds. This led to an upsurge in Polish underground activity and further German reprisals, which inflicted heavy losses on the Ukrainian peasants. In the summer of 1943 Soviet partisans also appeared in the Kholm region and Podlachia. In 1944, as the Soviet army advanced into the regions, Polish communist partisans became active there.

1944 to the present. In July 1944 the entire Kholm region and Podlachia were occupied by Soviet troops, and Kholm became the provisional capital of the Communist Polish People's Republic. In September 1944 a temporary Soviet-Polish border, following roughly the former *Curzon Line along the Buh River, was agreed upon. The border was settled in August 1945, and the Kholm region and Podlachia remained part of Poland as the eastern part of Lublin voivodeship.

On 3 September 1944 the Polish-Soviet authorities had signed an agreement in Lublin on the voluntary resettlement of Ukrainians living in Poland to Ukraine and of Poles living in Soviet Ukraine to Poland. The population transfer began in October 1944. By August 1946, 193,500 Ukrainians from the Kholm region and Podlachia had been resettled in Ukraine. Both the Polish Home Army and the UPA opposed the postwar regime and tried to sabotage the resettlement operation; in 1945 they even co-operated by restricting their operations to mutually agreed spheres of interest. Soviet and Polish government forces ensured the success of the resettlement operation, however, and only a small Ukrainian population – 25,000 to 40,000 – remained when it ended, in the southeastern part of Hrubeshiv county and in a thin strip along the Buh River in Biała Podlaska and Volodava counties.

In 1947 almost all of the remaining Ukrainians were forcibly resettled in the western and northern territories annexed by Poland after the war. Between 1953 and 1966 about 12,000 managed to return to their ancestral lands. Today they number about 20,000 and are concentrated in a strip along the Buh River, mostly in Podlachia. Although they belong to the *Polish Autocephalous Orthodox church, they lack many of the limited rights that are enjoyed by Ukrainians in other parts of postwar Poland; the Ukrainian language is not taught in any school, branches of the *Ukrainian Social and Cultural Society cannot be organized there, and persecution and discrimination have caused most Ukrainians to hide their ethnic identity and even to assimilate. The Ukrainian population in northern Podlachia is somewhat better off; most of it was not resettled, but it is officially considered to be Belorussian and is served by Belorussian schools and associations.

Population. In the second half of the 16th century, the Kholm land had 20 towns and 401 villages with a population of approximately 67,000. In 1867 the Ukrainian population was 217,300, of whom only 2,000 were Orthodox. In 1900 the population consisted of 463,902 Ukrainians and Belorussians (51.8 percent), 268,053 Poles (29.9 percent), 135,239 Jews (15.1 percent), and 29,123 others (3.2 percent). In 1939 the total population was 720,000, comprising 220,000 Ukrainians and 160,000 Kalakuty (together 52.8 percent), 260,000 Poles, 70,000 Jews, and 13,000 Germans. The most densely populated areas were the fertile chernozem parts of Hrubeshiv and Tomaszów counties, while the least populated was the sandy-soil area of Biłgoraj county. In 1931 only 18 percent of the population was urban; the largest towns were Kholm (1931 pop 38,600), Zamość (24,700), Hrubeshiv (12,600), Tomaszów (9,600), and outside Ukrainian ethnic territory, Krasnystaw (14,600) and Biłgoraj (13,800).

As a result of assimilation, the proportion of Ukrainian population in the Kholm region dropped over the years, though not as much as it did in Podlachia. Tables 1 and 2 show this decline in terms of religious affiliation. It must be pointed out, however, that many of those who were classified as Roman Catholics were of Ukrainian

TABLE 1
Orthodox inhabitants in Kholm region

		Orthodox pop	
County	Year	In 1000s	In %
Biłgoraj	1905	34.0	28.6
	1908	28.8	21.7
	1921	15.6	16.4
	1931	21.1	18.0
Hrubeshiv	1905	73.6	57.0
	1908	60.1	41.9
	1921	38.5	37.0
	1931	47.8	37.8
Zamość	1905	17.4	12.9
	1908	11.2	8.3
	1921	5.5	4.3
	1931	7.0	4.7
Krasnystaw (in part)	1905	10.1	26.0
	1908	6.4	17.0
	1921	4.0	11.6
	1931	4.3	11.0
Tomaszów	1905	50.6	43.6
	1908	42.1	33.8
	1921	23.3	23.8
	1931	32.5	26.8
Kholm	1905	60.2	44.4
	1908	48.1	27.4
	1921	25.1	20.6
	1931	36.8	22.6

TABLE 2
Changes in the Kholm region's religious populations

	Orthodox		Roman Catholics	
Year	In 1000s	In %	In 1000s	In %
1905	245.9	37.0	296.2	33.4
1908	196.7	26.2	421.7	56.1
1921	113.6	19.7	384.2	57.8
1931	149.5	20.9	487.3	68.1

origin. The Kholm region was a mixed Ukrainian-Polish ethnic territory. The Ukrainians were in a majority only in a narrow strip along the Buh River, particularly in Hrubeshiv county, but they were in a minority in every other county.

In 1931 the unreliable Polish census listed a population of 2,464,900 in Lublin voivodeship, of which Ukrainians made up 8.6 percent (212,000). Jews made up 12.8 percent (315,500), of whom about 70,000 lived in the Kholm region. Most of them lived in urban centers (up to the 20th century two-thirds of the region's urban population was Jewish). Most of them perished in the Nazi Holocaust. In 1931 there were only 13,000 Germans in Kholm county and the adjacent part of Volodava county. In 1914 there had been 31,500, most of whom had arrived after 1883 and settled on land as agricultural colonists. In 1915 all the Germans were deported by the Russian army, mostly to Siberia; only some of them were repatriated in 1920. In fall 1939 the German occupation authorities resettled them in the Third Reich. Thus, after the forced resettlement of Ukrainians in 1947, the Kholm region became an essentially Polish ethnic territory.

Economy. Throughout its history the Kholm region has been an agricultural land. Until 1939 about 80 percent of the population, including virtually all the Ukrainians, depended on subsistence farming for their livelihood. Large forests remained only in Biłgoraj county and the Roztochia Hills in the south. Arable land constituted 70 percent of the region's area; 51 percent of it was cultivated, 1.5 percent was orchards and gardens, 18 percent was meadows and hayfields, 24 percent was still forested, and 5.5 percent was wasteland. The principal crops grown were rye (30 percent of the seeded area), wheat (18 percent), potatoes (16 percent), oats (15 percent), fodder crops (11 percent), barley (8 percent), and industrial crops (mostly sugar beets, 2 percent). Dairy farming and hog raising were the only agricultural branches that generated large surpluses.

BIBLIOGRAPHY
Bańkowski, E. *Ruś Chełmska od czasu rozbioru Polski* (Lviv 1887)
Batiushkov, P. *Kholmskaia Rus'* (St Petersburg 1887)
Kolberg, O. *Chełmskie: Obraz etnograficzny*, 2 vols (Cracow 1890–1; repr: Wrocław-Poznań 1964)
Ploshchanskii, I. *Proshloe Kholmskoi Rusi* (Vilnius 1899)
Frantsev, V. *Karty russkogo i pravoslavnogo naseleniia Kholmskoi Rusi* (Warsaw 1909)
Dymcha, L. de. *La question de Chelm* (Paris 1911)
Wierciński, H. *Jeszcze z powodu wydzielenia Chełmszczyzny* (Cracow 1913)
– *Ziemia Chełmska i Podlasie* (Warsaw 1916)
Korduba, M. *Istoriia Kholmshchyny i Pidliashshia* (Cracow 1941)
Pasternak, Ie. *Narys istorii Kholmshchyny i Pidliashshia (novishi chasy)* (Winnipeg-Toronto 1968)
Kubiiovych, V. *Ukraïntsi v Heneral'nii Hubernii, 1939–1941* (Chicago 1975)
Nahaievs'kyi, I. 'Prychynky do istorii Kholms'koï zemli,' *Bohosloviia* 39 (1975)

V. Kubijovyč

Kholmsky, Ivan. See Krypiakevych, Ivan.

Kholodny, Hryhorii [Xolodnyj, Hryhorij], b 3 March 1886 in Tambov, Russia, d 1938. A mathematician and astronomer by training, Kholodny devoted himself to the development of Ukrainian scientific terminology. In 1918 he published a dictionary of Ukrainian physics terms. As secretary and then director of the VUAN *Institute of the Ukrainian Scientific Language and chief editor of its journal *Visnyk IUNM* (1928–30), he played an important role in defining the principles underlying the institute's work: a reliance on the popular language, especially in the formation of neologisms, and the extensive use of the results of terminological work in Galicia. Kholodny was arrested in 1929 during the *Union for the Liberation of Ukraine trials and charged with 'nationalist wrecking.' He survived many years in exile before he was reportedly executed.

Mykola Kholodny

Petro Kholodny Sr

Kholodny, Mykola [Xolodnyj], b 22 June 1882 in Tambov, Russia, d 4 May 1953 in Kiev. Plant physiologist, microbiologist; from 1929 full member of the AN URSR. After graduating from Kiev University in 1906, he taught there until 1941. From 1920 to 1949 he also worked at the AN URSR Institute of Botany. At the beginning of the 1920s he did important research on iron-fixing bacteria, and then pioneering work on plant hormones and their role in phytotropism. He also published work on ecology, soil science, the origin of life, and evolution. Besides writing numerous scientific articles, Kholodny wrote two important books – *Zhelezobakterii* (Iron Bacteria, 1921, 1953) and *Fitogormony* (Phytohormones, 1939) – and edited and wrote the commentary for the two botanical volumes of Darwin's collected works in Russian (1935–59). After his death the Institute of Botany at which he had worked was named in his honor.

Kholodny, Petro [Xolodnyj], b 18 December 1876 in Pereiaslav, Poltava gubernia, d 7 June 1930 in Warsaw. Distinguished painter, by profession a chemist. A graduate of the Kiev Drawing School, he began to exhibit his work in 1910. His early paintings include *Girl and Peacock*, *Ivasyk and the Witch*, *The Wind*, *Kateryna*, and *A Gray Day*. As a chemist, he was interested in paint manufacturing and application techniques. Attracted by ancient Galician icons in 1914, he became fascinated with the tempera technique and used it frequently. During the Revolution and Ukraine's independence, Kholodny worked in the Central Rada's Secretariat of Public Education and Ministry of Education. Under the Directory he was deputy minister of education. Leaving Ukraine with the UNR government in 1920, he was interned by the Poles in Tarnów and in 1921 settled in Lviv.

The subsequent period proved to be the most productive one in Kholodny's artistic career. In 1922 he helped found the Circle of Promoters of Ukrainian Art and took part in its exhibitions. He began to paint icons and churches and to design stained-glass windows. His principal works of this period are the icons and stained-glass windows of the Dormition Church in Lviv, the iconostasis and murals of the Chapel of the Greek Catholic Theological Seminary in Lviv, numerous icons of the parish churches in Radelychi, Kholoiv, Borshchovychi, and Zubrets, and the stained-glass windows of the church in Mraznytsia. The basic features of his work, rooted in Ukrainian artistic traditions that grew out of the synthesis of Byzantine iconography with folk art, were compositional unity, the primacy of the line, and harmonious, warm colors. In his stained-glass windows, Kholodny juxtaposed elements of pure colored glass to achieve lightness and transparency. He painted many portraits: V. Samiilenko, A. Nikovksy, Yu. Romanchuk, Rev Y. Slipy, and Ukrainian army officers such as generals M. Yunakiv, M. Bezruchko, V. Salsky, M. Omelianovych-Pavlenko, Yu. Tiutiunnyk, and V. Sinkler and Colonel D. Vitovsky. Historical compositions such as *Leaving the Castle*, *Prince Ihor's Campaign against the Cumans*, and *Oh, the Rye in the Field* are worthy of note.

Kholodny's style can be described as a mature impressionism of a Ukrainian variety that is profoundly lyrical. His neo-Byzantine works, which rivaled those of M. *Boichuk, revealed new potentialities of the ancient style, free of schematism or archaism. Kholodny also worked in graphic art, developing his own style of drawing. A posthumous exhibition of his works was held in Lviv in 1931. After the Red Army occupied Lviv, many of Kholodny's works were destroyed for their allegedly 'nationalist' spirit and his church murals were painted over.

S. Hordynsky

Petro Kholodny Jr

Kholodny, Petro [Xolodnyj], b 22 July 1902 in Kiev. Painter and graphic artist, son of P.*Kholodny. Having left Ukraine in 1920, he studied art at the Ukrainian Studio of Plastic Arts in Prague (1926–7) and the Warsaw Academy of Arts (1928–34), where, following his research tours of Italy and France, he taught drawing and tempera. As a member of the Spokii group of Ukrainian artists in Warsaw and of the Association of Independent Ukrainian Artists in Lviv, he took part in numerous exhibitions in Lviv and other European cities. In 1950 he immigrated to the United States, where he became a member of the Ukrainian Artists' Association in the USA. His main works are monumental – icons, stained-glass windows, and mosaics – and are done in a neo-Byzantine style. They include the iconostasis and mosaics of St Andrew's Church in Bound Brook, New Jersey; the stained-glass windows and mosaics of St John the Baptist's Church in Newark, New Jersey; the icons of the Ukrainian churches in Hunter and Glen Spey, New York, and Trenton, New Jersey; the stained-glass windows of St George's Church in New York; and the iconostasis of the Ukrainian Catholic Church in Lourdes, France. A versatile artist, Kholodny is also known for his landscapes and figural compositions such as his paintings of beetles. His work was influenced by modern trends, particularly by cubism and constructivism. Thus it is closely related to M. *Boichuk's school. In his search for maximal simplicity of form, Kholodny combines the flatness and colors of the Byzantine tradition with elements of modern painting. In graphic arts he has proved himself as an illustrator (for many years he illustrated the children's journal *Veselka*) and as a bookplate, logo, and monogram designer. His work is distinguished by its elegant, light line. One-man exhibitions of his work were held in New York, Philadelphia (1973 and 1977), and Chicago (1977), and a New York retrospective exhibition was held on his 80th birthday in 1982.

S. Hordynsky

Kholodnyi Yar [Xolodnyj Jar]. A landmark near the city of Chyhyryn and the Motronyn Trinity Monastery, now in Chyhyryn raion, Cherkasy oblast. The densely forested hills and gullies around Kholodnyi Yar for centuries served the local villagers as a refuge from Polish reprisals or Tatar invasions. The *Haidamakas gathered there to prepare their rebellions: in the 1730s under the leadership of the Zaporozhian Cossacks M. *Hryva and I. Zhyla, in the 1740s under H. *Holy, and in 1768 under M. *Zalizniak. From 1918 to 1924 Kholodnyi Yar was the operations base for contending Bolshevik and pro-UNR partisan detachments. The UNR partisans were commanded by a former teacher from the village of Melnyky, Otaman V. Chuchupaka, whose headquarters were at the Motronyn Monastery, and operated in the Cherkasy–Chyhyryn–Znamianka–Dnieper sector. Among the several thousand partisans there were soldiers from the Kuban (Otaman Uvarov), the Kiev region, and Galicia, as well as local peasants. During the Second World War, Soviet partisans under the command of P. Dubovy were active in the vicinity.

Kholop. The term designating a male slave (a female slave was called *roba*); it was used interchangeably with *cheliadnyk*. According to *Ruskaia Pravda* a *kholop* was an object, rather than a subject, of law: for taking the life of a *kholop* one paid a monetary fine known as **prodazha*, not a **vyra*, the fine for killing a freeman. A *kholop*'s master was responsible for any crime committed by him. One could become a *kholop* voluntarily or involuntarily. A freeman could assume the status by marrying a *roba*, by selling himself to a prince or boyar, or by serving in the capacity of a **tyvun* or of keeper of the keys. Involuntary *kholopy* were either war captives, **zakupy* who committed a crime, debtors unable to repay their debts, or descendants of *kholopy*. Voluntary *kholopy* and *kholopy* who were artisans had a higher value and received better treatment than ordinary *kholopy* (*riadovychi*). A master could dispose of his *kholopy* freely and could even sell or kill them. In fact they were often bought and sold. Yet *kholopy* enjoyed the right to own property. Their condition changed somewhat after the church promoted their redemption through monetary payments and provided protection to some categories of *kholopy* (see *Slavery). Full (*obelni*) *kholopy* were of a lower status than half-free individuals (*zakupy*). In Muscovy most *kholopy* became serfs in the 14th–15th centuries, but the institution survived, particularly in the form of debtor servitude. In the Polish Commonwealth the *khlop* (Polish: *chłop*) was not a slave, but a dependent peasant. In modern times the term has been applied to peasants in general.

BIBLIOGRAPHY
Zimin, A. *Kholopy* (Moscow 1973)

V. Markus

Kholostenko, Mykola [Xolostenko], b 7 December 1902 in Łódź, Poland, d 3 May 1978 in Kiev. Architect. A graduate of the Kiev State Art Institute (1929), he designed many residential buildings and high-rise developments in Kiev: Veteran's (1947–55) and Verstatozavod (1948–50) developments, Zhovtneve (1950–6), and the building complex of the Central Botanical Garden of the AN URSR (1951–64). He drew up the restoration plans for the ss Borys and Hlib Cathedral (1947–56), the Cathedral of the Transfiguration (1953–6), and the Church of Good Friday (1947–51) in Chernihiv, as well as St Cyril's Church in Kiev (1955) and the Great Belfry of the Kievan Cave Monastery (1959–60).

Kholostenko, Yevhen [Xolostenko, Jevhen], b May 1904 in Łódź, Poland, d 1945 in Yugoslavia. Monumentalist painter and art scholar. A graduate of the Kiev State Art Institute (1928) and a student of M. Boichuk, he was a member of the Association of Revolutionary Art of Ukraine. He was among the artists who in 1928 painted the Peasant Sanatorium in Odessa. He wrote a number of monographs: *V. Ovchynnikov* (1932), *B. Kratko* (1933), *M. Rokyts'ky* (1933), *V. Sedliar* (1934), *Monumental'ne maliarstvo radians'koï Ukraïny* (Monumental Painting of Soviet Ukraine, 1931), and *Ukraïns'kyi revoliutsiinyi pliakat* (The Ukrainian Revolutionary Poster, coauthor, 1933). He died at the front.

Khoma, Ivan [Xoma], b 27 November 1923 in Khyriv, Dobromyl county, Galicia. Clergyman and (since 1977) honorary archimandrite. Khoma studied theology in Peremyshl and at the Pontifical 'Urbaniana' University in Rome (1946–51). He has served as the secretary to Archbishop I. Buchko (1951–62), chancellor to Cardinal Y. Slipy (1963–84), professor at the Ukrainian Catholic University in Rome (1963–), and its rector since 1975. Coeditor of the journal *Bohosloviia*, he is the author of many articles on Ukrainian church history. He is one of the coeditors of the collected works of Cardinal Slipy (8 vols, 1968–76).

Khoma, Paraska [Xoma], b 10 November 1933 in Cherniatyn, Horodenka county, Galicia. Folk artist. Her paintings, done in pencil, watercolors, gouache, and occasionally in ink or distemper, depict mainly flowers and plants. Her numerous works are grouped in such series as *Garden Flowers*, *Poppies*, *My Land*, *Fantasy*, and *Songs*. An album of her work was prepared by V. Kachkan and published in 1983.

Khomenko, Arsenii [Xomenko, Arsenij], b 14 July 1891 in Baturyn, Konotip county, Chernihiv gubernia, d 1939 in prison. Demographer. A graduate of the physics and mathematics faculty of Kiev University, in 1923 he became head of the demography department of the Central Statistical Administration of Ukraine (TsSUU). During 1930–4, he headed the demographic section of the All-Ukrainian Institute of Socialist Health Care. Subjected to political persecution in 1934, he moved to Kharkiv and was arrested there in 1938. Khomenko oversaw the preparations for the 1926 census and supervised its implementation. He published many statistical surveys, and edited periodical publications of the TsSUU and the journal *Radians'kyi statystyk*, which contained many of his own studies. Besides population dynamics, he devoted much attention to Ukraine's national minorities. His ingenious projections of Ukraine's population are particularly important in that they make it possible to estimate the enormous loss of life in Ukraine during the 1930s. He wrote only in Ukrainian and, when research ceased to be published in Ukrainian after 1935, his work no longer appeared. Most of his manuscripts were seized by the NKVD and have disappeared. Along with O. Korchak-Chepurkivsky, he had a major influence on the younger generation of Ukrainian demographers. His most important works are *Do pytannia pro suchasnyi riven' zahal'noï smertnosty na Ukraïni* (On the Question of the Current Level of Mortality in Ukraine, 1925), *Naselennia Ukraïny 1897–1927 rr.* (The Population of Ukraine 1897–1927, 1927), *Natsional'nyi sklad liudnosty USRR* (The National Composition of the Population of the Ukrainian Socialist Soviet Republic, 1929), and *Suchasna smertnist' nemovliat v USRR* (Current Infant Mortality in the Ukrainian Socialist Soviet Republic, 1930). *Sem'ia i vosproizvodstvo naseleniia* (The Family and Population Reproduction) was published posthumously in Moscow in 1980.

S. Maksudov

Khomenko, Ivan [Xomenko], b 7 September 1882 in Kobi, Dushets county, Tbilisi gubernia, Georgia, d 7 August 1935 during an expedition to Sakhalin Island. Paleontologist. A graduate of Odessa University (1908), he was a professor at the Odessa Agricultural Institute (1918–25), then a research associate of the Geological Committee (1926–31) and Petroleum Institute (1931–5) in Leningrad. Khomenko researched the hipparion fauna of southern Ukraine and Moldavia, and paleolithic and neolithic mollusk fossils in southern Ukraine and on Sakhalin Island. Most of his work in paleontology was combined with research in stratigraphy to identify oil and coal deposits.

Khomenko, Ivan [Xomenko], b 11 November 1892 in Podilia gubernia, d 10 April 1981 on the Isle of Capri, Italy. Ukrainian Catholic priest and biblical scholar. He studied at Kiev and Vienna universities and theology in Rome. In 1918–20 he worked in the Ministry of Foreign Affairs in Kiev and in the embassy of the UNR in Vienna. Influenced by Metropolitan A. Sheptytsky, he became a priest in 1940. In 1945 he immigrated to Italy. There he translated the Bible into Ukrainian from the original Aramaic, Hebrew, and Greek texts. In 1963 the Basilian order in Rome published his complete translation of the Bible as *Sviate Pys'mo Staroho i Novoho Zavitu* (The Holy Scriptures of the Old and New Testament).

Khomenko, Varvara [Xomenko], b 12 December 1916 in Vertiivka, Nizhen county, Chernihiv gubernia, d 20 December 1974 in Kiev. Ethnographer and teacher. After graduating from the Nizhen Pedagogical Institute in 1938, she taught Ukrainian literature at the Konotip Teachers' Institute. In 1947 she completed her graduate studies at the Kiev Pedagogical Institute and became an associate of the AN URSR Institute of Fine Arts, Folklore, and Ethnography. From 1971 she taught at the Kiev Institute of Culture. Khomenko published over 50 studies, including monographs on the Cossack-Polish War in Ukrainian folklore (1953), the influence of the folk epic on M. Starytsky's and I. Karpenko-Kary's historical dramas (1958), B. Khmelnytsky in Ukrainian folklore (1970), and folk poetry of the October Revolution and the civil war in Ukraine (1971). She also edited, with introductions, the AN URSR collections of historical songs (1971) and dumas (1974).

Khomenko, Vasyl [Xomenko, Vasyl'], b 1 January 1912 in Tiflis, Georgia. Graphic artist. A graduate of the Kharkiv Polygraphic Institute (1937) and a student of V. Kasiian and M. Derehus, he designed books of various types: eg, *Ukraïns'ki narodni dumy* (Ukranian Folk Dumas, 1955), a three-volume collection of T. Shevchenko's works (1949), the six-volume *Istoriia ukraïns'koho mystetstva* (History of Ukrainian Art, 1966–70), and I. Kotliarevsky's *Natalka Poltavka* (Natalka from Poltava, 1957). He designed a new Ukrainian typeface.

Khomiak, Mykhailo [Xom'jak, Myxajlo], b 12 August 1905 in Stroniatyn, Lviv county, Galicia, d 16 April 1984 in Edmonton. Journalist and community leader. A graduate of Lviv University (1931), he worked as a correspondent and editor of *Dilo* (1928–39) and *Krakivs'ki visti* (1940–5). Immigrating to Canada in 1948, he contributed to the newspapers *Svoboda* in the United States and *Ukraïns'ki visti* in Edmonton (1981–2). Besides writing articles for the press, he edited a number of books: on the Plast Ukrainian Youth Association in Edmonton (1959, 1963), on the Ukrainian People's Home in Edmonton (1966), and on the painter Yu. Butsmaniuk (1982).

Khomychevsky, Mykola [Xomyčevs'kyj], 1898–? Orthodox church leader. A graduate of Kiev University, in 1921 he was ordained a priest of the Ukrainian Autocephalous Orthodox church in Kiev, eventually becoming an archpriest. He organized Ukrainian parishes in eastern Volhynia and served as the deputy chairman of the All-Ukrainian Orthodox Church Council (1924–6). He also contributed to the journal *Tserkva i Zhyttia* (1927–8). In 1929 he was arrested by the Soviet authorities and sentenced to 10 years' imprisonment in a concentration camp. His subsequent fate is unknown.

Khomyn, Petro [Xomyn], b 12 July 1890 in Piddnistriany, Bibrka county, Galicia. Clergyman and cultural figure. Khomyn studied theology and philosophy at Lviv and Vienna universities and law at Brno University in Czechoslovakia. Ordained in 1923, from 1924 he lived in Lviv, where he was a pastor and taught catechism in several Ukrainian secondary schools (until 1939) and served as secretary of the Greek Catholic Theological Academy (1928–39), coeditor of the quarterly *Bohosloviia* (1924–6), and editor of the clerical monthly *Nyva* (1929–39). From 1941 he edited the biweekly *Voskresennia* in Cracow. In 1944 he immigrated to Austria and in 1950 to Canada. In Toronto he has edited the Catholic weekly *Nasha meta* (1951–83) and the revived literary quarterly *Nyva* (1977–80). From 1971 he was the president of the *Ukrainian Catholic Press Association.

Rev Petro Khomyn

Metropolitan Hryhorii Khomyshyn

Khomyshyn, Hryhorii [Xomyšyn, Hryhorij], b 25 March 1867 in Hadynkivtsi, Kopychyntsi county, Galicia, d 17 January 1948 in Kiev. Ukrainian Catholic bishop and church leader. He studied theology in Lviv and at Vienna University (D TH 1899) before serving as rector of the Theological Seminary in Lviv (1902–4). In 1904 he was consecrated bishop of Stanyslaviv eparchy. As bishop he instituted significant reforms in religious and community life in his eparchy. He founded a theological seminary in 1906 and established the quarterly **Dobryi Pastyr* for priests in 1931. Khomyshyn also created a network of reading rooms called Skala, and encouraged charitable and relief work and the activity of various monastic orders and religious organizations. Politically, he supported the *Ukrainian Catholic People's party and its weekly **Nova Zoria*. For some time he also supported the pro-Polish policy of *normalization. As a Catholic hierarch, Khomyshyn was a 'Westerner' who favored the latinization of the rite. In 1916 he attempted to introduce the Gregorian calendar, which provoked great opposition from the faithful, and in 1921 he decreed obligatory celibacy for priests in his eparchy. Arrested in 1945 by the Soviet authorities, he was sentenced in March 1946 to 10 years' forced labor for 'anti-people's activity.' He died in a prison in Kiev.

V. Markus

Khorol [Xorol]. IV-14. Town (1971 pop 12,600) and raion center in Poltava oblast. First mentioned in 1083, from 1648 to 1782 it was a company town in Myrhorod regiment. From 1782, as part of the Russian Empire and the USSR, it was a county center in the Kiev (1782–5) and Chernihiv (1795–7) vicegerencies; in the Little Russia (1797–1802), Poltava (1802–1920), and Kremenchuk (1920–2) gubernias; and a raion center in Kremenchuk okruha (1923–32) and Kharkiv (1932–7) and Poltava (1937–) oblasts.

Khorol River [Xorol]. A right-bank tributary of the Psol River in Sumy and Poltava oblasts. It is 308 km long and drains a basin of 3,870 sq km; it has an average width of 40–80 m, a maximum width of 200 m, and an average depth of 3.5–5 m. It is fed mostly by meltwaters (85 percent). Seven sluices have been built on the river, and it is used for water supply and irrigation.

Khorosheve [Xoroševe]. IV-17. Picturesque town smt (1976 pop 5,900) on the Udy River in Kharkiv raion, Kharkiv oblast, 10 km south of Kharkiv. Much of its population works in Kharkiv. The town's chief architectural monument is St Michael's Church built in 1785.

Khoroshun, Antin [Xorošun], b 23 July 1893 in Tulyntsi, Kaniv county, Kiev gubernia, d 5 March 1970 in Dnipropetrovske. Dramatic actor. After acting in several amateur troupes, in 1914 he joined the Society of Ukrainian Actors in Kiev and then worked in the State People's Theater (1918–19) and the Shevchenko Ukrainian Drama Theater in Kiev (1921–6) and then in Dnipropetrovske. His repertoire included the leads in W. Shakespeare's *Othello* and H. Balzac's *Eugénie Grandet*, Gonta in the stage adaption of T. Shevchenko's *Haidamaky* (The Haidamakas), Hnat Holy in I. Tobilevych's *Sava Chalyi*, and Don Gonzago de Mendoza in Lesia Ukrainka's *Kaminnyi hospodar* (The Stone Host).

Metropolitan Mykhail Khoroshy

Khoroshy, Mykhail [Xorošyj, Myxajil], b 10 July 1885 in Fedorivka, Kherson gubernia, d 18 May 1977 in Toronto. Orthodox metropolitan. Following studies at the Kiev Theological Academy and Kiev University, Khoroshy was ordained in the Ukrainian Autocephalous Orthodox church (UAOC) in 1920. From 1920 to 1929 he was a pastor in Ternivka and Cherkasy and from 1923 head of the Cherkasy okruha church council. Arrested in 1929, he spent eight years in Soviet concentration camps. In May 1942 he was consecrated bishop of the Yelysavethrad (Kirovohrad) eparchy of the UAOC, and in November 1942 he became archbishop with duties in Mykolaiv (until 1944). As archbishop of the UAOC in Bavaria after the war, he helped establish the Ukrainian Orthodox Theological Academy in Munich and served as its first administrative curator (1946–8). From 1946 to 1951 he was vice-metropolitan and vice-chairman of the Holy Synod of the UAOC. He moved to Belgium in 1948. In 1951 he became archbishop of the Eastern eparchy and vice-metropolitan of the Ukrainian Greek Orthodox Church of Canada, and he was acting primate of the church from 1967 to 1975. He was elevated to metropolitan in 1975. Khoroshy is the author of religious texts and studies, poetry, and numerous musical compositions; he also completed one of the first translations of the Psalter into Ukrainian (1919).

Khorostkiv [Xorostkiv]. IV-6. Town smt (1973 pop 7,500) in Husiatyn raion, Ternopil oblast. It was first mentioned in 1564. Sugar, alcohol, and animal feed are produced in the town, and an oblast agricultural research station has been located there since 1962.

Khorovod. The most ancient form of Ukrainian *folk dance, which combines movement, singing, instrumental music, speech, and mime. Magic was once also an important component: in primitive Ukrainian society it was believed that *khorovody* could influence the gods to bring about a successful hunt, a bountiful harvest, family harmony, and the like. With the decline of pagan beliefs *khorovody* became simply a ritual form of entertainment that was performed by young maidens during calendric holidays, such as Christmas, Easter (see **Vesniankyhahilky*), and the *Kupalo festival, and during community or family celebrations, especially weddings (see *Wedding songs); married women and men in general rarely took part in them. Beginning in the second half of the 19th century, the relationship between ritual and *khorovody* was gradually severed.

Thematically, *khorovody* are divided into those depicting (1) the behavior of mammals and birds, anthropomorphizing them; (2) the work of artisans and farmers, using mime and dialogue-like, question-and-answer songs; (3) family and social relations, particularly courtship, betrothal, and married life, frequently in a humorous fashion; and (4) natural events or calendric rituals, using trees covered in garlands, masks, and bonfires. In terms of performance, *khorovody* are divided into those that are (1) mimetic and illustrative or (2) ornamental. Depending on the nature of the accompanying song, the dancers stand individually or in a group, file, row, semicircle, circle, or two circles, linked by holding hands or kerchiefs. The texts and melodies of the songs themselves are frequently ancient in origin. In the 20th century, *khorovody* have been a fundamental part of the repertoire of almost all professional and amateur Ukrainian dance and song ensembles.

BIBLIOGRAPHY
Humeniuk, A. (ed). *Ukraïns'ki narodni tantsi* (Kiev 1962)
Dei, O.; Humeniuk, A. (eds). *Ihry ta pisni* (Kiev 1963)

M. Hnatiukivsky

Khors. In Slavic mythology a god of the sun and the source of righteousness. According to the Primary Chronicle, an idol to Khors was located near the palace of Volodymyr the Great in Kiev. He is also mentioned in **Slovo o polku Ihorevi*. In the apocryphal *Khozhdeniia Bohorodytsi po mukakh* and other later sources he is sometimes referred to as Velykyi Khors (the Great Khors). Some scholars believe that Khors is of Iranian origin.

Khortytsia [Xortycja]. A co-operative publishing house in Lviv, founded and directed by members of the Ukrainian Society of Aid to Emigrants from Eastern Ukraine. During its existence (1928–39) it published the annual calendar *Dnipro*; some historical novels, such as A. Chaikivsky's *Polkovnyk Mykhailo Krychevs'kyi* (Colonel Mykhailo Krychevsky, 1935) and E. Borschak's *Voinarovs'kyi sestrinok Ivana Mazepy* (Voinarovsky, the Nephew of Ivan Mazepa, 1939); and biographical materials such as *Lystuvannia Lesi Ukraïnky z O. Makoveiem* (Lesia Ukrainka's Correspondence with O. Makovei, 1938), edited by V. Simovych, and S. Rusova's memoirs (1939). It also distributed the publications of other firms.

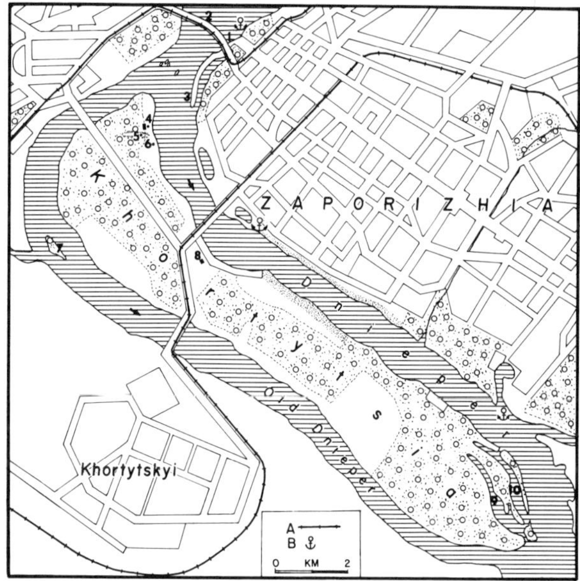

KHORTYTSIA

A. Railroad
B. Harbor

1. Lock
2. Dnieper Hydroelectric Station dam
3. Durna Skelia; according to legend, the cliff where Cossacks were punished
4. Sich Gate; the site of Cossack docks, now the site of the Zaporizhia City Museum
5. Zmiina Pechera ravine
6. Chorna Skelia; according to legend, the cliff where Grand Prince Sviatoslav I was killed by the Pechenegs in 972
7. Baida Island (Little Khortytsia)
8. Restaurant
9. Lake Richyshche
10. Lake Osokorove (Prohnii)

Khortytsia Island [Xortycja]. The largest island in the Dnieper River, situated south of the *Dnieper Hydroelectric Station and now a part of the city of *Zaporizhia. It is 12 km long and 2.5 km wide, and covers an area of over 3,000 ha. The island was located on 'the route from the Varangians to the Greeks' and was first mentioned as St Gregory's Island in the mid-10th century by Constantine VII Porphyrogenitus in his *De-administrando imperio*. In 972 Prince Sviatoslav I Ihorevych died in battle against the Pechenegs at the nearby Dnieper Rapids. The princes of Rus' under Sviatopolk II Iziaslavych gathered on the island in 1103 to begin their campaign against the Cumans. In 1224 the Rus' princes conferred there before engaging the Tatars in battle. The island played an important role in the Cossack wars with the Tatars and Poles. In the 1550s Prince D. *Vyshnevetsky built a Cossack fortress 10 km north on Mala Khortytsia Island, which served as a bulwark against various invaders. In 1557 a Tatar-Turkish army attacked the stronghold and eventually destroyed it. With brief intervals, a garrison of registered Cossacks was stationed on Khortytsia Island between 1596 and 1648. Hetmans T. Fedorovych (1630) and I. Sulyma (1635) launched their anti-Polish rebellions from there, and in 1648 Hetman B. Khmelnytsky routed its Polish garrison. In the 1660s and 1670s the Zaporozhian otaman I. Sirko used the island as his military base. The island was part of the territory held by the *Zaporozhian Sich until its destruction in 1775. During the Russo-Turkish War of 1735–9 a fortress and shipyard were built there in 1737; their remains have been preserved to this day.

The 18 September 1965 resolution of the government of the Ukrainian SSR entitled 'On Eternizing the Monumental Places Related to the History of the Zaporozhian Cossacks' decreed the island to be a historical-cultural preserve. It is not yet reconstructed and is used for recreational purposes.

BIBLIOGRAPHY
Evarnitskii, D. *Istoriia zaporozhskikh kozakov*, vol 1 (St Petersburg 1892)
Kytsenko, M.; Pieshchanov, V. *Khortytsia* (Kiev 1968)
A. Zhukovsky

Khorunzhy, Anatolii [Xorunžyj, Anatolij], b 5 November 1915 in Malomykhailivka, Katerynoslav gubernia. Writer of socialist-realist short prose. A graduate of the Kharkiv Institute of Journalism (1938), he is the author of over a dozen prose collections, including *Bukovyns'ki opovidannia* (Bukovynian Stories, 1949), *Vesnianyi doshch* (Spring Rain, 1954), and *Strohist'* (Severity, 1961), as well as of 10 short novels, including *Nezakinchenyi polit* (The Unfinished Flight, 1958), *Kovyla* (Feather Grass, 1960), *Try verby* (Three Willows, 1964), and *Duzhchyi za okean* (Mightier than the Ocean, 1978). In 1977 he was awarded the Aleksandr Fadeev Prize for his work.

Khorunzhyi [xorunžyj] (flag-bearer). Military rank or administrative title. In the Polish-Lithuanian Commonwealth, the *chorąży* was a county official in command of the recruitment of the *szlachta* or local military unit, or the king's flag-bearer. Modeled on this role, a rank was created in the 17th-century *Cossack *starshyna* and state administration. Attached to each regiment was a regimental (*polkovyi*) *khorunzhyi* who was responsible for the regimental flags, banners, and other regalia. A *heneralnyi khorunzhyi* was attached to the General Officer Staff; he was responsible for the flag in battle, and afterwards represented the hetman at various ceremonies. In Ukrainian military formations of the 20th century, a *khorunzhyi* was equivalent to a second lieutenant.

Khorvat, Ivan [Xorvat], ?–1780. Serbian colonel and nobleman who led a group of 218 Serbian immigrants to southern Ukraine in 1751. In 1752 he was appointed by Elizabeth I first Russian commander and lieutenant general of a corps of military settlers and governor of *New Serbia, to which extensive territories of the Zaporozhian Sich were annexed. In 1762 he was removed from office and exiled to Vologda, Russia, for his oppression of the military settlers and other abuses of authority.

Khotinok, Isaak [Xotinok], b 31 December 1908 in Borzna, Chernihiv gubernia. Graphic artist and medalist. A graduate of the Kharkiv Art Institute (1928) and student of I. Padalka and V. Yermilov, he works in printmaking and book graphics. He has illustrated and designed such books as I. Senchenko's *Dubovi hriady* (Oak Ranges, 1929), Sh. Rustaveli's *Vytiaz' u tyhrovii shkuri* (Knight in a Tiger Skin, 1950), *Ukraïns'ki narodni pisni* (Ukrainian Folk Songs, 1951), *Ukraïns'ke narodne dekoratyvne mystetstvo* (Ukrainian Folk Decorative Art, 1956), T. Shevchenko's *Kobzar* (1957), collections of translations from H. Heine (1956) and J. Słowacki (1959), and *Ukraïns'ki filihrani* (Ukrainian Filigree, 1972). His prints include *The Yard* (linocut, 1927), a landscape series (oil, gouache, 1968–9), and portraits of H. Barbusse (ink 1949) and I. Padalka (1970). Khotinok's work was displayed at the 1932 exhibition of the Association of Independent Ukrainian Artists in Lviv. He designed medals commemorating the centenary of T. Shevchenko's death and the jubilees of I. Franko, Dante, and I. Kotliarevsky.

Hnat Khotkevych

Khotkevych, Hnat [Xotkevyč], b 31 December 1877 in Kharkiv, d 8 October 1938. Modernist writer, scholar, composer, theater director, and civic figure. After graduating from the Kharkiv Technological Institute in 1900, he worked as a railway engineer. In 1899 he arranged a performance by *kobzars and *lirnyks at the 11th Archeological Conference in Kharkiv. Politically persecuted for being one of the leaders of a railwaymen's strike in Liubotyn in 1905, he was forced to emigrate to Galicia in 1906, where he lived in Lviv and then (1906–12) in Kryvorivnia, Kosiv county. He toured Galicia and Bukovyna with concerts of Ukrainian folk songs accompanied by the bandura and in 1910 founded the *Hutsul Theater in Krasnoilia, Kosiv county. Returning to Kharkiv in 1912, Khotkevych became involved in the cultural life there: he gave public lectures; founded a workers' theater, which in three years staged over 50 plays, mostly of Ukrainian classics; and in February 1913 became the editor of the literary journal *Visnyk kul'tury i zhyttia*. Again he came under political persecution and in 1915 was banished from Ukraine. Until the outbreak of the February Revolution he lived in Voronezh. He was opposed to the Bolshevik occupation of Ukraine, but from 1920 on was an active participant in Soviet cultural life. From 1920 to 1928 he taught Ukrainian literature and language at the Derkachi Zootekhnikum. Later he taught bandura-playing at the Kharkiv Music and Drama Institute. Throughout his life he worked at perfecting the art of bandura-playing and wrote a manual, *Pidruchnyk hry na banduri* (A Manual on Playing the Bandura, 1909; repr 1930), on the subject. He also composed a number of songs, including 'Baida,' 'Buria na Chornomu mori' (A Storm on the Black Sea), 'Sofron,' 'Nechai,' and 'A v poli korchomka' (There's a Tavern in the Field).

Khotkevych began writing in 1897; his first short story 'Hruzynka' (The Georgian Girl) appeared in the Lviv journal *Zoria*. His rich literary legacy, much of it published in contemporary periodicals, consists of such works as the stories 'Bludnyi syn' (The Prodigal Son, 1898) and 'Rizdvianyi vechir' (Christmas Eve, 1899); the cycle 'Zhyttievi analohiï' (Life's Analogies, 1897–1901); the novel *Berestechko*; the collection of stories *Hirs'ki akvareli* (Mountain Watercolors, 1914); stories written in 1914–15 and published under the title *Hutsul's'ki obrazy* (Hutsul Pictures, 1931); and the novelette *Aviron* (1917). His greatest literary achievement is the romantic novelette about Hutsuls, *Kaminna dusha* (The Stone Soul, 1st edn, 1911). Khotkevych also wrote a number of plays, including *Dovbush* (1909) and *Hutsul's'kyi rik* (The Hutsul Year, 1910). *Neproste* (Non-simple, 1911) and other plays were written especially for the Hutsul Theater. His historical plays – *O polku Ihorevim* (Ihor's Campaign, 1926) and the tetralogy *Bohdan Khmel'nyts'kyi* (1929) – were highly acclaimed by contemporary critics. In the last drama of the tetralogy, *Pereiaslav*, the playwright condemned the Treaty of *Pereiaslav of 1654 as an instrument of Russia's subjugation of Ukraine.

Khotkevych's literary and artistic interests were wide and varied. He wrote many studies, including *Hryhorii Savych Skovoroda* (1920), *Narodnyi i seredn'ovichnyi teatr u Halychyni* (Folk and Medieval Theater in Galicia, 1924), *Muzychni instrumenty ukraïns'koho narodu* (The Musical Instruments of the Ukrainian People, 1930), and *Teatr 1848 roku* (The Theater of 1848, 1932), and a series of articles on T. Shevchenko. In the Soviet period, he translated such world classics as the works of W. Shakespeare, Molière, F. Schiller, and V. Hugo.

Although he was politically suspect and stood aloof from Soviet literary discussions, Khotkevych remained one of the most popular writers in Ukraine. This is evident from the publication of an eight-volume collection of his works in 1928–32. Eventually, he again suffered persecution; his last novel, 'Dovbush,' was never published, and his tetralogy about T. Shevchenko, which he began in 1928, was never completed. During the *Yezhov terror he was arrested and perished under unknown circumstances. After Stalin's death he was posthumously rehabilitated, and two volumes of his works were published in 1966.

I. Koshelivets

Khotkevych, Volodymyr [Xotkevyč], b 11 April 1913 in Kiev, d 9 July 1982 in Kharkiv. Physicist and a corresponding member of the AN URSR from 1967; the son of H. *Khotkevych. A graduate of the Kharkiv Mechanics and Machine Building Institute (1935), he was a research associate at the Kharkiv Physical-Technical Institute of the AN URSR (1932–50). From 1950 he was a professor and rector (1966–75) at Kharkiv University. Khotkevych published over 70 scientific works dealing with superconductivity and low-temperature metal physics. Together with L. Shubnykov, he gave the first description of some of the magnetic properties of superconductive alloys.

Khotovytsky, Stepan [Xotovyc'kyj], b 1791–4 in Krasyliv, Podilia, d 11 March 1885 in St Petersburg. Pioneering physician and medical scientist. Khotovytsky graduated from the St Petersburg Medical Surgery Academy in 1817 and then studied in Vienna, Paris, Göttingen, Edinburgh, and London. He worked at the academy from 1822 to 1847, from 1832 as professor of gynecology, forensic medicine, and obstetrics. From 1828 to 1833 he was also the municipal obstetrician. He edited the Russian journal of military medicine, *Voenno-meditsinskii zhurnal*, in 1833–9, to which he contributed studies on gynecology, venereal disease, pediatrics, obstetrics, and social hygiene. He wrote the first Russian textbook of folk medicine (1844), a pediatrics textbook (1847), and monographs on pestilence in St Petersburg (1831) and cholera (1832), and translated European textbooks of gynecology and surgery.

Khotyn: northern tower of castle (13th century, rebuilt in 15th–16th century)

Khotyn [Xotyn]. v-7. Town (1970 pop 11,900) and raion center in Chernivtsi oblast. Founded by the Dacians and named after one of their leaders (Kotizon) Khotyn in the 10th century became part of Kievan Rus'; from the 12th century it belonged to the Principality of Galicia-Volhynia. In the second half of the 13th century the Genoese constructed a fortress there. In 1373 the town became part of the Moldavia principality.

From the turn of the 16th century to 1812 it remained, with intervals, a Turkish vassal; its stronghold played a key role in Turkey's control of Moldavia. In the 17th and 18th centuries Khotyn was an object of conquest in the Cossack, Polish, and Russian wars with Turkey. At the Battle of *Khotyn in 1621, the combined Cossack and Polish armies defeated the Turks, but the *Khotyn Peace Treaty left the citadel in Turkish hands. Cossack armies led by T. Khmelnytsky captured and held Khotyn in 1650 and 1652–3. After routing the Turkish army there on 11 November 1673 with the help of Moldavian and Cossack troops, the Polish hetman J. Sobieski took the citadel and revoked the *Buchach Peace Treaty of 1672. In 1711 the town was restored to Turkey. During the Russo-Turkish wars it was held by Russian troops in 1739, 1769–74, 1787–91, and 1806.

With the *Bucharest Peace Treaty of 1821, Khotyn came under Russian rule. Its citadel was dismantled in 1856. In 1873 Khotyn became a county center in Bessarabia gubernia. In 1897 its population was 23,800. Since most of the town's inhabitants were Jewish or Russian, Ukrainian cultural life was insignificant until the early 20th century.

In April 1918, during the Austrian occupation, Ukrainians held rallies in Khotyn and elsewhere in the county demanding that the region be annexed to the UNR, and the Central Rada sent its commissioner, I. Liskun, to Khotyn. Rumanian occupation of the region in November precipitated the January 1919 *Khotyn uprising. Its population declined from 24,000 in 1915 to 7,000 in 1940. In June 1940, the city was occupied by Soviet troops, but during the German-Soviet War, in July 1941, it was reoccupied by Rumania. In April 1944 it was incorporated into the Ukrainian SSR.

The war and Soviet rule brought about major changes in the city's ethnic composition. Whereas Ukrainians, Russians, Jews, and Rumanians constituted 15, 37, 38, and 9 percent of a 15,300 population in 1930, the respective figures in 1959 were 72, 16, 8, and 4 percent. The city's enterprises produce dairy and other food products, wood products, kilims, textiles, clothing, and handicrafts. An agricultural tekhnikum, a boarding school for handicapped children, and a museum are located there.

A. Zhukovsky

Khotyn, Battle of. A battle in 1621 during which joint Cossack and Polish forces defeated their Turkish enemy after 26 days of fighting near Khotyn in northern Bessarabia. This compelled Sultan Osman II to put an end to the Turkish-Polish War, which had begun with the Turkish victory at the Battle of *Cecora in 1620. The sultan had planned to conquer Ukraine, Poland, and eventually all of central Europe, and his army of 150,000 Turks and Tatars marched on Moldavia, which had allied with Poland. Unable to muster more than 30,000 soldiers to fight the Turks, the Polish government turned to the Ukrainian Cossacks for help. The Cossack council held on 15–17 June 1621 at Sukha Dibrova in the Cherkasy region decided to come to Poland's aid and sent a delegation headed by P. *Sahaidachny to Warsaw to petition for increased privileges for the Cossacks and recognition of the Orthodox hierarchy in Ukraine. Not waiting for the results, the Cossacks began attacking Turkish and Crimean Tatar coastal towns. A 40,000-man Cossack army commanded by the Zaporozhian hetman Ya. *Borodavka crossed the Dniester River into Moldavia and during August succeeded in slowing down the Turkish forces heading towards the Polish encampment near Khotyn. Distrusting the Poles, Borodavka refused to advance further until the Polish army began fighting the Turks. After Sahaidachny returned from Warsaw and informed the

Cossack council near Mohyliv-Podilskyi that the Sejm had agreed to their demands, the Cossacks deposed Borodavka and elected Sahaidachny hetman. On 1 September the Cossack forces broke through the Turkish lines and joined the Poles at Khotyn. Bearing the brunt of fierce battles from 2 to 28 September 1621, the Cossacks were instrumental in saving the Polish forces from destruction and repelling the sultan's army. Osman was forced to call a halt to the fighting and his expansionist plans and to negotiate the Peace Treaty of *Khotyn.

BIBLIOGRAPHY
Vasylenko, H. *Khotyns'ka viina* (Kiev 1960)
Meysztowicz, J. *Pod Cecorą i Chocimiem, 1620–1621* (Warsaw 1974)

A. Zhukovsky

Khotyn, Peace Treaty of. An agreement concluded in October 1621 after the Battle of *Khotyn, putting an end to the Polish-Turkish War of 1620–1. It designated the Dniester River as the border between Poland and Turkey. Turkey and the Crimean Khanate agreed to desist from raids on Ukraine and Poland in return for gifts of money and valuables; Poland undertook to return Khotyn to Moldavia, Turkey's vassal, and to curtail Cossack raids on the Crimea and Turkey. The Cossacks, who had fought bravely on the Polish side, were not party to the treaty. Their rights curtailed and their efforts not suitably rewarded, they felt that they had been treated unfairly and continued their sea raids on Turkey.

Khotyn uprising. An uprising from 23 to 31 January 1919 by the Ukrainian inhabitants of Khotyn county against the Rumanian occupation of Bessarabia. It was directed by the so-called Khotyn Directorate, whose members (chairman: M. Lyskun; secretary: L. Tokan) established friendly relations with the *Directory of the UNR. The UNR representative I. Maievsky supplied the three insurgent regiments – Rukshyn, Anadoly, and Dankivtsi – with arms. The rebels captured the town of Khotyn and most of the county's villages, and expelled the Rumanian authorities from the region. After fierce battles the Rumanian troops forced 4,000 rebels to retreat beyond the Dniester River together with about 50,000 refugees. The Rumanian authorities subjected eight villages (Rukshyn, Nedoboivtsi, Shyrivtsi, Kerstentsi, Stavchany, Dankivtsi, Vladychna, and Ataky) to severe reprisals. About 5,000 (15,000 according to Soviet sources) people were executed, 500 of them in Khotyn.

BIBLIOGRAPHY
Dembo, V. *Nikogda ne zabyt. Krovavaia letopis Bessarabii* (Moscow 1924)
Okhotnikov, J.; Batchinsky, N. *L'Insurrection de Khotine dans la Bessarabie et la paix européenne* (Paris 1927)
Heroïchna Khotynshchyna. Materialy naukovoï sesiï, prysviachenoï 50-richchiu Khotyns'koho povstannia (Lviv 1972)
Khotinskoe vosstanie: Sbornik dokumentov i materialov (Kishinev 1976)

A. Zhukovsky

Khotynsky, Yevhen [Xotyns'kyj, Jevhen], b 25 December 1877 in St Petersburg, d 30 June 1959 in Kharkiv. Organic chemist. After completing his higher education in Geneva, in 1909 he joined the faculty of Kharkiv University and in 1934 was appointed professor. He published about 60 works, including 20 secondary and advanced textbooks of organic chemistry. His *Kurs orhanichnoï khimiï* (Course in Organic Chemistry) went through several printings in Ukrainian and Russian, and was translated into Chinese. He studied bromination and reduction of pyrrole and its derivatives, and coal-tar aromatics, and he developed methods of analyzing organic compounds.

Khramatyka slovens'ka iazyka [*Khramatyka slovens'ka jazyka*] (Grammar of the Slavic Language). The earliest printed grammar for Ukrainian students based on the widespread manuscript treatise 'On Eight Parts of Speech' compiled in Serbia in the 14th century. It was commissioned by Prince K. Ostrozky for the Ostrih Academy and printed by the Mamonich brothers in Vilnius in 1586.

Khraplyva, Lesia [Xraplyva, Lesja] (married name: Shchur), b 27 May 1927 in Lviv. Writer and educator. A graduate of Columbia University (MS 1953), she edited the *Plast cubs' magazine *Hotuis'* (1953–70) and wrote literature for children and young people. She published collections of children's stories and fairy tales such as *Viter z Ukraïny* (The Wind from Ukraine, 2 vols, 1958, 1965) and *Kozak Nevmyraka* (The Cossack Nevmyraka, 1961), the novel *Otaman Volia* (1959), several children's plays, a book of children's verses, and a collection of poetry, *Dalekym i blyz'kym* (For the Distant and the Close, 1972).

Yevhen Khraplyvy

Khraplyvy, Yevhen [Xraplyvyj, Jevhen], b 22 June 1898 in Lysivtsi, Zalishchyky county, Galicia, d 6 May 1949 in Erlangen, Germany. Agricultural economist, co-operative leader; from 1935 full member of the Shevchenko Scientific Society. A graduate of the Higher School of Agriculture in Vienna (1924), he earned a doctorate in 1933 at the Ukrainian Husbandry Academy in Poděbrady, Czechoslovakia. From 1925 he worked as an inspector of dairy co-operatives at the Audit Union of Ukrainian Co-operatives (RSUK), and then as director of the Silskyi Hospodar society (1928–39). At the same time he edited a number of co-operative periodicals such as the weekly *Hospodars'ko-kooperatyvnyi chasopys* (1930–3), the semimonthly *Sil's'kyi hospodar* (1926–?), and the quarterly *Ukraïns'kyi agronomichnyi vistnyk* (1934–8). During the Second World War he taught agronomy at the Lviv Polytechnical Institute and the State Agricultural Courses in Dubliany (1942–4) and then emigrated to Germany, where he taught agricultural economics at the Ukrainian Technical and Husbandry Institute in Regensburg and at the Ukrainian Free University in Munich. Besides numerous articles, his publications include popular and scholarly monographs: for example, *Osnovy kooperatyvnoho molocharstva* (Foundations of Co-operative Dairying, 1927), *Sil's'ke hospodarstvo halyts'ko-volyns'kykh zemel'* (Agriculture in Galician-Volhynian Territories, 1936), and *Hospodarstvo Kholmshchyny i Pidliashshia* (Farming in the Kholm and Podlachia Regions, 1944). Only the first booklet of his *Ukraïns'ka sil's'ko-hospodars'ka entsyklopediia* (Ukrainian Agricultural Encyclopedia) appeared in print before the outbreak of the Second World War.

B. Krawchenko

Khrapovitsky, Antonii (Aleksei) [Xrapovickij, Antonij (Aleksej)], b 17 March 1863, d 8 August 1936 in Belgrade. Russian Orthodox metropolitan, ultraconservative Russian church and civic leader. In 1902 he became the bishop of Volhynia; in 1914, the archbishop of Kharkiv; and in 1917, the metropolitan of Kiev. He was known for his hostility to the Ukrainian national movement. In 1917–18 he staunchly opposed the proponents of an autocephalous Ukrainian Orthodox church. He was removed from his post by the Directory government in December 1918. From 1921 on he headed the Russian Orthodox hierarchy in emigration. Khrapovitsky is the author of many works on Eastern Orthodoxy. A nine-volume biography was published in 1956–63 by Bishop Nikon (Rklitsky).

Khrenov, Konstantin [Xrenov], b 25 February 1894 in Borovsk, Kaluga gubernia, d 11 October 1984 in Kiev. Specialist in electrical welding; from 1945 full member of the AN URSR. A graduate of the Petrograd Electrotechnical Institute (1918), he lectured at higher technical institutions in Moscow and Leningrad, and after 1945 worked in Kiev at the AN URSR Institute of Electric Welding, then at the Institute of Electrotechnics (1952–63). From 1947 he taught at the Kiev Polytechnical Institute and then at the Kiev Institute of Civil Aviation Engineers (1965–75). His main publications deal with arc welding, particularly underwater welding and metalcutting and cold-welding. His methods are used widely in restoring bridges and repairing ships.

Khreshchatyk [Xreščatyk]. The name of Kiev's main thoroughfare. Important administrative, economic, commercial, cultural, and educational institutions are located there. It runs through the center of the city from Komsomol Square and the Volodymyr Slope to Bessarabian Square and Shevchenko Boulevard; its overall length is 1.2 km. When the street was built, it replaced a forested valley (called Khreshchata Valley in the 17th century) with a stream flowing through it. The valley was used as a game preserve by the Kievan princes. In the early 18th century a road from the *Podil to the Pecherske district ran along the valley.

Construction of the first dwellings began in 1797. Most of the early buildings were one-story wooden houses. The city's development plan of 1837 determined the present course and length of Khreshchatyk. From the 1870s on mostly three-story stone structures with apartments, hotels, shops, government offices, banks, and theaters were built, predominantly in the eclectic or modern style.

Khreshchatyk: in September 1941

In 1876 the hall of the city duma was erected, and in 1892 the first electric tramline in the Russian Empire was installed, linking the street with the Podil district. By the beginning of the 20th century the street had become an important commercial center. In 1910 the first covered market in Ukraine was built on Bessarabian Square. In 1935 the street was paved with asphalt and the tramline was replaced by a trolleybus line. From 1936 to 1941 the street was radically reconstructed and built up. During the Second World War while the Soviets retreated from the advancing German army, Khreshchatyk was mined and most buildings destroyed (1941).

After the war Khreshchatyk was rebuilt. Multi-storied office and residential buildings went up, and the street was widened from 34–44 m to 75–100 m and was adorned with rows of chestnut and other trees and a boulevard. Today numerous institutions are located there, including nine ministries, the State Committee for Television and Radio Broadcasting, the Kiev Institute of Theater Arts, the central post office, the offices of the journals *Dnipro* and *Ranok*, the Ukrainian Association of Consumer Co-operatives, and various stores, offices, cinemas, and hotels.

A. Zhukovksy

Khrin. See Stebelsky, Stepan.

Khronika Katolyts'koï tserkvy na Ukraïni (Chronicle of the Catholic Church in Ukraine). A *samvydav* journal of the Initiative Group for the Defense of the Rights of Believers and the Church, which was formed in September 1982 in Ukraine. Between March and November 1984, eight issues, and a special unnumbered issue, appeared. Some of them were published in Ukrainian, others in Russian and Ukrainian. The journal had a militant religious profile and accepted the principle of Ukraine's independence. It published materials on a wide range of subjects: religious questions, the activities of the clandestine Ukrainian Catholic church, the sociopolitical situation in Ukraine, the persecution of various religious groups, and the arrests of Ukrainian human-rights activists. Some of the articles and petitions went beyond the limits of a religious journal; eg, the article on Raul Wallenberg (no. 2), Y. Terelia's letters to the president of Israel, to L. Wałęsa (no. 3), and to President R. Reagan (no. 4), and V. Kobryn's declarations to the Presidium

Khreshchatyk: after reconstruction

of the Supreme Soviet of the USSR (no. 5) and to the USSR minister of defense. The materials collected by the Initiative Group were confiscated, and announcement was made in the eighth issue that the *Khronika* ... would cease publication, but future issues of the *Khronika* ... continued to appear. Issues 11–13 did not get to the West, but beginning with spring 1987, issues 14 to 17 appeared.

O. Zinkevych

Khronika tekushchikh sobytii. See *Chronicle of Current Events*.

Khronoviat, Mykhailo [Xronov'jat, Myxajlo], b 18 January 1894 in Rybotychi, Dobromyl county, Galicia, d 20 July 1981 in Los Angeles. Officer of the Ukrainian Galician Army (UHA), agronomist, and civic leader. Having served as commander of a reserve platoon and the Sambir Officer Academy of the UHA, he was interned in Czechoslovakia and stayed there to complete his studies at the Higher Technical School in Prague (1926). Returning to Lviv, he assumed important positions in a number of Ukrainian organizations: in the *Maslosoiuz co-operative (1926–39) he became, eventually, executive director; in *Silskyi Hospodar he served on the Board of Directors; in *Prosvita he was a member of the Executive Committee; and in *Sokil-Batko he was president (1934–9). During the Second World War he headed the agricultural department of the Ukrainian Central Committee (1940–1) in Cracow, restored the co-operative Maslosoiuz in Lviv, and served on the Military Board of the Division Galizien (1943–5). After the war Khronoviat lectured at the Ukrainian Technical and Husbandry Institute in Germany and sat on the Presidium of the Ukrainian National Council. Immigrating to the United States in 1953, he presided over the Ukrainian Engineers' Society of America and a branch of the United Ukrainian War Veterans in America.

Khrukalova, Zinaida [Xrukalova, Zinajida], b 25 June 1907 in Novoiehorlyk, Salsk okrug, Don Cossack province. Actress. Upon graduating from the Lysenko Music and Drama Institute in Kiev in 1929, she joined the Kiev Ukrainian Drama Theater. Then she worked at the Theater of the Revolution in Odessa (1932–3) and the Dnipropetrovske Ukrainian Music and Drama Theater (1933–62). Her repertoire included the lead role in V. Hugo's *Marie Tudor*, Anna in I. Franko's *Ukradene shchastia* (Stolen Happiness), Marusia in M. Starytsky's *Marusia Bohuslavka*, Donna Anna in Lesia Ukrainka's *Kaminnyi hospodar* (The Stone Host), and Lady Milford in F. Schiller's *Kabale und Liebe*.

Khrushchev, Nikita [Xruščev], b 17 April 1894 in Kalinovka, Kursk gubernia, Russia, d 11 September 1971 in Moscow. Soviet political leader, first secretary of the CPSU, and premier of the USSR. Joining the Russian Communist Party (Bolshevik) in 1918 and the Red Army in 1919, he rose through the Party ranks to become a member of the CC by 1934. As head of the Moscow Party organization, he served J. Stalin zealously during the purges of the 1930s. From 1938 to 1949, except for nine months in 1947, he was first secretary of the CC CP(B)U. He presided over the forced introduction of Russian into Ukrainian schools, and the final year of the bloody purges known as the *Yezhov terror, in which thousands of Ukrainians, including Party members, were executed or imprisoned. In 1939 he was rewarded for these achievements with a seat on the Presidium. Under his secretaryship Galicia and Volhynia (1939), and then Bukovyna (1940), were incorporated into the Ukrainian SSR, and their inhabitants were subjected to repression and terror for two years. After the war his primary task was to restore agricultural production in Ukraine and to rebuild its industry as quickly as possible. At the same time he launched a propaganda campaign against Ukrainian nationalism and a military assault against UPA pockets of resistance. Writers and artists who dwelled on Ukraine's history or were influenced by European cultural currents came under severe criticism. Hundreds of Ukrainian intellectuals, including distinguished writers such as M. Rylsky, V. Sosiura, and O. Vyshnia, were persecuted.

After Stalin's death Khrushchev emerged victorious from a power struggle with G. Malenkov. On 25 February 1956 Khrushchev launched his de-Stalinization campaign with a secret speech to the 20th Party Congress in Moscow. His denunciation of Stalin's brutality, abuses of power, deportation of ethnic minorities, and mass terror had far-reaching effects. It not only led to a restriction of the powers of the secret police, greater freedom of expression, the release of thousands of political prisoners, and the 'rehabilitation' of some of the terror's victims, but also destroyed the cult of personality and faith in the Party's infallibility.

In 1958 Khrushchev unveiled his new seven-year plan, promising to overtake the United States in economic performance. Educational reforms were introduced to meet the demands of the new economic program. To Russify Ukraine's educational system, parents were allowed to choose their child's language of instruction in school, and Ukrainian was no longer a required subject in schools using Russian as the language of instruction. Khrushchev denied the need for languages other than Russian in scientific and technical fields. His ambitious agricultural plans, which opened up vast tracts of virgin land to cultivation, failed to achieve their production goals. A new scheme of industrial regionalization and a restructuring of the Party into industrial and agricultural sectors caused confusion and resentment. Reversing his policy of liberalization, in 1962 Khrushchev began to criticize writers, artists, and intellectuals for 'abstractionism,' 'modernism,' and 'formalism.' In Ukraine the Sixtiers, particularly I. Dziuba, Ye. Sverstiuk, and I. Svitlychny, came under increasing attack.

His frequent policy shifts and arbitrary administrative methods cost him the support of many Party and government officials, while the quarrel with China and the failures in agriculture led to widespread disillusionment among the people. Khrushchev's opponents steadily consolidated their power and in October 1964 ousted him from office. Confined to his *dacha* outside Moscow, he wrote his memoirs, which were smuggled to the West and published in two volumes entitled *Khrushchev Remembers* (1970, 1974).

BIBLIOGRAPHY
Maistrenko, I. *Istoriia Komunistychnoï partiï Ukraïny* (Munich 1979)
Lewytzkyj, B. *Politics and Society in Soviet Ukraine 1953–1980* (Edmonton 1984)
Krawchenko, B. *Social Change and National Consciousness in Twentieth-Century Ukraine* (Oxford 1985)

M. Stech

Khrushchev, Vasilii [Xruščev, Vasilij], b 12 June 1882 in St Petersburg, d 19 December 1941. Electrical engineer; full member of the AN URSR from 1939. A graduate of the Tomsk Technological Institute, he taught there from 1914 to 1923, and then was appointed professor of the Kharkiv Technological Institute. In 1930 he transferred to the Kharkiv Electrotechnical Institute and in 1939 became director of the AN URSR Institute of Power Engineering. His numerous publications, which include 16 monographs and textbooks, deal with such topics as AC machinery, power transmission, arc and mechanical rectifiers, and high-tension synchronous generators.

Khrutsky, Serhii [Xruc'kyj, Serhij], b 2 August 1887 in Kmichyn, Kholm region, d? Political and church figure. A gymnasium teacher, from 1922 to 1935 he was a deputy from the Kholm region in the Polish Sejm, the president of the Ukrainian Club in the Sejm, and vice-chairman of the Sejm Educational Commission. In 1925 he joined the *Ukrainian National Democratic Alliance and became a member of its Central Committee. He was a spokesman for Ukrainian autonomy in interwar Poland and spoke out against the persecution of the Ukrainians under Poland, Polonization, and the destruction and confiscation of Orthodox churches. A supporter of the movement to Ukrainianize the Russified Orthodox church in Volhynia, the Kholm region, and Podlachia, he became a member of the Ukrainian Church Committee in 1927. He and his family were arrested in 1939 during the Soviet occupation of Western Ukraine and imprisoned in concentration camps in Kazakhstan. His subsequent fate is unknown.

Pavlo Khrystiuk

Khrystiuk, Pavlo [Xrystjuk], b 1880 in the Kuban, d ? Co-operative organizer, political figure, and publicist. Before the Revolution he worked for the Kiev daily *Rada*, contributed to the organs of the *Ukrainian Party of Socialist Revolutionaries (UPSR) – *Borot'ba* and *Trudova respublika* – and served as an editor of the co-operative journal *Muraveinik-komashnia* (1916–17). During the revolutionary period he was a leading member of the central committees of the UPSR and the *Peasant Association. He served as a deputy of the *Central Rada and a member of its Little Rada. As general chancellor in the first UNR government (1917–18), led by V. Vynnychenko, he helped draft the land law of 31 January 1918. He served as minister of internal affairs and later state secretary (from the end of February 1918) in V. Holubovych's UNR government, and deputy minister of internal affairs in I. Mazepa's UNR government (1919). After the 4th Congress of the UPSR in May 1918, he joined the centrist faction. In 1919 he emigrated to Vienna, where he was a member of the foreign delegation of the UPSR and contributed to its journal *Boritesia–Poborete*. After returning to Ukraine in 1924, he worked for the Society of Scientific and Technical Workers for the Promotion of Socialist Construction (Kharkiv 1928–31) and contributed to the journal *Chervonyi shliakh*. His *Zamitky i materiialy do istoriï ukraïns'koï revoliutsiï 1917–1920 rr.* (Comments and Materials on the History of the Ukrainian Revolution, 1917–20, 4 vols, 1921–2) is a valuable source for the history of the Ukrainian revolution. He also authored several studies including *1905 rik na Ukraïni* (The Year 1905 in Ukraine, 1925) and *Istoriia kliasovoï borot'by (styslyi kurs)* (A History of Class Struggle [A Concise Course], 1927). Arrested in 1931, he disappeared without trace.

A. Zhukovsky

Khrystych, Zoia [Xrystyč, Zoja], b 1 November 1932 in Tiraspol, Moldavian ASSR. Soprano opera singer. A graduate of the Odessa Conservatory, in 1956 she was appointed soloist at the Kiev Theater of Opera and Ballet. Her classical repertoire includes Leonora in G. Verdi's *Il trovatore*, Marguerite in C. Gounod's *Faust*, Elsa in R. Wagner's *Lohengrin*, Queen of the Night in W. Mozart's *Magic Flute*, and Bianca in V. Shebalin's *Taming of the Shrew*. Her Ukrainian repertoire includes the heroine in M. Arkas's *Kateryna*, Helena in K. Dankevych's *Bohdan Khmelnytsky*, Oksana in S. Hulak-Artemovsky's *Zaporozhian Cossack beyond the Danube*, and Natalka in M. Lysenko's *Natalka from Poltava*. Since 1965 she has been teaching at the Kiev Conservatory. A book about her was written by E. Yavorsky in 1975.

Khrystyians'kyi holos (The Christian Voice). A Catholic religious weekly published since January 1949 in Munich. In 1959, it was adopted as the semiofficial newspaper of the Ukrainian Catholic exarchate in Germany. Its editors were P. Isaiiv (1949), R. Danylevych (1949–54), M. Konovalets (1954–65), and I. Voliansky (1965–). In 1957–8 a monthly supplement devoted to the Ukrainian Christian Movement appeared in the paper under the editorship of M. Zaiats. The supplement's better-known contributors have been Rev A. Velyky, I. Hvat, Rev R. Holovatsky, A. and O. Horbach, O. Zelenetsky, Rev I. Nazarko, Z. Pelensky, and S. Shakh.

Khrystynivka [Xrystynivka]. v-10. Town (1972 pop 12,100) and raion center in Cherkasy oblast, situated in the Dnieper Upland. First mentioned in 1574 as the town of Khrystyhorod, in 1793 it came under Russian rule. A railway junction since 1891, its enterprises service the railway and produce asphalt, mixed feed, and food and dairy products.

Khrystynopil *Apostol*. See Horodyshche *Apostol*.

Khrystynopil Monastery (Khrystynopilskyi sviatoiurskyi manastyr). A Basilian monastery founded in 1763 in Khrystonopil (also known as Krystynopil, now Chervonohrad), Galicia, by the Belz voivode S. Potocki. Its patron is St George. The large baroque church was famous for its icon of the Mother of God, which attracted numerous pilgrims. The monastery's valuable library contained several old parchment church books originally from the Basilian monastery in Horodyshche, eg, the *Horodyshche *Apostol* of the 12th century and the *Horodyshche (Buchach) Gospel of the 12th–13th centuries. The monastery was abolished in 1946 by the Soviet government. Since 1980 it has housed a branch of the Lviv Museum of the History of Religion and Atheism.

Khrzhonshchevsky, Nikanor [Xržonščevskij], b 7 July 1836 in Perm, d 1 September 1906 in Kiev. Pathologist; a founder of histophysiology. A graduate of Kazan University (1859), he taught at Kharkiv University (1867–8) and chaired the Department of Pathology of Kiev University (1869–1906). His research dealt with the structure and function of the liver, kidneys, lungs, and blood vessels. In 1886 he demonstrated, by injecting dyes, the capacity of liver cells to produce bile and determined the nature of the branching of the liver's bile ducts. He was one of the leading figures in Kiev's medical community, serving as president of the Kiev Medical Society (1869–72, 1886–9) and of the Kiev Society of Naturalists (1870–2).

Khudash, Mykhailo [Xudaš, Myxajlo], b 1925. Linguist. As a senior research associate of the AN URSR Institute of Social Sciences in Lviv, Khudash has published several articles and monographs on the history of Ukrainian. Using the documents of the Lviv Stauropegian Brotherhood, he published the monograph *Leksyka ukraïns'kykh dilovykh dokumentiv kintsia XVI–pochatku XVII st.* (The Vocabulary of Ukrainian Official Documents of the End of the 16th–Beginning of the 17th Centuries, 1961). He has also researched P. Berynda's language and anthroponymy of the 16th century, publishing the survey *Z istoriï ukraïns'koï antroponimiï* (From the History of Ukrainian Anthroponymy, 1977).

Khudorba, Arkhyp [Xudorba, Arxyp], b ca 1750 in Koman, near Novhorod-Siverskyi in the Chernihiv region, d early 19th century. Cossack officer, historian, and member of the *Novhorod-Siverskyi patriotic circle. He was appointed osaul (1769), otaman (1773), and captain of Sheptaky company, fellow of the standard (1783), and second major (1785) and first major (1790) of the Starodub Carabineer Regiment. He is the author of a lost history of 'Little Russia,' which was inspired by a liberal, anti-Russian spirit and, according to O. Ohloblyn, was an important source for **Istoriia Rusov*.

Khurgin, Ivan [Xurgin], ?–1926. Jewish socialist leader. A member of the Little Rada in 1917 from the United Jewish Socialist Workers' party and one of the architects of Jewish national autonomy in Ukraine, he participated actively in drafting the Central Rada's law on *national-personal autonomy. He served as deputy to the minister of Jewish affairs, M. *Silberfarb, in the governments of V. Vynnychenko and V. Holubovych. From 1919 he collaborated with the Bolsheviks.

Khust [Xust] (Hungarian: Huszt; Czechoslovak: Chust). v-4. City (1987 pop 34,000) and raion center in Transcarpathia oblast, situated on the Khustets River in the Maramureş Basin near the confluence of the Rika and Tysa rivers. It arose in the 10th century at the foot of a mountain of volcanic origin, on which a Hungarian castle was built from 1090 to 1191 to control access to salt mines 50 km away near the future town of Solotvyna. It was razed by the Mongols in 1242 but was soon rebuilt. Khust belonged to the Principality of Galicia-Volhynia from 1281. In 1321 Hungarian rule was restored. In the 16th and 17th centuries the Habsburgs and the Transylvanian princes fought each other for control of the town and its castle. It was besieged by the Crimean Tatars in 1594, 1659, and 1717, the Poles in 1657, and the Turks in 1661–2. Prince Ferenc Rákóczi II took the town in 1703 and convened a Transylvanian diet there in 1709. The castle burned down after lightning hit its gunpowder tower in 1766. A Ukrainian People's Council was founded there in November 1918. On 21 January 1919 the 425 delegates of the All-People's Congress of Hungarian Ruthenians in Khust created the *Central Ruthenian People's Council and voted to unite Transcarpathia with Ukraine. From 1919 to 1938 the city belonged to Czechoslovakia, from 1928 as a county center. Branches of the *Prosvita and *Dukhnovych societies were established there. After

Hungary occupied southwestern Transcarpathia, in November 1938, the autonomous Carpatho-Ukrainian government headed by A. *Voloshyn was evacuated from Uzhhorod to Khust, which became the capital of Carpatho-Ukraine. Congresses of the *Carpathian Sich National Defense Organization were held there in December 1938 and February 1939. In mid-March 1939 battles between *Carpathian Sich and Czech and Hungarian troops and the session of the Carpatho-Ukrainian Diet that proclaimed state independence took place there. In 1938–9 Khust was also the seat of Bishop D. Niaradi, the apostolic administrator of the Greek Catholic Mukachiv eparchy, and the home of the daily **Nova svoboda* and of the *Nova Stsena state theater. From March 1939 to October 1944 the city was under Hungarian rule. Since then it has been part of Soviet Ukraine. Felt hats, footwear, artistic wares, clothing, lumber, furniture, ceramics, bricks and tiles, and food products are made there. It has a small museum.

V. Markus

Khutir [xutir] (plural: *khutory*). A term used in the Russian Empire and the Soviet Union to denote a separate rural settlement built on privately owned land and consisting usually of a single farm. The name was also applied to offshoots of peasant villages and Don and Kuban Cossack **stanytsi* regardless of the number of farms. Similar settlements have existed in Europe and Central Asia for many centuries. Beginning in the 16th century Zaporozhian Cossacks built winter settlements (**zymovnyky*) to winter their horses and cattle. *Khutory* became widespread in Ukraine after serfdom was abolished in 1861 and spread throughout the empire during the *Stolypin agrarian reforms. The decree of 9 November 1906, which initiated the reforms, permitted a household head to demand of the village commune (**obshchina*) an allotment of land as his very own, to farm, lease, and sell as he pleased. If the household settled on this land, the new farmstead and land together were called a *khutir*; if the household remained in the village, the land it received was known as an *otrub* (plural: *otruby*).

During the reform years (1906–16) 400,000 *khutory* and *otruby* (14 percent of all peasant households), with a land area of 2.7 desiatins, were created in the Ukrainian gubernias. They were most widespread in Southern and Slobidska Ukraine. In Kherson and Kharkiv gubernias, for example, 22.5 percent of all farms were *khutory* or *otruby*, while in Poltava gubernia the number was only 12.9 percent. Better-off families or those large enough to be able to handle all the necessary farm work themselves settled on *khutory*. Often they leased or purchased other *khutory*; therefore, the land area at their disposal was often much larger than that of those who remained in the *obshchina*. Thus, in Poltava gubernia the average *khutir* household owned 26.7 ha while the average *obshchina* household had 7.7 ha of farmland. The rich *khutir* owners were often identified as *kulaks (kurkuls), and poor and middle peasants strenuously opposed the detachment of *khutory* from the *obshchina* by fighting, chasing away land surveyors, and resisting the police.

After the October Revolution, Soviet land redistribution affected gentry landowners and *khutir* owners alike. About 20 percent of the richest farms had half or more of their land redistributed among the poorer peasants. In 89 percent of the cases, the redistribution was forced and occurred only after violent struggle. By 1922 the proportion of *khutory* and *otruby* in the total number of farms had plummeted to 4 percent. During the Soviet *collectivization drive the victims of dekulakization measures were first and foremost peasant *khutir* owners. By the time collectivization was completed, the *khutir* as a form of farming had disappeared. Part of the population, however, continued living on *khutory* while working on collective farms. Because this arrangement enabled people to avoid the system of social control, in 1939, 1940, and after the Second World War farmers living on *khutory* were moved to collective-farm settlements. After the war, part of the private farmsteads in newly annexed Western Ukraine were also eliminated.

BIBLIOGRAPHY

Rubach, M. *Ocherki po istorii revoliutsionnogo preobrazovaniia agrarnykh otnoshenii na Ukraine v period provedeniia Oktiabr'skoi revoliutsii* (Kiev 1957)

Dubrovskii, S. *Stolypinskaia zemel'naia reforma* (Moscow 1963)

Rozvytok narodnoho hospodarstva Ukraïns'koï RSR, 1917–1967, 2 vols (Kiev 1967)

S. Maksudov

Khutorna, Yelysaveta [Xutorna, Jelysaveta] (real name: Ostroverkhova), b 11 June 1886 in Iznoskovo, Ivanovskoe county, Kursk gubernia, d 8 January 1980 in Kiev. Actress. From 1906 to 1920 she worked in the Sadovsky Theater in Kiev, then in various theaters in Vinnytsia, Odessa (1925), Poltava (1936), and Uzhhorod (1945), and finally in the Zaporizhia Ukrainian Music and Drama Theater (1947–57). Her repertoire included Vasylyna in I. Tobilevych's *Suieta* (Vanity), Khveska in M. Kropyvnytsky's *Dvi sim'ï* (Two Families), Zinka in L. Yanovska's *Lisova kvitka* (The Forest Flower), Dolores in Lesia Ukrainka's *Kaminnyi hospodar* (The Stone Host), Anna Andreevna in N. Gogol's *Revizor* (The Inspector General), and Sirchykha in M. Sadovsky's *Za dvoma zaitsiamy* (After Two Hares).

Khvastiv or **Fastiv** [Xvastiv]. III-10. City (1986 pop 54,000) and raion center in Kiev oblast, situated in the Dnieper Upland on the Unava River, a tributary of the Irpin. First mentioned in 1390, in 1601 it received the rights of Magdeburg law. From the mid-1680s to the beginning of the 18th century it was a Polish county town and the center of a Cossack regiment, whose Cossacks played a key role in Col S. *Palii's anti-Polish rebellion. Annexed by the Russian Empire in 1793, it became a town in Kiev gubernia in 1797 and an important gubernial grain-trade center. In 1923 the town became a raion center. In 1926 it had a population of 14,200, of which 66 percent was Ukrainian and 25 percent was Jewish. It is an important railway junction and depot; chemical machinery, electrothermal equipment, furniture, clothing, and food products are made there. A municipal museum, the wooden Church of the Holy Protectress (1779–81), and a large, beautiful Catholic stone church (1903–11) are located there.

Khvoika, Vikentii [Xvojka, Vikentij] (Czech: Chvojka), b 1850 in Semin, near Přelouč, Bohemia, d 2 November 1914 in Kiev. A pioneering Ukrainian archeologist of Czech origin. As an active member of the Kiev Society of Friends of Antiquities and Art, he helped found the Kiev City

Vikentii Khvoika

Oleksander Khvostenko-Khvostov

Museum of Antiquities and Art in 1899; he became the director of its archeological department in 1904.

From 1893 to 1903 Khvoika discovered, excavated, and studied the Kyrylivska settlement in Kiev and other Paleolithic sites (in Kiev's Protasiv ravine, Selyshche in Kaniv county, Korosten), sites of the Neolithic *Trypilian culture, Bronze and Iron Age tumuli and fortified settlements in Ukraine's forest-steppe (eg, *Pastyrske and Motronynske), and the 'burial fields' of cremation urns and settlements of the *Zarubyntsi and *Cherniakhiv cultures. He was a leading proponent of the theory that the Slavic inhabitants of the middle Dnieper Basin were autochthonous. He also excavated and studied medieval palaces, fortifications, and churches in Chyhyryn (1903), Kiev (*Kyselivka hill in 1894 and *Starokyivska Hora in 1907–8), and *Bilhorod.

Khvoika participated in the 11th to 14th All-Russian archeological congresses and published over 20 monographs and articles, including *Kamennyi vek Srednego Pridneprov'ia* (The Stone Age in the Middle Dnieper Region, 1901), *Raskopki v oblasti tripol'skoi kul'tury* (Excavations in the Area of the Trypilian Culture, 1901), *Polia pogrebenii v Srednem Pridneprov'e* (Burial Fields in the Middle Dnieper Region, 1901), *Kievo-Kirillovskaia paleoliticheskaia stoianka i kul'tura epokhi madlen* (Kiev's Kyrylivska Paleolithic Settlement and the Culture of the Magdalenian Epoch, 1903), *Gorodishcha Srednego Pridneprov'ia, ikh znachenie, drevnost' i narodnost'* (The Fortified Settlements of the Middle Dnieper Region, Their Significance, Antiquity, and Nationality, 1905), and *Drevnie obitateli Srednego Pridneprov'ia i ikh kul'tura v doistoricheskie vremena* (The Ancient Inhabitants of the Middle Dnieper Region and Their Culture in Prehistoric Times, 1913). For his archeological contributions he was elected a full or honorary member of 11 scholarly societies. Many of the artifacts he unearthed are preserved in the Historical Museum of the Ukrainian SSR in Kiev.

A. Zhukovsky

Khvorostetsky, Ivan [Xvorostec'kyj], b 18 April 1888 in Yurydyka, Kremianets county, Volhynia gubernia, d 19 November 1958 in Pochaiv, Ternopil oblast. Landscape painter and pedagogue. A graduate of the Kiev State Art Institute (1928), he belonged to the Association of Revolutionary Art of Ukraine, and later the Ukrainian Art Alliance, and took part in their exhibitions. He lectured at the Kiev Civil-Engineering and the Kiev State Art institutes. His paintings, which he began to exhibit in 1915, include *The Komsomol Girl in the Village* (1927), *Washerwomen* (1929), *The Lake in Ternopil* (1955), *Winter in Kremianets* (1957), and *Pochaiv Motif* (1958). In 1928 he won recognition at an international exhibition in Venice. His works are found in art museums in Kiev, Ternopil, Kamianets, and Mykolaiv. A monograph on Khvorostetsky was written in 1981 by V. Pavlov.

Khvostenko-Khvostov, Oleksander [Xvostenko-Xvostov] (real surname: Khvostenko), b 17 April 1895 in Borysivka, Hraivoron county, Kursk gubernia, d 16 February 1968 in Kiev. Stage designer and graphic artist, a founder of Ukrainian stage design. A graduate of the Moscow School of Painting, Sculpture, and Architecture (1917), he worked in book and newspaper graphics in Moscow and then in Ukraine. From the early 1920s he designed stage sets in Kharkiv. From 1925 he was the chief set designer of the Ukrainian State Metropolitan Opera in Kharkiv, preparing the sets for C. Gounod's *Faust* (1924), G. Rossini's *Barber of Seville* (1926), G. Bizet's *Carmen* (1934), R. Wagner's *Lohengrin* (1934), and I. Kotliarevsky's *Natalka from Poltava* (1934). At the Kiev Ukrainian Opera he designed the sets for R. Glière's *Red Poppy* (1928), B. Liatoshynsky's *The Golden Ring* (1930), S. Hulak-Artemovsky's *Zaporozhian Cossack beyond the Danube* (1935), B. Liatoshynsky's *Shchors* (1937), M. Verykivsky's *Servant Girl* (1943), M. Skorulsky's *The Forest Song* (1946), and M. Lysenko's *The Drowned Maiden* (1950). At the same time he drew satirical cartoons for a number of Kharkiv newspapers and taught at the Kharkiv Art Institute. A monograph on Khvostenko-Khvostov by A. Drak was published in 1962.

S. Yaniv

Khvylia, Andrii [Xvylia, Andrij] (real name probably Olinter), b 1898 in Khotyn county, Bessarabia gubernia, d ? Communist leader, journalist. A member of the Borotbists, he joined the CP(B)U in 1918 and later directed the Press Section (1926–8) and the Cultural Propaganda Section (1928–33) of its Central Committee. In 1933 he became Ukraine's deputy commissar of education. A Party loyalist, Khvylia was particularly opposed to what he regarded as Ukrainian nationalism. In print he attacked Ukrainian cultural organizations such as *Vaplite and the *Berezil theater, and prominent Ukrainian cultural and political figures such as M. *Khvylovy, L. *Kurbas, O. *Shumsky, and M. *Skrypnyk. He was responsible to a large extent for the death in the 1930s of many Ukrainian cultural activists. Besides numerous articles, he wrote books and booklets on Ukrainian nationalism; eg, *Natsional'nyi vopros na Ukraine* (The Nationality Question in Ukraine, 1926), *Vid ukhylu v prirvu: Pro 'Val'dshnepy' Khvyl'ovoho* (From Deviation to the Precipice: On Khvylovy's *Val'dshnepy*, 1928), and *Do rozv'iazannia natsional'noho pytannia na Ukraïni* (On the Solution to the Nationality Question in Ukraine, 1930). After M. Skrypnyk's suicide in 1933, Khvylia published a collection of articles, *Znyshchyty korinnia ukraïns'koho natsionalizmu na movnomu fronti* (To Destroy the Roots of Ukrainian Nationalism on the Linguistic Front, 1933), attacking the orthographic changes approved by Skrypnyk. Khvylia was arrested in 1937, and disappeared soon afterwards.

M. Stech

Khvylia, Oleksander [Xvylja], b 15 July 1905 in Oleksandro-Shuvetino in the Donets Basin, d October 1977. Stage and screen actor. He began his stage career in an amateur group, and in 1924 joined the Zankovetska Ukrainian Drama Theater. Then he worked in the Berezil theater and, finally, in the Kharkiv Ukrainian Drama Theater (to 1941). His repertoire included Husak in I. Mykytenko's *Dyktatura* (Dictatorship), the Balt in O. Korniichuk's *Zahybel' eskadry* (Destruction of the Squadron), and Kudriash in A. Ostrovsky's *Groza* (The Storm). In 1932 he made his film debut as the orator in O. Dovzhenko's film *Ivan*, and he played the leading roles in *Karmeliuk* (1938) and *Oleksander Parkhomenko* (1942).

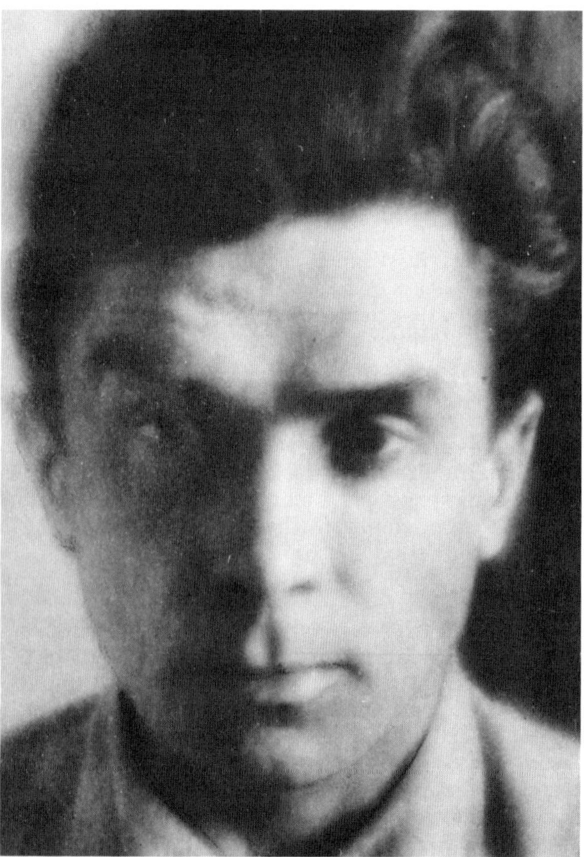

Mykola Khvylovy

Khvylovy, Mykola [Xvyl'ovyj], b 14 December 1893 in Trostianets, Kharkiv gubernia, d 13 May 1933 in Kharkiv. Prominent Ukrainian writer and publicist of the Ukrainian cultural renaissance of the 1920s. Born Mykola Fitilev, he graduated in 1916 as an extension student from the Bohodukhiv Gymnasium. In 1919 he joined the CP(B)U. In 1921 he moved to Kharkiv, where he worked as a millwright and also joined a body of writers grouped around V. *Blakytny and the newspaper *Visti VUTsVK*. In 1921, with V. *Sosiura and M. *Yohansen, he signed the literary manifesto 'Our Universal to the Ukrainian Workers and Ukrainian Proletarian Artists' (published in the collection *Zhovten'*). In the same year his poem 'V elektrychnyi vik' (In the Electrical Age) and his poetry collection *Molodist'* (Youth) were published.

After his second collection, *Dosvitni symfonii* (Twilight Symphonies, 1922), appeared, he switched to writing prose. His first short story, 'Zhyttia' (Life), was published in 1922. His first collections of short stories – *Syni etiudy* (Blue Etudes, 1923) and *Osin'* (Autumn, 1924) – immediately won him the acclaim of various critics including S. Yefremov, O. Biletsky, the party critic V. Koriak, and the émigrés Ye. Malaniuk and D. Dontsov.

The ornamental, impressionistic style of these and later lyrical-romantic stories – which exhibited the influence of expressionism (including its inherent naturalism) – became paradigmatic for most young Soviet Ukrainian writers then beginning their careers. Khvylovy experimented boldly in his prose, introducing into the narrative diaries, dialogues with the reader, speculations about the subsequent unfolding of the plot, philosophical musings about the nature of art, and other asides. In his brief period of creativity (less than five years) he masterfully depicted the revolution in Ukraine and the first hints of its degeneration, using a rich gallery of characters, most of them members of the intelligentsia. The characters' initial infatuation with the revolution ends in disillusionment, and their expected rebirth of Ukraine reifies into a new embodiment of the 'snout of the indomitable boor' in such stories as 'Redaktor Kark' (Editor Kark), 'Na hlukhim shliakhu' (On the Overgrown Path), and 'Synii lystopad' (Blue November). A later cycle of stories consists of merciless satires of insipid philistines and the transformation of former revolutionaries into bureaucrats and parasites. From 1924 on, Khvylovy's stories depict life much more psychodramatically and tragically, as in the novella 'Ia' (I) and 'Povist' pro sanatoriinu zonu' (Tale of the Sanatorium Zone).

At the same time Khvylovy played a key role in the life of literary organizations. One of the founders of the proletarian-writers' group *Hart in 1923, he soon became dissatisfied with its toeing of the official line and left it with a small group of writers to form the group Urbino. Later he opposed both Hart and the peasant-writers' group *Pluh for promoting mass participation in literary work instead of striving for artistic quality. He initiated and inspired with his ideas the group *Vaplite – the Free Academy of Proletarian Literature. Formed in November 1925, it numbered among its members the most talented writers, most of them former Pluh or Hart members. During Vaplite's brief existence (1925–8), Khvylovy tried his hand at large prose works. Around 1925 he began working on the novel 'Iraïda,' of which only one excerpt was published under the title 'Zav'iazka' (The Beginning). It reveals a change in Khvylovy's style: instead of being lyrical-ornamental and fragmentary, his narrative becomes balanced and more realistic. This change is also discernible in the novel *Val'dshnepy* (Woodcocks), of which only the first part was published (in the periodical *Vaplite*, no. 5, 1927); the second part, although it had been printed, was confiscated at the press by the authorities and destroyed. Despite diverse assessments of the purely literary aspects of the novel, Khvylovy's followers saw *Val'dshnepy* as the culmination of his literary work, while others, like Ye. Malaniuk, considered it an 'obvious failure.'

Khvylovy was a superb pamphleteer and polemicist. His polemical pamphlets provoked the well-known Ukrainian *literary discussion of 1925–8. In the first series of pamphlets, published in the supplement *Kul'tura i pobut* to *Visti VUTsK* in April–June 1925 and later that year separately as *Kamo hriadeshy?* (Whither Goest Thou?), he raised the decisive question 'Europe or "enlightenment"?' using the term 'enlightenment' to refer to Ukraine's provinciality and backwardness under Russian oppression. And his reply was, 'For art it can only be Europe.'

In the second series, 'Dumky proty techiï' (Thoughts against the Current), which appeared in *Kul'tura i pobut* in November–December 1925 and separately in 1926, Khvylovy further developed his argument against the 'cult of epigonism.' By adopting a psycho-intellectual orientation on Europe, he argued, Ukrainians can enter onto their own path of development. To this they have a perfect right, 'Insofar as the Ukrainian nation sought for several centuries its independence, we accept this as evidence of its unconquered desire to manifest and fully develop its national (not nationalist) being.' Again he underlined the necessity of overcoming its cultural backwardness and the psychological dependence on Moscow, in the belief 'that a nation can manifest itself culturally only if it finds its own, unique path of development.'

The third series of pamphlets, 'Apolohety pysaryzmu' (The Apologists of Scribbling), was published in *Kul'tura i pobut* in February–March 1926, but not separately. The idea of a completely independent development for Ukrainian literature, oriented 'at least not on Russian [literature],' was developed further, and the idea of Ukraine's right to sovereignty was formulated as follows: 'Is Russia an independent state? Yes, it's independent! Well then, we too are independent.' His last, and probably most radical, polemical work, 'Ukraïna chy Malorosiia?' (Ukraine or Little Russia?), was suppressed by the authorities; only a few quotations from it that appeared in the official critiques – A. *Khvylia's *Vid ukhylu v prirvu ...* (From Deviation to the Precipice ...) and E. Hirchak's *Na dva fronta v bor'be s natsionalizmom* (On Two Fronts in the Struggle with Nationalism) – are known.

Khvylovy's prose, particularly *Val'dshnepy*, which Khvylia described as antiparty, counterrevolutionary, and even fascist, and his polemical pamphlets make him the central figure in the above-mentioned literary discussion, which by its very nature turned into a political discussion of the direction Ukraine should take in its development. The National Communist opposition in the CP(B)U, led by O. *Shumsky, the *Neoclassicists (particularly M. *Zerov), and the entire nationally conscious, progressive Ukrainian intelligensia more or less openly sided with Khvylovy. On the opposing side were not only Khvylovy's literary opponents, such as S. *Pylypenko, S. Shchupak, and V. *Koriak, but also the party leaders A. Khvylia, L. *Kaganovich, V. *Chubar, H. Petrovsky, and other members of the Politburo of the CP(B)U. Moscow's chauvinistic proponents of a great (unitary 'Russian') state – V. Vaganian, Yu. Larin, and J. Stalin himself – threw their support behind Khvylovy's opponents. In a letter to Kaganovich, Stalin warned the CC CP(B)U against adopting Khvylovy's Western orientation and condemned it as 'bourgeois nationalism.'

Thenceforth Khvylovy was subjected to unrelenting persecution and was forced to move gradually from an offensive to a defensive tactic. To save Vaplite from forced dissolution, in December 1926 he was compelled to admit his 'errors,' and in January 1927 he, M. Yalovy, and O. Dosvitnii agreed to expulsion from Vaplite. From December 1927 to March 1928 Khvylovy lived in Berlin and Vienna, and according to some accounts in Paris. In January 1928, before returning to Ukraine, he sent an open letter from Vienna to the newspaper *Komunist* renouncing his slogan 'Away from Moscow' and recanting his views.

Yet he did not truly surrender: on his initiative an unaffiliated journal, **Literaturnyi iarmarok*, was established in 1928, and it continued Vaplite's orientation. In it Khvylovy's satirical stories 'Ivan Ivanovych' and 'Revizor' (The Inspector-general) appeared. In 1930 *Literaturnyi iarmarok* ceased publication, and Khvylovy inspired one last organization, the Union of Workshops of the Proletarian Literary Front, or *Prolitfront, which published a journal of the same name. None of his stories, but only his polemical articles refuting the hostile criticism of *Nova Generatsiia and the *All-Ukrainian Association of Proletarian Writers (VUSPP), appeared in the journal. When Prolitfront was disbanded in 1931 and many of its members joined VUSPP, Khvylovy no longer had a journal in which he could express his ideas. His attempts at writing on party-approved themes, as in the stories 'Maibutni shakhtari' (The Future Miners), 'Ostannii den'' (The Last Day), and 'Shchaslyvyi sekretar' (The Happy Secretary), were dismal failures. Thus, by the early 1930s Khvylovy's every opportunity to live, write, and fight for his ideas was blocked. Since he had no other way to protest against the Postyshev terror and famine that swept Ukraine in 1933, he committed suicide. This act became symbolic of his concern for the fate of his nation.

Immediately after his death, Khvylovy's works and even his name were banned from the public domain. Even after the post-Stalin thaw, when many other writers were 'rehabilitated' and selected works of some were published, the ban on his works and ideas has been enforced.

Khvylovy expressed in his works his own concept of Ukraine's renaissance spawned by the Revolution of 1917. Ukraine could overcome its slavishness and provinciality and 'catch up to other nations,' he believed, only by unreservedly breaking 'away from Moscow' and orienting itself psychologically and culturally on the progressive aspects of 'Europe.' As an alternative to both 'Moscow' and 'Europe' Khvylovy proposed the romantic idea of an 'Asiatic renaissance' – an awakening of Asia and other colonial, underdeveloped parts of the world. This renaissance was to begin in Ukraine, situated as it was between the West and the East, and spread to all parts of the world. Like M. Zerov, he considered Ukraine's orientation towards 'psychological Europe' a necessary precondition for Ukraine to fulfill its messianic role in this renaissance. As a romantic writer and thinker, Khvylovy believed that a 'vitalized romanticism' (*romantyka vitaizmu*) would be the literary style of the first period of the Asiatic renaissance.

Khvylovy's historiosophical vision has become known as Khvylovism, and his followers, as Khvylovists. They were physically destroyed during the Stalinist terror or were forced to reconstruct themselves as socialist realists. Several of them – Yu. Blokhyn, P. Holubenko, H. Kostiuk, Yu. Lavrinenko, A. Liubchenko, and P. Petrenko – emigrated during the Second World War to the West, where they popularized and studied Khvylovy's works. A first complete collection of his works has appeared (5 vols, 1978–86) under the editorship of H. Kostiuk.

BIBLIOGRAPHY
Leites, A.; Iashek, M. (eds). *Desiat' rokiv ukraïns'koï literatury (1917–1927)*, 2 vols (Kharkiv 1927–8)
Rudnyts'kyi, M. *Vid Myrnoho do Khvyl'ovoho* (Lviv 1936)
Hordyns'kyi, Ia. *Literaturna krytyka pidsoviets'koï Ukraïny* (Lviv 1939)
Han, O. *Trahediia Mykoly Khvyl'ovoho* (np 1947)
Holubenko, P. *Mykola Khvyl'ovyi i suchasnist'* (np 1947)
Luckyj, G. *Literary Politics in the Soviet Ukraine, 1917–1934* (New York 1956)
Lavrinenko, Iu. (ed). *Rozstriliane vidrodzhennia: Antolohiia, 1917–1933* (Paris 1959)
Khvylovy, M. *Stories from the Ukraine*, trans with an intro by G. Luckyj (New York 1960)
Sherekh, Iu. *Ne dlia ditei* (New York 1964)
Liubchenko, A. *Ioho taiemnytsia* (Paris 1966)
Smolych, Iu. *Rozpovid' pro nespokii* (Kiev 1968)
Lavrinenko, Iu. *Zrub i parosty* (Munich 1971)
Luts'kyi, Iu. (ed). *Vaplitians'kyi zbirnyk* (Edmonton and Toronto 1977)
Khvy'ovyi, M. *Tvory v p'iat'okh tomakh*, vols 1–5, ed H. Kostiuk; intros by H. Kostiuk, D. Ferguson, M. Shkandrij, and Iu. Shevelov (New York, Baltimore, and Toronto 1978–86)
Mace, J. *Communism and the Dilemmas of National Liberation: National Communism in Soviet Ukraine, 1918–1933* (Cambridge, Mass 1983)
Khvylovy, M. *The Cultural Renaissance in Ukraine: Polemical Pamphlets, 1925–1926*, trans with an intro by M. Shkandrij (Edmonton 1986)

I. Koshelivets

Khyliak, Volodymyr [Xyljak], b 27 July 1843 in Wierchomla Wielka, Nowy Sącz circle, Galicia, d 25 June 1893 in Litynia, Drohobych county. Greek Catholic priest, writer, feuilletonist, and ethnographer. He wrote under pseudonyms (Ieronim Anonim, Lemko-Semko, Ya-sam, Neliakh, and others). His works appeared in such newspapers as *Slovo* (1870–87) and *Russkii Sion*. He wrote an ethnographic study 'Svadebnye zvychai u lemkov' (Marriage Customs of the Lemkos, *Literaturnyi sbornik*, 1872). His realistic novelettes and short stories about everyday life, and his humorous stories, are written in the artificial, bookish language then popular in Galicia – *yazychie*. His collected works were published under the title *Povisti i rozskazy Ieronima Anonima* (Novelettes and Stories of Ieronim Anonim) in three volumes in 1882; a fourth volume, with a biographical sketch by I. Levytsky, came out in 1887. His most popular work was the novelette *Shybenychnyi verkh* (The Scaffold Hill, 1877–8), which was twice reprinted in literary Ukrainian.

Khymii, Yeronim Isydor. See Chimy, Isidore.

Khymych, Yurii [Xymyč, Jurij], b 12 April 1928 in Kamianets-Podilskyi. Architect and painter. A graduate of the Kiev Civil-Engineering Institute (1954) and the Academy of Architecture of the Ukrainian SSR (1958), he painted a series of watercolors of architectural monuments in Ukraine, particularly in old cities such as Kiev, Lviv, and Chernihiv.

Khyriv [Xyriv]. IV-3. Town (1970 pop 3,500) in Staryi Sambir raion, Lviv oblast, situated in Subcarpathia on the Stryvihor River. First mentioned in 1374 under Polish rule, it was razed by the Tatars in 1502–5. In 1528 it received the right of Magdeburg law. In 1939 its population was 4,250, of whom 1,900 were Poles and 1,000 were Jews. The town has remained undeveloped. Insulation, bricks, and furniture are made there.

Khyzhniak, Anton [Xyžnjak], b 8 December 1907 in Zachepylivka, Poltava gubernia. Writer. From 1950 to 1961 he was editor-in-chief of *Literaturna hazeta*. He is the author of several collections of short stories and essays, a play, the historic novels *Danylo Halyts'kyi* (Danylo of Halych, 1951) and *Kriz' stolittia* (Through the Centuries, 1980), and five novelettes – *Tamara* (1959), *Nevhamovna* (The Unrestrainable Woman, 1961), *Onuky spytaiut'* (Grandchildren Will Ask, 1963), *Nil's'ka lehenda* (The Nile Legend, 1965), for which he received the Nasser Prize in 1973, and *Kyivs'ka preliudiia* (Kievan Prelude, 1977). His works, in two volumes, were published in 1977.

Khyzhynsky, Leonyd [Xyžyns'kyj], b 3 January 1896 in Miastkivka, Olhopil county, Podilia gubernia. Graphic artist of Yu. *Narbut's school. A graduate of the Kiev Art School (1918), he studied with Narbut in 1920–1 and then at the Higher Artistic and Technical Institute in Leningrad (1922–7). He worked mostly in book graphics, designing such books as M. Rylsky's *De skhodiat'sia dorohy* (Where the Roads Meet, 1929) and M. Bazhan's *Poezii* (Poems, 1930), and illustrating a volume of selected short stories by H. Keller, a collection of C. Goldoni's comedies, and P. Mérimée's novel *La Chronique du temps de Charles IX* (1960). He was particularly innovative in the art of bookplate. His works were displayed at the exhibitions of the Association of Independent Ukrainian Artists held in Lviv in 1932 and 1933–4. From the 1930s Khyzhynsky worked in Leningrad. A monograph about him was written by K. Kravchenko in 1964.

Kibernetika (Cybernetics). Bimonthly, Russian-language journal of the *Institute of Cybernetics of the AN URSR in Kiev. It is devoted to the theoretical, methodological, and technical aspects of cybernetics and computers. Its editor in chief has been V. *Hlushkov since its inception in 1965. The journal appears in English in the United States under the title *Cybernetics*.

Kibzei, Ambrosii [Kibzej, Ambrosij], b 1888 in Myshkiv, Zalishchyky county, Galicia, d 25 April 1954 in Sault Sainte Marie, Michigan. Psychiatrist and community leader. Arriving in Canada in 1905, he completed college and worked as a teacher in Saskatchewan. Upon obtaining his medical degree from McGill University in 1922, he immigrated to the United States. From 1945 he specialized in psychiatry in Detroit. He was active in such Ukrainian organizations as the Mohyla Ukrainian Institute in Saskatoon, the Hrushevsky Institute in Edmonton, and the Ukrainian National Association. Kibzei wrote a popular medical handbook, *Ukraïns'kyi likar* (The Ukrainian Doctor, 1945; 2nd rev edn 1954).

Kiev [Kyjiv]. III-11. The historic and current political, religious, scientific, and cultural capital of Ukraine. It is also the largest city (1987 pop 2,559,000) in Ukraine and the third-largest in the USSR (with a metropolitan area of 780 sq km), one of the largest industrial centers, and an important transport and communications hub.

Location. Kiev is situated on the banks of the main river of Ukraine – the Dnieper. For over a millennium it has been the primary marketplace for the agricultural and forest products of the Dnieper Upland, Polisia, and the Dnieper Lowland. In the Middle Ages, however, far more significant was Kiev's location at the intersection of international trade routes: the *Varangian routes down the Dnieper and its tributaries to Constantinople; the overland *Zaloznyi route to the Azov Sea and Caucasia; the overland *Solianyi route to the Crimea; and the overland route to Galicia, Volhynia, Transcarpathia, and the rest of Europe. Consequently, by the 11th century Kiev was the largest economic and political center in eastern Europe. Its proximity to the Eurasian steppe, however, also rendered it vulnerable to the invasions of Asiatic hordes, which brought about its decline.

Plan of Kiev in A. Kalnofoisky's *Teraturgima* ... (1638)

The oldest part of Kiev lies along the high right bank of the Dnieper and its adjacent lower terrace among the picturesque hills between the Dnieper and the valley of its right-bank tributary, the Lybed. The highest points in the city are 200 m above sea level, 110 m above the Dnieper's surface; many of them rise steeply from the river, which is contained now by an embankment. The upper city was divided by the Khreshchatyi ravine; to the northwest was Old Kiev and the newer city to its west; to the southeast was the settlement of Pecherske. The main street of Kiev – *Khreshchatyk – runs along this ravine. The plateau on which the old city stands gradually drops towards the west and northwest into the wide Lybed Valley, which was built up only in the second half of the 19th century. On the other side of the valley, hills (up to 100 m high) again rise; there the settlements of Batyiova Hora, Solomianka, Chokolivka, Sovky, and Holosiieve arose. In the southwest periphery of the city the hills give way to relatively flat rolling land.

The most western and northwestern parts of Kiev (Sviatoshyno, Pushcha-Vodytsia) lie on a sandy plain amid pine forests. Northeastern Kiev is situated on a plain of the Dnieper Lowland and consists of a lower floodplain-meadow terrace and an upper wooded terrace with sandy soil and remnants of pine forests. On the Dnieper's right bank this plain covers only a small area; on its southern part lies *Podil, the old lower district closest to the river, while farther north lie Kurenivka and Priorka. Both terraces cover a larger area on the left bank; there, at some distance from the water, lies the new Darnytskyi city raion. The *Dnieper River serves as the city's main water source. The natural vegetation in Kiev's 66 parks is both coniferous (pine) and deciduous (oak and hornbeam).

History. The oldest human traces on the territory of Kiev date from the late Paleolithic period (see *Kyrylivska settlement). Traces of Neolithic Trypilian culture settlements are numerous, as are those of the Iron and Bronze ages. Excavated hoards of Roman coins and of burial grounds of the 2nd–4th centuries AD show that Kiev was already a large settlement and an important trading locus at that time.

According to the Rus' Primary Chronicle, the founders of Kiev were the brothers *Kyi, Shchek, and Khoryv, leaders of the Slavonic Polianian tribe, and the city was named after the eldest, Kyi. According to Soviet historiography, Kiev was founded in the latter half of the 5th, or the early 6th century, and in 1982 its 1,500th anniversary was officially celebrated.

The rise of Kiev. Kiev was the capital city of the *Polianians from the 8th century. At that time there were three distinct fortified settlements – one on St Andrew's Hill, one on Kyselivka Hill, and one in the vicinity of present-day Kyrylivska Street – which were amalgamated in the 10th century. The court of the princes was located in one of these settlements. The trading district was Podil, at the mouth of the now non-existent Pochaina River, where there was a landing.

With the founding of *Kievan Rus' in the second half of the 9th century, Kiev became its capital.

Grand Prince Volodymyr the Great (980–1015) extended the city's boundaries, and constructed the Church of the *Tithes and new, finely ornamented stone palace buildings. The houses of boyars and the royal retinue stood nearby, as did the tradesmen's quarters and the market square (Babyn Torzhok), which was decorated with trophies. Grand Prince Yaroslav the Wise (1019–54) extended the upper city onto a neighboring plateau and fortified it with a 14-m-high rampart with gates and palisades and a moat. In 1037 he built the *St Sophia Cathedral and many other churches and secular buildings. Under Yaroslav, Kiev became a trade and political center of international stature. The opulence of his court, the beauty and luxury of Kiev's buildings, and the city's populousness (50,000–100,000 by the 12th century) are documented in contemporary foreign travelers' accounts.

At that time Kiev was the religious center of Eastern Europe. A metropolitan's see, it had numerous churches and monasteries (the most famous being the *Kievan Cave Monastery). It was also a center of learning, writing, book transcribing, and painting. The first Rus' chronicles were written there (particularly at the Kievan Cave and *Vydubychi monasteries). The St Sophia Cathedral housed the prince's library – the first library in Ukraine.

For centuries, the upper city was primarily the administrative, military, and cultural center, while the more populous lower city (Podil) was mainly the commercial

A. City of Prince Volodymyr the Great (ca 1000)
B. City of Prince Yaroslav the Wise (ca 1050)
C. St Michael's Monastery
D. Kopyriv Kinets
E. Zamkova Hora hill
F. Shchekavytsia hill
G. Podil
H. Khorevytsia hill

KIEV IN THE 10TH–12TH CENTURIES

1. Church of the Tithes (989–96)
2–5. Princes' palaces (10th century)
6. St Theodore's Monastery
7. St Andrew's Church and Yanchyn Monastery (1131)
8. Church of the Three Saints (1183)
9. Church of the Elevation of the Holy Cross (1215)
10. Rotunda (12th–13th century)
11. St Sophia Gate (late 10th century)
12. St Sophia Cathedral (1037)
13. St George's Church and Monastery (1051–3)
14. St Irene's Church and Monastery (1051–3)
15. Church (11th century)
16. Stone palace (11th century)
17. Metropolitan's residence (11th century)
18. Golden Gate (1037)
19. Polish Gate (1037)
20. Jewish Gate (1037)
21. St Michael's Golden-Domed Cathedral (1108–13)
22. St Demetrius's Church (1062)
23. St Peter's Church (1085–7)
24–25. Churches of St Simeon's Monastery (second half of the 11th century)
26. St John's Church (1121)
27. Church (late 12th century)
28. Church of the Theotokos of Pyrohoshcha (1132–6)
29. St Michael's Church (mid-12th century)
30. Church of ss Borys and Hlib (mid-12th century)
31. Stone building
32. Church (1183)
33. St Nicholas's Church (12th century)
34. Stone building

and manufacturing district, with many shops, merchants' quarters, and foreign enclaves. The city's *viche* (popular assembly) took place in Podil. The prince's village of Berestove, the Kievan Cave Monastery, and, farther north, the Vydubychi Monastery stood outside the walls of the original city.

The richness and fame of Kiev attracted many plunderers, and it sustained numerous attacks and ruin by the *Pechenegs and the *Cumans. With the partition of Rus' among the various princes, Kiev was assigned to

View of Kiev from the Dnieper's Left Bank, a lithograph by P. Svinin (1840)

the eldest son of the grand prince. Incessant internecine battles for the throne of Kiev ensued. The sack of the city by Prince Andrei Bogoliubskii of Suzdal in 1169 and by Prince Riuryk Rostyslavych and his allies (the Olhovych princes of Chernihiv and the Cumans) in 1203 were particularly distructive.

Kiev in decline, 13th–16th centuries. A a result of the unceasing wars and plunderings, Kiev's importance dwindled. In December 1240, it was sacked by the Mongol-Tatar army of Batu Khan, which decimated its population. In the second half of the 13th century, the city underwent a revival under the rule of the vassal princes of the *Golden Horde. In 1362–3 Grand Duke Algirdas of Lithuania annexed the Kiev land to his realm as an appanage principality; it was governed by his son Volodymyr and the latter's descendants until 1470. From 1471 to 1569 Kiev was governed by Lithuanian viceroys. In 1471 it became the capital of *Kiev voievodeship. In the early 15th century, Kiev's trade and crafts revived to the extent that the burghers of Podil were granted self-government by Grand Duke Vytautas, and between 1494 and 1497 the entire city received the right of *Magdeburg law.

Kiev suffered greatly from Tatar depredations in the 15th and 16th centuries. In 1482, the Crimean khan Mengli-Girei, an ally of the Muscovite grand prince Ivan III, plundered Kiev and sent a golden chalice and dyskos taken from the St Sophia Cathedral to Moscow. The upper city lay in ruin for over a hundred years, during which time Podil was the center of activity. Above Podil, on a hill later called Kyselivka, the castle of the Lithuanian voievode was built in 1510. In 1569, in keeping with the provisions of the Union of *Lublin, Kiev and Kiev voievodeship came under Polish rule and cultural influence.

Maquette reconstruction of medieval Kiev

17th and 18th centuries. In the early 17th century, Kiev underwent a renaissance, becoming the political, religious, and cultural center of Ukraine. The Cossack hetman P. Sahaidachny (ca 1610–22) resided there and belonged to the Kiev Brotherhood. In 1615 the Kiev Epiphany Brotherhood School was founded in Podil and the Kievan Cave Monastery Press was established. In 1620 Patriarch Theophanes III of Jerusalem restored the Ukrainian Orthodox hierarchy and Kiev metropoly (after the 1596 Church Union of *Berestia, Kiev had been the see of only the Uniate metropolitan). As the archimandrite of the Kievan Cave Monastery (1627–32) and the metropolitan of Kiev (1632–47), P. Mohyla did much to make Kiev an important cultural center. The school he founded at the monastery in 1631 was amalgamated with the brotherhood school in 1633 to form the famous Kiev College (renamed the *Kievan Mohyla Academy in 1701). He initiated and funded the restoration of many of Kiev's old churches (particularly the St Sophia Cathedral) and the erection of many new ones.

Hetman B. Khmelnytsky and his army triumphantly entered Kiev in December 1648 to the joyful welcome of the populace. His army cleared the city of Polish forces in 1648, and Kiev became the capital of *Kiev regiment. In 1651, however, Kiev was ravaged by the Polish-Lithuanian army. After the 1654 Treaty of *Pereiaslav, a Muscovite garrison was stationed in Kiev, and a Muscovite fortress was built in the upper city. The Muscovite-Polish Treaty of Andrusovo (1667) granted Kiev to Muscovy for two years, but the Muscovites managed to retain it permanently and had their control formalized in the *Eternal Peace of 1686. Thenceforth until 1793, Kiev was an autonomous border town linked to the Muscovite-Russian state, the rest of Right-Bank Ukraine remaining under Poland.

Hetman I. Mazepa (1687–1709) contributed much to Kiev's cultural and architectural development. After his defeat by Peter I at the Battle of Poltava in 1709, Kiev's economic and religious importance was severely undermined by tsarist policies. The Russian monarchs, particularly Peter, Anna Ivanovna (1730–40), and Catherine II (1762–96), progressively eliminated Kiev's municipal autonomy, appointing their own functionaries to traditionally elective posts such as that of mayor (*viit*). Trading restrictions were imposed on Ukrainian merchants, while Russian merchants and artisans received preferential treatment and began settling in the city in increasing numbers. City-owned taverns (an important source of municipal revenue) were replaced by state-run ones. Outsiders and foreigners were allowed to reside in the city, changing its composition. In 1786 monastic properties were secularized.

In the late 18th century, Kiev still consisted of three separate, fortified, and built-up settlements: Podil, which had its own town council (*magistrat*); the fortified upper (old) city, where the metropolitan resided; and Pecherske, around the Kievan Cave Monastery and the *Kievan Cave Fortress (completed in 1723), where the Russian military and civil authorities were based from 1711. In 1782 Catherine II abolished the Cossack *regimental system, and Kiev became the capital of a vicegerency encompassing the Left-Bank lands of Kiev, Pereiaslav, Lubni, and Myrhorod regiments. After the second partition of Poland in 1793, Russia annexed much of Right-Bank Ukraine. In 1796 Kiev vicegerency was abolished, and Kiev became the capital of *Kiev gubernia in 1797.

below

The 19th and early 20th centuries. As the capital of Kiev gubernia, Kiev became the capital of Right-Bank Ukraine (the 'Southwest Region'). It attracted new residents, many of them Poles from the Right Bank, and its population rose steadily, from 30,000 in the late 18th century to 45,000 in 1840, despite cholera epidemics and a high mortality rate. Urban reconstruction, planning, and development began in earnest, particularly in Podil, after the great fire of 1811. The Kievan Cave Fortress was renovated and much enlarged in 1831–61. Residents displaced by this construction moved to the newly developed districts in the Lybed Valley and Khreschatyi ravine – upper-class Lypky, lower-class Shuliavka, and others. Old roads were repaired and new ones were built (eg, Khreshchatyk, Volodymyrska Street, and Bibikov [now Taras Shevchenko] Boulevard) in the 1830s and 1840s. The government and private individuals constructed new stone residences, churches (eg, one at Askoldova Mohyla, 1810; the Church of the Nativity in Podil, 1812), and public buildings (eg, the Contract Building in Podil [1801] and Kiev University [1837–43]) in the neoclassical style. The slopes of the hills along the Dnieper were reinforced, and the first suspension bridge spanning the river was built in 1848–53 (destroyed in 1929). As a result of all this development, the once separate districts began merging, and the suburbs began growing.

In the 1830s and 1840s, after the suppression of the Polish uprisings of 1830–1, intensive government-directed Russification of the city and of Right-Bank Ukraine occurred in an attempt to destroy the power of the Poles there; Ukrainians and their traditions were greatly affected by this process. In 1835 Kiev's right of *Magdeburg law was officially rescinded. The city *duma* (a council based on the Russian model), which replaced the *magi-*

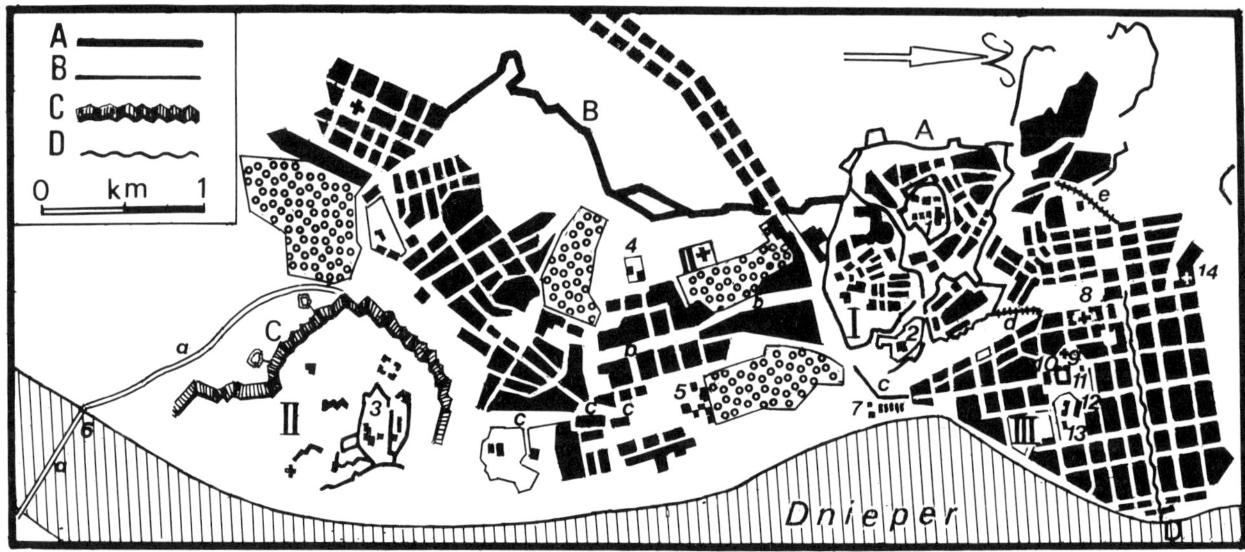

KIEV IN 1810

A. Wall around the old city
B. Münnich walls
C. Kievan Cave Fortress
D. Trench
a. Navodnytskyi floating bridge and road to Pecherske
b. Old Ivanivskyi road from Pecherske up to the old city
c. Road from Pecherske to Podil
d. Andriivskyi road from Podil up to the upper city
e. Kudriavets (or Voznesenskyi) road from the upper city down to Podil

I. Old upper city (Hora)
II. Pecherske
III. Podil (lower city)

1. St Sophia Cathedral
2. St Barbara's Church
3. Kievan Cave Monastery
4. Klov Palace
5. Mariinskyi Palace
6. Navodnytska dock
7. Lower monument to St Volodymyr, celebrating the restoration of Magdeburg law
8. St Florus's Monastery for women
9. Dormition Cathedral
10. Market Building (*hostynnyi dvir*)
11. City Hall (*magistrat*)
12. Contract Building (*kontraktovyi dvir*)
13. Brotherhood Building
14. Shchekavytsia Cemetery

strat in administrative matters in 1785 and in judicial matters in 1835, became dominated by Russian merchants. Russians were encouraged to settle in Kiev by the imperial government, which offered them tax exemptions and other economic incentives to do so, and their weight in the city's population rose swiftly. To promote Russification, the tsarist regime concentrated on education. It brought in Russian teachers and opened St Vladimir University (now Kiev University) and a second gymnasium (the first was opened in 1809) in 1834, an institute for girls of noble birth in 1838, and a military cadet school in 1852. Russification of religion was fostered at the Kiev Theological Academy, which replaced the Mohyla Academy in 1819. In 1838, the regime began publishing the Russian newspaper *Kievskie gubernskie vedomosti* (three issues per week).

Despite Russification and repression, a Ukrainian national movement arose in Kiev. The secret Society of United Slavs (1823–5) and the *Cyril and Methodius Brotherhood (1845–7) were based there, and the Ukrainian scholar M. Maksymovych was the first rector of Kiev University. In the late 1850s and 1860s, the **khlopoman* movement had a number of adherents among Kiev's university students and other members of the intelligentsia, as did the Kharkiv-Kiev Secret Society. The Ukrainophile student society, which later became the famous *Hromada of Kiev in 1859, had among its members many figures who came to play leading roles in Ukrainian life. In the years 1859–62, Kiev's Ukrainian intelligentsia organized the first *Sunday schools in the Russian Empire. In 1870, Galagan College was founded; many of its teachers were Ukrainophiles. Kiev became the center of revolutionary *Populism in Russian-ruled Ukraine; active there were such revolutionary groups as the Kiev Commune (1873–4), the South Russian Workers' Union (1880–1), and Narodnaia Volia (1884).

Kiev grew rapidly in the second half of the 19th century as a result of the general economic development of Russian-ruled Ukraine and the building of the first railway line, which connected it with Odessa and Moscow in 1869–70. The most important economic sector in Kiev continued to be trade, 50 percent of which was in beet sugar; Kiev was the main market of the sugar industry in the Russian Empire. The other 50 percent of Kiev's trade was in grain, machinery, and manufactured goods, which were sold at the *Kiev Contract Fair, at five smaller annual fairs, and at 1,060 (in the 1860s) trading houses. Kiev's commercial-financial center shifted from Podil to Khreshchatyk. Industry was of secondary importance in Kiev's economy: it consisted mainly of food processing

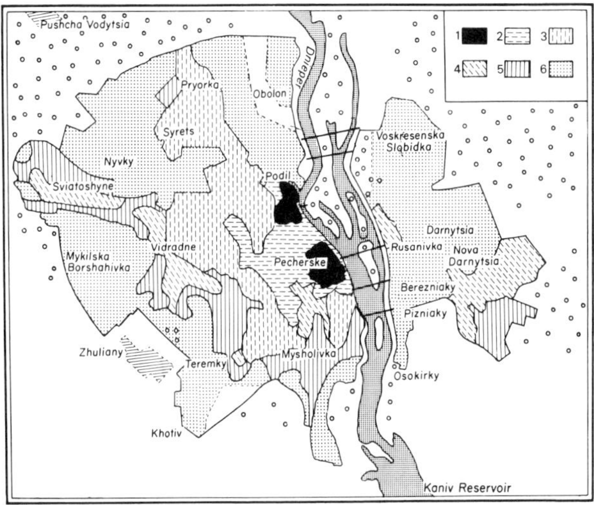

KIEV'S GROWTH

1. By 1650
2. By 1850
3. By 1917
4. By 1935
5. By 1945
6. By 1985

(62 percent of all production), distilling, tanning, metalworking, machine building (for the food-processing industry and water and railway transport), brickmaking, printing, and footwear and clothing manufacturing. Kiev's factories were relatively primitive and small; in 1900 there were 121, employing a total of 11,230 workers. In 1912, there were 14,600 industrial workers and 30,000 artisans and cottage-industry workers. As an industrial center, Kiev lagged behind such cities as Kharkiv, Katerynoslav, and Odessa, mainly because of its distance from the nearest sources of fuel (coal) and raw materials (iron ore).

Because it was an important administrative center, however, Kiev's population multiplied: from 65,000 in 1861 to over 127,000 in 1874 and 248,000 in 1897. Its various districts and main streets were increasingly built up. The city expanded mainly westward, absorbing adjacent villages and locales (Lukianivka, Shuliavka, Protasiv Ravine); at the turn of the 20th century it had an area of 18,000 ha. Limited public utilities were established in the central part of the city: a telegraph (1854), street gaslights (1872), a river water-supply system (1872), city hospital (1874), telephone system (ca 1886), electricity (1890), horse-drawn streetcars (1891), an electric tramway (1892, the first in the Russian Empire and the second in Europe), sewage system (1894), artesian water-supply system (1896), and new river port (1900). Poor sanitation, water shortages, cholera, urban poverty, and substandard housing, however, remained major problems, and labor conflict (over low wages, long hours, and unsafe conditions) was a common occurrence from the mid-1890s.

Many new buildings were erected in the 1890s and 1900s: banks, schools, libraries, a city museum (1899), theaters, an opera house, two People's homes (1897, 1902), a public auditorium (1895), hospitals, hotels, and a covered market. Their architecture was, in most cases, an eclectic combination of styles, ranging from Renaissance to Art Noveau and Modern. At the turn of the century, Kiev was considered to be in the vanguard of the Russian Empire's cities in terms of communal planning. Only its core districts, however, were well planned: in 1912, there were still more wooden (11,500) than stone (5,500) buildings; two-thirds of all homes were one- or two-story; and electric power, water supply, sewers, and paved roads existed only in the city's central area.

Russification did not diminish in the latter half of the 19th century. It was even intensified after the Polish Insurrection of 1863–4. The use of Polish was forbidden, and the government established a network of elementary schools, many secondary boys' and girls' schools, and several Russian libraries and professional cultural-educational societies; it also subsidized a new newspaper, **Kievlianin* (1864–1919). In an attempt to counteract official Russification, in 1873 members of the Kiev Hromada created the Southwestern Branch of the Imperial Russian Geographic Society, and in 1874 the Hromada turned the newspaper **Kievskii telegraf* into its semiofficial organ.

In 1875–6, the imperial government forbade all Ukrainophile activities and outlawed the Ukrainian language (see *Ems Ukase), forcing the Ukrainian movement underground. Thenceforth until the 1900s, a number of illegal, mostly student, political and educational organizations existed in Kiev; influenced mainly by the writings of M. *Drahomanov, an entire generation of Ukrainian activists matured within their ranks. The only legal Ukrainian-content periodical in Kiev in this period was the Russian-language **Kievskaia starina* (1882–1906), which was founded by the Hromada. From 1893 to 1898 Kiev was the center of the *Brotherhood of Taras, headed by B. Hrinchenko. In 1897, members of the Hromada founded the clandestine *General Ukrainian Non-Party Democratic Organization. The first Ukrainian revolutionary parties were established in Kiev: the Revolutionary Ukrainian party (1900), the Ukrainian Socialist party (1900), the Ukrainian People's party (1902), the Ukrainian Democratic party (1904), the Ukrainian Social Democratic Workers' party (1905), the Ukrainian Democratic Radical party (1905), the Ukrainian Social Democratic Spilka (1905), and the Ukrainian Party of Socialist Revolutionaries (1905).

During the liberal period after the *Revolution of 1905, Kiev was the focal point of Ukrainian cultural, scholarly, publishing, and political activity. Various periodicals were published: the daily *Hromads'ka dumka* (1906) and *Rada* (1906–14); the weekly *Slovo* (1907–9), *Ridnyi krai* (1908–14), *Selo* (1909–11), *Zasiv* (1911–12), *Muraveinyk-komashnia* (1912–19), and *Maiak* (1912–14); the semimonthlies *Rillia* (1911–18) and *Nasha kooperatsiia* (1913–14); and the monthlies *Literaturno-naukovyi vistnyk* (1907–14, 1917–19), *Ukraïns'ka khata* (1909–14), *Svitlo* (1910–14), *Dzvin* (1913–14), and *Siaivo* (1913–14). In 1906, a *Prosvita society was founded; in 1907 the *Ukrainian Scientific Society and the first permanent Ukrainian professional theater, the *Sadovsky Theater; and in 1908, the clandestine *Society of Ukrainian Progressives. Over 10 Ukrainian publishing houses (see *Publishers) were founded, numerous Ukrainian art exhibits were held, a literary-cultural Ukrainian Club was opened in 1908, and a committee to erect a monument to T. Shevchenko was struck. The Lysenko Music and Drama School (est 1904) became the main center of musical education.

The forces of Russian reaction (eg, the *Black Hundreds and the *Kiev Club of Russian Nationalists) tried to undermine and suppress this multifarious activity (a notable example was the official banning of celebrations of the 100th anniversary of Shevchenko's birth), but only after the outbreak of the First World War were most Ukrainian organizations and institutions closed down by the authorities. On the eve of the war, Kiev's population was 626,000, almost 10 times greater than it was in 1861 (65,000). In area it was the third-largest city in the Russian Empire.

Kiev as the capital of the independent Ukrainian state, 1917–20. After the February Revolution of 1917, Kiev became the center of the Ukrainian national revival, led by the Ukrainian Central Rada. The newspaper *Rada* was revived as *Nova rada.* A Provisional Ukrainian Military Council and various clubs (eg, Soldiers', Railway Workers') were established. On 1 April 1917, a massive Ukrainian national demonstration (estimated at 100,000 participants) took place. Several All-Ukrainian congresses followed (see *Central Rada); the All Ukrainian Orthodox Church Council was established; and education, art education, and theater arts training in Ukrainian and the Ukrainian co-operative movement flourished. The General Secretariat of the UNR was based in Kiev, and the formation of the *Ukrainian National Republic (20 November 1917) and its independence (25 January 1918 [predated to 22 January]) were both proclaimed there.

From 29 January to 8 February 1918, a Bolshevik uprising took place in Kiev (see *Arsenal); Soviet rule and terror lasted there until 2 March, when UNR and German troops regained the city. On 29 April a military coup took place in Kiev, and until 14 December 1918 Kiev was the capital of the conservative *Hetman government, which founded the Ukrainian Academy of Sciences, the National Library (now the AN URSR Central Scientific Library), the State Drama Theater, the State People's Theater, and other institutions there. On 14 December the anti-Hetman forces of the *Directory of the UNR took Kiev, and on 22 January 1919 the union of the UNR and the *Western Ukrainian National Republic was proclaimed there. On 5 February 1919, Bolshevik forces once again seized Kiev, and a *Cheka reign of terror ensued. On 30 August, combined forces of the UNR and Ukrainian Galician armies forced the Bosheviks to abandon Kiev, but they were themselves forced to withdraw by the advancing Russian Volunteer Army of Gen A. Denikin. On 16 December, the Bolsheviks again took Kiev. They were expelled on 6 May 1920 by a joint UNR-Polish offensive, but on 12 June they reoccupied the city.

The years of the war for Ukrainian independence and the frequent battles for control of Kiev caused much destruction and suffering to the city's residents, and many of them fled from the hunger and terror. As a result of wartime deaths and this exodus, Kiev's population fell from 544,000 (1919) to 366,000 (1920).

The interwar years. Although Kiev was rebuilt, its importance was diminished after Kharkiv became the capital of Soviet Ukraine in 1920. Kiev was neglected, and its economy and population (which reached 513,600 in 1926) grew at a slower pace than in the new capital and the cities of the industrial regions. Kiev remained, however, the focal point of Ukrainian scholarly life because the VUAN and numerous institutions of *higher education were established there. It also remained the main center of Ukrainian religious life, particularly of the *Ukrainian Autocephalous Orthodox church, which was established there in 1920. Kiev was also an important center of the literary and cultural renaissance that accompanied the policy of *Ukrainization in the 1920s. The *Neoclassicists and the writers' group Lanka-*MARS were based there, and the important cultural journal *Zhyttia i revoliutsiia* (1925–34) was published there. The famous *Berezil theater was founded in Kiev in 1922 and remained there until 1926, and the All-Ukrainian Photo-Cinema Administration was relocated to Kiev in 1928.

By the late 1920s, however, Kiev's intelligentsia was subjected to the first onslaught of Stalinist repressions and terror: the arrests and show trials of the alleged members of the *Union for the Liberation of Ukraine (1929–30). Ukrainization was abandoned in the early 1930s, and Russification of the Party and government apparats and of all educational institutions intensified. In most post-secondary and professional schools, instruction in Ukrainian virtually disappeared, and by the mid-1930s Ukrainian was rarely spoken in public.

In 1934, the Soviet regime decided to move the capital back to Kiev, 'the natural geographic center' of Ukraine, and began a program of intensive industrialization of the city. Consequently Kiev boomed, and its population grew from 578,000 in 1930 to 930,000 in 1940, much of it fed by peasants fleeing from the impoverished countryside. This transformation and growth necessitated the construction of new public and residential buildings. Much of Kiev's formerly undeveloped land was used for this purpose, and the city expanded east across the Dnieper, incorporating Darnytsia. In 1934–6, while the buildings and squares of the new government center were being designed, over two-dozen churches and other landmarks were senselessly destroyed in the old city, including St Michael's Golden-Domed Monastery, the Church of the Tithes, and the Church of the Three Saints. Iconostases were removed from many churches, including the churches of St George and St Michael at the Vydubychi Monastery. Landmarks were also destroyed in Podil (the Pyrohoshcha Church of the Dormition, St Flor's Monastery, and the Epiphany Church of the former Brotherhood Monastery), in Pecherske (St Nicholas's Military Cathedral), and in other parts of Kiev (St Cyril's Monastery); singled out for destruction were the churches whose construction had been funded by Hetman I. Mazepa. Several historic cemeteries, where many eminent Kievans were buried, were desecrated and paved or turned into parkland. Nevertheless, public utilities and the railway and public-transit networks in and around Kiev were improved; a second railway bridge (1929) and a new suspension bridge spanning the Dnieper (1925), a large new train station in the constructivist style (1932), a second airport (1933, in Brovary), a 150-kW radio station (1936), an automatic telephone exchange (1935), and a new thermal-power station (1936) were built.

The Second World War. After Nazi Germany invaded the USSR in June 1941, most of Kiev's intelligentsia and over 300,000 of its inhabitants were evacuated and 197 factories were dismantled and shipped to Soviet Asia. Before their final withdrawal, the Bolsheviks mined many public and residential buildings and destroyed the three bridges spanning the Dnieper, the railway station, and all railway shops, power stations, waterworks, and food and fuel depots. The Germans occupied Kiev on 19 September. Soviet mines began detonating on the 20th, and a huge fire raged for 10 days, destroying the buildings on Khreshchatyk and many adjacent streets. On 3 No-

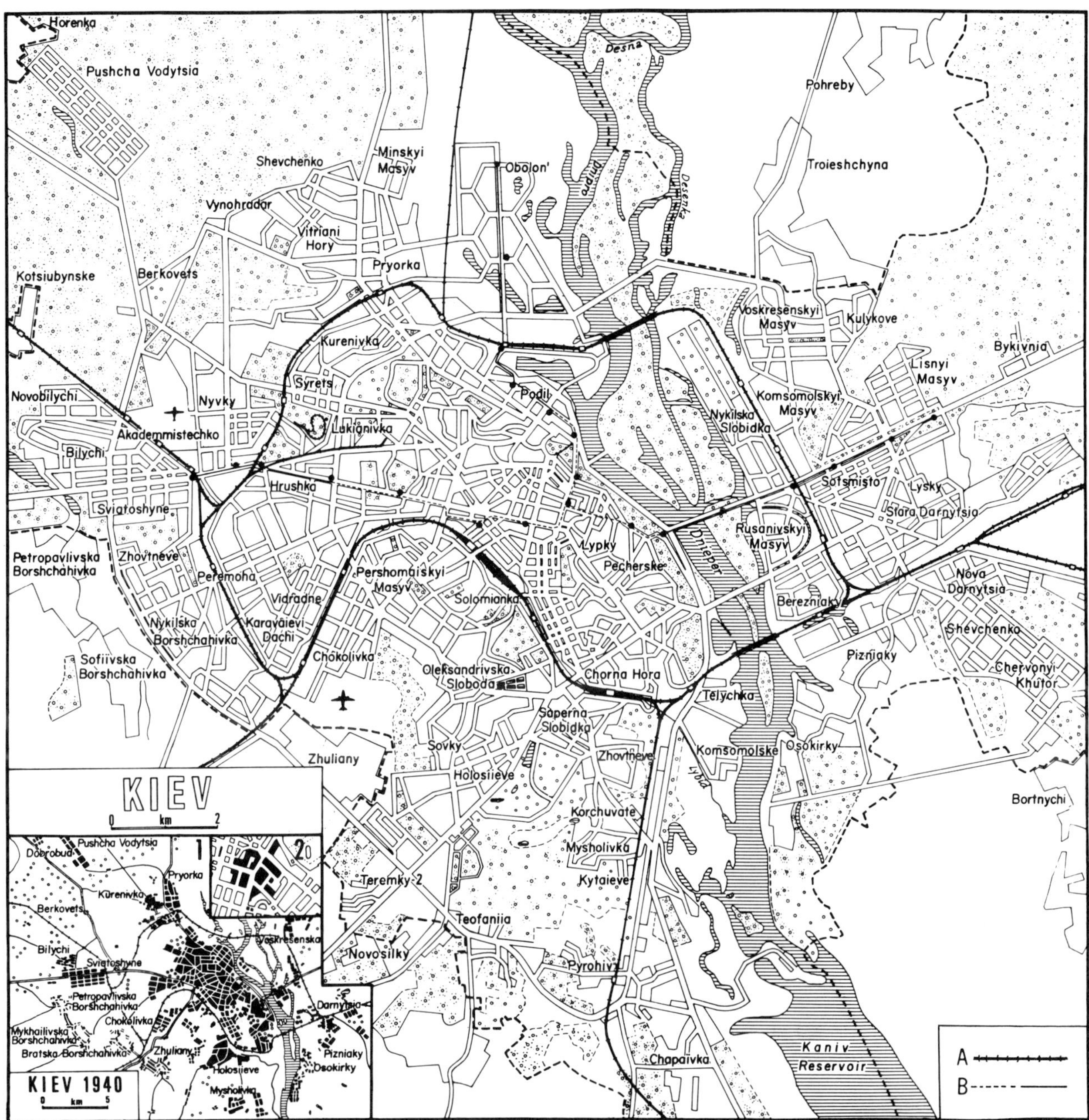

KIEV TODAY

1. Kiev in 1940 (inset)
2. Center of Kiev mined by retreating Soviet army in 1941 (inset)

A. Railway
B. Metro

vember a Soviet mine destroyed the Dormition Cathedral of the Kievan Cave Monastery.

Under the Germans, limited Ukrainian nationalist activity was briefly tolerated. A writers' and artists' associations were organized, and some publishing was allowed (eg, the dailies *Ukraïns'ke slovo* [1941] and *Nove ukraïns'ke slovo* [1941–3]). The Ukrainian Autocephalous Orthodox church, Ukrainian Red Cross, and Ukrainian co-operative movement were revived and a military club was founded by the new German-approved municipal administration headed by O. Ohloblyn and then V. Bahazii and L. Forostivsky. In October 1941 the OUN (Melnyk faction) created a *Ukrainian National Council in Kiev, headed by M. Velychkivsky, but it was soon outlawed by the Germans, who began a campaign of forced labor, terror, and suppression throughout the country. Many OUN activists were arrested, tortured, and shot. All schools were closed down, and no organized activity was allowed.

During the German occupation of Kiev, at least 200,000 of Kiev's residents, mostly Jews but also Ukrainians and Russians, were murdered (see *Babyn Yar). About 100,000 Ukrainians were forcibly sent as **Ostarbeiter* to Germany. About 100,000 Soviet soldiers died in German prisoner-of-war camps in Darnytsia and Syrets. During the winter of 1941–2, the Germans forbade the importation of food to Kiev and caused a famine there. By the summer of 1943, Kiev's population was only 305,000. Before the Germans withdrew from Kiev in November 1943, they looted its museums, libraries, factories, and homes, razed the settlements on the Dnieper's left bank, burned Kiev University and many other buildings, and destroyed the bridges they had rebuilt. Over 800 of Kiev's 1,176 enterprises, 42 percent of its living space, 940 government and public buildings, and most of its central streets lay in ruins. When the Red Army entered Kiev on 6 November, 80 percent of its residents were homeless.

The postwar period. After the war, Kiev's buildings, streets, public utilities, and industries were rebuilt and modernized. Kiev's population grew from 180,000 in 1943 to 472,000 in 1945 and 1,174,000 in 1961. New residential districts were created in the suburbs, and new industries were established. By 1949 industrial production attained the prewar level and it increased thereafter. The city's area increased from 680 sq km in 1940 to 769,000 sq km in 1960. In 1946–60, 5.2 million sq m of housing was built. By 1948 the city was utilizing the Kiev-Dashava gas pipeline. In 1949 construction of the *Kiev Metro began; it was opened in 1960. In 1951–8 the pavilions of the permanent Exhibition of Economic Achievements of the Ukrainian SSR were built.

Since the war Kiev has steadily expanded, annexing villages to its west, east, and north. Since 1957, and particularly in the 1970s, many large apartment complexes have been constructed in these new suburbs. Kiev's total housing fund rose from 6.74 million sq m in 1950 to 33.6 sq m in 1981. Kiev is one of the most verdant cities in Ukraine and the USSR. Its 'green zone' of 60 parks, suburban forested areas, and chestnut-, poplar-, and linden-lined boulevards and squares has a total area of 383,000 ha (1980), 18,300 ha of it in the city proper.

Economy. Since the 1930s the main economic sector in Kiev has been industry. After the consolidation of Soviet rule, it reached its pre–First World War level in 1925–6 and was significantly strengthened and modernized during the first two Five-Year Plans in the 1930s and again after the Second World War, particularly in the areas of machine building and light industry. Kiev's industry has grown thirtyfold since the Second World War. The main changes in output are shown in table 1. The importance of Kiev's heavy industry has grown even more in the last decade (see table 2).

Besides the main industrial branches listed in tables 1 and 2, other industries that are important in Kiev's economy include the building-materials, woodworking, medical-technology, pharmaceutical, and printing industries. The city is powered by two central thermoelectric stations (one of them, the TETs-5 [completed in 1971], is one of the largest in the USSR), the Kiev Hydroelectric Accumulation Station (HAES, completed in 1970, 37,500 kW), the *Kiev Hydroelectric Station (completed in 1968, 361,200 kW), and the thermal Trypillia Regional Electric Station (completed in 1972, 1.8 million kW).

A large part of Soviet Ukraine's industrial output is

TABLE 1
Changes in the weight of Kiev's industrial branches (% of total industrial output)

	1913	1957
Heavy industry	18.5	42.8
Light industry	14.3	35.6
Food industry	60.0	18.7
Other industries	7.2	2.9

TABLE 2
Changes in the weight of Kiev's industrial branches (% of total industrial output)

	1978	1983
Machine building and metalworking	45.0	47.0
Light industry	17.0	17.4
Food industry	15.0	12.5
Chemical and petrochemical industries	8.8	7.7
Other industries	14.2	15.4

produced by Kiev's enterprises: in 1983, 100 percent of all motorcycles, 40 percent of all tape recorders, 26.2 percent of all chemical fertilizers, 10.9 percent of all excavators, and 16.7 percent of all chemical fibers were produced there. Kiev's industries also account for a significant portion of Ukraine's industrial machines, precision tools and instruments, aircraft, hydraulic elevators, electrical equipment and instruments, armatures, audio and video equipment, textiles, wood products, furniture, building materials, cameras, clothing, foodstuffs, leather goods, consumer products, printed matter, and watercraft.

Kiev is the major transportation hub of Ukraine. It has five railway stations; the bus station Avtovokzal (from 1961), which services 50 intercity routes; a domestic airport near Zhuliany (from 1924) and an international one near Boryspil (from 1959); and an important river port, from which 22 million tons of cargo and 5 million passengers are transported per year (1979 figures). Six major bridges join Left- and Right-Bank Kiev: Paton (completed in 1953) and Moscow (1976) automobile bridges, the Podil and Darnytsia railway bridges (1949), the Metro Bridge (1965) and its extension the Rusanivka Bridge (1957), and the pedestrian Park Bridge (1957) from the center to Trukhaniv Island (and the Central Park of Culture and Recreation) in the Dnieper.

Ethnic composition. The first ethnic census of Kiev was conducted as part of the 1874 census by members of the Kiev Hromada. At that time, there were three major nationalities: Ukrainians, Russians, and Jews. Up to the 1917 Revolution and the subsequent formation of the Polish Republic, Kiev was also inhabited by many Poles, who played an important cultural and economic role there. The number of Jews rose steadily after they were allowed to leave the Pale of Settlement and settle there in 1856 and dropped drastically after many of them were murdered by the Nazis. Table 3 shows the change in Kiev's ethnic composition; the figures for the Russians include a sizable proportion of Russified Ukrainians ('Little Russians'), particularly in 1874, 1917, and 1920, which accounts for the significant drop in the percentage of Ukrainians between 1874 and 1917. In 1979, 52.8 percent

TABLE 3
Kiev's ethnic composition

	Total pop	Ukrainians (%)	Russians (%)	Jews (%)	Poles (%)	Others (%)
1874	127,500	30.3	47.0	11.0	8.2	3.5
1897	247,700	22.1	54.4	13.0	8.0	2.5
1917	430,500	16.4	50.0	18.6	9.1	5.9
1919	544,000	25.1	42.7	21.1	6.8	4.3
1920	366,000	14.3	46.8	32.0	3.8	3.1
1923	413,000	25.0	36.2	32.1	3.0	3.3
1926	513,000	41.6	25.5	26.3	3.3	3.3
1959	1,104,300	60.0	23.0	14.0	1.0	2.0
1970	1,632,000	64.9	22.0	9.3	0.6	2.3
1979	2,144,000	68.7	22.4	–	–	8.9

of Kievans claimed Ukrainian as their native language; 44.8 percent claimed Russian. The use of Russian, however, remains dominant in the city; 87.3 percent of the population spoke Russian, while only 76.3 percent spoke Ukrainian.

Education, science, and culture. Kiev is the cultural and academic center of Soviet Ukraine. The Presidium of the AN URSR, 43 of its 62 research institutes, the Central Scientific Library, the Central Republican Botanical Garden, and the Main Astronomical Observatory are located there. In 1954 the Ukrainian Agricultural Academy was founded in Kiev and the Academy of Construction and Architecture existed there from 1956 to 1964. Over 200 other research and planning and design institutes in the fields of economics, politics, pure and applied sciences, technology, and medicine that are under the jurisdiction of the CPU, Kiev University, the All-Union Academy of Agricultural Sciences, the various ministries, or other trade and industrial organizations are also based in Kiev. Kiev has 18 post-secondary schools: Kiev University, the Ukrainian Agricultural Academy; the Kiev Polytechnical, Art, Civil-Engineering, Automobile and Roads, Medical, Trade and Economics, and Pedagogical institutes; the Kiev Conservatory; the Kiev institutes of Theater Arts, Culture, Physical Culture, Civil-Aviation Engineers, and the National Economy; the Kiev technological institutes of the Food Industry and of Light Industry; and the Kiev Pedagogical Institute of Foreign Languages. The Higher Party School of the CC CPU was founded in Kiev in 1946. In 1983, 150,800 students were enrolled in Kiev's post-secondary schools. Another 61,900 attended 40 secondary specialized schools; 29,500, 41 vocational-technical schools; and 313,000, 308 elementary schools.

The executives of the Writers', Artists', Composers', Cinematographers', Journalists', and Architects' unions of Ukraine are based in Kiev. In 1980 there were 1,334 libraries in Kiev, including Ukraine's largest – the AN URSR Central Scientific Library (over 10 million volumes), the History Library of the Ukrainian SSR (over 650,000 volumes), the Republican Library (over 2.8 million volumes), the Kiev University Library (over 3 million volumes), republican Medical, Agricultural, and Technical libraries, libraries at the other 17 post-secondary schools, and city central libraries for adults, youths, and children.

In 1987 there were 28 government-funded museums in Kiev: the AN URSR Natural History Museum; the Historical Museum of the Ukrainian SSR; Kiev museums of Ukrainian Art, Ukrainian Decorative Folk Art, Russian Art, Western and Eastern Art, and Theater, Music, and Cinema Arts; Kievan Cave Historical-Cultural Preserve; St Sophia Museum; Museum of Kiev's History (opened in 1982); Museum of Ukraine's Literature (opened 1986); Taras Shevchenko Museum; the Ukrainian SSR museums of Historical Treasures, Sports Fame, Pedagogy, Book and Book Printing, and Folk Architecture and Folkways; literary-memorial museums dedicated to Lesia Ukrainka, T. Shevchenko, M. Lysenko, M. Rylsky, O. Korniichuk, H. Svitlytsky, P. Tychyna, and V. Kosenko; the Lenin Museum; the Kosyi Kaponir Museum (a former tsarist prison); and the Memorial Complex of the Great Patriotic War. There are also 40 smaller museums organized and run by private individuals, three observatories (the AN URSR Main Astronomical Observatory [est 1944], the Kiev University Astronomical Observatory [1845], and the Ukrainian Meteorological Observatory [1855]), a planetarium (1952), two botanical gardens (1839 and 1936), and a zoo (1908).

In 1987 there were 12 professional theaters in Kiev: the Kiev Theater of Opera and Ballet, Kiev Ukrainian Drama Theater, Kiev Russian Drama Theater, Kiev Operetta Theater, Kiev Young Spectator's Theater, Kiev Puppet Theater, Kiev Druzhba Theater, Kiev Theater of Comedy and Drama, Kiev Variety Theater, Kiev Theater of Historical Portrayal, Kiev Music Hall, and Kiev Young People's Theater. Professional musical ensembles include the Kiev State Philharmonic, DUMKA chorus, State Banduryst Kapelle of the Ukrainian SSR, Kiev Chamber Orchestra, Kiev Chamber Choir, Verovka State Choir, Symphony Orchestra of the Ukrainian SSR, Revutsky Men's Chorus, Virsky State Dance Ensemble, Dance and Song Ensemble of the Kiev Military District, Kiev Folk

Kiev: St Volodymyr's Hill

KIEV

1. Historical Museum of the Ukrainian SSR
1a. Historical Archive of the Ukrainian SSR
2. St Sophia Cathedral and Museum
3. St Cyril's Church
4. St Volodymyr's Cathedral
5. Kievan Cave Monastery
6. Vydubychi Monastery
7. St Andrew's Cathedral
8. Golden Gate
9. Building of the former Kievan Mohyla Academy
9a. Former building of the Central Rada (1917–18)
10. Natural science museums
11. Museum of the Book and Book Printing of the Ukrainian SSR
12. Museum of Theater, Musical, and Cinematic Arts of the Ukrainian SSR
13. Museum of Ukrainian Decorative Folk Art of the Ukrainian SSR
14. Museum of Ukrainian Art of the Ukrainian SSR
15. Museum of Western and Eastern Art
16. Archive-Museum of Literature and Art of the Ukrainian SSR
17. T.H. Shevchenko Literature and Art Museum
18. M.V. Lysenko Building and Museum
19. Lesia Ukrainka Literary-Memorial Museum
20. Exhibit of the Economic Achievements of the Ukrainian SSR
21. Planetarium (new building opened in 1984)
22. Museum of Historical Treasures of the Ukrainian SSR
23. Theater of Opera and Ballet of the Ukrainian SSR
24. Ukrainian Drama Theater
25. Russian Drama Theater
26. Young Spectator's Theater
27. Puppet Theater
28. Operetta Theater
29. Philharmonic
30. Circus
31. Kiev Artistic Film Studio
32. Television Center
33. Republican Library
34. University Library
35. Central Scientific Library of the AN URSR
36. Republican Medical Library
37. Scientific-Technical Library
38. History Library of the Ukrainian SSR
39. Republican Children's Library
40. Central City Library for Adults
41. University
42. Polytechnical Institute
43. Medical Institute
44. Institute of Culture
45. Ukrainian Agricultural Academy
46. Automobile and Roads Institute
47. Trade and Economics Institute
48. Institute of the National Economy
49. Technological Institute of the Food Industry
50. Technological Institute of Light Industry
51. Civil-Engineering Institute
52. Branch of the Kharkiv Institute of Railway-Transport Engineers
53. Institute of Civil-Aviation Engineers
54. Institute of Theater Arts
55. Pedagogical Institute
56. Conservatory (new building)
57. Art Institute
58. Pedagogical Institute of Foreign Languages
59. University Astronomical Observatory
59a. Ukrainian Hydrometeorological Observatory
60. Higher Party School of the CC CPU
61. Plant of Automatic Machine Tools
62. Bilshovyk Manufacturing Association of Polymer-Products Machine Building
63. Chervonyi Ekskavator Machine-building Plant
64. Leninska Kuznia Shipyard
65. Aviation Manufacturing Association
66. Motorcycle Plant
67. Transsyhnal Electromechanical Plant (railroad machinery)
68. Darnytsia Railway-Car Repair Plant
69. Electric Railway-Car Repair Plant
70. Tochelektroprylad Manufacturing Association (electric precision apparatuses)
71. Ukrkabel Electrotechnical Plant (cables)
72. Arsenal Plant
73. Darnytsia Chemical-Pharmaceutical Manufacturing Association
74. Slavutych Food Manufacturing Association
75. Silk Plant
76. Asbestos-Cement Manufacturing Complex
77. Relay and Automation Plant
78. Silk Plant
79. Chervonyi Humovyk Manufacturing Association of the Petroleum-Refining and Petrochemical Industry
80. Polihrafknyha Manufacturing Association of Book Printing Enterprises and the Radianska Ukraina Printing Complex
81. Khimvolokno Manufacturing Association (chemical fibers)
82. Knitted-Fabric Manufacturing Association
83. Confectionery Factory
84. Footwear Factory
85. Elektroprylad Plant (electric instruments)
86. Meat-Packing Complex
87. Clothing Factory
88. Vulkan Artificial Leather Plant
89. Metallic Products Plant
90. Leather Manufacturing Association
91. Furniture Factory
92. Medicinal Preparations Plant
93. Medaparatura Manufacturing Association (medical apparatuses)
94. Trade and Industry Palace of the Ukrainian SSR
95. Contract Building (19th century)
96. Red Cross Society of the Ukrainian SSR
97. Kiev Passenger Railway Station
98. Kiev-Moscow Railway Station
99. Darnytsia Railway Station
100. Zhuliany Airport
101. Nyvky Airport
102. Dnieper River Port
103. Funicular
104. Little Southwestern Railway (children's railway)
105. Avtovokzal (main bus depot)
106. Central Committee of the CPU
107. Supreme Soviet of the Ukrainian SSR
108. Council of Ministers of the Ukrainian SSR
109. Radio and Telegraph Agency of Ukraine (RATAU)
110. Telegraph Central
111. Telephone Central
112. Main Post Office
113. Presidium of the AN URSR
114. AN URSR Institute for Nuclear Research
115. Publishing House of the Ukrainian Soviet Encyclopedia
116. Central Department Store
117. October Department Store
118. Central Indoor Market and Central Collective-Farm Market
119. Children's Department Store
120. House of the Book
121. Sports Palace
122. Dynamo Stadium
123. Spartak Stadium
124. Baikove Cemetery
125. Lypky; the locale of mass executions of Ukrainians during the 1919 Bolshevik occupation
126. Babyn Yar; the locale of the mass murder of 150,000 Kievans, most of them Jews, by the Nazis in 1941–3
127. The locales of the mass destruction of prisoners of war by the Nazis in 1941–3
128. Lukianivka Cemetery
129. Central Park of Culture and Recreation
130. St Volodymyr's Hill Park
131. Eternal Glory Park
132. Shevchenko Park
133. Central Republican Botanical Garden of the AN URSR
134. Zoological Garden
135. Dnieper Park
136. Monument to St Volodymyr
137. Askoldova Mohyla Park

Abbreviations: Akad. = Akademik (Academician); Bd. = Boulevard; Gen. = General; N. = Nova (New); Naber. = Naberezhna (Shore Road); Nyzh. = Nyzhnia (Lower); Prosp., Pros., Pr. = Prospekt (Avenue); St. = Street; Verkh. = Verkhnia (Upper)

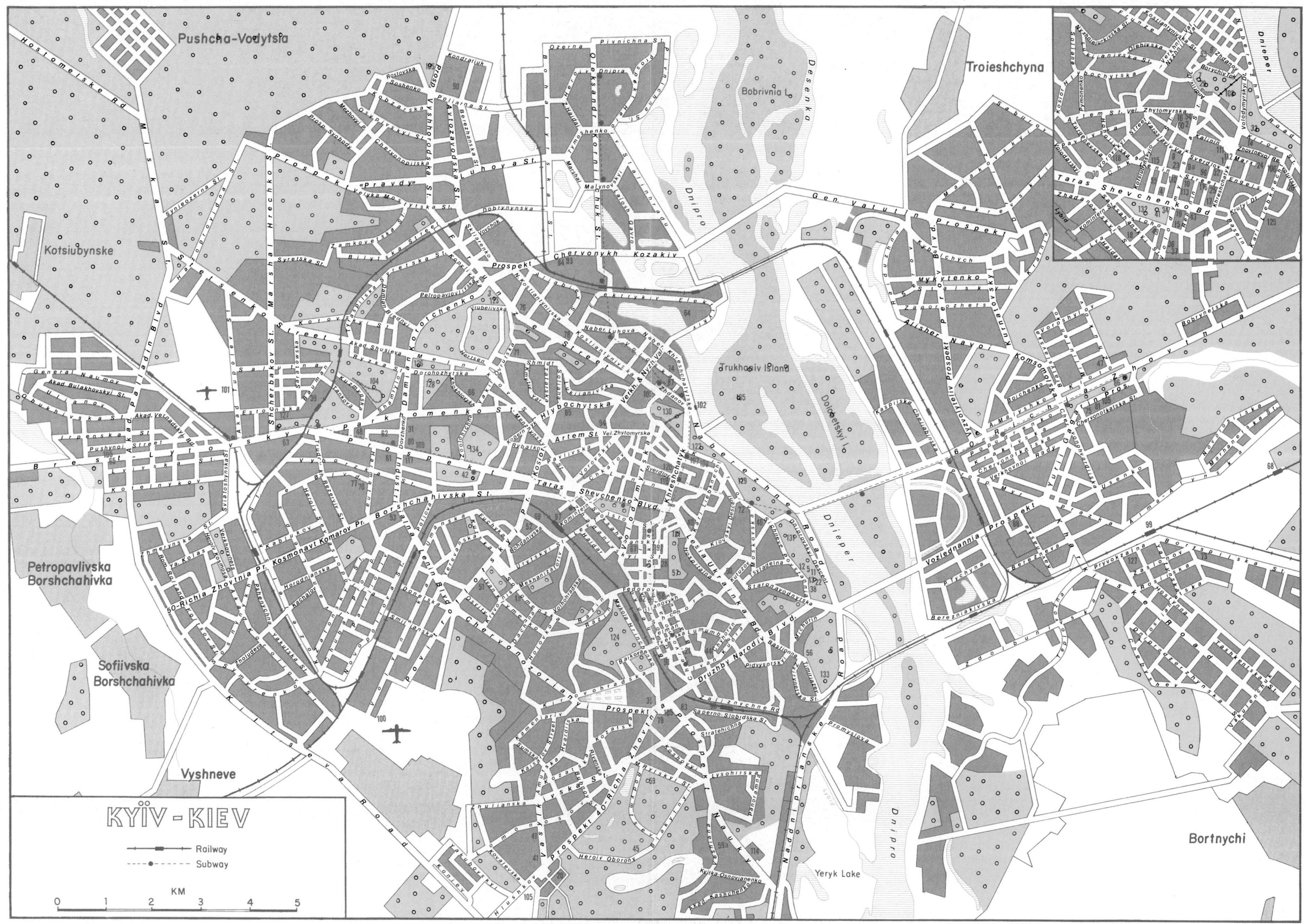

KYÏV - KIEV
Railway
Subway
KM
0 1 2 3 4 5
Pushcha-Vodytsia
Kotsiubynske
Troieshchyna
Petropavlivska Borshchahivka
Sofiivska Borshchahivka
Vyshneve
Bortnychi
Trukhaniv Island
Dolobetskyi I.
Bobrivnia I.
Desenka
Dnipro
Dnieper
Yeryk Lake
Taras Shevchenko Blvd.
Hostomelske Rd.
Kiltseva Road
Prospekt 40-Richia Zhovtnia
Vozziednannia Prospekt
Gen. Vatutin Prospekt
Prospekt Chervonykh Kozakiv

Instrument Orchestra, and Lysenko String Quartet. The Kiev Circus has existed since the 1860s.

Kiev has been the center of Ukrainian film and mass media. In 1928 the Dovzhenko Kiev Artistic Film Studio was founded there. Also located in Kiev are the Kiev Studio of Chronicle and Documentary Films, the Kiev Studio of Popular Science Films, and the Ukrtelefilm studio (est 1966). In 1981 there were 136 cinemas in Kiev. Kiev has had radio stations since 1927. Republican TV programs are broadcast daily in Ukrainian and Russian on three television channels from a telecenter established in Kiev in 1951.

Publishing. Kiev has always been an important publishing center in Ukraine; since the 1930s it has been the pre-eminent one. In 1917–18, there were 20 publishing houses, over 40 newspapers and journals, and 15 bookstores in Kiev. Today there are 16 publishing houses: Politvydav Ukrainy, Molod, Radianskyi Pysmennyk, Radianska Ukraina, Dnipro, Derzhavne Vydavnytstvo Ukrainy, Naukova Dumka, Vyshcha Shkola, Radianska Shkola, Mystetstvo, Tekhnika, Budivelnyk, Znannia, Muzychna Ukraina, Urozhai, and the publishing house of the Ukrainian Soviet Encyclopedia. Kiev is the major printing center in Ukraine. The association Polihrafknyha, consisting of six printing enterprises in Kiev and six elsewhere, prints and binds 95 percent of all the books published in Ukraine. Many newspapers and periodicals are based in Kiev: 14 republican newspapers (including the dailies *Radians'ka Ukraïna, Pravda Ukrainy, Robitnycha hazeta / Rabochaia gazeta, Sils'ki visti, Molod' Ukraïny*, and *Komsomol'skoe znamia*, the semiweekly *Radians'ka osvita*, and the weeklies *Kul'tura i zhyttia, Literaturna Ukraïna*, and *Druh chytacha*), the city dailies *Kyïv/Vechernii Kiev* and *Prapor komunizmu*, the oblast dailies *Kyïvs'ka pravda* and *Moloda hvardiia*, 55 republican periodicals (including the popular weekly *Ukraïna*, the biweeklies *Perets' and Pid praporom leninizmu*, and the monthlies *Komunist Ukraïny, Vitchyzna, Dnipro, Vsesvit, Kyïv, Raduga, Nauka i suspil'stvo, Novyny kinoekranu*, and *Radians'ka zhinka*), and 40 AN URSR periodicals. The Radio and Telegraph Agency of Ukraine has been based in Kiev since 1934.

Kiev: view of Podil

Religious life. In 1914 there were 7 men's and 3 women's monasteries, 4 cathedrals, 36 parish churches, and 40 other Orthodox churches in Kiev. The pillaging of churches by Bolshevik zealots in the 1920s and the wanton destruction and suppression of organized religion by the authorities left only a few small churches next to cemeteries and one church on the Trukhaniv Island open by the mid-1930s. After the Second World War, the authorities allowed a few more churches and monasteries to reopen. Currently functioning are two women's monasteries (the Holy Protectress and St Flor-Ascension monasteries) and five churches in addition to the ones at the monasteries (St Volodymyr's Cathedral, St Elijah's Church, ss Constantine and Helen's Church, St Nicholas's Prytyska Church, and the Holy Trinity Church). They are all administered by the Russian Orthodox church, the Ukrainian Autocephalous Orthodox church having been banned. *Pravoslavnyi visnyk*, the official organ of the Russian Orthodox metropolitan of Kiev and Halych, has been published in Kiev since 1971. A Russian Orthodox Theological Seminary was allowed to operate in Kiev from 1947 to 1960. The former St Nicholas's Roman Catholic Church (built in 1899–1909) was restored in 1979–80; it now houses the Republican Building of Organ and Chamber Music. The former St Alexander's Roman Catholic Church (built in 1817–42) has housed the Kiev Planetarium since 1952.

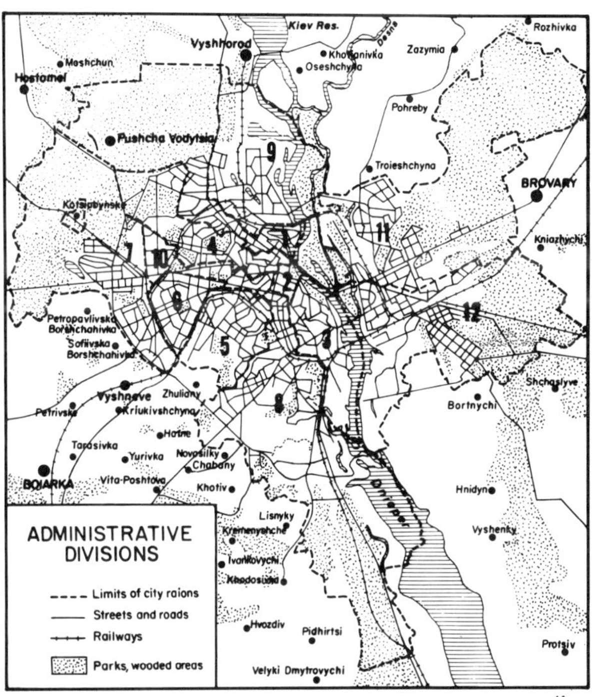

KIEV, ADMINISTRATIVE DIVISIONS

Raions

1. Podilskyi
2. Leninskyi
3. Pecherskyi
4. Shevchenkivskyi
5. Zaliznychnyi
6. Zhovtnevyi
7. Leninskyi
8. Moskovskyi
9. Minskyi
10. Radianskyi
11. Dniprovskyi
12. Darnytskyi

Kiev's city raions. Contemporary metropolitan Kiev is divided into 12 city raions (administrative districts).

Leninskyi raion (est 1921; 2.9 sq km) is Kiev's central district and is the administrative, cultural, commercial, and tourist hub of Kiev. Located there on Khreshchatyk, Kiev's main boulevard, are the buildings of the central post office, the Kiev City Soviet, and various ministries. Kiev's oldest architecture (eg, the Golden Gate) is found on Volodymyrska Street, the former center of the upper city during the reigns of princes Volodymyr the Great and Yaroslav the Wise. Also located in the raion are Kiev University; the AN URSR Central Scientific Library, Presidium, and five institutes; three other research institutes; the Conservatory; the Medical, Food Industry, and Party History institutes; the Fomin Botanical Garden and Shevchenko Park; the Litterateurs', Composers', Scholars', Teachers', and Architect's buildings; the Shevchenko, Tychyna, Russian Art, Western and Eastern Art, and Sports Fame museums; the Ukrainian Drama, Opera and Ballet, Drama and Comedy, Russian Drama, Puppet, and Young People's theaters; St Volodymyr's Cathedral; the Sports Palace; four hotels; eight cinemas; the Central Department Store and hundreds of stores; and monuments to T. Shevchenko, M. Lysenko, and I. Franko.

Pecherskyi raion (est 1921; 26.2 sq km) consists of the historical sites Pecherske, Lypky, Vydubychi, Klov, Zvirynets, and Telychka along the Dnieper. Many landmarks and cultural, educational, and government buildings, and 17 industrial enterprises, are found there, including the Kievan Cave Historical-Cultural Preserve (the Cave Monastery) and Kievan Cave Fortress; the Transfiguration Chruch in the Berestiv district; Vydubychi Monastery; the ruins of St Michael's Golden-Domed Monastery; Askoldova Mohyla; monuments to Lesia Ukrainka, Magdeburg law, St Volodymyr, and the Unknown Soldier; the Kiev Culture, Light Industry, and Automobile and Roads institutes; 12 AN URSR institutes; 36 other research and planning and design institutes; the Central Republican Botanical Garden; the History Library; the Young Spectator's Theater; the Philharmonic; the Planetarium; the Ukrainian Art, Historical Treasures, Book and Book Printing, Ukrainian Decorative Folk Art, Lenin, Kosyi Kaponir, Theater, Music, and Cinema Arts museums; the former buildings of the Ukrainian Central Rada and Pedagogical Museum; the 18th-century Mariinskyi and Klov palaces; the Council of Ministers and the Supreme Soviet of the Ukrainian SSR; Dynamo Stadium; Volodymyrska Hirka and five other parks; the Arsenal and Budindustriia plants; and cinemas.

Shevchenkivskyi raion (est 1937; 28.1 sq km) consists of part of the old upper city and the locales Lukianivka, Syrets, Nyvky, Berkovets, Vynohradar, and Babyn Yar. Landmarks there include the St Sophia Cathedral, Square, and Museum; St Andrew's Church; the B. Khmelnytsky, I. Kotliarevsky, and Babyn Yar monuments; Lukianivka Cemetery; the Art Institute; the Historical Museum, built where the Church of the Tithes once stood; the Trade and Industry Palace; the University Observatory; and Syrets Park. Eighteen industrial enterprises and 25 research and planning and design institutes are located in the raion.

Kiev: Bohdan Khmelnytsky Square

Podilskyi raion (est 1921; 88.6 sq km) consists of historic Podil and the locales Kurenivka, Vitriani Hory, and parts of Priorka, Pushcha-Vodytsia, Rybalky, and Trukhaniv Island. Located there are 50 industrial enterprises and associations, the River Station, the large Podil covered market, Spartak Stadium, Frunze Culture Park, and 2 research institutes. Notable landmarks include the building of the former Mohyla Academy, Kiev's first pharmacy (1728) and seminary, St Nicholas's Naberezhna Church, St Elijah's Church, the Kyrylivska settlement, the Svitlytsky Museum, Flor Monastery, St Cyril's Church, St Constantine and Helen's Church, and the ruins of the Pyrohoshcha Church of the Dormition.

Minskyi raion (est 1975; 57.3 sq km), the newest and northernmost area of the city, consists of the locales of Obolon and Priorka. Located there are the Minskyi Masyv, Obolon, and Vynohradar apartment subdivisions; 40 industrial enterprises, including Europe's largest window-and-door-block manufacturing complex; the AN URSR Institute of Superhard Materials; and the Ukrainian Scientific-Research Institute of the Leather and Shoe Industry.

Radianskyi raion (est 1933; 13.7 sq km) is immediately west of the center. From 1965 to 1973 it was extended along Shevchenko Boulevard and Brest-Litovsk Avenue for 14 km to Nyvky. Located there are over 30 industrial enterprises, including the Polihrafknyha association and the Polihrafist and Radianska Ukraina printing complexes; 7 AN URSR institutes; the Kiev Medical, Theater Arts, National Economy, and Pedagogical institutes; 28 other research and planning and design institutes; the editorial offices of the Ukrainian Soviet Encyclopedia; the Kiev Artistic Film Studio; the Zoo; the Circus; Kiev's largest department store, Ukraina; the Republican Children's Library; the Historical Portrayal Theater; 3 stadiums; 2 sports complexes; a velodrome; and 3 parks.

Zhovtnevyi raion (est 1921; 12.1 sq km) is west and southwest of the center and consists of the locales Shuliavka, Galagany, Hrushky, and Karavaievi Dachi. Located there are the Nyvky and Vidradnyi apartment subdivisions, 30 industrial enterprises and associations, several research institutes, the Kiev Polytechnical and Civil-Aviation Engineers institutes, 2 stadiums, and 2 public swimming pools.

Leninhradskyi raion (est 1973; 111.7 sq km), the westernmost district, consists of the locales Bilychi, Katerynivka, Sviatoshyne, and Mykilska Borshchahivka. Located there are the Novobilychi, Mykilska Borshchahivka, and Akademmistechko apartment subdivisions; 30 industrial enterprises, including the Kiev Aviation Manufacturing Association; 8 AN URSR institutes; an institute of the USSR Ministry of Fisheries; 8 other research institutes; 2 stadiums; a sports complex; and a forest park.

Zaliznychnyi raion (est 1938; 23.7 sq km), to the southwest of the center, consists of the locales Solomianka,

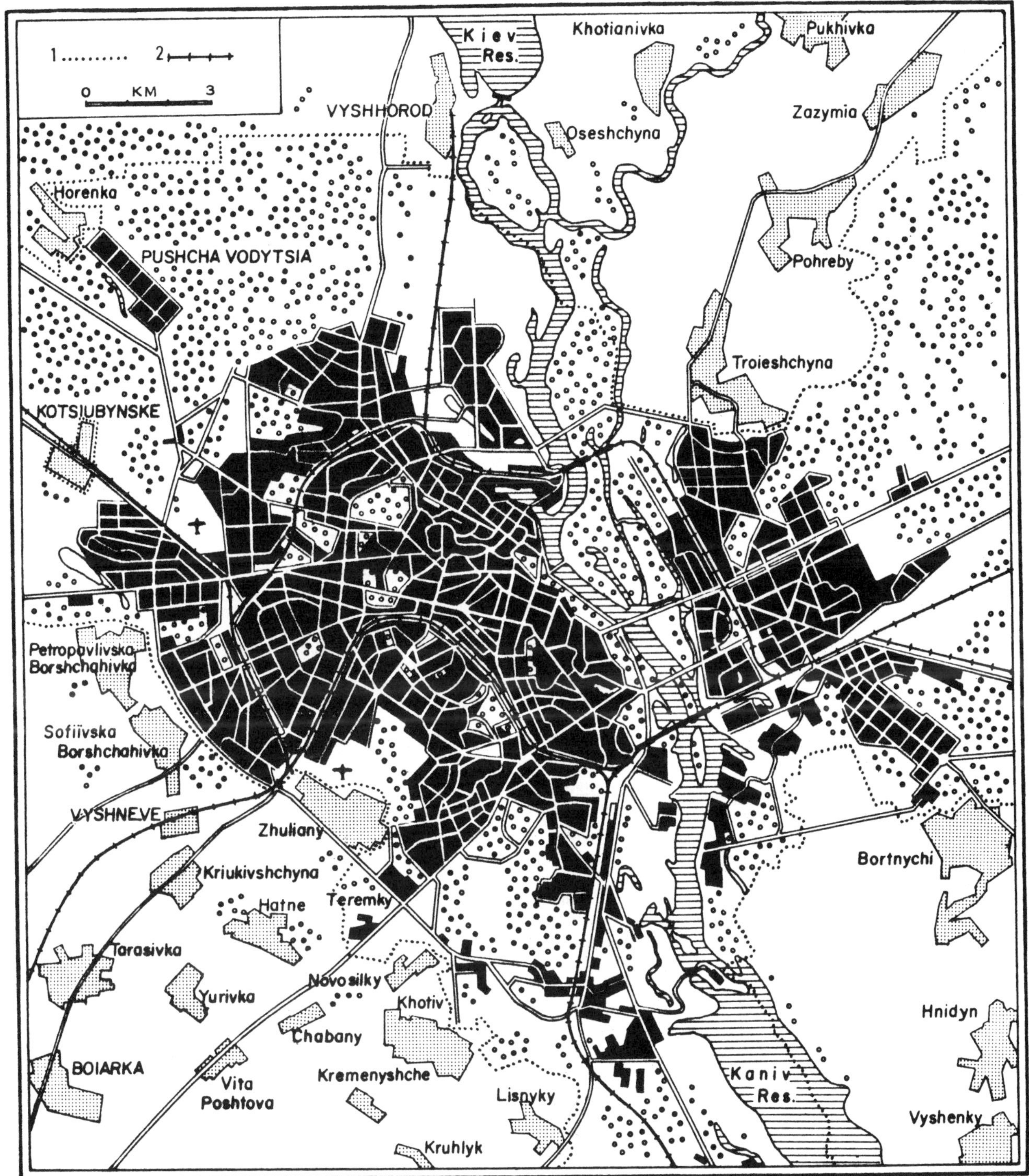

KIEV SUBURBS, 1975

1. City limits

2. Railway lines

Chokolivka, Batyieva Hora, Oleksandrivska Slobidka, and Sovky. Located there are the Pershotravnevyi, Solomianka, and Zaliznychnyi apartment subdivisions; 24 industrial enterprises, including railway-machine bulding and repair plants and a car plant; the Lysenko Museum; 31 research and planning institutes; the Kiev Civil-Engineering Institute; the Ministry of Health Protection institutes of Cardiology, Tuberculosis and Chest Surgery, and Epidemiology, Microbiology, and Parasitology; the Raduha Republican Mime Theater of the Ukrainian So-

Kiev: a modern development in Rusanivka

ciety for the Deaf; 4 sports complexes; and 3 public swimming pools.

Moskovskyi raion (est 1921; 146 sq km), the southernmost district, consists of the locales Baikova Hora, Demiivka, Saperna Slobidka, Holosiieve, Teremky, Korchuvate, Mysholovka, Kytaieve, Pyrohiv, Teofaniia, and Zhovtneve. Located there are 53 industrial enterprises; 38 planning institutes; a campus of Kiev University; the Kiev Institute of Physical Culture and Pedagogical Institute of Foreign Languages; the Ukrainian Agricultural Academy; the AN URSR Main Astronomical Observatory; 12 AN URSR institutes; a new building of the Central Scientific Library; the Republican Technical Library; the Studio of Chronicle and Documentary Films; the Operetta Theater; the Ukraina Palace of Culture; the Museum of Folk Architecture and Folkways; the Rylsky Museum; the Building of Chamber and Organ Music; the Exhibition of Economic Achievements of the Ukrainian SSR; Holosiieve Forest and Park; the historic Baikove Cemetery; the Kiev Hippodrome; a racetrack; the Avtovokzal bus station; the Republican Stadium (with a seating capacity of 100,000); and the first ice stadium in the USSR.

Darnytskyi raion (est 1935; 133.6 sq km), on the left bank, consists of Stara Darnytsia, Nova Darnytsia, Pizniaky, Chervonyi Khutir, Osokirky, and Lisky. Located there are the Berezniaky, Livoberezhnyi, and Rusanivka apartment subdivisions; 23 industrial enterprises; 8 research and planning institutes; 2 parks of culture and recreation; and the Ukrtelefilm studio.

Dniprovskyi raion (est 1969; 143.4 sq km), north of Darnytskyi raion on the left bank, consists of the locales Kylykove Pole, Bykivnia, Rybne, Voskresenska Slobidka, and Mykilska Slobidka. Located there are the apartment subdivisions Voskresenskyi, Lisovyi, Komsomolskyi, Livoberezhnyi, and Sotsmistechko; enterprises of the light, chemical, energy, building-materials, and printing industries; the Kiev Studio of Popular Science Films; two central thermoelectric stations (TETs-4 and TETs-6); 14 research and planning institutes; the AN URSR Institute of Organic Chemistry; the Kiev Trade and Economics Institute; the Republican Sports School; 4 large parks; and forested areas.

Many monuments have been erected in Kiev's squares, parks, and other public places. The oldest are the monuments to Magdeburg law on the right bank of the Dnieper (by A. Melensky, 1802–8), St Volodymyr in Volodymyrska Hirka park (by P. Klodt and V. Demut-Malynovsky, 1853), and B. Khmelnytsky in St Sophia Square (by M. Mikeshin, 1888). Most have been erected in the Soviet period, particularly after the Second World War, to honor Ukrainian cultural and scholarly figures, Soviet political figures, and the heroes and victims of the Second World War. They include monuments to T. Shevchenko near Kiev University (1939), I. Franko near the Ukrainian Drama Theater (1956), O. Dovzhenko (1964), M. Lysenko (1965), Lesia Ukrainka (1965, 1973), M. Rylsky (1968), M. Zankovetska (1974), I. Kotliarevsky (1975), H. Skovoroda (1976), and the Founders of Kiev (1982). There are also commemorative plates on hundreds of buildings where prominent individuals lived.

BIBLIOGRAPHY

Berlinskii, M. *Kratkoe opisanie Kieva* (St Petersburg 1820)
Zakrevskii, N. *Opisanie Kieva*, 2 vols (Moscow 1868)
Zakharchenko, M. *Kiev teper i prezhde* (Kiev 1888)
Petrov, N. *Istoriko-topograficheskie ocherki drevniago Kieva* (Kiev 1897)
Ikonnikov, V. *Kiev v 1654–1855 godakh* (Kiev 1904)
Sherotskii, K. *Kiev: Putevoditel'* (Kiev 1917)
Hrushevs'kyi, M. (ed). *Kyïv ta ioho okolytsia v istoriï i pam'iatkakh* (Kiev 1926)
Novi studiï z istoriï Kyïva Volodymyra Ivanovycha Shcherbyny (Kiev 1926)
Ernst, F. (ed). *Kyïv: Providnyk* (Kiev 1930)
Hrushevs'kyi, M. (ed). *Kyïvs'ki zbirnyky istoriï i arkheolohiï, pobutu i mystetstva*, 1 (Kiev 1930)
Voblyi, K. *Kyïv: Sertse Ukraïny* (Kiev 1944)
Mikorskii, B. *Razrushenie kul'turno-istoricheskikh pamiatnikov v Kieve v 1934–1936 godakh* (Munich 1951)
Forostivs'kyi, L. *Kyïv pid vorozhymy okupatsiiamy* (Buenos Aires 1952)
Povstenko, O. *Zolotoverkhyi Kyïv* (Washington 1954–62)
Havryliuk, V.; Rechmedin, I. *Pryroda Kyieva ta ioho okolyts'* (Kiev 1957)
Karger, M. *Drevnii Kiev*, 2 vols (Moscow-Leningrad 1958, 1961)
Shul'kevych, M. *Kyïv: Arkhitekturno-istorychnyi narys* (Kiev 1958)
Kasymenko, O. (ed). *Istoriia Kyieva*, 2 vols (Kiev 1960–1; Russian edn 1963–4)
Braichevs'kyi, M. *Koly i iak vynyk Kyïv* (Kiev 1963)
Shmorhun, P.; Korol'ov, B.; Kravchuk, M. *Kyïv u tr'okh revoliutsiiakh* (Kiev 1963)
Logvin, G. *Kiev: Kniga-sputnik po gorodu Kievu*, 2nd rev edn (Moscow 1967)
Istoriia mist i sil Ukraïns'koï RSR: Kyïv (Kiev 1968; Russian edn 1979)
Asieiev, Iu. *Mystetstvo starodavn'oho Kyieva* (Kiev 1969)
Tolochko, P. *Istorychna topohrafiia starodavn'oho Kyieva* (Kiev 1970)
Tolochko, P. (ed). *Starodavnii Kyïv* (Kiev 1975)
– *Arkheolohichni doslidzhennia starodavn'oho Kyieva* (Kiev 1976)
Belichko, Iu. *Izobrazitel'noe iskusstvo Kieva* (Moscow 1977)
Kyïv u tsyfrakh. Statystychnyi zbirnyk (Kiev 1977)
Tolochko, P. (ed). *Arkheolohiia Kyieva: Doslidzheniia i materialy* (Kiev 1979)
Vulytsi Kyieva: Dovidnyk (Kiev 1979)
Asieiev, Iu. *Dzherela: Mystetstvo Kyïvs'koï Rusi* (Kiev 1980)
Khinkulov, L. *Literaturni zustrichi: Rozpovidi pro pys'mennykiv u Kyievi* (Kiev 1980)
Tolochko, P. *Kiev i Kievskaia zemlia v epokhu feodal'noi razdroblennosti XII–XIII vekov* (Kiev 1980)
Borovs'kyi, Ia. *Pokhodzhennia Kyieva: Istoriohrafichnyi narys* (Kiev 1981)
Kudryts'kyi, A. (ed). *Kyïv: Entsyklopedychnyi dovidnyk* (Kiev 1981; Russian edn 1982)

Tolochko, P. (ed). *Novoe v arkheologii Kieva* (Kiev 1981)
Alferova, G.; Kharlamov, V. *Kiev vo vtoroi polovine XVII veka: Istoriko-arkhitekturnyi ocherk* (Kiev 1982)
Aseev, Iu. *Arkhitektura drevnego Kieva* (Kiev 1982)
Gupalo, K. *Podol v drevnem Kieve* (Kiev 1982)
Hewryk, T. *The Lost Architecture of Kiev* (New York 1982)
Ivakin, G. *Kiev v XIII–XV vekakh* (Kiev 1982)
Kondufor, Iu. (ed). *Istoriia Kyieva*, 3 vols in 4 bks (Kiev 1982–6)
Kudryts'kyi, A. (ed). *Kyïv: Istorychnyi ohliad (karty, iliustratsiï, dokumenty)* (Kiev 1982)
Logvin, G. *Kiev*, 3rd edn (Leningrad 1982)
Shul'kevich, M.; Dmitrenko, T. *Kiev: Arkitekturno-istoricheskii ocherk*, 6th edn (Kiev 1982)
Aseev, Iu. (ed) *Pamiatniki gradostroitel'stva i arkhitektury Ukrainskoi SSR, 1: Kiev, Kievskaia oblast'* (Kiev 1983)
Tolochko, P. *Drevnii Kiev* (Kiev 1983)
Kovalevskii, B. (ed). *Kiev v fondakh Tsentral'noi nauchnoi biblioteki AN USSR: Sbornik statei* (Kiev 1984)
Krasheninnikov, S. *Kyïv Shevchenkovykh chasiv* (New York-Paris-Sydney-Toronto 1984)
Tolochko, P. (ed). *Drevnerusskii gorod (Materialy Vsesoiuznoi arkheologicheskoi konferentsii, posviashchennoi 1500-letiiu goroda Kieva)* (Kiev 1984)
Veremeeva, I. et al. *Museums of Kiev: A Guide* (Moscow 1984)
Etnohrafiia Kyieva i Kyïvshchyny: Tradytsiï i suchasnist' (Kiev 1986)
Hamm, M.F. 'Continuity and Change in Late Imperial Kiev,' in *The City in Late Imperial Russia*, ed M.F. Hamm (Bloomington 1986)
Kiev: Architectural Landmarks and Art Museums: An Illustrated Guide (Leningrad 1987)

V. Kubijovyč, V. Pavlovsky, A. Zhukovsky

Kiev Academy. See Kievan Mohyla Academy.

Kiev Archeographic Commission (Vremennaia komissiia dlia razbora drevnikh aktov). A government institution affiliated with the governor-general's office in Kiev. It was established in 1843 at the initiative of M. *Maksymovych and existed until 1917. The task of the commission was to collect, research, and publish documents found in government archives, monasteries, and private collections in Ukraine and elsewhere. It concentrated on materials pertaining to the history of Right-Bank Ukraine (the Kiev region, Volhynia, and Podilia). The government's intention was to demonstrate that this territory had been Russian since ancient times and to justify the policy of *Russification implemented there after the Polish uprising of 1830–1. But Ukrainian cultural figures such as M. Maksymovych, M. Ivanyshev, P. Kulish, T. Shevchenko, M. Sudiienko, and N. Rigelman, who were associated with the commission, made important contributions to Ukrainian studies, especially regarding historical and archeological research. Eventually, some outstanding scholars became associated with it, among them V. Antonovych, M. Vladimirsky-Budanov, S. Golubev, M. Hrushevsky, M. Dovnar-Zapolsky, I. Kamanin, V. Kordt, O. Levytsky, N. Molchanovsky, A. and M. Storozhenko, S. Ternovsky, and V. Shcherbyna. The commission published collections of documents in Ukrainian history, archeology, paleography, and cartography, including *Drevnosti Iugo-Zapadnogo Kraia* (Antiquities of the Southwestern Krai, 3 fascicles, 1846), *Pamiatniki izdannye Kievskoi komissiei dlia razbora drevnikh aktov* (Memoirs Published by the Kiev Commission for the Study of Ancient Documents, 4 vols, 1845, 1846, 1852, 1859), *Arkhiv Iugo-Zapadnoi Rossii* (Archives of Southwestern Russia, 45 vols in 8 series, 1859–1914), S. Velychko's (4 vols, 1848, 1851, 1855, 1864) and H. Hrabianka's (1853) chronicles, *Materialy po istorii russkoi kartografii* (Materials on the History of Russian Cartography, 2 vols, 1899, 1910), *Paleograficheskii izbornik* (A Paleographic Collection, 1899), *Sbornik materialov dlia istoricheskoi topografii g. Kieva* (A Collection of Materials for the Historical Topography of the City of Kiev, 1874), and *Sbornik materialov po istorii Iugo-Zapadnoi Rossii* (A Collection of Materials on the History of Southwestern Russia, 2 vols, 1914, 1916). In 1921 the commission was merged with the Archeographic Commission of the Ukrainian Academy of Sciences. See also *Archeographic commissions and *Archeography.

A. Zhukovsky

Kiev Archeological Institute (Kyivskyi arkheolohichnyi instytut). An institution of higher learning founded in 1918 by a group of Kiev University professors headed by M. Dovnar-Zapolsky. At first the institute had two departments – archeology-history and archeography – and was one of the few institutions in Ukraine offering instruction in these disciplines. Reorganized several times beginning in 1920, in 1922 it was officially subordinated to the Ukrainian Academy of Sciences and F. Schmidt was appointed director. Other prominent scholars associated with the institute included S. Maslov, D. Shcherbakivsky, H. Pavlutsky, and N. Polonska-Vasylenko. The institute was abolished in 1925.

Kiev Army Group (Kyivska hrupa, aka Tsentralna armiiska hrupa). Formed in August 1919 under the command of Brig Gen A. Kravs, it consisted of the First and Third Corps of the Ukrainian Galician Army, the Zaporozhian Corps of the UNR Army, the insurgent units of otamans Sokolovsky and Mordalevych, and three artillery regiments. It was one of the three groups that were assigned the task of capturing Kiev. This task was accomplished on 30 August 1919.

Kiev Art School (Kyivske khudozhnie uchylyshche). A secondary art school that operated in Kiev from 1900 to 1920. During its first year it offered temporary classes in painting, drawing, and sketching. In 1901 the classes were reorganized into a regular program and the school was placed under the control of the St Petersburg Academy of Arts. It attracted students from the *Kiev Drawing School, reaching an enrollment of over 500 by 1902. It had a department of painting and of architecture. The school was organized by V. Menk, V. Nikolaev (director to 1911), V. Orlovsky, M. Pymonenko, Kh. Platonov, and I. Seleznov. Its faculty included F. Balavensky, M. Boichuk, H. Diadchenko, M. Kozyk, F. Krasytsky, F. Krychevsky, and O. Murashko. Among its graduates were A. Archipenko, I. Kavaleridze, L. Lozovsky, I. Padalka, A. Petrytsky, and V. Sedliar.

Kiev Artistic Film Studio (Kyivska kinostudiia khudozhnikh filmiv im. O. Dovzhenka). The chief motion-picture studio in Ukraine, established in 1928 as the Kiev Film Factory of the All-Ukrainian Photo-Cinema Administration (VUFKU). In 1930 it was renamed Ukrainfilm and in 1939 the Kiev Film Studio. The studio has a special department for television films, a museum (est 1957) for preserving the legacy of O. *Dovzhenko and other filmmakers, a permanent museum exhibition opened in 1962, and a film acting theater (est 1978). It conducts scientific research to improve the technology of filming and production. The studio is best known for its silent films, including D. Vertov's *Liudyna z kinoaparatom* (Man with a Movie Camera, 1929), a masterpiece of documentary filmmaking; and O. Dovzhenko's *Zemlia* (The Earth, 1930), the first film of the poetic cinema genre. The first sound films made at the studio were D. Vertov's *Symfoniia Donbasu* (Symphony of the Donbas, 1930) and O. Dovzhenko's *Ivan* (1932). The first Ukrainian color film was shot there – M. Ekk's *Sorochyns'kyi iarmarok* (The Sorochyntsi Fair, 1939). Many distinguished Ukrainian film directors worked at the studio: O. Dovzhenko, D. Vertov, I. Kavaleridze, I. Savchenko, H. Chukhrai, Yu. Illienko, and L. Osyka. Well-known cameramen such as D. Demutsky, M. Kauffman, Yu. Yekelchik, and Yu. Illienko were associated with the studio. Stage and film actors such as A. Buchma, S. Bondarchuk, Yu. Shumsky, I. Zamychkovsky, M. Nademsky, D. Kapka, I. Mykolaichuk, O. Hai, S. Shahaida, S. Shkurat, and N. Uzhvii starred in its productions. A number of films produced by the studio won international film awards: S. Paradzhanov's *Tini zabutykh predkiv* (Shadows of Forgotten Ancestors) at Mar del Plata, Argentina, and Rome in 1965, and Yu. Illienko's *Bilyi ptakh z chornoiu oznakoiu* (White Bird with a Black Mark) at Moscow in 1971. In 1958 O. Dovzhenko's *Zemlia* was named one of the 12 best films of all times by a panel of international film critics at the World Fair in Brussels. A large part of the studio's production consists of Russian and so-called counterpropaganda films. Seldom do its latest Ukrainian releases approach in quality Yu. Illienko's *Lehenda pro kniahyniu Ol'hu* (The Legend about Princess Olha, 1983).

V. Revutsky

Kiev Astronomical Observatory (Kyivska astronomichna observatoriia). A research institution of Kiev University founded in 1845. It consists of two separate facilities: one at Lisnyky and the other at Pylypovychi in Kiev oblast. The observatory is equipped with advanced astronomical instruments, including a meridian circle, astrograph, horizontal solar telescope, photospheric-chromospheric telescope, and meteor cameras. Besides mapping celestial bodies and tracking artificial earth satellites, the observatory conducts research on solar activity and solar forecasting. Noted astronomers such as V. Fedorov, R. Fogel, A. Shydlovsky, M. Khandrykov, S. Vsekhsviatsky, and O. Bohorodsky have worked there.

Kiev Automobile and Roads Institute (Kyivskyi avtomobilno-dorozhnyi instytut). A technical institution of higher education under the jurisdiction of the Ministry of Higher and Specialized Secondary Education of the Ukrainian SSR. Formed in 1944, it consists of the following departments: road building, automobile technology, mechanical engineering, engineering and economics, general technology, and qualifications upgrading. It has a graduate program. In 1980 its enrollment was 5,000.

Kiev Aviation Manufacturing Association (Kyivske aviatsiine vyrobnyche ob'iednannia im. 50-richchia zhovtnia). An airplane construction plant established in 1920 as the Rembovitria-6 plant; it assumed its present name in 1974. Originally the plant concentrated on repair work and the production of spare parts. Plane and glider construction began in 1923 under the direction of K. Kalinin. The first Soviet-designed plane, the K-1, was built here in 1925, as well as the first helicopter (1946) and the first airplane designed by O. Antonov, the AN-2 (1948). The conglomerate is one of the largest such plants in Ukraine, specializing in the construction of AN-24, AN-26, and AN-30 airplanes, many of which are exported abroad.

Kiev Branch of the Central V.I. Lenin Museum (Kyivskyi filial Tsentralnoho muzeiu V.I. Lenina). A museum dedicated to V. Lenin, established in 1938 by the Central Committee of the CPU. Until 1982 it was located in the former Pedagogical Museum, which also served as the *Central Rada's headquarters in 1917–18. Of the museum's total holdings of over 40,000 exponents, 8,000 items are on permanent display. These include works by and about Lenin, copies of his letters and telegrams, various documents on the activities of Ukrainian Bolsheviks and the CPU, and other memorabilia.

Kiev Brotherhood. See Kiev Epiphany Brotherhood.

Kiev Central Archive of Old Documents (Kyivskyi Tsentralnyi arkhiv davnikh aktiv). An archive founded in 1852 as the Central Archive of Old Record Books at Kiev University by the Temporary Commission for the Analysis of Old Documents (later the *Kiev Archeographic Commission) to collect and preserve 15th- to 18th-century documents and archives from Right-Bank Ukraine. By 1890 the archive contained 5,883 court record books and some 500,000 other documents. The material in the archive was used by the commission in the compilation and publication of **Arkhiv Iugo-zapadnoi Rossii* and its other publications. From 1921 to 1923 it was under the jurisdiction of the VUAN and after that, the state archival system. In the interwar years the archive assumed its present name and was enriched with other valuable documents and several family archives. During the Second World War, many of the documents were destroyed and part of the archive was taken by the Germans to the West. Most of the evacuated materials were recovered and returned to Kiev, where they are now housed in the *Central State Historical Archive of the Ukrainian SSR in Kiev.

BIBLIOGRAPHY

Romanovs'kyi, V. (ed). *Tsentral'nyi arkhiv starodavnikh aktiv u Kyievi. Zbirnyk stattiv* (Kiev, 1929)

Kiev Choreography School (Kyivske khoreohrafichne uchylyshche). Specialized secondary school under the Ministry of Culture of the Ukrainian SSR formed in 1938 out of the Ballet Studio of the Kiev Theater of Opera and Ballet (est 1934) and the Kiev Choreography Tekhnikum (est 1933). Since 1972 it has had two departments: classical ballet and folk dance. The school offers an eight-year program. Most of its principals – L. Zhukov (1938–41), A. Berezova (1945–66), and A. Vasylieva (1966–72) – were graduates of the Leningrad Choreography School, and passed on to their students the Russian tradition of classical ballet. The faculty included such teachers as P. Virsky, O. Potapova, B. Tairov, and A. Yarygina. Among its graduates are such well-known dancers as R. Khylko,

A. Havrylenko, L. Herasymchuk, V. Kalynovska, V. Kovtun, S. Kolyvanova, V. Kotliar, O. Kovalov, and A. Lahoda.

Kiev Chronicle (Kyivs'kyi litopys). One of the *chronicles, an important historical and literary monument of Kievan Rus'. Together with Nestor's **Povist' vremennykh lit* (Tale of Bygone Years) and the *Galician-Volhynian Chronicle it composes the *Hypatian Chronicle. The Kiev Chronicle covers the period from 1118 to 1200. It was compiled in the Vydubychi Monastery in Kiev using princely, monastery, and family chronicles and stories and accounts by various authors collected in Kiev, Chernihiv, Pereiaslav, Galicia, and Volhynia. Some sections were copied from the lost Chernihiv Chronicle and lost parts of the Galician Chronicle. Later, sections of the Kiev Chronicle were included in the Novgorod Chronicles.

The Kiev Chronicle is not a homogenous work, although there is a certain stylistic unity. In addition to short chronological entries, it contains accounts of the fate of Prince Iziaslav Mstyslavych, the killing of Prince Ihor Olhovych (1147), the death of Prince Rostyslav Mstyslavych (1168), the killing of Prince Andrei Bogoliubskii (1175), and the campaign of Prince Ihor Sviatoslavych (1185). The chronicle ends with a eulogy to Prince Riuryk Rostyslavych by Moses, the hegumen of Vydubychi Monastery. The entries for 1188 and 1190 are devoted to the crusades led by Frederick I Barbarossa. An account of the death of the Pereiaslav prince Volodymyr Hlibovych (ca 1187) contains the first use of the word *Ukraïna* (Ukraine) to refer to the southern territories of Rus'.

Stylistically, the Kiev Chronicle resembles the embellished style of the **Slovo o polku Ihorevi*. One of the outstanding features of the chronicle is the frequent use of dialogue to recount events. The tone of the chronicle is secular, although most of its authors were clerics. Military themes are very common, especially in the descriptions of the internecine struggles between the princes of Rus' for control over Kiev. Chivalry, glory, and honor are seen to influence the princes' conduct as much as material interests, and they are often protrayed as 'Christian knights' who appeal for God's help in the conviction that victory will come to those who fight for a just cause. At the same time, they exhibit a certain Rus' patriotism, even when this is combined with more narrow and local political goals.

The Kiev Chronicle was studied by M. Hrushevsky, M. Priselkov, D. Likhachev, B. Rybakov, A. Shakhmatov, and D. Chyzhevsky. Its relationship to Ukrainian historiography was examined by D. Bahalii and P. Klepatsky. It was published several times as part of the Hypatian Chronicle and a Ukrainian translation appeared in the journal *Kyïv*, 1984, nos 6–8. An English translation by L. Heinrich was published in 1978.

The so-called Short Kiev Chronicle is a 16th-century chronicle compiled mainly from Novgorod sources. It describes events in late 15th-century Ukraine and includes a panegyric to Prince K. Ostrozsky on the occasion of his victory over a Muscovite army in Orsha in 1515.

D. Chyzhevsky, A. Zhukovsky

Kiev Circus. The first wooden circus buildings were erected in Kiev in the 1860s. In the early 1870s a brick amphitheater was built for the circus. The horse trainer P. Krutikov built an amphitheater with 200 seats in 1890 and the Hippo Palace with 2,000 seats in 1903. Because of its excellent acoustics, this palace, the first two-story circus in Europe, served also as a concert and opera hall. It was destroyed during the Second World War. In the 1950s, circus performances were staged only in the summer. In 1960 a new building with 2,000 seats, one of the largest in the Soviet Union, was designed for the Kiev Circus by V. Zhukov. It contains not only an amphitheater but also a circus museum.

Kiev Civil-Engineering Institute (Kyivskyi inzhenerno-budivelnyi instytut). A technical institution of higher education under the Ministry of Higher and Specialized Secondary Education of the Ukrainian SSR. Formed in 1930 out of two departments of the Kiev Polytechnical Institute and the architecture department of the Kiev State Art Institute, it consists of departments such as civil engineering, architecture, construction, automatization and mechanization, urban planning, building technology, and sanitary engineering. It has a special preparatory department for foreign students, a graduate program, and a professional development program for teachers of specialized secondary and higher schools. In 1980 its enrollment was over 10,000.

Kiev Club of Russian Nationalists (Russian: Klub russkikh natsionalistov). A political and cultural organization established in 1908 to promote Russian national consciousness in the western borderlands and to defend Russian interests against 'Polish pressure and Ukrainophilism.' Headed by such noted Ukrainophobes as A. Savenko, Professor T. *Florinsky, V. Shulgin, I. Rakovich, and D. Pikhno, the publisher of the Russian nationalist daily **Kievlianin* and a member of the State Council, the club became one of the most powerful pressure groups in the Russian Empire owing to the unusually energetic political activity of its leadership and the social prominence of its members.

At its height, it numbered some 700 members, largely drawn from the Russian and Russified elite of Kiev. The club also cultivated a wide range of contacts with other conservative organizations and leaders throughout the empire, such as M. Menshikov, the influential columnist for the St Petersburg *Novoe vremia* and founder of the All-Russian National Union; Count A. Bobrinsky, president of the Congress of United Nobility; and Count V. Bobrinsky, head of the St Petersburg–based Galician-Russian Society.

From its inception, the Kiev Club of Russian Nationalists devoted considerable attention to Duma and local politics and was regarded as a relatively moderate element within the spectrum of Russian nationalist organizations because of its willingness to work within the new constitutional framework. The Nationalist party, founded in 1909 and a leading force in the Third and Fourth Dumas, was dominated by club members and their concerns. In 1909–12 the club lobbied to increase the political and economic positions of Russians in Right-Bank Ukraine and Belorussia and actively campaigned to restrict, by law, Jewish participation in trade and local politics.

The Kiev Club stood at the forefront of the struggle against the Ukrainian national movement before 1917. One of its first actions was a motion condemning the

1908 Duma bill to introduce Ukrainian as a language of instruction in elementary schools. Club leaders like Savenko and Florinsky always drew a sharp distinction, however, between the 'Mazepists,' ie, the Ukrainian intelligentsia, and the Ukrainian masses, considering the latter to be essentially loyal constituents of the all-Russian nation. Through its publications and lecture program, as well as newspaper articles in *Kievlianin* and *Novoe vremia*, the club attempted to raise public awareness concerning the dangers of the Ukrainian movement, which it viewed as a Polish-Austrian-German-Jewish intrigue. Kiev Club members also worked behind the scenes, with some success, to pressure the administration to close down Ukrainian organizations (the Kiev Ukrainian Club, 1912) and periodicals (*Rada*, 1914), and to prevent any public commemoration of the 50th anniversary of T. Shevchenko's death (1911) or the 100th anniversary of the poet's birth (1914). The government decision to shut down all Ukrainian institutions in January 1915 was the culmination of this campaign.

From 1909 to 1914 the club published five volumes of *Sbornik kluba russkikh natsionalistov* (Collection of the Club of Russian Nationalists). During the First World War, it gradually lapsed into inactivity, though formally the club continued to exist until 1917.

BIBLIOGRAPHY

Storozhenko, A. *Proiskhozhdenie i sushchnost' Ukrainofil'stva* (Kiev 1912)
Chykalenko, Ie. *Shchodennyk, 1907–1917* (Lviv 1931)
Edelman, R. *Gentry Politics on the Eve of the Russian Revolution: The Nationalist Party, 1907–1977* (New Brunswick, NJ 1980)

O. Andriewsky

Kiev Commercial Institute (Kyivskyi komertsiinyi instytut). A higher school of commerce and economics in Kiev founded in 1906 by M. Dovnar-Zapolsky as the Higher Commercial Courses and converted into an institute in 1908. Its charter was approved by the government in 1912. The institute consisted of two departments – commerce and technology, and economics – and a number of subdepartments such as railroads, insurance, banking, and pedagogy. It had laboratories, a museum, and library. Its director was M. Dovnar-Zapolsky, and many of its faculty were professors of Kiev University or Kiev Polytechnical Institute. It published its own scientific proceedings. In 1914 the enrollment was 4,000. Each year about 30 students were sent abroad for practical research. In 1920 the institute was reorganized into the Kiev Institute of the National Economy.

Kiev Commune. A group of Kievan populists (see *Populism) that existed from September 1873 until the end of 1874 when it had to stop its activity as a result of mass arrests. Ideologically, it was mainly influenced by M. Bakunin. The commune recruited its members (they numbered approx 30) from among the intelligentsia and the students of Kiev University; they included V. Debohorii-Mokriievych and Ya. Stefanovych. The members propagated populist and socialist ideas among the workers and peasants of the Kiev, Poltava, and Podilia regions, and the group maintained ties with populist circles in Kharkiv, Odessa, St Petersburg, and elsewhere.

Kiev Conservatory (Kyivska konservatoriia im. P. Chaikovskoho). A higher music school under the Ministry of Culture of the Ukrainian SSR. It was formed in 1913 out of the Kiev School of Music, which had existed from 1868 under the Kiev Branch of the Russian Music Society. The first principals were V. Pukhalsky (1913) and R. Glière (1914–20). In 1925 the conservatory was turned into a music tekhnikum, and it was restored in 1934. Today it is the largest music school and research center in Ukraine. It has six faculties: piano, vocal music, orchestra, conducting, composition, and history and theory, and an enrollment of 900 students (1980). Such distinguished Ukrainian musicologists and composers as L. Revutsky, B. Liatoshynsky, A. Shtoharenko, I. Patorzhynsky, and K. Dankevych have served on its faculty. Many of its graduates have distinguished themselves as musicians and composers; eg, H. and P. Maiboroda, D. Hnatiuk, Ye. Miroshnychenko, M. Kondratiuk, A. Filipenko, O. Bilash, and V. Kyreiko.

Kiev Conservatory

Kiev Construction- and Road-Machine-Building Plant. See Chervonyi Ekskavator.

Kiev Contract Fair in Podil (second building, 1817)

Kiev Contract Fair (Kyivskyi kontraktovyi yarmarok). An annual *contract fair held in Kiev from 1798 to 1927. It was transferred from Dubno in 1797 by Tsar Paul I to enliven the economic life of Kiev. The fair was first combined with the existing Vodokhreshchenskyi (Blessing of Water) Fair held during the Feast of the Epiphany (from 15 January to 1 February). From the middle of the 19th century, when the fair was held from 5 to 25 February, during the Feast of Christ's presentation at the Temple, it was also called the Stritenskyi (Candlemas) Fair. After a fire in 1811 destroyed the first hall built for the fair in 1801, in 1817 it moved to a two-story building designed by V. Heste and located in the center of Podil, the main trade sector in Kiev. The fair was an important commercial institution attended by merchants from throughout the Russian Empire and abroad and by burghers and estate owners, especially from Right-Bank Ukraine. The main objects of trade were wheat, manufactured goods, and, from 1840, sugar. In 1862 sales totaled 915,000 rubles. In addition, various financial matters were settled: loans and credit were secured, agreements for the future delivery of goods were concluded, and land was sold or leased. The importance of the fair fluctuated because of competition from fairs in Kharkiv and elsewhere; at the end of the 19th century 5–6 million rubles' worth of goods were traded at the Kiev fair. By that time it had lost most of its importance as a contract fair and had become a regular wholesale *fair. Under Soviet rule the significance of the fair continued to decline steadily until it was finally closed in 1927.

B. Krawchenko

Kiev Cossacks (Kyivska kozachchyna). Term given to a peasant revolt that began in Vasylkiv county in February 1855 and spread throughout the Kiev and Chernihiv regions. It lasted until the summer of 1855 and affected more than 500 villages. It began when Tsar Nicholas I issued a manifesto appealing to the population to join the army to fight in the *Crimean War. Many peasants did not understand the vague wording of the manifesto, and rumors began to circulate that the tsar wished them to organize Cossack regiments and that he would restore to them the privileges of the Cossack estate. The peasants refused to do corvée and to follow the orders of local authorities; some village *hromady* even seized control of the estates. In several areas the peasants beat the local priests, whom they accused of hiding the true manifesto granting their freedom. The revolt was eventually brutally suppressed by the army, and many of the leaders were beaten or deported to Siberia. According to official data, 39 people died, but the death toll was probably much higher. Although the Kiev Cossack movement was primarily a reaction against the inhuman conditions of serfdom, it nevertheless revealed the strength of Cossack traditions and consciousness among the Ukrainian peasantry in the 19th century.

BIBLIOGRAPHY
Tomashivs'kyi, S. *Kyïvs'ka kozachchyna 1855 r.* (Lviv 1902)
Shamrai, S. *Kyïvs'ka kozachchyna 1855 roku (Do istoriï selians'kykh rukhiv na Kyïvshchyni)* (Kiev 1928)
Hurzhii, I. *Borot'ba selian i robitnykiv Ukraïny proty feodal'no-kriposnyts'koho hnitu (z 80-kh rokiv XVIII st. do 1861 r.)* (Kiev 1958)

A. Zhukovsky

Kiev Division (Kyivska dyviziia). Formed in the summer of 1919 under the command of Otaman Yu. Tiutiunnyk, it was eventually designated as the Fourth Kiev Rifle Division of the UNR Army. It participated in the First Winter Campaign of 1919–20 and fought Bolshevik forces until the end of 1920.

Kiev Drawing School (Kyivska rysuvalna shkola). An art school that for one generation (1875–1901) played an important role in the development of art in Russian-ruled Ukraine. Founded and directed by M. *Murashko, it was first a private and then a city school. Most of its financial support came from I. *Tereshchenko. Its faculty included M. Murashko, M. Pymonenko, Kh. Platonov, and I. Seleznov. Its more distinguished students were S. Kostenko, O. Murashko, I. Izhakevych, H. Diadchenko, H. Svitlytsky, M. Zhuk, and F. Krasytsky. The school received support from non-Ukrainian artists such as N. Ge, I. Repin, M. Vrubel, and J. Stanisławski. Its teachers and pupils took part in the restoration of the frescoes of the Church of St Cyril's Monastery and in the painting of St Volodymyr's Cathedral in Kiev. Exhibitions of Ukrainian and Russian artists were held at the school.

Kiev Druzhba Theater (Kyivskyi teatr Druzhba). Founded in October 1979 by the Ukrainian Theatrical Society to present in Kiev the better plays of the USSR satellite countries and to promote Ukrainian plays outside Soviet Ukraine. So far, however, most of its imports have been productions by Russian (music and drama) theaters from Moscow and Leningrad. Guest performances have been given also by the Georgian Rustaveli Theater, the Estonian Vanemuine Theater, the Lithuanian Panevėžys Theater, and the Latvian Rainis Theater. No tours of the Druzhba Theater have been mentioned in the press. The director of the theater is M. Ravytsky.

Kiev eparchy. An eparchy of the Ukrainian church created after the Christianization of Ukraine in 988. Its bishop was also the Kievan metropolitan (see *Kiev metropoly) and head of the entire Ukrainian church province. The eparchy was one of the largest in Kievan Rus', its territory corresponding to the territory of *Kiev principality, centered primarily on the Right Bank. With the partition of Ukraine between Muscovy and Poland in the mid-17th century, most of the territory of the eparchy remained under Polish control, although the see was in the Russian-dominated Hetmanate. In the early 18th century the Kiev metropoly was abolished and the eparchy was placed directly under the Russian Holy Synod until 1743, when the metropoly was restored. After the incorporation of Right-Bank Ukraine into the Russian Empire, the eparchy's territory corresponded to the territory of *Kiev gubernia, created in 1797. Vicariates of the eparchy were established in Chyhyryn (1799), Uman (1874), and Kaniv (1884). From 1861 the eparchy published the journal *Kievskie eparkhial'nye vedomosti*, which contained much information on the history of the church and the Kiev region in general.

As the central eparchy in Ukraine and the metropolitan's see, Kiev eparchy contained many of the most important church institutions in Ukraine. Its 21 men's and 6 women's monasteries (1914) included the Kievan Cave, St Nicholas's, St Michael's Golden-Domed, Kiev Epiphany Brotherhood, St Flor's, Vydubychi, and Mezhyhiria Transfiguration monasteries. The Kievan Mohyla Academy (later the Kiev Theological Academy) and the Kiev Theological Seminary were also located there, and in 1913 there were six other higher schools administered by the eparchy. The eparchy's 1,710 churches (in 1913) were served by 1,435 priests.

In the 1920s there was a Kiev 'regional church' or eparchy of the *Ukrainian Autocephalous Orthodox church under Metropolitan V. Lypkivsky; it was liquidated along with the entire church in the 1930s. Since 1944 the eparchy has been under the Russian Orthodox church, and since 1966 the bishop has been F. Denysenko.

B. Balan

Kiev Epiphany Brotherhood (Kyivske Bohoiavlenske bratstvo). A church *brotherhood established ca 1615 at the *Kiev Epiphany Brotherhood Monastery in the Podil district by wealthy burghers, nobles, clerics, and Cossacks to defend the Orthodox faith from the onslaught of Polish rule and Catholicism. Hetman P. Sahaidachny gave it a great deal of support and joined it 'with the entire Zaporozhian Host' in 1620. That same year the Orthodox Kiev metropoly was restored and the brotherhood acquired stauropegion status and the right to establish a 'brotherhood for young men' from the visiting patriarch of Jerusalem, Theophanes. The Polish king Sigismund III granted the brotherhood a royal charter in 1629. The brotherhood became a cultural and educational center in Kiev. Many of Ukraine's leading figures were affiliated with it. To promote education, it founded the *Kiev Epiphany Brotherhood School in 1615. Granted a charter by Theophanes in 1620 to teach 'Helleno-Slavonic and Latin-Polish letters,' in 1631 the school was merged with the Kievan Cave Monastery School to form a college, which later became the *Kievan Mohyla Academy. Clerical involvement in the brotherhood forced its lay members – the burghers – into a secondary role. The brotherhood's 'elder brother,' Metropolitan P. *Mohyla, subordinated the brotherhood to the clergy in 1633, and the Epiphany Monastery gradually took over its functions.

Kiev Epiphany Brotherhood Monastery in the 1880s; the church and belfry were demolished by the Soviet authorities in 1935

Kiev Epiphany Brotherhood Monastery (Kyievo-Bratskyi or Bohoiavlenskyi manastyr). An Orthodox monastery established in 1616 in Kiev's Podil district after the noblewoman Ye. (H.) *Hulevychivna donated a lot and orchard for this purpose (15 October 1615). The *Kiev Epiphany Brotherhood, which was affiliated with the monastery, had built the original *Kiev Epiphany Brotherhood School on an adjacent lot in 1615. The Epiphany Church of the monastery was built in 1693. The monastery owned extensive property donated to it by Kievan metropolitans (P. Mohyla and R. Zaborovsky) and by Cossack hetmans (B. Khmelnytsky and I. Mazepa). The rector of the brotherhood school (later the *Kievan Mohyla Academy) was also the hegumen (from 1731, archimandrite) of the monastery; T. Prokopovych was its most famous hegumen. The monastery declined after its property was secularized in 1786. Its buildings on Alexander Square were destroyed several times during wars and by fire (1651, 1655, 1811). Hetman P. Sahaidachny and V. Hryhorovych-Barsky were buried at the monastery.

Kiev Epiphany Brotherhood School (Kyivska bratska shkola). One of the most important Orthodox *brotherhood schools in Ukraine. It was founded in 1615–16 by the *Kiev Epiphany Brotherhood, shortly after the brotherhood itself was organized. Modeled on the *Lviv Dormition Brotherhood School, its purpose was to diminish the enrollment of Orthodox children in Catholic schools. The school was open to boys from all estates. Its liberal arts program emphasized Church Slavonic and Greek. Its instructors came from Western Ukraine; they were graduates of the Ostrih Academy, the Lviv Dormition Brotherhood School, and various Polish and German institutions of higher learning. The school's rectors were prominent Orthodox churchmen and scholars: Y. Boretsky (1615–18), M. Smotrytsky (1618–20), K. Sakovych (1620–4), and T. Yevlevych (1628–32). Among its graduates were a number of prominent scholars and cultural figures of the 17th century. The school greatly benefited from Hetman P. Sahaidachny's protection and the financial support of the Epiphany Brotherhood. Patriarch Theophanes of Jerusalem, who visited Kiev in 1620, granted stauropegion to the Epiphany Brotherhood and praised its educational work. In 1632 the school was merged with the Kievan Cave Monastery School, which had been founded shortly before then by Archimandrite P. Mohyla, to form the Kievan Mohyla College (later the *Kievan Mohyla Academy).

BIBLIOGRAPHY

Kharlampovich, K. *Zapadnorusskie pravoslavnyie shkoly XVI i nachala XVII veka* (Kazan 1898)

Isaievych, Ia. *Bratstva ta ïkh rol' v rozvytku ukraïns'koï kul'tury XVI–XVII st.* (Kiev 1966)

N. Pylypiuk

Kiev Graphic Arts and Printing School (Kyivska shkola hrafiky i drukarskoi spravy). A vocational art school founded in 1903 and directed by V. Kulzhenko, a graduate of the Leipzig Polygraphic Academy. Artists such as F. Krasytsky, O. Sudomora, and H. Zolotov served on its faculty. Fine art publications were printed in the school's workshop. It closed in 1918.

Kiev gubernia. An administrative-territorial unit in Russian-ruled Ukraine. From 1708, it existed alongside the regimental system of the Hetmanate in Left-Bank Ukraine and in the non-Ukrainian territories of the Kursk, Briansk, and Orel regions. From 1719 the gubernia consisted of Kiev, Belgorod, Sevsk, and Orel provinces. The governor-general resided in Kiev. The Russian palatines and garrisons in Kiev, Pereiaslav, Nizhen, and Chernihiv were under his authority, but the administrative bodies of the Hetmanate were not. In 1781 the gubernia was replaced by Kiev vicegerency, which was abolished in

1796 after the second partition of Poland (1793) and replaced by a new gubernia, this time in Right-Bank Ukraine, on the territory of the former counties of Kiev vicegerency and one county of Volhynia vicegerency. From 1800 the gubernia's territory (50,957 sq km) was divided among 12 counties: Kiev, Vasylkiv, Zvenyhorodka, Radomyshl, Skvyra, Kaniv, Lypovets, Berdychiv, Cherkasy, Chyhyryn, Tarashcha, and Uman. Under Soviet rule, in 1925 the gubernia was abolished and replaced by Bila Tserkva, Berdychiv, Cherkasy, Kiev, and Uman okruhas.

The gubernias's population grew from 1,066,200 in 1811 to 1,459,800 in 1838, 1,635,800 in 1851, 2,012,100 in 1863, 2,847,600 in 1885, 3,559,200 in 1897, and 4,792,600 in 1914. It declined during the First World War and the revolutionary period. It was 4,258,800 in 1920 and 4,635,700 in 1924. In 1914 the population consisted of Ukrainians (78 percent), Jews (12 percent), Russians (7 percent), Poles (2 percent), and Germans (0.4 percent). The gubernia had the second-largest percentage of urban dwellers among the Ukrainian gubernias in 1914 – 18 percent, which rose to 25.4 percent in 1924. Ukrainians composed 51 percent of the urban population in 1923; Jews, 28.5 percent; and Russians, 16.5 percent. A large part of the urban population (48.3 percent in 1897) was born outside the gubernia.

The gubernia was primarily an agricultural region. In 1905 peasants (78 percent of the population) owned only 45.6 percent of the land; 45 percent was still owned by the gentry. Land hunger and poverty forced the peasants to seek seasonal work in Southern Ukraine and in the mines of the Donbas (200,000 annually) or to resettle in Siberia and the Far East (over 148,000 peasants resettled there in 1896–1912). Industry, with the exception of beet-sugar processing (in which the gubernia placed first in the empire), distilling, and flour milling, was poorly developed. There were only 75,700 industrial workers in the gubernia in 1912.

R. Senkus, A. Zhukovsky

Kiev Hills (Kyivski hory). Forming the eastern edge of the Dnieper Upland, the Kiev Hills near Kiev reach an elevation of 200 m and descend steeply to the Dnieper River (at 100 m). They are built of Tertiary and Quaternary strata (marls, clays, and sands) that are overlain with loess and dissected by rivers and ravines.

Kiev Historical Museum. See Historical Museum of the Ukrainian SSR.

Kiev hoards (Kyivski skarby). Treasures from the time of Kievan Rus' found in Kiev at various times since the 19th century. Over 50 hoards have been discovered, 48 of which were concealed during the Mongol siege of Kiev in 1240. The largest hoard was found in 1842 near the Church of the Tithes. Most of the hoards were found within the medieval inner city (*dytynets*), where the prince and boyars lived. The hoards consisted of Arab dirhems, silver **hryvnia*, and gold and silver bracelets, rings, necklaces, collars, earrings, and diadems. Some contained hundreds and even thousands of such articles. Most of these artifacts are preserved at the Museum of Historical Treasures in Kiev.

Kiev Hromada. See Hromada of Kiev.

Kiev Hydroelectric Station (Kyivska hidroelektrostantsiia im. Leninskoho komsomolu). Part of the *Dnieper Cascade of Hydroelectric Stations, the station was constructed between 1960 and 1968 on the Dnieper River near the city of Vyshhorod. With 20 generators, the Kiev HES has a capacity of 361,200 kW and an average annual output of 767 million kWh. Besides the station building, the Kiev HES includes 75 km of dams, which hold back the waters of the Kiev Reservoir, and a one-chamber lock.

The Kiev HES has a history of worker resistance to the Soviet regime's economic and nationality policies. In 1968 former workers of the station – Nazarenko, Kondriukov, and Karpenko – were arrested by the KGB for distributing leaflets at Kiev University and the Kiev Agricultural Academy calling for resistance to forced Russification. In May 1969 a major strike, led by I. Hryshchuk, occurred at the station. In 1969 a petition to the CC CPSU signed by over 600 workers of the Kiev HES and residents of Vyshhorod demanded I. Hryshchuk's release and an end to management and government violations of workers' rights. One of the most famous Ukrainian dissidents, V. Chornovil, served as secretary of the Komsomol Committee of the Kiev HES and as a journalist at the construction site; he was active in the struggle for better working and living conditions. In the early 1960s the labor force at the site consisted of 70–75 percent Ukrainians, 20 percent Russians, and 2 percent Belorussians. Yet, almost all of the top jobs (construction chiefs and engineers, sectional and divisional managers, etc) were held by Russians. Almost all the 127 Russian managers at the main installation came from Russia. Only 11 of them were born in Ukraine.

L. Szuch

Kiev Institute for the Upgrading of Physicians (Kyivskyi instytut udoskonalennia likariv). An institution of higher learning under the jurisdiction of the Ministry of Health Protection of the USSR. It was established in 1918 as a clinical institute of the Kiev Medical Society and was reorganized in 1930. The institute has 4 faculties (therapeutics, surgery, hygiene, and pharmacology), 60 chairs, a graduate program, a central research laboratory, and a library with about 180,000 volumes. Tens of thousands of physicians and pharmacists have attended the institute. Prominent medical specialists who have taught there include M. Amosov, O. Avilova, F. Bohdanov, O. Kolomiichenko, O. Lazariev, A. Nikolaiev, H. Pysemsky, A. Shalimov, T. Syvachenko, L. Tymoshenko, A. Vasiutynsky, and V. Vasylenko. It publishes in Russian textbooks, monographs, and serial collections of articles on surgery and human morphology.

Kiev Institute of Civil Aviation Engineers (Kyivskyi instytut inzheneriv tsyvilnoi aviiatsii). A technical institution of higher education under the USSR Ministry of Civil Aviation. Formed in 1933 out of a department at the Kiev Polytechnical Institute, until 1947 it was known as the Kiev Aviation Institute, then as the Kiev Institute of the Civil Air Fleet, and since 1964 by its present name. It consists of 11 departments, including aviational radioelectronics, aviational equipment, automation and computing, mechanics, and airport technology. It has a graduate program, a correspondence school, a professional development program for specialists, and a preparatory department for foreign students. The institute has branches in Irkutsk, Tashkent, and Rostov-na-Donu. In 1980 its enrollment was over 13,000.

Kiev Institute of Culture (Kyivskyi instytut kultury im. O. Korniichuka). An institution of higher education under the Ministry of Culture of the Ukrainian SSR. Formed in 1968 out of the Kiev branch of the Kharkiv Institute of Culture, it has two departments: library science, and culture and education. Its enrollment in 1980 was 6,000. The institute has a branch in Mykolaiv, a correspondence school, and a graduate program.

Kiev Institute of People's Education (Kyivskyi instytut narodnoi osvity or KINO). A post-secondary educational institution formed in 1920 out of the historical-philological and physical-mathematical-scientific faculties of *Kiev University. It was also known as the Kiev Higher Institute of People's Education. Consisting at first of three faculties, the institute was reorganized in 1921–2 into two faculties: social education and professional education. The former had a three-year program emphasizing practical pedagogy to prepare teachers for the higher grades of the unified labor schools, preschool institutions, and the Communist children's movement. The latter had a more academic four-year program to prepare teachers for vocational schools and tekhnikums. In 1922, 691 students were enrolled in a preparatory course, 191 in the social education faculty, and 835 in the professional education faculty of the institute. As a result of the *Ukrainization campaign, the proportion of courses taught in Ukrainian rose from 20 percent in 1922 to 40 percent in 1926. In 1927, 62 percent of the institute's 1,035 students were Ukrainians, 27 percent Jews, and 9 percent Russians. In 1930 KINO was reorganized into three separate institutes: the social education faculty became the Kiev Institute of Social Education (later the Kiev Pedagogical Institute), and the professional educational faculty was split into the Kiev Institute of Professional Education and the Kiev Physical-Chemical-Mathematical Institute. The first two institutes continued to train teachers; the last trained researchers for scientific institutions. Three years later the Kiev Institute of Professional Education and the Kiev Physical-Chemical-Mathematical Institute were merged to form Kiev University.

B. Krawchenko

Kiev Institute of Physical Culture (Kyivskyi instytut fizychnoi kultury). An institute of higher education under the Committee of Physical Culture and Sport of the Council of Ministers of the Ukrainian SSR. It was founded in 1930 as a section of the Kharkiv Institute of People's Education and reopened after the war (1944) on the basis of the Kiev Tekhnikum of Physical Culture. Since its establishment the institute has been the main center for the preparation of the best athletes, instructors, and coaches in Ukraine. It has five faculties (of sport, pedagogy, a correspondence program, and two for upgrading qualifications), 22 chairs, and a school for trainers. It also offers a graduate program. Research on training methods for athletes, the influence of exercise on children, nutrition, and physiotherapy is conducted there. Many Ukrainian, World, Olympic, and European champions and record holders have trained at the institute. Among the more prominent are V. Borzov, Ye. Bulanchyk, V. Holubnychy, V. Krepkina, L. Lysenko, N. Otkalenko, Yu. Siedykh in track and field; P. Astakhova, N. Bocharova, L. Latynina, Yu. Tytov, B. Shakhlin in gymnastics; H. Hamarnyk and P. Pinihin in wrestling; and O. Sydorenko and S. Fesenko in swimming. M. Bunchuk, the institute's long time director, favored the independent participation of Ukraine in the Olympic Games.

O. Zinkevych

Kiev Institute of the National Economy (Kyivskyi instytut narodnoho hospodarstva im. D. Korotchenka or KINH). An institution of higher learning under the Ministry for Higher and Specialized Secondary Education of the Ukrainian SSR. Formed in 1920 out of the Kiev Commercial Institute (est 1908), it had four faculties: industry, law, economics, and communications, all with a three-year program. In 1925 its enrollment was 1,400 and its teaching staff numbered 125. Before the institute was Ukrainized in 1923, its language of instruction had been Russian. In 1930 the KINH was reorganized into a number of higher educational institutions. One of them, the Kiev Financial and Economic Institute, was transferred to Kharkiv in 1934 and merged with the Kharkiv Financial and Economic Institute. In 1944 it was returned to Kiev, and in 1960 renamed the KINH. Today the institute consists of six faculties, including the faculty of economic planning. It is the only higher educational institution in Ukraine to prepare specialists for Ukraine's state planning agencies. In 1965, 78 percent of the students were Ukrainian, and 90 percent of the graduates obtained positions in Ukraine. However, only 18 (5 percent) of the 335 faculty members lectured in Ukrainian. Its enrollment in 1978–9 was 11,600. It publishes a collection of scientific papers (in Russian), *Mashinnaia obrabotka informatsii*. Noted scientists such as K. *Vobly, M. *Ptukha, and D. *Grave have worked at the institute.

B. Krawchenko

Kiev Institute of Theater Arts (Kyivskyi instytut teatralnoho mystetstva im. I. Karpenka-Karoho). A higher-educational institution within the theater and film system of the Ministry of Culture of the Ukrainian SSR. It was formed in 1934 out of the drama faculty of the Lysenko Music and Drama Institute, which was abolished. In 1934–41 the institute had two acting departments: a Ukrainian and a Jewish one. It did not operate in 1941–4 and its functions were assumed in 1941–2 by the Music and Drama Conservatory under the direction of O. Lysenko. When the institute was reopened in 1945, the Jewish department was replaced by a Russian one. The institute had three faculties – acting, stage directing, and theater studies – and from 1961 two departments – Ukrainian and Russian cinema. In 1968 six faculties were set up: acting, stage directing, theater studies, film directing, cinema studies, and cinematography. Correspondence courses in cinema and theater studies were available. The regular program required five years, with another year for specialization. In 1979–80 the institute was organized into two faculties: theater arts, which includes stage and film acting, stage directing, and theater studies; and cinema arts, which includes film and television directing, film and television-camera work, and film studies. There is also a correspondence school, a graduate program, and an apprenticeship program. Practical training is provided by the institute's teaching film studio (est 1961) and teaching theater (est 1965). The institute has been directed by S. Tkachenko (1947–60), I. Chabanenko (1961–5), and V. Kudyn (since 1965).

V. Revutsky

Kiev Juridical Society (Kievskoe yuridicheskoe obshchestvo). Association of lecturers of the Kiev University Faculty of Law and of other law scholars, established in 1877. In 1880 a department of customary law was set up within the society. The society's publications consisted of the *Code of Laws of 1743, university textbooks, and monographs. Its presidents included V. Demchenko, O. Huliaiev, O. Kistiakovsky, K. Mytiukov, Z. Synaisky, and V. Udintsev. The society's members were liberal in orientation. Its activities ceased in 1916.

Kiev Literacy Society (Kyivske tovarystvo hramotnosti). Society established in 1882 to promote literacy in Kiev, Podilia, and Volhynia gubernias. The society had branches in Uman, Smila, and other provincial centers. It operated libraries and reading rooms at parish schools, organized evening and Sunday courses for adults, provided financial assistance to primary-school teachers and students, sponsored literary and musical evenings, provided textbooks for schools, and published popular literature, including the works of T. Shevchenko. In 1902 the society built the Trinity People's Building in Kiev. The head of the society was V. Naumenko and its members included I. Luchytsky, the composer M. Lysenko, and the socialist activist O. Shlikhter. In 1904 it was one of the first organizations to advocate publicly the repeal of the Ems Ukase prohibiting the use of Ukrainian in the Russian Empire. This brought it the enmity of conservative Russian circles in Kiev, and the society was finally closed in 1908 by the Kiev governor-general.

Kiev Literary-Artistic Society (Kyivske literaturnoartystychne tovarystvo). An organization of artists, musicians, and writers established in Kiev in 1895. It arranged literary evenings, concerts, art exhibits, and anniversary celebrations. Among its members were such prominent figures as Lesia Ukrainka, O. Pchilka, I. Nechui-Levytsky, M. Lysenko, M. Starytsky, M. Sadovsky, P. Saksahansky, M. Murashko, and M. Zankovetska. The society was dissolved by imperial decree in 1905.

Kiev Manufacturing Association of Polymer-Products Machine Building (Kyivske vyrobnyche obiednannia polimernoho mashynobuduvannia or Kyivpolimermash). An industrial association created in 1975 from the merger of the Bilshovyk Machine-Building Plant with several experimental machine-building plants and research and design institutions. The Bilshovyk plant originated in Kiev in 1890, when the merchants Greter and Krivanek formed a joint-stock company and built a plant that produced machinery and parts for sugar refineries, breweries, distilleries, lumber and flour mills, and brick factories. Because of the long record of revolutionary activity engaged in by the plant's workers, it was given the name Bilshovyk in 1922. During the First Five-Year Plan, the plant was expanded and began producing parts and machinery for the chemical industry. During the Second World War the plant was dismantled and evacuated to the Urals, where it was reassembled to form the Uralkhimmash plant. In 1946 the plant was rebuilt in Kiev and subsequently expanded and modernized. Kyivpolimermash continues to produce numerous products for the chemical-plastics industry, many of which are exported to the Comecon countries.

Kiev Medical Institute (Kyivskyi medychnyi instytut im. akademika O.O. Bohomoltsia). An institution of higher learning under the jurisdiction of the Ministry of Health Protection of the Ukrainian SSR. It was founded in 1841 as the Medical Faculty of Kiev University, which was merged with the Kiev Woman's Medical Institute (from 1907 to 1916 the Medical Faculty of the Kiev Higher Courses for Women) to form the Kiev Medical Academy (renamed an institute in 1921). The institute has a teaching staff of over 500 in 5 faculties (therapeutics, pediatrics, hygiene, stomatology, and the upgrading of medical teachers), 67 chairs, a preparation department, a graduate program, courses for the upgrading of public health workers, a central research laboratory, 4 learning museums, and a library with over 620,000 volumes. So far it has granted about 50,000 degrees; in 1980 it had 6,300 students. The Museum of the History of Medicine of the Ukrainian SSR is run by the institute. Since 1937 it has published the newspaper *Meditsinskie kadry*. Many prominent medical specialists have taught at the institute (see *Medicine and *Medical education).

BIBLIOGRAPHY

Pliushch, V. *Narysy z istorii ukraïns'koï medychnoï nauky ta osvity*, 2 (Munich 1983)

Kiev Medical Society (Kyivske tovarystvo likariv). The first society of physicians in Ukraine, established in 1840 to promote medical research and health care in Kiev. Research papers were read and discussed at its meetings. Its members organized public vaccinations, lectures, and educational campaigns to fight infectious diseases, and founded hospitals, medical laboratories, night shelters, and a health-statistics office in Kiev. In 1881 the society was the first in the Russian Empire to promote emergency house-call services at night. It published educational pamphlets and a serial collection of research by its members and records of its meetings. The society ceased functioning during the First World War. Among its presidents were V. Karavaiv, C. Hübbenet, N. Khrzhonshchevsky, Yu. Matson, P. Peremezhko, G. Minkh, V. Vysokovych, M. Volkovych, and K. Tritshel.

Kiev metro (Kyivskyi metropolitan im. V. Lenina). An urban railway for passenger transport. Construction of the Kiev metro began in 1949 and the first section (5.2 km) was opened in 1960. The first line is now almost 20 km long, with 15 stations. It runs from the west (Sviatoshyne station) through the center of the city (Khreshchatyk station) to the east (Pionerska station). From Sviatoshyne to the Dnipro station the line is underground, and from there to the end it proceeds on the 700-m reinforced-concrete Metro Bridge over the Dnieper River and Rusaniv Channel. This line links the two banks of the Dnieper, the large residential areas, the industrial zones, and the main railway stations. In 1976 the first three stations of the Kurenivka–Chervonoarmiiske line were opened. When completed, this line will be about 20 km long and will cross the city from the Obolon apart-

Kiev Metro: Polytechnical Institute Station

ment subdivision in the north to the Teremky subdivision in the south. At present there are 12 stations on this line. Two further lines are planned: the Syrets–Pecherska (approx 28 km long), which will link the northwestern subdivision of Vynohradar to the Kharkiv Highway in the southeast of the city, and a line approx 26 km long, which will run in a north-south direction along the left bank of the Dnieper.

The metro transports about 20 percent of Kiev's urban commuters. With 800,000 passengers per day it is the third busiest metro in the USSR. The ornate stations are decorated with displays rich in historical and propagandistic motifs, many of which relate to local events.

A. Zhukovsky

Kiev metropoly. The central and original church organization on Ukrainian territory. It was established after the *Christianization of Ukraine in 988 and the organization of church hierarchy. From the 11th century, the metropoly was under the jurisdiction of the Patriarch of Constantinople.

The exact date of the establishment of the metropoly and the identity of its first hierarchs are unknown. Church tradition has it that the first metropolitan was a Greek named Michael who arrived in Kiev in 988 and died in 994. Some scholars, however, believe that the first metropolitan was the Greek Leontius or Theopemptos, who was sent to Kiev by the ecumenical patriarch in 1037.

The metropolitans of Kiev were, according to the 'law of the 34 apostles,' provincial metropolitans, or first hierarchs of an ecclesiastical province composed of a number of eparchies (see *Eparchy). They were also the titular bishops of *Kiev eparchy. At the time of the Mongol invasion (1240), there were 16 eparchies in the metropoly, of which 10 were on Ukrainian territory. The authority of the Patriarch of Constantinople included the power to (1) appoint and consecrate the metropolitan; (2) change the location of the metropolitan see or subdivide the metropoly; (3) try the metropolitan; (4) arbitrate in the case of disputes over theology or rite and issue patriarchal missives; (5) grant stauropegion; (6) make visitations; and (7) appoint exarchs to the metropoly.

In fact, the metropoly was really only subject to the canonical and spiritual authority of Constantinople. In its internal life and administration it enjoyed considerable autonomy. Yet only 2 of the first 24 metropolitans were of local origin (*Ilarion and *Klym Smoliatych). Their consecrations resulted from the desire of the Rus' princes and clergy to establish a native hierarchy. This circumstance has enabled many historians (eg, D. Doroshenko and N. Polonska-Vasylenko) to claim that Kiev metropoly actually constituted an autocephalous ecclesiastical body.

This independence of Constantinople enabled the church to spread Christianity among the people and serve as an important unifying factor in Kievan Rus', which was soon divided into various principalities. As Kiev declined in political significance in the 12th and early 13th centuries, a struggle for control over the metropoly ensued between the competing principalities. After the destruction of Kiev by the Mongols, the new metropolitan, *Cyril II (1243–81), moved to Vladimir on the Kliazma, which had not been conquered by the Mongols. His successor, the Greek Maximos (1283–1305), formally transferred the metropolitan's residence there in 1299. This led the Galician-Volhynian princes to establish a separate *Halych metropoly, which existed, with various interruptions, from 1303 until the end of the 14th century.

In the mid-14th century a third metropoly arose that claimed territories under Kievan jurisdiction, the *Lithuanian metropoly. In 1356 the Holy Synod in Constantinople granted the 'Metropolitan of Lithuania and Volhynia' jurisdiction over the eparchies of Polatsk and Turiv, Volodymyr, Lutske, Kholm, Halych, and Peremyshl, while Aleksei, the metropolitan of Kiev and all Rus', with his see in Moscow, retained control over the remaining eparchies of Rus'. By the end of the 14th century Metropolitan *Cyprian was able to reunite all of the eparchies formerly under the Halych or Lithuanian metropolitan. This unity, however, was shortlived. In 1415 a synod of the bishops of Polatsk, Smolensk, Lutske, Chernihiv, Volodymyr, Turiv, Peremyshl, and Kholm refused to recognize Cyprian's successor in Moscow as metropolitan and instead elected Hryhorii Tsamblak metropolitan. Although he was excommunicated by the patriarch he enjoyed the support of the hierarchs and the Lithuanian Grand Duke Vytautas until his death in 1419. At the time, the Kievan metropolitan in Moscow, Photius, was again able to reassert control over the Ukrainian and Belorussian eparchies in Lithuania.

The final split in the metropoly occurred in 1448 when Prince Vasilii of Moscow appointed Bishop Iona of Riazan metropolitan of Moscow with jurisdiction over several eparchies formerly under Kiev. Because this was done without consent of the Patriarch in Constantinople, under the terms of the Church Union of *Florence this act was considered schismatic. The Moscow church subsequently declared its autocephaly, which was recognized by Constantinople only in 1589. In the Polish-Lithuanian Commonwealth, Kiev metropoly was left with eight Ukrainian eparchies (Kiev, Chernihiv, Turiv-Pynske, Lutske, Volodymyr, Kholm, Peremyshl, and Lviv-Halych) and two Belorussian eparchies. Lviv-Halych eparchy, however, did not have a bishop from the beginning of the 15th century to 1539, because it had been given by the Polish king to the Roman Catholic archbishop of Lviv.

The first metropolitan of Kiev after the secession of Moscow metropoly was H. *Bolharyn, who arrived from Rome in 1458. In 1470 he was confirmed metropolitan by Patriarch Dionisios of Constantinople. His successors

– Mysail *Pstruch (1475–80), Symeon (1481–8), Iona Hlezna (1489–94), and *Makarii I (1495–7) – were all elected by sobors of the Rus' bishops. The appointment of the bishop of Smolensk, Y. *Bolharynovych, as metropolitan by the Lithuanian grand duke Alexander in 1498 ushered in a period of secular control over the metropoly and a period of decline for the Ukrainian Orthodox church. Some hierarchs were even raised to episcopal rank by the Polish king without any ecclesiastical vocation. Spiritual control over church life was progressively assumed by *brotherhoods and monasteries, many of which were granted *stauropegion by the patriarch. The growing rift between the clergy and faithful and the hierarchy led many bishops to adopt a pro–Roman Catholic orientation, which eventually culminated in their acceptance of the Church Union of *Berestia in 1596. Among the bishops who joined the new Uniate church was the Kievan metropolitan, M. Rahoza; the Polish king, Sigismund III, handed over the rights and privileges of the formerly Orthodox metropoly to the Uniate church.

The Orthodox forces in the metropoly, however, did not cease their activities, and the Patriarch of Constantinople continued to appoint exarchs to the metropoly. Under the leadership of the Cossack hetman P. Sahaidachny, the Orthodox hierarchy of Kiev metropoly was restored in 1620 by Patriarch Theophanes of Jerusalem. The new metropolitan was Y. *Boretsky, and bishops were consecrated for Polatsk (M. *Smotrytsky), Peremyshl (I. *Kopynsky), Volodymyr (Yo. Kurtsevych), Lutske (I. Boryskovych), and Kholm (P. Ipolytovych). The Polish government did not recognize the restored Orthodox metropoly and its hierarchy, but they continued to function under the protection of the Cossacks. After the death of Sigismund, King Władysław IV Vasa issued the 'Points of reconciliation with the Ruthenian people of Greek faith of 1632' legalizing the Kiev Orthodox metropoly and hierarchy headed by P. *Mohyla (1633–47). Under Mohyla and his successors in the 17th century – S. *Kosiv (1647–57), D. *Balaban (1657–63), Y. *Neliubovych-Tukalsky (1663–75), and A. *Vynnytsky – church life throughout the metropoly underwent a spiritual and institutional renaissance, supported by the Cossacks and burghers. An important issue in the uprising led by B. Khmelnytsky was the status of the church and Kiev metropoly. Under the terms of the Treaty of Zboriv (1649) between the Cossacks and the Poles, the Kievan metropolitan was to be guaranteed a seat in the Polish Sejm.

A major turning point in the history of the metropoly occurred in 1685–6. The bishop of Lutske, H. *Sviatopolk-Chetvertynsky, who had been elected metropolitan in 1679, at that time severed his ties with Constantinople, and placed himself under the jurisdiction of the Patriarch of Moscow. The formal subjugation of Kiev metropoly to Moscow Patriarchate was ratified in an agreement between the Muscovite tsar and Patriarch Dionisius IV of Constantinople (1686). This was supported by Hetman I. Samoilovych, and accompanied the growing political domination of the Hetman state by Muscovy following the Treaty of *Pereiaslav and of *Andrusovo, which formalized Russian rule over Left-Bank Ukraine. In 1924 Patriarch Gregory VII of Constantinople stated in a *Tomos* that this transfer of Kiev metropoly to the Moscow Patriarchate had not been canonical.

During the reign of Tsar Peter I, Kiev metropoly was abolished. It lost its status as an autonomous church province and became a mere local eparchy of the Russian church under the ultimate jurisdiction (from 1721) of the Holy Synod and headed by an archbishop. The title 'metropolitan of Kiev, Halych, and Little Russia' was restored in 1743, as a result of the efforts of R. *Zaborovsky, but under Empress Catherine II the words 'Little Russia' were dropped from the official title (1770). In the 18th century several Ukrainian-born clerics served as metropolitans, but most of them, eg, H. *Kremianetsky and S. *Myslavsky, did nothing to oppose the Russifying policies of the Holy Synod. Throughout the 19th century Russians occupied the post; some of these metropolitans proved to be capable defenders of the church; eg, E. Bolkhovitinov (1822–37), a noted historian of the church in Ukraine, F. Amfiteatrov (1837–57), and A. Moskvin (1860–76). Kievan metropolitans were permanent members of the Holy Synod throughout this period.

After the 1917 Revolution and the re-establishment of the Ukrainian Orthodox church as the *Ukrainian Autocephalous Orthodox church (UAOC), the head of the UAOC hierarchy had the title 'metropolitan of Kiev and all Ukraine.' This position was held by two metropolitans: V. *Lypkivsky (1921–7) and M. *Boretsky (1927–30). The liquidation of the UAOC in the early 1930s ended the short revival of Kiev metropoly. During the Second World War the UAOC was once again revived by the Synod of Bishops of the UAOC in Kiev on 9–17 May 1942, at which N. *Abramovych was elected archbishop of Kiev and Chyhyryn. The conference of delegates of the UAOC and the Ukrainian Autonomous Church, held on 8 October 1942 in Pochaiv, confirmed Metropolitan D. *Valedynsky as the provisional head of Kiev metropoly. After the war, however, the metropoly again became an integral part of the Russian Orthodox church, functioning as an exarchate of the Moscow Patriarchate.

The statute of the Russian Orthodox church of 1945 makes no mention of the autonomous status of the church in Ukraine, and assigns to the Kievan metropolitan ex officio membership in the Patriarchal Synod. The metropolitans of Kiev and Halych and the exarchs of Ukraine have been I. Sokolov (1944–64), Y. Leliukhin (1964–6), and F. *Denysenko (1966–), the last being the first metropolitan of Ukrainian origin in many years. Organizationally, and administratively, the Ukrainian exarchate, which includes 18 eparchies (of which 4 are unoccupied), has jurisdiction over the Kiev metropoly.

BIBLIOGRAPHY

Bolkhovitinov, E. *Opisanie Kievo-Sofiiskogo sobora i Kievskoi ierarkhii* (Kiev 1825)
Arkhiv Iugo-Zapadnoi Rossii, series 1, vols 1–12 (Kiev 1859–1904)
[Bulgakov], Makarii. *Istoriia Russkoi Tserkvi*, 12 vols (St Petersburg 1864–86)
Stroev, P. *Spiski ierarkhov i nastoiatelei monastyrei Rossiiskoi Tserkvi* (St Petersburg 1877)
Chistovich, I. *Ocherk istorii zapadno-russkoi Tserkvi*, 2 vols (St Petersburg 1882, 1884)
Spiski arkhiereev ierarkhii Vserossiiskoi i arkhiereiskikh kafedr ... (1721–1895) (St Petersburg 1896)
Hrushevs'kyi, M. *Istoriia Ukraïny-Rusy*, 10 vols (Lviv-Kiev 1898–1937)
Golubinskii, E. *Istoriia Russkoi Tserkvi*, 2 vols in 4 bks (Moscow 1901–17)
Titov, T. *Russkaia Pravoslavnaia Tserkov v pol'sko-litovskom gosudarstve v XVII–XVIII vekakh*, 3 vols (Kiev 1905–16)

Bednov, V. *Pravoslavnaia Tserkov v Pol'shche i Litve* (Katerynoslav 1908)
Chodynicki, K. *Kościół Prawosławny a Rzeczpospolita Polska: Zarys historyczny (1370–1632)* (Warsaw 1934)
Doroshenko, D. *Pravoslavna Tserkva v mynulomu i suchasnomu zhytti ukraïns'koho narodu* (Berlin 1940)
Hayer, F. *Die Orthodoxe Kirche in der Ukraine von 1917 bis 1945* (Köln-Braunsfeld 1953)
Vlasovs'kyi, I. *Narys istoriï Ukraïns'koï Pravoslavnoï Tserkvy*, 4 vols (Bound Brook, NJ 1953–66)
Lypkivs'kyi, V. *Istoriia Ukraïns'koï Pravoslavnoï Tserkvy* (Winnipeg 1961)
Polons'ka-Vasylenko, N. *Istorychni pidvalyny UAPTs* (Munich 1964)
Makarii. *Pravoslav'ia na Ukraïni* (Kiev 1980)

I. Vlasovsky, A. Zhukovsky

Kiev Missal (Kyivski lystky). One of the oldest Slavic literary monuments, written in the *Glagolitic alphabet, consisting of seven parchment sheets of undetermined origin. In 1872 it was deposited in the library of the Kiev Theological Academy (hence its name). The missal was published by I. Sreznevsky in 1874. Its language has been studied by such scholars as M. Hrunsky and G.Y. Shevelov. Today the document is preserved in the Central Scientific Library of the Academy of Sciences of the Ukrainian SSR.

Kiev Museum of Church Antiquities (Kyivskyi tserkovno-arkheolohichnyi muzei Dukhovnoi akademii). A collection of 20,000 church monuments, manuscripts, incunabula, and documents (icons, portraits, coins) established in 1878 by N. Petrov of the Kiev Society of Church History and Archeology (est 1872) at the Kiev Theological Academy. In 1923 it became part of the Lavra Museum of Cults and Way of Life (see *Kievan Cave Monastery). Eventually, the collection was dispersed among various museums.

Kiev Museum of Russian Art (Kyivskyi muzei rosiiskoho mystetstva). One of the largest art museums in Ukraine. It was set up in 1922 out of the nationalized private collections of the Tereshchenko family, dating back to the 1870s. Until 1934 it was known as the Kiev Picture Gallery. In the 1930s it acquired from the All-Ukrainian Historical Museum the works of V. Borovykovsky, D. Levytsky, I. Repin, and M. Yaroshenko and collections of N. Ge's and M. Vrubel's works. From the VUAN and the Art Cabinet of Kiev University, it obtained collections of old Rus' art. The collection is housed in a building built for M. Tereshchenko in 1880 by A. Hun and V. Nikolaev, and extended in 1882 by V. Shreter and V. Nikolaev. Its interior decorations were done by F. Melner. The museum is divided into three sections: old Rus' art, Russian art from the 18th to the early 20th centuries, and Soviet art. The exhibits consist of icons dating back to the 13th century, paintings, sculptures, prints, porcelain, china, and artistic glass from the 18th and 19th centuries. The museum holds frequent exhibitions to popularize Russian art. Its jubilee exhibitions include the better works of Ukrainian artists who had worked mostly in Russia. It publishes special art catalogs for students.

S. Yaniv

Kiev Museum of Theater, Music, and Cinema Arts (Kyivskyi muzei teatralnoho, muzychnoho ta kinomystetstva URSR). The largest collection of materials on the history of Ukrainian theater, music, and film in Ukraine. It was formed in 1926 as a theater museum out of the *Berezil theater's collection (est 1924), which in 1926 became part of the VUAN. In 1934 the museum was brought under the jurisdiction of the Committee for Artistic Affairs. In 1965 a cinema and a music department were added, and the museum was given its present name. By 1985 it possessed approximately 190,000 exhibits, including an 18th-century **vertep* with a set of puppets, folk-music instruments of the 18th and 19th centuries, manuscripts of plays and letters by M. Kropyvnytsky, I. Karpenko-Kary, M. Sadovsky, M. Zankovetska, and P. Saksahansky, the original music manuscripts of M. Lysenko, M. Arkas, B. Liatoshynsky, and L. Revytsky, costumes, stage decorations, posters, programs, personal collections such as V. Vasylko's with 5,000 items, and music publications from the mid-18th century. It has a photo, phono, film, and special-books library. The museum is situated on the grounds of the Kievan Cave Monastery. In 1960 the Zankovetska Museum and in 1980 the Lysenko Museum, branches of the Kiev Museum, were opened in M. Lysenko's former (1898–1912) residence.

V. Revutsky

Kiev Museum of Ukrainian Art

Kiev Museum of Ukrainian Art (Kyivskyi derzhavnyi muzei ukrainskoho obrazotvorchoho mystetstva, or DMUOM). The central art museum of Ukraine. It was founded in 1936 when the holdings of the All-Ukrainian Historical Museum were divided into a historical and an artistic collection. The former became the basis of the Kiev Historical Museum (see *Historical Museum of the Ukrainian SSR), the latter of the Kiev State Museum of Ukrainian Art, which received its present name in 1953. From 1954 to 1964 a collection of Ukrainian folk art, which became the Kiev Museum of Ukrainian Decorative Folk Art, constituted a branch of the Kiev Museum of Ukrainian Art. The museum is divided into three sections: old art, 19th- and early-20th-century art, and Soviet art. The first encompasses artistic works from the 12th to the 18th centuries: rare icons such as *Volhynian Mother of God* (14th century), *St George the Dragon-Slayer* (early 15th century), and *The Holy Protectress* (13th century); 17th- and 18th-century portraits, including the portraits of M. Myklashevsky, the colonel of Starodub (18th century), of D. Yefremov, the otaman of the Don Cossack Host (1752), of V. Hamaliia (mid-18th century), of P. Sulyma (mid-18th century), and *The Crucifixion with a Portrait of L. Svichka* (late 17th century); folk paintings titled *The Cossack Mamai*; and fine prints and samples of the earliest Ukrainian sculptures. The second section, devoted to the 19th and early 20th centuries, contains some valuable works of the portraitists D. Levytsky and V. Borovykovsky (most of their works are preserved at the Kiev Museum of Russian Art); the works of T. Shevchenko and his followers I. Sokolov, L. Zhemchuzhnikov, and K. Trutovsky; the paintings of P. Martynovych, N. Kuznetsov, M. Pymonenko, K. Kostandi, S. Svitoslavsky, P. Nilus, and P. Levchenko; the paintings and portraits of O. Murashko; the landscapes of S. Vasylkivsky; and the works of I. Trush, F. Krasytsky, H. Svitlytsky, M. Samokysha, and F. Krychevsky. The largest section is the one devoted to Soviet art. It contains posters of the revolutionary period; the works done in the 1920s and 1930s by prerevolutionary masters such as I. Izhakevych, M. Samokysha, F. Krychevsky, H. Svitlytsky, V. Kasiian, A. Petrytsky, O. Shovkunenko, K. Trokhymenko, M. Burachek, and I. Kavaleridze; works done after the war by S. Hryhoriev, M. Derehus, V. Kasiian, V. Kostetsky, O. Maksymenko, Yu. Melikhov, V. Lytvynenko, O. Kovalov, V. Myronenko, O. Pashchenko, and T. Yablonska; Transcarpathian and Galician art by Y. Bokshai, A. Kashshai, A. Kotska, F. Manailo, O. Kulchytska, and various socialist-realist artists; and contemporary works by M. Bozhii, V. Borodai, V. Borysenko, S. Huietsky, V. Znoba, V. Klokov, H. Kalchenko, O. Lopukhov, H. Tomenko, O. Fishchenko, V. Chekaniuk, V. Shatalin, and H. Yakutovych. In the exhibits preference is given to works on Leninist themes. The museum holds about 17,000 items. The museum building, which was erected in the Neoclassical style in 1897–1900 by V. Horodetsky and G. Boitsov and decorated by E. Sal, was enlarged in 1972 so that the exhibition area doubled.

S. Yaniv

Kiev Museum of Ukrainian Decorative Folk Art (Kyivskyi derzhavnyi muzei ukrainskoho narodnoho dekoratyvnoho mystetstva URSR). A museum located on the grounds of the Kievan Cave Historical-Cultural Preserve, in the former residence of the Kievan metropolitan. Many of its artifacts were originally in the Kiev Municipal Museum of Antiquities and Art, which was founded in 1899 and became the First State Museum in 1919, the All-Ukrainian Museum of History in 1924, and the *Kiev Museum of Ukrainian Art in 1936. A branch of the last museum from 1954, it became an independent institution in 1964. The museum has extensive collections of Ukrainian artistic folk kilims, printed and woven textiles, embroidery, needlework, dress, wood carvings, ceramics, pottery, glass, and decorative painting dating from the 15th century to the present. The paintings of K. *Bilokur are accorded an entire room in the museum.

Kiev Museum of Western and Eastern Art (Kyivskyi muzei zakhidnoho ta skhidnoho mystetstva). A state collection of art works from Western Europe and the Orient. It was founded in 1919 on the basis of B. and V. Khanenko's private collection, which originated in 1870 and was donated in 1919 to the VUAN by V. Khanenko. Its holdings grew in 1925–6 as other collections, particularly V. Shchavinsky's collection of about 200 paintings (mostly by Flemish masters), were donated, and in 1928–40 as collections from other Kiev and Leningrad museums were transferred to this depository. By the 1930s its collection, which at first numbered 1,200 exhibits, reached 6,500 art works and 33,000 prints. The museum has three sections: ancient, West European, and Eastern art. The exhibits include ancient Greek, Roman, and Byzantine art; paintings and sculptures by Italian masters such as P. Perugino, G. Bellini, A. Magnasco, F. Guardi, and J. Donatello; and the works of Spanish artists such as D. Velásquez, J. Zurbarán, and F. Goya; of Flemish masters such as P. Brueghel the Elder, F. Hals, P. Rubens, and J. Jordaens; and of French painters such as J. David, J. Greuze, and F. Boucher. The Eastern collection contains sculptures and drawings from ancient Egypt, Syria, Iran, Turkey, Central Asia, Caucasia, India, Nepal, Tibet, Mongolia, Thailand, Japan, China, and Indonesia. The museum is housed in a building built for the *Khanenko family by R. Meltser in the 1880s.

S. Yaniv

Kiev Music School (Kyivska muzychna shkola). The first professional music school in Kiev. It was founded in 1768 by the Kiev City Council to prepare musicians for the city orchestra. Besides music, students were taught mathematics, history, geography, and languages. In 1831 the school and orchestra were joined to form the Kiev City Kapelle, which gave concerts, accompanied theatrical performances, and played at official receptions. The kapelle and school were closed in 1852.

Kiev oblast. An administrative region in north-central Ukraine on both banks of the Dnieper River, formed on 27 February 1932. Its area is 28,900 sq km; in 1986 its population was 1,937,800 without Kiev, which was divided among 25 raions, 559 rural soviets, 23 cities, and 30 towns (smt). The oblast and national capital is Kiev.

Physical geography. The oblast is located on the rolling plain of the middle Dnieper Basin. Its northern part is located in the Polisia Lowland; it has coniferous and mixed forests, marshes, and soddy-podzolized, gley, meadow, and marshy soils. Its central part has podzolized chernozems, and solonets, solonchak, and gray forest soils; east of the Dnieper it lies in the Dnieper Lowland. Its highest (up to 273 m) southwestern part lies in the Dnieper Upland; the soils there are deep low-humus chernozems. The vegetation of the oblast's central and southern parts is of the forest-steppe variety. Forests cover 516,000 ha of the oblast's area. The climate is temperate-continental, with an average temperature of -6°C in January and 19.5°C in July. The annual precipitation is 500–600 mm. The average growing season is 198–204 days. The oblast has 177 rivers with lengths over 10 km; the principal ones are the Dnieper and its tributaries the Prypiat, Teteriv, Irpin, Stuhna, Desna, Trubizh, Ros, and Supii. The large Kiev and Kaniv reservoirs have been created on the Dnieper; there are 11 other reservoirs, 2,000 ponds, and 750 small floodplain lakes in the oblast.

History. The oblast's territory has been populated since late Paleolithic times. From the 9th to the 14th centuries it constituted parts of *Kiev and *Pereiaslav principalities of Kievan Rus'. From ca 1362 to 1569 it was ruled by Lithuania, from 1471 as part of *Kiev voivodeship. Under Polish rule from 1569, rebellions of *Cossacks took place

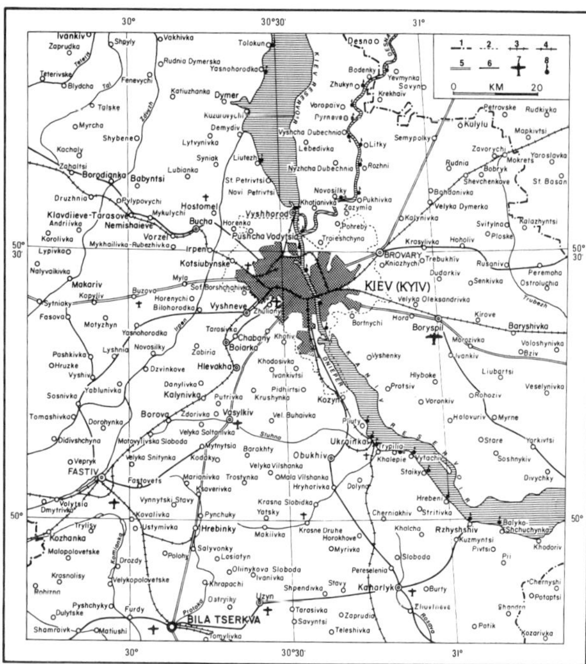

KIEV REGION

1. Boundary of Kiev oblast
2. Boundary of Kiev-Sviatoshynskyi raion
3. Multiple-track railway
4. Single-track railway
5. Main highway
6. Other highways
7. Airfields and airports
8. River ports

there in the late 16th and early 17th centuries. From 1648 to 1667 it was part of *Kiev regiment in the Hetman state. With the Treaty of *Andrusovo the Right Bank (except Kiev) remained under Poland, while the Left Bank and Kiev came under Muscovite rule. S. *Palii's rebellion (1702–4) and *Haidamaka uprisings occurred on the Right Bank in the 18th century. The Cossack Kiev regiment existed on the Left Bank until 1781. During the partitions of Poland in the late 18th century, all of the Right Bank was annexed by the Russian Empire, and the oblast's territory there made up a large part of *Kiev gubernia (1797–1925).

Under Soviet rule, Kiev gubernia was abolished in 1925, and its territory became part of Kiev, Cherkasy, Bila Tserkva, Berdychiv, Zhytomyr, and Korosten okruhas. Kiev oblast replaced the okruhas in February 1932; at that time the oblast incorporated a large part of Right-Bank Ukraine, including Soviet-ruled Volhynia (now Zhytomyr oblast). In October its northern raions became part of the new Chernihiv oblast. Other raions became part of the new Zhytomyr and Poltava oblasts in 1937, Vinnytsia and Kirovohrad oblasts in 1939, and Cherkasy oblast in 1954.

Population. In 1939 the population of the oblast within its present-day borders was 1,715,900 without Kiev and 2,562,600 with Kiev. Because of high mortality (including the destruction of many thousands of Jews in the Nazi Holocaust) during the Second World War, the population living outside Kiev had grown little by 1959, to 1,719,000. In 1970 it was 1,836,000. The city of *Kiev, however, has constantly attracted people from other parts of the oblast and elsewhere, and its population has grown substantially. By 1984 the population density of the oblast outside Kiev had increased, from 12.4 percent of the total population in 1939 to 26 percent in 1959, 36 percent in 1970, 45 percent in 1979, and 51 percent in 1984. Ukrainians constituted 93.2 percent of the population outside Kiev in 1959 and 90.5 percent in 1979; Russians, 4.8 percent in 1959 and 8.4 percent in 1979; Jews, 0.9 percent in 1959; and Poles, 0.4 percent in 1959. In 1984, the oblast's largest cities (with populations over 50,000) were Kiev, Bila Tserkva, Brovary, and Khvastiv.

Industry. In 1940 there were 797 large industrial enterprises in the oblast (including Kiev), which employed 210,000 workers and produced 12 percent of Soviet Ukraine's industrial output. Since the Second World War industry has been reconstructed and expanded. Much of it is concentrated in *Kiev. In 1984 the major branches were machine building and metalworking (22 percent of the oblast's total industrial output), food production (21.1 percent), energy production (13.9 percent), light industry (12.3 percent), and chemicals and petrochemicals manufacturing (10.5 percent).

Outside Kiev the food industry consists of sugar-beet processing (16 plants in Bila Tserkva, Hrebinky, Yahotyn, and elsewhere), dairy-products manufacturing (23 plants), distilling (in Stadnytsia, Chervona Sloboda, Tkhorivka, and Trylisy), and meat packing and vegetable and fruit canning (in Bila Tserkva). There are 21 animal-feed plants in the oblast. The main machine-building and metalworking industries are located in Brovary (mobile cranes, food-industry and lighting equipment), Bila Tserkva (electrotechnical equipment, agricultural machines), Khvastiv (electrotechnical and chemical-industry equipment), Irpin (peat-extraction machinery), Hrebinky (food-industry equipment), Borodianka (excavators), Vasylkiv (refrigerators, electric irons, and other appliances), and Rzhyshchiv (sanitation-technology equipment). A large powder-metallurgy plant is located in Brovary.

The oblast's light industry consists mainly of the manufacturing of clothing and textiles (in Bila Tserkva, Skvyra, Khvastiv, Poliske, Pereiaslav-Khmelnytskyi, Brovary, Bohuslav, and Berezan), leather goods and footwear (in Vasylkiv, Bila Tserkva, and Baryshivka), linen (in Ivankiv, Poliske, and Makariv), and wood products and furniture (in Khvastiv, Brovary, Bila Tserkva, Irpin, Komarivka, Motovylivka, and Klavdiieve). The main center of the chemical and petrochemical industries is Brovary (tires, rubber and asbestos products, plastics). Pharmaceuticals and biochemical preparations are made in Nemishaieve. Building materials produced include reinforced-concrete products (in Bila Tserkva, Vyshhorod, and elsewhere), bricks (in Staiky, Bila Tserkva, and Bucha), granite products (in Bucha), and glass (in Babyntsi, Bucha, Piskivka, and Hostomel). Granite is quarried near Bohuslav and Bila Tserkva.

Kiev oblast's industries are powered by the Kiev Thermal Central Station, Hydroelectric Station, and Water-Accumulating Electric Station. The Chornobyl Atomic Electric Station also provides energy despite the nuclear disaster there in April 1986. Sources of fuel include natural gas piped in from Dashava and Shebelynka and coal from the Donbas and local mines.

Agriculture. In 1985 there were 283 collective farms

and 164 state farms in the oblast. They had at their disposal 2,057,000 ha, of which 1,771,000 ha were used directly in agriculture; of the latter, 84.1 percent was tilled, 7.1 percent was hayfield, and 6.7 percent was pasture. Irrigated land amounted to 113,600 ha and drained land, to 161,900 ha. The main crops cultivated are high-quality grains (particularly winter wheat) and sugar beets in the forest-steppe raions, potatoes and *dovhunets* flax in the Polisian raions, vegetables, berries, and fruits.

In 1978 wheat took up 22.3 percent and barley 9.4 percent of the oblast's tilled land; other grains grown were pulses (14 percent in 1971), corn (7.2 percent in 1971), buckwheat, and millet. Fodder crops occupied 33.2 percent of the tilled land; vegetables, gourds, and potatoes, 10.3 percent; and industrial crops, 9.5 percent (in 1971, 82.1 percent of the latter consisted of sugar beets and 9 percent of flax). In 1978 berry crops and fruit orchards occupied 51,600 ha of land, of which 37,800 ha were productive.

Animal husbandry is also highly developed. It accounted for 54 percent of the total value of agricultural output in 1983. It consists of cattle farming in the Polisian raions, hog, cattle, and poultry farming (including 21 large poultry factories) in the forest-steppe raions, beekeeping, and rabbit and fish farming.

Transportation. In 1983 there were 880 km of railroad in the oblast. The main lines crossing the oblast are Moscow–Kiev–Odessa, Moscow–Kiev–Lviv, Kiev–Brest, Kharkiv–Kiev, and Kiev–Dnipropetrovske–Donetske. The main junctions are Kiev, Khvastiv, and Myronivka. There are 7,677 km of motor roads, of which 7,345 are paved. The main highways are Leningrad–Kiev–Odessa, Kiev–Kharkiv, Kiev–Dnipropetrovske, Kiev–Brest, and Kiev–Lviv. River transportation on the Dnieper, Desna, Prypiat, and part of the Teteriv is well developed. Airports are located in Boryspil, Zhuliany, Borodianka, Bila Tserkva, Hostomel, and Vasylkiv.

BIBLIOGRAPHY
Starovoitenko, I. *Kyïvs'ka oblast'* (Kiev 1967)
Rudych, F.; et al (eds). *Istoriia mist i sil Ukraïns'koï RSR: Kyïvs'ka oblast'* (Kiev 1971)
Pryroda Kyïvs'koï oblasti (Kiev 1972)
Kharchenko, A. (ed). *Atlas Kievskoi oblasti* (Moscow 1985)

I. Myhul, R. Senkus

Kiev Operetta Theater (Kyivskyi teatr operety). Founded in 1934 as the Kiev Theater of Musical Comedy, it was renamed in 1967. Its repertoire consists of Soviet operettas and classical operettas of J. Strauss, I. Kálmán, F. Lehár, and J. Offenbach. Its first stage director was S. Karhalsky; he was followed by V. Skliarenko, V. Kharchenko, B. Balaban, and V. Behma (1976–).

Kiev Pedagogical Institute (Kyivskyi pedahohichnyi instytut im. M. Gorkoho). An institution of higher education under the Ministry of Education of the Ukrainian SSR and one of the largest pedagogical institutes in Ukraine. It was organized in 1934 out of the Kiev Institute of Social Education (est 1920). In 1982 the institute consisted of nine faculties: physics and mathematics, general and technical studies, philology, history, natural science and geography, pedagogy, music teaching, and pedagogical training for teachers of Russian language and for teachers of the handicapped. Except for the music teaching faculty, all the faculties have a five-year program. There is also a correspondence and a graduate school. The total enrollment in 1980 was 8,500 and the faculty numbered 450.

Kiev Physics and Chemistry Society (Kyivske fizyko-khimichne tovarystvo). Society at Kiev University organized in 1910 on the basis of the chemistry section of the *Kiev Society of Naturalists. The society promoted the study of chemistry and organized public lectures. It published the journal *Protokoly fiziko-khimicheskogo obshchestva* (1911–15). In 1915 its activity was suspended because of the war, and in 1920 it resumed operation again as the chemistry section of the Society of Naturalists. It ceased operation in 1932, although it served as the basis for the newly formed Kiev chapter of the All-Union Chemistry Society. The society's president throughout its existence was S. Reformatsky; other prominent members were A. Dumansky, V. Izbekov, V. Plotnykov, and V. Shaposhnikov.

Kiev Physics and Mathematics Society (Kyivske fizyko-matematychne tovarystvo). A scholarly society at Kiev University organized in 1890 out of the mathematics section of the *Kiev Society of Naturalists. The society strove to popularize the study of mathematics and physics and to improve the teaching of these subjects in schools and universities. It held regular meetings throughout its existence (1890–1917), where more than 1,000 presentations were made on mathematics, physics, astronomy, and pedagogy. It published the journal *Otchety i protokoly fiziko-matematicheskogo obshchestva*. The society's founder and head until 1904 was the physicist N. Shiller. It had approx 350 members, including M. Avenarius, B. Bukreev, M. Khandrykov, V. Yermakov, and M. Vashchenko-Zakharchenko.

Kiev Polytechnical Institute

Kiev Polytechnical Institute (Kyivskyi politekhichnyi instytut im. 50-richchia Velykoi Zhovtnevoi sotsialistychnoi revoliutsii). An institution of higher education under the Ministry of Higher and Specialized Secondary Education of the Ukrainian SSR. It was founded in 1898 and its first director was V. Kirpichov. In 1909 the Kiev Society of Aerial Navigation was organized at the institute. In 1923–33 a number of specialized institutes were organized out of its departments. Its workshops formed the basis of several industrial concerns. Many famous scientists and engineers, such as N. Zhukovsky, D. Mendeleev, S. Korolov, A. Liulka, I. Sikorsky, K. Zvorykin, Ye. Paton, and L. Pysarzhevsky, either taught or studied at the institute. The institute consists of 19 faculties, including mechanics and machine building, chemical machine building, electrotechnology, electric power, thermal power, welding, electromechanics and automatization, electrical-equipment building and computing technology, and radiotechnology. It has two evening schools, a correspondence school, and a graduate school. Its branches in Zhytomyr and Chernihiv offer full-time, evening, and correspondence programs, while its Cherkasy branch offers only evening and correspondence programs. In 1980 the enrollment was over 30,000. The institute publishes several periodicals, all in Russian: *Izvestiia vysshikh uchebnykh zavedenii* MV *i* SSO SSSR, *Radioelektronika*, and *Vestnik Kievskogo politekhnicheskogo instituta*.

L. Onyshkevych

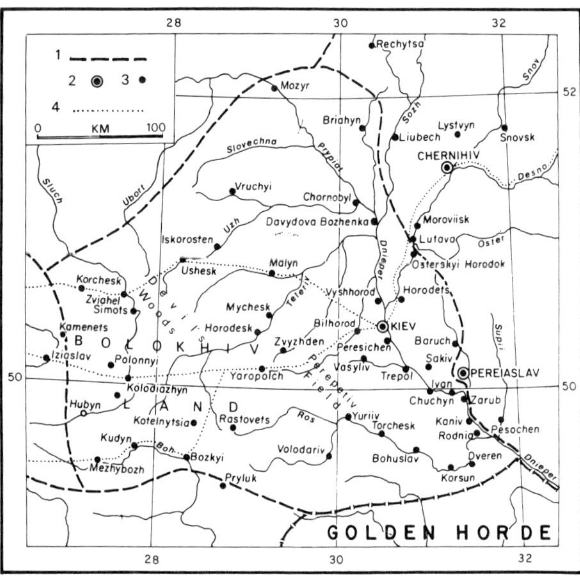

KIEV PRINCIPALITY, CA 1240

1. Borders
2. Capitals
3. Other towns
4. Trade routes

Kiev principality. The central principality in Kievan Rus'. It was formed in the mid-9th century and existed as an independent entity until the mid-12th century, when it became an appanage principality. Its basic territory consisted of the area of Right-Bank Ukraine inhabited by the *Polianians and *Derevlianians. The Prypiat River usually formed the northern boundary, the Dnieper River the eastern, and the Sluch and Horyn rivers the western. The southern boundary was the most dynamic; at times it was as far south as the southern Boh and Ros rivers, while at other times (end of the 11th century) it stopped at the Stuhna River. Kiev, the capital of the principality, lay on the crossroads of the trade routes from north to south and east to west that joined Asia to Europe. This favorable location fostered the development of trade and the prosperity of the principality. The oldest cities were Kiev, Vyshhorod, Ovruch, and Bilhorod.

Kiev principality in the 10th–12th centuries was the political center of *Kievan Rus'. At first, the senior member of the *Riurykide dynasty inhabited its throne with the title *grand prince. Beginning in the mid-11th century, however, a combination of factors initiated a long period of decline. The *Cumans, who settled on the steppes south of Kiev at this time, disrupted the flow of trade to the south and east and began a series of devastating attacks on Kiev that lasted for over a century and a half. Moreover, the shift in international economic patterns, which accompanied the decline of Constantinople and the Byzantine Empire, saw new trade routes opened that bypassed Kiev entirely. Finally, the long period of internecine war for control over Kiev between the various branches of the Riurykide dynasty who had established themselves in the other principalities of Rus' destroyed the political stability in Kiev and precipitated further economic decline. Kiev principality lost its leading position and the political center of Kievan Rus' moved west to the Principality of *Galicia-Volhynia. The Mongol invasion in 1240 caused enormous destruction throughout Kiev principality, but it continued to exist. In 1362 it fell under the rule of Lithuania and became an appanage principality in the *Lithuanian-Ruthenian state, ruled by princes of the *Gediminas family. In 1394 Lithuania abolished the principality and transformed it into a vicegerency. In 1440, Kiev principality was restored, but in 1471 it was finally transformed into *Kiev voivodeship.

At first, Kiev principality was ruled by the direct descendants of the Riurykide dynasty: Oleh (882–912), Ihor (912–45), Olha (945–62), Sviatoslav I (962–72), Yaropolk I Sviatoslavych (972–80), and Volodymyr I the Great (980–1015). Volodymyr's death began the struggle between the various brothers and cousins that characterized the rest of the history of the principality. Although Yaroslav the Wise's reign as the undisputed prince of Kiev (1036–54) briefly stopped these conflicts, his plan to divide political power between his sons and to re-establish the rotational system of rule, where the senior heir of the entire dynasty would rule in Kiev, greatly fostered political instability. The *Liubech Congress in 1097 formally recognized the independent patrimonies of the branches of the family, specifying, however, that each would recognize the primacy of Kiev. Unfortunately, this proved to be unenforceable, and the struggle for control over Kiev continued. Without a secure ruling family of its own, Kiev's throne changed hands numerous times and the principality declined both economically and politically.

Under Volodymyr Monomakh (1113–25) some stability in Kiev was re-established, but after his death the *Romanovychi of Galicia-Volhynia, the *Olhovychi of Chernihiv, the Vsevolodovychi in Rostov-Suzdal, and others resumed their destructive wars for control of Kiev. The city was sacked numerous times by the competing armies, and a succession of princes held sway in the principality, often intermittently: Vsevolod III Olhovych (1139–46), Ihor Olhovych (1146–7), Iziaslav II Mstyslavych (1146–54), Viacheslav Volodymyrovych (co-ruler with Iziaslav), Yurii Dolgorukii (1154–7), Iziaslav Davydovych (1157–62), Rostyslav Mstyslavych (1159–67), Mstyslav II Iziaslavych (1167–9), Hlib Yuriievych (1169–71), Roman Rostyslavych (1172–6), Sviatoslavych III Vsevolodovych (1176–94), Riuryk Rostyslavych (1194–1202), Roman Mstyslavych (1202–6), Vsevolod Sviatoslav Chermny (1206, 1210–12), and Mykhail Vsevolodovych (1238–9, 1241–6). (For bibliography, see *Kievan Rus'.)

A. Zhukovsky

Kiev Psalter. A monument of Old Ukrainian script and illumination. The work was commissioned by Bishop

Mykhail and composed in 1397 by the Kiev archdeacon Spyrydonii. Consisting of 228 large parchment sheets, its 293 rich miniatures belong to the highest achievements of 14th-century Ukrainian art and continue the artistic tradition of Kievan Rus'. The psalter, preserved in the Saltykov-Shchedrin Library in Leningrad, was reproduced photomechanically and published in Moscow in 1978.

Kiev Puppet Theater (Kyivskyi derzhavnyi teatr lialok). Founded in 1927 as a branch of the Kiev Young Spectator's Theater, it was turned into an independent theater in 1929. Its repertoire has included A. Shyian's *Ivasyk-Telesyk*, H. Usachov's *Kotyhoroshok* (Pea-roller), Yu. Chepovetsky's *Mysheniatko Mytsyk* (Mytsyk the Mouse) and *Dobryi Khorton* (The Good Khorton), B. Chaly's *Barvinok za synim morem* (The Periwinkle beyond the Blue Sea), S. Mikhalkov's *Tri porosenka i seryi volk* (The Three Little Pigs and the Gray Wolf, in Russian), V. Lopukhin's and V. Novatsky's *Pryhody dopytlyvoho charivnyka* (The Adventures of the Inquisitive Wizard, an adaptation of K. Čapek's story), D. Kardash's *Pryhody bilcheniatka Mishi* (The Adventures of the Little Squirrel Misha), V. Azov's and V. Tykhvynsky's *Lial'ka spadkoiemtsia Tutti* (The Doll of Crown Prince Tutti, an adaptation of Yu. Olesha's story), and *Mavgli* (based on R. Kipling's story in *The Jungle Book*). The repertoire for adults has included *Yosyp Shveik proty Frants Iosyfa* (Joseph Schweik against Francis Joseph, an adaptation of J. Hašek's *The Good Soldier Schweik*) and V. Maiakovsky's *Klop* (The Bedbug). In 1972 and 1976 the theater toured Poland. Since 1978 S. Yefremov has been its stage director.

Kiev regiment. Administrative-territorial and military unit in central Ukraine, created in 1648. At first its territory was mostly in Left-Bank Ukraine. In 1649 the regiment consisted of 17 companies (with 1,790 registered Cossacks), 4 of which were centered in the capital city of Kiev; the others were Bilohorodka, Vorsivka, Hostomel, Vasylkiv, Brovary, Makariv, Motovylivka, Obukhiv, Khodosivka, Trypillia, Ovruch, Perevarka, and Yasnohorodka. The first colonels were M. Krychevsky (1649) and A. Zhdanovych (1649–53). By 1654 it had acquired additional territory on the left bank and comprised 22 companies. When the right-bank territories were given to Poland under the terms of the Treaty of *Andrusovo (1667), parts of the Pereiaslav and Nizhen regiments were attached to the remaining left-bank territories. From 1687 to 1744 the regiment consisted of 8 companies: Kiev, Oster, Hoholiv, Kozelets, Bobrovytsia, Nosivka, Kobyzhcha, and Morozovsk. From the beginning of the 18th century its capital was Kozelets. In 1721 it had 6,910 male inhabitants, including 2,626 Cossacks. By 1764 it contained 3 cities, 14 towns, and 448 villages and farmsteads with a male population of 79,000, including 23,800 Cossacks. Kiev regiment took part in the Russian-Turkish wars of the 18th century. When it was abolished in 1781, its territory was incorporated into Kiev vicegerency and its Cossacks were reorganized into a carabineer regiment. Among the colonels who enjoyed longer tenures in the regiment were V. Dvoretsky (1659–60, 1663–8), K. Solonyna (1669–82, 1687–90), K. Mokiievsky (1691–1708), A. Tansky (1712–31), M. Tansky (1734–47), E. Daragan (1751–62), and L. Lukashevych (1779–83). O. Bezborodko, who later became a chancellor of the Russian Empire and a prince, was colonel in 1774–5.

B. Balan, A. Zhukovsky

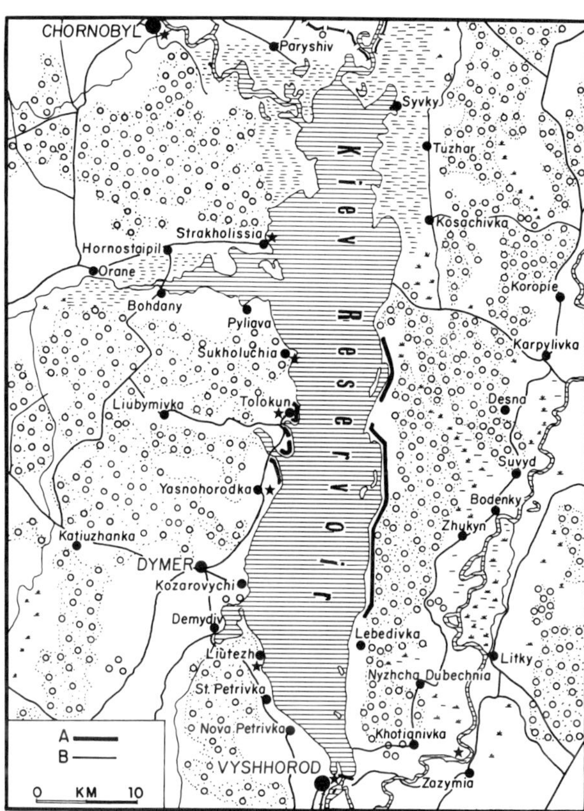

KIEV RESERVOIR

A. Levee B. Roads

Kiev Reservoir. The uppermost reservoir of the *Dnieper Cascade of Hydroelectric Stations. Created north of Kiev in 1960–6 after the dam of the *Kiev Hydroelectric Station was built, it is 110 km long and up to 12 km wide (average width 8.4 km). It has a surface area of 922 sq km, a volume of 3.7 cu km, and a usable volume of 1.2 cu km. Together with the *Kakhivka, *Kaniv, and *Kremenchuk reservoirs, it has facilitated long-term regulation of the Dnieper and created a deep-water route on the river, although it has also contributed to ecological problems (diminished flow velocity reduces water oxygenation, which has a deleterious effect on the balance of aquatic life forms). Its water is used for hydroelectricity generation, industrial and public consumption, and irrigation.

Kiev Russian Drama Theater (Kyivskyi rosiiskyi dramatychnyi teatr im. Lesi Ukrainky). Formed in 1926 out of the Second State Theater of the Ukrainian Soviet Republic, which had been organized in 1919 out of the Solovtsev Theater. In 1966 it was promoted to the status of an academic theater. Of all Kiev theaters it is most favored by the Party. The theater uses the stage to propagate Russian culture. Its repertoire consists of Russian classics and contemporary Soviet plays, including Ukrainian plays such as L. Dmyterko's *Naviky razom* (Together Forever), V. Sobko's *Zhyttia pochynaiet'sia znovu* (Life Begins Again), Yu. Yanovsky's *Dochka prokurora* (The Public Prosecutor's Daughter), O. Korniichuk's *Zahybel' eskadry* (The Destruction of the Squadron) and *Platon Krechet*, Ya. Halan's *Pid zolotym orlom* (Under the Golden Eagle), I. Mykytenko's *Solo na fleiti* (Flute Solo), and Yu. Shcherbak's *Spodivatys'!* (To Hope!). Of Ukrainian classics, Lesia Ukrainka's *Kaminnyi Hospodar* (The Stone Host) was staged in 1939 by K. Khokhlov (sets by A. Petrytsky), and her *U pushchi* (In the Wilderness) was staged in 1958 by M. Romanov. The repertoire contains a modest selection of world drama: W. Shakespeare's *Othello* and *Comedy of Errors*, B. Shaw's *Pygmalion*, and F. Schiller's *Don Carlos*. Quite a few Ukrainians work in the theater: eg, V. Dukler, V. Dobrovolsky, D. Franko, and A. Reshetchenko.

V. Revutsky

Kiev Shevchenko Museum (Kyivskyi muzei T.H. Shevchenka). A museum dedicated to T. Shevchenko administered by the Ministry of Culture of the Ukrainian SSR. Opened on 24 April 1949, it consists of the holdings of the former Central Shevchenko Museum (est 1941) and the Shevchenko collections at the Kharkiv Art Gallery and other museums. Over 4,000 objects are on display in the museum's 24 rooms. Over 800 items are linked directly with Shevchenko's life: his artworks, manuscripts, first editions, photographs, and personal belongings. A third of the 36,000 volumes in the museum library deal with Shevchenko. The museum's associates conduct bibliographic, literary, and art research on Shevchenko and organize conferences and commemorative events.

Kiev Silk Manufacturing Complex (Kyivskyi shovkovyi kombinat). A textile plant in Kiev established in 1946. It has spinning, weaving, drying, and decorating shops and specializes in raw silk, crepe, and chiffon textiles. In 1978 total production equaled 2.3 million sq m.

Kiev Society for the Advancement of Elementary Education (Kyivske tovarystvo spryiannia pochatkovii osviti). Society organized in 1882 by a group of Kiev University professors and local teachers to spread enlightenment among the population of Kiev and vicinity. Until 1902 it was called the Commission of Popular Readings. The society organized public readings (by 1900 over 700 had been held), literary evenings, and musical concerts, particularly by students from M. Lysenko's music school. In 1895 it built the People's Auditorium to house its events. From 1888 the society published 23 popular educational pamphlets with a total pressrun of over 130,000 copies. Many prominent Ukrainian activists and academics belonged to the society, including O. Andriievsky, V. Shcherbyna, and P. Tutkovsky. The society ceased to exist in 1918. In 1913 it published a book summarizing its first 30 years' work.

Kiev Society for the Preservation of Ancient and Artistic Monuments (Kyivske tovarystvo okhorony pamiatok starovyny i mystetstva). An association of historians, archeologists, and art scholars formed for the purpose of finding, preserving, studying, and recording the monuments of Ukrainian antiquity and art in 1910 in Kiev on the initiative of M. Biliashivsky and V. Khvoika. Its members were active in Kiev, Podilia, Volhynia, Chernihiv, Poltava, Katerynoslav, and Hrodna gubernias and Bessarabia province. Such prominent scholars as M. Dovnar-Zapolsky, M. Petrov, V. Ikonnikov, V. Shcherbyna, and V. Zavitnevych belonged to the society. In 1913 a branch was founded in Uman. The society was dissolved in 1919 upon the creation of the All-Ukrainian Committee for the Preservation of Ancient and Artistic Monuments.

Kiev Society of Aerial Navigation (Kyivske tovarystvo povitrianoi plavby). An amateur society for the advancement of flight and aviation, formed in 1909 out of a circle interested in flying at the Kiev Polytechnical Institute. The society was active until 1916, designing and testing flying machines, training pilots, and organizing competitions and exhibits. Its members included I. Sikorsky, P. Nesterov, A. Kudashev, and P. Skoropadsky. Some planes designed by its members were later built successfully.

Kiev Society of Naturalists (Kyivske tovarystvo doslidnykiv pryrody). An organization that promoted the study of natural sciences and the natural resources of Ukraine. It was established in 1869 at Kiev University on the initiative of P. Alekseev, K. Kessler, and A. Kovalevsky. Its first president was the botanist I. Borshchov. The society organized scientific research trips to various parts of Ukraine, the Caucasus, and abroad, and maintained a large library. Two sections of the society were separated from it to form the *Kiev Physics and Mathematics Society (1890) and the *Kiev Physics and Chemistry Society (1910). The society published *Zapiski Kievskogo obshchestva estestvoispytatelei* (Proceedings of the Kiev Society of Naturalists, 1870–1917 in Russian and 1926–8 in Ukrainian as *Zapysky Kyïvs'koho tovarystva pryrodoznavtsiv*), *Sbornik nauchnykh rabot Kievskogo obshchestva estestvoispytatelei* (Collection of Scientific Works of the Kiev Society of Naturalists, 1921–8), bibliographies, and geological maps. Its presidents included K. Feofilaktov (1877–98), S. Navashin, and M. Andrusiv. In 1897 it had 177 members; among the more active ones were the zoologists V. Sovynsky, A. Severtsov, and I. Shmalhauzen; the botanists O. Rohovych and M. Kholodny; the geologists P. Tutkovsky and V. Tarasenko; and the chemists N. Bunge and S. Reformatsky. The society was closed by the authorities in 1932.

Kiev State Art Institute (Kyivskyi derzhavnyi khudozhnii instytut). A higher educational institution under the Ministry of Culture of the Ukrainian SSR. It was formed in 1924 out of the Kiev Institute of Plastic Arts, which in 1922 replaced the Ukrainian State Academy of Arts, and the Kiev Architecture Institute (est 1918). It has five faculties: painting with its studios of easel painting, monumental painting, and set design, and the department of painting technique and restoration; sculpture with its studios of ordinary and monumental sculpture; graphic arts with its studios of printmaking, book graphics, and poster design; architecture with its studios of civic building, urban building, and residential building; and art studios. Since 1922 the faculty has included such artists and scholars as P. Aloshyn, O. Verbytsky, M. Boichuk, V. and F. Krychevsky, V. Kasiian, O. Shovkunenko, S. Hryhoriev, A. Petrytsky, M. Lysenko, H. Svitlytsky, I.

Pleshchynsky, T. Yablonska, Yu. Asieiev, and P. Biletsky. The institute's rector since 1973 has been O. Lopukhov. The institute is housed in the building of the former Kiev Theological Seminary, which was built in 1898 by S. Yermakov.

Kiev Studio of Popular Science Films (Kyivska kinostudiia naukovo-populiarnykh filmiv or Kyivnaukfilm). Motion-picture studio specializing in popular science, educational, technical, and propaganda films. It was organized in 1941 out of the technical films department of the Kiev Film Factory. During the war the studio was located in Tashkent, where it produced propaganda films for the Red Army. In 1966 it moved into a new building complex equipped with filming and sound studios, postproduction facilities, and laboratories. The studio produces over 400 films annually. Over 300 of its films have won prizes at USSR or international film competitions.

Kiev Technological Institute of Light Industry (Kyivskyi tekhnolohichnyi instytut lehkoi promyslovosti). A technical higher educational institution under the jurisdiction of the Ministry of Higher and Specialized Secondary Education of the Ukrainian SSR. Formed in 1930 out of certain departments of several technical institutes, it consists of eight departments, including sewing technology, leather technology, knitting technology, chemical engineering, and mechanical engineering. It has an evening and a correspondence school, a preparatory department, and a graduate program. In 1980 its enrollment was over 8,000.

Kiev Technological Institute of the Food Industry (Kyivskyi tekhnolohichnyi instytut kharchovoi promyslovosti). A technical higher educational institution under the jurisdiction of the Ministry of Higher and Specialized Secondary Education of the Ukrainian SSR. Formed in 1930 out of the department of sugar refining of the Kiev Polytechnical Institute, it consists of eight departments, including food machinery, baking technology, sugar technology, meat processing and dairy technology, and electric power. It has a graduate program and an experimental factory. In 1980 its enrollment was 8,500.

Kiev Theater of Musical Comedy. See Kiev Operetta Theater.

Kiev Theater of Opera and Ballet (Kyivskyi derzhavnyi akademichnyi teatr opery i baletu im. T.H. Shevchenka). The leading musical theater of Ukraine. Founded originally in 1856 as the Kiev City Theater, which in 1867 acquired a resident company and became known as the Kiev Russian Opera, it was nationalized in 1919 under the name of the Opera of the Ukrainian Soviet Republic, and in 1926 was Ukrainized and renamed the Kiev Ukrainian Opera. It acquired its present name in 1934. Thanks to its qualified staff and unusually talented performers, the theater has mounted many highly successful productions of classical and new Ukrainian operas. Its current opera repertoire includes M. Lysenko's *Natalka from Poltava*, *Christmas Night*, *Taras Bulba*, and *Aeneid*; S. Hulak-Artemovsky's *Zaporozhian Cossack beyond the Danube*; M. Arkas's *Kateryna*; B. Yanovsky's *Black Sea Duma*; V. Kostenko's *Karmeliuk*; B. Liatoshynsky's *Shchors* and *The Golden Ring*; M. Verykivsky's *Naimychka* (The Servant Girl); Yu.

Kiev Theater of Opera and Ballet

Meitus's *The Young Guard*; K. Dankevych's *Bohdan Khmelnytsky*; and H. Maiboroda's *Mylana*. The ballet repertoire includes M. Skorulsky's *The Forest Song*, K. Dankevych's *Lily*, M. Verykivsky's *The Nobleman Kanovsky*, H. Zhukovsky's *Rostyslava*, and A. Sviechnykov's *Marusia Bohuslavka*. Among the conductors who worked at the theater in the Soviet period were A. Margulian, V. Yorysh, V. Piradov, V. Dranishnikov, A. Rudnytsky, A. Pazovsky, B. Chystiakov, and O. Klymov. The choreographers were V. Lytvynenko, V. Verkhovynets, L. Zhukov, P. Virsky, and V. Vronsky. The stage directors included such names as V. Manzii, M. Smolych, M. Stefanovych, and V. Skliarenko; the stage designers, S. Evenbakh, O. Khvostenko-Khvostov, I. Kurochka-Armashevsky, A. Petrytsky, and F. Nirod. In the last few decades many outstanding singers have appeared at the Kiev theater: eg, M. Lytvynenko-Volhemut, O. Petrusenko, Z. Haidai, N. Zakharchenko, Ye. Chavdar, M. Skybytska, O. Ropska, L. Rudenko, Yu. Kyporenko-Domansky, V. Didkovsky, O. Kolodub, V. Kozeratsky, P. Bilynnyk, M. Zubarev, M. Hryshko, A. Ivanov, M. Donets, I. Patorzhynsky, M. Romensky, M. Chastii, and B. Hmyria. Russian and Western European guest soloists also appear on its stage.

In the early 1980s the company included such opera singers as Ye. Miroshnychenko, Ye. Kolesnyk, Z. Khrystych, H. Tsypola, K. Radchenko, M. Stefiuk, H. Tuftina, A. Solovianenko, V. Tretiak, V. Tymokhin, D. Hnatiuk, A. Mokrenko, and A. Kocherha, and such ballet soloists as V. Kovtun, V. Kalynovska, O. Potapova, A. Havrylenko, L. Smorhachova, and A. Lahoda. Its conductors were O. Riabov, I. Hamalko, A. Vlasenko, and R. Dorozhyvsky, and its choreographers were R. Kliavin and A. Shykero. The head conductor is S. Turchak, the head stage director D. Smolych, and the chief stage designer F. Nirod.

BIBLIOGRAPHY
Stefanovych, M. *Kyïvs'kyi derzhavnyi ordena Lenina akademichnyi teatr opery ta baletu URSR im. T.H. Shevchenka: Istorychnyi narys* (Kiev 1968)
Stanishevs'kyi, Iu. *Ukraïns'kyi radians'kyi muzychnyi teatr (1917–1947): Narysy istoriï* (Kiev 1970)

V. Revutsky

Kiev Theological Academy (Kyivska Dukhovna Akademiia). A higher theological school founded in 1819 at the Kiev Epiphany Brotherhood Monastery as the suc-

Kiev Theological Academy

cessor to the *Kievan Mohyla Academy. The academy developed religious scholarship, trained teachers for theological seminaries, and supervised eight seminaries. It was an important instrument in the Russification of the Orthodox church and rite in Ukraine. At first, it was organized according to the religious education statutes of 1808. It was headed by a rector (from 1874 the rectors were granted the title of bishop and made vicars of Kiev eparchy) and professors' council, and was supervised by the Commission of Theological Schools (to 1839) and then by the Holy Synod. In 1869 the rights of the professors' council were broadened and the qualifications for professors were raised. The new educational statutes of 1884 abolished secret elections to the professors' council and transferred supervision over the academy to the Kievan metropolitan. The provisional regulations of 1906 withdrew this supervision and returned the power to grant academic degrees to the professors' council (for some time this had been the prerogative of the Holy Synod).

The course of study lasted four years. From 1869 it covered three fields: theology, church history, and church rite. The students were graduates of theological seminaries, most of them sons of priests. Their number averaged approx 200 (in 1897 there were 175, and in 1913, 199). Students lived in a residence attached to the academy. Upon graduation many went on to work in the bureaucracy or in private careers. In 1913 there were 39 professors at the academy. Among the more distinguished faculty members were I. Borisov (rector 1830–6), M. Bulgakov, I. Malyshevsky, P. Ternovsky, Volodymyr Zavitnevych, M. Petrov, S. Golubev, F. Titov, O. Novytsky, P. Yurkevych, and P. Linytsky. Many important Ukrainian scholars and church and civic leaders graduated from the academy; eg, I. Nechui-Levytsky, P. Kozytsky, O. Koshyts, K. Voblyi, and P. Sikorsky. As a student there in the 1890s O. Lototsky organized an underground Ukrainian group that fostered the development of Ukrainian national consciousness among the students.

From 1837 the academy published the popular weekly journal *Voskresnoe Chtenie* and from 1860 the scholarly monthly **Trudy Kievskoi Dukhovnoi Akademii*. The academy's invaluable library, begun by P. Mohyla, had large collections of manuscripts, old documents, and early printed books; it is now part of the AN URSR Central Scientific Library. In 1872 the *Church-Archeological Society and an associated museum were established at the academy. The museum's long-time director was M. Petrov. Documents from the history of the academy were published in 10 volumes by M. Petrov (1904–8) and F. Titov (1910–15). Throughout its existence the Kiev Theological Academy was the only Orthodox higher school of theology in Ukraine. It was abolished by the Soviet authorities in 1920.

BIBLIOGRAPHY

Malyshevskii, I. *Istoricheskaia zapiska o sostoianii Akademii v minuvshee piatidesiatiletie* (Kiev 1869)
Piatydesiatiletnyi Iubilei Kievskoi Dukhovnoi Akademii (Kiev 1869)
Titov, Kh. *Stara vyshcha osvita v Kyïvs'kii Ukraïni kintsia XVI-pochatku XIX st.* (Kiev 1924)

I. Korovytsky, A. Zhukovsky

Kiev Trade and Economics Institute (Kyivskyi torhovelno-ekonomichnyi instytut). A higher educational institution under the Ministry of Trade of the Ukrainian SSR, formed in 1966 out of the Kiev branch of the Donetske Institute of Soviet Commerce. It has two faculties – economics and commerce – as well as a correspondence school, with branches in Vinnytsia and Chernivtsi, and a graduate program. In 1978–9 its total enrollment was close to 10,000. The institute publishes two collections: *Ekonomika torhivli* and *Suchasni pytannia tovaroznavstva*.

Kiev Ukrainian Drama Theater (1898)

Kiev Ukrainian Drama Theater (Kyivskyi derzhavnyi ordena Lenina akademichnyi ukrainskyi dramatychnyi teatr im. I. Franka). One of the leading drama theaters in Ukraine. It arose in January 1920 in Vinnytsia out of the union of the New Lviv Theater with a Molodyi Teatr group led by H. Yura. After touring Ukraine (Cherkasy, Kamianets-Podilskyi, and the Donets Basin) for three years, it performed in Kharkiv until 1926, then moved to Kiev. In this early period, it usually repeated plays from the *Molodyi Teatr repertoire. Although the company experimented with symbolism and expressionism, it adhered, generally, to realism, and in the early 1930s without much resistance adopted socialist realism. Hence it was spared political persecution, and after the suppression of the *Berezil theater, enjoyed official favor and attained the status of a national theater representing Ukraine. In the 1920s its Ukrainian repertoire included not only I. Karpenko-Kary's and M. Starytsky's but also V. Vynnychenko's plays, and some of M. Kulish's work: eg, *97*, *Komuna v stepakh* (Commune in the Steppes), and *Myna Mazailo*. One of its most successful productions of a drama classic was that of W. Shakespeare's *A Midsummer Night's Dream*. The theater produced over 20 modern plays by famous playwrights ranging from H. Ibsen to B. Shaw. One of the best productions among them was that of an adaptation of J. Hašek's *The Good Soldier Schweik*. In the 1929–41 period its repertoire consisted mostly of socialist-realist plays such as I. Mykytenko's *Dyktatura* (Dictatorship), *Kadry* (Cadres), *Divchata nashoï krainy* (Girls of Our Country), and *Solo na fleiti* (Flute Solo); O. Korniichuk's *Zahybel' eskadry* (The Destruction of the Squadron), *Platon Krechet*, *Pravda* (Truth), *Bohdan Khmel'nyts'kyi*, and *V stepakh Ukraïny* (In the Steppes of Ukraine); L. Pervomaisky's *Nevidomi soldaty* (Unknown Soldiers) and *Mistechko Ladeniu* (The Town of Ladeniu); I. Kocherha's *Maistry chasu* (Masters of Time); V. Sukhodolsky's *Ustym Karmeliuk*; and M. Irchan's *Pliatsdarm* (The Battle Zone). The number of Ukrainian and Russian classics and of contemporary Russian dramas in its repertoire increased. Of the world classics only F. Schiller's *Don Carlos* and W. Shakespeare's *Much Ado about Nothing* were staged. During the war the company was evacuated to Semipalatinsk, Kazakhstan, where it played for military and collective-farm audiences. In 1944 it returned to Kiev and continued its standard repertoire. It staged 10 plays by O. Korniichuk as well as plays by Ya. Bash and V. Mynko. Since 1956 the most often produced plays have been M. Zarudny's *Veselka* (The Rainbow), *Maryna* (an adaptation of T. Shevchenko's poem), *Na s'omomu nebi* (In Seventh Heaven), and *Za Sybirom sontse skhodyt'* (The Sun Rises beyond Siberia) and O. Kolomiiets's *Faraony* (The Pharaohs), *Planeta Speranta* (The Planet Speranta), *Dykyi Anhel* (The Wild Angel), and *Kamin' rusyna* (A Ruthenian's Stone). The most important plays in the company's repertoire are I. Kocherha's *Iaroslav Mudryi* (Yaroslav the Wise) and *Svichchyne vesillia* (Svichka's Wedding), Ya. Bash's *Profesor Buiko* (Professor Buiko), V. Sobko's *Za druhym frontom* (Beyond the Second Front), Yu. Yanovsky's *Duma pro Brytanku* (Duma about Brytanka), L. Dmyterko's *Divocha dolia* (Girls' Fate), V. Mynko's *Ne nazyvaiuchy prizvyshch* (Without Naming Names), S. Holovanivsky's *Istyna dorozhche* (Truth Is Dearer), and M. Rudenko's *Na dni mors'komu* (On the Sea Bed). Its repertoire includes Ukrainian classics such as Lesia Ukrainka's *U pushchi* (In the Wilderness) and *Kasandra* (Cassandra), and world classics such as Sophocles' *Antigone* and W. Shakespeare's *King Lear* and *Macbeth*. The Kiev company has produced contemporary plays such as J. Priestley's *They Came to a City*, J. Gow and A. d'Usseau's *Deep Are the Roots*, and F. Dürrenmatt's *Der Besuch der alten Dame*. It toured Poland in 1950.

The theater's artistic director was H. *Yura (1920–54). Its stage directors have been B. Glagolin, K. Koshevsky, B. Nord, M. Krushelnytsky (1954–61), V. Ohloblyn, V. Lyzohub, and S. Danchenko (from 1978). The sets have been designed by F. Nirod, A. Petrytsky, V. Meller, B. Erdman, M. Drak, M. Umansky, H. Tsapok, and D. Lider. Among its music directors have been H. and P. Maiboroda, I. Shamo, and N. Pruslin. Its distinguished actors have included A. Buchma, Yu. Shumsky, T. Yura, O. Yursky, D. Miliutenko, V. Dobrovolsky, O. Vatulia, O. Rubchak, T. Barvinska, N. Uzhvii, O. Kusenko, A. Hashynsky, Ye. Ponomarenko, V. Dalsky, N. Koperzhynska, S. Oleksenko, and B. Stupka. The theater building was designed by G. Shleifer and E. Bratman and completed in 1898. A third story was added by V. Kolchynsky in 1959–60. Today the theater seats 1,100 people.

BIBLIOGRAPHY
Ryl's'kyi, M. (ed). *Ukraïns'kyi dramatychnyi teatr*, vol 2 (Kiev 1959)
Boboshko, Iu. *Kyïvs'kyi derzhavnyi ordena Lenina akademichnyi ukraïns'kyi teatr im. Ivana Franka* (Kiev 1970)

V. Revutsky

Kiev University

Kiev University (Kyivskyi derzhavnyi universytet im. T.H. Shevchenka). Higher educational institution under the jurisdiction of the Ministry of Higher and Specialized Secondary Education of the Ukrainian SSR, and one of the oldest and most important scholarly and cultural centers in Ukraine.

Opened in 1834, it was the second university (after Kharkiv) to be established in Russian-ruled Ukraine. Several requests from the local nobility for a university in Kiev, dating back to 1765, were turned down by the imperial government, which until 1831 accepted the dominance of Polish culture in Right-Bank Ukraine and in 1803 even had established a Polish school system under the supervision of Vilnius University. The Polish Rebellion of 1830–1 convinced Nicholas I that the Right Bank had to be Russified, and to accomplish this the existing school system had to be replaced with a Russian one supervised from Kiev. Thus, Kiev University was established to oversee the new educational system. It inherited the library, collections, and faculty of the *Kremianets Lyceum, a higher Polish school that was abolished as a result of the rebellion. The university was named after St Vladimir and consisted, initially, of only one faculty – the philosophy faculty – which was subdivided into two departments – history and philology, and physics and mathematics. The following year the law faculty was added. The four-year program was designed to give a general, not a specialized, education. The university's autonomy was restricted: professors and faculty deans elected by the Professorial Council had to be approved by the minister of education, the elected rector had to be approved by the tsar, and the appointed curator of the school district kept a close watch over university affairs. Through a special school committee the university supervised all the schools in its school district until 1835. The first rector was a Ukrainian scholar, M. *Maksymovych, but most of the professors were Poles. Of the 62 original students, 34 were Catholics, mostly

Poles and some Uniates. Until the 1860s Poles from the Right Bank formed a majority of the student body, followed by Ukrainians from the Left Bank.

Although the university was intended to be an instrument of Russification, it became a center of revolutionary activity and national awakening. In 1838 a clandestine student society, a branch of the Union of the Polish People, was uncovered in Kiev. Many professors and students were expelled and the university was closed for half a year. New faculty were recruited among the German graduates of Dorpat University and the reduced student body was placed under stricter surveillance. In 1841 a medical faculty, formed out of the abolished Vilnius Medico-Surgical Academy, was added. In the following year enrollment rose to its 1838 level (ca 260). At the end of 1845 M. *Kostomarov, the professor of Russian history at Kiev University, founded the clandestine *Cyril and Methodius Brotherhood. The Russian government reacted to the revolutionary unrest in Central and Western Europe in 1848 by imposing new restrictions on the university: the rector and deans were appointed by the minister of education and approved by the tsar; lectures had to conform to a prescribed program and were monitored by the rector; the philosophy faculty was abolished; foreign scholars were denied teaching positions and Russian scholars were barred from studying abroad; and the enrollment of self-supporting students (excluding medical students) was restricted to 300. Student fees were doubled, while faculty salaries were cut. These measures had a disastrous effect on the quality of research and teaching at the university. Many chairs remained vacant, and many professors turned to outside work to supplement their income. The situation began to improve only at the end of the 1850s when the new tsar assumed a more liberal policy.

As restrictions on the freedom of association were lifted, students and faculty became involved in social issues. In 1859 a group of Kiev students, including M. *Drahomanov, organized *Sunday schools for workers and peasants, in which Ukrainian was used for the first time as the language of instruction. Two years later a number of students with a populist outlook, including V. *Antonovych, joined the group and formed the first clandestine *hromada of Kiev. The university reform of 1863 was intended to avoid the kind of student unrest that broke out in 1861. Universities were granted greater control of their curricula, research, and administration. Rectors, deans, and professors were again elected by the professorial councils. For the first time Kiev University was included under the general statute governing universities. In the next two decades the university expanded slowly but steadily. New chairs were established and the faculty expanded from 49 in 1863 to 66 in 1884. The number of works published by faculty members increased dramatically. The school's official monthly *Universitetskie izvestiia* began to appear (1861–1919). In spite of its social liberalism, the new regime disapproved of the fledgling Ukrainian movement: in 1862 the Sunday schools were suppressed and in the following year the student hromada was disbanded. The Polish insurrection of 1863–4 led to the expulsion of many Polish students from the university. Increasing political activity among university students aroused grave concern in government circles. New repressions against Ukrainians in the mid-1870s included M. Drahomanov's dismissal from his teaching position.

Following the assassination of Tsar Alexander II, a new statute adopted in 1884 sharply reduced the autonomy of universities. The minister of education assumed the right to appoint rectors, deans, and professors. State funds for universities were reduced, while student fees were raised. Student organizations and meetings were banned. In Kiev the new law provoked demonstrations, which led to the closing of the university for half a year. The general student strike in 1899 was supported by Kiev students. In 1900, 183 students of Kiev University were conscripted into the army as punishment for their participation in demonstrations. By 1905 the authorities realized that the 1884 university statute had to be replaced by a more liberal one. A number of drafts were prepared by successive education ministers, but none were signed into law. Although enrollment jumped from 2,313 in 1895 to 5,107 in 1910, the faculty grew only from 118 (in 1894) to 166 (in 1913) and the number of chairs did not change. Part of the faculty, particularly T. *Florinsky, was hostile to the Ukrainian movement. During the Revolution of 1905 Ukrainian students demanded four chairs with Ukrainian as the language of instruction, and a year later the university itself requested two such chairs, but nothing came of these efforts. In 1907 A. *Loboda and V. *Peretts decided to give their lectures in Ukrainian, but were forbidden to continue. It was only in September 1917 that limited use of Ukrainian at Kiev University was permitted. The Provisional Government approved its use as the language of instruction by four new chairs in Ukrainian studies: the chairs of literature, language, history, and the history of Western Ruthenian law. Under the changing regimes in 1917–20, the normal activities of the university were hampered by political interference and inadequate funding. According to Hetman P. Skoropadsky's Ukrainization policy, Kiev (or St Vladimir's) University was preserved as a Russian institution and a separate Ukrainian State University was established. In 1919 the Bolshevik authorities merged a number of institutes, higher schools for women, and the new Ukrainian university with the old university, which they renamed Kiev State University.

By the 20th century, Kiev University had established itself as one of the leading universities within the Russian Empire. It ran over 50 auxiliary facilities: 2 libraries, an astronomical and meteorological observatory, a botanical garden, various laboratories, cabinets, and 9 clinics. Its faculty included many prominent scholars, such as the historians M. Kostomarov, M. Drahomanov, V. Antonovych, M. Dovnar-Zapolsky, and I. Luchytsky; the literary scholar M. Dashkevych; the philologist V. Peretts; the jurist O. Kistiakovsky; the economist N. Bunge; the chemist S. Reformatsky; the physicists M. Avenarius and Y. Kosonohov; the mathematicians B. Bukreev and D. Grave; the zoologists A. Kovalevsky and A. Severtsov; the biologist S. Navashin; the anatomist V. Bets; and the pathologists G. Minkh and V. Pidvysotsky. Some of these professors were graduates of Kiev University. A number of learned societies were affiliated with the university: the Kiev Society of Naturalists (est 1869), the Historical Society of Nestor the Chronicler (est 1873), the Kiev Juridical Society (est 1877), the Kiev Midwifery and Gynecology Society (est 1885), the Kiev Physics and

Mathematics Society (est 1890), the Kiev Physico-Medical Society (est 1896), and the Kiev Physics and Chemistry Society (est 1910).

In 1920 the Soviet regime began a radical restructuring of Ukraine's educational system. The universities were replaced by institutes of people's education and Kiev University was reorganized into the *Kiev Institute of People's Education and the Kiev Institute of Health Care (later the Kiev Medical Institute). These institutes were Ukrainized rapidly. In 1933 Kiev University was restored by merging the Kiev Institute of Professional Education and the Kiev Physical-Chemical-Mathematical Institute. The university consisted of six faculties: physics and mathematics, chemistry, biology, geology and geography, history, and literature and language. In 1937 two new faculties were opened: law and Western languages and literatures. The university was named after T. Shevchenko in 1939. In the following year the physics and mathematics faculty was split into the mechanics and mathematics, and the physics faculties. Enrollment rose rapidly in the 1930s from 1,650 (1933) to 3,700 (1939). In spite of increasing funding and improved facilities, academic achievement was low because of countless political meetings, frequent revisions of the curriculum, and widespread purges. During the Second World War the university was evacuated to Kzyl-Orda in Kazakhstan, where it was amalgamated with Kharkiv University to form the Unified Ukrainian University (1941–3). When it was reopened in Kiev in 1945, the university consisted of 13 faculties and had an enrollment of 2,560. A strong emphasis was placed on making the university more responsive to the demands of industrial development.

Today Kiev University is the most prestigious higher educational institution in Ukraine. In 1979–80 the enrollment reached 21,000 and the faculty numbered 1,695. In 1982 it encompassed 16 faculties – philosophy, economics, history, (Slavic) philology, Romance-Germanic philology, journalism, law, international relations and law, mechanics and mathematics, cybernetics, physics, radio-physics, geology, geography, chemistry, and biology – as well as a graduate school, an evening school, and correspondence courses. It has published the journals *Naukovi zapysky* (1935–49) and *Visnyk Kyïvs'koho universytetu* (in seven series since 1957) and the newspaper *Za radians'ki kadry*.

During the Soviet period the faculty of Kiev University included many noted scholars, such as the linguists L. Bulakhovsky, M. Hrunsky, and P. Pliushch; the literary scholar O. Biletsky; the pedagogue M. Hryshchenko; the psychologist H. Kostiuk; the economist K. Vobly; the biologists D. Protsenko, D. Zerov, and O. Markevych; the physicists V. Lashkarov and S. Vsekhsviatsky; the geologists B. Chernyshov and V. Luchytsky; and the mathematician V. Hlushkov.

The main building of the university complex was built in 1837–42 by V. Beretti. Along with other buildings, it was heavily damaged during the Second World War, and was restored afterwards. In 1954 construction began on a new complex of buildings designed by V. Ladny, V. Kolomiiets, and V. Drizo.

BIBLIOGRAPHY
Vladimirskii-Budanov, M. *Istoriia Imperatorskogo universiteta sv. Vladimira* (Kiev 1884)
Zhmuds'kyi, O. (ed). *Istoriia Kyïvs'koho universytetu* (Kiev 1959)
Kyïvs'kyi universytet za 50 rokiv radians'koï vlady (Kiev 1967)
Belyi, M., et al (eds). *Kievskii universitet. Dokumenty i materialy, 1834–1984* (Kiev 1984)

B. Struminsky, T. Zakydalsky

Kiev Uprising of 1068–9. A popular uprising that took place in Kiev after the defeat of the forces of Grand Prince *Iziaslav Yaroslavych of Kiev and his brothers Sviatoslav of Chernihiv and Vsevolod of Pereiaslav by the *Cumans at the Alta River in September 1068. When Kiev's commoners asked Iziaslav to give them horses and arms to repel the Cumans, he refused, fearing the consequences of arming the population. The incensed populace turned against Kiev's patricians, freed the inmates of Kiev's prisons, including Prince Vseslav Briacheslavych of Polatsk, whom Iziaslav had imprisoned in 1067, and elected Vseslav as their ruler. Iziaslav's palace was plundered and he was forced to flee to Poland. In April 1069 he returned with the forces of his nephew Prince Bolesław II the Bold of Cracow. Vseslav fled to Polatsk, and Iziaslav and his son Mstyslav brutally suppressed their opponents.

Kiev Uprising of 1113. An uprising of the commoners of Kiev, and possibly of the rural populace of the Kiev region, which erupted upon the death of *Sviatopolk II Iziaslavych as a response to the corruption and injustices of his rule. The insurgents attacked and plundered Sviatopolk's officials and the local merchants and usurers, many of them Jews. Afraid that the unrest would grow and that the monasteries and they themselves would be the next victims, the intimidated boyars of Kiev offered the throne to the popular Prince *Volodymyr Monomakh of Pereiaslav, who quelled the uprising by granting legal concessions to the people (see *Volodymyr Monomakh's Statute).

Kiev voivodeship. Administrative-territorial unit in central Ukraine under the Lithuanian Grand Duchy (1471–1569) and then the Polish Kingdom (1569–1793). It was established after the abolition of *Kiev principality. The first voivode was M. Gasztołd, a Polonized Lithuanian magnate. Although a charter issued in 1507 assured local nobles the right to occupy administrative posts, in reality most of these posts were taken by Lithuanians. Under the terms of the Union of *Lublin (1569), the voivodeship was transferred to the Polish Kingdom. It was divided into *counties (Kiev, Zhytomyr, and Ovruch) and *starostvos (Bila Tserkva, Kaniv, Korsun, Romanivka, Cherkasy, and Chyhyryn). Part of Left-Bank Ukraine was also included in the voivodeship.

In the late 16th and 17th centuries, Kiev voivodeship was the scene of the social-national uprisings led by K. Kosynsky, S. Nalyvaiko, H. Loboda, I. Sulyma, D. Hunia, and Ya. Ostrianyn, and the major area of conflict in the *Cossack-Polish War, when the voivode was A. *Kysil. According to the Treaty of *Zboriv (1649), the Cossacks under B. Khmelnytsky acquired the voivodeship, which was divided among 12 *regiments, although Polish rule in the Right-Bank was restored in 1660. Under the terms of the Treaty of *Andrusovo (1667), the territory on the Left-Bank and the city of Kiev were acquired by the Muscovite-dominated Hetman state, and the capital of the restored voivodeship under Poland became Zhytomyr.

Peasant unrest continued in the 17th and 18th centuries; eg, the *Haidamaka uprisings and the *Palii and *Koliivshchyna rebellions. In 1793 Kiev voivodeship passed entirely under Russian rule and was divided between Kiev and Volhynia vicegerencies.

A. Zhukovsky

Kiev Young Spectator's Theater (Kyivskyi teatr yunoho hliadacha im. Leninskoho komsomolu). A leading theater for children and young people in Ukraine, founded in October 1924 as the Franko State Theater for Children. Its repertoire, consisting of folk tales, stage games, and adventure plays, is adapted to youth of different age groups. Beginning in 1928, besides European plays such as M. Maeterlinck's *L'Oiseau bleu* and J. Molière's *Les fourberies de Scapin*, Soviet plays such as O. Korniichuk's *Na hrani* (At the Limit), *Fioletova shchuka* (The Violet Pike), and *Shturm* (The Assault), Ya. Mamontov's *Kho*, and Yu. Mokriiev's *Reid* (Raid) and *Skrypka hutsula* (The Hutsul's Violin) were produced. In 1947 the theater was turned into a republican theater, and an emphasis was placed on war and political plays, mostly by Russian playwrights. The Ukrainian plays in its repertoire included I. Mykytenko's *Dvi iunosty* (Twice Youth), I. Kocherha's *Chornyi val's* (The Black Waltz), and P. Voronko's *Kazka pro Chuhaistra* (A Story about Chuhaister). Classical Ukrainian plays such as Lesia Ukrainka's *Lisova pisnia* (The Forest Song), I. Karpenko-Kary's *Sto tysiach* (One Hundred Thousand) and *Beztalanna* (The Hapless Girl), or dramatic adaptations of I. Franko's *Koval' Basim* (Basim the Blacksmith) and *Abukasymovi kaptsi* (Abu Kasim's Slippers) were rarely produced. In the 1970s and early 1980s the theater's repertoire included contemporary Ukrainian dramas such as O. Kolomiiets's *Planeta Speranta* (Planet Speranta) and *Sribna pavutyna* (The Silver Cobweb), and an adaptation of O. Honchar's *Bryhantyna* (The Brigantine); Russian classics by D. Fonvizin, A. Tolstoi, and M. Lermontov; and plays by M. Bulgakov and current Russian dramatists. O. Solomarsky (1924–31 and 1953–61), I. Deieva, and V. Nelli (1925–34), K. Koshevsky (1939–41), V. Dovbyshchenko (1947–52), and M. Merzlykin (from 1978) have directed the theater's productions. The theater is used to some extent as an instrument of Russification.

V. Revutsky

Kievan Cave Fortress (Kyievo-Pecherska fortetsia). A series of defensive fortifications surrounding the *Kievan Cave Monastery. The monastery was first fortified at the end of the 12th century, when a 2-m-wide, 5–6-m-high stone wall was erected. This wall was destroyed during the Tatar invasion and excavated in 1951. For the next four centuries the monastery was defended by a wooden wall. In 1679 Hetman I. Samoilovych had a moat and new ramparts constructed around the upper monastery. Under Hetman I. Mazepa, a thick stone wall with four towers was added. In 1706 Tsar Peter I ordered the construction of the so-called Old Cave Fortress. The first plans were prepared by an engineer named Gellert. Completed in 1723, this fortress consisted of a semicircular citadel with a 6-m-high earthen rampart, eight bulwarks, and other fortifications. Of its three original gates, two have survived (the Vasylkivska and Moskovska gates). The fortress was rebuilt several times in the 18th and 19th centuries. The Old Cave Fortress housed the administrative and military institutions of tsarist rule in Kiev.

Between 1831 and 1863 the so-called New Cave Fortress was built, under the direction of an engineer named Opperman. New ramparts (up to 15 m high, 1,039 m in length), barracks, and fortifications were added to the existing citadel, and the enclosed area of the lower monastery was greatly expanded. The main fortresses were the Vasylkivska, erected next to the Vasylkivska gates, and the Hospitalna, which also contained a military hospital and now houses the Kosyi Kaponir Museum. With the development of modern artillery, the fortress lost its defensive significance, and it was eventually turned into

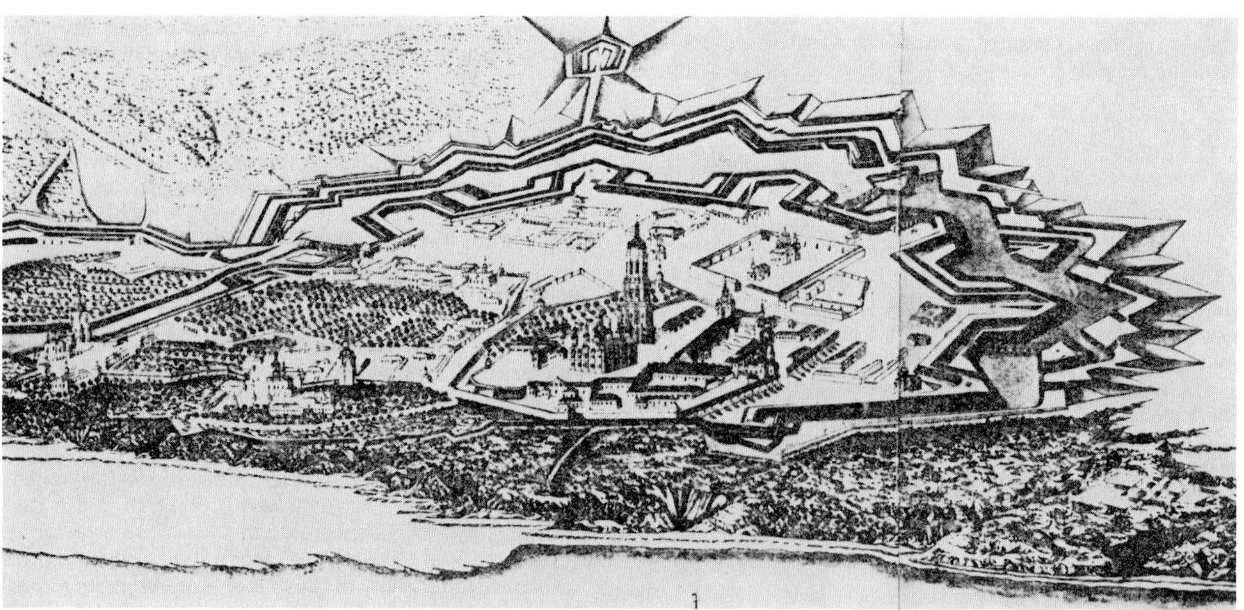

Kievan Cave Fortress (plan of 1783)

Kievan Cave Historical-Cultural Preserve

a military depot and then a garrison prison. The other surviving buildings of the New Fortress are the Mykilska gate and the Kruhla and Prozoriv towers.

Kievan Cave Historical-Cultural Preserve (Kyievo-Pecherskyi istoryko-kulturnyi zapovidnyk). An important historical preserve in Kiev, consisting of the entire complex of the former *Kievan Cave Monastery. The state-run preserve was organized in 1926, when the monastery was closed down by the Soviet authorities. On its 28-ha grounds there are over 80 cultural and public structures, 37 of them architectural and historical monuments from the 11th to 18th centuries. The most important are the Great Bell Tower (1731–44), the *Transfiguration Church in the Berestove district (early 12th century), the Trinity Church above the Main Gates (1108, restoration paid for by Hetman I. Mazepa in the early 18th century), and the *Dormition Cathedral of the Kievan Cave Monastery (1078, destroyed by a Soviet mine in 1941). The museums of the preserve contain many rare and valuable items from the 16th to 18th century: manuscripts, incunabula, and old books (many of them printed by the *Kievan Cave Monastery Press), and embroidery, precious metallic objects, engravings, printing blocks, and art works. During the civil war and the Second World War, many treasures were removed, destroyed, or stolen. During the Second World War over 30 monuments and buildings were destroyed; with the major exception of the Dormition Cathedral, almost all of them have been restored. Located at the preserve are the *Museum of the Book and Book Printing of the Ukrainian SSR, the *Museum of Historical Treasures of the Ukrainian SSR, the *Kiev Museum of Ukrainian Decorative Folk Arts, the *Kiev Museum of Theater, Music, and Cinema Arts, and the *History Library of the Ukrainian SSR.

Kievan Cave Monastery (Kyievo-Pecherska Lavra). An Orthodox monastery in Kiev. It was founded by *St Anthony of the Caves in the mid-11th century near the village of Berestove in a cave that the future metropolitan of Kiev, Ilarion, had excavated and lived in until 1051. The first monks excavated more caves and built a church above them. The monastery's first hegumen was Varlaam (to 1057). He was succeeded by *St Theodosius of the Caves (ca 1062–74), who introduced the strict Studite rule.

The Kievan princes and boyars generously supported the monastery, donating money, valuables, and land, and building fortifications and churches; some even became monks. Many of the monks were from the educated, upper strata, and the monastery soon became the largest religious and cultural center in Kievan Rus'. Twenty of its monks became bishops in the 12th and 13th centuries. St Theodosius's 'Teachings,' *Nestor the Chronicler's 'Story about Borys and Hlib,' 'Life of Theodosius of the Caves,' *Povist' vremennykh lit* (Tale of Bygone Years), and the *Kievan Cave Patericon were written there. Foreign works were translated, and books were transcribed and illuminated. Architecture and religious art (icons, mosaics, frescoes) – the works of Alimpii, Hryhorii, and others – developed there. Many folktales and legends eventually arose about its saintly figures and the miraculous construction of its main church. Early research on the monastery was done in the 17th century by S. Kosiv and A. Kalnofoisky.

The monastery was sacked several times, particularly

Kievan Cave Monastery: old engraving

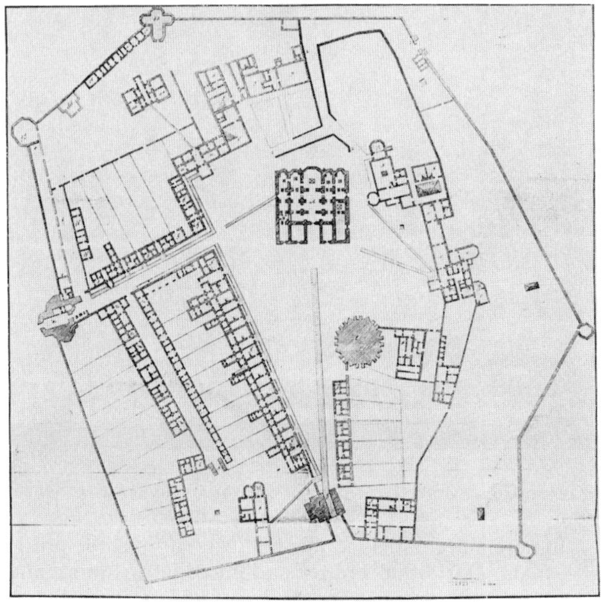

Kievan Cave Monastery: plan of buildings (1826)

in 1096 by the Cumans, in 1169 by Prince Andrei Bogoliubskii of Vladimir-Suzdal, in 1203 by Prince Riuryk Rostyslavych and the Chernihiv princes, and in 1240 by the Mongol Batu Khan. Each time it was rebuilt, new churches were erected, and the underground tunnels of caves and catacombs expanded. After a period of nonactivity it was rebuilt in 1470 by Prince Semen Olelkovych, but in 1482 the Tatars burned it down. It was eventually again rebuilt, and in the late 16th century it received *stauropegion status from the Patriarch of Constantinople, freeing it from the control of the local metropolitan. By that time consisting of six cloisters, the monastic complex was designated a **lavra*.

For a few years after the 1596 Church Union of Berestia the Uniate Catholics fought the Orthodox for control of the monastery, but the Orthodox retained control. In 1615 Archimandrite Ye. Pletenetsky established the first printing press in Kiev at the *Kievan Cave Monastery Press, which became an important center of publishing in Ukraine. Archimandrite (later Metropolitan) P. *Mohyla restored and embellished the monastery. In 1631 he opened the Kievan Cave Monastery School and introduced a 'western' curriculum; in 1632 it was merged with the *Kiev Epiphany Brotherhood School to form a college (later called the *Kievan Mohyla Academy). In 1688 the *lavra* became directly subordinate to the Moscow patriarch, retaining its stauropegion status.

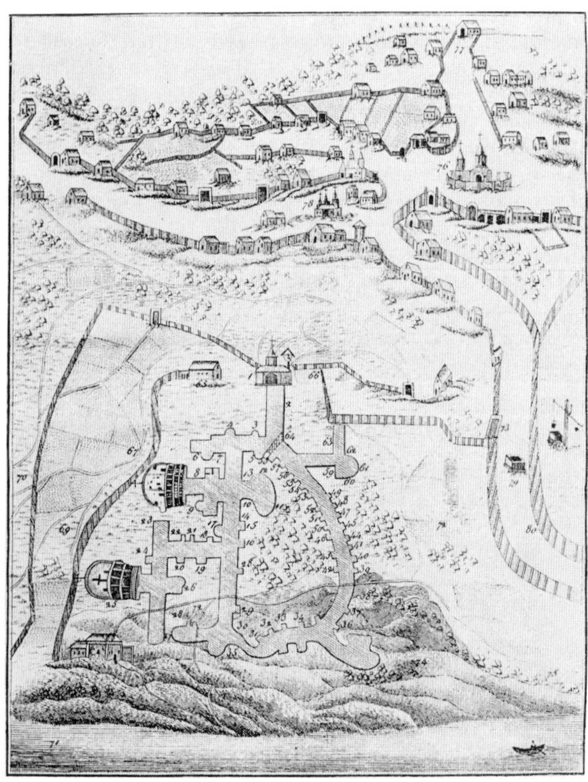

Kievan Cave Monastery: plan of the Far Caves (1638)

In 1718 a fire damaged most of its buildings, including the main (Dormition) church and the printing house, and destroyed the library and archive. Restorations lasted over 10 years. The monastery's cultural influence was later severely undercut by the Russian government's 1720 prohibition on the printing of new books and the imposition of synodal censorship on all publications. By the 18th century the monastery had acquired a great deal of wealth. It owned 3 cities, 7 towns, 200 villages and hamlets, 70,000 serfs, 11 brickyards, 6 foundries, over 150 distilleries, over 150 flour mills, and almost 200 taverns. In 1786 the Russian government secularized its property and made it a dependent of the state. At the same time the custom of electing the council elders, its governing body, was abolished. They were thereafter appointed by the Kiev metropolitan, who also became the archimandrite and had his residence within the monastery's precincts. Russification of the monastery began towards the end of the 18th century and increased with time.

Prior to the 1917 Revolution there were over 1,200 monks and novices at the monastery. It was one of the most famous centers of religious life in the Orthodox world and attracted hundreds of thousands of pilgrims. Its best-known sacred objects were the relics of its saintly monks who had been canonized by Metropolitan Mohyla in 1643. The caves (some of them dating from the Neolithic period) in which they lived and were buried, and from which the monastery's name is derived, form two underground labyrinths of tunnels, cells, and catacombs

Kievan Cave Monastery: passage in the Far Caves

excavated in soft sandstone and loess. The labyrinths (the Far and Near Caves) are 1.5 m wide, up to 2 m high, and 400 m apart. Burial niches in their walls are 0.5 m deep, 2 m long, and 1 m high; many still contain the mummified remains of monks and saints.

In 1921–2 the Soviet authorities confiscated many of the relics and precious historical and artistic objects belonging to the monastery and converted a number of buildings to commercial and other use. Many of the monastery's monuments and collections became part of the Lavra Museum of Religious Cults and Way of Life, which also contained the collections of several Kiev museums (eg, the Kiev Museum of Church Antiquities, the Kiev University Museum, and the All-Ukrainian History Museum). In 1926 the Soviet Ukrainian government closed down the monastery completely and turned its grounds (22 ha) into a state museum-preserve – the All-Ukrainian Museum Quarter (*Horodok*), which contained several museums (particularly of antireligious propaganda), archives, libraries, and workshops. In 1934 the museum quarter was abolished, and many of its collections were gradually transferred to new museums in Kiev. In 1941 Soviet forces retreating from the German advance mined the main church of the monastery, the *Dormition Cathedral, which once housed the legendary miracle-working icon of the Dormition; the mines exploded on 3 November 1941 after the Germans had occupied Kiev.

After the war the *lavra* preserve was restored and renamed the *Kievan Cave Historical-Cultural Preserve. Located there are several museums and institutions. Also on the preserve's grounds are the History Library of the Ukrainian SSR and the Ukrainian Society for the Protection of Historical and Cultural Monuments. From the Second World War to 1961 a Russian Orthodox monastery was allowed to function at the *lavra;* it had over 100 monks.

Dormition Cathedral of the Kievan Cave Monastery (1073–8; destroyed by Soviet mines in 1941)

RELIGIOSÆ
KIJOVIENSES
CRYPTÆ,
Sive
KIJOVIA SUBTERRANEA:
In quibus
LABYRINTHUS SUB TERRA
Et in eo emortua, à sexcentis annis, Divorum atque Heroum Græco-Ruthenorum, & nec dum corrupta, corpora, ex nomine atque ad oculum, è ΠΑΤΕΡΙΚΩ Sclavonica detegit.
M. JOHANNES HERBINIUS.
JENÆ,
Impensis MARTINI HALLERVORDI.
Literis JOHANNIS NISII.
ANNO M. DC. LXXV.

Herbinius's book on the Kievan Caves (1675)

The Cave Monastery is rich in architectural monuments. Thirty-seven of them were built before the 20th century. Some, like the Dormition Cathedral built in 1073–8 and the Main gate with the Trinity Church (1106–8) above it, have been rebuilt several times. After the 1718 fire these buildings were painted and ornamented in the baroque style; their frescoes depicted hetmans, princes, and metropolitans. Prior to its demolition in 1941 (it has not been rebuilt), the Dormition Cathedral contained the tombs of P. Berynda, Ye. Pletenetsky, K. Ostrozky, P. Mohyla, and other prominent nobles and personalities. Construction of the monastery's other churches was funded in the 17th and 18th centuries by Cossack hetmans and officers: the Church of the Elevation of the Cross, overlooking the Near Caves (1700); the All-Saints Church above the Economic Gate, funded by Hetman I. Mazepa (1696–8); the Tower-Church of St John the Calybite (Kushchnyk), Maliarna Tower, Onufriivska Tower, Hodynnykova Tower, and the fortified stone walls around the monastery; the Church of the Conception of St Anne (1679) and the Church of the Nativity of the Holy Mother of God (1696), both by the Far Caves; and the Resurrection Church (1698). In the 1720s cells for the council elders, a new printing house, a bakery, and other facilities were built. Many of the churches and buildings were altered by later restorations. The monastery's Great Bell Tower (96.5 m high), designed by the architect J.-G. Schädel, was built in 1731–44 in the classical style. Square bell towers near the Far (1754–61) and Near Caves (1759–63) were erected by the monastery's master builder S. Kovnir. All bells were removed by the Soviet authorities in 1931–2. In the 19th and 20th centuries many ancient buildings were torn down or rebuilt in the official Russian synodal style. Several new churches (eg, the Refectory Church, 1893–5) were built in this style.

BIBLIOGRAPHY
Bolkhovitinov, E. *Opisanie Kievo-Pecherskoi Lavry* (Kiev 1831)
'Kievo-Pecherskaia lavra v eia proshedshem i nynishnem sostoianii,' *KS*, 1886, nos 5–11
Goetz, L. *Das Kiever Höhlenkloster als Kulturzentrum des vormongolischen Russlands* (Passau 1904)
Titov, F. *Putevoditel' pri obozrenii Kievo-Pecherskoi lavry* (Kiev 1910)
Ripets'kyi, M; Popovych, D. *Kyïvo-Pechers'kyi monastyr i ioho podvyzhnyky* (Mundare 1954)
Kyïvs'kyi derzhavnyi zapovidnyk-muzei 'Kyievo-Pechers'ka Lavra': Korotkyi putivnyk (Kiev 1957)
Logvin, G. *Kievo-Pecherskaia Lavra* (Moscow 1958)
Kyievo-Pechers'kyi derzhavnyi istoryko-kul'turnyi zapovidnyk (Kiev 1971)
Kilesso, S. *Kievo-Pecherskaia lavra* (Moscow 1975)
Krykotun, V. *Za muramy lavry (Pro rol' Kyievo-Pechers'koï lavry u suspil'no-politychnomu zhytti Rosiï i Ukraïny u druhii polovyni XVIII–pochatku XX st.)* (Kiev 1979)
Petrenko, M. *Kyievo-Pechers'kyi derzhavnyi istoryko-kul'turnyi zapovidnyk: Putivnyk* (Kiev 1979)

V. Pavlovsky

Kievan Cave Monastery Gospel (Kyievo-Pecherskoi lavry yevanheliie). A Church Slavonic gospel transcribed before 1370 from a South-Slavic source. The manuscript consists of 181 sheets and is preserved in the museum of the Academy of Sciences in Kiev. Its language has a number of Ukrainian phonetic, morphological, and lexical features. Excerpts from it were printed in O. Shakhmatov and A. Krymsky's *Narysy z istoriï ukraïns'koï movy ta khrestomatiia z pam'iatnykiv pys'mens'koï staro-Ukraïnshchyny XI–XVIII vv.* (An Outline of the History of the Ukrainian Language and a Chrestomathy of the Texts of Old Ukrainian Writing of the 11th–18th Centuries, 1924).

Kievan Cave Monastery Icon Painting Studio (Lavrska ikonopysna maisternia). Main centre of Ukrainian icon painting for many centuries. Its founding at the end of the 11th century was connected with the painting of the Dormition Cathedral (1083–9) by Greek masters and the Kievan artists Olimpii and Hryhorii. The studio developed a distinctive style that is evident in its frescoes, icons, and book illuminations. From the late 16th century, collections of prints by western and local artists and of student drawings were kept for educational purposes. In the 18th century the studio was supervised by master Ivan (1724–30), T. Pavlovsky (1730–44), A. Halyk (1744–55), and B. Frederice (1760–?). Its finest masterpieces of the 18th century are the mural paintings of the Dormition Cathedral (1724–31) and the Trinity Church (1734–44) above the main gate of the Kievan Cave Monastery, which were done by I. Maksymovych, T. Pavlovsky, Z. Holubovsky, and A. Halyk. Many noted icon painters and engravers were trained at the studio. Towards the end of the 18th century the studio gradually lost its importance in the development of Ukrainian art. At the turn of the 19th century I. Izhakevych attempted to raise the artistic standard of the studio.

BIBLIOGRAPHY
Zholtovs'kyi, P. *Maliunky Kyievo-Lavrs'koï ikonopysnoï maisterni* (Kiev 1982)

Kievan Cave Monastery Press (Kyievo-Pecherska drukarnia). The first imprimery in Kiev and the most important center of printing and engraving in Ukraine in the 17th and 18th centuries. It was founded ca 1606–15 at the *Kievan Cave Monastery by the archimandrite Ye. *Pletenetsky, who purchased the equipment of the former press of H. *Balaban in Striatyn, Galicia. Later it was headed by, among others, Z. Kopystensky, P. Mohyla, I. Gizel (for over 30 years), V. Yasynsky, and Y. Krokovsky. Other prominent Ukrainian cultural figures – the writers Y. Boretsky, P. Berynda, L. Zyzanii, and I. Galiatovsky; the master printers S. Berynda, T. Zemka, and T. Verbytsky; and the engravers I. Shchyrsky, O. and L. Tarasevych, I. Myhura, N. Zubrytsky, Prokopii, Illia, A. Kozachkovsky, and H. Levytsky – also worked there. The oldest extant book printed by the imprimery is the *Chasoslov* (Horologion) of 1616. Other noteworthy books include **Antolohion* (1619), P. *Berynda's Slavonic-Ruthenian lexicon (1627), the *Kievan Cave Patericon (1661), I. Gizel's **Sinopsis* (Synopsis, 1674), and **Ifika iieropolitika* (1712). The imprimery issued several hundred titles on various subjects, both original works and translations, in Ukrainian, Church Slavonic, Polish, Russian, Latin, and Greek. The books printed included many ecclesiastical and liturgical texts, and also primers, hagiographic studies, Orthodox polemical treatises, didactic works, and literary works (panegyrics, emblems, epigrams) by such authors as S. Kosiv, P. Mohyla, L. Baranovych, I. Galiatovsky, I. Gizel, D. Tuptalo, A. Radyvylovsky, and T. Prokopovych. Beautifully engraved and ornamented, they were distributed throughout the Slavic countries, as well as Austria, Greece, and Moldavia. In the 16th and 17th centuries the imprimery played an important role in raising the level of education and culture in Ukraine and in aiding the Orthodox Ukrainians to defend themselves against the inroads of Polonization and Catholicism. The tsarist ukase of 1720 limited it to printing only religious works, which it continued to do until 1918. Its history, by F. Titov, was published in Kiev in 1916.

Kievan Cave Monastery Press; copper etching (1758)

Kievan Cave Patericon (Kyievo-Pechers'kyi pateryk). A collection of tales about the monks of the Kievan Cave Monastery. There exist two extant redactions: the Tver or Arsenian redaction of 1406, and the Kiev or Cassianian redaction of 1462. The original version arose after 1215 but not later than 1230 out of the correspondence of two

Kievan Cave Patericon

monks of the monastery – Simon (by then the bishop of Suzdal and Vladimir) and Polikarp, who used the epistolary form as a literary device. The letters contain 20 tales about righteous or sinful monks of the monastery based on oral legends and several written sources, such as the Life of St Anthony and the Kievan Cave and Rostov chronicles, which have not survived. The later redactions, it seems, did not change the original text significantly, but supplemented it with the Life of St Theodosius and the eulogy of him, the tale about St Isaac (from a chronicle), and stories from the monastery's history. The Kiev redaction contains information about the later influence of Byzantine Hesychasm. In 1635 the patericon was printed in Polish, and in 1661 in Ukrainian Church Slavonic. Several later editions were considerably corrupted by editorial changes.

Most of the original text deals with events of the 11th century. It varies from brief accounts of particular facts (Poemen and Kuksha) to novella-like or novel-like narratives ('Moses the Hungarian' and 'Theodore and Basil'). Most of the tales tend to be antisecular in tone and favor a strict, ascetic life. Nevertheless, some do testify to the decline of monastic life (some monks, for example, own property). Besides chronological data about the monastery, the text contains a wealth of historical and cultural information about monastic and secular life: such subjects as St Alimpii's icon painting, Armenian and Syrian physicians in Kiev, the cultural role of the Varangians, the fate of Kiev residents captured by King Bolesław I in his war with Grand Prince Yaroslav the Wise, bread made from pigweed during a famine, the princes' salt monopoly, the court system, private libraries, and the books read by monks. Only sporadically do the themes of wandering monks (a saint's encounter with devils and the magic treasure) occur, and demonology is mostly absent. Because of its relatively simple style, particularly in Simon, and its rich vocabulary, as well as its masterly characterization of individuals by means of dialogue, prayer, and 'internal monologue,' the patericon is one of the outstanding works of Old Ukrainian literature. It marked an important advance in the literary art of the period. A scholarly edition of the patericon was prepared by D. Abramovych and published in 1931.

BIBLIOGRAPHY

Shakhmatov, A. *Kievopecherskii paterik i Pecherskaia letopis'* (St Petersburg 1897)
Abramovich, D. *Izsledovanie o Kievo-Pecherskom paterike kak istoriko-literaturnom pamiatnike* (St Petersburg 1902)
Pechers'kyi Pateryk abo pravedni staroï Ukraïny: Davnie dzherelo staroukraïns'koï dukhovnosty, trans A. Velykyi (Rome 1973)

D. Chyzhevsky

Kievan chant (Kyivskyi naspiv or Kyivskyi rozspiv). A repertoire of melodies used in the liturgy in Kievan Rus'. It developed out of the earlier Byzantine and Bulgarian chants, and by the 11th century was characterized by a distinctive style. The Kievan chant was a homophonic diatonic melody based, like the Byzantine chant, on eight main modes, but its modes differed in structure from the Byzantine ones. The melodic motif could be employed in more than one mode, but some modes could be used only at the beginning, middle, or end of a chant. The Kievan chant was cultivated at the Kievan Cave Monastery and from there spread to other parts of Ukraine. The names of some of its adepts – the monks Stepan in Kiev, Dmytro in Peremyshl, and Luka in Volodymyr-Volynskyi – have been preserved in the historical record. Transmitted at first orally, the chant was written down, eventually, in neumatic notation, which conveyed only the general melody, leaving the pitch and length of sounds undetermined. The Kievan repertoire was subdivided into three distinct categories: the great chant (*velykyi rozspiv*), which was the original form and was used only on the most solemn feasts; the abbreviated chant (*skorochenyi rozspiv*), which was used on minor holidays; and the little chant (*malyi rozspiv*), which was used on Sundays. In the 15th and 16th centuries, the Kievan chant gave rise to several variations such as the Kievan Cave Monastery chant, the Volhynian (Pochaiv) chant, the Galician (Peremyshl and Lviv) chant, and the Subcarpathian (Basilian) chant. Minor variations in the Kievan chant led to the development of the Kharkiv, Poltava, and Horodyshche chants. The most developed variation was the Kievan Cave Monastery chant, which absorbed elements of western-European music and attained its full and final form in the 16th century. By this time the melody had evolved into a chromatic one. The leading voice was the second tenor, supported by the first tenor, alto, and two bass voices. Lacking a soprano voice, this choir produced music of a distinctive quality. The Kievan chant and the chants that evolved from it had a significant influence on the development of Ukrainian music.

M. Stech

Kievan Mohyla Academy (Kyievo-Mohylianska akademiia). The leading center of higher education in 17th- and 18th-century Ukraine, which exerted a significant intellectual influence over the entire Orthodox world at the time. Established in 1632 by the merging of the Kiev Epiphany Brotherhood School (est 1615–16) with the Kievan Cave Monastery School (est 1631 by P. *Mohyla), the new school was conceived by its founder, P. Mohyla, as an academy, ie, an institution of higher learning offering philosophy and theology courses and supervising a network of secondary schools. Completing the Orthodox school system, it was to compete on an equal footing with Polish academies run by the Jesuits. Fearing such competition, King Władysław IV granted the school the status of a mere college or secondary school, and prohibited it from teaching philosophy and theology. It was only in 1694 that the Kievan Mohyla College (Collegium Kijoviense Mohileanum) was granted the full privileges

Kievan Mohyla Academy; engraving by I. Shchyrsky (1698)

of an academy, and only in 1701 that it was recognized officially as an academy by Peter I.

In founding the school, Mohyla's purpose was to master the intellectual skills and learning of contemporary Europe and to apply them to the defense of the Orthodox faith. Taking his most dangerous adversary as the model, he adopted the organizational structure, the teaching methods, and the curriculum of the Jesuit schools. Unlike other Orthodox schools, which emphasized Church Slavonic and Greek, Mohyla's college gave primacy to Latin and Polish. This change was a victory for the more progressive churchmen, who appreciated the political and intellectual importance of these languages.

Slavonic, the sacral language, and Ruthenian, the literary language of Ukrainians and Belorussians closest to the vernacular, continued to be taught, while Greek was relegated to a secondary place. The undergraduate program, based on the liberal arts, was designed to develop the basic skills of public speaking rather than to pass on a body of knowledge, and was organized into five grades. The three lower grades were essentially grammarian. They were preceded by an introductory grade, *analog* or *fara*, devoted to reading and writing and elementary Latin, Polish, and Slavonic. The first grade, *infima*, provided an introduction to Latin grammar based on E. Álvarez's *De Institutione Grammatica Libri Tres*, the standard textbook adopted by the Jesuits. In the next grade, *grammatica*, Alvarez continued to be used for Latin syntax, readings from Cicero and Ovid were analyzed, and Greek grammar was introduced. In the *syntaxis* grade Alvarez was completed and Greek continued to be studied. Besides Ovid and Cicero, some works by Catullus, Virgil, Tibullus, and Aesop were read. Each grade required a year to complete and included some instruction in catechism, arithmetic, music, and painting.

The intermediate level consisted of two grades, in which students began to compose Latin prose and verse. The first, *poetica*, took one year and provided a grounding in the theory and practice of literature, and a close study of the writings of Caesar, Sallust, Livy, Curtius, Martial, Virgil, and Horace. Polish Renaissance and baroque poetry (J. Kochanowski, S. Twardowski) and, later in the century, some Ukrainian poetry (I. Velychkovsky) were also read. The two-year *rhetorica* grade completed the secondary-school program. Cicero and Aristotle's *Poetics* were studied in the course of mastering the rules of elegant composition. In both grades students absorbed much prose and verse information on secular and biblical history, mythology, and classical geography for the purpose of rhetoric, not of knowledge.

Kievan instructors, like the instructors of Polish and other European schools, prepared their own Latin manuals of poetics and rhetoric. Approximately 120 17th- and 18th-century manuals have survived, including T. *Prokopovych's *De Arte Poetica Libri III* (1705) and *De Arte Rhetorica Libri X* (1706). The remarkable efflorescence of Ukrainian *baroque literature was closely connected with the school's philological program.

Kievan Mohyla Academy: official seal

Higher education consisted of a three-year philosophy program that paved the way to four years of theology. In spite of the king's prohibition, some course in philosophy was usually taught, and in 1642–6 a theology course was offered. In the mid-1680s a full philosphy and theology program was given a permanent place in the curriculum. Logic, physics, and metaphysics were the main parts of the philosophy program. The philosophy manuals prepared by the school's professors, of which about 80 have survived, show that there was no uniform system of thought, but that each course reflected the preferences and abilities of the instructor. The basically Aristotelian philosophy taught in the school was derived not from Aristotle himself but from his medieval interpreters and was supplemented with doctrines from St Augustine, Thomas Aquinas, Duns Scotus, and William of Ockham, humanists such as L. Valla, L. Vives, and D. Erasmus and the Protestant scholar P. Melanchthon, and the Jesuits F. Suárez, P. Fonseca, and E. Molina. At the beginning of the 18th century T. Prokopovych showed an interest in R. Descartes and F. Bacon. From the middle of the 18th century on orders from the Holy Synod the academy adopted C. Wolff's philosophy. The theological courses at the academy consisted of commentaries on Catholic theologians such as R. Bellarmine, F. Suárez, T. González, and the Polish Jesuit T. Mło dzianowski. In method, if not in content, they were very Thomistic. The only attempt to work out an independent theological system was P. Mohyla's *Pravoslavnoe ispovedanie* ... (Orthodox Confession ..., 1640).

From its beginnings, the academy had close ties with the Cossack *starshyna*, which provided it with moral and material support. Hetman I. Petrazhytsky-Kulaha approved P. Mohyla's plans for the new school in 1632 and granted it a charter. The school, in turn, educated the succeeding generation of the service elite. In the 1640s, when the Orthodox hierarchy sided with the Polish Crown against the rebellious Cossacks, Cossack sons continued to attend the college. Among them were the future hetmans I. Vyhovsky, I. Samoilovych, P. Teteria, I. Mazepa, and P. Polubotok. B. Khmelnytsky established the tradition of hetman grants in money, lands, and privileges to the college. The Kiev clergy's opposition to the Treaty of *Pereiaslav (1654) severely strained their relation with the Cossacks. During the *Cossack-Polish wars (1648–57) and the Ruin period (1657–87), the activities of the college were severely disrupted. Its buildings and property were looted and destroyed several times by Muscovite and Polish armies. The strong Hetman state that emerged in Left-Bank Ukraine after the Ruin period provided favorable conditions for the college's growth. Supported generously by Hetman I. Samoilovych (1672–87), the school began to flourish towards the end of his rule, and during I. Mazepa's reign (1687–1709), enjoyed its golden age. The enrollment at the time exceeded 2,000. Some of the students, including S. Maksymovych, O. Turansky, and A. Runovsky, later gained prominence as Cossack officers.

Many of the most accomplished Ukrainian authors and churchmen of the time served on the school's faculty: L. Baranovych, Ioan Maksymovych, D. Tuptalo, S. Yavorsky, and T. Prokopovych. Some of them played instrumental roles in Peter I's educational reforms in Russia. The Moscow academy was patterned after the Kievan one and numerous Russian schools were organized by bishops who were graduates of the Kiev academy. Open to young men from all social strata, the academy attracted students from various regions of the Orthodox world. Some of its graduates, Ukrainian or foreign, continued their studies in Polish or European academies and universities, and returned home to weave Kievan and European thought patterns into their native tradition.

At the same time, Moscow's expanding political power and increasing interference in Ukrainian affairs threatened the academy's freedom and well-being. Gaining control of Kiev metropoly in 1686, the Patriarch of Moscow attempted to end the intellectual influence of Kiev on Muscovite society by placing almost all Kiev publications on an index of heretical books. It was forbidden to print books in Ruthenian. Although in 1693 Patriarch Adrian eased the linguistic restrictions, Ukrainian books were denied entry into Muscovy. The academy's golden age came to an abrupt end with Mazepa's defeat at Poltava in 1709. The school's properties were plundered by Russian troops. Students from Right-Bank Ukraine, which was under Polish rule, were no longer admitted. By 1711 the enrollment fell to 161. Graduates of the academy were encouraged to seek positions in Moscow or St Petersburg. Peter I's ban on Ruthenian publications and religious texts in the Ukrainian recension of Church Slavonic was a heavy blow to the academy.

After Peter's death, Mazepa's endowments were returned to the academy. Thanks to the support of Hetman D. Apostol and the administrative talents of Metropolitan R. Zaborovsky (1731–42), the school revived. New courses in modern languages, history and mathematics, medicine, and geography were added to its curriculum. The enrollment rose steadily from 490 in 1738–9 to 1,110 in 1744–5. Graduates were encouraged to complete their education in European universities and many sons of wealthy Cossack families studied abroad. The academy continued to educate the civil and ecclesiastical elite of the Hetman state and the Russian Empire. Catherine II's abolition of the Hetmanate in 1764 and secularization of the monasteries in 1786 deprived the academy of its chief sources of financial support. The school became a ward of the Russian imperial government and its importance declined rapidly. By the end of the century it was reduced to an eparchial seminary. In 1811, 1,069 of its 1,198 students were candidates for the priesthood. In 1817 the academy was closed down, and two years later a theological academy was opened in its place.

The academy's adaptation of European education was largely conditioned by the social and religious demands of early 17th-century Ukrainian society. Hardly touched by the Renaissance and Reformation movements, it placed little value on the Ukrainian vernacular and felt no need for a secular culture. It defined itself mostly in religious terms and, therefore, made the preservation of the Orthodox faith its primary concern. By arming the Ukrainian members of the leading estates in the Polish Commonwealth with the languages and intellectual tools of the dominant culture, the academy fulfilled the demands placed on it by society. Accustomed to a defensive, conservative posture, the intellectual elite nurtured by the academy failed to capitalize on the new opportunities offered by the Hetman state. In the 18th century the academy adjusted itself as best it could to the increasing restrictions placed on it by an alien church hierarchy and imperial power. Its literary and scholarly achievement had a decisive impact on the development of Ukrainian culture and provided a firm foundation for later accomplishments.

BIBLIOGRAPHY

Golubev, S. *Istoriia Kievskoi akademii*, 1 (Kiev 1866)

Jabłonowski, A. *Akademia Kijowsko-Mohilańska: Zarys historyczny na tle rozwoju ogólnego cywilizaciji zachodniej na Rusi* (Cracow 1900)

Titov, Kh. *Stara vyshcha osvita v Kyïvs'kii Ukraïni XVI–poch. XIX v.* (Kiev 1924)

Khyzhniak, Z. *Kyievo-Mohylians'ka akademiia*, 2 edns (Kiev 1970 and 1981)

Joukovsky, A. 'Contributions à l'histoire de l'Académie de Kiev (1615–1817): Centre culturel et d'enseignement en Europe orientale,' PH D diss., Sorbonne University 1975
Sydorenko, A. *The Kievan Academy in the Seventeenth Century* (Ottawa 1977)
Belodid, I. *Kievo-Mohylianska akademiia v istorii skhidno-slav'ianskykh literaturnykh mov* (Kiev 1979)
Stratii, Ia.; Litvinov, V.; Andrushko, V. *Opisanie kursov filosofii i ritoriki professorov Kievo-Mogilianskoi akademii* (Kiev 1982)
The Kiev Mohyla Academy. Special issue of *Harvard Ukrainian Studies*, 8, no. 1/2 (June 1984)

N. Pylypiuk

Kievan Rus'. The first state to arise among the Eastern Slavs. It took its name from the city of Kiev, the seat of the grand prince from about 880 until the beginning of the 13th century. At its zenith, it covered a territory stretching from the Carpathian Mountains to the Volga River, and from the Black Sea to the Baltic Sea. The state's rapid rise and development was based on its advantageous location at the intersection of major north-south and east-west land and water trade routes with access to two major seas, and favorable local conditions for the development of agriculture. In the end, however, the state's great size led to the development of centrifugal tendencies and local interests that limited its political and social cohesion. This, and its proximity to the Asian steppes, which left it vulnerable to invasions of nomadic hordes, eventually contributed to the decline of Kievan Rus'.

In the 8th century, the territory of Kievan Rus' was inhabited by a number of tribes who shared a common proto-Slavic language, pagan beliefs, and life-style. The ancestors of the Ukrainians included the *Polianians, *Siverianians, *Derevlianians, *Dulibians, *White Croatians, *Ulychians, and *Tivertsians. The proto-Russian *Krivichians, *Viatichians, and *Radimichians and the proto-Belorussian *Drehovichians also lived on the lands that eventually constituted Kievan Rus'. The Polianians were the largest and most developed of the tribes; according to the Rus' Primary Chronicle, their prince *Kyi founded the city of Kiev in the 6th century. None of the tribes, however, was able to create a viable state, and in the 9th century the *Varangians from Scandinavia conquered the tribes and laid the groundwork for the Kievan Rus' state.

History. According to some sources, the first Varangian rulers of Rus' were *Askold and Dyr. In 882 they were killed by Prince *Oleh, the son of *Riuryk. From that time, descendants of the *Riurykide dynasty ruled Kievan Rus' and other east-European territories until 1596.

Oleh was soon able to consolidate his rule in Kiev and defeated the *Khazars, who had been threatening the individual tribes from the east. In 907 he led a campaign against Constantinople and four years later concluded an important trade agreement that laid the basis for a permanent relationship between Rus' and the *Byzantine Empire. Oleh's son *Ihor (912–45) expanded the territory under his control to include the northern Pontic littoral. His attempts to extend his rule over all of the tribes in the region, however, were resisted and he was eventually killed by the Derevlianians, who refused to pay him tribute. His widow *Olha (945–62) ruled as regent until their son came of age. She was the first Rus' ruler to convert to Christianity and to establish direct ties with central and western-European rulers. The reign of *Sviatoslav I (962–72) was marked by almost uninterrupted warfare. Known as 'the Conqueror,' Sviatoslav attempted to expand his territory to the Danube River, defeating the Bulgarians and establishing Pereiaslavets on the Danube.

If the first period of Kievan Rus' history can be characterized as the era of expansion, which saw Kiev extend its authority over all of the east-Slavic tribes and witnessed the attempts of the rulers to expand their realm to the Danube and Volga basins, then the second period, beginning with the reign of *Yaropolk I Sviatoslavych (972–80), may best be described as the era of internal consolidation. However, it was under Yaropolk's brother *Volodymyr I the Great, who seized power with the help of Varangian mercenaries and killed his brother in 980, that Kievan Rus' became one of the pre-eminent states of Europe. The most important achievement of Volodymyr's rule was the adoption of Christianity in 988 as the official religion of Rus' (see *Christianization of Ukraine), which facilitated the spread of Byzantine culture throughout the state (see *Byzantine art, *Byzantine law) and served to reinforce the political unity and cultural cohesion of Rus'.

After Volodymyr's death in 1015, his son *Sviatopolk I seized power, but he was opposed in a bitter internecine war. Sviatopolk was initially helped by the Polish prince *Bolesław I the Brave, who took the opportunity to capture the *Cherven towns from Rus'; however, when he abandoned this alliance, his brother *Yaroslav the Wise, aided by an army of Varangians, captured Kiev. A second series of wars ensued between Yaroslav and his brother *Mstyslav, who had developed an important power base as prince of Tmutorokan. The two brothers ruled jointly until Mstyslav died in 1036 without an heir, leaving Yaroslav as grand prince of a reunited Rus'. Yaroslav's reign as unchallenged grand prince (1036–54) was one of the highest points in the history of Rus'. The process of internal consolidation begun earlier was greatly furthered by Yaroslav's codification of the law in **Ruskaia Pravda*. Culture flourished: the magnificent St Sophia Cathedral was built in Kiev, the Kievan Cave Monastery was founded, a library was established, and learning and education were encouraged. Yaroslav also appointed the first local hierarch as Kievan metropolitan (see *Ilarion), thus asserting Kiev's independence of Constantinople. Yaroslav's death initiated another round of civil war and internecine struggle, although he had tried to prevent this effect by preparing a plan for dividing up political power between his sons and re-establishing the seniority-rotation system devised by Volodymyr the Great. By this time, the interests of the individual princes were too disparate to be easily reconciled and none respected the others' domains or the ultimate authority of the Kievan prince. The situation was further complicated by the presence of the *Cumans, who in the middle of the 11th century had replaced the *Pechenegs on the southern border of Rus'. For the next century and a half they waged continuous war against Rus' and became involved in the internecine wars, serving as allies of one branch of the dynasty or another. The princes attempted to solve their differences in a series of conferences, especially the *Liubech congress in 1097, which altered the patrimonial system of decreeing that sons could rightfully inherit their father's lands, although they would all

KIEVAN RUS'

1. Borders of Kiev Principality
2. Borders of the expanded Kiev Principality (1054)
3. Borders of other states
4. Campaigns of Sviatoslav I
5. Campaigns of Volodymyr the Great
6. Campaigns of Yaroslav the Wise
7. Western territories annexed by Volodymyr the Great (980 to 1015)
8. Northwestern territories annexed by Yaroslav the Wise (1019 to 1054)
9. The southern border of Kievan Rus' under Sviatoslav I
10. Fortification walls
11. Varangian trade route from Scandinavia to Constantinople
12. Pecheneg and Polovtsian raids
13. Pecheneg and Polovtsian migrations

respect the authority of the Kievan prince. All of these solutions were short-lived, however, and the civil wars continued.

A brief respite occurred during the reign of *Volodymyr Monomakh. Under Monomakh (1113–25) Kiev once again flourished and the internecine wars abated. *Ruskaia Pravda* was amended (see *Statute of Volodymyr Monomakh), and several valuable works of literature, *hagiography, and *historiography were composed, including the important *Kievan Cave Patericon. Monomakh himself wrote his famous testament **Pouchennia ditiam*, in which he told his sons how to be just and powerful rulers. His son *Mstyslav I Volodymyrovych (1125–32) inherited the principal lands of Rus', while the remaining territories were distributed among his brothers. Neither Mstyslav nor his brother and successor in Kiev, Yaropolk Volodymyrovych (1132–9), was able to prevent the dynastic rivalry for the title of 'grand prince of Kiev and all Rus'.' The Kievan Rus' federation continued to disintegrate and Kiev itself lost its primacy: the city was sacked several times by feuding princes, most notably in 1169 by Andrei Bogoliubskii of Vladimir, Rostov, and Suzdal. The principalities of *Kiev, *Polatsk, *Turiv-Pynske, Volodymyr-Volynskyi (see *Volhynia), Halych (see *Galicia), *Chernihiv, and *Pereiaslav emerged as independent and separate entities, with their own political and economic peculiarities, as did *Novgorod, Suzdal, Vladimir, and others that later constituted Muscovy and then *Russia. The quarreling between the princes left Rus' vulnerable to foreign attacks, and the invasion of the *Mongols in 1236–40 finally destroyed the state. The principalities never organized a common defense, and in turn each was conquered and pillaged. Kiev was thoroughly sacked in 1240 and reduced to a shadow of its former self.

Origins. The question of the origins of Kievan Rus' still produces controversy among historians. The oldest, or *Normanist, theory rests mainly on a literal interpretation of the Primary Chronicle and stresses the role of the Varangians as the first leaders and organizers of the state. Ukrainian historians, beginning with M. Maksymovych and followed by M. Kostomarov, V. Antonovych, M. Hrushevsky, D. Bahalii, D. Doroshenko, M. Chubaty, and others, have generally downplayed the Varangian influence on the formation of Rus'. Contemporary Soviet historiography categorically rejects the Normanist theory, considering it bourgeois. However, it remains, with certain modifications, the basis of Western historiography of Russia and Ukraine.

The issue of the nationality of the inhabitants of the Kievan state is also a matter of continuing controversy. The discussion was initiated by the Russian historian M. Pogodin, who claimed that the original inhabitants of contemporary Ukraine fled north under pressure from the Mongols, and that they later became the modern Russian nation. The Ukrainians, meanwhile, arrived much later from somewhere in the Carpathian Mountains. Pogodin's views were expanded on by the philologist O. Sobolevsky. This theory was disputed by Ukrainian historians such as M. Maksymovych, M. Dashkevych, P. Zhytetsky, and A. Krymsky. M. Hrushevsky sought to demonstrate that Ukrainians were autochthonous in their territories, and that the Principality of Galicia-Volhynia was the successor to the Kievan state. Hrushevsky's theories were for the most part adopted by Ukrainian historians and by some others. Because these theories do not correspond to the political objectives of the Soviet leadership, a panel of historians was commissioned in the 1930s by the Communist Party to draw up a new historical schema of Eastern Europe; its basic premise was that Kievan Rus' had been founded by a single old Rus' nationality, out of which Ukrainians, Russians, and Belorussians developed in the 14th and 15th centuries. This theory was given official approbation with the publication of *Tezy pro 300-richchia vozz'iednannia Ukraïny z Rosiieiu, 1654–1954* (Theses about the 300th Anniversary of the Reunification of Ukraine with Russia, 1954). Contemporary émigré Ukrainian scholarship bases itself on Hrushevsky's approach, and continues to expand its corollaries along historical (M. Chubaty, N. Polonska-Vasylenko, M. Zhdan, O. Pritsak), archeological (Ya. Pasternak), and linguistic (S. Smal-Stotsky, G.Y. Shevelov) lines.

The political and social institutions of Kievan Rus'. From the 10th to the 12th century the Kievan state underwent significant sociopolitical changes. Its original component tribes had no political tradition, and its first rulers viewed their domain simply as an object of exploitation, at best as a clan possession. Volodymyr the Great was the first ruler to give Rus' political unity, by way of organized religion. The church provided him with the concepts of territorial and hierarchical organization; Byzantine notions of autocracy were adopted by him and his successors to give them the equivalent of imperial authority. The political traditions introduced by Volodymyr were based on the principles of territorial indivisibility and dynastic sovereignty. The seniority system of rule – ascension from elder brother to younger and from the youngest uncle to the eldest nephew – provided the Riuryk dynasty with a rotating system of advancement of its members, gave them political experience in lands they could someday expect to rule from Kiev, and assured control, by way of traditional sanctions, of key points of the realm. This system served well until the reign of Monomakh, but did not survive Kiev's decline.

The power of the grand prince was maintained by his military strength, particularly that of his **druzhyna*, or retinue. Ideologically, his power was upheld by the church, whose teachings gave him the attributes and responsibilities of a national leader, judge, and first Christian of the realm. The grand prince ruled and dispensed justice with the help of viceroys appointed by him, who were often the sons of the grand prince, of other princes, of governors, or of military commanders. These representatives of the grand prince's central power were aided by local administrators – the **desiatski*. The grand prince consulted on important state matters with the *Boyar Council, which consisted of his senior retainers and the local aristocracy of power and wealth.

The **viche* (assembly), an important organ already within the tribal network, resolved all matters on behalf of the population. The city *viche*, composed of freemen, decided mainly on questions of war and peace and on the invitation, recognition, or expulsion of a prince. It became particularly important in the 12th century during the internecine wars of the princes for the throne of Kiev.

In the Princely era, Ukrainian society had its own peculiarities. Its privileged elite (the *boyars and the 'better people'), which enjoyed full protection of the law, was not a closed estate; based, as it was, on merit, which the prince rewarded with grants of land, its membership was dependent on the will of the prince. Thus even priests' sons and commoners could become boyars. The townsfolk consisted of *burghers – mostly merchants and craftspeople – and paupers. There was little difference in status between the wealthy *merchants and the landed boyars. Most freemen were yeomen called *smerds, who lived on their own land or on the land of the prince, paid taxes, and performed certain duties, such as building fortifications, bridges, and roads and serving in the *levy en masse in times of war; gradually the smerds became dependent on their lords, and some became tenants or hired laborers on the land. A smaller category of peasants consisted of zakups – impoverished smerds who had become indentured and half-free. The lowest social stratum in Rus' consisted of slaves (see *Slavery). Male slaves were called **kholopy*; usually prisoners of war or the offspring of slaves, they had no rights as persons and were considered the legal, movable property of their masters. Certain churchmen and princes, eg, Monomakh in his statute, tried to improve the lot and legal status of the slaves.

The economy of Kievan Rus'. Relatively little is known about the economy of Kiev, although there is no doubt that *agriculture was the main activity of the inhabitants. Farming techniques and implements were naturally primitive and the peasants lived mostly at a subsistence level. Some animal husbandry was practiced, as was extensive grain cultivation. Land, particularly after the 11th century, was privately owned. Most peasants supplemented their agricultural activities with fishing, trapping, and hunting, especially in the northern forest and forest-steppe regions. The forests also supplied wood, the major source of fuel. The peasants generally lived in small, scattered villages.

The second major component of Kiev's economy was foreign trade. Not only were local goods, particularly furs, traded for important items, but much profit was made from the simple transshipment of goods along the great trade routes linking first east and west and later north and south. In the end, it was the breakdown of the trade route from 'the Varangians to Byzantium' that partially initiated Kiev's decline, and it was the emergence of specialized routes linking the northern principalities to the Hanseatic League of states that furthered the disintegration of the state.

BIBLIOGRAPHY
Hrushevs'kyi, M. *Istoriia Ukraïny-Rusy*, vols 1–3 (Lviv 1898–9)
Grekov, B. *Kievskaia Rus'* (Moscow 1949; English trans *Kiev Rus* [Moscow 1959])
Paszkiewicz, H. *The Origin of Russia* (London 1954)
Vernadsky, G. *The Origins of Russia* (New Haven 1959)
Rybakov, B. *Drevnaia Rus'* (Moscow 1963)
Shekera, I. *Mizhnarodni zv'iazky Kyïvs'koï Rusi* (Kiev 1963)
Chubatyi, M. 'Kniazha Rus'-Ukraïna ta vynyknennia tr'okh skhidn'o-slovians'kykh natsii,' in *ZNTSh*, vol 178 (New York-Paris 1964)
Polons'ka-Vasylenko, N. *Dvi kontseptsiï istoriï Ukraïny i Rosiï* (Munich 1964; English trans *Two Conceptions of the History of Ukraine and Russia* [London 1968])
Braichevs'kyi, M. *Pokhodzhennia Rusi* (Kiev 1968)
Pashuto, V. *Vneshniaia politika Drevnei Rusi* (Moscow 1968)
Froianov, I. *Kievskaia Rus': Ocherki sotsial'no-politicheskoi istorii* (Leningrad 1980)
Tolochko, P. *Kiev i Kievskaia zemlia v epokhu feodal'noi razdroblennosti XII–XIII vekov* (Kiev 1980)
Pritsak, O. *The Origin of Rus'*, vol 1 (Cambridge, Mass 1981)
Rybakov, B. *Kievs'kaia Rus' i russkie kniazhestva XII–XIII vekov* (Moscow 1982)
Rybakov, B.; Selov, V. *Vostochnye slaviany v VI–XIII vv.* (Moscow 1982)

M. Zhdan

Kievlianin: title page (1840–50)

Kievlianin (The Kievan). An almanac published and edited by M. *Maksymovych. Only three volumes appeared: the first in 1840, the next in 1841 (both in Kiev), and the last in 1850 (in Moscow). They contained many articles on the history of Kiev (some of them by Maksymovych himself), Pereiaslav, Volhynia, and Transcarpathia. In his articles on literature, Maksymovych stressed the distinctiveness of the Ukrainian language and its great literary potential, and strongly condemned the attacks of the Russian chauvinist press on Ukrainian. The almanac published historical documents and charters, and the literary works of Ye. Hrebinka, H. Kvitka-Osnovianenko, P. Kulish, and some Russian poets.

Kievlianin (The Kievan). A conservative Russian newspaper published thrice weekly (1864–79) and then daily (to 1919) in Kiev (interrupted from February 1917 to August 1919). Subsidized by the tsarist government, it advocated a rigid anti-Ukrainian and anti-Polish policy. It attacked any expression of Ukrainophilism as Ukrainian separatism. Its founder and first editor was V. Shulgin (1864–78), who was succeeded by D. Pikhno (1878–1911) and then by his son V. Shulgin (1911–19). In 1869–72 it published A. Svydnytsky's stories about everyday life in Ukraine.

Kievskaia mysl' (Kievan Thought). A liberal Russian daily published in Kiev from 12 January 1907 to December 1918. Representing the democratic intelligentsia, it advocated a moderate anti-Ukrainian policy. It had the largest circulation of any Russian newspaper in Ukraine. Besides political news, it published literary works. In 1906–15 it had an illustrated weekly supplement. In 1917–18 a morning and an evening edition were published.

Kievskaia starina (Kiev Antiquity). A learned monthly for Ukrainian studies printed in Russian and published in Kiev from 1882 to 1906. In 1907 it was renamed *Ukraïna*

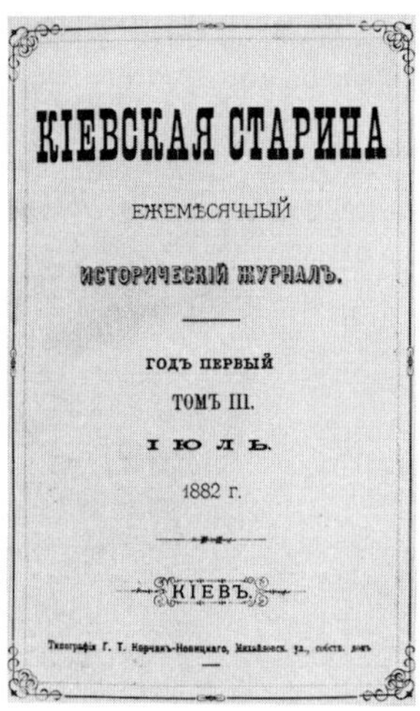
КІЕВСКАЯ СТАРИНА

ЕЖЕМѢСЯЧНЫЙ

ИСТОРИЧЕСКІЙ ЖУРНАЛЪ.

ГОДЪ ПЕРВЫЙ

ТОМЪ III.

ІЮЛЬ.

1882 г.

КІЕВЪ.

Kievskaia starina: cover in 1882

and appeared in Ukrainian. The journal was founded by T. Lebedyntsev, V. Antonovych, O. Lazarevsky, and P. Zhytetsky, and was financed mostly by V. Symyrenko. As the unofficial organ of the *Hromada of Kiev, which in 1893 became its real owner, it was published and edited by T. Lebedyntsev (1882–7), O. Lashkevych (1888–9), Ye. Kyvlytsky (1889–92), and V. Naumenko (1893–1907). For over 25 years *Kievskaia starina* was the only printed medium of Ukrainian scholarship in Russian-ruled Ukraine. It published a wealth of research and documentary materials in history, archeology (particularly its supplement *Arkheologicheskaia letopis' iuzhnoi Rossii*, 1899–1901), ethnography, philology, and bibliography. In 1890 it began to publish belles-lettres, which from 1897 appeared in Ukrainian, and literary criticism. The leading Ukrainian scientific minds and cultural figures of the time were grouped around the journal, forming something like a learned society. At the turn of the century *Kievskia starina* became a sort of encyclopedia of Ukrainian studies. Among its contributors were the following scholars: M. Kostomarov, V. Antonovych, M. Drahomanov (whose articles appeared under the nom de plume of P. Kuzmychevsky as well as others), P. and O. Yefymenko, O. Lazarevsky, M. and A. Storozhenko, M. Dashkevych, P. Zhytetsky, K. Mykhalchuk, O. Rusov, I. Manzhura, A. Vostokov, Ya. Shulhin, N. Molchanovsky, V. Horlenko, V. Naumenko, I. Luchytsky, M. Petrov, S. Golubev, V. Ikonnikov, D. Bahalii, M. Sumtsov, I. Franko, A. Skalkovsky, V. Shcherbyna, I. Novytsky, O. Levytsky, M. Vasylenko, M. Hrushevsky, A. Krymsky, M. Biliashivsky, and V. Hnatiuk.

The journal published such historical materials as the diaries of M. Khanenko (1884–6), Ya. Markovych (1893–7), S. Oświęcim (1882), K. Chojecki (1883), I. Ostrozhsky-Lokhvytsky (1886), and P. Seletsky (1884); memoirs of M. Tyshkevych (1889) and M. Chalyi (1890–6); and correspondence of several prominent Ukrainians in the nineteenth century, including the letters of P. Kulish and the Myloradovych Liubetskyi archives (1897). It made an enormous contribution to the development of Ukrainian learning and culture. A systematic index to the journal was published in 1911.

O. Ohloblyn

Kievskie gubernskie vedomosti (Kiev Gubernia News). An official government newspaper published in Kiev from 1838 to 1917, thrice weekly from 1866. In its official section it published administrative decrees and notices, and in its non-official section local news; articles on archeology, ethnography, history, geography, economics, and politics in Kiev gubernia and its neighbors; and world news. Some Ukrainian scholars, such as O. Lazarevsky, D. Bahalii, and P. Yefymenko, contributed articles to the paper. In 1917 it began to be published in both Russian and Ukrainian.

Kievskii telegraf (Kiev Telegraph). Kiev's first newspaper, a political, scientific, and literary semiweekly published from August 1859 to July 1876. It was founded by A. Yunk, who was its first publisher and editor. Printed in Russian, from 1864 it began to appear thrice weekly. In 1860–3 it published a literary supplement. It lacked any clear editorial policy, but showed a pro-Ukrainian attitude. In 1874 the paper was purchased by Ye. Hohotska, the wife of S. Hohotsky, who relied on Yu. Tsvitkovsky and his Ukrainophile friends to edit the paper. *Kievskii telegraf* became the unofficial paper of the *Hromada of Kiev. Its new policy was worked out by M. *Drahomanov. Ukrainian scholars such as V. Antonovych, V. Berenshtam, F. Vovk, M. Drahomanov, M. Ziber, V. Navrotsky, S. Podolynsky, O. Rusov, P. Zhytetsky, P. Chubynsky, and Ya. Shulhin became its main contributors. It covered political developments in the Russian Empire and in other Slavic countries, the Ukrainian literary movement, the theater in Kiev and the gubernia, and the evolution of Ukrainian culture and language. Constant denunciations by influential Russian reactionaries prompted the authorities to apply the provisions of the *Ems Ukase and to close down the paper on 5 July 1876.

Kiik-Koba (also Kiikkoba). A Lower Paleolithic settlement located in caves on the right bank of the Zuia River, 25 km east of Symferopil in the Crimea. Kiik-Koba was discovered by G. Bonch-Osmolovsky and excavated by him in 1924–6. The lower cultural layer was dated to the late Acheulean–early Mousterian period and contained flint tools of indeterminate form and animal bones (giant deer, wild ass, saiga). The upper cultural layer belonged to the middle Mousterian period and contained flint points and scrapers as well as bones of giant deer, wooly rhinoceros, saiga, cave bear, mammoth, and other animals. There were also remnants of walls, which had been constructed in the Mousterian period to block drafts. Graves dug in the stone floor contained the remains of a Neanderthal adult male and a year-old infant. These were the first remains of early man discovered in Ukraine.

Kikot, Andrii [Kikot', Andrij], b 27 November 1929 in Kamianka, Poltava oblast, d 13 October 1975 in Kiev. Operatic bass. A student of I. *Patorzhynsky and a graduate of the Kiev Conservatory (1959), he joined the Kiev Theater of Opera and Ballet. His repertoire included Sarastro in A. Mozart's *Magic Flute*, Mephistopheles in C. Gounod's *Faust*, Karas in S. Hulak-Artemovsky's *Zaporozhian Cossack beyond the Danube*, Taras in M. Lysenko's *Taras Bulba*, the General in H. Maiboroda's *Arsenal*, Kryvonis in K. Dankevych's *Bohdan Khmelnytsky*, and Godunov in M. Mussorgsky's *Boris Godunov*. He won several silver and gold medals at international competitions.

KILIMS 1) 17th-century fragment, from Kiev (Lviv Museum of Ukrainian Art). 2) 18th-century fragment, from the Kiev region (Lviv Museum of Ukrainian Art). 3) 18th century, from the Poltava region (Kiev Museum of Ukrainian Art). 4) Late 18th century, from the Poltava region (Poltava Art Museum). 5) 18th century, from the Poltava region (Kiev Museum of Ukrainian Art). 6) 18th century, from the Hutsul region (Lviv Museum of Ukrainain Art). 7) Late 18th century, from Podilia (Ukrainian Museum, New York City). 8) 19th century, from the Kiev region (Museum of the Ethnography of the Peoples of the USSR, Leningrad). 9) Late 19th century, from Podilia (Kamianets-Podilskyi Museum). 10) 19th century, from the Poltava region (Poltava Art Museum). 11) 19th century, from Volhynia (Lviv Museum of Ukrainian Art).

Mykola Kilchevsky

Kilchevsky, Mykola [Kil'čevs'kyj], b 15 June 1909 in Kamianets-Podilskyi, Podilia gubernia, d 14 June 1979 in Kiev. Specialist in mechanics and mathematics; full member of the AN URSR from 1969. A graduate of the Kiev Physical-Chemical-Mathematical Institute, he taught at various institutes in Kiev and Tashkent. In 1945 he was appointed professor at Kiev University and in 1958 chairman of a department of the Institute of Structural Mechanics. His main publications deal with general mechanics, the theory of membranes, the theory of elasticity, and the analysis of solid body collisions.

Kiliia [Kilija]. VIII-10. City (1969 pop 24,500), fluvial port, and raion center in Odessa oblast situated on the left bank of the Kiliia Channel of the Danube Delta 40 km from the Black Sea. It was first mentioned in the late 7th century BC as the Greek polis of Licostomo. Kiliia belonged to Kievan Rus' from the 10th century AD and the Principality of Galicia-Volhynia from the early 13th century. Because of its commercial importance and strategic location on the delta it was an object of conquest, and from the 14th century on it was besieged and changed hands numerous times. It was ruled by Hungary (1353–9, 1448–65), Wallachia (1404–27), and Moldavia (1359–1403, 1427–48, 1465–84) before falling to Turkey (1484–1812). Its citadel (built in 1479) controlled traffic on the delta. As a Turkish port, Kiliia was plundered by Cossacks led by H. Loboda and S. Nalyvaiko (1594–5), I. Sulyma (1635), and S. Palii (1693). During the Russo-Turkish wars it was held by Russian forces in 1770–74, 1790–1, and 1806–12. Formally ceded to the Russian Empire in 1812, it was restored to Turkey after the Crimean War (in 1856), but was again ceded to Russia in 1878. In 1897 its population of 11,600 consisted of 4,500 Ukrainians, 2,500 Moldavians, 2,200 Russians, and 2,150 Jews. One of the largest trading cities on the Danube, after the First World War Kiliia was ceded to Rumania. From June 1940 to July 1941 it was occupied by Soviet troops, and since August 1944 it has remained a Soviet city. It is one of the major shipping and fishing centers on the Danube. Ship-repair yards are located in its harbor, and its industries manufacture bricks, asphalt, flax fiber, essential oils, and food products. A monument to B. Khmelnytsky, remains of the citadel, a 16th-century Greek church, St Nicholas's Church (1648), and the Holy Protectress Cathedral (1836) are found there.

Kilim weaving. The term 'kilim' (Ukrainian: *kylym*) is of Turkic origin and denotes an ornamented woven fabric used to cover floors or to adorn walls. The earliest references to kilims date back to the chronicles of Kievan Rus' and link them to burial rites. The princes used kilims also as chair covers. References to kilims are found in *bylyny* and historical songs. Kilims are depicted in the frescoes of St Cyril's Church in Kiev and in portraits of the late 17th and early 18th centuries.

Nothing definite can be said about kilim weaving in Ukraine before the 16th century. The earlier kilims belonging to the ruling class most likely had been imported. The earliest references to kilim imports from eastern countries occur in 15th-century sources. Kilim production in Volhynia in the 16th century is well documented; eg, a 1578 document listing M. Holshanska's dowry mentions two serf weavers, Yurko and Fedir. There are many 17th-century references to both locally produced and imported kilims. By the 18th century, kilim weaving was widespread: in Right-Bank Ukraine the mills owned by the Czartoryski and Potocki families, and in Left-Bank Ukraine Col P. Polubotok's mill, were well known. Although kilim weaving may have been taken up by peasants much earlier, in the 18th century it became widespread among them. Monks and town craftsmen also engaged in weaving. The industry grew rapidly at the end of the 18th century and in the first half of the 19th century. New mills were opened by landowners on their estates, especially in Left-Bank Ukraine, and in the towns. By the mid-19th century, Kharkiv's yearly production of kilims and woolen caparisons amounted to 25,000 pieces.

During the second half of the 19th century the kilim industry in Ukraine suffered an abrupt decline. Kharkiv's annual output, for example, fell to 4,000 kilims. Some measures were taken by individual manufacturers and zemstvos to counteract this trend. The Poltava zemstvo opened a kilim-weaving school, promoted kilim sales, and set up a collection of traditional kilims. In 1905 V. Khanenko organized a cottage weaving industry in Helenivka village, Vasylkiv county, Kiev gubernia. His craftsmen served a two-year apprenticeship. V. Fedorovych started a kilim-weaving school and workshop in the late 1880s in Vikno village, Ternopil region. At the beginning of the 20th century the main kilim-weaving districts in Left-Bank Ukraine were Myrhorod, Zinkiv, Romne, Poltava, and Pryluka counties. Thanks to the efforts of the artist O. Prybylska, a cottage weaving industry sprang up in 1913 in Skoptsi village, Kiev gubernia. Kilim weaving prospered also in the Katerynoslav region, Podilia, and the Ternopil region (Zbarazh, Zalozhtsi, Tovste, and Vikno).

In the late 19th and the beginning of the 20th century, new kilim-weaving centers sprang up in Galicia under the influence of the developing kilim industry in western Podilia. The Weaving Society, founded in 1886, began to produce kilims in 1890. In 1894 the society opened a weaving school, which in the 1920s was transformed into a kilim factory. A number of short-lived kilim mills were set up in the vicinity of Kosiv, Ternopil, Chortkiv, Zbarazh, Zhydachiv, and Lviv. A kilim industry existed in Transcarpathia in the 19th century, although information about it is sparse. In 1905 a co-operative kilim mill was organized in Hanychi village, Tiachiv county. Another mill appeared in Ardanove village, Irshava county. Bukovyna had a well-developed kilim industry in the 19th century. In the 1920s a kilim weaving school was opened in Ataky, Bessarabia.

At the beginning of the Soviet period the kilim industry in Ukraine experienced some serious difficulties: there was a shortage of equipment and raw materials, and private mills had closed down. With much effort the new authorities restored kilim weaving in its traditional centers. Workshops and art schools were set up in the Poltava, Chernihiv, and Kiev regions and in eastern Podilia to train qualified workers for the kilim industry. The industry was organized into handicraft (or the so-called artcraft) artels and was encouraged to produce kilims for export. Between 1928 and 1930 its output increased from 40,000 to 100,000 rubles' worth. In the 1930s the artels were turned into large state enterprises and were brought under the Ukrainian Handicraft Association (est 1936). Their production was regulated by the five-year plans. Today the more important kilim enterprises are located in Reshetylivka, Dihtiari, Hlyniany, Kolomyia, Khotyn, and Kosiv. Since the Second World War kilim production at these centers has grown steadily, with geometric kilims outweighing floral ones. Hlyniany's output increased from 15,000 sq m in 1945 to 49,000 sq m in 1960 and 82,000 sq m in 1970; Kosiv's from 95,000 sq m in 1955 to 120,000 sq m in 1965; and Khotyn's from 10,600 sq m in 1950 to 17,000 sq m in 1960 and 46,000 sq m in 1970.

Kilim making is a complex and labor-intensive process that includes yarn spinning, dyeing, and weaving. Traditionally, the necessary skills were passed on from generation to generation. Originally, the basic material was sheep's wool. Later on cotton and flax yarns were introduced, and in recent times synthetic fibres that are resistant to rot, mold, and moths have been adopted. Until the second half of the 19th century only natural dyes, mostly from local plants, were used. Yellow and green dyes were obtained from onion husks and blackthorn berries, red dyes from cochineal insects, black and gray dyes from oak gall, brown dyes from young alder bark, and blue dyes from indigo shrubs. These natural dyes produced pleasant soft colors that were very fast. Today, synthetic dyes have replaced the traditional natural dyes. Two basic types of looms – vertical and horizontal – have been used in kilim weaving. Flat-woven as well as knotted kilims were prepared on vertical looms. Patterns were produced by the interlocked tapestry weave: the wefts were woven back and forth into the warp by hand until the desired color area was defined. Then the background was woven in mechanically. Horizontal looms, which are mainly for geometric patterns, were introduced later. Today kilims are produced in the traditional way and on the somewhat more modern Axminster and Jacquard machines.

The oldest record about the ornamentation of Ukrainian kilims dates back to the 16th century. It describes kilims 'with various flowers,' two of them with a light blue, two with a white, one with a yellow, and five with a black background. Three 17th-century kilims have been preserved. One of them, a piled kilim with a floral ornament, was produced in 1698 at S. Koniecpolski's mill, which was built in Brody in the mid-17th century.

The ornamentation of 18th-century kilims consisted mostly of plant designs, which display much originality and local variations. The plants depicted on Right-Bank kilims tend to be slenderer and more stylized than those on Left-Bank kilims. Geometrical ornaments were more widespread than floral ones. As the market for the geometrically ornamented kilims grew, the floral ornamentation evolved towards a more geometric, stylized pattern. The geometrically ornamented kilim was and continues to be the basic type of kilim produced in Galicia, Bukovyna, Polisia, Podilia, and the Hutsul region of the Carpathian Mountains. Many motifs on these kilims symbolize natural phenomena as they appeared to a primitive mind. For centuries the magical symbols revered by the common people were depicted in folk art. In time they lost their original meaning and became simply decorative elements. In addition to geometrical and floral designs, Ukrainian kilims in the past also depicted coats of arms, emblems, scenes from gentry life, and religious images. In the Soviet period such themes have been replaced by portraits of Soviet leaders and scenes from Soviet life.

BIBLIOGRAPHY
Zhuk, A. *Ukraïns'ki narodni kylymy (XVII–poch. XX st.)* (Kiev 1966)
Zapasko, Ia. *Ukraïns'ke narodne kylymarstvo* (Kiev 1973)
Zhuk, A. *Ukraïns'kyi radians'kyi kylym* (Kiev 1973)

B. Medwidsky

Kimmerikon (Kimmeryk). An ancient Greek colony from the 6th century BC to the 3rd century AD on the Kerch Peninsula in the Crimea, and the southwestern outpost and harbor of the *Bosporan Kingdom. Remains from the colony's fort have been found on Mt Opuk. Older remains dating from the late Bronze Age were discovered on the east ridge of Mt Opuk and suggest that the settlement may have been founded by the *Cimmerians, the people who lived in the area before the Greeks. Excavations began in the late 19th century and since 1927 have proceeded systematically. In the 1st century AD Kimmerikon reached its zenith as a commercial and agricultural center. The town is mentioned by such classical writers as Strabo, Ptolemy, and Pliny.

Kinakh, Hlib [Kinax], b 5 October 1888 in Zbarazh, Galicia, d 29 January 1980 in Rome. Basilian priest; church historian. From 1920 he was active in Transcarpathia. In 1939 he was transferred to Prešov to oversee the eparchial library and to edit the eparchy's publications. From 1946 he lived in Rome, where he held various offices on the executive of the Basilian order, including archimandrite. He contributed to *Naukovyi zbirnyk Tovarystva Prosvita*, in which his materials on Transcarpathian church history appeared, and to *Analecta Ordinis S Basilii Magni*, in which his most important work, 'Zapysnyk' (Notebook), on early Basilian reform in Transcarpathia, appeared posthumously (1985).

Kinburn. A fortress that was located on Kinburn Spit in the mouth of the Dnieper River opposite Ochakiv, now in Mykolaiv oblast. Kinburn was built by the Turks in the 15th century. Later, it denied the Zaporozhian Cossacks access to the Black Sea from the Dnieper Estuary. In 1774 it was captured by a Russian army that included a large detachment of Zaporozhian Cossacks. Russia acquired the entire region under the terms of the Treaty of *Küçük Kaynarca, although the Turks attempted unsuccessfully to regain the fortress in 1787. Kinburn was attacked by the French during the Crimean War, and fell into disuse after the war.

Kinburn Spit. VII-12. A sand spit, 40 km long and 8–10 km wide, lying between the Dnieper-Boh Estuary and Yahorlytskyi Liman. The spit is dotted by 400 small, shallow fresh- and salt-water lakes. Its sand dunes are covered with steppe vegetation, while its marshy depressions are forested, partly with northern species. A part of the spit belongs to the *Black Sea Nature Reserve.

Kindrat, Peter, b 15 November 1892 in Chemeryntsi, Peremyshliany county, Galicia, d 22 June 1972 in Winnipeg. Religious leader and author. Immigrating to Canada in 1910, Kindrat studied at McMaster University and, after meeting I. Kolesnykiv, joined a group of Baptists in Toronto. After 1921 he served as a pastor in Montreal, Ottawa, Dauphin, Swan River, Prince Albert, and Winnipeg. A founder of the Ukrainian Baptist press in Canada, he was coeditor of *Khrystyians'kyi visnyk* (1942–52), secretary-general and president of the Ukrainian Evangelical Baptist Convention of Canada, and president of the All-Ukrainian Evangelical Baptist Fellowship (1949–59). Kindrat wrote *Ukraïns'kyi Baptysts'kyi Rukh u Kanadi* (Ukrainian Baptist Movement in Canada, 1972).

Kino (Cinema). A monthly magazine published in 1925 and in 1932–3 in Kharkiv and in 1926–32 in Kiev, first by the All-Ukrainian Photo-Cinema Administration (VUFKU) and then by Ukrainfilm. In 1927, 1929, 1930, and 1932 it came out twice a month. The magazine published articles on the history and theory of cinema, but devoted more space to film actors, film reviews, and the problems of filmmaking in Ukraine and abroad. Its editorial board was chaired by D. Falkivsky, and its main contributors included M. Bazhan, O. Vlyzko, O. Dovzhenko, H. Epik, M. Irchan, V. Krychevsky, O. Kopylenko, V. Polishchuk, H. Tasin, M. Trublaini, N. Ushakov, and Yu. Yanovsky. Altogether 135 issues appeared. In 1935–8 *Kino* was replaced by the magazine *Radians'ke kino*.

Kino (Cinema). A semimonthly magazine published in Lviv from 1930 to 1936 by D. Krenzhalovsky. It published reports and reviews of films playing at home and abroad.

Kino-hazeta (Cinema Newspaper). A periodical published semimonthly in Kiev from 1928 to 1931, and every 10 days in Kharkiv in 1931–2. It published news about the film industry in the Soviet Union, reviews of new films, and discussions of techniques for filming towns and villages. Its predecessor was the weekly *Kinotyzhden'* (1927–8).

Kinship. System of human relationships derived from procreation (consanguinity) and marriage (affinity). It plays a major role in all societies by regulating individual behavior and affecting social, economic, and political organization. Although in the past Ukrainians lived in extended or joint families, today their principal kinship ties are restricted to the nuclear family consisting of a married couple and their children. Marriage between two individuals is restricted within kinship groups by incest rules and is the way in which new kinship units based on affinity are formed.

Historically, Ukrainians lived in extended domestic units or joint families called *rody* (singular: *rid*). There are various theories about the extension and the legal status of this family unit. Strictly speaking, it consists of several families under the authority of an elder, and is unified by the right to blood vengeance. According to Ukraine's first code of law, **Ruskaia Pravda*, the right to blood vengeance seems to have extended over the whole *rid*. Thus the father, sons, brothers, and cousins of the wronged party had the right to vengeance. The feeling of family solidarity, however, extended beyond mentioned relatives. Various economic and juridical relations such as the shared homestead and property, as well as the authority of the family head, made the extended family in Ukraine a very tightly knit and culturally cohesive entity. The family's historical persistence testifies to the strength of the internal ties among its members. Federations of families with common property and a single head (generally, an elder), known as *dvoryshcha* (singular: *dvoryshche*), existed in Ukraine as late as the 14th–16th centuries. Some *dvoryshcha* survived into the 18th century, and remnants of this social entity were observed in the Boiko region in the 19th century.

Expressions of kinship mores have been preserved to this day in many Ukrainian folk songs, particularly traditional wedding songs, which stress the idea of family honor. The solitary, kinless individual is utterly wretched and defenseless according to such songs: 'Oi tym zhe ia pohybaiu bo rodu na maiu' (Oh I Am Perishing because I Have No Kin) and 'Duma pro buriu na Chornomu mori' (Duma about the Storm on the Black Sea). To reject one's kinship bonds is the ultimate wrong, as these proverbs claim: 'There is no greater sin or shame than to disown one's kin' and 'If I renounced my father and mother, then God would renounce me.' Unmarried and childless members were disapproved of by their kinsmen. According to some folk songs such individuals were not admitted to heaven because they had no offspring to pray for them. Traditionally, birth control was condemned.

The scope of the Ukrainian kinship network is reflected in the language. Current dictionaries provide distinct terms for the following lineal relationships in ascending order: *bat'ko* (father), *maty* (mother), *did* (grandfather), *baba* (grandmother), *pradid* (great-grandfather), *prababa* (great-grandmother), *prapradid* (great-great-grandfather), and *praprababa* (great-great-grandmother). More remote lineal antecedents are simply described as ancestors. In descending order the following terms are used: *syn* (son), *dochka* (daughter), *unuk* (grandson), *unuka* (granddaughter), *pravnuk* (great-grandson), *pravnuka* (great-granddaughter), *prapravnuk* (great-great-grandson), and *prapravnuka* (great-great-granddaughter). Their successors are described simply as descendants. In the lateral direction the common terms are *brat* (brother), *sestra* (sister), *diad'ko* (uncle), and *titka* (aunt), although in the dialects there are special terms for the father's brother (*stryiko*), the father's sister (*stryina*), the mother's brother (*vuiko*), and the mother's sister (*vuina*). In the literary language there is but one masculine and one feminine term for cousins (masculine: *dvoiuridni braty*, and feminine: *dvoiuridni sestry*) and nephews (masculine: *pleminnyky*, and feminine: *pleminnytsi*), but in the dialects there is a much richer vocabulary for these relations. Other collateral relations are identified by descriptive phrases such as 'grandmother's brother's son.'

There are a great number of affinal terms in Ukrainian. The central ones are *cholovik* (husband) and *zhinka* (wife). Parents of newlyweds (in-laws) laterally recognize each other as *svaty* (masculine sing: *svat*, and feminine sing: *svakha*). There are special terms for the father and mother of the groom (*test'* and *teshcha*) and the father and mother of the bride (*svekor* and *svekrukha*). Ukrainian also has a distinct term for the son-in-law (*ziat'*) and the daughter-in-law (*nevistka*), the husband's brother and sister (*diver* and *zovytsia*), and the wife's brother (*shvager*), but the term for the wife's sister (*svist'*) is archaic. Although Ukrainian dialects contain specific terms for other affinal relations, in the literary language such terms have been replaced by the general *svoiak* (masculine relative) and *svoiachka* (feminine relative) or by descriptive phrases such as 'wife of wife's brother.'

Traditionally, the most prevalent form of fictive kinship in Ukrainian society has been the institution of godparents (*kumy*). The godparents are also fictive relatives to the parents of the godchild. Because of this quasi-kinship, marriage between a godparent and a godchild was prohibited, and sexual intimacy between a parent and a godparent was considered a cardinal sin. Sexual relations between godparents, however, were treated as a less serious transgression and were mentioned often in folk songs and proverbs.

BIBLIOGRAPHY
Buriachok, A. *Nazvy sporidnenosti i svoiatstva v ukraïns'kii movi* (Kiev 1961)

B. Medwidsky

Vadym Kipa

Andrii Kiprianov

Kipa, Vadym (Kippa), b 13 May 1912 in Kuchmisterska Slobodka, a suburb of Kiev, d 31 August 1968 in New York. Pianist, composer, and educator. A graduate of the Kiev Conservatory (1937), he joined its teaching staff and in 1941 completed its graduate program. He was one of 10 finalists at the First All-Soviet Piano Competition in Moscow (1937). Deported to Germany in 1943, he was appointed accompanist at the opera studio of the Klindworth-Scharwenka Conservatory in Berlin and then professor of music. In 1951 he immigrated to the United States and established his own piano studio in New York. In his recitals and solo appearances he impressed critics with his perfect technique and unique emotional power. Kipa's compositions, dating back to 1939, consist mostly of works for piano (including an album for young pianists and *Variations Phantastique*) and for voice and piano (art songs). His style evolved from Neoromanticism to Impressionism and Neoclassicism with tonal and rhythmic autonomy.

Kipchaks. See Cumans.

Kiprianov, Andrii, b 16 July 1896 in Ruski Tyshky, Kharkiv county, Kharkiv gubernia, d 29 September 1972 in Kiev. Organic chemist; full member of the AN URSR from 1945 and vice-president from 1946 to 1948. He graduated from Kharkiv University in 1919 and worked there until 1941. From 1945 to 1960 he was the director of the AN URSR Institute of Organic Chemistry and a professor at Kiev University. Kiprianov published some 200 papers. Most of his research dealt with organic dyes. He resolved a number of problems in color theory, establishing, for example, that changing the electronic symmetry in a dye displaces the absorption maximum towards shorter wavelengths. He also explained the solvatochromic behavior of dyes, and discovered and elucidated the phenomenon of interaction between conjugated chromophores. A number of new dyes that he discovered found industrial use.

Kirgizia or **Kirgiz** SSR. A Soviet republic in Central Asia with an indigenous Turkic population. It is bounded by Kazakhstan to the north, Uzbekistan to the southwest, Tadzhikistan to the south, and China to the southeast. It has an area of 198,500 sq km divided into three oblasts. In 1986 its population was estimated at 4,051,000. Urban dwellers (39.7 percent of the total population) live in 21 cities and 20 towns. The average density in 1981 was 20.4 inhabitants per sq km. The capital and largest city is Frunze (1986 pop 617,000). In 1979 about 1.7 million Kirgiz lived in the republic; about 219,000 others lived elsewhere in the USSR (the RSFSR; the Uzbek, Tadzhik, and Kazakh republics; and Ukraine [2,370]). About 80,000 live in China, 25,000 in Afghanistan, and 1,000 in Turkey. In 1970, 85.5 percent of the republic's Kirgiz were rural dwellers; in contrast, 66 percent of the republic's Russians and 51 percent of its Ukrainians were urban dwellers. In 1979, 98 percent of the Kirgiz claimed Kirgiz as their native language.

Kirgizia is a rugged, mountainous country lying in the center of the Tian Shen mountain system. Some of the highest mountains in the USSR are found there (7,439 m). Lowlands occupy only 15 percent of the total area. The main ones are the Chui and Talas valleys in the north, the Fergana Valley in the southwest, and the Issyk-Kul Depression in the south. Kirgizia is landlocked and much higher than the central-Asian plains and deserts to its northwest and southeast. The climate is relatively harsh and dry and varies with altitude. In the lowland areas of Ukrainian settlement, the average temperature is −6 to −8°C in January and +20–25°C in July; the total annual precipitation is 300–400 mm, and the soil consists of sierozems.

The nomadic Kirgiz were vassals of the Khanate of Kokand when it became a Russian protectorate in 1868 and was integrated into the Russian Empire in 1876 as part of Semerechenskaia and Fergana provinces of *Turkestan general gubernia. During the 1917 Revolution a Kirgiz independence movement arose, but it was suppressed by the Bolsheviks in 1920–3. Kirgizia became part

The ethnic composition of Kirgizia, 1926–79 (percentages in parentheses)

	1926		1959		1970		1979	
Kirghiz	661,000	(66.6)	837,000	(40.5)	1,285,000	(43.8)	1,687,000	(47.9)
Russians	116,000	(11.7)	624,000	(30.2)	856,000	(29.2)	912,000	(25.9)
Ukrainians	64,000	(6.4)	137,000	(6.6)	120,000	(4.1)	109,000	(3.1)
Uzbeks	110,000	(11.1)	219,000	(10.6)	333,000	(11.4)	426,000	(12.1)
Others	42,000	(4.2)	249,000	(12.1)	339,000	(11.5)	389,000	(11.0)*
Total	993,000	(100)	2,066,000	(100)	2,933,000	(100)	3,523,000	(100)

*101,000 Germans, 72,000 Tatars, 30,000 Uigurs, 27,000 Kazakhs, 27,000 Dungans, 23,000 Tadzhiks

of the Kara-Kirgiz autonomous oblast in 1924; it became the Kirgiz ASSR in 1926 and the Kirgiz SSR in 1936. In the Soviet period Kirgizia's population has quadrupled; it grew from 1 million in 1926 to 1.5 million in 1939, 2 million in 1959, and 3.5 million in 1979.

Until the Soviet period virtually all Kirgiz lived by nomadic herding. Since the 1920s the republic's economy has been extensively transformed. Agriculture is collectivized and mechanized. The main branches are pasture-based livestock raising (beef cattle and sheep for wool) and the cultivation of food grains, cotton, sugar beets, tobacco, and opium poppies, much of it on land that is irrigated. In 1978, industry produced 57.4 percent of the total value of the republic's output; the main branches are coal mining, metalworking, machine building, food processing, and textile and clothing manufacturing.

Beginning in the late 19th century many Russian and Ukrainian peasants began settling in Kirgizia, particularly in the cities and arable lowlands. Their influx increased in the Soviet period. Consequently, the Kirgiz have become a minority in their own republic even though their number has almost tripled (see table).

Cumulative immigration estimates indicate that the number of Ukrainians in Kirgizia is much greater than official statistics show: about 250,000 to 300,000. They live mainly in the north in the Chui and Talas valleys (two-thirds of all Ukrainians in Kirgizia were living there in 1926), but also in the south in the Issyk-Kul Depression and the Fergana Valley, and in the larger cities. Most of the Ukrainians have become Russified and identify themselves as Russian. In the 1979 census only 38 percent of them claimed Ukrainian as their native language; 62 percent claimed Russian. In 1970 Ukrainians constituted 5.6 percent of the total urban population.

Kirgiz-Ukrainian relations have been primarily literary. T. Shevchenko's *Kobzar* was published in Kirgiz in 1939, another collection of his poems appeared in 1959, and Kirgiz scholars have written about Shevchenko. The works of Lesia Ukrainka, I. Franko, P. Hrabovsky, P. Tychyna, and N. Rybak have been translated into Kirgiz. Works by the Kirgiz writers Ch. Aitmatov, T. Sidibekov, T. Satylganov, A. Usebaiev, Dzh. Bokonbaiev, and A. Tokombaiev have been translated into Ukrainian. I. Le's *Roman mizhhir'ia* (A Novel of the Mountain Valley, 1929–30) is set in Soviet Kirgizia.

BIBLIOGRAPHY

Korbut, S. *Siryi Klyn i ukraïns'ka kolonizatsiina sprava* (Lviv 1937)

Marunchak, M. *Ukraïntsi v SSSR poza kordonamy URSR* (Winnipeg 1974)

V. Kubijovyč, R. Senkus, A. Zhukovsky

Illia Kiriak

Watson Kirkconnell

Kiriak, Illia [Kyrijak, Illja], b 29 May 1888 in Zavallia, Sniatyn county, Galicia, d 28 December 1955 in Edmonton. Teacher and novelist. Kiriak immigrated to Canada in 1907 and settled in Alberta. Until 1936 he taught school in rural Ukrainian districts. He was secretary of the Ukrainian Self-Reliance League (1936–42) and rector of the Hrushevsky Institute (now St John's Institute) in Edmonton (1940–2). His three-volume epic novel *Syny zemli* (1939–45), which appeared also in an abridged translation titled *Sons of the Soil* (1959), is a valuable sociological document about Ukrainians in Alberta during the half-century before the Second World War.

Kirichenko, Aleksei. See Kyrychenko, Oleksii.

Kirkconnell, Watson, b 16 May 1895 in Port Hope, Ontario, d 26 February 1977 in Wolfville, Nova Scotia. Literary scholar, writer, and translator. Educated at Queen's University and Lincoln College, Oxford, Kirkconnell taught English literature and classics at Wesley College, Winnipeg, McMaster University, and Acadia University. Living in Winnipeg (1922–40), he became interested in the languages and literatures of the city's ethnic groups. In 1935 he edited *Canadian Overtones*, the first anthology of 'New Canadian' writings in English translation. Between 1937 and 1965 he contributed an annual review 'Publications in Other Languages' to the *University of Toronto Quarterly*. During the Second World War he helped organize the Department of National War Services and served on advisory committees of its Nationalities Branch. He played an important role in the founding of the Ukrainian Canadian Committee (UCC). In pamphlets such as *Our Ukrainian Loyalists* (1943) he emphasized the dedication of the UCC and non-communist Ukrainian Canadians to the Allied war effort and criticized the pro-Communist Association of United Ukrainian Canadians. Kirkconnell collaborated with C.H. Andrusyshen to produce two volumes of Ukrainian poetry in translation: *The Ukrainian Poets 1189 1962* (1963) and *The Poetical Works of Taras Shevchenko* (1964).

Kirkor, Adam, b 21 January 1818 in Slyvyn, now in Mohiliou oblast, Belorussian SSR, d 23 November 1886 in Cracow. Polish scholar, specializing in the history, archeology, ethnography, literature, and language of Lithuania, Belorussia, and Ukraine. Kirkor excavated *kurhans in western Podilia and Pokutia, and made important archeological findings in Vasylkivtsi and Kotsiubyntsi, in the Ternopil region. He explored the artificial caves (Dovbush's Caves) near Stryi in the Lviv region. He is the author of *Litwa i Ruś pod względem historycznym, geograficznym, statystycznym i archeologicznym* (Lithuania and Rus' from a Historical, Geographical, Statistical, and Archeological Viewpoint, 1875) and of an outline of Ukrainian literature, *O literaturze pobratymczych narodów słowiańskich* (Concerning the Literature of the Fraternal Slavic Peoples, 1874).

Kirove. V-18, DB III-3. Town smt (1979 pop 11,100) in Donetske oblast, under the jurisdiction of the Dzerzhynske city soviet. Founded in the 18th century, its main industry is anthracite mining.

Kirovohrad: model of the original St Elizabeth Fortress

Kirovohrad. V-13. City and oblast capital (1986 pop 266,000) in the southeastern Dnieper Upland on the Inhul River. It is divided into two city raions.

The city was founded in 1754 on Zaporozhian Cossack territory as the St Elizabeth Fortress, which was built to protect the Russian Empire's southern frontier and the Balkan colonists of *New Serbia from raids of Turks and Crimean Tatars. During the Russo-Turkish War of 1768–74 the fortress was the operational base of the Russian army. In 1775 the town that grew up around the fortress was named Yelysavethrad; it had a population of 4,750 in 1787 and 9,300 in 1823. The town became a county center in New Russia gubernia (1764–83, 1797–1801), Katerynoslav and Voznesensk vicegerencies (1784–97), and Kherson gubernia (1802–28, 1865–1925). Until the First World War it was an important center of trade in grain, wool, lard, flour, timber, cattle, and horses, much of which was exported via Odessa and Mykolaiv.

From 1828 to 1860 Yelysavethrad was a major garrison city under strict martial law and the center of *military settlements in Southern Ukraine. During that time it declined economically. It experienced growth only after a railway link was established with Odessa, Mykolaiv, Kremenchuk, and Khvastiv in the late 1860s and the British-owned Ellworthy agricultural-machinery plant was founded in 1874. By the 1890s there were eight such plants; they employed 58 percent of the city's workers. Many flour mills and distilleries were located in the city, and each year it was visited by thousands of migrant laborers seeking work during the harvest in Southern Ukraine. Its population grew from 15,000 in 1850 to 23,700 in 1861 and 61,500 in 1897 despite recurrent fires, river floods, and epidemics. Until the late 19th century public utilities were sorely lacking. There were few elementary schools (only 12 in the 1890s); consequently there was a high illiteracy rate. A waterworks was built only in 1892, an electric tramway in 1897, and a power station in 1908. The first newspaper in the city, *Elisavetgradskii gorodskoi listok*, was published in 1874–6. Others followed: *Elisavetgradskii vestnik* (1876–mid-1890s), *Vedomosti Elisavetgradskogo gorodskogo upravleniia* (1892–1917), *Golos iuga* (1905–14), and several short-lived papers. There were few physicians and public health care was poor; between 1902 and 1912 the mortality rate from infectious diseases was 21–29 percent of the population in general and 51 percent of the non-adult population.

From the 1870s the city was a regional center of cultural and revolutionary activity. Ukrainian theatrical productions were performed on an ongoing basis; such prominent figures as I. Karpenko-Kary, M. Sadovsky, P. Saksahansky, M. Kropyvnytsky, M. Zankovetska, and P. Nishchynsky were instrumental in their mounting. Populist and, later, Marxist cells sprang up; their members were instrumental in educating and politicizing the local population. From the late 19th century, workers' unrest was a recurring phenomenon. In 1913 the city had 64 factories employing 4,300 workers; 2,300 of them worked at the Ellworthy plant, which produced a 10th of the empire's agricultural machines.

The turmoil of the 1917 Revolution and subsequent strife did not bypass the city. It was occupied by units of the Free Cossacks in 1917 and by the Ukrainian Sich Riflemen in 1918. Prolonged fighting took place there between the insurgent forces of Otaman N. Hryhoriiv and the Red Guards in spring 1919. After Soviet rule was established the population declined from 77,100 in 1920 to 50,300 in 1923; it then grew to 66,500 by 1926, of which 44.5 percent was Ukrainian, 27.6 percent was Jewish, and 25 percent was Russian. By 1925 the city and its industries had been rebuilt. It was renamed Zinovivske in 1924, Kirove in 1934, and Kirovohrad in 1939. It was an okruha center from 1923 and a raion center from 1930. Industrial growth intensified in the 1930s, and the population grew to 100,000 by 1939. In 1939 the city became the capital of a new oblast. From August 1941 to January 1944 it was occupied by the German army. Much of its population fled, but much of it was also killed, and the city's buildings and industries were largely destroyed. Postwar reconstruction ended in late 1948, after which industrial expansion occurred.

Kirovohrad: military training post of the Ukrainian Sich Riflemen, 1918

In the postwar period Kirovohrad has been an important industrial city. Its output consists of agricultural machines (40 percent of all Soviet seeders in the 1960s), tractor parts, radio components, typewriters, food products, pig iron, filtering kieselguhr, clothing, footwear, furniture, and building materials. Its population has grown steadily, reaching 132,000 in 1959 (75 percent Ukrainian, 19 percent Russian) and 189,000 in 1970. In 1979 there were 9 secondary-specialized schools, 11 vocational-technical schools, and 3 post-secondary schools – a pedagogical institute, an institute of agricultural machine building, and a civil-aviation pilots' school – in the city. Several institutes that plan and design agicultural machines and tractors, a Ukrainian music and drama theater, a puppet theater, an oblast philharmonic, and a regional museum are also located there. Buildings and walls of the fortress, a Greek church (1812), the Church of the Holy Protectress (1850s), and several 19th-century buildings have been preserved.

BIBLIOGRAPHY
Pashutin, A. *Istoricheskii ocherk g. Elisavetgrada* (Yelysavethrad 1897)
Hvozdets'kyi, V. *Kirovohrad* (Kiev 1964)
Syvolap, D.; et al (eds). *Istoriia mist i sil Ukraïns'koï* RSR: *Kirovohrads'ka oblast'* (Kiev 1972)

R. Senkus, A. Zhukovsky

Kirovohrad Agricultural Machines Plant (Kirovohradskyi zavod silskohospodarskykh mashyn Chervona zirka). Established in Yelysavethrad (now Kirovohrad) in 1874 by T. and R. Allworthy as an agricultural-machinery repair shop, it developed by the end of the century into an agricultural-implements plant. It played an important role in the mechanization of agriculture in the steppe region. It was nationalized in 1920, and in the 1930s underwent major reconstruction. Today it produces all the sugar-beet, corn, and vegetable seed sowers in the USSR as well as 25 percent of the grain sowers.

Kirovohrad Institute of Agricultural Machine Building (Kirovohradskyi instytut silskohospodarskoho mashynobuduvannia). Technical school of higher education under the Ministry of Higher and Specialized Secondary Education of the Ukrainian SSR. Formed in 1967 out of several sections of the Kharkiv Polytechnical Institute, it consists of five departments – agricultural machine building, mechanical engineering, road-construction machinery, road repair, and general technology – and an evening school. In 1979–80 the enrollment was 5,300.

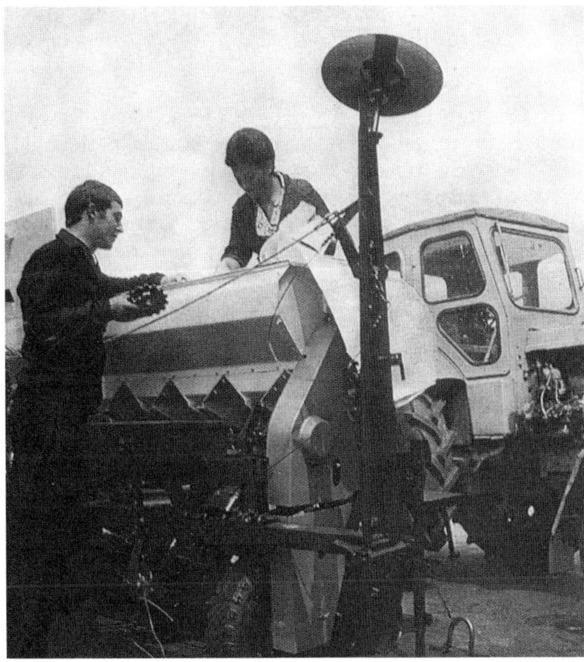

At the Kirovohrad Agricultural Machines Plant

Kirovohrad oblast. An administrative region (1986 pop 1,228,700) in south-central Ukraine, formed on 10 January 1939. It has an area of 24,600 sq km, divided among 21 raions, 315 rural soviets, 12 cities, and 26 towns (smt). The capital and largest city is Kirovohrad.

Physical geography. The oblast is essentially a fertile elevated plain located in the steppe and forest-steppe of the southern Dnieper Upland between the Dnieper and Buh rivers; it is dissected by deep river valleys and ravines. In the north the soils are mostly deep and podzolized chernozems, with gray podzolized soils in the forest-steppe. In the south they are mostly medium- and low-humus chernozems. The *Dnieper Lignite Coal Basin and sizable nickel, iron-ore, marl, kaolin, amphibolite, chromite, graphite, peat, quartzite, granite, labradorite, marble, and oil-shale deposits are found in the oblast. Broad-leaved and pine forests cover 150,500 ha of the area; nature reserves cover 4,100 ha.

There are 207 rivers longer than 10 km in the oblast. The principal ones are the Dnieper and its tributaries, the Tiasmyn, Tsybulnyk, and Inhulets, and the Boh and its tributaries, the Inhul, Syniukha, and Synytsia. Fifty-four river reservoirs have been built; the largest are the Novoarkhanhelske, Chervonokhutirske, Iskrivka, and Ternivka reservoirs. Parts of the Dnieper's Kremenchuk and Dniprodzerzhynske reservoirs lie on the oblast's eastern periphery. A large aqueduct runs from Svitlovodske on the Dnieper to Kirovohrad. The oblast's climate is temperate-continental. Winters are short and mild, and summers are hot, with dry winds and occasional droughts. The average temperature is −5°C in January and +20°C in July. The annual precipitation is 400–470 mm.

History. From the 9th to 14th centuries, the oblast's northern parts belonged to Kievan Rus'. Then the territory came under Lithuanian rule in 1362 and Polish rule in 1569. By and large it was wild, unpopulated steppe. From the late 16th to the mid-18th centuries it was part of the lands of the Zaporozhian Cossacks, and Ukrainian peasants began settling there. In 1648 the Cossack-Polish Battle of Zhovti Vody took place there. In 1739 Russia acquired nominal rule over the territory and in 1752 created a region called *New Serbia for Balkan military settlers. In 1754 the city of Yelysavethrad (Kirovohrad) was founded.

During the revolutionary years of 1918–20 various armed conflicts took place on the territory, involving, at various times, UNR and German troops, the Bolsheviks, N. Hryhoriiv's partisans, N. Makhno's partisans, and the Denikin army. Under Soviet rule, the territory was divided among Yelysavethrad, Oleksandriia, Pervomaiske, Kremenchuk, Uman, and Dnipropetrovske okruhas in 1925 and between Kiev and Odessa oblasts in 1932. In 1937 the raions in Odessa oblast were transferred to the restructured Dnipropetrovske oblast and the new Mykolaiv oblast. Kirovohrad oblast was created in 1939. From August 1941 to March 1944 the oblast was occupied by the German army.

Population. The oblast's population increased from 1,176,900 in 1940 to 1,241,000 in 1970 and 1,265,700 in 1974. Between 1974 and 1984 it decreased by 2.6 percent. The urban share of the population has increased significantly, from 14.7 percent in 1940 to 31 percent in 1959, 44 percent in 1970, and 56.6 percent in 1984. Ukrainians composed 88.7 percent of the population in 1959 and 86.8 percent in 1979; in 1979, 97 percent of them considered Ukrainian their native language. Russians composed 8.4 percent in 1959 and 10 percent in 1979. In 1959 Belorussians composed 0.8 percent; Jews, 0.8 percent; and Moldavians, 0.5 percent. Cities with populations over 50,000 are Kirovohrad, Oleksandriia, and Svitlovodske.

Industry. The main branches of industry are food production (31.8 percent of total output in 1983), machine building and metalworking (28 percent), non-ferrous metallurgy (7.3 percent), fuel production (6.8 percent), light industry, and building-materials production. Sugar, the oblast's most important food product, is made by plants in Ulianivka, Oleksandriia, Dolynske, Oleksandrivka, Mala Vyska, and Novoukrainka. Vegetable oils and animal fats are rendered in Kirovohrad. Distilleries are found in Kirovohrad, Mala Vyska, Oleksandriia, Znamianka, and Mezhyrichka. Flour mills and meat-packing plants are located mostly in Kirovohrad. The principal output of the machine-building and metalworking industries is the production of agricultural machines and equipment. The *Kirovohrad Agricultural Machines Plant is one of the largest in Ukraine. Other plants in Kirovohrad make parts for diesel engines and combines and equipment for the sugar industry and repair automobiles and farm machines. Large cranes, mining equipment, and machine parts are made in Oleksandriia. Steam engines are repaired in Haivoron.

Iron and nickel are smelted in Pobuzke. Semiconductors are produced in Svitlovodske. The oblast has the largest lignite reserves in Ukraine; several open pits and mines are found around Oleksandriia. Iron-ore quartzites are mined near Petrove. Coal briquettes are made in Semenivka-Holovkivka and Baidakove. Chemical products (mineral waxes and coal-derived reagents) are made in Oleksandriia. A huge graphite-mining and enrichment complex is located near Zavallia; it produced 60 percent of Soviet graphite in 1968. Using locally quarried granite, refractory clays, labradorite, and gravel, reinforced concrete and other building materials are made in Kirovohrad, Svitlovodske, Znamianka, Vlasivka, and elsewhere. The oblast's light industry produces clothing, cord and twine, and leather goods. Wood products and furniture are made in Znamianka, Kirovohrad, Oleksandriia, and Svitlovodske. The oblast's industries are powered by the Kremenchuk, Novoarkhanhelske, Haivoron, Chervonokhutirska, and Ternivka hydroelectric stations and Kirovohrad and Oleksandriia thermal stations.

Agriculture. In 1983 there were 315 collective farms and 47 state farms in the oblast. They had at their disposal 2,225,600 ha of land, of which 2,057,000 ha were farmed; of the latter, 90 percent were cultivated, 7.6 percent were pastures, and 0.7 percent were hayfields. The entire seeded area was 1,752,000 ha.

Of the entire seeded area in 1971 (1,732,000 ha), 50.2 percent was sown with grains, 28 percent with fodder crops, and 17 percent with industrial crops. Winter wheat was the main grain crop (482,200 ha), followed by corn (182,300 ha), spring barley (130,900 ha), pulses, millet, and buckwheat. The main industrial crops in 1971 were sugar beets (122,700 ha) and sunflowers (142,900 ha); coriander and soybeans are grown in the oblast's southeast. Fruits grown (on 39,000 ha in 1978) include apples, pears, cherries, plums, and various berries.

In 1983 animal husbandry accounted for 54.7 percent of the total value of agricultural production. It consisted mostly of beef and dairy cattle, sheep, and goat farming and some fish and rabbit farming, beekeeping, and sericulture.

Transportation. In 1983 there were 869 km of railroad in the oblast. The main lines crossing it are Kiev–Dnipropetrovske, Moscow–Odessa, Kiev–Kherson, Kharkiv–Odessa, and Znamianka–Mykolaiv. The main junctions are Znamianka, Pomichna, Korystivka, Dolynska, and Haivoron. In 1983 there were 5,400 km of motor roads, of which 4,500 were paved. The main highways are Kiev–Odessa, Kirovohrad–Mykolaiv, Kiev–Dnipropetrovske, Kharkiv–Odessa, and Poltava–Kishinev. River transport on the Dnieper is well developed; the main port is Svitlovodske. Airports located in Kirovohrad oblast are Kamatovo near Kirovohrad and smaller ones in Mala Vyska, Chervona Kaminka, and Dolynska.

BIBLIOGRAPHY

Rozvytok ekonomiky i kul'tury Kirovohradshchyny za 40 rokiv (1917–1957) (Kirovohrad 1957)
Mishchenko, H. *Kirovohrads'ka oblast'* (Kiev 1961)
Syvolap, D.; et al (eds). *Istoriia mist i sil Ukraïns'koï RSR: Kirovohrads'ka oblast'* (Kiev 1972)

I. Myhul, R. Senkus

Kirovohrad Pedagogical Institute (Kirovohradskyi pedahohichnyi instytut im. O.S. Pushkina). An institution of higher learning under the jurisdiction of the Ministry of Education of the Ukrainian SSR. At first a pedagogical tekhnikum (established 1923), it was reorganized into an institute of social education in 1930 before assuming its present form in 1933. The institute has seven faculties – history, philology, English language, physics and mathematics, pedagogy, music, and physical education – and an extension department offering preparatory and correspondence courses. Its enrollment was 3,800 (1978–9). The institute's library holdings number over 415,000.

Kirovohrad Regional Museum

Kirovohrad Regional Museum (Kirovohradskyi kraieznavchyi muzei). Founded in 1883, the museum has departments for the natural history of the region, prerevolutionary Ukrainian history, and Soviet history; a picture gallery; and a branch, the Karpenko-Kary Museum and Nature Reserve. It also maintains a special collection relating to Yu. *Yanovsky. By 1979 the museum had over 50,000 exponents, many relating to the history of the Ukrainian theater, including materials on I. Karpenko-Kary, M. Kropyvnytsky, and I. Mykytenko. The art collection includes works by I. Aivazovsky, V. Makovsky, and K. Trutovsky.

Kirovohrad Ukrainian Music and Drama Theater (Kirovohradskyi ukrainskyi muzychno-dramatychnyi teatr im. M. Kropyvnytskoho). Founded in 1938 as an oblast collective farmers' theater in Oleksandriia, it was evacuated during the war and then relocated to Kirovohrad. Its repertoire includes Ukrainian and world classics such as M. Kropyvnytsky's *Dai sertsiu voliu, zavede v nevoliu* (Give the Heart Freedom and It Will Lead to Slavery) and *Zamuleni dzherela* (The Silted Springs), M. Starytsky's *Talan* (Talent), Lope de Vega's *Fuente ovejuna*, and W. Shakespeare's *King Lear*, as well as contemporary plays such as Yu. Yanovsky's *Duma pro Brytanku* (Duma about Brytanka) and O. Kolomiiets's *Dykyi anhel* (The Wild Angel). Its stage directors have included H. Volovyk, I. Kaznadii, and M. Hiliarovsky (1976–8).

Kirovske [Kirovs'ke]. V-19, DB II-5. City (1976 pop 60,500) under the jurisdiction of Voroshylovhrad oblast, situated on the Luhanka River. Founded in 1764 as Holubivka, until 1944 it was called Holubivskyi Rudnyk. It has eight anthracite mines, a winery, a clothing factory, a manufacturing complex, and a mining-transport tekhnikum.

Kirovske [Kirovs'ke]. V-15. Town smt (1979 pop 7,900) on the Dnieper River's left bank in Dnipropetrovske raion. Founded in the 18th century, until 1938 this river port was called Obukhivka.

Kirovske [Kirovs'ke]. VIII-16. Town smt (1979 pop 6,700) and raion center in the eastern Crimea. It was first mentioned in 1783 as Islam-Terek. A German colony was founded there in the 1840s. The town was renamed in 1945.

Kirsanov, Oleksander, b 2 November 1902 in Moscow. Organic chemist; since 1961 full member of the AN URSR. After completing his studies he worked at scientific institutes in Moscow (1924–32), Sverdlovsk (1932–44), and Dnipropetrovske (1944–56). In 1956 he was appointed department chairman, and in 1960 director, at the AN URSR Institute of Organic Chemistry. Most of his 400 papers deal with the chemistry of organophosphorus and organosulfur compounds. He discovered a number of methods to synthesize new classes and types of compounds. The phosphazo-reaction, a method of synthesizing compounds with a nitrogen-phosphorus double bond, and the direct amidation of carboxylic acids were named after him. His synthesis of phosphorus isocyanates led to the production of new insecticides.

Kish [kiš] (from the Turkic *koš* or *goš*, meaning camp, group of yurts, stable stall, or troop). A Cossack encampment or settlement of Zaporozhian Cossacks. The title given to the leader of the Zaporozhian Sich – *Kish otaman – is derived from the word.

Kish of Ukrainian Sich Riflemen. See Ukrainian Sich Riflemen.

Kish otaman (*koshovyi otaman*). The elective leader of the *Zaporozhian Sich and chief executive officer in the 16th–18th centuries. Until the end of the 17th century he was also called hetman. The Kish otaman was elected for a one-year term by the *Sich Council from among the more respected and influential Cossacks. He could be dismissed before the end of his mandate or re-elected; eg, the last Kish otaman, P. Kalnyshevsky, retained his post almost without interruption from 1765 to 1775. The Kish otaman, aided by the *starshyna*, wielded ultimate military and political power and was responsible for maintaining external diplomatic relations. He was the chief magistrate and had the power of final decision during wartime. In peacetime, his decisions could be appealed to the Sich Council. His symbol of authority was the **bulava*. The office of Kish otaman was retained by the Black Sea Cossacks until 1797.

Kishinev [Kišinev] (Rumanian: Chişinău). VI-9. Capital (1985 pop 624,000) of the Moldavian SSR since 1940. In 1970, 14.2 percent (50,500) of its population was Ukrainian. The town is first mentioned in historical documents in 1420, when it belonged to the Moldavian principality. In 1812, with the rest of Bessarabia, it was annexed by Russia and in 1818 it became the capital of Bessarabia oblast. From 1918 to 1940 Kishinev was part of Rumania. I. *Nechui-Levytsky taught at the gymnasium in Kishinev (1873–84) and in the 1890s M. *Kotsiubynsky stayed there. In the 1930s there was a community of Ukrainian political émigrés in Kishinev.

Kishka, Samiilo [Kiška, Samijlo] (Koshka, Kushka, Koshych), ?–1602. A Ukrainian nobleman and Cossack leader from the Bratslav region. During a Zaporozhian Cossacks sea campaign in the 1570s, he was captured and spent about 25 years in Turkish captivity. In 1599 he led a rebellion of Cossack slaves (immortalized in a *duma named after him) on a Turkish galley near Gezlev (now Yevpatoriia in the Crimea). He escaped back to Ukraine and became the leader of the *Registered Cossacks. In return for their participation in Poland's wars, he secured the abolition of the Polish proclamation of the Cossacks as outlaws and the restoration of their former rights and privileges. In 1600 he led the Cossack troops during the Polish campaign against the Turks in Moldavia. In 1601–2 he commanded the 2,000 Cossacks who took part in the Polish-Swedish War in Livonia. He died in the Battle of Fellin.

Bohdan Kistiakovsky

Kistiakovsky, Bohdan [Kistjakovs'kyj], b 4 November 1868 in Kiev, d 16 April 1920 in Katerynodar (today Krasnodar) or Novorosiiske in the Kuban. Influential jurist, sociologist, and philosopher of law; the son of O. *Kistiakovsky, father of G. *Kistiakowsky, and nephew of V. Antonovych. He studied at the universities of Kiev (1888–90), Kharkiv (1890), and Dorpat (Tartu, 1890–2). He received his PH D from Strasbourg University in 1899. By 1902 he had abandoned Marxism and philosophical materialism, becoming an avowed neo-Kantian, and developed a profound interest in the epistemological and methodological foundations of the social sciences and social theory.

Kistiakovsky had close contacts with the Galician Radicals (including I. Franko and M. Pavlyk) and the Russian liberal émigrés grouped around P. Struve; he helped Struve to edit the well-known journal *Osvobozhdenie* (1902–5). He also developed a mutually beneficial association with the social philosopher M. Weber.

Kistiakovsky taught at the Moscow Commercial Institute (1906–11), Moscow University (1909–10), and the Demidov Juridical Lyceum in Yaroslavl (1911–17). In 1912 he became the editor of the influential law journal *Iuridicheskii vestnik* (Moscow 1913–17). A lifelong supporter of the Ukrainian movement, he returned to Kiev in 1917 and became a professor at Kiev University. In 1918 he was appointed to the State Senate and the General Administrative Court of the Hetman government and served on the commissions for drafting the law on Ukrainian citizenship and the statute of the newly founded Ukrainian Academy of Sciences (UAN). In 1919 he was elected a full member of the UAN; he sat on its Legal Terminology Commission and the Commission for the Study of Social Movements and held the chairs of state, administrative, and international law and of sociology.

Kistiakovsky contributed many articles (some under the pseudonym Ukrainets) to Russian scholarly, popular, and political periodicals. He edited Russian translations of Western scholarship and the bibliographic journal *Kriticheskoe obozrenie* (Moscow 1907–10). His chief works include his well-received dissertation *Gesellschaft und Einzelwesen: Eine methodologische Untersuchung* (1899), *Stranitsy proshlogo: K istorii konstitutsionnogo dvizhennia v Rossii* (Pages from the Past: Towards a History of the Constitutional Movement in Russia, 1909), and *Sotsial'nye nauki i pravo* (The Social Sciences and Law, 1916), an important compendium of his sociological articles that earned him another PH D (from Kharkiv University). He also contributed articles (under the pseudonym Khatchenko) to the Moscow Ukrainophile journal *Ukrainskaia zhizn'* (1912–17) and edited and wrote long introductory essays to the political works of M. *Drahomanov, who influenced his views.

Kistiakovsky is regarded as having been an original and leading proponent of neo-Kantianism and formal sociology in Western Europe and in the Russian Empire. A. Vucinich has devoted a chapter to his life and ideas in his *Social Thought in Tsarist Russia: The Quest for a General Science of Society, 1861–1917* (1976).

R. Senkus

Kistiakovsky, Ihor [Kistjakovs'kyj], b 1876 in Kiev, d 1941 in Paris. Lawyer, educator, and political figure; the son of O. *Kistiakovsky. A graduate of Kiev University, he studied Roman and civil law in Germany and taught briefly at Kiev University. In 1903 he moved to Moscow to practice law and taught at the university (1903–10) and commercial institute (1910–17) there. From May 1918 he was state secretary in P. Skoropadsky's Hetman government and deputy head of the Ukrainian Peace Delegation that negotiated a truce with Soviet Russia; in July he was appointed minister of internal affairs. He was one of a group of ministers (with V. Liubynsky, D. Doroshenko, B. Butenko, and O. Rohoza) that advocated an independent course and opposed federation with a non-Bolshevik Russia. In 1919 he fled to Istanbul, where he worked as a lawyer and assisted refugees. Later he immigrated to Paris, where he was active in the Russian White émigré community. Kistiakovsky wrote several Russian-language works in the field of law, including studies on heirs' responsibilities for debts in Roman law (1900) and on the concept of the legal subject (1903).

Kistiakovsky, Oleksander [Kistjakovs'kyj], b 26 March 1833 in Horodyshche, Sosnytsia county, Chernihiv gubernia, d 25 January 1885 in Kiev. Noted jurist and historian of law. He graduated from Kiev University and

Oleksander Kistiakovsky

Volodymyr Kistiakovsky

George Bohdan Kistiakowsky

taught there from 1864. In 1869 he was appointed professor of criminal law and procedure. He cofounded and for a time presided over the *Kiev Juridical Society. He was an assistant editor of the journal *Osnova* and active in the old *Hromada. In his research he focused on the history of law and the court system of the Hetman state, on *Magdeburg law, and on common law. The *Code of Laws of 1743 was published by him with a scholarly commentary in 1879. His other legal works include *Issledovanie o smertnoi kazni* (Research on the Death Penalty, 1867), *Elementarnyi uchebnik obshchogo ugolovnogo prava* (Elementary Textbook of Common Criminal Law, 1875), and over 70 articles in such journals as *Kievskaia starina* and *Kievskie Universitetskie izvestiia*.

Kistiakovsky, Volodymyr [Kistjakovs'kyj], b 12 October 1865 in Kiev, d 19 October 1952 in Moscow. Physical chemist; full member of the AN URSR from 1919 and of the USSR Academy of Sciences from 1929; the son of O. *Kistiakovsky. A graduate of St Petersburg University (1889), he was a professor at the Leningrad Polytechnical Institute (1903–34) and then director of the USSR Academy of Sciences' Colloid-Electrochemical Institute (from 1945 the Institute of Physical Chemistry). He developed the surface-film theory of metal corrosion, and his work found practical applications in the passivation of metals through electrolytic plating. He published numerous papers, mostly in the areas of electrochemistry, colloid chemistry, metal corrosion, and the theory of liquids.

Kistiakowsky, George Bohdan [Kistjakovs'kyj, Jurij], b 18 November 1900 in Kiev, d 7 December 1982 in Cambridge, Massachusetts. Physical chemist; member of the National Academy of Sciences of the United States (vice-president, 1965–71) and full member of the Shevchenko Scientific Society; son of B. *Kistiakovsky. He fled from Ukraine after the Bolshevik takeover and obtained a PH D from the University of Berlin (1925). He immigrated to the United States and taught at Princeton University (1926–30) and at Harvard University, where he became professor of chemistry in 1938, chairman of the Chemistry Department (1947–50), and professor emeritus in 1971. Kistiakowsky was the chief of the explosives division of the National Defense Research Committee during the development of the atomic bomb (1944–6), for which he developed the detonator. In addition to his academic work, much of it related to explosives, he often advised the federal government, serving as science adviser to President D. Eisenhower (1959–61) and as a member of the United States Arms Control and Disarmament Agency (1961–9), where he devoted all of his efforts to the prevention of nuclear war through arms control. He received numerous awards and honorary degrees, and published over 150 articles, mainly in the areas of chemical kinetics, thermodynamics of organic molecules, molecular spectroscopy, and shock and detonation waves.

Kistiakowsky, Vera, b 7 September 1928 in Princeton, New Jersey. Experimental physicist; daughter of G.B. *Kistiakowsky. A graduate of Mount Holyoke College and the University of California at Berkeley (PH D 1952), she did research at Columbia (1954–9) and Brandeis universities before joining the faculty of the Massachusetts Institute of Technology. Her research has focused on experimental elementary particle physics and on neutrino form factors (at the Fermi National Accelerator Laboratory). She also participated in the design of the second-generation detector at the Stanford Linear Collider.

Kitsman [Kicman']. v-6. Town (1969 pop ca 7,500), and raion center in Chernivtsi oblast, situated on the Sovytsia River in Bukovyna. First mentioned in 1413, it was a part of Moldavia from the 14th to the mid-16th century, and then until 1774 it belonged to Turkey. Under Austria (1774–1918) it was a Ukrainian cultural and educational center. In November 1918 it was briefly the seat of the Ukrainian-Bukovynian government, then it was annexed by Rumania and, in June 1940, by the USSR, when it ceased being an important Ukrainian cultural center in northern Bukovyna. It has a state-farm tekhnikum (formerly a Ukrainian agricultural school).

Kivertsi or **Kyvertsi** [Kiverci]. III-6. City (1969 pop 11,400) and raion center in Volhynia oblast. First mentioned in 1583, it became a railroad junction in the 1870s on the Kobel–Zhytomyr line. Wood products, lumber, and consumer products are made there.

Klebanov, Dmytro, b 25 July 1907 in Kharkiv. Composer, violinist, conductor, and educator. A student of S. Bohatyrov and graduate of the Kharkiv Music and Drama Institute (1926), he was appointed lecturer (1934) and professor (1960) at the Kharkiv Conservatory and then at the Kharkiv Institute of Arts (1963–73). His compositions include the operas *Communist* (1967) and *Red*

Cossacks (1972), two ballets, five symphonies, suites for symphony and chamber orchestras, concertos for violin, cello, flute, and harp, and vocal music.

Klebanov, Vladimir, b 14 June 1932 in Belorussia. Soviet workers' rights activist. A foreman at the Blazhanova coal mine in the Donets Basin, in 1960 he tried to organize an independent trade union at his mine but was stopped by the authorities. For protesting against unsafe working conditions he was dismissed from his job and then confined in a psychiatric hospital from 1968 to 1973. Upon his release he organized a workers' group to protest the abuses and persecution suffered by workers. In January 1978 the group formed the Association of Free Trade Unions in Moscow and claimed to represent about 200 workers. Its leaders were detained immediately by the police, and Klebanov was taken to a psychiatric hospital in Donetske.

Kleinwächter, Friedrich, b 25 February 1838 in Prague, d 12 December 1927 in Chernivtsi. Political economist. A graduate of Charles University (JD 1871), he taught in Prague and Riga before becoming the first professor of political economy at Chernivtsi University (1875–1909). He was also involved in various imperial Austrian government and civic bodies. A specialist in industrial organization and comparative economic systems, he wrote many books and articles.

Klembivka. V-9. Village (1972 pop 5,100) on the Rusava River in Yampil raion, Vinnytsia oblast, and a center of traditional gold-and-silver silk embroidery and *kilim making. It was first mentioned in the early 17th century. The Zhinocha Pratsia kilim factory was established there in 1870; it manufactures custom-made as well as mass-produced items. The factory's kilims were awarded the gold medal at the Leipzig International Fair in 1968. O. Khomenko and M. Seniuk are the village's most original weavers.

Yurii Klen

Klen, Yurii (pseud of Oswald Burghardt), b 4 October 1891 in Serbynivtsi, Podilia gubernia, d 30 October 1947 in Augsburg, West Germany. Writer, poet, literary scholar, and translator. After graduating from Kiev University, he published in Russian a study on the latest analyses of poetic style (1915). Because he was the son of German colonists, he was exiled during the First World War to a village in the Arkhangelsk region of northern Russia. Returning to Ukraine after the 1917 Revolution, he worked as a teacher in Baryshivka. There he renewed his friendship with the scholar and poet M. *Zerov and began writing poetry in Ukrainian. Klen became one of the unofficial five-member group called the *Neoclassicists. Although his poems began to appear in the periodical press beginning in 1924, his major contributions were his translations of German, French, and English poetry; a separate collection of translated German poetry, *Zalizni sonety* (Iron Sonnets), appeared in 1926. In 1931 Klen managed to emigrate to Germany and taught Slavic literatures at the universities of Münster, Innsbruck, and Prague. His literary output in both German and Ukrainian (as Yu. Klen) increased in the 1930s. In Ukrainian journals in Prague and Lviv, he revealed himself as an erudite, technically masterful writer of short stories, epic poems, and lyrics marked by precision of language, plastic imagery, and thematic heterogeneity. Although neoclassicist in their mastery of form, his poems are permeated with a neoromantic drive reflecting the turbulent epoch of the Second World War. His long poem *Prokliati roky* (The Accursed Years, 1937; 2nd edn, 1943) was followed by his sole collection of lyrics, *Karavely* (Caravels, 1943). Before his untimely death he managed to complete four parts of his monumental epic poem, *Popil imperii* (The Ashes of Empires, 1946), as well as the invaluable first-hand account *Spohady pro neokliasykiv* (Memoirs about the Neoclassicists, 1947).

Klen's literary parodies, written together with L. *Mosendz under the joint pseudonym of Porfyrii Horotak, were published in 1947 as *Dyiabolichni paraboly* (Diabolic Parables). His Ukrainian translations of W. Shakespeare's *Hamlet* and *Tempest* appeared together with most of his other Ukrainian works in the posthumously published *Tvory* (Works, vols 2–4, 1957–60); vol 1, which was to include his lyrical poetry, has not been published. A German-language study of his life and works by his sister, J. Burghardt, *Oswald Burghardt: Leben und Werke*, appeared in 1962.

D.H. Struk

Kleopov, Yurii, b 9 August 1902 in Horodyshche, Cherkasy county, Kiev gubernia, d 1943 in Smila, Cherkasy oblast. Botanist. Kleopov studied under O. Fomin at Kiev University before becoming a professor at Kharkiv University. From 1931 he directed the department of geobotany of the AN URSR Institute of Botany. A specialist in floristics, taxonomy, and geobotany, he dealt in his research both with the contemporary flora of Ukraine (especially Southern Ukraine) and with the flora of the Tertiary and Quaternary periods. Kleopov described six new types of plants and developed the theory of coenoelements in botany. He published many articles and studies, mostly in the journals *Visnyk Kyïvs'koho botanichnoho sadu* and *Ukraïns'kyi botanichnyi zhurnal*.

Klepatsky, Pavlo [Klepac'kyj], b 12 January 1885 in Puhachivka, Tarashcha county, Kiev gubernia, d ? Historian. He was a professor at the Kamianets-Podilskyi Ukrainian State University and then at the Poltava Institute of People's Education. His main works include *Ocherki po istorii Kievskoi zemli: Litovs'kii period* (Essays on the History of the Kiev Region: The Lithuanian Period, 1912), *Ohliad dzherel do istoriï Ukraïny* (A Survey of Sources on the History of Ukraine, 1920), and articles on the historian M. Maksymovych, on economic and social history of the first half of the 19th century, and on the plan to create a Cossack army during the Napoleonic Wars in the journal *Ukraïna* and elsewhere. He was arrested in the Stalinist terror of the 1930s and disappeared without a trace.

Kletsky, Lev [Klec'kyj], b 18 March 1903 in Oleksandrivka, Perekop county, Tavriia gubernia. Agricultural economist. A graduate of the Kharkiv Agro-economic Institute (1928), he worked in it until he became department chairman at the Kharkiv Agricultural Institute (1933–59). From 1963 to 1979 he was academic secretary of the sector of agricultural economy and organization and member of the Presidium of the Ukrainian Academy of Agricultural Sciences. He has published over 100 works on productivity, profitability, and accountancy in Soviet agriculture.

Klevan [Klevan']. III-6. Town smt (1979 pop 8,400) in Rivne raion, Rivne oblast, situated in western Volhynia on the Stuhla River. It was first mentioned in 1458. It has a woodworking and a food-processing industry. Ruins of a castle (built in the 15th century and reconstructed in the 17th century) owned by the Czartoryski family and a stone Roman Catholic church built in 1630 are located there.

Kleven River [Kleven']. A right-bank tributary of the Seim River, the Kleven flows for 143 km through the East-European Central Upland and drains a basin of 2,660 sq km. The waters of this gently sloping river supply the local population and industry and are used for irrigation.

Kliachkivsky, Dmytro. See Savur, Klym.

Klintsy [Klincy]. I-13. City (1984 pop 71,000) under oblast jurisdiction and a raion center in Briansk oblast, Russian SFSR. It was founded in the early 18th century on mixed Ukrainian-Russian territory, and under the Hetman state (1663–1781) it was on the territory of the Starodub regiment. From 1802 to 1917 it was a major manufacturing center in Chernihiv gubernia, producing woolens, linen, sheepskin, boots, cast iron, and bricks.

Kliuchevsky, Vasilii [Ključevskij, Vasilij], b 28 January 1841 in Voskresenskoe, Penza gubernia, Russia, d 25 May 1911 in Moscow. Prominent Russian historian; full member of the St Petersburg Academy of Sciences from 1900. A professor at Moscow University, Kliuchevsky was one of the most important figures in the development of Russian historiography. In his broad syntheses (eg, *Kurs russkoi istorii* [A Course in Russian History], 5 vols, 1904–21) he traced the history of the Russian nation back to Kievan Rus' and developed a systematic presentation stressing the continuity of Russian history to the modern period. In this 'imperialistic' approach he paid no attention to the experiences of the other nations in the Russian Empire, including Ukrainians. However, his works on social and economic history contain much important information relating to Ukraine: eg, *Proiskhodzhdenie krepostnogo prava v Rossii* (The Origins of Serf Law in Russia, 1885), *Podushnaia podat' i otmena kholopstva v Rossii* (The Poll-tax and the Abolishment of Serfdom in Russia, 1885), and *Istoriia soslovii v Rossii* (A History of Social Classes in Russia, 1913).

Klochkovsky, Viacheslav [Kločkovs'kyj, Vjačeslav], 1873–1931. Rear admiral of the Ukrainian navy. In 1917–18 he was port commander of Sevastopil and in charge of the submarine division. On 12 November 1918 he was appointed commander of the Black Sea Fleet under the Hetman government.

Stepan Klochurak

Klochurak, Stepan [Kločurak], b 27 February 1895 in Yasinia, Máramaros county, Transcarpathia, d 1980 in Prague. Political activist and journalist. In 1918–19 he organized local Ukrainian national councils and a Hutsul army, with which he defended the short-lived Hutsul Republic (see *Hutsuls) from the Hungarians. After the war he helped found the Subcarpathian Social Democratic party, and edited its newspapers *Narod* (1920–1) and *Vpered* (1922–34). Joining the Ukrainian branch of the pro-government Czechoslovak Agrarian party in 1934, he edited its organ *Zemlia i volia* (1934–8). He sat on the presidium of the Prosvita society and organized rural branches of the society. In the autonomous Carpatho-Ukrainian state within Czechoslovakia, Klochurak served as secretary to the prime minister and delegate to the *Vienna Arbitration. In the independent republic of Carpatho-Ukraine, he briefly held the office of defense minister (15 March 1939). In 1945 he was arrested by Soviet authorities in Prague; he returned there after serving 11 years in prison. His memoirs *Do voli* (To Freedom, 1978) were published in the West.

Klokov, Mykhailo. See Dolengo, Mykhailo.

Klokov, Viacheslav, b 19 February 1928 in Kharkiv. Sculptor; son of M. Klokov. A graduate of the Kiev Art Institute (1953), he works in monumental and easel sculpture. His works include *Before the Start*, *By the Stream*, *Yaroslavna* (1979), and the reliefs of the Myr Hotel in Kharkiv and *Scythians* of the Pektoral restaurant in Kiev. An album of his work was published in 1980.

Klokov, Vsevolod, b 25 June 1917 in Ust-Katav (now in Cheliabinska oblast), Russia. Historian; corresponding member of the AN URSR since 1978. A veteran of the Soviet partisans during the Second World War, in 1945–9 Klokov directed a department of the AN URSR Commission for the History of the 'Great Fatherland' War. He has been an associate of the AN URSR Institute of History since 1950 and director of a department there since 1962. Since 1965 he has also been a professor of the history of the CP(U) at the Kiev Institute of Civil-Aviation Engineers. Klokov is the author of several propagandistic monographs on the partisans in Ukraine during the Second World War. His memoirs of the war, *Kovel'skii uzel* (The Kovel Junction), were published in 1981.

Klosovsky, Oleksander [Klosovs'kyj], b 1846 in Zhytomyr, Volhynia gubernia, d 13 April 1917 in Petrograd. Meteorologist and geophysicist; corresponding member of the Russian Imperial Academy of Sciences from 1910. Klosovsky graduated from Kiev (1868) and Odessa (PH D 1884) universities and was professor at Odessa (1880–1907) and St Petersburg (1909–17). In 1886 he began the organization of the Metereological Network in the south-western part of the Russian Empire, which by 1896 had over 1,000 weather stations throughout Russian-ruled Ukraine. Research conducted at these stations was published in a regular serial. In 1892 Klosovsky founded a magneto-meteorological observatory in Odessa. In his work he combined theoretical and experimental approaches to the study of the earth's atmosphere. His publications include general works on metereology as well as studies on the climate of Kiev (published in *Zapiski Iugo-Zapadnogo otdela Russkogo geograficheskogo obshchestva*, 1874 and 1898) and Odessa (1893).

Klym, Ivan, 1909–44. OUN and UPA figure. A political prisoner in Poland before the Second World War, Klym was active in the Ukrainian Relief Committee in Peremyshl (1939–41). In 1941 he went to the Donbas to organize Ukrainian workers for the OUN. Later he organized UPA radio broadcasts in the Carpathian Mountains. He was arrested by the Gestapo and executed.

Klym (Klymentii) Smoliatych [Klym Smoljatyč]. A Kiev metropolitan (1147–54) and church figure from the Smolensk region (from which his surname is derived), Belorussia. A monk of the Zarub Monastery, Klym was elected metropolitan by a synod of the hierarchy of the Rus' church under pressure from Prince Iziaslav Mstyslavych. However, his election was never confirmed by the Patriarch of Constantinople. Klym was also opposed by Prince Yurii Dolgorukii, Iziaslav's rival, and the bishop of Novgorod, Niphont. After Iziaslav's death he was forced to abdicate as metropolitan and became bishop of Volodymyr-Volynskyi. Klym was an erudite sermonizer and philosopher. His best-known work is 'Poslaniie do presvitera Khomy' (Letter to Presbyter Khoma), which has survived in two manuscript forms. It contains a symbolic explanation of the Holy Scriptures, and demonstrates his knowledge of Homer, Plato, and Aristotle. Other works are also attributed to him. The most extensive biography and bibliography of Klym is N. Nikolsky's *O literaturnykh trudakh mitropolita Klimenta Smoliaticha, pisatelia XII veka* (The Literary Works of Metropolitan Klyment Smoliatych, a Writer of the 12th Century, 1892). His election as metropolitan is described in a monograph by T. Kostruba.

A. Zhukovsky

Klymasz, Robert [Klymaš, Bohdan], b 14 May 1936 in Toronto. Folklorist. Educated at the universities of Toronto, Manitoba, Harvard, and Indiana (PH D 1971), Klymasz is a specialist on Ukrainian-Canadian folklore and the author of *An Introduction to the Ukrainian-Canadian Immigrant Folksong Cycle* (1970) and *Ukrainian Folklore in Canada* (1980). He was executive director of the Ukrainian Cultural and Educational Centre in Winnipeg (1976–8). Currently, he is curator for the East European Programme at the Canadian Centre for Folk Culture Studies in Ottawa.

Klymchenko, Kostiantyn [Klymčenko, Kostjantyn], b 1816, d 29 August 1849 in Moscow. Sculptor. A graduate of the St Petersburg Academy of Arts (1839), he settled in Rome in 1842 and did most of his work there. His sculptures, done in a classicist style, include *Paris with Apple, Narcissus Gazing into the Water* (1842–5), *The Bacchante* (1846), *Girl with Mirror* (1840s), *Abraham's Sacrifice*, and a portrait of Catherine II. His early work was influenced by I. Martos.

Klymenko, Pylyp, b 5 July 1887 in Kozelets, Chernihiv gubernia, d 8 July 1955. Historian. He graduated from the St Petersburg Polytechnical and Kiev University, where he studied under M. Dovnar-Zapolsky. After teaching for a short time at the Kamianets-Podilskyi Ukrainian State University, he worked at the VUAN Archeographic Commission and lectured at the Kiev Archeological Institute. From 1925 he was associated with several institutes of VUAN, including the Institute of History. A prolific writer, in his research Klymenko focused on the economic and social history of 17th–19th-century Ukraine. His most important works include *Tsekhy na Ukraïni* (Guilds in Ukraine, 1929), 'Misto i terytoriia na Ukraïni za Het'manshchyny, 1654–1764' (The City and Territory in Ukraine during the Hetmanate, 1654–1764, *Zapysky Istorychno-Filolohichnoho Viddilu VUAN*, 1926, and separately), 'Komputy ta revizii XVIII st.' (Registers and Revisions of the 18th Century, *Ukraïns'kyi Arkheohrafichnyi Zbirnyk*, 1930), and works on the history of Nizhen, Dubno, and trade and industry in Podilia gubernia in *Visnyk tsukrovoï promyslovosti* and elsewhere. Klymenko also published several important historical documents with his own annotations and a number of articles on the history of Ukrainian culture. Arrested in 1936, he was exiled to a labor camp, where he died. An attempt was made to 'rehabilitate' him in 1967.

B. Balan

Klymentii, Zynovii's son [Klymentij Zynovijiv syn], b mid-17th century, d after 1712. Monk, poet, and ethnographer. He traveled throughout Ukraine and visited Russia and Poland while collecting donations for his monastery. Between 1700 and 1709 he wrote about 400 poems (published in their entirety by V. Peretts, 1912) depicting the life of Cossacks, artisans, and migrant workers and satirizing the behavior of the clergy, merchants, and functionaries. His poetry is rich in social and ethnographic detail. About 2,000 proverbs collected by Klymentii were published in 1971. A study of him by V. Kolosova appeared in 1964.

Klymiv, Ivan (pseud: Legenda), b 1909 in Silets, Sokal county, Galicia, d December 1942. Leader of the OUN (Bandera faction). He was arrested by the Polish authorities in 1935 and sentenced to 10 years in the Bereza Kartuzka concentration camp. Freed after the collapse of the Polish state, in the first half of 1941 he headed the

OUN territorial executive in Western Ukraine and participated in the OUN anti-Nazi underground. He was arrested by the Gestapo in December 1942 and tortured to death.

Klymko, Nykyfor, b 22 February 1904 in Landari, Poltava county, Poltava gubernia, d 29 June 1979 in Kiev. Economist. A senior researcher at the International Agricultural Institute of the Executive Committee of the Comintern (1930–9), he chaired (from 1944) the department of political economy at the Kiev Technological Institute of the Food Production Industry, and directed (1963–70) the Ukrainian section of the Institute of the Economy of the World Socialist System of the USSR Academy of Sciences. He has published over 60 works dealing with economic problems of socialist countries.

Klymko, Oleksander, b 1906 in Galicia, d 27 November 1970 in Elizabeth, New Jersey. Painter, caricaturist, and stage designer. Having studied art in Lviv and Vienna, he worked in Lviv as an illustrator of the humor magazines *Zyz* and *Komar*. After the Second World War he emigrated to Argentina, where he illustrated the satirical almanac *Mitla* and designed sets for the National Theater in Buenos Aires. Having immigrated to the United States in 1956, he designed sets for the National Ballet Company in Washington, DC, and the New York Metropolitan Opera. As a painter he specialized in landscapes and battle scenes.

Klymkovych, Ksenofont [Klymkovyč], b 17 January 1835 in Khotymyr, Tovmach circle, Galicia, d 19 October 1881. Populist poet, journalist, and translator. He edited and published the Lviv periodicals *Meta* (1863–5) and *Osnova* (1872) and the Ruska Chytalnia literature series (1865). He popularized and published T. Shevchenko's poetry, including the first edition of *Son* (The Dream, 1865). His Romantic poetry appeared from 1855 in *Pravda* and other Galician periodicals. He also translated works by N. Gogol, Lord Byron, A. Mickiewicz, and others into Ukrainian, as well as some works by Shevchenko and Marko Vovchok into German.

Klymov, Oleksander, b 12 September 1898 in Kustanai, Turgai oblast, Russia, d 22 June 1974 in Leningrad. Conductor and educator. A graduate of the Lysenko Music and Drama Institute (1928), where he studied under V. Berdiaiev, he worked as a conductor in Donetske, Saratov, Kharkiv, and Odessa. During the Second World War he was the principal conductor of the State Symphony Orchestra of the Ukrainian SSR (1942–5), then of the Symphony Orchestra of the Odessa Philharmonic (1945–8), and of the Kiev (1954–61) and Leningrad (1961–7) theaters of opera and ballet. At the same time he taught at the Lysenko Music and Drama Institute (1928–31), the Odessa Conservatory (1945–8), and the Kiev Conservatory (1948–54).

Klymovsky, Semen [Klymovs'kyj] (Klymov), b and d ? Poet. A Cossack in the Kharkiv regiment, in 1724 he dedicated two didactic poems to Peter I: 'O pravosudii nachal'stvuiuchykh' (On the Justice of the Rulers) and 'O smirenii vysochaishikh' (On the Humility of the Powerful). Prince A. Shakhovsky's *Kazak-stikhotvorets* (The Cossack Versifier, 1812), a comic opera about Klymovsky, had an influence on I. Kotliarevsky's dramatic works. It is believed that Klymovsky was the author of a number of folk songs, such as 'Ïkhav kozak za Dunai' (The Cossack Was Traveling beyond the Danube).

Klymovych, Petro [Klymovyč], b 1855, d 1920 in Odessa. Lawyer and political leader. He joined the Odessa Hromada in the 1870s as a university student and took an active part in Ukrainian community life in Odessa. Under the Central Rada he served as deputy finance minister in V. Holubovych's cabinet. He was executed by the Bolsheviks.

Klymyshyn, Mykola [Klymyšyn], b 25 February 1909 in Mostyshche, Kalush county, Galicia. Community and OUN activist. He studied at Cracow University and the Ukrainian Free University in Munich. In 1934 he was implicated in the assassination of the Polish minister B. *Pieracki, and was tried in Warsaw and sentenced to death. The sentence was commuted to life imprisonment, and until 1939 he was held in various Polish prisons. In 1940 he became one of the leaders of the OUN (Bandera faction), and in 1941–2 he commanded its northern task force. He was arrested by the Germans in Zhytomyr and sent to the Auschwitz concentration camp. From 1945 to 1962 he was a member of the Leadership of the Bandera faction abroad while living in Munich and, since 1949, the United States. He has worked as a Ukrainian émigré journalist and has been the vice-president of the Association of Activists of Ukrainian Culture. His memoirs, *V pokhodi do voli* (The March to Freedom), appeared in 1975.

Klynovy, Yurii. See Stefanyk, Yurii.

Kmet [kmet'; Polish: *kmieć*]. A historical term used by various Slavic groups, its meaning differing with time and place. In the *Pouchennia ditiam* of Volodymyr Monomakh and in such works as *Slovo o polku Ihorevi*, *kmet* meant a cavalryman, a member of a prince's **druzhyna*. In the western Ukrainian and Belorussian lands under Poland in the 14th–16th centuries the word indicated a free peasant, who paid only a state tax. By the early 17th century, when the peasantry had become enserfed, *kmet* meant a serf attached to the land. The obligations of a *kmet* consisted of the payment of a quit-rent for the land, payment-in-kind, and compulsory labor for the lord. The right of the *kmet* to become independent of the lord was limited, and a *kmet* was subject to the lord's private court (see *Domanial jurisdiction). *Kmet*, signifying serf, gradually fell into disuse and was replaced with the word **kholop*. The term *kmet* and a remnant of this institution were preserved in customary law in Transcarpathia into the 20th century. The word denoted a poor peasant who lived in another's house and was obligated to work the land.

Kmeta, Arkhyp, b 3 March 1891 in Ichnia, Borzna county, Chernihiv gubernia, d 3 June 1978 in New York. Military officer. After graduating from the Alexandrian Military School in Moscow in 1913, Kmeta served in the Russian army during the First World War. In November 1917 he joined the newly created Army of the UNR, rising quickly through the ranks until he became in 1919 the commander-in-chief of the 4th Regiment of the Sich Riflemen. After crossing with the army into Poland, he headed the department of statutes and regulations of the General Staff (1920–2), then occupied other posts in the military organs of the UNR Government-in-exile and helped found the Brotherhood of Ukrainian Statists. From 1935 Kmeta worked as a contract officer for the Polish army. After the Second World War he immigrated to the United States.

Kmeta-Ichniansky, Ivan. See Ichniansky, Myroslav.

Mykhailo Kmit: *Self-Portrait* (1946)

Kmit, Mykhailo, b 25 July 1910 in Stryi, Galicia, d 22 May 1981 in Sydney, Australia. Modernist painter. After completing O. *Novakivsky's school in Lviv (1932), he studied under F. Pautsch at the Cracow Academy of Arts (1933–9) and did art research in Italy, Germany, and Czechoslovakia. During the Second World War he taught at an elementary school in Biała Podlaska and at the Art and Trade School in Lviv. Emigrating to Australia in 1949, he quickly gained recognition for his work. He won a number of prizes, and his paintings were acquired by public galleries in Sydney and Melbourne and by the National Gallery in Canberra. An attempt to establish himself as a painter in the United States (1958–65) did not succeed, and he returned to Australia. Almost all of Kmit's paintings deal with the human, mostly female, figure. Some of his works have a religious theme: his *Amen* was reproduced on a postcard published by UNESCO. Kmit's style is expressionistic, complicated sometimes with cubist or neo-Byzantine traits. His forte was color.

Kmit, Yurii, b 1872 in Koblo-Stare, Sambir county, Galicia, d 25 June 1946 in Kulchytsi, Sambir raion, Lviv oblast. Writer, literary scholar, ethnographer, priest. His ethnographic research focused on the culture and lifestyle of the *Boikos about whom he wrote such literary works as *Z hir* (From the Mountains), *V zatinku i na sontsi* (In the Shade and in the Sun, 1910), a collection of short stories, and *Tremtinnia dushi* (The Trembling of the Soul, 1922). Some of these works were written in the *Boiko dialect. He also wrote articles popularizing the work of various Ukrainian and European writers.

Kmitsykevych, Volodymyr [Kmicykevyč], b 28 August 1863, d 29 July 1942 in Chernivtsi. A gymnasium teacher in Galicia and Chernivtsi, he compiled a German-Ukrainian dictionary (1912) and Greek-Ukrainian dictionary (1922–3), contributed articles on cultural and educational issues to the Bukovynian Ukrainian press, and translated F. Schiller's *William Tell* (1887) and Plato's *Apology* (1898) into Ukrainian.

Kniahynytsky, Yov [Knjahynyc'kyj, Jov] (secular name: Ivan), b ca 1550 in Tysmenytsia, near Stanyslaviv (present-day Ivano-Frankivske), d 1621. Hegumen and churchman. He probably studied at the Ostrih Academy before becoming a monk on Mount Athos. Returning to Ukraine in the early 17th century, he played an important role in the Orthodox struggle against the Church Union of *Berestia. As a monk in the Uhornyk Monastery (near present-day Ivano-Frankivske) and the Maniava Hermitage he became famous for reviving Orthodox monasticism. He worked with I. Vyshensky, Z. Kopystensky, and other church leaders and was considered an authority on the purity of the faith and ascetism. In 1619 Kniahynytsky wrote an important critique of K. Stavrovetsky-Trankvilion's *Zertsalo bohosloviia* (The Mirror of Theology, 1618) from an Orthodox perspective.

Kniaz. See Prince.

Kniazha Hora: Encolpion with St John the Evangelist

Kniazha Hora [Knjaža Hora]. A landmark near Kaniv, Cherkasy oblast, and the site of the fortified Rus' city of Roden (Rodnia), which is mentioned in the chronicles under the year 980. Excavations carried out in 1870–1900 and 1958–65 uncovered the remains of wooden and earthen dwellings, various workshops, other buildings, many farm and artisans' implements, domestic utensils, weapons, and 12 hoards of gold and silver ornaments. Roden's inhabitants were artisans and traders. The city was destroyed during the Mongol invasion of 1240. A monograph about Roden by H. Mezentseva was published in Kiev in 1968.

Kniazhdvir. See Verkhnie.

Kniazhevych, Dmytro [Knjaževyč], b 6 May 1788 in St Petersburg, d 13 October 1844 in Velyka Buromka, Zolotonosha county, Poltava gubernia. Prominent figure in educational and cultural affairs. From 1802 he held various government positions at home and abroad, and in 1837 he became a trustee of the Odessa school district, assisting in the reorganization and expansion of the Richelieu Lyceum. He founded (1839) and headed the Odessa Society of History and Antiquities and was editor of its *Zapiski*. In addition to writing many works on philology, literature, agriculture, education, and history, he headed archeological explorations on the Black Sea coast.

Kniazhynsky, Antin [Knjažyns'kyj], b 11 February 1893 in Tysovytsia, Turka county, Galicia, d 12 February 1960 in Philadelphia. Educator. A graduate of Lviv University, he taught at several Galician gymnasiums. During the Second World War he organized cultural and educational work in Kolomyia county. In 1944 he fled to Vienna, but was apprehended by the NKVD and from 1945 to 1955 he was incarcerated in Soviet prison camps. He subsequently emigrated to the United States. Kniazhynsky wrote several works, including *Na dni SSSR* (On the Bottom of the USSR, 1959) and *Dukh natsiï: Sotsiolohichno-etnopsykholohichna studiia* (The Spirit of a Nation: A Sociological-Ethnopsychological Study, 1959).

Knitwear industry. A branch of the textile industry that produces cotton, wool, linen, and synthetic knitted clothing and other knitted goods. Until the First World War, large-scale knitwear production did not exist in Ukraine; only small quantities were produced by cottage enterprises, while most knitwear was imported from textile centers in central Russia. In 1915, knitwear factories were established in Poltava and Kharkiv on the basis of plants evacuated from Russian-ruled Poland.

By 1925, 11 factories existed; in 1928 they produced about 14 percent of Soviet hose, underwear, and other clothing. Large plants were built during the First and Second Five-Year plans in Kharkiv, Kiev, and Poltava; in the late 1930s they produced over 80 percent of Soviet Ukraine's knitwear. While other branches of Ukraine's textile production remained underdeveloped, the knitwear industry received relatively large investments (37.7 million rubles during the First and Second Five-Year plans), and its output increased significantly. By 1940 it was producing 16.4–24.4 percent of all Soviet assorted knitwear. Because other textile branches were underdeveloped, much of the thread used in production had to be imported from Russia. The Poltava Cotton-Spinning Factory supplied only 50 percent of Ukraine's needs.

The industry was devastated during the Second World War, and only 9 percent of prewar output was attained in 1945. Although it was one of the most quickly reconstructed branches of Ukraine's light industry, it only gradually attained its prewar level of output. In the early 1970s there were 60 knitwear plants in Ukraine. Their share in total Soviet output has stabilized at 16 percent (50 million items in 1968 and 75 million in 1982), 19 percent of underwear (162 and 219 million items), and 21 percent of hose and socks (307 and 369 million pairs). The largest factories are in Kiev, Donetske, Voroshylovhrad, Odessa, and Mykolaiv; the largest hose factories are in Kharkiv, Zhytomyr, Chernivtsi, Lviv, and Chervonohrad.

B. Somchynsky

Knyhar (Bookseller). A monthly literary magazine of criticism and bibliography published by the Chas publishing house in Kiev from September 1917 to March 1920 and edited by V. Koroliv-Stary and M. Zerov. Thirty-one issues appeared. Besides a large section devoted to book reviews and bibliography, it contained articles on various aspects of book production: eg, V. Modzalevsky's study of the history of the book trade in Ukraine, V. Miiakovsky's review of the history of Russian censorship of Ukrainian books, S. Kondra's analysis of Ukrainian journalistic bibliography, H. Hasenko's assessment of Ukraine's image in the European press, and A. Yarynovych's survey of the Ukrainian press in North America. Besides these contributors, many other critics and literary historians contributed to the journal: S. Yefremov, M. Zerov, A. Nikovsky, M. Shapoval, D. Doroshenko, S. Cherkasenko, M. Sadovsky, P. Zaitsev, L. Starytska-Cherniakhivska, Mykola Levytsky, Orest Levytsky, S. Rusova, Yu. Tyshchenko, O. Mytsiuk, and O. Koshyts.

Knyholiub (Bibliophile). An irregular journal of the Ukrainian Society of Bibliophiles in Prague published from 1927 to 1932. Its editor was S. Siropolko. Devoted to the history of Ukrainian book publishing, the journal printed mostly the lectures presented to the society by its members: V. Simovych's bibliography of O. Kobylianska's works, D. Chyzhevsky's survey of Ukrainian philosophical literature in 1920–6, V. Bidnov's review of religious publications in Ukraine, S. Narizhnyi's survey of Slavica including Ucrainica, D. Antonovych's study on the cult of Narbut and modern Ukrainian book design, V. Sichynsky's survey of literature on Ukrainian fine art, and S. Siropolko's study of bibliology in Soviet Ukraine. The journal contained special sections devoted to library affairs, publishing news, Ucrainica, and new Ukrainian publications in Czechoslovakia. Altogether 15 issues of *Knyholiub* appeared.

Knyhospilka (aka Ukrainian Co-operative Publishing Union [Ukrainska kooperatyvna vydavnycha spilka]). The largest book publishing and distributing firm in Soviet Ukraine in the 1920s. Organized in Kiev in 1918 under the direction of M. Stasiuk, it published literary works, scientific books, and school textbooks. It was closed in 1920 when the Bolsheviks occupied Ukraine, and was reopened in November 1922 with the head office in Kharkiv and branch offices in Kiev and Odessa. Its chief managers were M. Ahuf, S. Pylypenko, and V. Tselarius. By the end of 1924 branches were established also in Vinnytsia, Uman, Sumy, and Zhytomyr. The main publications in this period were Literaturna biblioteka (Literary Library), a series of Ukrainian literary classics; Svitova literatura (World Literature), a translation series including the works of H. de Balzac, A. France, and G. de Maupassant; an academic edition of Lesia Ukrainka's and M. Kotsiubynsky's works; school textbooks; practical manuals for farmers; booklets on co-operation; and a music library edited by L. Revutsky. The firm also published book magazines such as *Knyha* and *Kooperatyvnyi knyhar*. Its book output rose rapidly from 26 titles (229,000 copies) in 1923 to 534 titles (5,350,000 copies) in 1926–7. Ninety to 95 percent of the books were published in Ukrainian. In 1931 Knyhospilka was abolished by the authorities as part of the campaign to suppress Ukrainian culture.

S. Yaniv

Knyhospilka (Book Union). A publishing house founded in New York in 1952 by A. Bilous, O. Balynsky, and I.

Krylov. It reprinted by offset M. Hrushevsky's *Istoriia ukraïns'koï literatury* (The History of Ukrainian Literature, 5 vols, 1959–60) and *Istoriia Ukraïny-Rusy* (The History of Ukraine-Rus', 10 vols, 1954–8) and H. Holoskevych's *Pravopysnyi slovnyk* (Orthographic Dictionary, 1952), and published I. Franko's works in 20 volumes (1956–62), M. Kotsiubynsky's works in two volumes (1955), and some children's literature.

Knyhy bytiia ukraïns'koho narodu (The Books of Genesis of the Ukrainian People). The main ideological and programmatic statement of the *Cyril and Methodius Brotherhood, written by M. *Kostomarov in 1846 and called the *Zakon Bozhyi* (Divine Law) in the official police investigation of the brotherhood. The *Knyhy* was the political culmination of the Ukrainian national renaissance of the early 19th century. It was greatly influenced by the ideas of Western European romanticism, Slavophilism, the *Decembrist movement and the *Society of United Slavs, the historical concepts of **Istoriia Rusov* (The History of the Rus' People), and the revolutionary ideas of T. Shevchenko. The title of the work and its literary style, especially in the first half, are reminiscent of A. Mickiewicz's *Księgi narodu polskiego i pielgrzymstwa polskiego* (Books of the Polish People and of the Polish Pilgrimage).

In the context of a broad 'Christian' interpretation of world history, the *Knyhy* chronicles how each nation in turn fell from grace by succumbing to despotic monarchs or foreign domination. In the end, only the Ukrainians founded a democratic Christian society, the Cossack Host, the idealization of which is a prominent theme of the book. In a biblical style equating democracy with Christianity, the *Knyhy* stresses the mystical mission of the Slavs and the messianic role of the Ukrainians in particular. It calls for an end to the national oppression of Ukraine and advocates the establishment of a union of autonomous Slavic states under the leadership of a 'resurrected' Ukrainian nation.

Besides its message of Ukrainian nationalism, the *Knyhy* advocates a radical social program, calling for the emancipation of the serfs and an end to monarchism and privileges for the nobility.

Two versions of the *Knyhy* were uncovered during the police investigation of the Cyril and Methodius Brotherhood, one consisting of 104 paragraphs and the other of 109 paragraphs in Russian translation. The manuscripts were kept in the secret-police archives in St Petersburg until the 1917 Revolution and have been preserved in the Central State Historical Archive in Moscow since then. The first unabridged edition of the *Knyhy* was published, with notes by P. Zaitsev, in the Kiev journal *Nashe mynule*, 1 (1918). Later editions were published by M. Vozniak in Lviv (1921) and by I. Borshchak in Paris (1946). A French translation by G. Luciani was published in 1956, and an English one by B. Yankivsky in 1954.

BIBLIOGRAPHY

Semevskii, V. *Kirillo-Mefodievskoe obshchestvo 1846–47 gg.* (Moscow 1918)
Luciani, G. *Le Livre de la Genèse du peuple ukrainien* (Paris 1956)
Zaionchkovskii, P. *Kirillo-Mefodievskoe obshchestvo* (Moscow 1959)
Kostiv, K. *Knyhy buttia ukraïns'koho narodu* (Toronto 1980)

A. Zhukovsky

Knysh, Irena [Knyš] (née Shkvarok), b 20 April 1909 in Lviv. Feminist and author. Since immigrating to Canada in 1950, she has worked as a journalist and has written extensively on the Ukrainian women's movement. Her major works include *Ivan Franko ta rivnopravnist' zhinky* (Ivan Franko and Equal Rights for Women, 1956); *Smoloskyp u temriavi* (A Torch in the Darkness, 1957), a study of N. Kobrynska and the origins of the Ukrainian women's movement; and *Try rovesnytsi: 1860–1960* (Three [Ukrainian] Contemporaries: 1860–1960, nd), a collection of biographical studies of U. Kravchenko, M. Bashkirtseva, and M. Zankovetska. She edited a collection of reminiscences, *Nezabutnia Ol'ha Basarab: Vybrane* (The Unforgettable Olha Basarab: Selections, 1976), and has published two collections of her journalistic articles.

Zynovii Knysh

Knysh, Zynovii [Knyš, Zynovij], b 16 June 1906 in Kolomyia, Galicia. Political and community activist, author, and publisher (pen name: B. Mykhailiuk). A graduate of Lviv University (PH D 1930), in the late 1920s he was a leading member of the Ukrainian Military Organization (UVO). In 1930 he was put in charge of OUN 'combat' activities but was soon arrested and imprisoned by the Polish authorities until 1936. He then worked as a secretary of the Tsentrosoiuz co-operative union in Lviv (1936–9), director of the office of the Ukrainian Central Committee in Cracow (1940–1), secretary of the Narodna Torhovlia consumer co-operative in Lviv (1941–2), the mayor of Kalush (1942), and director of the Zolochiv circle administration (1943–4). From 1940 to 1978 he was a member of the Leadership of the OUN (Melnyk faction). A refugee in Austria in 1944–6, he was secretary of the Greek Catholic Mission for Ukrainians in Western Europe in Paris (1946–8) before immigrating to Canada. In 1949–52 he was secretary of the National Executive of the Ukrainian National Federation in Winnipeg. He is the author of over 60 brochures, books, and memoirs, mostly about the UVO and OUN, including *Bunt Bandery* (Bandera's Revolt, 1950), *Dukh, shcho tilo rve do boiu* (The Spirit That Spurs the Body on to Battle, 1951), *Dryzhyt' pidzemnyi huk* (The Underground Din Resounds, 1953), *Pered pokhodom na Skhid* (Before the March to the East, 2 vols, 1959), *Sribna surma* (The Silver Bugle, 5 vols, 1962–7), and *Na povni vitryla!* (At Full Sail! 1970). Among his publicistic works are *Istoriia ukraïns'koï politychnoï dumky do kintsia XVIII st.* (A History of Ukrainian Political Thought to the End of the 18th Century, 1952), *U trystarichchia*

Pereiaslavs'koho dohovoru (On the Occasion of the Tricentennial of the Pereiaslav Treaty, 1954), and *Pip Hapon* (The Priest Gapon, 1977).

R. Senkus, A. Zhukovsky

Knyzhka (Book). A monthly journal of literary criticism and bibliography published from 1921 to 1923 by the Bystrytsia publishing house in Stanyslaviv. It was edited by I. Chepyha. Its supplement *Vseukraïns'ka bibliohrafiia* was edited by I. Kalynovych. Besides bibliographies, it published news about Ukrainian publishers at home and abroad, articles about books, and reviews of new publications. Its contributors included V. Doroshenko, O. Zalesky, S. Siropolko, V. Koroliv-Stary, Z. Kuzelia, and L. Bachynsky.

Knyzhochky myssiiny (Missionary Booklets). Popular educational and religious booklets published monthly by the Rev L. Dzhulynsky from 1890 to 1911 in Berezhany, Lviv, Peremyshl, and Ternopil. They contained short articles in verse or prose written mostly by priests, such as S. Lepky, Ye. Lutsyk, Yu. Nasalsky, D. Tretiak, Ya. Zrobek, I. Byrchak, I. Ozarkevych, V. Chernetsky, and E. Tsurkovsky.

Kobelev, Aleksandr [Kobeljev], b 1860 in Tsarskoe Selo, St Petersburg gubernia, d 1942 in Kiev. Architect. A graduate of the St Petersburg Civil-Engineering Institute (1887), he worked as an engineer for the Administration of Southern Railways in Kiev. From 1899 he taught architectural design at the Kiev Polytechnical Institute. He built the railway stations in Bendery, Koziatyn, and Sarny and a number of buildings in Kiev, including the State Bank (1902–5, with O. Verbytsky), the Central Telegraph (1903), the Commercial Institute (1906, with V. Obremsky), and the building of the Higher Courses for Women (1911–13). His book on general civil architecture was published in 1907.

Kobeliaky [Kobeljaky]. IV-15. Town (1970 pop 10,800) and raion center in Poltava oblast, situated on the Vorskla River, in the Dnieper Lowland. Known since the early 17th century, from 1648 to 1764 it was a Cossack company town in the Poltava regiment, and from 1802 to 1917 a county town in Poltava gubernia. It has a clothing factory, a large sugar refinery, a brickyard, and food-processing and light industries.

Kobersky, Karlo [Kobers'kyj] (pseud: K. Pushkar), b 5 October 1890 in Zalesie, Rzeszów county, Galicia, d 1940. Civic and political leader, theoretician of co-operation, and publicist. A graduate of Lviv University, he was docent at the Ukrainian Husbandry Academy at Poděbrady (from 1926) and a full member of the Shevchenko Scientific Society (from 1935). He edited the journal *Kooperatyvna respublyka* (1928–39) as well as other publications of the Audit Union of Ukrainian Co-operatives in Lviv. A member of the Supreme Secretariat of the Ukrainian Radical party, Kobersky wrote many articles on political and economic issues, and such larger works as *Ukraïns'ke narodnytstvo po obokh bokakh Zbrucha* (Ukrainian Populism on Both Sides of the Zbruch River, 1924), *Ukraïna v svitovomu hospodarstvi* (Ukraine in the World Economy, 1933), and *Kooperatyvnyi bukvar* (A Co-operative Alphabet, 1928, 2nd edn, 1939). He was killed by the NKVD.

Karlo Kobersky

Kobersky, Ostap [Kobers'kyj], b 1895 in Sianik, Galicia, d 19 November 1944 in Trnava, Czechoslovakia. Political leader; brother of K. *Kobersky. He was one of the organizers of the Galician youth movement before the First World War, and was particularly active in the Sich sports association. During the war he rose from the ranks to become a lieutenant in the Ukrainian Sich Riflemen and was twice wounded in battle. A founding member of the Ukrainian Military Organization, he was implicated in S. Fedak's attempt on the life of the Polish president J. Piłsudski. After studying in Prague (1922–5), he worked in a co-operative in Sambir and served on the executive of the Ukrainian Social Radical party.

Kobets, Oleksii [Kobec', Oleksij] (pseud: Oleksa Varavva), b 1889, d 5 September 1967 in Buffalo, New York. Writer and journalist. During the First World War Kobets carried on cultural and educational work with Ukrainian POWs at Freistadt on behalf of the Union for the Liberation of Ukraine. In the 1920s and 1930s he worked for various publishers, particularly in the co-operative press. After the Second World War he immigrated to the United States. Kobets is the author of several poetry collections, movie scripts, and the autobiographical prose work *Zapysky polonenoho* (Memoirs of a Prisoner, 1931), which won him critical acclaim at home and abroad.

Kobiak [Kobjak]. Khan of the *Cumans. Kobiak, together with Khan Konchak, led a number of raids on Kievan Rus' in the 1170s and took part in the internecine struggle among the Rus' princes in 1180–1. During a major assault on Rus' in 1184 Konchak and Kobiak were defeated by the princes and the latter was taken prisoner.

Kobryn, Vasyl, b 1938 in Tuchne, Peremyshl county, Galicia. Religious dissident. A graduate of a tekhnikum in Lviv, he headed the Initiative Group for Defending the Rights of Believers and the Church in Ukraine (1983–4) and wrote several articles and declarations protesting Soviet religious policy. He collaborated with the *samvydav* journal *Khronika Katolyts'koï tserkvy na Ukraïni*. In March 1985, he was sentenced to three years' imprisonment for his defense of religious rights.

Kobrynska, Nataliia [Kobryns'ka, Natalija] (née Ozarkevych), b 8 June 1851 in Beleluia, Sniatyn circle, d 22 January 1920 in Bolekhiv, Dolyna county, Galicia. Writer and pioneer of the Ukrainian *women's movement in

Nataliia Kobrynska

Galicia. In 1884 she organized the Society of Ruthenian Women in Stanyslaviv. Three years later she edited and published, with O. Pchilka, the first feminist almanac, **Pershyi vinok* (The First Garland). In 1891 she convened in Stryi the first public feminist meeting, at which she raised the issue of day-care centers. In 1893 she published a second almanac, *Nasha dolia* (Our Fate, further issues in 1895 and 1896), and in 1907 a third almanac, *Zhinocha dolia* (Women's Fate). Kobrynska's short stories deal with women's and social issues, psychological themes, folk beliefs, and the First World War. They were also published in several collections – *Zadlia kusnyka khliba* (For the Sake of a Piece of Bread, 1884), *Dukh chasu* (The Spirit of the Times, 1889), *Vyborets'* (The Elector, 1904), *Kazky* (Fairy Tales, 1904), *Iadzia i Katrusia ta inshi opovidannia* (Yadzia and Katrusia and Other Stories, 1904) – and in editions of collected or selected works (1930, 1954, 1958). A commemorative biography – *Smoloskyp u temriavi: Nataliia Kobryns'ka i ukraïns'kyi zhinochyi rukh* (A Torch in the Darkness: Nataliia Kobrynska and the Ukrainian Women's Movement, 1957) by I. Knysh – appeared in Canada. A bibliography of her works by P. Babiak was published in 1967.

D.H. Struk

Kobrynsky, Illia [Kobryns'kyj, Illja], b 23 December 1904 in Shyroke, Kryvyi Rih county, Kherson gubernia, d 4 November 1979 in Dnipropetrovske. Stage director and actor. Upon graduating from the Moscow Institute of Theater Art (1935), he began to direct plays in such theaters as the Dnipropetrovske Ukrainian Music and Drama Theater (1935–41, 1950–5, and 1961) and the Dnipropetrovske Russian Drama Theater (1944–50, 1955–60), where in 1962 he was appointed principal stage director. He produced such plays as O. Korniichuk's *Pravda* (Truth) and L. Dmyterko's *Na viky razom* (Forever Together) and many Russian classics. From 1935 to 1956 he lectured at the Dnipropetrovske Theater School.

Kobrynsky, Volodymyr [Kobryns'kyj], b 16 October 1873 in Bilozirka, Zbarazh county, Galicia, d 17 October 1958 in Kolomyia, Ivano-Frankivske oblast. Civic and cultural figure; ethnographer. Under the Western Ukrainian National Republic he was active in Kolomyia's local government. He founded a branch of the Lviv *Silskyi Hospodar society in the Hutsul region and was a member of the National Committee of the Ukrainian National Democratic Alliance. In 1926 Kobrynsky founded the Hutsulshchyna Museum in Kolomyia (today the Kolomyia Museum of Hutsul Folk Art), which he directed for many years. He collected Hutsul folklore and folk art and wrote a book on Hutsul brass handicrafts.

Kobrynsky, Yosafat [Kobryns'kyj, Josafat], b 15 September 1818 in Kolomyia, Galicia, d 14 March 1901 in Myshyn, Kolomyia county. Greek Catholic priest, pedagogue, and community leader. After studying theology in Vienna (1837–9), he served as a priest in the Kolomyia region and promoted popular education. He founded the first reading room and the People's Home in Kolomyia, donating to it a considerable sum of money. In 1842 he published a primer designed for home use and a handbook on speed-reading. He was first to introduce the *Hrazhdanka alphabet and a progressive method for teaching literacy. In 1848 he took part in the Congress of Ruthenian Scholars. He contributed articles on pedagogy and economics to *Slovo* and Catholic newspapers.

Kobyletsky, Yurii (Ivan) [Kobylec'kyj, Jurij], b 11 August 1906 in Zvenyhorodka, Kiev gubernia. Literary scholar. A graduate of Kiev University (1934), he taught there from 1935 and at the Kiev Pedagogical Institute from 1958. He is the author of books about O. Kobylianska (1944), I. Franko (1946, 1951, 1956, 1964), A. Malyshko (1947), O. Korniichuk (1965), and the history of Ukrainian literature of the first (1965) and second (1966) halves of the 19th century, and numerous articles.

Olha Kobylianska

Kobylianska, Olha [Kobyljans'ka, Ol'ha], b 27 November 1863 in Gura Humorului, Bukovyna, d 21 March 1942 in Chernivtsi. A pioneering Ukrainian modernist writer. A self-educated and well-read woman, her first *novellen* were written in German, beginning in 1880. From 1891 she lived in Chernivtsi. Her travels and acquaintance with Lesia Ukrainka, N. Kobrynska, O. Makovei, I. Franko, V. Stefanyk, and M. Kotsiubynsky changed her cultural and political outlook, and she became involved in the Ukrainian women's movement in Bukovyna and began writing in Ukrainian. Many of her works – including the novels *Liudyna* (A Person, 1891) and *Tsarivna* (The Princess, 1895) – have as their protagonists cultured, emancipated women oppressed in a philistine, provincial society; semiautobiographical elements and the influence of the writings of George Sand and F. Nietzsche are evident. A neoromantic symbolist, she depicted the struggle between good and evil and the mystical force of nature (eg, the short story 'Bytva' [Battle]), predestination, magic, and the irrational in many of her stories of peasant life and in her most famous novels, *Zemlia* (Land, 1902) and *V nediliu rano zillia kopala* (On Sunday Morn She Gathered Herbs, 1909). Her works are known for their impressionistic, lyrical descriptions of nature and subtle psychological portrayals.

Kobylianska's works have been published in many editions and selections. The fullest collections were published in 1927–9 (9 vols) and 1962–3 (5 vols). In 1944 a literary-memorial museum dedicated to her was opened in Chernivtsi.

BIBLIOGRAPHY
Kohut, L. (ed). *Ol'ha Kobylians'ka: Al'manakh u pam'iatku ïï soroklitn'oï pys'mennyts'koï diial'nosty (1887–1927)* (Chernivtsi 1928)
Ol'ha Kobylians'ka: Statti i materialy (Chernivtsi 1958)
Kushch, O. *Ol'ha Kobylians'ka: Bibliohrafichnyi pokazhchyk* (Kiev 1960)
Babyshkin, O. *Ol'ha Kobylians'ka* (Lviv 1963)
Ol'ha Kobylians'ka v krytytsi ta spohadakh (Kiev 1963)
Tomashuk, N. *Ol'ha Kobylians'ka* (Kiev 1969)
Kopach, O. *Movostyl' Ol'hy Kobylians'koï* (Toronto 1972)

R. Senkus

Kobylianska Museum (Muzei O.Yu. Kobylianskoi). Museum founded in 1944 in Chernivtsi to honor the writer O. *Kobylianska. The museum occupies a building where she resided from 1928 to 1942. The exhibits include editions of her works, photographs, documentary materials, and personal belongings. A second memorial museum dedicated to Kobylianska has been established in the village of Dymka, Chernivtsi oblast, where she resided for a long period of time.

Kobyliansky, Antin [Kobyljans'kyj], b 29 January 1837 in Pererisl, Nadvirna county, Galicia, d 8 February 1910 in Lviv. A civic figure, physician, and inventor. In 1861 in his article 'Slovo na Slovo do Redaktora *Slova*' (A Word on the Word to the Editor of *Slovo*) and brochure *Holos na holos dlia Halychyny* (A Voice on the Voice for Galicia, 1861) he protested against B. Didytsky's Russification of the Ukrainian language. Kobyliansky also urged Yu. *Fedkovych to write in Ukrainian instead of German.

Kobyliansky, Bronyslav [Kobyljans'kyj], b 1896. Linguist. A specialist in Hutsul dialects, he was a docent at the Lviv Pedagogical Institute. He published a general description of the Hutsul and Pokutian dialects in *Ukraïns'kyi diialektolohichnyi zbirnyk*, no. 1 (1928), and then attempted to explain their origin in *Dialekt i literaturna mova* (Dialect and Literary Language, 1960). He also wrote etymological studies and popular articles.

Kobyliansky, Liutsii [Kobyljans'kyj, Ljucij], b 1855 in Zolotonosha, Poltava gubernia, d 15 March 1941 in Prague. A physician and cultural figure. During his medical studies in Kiev (1871–7) he sang in M. Lysenko's choir and belonged to the Kiev Hromada. Working as a gubernial medical inspector in Caucasia, he organized Sunday schools, a choir, and a Prosvita society in Baku. In 1917 he was elected deputy from the Ukrainian Party of Socialist Revolutionaries to the Central Rada. In 1918–19 he served as adviser to the Ukrainian consulates in Istanbul and Budapest. Immigrating to Czechoslovakia after the war, he worked in a sanatorium and belonged to the Ukrainian Physicians' Association in Czechoslovakia. Kobyliansky's publications include articles on music and medicine and a monograph on M. Lysenko (1930).

Volodymyr Kobyliansky

Lukian Kobylytsia

Kobyliansky, Volodymyr [Kobyljans'kyj], b 27 August 1895 in Iaşi, Moldavia, d 10 September 1919 in Kiev. Symbolist poet, translator, and critic. His first poems appeared in 1913 in the Chernivtsi paper *Nova Bukovyna* while he was a Bukovynian village teacher. From 1913 he lived in Kiev and contributed to journals there. He translated into Ukrainian much of H. Heine's *Buch der Lieder* and individual works by F. Schiller. In the last months of his life he belonged to the writers' group *Muzahet. Collections of his works, *Mii dar* (My Gift, 1920) and *Tvory* (Works, 1930), were published after his death from typhus.

Kobyliansky, Yuliian [Kobyljans'kyj, Julijan], b 26 December 1859 in Gurahumora, Bukovyna, d 11 November 1922 in Chernivtsi. Classical philologist and educator; brother of O. *Kobylianska. A graduate of Chernivtsi University (1883), he taught classical languages at the Chernivtsi Ukrainian Gymnasium. One of the first scholars to work on Latin-Ukrainian lexicography, he is the author of several high-school Latin textbooks, a Ukrainian-Latin dictionary (1907), and a Latin-Ukrainian dictionary (1912).

Kobylytsia, Lukian [Kobylycja, Lukjan], b ca 1803 (1812 according to some sources) in Storonets-Putyliv, Vyzhnytsia region, Bukovyna, d 24 October 1851 in Solca (Gura-Humorolui according to other sources), Bukovyna. Peasant revolutionary and political leader in the Hutsul region of Bukovyna. In the 1840s Kobylytsia led several popular rebellions against the landowners in the Hutsul (Vyzhnytsia, Putyliv, and Câimpulung) region, for which he was twice imprisoned (1842–4, 1847). In 1848 he was elected to the Austrian Parliament. There he campaigned for the political autonomy of Bukovyna and its attachment to Galicia, and for the distribution of land to the peasants without compensation for the landlords. During the Revolutions of 1848–9, he struggled against Rumanian leaders in Bukovyna and organized 'Hutsul councils,' institutions of local administration. He traveled throughout the Hutsul region with groups of armed Hutsuls, presenting himself as the official envoy of the

Austrian emperor and fomenting revolution against the local nobles. By the end of 1848, the uprising had embraced all of Bukovyna and spread to Galicia. According to some historians, Kobylytsia was even allied with the leader of the Hungarian revolution, L. Kossuth. In spring 1849 the uprising was finally quelled by the Austrian army and in April 1850 Kobylytsia was arrested in Zhabie. Released in 1851, he was not permitted to return to the Hutsul region, but forced to remain under police surveillance in Solca. Kobylytsia became a folk hero, immortalized in folk songs and legends and in a popular poem by O. Fedkovych.

BIBLIOGRAPHY
Franko, I. 'Lukian Kobylytsia: epizod z istorii Hutsul'shchyny v pershii polovyni XIX st.,' *ZNTSh*, 49 (1902)
Revakovych, T. 'Luk'ian Kobylytsia.' *ZNTSh*, 126–7 (1918)
Balan, T. *Luchian Cobiliţa* (Chernivtsi 1926)
Selians'kyi rukh na Bukovyni v 40-kh rokakh XIX st.: Zbirnyk dokumentiv (Kiev 1949)
Shevchenko, F. *Luk'ian Kobylytsia* (Kiev 1958)
Narod pro Kobylytsiu (Kiev 1968)

A. Zhukovsky

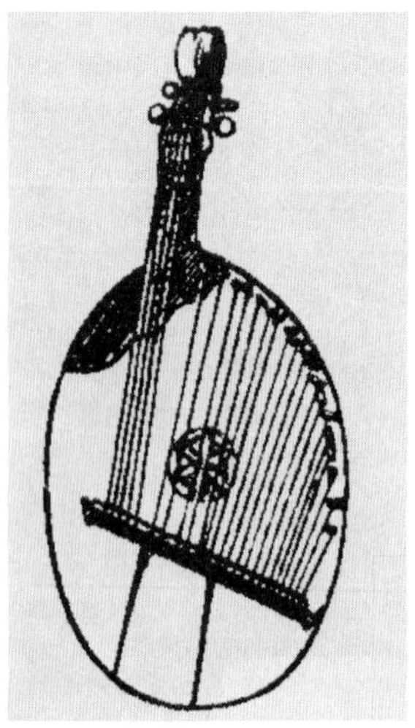

Kobza

Kobza. An ancient string instrument of the lute family. Of eastern origin, it was known in Ukraine as early as the 11th century, but became popular only in the 16th century, when it was used to accompany the recitation of *dumas. Eventually, it was supplanted by the *bandura, which has a larger body, longer neck, and more strings. Today 'kobza' and 'bandura' are often used synonymously.

Kobzar (literally the 'kobza player' or 'minstrel'). Originally the title of the first collection of poems by T. *Shevchenko, consisting of eight poems, mainly Romantic ballads, published by P. Martos in St Petersburg in 1840 (the most recent offset facsimile in 1976). The title has, with time, been applied to Shevchenko's poetic works in general. It has acquired a meaning symbolic of the Ukrainian literary and national rebirth because of the national spirit of Shevchenko's poetry and of the fact that two other editions of his works incorporating the title 'Kobzar' but including newer works appeared during his lifetime: *Chyhyrynskii Kobzar i Haidamaky* (The Chyhyryn *Kobzar* and *Haidamaky*, St Petersburg, 1844)

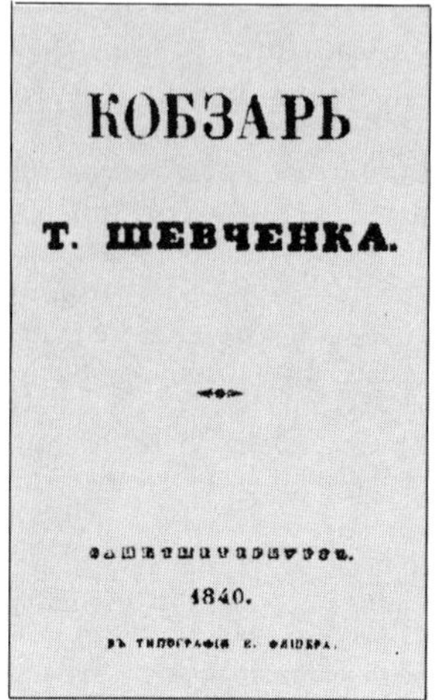

Title page of the first edition of T. Shevchenko's *Kobzar* (1840)

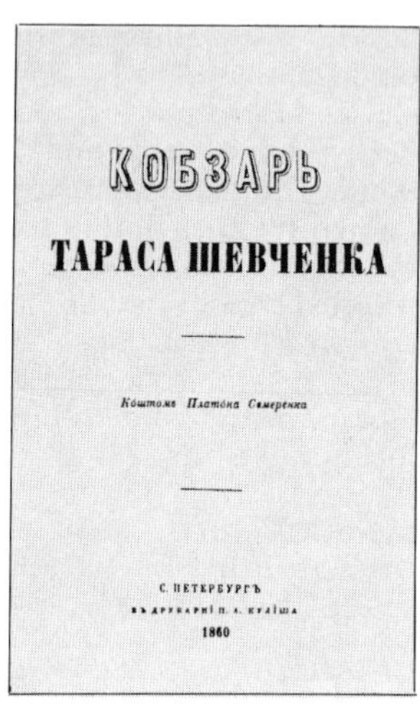

Title page of the 1860 *Kobzar*

and *Kobzar Tarasa Shevchenka* (The *Kobzar* of Taras Shevchenko, St Petersburg, 1860; an offset facsimile appeared in 1981). Shevchenko's exile, when he was forbidden to write, and the strict censorship of his poetry made it impossible for a complete edition of his works to appear until after his death. Subsequently many editions of *Kobzar* were published, each of which included previously unpublished poems. The most notable are the Osnova (1861–2) and D. Kozhanchikov (1867) editions. The *Ems Ukase (1876), which prohibited publications in Ukrainian, brought about the first editions outside Ukraine – O. Rusov's (Prague, 1876) and the Shevchenko Scientific Society's (Lviv, 1893). However it was not until 1907 that a relatively complete edition appeared, in St Petersburg under the editorship of V. Domanytsky (2nd edn, 1908; 3rd edn, 1910).

Attempts at publishing a complete and definitive version resulted in the five-volume Kiev-Leipzig edition (1918–21); the first Soviet 'canonic' edition (edited by I. Aizenshtok and M. Plevako, 1925); the first academic edition (edited by S. Yefremov and M. Novytsky, vols 1–2, 1927; vol 3, 1929); and the first 'full' edition in 14 vols (vols 2–15), edited by P. Zaitsev and published by the Ukrainian Scientific Institute in Warsaw (1934–7, rev edn in 14 vols published by M. Denysiuk Publishers, Chicago, 1959–61). In Soviet Ukraine there appeared a censored jubilee edition (edited by V. Zatonsky, A. Khvylia, and Ye. Shabliovsky, 2 vols, 1935, 1937) and an equally 'selected' academic edition (edited by O. Korniichuk, P. Tychyna, M. Rylsky, et al, 5 vols, 1939). During the Second World War a jubilee edition under L. Biletsky's editorship had been prepared, but only one volume appeared, in 1942 in Prague; the remaining volumes were issued as a revised edition in Winnipeg (4 vols, 1952–4). A full but censored Soviet 10-volume academic edition was published under the editorship of O. Biletsky (1949–53). It was not until the six-volume collected works of Shevchenko were published in Kiev in 1964 that the first full, uncensored edition of Shevchenko's poetry appeared in Soviet Ukraine. Thus, censorship of *Kobzar* has taken various forms, from outright prohibition in Ukraine under tsarist Russia to selective cuts or the use of more suitable variants and tendentious explanatory notes under the Soviet regime.

Kobzar has been translated into all of the world's major languages. The most comprehensive English version appeared in Canada as *The Poetical Works of Taras Shevchenko: The Kobzar* (translated by C. Andrusyshen and W. Kirkconnell, Toronto 1964).

BIBLIOGRAPHY
Bohats'kyi, P. *'Kobzar' T. Shevchenka za sto rokiv: 1840–1940* (Lviv-Cracow 1942)
Doroshenko, V. *Zhenevs'ki vydannia Shevchenkovykh poezii* (Lviv-Cracow 1942)
Žukovsky, A. *Catalogue des éditions concernant Taras Ševčenko dans les bibliothèques de Paris* (Paris 1961)
Bachyns'kyi, L. *Shevchenkiiana v SShA i Kanadi v rr. 1960 i 1961* (Cleveland 1962)
– *Vydannia tvoriv T. Shevchenka v S. Sh. A. Bibliohrafichni materiialy do 1960 roku vkliuchno* (Cleveland 1962)
Rudnyćkyj, J.B. *Shevchenkiana Helvetica* (Winnipeg 1962)
Velinská, E; Zilynskyj, O. *Taras Ševčenko v české kultuře. Bibliografie* (Prague 1962)
Hres'ko, M. *T.H. Shevchenko frantsuz'koiu movoiu 1847–1967. Bibliohrafichnyi pokazhchyk* (Lviv 1967)
– *T.H. Shevchenko italiis'koiu, ispans'koiu, portuhal's'koiu ta esperanto movamy. Bibliohrafichnyi pokazhchyk* (Lviv 1968)
Hres'ko, M.; et al. *T.H. Shevchenko v nimets'kykh perekladakh ta krytytsi (1843–1917). Bibliohrafichnyi pokazhchyk* (Lviv 1968)
Shevchenkivs'kyi slovnyk, vol 1 (Kiev 1976)

D.H. Struk

Kobzar brotherhoods. County organizations of *kobzars and *lirnyks that were widespread in the mid-19th century. Modeled on artisans' guilds, they protected their members' interests. Some ran kobza schools. Every brotherhood had its own secret traditions and regulations. Its members collectively chose as their center a church, for which they bought icons, candles, and oil. They met at the church on certain holy days to attend requiem services for deceased members and to settle urgent matters. In the spring they secretly gathered elsewhere (usually in the forests near Brovary outside Kiev) to elect their officers, to define the territory on which individual kobzars could operate, and to initiate new members according to a prescribed ritual. If necessary, the elected leader (*pan otets*) would call additional meetings. To become a member one had to have a physical handicap, to study kobza playing with a master (usually for at least two years) and obtain permission (*vyzvilka*) to perform independently, to know the kobzars' *lebiiskyi* jargon, and to pay dues regularly.

Only kobzars with good reputations were accepted into a brotherhood. A member who violated a brotherhood's moral code was tried by a brotherhood court. The severest punishment was ostracism. Lesser transgressors were whipped or fined. Civil judges in rural counties did not try kobzars, but handed them over to the brotherhood courts. A member who chose to marry received a dowry from the brotherhood's treasury and was thereafter addressed in the polite second person plural by other members. If members caught a kobzar performing who had not received a *vyzvilka*, they destroyed his bandura, and he was fined and even beaten. The brotherhoods propagated the idea that kobzars were not beggars but professional artists, and instilled a sense of pride among their members; eg, in asking or waiting for a reward, a member was forbidden to fall to his knees.

M. Hnatiukivsky

Kobzars (*kobzari*). Wandering folk bards who performed a large repertoire of epic-historical, religious, and folk songs while playing a *kobza or *bandura. Kobzars first emerged in Kievan Rus' and were popular by the 15th century. Some (eg, Churylo and Tarashko) performed at Polish royal courts. They lived at the Zaporozhian Sich and were esteemed by the Cossacks, whom they frequently accompanied on various campaigns against the Turks, Tatars, and Poles. The epic songs they performed (see *Duma) served to raise the morale of the Cossack army in times of war, and some (eg, P. Skriaha, V. Varchenko, and Mykhailo, 'Sokovy's son-in-law') were even beheaded by the Poles for performing dumas that incited popular revolts.

As the Hetman state declined, so did the fortunes of the kobzars, and they gradually joined the ranks of mendicants, playing and begging for alms at rural marketplaces. In the late 18th century the occupation of kobzar became the almost exclusive province of the blind and crippled, who organized *kobzar brotherhoods to protect their corporate interests. A few performed at the Russian courts of Peter I, Elizabeth I, and Catherine II (eg, H. Liubystok and O. Rozumovsky). In the 19th and 20th centuries, particularly from the 1870s, the kobzars, including the virtuosos O. *Veresai and H. *Honcharenko, were persecuted by the tsarist regime as the propagators of Ukrainophile sentiments and historical memory. (Kobzars are immortalized in the poetry and drawings of T. Shevchenko and he titled his poetic works **Kobzar*.) The few hundred remaining kobzars in Poltava, Kharkiv, and Chernihiv gubernias and their artistry aroused the interest of various ethnographers, composers, and painters, including M. Lysenko, O. Rusov, O. Slastion, Lesia Ukrainka, K. Kvitka, M. Sumtsov, V. Horlenko, V. Borzhkovsky, O. Borodai, F. Kolessa, and D. Revutsky. At the 12th Russian Archeological Congress in Kharkiv in 1902, the kobzars T. Parkhomenko, H. Honcharenko, M. Kravchenko, I. Kucherenko-Kuchuhura, P. Hashchenko, P. Drevchenko, and I. Netesa, accompanied by H. *Khotkevych, the 'first seeing kobzar' (he composed 69 works for the bandura) and the leading authority on kobzar artistry, performed to great acclaim, and the congress participants passed a resolution concerning the great value of the kobzars' art. Government attitudes toward the kobzars softened, and thereafter kobzar concerts became frequent events in many Ukrainian and Russian cities. Bandura schools were established, and in 1907 Khotkevych published the first history and manual of bandura playing; V. Shevchenko's and V. Ovchynnykov's manuals followed in 1914.

After the Revolution of 1905 the kobzars again flourished. From 1908 bandura playing was taught at the Lysenko Music and Drama School in Kiev. The kobzar artistry spread into the Kuban, where it had not existed before. The Kuban kobzars A. Chorny, V. Liashchenko, and D. Darnopykh became famous, and the bandura was introduced into the military orchestras of the Kuban Cossacks. During the 1917 Revolution and subsequent Ukrainian-Russian War, kobzars composed and performed songs promoting the Ukrainian national cause and smuggled political literature; many paid for this with their lives. From July 1918 to 1919 the first Ukrainian banduryst ensemble existed briefly in Kiev.

Under Soviet rule, the *State Banduryst Kapelle of the Ukrainian SSR was established in Kiev in 1927. The VUAN

Kobzar Hnat Honcharenko; woodcut by O. Danchenko (1961)

Ethnographic Commission and Cabinet of Musical Ethnography, particularly the members K. Kvitka, M. Hrinchenko, and K. Hrushevska, conducted important studies of the kobzars in the 1920s. In 1929 H. Epik published the novel *Zustrich* (The Rendezvous) depicting the persecution of the kobzars. In the 1930s, with forced collectivization, the man-made famine of 1932–3, and the Stalinist suppression of Ukrainian culture, the kobzars were again repressed. Party directives to create a new socialist folklore and 'Soviet' kobzars resulted in the AN URSR Institute of Folklore–Sponsored First Republican Conference of Kobzars and Lirnyks in April 1939. Thirty-seven kobzars, including P. Huz, F. Kushneryk, Ye. Movchan, P. Nosach, O. Markevych, Ye. Adamtsevych, S. Avramenko, and V. Perepeliuk, were brought together to discuss 'the first examples of Soviet dumas and heroic songs and the task of creating a Soviet epos.' A number of such examples (eg, 'Duma about the Communist Party,' 'Duma about Lenin') were composed with the institute's workers and members of Ukraine's writers' and composers' unions and performed at the conference's closing concert. The 'creators' were immediately inducted into the writers' union, and a Section of Folk Arts was formed in the union to 'organize systematic creative and methodological assistance for kobzars and *lirnyks.' Yet, as composer D. Shostakovich testifies in his memoirs (*Testimony*, 1979), several hundred kobzars and lirnyks were brought to the congress from all parts of Ukraine and after the congress ended almost all of them were shot.

To hide this tragedy, the Institute of Folklore and the Kiev Philharmonic jointly set up a State Ethnographic Kobzar Ensemble in early 1941, consisting of Ye. Movchan, P. Nosach, P. Huz, O. Markevych, V. Perepeliuk, and I. Ivanchenko; M. Hrinchenko was appointed artistic director. During its brief existence, the ensemble performed throughout Ukraine and in Moscow until the German invasion of the Soviet Union in June 1941.

During the Second World War, kobzars fought in the Red Army and various Soviet partisan units (eg, O. Chupryna, S. Vlasko, D. Vovk, A. Bilotsky) and composed military-patriot songs. Since the war, many professional *bandurysts (eg, F. Zharko, V. Perepeliuk, and A. Hryshyn) have supplemented the folk kobzars. Bandura playing has been widely taught, and many amateur and professional ensembles have been created. In 1969 a large kobzar concert took place in Kiev and the Alliance of Folk Bards-Kobzars was formed under the auspices of the Music Society of the Ukrainian SSR. In 1974 the alliance was transformed into a Section of Kobzars and Bandurysts, with professional and amateur members. In 1975 an artistic council of bandurysts was formed from among its members.

Kobzar artistry has been cultivated among Ukrainians in the West, thanks to the efforts of V. Yemets, J. and H. *Kytasty, P. Honcharenko, V. Kachurak, Z. Shtokalko, V. Levytsky, V. Lutsiv, V. Michalov, and other masters. Various bandurist ensembles exist in many countries in Europe and North America. In New York, Detroit, Chicago, and Toronto, there are bandura schools. Since 1982 the school in New York has published the journal *Bandura*. In Poland, kobzar artistry has successfully been propagated among Ukrainians through the efforts of A. Khraniuk. In Slovakia, there has been a group of female bandurysts within the Duklia Ukrainian Folk Ensemble in Prešov.

BIBLIOGRAPHY
Speranskii, M. *Iuzhnorusskaia pesnia i sovremennye ee nositeli (po povodu bandurista T.M. Parkhomenko)* (Kiev 1904)
Iemets', V. *Kobza ta kobzari* (Berlin 1922)
Kyrdan, B.; Omel'chenko, A. *Narodni spivtsi-muzykanty na Ukraïni* (Kiev 1980)
Lavrov, F. *Kobzari: Narysy z istoriï kobzarstva Ukraïny* (Kiev 1980)
M. Hnatiukivsky

Kobzei, Toma [Kobzej], b 30 June 1895 in Kniazhe, Sniatyn county, Galicia, d 17 August 1972 in Winnipeg.

Toma Kobzei

Community leader and writer. Immigrating to Canada in 1911, Kobzei joined the Ukrainian Social Democratic Party of Canada. During the 1920s he was secretary-general of the Ukrainian Labour-Farmer Temple Association and a member of the Politburo of the Communist Party of Canada. In 1935 he and a group of Ukrainians left the Communist movement, protesting against the man-made famine and terror in Soviet Ukraine. He helped found the League of Ukrainian Organizations (renamed the Ukrainian Workers' League in 1940), and was a contributing editor of its papers *Pravda* (1936–8) and *Vpered* (1938–40). A founding member of the Ukrainian Canadian Committee, he sat on its central executive and headed its Workers' Commission. Kobzei wrote a monograph on V. Stefanyk, *Velykyi riz'bar ukraïns'kykh selians'kykh dush* (The Great Sculptor of Ukrainian Peasant Souls, 1966), and his memoirs *Na ternystykh ta khreshchatykh dorohakh* (On the Thorny Way and Crossroads, 2 vols, 1972–3).

Koch, Erich, b 19 June 1896 in Prussia, d 12 November 1986 in Barczewo, Poland. German Nazi leader and war criminal. Koch joined the Nazi movement in the early 1920s and from 1933 served as party leader and *Gauleiter* (governor) of East Prussia. In 1941 he was appointed Reich commissioner of the *Reichskommissariat Ukraine. Until the end of 1944 he ruled most of German-occupied Ukraine with an iron fist, and then served again as *Gauleiter* in East Prussia (1944–5). Koch was responsible for the death of 4 million people in Ukraine by starvation or execution, including almost the entire Ukrainian Jewish population. Several villages in Ukraine were destroyed in reprisals against Ukrainian nationalist and Soviet guerrilla activites. Under his rule, another 2.5 million Ukrainians were deported to Germany to work as slave laborers. Koch viewed Ukrainians as an inferior race to be used solely as a source of manpower in agriculture and industry for the German war effort.

After Germany's capitulation, Koch lived incognito in the British occupation zone of Germany until 1949, when he was discovered and extradited to Poland for trial. In 1959 he was convicted for war crimes he committed as *Gauleiter* of East Prussia and sentenced to death, but the sentence was never carried out, allegedly because of his poor health. Koch was allowed to spend the rest of his life in prison in relatively comfortable surroundings. Inexplicably, the Soviet authorities never requested his extradition to stand trial for the heinous crimes he committed as Reich commissioner of Ukraine, and they never openly pressured the Polish government to carry out his death sentence.

V. Markus

Koch, Hans, b 7 July 1894 in Lviv, d 9 April 1959 in Munich. German historian; full member of the Shevchenko Scientific Society from 1949. A graduate of the University of Vienna (PH D 1924), he was a professor of East European history at Königsberg, Breslau, Vienna, and Munich universities and director of the East European institutes in Breslau (1937–40) and Munich (from 1952). Koch took part in the Ukrainian independence struggle of 1918–20 as a captain in the Ukrainian Galician Army. During the Second World War he was an officer in the German army involved in Ukrainian affairs; in

Hans Koch

Ivan Kocherha

1939–40, as a member of the German repatriation commission, he helped many Ukrainians escape the Soviet occupation of Western Ukraine. In 1952–4 he was a founder and chairman of the Herder German-Ukrainian Society. A specialist on the history of the church in Ukraine, he published articles on the Ukrainian Autocephalous Orthodox church (1928), the early relationship between Byzantium, Ochrid, and the church in Kiev (1938), and the theory of 'Moscow as the Third Rome' (1953), and the monograph *Ukraine und Protestantismus* (1954). Koch also published German translations of Ukrainian literature (1955). His memoirs focusing on the struggle for Ukrainian independence, *Dohovir z Denikinom* (The Agreement with Denikin), were published in 1931. His biography and complete bibliography are found in *Jahrbücher für Geschichte Osteuropas*, 7 (1959), no. 2.

A. Zhukovsky

Kochan, Volodymyr. See Kokhan, Volodymyr.

Kocherha, Ivan [Kočerha], b 6 October 1881 in Nosivka, Chernihiv gubernia, d 29 December 1952 in Kiev. Playwright and theater critic. He studied law at Kiev University and then lived in Chernihiv (1903–14), Zhytomyr (1914–34), and Kiev (1934–41, 1945–52). His first theater reviews appeared in 1904 in *Chernigovskie gubernskie vedomosti*. His first play, *Pesnia v bokale* (Song in a Wineglass, 1910), was first staged in 1926, in his own Ukrainian translation. Because of his unique style and experimental form, his plays were ignored until his *Maistry chasu* (Masters of Time) won third prize in an All-Union competition in 1933. Kocherha wrote over 30 comedies, satires, and historical plays, including *Feia hirkoho myhdaliu* (The Fairy of the Bitter Almond, 1926), *Almazne zhorno* (The Diamond Millstone, 1927), *Marko v pekli* (Marko in Hell, 1928), *Svichchyne vesillia* (Svichka's Wedding, 1930), *Pidesh–ne verneshsia* (If You Go You Won't Return, 1935), and *Yaroslav Mudryi* (Yaroslav the Wise, 1944). The most complete edition of his works (25 plays) appeared in three volumes in 1956. Because of the unique style, form, and philosophical symbolism of his plays, official Soviet critics have tended to undervalue them vis-á-vis the plays of someone like the less talented but more politically engagé O. Korniichuk. Monographs on his works have been written by Ye. Starynkevych (1947), N. Andrianova (1963), and N. Kuziakina (1968).

I. Koshelivets

Kochevsky, Viktor [Kočevs'kyj], b 15 November 1923 in Rizunenkove, Valky county, Kharkiv gubernia. Poet. A graduate of Kiev University (1956). First published in 1948, he has authored several collections of poetry, including *Hospodari vesny* (Masters of Spring, 1951), *Zemliaky* (Countrymen, 1957), *Kolosky i suzir'ia* (Grain Ears and Constellations, 1964), *Mii Dyvokrai* (My Wonderland, 1973), and *Na krutoskhylakh lit* (On the Steep Slopes of Time, 1973). He has also translated a number of classics of Armenian literature into Ukrainian.

Kochubei [Kočubej]. A family of Cossack officers descended from the Tatar Kuchukbei, who became a Christian and took the name Andrii. Andrii's grandson, Vasyl *Kochubei, was the general chancellor (1687–99) and general judge (1699–1708) under Hetman I. Mazepa. Vasyl's son, also Vasyl (ca 1680–1743), was the colonel of Poltava regiment from 1729 to 1743. His grandson, Semen (1725–79), was the colonel of Nizhen regiment (1746–51), the last general quartermaster (1756–79) and the actual head of the government under Hetman K. Rozumovsky, and, from 1764, a member of the *Little Russian Collegium. Semen's grandson, also named Semen (ca 1778–1835), was the marshal of the nobility in Poltava gubernia and a member of the Love of Truth masonic lodge in Poltava. A relative, Viktor Kochubei (1768–1834), became a Russian count in 1799 and a prince in 1831 and was a prominent Russian statesman and diplomat. He was appointed imperial vice-chancellor in 1798 and senator in 1801, and served as the minister of internal affairs (1802–12, 1819–25) and chairman of the State Council and the Committee of Ministers (1827–34). Viktor's son, Vasilii, was a famous numismatist. The noble family owned estates in Poltava, Chernihiv, and St Petersburg gubernias.

Kochubei, Motria [Kočubej, Motrja], b ca 1688, d ? The daughter of General Judge V. *Kochubei. Her godfather, Hetman I. *Mazepa, wanted to marry her in 1704 but failed to win her parents' consent. Nevertheless, Motria went to live with Mazepa. In 1707 she married General Judge V. Chuikevych. After Mazepa's defeat in 1708, she and her husband were exiled to Siberia. Upon returning to Ukraine, she entered a monastery. Mazepa's interesting, poetic letters to her have been preserved, and their love affair is portrayed in B. Lepky's trilogy *Mazepa*, A. Pushkin's poem *Poltava*, P. Tchaikovsky's opera *Mazepa*, and I. Repin's painting *Motrona Kochubei*.

Kochubei, Vasyl [Kočubej, Vasyl'], b ca 1640, d 25 July 1708. Statesman. Under Hetman P. Doroshenko he carried out diplomatic assignments such as the mission to Adrianople in 1675. Under Hetman I. Samoilovych he was the supervisor of the general chancellery and in 1685 his envoy in Moscow. He helped Hetman I. *Mazepa to come to power. Under Mazepa he was general chancellor (1687–99) and general judge (1699–1708), and on occasion he served as acting hetman. Kochubei led the Poltava Cossack officers' opposition to Ukraine's participation in the anti-Turkish coalition at the end of the 17th century, which culminated in P. *Petryk's rebellion against Mazepa and Peter I. This affected his hitherto friendly relations with Mazepa. Mazepa's love affair with Kochubei's daughter, Motria, further strained relations between the two men in 1704. Upon learning of Mazepa's secret negotiations with King Stanislaus I Leszczyński of Poland,

Vasyl Kochubei

Kochubei and the colonel of Poltava, I. *Iskra, denounced Mazepa's political plans to Peter, possibly in the hope of winning the hetman's office. Peter initiated an investigation, which found nothing to prove Kochubei's accusations. Trusting Mazepa, Peter had Kochubei and Iskra arrested and taken to Vitebsk where, under torture, they were forced to recant. Peter had them returned to Ukraine and beheaded. They were buried at the Kievan Cave Monastery.

O. Ohloblyn

Kochubinsky, Aleksandr [Kočubinskij], b 3 November 1845 in Kishinev, d 28 May 1907 in Odessa. Russian Slavist. A graduate of Warsaw and Kiev universities, in 1871 he was appointed docent at Odessa (New Russia) University. His works, written in a pre-Neogrammarian spirit, dealt with the history of eastern Slavic languages and with toponymy (the historical boundaries of Baltic and Slavic tribes in the Dnieper Basin and the Slavic colonization of Transylvania). His theory of the development of Ukrainian was set forth in his doctoral dissertation, *K voprosu o vzaimnykh otnosheniiakh slavianskikh narechii* (On the Question of Mutual Relations among Slavic Dialects, 1877), and in his extensive review of P. Zhytetsky's *Ocherk literaturnoi istorii malorusskogo narechiia v XVII v.* (Outline of the Literary History of the Little Russian Dialect in the 17th century, 1889) in *Otchet o … prisuzhdenii nagrad grafa Uvarova*, 32 (1892). In his *Otchet o zaniatiiakh …* (Report on the Activities …, 1876) he summarized his studies on Galician dialects and described several manuscript collections in Lviv. A bibliography of his publications can be found in *Sbornik v pamiat' A.A. Kochubinskogo* (A Collection in Memory of A.A. Kochubinsky, 1909).

Kochur, Hryhorii [Kočur, Hryhorij], b 17 November 1908 in Feskivka, Chernihiv gubernia. Pedagogue and translator. A graduate of Kiev University (1932), he taught foreign languages at the Tyraspil and Vinnytsia pedagogical institutes, translated ancient Greek, Czech, Slovak, Polish, and French literature and W. Shakespeare's *Hamlet* (1964) into Ukrainian, and wrote literary criticism. In 1968 he signed an open letter from 139 Ukrainians protesting the arrests and secret trials of Ukrainian intellectuals in 1965–7. Subsequently he was persecuted by the KGB. In 1973 he was expelled from the Writers' Union for offering to serve I. *Dziuba's sentence.

Koćura (aka Kucura). Village (1986 pop over 5,000) in the *Bačka region, Yugoslavia. With 75 percent of its inhabitants being Rusyn-Ukrainians, it is after Ruski Krstur the second largest Rusyn-Ukrainian cultural and educational center in Bačka. Rusyn-Ukrainians from northern Hungary began to settle here in 1762. At the beginning of the 19th century a large Greek Catholic church and a primary school were built in Koćura. The local dialect was the language of instruction in the school. In 1933 the Cultural-National Union of Yugoslav Rusyns, a Russophile organization, was founded in the village. It published the newspaper *Zoria* (1934–7).

Kodak, Yurii (pseud of Panasenko), b 10 March 1916 in Myrhorod, Poltava gubernia. Architect. A graduate of the Kiev State Art Institute (1940), he established his own architectural firm in Germany in 1946 and then in Canada in 1949. He designed and built a number of Ukrainian Orthodox churches such as the Church of the Descent of the Holy Ghost in Regina, Saskatchewan, St Andrew's Memorial Church in South Bound Brook, New Jersey, and St Demetrius's Church in Long Branch, Ontario. He also designed the iconostases of Orthodox churches in Grimsby (Ontario), Toronto, Boston, Hamilton, Winnipeg, and Montreal. In his buildings he blends the traditional forms of Ukrainian architecture, especially the baroque, with modern forms and techniques.

Kodak (Kudak). A fortress located on the right bank of the Dnieper River near the Kodak rapids, 10 km south of present-day Dnipropetrovske. It was completed in July 1635 by the Polish government on the design of G. de Beauplan to secure the southern frontier of the Commonwealth and the route to the Don River and the Black Sea, and to prevent escaping serfs from joining the Cossacks in Zaporizhia. Razed in August 1635 by Cossacks under Hetman I. Sulyma, it was rebuilt in 1639 to control the growing Cossack unrest. The garrison of some 600 soldiers included many German mercenaries. In 1648, after a four-month siege, the fortress was seized by a Cossack army commanded by Col M. Nesterenko. In the latter half of the 17th century, Kodak had a garrison of Cossacks. River pilots who guided boats through the *Dnieper rapids also lived there. Under the terms of the 1711 Prut Treaty between Russia and the Ottoman Empire, the fortress was destroyed.

KoDUS. See Ukrainian Students' Aid Commission.

Kodyma. V-10. Town smt (1979 pop 10,900) in southeastern Podilia and a raion center in Odessa oblast. It was founded in 1754. In 1919 the UNR Army, Bolshevik forces, and A. Denikin's Volunteer Army fought each other there. From 1930 to 1940 it was a raion center in the Moldavian ASSR.

Kodyma River. A right-bank tributary of the Boh River, 149 km in length, flowing through the Podolian Upland and the Black Sea Lowland and draining a basin of 2,470 sq km. From the 16th to the 18th centuries the Kodyma marked the border between the Lithuanian-Polish state and Turkey; later it separated Podilia and Kherson gubernias. In 1693 Ukrainian-Cossack forces, consisting of Right-Bank regiments led by S. Palii and Left-Bank regiments, crushed an invading Tatar army there. In 1738 a decisive battle between Russian-Ukrainian and Turkish-Tatar forces took place there.

Kohl, Johann Georg, b 28 April 1808 in Bremen, d 28 October 1878 in Bremen. German geographer and traveler, who visited Ukraine in 1838. His *Reisen in Südrussland* (2 vols, 1841) and *Reisen im Innern von Russland und Polen* (pts 2–3, 1841) provide valuable descriptions of Ukraine and its people in the first half of the 19th century.

Kohuska, Natalia [Kohus'ka, Natalja] (née Levenets), b September 1905 in Lozy, Kremianets county, Volhynia gubernia. Journalist. A member of the Ukrainian Greek Orthodox church and president of the Ukrainian Women's Association of Canada (SUK) (1942–8), she has edited a number of jubilee books on SUK and the Canadian Ukrainian Youth Association. She has written some fictional works and a literary study, *Vydatni postati ukraïns'koï literatury* (Selected Luminaries of Ukrainian Literature, 1984). Since 1960 she has edited *Promin'*, a monthly magazine published by SUK.

Lev Kohut

Osyp Kohut

Kohut, Lev, b 7 February 1878 in Monastyrska, Bukovyna, d 26 October 1947 in Graz, Austria. Lawyer; political and co-operative leader; journalist and publisher. In 1902–3 he edited publications of the Revolutionary Ukrainian party in Chernivtsi: the monthlies *Haslo* and *Selianyn*, and various brochures. In 1903 he became the first director of the Selianska Kasa association of Ukrainian Raiffeisen co-operatives for farmers in Bukovyna, which he had founded with S. Smal-Stotsky. At the same time he edited a number of books in its book series. A founding member of the Ukrainian People's Organization of Bukovyna (1922–7), he edited its newspaper *Ridnyi krai* (1926–30). Then he served as vice-president of the Ukrainian National party (1927–38) and editor of the daily *Chas* (1932–40). Sentenced to death by the Soviets in 1940, he was released eventually and emigrated to Austria, where he lectured at the Slavic Institute of Graz University. Kohut wrote numerous articles on economic and cultural topics and planned a four-volume study, *Ukraïna i moskovs'kyi imperiializm* (Ukraine and Muscovite Imperialism), of which he published only the first volume in 1916.

Kohut, Osyp, b 2 February 1891 in Buchach, Galicia, d ca 15 October 1941 in a Soviet labor camp. Lawyer; political and civic leader. As a young man, he was an organizer of radical students. Later he helped organize the Ukrainian Sich Riflemen. In the 1920s he practiced law in Bohorodchany, Stanyslaviv county, and sat on the supreme executive council of the Ukrainian Social Radical party (USRP). From 1928 to 1930 he was a USRP deputy to the Polish Sejm. He was imprisoned by the Polish authorities during the *Pacification campaign in 1930. In the mid-1930s Kohut broke with the USRP and published an antiradical newspaper, *Bohorodchans'kyi tsip*. In 1939, when Galicia became part of the USSR, he was imprisoned in a labor camp by the Soviets.

Kohutiak, Ivan [Kohutjak], b 4 April 1893 in Knihynyn, Stanyslaviv county, Galicia, d 29 November 1968 in Ivano-Frankivske. Stage producer and actor. He was director of the Ukrainian Touring Drama Theater of Stanyslaviv (est 1920), which in the interwar period toured Galicia and Volhynia presenting mostly populist-realist plays. In 1939–44 he was director of the resident theater in Kolomyia, which had a varied musical and dramatic repertoire.

Kohylnyk River [Kohyl'nyk] (also known as the Kunduk River). A river flowing for 243 km through the Bessarabian Upland and the Black Sea Lowland and draining a basin of 3,910 sq km. It empties into Sasyk Lake.

Koialovich, Mikhail [Kojalovič, Mixail], b 2 October 1828 in Kuznitsa, Sokolka county, Hrodna gubernia, d 4 September 1891 in St Petersburg. Russian historian. He was a graduate, then professor (from 1862), of the St Petersburg Theological Academy. Koialovich's works, mainly devoted to the history of the Ukrainian-Belorussian church, were written from the viewpoint of Russian imperialism and Slavophilism. His works include *Litovskaia Tserkovnaia Uniia* (The Lithuanian Church Union, 2 vols, 1859, 1862), 'Istoriia Basilianskogo ordena' (The History of the Basilian Order, *Khristianskoe Chtenie*, 1864), his PH D dissertation *Istoriia vossoedineniia zapadnorusskikh Uniatov starykh vremen* (The History of the Reunification of the Western Russian Uniates of Ancient Times, 1873), and *Istoriia russkogo samosoznaniia po istoricheskim pamiatnikam i nauchnym sochineniiam* (The History of Russian Consciousness on the Basis of Historical Sources and Scholarly Studies, 1884). His essays on the history of Right-Bank Ukraine and on the church brotherhoods there appeared in the Slavophile journal *Den* (1862–4) and elsewhere. Koialovych also compiled and edited *Dokumenty, obiasniaiushchie istoriiu Zapadnoi Rossii i eia otnosheniia k Vostochnoi Rossii i k Pol'she* (Documents Explaining the History of Western Russia and Its Relationship to Eastern Russia and Poland, 1865) and *Dnevnik Liublinskogo seima 1569 g.* (The Minutes of the Lublin Sejm of 1569, 1869).

A. Zhukovsky

Kokel, Oleksa [Kokel'], b 13 March 1880 in the Chuvash region, Russia, d 4 February 1956 in Kharkiv. Painter. A graduate of the St Petersburg Academy of Arts (1912), he settled in Kharkiv in 1916 and lectured at the Kharkiv Art School (later the Kharkiv Art Institute). He was a founding member of the Association of Artists of Red Ukraine. Kokel's style evolved from an impressionistic to a realist one. His works include landscapes such as *Izium: A View of Kremianets Hill* (1936), still lifes, portraits, and depictions of Soviet life such as *The Collective-Farm Market* (1930).

Kokhan, Hryhorii [Koxan, Hryhorij], b 23 June 1931 in Bortkiv, Zolochiv county, Galicia. Filmmaker. A graduate of the Lviv Polygraphic Institute (1955) and the All-Union Institute of Cinematography (1964) in Moscow, he worked at the Kiev Studio of Popular Science Films (1964–9) and then at the Kiev Artistic Film Studio. He directed such films as *Khlib i sil'* (Bread and Salt, 1970), *Narodzheni revoliutsiieiu* (Born of the Revolution, 1973–7), and *Iaroslav Mudryi* (Yaroslav the Wise, 1981).

Volodymyr Kokhan

Kokhan, Volodymyr [Koxan] (Kochan), b 4 December 1898 in Tudorkovychi, Sokal county, Galicia, d 13 June 1966 in Winnipeg. Politician and community leader. During the First World War he served in the Austrian and the Ukrainian Galician armies. After the war he was director of the Ukrainian Bank in Sokal and an active organizer of the Ukrainian co-operative movement in Galicia. A member of the *Ukrainian National Democratic Alliance (UNDO), in 1928 he was elected to the Polish Sejm. His political speeches led to his arrest and imprisonment. In 1930 he was re-elected but resigned from the Sejm and the UNDO in protest against the new policy of 'normalization' of Ukrainian-Polish relations. With other UNDO dissidents he participated in founding the *Front of National Unity and in 1936 was elected to its central executive. During the Second World War Kokhan was active in the co-operative movement. After the war he served as general secretary of the Ukrainian Coordinating Committee in Bavaria and edited the journal *Na chuzhyni*. Immigrating to Canada in 1948, he served as executive director of the *Ukrainian Canadian Committee (1948–66) and director of the Ukrainian Canadian Relief Fund as well as the Ukrainian Canadian Foundation of Taras Shevchenko. He was one of the founders of the World Congress of Free Ukrainians.

Kokhanenko, Yevhen [Koxanenko, Jevhen] (real name: Kokhan), b 10 February 1886 in Vyniatyntsi, Zalishchyky county, Galicia, d 16 October 1955 in Poltava. Stage director and character actor. From 1905 to 1918 he worked, intermittently, with the Ruska Besida theater in Lviv (1905–18), then with the Sadovsky Theater (1919) and, finally, with the Kiev Ukrainian Drama Theater (1922–48). For the latter in 1922 he directed J. Gordin's *Got, Mensch und Teivel*, Molière's *Tartuffe*, Lesia Ukrainka's *Lisova pisnia* (The Forest Song), and H. Sudermann's *Johannisfeuer*. Later he directed C. Goldoni's *La Locandiera* and Ya. Mamontov's *Kniazhna Viktoriia* (Princess Victoria). His acting repertoire included Khlopov in N. Gogol's *Revizor* (The Inspector General), Antonio in P. Beaumarchais's *Le Mariage de Figaro*, Piven in I. Mykytenko's *Dyktatura* (Dictatorship), Lundyshev in I. Kocherha's *Maistry chasu* (The Masters of Time), and Antonio in W. Shakespeare's *Much Ado about Nothing*.

Kokhanovska, Avhusta [Koxanovs'ka], b 6 July 1863 in Cîmpulung, Rumania, d 7 December 1927 in Toruń, Poland. Painter. A graduate of the Vienna Academy of Arts (1899), she lived in Chernivtsi, where she became friends with O. *Kobylianska. Many of her works deal with the everyday life of the Hutsuls: eg, *Hutsuls Returning from the Market* (1906), *The Blessing of Paskas in the Hutsul Region* (1907), *The Old Hutsul* (1910), and *Easter* (1911). She was also a portraitist (eg, a self-portrait [1896] and a portrait of O. Kobylianska [1926]) and a book illustrator (eg, illustrations to O. Kobylianska's stories [1901] and to I. Franko's *Petrii i Dovbushchuky* [1913]). She wrote some articles on peasant life in Bukovyna.

Kokhanovych, Hryhorii Onufrii [Koxanovyč, Hryhorij Onufrij], b before 1750 in Belorussia, d 1814 in Zhydychyn, Lutske county, Volhynia gubernia. Uniate Catholic metropolitan. He probably studied theology in Vilnius before being ordained and posted to Polatsk eparchy, where he soon became the delegate of Kievan metropolitan I. Lisovsky. In 1807 he was appointed bishop of Lutske. Before his death Metropolitan Lisovsky named Kokhanovych as his successor, and he was granted the title 'metropolitan of the Uniate churches in Russia' by Tsar Alexander I in 1809. However, because of the Napoleonic wars and the transfer of Pope Pius VII to France, Kokhanovych was unable to correspond with the pope and his nomination as Kievan metropolitan was not officially recognized by the Vatican. Throughout his tenure as metropolitan he waged a campaign to limit the powers of the Basilian monastic order and to stop the acceptance of Roman Catholic nobles into the order.

Kokhovsky, Vsevolod [Koxovs'kyj] (pseuds: Danylo Medovyk, Pohonets), b 14 March 1835 in Starodubivka, Slavianoserbsk county, Katerynoslav gubernia, d 14 May 1891 in St Petersburg. Writer and pedagogue. A graduate of St Petersburg Military Academy, he founded and headed a cadet pedagogical museum in St Petersburg. An early organizer of popular reading rooms, he wrote a number of articles on education. His earliest literary works, consisting of stories and sketches, appeared in the journal *Osnova*. *Narodoliubets'* (Lover of the People, 1870), a novel, is his most notable literary work.

Kokorudz, Illia, b 1857 in Yavoriv, Galicia, d 1933. Educator, philologist, and specialist in Ukrainian language and literature. Kokorudz was the director of the *Academic Gymnasium of Lviv (1911–27), where he taught from 1896. He was also head of the Ridna Shkola society and one of its benefactors. During the First World War he organized courses for Ukrainian students in Vienna, and after the war he headed the Ukrainian Besida Theater. He wrote several articles on Classical culture, pedagogy, and the history of Ukrainian literature (in particular, on T. Shevchenko, M. Shashkevych, O. Ohonovsky, and Old-Ukrainian legal texts).

Illia Kokorudz

Kolas, Yakub (pseud of Kanstants Mitskevich), b 3 November 1882 on Akinchytsy khutir in Minsk county, Belorussia, d 13 August 1956 in Minsk. Belorussian poet, writer, playwright, and cultural figure; one of the founders of modern Belorussian language and literature. His prerevolutionary writings are imbued with the ideas of Belorussia's social and national liberation and national renaissance. From the 1930s on he wrote in the officially approved Soviet style. His poetry appeared in several collections. A popularizer of Ukrainian literature, he wrote *T. Shevchenko i bilorus'ka literatura* (T. Shevchenko and Belorussian Literature, 1939). Kolas's works have been popular among Ukrainian readers; Ukrainian translations include *Vybrani tvory* (Selected Works, 1951) and *Na rozstaniakh* (At Partings, 1970).

Kolasky, John [Koljaska, Ivan], b 5 October 1915 in Cobalt, Ontario. Educator and author. Educated at the universities of Saskatchewan, Toronto (MA 1950), and Manitoba, he taught high school and was active in the Association of United Ukrainian Canadians (AUUC) and the Communist Party of Canada (CPC). In 1963–5 he attended the Higher Party School of the Central Committee of the Communist Party of Ukraine in Kiev, where he observed the Russification of Ukrainian institutions. For unmasking Soviet nationality policy in his *Education in Soviet Ukraine* (1968), he was expelled from the AUUC and the CPC. He also wrote *Two Years in Soviet Ukraine* (1970) and *The Shattered Illusion* (1979), and translated V. Moroz's *Report from the Beria Reserve* (1974).

Kolberg, Oskar, b 22 February 1814 in Przysucha, Poland, d 3 June 1890 in Cracow. Prominent Polish ethnographer; folk musicologist and minor composer. For 50 years (until 1885) he conducted fieldwork as an independent scholar and as a member of the Anthropological Commission of the Polish Academy of Sciences throughout Poland, Western Ukraine, Belorussia, and Lithuania and amassed a huge amount of ethnographic data on these regions. Much of it was published as *Lud: Jego zwyczaje, sposób życia, mowa, podania, przysłowia, obrzędy, gusła, zabawy, pieśni, muzyka i tańce* (The Folk: Its Customs, Way of Life, Language, Legends, Proverbs, Rituals, Magic, Games, Songs, Music, and Dances, 23 vols, 1867–90) and *Obrazy etnograficzne* (Ethnographic Images, 10 vols, 1882–90); of the latter, five volumes were devoted to regions of Ukraine. When Kolberg died, more than half of his research remained in manuscript and unedited form.

In 1961 the Polish Folklore Society and Academy of Sciences began publishing Kolberg's complete works, including previously published volumes and all unedited manuscripts, notes, and correspondence. By 1986, 67 volumes had appeared. The volumes on Ukrainian regions are *Pokucie* (Pokutia, vols 29–32, 1962–3), *Chełmskie* (The Kholm Region, vols 33–4, 1964), *Przemyskie* (The Peremyshl Region, vol 35, 1964), *Wołyń* (Volhynia, vol 36, 1964), and the previously unpublished *Sanockie-Krośnieńskie* (The Sianik-Krosno Region, vols 49–51, 1972), *Białoruś-Polesie* (Belorussia-Polisia, vol 52, 1968), *Ruś Karpacka* (Carpathian Ruthenia, vols 54–5, 1970–1, on the Hutsul region), and *Ruś Czerwona* (Red Ruthenia, vols 56–7 [3 bks], 1976–9, on central Ukrainian Galicia).

BIBLIOGRAPHY

Górski, R. *Oskar Kolberg: Zarys życia i działalności* (Warsaw 1974)

Boltarovych, Z. *Ukraïna v doslidzhenniakh pol's'kykh etnohrafiv* XIX *st.* (Kiev 1976)

Millerowa, E.; Skrukwa, A. 'Oskar Kolberg (1814–1890),' in *Dzieje folklorystyki Polskiej 1864–1918*, ed H. Kapełuś and J. Krzyżanowski (Warsaw 1982)

M. Hnatiukivsky

Kolchak, Aleksandr [Kolčak], b 4 November 1873 in St Petersburg, d 7 February 1920 in Irkutsk. Russian admiral and political leader. In 1916–17 Kolchak commanded the Black Sea Fleet. With British backing he overthrew the Omsk Directorate and in November 1918 installed himself as dictator and supreme ruler of the White forces in Siberia. His goal was to restore the Russian Empire. When the Allies recognized him in 1919 as the chief anti-Bolshevik leader in Russia, the action provoked protests from the Ukrainian and other national governments. The ineptness and brutality of Kolchak's regime alienated the population, and by the end of 1919 he was pushed out of western Siberia by the Red Army. The Czechoslovak Legion turned Kolchak over to the Bolsheviks, who executed him.

Kolchynsky, Oleksander [Kol'čyns'kyj], b 20 February 1955 in Kiev. Wrestler. A graduate of the Kiev Institute of Physical Culture (1978), Kolchynsky was the gold medalist in Greco-Roman wrestling at the 1976 and 1980 Olympic Games. He was World champion in 1978 and Ukrainian and USSR champion several times between 1974 and 1980.

Kolenska, Liubov [Kolens'ka, Ljubov], b 17 April 1923 in Stanyslaviv (now Ivano-Frankivske), Galicia. Writer. A graduate of the Faculty of Philosophy, Innsbruck University (1949), she has written three collections of short stories since immigrating to the United States in 1949: *Samotnist'* (Solitude, 1966), *Pavliv triiumf* (Pavlo's Triumph, 1971), and *Dzerkala* (Mirrors, 1981). Her works, which convey fragmentary impressions and moods, are fine examples of the neo-impressionistic style. Since 1971 she has been a member of the editorial staff of the newspaper *Svoboda*.

Kolesar, Julian, b 15 July 1927 in Djurdjevo, Bačka, Yugoslavia. Artist. A graduate of the Novi Sad Art School (1953), he immigrated to the United States in 1968 and later moved to Montreal. Besides painting, Kolesar designed advertisements for RCA, Wanamaker's, and the Philadelphia Opera. In 1970 he had his first one-man show in Philadelphia and another at the Ukrainian Institute of America in New York. His surrealistic paintings, such as *Girl-Like White Peacocks, Firebird, Poet and Moon, Imaginary Figures, Man Crucified*, and *Blooming Reverie*, combine motifs drawn from folk art with expressionistic, deformed forms.

Julian Kolesar: *On the Wings of Poetry*

Kolesnychenko, Trokhym [Kolesnyčenko, Troxym], b 1876 in Yelysavethrad, Kherson gubernia, d 1941 in Kiev. Stage actor, director, producer, and playwright.

After acting in O. Suslov's (1898), M. Ponomarenko's (1902), V. Zakharenko's (1904), and D. Haidamaka's (1905) troupes, he directed various provincial troupes. From 1925 to 1941 he worked with the Zankovetska Ukrainian Drama Theater. Kolesnychenko's repertoire included heroic roles such as Sava Chalyi in I. Tobilevych's *Sava Chalyi* and Sirko in S. Cherkasenko's *Pro shcho tyrsa shelestila* (What the Steppe Grass Murmured About). He directed such plays as H. Ibsen's *Gengangere* (Ghosts), N. Gogol's *Revizor* (The Inspector General), and M. Gorky's *Na dne* (The Lower Depths), and wrote several plays, including *Za voliu i pravdu* (For Freedom and Truth, 1907), *Novyi zakon* (The New Law, 1917), *Perepolokh* (The Scare, 1917), and *Chad* (Fumes, 1918). In spite of prohibitions, Kolesnychenko gave a free Sunday performance each year to honor T. Shevchenko.

Kolesnyk, Hanna, b 3 June 1935 in Styla, Starobesheve raion, Staline oblast. Opera and concert mezzo-soprano. A graduate of the Kiev Conservatory (1963), where she studied under Z. Haidai, she joined the Kiev Theater of Opera and Ballet as a soloist. She sang the leading lady in such operas as G. Verdi's *Il Trovatore* and *Aida*, P. Mascagni's *Cavalleria Rusticana*, P. Tchaikovsky's *Queen of Spades* and *Evgenii Onegin*, S. Hulak-Artemovsky's *Zaporozhian Cossack beyond the Danube*, and M. Lysenko's *Taras Bulba*. After defecting from the USSR in 1972 with her husband, conductor V. *Kolesnyk, she made a concert tour of the United States and Canada, and appeared as Halia in A. Vakhnianyn's *Kupalo* (1979) and as Odarka in *Zaporozhian Cossack beyond the Danube* (1981).

Kolesnyk, Petro, b 28 January 1905 in Baryshivka, Poltava gubernia, d 8 August 1987 in Kiev. Writer and literary scholar. A graduate of the Kiev Institute of People's Education (1928), he was an associate of the Shevchenko Institute of Literature and belonged to the *Molodniak writers' group and the All-Ukrainian Association of Proletarian Writers. He helped annotate the 1935 edition of T. Shevchenko's complete works. In 1937 he was accused of belonging to a fictional National Fascist Organization and was imprisoned in a Soviet concentration camp. He was rehabilitated in 1956 and became an associate of the AN URSR Institute of Literature. He is the author of books about V. Pidmohylny (1931), I. Franko (1956, 1957, 1964, 1966), T. Shevchenko (1961), M. Kotsiubynsky (two in 1964), and S. Rudansky (1971), and of the novels *Borot'ba* (Struggle, 1932), *Na fronti stalysia zminy* (Changes Occurred on the Front, 1935), *Teren na shliakhu* (Blackthorns on the Road, 1959), and *Poet pid chas oblohy* (The Poet during the Siege, 1980).

Kolesnyk, Volodymyr, b 7 September 1928 in Dnipropetrovske. Choirmaster and conductor. A graduate of the Kiev Conservatory (DMA 1954), where he had studied under H. Verovka, Kolesnyk lectured at the conservatory and conducted the chorus of the Kiev Theater of Opera and Ballet. In 1969 he was appointed the theater's director. Defecting in 1972, he spent three years in Australia and then settled in Canada. He has appeared as guest conductor with the Australian Opera Company, the Symphony Orchestra of the Australian Broadcasting Corporation, the Edmonton Symphony Orchestra, the Hamilton Philharmonic Orchestra, and the CBC Vancouver Orchestra. As conductor of the Canadian Ukrainian

Volodymyr Kolesnyk

Yevdokiia Kolesnyk

Opera Chorus, which he helped found, he directed highly successful productions of *Kupalo*, *Natalka from Poltava*, and *Zaporozhian Cossack beyond the Danube*. He also conducts the Ukrainian Bandurist Chorus of Detroit and the Millennium Choir organized in Canada to celebrate the millennium of Christianity in Ukraine. Kolesnyk has compiled a three-volume anthology of operatic choral compositions, and has recorded a number of Ukrainian operas.

Kolesnyk, Yevdokiia, b 1 May 1942 in Pustelnykove, Oleksandriia raion, Kirovohrad oblast. Dramatic soprano. Upon graduating from the Kiev Conservatory (1968), she became a soloist of the Kiev Theater of Opera and Ballet. Her repertoire includes Oksana in S. Hulak-Artemovsky's *Zaporozhian Cossack beyond the Danube*, Mylana in H. Maiboroda's *Mylana*, Katerina in D. Shostakovich's *Katerina Izmailova*, Liza in P. Tchaikovsky's *The Queen of Spades*, and Leonora in G. Verdi's *Il trovatore*. She has won international competitions and performed outside the USSR.

Kolesnykov, Arkadii, b 5 December 1907 in Jurbarkas, Lithuania, d 4 March 1978 in Sevastopil. Geophysicist; full member of the AN URSR from 1967. A graduate of the Moscow Higher Technical School (1930), Kolesnykov was an associate of the USSR Academy of Sciences' Institute of Theoretical Geophysics (1938–42), then director of its Laboratory of Marine Geophysics (1942–54) and a professor at Moscow University (1947–62). From 1963 to 1975 he was director of the AN URSR Marine Hydrophysical Institute in Sevastopil. Kolesnykov published over 100 scientific works on the mechanics of thermal exchange in oceans, seas, and water reservoirs, and on the radioactive contamination of the oceans and nuclear-waste management. He also developed a theory of the crystallization of ice in turbulent water.

Kolesnykov, Stepan, b 11 July 1879 in Adrianopil, Bakhmut county, Katerynoslav gubernia, d May 1955 in Belgrade. Realist painter. A graduate of the Odessa Art School (1903) and the St Petersburg Academy of Arts (1909), he lived in Odessa and participated in the exhibitions of the Society of South Russian Artists. In 1920 he emigrated and settled in Belgrade. Kolesnykov did landscapes, genre paintings, and decorative murals. His works include *Spring* (1909), *By a House* (1912), *Caroling*

(1915), *Oxen Plowing* (1915), and *Windmills* (1917). He painted 17 panels for the Palace Hotel and the ceiling of the opera theater in Belgrade.

Filaret Kolessa

Liubka Kolessa

Kolessa, Filaret, b 17 July 1871 in Tatarske, Stryj county, Galicia, d 3 March 1947 in Lviv. Musicologist, folklorist, and composer; from 1909 full member of the Shevchenko Scientific Society and from 1929 of the VUAN; brother of O. *Kolessa. A graduate of the universities of Lviv (1896) and Vienna (PH D 1918), he taught at several gymnasia in Galicia before being appointed in 1939 professor at Lviv University. In the following year he became director of the Lviv Branch of the Institute of Fine Arts, Folklore, and Ethnography of the AN URSR and of the Ukrainian State Museum of Ethnography and Crafts. His publications deal mainly with the origin and development of Ukrainian folklore, particularly of Ukrainian *dumas. Kolessa defended the view that dumas are of folk origin. His works on Ukrainian folk songs and dumas include *Ohliad ukraïns'ko-rus'koï narodnoï poeziï* (A Survey of Ukrainian-Rus' Folk Poetry, 1905), *Rytmika ukraïns'kykh narodnykh pisen'* (The Rhythmics of Ukrainian Folk Songs, 1906–7), *Melodiï ukraïns'kykh narodnykh dum* (Melodies of Ukrainian Folk Dumas, 2 vols, 1910, 1913), 'Variianty melodii ukraïns'kykh narodnykh dum, ïkh kharakterystyka i hrupuvannia' (Variants of the Melodies of Ukrainian Folk Dumas, Their Characterization and Grouping, *ZNTSh*, nos. 116–17 [1913]), 'Pro henezu ukraïns'kykh narodnykh dum' (On the Genesis of Ukrainian Folk Dumas, *ZNTSh*, nos 130–2 [1920–2]), 'Narodni pisni z halyts'koï Lemkivshchyny' (Folk Songs from the Galician Lemko Region, *Etnolohichnyi zbirnyk NTSh*, nos 39–40 [1929]), and *Ukraïns'ka usna slovestnist'* (The Ukrainian Oral Literature, 1938; repr, 1983). His studies on Subcarpathian, Polisian, and Lemko folk songs were pioneering works on Ukrainian musical dialects. His own compositions include choral works and arrangements of folk melodies. Some of his studies have been collected and republished posthumously in three volumes: *Muzykoznavchi pratsi* (Musicological Works, 1970), *Fol'klorystychni pratsi* (Folkloristic Works, 1970), and *Muzychni tvory* (Musical Compositions, 1972).

BIBLIOGRAPHY

Hrytsa, S. *Filaret Mykhailovych Kolessa* (Kiev 1962)

W. Wytwycky

Kolessa, Khrystia, b 15 October 1915 in Vienna, d 22 July 1978 in Ottawa. Cellist and educator; daughter of O. *Kolessa. A student of H. Bekker, she began to give concerts in 1926, first in Europe and then in North America. After the Second World War she immigrated to Canada. Her repertoire included works by Ukrainian composers, particularly by V. Barvinsky, M. Fomenko, and A. Rudnytsky. Some of her recitals were recorded by the German firm Electrola.

Kolessa, Liubka, b 19 May 1904 in Lviv. Pianist and educator; daughter of O. *Kolessa. Upon graduating from the Vienna Academy of Music (1920) where she studied under L. Thern and E. von Sauer, she made the first of several European concert tours. She performed frequently in Lviv, and in 1929 she toured Soviet Ukraine. She was the first Ukrainian pianist to be recorded by European firms; in 1938 His Masters' Voice and Electrola recorded her recitals of works of L. Beethoven, G. Hummel, F. Chopin, and W. Mozart. In 1940 Kolessa immigrated to Canada. She taught at the Toronto Conservatory of Music, and continued to perform on stage until 1950. Her repertoire consisted mostly of classical and romantic music, and included the works of Ukrainian composers such as V. Barvinsky and N. Nyzhankivsky. She was noted for her fluent technique and subtle tone modulation.

Mykola Kolessa

Kolessa, Mykola, b 6 December 1903 in Sambir, Galicia. Composer, conductor, and educator; son of F. *Kolessa. A graduate of the Prague Conservatory (1928) and its School of Master Artists (1931), where he studied under V. Novák. Kolessa taught at the Lysenko Higher Institute of Music (1931–9) and then at the Lviv Conservatory, where he also served as rector (1953–65). Among his students were S. Turchak and Yu. Lutsiv. At the same time he conducted the Lviv Symphony Orchestra (1940–53), the orchestra of the Lviv Theater of Opera and Ballet (1944–7), and Boian, Banduryst, and Trembita choirs. As a composer, Kolessa used Lemko and Hutsul folklore material, to which he applied modern technique. His compositions include two symphonies, *The Ukrainian Suite* (1928), *Symphonic Variations* (1931), a suite for string orchestra *In the Mountains* (1935), a piano quartet, a piano suite *Portraits of the Hutsul Region* (1934), *Fantastic Prelude* (1938), *Autumn Prelude* (1969), and other piano pieces, arrangments of folk songs, and *The Lemko Wedding* for a mixed choir and a string quartet. He wrote *Osnovy tekhniky dyryhuvannia* (The Foundation of Conducting Technique, 1960; repr, 1973).

BIBLIOGRAPHY
Volyns'kyi, I. *Kompozytor Mykola Kolessa* (Lviv 1954)
W. Wytwycky

Kolessa, Oleksander, b 24 April 1867 in Khodovychi, Stryi county, Galicia, d 23 May 1945 in Prague. Linguist, literary historian, ethnographer, and civic leader; brother of F. *Kolessa. In 1895 he was appointed lecturer and in 1898 professor at Lviv University. In 1899 he was elected a full member of the Shevchenko Scientific Society. As a member of the Austrian Parliament in 1907 and from 1911 to 1918, he defended the educational rights of Ukrainians, including the right to have a Ukrainian university. He was one of the founders in 1915 and the vice-president of the *Ukrainian Cultural Council in Vienna, which organized Ukrainian émigré schools. From 1921 he headed the Western Ukrainian National Republic's diplomatic mission to Rome. He was a central figure in émigré scholarly life in Prague: organizer, professor, and rector (1921–2, 1925–8, 1935–7) of the *Ukrainian Free University; a founder and vice-president (1923–32) of the *Ukrainian Historical-Philological Society; and first president (1924) of the *Ukrainian Academic Committee. From 1926 to 1939 he was also a professor at Prague University, and from 1929 a member of the Slavic Institute in Prague.

Kolessa belonged to F. Miklosič's linguistic school. He investigated old Ukrainian paleography, historical phonology, and morphology particularly in the Horodyshche manuscripts, the Uzhhorod *Poluustav*, and the life of St Sava. From the study of the last (1896) he drew some important generalizations about the distinctive characteristics of old Ukrainian texts in relation to old Russian texts. In his *Pohliad na istoriiu ukraïns'koï movy* (A View of the History of the Ukrainian Language, 1924) he gave a general survey of the history of the Ukrainian language.

As a literary scholar he studied Ukrainian-Polish literary relations (he wrote articles on Ukrainian folk songs in the poetry of B. Zaleski and on A. Mickiewicz's influence on T. Shevchenko). He is the author of studies of Yu. Fedkovych (1893). He also wrote about the genesis of the modern Ukrainian novella (1924). His *Pohliad na suchasnyi stan istorychnykh rozslidiv ukraïns'ko-rus'koï literatury, Naidavnishyi peryod: Kil'ka probliem i deziderativ* (A View on the Present State of Historical Research on Ukrainian-Ruthenian Literature; The Earliest Period: Several Problems and Desiderata, 1901) summarizes his general views. In the field of folklore studies he contributed *Holovni napriamy i metody v rozslidakh ukraïns'koho fol'kl'oru* (The Main Directions and Methods in the Study of Ukrainian Folklore, 1927) and articles on apocrypha and solar and lunar motifs in Ukrainian Christmas carols.

V. Kubijovyč, G.Y. Shevelov

Oleksander Kolessa

Kolhosp. See Collective farm.

Kolhospne Selo. See *Sil's'ki visti.*

Kolhospnyk Ukraïny (Collective Farmer of Ukraine). Popular agricultural monthly published in Kiev from 1 April 1939 to August 1949, first by the People's Commissariat of Agriculture of the Ukrainian SSR and from 1944 by Ukraine's Ministry of Agriculture. In 1949 it was renamed *Kolhospne selo.*

Kolhospnytsia Ukraïny (Collective-Farm Woman of Ukraine). A semimonthly organ of the CC CP(B)U, which was separated from the journal *Komunarka Ukraïny* and was published in Kiev from 1924 to 1941. Until 1931 it was called *Selianka Ukraïny.*

Koliada, Hryhorii [Koljada, Hryhorij], b 26 November 1896 in Chornukhy, Lokhvytsia county, Poltava gubernia, d 20 February 1977 in Tashkent. Bibliologist. A graduate of Moscow University (1917) and the Kiev Institute of the National Economy (1926), he lectured at Kiev Pedagogical Institute and then at Tadzhik (1949–54) and Tashkent universities. His publications deal with the history of book printing in Ukraine, particularly with the contributions of I. Fedorovych and P. Berynda to the development of printing.

Koliada, Hryhorii (Heo) [Koljada, Hryhorij], b 21 January 1904 in Valky, Kharkiv gubernia, d ? Futurist poet. In 1921–3 he taught in Kharkiv and ran the Petrovsky Children's Commune and the VUTsVK Children's Town. Then he studied at the Academy of Communist Education (1923–6) and the Institute of Transport (1926–30) in Moscow. He was a member of the literary organizations *Pluh and *Hart and while in Moscow joined the group Selo i Misto. Koliada debuted as a poet in 1922. In 1923 he coauthored a poetry collection, *Shturma* (The Storm), with O. Kopylenko and I. Senchenko in Kharkiv. In Moscow six collections of his poetry were published by K. *Burevii's Ukrainian publishing concern Selo i Misto: *Olenka* (1925), *Shturm i natysk* (Assault and Pressure, 1926), *Prekrasnyi den'* (A Beautiful Day, 1926), *Zoloti kucheri* (Golden Curls, 1926), *Futur-extra* (1927), and *Arsenal syl: Roman novoï konstruktsiï* (Arsenal of Forces: A Novel of New Construction, 1929). Nothing he wrote was published during the Stalinist terror of the 1930s. Koliada disappeared without trace after joining the Soviet levy en masse during the German invasion of the USSR.

Koliada, Mykola [Koljada], b 4 April 1907 in Berezivka, Pyriatyn county, Poltava gubernia, d 30 July 1935 in Kharkiv. Composer. A graduate of the Kharkiv Music and Drama Institute (1931), where he studied under S. Bohatyrov, Koliada worked as a composer in the Kharkiv Theater of Working Youth. He was a founding member of the Association of Proletarian Musicians of Ukraine. His works include a symphonic suite on Ukrainian themes (1927), a vocal-symphonic poem *Tractor Attack* (1932), a piano quintet, a sonata, variations and pieces for violin

Mykola Koliada

and piano, arrangements of folk songs, and stage and film scores. O. Arnautov wrote a monograph on Koliada in 1936.

Koliada. The name of a cycle of Ukrainian winter rituals stemming from ancient Greek *kalandai* and the Roman *calendae*. In Christian times it has been performed between Christmas Eve (6 January) and Epiphany (19 January). The *koliada* incorporated certain fall harvest rituals (such as the laying out of harvested produce and the bringing in of the last grain sheaf to the house), livestock-fertility rituals (the feeding of bread, garlic, and rose hips to livestock, feeding chickens in a chain, bringing a lamb into the house), and spring rituals (the sowing of grain, the plowing of furrows, and visiting with the **koza*). It was believed to be a personification capable of influencing the future harvest. Thus arose the customs of 'calling *koliada* to partake in the Christmas **kutia*' and the 'shooing away of *koliada*.' The *koliada* cycle was a time of general merriment, during which generous helpings of food (9 or 12 dishes) were consumed. Even the poorest of families tried to maintain the eating ritual. The visiting of each other's homes and gift giving, particularly among family members but also among neighbors, were customary.

Since *koliada* rituals were originally pagan, the church tried to supplant them with Christian ones. Many rituals of *koliada* were incorporated in the celebration of *Christmas and persist until today.

M. Hnatiukivsky

Koliadky. See Carols.

Koliankivsky, Mykola [Koljankivs'kyj], b 19 June 1912 in Panivtsi, Borshchiv county, Galicia, d 28 October 1985 in Niagara Falls, Ontario. Journalist, publisher, and art collector and dealer. A graduate of the Greek Catholic Theological Academy in Lviv (1936), he worked on the newspaper *Krakivs'ki visti*. After the war he edited and published the paper *Chas* and the journal *My i svit* in Germany. Immigrating to Canada in 1955, he edited the newspaper *Nasha meta* (1955–8) and then opened an art gallery in Toronto, while continuing to publish *My i svit*. In 1970 he founded the Niagara Falls Arts Gallery and Museum, and in 1975 he published W. Kurelek's *The Passion of Christ*. Two collections of his satire on Ukrainian-Canadian life – *Ambasadory* (The Ambassadors, 1968) and *Tovpa* (The Crowd, 1979) – appeared under the pseudonym M. Tochylo.

Kolienda, Havryil [Koljenda, Havryjil], 1606–74. Kievan Uniate metropolitan. Kolienda was probably born in Belorussia. After joining the Basilian order, he studied philosophy and theology in Braunsberg, Prussia (1627–30), Vienna (1633–6), and at the Greek College in Rome (1636–9). He served as coadjutor (1652–5), then bishop (1655–74) of Polatsk eparchy, although he was not able to assume his post because of the incessant wars between the Cossacks, Poland, and Muscovy. After the death of A. Seliava, he administered the Kiev metropoly (1656–65), as Polish King Jan II Casimir Vasa had promised the Cossacks not to appoint a new Uniate metropolitan; it was only in 1665 that the Vatican appointed him metropolitan; in 1667, after the Treaty of *Andrusovo, this appointment was confirmed by the Polish government. At the same time, he was protoarchimandrite of the Basilian order. Kolienda's correspondence with the Vatican was published by A. Velyky in two volumes in 1956.

Koliivshchyna rebellion. A major *haidamaka rebellion that broke out in Right-Bank Ukraine in May 1768 against social and national-religious oppression by the Polish administration and nobility. The word Koliivshchyna is probably derived from *kil* (pike or lance), the weapon used by the rebels (called *kolii*).

The underlying causes of the rebellion were the social unrest created by the difficult conditions of serfdom in Right-Bank Ukraine and the religious oppression of the Orthodox peasants and Cossacks by the Polish Roman Catholic church and nobles (see *Haidamaka uprisings). The rebellion was provoked by the Confederation of *Bar and the antipeasant and anti-Orthodox positions taken by the Polish nobles there. The center of the rebellion was *Kholodnyi Yar and its leader was M. *Zalizniak, a Zaporozhian Cossack from Medvedivka, near Chyhyryn. The haidamakas soon captured the towns of Zhabotyn, Smila, Cherkasy, Korsun, Kaniv, Bohuslav, Moshyn, and Lysianka. Following these first successes, the number of haidamakas increased at the beginning of June, and separate groups dispersed in various directions, seizing centers in the Kiev and Bratslav regions and then in Podilia and Volhynia. An important factor in the spread of the rebellion was the anti-Catholic propaganda that emanated from the Orthodox monasteries of the area. The hegumen of the Motronynskyi Monastery near Chyhyryn, M. *Znachko-Yavorsky, played a particularly influential role in fomenting the rebellion, and many rebels hid from the authorities in the monasteries.

A major achievement of the uprising was the capture of the fortified town of Uman (20–21 June 1768), an important trading center in Right-Bank Ukraine. The captain of the Uman militia under the local magnate F. Potocki, I. *Gonta, joined the insurgency with the Cossacks under his command. A major demand of the insurgents was the restoration of the Cossack political and social order established under B. Khmelnytsky, but which persisted only in Left-Bank Ukraine (the *Hetman state) and in Zaporizhia. Among the more renowned leaders of haidamaka detachments were S. Nezhyvy, M. Shvachka, A. Zhurba, I. Bondarenko, and M. Moskal. The haidamakas inflicted great losses, killing hundreds of Polish nobles, Catholic clerics, and Jewish stewards and moneylenders, and burning scores of estates.

The Koliivshchyna rebellion provoked grave concern

in the Ottoman Empire, Poland's neighbor, which feared the spread of peasant unrest and was particularly angered when haidamaka detachments entered Turkish frontier towns in pursuit of their enemies. Russian policy toward the haidamakas was more ambiguous. Although Empress Catherine II clearly supported the Orthodox cause and the haidamakas believed a fictitious proclamation of her support and call to arms that circulated widely in Right-Bank Ukraine (see *Golden Charter), eventually she ordered Gen M. Krechetnikov to put an end to the uprising. Russian troops began to advance against the haidamaka detachments in late June 1768 and quickly routed them. During a meeting with the Russian high command, M. Zalizniak, I. Gonta, and S. Nezhyvy were arrested and their detachments were disarmed. The Russian army was helped by the Polish army, which brutally tortured, then killed, the captured insurgents (eg, in Kodna, near Zhytomyr). Even many peasants who had not taken part in the uprising were severely repressed. I. Gonta was tortured to death in the village of Serby near Mohyliv-Podilskyi and M. Zalizniak was exiled to Siberia.

The Koliivshchyna insurgents were idealized and immortalized in folk songs and legends, and especially in the poetry of T. Shevchenko, whose famous poem 'Haidamaky' is devoted to the rebellion. The rebellion was also a popular subject in Polish literature, although most Polish writers (eg, S. Goszczyński, M. Czajkowski, J. Słowacki) berated the haidamakas and Cossacks as bandits and religious fanatics under the influence of the Russians. Populist Ukrainian historians (eg, V. Antonovych) generally idealized the haidamakas.

BIBLIOGRAPHY

Shul'gin, Ia. *Ocherk Koliivshchiny po neizdannym i izdannym dokumentam 1768 i blizhaishikh godov* (Kiev 1890)
Huslystyi, K. *Koliïvshchyna* (Kiev 1947)
Serczyk, W. *Koliszczyzna* (Warsaw 1968)
Koliïvshchyna 1768: Materialy iuvileinoï naukovoï sesiï, prysviachenoï 200-richchiu povstannia (Kiev 1970)
Mirchuk, P. *Koliïvshchyna: Haidamats'ke povstannia 1768 r.* (New York 1973)

A. Zhukovsky

Kolisnyk, Peter, b 30 November 1934 in Toronto. Artist and educator. His modernistic sculptures and paintings have been widely exhibited in North America at such institutions as the Montreal Museum of Fine Art, the Museum of Contemporary Art in Chicago, the Art Gallery of Ontario, the Royal Canadian Academy, and the Ukrainian Institute of Modern Art in Chicago. He has received several awards for his watercolors and sculptures and has served as curator of the Cobourg Art Gallery (1964–9) and trustee of the Art Gallery of Ontario (1982). Kolisnyk has taught art at York University since 1975 and has lectured at many Ontario colleges. Besides doing paintings and sculptures, he has designed stage sets.

Kolisnyk, William, b 1887 in Demyche, Sniatyn county, Galicia, d 4 November 1967 in Vancouver. Political activist. He came to Canada with his parents in 1898 and settled in rural Manitoba. A few years later he moved to Winnipeg, joined the Shevchenko Educational Association, and became active in the Ukrainian socialist movement. He was a member of the Ukrainian Social Democratic Party of Canada, its successor the Ukrainian Labour-Farmer Temple Association, and the Communist Party of Canada (CPC). As alderman for Winnipeg's Ward 3 (1926–30), he was the first Communist to be elected to public office in North America. From 1940 to 1942 he was interned as a CPC activist.

Koliukh, Dmytro [Koljux], b ca 1882 in Rossosh, Ostrogozhsk county, Voronezh gubernia, d ca 1937. Civic and co-operative leader. An organizer of Ukrainian consumer co-operatives, he took part in the Second All-Russian Co-operative Congress in Kiev (1913), where he made the proposal to set up a central Ukrainian co-operative union. In summer 1917 he served in the municipal government of Kiev. From 1917 to 1920 Koliukh was the executive president of Dniprosoiuz, and at the same time minister of food supplies in V. Holubovych's cabinet (1918). In 1920 he was appointed vice-president of Vukoopspilka (All-Ukrainian Co-operative Union). In about 1930 he was arrested and deported to Central Asia, where he died.

Kolky. II-6. Town smt (1979 pop 4,000) on the Styr River in Manevychi raion, Volhynia oblast. In 1915 fierce battles between Russian and Austrian-German forces took place there. In 1943–5 it was the center of the Northern group of the UPA, and had several field hospitals.

Kollard, Yurii, b 2 January 1875 in Morachiv, Poltava gubernia, d 3 January 1951 in Augsburg, Germany. Civil engineer; civic and political leader. He was a founding member of the *Revolutionary Ukrainian party. In 1917–19 he belonged to the Ukrainian Party of Socialist Independentists. Under the Central Rada he served as commissar of railways in Polisia, under the Hetman government as senior inspector of railways, and under the Directory as deputy minister of transport. After the First World War he lived in Czechoslovakia, Poland, and Germany. His memoirs, 'Spohady iunats'kykh dniv' (Recollections of Days of Youth), were serialized in *Literaturno-naukovyi vistnyk* (1928–31) and were reprinted in book form in 1972.

Koloda. See Weights and measures.

Kolodiazhyn [Kolodjažyn]. A fortified town and castle in 12th–13th century Kievan Rus', located on the Sluch River near the present-day village of Kolodiazhne, Zhytomyr oblast. Kolodiazhyn was part of the system of city-fortresses that protected Rus' from the nomads, and an economic and administrative center. The main occupations of its inhabitants were agriculture and animal husbandry. The town was sacked by the Mongols in 1241. Remnants of the fortifications, covering an area of 1.5 ha, still remain. In 1948–53 the Institute of Archeology of the AN URSR investigated the site. The town was fortified with earthworks and a ditch. Uncovered were the remains of 22 burnt wooden dwellings, craftsmen's workshops, and buildings with defense or commercial purposes; 16 semi-pit dwellings; charred supplies of cereal and industrial crops (rye, wheat, barley, oats, millet, peas); and assorted tools, weapons, ornaments, religious articles, and the like. It is thought that in the town below the castle lived the retinue and guards of the city's ruler, who was probably an appanage prince.

Kolodka. A ritual folk game. On the Monday of the last week before Lent (the so-called Kolodii festival), married women would tie a small log (*kolodka*) to the legs of young men and women who had not married before Carnival Sunday. Those thus 'punished' had to buy their 'freedom' through gifts or money. In the Poltava region, logs were also tied to the legs of parents for not having arranged marriages for their unmarried children. In more recent times, the log was replaced by symbolic ribbons, kerchiefs, or bundles of flowers. Because shepherds tied small logs to the feet of their herd animals to prevent them from jumping over fences and straying, certain ethnographers have hypothesized by analogy that the custom was applied to feisty young bachelors during the days of greatest festivity as a moral restraint against promiscuity. Others have argued that the game is a remnant of the ancient punishment of pillorying for nonperformance of duties.

Kolodub, Lev, b 1 May 1930 in Kiev. Composer and teacher. After graduating from the Kharkiv Conservatory (1954), where he studied under M. Tits, Kolodub worked as sound director in the Kiev Recording Studio (1955–6). Then he taught musical theory at the Kiev Institute of Theater Arts (1958–60), and since 1966 he has been teaching composition and instrumentation at the Kiev Conservatory. He has served on the executive of the Union of Composers of Ukraine since 1962. His works include an operetta, *City of Lovers* (1969); a cantata for soloists, chorus, and orchestra, *Glory to the Fatherland* (1951); a poem for orchestra, *The Great Stonemason* (1953–5), dedicated to I. Franko; a symphony (1958); *The Ukrainian Carpathian Rhapsody* (1960); a symphony-duma, *Shevchenko Pictures* (1964); a suite, *Hutsul Images* (1966); a concerto for french horn and orchestra (1972); chamber works; choral pieces; arrangements of folk songs; art songs; and radio and film music.

BIBLIOGRAPHY

Zahaikevych, M. *Levko Kolodub* (Kiev 1973)

Kolodub, Zhanna, b 1 January 1930 in Vinnytsia. Composer. A graduate of the Kiev Music School (violin and piano) and the Kiev Conservatory (1954), she has taught piano at the conservatory since 1952. Her works (some in collaboration with L. *Kolodub) include a ballet for children, *Thumbelina* (1969), based on H. Andersen's story; a musical comedy *Merry Girls* (1968); a musical, *Adventure on the Mississippi*, based on Mark Twain's *Huckleberry Finn* (1971); a suite for symphony orchestra, *Kiev Lyrical Portraits* (1976); two dance suites (1961, 1965); *Nocturne* for flute and harp (1965); *Poem* for flute and piano (1966); and children's songs and folk-song arrangements.

Kolody, Helena [Kolodij, Olena], b 12 October 1912 in Cruz Machado, Paraná, Brazil. Brazilian poet. The daughter of Ukrainian immigrants, she was a teacher in Rio Negro, Ponta Grossa, and Curitiba. She made her debut as a poet in the 1930s; between 1941 and 1986 she published 14 collections of crafted philosophical and mystical verse of which the first was *Paisagem Interior* and the latest, *Poesia Minima*. She has translated Ukrainian poetry into Portuguese for the anthologies *Antologia da Literatura Ucraniana* (1959), *Girassol* (1966), and *Viburno Rubro* (1977).

Mykhailo Kolodzinsky

Kolodzinsky, Mykhailo [Kolodzins'kyj, Myxajlo] (pseuds: Kum, Huzar), b 26 July 1902 in Potochyska, Horodenka county, Galicia, d 18 March 1939 in Bushtyna, near Khust in Carpatho-Ukraine. Prominent OUN military leader. He was a member of the Ukrainian Military Organization from 1922 and a key leader of the OUN in Galicia from 1929. In 1932–3 he served on the OUN Executive for Galicia as chief of military training. In 1938–9 he helped organize the Carpathian Sich and became its chief of staff with the rank of colonel. He was killed in combat with the Hungarian army. Kolodzinsky wrote a number of works on military strategy.

Kolokoltsov, Vasilii [Kolokol'cov, Vasilij], b and d ? Political figure, agronomist. A landowner in Kharkiv gubernia, he was zemstvo president of the Vovchanske county zemstvo. Under the Hetman government he served as minister of land affairs in F. Lyzohub's cabinet and introduced the law on land sales (1918). In October 1918 he signed the so-called *Note of the Nine* rejecting the idea of Ukrainian autonomy and arguing for the restoration of the Russian Empire.

Kolomak. IV-16. Town smt (1979 pop 5,400), in Valky raion, Kharkiv oblast, situated on the Kolomak River. The town was founded in the mid-17th century on the site of the Kolomak fortified settlement (first mentioned in 1571). A sugar refinery and a brick plant are located there.

Kolomak Articles (Kolomatski statti). Ukrainian-Russian treaty concluded on 4 August 1687 at the Cossack general council held on the Kolomak River, which formed the boundary of the Hetman state. The council, attended by a limited number of Cossacks, was surrounded by Muscovite troops under the command of Prince V. Golitsyn. Under Russian pressure the council deposed and arrested Hetman I. Samoilovych, elected I. Mazepa hetman, and accepted a previously prepared agreement.

The treaty consisted of 22 articles and was based on the *Hlukhiv Articles of 1669, supplemented with articles accepted during Samoilovych's rule. Although the treaty reasserted Ukrainian rights and privileges and preserved the 30,000-man Cossack register, it also required that the hetman obtain the tsar's approval for any changes in high offices, thus defending the interests of the *starshyna*. Furthermore, it entrenched Muscovy's military and political supremacy over Ukraine: the hetman could not establish diplomatic relations with other countries; he had to maintain an 'eternal peace and alliance' with Poland, thus recognizing in effect Poland's right to Right-Bank Ukraine; he had to provide troops for campaigns against the Crimean Tatars and Turkey; and Muscovite soldiers were to be stationed in Baturyn, capital of the Hetman state. By this treaty the Hetman state was obliged for the first time 'to unite by every method and means the Little-Russian people with the Great-Russian people and to lead them by intermarriage and other measures to an indestructible and firm harmony.' These articles marked another step in the erosion of Ukraine's independence to the advantage of Muscovy.

O. Ohloblyn

Kolomak Petitions (Kolomatski cholobytni). Two petitions sent by senior Cossack officers to Tsar Peter I. They were drafted on the initiative of the Myrhorod colonel D. *Apostol during the Persian campaign on the Kolomak River in summer 1723. The petitions demanded the restoration of Cossack rights, permission to elect a new hetman, and the abolition of requisitions from estates as practiced by the *Little Russian Collegium. The Russian government responded to these and other similar petitions by arresting the acting hetman P. *Polubotok, D. Apostol, and several senior officers (Ya. Lyzohub, V. Zhurakovsky, M. Khanenko, H. Hrabianka, etc). Most of the officers were released in 1725, but Polubotok died in prison.

Kolomak River. A left tributary of the Vorskla River in Kharkiv and Poltava oblasts, 102 km long and with a basin area of 1,650 sq km.

Kolomiichenko, Oleksii [Kolomijčenko, Oleksij], b 30 March 1898 in Shpola, Zvenyhorodka county, Kiev gubernia, d 17 September 1974 in Kiev. Otolaryngologist; corresponding member of the AN URSR from 1967. A graduate of the Kiev Medical Institute (1924), he worked at the Shepetivka hospital (1924–8), the Kiev Institute for the Upgrading of Physicians (1928–35), and various hospitals in Kiev (1936–44, 1952–60). He also held the chairs of otorhinolaryngology at the Kiev Medical Institute (1943–44) and the Kiev Institute for the Upgrading of Physicians (1944–74) and founded and directed the Kiev Scientific Research Institute of Otorhinolaryngology (1960–74). His scientific works deal with otosclerosis; ear, throat, and nose tumors; and the restoration of hearing. He was the first in the USSR to perform a successful microsurgical operation on the inner ear to restore hearing.

Kolomiiets, Inna [Kolomijec'], b 8 March 1921 at Aleiskaia stanitsa, Altai krai. Sculptor. A graduate of the Kiev State Art Institute (1951), she works in monumental, easel, and decorative sculpture. Her major works include *The Only Son* (1964), *The Victors* (1971), ceramic bas-reliefs on themes from I. Kotliarevsky's *Eneida* (1961), and several series such as *Around Italy* (1962–4), *Around Japan* (1966–7), and *Vechornytsi* (1965).

Kolomiiets, Oleksii [Kolomijec', Oleksij], b 17 March 1919 in Kharkivtsi, Poltava gubernia. A leading Soviet Ukrainian playwright. His plays include *Faraony* (The Pharaohs, 1961), *De zh tvoie sontse?* (Where Is Your Sun? 1963), *Planeta Speranta* (Planet Speranta, 1966), *Spasybi tobi, moie kokhannia* (Thank You, My Love, 1967), *Horlytsia* (The Turtle Dove, 1969), *Pershyi hrikh* (The First Sin, 1971), *Odisseia v sim dniv* (An Odyssey in Seven Days, 1974), *Holubi oleni* (Azure Stags, 1973), *Sribna pavutyna* (The Silver Cobweb, 1977), *Dykyi anhel* (The Wild Angel, 1978), and *Ubyi leva* (Kill the Lion, 1985).

Kolomiiets, Volodymyr [Kolomijec'], b 2 November 1935 in Vovchkiv, Kiev oblast. Poet. From 1979 to 1984 he was the editor in chief of the literary journal *Dnipro*. His first collection, *Do sertsia liuds'koho* (To the Human Heart), appeared in 1959. In 1981 the best poetry from his previous 13 collections was reprinted as the large collection *Vid obriiu do obriiu* (From Horizon to Horizon). Between 1981 and 1987 he published five more collections, including *Vybrane* (Selected Works, 1985). He has also written several collections of poetry for children.

Kolomiiets, Yurii [Kolomijec', Jurij], b 25 October 1925 in Khrystynivka, Cherkasy oblast. Soviet Ukrainian Party and government figure. An agronomist by profession, he was a CPU raion committee secretary before becoming secretary of the Cherkasy Oblast Committee in 1965, deputy minister of agriculture of the Ukrainian SSR in 1970, minister of state farms in 1977, first deputy chairman of the State Planning Committee in 1979, and first deputy chairman of the Council of Ministers in 1980. He was elected a candidate member of the CC CPU in 1976 and a full member of its Politburo in 1980.

Kolomyia [Kolomyja]. V-6. City (1985 pop 60,000) on the Prut River in southeastern Galicia and a raion center under oblast jurisdiction in Ivano-Frankivske oblast. The principal city of *Pokutia, it is an important transport junction. First mentioned in the Hypatian Chronicle under the year 1240, it was granted the rights of Magdeburg law in 1405. Salt was mined in the vicinity from the Middle Ages, and Kolomyia became an important salt-trading center (with special privileges granted by the Polish king Casimir IV Jagiellończyk). Because of its proximity to the Moldavian border, the town suffered frequent attacks by the Moldavians, Tatars, and Turks. Under Austrian rule (1772–1918) it was a circle and county center (1815–1918). Owing to its importance as a commercial and administrative center it grew rapidly, reaching a population of 23,100 in 1880, 34,200 in 1900, and 42,700 in 1910, of which Jews constituted a large part. After the First World War its commercial importance diminished. Consequently, by 1931 its population had fallen to 33,400, of which Ukrainians constituted 18.6 percent; Jews, 42.3; Poles and Roman Catholic Ukrainians, 33.7; and Germans, 5.1. In 1943, after the Nazis had exterminated the Jewish population, only 18,500 inhabitants remained in the city.

Until 1914 (and to a lesser extent even until 1939), Kolomyia was a major center of Ukrainian culture in Galicia. Until the early 20th century its role in publishing in Galicia was second only to Lviv's. Yu. Nasalsky published the brochure series *Biblioteka dlia Ruskoi Molodezhy there (1894–1913). The major publishing houses up to 1914 were M. Bilous's press, Ya. Orenshtain's Halytska Nakladnia, and the Zhinocha Biblioteka press. In the 1920s and 1930s the major publishing houses were Zahalna Knyhozbirnia, Ukrainska Zahalna Entsyklopediia, OKA, and Rekord. In 1875, 17 individual Ukrainian

Kolomyia: city hall

publications came out in Kolomyia (compared to 42 in Lviv), but in 1913 only 28 publications appeared (compared to 238 in Lviv). Of all of Galicia's provincial cities Kolomyia had the most (over 30) newspapers and journals. Among them were *Holos narodnyi* (1865–8), the humor magazine *Kropylo* (1869), the Russophile monthly **Nauka* (1871–6) and biweekly *Russkaia rada* (1871–1912), the Radical biweeklies **Khliborob* (1891–3) and *Narod* (1892–4), the popular biweeklies *Vesna* (1878–80) and *Khlops'ka pravda* (1903, 1909), the educational weekly **Postup* (1903–5), and the women's biweekly **Zhinocha dolia* (1925–39). The first Ukrainian drama society in Galicia was established there in 1848 by I. Ozarkevych. The third-oldest Ukrainian gymnasium in Galicia (est 1894 after Lviv's and Peremyshl's) and a branch of the Lysenko Music Institute were located in Kolomyia. The city was also an important center of the *Ukrainian Radical party and the *Sich movement, which were organized by K. *Trylovsky.

Under the Soviet regime Kolomyia's population has grown: by 1959 it was 31,300, and by 1970, 41,000. Its national composition changed radically because of the Second World War and its aftermath; in 1959 Ukrainians composed approximately 72 percent of its inhabitants; Russians, 20; Poles, 4; and Jews, 2. Today Kolomyia is a regional industrial and cultural center. Its population is employed in light industries. Kolomyia has long been famous for its Hutsul crafts (wood carving, weaving, kilim making, embroidery, and ceramics). The city has a mechanized-woodworking tekhnikum and four vocational-technical schools (medical, pharmaceutical, technical, and pedagogical). The Kolomyia Museum of Hutsul Folk Art was founded there in 1926 by V. Kobrynsky. The wooden Church of the Annunciation and its belfry (built in 1587) are the city's oldest architectural monuments.

V. Kubijovyč

Kolomyia Brigade of the Ukrainian Galician Army (Kolomyiska 2-ha brygada UHA). Formed in January 1919 out of the Stare Selo Group, the brigade consisted of three infantry regiments and an artillery regiment, and was part of the Second Corps of the UHA. Its commanders were Majs F. Tinkel (to June 1919) and R. Dudynsky, Col A. Vymetal, and Capt O. Revniuk. The brigade distinguished itself in combat against the Poles near Lviv, and later during the Chortkiv offensive. It took part in the Kiev offensive against the Bolsheviks and entered Kiev on 30 August 1919. Subsequently, it fought against Denikin's army. When the UHA allied itself with the Red Army, the brigade was reorganized in the spring of 1920 into the Second Infantry Regiment of the Third Brigade of the Red UHA. In April 1920 the regiment along with the rest of the Third Brigade turned against the Bolsheviks, but was captured by the Poles and interned by them near Proskuriv.

Kolomyia Museum of Hutsul Folk Art

Kolomyia Museum of Hutsul Folk Art (Kolomyiskyi muzei narodnoho mystetstva Hutsulshchyny). A museum originally established in 1926 by its first director V. *Kobrynsky, who collected its original artifacts. It was opened to the public in 1935; initially it consisted of one room in the Kolomyia People's Home. Until 1944 the museum was run by volunteers and opened only on

Sunday. Today the museum has 18 halls and exhibits over 18,000 items of Hutsul folk art and handicrafts. It is visited by over 70,000 people annually. The museum's scholarly associates conduct research on the ethnography of the Hutsul region, which is published in article and book form, and organize conferences, special events, and touring exhibits. A branch of the museum was founded in Kosiv in 1971. A guide to the museum was published in Uzhhorod in 1970.

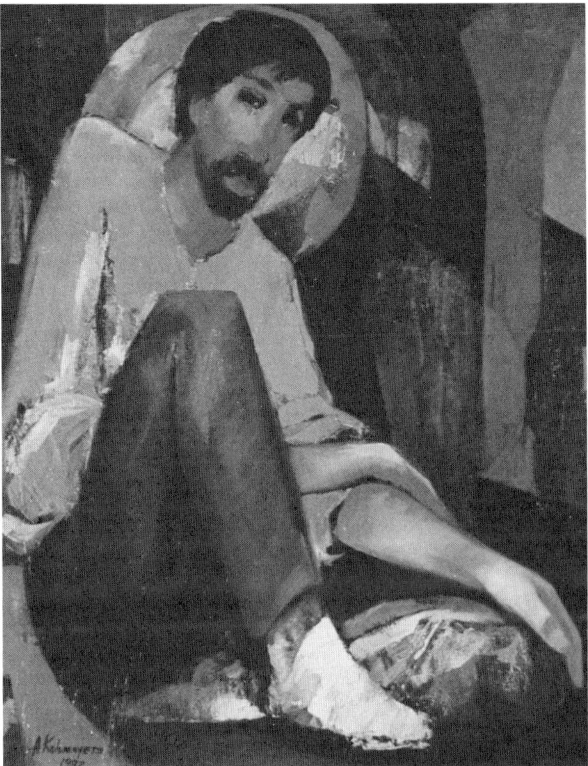

Anatole Kolomayets: *Apostle* (oil)

Kolomyiets, Anatol [Kolomyjec', Anatol'] (aka Kolomayets, Anatole), b 12 February 1927 in the Poltava region. Painter. From 1948 to 1953 he studied painting at St Luke's Institute and at the Royal Academy of Fine Arts in Liège, Belgium. In 1954 he came to the United States and settled in Chicago, where he has worked as a commercial artist for the *Chicago Sun-Times* and the *Chicago Tribune*. He was a founder of the Monolith group of Ukrainian artists. Specializing in oils and watercolors, he has held over 20 one-man exhibits in North America and has participated in many group shows. His paintings, such as *Mother of Sorrows* and *Hutsul*, are expressionistic, but retain a strong grasp of the object. He has done some icon painting and has designed a number of iconostases.

Kolomyiets, Anatolii [Kolomyjec', Anatolij], b 4 October 1918 in Savyntsi, Myrhorod county, Poltava gubernia. Composer. Studying composition under L. Revutsky, he graduated from the Tashkent Conservatory (1943) and the Kiev Conservatory (PH D 1951). Since then he has taught at the Kiev Conservatory, obtaining the rank of full professor by 1971. His compositions include *Variations on a Ukrainian Theme* (1956) for orchestra, a ballet *Ulianka* (1959), a cantata *In Memory of I. Kotliarevsky* (in collaboration with V. Kyreiko, text by M. Rylsky, 1969), a piano sonata (1941) and various other piano pieces, *The Ukrainian Sonata* (1968) for bandura and piano, several bandura pieces, compositions for mixed choir, and music to various verses by Ukrainian poets.

Avenir Kolomyiets

Kolomyiets, Avenir [Kolomyjec'], b 19 February 1906 in Horodets, Volhynia, d 22 July 1946 in Salzburg, Austria. Journalist and poet. After graduating from Warsaw University in 1930, he contributed literary criticism and poetry to *Novi shliakhy* and other pro-Soviet periodicals in Lviv until he broke with the Sovietophiles in 1933. He studied directing at the Warsaw Institute of Theater Arts for three years and traveled abroad. From 1936 he worked in education and theater in Volhynia, promoted Esperanto, and contributed poetry and articles to Western Ukrainian journals. His varied legacy consists of the poem 'Deviatyi val' (The Ninth Wave, 1930), the poetry collection *Provisni kadry* (Prophetic Cadres, 1932), unpublished novellas, *Ieretyk* (The Heretic, 1936) and other plays, stories and plays for children, a libretto, school textbooks, and the essay collection *Shevchenkova era* (Shevchenko's Era, 1942).

Kolomyiets, Yurii [Kolomyjec', Jurij], b 1930 in Kobeliaky, Poltava oblast. Poet. A postwar refugee, he lived in Germany until 1947 and in Belgium until 1952, when he immigrated to the United States. He lives in Chicago and has published two collections of modern poetry: *Hranchaste sontse* (The Faceted Sun, 1965) and *Bili temy* (White Themes, 1983).

Kolomyika [kolomyjka]. The most popular form of Ukrainian folk ditty. It consists usually of two rhyming lines with a set rhythmic pattern: a 14-syllable line with feminine ending and a caesura after the eighth syllable (4 + 4 + 6). *Kolomyiky* are widespread throughout Ukraine. The Carpathian Hutsul region, however, is considered their epicenter, and the name is believed to be derived from the Hutsul city of Kolomyia.

Tens of thousands *kolomyiky* have been transcribed and published. The oldest transcriptions are in 16th-century compilations of songs for the lute. The oldest written text – 'Chy ia tobi ne movyla, ne bery voloshky' ('Didn't I Tell You, Don't Take a Wallachian Girl') – is found in a 1659 Polish letter from M. Zamoyska to King Jan III

Sobieski. Thousands of *kolomyiky* were written down and studied in the 19th century by Ukrainian and Polish ethnographers (Z. Dołęga-Chodakowski, P. Lukashevych, P. Chubynsky, Ya. Holovatsky, V. Shukhevych, and others). The largest number (8,622) is in V. *Hnatiuk's *Kolomyiky* (3 vols, 1905–7). N. Shumada and Z. Vasylenko's *Kolomyiky* (1969) contains 4,814 texts and 452 melodies.

Kolomyiky treat literally every facet of everyday folk life, both familial and social, in a humorous fashion. *Kolomyiky* are one of the few folk-song genres still being improvised in Soviet Ukraine. Contemporary versions, however, while also heavily propagandistic, are often similar to the Russian *chastushka* and are now studied in the Soviet Union with the latter as one genre, downplaying the uniquely Ukrainian character of the *kolomyiky*.

Kolomyika is also the name of a mimetic circular Hutsul dance in 2/4 time, of which there are many variants.

M. Hnatiukivsky

Kolomyishchyna [Kolomyjščyna]. A landmark near Khalepia, Obukhiv raion, Kiev oblast. Excavations in 1934–9 revealed two settlements: one, designated Kolomyishchyna I, from the late stage of the Neolithic *Trypilian culture, and the second, Kolomyishchyna II, from the middle stage of the Trypilian culture. The first consisted of 39 ground dwellings arranged in two concentric circles around communal buildings at the center. Each dwelling contained several rooms and stoves. The second consisted of similar dwellings arranged in a circle.

Joanne Kolomyjec

Kolomyjec, Joanne [Kolomyjec', Ivanka], b 23 April 1955 in Sudbury, Ontario. Operatic soprano. A graduate of the University of Toronto (BM 1976) and of its Opera Division (1980), she won the Metropolitan Opera Auditions in New York in 1983. She has performed as a soloist with the Canadian, Vancouver, Edmonton, and Santa Fe opera companies, the Toronto Symphony Orchestra, and the Canadian National Ballet. Her repertoire includes Mimi in G. Puccini's *La Bohème*, Violetta in G. Verdi's *La Traviata*, Anna Glawari in F. Lehár's *Merry Widow*, Fiordiligi in W. Mozart's *Cosi fan tutte*, and the Countess in his *Marriage of Figaro*.

Kolubovsky, Yakiv [Kolubovs'kyj, Jakiv], b 1863 in Hlukhiv, Chernihiv gubernia, d 1930. Bibliographer and historian of Ukrainian and Russian philosophy. A graduate of St Petersburg University (1866), he studied philosophy and pedagogy in Leipzig before becoming an assistant to the editor of *Voprosy filosofii i psikhologii* (1891) and a lecturer in the history of pedagogy (1892) and logic (1894) at the St Petersburg Pedagogical Courses. During the Revolution of 1917 he was director of the Galagan College in Kiev and then professor at the Nizhen Institute of People's Education. His bibliographic surveys of Russian publications in philosophy appeared in *Voprosy filosofii i psikhologii*. Later he contributed articles to *Knyzhnyi vistnyk* in Kiev (1919).

Kolyma region. The area along the Kolyma River in the eastern part of the Yakut ASSR and the southern part of Magadan oblast, RSFSR. Because of its severe climate (temperatures in January reach −70°C), the region was completely uninhabited until the Soviet government decided to develop it by means of forced labor. The northern group of concentration camps belonging to the Dalstroi system began to be built along the Kolyma River in the early 1930s. By the 1950s these camps held up to 3 million prisoners, a large percentage of them Ukrainians. The inmates are employed mostly in gold mines. The Kolyma concentration camps are the cruelest and deadliest camps in the USSR: millions of people have perished there.

BIBLIOGRAPHY

Conquest, R. *Kolyma: The Arctic Death Camps* (London 1978)

Kolyvanova, Svitlana, b 26 September 1940 in Kiev. Ballet dancer. A graduate of the Kiev Choreography School (1959), she danced briefly with the Kiev Theater of Opera and Ballet, and then at the Uzbek Opera and Ballet Theater in Tashkent. Since 1964 she has worked at the Kharkiv Theater of Opera and Ballet. Her repertoire includes such roles as Odette and Aurora in P. Tchaikovsky's *Swan Lake* and *The Sleeping Beauty*, Mavka in M. Skorulsky's *The Forest Song*, Donna Anna in V. Hubarenko's *The Stone Master*, and Cinderella, Juliet, and the Mistress of Copper Mountain in S. Prokofiev's *Cinderella, Romeo and Juliet*, and *Stone Flower*. In 1966 she won first prize at an international dance competition in Varna, Bulgaria.

Kolyvo. A traditional funeral dish made of boiled wheat kernels and honey (nowadays, rice, raisins, plums, apples, and nuts are used) that is placed next to the coffin of the deceased. After the interment, those attending the funeral each ritually eat a spoonful of the *kolyvo*, which symbolizes resurrection. The practice was originally a pagan one adopted from the ancient Greeks, who brought boiled wheat as an offering to Apollo. In certain parts of Ukraine bread was used instead of *kolyvo*. Sometimes the dish was eaten on Pentecost.

Komar, Anatolii, b 25 December 1909 in Kiev, d 26 October 1959 in Kiev. Civil engineer; from 1956 a full member and president (1956–9) of the Academy of Construction and Architecture of the Ukrainian SSR, and from 1957 member of the Academy of Construction and Architecture of the USSR. He helped design the blast furnaces of the Zaporizhstal metallurgical plant and similar plants in the Urals and directed construction of hydraulic projects, roads, and public buildings in Ukraine. His publications deal with the organization and mechanization of construction.

Komar, Antin, b 30 January 1904 in Berezna, Skvyra county, Kiev gubernia. Physicist; full member of the AN URSR from 1948. A graduate of the Kiev Polytechnical

Institute (1930), he worked at the USSR Academy of Sciences' Physico-Technical Institute in Sverdlovsk (1936–47) before joining the academy's Physico-Technical Institute in Leningrad in 1950. He was director of the institute (1950–7) and also served on the faculty of Leningrad Polytechnical Institute (1950–69). Komar made significant contributions to the physics of metals and ferrites, nuclear-accelerator technology, instrumentation, and nuclear-structure research.

Komar, Ted, b 6 June 1929 in Winnipeg. Accordionist, arranger, teacher. From 1947 to 1958 he performed as an accordion soloist on the CBC radio's *Prairie Schooner*. In 1952 he formed the Ted Komar Orchestra, which has appeared widely in Canada and the United States featuring old-time music. In 1975 it recorded *Happiness Is Resi* and *Reflections*. Komar has conducted a number of studio orchestras on CBC radio and TV. In 1975 he performed his own arrangement of *Three Ukrainian Dances* with the Winnipeg Symphony Orchestra. Komar has published accordion instruction books and founded two music schools in Winnipeg.

Komar (Mosquito). An illustrated semimonthly of humor and satire published in Lviv from 22 January 1900 to 1906. The publisher and editor was I. Kuntsevych, the illustrator Ya. Pstrak, and the caricaturist Ya. Strukhmanchuk.

Komar (Mosquito). A weekly paper of humor and satire, published from 1933 to 1939 in Lviv by Ukrainska Presa publishers. The editor and chief caricaturist was E. *Kozak. Its principal contributors were M. Holynsky, I. Hirny, I. Kernytsky, L. Senyshyn, M. Levytsky, and T. Kurpita.

Komaretsky, Serhii [Komarec'kyj, Serhij], b 1881 in Poltava gubernia, d 1 August 1952 in Haar, Germany. Chemist. In 1922 he was appointed lecturer, and in 1927 professor, at the Ukrainian Husbandry Academy in Poděbrady, Czechoslovakia. From 1942 to 1945 he served as director of the Ukrainian Technical and Husbandry Institute. His publications include chemistry textbooks and papers on inorganic chemistry; eg, on obtaining iodine from Black Sea seaweed.

Komarevych, Vasyl [Komarevyč, Vasyl'], 1891–1927. Community and church leader in Volhynia. A lawyer by profession, in 1918 he served as an officer in the UNR Army. He founded and headed the Prosvita society in Volodymyr-Volynskyi in 1918, and was elected to the Polish Sejm in 1922.

Komariv culture. An archeological culture of the middle and late Bronze Age (17th–12th centuries BC), named after a settlement and a burial site excavated in 1886 and 1934–6 near Komariv, Stanyslaviv county, Galicia (present-day Ivano-Frankivske oblast). The culture existed throughout Subcarpathia, Podilia, Volhynia, and part of the middle Dnieper region. Its people lived in patriarchal clans and practiced crop cultivation and herding. They rarely interred their dead; instead corpses were covered with mounds of earth, frequently after a cremation ritual. Their houses were built of wood and earth on a stone and oak foundation. Flint, stone, and bronze weapons and tools, corded earthenware, and bronze ornaments were discovered during excavations. Scholars believe that the people were the ancestors of either the Thracians or the proto-Slavs.

Komarne. IV-4. Town (1970 pop 3,300) in Horodok raion, Lviv oblast. It arose in the 12th–13th century. In 1473 the town was granted the rights of Magdeburg law and a castle was built. An Orthodox brotherhood was established there in 1592. In the 19th century it was an important crafts (particularly weaving) and trading center in Galicia. From 1939 to 1959 it was a raion center. Komarne's main industries are natural-gas extraction and processing, food processing, tree farming, woodworking, and fish farming. Its oldest architectural monuments are a Roman Catholic church (built in 1473 and reconstructed in 1657) and the wooden St Michael's Church (built in 1754 and decorated with frescoes).

Komarnytsky, Yosyf [Komarnyc'kyj, Josyf], b 17 August 1852 in Roliv, Sambir circle, Galicia, d 1920. Uniate priest and professor. He attended the Central Seminary in Vienna and studied canon law at Vienna University (PH D 1883). From 1891 he was a professor of biblical studies at Lviv University, serving as rector in 1896–8. He wrote a treatise on the Gospel according to St Matthew and a number of scholarly and popular studies and articles for the journals *Dushpastyr* (which he edited) and *Ruskii Sion*. Komarnytsky also edited the newpaper *Myr* (1885–7).

Mykhailo Komarov

Komarov, Mykhailo, b 23 January 1844 in Dmytrivka, Pavlohrad county, Katerynoslav gubernia, d 19 August 1913 in Odessa. Bibliographer, ethnographer, critic, and historian. He studied at Kharkiv University. A public notary, he lived in Kiev, Uman, and (from 1880) Odessa where he was a central figure in community life. He used his legal training to fight tsarist censorship. He wrote valuable bibliographic guides, including bibliographies of Ukrainian literature (1798–1883) in the almanac *Rada* (1883); of Ukrainian drama and theater from 1815 (1906, revised 1912); and of such figures as I. Kotliarevsky (1904), T. Shevchenko (1903), I. Nechui-Levytsky, M. Lysenko (1904), and S. Rudansky (1895). He also compiled *Nova zbirka malorus'kykh prykazok, prysliv'ïv, pomovok, zahadok i zamovlian'* (A New Collection of Little-Russian Proverbs, Maxims, Sayings, Riddles, and Incantations, 1890) and *Russko-ukrainskii slovar'* (Russian-Ukrainian Dictionary, 4 vols), which was published in Lviv in 1893–8 under the pseudonym M. Umanets; contributed literary criticism to the newspapers *Zoria* and *Dilo*; wrote historical studies on A. Holovaty (1891), B. Khmelnytsky (1901), Zaporozhian liberties (1907), and censorship in Ukraine; and published popular literature.

Komarynsky, Volodymyr [Komaryns'kyj], b 4 June 1906 in Sokal, Lviv county, Galicia, d 4 November 1981 in Albany, New York. Lawyer; community activist. He studied law in Prague, and in 1935 opened a legal practice in Mukachiv, where he served as defense counsel for Ukrainians in various political trials. In 1938–9 he was the press secretary for the autonomous government of Carpatho-Ukraine and a member of its parliament. After the Second World War he lived in Germany and served as a legal adviser to the International Refugee Organization. He later immigrated to the United States, where he became president of the *Carpathian Alliance.

Kombinat. See Manufacturing complex.

Kominternivske. VII-11. Town smt (1979 pop 4,700) and raion center in Odessa oblast. Founded in 1802, until 1933 it was called Antonove-Kodyntseve. Food products are manufactured there.

Komisarenko, Vasyl, b 14 January 1907 in Cherniakhiv, Kiev county, Kiev gubernia. Endocrinologist; from 1951 full member of the AN URSR. A graduate of the Kharkiv Medical Institute (1932), he was director of the Institute of Endocrinology in Kharkiv (1937–40). From 1945 to 1965 Komisarenko headed the endocrinology laboratory of the Institute of Experimental Biology and Pathology of the republic's Ministry of Public Health (from 1953, the AN URSR Institute of Physiology). He also served as a department chairman at the Kiev Medical Institute (1950–4). He was the first director of the Kiev Scientific Research Institute of Endocrinology and Metabolism (est 1965) of the Ministry of Public Health. His research dealt with the mechanisms of hormonal action and the effect of insulin on the nervous system.

Komitat (from the Latin *comitatus*). An administrative-territorial unit in the kingdom of Hungary. The concept was derived from the South-Slavic *zhupa* (*župa*), an early medieval alliance of clans that later designated a group of peasant communities. The komitat (Hungarian: *vármegyék*) was introduced in Hungary in the 13th century. Its head was a royal official (Hungarian: *ispán*; Slavic: *zhupan*) who represented the king's authority, administered the population, and collected taxes with the aid of various underlings and an armed force of free men. In Transcarpathia and the Prešov region, the Ukrainians under Hungarian rule lived in Szepes, Sŕos, Zemplén, Ung, Bereg, Ugocsa, and Máramoros komitats; their capitals were Levoča, Prešov, Nové Mesto, Uzhhorod, Berehove, Sevliush, and Syhit. In the last four komitats Ukrainians constituted the majority of the population. The komitats were retained in the interwar Czechoslovak Republic under the name of *župa* until 1928. The Slovak names of the Ukrainian-populated komitats were Spiš, Šariš, Zemplin, Už, Berehovo, and Marmaroš.

Komnezam. See Committee of Poor Peasants.

Komornyk. A category of dependent people in the Grand Duchy of Lithuania and later in the Polish-Lithuanian Commonwealth who did not own land or a house. They performed pedestrian corvée or paid taxes in cash or in kind to landlords, who provided them with accommodation in their houses or outbuildings (hence the term *komornyk*, from *komora*, meaning barn or storehouse). In the 15th and 16th centuries the term was also applied to the urban poor – beggars, workmen engaged in handicrafts or as day laborers, and even poor people engaged in petty commerce. *Kormornyky* ceased being regarded as such if they acquired a plot of land with a house or if they were able to rent such property.

Kompan, Olena, b 19 March 1916 in Yenakiieve, Katerynoslav gubernia. Historian. Since 1950 she has worked as a research associate of the AN URSR Institute of History. Most of her works deal with Ukraine up to the 18th century, particularly with the history of cities and the working class. One of her more important works is *Mista Ukraïny v druhii polovyni XVII st.* (The Cities of Ukraine in the Second Half of the 17th Century, 1963).

Kompaniitsi. See Mercenary regiments.

Kompaniivka [Kompanijivka]. V-13. Town smt (1979 pop 5,000), raion center in Kirovohrad oblast. It was founded in the mid-18th century. It has a mixed-feed plant, a poultry hatchery, a forest-reclamation station, and a veterinary tekhnikum.

Komput (from the Latin *computo*: to calculate, reckon). A register of names that defined the social position of an individual within Cossack society. *Komputy* were introduced while Ukraine was under Polish rule. After 1648 the register also contained information regarding a Cossack's military service and his property. Compiled by regimental clerks, the *komput* had judicial authority and was the basis for deciding who had official Cossack status. It was abolished in Slobidska Ukraine in 1765 and in Left-Bank Ukraine in the 1780s, when Ukrainian autonomy was eliminated by the tsarist state. The register constitutes an important historical source for the social and economic history of Ukraine of the 17th and 18th centuries. (See also *Registered Cossacks.)

Komsomol. See Communist Youth League of Ukraine.

Komsomolets' Ukraïny. See *Molod' Ukraïny*.

Komsomolske [Komsomol's'ke]. IV-17. Town smt (1980 pop 14,100) in Hotvald raion, Kharkiv oblast, situated near Lyman Lake. The town was founded in 1956. The Zmiiv Regional Electric Station is located there.

Komsomolske [Komsomol's'ke]. VI-19, DB IV-4. Town (1970 pop 15,800) in Starobesheve raion, Donetske oblast, situated on the Kalmiius River. It was founded as a mining settlement called Karakubbud in 1933. Its main industry is the quarrying of limestone and broken stone. An industrial tekhnikum is located there.

Komunarske [Komunars'ke]. V-19, DB III-5. City (1986 pop 125,000) under oblast jurisdiction in Voroshylovhrad oblast. It was established in 1895 as a workers' settlement of the Donetsko-Yurievske Metallurgical Company. Called Alchevske until 1931, from 1931 to 1961 it was called Voroshylovske. It became one of the largest metallurgical centers in the Donbas. Building systems and materials, coke-chemical products, clothing, and food products are also manufactured there, and a mining and metallurgical institute and museums of history, the history of metallurgy, and geology and mineralogy are located in the city. The city has grown substantially in the Soviet period. In 1923 it had a population of only 9,300.

Komunarske Metallurgical Plant (Komunarskyi metalurhiinyi zavod). A large ferrous metallurgy plant located in Komunarske, Voroshylovhrad oblast. It was founded in 1895 by the Donetsko-Yurievske Metallurgical Society. Now its basic production consists of cast iron, steel, and rolled steel. In 1979 the plant included a large agglomerating workshop, five blast furnaces (the largest with a capacity of 3,000 cu m), nine open-hearth ovens using the Martin process to make steel from pig iron, a continuous steel-pouring aggregate, Blooming mills, and a variety of other furnaces.

Komunarske Mining and Metallurgical Institute (Komunarskyi hirnycho-metalurhiinyi instytut). A technical school of higher education under the jurisdiction of the Ministry of Higher and Specialized Secondary Education of the Ukrainian SSR, established in 1957. It has eight departments (including departments of mining, metallurgy, civil engineering, and automation), an evening school, preparatory courses, and a branch in Stakhanov. The institute's enrollment is over 12,000 (1980) and over 20,000 engineers have graduated from it since its establishment.

Komunist. See *Radians'ka Ukraïna.*

Komunist Ukraïny (Communist of Ukraine). The theoretical and political monthly journal of the CC CPU. First published in 1925 as *Bilshovyk*, it was renamed *Bilshovyk Ukraïny* in 1926 and acquired its present title in 1952. It did not appear from 1941 to 1945. It has been published in Ukrainian and in Russian since 1950.

Komunistychna osvita. See *Radians'ka shkola.*

Komyshany [Komyšany]. VII-13. Town smt (1983 pop 9,500) in Kherson oblast, situated 4 km from Kherson and under the jurisdiction of the Komsomolskyi raion soviet of the city of Kherson. First mentioned in 1795, its earliest inhabitants were settlers from the Balkans. Until 1946 this agricultural town was called Arnautka.

Komysh-Buruny Iron-ore Complex (Komysh-Burunskyi zalizorudnyi kombinat im. S. Ordzhonikidze). Industrial concern specializing in ferrous metallurgy, located in the Kerch Iron-ore Basin. Built in 1931 and rebuilt in 1951, the complex consists of mines, limestone quarries, and sorting and enrichment plants. Its main products are iron, cinder, and niello.

Kon, Felix, b 30 May 1864 in Warsaw, d 28 July 1941 in Moscow. A Bolshevik figure of Polish-Jewish origin. A member of the Polish Proletariat party from 1882, he was imprisoned in a labor camp in Siberia in 1886. He belonged to the Polish Socialist party from 1904 and was a member of the CC Left Faction from 1906. During the Revolution of 1905, he was active in Odessa and Mykolaiv and then lived in Switzerland, where he had close ties with émigré Mensheviks. In late 1917 and 1918 he was the Bolshevik commissar for Polish Affairs in Kharkiv gubernia. In 1919 he edited the Polish-language Bolshevik newspaper in Kiev and became a member of the Collegium of the People's Commissariat of External Affairs of the Ukrainian SSR. During the Polish-Soviet War of 1920, he was a member of the Provisional Polish Revolutionary Committee in Białystok and then the head of the Galician Organizing Committee of the CP(B)U and one of the organizers of the Foreign Section of the CP(B)U Central Executive Committee (CEC). He was also a CEC candidate member in 1920–1, a member of the CP(B)U Organizational Bureau and Kiev Gubernial Committee in 1920, a CP(B)U secretary in charge of agitation and propaganda in 1921, and chief of the Ukrainian Political Administration of the Red Army in 1922. In 1922 Kon was the last plenipotentiary representative of the Soviet Ukrainian government in Moscow; thereafter he held various Party, government, Comintern, and editorial posts there.

V. Markus

Konash-Konashevych, Vasyl [Konaš-Konaševyč, Vasyl'] (Konarz-Konarzewski, Stanisław), b 22 January 1914 in Warsaw. Painter, graphic artist, miniaturist, and mu-

Vasyl Konash-Konashevych: illustration for Petrarch's Sonnets

ralist. Having graduated from the Cracow Academy of Fine Arts (1936), he studied art in Munich and Paris (1936–8) and then taught drawing at the Lviv Institute of Applied Art (1942–4). Having moved to Warsaw in 1945, he was turned over to the Soviets in 1947 and sentenced to 10 years in a labor camp. Released in 1956, he emigrated in 1973 and lived in Paris and Munich before settling in Montreal (1984). His works include a number of series: on the history of Jews in Poland, on biblical themes, on Polish customs and rites, on the Warsaw Uprising, on *Anna Yaroslavna the Queen of France, and on the millennium of Ukraine's Christianization. Most of his paintings take the form of large illuminations. His works have appeared in many exhibitions in Europe and North America, and have received wide acclaim.

Konashevych-Sahaidachny, Petro. See Sahaidachny, Petro.

Konchak [Končak]. Khan of the *Cumans. In the latter half of the 12th century Konchak united the tribes of the eastern Cumans, and in the 1170s and 1180s carried out a number of attacks on settlements in the regions of Pereiaslav, Kiev, and Chernihiv. The raids were particularly destructive along the Sula River. In 1171 and 1180–1 he aided the princes of Novhorod-Siverskyi in their internecine struggle for power with other Rus' princes. In 1184 he and the Cuman khan *Kobiak were routed on the Khorol River during an assault on Rus', but in 1185, at the Kaiala River, he defeated the forces of Prince *Ihor Sviatoslavych, who was taken prisoner. Konchak proceeded to ravage the Kiev and Chernihiv regions, and to lay seige to Pereiaslav. The struggle of Ihor Sviatoslavych and the princes of Rus' to repel Konchak is immortalized in the epic **Slovo o polku Ihorevi*.

Kondra, Peter, b 30 July 1911 in Mikado, Saskatchewan. Poultry scientist and community leader. Educated at the universities of Manitoba and Minnesota (PH D 1953), Kondra joined the faculty of the University of Manitoba in 1946 as a specialist in poultry genetics. He has published numerous articles on poultry breeding, incubation, and housing. An active member of the Ukrainian Greek Orthodox church, the Ukrainian Self-Reliance League, and the Ukrainian Canadian Professional and Business Federation, he served as president of the Ukrainian Canadian Committee (1971–4) and at the same time sat on the executive of the World Congress of Free Ukrainians.

Kondratenko, Hennadii, b 14 September 1920 in Mariiupil (now Zhdanov). Physician and microbiologist. A graduate of the Donetske Medical Institute (1941), he has taught there since 1946; he became its rector in 1964. His research is devoted to salmonellae and staphylococcal infections.

Kondratiev [Kondrat'jev]. Family of Cossack officers in Slobidska Ukraine. Herasym, the otaman of Stavyshch on the Right Bank, settled in Slobidska Ukraine in 1655. He founded the town of Sumy and became the first colonel of Sumy regiment (1658–1701). His son, Andrii, who was killed by K. Bulavin's Don Cossacks, and his grandson, Ivan (d 1726/7), were both colonels of Sumy regiment. The family was closely tied to the Cossack *starshyna* of the Hetman state. They also enjoyed the favor of several Russian tsars, whose generous grants of estates allowed them to become one of the wealthiest families in Slobidska Ukraine; in 1785 members of the family owned over 130,000 ha in Kharkiv gubernia alone.

Kondratiuk, Mykola [Kondratjuk], b 5 May 1931 in Starokostiantyniv, Starokostiantyniv raion. Baritone singer; educator. A soloist of the Ukrainian People's Choir from 1957, he graduated from the Kiev Conservatory in 1958 and joined the Kiev Theater of Opera and Ballet in 1959. Since 1966 he has been a soloist with the Ukrkontsert company and the Kiev Philharmonic, and since 1968 he has taught at the Kiev Conservatory, where he was rector in 1974. His repertoire includes Prince Igor in A. Borodin's *Prince Igor*, Ostap in M. Lysenko's *Taras Bulba*, Maksym in H. Maiboroda's *Arsenal*, and Figaro in G. Rossini's *The Barber of Seville*. In 1963–4 he performed at La Scala in Milan.

Yurii Kondratiuk

Kondratiuk, Yurii [Kondratjuk, Jurij], b 21 June 1897 in Poltava, d 1941 or 1942 in Kozelsk raion, Kaluga oblast, RSFSR. Scientist and inventor; pioneer in rocketry and space technology. After studying at the St Petersburg Polytechnical Institute, he worked at various plants in Ukraine, Russia, Northern Caucasia, and Siberia. From 1933 he headed a task force at the Ukrainian Scientific Research Institute of Industrial Power Engineering in Kharkiv designing the largest wind-powered electric station in the world. In 1919 he published *Tem, kto budet chitat', chtoby stroit'* (To Those Who Will Read in Order to Build), which was expanded into *Zavoievanie mezhplanetnykh prostranstv* (The Conquest of Interplanetary Space, 1929). In this work Kondratiuk developed the basic equations for rocket motion, calculated optimal flight trajectories, explained the theory of multistage rockets, and advocated the use of new rocket fuels, including the boron fuels used today. He proposed that orbiting supply bases be used to supply spacecraft, that atmospheric drag be used for braking descending spacecraft, that small excursion vehicles be used to land men on planets and return them to spaceships, and that the gravitational fields of celestial bodies be used for accelerating and braking spaceships. Kondratiuk's ideas and equations are used widely today by both Soviet and American engineers. The National Aeronautic and Space Administration has translated his work into English and has used many of his concepts in the Apollo moon flights. One of the craters on the far side of the moon is named after him. During the Second World War he reportedly was drafted into the army and died under undisclosed circumstances.

L.S. Onyshkevych

Kondratovych, Irynei [Kondratovyč, Irynej] (Kontratovych), b 1878 in Dubrynych, Trancarpathia, d 1957. Greek Catholic priest and historian. A graduate of the Uzhhorod Theological Seminary, he served as a parish priest in several Transcarpathian villages. During the Hungarian occupation of Transcarpathia, Kondratovych was the vice-president of the Subcarpathian Academy of Sciences. He wrote the popular textbook *Istoriia Podkarpats'koi Rusy* (The History of Subcarpathian [Transcarpathian] Rus', 3rd edn 1930), *K istorii starodavniago Uzhgoroda i Podkarpatskoi Rusy do XIV vieka* (To the History of Ancient Uzhhorod and Subcarpathian [Transcarpathian] Rus' to the 14th Century, 1928), and numerous articles. In 1949 he converted to Orthodoxy and led the campaign to 'reunite' the Uniate Church of Transcarpathia with the Russian Orthodox church, serving as provisional administrator of the Orthodox Mukachiv eparchy.

Kondratowicz, Ludwik. See Syrokomla, Władysław.

Kondufor, Yurii, b 30 January 1922 in Zubani, Hlobyne raion, Poltava oblast; full member of the AN URSR since 1985. Historian and Party functionary. A lecturer at Kharkiv University after 1952, from 1958 to 1968 he directed the Department of Science and Culture of the CC CPU. Since 1960 he has been a candidate member of the CC CPU. In 1968 he was appointed professor and director of the Chair of Soviet Social History at Kiev University. In 1978 he became the director of the AN URSR Institute of History. His books and articles deal mainly with the history of the CPU and the working class and are propagandist in nature.

Kondzelevych, Yov [Kondzelevyč, Jov], b 1667 in Zhovkva, Galicia, d ca 1740 in Lutske, Volhynia. Noted icon painter and elder of the Bilostok Monastery in Volhynia. After his training at the Zhovkva Icon Painting Studio, he probably studied painting at the Kiev Cave Monastery Icon Painting Studio and abroad. Some of his numerous works have survived, including a fragment of the Bilostok Monastery iconostasis with depictions of six apostles and of the Dormition; the tabernacle of the Zahoriv Monastery (1695) with paintings of Joachim and Anna, the Trinity, the Baptism, St Barbara the Martyr, and Archdeacon Steven; and the famous iconostasis of the Maniava Hermitage, painted in 1698–1705 and transferred in 1785 to the church in Bohorodchany upon the dissolution of the hermitage. In 1923 the iconostasis was deposited in the National Museum in Lviv under the name the *Bohorodchany* iconostasis. *The Dormition, The Assumption, The Last Supper, The Crucifixion, Christ and the Samaritan Woman, Christ and Nicodemus,* and the archangels Michael and Gabriel on the Deacon Doors are those parts of the iconostasis painted by Kondzelevych himself; the rest of the icons were done by his subordinates. In 1722 Kondzelevych took part in painting the iconostasis of the Zahoriv Monastery. He did the Deacon Doors,

Yov Kondzelevych: detail of city life from the icon of the Dormition (1690; at the Bilostok Monastery in Volhynia)

Christ's Presentation at the Temple, and the Vernicle. His last work was *The Crucifixion* (1737) for the Lutske Monastery. Kondzelevych broadened the traditional scheme of the icon significantly: he devoted much attention to the surroundings, particularly to the landscape, which he filled with distinctive architectural ensembles.

BIBLIOGRAPHY
Batih, M. *Iov Kondzelevych i Bohorodchans'kyi ikonostas* (Lviv 1957)

S. Hordynsky

Koniecpolski, Stanisław, b ca 1590, d 12 March 1646 in Brody. Polish magnate and military figure. One of the largest landowners in Bratslav voivodeship, he was the Polish Field Hetman (1619–32), then Grand Hetman (from 1632). From 1625 he also headed the commission for the regulation of Cossack affairs. He negotiated the *Kurukove Treaty in 1625 that ended the Cossack uprising led by Zhmailo. Although the Poles had been defeated in the Battle of Borovytsia, Koniecpolski was able to limit the number of *registered Cossacks allowed under the terms of the treaty to 6,000. He was again defeated by the Cossacks under T. Fedorovych at Pereiaslav and concluded the *Pereiaslav Treaty of 1630, which increased the number of registered Cossacks to 8,000. He initiated the construction of the *Kodak fortress in 1635 and managed to quell the Cossack uprisings led by Ya. Ostrianyn and P. Pavliuk (1637–8).

Königsek, Friedrich von, ?–1708. Military engineer from Saxony, an *osaul of the general artillery and an aid to Hetman I. Mazepa during the war of 1708 with Russia. He helped improve the artillery of the Hetman state and was one of the leaders of the defense of Baturyn in October 1708. He died of his wounds on the way to Hlukhiv, where he was being taken by the Russians for execution.

Konka River (also known as the Kinska River and Kinski Vody). A left-bank tributary of the Dnieper River, which it once joined in the Velykyi Luh floodplain (now the Kakhivka Reservoir). The Konka is 150 km long (240 km previously) and drains a basin of 2,600 sq km. In its upper stretch the river flows through a narrow valley in the Azov Upland; it then broadens out and divides into channels. Its waters are used for irrigation.

Kononenko, Hryhorii, b 13 March 1938 in Zolota Nyva, Velyka Novosilka raion, Donetske oblast. Theater director. Graduating from the Kharkiv Institute of Arts (1965), he joined the Kharkiv Ukrainian Drama Theater as a director. In 1969 he was appointed principal director at the Dnipropetrovske Young Spectator's Theater, and then in 1985 at the Kiev Russian Drama Theater. He has staged such plays as *Taras Bul'ba*, an adaptation of N. Gogol's novel, N. Zabila's *Koly misiats' ziide* (When the Moon Rises), P. Zahrebelny's *Khto za, khto proty* (Who's For, Who's Against), and *Skarby Flinta* (Flint's Treasure, an adaptation of R. Stevenson's *Treasure Island*).

Kononenko, Kharytia, b 18 October 1900 in Mykolaivka, Poltava gubernia, d 15 October 1943 in Rivne, Volhynia. Civic leader. An agronomist by profession, she was active in the Ukrainian women's movement in Czechoslovakia and Galicia. In the 1930s she organized the Farm Women's Section of the Silskyi Hospodar society in Lviv. In 1941 she was the head of the Ukrainian Red Cross and the Ukrainian Relief Committee in Rivne. She was executed by the German police.

Kononenko, Konstantyn, b 3 June 1889 in Rylsk, Slobidska Ukraine, d 28 August 1964 in Boonton, New Jersey. Economist; civic and political figure. A member of the Russian Social Democratic Workers' party (Menshevik), he was a member of the Central Rada. In 1919–20 he headed the Kharkiv Association of Agriculture, and from 1921 to 1924 the finance department of the People's Commissariat of Land Affairs of the Ukrainian SSR. Until 1930 he served as director of the All-Ukrainian Agricultural Bank and as a research consultant to the State Planning Committee. Kononenko was arrested in 1930 and sentenced to eight years of forced labor. He immigrated to Germany in 1944 and to the United States in 1951. As an émigré he was involved in the OUN (Bandera faction). Among his numerous articles and studies are *Agrarna polityka bol'shevykiv* (The Agrarian Policy of the Bolsheviks, published under the pseud N. Olezhko, 1948) and *Ukraine and Russia: A History of the Economic Relations between Ukraine and Russia, 1654–1917* (1958); a second volume, covering economic relations between 1917 and 1960, was published in Ukrainian as *Ukraïna i Rosiia* (Ukraine and Russia, 1965). Kononenko also coauthored and edited *Orhanizatsiia sil's'koho hospodarstva v Lisostepu i Polissi Ukraïny* (The Organization of Agriculture in Ukraine's Forest-Steppe and Polisia, 1924).

Konstantyn Kononenko

Viktor Kononenko

Kononenko, Musii (pseud: Shkolychenko), b 21 August 1864 in Turkivka, Pryluka county, Poltava gubernia, d 14 June 1922. Poet and writer. He contributed populist verses to Western Ukrainian periodicals, beginning in 1883 with the poem 'Neshchaslyve kokhannia' (Unhappy Love). His poetry collections include *Lira* (Lyre, 1885), *Struna* (String, 1908), and *Khvyli* (Waves, 3 vols, 1917–18). He also wrote several short stories.

Kononenko, Mytrofan, b 17 June 1900 in Kaharlyk, Kiev county, Kiev gubernia, d 1 January 1965 in Kharkiv. Stage actor specializing in heroic roles. Graduating from the Lysenko Music and Drama Institute (1923), he worked in the Berezil theater and then in the Kharkiv Ukrainian Drama Theater. His principal roles were Hapon in L. Kurbas's and S. Bondarchuk's *Proloh* (Prologue), Satan in I. Dniprovsky's *Iablunevyi polon* (Apple-Blossom Captivity), the professor in A. Sullivan's *Mikado* (text by M. Khvylovy, M. Yohansen, and O. Vyshnia), Velzevul in *Allo na khvyli 477* (Hello on Frequency 477; by the same authors), Gianettino in F. Schiller's *Die Verschwörung des Fiesko zu Genua*, and Tur in O. Korniichuk's *Bohdan Khmel'nyts'kyi*.

Kononenko, Viktor, b 11 September 1918 in Korocha, Kursk gubernia, d 29 July 1975 in Kiev. Mechanical engineer; from 1964 full member of the AN URSR. After graduating from the Kharkiv Institute of Railway-Transport Engineers he worked at various institutes in Moscow and Kiev. From 1965 to 1975 he served as director of the AN URSR Institute of Mechanics and taught at Kiev University. His publications deal with the theory of non-linear oscillations, particularly the theory of auto-oscillation, and parametric oscillations, and the theory of interaction of oscillating systems with energy sources.

Kononovych, Oleksander [Kononovyč], b 31 January 1850 in Tahanrih, d 5 May 1910 in Odessa. Astronomer.

A graduate of New Russia (Odessa) University (1871), from 1886 he was a professor at that university. From 1881 he also headed the Odessa Astronomical Observatory, which, under his leadership, became an important scientific research facility. A pioneer of astronomy in the Russian Empire, Kononovych contributed mainly in the areas of solar-system studies and studies of binary star systems.

Kononovych-Horbatsky, Yosyf [Kononovyč-Horbac'kyj, Josyf], b ?, d ca 1653. Orthodox bishop and educator. A graduate of the Zamość Academy, he was one of the first scholars from Western Ukraine to be invited by P. Mohyla to teach in Kiev. He lectured on rhetoric (1635–6) and philosophy (1639–42), and served as rector (1642–6) of the Kievan Mohyla College. In 1642 he headed the Ukrainian delegation to the Council of Iaşi, where he defended the use of Jesuit pedagogical methods and of Latin in Orthodox education. After serving as hegumen of the St Michael's Golden-Domed Monastery in Kiev, he was consecrated bishop of Vitsebsk, Orsha, Mstsislau, and Mahiliou in 1650.

Kononovych-Horbatsky's course manuals *Orator Mohileanus Marci Tullii Ciceronis apparatisimis partitionibus excultus* (1635–6), *In dialecticarum institutionum disputationes prooemium* (1635–6), and *Subsidium logicae* (1639–40) are the earliest records of courses taught at the college. The logic course, which is the first part of a three-year philosophy course, is based on Aristotle's *Organon* and shows a nominalist tendency. Excerpts from the three courses have been translated into Ukrainian and published in *Filosofs'ka dumka*, nos 1–3 (1972).

N. Pylypiuk

Konotip or **Konotop.** II-14. City (1982 pop 86,000) and raion center in Sumy oblast under oblast jurisdiction, situated on the Yezuch River. Konotip was founded in 1634. From 1654 to 1781 it was a fortified company town in Nizhen regiment. In the summer of 1659 during the Ukrainian-Muscovite War, it was besieged for three months by Prince A. Trubetskoi's army and defended by Col H. Hulianytsky. On 8 July 1659 Hetman I. Vyhovsky, who came to the town's aid, scored his first great victory, killing or scattering 30,000 Russians and capturing 5,000. In 1664 Konotip was destroyed by the Poles. From 1782 to the early 1920s it was a county town, from 1802 in Chernihiv gubernia. From 1923 to 1932 it was an okruha center, and from 1932 to 1939 a raion center, in Chernihiv oblast. Its development began only after it became a junction on the Kiev–Voronezh railway: in 1859 its population was 9,000; in 1897, 18,440; in 1926, 33,600; in 1959, 54,100; and in 1970, 68,400. Its major industries are machine building and metalworking. The electromechanical plant Chervonyi Metalist (est 1916) produces automated mining equipment. The city also has a repair plant for locomotive and railroad cars, firms servicing railway transport, a food industry, a piston plant, a clothing factory, and a construction-materials industry. Several educational institutions are located there; among them the Avtomatvuhlerudprom design-and-construction institute, a general technical faculty of the Sumy branch of the Kharkiv Polytechnical Institute. Its regional museum was founded in 1900.

V. Kubijovyč

Konotip Articles (Konotopski statti). An agreement between the Cossacks and Muscovy, concluded in Kozatska Dibrova, between Konotip and Putyvl, on the occasion of the election of Hetman I. Samoilovych (June 1672). Although the articles, consisting of 10 points, formally ratified the *Hlukhiv Articles, in practice they further limited Ukraine's rights, particularly in foreign affairs, by prohibiting the hetman from having direct diplomatic relations with neighboring states. They also strengthened the interference of Muscovy in Ukrainian internal affairs by limiting the hetman's judicial powers and limiting the number and autonomy of the *kompaniitsi* (*Mercenary regiments). The Konotip Articles were published in *Akty otnosiashchiesia k istorii Iuzhnoi i Zapadnoi Rossii*, vol 9, and by A. Yakovliv in *Ukraïns'ko-Moskovs'ki dohovory v XVII–XVIII vikakh* (Ukrainian-Muskovite Agreements in the 17th–18th Centuries, 1934).

Konovalets, Myron [Konovalec'] (pseud: Zashkivsky), b 22 July 1894 in Zashkiv, Lviv county, Galicia, d 14 October 1980 in Munich. Journalist and civic figure; a lawyer by profession; brother of Ye. *Konovalets. In 1918–20 he served as a lieutenant in the Ukrainian Galician Army. In the interwar period he was a coeditor (1926–39) of the Lviv daily *Novyi chas* and secretary (1927–39) of the Supreme Executive of the Ridna Shkola society in Lviv. In 1940–5 he worked with the Ukrainian Central Committee as its office manager, legal adviser, and editor of *Visnyk*. After the Second World War he edited (1954–65) the weekly **Khrystyians'kyi holos* in Munich, and presided (1950–5) over the Ukrainian Journalists' Association Abroad. He wrote numerous articles and pamphlets on current affairs.

Konovalets, Yevhen [Konovalec', Jevhen], b 14 June 1891 in Zashkiv, Lviv county, Galicia, d 23 May 1938 in Rotterdam. Military commander with the rank of colonel in the UNR Army, and political leader of the nationalist movement. Studying law at Lviv University, he was active in the Prosvita society and in the campaign for a Ukrainian university. He became active in politics as a student representative on the executive committee of the National Democratic party.

Serving as a second lieutenant in the Austrian army during the First World War, he was captured in 1915 by the Russians and interned in a POW camp near Tsaritsyn. There he joined a group of Galician officers (A. Melnyk, R. Sushko, V. Kuchabsky, I. Chmola, and F. Chernyk), escaped with them to Kiev, and organized the Galician-Bukovynian Battalion of Sich Riflemen in November 1917. Two months later Konovalets assumed command of the battalion, which was reorganized and renamed the First Battalion of Sich Riflemen. Committed to the idea of an independent and unified Ukraine, this force distinguished itself in suppressing the Bolshevik uprising in Kiev, in resisting M. Muravev's offensive, and in liberating Kiev by March 1918. Because they refused to recognize the new *Hetman government, the Sich Riflemen were disarmed and disbanded by the hetman's German allies. Prompted by the Ukrainian National Union, Konovalets obtained the hetman's permission to re-establish his unit and formed the Separate Detachment of Sich Riflemen in Bila Tserkva. In November 1918 this force played a key role in overthrowing P. Skoropadsky and restoring the UNR. Later Konovalets expanded the de-

Yevhen Konovalets

tachment into a division, corps, and finally, a group. In December 1919 the force was demobilized, and its commander was interned in a Polish POW camp in Lutske. With S. *Petliura's blessing he went to Prague in spring 1920 to win Galician support for a brigade formed of Ukrainian soldiers held in Czechoslovak internment camps and Italian POW camps. Ye. *Petrushevych's strong opposition put an end to this plan.

With the cessation of war, Konovalets decided to continue the struggle for independence by underground means. In summer 1921 he returned to Lviv to take charge of the *Ukrainian Military Organization (UVO) and to build up its organizational network. Emigrating in December 1922, he lived with his family (wife Olha and son Yurii) in Berlin (1922–9), Geneva (1929–36), and Rome. He maintained control of the UVO and established contacts with foreign, particularly German and Lithuanian, intelligence and military circles. To win political support from Western governments and public sympathy for the cause of Ukrainian independence, he promoted the setting up of foreign-language press bureaus and publishing houses abroad. Recognizing the various groups of young nationalists at home as his natural allies in the struggle for independence, he unified them into one organization, the *Organization of Ukrainian Nationalists (OUN est 1929), and as the head of the Leadership of Ukrainian Nationalists (PUN), channeled their activities to politically motivated goals.

During a visit to the United States and Canada, Konovalets encouraged his followers to establish Ukrainian veterans' associations, which became the nuclei of nationalist community organizations: the *Organization for the Rebirth of Ukraine in the United States and the *Ukrainian National Federation in Canada.

In the 10 years in which he led the OUN, Konovalets consolidated its position in Ukraine and abroad, promoted the development of all-Ukrainian community organizations in France, Germany, and Austria, and tried to bring the Ukrainian national question to the attention of the League of Nations. His persistent efforts to revive the nationalist underground in Soviet Ukraine led to his assassination by a Bolshevik agent.

Konovalets was one of the most prominent figures in 20th-century Ukrainian history. As a military officer he was noted for his organizational abilities and loyalty to the UNR. As a political leader he was able to unite high principles with operational flexibility and to combine creative thinking with intricate organization and effective action. He enjoyed enormous personal authority among OUN cadres, and the respect of even his political adversaries.

Konovalets set down his recollections about the war period in *Prychynky do istorii ukraïns'koï revoliutsiï* (Materials for the History of the Ukrainian Revolution, 1928; 2nd edn, 1948). A special foundation, set up on the 20th anniversary of his death, published a collection of materials on his life and work, *Ye. Konovalets' ta ioho doba* (Ye. Konovalets and His Era, 1974), edited by Yu. Boiko and M. Borys.

V. Yaniv

Konowal, Filip [Konoval, Fylyp], b 15 September 1888 in Kudkiv, Podilia gubernia, d 3 June 1959 in Ottawa. War hero. Konowal immigrated to Canada in 1913 and joined the Canadian infantry in 1915. In August 1917, near Lens, France, he single-handedly destroyed two German machine-gun nests and killed 16 German soldiers before being severely wounded. For his bravery he was promoted from corporal to sergeant and awarded the Victoria Cross. He was patron of Ukrainian Branch No. 360 of the Royal Canadian Legion in Toronto.

Konrad, Mykola, b 16 May 1876 in Strusiv, Terebovlia county, Galicia, d 27 June 1941 in Stradch, Horodok county, Galicia. Ukrainian Catholic priest, pedagogue, and scholar. A graduate of the De Propaganda Fide College in Rome (PH D 1895 and D TH 1899), he taught catechism in Terebovlia and Ternopil. In 1930 he was invited to teach sociology and ancient and modern philosophy at the Greek Catholic Theological Academy in Lviv, and by 1937 he had attained the rank of full professor. At the same time he served as rector of the philosophy faculty and spiritual adviser to the Obnova Society of Ukrainian Catholic Students. His main publications are *Narys istorii starodavn'oï filosofiï* (Survey of the History of Ancient Philosophy, 1934–5; repr, 1974) and *Osnovni napriamky novitn'oï sotsiolohiï* (The Basic Trends in Modern Sociology, 1936). He was shot by agents of the Soviet secret police.

Konstankevych, Ivan [Konstankevyč], b 10 October 1859 in the Lemko region, d 19 April 1918 near Shamokin, Pennsylvania. Greek Catholic priest; church and community leader among Ukrainian immigrants in the United States. A member of the *American circle, he came to the United States in 1893 and served the predominantly Galician parish of Shamokin. He was a founding member and the first secretary of the Ruthenian National Association (est 1894), and edited its newspaper *Svoboda* (1895–6). Konstankevych sharply attacked the Russophile and Magyarophile tendencies among the Galician and Transcarpathian immigrants, particularly the orientation of the *Greek Catholic Union. In 1901–7 he presided over the Sacerdotal Council, which demanded a separate Ukrainian episcopate from Rome. In 1910 he became Bishop S. Ortynsky's vicar-general. He established in Shamokin one of the first Ukrainian parish schools in the United States.

Konstantyn I, d 1159. The metropolitan of Kiev and All Rus'; by origin a Greek. In 1155 he was appointed metropolitan by the Patriarch of Constantinople in place of *Klym Smoliatych. When this led to popular dissatisfaction in Kiev, he willingly abdicated and moved to Chernihiv, where he died.

Konstantynohrad. See Krasnohrad.

Konstantynovych, Yaroslav [Konstantynovyč, Jaroslav], b 13 March 1893 in Torky, Peremyshl county, Galicia, d 1972 in Żelechów, Warsaw voivodeship, Poland. Art historian, critic, and educator. Completing his higher education in Munich, Vienna, and Lviv, he studied church art in Galicia, Austria, Yugoslavia, and Italy. His works include *Wychowanie estetyczne w nowoczesnej szkole* (Esthetic Education in the Modern School, 1936), *Ikonostasis: Studien und Forschungen* (1939), and 'Prychynky do studiï ukraïns'koï ikony XIV–XVI st.' (Materials for the Study of Ukrainian Icons of the 14th–16th Centuries, *Bohosloviia*, vol 42 [1978]). He left unpublished manuscripts on Ukrainian iconostases of the 14th–16th centuries in Poland and 17th-century iconostases in Lviv, Peremyshl, Belz, and Kholm eparchies. He also photographed and described the abandoned churches in the Lemko region.

Archbishop Heorhii Konysky

Oleksander Konysky

Konysky, Heorhii [Konys'kyj, Heorhij] (secular name: Hryhorii; aka Yurii), b 20 November 1717 in Nizhen, d 13 February 1795 in Mahiliou, Belorussia. Orthodox bishop and church figure of noble descent. Konysky graduated from the Kiev Mohyla Academy in 1743, then served there as a professor of poetics, rhetoric, philosophy, and theology (1745–55) and as rector (1752–5). He was consecrated bishop of Mahiliou and Belorussia in 1775 and elevated to archbishop in 1783. In these posts he tried to return Uniates to the Orthodox church. In 1757 he founded a theological seminary in Mahiliou. A prolific writer, Konysky wrote many baroque poems; the play *Voskreseniie mertvykh* (Resurrection of the Dead, published in *Letopisy russkoi literatury*, 1860); a philosophical textbook *Philosophia peripatetica quadripartita* (1747–51), which remained unpublished; and historical works such as *Prawa i wolności obywatelów Korony Polskiej i Wielkiego Księstwa Litewskiego* (The Rights and Freedoms of the Citizens of the Polish Kingdom and the Grand Duchy of Lithuania, 1767), *Istoricheskoe izvestie o Belorusskoi eparkhii* (Historical Information about the Belorussian Eparchy, 1776), *Zapyska ... o tom, chto v Rossii do kontsa XVI veka ne bylo nikakoi unii s Rimskoi Tserkoviu* (A Note ... about the Fact That until the End of the 16th Century There Was No Union with the Roman Church in Russia, published in 1847). Konysky was also considered by some scholars to have been the author of **Istoriia Rusov*. His collected works, in two volumes, were published in 1835 (2nd edn 1861) and his sermons in 1892.

BIBLIOGRAPHY
Kashuba, M. *Georgii Konisskii* (Moscow 1979)

A. Zhukovsky

Konysky, Oleksander [Konys'kyj], b 18 August 1836 at Perekhodivtsi khutir, Nizhen county, Chernihiv gubernia, d 11 December 1900 in Kiev. Populist writer, lawyer, scholar, and community leader. From 1856 he worked in Poltava for the gubernial administration and as a lawyer. A leading member of the secret Poltava Hromada, he helped organize Sunday schools, prepared textbooks for them, initiated the creation of the Poltava Literary Society, and wrote articles on church affairs. Much of his time was also devoted to Ukrainian-language publishing, both in Russian-ruled Ukraine and in Galicia. During the suppression of Ukrainian culture in 1863 (see P. *Valuev), Konysky was arrested and exiled without a trial to Vologda in northern Russia. In 1865 he was allowed to move to Voronezh and then to go abroad. He stayed for several months in Galicia and Bukovyna and developed close ties with leading cultural figures there. He lived from 1866 in Katerynoslav and from 1872 until his death in Kiev, maintaining close ties with Galicia. He was active in the Kiev *Hromada. As a member of the Kiev city council, he tried to get Ukrainian introduced into the city's schools. One of the patrons of the literary Shevchenko Society in Lviv from 1873, he initiated its transformation into the *Shevchenko Scientific Society in 1893 and bequeathed 10,000 rubles to it.

As a writer, Konysky used over 100 pseudonyms (eg, Vernyvolia, O. Horovenko, F. Perebendia, O. Khutorny). His writing first appeared in *Chernigovskie gubernskie vedomosti* in 1858. In his day his poetry (he was an epigone of T. Shevchenko) was very popular (eg, 'Ia ne boius' tiurmy i kata' [I'm Not Afraid of Prisons or Torturers] and 'Na pokhoron T. Shevchenka' [On the Occasion of T. Shevchenko's Funeral]). His more than 50 short stories and novelettes had more lasting value. They dealt primarily with peasant life and tribulations (eg, 'Khvora dusha' [A Sick Soul], 'Startsi' [Oldsters], and 'Za kryhoiu' [After the Ice]), and the social and national oppression of Ukraine (eg, 'Pivniv praznyk' [The Cock's Holiday], 'Mlyn' [The Mill], and 'Spokuslyva nyva'

[The Seductive Field]). In the novelettes *Semen Zhuk i ioho rodychi* (Semen Zhuk and His Relatives, 1875) and *Iurii Horovenko* (1885) he depicted the problems encountered by the Ukrainophile intelligentsia. In 1881 he published the literary almanac *Luna*, the first Ukrainian publication after the *Ems Ukase in Russian-ruled Ukraine.

Konysky also wrote many literary articles and studies. The best known are 'Vidchyty z istoriï rus'ko-ukraïns'koho pys'menstva XIX v.' (Lectures on the History of Ruthenian-Ukrainian Literature of the 19th Century,' *S'vit*, 1881, nos 1–2, 8–10) and a fundamental biography of T. Shevchenko, *Taras Shevchenko-Hrushivs'kyi: Khronika ioho zhyttia* (Taras Shevchenko-Hrushivsky: A Chronicle of His Life, 2 vols, 1898, 1901). Most of the latter was published in the Lviv periodicals *Slovo, Halychanyn, Pravda, Zoria, S'vit, Zapysky NTSh*, and *Literaturno-naukovyi vistnyk*. He also translated Russian works by and about Shevchenko into Ukrainian. His collected belletristic works were published as *Opovidannia* (Stories, 4 vols, 1899–1903), *Opovidannia ta virshi* (Stories and Poems, 4 vols, 1918–19), and *Vybrani tvory* (Selected Works, 2 vols, 1927). In Soviet scholarship Konysky has been denigrated as a nationalist, and apart from a few small excerpts, his works were not published from the late 1920s until 1986, when an edition of his selected works appeared in Kiev. V. Domanytsky's bibliography of his writings appeared in *Kievskaia starina*, 1901, no. 1.

BIBLIOGRAPHY
Franko, I. *Pro zhytie i diial'nist' Oleksandra Konys'koho* (Lviv 1901)
Hrushevs'kyi, M. 'Pamiaty Oleksandra Konys'koho,' *ZNTSh*, 39 (1901)
Iefremov, S. Introduction to O. Konys'kyi, *Vybrani tvory*, 1 (Kiev 1927)

I. Koshelivets

Kooperatyvna respublyka (Co-operative Republic). Monthly journal published from 1928 to 1939 by the Audit Union of Ukrainian Co-operatives in Lviv. Edited by K. *Kobersky, the journal was devoted to theoretical problems of co-operation and to general economic questions. It ceased publication when Western Ukraine was occupied by Soviet troops.

Kooperatyvna rodyna (Co-operative Family). A popular co-operative educational monthly published from 1934 to 1939 by the *Audit Union of Ukrainian Co-operatives in Lviv. Aimed at members of Ukrainian co-operative unions, it had a circulation of 50,000. Its editors were O. Lutsky and R. Kupchynsky. A special section of the paper, *Dlia nashoï khaty*, was edited by the Ukrainske Narodne Mystetstvo co-operative.

Kooperatyvna zoria (Co-operative Star). A semimonthly magazine for Ukrainian consumer co-operatives, published by the *Dniprosoiuz union in Kiev. Fifty-six issues were published from 1918 to 1920. The contributors included Kh. Baranovsky, A. Serbynenko, I. Chopivsky, P. Vysochansky, D. Koliukh, and A. Kharchenko.

Kooperatyvne budivnytstvo (Co-operative Construction). The official journal of the *All-Ukrainian Association of Consumer Co-operative Organizations, published from 1923 to 1935, mostly in Kharkiv and in the final year in Kiev. First it came out monthly in Russian under the name *Kooperativnyi biulieten'* (Co-operative Bulletin, 1923–6). At the beginning of 1927 it was renamed and converted into a Ukrainian semimonthly. In 1931–3 it came out every 10 days, and starting with the ninth issue in 1933 once a month. *Kooperatyvne budivnytstvo* included the supplements *Kooperatyvno-osvitnia robota* (Co-operative Educational Work, 27 issues from 1927 to 1929) and *Informatsiinyi biuleten' Vukoopspilky* (Information Bulletin of the Vukoopspilka, 31 issues from 1930 to 1931).

Kooperatyvne molocharstvo (Co-operative Dairying). A popular monthly for members of dairy co-operatives published from 1926 to 1939 by the *Maslosoiuz dairy union in Lviv. At first it was a supplement to **Hospodars'ko-kooperatyvnyi chasopys*. Its editors were A. Mudryk, A. Palii, and M. Khronoviat.

Kooperatyvne zhyttia (Co-operative Life). The leading newspaper for activists in all branches of the co-operative movement, published in Kharkiv semiweekly (1926–7) and then three times a week (1928) by Knyhospilka. Its circulation was 10,000. In 1929 it was reduced to a one-page section of *Visti VUTsVK*.

***Kopa* court.** See Community court.

Kopach, Ivan [Kopač], b 4 March 1870 in Hrozova, Turka county, Galicia, d 7 October 1952 in Lviv. Classical philologist, philosopher, educator, and civic leader. Kopach received a PH D from the University of Vienna (1901), then taught at the Academic Gymnasium of Lviv before becoming the regional inspector of Ukrainian gymnasia in Galicia (1908–29). He was the president of the Boian music society and the Ukrainska Besida club. After the Soviet occupation of Western Ukraine he was appointed professor of philosophy at Lviv University. Kopach wrote a number of articles on Greek philosophy, Latin philology, and pedagogical and philosophical issues, and coauthored a secondary-school Latin grammar and a Ukrainian reader.

Kopaihorod [Kopajhorod]. V-8. Town smt (1979 pop 2,000) in Bar raion, Vinnytsia oblast, situated on the Nemiia River in eastern Podilia. First mentioned in the early 17th century as Novhorod, in 1624 it received the rights of Magdeburg law and was renamed. It was the site of several battles: in July 1919 Otaman Yu. Tiutiunnyk's units, and in November 1919 the Sich Riflemen, fought the Bolsheviks; and in 1920 the UNR forces defeated the Bolsheviks there.

Kopelev, Lev, b 9 April 1912 in Kiev. Writer and political dissident of Jewish descent. Kopelev was active in the Jewish sections of the CP(B) in the 1920s and as a Party agitator during the collectivization of agriculture in Ukraine. During the Second World War he was imprisoned for trying to prevent his detachment in Germany from committing acts of rape and pillage. In the 1950s he became active in the dissident movement and began writing novels. In 1980 he emigrated to West Germany. Kopelev's three volumes of memoirs – translated into English as *To be Preserved Forever* (1977), *The Education* *of a True Believer* (1980), and *Ease My Sorrows* (1983) – contain much information on life in Soviet Ukraine in the 1920s, particularly on the forced collectivization of agriculture that precipitated the man-made *famine of 1932–3.

Kopernicki, Izydor, b 17 April 1825 in Chyzhivka, Zvenyhorodka county, Kiev gubernia, d 17 April 1891 in Cracow. Polish physician, anthropologist, and ethnographer. A graduate of Kiev University (1849), he was a military doctor in Ukraine and became a teacher of anatomy at Kiev University in 1857. He took part in the Polish Insurrection of 1863–4 as a commissioner in Lviv, was imprisoned, and then lived as a refugee in Paris, Belgrade, and Bucharest, where he founded and directed the Anatomy Museum. From 1871 he worked as a physician in Cracow. He also studied (PH D 1876) and taught anthropology at Cracow University, from 1886 as a professor. In 1875 he became the secretary of the Anthropological Commission of the Polish Academy of Learning. He edited many ethnographic publications and the journal *Zbiór Wiadomości do Antropologii Krajowej* (1877–91), to which he contributed valuable studies on the anthropology and ethnography of Ukraine, particularly of the inhabitants of the Carpathians, where he spent much of his time. In 1889 he published *O góralach ruskich w Galicyi: Zarys etnograficzny* (On the Ruthenian Mountaineers in Galicia: An Ethnographic Sketch). He is the author of over 120 works; most of his research on Ukraine remains unpublished. In 1891 Kopernicki published O. *Kolberg's books on the Kholm and Peremyshl regions. He had cordial relations with I. Franko, F. Vovk, and other Ukrainian scholars.

M. Hnatiukivsky

Koperzhynska, Nonna [Koperžyns'ka], b 1 May 1920 in Kiev. Character actress; daughter of K. *Koperzhynsky. A graduate of the Kiev Institute of Theater Arts (1941), since 1946 she has worked in the Kiev Ukrainian Drama Theater. Her main roles include Vustia Shurai in M. Starytsky's *Oi ne khody, Hrytsiu, ta i na vechornytsi* (Don't Go to the Party, Hryts) and Stepanyda in his *Ne sudylos'* (It Was Not Fated), Hanna in I. Tobilevych's *Beztalanna* (The Hapless Woman), Nastia in M. Kulish's *Patetychna Sonata* (Sonata Pathétique), Varvara in O. Korniichuk's *Kryla* (Wings), and Claire Zachanassian in F. Dürrenmatt's *Der Besuch der alten Dame*. She has appeared also in films; eg, in *Dolia Maryny* (Maryna's Fate, an adaptation of T. Shevchenko's poem), *Ukradene shchastia* (Stolen Happiness, an adaptation of I. Franko's play), and *Za dvoma zaitsiamy* (Chasing Two Hares, an adaptation of M. Starytsky's play).

Koperzhynsky, Kostiantyn [Koperžyns'kyj, Kostjantyn], b 4 November 1894 in Hlibiv, Nova Ushytsia county, Podilia gubernia, d 18 March 1953 in Leningrad. Folklorist, literary and theater scholar, and bibliographer. A student of V. Peretts, he graduated from Petrograd University in 1918 and taught at Leningrad (1923–5) and Odessa (1925–8) universities. From 1928 to 1934 he was a member of the VUAN Ethnographic Commission and an associate of the Commission for Old Ukrainian Literature. In 1934 he was imprisoned in a Stalinist concentration camp. After his release he taught at Irkutsk (1937–45) and Leningrad (1945–53) universities, but no longer wrote in Ukrainian or on Ukrainian subjects. From the mid-1920s to the early 1930s his articles and reviews appeared in several VUAN periodicals and collections. They include articles on late-18th/early-19th–century theater life in Podilia and the Chernihiv region; M. Kotsiubynsky; the 16th-century writer V. Surazky; ancient Slavic harvest and new-year rituals and the concept of time; M. Komarov; Ukrainian magic, acrobatic, and pantomime performances in the late 18th and early 19th centuries; and M. Drahomanov's political tactics. He wrote several survey articles on contemporary Ukrainian literary and theater scholarship. Some of his articles also appeared as offprints. He is the author of *Obzhynky: Obriady zboru vrozhaiu u slov'ians'kykh narodiv u naidavnishu dobu rozvytku* (*Obzhynky*: Harvest Rituals among the Slavic Peoples during the Earliest Period of Development, 1926).

M. Hnatiukivsky

Kopniaiev, Pavlo [Kopnjajev], b 27 February 1867 in Uralsk, d 3 June 1932 in Kharkiv. Electrical engineer. He taught at the Kharkiv Technological Institute, where in 1898 he introduced a specialization in electrical engineering and in 1921 a separate faculty of electrical engineering. His publications deal with the theory of electric machinery, particularly trolley motors. He wrote the first textbooks in electrical engineering in the Russian Empire.

Kopnin, Pavel, b 27 January 1922 in Gzhel, Moscow gubernia, d 27 June 1971 in Moscow. Soviet philosopher; from 1967 full member of the AN URSR. A graduate of Moscow University (1944), he held the Chair of Philosophy at Tomsk University and at the USSR Academy of Sciences before coming to Ukraine in 1958 to head the philosophy department at the Kiev Polytechnical Institute and at Kiev University. In 1962 he was appointed director of the Institute of Philosophy of the AN URSR, and in 1968 director of the Institute of Philosophy of the USSR Academy of Sciences in Moscow. His main contributions are in the philosophy of science, dialectical materialism, and the history of philosophy. Besides numerous articles, Kopnin wrote *Dialektika kak logika* (Dialectics as Logic, 1961), *Gipoteza i poznanie deistvitel'nosti* (Hypothesis and Knowledge of Reality, 1962), and *Ideia kak forma myshleniia* (Idea as a Form of Thought, 1963).

Köppen, Peter (Keppen, Petr), b 2 March 1793 in Kharkiv, d 4 June 1864 in Karabah in the Crimea. Statistician, bibliographer, geographer, and ethnographer; full member of the Russian Academy of Sciences. From 1829 to 1834 he worked in the Crimea and traveled annually through southern Ukraine, where he collected a great deal of information on its geography and natural history. Among his numerous works are an ethnographic map of Russia (1851), pioneering population studies of Russia, studies of Tavriia gubernia, and *Materiialy dlia istorii prosveshcheniia v Rosii* (Materials for the History of Education in Russia, 3 vols, 1819, 1825, 1827). His research served as the model for the 69-volume register of Russia's towns and villages.

Koptilov, Viktor, b 3 July 1930 in Kiev. Literary critic, linguist, and translator. A doctor of philological sciences, he teaches at Kiev University. He is the author of three books on literary translation and stylistics (1971, 1972, 1982) and has translated the works of E. Whitman, F. Sagan, and several Polish writers.

Kopychyntsi [Kopyčynci]. IV-6. Town (1973 pop 7,500) in Husiatyn raion, Ternopil oblast, situated on the Nichlava River in western Podilia. It was first mentioned in the early 14th century. It has a toy factory, a canning plant, and an agricultural tekhnikum.

Oleksander Kopylenko

Kopylenko, Oleksander, b 1 August 1900 in Kostiantynohrad (now Krasnohrad), Poltava gubernia, d 1 December 1958 in Kiev. Writer. In the 1920s he belonged to the writers' groups *Pluh, *Hart, *Vaplite, and *Prolitfront. His prose works of the 1920s – including the story collections *Kara-Krucha* (1923) and *Imenem ukraïns'koho narodu* (In the Name of the Ukrainian People, 1924), the novel *Buinyi khmil'* (Wild Hops, 1925), the story collection *Tverdyi materiial* (Hard Material, 1928), and the novel *Vyzvolennia* (Liberation, 1930) – depict the revolutionary and early Soviet years in Ukraine in the expressionistic manner of M. *Khvylovy. The last two publications were subjected to severe Party criticism for their 'pessimistic' and 'individualistic' approach.

Kopylenko was one of the first members of Vaplite to accept the Party's dictates on literature, and he managed to survive the Stalinist terror as one of the organizers of the Writers' Union of Ukraine. His novel *Narodzhuiet'sia misto* (The City Is Born, 1932) was an early socialist-realist work about industrialization. His novels for adolescents – *Duzhe dobre* (Very Good, 1935) and *Desiatyklasnyky* (The Tenth Graders, 1938) – are considered his best works. His postwar novel *Leitenanty* (Lieutenants, 1947) is a typical hackneyed Soviet work about postwar reconstruction. His last novel, *Zemlia velyka* (The Great Earth, 1957), is an attempt at a more serious treatment of the life of the rural intelligentsia, careerism, and bureaucratization. In addition to many stories for adults and children, Kopylenko wrote several plays, including *Khurtovyna* (The Tempest, 1943) and *Chomu ne hasnut' zori* (Why the Stars Don't Go Out, 1944). His expurgated works in four volumes were published posthumously in 1961–2.

BIBLIOGRAPHY
Svider, P. *Oleksandr Kopylenko: Zhyttia i tvorchist'* (Kiev 1960)
– *Oleksandr Kopylenko (1900–1958)* (Kiev 1962)
Kopylenko, Ts. and L. (eds). *Pro Oleksandra Kopylenka: Spohady* (Kiev 1971)

I. Koshelivets

Kopynsky, Isaia [Kopyns'kyj, Isaija], b ? in Galicia, d 5 October 1640. Orthodox church figure and Kievan metropolitan. He studied at the Lviv Brotherhood School and entered a monastery as a youth. Eventually he became the hegumen of the Kiev Epiphany Brotherhood and Mezhyhiria Transfiguration monasteries and one of the founders of the Kievan Epiphany Brotherhood School. In 1620, when the Orthodox hierarchy was renewed by Patriarch Theophanes of Jerusalem, Kopynsky was consecrated bishop of Peremyshl and Sambir; however, he was not permitted to assume his post by the Polish king, and he was instead named bishop of Chernihiv and Smolensk. He was well known as an organizer of monasteries; through his efforts the Uhar Transfiguration, Hustynia Trinity, and other monasteries were founded. In 1631 he succeeded Metropolitan Y. Boretsky as Kievan metropolitan.

Kopynsky was a conservative and a decided foe of Catholicism and the Uniate church. He was also pro-Muscovite and favored conciliation with the tsar and the Moscow metropolitan. After the legalization of the Orthodox hierarchy by Poland in 1632 and the election of P. *Mohyla as metropolitan of Kiev, Kopynsky was forced by the latter to relinquish his post. He became the supervisor of the Kiev Saint Michael's Golden-Domed Monastery in 1633, and lobbied unsuccessfully to regain his title from Mohyla, supported by many monasteries and Cossacks. In 1635 he moved to Polisia, and in 1638 back to Kiev, where he probably died.

Kopystensky, Mykhail [Kopystens'kyj, Myxajil] (secular name: Matei), ?–1610. Orthodox bishop. A member of the Peremyshl aristocracy, he became the bishop of Peremyshl eparchy in 1591. In 1596 he refused to support the Church Union of *Berestia and remained Orthodox. He continued consecrating priests for other Orthodox eparchies and defending Orthodox interests. In 1606 he addressed a letter to a congress of Orthodox nobles in Lublin who opposed the Church Union, in which he described the persecution of Orthodox faithful. After his death, the Ukrainian Orthodox church was left with only one bishop.

Archimandrite Zakhariia Kopystensky

Teofil Kopystynsky

Kopystensky, Zakhariia [Kopystens'kyj, Zaxarija], b ? in Peremyshl, d 21 March 1627 in Kiev. Outstanding Orthodox theologian, writer, and churchman; nephew of M. *Kopystensky. He probably studied at the Lviv Dormition Brotherhood School before traveling throughout the Balkans and moving to Kiev in 1616, where he joined the Kiev Epiphany Brotherhood. Fluent in Greek and Latin, in Kiev he engaged in publishing and writing, especially *polemical literature. On 20 November 1624, he became the archimandrite of the Kievan Cave Monastery. He published several translations of Greek religious books, including **Chasoslov* (1617), *Nomokanon* … (Nomocanon …, 1625), and the works of St John Chrysostom. His major work is **Palinodiia, ili kniga oborony … vskhodnei tserkvy* … (A Palinode, or a Book in Defense … of the Eastern Church …, 1621). Although this work was only published in 1876, it was widely read in Orthodox circles in manuscript. *Palinodiia* is a comprehensive exposition of the Orthodox theology of the Kiev school, written in response to *Obrona jedności cerkiewnej* (A Defense of Church Unity) by the Uniate hegumen of Vilnius monastery, L. Krevza. This work not only showed his skill as a polemicist, but also demonstrated his great erudition and knowledge of church history and theology. His sermons on the grave of Ye. Pletenetsky, his predecessor as archimandrite of the Kievan Cave Monastery, were published in 1625, and *Kniga o vere iedinoi* … (A Book on the True Faith …, ca 1620) has been attributed to him.

A. Zhukovsky

Kopystiansky, Adriian [Kopystjans'kyj, Adrijan], b 1871 in Lisko county, Galicia, d 1934 in Lviv. Historian. Kopystiansky taught in the gymnasium in Stanyslaviv (now Ivano-Frankivske) and at the Academic Gymnasium of Lviv. A Russophile, he headed the *Kachkovsky Society in Lviv and published popular histories of Galicia in Russian, including the three-volume *Istoriia Rusi* (A History of Ruthenia, 1931–3). He also published a collection of documents on the Lviv Stauropegian Brotherhood and *Istoriia Volyns'koi Tserkvy* (A History of the Volhynian Church, 1929).

Kopystynsky, Teofil [Kopystyns'kyj], b 15 April 1844 in Peremyshl, Galicia, d 5 July 1916 in Lviv. Monumentalist painter and portraitist. A graduate of the Cracow School of Fine Arts (1871) and the Vienna Academy of Art (1872), he spent his life painting churches, iconostases, and icons in Lviv and the surrounding villages. His more important works have been preserved: the murals of the wooden church in Batiatychi, the altar icon of the Transfiguration in the Church of the Transfiguration in Lviv, *The Crucifixion* (1902) in ss Cyril and Methodius's Church in Sokolia near Buzk, the murals (1911–12) of St Michael's Church in Rudnyky, and the iconostases in the churches in Zhovtantsi, Batiatychi, Zhydachiv, Myklashiv (1908), and Synevidsko Vyzhnie. He was also recognized as a restorer and conservator of old art. From 1878 to 1899 Kopystynsky restored a number of religious masterpieces: the Byzantine altar icon of the Annunciation in Zahiria; two 17th-century paintings under the arcades of the Dormition Church in Lviv, *Jerusalem and the Holy Land* and *Atons'ka Hora* (Mount Athos); the frescoes in St Martin's Church and the altar of the Church of Our Lady of the Snows (both Roman Catholic churches in Lviv); the frescoes of the Wawel Cathedral in Cracow; the murals of the Lubomirski chapel at the Dominican Church and the 17th-century sacristy of St Mary's Church in Cracow. In 1888 he cleaned and restored 150 old Ukrainian icons at the Stauropegion Museum in Lviv. Kopystynsky established a reputation as a master portraitist with such works as the portraits of I. and L. Kovshevych (1867), A. Yanovsky, Bishop I. Stupnytsky, and a Dalmatian lady (1872). From 1872 to 1895 he painted 17 portraits of prominent Ukrainian social and cultural figures of the 19th century, as well as Hetman P. Sahaidachny and Metropolitan P. Mohyla.

Kopystynsky was a leading illustrator in Western Ukraine. He illustrated the religious semimonthly *Poslannyk* (1889–1911), the children's magazine *Dzvinok* (Bell, 1890–1914), the Prosvita calendar, and I. Franko's *Lys Mykyta* (Mykyta the Fox) and *Pryhody Don Kikhota* (The Adventures of Don Quixote). He painted numerous canvases, including *Hutsul from Lypovytsia, Grandfather, Blind Man with Guide, In a Peasant Cottage,* and *Kolomyiky*. Kopystynsky taught drawing in secondary schools in Lviv and participated in the exhibitions of the Society of Friends of the Fine Arts. His works have been preserved in the Lviv Museum of Ukrainian Art and in private collections.

BIBLIOGRAPHY
Tkachenko, M. *Teofil Kopystyns'kyi* (Kiev 1972)

S. Hordynsky

Kopytov, Viktor, b 21 November 1906 in Kurgan, Tobolsk gubernia. Specialist in metallurgy, thermal engineering, and industrial furnaces; since 1967 full member of the AN URSR. A graduate of the Ural Polytechnical Institute, in 1950 he joined the AN URSR Institute of Gas, and in 1952 became its director. His publications deal with coal gasification, heat transfer in furnaces, new industrial uses of gases, and air pollution.

Kopytsia, Davyd [Kopycja], b 7 July 1906 in Sloboda, Lityn county, Podilia gubernia, d 15 December 1965 in Kiev. Writer and literary critic. After graduating from the Kharkiv Institute of People's Education (1929), he worked as an editor in Kharkiv and belonged to the writers' group *Molodniak. He also worked as a scenarist and was the deputy director and director of the Odessa Artistic Film Studio (1932–4), a docent and dean of the Kiev Film Institute (1934–6), and head of the screenplay department at the Kiev Artistic Film Studio (1936). In 1938 he became a senior research fellow and deputy director of the AN URSR Institute of Literature. He was the head of propaganda for the CC CP(B)U (1946–8), the Ukrainian deputy minister of culture (1948–57), a candidate member of the CC CPU from 1952, and the director of the Kiev Artistic Film Studio from 1957.

Kopytsia debuted as a literary critic of the vulgar Marxist variety in the early 1930s. He wrote several stories and many articles on 19th-century and Soviet Ukrainian writers. He also coedited the editions of the works of T. Shevchenko (10 vols, 1939–44) and I. Franko (20 vols, 1950–6) that were prepared by the Institute of Literature. A selection of his criticism was published posthumously in 1968.

I. Koshelivets

Korablov, Ipolit [Korabl'ov], b 9 February 1871 in Gorodok, Dukhovshchina county, Smolensk gubernia, d 7 July 1951 in Uman, Cherkasy oblast. Apiarist. After graduating from the Petrovskoe Agricultural Academy in Moscow (1902), he conducted research on beekeeping and silkworm breeding in Poltava, Chernihiv, and Kharkiv gubernias. He lectured for many years at the Uman School of Orcharding and in 1921 was appointed professor at the Uman Agricultural Institute. He directed an experimental apiary and wrote numerous works on beekeeping.

Korba, Yosyp, b 13 May 1921 in Chmelova, Bardějov county, Slovakia. Character actor. Since 1946 he has worked in the Ukrainian National Theater in Prešov. His repertoire includes Uncle Lev in Lesia Ukrainka's *Lisova pisnia* (The Forest Song), Ivonika in *Zemlia* (Earth, an adaptation of O. Kobylianska's novel), Zadorozhnyi in I. Franko's *Ukradene shchastia* (Stolen Happiness), Chasnyk in O. Korniichuk's *V stepakh Ukraïny* (In the Steppes of Ukraine), Lear in W. Shakespeare's *King Lear,* and Dr Galen in K. Čapek's *Bílá nemoc* (The White Plague).

Korbutiak, Vasyl [Korbutjak, Vasyl'], b 27 November 1883 in Balyntsi, Kolomyia county, Galicia, d 1937? in Soviet Ukraine. Communist activist. From 1912 to 1920 he lived in Canada and the United States, joining the Ukrainian Federation of the Socialist Party of America in 1916. In 1920 he returned to Galicia, joined the underground Communist Party of Eastern Galicia (renamed the *Communist Party of Western Ukraine), and organized its cells in the Kolomyia region. He was elected to the party's CC in 1924. In 1930 he moved to Soviet Ukraine. Arrested during the Stalinist terror ca 1933, he died in a concentration camp or was shot.

Korchak burial site. An early Slavic burial ground of the middle of the first millennium AD situated on the Teteriv River near Korchak in Zhytomyr raion. The kurhans at the site were excavated in 1921. The dead had been cremated. A settlement contemporary with the burial ground was discovered adjacent to it. Similar burial sites and settlements were excavated in 1925, 1946–7, and 1956 in Volhynian Polisia. They are believed to be associated with the *Derevlianians, one of the East Slavic tribes, and form part of the *Korchak culture.

Korchak culture. An archeological culture of the late 5th to 7th centuries AD, discovered in 1921 by S. Hamchenko near the village of Korchak in Zhytomyr county (see *Korchak burial site). It was a variation of the Prague culture (of the middle of the 1st millennium AD) and spread to Ukraine from the territories of Poland and Czechoslovakia. The Korchak culture was widespread in eastern Volhynia. Monuments of the culture were excavated in the 1950s and 1960s by I. Rusanova and described by her in a series of articles. The population of the Korchak culture lived in pit dwellings with stone ovens in predominantly unfortified settlements. Only one hill fort, near Zymne, Volodymyr-Volynskyi county, is known. The dead were cremated and buried in small kurhans and in moundless burial grounds. A pagan sanctuary on the Hnylopiad River near Zhytomyr was uncovered in 1964. The tribes of the Korchak culture practiced agriculture and animal husbandry. Crafts were well developed, especially at the Zymne hill fort, which was a center of blacksmithing and jewelry production. The Korchak culture is the earliest archeological culture discovered in Eastern Europe that scholarly consensus positively indentifies with the ancient Slavs. Its features are visible in the subsequent cultures of the early medieval Slavs and Kievan Rus'.

V. Mezentsev

Ovksentii Korchak-Chepurkivsky

Korchak-Chepurkivsky, Ovksentii [Korčak-Čepurkivs'kyj, Ovksentij], b 28 February 1857 in Kostiantynohrad, Poltava gubernia, d 27 November 1947 in Kiev. Hygienist and epidemiologist; from 1921 full member of the AN URSR. After graduating from Kharkiv University (1883) and working as a sanitation and public-health physician in several gubernias, from 1903 he was a lecturer and then professor of hygiene at Kiev University. During the Hetman government he headed the sanitation department of the Ministry of Health and served as chairman of the medical faculty of Kiev University; while under the Directory he served as minister of national health. He held the Chair of Public Health (renamed the Chair of Hygiene and Sanitation) at the AN URSR (1921–34) and chaired a department of the academy's Institute of Demography and Sanitation Statistics (1934–8). He also served as the academy's permanent secretary (1928–34). His numerous publications deal with diphtheria epidemics, the antagonistic relationship between diphtheria and other infectious childhood diseases, sanitation, and the history of zemstvo medicine. In 1927 he proposed the first systematic Ukrainian nomenclature of diseases.

Korchak-Chepurkivsky, Yurii [Korčak-Čepurkivs'kyj, Jurij], b 15 December 1896 in Kishinev, Bessarabia, d 20 August 1967 in Kiev. Demographer; the son of O. *Korchak-Chepurkivsky. A graduate of the Kiev Institute of the National Economy (1922), while still a student he began working for the VUAN Demographic Institute (see *Demography). In 1925–8, he worked at the demographic department of the Central Statistical Administration of Ukraine. He became a scholarly associate of the VUAN Chair of Hygiene and Sanitation and institutes of Maternity Care and of Socialist Health Protection in 1928 and a senior associate of the AN URSR Institute of Demography and Sanitation Statistics in 1934. In 1938 the institute was closed down and its staff, including Korchak-Chepurkivsky, were arrested and imprisoned.

After the Second World War Korchak-Chepurkivsky was allowed to set up and direct a methodological bureau of health statistics in Samarkand, Uzbekistan, and then to move to Moscow, where he worked in the statistical department of the Rusakov Children's Hospital. He was permitted to retire in Kiev in 1957. There he continued his research and published his invaluable theoretical and applied population studies. Korchak-Chepurkivsky's studies on mortality among various age and occupational groups in Ukraine are particularly significant. He devised original research methods and determined the reliability of the statistical materials he used. His last work, which he did not manage to complete, was devoted to analyzing the losses in Ukraine's population during the man-made *famine of 1932–3 and the Stalinist terror of the 1930s. A volume of his *Izbrannye demograficheskie issledovaniia* (Selected Demographic Studies) was published posthumously in 1970. His other major works are *Materiialy sanitarnoï statystyky Ukraïny 1876–1914 rr.* (Materials on the Sanitation Statistics of Ukraine in 1876–1914, 1926), *Tablytsi dozhyvannia i spodivanoho zhyttia liudnosty USRR* 1925–1926 (Tables of Life Spans and Life Expectancies of the Population of the Ukrainian SSR for 1925–1926, 1929), and *Pryrodnyi rukh naselennia Ukraïny v 1926 rotsi* (Natural Population Changes in Ukraine in 1926, 1929).

S. Maksudov

Korchev (also K"rchev, Kr"chev). The old Slavic name for a 10th–12th-century city in Tmutorokan principality, now the city of Kerch. It was an important trade center linking Kievan Rus' with the Crimea, the Caucasus, and the Mediterranean Sea. Earlier, the city was known as *Panticapaeum.

Korchuvate burial site. An early Slavic burial ground of the *Zarubyntsi culture (2nd century BC to 1st century AD), discovered in Korchuvate near Kiev in 1937 and excavated in 1940–1. Over 100 moundless burials, most of them with cremated remains, earthenware, iron knives, bronze ornaments, beads, ceramics similar to those of the Scythians, and animal bones, were found.

Korchynsky, Michael [Korčyns'kyj, Myxajlo], b 11 April 1918 in Kiev. Metallurgist. Korchynsky completed his engineering studies at the Lviv Polytechnical Institute in 1942 and remained as an associate there until 1944. Employed as an engineer by the US Army in Regensburg (1945–50), he immigrated to the United States in 1950 and began a long career as a researcher and alloy developer with Union Carbide. The holder of several US and international patents and a recipient of the prestigious Eisenman Award of the American Society of Metallurgists (1986), Korchynsky has done research on materials for high-temperature service, nuclear fuels, and particularly the technology and application of high-strength, low-alloy steel.

Korchynsky, Mykhailo [Korčyns'kyj, Myxajlo], b 27 March 1885 in Zaluchia, Kamianets-Podilskyi county, Podilia gubernia, d 7 October 1937 in Lviv. Political and civic leader. A lawyer by profession, from 1908 to 1917 he was active in the Ukrainian community in St Petersburg, serving as chairman of the local young hromada, of the Society of Ukrainian Progressives, and of the Ukrainian Civic Club. Under the Provisional Government he was appointed deputy to the gubernial commissar of Bukovyna. Korchynsky sat in the Central Rada

Mykhailo Korchynsky

as a deputy from the Ukrainian Party of Socialists-Federalists. Under the Directory he served as state secretary in V. Chekhivsky's and S. Ostapenko's cabinets. He was one of the advocates and then a member of the Council of the Republic, which convened in Tarnów in 1921. After the First World War Korchynsky worked in Ukrainian institutions in Galicia: he headed the legal department of the Audit Union of Ukrainian Co-operatives in Lviv from 1922, served on the Supreme Executive of the Prosvita society (1932–7), sat on the legal commission of the Shevchenko Scientific Society, and belonged to the Ukrainian Society of Aid to Emigrants from Eastern Ukraine. His articles appeared in the co-operative and general Ukrainian press.

Kordiuk, Bohdan [Kordjuk], b 17 January 1908 in Lviv. Geologist; political figure and publicist. He studied at Lviv and Berlin universities. An active member of the *Ukrainian Military Organization and the OUN, he headed the latter's Home Executive in 1932–3 before being imprisoned by the Polish police. For most of 1941–5 he was imprisoned in German concentration camps. Since the Second World War he has lived in Munich, where he headed the Political Council of the OUN Abroad faction (1958–79), was the chief editor of the monthly *Ukraïns'kyi samostiinyk* (1958–75), and was a professor at the Ukrainian Technical and Husbandry Institute and the Ukrainian Free University from the 1960s. In 1976 he was one of the founders of the *Ukrainian Democratic Alliance. He is the author of many publicistic articles, mainly on Ukrainian-Jewish relations and the need for mutual dialogue.

Kordium, Arnold [Kordjum, Arnol'd], b 13 July 1890 in Stanyslaviv (now Ivano-Frankivske), d 29 August 1969 in Kiev. Film director and screenwriter. From 1924 to 1935 he worked as a filmmaker in Yalta, Odessa, and Kiev, and in Tashkent from 1936 to 1939. After the war he worked at the Kiev Studio of Popular Science Films (1947–57). He directed such films as *Za lisom* (Beyond the Forest, 1926), *Sprava ch. 128* (Case No. 128, 1927), *Ostannii lotsman* (The Last Pilot, 1930), *Askaniia Nova* (1947), and *Soniashnyk* (The Sunflower, 1949). Kordium usually wrote the screenplays of films he directed.

Kordt, Veniiamyn, b 19 February 1860 in Tartu, Estonia, d 24 December 1934. Historian, cartographer, and bibliographer, of German descent. A graduate of Yurev (Tartu) University (1888), from 1894 he lectured at Kiev

University and was the director of the university's library. Kordt was a member of the *Kiev Archeographic Commission and the VUAN Archeographic Commission, and one of the organizers in 1918 of the National Library of the Ukrainian State (later the *Central Scientific Library of the AN URSR), where he headed the cartography department. Kordt's main works deal with the history of Ukrainian cartography: *Materialy po istorii russkoi kartografii* (Materials on the History of Russian Cartography, 2 vols, 1899, 1910) and *Materiialy do istorii kartohrafii Ukraïny* (Materials for the History of Ukrainian Cartography, 1931). He also wrote *Chuzhozemni podorozhi po Skhidnii Ievropi do 1700 r.* (Foreign Travels in Eastern Europe up to 1700, 1926), articles on Swedish sources to Ukrainian history in *Zapysky Istorychno-filolohichnoho viddilu VUAN* and *Ukraïns'kyi arkheohrafichnyi zbirnyk*, and several bibliographic studies.

Korduba, Feliks, b 28 May 1908 in Ternopil, d 21 January 1987 in Munich. OUN activist, editor, journalist, civic leader. In 1930 Korduba was arrested by the Polish authorities for his involvement in the OUN in Galicia and was imprisoned until 1939. In 1943 he joined the *Division Galizien. A postwar refugee in Austria and Bavaria, from 1951 he worked for the Logos Ukrainian publishing house in Munich, of which he became director in 1977. For many years he was the secretary of the Ukrainian Journalists' Association Abroad. From 1961 to 1968 he was the president of the Supreme Council of the *Central Representation of the Ukrainian Emigration in Germany. He was the author of numerous articles dealing with historical and sociopolitical issues.

Myron Korduba

Korduba, Myron, b 7 March 1876 in Ostriv near Ternopil, d 2 May 1947 in Lviv. Historian. He studied at the universities of Lviv (1893–5, under M. Hrushevsky) and Vienna (1895–8). He worked as a gymnasium teacher in Chernivtsi (1900–18), Lviv, and Kholm and was a professor at Warsaw (1929–39) and Lviv (1944–7) universities. In 1903 he was elected full member of the Shevchenko Scientific Society, and in 1923 he became director of its historical-philosophical section. After the Second World War he was a research associate of the Lviv Branch of the Institute of History of the AN URSR. He wrote works on the history and historical geography of medieval Ukraine: they include, in *ZNTSh*, 'Persha derzhava slov'ians'ka' (The First Slavic State, vol 13 [1896]), 'Suspil'ni verstvy ta politychni partiï v Halyts'kim kniazivstvi do polovyny XIII st.' (Social Strata and Political Parties in Halych Principality to the Mid-13th Century, vols 31–2 [1899]), and 'Zakhidne pohranychchia Halyts'koï derzhavy mizh Karpatamy ta dolishnym Sianom v XIII st.' (The Western Frontier of the Galician State between the Carpathians and the Lower Sian River in the 13th Century, vols 138–40 [1925]). He wrote a number of important studies of the Khmelnytsky period: 'Venetsiis'ke posol'stvo do Khmel'nyts'koho (1650)' (The Venetian Legation to Khmelnytsky [1650], *ZNTSh*, vol 78 [1907]), 'Proba avstriis'koho poserednytstva mizh Khmel'nyts'kym i Pol'shcheiu' (The Austrian Attempt at Mediation between Khmelnytsky and Poland, *ZNTSh*, vol 84 [1908]), 'Borot'ba za pol's'kyi prestol po smerti Volodyslava IV' (The Struggle for the Polish Throne after the Death of Władysław IV, *Zherela do istoriï Ukraïny-Rusy*, vol 12 [1912]), 'Mizh Zamostiam ta Zborovym (storinka znosyn Semyhorodu z Ukraïnoiu i Pol'shcheiu)' (Between Zamostia and Zboriv [On Transylvania's Relations with Ukraine and Poland], *ZNTSh*, vol 133 [1922]), and *Bohdan Khmel'nyts'kyi u Belzchyni i Kholmshchyni* (Bohdan Khmelnytsky in the Belz and Kholm Regions, 1941). He also authored many works on Ukrainian historiography and several on geography, toponymy, and statistics. They include *La littérature historique ukrainienne en Pologne et dans l'émigration ukrainienne* (1929), *La littérature historique soviétique ukrainienne: Compte-rendu 1917–1931* (1938; repr, 1972), and *Terytoriia i naselennia Ukraïny* (The Territory and Population of Ukraine, 1917). Besides these and many other scholarly works (including articles on M. Maksymovych, P. Kulish, V. Antonovych, and M. Hrushevsky), he wrote a number of popular histories, such as *Istoriia Kholmshchyny i Pidliashshia* (A History of the Kholm Region and Podlachia, 1941), *Pivnichno-zakhidna Ukraïna* (Northwestern Ukraine, 1917), and *Iliustrovana istoriia Bukovyny* (An Illustrated History of Bukovyna, 1906), and was a coauthor of *The Cambridge History of Poland*, vol 1 (1950).

A. Zhukovsky

Kordysh, Leon [Kordyš], b 22 July 1878 in Kiev, d 11 July 1932 in Kiev. Theoretical physicist. He graduated from Kiev University in 1900, then conducted research in Berlin with M. Planck (1904), in Paris with H. Poincaré (1911–12), and in Munich with A. Sommerfeld (1913). In 1918 Kordysh helped organize the Physics Department at Kiev University's Crimean Branch, where he taught until 1921. In 1922 he was appointed professor of theoretical electrical engineering at the Kiev Polytechnical Institute. His research dealt with Bremsstrahlung components of X-ray spectra, superconductivity, the Zeeman effect, and early applications of special relativity and quantum theory. Kordysh wrote several advanced textbooks in Ukrainian that were widely used in Soviet Ukraine in the 1930s, including *Elektrotekhnika: Osnovy teoretychni* (Theoretical Foundations of Electrical Engineering, 1927) and *Elektrotekhnika vysokoï chastoty: Zahal'ni teoretychni osnovy* (General Theoretical Foundations of High-frequency Electrical Engineering, 1934).

Koreiz [Korejiz]. IX-15. Town smt (1979 pop 6,300) on the southeastern shore of the Crimea at the foot of Mt Ai-Petri. Founded in the late 17th century, it is a health-resort center administered by the Yalta city soviet. About 50,000 people stay there each year.

Denys Korenets

Volodymyr Koretsky

Korenets, Denys [Korenec'], b 3 April 1875 in Rozvadiv, Zhydachiv county, Galicia, d 6 March 1946 in Munich. Pedagogue, leader in the co-operative movement. Korenets was an early advocate of Ukrainian commercial and vocational education. After graduating from Lviv University (1897), he taught at various gymnasiums, including the Ukrainian gymnasium in Peremyshl (1904–13) and the Academic Gymnasium of Lviv. He was the director (1917–34) of the Commercial School of the Prosvita (and later Ridna Shkola) society in Lviv, and an organizer of the Husbandry and Trade Association (later *Tsentrosoiuz) in Peremyshl and Lviv. With the Soviet occupation of Western Ukraine in 1944, Korenets fled to Germany. He is the author of economic and educational articles in various Galician periodicals. Korenets is the subject of a biography by A. Kachor (Winnipeg, 1955).

Korenytsky, Porfyrii [Korenyc'kyj, Porfyrij], b ca 1815 in the Kharkiv region, d January 1854 in Kharkiv. Writer. He composed poetry and fables in which he used folkloric material and depicted the life of the common people. In such poems as 'Vechornytsi: Satyrychna poema' (Evening Parties: A Satirical Poem, *Snip*, 1841) he imitated the burlesque style of I. Kotliarevsky's *Eneida* (The Aeneid). Except for 'Vechornytsi' and 'Pan'ko ta verstva' (Panko and the Mile Pole, *Lastivka*, 1841), his poems were all published posthumously. His collected works, with an introduction by M. Sumtsov, appeared in Kharkiv in 1919.

Korets [Korec']. III-8. Town (1970 pop 7,100) and raion center in Rivne oblast, situated on the Korchyk River in Volhynia. It was first mentioned as Korchesk in the Hypatian Chronicle under the year 1150. In 1494 a Tatar army was defeated there. The town was the seat of the Volhynian Koretsky princes. In the late 18th and early 19th centuries the town's large porcelain factory was famous for its fine wares. In March and April 1919 the Northern Group of the UNR Army fought the Bolsheviks there. The city has a plastics plant and a sugar refinery. Among its architectural monuments are the ruins of a 16th-century castle, 16th–19th-century convent buildings, a 17th-century Roman Catholic church, and several 18th-century churches.

Koretsky, Volodymyr [Korec'kyj], b 18 February 1890 in Katerynoslav (now Dnipropetrovske), d 25 July 1984 in Kiev. Soviet specialist in international law; full member of the AN URSR from 1948. A graduate of the Law Faculty of Kharkiv University, he taught law at several institutes in Kharkiv from 1919 to 1949. In 1949 he became director of the AN URSR Sector (later Institute) of State and Law. He sat on many international commissions, such as the Permanent Chamber of the Arbitration Court at the Hague (1957–69) and the UN International Court (1961–70). Koretsky wrote over 50 studies on international public and private law, and on the history of law and the concept of state, including *Ocherki mezhdunarodnogo khoziaistvennogo prava* (Outlines of International Economic Law, 1928), *Obshchie printsipy prava v mezhdunarodnom prave* (Universal Principles of International Law, 1957), and *Deklaratsiia prav i obiazannostei gosudarstv* (Declaration of the Rights and Obligations of States, 1962).

Koretsky, Yurii [Korec'kyj, Jurij], b 24 May 1911 in Katerynoslav (now Dnipropetrovske), d 19 September 1941 in Kiev. Poet, translator; son of V. *Koretsky. He was the author of *My shche povernemos'* (We Shall Yet Return, 1934), a collection of stories in verse, and of *Plem'ia vidvazhnykh* (The Tribe of the Brave, 1935), a collection of children's poetry. His translations into Ukrainian include works by Byron, Shakespeare, and Schiller. Koretsky was killed during the Second World War. His selected works were published in Kharkiv in 1967.

Koretsky-Satanovsky, Arsenii [Korec'kyj-Satanovs'kyj, Arsenij], b ? in Sataniv, Podilia, d after 1653. Lexicographer. Of noble origin and a monk at the Kiev Epiphany Brotherhood Monastery, he taught at the monastery's school until 1649, when he and Hieromonach Ye. *Slavynetsky were summoned to Moscow. There he helped Slavynetsky to prepare a Russian version of the latter's Latin-Slavonic dictionary (compiled ca 1642 in Kiev). At the same time both men worked on a Slavonic-Latin dictionary (1650), six known manuscript copies of which are preserved in Paris, Uppsala, Leningrad, and Moscow (three copies). It has been published by O. Horbach (Rome 1968) and V. Nimchuk (Kiev 1973). The dictionary's Slavonic part relies heavily on P. *Berynda's lexis, while its Latin part is based on *Thesaurus Polono-Latino-Graecus* by G. Cnapius (Knapski). It is a valuable source on the vocabulary of mid-17th-century literary Ukrainian. Koretsky also translated from the Latin. In 1653 he was exiled to a monastery in northern Russia, and his fate is unknown.

BIBLIOGRAPHY

Nimchuk, V. *Staroukraïns'ka leksykohrafiia v ïï zv'iazkakh z rosiis'koiu ta bilorus'koiu* (Kiev 1980)

G.Y. Shevelov

Korf, Nikolai, b 14 July 1834 in Kharkiv, d 25 November 1883 in Kharkiv. Zemstvo leader and prominent proponent of universal education. A Russian baron of German origin, he organized zemstvo schools and Sunday schools, and invented the three-year village school. He conducted numerous teachers' courses and congresses in the Kherson, Mariiupil, and Berdianske regions. Although he did not accept the equality of Ukrainian with Russian, he proposed to begin elementary education for Ukrainian children in the Ukrainian language. At the time, this was a significant departure from official policy. He wrote a number of textbooks for teachers and students, and numerous articles on educational matters.

Koriak, Volodymyr [Korjak] (pseud of V. Blumstein), b 14 January 1889 in Slovianske, Kharkiv gubernia, d 12 April 1939? Jewish-Ukrainian literary critic and publicist. Koriak was exiled to Kazakhstan in 1915 for belonging to the outlawed Ukrainian Party of Socialist Revolutionaries. He returned to Ukraine after the February Revolution of 1917 and joined the Ukrainian Party of Socialist Revolutionaries-Borotbists. In 1920 he joined the CP(B)U and became a leading exponent of the Party line on literature. A founding member of the writers' organizations *Hart (1923) and the All-Ukrainian Association of Proletarian Writers (1927), he worked for the People's Commissariat of Education (1919–25) and taught at the Kharkiv Institute of People's Education (1925–33) and Kharkiv University (1933–6). During the *Literary Discussion in Ukraine (1925–7) he was a major opponent of M. *Khvylovy, and in 1932 he was one of the organizers of the Writers' Union of Ukraine. Koriak was the author of Marxist literary criticism, polemical articles, and literature textbooks; the latter (eg, his two-volume history of Ukrainian literature, 1925, 1929), though lacking in scholarly value, were widely used in the 1920s and 1930s. In 1937 he was accused of being a Trotskyist, fascist, and 'nationalist deviationist' and arrested. He was most likely shot by the NKVD.

I. Koshelivets

Prince Fedir Koriiatovych

Koriiatovych, Fedir [Korijatovyč], ?–ca 1417. The nephew of Grand Duke *Algirdas of Lithuania, in the 1380s Koriatovych became a voivode of Podilia. In 1393 he was attacked by Grand Duke Vytautas and fled to Hungary. There he was granted the city of Mukachiv by the Hungarian king and became the ruler of Berehove, Zemplyn, and Máramaros *zhupy* (counties) in Transcarpathia. Koriatovych founded Saint Nicholas's Monastery in Mukachiv. According to ancient chronicles, thousands of Ukrainians accompanied Koriatovych to Transcarpathia from Podilia, thus giving rise to the theory of the Ukrainian colonization of the Hungarian foothills of the Carpathian Mountains.

Koriukivka [Korjukivka]. II-13. Town (1972 pop 9,800) and raion center in Chernihiv oblast, situated on the Brech River. It was founded in 1657. Up to the Second World War it had one of the best sugar refineries in the USSR. A paper mill is located there.

Kormchaia kniga. In Church Slavonic a term, which means literally 'a pilot's book,' referring to a Church Slavonic redaction of the Greek *Nomocanon*. This was a digest of church canons, consisting of apostolic, conciliar, and episcopal instructions for conducting administrative and judicial affairs in the church. The earliest Slavic translation is believed to have been done by St Methodius in the second half of the 9th century. The chief recensions of the *Kormchaia kniga* known in Kievan Rus' were the Serbian (a 13th-century translation by Archbishop Sava of the *Nomocanon of Fourteen Titles*), the Vladimir or the Russian (containing the resolutions of the sobor in Vladimir-on-Kliazma, held in 1274), the Novgorod (ca 1280), the Volodymyr-Volynskyi (common in Ukraine, written in 1286 on the basis of the Vladimir recension), and the Lukashevych (written in the 14th century on the basis of the Vladimir recension and preserved in transcriptions from the 16th century). Some redactions contain particular laws from *Ruskaia Pravda* and elements of customary law. Such digests were important sources of law for the southern and eastern Slavs after their Christianization (see *Canon law).

Kormosh, Teofil [Kormoš, Teofil'], b 26 January 1861 in Galicia, d 26 November 1927 in Peremyshl. Civic and political leader. A lawyer by profession, he was an active organizer of Ukrainian economic institutions. In Peremyshl he founded the Vira savings society (1894) and the Ruska Shchadnytsia bank (1907). In Lviv he helped organize the Dnister co-operative bank (1895), the Tsentrobank (1899), and the Land Mortgage Bank (1910). In 1913 he was elected to the Galician Diet. He was active in the Ukrainian National Democratic party, and later in the Ukrainian National Democratic Alliance. Furthermore, he was involved in the work of the Prosvita society and the Ridna Shkola pedagogical society.

Konstiantyn Korniakt

Korniakt, Konstiantyn [Kornjakt, Konstjantyn], 1517–1603. Merchant and philanthropist. A Greek by origin, in the mid-16th century he worked at the court of the Moldavian hospodar A. Lapuşneanu. In the 1560s he moved to Lviv, where he became one of the city's wealthiest merchants. He conducted extensive trade with the territories under Ottoman rule and with Germany, and eventually owned over 40 villages in the Lviv and Peremyshl areas. In 1589 he became a member of the *Lviv Dormition Brotherhood, although he later supported Bishop H. *Balaban in his struggle with the brotherhood. He personally financed the construction of the belfry of the Lviv Dormition Church (1572–8). The belfry and his house, the famous *Korniakt Building, are among the finest examples of Ukrainian Renaissance architecture.

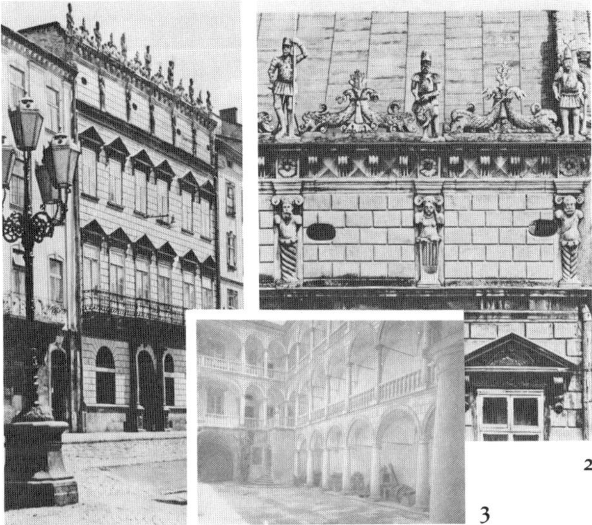

Korniakt Building: 1) main facade; 2) detail of frieze on the roof; 3) courtyard in the Italian style

Korniakt building. One of the finest monuments of Renaissance architecture in Ukraine. It was built for K. Korniakt in 1580 at no. 6 Rynok Square in Lviv by the architect P. di Barbone. In 1623 the building was acquired by the Carmelite monastic order, and in 1640 by voivode J. Sobieski. The Eternal Peace of 1686 was ratified there by Poland and Russia. In 1908 the building was bought by the city and after extensive renovation became the King Jan III Sobieski Museum. Since 1940 it has housed the Lviv Historical Museum. The structure consists of three stories and an attic. The lowest stage of the facade has three windows and an impressive portal framed by two Corinthian columns, surmounted by mascarons, and topped by a lion's mask flanked by two garlands. This entrance was added in 1678 and is the work of local sculptors. The second and third stories have six windows each. The attic, added to the building in 1678, is adorned with seven caryatids and atlantes supporting an architrave and Ionic frieze with consoles, and is topped with statues of a king and six fully armed knights, which are tied together by volutes of stylized dolphins. The rear facade, facing Fedorov Street, has an inscription of the construction date and a simpler portal consisting of two pairs of columns and a cornice with a cartouche, volutes, and the family coat of arms. The first floor of the interior consists of a vestibule with a Renaissance ceiling, two large Renaissance halls on the right, and a Gothic hall, dating back to the 16th century, on the left. The staircase on the left was built in the late classical style of the 18th century and the iron balustrade was made by Lviv craftsmen. The halls on the second story are more elaborate and were designed in the 18th century. The Italian Renaissance courtyard is enclosed in a graceful three-tier loggia with Tuscan columns. The Korniakt building is often compared to Palazzo Avignonensi in Montepulciano, Italy.

S. Hordynsky

Korniev, Kostiantyn [Kornjev, Kostjantyn], b 28 May 1908 in Sosnytsia, Chernihiv gubernia, d 8 October 1974 in Sosnytsia. Organic chemist; from 1961 corresponding member of the AN URSR. After graduating from the Kiev Pharmaceutical Institute in 1930, he worked at the Institute of Chemistry for nine years and then at the AN URSR Institute of Organic Chemistry and Technology. In 1958 he was appointed director of the academy's Institute of Macromolecular Chemistry, and in 1965 chairman of its department for synthesizing thermally stable polymers. His publications deal with various aspects of specialized organic syntheses. He studied anticancer agents and synthesized new chloralkylamines, ethyleneimines, and thermally stable polymeric resins. He was the discoverer of the Korniev reaction.

Oleksander Korniichuk

Korniichuk, Oleksander [Kornijčuk], b 25 May 1905 in Khrystynivka, Kiev gubernia, d 14 May 1972 in Kiev. Dramatist and prominent Soviet Ukrainian political figure. He worked as a scenarist at the Kiev (1929–31), Kharkiv (1931–2), and Odessa (1932–4) artistic film studios. In 1934 he became a member of the executive of the newly created Writers' Union of Ukraine (WU). A protégé of J. Stalin, he was promoted to numerous positions: deputy to the supreme soviets of the USSR (from 1937) and Ukrainian SSR (from 1938); head of the WU (1938–41, 1946–53); full member of the AN URSR (from 1939) and USSR Academy of Sciences (from 1943); USSR deputy people's commissar of foreign affairs (1943); Ukrainian SSR people's commissar of foreign affairs (1944); president of the Ukrainian SSR Supreme Soviet (1947–55, 1959–72); member of the CC CPU (from 1949) and CC CPSU (from 1952); member of the World Peace Council bureau (from 1950) and presidium (from 1959); and first deputy chairman of the Ukrainian SSR Council of Ministers and member of the CC CPU Presidium (1953–4). After Stalin's death he supported de-Stalinization and the cultural thaw.

Korniichuk's first plays, *Na hrani* (On the Edge, 1928), *Kam'ianyi ostriv* (The Stone Island, 1929), and *Shturma* (The Storm, 1930), attracted little attention. He garnered fame with his play about the Civil War, *Zahybel' eskadry*

(The Destruction of the Squadron, 1933), which was staged throughout the USSR. His subsequent plays were formulaic and written in conformity with the Party's political imperatives and propagandistic needs: *Pravda* (Truth, 1937), in which Korniichuk was one of the first to write about the Russian people's 'fraternal assistance' to Ukraine; *V stepakh Ukraïny* (On the Steppes of Ukraine, 1941); the anti-American *Misiia mistera Perkinsa v kraïnu bil'shovykiv* (The Mission of Mr Perkins in the Land of the Bolsheviks, 1944); *Pryïzdit' u Dzvinkove* (Come to Dzvinkove, 1947); *Makar Dibrova* (1948); *Kalynovyi hai* (The Viburnum Grove, 1950); *Kryla* (Wings, 1954); *Pam'iat' sertsia* (Memory of the Heart, 1969); and others. His only epic historical play, *Bohdan Khmel'nyts'kyi* (1939), is an apologia for the 'unification' of Ukraine and Russia; it served as the basis for a feature film (1939) and for K. Dankevych's opera of the same name (1951). The popularity of Korniichuk's plays was heightened by their seemingly pointed criticisms of the flaws in the Soviet system (particularly in *Kryla*); these criticisms, however, never exceeded the bounds set by the Party censors.

Korniichuk's plays have been staged many times, have been published in many editions (the fullest being in five volumes in 1985–7), and have been the subject of a large body of Soviet literary commentary.

BIBLIOGRAPHY
Kobylets'kyi, Iu. *Dramaturh i chas: Tvorchist' Oleksandra Korniichuka* (Kiev 1965)
– *Kryla Krecheta* (Kiev 1975)
Vakulenko, D. *Oleksandr Korniichuk: Narys zhyttia i tvorchosti* (Kiev 1980)

I. Koshelivets

Korniienko, Vasyl [Kornijenko, Vasyl'], b 22 April 1867 in Manuilivka, Verkhnodniprovske county, Katerynoslav gubernia, d 24 December 1904 in Odessa. Painter, graphic artist, and children's writer. A graduate of the St Petersburg Academy of Arts (1896), he settled and worked in Odessa. His artistic works include illustrations to I. Kotliarevsky's *Eneïda* (Aeneid, 1904); historical paintings such as *B. Khmelnytsky's Entry into Kiev* (1904) and *Holota the Cossack and the Tatar*; genre paintings such as *By a Tavern* (1902) and *Charms*; paintings on duma themes, reproduced on postcards; and a portrait of T. Shevchenko (end of the 19th century). He wrote stories for children: eg, 'Zaporoz'kyi klad' (The Zaporozhian Treasure).

Korniiets, Leonid [Kornijec'], b 21 August 1901 in Bobrynets, Kherson gubernia, d 29 May 1969 in Moscow. Soviet political figure: member of the Politburo of the CC CP(B)U (1938–53), president of the Presidium of the Supreme Soviet (1938–9), president (1939–44) and first vice-president (1944–6) of the Council of People's Commissars, and first vice-president of the Council of Ministers of the Ukrainian SSR (1946–53). He was also the minister of procurement (1953–6) and of grain products (1956–8) for the USSR, the chairman (1958–61) of the State Committee for Grain Products of the USSR Council of Ministers, and first vice-chairman (1961–3) and chairman (1963–) of the latter council's State Committee for Grain Procurement.

Kornoukhov, Mykola [Kornouxov], b 23 October 1903 in Nizhen, Chernihiv gubernia, d 2 June 1958 in Kiev. Civil engineer; from 1951 full member of the AN URSR. After graduating from the Kiev Polytechnical Institute, he lectured at the Kiev Institute of Civil Engineering and worked at the AN URSR Institute of Mechanics, where he served as director from 1940 to 1944. He developed a composite method of determining the strength and stability of truss systems and precise methods for measuring the stability of frames, columns, and other structural members.

Mykola Kornoukhov

Kornyliak, Platon [Kornyljak], b 6 September 1920 in Stebni, Vyzhnytsia county, Bukovyna. Ukrainian Catholic bishop. He studied at the Urban and Gregorian universities in Rome, obtaining his D TH in 1946 and PH D in 1948. Ordained in 1945, he immigrated to the United States in 1948, where he became the chancellor of Philadelphia eparchy in 1952. In 1959 he was consecrated bishop and appointed apostolic exarch for Ukrainian Catholics in Germany. This exarchate's jurisdiction was extended to include the Scandinavian countries in 1982. Kornyliak participated in the Second Vatican Council and was a member of the Theological Preparatory Commission for the council from 1960. He commissioned the building of the St Andrew's Cathedral in Munich as well as numerous other churches throughout Germany, and has published a number of theological studies, including *La dialettica esistenziale del divino e dell'umano secondo Nicola Berdiaeff* (1948) and *Sancti Augustini de efficacitate sacramentorum doctrina contra Donatistas* (1953).

Korobchansky, Ivan [Korobčans'kyj], b 16 January 1895 in Kekyne, Sumy county, Kharkiv gubernia, d 1 April 1956 in Donetske. Specialist in fuel technology; from 1951 corresponding member of the AN URSR. After graduating from the Kharkiv Technological Institute, he worked in various industrial plants in Kharkiv and in the Donbas region. From 1935 to 1956 he chaired a department of the Donetske Industrial Institute. He did research on coking technology, coal enrichment, and the underground gasification of coal.

Korobka, Fedir, b and d ? Cossack leader and diplomat. He was the acting colonel of Chyhyryn regiment (1649–50) and general quartermaster of the Hetmanate (1650–4, 1669). He made important diplomatic missions for hetmans B. and Yu. Khmelnytsky and I. Vyhovsky to Moscow (1657), Sweden (1657–8), Turkey (1657), and

Moldavia (1657), and served on the staff of Hetman P. Doroshenko.

Korobka, Fedir, b and d ? Kiev goldsmith of the early 19th century. He was president of the silversmith's guild a number of times, and a municipal councilman. Many of his works were done for the Kievan Cave Monastery: eg, the copper iconostases of St Barlaam's Church (1819) and the Church of the Presentation; silver casings for the icons of St Anthony (1818–19), St Barbara (1822), and the *Council of Holy Fathers* (1822); five silver lamps; and an engraving of the plan and facade of the Main Bell Tower (1817). Some of these works have been preserved in the Historical Museum of the Ukrainian SSR in Kiev. Korobka's house, built in the classicist style (1830–1), has been preserved.

Korobka, Mykola, b 6 May 1872 in Kremianets, Volhynia gubernia, d 1921. Folklorist and literary scholar. He studied at Kiev University and graduated from St Petersburg University (1894). He collected and studied the folklore of Volhynia and Podilia, publishing it as *Pesni Kamenetskogo uezda, Podol'skoi gubernii* (Songs of Kamianets County, Podilia Gubernia, 1895), *Vostochnaia Volyn'* (Eastern Volhynia, 1895), *Koliadki i shchedrovki, zapisannye v Volyn'skom Poles'e* (Christmas and Epiphany Carols Recorded in Volhynian Polisia, 1901), and *K izucheniiu malorusskikh koliadok* (Toward a Study of Little Russian Christmas Carols, 1902). A contributor to the journals *Zhivaia starina, Izvestiia otdeleniia russkogo iazyka i slovesnosti,* and *Russkoe bogatstvo,* he also wrote a survey of the history of Russian literature (3 vols, 1907–14) and monographs on N. Gogol (1902), A. Puskhin and M. Lermontov (1903), and M. Gorky (1901), and edited an uncompleted nine-volume edition of Gogol's works (1912–14).

Koroed, Aleksei [Korojed, Aleksej], b 10 July 1911 in Sliudianka, Irkutsk county, Irkutsk gubernia. Economist and Party administrator; since 1961 corresponding member of the AN URSR. A graduate of Kharkiv University (1933), he served as deputy director of the AN URSR Institute of Economics (1955–65) and head of the Section of Social Sciences (1957–63), and then as rector (1965–72) and department head (1972–9) at the Kiev Institute of the National Economy. His works deal with problems of technological progress, the development of Ukraine's productive potential, and the political economy of socialism.

Korol, Mykhailo [Korol', Myxajlo], b 15 September 1856 in Neslykhiv, Kamianka-Buzka county, Galicia, d 15 July 1925 in Zhovkva. Political and civic leader. A graduate of Lviv University, he opened a law practice in Zhovkva in 1888 and in the following year was elected to the Galician Diet. Although he sided with the Old Ruthenians, he was opposed to Russophilism. In 1907 he won a seat in the Austrian Parliament, where he joined the Ruthenian caucus. Elected to the Galician Diet as an independent candidate in 1913, he voted with the Ukrainian National Democratic party. In 1918–19 he served as commissioner of Zhovkva county, and after the war he was active in several Ukrainian cultural and financial institutions.

Korol, Mykhailo [Korol', Myxajlo], b 25 October 1911 in Zarubyntsi, Lypovets county, Kiev gubernia. Pro-Communist community leader in Canada. Arriving in Canada in 1924, he helped organize the youth section of the Ukrainian Labour-Farmer Temple Association. In 1928 he joined the Young Communist League of Canada (YCLC) and set up branches of the league in Montreal and Sudbury. After being admitted to the Communist Party of Canada (1931), he edited the YCLC newspaper *Young Worker* in Toronto. In 1946 he became a member of the National Executive Committee of the Association of United Ukrainian Canadians. From 1956 to 1965 he served as the manager of the newspaper *Ukraïns'ke zhyttia* and afterwards of *Zhyttia i slovo.*

Oleksander Korolchuk

Vladimir Korolenko

Korolchuk, Oleksander [Korol'čuk], b 12 October 1883 in Volhynia, d 3 March 1925 in Zaporizhia. Actor specializing in heroic and character roles and play director of the Mykola Sadovsky school. He began to act in 1905 in I. Sahatovsky's company, and then joined the *Sadovsky Theater (1907–17). In the UNR period he worked in the State Drama Theater (1918–19) and was an instructor of theater arts. In 1920 with I. *Kavaleridze he founded a Ukrainian drama company in Romen. In the following year he worked with P. *Saksahansky in the State People's Theater, and in 1922 became one of the founders of the *Zankovetska Ukrainian Drama Theater. He directed such plays as *Chorna rada* (The Black Council, an adaptation of P. Kulish's novel), S. Cherkasenko's *Zemlia* (The Earth), Lesia Ukrainka's *U pushchi* (In the Wilderness), V. Vynnychenko's *Memento,* Ya. Mamontov's *Ave Maria,* J. Słowacki's *Mazepa,* J. Synge's *The Playboy of the Western World,* and N. Gogol's *Revizor* (The Inspector General). His actor's repertoire included the title roles in I. Tobilevych's *Sava Chalyi* and M. Starytsky's *Bohdan Khmel'nyts'kyi,* Franz Moor in F. Schiller's *Die Räuber,* and Pastor Manders in H. Ibsen's *Gengangere* (Ghosts). Korolchuk was also a coeditor of the literary and artistic magazine *Siaivo* (1913–14).

V. Revutsky

Korolenko, Vladimir, b 27 July 1853 in Zhytomyr, d 25 December 1921 in Poltava. Russian Populist writer and publicist of Ukrainian-Polish parentage. As a student in St Petersburg and Moscow (1871–9) he became an avowed opponent of tsarism. He was imprisoned for his beliefs in Viatka (1879–80) and exiled to Yakutia in eastern Siberia (1881–4). From 1900 to the end of his life he lived in Poltava, where he wrote his greatest work, the autobiography *Istoriia moego sovremmenika* (The History of My Contemporary, 1922; English trans, 1972), and served as the chief editor of *Russkoe bogatstvo* (1904–18). He was renowned as a champion of the oppressed and a democrat. He did not support the Bolshevik regime.

From 1878 Korolenko published over 100 stories and short novels and 600 articles and sketches. His realistic prose is characterized by its lyricism, moral outlook, delicate humor, and humane portrayals of the common folk and the oppressed, mostly in Siberia and Ukraine. Twenty of his stories (some of them his best) deal with Ukrainian subjects: eg, 'V durnom obshchestve' (In Bad Company, 1885), about the persecuted Uniate Catholics in Volhynia; 'Slepoi muzykant' (The Blind Musician, 1886; English trans, 1925), about Populists in Ukraine 'going to the people'; 'Les shumit' (The Murmuring Forest, 1886), about Polisian peasants avenging themselves on a Polish landlord; and 'Bez iazyka' (Without the Language, 1895; English trans: *In a Strange Land*, 1925 and 1975), about the trials and tribulations of a Volhynian peasant immigrant in America.

Almost 250 of Korolenko's articles deal with Ukraine. He spoke out against the persecution of the Uniates in Volhynia and the Kholm region, the repression of Ukrainian peasant rebels in Sorochyntsi and elsewhere in 1906, the oppression of the Ukrainians and the imprisonment of Metropolitan A. Sheptytsky during the Russian occupation of Galicia in the First World War, and injustice in general.

Although Korolenko was involved in community affairs in Poltava, had a great love for Ukraine, its peasantry, and their folklore, and counted many Ukrainian intellectuals and writers among his friends, because of his mixed background and philosophical outlook he was indifferent to the Ukrainian national movement. His works have appeared in many editions in Russian. The major editions in Ukrainian were published in three volumes in 1923 (ed S. Yefremov) and in four volumes in 1953–4.

BIBLIOGRAPHY

Boiko, I. *Korolenko i Ukraïna: Bibliohrafichnyi pokazhchyk* (Kiev 1957)

Malyi, P. *V. H. Korolenko i Ukraïna* (Lviv 1958)

– *Ukraïna v publitsystytsi V.H. Korolenka* (Kiev 1958)

Donskoi, Ia. *V.G. Korolenko: Ocherk poltavskogo perioda zhizni i deiatel'nosti pisatelia, 1900–1921* (Kharkiv 1963)

Mukhyn, I. *Za viru bat'kiv (Uniiaty v khudozhnikh tvorakh V.H. Korolenka)* (Chicago 1976)

R. Senkus

Korolenko museums (Muzei V.H. Korolenka). There are two memorial museums in Ukraine dedicated to the Russian writer of Ukrainian origin V. *Korolenko. The museum in Poltava was established in 1928 in a building occupied by Korolenko from 1903 to 1921. Its holdings consist of over 8,000 items – manuscripts, paintings, books, photographs, letters from M. Kotsiubynsky, and personal belongings. Two sections of its exhibition are 'Korolenko in Ukraine' and 'Korolenko and Ukrainian Literature.' The museum in Zhytomyr was opened in 1973 in the building where Korolenko was born. It houses over 550 exponents, including letters, photographs, and first editions of the author's works.

Koroleva, Natalena (née Dunin-Borkowska), b 3 March 1888 in San Pedro-de-Cordena near Burgos, Spain, d 1

Natalena Koroleva

July 1966 in Mělník, Czechoslovakia. Writer. She grew up in Spain, France, and Italy; studied archeology and history in Paris, Rome, and St Petersburg; and took part in archeological digs in Pompei, Alexandria, Armenia, and Iran. In 1919 she immigrated to Czechoslovakia and married V. Koroliv-Stary. Her first works were written in French and appeared in 1904. In 1919 her first story in Ukrainian was published in the Vienna weekly *Volia*. Some of her writings are based on her historical and archeological studies. Her works consist of autobiographic stories, recollections, legends, and exotic stories set in biblical or medieval times in such places as Caucasia or Persia. Among them are the collection *Vo dni ony* (Once upon a Time, 1935), the novella *1913* (1935), the autobiographic novella *Bez korinnia* (Without Roots, 1936; 3rd rev edn, 1968), the collection *Legendy starokyïvs'ki* (Ancient Kievan Legends, 2 vols, 1942–3), and the historical novella *Quid est veritas?* (1961). Many of her stories appeared in Western Ukrainian and émigré periodicals, particularly in the journal *Dzvony*. She also translated works into Ukrainian, including Thomas à Kempis's *Imitation of Christ* (1923).

Koroleve. V-4. Town smt (1979 pop 6,800) and railway depot in Vynohradiv raion, Transcarpathia oblast, on the Tysa River. It was first mentioned in 1262. A Hungarian castle was built there in the 13th century. Its inhabitants manufacture clothing, artistic wares, and bread products. The oldest Paleolithic site in Ukraine, with 11 strata of the Acheulean and Mousterian cultures, has been under excavation nearby since 1974.

Korolevskij, Cyrille (real name: Jean Francois Joseph Charon), b 16 December 1878 in Caen, France, d 19 April 1959 in Rome. French priest and historian of the Eastern Catholic churches. He studied Eastern theology and rite at the Patriarchal College in Beirut, Lebanon, and was admitted to the Melchite order in 1902. After writing several works on the history of the Melchites, he turned his attention to the Ukrainian Catholic church. During his extensive travels in Ukraine and Eastern Europe he met Metropolitan A. Sheptytsky, who commissioned him to collect documents in Rome about Metropolitan V. Rutsky and the history of the Ukrainian church. He compiled a catalogue to the documents of the Basilian order, published in *Zapysky chyna sv. Vasyliia Velykoho* (1926–8, 1949), began the compilation of *Monumenta Ucrainae His-*

torica, and wrote *Métropolite André Szeptyckyj, 1865–1944* (1964). Korolevskij also worked with the Congregation for Eastern Churches as a member of the commissions on eastern law and on the revision of eastern liturgical books, and coauthored the rules of the Studite order (1943–4). In his studies of the eastern rite, Korolevskij opposed the concept of Uniatism and the Latinization of the eastern churches.

Koroliuk, Volodymyr [Koroljuk], b 19 August 1925 in Kiev. Mathematician; full member of the AN URSR since 1976. A graduate of Kiev University (1950), in 1954 he joined the staff of the AN URSR Institute of Mathematics, serving as the head of the section of probability and mathematical statistics since 1960 and as assistant director since 1966. He has also been a professor at Kiev University since 1965. Koroliuk has published over 200 articles and 10 monographs, some of which have been translated into other languages. His main publications deal with various problems in the theory of probability, mathematical statistics, computational mathematics, and mathematical programming. He is particularly known for his contributions to the development of analytic and asymptotic methods for solving boundary-value problems for homogeneous processes with independent increases, and for his work on phase methods in the study of Markov and semi-Markov processes.

Koroliv, Fedir, b 1886, d 14 February 1935 in Berlin. Political figure. A member of the Ukrainian Party of Socialist Revolutionaries in Russian-ruled Ukraine, he emigrated to Galicia in 1906 and then lived in Chernivtsi and, from 1914, Vienna. Returning to Ukraine after the February Revolution of 1917, in 1918 he became a department director in the UNR Ministry of the National Economy in Kiev and was a member of the Economic Commission in the Hetman government that negotiated with the Central Powers. In 1919 he headed the UNR trade commission in Switzerland and then lived in Berlin, where he headed the Relief Committee for Emigrants from Ukraine. He was a cofounder of the *Ukrainian National Alliance in Germany and its head in 1933–5.

Vasyl Koroliv-Stary

Koroliv-Stary, Vasyl [Koroliv-Staryj, Vasyl'], b 17 February 1879 in Dykanka, Poltava county, Poltava gubernia, d 11 December 1941 in Mělník, Czechoslovakia. Writer, publisher, and civic figure. A graduate of the Kharkiv Veterinary Institute (1904), he helped found and direct the Chas publishing house in Kiev. In 1917–19 he edited the monthly *Knyhar*. Sent to Czechoslovakia in 1919 as a member of the UNR diplomatic mission, he remained there after the war and became a lecturer at the Ukrainian Husbandry Academy. He wrote textbooks on zoology and animal physiology; children's stories and plays; a children's novelette, *Chmelyk* (The Bumblebee, 1923); and a book of memoirs, *Zhadky pro moiu smert'* (Memories about My Death, 1942; repr, 1961). He also translated Czech writers.

Korolivsky, Stepan [Korolivs'kyj], b 16 August 1904 in Katerynivka, Pavlohrad county, Katerynoslav gubernia, d 1 November 1976 in Kharkiv. Historian. After completing his studies in 1927, he lectured at higher educational institutions in Kharkiv (from 1933 to 1940 at Kharkiv University). In 1945 he was appointed to the Chair of Soviet History at Kharkiv University. Most of his published works deal with the 1917 Revolution in a propagandist way. He is the author of books on the First Congress of Soviets in Ukraine (1947) and the First All-Ukrainian Peasant Conference (1958).

Korolko, Mykola [Korol'ko], b 25 November 1905 in Juriw, Tomaszów county, Lublin gubernia, d 20 March 1986 in Lublin. Political and community leader. A regional organizer of the Communist Party of Western Ukraine, he was arrested in 1926 by the Polish police and sentenced to seven years in prison for his political activities. Upon his release he went underground. Korolko spent the Second World War in German prisons and concentration camps. After the war he worked in the county Party organization, and in 1956 helped found the Ukrainian Social and Cultural Society (USKT). From 1957 to 1960 he was a special ministerial assistant for Ukrainian affairs. In 1967 Korolko was elected president of the USKT. During his term in office, which lasted for over 10 years, the society made some important advances in the fields of Ukrainian education and culture.

Serhii Korolov

Korolov, Serhii [Korol'ov, Serhij], b 12 January 1907 in Zhytomyr, Volhynia gubernia, d 14 January 1966 in Moscow. Aeronautical engineer, designer of the first Soviet guided missiles and spacecraft; from 1958 full member of the AN URSR. After studying engineering in Odessa, Kiev, and Moscow, he began to design gliders and airplanes at the Central Aerodynamics Institute. His interest in rocketry led him to organize, with F. Tsander, the Group for the Study of Jet Propulsion, which in 1933 launched the first Soviet liquid-fueled rocket, the GIRD-

09. In late 1933 he was appointed deputy scientific director of the Jet Scientific Research Institute. He was arrested in 1937 or 1938, and sent first to a concentration camp and then to a special work camp for scientists. There he worked on rocket boosters for airplanes. After the war he tested and improved the German V-2 missile. During the Khrushchev era Korolov headed many research and design teams developing ballistic missiles, launch vehicles, and spacecraft. He was in charge of designing, constructing, and launching the Vostok and Voskhod manned spacecraft, and the Electron, Kosmos, and Molniia earth satellites, as well as the first space stations. Rockets developed by him launched the first artificial earth satellite (Sputnik), the first astronauts in earth orbit, the first probes to the moon, Mars, and Venus, and the first unmanned soft landing on the moon. During his lifetime his name was kept secret and he was referred to only as the Chief Designer. After his death his name became widely known and honored: a museum in Zhytomyr and a monument in Moscow were dedicated to him, and a large crater on the far side of the moon was named after him.

L.S. Onyshkevych

Korolyk, Volodymyr, b 17 December 1907 in Boryslav, Drohobych county, Galicia, d 27 January 1987 in New York. Character actor. He began his stage career in 1929 in Stadnyk's touring theater. Then he performed with the Tobilevych Ukrainian People's Theater, the Zahrava Young Ukrainian Theater, V. Blavatsky's Ensemble of Ukrainian Actors in Germany, and the Novyi Teatr group in New York. His main roles were Ovid in *Kamo hriadeshy* (an adaptation of H. Sienkiewicz's *Quo Vadis*), Mokii in M. Kulish's *Myna Mazailo*, Major Kharin-Geroiev in Yu. Kosach's *Orden* (The Medal), and Voinarovsky in *Motria* (an adaptation of B. Lepky's novel).

Korop. II-13. Town smt (1983 pop 5,300) and raion center in Chernihiv oblast, situated in the Desna River valley. First mentioned in the Hypatian Chronicle under the year 1153 as Khorobor, Korop was a company town in Nizhen regiment and the seat of the Hetman state's artillery from 1659 to the mid-18th century; its company was commanded directly by the hetman. It had the only fortified church in Left-Bank Ukraine. The town was granted the rights of Magdeburg law in the early 18th century. From 1782 to 1797 it was a county town in Novhorod-Siverskyi vicegerency. Korop has a food industry and a flax mill.

Koropchevsky, Pavlo [Koropčevs'kyj], b 1741, d 16 March 1808 in Banychi, Hlukhiv county, Chernihiv gubernia. Cossack officer. He studied at the Kievan Mohyla Academy before becoming chancellor of Myrhorod regiment and then general chancellor (1761–8). In 1768 he was arrested for his involvement in the rebellion of the *Pikeman regiments, but was soon released. From 1769 to 1774 Koropchevsky was registrar of the *Little Russian Collegium. In the 1780s and 1790s he was a prominent official in *Novhorod-Siverskyi vicegerency and then vice-governor of Little Russia gubernia (1797–9). Koropchevsky was also a member of the *Novhorod-Siverskyi patriotic circle.

Koropeckyj, Iwan [Koropec'kyj, Ivan], b 24 June 1921 in Strupkiv, Tovmach county, Galicia. Economist. He began his studies after the Second World War in Germany and, following immigration to the United States, completed them with a PH D in economics from Columbia University in 1964. At present, he is a professor of economics at Temple University and a member of the Ukrainian Academy of Arts and Sciences. He is the author of *Location Problems in Soviet Industry before WW II* (1971) and editor of *Selected Contributions of Ukrainian Scholars to Economics* (1984), *Selected Works of Vsevolod Holubnychy – Soviet Regional Economics* (1982), and *The Ukraine within the USSR: An Economic Balance Sheet* (1977).

Koropets River [Koropec']. A left-bank tributary of the Dniester River, flowing for 78 km through Podilia and draining a basin of 511 sq km. Its waters are used for irrigation and to supply industry.

Koropetsky, Ivan. See Koropeckyj, Iwan.

Korosno. See Krosno.

Korosten [Korosten']. III-9. Industrial city (1982 pop 67,000) and raion center in Zhytomyr oblast on the Uzh River. It was first mentioned in 945 as Iskorosten, the capital of the *Derevlianians destroyed by Princess Olha. Since the late 19th century it has been an important railway and highway junction, and its population grew from 2,600 in 1897 to 12,000 in 1926 and 34,000 in 1956. Because of its strategic importance, the UNR and Red armies fought for its control in 1918, in February and the summer of 1919, and during the Second Winter Campaign in November 1921. Its plants manufacture road-construction and chemical-industry machinery, reinforced-concrete railway ties, porcelain products, silos, household chemicals, lumber, granite, clothing, cotton thread, meat and dairy products, and wine. Four Rus' settlements have been excavated there.

Korostovets, Ivan [Korostovec'], b 1862 in the Chernihiv region, d 1932. Career diplomat. He headed the Russian diplomatic chancellery in Port Arthur (1899–1902), was Count S. Witte's secretary at the Portsmouth Conference (1905), and was the Russian ambassador in Peking (1907–12) and Tehran (1913–17). As a plenipotentiary of the *Hetman government, he met with representatives of the Entente Powers in Iaşi in November 1918. His diary of the Portsmouth Conference was published in English in 1920. He also wrote a book on Russia in the Far East (in Russian, 1922) and a history of Mongolia (in German, 1926).

Korostovets, Volodymyr [Korostovec'], b 16 July 1888 in Peresazh, Chernihiv county, Chernihiv gubernia, d 29 September 1953 in London. Journalist and political figure. He completed his higher education at Kiev and St Petersburg universities with a doctorate in political science and international law. From 1912 to 1917 he served in the diplomatic corps of the Russian Ministry of Foreign Affairs. When the Bolsheviks came to power, he emigrated to Poland and then (1925) to Germany, where he was active in the Hetmanite movement and served as curator of the Ukrainian Scientific Institute in Berlin. Moving to London in 1932, he published *The Investigator* (1932–4), in which he argued that an independent Ukraine was necessary for the achievement of peace in Eastern Europe. From 1949 he sat on the presidium of the Association of Ukrainians in Great Britain. Besides articles in the British and American periodical press, his publications include *The Re-birth of Poland* (1928), *Quo Vadis Polonia?* (1929), *Graf Witte, der Steuermann in der Not* (1929), and *Europe in the Melting Pot* (1938).

Korostyshiv [Korostyšiv]. III-10. City (1972 pop 22,200) and raion center in Zhytomyr oblast, situated on the Teteriv River in eastern Volhynia. It was first mentioned in the 13th century. In 1649 it became a company town in Bila Tserkva regiment. It was granted the rights of Magdeburg law in 1779. In the 19th century it was a popular health resort. In the summer of 1919 the UNR troops defended the town from invading Bolshevik forces. A cotton mill, the Elektroprylad plant, and granite quarrying play an important role in its economy.

Korotchenko, Demian [Korotčenko, Demjan], b 10 November 1894 in Pohribky (today Korotchenkove), Hlukhiv county, Chernihiv gubernia, d 7 April 1969 in Kiev. Soviet state and party official. He worked as a party functionary in Ukraine (1924–8) and Russia (1931–7) before becoming chairman of the Council of People's Commissars (1938–9), secretary of the CC CP(B)U (1939–47), chairman of the Council of Ministers (1947–54), and president of the Supreme Soviet of the Ukrainian SSR (1954–69). He was also a member of the Presidium and Politburo of the CC CP(B)U from 1938, vice-president of the Supreme Soviet of the USSR from 1954, and member (1952–3) and candidate member (1957–61) of the Presidium of the CC CPSU.

Korotych, Vitalii [Korotyč, Vitalij], b 26 May 1936 in Kiev. Physician, poet, publicist, and Soviet media personality. The poetry in his first collections, *Zoloti ruky* (Golden Hands, 1961), *Zapakh neba* (The Scent of the Sky, 1962), and *Vulytsia voloshok* (The Street of Cornflowers, 1963), was similar in spirit to that of the *Shestydesiatnyky. Since 1965, however, his dozen or so subsequent 'engagé' collections have been produced in conformity with the Party line on literature. In the latter half of the 1960s Korotych also began writing propagandistic biographical and travel essays (reprinted in several collections) and prose. His first novella, *Taka lykha pamiat'* (Such a Bad Memory), appeared in 1970, and his first novel, *Desiate travnia* (The Tenth of May), appeared in 1979. The 'publicistic novel' *Lytse nenavysti* (The Face of Hatred, 1984) and novella *Trava bilia poroha* (The Grass near the Threshold, 1985) most strongly reflect current Party attitudes toward the West. A two-volume selection of his *Tvory* (Works) appeared in 1986.

As the chief editor of the journal *Vsesvit* from 1979 to 1986, Korotych did much to promote foreign literature in Ukraine. The editor of the popular biweekly Moscow magazine *Ogonëk* since 1986, he is now a prominent spokesman for cultural liberalization in the USSR. The Ukrainian equivalent of Ye. Yevtushenko, since the 1960s Korotych has traveled widely in the West as an official representative of the USSR. He is the deputy head of the Ukrainian Committee for the Preservation of Peace and, since 1983, vice-president of the international Artists for Nuclear Disarmament. A book about him by V. Zdoroveha appeared in 1986.

I. Koshelivets, R. Senkus

Korotych [Korotyč]. IV-17. Town smt (1979 pop 5,900) in Kharkiv raion, Kharkiv oblast. It was founded in the second half of the 17th century. Most of its inhabitants work in nearby Kharkiv. The Komunar experimental base of the Ukrainian Scientific Research Institute of Soil Science and Agrochemistry is located there.

Korovai Being Decorated; pencil drawing by I. Batechko (1968)

Korovai. A traditional braided wedding bread baked from wheat flour embellished with little dough flags and figurines (sun, moon, birds, animals, etc). Its origin is ancient, and it is a relic of the pagan belief in the magical properties of grain. Women prepared it while singing traditional songs at the new home of the couple about to be married. The bride and groom were blessed with it before their marriage ceremony. At the wedding the *korovai* was kept in a prominent place, and the bride was greeted with it when she arrived at her new home. After the nuptials, the best man served it to all the guests; some scholars consider this ritual a manifestation of collective communion.

Korovytsky, Ivan [Korovyc'kyj], b 4 June 1907 in Volhynia. Writer, scholar, and bibliographer. After receiving an MA in theology from Warsaw University, he taught Old Church Slavonic and the history of the Ukrainian Orthodox church there and ran the Orthodox Metropolitan's Museum in Warsaw. A postwar refugee, he taught at the Theological Academy of the Ukrainian Autocephalous Orthodox church in Munich (1946–8). After immigrating to the United States in the late 1940s, he taught at the St Sophia Seminary in South Bound Brook, New Jersey. He is the author of a poetry collection (1936), stories for children, and a work on the destruction of churches in the Kholm region (under the pseudonym Zhukiv, 1940). In the United States he has edited several Ukrainian monographs and written many articles on Ukrainian church history and literature, many of them for the émigré *Entsyklopediia ukraïnoznavstva*. A full member of the Ukrainian Academy of Arts and Sciences in the United States and an associate of the Lypynsky East European Research Institute in Philadelphia, he heads the Ukrainian Orthodox Church in America Library in South Bound Brook.

Korovytsky, Leonid [Korovyc'kyj], b 4 February 1890 in Zhytomyr, d 8 December 1976 in Odessa. Physician and medical scientist. A graduate of Odessa University (1913), he was in charge of the chair of propaedeutic therapy at Odessa University from 1934 and then the director of the Infectuous Disease Clinic at the Odessa Medical Institute. His works deal with the diagnosis and cure of infectious, parasitic, and tropical diseases, particularly malaria, brucellosis, and toxoplasmosis.

Carved wooden bottle and tumbler by Yu. Korpaniuk

Carved and inlaid wooden plate by S. Korpaniuk

Korpaniuk [Korpanjuk]. The family name of Hutsul master wood-carvers living in Yavoriv (now in Kosiv raion, Ivano-Frankivske oblast): Yu. *Shkribliak's grandsons, the brothers Yurii (12 September 1892–19 April 1977), Semen (14 September 1894–20 November 1970), Petro (1897–12 February 1961); and Semen's son Vasyl (b 18 May 1922). Their finely engraved and encrusted wooden plates, boxes, chests, barrels, and walking sticks have been widely exhibited since the 1920s in Ukraine and abroad and are preserved in ethnographic museums in Kolomyia, Lviv, Kiev, and elsewhere and in private collections. Yurii and Semen were awarded the title Merited Master of Folk Creativity of the Ukrainian SSR.

Korsak, Rafail (secular name: Mykola), b ca 1600, d 1640 in Rome. Uniate Catholic church leader of Belorussian noble descent. As a young man he converted to Catholicism. He studied at the Jesuit Zamostia Academy and at Catholic colleges in Braunsberg and Prague before joining the Basilian monastic order and continuing his studies at the Greek Collegium in Rome (1621–4). Korsak became the protoarchimandrite of the Basilian order in 1625, and the next year the Kievan metropolitan Y. Rutsky named him bishop of Halych, although his appointment was delayed by the Polish king. In 1631–7 he was bishop of Turiv-Pynske eparchy and coadjutor to Metropolitan Rutsky. When Rutsky died in 1637, Korsak became metropolitan of Kiev. As metropolitan, he defended the rights of Uniates in Poland and attempted to extend the Church Union. He translated the works of M. Smotrytsky into Latin, and wrote a biography of Metropolitan Rutsky. He was buried in the Church of SS Sergius and Bacchus in Rome. His correspondence with the Vatican has been published in *Epistolae Metropolitarum Kioviensium Catholicorum R. Korsak, A. Sielava, G. Kolenda (1637–1674)* (1956).

Fedor Korsh

Korsh, Fedor [Korš], b 4 May 1843 in Moscow, d 1 March 1915 in Moscow. Noted Russian Classical philologist, Slavist, and Orientalist; full member of the Russian Imperial Academy of Sciences from 1900 and of the Shevchenko Scientific Society. A graduate of Moscow University (PH D 1877), he was a professor at Moscow (1877) and Odessa (1890–2) universities and at the Lazarev Institute of Oriental Languages in St Petersburg. In addition to works on Roman metrics and literature, he wrote important studies of Slavic song metrics, *O russkom narodnom stikhoslozhenii* (On Russian Folk Versification, 1896, 1901) and *Vvedenie v nauku o slavianskom stikhoslozhenii* (Introduction to the Study of Slavic Versification, 1906), and a monograph on historical-comparative syntax, *Sposoby otnositel'nogo podchineniia* (Types of Relative Subordination, 1877). As a supporter of the Ukrainian cultural movement and a defender of Ukrainian linguistic rights, he coauthored the memorandum of the Imperial Academy of Sciences urging the repeal of the *Ems Ukase, which prohibited the use of Ukrainian in publications (1905). He also wrote articles on the history of the Ukrainian language and literature; eg, on the genesis of Ukrainian, on Turkic elements in *Slovo o polku Ihorevi* (The Tale of Ihor's Campaign), and on T. Shevchenko. He also attempted writing poetry in Ukrainian under the pseudonym Khvedir Korzh.

G.Y. Shevelov

Korshykov, Oleksander [Koršykov], b 28 October 1889 in Sumy, Kharkiv gubernia, d 1942. Botanist. A graduate of Kharkiv University (1915), Korshykov became a professor at that university in 1926 and director of its Scientific Research Institute of Biology in 1930. A specialist in the algology of Ukraine, he focused his research on the morphology and taxonomy of freshwater plants. He described 60 new species and 300 subspecies of water plants. His publications include a guide to the Volvocaceae of Ukraine (1938) in the 12-volume *Vyznachnyk prisnovodnykh vodorostei URSR* (Guide to Freshwater Plants of the Ukrainian SSR, 1953). He was killed by the Nazis.

Korsun. See Chersonese Taurica.

Korsun. See Korsun-Shevchenkivskyi.

Korsun, Oleksander, b 8 June 1818 in Bogdanovska Antypovka, Rostov county, Don Cossack province, d 6 November 1891 in Bogdanovska Antypovka. Poet and publisher. A graduate of Kharkiv University (1842), he wrote *Ukrainskie pover'ia* (Ukrainian Mythology, 1839), a collection of popular works of mythology set to verse. In the early 1840s he composed nostalgic poetry of a Romantic nature, some examples of which appeared in the almanac *Snip*, which he edited and published in 1841. His recollections about M. Kostomarov were published in *Russkii arkhiv* in 1890.

Korsun, Battle of 1648. One of the major battles of the *Cossack-Polish War of 1648–57, which took place near the town of Korsun (now Korsun-Shevchenkivskyi, in Cherkasy oblast). The battle followed the defeat of the Poles at *Zhovti Vody on 16 May 1648. The Polish hetmans M. Potocki and M. Kalinowski led an army of 20,000 men against 15,000 Cossacks led by Hetman B. *Khmelnytsky and 4,000 Tatars under the Crimean khan Tuhai-Bei. On 26 May the Polish forces were routed and more than 8,700 prisoners were taken, including Potocki and Kalinowski. The Cossack victory at Korsun helped launch a national uprising against Polish domination.

Korsun Council (1657). A council of the Cossack *starshyna* that took place in October 1657 after the death of Hetman B. *Khmelnytsky. It confirmed the election of general chancellor I. *Vyhovsky as the new hetman of Ukraine, and confirmed the relationship with the tsar in accordance with the Pereiaslav treaty.

Korsun-Shevchenkivskyi [Korsun'-Ševčenkivs'kyj]. IV-12. City (1972 pop 17,300) and raion center in Cherkasy oblast, situated on the Ros River. Founded as a fortress by Grand Prince Yaroslav the Wise in 1032, until 1944 it was called Korsun. It was destroyed by the Mongols in 1240. A Polish fortress was built there in 1584, and the town received the right of Magdeburg law. In 1630 Cossack rebels led by T. Fedorovych attacked the town and destroyed its Polish garrison. The town was razed by the Polish forces during the 1637 Cossack rebellion led by P. Pavliuk. During the Cossack-Polish War the Battle of *Korsun took place there in 1648, and the town was the center of Korsun regiment from 1648 to 1712. In 1702–4 the Korsun colonel Z. Iskra was one of the leaders of a popular rebellion. In 1768, during the Koliivshchyna rebellion, the Polish garrison was destroyed by the forces of M. Zalizniak. The town came under tsarist rule in 1793. In 1903 one of the largest paint factories in the Russian Empire was built there. In January-February 1944 a 80,000-man German force was encircled and destroyed by the Red Army during the Battle of Korsun-Shevchenkivskyi.

The city's plants produce automobile and tractor machine tools, machine parts, bricks, building materials, canned fruit and vegetables, dairy products, feed, clothing, and furniture; and repair automobiles and tractors. A hydroelectric station and the Museum of the History of the Korsun-Shevchenkivskyi Battle (in a palace built by S. Poniatowski in 1785–9) are located in the city, and a late-18th-century park, the remains of old settlements and fortifications, and Scythian and Cossack burial mounds are preserved there.

Oleksander Korsunsky

Korsunsky, Oleksander [Korsuns'kyj], b 18 October 1893 in Pishchane, Poltava county, Poltava gubernia, d 25 October 1984 in Minneapolis. Microbiologist and bacteriologist. Korsunsky was a professor at the Kiev Veterinary Zootechnical Institute (1922–30), the Kamianets-Podilskyi (1930–3) and Bila Tserkva (1934–41) agricultural institutes, and the Ukrainian Technical and Husbandry Institute in Regensburg (1945–9). He immigrated to the United States in 1952. Korsunsky published over 20 works dealing mostly with the problem of immunization of birds and fish. Korsunsky was also a member of the Ukrainian National Council in Kiev in 1941 and a founder and head of the Relief Committee in Munich after the Second World War.

Korunka. A family of Lviv craftsmen and painters in the second half of the 16th and the first half of the 17th centuries. Semen (aka Senko), a cobbler, was active in printing and book selling, and became a close associate of I. *Fedorovych. Semen's son Ivan (d 1657) was a painter;

his name began to appear in historical documents in 1624. Semen's second son, Oleksander (d 1648), was also a painter. Ivan's son Ivan (1594–1665), also a painter, was a prominent member of the Lviv Dormition Brotherhood. Semen's brother, Sevastian (d 1668), painted churches and served as an officer of the painters' guild (1662–6); he drew eight illustrations for the triodion (Lviv 1664), which were engraved in wood by V. Ushakevych.

Korytnyk, Walter [Korytnyk, Vsevolod], b 21 April 1929 in Časlav, Czechoslovakia, d 31 October 1985 in Buffalo, New York. Medical chemist and biochemist; full member of the Shevchenko Scientific Society. A graduate of the University of Adelaide (PH D 1957), he emigrated to the United States in 1958 and two years later was appointed senior cancer research scientist at the Roswell Park Memorial Institute. In 1981 he became director of graduate studies in medical chemistry at the State University of New York at Buffalo. Korytnyk published over 83 papers and chapters in the field of carbohydrate chemistry and biochemistry, plasma membrane modifiers and inhibitors, vitamin B-6 and anti-cancer agents, and the application of nuclear magnetic resonance to chemistry and pharmacology.

Korzeniowski, Józef, b 19 March 1797 near Brody, Galicia, d 17 September 1863 in Dresden, Germany. Polish playwright and pedagogue. He taught Polish literature at the Kremianets Lyceum (1823–32) and philology at Kiev University (1833–8) before becoming the director of a gymnasium in Kharkiv (1838–46). Ukrainian subject-matter and themes are prevalent in many of his works, most particularly in his drama *Karpaccy górale* (Carpathian Highlanders, 1843). This work underwent several translations and adaptations into Ukrainian. The first was M. Ustyianovych's 'Verkhovyntsi Beskydiv' (The Highlanders of the Beskyds, 1848); the song from the play, 'Hei, brattia opryshky' (Hey, Fellow Opryshoks), became extremely popular in Western Ukraine. Other translations followed: K. Klymkovych's 'Verkhovyntsi' (staged in 1864); V. Derzhyruka's, under the same title (1909); and an anonymous translation (1924, republished in 1927). In Russian-ruled Ukraine the play was translated by S. Tobilevych as 'Hutsuly' (Hutsuls, 1890) and by H. Khotkevych as 'Antin Revizorchuk' (1910).

Korzh, Kuzma [Korž, Kuz'ma], b ? in the Katerynoslav region, d 1919 in Kiev. Community and political activist. A member of the CC of the Ukrainian Party of Socialist Revolutionaries, he was elected to the Ukrainian Central Rada in 1917 and was the secretary of its Information Bureau. He was shot by the Bolsheviks during their occupation of Kiev in summer 1919.

Korzh, Oleksii [Korž, Oleksij], b 23 April 1924 in Obolon, Poltava gubernia. Medical scientist; corresponding member of the USSR Academy of Medical Sciences since 1967. Upon graduating from the Kharkiv Medical Institute in 1951, he began working at the Kharkiv Institute of Orthopedics and Traumatology, becoming its director in 1965. Since 1966 he has also been a professor of orthopedics and traumatology at the Ukrainian Institute for the Upgrading of Physicians. He has written on the surgical treatment of traumatic swelling, bone and joint tuberculosis, and regeneration.

Kos, Andrii, 1864–1918. Political and civic leader. He practiced law in Lviv (1893–6) and Kalush (1896–1918). Together with I. Kurovets, he organized Ukrainian institutions in Kalush county. Serving as a deputy in the Austrian Parliament (1900–7), he attacked the enormous influence of Polish landowners in Galician politics. During the Russian occupation of Galicia Kos was arrested and exiled to Siberia for two years. Released in 1917, he returned to Kalush.

Kos, Mykhailo, b 1863 in Komarno, Rudky county, Galicia, d 12 February 1930 in Peremyshl. Ophthalmologist and civic leader; from 1911 full member of the Shevchenko Scientific Society. Upon completing his medical studies, he served as a physician in the Austrian army. He promoted medical care and first-aid services for the people, and for 30 years played a prominent role in the Ukrainian community in Peremyshl. Kos wrote a number of scientific and popular articles on ophthalmology. He was a frequent contributor to various Galician newspapers.

Anatol Kos-Anatolsky

Yurii Kosach

Kos-Anatolsky, Anatol [Kos-Anatol's'kyj, Anatol'] (real surname: Kos), b 1 December 1909 in Kolomyia, Galicia, d 30 November 1983 in Lviv. Composer and educator. A graduate of the law faculty of Lviv University (1931) and Lviv Conservatory (1934), he taught at the Stryi Branch of the Lysenko Higher Institute of Music (1934–7) and later at the Lviv Conservatory (1952–83). His works include the opera *To Meet the Sun* (1957, revised as *The Fiery Sky*, 1959); the ballets *Dovbush's Kerchief* (1951), *The Jay's Wing* (1956), and *Orysia* (1964); the operetta *Spring Storms* (1960); the cantatas *It Passed a Long Time Ago* (1961) and *The Immortal Testament* (1963); the oratorio *From the Niagara to the Dnieper* (1969); two piano concertos and two violin concertos; chamber music; piano pieces; and choral works.

BIBLIOGRAPHY

Volyns'kyi, I. *Anatolii Iosypovych Kos-Anatol's'kyi* (Kiev 1965)
Kolodii, Ia.; Polek, V. *Kompozytor Anatolii Kos-Anatol's'kyi: Materialy do notohrafiï ta bibliohrafiï, 1947–1972 rr.* (Lviv 1974)

Kosach, Mykhailo [Kosač, Myxajlo] (pseud: Obachny), b 30 July 1869 in Kolodiazhne, Kovel county, Volhynia gubernia, d 16 October 1903 in Kharkiv. Writer and mathematician; brother of Lesia *Ukrainka. A graduate of Yuriev (Tartu) University (1894), he lectured on physics and metereology at Kharkiv University. His contribution to Ukrainian literature consists of short stories such as *Rizdvo pid Khrestom Poludnevym* (Christmas under the Southern Cross), *Khmary* (Clouds), and *Hist'* (The Guest), published in *Zoria*, and Ukrainian translations of V. Korolenko, N. Gogol, and other Russian writers.

Kosach, Oleksandra. See Hryhorenko, Hrytsko.

Kosach, Olha. See Pchilka, Olena.

Kosach, Yurii [Košač, Jurij] (Kossatch; pseuds: Ya. Kosarych, H. Roslavets, A. Zhorianych), b 5 December 1909 in Kiev. Poet, writer, and dramatist; nephew of Lesia Ukrainka. Kosach studied at Warsaw University and in Paris. After the war he lived in displaced persons camps in Germany and was an active member of the writers' organization *MUR. In 1949 he immigrated to the United States. While in New York he began publishing a pro-Soviet journal, *Za synim obriiem*, which was notable primarily for its strident anti-émigré attacks. A prolific author excelling in the genre of the historical novel, he is also the author of several collections of rather average poetry, often marked by his interest in history and mythology. His dramatic works consist of *Obloha* (The Siege, 1943) – a dramatic poem – and the tragedy *Diistvo pro Iuriia Peremozhtsia* (Play about Yurii, the Conqueror, 1947).

By far the largest and most interesting body of work is Kosach's prose, written prior to his emigration to the United States. Dynamic and with a great emphasis on plot, it consists of several collections of historical novellas and short stories – *Chorna pani* (The Black Lady, 1932), *Charivna Ukraïna* (Enchanting Ukraine, 1937), *13-ta chota* (The Settlement of the 13th Platoon, 1937), *Klubok Ariadny* (Ariadne's Thread, 1937), *Hlukhivs'ka pani* (The Lady of Hlukhiv, 1938), and others; as well as novelettes and novels – *Sontse skhodyt' v Chyhyryni* (The Sun Rises in Chyhyryn, 1934), *Dyvymos' v ochi smerti* (We Look Death in the Eyes, 1936), *Chad* (The Fumes, 1937), *Rubikon Khmel'nyts'koho* (Khmelnytsky's Rubicon, 1941), *Enei i zhyttia inshykh* (Aeneas and the Lives of Others, 1947), *Den' hnivu* (The Day of Wrath, 1947), and others. His work weakened in the United States; as his political views changed, he began to write in the style of socialist realism, and was published in Soviet Ukraine. His latest novel, *Suziria Lebedia* (The Constellation Cygnus, 1983) – a family chronicle published in the West – is Chekhovian in atmosphere and reflects the ambivalent political stance of the author.

D.H. Struk

Kosach-Kryvyniuk, Olha [Kosač-Kryvynjuk, Ol'ha], b 26 May 1877 in Zviahel (now Novohrad-Volynskyi), Volhynia gubernia, d 11 November 1945 in Augsburg, West Germany. Physician, community figure, ethnographer, and writer; the daughter of Olena *Pchilka and sister of Lesia *Ukrainka. She taught in Sunday schools in Kiev. While studying at the St Petersburg Women's Medical Institute (1899–1903), she was active in the St Petersburg Ukrainian Student Hromada and was imprisoned for her involvement. From 1910 to 1922 she was a zemstvo physician in Lotsmanska Kamianka near Katerynoslav, directed an orphanage there, published several of her sister's works, and translated Russian and French literature (by V. Hugo, George Sand, and others) into Ukrainian (under the pseudonym Olena Zirka). She amassed a large collection of Ukrainian embroidery, which served as the basis for her collection *Ukraïns'ki narodni vzory z Kyïvshchyny, Poltavshchyny, i Katerynoslavshchyny* (Ukrainian Folk [Embroidery] Patterns from the Kiev, Poltava, and Katerynoslav Regions). The last years of her life were devoted to collecting and studying materials about her sister. Her monumental *Lesia Ukraïnka: Khronolohiia zhyttia i tvorchosty* (Lesia Ukrainka: A Chronology of Her Life and Work) was published posthumously in 1970 in New York.

M. Stech

Kosach-Kvitka, Larysa. See Ukrainka, Lesia.

Kosarenko-Kosarevych, Vasyl [Kosarenko-Kosarevyč, Vasyl'], b 23 March 1891 in Lany, Kaminka-Strumylova county, Galicia, d 30 September 1964 in New York. Publicist and political figure. In 1918 he served in the UNR Ministry of Foreign Affairs as a member of the delegation to Brest-Litovsk, then as the chargé d'affaires in Berlin, and, finally, as the secretary of the mission in Stockholm. Under the Directory he was entrusted with special assignments by the ministries of highways, foreign affairs, and finances. After the war he completed his studies in engineering and political science in Berlin, established a successful business, and devoted himself to philosophical and historical research. He was arrested in 1943 by the Gestapo for his sharp criticism of Hitler's eastern policy and spent two years in concentration camps. In 1952 he immigrated to the United States. Besides articles in the Ukrainian and German press, he wrote *Die Moskauer Sphinx: Mythos und Macht in den Vorstellungen über Osteuropa* (1955), which was revised and published also in Ukrainian (1957) and English (1961).

Kosariev, Borys [Kosarjev], b 4 August 1897 in Kharkiv. Stage designer and pedagogue. Upon graduating from the Kharkiv Art School (1918), he worked with various theater groups in Odessa. In 1920 he returned to Kharkiv and worked in the Chervonyi Fakel theater, the children's theater, the Kharkiv Chervonozavodskyi Ukrainian Drama Theater, the Kharkiv Young Spectator's Theater, and the Kharkiv Ukrainian Drama Theater. From 1931 he taught at the Kharkiv Art Institute. His most successful sets were designed for M. Starytsky's *Za dvoma zaitsiamy* (After Two Hares), I. Kocherha's *Iaroslav Mudryi* and *Marko v pekli* (Marko in Hell), and J. Molière's *L'Avare*.

Kosaryk, Dmytro (pen name of Dmytro Kovalenko), b 31 October 1904 in Fydrivka in the Poltava region. Prose writer and literary critic. A member of the *Pluh writers' group, his first collection, *Chervona kupil'* (The Red Bath, 1925), was followed by the collection *Mii azymut* (My Azimuth, 1931) and five short novels (1932, 1961, 1962, 1964, 1971). He has also produced popular propagandistic-literary works, including *Literaturna tvorchist' voïniv hromadians'koï viiny* (The Literary Creativity of the Soldiers of the Civil War, 1936) and books on A. Pushkin, T. Shevchenko, and M. Gorky.

Kosenko, Ilarion, b 19 October 1888 in Zinkiv, Poltava gubernia, d 10 October 1950 in Paris. Political and civic figure. A member of the Ukrainian Party of Socialist Revolutionaries, he was elected to the Labor Congress, convened by the Directory in January 1919. Then he was in charge of the Kiev postal and telegraph district. In 1920 he served briefly as minister of postal and telegraph services in V. Prokopovych's cabinet. Emigrating in 1920, he settled in Paris and was active in the Ukrainian community. He was the business manager of the weekly *Tryzub* (1925–40) and chairman of the Board of Directors of the *Petliura Ukrainian Library (1942–50).

Viktor Kosenko

Ivan Koshelivets

Kosenko, Viktor, b 23 November 1896 in St Petersburg, d 3 October 1938 in Kiev. Pianist, composer, and educator. A student of A. Michałowski and a graduate of the Petrograd Conservatory (1918), where he studied under I. Myklashevsky, Kosenko began to lecture at the Zhytomyr Music Tekhnikum in 1918, at the Lysenko Music and Drama Institute in 1929, and at the Kiev Conservatory in 1934. At the same time he gave piano concerts in different cities of Ukraine. His works include a sonata for cello and piano (1923), *Classical Trio* for piano, violin, and cello (1927), a sonata for violin and piano (1927), *Heroic Overture* (1932), *Moldavian Poem* (1937), a piano concerto, three piano sonatas, a trio, a violin concerto, about 100 piano pieces, including 24 pieces for children (1936), and many songs.

BIBLIOGRAPHY
Kosenko, A. (ed). *V.S. Kosenko u spohadakh suchasnykiv* (Kiev 1967)
Stetsiuk, R. *Viktor Kosenko* (Kiev 1974)
Oliinyk, O. *Fortepianna tvorchist' V.S. Kosenka* (Kiev 1977)

Koshelivets, Ivan [Koševivec'] (Koszeliwec, Iwan), b 10 November 1907 in the Chernihiv region. A leading émigré literary scholar and critic; full member of the Shevchenko Scientific Society and the Ukrainian Academy of Arts and Sciences. A graduate of the Nizhen Institute of People's Education (1930), he worked as a teacher in Kremenchuk and Nizhen in the 1930s and was a graduate student at the AN URSR Institute of Literature in 1940–1. As a postwar refugee, he has lived in Munich since 1947. He was the editor in chief of the monthlies *Ukraïns'ka literaturna hazeta* (1955–60) and *Suchasnist'* (1961–6, 1976–7, 1983–4) and, with a few breaks, a member of the latter's editorial board. Since the late 1950s he has also been a member of the editorial board of *Entsyklopediia ukraïnoznavstva* (Encyclopedia of Ukraine). Koshelivets has written many articles on literature and the arts. He compiled and edited the anthology *Panorama nainovishoï literatury v URSR* (Panorama of the Newest Literature of the Ukrainian SSR, 1963; rev edn, 1974); wrote the monographs *Suchasna literatura v URSR* (Contemporary Literature in the Ukrainian SSR, 1964), *Mykola Skrypnyk* (1972), and *Oleksander Dovzhenko* (1980); edited a Polish collection of Soviet Ukrainian dissident documents, *Ukraina 1956–1968* (Ukraine, 1956–1968, 1969); and has translated into Ukrainian literary works from Russian, Belorussian, German (F. Kafka's short prose), and French (including D. Diderot's *Jacques Fataliste et son Maître*). His memoirs, *Rozmovy v dorozi do sebe* (Conversations on the Way to Myself), appeared in 1985.

Koshevsky, Kost [Koševs'kyj, Kost'] (real name: Shkliar), b 30 September 1895 in Shulhivka, Novomoskovske county, Katerynoslav gubernia, d 14 March 1945 in Kiev. Actor, dramatist, and stage director. From 1914 to 1918 he acted with various amateur groups, and then joined the Molodyi Teatr company. After working briefly at the Shevchenko Kiev Ukrainian Drama Theater (1920–1), he stayed with the Kiev Ukrainian Drama Theater (1922–39), except for short periods with the Odessa Theater of the Revolution (1930–1) and the Dnipropetrovske Ukrainian Music and Drama Theater (1932–3). He was appointed artistic director of the Kiev Young Spectator's Theater in 1939, but was dismissed in 1941 for criticizing contemporary Soviet drama. His more successful productions were O. Korniichuk's *Platon Krechet* and J. Molière's *Les Fourberies de Scapin*. His actor's repertoire included Perelesnyk in Lesia Ukrainka's *Lisova pisnia* (The Forest Song), Mokii in M. Kulish's *Myna Mazailo*, the title role in K. Gutzkow's *Uriel Acosta*, Creon in Sophocles' *Oedipus Rex*, and Möbius in W. Hasenclever's *Ein besserer Herr*. He also wrote several plays: *Kooperatory* (Co-operative Managers), *Budni* (Everyday Life), and *Bludni vohni* (Wayward Fires), an adaptation of M. Kotsiubynsky's *Fata morgana*.

Oleksander Koshyts

Koshyts, Oleksander [Košyc'] (Koshetz, Alexander), b 14 September 1875 in Romashky, Kaniv county, Kiev gubernia, d 21 September 1944 in Winnipeg. Composer, choirmaster, and ethnographer. A graduate of the Kiev

Theological Academy (1901), he studied composition with H. Liubomyrsky at the Lysenko Music and Drama School (1908–10) and served as assistant choirmaster at the school. During that period he conducted the Boian choir, organized two student choirs (one consisting of students of Kiev University, the other of students of the Higher Courses for Women), taught choral music at the Kiev Conservatory, conducted the orchestra of the Sadovsky Theater (1912–16), and served as conductor and choirmaster of the Kiev Opera (1916–17). He collected Ukrainian folk songs in the Kiev region (1893–1900) and in the Kuban (summers of 1903, 1904, and 1905). In 1918 Koshyts cofounded the *Ukrainian Republican Kapelle (reorganized in 1920 into the Ukrainian National Choir), which for seven years toured Europe and North and South America to win public support for the Ukrainian National Republic. In 1926 he settled in New York, where he taught choir conducting, and in 1941 moved to Winnipeg. A leading popularizer of Ukrainian folk songs and liturgical music, Koshyts composed five liturgies, arranged numerous folk songs, and published a number of collections and musical studies. His memoirs were published in 1947–8 in two volumes.

BIBLIOGRAPHY

Koshyts', O. *Z pisneiu cherez svit*, 3 vols (Winnipeg 1952–74)
Antonovych, M. *O.A. Koshyts', kompozytor tserkovnoï muzyky i dyrygent* (Winnipeg 1975)

W. Wytwycky

Koshyts, Tetiana [Košyc', Tetjana] (Koshetz, Tatiana; née Heorhiievska), b 25 January 1892 in Vinnytsia, Podilia gubernia, d 26 March 1966 in Winnipeg. Voice teacher and museum curator; wife of O. *Koshyts. In 1918 she joined the Ukrainian Republican Kapelle and toured Western Europe and North America. From 1926 she taught voice in New York. As director of the *Ukrainian Cultural and Educational Centre (Oseredok) in Winnipeg (1943–66), she offered courses on Ukrainian folk arts and collected valuable artifacts and archives for the museum.

Kosiachenko, Hryhorii [Kosjačenko, Hryhorij], b 29 September 1903 in Cherniakhivka, Poltava gubernia, d 19 October 1936 in Yahotyn, Kiev oblast. Poet and journalist. A member of the writers' groups *Hart and the All-Ukrainian Association of Proletarian Writers in Kiev in the 1920s, he wrote the poetry collections *Vikholy* (Snowstorms, 1927), *Zalizna krov* (Iron Blood, 1927), *Malyi Kobzar* (Small Kobzar, 1928), *Skhid sontsia* (Sunrise, 1928), *Shtorm* (The Assault, 1929), *Polustanok* (The Railway Stop, 1930), *Doroha* (The Road, 1931), and *Bornia i dni* (The Struggle and the Days, 1932). He disappeared during the Stalinist terror in 1932.

Košice (Ukrainian: Koshytsi). A city (1987 pop 222,200) on the Hornád River; the capital of the Eastern Slovak Region of Czechoslovakia. It is inhabited mostly by Slovaks, some Hungarians, and about 3,000 Ukrainians and Slovakized Ukrainians. In the 1850s Transcarpathia belonged briefly to the Košice administrative district. From 1929 to 1939 the city served as the seat of the Czechoslovak Higher Court for Transcarpathia. In 1968 the Greek Catholic parish in Košice was restored, and a local branch of the Cultural Association of Ukrainian Workers was set up.

Kosior, Stanislav, b 18 November 1889 in Węgrów, Poland, d 26 February 1939. Soviet state and Party official. A Donbas worker who was active in the Bolshevik underground in Ukraine before the 1917 Revolution, he became a member of the Petrograd Military Revolutionary Committee in 1917. From 1918 he held several important state, party, and military posts in Ukraine, including membership in the CP(B)U Politburo. After a stint in the Siberian party organization and in Moscow (1922–8), he returned to Ukraine and was general secretary (1928–34) and first secretary (1934–8) of the CP(B)U. Under Kosior's administration, during which the second secretary P. *Postyshev had a great influence, Ukraine suffered a shift in policy from *Ukrainization to Russification, forced *collectivization of the peasantry, the man-made *famine of 1933, the Stalinist *terror, and the physical destruction of the Ukrainian intelligentsia. Transferred in 1938 to Moscow, Kosior was himself arrested and shot in 1939. He was rehabilitated posthumously in the 1960s.

Kosiv, Sylvestr, b ? in the Vitsebsk region, Belorussia, d 13 April 1657. Prominent Orthodox church leader, metropolitan, and writer. He studied at the Vilnius Brotherhood School and at the Catholic academies in Lublin and Zamostia, then taught at the Lviv Dormition Brotherhood School. In 1631 Metropolitan P. Mohyla invited him to become a lecturer at the Kievan Cave Monastery School, which in 1632 became a college (later called the *Kievan Mohyla Academy). He soon became the prefect of the college and a close collaborator of Mohyla's. In 1635 he was appointed bishop of Mstsislau, Orsha, and Mahiliou and began implementing sweeping reforms of church administration. In 1647 he became the metropolitan of Kiev. Kosiv's tenure as metropolitan, which coincided with the Khmelnytsky rebellion, was a greatly unsettled period in the history of the Ukrainian church. In politics Kosiv opposed a union with Moscow as well as an unconditional alliance with Poland; although he gave a lavish greeting to B. *Khmelnytsky upon the latter's arrival in Kiev in December 1648, he was also critical of Cossack policies. He favored an independent Ukrainian Orthodox church under the ultimate jurisdiction of the Patriarch of Constantinople and resisted pressures for the subjugation of Kiev metropoly to Moscow. He was the author of *Exegesis* ... (1635), an essay in defense of Orthodox schools, and *Didaskaliia* ... (1637), an essay about the seven sacraments. He also published a Polish translation of the Kievan Cave Patericon (1635).

A. Zhukovsky

Kosiv. V-6. Town (1970 pop 8,100) and raion center in Ivano-Frankivske oblast. It was first mentioned in 1424. From 1869 to 1939 it was a county town and the administrative and commercial center of the Hutsul region. In the past its main industry was salt extraction; today it is sawmilling, woodworking, and furniture making. Because of its mild climate, Kosiv is a popular health resort. The city has long been known for its artistic handicrafts. Before the Second World War its most important handicraft manufacturers were the Hutsulske Mystetstvo kilim mill and the Hutsulshchyna co-operative. Today the Hutsulshchyna artistic crafts association produces finely carved and inlaid wood, metal, and leather objects, kilims, other woven and embroidered articles, and ceramic

Kosiv

wares. Artisans are trained at a tekhnikum of applied folk handicrafts. A branch of the Museum of Hutsul Folk Art and the M. Pavlyk Literary Museum are located in Kosiv.

Kosmatenko, Anatolii, b 3 October 1921 in Vremivka, Mariiupil county, Katerynoslav gubernia, d 6 April 1975 in Kiev. Fabulist. A graduate of Kiev University (1953), he worked for the paper *Literaturna Ukraïna*, the journal *Dnipro*, and the Radianskyi Pysmennyk publishing house. From 1947 his satirical and humorous fables appeared regularly in Soviet Ukrainian periodicals. Between 1953 and 1977, 11 of his fable collections were published. Kosmatenko's fables have been acclaimed for their originality, freshness, intellectual and linguistic sophistication, and structural innovativeness.

Kosonocky, Walter F. [Kosonots'kyj, Volodymyr], b 15 December 1931 in Sieradz, Poland. Ukrainian-American inventor in the fields of electronics and solid-state physics. A graduate of Columbia University (he received his doctorate in 1965), since 1955 he has worked at the RCA Laboratories in Princeton, New Jersey, becoming a Fellow of the Laboratories in 1975. In 1987 he was also appointed professor of optic electronics at the New Jersey Technological Institute. He is the author of over 75 technical papers and holds over 40 US patents. His main contributions are in the development of various solid-state devices and systems, including lasers, holographic memories, charge-coupled devices (an area in which he is considered a world expert), and Schottky-barrier image sensors.

Kosonohov, Yosyf, b 31 March 1866 in Stanytsia Kamenska (now Kamensk-Shakhtinskii), Don Cossack province, d 22 March 1922. Physicist and meteorologist; elected full member of the Ukrainian Academy of Sciences in 1922. He graduated in 1889 from Kiev University, where he studied under M. Avenarius, and remained there as a lecturer and then professor (1903–22) and holder of the Chair of Physical Geography and Meteorology. From 1895 he also directed the Kiev Meteorological Observatory. His publications include works on electric oscillation and optical resonance, as well as several textbooks and popular surveys.

Kosonotsky, Volodymyr [Kosonoc'kyj], b 21 September 1886 in Dub, Tomaszów county, Lublin gubernia, d 24 April 1942 in Kholm. Orthodox church and community leader. A graduate of the law faculty at Kiev University (1910), he served to 1914 as an examining judge in Uman. From 1922 to 1934 he was the secretary of the Ukrainian Parliamentary Representation in Warsaw and a member of the Ukrainian Church Committee. In 1939 he became active in the Orthodox church of the Kholm region, and played an important role in establishing a separate Kholm-Podlachia eparchy. He served as director of the eparchy's press department and edited *Kholms'kyi pravoslavno-narodnii kalendar* (1941–2) and other eparchial publications. To refute Polish claims to various churches and monasteries held by the Orthodox church he wrote *Protses za pravoslavni tserkvy* (Legal Action on Behalf of Orthodox Churches, 1930).

Hryhorii Kossak

Kossak, Hryhorii, b 7 March 1882 in Drohobych, Galicia, d 1931? in Kharkiv. Senior officer of the Ukrainian Galician Army (UHA) with the rank of colonel. As a reserve officer of the Austrian army, in 1914 he was put in charge of a field unit of the Ukrainian Sich Riflemen (USS). In 1915 he commanded the First Kurin and then the First Regiment of the USS, which fought in the Carpathians. In 1917–18 Kossak was responsible for recruit training in the USS. During the *November Uprising in 1918, he commanded (3–9 November) the Ukrainian forces in Lviv. Subsequently, he commanded the Third Corps of the UHA. In June 1919 he was appointed commander of the short-lived Fifth Corps and then commander of the army's rear guard. In November 1919 Kossak emigrated to Austria with the UNR government and then settled in Czechoslovakia. He returned to Ukraine in 1924 during the Ukrainization period and served as an instructor at the Red Officer School in Kharkiv. Arrested in 1931 and accused of belonging to the so-called Ukrainian National Center, he was executed by the Soviet secret police.

Kossak, Ivan, b 11 September 1876 in Drohobych, Galicia, d 15 January 1927 in Kiev. Military and civic leader; brother of H. *Kossak. He was a teacher at the Chortkiv Teacher's Seminary and was active in the Prosvita, Silskyi Hospodar, and Sokil societies. During the First World War he served as a captain in the Ukrainian Sich Riflemen and saw action in the Carpathians. In 1919, during the Ukrainian-Polish War, Kossak was the commander of the Zhovkva sector and was wounded in combat. In

1920 he served as a UNR military attaché in Rome. Then, in Vienna, he was active in the Western Ukrainian Association of the League of Nations. In 1925 he immigrated to the Ukrainian SSR, where he worked in co-operative banking.

Kossak, Juliusz, b 15 December 1824 in Vyzhnytsia, Bukovyna, d 3 February 1899 in Cracow. Polish painter of Ukrainian origin. He studied in Lviv, St Petersburg (1851), and Paris, then worked as an illustrator for the newspaper *Tygodnik ilustrowany* in Warsaw. He subsequently moved to Cracow. His works on Ukrainian themes include *Cossacks in the Steppe* (1884), *The Meeting of Bohdan Khmelnytsky with Tuhai-Bei* (1885), and various Volhynian and Podilian landscapes.

Kossak, Vasyl, b 12 February 1886 in Chortkiv, Galicia, d 23 May 1932 in Stryi, Galicia. Actor, singer (tenor), and stage director. Joining the Ruska Besida theater as an actor in 1904, he worked his way to director of the company (1915–18). In 1918–22 he worked with his own troupe in Kolomyia, and then with Y. Stadnyk's touring theater (1924–7) and with the Starytsky theater in Stryi (1928–32). His repertoire included such roles as Andrii in S. Hulak-Artemovsky's *Zaporozhian Cossack beyond the Danube*, Petro in M. Lysenko's *Natalka from Poltava*, Suleiman in D. Sichynsky's *Roksoliana*, Barinkey in J. Strauss's *Zigeunerbaron*, Antos in S. Moniuszko's *Halka*, the title role in C. Gounod's *Faust*, and Stepan in M. Kropyvnytsky's *Nevol'nyk* (The Captive).

Zenon Kossak

Volodymyr Kossar

Kossak, Zenon, b 1 April 1907 in Drohobych, d 19 March 1939 in Solotvyna, Transcarpathia. Nationalist activist. He studied law at Lviv University and was a member of the Ukrainian Military Organization in the late 1920s. He directed the 'combat,' then the organizational, activities of the OUN in 1929–32 as a member of its Home Executive. A Polish political prisoner in 1931–8, after his release he became an ideological instructor and later the deputy commander of the *Carpathian Sich National Defense Organization in Carpatho-Ukraine. He and Col M. Kolodzinsky were captured in battle and murdered in a salt mine by Hungarian troops.

Kossar, Volodymyr (Wolodymyr), b 23 November 1890 in Rusyliv, Kamianka Strumylova county, Galicia, d 11 May 1970 in St Catharines, Ontario. Community leader and agronomist. Kossar served in the Austrian and Ukrainian Galician armies during the First World War. In 1920 he emigrated to Czechoslovakia, where he studied agricultural engineering in Prague and lectured in Transcarpathia. A member of the *Ukrainian Military Organization, he came to Saskatoon in 1927, where he worked as a plant ecologist at the University of Saskatchewan (1935–42). He helped found the *Ukrainian War Veterans' Association (1928) and the *Ukrainian National Federation (1932), whose executive he headed (1937–53). Kossar helped form the *Ukrainian Canadian Committee in 1940 and served as its second vice-president for many years.

Kyriak Kostandi

Kostandi, Kyriak, b 3 October 1852 in Dofinivka, Odessa county, Kherson gubernia, d 31 October 1921 in Odessa. Realist painter and art scholar. After graduating from the Odessa Drawing School (1874) and the St Petersburg Academy of Arts (1882), he returned to Odessa, where he painted and taught at the drawing school. In 1897 he joined the *Peredvizhniki and began to take part in their exhibitions. Having helped found the Society of South Russian Artists, he served from 1902 to 1920 as its president. In 1907 he was elected full member of the St Petersburg Academy of Arts. From 1917 he served as director of the Odessa City Museum. Kostandi was opposed to every formalist trend. Adhering to a strictly realist style, he devoted himself to genre painting, but did some landscape and portrait painting as well. His works include *At a Friend's Sickbed* (1884), *Geese* (1888), *Early Spring* (1892), *Little Bright Cloud* (1906), and *Little Blue Cloud* (1908). V. Afanasiev wrote a critical biography of Kostandi in 1955.

Kostandi Society of Artists (Tovarystvo khudozhnykiv im. K. Kostandi). A society of realist painters and art lovers that was active in Odessa from 1922 to 1929. Some of its chief members formerly belonged to the Society of South Russian Artists. The society adhered to the artistic principles of the *Peredvizhniki, a group of realist painters with populist sympathies (est 1870). Its better-known members were artists such as D. Krainev, V. Zauze, Y. Bukovetsky, P. Vasilev, P. Volokydin, and O. Shovkunenko. Other members, such as the writer A. Kipen (the society's president) and the professors of medicine V. Filatov and V. Snezhkov, were devoted supporters of the arts. Owing to its realist style and ideological orientation, the Kostandi Society served as a precursor of socialist realism in art.

Myrna Kostash

Havryil Kostelnyk

Kostash, Myrna [Kostaš], b 2 September 1944 in Edmonton. Canadian writer of Ukrainian origin. Kostash has written short stories and many articles on Canadian feminism, regionalism, ethnicity, literature, and radical politics. Her *All of Baba's Children* (1977) – a subjective account of the Ukrainian immigrant experience in western Canada – was a Canadian best-seller. She is also the author of *Long Way from Home: The Story of the Sixties Generation in Canada* (1980), two story collections, several film scripts, including *Teach Me to Dance* (NFB, 1978), and a stage play.

Kostelnyk, Havryil [Kostel'nyk, Havryjil], b 1886 in Ruski Krstur, Bačka region, Serbia, d 20 September 1948 in Lviv. Priest, writer, journalist, philosopher, and theologian. He studied philosophy and theology at Zagreb, Lviv, and Freibourg (PH D 1913) universities. Ordained in 1913, after the First World War he moved to Lviv, where he was a professor of theology and philosophy at the Greek Catholic Theological Seminary (1920–8) and the Greek Catholic Theological Academy (1928–30). He also edited the religious journal *Nyva* (1922–32). In the late 1920s, Kostelnyk emerged as a critic of the Vatican's Uniate policy and the leading representative of the 'Eastern' (anti-Latinization) orientation among the Greek Catholic clergy. His position made him a target of NKVD pressure and blackmail during the 1939–41 Soviet occupation of Galicia, when the authorities tried unsuccessfully to have Kostelnyk organize an 'away from Rome' schism in the Ukrainian Catholic church. After the Soviets reoccupied Galicia in 1944 and arrested the entire Ukrainian Catholic episcopate, Kostelnyk was finally compelled by the authorities to assume chairmanship of the so-called Initiating Committee for the Reunification of the Greek Catholic Church with the Russian Orthodox Church. In this capacity, Kostelnyk presided over the Soviet-staged 'Reunion Sobor' in Lviv in March 1946, designed to supply the pseudo-canonic, voluntary facade to the Soviet suppression of the Ukrainian Catholic church. He was killed under mysterious circumstances; while Soviet authorities have blamed his murder on the Vatican and Ukrainian nationalists, the evidence suggests that the assassination was masterminded by the Soviet police.

Kostelnyk's early poetry and prose were written in his native dialect, and he is considered the creator of the *Bačka literary language. His first literary work, *Z moioho valala* (From My Village), appeared in 1904, and in 1923 he published *Hramatyka bachvan'sko-ruskei besedy* (Grammar of the Bačka Ruthenian Language), the first work of its kind. His collected works in the Bačka dialect were published in two volumes in Novi Sad (1970, 1975). Later he began to write prose and poetry in Ukrainian. His scholarly works include *Try rozpravy pro piznannia* (Three Tracts on Understanding, 1925), *Spir pro epiklezu mizh Skhodom i Zakhodom* (The Disagreement about Epiclesis between East and West, 1928), and articles in the journals *Nyva* and *Bohosloviia*.

B.R. Bociurkiw

Kostenko, Anatol, b 17 August 1908 in Balakliia, Poltava gubernia. Literary scholar. A graduate of the Poltava Institute of People's Education (1931), he began publishing literary criticism in 1932. An associate of the Shevchenko Institute, he was arrested in 1936/7 and most likely imprisoned in a Stalinist concentration camp. He was 'rehabilitated' in 1956. He is the author of numerous articles about T. Shevchenko and Lesia Ukrainka and of the books *Shevchenko v memuarakh* (Shevchenko in Memoirs, 1965), *Spivachka dosvitnikh vohniv* (The Songstress of Twilight Fires, 1963), *Lesia Ukraïnka* (1971, 1984), and *Za moriamy, za horamy* (Beyond Seas, beyond Mountains, 1984). He also edited, with introductions and notes, Shevchenko's diary (1936) and *Spohady pro Shevchenka* (Reminiscences about Shevchenko, 1958).

Lina Kostenko

Kostenko, Lina, b 19 March 1930 in Rzhyshchiv, Kiev oblast. Poet; one of the earliest and most outstanding of the *Shestydesiatnyky, the Soviet Ukrainian writers of the post-Stalin thaw. She studied at the Kiev Pedagogical Institute and graduated from the Gorky Institute of Literature in Moscow in 1956. Her first poems were published in the early 1950s. She is the author of the collections *Prominnia zemli* (Rays of the Earth, 1957), *Vitryla* (Sails, 1958), and *Mandrivky sertsia* (Wanderings of the Heart, 1961). The collection 'Zorianyi integral' (The Stellar Integral) was ready for publication in 1962, but the censors judged it ideologically harmful and a departure from socialist realism and suppressed it. Twelve of the poems from the collection appeared in the anthology of Ukrainian samvydav *Shyroke more Ukraïny* (The Wide Sea of Ukraine, Paris-Baltimore 1972), and a volume encompassing her work to date was published in the West in 1969 as *Poeziï* (Poems). In 1965 and 1968 Kostenko signed several open letters protesting the arrests and secret trials of Ukrainian intellectuals. Her poetry was not published in Ukraine again until 1977, when her collection *Nad berehamy vichnoï riky* (On the Banks of the Eternal River) appeared. A novel in verse, *Marusia Churai* (1979), and the collection *Nepovtornist'* (Uniqueness, 1980) followed.

Kostenko's poetry consists primarily of intimate, lyric poems and 'social' poems on the role and responsibility of a poet, particularly in a totalitarian society. Employing diverse rhythms, sophisticated language, a colloquial and aphoristic manner of writing, and a subtle emotivity, ranging from playful irony and humor to scathing satire, she is acknowledged as one of the better contemporary Ukrainian poets. *Marusia Churai* is a unique work in Ukrainian literature. In it Kostenko depicts the tragic fate of a semilegendary figure in Ukrainian history against the background of the Cossack-Polish War. Two new collections – 'Sad netanuchykh skul'ptur' (The Garden of Unmelting Sculptures) and, for children, 'Buzynovyi tsar' (The Lilac Emperor) – are scheduled to be published in 1987.

I. Koshelivets

Serhii Kostenko

Valentyn Kostenko

Kostenko, Serhii, b 1868 in Kiev, d 1900 in Paris. Realist painter. After graduating from the Kiev Drawing School in 1889, he taught there and took part in painting St Volodymyr's Cathedral in Kiev, where he did the murals *Volodymyr's Baptism* and *Blessedness of Paradise*. He also painted *The Last Supper* in the Askoldova Mohyla Church. His easel paintings *Faust and Margaret, The Dnieper*, and *Self-portrait* were displayed in 1889 at the exhibitions of the *Peredvizhniki in Kiev. In 1893 he went to Paris, where his works were exhibited in salons. He fell ill and died in a mental hospital.

Kostenko, Valentyn, b 28 July 1895 in Urazovo, Valuiki county, Voronezh gubernia, d 14 July 1960 in Kharkiv. Composer, musicologist, and educator. As a youth he sang in the court kapelle, and in 1921 he graduated from the St Petersburg Conservatory. From 1923 he taught at the Kharkiv Music and Drama Institute and served as musical director of Kharkiv Ukrainian Radio. In 1927–32 he headed the Association of Revolutionary Composers of Ukraine. His compositions, which were influenced by contemporary European music, include the operas *Karmeliuk, Nazar Stodolia*, and *The Carpathians*; the ballet *Reborn Steppe*; the symphony *The Year 1917*; a suite for symphony orchestra; violin, piano, and choral pieces; and six string quartets. His scholarly publications include studies of P. Senytsia (1922), the role of folk songs in Ukrainian music (1928), and the influence of German expressionism on Ukrainian music (1929). He also prepared a textbook on musical theory.

Ihor Kostetsky

Kostetsky, Ihor [Kostec'kyj] (Kostetzky, Eaghor; pen name of Ivan Merzliakov), b 14 May 1913 in Kiev, d 14 June 1983 in Schwaikheim, West Germany. Writer, translator, critic, and publisher. He grew up in Volhynia and Kiev. In the 1930s he studied stage directing in Leningrad and Moscow and spent two years as an actor in Siberia. A postwar refugee in West Germany, he was active in the writers' association *MUR. He and his wife, the German poet and translator E. *Kottmeier, established the Na Hori publishing house.

Kostetsky first published in 1941. He combined traditional and modernist (expressionist, surrealist, dadaist) forms of expression in his prose collections *Opovidannia pro peremozhtsiv* (Tales about the Victors, 1946) and *Tam de pochatok chuda* (There, Where the Miracle Begins, 1948) and in a collection of three plays, *Teatr pered tvoïm porohom* (The Theater on Your Doorstep, 1963). He also wrote the study *Sovetskaia teatral'naia politika i sistema Stanislavskogo* (Soviet Theater Policy and Stanislavsky's System, 1956). A great translator and promoter of literary classics, Kostetsky translated into Ukrainian and published W. Shakespeare's sonnets (1958) and *King Lear* (1969), T.S. Eliot's poetry (1960) and *Murder in the Cathedral* (1963), P. Verlaine's poems (1979), E. Pound's works (1960), F. Garcia Lorca's poems (1958), Québecois poetry (1972), and R.M. Rilke's poems (1971). He was a member of International PEN, the German Shakespeare Society, and the Teilhard de Chardin Society. A collection of works by and about him was published in Munich in 1964.

D.H. Struk

Kostetsky, Pliaton [Kostec'kyj, Pljaton], b 2 July 1832 in Viatskovychi, Sambir circle, Galicia, d 1 May 1908 in Lviv. Publicist and writer. Graduating from the law faculty of Lviv University (1853), he edited the first Ukrainian weekly *Zoria halyts'ka* (1855–6) and contributed to the periodicals *Halychanyn* (1868) and *Rus'ka chytanka* (1871). In the 1860s he became a proponent of the Polish cause and began to collaborate with various Polish newspapers. He edited the Polish daily *Gazeta narodowa* in Lviv (1869–1908). In Ukrainian he published the collection *Poezii rus'ki* (Ruthenian Poems, 1862) and several short stories about the Lemkos under the pseudonym Vasyl Suskii.

Kostetsky, Volodymyr [Kostec'kyj], b 10 September 1905 in Kholmy, Sosnytsia county, Chernihiv gubernia, d 26 May 1968 in Kiev. Realist painter. A graduate of the Kiev State Art Institute (1928) and a student of F. *Krychevsky, he depicted the life of Donbas miners in his earliest works. In the 1930s he converted to socialist realism and in this style produced such propagandistic works as *Interrogation of the Enemy* (1937), *The Return* (1947), *The Scouts* (1950), and *Presentation of the Party Card* (1959). From 1937 he lectured at the Kiev State Art Institute. H. Portnov published a monograph on Kostetsky in 1958.

Kostiamin, Nikolai [Kostjamin, Nikolaj], b 9 September 1868 in Velikii Ustiug, Vologda gubernia, Russia, d 26 February 1958 in Odessa. Russian hygienist. Kostiamin graduated from St Petersburg University (1890) and the Military Medical Academy there in 1896. In 1914 he became a professor at Odessa University. Later he taught at the Odessa Medical Institute. He wrote works on military, occupational, and nutritional hygiene and several textbooks.

Kostiantynivka [Kostjantynivka]. v-18, DB II-3. City (1984 pop 114,000) and raion center under oblast jurisdiction in Donetske oblast, situated on the Kryvyi Torets River. The city is an important transport junction and industrial center in the Donbas. Founded in 1859, Kostiantynivka had a population of 3,100 in 1897. Thereafter it grew rapidly, reaching a population of 25,400 in 1926, 96,000 in 1939, 89,000 in 1959, and 106,000 in 1970. From the late 1890s to the 1917 Revolution it was a center of working-class unrest. The city was destroyed during the Second World War; over a third of its population was killed. The city's main industries, which are based on local raw materials, are ferrous metallurgy (the Vtorchormet Plant), non-ferrous metallurgy (the Ukrtsynk Plant), chemicals production, window and industrial-glass manufacturing (the Avtosklo Plant and the Mechanized Glass Plant), and refractory- and other building-materials manufacturing (the Chervonyi Zhovten Plant). It also has a food industry, a leather-manufacturing complex, and railway-transport servicing shops. Institutions in the city include the Scientific Research Institute of Glass Products and the General-Technical Faculty of the Ukrainian Polytechnical Correspondence Institute.

Kostiantynivka Avtosklo Plant. A large glass factory located in Kostiantynivka, Donetske oblast. Opened in 1899 by a Belgian firm, it originally produced mirrors. Rebuilt after the Second World War, the plant produces over 200 glass products, including plate glass, windshields, portholes, and mirrors.

Kostiantynivka Ukrtsynk Plant. A metal-processing plant located in Kostiantynivka, Donetske oblast. Construction of the plant began in 1928, and the first zinc was produced in 1930. Since then it has been reconstructed several times, especially in 1943. Its highly diversified production includes zinc, stibrite lead, tin, cadmium, indium, and sulfuric acid.

Kostiuk, Hryhorii [Kostjuk, Hryhorij], b 5 December 1899 in Mohylne, Olviopil county, Podilia gubernia, d 25 January 1982 in Kiev. Psychologist; full member of the USSR Academy of Pedagogical Sciences from 1967. A graduate of Galagan College (1919) and the Kiev Institute of People's Education (1923), Kostiuk was a lecturer (1930–5) and professor (1935–45) at the Kiev Pedagogical Institute and a researcher at the Ukrainian Scientific Research Institute of Pedagogy. In 1945 he became director of the Ukrainian Scientific Research Institute of Psychology and of the Kiev laboratory of pedagogical psychology of the USSR Academy of Pedagogical Sciences. Kostiuk's principal works deal with the psychology of thought, the relationship between schooling and upbringing and the development of the child's personality and abilities, and the theory and history of psychology. He is the author of the textbook *Psykholohiia* (Psychology, 5th edn, 1968) and *Zdibnosti ta ikh rozvytok u ditei* (Abilities and Their Development in Children, 1963), and editor of *Narysy z istorii vitchyznianoi psykholohii* (Outlines of the History of Psychology in Our Homeland, 3 vols, 1952–5).

Hryhory Kostiuk

Kostiuk, Hryhory [Kostjuk, Hryhorij] (pseud: B. Podoliak), b 25 October 1902 in Boryshkivtsi, Podilia gubernia. Prominent émigré literary scholar and publicist; full member of the Ukrainian Academy of Sciences in the United States. He studied at the Kiev Institute of People's Education (1925–9) and was a graduate student at the Shevchenko Institute of Literature in Kharkiv in the early 1930s. From 1927 to 1931 his literary reviews and essays appeared in *Zhyttia i revoliutsiia, Molodniak, Chervonyi shliakh, Krytyka, Prolitfront*, and other journals. He taught Ukrainian literary history at Kharkiv University (1932–3) and the Luhanske Pedagogical Institute (1933–4). Arrested in Kiev during the Stalinist terror and accused of 'nationalism' and 'Khvylovyism,' he spent the years 1935–40 in a Soviet prison and concentration camps, mostly at Vorkuta. A postwar refugee in West Germany from 1944, he helped found the *MUR literary organization and was one of the founding members of the *Ukrainian Revolutionary Democratic party and its secretary in 1948. As a member of its left-wing faction, he cofounded the monthly **Vpered* in 1949. Since 1952 he has lived in the United States. There he headed the *Slovo Association of Ukrainian Writers in Exile from 1955 to 1975. In the late 1950s he brought the archives of V. *Vynnychenko from France and became their curator at Columbia University. He has edited several volumes of Vynnychenko's previously unpublished literary works and diaries.

Since the war Kostiuk has written extensively on Ukrainian literature and politics in interwar Soviet Ukraine and in the postwar West. Many of his essays, which appeared in several émigré periodicals, were republished in his collections *Volodymyr Vynnychenko ta ioho doba* (Volodymyr Vynnychenko and His Age, 1980), *Na magistraliakh doby* (On the Thoroughfares of an Age, 1983), and *U sviti idei i obraziv* (In the World of Ideas and Images, 1983). He has been instrumental in keeping alive the memory of Ukrainian writers who were victims of the Stalinist terror. He collected and was the editor in chief of the complete edition of M. *Khvylovy's works (5 vols, 1978–86), which have been banned in Soviet Ukraine since the early 1930s. He also edited new editions of V. Pidmohylny's *Misto* (The City, 1954) and the works of M. Kulish (1955), M. Plevako (1961), P. Fylypovych (1971), and M. Drai-Khmara (1979). He is the author of the seminal *Stalinist Rule in the Ukraine: A Study of the Decade of Mass Terror, 1929–39* (1960) and of *Teoriia i diisnist': Do problemy vyvchennia teorii, praktyky i stratehii bil'shovyzmu v natsional'nomu pytanni* (Theory and Reality: On the Problem of Studying the Theory, Practice, and Strategy of Bolshevism vis-á-vis the National Question, 1971). Memoirs of his imprisonment, *Okaianni roky* (The Accursed Years), appeared in 1978. His autobiography is forthcoming.

BIBLIOGRAPHY
'Bibliohrafiia prats' H.O. Kostiuka (1927–1972),' *Slovo: Zbirnyk*, 5 (Edmonton 1973)
Holubenko, P. 'Na poli boiu: Zhyttievyi i tvorchyi shliakh Hryhoriia Kostiuka (slovo z nahody 80-littia),' *Novi dni*, December 1982–January 1983
Husar-Struk, D. 'Khto takyi Borys Podoliak?' *Slovo: Zbirnyk*, 10 (Edmonton 1983)
'Hryhorij Kostiuk: A Bibliography (1972–85),' AUA, 16 (1984–5)
I. Koshelivets, R. Senkus

Kostiuk, Platon [Kostjuk], b 20 August 1924 in Kiev. Neurophysiologist, son of the psychologist H. *Kostiuk; since 1969 full member of the AN URSR, and since 1974 full member of the USSR Academy of Sciences. A graduate of Kiev University (1946) and the Kiev Medical Institute (1949), he joined the staff of the university's Institute of Animal Physiology. In 1966 he was appointed director of the AN URSR Institute of Physiology, and in 1975 academic secretary of the physiology division of the USSR Academy of Sciences. Kostiuk has led Soviet research in the use of techniques of molecular biology and biophysics in the study of the nervous system and the brain. He was first in the USSR to use intracellular measurement of electrical potentials in brain studies and has published a book on the subject – *Mikroelektrodnaia tekhnika* (Microelectrode Technology, 1960). He has served as vice-president of the International Organization for Brain Research and the International Union of Theoretical and Applied Biophysics.

Kostiuk, Yurii [Kostjuk, Jurij], b 3 March 1912 in Drotyntsi, Transcarpathia. Folklorist, conductor, music teacher. A graduate of the Prague Conservatory (1938) and Charles University (1947), in 1958 he was appointed docent in the Pedagogical Faculty of Šafařík University in Prešov. He organized and conducted over 30 amateur choirs, and served as artistic director of two professional ensembles that he helped to establish: the Ukrainian Song and Dance Ensemble in Medzilaborce and the Duklia Ukrainian Folk Ensemble in Prešov. Kostiuk compiled several folklore collections: *Narodni pisni pidkarpats'kykh rusyniv* (Folk Songs of Transcarpathian Ruthenians, coauthor, 1944), *Pisni dlia dytiachoho-zhinochoho khoru* (Songs for a Children's and Women's Choir, 1952), and *Ukraïns'ki narodni pisni Priashivs'koho kraiu* (Ukrainian Folk Songs of the Prešov Region, 1958). He wrote a textbook (*Muzychne vykhovannia* [(Musical Education, 1959, 1966]), music-studies curricula, and dozens of articles. His compositions include several cantatas, instrumental pieces, arrangements of folk songs, and songs based on published poetry. V. Liubymov's monograph on Kostiuk was published in 1982.

M. Hnatiukivsky

Kostiukov, Oleksander [Kostjukov], b 10 September 1909 in Sevastopil, Tavriia gubernia, d 29 April 1976 in Odessa. Shipbuilding engineer. Professor (from 1958) and rector (1960–71) of the Odessa Institute of Naval Engineers. His publications deal with the theory of ship's waves and wave resistance of vessels.

Kostiv, Kostiantyn, b 1917 in Rivne, Volhynia. Sociologist, researcher of religious movements in Ukraine, and translator; full member of the Shevchenko Scientific Society and a lecturer at the Ukrainian Technical and Husbandry Institute. A postwar refugee, he studied at Erlangen University and the Ukrainian Free University and received doctorates in philosophy and law. He is the author of works about Metropolitan I. Ohiienko as a translator of the Bible (1950), the Reformation (1956), and the constitutional acts of the UNR and the Hetman government (1964); a Ukrainian biblical reference book (1971); the religious-sociological study *Knyhy buttia ukraïns'koho narodu* (Books of Existence of the Ukrainian People, 1980); and a Ukrainian dictionary of biblical figures, tribes, and peoples (1982).

Kostiv, Vasyl. See Verkhovynets, Vasyl.

Mykola Kostomarov

Kostomarov, Mykola (pseuds: Iieremiia Halka, Ivan Bogucharov), b 16 May 1817 in Yurasivka, Ostrohozke county, in Voronezh gubernia, d 19 April 1885 in St Petersburg. Historian, publicist, and writer. He graduated from the Voronezh gymnasium and then in 1837 from Kharkiv University. From 1844 to 1845 Kostomarov taught history at the Rivne and at the First Kiev gymnasiums. In 1846 he was appointed assistant professor in the Department of Russian History at Kiev University. That year, along with V. Bilozersky, M. Hulak, P. Kulish, T. Shevchenko, and others, he formed the *Cyril and Methodius Brotherhood. In *Knyhy bytiia ukraïns'koho narodu* (*Books of the Genesis of the Ukrainian People), *Ustav Slov'ians'koho tovarystva sv Kyryla i Metodiia: Holovni ideï* (The Statute of the Slavic Society of ss Cyril and Methodius: Its Main Ideas), and two proclamations, Kostomarov formulated the society's program and basic ideas: Christian piety, democratic republicanism, a Ukrainian national renaissance, Ukrainian messianism, and pan-Slavic federalism. In 1847 he was arrested along with all the other members of the society and sentenced to one year's imprisonment in the ss Peter and Paul Fortress in St Petersburg, followed by exile.

Until 1856 he lived in exile in Saratov, serving as a chancellery clerk. Three years later he moved to St Petersburg, where he was appointed to the Chair of Russian History at the university. Because of his political involvements he had to resign his university position in 1862 and could not accept offers from other universities. From then on he devoted himself exclusively to research.

Kostomarov wrote a number of fundamental works on the history of Ukraine in the 16th–18th centuries. Among them were *Bogdan Khmel'nitskii i vozvrashchenie Iuzhnoi Rusi k Rossii* (Bohdan Khmelnytsky and the Return of Southern Rus' to Russia, 1st edn in *Otechestvennye zapiski*, 1857, vols 110–13; 2nd edn in 2 vols, 1859; 3rd edn in 3 vols, 1876), *Ruina, istoricheskaia monografiia iz zhizni Malorossii 1663–1687 gg.* (The Ruin: A Historical Monograph on the Life of Little Russia from 1663 to 1687, 1st edn in *Vestnik Evropy*, nos 4–9 [1879] and nos 7–9 [1880]), and 'Mazepa i Mazepintsy' (Mazepa and the Mazepists, in *Russkaia mysl'* [1882–4]). These works are based on extensive documentary material that, as a member of the St Petersburg Archeographic Commission, Kostomarov collected in St Petersburg and Moscow archives and partly published in *Akty, otnosiashchiesia k istorii Iuzhnoi i Zapadnoi Rossii* (Documents on the History of Southern and Western Russia, 10 vols, 1861–78). He also wrote a series of books on Russian history. His historical monographs and articles were published by the Literary Fund in St Petersburg. Its last edition of his works, in eight volumes, came out in 1903–6. He was the author of *Russkaia istoriia v zhizneopisaniiakh eia vazhneishikh deiatelei* (Rus' History in the Biographies of Its Important Figures, 1874–6), which was devoted mostly to Ukrainian historical figures. This work was translated into Ukrainian and published in *Pravda* and separately under the title *Rus'ka istoriia v zhyttiepysakh ïï naiholovnishykh diiateliv* (1875–7), then republished as *Ukraïns'ka istoriia v zhyttiepysakh ïï naiznamenytnishykh diiachiv* (1918).

Kostomarov was the founder of the populist trend in Ukrainian historiography. He believed that the purpose of the historical sciences was to describe the past of human communities. In his historicophilosophical studies, such as 'Mysli o federativnom nachale v drevnei Rusi' (Reflections on the Federative Principle in Ancient Rus'), 'Dve russkie narodnosti' (Two Rus' Peoples), and 'Cherty narodnoi iuzhnorusskoi istorii' (Characteristics of Popular South-Rus' History), which were all published in *Osnova*, nos 1–3 (1861), and in his journalistic articles, such as 'Pravda moskvicham o Rusi' (The Truth about Rus' for Muscovites), 'Pravda poliakam o Rusi' (The Truth about Rus' for Poles), and his letter to the editor of *Kolokol* in 1860, as well as in his historical monographs, Kostomarov argued for the national distinctiveness of the Ukrainian people and the uniqueness of their historial development, which, unlike for the Poles and Russians, was manifested in the Ukrainian freedom-loving, democratic, and individualistic spirit.

The same ideas formed the basis of his ethnographic research. He published a series of ethnographic studies, including 'Istoricheskoe znachenie iuzhnorusskogo narodnogo pesennogo tvorchestva' (The Historical Significance of the South-Rus' Folk Song Tradition, in *Beseda*, vols 4–12 [1872]) and 'Istoriia kozachestva v pamiatkakh iuzhnorusskogo narodnogo pesennogo tvorchestva' (The History of the Cossacks in the Monuments of the South-Rus' Folk Song Tradition, in *Russkaia mysl'*, nos 1–8 [1880], nos 7–8 [1883]), and he edited vols 3, 4, and 5 of the papers of P. *Chubynsky's ethnographic and statistical expedition to Right-Bank Ukraine. Some of Kostomarov's ethnographic works were republished by M. Hrushevsky in a separate collection, *Etnohrafichni pysannia* (Ethnographic Writings, 1930).

Kostomarov's numerous journalistic articles appeared in the 1860s–1880s in such journals as *Osnova*, *Otechestvennye zapiski*, *Sovremennik*, and *Vestnik Evropy*. Some of them were collected and republished by M. Hrushevsky as *Naukovo-publitsystychni i polemichni pysannia Kostomarova* (Scholarly-Publicistic and Polemical Writings of Kostomarov, 1928).

As a writer, Kostomarov is classified as a member of the *Kharkiv Romantic School. His poetry collections, *Ukraïns'ki baliady* (Ukrainian Ballads, 1839) and *Vitka* (The Branch, 1840, both published under the pseud Iieremiia Halka), contain historical poems about the Princely era and the Khmelnytsky period (eg, 'Did pasichnyk' [The Old Beekeeper]). The language of his poetry is marked on the one hand by an extensive use of the vocabulary and phraseology of folk songs, and on the other by a striving to elevate it to the level of a literary language. His historical dramas, *Sava Chalyi* (1838) and *Pereiaslavs'ka nich* (The Pereiaslav Night, 1841), are attempts at 'high tragedy.' Lacking in dramatic qualities, however, Kostomarov's plays have left no noticeable mark on the subsequent development of the Ukrainian theater. His prose written in Russian (the novelette *Kudeiar*, 1875) or in Russian interspersed with dialogues in Ukrainian (*Chernigovka*, 1881) is even less significant than his dramas. His literary works were published in two volumes in 1967. A bibliography of his works appeared in *Kostomarov N.I.: Literaturnoe nasledie* (Kostomarov N.I.: The Literary Legacy, 1890).

BIBLIOGRAPHY

Antonovich, V. 'Kostomarov, kak istorik,' *KS*, 5 (1885)

Drahomanov, M. *Mykola Ivanovych Kostomarov* (Lviv 1901)

Hrushevs'kyi, M. 'Ukraïns'ka istoriohrafiia i Mykola Kostomarov,' *LNV*, 5 (1910)

Krypiakevych, I. 'Arkheohrafichni pratsi Kostomarova,' *ZNTSh*, vols 126–7 (1918)

Kostomarov, N. *Avtobiografiia* (Moscow 1922)

Doroshenko, D. *Mykola Ivanovych Kostomarov* (Leipzig 1924)

Hrushevs'kyi, M. 'Kostomarov i novitnia Ukraïna,' *Ukraïna*, 3 (1925)

Polukhin, L. *Formuvannia istorychnykh pohliadiv M.I. Kostomarova* (Kiev 1959)
Papazian, D. 'N.I. Kostomarov: Russian Historian, Ukrainian Nationalist, Slavic Federalist,' PH D diss, University of Michigan (1966)
Pinchuk, Iu. *Istoricheskie vzgliady N.I. Kostomarova* (Kiev 1984)
A. Zhukovsky

Kostopil [Kostopil']. III-7. City (1970 pop 17,500) and raion center in Rivne oblast, situated on the Zamchyske River in Volhynian Polisia. It was founded in the late 18th century. UNR and Bolshevik forces fought there in 1919, and Yu. Tiutiunnyk launched the Second Winter Campaign from there in October 1921. Its main industries are woodworking and lumbering. The city has a construction and a construction-materials complex. Basalt is quarried nearby in Berestovets.

Kostoprav, Heorhii (Georgii), b 9 November 1903 in Maloianysol (now Kuibysheve), Mariiupil county, Katerynoslav gubernia, d 23 July 1944? Soviet poet and translator of Greek origin. His poetry was first published in the mid-1920s in Russian. From 1931 he wrote mostly in Greek. He translated poems by T. Shevchenko, P. Tychyna, and M. Rylsky into Greek. He was arrested and disappeared during the Stalinist terror.

Kostromenko, Vadym, b 26 September 1934 in Artemivske, Staline oblast. Cameraman and film director. A graduate of the All-Union Institute of Cinematography (1957), he worked as a cameraman at the Odessa Artistic Film Studio shooting such films as *Spovid'* (Confession, 1962), *Samotnist'* (Solitude, 1964), and *Virnist'* (Fidelity, 1965). In 1971 he began to direct television films such as *Vershnyky* (The Horsemen) and feature films such as *Sto pershyi* (The Hundred and First, 1983). He is first secretary of the Odessa Branch of the Union of Cinematographers of Ukraine.

Kostruba, Petro, b 1902. Linguist; a docent at Lviv University. His annotated translation into modern Ukrainian of the epic poem *Slovo o polku Ihorevi* appeared in Lviv in 1928. After the Second World War his academic career was interrupted by arrest and imprisonment in the 1940s and 1950s. A specialist in Ukrainian phonemics and phonetics, he is the author of several articles, the monograph *Fonetyka suchasnoï ukraïns'koï literaturnoï movy* (The Phonetics of Contemporary Literary Ukrainian, 1963), and the chapters on phonemics in the collective work *Suchasna ukraïns'ka literaturna mova: Vstup, Fonetyka* (Contemporary Literary Ukrainian: Introduction, Phonetics, 1969), published by the AN URSR Institute of Linguistics. Because the editor of the latter work, I. Bilodid, distorted some of Kostruba's views in order to bring Ukrainian closer to Russian, Kostruba addressed a letter of protest to Ukrainian linguists abroad. Among his contributions are also works on modern Ukrainian syntax.

Kostruba, Teofil (monastic name: Teodosii), b 26 May 1907 in Yaholnytsia Stara, Chortkiv county, Galicia, d 3 March 1943 in Lviv. Basilian monk, historian, and journalist. Kostruba studied philosophy and theology at Lviv University (1935–9) and worked with the Commission on Ancient Ukrainian History of the Shevchenko Scientific Society. His major works focused on the early history of the church in Ukraine and the history of Galicia. His monographs included *Narysy z tserkovnoï istoriï Ukraïny X–XIII stolittia* (Essays on the Church History of Ukraine from the 10th to 13th Centuries, 1939; 2nd edn 1955), *Narys istoriï Ukraïny* (A Survey of the History of Ukraine, 1961), which provided an overview of Ukrainian history to the reign of Prince Danylo Romanovych, and *Iak Moskva nyshchyla ukraïns'ku tserkvu* (How Moscow Destroyed the Ukrainian Church, 1961). His translation of the Galician-Volhynian Chronicle into contemporary Ukrainian was published in 1936. Kostruba's articles appeared in the journals *Dzvony, Zapysky Naukovoho tovarystva im. Shevchenka,* and *Litopys Chervonoï Kalyny* and the newspapers *Khliborobs'kyi Shliakh, Nova Zoria, Novyi Chas,* and others.

Teofil Kostruba

Hryhorii Kosynka

Kostyniuk, Ronald [Kostynjuk], b 8 July 1941 in Wakaw, Saskatchewan. Sculptor and educator. Educated at the universities of Saskatchewan, Alberta, and Wisconsin, since 1971 he has taught design and sculpture at the University of Calgary. He has had over 25 solo exhibitions in Canada. Most of Kostyniuk's sculptures are large relief structures built of plexiglass with multiple colored planes arranged in a complex geometric composition. They suggest that there is an affinity between pure science and abstract art. Kostyniuk is a member of the Royal Canadian Academy of Arts.

Kostyrko, Petro, b 14 February 1897 in Lavy, Sosnytsia county, Chernihiv gubernia, d 13 February 1982 in Kiev. Architect. Upon graduating from the Kiev State Art Institute (1930), where he had studied with V. *Krychevsky and P. Aloshyn, he became a lecturer (later director) at the Kiev Civil-Engineering Institute, and in 1937 a lecturer at the Kiev State Art Institute. He reconstructed the City Soviet building in Kiev. He collaborated with V. Krychevsky in designing the first central thermoelectric station in Kiev (1931–6), the building of the Rolit writers' association, and the Kaniv Museum-Preserve (1936–8). In 1960–4 he supervised the reconstruction of the Poltava Regional Museum. Kostyrko did the architectural design for a number of monuments, such as the O. Verbytsky (1960) and Yu. Yanovsky (1961) monuments in Kiev and the P. Zaporozhets monument (1971) in Bila Tserkva.

Kosynka, Hryhorii (pseud of Hryhorii Strilets), b 29 November 1899 in Shcherbanivka, Kiev gubernia, d 17

December 1934 in Kiev. Writer. From 1920 he lived in Kiev and belonged to the writers' groups Lanka and *MARS. His first story, 'Na buriaky' (At Beet Harvest), appeared in 1919 in the paper *Borot'ba*. About 20 of his story collections appeared during his life, including *Na zolotykh bohiv* (Against the Golden Gods, 1922), *Zakvitchanyi son* (The Florid Dream, 1923), *Za vorit'my* (Behind the Gates, 1925), *Maty* (Mother, 1925), *V zhytakh* (In the Wheat Fields, 1926), *Polityka* (Politics, 1927), *Vybrani opovidannia* (Selected Stories, 1928 and 1929), and *Tsyrkul'* (The Compass, 1930). Publication of the collection 'Sertse' (The Heart, 1933) was prevented by the censors. Party critics accused Kosynka of propagating 'kulak ideology,' 'counterrevolutionary tendencies,' and 'banditry' in his stories. Publishing his stories was forbidden in the early 1930s, and he was forced to work as a scenarist. Arrested during the Stalinist terror, he and 36 others were tried on fabricated charges of terrorist activity by a military tribunal, and he and 27 others were summarily shot.

Kosynka was one of the more outstanding Soviet Ukrainian story writers of the 1920s and early 1930s. His stories captured the prevalent attitudes, relations, and political shifts among the Ukrainian peasantry during the 1917–21 period of revolutionary upheaval and war. Although Soviet criticism today views him as merely an epigone of M. Kotsiubynsky, S. Vasylchenko, and V. Stefanyk, this view is belied by an analysis of his unique style, in which examples of expressionism and experimentation, not unlike those of his contemporary M. Khvylovy, abound. Kosynka was posthumously 'rehabilitated' after Stalin's death. Selected editions of his works appeared in New York in 1955, in Kiev in 1962, 1967, and 1972, in Lviv in 1971, and (in Russian) in Moscow in 1930 and 1966. A book of memoirs about him was published in Kiev in 1969.

I. Koshelivets

Kosynov, Oleksander, b 28 July 1936 in Stavropol, Stavropol krai, RSFSR. Film director. A graduate of the All-Union Institute of Cinematography (1964), he works at the Kiev Studio of Chronicle and Documentary Films and has directed such films as *Muzhnist'* (Manliness, 1967), *Ukraïna, zemlia i liudy* (Ukraine, the Land and the People, 1968), *Poema pro Donets'kyi krai* (Poem about the Donets Land, 1974), *Dorohoiu bat'kiv* (Along the Parents' Road, 1978), and *Ptakhy letiat' nado mnoiu* (The Birds Fly above Me, 1983), a film about O. Dovzhenko.

Kryshtof Kosynsky; a medal by V. Masiutyn

Kosynsky, Kryshtof [Kosyns'kyj, Kryštof], ?–1593. Ukrainian nobleman from Podlachia, hetman of the Zaporozhian Cossacks (1586) and then of the *registered Cossacks in the early 1590s. Kosynsky was the leader of the first large-scale uprising of the Ukrainian peasantry and Cossacks against the Polish nobility, in 1591–3. He was killed in May 1593 during the siege of Cherkasy.

Kosynsky, Volodymyr [Kosyns'kyj], b 1866 in Hlukhiv county, Chernihiv gubernia, d ? Economist. A graduate of Moscow University (MA, 1901), he was a professor of economics at the Riga Polytechnical Institute, Odessa University (1905–9), the Kiev Polytechnical Institute, and the Kamianets-Podilskyi Ukrainian State University. A member of the Kiev Hromada, in 1917 he was elected to the Central Rada from the Russian Constitutional Democratic party. In November 1918 he became the third minister of labor in the Hetman government and a full member of the newly created Ukrainian Academy of Sciences and head of its Chair of Agriculture. A leading scholar of agrarian relations in the Russian Empire, his many works include *O priemakh nauchnoi razrabotki statisticheskikh dannykh* (On Methods for Processing Statistical Data, 1890), *K agrarnomu voprosu* (On the Agrarian Question, 1906), and *O merakh k razvitiiu proizvoditel'nykh sil Rossii* (On the Measures for Developing the Productive Forces of Russia, 1904). In 1913 he was attacked by V. Lenin for his criticism of the theory of rural 'proletarianization.'

Koszeliwec, Iwan. See Koshelivets, Ivan.

Kot, Stanisław, b 22 October 1885 in Ruda, near Ropczyce, Poland, d 26 December 1975 in London. Polish historian, politician, and diplomat. Kot was a professor at Cracow University from 1920, a member of the Polish Academy of Sciences from 1921, and a full member of the Shevchenko Scientific Society from 1952. During the Second World War he worked with the Polish government-in-exile in London and as its ambassador to the USSR. In 1947 he moved permanently to London. He was a specialist in the history of culture, education, and intellectual thought, particularly during the Reformation. His works, such as *Z dziejów kultury humanizmu w Polsce* (From the History of the Culture of Humanism in Poland, 1920), *Historia wychowania* (The History of Education, 2 vols, 1934), and especially *Georges Niemirycz et la lutte contre l'intolérance au XVII siècle* (1960), contain much material on Ukraine and Belorussia.

Kotarbiński, Wilhelm, b 30 November 1849 in Nieborów, Łowicz county, Warsaw gubernia, d 4 September 1921 in Kiev. Polish painter of Ukrainian origin; from 1905 full member of the St Petersburg Academy of Arts. A graduate of the Warsaw Art School (1871), St Luke's Academy in Rome (1875), and the St Petersburg Academy of Arts (1882), he worked many years in Kiev and was a founding member of the Society of Kiev Artists (1893). Collaborating with A. and P. Svedomsky, he painted St Volodymyr's Cathedral in Kiev (1885–96), including such murals as *The Last Supper, The Entry into Jerusalem, Ascension,* and *Judgment of Pilate*. He also painted the ceilings of M. Tereshchenko's and B. Khanenko's residences in Kiev. Many of his canvases deal with mythological themes and are highly symbolic; eg, *Prometheus and Vulcan* (1881), *Roman Orgy, The Battle of the Centaurs and Amazons,* and *Sacrifice to Nilus*. He also illustrated the Bible.

Kotelnia [Kotel'nja]. A fortified Rus' city and capital of an appanage principality in Kiev principality. It was first mentioned in the chronicles as Kotelnych under the year 1143; it was also called Kotelnytsia in that period. Until the 1930s Kotelnia was a small town. It is now the village of Stara Kotelnia in Andrushivka raion, Zhytomyr oblast. The ruins of medieval fortifications remain there.

Kotelnykov, Oleksander [Kotel'nykov], b 18 March 1877 in Nizhnii Novgorod (now Gorkii), Russia, d 23 January 1964 in Kiev. Electrical engineer; corresponding member of the AN URSR from 1939. Kotelnykov studied and taught (1913–31) at the Kiev Polytechnical Institute. Then he worked at the Odessa Institute of Communications Engineers and, starting in 1938, at various institutes in Kiev: the Institute of the Food Industry, the Institute of Power Engineering, and the Institute of Electrotechnology. His main publications deal with the technology of weak currents, electrodynamics, and the theory of long transmission lines.

Kotelva [Kotel'va]. III-15. Town smt (1979 pop 12,000) and raion center in Poltava oblast. It was founded in the late 16th century and was a company town in Poltava (1654–62), Zinkiv (1662–72), and Hadiache (1648–9, 1672–1724) regiments. In 1724 it became the only Cossack company town ever transferred from the jurisdiction of the Hetmanate to the government of Slobidska Ukraine (as a company town in Okhtyrka regiment). Until the early 1930s Kotelva was one of the largest villages (pop ca 20,000) in Ukraine and had a well-developed cottage industry (primarily weaving). The Holy Trinity Church (built in 1812) is its chief architectural monument.

Kotian (Sutoiovych), b and d ? Khan of the *Cumans, father-in-law and ally of *Mstyslav Mstyslavych. Kotian is mentioned in the chronicles under the years 1202, 1225, and 1228, when he participated in the internecine power struggles between the princes of Rus'. After the defeat of the Cumans by the Mongols in 1222, Kotian left the Dnieper region and sought the aid of the princes of Rus'. They were all defeated, however, by the Mongols at the Battle of *Kalka River in 1223. In 1238 Kotian was again defeated by Khan *Batu on the Astrakhan steppes. He settled with the remainder of the Cumans in Hungary, under the protection of the Hungarian king.

Kotko, Dmytro, b 17 January 1892 in Balky, Melitopil county, Tavriia gubernia, d 18 November 1982 in Lviv.

Dmytro Kotko

Choir conductor. Having studied conducting in Moscow, he emigrated to Galicia after the First World War and organized the Ukrainian Choir, a male choir consisting of former UNR Army soldiers. Reorganized in 1925 into a mixed choir, it toured Western Ukraine and the major cities of Poland and Germany a number of times. Everywhere it received enthusiastic reviews, and Kotko's conducting was praised highly. Some of the performances were recorded. Much of the music sung by the Ukrainian Choir was arranged by Kotko himself.

Kotko, Kost. See Liubchenko, Mykola.

Ivan Kotliarevsky

Kotliarevsky, Ivan [Kotljarevs'kyj], b 9 September 1769 in Poltava, d 10 November 1838 in Poltava. Poet and playwright; the 'founder' of modern Ukrainian literature. After studying at the Poltava Theological Seminary (1780–9), he worked as a tutor at rural gentry estates, where he became acquainted with folk life and the peasant vernacular, and then served in the Russian army (1796–1808). In 1810 he became the trustee of an institution for the education of children of impoverished nobles. In 1812 he organized a Cossack cavalry regiment to fight Napoleon and served in it as a major. He helped stage theatrical productions at the Poltava governor-general's residence and was the artistic director of the Poltava Theater (1812–21). From 1827 to 1835 he directed several philanthropic agencies.

Kotliarevsky's greatest literary work is his travesty of Virgil's *Aeneid, Eneïda,* which he began writing in 1794. Publication of its first three parts in St Petersburg in 1798 was funded by M. Parpura. Part four appeared in 1809. Kotliarevsky finished parts five and six around 1820, but the first full edition of the work (with a glossary) was published only after his death, in Kharkiv in 1842. *Eneïda* was written in the tradition of several existing parodies of Virgil's epic, including those by P. Scarron, A. Blumauer, and N. Osipov and A. Kotelnitsky. Although the Osipov-Kotelnitsky travesty served as a model for Kotliarevsky's mock-heroic poem, the latter is, unlike the former, a completely original work and much better from an artistic point of view. In addition to the innovation of writing it in the Ukrainian vernacular, Kotliarevsky used a new verse form – a 10-line strophe of four-foot iambs with regular rhymes – instead of the then-popular syllabic verse.

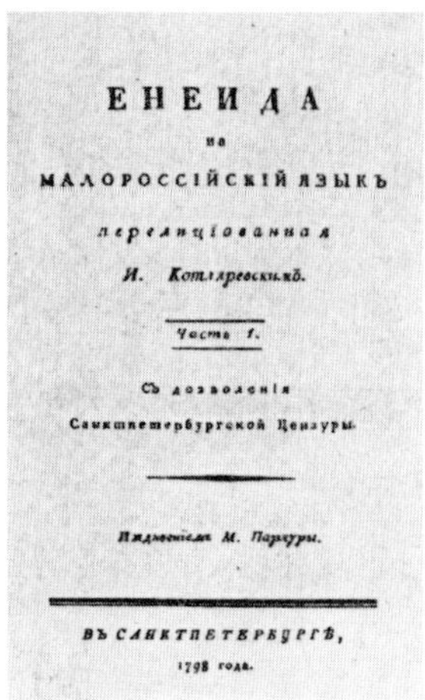
ЕНЕИДА
на
МАЛОРОССІЙСКІЙ ЯЗЫКЪ
перелицїованная
И. Котляревскимъ.
Часть I.
Съ дозволенія
Санктпетербургской Цензуры.
Иждивеніемъ М. Парпуры.
ВЪ САНКТПЕТЕРБУРГѢ,
1798 года.

Title page of the first edition of *Eneïda*

Eneïda was written at a time when popular memory of the Cossack Hetmanate was still alive and the oppression of tsarist serfdom in Ukraine was at its height. Kotliarevsky's broad satire of the mores of the social estates during these two distinct ages, combined with the in-vogue use of ethnographic detail and with racy, colorful, colloquial Ukrainian, ensured his work's great popularity among his comtemporaries. It spawned several imitations (by P. Hulak-Artemovsky, K. Dumytrashko, P. Biletsky-Nosenko, and others) and began the process by which the Ukrainian vernacular acquired the status of a literary language, thereby supplanting the use of older, bookish linguistic forms.

Kotliarevsky's operetta *Natalka Poltavka* (Natalka from Poltava) and vaudeville *Moskal'-charivnyk* (The Muscovite-Sorcerer) were landmarks in the development of Ukrainian theater. Written ca 1819, they were first published in vols 1 (1838) and 2 (1841) of the almanac *Ukrainskii sbornik* edited by I. Sreznevsky. Both were written for and performed at the Poltava Theater; both, particularly the first, were responses to the caricatures of Ukrainian life in Prince A. Shakhovskoi's comedy *Kazak-stikhotvorets* (The Cossack Poetaster), which was also staged at the Poltava Theater. As a playwright, Kotliarevsky combined the **intermede* tradition with his knowledge of Ukrainian folkways and folklore.

Kotliarevsky's influence is evident not only in the works of his immediate successors (H. Kvitka-Osnovianenko, T. Shevchenko, Ya. Kukharenko, K. Topolia, S. Pysarevsky, and others), but also in the ethnographic plays of the second half of the 19th century and in Russian (the works of the ethnic Ukrainians N. Gogol and V. Narezhny) and Belorussian (the anonymous *Eneida navyvarat* [The Aeneid Travestied]) literature. In his use of genres and poetics he was more a Baroque-influenced Classicist than an incipient Romantic. His view of the world was guided by moral rather than by sociopolitical criteria, and his sympathy for the socially and nationally oppressed Ukrainian peasantry was subordinated to his loyalty to tsarist autocracy. Full editions of his works appeared in Kiev in 1952–3 and 1969. The Kotliarevsky Literary-Memorial Museum was opened in Poltava in 1952.

BIBLIOGRAPHY
Zhitetskii, P. *'Eneida' Kotliarevskogo i drevneishii spisok ee v sviazi s obzorom malorusskoi literatury XVIII v.* (Kiev 1900)
Zerov, M. *Nove ukraïns'ke pys'menstvo* (Kiev 1924; Munich 1960)
Aizenshtok, Ia. *I. Kotliarevs'kyi i ukraïns'ka literatura* (Kiev 1928)
Zalashko, A. (ed). *I.P. Kotliarevs'kyi u krytytsi ta dokumentakh* (Kiev 1959)
Ivan Kotliarevs'kyi u dokumentakh, spohadakh, doslidzhenniakh (Kiev 1969)
Kyryliuk, Ie. *Zhyvi tradytsiï: Ivan Kotliarevs'kyi ta ukraïns'ka literatura* (Kiev 1969)
Moroz, M. *Ivan Kotliarevs'kyi: Bibliohrafichnyi pokazhchyk* (Kiev 1969)
Čyževs'kyj, D. *A History of Ukrainian Literature (From the 11th to the End of the 19th Century)* (Littleton, Colo 1975)
Sverstiuk, Ie. 'Ivan Kotliarevs'kyi Is Laughing,' in his *Clandestine Essays*, trans and ed G.S.N. Luckyj (Cambridge, Mass 1976)
Iatsenko, M. *Na rubezhi literaturnykh epokh: 'Eneïda' Kotliarevs'koho i khudozhnii prohres v ukraïns'kii literaturi* (Kiev 1977)

P. Petrenko

Kotliarevsky, Oleksander [Kotljarevs'kyj], b 1837 in Kriukiv (now part of Kremenchuk), Kremenchuk county, Poltava gubernia, d 11 October 1881 in Pisa, Italy. Philologist, archeologist, and ethnographer; corresponding member of the Imperial Academy of Sciences from 1875. A graduate of Moscow and St Petersburg (PH D 1874) universities, he was a professor at Dorpat (Tartu) University (1868–72) and at Kiev University (1875–81). He was a founding member and head of the Historical Society of Nestor the Chronicler at Kiev University. Kotliarevsky wrote over 100 scholarly bibliographies, articles, and monographs, including *O pogrebal'nykh obychaiakh iazycheskykh Slavian* (On the Burial Rites of Pagan Slavs, 1868). As a student he wrote Ukrainian literary criticism under the pseudonym Skubent Chupryna.

Kotliarevsky Museum (Muzei I.P. Kotliarevskoho). Literary memorial museum in Poltava dedicated to I. *Kotliarevsky. It was opened in 1952. The exhibits, which are arranged in six rooms, consist of manuscripts, books, photographs, paintings, and the writer's personal belongings. The exhibits that relate to his work *Eneida* (The Aeneid) are located in a separate room.

Kotliarevsky Theater. See Tobilevych Ukrainian People's Theater and Zahrava Young Ukrainian Theater.

Kotorovych, Bohodar [Kotorovyč], b 3 July 1941 in Hrubeshiv, Kholm region (now in Poland). Violinist. Upon graduating from the Moscow Conservatory in 1966, he was appointed concertmaster of the Symphony Orchestra of the Ukrainian SSR and soloist of the Kiev Philharmonic Orchestra. Since 1967 he has lectured at the Kiev Conservatory. He has won a number of international violin competitions; eg, in Bucharest (1967) and in Genoa (1971).

Kotov, Mykhailo, b 9 November 1895 in Zadonsk, Voronezh gubernia, d 25 August 1978 in Kiev. Botanist. A graduate of the Kharkiv Institute of People's Education (1922), he worked in various scientific institutions in Kharkiv before joining the staff of the AN URSR Institute of Botany in 1939. As a taxonomist specializing in Ukrainian flora, he described 36 new species and edited as well as coauthored vols 3, 4, and 8 of *Flora URSR* (Flora of the Ukrainian SSR, 12 vols, 1936–65). He was active in the conservation movement.

Kotovske [Kotovs'ke]. VI-10. City (1970 pop 37,100) and raion center under oblast jurisdiction in Odessa oblast. It was founded in the mid-18th century and until 1935 was called Birzula. The UNR Army fought several battles against Bolshevik forces there in 1919. On 2 September 1919 Ukrainian troops led by generals P. Yeroshevych and O. Udovychenko routed the Bolsheviks and captured 3,000 prisoners. In that period Otaman Zabolotny's Ukrainian partisans and G. Kotovsky's Bolshevik partisans also operated in the region. Kotovske is an important railroad and highway junction.

Kotovsky, Hryhorii [Kotovs'kyj, Hryhorij], b 24 June 1881 in Hancheshti, Bessarabia gubernia, d 6 August 1925 in Chebanka near Odessa. Soviet military commander. In 1918–19, he commanded a partisan unit that fought in southern Ukraine against UNR and Denikin forces. Then, as commander of the Second Red Cavalry Brigade and of the Seventeenth Red Cavalry Division, he continually fought UNR troops and insurgents. From 17 November 1921 Kotovsky commanded the Third Cavalry Brigade, which slaughtered near *Bazar the surviving participants of the Second Winter Campaign. In 1922 he took command of the Second Red Cavalry Corps. Kotovsky was one of the leading founders of the Moldavian ASSR. He was murdered by a former subordinate.

Kotsak, Arsenii [Kocak, Arsenij], b 14 March 1737 in Bukovets, Prešov region, d 12 April 1800 in Mukachiv. Priest of the Basilian monastic order, writer, and pedagogue. After obtaining the degree of doctor of theology at Trnava University, he taught languages, history, and theology at monastery schools in Transcarpathia. He compiled a grammar of the Slavonic-Ruthenian language, *Hrammatyka russkaia ...* (1788), based on M. Smotrytsky's well-known grammar and the local dialect. Kotsak also composed poetry. His works were never printed, but have been preserved in manuscript form.

Kotsevalov, Andrii [Kocevalov, Andrij], b 22 October 1892 in Kharkiv, d 26 February 1960 in New York. Classical philologist. A graduate of Kharkiv University, he was a research associate at several academic institutions in Kharkiv and at the AN URSR Institute of Archeology (1935–41) and professor at Kharkiv University (1937–41). He emigrated from Ukraine in 1943 and, after teaching at the Ukrainian Free University in Munich, moved to New York in 1952. A specialist in the history of Greek grammar and in ancient Greek inscriptions on the Black Sea coast, he is the author of several works, most notably *Syntaxis inscriptionum antiquarum coloniarum Graecarum orae septenrionalis Ponti Euxini* (1935).

Kotsiuba, Hordii [Kocjuba, Hordij], b 14 January 1892 in Kostiv, Kharkiv gubernia, d 22 March 1939? Writer. A graduate in law from Petrograd University in 1917 and a member of the Borotbist party during the revolutionary period, he first published in 1919. In 1921 he cofounded and edited the journal *Shliakhy mystetstva*. In the 1920s he belonged to the writers' groups *Hart and *Vaplite. In 1934 he was elected to the executive of the new Writers' Union of Ukraine. Between 1924 and 1934, 18 of his story collections appeared, including *Sviato na budniakh* (A Celebration during Workdays, 1927), *Zmova masok* (Conspiracy of the Masks, 1929), *Dniprovi sagy* (Dnieper Sagas, 1931), *Na terezakh* (On the Scales, 1931), and *Bronzovi liudy* (Bronze People, 1931). He also wrote the novels *Novi berehy* (New Shores, 2 vols, 1932, 1937), *Rodiuchist'* (Fertility, 1934), and *Pered hrozoiu* (Before the Storm, 1938). He was arrested during the Yezhov terror and most likely shot. He was posthumously 'rehabilitated' in 1956, and his novels *Pered hrozoiu* (1958) and *Novi berehy* (1959) were reprinted.

Kotsiuba, Mykhailo [Kocjuba, Myxajlo], b 20 October 1855 in Verchany, Stryi county, Galicia, d 1 December 1931 in Lviv. Educator; organizer of agricultural schooling. After studying zoology at the University of Vienna and agronomy at the Farming Academy in Dubliany and the Higher School of Agriculture in Vienna, he received a PH D (1885) and an MD (1893) from Cracow University. While serving as a senior lecturer in agricultural studies at the state college for men teachers in Stanyslaviv (1893–1902), Kotsiuba was active in the cultural and economic life of the Ukrainian community: he presided over the Ukrainska Besida society and the local Prosvita branch (1895–1902) and founded the Narodnyi Dim credit association and a pork marketing union. He founded and directed (1903–9) in Lviv a teacher's college for women within the private system run by the Ukrainian Pedagogical Society. He served on the Board of Directors of the Silskyi Hospodar society and in the supreme executive of the Prosvita society for many years. In 1904 he edited the monthly *Ekonomist*. In 1910 the Provincial School Board appointed him inspector of agricultural studies in the public schools and teachers' colleges. After the war he was in charge of the board's hygienic and medical program in primary and secondary schools and served on the Auditing Council of the Provincial Union of Farming and Trading Associations (from 1924 Tsentrosoiuz).

Kotsiubynska, Nataliia [Kocjubyns'ka, Natalija], 1890–1939. Art historian and ethnographer. She wrote a number of studies in the history of Ukrainian art, including 'Pelikan v ukraïns'komu mystetstvi' (The Pelican in Ukrainian Art, *ZIFV*, no. 9 [1926]) and 'Reshtky zamkovykh budov u Khmil'nyku na Podilli' (Remnants of Castle Structures in the Town of Khmilnyk in Podilia, *Khronika arkheolohiï ta mystetstva*, no. 3 [1931]). She was arrested by the secret police in 1937 and died in a labor camp.

Kotsiubynsky, Florian [Kocjubyns'kyj], b 24 February 1921 in Kazan, RSFSR. Sculptor. A graduate of the Kiev State Art Institute (1952) and a student of M. Lysenko, he has specialized in portraits and monuments. He has done busts of V. Maiakovsky (1957), Yu. Kotsiubynsky (1963–5), T. Shevchenko (1964), and V. Poryk. His monuments include S. Kovpak's gravestone in Kiev (1968), *Glory* in Kalush (1970), and the bust of Yu. Kotsiubynsky in Chernihiv (in collaboration with K. Kuznetsov, 1970).

Kotsiubynsky, Mykhailo [Kocjubyns'kyj, Myxajlo] (pseud: Zakhar Kozub), b 17 September 1864 in Vinnytsia, d 25 April 1913 in Kiev. One of the finest Ukrainian writers of the late 19th and early 20th centuries. As a child he lived in Vinnytsia, Bar, and elsewhere in Podilia. After graduating from the Sharhorod Religious Boarding School in 1880, he continued his studies at the Kamianets-Podilskyi Theological Seminary. Expelled from the school in 1882 for his Populist involvement, he remained

Mykhailo Kotsiubynsky

under police surveillance for the rest of his life. After his father lost his government job and his mother went blind, he supported his family by working as a private tutor in and near Vinnytsia. A self-taught intellectual, as a young man he was influenced by the works of T. Shevchenko, Marko Vovchok, F. Dostoevsky, H. Heine, E. Zola, V. Hugo, and G. de Maupassant. His reading of the works of L. Feuerbach and C. Fourier contributed to his becoming an atheist and a socialist, and Ukrainian literature awakened in him a national consciousness and a desire to work for his people at an early age. In 1892–7 he was a member of the secret *Brotherhood of Taras. In 1888–90 he was a member of the Vinnytsia Municipal Duma. For large parts of the years 1892–7 he worked for a commission studying phylloxera in Bessarabia and the Crimea. In 1898 he moved to Chernihiv and worked there as a zemstvo statistician. He was active in the Chernihiv Gubernia Scholarly Archival Commission and headed the Chernihiv Prosvita society in 1906–8.

Kotsiubynsky first visited Galicia in 1890 and became acquainted with many Ukrainian cultural figures there, including I. Franko and V. Hnatiuk. He maintained contact with many Galician intellectuals and editors of journals, who published his stories beginning in 1890. In 1905 he traveled to Germany, Austria, Italy, Switzerland, and southern France. Suffering from heart disease, he rested on the Isle of Capri in the years 1909–11. He visited Greece in 1910 and stayed in the Carpathian village of Kryvorivnia in 1910 and 1912. His exhausting job and community involvement made it difficult for Kotsiubynsky to write and contributed to his early demise from heart disease. It was not until 1911 that the Ukrainian Society for the Support of Literature, Science, and Art granted Kotsiubynsky a pension enabling him to quit his job, but he was already in poor health and died two years later.

About two dozen books of his prose were published during his lifetime, ranging from individual stories to the large collections *V putakh shaitana i inshi opovidannia* (In Satan's Clutches and Other Stories, 1899), *Po-liuds'-komu: Opovidannia z bessarabs'koho zhyttia* (In a Civilized Way: Stories from Bessarabian Life, 1900), *Opovidannia* (Stories, 1903), *Poiedynok i inshi opovidannia* (The Duel and Other Stories, 1903), *U hrishnyi svit* (Into the Sinful World, 1905), *Z hlybyn* (From the Depths, 1909), *Debiut* (Debut, 1911), and *Tini zabutykh predkiv* (Shadows of Forgotten Ancestors, 1913). A three-volume Russian edition of his works, translated by M. Mohyliansky, appeared in 1911–14. Many of his stories were translated into several European languages during his lifetime.

Kotsiubynsky's early stories – 'Andrii Soloveiko' (1884), '21 hrudnia, na Vvedeniie' (The 21st of December on the Day of the Presentation at the Temple, 1885), 'Na viru' (A Common-Law Marriage, 1891), 'P''iatyzlotnyk' (The Five Zloty Coin, 1892), 'Tsipov'iaz' (The Flail Maker, 1893), 'Kho' (1894), 'Dlia zahal'noho dobra' (For the Common Good, 1895), and others – are examples of ethnographic realism and show the influence of I. *Nechui-Levytsky and Populist ideas. In the late 1890s, however, his themes and subjects became more varied and his approach more sophisticated, and he evolved into one of the most talented Ukrainian modernist writers. Lyrical impressionism was already apparent in his *V putakh shaitana*, and his 'exotic études' 'Na kameni' (On the Rock, 1902) and 'Pid minaretamy' (Under the Minarets, 1904) are masterpieces of that style.

Kotsiubynsky's morally healthy estheticism and abiding interest in internal, spiritual states are reflected in 'Lialechka' (The Little Doll, 1901), an ironic depiction of an intellectual disillusioned with the passions of his youth; in 'Tsvit iabluni' (The Apple Blossom, 1902), a story about the divided psyche of a writer watching his young daughter die and recording his observations for use in a future work; and in 'Son' (The Dream, 1904), a story about a man's escape from the oppressiveness of everyday life into dreams. Subtle psychological realism is also characteristic of the works Kotsiubynsky wrote after the Revolution of 1905. These stories are his most original contributions on another recurring theme: tsarist national and social oppression in Ukraine. They include 'Vin ide!' (He Is Coming! 1906), 'Smikh' (Laughter, 1906), 'Persona grata' (1907), 'Podarunok na imenyny' (The Name-Day Gift, 1912), and the artistically powerful unfinished novella *Fata morgana* (1903–10; English trans, 1976).

Kotsiubynsky's most artistic works are 'Intermezzo' (1908), in which he depicted, using a combination of naturalism and impressionism, the healing powers of nature for a neurasthenic author, reminding him of his duty to his people; and *Tini zabutykh predkiv* (1911; English trans, 1981), a psychological novella about Hutsul life that draws widely on pagan demonology and folk legends. His masterfully written, linguistically sophisticated works had a great influence on early-20th-century Ukrainian prose writers and poets (eg, P. *Tychyna). His works have been republished many times. The fullest editions appeared in 1929–30 (5 vols), 1961–2 (6 vols), and 1973–5 (7 vols). Since the 1930s Soviet criticism has promoted a simplistic interpretation of Kotsiubynsky as merely a 'realist' and a 'revolutionary democrat' and has emphasized his friendship with M. Gorky. Several Soviet films have been based on his works: *Koni ne vynni* (Horses Aren't to Blame, 1956), *Kryvavyi svitanok* (Bloody Dawn, 1956), *Pe-kopt'or* (1957), *Dorohoiu tsinoiu* (At a High Price, 1957), and the acclaimed *Tini zabutykh predkiv* (1967). Literary-memorial museums were opened in Vinnytsia in 1927 in the building where Kotsiubynsky was born, and in Chernihiv in 1934 in the building he lived in.

BIBLIOGRAPHY

Kotsiubyns'kyi, M. *Lysty do Volodymyra Hnatiuka*, ed with an intro by V. Hnatiuk (Lviv 1914)

Fedun, F. (ed). *Mykhailo Kotsiubyns'kyi (do 75-richchia z dnia*

narodzhennia): Zbirnyk materiialiv, stattei, virshiv ta narysiv (Vinnytsia 1939)
Kotsiubyns'kyi, Kh. (ed). *Do 75-richchia z dnia narodzhennia M.M. Kotsiubyns'koho*, 2 vols (Chernihiv 1940–1)
Vozniak, M. *Do zv'iazkiv M.M. Kotsiubyns'koho z Halychynoiu* (Lviv 1941)
Kotsiubyns'ka-Iefimenko, Z. *Mykhailo Kotsiubyns'kyi: Zhyttia i tvorchist'* (Kiev 1955)
Moroz, M. *Mykhailo Kotsiubyns'kyi: Bibliohrafichnyi pokazhchyk* (Kiev 1964)
Kup'ians'kyi, I. *Litopys zhyttia i tvorchosti Mykhaila Kotsiubyns'koho* (Kiev 1965)
Kalenychenko, N. *Velykyi sontsepoklonnyk: Zhyttia i tvorchist' Mykhaila Kotsiubyns'koho* (Kiev 1967)
Kostenko, M. *Khudozhnia maisternist' Mykhaila Kotsiubyns'koho* (Kiev 1969)
Wiśniewska, E. *O sztuce pisarskiej Mychajla Kociubyńskiego* (Wrocław 1973)
Chernenko, O. *Mykhailo Kotsiubyns'kyi – impresionist: Obraz liudyny v tvorchosti pys'mennyka* ([Munich] 1977)
Rubchak, B. 'The Music of Satan and the Bedeviled World: An Essay on Mykhailo Kotsiubynsky,' in M. Kotsiubynsky, *Shadows of Forgotten Ancestors*, trans M. Carynnyk (Littleton, Colo 1981)

I. Koshelivets, R. Senkus

Yurii Kotsiubynsky

Kotsiubynsky, Yurii [Kocjubyns'kyj, Jurij], b 7 December 1896 in Vinnytsia, d 8 March 1937. Soviet political figure; the son of M. *Kotsiubynsky. He joined the Bolshevik party in 1914. In 1917 he was a member of the Petrograd Military Revolutionary Committee; he became secretary for military affairs in the first Soviet Ukrainian government (1917–18) and the commander of the Bolshevik army in Ukraine (1918). A diplomat from 1920, he represented Soviet Ukraine in Austria (1921–2) and was consul there and in Poland (1927–30). He was deputy chairman (1930–4) and chairman (1934–6) of the State Planning Commission, and a member of the All-Ukrainian Central Executive Committee. He was arrested in April 1936 and shot without trial for being a 'leader of a Ukrainian Trotskyist Center.' He was rehabilitated posthumously in the 1960s. Two biographies of him, by A. Yaroshenko (1977) and I. Tsiupa (1966), were published in Kiev.

Kotska, Andrii [Kocka, Andrij], b 23 May 1911 in Uzhhorod, Transcarpathia. Painter. Having studied with A. *Erdeli in Uzhhorod (1927–31) and with F. Ferrazzi at the Rome Academy of Fine Arts (1940–2), Kotska specializes in portraits and landscapes, and deals mostly with the Hutsuls and the Hutsul region: eg, *Hutsul Girl* (1949), *Highland Girl* (1956), *The Milkmaid Odotia Polianska* (1966), *Autumn* (1954), *Reservoir at the Foot of Hoverlia* (1957), and *Early Spring* (1969). His style shows an inclination towards expressionism. An album of his work was published in Kiev in 1973.

Andrii Kotska: *Hutsuls* (oil, 1972)

Adam Kotsko

Kotsko, Adam [Kocko], b 24 December 1882 in Sholomyia, Bibrka county, Galicia, d 1 July 1910 in Lviv. Student activist. He was a member of the clandestine Committee of Ukrainian Youth (KUM), which spearheaded the campaign for a Ukrainian university in Lviv. Killed in a clash with Polish students at the university, he is remembered as a martyr by generations of Ukrainian students.

Kotsylovsky, Yosafat [Kocylovs'kyj, Josafat] (secular name: Yosyf), b 3 March 1876 in Pakoshivka, Sianik county, Galicia, d 17 November 1947. Uniate bishop. He studied at the Pontifical Urban University in Rome (PH D 1903, D TH 1907). After ordination (1907), he was a professor of theology and prorector of the seminary in Stanyslaviv

Bishop Yosafat Kotsylovsky

(Ivano-Frankivske). He entered the Basilian order (1911) and taught theology in the Lavriv monastery before serving as rector of the evacuated Ukrainian seminary in Moravia (1914–16). In 1917 Kotsylovsky was appointed bishop of Peremyshl. He established several eparchial clerical organizations and funded the weekly *Ukraïns'kyi Beskyd*. In 1921 he revived the Peremyshl Seminary as a complete seminary (from 1845 it had only offered one year of study). In 1945 he was arrested by Polish authorities and handed over to the Soviets; released briefly, he was rearrested in 1946 and sent to a Siberian concentration camp, where he died.

Kottmeier, Elisabeth, b 31 July 1902, d 11 January 1983. German writer and translator; the wife of I. *Kostetsky. She was a coeditor of the irregular journal *Ukraïna i svit* (Hannover, 1946–69) and translated Ukrainian literature into German: V. Barka's *Troiandnyi roman* (*Trojandenroman*, 1956), the poetry anthology *Weinstock der Wiedergeburt: Moderne ukrainische Lyrik* (1957), and a selection of Lesia Ukrainka's works, *Auf dem Blutacker*. She and her husband cotranslated an anthology of old Ukrainian literature (*Aus dem Alten Russland*, 1968) and O. Honchar's novel *Sobor* (The Cathedral, under the title *Der Dom von Satschipljanka*, 1970).

Kouzan, Marian [Kuzan, Marijan], b 29 September 1925 in Isai, Turka county, Galicia. Composer and conductor. Arriving in France at the age of two, he studied violin under O. Messiaen at the Paris Conservatory and then turned to conducting and composing. In 1966 he organized and conducted the Alpha-Omega Orchestra of Paris; later he became music director of the Compagnie Luxembourgeoise de Télédiffusion. He specializes in conducting medieval and Renaissance music. Kouzan's development as a composer was influenced by Ukrainian folk music and such masters as E. Varèse, A. Schoenberg, and B. Bartók. His compositions, which are written mostly in the modern idiom, include orchestral and other instrumental music, vocal music, and incidental music for films. In 1984 Kouzan's cantata *L'amour de l'homme* was performed in Chartres Cathedral.

Kovach, Fedir [Kovač], b 7 March 1931 in Humenský Rokytov in the Prešov region of eastern Slovakia. Literary scholar and community figure. A graduate of Kiev University (1958), he worked in the Ukrainian department of the Slovak Pedagogical Publishing House. He has taught Ukrainian literature at Prešov University since 1969 and headed the Cultural Association of Ukrainian Workers in Czechoslovakia since 1979. From 1972 to 1986 he was the editor in chief of the journal *Duklia*. He has also been a deputy in the Slovak National Council. He has written many articles on Ukrainian literature in the Prešov region, two books about the 19th-century Transcarpathian poet O. Pavlovych (1969 and [in Russian] 1970), and the collection of literary criticism *Slovo pro poeziiu ta poetiv* (A Word about Poetry and Poets, 1978). He has also translated Ukrainian works into Czech and Slovak and edited several books and anthologies.

Kovach, Mykhailo (Mihajlo) [Kovač, Myxajlo], b 2 October 1909 in Šid in the Srem region of Yugoslavia. Writer, ethnographer, and pedagogue. Since 1927 he has published in Srem-Bačka periodicals, including *Ruski novini* (1921–41), *Nasha Zahradka* (1937–41), *Pionirska Zahradka* (since 1947), and *Švetlošc* (since 1952). He writes in the *Bačka dialect (Rusyn). Seven of his plays (1939–71), the poetry collection *Moi shvet* (My World, 1964), three collections of stories for children (1971–81), a collection of poetry for children (1979), the novel *Hrits Bandurik* (1972), and the novella *Tsehliarnia* (The Brickyard, 1982) have been published separately. He has also prepared school textbooks and collected folk songs and melodies.

Koval, Alla [Koval'], b ? Linguist. Associated with Kiev University, Koval specializes in prescriptive linguistics for the general reader. Since 1960 she has published several manuals of 'practical stylistics,' including *Praktychna stylistyka suchasnoï ukraïns'koï movy* (Practical Stylistics of the Contemporary Ukainian Language, 2nd edn, 1978). These large-edition works are slanted towards bringing Ukrainian as close to Russian as possible.

Koval, Volodymyr [Koval'], b 14 February 1885 in Kulchyny, Starokostiantyniv county, Volhynia gubernia, d 21 March 1927 in Prague. Co-operative leader and agronomist. He graduated from the Kiev Polytechnical Institute (1912) and then worked in St Petersburg and Kiev, where he served on the executive of the Society of Western Zemstvos, popularizing the use of agricultural machines and teaching modern farming techniques. During the struggle for Ukrainian independence he was a member of the Central Rada and president of the *Tsentral union of agricultural co-operatives. In 1920 he became a professor at the Kiev Polytechnical Institute and the Kiev Commercial Institute. In 1921 he immigrated to Germany, and in 1924 to Czechoslovakia. Koval was the author of over 30 works on agriculture.

Kovalenko, Anatolii, b 16 January 1905 in Kiev, d 19 September 1973 in Kiev. Specialist in mechanics; full member of the AN URSR from 1961. A graduate of the Kiev Polytechnical Institute, he taught there from 1935 to 1949 and then at Kiev University. From 1936 he also worked at the AN URSR Institute of Structural Mechanics (later the Institute of Mechanics), serving as director from 1959 to 1965. He founded a branch of thermomechanics, and published important works on the theory of thermoelasticity and thermal stress and the theoretical basis of turbine-blade design.

Kovalenko, Borys, b 25 November 1903 in Khotunychi, Chernihiv gubernia, d 24 August 1938? Literary critic. A member of the writers' groups *Pluh and *Hart in the early 1920s, in 1926 he was one of the founders of the Communist writers' group *Molodniak. From 1927 he was a leading spokesman of the *All-Ukrainian Association of Proletarian Writers. An orthodox Marxist, Kovalenko promoted 'proletarian realism' and was one of the fiercest critics of M. *Khvylovy and other writers, beginning with the *Literary Discussion in 1925. Many of his articles were reprinted in the collections *V borot'bi za proletars'ku literaturu* (In the Struggle for a Proletarian Literature, 1928), *Pershyi pryzov* (The First Call-up, 1928), *Proletars'ki pys'mennyky* (Proletarian Writers, 1931), and *Za mahnetobuda literatury* (For the 'Magnetostroi' of Literature, 1932). From 1931 he worked as a Stalinist publicist in Moscow. In 1934 he was elected to the executive of the new Writers' Union of Ukraine, and in 1935 he was sent to Kiev to head the Chair of Contemporary Ukrainian Literature at Kiev University and to teach at a Party institute. Although he played an important part in the Party witch-hunt to 'root out the remnants of Ukrainian nationalism,' in 1937 he himself was accused of being a Trotskyist, fascist, and a member of a fascist organization and arrested. He was most likely shot. In 1956 he was posthumously 'rehabilitated,' and a volume of his articles was published in 1962.

I. Koshelivets

Kovalenko, Hryhorii, b 24 January 1868 in Baryshivka, Poltava gubernia, d 28 October 1937? Writer, ethnographer, artist, and community figure. In the years 1896–1905 he lived in Chernihiv and helped B. *Hrinchenko publish educational literature for the masses. There he became a close friend of M. Kotsiubynsky and V. Samiilenko and a supporter of the Revolutionary Ukrainian party. He was also an active member of the Poltava Scholarly Archival Commission and published his research on the Ukrainian peasant home in its *Trudy*. He edited the journal *Ridnyi krai* in 1906 and published the journal *Zhyttia i znannia* in 1913–14. In the 1920s he traveled through the local countryside and continued his research on the peasant home.

Kovalenko's articles, poems, stories, and illustrations appeared from 1891 in many periodicals. Published separately were his story collection *Zharty zhyttia* (Life's Jokes, 1911), plays for children, his and Hrinchenko's book on I. Kotliarevsky (1898), and many educational brochures on medicine and Ukrainian writers and history. After the February 1917 Revolution he published a book about Ye. Hrebinka (1918), his comedy *Vorozhka* (The Fortuneteller, 1918), and sketches of H. Skovoroda and I. Kotliarevsky (1919). In the 1920s he contributed to several popular journals and to the Kiev daily *Proletars'ka pravda*. Arrested during the Yezhov terror, he died in prison. Many of the works he wrote in the Soviet period – novellas, plays, and the historical novel 'Iurko Sokolenko' – remain unpublished. He left behind many paintings, sketches, and photos of Ukrainian folk architecture.

R. Senkus

Kovalenko, Ihor, b 16 March 1935 in Kiev. Mathematician and cyberneticist; full member of the AN URSR since 1978. A graduate of the University of Kiev (1957), he worked at the AN URSR Institute of Mathematics (1957–61) and the Moscow Institute of Electronic Machine Building (1962–71). Since 1971 he has been the head of a department of the AN URSR Institute of Cybernetics and a professor at Kiev University. Most of his research deals with probability, queuing theory, and reliability.

Ihor Kovalenko

Liudmyla Kovalenko

Kovalenko, Leonid, b 12 March 1907 in Stupychne, Zvenynhorodka county, Kiev gubernia, d 22 June 1985 in Kamianets-Podilskyi. Historian. He was a senior research associate at the AN URSR Institute of History from 1945 to 1947 and then taught at the Zhytomyr Pedagogical Institute (1947–56), Uzhhorod University (1956–61), and the Kamianets-Podilskyi Pedagogical Institute (1961–85). He wrote over 100 works devoted to Ukrainian historiography and the history of Western Europe and Hungary, including a conspectus of lectures on 19th-century Ukrainian historiography (1964), a book on the French Revolution and political movements in Ukraine (1973), and a book on the historiography of Ukraine to the 1917 Revolution (1983).

Kovalenko, Liudmyla, b 1898 in the Azov region, d 13 June 1969 in Trenton, New Jersey. Writer, journalist, and community figure. Her short stories and translations of such French writers as E. Zola, H. de Balzac, Voltaire, and G. de Maupassant appeared from 1926 in the Soviet Ukrainian journals *Nova hromada, Chervonyi shliakh*, and *Zhyttia i revoliutsiia*. After her husband M. *Ivchenko was arrested in 1929, she did not publish prose again until she was in Lviv during the German occupation in 1943. She was an organizer of the Ukrainian Red Cross in Kiev in 1941. As a postwar refugee in Germany, she edited the women's journal *Hromadianka* (1946–9), was vice-president of the Ukrainian Women's Alliance, and belonged to the literary organization *MUR. In 1950 she immigrated to the United States, where she worked for the Voice of America, contributed to émigré periodicals, and headed the Ukrainian Orthodox Sisterhood. She was a member of the Ukrainian Academy of Arts and Sciences in the United States, the Association of Ukrainian Journalists in America, the Slovo Association of Ukrainian Writers in Exile, and International PEN. Her major works are the collection of six plays *V chasi i prostori* (In Time and Space, 1950); the science fiction novel *Rik 2245* (The Year 2245, 1958); three story collections on religious themes – *Vita nova* (1957), *Davni dni* (Olden Days, 1961), and *Dvi krasy* (Two Beauties, 1965); and the historical trilogy *Nasha ne svoia zemlia* (Our Native Land That Is Not Ours), consisting of *Stepovi obrii* (Steppe Horizons, 1964), *Prorist'* (Sprout, 1966), and *Ïï okradenu zbudyly* (Awakened in Flames, 1968).

D.H. Struk

Kovalenko, Mykhailo, ?–1919. Politically active landowner of Kostiantynohrad county, Poltava gubernia. In 1917 in the Poltava region he founded the *All-Ukrainian Union of Landowners, which opposed the confiscation of private property. On 20 October 1918 Kovalenko presented Hetman P. Skoropadsky with a memorandum from the small landholders' faction of the union demanding independence and sovereignty for Ukraine.

Kovalenko, Oleksa, b 1880 in Voronezh gubernia, d 1927. Poet. He lived in Kiev. From 1903 his poetry appeared in Ukrainian periodicals and in over 10 large prerevolutionary anthologies of Ukrainian literature, three of which he edited: *Rozvaha* (Amusement, 2 vols, 1905–6), *Ternovyi vinok* (Crown of Thorns, 1908), and *Ukraïns'ka muza* (The Ukrainian Muse, 1908). Published separately were his collections *Zolotyi zasiv* (The Golden Sowing, 1910), *Spiv solov'ia* (The Nightingale's Singing, 1911), and *Sribni rosy* (Silver Dews). He also translated foreign and Russian works into Ukrainian, including N. Gogol's *Revizor* (Inspector General) and K. Ryleev's *Voinarovskii*. In 1906 he founded the Ranok publishing house in Kiev.

Kovalenko, Oleksander, b 10 August 1875 in Romen, Poltava gubernia, d 17 October 1963 in Geneva. Engineer and political activist. While studying at the Kharkiv Technological Institute, he helped found the *Revolutionary Ukrainian party (RUP). Upon graduating he worked as a mechanical engineer on the battleship *Prince Potemkin*, and in 1905 played an important part in its uprising. He escaped abroad and did not return to Ukraine until 1917. In early 1918 Kovalenko was one of the organizers of the UNR Naval Ministry. From 1919 to 1922 he served on the UNR missions in Geneva and Paris, and after that lectured in mathematics at the Ukrainian Husbandry Academy and the Ukrainian Technical and Husbandry Institute. At the end of the Second World War he moved to Geneva. Kovalenko's publications include textbooks in mechanics and mathematics, and personal recollections.

Prokhor Kovalenko

Kovalenko, Prokhor, b 23 February 1884 in Yaroslavets, Hlukhiv county, Chernihiv gubernia, d 16 October 1963 in Kiev. Character actor and educator. Upon graduating from the Lysenko Music and Drama School (1910), he joined the Sadovsky Theater in Kiev and worked there until 1917. After a brief period at the State People's Theater in Kiev, he played with various provincial companies before committing himself permanently to the Kiev Ukrainian Drama Theater (1926–48). At the same time he lectured at the Kiev Institute of Theater Arts (1934–60). His repertoire included such roles as Zolotnytsky in B. Hrinchenko's *Stepovyi hist'* (Steppe Guest), Kramariuk in I. Tobilevych's *Zhyteis'ke more* (The Sea of Life), Tataryn in S. Vasylchenko's *V kholodku* (In the Shade), and Dobchinsky in N. Gogol's *Revizor* (Inspector General). He wrote two books of memoirs: *Nezabutnie* (The Unforgettable, 1962) and *Shliakhy na stsenu* (Paths to the Stage, 1964).

Kovalevska, Mariia [Kovalevs'ka, Marija] (née Vorontsova), b August 1849 in Katerynoslav gubernia, d 19 November 1889 in Kara, Transbaikal region. One of the most active revolutionary populists of the 1870s and wife of Mykola *Kovalevsky. From 1874 she was involved with revolutionary circles in Odessa and Kiev opposed to the tsarist government, especially the Kiev group of 'southern rebels,' who believed in encouraging peasant uprisings. In 1876 she was arrested in connection with a trial of populists, the so-called Trial of the 193, but released. In February 1879 she was rearrested in Kiev and sentenced to nearly 15 years of hard labor in Siberia, where she committed suicide.

Kovalevsky, Aleksandr [Kovalevskij], b 7 November 1840 in Shustianka, Dinabur county, Vitsebsk gubernia (now Latvia), d 9 November 1901 in St Petersburg. Russian zoologist; member of the Russian Imperial Academy of Sciences from 1890. Kovalevsky received his PH D from St Petersburg University in 1867 and was a professor at Kiev (1869–74), Odessa (1874–91), and St Petersburg (1891–4) universities. He also cofounded and directed the Sevastopil Biological Station (1892–1901), which is now named in his honor. An evolutionist, he was the founder of comparative embryology and experimental and evolutionary histology. Kovalevsky's work dealt with the embryonic growth and the physiology and anatomy of invertebrate and chordate animals. He first established the existence of a common pattern of development in all multicellular animals, providing important evidence of evolution. Kovalevsky's collected works, *Izbrannye raboty*, were published in 1951.

Kovalevsky, Ivan [Kovalevs'kyj], b 7 February 1882 in Monastyryshche, Lypovets county, Kiev gubernia, d 22 November 1955 in Ingolstadt, West Germany. Comic actor of the Sadovsky school. From 1906 to 1920 he worked as an actor and an administrator in the Sadovsky Theater in Kiev. Then he acted in the State People's Theater, the Shevchenko Kiev Ukrainian Drama Theater (1922–5), the Odessa Theater of the Revolution (1925–9), and the Zhytomyr Oblast Theater (1933–43). In 1945 he emigrated to West Germany. His repertoire included such roles as Tereshko in I. Karpenko-Kary's *Suieta* (Vanity), Omelko and Stopa in his *Martyn Borulia*, Shpak in H. Kvitka-Osnovianenko's *Shel'menko-denshchyk* (Shelmenko the Orderly), Andrii Karpovych in V. Vynnychenko's *Brekhnia* (The Lie), Shanarel in Lesia Ukrainka's *Kamianyi hospodar* (The Stone Host), Pastor Moser in F. Schiller's *Die Räuber*, the Marquise of Forlipopoli in C. Goldoni's *La locandiera*, and the cantor Havrylo in O. Korniichuk's *Bohdan Khmel'nyts'kyi*.

Maksym Kovalevsky

Kovalevsky, Maksym [Kovalevs'kyj], b 8 September 1851 in Kharkiv, d 5 April 1916 in Petrograd. Renowned historian, sociologist, ethnographer, jurist, and politician. As a law student at Kharkiv University, he was greatly influenced by D. Kachenovsky's lectures on the history of international law and state institutions. In 1877 he became a docent in European state law at Moscow University. In 1880 he received his doctorate and became a full professor. Because he promoted constitutional government and socioeconomic change in his lectures, he was forced to resign his post by the tsarist government in 1887. He went abroad and gave university lectures in Stockholm, Oxford, Paris, Brussels, and Chicago. He was one of the founders of the International Institute of Sociology and was elected its vice-president in 1895 and president in 1907. In 1901 he founded and directed the Russian Higher School of Social Sciences in Paris; many prominent figures, including M. Hrushevsky, M. Tuhan-Baranovsky, F. Vovk, P. Struve, P. Miliukov, and V. Lenin, were guest lecturers there.

In 1905 Kovalevsky returned to Russia and was appointed a professor at the St Petersburg Polytechnical Institute. At the private Psychoneurological Institute he taught the first systematic course in sociology to be offered at a post-secondary school in the Russian Empire. In 1906 he cofounded the Party of Constitutional Monarchy and Democratic Reforms and was elected to the First Russian State Duma as a representative of Kharkiv gubernia. In 1907 he was chosen as the representative of the academic curia in the State Council. From 1909 he also edited the prestigious journal *Vestnik Evropy*. In 1914 he was elected a full member of the Imperial Academy of Sciences. Kovalevsky co-operated with the Ukrainian faction in the Duma. In 1907 he became the head of the Shevchenko Philanthropic Society, which aided Ukrainian students in St Petersburg. He also headed the editorial committee of the encyclopedic *Ukrainskii narod v ego proshlom i nastoiashchem* (The Ukrainian People in Its Past and Present, 2 vols, 1914, 1916) and prepared a study of the origin of land ownership in Slobidska Ukraine for the third volume, which was never published.

As a scholar, Kovalevsky was fundamentally a Comtian positivist. His studies in comparative history and evolutionary sociology were based largely on the ethnographic approach. He wrote many internationally acclaimed studies on a vast range of subjects. In his empirical and theoretical works and formulations of a universal law of development, he took into account many factors: social and cultural forces, ethnocultural identity, language, psychology, and even biology. He generally believed in plural causation and firmly opposed K. Marx's economic determinism and views of the state.

Kovalevsky's numerous works were published in many Russian and Western journals. He wrote, in Russian, monographs on primitive law (2 vols, 1876), Russian peasant-commune land ownership (1879), the historical-comparative method in jurisprudence and means for studying the history of law (1880), law and custom in the Caucasus (2 vols, 1890), the origins of contemporary democracy (4 vols, 1895–7), economic growth in Europe to the appearance of capitalist economy (3 vols, 1898–1900; rev German edn, 7 vols, 1901–14), Russian political institutions (1902), family life in the past and present from the perspective of comparative ethnography and the history of law (2 vols, 1905), contemporary sociologists (1905), social evolution from direct to representational popular rule and from patriarchal monarchy to parliamentarism (3 vols, 1906), sociology (2 vols, 1910), and the origin of the family, clan, tribe, state, and religion (1914).

BIBLIOGRAPHY

M.M. Kovalevskii – uchenyi, gosudarstvennyi i obshchestvennyi deiatel' i grazhdanin: Sbornik statei (Petrograd 1917)

Safronov, B. *M.M. Kovalevskii kak sotsiolog* (Moscow 1960)

Vucinich, A. 'Comparative History and Sociology: M.M. Kovalevskii,' in his *Social Thought in Tsarist Russia: The Quest for a General Science of Society, 1861–1917* (Chicago and London 1976)

Kaloev, B. *M.M. Kovalevskii i ego issledovaniia gorskikh narodov Kavkaza* (Moscow 1979)

V. Markus, R. Senkus

Kovalevsky, Mykola [Kovalevs'kyj], b 1841 near Hadiache, Poltava gubernia, d 1897 in Kiev. Teacher and community leader. A graduate of Kiev University and the Higher Pedagogical Courses in St Petersburg, he taught in the Cadet School in Kiev before he was fired for political reasons and moved to Odessa, where he worked as a private tutor. A close friend of M. *Drahomanov, he taught in the *Sunday school movement (1859–60) and was a member of the Kiev and Odessa *hromadas. Kovalevsky was arrested in June 1879 and exiled to Siberia until 1882. There he became acquainted with the American G. Kennan and provided him with much information for his book *The Siberian Exile System* (2 vols, 1891). From 1882 Kovalevsky helped raise money to support Drahomanov's political and publicistic work in Geneva. He also wrote a popular history of Ukraine, published in Lviv under the pseudonym I. Markevych, and raised money for the Galician radicals. His memoirs were published in the journal *Literaturno-naukovyi vistnyk* (1901). He is buried in the Baikove cemetery in Kiev.

Kovalevsky, Mykola [Kovalevs'kyj], b 3 September 1892 in Krupe, Lublin gubernia, d 18 August 1957 in Innsbruck. Political leader, co-operative organizer, and publicist. As a student he headed the Ukrainian student hromada in Moscow (1912) and then in Kiev (1915). In 1917 he played a leading role in the Ukrainian Party of Socialist Revolutionaries and the Peasant Association, and edited the latter's daily *Narodna volia*. A member of the *Central Rada, he served in V. Vynnychenko's cabinet as minister of food supplies and in V. Holubovych's

Mykola Kovalevsky

cabinet as minister of agrarian affairs. In 1919 under the *Directory he was minister of agrarian affairs in B. Martos's and I. Mazepa's cabinets. Emigrating in 1920, he moved from Warsaw to Bucharest, and then to Innsbruck. A prolific writer, particularly on Soviet policy, he contributed to many journals, including *Literaturno-naukovyi vistnyk*, *Biuletyn Polsko-Ukraiński*, and *Sprawy Narodowościowe*. In 1940–2 he was a coeditor of *Nashe zhyttia* in Bucharest, and from 1950 an editor of the Express-Pressedienst in Innsbruck. Besides newspaper and journal articles and entries for *Entsyklopediia ukraïnoznavstva* (Encyclopedia of Ukraine), he wrote a number of monographs: *Ukraïna pid chervonym iarmom* (Ukraine under the Red Yoke, 1936), *Opozytsiini rukhy v Ukraïni i natsional'na polityka SSSR (1920–1954)* (Opposition Movements in Ukraine and the Nationality Policy of the USSR [1920–1954], 1955), and a book of memoirs, *Pry dzherelakh borot'by* (At the Sources of Struggle, 1960).

A. Zhukovsky

Kovalevsky, Oleksander [Kovalevs'kyj], 1890–? Political and civic leader, co-operative organizer, and publicist. A founder and leading member of the Ukrainian People's Republican party (est 1918), he served as UNR minister of agriculture in 1920. After the war he was active in the co-operative movement in Volhynia and was director of the Ukrainbank in Lutske. In the 1930s he edited the progovernment paper *Volyns'ke slovo*. When Soviet troops occupied Volhynia in 1939, he was arrested and disappeared.

Kovalevsky, Pavlo [Kovalevs'kyj], b 1849 in Kharkiv, d 1923 in Petrograd. Psychiatrist and psychologist. After receiving his PH D in medicine from Kharkiv University, he taught there from 1877 to 1892 and founded the first chair of psychiatry and psychology laboratory in Ukraine. In 1883–98 he published the first journal of psychiatry in the Russian Empire, *Arkhiv psikhiatrii, neirologii i sudebnoi psikhopatologii*. He was also the rector of Warsaw University (1893–7) and a professor of psychiatry at Kazan (1903–6) and St Petersburg universities. He wrote a two-volume psychiatry textbook and many works in the field of psychiatry, most of them based on clinical research.

Kovalevsky, Volodymyr [Kovalevs'kyj], b 29 May 1905 in Sosnytsia, Chernihiv gubernia, d 10 November 1970 in Kiev. Literary scholar and journalist. He began publishing in 1924. His most important works are *Rytmichni zasoby ukraïns'koho literaturnoho virsha* (The Rhythmic Devices of Ukrainian Literary Verse, 1960) and *Ryma* (Rhyme, 1965).

Kovalevsky, Yevhraf [Kovalevs'kyj, Jevhraf], b 21 December 1790 (1792 according to some sources) in Kharkiv, d 30 March 1867 in St Petersburg. Engineer and government official; honorary member of the St Petersburg Academy of Sciences from 1856. He graduated from the Cadet School in St Petersburg in 1810 and began to work in the Department of Mining in 1819. In 1826 he was sent to expand the Luhanske smelting refinery. He then conducted important studies on coal and salt reserves in the *Donets Basin, and compiled the first stratographic map of the basin. He occupied a number of positions in the mining department before becoming minister of education in 1858. As minister he carried out several significant reforms and drafted a new liberal law on censorship; eventually, opposition to him in reactionary circles forced him to retire as minister in 1861. In 1862 he was elected president of the Free Economic Society.

Kovalevych, Ivan Robert [Kovalevyč], b 4 March 1896 in Verkhnyi Stumyn, Stanyslaviv county, Galicia, d 7 January 1978 in Winnipeg. Religious leader and editor. Kovalevych immigrated to South America in 1911 and came to Canada during the First World War. In 1929 he was ordained in the United church. From its inception in 1922, he was active in the Ukrainian Evangelical Alliance of North America and served Ukrainian congregations in Saskatchewan, Toronto, and the Winnipeg region. He edited **Kanadiis'kyi ranok* (1947–58) and after 1961 helped edit its successor *Ievanhels'kyi ranok*. For 23 years he represented the Ukrainian Evangelical Alliance on the Presidium of the Ukrainian Canadian Committee.

Kovalinsky, Mykhailo [Kovalins'kyj, Myxajlo] (Kovalynsky), b 1757 in the Kharkiv region, d 1807. Writer and pedagogue. He studied with H. *Skovoroda and at Strasbourg University, and traveled throughout western Europe with O. Rozumovsky. Empress Catherine II appointed him vicegerent of Riazan and Tsar Paul named him curator of Moscow University (1801–4). Kovalinsky's writings are the main source of biographical data on Skovoroda. His biography of Skovoroda, *Zhitie Grigoriia Skovorody*, was written in 1796 but published only in 1886 in the journal *Kievskaia starina*; a second version, edited by the historian D. Bahalii, was published in *Sbornik Kharkovskogo Istoriko-filologicheskogo obshchestva* in 1894. His correspondence with Skovoroda was published in that same journal and in a two-volume edition of Skovoroda's complete works (1973). Kovalinsky also wrote two odes to Empress Catherine (1774).

Kovaliv, Levko, b ca 1890, d ? Revolutionary figure. In 1917–18 he was a member of the CC of the Ukrainian Party of Socialist Revolutionaries and of the Ukrainian Central Rada. In 1919, as a member of the CC of the *Borotbists, he and H. Hrynko negotiated unsuccessfully with the Comintern executive in Moscow in an effort to obtain admission of the Borotbist party into the Comintern, and in December of that year he signed the compact between the Borotbists and the CP(B)U. After the dissolution of the Borotbist party in 1920, he did not join the CP(B)U. Forsaking politics altogether, he worked as a mathematician, chemist, and book illustrator. He was arrested during the Stalinist terror in 1934 and was shot in a concentration camp.

Kovaliv, Panteleimon, b 9 August 1898 in Brailiv, Vinnytsia county, Podilia gubernia, d 15 November 1973 in Washington, DC. Linguist; full member of the Shevchenko Scientific Society from 1949. A graduate of the Kiev Institute of People's Education (1930), he was a docent at the Kiev Pedagogical Institute and at Kiev University. After immigrating to Germany in 1944, he became professor at the Ukrainian Free University in 1945 and professor and rector at the Theological Academy of the Ukrainian Autocephalous Orthodox Church in Munich (1946–51). In 1952 he immigrated to the United States. His publications include works in the history of Ukrainian such as *Narysy z istoriï ukraïns'koï movy* (Sketches on the History of the Ukrainian Language, 1941), coauthored with M. Hrunsky; studies of the descriptive and historical morphology of Russian and Ukrainian (prefixes, participles, stress); and *Leksychnyi fond literaturnoï movy kyïvs'koho periodu x–xiv st.* (The Lexical Fund of the Literary Language of the Kievan Period, x–xiv Centuries, 2 vols, 1962, 1964). He defended the authenticity of *Molytovnyk-sluzhebnyk: Pam'iatka xiv st.* (The Prayer Book-Missal: A Memorial of the 14th Century, 1960).

Kovaliv, Stepan (pseud: Stefan Piatka), b 25 December 1848 in Bronytsia, Sambir circle, Galicia, d 26 April 1920 in Boryslav. Populist writer and teacher. A graduate of the Lviv Teachers' Seminary, from 1879 he taught in Boryslav. He first published in 1881. Beginning in 1891, 14 of his story collections appeared during his lifetime. Some – eg, *Charodiina skrypka* (The Magic Violin, 1910) and *V ostannii lavtsi* (In the Last Row of Desks, 1911) – were written for children. Many of his stories, particularly those in the collections *Hromads'ki promyslovtsi* (Community Industrialists, 1899) and *Obrazky z halyts'koï Kaliforniï* (Pictures from Galician California, 1913), depict the lives of the impoverished Galician peasantry and the exploited workers of Boryslav. An edition of his complete works appeared in 1958. I. Franko had an important influence on his writing.

Kovalivsky, Andrii [Kovalivs'kyj, Andrij], b 1 February 1895 in Rozsokhovate near Zolochiv, Kharkiv gubernia, d 29 November 1969 in Kharkiv. Historian and specialist on Oriental sources of Slavic history. He was one of the founders of the All-Ukrainian Learned Association of Oriental Studies. He worked at the Institute of Oriental Studies in Leningrad (1934–9) and at the Saransk Pedagogical Institute in Mordovia (1939–44). In 1947 he returned to the Institute of Oriental Studies in Leningrad and lectured at the university there. In 1951 he received his doctorate from Kharkiv University, and in 1964 he was appointed head of the Chair of Medieval History. Apart from Middle Eastern studies, he was interested in the history of Kievan Rus' and 18th-century Ukraine. He is the author of over 90 works, including *Rozvytok etychnykh pohliadiv Hryhoriia Skovorody v zv'iazku z ioho zhyttiam* (The Development of H. Skovoroda's Ethical Views in Relation to His Life, 1923), *Kniga Akhmeda Ibn-Fadlana o ego puteshestvii na Volgu v 921–922 gg.* (Ahmad Ibn-Faḍlān's Book on His Travels to the Volga in 921–2, 1956), *Antolohiia literatur Skhodu* (Anthology of Oriental Literatures, 1961), translations of medieval Arabic accounts and works by Middle Eastern writers, and studies of Ukrainian folk beliefs, A. Krymsky, P. Ritter, and Paul of Aleppo. Kovalivsky is the subject of a biobibliography published in Kharkiv in 1966.

Kovalivsky, Ivan [Kovalivs'kyj], b and d ? *General osaul (1648–59) and diplomat in the administrations of hetmans B. Khmelnytsky and I. Vyhovsky. He was Ukraine's signatory in the treaties concluded with Moldavia (1654), Transylvania (1656), and Sweden (at Korsun, 1657). In 1663 Kovalivsky was the captain of Hlynske company of the Lubni regiment. His subsequent fate is unknown.

Kovalivsky, Petro [Kovalivs'kyj], 1865–1942. Educator. He was a professor at the Kharkiv Institute of People's Education and a research associate of the Ukrainian Scientific Research Institute of Pedagogy. He wrote a number of studies on professional education, regional industry, labor, and the economy of Slobidska Ukraine. Kovalivsky founded the Kharkiv branch of the Prosvita society.

Kovalnytsky, Dmytro [Koval'nyc'kyj], b 1839 in Volhynia, d 1913. Church figure and historian. A graduate of the Volhynian Theological Seminary (1859) and the *Kiev Theological Academy (1868), he taught at the academy from 1869 to 1902 and served as rector (1898–1902). He encouraged the study of the academy's history and in 1901 initiated the publication of documents on the academy. He was ordained as the bishop of Chyhyryn and vicar of Kiev eparchy in 1898, as bishop of Tambov in 1902, as archbishop of Kazan in 1903, and finally, as archbishop of Kherson and Odessa in 1904.

Kovalov, Oleksander [Koval'ov], b 31 December 1915 in Rohachou, Mahiliou gubernia. Realist sculptor. He graduated in 1942 from the Kiev State Art Institute, where he had studied with B. Kratko. In the late 1940s and the 1950s he did portraits, producing busts of L. Revutsky, P. Tchaikovsky, V. Filatov, B. Khmelnytsky, T. Shevchenko, M. Rylsky, and B. Hmyria. Later he sculpted many monuments, including those to M. Lysenko in Kiev (1965), V. Filatov in Odessa (1966), I. Karpenko-Kary at the Khutir Nadiia Museum-Reserve in Kirovohrad oblast (1969), M. Rylsky in Romanivka, Zhytomyr oblast (1970), and A. Pushkin in Kiev (1964) and in New York (1970). D. Yanko has published a monograph on Kovalov and an album of his work (1977).

Kovalsky, Ivan [Koval's'kyj], b 1850 in Sobolivka, Haisyn county, Podilia gubernia, d 14 August 1878 in Odessa. Revolutionary populist. With other students who wanted to devote themselves to improving the lives of the peasants, he went 'among the people.' After serving a year in prison, he organized a populist circle in Odessa that advocated terrorism and worked primarily among the *Stundists and *Molokane sects. In 1877 he established an underground press and coauthored the proclamation 'The Voice of Honest Men.' He was arrested for armed resistance to the police and was hanged.

Kovalsky, Mykola [Koval's'kyj], b 1885 in Volhynia, d 28 December 1944 in Dachau, Germany. Political figure. Before the 1917 Revolution he was a member of the Revolutionary Ukrainian party and the Ukrainian Social Democratic Workers' party. He was elected to the Ukrainian Central Rada in 1917 and directed the UNR government's Department of State Control in 1918–20. An émigré in Warsaw from 1921, he headed the Ukrainian Central Committee there. Arrested by the Germans during the Second World War, he died in a concentration camp. A monograph on him was written by M. Sadovsky (New York-Toronto, 1954).

Kovalsky, Mykola [Koval's'kyj], b 24 October 1899 in Kiev, d 20 September 1976 in Courbon, Seine-et-Marne, France. Civic and political figure; publicist. As a member of the UNR diplomatic corps, he served in the mission in Istanbul and on the delegation to the peace negotiations in Brest-Litovsk. In 1924 he arrived in France with a contingent of UNR Army veterans and became active in the Ukrainian community in Paris. For many years he was secretary of the General Council of the Union of Ukrainian Emigré Organizations in France and of the Society of Former Combatants of the Ukrainian Republican Democratic Army in France, and president of the Circle of Ukrainians in Paris. He contributed articles and verses to *Literaturno-naukovyi vistnyk* and *Tryzub*. His publications include an essay on the political situation of Ukraine on the eve of the Second World War (1939) and a collection of verses on diverse themes titled *Etiudy: Poezii* (Etudes: Poems, 1978).

Kovalsky, Vasyl [Koval's'kyj, Vasyl'], 1826–1911. Jurist, civic leader, publicist. Starting as a judge in Peremyshl, Kovalsky rose to become a member of the Supreme Court in Vienna. He was the first Ukrainian translator of the official gazette for legislative acts. In the 1850s he was an active publicist whose articles appeared in such papers as *Zoria halyts'ka*. He also prepared Ukrainian textbooks; for example *Rus'ka chytanka dlia nyzshoï gimnazii* (A Ruthenian Reader for the Lower Gymnasium, 1852). As deputy to the Galician Diet (1860s–1870s) and the Austrian Parliament (1880s), he defended the rights of the Ukrainian population in Austria-Hungary. He was a founding member of the *People's Home and the *Halytsko-Ruska Matytsia society in Lviv. Towards the end of his life he became a Russophile.

Kovalsky, Viktor [Koval's'kyj], b 28 January 1899 in Odessa. Biochemist and biogeochemist. A graduate of the university in Odessa (1921), he chaired the department of comparative and evolutionary biochemistry at the AN URSR Institute of Biochemistry (1933–44) and the biochemistry department of the Ukrainian Stomatological Institute in Kiev (1935–41). In 1946 he organized and became director of the Odessa Marine Ecology Laboratory. From 1954 he headed the biogeochemical laboratory at the Institute of Geological and Analytical Chemistry of the USSR Academy of Sciences. Much of Kovalsky's work has dealt with the biological importance of trace elements, their ecological recycling, and their use in evolutionary and climatic research.

Kovalyk, Ivan, b 16 November 1907 in Mlyny, Yavoriv county, Galicia. Linguist. Having studied linguistics at Lviv University under J. Janów and W. Taszycki, he became a docent at that university and later at the Drohobych Pedagogical Institute. He has published works on word derivation, phonetics, the language and style of Western Ukrainian writers (eg, the function of dialectisms in V. Stefanyk), 17th-century Ukrainian syntax, and the application of phonology to the history of Ukrainian.

Kovalyk, Serhii, b 25 October 1846 in the Poltava region, d 26 April 1926 in Minsk. Populist revolutionary. A graduate of Kiev University (1869), he advocated the idea of 'going to the people' and in 1872 spread revolutionary propaganda among the peasants of Mhlyn county in Chernihiv gubernia. Then he organized a number of anarchist circles in Kiev, Kharkiv, Moscow, and villages of the Volga region. He was arrested in 1874 and sentenced to 10 years of hard labor. Returning from exile in 1898, he did not resume political activity. His memoirs, 'Dvizhenie semidesiatykh godov po Bol'shomu protsessu' (The Movement of the Seventies according to the Great Trial), appeared in *Byloe* in 1928.

Kovanko-Kovankovsky, Petro [Kovan'ko-Kovan'-kovs'kyj], b 10 July 1876, d ? Economist. A graduate of the Kiev University law school (1899), he taught financial law there from 1909. Receiving a PH D in 1919, he was a professor at the Kuban Polytechnical Institute in Katerynodar (now Krasnodar) in 1921–2. In the 1920s and 1930s he taught at the Kiev Agricultural Institute and was an associate of the VUAN Commission for the Study of Financial Matters; he edited and contributed to no. 5 of the commission's *Trudy* (1929), which was devoted to Kiev's economy. A wartime refugee, he was a consultant on Soviet finance at Breslau University in 1942–5. After the war he was an associate of the Institute for the Study of the USSR in Munich and a member of the Ukrainian Free Academy of Sciences (from 1948). He wrote several monographs in Russian on such subjects as peasant emancipation and compulsory redemption payments in Russia (1912), the 1861 reform and its financial consequences (1914), the productive forces of Ukraine (1922), the budgets of zemstvos and cities in Russia in 1912–14 (1922), and the finances of the USSR during the Second World War (1951) and after it (1954). He also wrote a commerce textbook (7 edns, 1911–19) and a study of Kiev's economy in the last 100 years, which perished while being typeset in Germany in 1945.

Kovbasiuk, Mykola [Kovbasjuk], b 1817 in Verbizh near Kolomyia (now Verkhnii Verbizh, in Ivano-Frankivske oblast), d 1889. Civic leader in Galicia, of peasant background. In the 1860s and 1870s Kovbasiuk was elected to the Galician Diet, and in 1861 to the Austrian Parliament. He was a tireless defender of the Western Ukrainian peasantry in the Austrian Empire, speaking out on economic issues, for village self-government and for the use of Ukrainian as the language of instruction in eastern Galicia and in the Diet.

Kovbel (Kowbell), Semen [Kovbel'], b 25 January 1877 in Borshchiv, Galicia, d 3 January 1966 in Toronto. Ukrainian-Canadian playwright, poet, prosaist, and community figure. Emigrating to Montreal in 1909, Kovbel settled in Winnipeg during the First World War and became one of the leading organizers of the Ukrainian People's Home there. His primary literary interest, and the genre in which he was most successful, was drama. All of his 17 plays were staged, but only 6 were published: *Divochi mrii* (A Maiden's Daydreams, 1920), *Virna sestra – to zoloto* (A Faithful Sister Is a Treasure, 1938), *Ukraïnizatsiia* (Ukrainization, 1938), *Delegatsiia do raiu* (A Delegation to Paradise, 1938), *Povisyvsia* (He Hanged Himself, 1938), and *Parubochi mrii* (A Bachelor's Daydreams, 1942). Four of his unpublished plays were adaptations of B. Lepky's historical novels. His lyrical and political poems and short stories appeared in Ukrainian-Canadian newspapers and almanacs.

Kovcheh (The Ark). A bilingual (Ukrainian-English) Catholic religious and educational monthly published from 1946 to 1956 in Stamford, Connecticut.

Kovel [Kovel']. II-5. City (1984 pop 61,000) and raion center in Volhynia oblast, situated in Polisia on the Turiia River. First mentioned in 1310, in 1518 it was granted the rights of Magdeburg law. It became a county town of Volhynia vicegerency in 1795 and of Volhynia gubernia in 1797. In 1919 the Volhynian Division of the UNR Army fought the Polish army there. From 1921 to 1939 Kovel was under Polish rule. The city is an important railway junction. Among its industries are agricultural-machinery, reinforced-concrete, and food- and feed-processing plants. Its architectural monuments – the wooden Annunciation Cathedral (built in 1505) and the railway station (1905, architect O. Verbytsky) – were damaged during the Second World War.

Kovenko, Mykhailo, b and d ? Political figure. An engineer, he was an active participant in the Ukrainian struggle for independence of 1917–20 as a member of the Ukrainian Social Democratic Workers' party and then the Ukrainian Party of Socialists-Independentists. In 1917 he organized a regiment of *Free Cossacks from among Kiev's workers, and in January 1918 he commanded the UNR forces defending Kiev during the Bolshevik uprising and offensive. Under the UNR Directory he headed the Supreme Investigative Commission to Fight Counterrevolution. In the fall of 1919 he edited the newspaper *Ukraïna* in Kamianets-Podilskyi. From 1920 he lived in Rumania.

Koverko, Andrii, b 28 August 1893 in Ostriv, Lviv county, Galicia, d 19 July 1967 in Kishinev, Moldavian SSR. Sculptor. A graduate of the Kolomyia Industrial Design School (1914), he did mostly monumental sculptures in wood. In 1926–7 he carved the altar and iconostasis of the Church of the Holy Spirit at the Greek Catholic Theological Seminary in Lviv and the iconostasis of the village church in Sokal. The T. Shevchenko monument in Vynnyky (1924) and the A. Sheptytsky monument at the Greek Catholic Theological Seminary in Lviv were done by Koverko. In the 1920s and 1930s he carved many bas-relief portraits in wood, including portraits of I. Franko, I. Svientsinsky, M. Vorony, I. Trush, and O. Novakivsky. Until 1939 he took part in the exhibitions organized by the Circle of Promoters of Ukrainian Art and by the Association of Independent Ukrainian Artists in Lviv.

Kovhaniuk, Stepan [Kovhanjuk], b 26 April 1902 in Onopriivka, Uman county, Kiev gubernia, d 26 August 1982 in Odessa. Writer and translator. In the 1920s he worked as a teacher and editor in Kharkiv and Odessa. He is the author of the story collection *Manevry* (Maneuvers, 1930), many Ukrainian translations of Polish and Russian literature, and the work *Praktyka perekladu* (The Practice of Translation, 1968).

Kovinka, Oleksander [Kovin'ka], b 14 January 1900 in Ploske, Poltava gubernia, d 25 July 1985 in Poltava. Writer of humorous and satiric, often autobiographical, prose. His first collection of stories, *Industriial'na tekhnika* (Industrial Technology), appeared in 1929. He did not publish during the Stalinist period. Between 1958 and 1980, 30 collections of his stories were published, including a two-volume edition of his selected works (1980).

Kovner, Savelii, b February 1837 in Vilnius, Lithuania, d 22 September 1896 in Kiev. Physician and historian of medicine. A graduate of Kiev University (1865), from 1868 to 1890 he worked as a physician, mostly in Nizhen. He knew several ancient languages and studied original Oriental, Greek, Roman, and Arabic sources on medicine. He wrote a number of works on the history of medicine, including *Istoriia meditsiny* (A History of Medicine, 3 vols, 1878–88) and *Istoriia srednevekovoi meditsiny* (A History of Medieval Medicine, 2 vols, 1893, 1897).

Kovnir, Stepan, b 1695 in Hvizdiv, Kiev county, Kiev gubernia, d 1786 in Kiev. Master builder. For over 60

Stepan Kovnir: belfry at the Far Caves of the Kievan Cave Monastery (1754–61)

years he worked under various architects on building projects of the Kievan Cave Monastery – the so-called Kovnir building (1744–5) and the belfries of the Near (1759–63) and Far (1754–61) Caves (designed by I. Hryhorovych-Barsky) – on the belfry of the Kiev Epiphany Brotherhood Monastery (1756–9), on the Klov Palace in Kiev (1752–6, designed by P. Neelov), on the church and belfry in Vasylkiv (1756–9), and on the Trinity Church of the Kytaieve Hermitage near Kiev (1763–7). With their elaborate plaster facades Kovnir's buildings are fine examples of the Ukrainian baroque style.

Kovpak, Sydir, b 13 May 1887 in Kotelva, Bohodukhiv county, Kharkiv gubernia, d 11 December 1967 in Kiev. Prominent Soviet partisan commander during the Second World War. He commanded a Communist partisan unit fighting Ukrainian nationalist forces during 1918–19 and then served as a Red Army political commissar. From 1926 to 1941 he worked in Party administration in Sumy oblast. In 1941 Kovpak organized a partisan unit in the Putyvl area, Sumy oblast. It quickly grew in size and importance, recruiting mostly Party and government officials and Russian peasants from the region. In 1942 the unit raided west through Polisia and conducted acts of sabotage to disrupt German supply lines. In June 1943 during a raid through Galicia to the Carpathian mountains, the detachment (numbering some 1,600 partisans) was decimated in battles with German units and later harassed by the UPA. Remnants returned to Polisia, where Kovpak reactivated his unit by mobilizing local inhabitants. For his exploits he was promoted to brigadier general and his unit was expanded to division size and named after him. In 1946 Kovpak became defense minister of the Ukrainian SSR, and from 1947 to 1967 he served as deputy chairman of the Presidium of the Supreme Soviet of the Ukrainian SSR and as a member of the CC CPU. His memoirs, *Vid Putyvlia do Karpat* (From Putyvl to the Carpathians), were first published in 1946.

P. Sodol

Kovshevych, Roman [Kovševyč], b 22 July 1873 in Jarosław, Galicia, d 3 March 1932 in Lviv. Lawyer, jurist, and educator. A graduate of Lviv University (LL D 1898), he served as a court official and continued to study canon law. During the war he fought in the ranks of the Ukrainian Sich Riflemen, and after the war he served as professor and dean of the law department at Lviv (Underground) Ukrainian University. In 1930 Kovshevych was invited by Metropolitan A. Sheptytsky to teach canon law at the Greek Catholic Theological Academy in Lviv. His publications include 'De primis litibus ex antiquae Poloniae dioecesibus apud Romanam Rotam iudicatis' and 'De primis litibus Ucrainorum apud Romanam Curiam iudicatis' (in *Bohosloviia*, 7 [1929]).

Kovtun, Valerii, b 22 October 1944 in Yasynuvata, Staline oblast. Ballet dancer. A graduate of the Kiev Choreography School (1965), he danced with the Kharkiv Theater of Opera and Ballet and in 1968 became a soloist at the Kiev Theater of Opera and Ballet. He has appeared in such roles as Lukash in M. Skorulsky's *The Forest Song*, Don Juan in V. Hubarenko's *The Stone Master*, Daphnis and the Youth in M. Ravel's *Daphnis et Chloé* and *Boléro*, and Romeo in S. Prokofiev's *Romeo and Juliet*. He has won recognition at international ballet competitions: first prize at Varna, Bulgaria, in 1970, and the Nijinsky Prize in Paris in 1977.

Kovui [Kovuji] (also: Koui). Nomadic Turkic tribes living on the southeastern borders of Kievan Rus'. In the ancient chronicles the Kovui are described as part of the *Chorni Klobuky people. It is possible that the tribes belonged to the *Cumans who settled in Rus'. The chronicles first mention the Kovui in the year 1151 in connection with their support of the Kievan prince Viacheslav Volodymyrovych's struggle with the Olhovych dynasty. Further mention is made of the Kovui for the years 1162, 1170, and 1185. The epic **Slovo o polku Ihorevi* refers to their participation in the campaign of Olstyn Oleksych and the Siverian princes against the Cumans in 1185.

Pavlo Kovzhun: cover for I. Franko's *Iz dniv zhurby*

Kovzhun, Pavlo [Kovžun], b 3 October 1896 in Kostiushky, Ovruch county, Volhynia gubernia, d 15 May 1939 in Lviv. Noted graphic artist, painter, and art scholar. His graphic works began to appear in Kiev journals while he was still a student at the Kiev Art School. By 1914 his work began to attract wide attention. Sent to the front in 1915, at the outbreak of the 1917 Revolution he joined the Ukrainian movement in the armed forces and edited

Ukrainian military newspapers, such as *Ukraïna, Holos chasu*, and *Volia*. During the UNR period he helped to set up the Grunt publishing house, served as secretary of *Universal'nyi zhurnal*, and belonged to the *Muzahet artistic and literary alliance in Kiev. Finding refuge in Poland with the remnants of the UNR Army, in 1922 Kovzhun settled in Lviv, where he became a leading figure in the artistic community. With V. Sichynsky, P. Kholodny, S. Tymoshenko, and M. Holubets, he founded the Circle of Promoters of Ukrainian Art (HDUM), and in 1931 helped organize the Association of Independent Ukrainian Artists (ANUM), whose journal he edited (1932–6). His graphic work was displayed at exhibitions in Lviv, Warsaw, Prague, Brussels, Berlin, Rome, and Naples, and had a major impact on book graphics in Western Ukraine. Kovzhun ranks with Yu. *Narbut as the leading Ukrainian graphic artist of the 20th century. He was thoroughly modern and yet closely bound to Ukrainian artistic traditions. His early work was influenced by symbolism, futurism, and to some extent by Narbut, but after 1924 he developed his own style, which was at first expressionistic and then constructivist. Kovzhun was also a noted muralist: with M. Osinchuk he painted a number of churches in Ozirna, Sokal, Zashkiv, Dolyna, Myklashiv, Kalush, and Stoianiv in a modernized neo-Byzantine style. Kovzhun was a tireless organizer of exhibitions, and an editor and writer. He wrote several monographs about contemporary artists, such as M. Hlushchenko, O. Hryshchenko, and L. Gets, and numerous articles on art. He edited a collection of bookplates, *Ekslibris: Zbirnyk Asotsiiatsiï nezalezhnykh ukraïns'kykh mysttsiv* (Bookplates: A Collection of the Association of Independent Ukrainian Artists, 1932), in which his own work appeared.

BIBLIOGRAPHY

Fediuk, M. *Hrafika P. Kovzhuna* (Lviv 1924)
Sichyns'kyi, V. 'Knyzhna hrafika Pavla Kovzhuna,' *Bibliohrafichni visti*, 2 (1927)
Holubets', M. *Pavlo Kovzhun* (Lviv 1939)
Masjutin, W. 'Pavlo Kowzun,' *Gebrauchsgraphik*, 9 (1939)
Hordyns'kyi, S. *Pavlo Kovzhun* (Lviv 1944)

S. Hordynsky

Kowalchuk, John [Koval'čuk], b 30 August 1921 in Goodeve, Saskatchewan. Farmer and politician. Educated at the University of Saskatchewan, Kowalchuk served as reeve of Stanley Municipality in 1965–6. He was elected to the Saskatchewan legislature in 1967 as a New Democratic Party member from the constituency of Melville. Re-elected in 1971, 1975, and 1978, he served as minister of tourism and renewable resources in 1974–5.

Koza (Goat). A traditional mimetic folk play that was acted out during the Christmas cycle by young men, who visited all the houses in a village. The Goat – a youth wearing an inverted sheepskin coat and a mask resembling a goat's head – entered a house, bowed to the head of the household, and performed a ritual dance to bring about an abundant harvest. The other youths sang an accompanying ditty: 'De Koza khodyt', tam zhyto rodyt', de Koza tup-tup, tam zhyta sim kup' (Where the Goat goes, there wheat grows; where the Goat stamps its feet, there are seven sheaves of wheat). A dramatization of a goat being pursued by hunters and wolves, killed, and gutted followed. At the singers' call 'Bud', Kozo, zhyva!' (Come alive, Goat!) the Goat rose from the dead and returned to its 'field,' which then came to life (as acted out by the chorus). The game ended with the Goat delivering a wish: 'Shchob ts'omu hospodariu i korovky buly nevrochlyvii i molochlyvii, i oves – samosii, i pshenytsia – sochevytsia' (May this farmer's cattle be unbedeviled and full of milk, and may his oats sow themselves and his wheat be of the best sort). In the Hutsul region the Goat was 'led around' by children, who 'sowed' grain kernels throughout the house; the Goat's ears were made of grain spikes. Occasionally, the Goat was accompanied by others disguised as the Old Man, the Gypsy, Malanka (the New Year's Eve maiden), the Bear, and other characters. The original purpose of *Koza* was the same as that of carols: to invoke a successful year for the peasant household. With time, belief in its magical function disappeared, and the game became simply a form of entertainment in the repertoires of Christmas parties.

M. Hnatiukivsky

Kozacha Lopan [Kozača Lopan']. III-17. Town smt (1979 pop 8,800) on the Lopan River in Derkachi raion, Kharkiv oblast. It was founded in the 17th century. An important battle took place here at the end of 1918, in which UNR forces were defeated, enabling the Red Army to take over the Kharkiv region.

Hryhorii Kozachenko

Kozachenko, Hryhorii [Kozačenko, Hryhorij], b 2 January 1901 in Trushky, Vasylkiv county, Kiev gubernia, d 1 June 1970 in Kharkiv. Character actor of L. *Kurbas's school. On completing his training at the drama studio of the Berezil theater (1924), he acted with *Berezil and its successor, the Kharkiv Ukrainian Drama Theater. His repertoire included such roles as Omelko in M. Kropyvnytsky's *Dai sertsiu voliu, zavede v nevoliu* (Give the Heart Freedom and It Will Lead You into Slavery), Knur in P. Myrny's *Lymerivna* (The Saddler's Daughter), Kotenko in M. Starytsky's *Talan* (Destiny), Sylvester the monk in I. Kocherha's *Iaroslav Mudryi* (Yaroslav the Wise), and Kobza the boatswain in O. Korniichuk's *Zahybel' eskadry* (The Destruction of a Squadron).

Kozachenko, Vasyl [Kozačenko, Vasyl'], b 25 March 1913 in Novoarkhanhelske, Kherson gubernia. Stalinist writer and Party bureaucrat. In the 1960s and 1970s he was the Party's watchdog in literature and launched the campaigns against the literary critics I. Dziuba, Ye. Sverstiuk, and I. Svitlychny; O. Honchar's novel *Sobor* (The

Cathedral); and such writers as V. Drozd, V. Maniak, R. Andriiashyk, I. Chendei, O. Berdnyk, and I. Bilyk. In 1973–8 he was the first secretary of the Writer's Union of Ukraine. His first novella, *Pegas* (Pegasus), appeared in 1938. Since that time he has published over 30 books of ideological prose, publicism, and literary criticism. A four-volume edition of his selected works was published in 1979–80.

Averkii Kozachkivsky: *Christ Taken down from the Cross* (1726)

Kozachkivsky, Averkii [Kozačkivs'kyj, Averkij], b and d ? Noted Kiev engraver of the early 18th century. From 1721 to 1737 he did over 40 engravings – copper engravings, etchings, and mezzotint – most for the Kievan Cave Monastery Printing House. The better-known ones are *The Crucifixion* (mezzotint), *The Interment of Jesus Christ, King David,* two views of the Kievan Cave Monastery, the illustrations to the psalter with explanations of 1728, illustrations to the New Testament with a psalter of 1732, and the frontispiece to the *Apostol* of 1722.

Kozachkivsky, Domian [Kozačkivs'kyj, Domjan], b 13 November 1896 in Lysycha, Poltava county, Poltava gubernia, d 17 March 1967 in Lviv. Comic and character actor and stage director. Making his debut on the stage in 1914 with L. Leonidov's and P. Kahanets's Ukrainian troupe, he became stage director at the Poltava Ukrainian Drama Society (1915–17). After the Revolution he worked in the Franko Ukrainian Drama Theater in Kharkiv, the Kiev Ukrainian Drama Theater, the Kharkiv Theater of the Revolution (1934–9), the Sumy Ukrainian Music and Drama Theater (artistic director, 1939–44), the Lviv Theater of Musical Comedy (1945–50), and the Lviv Ukrainian Drama Theater (1957–67). His repertoire included such roles as Holokhvosty in M. Starytsky's *Za dvoma zaitsiamy* (After Two Hares), Podkolesin in N. Gogol's *Zhenit'ba* (Marriage), Bulava in I. Mykytenko's *Solo na fleiti* (Flute Solo), and Dmytro in his *Marusia Shurai*, Peterson in Ya. Halan's *Pid zolotym orlom* (Under the Golden Eagle), and the title role in J. Molière's *Tartuffe*.

Kozachkovsky, Andrii [Kozačkovs'kyj, Andrij], b 16 August 1812 in Pereiaslav (now Pereiaslav-Khmelnytskyi, Kiev oblast), d 20 August 1889 in Pereiaslav. Physician and friend of T. Shevchenko. Kozachkovsky completed his studies in St Petersburg in 1835. From 1842 he was a county physician in Kursk, and from January 1844 a doctor and lecturer in medicine at the Pereiaslav seminary. Shevchenko visited Kozachkovsky in Pereiaslav in August 1845, and from October 1845 lived in his home intermittently until the beginning of January 1846. There he wrote the poems 'Naimychka' (The Servant-Girl), 'Zapovit' (Testament), and 'Kavkaz' (The Caucasus), and began writing 'Ieretyk' (The Heretic). Kozachkovsky corresponded with Shevchenko while the poet was in exile and gave him financial help. He published valuable memoirs about Shevchenko in *Kievskii telegraf* (1875; reprinted in *T.G. Shevchenko v vospominanniakh sovremennikov* [T.H. Shevchenko in the Reminiscences of His Contemporaries, 1962]). Kozachkovsky's home in Pereiaslav-Khmelnytskyi is now a historical museum.

Kozachok (Little Cossack). A folk dance for male-female pairs, which emerged among the Cossacks in the 16th century; hence its name. In the 17th and 18th centuries it was performed throughout Ukraine and also in the noble courts of Poland, Hungary, Russia, France, and other countries. The dance has a rapid to very rapid tempo and is at times accompanied by a contrasting slow, lyrical, musical introduction. The basic moves are *bihunok, dorizhka, vykhyliasnyk, virovochka, prystup, prypadannia,* and (for males only) *prysiadka*. Their dynamic interplay in various formations produces a sophisticated and complex choreographic image. The main weight falls on the women's parts, and competitions between groups of dancers and individuals frequently occur in the dance. The accompanying music is rhythmic and is played at 2/4 time. *Kozachok* melodies were used in Polish operas and ballets of the 18th century and by M. Arkas, L. Revutsky, R. Simovych, A. Kolomyiets, S. Liudkevych, V. Kyreiko, and other Ukrainian composers.

Kozachynsky, Mykhail (Manuil) [Kozačyns'kyj, Myxajil], b 1699 in Yampil, Podilia, d 27 August 1755 in Slutsk, Belorussia. Pedagogue and writer. After graduating from the Kievan Mohyla Academy in 1733, he was a teacher and prefect in Karlovac, Croatia. In 1737 he entered the Vydubychi Monastery in Kiev, and from 1739 to 1746 he was a prefect and lecturer at the Kievan Mohyla Academy. From 1748 he was the archimandrite of

ART 1) O. Hryshchenko: *Fishes* (oil, 1939; private collection). 2) V. Khmeliuk: *Flowers* (oil; private collection). 3) F. Krychevsky: *The Family* (tempera, 1925–7; Kiev Museum of Ukrainian Art). 4) F. Humeniuk: *County Fair* (watercolor; private collection). 5) P. Kholodny, Jr: *Girl with Scarf* (tempera; courtesy of G. Saj). 6) E. Kozak: *Hutsul Brothers* (acrylic). 7) N. Husar: *Deepest Sympathy* (acrylic, 1986). 8) A. Kolomayets: *Bandura Player* (oil; courtesy of G. and M. Honcharenko).

the Slutsk Monastery. He wrote panegyrical poetry, two plays – about the fall of the Serbian Kingdom (1733; pub, 1798) and Marcus Aurelius Antoninus (1745) – and a disputation on Aristotelean philosophy (1745).

Edvard Kozak

Kozak, Edvard (pseuds: EKO, Mamai, Hryts Zozulia, Maik Chichka, Avenir Lushniak, Kosy), b 26 January 1902 in Hirne, Stryi county, Galicia. Caricaturist, illustrator, and painter; feuilletonist, satirist, and editor. He studied at the Vienna Art School (1917) and O. *Novakivsky's art school in Lviv (1926), illustrated and edited the satirical periodicals *Zyz* (1926–33) and *Komar* (1933–9) in Lviv, and illustrated the children's magazines *Svit dytyny*, *Dzvinochok* (1931–9), and *Iuni druzi* (1933–4) and the books published by I. *Tyktor. At the same time, he painted and participated in the exhibitions of the Association of Independent Ukrainian Artists (1933–6) in Lviv. Emigrating to Germany at the end of the Second World War, he founded the humor magazine **Lys Mykyta* (1948) and headed the Ukrainian Association of Artists (USOM). In 1949 he settled in the United States, where he worked in animated television films, receiving an award for his work from the National Educational Association in 1957. He resumed publishing *Lys Mykyta* in 1951, and exhibited his paintings in Detroit, Chicago, Buffalo, Toronto, Edmonton, and Hunter (New York). For a time he illustrated the children's magazine *Veselka*.

Kozak is best known for his satirical drawings and writings, which amount to a running commentary on political and social developments in the Ukrainian community for over half a century. His caricatures of J. Stalin, which were reprinted in the German, French, Italian, English, Dutch, Polish, and Yugoslavian press, are recognized classics in the field. Many of his paintings deal with folk motifs and display a light-hearted humor and expressive colors; eg, *The Market*, *Sich*, *Old Inn*, and *Village*. He has published two albums of drawings with witty captions: *Selo* (The Village, 1949) and *EKO* (1949). As a satirical writer, he has created the incisive peasant philosopher Hryts Zozulia, under whose name he has published two collections of humorous sketches: *Hryts' Zozulia* (1973) and *Na khlops'kyi rozum Hrytsia Zozuli* (According to Hryts Zozulia's Common Sense, 1982). He has written numerous feuilletons and verses under different pen names. Some of the verses are printed in the collection *Virshi ironichni, satyrychni i komichni* (Ironic, Satiric, and Comic Verses, 1959).

S. Hordynsky

Yurii Kozak: *St George* (oil)

Kozak, George (Yurii), b 14 December 1933 in Stryi, Galicia. Painter and sculptor; son of E. *Kozak. Having studied at the Center for Creative Studies in Detroit, he works as an industrial sculptor for General Motors Corp. and as a freelance painter in oil and acrylic. He is also a master of stained glass and mosaics. His paintings often deal with religious themes, and have been awarded first prize at several exhibitions of religious art. His monumental painting of Ukraine's baptism is in the collection of the Ukrainian Canadian Art Foundation in Toronto.

Kozak, Ivan, b 8 August 1891 in Hichva, Lisko county, Galicia, d 27 December 1978 in New York. Civic and military figure; by profession a lawyer. After studying law at Lviv, Prague, and Cracow universities he practiced law in Uhniv, Galicia. During the First World War he served in the Austrian infantry and, having been wounded, was reassigned to the gendarmerie. In 1918–20 he served in the Ukrainian Galician Army (UHA) with the rank of captain, organizing and then commanding its gendarmerie. Joining the UNR Army in 1920, he served as staff commander of its Kherson Division. With A. Kravs's group he retreated to Czechoslovakia, where he was interned and was appointed commander of the Josefov internment camp (1923–6). Leaving Galicia after the Second World War, he immigrated in 1949 to the United States, where he helped found the United Ukrainian War Veterans in America and served as its vice-president. He chaired the committee that erected the T. Shevchenko monument in Washington, DC. Kozak wrote some articles on military subjects and recollections.

Yarema Kozak: *Forest Fantasy* (acrylic)

Kozak, Jerome (Yarema), b 17 April 1941 in Cracow, Poland. Expressionist painter; son of E. *Kozak. A graduate of Wayne State University in Detroit (MA 1966, MFA 1971), he specializes in oils and acrylics. His work, which has been exhibited at over 30 group and one-man shows, is characterized by vibrant colors.

Kozak, Serhii, b 14 March 1921 in Kryvyn near Slavuta, Volhynia gubernia. Baritone singer and composer. Upon graduating from the Moscow Conservatory in 1950, he joined the Kiev Theater of Opera and Ballet as a soloist. His repertoire consists of over 60 roles, including Ostap in M. Lysenko's *Taras Bulba,* the title roles in K. Dankevych's *Bohdan Khmelnytsky* and P. Tchaikovsky's *Eugene Onegin,* Martyn in H. Maiboroda's *Mylana* and Horbenko in his *Arsenal,* and Telramund in R. Wagner's *Lohengrin.* He has composed numerous songs and choral works, and has written books on M. Hryshko and H. Verovka.

Kozak, Stepan, b 11 July 1937 in Verbytsia, Tomaszów county, Kholm region. Literary historian. He studied at Kiev University (1957–62, 1964–7) and received a candidate of sciences degree there. He then worked as a research associate of the Institute of Slavic Studies of the Polish Academy of Sciences. In 1970–5 he was the scholarly secretary of the journal *Slavia Orientalis.* For over a decade he has taught Ukrainian literature at Warsaw University. In 1982 he was appointed head of the Chair of Comparative Slavic Literature at Warsaw University. He is the author of over 100 articles and reviews on 19th- and 20th-century Ukrainian literature and a monograph based on his doctoral dissertation, *U źródeł romantyzmu i nowożytnej myśli społecznej na Ukrainie* (At the Sources of Romanticism and Modern Social Thought in Ukraine, 1978). He has also coedited Polish books on the history of Ukrainian-Polish literary relations (1974) and the Napoleonic epoch and the Slavs (1982) and edited books of O. Dovzhenko's (1976) and Lesia Ukrainka's (1982) selected works in Polish translation. An active member of the Ukrainian Social and Cultural Society in Poland, he has contributed over 50 articles to its newspaper *Nashe slovo.*

Kozak, Yevhen, b 21 December 1857 in Sloboda-Banyliv, Vashkivtsi county, Bukovyna, d 5 September 1933 in Chernivtsi. Slavicist. He studied theology and philology at Chernivtsi and Vienna (with V. Jagić) universities before receiving his PH D from Chernivtsi in 1891 for his dissertation on the 'Chernivtsi Collection of 1359.' He was a professor of Old Church Slavonic language and literature in the theological faculty of Chernivtsi University (1899–1919). His publications include *Die Inschriften aus der Bukovina ...* (1903), a study of old manuscripts found in the Putna monastery, and works on the history of the Orthodox church in Bukovyna. Kozak argued that Ukrainians were autochthonous in Bukovyna, and in church affairs opposed the Rumanianization of Bukovynian Orthodox eparchies in the interwar period.

Kozak, Yevhen, b 22 April 1907 in Lviv. Conductor, composer, and educator. As a student of the Polish Music Society Conservatory and the Lysenko Higher Institute of Music in Lviv, he organized a popular male quartet, for which he arranged and composed tunes. In 1939 he was appointed choir conductor and musical director of Lviv Radio. After the war he taught at the Lviv Music School (1951–5), the Lviv Pedagogical Institute (1956–9), and the Lviv Conservatory. He has composed many choral works, such as *Under Ukraine's Sky,* and arranged numerous Ukrainian folk songs, some of which belong to the cycle *A Garland of Lemko Songs.* He has written scores for such plays as I. Franko's *Uchytel'* (The Teacher).

Kozak-Mamai

Kozak-Mamai (the Cossack Mamai). The most popular figure in Ukrainian folk painting of the 17th–20th centuries. Paintings of Kozak-Mamai were done in various media (mostly in oil and tempera) on wood, canvas, paper, walls of peasant houses, dishes, and ceramic tiles. He is portrayed as a serene and likable Cossack smoking a pipe and playing a bandura while squatting in an Oriental manner. His horse stands saddled alongside tied to his spear, and his weapons hang on a nearby tree. Often, along the bottom or the sides of the painting, there is a versified account of Cossack life and feats; usually it is taken from the monolog of the Cossack character in the **vertep* play. Most paintings were done by wandering icon painters or by students (usually of the Kiev Theological Academy) and sold at markets. They were then copied by various peasant artists, who would add details from local life to their versions. Kozak-Mamai came to represent the generalized, popular image of the Ukrainian Cossacks, particularly after the destruction of the Zaporozhian Sich and the Russian conquest of most of Ukraine. He also became a theme in literature, drama, and fine art (eg, in the works of M. Kulish, I. Repin, Yu. Narbut, and M. Butovych). There are Kozak-Mamai paintings in many Ukrainian museums; the largest collections are in the Kiev Museum of Ukrainian Art, the Kiev Museum of Ukrainian Decorative Folk Art, the Dnipropetrovske Art Museum (the D. Yavornytsky collection), and the private museum of I. Honchar in Kiev. A book about Kozak-Mamai in Ukrainian folk art, by P. Biletsky, was published in Lviv in 1960.

M. Hnatiukivsky

Kozakovsky, Yurii [Kozakovs'kyj, Jurij], b 16 February 1902 in Kharkiv, d 3 September 1980 in Chernivtsi. Actor specializing in heroic and character roles. He worked in the Kiev Ukrainian Drama Theater (1923–31), the Kharkiv Theater of the Revolution (1933–40), and the Chernivtsi Oblast Ukrainian Music and Drama Theater (artistic director in 1959–65). His repertoire included such roles as Andronati in an adaptation of O. Kobylianska's *V nediliu rano zillia kopala* (On Sunday Morn She Gathered Herbs), Hurman in I. Franko's *Ukradene shchastia* (Stolen Happiness), Iago in W. Shakespeare's *Othello*, and the title role in V. Hugo's *Angelo, tyran de Padoue*.

Kozatski Mohyly Museum and Preserve. A historic site and museum on Zhuravlykha Island on the river Styr near the village of Pliasheva, Rivne oblast, established in 1966. Located on the grounds of the preserve is the Church of the Holy Protectress, designed by V. Maksimov, with frescoes by I. Izhakevych. The church was built in 1912–14 with money donated by the local population. It is dedicated to the memory of the more than 10,000 Cossacks who died in the Battle of *Berestechko (1651) and located on a mass grave of Cossacks (from which the entire preserve takes its name). Also located on the site are the Kozatski Mohyly Pliasheva Ethnographic Museum, which houses numerous artifacts from the Cossack period, and the wooden Church of St Michael (1650), which was moved from the village of Ostriv. B. Khmelnytsky is said to have prayed in this church before going to battle against the Poles. Throughout the centuries, the local villagers staged annual commemorations of the Cossack struggle against social and national oppression at the mass graves on the site, and now the entire complex is a major tourist attraction.

Kozelets [Kozelec']. III-12. Town smt (1983 pop 8,400) and raion center in Chernihiv oblast. First mentioned in 1098, it was a fortified town in Kievan Rus'. In 1656 it was granted the rights of Magdeburg law. It was a company town in the Pereiaslav (1648–67) and Kiev (1667–1782) regiments, and from 1708 served as the administrative center of the latter. It then was a county town in Kiev vicegerency (1782–97) and Little Russia (1797–1802) and Chernihiv (1802–1917) gubernias. It has a flax-processing plant, food and feed industry, and a veterinary tekhnikum. Several of the town's architectural monuments have been preserved: the baroque Cathedral of the Nativity of the Mother of God (designed by V. Rastrelli and built by A. Kvasov and I. Hryhorovych-Barsky in 1752–63) with a finely engraved bronze iconostasis, the town hall (designed and built by A. Kvasov in 1756–60), and the Darahan building.

Kozelsky, Yakiv [Kozel's'kyj, Jakiv], b ca 1729 in Keleberda, Kaniv county, Kiev gubernia, d after 1795 in Krutyi Bereh, Lubni county, Poltava gubernia. Enlightenment thinker. Having studied at the Kievan Mohyla Academy (1744–50) and the Academic University of the St Petersburg Academy of Sciences (1751–7), he taught at the St Petersburg artillery and engineering schools and then served as a secretary of the Senate (1767–70). From 1770 to 1778 he sat on the Little Russian Collegium in Hlukhiv. Kozelsky wrote handbooks on mathematics, mechanics, military science, and economics. Influenced by J. Rousseau's ideas of the social contract and natural law, he criticized the existing system of serfdom. In his major work *Filosoficheskie predlozheniia* (Philosophical Propositions, 1768) he rejected religious dogma and stressed the practical, moral function of philosophy.

Kozeratsky, Vasyl [Kozerac'kyj, Vasyl'], b 13 January 1906 in Hruzke, Balta county, Podilia gubernia, d 29 December 1982 in Kiev. Singer (dramatic tenor). Graduating from the Odessa Music and Drama Institute in 1931, he appeared in musical-comedy theaters in Odessa, Kiev, and Dnipropetrovske. In 1951 he joined the Kiev Theater of Opera and Ballet as a soloist, and in 1963 he turned to teaching. From 1965 he taught at the Kiev Conservatory. His repertoire included such parts as Andrii in M. Lysenko's *Taras Bulba*, Bohun in K. Dankevych's *Bohdan Khmelnytsky*, Vasyl in H. Maiboroda's *Mylana*, and Herman in P. Tchaikovsky's *The Queen of Spades*.

Kozhevnykov, Serhii [Koževnykov, Serhij], b 23 September 1906 in Katerynoslav (now Dnipropetrovske). Specialist in mechanics; corresponding member of the AN URSR since 1951. After graduating from the Moscow Industrial Pedagogical Institute, he worked at various institutes in Moscow, Dnipropetrovske, and Kiev. In 1970 he became chairman of a department at the AN URSR Institute of Mechanics. His publications deal with the mechanization and automatization of mining operations and the dynamics of machines.

Kozhukhar, Volodymyr [Kožuxar], b 16 March 1941 in Vinnytsia. Conductor and educator. Upon graduating from the Kiev Conservatory in 1963, he was appointed conductor of the Symphony Orchestra of the Ukrainian SSR, and in 1973 conductor of the Kiev Theater of Opera and Ballet as well. Since 1977 he has served as chief conductor of the Moscow Music Theater. His repertoire includes F. Haydn, W.A. Mozart, L. Beethoven, C. Debussy, G. Gershwin, P. Tchaikovsky, S. Prokofiev, and D. Shostakovich. He has recorded systematically the works of such Ukrainian composers as L. Revutsky, B. Liatoshynsky, H. Maiboroda, A. Shtoharenko, L. Kolodub, V. Hubarenko, and M. Skoryk. He taught opera and orchestra conducting at the Kiev Conservatory (1965–77) and then held the chair of orchestra conducting at the Gnesin Music and Pedagogy Institute in Moscow.

Kozhukhivka [Kožuxivka]. III-11. A village in Vasylkiv raion southwest of Kiev. Battles took place there between the Sich Riflemen and the Russian Volunteer Army (November 1918) and the Red Army (February 1919), and between the Ukrainian Galician Army and the Red Army (August 1919).

Kozhukhov [Kožuxov]. Soviet concentration camp near Moscow. In spring 1920 approximately 250 officers and soldiers of the Ukrainian Galician Army were interned there, among them Gen O. Mykytka and Gen H. Tsirits. At the beginning of July 1920, 217 officers were deported, probably to Arkhangelsk. None were ever heard from again.

Koziak, Brother Methodius, [Kozjak], b 7 May 1904 in Leeshore, Alberta, d 4 April 1981 in Yorkton, Saskatchewan. Educator. Educated at St Joseph's College in Yorkton, Koziak joined the Order of Christian Brothers in 1923 and served as principal of St Joseph's College for 35 years. While chairman of the Ukrainian Curriculum Committee, he helped to make Ukrainian an accredited language option in most provincial high schools. A founder of the *Ukrainian Catholic Brotherhood, Koziak was coeditor of **Svitlo* (1950–65). In 1973 he was appointed to the Order of Canada.

Koziak, Julian (Gregory) [Kozjak], b 16 September 1940 in Edmonton. Lawyer and politician. A graduate of the University of Alberta, Koziak was elected in 1971 to represent Edmonton-Strathcona in the Alberta legislature as a Progressive Conservative. He has served as minister of education (1975–9), minister of consumer and corporate affairs (1979–82), and minister of municipal affairs (1982–6). Under his tenureship as minister of education, the Ukrainian bilingual program became a permanent feature of the Alberta school system. Koziak is active in many Ukrainian Catholic organizations. He was a candidate for the leadership of the Alberta Progressive Conservative party in 1985.

Koziatyn [Kozjatyn]. IV-9. City (1970 pop 26,600) and raion center in Vinnytsia oblast. An important railroad junction, it is known to have existed during the *Haidamaka uprising of 1734. In late 1918 Ukrainian insurgent forces clashed with the German army there; in February 1919 the Sich Riflemen Corps battled the Red Army; and in the summer of 1919 the Ukrainian Galician Army fought the Bolsheviks there during its advance on Kiev. Today the city's main industries are food processing and railroad-transport servicing.

Koziurenko, Oleksander [Kozjurenko], b 22 February 1892 in Hnyliakove, Odessa county, Kherson gubernia, d 28 May 1959 in Kiev. Graphic artist and caricaturist. A graduate of the Odessa Art School (1915), he established himself in Kiev, designing propaganda posters and drawing satirical sketches and caricatures for newspapers and magazines such as *Komunist, Bil'shovyk, Chervonyi perets'*, and *Vsesvit*. During the Second World War he worked in his profession at the front. From 1943 to 1959 he was on the staff of the satirical magazine *Perets'*.

Kozlaniuk, Petro [Kozlanjuk], b 12 August 1904 in Pereriv, Kolomyia county, Galicia, d 19 March 1965 in Lviv. Galician Sovietophile writer. He began publishing political feuilletons and stories about the Galician working class in 1926 in the periodicals *Hromads'kyi holos* and *Sel'-Rob*. A member of the editorial board of the journal *Vikna* (1927–32), he cofounded the literary organization *Horno in 1929 and was an editor of the weekly *Syla* (1930–2). During the 1939–41 Soviet occupation of Galicia, he wrote for the newspaper *Vil'na Ukraïna*. During the Second World War he was a Soviet radio commentator, and after the war he headed the Lviv branch of the Writer's Union of Ukraine (1944–52, 1954–65). He wrote many works, mostly of a propagandistic and socialist-realist nature, set in interwar Galicia. Over 30 collections of his stories and feuilletons appeared during his lifetime. His largest work is the trilogy *Iurko Kruk* (1946–56). Collected editions of his works appeared in 1960 (3 vols) and 1974–5 (4 vols). Books about him have been written by Yu. Baida (1959) and V. Kachkan (1980).

Kozlov, Petr, b 15 October 1863 in Dukhovshchina, Smolensk gubernia, d 26 September 1935 in Petergof, Leningrad oblast. Naturalist, geographer, and explorer; from 1928 full member of the AN URSR. Having participated in several expeditions, he led expeditions to the Altai, Gobi, and Tibet (1899–1901), and to Mongolia and Szechuan (1907–9). After the Revolution he worked at the Askaniia-Nova Nature Reserve and in 1923–6 led the first Soviet expedition to Central Mongolia. Kozlov helped to establish the geography of lakes, rivers, and mountains of Central Asia and Mongolia, and assembled a rich collection of mammals, birds, and fish of the region. He made important finds of Tertiary fossils in the northern Gobi Desert.

Valeriia Kozlovska

Kozlovska, Valeriia [Kozlovs'ka, Valerija], b 20 June 1889 in Kiev, d 6 May 1956 in Utica, New York. Archeologist. After graduating from Kiev University in 1915, she studied under V. *Khvoika and assisted him in his archeological work. In 1914 she became director of the archeology department of the Kiev Museum of Antiquities and Art (now the Kiev Historical Museum). She was a member of the All-Ukrainian Archeological Committee (VUAK) and a senior research associate of the AN URSR Institute of Archeology. She participated in over 40 excavations of Trypilian and medieval sites and edited *Khronika arkheolohiï ta mystetstva* (3 issues, 1930–1). She wrote over 40 articles based on her investigations and on archeology in general; a bibliography can be found in *Rozvytok radians'koï arkheolohiï na Ukraïni (1917–1966)* (The Development of Soviet Archeology in Ukraine [1917–1966], 1966). After the Second World War she lived in

Aschaffenburg and Munich and took part in émigré scholarly life. She immigrated to the United States in 1950.

Ivan Kozlovsky

Vsevolod Kozlovsky

Kozlovsky, Ivan [Kozlovs'kyj], b 24 March 1900 in Marianivka, Vasylkiv county, Kiev gubernia. Opera and concert singer (lyrical tenor). A graduate of the Lysenko Music and Drama Institute in Kiev (1919), he performed as a soloist in the Poltava Touring Music and Drama Theater, the Kharkiv (1924) and Sverdlovsk (1925) opera theaters, and the Bolshoi Theater in Moscow (1926–54). His major roles were Lensky in P. Tchaikovsky's *Eugene Onegin*, the Fool in M. Mussorgsky's *Boris Godunov*, Levko in N. Rimsky-Korsakov's *A May Night* and Berendei in his *Snow Maiden*, and the title roles in R. Wagner's *Lohengrin* and J. Massenet's *Werther*. His Ukrainian repertoire included Levko in M. Lysenko's *The Drowned Girl* and Petro in his *Natalka from Poltava*, Andrii in M. Arkas's *Kateryna*, and Andrii in S. Hulak-Artemovsky's *Zaporozhian Cossack beyond the Danube*. He began giving concerts in 1919, including in them arias from Ukrainian operas and songs by Ukrainian, Russian, and other composers, such as L. Beethoven, F. Schubert, R. Schumann, and F. Liszt. His recordings have earned him an outstanding reputation in the United States.

BIBLIOGRAPHY

Polianovskii, H. *Ivan S. Kozlovskii* (Moscow-Leningrad 1945)
Kuznetsova, A. *Stranitsy zhizni i tvorchestva I.S. Kozlovskogo* (Moscow 1964)

Kozlovsky, Oleksii [Kozlovs'kyj, Oleksij], b 17 March 1892 in Isakivtsi, Kamianets-Podilskyi county, Podilia gubernia. Civic and political figure. Completing his law studies at Kiev University, he served in the Russian army. In 1918 he joined the Karmaliuk Haidamaka Battalion of the UNR Army. When the Directory came to power, he worked at the Defense Ministry in Kiev. Emigrating in 1920 to Czechoslovakia, he served from 1922 to 1951 as lecturer and secretary of the Ukrainian Husbandry Academy and the Ukrainian Technical and Husbandry Institute. At the same time he belonged to the external delegation of the Ukrainian Social Democratic Workers' party and edited and published its central organ *Sotsiial-Demokrat* in Poděbrady, Czechoslovakia. In 1951 he immigrated to the United States.

Kozlovsky, Vsevolod [Kozlovs'kyj], b 18 April 1877 in eastern Podilia, d ? Librarian and civic figure. In 1906 he was secretary of *Hromads'ka dumka*, the first Ukrainian daily newspaper in Kiev. Having emigrated to Galicia, he served as secretary of the Union for the Liberation of Ukraine (1914–17) and of the UNR diplomatic legation in Berlin (1918). Upon returning to Ukraine in 1920, he worked in the National Library of Ukraine. In the 1930s he moved to Alma-Ata, Kazakh SSR.

Kozlovsky-Trofymovych, Isaia [Kozlovs'kyj-Trofymovyč, Isaja], b ?, d 15 March 1651 in Kiev. Renowned Orthodox theologian and pedagogue of Galician origin. He studied at the Vilnius Brotherhood School, then at the Jesuit College in Lublin and the Zamostia Academy. From 1631 he lived in Kiev, where he was a professor and rector at the Kievan Mohyla College (later the Kievan Mohyla Academy). Kozlovsky-Trofymovych was a close collaborator of Metropolitan P. *Mohyla. In 1633 he was sent as an envoy to gain Patriarch Cyril Lucaris's confirmation of Mohyla's election as metropolitan. He was an active participant in the church councils in Kiev (1640) and Iaşi (1642), and coauthor with Mohyla of *Pravoslavne Ispovidannia Viry* (Orthodox Confession of Faith, published in 1696), for which he was awarded the title 'Doctor of Theology' by the Kiev church council in September 1640. *Pravoslavne Ispovidannia Viry* was approved in 1643 by the four Eastern patriarchs and became a cornerstone of the entire Orthodox church. An abridged version was published in Polish (1645) and in Ukrainian as *Sobranie korotkoi nauky o artykulakh viry pravoslavnokafolicheskoi ...* (A Collection of Short Lessons on the Articles of the Universal Orthodox Faith ..., 1645). Kozlovsky-Trofymovych also assisted Mohyla in compiling the **Trebnyk* (Euchologion) of 1646. From 1638 until his death he was hegumen of the Kiev St Nicholas's Monastery.

BIBLIOGRAPHY

Kharlampovich, K. *Zapadnorusskie pravoslavnye shkoly XVI i nachala XVII veka* (Kazan 1898)
Vozniak, M. *Istoriia ukraïns'koï literatury*, 2 (Lviv 1921)

A. Zhukovsky

Kozlovych, Ioan [Kozlovyč], b ?, d 17 March 1757. Orthodox churchman and bishop. He was a professor of poetics and rhetoric at the Kievan Mohyla Academy before moving to Moscow, where he was professor of philosophy and prefect (from 1742) and then rector (1748–53) at the Slavonic-Greek-Latin Academy. He was also archimandrite of the Donskoi Monastery of the Mother of God and the Zaikonospasskii Monastery in Moscow. In 1753 he was appointed bishop of Pereiaslav and Boryspil. As bishop, he improved education in his eparchy and built hospices for the poor.

Kozłowski, Leon, b 1892 in Rembieszyce, Jędrzejów county, Poland, d 11 May 1944 in Berlin. Polish archeologist and politician. He held the Chair of Archeology at Lviv University (1922–39), and served as a senator (1935–9) and a member (1929–32), minister (1930–2), and chairman (1934–5) of the Polish Sejm. He excavated Neolithic and Trypilian sites in Galicia (Buchach, Koshylivtsi, and Nezvysko) and wrote several important books on Polish archeology, including *Zarys pradziejów Polski południowo wschodniej* (An Outline of the Prehistory of Southeastern Poland, 1939).

Kozoris, Mykhailo, b 1882 in Kalush, Galicia, d 1937. Writer. A graduate of Lviv University, whose short stories, fables, and children's plays began to appear in 1907 in the Bukovynian and Galician press. After the First World War he settled in Soviet Ukraine and joined the Zakhidnia Ukraina writers' union in 1925. He authored two collections of short stories, *Viche* (The Public Meeting, 1928) and *Po kam'ianii stezhtsi* (Along the Rocky Path, 1931), and three novels, *Selo vstaie* (The Village Is Rising, 1929), *Chornohora hovoryt'* (Chornohora Speaks, 1931), and *Holuba krov* (Azure Blood, 1932). He also wrote a literary study, *Sotsial'ni momenty v tvorchosti V. Stefanyka* (Social Elements in the Works of V. Stefanyk, 1932). Kozoris was arrested in 1933, and his subsequent fate is unknown.

Kozova. IV-6. Town smt (1979 pop 7,700) and raion center in Ternopil oblast, situated on the Koropets River. It was first mentioned in 1440. Sugar, bricks, furniture, and wood and dairy products are made there.

Borys Kozubsky

Kozubsky, Borys [Kozubs'kyj], b 19 February 1886 in Vyshnivets, Kremianets county, Volhynia gubernia, d ? Civic and political figure. He studied law at Kiev University, but was forced to return to Volhynia in 1907 because of his membership in the Revolutionary Ukrainian party and the Ukrainian Social Democratic Workers' party, to whose weekly, *Slovo*, he contributed articles. In 1909 he was permitted to continue his studies at Kharkiv University, and he graduated in 1912. He then practiced law and worked as a local official in Kremianets. In 1917 he was a delegate to the Central Rada. When Polish rule was established in Volhynia he was arrested but released soon afterwards. He returned to Kremianets to continue his law practice and work in the Ukrainian co-operative movement. He was twice elected as a delegate to the Polish Sejm (1922 and 1927) and he became a leading member of the Ukrainian National Democratic Alliance.

Kozyk, Mykhailo, b 2 October 1879 in Semenivka, Novozybkiv county, Chernihiv gubernia, d 2 January 1947 in Lviv. Realist painter. A graduate of the Kiev Art School (1909), where he studied under H. *Diadchenko, and of the Moscow School of Painting, Sculpture, and Architecture (1913), Kozyk taught at the Kiev Art School (1915–25), the Kiev State Art Institute (1925–32), and the Kharkiv Art Institute (1932–41). He was an active member of the *Association of Artists of Red Ukraine. His works include portraits of M. Biliashivsky, V. Krychevsky, I. Steshenko, M. Hrinchenko, and V. Drukivsky with children; landscapes of orchards, Kiev parks, and industrial areas; and children's book and textbook illustrations.

Kozyrky fortified settlement. An archeological site near Kozyrky, Ochakiv raion, Mykolaiv oblast, situated on the right shore of the Boh River estuary not far from the former Greek colony of *Olbia. The settlement dates back to the 1st–3rd centuries AD. Excavations of the site in 1954–67 uncovered the remains of stone dwellings, farm buildings, and workshops with numerous weaving and milling implements. The walls of some ceremonial buildings were decorated with frescoes and plaster cornices. Under the floors pots or shallow pits with the skeletal remains of children were found. A Sarmatian burial ground from the 2nd century AD with wooden coffins containing skeletons and various artifacts was discovered nearby. The inhabitants depended on land cultivation and animal herding for their livelihood.

Kozytsky, Hryhorii [Kozyc'kyj, Hryhorij], b ca 1725 in the Hetmanate, d 6 January 1776 in St Petersburg. Writer and civic figure. He studied at the Kievan Mohyla Academy and at Leipzig University before becoming a professor of philosophy and oral literature at the Academic University of the St Petersburg Academy of Sciences (1758). In ca 1765 he was appointed secretary to Empress Catherine II. He participated in the drafting of her 'Instruction' to the Legislative Commission of 1767–9 and in the preparation of the Latin text of the commission's resolutions. In 1768 Catherine appointed him as her representative to the Society for the Translation of Foreign Books into Russian. He oversaw the work of the society and prepared several translations himself, including Ovid's *Metamorphoses* (1772) and F. Aepinus's *Beschriebung d. Weltgebäudes* (1770). He also edited the first Russian weekly, *Vsiakaia vsiachina* (1769), and translated several works by M. Lomonosov into Latin.

Pylyp Kozytsky

Kozytsky, Pylyp [Kozyc'kyj], b 23 October 1893 in Letychivka, Lypovets county, Kiev gubernia, d 27 April 1960 in Kiev. Composer and educator. A graduate of the Kiev Theological Academy (1917) and the Kiev Conservatory (1920), where he studied under B. Yavorsky and R. Glière, he taught at the Lysenko Music and Drama Institute in Kiev (1918–24), the Kharkiv Music and Drama

Institute (1925–35), and the Kiev Conservatory. He was a founding member of the *Leontovych Music Society, whose magazines *Muzyka* (1923–7) and *Muzyka masam* (1928–31) he edited, and president of the Union of Composers of Ukraine (1952–6). His works include the operas *Unknown Soldiers* (1934) and *For the Fatherland* (1941), the orchestral suite *Kozak Holota* (1925), the poem *Partisan's Daughter* (1938), string quartets, preludes for piano, choral works, church music, arrangements of folk songs, and film and drama scores (to Berezil's *Sava Chalyi* and *Le Roi s'amuse*). Kozytsky's work is based on Ukrainian folk songs and is tied to the traditions of Ukrainian classical music. His themes are mostly social and patriotic. In addition to composing, he wrote many articles and published studies on the work of such composers as M. Leontovych, K. Stetsenko, B. Liatoshynsky, and B. Smetana.

BIBLIOGRAPHY

Hordiichuk, M. *P.O. Kozyts'kyi* (Kiev 1959)
Honcharenko, M. *P. Kozyts'kyi* (Kiev 1985)

Kozytsky, Serhii [Kozyc'kyj, Serhij], b 7 October 1883 in Volodymyr-Volynskyi, Volhynia gubernia, d 1941. Political and civic leader. He studied at the Moscow Pedagogical Institute and at the Kamianets-Podilskyi Ukrainian State University. In 1918–19 he served as the UNR commissar of education in Kamianets-Podilskyi county. In 1922–7 he was a deputy to the Polish Sejm and president of the Ukrainian Club (1926). Joining *Sel-Rob in 1927, he sat in the Polish Senate as a deputy of Sel-Rob's right wing (1928–30). In the Sejm he was a member of the Educational Commission. He was also the president of the Prosvita society branch in Ostrih.

Krai. The term for an administrative-territorial unit, from the Slavic word for a locale, country, or province. In the Russian Empire it was used to designate large border regions made up of several gubernias or provinces (oblasts) and was synonymous with a general-gubernia (eg, the Southwestern krai, consisting of Kiev, Podilia, and Volhynia gubernias). Since 1924 the term has been used in the RSFSR for six regions made up of autonomous oblasts and okrugs for national minorities. *Krasnodar and *Stavropol krais lie within Ukrainian ethnic territory, and Altai krai in *Siberia and Khabarovsk and Primore krais in the Soviet *Far East have sizable Ukrainian populations.

Kraikivsky, Yuliian [Krajkivs'kyj, Julijan], b 12 August 1892 in Rizdviany, Rohatyn county, Galicia, d 14 September 1975 in Edmonton. Painter specializing in battle scenes. A graduate of the Vienna Academy of Arts (1920), in the interwar period he taught art in gymnasiums in Stanyslaviv and Rohatyn and worked as an illustrator for the Chervona Kalyna publishing cooperative. He left Ukraine in 1944 and settled in Edmonton in 1948. Some of his better-known works are *Bohdan Khmelnytsky's Campaign*, *The Cavalry Attack*, *Satan's Raid*, *Arkan*, and *Hahilky* from his Hutsul cycle, and a portrait of V. Stefanyk. He took part in 19 exhibitions. A posthumous exhibition, consisting of 51 works, was held in his memory in 1976 in Edmonton.

Krainiev, Danylo [Krajnjev], b 13 December 1872 in Bosarevo, Orel gubernia, d 2 June 1949 in Odessa. Realist painter and educator. A graduate of the Odessa Drawing School (1890) and the St Petersburg Academy of Arts (1901), he worked most of his life in Odessa, painting and lecturing at the Odessa Art School (later Institute). He painted portraits, including a self-portrait; genre paintings such as *Punishment by the Rod at Zaporizhia* (1935), *Cadres* (1925), and *Friends at T. Shevchenko's Sickbed* (1939); still lifes; and landscapes.

Krainsky, Mykola [Krajins'kyj], b 1869 in Kiev, d 18 July 1951 in Kharkiv. Psychiatrist and psychologist. A graduate of Kharkiv University (1893), from 1894 he worked at P. Kovalevsky's psychiatric clinic in Kharkiv. He taught psychiatry at Kiev (1918–19), Zagreb (1921–8), and Belgrade (1928–41) universities. He returned to Ukraine in 1946 and directed the biophysiological laboratory at the Ukrainian Institute of Psychoneurology. He wrote works on syphilis of the brain, hallucination, the theory of nervous and mental processes, and epilepsy; the books *Energetik der mechanischen Erscheinungen* (1924) and *Matematicheskie osnovy estestvoznaniia* (The Mathematical Foundations of Natural Science, 1927); and an introductory textbook on teaching forensic experimental psychology (1930), written in Serbian.

Krainychenko, Volodymyr [Krajnyčenko], b 6 August 1925 in Verkhnie, Pervomaiske okruha, d 11 May 1964 in Kharkiv. Stage director. Upon graduating from the Kharkiv Theater Institute, where he studied under M. Krushelnytsky, he worked as a stage director with the Kharkiv Ukrainian Drama Theater (1952–64). He directed such plays as P. Myrny's *Lymerivna* (The Saddler's Daughter, 1952), T. Shevchenko's *Nazar Stodolia*, his own stage adaptations of P. Myrny's *Poviia* (The Strumpet) and M. Stelmakh's *Krov liuds'ka – ne vodytsia* (Human Blood Is Not Water), M. Pechenizhsky's *Den' narodzhennia* (Birthday, 1960), and M. Zarudny's *Maryna* (1964).

Krainyk, Mykola [Krajnyk], b 20 April 1935 in Galicia. Ukrainian dissident; by profession a teacher. He was arrested on 29 September 1979 and accused of organizing the Ukrainian National Front, publishing a *samvydav* anthology, *Prozrinnia* (The Recovery of Sight), and circulating the underground journal *Ukraïns'kyi visnyk*. He was sentenced to seven years' imprisonment and three years' internal exile for 'anti-Soviet agitation and propaganda' and 'participation in anti-Soviet organizations.'

Kraiovyi Soiuz Reviziinyi. See Audit Union of Ukrainian Co-operatives.

Krakaliia, Kost [Krakalija, Kost'], b 1884. Bukovynian political leader and journalist. Until 1922 he was a leading member of the Ukrainian section of the Social Democratic Party of Bukovyna. Then, abandoning the interests of the Ukrainian population of Bukovyna, he joined the Rumanian National Farmer's party and headed its Ukrainian section (1922–30). During this period he edited the Ukrainian-language weekly *Khliborob* (1923) and *Khliborobs'ka pravda* (1924–38), in which he attacked the Ukrainian nationalist movement and supported the government's anti-Ukrainian policies. In 1920–2 and 1928–31 Krakaliia was a deputy to the Rumanian Parliament. Breaking with the National Farmer's party in 1930, he collaborated with various other Rumanian political parties. Besides being involved in political life, he translated many Ukrainian works into German and prepared the language handbook *Ukrainisch (Ruthenisch): Methode Toussaint-Langenscheidt Sprachführer* (1915).

Krakivs'ki visti

Krakivs'ki visti (Cracow News). A daily newspaper published from 1940 to 1944 in Cracow (semiweekly from 7 January to 1 May 1940 and then triweekly to 30 October 1940), and from 10 October 1944 to 4 April 1945 in Vienna. The unofficial organ of the *Ukrainian Central Committee, it was published by the Ukrainske Vydavnytstvo publishing house. Its chief editors were B. Levytsky (briefly) and M. Khomiak (assisted by L. Lepky), and its staff included journalists such as I. Kedryn, I. Durbak, M. Kozak, and P. Sahaidachny. Altogether 1,400 issues came out, and the circulation ranged from 7,200 to 22,500. The paper was published for the Ukrainian population in the Nazi-ruled *Generalgouvernement, but it was read also by Ukrainians in Germany and Czechoslovakia. *Krakivs'ki visti* was the most influential Ukrainian daily published during the Second World War and, in spite of severe German censorship, it was an important source of information about developments at the time on all Ukrainian territories. Concurrently, a popular weekly aimed at Ukrainian farmers was published under the same title as the daily from 1 November 1940 to the end of 1944 (200 issues in all). Its circulation ranged from 6,000 to 27,000. Its chief editor was Yu. Tarnovych. A somewhat revised version of the weekly, titled *Kholms'ka zemlia*, was published for the Kholm region.

S. Yaniv

Král, Jiří, b 31 October 1893 in Prague. Czech geographer and anthropologist; full member of the Shevchenko Scientific Society. A graduate of Prague University (1917), in the 1920s he lectured at Prague University, then at Bratislava University (1929–38), and after the Second World War again at Prague University. Specializing in the geography and anthropology of Transcarpathia, he wrote *Podkarpatská Rus* (1924) and *Nejnovější mapy antropologické Slovenska a Podkarpatské Rusi* (1933).

Kralytsky, Anatol [Kralyc'kyj, Anatol'], b 13 February 1835 in Čabiny, Humenne circle, Slovakia, d 30 January 1894 in Mukachiv, Transcarpathia. Writer and historian. In 1858 he entered the Basilian order, later serving as the hegumen of a monastery in Mukachiv. He organized the educational and publishing Society of St Basil the Great. A number of old documents in the history of Transcarpathia as well as a history of Ukrainian monasteries of the region were published by Kralytsky. He collected ethnographic materials for M. Drahomanov and contributed historical and biographical articles to the Galician and Transcarpathian press. His fiction consists of short stories and novels, of which the best known is *Kniaz' Laborets'* (Prince Laborets, 1863).

Kramar, Yevhen, b 18 February 1933 in Psary (now Pryozerne), Rohatyn county, Galicia. Lawyer, historian, and publicist. He completed his law studies at Lviv University (1956), then practiced in Moldavia and Odessa and Volhynia oblasts. His popular articles on Ukrainian history – on topics as diverse as the *Slovo o polku Ihorevi*, the etymology of the word *kozak* ('Cossack'), and I. Franko – have appeared in Soviet Ukrainian journals as well as in *Nashe slovo* in Warsaw and Ukrainian periodicals in Yugoslavia. He has also written studies of the Gagauzy, Karaites, and Gypsies in Ukraine, and on the history of Ukrainian-Bulgarian relations. A selection of his essays was published in the West as *Doslidzhennia z istoriï Ukraïny* (Studies in Ukrainian History, 1984).

Kramarenko, Andrii, b 16 October 1897 in Vilshany, Kharkiv county, Kharkiv gubernia, d 1 April 1976 in Odessa. Character actor. A graduate of the drama studio of the Chief Political-Educational Committee in Kharkiv (1921), Kramarenko first worked with I. Yukhymenko and then at the Kharkiv Chervonozavodskyi Ukrainian Drama Theater (1927–33) and the Odessa Ukrainian Drama Theater of the October Revolution (1934–60). He appeared in a wide range of plays: from populist-realist to socialist-realist plays, to world classics. For example, he played Cherevyk in M. Starytsky's *Sorochyns'kyi iarmarok* (The Sorochyntsi Fair), Yarchuk in I. Mykytenko's *Solo na fleiti* (Flute Solo), and Benedick in W. Shakespeare's *Much Ado about Nothing*. Kramarenko also directed plays.

Kramarenko, Leonid, b 15 December 1881 in Balta, Podilia gubernia, d 14 May 1960 in Kharkiv. Specialist in agricultural machine building; corresponding member of the AN URSR from 1939. A graduate of Kiev University, he taught at the Kiev Polytechnical Institute (1915–29) and then at the Kharkiv Institute of Mechanics and Machine Building. In 1945 he joined the Kharkiv Scientific Research Institute of Animal Husbandry of the Forest-Steppe and Polisia. His publications deal with the theory and design of various agricultural machines and processes.

Lev Kramarenko: *Factory Town in the Donbas* (oil, 1937)

Kramarenko, Lev, b 13 January 1888 in Uman, Kiev gubernia, d 5 March 1942 in Samarkand, Uzbek SSR.

Monumentalist painter and pedagogue. A graduate of the St Petersburg (1908) and Paris (1911) academies of art, he was a lecturer of the Kiev (1923–30) and Kharkiv (1931–2) art institutes. From 1927 he belonged to the Union of Contemporary Artists of Ukraine. He took part in decorating the clubhouse and cafeteria of the Children's Village in Kiev (1924), the Academy of Sciences conference hall in Kiev (1930), the Serp i Molot club in Moscow (1934), and the Kiev Russian Drama Theater (1936–7). His easel paintings include frescoes such as *Working Woman* (1927), still lifes such as *Still Life with Samovar* (1929), and landscapes of the Donets Basin, the Crimea, and Central Asia. L. Lohvynska and O. Malashenko wrote a monograph about Kramarenko in 1975.

Kramatorske or **Kramatorsk** [Kramators'ke], V-18, DB II-3. City (1985 pop 192,000) in Donetske oblast, situated on the Kazennyi Torets River, a tributary of the Dinets. It is one of the largest centers of the heavy-machine-building industry in Ukraine and an important railway junction linking Lozova, Popasna, Rostov-na-Donu, Artemivske, and Krasnyi Lyman. Kramatorske arose in the second half of the 19th century, when a station of the Kursk–Azov railway was established on the city's present site and the town grew up around it. Over time, several settlements established in the late 18th century were incorporated into the new town. The city grew as the entire *Donets Basin was developed. In 1896 a German firm opened a factory to produce machinery for the mining and railway industries (now the Old Kramatorske Machine-Building Plant). By 1914 the city had 4,000 inhabitants. Its population grew quickly with the industrialization of the entire region, reaching 12,000 in 1926, 93,000 in 1939, and 115,000 in 1959. The large New Kramatorske Machine-Building Plant was opened in 1934. Today the city's industries produce equipment for the metallurgical, coal, mining, and heavy-machine-tool-building industries and building materials (cement, slate, and slagwood). The coke-chemicals, casting and forging, food, and light industries are also developed. Kramatorske has a scientific-research and technological-planning institute of machine building, an industrial institute, two tekhnikums, and a museum of revolutionary and labor glory.

Kramatorske Industrial Institute (Kramatorskyi industrialnyi instytut). A technical school of higher education under the jurisdiction of the Ministry of Higher and Specialized Secondary Education of the Ukrainian SSR. Formed in 1953 as a branch of the Donetske Polytechnical Institute, it was transformed into an independent evening school in 1960, and into a complete institute, with day, evening, and correspondence sections, in 1963. It has departments of mechanical engineering, metallurgy, and automatization, among others, and graduate and preparatory programs. The institute's enrollment is approximately 5,000, and over 12,000 engineers have graduated from it since its establishment.

Kramskoi, Ivan [Kramskoj] (Kramsky), b 8 June 1837 in Ostrohozke, Voronezh gubernia, Russia, d 5 April 1887 in St Petersburg. Russian realist painter of Ukrainian origin. A graduate (1863) and faculty member (1869–87) of the St Petersburg Academy of Arts, he was one of the founders and ideologists of the *Peredvizhniki. In the 1850s he visited Kharkiv, and in 1871 he worked in Khotin village in the Sumy region. He made frequent trips to the Crimea. His works include canvases on religious themes such as *Christ in the Desert* (1872) and *Inconsolable Grief* (1884); a collection of portraits, including portraits of T. Shevchenko (1871), P. Martynovych (1876), O. Lytovchenko (1878), and a self-portrait (1867); and a series of genre paintings, such as *Forester* (1874), *Peasant with Bridle* (1883), and *Rural Smithy* (1885). His *Nymphs* (1871) and *Moonlit Night* (1880) were based on his memories of Ukraine and the impact of N. Gogol's writings on him.

Ivan Kramskoi: *Portrait of T. Shevchenko* (oil, 1871)

Krasheninnikov, Serhii [Krašeninnikov, Serhij], b 25 October 1895 in Slutsk, Belorussia, d 27 August 1987 in Philadelphia. Zoologist; full member of the Shevchenko Scientific Society and of the Ukrainian Academy of Arts and Sciences in the United States. A graduate of Kiev (1924) and Moscow (1937) universities and the Ukrainian Free University in Munich (PH D 1949), Krasheninnikov taught zoology at Kiev University (1936–7), the Bila Tserkva Agricultural Institute (1934–41), and the Ukrainian Technical and Husbandry Institute in Regensburg (1945–9). After immigrating to the United States in 1949, he worked as a researcher at the University of Pennsylvania (1955–62) and as a professor at the University of Miami (1962–3). He published over 40 scientific papers, mostly dealing with parasitic Ciliata (Protozoa). He also edited the album *Kyïv Shevchenkovykh chasiv* (Kiev during Shevchenko's Times, 1984).

Krasivsky, Zinovii [Krasivs'kyj, Zinovij], b 12 November 1929 in Vytvytsia, Dolyna county, Galicia. Poet; Ukrainian dissident and human-rights activist. Deported

Zynovii Krasivsky

with his whole family to Kazakhstan in 1947, he escaped and took part in the resistance movement in Ukraine. He was sentenced in 1949 to five years' imprisonment and perpetual exile. Released in 1953, he joined his family in Karaganda, where he was crippled in a mining accident. In 1959 he returned to Ukraine. After receiving a degree in philology at Lviv University (1962), he became active in the Ukrainian National Front and helped publish its underground journal *Volia i bat'kivshchyna*. For this he was sentenced in 1967 to five years' imprisonment, seven years' hard labor, and five years' exile. For writing a verse collection *Nevil'nychi plachi* (Slave Lamentations), the poem 'Triumf satany' (Satan's Triumph), and protest letters, and participating in hunger strikes, he was transferred in 1972 to a psychiatric hospital in Smolensk and in 1976 to a similar institution in Lviv. After being released he joined the *Ukrainian Helsinki Group in 1979. In March 1980 he was rearrested and forced to complete his earlier sentence. He was released in 1985.

Kraskovsky, Ivan [Kraskovs'kyj], b 1882 in the northern Podlachia region, d ? Political figure of Ukrainian-Belorussian background. He studied at Warsaw University. During the First World War he was a representative of the All-Russian Union of Cities in Galicia. A member of the Ukrainian Party of Socialist Revolutionaries, in 1917 he was a gubernial commissar of the Russian Provisional Government in the Ternopil region. In January 1918 he became a deputy minister under the UNR prime minister, V. Vynnychenko. During the Hetman government he was a member of the Council of the Ministry of Foreign Affairs, then the representative of the UNR in Georgia and Kuban. In 1920 he moved to Belorussia and became a lecturer at the State University in Minsk. He was arrested in the 1930s and his fate is unknown.

Krasna or **Polonyna Krasna.** A mountain ridge in the *Polonynian Beskyd between the Tereblia and Teresva rivers. In its southwestern part it joins the Menchul (Menchiv) mountain group. This broad, uniform ridge reaches an elevation of 1,719 m (Mt Strymba) and is covered with meadows. Its steep slopes are forested with beech and (in the northeast) evergreens.

Krasna River. A left-bank tributary of the Donets River, flowing for 130 km through the Central Upland and the Donets Lowland and draining a basin of 2,710 sq km.

Krasne. IV-5. Town smt (1979 pop 5,700) in Buzke raion, Lviv oblast. It was first mentioned in 1476. During the Ukrainian-Polish War of 1918–19 the town served as an air base of the Ukrainian Galician Army (UHA); there the UHA *Chortkiv offensive was broken by the Poles on 28 June 1919. Since the 1870s Krasne has been a railroad junction; it has a sugar refinery and a mixed-feed plant.

Krasni Okny. VI-10. Town smt (1979 pop 5,300) and raion center in Odessa oblast. It was founded in the late 18th century and was called Okny until 1919. The town has a local food and mixed-feed industry.

Krasnoarmiiske [Krasnoarmijs'ke]. V-18, DB III-2. City (1984 pop 65,000) and raion center under oblast jurisdiction in Donetske oblast. Established as a railroad construction settlement in the early 1880s, it was called Hryshyne until 1934 and Postysheve in 1934–8. By the turn of the century it was an important railroad junction and coal-mining center in the Donbas. From a population of 4,500 in 1913 it grew to 11,400 in 1926, 16,500 in 1933, over 30,000 in 1939, 48,000 in 1959, and 55,000 in 1970. It has six coal mines, railway-servicing firms, the plants Elektrodvyhun and Metalist, a dairy, clothing factory, and several food-processing plants. Among its educational institutions are a branch of the Donetske Polytechnical Institute and a pedagogical school. From 1904 to 1908 the composer M. Leontovych worked there and conducted the first railwaymen's choir in Ukraine.

Krasnodar. VIII-19. City (1985 pop 609,000) and capital of *Krasnodar krai, located on the Kuban River. It was founded in 1794 as Katerynodar and assumed its present name in 1920. The city was settled by former Zaporozhian Cossacks and was the main center of the *Black Sea Cossacks and then the *Kuban Cossack Host (from 1860). At the end of the 19th century it became an important trade and transport center, through which much of the agricultural produce of *Kuban passed. There was also some local industry, mainly food processing, located there. In 1897 the population was 66,000. The capital of the *Kuban People's Republic in 1918–20, it was an important center of Ukrainian life in the early 20th century. Under Soviet rule the machine-building (lathes, compressors, electronic-testing equipment), chemicals, petroleum-processing, food-processing, and textile industries have been developed. Krasnodar is also home to Kuban University (from 1920 to 1970 the Kuban Pedagogical Institute), three other institutions of higher education, and historical-regional and art museums.

Krasnodar krai. An autonomous region of the RSFSR in northwestern Caucasia, established in September 1937. It has an area of 83,600 sq km and a population (1979) of 4,814,000, 52 percent of which is urban. The region is divided into 41 raions and has 28 cities and 28 towns smt. It includes within its borders the *Adygei Autonomous oblast. The capital city is *Krasnodar (1985 pop 609,000). Krasnodar krai extends northward from the Caucasus Mountains across the steppes of Subcaucasia east of the Black and Azov seas as far as Tahanrih Bay. It is separated from Crimea by the Kerch Strait. It borders with Georgia in the south, the Karachai-Cherkess Autonomous oblast in the southeast, Stavropol krai in the east, and Rostov oblast in the north.

It was established as a separate administrative unit on the basis of the Kuban–Black Sea oblast of the RSFSR, which had been abolished in 1924 and reorganized several times in the 1920s. Its borders were approximately the same as those of the independent *Kuban People's Republic (est January 1918) and the Kuban–Black Sea Soviet Republic (est July 1918). (For the history of Krasnodar krai to 1937 and for a description of its physical geography, see *Kuban.)

Population. The inhabitants of Krasnodar krai today are mostly Russians or Russified Ukrainians, but they include Adygeians, Cherkassians, and some Armenians, Belorussians, Greeks, Tatars, and others. The distribution of the population is uneven. The most densely populated areas are the northern part of the Kuban Lowland and the Black Sea coast. The least populated areas are in the higher parts of the Caucasus Mountains. In addition to Krasnodar, other cities with a population of over 100,000 (1983) are Sochi (304,000), Novorossiiske (171,000), Armavir (167,000), and Maikop (135,000). The cities are generally concentrated on the southern edge of the Kuban Lowland and on the Black Sea coast. In 1926 Ukrainians constituted 47 percent of the entire population of the Kuban–Black Sea oblast. However, many of them were forced to flee to Asia or Transcaucasia during the forced *collectivization of agriculture in the 1930s. Many others died during the resulting famine. Those who remained were denied national rights (Ukrainian-language schools, newspapers, institutions, etc were closed) and exposed to continuous Russification. Thus, assimilation and the continual immigration of Russians and people of other nationalities have caused the proportion of Ukrainians in Krasnodar krai to decline steadily. In 1979 approx 3.9 percent of the population was Ukrainian.

Economy. Krasnodar krai is primarily an agricultural region. Approximately 62 percent of its entire area is farmland and 52.3 percent is cultivated. There are two distinct agricultural regions: the Kuban Lowland in the north, where the fertile chernozem steppe supports extensive grain production, and the Black Sea coast with its Mediterranean climate, where fruits are cultivated. The grains produced are winter wheat, winter barley, and corn. Along the lower Kuban River, much swampland has been reclaimed for rice growing. Sunflowers are the most important industrial crop of Krasnodar krai; others include sugar beets and tobacco. Vegetables are grown in the regions along the Kuban River. In the Caucasus foothills, fruit (particularly apples, cherries, pears, and apricots) and vines are cultivated. Tea and citrus fruit are grown along the Black Sea coast.

Large numbers of cattle, pigs, and poultry are raised, particularly in the Kuban Lowland. The alpine meadows in the Caucasus Mountains are used for grazing. Fish farming is practiced, and some fur-bearing animals (eg, mink) are kept.

The major industry is food processing. Wine making, including high-quality wines and cognacs (Abrau-Diurso), meat processing (Krasnodar, Armavir, etc), the fishing industry (Yeiske, Temriuk, Novorossiiske), oil pressing (Krasnodar, Kropotkin), and sugar, margarine, tobacco, and tea processing are all developed. Petroleum and natural gas are exploited near Maikop, on the Taman Peninsula, and in the north, and refined in Tuapse, Krasnodar, and Afypskyi. Salt, mercury, and other minerals are mined. Manufactured in Krasnodar krai are machine tools (Krasnodar, Maikop), tractor and automobile parts (Krasnodar, Armavir, Novorossiiske), transport machines (Tykhoritske, Novorossiiske), machines for the oil industry (Krasnodar, Armavir), printing machines (Yeiske), and other products. The chemical industry, concrete production (the Novorossiske region), woodworking and furniture manufacturing (Krasnodar, Maikop, Armavir), as well as wool, cotton, leather, and other branches of light industry (Krasnodar) are developed. Energy for the industry of Krasnodar krai comes from a network of thermoelectric stations using natural gas (Krasnodar), coal (Armavir), and oil (Novorossiiske), as well as a number of hydroelectric stations (Beleoechensk, Krasnopol, and others).

Transportation. The main railway lines in the krai are Rostov-na-Donu–Armavir–Adler-Sukhumi and Volgograd–Krasnodar–Novorossiiske. A new electric railway line from Krasnodar to Tuapse is being completed. Auto transport is more important on the Black Sea coast. The main highways are Krasnodar–Sochi–Adler and Anapa–Novorossiiske–Tuapse. Boats travel the Kuban River and the coastal waters. The main seaports are Novorossiiske (for the export of grain and concrete), Tuapse (oil products), Sochi, and Anapa on the Black Sea, and Yeiske and Temriuk on the Sea of Azov.

Resorts and tourism. Krasnodar krai is one of the most important resort and tourist regions in the USSR. It has 92 sanatoriums and 120 rest homes on the sea coast and in the Caucasus Mountains, often with mineral springs and mud baths. The most important resort region is the Black Sea coast between Tuapse and Adler, centered in Sochi. On the Azov coast, the largest resort center is Yeiske, with its sulfur-hydrogen mineral springs and mud baths. In the Caucasus Mountains the best-known resort is Hariachyi Kliuch. The *Caucasus Nature Reserve is located in the southwest corner of Krasnodar krai.

M. Stech

Krasnodon. V-20, DB III-7. City (1986 pop 51,000) and raion center under oblast jurisdiction in Voroshylovhrad oblast. It was founded in 1914 as a mining settlement and was called Sorokyne until 1938. The city is a coal-mining center. It also has an automotive-parts plant and a building-materials plant. A war museum highlights the activities of the Soviet underground during the Second World War, in particular the Moloda Gvardiia group.

Krasnogvardiiske [Krasnogvardijs'ke]. VIII-15. Town smt (1979 pop 9,100) and raion center in Crimea oblast. It has been known since the mid-19th century and until 1945 was called Kurman-Kemelchi. The food industry is the mainstay of its economy.

Krasnohorivka. V-18, DB III-3. City (1970 pop 19,600) in Marinka raion, Donetske oblast, situated on the Lozova River 25 km northwest of Donetske. Krasnohorivka was founded in the 1870s. Today it has a plant that manufactures refractory materials and an automobile-repair plant.

Krasnohrad. IV-16. City (1972 pop 19,500) and raion center in Kharkiv oblast. In 1731 the Bielovska Fortress, which became the seat of the *Ukrainian Line of frontier fortifications, was erected at its site. In 1784 the fortress became the town of Kostiantynohrad. In the 18th and 19th century it produced textiles, especially silk. The town kept this name until 1922; from 1802 to 1917 it was a county town in Poltava gubernia. Today Krasnohrad is a railroad junction. It has a food industry, building-materials industry, and a mechanized-agriculture tekhnikum.

Krasnoilske or **Krasnoilsk** [Krasnojil's'ke]. v-6. Town smt (1979 pop 7,200) in Storozhynets raion, Chernivtsi oblast, situated on the Sireteli River. First mentioned in a document from 1431, the town has wood-processing and household-products factories.

Krasnokutske or **Krasnokutsk** [Krasnokuc'ke]. III-16. Town smt (1986 pop 7,700) and raion center in Kharkiv oblast, situated on the Merla River. One of the oldest towns in Slobidska Ukraine, Krasnokutske was founded as Krasnyi Kut in 1651 by Cossacks from the Korsun region. A company town in Okhtyrka regiment until 1765 and then a county town in Kharkiv gubernia at the end of the century, it assumed its present name in 1780. In 1897 it had 6,860 inhabitants, most of whom were engaged in agriculture. Today it has a creamery, building-materials plant, and a furniture factory.

Krasnokutskyi kurhan. A Scythian kurhan, also known as Tovsta Mohyla, from the 4th to the early 3rd centuries BC situated near Loshkarivka, Nykopil raion, Dnipropetrovske oblast. I. Zabelin's excavation of the kurhan in 1860 uncovered the pillaged grave of a Scythian chieftain, the skeletons of four horses, horse armor with silver ornaments, and parts of two wooden carts.

Krasnopavlivka. IV-17. Town smt (1979 pop 8,600) in Lozova raion, Kharkiv oblast. The town was founded in 1874–5 as a railway station on the Kursk–Azov railroad. Food-processing factories and machine-repair shops are located there. The Krasnopavlivka Reservoir on the Dnieper-Donbas Canal is located nearby.

Krasnoperekopske or **Krasnoperekopsk** [Krasnoperekops'ke]. VIII-14. City (1974 pop 16,000) and raion center in northern Crimea oblast. The city is located on the southern Perekop Isthmus. It was founded in 1932 with the establishment there of a bromide factory that used raw materials from Syvash Lake. The city also has a soda plant, several food-processing plants (a juice and wine plant, a cannery, and a dairy), and a reinforced-concrete plant.

Krasnopilia [Krasnopilja]. III-16. Town smt (1979 pop 9,200) and raion center in Sumy oblast. It was established ca 1640 as a fortress, and after the abolition of the Slobidska Ukrainian regiments in 1765 it became a *sloboda* (self-governing settlement). Today the town has several food-processing plants and a furniture factory.

Krasnopushcha [Krasnopušča]. Village in Berezhany raion, Ternopil oblast. A Basilian monastery was built there in 1664 and functioned until 1945. During the years 1771–2 and 1809–14 it had a noviciate. The monastery had a famous iconostasis decorated by the Lviv painter Vasyl; it perished in a fire in 1899 except for the royal door and some small medallions. A scaled-down version of the iconostasis was constructed in the 1890s at St Onuphrius's Monastery in Lviv.

Krasnoselsky, Oleksander [Krasnosel's'kyj], b 7 July 1877 in Moscow, d 19 March 1944 in Dnipropetrovske. Architect. A graduate of the Riga Polytechnical Institute (1906), from 1912 he worked in Dnipropetrovske, where he designed a children's residence (1914–15), a residential building with a pharmacy (1915–16), the Anatomy Building of the Medical Institute (1916), the Second Workers' Polyclinic (1924–7), the Illich Palace of Culture (1926–32), the university complex (in collaboration with V. Samodryga, 1936), and a theater (1941). His buildings vary in style: some are classicist and some are modernist.

Krasnov, Andrei, b 8 November 1862 in St Petersburg, d 1 January 1915 in Tbilisi. Russian botanist and geographer. A graduate of St Petersburg University (1885), Krasnov was a professor at Kharkiv University (1889–1911). He organized expeditions to carry out research on the soils and flora of southeastern Ukraine (the Katerynoslav, Kryvyi Rih, and Donetske regions) and the Caucasus. He also led many scientific expeditions to Central Asia, the Far East, and the Indian subcontinent. Krasnov's works were devoted to the problems of natural zones and the origin of soils, forests, and the steppe. He also wrote several textbooks. In 1912 he established the Batumi Botanical Garden in Georgia for the purpose of acclimatizing tropical plants (eg, tea) in the Russian Empire.

Krasnoznamianka Irrigation System. An irrigation system constructed in 1953–75 that uses water from the Dnieper River to irrigate the southern coast of Kherson oblast on the Black Sea. The North Crimean Canal takes water from the *Kakhivka Reservoir to feed a network of interfarm supply and field canals (total length 166 km) and 18 water stations. The total irrigated area under cultivation is 62,500 ha.

Krasny, Pinkhas, b 1881 in the Kiev region, d 1939 in Kiev. Jewish civic and political leader. He was a member of the executive of the Jewish People's party, an organizer of Jewish schools in Ukraine, and in 1919 the minister for Jewish affairs in the cabinets of B. Martos and I. Mazepa under the *Directory of the UNR. Together with other members of the UNR government, he issued numerous proclamations against pogroms carried out by some military units and civilians. He was shot in a Soviet prison in Kiev in 1939.

Ruins of Krasný Brod Monastery

Krasný Brod. Village (1970 pop 1,000) near Medzilaborce in the Prešov region of Czechoslovakia. In the 16th century a Basilian monastery was built there. In the 17th and 18th centuries the monastery ran a well-known school offering also instruction in philosophy. Later it became a place of pilgrimage. In 1915 the monastery and its church were devastated. From 1958 to 1964 the Museum of Ukrainian Culture, which later was transferred to *Svydnyk, was located in the village.

Krasnyi Luch [Krasnyj Luč]. V-19, DB III 5. City (1984 pop 110,000) under oblast jurisdiction in Voroshylovhrad oblast, situated in the central Donbas. It arose as a miners' settlement in the late 1880s and was called Kryndachivka until 1920. Krasnyi Luch is an important coal-industry center. It has five anthracite mines, three enrichment plants, an automobile-repair plant, a machine-building plant, a building-systems plant, a building-supplies plant, two reinforced-concrete plants, a metalworking plant, a furniture factory, a clothing factory, and several food-processing plants. Among its institutions are a power-engineering tekhnikum, a mining tekhnikum, and nine vocational-technical schools.

Krasnyi Lyman [Krasnyj Lyman]. V-18, DB II-3. City (1971 pop 31,000) and raion center in Donetske oblast. It was founded as a frontier *sloboda* (self-governing settlement) in 1667 and until 1938 was called Lyman. Today it is a large railroad-distribution center through which raw materials and products pass on their way out of the Donbas. It has a food industry, a building-materials industry, a railway-servicing industry, a medical school, and a technical school.

Krasnystaw (Ukrainian: Krasnostav). III-4. City (1977 pop 14,000) in the Kholm region on the Vepr (Wieprz) River, now in Chełm voievodship, Poland. One of the oldest cities of the Kholm region, it was an important center (known as Shchekariv) in the Principality of Galicia-Volhynia. It is mentioned in the Galician-Volhynian Chronicle of the 13th century. At the end of the 14th century it came under Polish rule, and in 1394 the city was granted the rights of Magdeburg law. The city prospered in the 15th and 16th centuries, when it was a major stop on the trade route between Right-Bank Ukraine and the Baltic port of Gdańsk (Danzig), but it entered a long period of decline in the 17th century. A Uniate Gothic-style church was built there in the 1540s, but neither the Uniates nor the sizable Ukrainian Orthodox population could withstand the Polonizing pressures. In 1940 there were only about 5,000 Polonized Ukrainians living in the Krasnystaw district, and they were deported to the Ukrainian SSR in 1945–6.

Krasovsky, Andrii [Krasovs'kyj, Andrij], b 1822 in Kiev, d 1868. Lieutenant colonel in the Russian army and political activist. Sometime in 1842 or 1843 Krasovsky became friends with T. *Shevchenko, whose poetry and radical ideas were to influence him greatly. In 1861 Krasovsky moved to Kiev, where he met many prominent Ukrainian intellectuals, among them O. Markovych, Marko Vovchok, and other friends of Shevchenko. Krasovsky helped organize an underground circle and a clandestine printing press and began to distribute materials and the banned poetry of Shevchenko among the peasants of Korsun and Bohuslav. Later he joined the political terrorist organization *Zemlia i Volia. In June 1862 he was arrested for writing and distributing an appeal to the soldiers of Zhytomyr regiment, dissuading them from participating in the suppression of a peasant uprising in Bohuslav. His death sentence was commuted to 12 years' hard labor, which he partially served in Nerchynsk, Chita region. He died while trying to escape.

Krasovsky, Ivan [Krasovs'kyj], b 22 October 1927 in Doshno, Sianik county, Galicia. Ethnographer, historian, specialist in Lemko history and culture. A graduate of Lviv University (1957), since 1969 he has been senior research associate of the Lviv Museum of Folk Architecture and Folkways. Most of his scholarly articles have appeared in *Nashe slovo*, published in Warsaw.

Krasovsky, Mykola [Krasovs'kyj], b 1876 in Kostiukovichy, Mahiliou gubernia, d 1953 in Kharkiv. Pharmacologist and educator. Krasovsky graduated from Kharkiv University in 1899 and became a docent there in 1909 and a professor in 1917. From 1913 to 1922 he was the president of the Kharkiv Pharmaceutical Society. In 1921 he helped organize the Kharkiv Pharmaceutical Institute, where he served as professor and assistant director for many years. He is the author of some 40 scientific works and a pharmacology textbook.

Krasovsky, Oleksander [Krasovs'kyj], 1891–1921. Political activist. He was a member of the Kiev Gubernial Executive Committee in 1917, and in 1919 an assistant inspector of the UNR Army. In October 1919 he was sent by the UNR Directory to Moscow to negotiate an alliance against the Whites led by Gen A. Denikin. He was killed while participating in the partisan struggle against the Bolsheviks.

Petro Krasovsky: Belfry of the Armenian Church in Lviv (1571)

Krasovsky, Petro [Krasovs'kyj], b and d ? Noted architect of the second half of the 16th century. He worked mostly in Lviv, where he built the belfry of the Armenian Cathedral in 1570 and the belfry (not preserved) of the Dormition Cathedral. Art historians attribute the so-called Black Building (1577) on Rynok Square and the Chapel of the Three Saints (1578) to Krasovsky. His buildings display an original synthesis of local architectural traditions with the Italian Renaissance style.

Krasusky, Konstantin [Krasuskij], b 14 September 1867 in Zaraisk county, Moscow gubernia, d 7 April 1937. Russian organic chemist; corresponding member of the AN URSR from 1926 and of the USSR Academy of Sciences from 1933. He studied at St Petersburg and Heidelberg (1892–3) universities, then taught at St Petersburg (1894–1902) and Warsaw (1902–7) before moving to Kiev. There he was a professor of organic chemistry at the Kiev Polytechnic (1907–12) and Kiev University (1912–16). He then served as professor at Kharkiv University (1916–29) before moving to Azerbaidzhan. Krasusky published over 40 papers, mainly on alpha-oxy-compounds and amino alcohols and their isomerization reactions.

Krasyliv. IV-7. City (1971 pop 13,500) and raion center in Khmelnytskyi oblast, situated on the Sluch River. First mentioned in a document from 1444, for most of the 16th and early 17th centuries it was owned by the Ostrozky family and was a small trading and crafts center. Acquired by the Russian Empire in the Second Polish Partition (1793), from 1797 it was a volost center in Starokostiantyniv county, Volhynia gubernia. Now the city has a sugar refinery, machine-construction plant, and food-processing factories.

Fotii Krasytsky: *Guest from the Zaporizhia* (oil, 1910)

Krasytsky, Fotii [Krasyc'kyj, Fotij], b 24 August 1873 in Zelena Dibrova, Zvenyhorodka county, Kiev gubernia, d 2 June 1944 in Kiev. Painter, graphic artist, and pedagogue. Having studied with M. Pymonenko at the Kiev Drawing School (1888–92), with K. Kostandi at the Odessa Drawing School (1892–4), and with I. Repin at the St Petersburg Academy of Arts (1894–1901), he settled and worked in Kiev. From 1927 to 1937 he taught at the Kiev State Art Institute. A realist painter with an inclination towards impressionism, Krasytsky produced a series of genre and landscape paintings with painstaking attention to ethnographic detail, including *Beside the Well* (1901), *Guest from Zaporizhia* (1901, variant 1916), *Old Man, Beehives, At Dinner, Road to Kozatske Village* (1899), and *Kyrylivka Village* (1901). His numerous portraits include M. Starytsky, M. Sadovsky, Lesia Ukrainka, M. Hrushevsky, I. Franko, T. Shevchenko, and a series devoted to Soviet writers (1933–4). He designed the stage sets for M. Lysenko's opera *Christmas Night*, performed in Kiev in 1903. His caricatures appeared in the satirical magazine *Shershen'* (1906) and in the handbook *Rysuvannia i maliuvannia* (Drawing and Painting, 1929).

Kraszewski, Józef, b 28 July 1812 in Warsaw, d 19 March 1887 in Geneva. Polish novelist, poet, dramatist, literary critic, historian, and journalist. A prolific writer, he is best known for his historical novels written in the Romantic spirit. He lived almost 20 years in rural Volhynia and acquired a deep sympathy for the Ukrainian peasantry and an intimate knowledge of its folkways. He wrote a cycle of novelettes dealing with the life of Ukrainian peasants, including such works as *Historia Sawki* (The Story of Savka, 1842), *Ulana* (1843), *Ostap Bodnarczuk* (1847), *Jaryna* (1850), *Chata za wsią* (The House beyond the Village, 1853–4), *Jermoła* (1857), and *Historia kołka w płocie* (The Story about a Stake in the Fence, 1860). His observations about Ukraine were collected in *Wspomnienia z Polesia, Wołynia i Litwy* (Recollections from Polisia, Volhynia, and Lithuania, 1840). M. Starytsky's play *Tsyhanka Aza* (Aza the Gypsy) was based on Kraszewski's *Chata za wsią*. A number of Ukrainian writers, including T. Shevchenko and I. Franko, valued highly Kraszewski's literary works.

Krat, Mykhailo, b 6 August 1892 in Hadiache, Poltava gubernia, d 8 August 1979 in Detroit. Prominent Ukrainian army officer. After years of distinguished service in the Russian army, he joined the UNR Army in 1917, where he attained the rank of colonel. In 1917–18 he held various staff appointments and in 1919 commanded the Eighth Black Sea Regiment. In the First Winter Campaign, Krat was first chief of staff of the Third Iron Rifle Division and then of the Zaporozhian Division. After the war he was released from Polish internment and lived in Poland. In 1944–5, Krat served as a staff officer of the First Division of the Ukrainian National Army. Upon surrendering to the British, the division was interned and Krat was appointed commander of the POW camps near Bellaria and Rimini, Italy. During this time he was promoted to brigadier general by the UNR government-in-exile. After being released by the British, he immigrated to the United States.

Pavlo Krat

Krat, Pavlo (Crath, Paul), b 10 October 1882 in Krasna Luka, Hadiache county, Poltava gubernia, d 25 December 1952 in Toronto. Socialist and Protestant leader, writer, poet, journalist, and translator. Active in the Revolutionary Ukrainian party in Poltava gubernia in the years 1901–4, Krat helped to form the Ukrainian Social Democratic Union (Spilka) in 1905. He fled to Galicia during the 1905 Revolution and in 1906 enrolled at Lviv University, where he was arrested while agitating for a Ukrainian university.

In 1907 Krat escaped to Canada. There he became active in the Federation of Ukrainian Social Democrats in Canada (later the Ukrainian Social Democratic party) in Winnipeg and Toronto and edited the periodicals *Chervonyi prapor* (1907–8), *Robochyi narod* (1914–16), *Robitnyche slovo,* and *Kadylo* (1913–18). In 1914 he founded the Society for an Independent Ukraine, and in the years 1915–16 he translated for the Office of the Press Censor for Western Canada. Ordained as a Presbyterian minister in 1917, Krat became pastor of the Ukrainian Evangelical church in Toronto in 1918. From 1923 to 1938, as a missionary, he helped to organize the Ukrainian Evangelical Reformed church in Western Ukraine. He is the author of *Robitnychi pisni* (Workers' Songs, 1911), *Vizyta 'Chervonoï druzhyny'* (Visit of the 'Red Detachment,' 1912), *Poslidnie khozhdeniie Boha po Zemli* (God's Last Wanderings on Earth, 1915), *Ukraïns'ka starodavnist'* (Ukrainian Antiquity, 1958), and other stories, satires, poems, translations, and articles.

Kratkaia letopis' Malyia Rossii (A Short Chronicle of Little Russia). A book published in 1777 by V. *Ruban in St Petersburg. The body of the book is a Cossack *chronicle covering the period from 1506 to 1734 that circulated widely in the mid-18th century in the Hetmanate. It was based on H. *Hrabianka's chronicle and perhaps a number of chronicles of the 16th–18th centuries. Known as *Kratkoe opisanie Malorossii* (A Short Description of Little Russia), it focused on the period from the Khmelnytsky uprising to the early 18th century and was later published as a supplement to the *Samovydets Chronicle. The anonymous compiler, who also wrote the section covering the years 1709–34 himself, was inspired by the idea of Ukrainian Cossack autonomism. A second section, by O. Bezborodko, provides an overview of events in Ukraine from 1735 to 1770 and summarizes the method of government in the Hetmanate. This includes a list of hetmans, senior Cossack officers, and tsarist generals and administrators in Ukraine, and is intended to raise the prestige of the Cossack *starshyna* in the Russian Empire. The final component of the book is *Zemleopisania Malyia Rossii,* which contains a description of the geography, administrative districts, population, and cities of Left-Bank Ukraine.

Kratko, Bernard, b 17 January 1884 in Warsaw, d 1 August 1960 in Kiev. Impressionist sculptor. Having studied art with K. Dunikowski at the Warsaw School of Fine Arts (1901–6), he worked as a sculptor in Warsaw and from 1916 in Petrograd. Settling in Ukraine, he became lecturer at the Kharkiv (1920–5) and Kiev (1925–35) art institutes. At the same time (1921–4) he was on the faculty of the Ukrainian State Academy of Arts in Kiev. He did many large busts for monuments: of T. Shevchenko in Kiev (1920, destroyed) and Kharkiv (1921), of H. Skovoroda in Skovorodyntsi (1923), of M. Zankovetska (1928), of M. Boichuk (1934), and of F. Krychevsky (1935). His works also include decorative bas-reliefs on the monument to the executed Decembrists in Kiev (1925) and on the portal of the Peasant Sanatorium in Odessa (1928). In 1937 Kratko was exiled to Central Asia, but he returned after the war, settled in Staline (now Donetske), and resumed sculpting. The composition *Miners* (1946) and the monuments to Ya. Sverdlov in Yenakiieve (1951) and to Lenin in Cheliuskinets are examples of his later work.

Kratokhvylia-Vidymska, Yuzefa [Kratoxvylja-Vidyms'ka, Juzefa] (Polish: Kratochwila-Widymska, Józefa), b 18 May 1878 in Lviv, d 19 December 1965 in Lviv. Painter and graphic artist. Until 1918 she studied at the Higher Art School in Vienna, and then (1921–3) at the State School of Decorative Arts and Artistic Handicrafts in Lviv (painting under K. Sichulski and graphic arts under L. Tyrowicz). In 1934 she became a member of the Association of Lviv Graphic Artists. Her paintings are devoted to landscapes, portraits, and still lifes, and include such works as *Still Life with a Violin* (1931) and views of Paris, Dalmatia, and Salzburg. In her graphic work she used various techniques, and her favorite themes were the city of Lviv and the Hutsuls. The series *Lviv Alleys, Old Lviv,* and *Old Lviv Stalls* (1934–6) consist of etchings, drypoints, aquatints, and monoprints. Her monoprint series *Hutsul Motifs* (1930s) includes such masterpieces as *Old Hutsul with Pipe, The Road to Church, Musicians from Vorokhta, Hutsul Girls, Bridesmaids, Church in Vorokhta,* and *The Lirnyk.* She also did the monoprint series *Winter in Lviv* and *Old Drohobych.* Her works were exhibited often, not only in Lviv but also in Warsaw, Cracow, Stanyslaviv, Vienna, Kiev, and Kharkiv. H. Ostrovsky published a monograph on her in 1967.

Kravchenko, Ivan [Kravčenko], b 20 July 1899 in Dovhalivske, Bila Tserkva county, Kiev gubernia, d 18 February 1953. Party historian. A graduate of the Kiev Institute of People's Education (1924), he was a research associate of the Kiev Oblast State Archives (1928–37) and the AN URSR Central Scientific Library (1938–40). In 1935–6 he also headed the VUAN Historical-Archeological Institute that was established in 1934 to fight 'Ukrainian bourgeois historiography.' In 1944 he was sent to help 'Sovietize' Chernivtsi University, serving as a lecturer and then professor of Soviet history, dean of the history faculty, and finally the prorector of the university. Kravchenko wrote works on the economic history of 18th- and 19th-century Ukraine and on the history of the 1831 Polish uprising in Ukraine.

Mykhailo Kravchenko

Kravchenko, Mykhailo [Kravčenko, Myxajlo], b 1858 in Velyki Sorochyntsi, Poltava gubernia, d 21 April 1917 in Velyki Sorochyntsi. A famous folk *kobzar. Blind from the age of 15, he learned his craft from the kobzars S. Yashno and F. Hrytsenko-Kholodny. He performed at the 12th Russian Archeological Congress in Kharkiv and the All-Russian Cottage-Industry Exhibition in St Petersburg in 1902 and gave several concerts in Moscow, Kiev, Katerynoslav, and Poltava. Two of his own *dumas deal with the 1905 peasant uprising in Sorochyntsi. Lesia Ukrainka, V. Korolenko, O. Slastion, P. Martynovych, and particularly F. Kolessa recorded the dumas he sang. He taught the famous kobzar P. *Huz.

Uliana Kravchenko

Kravchenko, Uliana [Kravčenko, Uljana] (pen name of Yuliia Schneider), b 18 April 1860 in Mykolaiv, Zhydachiv county, Galicia, d 31 March 1947 in Peremyshl. Writer and village school teacher. Her first work – the story 'Kalytka' (The Purse) – was published in 1881 in the journal *Zoria*. As a writer she was strongly influenced by I. *Franko. She was active in the Ukrainian women's movement in Galicia, and much of her poetry deals with the theme of women's liberation. Her separate poetry collections are *Prima vera* (1885, 1925), *Na novyi shliakh* (Onto a New Road, 1891, 1928), *V zhytti ie shchos'* (There Is Something in Life, 1929), *Dlia neï – vse!* (For Her – Everything! 1931), and *Vybrani poeziï* (Selected Poems, 1941). Her poetry for children was published as the collections *Prolisky* (Anemones, 1921), *V dorohu* (On Our Way, 1921), *Lebedyna pisnia* (The Swan Song, 1924), and *Shelesty nam barvinochku* (Rustle for Us, Little Periwinkle, 1932). She also published the story *Holos sertsia* (Voice of the Heart, 1923), the collection of lyrical sketches *Moï tsvity* (My Flowers, 1933), and two volumes of memoiristic stories: *Zamist' avtobiohrafiï* (Instead of An Autobiography, 1934) and *Spohady uchytel'ky* (Memoirs of a Teacher, 1935). Her autobiographic novella *Khryzantemy* (Chrysanthemums, 1961) was published posthumously in Chicago, as were two selected Soviet editions of her works (1956, 1958). A complete edition of her works appeared in Toronto in 1975.

D.H. Struk

Kravchenko, Vasyl [Kravčenko, Vasyl'], b 8 May 1862 in Berdianske, Tavriia gubernia, d 20 March 1945 in Rostov-na-Donu, Russia. Ethnographer and writer. He was one of the founders of the Society of Researchers of Volhynia and the director of its ethnographic section. By the end of the 19th century he had amassed a considerable collection of ethnographic materials, part of which was published by B. Hrinchenko in his *Etnograficheskie materialy sobrannye v Chernigovskoi i sosednikh s nei guberniiakh* (Ethnographic Materials Collected in Chernihiv and Neighboring Gubernias, 3 vols, 1895–9). Kravchenko directed the ethnographic department of the Volhynian Scientific Research Museum in Zhytomyr from 1920 to 1932, taught various courses there in 1922–4, and founded an ethnographic club (40 members) which published 13 issues of the handwritten journal *Etnohraf*. In 1932 Soviet authorities had him fired from his job and transferred to Dnipropetrovske. His house and private archives and library were confiscated. Later he was exiled to Russia. His primary works are *Etnohrafichni materiialy zibrani Kravchenkom Vasyl'om* (Ethnographic Materials Collected by Vasyl Kravchenko, 1911–20) and the story collection *Budenne zhyttia* (Everyday Life, 1902).

Kravchenko, Viktor [Kravčenko], b 1905 in Katerynoslav, d 26 February 1966 in New York. Soviet defector. He served as director of several metallurgical enterprises in Ukraine and the Ural region. In 1943 he was sent to the United States as a member of the Soviet Purchasing Commission. In the following year he renounced his Soviet citizenship and wrote an autobiography, *I Chose Freedom* (1946), in which he exposed the terror and crimes committed by the Soviet regime. In 1949 Kravchenko filed a libel suit against the Communist magazine *Les Lettres Françaises*, which had called his book a fraud. He described the trial in his second book, *I Chose Justice* (1950). Living in continuous hiding and always fearful of Soviet vengeance, he committed suicide.

Kravchenko, Yevhen [Kravčenko, Jevhen], b 25 December 1907 in Volodymyrivka, Kherson gubernia, d 28 June 1975 in Kiev. Writer; literary and theater reviewer. He published over 12 plays (from 1939), over 10 collections of stories and humorous sketches (from 1954), and the novella *Na svitanni* (At Daybreak, 1967). Collections of his plays were published in 1957, 1959, 1961, 1962, and 1978.

Mykhailo Kravchuk

Antin Kravs

Kravchuk, Mykhailo [Kravčuk, Myxajlo], b 12 October 1892 in Chovnytsia, Lutske county, Volhynia, d 9 March 1942? Mathematician; full member of the AN URSR from 1929 and of the Shevchenko Scientific Society from 1925. A graduate of Kiev University (1914), he taught mathematics in various higher schools in Kiev before receiving his PH D from Kiev University in 1924 and joining the faculty there in 1925. In 1917 he compiled the first Ukrainian mathematics dictionary. He headed the VUAN Commission of Mathematical Statistics (1923–33), then directed the Section of Mathematical Statistics of the AN URSR Institute of Mathematics (1934–8). Kravchuk is regarded as one of the most influential Ukrainian mathematicians. He published more than 80 papers that made original contributions in such diverse fields as advanced algebra, mathematical analysis, differential and integral equations, analytic functions and functions of real variables, probability theory, mathematical statistics, problems of moments, and approximation methods. Kravchuk also wrote or coauthored several monographs, including *Algebraïchni studiï nad analitychnymy funktsiiamy* (Algebraic Studies on Analytical Functions, 1929) and *Zastosuvannia sposobu momentiv do rosv'iazuvannia liniinykh ta intehral'nykh problem* (The Application of the Method of Moments to the Solving of Linear and Differential Equations, 1932), and the textbook *Vyshcha matematyka* (Advanced Mathematics, 1934, with P. Kasiianenko, S. Kulyk, V. Mozhar, and O. Smohorzhevsky). Kravchuk was arrested in 1938 and sent to a labor camp, where he presumably died. His name was 'rehabilitated' in the 1960s and he was the subject of two biographical novels by M. Soroka: *Poet nimoho chysla* (Poet of the Silent Number, 1967) and *Mykhailo Kravchuk* (1985).

V. Petryshyn

Kravets, Mykola [Kravec'], b 24 November 1928 in Babice, Biłgoraj county, Poland. Historian. After graduating from the Lviv Pedagogical Institute in 1949, he worked as a teacher and principal in Volhynia. In 1955 he was appointed research associate of the AN URSR Institute of Social Sciences in Lviv. In 1968 he became head of the Chair of Ukrainian History at Lviv University. His works deal with the social history and historiography of Western Ukraine. They include *Narysy robitnychoho rukhu v Zakhidnii Ukraïni v 1921–1939 rr.* (Essays on the Workers' Movement in Western Ukraine in 1921–39, 1959), *Selianstvo Skhidnoï Halychyny i pivnichnoï Bukovyny u druhii polovyni XIX st.* (The Peasantry of Eastern Galicia and Northern Bukovyna in the Second Half of the 19th Century, 1964), and *Ivan Franko – istoryk Ukraïny* (Ivan Franko – A Historian of Ukraine, 1971).

Kravs, Antin, b 23 November 1871 in Berhomet, Bukovyna, d 13 November 1945 in Vienna. General of the Ukrainian Galician Army (UHA). A graduate of the cadet school in Vienna (1891), he served in the Austrian army, attaining by 1918 the rank of lieutenant colonel and command of the 55th Berezhany Infantry Regiment. With the collapse of the Austrian Empire, he volunteered in November 1918 to serve in the UHA and was appointed commander of the Khyriv Group, which later became the Sambir Brigade. In the spring of 1919 he was given command of the Third Corps, and in June 1919 was promoted to brigadier general. As commander of the Kiev Army Group, he captured Kiev on 30 August 1919. In 1920 Kravs commanded a unit of the Kherson Division of the UNR Army composed of UHA soldiers who had avoided capture by the Poles. Unwilling to fight alongside the Polish army, this unit left the UNR Army in August 1920 and made its way to Czechoslovakia, where it was interned until 1924. Kravs wrote a volume of memoirs: *Za ukraïns'ku spravu* (For the Ukrainian Cause, 1937).

Bohdan Kravtsiv

Bohdan Krawchenko

Kravtsiv, Bohdan [Kravciv], b 5 May 1904 in Lopianka, Dolyna county, Galicia, d 21 November 1975 in Rutherford, New Jersey. Poet, journalist, and community and political figure; full member of the Shevchenko Scientific Society. A member of the Ukrainian Military Organization and a student activist, he headed the Union of Ukrainian Nationalist Youth (1928–9). In the 1930s he edited several nationalist periodicals in Galicia – *Visti, Holos natsiï,* and *Holos* – as well as the literary journals *Dazhboh* and *Obriï.* From 1940 to 1945 he edited the daily *Holos* in Berlin and other publications for Ukrainians working in Germany. In 1949 he immigrated to the United States, where he worked on the editorial boards of the newspapers *Ameryka* and *Svoboda* (from 1955). He served several times as the editor of the Plast journal *Molode zhyttia* and was a member of the editorial boards of the journal *Suchasnist'* and *Entsyklopediia ukraïnoznavstva* (Encyclopedia of Ukraine).

Kravtsiv's poetry was published in periodicals (beginning in 1922) and in the collections *Doroha* (The Road, 1929), *Promeni* (Rays, 1930), *Sonety i strofy* (Sonnets and Strophes, 1933), *Ostannia osin'* (The Last Autumn, 1940), *Pid chuzhymy zoriamy* (Under Foreign Stars, 1941), *Korabli* (Ships, 1948), *Zymozelen'* (Wintergreen, 1951), *Dzvenyslava* (1962), and *Hlosarii* (Glossary, 1974). From the 1930s on, his poetic style evolved towards a classicist form. He translated into Ukrainian 'The Song of Songs' (1934) and R.M. Rilke's poems, under the title *Rechi i obrazy* (Things and Images, 1947). He edited several key anthologies of poetry: *Obirvani struny* (Broken Strings, 1955), *Poety chumats'koho shliakhu* (Poets of the Milky Way, 1962), and *Shistdesiat' poetiv shistdesiatykh rokiv* (Sixty Poets of the Sixties, 1966). He also authored studies of contemporary Ukrainian literature, such as *Na bahrianomu koni revoliutsiï* (On the Crimson Horse of the Revolution, 1960), as well as bibliographic guides and articles on old maps of Ukraine and old Ukrainian mythology. His collected works appeared posthumously in two volumes, *Zibrani tvory* (1978, 1980).

D.H. Struk

Krawchenko, Bohdan [Kravčenko], b 29 December 1946 in Gunsburg, Germany. Political economist. Educated at Bishop's University, the University of Toronto, Glasgow University, and Oxford University, Krawchenko was active in the multicultural and Ukrainian student movements of the late 1960s and early 1970s. In 1969–70 he was president of the *Ukrainian Canadian

Students' Union (SUSK). Krawchenko joined the staff of the *Canadian Institute of Ukrainian Studies in 1976 and became director in 1986. A specialist on contemporary Ukraine and the USSR, he is the author of *Social Change and National Consciousness in Twentieth-Century Ukraine* (1985).

Peter Krawchuk

Krawchuk, Peter [Kravčuk, Petro] (pseuds: Peter Arsen, Marko Terlytsia), b 6 July 1911 in Stoianiv, Radekhiv county, Galicia. Community leader, journalist, and author. He was active in Sel-Rob and the Communist Youth Association of Western Ukraine before immigrating to Canada in 1930. In Winnipeg he joined the Ukrainian Labour-Farmer Temple Association (ULFTA), the Workers' Benevolent Association, and the Communist Party of Canada. A member of the Young Communist League, Krawchuk was active before the Second World War in the ULFTA's youth section and in the Association to Aid the Liberation Movement in Western Ukraine. He worked on the editorial board of *Ukraïns'ke zhyttia* (1946–65) and then *Zhyttia i slovo*. He opposed, on grounds of 'bourgeois nationalism' and collaboration with the enemy, the admission of Ukrainian refugees to Canada after the war. In the 1960s he criticized Soviet travel restrictions, Russification in Ukraine, and the Soviet invasion of Czechoslovakia, but did not comment on the Ukrainian dissident movement. Since 1979 he has been president of the pro-Communist Association of United Ukrainian Canadians. Krawchuk has written or edited some 15 books on the history and literature of Ukrainians in Canada.

Krawciw, Nicholas [Kravciv, Mykola], b 28 November 1935 in Lviv, Galicia. United States army general officer; son of B. *Kravtsiv. A graduate of the US Military Academy at West Point (1959), he served with distinction in Vietnam (1962–3 and 1968–9). He was appointed military observer in the Middle East: first for the Israel-Syria Mixed Armistice Commission and then for the United Nations Truce Supervision Organization (1972–4). Having served as assistant to the deputy secretary of defense (1982–3) and assistant division commander with US forces in West Germany (1984–5), he was promoted to major general and appointed executive to the Supreme Commander of NATO in Europe.

Nicholas Krawciw

Krechetnikov, Mikhail [Krečetnikov, Mixail], b 1729, d 20 May 1793. Russian general and statesman. He fought in the Russo-Turkish wars and commanded the army that suppressed the *Koliivshchyna rebellion in 1768. In 1790 he replaced P. Rumiantsev as the governor-general of Little Russia (Left-Bank Ukraine). He commanded one of the armies that invaded Poland following the creation of the Torhovytsia Confederacy in 1792, and in 1793 he was named the governor-general of the Right-Bank Ukrainian territories acquired by Russia in the Second Polish Partition. He died soon afterwards.

Krein, Marko [Krejn], b 3 April 1907 in Kiev. Mathematician; corresponding member of the AN URSR since 1939. A graduate of the Odessa Institute of People's Education (1929), from 1934 to 1944 he taught at various technological institutes in Odessa and was associated with the Mathematics Research Institute at Kharkiv University. He then worked at the AN URSR Institute of Mathematics in Kiev (1944–51) and at the Odessa Civil Engineering Institute (1954–74). Since the early 1930s, Krein's fundamental contributions to functional analysis have made him one of the world's leading specialists in this area. He has done pioneering work on problems of moments and, in particular, the theory of Hermitian operators and its applications to the spectral theory of differential operators and scattering theory. Krein has also made some fundamental contributions to Sturm-Liouville problems, extrapolation theory, stability theory, and the solvability of boundary-value problems. Because of these contributions he is regarded as the founder of the functional analysis school in Ukraine, the first such school in the USSR.

Kreitsarova Biblioteka (The Kreutzer Library). A children's book series published from 1902 to 1908 by the Chernivtsi branch of the Ruska Shkola pedagogical association. Its editors were I. Karbulytsky, I. Syniuk, I. Iliuk, and D. Pihuliak.

Krekhiv *Apostol*. An important monument of literary Middle Ukrainian when it was most like the vernacular. It consists of the Acts and Epistles, translated in 1563–72 mostly from the Polish Bible of 1563, and a commentary. The 663-page manuscript was discovered in the Krekhiv Monastery in Galicia, and has been described by V. Lev, I. Ohiienko, and J. Jánow.

Krekhiv Monastery (Krekhivskyi Sviato-Mykolaivskyi manastyr). Famous monastery in the village of Krekhiv in the Zhovkva region (now in Nesteriv raion, Lviv oblast). The monastery's patron saint was St Nicholas. It was founded at the beginning of the 17th century by the

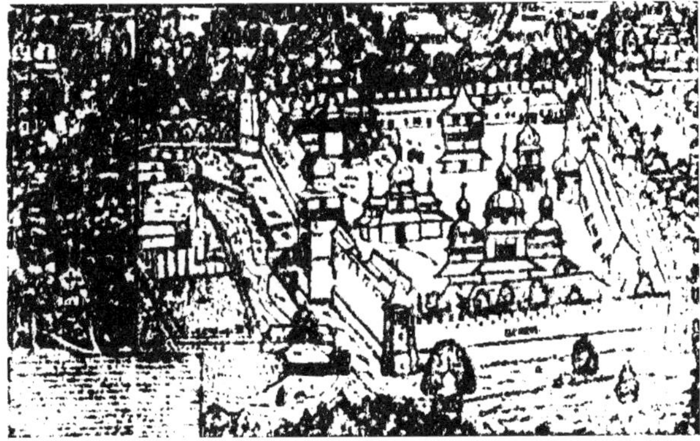

Krekhiv Monastery; engraving by D. Sinkevych (1699)

monk Yoil, and the large complex of churches and other structures was built in 1619–58. A stone wall surrounding the monastery was completed in 1669. In 1628 the monastery was granted the right of *stauropegion, or autonomy, and at the beginning the 18th century it joined the Church Union of *Berestia.

The Krekhiv Monastery is a typical Ukrainian wooden monastery-fortress. Its early patrons included the hetmans B. Khmelnytsky, P. Doroshenko, and I. Mazepa. The Church of the Assumption and its bell tower, dating from 1658, which were moved to the village of Krekhiv in 1775, are excellent examples of wooden church architecture of the period. There is a valuable iconostasis by the artist Vasyl from Lviv and a famous woodcut of the monastery by D. Sinkevych (1699). The monastery had a large library, which housed the famous *Krekhiv *Apostol* and *Krekhiv *Paleia*. From 1902 it was the novitiate for the Basilian order in Galicia. Its two famous icons, one of the Virgin Mary and one of St Nicholas, attracted many pilgrims. Under Soviet rule the monastery was closed; its towers and walls were dismantled and many of its artistic treasures were destroyed.

Krekhiv *Paleia*. A monument of 15th-century Ukrainian apocryphal literature. It was discovered in the Krekhiv Monastery by I. Franko, who published a description of it and some excerpts in his *Pam'iatky ukraïns'ko-rus'koï movy i literatury* (Monuments of the Ukrainian-Ruthenian Language and Literature, 1906).

Krekhovetsky, Ivan [Krexovec'kyj], b and d ? Galician nobleman and Cossack officer. Krekhovetsky conducted several diplomatic missions for B. Khmelnytsky: to Poland (1650), Transylvania (1655), and Sweden (1656). He was later colonel of Korsun regiment (1658), then general judge under Hetman P. Teteria (1665). He was captured by I. Briukhovetsky's forces in Korsun in 1665 and exiled to Moscow.

Kremar, Roman (pseud of Mykhailo Solodukha), b 5 February 1885 in Verbytsi, Rava Ruska county, Galicia, d 13 January 1953 in Edmonton. Journalist. A lawyer educated at the University of Lviv and a socialist sympathizer, Kremar emigrated to Edmonton in 1909. As secretary of the *Federation of Ukrainian Social Democrats in Canada in 1910, he quarreled with the editors of *Robochyi narod* in Winnipeg and precipitated a schism in 1911 by publishing his own paper, *Nova hromada*, and organizing a rival *Federation of Ukrainian Socialists in Canada (FUS). Within a year both the paper and the FUS collapsed and Kremar left the socialist camp. Between January 1913 and October 1918 he edited the newspaper *Novyny*, and in 1918–19 the Ukrainian Catholic *Kanadiis'kyi rusyn*. Later he edited *Kanadiis'kyi ukraïnets'*.

Kremenchuk [Kremenčuk]. IV-14. City (1986 pop 227,000), raion center, and river port in Poltava oblast, situated on both banks of the Dnieper River; until 1796 the settlement on the Right Bank was the separate town of Kriukiv. Kremenchuk was founded in 1571. A Polish castle was built there in 1596. In the Hetman state the town was a Cossack company center in Chyhyryn regiment (1648–61, 1663–7), the capital of a separate Kremenchuk regiment (1661–3), and a company center in Myrhorod regiment (1667–1765). Under Russian rule it was the capital of New Russia gubernia in 1765–83 and the administrative center of Katerynoslav vicegerency in 1784–9; thereafter it was a county center from 1802 to 1920 in Poltava gubernia.

In the second half of the 19th century, Kremenchuk became an important trade and manufacturing center. Consequently its population grew from 24,000 in 1860 to 63,000 in 1897 and 88,400 in 1910. In 1913 it had 95 enterprises, which employed almost half (6,000) of the industrial workers in Poltava gubernia. Under Soviet rule the city was a gubernia capital in 1920–2, an okruha capital in 1922–30, and a raion center in Kharkiv oblast in 1932–7. In 1937 it became part of Poltava oblast. After the 1917 Revolution its economy declined, and in 1926 its population was only 58,800 (40.6 percent Ukrainian, 49.2 percent Jewish, and 8.4 percent Russian). Its economy revived during the period of industrialization in the 1930s, and by 1939 its population had grown to 89,700. During the Second World War the city was devastated, and much of its Jewish population perished in the Nazi Holocaust. After the war the city was extensively reconstructed, and its population increased to 93,000 in 1959 and 166,000 in 1970.

Today Kremenchuk is an important center of heavy industry, with six truck plants, the *Kriukiv Freight-Car Plant, a mineral-enrichment complex, a petroleum refinery, and plants producing petrochemicals, steel, road-building machines, wheels, silicates, and reinforced-concrete sleepers. Food products, clothing, furniture, leather goods, and footwear are also manufactured there. Institutions in the city include an all-Union planning and technology institute of freight-car construction, a branch of the Kharkiv Polytechnical Institute, a regional-history museum, the A. Makarenko Pedagogical-Memorial Museum, and a civil-aviation pilots' school. Most of its architectural monuments were destroyed during the Second World War.

Kremenchuk Hydroelectric Station (Kremenchutska HES). One of the largest stations of the *Dnieper Cascade of Hydroelectric Stations. It was built in 1954–60 near Kremenchuk and has a general output capacity of 625,000 kW, producing annually an average of 1.5 billion kWh. The station's 12 generating plants, one-chamber shipping lock, concrete dam, and several earthen levees occupy a 12.6-km-long pressure front. The station is the first in the USSR to operate without an engine room; its generators are built beneath special metal hoods, and all operations are automated. The Kremenchuk Reservoir was created with the completion of the station's dam.

Kremenchuk Iron-ore Region. A major iron-ore deposit located in Poltava oblast. The geological continuation of the *Kryvyi Rih Iron-ore Basin onto the Left Bank of the Dnieper River, the Kremenchuk Basin is a narrow strip 45 km long and 1–3.5 km wide. In 1968 its reserves were estimated at 2 billion t (6.1 percent of Ukraine's total iron-ore reserves). Three of the basin's four known deposits contain ferruginous quartzites with an average iron content of 35 percent. These deposits reach a depth of 300 m. The fourth deposit contains rich martite and hematite-martite ores with an average iron content of 58.2 percent. This deposit reaches a depth of 2,000 m or more. First discovered in 1928, the deposits were initially exploited in the 1950s. The huge Komsomolsk pit, which yielded its first ore in 1970 and now approaches 200 meters, produced 34 million t of crude ore in 1984. The crude ore was converted into 14 million t of concentrate at the Dnieper Mineral-Enrichment Complex, accounting for 11.4 percent of total Ukrainian production.

Kremenchuk Petroleum Refinery (Kremenchutskyi naftopererobnyi zavod). One of the largest petroleum refineries in Ukraine, located near Kremenchuk, Poltava oblast. Construction of the plant began in 1961, and it is still being enlarged. The principal products are gasoline, diesel fuel, fuel oil, gas, and a number of petrochemicals.

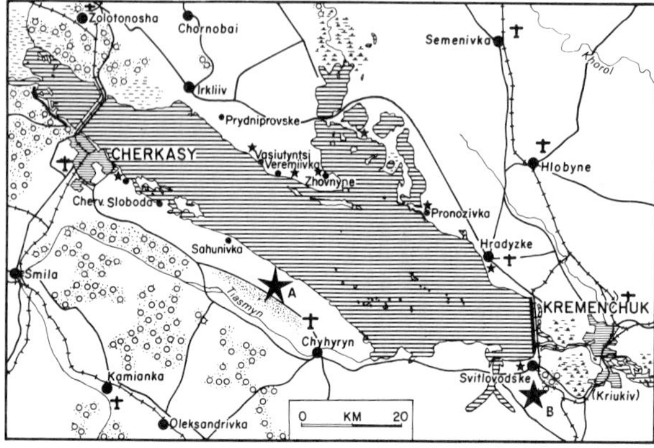

KREMENCHUK RESERVOIR

A. Site of future atomic power station
B. Hydroelectric station

Kremenchuk Reservoir. The largest water reservoir located on the Dnieper River, covering an area of 2,250 sq km on the territories of Poltava, Cherkasy, and Kirovohrad oblasts. The reservoir was formed as a result of the construction of the *Kremenchuk Hydroelectric Station in 1959. It is 149 km long and up to 28 km wide (with an average width of 13.2 km), and averages 6 m in depth. Its water volume is 13.5 billion cu m. The reservoir is used for irrigation, flood control, fishing, and transport. Its principal ports are Cherkasy and Svitlovodske.

Kremianets: Bona Mountain with ruins of a castle

Kremianets or **Kremenets** [Krem'janec' or Kremenec']. III-6. City (1972 pop 20,300) and raion center in Ternopil oblast. It is located on the site of Ostra Hora, one of the oldest known settlements in Ukraine, which dates from the Paleolithic period. Unearthed Greek and Roman coins indicate that inhabitants in the area had trade relations with the Dnieper region in ancient times. Kremianets was first mentioned in the Hypatian Chronicle under the year 1226. It was one of the strongholds of the Principality of Galicia-Volhynia and withstood several sieges, by Hungarians, Poles, Mongols, and Tatars, before being destroyed in 1261. In 1366 it came under Lithuanian rule. In 1438 it was granted the rights of Magdeburg law. The town flourished in the 15th and 16th centuries. During the years 1536–66 it belonged to the Polish queen Bona, who strengthened its castle and expanded the town. Under Polish rule from 1569, Kremianets was a county town in Volhynia voivodeship and played an important role in Poland's wars against the Tatars and Turks. The Orthodox Epiphany Monastery – with a brotherhood school, printing press, and hospital – was founded there in 1633 (in the years 1725–1839 it was a Uniate monastery run by the Basilian monks). In 1648, during the Cossack-Polish War, it was captured by the Cossacks. From the second half of the 17th century the town declined.

In 1793 Kremianets came under Russian rule; from 1797 to 1917 it was a county town in Volhynia gubernia. With the establishment of the *Kremianets Lyceum, the town became an important cultural center in the first half of the 19th century and was known as the 'Volhynian Athens.' In 1895 it had 13,300 inhabitants, 5,300 of whom were Jews. In 1919 UNR and Bolshevik forces battled each other for its control. From 1920 to 1939 the town belonged to Poland. Kremianets was an important Orthodox center: it was an eparchial see and located there were a theological seminary, a brotherhood (revived in 1880), and a religious press, which published the periodicals **Dukhovnyi siiach* and **Pravoslavna Volyn'* and liturgical books. It was also an educational center for western Volhynia; a Ukrainian gymnasium and Polish secondary schools were located there.

Today Kremianets has several food-processing and

textile plants. Among its institutions are a forestry tekhnikum, a pedagogical school, a medical school, a vocational-technical school, and a regional museum. The city is rich in architectural monuments: ruins of a castle (13th–17th centuries); the Epiphany Monastery (built in the baroque style in 1633); St Nicholas's Cathedral (1636); a Jesuit building complex (built in 1731–43), including a lyceum, college, and church; and a number of religious and residential buildings of the 16th to 18th centuries.

BIBLIOGRAPHY
Elhart, B. *Kremianets'. Istoryko-kraieznavchyi narys* (Lviv 1969)

V. Kubijovyč

Kremianets Grammar. A grammar compiled in 1638 by an anonymous author under the probable sponsorship of the brotherhood school at the Kremianets Epiphany Monastery and published as *Hrammatiky yly pysmennytsa iazyka slovenskaho.* It is a radically abridged version of M. Smotrytsky's grammar with some modifications, particularly in the theory of verse. Only six copies of the book have been preserved. The text was reprinted with comments by O. Horbach in 1977.

Kremianets Lyceum. A Polish higher school in Kremianets, formed in 1819 out of the local gymnasium, which had been established in 1805 by T. Czacki to serve as a university for the young nobles of the Kiev region, Podilia, and Volhynia. The reorganization of the school into a lyceum did not entail any significant change in its program. It offered a general education consisting of four one-year grades (languages, mathematics, geography, calligraphy) and three upper two-year grades (languages, theology, history, algebra, geometry, trigonometry, botany, physics, chemistry, mineralogy, civil architecture, and technology). Besides Polish, which was the language of instruction, Russian, Latin, and German were taught (English and Greek were optional). The lyceum had a large library and several natural science collections. Members of its faculty, such as A. Andrzejowski and W. Besser, did some important research on the fauna and flora in Right-Bank Ukraine. Most of the students were Poles: in 1821 only 34 of the 600 enrolled students were Ukrainian. Because many of the lyceum students took part in the Polish uprising of 1830–1, the authorities closed the school and in 1832 transferred its library, collections, and faculty to Kiev, where they became the foundation on which Kiev University was established. In the 1920s another lyceum was established in Kremianets by the Polish authorities. It was a secondary-school complex consisting of a teachers' seminary, gymnasium, and vocational schools.

Kremianets Mountains. Chain of low mountains in the northern part of the Podolian Upland in Ternopil oblast. The Kremianets Mountains extend approx 20 km between the valleys of the Ikva and Viliia rivers. They rise to 300–400 m above sea level (the highest peak reaches 408 m), or 150–200 m in relative height. The mountains are highly eroded, built mostly of chalk, clay, sand, and limestone. They include low mountain chains, outliers, and flat plateaus separated by river valleys, ravines, and gullies. In the north, they descend in a steep incline to the plains of Little Polisia. They are located in the northern region of the forest-steppe and are covered partly with oak, elm, and pine forests and partly with steppe vegetation. Agriculture is well developed in the area. The mountains are especially famous for their picturesque landscapes.

Kremianetsky, Havryil [Kremjanec'kyj, Havryjil] (secular name: Hryhorii), b ca 1715 in Nosivka, Kiev regiment, d 9 August 1783 in Kiev. Orthodox church figure and metropolitan. After studying at the Kievan Mohyla Academy, Kharkiv College, and the Moscow Greek-Slavonic-Latin Academy, he was a professor and rector of the Aleksandro-Nevskii Seminary in St Petersburg (1743–8) and then archimandrite of the Novospaskii Monastery in Moscow (1748–9). A member of the Holy Synod from 1748, Kremianetsky was bishop of Kolomna (1749–55) and Kazan (1755–62) and archbishop of St Petersburg (1762–70) before being appointed metropolitan of Kiev, a post he held until his death. He wilfully implemented the government's and Holy Synod's Russification policy and tried to destroy the individuality of the Ukrainian church and its traditions. He is the author of *Pouchenie o obriadakh khrystianskikh ... ili Slovo k narodu kafolicheskomu* (A Sermon on Christian Rites ... or A Word to the Catholic People, 1779).

Kreminna. IV-19, DB I-4. City (1972 pop 25,000) and raion center in Voroshylovhrad oblast, situated on the Krasna River. A group of Don Cossacks settled there in 1680, followed by peasants from Right-Bank Ukraine. In 1688 a company of Izium regiment was established there. Coal was discovered nearby in the late 19th century and many of the town's inhabitants began to work in the mines. The city is still a coal-mining center. Furniture, household-products, and building-materials plants are located there, and natural gas is extracted nearby. Kreminna is also a center of the logging and woodworking industries.

Kremnov, Oleh [Kremn'ov], b 13 March 1919 in Kriukiv (now part of Kremenchuk), Poltava gubernia. Specialist in theoretical and industrial thermodynamics; since 1976 a full member of the AN URSR. A graduate of the Kiev Polytechnical Institute, from 1949 he has worked at the AN URSR Institute of Technical Thermophysics. His main publications deal with the intensification of heat and mass transfer, the use of geothermal and solar energy, and heat management in mines.

Krendovsky, Yevhraf [Krendovs'kyj, Jevhraf], b 1810 in Kremenchuk, Poltava gubernia, d after 1853 in Kremenchuk. Painter of Venetsianov's school. A student of A. Stupin at the Arzamas Art School and of A. Venetsianov, he attended drawing classes at the St Petersburg Academy of Art (1830–5) and attained the title of independent artist (1839). He settled in Manuilivka, Poltava gubernia, and taught painting. Most of his works were done in Ukraine. They include *Pipe Players* (1835), *Gathering for the Hunt* (1836), *Square of a Provincial Town, A Ukrainian Woman,* and *Girl Friends.* He spent the last years of his life in Kremenchuk, where he ran his own art school.

Krestianskii Pozemelnyi Bank. See Peasant Land Bank.

Krett, James [Kret, Jakiv], b 1883 in Pechenizhyn, Kolomyia county, Galicia, d 23 May 1965 in Winnipeg. Editor and lexicographer. Krett studied at Manitoba College and was briefly associated with the *Independent Greek Church. In 1911 he edited *Khata*, an illustrated journal of literature, politics, and contemporary affairs. The following year he published the first pocket-sized Ukrainian-English dictionary in Canada. He later assisted C.H. Andrusyshen in compiling the *Ukrainian-English Dictionary* (1955).

Ivan Krevetsky

Krevetsky, Ivan [Krevec'kyj], b 14 October 1883 in Ivanivtsi, Zhydachiv county, Galicia, d 27 June 1940 in Rozdil, Zhydachiv county. Historian and bibliographer; full member of the Shevchenko Scientific Society (NTSh) from 1907. After studying with M. Hrushevsky at Lviv University, he directed the NTSh library in Lviv (1905–14, 1921–37) and edited its historical monthly *Stara Ukraïna* (1924–5). He also edited the journal *Nasha shkola* in Lviv (1909–12) and *Respublyka*, the press organ of the Western Ukrainian National Republic in Stanyslaviv (1919). Krevetsky published some 40 articles on Galician history, mainly in the journal *Zapysky NTSh*. Many of these dealt with the Revolution of 1848–9 in Galicia, especially with the organization of Ukrainian military units, the attempts to divide Galicia between the Poles and Ukrainians, and the election of 1848. He also wrote the monograph *Agrarni straiky i boikoty u skhidnii Halychyni v 1848–1849 rr.: Do istoriï borot'by za suspil'no-ekonomichne vyzvolenie ukraïns'kykh mas u skhidnii Halychyni* (Agrarian Strikes and Boycotts in Eastern Galicia in 1848–9: Toward the History of the Struggle for the Socioeconomic Liberation of the Ukrainian Masses in Eastern Galicia, 1906) and several articles on the history of the Ukrainian press in Galicia and on Ukrainian historiography. Krevetsky also contributed entries on the press to *Ukraïns'ka zahal'na entsyklopediia* (Ukrainian General Encyclopedia, 1930–5).

A. Zhukovsky

Krevo, Union of (Ukrainian: Krevska uniia). A treaty between the Kingdom of Poland and the Grand Duchy of Lithuania, signed 14 August 1385 (in Krevo, now in the Belorussian SSR). It created a dynastic link of the two states through a marriage between the Polish queen Jadwiga and the Lithuanian prince Jagiełło. It also united the two countries in their struggle against the invading *Teutonic knights. With the Union of Krevo, Ukrainian and Belorussian lands under the rule of Lithuania were incorporated into the Kingdom of Poland. Ukrainian and Belorussian nobles opposed the union, but to no avail.

Krezub, Antin. See Dumin, Osyp.

Krilyk, Osyp. See Vasylkiv, Osyp.

Kripatstvo. See Serfdom.

Kripenskyi [Kripens'kyj]. V-20, DB III-6. Town smt (1979 pop 9,700) under the jurisdiction of the Antratsyt city soviet in Voroshylovhrad oblast. It was founded in the early 20th century. Now three coal mines are located there.

Kriukiv. See Kremenchuk.

Kriukiv Freight-Car Plant (Kriukivskyi vahonobudivnyi zavod). A manufacturing plant located in Kremenchuk, Poltava oblast. It was founded in 1896 in Kriukiv, now a suburb of Kremenchuk. Until 1926 the plant only repaired railway cars on the Kharkiv-Mykolaiv railroad. Since that time it has also manufactured cars. Now the plant produces primarily 4-axle universal and 8-axle grain and cement cars.

Borys Kriukov: *Self-Portrait* (oil, 1963)

Kriukov, Borys [Krjukov], b 19 January 1895 in Orgeev, Bessarabia gubernia, d 6 March 1967 in Buenos Aires. Painter. A student of F. *Krychevsky at the Kiev Art School (1913–17), he taught painting and drawing at that school. Concentrating on graphic art, in the interwar period he illustrated over 500 books and was recognized as one of the leading graphic artists in Ukraine. From 1923 he also designed sets for the Kiev Theater of Opera and Ballet. In 1943 he immigrated to Lviv, then to Cracow, and in 1944 to Austria, where he painted under the pseudonym Ivan Usatenko. In 1948 he settled in Buenos Aires and returned to book graphics. As the chief illustrator of the large Argentinian printing house Ateneo, he illustrated such world classics as *Arabian Nights* (1950), Dante's *Divine Comedy* (1952), and M. de Cervantes's *Don Quixote* (1952–4), and the selected works of E.A. Poe, A. France, and E. Zola. His work for *Don Quixote* won first prize in 1964 at an international art competition in Madrid. His caricatures appeared in the Ukrainian humor magazine *Mitla* and in a separate collection *Smikholina* (Laughter, 1966). Kriukov also executed a number of icons and mosaics in local Ukrainian churches. His canvases, depicting romantic heroes from many lands, including Ukrainian Cossacks, were done by various techniques, mostly in oil. Kriukov's works can be found in Argentina, the United States, and many European countries, where his exhibitions were held. A monograph about him in Ukrainian, Spanish, and English was published by his wife, O. Hurska, in 1970.

S. Hordynsky

Krivichians (Ukrainian: *Kryvychi*). An Eastern Slavic tribe (or union of tribes) of the 6th–9th centuries AD, mentioned in the chronicles of Kievan Rus'. They lived along the upper reaches of the Dnieper, western Dvina, and Volga rivers, and in the southern basin of Chudskoe (Peipus) Lake in the Baltic region. The Krivichians migrated there either from the south in the 6th century or possibly from the west in the 8th century. Their principal cities were Smolensk, Polatsk, Izborsk, Toropetsk, Kryvychi, and, possibly, Pskov. They apparently engaged in trade with Byzantium. Their primary occupations were farming and cattle breeding and some crafts. At the end of the 9th century the Krivichian territories were incorporated into Kievan Rus'. Their lands were transformed into the Smolensk and Polatsk principalities; the northwestern portion of their territory was absorbed by Novgorod principality. They took part in the campaigns of *Oleh and *Ihor against Constantinople. The Krivichians (together with the *Drehovichians) are the ancestors of the Belorussians and Russians.

Križanić, Jurai, b ca 1618 in Obrh, Croatia, d 12 September 1683 in Vienna. Croatian political thinker, writer, linguist, and Catholic missionary. He studied in Graz, Bologna, and Rome. While in Rome he met Ukrainians who were studying at the Collegium Graecum and developed an interest in Old Church Slavonic, Kievan Rus', and Ukrainian folklore. Križanić was a pan-Slav who hoped to create a federated Slavic state led by a reformed Muscovy; he even devised a 'Slavic Esperanto' called *Križanica,* which he used to write most of his works. In 1659, on his way to Moscow, he spent a few months traveling in Ukraine writing two accounts that contain valuable information on the everyday lives of Ukrainians and arguments that Ukrainians, like all Slavs, should strengthen their ties with Muscovy. In Moscow he served at the court of Tsar Aleksei, but he was eventually arrested and exiled to Siberia, although he was allowed to continue writing. In his writings he argued that Muscovy should accept a Church Union with Rome. He also criticized the *Normanist theory of Kievan Rus' history.

Križevci eparchy. Greek Catholic eparchy in Yugoslavia that takes its name from its see, located in southern Croatia. It was founded in 1777 by Pope Pius VI on the urging of Maria Theresa out of the Marče-Svidník vicariate of the Roman Catholic diocese of Zagreb. This diocese had been established in the 17th century out of a separate Uniate eparchy founded in 1611, when Bishop Simeon Vratania accepted the Church Union along with his faithful, Orthodox émigrés from Bosnia and Montenegro. Prominent Ukrainians active in the eparchy in the 18th century included M. Terletsky, who later became the bishop of Kholm; H. Bulo, the eparchy's vicar in the 1730s; and Bishop H. Palkovych (1751–9) (the last two were from Transcarpathia).

In addition to the Greek Catholics of Croatia, the eparchy had jurisdiction over the Ukrainians in the *Bačka region, which included parishes in Ruski Krstur and Koćura, and Slovenia (from the late 19th century). In 1920 Ukrainians in Bosnia and Greek Catholic Macedonians (in Macedonia) and Rumanians (in the Banat) were also placed under its jurisdiction. While all the eparchy's bishops in the 19th century were Croatians, since then a number of Ukrainians have held this post: Yu. Drohobetsky (1891–1920), who was born in the Prešov region; and D. *Niaradi (1920–40), Archbishop H. *Bukatko (1950–81), and Y. Segedi (1981–3), all from Ruski Krstur. Since 1983 the bishop has been S. Miklovsh.

Today, all 50,000 Greek Catholics in Yugoslavia are under Križevci eparchy, including 35,000 Ukrainians, 10,000 Croatians, 4,000 Macedonians, and a few hundred Rumanians. There are 50 parishes, of which 30 are Ukrainian, 13 are Croatian, 8 are Macedonian, and 1 is Rumanian. The eparchy operates a theological seminary in Zagreb. Located in Kula are a Basilian men's monastery, 11 Ukrainian women's monasteries (6 of the Basilian order and 5 under the Sister Servants of Mary Immaculate), and 5 other women's monasteries. Since 1969 the annual *Khrystiians'kyi kalendar* has been published in Ukrainian and in the local Ruthenian dialect.

M. Busko, R. Miz

Krman, Daniel (aka Kerman), b 28 August 1663 in Mšeno, Trenčín district, Slovakia, d 23 September 1740 in Bratislava. Slovak scholar, writer, and civic figure. As the representative of the Evangelical church on a diplomatic mission to King Charles XII of Sweden, who was then at war with Peter I of Russia, he visited Ukraine in 1708–9 and left a detailed account of the visit in his diary *Itinerarium* (1709–11). He devotes considerable space to Hetman I. *Mazepa, whom he saw frequently, his negotiations with Charles, and the Battle of Poltava. He describes the Cossack army, the culture and way of life of the Ukrainian population, and the natural environment. The 256-page manuscript, which has been published a number of times in Latin and in Slovak translation, is preserved at the State Archive in Prešov. Krman was arrested for anti-Habsburg activity, sentenced to death, and executed.

Kroitor, Roman [Krojtor], b 12 December 1926 in Yorkton, Saskatchewan. Leading Canadian filmmaker of Ukrainian descent. Upon graduating from the University of Manitoba (MA 1949) he joined the National Film Board of Canada. One of his first films, *Paul Tomkowicz* (1954), which deals with the life of a Canadian railway worker, is recognized as a milestone in the development of the documentary film. Another of his early films, *City of Gold*, a chronicle of the Yukon gold rush, was acclaimed for its innovative camera work. In 1960 he co-produced *Universe*, a pioneer film on space exploration, which won numerous awards and had a strong influence on S. Kubrik's title sequence to *2001: A Space Odyssey*. In the early 1960s, with W. Koenig, he produced and directed *Candid Eye*, the world's first cinema vérité television series. Kroitor's *Labyrinth* (1967), a multi-image film created for Expo 67 in Montreal, was an enormous success and eventually led to the formation of Imax Systems Corporation, of which he is senior vice-president and director. At Imax he produced *Tiger Child* for Expo 70 in Osaka and co-produced *Man Belongs to the Earth* for the 1974 World's Fair at Spokane and *Hail Columbia* (1982), employing in all of them the revolutionary giant screen IMAX system, which he had helped design. A restless innovator, he produced and directed the first OMNIMAX 3-D movie, *We Are Born of Stars*, for Expo 85 and *A Freedom to Move* for Expo 86. His latest film, of which he is executive producer, is *Heart Land* (1987).

Krokhmaliuk, Yurii. See Tys, Yurii.

Krokos, Volodymyr, b 26 June 1889 in Odessa, d 28 November 1936 in Odessa. Geologist. A graduate of Odessa University (1912), he worked at the Odessa Agricultural Institute and Odessa University before becoming an associate of the VUAN Geological Institute (1926–36), later the AN URSR Institute of Geological Sciences. He also served on the faculty of Kiev University. Krokos was a specialist in mammal paleontology and the geology of the Quaternary period. His publications include numerous papers; the monographs *Materialy do kharakterystyky chetvertynnykh pokladiv Skhidnoï ta Pivdennoï Ukraïny* (Materials toward a Characterization of the Quaternary Deposits of Eastern and Southern Ukraine, 1927), and *Kurs paleozoolohiï* (A Course in Paleozoology, 2 vols, 1931, 1936); and the popular survey *Zemlia (ïï pokhodzhennia i naidavnisha istoriia)* (The Earth [Its Origins and Earliest History], 1936).

Krokovsky, Yoasaf [Krokovs'kyj, Joasaf], b ?, d 1 July 1718 in Tver. Orthodox theologian and metropolitan of Kiev. He studied in the Kievan Mohyla College until 1673 and in Rome. He was prefect (1683–5), lecturer in theology (1689–93), and rector (1693–7) of the college, which under his leadership was transformed into the *Kievan Mohyla Academy in 1694. He was also hegumen of the Kiev St Nicholas's Monastery (1689–93) and the Kiev Epiphany Brotherhood Monastery (1693–7), and from 1697 archimandrite of the Kievan Cave Monastery. In 1707, with the support of Hetman I. Mazepa, he was elected metropolitan of Kiev. In 1708, on the orders of Tsar Peter I, he was abducted because he 'was known to be a supporter of Mazepa' and taken to Hlukhiv, where he was forced to take part in the pronouncement of anathema on Mazepa. In 1718 Peter I suspected him of opposition and summoned him to St Petersburg; however, he died under mysterious circumstances in Tver en route. Krokovsky wrote a rhetoric textbook for use at the Kievan College (1683), the philosophical work *Disputationes logicae per consonam dispositionem Organi Aristotelici* (1686), *Tractus theologia speculative et theologiae controversae* (1693–7), and several shorter works.

Metropolitan Yoasaf Krokovsky (portrait from the 18th century)

Krolevets [Krolevec']. II-14. Town (1970 pop 18,300) and raion center in Sumy oblast. Established in 1601, it was mentioned in 1638 in Hetman Ya. Ostrianyn's decree as a county town. In 1644, under Polish rule, it was granted the rights of Magdeburg law and was fortified. Under the Hetman state it was a company center in the Nizhen regiment (1650–1781). Under Russian rule it was a county town in Chernihiv gubernia (beginning in 1802). In the 18th and 19th centuries it was an important commercial center as the site of a large annual fair. Since the 16th century Krolevets and its vicinity have been known for their decorative weaving of embroidered cloths (*rushnyky*), shirts, kerchiefs, and spreads. In the Soviet period this cottage industry was replaced by a weaving artel and, in the 1960s, by a factory. A trade school trains future artisans. The city's industries also produce metal parts, moldings, bricks, hemp products, and foodstuffs.

Krone (crown; Ukrainian: *korona*). The basic monetary unit of the Austro-Hungarian Empire from 1892, when it replaced the gulden (1 gulden for 2 krone). A krone was divided into 100 haller. In 1913 the krone was equal to 0.20 US dollars. After the establishment of the UNR in 1918, the Central Rada and the Central Powers fixed the exchange rate between the Austrian gold krone and the Ukrainian gold *karbovanets* at the 1913 foreign-exchange level of the tsarist ruble: ie, 1 krone (valued at 0.3018 gram of gold) for 0.4 *karbovanets*. After the collapse of the Austro-Hungarian Empire, Austria and Hungary each issued separate krone until 1924, when the schilling became the basic monetary unit in Austria and the pengö in Hungary. In Czechoslovak-ruled Transcarpathia (1918–38), the basic monetary unit from 1919 was the Czechoslovak koruna. It was based on the Swiss franc and the American dollar until 1929 when it was placed on the gold standard (1 koruna equal to 0.04458 gram of gold).

Krontovsky, Oleksii [Krontovs'kyj, Oleksij], b 24 March 1855 in Penza, Russia, d 15 August 1933 in Kiev. Physician and pathologist. He graduated from Kiev University (1911) and was a professor of bacteriology there from 1921. From 1924 he was also associated with the Kiev institutes of Bacteriology and Roentgenology. Krontovsky wrote a number of works in the fields of oncology, the pathology of heredity, endocrinology, and regeneration. He studied the influence of x-rays and bacterial toxicosis on the growth of tissues, and was one of the first to work on methods of cultivating tissues outside of living organisms.

Kropyviansky, Mykola [Kropyv'jans'kyj], b 28 December 1889 in Volodkova Divytsia, Nizhen county, Chernihiv gubernia, d 21 October 1948 in Nizhen. Soviet military commander and state security officer. A colonel major of the tsarist army, he was a communist organizer on the southwestern front in 1917. After the October Revolution he served as commander of the Twelfth Army Corps, chief of staff of the Second Ukrainian Soviet Army, commander of the First Ukrainian Soviet Division, commander of the 60th Rifle Division and then the 47th Rifle Division, and chief of staff of the Twelfth Army. In 1921–8 Kropyviansky commanded special counter-insurgency troops in Ukraine. Subsequently he served as a senior inspector of border troops and as a senior official in the USSR Ministry of Internal Affairs.

Marko Kropyvnytsky

Kropyvnytsky, Marko [Kropyvnyc'kyj], b 22 May 1840 in Bezhbairaky (now Kropyvnytske), Yelysavet county, Kherson gubernia, d 21 April 1910 en route from Mykolaiv to Kharkiv, buried in Kharkiv. Renowned actor, stage director, playwright, and composer; a founder and director of the first professional Ukrainian theater in Russian-ruled Ukraine. Working as a petty official of the county court or the municipal government in Bobrynets and Yelysavet, for 10 years he was active as an actor and play director in amateur drama groups with I. Tobilevych (see I. *Karpenko-Kary). In 1871 he moved to Odessa and joined the professional theater of Russian popular drama owned by the brothers I. and D. Morkov and M. Chernyshov, where he played mostly the roles of Ukrainian characters. For the next decade he worked in Ukrainian and Russian provincial troupes, appearing mostly in Odessa, Kharkiv, Kherson, Yelysavet, and Katerynoslav, and occasionally in Galicia (1875), the Crimea, and St Petersburg (1874). In 1882 Kropyvnytsky organized his own troupe in Yelysavet. As the first Ukrainian professional troupe, it marks the beginning of a new period in the history of the Ukrainian theater. Drawing on the talent of such actors as M. Zankovetska, M. Sadovsky, L. Manko, O. Viryna, and A. Maksymovych, the troupe toured Ukraine and some Russian cities (Rostov-na-Donu) with a populist-realist repertoire, and was acclaimed highly by both Ukrainian and Russian critics. In 1883 M. *Starytsky assumed control over the troupe, but Kropyvnytsky stayed on as a stage director. For over 20 years he continued to work as an actor and play director in various Ukrainian troupes, some of which he himself had organized and managed (1885–8 and 1894–1900). Retiring in early 1903 to his estate Zatyshok in the Kharkiv region, he continued writing plays, worked on his memoirs, and occasionally acted with touring companies.

Kropyvnytsky performed diverse character roles, ranging from the dramatic to the comedic genre, in which he excelled. His repertoire included such roles as Stetsko in *Svatannia na Honcharivtsi* (Matchmaking at Honcharivka), Makohonenko in *Natalka Poltavka* (Natalka from Poltava), Karas in *Zaporozhian Cossack beyond the Danube*, Bychok in *Hlytai, abo zh pavuk* (The Profiteer, or the Spider), the title roles in *Taras Bul'ba* and *Othello*, and Talbot in *Maria Stuart*. Creating his own school of acting, Kropyvnytsky perpetuated the traditions of K. *Solenyk and M. *Shchepkin and promoted the trend to realism on the stage. Several generations of populist-realist actors of the prerevolutionary period, including the stars of the Ukrainian stage, were trained by him.

Kropyvnytsky's work as a dramatist, which began in 1863, was determined to a large extent by the immediate demands of the stage. Accepting the principles of the romantic-populist theater, Kropyvnytsky subordinated his depiction of reality to the standards of romantic theater. His best plays are *Dvi sim'ï* (Two Families, 1888) and *Zaidyholova* (The Dreamer, 1889). The comedic opera *Poshylys' u durni* (They Made Fools of Themselves, 1882) is a witty composition in the style of Molière. Kropyvnytsky successfully adapted for the stage O. Storozhenko's story 'Vusy' (Whiskers, 1885), depicting the life of Ukrainian landowners in the 1840s. The comedy *Chmyr* (The Dirty Fellow, 1890) presents a gallery of village characters. His most popular plays with social significance were *Hlytai, abo zh pavuk* (1882) and *Po revizii* (After the Inspection, 1882). His first play, *Dai sertsiu voliu, zavede v nevoliu* (Give the Heart Freedom and It Will Lead You into Slavery, 1863), is interesting for its vivid portrayal of folk customs. Besides the plays already mentioned, *Olesia* (1891), *Doky sontse ziide, rosa ochi vyïst'* (By the Time the Sun Rises, the Dew Will Devour the Eyes, 1882), *Vii* (an adaptation of N. Gogol's story, 1894), *Eneïda* (Aeneid, an adaptation of I. Kotliarevsky's poem, 1898), and *Nevol'nyk* (The Captive, 1872) and *Tytarivna* (The Sexton's Daughter, 1891), both adaptations of T. Shevchenko's poems, are still performed. Kropyvnytsky wrote over 40 original plays and stage adaptations, which are recognized as classics of 19th-century Ukrainian drama.

BIBLIOGRAPHY

Kropyvnyts'kyi, M. *Povnyi zbirnyk tvoriv*, 3 vols (Kharkiv 1895–1903)

Sadovs'kyi, M. *Moï teatral'ni zhadky* (Kiev-Kharkiv 1919)

Slabchenko, T. *Z Lystuvannia M. Kropyvnyts'koho* (Kiev 1927)

Kropyvnyts'kyi, M. *Tvory*, 7 vols (Kharkiv-Kiev 1929–31)

Kyryliuk, Ie. *Marko Lukych Kropyvnyts'kyi: Aktor i dramaturh* (Kiev 1943)

Kropyvnyts'kyi, M. *P'iesy* (Kiev 1950)
Marko Lukych Kropyvnyts'kyi: Zbirnyk statei, spohadiv i materialiv (Kiev 1955)
Mar'ianenko, I. *Stsena, aktory, roli* (Kiev 1964)
Iosypenko, M. *Marko Lukych Kropyvnyts'kyi* (Kiev 1969)
Kyrychok, P. *Marko Kropyvnyts'kyi: Narys zhyttia i tvorchosti* (Kiev 1985)

V. Revutsky

Krosno or **Korosno.** IV-2. City (1983 pop 42,900) and voivodeship capital in southeastern Poland. Krosno was a town in Peremyshl principality near the Polish border. It received the rights of Magdeburg law, probably in the mid-14th century. From the 15th to 17th century it was a famous trade center with strong commercial ties to Hungary. The Krosno region was Polonized long ago, except for its southern part (several Ukrainian [Lemko] islands), which in 1939 had 8,700 Ukrainian inhabitants among a total population of 9,400 and remained Ukrainian ethnic territory until 1945.

Krotevych, Kostiantyn [Krotevyč, Kostjantyn], b 1872 in the Poltava region, d ? Orthodox church leader and lawyer. He attended the Kharkiv Theological Seminary, studied law at Kharkiv University, and then served as a prosecutor in the Poltava district court until 1917. In 1918 he was ordained a priest of the Ukrainian Autocephalous Orthodox church (UAOC). In March 1922 he was consecrated bishop, serving in Poltava (until 1924) and then Vinnytsia (1924–30) eparchies. In 1924 he made a missionary visit to the Ukrainian faithful in Kazakhstan. He was arrested in 1930 and exiled; his subsequent fate is unknown. Krotevych was one of the chief ideologists of the UAOC and a noted sermonizer. In the journal *Tserkva i zhyttia* he published the essays 'Do pytannia pro relihiiu Khrysta' (On the Religion of Christ, 1927) and 'Do ideolohiï UAPTs' (On the Ideology of the UAOC, 1928).

Krotevych, Yevhen [Krotevyč, Jevhen], b 23 January 1884 in Zhuravka, Cherkasy county, Kiev gubernia, d 29 May 1968 in Kiev. Writer. He was first published in 1906. His works consist of plays, such as *Santymental'nyi chort* (The Sentimental Devil, 1923), *Syn sovy* (The Owl's Son, 1924), and *Sekretar prem'ier ministra* (The Prime Minister's Secretary, 1924); novels, such as *Zvil'nennia zhinky* (Woman's Liberation, 1930), *Syny zemli* (Sons of the Soil, 1948), and *Ponad Slavutychem-Dniprom* (Along the Slavutych-Dnieper, 2 vols, 1955, 1963); short stories, which were collected in *Noveli* (Novellas, 1957) and *Vybrane* (Selections, 1959); and recollections about Ukrainian writers and contemporaries, *Kyïvs'ki zustrichi* (Kievan Encounters, 1965). He was imprisoned in the 1930s, but was rehabilitated later.

Krotiuk, Serhii [Krotjuk, Serhij], b 24 September 1903 in Rivne, Volhynia gubernia, d 14 June 1980 in Denver. Economist and civic leader. He served as a co-operative inspector in the Kholm region (1940–1), ran his own construction firm in Volhynia (1941–3), and then oversaw a department of the Union of Co-operatives in Peremyshl (1943–4). As an émigré in Munich and from 1949 in the United States, he was an active OUN member. He wrote *Sil's'kohospodars'ka tekhnichna syrovyna na ukraïns'kykh zemliakh na tli rozvytku sil's'koho hospodarstva Ukraïny* (Agricultural Technical Raw Materials on Ukrainian Territories in Relation to the Development of Agriculture in Ukraine, 1982).

Kruglov, Venir, b 18 September 1936 in Perm, RSFSR. Ballet dancer. A graduate of the Perm Choreography School (1956), he danced with the Sverdlovsk Theater of Opera and Ballet before joining the Kiev Theater of Opera and Ballet in 1963. He has appeared in such roles as Stepan in K. Dankevych's *The Lily*, Lukash in M. Skorulsky's *The Forest Song*, Molfar in V. Kyreiko's *Shadows of Forgotten Ancestors*, Spartacus in A. Khachaturian's *Spartacus*, and Albert in A. Adam's *Giselle*.

Hryhorii Kruk

Hryhorii Kruk: *Maiden* (bronze, 1972)

Kruk, Hryhorii, b 30 October 1911 in Bratyshiv, Tovmach county, Galicia. Sculptor. A graduate of the Lviv School of Decorative Art (1934), the Cracow Academy of Arts (1937), and the Berlin Academy of Arts (1940), where he studied under A. Focke and A. Breker, he settled in Munich at the end of the war and devoted himself to sculpture. By 1960 he had produced up to 200 sculptures and had established a Europe-wide reputation. His works were displayed at one-man shows: in Munich (1952, 1963, 1969), Paris (S. Badinier Gallery, 1954), London (1954), Edinburgh (1954), Bonn (1955), Rome (1957), New York and Philadelphia (1961), Vienna (1962), Toronto (1964, 1981), and Geneva (1971). Kruk is a thoroughly modern artist, who attempts to go beyond the traditional norms in search of the immediate, instinctive impression evoked by an expressive, suitably deformed form. He remains true to his peasant origins: his strong bond with the earth is expressed through the massiveness, heaviness, and brutal vitality of his figures. He has sculpted many portraits, including those of Pope Paul VI and Cardinal Y. Slipy, and figures of peasants, monks, Cossacks, bandura players, rabbis, working women, and dancers. His favorite subject is woman. Kruk's sculptures have been presented in two albums: S. Hordynsky's *Kruk, Pavlos', Mukhyn* (1947) and *Gregor Kruk* (1969, with an introduction by I. Bauer). His drawings, which have been published in a special album (1980), are distinguished also by immediacy and spontaneity.

S. Hordynsky

Krukenychi Group. Formed in December 1918 as an operational unit of the Ukrainian Galician Army (UHA), it was given the task of defending the western approaches to Sambir and Drohobych against the Polish army. Its headquarters were located in Krukenychi village, Mostyska county, Galicia. At its peak the group consisted of four infantry kurins with four companies each, a cavalry troop, and three artillery batteries. Its commanders were Lt M. Stakhiv, Capt Kravchuk, Col Shepel, and Lt Col Fedorovych. In June 1919 it was forced to retreat into Czechoslovakia. Later, soldiers from the Krukenychi Group were assigned to the Stryi Brigade of the UHA.

Krupetsky, Atanasii [Krupec'kyj, Atanasij] (secular name: Oleksander), ca 1570–1652. Uniate bishop. He worked first in the chancellery of King Sigismund III Vasa. In 1610, after joining the Basilian order, he was consecrated the Uniate bishop of Peremyshl. Throughout his entire tenure he was opposed by Orthodox clergy and nobles who fought to maintain control over the eparchy. In 1612 he attempted unsuccessfully to bring the Prešov region into the Church Union and was even briefly named Uniate bishop of Mukachiv.

Borys Krupnytsky

Solomiia Krushelnytska

Krupnytsky, Borys [Krupnyc'kyj], b 24 July 1894 in Medvedivka, Chyhyryn county, Kiev gubernia, d 5 June 1956 in Himmelpforten, Germany. Historian; full member of the Shevchenko Scientific Society and of the Ukrainian Academy of Arts and Sciences. He studied at Kiev University before the 1917 Revolution, then immigrated to Germany, where he continued his studies at Berlin University (PH D 1929). Krupnytsky was a research associate and professor (from 1932) at the Ukrainian Scientific Institute in Berlin and from 1941 at the Ukrainian Free University. A specialist in 17th- and 18th-century Ukrainian history, he wrote over 150 works. The most noteworthy of these were *Het'man Pylyp Orlyk (1672–1742)* (1938), *Hetman Mazepa und seine Zeit (1687–1709)* (1942), and *Het'man Danylo Apostol i ioho doba* (Hetman Danylo Apostol and His Era, 1948). He also wrote several works based on Swedish and other Western European sources, and a number of historiographical surveys: *Johann Christian von Engel und die Geschichte der Ukraine* (1931, based on his PH D dissertation), *Ukraïns'ka istorychna nauka pid Sovietamy (1920–1950)* (Ukrainian Historical Scholarship under the Soviets [1920–1950], 1957, which contains a bibliography of his works), *Istorioznavchi problemy istoriï Ukraïny* (Historiographic Problems in the History of Ukraine, 1959), and *Osnovni problemy istoriï Ukraïny* (Fundamental Problems in the History of Ukraine, 1955). His most noted work in German was a survey of Ukrainian history: *Geschichte der Ukraine von den Anfängen bis zum Jahre 1917* (1943; 2nd edn, 1963).

O. Ohloblyn

Krushelnytska, Lidiia [Krušel'nyc'ka, Lidija] (née Karatnytska), b 1 May 1915 in Kuty, Kosiv county, Galicia. Actress and play director. A graduate of the Lviv Conservatory (1939), she appeared in several operas in Stanyslaviv and Lviv, and after the war performed as a soloist with the Muza performing arts group in Austria. Immigrating to the United States in 1949, she joined the Theater-Studio of Y. Hirniak and O. Dobrovolska and appeared in many of its productions. In 1966 she became director of the Studio of the Oral Arts in New York, where she has been working with young actors as an educator and play director. She has directed children's plays such as the adaptation of H.C. Andersen's tale 'The Flying Ship' and of the folk tale 'Lisovyi Tsar Okh' (The Forest King Okh); dramatizations of poems by Lesia Ukrainka, T. Shevchenko, I. Franko, and L. Kostenko; and now rarely performed plays such as S. Cherkasenko's *Kazka staroho mlyna* (Tale of the Old Mill), V. Vynnychenko's *Chorna pantera i bilyi vedmid'* (Black Panther and White Bear), and E. Scribe's *Le verre d'eau*.

Krushelnytska, Mariia [Krušel'nyc'ka, Marija], b 31 December 1934 in Kharkiv. Pianist. A graduate of the Moscow Conservatory and a student of G. Neigauz, she has lectured at the Lviv Conservatory since 1963. In 1962 she won the All-Ukrainian M. Lysenko contest. The Ukrainian composers L. Revutsky, S. Liudkevych, V. Kosenko, A. Shtoharenko, and M. Kolessa have a special place in her repertoire.

Krushelnytska, Solomiia [Krušel'nyc'ka, Solomija], b 23 September 1872 in Biliavyntsi, Buchach county, Galicia, d 16 November 1952 in Lviv. World-famous singer (dramatic soprano). Upon graduating from the Lviv Conservatory (1893), where she studied under W. Wysocki, she made her debut with the Lviv Opera as Leonora in G. Donizetti's *La favorita* and went to Milan to study under F. Crespi (1893–6). From 1896 she performed with most of the great opera companies of Europe and South America: Odessa (1896–7), Warsaw (1898–1902), St Petersburg (1901–2), Paris (1902), Naples (1902, 1904), Rome (1904–5), Milan (La Scala, 1898, 1904, 1907, 1909, 1915), and Buenos Aires (1906, 1908, 1910–13). Her performance as Aida (1903) was a triumph, and her rendition of the title role in G. Puccini's *Madame Butterfly* in 1904 contributed to its admission to the world repertoire. Because of her and A. Toscanini, R. Strauss's *Salome* was a great success at La Scala (1906). In 1915 she sang the title role in the world premiere of I. Pizzetti's *Fedra* at La Scala. Her operatic repertoire numbered close to 60 roles, including the title roles in R. Strauss's *Salome* and *Elektra*, Brünnhilde in R. Wagner's *Die Walküre* and Isolde in his *Tristan und Isolde*, and the title roles in A. Ponchielli's *La Gioconda* and S. Moniuszko's *Halka*. Many of the performances in which she starred were conducted by A. Toscanini. Krushelnytska combined a colorful voice of great range (three octaves) with a fiery temperament and enormous acting ability. In the mid-1920s she turned from opera to concert recitals. Her concert repertoire included works by C. Monteverdi, C. Gluck, W. Mozart, M. Mussorgsky, M. Lysenko, D. Sichynsky, and S. Liudkevych. She enjoyed performing Ukrainian folk songs to her own piano accompaniment. Returning to Lviv in 1939, she taught solo singing at the Lviv Conservatory (1944–52).

BIBLIOGRAPHY
Holovashchenko, M. (ed). *Solomiia Krushel'nyts'ka. Spohady, materialy, lystuvannia*, 2 vols (Kiev 1978–9)
Vrublevs'ka, V. *Solomiia Krushel'nyts'ka* (Kiev 1979)

W. Wytwycky

Antin Krushelnytsky

Marian Krushelnytsky

Krushelnytsky, Antin [Krušel'nyc'kyj], b 4 August 1878 in Łańcut, Poland, d 13 November 1941. Writer, educator, journalist; political and civic figure. As a student he was associated closely with the monthly *Moloda Ukraïna* and helped I. Franko in editing *Literaturno-naukovyi vistnyk*. Later, he worked as a secondary-school teacher and principal, and played a prominent role in the Ukrainian Radical party. In 1919 he served as minister of education in B. Martos's cabinet under the *Directory of the UNR. After the war he worked as an editor at the Chaika publishing house in Vienna, which specialized in Ukrainian textbooks and translations of world classics. Returning to Galicia in 1925, he could not obtain a teaching position. From 1929 to 1933 he edited the pro-Soviet journals *Novi shliakhy* and *Krytyka*. Persecuted and repeatedly arrested by Polish authorities, he immigrated with his family to the Ukrainian SSR in 1934. Soon, all of them were arrested: Antin and his wife, Mariia, were sent to concentration camps, while their sons Ivan and Taras were executed. Krushelnytsky died in prison and was posthumously 'rehabilitated' after Stalin's death.

As a prose writer Krushelnytsky was influenced by Western European modernism. His rich literary legacy includes collections of short stories such as *Proletari* (Proletarians, 1899) and *Svitla i tini* (Lights and Shadows, 1900); dramas such as *Semchyshyny* (The Semchyshyns, 1900), *Cholovik chesti* (Man of Honor, 1904), *Artystka* (Actress, 1901); the comedy *Orly* (Eagles, 1906); novels such as *Rubaiut' lis* (They Are Cutting the Forest, 1914), *Homin Halyts'koï zemli* (Echo of the Galician Land, 1918–19), *Iak promovyt' zemlia* (When the Land Will Speak, 1920), *Iak pryhorne zemlia* (When the Land Will Embrace, 1920), and *Budennyi khlib* (Daily Bread, 1920); literary surveys and criticism; school readers such as *Vybir z ukraïns'koho narodnoho pys'menstva* (Selections from Ukrainian Folk Literature, 2 vols, 1918, 1922); and translations.

A. Zhukovsky

Krushelnytsky, Ivan [Krušel'nyc'kyj], b 12 November 1905 in Rohatyn, Galicia, d 17 December 1934 in Kharkiv. Poet, graphic artist, and art critic; son of A. *Krushelnytsky. After graduating from the University of Vienna (1927), he taught at the Ridna Shkola seminary in Stryi. From 1929 he helped his father publish the Sovietophile journal *Novi shliakhy*. He published several collections of modernist poetry, including *Vesniana pisnia* (Spring Song, 1924), *Iunyi spokii* (Youthful Serenity, 1929), and *Buri i vikna* (Storms and Windows, 1930), and the dramatic poems *Spir za Madonnu Sil'viiu* (The Dispute over Madonna Silvia, 1930) and *Na skeliakh* (On the Cliffs, 1931). His graphic works were published in a separate collection. Immigrating to Soviet Ukraine in 1934 with his family, he worked briefly at the VUAN Institute of the History of Material Culture. He was shot by the Soviets in 1934 and was posthumously 'rehabilitated' after Stalin's death. A selection of his poetry was published in Kiev in 1964.

Krushelnytsky, Marian [Krušel'nyc'kyj, Mar'jan], b 18 April 1897 in Pyliava, Buchach county, Galicia, d 5 April 1963 in Kiev. Actor and play director of L. Kurbas's school; educator. Making his stage debut in 1915 in the Ternopilski Teatralni Vechory theater, he subsequently acted in the Ukrainian Theater in Ternopil (1918, 1920–1), the New Lviv Theater (1919), the Franko Ukrainian Drama Theater in Vinnytsia (1920), and the Ukrainska Besida theater in Lviv (1922–4). Then he was one of the leading actors of the *Berezil theater, and after L. Kurbas's arrest and the dissolution of Berezil, Krushelnytsky was appointed in 1934 artistic director and chief play director of the Kharkiv Ukrainian Drama Theater. He modified the theater's profile, particularly its repertoire, according to the demands of socialist realism: preference was given to O. Korniichuk's and L. Dmyterko's plays and Russian classics. Joining the Kiev Ukrainian Drama Theater in 1952, he eventually became its chief stage director (1954–63). After the war, he also taught acting at the Kharkiv (1946–52) and Kiev (1952–63) theater institutes.

As an actor Krushelnytsky distinguished himself under L. *Kurbas's direction in the Berezil theater. He played a wide range of roles, including Honoré d'Apremout in P. Mérimé's *La Jacquerie*, Barbulesque in F. Crommelynck's *Tripes d'or*, and Maloshtan in I. Mykytenko's *Dyktatura* (Dictatorship). He was particularly impressive in M. Kulish's plays: as Malakhii in *Narodnyi Malakhii* (The People's Malakhii), Uncle Taras in *Myna Mazailo*, and Padura in *Maklena Grasa*. In the post-Berezil period his better roles were comedic ones such as Kuksa in M. Kropyvnytsky's *Poshylys' u durni* (They Made Fools of Themselves) and Ivan Nepokryty in his *Dai sertsiu voliu zavede v nevoliu* (Give the Heart Freedom and It Will Lead You into Slavery), the title role in I. Karpenko-Kary's *Martyn Borulia*, Kindrat Halushka in O. Korniichuk's *V stepakh Ukraïny* (In Ukraine's Steppes), and cantor Havrylo in *Bohdan Khmel'nyts'kyi*. Krushelnytsky won acclaim for his original interpretation of Tevie in *Tevie-molochnyk* (Tevie, the Milkman, based on the story by

Sholem Aleichem) and of Lear in W. Shakespeare's *King Lear*.

BIBLIOGRAPHY
Han, Ia. *Mar'ian Mykhailovych Krushel'nyts'kyi* (Kiev 1960)
Taniuk, L. *Mar'ian Krushel'nitskii* (Moscow 1974)
Hirniak, I. *Spomyny* (New York 1982)

V. Revutsky

Kruty, Battle of. A battle near Kruty on 29 January 1918. As a Bolshevik force of about 4,000 men commanded by M. Muravev advanced toward Kiev, a small contingent of 500 men was hastily organized and sent to the front. It consisted mainly of a company of the Student Kurin of Sich Riflemen, a company of the Khmelnytsky Cadet School, and a Haidamaka detachment. Commanded by Capt A. Honcharenko, this force attempted to block the Bolshevik advance on the capital at Kruty, a railroad station 130 km northeast of Kiev. In a bitter battle about half of the Ukrainian soldiers were killed, but their resistance delayed Muravev's capture of Kiev and enabled the Ukrainian government to conclude the Peace Treaty of Brest-Litovsk. The battle is commemorated as a symbol of patriotic self-sacrifice and is immortalized in numerous literary and publicistic works.

Krutykova, Nina, b 27 January 1913 in Łodz, Poland. Literary scholar; corresponding member of the AN URSR since 1957. After completing graduate studies at Kiev University, she taught at Kiev University (from 1938) and was an associate of the AN URSR Institute of Literature (from 1941). She has written, in the spirit of official Soviet scholarship, numerous studies on Ukrainian and Russian literature, including monographs on the works of I. Nechui-Levytsky (1961), on Marko Vovchok (1965), on N. Gogol and Ukrainian literature (1949, 1957, 1984), on A. Chekhov's works and their importance for the development of Ukrainian literature (1954), on V. Korolenko and Ukrainian literature (1955), on L. Tolstoy and Ukrainian literature (1958), on the literary relations of the Ukrainian and Russian peoples (1954), and on Russian realism and the establishment of Ukrainian realist prose (1963).

Krvavych, Dmytro [Krvavyč], b 28 September 1926 in Kniazhpil, Dobromyl county, Galicia. Sculptor. After graduating from the Lviv Institute of Applied and Decorative Arts (1953), he chaired the Department of Russian Art at the Lviv Painting Gallery and taught at the Lviv Children's Art School. In 1958 he published a monograph on his teacher, I. Seveva. His sculptures include portraits of M. Lysenko (1954), I. Vyshensky (1964), and S. Tudor (1972); monuments to I. Franko (1964), to M. Shashkevych (1960) in Pidlysia, as well as some dedicated to the armed forces of the USSR (1970) in Lviv; and majolica figures such as *Kozak-Mamai* (1959), *Carpathian Legend* (1959), *Ksenia* (1962), *A Memory* (1962), and *The Sun Is Low* (1963). M. Batih published a monograph on Krvavych in 1968 in Kiev.

Krychevsky, Fedir [Kryčevs'kyj], b 22 May 1879 in Lebedyn, Kharkiv gubernia, d 30 July 1947 in Irpin, Kiev oblast. Painter and pedagogue; brother of V. *Krychevsky, Sr. A graduate of the Moscow School of Painting, Sculpture, and Architecture (1901) and the St Petersburg Academy of Arts (1910), he traveled in Western Europe for a year and then settled in Kiev, where he served as professor and director at the Kiev Art School (1914–18). In 1917 he was one of the founders of the Ukrainian State Academy of Arts, at which he taught genre and historical painting and portraiture, and of which he served as director (1920–2) and rector (1918, 1920–2). When the academy was abolished, he was appointed professor at the Kiev (1922–32, 1934–41) and the Kharkiv state art institutes. Fleeing west in 1943, he fell ill and was overtaken by advancing Soviet troops. After prolonged interrogation and torture he was released in a hopelessly weakened condition, and stripped of all his titles and honors. Twelve years after his death Krychevsky was 'rehabilitated': in 1959 the first posthumous retrospective exhibition of his works was held in Kiev, and albums and monographs about his work began to be published.

Fedir Krychevsky

Krychevsky was a prolific artist: he produced close to a thousand works (compositions, portraits, landscapes, sketches, and studies). He preferred large canvases and enjoyed grappling with the stylistic problems they presented. At one time he came close to the Neo-Byzantinism of M. *Boichuk's school but, eventually, he turned to a more realist style based on patches of vivid color. His more important works are *Three Ages* (1913), *Life: Triptych* (1925–7), which was highly praised at the 1928 Venice Biennial, *Matchmakers* (1928), *Merry Milkmaids* (1937), *Dovbush* (1932), *Conquerors of Wrangel* (1934), a cycle of temperas based on T. Shevchenko's poem *Kateryna* (1937–40), and a series of portraits (of his mother, wife, son, L. Starytska, H. Pavlutsky, and several self-portraits). For 30 years Krychevsky was one of the leading figures in Ukrainian art. He organized the first strictly Ukrainian art exhibitions in 1911 and 1913, and his work was exhibited, beginning in 1897, at over 34 individual and group shows in and outside Ukraine. He was also a successful teacher, whose students included M. Dmytrenko, L. Morozova, T. Yablonska, S. Hryhoriev, and Yu. Melikhov.

BIBLIOGRAPHY
Vystavka tvoriv zasluzhenoho diiacha mystetstv URSR Fedora Hryhorovycha Krychevs'koho (1879–1947). Kataloh (Kiev 1960)
Musiienko, P. *Fedir Hryhorovych Krychevs'kyi* (Kiev 1966)
Chlenova, L. *Fedor Krichevskii* (Moscow 1969)
Pianida, B. (ed). *Fedir Krychevs'kyi. Spohady, statti, dokumenty* (Kiev 1972)
Chlenova, L. *Fedir Krychevs'kyi. Al'bom* (Kiev 1980)

S. Hordynsky

Mykhailo Krychevsky

Krychevsky, Mykhailo [Kryčevs'kyj, Myxajlo], b ?, d 24 July 1649 in Loev, Belorussia. Nobleman from the Berestia region and Cossack officer. He was the colonel of the Chyhyryn registered Cossacks from 1643. In 1647 he convinced S. Koniecpolski to release B. Khmelnytsky from prison by guaranteeing his conduct. He then helped Khmelnytsky to escape to Zaporizhia, and the next year he joined the rebellion led by him. He became the colonel of Kiev regiment and in 1649 he led a 30,000-man Cossack army to repel a Polish-Lithuanian invasion of Ukraine. He was killed at the Battle of Loev, where his army was defeated. Krychevsky is the subject of a biography by V. Lypynsky in *Z dziejów Ukrainy* (From the History of Ukraine, 1912).

Krychevsky, Mykola [Kryčevs'kyj], b 24 November 1898 in Kharkiv, d 11 September 1961 in Paris. Impressionist painter; son of V. Krychevsky, Sr. After studying art with his father, and with Y. Bokshai in Uzhhorod, he graduated from the School of Industrial Design in Prague. In 1929 he moved to Paris. Krychevsky is best known for his watercolors: his scenes of Paris and Venice earned him international acclaim. His work was exhibited at the Salon des Indépendents in Paris, and in various cities of Western Europe and North America. Krychevsky also designed stage sets for the Prosvita Theater (1921–3) and O. Zaharov's company (1921–5) in Uzhhorod, and the Théatre des Arts (1939) and the Théatre Hébertot (1942) in Paris.

Krychevsky, Vasyl [Kryčevs'kyj, Vasyl'], b 12 January 1873 in Vorozhba, Lebedyn county, Kharkiv gubernia, d 15 November 1952 in Caracas. Outstanding art scholar, architect, painter, graphic artist, set designer, and a master of applied and decorative art; brother of F. *Krychevsky. He received little formal education. Interested deeply in Ukrainian folklore and art history, he audited M. Sumtsov's, D. Bahalii's, and Ye. Riedin's classes at Kharkiv University. Working as an independent architect and artist, he achieved a national reputation by the time of the outbreak of the First World War. During the revolutionary period he was a founder and the first president of the Ukrainian State Academy of Arts. In the 1920s he taught at the Kiev Institute of Plastic Arts and the Kiev Architectural Institute. In 1927 he taught for a year at the Odessa Art Institute, and then served in the architectural department of the Kiev State Art Institute until 1941. Moving to Lviv in 1943, he was appointed rector of a new Ukrainian art school, the Higher Art

Vasyl Krychevsky: cover design

Studio. After the war he lived briefly in Paris before immigrating in 1947 to South America.

Krychevsky first achieved public recognition in 1903 by winning the architectural competition to build the Poltava Zemstvo Building (now the Poltava Regional Museum). His design of the building inaugurated a new style based on the traditions of Ukrainian folk architecture, and set a new trend among young architects in Ukraine. He continued to work in this style, using it for a number of public and private buildings and monuments, such as the People's Home in Lokhvytsia (1904); the residences of D. Myloradovych (1905), I. Shchitkivsky (1907), and M. Hrushevsky (1908–9); the Shevchenko Memorial Museum in Kaniv (1931–4); and monuments to M. Myloradovych (1908), M. Kotsiubynsky (1928), D. Zabolotny (1932), and M. Hrushevsky (1935). This distinctive Ukrainian style marked his interior designs for private homes and exhibition halls.

As a painter Krychevsky was deeply influenced by French impressionism. The pure and harmonious colors of his south-Ukrainian landscapes (done in oils and watercolors) convey a lyrical atmosphere. His paintings were first exhibited in Kharkiv in 1897. He participated in the annual exhibitions of the Society of Russian Watercolorists in St Petersburg (1899–1902) and, later, in the exhibitions of the Kiev painters (1910–13). Altogether he did about 300 paintings. Krychevsky is one of the main founders of modern Ukrainian book design. In his work he used traditional folk ornamentation and motifs in old Ukrainian books, and revived the old techniques of wood engraving, etching, and lithography. He designed over 80 bookcovers, some bookplates, and a number of entire books, including the deluxe edition of *Ukraïns'ka pisnia* (Ukrainian Song, 1935). At M. Hrushevsky's request he designed the state emblems and seals of the UNR and

Vasyl Krychevsky: cover designs and bookplates

a number of bank notes. From 1907 through to 1910, Krychevsky designed sets and costumes for some 15 plays and operas produced by the Sadovsky Theater in Kiev, including M. Starytsky's *Bohdan Khmel'nyts'kyi*, I. Karpenko-Kary's *Sava Chalyi*, B. Smetana's *The Bartered Bride*, and S. Moniuszko's *Halka*. Then in 1917–18 he worked with the Ukrainian National Theater. Noted for their realism and attention to detail, his sets occasionally assumed an abstract or grotesque character to match the atmosphere of the drama. In the Soviet period he served as a consultant or artistic director for 12 films shot in Ukraine, including *Taras Shevchenko* (1926), *Taras Triasylo* (1927), *Zvenyhora* (1928), and *Sorochyns'kyi iarmarok* (The Sorochyntsi Fair, 1939), the first Ukrainian color film.

Krychevsky was an enthusiastic collector and student of Ukrainian folk art. Agreeing fully with J. Ruskin's and W. Morris's views on the relation of art to everyday life, he played an important role in promoting handicrafts among the people. He served as instructor in B. Khanenko's kilim-weaving and cloth-printing workshop in Olenivka (1912–15) and as director of a ceramics school in Myrhorod (1918–19). He created his own designs for kilims, printed fabrics, embroideries, ceramic products, and furniture. Over 1,100 samples of his work were displayed at a retrospective exhibition in Kiev in 1940.

Krychevsky's articles on art and reviews appeared in the leading journals in Ukraine. His more important contributions to art criticism and history are 'Pro rozuminnia ukraïns'koho styliu' (On Understanding the Ukrainian Style, *Siaivo*, no. 3 [1914]), 'Budynok, de zhyv T.H. Shevchenko u Kyïvi' (The Building Where T. Shevchenko Lived in Kiev, *Ukraïna*, 1925, nos 1–2), and 'Arkhitektura doby' (The Architecture of the Age, *Chervonyi shliakh*, 1928, no. 3).

BIBLIOGRAPHY
Pavlovs'kyi, V. *Vasyl' Hryhorovych Krychevs'kyi. Zhyttia i tvorchist'* (New York 1974)

S. Hordynsky, V. Pavlovsky

Krychevsky, Vasyl [Kryčevs'kyj, Vasyl'], b 18 March 1901 in Kharkiv, d 16 June 1978 in Mountain View, California. Painter; son of Vasyl Krychevsky, Sr. A graduate of the Ukrainian State Academy of Arts in Kiev, where in 1917–23 he studied under V. and F. Krychevsky, he became a lecturer at the Kiev Industrial Design School and film editor at the Kiev Film Factory and Ukrainfilm. His first exhibition was in 1937. Leaving Ukraine in 1943, he settled in the United States in 1949. He painted portraits and landscapes, illustrated books and posters, designed stage and film sets, and made artistic porcelain.

Krylati (The Winged Ones). An illustrated monthly published since 1963 in New York, and since 1973 in Brussels, for members of the *Ukrainian Youth Association (SUM).

Krylos. IV-5. Village (1971 pop 1,700) in Halych raion, Ivano-Frankivske oblast, located on Krylos Mountain near the Lukva River (a tributary of the Dniester River), 5 km from the center of present-day Halych. Krylos was originally at the center of the complex of villages that formed the princely capital of *Halych.

Krylos Gospel. See Halych Gospel (1144).

Krylov, Mykola, b 29 November 1879 in St Petersburg, d 11 May 1955 in Moscow. Mathematician, specialist in mechanics; full member of the AN URSR from 1922, of the Shevchenko Scientific Society, and of the USSR Academy of Sciences from 1929. A graduate of the St Petersburg Mining Institute and of St Petersburg University (PH D 1917), he was a professor at Crimea University (1917–22), then head of the Chair of Mathematical Physics at the Institute of Technical Mathematics (later the Institute of Construction Mechanics, now the AN URSR Institute of Structural Mechanics) in Kiev. Krylov published some 180 papers and 4 monographs. He made significant contributions to the theory of interpolation and mechanical quadrature, variational methods, approximation solvability of differential equations of mathematical physics, and convergence and error estimates of the Ritz and of his own methods. From 1932 his work with N. Bogoliubov provided the foundation for non-linear mechanics, and the two established the Kiev school of non-linear mechanics. Krylov's basic works deal with the theory of mechanics and of dynamic systems.

Krylov, Vladimir, b 16 April 1841 in Pokrovskoe-Ramenia, Yaroslavl gubernia, Russia, d 6 February 1906 in Kharkiv. Physician and medical scientist. A graduate of the St Petersburg Medical-Surgical Academy (1868), he was the vice-president of the Kharkiv Medical Society and the first professor of pathological anatomy at Kharkiv University (1872–1902). He founded the Kharkiv Bacteriological Station and several prosectoriums in Kharkiv and was the first in the Russian Empire to introduce practical assignments in pathological histology. His works deal with infections of the brain membrane, heart disease, typhoid, the effects of syphilis on the lungs, trichinosis, and anthropometry.

Krylovsky, Amvrosii [Krylovs'kyj, Amvrosij], b 1853 in Galicia, d 1930 in Kiev. Historian and librarian. He served as director of the Library of the Kiev Theological Academy and then as head of a section of the National Library of Ukraine, which absorbed the former library. He collaborated with the Temporary Commission for the Analysis of Ancient Documents and published his studies on 16th- and 17th-century church and civic organizations in Ukraine, including the Lviv Dormition Brotherhood, in its *Arkhiv Iugo-Zapadnoi Rossii*. During the period of Ukraine's independence he was a full member of the Archeographic Commission of the Ukrainian Academy of Sciences.

Krym (Crimea). An irregular literary and artistic almanac of the Crimean branch of the Writers' Union of Ukraine published from 1948 to 1962 in Symferopil. Altogether 31 volumes came out. They consist of works by Crimean Ukrainian and Russian writers such as M. Biriukov, I. Nekhoda, P. Pavlenko, and E. Popovkin, translations of Soviet writers of other nationalities, regional materials, and articles in literary history and criticism.

Krymchaks. Turkic-speaking Jews in the Crimea who are believed to be descendants of the *Khazars. They professed Orthodox, Talmudic Judaism and had their own form of ritual and their own dialect, written mostly in the Hebrew script. Their major centers were Bilohirske (Karasu-Bazar) and Symferopil. In 1926 they numbered 6,400. Many were killed by the Nazis during the Second World War, and others emigrated or assimilated, or fled to other parts of the USSR. In 1974, estimates placed their number at 2,500 in the USSR, most of them in the Crimea.

Oleksii Krymov

Ahatanhel Krymsky

Krymov, Oleksii (Aleksei), b 30 July 1872 in Moscow, d 11 December 1954 in Kiev. Surgeon; full member of the USSR Academy of Medical Sciences from 1945. A graduate of Moscow University (1898), he taught there (1906–12) and was a professor at Kiev University (1912–21) and the Kiev Medical Institute (from 1921). In 1936 he became the president of the Ukrainian Society of Surgeons. He wrote 135 works in the field of surgery, including *Ognestrel'naia anevrizma* (Bullet-Wound Aneurysms, 1948), *Spetsiial'na khirurhiia* (Special Surgery, 1948), and *Briushnye gryzhi* (Stomach Ruptures, 1950), and one of the first surgery textbooks in Ukrainian. He developed new methods for the treatment of ruptures and aneurysms.

Kryms'ka pravda (Crimean Truth). Official newspaper of the Crimean Oblast Committee of the CPU and of the Crimean Oblast Soviet of People's Deputies. It is published six times weekly in Symferopil. Its first issue appeared on 6 February 1918 under the name *Tavricheskaia pravda* (Tavriia Truth). In 1919 its name was changed to *Krymskii kommunist* (Crimean Communist), and on 17 November 1920 it became *Krasnyi Krym* (Red Crimea). During the war years (1941–5), it was published in the form of a leaflet in different cities as the Soviet forces retreated: in Sevastopil, Kerch, Krasnodar, and Sochi. Returning to Symferopil on 15 April 1944, it was renamed *Kryms'ka pravda* on 18 January 1952. Since 16 December 1959 the daily has been published in Ukrainian.

Krymsky, Ahatanhel [Kryms'kyj], b 15 January 1871 in Volodymyr-Volynskyi, d reportedly 25 January 1942 in Kustanai, Kazakhstan. Eminent Ukrainian Orientalist, belletrist, linguist, literary scholar, folklorist, and translator; full member of the VUAN and AN URSR from 1918 and the Shevchenko Scientific Society from 1903. A graduate of Galagan College in Kiev (1889), the Lazarev Institute of Oriental Languages in Moscow (1891), and Moscow University (1896), he conducted research in Syria and Lebanon (1896–8) and then taught at the Lazarev Institute, from 1900 as professor of Arabic literature and from 1902 also as professor of Oriental history. He was an active member of Moscow's Ukrainian Hromada. His political views were greatly influenced by M. Drahomanov, I. Franko, and P. Tuchapsky. In July 1918 Krymsky moved to Kiev. There he helped to found the VUAN and its library and served as the first VUAN permanent secretary and de facto director until the Soviet government brought about his defeat in the VUAN elections of 1929. He edited 20 of the 25 volumes of **Zapysky Istorychno-filolohichnoho viddilu VUAN* (1920–9) and was a professor at Kiev University as well as the vice-president of the Ukrainian Scientific Society in Kiev (from 1918). Krymsky survived the Stalinist terror of the 1930s although for nearly 10 years he was removed from scholarly and pedagogical activity. Apparently rehabilitated in 1939, he was, however, arrested by the NKVD in July 1941, and disappeared.

As an Orientalist (an expert in up to 34 languages) Krymsky contributed several hundred entries to the prerevolutionary Brockhaus and Efron and Granat Russian encyclopedias and wrote many other works on Arabic, Turkish, Turkic, Crimean Tatar, and Iranian history and literature. He wrote, in Russian, pioneering textbook histories of Islam (3 parts, 1904–12); of Turkey and its literature (2 vols, 1910, 1916); of the Arabs and their literature (3 parts, 1911–13); of Persia, its literature, and Dervish theosophy (3 vols, 1901–6, 1909–14); and a study of the Semitic languages and peoples (3 parts, 1903–12). In Ukrainian he also wrote histories of Turkey and its literature (2 vols, 1924, 1927) and of Persia and its literature (1923); monographs on Ḥāfiẓ and his songs (1924) and on the Turkic peoples, their languages, and literatures (1930); edited a collection of articles on the Crimean

Tatars (1930); and wrote, with O. Boholiubsky, a study of Arab higher education and the Arabian Academy of Sciences (1928). During the last years of his life he wrote a six-volume history of the Khazars; it was never published.

Krymsky's research on the history of the Ukrainian language was sparked by his desire to refute A. Sobolevsky's claim that the language of ancient Kiev was Russian, not Ukrainian. After painstaking, though insufficiently critical and one-sided, investigations of Old Ukrainian texts, he wrote three polemical studies – *Filologiia i pogodinskaia gipoteza* (Philology and Pogodin's Hypothesis, 1904), *Deiaki nepevni kryterii dlia diialektolohichnoï kliasyfikatsiï staro-rus'kykh rukopysiv* (Some Questionable Criteria for the Dialectological Classification of Old Rus' Manuscripts, 1906), and *Drevne-Kievskii govor* (The Ancient Kievan Dialect, 1907) – and the historical *Ukrainskaia grammatika dlia uchenikov vysshikh klassov gimnazii i seminarii Pridneprov'ia* (Ukrainian Grammar for Students of Higher Grades in the Dnieper Region's Gymnasiums and Seminaries, 2 parts, 1907–8). His views on the language of Kievan Rus' are summarized in 'Ukraïns'ka mova, zvidkilia vona vzialasia i iak rozvyvalasia' (The Ukrainian Language: Whence It Came and How It Developed) in his and A. Shakhmatov's *Narysy z istoriï ukraïns'koï movy ta khrestomatiia z pam'iatnykiv pys'mens'koï staro-ukraïnshchyny XI–XVIII vv.* (An Outline of the History of the Ukrainian Language and a Chrestomathy of Texts of Literary Old-Ukrainian Writing of the 11th–18th Centuries, 1924). Together with K. Mykhalchuk, Krymsky published a program for collecting the distinctive features of Ukrainian dialects (1910). As the director of the *Institute of the Ukrainian Scientific Language (1921–9), he was actively involved in the work of standardizing the vocabulary and orthography of literary Ukrainian. In this activity he vehemently rejected the Galician orthographic tradition. He was the editor in chief of vols 1–2 (4 issues) of the VUAN Russian-Ukrainian dictionary (1924–33) and of the Russian-Ukrainian dictionary of legal language (1926).

As a belletrist Krymsky is known for his three books of lyrical poetry on Oriental themes entitled *Pal'move hillia: Ekzotychni poeziï* (Palm Branches: Exotic Poems, 1901, 1908, 1922), the novella *Andrii Lahovs'kyi* (1905, 1972), the collection *Povistky i eskizy z ukraïns'koho zhyttia* (Narratives and Sketches from Ukrainian Life, 1895), and the collection *Beiruts'ki opovidannia* (Beirut Stories, 1906).

Krymsky translated many Arabic and Persian literary works into Ukrainian, including *The Rubáiyát of Omar Khayyam*, *A Thousand and One Nights*, and Ḥāfiẓ's songs. He also translated the poetry of H. Heine, Byron, Sappho, F. Rückert, and other European writers. He published articles and reviews on Ukrainian writers and their works (eg, I. Vyshensky, O. Kobylianska, I. Franko) and on Ukrainian theater in Lviv and Kiev periodicals (*Zhytie i slovo*, *Zoria*, *Pravda*, *Dzvin*, *Literaturno-naukovyi vistnyk*, *Kievskaia starina*, and others). He published, with M. Levchenko, two volumes of materials on S. Rudansky (1926–9).

As an ethnographer, Krymsky was an advocate of migration theory. He translated into Ukrainian and annotated W.A. Clouston's *Popular Tales and Fictions* ... (1896). A great deal of ethnographic material is found in his Orientalist works. He also wrote articles about such Ukrainian ethnographers as M. Drahomanov, M. Lysenko, and V. Miller. Twenty-seven of his ethnographic articles were republished as *Rozvidky, statti ta zamitky* (Studies, Articles, and Comments, 1928). Of particular importance is his *Zvenyhorodshchyna z pohliadu etnohrafichnoho ta diialektolohichnoho* (The Zvenyhorod Region from an Ethnographic and Dialectological Perspective, 1928). The second volume of this work, like many of his other manuscripts, was never published.

Krymsky donated his valuable 30,000-volume library to the VUAN; it is now part of the Central Scientific Library of the AN URSR. His personal archive – consisting of thousands of manuscripts and the papers of M. Bilozersky, P. Zhytetsky, S. Rudansky, A. Dyminsky, and others – is preserved at this library and at the Institute of Fine Arts, Folklore, and Ethnography. His works appeared in a five-volume edition in Kiev (1972–3).

BIBLIOGRAPHY

Babyshkin, O. *Ahatanhel Kryms'kyi: Literaturnyi portret* (Kiev 1967)
Hurnyts'kyi, K. *Kryms'kyi iak istoryk* (Kiev 1971)
Skokan, K.; Derkach, N.; Isaieva, N.; Martynenko, H. (comps). *A. Iu. Kryms'kyi: Bibliohrafichnyi pokazhchyk (1889–1971)* (Kiev 1972)
Bilodid, I. (ed). *A. Iu. Kryms'kyi – ukraïnist i oriientalist* (Kiev 1974)

M. Hnatiukivsky, R. Senkus, G.Y. Shevelov

Krynica. See Krynytsia.

Krynytsia [Krynycja] (Polish: Krynica). IV-1. Town (1977 pop 11,700) in the western Lemko region. From the 19th century it had a large spa that in the interwar years attracted 60,000 visitors annually to its six therapeutic mineral springs. At one time Krynytsia was inhabited exclusively by Ukrainians; in 1860 they constituted 92 percent of its 1,100 inhabitants. With time its population became mixed, and in 1939 there were 2,900 Ukrainians, 4,300 Poles, and 1,600 Jews in the town. From 1940 to 1944 it was an important Ukrainian center; a Ukrainian teachers' college and various Ukrainian cultural and economic institutions were located there. After the war the Polish authorities forcibly resettled the Ukrainian population in western and northern Poland.

Krynytsia (Well). Publishing company operating in Kiev in 1912–14 and 1917–20. By 1914 it had published a series of inexpensive books, such as M. Drahomanov's *Chudats'ki dumky pro ukraïns'ku natsional'nu spravu* (Eccentric Thoughts on the Ukrainian National Cause) and *Shevchenko, ukraïnofily i sotsiializm* (Shevchenko, the Ukrainophiles, and Socialism), and a complete edition of T. Shevchenko's *Kobzar*. The publishing house was closed down at the beginning of the First World War. It was revived in 1917 and in the next three years it issued numerous books on various subjects. Its publications included works by I. Karpenko-Kary, M. Kotsiubynsky, O. Oles, H. Chuprynka, and S. Vasylchenko, textbooks, children's books, and the Muzychna biblioteka (Music Library) series edited by O. Koshyts. During the period of Ukrainian independence Krynytsia acquired its own printing press and bookstore. The company was abolished by the Bolsheviks in 1920.

Krynytska, Lidiia [Krynyc'ka, Lidija], b 5 July 1898 in Tomaszów, Lublin gubernia (now Poland), d 23 August

1966 in Kharkiv. Character actress. Upon graduating from the Lysenko Music and Drama Institute in Kiev (1923), she joined the *Berezil theater. After working briefly with the Odessa Ukrainian Drama Theater (1929–31), she acted for many years with the Kharkiv Ukrainian Drama Theater. Her repertoire included the Strumpet in V. Yaroshenko's *Shpana* (Riffraff), the noble's daughter in I. Tobilevych's *Sava Chalyi*, Ingiherda in I. Kocherha's *Iaroslav Mudryi* (Yaroslav the Wise), and the title role in V. Hugo's *Marie Tudor*. She also acted in films.

Krynytsky, Ivan [Krynyc'kyj], b 13 July 1797 in Zvenyhorodka, Kiev gubernia, d 12 October 1838 in the Caucasus Mountains. Zoologist and mineralogist. Krynytsky studied at Vilnius University, then worked there as a professor of agriculture (1823–5). In 1825 he became a professor of mineralogy and zoology at Kharkiv University, the first Ukrainian-born professional zoologist. Krynytsky completed several research trips to southern Ukraine, the Caucasus, and the shore of the Caspian Sea and wrote over 30 scientific studies describing over 70 species of insects, birds, and amphibians. During one of his research trips, Krynytsky fell ill and died.

Krynytsky, Onufrii [Krynyc'kyj, Onufrij], b 12 June 1791 in Kryva, Jasło circle, Galicia, d 8 April 1867 in Zhovtantsi, Zhovkva county, Galicia. Theologian. He studied at the Greek Catholic Theological Seminary in Lviv, and, after being ordained, at Vienna University (D TH 1815). Krynytsky taught Church history and Eastern languages at Lviv University from 1819 to 1861, serving as rector several times. He also taught these subjects at the Greek Catholic seminary. During the Revolution of 1848–9 he sided with the Poles in their conflicts with the Ukrainians and lost the confidence of the Greek Catholic hierarchy.

Ivan Krypiakevych

Krypiakevych, Ivan [Kryp'jakevyč], b 25 June 1886 in Lviv, d 21 April 1967 in Lviv. Noted historian; full member of the Shevchenko Scientific Society (NTSh) from 1911 and of the AN URSR from 1958. He received his doctorate from Lviv University in 1911 and from 1911 to 1939 taught history in Polish gymnasiums in Zhovkva, Rohatyn, and Lviv, and at the Academic Gymnasium of Lviv. He also taught Ukrainian history at the Kamianets-Podilskyi Ukrainian State University (1919), the Lviv (Underground) Ukrainian University (1921–4), and the Greek Catholic Theological Academy (1934–9). From 1913 to 1914 he edited *Iliustrovana Ukraïna*, a popular semimonthly. For many years he served as director of the historical-philosophical section of NTSh, and in 1934 he became the editor of its periodical, *Zapysky Naukovoho tovarystva im. Shevchenka* (*ZNTSh*). In 1939 he was appointed professor at Lviv University, and in 1940 he became the director of the Lviv Branch of the AN URSR Institute of History. From 1946 to 1951 he was politically persecuted by the Soviet regime, but in 1953 he became the director of the AN URSR Institute of Social Sciences in Lviv.

Krypiakevych began his career as a historian under the tutelage of M. *Hrushevsky. At first he devoted himself to the socioeconomic and cultural history of Lviv and Galicia in the 16th and 17th centuries. His main publications in this period were 'Materiialy do istoriï torhivli L'vova' (Materials on the History of Trade in Lviv, *ZNTSh*, vol 65 [1905]) and 'L'vivs'ka Rus' v pershii polovyni XVI v.' (Lviv Rus' in the First Half of the 16th Century, *ZNTSh*, vols 77–9 [1907]). Soon, however, his attention focused on the history of the Cossacks and the Hetman state, and his major works are devoted to this subject. Among them are 'Kozachchyna i Batoriievi vol'nosti' (The Cossacks and Bathory's Privileges, *Zherela do istoriï Ukraïny-Rusy*, vol 8, 1908), 'Kozachchyna v politychnykh kombinatsiiakh 1620–1630 rr.' (The Cossacks in the Political Combinations of the 1620s–1630s, *ZNTSh*, vols 117–18 [1914]), 'Studiï nad derzhavoiu Bohdana Khmel'nyts'koho' (Studies of Bohdan Khmelnytsky's State, *ZNTSh*, vols 138–40, 144–5, 147, 151 [1925–31]), and the large monograph *Bohdan Khmel'nyts'kyi* (1954), which was written in conformity with official Soviet historiography. His monograph *Halyts'ko-Volyns'ke kniazivstvo* (The Principality of Galicia-Volhynia, 1984) appeared posthumously.

Krypiakevych is the author of over 500 works on historiography, archeography, sphragistics, the study of primary sources, numismatics, historical geography, and cultural history. They include *Ukraïns'ka istoriohrafiia* (Ukrainian Historiography, 1923), *Istoriia ukraïns'koï kul'tury* (The History of Ukrainian Culture, 1937), and *Dzherela z istoriï Halychyny periodu feodalizmu (do 1772 r.)* (Sources for the History of Galicia in the Feudal Period [to 1772], 1962). He was a brilliant popularizer and wrote many popular surveys and accounts of Ukraine's history. The best known among them are *Velyka istoriia Ukraïny* (The Great History of Ukraine, 1935) and *Istoriia ukraïns'koho viis'ka* (A History of Ukrainian Armed Forces, 1936), written in collaboration with other historians, and *Istoriia Ukraïny* (The History of Ukraine, 1949, under the pseudonym Ivan Kholmsky). Under the pseudonym Ivan Petrenko he wrote stories with historical themes for children and youth; they appeared in *Dzvinok* (which he edited in 1911–14) and as separate booklets. A bibliography of his writings by O. Kizlyk was published in 1966 in Lviv.

O. Ohloblyn

Krys, Hryhorii, b 24 December 1940 in Kiev. World and Olympic fencing champion. A graduate of the Kiev Institute of Physical Culture (1972), he won the gold medal at the 1964 Olympic Games and two silver medals at the 1968 Olympic Games. He was a member of the world champion USSR fencing team (1967–71) and individual champion of Ukraine and the USSR several times between 1964 and 1972. He now works as a coach.

Krysa, Herasym, b and d ? *Kish otaman of the *Zaporozhian Sich in 1703. Krysa was Hetman I. *Mazepa's candidate and a spokesman for the Cossack faction favoring rapprochement with the Russian tsar. He replaced K. *Hordiienko, who represented those Cossacks hostile to Mazepa and the tsar. However, the Hordiienko faction won out, and in December 1703 Hordiienko was again elected Kish otaman.

Krysa, Oleh, b 1 June 1942 in Małe Uchanie in the Kholm region. Violinist and teacher. A graduate of the Moscow Conservatory (1965), where he studied under D. Oistrakh, Krysa has won several international awards: second prize at the Wieniawski competition (Poznań 1962), first prize at the Paganini competition (Genoa 1963), and first prize at the International Institute of Music competition (Montreal 1969). He has given concerts in most European countries and in Japan, and in 1971 he toured Canada and the United States. His repertoire includes works by A. Vivaldi, J. Bach, L. Beethoven, N. Paganini, J. Brahms, P. Tchaikovsky, E. Lalo, C. Debussy, M. Ravel, S. Prokofiev, J. Sibelius, and D. Shostakovich, as well as the Ukrainian composers A. Shtoharenko, V. Hubarenko, and M. Skoryk. After teaching at the Kiev Conservatory (1968–73), he moved to Moscow, where he has been teaching at the Gnesin Music and Pedagogic Institute and the Moscow Conservatory.

Kryshtofovych, Afrykan [Kryštofovyč], b 8 November 1885 in Kryshtopivka, Pavlohrad county, Katerynoslav gubernia, d 8 November 1953 in Leningrad. Paleobotanist; from 1945 full member of the AN URSR and from 1953 corresponding member of the USSR Academy of Sciences. A graduate of New Russia (Odessa) University (1908), he chaired the Department of Paleobotany at the AN URSR Institute of Botany from 1945 to 1948. Kryshtofovych studied plant fossils of the USSR and Asia from the Cenozoic, Mesozoic, and Paleozoic eras. He delineated the floral zones and climates of past eras and established that the Ukrainian forests of the Miocene epoch consisted mostly of deciduous plants.

Kryster, Arnold, b 30 October 1886, d ? Lawyer and historian of law. Kryster was a professor at the Kiev Institute of the National Economy and president of the VUAN commissions of Customary Law in Ukraine and Soviet Law. He was also the vice-president of the Society of Ukrainian Lawyers. Kryster published several works in the field of customary law, most of them appearing in journals of the VUAN, some of which he also edited. Kryster was arrested by the Soviet authorities in 1937 and sent to Siberia. His subsequent fate is unknown.

Krystynopil. See Chervonohrad.

Krytyka. See *Literaturna krytyka.*

Kryva Spit. VI-19. A sandy spit located on the northern coast of Tahanrih Bay of the Sea of Azov, in Donetske oblast. The spit is approximately 10 km long. Its width varies considerably; at its narrowest point it is approx 100 m wide. The town smt Siedove is located on the spit.

Kryvche [Kryvče]. V-7. Village (1973 pop 2,400) in Borshchiv raion, Ternopil oblast, located on the Tsyhanka River. Kryvche is the site of ruins dating from the princely era (11th–13th centuries) and of a castle from the 17th century that was destroyed by the forces of the Turkish sultan Mahomet IV.

Kryvchenia, Oleksa [Kryvčenja], b 12 August 1910 in Odessa, d 10 March 1974 in Moscow. Singer (bass). A graduate of the Odessa Conservatory (1938), he performed for 10 years with opera companies in Voroshylovhrad, Dnipropetrovske, and Novosibirsk. In 1949 he was appointed soloist with the Bolshoi Theater in Moscow. His repertoire included such roles as Karas in S. Hulak-Artemovsky's *Zaporozhian Cossack beyond the Danube,* the title role in M. Lysenko's *Taras Bulba,* Cherevik in M. Mussorgsky's *Sorochyntsi Fair,* and Don Basilio in G. Rossini's *Il barbiere di Siviglia.* Kryvchenia also performed abroad: in France, Germany, Poland, Rumania, and Japan.

Kryvchenko, Heorhii (Yurii) [Kryvčenko, Heorhij], b 15 April 1883 in Kybyntsi, Myrhorod county, Poltava gubernia, d 11 April 1960 in Kiev. Economist, geographer, and statistician. Kryvchenko studied at the St Petersburg Polytechnical and then graduated from the University of Munich (1910). After working for government statistical offices in Saratov and Penza, he was an associate of the VUAN Institute of Demography (1919–20) and a professor at the Kiev Institute of the National Economy (1922–31). Repressed during the Stalinist terror of the 1930s, he was a professor at Kiev University (1943–52) before returning to the Institute of the National Economy (1956–60). Kryvchenko published a number of monographs and statistical surveys of Ukraine and other countries, primarily concerning the development of agriculture. His most notable works include *Zbirnyk statystychnykh vidomostei po narodnomu hospodarstvu Ukraïny* (Collection of Statistical Data on the National Economy of Ukraine, 1919), *Vneshniaia torgovlia Ukrainy v nastoiashchee vremia i do voiny* (The Foreign Trade of Ukraine at the Present Time and before the War, 1923), *Stanovyshche sil's'koho hospodarstva stepovoï Ukraïny* (Agricultural Conditions in the Steppe Region of Ukraine, 1927), and *Slovnyk ekonomichnoï terminolohiï* (Dictionary of Economic Terminology, 1931; with V. Ihnatovych).

B. Krawchenko

Kryve Ozero. VI-11. Town smt (1979 pop 12,000) and raion center in Mykolaiv oblast, situated on the Kodyma River in the Dnieper Lowland. It was founded in the 1850s. Today food processing is its main industry.

Kryvetsky, Mykhailo [Kryvec'kyj, Myxajlo], b ?, d 27 August 1929 in Clamart, France. Economist. Before the 1917 Revolution Kryvetsky worked in the Russian Ministry of Finance. A member of the Ukrainian Party of Socialists-Independentists, Kryvetsky was deputy minister of finance and head of the State Bank under the Central Rada and then finance minister in the government of S. Ostapenko (1919). His signature appears on the 1917 Central Rada issue of Ukrainian *currency. He emigrated after the fall of the Directory and lived in Vienna and later in France.

Kryvohlaz, Mykhailo, b 18 May 1929 in Kiev. Physicist; corresponding member of the AN URSR since 1978.

A graduate of Kiev University (1950), since 1951 he has worked at the AN URSR Laboratory (later Institute) of Metal Physics, becoming the head of a department in 1964. He was also a professor at Kiev University (1963–70). He has written a number of works in solid-state theory and developed a full kinematic theory of the refraction of x-rays and neutrons by imperfect crystals, and devised methods for the refractrometric analysis of crystals and alloys.

Kryvonis, Maksym, b ?, d November 1648 near Zamostia (Zamość). Prominent Cossack military leader of the *Cossack-Polish War. Little is known about Kryvonis's early years. According to various sources he was either a peasant from Vilshane near Cherkasy or from near Zhytomyr, or a townsman from Ostrih or Mohyliv-Podilskyi. As a Zaporozhian Cossack, he took part in Cossack campaigns against the Crimean Tatars and Turkey. Kryvonis was one of the first to join B. Khmelnytsky's uprising and quickly became a close associate of the hetman's. He gained distinction as a cavalry commander in the Battle of *Korsun (May 1648). Following Khmelnytsky's orders, in summer 1648 Kryvonis organized mass peasant uprisings in Bratslav and Kiev regions and even in Left-Bank Ukraine, and engaged in a series of bloody battles with the Polish nobility's forces led by J. Wiśniowiecki. He later took part in the fighting on the Right Bank, according to some sources as the colonel of Cherkasy regiment. He distinguished himself in the Battle of *Pyliavtsi, and was wounded near Starokonstantyniv. Later he took part in the Galician campaign, gaining great fame when Cossacks under his command stormed the Vysokyi Zamok castle in Lviv (5 October 1648). He died of the plague during the siege of Zamostia. Kryvonis was immortalized in folk songs and legends, some of which claim he was of Scottish descent. Many sources refer to him as Perebyinis. Kryvonis is the hero of V.M. Kulakovsky's historical novel *Maksym Kryvonis* (1983).

BIBLIOGRAPHY
Polukhin, L. *Maksym Kryvonis – heroi vyzvol'noï viiny ukraïns'koho narodu, 1648–1654* (Kiev 1952)
Lola, A. *Maksym Kryvonis* (Kiev 1957)
Vynar, L. 'Pytannia pokhodzhennia polkovnyka M. Kryvonosa,' *Ukraïns'kyi istoryk*, 1971, nos 3–4

A. Zhukovsky

Kryvorivnia [Kryvorivnja]. v-5. Carpathian village (1971 pop 1,200) in Verkhovyna (Zhabie) raion, Ivano-Frankivske oblast, situated in the Hutsul region. Kryvorivnia was first mentioned in 1717. At the turn of the 19th century it was a favorite summer resort for I. Franko and other Ukrainian scholars and writers, such as V. Hnatiuk, M. Hrushevsky, M. Kotsiubynsky, Lesia Ukrainka, O. Kobylianska, L. Martovych, V. Stefanyk, and H. Khotkevych. In 1953 a literary-memorial museum dedicated to Franko was opened there. In the early 1970s the village's name was changed to Kryvopillia.

Kryvy (Krevey), Yefrem [Kryvyj, Jefrem], b 12 December 1928 in Ivaí, Paraná, Brazil. Ukrainian Catholic bishop. He studied at the Gregorian University in Rome (1948–52) and was ordained a priest of the Basilian order in 1951. In 1972 Pope Paul VI consecrated him as auxiliary bishop of St John eparchy in Curitiba, and in 1978 he became the full bishop of the eparchy. Kryvy has successfully organized pastoral care for the Ukrainian population in Brazil.

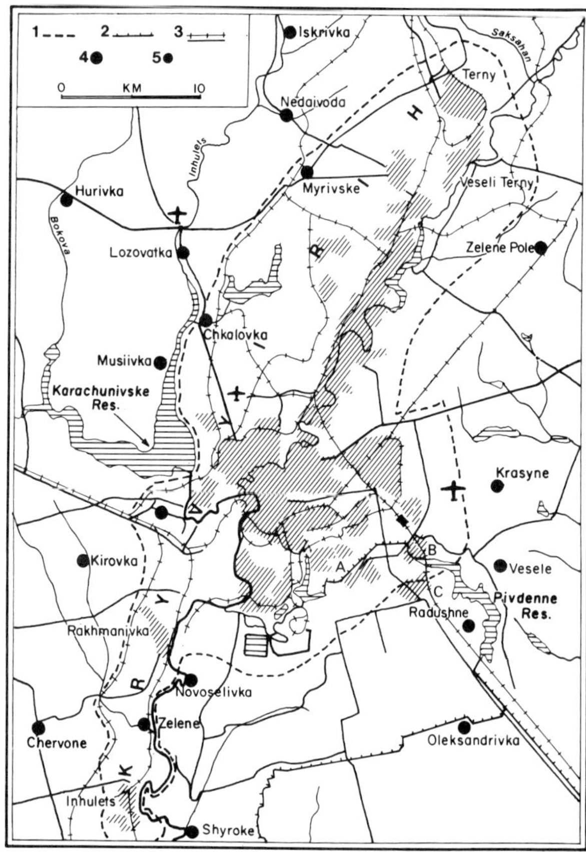

KRYVYI RIH

1. Boundaries of Greater Kryvyi Rih
2. Canals
3. Railways and roads
4–5. Villages and semirural settlements

Workers' boroughs
A. Suvorove
B. Kalynine
C. Zaliznychne

Kryvyi Rih [Kryvyj Rih]. VI-14. City (1986 pop 691,000) and raion center in Dnipropetrovske oblast, situated at the confluence of the Inhulets and Saksahan rivers. The eighth-largest city in Ukraine, it is divided into six city raions. It arose in the 17th century as a concentration of Zaporozhian Cossack winter homesteads. It came under Russian rule in 1774 and from 1803 was part of Kherson gubernia. From 1829 to 1860 it was a *military settlement. The beginnings of its industrial growth coincided with the exploitation of the *Kryvyi Rih Iron-ore Basin from 1881 and the construction of a railroad linking the basin with the Donbas. Consequently its population increased from 3,650 in 1859 to 15,000 in 1897 and 18,000 in 1910. Under Soviet rule the city was an okruha center in 1923–

32. It underwent intensive industrialization in the 1930s, and its population multiplied from 19,000 in 1923 to 31,300 in 1926 (69 percent Ukrainian, 18 percent Jewish, 10 percent Russian), 197,600 in 1939, and 212,900 in 1941. During the Second World War the city's industries were evacuated to the east and its mines were dynamited before it was occupied by German troops (August 1941–February 1944).

After the Second World War, Kryvyi Rih was extensively rebuilt and developed, and its population grew to 408,000 in 1959 and 581,000 in 1970. A major center of mining and ferrous metallurgy in the USSR, it has 24 mines, 4 mineral-enrichment complexes, a mining-equipment plant, a coke-chemical plant, and numerous factories producing machinery, metal products, and building materials. Wool, footwear, clothing, food, and wood products are also manufactured there. Located in the city are 7 scientific-research and planning-and-design institutes, including a mining and a pedagogical institute, a branch of the Kiev Institute of the National Economy, and an evening faculty of the Dnipropetrovske Metallurgical Institute; 17 specialized secondary schools; 18 vocational-technical schools; a Russian music-and-drama and a puppet theater; a regional-history museum; and a circus. In 1959, 73 percent of its population was Ukrainian, 21 percent Russian, and 3 percent Jewish.

Kryvyi Rih Iron-ore Basin. The most important Ukrainian iron-ore–producing region and the largest single source of iron in the Soviet Union. A narrow strip about 100 km long and 2–7 km wide, extending through western Dnipropetrovske oblast from the town of Zhovti Vody in the north to Inhulets in the south, the basin covers an area of approximately 300 sq km. The city of Kryvyi Rih is the major industrial center in the region.

The Kryvyi Rih Basin contains mostly Precambrian sedimentary-metamorphic rocks and is divided into three suites. The middle suite, with a thickness of up to 2,000 m, is the main ore-bearing formation. It consists of seven to eight seams of ferruginous quartzites (represented by hematites, magnetites, and mixed hematite-magnetite varieties) and schists. The average iron content is 30–40 percent in the ferruginous quartzites and 25–30 percent in the magnetite varieties (which compose 20 percent of the total quartzite reserves). Rich iron-ore bodies are dispersed throughout the ore-bearing formation. The ore is formed in columnar, lenticular, and pocket-like bodies that descend to a depth of over 1,000 m. In several places the bodies merge into large sloping ore beds. The rich ores are divided into magnetite, martite, and hematite-martite ores. The last two varieties have an average iron content of 63.7 percent and make up more than half of all reserves.

The Kryvyi Rih Basin has been excavated for iron since the time of the Scythians, but detailed prospecting and commercial exploitation began only in the second half of the 19th century. In 1881 O. *Pol founded a joint-stock company with French capital to develop mining in the basin. In its first year the company mined 37,400 t of iron ore. Production rose rapidly when a railway was constructed in 1884 connecting Kryvyi Rih with the coal-producing region of the Donets Basin. By 1913 the Kryvyi Rih Basin provided 6.4 million t, or 74.5 percent of all the iron ore produced in the Russian Empire. Fifty-one mines had been sunk and 23,600 miners worked in the region, making the area one of the largest industrial centers in Ukraine.

During the Revolution of 1917 and the subsequent struggle for Ukrainian independence, many of the mines and machines were destroyed and production fell drastically. The prewar level of production was not reached again until 1931. However, efficiency was greatly disrupted by the forced rate of industrialization, and more workers (77,339 in 1932) were needed to reach the same level of output.

In 1940, production reached 18.9 million t, or 63 percent of the Soviet total. After the Second World War the mines were increasingly mechanized and the problems of beneficiating ferruginous quartzites were overcome. The basin produced 80 million t, or 52 percent of Soviet production, in 1965 and 58 percent of total Soviet output in 1972. Since then, however, its proportion of Soviet production has declined as the rich deposits in Kryvyi Rih have been exhausted and new sources have been developed. In 1984 the basin accounted for 46 percent of all Soviet production, although total output increased to 103 million t.

Annual production now consists of 38 million t of deep-mined ore excavated from 23 mines extending down to 1,200 m. Another 65 million t are mined from 11 open pits. The rich iron-ore bodies are becoming depleted and reserves (1.5 billion t in 1968) are expected to last only another 25–35 years. The lower-grade quartzite ores that are mined in open pits are becoming increasingly important and are beneficiated in five large complexes, including the Southern and New Kryvyi Rih mineral-enrichment complexes. A sixth concentrator is being built jointly by the Comecon countries. This reflects the importance of Ukrainian iron ore for the east-European countries, which import one-quarter of Ukraine's production. The new concentrator will reprocess inferior-grade quartzites that are now discarded as tailings and will have an annual capacity of 14 million t. Total industrial reserves in the basin are estimated at 16 billion t (1979) and are expected to last several hundred years.

The Kryvyi Rih Basin, producing 85 percent of total Ukrainian output, supplies iron ore to several metallurgical plants in the *Dnieper Industrial Region and the *Donets Basin. The extractive industry employs 62.5 percent of the work force in the city of Kryvyi Rih and 93 percent in the towns of Zhovti Vody and Inhulets.

B. Somchynsky

Kryvyi Rih Metallurgical Plant (Kryvorizkyi metalurhiinyi zavod im. V.I. Lenina or Kryvorizhstal). A metallurgical plant located in Kryvyi Rih that mainly processes the rich local resources of the *Kryvyi Rih Iron-ore Basin. Construction of the plant began in 1931, and the first blast furnace was put into operation in 1934. Before the Second World War, the complex consisted of three blast furnaces, a Bessemer department with two converters, two coke-chemical batteries, and fuel and mechanical divisions. At the outbreak of war, most of the plant's machinery was evacuated to the Ural region. The remaining facilities were completely destroyed during the war. After the war, the plant was reconstructed and significantly expanded, especially during the 1959–65 period when new facilities were constructed every year. At the same time, new technological processes and computerization were introduced. Now, the enterprise consists of an agglomerating plant, 9 blast furnaces, an open-hearth furnace, 2 oxygen converters, 3 continuous blooming mills, and 10 rolling mills. The basic output of the enterprise is pig iron, steel, and rolled metal (strips, wound wire, angle iron, and fitting, round, and sheet steel). The Kryvyi Rih Metallurgical Plant is the largest producer of pig iron and the second largest producer of steel and rolled metal in the USSR.

I. Koropeckyj

Kryvyi Torets River [Kryvyj Torec']. A right-bank tributary of the Kazennyi Torets River, flowing for 88 km through the Donets Ridge and draining a basin of 1,590 sq km. The waters of this gently sloping river are used for irrigation and to supply the population and industry.

Oleksandra Kryvytska

Kryvytska, Oleksandra [Kryvyc'ka], b 16 January 1899 in Chyhyryn, Kiev gubernia, d 24 February 1981 in Lviv. Stage actress. Making her debut in 1916 with S. Pronsky's troupe, in 1918 she joined the Sadovsky Theater in Kiev. From 1921 she worked with various provincial troupes in Galicia. In 1928 she joined the new Tobilevych Ukrainian People's Theater in Stanyslaviv, which she left for the Zahrava Young Ukrainian Theater in 1933. Then she worked with the Kotliarevsky Theater, which arose in 1938 from the merger of the Tobilevych and Zahrava theaters, the Lesia Ukrainka Theater (1939–41), and the Lviv Opera Theater (1941–4), all of which were directed by V. Blavatsky. From 1945 to 1973 she worked with the Zankovetska Ukrainian Drama Theater. Kryvytska played lead roles in Ukrainian, European, and Soviet plays, including Beatriche in Yu. Kosach's *Obloha* (The Siege), Predslava in I. Franko's *Son kniazia Sviatoslava* (Prince Sviatoslav's Dream), Lady Milford in F. Schiller's *Kabale und Liebe*, and Lida in O. Korniichuk's *Platon Krechet*.

Kryzhanivsky, Stepan [Kryžanivs'kyj], b 8 January 1911 in Novyi Buh, Kherson gubernia. Poet and literary scholar. Since 1940 he has been associated with the AN URSR Institute of Literature. Between 1930 and 1981 he published 20 poetry collections. A large edition of his selected poetry appeared in 1957. He has also written short books about V. Stefanyk (1946), A. Malyshko (1951), A. Teslenko (1949), M. Bazhan (1954), and M. Rylsky (1955), literary articles, introductions to editions of works by various Soviet Ukrainian writers, and chapters in multiauthor, multivolume histories of Ukrainian literature. His theoretical-critical works on socialist realism include *Osnovni rysy radians'koï literatury* (The Fundamental Traits of Soviet Literature, 1954), *Problemy typovosty v khudozhnii literaturi* (The Problems of Types in Creative Literature, 1961), *Vykhovannia pravdoiu i krasoiu (Rol' radians'koï literatury u formuvanni novoï liudyny)* (Upbringing on Truth and Beauty [The Role of Soviet Literature in the Formation of the New Person], 1962), *Robitnycha tema v radians'kii literaturi* (The Theme of Labor in Soviet Literature, 1979), and *Khudozhni vidkryttia i literaturnyi protses* (Artistic Discoveries and the Literary Process, 1979).

Kryzhanovsky, Navkratii [Kryžanovs'kyj, Navkratij], b 22 May 1876 in Verkhobuzh, Zolochiv county, Galicia, d 10 April 1940 in Stamford, Connecticut. Missionary priest. He entered the Basilian monastic order in 1896 and was ordained in 1903, a few months before coming to Canada. Until 1910 he ministered to Ukrainian Catholics in Winnipeg and its environs, and he then established a mission in Mundare, Alberta. In 1923 he built a monastery there and directed the Basilian Mission in Canada. In 1932 Kryzhanovsky became the first protohegumen of the new American-Canadian Province of the Basilian order.

Kryzhopil [Kryžopil']. V-9. Town smt (1979 pop 8,500) and raion center in Vinnytsia oblast. The town was established in 1866. During the struggle for Ukrainian independence it was the site of battles between the Ukrainian Galician Army and the Red Army, the UNR Army and A. Denikin's Volunteer Army, and the UNR Army and the Red Army. Now several small food-processing plants are located there.

Kryzhytsky, Kostiantyn [Kryžyc'kyj, Kostjantyn], b 29 May 1858 in Kiev, d 17 April 1911 in St Petersburg. Landscapist; from 1900 full member of the St Petersburg Academy of Arts. After attending the Kiev Drawing School, he completed his studies under M. Klodt at the St Petersburg Academy of Arts (1877–85). His canvases, done in a realist style, include *Oaks* (1911), *Mowers in Ukraine* (1884), *Before the Storm* (1885), *A Farmstead in Ukraine*, *Village*, *Bank of the Dnieper*, *A Summer Day in the Steppe*, *A Market*, and *Grain Harvesting*.

Kuba, Ludvik, b 16 April 1863 in Poděbrady, Czechoslovakia, d 30 November 1956 in Prague. Czech painter, ethnographer, and musicologist. After graduating from a teacher's college (1883), he worked as a rural teacher. Inspired by the idea of Slavic unity, he devoted his life to collecting and publishing the folk songs of all the Slavic nations. From 1884 to 1929 he published the monumental, 15-volume *Slovanstvo ve svých zpěvech* (Slavdom in Its Songs), in which each song is given in its original and in Czech translation, and is accompanied with a vocal and piano score. Many of the songs were written down by Kuba himself on his frequent expeditions. Volume 6 (1885–8; repr, 1922, 1944) is devoted to the eastern Slavs and contains over a hundred Ukrainian folk songs. During his travels (in Ukraine 1886, 1887) Kuba also collected ethnographic materials and painted. On the basis of his observations he published many articles on the folkways and folklore of the various Slavic nations, including the Ukrainians. As an artist he produced over 2,200 paintings, sketches, and drawings, some of which were published in Czech journals or in his monographs. In 1963 a collection of Kuba's works dealing with Ukrainian songs and folklore, titled *Liudvik Kuba pro Ukraïnu* (Ludvik Kuba on Ukraine), was compiled by M. Molnar.

Kubala, Ludwik, b 9 September 1838 in Kamienica, Cracow county, d 30 September 1918 in Lviv. Prominent Polish historian and political figure. Kubala studied at the universities of Cracow and Vienna. He was a participant in the Polish uprising of 1863–4. From 1875 to 1906 he taught in a gymnasium in Lviv. Kubala was a member of the Polish Academy of Sciences from 1884 and a full member of the Shevchenko Scientific Society. He specialized in the history of Poland and in Ukrainian-Polish relations during the time of the *Cossack-Polish War of 1648–57; he was particularly interested in military history and the personalities of such major figures as Hetman B. *Khmelnytsky. His publications include *Szkice historyczne* (Historical Sketches, 6 vols, 1881–1922), *Jerzy Ossoliński* (2 vols, 1883), *Wojna moskiewska r. 1654–55* (The Muscovite War, 1654–5, 1910), *Wojna szwedzka r. 1655–56* (The Swedish War, 1655–6, 1913), *Wojna brandenburska i najazd Rakoczego w r. 1656–57* (The Brandenburg War and the Invasion of Ráköczi in 1656–7, 1917), and *Wojna duńska i pokój oliwski 1657–60* (The Danish War and the Peace of Oliwa, 1657–60, 1922).

Kuban [Kuban']. A historical-geographical region in northwestern *Caucasia. Kuban is the southernmost Ukrainian ethnographic territory, separated from the rest of Ukraine by the Sea of Azov and the Russian *Don region. It encompasses the western part of the steppes of *Subcaucasia and the main massif of the Caucasus Mountains, their foothills, and their western slopes. Historically, in the west, Kuban was bordered by the Black and Azov seas and the Kerch Strait; in the north, by the Don region at the Yeia River; in the east, by the *Stavropol and *Terek regions; and in the south, by Georgia and the main Caucasian Mountain range from Mount Elbrus to the Black Sea near Sochi. Kuban covers an area of about 100,000 sq km and has a population (1985) of approx 5.8 million.

Until the end of the 18th century, ties between Kuban and the rest of Ukraine were weak because of the great distances separating the two. In the course of Russia's struggle to control Caucasia and extend its influence into Asia Minor, Kuban, because of its location on the route to Baku, the Caspian Sea, and the warmwater ports of the Black Sea (Novorossiiske), gained in significance. Kuban has great geopolitical importance for Ukraine. It strengthens its position on the Black Sea, cutting Russia off from it entirely, and provides a direct link to Transcaucasia.

Kuban emerged as a political and administrative unit in 1860 after the unification of the territories of the *Black Sea Cossacks with the eastern regions of Kuban to create Kuban oblast. The new territory was mostly inhabited by the *Kuban Cossack Host. In the 1860s the territory on the left bank of the Kuban River (the Transkuban) was joined to Kuban oblast. In 1896, the Black Sea coast was separated from the oblast to form the Black Sea gubernia. Most of the territory of Kuban was claimed after the First World War by the *Kuban People's Republic, but in 1920 the region was incorporated by the Bolsheviks into the RSFSR as Kuban–Black Sea oblast. Reorganized several times in the 1920s, the territory of Kuban corresponds largely to the present-day *Krasnodar krai (formed in 1937) and the *Karachai-Cherkess Autonomous oblast on the upper reaches of the Kuban River, which was historically inhabited by Cherkessian (Circassian) tribes.

Geography. Kuban consists of several distinct geographic regions. The *Kuban Lowland (up to 120 m in elevation) in the north is a poorly differentiated plain of fertile, chernozem-covered arable steppe. Its uniformity is only interrupted by occasional minor depressions. The southern region, on the left bank of the Kuban River, is called Transkuban (*Zakubannia*). It is more elevated and forested and broken by tributaries of the Kuban. A somewhat different relief is found on the *Taman Peninsula, a part of the Kuban Lowland that separates the Azov from the Black Sea. It is covered by floodplains, and mud volcanoes are encountered. The Azov coast is characterized by widespread salt marshes and lagoons, and the Black Sea coast is distinguished by its clayey and sandy soils and Mediterranean climate and flora. In the east, the Kuban Lowland rises slightly to join the *Stavropol Upland.

In the south, the Black Sea range of the Caucasus Mountains rises from the Kuban Lowland. Its elevation averages 300 m. The Vovchi Vorota and Hoitkh passes permit travel between the interior and the Black Sea coast. The Abkhaz and Central Caucasian ranges on the east are only partially situated on Kuban territory, and even less so on Ukrainian ethnographic territory. Asymmetrical spurs with steep southern and gentle northern slopes extend to the northeast. Two of these run parallel to the Black Sea range, and three run towards the east. The lower slopes of the mountains are covered by deciduous forests and the peaks are covered by coniferous forests and occasional alpine meadows. January temperatures average −5°C in northern and central Kuban and 5°C on the Black Sea coast, while July temperatures average 22–24°C. In the mountains, temperatures average −7 to −8°C in January and 12–13°C in July. Rainfall averages 400–600 mm in the lowlands and much higher in the mountains. The largest rivers are the *Kuban and its tributaries the Laba, Urup, and Bila, and the Protoka. Deposits of oil, natural gas, and rock salt are found there.

History

To the end of the 18th century. Kuban has been inhabited without interruption since the Paleolithic era. The region is rich in artifacts from the Neolithic and Bronze ages, especially the 'Great Kuban graves,' which contain the remains and riches of deceased chieftains. In the first half of the first millennium BC Kuban was one of the first centers of bronze making; from there the craft spread to Ukraine up to the Dnieper River. The first inhabitants were probably the Indo-European Cimmerians. In the 7th century BC they were pushed out by the Scythians. From that time, the region was populated by several interrelated peoples: the Scythians, the Sindians, who were centered south of the Kuban River and on the Taman Peninsula, and various Maeotian tribes on the shores of the Azov Sea. They farmed and fished and conducted extensive trade with Byzantium. The Scythian culture flourished throughout Kuban, and many grave sites and artifacts have been excavated. A number of Greek city-states, centered chiefly on the Taman Peninsula, were established in the 6th–5th centuries BC. The most important of these were *Phanagoria, Hermonassa, and Cepi. These colonies, as well as the territories of the Sindians and Maeotians, were subsequently incorporated into the *Bosporan Kingdom and the entire coastal region was largely Hellenized. After the 2nd century AD, the nomadic Sarmatians and Alans pushed the Scythian tribes out of the steppes. The invasion of the Huns in the 4th century AD destroyed the Bosporan Kingdom. The local inhabitants integrated with the Huns and other later invaders. In the west, the Maeotians and Sindians eventually became the Cherkessians (also known as the Circassians, they are the modern Adygeians and Kabardians), and in the central Caucasus, the Ossetes emerged from the Alans. In the 5th century some Goths came to Taman from Crimea. In the 7th century, the entire Kuban region was incorporated into the Khazar kaganate. During this period, the Greek colonies on the Taman Peninsula and the Caucasian Black Sea coast remained as links to Byzantine culture and Christianity.

In the 9th century, colonies were established by the proto-Ukrainian Siverianians, who moved along the Donets River to the lower Don, and from there to the shores of the Sea of Azov, Taman, and up the Kuban River. After Prince Sviatoslav's defeat of the Khazars, Ossetians (known in Rus' sources as the Yasy), and Cherkessians (known as the Kasohy), the *Tmutorokan principality of Kievan Rus' was established in Taman. It was under the control of the Chernihiv princes, and the Cherkessians were its vassals. In the 12th century, the Cumans cut Kuban off from the rest of Ukraine and ended Rus' control over Tmutorokan. However, Rus' settlements on the shores of the Sea of Azov were still mentioned in 13th-century chronicles as vassals of the Cumans.

In the first half of the 13th century, Kuban was conquered by the Mongols. Many local inhabitants sought refuge in the mountains (see *Caucasian Mountain peoples). When Mongol influence declined, several Italian (mainly Genoese) colonies were established on the Black Sea, most notably Mapa (present-day Anapa), Bata (Novorosiiske), Matriga (Tmutorokan), and Kopa (near the mouth of the Kuban River). They were important centers of trade and culture. After the disintegration of the Golden Horde in the 15th century, the Nogay Tatars settled on the Kuban steppes and allied themselves with the *Crimean Khanate. In the 1470s–1480s the Genoese colonies were captured by the Turks. The Crimean Khanate, which became a Turkish vassal, gained control over northern Kuban through the Nogay Tatars, and the Taman towns of Temriuk, Taman, and Anapa came under direct Turkish control. Only in the mountains were the Cherkessians able to remain independent. However, even they came under Turkish cultural influence and adopted Islam. Muscovite influence, which began to penetrate the Caucasus in the mid-16th century, became very pronounced in the 18th century. The Russians hoped to gain control over all of Caucasia. Throughout this period, the Kuban steppes were the scene of fierce conflict between the Cherkessians and the Nogay Tatars. Zaporozhian Cossacks began to dock on the eastern shore of the Sea of Azov and establish fishing ports in Taman.

During the Russo-Turkish War of 1768–74, the Nogay Tatars were pushed out of northern Kuban and the area was nearly depopulated. In 1774, the Turks relinquished control over the Crimean Khanate, and thus over northern Kuban, under the terms of the Treaty of *Küçük-Kaynarca, and in 1783 northern Kuban was incorporated into the Russian Empire. The Kuban and Laba rivers served as the new border between Russia and the still autonomous Cherkessian tribes.

From 1792 to 1917. In order to secure control over the new territory, Empress Catherine II gave the remaining Zaporozhian Cossacks, who had been reorganized as the *Black Sea Cossacks, the lands between the Kuban and Yeia rivers. There they were granted extensive autonomy. Totaling some 30,000 sq km, these lands constituted about one-third of the territory of the future Kuban Cossack Host. The colonization began in 1792, and by 1795, 20,000 Cossacks and some Russians lived in the territory. The Zaporozhian Cossack administrative system and social order were reconstituted, and 40 *kurins (companies) were established and named for the original kurins of Zaporizhia. The Cossacks were given the responsibility of defending the new border, the so-called Black Sea Line (*Chornomorska liniia*) that followed the Kuban River from the Black Sea to Ust-Labynsk, a distance of some 320 km. In 1794 the town of Katerynodar (now *Krasnodar) was founded as the Cossack headquarters.

Because of the difficult climate, diseases such as malaria, and the never-ending conflicts with the Cherkessians, the Cossacks suffered many casualties. Their numbers were bolstered by the arrival of Cossacks and escaping serfs from Left-Bank and Slobidska Ukraine. From 1809 to 1811, around 41,000 new immigrants arrived in northern Kuban, followed by about 48,000 in 1821–5 and 16,000 in 1848–50. In total, 100,000 settlers arrived, almost all of them Ukrainians. These, too, suffered a high mortality rate, however, and in 1861 the population of the region stood at only 189,000, including 5,000 non-Cossacks (upon arriving in Kuban most serfs joined the Cossacks). The population density was low, barely 6 persons per sq km. Because most able-bodied males served in the military, the main industries were animal husbandry, extensive agriculture, and fishing.

Beginning in 1794 colonization of northeastern Kuban (the area between Stavropol and Ust-Labynsk) began. The first settlers were mostly from the Katerynoslav and Voronezh regions and included many Ukrainians and Don Cossacks. They were soon organized into the Kuban Cossack regiment, and bolstered by the arrival in 1802 of the 3,000-man *Katerynoslav Cossack Army. In the early 19th century, the population of this region reached 25,000. In 1832, all the varied Cossack units and colonies there were united with the Terek Cossack Host to the east to form the Caucasian Cossack *Frontier Army (*liniitsi*). Several new units composed mostly of Russian and Ukrainian peasants and Cossacks from Left-Bank Ukraine were settled in the region in 1831–4. They defended the so-called Old Line, running from Stavropol northwest and joining the eastern frontier of the Black Sea Cossack territory. In 1840 the frontier was moved south to run from the Kuban River south along the Laba and Bila (the so-called New Line). The 'New Frontier' was settled by a variety of Kuban, Caucasian, and Terek Cossacks. None of these units enjoyed the same autonomy that the Black Sea Cossacks did, and they were all directly or indirectly under regular Russian army control.

A major reorganization of the territory occurred in 1860

when the *Kuban Cossack Host was created out of the Black Sea Cossacks and the six western regiments in the 'New Frontier.' The Terek Cossack Host was created in the eastern half of northern Caucasia. Both of these hosts were part of the Caucasus vicegerency. In the 1860s, the Russian Empire began acquiring the Transkuban territories south of the Kuban River. The Adrianopol Treaty of 1829 with Turkey had already granted Russia the entire Black Sea coast from Anapa to Gagra and recognized Russian dominance over the entire Caucasus. Colonization began soon afterwards, and in 1862–4 the Ukrainian *Azov Cossack Host was forcibly settled there. Russian pressure on the Cherkessian tribes, who by this time were concentrated in the mountains, intensified, and fierce fighting raged on the borders. In 1864 Cherkessian resistance was finally broken, and most of the Cherkessians either emigrated voluntarily or were forcibly removed to Turkey; by 1865 only 74,000 remained in Kuban. Transkuban was then settled by Black Sea Cossacks, Cossacks of the Frontier Army, and peasants from Ukraine and the Azov region – between 1861 and 1865 a total of 16,000 families. In 1865 the population of the entire Kuban was 557,000, of which 90.1 percent were Cossacks or Caucasian mountain peoples. The population began to grow significantly after 1868, when non-Cossacks were first permitted to acquire land. Over the next 15 years, about 250,000 settlers arrived in Kuban, primarily Ukrainian peasants fleeing overcrowded conditions at home. Upon arrival, some of the peasants became Cossacks, but this was not officially allowed after 1870. From then on, the Cossack estate became closed, and the Cossack proportion of the population dropped gradually. By 1897 the total population reached 1,919,000, and by 1914, 3,051,000 (excluding Black Sea gubernia).

On the eve of the 1917 Revolution, Cossacks composed 49 percent of Kuban's population and the mountain peoples 7 percent. The rest of the population was referred to as *horodovyky*, from the Russian *inogorodnye* (outlanders). The Cossacks lived in *stanytsias (garrisons) ranging in size from 5,000 to 20,000 or more. These stanytsias were self-administered, and the Cossacks owned 79 percent of the land (for a more detailed account of the agrarian and military organization of the Kuban army, see *Kuban Cossack Host). The *horodovyky* were either *korinni* or *nekorinni*. The former (9 percent of the population) lived in separate villages and owned their own land (9 percent of that available), and enjoyed some autonomy. The *nekorinni* peasants rented land from landlords or Cossacks, or simply worked as laborers. They lived in the stanytsias or rented homesteads and had no rights of self-government. Great differences in political status between the Cossacks and non-Cossacks were accompanied by considerable socioeconomic differences.

From the beginning of the colonization of Kuban by Black Sea Cossacks, the tsarist government systematically restricted Cossack autonomy and the traditional Zaporozhian way of life and worked to Russify the Cossacks. As early as 1794, the convocation of Cossack councils was prohibited, as was the election of senior officers and the judiciary. Russian generals were appointed as otamans; only the last otaman before the 1917 Revolution, the Russified M. Babych, was a Ukrainian. The state confiscated about 1 million ha of Cossack land for distribution among Russian functionaries and officers or loyal Cossacks. In 1896, when a section of the Black Sea coast was detached from Kuban and transformed into a separate Black Sea gubernia, the stanytsias there were simply closed.

The merger of the Ukrainian Black Sea Cossacks with the mixed Frontier Army served the cause of Russification. The government also hoped to alienate the Cossack officers from the rank and file by granting them large estates, although none of them displayed any desire to engage in agriculture, creating a kind of Cossack aristocracy. On the whole, the officers displayed great loyalty to the tsar and the Russian government. In order to further shelter Kuban Cossacks from Ukrainian influence, they were often sent to borderlands of the empire, particularly Turkestan, Poland, and Transcaucasia. Conversely, Russian Cossacks were stationed in Ukraine. The government did not establish any military academies for Kuban Cossacks, as it did for other Cossack hosts, and local aspirants had to go for training to Stavropol, Orenburg, Tiflis (now Tbilisi), or elsewhere. In the first years following the settlement of Kuban, the Cossacks elected their own priests and sent them to seminaries in Teodosiia. This practice was soon prohibited by the government, however, which gave the right to designate and ordain priests for the region to the bishops of Rostov and Stavropol. A separate eparchy was never created for Kuban, no seminary was established, and its priests were mainly Russians. Kuban also lacked formal institutions such as a supreme court or a true capital city. Since there were only four teachers' colleges, most teachers came from Russian gubernias, and although Kuban was a leading agricultural producer, it lacked even a secondary school in agriculture. It also lacked any institution of higher learning.

The official policy of colonial exploitation was particularly evident in tsarist taxation practices. In 1913, 34.3 million rubles were collected for the state treasury in the region, but total expenditures came to only 15.4 million rubles. Thus, about 19 million rubles were drained from Kuban in that one year alone.

An important factor contributing to the underdevelopment of Kuban was the lack of *zemstvos like those that were established in Left-Bank Ukraine. The fact that Cossack autonomy was limited to the stanytsias meant that local administrations (both civilian and Cossack) had to deal with problems that would have been better dealt with by a united zemstvo system. Agriculture, medical and veterinary care, education, and public works could not be adequately developed, and there were no institutions in Kuban in which both non-Cossacks and Cossacks could co-operate.

Despite all these obstacles, the years immediately preceding the First World War saw a marked increase in the political and social initiative of the population, and particularly the Cossacks. Cossack stanytsias set up their own elementary schools, which were often better than their counterparts elsewhere in the empire. Credit and agricultural co-operatives were established, and Kuban became a leader in agricultural production in the empire. During the Revolution of 1905, there were signs of Cossack opposition to the central government, and in 1906 Otaman Mikhailov convened a Kuban Military Council (after 110 years of inactivity) for the settling of land rights, for which he was dismissed. Kuban sent progressive delegates to all four state dumas, among them the Ukrainian K. Bardizh.

The Ukrainian national movement in Kuban was rather weak. Most of the intelligentsia, particularly government functionaries, priests, and teachers, were from Russia proper or drawn from the local Russified population. Although the Cossacks and many peasants retained Ukrainian traditions and the language, they did not participate in organized Ukrainian life and very few developed a modern Ukrainian national consciousness. There was, however, a conscious Ukrainian element among some of the intelligentsia. A number of Kuban writers, influenced by T. Shevchenko and P. Kulish, wrote in Ukrainian; these included Ya. *Kukharenko, a friend of Shevchenko's and the otaman of the Black Sea Cossacks, and V. Mova (Lymansky). Students from Kuban who studied in Kharkiv, Kiev, or St Petersburg often joined Ukrainian groups. Many Ukrainian writers went to Kuban, including M. Vorony, A. Kashchenko, V. Samiilenko, and V. Potapenko. The development of the Ukrainian movement was also influenced by the various Ukrainian theatrical troupes that toured Kuban. Some political relations between Kuban and Ukraine were established after the creation of the Revolutionary Ukrainian party (RUP). In Katerynodar, the local RUP group, known as the Chornomorska Hromada, was headed by S. Erastiv. Many RUP leaders – including I. Rotar, S. Petliura, P. Poniatenko, B. Martos, A. Kucheriavenko, P. Suliatytsky, I. Ivasiuk, M. Bilynsky, and Yu. Kollard – fled to Kuban to escape tsarist repression. In Katerynodar, a large Ukrainian library was established by Yu. Tyshchenko with funds provided by the Shevchenko Scientific Society. Shevchenko commemorations were held and amateur Ukrainian theater ensembles were organized. The repertoire of the Kuban Army Chorus (conducted by the composer H. Kontsevych), which comprised the best singers of Kuban, was almost exclusively Ukrainian.

From 1917 to 1920. After the February Revolution of 1917, four tendencies manifested themselves in Kuban political life: (1) a pro-Russian movement, with adherents mainly among the Russian and Russified non-Cossack intelligentsia, saw Kuban as a strictly Russian territory and opposed any distinct recognition for the Cossacks; (2) the strongest movement, supported by the majority of the Cossack intelligentsia, hoped simply to preserve the Kuban Cossack Host and expel the *horodovyky* from the region; (3) an autonomist trend favored ties to a federated Russian republic but with considerable political autonomy for the Cossacks; and (4) a pro-Ukrainian faction aimed to join Kuban to Ukraine in a federation without ties to Russia. The latter two movements, which had the fewest supporters, were also those with a largely Ukrainian Cossack or *horodovyk* constituency. They believed in granting the two groups equal rights. These different visions of Kuban's future reflected serious differences in class and national consciousness and the deep-rooted antagonisms between the Cossacks, who jealously guarded their special status and privileges, and the *horodovyky*, who hoped to be placed on an equal footing with the Cossacks and especially hoped for a major redistribution of land that would benefit the land-hungry peasants.

In May 1917, a congress in Katerynodar elected a Provincial Council and Executive Committee, which, along with a commissioner (K. Bardizh) of the Russian Provisional Government, carried out the duties of a territorial government. At this same conference, the delegates also endorsed the creation of a separate Cossack Military Council and Military Government. Later, the Cossacks joined the Southeastern Union of the three larger Cossack hosts: the Don, Kuban, and Terek. Because of differences with the Provincial Executive Committee, which insisted on recognizing central Russian authority, the Kuban Cossacks left the Provincial Council in June 1917, thus initiating a period during which two centers of political power coexisted.

In September 1917, the Military Council, sitting in its second session, added delegates from the mountain peoples and the urban and *nekorinni* non-Cossack populations and proclaimed itself a Territorial Council. A constitution was passed, and the creation of the Kuban Krai Republic, which would join a future Russian federated republic, was proclaimed. A Legislative Council was to act as a parliament and elect the Territorial Government and the otaman as the commander in chief of the army and head of state. The first otaman was A. Filimonov (a Russophile and descendant of a Frontier Army Cossack), and the first prime minister was L. *Bych (a Ukrainian). The first constitution did not guarantee full rights to the *nekorinni horodovyky*, and this widened the rift between them and the Cossacks.

The Kuban Territorial Government did not recognize the Bolshevik seizure of power in Petrograd in November 1917 and assumed full legal power. At its December session, the Territorial Council proclaimed that 'the highest institutions of government of the Kuban territory are the Kuban Territorial and Legislative Councils, elected on the basis of a universal, equal, direct, and secret vote.' This declaration finally recognized the equality of the *horodovyky* and the Cossacks. On 28 January 1918, the Legislative Council, consisting of 46 representatives from the Cossacks, 46 from the *horodovyky*, and 8 from the mountain peoples, organized a new Territorial Government, headed by L. Bych, consisting of 5 Cossacks, 5 *horodovyky*, and 1 representative from the mountain peoples. These developments were partly motivated by a fear of the imminent Bolshevik invasion and the prospect that many Cossacks and *horodovyky* would join the Bolsheviks. On 16 February, the Legislative Council unanimously proclaimed the independent Kuban People's Republic. Under the pressure of the overwhelming Bolshevik forces, the Legislative Council, the military otaman, the government, and the army of some 3,000 volunteers were forced to retreat from Katerynodar. On 17 March, they entered into an anti-Bolshevik alliance with Gen L. Kornilov, the commander of the Russian Volunteer Army. After the death of Kornilov near Katerynodar on 31 March, he was succeeded by A. *Denikin, who also assumed command of the Kuban army.

Before its departure from Katerynodar, the Legislative Council had voted for federation with Ukraine. On 15 May 1918, a delegation headed by M. Riabovol was sent to Kiev, but it did not reach an accord with Hetman P. Skoropadsky. After its return, the Territorial Council (consisting of 10 members at the time) decided on 23 June not to federate with Ukraine but to join Denikin's White forces.

After the 2 August 1918 occupation of Katerynodar and the expulsion of the Bolsheviks from the Kuban in October, Denikin attempted to impose a dictatorship in the region. This was supported in part by the Entente

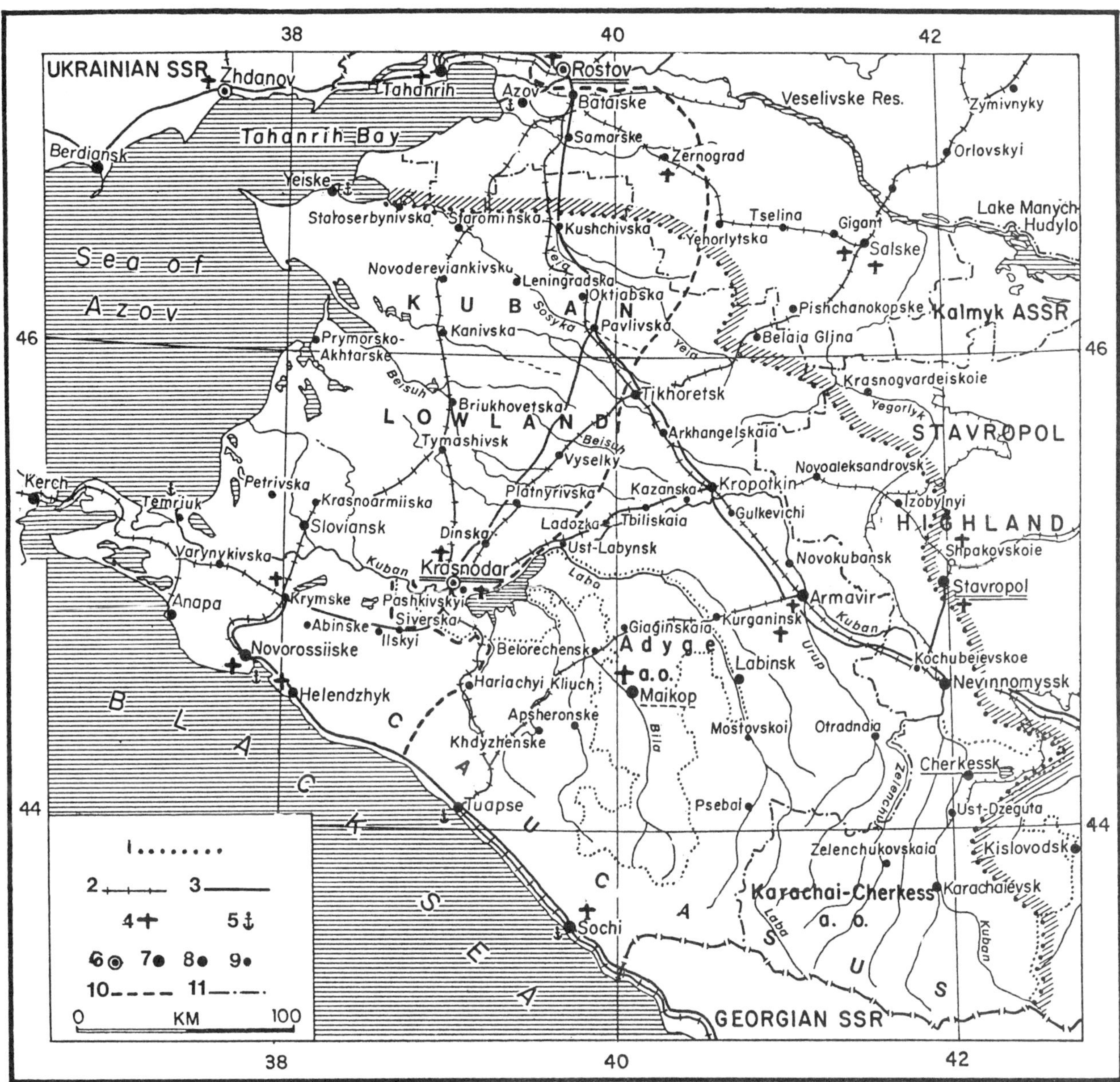

KUBAN

1. Geographic boundary
2. Railways
3. Highways
4. Airports
5. Seaports
6. Cities with a population over 500,000
7. Cities with a population over 100,000
8. Cities with a population of 50,000–100,000
9. Other cities and towns
10. Limit of compact Ukrainian ethnic territory in 1926
11. Borders of oblasts, krais, and autonomous SSR

powers, who favored a single and undivided Russia, and who supported only the Volunteer Army, providing supplies such as medication, clothing, and ammunition. Yet the Kuban Territorial Council adopted the second Kuban constitution (28 October–8 November 1919) that declared Kuban an independent, democratic, parliamentary republic. The constitution also restated Kuban's willingness to join a future federated Russian republic.

In this period, two political factions emerged among the Cossacks. The Black Sea Ukrainian Cossacks opposed Denikin and wished to establish an independent Kuban within an alliance of Cossack states consisting of Kuban, Ukraine, and the Caucasus. The Russophile faction, consisting primarily of Frontier Army Cossacks and headed by Otaman A. Filimonov and Premier P. Sushkov (elected in December 1918), proposed a union of the Don, Kuban, and Terek Cossack territories that would serve as a base for the renewal of a single and undivided

Russia. This faction organized the Congress of the Don, Kuban, and Terek (DKT) in Rostov-na-Donu (13 June 1919). The Kuban delegation to this congress was headed by M. Riabovol. He was murdered by Denikin supporters after he gave a speech proposing an alliance of all anti-Bolshevik forces in which he expressed reservations about the Volunteer Army. After his assassination, the DKT Congress became the 'South Russian' conference. In addition to the Cossacks, the conference accepted delegates from the Volunteer Army and took on a Russophile character. It called for the establishment of a single Russian state formation that would include the Cossack territories, Ukraine, and the Caucasus. These plans were opposed by the Kuban delegates who supported the Legislative Council and the new pro-Ukrainian government of P. Kurhansky (who had replaced P. Sushkov). Denikin decided to organize a coup d'état in Kuban. As a pretext, he chose the projected mutual friendship agreement reached at the Paris Peace Talks in July 1919 between the Kuban delegation headed by L. Bych and the Republic of the Mountain Peoples of the Northern Caucasus, which was occupied by the Volunteer Army. He arrested the Kuban delegation and ordered that Gen P. Wrangel, Otaman A. Filimonov, and V. Naumenko, an ex-minister of the Kuban Republic, carry out the coup. On 6 November 1919, V. Pokrovsky surrounded the Territorial Council with an armed detachment and forced them to make the changes to the constitution that Denikin demanded. A member of the Kuban delegation to Paris, Rev O. Kulabukhiv, was publicly hanged. This prompted the resignation of Filimonov and the government of P. Kurhansky. M. Uspensky was appointed as the new military otaman, while the government was once again headed by P. Sushkov.

As a result of this coup, the Kuban Cossack forces stopped fighting the Bolsheviks. The Volunteer Army alone was not capable of maintaining the fronts against the Bolshevik forces, mainly because it also had to contend with the partisan movement in Ukraine. This resulted in the total demoralization of the Volunteer Army, which began disintegrating; its remnants, along with thousands of refugees, ended up in Crimea and Kuban in February 1920. Meanwhile, M. Uspensky had died in December 1919 and the Kuban Territorial Council reconvened on 1 January 1920. It removed the pro-Denikin government, reinstated the constitution, and appointed M. Bukretov military otaman. On 4 January, V. *Ivanys, a Ukrainian separatist and former minister of trade and commerce in Kurhansky's cabinet, was asked to form a new government.

The first task of the new government was to sever its ties with Denikin's forces and to continue the struggle against Russia together with Ukraine and the Caucasian republics. However, the Bolshevik front was moving southward too quickly to carry out this plan. On 4 March 1920, Katerynodar was evacuated and the otaman, the government, and the Legislative Council were forced to retreat to the Black Sea coast. Because of a lack of ammunition and food, when Georgia refused to intern the Kuban forces, about 15,000 troops of the army were transferred to Crimea, where they ended up joining Gen Wrangel, who had assumed command of the Volunteer Army. On 19 May, the Legislative Council issued its final proclamation in Adler, stating that 'the Military Otaman and the government must preserve the Kuban institutions of statehood and continue the fight for the liberation of Kuban to the end.' After the resignation of Gen Bukretov on 27 May, the duties of the military otaman were assumed by V. Ivanys.

In order to save the remnants of the Kuban army in Crimea, on 22 July 1920 in Sevastopil Ivanys was forced to sign a treaty with Wrangel and agree to recognize his military command. Soon after, a Kuban delegation in Warsaw also signed an agreement with the government of the UNR (9 August). In November 1920, the armies of the UNR and Kuban went into exile.

It should be noted that the Ukrainian movement in Kuban did not grow as quickly as it did in central Ukraine during the revolutionary period. Ukrainian activists did not actively co-operate with the Ukrainian *horodovyky*, who were often under the influence of Bolshevik agitators. No proclamations of independence from Russia were issued, nor was a clear desire to establish closer ties to Ukraine articulated. The Third Universal of the Ukrainian Central Rada, issued on 20 November 1917, did not even mention Ukrainian claims to Kuban. Contact between Kuban and Ukrainian authorities in central Ukraine was weak and sporadic. The trip of the Central Rada representative M. Halahan to Kuban in December 1917, the meetings of Kuban delegations in Kiev with Hetman P. Skoropadsky, and the contacts between the Kuban and Ukrainian delegations at the Paris Peace Conference were the main opportunities for discussion. After M. Halahan, F. Borzhynsky represented the UNR in Kuban, V. Tkachov was the emissary of the Hetman government, and I. Krasovsky, the Ukrainian ambassador to Georgia, represented the Directory.

The Ukrainianization of Kuban in 1917–20 was incomplete. It was limited to the Ukrainianization of a small number of primary schools mainly through the efforts of the Kuban Ukrainian Association for Education, which prepared course outlines in Katerynodar and the publication of a Ukrainian reader, and initiated the opening of two Ukrainian secondary schools (with 151 students) and the Ukrainianization of a teachers' college in stanytsia Poltava. The Ukrainianization of education was retarded by the dearth of teachers who had an adequate command of Ukrainian. Approximately 40 Prosvita societies were active in the various stanytsias. The Ukrainian press also did not develop in Kuban: *Chornomorets'* (6 issues) and *Kubans'ka zoria* (10 issues) appeared sporadically.

Kuban under the Bolsheviks. During the first Bolshevik occupation of Kuban, from March to July 1918, the Bolsheviks controlled the area through local Communist cells. This was the period of War Communism and the settling of scores with the Cossacks, often of a personal nature. The Bolsheviks established the Kuban–Black Sea Soviet Republic (which lasted from 30 May to 6 July 1918). It consisted of lands on the Black Sea coast and parts of the Stavropol and Terek regions. It was subsequently incorporated into the North Caucasian Soviet Republic, which was abolished in November 1918.

After the second Soviet occupation in May 1920, Kuban was annexed to the RSFSR as the Kuban–Black Sea oblast. The mountain people were first granted considerable autonomy, then in 1922 their own Adygei and Karachai-Cherkess autonomous oblasts. In 1924, the Kuban–Black Sea oblast was abolished and divided into separate okruhas (regions): Armavir, Kuban, Maikop,

Black Sea, and parts of the Don and Terek regions. These okruhas were abolished in 1929 and the entire area was incorporated into the North Caucasian krai.

In the 1920s, Kuban benefited from the policy of *indigenization, and schools and public life were *Ukrainized. By 1930–1, most schools in Ukrainian districts offered instruction in Ukrainian. A Ukrainian section was established at the Kuban Pedagogical Institute and many teachers arrived from central Ukraine. Most areas with a Ukrainian population had their own newspapers: in 1931 there were 20 raion and collective-farm newspapers. Yet armed resistance to Bolshevik rule continued throughout the 1920s. Large Cossack uprisings occurred in 1922–3 and 1928, and small Cossack bands hid in the mountains and conducted periodic raids. Repressions began in earnest in 1929. Former officers of the Kuban army and remaining members of the Territorial Council were deported, the Cossacks lost their special status, and the stanytsias were stripped of their political autonomy and subordinated to raion committees. The Cheka and local revolutionary committees also increased their activity.

In 1929 the *collectivization of agriculture began, bringing great suffering and hardship. Thousands of 'kulaks' were deported, as well as entire stanytsias of Cossacks (as many as 200,000 people in total). Although some people managed to escape to Asia, Transcaucasia, or the north, hundreds of thousands of people died from the resulting famine. They were replaced in part by Russian immigrants, who began flooding into the area. In 1934, the teaching of Ukrainian was abolished (over 700 Ukrainian primary schools were Russified), and all Ukrainian-language newspapers were closed down. Ukrainian activists were repressed, particularly the faculty and students of the Katerynodar Pedagogical Institute. Since then, the Ukrainian population of Kuban has not been granted any national or cultural rights and has been exposed to constant official Russification.

The Kuban emigration. After the victory of the Bolsheviks, about 17,000 Kuban troops with Gen Wrangel's army were transported by the Western allies to the island of Lemnos in the Aegean Sea. There, under pressure from Wrangel and the pro-Russian members of the Kuban Territorial Council, some Cossack delegates chose V. Naumenko as the new military otaman. This act was not recognized by the Kuban separatists.

Many Kuban and other Cossacks found themselves in Yugoslavia and Bulgaria. There they maintained their military organizations and were employed in public works. From there some moved to France, some to Czechoslovakia (mainly members of the intelligentsia and students), and some returned to Kuban. Most Kuban Cossacks lived in communities modeled on their native stanytsias, led by elected otamans.

The Kuban emigration (which included few *horodovyky*) had no distinct political parties. However, political groupings or currents did manifest themselves. There were the Kuban independentists, the Russophiles, and the Cossack independentists. They all adhered to a Cossack ideology, but its form varied in each current.

The Kuban independentists favored full Kuban statehood and independence from Russia, but with federative ties to the various Caucasian states, the Don, Terek, and Ukraine. They aimed to unite all three nationalities that populated Kuban: the Ukrainians, Russians, and the mountain peoples. Most supporters of this orientation ended up in Czechoslovakia: V. Ivanys, B. Balabas, K. Bezkrovny, I. Ivasiuk, S. Manzhula, H. and M. Omelchenko, K. Plokhy, P. Suliatytsky, and F. Shcherbyna. They maintained ties to both the Kuban and UNR governments in exile and published periodicals in Prague, such as *Kubans'kyi krai* (1929–33, 12 issues), *Nash krai* (1927–8, 2 issues), and *Kubans'ki dumky* (1928, 3 issues), and brochures on issues of general interest to the Cossack community. The Kuban Hromada relief organization for all Kuban émigrés in Czechoslovakia was set up in 1921. It was headed by P. Makarenko and maintained close ties with the Ukrainian Civic Committee in Prague. Over 100 Kuban natives studied in the Ukrainian higher educational institutions in Czechoslovakia and formed their own student organizations. There were 10 professors and lecturers of Kuban origin. The Hromada published the collection *Kuban'* (1927). The Ukrainian Institute of Sociology in Prague published an economic study of Kuban by I. Ivasiuk (1925) and P. Suliatytsky's *Narysy z istoriï revoliutsiï na Kubani* (Surveys of the History of the Revolution in Kuban, 1926).

A small number of Kuban émigrés, led by I. Bily, believed that the Cossacks constituted a distinct people and hoped to establish an independent 'Cossackia,' uniting all the Cossack territories. The largest and most active element in the Kuban emigration was the pro-Russian faction that sought autonomy for Kuban within a Russian state. This group worked closely with the Russian émigré community. Their center was Belgrade, and their leaders were mostly officers of the Kuban armies such as V. Naumenko, A. Filimonov, and D. Skobtsov.

Population. Before the acquisition of Transkuban by Russia, Kuban was sparsely populated by Nogay Tatars. After their departure and the arrival of Cossack settlers, the population of the region began to rise dramatically, reaching 390,000 by the early 1860s (6 persons per sq km). Higher population densities were found in the regions inhabited by the Cherkessians. After their emigration in 1864, the population of Kuban decreased and did not begin to increase until the mass peasant immigration began in 1868; as late as 1897, 52,000 immigrants arrived in the region. In that year, Kuban's total population stood at 1,976,000 (including Black Sea gubernia). There were few large cities (the largest, Katerynodar [now *Krasnodar], had a population of approx 66,000), and most of the population lived in stanytsias of 10,000 or less. Some cities on the Black Sea coast (Sochi, Novorosiiske, Armavir) were important as trade centers and forts. According to the 1897 census, 49.1 percent of the population considered their native language to be Ukrainian, and 41.8 percent considered it to be Russian (not including Black Sea gubernia). Over one-third of the inhabitants were born outside Kuban. Of these, 24.2 percent were born in the ethnically mixed Voronezh and Kursk gubernias and 40.1 percent were born in the Ukrainian gubernias of Kharkiv, Poltava, Katerynoslav, and Chernihiv; the number of immigrants from Kiev and Kherson was also significant. By 1926, the total population of Kuban was 3,557,000 (including Black Sea gubernia). Of these, 47.1 percent (1,674,000) were Ukrainians, 41 percent (1,460,000) Russians, 4.9 percent (172,000) various mountain peoples, 2.2 percent (79,000) Armenians, 1.1 percent (38,000) Germans, and 0.9 percent (35,000) Greeks. Analysis of the history of Kuban's settlement led some researchers (eg, F. Shcherbyna and

O. Rusov) to argue that ethnic Ukrainians actually constituted 60–62 percent of the population and Russians only 28–30 percent, but that many Ukrainians had become Russified. A sharp decline in the proportion of Ukrainians in Kuban began in the 1930s. The end of Ukrainization unleashed strong pressures for Russification. The forced collectivization of agriculture saw as many as 200,000 people deported from Kuban and the resulting famine claimed tens of thousands more lives. They were replaced by peasants and former Red Army soldiers from Russia. Many Russian Party and government functionaries and specialists also flooded the cities of Kuban. By 1979, only 3.6 percent of the region's inhabitants considered themselves to be Ukrainian.

Economy. The main activity of the Nogay Tatars who lived in Kuban before it was acquired by Russia was nomadic herding. The Cossacks introduced an extensive system of agriculture using the three-field rotation method. The main crops were wheat, rye, millet, and barley. In the mid-19th century, only 12 percent of the total land, and one-fifth of the arable land, was under plow. Because of the Cossacks' military obligations, a shortage of labor was common and hindered the development of agriculture and industry. The region was often plagued by grain shortages and had to import it from the Stavropol and Don regions. Animal husbandry continued to be more important to the region's economy. The Black Sea Cossacks brought from Ukraine *great horned cattle, which were good as draft animals and for beef. Horse raising and sheep herding (at first local Cherkessian breeds were raised, later merino sheep were introduced) were widely practiced. In the mid-19th century there were 25 horses, 104 head of cattle, and 264 sheep per 100 inhabitants in the region. Also important to the Cossacks was fishing and the salt trade. Agriculture was more intensive among the Cherkessians of Transkuban. Their main crop was millet and they maintained a very productive system of orchards.

After the Russian acquisition of Transkuban in 1864 and the emigration of the Cherkessians, agriculture in the region went into a temporary decline. Most of the tilled soil, and particularly the famous Cherkessian orchards, lay fallow. Agricultural production did not start increasing until the 1870s, with the large influx of peasants, the building of the Rostov-Vladikavkaz (1875) and Tykhoritske-Katerynodar-Novorosiiske (1887–8) railway lines, and the growth in demand for grain in Western Europe. The area under plow increased by 2.4 times between 1875 and 1894, and by the First World War 40 percent of the region's land was tilled. Cash crops such as winter wheat (36.3 percent of sown land), spring wheat (22.8 percent), and barley (26.6 percent) increased in importance; less popular were oats (6.6 percent), corn (2.6 percent), and millet (1.2 percent). The average annual harvest (1911–15) produced 3.5 million t of grain, of which 42 percent was exported from Kuban (47 percent of the hard wheat and 53 percent of the barley). Of this, 75 percent was exported beyond the borders of the Russian Empire. After Southern Ukraine, Kuban was the most important territory for the production of grain for export from the empire. Because of the favorable natural conditions, grain yields in Kuban were unparalleled in the Russian Empire (10 centners per ha in Kuban compared to 9.7 in central Ukraine). The use of machines was widespread. Sunflowers (by 1917 they covered 340,000 ha of land, or 8 percent of all tilled land), tobacco (which used valuable yellow Turkish strains), melons, and grapes were also grown.

In 1916–17 there were 999,000 horses, 1,523,000 cattle, 2,164,000 sheep and goats, and 967,000 pigs in Kuban, but little meat or livestock was exported. Seventy-five percent of the population was engaged in agriculture and only 10 percent in industry, mainly the food industry (milling and oil pressing). Cement was produced in Novorosiiske, and petroleum was discovered southwest of Maikop in 1909; production increased from 150,000 t of crude oil in 1911 to 1 million t in 1930. The larger industrial centers were Katerynodar, Armavir, and Novorosiiske. There were also a number of health sanatoriums established on the Black Sea coast. Kuban primarily exported agricultural produce such as grain, flour, oils, poppyseed, and tobacco, and some cement and petroleum. Imports included manufactured goods, metals, sugar, and fish. Exports went mostly outside the Russian Empire, but imports came from within it.

The economy of Kuban followed the same pattern of changes after the 1917 Revolution that occurred in central Ukraine. The sharp decline in production and hardships of 1919–22 were followed by a major economic reconstruction under the New Economic Policy. Agricultural devastation accompanied the collectivization drive of the early 1930s, and the authorities gave priority to the development of heavy industry, which still remained limited. Grains, especially barley, declined in importance, while corn, rice, and tobacco increased. (For current conditions in Kuban, see *Krasnodar krai.)

BIBLIOGRAPHY

Lichkov, L. 'Ocherki iz proshlago i nastoiashchago chernomorskago poberezh'ia Kavkaza,' *KS*, 1905, nos 6–8, 10–12

Shcherbina, F. *Estestvenno-istoricheskiia usloviia i smena narodnostei na Kubani* (Katerynodar 1906)

Makedonov, L. *V gorakh Kubanskogo kraia: Byt i khoziaistvo zhitelei nagornoi polosy Kubanskoi oblasti* (Voronezh 1908)

Kapel'horods'kyi, P. *Ukraïntsi na Kubani* (Kiev 1909)

Shcherbina, F. *Istoriia Kubanskogo Kazach'ego Voiska*, 2 vols (Katerynodar 1910, 1913)

Spravochnaia kniga: Kuban' i Chernomorskoe poberezh'e (Katerynodar 1914)

Hnatiuk, V. *Kuban'shchyna i kubans'ki ukraïntsi* (Lviv 1920)

Ivasiuk, I. *Kuban'* (Prague 1925)

Suliatyts'kyi, P. *Narysy z istoriï revoliutsiï na Kubani* (Prague 1926)

Bych, L. *Kuban' u kryvomu dzerkali* (Prague 1927)

Kuban': Zbirnyk stattiv pro Kuban' i kubantsiv (Prague 1927)

Suliatyts'kyi, P. *Kubań* (Warsaw 1930)

Sanders [Nikuradse], A. *Kaukasien, Nordkaukasien, Aserbeidschan, Armenien, Georgien: Geschichtlicher Umriss* (Munich 1944)

Volyniak, P. *Kuban' – zemlia ukraïns'ka, kozacha* (Buenos Aires 1948)

Kotel'nikov, V. *Don, Kuban', Terek* (Moscow 1950)

Bolotenko, O. *Kozatstvo i Ukraïna* (Toronto 1951)

Golobutskii, V. *Chernomorskoe kazachestvo* (Kiev 1956)

Maslov, E. *V stepakh i predgor'iakh Kavkaza* (Moscow 1956)

Fadeev A. *Ocherki ekonomicheskogo razvitiia stepnogo Predkavkaz'ia v doreformennyi period* (Moscow 1957)

Kuban' rodnaia (Krasnodar 1957)

Temnikova, N. *Klimat Severnogo Kavkaza i prilezhashchikh stepei* (Moscow 1959)

Skobtsov, D. *Tri goda revoliutsii i grazhdanskoi voiny na Kubani* (Paris 1961)

Gvozdetskii, M. *Kavkaz* (Moscow 1963)

Varavva, I. *Pesni kazakov Kubani* (Krasnodar 1966)
Chistov, K. (ed). *Kubanskie stanitsy: Etnicheskie i kul'turno-bytovye protsessy na Kubani* (Moscow 1967)
Kuban' za piat'desiat sovetskikh let (Krasnodar 1967)
Ivanys, V. *Borot'ba Kubani za nezalezhnist'* (Munich 1968)

V. Ivanys, V. Kubijovyč, M. Miller

Officer of the Kuban Cossack Host

Kuban Cossack Host. The only formation of Ukrainian Cossacks that existed until the final days of tsarist rule, and one of the 12 Cossack armies in the Russian Empire. The Kuban Cossack Host was created in 1860 out of the *Black Sea Cossacks, the remnants of the Zaporozhian Cossacks, and the six western units of the *Frontier Army. Numbering 400,000 people in 1860, by 1912 the total number had grown to 1,392,000 (including both Cossacks and their families). While the Black Sea Cossacks had originally enjoyed considerable autonomy and were permitted to retain Zaporozhian traditions and practices, these rights were increasingly restricted in the early 19th century. The organization of the Kuban host was modeled after that of Russian Cossack hosts, and regular Russian army institutions and discipline were slowly introduced. Election of senior officers was not allowed, and the host was usually headed by a Russian general appointed by the government. He took the title of acting otaman and also exercised civilian authority in the Kuban provincial government. Autonomy was limited to the *stanytsia (garrison) level, where officers, including the local otaman, his staff, and judges, were elected.

Military training for the Cossacks was very demanding. It included three years of basic training in the stanytsias, four years of active service in the various regiments, four years in the reserve units with annual summer exercises, four years in secondary reserve units with one major exercise during that period, and five years in the general reserve corps, when the Cossacks could be mobilized in an emergency. The Cossacks provided their own uniforms, swords, and horses. Compared to other Cossack armies, the Kuban host mobilized many units. In 1860 it mustered 22 cavalry regiments, 3 cavalry squadrons, 13 scout (*plastun*) battalions, and 5 artillery batteries. Later, Kuban Cossacks were often posted in Warsaw and elsewhere in the empire to suppress revolts and serve as special guard units. In 1914 the host comprised 37 cavalry regiments, 22 *plastun* battalions, 6 artillery batteries, and 47 various other units, for a total of about 90,000 men in active service.

At first, landownership was determined according to the traditions of the Zaporozhian Cossacks. The host was granted 7.4 million ha of land out of the 9.4 million ha in the entire province. The host then divided this land among the stanytsias. Every Cossack over 16 years of age was guaranteed his own plot of land, and a tenth of the land remained in reserve for later distribution. Periodically the land was redistributed, based on need. Land was especially plentiful after Russia acquired the area to the south of the Kuban River (Transkuban), expelling the native Cherkessians (Circassians) and establishing new stanytsias in the 1860s and 1870s. The tsarist government granted hereditary holdings of 28–55 ha to faithful officers. The obligations of military service forced many Cossacks to neglect their farms, however, and the constant redistribution retarded the development of modern agricultural practices. Yet, many officers prospered, often renting their land to peasants to work. The main crops grown were winter wheat, rice, barley, oats, and flax. Cattle raising served mainly local needs, and large-scale horse breeding began only in the late 19th century. Many Cossacks fished in the Black Sea and inland waters. The Kuban host also had its own treasury and collected taxes to pay for provincial administration, education, health care, and public works. In 1912, it had a capital base of 16.3 million rubles.

During the First World War the Kuban Cossacks fought on various fronts. After the 1917 Revolution, most eventually joined the Volunteer Army under Gen A. *Denikin, but their support waned as disenchantment grew with Denikin's plans to restore a 'single, undivided' tsarist Russia and with his mistreatment of the Kuban population. The host was finally dissolved by the Bolsheviks in 1920, and many Cossacks emigrated to Western Europe. (See also *Kuban.)

BIBLIOGRAPHY

Felitsyn, E. (ed). *Kubanskoe Kazach'e Voisko, 1696–1888 g: Sbornik kratkikh svedenii o voiske* (Voronezh 1888)
Dmytrenko, I. *Sbornik istoricheskikh materialov po istorii Kubanskogo Kazach'ego Voiska*, 4 vols (St Petersburg 1896–8)
Shcherbina, F. *Istoriia Kubanskogo Kazach'ego Voiska*, 2 vols (Katerynodar 1910, 1913)

Kuban Legislative Council (Kubanska Zakonodavcha Rada). Legislative organ of the *Kuban People's Republic in 1917–20. The Kuban Legislative Council (KLC) was to be re-elected at three-year intervals. Its mandate was determined by the *Kuban Territorial Council (KTC). Its jurisdiction included the review and approval of the regional budget; the election of the state comptroller; the approval of state loans; the drawing up of annual lists of people eligible for military service; the ratification of treaties; and the review of and debate on the performance of the KTC, which was responsible to the KLC and which could receive a vote of non-confidence from the

KLC. There were approximately 80 members of the KLC; they also participated in KTC assemblies, in an advisory capacity. The KLC met annually on 15 November. An extraordinary session could be called on the initiative of the military otaman, or at the request of not less than one-third of the KLC itself. In 1918 the KLC was elected for a one-year term only, from members of the KTC, but later its authority was extended.

Kuban Lowland. An extensive plain located in the western part of Subcaucasia within the borders of Rostov oblast and Krasnodar krai in the RSFSR. It extends to the Azov Sea in the west, to the Stavropol Upland in the east, to the Kuma-Manych Upland in the north, and to the foothills of the Causasus Mountains in the south, and occupies three-quarters of the territory of *Kuban.

The Kuban Lowland is a tectonic depression built of chalk and tertiary strata that cover the layered Hercynian foundation. The upper layers are composed of sedimentary deposits (mainly sand and clay) accumulated by the rivers flowing from the Caucasus Mountains. In the south these upper layers are built of fluvioglacial strata. On the surface, the lowland is covered with a 20–50-m layer of loess. In its central part, the plain has an average elevation of 100–150 m. The land gradually decreases in height toward the coast of the Azov Sea in the west and rises gently (to a maximum of 300 m) toward the foothills of the Caucasus Mountains south of the Kuban River. It is an almost perfectly flat plain with some shallow, swampy depressions. On the coast of the Azov Sea, limans have formed. In this region there are also numerous lakes (the largest is the saline Khanske Lake), floodplains, and marshlands, located mainly in the vast delta of the Kuban River. In the east and south the plain is dissected by rivers into a number of flat plateaus. There are chains of low anticlinal hills (up to 162 m in height) on the *Taman Peninsula, which is connected to the Kuban Lowland by the Kuban Delta.

The Kuban Lowland has a continental climate, similar to the climate of the Ukrainian steppe, but warmer and more humid (the yearly average temperature is 10–12°C). It results in relatively cold winters and long and hot summers. Most precipitation occurs from May to July. The summers are conducive to the cultivation of some subtropical crops (eg, rice) as well as to fruit growing and viticulture. The lowland's only large river is the *Kuban River. There are no major rivers in the northern part of the plain, and the existing ones often dry out in the summer.

The Kuban Lowland has mainly carbonated chernozem soils. Other types of soils encountered in the plain are peat-meadow soils in the delta of the Kuban River and dark-chestnut saline soils in the Taman Peninsula. The Kuban Lowland is a region of highly developed agriculture. Its main cultures are grains, melons, and fruits. In the northwestern part of the plain there are rich deposits of natural gas. The fauna of the Kuban Lowland is similar to that of the Ukrainian steppe. The most common animals encountered in the region are gophers, field mice, and polecats.

V. Kubijovyč, M. Stech

Kuban People's Republic. The name of the state formed on 16 February 1918 that existed in several forms until the Bolshevik consolidation of power in *Kuban in May 1920. It was established as a sovereign state on the territory of the former Kuban oblast of the Russian Empire by a proclamation of the *Kuban Legislative Council. On 4 December 1918, a new constitution, adopted in an extraordinary session of the *Kuban Territorial Council, changed the name of the republic to Kuban Krai. The constitution also contained a declaration stating that the krai would be independent until order was restored in Russia and it could join a future Russian Federated Republic. The Territorial Council was the state's constituent assembly and the Legislative Council was the legislative organ. The chief executive officer was the military otaman, who was elected for a four-year term by the Territorial Council but was responsible to the Legislative Council. He was the commander in chief of the armed forces and the head of government.

Kuban River. River in Krasnodar and Stavropol krais. It is the longest river in northern Caucasia (approx 870 km) and drains approx 57,900 sq km. It originates with the Ullukam and Uchkulan rivers, which arise from glaciers on Mt Elbrus in the Caucasus Mountains, and flows to the Sea of Azov. Its upper part (to Nevinnomyssk) runs northwest and is a typical mountain river flowing quickly through narrow gorges with many rapids. Near Nevinnomyssk a dam (built in 1948) leads some water into the Nevinnomyssk Canal. Farther down its course, the river encounters the Stavropol Upland and turns west. From there it meanders slowly through the Subcaucasian steppe. It contains many small islands and sandbanks and runs through marshy floodplains. The Protoka River branches off on the right bank approx 116 km from the Kuban's mouth. At its mouth, the river forms a large marshy delta. All its main tributaries – Teberda, Malyi Zelenchuk, Velykyi Zelenchuk, Urup, Laba, Bila, and Pshysh – are left tributaries. The Kuban reaches its highest water level in the summer, when it is fed by melting snow and glaciers in the Caucasus Mountains. The river is regulated by the Tshchytske, Shapsuhske, and Krasnodarske reservoirs and much of its water is diverted for irrigation. It is navigable from the mouth to Ust-Labynsk and is ice-free 340–350 days a year. The Kuban is rich in fish, especially carp, perch, and pike, and its large delta serves as a nesting place for many species of birds. The main cities on the river are Cherkessk, Nevinnomyssk, Armavir, Kropotkin, Ust-Labynsk, and Krasnodar.

Kuban Territorial Council (Kubanska Kraiova Rada). Constituent assembly of the *Kuban People's Republic. The Kuban Territorial Council (KTC) consisted of approximately 600 representatives, and was elected by male citizens only. The great majority of elected representatives were of peasant or rank-and-file Cossack origin (60 percent); the remainder were Cossack or *horodovyk* (outlander) intellectuals (15 percent) and officers (25 percent). The KTC was formed in the spring of 1917. It convened to choose a military otaman (president of the Kuban Republic, elected for four years), to review and approve new legislation, and to resolve problems brought forward for its consideration by the military otaman or the *Kuban Legislative Council (KLC) (at the request of two-thirds of its members) or at its own behest. The KTC was convened by the military otaman or the KLC. Its authority did not extend to deciding matters proposed by itself. The KTC could not meet with less than two-thirds of its members present. There were three sessions of the KTC: in 1918, 1919, and 1920.

Volodymyr Kubijovyč

Kubijovyč, Volodymyr, b 23 September 1900 in Nowy Sącz, Poland, d 2 November 1985 in Paris. Geographer, demographer, and encyclopedist. From 1928 to 1939 he lectured at Cracow University; in 1940 he was appointed professor at the Ukrainian Free University in Prague. In 1931 he was elected full member (in 1981 he became an honorary member) of the Shevchenko Scientific Society and headed its geographic commission. He was the society's general secretary from 1947 to 1963, and from 1952 president of its European branch. During the Second World War he headed the *Ukrainian Central Committee (UCC) in Cracow and in 1943 took part in organizing the *Division Galizien. In his role as head of the UCC, Kubijovyč revealed his exceptional ability as an organizer and statesman. After the war he emigrated to Germany and then France. He published over 80 works on the anthropogeography and demography of Ukraine, particularly of the Carpathian region. They include *Życie pasterskie w Beskidach Wschodnich* (Pastoral Life in the Eastern Beskyds, 1926), *Rozšiření kultur a obyvatelstva v Severních Karpatech* (The Spread of Cultures and Society in the Northern Carpathians, 1932), *Pastoritul in Maramureş* (Pastoral Life in the Maramureş Region, 1935), *Pastushstvo Bukovyny* (Pastoral Life in Bukovyna, 1935), *Pastýřský život v Podkarpatské Rusi* (Pastoral Life in Subcarpathian Ruthenia, 2 vols, 1935–7), *Terytoriia i liudnist' ukraïns'kykh zemel'* (The Territory and Population of the Ukrainian Lands, 1935), and *Etnichni hrupy Pivdenno-zakhidn'oï Ukraïny (Halychyny) na 1.01.1939: Natsional'na statystyka i etnohrafichna karta* (Ethnic Groups of Southwestern Ukraine [Galicia] on 1 January 1939: Nationality Statistics and an Ethnographic Map, 1983).

Together with other specialists Kubijovyč prepared and edited *Atlas Ukraïny i sumezhnykh kraïv* (An Atlas of Ukraine and Adjacent Countries, 1937) and *Heohrafiia Ukraïny i sumezhnykh zemel'* (A Geography of Ukraine and Adjacent Lands, 1938 and 1943), securing his reputation as one of the founders of Ukrainian geography. He contributed numerous demographic and statistical surveys to Ukrainian, Polish, and Czech serials, and with the help of M. Kulytsky, and later A. Zhukovsky, produced several maps of Ukraine and its regions. From their inception he was the chief editor of *Entsyklopediia ukraïnoznavstva* (Encyclopedia of Ukraine, 1949–), *Ukraine: A Concise Encyclopaedia* (2 vols, 1963, 1971), and *Encyclopedia of Ukraine* (1984–), to which he contributed numerous entries. His contribution in this regard cannot be overestimated. His conceptualization of the *Entsyklopediia ukraïnoznavstva* provided a sorely needed structure to Ukrainian scholarship in the West. Overcoming great obstacles, Kubijovyč organized the scattered intellectual resources in time to ensure that the rich knowledge of Ukraine carried out by the various scholars forced to emigrate during the Second World War be passed on to future generations. His memoirs include *Ukraïntsi v Heneral'nii Hubernii 1939–1941* (Ukrainians in the Generalgouvernement 1939–41, 1975), *Meni 70* (I Am 70, 1970), and *Meni 85* (I Am 85, 1985, with a selected bibliography).

D.H. Struk, A. Zhukovsky

Kuch, Peter [Kuc', Petro], b 1917 in Winnipeg, d 14 June 1980 in Winnipeg. Painter, political cartoonist, and illustrator. A veteran of the Royal Canadian Air Force, in 1945 he joined the *Winnipeg Free Press* and in 1952 became its political cartoonist. He painted landscapes and portraits. His cartoons of J. Diefenbaker were published as a separate collection, *Five Years of Following John* (1962). Besides two Ukrainian-language children's books he illustrated *The Flying Ship* (1975), a selection of Ukrainian folk tales in English translation.

Kuchabsky, Vasyl [Kučabs'kyj, Vasyl'], b 1895 in Volytsia, Lviv county, Galicia, d ? Historian, publicist, and military figure; from 1935 full member of the Shevchenko Scientific Society. An officer of the Ukrainian Sich Riflemen and the Sich Riflemen (commander of the 2nd Infantry), he was a member of the Riflemen Council. After the war he emigrated and lived in Berlin, then in Kiev, working as a librarian. Besides articles on Ukrainian history and politics for German journals, Kuchabsky wrote a number of monographs about the Sich Riflemen and Ukraine's wars for independence, including 'Ukraïns'ki Sichovi Stril'tsi i Sichovi Stril'tsi' (The Ukrainian Sich Riflemen and the Sich Riflemen, *Kalendar Chervonoï Kalyny*, 1924), *Bol'shevyzm i suchasne zavdannia ukraïns'koho zakhodu* (Bolshevism and the Current Task of the Ukrainian West, 1925), *Ukraïna i Pol'shcha: Otverta vidpovid' pol's'komu konservatystovi* (Ukraine and Poland: A Frank Answer to a Polish Conservative, 1933), and *Die West-Ukraine im Kampfe mit Polen und dem Bolschewismus in den Jahren 1918–23* (1934). He disappeared without a trace in 1945.

Kucher, Roman [Kučer], b 12 March 1925 in Lviv. Physical chemist; full member of the AN URSR since 1972. He graduated from Lviv University (1947) and stayed there as a researcher, eventually becoming professor of physical and colloid chemistry (1964–5). Since 1966 he has been director of the radicals department at the Donetske branch of the AN URSR Institute of Physical Chemistry (now the separate Institute of Physical-Organic Chemistry and Coal Chemistry). He has published over 70 papers dealing with kinetics and the mechanism of hydrocarbon oxidation in liquid phase, and has made several important discoveries in the area of emulsions.

Kucher, Vasyl [Kučer, Vasyl'], b 20 July 1911 in Viitivtsi, Volhynia gubernia, d 18 April 1967 in Kiev. Socialist-realist writer. In 1930–4 he studied at Kharkiv University and belonged to the writers' group Traktor. Between 1932 and 1940 he published eight story collections about collectivization and industrialization and the historical novella *Karmaliuk* (1940). After the Second World War he published several short biographies of Soviet working-class heroes, over 10 other story collections, and several long novels about 'positive heroes': *Chornomortsi* (Black Sea Sailors, 2 vols, 1948, 1952) and *Holod* (Famine, 1961), about Soviet sailors and citizens defending Sevastopil and Odessa from the Germans; *Ustym Karmaliuk* (1954), about the 19th-century folk hero; *Proshchai, more* (Farewell, Sea, 1957) and *Trudna liubov* (A Difficult Love, 1960), which are set on collective farms; *Namysto* (The Necklace, 1964) and *Orly vodu p'iut'* (The Eagles Drink Water, 1966), about life in the postwar years; and *My ne spymo na troiandakh* (We Do Not Sleep on Roses, 1967), about the Bolshevik leader Artem. His collected works in five volumes appeared in 1970–1.

Kucherenko, Illia [Kučerenko, Illja], b 1923 in Nova Orzhytsia near Yahotyn, Kiev region. Linguist. Kucherenko is a professor of Kiev University and editor of the interuniversity annual *Ukraïns'ke movoznavstvo* (1973–). He has devoted special attention to the problem of grammatical meaning in relation to the classification of grammatical categories and parts of speech in modern standard Ukrainian. The most systematic presentation of his morphological theory appears in the two-part *Teoretychni pytannia hramatyky ukraïns'koï movy* (Theoretical Questions of the Grammar of the Ukrainian Language, 1961, 1964). He has also written articles on morphology and syntax.

Kucherenko, Pavlo [Kučerenko], b 27 October 1882 in Rostov-na-Donu, d 28 May 1936 in Kiev. Pathologist. A graduate of the St Petersburg Military Medical Academy (1908), in 1910 he began working at Kiev University under the supervision of V. Vysokovych. From 1921 he was the professor of pathological anatomy at the Kiev Medical Institute and later he became a professor at the Kiev Institute for the Upgrading of Physicians. In 1927 he was one of the organizers of the VUAN Chair of Pathological Anatomy. He wrote 70 works dealing with changes in kidney functions in diabetics, pathological glycogenesis, endemic goiter, lymphogranulomatosis, oncology, and physical chemistry, and a pathological-anatomy textbook (1936).

Kucherenko-Kuchuhura, Ivan [Kučerenko-Kučuhura], b 7 July 1878 in Murafa, Bohodukhiv county,

Ivan Kucherenko-Kuchuhura

Kharkiv gubernia, d 1943 in a prison camp. Kobzar. Blinded in childhood, he learned to sing and play the bandura from the kobzar P. Hashchenko. With a repertoire of over 500 songs and dumas, he was invited by H. *Khotkevych to teach bandura at the Lysenko Music and Drama School in Kiev (1908–10). As his reputation grew, he staged concerts in Kharkiv, Kiev, Odessa, Katerynoslav, Poltava, Rostov-na-Donu, Minsk, St Petersburg, Moscow, and Warsaw. Many songs in his repertoire were of his own composition. Some of the dumas he sang were written down by F. Kolessa. In 1939 Kucherenko-Kuchuhura was arrested and sent to a distant labor camp.

Kucherepa, John [Kučerepa, Ivan], b 27 May 1919 in Toronto. Community and political leader. A graduate of the University of Toronto (1945), he practiced medicine in Toronto and was active in the Ukrainian community, serving as president of the Ukrainian Business and Professional Men's Association of Toronto (1948) and of the Ukrainian Catholic Council of Eastern Canada (1956–8). From 1952 to 1957 he served as alderman. In 1957 and 1958 he was elected from the Progressive Conservative party to the House of Commons.

Kucherov, Panteleimon [Kučerov, Pantelejmon], b 9 August 1902 in Kazanska stanitsa, Donets okrug, Don Cossack province, d 25 June 1973 in Kiev. Specialist in mining mechanics; from 1939 corresponding member of the AN URSR. He studied and then taught at the Donetske Mining Institute. From 1939 to 1940 and again from 1945 to 1958 he served as director of the AN URSR Institute of Mining. From 1958 he worked at the academy's Institute of History. His main publications deal with the theory of coal extraction, the automation of mining machines, and the history of mining in Ukraine. He supervised the design of coal-mining machinery.

Kuchmanskyi Route (Kuchmanskyi shliakh). An invasion and trade route along the watershed separating the Boh and Dniester rivers. From the 16th to the mid-18th century the Tatars followed this route, which was one of the branches of the *Black Route, during their raids into Podilia and Galicia. In the 19th century the *chumaks used it to get to Odessa. The route passed through large tracts of forest.

Kuchmij, Halya [Kučmij, Halja], b 2 May 1951 in Keighly, England. Filmmaker. Coming to Canada with her parents in 1952, she was educated at Toronto and York universities. In 1978–9 she studied at the Center for Advanced Film Studies of the American Film Institute in Los Angeles. Her first film, *Streetcar* (1977), won First Prize (Drama) at the Canadian National Exhibition in 1977. *The Strongest Man in the World* (1980) won the Best Producer award at the Yorkton International Film Festival in 1980 and the Genie Award for the Best Canadian Theatrical Short in 1981. She has also produced *Laughter in My Soul* (1983) about Ya. Maidanek, a Ukrainian Canadian artist and humorist, and a number of prize-winning features for CBC-TV's news magazine 'The Journal.'

Kuchuk-Yatsenko, Serhii [Kučuk-Jacenko, Serhij], b 2 August 1930 in Zhytomyr. Specialist in electric welding; since 1978 corresponding member of the AN URSR. A graduate of the Kiev Polytechnical Institute, since 1958 he has worked at the academy's Institute of Electric Welding. He has developed new techniques of resistance welding.

Kuchurhan Estuary [Kučurhans'kyj lyman]. VII-10. Flooded mouth of the Kuchurhan River located on the border of Odessa oblast and the Moldavian SSR, where the Kuchurhan flows into the Rukav Turunchuk, a branch of the Dniester River. The estuary is approx 15 km long, up to 3 km wide, and up to 5 m deep. Burial sites dating back to the 9th–12th centuries have been excavated on its banks.

Küçük Kaynarca, Peace Treaty of. Treaty marking the end of the Russo-Turkish War of 1768–74. It was signed by the two former adversaries in the village of Küçük Kaynarca in southeast Bulgaria on 21 July 1774. By the terms of the treaty Turkey relinquished control of the northern coast of the Black Sea and left Russia in possession of the lower reaches of the Dnieper and Boh rivers, including Oziv and the fortresses of Kerch, Yenikale, and Kinburn. Russia obtained the right to maintain a fleet on the Black Sea and rights of protection over the Christian population of European countries under Turkish rule. The *Crimean Khanate was acknowledged to be independent of Turkey in all except religious matters.

Kuczer, Michael [Kučer, Myxajlo], b 23 October 1910 in Winnipeg, d 2 September 1975 in Toronto. Painter and violinist. Having studied for three years under L. Fitzgerald at the Winnipeg School of Art, in 1929 he won a scholarship to the Royal College of Music in London, where he continued to study painting at the St John's Wood School of Art. In 1949 he returned to Canada and settled in Toronto. Teaching music to support himself, Kuczer experimented with various painting styles and media. His works include abstract compositions such as *Softly Flowing* (1951) and *Mischief* (1959), a number of portraits, usually in a post-impressionist style, and landscapes such as *Summer Day in the Woods* (1952).

Kudryk, Borys, b 1897 in Rohatyn, Galicia, d 1950 in a prison camp in Siberia. Composer, musicologist, and educator. His music studies, begun under Ye. Mandychevsky at the University of Vienna, were completed only after the First World War under A. Chybiński at Lviv University (PH D). From 1926 to 1939 he taught the history and theory of music at the Lysenko Higher Institute of Music, and the history of church music at the Greek Catholic Theological Academy (1933–9) in Lviv. In 1941–4 he wrote stage scores for the Lviv Opera Theater and songs for the Veselyi Lviv Theater. Emigrating to Vienna at the end of 1944, he was arrested there by Soviet authorities and sent to a concentration camp. Besides reviews and articles on music, he wrote *Ukraïns'ka narodnia pisnia i vsesvitnia muzyka* (The Ukrainian Folk Song and World Music, 1927) and 'Ohliad istoriï ukraïns'koï tserkovnoï muzyky' (A Survey of Ukrainian Church Music, *Pratsi Hreko-katolyts'koï bohoslovs'koï akademiï u L'vovi*, 39 [1937]). Stylistically, Kudryk's music is close to classical Viennese music. His works include piano music (three sonatas, a rondo, and variations), violin pieces (sonatinas, three sonatas), a string quartet, a piano trio, vocal solos, choral music, the cantata *Election of a Hetman*, church music, and arrangements of folk songs.

W. Wytwycky

Borys Kudryk

Vasyl Kudryk

Kudryk, Vasyl, b 13 October 1880 in Tsebriv, Ternopil county, Galicia, d 7 October 1963 in Winnipeg. Educator, author, journalist, and priest. Kudryk immigrated to Canada in 1903 and settled near Tolstoi, Manitoba. He taught in several Ukrainian rural school districts. His short stories and articles appeared in the Ukrainian press, while his poetry came out in a separate collection: *Vesna* (Spring, 1911). As editor of *Ukraïns'kyi holos* from 1910 to 1921, he played a prominent role in founding the Ukrainian Greek Orthodox church. In 1923 he was ordained, and he then served as a priest in Alberta and Saskatchewan. From 1941 to 1954 he edited **Visnyk*, the official semimonthly of the Ukrainian Greek Orthodox church. His publications include a number of polemical works, such as *Chuzha ruka* (The Foreign Hand, 1935) and *Malovidome z istorii uniiats'koi tserkvy* (Little-Known Facts from the History of the Uniate Church, 4 vols, 1952–6).

Kudryn, Arsenii, 1887–? Organizer of Ukrainian opera. Kudryn served as director of the Ukrainian Capital Opera in Kharkiv (1925–7) and of the Kiev Ukrainian Opera (1927–37). An active supporter of Ukrainization in the 1920s, he promoted the development of Ukrainian opera. He was arrested in 1937 during the Great Terror and disappeared.

Kudrytsky, Mykhailo [Kudryc'kyj, Myxajlo], b 23 February 1856 in Ohiivka, Skvyra county, Kiev gubernia, d 27 December 1933 in Zhytomyr. Meteorologist; an organizer of the first meteorological network in Ukraine. A graduate of Kiev University, from 1882 to 1901 he trained meteorological observers and set up an agrometeorological network in Polisia. In the early 1920s he worked at the Institute of People's Education in Zhytomyr and served as director of a branch of the Agricultural Scientific Committee of Ukraine.

Kudrytsky, Mykola [Kudryc'kyj], 1884–? Political figure. A member of the Ukrainian Social Democratic Workers' party, in 1917–18 he was a representative to the Central Rada. In the 1920s he worked as a research associate of the All-Ukrainian Academy of Sciences and lectured at the Kiev Medical Institute. Tried and sentenced in 1930 for belonging to the *Union for the Liberation of Ukraine, he disappeared in prison without trace.

Kudrytsky, Yevhen [Kudryc'kyj, Jevhen], b 19 February 1894 in Korostyshiv, Radomysl county, Kiev gubernia, d 15 January 1976 in Zhytomyr. Linguist. Although he graduated from Kiev University in 1917 as a specialist in Ancient Greek and Latin, he taught Ukrainian and its history at pedagogical institutes in Zaporizhia, Poltava, and Zhytomyr (1930–). His publications deal with 18th-century literary Ukrainian, particularly the works of H. Skovoroda (including his Latin works). He also translated from Latin and commented on the text of I. Uzhevych's Grammar of 1643 (1970).

Kuialnyk Estuary [Kujal'nyc'kyj lyman]. VII-11. A salty estuary on the northwest coast of the Black Sea near Odessa. Separated from the Black Sea by a sandy spit up to 3 km wide, the liman is 28 km long, up to 3 km wide, and up to 3 m deep. The Velykyi Kuialnyk River flows into the liman. Several health resorts have been established on its banks to take advantage of the liman's warm water temperature (28–30°C) and high salt content (averaging 74.3 parts per thousand). Salt was mined there between 1860 and 1931.

Kuibysheve [Kujbyševe]. VI-17. Town smt (1979 pop 7,900), and raion center in Zaporizhia oblast. It was founded circa 1782 as Kamianka. By the mid-19th century the name had changed to Belmanka; later it became Tsarekostiantynivka (until 1926) and Pershotravneve (until 1935). It has a granite quarry and plants that produce electrical appliances, building materials, and crushed stone.

Kuilovsky-Sas, Yuliian [Kujilovs'kyj-Sas, Julijan], b 1 May 1826 in Koniushky, Peremyshl circle, Galicia, d 4 May 1900 in Lviv. Ukrainian Greek Catholic metropolitan. As a young student, he was arrested for participating in the Revolution of 1848–9 and fled to Paris, where he studied theology. He was ordained in 1854. In 1857 he obtained an amnesty from the Austrian government and returned to Galicia. He served as a priest in Peremyshl eparchy, then as rector of the Peremyshl Theological Seminary and pastor at the cathedral. He was then appointed archpresbyter of Stanyslaviv eparchy (1887–90), assistant bishop of Peremyshl eparchy, and bishop of Stanyslaviv (from 1891). Kuilovsky-Sas was a conservative bishop who did not support the attempts at major reform of the church. In 1899 Pope Leo XIII appointed him Galician metropolitan, but he died soon afterwards.

Arkhyp Kuindzhi: *Evening in Ukraine* (oil, 1878)

Kuindzhi, Arkhyp [Kujindži, Arxyp], b January 1842 in Mariiupil, Katerynoslav gubernia, d 24 July 1910 in St Petersburg. Landscape painter of Greek origin; from 1893 full member of the St Petersburg Academy of Arts. Having studied with I. Aivazovsky and at the St Petersburg Academy of Arts (1868–72), he joined the *Peredvizhniki. From 1894 to 1897 he directed the landscape workshop at the academy, but was dismissed for supporting a student strike. Many of his works depict Ukrainian landscapes: *Chumak Route* (1875), *Ukrainian Night* (1876), *Evening* in Ukraine (1878), *The Steppe* (1875), *Birch Grove* (1879), *Moonlit Night on the Dnieper* (1880), and *The Dnieper in the Morning* (1881). His paintings are noted for the lively play of sunlight and moonlight. In 1909 a group of artists in St Petersburg formed the Kuindzhi Society, which existed until 1930.

Kuk, Vasyl (pseuds: Yurii Lemish, Vasyl Koval), b 1913 in Krasne, Zolochiv county, Galicia. Political and military leader. A law student at the Catholic University of Lublin, he joined the OUN and in 1937, when the Polish police began to hunt for him, he went underground. In 1941 he was promoted to the OUN Leadership. In 1942–3 Kuk headed the OUN-organized anti-Nazi underground in the Dnipropetrovske region, which encompassed the southern part of the Reichskommissariat Ukraine. After the war he was a member of the OUN Leadership in Ukraine. When R. *Shukhevych was killed in 1950, Kuk (as Yurii Lemish) assumed his positions as leader of the OUN in Ukraine and (as Col Vasyl Koval) commander in chief of the UPA. According to Soviet sources, he was arrested by the secret police in the mid-1950s and repudiated his anti-Soviet activities.

Kukhar, Roman [Kuxar] (pseud: R. Volodymyr), b 21 February 1920 in Lviv. Emigré writer and singer. He studied at Lviv University (1939–41) and the Vienna Conservatory (1943–5). As a postwar refugee, he studied at the University of Colorado, the Pratt Institute, and the Ukrainian Free University (PH D 1962). Since 1962 he has taught at Fort Hays State University in Kansas. He is the author of articles on Ukrainian literature and of 12 volumes of poetry, prose, plays, and essays, including the poetry collection *Palki sertsia* (Passionate Hearts, 1964), the essay collection *Prostir i volia* (Space and Freedom, 1972), the drama collection *Suchasnyi vertep* (A Contemporary *Vertep*, 1973), and the novel *Natsiia na svitanku* (Dawning of a Nation, 2 vols, 1973–4). In 1943–56 he performed in Ukrainian operettas and as a concert soloist.

Kukhar, Valerii [Kuxar, Valerij], b 26 January 1942 in Kiev. Organic chemist; since 1985 full member of the AN URSR. After graduating from the Dnipropetrovske Institute of Chemical Technology in 1963, he joined the AN URSR Institute of Organic Chemistry and in 1975 was appointed chairman of a department at the institute. In 1978 he became a member of the academy's presidium and academic secretary of the Division of Chemistry and Chemical Technology. His most important research deals with polyhalo-organic and phospho-organic compounds.

Kukharenko, Ivan [Kuxarenko], 1880–? Engineer and agronomist. He was a professor of the Kiev Polytechnical Institute and the Kiev Agricultural Institute, and head of the VUAN Chair of Agricultural Technology. From 1927 he was associated with the All-Union Scientific Research Institute of the Sugar Industry in Kiev and editor of its journal *Nauchnye zapiski po sakharnoi promyshlennosti*. He wrote several works on sugar-beet cultivation and processing, including the monograph *Materialy k poznaniiu roli kolloidov v sakharnom proizvodstve* (Materials for Understanding the Role of Colloids in the Sugar Industry, 1931). Kukharenko was arrested in the late 1930s and his further fate is unknown.

Kukharenko, Lidiia [Kuxarenko, Lidija], b 21 January 1906 in St Petersburg, d 10 March 1971 in Kiev. Economist and Party activist. A graduate of the Leningrad Institute of People's Education (1930), from 1931 she taught at Kiev University, becoming director of its Chair of Political Economy in 1953. She was a member of the CC CPSU (1949–66) and head of the Znannia Society of the Ukrainian SSR. Her propagandistic 'studies' include *Lenins'ko-stalins'kyi plan elektryfikatsiï SRSR* (The Leninist-Stalinist Plan for the Electrification of the USSR, 1951) and *Peretvorennia Ukraïny z ahrarnoï v mohutniu industrial'no-kolhospnu respubliku* (The Transformation of Ukraine from an Agrarian into a Strong Industrial, Collective-Farm Republic, 1959).

Kukharenko, Yakiv [Kuxarenko, Jakiv], b 1799 or 1800 in Yeiske in Kuban, d 8 October 1862. Writer, ethnographer, and major-general. He attended the Katerynodar Military Gymnasium and became a career army officer in 1823. In 1851 he became the acting otaman of the Black Sea Cossack Army. In 1842 he met T. Shevchenko and

Yakiv Kukharenko

they became lifelong friends; Shevchenko dedicated his poem 'Moskaleva krynytsia' (The Soldier's Well, 1857) to him. Kukharenko's ethnographic play 'Chornomors'kyi pobut na Kubani' (Black Sea Cossack Life in Kuban, 1836) was published in *Osnova* in 1861 and adapted in 1877 by M. Starytsky as the opera *Chornomortsi* (The Black Sea Cossacks), with music by M. Lysenko. *Osnova* also published his ethnographic studies about Kuban Cossack volunteer guards (1862) and shepherds on the Black Sea littoral (1861), and the folk tale 'Voronyi kin'' (The Black Horse, 1861). He died as a prisoner of the Caucasian Abkhazians and was buried in Katerynodar. Posthumous collections of his works were published in Kiev in 1880 and in Prague in 1928.

Kukhtenko, Oleksander [Kuxtenko], b 11 March 1914 in Horodnia, Chernihiv gubernia. Specialist in automation and technical cybernetics; since 1972 full member of the AN URSR. He graduated from and then taught at the Donetske Industrial Institute (1937–41). After the war he worked at the AN URSR Institute of Mining. In 1955 he was put in charge of a department at the Kiev Institute of Civil Aviation Engineers. Since 1963 he has been chairman of a department at the Institute of Cybernetics. His main publications deal with automatic control systems and their application to aircraft motion, problems of invariance in automation, and the dynamics of machines.

Kukolnyk, Vasyl [Kukol'nyk, Vasyl'], b 1765 in Transcarpathia, d 1821 in Nizhen. Jurist, natural scientist, economist. After completing his studies in Hungary Kukolnyk taught physics, natural history, and agriculture at Zamostia Academy. In 1803–4 he edited *Dziennik Ekonomiczny*. He published several books on Russian civil law and Roman law. In 1816 he took up the Chair of Roman Law at the St Petersburg Pedagogical Institute. In 1820 he became director of the new Nizhen Lyceum.

Kukuruza, Pavlo, b 4 March 1896 in Nova Ushchytsia, Podilia gubernia, d 14 February 1978 in Minneapolis. Publisher, editor, and pedagogue. He immigrated to Warsaw in 1920, and later to Slovakia. In Uzhhorod he organized the Pchilka Publishing House, which published some 80 monographs as well as the youth journal *Pchilka* (1922–32), the monthly *Pidkarpatske pcholiarstvo* (1923–6), and a series of children's books. He also edited almanacs of the Prosvita society and various textbooks. He was imprisoned in Hungary (1939) and Germany (1941–2). In 1945–9 he organized the publishing activities of the Ukrainian Technical and Husbandry Institute in Munich. He immigrated to the United States in 1949.

Golden vase from the Kul Oba barrow

Kul Oba. A Scythian kurhan from the 4th century BC 6 km from the city of Kerch in the Crimea. P. Dubrux and I. Stempkovsky's excavation of the kurhan in 1830 uncovered a pyramid-shaped stone vault containing the skeletons of a Hellenized Scythian chieftain, his wife or courtesan, and his servant, and a rich hoard of several hundred gold trinkets, two gold diadems with gold tablets depicting Scythians, weapons with gold ornamentation, two gold collars and bracelets, medallions depicting Athena's head, earrings, gold, silver, and bronze ware, and hundreds of bronze arrowheads and spearheads. The most valuable artifact discovered there was a gold and silver bowl ornamented with scenes of Scythian life. Much of the jewelry is held at the Hermitage Museum in Leningrad.

Kulabukhiv, Oleksa [Kulabuxiv], b ca 1880 in Novopokrovska stanytsia, Kuban, d 7 November 1919 in Katerynodar (now Krasnodar). Priest and political figure in Kuban. He graduated from the Stavropol Theological Seminary. After the Revolution of 1917 he was a member of the *Kuban Legislative Council and minister of internal affairs in the government of L. Bych. Kulabukhiv was a supporter of the Kuban independence movement and spoke out against the Bolsheviks and the Whites under Gen A. Denikin. In 1919 he was a member of the Kuban Territorial Council delegation to the Paris Peace Conference, where he signed a draft peace treaty between the Kuban Krai Republic and the Republic of the Mountain Peoples of the Northern Caucasus. After his return he was arrested by Denikin's Volunteer Army, tried by a military court, and hanged 'for the betrayal of Russia and the Cossacks.' Kulabukhiv's brutal execution created great resentment towards Denikin in Kuban. As a result, many Kuban Cossacks abandoned Denikin's anti-Bolshevik front, thus contributing to the collapse of Denikin's army and the Bolshevik victory in Kuban.

Kulachkovsky, Yaroslav [Kulačkovs'kyj, Jaroslav], 1863–1909. Economist, lawyer, and community activist in Galicia. He was founder and director of the *Dnister insurance company (1892–1909) and of the Dnister co-operative bank. In 1898 he helped found the Provincial Credit Union (see *Tsentrobank) and later the *Audit Union of Ukrainian Co-operatives, the main organizational center of the Ukrainian co-operative movement.

Kulak (Ukrainian: *kurkul, hlytai*). A Russian term, now part of the English lexicon, for a peasant who owns a prosperous farm and a substantial allotment of land, which he works with the help of hired labor. The *Stolypin agrarian reforms of 1906, which permitted well-to-do peasants to withdraw from the village commune (**obshchina*) and to purchase up to five allotted parcels of land, strengthened the position of such peasants. They were able to lease land, to hire seasonal and permanent farm laborers, and to buy farm machinery; their method of production began to resemble capitalist farming.

In the Soviet period the term 'kulak' became an ambiguous Party construct but with a fundamentally negative connotation. At times it was applied to all well-to-do peasants; at other times it was used to tar all peasants who opposed Soviet rule. According to Soviet sources, in 1917 there were 518,400 kulak households – ie, owning over 6 desiatins in the steppe region and over 10 desiatins elsewhere – in Ukraine; they constituted 12.2 percent of all peasant households. During the Ukrainian-Russian War (1918–19) the kulaks' farms were completely destroyed. The Bolsheviks confiscated all their 'surplus' grain, land, and in many cases, even means of production (livestock and machines). During the period of *War Communism, Soviet decrees prohibited the exploitation of other people's labor and abolished the leasing of land, and the term 'dekulakization' was introduced to designate the official confiscation of land and property. In Ukraine the First Congress of *Committees of Poor Peasants passed a resolution on 18 October 1920 'to eliminate kulak farms as landowners' farms,' to confiscate the kulaks' properties, and to drive the kulaks out of the villages. In practice the campaign resulted only in land redistribution and in the confiscation of the properties of only those farmers who had put up armed resistance to Soviet rule. Soviet leaders regarded the prosperous peasant strata as their chief internal enemy. Any rural revolt, including those led by N. *Makhno and N. *Hryhoriv, was attributed to 'kulaks.' Armed Bolshevik surplus-procurement detachments confiscated massive amounts of grain, which naturally aroused the hostility of not only those peasants who were directly affected but the rural population at large.

During the period of the *New Economic Policy, restrictions on land leasing and labor hiring were gradually lifted. In 1922, 6-year leases, and later 12-year leases, were permitted. Laborers could be hired as seasonal farm help or as permanent farmhands. In 1925 the Third Congress of Soviets permitted the hiring of 12–14-year-olds. However, the equal distribution of land among the peasantry had undermined the economic basis of hired labor, and the dominant figure in the village at that time became the middle peasant, ie, a peasant who farmed the land he owned by himself. In 1926, 10 percent of the peasants in Ukraine owned less than 1 desiatin of sown or unsown land, compared to 32 percent in 1917; 70 percent owned 2–8 sown desiatins, compared to 39 percent in 1917; and only 8 percent owned over 8 desiatins, compared to 16 percent in 1917. According to the Soviet census of 1926, 738,000 farming families, 120,000 of them in Ukraine, used hired labor, and there were 883,000 farm laborers in the USSR, 122,000 of them in Ukraine. Most of the hired laborers were shepherds, blacksmiths, agronomists, and children's nurses. The principal employers were not rich but poor peasants: single women who needed male workers, juvenile and aged heads of households, and farmers who did not own a horse and depended on their neighbor's draft animals to plow their fields. The formerly rich peasants, having had their surplus land confiscated but still having large families to support, were forced to sell their labor to make ends meet.

Compared to the total population occupied in farming, the number of hired hands was trivial. In Ukraine, excluding shepherds and youngsters, there were 66,000, or 0.3 percent of all those engaged in farming. The sample agricultural census of 1927 showed that outside help played practically no role in agricultural production and amounted to only 1.5 percent of all labor expended per household. Even among the most prosperous peasant households – those with over 1,600 rubles' worth of the basic means of production – half did not use hired help at all; among the other half, in the USSR hired labor accounted for only 7 percent, and in Ukraine for only 5 percent, of their work force. After deducting expenses, hired labor provided only 1–2 percent of a 'kulak' family's net income.

Although Soviet policies had deprived them of their economic status, the 'kulaks' continued to be regarded as class enemies by the authorities and were not allowed to vote in elections to the rural soviets, to hold governing positions in co-operatives, or to receive bank loans or tax reductions. Their children were not allowed to join the Red Army or be admitted to post-secondary schools. Local security police agents (see *GPU) and their secret informers were ordered to keep expropriated 'kulaks' under close secret surveillance. Soviet propaganda continuously heaped abuse on the 'kulaks,' blaming them for every economic difficulty and accusing them of criminal designs. Yet, there were no objective criteria for identifying who was a 'kulak.' A Party commission estimated on the basis of the sample agricultural census of 1927 that 3.9 percent of peasant households were 'kulak' because they employed hired labor and owned a relatively large share of the means of production. This estimate was applied in making all subsequent Party decisions; eg, in 1929 higher taxes were levied on 3 percent of peasant households, and 4 percent of the peasantry were deprived of the right to vote in elections to the rural soviets.

The peasants who were classified as 'kulaks' were not rich in the usual sense of the word. The value of their property, including their house and other buildings, was about 1,000 rubles, their average annual income was 1,200 rubles (190 rubles per family member), and they lacked farm machines and draft animals. Individual incomes among the rural proletariat were only half that of the 'kulaks,' but poor peasants and village leaders of poor-peasant backgrounds paid lower taxes, did not bear any production costs, and hence could afford to buy more manufactured goods. Urban residents could afford to spend several times more than the 'kulaks'; they consumed more meat, butter, and fruit, bought more consumer goods, and received better medical care. In comparison to a Soviet urban functionary, a 'kulak' was practically a pauper.

On 21 May 1929 the USSR government defined a kulak farm as one that (1) had a minimum annual income of 300 rubles per person and 1,500 per family and (2) used hired labor, or owned a motorized farm machine (mill, churn, fruit dryer), or rented out its farm inventory or buildings, or engaged in trade, or had income not derived from work (as was the case with clergy). A personal income of 300 rubles was not high at the time; it was about the same as that of an average industrial worker. Yet, few peasant families made even that much, and the government soon had to set aside its definition, allowing local authorities to set their own criteria in defining who was a 'kulak.'

In 1928 and 1929 the government introduced special measures against the 'kulaks.' Their agricultural taxes were increased from 100 to 267 rubles per household. Their state grain-delivery quotas were also raised, and the family head became subject to criminal prosecution for non-fulfillment. Thus, thousands of individuals had their property confiscated. According to a report given at the 11th CP(B)U Congress, in 22 of Ukraine's 41 okruhas, 33,000 people had been prosecuted and lost their farms in 1929. An even larger number of peasants were fined, and rural officials were empowered to impose fines equaling five times the amount of the unfulfilled quotas. Consequently, many peasants abandoned their farms and fled to the cities to work in construction or moved to other regions of the USSR. The number of 'kulaks' thus fell rapidly. By spring 1929 a sample census gave the figure as 71,500 (1.4 percent of all households compared to 3.8 percent in 1927) in Ukraine.

At the beginning of the *collectivization drive in 1929 the party decided to 'liquidate the kulak as a class,' and a special commission headed by V. Molotov was established to determine what to do with the 'kulaks.' According to Party and government decrees issued in January and February 1930, in regions targeted for 'total collectivization' the law allowing land leasing and hired labor was abolished and the confiscation of the 'kulaks' ' property and their deportation was allowed. Molotov's commission divided the 'kulaks' into three categories: those who were to be arrested and imprisoned in *concentration camps or shot; those who were to be deported to Siberia; and those whose property, including their homes, was to be confiscated and who were to be resettled in other regions in their oblast. In Ukraine alone the first and second groups encompassed 40,000–50,000 households, while the third group included about 200,000 individuals.

The decisions of the Molotov commission were implemented almost immediately, beginning in February 1930, and were zealously pursued by special armed dekulakization brigades made up of Party activists, Komsomol members, urban residents, and employees of the

Dekulakization in Ukraine as of 10 March 1930

Region	Total no. of raions	Raions affected	Families affected	% of all households	Value of confiscated property (in rubles)	Value of property per family (in rubles)
Polisia	60	4	987	2.1	1,125,000	1,140
Right Bank	182	96	14,419	1.4	7,768,478	539
Left Bank	151	72	12,934	2.4	7,423,172	574
Steppe	199	133	33,557	3.6	23,984,284	715
Total for Ukraine	592	305	61,897	2.4	40,300,934	742

OGPU and the Party apparat. Peasants were informed that their property no longer belonged to them and were forbidden to slaughter or sell livestock and to leave their villages without permission. All confiscated property was transferred to the newly formed collective farms. To prevent kulaks from divesting themselves of their property before it could be confiscated, Stalin ordered collectivization to be speeded up. Dekulakization became a powerful inducement for all peasants to join collective farms, for they thus avoided being branded enemies of the state and sharing the tragic fates of those who had already become victims.

Rural Party activists needed little encouragement to participate in sanctioned robbery of their neighbors. In the first two months of the dekulakization campaign, 3–4 percent of the peasants in the grain-growing regions of Ukraine were expropriated. By 10 March 1930, in the 305 raions of Ukraine 58,520 horses and oxen and 586,400 ha of land were confiscated from 61,897 dekulakized households. Figures in the accompanying table show that, except in Polisia, where the number of those dekulakized was small, a 'kulak's' property was worth less than the Soviet average of 770 rubles. In other words, at the time they were robbed the 'kulaks' were not rich but poor peasants. A 'twenty-five thousander,' one of the 25,000 industrial workers who were Party members and usually led dekulakization brigades, could buy two or three 'kulak' farms with his annual salary. At the same time that targeted peasants were being openly robbed, other well-to-do peasants were subjected to increasingly heavy taxes. Thus, in 1931 a 'kulak' whose annual income was 1,000 rubles paid 840 rubles in taxes, while urban workers and functionaries with salaries of 1,200 rubles paid only 22 rubles, thus giving them a net income 7.4 times greater than that of their rural counterparts. This injustice was made even graver by the fact that the purchasing power of the ruble in the rural private sector amounted to only 16 percent of that in the urban state sector; in other words, a peasant's ruble bought only one-sixth the goods a worker's did.

By 1 July 1930, 93,000 peasant households had been dekulakized in Soviet Ukraine; the value of their confiscated property amounted to nearly 50.2 million rubles. A comparison with the figures for 10 March 1930 shows that increasingly poorer peasants were dekulakized. By the end of 1930 dekulakized households numbered 160,000–200,000 in Ukraine. An additional 50,000 farms were confiscated for non-payment of taxes. Hundreds of thousands of peasant families 'dekulakized' themselves: they abandoned their farms and fled to the cities. Dekulakization continued in 1931, mostly in the form of confiscation of property of those who owed taxes. A total of 200,000 households in Ukraine were taxed individually, and 110,000 of them disappeared in the course of the year. Thus, in 1930–1 the total number of those dekulakized in Ukraine amounted to 300,000 families, or almost 1,500,000 people.

By 10 March 1930, 11,374 peasant families – one-third of all those dekulakized – had been arrested and deported from the 11 regions targeted for rapid collectivization in Ukraine. During the entire collectivization period the number of families deported from Ukraine was 60,000–100,000 (300,000–400,000 people). Many of those inhumanely deported ended up in prisons or concentration camps; others died in transit or during the first months or years of exile. A secret instruction issued by J. Stalin and V. Molotov on 8 May 1933 ordered an end to the mass deportation of peasants and set a final limit of 2,000 for Ukraine.

In the 1930s the term 'kulak' thus ceased to have any economic significance and was used only as a political label. A new term, 'subkulak' (*podkulachnik*), was applied to anyone, including collective farmers and poor peasants, who sympathized with the plight of the persecuted and disagreed with the actions of the authorities. At the same time, incompetent or dishonest collective-farm managers, bookkeepers, and clerks were labeled kulaks and accused of treacherous designs. Later, the term was applied to the helpless poor who lived on charity and thus unintentionally exposed the state of economic conditions in the countryside.

The peasant deportees were resettled in the wilderness of sub-Arctic Russia, the northern Urals, western Siberia, and Kazakhstan. There they lived in special colonies run by the OGPU. Most were organized into collective farms called statuteless artels, which did not have an elected leader. Others were forced to work in dangerous mines. Treated as subhumans, many of them died from starvation, cold, or disease. In spring 1930 the rate of collectivization was reviewed, and special commissions 'rehabilitated' about 10 percent of the deportees and permitted them to return home. With time, the situation of the deportees was normalized. The 1936 Constitution granted them the right to vote. In 1938 their collective farms became normal artels, and after the Second World War they were allowed to return home.

It should be noted that the position of the ordinary collective farmer who had not been deported was not much different from that of the 'kulak' who was. In 1932–3 the confiscation of surplus grain was extended to all peasants and not just 'kulaks.' Gradually the special measures used to repress the latter were applied to all economically independent peasants who did not join the collective farms; later all peasants were saddled with excessive taxes and compulsory deliveries of meat, milk, and agricultural produce. In the mid-1930s all rural residents in the USSR were deprived of internal passports and thus of the possibility of leaving their places of residence.

Dekulakization was an essential element in the collectivization drive. It ensured the Stalinist regime's victory in the countryside and its complete control over the peasantry. It also undermined agricultural productivity and significantly depressed the living standard. The peasantry lost interest in and the incentive to work. Dekulakization had tragic consequences for the Ukrainian nation and economy (see *Famine and *Genocide).

BIBLIOGRAPHY

Jasny, N. *The Socialized Agriculture of the USSR: Plans and Performance* (Stanford 1949)
Slyn'ko, I. *Sotsialistychna perebudova i tekhnichna rekonstruktsiia sil's'koho hospodarstva Ukraïny (1927–1932 rr.)* (Kiev 1961)
Danilov, V. (ed). *Ocherki istorii kollektivizatsii sel'skogo khoziaistva v soiuznykh respublikakh* (Moscow 1963)
Problemy agrarnoi istorii sovetskogo obshchestva (Moscow 1971)
Ivnitskii, N. *Klassovaia bor'ba i likvidatsiia kulachestva kak klassa, 1929–1932* (Moscow 1972)
Danilov, V. *Sovetskaia dokolkhoznaia derevnia*, 2 vols (Moscow 1977, 1979)
Conquest, R. *The Harvest of Sorrow: Soviet Collectivization and the Terror–Famine* (New York and Edmonton 1986)

S. Maksudov

Kulakovsky, Yulian [Kulakovskij, Juljan], b 25 July 1855 in Panevežys (now in the Lithuanian SSR), d 21 February 1919 in Kiev. Russian historian, classical philologist, and archeologist. Kulakovsky finished his studies at Moscow University in 1876. In 1881 he became a lecturer at Kiev University and in 1888, a professor. He specialized in the ancient history and geography of the northern Black Sea coast area and in the history of Byzantium and ancient Rome. He conducted archeological digs on old monuments in southern Ukraine covering the period from the Greek settlements to the late Middle Ages. Among his principal works are *Alany po svedeniiam klassicheskikh i vizantiiskikh istochnikov* (The Alans According to Information in Classical and Byzantine Sources, 1899), *Proshloe Tavridy* (The Past of Taurida, 1906), and *Istoriia Vizantii* (The History of Byzantium, 3 vols, 1910–15).

Kulas, Julian [Kuljas, Julijan], b 5 June 1934 in Boratyn, Jarosław county, Galicia. Community leader. Coming to the United States with his parents in 1950, he graduated from De Paul University Law School in Chicago (1959). He is active in the Ukrainian community in Chicago: he served as president of the local branch of the Ukrainian Congress Committee (1975–7) and of the Ukrainian-American Democratic Party Organization (since 1974). He is a member of the United States Holocaust Memorial Council (since 1978) and of the Chicago Commission on Human Relations (since 1979). As V. Polovchak's attorney (1980–6), he successfully defended the Ukrainian teenager from deportation to the USSR. In 1986 he was a member of the United States delegation to the Helsinki Accords Review Conference in Vienna.

Kulbakin, Stepan [Kul'bakin], b 9 August 1873 in Tbilisi, Georgia, d 22 December 1941 in Belgrade. Russian Slavist. A graduate of New Russia (Odessa) University (1897), Kulbakin was a professor at Kharkiv (1905–19), Skopje, and Belgrade (1924–) universities. A Neogrammarian, he wrote valuable textbooks of Old Church Slavonic and of various Slavic languages, including *Ukrainskii iazyk: Kratkii ocherk istoricheskoi fonetiki i morfologii* (The Ukrainian Language: A Short Outline of Historical Phonetics and Morphology, 1919). His publications also include studies of Old Church Slavonic, Polish dialects, and Slavic accentuation.

Kulchynsky, Ihnatii [Kul'čyns'kyj, Ihnatij], b 1694 in Volhynia, d 1741 in Hrodna, Belorussia. Uniate Church activist and historian. Kulchynsky graduated from the Urban College in Rome and was ordained in 1720. He served as a secretary to the protoarchimandrite of the Basilian order in Byten, Volhynia, and then as procurator of the order and rector of the SS Sergius and Bacchus Church in Rome (1729–36). In 1737 he was appointed archimandrite of the Basilian order in Hrodna. Kulchynsky published the first history of the Ukrainian Catholic church, *Specimen Ecclesiae Ruthenicae* (1733). The next year he wrote *Appendix ad Specimen Ecclesiae Ruthenicae* (1734), an expanded version of the first book that included archival documentation. In Hrodna, he wrote his best works, including hagiographies of the saints of the Basilian order, *Monologium Bazyliańskie* ... (Basilian Monologium ..., published posthumously in 1771).

Kulchytska, Olena [Kul'čyc'ka], b 15 September 1877 in Berezhany, Galicia, d 8 March 1967 in Lviv. Painter,

Olena Kulchytska: *Self-Portrait* (1917)

graphic artist, master of applied arts, and pedagogue. Completing her art studies at the studio of R. Bratkowski and S. Batowski-Kaczor in Lviv (1901–3), and the Vienna School of Industrial Design (1903–8), she taught secondary school in Peremyshl (1910–38). In 1939 she joined the ethnographic department of the Museum of the Shevchenko Scientific Society in Lviv. After the war she taught book graphics at the Lviv Polygraphic Institute (1945–51) and in 1950 she was elected corresponding member of the Academy of Architecture of the Ukrainian SSR. Most of her artistic work consists of oils, watercolors, and illustrations, particularly of children's books. As a graphic artist she used various techniques, such as woodcut, linocut, copper engraving, and etching. Her chief oil paintings are *Children in a Meadow* (1908), *Harvest* (1913), *Children with Candles* (1913), portraits of her sister Olha (1912), a self-portrait (1917), and the series *Christ's Passion*, *Spring*, and *Landscapes*. Besides such well-known individual watercolors as *Apple Trees in Bloom* (1928), *Mountain Meadows* (1925), and *Mikhova Village* (1930–1), she did several watercolor series, including *Folk Costumes of the Western Regions of the Ukrainian SSR* (1959) and *Folk Architecture of the Western Regions of Ukraine*. Her mastery of the woodcut and linocut techniques is evident in such print series as *Ukrainian Writers* (1920), *Folk Architecture* (1931), *The Hutsul Region* (1935), *Legend of the Mountains and Forests* (1936), and *Dovbush* (1940). Her etchings, such as *Beyond the Sea* (1915), *Under a Foreign Sky* (1915), *The Moloch of War* (1915), *The Black Clouds of War* (1915), and *Vengeance* (1917), are a powerful condemnation of the exploitation of Ukrainian peasants and of war. She has illustrated numerous books: *Ukraïns'ka narodna mitolohiia* (Ukrainian Folk Mythology, 1922), I. Franko's poems *Lys Mykyta* (Fox Mykyta, 1951, 1962) and *Moisei* (Moses, 1939), *Slovo o polku Ihorevi* (The Tale of Ihor's Campaign), and various works by M. Kotsiubynsky, V. Stefanyk, and Yu. Fedkovych. Her contribution to children's literature consists of illustrations to the book series Nashym naimenshym (For Our Smallest Ones, 1915–28) and to the books and magazine published by Svit Dytyny. In the field of applied arts, collaborating with her sister Olha, she designed 80 kilims. Her skillful blending of modernist Viennese trends with Ukrainian folk art made her art extremely popular. From 1908 Kulchytska took part in numerous exhibitions in Lviv, Cracow, Warsaw, Poznań, Kiev (1911, 1913), Poltava, Vienna, Berlin, Kharkiv, and Prague. In 1950 she donated her own collection consisting of over 3,000 of her works (paintings, prints, and kilims) to the Lviv Museum of Ukrainian Art. The Kulchytska Memorial Museum was opened in Lviv in 1971.

BIBLIOGRAPHY

Holubets', M. *Olena Kul'chyts'ka* (Lviv 1933)
Seniv, I. *Tvorchist' Oleny L'vivny Kul'chyts'koï* (Kiev 1961)
Batih, M.; Hurhula, I. *Olena Kul'chyts'ka. Kataloh vystavky 1968* (Lviv 1969)
V'iunyk, A. *Olena Kul'chyts'ka. Al'bom* (Kiev 1969)

S. Hordynsky

Kulchytsky, Inokentii [Kul'čyc'kyj, Inokentij] (secular name: Ivan), b 1680?, d 6 December 1731. Orthodox church figure, bishop, and saint. Of noble descent from Volhynia, he studied at the Kievan Mohyla Academy until 1706 and in 1708 became a monk in the Kievan Cave Monastery. He lectured at the Moscow Greek-Slavonic-Latin Academy (ca 1711–18), serving for some time also as the academy's prefect. Kulchytsky was consecrated bishop of Pereiaslav in 1721 and assigned to missionary work in Peking. When he was barred entry to China, in 1727 he became the bishop of Irkutsk eparchy. There he did missionary work among the local population and expanded the local school system. Kulchytsky's remains were found in 1764, and his relics became so famous that in 1805 Kulchytsky was canonized.

Kulchytsky, Oleksander (Les) [Kul'čyc'kyj], b 26 November 1859 in Kolomyia, d 21 November 1938 in Lviv. Economist and community leader in the Kolomyia region. He studied law at Chernivtsi University and worked in local government in Kolomyia. There he was the organizer and first director of the Pokutia Credit Union, and a founder of the local Prosvita society branch and People's Home. He also helped found the weekly *Postup* (1903) and headed the Kolomyia branch of the National Democratic party. In Lviv Kulchytsky was a founding member of the newspaper *Dilo and the first director (1910–30) of the Land Mortgage Bank, a general credit joint-stock company. He was also a member of the governing board of the Provincial Audit Union (1920) and a leading member of the control commission of Tsentrobank.

Oleksander Kulchytsky

Yurii Frants Kulchytsky

Kulchytsky, Oleksander [Kul'čyc'kyj] (Kultschytzkyj), b 8 February 1895 in Skalat, Galicia, d 30 April 1980 in Sarcelles, France. Psychologist and educator; full member of the Shevchenko Scientific Society from 1947 and vice-president of its European branch (1952–80). After graduating in psychology from Lviv University (PH D 1930), he taught secondary school in Krosno, Zolochiv, Kolomyia, and Lviv. Appointed professor at the State Pedagogical Lyceum in Lviv for his contributions to educational psychology, a year later he fled the Soviet-occupation regime and worked in Munich, where in 1945 he became a professor of psychology at the Ukrainian Free University (UVU). Settling in Sarcelles in 1951, he chaired the Ukrainian Students' Aid Commission (1952–80), belonged to the Free International Academy of Sciences and Letters, founded and headed the Ukrainian-Polish Society in Paris, conducted research on Ukrainian emigrants in France for the National Center for Scientific Research, and served as rector (1962–3) and dean of the philosophical faculty (1972–4) of the UVU. His publications include numerous monographs, such as *Narys* *strukturnoï psykholohiï* (Outline of Structural Psychology, 1949), *Osnovy psykholohiï i filosofichnykh dystsyplin* (Foundations of Psychology and Philosophical Disciplines, 1953), *Die marxistisch-sowjetische Konzeption des Menschen im Lichte der westlichen Psychologie* (1956), *Das operative Schema der somatopsychischen Erfassung des ukrainischen Ethnotypus* (1966), *Vvedennia u filosofichnu antropolohiiu* (Introduction to Philosophical Anthropology, 1973), and posthumously, *Ukraïns'kyi personalizm – filosofs'ka i etnopsykholohichna synteza* (The Ukrainian Personality – Philosophical and Ethnopsychological Synthesis, 1985).

B. Krawchenko

Kulchytsky, Yevhen [Kul'čyc'kyj, Jevhen] (Gut Kulchytsky), b 12 April 1903 in Lviv, d 23 March 1982 in Detroit. Forester, youth organizer, and journalist. A graduate of the Prague Polytechnical Institute (1929), he was an organizer of the Ukrainian scouting movement for many years. In 1924 he was elected to the Supreme Plast Command in Lviv, and organized the Rovers' Club. In Prague he helped found the Union of Ukrainian Emigrant Scouts and served as its president (1931–4). A member of the Ukrainian Military Organization (UVO) and then of the OUN, he was in charge of organizational matters for the Chief Command of the Carpathian Sich in Khust (1938–9) and commander of the OUN in Czechoslovakia (1940). He spent much of the war in a Hungarian concentration camp. Emigrating in 1950 to the United States, he organized and headed the Ukrainian youth association *Plast there. Kulchytsky translated R. Baden-Powell's *Scouting for Boys* into Ukrainian and wrote many technical and educational handbooks for Plast. His articles on current Ukrainian issues appeared in newspapers such as *Svoboda, Novyi shliakh,* and *Ukraïns'ke slovo.* As a member of the *Organization for the Rebirth of Ukraine, he continued to be active in Ukrainian political life.

Kulchytsky, Yurii [Kul'čyc'kyj, Jurij], b 15 December 1912 in Pidbyzh, Drohobych county, Galicia. Graphic artist and ceramicist. While studying at the Cracow Academy of Fine Art (1933–8), he belonged to the *Zarevo art group and took part in its exhibitions. Immigrating to Austria (1945) and then Paris (1948), in 1960 he settled in Mougins near Cannes and set up a modern ceramics atelier with I. *Vynnykiv. Until the mid-1950s Kulchytsky did mostly woodcuts, including prints such as *Three Cossacks, The Pursuit, Kozak-Mamai,* and *Fist Fight,* and illustrations to K. Malytska's *Harfa Leili* (The Harp of Leila, 1953). By linocut he produced prints such as *The Collectivization.* He has also done some woodcut bookplates. In ceramics he has introduced new modern forms based on elements of Ukrainian folk ceramics, an art particularly rich in linear rhythm, which can be described as musical. His fantastic depictions of birds, animals, and human beings are almost surrealistic, but preserve that esthetic quality characteristic of folk art.

Kulchytsky, Yurii Frants [Kul'čyc'kyj, Jurij Franc], b ca 1640 in Kulchytsi, in the Sambir region, Galicia, d 20 February 1694 in Vienna. Traveler and merchant; hero of the defense of Vienna during the Austrian-Turkish War of 1683–99. Kulchytsky came from the ranks of the petty nobility. According to some sources, he joined the Zaporozhian Cossacks and was captured and imprisoned by the Turks. He had an excellent knowledge of the Turkish language and customs, and in the 1760s he worked as a translator for the Eastern Trading Company in Belgrade and Vienna. He later became a merchant himself. In July 1683 the Turks had advanced through Central Europe as far as Vienna, to which they laid siege. Defended by a small garrison of 10,000 men, the Viennese were soon in desperate straits: famine and disease ravaged the city and panic was beginning to spread. Disguised as a Turk, on 13 August 1683 Kulchytsky stole through the enemy lines to the Austrian army. He told the Austrians of the city's critical situation, gave them information necessary for a co-ordinated plan of action against the Turks, and returned to Vienna with the news that the Polish king Jan III Sobieski and an army of Ukrainian Cossacks were coming to rescue the city. Their hope renewed, the Viennese continued to resist the Turks, and on 12 September the combined Christian armies defeated the Turks and raised the siege. According to tradition, the grateful Viennese, or even Jan Sobieski himself, gave Kulchytsky coffee captured from the Turks, with which he opened the first coffee house in Vienna. In 1885 the sculptor I. Pendl created a monument to Kulchytsky on a street named after him. A fictionalized biography of Kulchytsky was written by I. Fylypchak (1933; 2nd edn, 1983).

Kuleshov, Mykola [Kulešov], b 17 December 1890 in Novyi Margelan, Fergana oblast, Turkestan general gubernia, d 19 January 1968 in Kharkiv. Plant breeder; from 1951 full member of the AN URSR. A graduate of the Kiev Polytechnical Institute (1913), he became director of the Central Seed Testing Station of the Ukrainian SSR (1920–6) and assistant director of the All-Union Institute of Plant Breeding (1926–34). He headed plant-breeding departments at agricultural institutes in Irkutsk (1934–8), Omsk (1938–45), and Kharkiv (1945–68). From 1947 to 1960 he was head of the ecology laboratory of the Ukrainian Research Institute of Plant Breeding, Selection, and Genetics. Kuleshov developed methods for improving and testing grain seed, particularly spring and winter wheat seed.

Kulets, Ivan [Kulec'], b 24 June 1880 in Kholoiv (now Vuzlove), Zolochiv county, Galicia, d 11 March 1952 in Prague. Artist and pedagogue. A graduate of the Cracow Painting Academy (1909), he moved to Bohemia in 1914. In 1924 he began to teach at the Ukrainian Studio of Plastic Arts in Prague, which became his private art school following elimination of government subsidies (1932). In 1939 he renamed it the Ukrainian Painting Academy, and in 1946 the school was nationalized. Kulets trained hundreds of painters, some of whom later received international recognition. At first his painting was influenced by the Secession movements, but by the beginning of the 1920s his style reflected experimental innovations in technique and media. His notable paintings include *Antichrist, Revolution, Christ,* and *Lovers.* Twenty of his paintings are located at the Prague National Gallery, and 164 works are at the Museum of Ukrainian Culture in Svydnyk, where his first posthumous exhibition was held in 1980.

Kuliabka [Kuljabka]. Name of a prominent Cossack family in the Lubni region. Sylvester *Kuliabka (1701–

61) was a noted theologian. His brother Ivan (ca 1705–73) was colonel in Lubni regiment (1757–71). Ivan's son Pavlo was quartermaster of the regiment (1775–82) and several other members of the family served as captains of Lubni company or as regimental officers.

Kuliabka, Sylvester [Kuljabka, Syl'vester] (secular name: Semen), b 1701 (1704 according to some sources) in Lubni, d 17 April 1761 in St Petersburg. Churchman and theologian. The son of a Cossack officer and grandson of Hetman D. Apostol, he graduated from the Kievan Mohyla Academy in 1726. He was a professor (from 1727), prefect (1737–40), and rector (1740–5) of the academy before being appointed bishop of Kostroma (1745–50). As bishop he founded the first theological seminary in the eparchy. In 1750 he was appointed archbishop of St Petersburg and a member of the Holy Synod. An erudite scholar and sermonizer, he was known as *aureus benedicendus magister*. Thirteen of his popular sermons were published.

Kulik, Stephen [Kulyk, Stepan], b 6 January 1899 in Popivka, Konotip county, Chernihiv gubernia. Mathematician; full member of the Shevchenko Scientific Society. Kulik was a research associate of the AN URSR Institute of Mathematics (1932–7, 1941–2) and a docent at Kiev University (1930–43). As a postwar refugee in Germany and then in Great Britain, he worked as a researcher in industry. Immigrating to the United States in 1951, Kulik has taught at Claremont Men's College in California (1951–3), the University of South Carolina in Columbia (1953–8), and Long Beach State College in California (1959–64). He has written works in Ukrainian, Russian, and English dealing with the theory of probability, statistics, numerical methods for calculating roots of algebraic and transcendental equations, and polynomials.

Mykola Kulish

Kulish, Mykola [Kuliš], b 18 December 1892 in Chaplyntsi, Tavriia gubernia, d 1937? Renowned playwright. Kulish began writing satirical poetry and plays as a gymnasium student in Oleshky. In 1924 he joined the proletarian writers' group *Hart, and in Kharkiv he met its other members; one of them, M. *Khvylovy, thereafter had a great impact on his writing and views. In 1925 he was elected a member of the presidium of the writers' group *Vaplite; from November 1926 to its forced dissolution in January 1928 he was its president. In 1926 he founded and headed the Ukrainian Society of Dramatists and Composers. In 1927–8 he was also a member of the editorial board of the prominent cultural journal *Chervonyi shliakh*. In late 1929 he became a member of the presidium of the new writers' organization *Prolitfront. After its forced dissolution in January 1931, he was not allowed to join the only regime-sanctioned writers' organization, the All-Ukrainian Association of Proletarian Writers. Prevented from publishing, he made his living as a film scenarist. In June 1934 his plays were condemned as nationalist and harmful and he was purged from the CP(B) as a 'counterrevolutionary.' In December 1934 he was arrested by the NKVD, tried as a member of an 'All-Ukrainian Borotbist Terrorist Center,' and sentenced to 10 years in an isolation cell in a concentration camp on the Solovets Islands. He was last heard from in 1937.

Kulish wrote 13 plays, of which 6 were published during his lifetime: *97* (1925), *Khulii Khuryna* (1926), *Myna Mazailo* (1929), *Narodnii Malakhii* (The People's Malakhii, in *Literaturnyi iarmarok*, no. 9 [1929]), *Komuna v stepakh* (Commune in the Steppes, 1931), and *Povorot Marka* (Marko's Return, 1934). The first five as well as two others – *Patetychna sonata* (Sonata Pathétique, 1930) and *Maklena Grassa* (1932) – were staged and received critical acclaim. Most of them were staged by the *Berezil theater in Kharkiv under the direction of L. *Kurbas. Forbidden to be staged in Ukraine by the censors, *Patetychna sonata* was translated into Russian and staged at the Moscow Kamernyi Theater by A. Tairov and at the Leningrad Bolshoi Drama Theater by K. Tvertsov simultaneously from December 1931 to March 1932.

Kulish became famous after the stage success in 1924 of his first play, *97*, a portrayal of peasant life after the Revolution. It was, however, in his 'national' trilogy – *Narodnii Malakhii*, *Myna Mazailo*, and *Patetychna sonata*, written while Kulish was a close associate of Kurbas – that his exceptional talent and originality as a dramatist became evident. In *Narodnii Malakhii* Kulish satirized the contradictions between Ukrainian national aspirations and Soviet reality. In *Myna Mazailo* he satirized the political and social impact of the policy of *Ukrainization. In *Patetychna sonata* he depicted, using elements of both modern experimental theater and traditional Ukrainian puppet theater (**vertep*), the chaos and political conflicts of the revolutionary period in Ukraine. The content of the trilogy was subject to a great deal of Stalinist invective, and it was for writing those plays and his close association with Khvylovy that Kulish became a victim of the terror.

Kulish was posthumously 'rehabilitated' in 1956, and editions of his selected plays – including the previously unpublished *Patetychna sonata*, *Otak zahynuv Huska* (That's How Huska Died), and *Maklena Grassa* – appeared in Kiev (1960, 1969) and in Russian in Moscow (1964, 1980).

BIBLIOGRAPHY
Kulish, M. *Tvory*, ed H. Kostiuk (New York 1955)
Kuziakina, N. *Dramaturh Mykola Kulish: Literaturno-krytychnyi narys* (Kiev 1962)
– *P'iesy Mykoly Kulisha: Literaturna i stsenichna istoriia* (Kiev 1970)
Revutsky, V. 'Mykola Kulish in the Modern Ukrainian Theatre,' *SEER*, 49, no. 116 (July 1971)

V. Revutsky, R. Senkus

Kulish, Oleksandra. See Barvinok, Hanna.

Panteleimon Kulish

Kulish, Panteleimon [Kuliš, Pantelejmon], b 8 August 1819 in Voronizh, Chernihiv gubernia, d 14 February 1897 in Motronivka, Chernihiv gubernia. Prominent writer, historian, ethnographer, and translator. He was born into an impoverished Cossack-gentry family. After completing only five years at the Novhorod-Siverskyi gymnasium he enrolled at Kiev University in 1837 but was not allowed to finish his studies because he was not a noble. He obtained a teaching position in Lutske in 1840. There he wrote his first historical novel in Russian, *Mikhail Charnyshenko, ili Malorossiia vosem'desiat let nazad* (Mykhailo Charnyshenko, or Little Russia Eighty Years Ago, 2 vols, 1843). M. *Maksymovych promoted Kulish's literary efforts and published several of his early stories. His first longer work written in Ukrainian was the epic poem 'Ukraïna' (Ukraine, 1843). In 1843–5 Kulish taught in Kiev and studied Ukrainian history and ethnography. There he befriended T. Shevchenko, M. Kostomarov, and V. Bilozersky; their circle later became the nucleus of the secret *Cyril and Methodius Brotherhood. Another new friend, the Polish writer M. Grabowski, also had a great influence on him.

In 1845 P. Pletnev, the rector of St Petersburg University, invited Kulish to teach at the university. In St Petersburg Kulish finished in Ukrainian his major historical novel, *Chorna rada, khronika 1663 roku* (The Black Council, a Chronicle of the Year 1663), of which excerpts were published in Russian translation in Muscovite journals in 1845–6. To prepare him for a professorial career, the Imperial Academy of Sciences granted him a scholarship to do research abroad. In 1847 he married O. Bilozerska (the future writer Hanna *Barvinok) and set out with her for Prague. En route he was arrested by the tsarist police in Warsaw for belonging to the Cyril and Methodius Brotherhood, which had been uncovered at the time. After two months in prison he was exiled for three years to Tula. Because his main offence had been writing a 'Tale of the Ukrainian People,' Kulish was forbidden to write. He maintained his innocence, but his interrogation and closed trial and subsequent loss of freedom were for him a deep trauma.

In 1850 he was allowed to return to St Petersburg. While working as an editor there, he tried, unsuccessfully, to establish himself as a Russian littérateur, publishing in the journal *Sovremennik* the autobiographical novella 'Istoriia Uliany Terent'evny' (The History of Uliana Terentevna, 1852), the historical novel 'Aleksei Odnorog' (1852–3), and the novella 'Iakov Iakovlevich.' He worked on a long biography of N. Gogol, finishing it in 1856 while visiting S. Aksakov.

Soon his Ukrainian interests took the upper hand. After living for a while on a *khutir* in Ukraine and in Kiev, Kulish returned to St Petersburg. There he established a Ukrainian printing press and, after being allowed to publish under his own name, issued two splendid volumes of **Zapiski o Iuzhnoi Rusi* (Notes on Southern Rus', 1856–7), a rich collection of Ukrainian folklore, ethnography, and literature in which he introduced a new orthography (**Kulishivka*). In 1857 he finally published *Chorna rada* in its entirety, in both Ukrainian and Russian. In the epilogue to the Russian edition he pleaded for the first time for the political unity of Ukraine and Russia while stressing their cultural separateness. He also published a primer (*Hramatka*, 1857) for use in Sunday schools, a volume of Marko Vovchok's folk tales (1858), and the Ukrainian almanac **Khata* (Home, 1860). 'Maior' (Major), his Russian novella about his life in Ukraine, appeared in *Russkii vestnik* in 1859. In 1860–2 he was actively involved in **Osnova*, the Ukrainian journal published in St Petersburg. In 1862 he published a separate collection of his own poems, *Dosvitky* (Glimmers of Dawn).

In 1864 Kulish accepted a high Russian official post in Warsaw. From there he developed further the contacts he had made earlier with Galician intellectuals and contributed to several Lviv periodicals. When he was asked to end these contacts he refused and resigned in 1867. After traveling abroad he returned to St Petersburg. For a while he edited a Russian government publication. Most of his time he devoted to the study of Ukrainian history, particularly of the Cossack period. His earlier romantic view of the Cossacks gave way to a new and very critical appraisal of them, which had already been evident in *Chorna rada*. He published several long articles on the Cossacks entitled 'Mal'ovana haidamachchyna' (The Painted Haidamaka Era, 1876) and a major study in three volumes, *Istoriia vossoedineniia Rusi* (The History of the Reunification of Rus', 1874–7). In the latter he expressed admiration for Peter I and Catherine II and made some uncomplimentary remarks about T. Shevchenko, thereby alienating most of the Ukrainian reading public. At about the same time, Kulish began translating the *Bible, a work that, with the help of I. Puliui and I. Nechui-Levytsky, was finally completed only after his death. His translation of the Psalter was published in Galicia in 1871.

After the 1876 *Ems Ukase forbade Ukrainian publications in the Russian Empire, Kulish strengthened his ties with Galicia. In 1881 he went to Lviv, and in 1882 his collection of poems and essays, *Khutorna poeziia* (*Khutir* Poetry), his Ukrainian translations of Shakespeare's *Othello, Troilus and Cressida*, and *Comedy of Errors*, and an appeal for Ukrainian-Polish understanding, *Krashanka rusynam i poliakam na Velykden' 1882 roku* (A Painted Egg for the Ruthenians and the Poles at Easter 1882), were published there. In 1883 he published his long poem 'Mahomet i Khadyza' (Muhammad and Khadijah), showing his deep interest in Islam. He seriously considered renouncing his Russian citizenship and remaining in Austria-Hungary, but government policies there changed his mind. Disheartened but not dejected, Kulish returned to Russian-ruled Ukraine, settled on his *khutir* Motronivka, and remained there with his wife until his death. Cut off from most Ukrainian activists, he conducted a wide correspondence and worked on translations of the Bible and the works of Shakespeare, Goethe, and Byron. He wrote two more collections of poetry, *Dzvin* (The Bell, 1893) and *Pozychena kobza* (The Borrowed Kobza, 1897), which were published in Geneva. A major historical study, 'Otpadenie Malorossii ot Pol'shi' (The Separation of Little Russia from Poland, 1888–9), was also completed on his *khutir*.

Both during his life and after his death Kulish was a controversial figure. His emphasis on the development of a separate, indigenous Ukrainian high culture while advocating political union with Russia found little sympathy among Ukrainian populists. After 1850, during his intense writing and publishing activity, he remained aloof from organized Ukrainian community life. His attempts at influencing Ukrainian cultural activities in Austrian-ruled Galicia were often misunderstood. Kulish's uncompromising attitude and his egocentrism were often stumbling blocks in his relations with others. Yet even his opponents granted him his achievements. During the modernist period of Ukrainian literature interest in Kulish was revived by M. Sribliansky and M. Yevshan. *Dubove lystia* (Oak Leaves), an almanac in his memory, appeared in Kiev in 1903, and editions of his works were published in Kiev (5 vols) and Lviv (6 vols) in 1908–10. In Soviet Ukraine some of his works were republished, new research about him (by V. Petrov, O. Doroshkevych, M. Mohyliansky, Ye. Kyryliuk, M. Zerov, M. Vozniak, and others) appeared, and the publication of a complete edition of his works was begun (2 vols, 1930, 1934) in Kiev but not completed. During the *Literary Discussion of 1925, M. Khvylovy defended Kulish as a 'truly European intellectual.' From 1933 on, however, Kulish's works were virtually proscribed in the USSR until a volume of his selected writings appeared in Kiev in 1969, followed by a small volume of his poetry in 1970. Soviet literary critics have wrongly accused Kulish of 'bourgeois nationalism.' In the West, interest in Kulish has existed mainly among academics. An abridged English translation of his *Chorna rada* was published in Littleton, Colorado, in 1973, and a Ukrainian volume of his selected letters appeared in New York in 1984.

BIBLIOGRAPHY

'Zhyzn' Kulisha,' *Pravda* (Lviv), 1868, nos 2–4, 7, 24–8
Shenrok, V. *P.A. Kulish (Biograficheskii ocherk)* (Kiev 1901)
Doroshenko, D. *Panteleimon Kulish* (Berlin [1923])
Hrushevskyi, M. 'Sotsiial'no-tradytsiini pidosnovy Kulishevoï tvorchosty,' *Ukraïna*, 1927, nos 1–2
Iefremov, S.; Doroshkevych, O. (eds). *Panteleimon Kulish* (Kiev 1927)
Kyryliuk, Ie. *Bibliohrafiia prats' P.O. Kulisha ta pysan' pro n'oho* (Kiev 1929)
Petrov, V. *Panteleimon Kulish u p'iatdesiati roky* (Kiev 1929)
Luckyj, G. *Panteleimon Kulish: A Sketch of His Life and Times* (Boulder, Colo 1983)

G.S.N. Luckyj

Kulish, Yaroslava. See Kerch, Oksana.

Kulishivka [Kulišivka]. A Ukrainian alphabet and orthography used for the first time by P. *Kulish in his *Zapiski o Iuzhnoi Rusi* (Notes on Southern Rus', 1856) and adopted in the 1860s by Populist publications in Galicia. Kulishivka retained *ь* at the end of words and often after labials (*pьjut'* – they drink) and after *r*; replaced the old *ѣ* as well as *o* in closed syllables with *i*; introduced *є* after soft consonants – *davnie* (old), but *est'* (is) and *svoe* (one's own) – while rendering the *e* in such cases as э – э*he* (yes), *po*э*ta* (poet); introduced *ë* – *ëho* (his), *slëzy* (tears); eliminated the letter ы, replacing the old ы and *i* by и – *vyvčyv* (learned); and used the Latin *g* – *grunt* (land). This became the foundation of a systematized way of writing contemporary Ukrainian orthography (see *Zhelekhivka), which is sometimes also called *Kulishivka*. From the 1880s Kulish modified his orthography extensively in the phonetic direction – *occja* to replace *otcja* ('father' gen sg), *ticci* to replace *titci* ('aunt' dat sg), *š čereva* instead of *z čereva* ('from the belly'), *ž žonoju* instead of *z žonoju* ('with the wife'), *bež žalju* instead of *bez žalju* ('without pity') – but this reform was not widely adopted.

Kulka, Marshall, b 1 March 1911 in Warspite, Alberta. Organic chemist. A graduate of the University of Alberta (1936) and McGill University (PH D 1942), Kulka was a research scientist with the Dominion Rubber Company (1943–63) and the Uniroyal Research Labs (1963–76). He discovered agricultural chemicals to combat fungal pathogens and has written over 80 scientific papers.

Kulsky, Leonid [Kul's'kyj], b 10 April 1903 in Nowo-Radomsk, Piotrków gubernia. Chemist; since 1969 full member of the AN URSR. After graduating from the Kiev Institute of People's Education (1925) and Leningrad University (1928), he worked at various institutes in Kiev. From 1937 to 1965 he headed the laboratory of hydrochemistry and hydrotechnology at the AN URSR Institute of General and Inorganic Chemistry. Then for three years he oversaw the academy's hydrochemistry and hydrotechnology sector. Until 1973 he served as deputy director of the Institute of Colloidal Chemistry and Hydrochemistry, and then as chairman of a department at the institute. His numerous publications include monographs and textbooks. He has done pioneering work in the chemistry and technology of water purification. His methods of water treatment have been applied widely in the USSR to improve the quality of potable and industrial water.

Kul'tfront (Cultural Front). A popular educational magazine published from 1931 to 1935 in Kharkiv by the Council of Trade Unions of Ukraine. Its name, language, and periodicity changed many times. The purpose of the magazine was to propagate 'Ukrainian Soviet Socialist culture among the workers of Ukraine.' Its predecessors were the irregular Russian-language magazine *Put' k kommunizmu* (1921–4), the Russian monthly *Rabochii klub* (1925–6), the Russian semimonthly *Kul'trabotnik* (1927), and the Ukrainian-language semimonthly *Kul'trobitnyk* (1928–30). At first *Kul'tfront* was a trimonthly; in 1934 it became a monthly. It was replaced by the magazine *Sotsialistychna kul'tura* (1936–41), issues 1–9 of which were published under the name *Kolbud*.

Kul'tura (Culture). A literary and political monthly of a Marxist profile published from 1926 to 1931 in Lviv. It was preceded by *Nova kul'tura* (1923–6). From 1928 *Kul'tura* defended Shumskyism and Khvylovism (see O. *Shumsky and M. *Khvylovy) and criticized Stalinist nationality policy in Ukraine. Its editor in chief was S. Rudyk and the coeditors were V. Bobynsky, O. Vasylkiv, M. Irchan,

N. Lazarkevych, V. Levynsky, M. Tarnovsky, and M. Vozniak.

Kultura. Polish monthly journal of politics, arts, and literature published in Paris since 1947 by the Instytut Literacki under the editorship of J. Giedroyc. The journal deals primarily with issues concerning Eastern Europe. It devotes considerable attention to Ukrainian issues, especially in articles by R. Wraga, and publishes translations of Ukrainian literature by J. Łobodowski, S. Baranczak, and others. In its 'Ukrainian Chronicle,' *Kultura* surveys significant developments in Ukrainian life in Ukraine and the West. Matters concerning the Ukrainian Catholic church are dealt with by D. Morawski in the section 'Correspondence from Rome.' Among the Ukrainians who have contributed articles to *Kultura* are B. Levytsky, B. Osadchuk, B. Struminsky, W. Wytwycky, I. Ševčenko, I. Koshelivets, and G.Y. Shevelov. The Instytut Literacki also publishes a monograph series under the title Kultura Library. This series has included several books in Ukrainian or on Ukrainian topics, such as Yu. Lavrinenko's *Rozstriliane Vidrodzhennia* (The Rebirth That Was Executed, 1959) and *Ukraina, 1956–1968* (Ukraine, 1956–1968, 1969), a collection of documents edited by I. Koshelivets.

Kultura i Osvita (Culture and Education). The publishing house of the Ukrainian Cultural and Educational Centre in Winnipeg. Since 1944 it has published over 50 book titles, some music collections, and plays.

Kul'tura i pobut. See *Visti VUTsVK.*

Kul'tura i zhyttia (Culture and Life). A newspaper published in Kiev since 1965 by the Ministry of Culture of the Ukrainian SSR and the Republican Committee of the Trade Union of Cultural Workers. It publishes news about artistic developments in Ukraine and abroad. It reports on the latest achievements in fine art, folk art, music, theater, and film, and on the activities of amateur groups, museums, clubs, and libraries. It was preceded by a number of newspapers published by various institutions in Kharkiv: *Literatura, nauka, i mystetstvo* (1923–4), *Kul'tura i pobut* (1924–8), and *Literatura i mystetstvo* (1929–30), all weekly supplements to *Visti VUTsVK*, the weekly *Radians'ke mystetstvo* (1941–3 in Voroshylovhrad, Ufa, Moscow, and Kharkiv; 1945–54 in Kiev), and the semiweekly *Radians'ka kul'tura* (1955–64).

Kulturna Spilka Ukrainskykh Trudiashchykh. See Cultural Association of Ukrainian Workers.

Kulyk, Ihor, b 19 November 1935 in Kharkiv. Solid-state physicist; corresponding member of the AN URSR since 1970. A graduate of Kharkiv University (1959), since 1960 he has been a research associate at the AN URSR Physical-Technical Institute of Low Temperatures. He has achieved significant research results in the fields of superconductivity and surface physics.

Kulyk, Ivan, b 26 January 1897 in Shpola, Kiev gubernia, d 14 October 1941? Soviet Ukrainian writer and political figure; the husband of L. *Piontek. In 1914 he joined the Bolshevik party and emigrated to Pennsylvania, where he was active in the Russian and Ukrainian socialist movements. He returned to Ukraine in June 1917 and became a member of the first Soviet government in Ukraine in Kharkiv in 1918. In 1919, as a member of the Collegium of the People's Commissariat of Foreign Affairs, he was engaged in underground work in Western Ukraine. In 1920 he was a member of the *Galician Revolutionary Committee. A member of the proletarian writers' group *Hart from 1923, in 1924–7 he was a Soviet consul in Montreal. In 1927 he became a founding member of the All-Ukrainian Association of Proletarian Writers and edited its journal *Hart*. From 1932 he headed the organizing committee of the Writers' Union of Ukraine; in 1934 he became the head of the new union but was removed in 1935. In 1936–7 he directed the Radio Committee of Ukraine, and in 1937 he was elected to the CC CP(B)U and the All-Ukrainian Central Executive Committee. Despite his loyal service to the Party and denunciation of numerous 'nationalist' writers, however, he too was arrested by the NKVD and disappeared during the Yezhov terror of 1937.

Ivan Kulyk

Kulyk began publishing poetry and political articles in the Ukrainian socialist periodicals *Robitnyk* (Cleveland) and *Robochyi narod* (Winnipeg) under the pseudonym R. Rolinato before the 1917 Revolution. Between 1920 and 1935 he published in Ukraine eight collections of poetry, several long poems (including a collection of six of them in 1930), and several collections of short stories, most notably *Zapysky konsula* (Notes of a Consul, 2 vols, 1934). His political articles appeared in the Soviet press and in the Winnipeg paper *Ukraïns'ki robitnychi visti*. He also wrote several articles about the history of the CP(B)U and the revolutionary period in Ukraine and translated a large anthology of 33 American poets into Ukrainian (1928). He was posthumously 'rehabilitated' after Stalin's death, and books of his selected works (1958, 1962, 1967) and a volume of memoirs about him (1971) were published in Kiev.

I. Koshelivets, R. Senkus

Kulyk, Vasyl, b 1830 in Kovalivka, Poltava gubernia, d 1870 in Kovalivka. Poet. Inspired by populist ideas, he spent several years wandering through Southern Ukraine studying the life and the lore of the common people. After settling in Poltava, he began writing poems about contemporary peasant life, Romantic ballads, fables, and sketches, selections of which were subsequently published in *Osnova*. A collection of his poetry, *Pysannia Vasylia Kulyka* (The Writings of Vasyl Kulyk, 1894), appeared posthumously in Lviv.

Kulyk, Yakiv (Kulik, Jakub), b 1 April 1783 in Lviv, d 28 February 1863 in Prague. Mathematician. He graduated from the law and philosophy faculties at Lviv University (1814), then taught at a gymnasium before completing his PH D in 1822. He was a professor of mathematics at Charles University in Prague from 1826, and a member of the Royal Czech Scientific Society and its head from 1835. He wrote a number of mathematics and mechanics texts and edited numerous tables; his table of divisors of integers consists of 4,212 pages. After the destruction of the Lviv University library by fire in 1848, he donated 1,000 books to it. His most important works are *Lehrbuch der höheren Mechanik* (1846) and *Der tausendjährige Kalender*.

Kulykivka. II-12. Town smt (1983 pop 5,300) and raion center in Chernihiv oblast. It was founded as a Cossack village in Nizhen regiment in the mid-17th century.

Kulynych, Yaroslav [Kulynyč, Jaroslav], b 21 March 1926 near Ternopil, Galicia. Film director and producer. After 1945 he worked in the UFA film studio in Munich before immigrating to Australia, where he studied at the University of Adelaide. Since 1961 he has lived in the United States. Kulynych produced and directed several documentary films dealing with Ukrainian life in the West, including two films about the Ukrainian community in Australia, the opening of the monument to T. Shevchenko in Washington, the Plast Ukrainian Youth Association, the Ukrainian Youth Association, and the World Congress of Free Ukrainians. He has also made several films on the life of Cardinal Y. Slipy and on the Ukrainian Catholic church.

Kulytsky, Mykola [Kulyc'kyj], b 1903 in Hlyniany, Peremyshliany county, Galicia, d 26 May 1970 in Chicago. Cartographer and geographer. He studied at Cracow University and in the 1930s and 1940s helped V. *Kubijovyč prepare various maps and his atlas of Ukraine. During the Second World War he directed the cartography and statistics office of the Ukrainian Central Committee in Cracow and Lviv. A postwar refugee, he received a PH D from the Ukrainian Free University and was a full member of the Shevchenko Scientific Society. He emigrated to Chicago in the early 1950s.

Kulzhenko, Vasyl [Kul'ženko, Vasyl'], b 11 February 1865 in Kiev, d 7 September 1934 in Kiev. Publisher and printer. He studied at the Leipzig Polygraphic Academy before taking over control of his father's printing company in Kiev. In 1903 he established and began lecturing at the Kiev Graphic Arts and Printing School and from 1908 to 1914 he published the journal *Iskusstvo i pechatnoe delo* (later renamed **Iskusstvo v Iuzhnoi Rossii*). From 1924 to 1928 he lectured at the Kiev Art Institute. Kulzhenko's firm printed the currency, official documents, and postage stamps issued by the UNR and Hetman government between 1917 and 1919.

Kulzhynsky, Ivan [Kul'žyns'kyj], b 26 April 1803 in Hlukhiv, Chernihiv gubernia, d 4 April 1884 in Nizhen. Literary scholar, ethnographer, and educator. A graduate of the Chernihiv seminary (1823), he taught at Chernihiv (1823–5), Nizhen (1825–9), and Kharkiv gymnasiums (1829–32), lectured at Kharkiv University on folk oral literature, directed the Lutske (1832–9) and Nemyriv (1839–41) gymnasiums, was an inspector of the Nizhen Lyceum (1841–3), and directed schools in Transcaucasia (1843–7). His Russian historical, literary, and ethnographic articles, poetry, short stories, plays, and novellas appeared from 1825 in various periodicals, including *Ukrainskii vestnik* and *Ukrainskii zhurnal* in Kharkiv. Published separately were his history of the world (3 vols, 1859), a history of Poland (1864), narratives on Russian history (1863), and several other works. His works dealing with Ukraine include the novella 'Tereshko,' the drama 'Kochubei' (1841), the novel *Fediusha Motovil'skii* (1833), and the polemical works *O zarozhdaiushcheisia tak nazyvaemoi malorossiiskoi literature* (On Nascent So-Called Little Russian Literature, 1863) and *Novyi vzgliad na khokhlomanstvo* (A New Look at *Khokhol*-Mania, 1864). His study of Ukrainian folk customs, rituals, songs, poems, and anecdotes, *Malorossiiskaia derevnia* (The Little Russian Village, 1827), influenced the early works of the writers N. Gogol and Ye. Hrebinka, who were his pupils at the Nizhen Gymnasium. A Russified obscurantist and supporter of tsarist centralism, Kulzhynsky was condescendingly critical of T. Shevchenko, Marko Vovchok, P. Kulish, and others who wrote in Ukrainian, which he viewed as a quaint but spoiled dialect of Russian.

Kumanchenko, Polina [Kumančenko], b 21 October 1910 in Muzykivka, Kherson county, Kherson gubernia. Actress specializing in lyrical roles. Graduating from the studio of the Mykolaiv Russian Drama Theater in 1928, she worked with the Mykolaiv Ukrainian Workers' and Peasants' Touring Theater (1929–31), the Kharkiv Theater of Working Youth (1932–7), the Kharkiv Ukrainian Drama Theater (1937–61), and the Kiev Ukrainian Drama Theater. Her repertoire includes roles such as Yelyzaveta in I. Kocherha's *Iaroslav Mudryi* (Yaroslav the Wise), Kharytyna in I. Tobilevych's *Naimychka* (The Servant Girl), Sylvette in E. Rostand's *Les romanesques*, and Inés in P. Calderón's *No hay burlas con el amor*. She has also appeared in films. Yu. Martych wrote a monograph about her career in 1964.

Kumans. See Cumans.

Kumeiky, Battle of 1637. Battle between Ukrainian peasant and Cossack forces and the army of the Polish nobility, which ended the Pavliuk rebellion. In the spring of 1637 P. *Pavliuk led an insurrection of the Ukrainian peasantry in Right-Bank Ukraine against the Polish lords. The uprising spread to a substantial portion of Left-Bank Ukraine. On 16 December 1637 near Kumeiky (now in Cherkasy oblast) Polish forces led by Hetman M. Potocki engaged the Ukrainians. On 20 December the Polish army surrounded the insurgents at Borovytsia. Unable to capture the town, Potocki proposed negotiations, to which the Cossack *starshyna* agreed. During the talks, Pavliuk and the other leaders of the rebellion were taken prisoner, sent to Warsaw, and executed. Despite the defeat at Kumeiky, another rebellion arose in the spring of 1638 (see Ya. *Ostrianyn).

Kuna. Monetary unit in Kievan Rus'. The word *kuna* is derived from the word for a marten pelt. Pelts were used as money before the introduction of metallic currency. When foreign silver coins (Arabic dirhams and Roman denarii) came into Rus', they were referred to as *kuny*. The value of *kuny* differed in various regions and changed over time. In the 9th–11th centuries, 25 *kuny* were equal to one **hryvnia*, while in the 12th–13th centuries 50 *kuny* equaled a *hryvnia*. The term *kuny* in the general sense of money was used in Rus' throughout the 10th–14th centuries; it was only later that the word was replaced by the *dengi* and *serebro*.

Kundiiev, Yurii [Kundijev, Jurij], b 2 October 1927 in Troiany, Kirovohrad okruha. Public-health physician; since 1979 full member of the AN URSR. Upon graduating from the Kiev Medical Institute (1951), he joined the staff of the Kiev Scientific Research Institute of Labor Hygiene and Occupational Illnesses of Ukraine's Ministry of Public Health. By 1955 he was promoted to a laboratory head and by 1964 to director of the institute. Most of his research deals with pesticide toxicology and the safety of farm workers.

Kundriucha River [Kundrjuča]. River in Voroshylovhrad and Rostov oblasts in the RSFSR. A right-bank tributary of the Donets, it is 244 km long and has a basin area of 2,320 sq km. The Kundriucha originates in the Donets Ridge and is fed primarily by melting snow.

Kunduk Estuary. See Sasyk Estuary.

Kunduk River. See Kohylnyk River.

Kundzich, Oleksii [Kundzič, Oleksij], b 22 April 1904 in Pavlivka, Podilia gubernia, d 20 June 1964 in Kiev. Writer, literary critic, and translator. In the 1920s he belonged to the literary organizations *Molodniak and the All-Ukrainian Association of Proletarian Writers. His first story collection, *Chervonoiu dorohoiu* (Along the Red Road, 1926), was followed by 16 others, including the large collections *Noveli* (Novellas, 1929) and *Chervonoiu dorohoiu* (1929, 1931). He also wrote the novels *Okupant* (The Occupier, 1930), *De facto* (1930), and *Rodychi* (Relatives, 1936) and translated works by M. Lermontov, L. Tolstoy, and N. Leskov into Ukrainian. Books of his selected prose (1932, 1938, 1951) and selected literary criticism and articles about translation (1956, 1966, 1973) have been published.

Kuntsevych, Vsevolod [Kuncevyč], b 15 March 1929 in Kiev. Specialist in automatic control systems. A graduate of the Kiev Polytechnical Institute, since 1966 he has chaired the Department of Digital Control Systems at the AN URSR Institute of Cybernetics. His main publications deal with the analysis and synthesis of non-linear control systems, including digital control systems.

Kuntsevych, Yosafat [Kuncevyč, Josafat] (secular name: Ivan), b ca 1580 in Volodymyr-Volynskyi, Volhynia, d 12 November 1623 in Vitsebsk, Belorussia. Uniate archbishop and polemicist; Catholic saint. Kuntsevych entered the Holy Trinity Basilian Monastery in Vilnius in 1604. Ordained in 1609, he became the archimandrite of the monastery in 1614. He was consecrated bishop of Polatsk in 1617 and elevated to archbishop in 1618. Kuntsevych raised the educational and moral standards of the Uniate clergy in his eparchy, implementing rigorous new rules for their conduct, and together with Y. Rutsky, initiated a major reform of the Basilian order. He was one of the most active propagators of Catholicism and the Church Union among the Orthodox population. Supported by the Polish king and the Vatican, Kuntsevych took over many Orthodox churches and transformed them into Uniate ones. The re-establishment of the Orthodox hierarchy in 1620 and the appointment of a new Orthodox bishop for Polatsk resulted in intensified religious conflict in the region. The forced implementation of Catholicism had antagonized the Orthodox archbishop M. Smotrytsky and many lay people, especially the burghers, and Kuntsevych was killed by enraged Orthodox followers on 12 November 1623. He was beatified by the Vatican on 16 May 1642. His canonization by Pope Pius IX took place on 29 June 1867 and he became the first eastern-rite saint in the Catholic church. Saint Josaphat's remains were moved from Biała Podlaska to St Barbara's Church in Vienna in 1917, and since 1946 they have been on display at St Peter's Basilica in Rome. Kuntsevych wrote many polemical articles in Ukrainian and Polish; they, and many of his sermons, have been reprinted several times in various biographies and collections.

Saint Yosafat Kuntsevych

BIBLIOGRAPHY

Susza, I. *Cursus vitae et certamen martyrii B. Josaphat Kuncevicii* (Rome 1665, Paris 1865)

Guépin, A. *Un apôtre de l'Union des Eglises au XVII siècle: Saint Josaphat et l'Eglise Gréco-slave en Pologne et en Rusie*, 2 vols (Paris 1897–8)

Slipyi, I. (ed). *Sviatyi sviashchenomuchenyk Iosafat Kuntsevych: Materialy i rozvidky* (Lviv 1925)

Gerych, Iu. *Ohliad bohoslovs'ko-literaturnoï diialnosty sv. Iosafata Kuntsevycha* (Toronto 1960)

Solovii, M.; Velykyi, A. *Sviatyi Iosafat Kuntsevych: Ioho zhyttia i doba* (Toronto 1967)

Kunytsky, Dionysii [Kunyc'kyj, Dionysij] (secular name: Kyrylo), b 1781, d 16 April 1836. Orthodox church figure. He was rector of a Kiev seminary and then professor and rector (1827–8) at the Kiev Theological Academy. From 1828 to 1835 he was the bishop of Chyhyryn and vicar of Kiev metropoly.

Kunytsky, Leontii [Kunyc'kyj, Leontij], b 20 June 1876 in Orikhovets, Skalat county, Galicia, d 25 September 1961 in Mostysky, Lviv oblast. Ukrainian Catholic priest, and church and political figure. He studied in Lviv, Vienna, Rome, and Innsbruck (D TH 1904). Ordained in 1901, he ministered to the Galician immigrants in North America until 1914. After his return to Lviv (1917), in an unusual act, the government of the Western Ukrainian National Republic appointed him canon of Lviv eparchy (1918). He was also pastor of Saint George's Cathedral in Lviv and taught theology at the Lviv Theological Academy. In the 1920s he was a prominent member of the *Ukrainian Labor party and published its journals *Nova rada* (1919–20) and *Nash prapor* (1923–4). A founding member of the *Ukrainian National Democratic Alliance and a member of its Central Committee, he represented that party as a deputy to the Polish Sejm (1928–30). In 1937–9 he headed an aid committee for Ukrainian political prisoners. He was arrested by the NKVD and sent to the GULAG until 1956.

Kunytsky, Stepan [Kunyc'kyj], b and d ? Hetman of the *registered Cossacks in 1683. Kunytsky was a noble in the Cossack *starshyna* during the rule of Hetman P. Doroshenko (1672). He was appointed hetman of Right-Bank Ukraine by the Polish king Jan III Sobieski, with the object of reorganizing the Cossack forces for Sobieski's struggle against the Turks. Kunytsky had some success in attracting settlers to Right-Bank Ukraine and reviving such Cossack cities as Bohuslav, Moshny, and Korsun, which were ruined by the internecine struggle of hetmans Doroshenko and Yu. Khmelnytsky. At the end of 1683 Sobieski attacked the Turks near Vienna. To create a diversion, Kunytsky led a Cossack campaign against Turkish-held Moldavia. However, the Turks defeated Kunytsky, and he fled to Ukraine. The Cossacks rebelled against Kunytsky and killed him in Mohyliv.

Kupala, Yanka (pen name of Ivan Lutsevich), b 7 July 1882 in Viazynka, Vileika county, Belorussia, d 28 June 1942 in Moscow. Noted Belorussian poet; full member of the Academy of Sciences of the Belorussian SSR and of the AN URSR from 1929. His prerevolutionary poetry focused on the social and national oppression of the Belorussians. The influence of T. Shevchenko on his poetry is evident in the poem 'Bandaroŭna' (The Cooper's Daughter, 1913). After the 1917 Revolution, particularly in the 1930s, he wrote in the socialist-realist style. He also translated the Rus' epic *Slovo o polku Ihorevi* (The Tale of Ihor's Campaign) and over a dozen of Shevchenko's long poems into Belorussian. He was arrested in 1930 and unsuccessfully attempted suicide; he tried again and succeeded. Books of his selected poetry were translated into Ukrainian and published in 1937, 1947, 1953, and 1967.

Kupalo festival (also Kupailo, Ivan Kupalo). A Slavic celebration of ancient pagan origin marking the end of the summer solstice and the beginning of the harvest (midsummer). In the western Ukrainian Lemko and Prešov regions it was called Sobitka. In Christian times, the church tried to suppress the tradition, substituting it with the feast day of the Nativity of St John the Baptist (24 June), but it remained firmly part of folk ritual as the festival of Ivan (John, from St John) Kupalo.

Kupalo was believed to be the god of love and of the harvest and the personification of the earth's fertility. According to popular belief, 'Kupalo eve' ('Ivan's eve') was the only time of the year when the earth revealed its secrets and made ferns bloom to mark places where its treasures were buried, and the only time when trees spoke and even moved and when witches gathered. It was also the only time of the year when free love received popular sanction. On the eve unmarried young men and women gathered outside the village in the forest or near a stream or pond. There they built 'Kupalo fires' – a relic of the pagan custom of bringing sacrifice – around which they performed ritual dances (see *Khorovod*) and sang ritual, often erotic, songs. They leaped over the fires, bathed in the water (an act of purification), and played physical games with obviously sexual connotations. The fires were also used to burn herbs gathered in the previous year and various items of no further use, particularly those that had been blessed with holy water and could therefore not be discarded by normal means. The fires were never extinguished, but were always allowed to smolder out. On the eve female participants wore scented herbs and flowers to attract the males and adorned their hair with garlands of freshly cut flowers. Later they divined their fates according to what happened to the garlands which they had sent flowing on the water.

An integral part of the festivities was a supper of eggs, **varenyky*, and liquor. An anthropomorphic effigy of Kupalo or a decorated sapling representing him was burned, drowned, buried, or torn apart and scattered in the fields as a symbol of the impending decline in the earth's fertility. In some regions Kupalo was represented by a wheel laced with dry grasses or straw, which was set on fire and rolled down a hill as a symbol of the declining life-giving powers of the sun after the solstice. The representation of Kupalo was frequently identified with Kostrub, the pagan god of winter, or with Marena, the goddess of spring.

Magical properties were ascribed to the plants and herbs gathered on Kupalo eve. It was believed that such herbs could protect one from the evil forces of nature and even cure illnesses in humans and animals. Local priests seemingly sanctioned this belief by blessing the herbs in church on the day of the Nativity of St John the Baptist. On the morning of that day girls washed themselves with the dew that had fallen on Kupalo eve, which they collected in a bowl left outside overnight, and ran barefoot through the bedewed fields in the belief that doing so would improve their opportunity to get married. The sick would roll naked in the dewy meadows in the belief that this action would help them get well, and farmers would run their cattle through such meadows in the belief that this routine would prevent disease.

Written references to the festival date from the 11th century. Its origins are much earlier, however. On a 4th-century calendar pot found in the middle-Dnieper region once inhabited by the Slavic Polianians, for example, the time of the festival was already marked by two crosses. The term 'Kupalo' was itself first mentioned in the Hypatian Chronicle under the year 1262. In medieval and early-modern church documents – eg, 'The Sermon of St John Chrysostom' and the 'Epistle of Hegumen Pamphil' of Pskov Monastery (1515) – there are fairly detailed descriptions of the lascivious festivities. Despite the efforts of the church and secular rulers – eg, Hetman I. Skoropadsky issued a decree in 1719 categorically forbidding it, and many similar decrees were later issued – the tradition proved too old and too well rooted to disappear. By the late 19th century most of the pagan beliefs connected with the Kupalo rituals had vanished, but the festival was still widely celebrated to mark the beginning of the harvest (see *Harvest rituals). As a theme it has figured in the writings of N. Gogol, M. Starytsky, Lesia Ukrainka, O. Kobylianska, and M. Kotsiubynsky, in the music of M. Lysenko and A. Vakhnianyn, in the paintings of O. Kulchytska, and in an early film by D. Sakhnenko.

In postwar Soviet Ukraine, efforts have been made to revive a Sovietized, politicized version of Kupalo rituals. In 1958 the Supreme Soviet of the Ukrainian SSR designated the last Sunday in June the 'Day of Soviet Youth' and recommended that it become a youth holiday throughout the USSR. Attempts at incorporating traditional rituals into the celebration of this day have not been widely accepted, however, because of the contrived nature of the Soviet Kupalo festival.

BIBLIOGRAPHY
Potebnia, A. *O kupal'skikh ogniakh i srodnykh s nimi predstavleniiakh* (Moscow 1867; Kharkiv 1914)
Ukraïnka, L. 'Kupala na Volyni,' *Zhytie i slovo*, 1 (Lviv 1894)
Dei, O. (ed). *Ihry ta pisni* (Kiev 1963)
Shmaida, M. *Sobitky* (Prešov 1963)
Dei, O. (ed). *Kupal's'ki pisni* (Kiev 1970)
Sviata ta obriady Radians'koï Ukraïny (Kiev 1971)

M. Hnatiukivsky

Kupchanko, Hryhorii [Kupčanko, Hryhorij], b 1849 in Berehomet, Bukovyna, d 10 May 1902. Ethnographer, publicist, and Russophile community leader in Bukovyna. He began collecting Ukrainian folklore in the 1870s and published it in the Bukovynian press, mostly in *Bukovynskaia zoria*. In the 1880s and 1890s he edited the Russophile journals *Russkaia pravda, Prosveshchenie*, and *Venochok* in Vienna. His major ethnographic works, about Bukovynian folk songs and the history and geography of Bukovyna, appeared in volume 2 of *Zapiski* of the Southwestern Branch of the Imperial Russian Geographic Society in 1875 and the book *Nasha rodina* (Our Homeland, 1896).

Roman Kupchynsky

Kupchynsky, Roman [Kupčyns'kyj] (pseud: Halaktion Chipka), b 24 September 1894 in Rozhadiv, Zboriv county, Galicia, d 10 June 1976 in New York. Writer, journalist, and feuilletonist. A former officer in the Ukrainian Sich Riflemen and the Ukrainian Galician Army, he cofounded in 1922, the neosymbolist group Mytusa, consisting mostly of poets who were army veterans. In Lviv, he worked for the newspaper *Dilo* as a feuilletonist (1924–39) and for such journals as *Chervona Kalyna*, and headed (1933–9) the Society of Writers and Journalists. He emigrated to the United States in 1949 and contributed to various periodicals, particularly the newspaper *Svoboda*. He is the author of two dramatic narrative poems, *Velykyi den'* (The Great Day, 1921) and *Skoropad* (Fast-fall, 1965). His prose consists of the trilogy *Zametil'* (The Snowstorm, 1928–33) and two collections of stories: *U zvorakh Beskydu* (In the Valleys of the Beskyds, 1933) and *Myslyvs'ki opovidannia* (Hunting Stories, 1964). He is most noted for the 80-odd songs he has composed; some of them, like 'Bozhe Velykyi, Tvorche vsesvitu' (O Great God, Creator of the Universe), have attained wide popularity. A collection of his songs, *My idemo v bii* (We Go into Battle), was published posthumously in 1977. A collection of his poems and prose, *Nevyspivani pisni* (Unsung Songs), appeared in 1983.

D.H. Struk

Kupianka or **Kupiansk** [Kup'janka or Kup'jans'k]. IV-18. City (1977 pop 58,000) and raion center under Kharkiv oblast jurisdiction, situated on the Oskil River. It was founded in 1655 as a *sloboda* (self-governing settlement) and was a company town in the Kharkiv and Izium regiments of Slobidska Ukraine (1685–1765). It became a county town in Voronezh vicegerency in 1780, in Slobidska Ukraine gubernia (1797), and in Kharkiv gubernia (1835). Since the late 19th century Kupianka has been an important railway junction: five lines intersect there and at the adjacent town of Kupianka-Vuzlova. The city has an agricultural-machinery factory and food-processing industry. There is a historical-regional museum and an automobile-transportation tekhnikum.

Kupianka Vuzlova [Kup'janka Vuzlova]. IV-18. Town smt (1980 pop 13,000) in Kharkiv oblast, situated on the Oskil River. Founded in 1895, the town is now an important railroad junction. Railway depots and a building-materials plant are located there.

Kupynos, Voitykh. See Kapynos, Voitykh.

Kurakh, Ivan [Kurax], b 1909 in Galicia, d 15 January 1968 in Zurich. Impressionist painter. Having studied art in Warsaw, Rome, and Milan, in 1939 he became an assistant and later a lecturer at the Brera Academy in Milan. During the war he fought with the Italian Legion on the Soviet front, and his experience had a determining impact on his artistic work. Restricting himself to gray and brown tones and using only the simplest technical devices, he created a mood of profound sorrow. From 1956 he had a studio in New York and Zurich, and exhibited his work in over a hundred shows in the United States and Europe.

Kurakhivka [Kuraxivka]. V-18, DB III-2. Town smt (1980 pop 6,300) in Donetske oblast, situated on the Vovcha River in the western Donbas and administered by the city soviet of Selydove. Founded as a mining settlement in 1924, it has two coal mines and a coal-enrichment plant.

Kurakhove [Kuraxove]. VI-18, DB IV-2. City (1970 pop 15,600) in Marinka raion, Donetske oblast. It arose as a workers' settlement during the construction of the Kurakhivka Regional Electric Station and Reservoir on the

Vovcha River, which began in 1936. Construction was completed in 1952, and the city was incorporated in 1956. Boilers, reinforced-concrete panels, and food products are made there.

Kuraszkiewicz, Władysław, b 22 February 1905 in Włodawa, Poland. Polish linguist and philologist. A graduate of Lviv University and the Jagellonian University in Cracow (1934), he was a professor at Poznań University from 1950 to 1975. The author of several important studies on the history of Polish and East-Slavic languages, his contributions to Ukrainian linguistics include the monograph *Gramoty halicko-wołyńskie XIV–XV wieku: Studium językowe* (Galician-Volhynian Charters of the 14th and 15th Centures: A Linguistic Study, 1934) and numerous studies of Podlachian, Kholm, and Carpathian dialects. Based on his own field research, these latter studies combine precise and detailed observations with polemics against V. Hantsov's, O. Kurylo's, and later G. Shevelov's conceptions of the aboriginal distinctions between northern and southern Proto-Ukrainian dialects. They have been summarized in his books *Zarys dialektologii wschodnio-słowiańskiej* (Outline of East-Slavic Dialectology, 1954) and *Ruthenica* (1985).

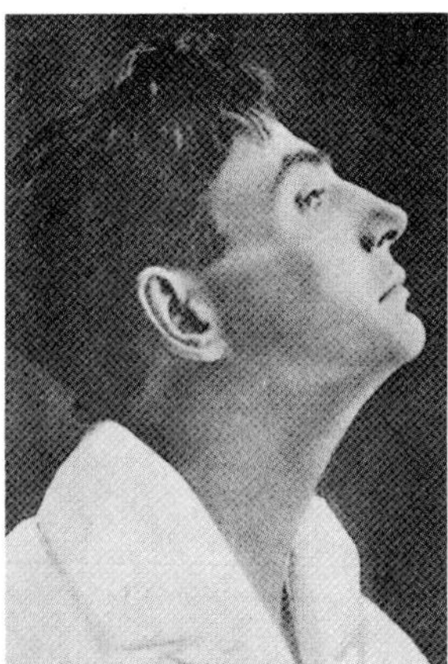

Les Kurbas

Kurbas, Les (Oleksander), b 25 February 1887 in Sambir, Galicia, d 15 October 1942? An outstanding organizer and director of Ukrainian avant-garde theater, actor, and pedagogue; the son of the Galician actor S. *Yanovych (stage name: Kurbas). In 1907–8 he studied philosophy at the University of Vienna and drama with the famous Viennese actor J. Kainz. Graduating from Lviv University in 1910, he worked as an actor in the troupes of the *Hutsul Theater (1911–12) and Ruska (*Ukrainska) Besida theater (1912–14), founded and directed the *Ternopil Teatralni Vechory theater (1915–16), and worked at the *Sadovsky Theater in Kiev (1916–17).

After the February Revolution of 1917 Kurbas reorganized an actors' studio he had founded in 1916 into the *Molodyi Teatr theater (1917–19) in Kiev and became the secretary of the journal **Teatral'ni visti*. With the Molodyi Teatr productions, which included the first production in Ukrainian of a classical Greek play, Sophocles' *Oedipus Rex*, Kurbas revolutionized Ukrainian theater, elevating it in style, esthetics, and repertoire from the provincial to the level of modern Western European theater. He placed much emphasis on his actors' intellectual and technical training, using in the latter the systems of gestures developed by F. Delsarte and E. Jaques-Dalcroze, and on architectural design, using the talents of A. *Petrytsky and M. *Boichuk. In 1919 Molodyi Teatr was forced by the Bolshevik authorities to merge with the *State Drama Theater, and Kurbas became the co-director, with O. Zaharov, of the new Shevchenko Theater. There he dramatized, to great acclaim, T. Shevchenko's epic *Haidamaky* (The Haidamakas); this monumental production, with music by R. Glière, became the standard by which all Ukrainian theatrical productions were measured in the 1920s. In 1920 Kurbas formed the *Kyidramte theater, which toured Bila Tserkva, Uman, and Kharkiv. He then gave up acting to concentrate solely on teaching and directing. In 1922, having become convinced that theater was a powerful political instrument, he founded the *Berezil artistic association in Kiev.

It was at the Berezil theater in both Kiev (1922–6) and Kharkiv (1926–33) that Kurbas's creative genius became most evident. There he perfected his rigorous system for the intellectual and technical training of actors, encouraging them to think independently. One of the basic principles of his system was that the stage image, although it is created by the actor's emotions, nerves, voice, gestures, and temperament, must be objectivized and remain separate from the actor's frame of mind and personal experiences. The image created is successful only when it can be presented in a consistent, concrete form. With its over 300 actors and staff members, 6 actors' studios, directors' lab, design studio, theater museum, and 10 committees, the Berezil association became the focal point of theater in Ukraine. In 1933, Kurbas, his ideas, and his dynamic, innovative, and often controversial productions were condemned as nationalist, rationalist, formalist, and counterrevolutionary. In October he was dismissed as the director of Berezil, and all of his productions were banned from the Soviet Ukrainian repertoire. He moved to Moscow, where he was arrested in December and imprisoned on the Solovets Islands. He was last heard from in 1937.

Kurbas left his mark in the history of Ukrainian theater as an innovative organizer and teacher, and daring experimental director. At Molodyi Teatr he introduced a modern European repertoire and style of acting. At Berezil he broke down the old forms of Ukrainian theater and, after a long period of searching and enthusiastic experimentation with German Expressionist theater and the theories of Constructivism, succeeded, in his productions of M. *Kulish's plays, in creating a unique, Ukrainian Expressionist theater. With his production of G. Kaiser's *Gas* in 1922, Kurbas broke completely with traditional Ukrainian realistic, ethnographic theater to present spectacles that forced the audience to think instead of simply watching passively. This intellectualism was combined with a brilliant synthesis of rhythm, movement, and avant-garde theatrical and visual devices, including montage. He managed to concentrate around himself the best actors, directors, set designers (eg, V. Meller), and playwrights (eg, M. Kulish) in Ukraine. At the Berezil studios and the Kiev (1922–6) and Kharkiv (1926–33) music and drama institutes, he trained an entire generation of Ukrainian actors and directors, including D. Antonovych, B. Balaban, Ye. Bondarenko, A. Buchma, his wife V. Chystiakova, S. Fedortseva, O. Dobrovolska, L. Dubovyk, L. Hakkebush, Y. Hirniak, D. Kozachkovsky, L. Krynytska, M. Krushelnytsky, I. Marianenko, D. Miliutenko, F. Radchuk, P. Samiilenko, V. Serdiuk, V. Skliarenko, N. Tytarenko, B. Tiahno, N. Uzhvii, and V. Vasylko. His theoretical and polemical articles about theater appeared in journals such as *Teatral'ni visti, Nove mystetstvo, Muzahet, Hlobus, Vaplite, Radians'kyi teatr,* and Berezil's *Barykady teatru* (1923–4), which he edited. He was posthumously 'rehabilitated' after Stalin's death.

BIBLIOGRAPHY
Hirniak, Y. 'Birth and Death of the Modern Ukrainian Theater,' in *Soviet Theaters 1917–1941: A Collection of Articles,* ed M. Bradshaw (New York 1954)
Vasyl'ko, V. (ed). *Les' Kurbas: Spohady suchasnykiv* (Kiev 1969)
Smolych, Iu. *Pro teatr* (Kiev 1977)
Hirniak, I. *Spomyny* (New York 1982)
Boboshko, Iu. *Rezhyser Les' Kurbas* (Kiev 1987)

V. Haievsky

Kurdiumov, Georgii [Kurdjumov, Georgij], b 14 February 1902 in Rylsk, Kursk gubernia. Metal physicist; full member of the AN URSR since 1939 and the USSR Academy of Sciences since 1953. A graduate of the Leningrad Polytechnical Institute (1926), from 1932 to 1944 he taught at Dnipropetrovske University and worked in the Dnipropetrovske Physico-Technical Institute. When this institute was expanded into the Scientific-Research Institute of Metal and Materials Science he became its director (1945–78). Kurdiumov also founded and directed (1945–51) the AN URSR Laboratory of Metal Physics in Kiev (later the Institute of Metal Physics), which under his leadership became one of the leading metal physics research centers in the USSR, and was director of the Institute of Solid State Physics of the USSR Academy of Sciences (1962–73). His scientific accomplishments include the determination of the structure and properties of martensite, the hard constituent of quenched steel. His work has played an important role in the development of Soviet metallurgy.

Anatol Kurdydyk

William Kurelek: *Self-Portrait* (watercolor, 1957)

Kurdydyk, Anatol, b 24 July 1905 in Pidhaitsi, Galicia. Journalist and writer. Kurdydyk completed his law studies at Lviv University in 1928. He coedited the Peremyshl newspaper *Ukraïns'kyi holos* (1928–9), then worked as a writer with *Nedilia* (1929–34) and *Dilo* (1934–9) in Lviv. During the Second World War he was a correspondent for *Krakivs'ki visti* in Vienna. Settling in Canada after the war, he founded and edited *Vil'ne slovo* (1956–9) in Toronto and then edited *Novyi shliakh* (1959–62) and *Postup* (1962–70) in Winnipeg. He was the organizer and head of the literary group '12' in Lviv and debuted as a writer in 1924. His collection of legends, *Iasni vohni* (Bright Fires), appeared in Lviv in 1929; it was followed by a collection of stories, *Taina odnoho znaiomoho* (The Secret of an Acquaintance, 1935); the novelette *Try koroli i dama* (Three Kings and a Queen, 1943); and several volumes of publicistic prose. Together with L. Lisevych he wrote the operetta *Zalizna ostroha* (The Iron Stirrup, 1934) and the comedy *Oi, ta Prosvita* (Oh, That Prosvita, 1938). He edited the biobibliographic anthology *Knyha mysttsiv* (A Book of Artists, 1954) as well as T. Kobzei's memoirs (2 vols, 1972, 1974). His poems, articles, novellas, and stories were published in various newspapers in the interwar period.

D.H. Struk

Kurdydyk, Yaroslav (pseuds: Yaroslav Petrovych, Slavko, Maksym Bul'ka), b 6 March 1907 in Pidhaitsi, Galicia. Journalist and writer; brother of A. *Kurdydyk. Having studied journalism at the Free Polish University in Warsaw (1929–31) and law at the University of Vienna (1932–3), he belonged to the literary group '12' in Lviv and specialized in writing poetry and prose miniatures. He contributed literary pieces to the Lviv dailies *Chas* (1933–4) and *Novyi chas* (1934–9), and humorous sketches to *Zyz.* Emigrating to the United States after the war, he contributed articles on military and political affairs to *Svoboda* and *Vyzvol'nyi shliakh,* and coedited the veterans' monthly *Peremoha.* He wrote two collections of prose miniatures, *Dva kulemety* (Two Machine Guns, 1954) and *Etiudy, Miniiatury* (Etudes, Miniatures, 1955), and a collection of war poetry, *Sertse i zbroia* (Heart and Arms, 1976).

Kurelek, William [Kurylyk, Vasyl'], b 3 March 1927 in Whitford, Alberta, d 3 November 1977 in Toronto. Painter. Son of a Ukrainian immigrant farmer, he was raised in rural Manitoba, attended high school and university in Winnipeg, and then studied art at the Ontario College of Art and the Instituto Allende in Mexico. During his stay in England (1952–9), he was hospitalized for

William Kurelek: *Manitoba Party* (National Gallery of Canada)

chronic depression and found solace in the Roman Catholic faith. After visiting the Holy Land (1959, 1964), he depicted the Passion of Christ in a series of 160 paintings, which he considered to be his most important work. His most popular works, however, were paintings of life on the prairies. He created a series of intricate works depicting various ethnic groups of Canada, among them Ukrainians, Poles, Irish, Jews, and Eskimos. His personal and artistic development is outlined in his candid autobiography *Someone with Me* (1973; rev edn, 1980). At least 17 volumes of his plates and illustrations have been published, including the award winning *A Prairie Boy's Winter* (1973), *Lumberjack* (1974), *The Passion of Christ* (1975), and *Fox Mykyta* (1978). Kurelek has been the subject of several films and a biography by P. Morley (1986). His realistic and symbolic works convey through vivid colors and simple lines an intense, personal vision. Leading art critics called him the Breughel of the North. His works are on display in 15 museums and galleries in North America, including the Museum of Modern Art in New York, the National Gallery of Canada in Ottawa, the Art Gallery of Ontario in Toronto, and the Kurelek Art Gallery in Niagara Falls, Ontario.

S. Hordynsky

Kurensky, Maksym [Kurens'kyj], b 8 April 1895 in Atiusha, Krolevets county, Chernihiv gubernia, d 4 September 1940. Noted mathematician. He graduated from Kiev University in 1918, then worked at various institutions at the VUAN (1920–32) and as a professor at Kiev University (1926–32). He also directed seminars in differential equations with Yu. Pfeiffer. In 1933–7 he taught in Leningrad before becoming professor of mathematical analysis at the Karelo-Finnish Pedagogical Institute (1938). Kurensky's principal works include two volumes on differential equations and research papers on partial differential equations and mathematical physics. Many of his publications appeared in the journal *Zapysky Fizychno-matematychnoho viddilu* VUAN (1926–31) and in Western European mathematics journals.

Kurhan or **kurgan.** A term from the Turkic word for mound or stronghold, used in Eastern Europe for a tumulus or barrow, that is, an earthen or stone mound built over a grave. Kurhans first appeared in the steppes north of the Caspian and Black seas and in Subcaucasia and Transcaucasia during the upper Neolithic and the Eneolithic ages (3rd century BC). They vary in height from 3 to over 20 m, and in diameter from 3 to over 100 m. The oldest kurhans in present-day Ukraine date from the early period of the Pit-Grave culture. The most famous ones are the so-called Scythian royal kurhans. Sometimes the mound was encircled by a cromlech and topped by a *stone *baba*, an anthropomorphic statue. The dead were interred or cremated and deposited together with their worldly goods and valuables in timber graves, vaults, catacombs, or pits. Kurhans were then thrown up over them. They usually occur in groups, indicating that clans and tribes had designated burial grounds. Until the 18th century the Cossacks also buried their dead beneath them. At one time, kurhans were used as military lookouts.

Kurin [Kurin']. A type of barracks at the Zaporozhian Sich as well as a military and administrative unit consisting of several companies. There were 38 kurins at the Zaporozhian Sich, each commanded by an elected otaman, who had both administrative and military functions. In the Ukrainian armies of the 20th century a kurin was a battalion-size unit consisting usually of two or more companies.

Petro Kurinny

Kurinny, Petro [Kurinnyj], b 1 May 1894 in Uman, Kiev gubernia, d 25 November 1972 in Munich. Historian, archeologist, ethnographer, and art scholar. He served as academic secretary of the All-Ukrainian Archeological Committee (VUAK), director of the All-Ukrainian Museum Quarter at the Kievan Cave Monastery, and senior research associate of the Institute of Archeology of the Academy of Sciences of the Ukrainian SSR. He excavated sites of the Trypilia and Bilohrudivka cultures, and of the medieval period in Kiev. He was a cofounder of museums in Uman and Berdychiv, and of the All-Ukrainian Museum Quarter in Kiev. In 1943 he emigrated to Germany, where he served as professor at the Ukrainian Free University, president of the Ukrainian Academy of Arts and Sciences in Germany, and editor of *Ukraïns'kyi zbirnyk* of the Institute for the Study of the USSR in Munich. He was a full member of the Shevchenko Scientific Society. He is the author of articles based on his archeological research and *Narysy z istoriï ukraïns'koï arkheolohiï* (Studies on the History of Ukrainian Archeology, 1947).

Khrystyna Kuritsa-Tsimmermann: *Flower Ornament* (Gobelin)

Kuritsa-Tsimmermann, Khrystyna [Kurica-Cimmermann, Xrystyna] (Kurica-Zimmermann, Chrystyna), b 1937 in Nastasiv, Ternopil region, Galicia. Painter and tapestry designer. Emigrating to Austria with her parents in 1943, she graduated from the Vienna Academy of Applied Art (1963) and continued to study sculpture and ceramics with H. Leinfellner (1963–7) and tapestry weaving with Rader-Soulek (1974). Her paintings, including works such as *My Road, The Sun is Rising, Recollection of Ukraine, Tree of My Life*, and *Recollection of Calabria*, are marked by a striking use of color and semiabstract forms. In her tapestries she skillfully uses geometric elements, which are typical of Ukrainian kilims, to achieve novel and startling effects. Her work has been displayed at numerous shows in Austria, including a one-woman show at the Ukrainian Free University in 1980.

Kurkul. See Kulak.

Viktor Kurmanovych

Kurmanovych, Viktor [Kurmanovyč], b 26 November 1876 in Vilshanytsia, Zolochiv county, Galicia, d 18 October 1945 in Odessa. General of the Ukrainian Galician Army (UHA). A graduate of the Austrian Military Academy in Vienna (1912), he served in the intelligence division of the Austrian General Staff. In 1914 he was captured by the Russians and imprisoned for spying. Exchanged for a Russian officer in 1915, he commanded Austrian troops on the Bukovynian and Italian fronts until 1918. After the collapse of the Austrian Empire, Kurmanovych enlisted in the UHA. He was appointed commander of the Zhovkva Group and then the Southern Group at the front. Subsequently he was assigned to the Supreme Command of the UHA, promoted to colonel, and appointed chief of staff (13 February–7 June 1919). For a few months he served also as state secretary for military affairs. After the UHA retreated to the territory of the UNR, Kurmanovych was promoted to brigadier general and appointed (11 August) general quartermaster on the Staff of the Supreme Otaman, which directed the operations of the unified Ukrainian armies. Because of disagreements over strategy and illness, he left the army and in September 1919 immigrated to Austria. He lived in Vienna until April 1945, when he was arrested by Soviet authorities and deported to Odessa. He died there in a prison hospital.

P. Sodol

Kurochka-Armashevsky, Ivan [Kuročka-Armaševs'kyj], b 15 June 1896 near Chernihiv, d 9 August 1971 in Toronto. Stage designer and painter. A graduate of the Kiev Art Institute, he designed sets for the Kiev Theater of Opera and Ballet (1927–41, 20 productions) and the Subcarpathian Theater in Drohobych (1943–4). In 1948 he emigrated to Canada. His sets contributed to the success of productions such as M. Lysenko's *Taras Bulba* and *Christmas Night* (1929), V. Kostenko's *Karmeliuk*, M. Verykivsky's *Pan Kanovs'kyi*, V. Yorysh's adaptations of *Zaporozhian Cossack beyond the Danube* and *Natalka from Poltava*, G. Puccini's *Turandot*, R. Wagner's *Lohengrin*, and S. Prokofiev's *The Tale of the Buffoon*. In Canada he painted churches.

Kuroedov, Vladimir, b 1906 in Nizhnii Novgorod gubernia. Soviet political figure. A teacher by profession, Kuroedov advanced through the Communist Party ideological apparatus to become secretary of the Gorky oblast Party committee and then a science editor of the daily *Sovetskaia Rossiia*. Appointed chairman of the Council on the Affairs of the Russian Orthodox Church (CAROC) in 1960, he played a leading part in Khrushchev's antireligious campaign that by 1964 led to the closing in Ukraine of some 3,500 Orthodox churches as well as the liquidation of some 29 monasteries (including the Kievan Cave Monastery and two [Kiev and Lutske] out of three theological seminaries). From 1966 to 1984 he headed the *Council on Religious Affairs, which oversees the implementation of religious policy for all denominations in the Soviet Union. Kuroedov wrote several propaganda brochures on church-state relations in the USSR.

Kuropas, Myron [Kuropas'], b 15 November 1932 in Chicago. Political and community leader, educator, historian, and journalist; son of S. *Kuropas. A graduate of the University of Chicago (PH D 1973), he was president of the Ukrainian National Youth Federation (MUN) (1960–2) and editor of its periodicals *Scope* (1959–60) and *The Trident* (1960–2). An active member of the Republican party in the United States, he served as regional director of the Action Program (1971–5), special assistant for ethnic affairs to President G. Ford (1976–7), and legislative assistant to Sen R. Dole (1977). Since 1978 he has been supreme vice-president of the Ukrainian National Association. He has written several books on the history of Ukrainians in North America, such as *The Ukrainians in America* (1972) and *To Preserve a Heritage: The Story of the Ukrainian Immigration in the United States* (1984). He contributes frequently to the Ukrainian press, particularly to *The Ukrainian Weekly*.

Kuropas, Stepan [Kuropas'], b 1 October 1900 in Peremyshl, Galicia. Community leader and journalist. A graduate of the Agricultural Engineering Institute in Czechoslovakia (1924), he served as an officer in the Austrian army (1918), the Ukrainian Galician Army (1918–20), and the Polish army (1924–5). Immigrating to the United States, in 1930 he became an activist in Ukrainian organizations, such as the Ukrainian Professional Association of the United States, the Organization for the Rebirth of Ukraine, and the Ukrainian Congress Committee of America. He was also vice-president and auditor of the Ukrainian National Association (1938–69). Kuropas contributed a regular column to *Svoboda* (1938–70) and edited *Samostiina Ukraïna*.

Kurovets, Ivan [Kurovec'], b 17 January 1863 in Batiatyche, Kaminka-Strumylova county, Galicia, d 13 May 1931. Physician; civic and political activist. A graduate of the Medical Academy in Vienna (1887), Kurovets worked as a physician in Kalush, where he helped establish the Peasant's Bank and People's Home, and was a delegate to the Galician Sejm (1908–14). In 1918–19 he served as secretary of health in the government of the Western Ukrainian National Republic. After that he was the director of the Narodna Lichnytsia society in Lviv (1923–31). As a leading member of the Ukrainian Labor party, he was an influential figure in the establishment of the Ukrainian National Democratic Alliance (UNDO). He was elected a delegate from UNDO to the Polish Sejm in 1928, but resigned shortly afterwards. Kurovets was also a member of the Shevchenko Scientific Society and the Ukrainian Physicians Society, and chairman of the advisory council of the Dilo publishing house (1921–31). He published many scholarly and popular articles and pamphlets on medical and other topics.

Kurpita, Teodor (pseud: Teok), b 1913 in Galicia, d 1974 in Chicago. Poet, writer, editor. He edited the literary-artistic journal *Ridne slovo* and the satirical magazine *Izhak-Komar*. His poetry was published in a number of collections, including: *Na dospivakh vesnianykh* (At Spring Songfests, 1934), *Not e pess: liryka* (Not a Pass: Lyrics, 1946), and *Blakytni troiandy* (Blue Roses, 1966). He also published a collection of short stories, *Otets' z zolotym sertsem* (A Father with a Heart of Gold, 1937), and a collection of satirical sketches, *Karykatury z literatury* (Caricatures from Literature, 1947).

Kursk. II-17. City (1985 pop 420,000) and oblast capital in the Russian SFSR. It was first mentioned in the chronicles in 1032 as a fortified town in Chernihiv principality and a defense outpost against the Cumans. Later the capital of an appanage principality, it was razed in 1240 by the Mongols. Rebuilt in 1582 as a fortified town on Muscovy's frontier with the Crimean Khanate, from 1708 to 1727 it belonged to Kiev gubernia. From 1780 to 1797 it was a vicegerency capital, and from 1797 to 1917, a gubernia capital. Today Kursk is an important transport, industrial, and cultural center. Of its 98,800 inhabitants in 1926, 2,400 were Ukrainian.

Kursk Magnetic Anomaly. The largest magnetic anomaly and iron-ore basin in the USSR. Covering an area of 80,000 sq km, most of it lies within Kursk, Belgorod, and Orel oblasts, but its southern part extends into Ukrainian ethnic territory within the borders of the RSFSR (the upper Oskil River region south of Belgorod) and into Kharkiv oblast (Vovchanske raion). The magnetic anomaly is caused by iron-ore deposits lying close to the surface; they consist mostly of Precambrian ferruginous quartzites whose basic ores are magnetite and hematite. The anomaly's ore reserves in 1980 were estimated to be 44.8 billion t, of which 29.4 billion t were high grade. Mining began there in 1952. Further exploitation of the resources of the anomaly will continue to have a great impact on the growth of heavy industry in the Donbas and the USSR as a whole.

Kursk region (Kurshchyna). A mixed Russian-Ukrainian region northeast of *Slobidska Ukraine. In the 16th century it became part of Muscovy. In the 19th and early 20th centuries it constituted Kursk gubernia, which bordered on Chernihiv, Poltava, and Kharkiv gubernias. In 1934, with somewhat changed borders, it made up Kursk oblast in the RSFSR, with an area of 50,800 sq km. The region's southern part (11,100 sq km) lies on Ukrainian ethnic territory and was inhabited by 554,700 Ukrainians (19.1 percent of the oblast's population) in 1926. In 1954 almost all of this southern part, of which about half of the population was Ukrainian, was incorporated into newly created *Belgorod oblast. Since that time Kursk oblast has had an area of 29,800 sq km, of which only 1,200 sq km lies on Ukrainian ethnic territory. In 1979 Kursk oblast had a population of 1,395,400; only 19,500 identified themselves as Ukrainians, of which only 9,300 stated that Ukrainian was their native language.

Kurtiak, Ivan [Kurtjak], b 1888 in Khust, Transcarpathia, d 2 January 1933 in Sevliush (now Vynohradiv), Transcarpathia. Pro-Hungarian Transcarpathian community and political figure. A school teacher before the First World War, in November 1918 he was appointed school inspector for Khust by the Hungarian authorities. After Transcarpathia was incorporated into Czechoslovakia, he refused to pledge allegiance to the new government and entered politics full time. He cofounded and headed the Subcarpathian Agricultural Union (1920–3) and its successor the Autonomous Agricultural Union (1924–33), serving as a deputy from that party to the Prague parliament from 1924 to his death. He demanded autonomy for Transcarpathia (Subcarpathian Ruthenia) from the central government in Prague.

Kurukove Treaty. An agreement between the Polish government (represented by Hetman S. Koniecpolski) and the Cossacks (led by M. Doroshenko), concluded during the successful Zhmailo uprising of the Cossacks against the Poles. The treaty was signed 5 November 1625 beside Lake Kurukove, near present-day Kremenchuk. The terms of the treaty were as follows: all the insurgents were granted amnesty; the list of *registered Cossacks was increased to 6,000 men; those registered were to receive from the Polish crown an annual salary for service; and they retained the right to elect their leader. The Cossacks were forbidden to enter into relations with other countries or to undertake military campaigns against the Turks.

Kurylas, Osyp, b 7 August 1870 in Shchyrets, Lviv county, Galicia, d 25 June 1951 in Lviv. Painter and graphic artist. A graduate of the Lviv Industrial Design School (1890) and the Cracow Academy of Fine Art (1900), he specialized in genre painting and portraiture. He did portraits of T. Shevchenko (1918), Metropolitan A. Sheptytsky, Prince Volodymyr the Great, Prof Yavorsky, his wife (1918), and V. Shukhevych, and a self-portrait. Many of his paintings depict the Hutsuls in their everyday life: *A Hutsul Pair* (1937), *Blahodatka Village*, *View of Chernivtsi*, *Wooden Church in Zhyravka*, *Hutsuls Reading a Newspaper* (1945), *Woodsmen* (1947), and *The Homeless*. He also illustrated children's books, such as *Pryhody Iurchyka kucheriavoho* (The Adventures of Curly-Haired Yurchyk), *Kazka didusia Tarasa* (Grandfather Taras's Story), and *Hav na vakatsiiakh* (Hav on Vacation); the children's magazine *Svit dytyny*; a number of Ukrainian readers and primers; and V. Stefanyk's novellas *Klenovi lystky* (Maple Leaves) and *Novyna* (News). His postcards on historical themes and drawings depicting the period of the wars for Ukraine's independence were very popular. Kurylas was

Osyp Kurylas: *Hutsul Types* (oil, 1945)

one of the pioneers of the new movement in Ukrainian religious painting. His icons of the Mother of God and Christ are distinctively Ukrainian. He designed many iconostases in Galicia. A. Viunyk (1963) and S. Kostiuk (1970) have written monographs on Kurylas.

S. Hordynsky

Kurylenko, Onysym, b 16 March 1904 in Borivka, Mykolaiv county, Podilia gubernia, d 25 September 1982. Physical chemist; corresponding member of the AN URSR from 1969. After graduating from the Kiev Polytechnical Institute in 1930, he lectured at the Kiev Technological Institute of the Food Industry. After the war he worked at the AN URSR Institute of General and Inorganic Chemistry until 1951 when he returned to the Kiev Technological Institute of the Food Industry to chair a department. In 1962 he was appointed deputy director of the Institute of General and Inorganic Chemistry and in 1968 director of the Institute of Colloidal Chemistry and Hydrochemistry. He did research on the stability of dispersed systems, the electrochemistry of polyelectrolytes, the hydration of macromolecular compounds, the chemistry of surface phenomena, and the interaction between water and hydrophilic substances.

Kurylo, Olena, b 6 October 1890 in Slonim, Belorussia, d reportedly in 1937. Linguist. Kurylo studied with Ye. *Tymchenko at Warsaw University. After the 1917 Revolution she became a senior associate of the VUAN in Kiev, a member of its Ethnographic, Regional Studies, and Dialectological commissions, and a consultant to its Institute of the Ukrainian Scientific Language. She played an important role in the normalization of literary Ukrainian and Ukrainian scientific terminology (particularly of chemistry and botany), which she approached from a puristic and ethnographic position. Her contributions to the standardization of Ukrainian literary language include a widely used elementary Ukrainian grammar (1918; 11th edn, 1926) and *Uvahy do suchasnoï ukraïns'koï literaturnoï movy* (Remarks on the Contemporary Ukrainian Literary Language, 1920; 3rd edn, 1925).

From her systematic study of the phonetics of northern and southwestern Ukrainian dialects, particularly of their accentuation, which expanded on V. *Hantsov's research, Kurylo concluded that Ukrainian arose from the merging of two originally distinct dialectal groups. In several articles and the monograph *Sproba poiasnyty protses zminy* e, o *v novykh zakrytykh skladakh u pivdennii hrupi ukraïns'kykh diialektiv* (An Attempt at Explaining the Process of Change of *e, o* in New Closed Syllables of the Southern Group of Ukrainian Dialects, 1928), she showed that the alternation of *o, e* with *i* developed independently in these groups through diphthongization in the north and assimilation in the south. Kurylo gave new explanations for the transition of *o* into *a* in such words as *bahatyj* ('rich') and of the transition in Western Ukraine of *a* into *e* preceded by a soft consonant (eg, *žal'* to *žiel'*, 'grief'). She also wrote works on the history of Russian (she contributed a new theory of the rise of dissimilatory *akan'e*), on Moldavian dialects, and on phonetics in general, as well as the first program for collecting Ukrainian folk gestures, facial expressions, children's exclamations and language, jargon, and nicknames (1923). Her approach gradually evolved from a purely phonetic one characteristic of the Neogrammarians into a structuralist-phonological one.

During the purge of the VUAN in the early 1930s, Kurylo sought refuge in Moscow, where she taught until her arrest in 1937. Her subsequent fate is unknown. A detailed analysis of her contributions is found in Yu. Sherekh's (G.Y. Shevelov's) *Vsevolod Hantsov. Olena Kurylo* (1954).

G.Y. Shevelov

Yevhen Kurylo

Kurylo, Yevhen, b 18 October 1912 in Chortkiv, Galicia. Stage and screen actor specializing in heroic roles. He began his acting career in 1928 with the Tobilevych Ukrainian People's Theater in Stanyslaviv. Then he worked under V. Blavatsky's direction in the Zahrava Young Ukrainian Theater (1935–8), the Kotliarevsky Theater (1938–9), the Lesia Ukrainka Drama Theater (1939–41), and the Lviv Opera Theater (1941–4). Upon emigrating to Germany, he joined the Ukrainian Actors' Ensemble led by V. *Blavatsky. In 1949 he settled in the United States. His stage repertoire included Sokhron in M. Starytsky's *Marusia Bohuslavka*, Prince Ihor in H. Luzhnytsky's *Slovo o polku Ihorevi* (The Tale of Ihor's Campaign), Mazepa in B. Lepky's *Baturyn*, Mokii in M. Kulish's *Myna Mazailo*, Bernardo del Aqua in Yu. Kosach's *Obloha* (Siege), Count Riccardo in Goldoni's *I rusteghi*, and Don Alvaro di Castiglia in his *La vedova scaltra*. Kurylo appeared in the films *Dovbush* and *Viter zi skhodu* (Wind from the East).

Kurylyk, Vasyl. See Kurelek, William.

Kuryshko, Kateryna [Kuryško] (née Nahirna), b 12 April 1949 in Vepryk, Hadiache raion, Poltava oblast. Athlete. A graduate of the Kiev Institute of Physical Culture (1973), she was a gold medalist in two-man canoeing at the 1972 Olympics and World and European champion in four-man canoeing in 1971. Kuryshko was also the Ukrainian and USSR champion in various canoeing categories several times. She now works with the Committee of Sports and Physical Culture of the Ukrainian Council of Ministers.

Kusenko, Olha, b 11 November 1919 in Kaniv, Kiev gubernia. Stage actress. A graduate of the Kiev Institute of Theater Arts (1941), she worked in theaters at the front during the war and in 1944 joined the Kiev Ukrainian Drama Theater. She is a versatile actress, who has proved herself in such varied roles as Melanka in I. Kocherha's *Svichchyne vesillia* (Svichka's Wedding) and Mariia Krzhysevych in his *Prorok* (Prophet), Varka in Yu. Yanovsky's *Duma pro Brytanku* (Duma about Brytanka), Varia in A. Chekhov's *Vishnëvyi sad* (Cherry Orchard), Beatrice in W. Shakespeare's *Much Ado about Nothing*, and Regan in his *King Lear*. Since 1973 Kusenko has served as president of the presidium of the Ukrainian Theatrical Society.

Kushch, Viktor [Kušč], 1878–1942. Senior officer in the UNR Army. Having served as a general staff officer in the Russian army, in 1919–20 he was an operations officer on the staff of the UNR Army. In the fall of 1920 he was promoted to brigadier general. After the war he edited the military journal *Tabor* and wrote articles on military subjects. In 1927 he served briefly as chief of staff of the UNR Ministry of Military Affairs, which was established secretly in Warsaw.

Kushchak, Andrii [Kuščak, Andrij], b 12 December 1901 in Leshchakiv, Sokal county, Galicia, d 17 November 1986 in New York. Metropolitan of the *Ukrainian Orthodox Church of America. He immigrated to Canada in 1928, and then to the United States in 1932. That year he was ordained a priest. On 28 January 1967 he was consecrated bishop by Archbishop Palladius and confirmed by the Patriarch of Constantinople, succeeding B. Shpylka as head of the church. In 1983 Patriarch Demetrius of Constantinople elevated him to metropolitan.

Kushnir, Ivan [Kušnir], b 17 June 1877 in Lviv, d 1 January 1940 in Lviv. Political activist. He was a leading member of the Ukrainian Social Democratic party in Galicia. From 1905 he worked in the trade union movement in Lviv. He was arrested by the Soviet authorities during the first occupation of Galicia and died in prison.

Kushnir, Makar [Kušnir] (pseuds: Bohush, Yakymenko, B. Dniprovy), b 10 August 1890 in Cherkasy, Kiev gubernia, d 16 September 1951 in Pomerolle, Belgium. Political figure and journalist. He studied at St Petersburg University. At the beginning of the 1917 Revolution he moved to Kiev, where he was a delegate from the Ukrainian Party of Socialists-Federalists to the *Central Rada and the Mala Rada. He also contributed to the journal *Nova Rada* and the daily *Trybuna*. At the end of 1918 he was a member of the UNR delegation to the Paris

Makar Kushnir

Peace Conference. From 1920 he lived in Vienna and then Geneva, where he wrote for the Ukrainian (*Volia*) and foreign press, and contributed to such nationalistic publications as *Rozbudova Natsiï*. Kushnir was also a founding member of the OUN, the organization's chief judge, and a close adviser to Ye. *Konovalets. After the Second World War he settled in Belgium.

Kushnir, Mykhailo [Kušnir, Myxajlo], b 23 August 1897 in Stanyslaviv, Galicia. Painter and art critic; a publicist and community leader. Having served as a captain in the Ukrainian Galician Army (1918–19), he studied art at the Vienna Academy of Arts (1919–20) and philosophy at Lviv and Heidelberg (PH D 1950) universities. A member of the Ukrainian Military Organization (UVO) and then of the OUN, he organized Prosvita branches and theater groups in the Stanyslaviv region and Lviv. In 1941–5 he headed the department of culture of the *Ukrainian Central Committee and belonged to the Military Board of the Division Galizien. Immigrating to the United States in 1951, he was active in the Ukrainian Youth Association (SUM) and the Organization for the Defense of Four Freedoms, and was president of the Association for the Advancement of Ukrainian Culture (1965–70). His publications include four albums of woodcuts (1927, 1931, 1935, 1956); monographs on art theory, such as *Der Sinn im Gegenstand* (1929), *Das Problem der Stilenwicklung in der modernen Kunst* (1950), and *Velych mystetstva i vidrodzhennia kul'tury* (The Greatness of Art and the Revival of Culture, 1968); and numerous articles on philosophical, artistic, educational, and political questions in the Ukrainian press. He is a proponent of Christian nationalism.

Kushnir, Vasyl (Basil) [Kušnir, Vasyl'], b 17 September 1893 in Vikno, Skalat county, Galicia, d 25 September 1979 in Winnipeg. Community leader and priest. After serving in the Austrian army during the First World War, Kushnir studied at the Catholic Theological Seminary in Lviv and at the University of Innsbruck (DD 1929). Ordained a priest in 1927, he taught at the Catholic Theological Seminary in Stanyslaviv (1930–4). In Canada he was parish priest of SS Vladimir and Olga Ukrainian Catholic Cathedral in Winnipeg (1934–79) and chancellor (1947–57) and vicar general (1957–79) of Winnipeg eparchy. He helped form the Ukrainian Canadian Committee (UCC). Representing the Ukrainian Catholic Brotherhood of Canada, Kushnir was president of the UCC for 26 years (1940–52, 1957–71). In 1944 he worked with the Ukrainian Canadian Relief Fund, which assisted the Ukrainians in

Vasyl Kushnir

Volodymyr Kushnir

displaced persons camps in Germany to resettle in Canada. A founding member of the Pan-American Ukrainian Conference in 1946, he was its chairman (1947–67) and the first president of the *World Congress of Free Ukrainians (1967–78). In 1972 Kushnir was appointed to the Order of Canada.

Kushnir, Volodymyr [Kušnir] (Kuschnir, Vladimir), b 1881 in Galicia, d 25 October 1933 in Prague. Publicist and journalist. In the early 20th century he moved to Vienna, where he worked on *Ruthenische Revue*, co-founded and edited *Ukrainische Rundschau* (1906–10), and founded and headed the Ukrainian Press Bureau there (1907). All of these organs worked to inform the West about the Ukrainian question. In 1912 he was the editor of the Lviv newspaper *Dilo*, then he edited *Bukovyna* and *Narodnyi Holos* (1913–14) in Chernivtsi. During the First World War, he returned to Vienna, where he edited *Ukrainische Korrespondenz* (1917–18), published by the General Ukrainian Council, and then worked for the journals *Volia* (1919) and *Na Perelomi* (1920) in Vienna and *Die Ukraine* in Berlin. He was the first head of the *Union of Ukrainian Journalists and Writers Abroad. From 1923 he lived in Prague, where he taught at the Ukrainian Higher Pedagogical Institute. Kushnir contributed articles to numerous Ukrainian and Western publications and wrote several political essays and studies, including *Der Neopanslawismus* (1908). He also compiled and edited a collection of documents on the Polish *Pacification of Galicia, published in English as *Polish Atrocities in the West Ukraine* (1931).

Kushtanovytsia culture. An archeological culture named after a burial mound site of the 6th–3rd centuries BC widespread in Transcarpathia. It is situated near Kushtanovytsia, Mukachiv raion, Transcarpathia oblast. The site was excavated in 1898 by T. Lehotsky and in 1929–31 by J. Jankovich and J. Böhm, who uncovered the remains of cremations in urns and in shallow pits, hand-molded pottery, tools, iron weapons, bronze, glass, and bone ornaments, a gold disc, and other artifacts. The people buried there were Thracian farmers and herders who were influenced by the Scythians. Similar burial grounds in Transcarpathia were excavated later on. The pottery discovered there is similar to pottery found in Scythian kurhans in western Podilia.

Kushuhum [Kušuhum]. VI-16. Town smt (1980 pop 9,300) in Zaporizhia raion, Zaporizhia oblast, situated 10 km south of Zaporizhia. It was established in 1770 and until 1927 was called Velyka Katerynivka. It has a lime plant.

Kut burial site. A burial ground of 32 kurhans excavated in 1951–2 near the former village of Kut, Apostolove raion, Dnipropetrovske oblast (now inundated by the Kakhivka Reservoir). Over 200 graves belonging to the Pit-Grave, Catacomb, and Timber-Grave cultures of the Bronze Age and to the Scythian period (4th–3rd centuries BC) were uncovered. The burials contained stone and flint axes, tools, knives and arrowheads, clay pottery, and various ornaments.

Kutia [kutja]. Ritual dish made with wheat or barley grain and ground poppy seeds that is eaten with a honey sauce on Christmas Eve (*bahata kutia*) and Epiphany Eve (*holodna kutia*). It is one of the oldest of the 12 traditional dishes and is served to begin or end the Christmas and Epiphany dinners. The exact recipe and its use in ritual differed in the various regions of Ukraine. *Kutia* was usually used to foretell a plentiful harvest and family happiness (see *Christmas). On Christmas Eve children often took servings of *kutia* to their godparents, and after dinner a portion was left on the table for the souls of the deceased.

Kutkin, Volodymyr, b 12 November 1926 in Zhytomyr. Graphic artist. A graduate of the Kiev State Art Institute (1959), he works mainly in printmaking, book graphics, and monumental decorative art. His chief works are the linocut series *On Motifs from T. Shevchenko's Works* (1959–65), illustrations and ornamental designs for T. Shevchenko's *Kobzar* (with others, 1963), illustrations to O. Honchar's novel *Tronka* (1966), the linocut series *My Land* (1966–7), the mosaic panel *The Great Kobzar* (1969–71) in Tashkent, and illustrations to H. Kosynka's short stories (1970). He has also done bookplates. Kutkin has participated in many exhibitions in the USSR and abroad: in San Francisco (1963), Leipzig (silver medal, 1965), and at Expo 67 in Montreal. In 1968 I. Buhaienko wrote a monograph on Kutkin.

Kuts, Valentyn [Kuc] (pseud of Parfenii Smola), b 17 December 1883 in Dudchany, Kherson gubernia, d 15 September 1948 in Curitiba, Brazil. Community leader and organizer of co-operatives. For his participation in the Ukrainian revolutionary movement Kuts was forced to change his name and in 1911 emigrate to the state of Paraná in Brazil. There he taught in many Ukrainian settlements and organized co-operatives for the marketing of agricultural produce. In 1931 he worked for the journal *Ukraïns'kyi khliborob*, editing its Portuguese-language supplement, *A Vida Ucraina* (22 issues in all). Kuts was the author of the poem *Rus'kyi Moisei* (The Ruthenian Moses, 1925) and a Ukrainian textbook on learning Portuguese.

Kuts, Volodymyr [Kuc], b 7 February 1927 in Oleksyne, Sumy okruha, d 16 August 1975 in Moscow. Noted track-and-field athlete. Kuts moved to Leningrad at an early age while serving in the military. Afterwards, he settled in Moscow and was denied permission to return

Volodymyr Kuts

Zenon Kuzelia

to Ukraine. He is among the few athletes in the world who established new records in both the 5,000- and 10,000-meter runs. At the 1956 Olympic Games he won the gold medal in both events. He set the world record for the 5,000-meter run 4 times and between 1954 and 1957 he surpassed his own USSR records 12 times. In 1961 he graduated from the Leningrad Institute of Athletics and became a coach. Although he lived outside Ukraine, Kuts always emphasized his Ukrainian nationality during international meets. He died under mysterious circumstances. Kuts is the author of the book *Povest' o bege* (A Story about Running, 1964).

Kutsenko, Pavlo [Kucenko], b 14 November 1908 in Kamianka, Chyhyryn county, Kiev gubernia, d 30 June 1983 in Kiev. Graphic artist. In 1937 he graduated from the Kiev State Art Institute where he had studied under S. Naliepinska-Boichuk and F. Krychevsky. His works consist mainly of lyric landscapes and experiments with various etching techniques. His prints include *The Beginning of the Spring* (aquatint, 1937), the series *Donbas* (drypoint, 1944), *Autumn on the Dnieper* (cardboard cut, 1963), *Kiev Slopes* (etching, 1970), and *Old Apple Trees* (1974). A catalog of his work was published in Kiev in 1971.

Kutsenko, Volodymyr [Kucenko], b 18 February 1921 in Blahodatne, Pavlohrad county, Katerynoslav gubernia. Soviet philosopher; since 1985 full member of the AN URSR. A graduate of Kiev University (1948) and the Academy of Social Sciences of the CC CPSU (1953), he taught at and chaired a department of the Higher Party School of the CC CPU (1953–70). Then he served as a department chairman and academic secretary (1975) of the AN URSR Institute of Philosophy. As the chief editor of *Filosofs'ka dumka* (1972–8), he was largely responsible for the decline in the journal's intellectual quality. Kutsenko specializes in the methodology of the social sciences. He is the author of *Sotsial'naia zadacha kak kategoriia istoricheskogo materializma* (The Social Task as a Category of Historical Materialism, 1972), the coauthor of *Sotsial'noe poznanie i sotsial'noe upravlenie* (Social Knowledge and Social Control, 1979), and the editor of several collections of papers on methodological problems.

Kutsenko, Yakiv [Kucenko, Jakiv], b 20 November 1915 in Kiev. Weight lifter. He studied at the Kiev Institute of Physical Culture in the 1930s. He was twice European champion (1947 and 1950) and the silver medalist at the 1946 and 1950 World championships. Kutsenko set 10 world and 58 USSR records and was Ukrainian champion 12 times and USSR champion 14 times in his career. He also wrote the books *Zoloti kilohramy* (Golden Kilograms, 1968) and *U velykomu tryborstvi* (In the Great Weight-Lifting Competition, 1968).

Kuty. V-6. Town smt (1980 pop 4,400) in Kosiv raion, Ivano-Frankivske oblast. It was first mentioned in 1448. In the early 18th century O. Dovbush and his *opryshoks were active in the vicinity. From 1772 to 1918 the town was under Austrian rule, and in the interwar period, under Poland. Owing to its mild climate Kuty is a popular resort town. A colony of Armenians from Moldavia was founded there in the early 18th century.

Kuzelia (Kuzela), Zenon [Kuzelja], b 23 June 1882 in Poruchyn, Berezhany county, Galicia, d 24 May 1952 in Paris. Ethnographer, lexicographer, bibliographer, journalist, and community figure; full member of the Shevchenko Scientific Society (NTSh) from 1909. In 1898 he founded and headed the Moloda Ukraina secret society at the Berezhany Polish gymnasium. He studied at Lviv (1900–1) and Vienna (1901–6) universities. At the latter he was V. Jagić's personal secretary, the librarian of the Slavic Seminar, and an official Slavic translator from 1903. He headed the Sich Ukrainian student society in Vienna in 1902–4 and coedited its jubilee almanac in 1908. He also did volunteer work at the Ethnographic and Anthropological Department of the Imperial Court Museum (1904–6) and the Museum of Austrian Ethnography (1904–7). In 1904–6 he took part in three NTSh ethnographic-anthropological expeditions to the Carpathian Mountains led by F. Vovk and I. Franko.

After obtaining a doctorate in philology and history, Kuzelia worked as a Slavic librarian at the University of Vienna (1906–9) and contributed to *Ukrainische Rundschau* and *Zeitschrift für österreichische Bibliographie* in Vienna and *Dilo* in Lviv. From 1909 to 1914 he was the chairman of the Slavic Department at Chernivtsi University, lectured on the Ukrainian language there (1913–14), headed the Chernivtsi branch of the Ruska Besida society, and edited the weekly *Ukraïna* (1913–14) and the Ukrainian supplement to *Czernowitzer Allgemeine Zeitung*.

From the outbreak of the First World War to his death, Kuzelia lived outside Ukraine. In 1914–16 he worked at the Institute of East European History in Vienna. In 1916–20 he directed educational work among the Ukrainians in the Russian army who were held in the POW camp in *Salzwedel, Germany, and edited the papers *Vil'ne slovo* (1918) and *Shliakh* (1919–20) there. From 1920 he lived in Berlin, where he edited the papers *Ukraïns'ke slovo* (1921–3), *Osteuropäische Korrespondenz* (1926–30), and *Ukrainische Kulturberichte* (1933–40) and books of the publishing houses Ukrainske Slovo and Ukrainska Nakladnia. He headed the Ukrainska Hromada community organization (1924–33) and the Union of Foreign Journalists (1930–6), was a correspondent of the Lviv daily *Dilo* and a member of the Ukrainian Scientific Institute in Berlin (1926–45), and lectured at Berlin University. As a postwar refugee in Fürth, Bavaria, he edited the newspaper *Chas* and the NTSh journal *S'ohochasne i mynule*, headed the Ukrainian Students' Aid Commission (KoDUS), and was the coeditor, with V. Kubijovyč, of the *Entsyklopediia ukraïnoznavstva* (Encyclopedia of Ukraine) and served as president of NTSh (from 1949). In 1951 he moved to France to work at the new NTSh center in Sarcelles near Paris.

Up to the First World War Kuzelia published over 200 reviews and surveys of West European scholarly books in *Zapysky NTSh*. As an ethnographer he was, with I. Franko and V. Hnatiuk, an adherent of the comparative school and later of the Finnish school (the historical-geographic approach). He published, in NTSh serials, valuable studies on the motif of wandering in Slavic folklore, on Ukrainian burial, courting, wedding, and birth customs and rituals, on folk medicine and folk theater, on the belief in vampires, and on Ukrainian emigration. He also compiled, with M. Chaikovsky, the first two Ukrainian dictionaries of foreign words (1910, 1919) and, with J. Rudnyckyj, a Ukrainian-German dictionary (1943); published articles in Austrian, German, Polish, and Czech scholarly periodicals, in the German scholarly yearbook *Minerva* (1926–35), and in the collections *Ukraine und die kirchliche Union* (1930) and *Die Westukraine*, which he edited; and wrote several chapters for the encyclopedic *Handbuch der Ukraine* (1941) and *The Ukraine and Its People* (1949) edited by I. Mirchuk. His survey articles on Ukrainian ethnography can be found in vol 1 of *Ukraine: A Concise Encyclopaedia* (1963). Articles about his life and contributions and a select bibliography of his writings were published in a festschrift edited by V. Yaniv as vol 169 of *Zapysky NTSh* (1962).

M. Hnatiukivsky

Mykhailo Kuzemsky

Alex Kuziak

Kuzemsky, Mykhailo [Kuzems'kyj, Myxajlo], b 1809, d 1879 in Galicia. Religious and community leader, canon of Lviv eparchy. Kuzemsky was the most active member of the *Supreme Ruthenian Council and later the main organizer of its branches in the provinces. He was a founder and the first head of the *Halytsko-Ruska Matytsia educational-publishing society. For 15 years he was a leader and trustee of Ukrainian popular education in eastern Galicia, defending the use of the Ukrainian language in schools and the right to Ukrainian political and administrative independence in Galicia. From 1868 to 1871 he was the last Greek Catholic archbishop of *Kholm eparchy.

Kuziak, Alex Gordon [Kuzjak], b 15 October 1908 in Canora, Saskatchewan. Businessman and politician. Kuziak was elected to the Saskatchewan legislature (1948–64) as the Co-operative Commonwealth Federation (CCF) member in the constituency of Canora. As minister of telephones and minister in charge of the Government Finance Office (1952), he was the first MLA of Ukrainian origin to hold cabinet office in Saskatchewan. He was also minister in charge of the Northern Crown Corporation and Natural Resources (1956–62) and of Mineral Resources (1962–4), until his defeat in 1964.

Kuziakina, Natalia [Kuzjakina, Natalja], b 5 September 1928 in Kiev. Specialist on the history of Soviet Ukrainian theater. After completing graduate studies in Ukrainian literature at Kiev University (1951), she taught Ukrainian literature at the Izmail Pedagogical Institute and Odessa University. In 1962 she became a senior scholarly associate in the theater department of the AN URSR Institute of Fine Arts, Folklore, and Ethnography. Her articles and reviews were first published in 1950. She has written monographs about the playwright M. Kulish (1962) and his plays (1970), the playwright I. Kocherha (1968), and Ukrainian dramaturgy in the years 1917–60 (2 vols, 1958, 1963).

Vasyl Kuziv

Kuziv, Vasyl, b 3 February 1887 in Denysiv, Ternopil county, Galicia, d 24 July 1958 in Crenford, New Jersey. Protestant church figure. He graduated from the theological seminary in Bloomfield, New Jersey, in 1910, and for the next 30 years served intermittently as the pastor of the Ukrainian Presbyterian Church in Newark and as a professor at the seminary in Bloomfield. He also traveled extensively, organizing Protestant parishes throughout North America. In 1922 he was a cofounder of the Ukrainian Evangelical Alliance of North America, an organization he headed for several years. In 1935 he moved to Kolomyia, where he was consecrated a bishop and chosen head of the Ukrainian Evangelical Reformed church in Western Ukraine. After the war Kuziv worked among the displaced persons in Germany as a representative of the World Council of Churches. He wrote numerous articles on religious themes and is the subject of a biography by L. Bykovsky (1966).

Kuzma, Liubomyr [Kuz'ma, Ljubomyr], b 24 May 1913 in Galicia. Neorealist painter. Having studied with W. Lam, he enrolled in 1938 in the Warsaw Academy of Fine

Arts. Since 1949 he has resided in the United States and participated in the exhibitions of the Ukrainian Artists' Association there, and in exhibitions organized by American museums. Kuzma directs an art school for young people in New York. Most of his work – still lifes, landscapes, and portraits – is done in tempera.

Kuzma, Oleksa [Kuz'ma], b 1875 in Galicia, d 1941 in Lviv. Journalist. He was a longtime contributor and member of the editorial board of the newspaper *Dilo* (1902–38) and the editor of *Svoboda* (1922–38), the official organ of the Ukrainian National Democratic Alliance (from 1925). A captain of the Ukrainian Galician Army (UHA) during the struggle for Ukrainian independence, he wrote the monograph *Lystopadovi dni 1918 r.* (The Days of November 1918, 1931; repr, 1960), an account of the Ukrainian siezure of power in Lviv, and numerous articles and essays on the history of the UHA in *Dilo* and elsewhere. He also published a collection of essays, *Nacherky Oleksy Kuz'my* (Sketches by Oleksa Kuzma, 1902), and several translations of foreign works for the Dilo book series of world literature.

Kuzmenko, Andrii [Kuz'menko, Andrij], b 1903 in Kharkiv gubernia. Biochemist. He studied at the Kharkiv Agricultural Institute with V. Liubymenko, then worked at the Kharkiv Institute of Applied Botany (1928–31) and edited the journal *Visnyk prykladnoï botaniky*. He headed the Department of Physiology at the Kiev Institute of the Tobacco Industry (1931–4) before becoming a professor of physiology at the Kiev Agricultural Institute. Kuzmenko's research, which focused on the exchange of fluids in plants, is summarized in over 60 papers.

Kuzmenko, Petro [Kuz'menko], b 1831 in Ponornytsia, Novhorod Siverskyi county, Chernihiv gubernia, d 1874 at Potitkivskyi khutir, Chernihiv gubernia. Writer and ethnographer. A teacher by vocation, he composed poems in the Romantic style and wrote a novel about peasant life, *Ne tak zhdalosia, da tak sklalosia* (It Did Not Turn Out as Expected, 1861). His literary works and his ethnographic studies appeared in the almanac *Khata*, the journal *Osnova*, and the newspaper *Chernigovskii listok*.

Kuzmovych, Olha [Kuz'movyč, Ol'ha] (née Sheparovych), b 24 November 1917 in Lviv. Journalist and community leader. A graduate of the Higher School of Journalism in Warsaw (1939), she was coeditor of the youth magazine *Doroha* (1942–4). Immigrating to the United States in 1947, she edited the Plast magazines *Molode Zhyttia* (1952–3), *Iunak* (1968–9), and *Plastovyi shliakh* (1980–4), and the 'Plastova vatra' section in *Svoboda* (1964–8). She was also active in *Plast as president of its national executive (1960–3) and president of the Supreme Plast Council (1970–4). A coeditor of the daily *Svoboda*, she has served since 1976 as president of the Association of Ukrainian Journalists in America. She is a member of the Presidium of the Ukrainian American Coordinating Council. Her publications include numerous essays and short stories.

Kuzmovych, Volodymyr [Kuz'movyč], b 30 November 1886 in Bolekhiv, Dolyna county, Galicia, d December 1943? in Utvin, Komi Republic. Political activist, pedagogue, and journalist. He studied mathematics and physics at the University of Vienna before becoming a teacher at a women's seminary and gymnasium. During the First World War, he was arrested by the Russian authorities and deported to Tashkent. After his return to Lviv he lectured at the Lviv (Underground) Ukrainian University (1922–3), then became a school inspector for the Ridna Shkola society. He was the longtime secretary of the Ukrainian Catholic Union and editor of its organ *Meta* (1931–9). He was also a member of the Central Committee of the Ukrainian National Democratic Alliance (UNDO), its general secretary in 1938–9, and an UNDO delegate to the Polish Sejm (1935–8). In 1939 he was arrested during the Soviet occupation of Western Ukraine and exiled to Siberia, where he died in a concentration camp.

Volodymyr Kuzmovych

Kuzmych, Volodymyr [Kuz'myč], b 27 June 1904 in Bakhmach, Chernihiv gubernia, d 4 October 1943? Writer. In the 1920s he was a member of the writers' group *Molodniak. He began publishing in 1925 and wrote the novella *Italiika z Madzhento* (The Italian Woman from Magento, 1927) and 13 story collections, including *Nahan* (The Revolver, 1927), *Khao-Zhen'* (1928), and *Korabli* (Ships, 1931). In his 'industrialization' novels *Kryla* (Wings, 1930) and *Turbiny* (Turbines, 1932) he provided, despite their ideological overtones, insights into the development of the aviation industry in Ukraine and the construction of the Dnieper Hydroelectric Dam and revealed his mastery in writing prose. He also wrote prose for children; eg, the novella *Okean* (The Ocean, 1939).

Kuzmyn, Mykola [Kuz'myn], b 25 May 1881 in Ozirna, Zboriv county, Galicia, d 27 May 1955 in Cleveland. Civic and political leader. In the interwar period Kuzmyn was active in the co-operative movement in the Zboriv region, and president of the Prosvita and Ridna Shkola societies in Ozirna. A member of the Central Committee of the Ukrainian National Democratic Alliance, between 1928 and 1930 he was a delegate from that party to the Polish Senate. He was vice-president of the *Silskyi Hospodar society in Lviv from 1936. In 1939 he was arrested by the Polish authorities and imprisoned in the Bereza Kartuzka concentration camp. After he was released, Kuzmyn fled to the West and eventually immigrated to the United States.

Kuzmyn, Yevhen [Kuz'myn, Jevhen], b 22 October 1871 in Lucerne, Switzerland, d 9 July 1942 in Kazalinsk,

Kzyl-Orda oblast, Kazakh SSR. Art scholar and critic. A graduate of the Kiev Drawing School (1893), he was professor of art history at the Lysenko Music and Drama School in Kiev (1914–25). He wrote studies of Ukrainian art, including studies of Ukrainian kilims, pottery, and Kiev icons, and monographs on painters such as M. Vrubel, T. Shevchenko (1900–11), Yu. Narbut (1927), and O. Murashko. Arrested in 1933, he died in prison.

Kuznetsov, Anatolii [Kuznecov, Anatolij] (pseud: A. Anatolii), b 18 August 1929 in Kiev, d 13 June 1979 in London, England. Russian writer of Jewish origin. He grew up in Kiev and graduated from the Gorky Institute of Literature in Moscow. In 1969 he was granted asylum in London while visiting there. He was the author of two story collections and three novels, the most famous of which was *Babii Iar* (1967; uncensored English trans: *Babi Yar*, 1970), a documentary novel about the mass murders committed by the Nazis at the *Babyn Yar ravine in Kiev.

Kuznetsov, Mykola [Kuznecov], b 14 December 1850 in Stepanivka, Melitopil county, Tavriia gubernia, d 2 March 1929 in Sarajevo, Yugoslavia. Painter. Upon graduating from the St Petersburg Academy of Arts (1879), where he had studied under P. Chistiakov, he traveled in France and Italy. He lectured briefly at the St Petersburg Academy of Arts (1895–7) and then lived in Odessa, where he participated in the exhibitions of the Society of South Russian Artists and the *Peredvizhniki group. His works consist of genre paintings, such as *On a Holiday* (1881), *Hired Labor* (1882), and *After Dinner* (1888), and portraits, including those of P. Tchaikovsky and I. Mechnikov. In 1920 he immigrated to Yugoslavia. L. Chlenova published a monograph on Kuznetsov in 1962.

Hryhorii Kuznevych: marble portrait on a gravestone (1903)

Kuznevych, Hryhorii [Kuznevyč, Hryhorij], b 30 September 1871 in Stare Brusno, Liubachiv county, Galicia, d 9 January 1948 in Hanachivka, Peremyshliany raion, Lviv oblast. Sculptor. After studying at the Lviv School of Industrial Design and J. Markowski's studio, he spent two years (1899–1901) at the Rome Institute of Fine Arts and carved the statues *The First Farmer* (1900) and *The Potter* (1901) there. Returning to Lviv he did the monuments to S. Szczepanowski (1905) and B. Głowacki (1906) at Lychakiv Cemetery in Lviv. His early works include *Fortuna* (1892) for a savings bank and a decorative composition for the Arts Palace in Lviv (1894), both in collaboration with J. Markowski. During his stay in the United States (1907–12) he produced a bust of T. Shevchenko (1908, another in 1914) and designed a monument to Shevchenko for Kiev (1910). Upon his return he carved a number of works in honor of the great poet, including a medallion with an image of Shevchenko, and a bust of M. Lysenko (1914) for the Lysenko Music Society in Lviv.

Kuzyk, Dmytro, b 20 December 1906 in Pechenizhyn, Kolomyia county, Galicia, d 13 March 1982 in Trenton, New Jersey. Journalist and community activist; by profession an engineer. He graduated from the Lviv Polytechnic in 1931. He was a member of the Ukrainian National Democratic Alliance (UNDO) and helped edit its journal *Svoboda*. In 1938 he left UNDO and joined the Front of National Unity. He emigrated to Germany in 1945, where he coedited *Na Chuzhyni* (1946–8). In 1948 he immigrated to the United States. He was the cofounder of the Association of Ukrainian Americans and the editor and publisher of its journal *Nash Holos* from 1972 until his death.

Kuzyk, Stepan, b 7 January 1888 in Galicia, d 1947 in Berchtesgaden, Germany. Lawyer and civic leader. Kuzyk was a director of the Dilo publishing house and a deputy to the Polish Sejm from the Ukrainian National Democratic Alliance (1928–35). During the Second World War he was the director of Tsentrobank in Lviv. For many years he was director of the Audit Union of Ukrainian Co-operatives and an executive member of the Prosvita society.

Kuzyk, Sydir, b 5 January 1885, d 11 May 1925 in Lviv. Agronomist and co-operative activist. He studied agronomy at Cracow University. After graduating (1909) he worked for the Prosvita society as the director of its economic section and then head of the commission that oversaw the society's holdings. He also served as a director of the Provincial Audit Union and the Silskyi Hospodar society. After the First World War he was a founder and director of the Vidbudova commercial trade association. Kuzyk contributed numerous articles on the co-operative movement and other issues (under the pseud Khliborob) to the journals *Ekonomist* and *Samopomich* and the newspaper *Dilo*.

Kvachevsky, Oleksander [Kvačevs'kyj], ?–1890. Legal scholar and lawyer. He took part in drafting the 1864 Russian statutes of judicial institutions, and then worked as a procurator and attorney in the reformed court system. From 1873 he practiced law in Kiev and Poltava. He wrote on Russian procedural and criminal law, law reforms, the new jury courts (*prisiazhnye sudi*), the Lithuanian statute, and the local laws of Chernihiv and Poltava gubernias.

Kvasnytsia, Ivan [Kvasnycja], b 1893 in Galicia. Journalist and political leader. Kvasnytsia was a prominent member of the Ukrainian Social Democratic party and the secretary of its Central Committee. He was a coeditor of the party's organ *Vpered* (1919–21), and a contributor to several socialist newspapers, including *Svit* and *Profesional'nyi visnyk*. Between 1927 and 1935 he was the editor of the journal *Ukraïns'kyi emigrant*. In December 1939 he was arrested by the Soviets. Released in 1955, Kvasnytsia settled in Lviv.

Kvasnytsky, Oleksii [Kvasnyc'kyj, Oleksij], b 25 February 1900 in Lysa Hora, Yelysavethrad county, Kherson gubernia. Physiologist; from 1951 full member of the AN URSR. After graduating from the Kamianets-Podilskyi Agricultural Institute in 1925, he taught for five years at the Vinnytsia Agricultural Tekhnikum. From 1931 he worked at the Poltava Scientific Research Institute of Hog Raising, where in 1937 he became head of the physiology laboratory. From 1936 to 1972 he also chaired a department at the Poltava Agricultural Institute. His research dealt mostly with the physiology of digestion, reproduction, and lactation in farm animals. In 1945 he proposed a method of intervarietal transplantation of zygotes in swine, sheep, and rabbits.

Kvasov, Andrei, b and d ? Russian architect of the 18th century. He came to Ukraine in 1748 and designed the Rozumovsky palaces and park grounds in Kozelets (1744), Hlukhiv (1751–7), and Baturyn (1760s). He also designed the gardens in Adamivka (1748–50s) and, together with I. *Hryhorovych-Barsky, the regimental chancellery (1756) and the Church of the Nativity of the Mother of God in Kozelets (1752–64). He built four stone monuments in Nizhen during the 1760s and the municipal council building in the 1770s. He also designed the chancellery, Trinity Cathedral, palace and grounds of P. Rumiantsev, and several other official buildings in Hlukhiv, most of which have not survived. Kvasov's style combined baroque and classical elements.

Kvetsko, Dmytro [Kvec'ko], b 1935 in Stanyslaviv (now Ivano-Frankivske), Galicia. Human-rights activist. He studied history at Lviv University and worked as a history teacher. In 1967 he was tried for belonging to the *Ukrainian National Front and sentenced to 15 years' imprisonment and 5 years' exile. In 1970 he participated in a mass hunger strike of political prisoners, and in 1977 he made a declaration to the Presidium of the Supreme Soviet of the USSR renouncing his Soviet citizenship.

Kviring, Emmanuil, b 13 September 1888 in Frezental, Samara gubernia, d 26 November 1937. Soviet party and state official of German origin. Before the 1917 Revolution he was the secretary of the Russian Bolshevik faction in the 4th Russian State Duma. As secretary of the Bolsheviks' Katerynoslav ('right') faction in 1918, he advocated the separation of the Katerynoslav region from Ukraine and its unification with the *Donets–Kryvyi Rih Republic. Kviring opposed the establishment of a separate Communist party in Ukraine and, as first secretary of the CP(B)U in 1923–5, he was reluctant to pursue the policy of *Ukrainization and even condemned it. From 1925 he held important USSR government posts. Arrested during the *Yezhov terror, he disappeared without trace. He was posthumously rehabilitated in 1956.

Kvitka. Name of a prominent Cossack family in Slobidska Ukraine. Semen was the captain of Kharkiv regiment (1672), then a regimental judge. His son Hryhorii (ca 1670–1734) was also a colonel of Kharkiv regiment (1713). Ivan (d 1751), Hryhorii's son, was a colonel of Izium regiment in 1743 and the grandfather of H. *Kvitka-Osnovianenko.

Klyment Kvitka

Hryhorii Kvitka-Osnovianenko

Kvitka, Klyment, b 4 February 1880 in Khmeliv, Poltava gubernia, d 19 September 1953 in Moscow. Noted ethnomusicologist and founder of the sociological approach in the study of Ukrainian music. After studying law at Kiev University (1897–1902), he worked as a lawyer until 1917 in Tbilisi, Kiev, and elsewhere in Ukraine, and published a two-volume study on electoral rights (St Petersburg 1906). At the same time he avidly pursued his lifelong metier of transcribing and publishing folk songs and music he collected throughout Ukraine. In 1907 he married the writer Lesia *Ukrainka. He transcribed and edited a two-volume collection of 229 folk melodies sung by his wife (Kiev 1917–18). In September 1917 he became a member of the Music Division of the Arts Administration of the UNR Secretariat of Education. In 1918 he became a professor at the Lysenko Music and Drama Institute in Kiev.

Under Soviet rule, he became the deputy head of the Ethnographic Section of the VUAN Ukrainian Scientific Society in 1920. He founded the VUAN Cabinet of Musical Ethnography in 1922 and directed it until 1933. In 1922 he also published an important collection of 743 Ukrainian folk melodies, 685 of which he himself collected and transcribed. Over 40 of his ethnomusicological works appeared in Kiev during the years 1923–30: a pioneering program for studying the activities and way of life of professional folk bards and musicians in Ukraine (1924) and seminal articles in serials such as *Pervisne hromadianstvo ta ioho perezhytky na Ukraïni*, *Muzyka*, *Etnohrafichnyi visnyk*, *Ukraïna*, *Zapysky Etnohrafichnoho tovarystva*, *Pobut*, and *Zapysky Istorychno filolohichnoho viddilu VUAN*. In 1930 he published a long article about M. Lysenko's folkloric legacy in *Zbirnyk Muzeiu diiachiv nauky ta mystetstva Ukraïny*. He also annotated the 1923–4 seven-volume edition of Lesia Ukrainka's works.

In 1933, during the Stalinist terror, Kvitka was forced to move to Moscow and then was exiled to Karaganda and Alma-Ata in Kazakhstan. In 1936 he was allowed to return to Moscow, where he became an associate of the Music Institute at the conservatory, organized and directed there, from 1937, the Cabinet for the Study of the Musical Creativity of the Peoples of the USSR, and became, in 1940, a member of the Chair of Musical Folklore. After 1930 he published only two brief articles. After his death, his articles about I. Franko as a performer of folk songs and about Lesia Ukrainka's musical-folklore legacy appeared in collections in Kiev in 1956.

Kvitka left behind an archive of almost 6,000 folk songs and 74 scholarly works, totaling 3,364 manuscript pages; they are preserved at the archives of the Cabinet of Folk Music, the Conservatory, the Central Museum of Musical Culture of the USSR (which he founded) in Moscow, and at the AN URSR Institute of Fine Art, Folklore, and Ethnography in Kiev. After Stalin's death, several articles about him were published in Ukraine, particularly in the magazine *Narodna tvorchist' ta etnohrafiia*, but it was not until the 1960s that one of his ethnomusicological works was published again.

BIBLIOGRAPHY

Kvitka, K. *Izbrannye trudy v dvukh tomakh*, ed V. Goshovskii, 2 vols (Moscow 1971, 1973)
Ivanyts'kyi, A. 'Klyment Vasyl'ovych Kvitka (Do 100-richchia z dnia narodzhennia),' *Ukraïns'ke muzykoznavstvo*, 15 (1980)
Kvitka, K. *Vybrani pratsi* (Kiev 1985)

M. Hnatiukivsky

Kvitka-Osnovianenko, Hryhorii [Kvitka-Osnov'janenko, Hryhorij], b 29 November 1778 in Osnova, now a suburb of Kharkiv, d 20 August 1843 in Kharkiv. Writer; cultural and civic figure. At the age of 23 he entered the Kuriazh Monastery, but after serving as a novice for 10 months he returned to secular life. His religiosity remained a constant throughout his life and is evident in his writings. On his initiative the Kharkiv Theater was established in 1812, and he served as its first director. That year he also helped found and headed the Society of Benevolence, which provided aid to indigent children. He was a benefactor of an institute for girls and served as a county marshal of the nobility (1816–28), president of the Kharkiv chamber of the criminal court (1840–3), and curator of the first public book collection in Kharkiv.

Kvitka began writing rather late in his life, first in Russian and then in Ukrainian. His *Malorossiskie anekdoty* (Little Russian Anecdotes) was written in 1820–2 and published in 1822. Being a member of the provincial nobility, which accepted the existing social and political order as unchangeable, Kvitka never raised in his writings the issue of social or national injustice. At first he wrote in the tradition of literary travesty represented by I. *Kotliarevsky, which viewed writing in Ukrainian merely as a pleasant pastime. His first Ukrainian short story, and the first story in modern Ukrainian literature – 'Saldats'kyi patret: Latyns'ka pobrekhen'ka po nashomu rozkazana' (A Soldier's Portrait: A Latin Tall Tale Told in Our Tongue, 1833) – is written à la Kotliarevsky. To some extent his other humorous novelettes – *Parkhymove snidannia* (Parkhym's Breakfast, 1841), *Pidbrekhach* (The Second Matchmaker, 1843), and *Kupovanyi rozum* (Purchased Intelligence, 1842) – belong to the same genre.

Much more important was his collection *Malorossiskie povesti* (Little Russian Novelettes, 2 vols, 1834, 1837), which included 'Marusia,' 'Serdeshna Oksana' (Poor Oksana), 'Shchyra liubov' (True Love), 'Bozhi dity' (God's Children), 'Perekotypole' (The Tumbleweed), and other stories. In them he moved beyond anecdote and travesty and showed that the Ukrainian language can also be used for serious subjects. These tales had a great influence on the subsequent development of Ukrainian literature and won their author the honorary title of the 'father of Ukrainian prose.' Having plots without any social conflict, and characters who are paragons of chastity and piety, Kvitka's serious tales are typical examples of Ukrainian sentimentalism, based on both the literary and the oral tradition. Kvitka's predilection for ethnographic detail left a mark on Ukrainian prose of the 19th and even 20th century. His simple style is attributable to the generally accepted belief that to write in Ukrainian one had to view the subject through the eyes of simple folk.

Kvitka's enduring popularity as a playwright rests on the comedies *Svatannia na Honcharivtsi* (Matchmaking at Honcharivka, 1836), *Shel'menko, volostnoi pysar* (Shelmenko, the District Scribe, 1831), and *Shel'menko-denshchyk* (Shelmenko the Orderly, 1837). He also wrote several comedies in Russian, including *Priezzhii iz stolitsy, ili sumatokha v uezdnom gorode* (The Newcomer from the Capital, or the Hubbub in the County Town, 1840), which some critics consider the precursor of N. Gogol's *Revizor* (The Inspector-General). His most popular work in Russian was the novel *Pan Khaliavskii* (Master Khaliavsky, 1839).

Kvitka's works have appeared in numerous editions. They belong to the Classicist period and are quite free of Romanticism, which was then coming into vogue. His major contribution was to extend the use of the Ukrainian language to 'serious' prose and to promote an interest in ethnography among his literary successors. He also wrote several historical studies of Slobidska Ukraine; most of them were published in the journal *Sovremennik*.

BIBLIOGRAPHY

Chalyi, D. *H.F. Kvitka-Osnov'ianenko (Tvorchist')* (Kiev 1962)
Honchar, O. *Hryhorii Kvitka-Osnov'ianenko: Zhyttia i tvorchist'* (Kiev 1969)
Sulyma-Blokhyn, O. *Kvitka i Kulish: Osnovopolozhnyky ukraïns'koï noveli* (Munich 1969)
Honchar, O. *Hryhorii Kvitka-Osnov'ianenko: Seminarii*, 2nd rev edn (Kiev 1978)
Luts'kyi, Iu. *Dramaturhiia H.F. Kvitky-Osnov'ianenka i teatr* (Kiev 1978)
Zubkov, S. *Hryhorii Kvitka-Osnov'ianenko: Zhyttia i tvorchist'* (Kiev 1978)

I. Koshelivets

Kvitko, Leib, b 15 October 1890 in Holoskiv, Podilia gubernia, d 12 September 1952. Yiddish poet and novelist. Together with the poets D. Hofstein and P. Markish he made up the so-called Kiev lyric triad of Yiddish poets. His poem 'Royter Shturm' (The Red Storm, 1918) was the first Yiddish work about the October Revolution. From 1920 to 1925 Kvitko lived and published in Germany. From 1926 to 1936 he lived in Kharkiv, working as a journal editor, and wrote mostly children's stories and poems. Four collections of his work were translated into Ukrainian and published in 1930–2 and 1958. He was arrested in Moscow in 1949 during one of Stalin's purges and executed with 30 other Yiddish writers. He was posthumously 'rehabilitated' in 1954.

Kvitkovska, Mariia [Kvitkovs'ka, Marija], b 19 February 1915 in Chernivtsi. Community activist and pedagogue; wife of D. *Kvitkovsky. She studied at the University of Chernivtsi before emigrating to Germany in 1941 and to the United States in 1949. She continued her studies at the University of Detroit and was a professor of sociology there from 1962 to 1980. She was the head of the *Ukrainian Gold Cross of America in 1958–82 and since 1982 has been the head of the *World Federation of Ukrainian Women's Organizations.

Denys Kvitkovsky

Mykola Kybalchych

Kvitkovsky, Denys [Kvitkovs'kyj] (pseud: D. Kyrylchuk), b 22 May 1909 in Sherivtsi Dolishni, Bukovyna, d 15 March 1979 in Detroit. Lawyer, editor, and political activist. He became a leading member of the Ukrainian nationalist movement in Bukovyna while still a student at Chernivtsi University. He was the editor of the nationalist weekly **Samostiinist'* (1934–7) and a coeditor of the monthly **Samostiina dumka* (1931–7) in Chernivtsi. Imprisoned for his activities by the Rumanian authorities, he emigrated to Germany in 1940 and joined the executive of the Ukrainian National Alliance in Berlin. In 1949 he immigrated to the United States and started a law practice in Detroit. He was a contributor to *Ukraïns'ke slovo* in Paris and the editor of *Samostiina Ukraïna* in Chicago (1976–9). He was a leading member of the OUN (Melnyk faction) and head of the Leadership of Ukrainian Nationalists in 1977–9. He wrote a number of political essays, including *Natsiia, derzhava, i provid u 'Natsiiokratiï' Mykoly Stsibors'koho* (Nation, State, and Leadership in Mykola Stsiborsky's 'Nationocracy,' 1943) and *Represiï v Ukraïni v svitli mizhnarodnoï konventsiï pro zlochyn genotsydu* (Repressions in Ukraine from the Perspective of the International Convention on Genocide, 1968). He was the coeditor of *Bukovyna: Ïï mynule i suchasne* (Bukovyna: Its Past and Present, 1956).

A. Zhukovsky

Kybalchych, Mykola [Kybal'čyč], b 31 October 1853 in Korop, Chernihiv gubernia, d 15 April 1881 in St Petersburg. Inventor and revolutionary. While studying in St Petersburg at the Institute of Railroad Engineers and then at the Medical-Surgical Academy, he became active in the revolutionary movement and was imprisoned in 1875 in Kiev's Lukianivka Prison. A year after his release in 1878, he organized an explosives laboratory for *Narodnaia Volia. A bomb built by him was used in the assassination of Alexander II in 1881. He was arrested, tried, and executed at the Peter and Paul Fortress in St Petersburg. While awaiting execution he wrote a letter to the Academy of Sciences outlining his design of a rocket-propelled aircraft capable of rising beyond earth's atmosphere. This is the first recorded proposal of its kind. Kybalchych developed the idea of jet propulsion, theoretically and experimentally, before his imprisonment, but did not work out the details. Though simple, his ideas are basic to space technology. A crater on the far side of the moon has been named after him.

Kybalchych-Kozlovska, Nadiia [Kybal'čyč-Kozlovs'ka], b 8 May 1878 in Yasnohorod, Volhynia gubernia, d 19 September 1914 in Poltava gubernia. Writer; the daughter of M. *Nomys. She began publishing poems and stories in 1899 in *Literaturno-naukovyi vistnyk*. During 1905–13 she lived in Italy and Austria with her husband and corresponded with Lesia Ukrainka. A collection of her poems (1913) and two collections of her stories (1914) were published in Kiev.

Kyi [Kyj]. Semi-legendary prince of the Polianians who, according to the Rus' Primary Chronicle, together with his brothers Shchek and Khoryv and his sister Lybed, founded the city of Kiev, which was named after him. The chronicle rejects another account that referred to him as a ferryman on the Dnieper River and relates that he had been received by the Byzantine emperor and later tried to establish the town of Kyievets on the Danube before returning to Kiev, where he died. On the basis of the legend told in the Primary Chronicle, archeological digs conducted in Kiev in 1908 uncovered traces of settlements and fortifications. Some historians believe that Kyi lived in the early 6th century and did in fact maintain contact with the Byzantine emperor and attempt to extend his rule to the Danube.

Kyiak, Hryhorii [Kyjak, Hryhorij], b 2 January 1910 in Vynnyky, Lviv county, Galicia. Agronomist; corresponding member of the AN URSR since 1951. He finished his studies at the Lviv Polytechnical Institute in 1934 and since 1944 has directed the Chair of Crop and Meadow Culture at Lviv University. He received his doctorate in agronomy in 1956 and headed a department of the AN URSR Institute of Agrobiology (1951–60). Kyiak's scholarly works deal with crop cultivation, selective breeding, and meadow cultures. He has successfully bred several hybrids, including Halytska winter wheat, Dublianka 4 spring wheat, Lviv winter rye, and the Korychnevi feed beans. He is the author of two textbooks: *Roslynnytstvo* (Crop Cultivation, 1964) and *Lukivnytstvo* (Meadow Culture, 1976).

Kyianytsia, Petro [Kyjanycja], b ? d 1933. Member of the Ukrainian Communist party and later of the CP(B)U. Kyianytsia worked with the historical sections of the All-Ukrainian Academy of Sciences and the All-Ukrainian

Association of Marxist-Leninist Scientific Research Institutes. He specialized in modern history. In July 1933 he was arrested and shot for belonging to the fictitious Bloc of Ukrainian Nationalist Parties.

Kyidramte or **Kiev Drama Theater.** An experimental theater company formed by L. *Kurbas in May 1920 from among the members of the Shevchenko First Theater of the Ukrainian Soviet Republic, who left the latter as a result of artistic differences with the director, O. *Zaharov. Kyidramte's 36 members included Kurbas, D. Antonovych, H. Babiivna, L. Boloban, Ya. Bortnyk, V. Vasylko, L. Hakkebush, P. Dolyna, P. Haivoronsky, H. Ihnatovych, V. Kalyn, F. Lopatynsky, R. Neshchadymenko, A. Smereka, V. Chystiakova, S. Levchenko, K. Hrai, O. Lypkivsky, and L. Predslavych. The company organized an acting studio and courses in directing. For a year and a half it toured the Bila Tserkva and Uman areas, performing for Red Army units and public audiences; from April to July 1921 it performed in Kharkiv as the 'Ukrainian State Exemplary Theater' under the egis of the People's Commissariat of Education. Kyidramte's repertoire included plays originally performed by Kurbas's *Molodyi Teatr theater in 1917–18: *Vertep* and Ukrainian versions of F. Grillparzer's *Weh dem, der lügt*, Sophocles' *Oedipus Rex*, and M. Halbe's *Jugend*; the first Ukrainian production of Shakespeare's *Macbeth*, with Kurbas in his last stage role; C. Goldoni's *Mirandolina*; *Haidamaky* (The Haidamakas), based on T. Shevchenko's poem; *Novyi redaktor* (The New Editor), based on a story by Mark Twain; plays by N. Gogol, M. Kropyvnytsky, and one-act études by O. Oles and S. Vasylchenko. In July 1921 the company fell apart because of a famine in Kharkiv. Most of its actors joined Kurbas's new *Berezil theater in March 1922.

V. Revutsky

Kyiv. See Kiev.

Kyïv (Kiev). A bimonthly journal of literature, scholarship, art, criticism, and community life published in Philadelphia from 1950 to 1964. Edited and published by B. *Romanenchuk, its contributors included M. Andrusiak, S. Hordynsky, O. Dombrovsky, V. Doroshenko, R. Klymkevych, P. Kovaliv, M. Kushnir, H. Luzhnytsky, M. Ostroverkha, O. Tarnavsky, V. Chaplenko, and I. Shankovsky. It was an important forum for contemporary Ukrainian prose and poetry and translations of world literature. It was especially known for its literary criticism and reviews. Several valuable memoirs were published in it, including those of V. Blavatsky and H. Nychka.

Kyïv (Kiev). A journal of arts, literature, and politics published in Kiev in 1978–82 by the Radianskyi Pysmennyk press. The editor in chief was Yu. Bedzyk, and the editorial board consisted of P. Zahrebelny, Yu. Zbanatsky, B. Oliinyk, and P. Osadchuk. It contained original works by Ukrainian writers, art reproductions, literary criticism, publicistic works, and news of the Kiev literary scene. It served as a forum for works on or about the city of Kiev, publishing articles such as P. Biletsky's review of paintings and etchings of Kiev and H. Ivakin's article on the libraries of ancient Kiev. The journal published poetry by I. Drach, V. Kolomiiets, M. Nahnybida, B. Oliinyk, P. Perebyinis, M. Upenyk, V. Shvets, and P. Voronko; prose by Ye. Hutsalo, I. Senchenko, and V. Zemliak; and literary criticism and humor. In 1983, a monthly journal with a similar profile began publication under the same title.

Kyïv (Kiev). A monthly journal of literature, the arts, politics, and community affairs. It is the official organ of the Writers' Union of Ukraine and of the Kiev Writers' Organization. Published since 1983 in Kiev by the Radianskyi Pysmennyk publishing house, it is a forum for the latest works by Kievan writers, including poetry, prose, publicistic works, criticism, art history, essays, and memoirs. It has a children's and a humor section. The editor in chief was initially V. Drozd, but he was replaced by P. Perebyinis in March 1986. The editorial board has included some of the most influential and popular writers and critics in Ukraine today, such as M. Vinhranovsky, D. Holovko, Ye. Hutsalo, M. Zhulynsky, P. Zahrebelny, D. Mishchenko, Yu. Mushketyk, Yu. Shcherbak, D. Pavlychko, and Yu. Serdiuk. Most of these people are also regular contributors to the journal. An important feature in the journal is its translations into modern Ukrainian of several historical sources, including the *Kiev Chronicle and the Cossack chronicle of S. *Velychko (by Valerii Shevchuk).

Kyïvs'ka pravda (Kiev Truth). The official organ of the Kiev oblast CPU and the oblast and city soviets in Kiev. It has been published every weekday since 28 October 1943. Earlier organs of the Kiev oblast or city Party organization included *Golos sotsial-demokrata* and *Proletarskaia mysl'* (1917), *Kievskii kommunist* (1918–19), *Kommunist* (1919–21), and *Proletars'ka pravda* (1921–41), which was published in Russian until 1925.

Kylymnyk, Oleh, b 26 July 1913 in Yampil, Kiev gubernia. Soviet literary scholar. A graduate of the Odessa Pedagogical Institute, he completed graduate work at the AN URSR Institute of Literature in 1948 and worked there as a learned secretary and senior scholarly associate. From 1949 to 1960 he also directed the Chair of Literature at the CC CPU Higher Party School and then directed the Chair of Editing Theory and Practice at the Ukrainian Printing Institute before becoming the director of the Chair of Literature at the Kiev Institute of Culture. He has written many articles about Soviet Ukrainian literature, books about A. Holovko, O. Honchar, H. Epik, O. Kopylenko, and Yu. Yanovsky, and a monograph about Soviet Ukrainian literature, *Romantyka pravdy* (The Romanticism of Truth, 1964). Seven collections of his literary criticism have also been published.

Kylymnyk, Stepan, b 5 January 1890 in Yakushyntsi, Vinnytsia county, Podilia gubernia, d 9 May 1963 in Toronto. Ethnographer and publicist. Kylymnyk studied history and ethnography at the Vinnytsia Pedagogical Institute and at Kharkiv University. In the interwar period he worked for the Commissariat of Education of the Ukrainian SSR. He moved to Galicia in 1943 and in 1949 emigrated to Canada. He is the author of *Ukraïns'kyi rik u narodnykh zvychaiakh v istorychnomu osvitlenni* (Folk Customs of the Ukrainian Calendar Year in Historical Perspective, 5 vols, 1955–62) and numerous popular articles on history and ethnography in such journals as *Novi dni* and *Porohy*.

Kymbarovsky, Mykhailo [Kymbarovs'kyj, Myxajlo], b 15 December 1897 in Katerynoslav (now Dnipropetrovske), d 5 November 1966 in Dnipropetrovske. Physician. A graduate of the Dnipropetrovske Medical Institute (1923), Kymbarovsky was a professor of surgery at the Ivanovo (1935–44) and Dnipropetrovske (1944–66) medical institutes. He wrote a number of works dealing with the surgical treatment of groin ruptures, stomach resection, and the use of Filatov pedicles for the surgical treatment of cleft palate.

Yurii Kyporenko-Domansky Vitalii Kyreiko

Kyporenko-Domansky, Yurii [Kyporenko-Domans'kyj, Jurij], b 24 March 1888 in Kharkiv, d 6 August 1955 in Kiev. Opera singer (dramatic tenor). He made his debut with O. Sukhodolsky's troupe in 1907, then worked with the companies of P. Saksahansky and D. Haidamaka. After singing with Russian companies in Moscow (1913–17) and Saratov (1918–21), he returned to Ukraine, where he performed with the Odessa and Kharkiv operas before becoming a permanent soloist at the Kiev Theater of Opera and Ballet in 1939. His main roles included José in Bizet's *Carmen*; the title roles in R. Wagner's *Lohengrin, Tristan und Isolde,* and *Tannhäuser*, and G. Verdi's *Othello*; and Andrii in *Taras Bulba* and Taras in *Christmas Night*, both by M. Lysenko.

Kypriian, Myron [Kyprijan], b 27 July 1930 in Lviv. Stage designer. A graduate of the Lviv Institute of Applied and Decorative Art (1954), where he studied with V. Manastyrsky, Kypriian first worked in the Lviv Puppet Theater, and in 1957 was appointed chief set designer of the Lviv Ukrainian Drama Theater. He designed the sets for classics of Ukrainian drama such as an adaption of T. Shevchenko's *Haidamaky* (Haidamakas, 1964), I. Tobilevych's *Khaziaïn* (The Master, 1970), and I. Franko's *Ukradene shchastia* (Stolen Happiness, 1976); for Soviet plays such as M. Zarudny's *Veselka* (The Rainbow, 1958), I. Kocherha's *Im'ia* (Name, 1959), O. Levada's *Favst i smert'* (Faust and Death, 1960), and M. Kulish's *Maklena Grassa* (1966); and for European plays such as E. Remarque's *Die letzte Station* (1958), H. Lovinescu's *Citadela sfărîmată* (The Crumbling Citadel, 1961), W. Shakespeare's *Romeo and Juliet* (1964, at the Lviv Young Spectator's Theater), *King Lear* (1969), and *Richard III* (1974), A. Fredro's *Damy i huzary* (Ladies and Hussars, 1976), and an adaptation of G. Boccaccio's *Decameron* (1982).

Kyrchiv, Bohdan [Kyrčiv], b 12 June 1856 in Korchyn, Stryi county, Galicia, d 19 October 1900 in Dovhe, Stryi county. Writer. In the 1880s and 1890s his poetry and stories appeared in *Zoria* and other Galician periodicals. He also translated Russian and German plays that were staged in Galicia. Some of his poems were put to music by O. Nyzhankivsky and V. Matiuk.

Kyrchiv, Roman [Kyrčiv], b 14 April 1930 in Korchyn, Sokal county, Galicia. Ethnographer and literary scholar. He is chairman of the Ethnography Department of the Lviv branch of the AN URSR Institute of Fine Arts, Folklore, and Ethnography. A specialist in the history of the theater in Western Ukraine and on the work of P. Saksahansky, I. Rubchak, and Y. Stadnyk, Kurchiv has written such works as *Komediï Ivana Franka* (The Comedies of Ivan Franko, 1961), *Ukraïnika v pol's'kykh al'manakhakh doby romantyzmu* (Ucrainica in Polish Almanacs of the Romantic Period, 1965), *Ukraïns'kyi fol'klor u pol's'kii literaturi* (Ukrainian Folklore in Polish Literature, 1971), and *Etnohrafichne doslidzhennia Boikivshchyny* (Ethnographic Research on the Boiko Region, 1978).

Kyrdan, Borys, b 25 September 1922 in Hanno-Leontovycheve, Kherson gubernia. Folklorist; literary scholar. A graduate of Moscow University (1951), in 1953 he joined the Institute of World Literature of the USSR Academy of Sciences in Moscow. At present, he chairs the Department of Russian Literature at Moscow Pedagogical Institute. Noted for his thorough use of archival materials, his chief works are *Ukrainskie narodnye dumy XV–nach. XVII v.* (Ukrainian Folk Dumas of the 15th–Early 17th Centuries, 1962), *Ukrainskii narodnyi epos* (The Ukrainian Folk Epos, 1965), and *Sobirateli narodnoi poezii: Iz istorii ukrainskoi fol'kloristiki XIX v.* (Collectors of Folk Poetry: From the History of Ukrainian Folklore Studies, 19th Century, 1974). He also coauthored *Narodni spivtsi-muzykanty na* Ukraïni (Folk Bards-Musicians in Ukraine, 1980) and compiled the collection *Ukrainskie narodnye dumy* (Ukrainian Folk Dumas, 1972).

Kyreiko, Vitalii [Kyrejko, Vitalij], b 23 December 1926 in Shyroke, Dnipropetrovske oblast. Composer and pedagogue. Upon graduating in 1949 from the Kiev Conservatory, where he studied with L. Revutsky, he became a lecturer there. He has written the operas *Forest Song*, an adaptation of the play by Lesia Ukrainka (1957), *On Sunday Morning She Gathered Herbs*, an adaptation of the novelette by O. Kobylianska (1966), and *Marko in Hell* (1966); the ballets *Shadows of Forgotten Ancestors*, an adaptation of the novelette by M. Kotsiubynsky (1960), *The Witch* (1967), and *The Orgy* (1977), based on the play by Lesia Ukrainka; a choral cantata for male voice in memory of M. Kropyvnytsky (libretto by M. Rylsky, 1965); concertos for cello and orchestra (1961) and for violin and orchestra (1967); and piano variations on the themes of L. Revutsky (1952). He has also written a number of symphonies, overtures, string quartets, and piano, choir, and solo voice compositions to the words of T. Shevchenko, I. Franko, Lesia Ukrainka, and others, and several arrangements of folk songs and music.

Kyrnarsky, Marko [Kyrnars'kyj], b 23 May 1893 in Pohar, Briansk county, Orel gubernia, Russia, d 1941 in Leningrad. Graphic artist. A student of Yu. *Narbut, in

1920–3 he worked in Kiev as a book designer. He designed the covers for T. Shevchenko's *Kobzar* (1921) and *Persha v'iazochka bublykiv* (The First String of Rolls, 1921), a frontispiece for the journal *Grono* (1920), and the cover for the journal *Shliakhy mystetstva* (1922). Moving to Leningrad in 1923, he continued to work for Ukrainian publishers, designing such books as the works of T. Shevchenko, I. Tobilevych (6 vols, 1929–31), and M. Kotsiubynsky (1929). He also designed Russian books such as E. Gollerbakh's *Syluety Narbuta* (Narbut's Silhouettes, 1926) and A. Blok's *Neizdannye Stikhotvoreniia, 1897–1919* (Unpublished Poems, 1897–1919, 1926). In 1928 E. Gollerbakh published a monograph on Kyrnarsky's graphic art.

Kyrnasivka. Town smt (1979 pop 6,000) in Tulchyn raion, Vinnytsia oblast. It was first mentioned in the early 18th century as the town of Krasnopilia. It has two sugar refineries and plants producing reinforced-concrete structures and asphalt.

Kyrychenko, Fedir [Kyryčenko], b 1 March 1904 in Vladyslavka, Kaniv county, Kiev gubernia. Agricultural biologist; full member of the All-Union Academy of Agricultural Sciences since 1956. A graduate of the Maslivka Institute of Selection and Seeding (1928), he was an associate of the Odessa Institute of Selection and Seeding from 1944, serving as its director in 1954–69. Kyrychenko's research has focused on the seeding of grain crops. He developed a number of methods for hybridization with free fertilization and for selecting crops according to the strength of their root systems. Under his direction, the Odessa institute developed several new varieties of high-yield and cold- and drought-resistant winter wheat. Kyrychenko also developed new varieties of hard winter wheat for the steppes; his Odessa Jubilee yields 35–40 centners of grain per ha.

Kyrychenko, Illia [Kyryčenko, Illja], b 19 July 1889 in Riabukhy, Konotip county, Chernihiv gubernia, d 13 July 1955 in Kiev. Lexicographer; corresponding member of the AN URSR from 1951. A graduate of the Nizhen Institute (1914), from 1918 he worked as a teacher in Lubni and Kiev. In 1931 he joined the AN URSR Institute of Linguistics, becoming the director of its dictionary department in 1946. From 1936 he was also a professor of classical philology at Kiev University. Kyrychenko wrote or compiled over 40 lexicographic works and edited many others. He was the author of the institute's Ukrainian dictionary of medical terminology (1936); co-compiler of its Russian-Ukrainian dictionary (1948); the chief editor of its Ukrainian-Russian dictionary (6 vols, 1953–63; vols 2–6 published posthumously) and Ukrainian-Russian dictionary of personal names (1954); coauthor of the official Soviet Ukrainian orthography of 1946; and author of several editions of a Soviet Ukrainian orthographic dictionary from 1946, the fullest being the 1955 edition. He also founded and edited the first five issues of the AN URSR serial *Leksykohrafichnyi biuleten'* (1951–5).

Kyrychenko, Oleksii [Kyryčenko, Oleksij], b 25 February 1908 in Chornobaivka khutir, near Kherson, d 29 December 1975 in Moscow. Soviet party and state official. He worked in the CC CP(B)U apparat from 1938 and as a political officer in the armed forces during the Second World War. He was second secretary of the CC CPU (1949–53). After J. Stalin's death he was the first Ukrainian head of the CC CPU (1953–7), member of the CC CPU Presidium (1952–7), and candidate member (1953–5) and full member (1955–60) of the CC CPSU Presidium. N. Khrushchev's protégé and a very influential member of the CPSU secretariat, he was demoted in 1960.

Kyrychenko, Stepan [Kyryčenko], b 9 April 1911 in Chopovychi, Radomyshl county, Kiev gubernia. Monumentalist painter and mosaicist. A graduate of the Kiev State Art Institute (1949), where he studied with F. Krychevsky, S. Naliepinska-Boichuk, and M. Rokytsky, he prefers to do mosaics and often collaborates with N. Klein. He took part in painting the main pavilion and the Ukrainian pavilion at the Exhibition of Economic Achievements of the USSR in Moscow in 1955. With N. Klein he made mosaics such as *The Harvest* (1957), *Our Duma, Our Song* (1960), *A Hutsul Melody* (1963), *Shevchenko* (a triptych by N. Klein and S. and R. Kyrychenko, 1964), and *Ukraine* (1969). An album of Kyrychenko and Klein's works was published in 1970.

Kyrylenko, Ivan, b 2 December 1902 in Viazivok, Katerynoslav gubernia, d 20 October 1939? Socialist-realist writer. In the 1920s he belonged to the writers' groups *Pluh and the All-Ukrainian Association of Proletarian Writers. He began publishing in 1923 and wrote several story collections; the novellas *Kursy* (Courses, 1927), *Kucheriavi dni* (Luxuriant Days, 1928), *Natysk* (Pressure, 1930), *Pereshykhtovka* (The Shift Change, 1932), and *Avanposty* (Outposts, 1933); and the novel *Vesna* (Spring, 1936). A member of the presidium of the Writers' Union of Ukraine, he was arrested and disappeared during the Yezhov terror. A book of his selected works was published in 1960 in Kiev.

Yevhen Kyryliuk

Kyryliuk, Yevhen [Kyryljuk, Jevhen], b 18 March 1902 in Warsaw. Slavist and literary critic; professor at Kiev University from 1944 and corresponding member of the AN URSR from 1957. A graduate of the Kiev Institute of People's Education (1926), he became an associate of the AN URSR Institute of Literature; from 1944 he headed its Department of Shevchenko Studies. A prominent specialist in 19th-century Ukrainian literature, he has written books on P. Kulish (1929) (and compiled a bibliography of his works [1929]), P. Myrny (1930, 1939), T. Shevchenko (1951), I. Franko (1956, 1966), Lesia Ukrainka

(1966), V. Karadžić and Ukrainian literature (1978), and I. Kotliarevsky (1969, 1982). He has also written the studies *Ukraïns'ki pys'mennyky – revoliutsiini demokraty i literatury zakhidnykh i pivdennykh slov'ians'kykh narodiv u XIX stolitti* (Ukrainian Writers – Revolutionary Democrats and the Literatures of the West and South Slavic Peoples in the 19th Century, 1963) and *Ukraïns'kyi romantyzm u typolohichnomu zistavlenni z literaturamy zakhidno- i pivdennoslov'ians'kykh narodiv* (Ukrainian Romanticism in Typological Comparison with the Literatures of the Western and Southern Slavic Peoples, 1973). A study of Ukrainian literature (1945) he wrote with S. Maslov was harshly criticized as 'nationalist' and banned. He was also the editor in chief of the complete edition of Shevchenko's works (6 vols, 1963–4) and the Shevchenko dictionary (2 vols, 1976–7). Collections of his literary articles were published in 1969, 1972, and 1977.

I. Koshelivets

Kyrylivka. See Shevchenkove.

Kyrylivska settlement. A late paleolithic archeological site discovered on Kyrylivska (now Frunze) Street in Kiev. It was excavated by V. Khvoika and Ya. Armashevsky in 1893–1903. They found two archeological strata. The lower stratum, from the early Magdalenian period, contained traces of fires, flint implements, piles of mammoth bones, some of them with ornamental carvings, and other animal bones. The upper stratum, from the late Magdalenian period, yielded implements, the bones of bears, lions, wolves, and gluttons, and petrified coal. The bones were used to build shelters.

Kyrylo Kozhumiaka [Kožum'jaka]. A mythical dragon slayer in Ukrainian folk legends dating from the time of Kievan Rus'. Numerous tales about him were written down in the 19th and 20th centuries. As a symbol of the might of the Ukrainian people, he was endowed with tremendous physical strength, which enabled him to kill in a duel the dragon (ie, Asiatic hordes) that had conquered Kiev, thus freeing the Kievan lands from rendering tribute (in the form of human sacrifice) and a princess from certain death. Variations of the legend have connected the locale of Kozhumiaky in Kiev and the ancient Zmiiovi Valy ('Dragon's Ramparts') south of Kiev with the legend. The figure of Kyrylo Kozhumiaka was re-created in the works of O. Oles, P. Tychyna, I. Kocherha, and other writers.

Kyselivka (also known as Zamkova Hora and Florivska Hora). A hill rising above the Podil district of Kiev on the right bank of the Dnieper River. Excavations at the end of the 19th century uncovered traces of a settlement from the period of the *Trypilian culture (3rd millennium BC), one from the early Iron Age (5th–4th centuries BC), and another from the early Slavic period of the Zarubyntsi culture. Scholars believe that the founder of Kiev, *Kyi, had a residence there. Archeologists discovered that in the period of Kievan Rus' a princely palace stood on the hill and that the vicinity was inhabited by merchants and artisans who manufactured bone, clay, copper, bronze, and iron articles. In the 1470s a large wooden castle was built there for the Lithuanian palatine (hence the name Zamkova Hora [Castle Hill]), and the Podil became the administrative center of Kiev. In the mid-17th century the hill came to be known as Kyselivka after the Polish palatine A. *Kysil. The castle was destroyed by rebellious Cossacks in 1651. From 1816 a cemetery existed there. In the mid-19th century the hill was acquired by the St Florus Women's Monastery (hence the name Florivska Hora [Florus's Hill]).

Kyselov (Kiselev), Leonid [Kysel'ov] (Kiseljov), b 1946 in Kiev, d October 1968 in Kiev. Poet. The son of a Russian writer, he began writing in Russian in 1959 and published his first poems in the journal *Novyi mir* in 1963. His Shevchenko-like negative portrayal of Peter I and the Russian tsars in general in his poem 'Tsari' (The Tsars, 1963) elicited indignant hostility from Russian chauvinist circles. His critically acclaimed Russian and Ukrainian verse was published in two bilingual collections: *Stikhi – Virshi* (Poems, 1970) and *Poslednaia pesnia – Ostannia pisnia* (The Last Song, 1979). His Ukrainian poems show the influence of T. Shevchenko and the early P. Tychyna. Kyselov's switch from writing in Russian to writing in Ukrainian in the last years before his death from leukemia was an exception to recent trends.

Kyselov, Oleksander [Kysel'ov], b 29 March 1903 in Satanivka, Podilia gubernia, d 24 February 1967 in Kiev. Literary critic. After completing graduate studies at Kiev University (1936), he worked as a senior scholar at the AN URSR Institute of Literature. His first essay was published in 1926. He wrote books on P. Hrabovsky (1940, 1948, 1951, and 1959) and coauthored a book about I. Franko (1956) with O. Biletsky and I. Bass.

Kyselov, Yosyp [Kysel'ov, Josyp], b 15 March 1905 in Shyraivka, near Briansk, Russia, d 3 June 1980 in Kiev. Writer and literary critic. His first collection of poetry was published in Russian in 1928. After the Second World War, his writing consisted mainly of literary and dramatic criticism, which was published in several collections, including *Konflikty i kharaktery* (Conflicts and Characters, 1953), *Teatral'ni portrety* (Theatrical Portraits, 1955), *Epichna poeziia* (Epic Poetry, 1958), *Dramaturhy Ukraïny* (Ukraine's Playwrights, 1967), *Razom z zhyttiam* (Together with Life, 1972), and *Maistry teatral'noï literatury* (Masters of Theatrical Literature, 1976).

Kyshka or **Kishka, Lev** [Kyška] (secular name: Luka), b 1663 (1668 according to other sources) in Kovel, Volhynia, d 1728 in Volodymyr-Volynskyi, Volhynia. Uniate metropolitan of Kiev. After his ordination he studied at the Collegium Propaganda Fide in Rome (1687–91). He was protoarchimandrite of the Basilian order in 1703–13 and consecrated bishop of Volodymyr and Berestia in 1711. As bishop he proved to be an able administrator and organizer of religious education; among other schools he founded a theological seminary in Volodymyr-Volynskyi. In 1714 he was elected metropolitan of Kiev. His most important act as metropolitan was the organization of the *Synod of Zamostia in 1720, which ratified several reforms in the organization and creed of the Uniate church. His works include *O Sakramentakh* (About the Holy Sacraments, 1697), a Polish translation of the sermons of Metropolitan I. Potii (1714), and a book about the Zamostia Synod, published in Rome in Latin (1724). His correspondence with the Vatican was published by A. Velyky (Welykyj) in 1959.

Kyshynivsky, Solomon [Kyšynivs'kyj], b 1862 in Odessa, d 1942 in Odessa. Painter. He studied at the Odessa School of Painting (1879–83) and at art academies in Munich, Paris, and Rome. His early genre paintings were influenced by the *Peredvizhniki – eg, *The Request* (1889), *A Morning in the Cold* (1897), *The Quarrel* (1904), and *The Card Game* (1906) – but later his work became more impressionistic. He joined the Association of Revolutionary Art of Ukraine in 1925 and the Union of Contemporary Artists of Ukraine in 1934 and participated in their exhibitions. In 1927–9 he painted a series of three works about the Revolution of 1905: *The Revolt on the Battleship Potemkin, The Final Minutes of Matiushenko,* and *Lieutenant Shmidt Bids His Son Farewell.*

Adam Kysil

Kysil, Adam [Kysil'], b 1600, d 3 May 1653. Ukrainian statesman and diplomat in the Polish Commonwealth. Kysil was born into a prominent Orthodox noble family in Volhynia. He was educated at the Zamostia Academy, where he befriended the famous Polish statesman T. Zamoyski, who later helped him in his political and diplomatic career. From 1617 he served in the military, gaining prominence for his successes in the Polish wars with the Ottoman Empire, Muscovy, and Sweden. He also gained a reputation at the court as an effective negotiator. He was sent as the envoy of King Zygmunt III to the Kiev Church Synod of 1629, which had been convened to reconcile the Orthodox and Uniate churches. In local dietines and in the Diet, he defended the interests and rights of the Orthodox church, although he was always able to maintain close contacts with Uniate and Roman Catholic leaders, despite the atmosphere of distrust that existed at the time. In 1637 he was sent to negotiate an end to the Cossack rebellion led by P. Pavliuk, but Poland later reneged on the agreements and ruthlessly repressed the Cossacks. From 1649, he was one of the central figures in the negotiations to end the uprising led by B. Khmelnytsky. He helped conclude the agreements reached in Pereiaslav (February 1649), Zboriv (August 1649), and Bila Tserkva (September 1651), and tried to find a compromise between the Poles and the Cossacks. Following the signing of the Treaty of *Bila Tserkva, he was appointed voivode of Kiev to supervise the implementation of the terms of the agreement. During his career, Kysil received many honors and was appointed to a variety of administrative posts: castellan of Chernihiv (1639), senator (1641), castellan of Kiev and Bratslav voivodeships (1646), and Kievan voivode. He was able to use his positions to amass a great fortune and became one of the richest men in Ukraine with large estates in Volhynia, Kiev, and Chernihiv voivodeships. He was buried in his family's church in Nyzkynychi, Volhynia. A supporter of the political and social system of the Polish Commonwealth, Kysil strove unsuccessfully to find a compromise between the Orthodox and the Uniates, and between the Polish government and the Zaporozhian Host.

BIBLIOGRAPHY

Sysyn, F. *Between Poland and Ukraine: The Dilemma of Adam Kysil, 1600–1653* (Cambridge, Mass 1985)

A. Zhukovsky

Kysil, Oleksander [Kysil'] (pen name of O. Kyselov), b 27 March 1889 in Krasylivka, Chernihiv gubernia, d 28 November 1942? Theater critic and pedagogue. He developed an interest in Ukrainian culture under the influence of M. *Kotsiubynsky. He studied at St Petersburg University (1907–12) and was involved in St Petersburg in the *Philanthropic Society for Publishing Generally Useful and Inexpensive Books. He lectured on the history of Ukrainian theater at Kiev University (1918) and the Kiev Music and Drama Institute (from 1922), directed the Theater Section of the VUAN Institute of the Ukrainian Language, and was a senior associate of the VUAN Museum of Theater. He is the author of the popular studies *Ukraïns'kyi vertep* (The Ukrainian *Vertep* Theater, 1918) and *Shliakhy rozvytku ukraïns'koho teatru* (The Paths of Development of Ukrainian Theater, 1920); the monographs *Ukraïns'kyi teatr* (Ukrainian Theater, 1925) and *Karpo Solenyk* (1928); and articles on the history of theater and reviews in Soviet Ukrainian periodicals. He was arrested during the Stalinist terror in 1937 and his further fate is unknown. A collection of his selected works, many of them abridged, was published in Kiev in 1968.

Olena Kysilevska; portrait by M. Dmytrenko

Kysilevska, Olena [Kysilevs'ka] (née Simenovych; pseuds: O. Halychanka, Kalyna, Neznana), b 24 March 1869 in Monastyryska, Buchach county, Galicia, d 29 March 1956 in Ottawa. Editor, community activist, and writer. She became active in the Ukrainian women's movement as a gymnasium student in Stanyslaviv when she joined the Society of Ruthenian Women organized by N. *Kobrynska in 1884. She began publishing short stories and articles on education and women's rights in almanacs and journals in 1910, and from 1912 she edited a women's page in the newspaper *Dilo*. During the First

World War she was a member of the Red Cross relief committee for prisoners and the wounded in Vienna. After the war she became a member of the executive of the Union of Ukrainian Women in Lviv. In 1925–39 she published and edited the semimonthly *Zhinocha dolia* in Kolomyia. She traveled extensively throughout Western Europe and North America (1924), participating in the international women's movement and organizing Ukrainian women's organizations. Several of these trips were described in the travelogues *Lysty z-nad Chornoho moria* (Letters from the Black Sea Coast, 1939) and *Po ridnomu kraiu* (Around My Native Land, 1951). She was an active member of the Ukrainian National Democratic Alliance and was elected to two terms in the Polish Senate (1928–35). From 1935 she headed the women's section of the *Silskyi Hospodar society in Lviv. After fleeing Ukraine during the Second World War, she lived as a displaced person in Western Europe until she immigrated to Canada in 1948 and joined her son V. *Kaye-Kysilewsky. That same year she was elected the first president of the *World Federation of Ukrainian Women's Organizations, a position she held until her death. Her personal archive is now located in the Public Archives of Canada and its holdings are described in a research report, *The Olena Kysilevska Collection* (1985), published by the Canadian Institute of Ukrainian Studies.

B. Balan

Kysilevsky, Kost [Kysilevs'kyj, Kost'], b 23 February 1890 in Roshniv, Tovmach county, Galicia, d 20 September 1974 in Irvington, New Jersey. Linguist and pedagogue; full member of the Shevchenko Scientific Society from 1932 and of the Ukrainian Academy of Arts and Sciences from 1948. A graduate of the Universities of Leipzig and Vienna (PH D 1912), Kysilevsky taught in several gymnasiums and teachers' seminaries in Galicia in the interwar period. He immigrated to Germany in 1944, where he was appointed professor of the Ukrainian Free University in 1945. In 1949 he moved to the United States. His publications include a number of textbooks of Ukrainian, didactic works, and a Ukrainian-Polish-Ukrainian dictionary (compiled with Ye. Hrytsak, 1930–1). His study of the language of the *Hankenstein Codex appeared in *Zapysky Naukovoho tovarystva im. Shevchenka*, vol 161, and his description of the dialects of the Dniester and Prut basins appeared in vol 162. He also proposed a revision of the classification of Ukrainian dialects.

Kysilevsky, Volodymyr. See Kaye-Kysilewsky, Vladimir.

Kytasty, Hryhorii [Kytastyj, Hryhorij], b 17 January 1907 in Kobeliaky, Poltava gubernia, d 6 April 1984 in San Diego, California. Banduryst, composer, and conductor. He studied at the Poltava Musical Tekhnikum (1927–30) and the Lysenko Music and Drama School in Kiev (1930–5, under M. Hrinchenko, L. Revutsky, and V. Kosenko). He was a member of the State Banduryst Kapelle of the Ukrainian SSR from its inception in 1935, serving as concertmaster and assistant artistic director (from 1937). In 1941 Kytasty was conscripted into the Red Army and captured by the Germans. He soon managed to escape and return to Kiev, where he founded and became the first director of the Shevchenko Ukrainian Banduryst Kapelle, which reunited many of the original members of the State Banduryst Kapelle. This group was for a time interned in a Nazi concentration camp, but was subsequently allowed to tour Ukrainian *Ostarbeiter* camps in Western Europe. A displaced person after the war, he performed as a soloist and with the kapelle throughout Western Europe, touring Ukrainian displaced persons camps and organizing bandura classes. He immigrated to the United States in 1949 and settled in Detroit with the entire ensemble, which was renamed the *Ukrainian Bandurist Chorus. He served as the conductor and director of the chorus to 1954, in 1958–9, and from 1967 to his death. Kytasty wrote countless original works and arrangements of folk songs for choir and bandura accompaniment, solo bandura, choir and piano, and bandura orchestra. He also composed several dumas and put the works of various Ukrainian poets to music, including T. Shevchenko, I. Bahriany, O. Oles, B. Oleksandriv, and V. Symonenko. Many of his compositions have entered the repertoire of almost every bandura ensemble in the West, especially the haunting instrumental piece *Sound of the Steppe*. Kystasty was a tireless propagator of the bandura art. He taught numerous courses and seminars on the bandura and influenced an entire generation of bandurysts in North America.

Hryhorii Kytasty

BIBLIOGRAPHY

Samchuk, U. *Zhyvi struny. Bandura i bandurysty* (Detroit 1976)
Hurs'kyi, Ia. (ed). *Zbirnyk na poshanu Hryhoriia Kytastoho u 70-richchia z dnia narodzhennia* (New York 1980)

W. Wytwycky

Kyveliuk, Ivan [Kyveljuk], b 1866 in Galicia, d 1 March 1922 in Lviv. Civic and political leader. From 1908 to 1918 Kyveliuk was a deputy to the Galician Sejm. He was also a leading member of the *Prosvita society in Lviv and its president from 1910 to 1922. Under his presidency, the society reached the peak of its development. Its educational programs were expanded and the society began working with the Lviv Silskyi Hospodar society in improving agriculture. In the early 1920s Kyveliuk was imprisoned by the Polish authorities and he died shortly after his release.

Kyzia, Luka [Kuzja], b 21 February 1912 in Zhykhove, Novhorod-Siverskyi county, Chernihiv gubernia, d 29 December 1974 in Kiev. Party functionary and Soviet diplomat. During the Second World War he was the political commissar of a partisan detachment in Volhynia and the secretary of the underground Rivne oblast committee of the CP(B)U. He was the head of the Ukrainian Society for Cultural Relations with Foreign Countries (1951–6), deputy minister of higher and specialized secondary education (1956–9, 1964–7), and permanent representative of the Ukrainian SSR at the United Nations (1961–4). He was also associated with the AN URSR Institute of History. There he wrote several propagandistic works on the partisan movement during the Second World War and the anti-émigré *Pravdy ne zat'maryty: Proty burzhuaznoï fal'syfikatsiï istoriï partyzans'koho rukhu* (One Cannot Obscure the Truth: Against Bourgeois Falsification of the History of the Partisan Movement, 1965).

Kyzym (Kizim), Leonid, b 5 August 1941 in Krasnyi Lyman, Donetske oblast. Soviet cosmonaut and air force colonel. A graduate of the Chernihiv Higher Military Aviation School (1963), he received cosmonaut training at the Gagarin Air Force Academy from 1975. He commanded the three-man crew of the Soyuz T-3 spacecraft during its orbit of the Earth and docking with the Salyut-6 space station. He was also a member of the three-man crew of Soyuz T-10 that spent a record 237 days in space. During their time in space they spent more than 19 hours performing five extravehicular space walks to maintain and repair the space station Salyut-7. In 1986 Kyzym and V. Solovev – the crew of Soyuz T-15 – spent 125 days in orbit. They docked with the newest space station, Mir, and then flew Soyuz T-15 to Salyut-7, boarding it in the first station-to-station transfer ever accomplished. On 28 and 31 May the two men staged spacewalks, during which they deployed a 15-m metal lattice tower to demonstrate space construction techniques.